2008 ESPN
SPORTS ALMANAC

**With Exclusive Year in Review Commentary
from ESPN Anchors and Analysts, Writers
from ESPN The Magazine and ESPN.com**

Stuart Scott

Chris Berman

Mike Golic

Dick Vitale

Mike Greenberg

John Anderson

Lee Corso

Chris Fowler

Rusty Wallace

Trey Wingo

ALSO CONTRIBUTING

YEAR IN
REVIEW

BASEBALL

COLLEGE
FOOTBALL

PRO
FOOTBALL

COLLEGE
BASKETBALL

PRO
BASKETBALL

HOCKEY

FANTASY
SPORTS

COLLEGE
SPORTS

HALLS OF
FAME &
AWARDS

WHO'S
WHO

The Champions of 2007

Auto Racing

For all the statistics, see the Auto Racing section.

NASCAR Circuit
Daytona 500	Kevin Harvick
Coca-Cola 600	Casey Mears
Allstate 400 at the Brickyard	Tony Stewart
UAW-Ford 500	Jeff Gordon
Chase For The Nextel Cup Leader	Jeff Gordon, 6201 pts
	(through Oct. 29)

Champ Car World Series Circuit
Points Championship	Sebastien Bourdais, 332 pts
	(through Oct. 29)

Indy Racing League Circuit
Indianapolis 500	Dario Franchitti
IndyCar Championship	Dario Franchitti, 637 pts

Formula One Circuit
U.S. Grand Prix	Lewis Hamilton
World Driving Champion	Kimi Raikkonen, 110 pts

Baseball

For all the statistics, see the Baseball section.

World Series	Boston def. Colorado, 4 games to 0
MVP	Mike Lowell, Boston, 3B
ALCS	Boston def. Cleveland, 4 games to 3
NLCS	Colorado def. Arizona, 4 games to 0
All-Star Game	American League 5, National League 4
MVP	Ichiro Suzuki, AL (Seattle), OF
Coll. World Series	Oregon St. def. UNC, 2 games to 0

College Basketball

For all the statistics, see the College Basketball section.

Men's NCAA Tournament
Championship	Florida 84, Ohio St. 75
MVP	Corey Brewer, Florida, F

Women's NCAA Tournament
Championship	Tennessee 59, Rutgers 46
MVP	Candace Parker, Tennessee, F

Pro Basketball

For all the statistics, see the Pro Basketball section.

NBA Finals	San Antonio def. Cleveland, 4 games to 0
MVP	Tony Parker, San Antonio, G
Eastern Final	Cleveland def. Detroit, 4 games to 2
Western Final	San Antonio def. Utah, 4 games to 1
All-Star Game	West 153, East 132
MVP	Kobe Bryant, West (LA Lakers), G
Regular Season MVP	Dirk Nowitzki, Dallas, F
FIBA Americas Champ's	USA 118, Argentina 81

College Football (2006)

For all the statistics, see the College Football section.

National Champions
AP	Florida (13-1)
USA Today Coaches'	Florida (13-1)

Major Bowls
BCS Title Game	Florida 41, Ohio St. 14
Rose	USC 38, Michigan 18
Orange	Louisville 24, Wake Forest 13
Fiesta	Boise St. 43, Oklahoma 42 OT
Sugar	LSU 41, Notre Dame 14
Heisman Trophy	Troy Smith, Ohio St., QB

Pro Football (2006)

For all the statistics, see the Pro Football section.

Super Bowl XLI	Indianapolis 29, Chicago 17
MVP	Peyton Manning, Indianapolis, QB
AFC Championship	Indianapolis 38, New England 34
NFC Championship	Chicago 39, New Orleans 14
Pro Bowl	AFC 31, NFC 28
MVP	Carson Palmer, Cincinnati, QB
CFL Grey Cup Final	British Columbia 25, Montreal 14
MVP	Dave Dickenson, British Columbia, QB

Golf

For all the statistics, see the Golf section.

Men's Major Championships
Masters	Zach Johnso
U.S. Open	Angel Cabrer
British Open	Padraig Harringto
PGA Championship	Tiger Wood

Champions (Seniors) Major Championships
The Tradition	Mark McNul
Senior PGA Championship	Denis Watso
U.S. Senior Open	Brad Bryar
Senior Players Championship	Loren Rober
Senior British Open	Tom Watso

Women's Major Championships
Kraft Nabisco Championship	Morgan Presse
LPGA Championship	Suzann Petterse
U.S. Women's Open	Cristie Ke
Women's British Open	Lorena Ocho

National Team Competition
Solheim Cup	United States 16, Europe 1
Presidents Cup	United States 19½, International 14½

Hockey

For all the statistics, see the Hockey section.

Stanley Cup	Anaheim def. Ottawa, 4 games to
MVP	Scott Niedermayer, Anaheim,
Eastern Final	Ottawa def. Buffalo, 4 games to
Western Final	Anaheim def. Detroit, 4 games to
All-Star Game	West 12, East
MVP	Daniel Briere, East (Buffalo),

Horse Racing

For all the statistics, see the Horse Racing section.

Triple Crown Champions
Kentucky Derby	Street Sense (Calvin Bore
Preakness Stakes	Curlin (Robby Albarad
Belmont Stakes	Rags to Riches (John Velazque

Harness Racing
Hambletonian	Donato Hanover (Ron Pierce
Little Brown Jug	Tell All (Jody Jamieso

Soccer

For all the statistics, see the Soccer section.

FIFA Women's World Cup 2007	Germany 2, Brazil
MVP	Marta, Brazil,
MLS Cup 2006	Houston 1, New England
	Houston won on penalty kicks, 4-
MVP	Brian Ching, Houston,

Tennis

For all the statistics, see the Tennis section.

Men's Grand Slam Championships
Australian Open	Roger Federe
French Open	Rafael Nad
Wimbledon	Roger Federe
U.S. Open	Roger Federe

Women's Grand Slam Championships
Australian Open	Serena William
French Open	Justine Heni
Wimbledon	Venus William
U.S. Open	Justine Heni

Miscellaneous Champions

For more, see the Miscellaneous & Int'l Sports sections.

PBA Bowler of the Year	Doug Ke
Little League World Series	Warner Robbins, G
Tour de France	Alberto Contador (Spai
Iditarod	Lance Macke
World Series of Poker	Jerry Yan
Boston Marathon	Robert Cheruiyot (Keny
Bassmasters Classic	Boyd Ducke
Ironman Triathlon	Chris McCormack (Me
	Chrissie Wellington (Wome

2008

ESPN

SPORTS

ALMANAC

Gerry Brown
Michael Morrison
EDITORS

ESPN
BOOKS

Editors

Gerry Brown

Michael Morrison

Contributing Writers

Andy Katz	Chris Broussard
Jerry Crasnick	E.J. Hradek
Gene Wojciechowski	Dan Rafael
Mary Fenton	Russell Baxter
Mark Ashenfelter	

Comments and suggestions from readers are invited. Because of the many letters received, however, it is not possible to respond personally to every correspondent. Nevertheless, all letters are welcome and each will be carefully considered. The **ESPN Sports Almanac** does not rule on bets or wagers. Address all correspondence to: Sports Almanac, Inc., P.O. Box 542281, Lake Worth, FL 33454-2281.
Email: info@espnsportsalmanac.com.

ISBN13: 978-1-933060-38-5

ISBN: 1-933060-38-7

FIRST EDITION

10 9 8 7 6 5 4 3 2 1

CONTENTS

6 CONTENTS

EDITORS' NOTE

RECORDS ARE MADE TO BE BROKEN.

This year the biggest record of them all was broken (see page 124). You won't find an asterisk there. Should there be? Depends on who you talk to. If you really feel the need, pick up a pen and draw in your own.

There's no way to know exactly how much the sports world has been impacted by performance-enhancers. Technology has changed sports from swimming to speed skating. Are all the world records broken by swimmer Michael Phelps tainted because today's pools are designed to offer less resistance and faster times? Maybe. But if it were only that simple, things would be easier to swallow. We're not just talking faster pools and clap skates. We're talking the clear, the cream, EPO, HGH, syringes, test-tube champions, false positives, tainted samples, and on and on.

Drugs, and the overarching suspicion of everyone who does something special, are responsible for soiling baseball, killing the Tour de France, and tarnishing the Olympic Rings. What's next? The UFC?!?!?

In the fall of 2007, George Mitchell's report on baseball's steroid users was looming. In fact, it was due to come out just after this book hit the shelves. Whose names will appear on his list? Unknown. But is a witch hunt a witch hunt when you're surrounded by witches? The questions continue...

One thing that is beyond question is the help offered by the following fine folks...

ESPN director of research Craig Winston is always quick with a solution, or just some helpful advice. Craig's team, including Anna Clemmons, Simon Brennan, Mary Fenton, Adesina Koiki, Gueorgui Milkov and Michael Woods, is a true all-star lineup.

Thanks to ESPN Books big wig Chris Raymond for making all the right moves. Big thanks also to production manager John Glenn and designer Henry Lee.

Thanks to former editor John Hassan for being more valuable than ever before, and also to Russell Baxter, Mark Ashenfelter, John Broder and Tommy Craggs for gathering some hard-to-find information when we needed it.

The precedent set by founding editor Mike Meserole continues to push us to go above and beyond.

Thank you as well to Kevin O'Sullivan at AP/Wide World, Barbara Zidovsky at Nielsen Media Research, Rick Sommers at Command Web and the media relations folks from coast to coast.

Thanks also to our wives, Lisa and Lori for picking up the slack (and slacks...and socks...and shoes) at home during crunch time.

Gerry Brown
Michael Morrison
October 28, 2007

Major League Cities & Teams

As of Oct. 31, 2007, there were 134 major league teams playing or scheduled to play baseball, men's basketball, NFL football, hockey and soccer in 53 cities in the United States and Canada. Listed below are the cities and the teams that play there.

Anaheim
AL   Los Angeles Angels of Anaheim
NHL   Ducks

Atlanta
NL   Braves   NFL   Falcons
NBA   Hawks   NHL   Thrashers

Baltimore
AL   Orioles   NFL   Ravens

Boston
AL   Red Sox
NBA   Celtics
NFL   N.E. Patriots (Foxboro)
NHL   Bruins
MLS   N.E. Revolution (Foxboro)

Buffalo
NFL   Bills (Orchard Park)
NHL   Sabres

Calgary
NHL   Flames

Charlotte
NBA   Bobcats
NFL   Carolina Panthers

Chicago
AL   White Sox
NL   Cubs
NBA   Bulls
NFL   Bears
NHL   Blackhawks
MLS   Fire (Bridgeview)

Cincinnati
NL   Reds   NFL   Bengals

Cleveland
AL   Indians   NBA   Cavaliers
NFL   Browns

Columbus
NHL   Blue Jackets
MLS   Crew

Dallas
AL   Texas Rangers (Arlington)
NBA   Mavericks
NFL   Cowboys (Irving)
NHL   Stars
MLS   FC Dallas (Frisco)

Denver
NL   Colorado Rockies
NBA   Nuggets
NFL   Broncos
NHL   Colorado Avalanche
MLS   Colo. Rapids (Commerce City)

Detroit
AL   Tigers
NBA   Pistons (Auburn Hills)
NFL   Lions
NHL   Red Wings

East Rutherford
NBA   New Jersey Nets
NFL   New York Giants
NFL   New York Jets
MLS   Red Bull New York

Edmonton
NHL   Oilers

Green Bay
NFL   Packers

Houston
NL   Astros
NBA   Rockets
NFL   Texans
MLS   Dynamo

Indianapolis
NBA   Indiana Pacers
NFL   Colts

Jacksonville
NFL   Jaguars

Kansas City
AL   Royals
NFL   Chiefs
MLS   Wizards

Los Angeles
NL   Dodgers
NBA   Clippers
NBA   Lakers
NHL   Kings
MLS   Galaxy (Carson)
MLS   Club Chivas USA (Carson)

Memphis
NBA   Grizzlies

Miami
NL   Florida Marlins
NBA   Heat
NFL   Dolphins
NHL   Florida Panthers (Sunrise)

Milwaukee
NL   Brewers
NBA   Bucks

Minneapolis
AL   Minnesota Twins
NBA   Minnesota Timberwolves
NFL   Minnesota Vikings

Montreal
NHL   Canadiens

Nashville
NFL   Tennessee Titans
NHL   Predators

New Orleans
NBA   New Orleans Hornets
NFL   New Orleans Saints

New York
AL   Yankees
NL   Mets (Flushing)
NBA   Knicks
NHL   Rangers
NHL   Islanders (Uniondale)

Newark
NHL   New Jersey Devils

Oakland
AL   Athletics
NBA   Golden St. Warriors
NFL   Raiders

Orlando
NBA   Magic

Ottawa
NHL   Senators (Kanata)

Philadelphia
NL   Phillies
NBA   76ers
NFL   Eagles
NHL   Flyers

Phoenix
NL   Arizona Diamondbacks
NBA   Suns
NFL   Arizona Cardinals (Glendale)
NHL   Coyotes (Glendale)

Pittsburgh
NL   Pirates
NFL   Steelers
NHL   Penguins

Portland
NBA   Trail Blazers

Raleigh
NHL   Carolina Hurricanes

Sacramento
NBA   Kings

St. Louis
NL   Cardinals
NFL   Rams
NHL   Blues

St. Paul
NHL   Minnesota Wild

Salt Lake City
NBA   Utah Jazz
MLS   Real Salt Lake

San Antonio
NBA   Spurs
NFL   New Orleans Saints

San Diego
NL   Padres
NFL   Chargers

San Francisco
NL   Giants
NFL   49ers

San Jose
NHL   Sharks

Seattle
AL   Mariners
NBA   SuperSonics
NFL   Seahawks

Tampa
AL   T.B. Devil Rays (St. Petersburg)
NFL   T.B. Buccaneers
NHL   T.B. Lightning

Toronto
AL   Blue Jays
NBA   Raptors
NHL   Maple Leafs
MLS   Toronto FC

Vancouver
NHL   Canucks

Washington
NL   Nationals
NBA   Wizards
NFL   Redskins (Raljon, Md.)
NHL   Capitals
MLS   D.C. United

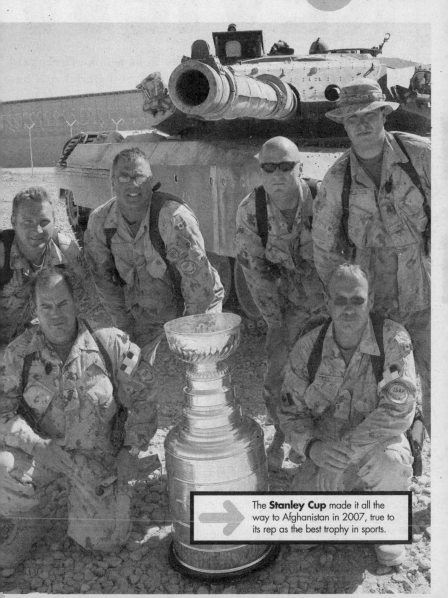

YEAR IN REVIEW

2006 / 2007

The **Stanley Cup** made it all the way to Afghanistan in 2007, true to its rep as the best trophy in sports.

THE YEAR IN REVIEW

We sat down with ESPN Radio's Mike Golic & Mike Greenberg to get them to weigh in on some of the biggest stories and best performers of the year in sports.

Almanac: In 2007, it seemed like the middle of the year was dominated by all that bad news from Michael Vick and dog fighting to the Tim Donaghy scandal, and even Bonds had a negative tint to him. So, is that your impression, your takeaway from this year, that it was kind of a down year?

Greenie: "Yes. I think it was a bad year in sports. I think, all things considered, it was a bad year in sports because an increasing amount of the media coverage involves things that take place away from the playing field. And certainly the two dominant stories off the field in sports this year

Golic

Greenie

were Michael Vick and T Donaghy. And those were ba extraordinarily negative, and co both of their leagues in a very b light."

Golic: "And I think you throw the Bonds saga and the steroi story in baseball. I think it's leavi the fans more than ever asking t question, 'What's real? What real in sports anymore? What c we trust that we're watching.' S either they're going to be involv and want it cleaned up, or say, 'y know what, I'm just going to wat and enjoy what I see on the fie and not get caught up in anythi else.'"

Atlanta Falcon **Michael Vick**'s involvement with dog-fighting, and the legal woes that ensued, cast a shadow of doubt on his long-term future as an NFL player.

MICHAEL VICK
INDICTED BY A GRAND JURY

Almanac: What's your opinion at this point regarding Michael Vick? Where do you sit on it right now?

Greenie: "I don't think he'll ever play pro football again. I think he made a colossal mistake and it would be selling short what he did to suggest that his biggest mistake was not coming clean sooner than he did. But the reason he'll never play football again is that he didn't come clean sooner than he did. Qyntel Woods played in the NBA after having been involved in relatively similar things.

Michael Vick would still be playing in the NFL if he had just acknowledged his role in this thing initially. The seriousness of the crime followed by the cover-up are the reasons that you have seen the last of Michael Vick."

Golic: "I disagree with that. I don't think you've seen the last of him. He'll play again. If a team wants to take a chance on him, he'll get the opportunity to. It may not be until 2010. But if a team wants to sign him, he'll get a chance to

Mike &
MIKE
in the morning

NBA official **Tim Donaghy** gave the NBA a big punch in the gut in 2007.

AP/Wide World Photos

ter of how much they'll get. But they'll get some."

Greenie: "And the should. They should. Just the Dolphins should get bunch of Ricky William money back. You get pai that money because you mak a commitment when you g that money. And that comm ment—and the signin bonus—is not just to sign you name. I think that the tea has a right to expect mo than just a signature for th signing bonus. I think the should get money back."

TIM DONAGHY CASTS A SHADOW OF DOUBT ON THE NBA

Almanac: *NBA offici Tim Donaghy was at the ce ter of a huge gambling sca dal this year...*

Golic: "Every year I end u screaming when the post-seaso starts because we get so many pe ple emailing or calling the rad show that talk about the conspirac theories in the NBA claiming th league wants this team or this pla er to move forward in the playoff And I scream and scream and sa 'How are they going to do it? The can't do it. There's no way w wouldn't know about it now.'

And then the Donaghy thing com out, and you know what, it makes m have to say it a little lighter and a l tle quieter, because I don't kno what we can believe anymore."

play in the NFL again. And I do think he will get that chance.

He's doing what most athletes do in this situation. When you hear them with a heartfelt apology is it genuine? Or is it, 'I'm sorry that I got caught' more than 'I'm sorry for what I did?'"

Almanac: *Do you think the Falcons will get any of that money back?*

Golic: "They'll get some of it back, absolutely. It's just a mat-

"Now, again, David Stern is
[sa]ying this is the only one. It's
[iso]lated. But the fan will say,
[h]ow do we know?' When that
[ca]ll is made in the game,
[th]ey're going to say, 'How do
[w]e know?' And how can we
[bl]ame them for that?"

Greenie: "That said, I think
[th]e NBA and Stern did a good
[jo]b of minimizing the damage.
[C]ertainly there was damage,
[a]nd there will be damage still
[to] come. But I do not think the
[d]amage will be of the cata-
[st]rophic nature that a gambling
[s]candal could potentially have
[fo]r a league. I do not think this
[is] 'stop the presses', 'stop the
[le]ague', 'the league will never
[r]ecover from it' news.
[B]asketball has gone through
[m]ultiple gambling scandals in
[th]e past. It has always come
[b]ack from it, and it will again."

AP/Wide World Photos

Colts QB **Peyton Manning**
went from the dog house to
The White House in 2007.

PEYTON MANNING FINALLY WINS THE 'BIG' ONE

Almanac: Peyton Manning
[s]ilenced his critics this year...

Greenie: "Legitimized his name
[i]n the discussion with the greatest
[q]uarterbacks of all time."

Golic: "To me, it was a matter of
[t]ime. I knew they were going to win
[i]t. And as bad as it is to say, I agree
[w]ith Greenie that if you need some-
[t]hing to legitimize your career, that's
[w]hat you need. Because that's some-
[t]hing that will follow Dan Marino for
[t]he rest of his life.

He's already in rarefied air, and if
Peyton were to win another one, he
could be standing alone very soon."

Greenie: "I'll take it a step further. In the year 2007, we were privileged to see two guys who are
going to go down as absolutely as
good as any two quarterbacks who
have ever played the game, in
Peyton Manning and Tom Brady.
Both were playing at their very
best."

What was an off-year for **Tiger Woods**, winning just one Major, made **Angel Cabrera** the happiest guy around in 2007.

TIGER WOODS

Almanac: *Somebody who does-n't need legitimizing, Tiger Woods had a pretty good year. He's a little bit closer to Jack's major record. So again, what do you think about watching the prime of that guy's career?*

Greenie: "It's a treat to be able to watch. And I'll tell you what, I think Tiger Woods has handled him-self exceptionally well. If you look at the attention that he has brought to golf—an individual sport—that never existed before, the attention that he has received himself that almost no other athlete could ev deal with. Few other athletes in t world today have had to deal wi that kind of fame. I don't know ho much better you could handle it th he's handled it, you know? I thi the guy is really remarkable. And think he's one of these guys wh like Muhammad Ali, is someone th to his dying day and long beyond going to be beloved and revered people, even people that don't ca a lick about golf."

Golic: "This guy's flat out goi to go down as the greatest golfer the history of the game. There's doubt about it, and he's handli imself incredibly, incredibly well. The other golfers should all thank im for how much he's helped the PGA Tour as far as the money and everything. The guy, I love his attitude. I love his preparation. He knows what he wants to do. He's the best golfer in the world.

A lot of times people root for the underdog. But I really think with Tiger you get a lot of people that are rooting for him. He's never an underdog. He's going to be the greatest ever and when he's winning a tournament, I really think more people tune in to see him and by just how much he's going to dominate."

APPALACHIAN STATE PULLS *HOOSIERS*-TYPE UPSET

Almanac: *Appalachian State from the I-AA, er, football championship subdivision ranks, knocks off Michigan, the winningest program in major college history...*

Golic: "It was one of the greatest upsets ever. Usually, the best time of the year is the NCAA college basketball tournament, when you get the unknowns to beat the big programs. That's what you get in the NCAA tournament every year. And you got it on the college football level this time around with Appalachian State. It was huge for college football, huge for that pro-

→ **Appalachian State** coach Jerry Moore was carried off the field at Michigan Stadium after his Mountaineers pulled off the upset of the year.

that team that would neve
have been on that team 2
years ago. And that's a good
reason why you saw so man
upsets in the 2007 colleg
football season, none of th
magnitude of Appalachia
State, of course. But general
speaking, the distanc
between number one an
number 50 in college footba
has never been shorter than
is right now."

FLORIDA

Almanac: Speaking o
college sports, Florida
repeat in basketball and th
team having a two-fer wit
the football and basketba
teams, what do you think o
that?

Golic: "Well, it's rare to b
that dominant. I mean, it'
unbelievably impressive, yo
know? To get the guys to wi
in Florida in basketball, and
then all come back to want to do i
again, that to me was a cool thing
Because these guys would have
been high NBA draft picks. The
could have gone and grabbed the
money, but decided instead, 'You
know what, we've got another yea
of this. Let's try and do this again.
And to me, I think that was a grea
message to send.

Other than the guys that you
know are only going to school for o
year and then to jump to the NBA—
the Kevin Durants and the Greg
Odens of the world and I'm not say
ing that's a wrong decision—it was

The **Florida Gators** ate up the rest of the college sports world in 2007.

gram, huge for those kids. I mean,
that, when you think of college
sports, you think of games like that,
of teams that supposedly have no
business being there. They didn't
get lucky with the win. They flat-out
outplayed a team that's considered
one of the best programs in the history of college sports."

Greenie: "And it's also, I think,
illustrative of what we have now,
which is an era of unprecedented
parity in college football because of
the limitations on scholarships and
things like that. There are players on

refreshing to see guys who were going to go make a lot of money still say, 'You know what? We want to go try and do this again on the college level.'"

Greenie: "Yeah, I would agree. I thought that Billy Donovan's flirtation with the NBA, or beyond flirtation—he had an actual signed contract with the Orlando Magic—and then going back to Gainesville put a little bit of a damper on that for me. I thought that was just handled so incredibly badly. But at the same time, there was a degree of earnest love for the college game and for the school that he displayed that sort of mirrored what we saw from his players. So, overall, there's no question the predominant college athletic program right now is at the University of Florida."

AP/Wide World Photos

Mixed Martial Arts forced its way into the mainstream, racking up huge TV ratings

THE METEORIC RISE OF MIXED MARTIAL ARTS

Almanac: *Mixed Martial Arts, Ultimate Fighting, whatever you call it, it seems to have caught the nation by storm.*

Greenie: "I love it. I'm telling you, to me it has surpassed boxing. I watched an MMA pay-per-view event, and I watched every one of the five or six fights. And I didn't know a person in it outside of Chuck Liddell. I mean, that's why I got it [because of Liddell], but the other guys I didn't know. What do you do when you buy a boxing pay-per-view? You sit around, and you drink and eat wings and wait until the main event. You barely watch the undercard. This, I watched them all. I didn't know anybody. There's a lot of action. It keeps moving all the time. I think they promote it extremely well, and I like it a lot better than boxing. I think it has surpassed boxing, without a doubt."

Golic: "Nothing has ever made me feel older than MMA. I've never seen one second of it, and I recognize that that makes me an old fart, because it is clear that that is a sport of the future, and that is what peo-

Giants slugger **Barry Bonds** seemed to know something we didn't on his long march to 756.

ple a generation younger than I am are getting into."

ROGER FEDERER

Almanac: *Roger Federer just keeps rolling along...*

Greenie: "He is just one win away from being the greatest tennis player that ever lived. And he can win on clay, unlike Pete Sampras. He gets to the finals at Roland Garros every year. He's the second best player in the world on clay right now. That's a lot better than Pete Sampras ever was [on clay]. Roger Federer probably doesn't need to win the French Ope in order to be the greate player that ever lived. But he does win that tournamen then he locks it up."

Golic: "Well, my though on it are 'see Tiger Woods'. mean, it's the same thing We're seeing the greates player of all time. We're see ing a guy handle the stardo incredibly well; a guy that going to buy pizzas for th ball boys and the ball girls; guy that doesn't have a entourage around him or whole management grou behind him; a guy that play it like a regular guy, sincere ly the way he handles him self. It's just—and I know Tiger does have a entourage around him, bu just the way they're both ha dling their greatness, to me is very, very impressive. He's anoth er one, I watch him play to see how much he's going to dominate, whe normally people are going to roc for the underdog."

BARRY BONDS

Almanac: *Finally, we can ta about this for the last time, Barr Bonds passing Hank Aaron, what your takeaway at this point?*

Greenie: "It's a sad day i sports..."

Golic: "I don't have a proble with it. Greenie and I disagree o this. You know what, there hav been things that have gone on i aseball since the start of aseball. And certainly this is a steroid era, and certainly we know what's going on. But, you know what, let the history books talk about it. I don't have a problem with it. We're going to see more records broken, and maybe more people are going to be questioned in this as we go down the line. But, you know what, let fathers and mothers tell sons and daughters of what their opinion of it is, and let these people grow up and form their own opinions as well."

Greenie: "The one good thing that came out of it is that we got to see the extraordinary grace and decency of Hank Aaron on full display one more time, the way he handled it, I thought, was magnificent."

→ **David Beckham**, and wife **Victoria**, made a big splash when they landed in L.A.

DAVID BECKHAM

Almanac: *What about David Beckham's arrival in the United States, the latest candidate to try to make soccer popular in this country?*

Golic: "Well, even if he was healthy and playing in every game... You know, all right, it was going to add a few thousand to the attendance. I certainly understand that. But unfortunately, I don't think it's going to make soccer any more popular. *He's* going to be more popular on the red carpet, he and his wife, for television commercials or ads or movies. I think that's where he's going to make his biggest impact. It's not going to be his impact on Major League Soccer in the United States. I just don't think it's going to happen."

Greenie: "He did make a little more impact than I thought he would. I have to confess I didn't expect the jam-packed stadiums that we saw when he first arrived. So I think he made more of an impact on actual on-the-field interest than I expected. That said, I certainly don't expect it to go much further.

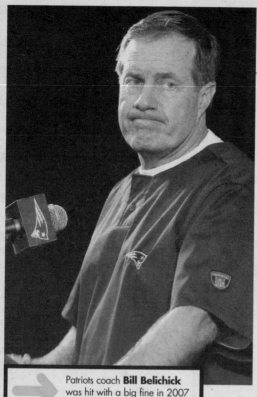

Patriots coach **Bill Belichick** was hit with a big fine in 2007 for videotaping opponents.

BILL BELICHICK AND SPYGATE

Almanac: What about the Bill Belichick videotaping scandal? What's your feeling about that and its effect on his and the team's legacy?.

Golic: "None. Listen, stuff like this has been going on forever, teams, players trying to find an edge. And Bill Belichick went too far, and he got caught. It's not to say that other teams haven't done that or done things like that. I don't think it affects his legacy. I don't think it affects the team's legacy. I think he's a great coach. And I think this is something that's gone on for years, and he got caught doing it. There's no doubt about it, he got caught doing it. But, you know, there's no way we're going to say, 'Wow, look at that. I mean, let's nullify everything` he's done,' when there's a whole lot of other teams out there that try and find that edge as well."

Almanac: It'll never become a big TV sport.

Greenie: "Never say never, but I wouldn't expect that any time in the foreseeable future."

Golic: "I don't think it will. Just for the fans of today, there's not enough action or scoring, you know? There's just not enough for what people want today in our microwave society.

Greenie: "I will say, however, that his complete refusal to ever really explain it, and the NFL's refusal to ever tell us exactly what they were investigating—and to this point what their investigation turned up—leave a lot of questions. And it is not our fault that we're asking those questions. It's their fault."

Golic: "And you know what, no one outside of us is asking the questions. The fans, they don't care. They want to go see the most popular sport around, and they don't want to see it tarnished."

Almanac: What do you guys think of new NFL Commissioner Roger Goodell, by the way?

Golic: "I think he's done a great job. I think he's a guy that came in and had some tough situations right off the bat. So you wondered, how was he going to react? You know how you can tell he did a good job? Everybody, from union to management, was in agreement with what he was doing. Everybody stood behind it and said, 'Even though maybe we want to tweak here or there, we like what you're doing. We like the direction you're going.'"

Because normally you expect the the union reps to jump in and say, 'You can't do this to our players.' I think even players are sick of some of the things that have been going on, and don't mind that someone is stepping in and saying, 'You know what, enough is enough. You have to act differently.'"

Greenie: "Yeah, he's the new sheriff in town. I mean, it's a shame that the sport was in a place where those were the first and most pressing needs that he had to deal with. But I think they were, and I thought he handled them extremely well. Now we'll see how he handles more routine matters, but I think he handled all those situations very well.

METS COLLAPSE

Almanac: The Mets collapse. When you look back on where the Mets were—seven games up, how do you rank this one?

Greenie: "Yeah, it is the worst collapse in the history of Major League Baseball, both literally and figuratively. And it is something from which I do not think the organization will recover fast. I think things like that don't just go away. I think scars from things like that remain. And I do not think the organization will just bounce back as though it never happened."

Golic: "I think it is a classic example of—and I talk about this a lot, but it's not a tangible thing for people to grasp—is you were seeing how athletes handle things mentally. Because it's not like at the end of the year these guys forgot how to field a grounder, forgot how to hit, or forgot how to pitch. They were doing it all pretty well for just about the entire season to put themselves in the position they were. Then, all of a sudden, it started going bad, and it kept going bad.

You saw how you can be beaten mentally by—all of a sudden—gripping the bat a little tighter, trying to make the perfect throw from the field, trying to make a different pitch than you are normally used to. You saw a team collapse on the field, but I think you saw a team mentally collapse more than anything."

Overheard in Bristol...

"O.J. Simpson, Pete Rose, and **Michael Vick**. In the history of all-time falls from sporting grace, that's the list. And you could make a fairly compelling argument that neither Rose nor Simpson fell as hard, or as fast, as Michael Vick. Simpson was never convicted in criminal court. Rose, to this day, despite finally coming clean about betting on baseball still has his ardent supporters. Michael Vick is going to jail as a convicted felon on **federal dog fighting and gambling charges**. Unless your last name is Vick, or you are one of his very few close personal friends, his supporters are few and far between.

Less than six months ago, Michael Vick was one of the very few stars in the NFL that the league chose to market its sport around. He was the face of a franchise, and one of the priviledged few with a contract north of $100 million. **Now he's disgraced**, his team is trying to get back most of the money they've paid him and he will be serving time in a federal penitentiary. Just think on that for a few minutes. A man who had it all will be issued prison wear. They say America loves a good comeback story. A few years from now, Michael Vick will have a shot, at writing the greatest one we've ever seen."

—Trey Wingo

"We hear it but don't neccesarily believe it. Sure, the idea forms in our minds but an idea rarely becomes reality unless you FULLY believe it. Commit to it. Make it a part of WHO and WHAT you are. 'On any given day, any football team can beat any other.'

Yeah...right. Maybe in the NFL but not in college football when one school is one of the most prestigious programs in college football history. The home of national champions, Heisman Trophy winners and a home stadium that seats more people than many mid-size American cities.

A place that EVERY YEAR recruits the very best high school athletes in the nation. A locker room full of young men who arrive on campus seemingly ready to play in the NFL. How can a Division I-AA school even compete or whatever politically correct thing we call Division I-AA these days. Sure they may have won some I-AA national championships in the last few seasons. But they were playing MICHIGAN, the #5 team in the nation and, after all, it's Division I-AA!

Appalachian State

usually gets the rejects of the guys North Carolina, Duke, and Wake Forest didn't want. And what have those big name ACC schools done lately in football? Not much. So how could they will themselves to **beat Michigan**—AT MICHIGAN?? Because they BELIEVED they could. They didn't HOPE they would. They didn't FIGURE they could. They didn't PRAY the could. They KNEW it. Fully believed it. Committed to it . . . a n d then...did it. It's the size of the heart, not the size of the young man."

–Stuart Scott

"Faster, higher, stronger. Even if it takes a syringe.

Marion Jones wowed us in 2000 with her three gold and five medal performance in Sydney, Australia. She made headlines again when she finally acknowledged in a courtroom the BALCO **drug use** that led to those top-of-the-podium, national anthem finishes.

Jones is not, despite years of vigorous and angry denials, a golden girl but rather an ordinary drug cheat and an extraordinary liar.

Her public apology, while tearful and dramatic, did little to stir sympathy from any of us who love track and field or who have spent an afternoon running quarter mile repeats. She failed to explain record setting years on her timeline leading up to Sydney. She likely cost her relay teammates their medals. And would there have been a confession at all if the Feds hadn't forced it out of her in the face of overwhelming evidence?

Jones returned her precious medals to Olympic organizers and what hangs around her neck now are disgrace and shame."

–John Anderson

"There was the heat at the PGA Championship: triple digit temperatures all week in Tulsa. And then there was the *h e a t*: **T i g e r Woods'** five-stroke final-round lead down to one as he stepped to the 15th tee **at Southern Hills Country Club**. Woody Austin had momentum, Woods had gone shaky and those with a five-month memory couldn't shake the thought of the Big Red Shirt's second place Sunday finishes at Augusta and Oakmont.

Quiet please.

4-iron, 7-iron, putt. Birdie. Ball game. **Major championship number 13 in the books**. His first of fatherhood.

It's why he's the Babe Ruth of this generation and Rory Sabbatini is…whatever.

Jack Nicklaus's record of 18 professional major championships is now in plain sight and sure to fall by Tiger's 40th birthday.

Now how many FedEx Cup points is that worth?

–John Anderson

It was a banner year for Red Sox pitchers **Daisuke Matsuzaka** and **Hideki Okajima**. Except probably for *this* day.

EXTRA POINTS

A look back at some of the more offbeat sports moments, quotes and personalities from the past year.

From West Wing To Clipped Wing

In June, a ball hit by Rob Lowe during a celebrity golf game in Iowa hit a goldfinch, the Iowa state bird, in mid-flight.

Reportedly, the rest of the players in his group (none of which included Randy Johnson or Dave Winfield) broke out in laughter and applause.

"That's unbelievable," he said. "Who comes here and kills the state bird? Only me." He also added, "That's my birdie."

What Would Mickey Say?

In May, 60-year-old actor Sylvester Stallone, on tour to promote his upcoming movie Rocky Balboa, pleaded guilty to importing 48 vials of the human growth hormone, Jintropin, into Australia, as well as possessing four vials of testosterone.

He of course claimed the substances were to treat a medical condition, and that he was unaware that he was breaking Australian law. Ultimately he paid fines of just under $3,000, plus court costs of $10,000.

He's Baaaaack!

In September, NFL Hall of Famer O.J. Simpson was arrested for breaking into a Las Vegas hotel room and attempting to steal back memorabilia that he claims was originally stolen from him.

In an audiotape of the break-in released by the celebrity news Web site TMZ.com, Simpson could be heard yelling, "Think you can steal my [expletive] and sell it?" as well as the more ominous statement, "Don't let nobody out of here!"

He was booked on two counts of robbery with a deadly weapon, two counts of assault with a deadly weapon, and conspiracy to commit a crime and burglary with a firearm.

Zany Tennessee men's head basketball coach **Bruce Pearl**, is the "V" in "Volunteers" as he cheers along with students at the Tennessee women's game against Duke on Jan. 22.

Get Up in Manny's Grill!

The following is an actual eBay Listing from March 2007:

"Hi, I'm Manny Ramirez. I bought this AMAZING grill for about $4,000 and I used it once. … But I never have the time to use it because I am always on the road. I would love to sell it and you will get an autographed ball signed by me. Enjoy it, Manny Ramirez."

The original listing included seven photos of the grill, two with Ramirez next to it. Opening bid for the grill was $3,000 (plus shipping), but the bids quickly shot up to over $20,000. The listing was eventually pulled from eBay, because site administrators couldn't verify whether Ramirez was the grill's owner.

Just Manny being Manny.

A Side of Bill We Don't Know?

"I think Coach Belichick is one of those people who is a great feeler of people." – Patriots rookie DB Brandon Meriweather

There's An "I" in Pierce.

"I'm the classic case of a great player on a bad team, and it stinks."
– Celtics F Paul Pierce

AP/Wide World Photos

Seahawks attacked by Peacock! An **NBC overhead camera** fell to the turf at Qwest Field during a game between the Saints and the Seahawks on Oct. 14. It just missed landing on Seattle quarterback Matt Hasselbeck.

Forget Something?

Kelly Pavlik earned a gross purse of $1.05 million for beating Jermain Taylor in their middleweight title bout in late September. One problem — Pavlik and his father/co-manager Mike left their winnings on the counter of their Atlantic City hotel room. D'oh!

Kelly's check was for $666,750 and Mike's was for $105,000. No worries — fight promoter Bob Arum simply stopped payment on the checks and issued new ones. "I think I gave that maid probably the best tip she ever got," said Mike.

Lose Something?

For some reason, sprinter Sanya Richards decided to run her 200m preliminary heat at the World Championships in Osaka...with a $20,000 diamond broach pinned to her chest. And she almost lost it.

"I'm coming off the turn, it clinks off my knee and it goes over to lane eight," Richards explained. "And I'm looking like: 'No!' But I have to be focused and finish the race."

Volunteers scoured the area and, fortunately, recovered the jewel. Perhaps just as fortunate, there was a second heat, which Richards won in 22.31.

Injuries of the Year

) While practicing his swing in his otel room, Scottish golfer **Marc Varren** accidentally smashed a chandelier and was taken to a hospital where he received stitches for a deep ut in his abdomen. He also had minor uts on his arms and head. He was back playing at the Seve Trophy tournament the next day.

2) Two New Orleans Saints players, linebacker **Scott Fujita** and tight end **Billy Miller**, were injured during a preseason visit to Rapids On the Reservoir water park in Mississippi. Fujita suffered a bruised heel and Miller received a gash on his forehead.

3) Cubs reliever **Bobby Howry** suffered an upper-back strain while moving his barbecue grill.

4) Giants LB **Chase Blackburn** was cleaning his ear with a Q-tip after a game in September when an overzealous reporter ran into him, causing the Q-tip to jam into his ear. He suffered temporary hearing loss.

5) Australian rugby player **Ben Czislowski** had his head stitched up after battling with an opponent in an April match. In July, after months of continuous headaches and an eye infection, his doctor discovered the culprit — he found a tooth embedded in Czislowski's head. "I can laugh about it now, but the doctor told me it could have been serious, with teeth carrying germs," he said.

Bridgewater State Wins a Squeaker

The Division III Bridgewater State (Mass.) baseball team pasted Newbury College, 57-1, on April 9, breaking far too many NCAA records to list in this space.

Bridgewater St 57, Newbury 1

April 9, at Bridgewater, Mass.

Newbury	AB	R	H	RBI	Bridgewater	AB	R	H	RBI
Fish, c-p	4	0	1	0	Koneski, rf	2	4	1	2
Carroll, 1b-ss	2	1	1	0	Mooney, ph-rf	6	3	3	4
Torres, p-lff	3	0	0	0	Claffey, 3b	8	7	6	7
Maddock, cf-p	3	0	2	0	Smith, lf	8	7	7	10
Siedlecki, 2b-lf	3	0	1	0	Dillon, cf	8	6	5	9
Mathew, ss-3b	2	0	0	1	LaDow, c	4	4	4	3
McKechnie, 1b	0	0	0	0	Sousa, c	2	4	0	1
DiClemente,p-cf	3	0	0	0	Hansen, dh	5	3	3	3
Cooper, 3b	0	0	0	0	Clough, dh	3	3	2	2
Picanco, rf	1	0	0	0	Kiloski, 1b	3	3	2	2
Chiem, 2b	2	0	0	0	Couet, 1b	4	4	2	2
Kazin, lf-rf	3	0	0	0	Lamoureux, ss	5	3	3	3
					Medairos, ss	4	2	3	2
					Karngioze, 2b	1	2	0	2
					Downey, 2b	4	2	3	3
					Altman, p	0	0	0	0
					Higham, p	0	0	0	0
Totals	**26**	**1**	**5**	**1**	**Totals**	**67**	**57**	**44**	**55**

						R	H	E
Newbury	0	0 0	0 0	1 0	—	1	5	5
Bridgewater	13	9 9	16 8	2 x	—	57	44	2

2B: Claffey, Smith 2, LaDow 2, Clough, Lamoureux. **HR:** Smith, Dillon 2. **HBP:** Clough, Karangioze2, Downey. **SF:** Mathew. **SB:** Koneski.

Newbury	IP	H	R	ER	BB	SO	BF	ERA
DiClemente (L, 0-1)	0	4	7	7	3	0	7	—
Maddock	1	4	6	5	4	1	12	45.00
Torres	2	16	22	19	5	3	32	85.50
Mathew	2	15	30	11	8	2	32	49.50
Fish	1	5	2	2	0	1	8	18.00

Bridgewater	IP	H	R	ER	BB	SO	BF	ERA
Altman (W, 2-0)	5	3	0	0	1	7	19	0.00
Higham	2	2	1	0	0	1	9	0.00

WP: Maddock. **HBP:** by Torres (Karangioze); by Torres (Karangioze); by Torres (Clough); by Mathew (Downey). **PB:** Fish.

Bobby Howry   **Chase Blackburn**

Mother of the Year Nominee

A 42-year-old Nebraska woman, upset with her teenage daughter's play in a soccer game, pulled over on the way home and left her on the side of I-80.

Father of the Year Nominee

A 37-year-old Connecticut dad, reportedly in an attempt to impress his 7-year-old, jumped onto the field at Fenway Park during the ninth inning of a Red Sox game. Not surprisingly, he was arrested.

Cincinnati Red-Faced

At a U.S. Army-sponsored baseball camp for kids age 7 to 14, guest speaker Pete Rose angered parents and Army officials with his unnecessarily salty language.

He "was a complete embarrassment," Staff Sgt. Steven Tischer told the *Cincinnati Enquirer*. "You don't swear in front of kids, that's just common sense. He dropped the F-bomb and the S-bomb. He told them winning is everything and if you get second place you're just losers."

Say What?

In other kid-friendly quotes, Cleveland Cavaliers center Scot Pollard looked into the camera during a game in March and said, "Hey kids, do drugs." He later apologized.

Baby Name of The Year

Born on Sept. 12 to Indiana couple and devoted Cub fans, Paul and Teri Fields,

Wrigley Fields

A Hard Day's Work

As the Colorado Rockies grounds crew attempted to pull the tarp onto the field during a rain delay on July 8, a strong wind gust quickly caused the tarp to fly out of control. Enter...the Philadelphia Phillies, most of whom were sitting in the dugout and leapt onto the field to help the flailing crew. "One guy flew 10 feet in the air," said pitcher Adam Eaton.

Head Groundskeeper Mark Razum added, "The wind was so strong, we couldn't hold it. When it draped over the guys, I was worried that somebody might suffocate. It was really cool the Phillies came out and gave us a hand."

The Phillies went on to beat the Rockies, 8-4. All in a day's work.

In Other Groundskeeping News

The New Hampshire Fisher Cats, a double-A minor league baseball team, offered free tickets to anyone who came out to help shovel snow off the field before a post-snowstorm April game.

Just one fan accepted the offer.

Scot Pollard   Adam Eaton

INF Photos

AP/Wide World Photos

Which Yankee Hat is More Offensive??

On one side, we have **Tom Brady** — quarterback extraordinaire for the New England Patriots, who happen to play in the same state as the Boston Red Sox, who just happen to be division rivals and sworn mortal enemies of the New York Yankees.

On the other side, we have **LeBron James** — NBA superstar for the Cleveland Cavaliers and long-time Yankee fan, despite growing up in Akron, Ohio, which is smack dab in the middle of Indians territory.

And the verdict is...LeBron's

Sorry Red Sox fans. The very site of Tom Terrific in the "forbidden lid" may make you gasp (and the man-purse doesn't help either). But look at it this way: this shot was snapped in New York City. He's probably just trying to avoid being noticed, by blending in with the millions of others also in Yankee hats. Plus maybe Gisele made him wear it.

However...LeBron's photo was taken *at Jacobs Field* during an Indians-Yankees playoff game! Hey LeBron, be a fan of whichever team you want. Just don't stick it in the face of the very people that fill the arena in which you play your home games.

Heisman Shipped

Former Ohio State quarterback Troy Smith had to ship his brand new Heisman Trophy from New York to Columbus because airport security would not allow him to take it on the plane.

It's probably just as well. Eddie George, the last Buckeye to win the Heisman in 1995, had his trophy get stuck in an airport X-ray machine, losing the tip of its right index finger and bending the middle finger.

Lesser-Known Records Set in 2007

Barry Bonds and Brett Favre weren't the only athletes to break important records in 2007. Below is a top-10 list of some of the records that captured a little less attention than the ones just mentioned.

10 On March 9, Super heavyweight boxers Eric "Butterbean" Esch and Joe Siciliano establish what is believed to be a record for total poundage in a boxing match, weighing in at a combined 730.5 pounds, 417 of which belong to Esch.

09 On Jan. 3, Michael Perham, 14, from Hertfordshire, England, sails into Nelson's Dockyard in Antigua, becoming the youngest person to cross the Atlantic single-handed.

08 On July 14, George Hood, of Aurora, Ill., sets the world record for stationary cycling, completing his 111th straight hour on an exercise bike. The previous record was 83 hours.

07 On Oct. 6, harness racing's Donato Hanover wins the mile-long Kentucky Futurity in a record-tying 1:50.1. It's his 11th consecutive victory (see the Horse Racing chapter for more).

06 On Aug. 4, Isabella Wagner, of Germany, runs 100 meters backward in 16.8 seconds, breaking the previous record by nearly a second. Wagner also sets the backward 400-meter mark, finishing in 1:29.

05 On Jan. 22, British skateboarder Dave Cornthwaite completes a five-month, 3,638-mile trek across Australia, setting a record.

04 On Oct. 20, Steven Purugganan, 10 years old, of Longmeadow, Mass., establishes a new record for individual cycle at the WSSA New York State Sports Stacking Championships. His time in the event, which entails stacking 12 plastic cups in a sequence of positions, is 7.23 seconds, besting by .02 seconds the record established in April by 11-year-old David Wolf of Germany.

03 On Aug. 19, Sheila Drummond, 53, blinded by diabetes more than two decades ago, hits a hole-in-one on the 144-yard, par-three fourth hole at Mahoning Valley Country Club, near Lehighton, Pa.

02 On Oct. 14, Erik Akkersdijk, of the Netherlands, solves a Rubik's Cube in a record 9.77 seconds at the Dutch Open.

01 On Aug. 4: Kevin Taylor, of Michigan, sets a speed brick-breaking record, smashing 584 cement bricks in 57.5 seconds.

LeBron James dropped 48 points on the Detroit Pistons in the Cavs' double-overtime win on May 31.

November 2006

Sun	Mon	Tue	Wed	Thu	Fri	Sat
			1	2	3	4
5	6	7	8	9	10	11
12	13	14	15	16	17	18
19	20	21	22	23	24	25
26	27	28	29	30		

What's Up Knight?

Did Bobby Knight cross the line when he used his hand to push one of his player's chin up to get his attention on Nov. 13?

72% — Yes
28% — No

A Sampling of SportsNation feedback:

Darren (Lebanon, Ohio): Coach Knight did nothing wrong. He is in an authoritative roll [sic] and when he speaks to a player he deserves the player's attention. If he needs to lift the chin of a player for that player to look him square in the eyes, he has every right to do that.

Paul (Flanders, NJ): With all due respect to coach Knight, he was out of line. You don't touch players. Period.

Ramsey (Seattle): Clearly unacceptable. It's a shame people are defending Knight. Why don't all coaches (girls, boys, college, NBA) smack their players around? Because it's physical assault and inhumane.

Kevin (Long Island): If anything, Knight should be commended for his actions. Coaches need to be able to discipline their players if they are to command respect.

2 Detroit Tigers catcher Ivan Rodriguez highlights the list of American League Gold Glove Award winners with his record (for a catcher) 12th. A day later, pitcher Greg Maddux wins his 16th, tying the record for pitchers with Jim Kaat.

4 Invasor, trained by Kiaran McLaughlin and ridden by 18-year-old Fernando Jara, chases down Preakness winner Bernardini to win the $5 million Breeders' Cup Classic at Churchill Downs by a length. Tragedy strikes, however, as Pine Island breaks down during the $2.2 million distaff and is later euthanized.

Penn State football coach Joe Paterno breaks his shin bone and injures a knee ligament when two players run into him on the sidelines. The 79-year-old promises the injury won't slow him down, but sadly his doctors feel otherwise. A week later, Paterno misses his first Penn State game since 1977.

5 Marilson Gomes dos Santos of Brazil becomes the first South American to win the New York City Marathon, clocking in at 2:08:58. Jelena Prokupcuka of Latvia successfully defends her title in the women's division with a time of 2:25:05.

6 Former Oakland A's coach Ron Washington is named manager of the Texas Rangers.

7 Bud Black, former pitching coach of the Los Angeles Angels, is named manager of the San Diego Padres, replacing Bruce Bochy who left a month ago to manage the San Francisco Giants.

9 Jeremy Ito kicks a 28-yard field goal with 13 seconds remaining to lift No. 15 Rutgers over No. 3 Louisville, 28-25. It sets off a week that also sees No. 4 Texas lose, 45-42, to Kansas St. and No. 5 Auburn lose, 37-15, to Georgia.

12 Manny Acta, the New York Mets 3rd base coach, is named manager of the Washington Nationals.

The San Diego Chargers score 42 points in the second half and storm from behind to beat the Cincinnati Bengals, 49-41. The Chargers trailed by 21 at halftime.

The Houston Dynamo beat the New England Revolution on penalty kicks, 4-3, in the MLS Cup, after a 1-1 standoff.

13 Legendary coach Bobby Knight makes headlines once again for the wrong reasons after he lifts/slaps/pops (you decide) the chin of sophomore Michael Prince, to tell him to keep his head up.

AP/Wide World Photos

Emmitt Smith and Cheryl Burke celebrate their win, and display the mirrorball trophy on "Dancing with the Stars" on Nov. 15.

Florida Marlins shortstop Hanley Ramirez tops Washington 3rd baseman Ryan Zimmerman as NL Rookie of the Year.

14 Arizona ace Brandon Webb wins the NL Cy Young Award.

The Boston Red Sox pay $51.1 million for the rights to negotiate exclusively with Japanese pitching phenom Daisuke Matsuzaka.

15 Recently fired Florida Marlins manager Joe Girardi wins the NL Manager of the Year award. Detroit Tigers' Jim Leyland wins the AL award.

16 Uh oh, here it comes. MLS team Real Salt Lake becomes the first team in a major American sports league to display the name of a sponsor (juice company XanGo) on the front of its jersey.

Ace Johan Santana of the Minnesota Twins wins the AL Cy Young Award for the second time in three years.

Bench coach Bob Geren is promoted to manager of the Oakland A's.

17 Michigan football coaching great Bo Schembechler dies at 77 on the eve of the highly anticipated Michigan-Ohio State matchup. He was 234-65-8 in 26 seasons as coach of Michigan and Miami (Ohio).

18 Top-ranked Ohio State defeats Michigan, 42-39, to solidify its spot in the BCS Title Game.

19 Jimmy Johnson finishes ninth at the season-ending Ford 400 outside of Miami, but that's enough to clinch his first season-long NASCAR points championship.

The Chicago Cubs sign Alfonso Soriano to an eight-year, $136 million deal.

20 Phillies slugger Ryan Howard wins the NL MVP award.

21 Justin Morneau edges Derek Jeter for the AL MVP award.

26 Glidemaster wins the Yonkers Trot to become just the eighth horse to win the Trotting Triple Crown (he had previously won the Hambletonian and Kentucky Futurity).

December 2006

Sun	Mon	Tue	Wed	Thu	Fri	Sat
					1	2
3	4	5	6	7	8	9
10	11	12	13	14	15	16
17	18	19	20	21	22	23
24/31	25	26	27	28	29	30

ESPN sportsnation

Brawling at the Garden

How do you rate the league's overall reaction to the Dec. 16 brawl between the Knicks and the Nuggets?

49.8% — *About right*
26.7% — Too soft
23.5% — Too harsh

What do you think of Isiah Thomas not drawing a fine or suspension?

55.5% — *Should have been suspended*
27.5% — Should have been fined
17.0% — Right call

In the wake of the brawl and a 9-17 start, should the Knicks fire Thomas?

74.1% — *Yes*
25.9% — No

Total Votes: 74,991

1 Jockey Russell Baze, aboard Butterfly Belle, wins the fourth race at Bay Meadows in San Mateo, Calif. to become thoroughbred racing's all-time winningest jockey. It is the 9,531st win of his career, breaking Laffit Pincay Jr.'s former mark.

2 No. 2 USC's title hopes are dashed and the BCS rankings are thrown for a loop as the Trojans are stunned, 13-9, by Pac-10 rival UCLA. Florida, meanwhile, wins the SEC title game, 38-28, over Arkansas.

Ohio State freshman Greg Oden makes his college basketball debut in impressive fashion, scoring 14 points and grabbing 10 rebounds in a 78-58 win over Valparaiso.

3 Florida edges Michigan in the BCS rankings by mere percentage points to secure their spot in January's inaugural BCS Title Game against Ohio State.

7 The Phoenix Suns beat the New Jersey Nets, 161-157, in double overtime. The game features 224 shots, 27 successful three-pointers and 57 fouls.

9 Ohio State quarterback Troy Smith runs away with the 2006 Heisman Trophy, amassing 2,540 points to defeat runner-up Darren McFadden of Arkansas (878) and Notre Dame quarterback Brady Quinn (782). It is Ohio State's seventh.

10 Running back LaDainian Tomlinson scores his 29th touchdown of the season in a 48-20 Chargers win over the Broncos, breaking Shaun Alexander's all-time single-season touchdown record. He would add two more over the final two weeks of the season to put the new mark at 31.

11 Freddy Adu, 17, is traded from the D.C. United to Real Salt Lake.

13 Japanese pitcher Daisuke Matsuzaka signs a six-year, $52 million deal with the Boston Red Sox. The amount is in addition to the $51.1 million the Red Sox must now pay to his former team, the Seibu Lions.

Lamar Hunt, NFL pioneer and owner of the Kansas City Chiefs, dies of complications from prostate cancer at age 74. Hunt founded the AFL in 1960 and was a pivotal force behind the AFL-NFL merger and the Super Bowl.

16 Morten Andersen becomes the NFL's all-time leading scorer with 2,437 points, and Michael Vick breaks the single-season record for rushing yards in a season by a quarterback, but the Atlanta Falcons lose, 38-28, to the Dallas Cowboys.

AP/Wide World Photos

Knicks' guard **Nate Robinson**, second from left, and Denver Nuggets' J.R. Smith exchange words, while Carmelo Anthony is restrained during a fight that broke out on Dec. 16.

Carmelo Anthony and nine other players are ejected for a nasty, fist-flying brawl between the Denver Nuggets and New York Knicks, after a flagrant foul by Knicks guard Mardy Collins. Anthony, the league's top scorer, is later suspended for 15 games.

18 **Italy's Fabio Cannavaro** and Brazil's Marta are voted FIFA Men's Player of the Year and Women's Player of the Year, respectively.

19 **After weeks of speculation,** Allen Iverson is finally traded from the Philadelphia 76ers to the Denver Nuggets for Andre Miller, Joe Smith and two 2007 1st round picks.

22 **Rape charges are dropped** against three former Duke lacrosse players, but District Attorney Mike Nifong continues to press on with sexual offense and kidnapping charges, despite a stunning lack of evidence and a growing list of inconsistencies by the accuser.

25 **Tiger Woods is named** AP Male Athlete of the Year over runner-up LaDainian Tomlinson and third-place Roger Federer.

Hawaii quarterback Colt Brennan throws five touchdown passes in a 41-24 win over Arizona State, giving him 58 for the season — a new NCAA record.

26 **Former President Gerald Ford dies** at the age of 93. Ford was a center at the University of Michigan, and turned down offers from the Lions and Packers to play in the NFL.

Golfer Lorena Ochoa is named AP Female Athlete of the Year.

29 **Mike Tyson is arrested** in Phoenix. After nearly ramming a police SUV, he is found to be in possession of two bags of cocaine in his back pocket.

29 **Down 31 points** in the third quarter, Texas Tech rallies for a stunning 44-41 win over Minnesota in the Insight Bowl.

30 **Boston College beats Navy,** 25-24 on the final play of the Meineke Bowl, Texas defeats Iowa, 26-24, in the Alamo Bowl and Georgia upsets Virginia Tech, 31-24, in the Chick-fil-A Bowl.

January 2007

Sun	Mon	Tue	Wed	Thu	Fri	Sat
	1	2	3	4	5	6
7	8	9	10	11	12	13
14	15	16	17	18	19	20
21	22	23	24	25	26	27
28	29	30	31			

Was the Fiesta Bowl the best college football game ever?

Where does this game stand, in terms of the greatest college football games of all-time?

47.9% — Top 5
25.0% — It's the best
20.4% — Top 10
6.7% — It's not in the top 10

Which was the best play of the game?

51.9% — "Hook and Ladder" to tie it
48.9% — "Statue of Liberty" to win it

Does Boise State deserve a shot at Ohio State for the national championship?

76.1% — Yes, they are the only other unbeaten and showed they belong in that game
23.9% — No, the BCS system worked fine and Florida is more deserving than Boise State

Total Votes: 229,035

1 In the college football game of th year, Boise St. stuns Oklahoma, 43-42, in th Fiesta Bowl on a "Statue of Liberty" two-poi conversion by Ian Johnson. He then proposes his girlfriend for the cameras.

Among other Bowl game action, US beats Michigan, 32-18, in the Rose Bowl, Pen State gets by Tennessee, 20-10, in the Outbac Auburn edges Nebraska in the Cotton Bowl, 1 14, and West Virginia edges Georgia Tech, 3 35, in the Gator Bowl.

Bobby Knight becomes the NCAA al time winningest basketball coach in NCAA hi tory with Texas Tech's 70-68 nailbiter over Ne Mexico. It's win no. 880 for the highly successf yet controversial coach as he passes North Ca olina legend Dean Smith.

3 Bama-Boozled! Nick Saban bolts th Miami Dolphins to become head coach c Alabama. The departure comes just two week after Saban claimed, "I'm not going to be th Alabama coach. I shouldn't even have to con ment on this. I think I've said this over and ove again."

4 LaDainian Tomlinson is selected as th runaway winner of the AP NFL Most Valuabl Player award.

5 Bill Cowher resigns as coach of the Pitts burgh Steelers after 15 seasons and a Supe Bowl title.

6 Tony Romo botches the snap on who could have been a game-winning field goal t seal the Cowboys' 21-20 loss to the Seattle Sec hawks in their NFL Wild Card game.

New Orleans Saints coach Sean Payto is the landslide winner of the AP NFL Coach c the Year award.

8 Chomp! The Florida Gators rout the top ranked Ohio State Buckeyes, 41-14, in the BC Title Game to win their second national footba championship. Quarterback Chris Leak com pletes his first nine passes (25 of 36 overall) an the stifling Gator defense forces Heisman winne Troy Smith into the worst game of his colleg career. Florida becomes the first Division I schoc to hold the NCAA basketball and football titles i the same year.

9 Cal Ripken and Tony Gwynn are elec ed for induction into the Baseball Hall of Fam with 98.5 percent and 97.6 percent of the vote respectively. Perhaps just as noteworthy, Mar McGwire is nowhere even close, garnering onl 23.5 percent, well short of the 75 percer required for induction.

AP/Wide World Photos

 Boise State tailback **Ian Johnson** proposes to his girlfriend, cheerleader Chrissy Popadics, after Boise State beat Oklahoma, 43-42, in the Fiesta Bowl.

11 English soccer star and international celebrity David Beckham signs a five-year, $250 million deal to play with the MLS' Los Angeles Galaxy.

13 The New Orleans Saints defeat the Philadelphia Eagles, 27-24, to advance to the NFC Championship Game, while the Indianapolis Colts use five Adam Vinatieri field goals to beat Baltimore, 15-6, to reach the AFC Championship Game.

14 The New England Patriots rally to defeat the San Diego Chargers, 24-21, to set up a battle with the Colts, while the Chicago Bears nip Seattle, 27-24 in overtime.

17 Pete Sampras and Arantxa Sanchez-Vicario are among four elected to the International Tennis Hall of Fame in Newport, R.I.

21 The Indianapolis Colts, down 21-6 at halftime, stage a ferocious comeback with 32 points in the second half to beat the New England Patriots, 38-34, and advance to Super Bowl XLI.

The Chicago Bears defeat the New Orleans Saints, 39-14, in snowy Soldier Field to advance to their first Super Bowl since 1986. The Bears score three fourth-quarter touchdowns to pull away.

22 Cowboys coach Bill Parcells announces his retirement. He leaves with a 172-130-1 regular season record and two Super Bowl titles.

23 Yankee Stadium is chosen to host the 2008 MLB All-Star Game.

24 The Western Conference beats the East, 12-9, in the NHL All-Star Game.

27 Serena Williams tops Maria Sharapova, 6-1, 6-2, in the finals of the Australian Open. It's her eighth Grand Slam singles title.

28 Roger Federer cruises to his tenth Grand Slam singles title, beating Chile's Fernando Gonzalez, 7-6, 6-4, 6-4, in the Australian Open final.

29 Barbaro is euthanized after his long struggle since the 2006 Preakness.

February 2007

Sun	Mon	Tue	Wed	Thu	Fri	Sat
				1	2	3
4	5	6	7	8	9	10
11	12	13	14	15	16	17
18	19	20	21	22	23	24
25	26	27	28			

What did you think of Super Bowl XLI?

Which was better?

83.7% — The game
16.3% — The commercials

Does Peyton Manning vault into the Top 5 quarterbacks of all time.

70.1% — Yes
29.9% — No

Total Votes: 59,508

John Amaechi — your reaction

Is Amaechi coming out a big story?

36.1% — No, because being gay is not a story
26.2% — Yes, any pro athlete that comes out is a big story
21.1% — Yes, because he is the first NBA player to do so
16.6% — No, because he was not a star player

If your favorite player announced he was gay, would you care?

54.0% — No
46.0% — Yes

Total Votes: 15,965

3 **Former Cowboys wide receiver Michael Irvin** is voted into the Pro Football Hall of Fame in Canton on his third try. He'll be enshrined with former Bills running back Thurman Thomas and four others.

4 **Peyton Manning,** Tony Dungy and the Indianapolis Colts beat the Chicago Bears, 29-17 in rainy Super Bowl XLI in Miami for the franchise's first NFL title since 1970. The underrated Colts defense forces five Bears turnovers, while Manning throws for 247 yards and a touchdown en route to being selected as the game's MVP. Dungy becomes the first African-American head coach to win the Super Bowl, and becomes the third man to win the title as a player and coach (Tom Flores and Mike Ditka are the others).

6 **Stephon Marbury debuts** the Starbury Team, his latest pair of sneakers that sell for just $14.98.

7 **The rich get richer,** as defending champion Florida inks what experts believe to be the top recruiting class on national football signing day.

11 **John Amaechi,** who retired from the NBA in 2003, publicly announces that he's gay in advance of his upcoming autobiography, Man In The Middle. He saves his harshest words for former teammate Karl Malone ("a xenophobe"), Jazz owner Larry Miller ("a bigot") and coach Jerry Sloan, who Amaechi claimed "hated" him.

Chargers kicker Nate Kaeding boots a 21-yard field goal with no time left on the clock to lead the AFC to a 31-28 win over the NFC in the NFL Pro Bowl. Bengals quarterback Carson Palmer throws for 190 yards and two touchdowns, and is selected as the game's MVP.

12 **Despite a 14-2 regular season record,** head coach Marty Schottenheimer is fired from the San Diego Chargers after a disappointing playoff loss to New England.

Junior Brian McGuirk nets the game-winner at 5:06 of overtime to lead BU to a 2-1 win over BC and their 28th Beanpot title.

14 **Former NBA guard Tim Hardaway** announces, "I hate gay people" in a radio interview with 790 The Ticket in Miami, amidst the release of John Amaechi's book. He also adds that he would not speak to a gay family member. Commissioner David Stern immediately distances himself and the league from the comments.

15 **Barry Bonds,** looking to break Hank Aaron's all-time career home run mark in 2007, signs a one-year, $15.8 million deal with the San Francisco Giants.

Retired NBA basketball player **John Amaechi** autographs his book *Man In The Middle* for a well-wisher.

18 **Kevin Harvick vaults** from seventh place to first on the crash-marred final lap and wins the Daytona 500 by just 0.02 seconds, the tightest margin of victory in race history. Veteran Mark Martin finishes in a disappointing second and Jeff Burton places third as Chevrolet grabs the top four spots and six of the top 10.

Kobe Bryant scores a game-high 31 points and Phoenix forward Amare Stoudemire adds 29 and nine rebounds to lead the West to a 153-132 win in the NBA All-Star Game in Las Vegas. Bryant is named the game's MVP. LeBron James paces the East with 28 points.

19 **Titans oft-troubled cornerback** Adam "Pacman" Jones is involved in a triple shooting at a Las Vegas nightclub that leaves one club employee paralyzed. Reportedly, Jones had been showering more than 40 strippers with $81,000 in cash — or as he calls it, "making it rain" — and when some tried to take handfuls of money, a melee ensued.

22 **Wimbledon becomes** the last of the four Grand Slam tennis tournaments to award equal compensation for its male and female champions. The announcement marks a departure from the world's most prestigious tournament's 123-year tradition of paying women less.

25 **Alabama angler Boyd Duckett** wins the Bassmaster Classic in his home state, surging ahead on the final day to amass a three-day total of 48 lbs, 10 oz. He wins the grand prize of $502,000.

26 **The Honus Wagner T206,** considered the "Mona Lisa of baseball cards," is sold for a record $2.35 million. The card was once co-owned by hockey legend Wayne Gretzky.

ATP tennis rankings are released and Roger Federer is the No. 1 ranked men's player for the 161st consecutive week, breaking the all-time record held for the last 30 years by Jimmy Connors.

27 **Mia Hamm and Julie Foudy** are elected to the National Soccer Hall of Fame.

March 2007

Sun	Mon	Tue	Wed	Thu	Fri	Sat
					1	2	3
4	5	6	7	8	9	10
11	12	13	14	15	16	17
18	19	20	21	22	23	24
25	26	27	28	29	30	31

Violence in the NHL

How long should the NHL suspend Chris Simon?

29.9% — *All of this season, the play-offs, and a percentage of next season*

28.9% — All of this season, plus the playoffs

22.3% — He should be expelled from the league

19.0% — All of this season

Do you think the NHL has done enough to discourage such reactionary behavior in the game?

62.9% — *No*

37.1% — Yes

What do you believe is the league's current stance on "revenge" hits since the Bertuzzi-Moore incident?

52.2% — *The same*

39.2% — More strict

8.6% — More lenient

Total Votes: 29,405

4 **American speedskater Shani Davis,** gold medalist in the 2006 Turin Olympics, breaks his own record in the 1,500 meters at the World Cup final in Calgary.

Colombian Juan Pablo Montoya goes from 19th to first in the final 26 laps of the Busch Telcel-Motorola Mexico 200 for the first NASCAR win of his blossoming career.

Fiery bowler Pete Weber beats Wes Malott, 210-204, to win the 64th U.S. Open in North Brunswick, N.J. It is Weber's fourth U.S. Open victory and record-tying eighth career major title.

11 **Kansas, North Carolina, Ohio State,** and defending champion Florida are awarded the top seeds for the upcoming NCAA Division I Men's Basketball Tournament. Syracuse is perhaps the most notable "bubble" team not invited to the dance.

Guillermo Canas shocks top-ranked Roger Federer, 7-5, 6-2, in the third round of the Pacific Life Open at Indian Wells, snapping Federer's 41-match winning streak.

The NHL suspends Islanders enforcer Chris Simon for 25 games, following his vicious two-hand stick swing to the face of the Rangers' Ryan Hollweg.

12 **Five-time world champ Johnny Tapia** is hospitalized and in critical condition after an apparent cocaine overdose.

Jody Conradt, the second winningest coach in Division I women's basketball history with 900 wins, resigns from the University of Texas after the Longhorns fail to make the NCAA tournament for the second year in a row.

13 **Lance Mackey crosses under** the burled arch in downtown Nome and wins the Iditarod Trail sled Dog Race in just over nine days.

Chief Illiniwek, long considered demeaning to some American Indians, is no more as the University of Illinois votes to retire the mascot's name, regalia and image.

14 **Pete Rose, in an interview with ESPN Radio,** claims "I bet on my team to win every night because I love my team, I believe in my team."

15 **The NCAA Men's Basketball tournament** tips off with VCU stunning Duke, 79-77, on Eric Maynor's 15-footer with under two seconds on the clock.

Bowie Kuhn, former Major League Baseball commissioner, dies at the age of 80 following a bout with pneumonia. He served as commissioner from 1969 to 1984.

AP/Wide World Photos

Lance Mackey gets a kiss from a his lead dog Larry, left, with Lippy right, after his win at the Iditarod Trail Sled Dog Race victory in Nome, Alaska.

18 The Boston Celtics are fined $30,000 after general manager Danny Ainge sits next to the mother of Texas Longhorns star Kevin Durant at the Big 12 Tournament.

19 Newly-signed Miami Dolphin linebacker Joey Porter is accused of sucker punching Cincinnati Bengal Levi Jones at a blackjack table in a Las Vegas casino. Reportedly members of Porter's entourage were also involved in the attack of the six-foot-five, 305-pound lineman.

21 St. Louis Cardinals manager Tony La Russa is arrested after being found slumped over the steering wheel of his car with the engine running, the car in "drive," and his foot on the brake.

22 Brian Joubert becomes the first Frenchman in 42 years to win the men's title at the World Figure Skating Championships in Tokyo. American Evan Lycacek places fifth.

23 Tubby Smith announces his decision to resign as coach of the Kentucky hoops team to assume the same role with Minnesota.

24 Sergio Garcia draws the ire of many after he knocks in a bogey putt at the CA Championship at Doral, then retrieves his ball, and spits into the cup.

25 The Final Four pairings are set as Florida knocks off Oregon, 85-77, and will face UCLA, while Georgetown takes down North Carolina in overtime, 96-84, to set up a Final Four matchup with Ohio State.

28 Former major league pitcher Ugueth Urbina is sentenced to 14 years in prison for attempted murder, after he is found guilty of attacking five people with machetes and then pouring gasoline on them.

31 First football, now basketball. Ohio State and Florida will square off in the men's basketball championship game in a repeat of their BCS Title Game matchup three months earlier. Florida beats UCLA, 76-66, while Ohio State takes care of Georgetown, 67-60 to advance.

Invasor wins the $6 million Dubai Cup, thoroughbred racing's richest event.

April 2007

Sun	Mon	Tue	Wed	Thu	Fri	Sat
1	2	3	4	5	6	7
8	9	10	11	12	13	14
15	16	17	18	19	20	21
22	23	24	25	26	27	28
29	30					

Pacman is Suspended...

Is a one-season suspension for Adam "Pacman" Jones appropriate?

66.4% — It's about right
19.3% — It's too severe
14.3% — It's too light

Do you believe commissioner Roger Goodell is committed to eliminating off-field behavioral issues in the NFL?

93.9% — Yes
6.1% — No

Total Votes: 115,546

...and Imus is Fired

Should Imus have been fired?

61.7% — No
38.3% — Yes

Total Votes: 62,304

1 Texas hoops star Kevin Durant becomes the first freshman to be named the Naismith Player of the Year.

The World Swimming Championships come to a conclusion in Melbourne with American Michael Phelps setting five world records and taking home seven gold medals.

2 The Florida Gators defeat the Ohio State Buckeyes, 84-75, for their second consecutive NCAA Division I men's basketball title. Forward Corey Brewer scores 13 points and hauls in eight rebounds in the final to earn the Final Four's Most Outstanding Player award. Buckeye freshman phenom Greg Oden scores 25 points and grabs 12 boards in what turns out to be his final college game.

The Major League Baseball season is underway with the New York Yankees defeating Tampa Bay, 9-5, Seattle ace Felix Hernandez shutting down the Oakland A's and AL MVP Justin Morneau picking up where he left off, going 3-for-4 with a homer in the Twins' 7-4 win over the Orioles.

3 Candace Parker scores 17 points to lead Tennessee to its seventh NCAA women's basketball title with a 59-46 win over Rutgers. It is Tennessee's first title since 1998. Nicky Anosike grabs 16 rebounds for the Volunteers, while Kia Vaughn leads Rutgers with 20 points.

Legendary Grambling football coach Eddie Robinson dies at the age of 88. He sent more than 200 players to the NFL and retired in 1997 with 408 wins, at that time the most in NCAA history.

5 Daisuke Matsuzaka lives up to the incredible preseason hype, whiffing 10 in his debut and allowing just one run on six hits over seven innings in the Red Sox' 4-1 victory over Kansas City.

8 Iowan Zach Johnson shoots a 1-over-par 289 to win the Masters by two strokes over Rory Sabbatini, Retief Goosen and Tiger Woods. Thanks in part to a rough wind and biting cold, it is tied for the highest winning score in Masters history.

9 The New York Islanders win a thrilling 3-2 shootout over the New Jersey Devils to secure the Eastern Conference's last playoff berth and bump out the Toronto Maple Leafs.

10 NFL commissioner Roger Goodell lays down the law, suspending Titans cornerback Adam "Pacman" Jones for the entire season and Bengals receiver Chris Henry for eight games for committing a long list of infractions.

AP/Wide World Photos

> A school and the nation mourned when a gunman killed 32 people at Virginia Tech (and took his own life) on April 16 in the deadliest shooting rampage in modern U.S. history.

11 Quarterback Drew Bledsoe, announces his retirement after 15 years in the NFL with the Patriots, Bills and Cowboys. he threw for 44,611 yards and 251 touchdowns over his career.

All charges are dropped against former Duke lacrosse players Reade Seligmann, David Evans and Collin Finnerty, as North Carolina Attorney General Roy Cooper claims the three were railroaded in a "tragic rush to accuse." Former DA Mike Nifong is brought up on charges and later serves a day in jail.

12 Longtime New York radio host Don Imus is fired after referring to the Rutgers women's basketball team as "nappy-headed hos" the day after the team's loss to Tennessee in the championship game.

15 Major League Baseball celebrates the 60th anniversary of Jackie Robinson's breaking of the color barrier.

16 A horrific shooting on the campus of Virginia Tech leaves 33 dead. It's the deadliest shooting rampage in American history.

Kenyan Robert Cheruiyot and Russian Lidiya Grigoryeva brave the wind, cold and occasional driving rain to win the men's and women's titles at the Boston Marathon.

17 NBA referee Joey Crawford is suspended for his overly aggressive conduct in ejecting San Antonio star Tim Duncan.

18 Chicago White Sox hurler Mark Buehrle throws the season's first no-hitter in a 6-0 win over the Texas Rangers.

26 Police conducting a drug investigation raid quarterback Michael Vick's house in Virginia and discover dozens of dogs, some injured and emaciated.

28 The Oakland Raiders select LSU quarterback JaMarcus Russell with the top pick in the NFL draft. The following day, the Raiders trade talented but troubled receiver Randy Moss to the New England Patriots for a fourth-round pick.

29 Colorado rookie shortstop Troy Tulowitzki turns an unassisted triple play against the Atlanta Braves.

May 2007

Sun	Mon	Tue	Wed	Thu	Fri	Sat
		1	2	3	4	5
6	7	8	9	10	11	12
13	14	15	16	17	18	19
20	21	22	23	24	25	26
27	28	29	30	31		

Roger Returns to the Yankees

Are you surprised Clemens is returning to the Yankees?

68.8%	—	*No*
15.2%	—	Yes, I thought he would come back with the Astros
9.4%	—	Yes, I thought he would come back with the Red Sox
6.6%	—	Yes, I thought he was retired for good

Is Roger Clemens the greatest pitcher of all-time?

66.6%	—	*No*
33.4%	—	Yes

Total Votes: 57,326

Dale Jr. Leaves DEI

Who is to blame for Dale Earnhardt Jr. leaving DEI?

78.4%	—	*Teresa Earnhardt*
13.4%	—	All four share in the blame
2.9%	—	Kelly Earnhardt Elledge
2.9%	—	Dale Earnhardt Jr.
2.4%	—	Max Siegel

Total Votes: 78,449

2 Portland Trail Blazers guard Brandon Roy is chosen as the NBA's Rookie of the Year.

Half and Half! Rafael Nadal defeats Roger Federer, 7-5, 4-6, 7-6, in a strange exhibition match in Mallorca played on a customized half-grass, half-clay court.

The Phoenix Suns win Game 5 of their Western Conference semifinal matchup, 119-110, to oust Kobe Bryant and the Los Angeles Lakers from the playoffs.

5 Street Sense, under jockey Calvin Borel, races from 19th place to first in a hurry to win the 133rd Kentucky Derby at Churchill Downs. Trained by Carl Nafzger, he becomes the first horse to win the Derby after also winning the Breeders' Cup Juvenile race. Hard Spun finishes in second while Curlin places third. Despite entering five horses, trainer Todd Pletcher once again misses out on his elusive first Triple Crown victory.

Floyd Mayweather Jr. wins a split-decision over the Golden Boy, Oscar De La Hoya in their WBC Super Welterweight championship bout. With 2.15 million pay-per-view buys and $120 million in pay-per-view revenue, the fight is the richest in boxing history.

6 Oh my goodness gracious! Future hall of famer Roger Clemens, 44, signs a deal worth approximately $18.5 million (prorated from $28 million) to pitch for the New York Yankees for the remainder of the season. Clemens dramatically announces his return to the Yankee Stadium crowd with a speech from owner George Steinbrenner's box during the seventh-inning stretch of the Yankees-Mariners game.

10 Dale Earnhardt Jr. announces his decision to part ways with Dale Earnhardt Inc., the company founded by his father. The breakup is due in large part to a strained relationship he has with his step-mother Teresa.

11 Dolphins' running back Ricky Williams fails the fifth drug test over his tumultuous seven-year career and now must wait several months before even applying for possible reinstatement to the NFL.

14 Dallas Mavericks forward Dirk Nowitzki becomes the first European player to win the NBA Most Valuable Player award.

15 Phoenix Suns Amare Stoudemire and Boris Diaw are suspended for Game 5 of their playoff series with the San Antonio Spurs after leaving "the vicinity of the bench" in response to a body check by Robert Horry on Suns star Steve Nash. Horry is suspended for two games.

Boston Celtics head coach **Doc Rivers**, left, and GM **Danny Ainge** can't hide their disappointment after the team slipped out of the top three in the NBA draft lottery.

16 **The Atlanta Braves are sold** from Time Warner Inc. to Liberty Media Corp.

18 **Jason Giambi** raises some eyebrows and once again puts himself under the steroid microscope by claiming he was "wrong for doing that stuff." He also adds, "What we should have done a long time ago was stand up — players, ownership, everybody — and said: 'We made a mistake.'"

19 **Curlin, ridden by** Robby Albarado and trained by Steven Asmussen, chases down Kentucky Derby winner Street Sense to win the Preakness by a head. Street Sense's loss eliminate's any chance of seeing thoroughbred racing's first Triple Crown winner since Affirmed in 1978. Derby runner-up Hard Spun places third.

20 **Roger Federer beats** Rafael Nadal, 2-6, 6-2, 6-0, in the final of the Hamburg Masters to snap Nadal's 81-match winning streak on clay. It's Federer's first clay-court title in two years and it's also the first time he's ever beaten Nadal on the surface.

22 **Jackpot!** The Portland Trail Blazers win the top pick at the NBA Draft Lottery and the right to draft either Greg Oden or Kevin Durant. Seattle wins the second pick.

24 **One game after he passes up** the potential game-winning shot, LeBron James this times opts to take the final shot — and misses — as the Pistons win, 79-76, and go up 2 games to 0 in their Eastern Conference Final matchup.

27 **Dario Franchitti wins** the rain-shortened Indianapolis 500. The win is also marked by a spectacular late crash by Marco Andretti that allowed Franchitti to cruise to the win under caution.

Casey Mears grabs his first Nextel Cup victory at the Coca-Cola 600 in Charlotte. J.J. Yeley and Kyle Petty finish second and third, respectively.

31 **LeBron James dominates**, scoring 48 points — including 29 of his team's final 30 — to lead the Cavaliers to a 109-107 double-overtime thriller over the Pistons.

June 2007

Sun	Mon	Tue	Wed	Thu	Fri	Sat
					1	2
3	4	5	6	7	8	9
10	11	12	13	14	15	16
17	18	19	20	21	22	23
24	25	26	27	28	29	30

The NBA Class of 2007

Which player would you rather build around?

61.2% — *Greg Oden*
38.8% — Kevin Durant

What does the future hold for Oden and Durant?

86.9% — *Both will be stars*
7.4% — Only Durant will be a star
4.4% — Only Oden will be a star
1.4% — Both will be busts

Which team made the biggest reach in the lottery?

26.5% — *Chicago: Joakim Noah*
20.4% — Milwaukee: Yi Jianlian
10.3% — Philadelphia: Thaddeus Young
10.0% — Sacramento: Spencer Hawes
7.0% — Seattle: Jeff Green
5.7% — Memphis: Mike Conley
5.4% — Atlanta: Acie Law
5.0% — Atlanta: Al Horford
2.7% — Minnesota: Corey Brewer
2.7% — Charlotte: Brandan Wright
2.5% — LA Clippers: Al Thornton
1.8% — New Orleans: Julian Wright

Total Votes: 119,575

1 Chicago Cubs catcher Michael Barrett needs six stitches after his in-game, clubhouse mini-brawl with team ace Carlos Zambrano.

2 LeBron James takes the next step, carrying the Cleveland Cavaliers to the NBA Finals in his fourth season. The Cavs beat the Pistons, 98-82, in Game 6 of the Eastern Conference Finals and now have the daunting task of facing Tim Duncan, Tony Parker and the San Antonio Spurs, who easily dispatched the Utah Jazz in five games.

4 Florida Gators hoops coach Billy Donovan, just days after accepting the head coaching job with the NBA's Orlando Magic, gets cold feet and opts to back out of his contract and remain the head coach at Florida. Stan Van Gundy is later hired as Donovan's replacement.

Auto racing pioneer Bill France Jr., who directed NASCAR for 31 years and turned it into the major national sport that it is today, dies at 74.

6 The Anaheim Ducks beat the Ottawa Senators, 6-2, to win their first Stanley Cup in five games. They become the first team from California to win the Cup. Defenseman and team captain Scott Niedermayer wins the Conn Smythe Trophy as playoff MVP and has the rare honor of accepting the cup from the commissioner, then passing it directly to his brother, Rob. Goalie Jean-Sebastien Giguere stops 11 shots, including a penalty shot in the third period.

9 Rags to Riches edges Preakness winner Curlin at the wire to win the Belmont Stakes by a head. She becomes the first filly to win the Belmont in 102 years. The win also earns Todd Pletcher his first win in a Triple Crown race, snapping an 0-for-28 drought. Jockey John Velazquez snaps a Triple Crown drought of his own with his first win in 21 races.

Belgian Justine Henin defeats Ana Ivanovic, 6-1, 6-2, in the women's singles final of the French Open for her third straight French Open title and fourth overall.

Roger Clemens wins his season debut, allowing three runs in six innings in a 9-3 Yankee win over the Pirates.

10 Roger Federer can't solve Spaniard Rafael Nadal once again at Roland Garros, losing, 6-3, 4-6, 6-3, 6-4, in the French Open men's final. It's Nadal's third consecutive French Open title.

11 Chamique Holdsclaw, a six-time WNBA all-star, announces that she's retiring immediately, just five games into the season.

Craig Biggio connects for his 3,000th career hit during the seventh inning of the Astros-Rockies game on June 28.

12 **Flame-thrower Justin Verlander** throws the second no-hitter of the MLB season, blanking the Milwaukee Brewers, 4-0. He walks four and fans 12.

13 **Dale Earnhardt Jr. announces** his plans to join rivals Jeff Gordon and Jimmie Johnson at Hendrick Motorsports for the 2008 season.

14 **The San Antonio Spurs** edge the Cleveland Cavaliers, 83-82, to complete their four-game sweep and win their fourth NBA championship in nine years. Manu Ginobili scores 27 points and Finals MVP Tony Parker adds 24, then kisses fiance Eva Longoria.

Penguins star Sidney Crosby is awarded the Hart Trophy as the league MVP. New Jersey goalie Martin Brodeur wins the Vezina Trophy for the third time in four seasons, Detroit Red Wings defenseman Nicklas Lidstrom wins his fifth Norris Trophy.

17 **Affable Argentine Angel Cabrera** holds off Tiger Woods and Jim Furyk to win the U.S. Open by a stroke.

Britain's Lewis Hamilton makes it two-for-two in North America, winning Formula One's U.S. Grand Prix in Indianapolis, just a week after winning the inaugural Canadian Grand Prix.

"The more I thought about the future, the more I became convinced that the Lakers and me just have two different visions for the future," writes Kobe Bryant on his website.

The Baltimore Orioles fire manager Sam Perlozzo after a 29-40 start.

20 **Sammy Sosa becomes** the fifth major leaguer to hit 600 home runs with his fifth-inning blast in the Rangers' 7-3 win over the Cubs.

24 **Former major leaguer Rod Beck** is found dead at the age of 38.

28 **Greg Oden is selected** first overall by the Portland Trail Blazers, while Seattle follows with Kevin Durant. The Sonics also make noise by trading guard Ray Allen to the Celtics.

Houston's Craig Biggio becomes the 27th player to reach 3,000 hits.

July 2007

Sun	Mon	Tue	Wed	Thu	Fri	Sat
1	2	3	4	5	6	7
8	9	10	11	12	13	14
15	16	17	18	19	20	21
22	23	24	25	26	27	28
29	30	31				

What Should Happen to Michael Vick?

Will Michael Vick ever play in the NFL again?

54.3% — No
45.7% — Yes

Would you want Vick to play for your favorite NFL team after he completes his still to be determined jail sentence?

79.5% — No
20.5% — Yes

How should the NFL punish Vick in addition to whatever time he might spend in jail?

41.5% — Lifetime ban
20.3% — One-year suspension
16.5% — Two-year suspension
13.7% — No additional punishment
7.9% — More than two-years

How serious a crime is dogfighting?

62.9% — Very serious
27.3% — Moderately serious
6.6% — Not serious
3.3% — Dogfighting should not be a crime

Total Votes: 65,211

---

1 **Cristie Kerr cards** a two-under-par 279 defeat Lorena Ochoa and Angela Park by two strokes at the U.S. Women's Open at Southern Pines, N.C. It is the first major title of her career

Mike Hargrove abruptly and surprisingly resigns as manager of the Seattle Mariners winners of eight in a row. He is replaced for the remainder of the season by bench coach John McLaren.

Alex Rodriguez' wife, Cynthia, causes quite a stir when she shows up to a game at Yankee Stadium wearing a white tank top with an obscenity on the back.

2 **Roger Clemens allows** just two hits over eight innings to beat the Minnesota Twins, 5-1 and earn his 350th career win.

3 **Alinghi wins** a thrilling photo finish over Team New Zealand to retain the America's Cup The overall margin of victory is just one second as the Swiss take the best-of-nine series, 5-2.

4 **The 2014 Winter Olympic Games** are awarded to Sochi, Russia. Sochi edges Pyeongchang, South Korea, 51-47, in the final round of voting.

Joey Chestnut brings the Mustard Yellow Belt back to America by downing a record 66 hot dogs to beat defending champ Kobayashi (63) at the annual Nathan's Famous Fourth of July International Hot Dog Eating Contest at Coney Island.

6 **Sabotage in Formula One!** A Ferrari employee is fired after allegedly sending a package of technical information to the rival McLaren team.

Court documents show that a house owned by Falcons quarterback Michael Vick was used as the "main staging area for housing and training the pit bulls involved" in a widespread dogfighting operation.

7 **Venus Williams is back,** beating Marion Bartoli, 6-4, 6-1, in just 90 minutes in the women's Wimbledon final. It's the fourth Wimbledon singles title of her career and her sixth major singles title overall. She was just the 23rd seed entering the tournament.

8 **Roger Federer outlasts Rafael Nadal** in five sets to win his fifth consecutive Wimbledon singles title and 11th major title overall

10 **Ichiro Suzuki hits** the first inside-the-park home run at a Major League Baseball All-Star Game to lead the American League to a 5-4 victory. Carl Crawford and Victor Martinez later add conventional homers. It is the AL's fifth consecutive win since 2002's tie.

AP/Wide World Photos

→ **Jimmie Johnson** leaps from his car after colliding into the wall on turn 3 during the Allstate 400 at the Brickyard on July 29.

13 Gary Sheffield rips the New York Yankees and specifically, manager Joe Torre, in an episode of HBO's *Real Sports*. He claims, among other things, that "[Black players] weren't treated like everybody else," that Derek Jeter "ain't all-the-way black," and that "steroids is something you shoot in your butt."

15 The Philadelphia Phillies are crushed by the St. louis Cardinals, 10-2, for the organization's 10,000th loss.

17 Michael Vick is indicted by a federal grand jury on charges stemming from his role in an illegal dogfighting ring. The indictment reveals a number of gruesome details and alleges that losing dogs were sometimes electrocuted, drowned, hung or shot.

18 Jerry Yang, a psychologist and social worker from California, draws a straight on the river to win the $8.25 million grand prize at the World Series of Poker in Las Vegas.

21 David Beckham makes his debut with the Los Angeles Galaxy in an exhibition match and plays an uneventful 12 minutes.

22 Ireland's Padraig Harrington tops Sergio Garcia in a four-hole playoff to win the British Open and become the first Irish winner of the Claret Jug in 60 years. Two Harrington shots into the Barry Burn and a Garcia miss of an eight-foot putt on the final hole of regulation forces the playoff.

24 NBA Commissioner David Stern holds a news conference to address the fact that former referee Tim Donaghy is being investigated not only for betting on NBA games, but also for providing "information to others for the purpose of allowing them to profit on betting on NBA games." Stern also refers to the incident as an "isolated instance."

29 Alberto Contador wins the drug-plagued Tour de France after race leader Michael Rasmussen is booted by his own team for lying about missing drug tests.

30 Legendary NFL coach Bill Walsh dies of leukemia at age 75.

Kevin Garnett is traded from the Minnesota Timberwolves to the Boston Celtics.

August 2007

Sun	Mon	Tue	Wed	Thu	Fri	Sat
			1	2	3	4
5	6	7	8	9	10	11
12	13	14	15	16	17	18
19	20	21	22	23	24	25
26	27	28	29	30	31	

NBA Game Fixing?

Which scandal has affected its particular sport the most?

- 44.8% — *MLB: Steroids*
- 38.7% — *NBA: Tim Donaghy/fixing*
- 16.4% — *NFL: Michael Vick*

Which statement best fits your view of the Tim Donaghy story?

- 58.5% — *This report is just the tip of the iceberg*
- 30.9% — *This is probably an isolated incident*
- 10.6% — *I have no opinion*

How will this affect your interest in the NBA?

- 55.7% — *It won't affect my interest*
- 23.2% — *I'll still be interested but probably not be as big a fan as before*
- 21.1% — *My interest will decline significantly*

Total Votes: 50,358

2 **The Minnesota Twins**-Kansas City Royal game is postponed a day after the devastating 35W Bridge collapse not far from the Metrodome.

Skateboarder Jake Brown freefalls 40 feet and slams to the floor with such force that his shoes pop off during the Skateboard Big Air competition at the Summer X Games in Los Angeles. He walks away with a broken wrist, a bruised lung and a bruised liver. But he walks away.

4 **Barry Bonds launches** home run No. 755 off San Diego hurler Clay Hensley to tie Hank Aaron's all-time career home run mark.

Former Dallas Cowboys wide receiver Michael Irvin delivers a stirring and at times, tearful speech at his induction into the Pro Football Hall of Fame in Canton.

Alex Rodriguez hits home run No. 500, becoming the youngest player to reach that plateau in major league history.

5 **Tom Glavine becomes** the 23rd pitcher to win 300 games in a career, with the Mets' 8-3 victory over the Chicago Cubs at Wrigley Field. He's only the fifth lefthander to reach that milestone.

"I opened my eyes and I was upside down," said Dario Franchitti. "It looked like I was 30 feet in the air. My first thought was 'This isn't good.'" This comes after Franchitti gets the worst of a seven-car pileup at the Firestone Indy 400 at Michigan.

6 **Jockey Jose Santos** and former Preakness winner Silver Charm highlight the inductees into the National Museum of Racing and Hall of Fame.

7 **Barry Bonds hits home run No. 756** to become Major League Baseball's all-time home run king. The inning was the fifth, the count was 3-2, the pitcher was Washington's Mike Bacsik and the blast cleared the left-centerfield wall at San Francisco's AT&T Park. The Giants would go on to lose the game, however, 8-6.

The Tampa Bay Lightning are sold to Absolute Hockey Enterprises, a group led by former Florida Panthers head coach Doug MacLean.

9 **St. Louis'** Rick Ankiel returns to the major leagues as an outfielder and hits a home run to lead the Cardinals to a 5-0 win over the San Diego Padres.

The D.C. United blank the Los Angeles Galaxy, 1-0, in David Beckham's MLS debut. he plays 21 minutes in the loss.

Long Island Duck **Jose Offerman** pulled a nutty on Aug. 14, attacking pitcher Matt Beech with a bat during an Atlantic League game in Connecticut. He was later charged with assault, and pleaded...not guilty!?!?

12 Tiger Woods wins the PGA Championship at Southern Hills by two strokes over Woody Austin for his 13th major victory. With four PGA Championships, four Masters, three British Opens and two U.S. Opens, he now stands just five back of Jack Nicklaus's all-time major record of 18.

13 Pat Riley announces his intentions to coach the Miami Heat for three more seasons.

Phil Rizzuto, hall of famer, former Yankee shortstop and long-time announcer, dies in his sleep at the age of 89.

15 Former NBA referee Tim Donaghy officially pleads guilty to two felony charges: conspiracy to engage in wire fraud and transmitting betting information through interstate commerce. NBA Commissioner David Stern again refers to Donaghy as a "rogue, isolated criminal."

16 David Beckham finally shows flashes of brilliance, scoring a goal on a free kick and assisting on another to lead the Galaxy to a 2-0 win over D.C. United.

18 Italian defender Marco Materazzi, after more than a year of guessing and speculation, finally reveals what he said to French star Zinedine Zidane to cause the headbutt heard 'round the world at the 2006 World Cup — "I prefer the whore that is your sister."

Roger Federer beats James Blake, 6-1, 6-4 in Cincinnati for the 50th tournament win of his career.

20 Michael Vick pleads guilty to the federal dogfighting charges against him and faces up to 18 months, or more, in prison. Four days later, he is suspended from the NFL.

22 The Texas Rangers crush the Baltimore Orioles, 30-3, setting a new modern-day record for runs scored in a nine-inning game. The Orioles actually held a 3-0 lead at one point. Despite the lopsided score, reliever Wes Littleton still earns a save.

26 Dalton Carriker hits a walk-off homer to propel Warner-Robbins, Ga. to a 3-2 win and the Little League World Series title over Tokyo.

September 2007

Sun	Mon	Tue	Wed	Thu	Fri	Sat
						1
2	3	4	5	6	7	8
9	10	11	12	13	14	15
16	17	18	19	20	21	22
23/30	24	25	26	27	28	29

Oklahoma State Coach Mike Gundy's RANT!

What did you think of Mike Gundy's rant against reporter Jenni Carlson's critical column?

66.6% — *It was appropriate*

25.7% — He overreacted, but he was trying to protect his player

5.9% — Completely inappropriate

1.8% — He underreacted

Which press conference coaching rant is your favorite?

40.7% — *Mike Gundy (I'm a man! I'm 40!)*

25.1% — Jim Mora (Playoffs!?)

15.0% — Dennis Green (The Bears are who we thought they were!)

12.5% — Herm Edwards (You play to win the game!)

4.3% — Rick Pitino (Larry Bird isn't walking through that door!)

2.4% — Lee Elia (#$^*@#$!!)

Total Votes: 45,633

---

1 **Appalachian State stuns** Michigan, 34-32, at the Big House in Michigan. The Wolverines become the first ranked Division I-A team (now known as the Football Bowl Subdivision) to lose to a team from I-AA (now known as the Football Championship Subdivision). The loss drops Michigan from No. 5 in the country to all the way out of the AP Top 25 poll.

Boston rookie Clay Buchholz fires the third no-hitter of the year in a Red Sox 10-0 win over Baltimore.

3 **Pedro Martinez returns** to the New York Mets for the first time of the season and leads his team to a 10-4 win over Cincinnati. He also gets his 3,000th career strikeout for good measure.

5 **The United States women's squad** comes from behind to win the title at the World Gymnastics Championship in Stuttgart, Germany. Shawn Johnson and Alicia Sacramone deliver dazzling performances in the floor exercise routine to bolster the win.

The 1909 Honus Wagner T206 baseball card, sold for $2.35 million in February, is sold once again, this time for $2.8 million.

6 **The 2007 NFL season kicks off** with Peyton Manning and the defending champion Indianapolis Colts picking up right where they left off with a 41-10 win over the Saints.

St. Louis slugger Rick Ankiel continues his rampage on National League pitching as he blasts two home runs and drives in seven in a 16-4 Cardinals win over the Pirates.

The New York Rangers announce plans to retire Brian Leetch's No. 2 at a ceremony on January 24 at Madison Square Garden.

8 **Justine Henin** wins the 2007 U.S. Open without dropping a single set. She pastes Svetlana Kuznetsova, 6-1, 6-3 in the finals. It is her second Grand Slam title of the year and seventh of her career.

9 **Roger Federer makes it a dozen** with a 7-6, 7-6, 6-4 win over Novak Djokovic at the finals of the U.S. Open. It is his fourth consecutive U.S. Open title and 12th major title overall. He now trails only Pete Sampras (14) for the most career men's Grand Slam singles.

Jamaica's Asafa Powell, the world's fastest man, gets even faster, lowering his world record in the 100-meters from 9.77 to 9.74 at the Rieti Grand Prix in Italy.

Dario Franchitti wins his first IndyCar Series points title with his victory at Chicagoland Speedway when race leader Scott Dixon runs out of fuel on the final lap.

AP/Wide World Photos

➡ "Come after me! I'm a man! I'm 40!" Oklahoma State coach **Mike Gundy** took exception to a column written about one of his players in September. And he let everyone know it.

11 Great news for Kevin Everett. Just two days after the Bills tight end suffers what looks to be a life-threatening on-field spinal injury that leaves him with no movement below the shoulders, his prognosis takes a sharp positive turn, as all signs now point to him regaining full movement and eventually walking out of the hospital.

12 Spygate! Three days after the Patriots easily dispose of the Jets, 38-14, the league begins to investigate Jet claims that Patriots video assistant Matt Estrella was specifically given the assignment of videotaping the Jets' defensive coaches as they signaled plays onto the field. Pats coach Bill Belichick offers a terse apology and — no surprise — declined to discuss the matter. A day later, he is fined $500,000, and the team is fined $250,000 and ordered to forfeit their 2008 first-round draft choice (assuming they make the playoffs).

13 It is announced that Portland Trail Blazer Greg Oden will miss the entire 2007-08 season with a knee injury.

15 Dottie Pepper, a former American golfer and current Golf Channel analyst, refers to the American Solheim Cup team as "chokin' freakin dogs."

16 Tiger Woods wins the Tour Championship, and with it, the inaugural FedExCup and its accompanying $10 million top prize.

19 Hendrick Motorsports unveils Dale Earnhardt Jr.'s snazzy green '88' car, sponsored by Pepsi and the National Guard.

20 An arbitrator rules that Floyd Landis must forfeit his 2006 Tour de France title, meaning the official race winner is now Spain's Oscar Pereiro.

27 United States World Cup goalie Hope Solo is benched, and the team is crushed, 4-0, by Brazil. She responds with scathing criticism of coach Greg Ryan.

31 The Mets' stunning collapse is complete as the Phillies win the NL East.

Brett Favre's first of two touchdown passes gives him 421, pushing him over Dan Marino as the NFL's all-time leader.

October 2007

Sun	Mon	Tue	Wed	Thu	Fri	Sat
	1	2	3	4	5	6
7	8	9	10	11	12	13
14	15	16	17	18	19	20
21	22	23	24	25	26	27
28	29	30				

What Does Cheating Mean To You?

What is your first reaction when you see an extraordinary feat by an athlete?

65.4% — *Amazing! That athlete has incredible talent!*

31.1% — That's impressive but I wonder if it is natural.

3.5% — That athlete must be using performance-enhancing drugs.

How do you feel the amount of cheating in professional sports today compares to 20 years ago?

43.9% — *Significantly more now*

25.5% — Slightly more now

25.1% — About the same

4.0% — Slightly less now

1.5% — Significantly less now

Which form of cheating by athletes bothers you more as a fan?

80.6% — *Off-field (drugs, point-shaving)*

13.6% — On-field (stealing signs, flops)

5.8% — Neither bothers me

Total Votes: 89,850

1 **The Colorado Rockies defeat** the San Diego Padres, 9-8, in 13 innings, in a one-game, winner-take-all playoff and advance to the post-season as the National League wild card representative. The Rockies score three in the bottom of the 13th off closer Trevor Hoffman.

2 **A federal jury rules** that Knicks coach Isiah Thomas did, in fact, sexually harass former team executive Anucha Browne Sanders and orders team parent company Madison Square Garden to pay her $11.6 million.

4 **American Olympian Marion Jones,** in a tearful confession, admits to using steroids during the 2000 Summer Games in Sydney, in which she won five gold medals. Her admission comes after years of adamant and often angry denials. "I am sorry for disappointing you all in so many ways," she says. Days later, she publicly returns all of her medals and accepts a two-year ban.

6 **Maybe next year.** The Chicago Cubs lose, 5-1, to the Arizona Diamondbacks and are eliminated from the playoffs in a three-game sweep, extending their World Series drought to 99 years. Elsewhere, the Colorado Rockies complete their sweep of the Philadelphia Phillies.

7 **The Red Sox easily** complete their three-game sweep of the Los Angeles Angels, 9-1.

8 **The Yankees are eliminated** from the postseason in four games by the Cleveland Indians, days after owner George Steinbrenner issues what sounds like a win-or-you're-fired ultimatum for manager Joe Torre. The Indians advance to the American League Championship Series.

9 **An arbitrator rules** that Michael Vick must repay nearly $20 million in bonus money to the Atlanta Falcons.

10 **"Getcha popcorn ready,"** writes Terrell Owens in a note placed in his locker, in anticipation of the Cowboys upcoming game with the New England Patriots. The Pats would go on to defeat the Cowboys, 48-27, for their first loss of the season.

13 **The season of upsets continues** in college football as top-ranked LSU falls to Kentucky, 43-37, in a triple overtime thriller, a week after USC is shocked by Stanford, 24-23.

Evander Holyfield, 44, loses a unanimous decision to WBO heavyweight champ Sultan Ibragimov in Moscow.

14 **Lorena Ochoa wins** the Samsung World Championship by four strokes and clinches her second straight LPGA Player of the Year award.

AP/Wide World Photos

→ The Patriots got some new receivers for the 2007 season, and quarterback **Tom Brady** seemed to gel pretty well with them, throwing for 30 touchdowns by the end of October.

Minnesota rookie Adrian Peterson explodes for 224 rushing yards and three touchdowns in the Vikings' win over the Bears.

15 Dusty Baker is hired as manager of the Cincinnati Reds.

The Colorado Rockies continue their amazing late-season run, winning the 21st of their last 22 games and completing a four-game sweep of the Arizona Diamondbacks to advance to the World Series.

18 Joe Torre rejects New York's one-year, $5 million offer — a $2.5 million pay cut — and is out as manager of the Yankees after a 12-year run that saw him win four World Series titles and advance to the postseason in all 12 years.

20 Notre Dame is pounded, 38-0, at home by USC and falls to an unsightly 1-7.

21 Ferrari's Kimi Raikkonen wins the Brazilian Grand Prix and vaults past McLaren drivers Lewis Hamilton and Fernando Alonso to take the season-long points championship by a single point.

The Red Sox complete their ALCS comeback with a definitive Game 7, 11-2 pasting of the Cleveland Indians to advance to the World Series against the Rockies. Down three games to one, Boston outscores Cleveland, 30-5, over the last three games.

22 Greg Ryan is fired as coach of the U.S. women's national soccer team.

27 Preakness winner Curlin rolls to a victory in the $5 million Breeders' Cup Classic at Monmouth Park and stakes his claim as the 2007 Horse of the Year.

28 The New England Patriots continue to impress, rolling up the points in a 52-7 rout of the Washington Redskins.

The Boston Red Sox win their second World Series title in the last four years with a 4-3 win in Game 4 over the Colorado Rockies. Mike Lowell is named World Series MVP

Alex Rodriguez opts out of his contract with the New York Yankees.

30 Joe Girardi, former NL Manager of the Year, is hired as manager of the NY Yankees.

W2W4: What To Watch For in 2008

AP/Wide World Photos

Tiger Woods *looks to close the gap between his 13 major titles and Jack Nicklaus' 18.*

AP/Wide World Photo.

*Can **Dale Earnhardt Jr.** play nice with his new teammates at Hendrick Motorsports?*

AP/Wide World Photos

*We may have lost Greg Oden for the year, but we still have the NBA arrival of **Kevin Durant**.*

AP/Wide World Photos

*Just how big of a medal haul will **Michael Phelps** grab at the 2008 Olympics in Beijing?*

BASEBALL

Barry Bonds hit his 756th home run on August 7 to pass Hank Aaron and become MLB's all-time home run king.

SOX ROCK

Red Sox Nation rejoices as Boston rolls past Colorado for its second World Series sweep in the last four years.

REMEMBER THE DAYS WHEN BOSTON RED SOX FANS WERE UNIVERSALLY DESCRIBED AS "LONG-SUFFERING?"

And every retrospective of the team's history was sure to include a mention of Bucky Dent's home run off Mike Torrez, Mookie Wilson's groundball through Bill Buckner's legs and Harry Frazee selling Babe Ruth to the Yankees to finance "No No Nanette?"

File that fatalistic mindset under past tense. These days, the suffering is limited strictly to Boston's opponents.

The 2007 Red Sox became the first Major League Baseball team to win two championships this decade by defeating the Colorado Rockies 4-0 in the World Series. The Red Sox outhit the Rockies .333 to .220 and outscored them 29-10 to complete the third Series sweep in four years.

Most observers considered that a fitting conclusion to the season, given the pronounced talent gap between the American and National Leagues.

After being swept by Boston in the Division Series, the Los Angeles Angels of Anaheim entered the off-season looking for a power hitter to complement outfielder Vladimir Guerrero. The New York Yankees cut their ties with manager Joe Torre after losing to Cleveland in the first round. And the Indians, who blew a 3-1 lead to Boston in the American League Championship Series, lamented their 59th straight season without a title.

In the National League, the Philadelphia Phillies became the first professional sports franchise to reach 10,000 losses, but overcame a multitude of injuries to win the NL East for the first time since 1993. They received lots of help from the New York Mets, who blew a seven-game lead with 17 to play to surrender the division.

New York's collapse rivaled that of the 1964 Phillies, who relinquished a 6.5 game lead with 12 to play to fin-

Jerry Crasnick covers baseball for ESPN Insider and is the author of *License To Deal*.

AP/Wide World Photos

Closer **Jonathan Papelbon**, left, and catcher **Jason Varitek** start the Red Sox celebration after the final out of the 2007 World Series.

ish second to St. Louis. As center fielder Carlos Beltran told reporters, "I would have said you're crazy or hated the Mets if you would have said this was going to happen."

The Mets' late fold prompted many New York diehards to turn on manager Willie Randolph for his low-key style and inability to inject his team with the requisite sense of urgency. But shortly after the Mets were eliminated, general manager Omar Minaya announced that Randolph — who still has two years and $4.25 million left on his contract — will be back to manage the Mets in 2008.

The 2007 season brought about a resurgence at Wrigley Field — sort of. The Cubs, whose off-season investment of almost $300 million on free agents produced heightened expectations under new manager Lou Piniella, claimed their first division title since 2003. But the euphoria died when they were swept by Arizona in the opening round.

The National League West, until recently a source of derision in baseball circles, enjoyed a comeback thanks to an influx of young talent. The Rockies posted the best record in franchise history thanks to a largely homegrown roster and a 14-1 run down the stretch, and Arizona tied for the league lead with 90 victories despite being outscored 732-712. Centerfielder Chris Young and shortstop Stephen Drew were among the

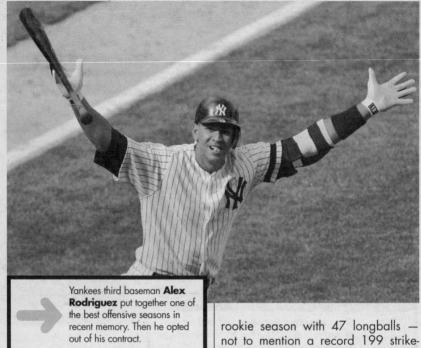

Yankees third baseman **Alex Rodriguez** put together one of the best offensive seasons in recent memory. Then he opted out of his contract.

AP/Wide World Photos

everyday fixtures for manager Bob Melvin's young club.

While Craig Biggio retired and the end appeared to draw near for Roger Clemens, Randy Johnson and other future Hall of Famers, several players in their 20s had coming-out parties.

Detroit outfielder Curtis Granderson and Philadelphia shortstop Jimmy Rollins joined Willie Mays and Frank "Wildfire" Schulte as the only players in history to amass 20 homers, doubles, triples and stolen bases in the same season. Milwaukee first baseman Prince Fielder hit 50 homers, one short of the single-season high posted by his dad, Cecil, with Detroit in 1990. Philadelphia's Ryan Howard followed up his 58-homer

rookie season with 47 longballs — not to mention a record 199 strikeouts. And Milwaukee third baseman Ryan Braun and Colorado's Troy Tulowitzki staged a spirited competition for the National League Rookie of the Year award.

Several young pitchers also made their mark. San Diego's Jake Peavy led the National League with 19 wins and 240 strikeouts, and Boston's Josh Beckett was the only big leaguer to reach 20 victories. In Cleveland, C.C. Sabathia and Fausto Carmona combined to go 38-15 to bring the Indians their first division title since 2001.

In the most bizarre game of the season, Texas beat Baltimore 30-3 in August on the same day the Orioles announced that manager Dave Trembley would be returning in 2008. Best of luck in Baltimore, Skip.

JERRY CRASNICK'S

Biggest Stories of the Year in **Baseball**

10 Cardinal Trouble.

It's a turbulent season for Major League Baseball's defending champions in St. Louis, beginning with manager Tony La Russa's spring training arrest for drunk driving, and ending with his decision to return under a two-year contract.

During the intervening months, reliever Josh Hancock died in an automobile accident, Scott Spiezio entered a drug and alcohol rehab facility, Juan Encarnacion suffered a potentially career-ending eye injury, Rick Ankiel's magical comeback story ended with news that he had received eight shipments of human growth hormone in 2004, and GM Walt Jocketty was fired after 13 seasons running the Cardinals. Oh yeah — St. Louis finished out of the playoffs for only the second time since 2000.

09 All Class.

A record crowd of 75,000 shows up to watch Cal Ripken Jr. and Tony Gwynn deliver their induction speeches as this year's honorees at the Baseball Hall of Fame. Mark McGwire, who should have made it three based on his 583 career home runs, falls victim to steroid allegations and receives a mere 23.5 percent of the vote — far short of the 7.5 percent required for induction.

08 Changes at the Top.

Running a big league team is a bigger challenge than ever, and the position takes its toll on several prominent executives in 2007. Minnesota general manager Terry Ryan calls it quits in mid-September, citing his waning enthusiasm for the job after 13 seasons, and gives way to long-time assistant Bill Smith. In October, Atlanta's John Schuerholz and the Angels' Bill Stoneman move upstairs and pass along their job titles to Frank Wren and Tony Reagins, respectively.

07 No-No's.

Chicago's Mark Buehrle, Detroit's Justin Verlander and Boston rookie Clay Buchholz throw no-hitters, giving baseball three no-nos for the first time since 2001 — when A.J. Burnett, Hideo Nomo and Bud Smith achieved the feat. In addition, Boston's Curt Schilling, Toronto's Dustin McGowan and Minnesota's Scott Baker all have no-hit bids broken up in the ninth inning.

06 Steroids Won't Go Away.

Major League Baseball's steroid saga continues to drag on, with Rick Ankiel, Troy Glaus, Jay Gibbons and Paul Byrd among the players reported to have received shipments of performance enhancing drugs from an anti-aging clinic in Florida. In addition, Yankees first baseman Jason Giambi is hauled into the commissioner's office to explain himself after telling *USA Today* that MLB should apologize to fans for the excesses of the steroid era. Former U.S. Senator George Mitchell's investigation was expected to conclude after the World Series, with the promise of more names, more bombshells and more controversy as baseball tries to put the 90s in proper context and move forward.

05 End of an Era.

Joe Torre's memorable 12-year run in the Bronx comes to an end when he rejects a one-year, $5 million offer to return to the club in 2008. Torre led the Yankees to 12 straight postseason appearances since his arrival in late 1995, when the New York Daily News christened him "Clueless Joe." But owner George Steinbrenner runs out of patience after the Yankees fail to make it out of the Division Series for the third straight season. Twelve days later, he hires Joe Girardi, former N.L. Manager of the Year with the Florida Marlins.

04 Escape From New York.

A-Rod leads the major leagues with 54 homers, 156 RBIs, 143 runs scored and a combined OBP of 1.067. He also prompts agent and master salesman Scott Boras to label him an "IPN" player, short for "Iconic" magnetism, historic "Performance" and "Network" value. The one thing A-Rod lacks, it appears, is timing. Before the Yankees even had a chance to make him an offer, Rodriguez notifies the club of his intention to exercise an opt-out clause in his contract and become a free agent. Strangely enough, Boras and A-Rod make their feelings known just as Boston was winning the deciding game of the World Series.

03 Milestones.

Tom Glavine joins former Atlanta teammate Greg Maddux and 21 others in the 300-win club, and Trevor Hoffman becomes the first closer to record 500 saves. Houston's Craig Biggio logs his 3,000th career hit against Colorado's Aaron Cook, becoming the 27th player to achieve the feat and only the ninth to record all 3,000 for a single club. Sammy Sosa, making a comeback in Texas, passes the 600-homer mark, while Frank Thomas, Jim Thome and Alex Rodriguez expand the list of players in the 500-home run club to 23.

02 Home Run King.

Barry Bonds' long-running pursuit of Hank Aaron comes to a merciful end on Aug. 7 in San Francisco, when he goes deep against Washington's Mike Bacsik for his 756th career homer. While many fans, media members and baseball insiders view the record as tarnished because of Bonds' alleged use of performance-enhancing drugs, Aaron lends the achievement some credibility when he appears via taped message on the outfield scoreboard and offers Bonds his congratulations.

01 Boston Two Party.

The Boston Red Sox beat the upstart Colorado Rockies in four straight games to win their second World Series in four seasons. Third baseman Mike Lowell wins the Series MVP award, and the Red Sox display an effective blend of experience mixed with youth. David Ortiz and Manny Ramirez lead the offense, Josh Beckett anchors the pitching staff, and homegrown players like Dustin Pedroia, Jacoby Ellsbury, Kevin Youkilis and Jonathan Papelbon bring youth, enthusiasm, and a sense of fiscal sanity to the operation.

2007
Season in Review

SPORTS ALMANAC

Final Major League Standings

Division champions (*) and Wild Card (†) winners are noted. Number of seasons listed after each manager refers to current tenure with club.

American League
East Division

	W	L	Pct	GB	Home	Road
*Boston	96	66	.593	—	51-30	45-36
†New York	94	68	.580	2	52-29	42-39
Toronto	83	79	.512	13	49-32	34-47
Baltimore	69	93	.426	27	35-46	34-47
Tampa Bay	66	96	.407	30	37-44	29-52

2007 Managers: Bos—Terry Francona (4th season); **NY**—Joe Torre (12th); **Tor**—John Gibbons (4th); **Bal**—Sam Perlozzo (3rd, 29-40) was fired on June 18 and replaced by bullpen coach Dave Trembley (40-53); **TB**—Joe Maddon (2nd).
2006 Standings: 1. New York (97-65); 2. Toronto (87-75); 3. Boston (86-76); 4. Baltimore (70-92); 5. Tampa Bay (61-101).

Central Division

	W	L	Pct	GB	Home	Road
*Cleveland	96	66	.593	—	51-29	45-37
Detroit	88	74	.543	8	45-36	43-38
Minnesota	79	83	.488	17	41-40	38-43
Chicago	72	90	.444	24	38-43	34-47
Kansas City	69	93	.426	27	35-46	34-47

2007 Managers: Cle—Eric Wedge (4th season); **Det**—Jim Leyland (2nd); **Min**—Ron Gardenhire (6th); **Chi**—Ozzie Guillen (4th); **KC**—Buddy Bell (3rd).
2006 Standings: 1. Minnesota (96-66); 2. Detroit (95-67); 3. Chicago (90-72); 4. Cleveland (78-84); 5. Kansas City (62-100).

West Division

	W	L	Pct	GB	Home	Road
*Los Angeles	94	68	.580	—	54-27	40-41
Seattle	88	74	.543	6	49-33	39-41
Oakland	76	86	.469	18	40-41	36-45
Texas	75	87	.463	19	47-34	28-53

2007 Managers: LAA—Mike Scioscia (7th season); **Sea**—Mike Hargrove (3rd, 45-33) resigned on July 1 and was replaced by bench coach John McLaren (43-41); **Oak**—Bob Geren (1st); **Tex**—Ron Washington (1st).
2006 Standings: 1. Oakland (93-69); 2. Los Angeles (89-73); 3. Texas (80-82); 4. Seattle (78-84).

National League
East Division

	W	L	Pct	GB	Home	Road
*Philadelphia	89	73	.549	—	47-34	42-39
New York	88	74	.543	1	41-40	47-34
Atlanta	84	78	.519	5	44-37	40-41
Washington	73	89	.451	16	40-41	33-48
Florida	71	91	.438	18	36-45	35-46

2007 Managers: Phi—Charlie Manuel (3rd season); **NY**—Willie Randolph (3rd); **Atl**—Bobby Cox (18th); **Wash**—Manny Acta (1st); **Fla**—Fredi Gonzalez (1st).
2006 Standings: 1. New York (97-65); 2. Philadelphia (85-77); 3. Atlanta (79-83); 4. Florida (78-84); 5. Washington (71-91).

Central Division

	W	L	Pct	GB	Home	Road
*Chicago	85	77	.525	—	44-37	41-40
Milwaukee	83	79	.512	2	51-30	32-49
St. Louis	78	84	.481	7	43-38	35-46
Houston	73	89	.451	12	42-39	31-50
Cincinnati	72	90	.444	13	39-42	33-48
Pittsburgh	68	94	.420	17	37-44	31-50

2007 Managers: Chi—Lou Piniella (1st season); **Mil**—Ned Yost (5th); **St.L**—Tony La Russa (12th); **Hou**—Phil Garner (4th, 58-73) was fired on Aug. 27 and replaced by Cecil Cooper (15-16); **Cin**—Jerry Narron (3rd, 31-51) was fired on July 1 and replaced by Pete Mackinen (41-39); **Pit**—Jim Tracy (2nd).
2006 Standings: 1. St. Louis (83-78); 2. Houston (82-80); 3. Cincinnati (80-82); 4. Milwaukee (75-87); 5. Pittsburgh (67-95); 6. Chicago (66-96).

West Division

	W	L	Pct	GB	Home	Road
*Arizona	90	72	.556	—	50-31	40-42
†Colorado	90	73	.552	½	51-31	39-42
San Diego	89	74	.546	1½	47-34	42-40
Los Angeles	82	80	.506	8	43-38	39-42
San Francisco	71	91	.438	19	39-42	32-49

2007 Managers: Ari—Bob Melvin (3rd season); **Col**—Clint Hurdle (6th); **SD**—Bud Black (1st); **LA**—Grady Little (2nd); **SF**—Bruce Bochy (1st).
2006 Standings: 1. San Diego (88-74); 2. Los Angeles (88-74); 3. San Francisco (76-85); 4. Arizona (76-86); 5. Colorado (76-86).
Note: Colorado won the wild card berth with a 9-8, 13-inning victory over San Diego in a one-game playoff.

Interleague Play Standings

American League

	W-L	Pct			W-L	Pct
Detroit	14-4	.778	Cleveland		9-9	.500
Los Angeles	14-4	.778	Seattle		9-9	.500
Boston	12-6	.667	Tampa Bay		7-11	.389
Minnesota	11-7	.611	Baltimore		6-12	.333
Texas	11-7	.611	Chicago		4-14	.222
New York	10-8	.556	**Totals**		**137-115**	**.544**
Toronto	10-8	.556				
Kansas City	10-8	.556				
Oakland	10-8	.556				

National League

	W-L	Pct			W-L	Pct
Chicago	8-4	.667	St. Louis		6-9	.400
Colorado	10-8	.556	San Diego		6-9	.400
Milwaukee	8-7	.533	Cincinnati		7-11	.389
Philadelphia	8-7	.533	Pittsburgh		5-10	.333
New York	8-7	.533	Los Angeles		5-10	.333
Arizona	8-7	.533	San Francisco		5-10	.333
Washington	9-9	.500	Atlanta		4-11	.267
Florida	9-9	.500	**Totals**		**115-137**	**.456**
Houston	9-9	.500				

Detroit Tigers
Magglio Ordonez
Batting Avg.

New York Yankees
Alex Rodriguez
HR, RBI, Runs, SLG, TB

Los Angeles Angels
John Lackey
ERA

Boston Red Sox
Josh Beckett
Wins

American League Leaders

(*) indicates rookie.

Batting

	Bat	Gm	AB	R	H	Avg	TB	2B	3B	HR	RBI	BB	SO	SB	Slg Pct	OBP
Magglio Ordonez, Det	R	157	595	117	216	**.363**	354	54	0	28	139	76	79	4	.595	.434
Ichiro Suzuki, Sea	L	161	678	111	238	**.351**	292	22	7	6	68	49	77	37	.431	.396
Placido Polanco, Det	R	142	587	105	200	**.341**	269	36	3	9	67	37	30	7	.458	.388
Jorge Posada, NY	S	144	506	91	171	**.338**	275	42	1	20	90	74	98	2	.543	.426
David Ortiz, Bos	L	149	549	116	182	**.332**	341	52	1	35	117	111	103	3	.621	.445
Chone Figgins, LA	S	115	442	81	146	**.330**	191	24	6	3	58	51	81	41	.432	.393
Mike Lowell, Bos	R	154	589	79	191	**.324**	295	37	2	21	120	53	71	3	.501	.378
Vladimir Guerrero, LA	R	150	574	89	186	**.324**	314	45	1	27	125	71	62	2	.547	.403
Derek Jeter, NY	R	156	639	102	206	**.322**	289	39	4	12	73	56	100	15	.452	.388
Dustin Pedroia*, Bos	R	139	520	86	165	**.317**	230	39	1	8	50	47	42	7	.442	.380
Carl Crawford, TB	L	143	584	93	184	**.315**	272	37	9	11	80	32	112	50	.466	.355
Michael Young, Tex	R	156	639	40	201	**.315**	267	37	1	9	94	47	107	13	.418	.366
Alex Rodriguez, NY	R	158	583	143	183	**.314**	376	31	0	54	156	95	120	24	.645	.422
Jose Vidro, Sea	D	147	548	78	172	**.314**	216	26	0	6	59	63	57	0	.394	.381
Robinson Cano, NY	L	160	617	93	189	**.306**	301	41	7	19	97	39	85	4	.488	.353

Note: Batters must have 3.1 plate appearances per their team's games played to qualify.

Home Runs

Rodriguez, NY	54
Pena, TB	46
Thome, Chi	35
Ortiz, Bos	35
Konerko, Chi	31
Morneau, Min	31
Dye, Chi	28
Hunter, Min	28
Ordonez, Det	28
Guerrero, LA	27

Triples

Granderson, Det	23
Iwamura*, TB	10
Guillen, Det	9
Crawford, TB	9
DeJesus, KC	9
Three tie with 8 each.	

On Base Pct.

Ortiz, Bos	.445
Ordonez, Det	.434
Posada, NY	.426
Rodriguez, NY	.422
Pena, TB	.411
Thome, Chi	.410
Cust, Oak	.408
Guerrero, LA	.403
Suzuki, Sea	.396

Runs Batted In

Rodriguez, NY	156
Ordonez, Det	139
Guerrero, LA	125
Pena, TB	121
Lowell, Bos	120
Ortiz, Bos	117
Martinez, Cle	114
Markakis, Bal	112
Morneau, Min	111
Hunter, Min	107

Doubles

Ordonez, Det	54
Ortiz, Bos	52
Hill, Tor	47
Guerrero, LA	45
Hunter, Min	45
Rios, Tor	43
Markakis, Bal	43

Slugging Pct.

Rodriguez, NY	.645
Pena, TB	.627
Ortiz, Bos	.621
Ordonez, Det	.595
Thome, Chi	.563
Granderson, Det	.552
Guerrero, LA	.547
Posada, NY	.543

Hits

Suzuki, Sea	238
Ordonez, Det	216
Jeter, NY	206
Young, Tex	201
Polanco, Det	200
Cabrera, LA	192
Lowell, Bos	191
Rios, Tor	191
Markakis, Bal	191
Cano, NY	189

Runs

Rodriguez, NY	143
Abreu, NY	123
Granderson, Det	122
Sizemore, Cle	118
Ordonez, Det	117
Ortiz, Bos	116
Rios, Tor	114
Suzuki, Sea	111
Sheffield, Det	107

Walks

Ortiz, Bos	111
Cust, Oak	105
Pena, TB	103
Hafner, Cle	102
Sizemore, Cle	101
Swisher, Oak	100

Stolen Bases

	SB	CS
Roberts, Bal	50	7
Crawford, TB	50	10
Figgins, LA	41	12
Patterson, Bal	37	9
Suzuki, Sea	37	8
Lugo, Bos	33	6
Sizemore, Cle	33	10
Owens*, Chi	32	8
Crisp, Bos	28	6

Total Bases

Rodriguez, NY	376
Ordonez, Det	354
Ortiz, Bos	341
Granderson, Det	338
Rios, Tor	320
Guerrero, LA	314
Markakis, Bal	309
Pena, TB	307
Hunter, Min	303

Strikeouts

Cust, Oak	164
Sizemore, Cle	155
Upton, TB	154
Inge, Det	150
Peralta, Cle	146

Pitching

	Arm	W	L	ERA	Gm	GS	CG	ShO	Sv	IP	H	R	ER	HR	HB	BB	SO	WP
John Lackey, LA	R	19	9	3.01	33	33	2	2	0	224.0	219	87	75	18	12	52	179	9
Fausto Carmona, Cle	R	19	8	3.06	32	32	2	1	0	215.0	199	78	73	16	11	61	137	5
Dan Haren, Oak	R	15	9	3.07	34	34	0	0	0	222.2	214	91	76	24	3	55	192	10
Erik Bedard, Bal	L	13	5	3.16	28	28	1	1	0	182.0	141	66	64	19	5	57	221	3
C.C. Sabathia, Cle	L	19	7	3.21	34	34	4	1	0	241.0	238	94	86	20	8	37	209	1
Josh Beckett, Bos	R	20	7	3.27	30	30	1	0	0	200.2	189	76	73	17	5	40	194	3
Johan Santana, Min	L	15	13	3.33	33	33	1	1	0	219.0	183	88	81	33	4	52	235	7
Kelvim Escobar, LA	R	18	7	3.40	30	30	3	1	0	195.2	182	79	74	11	3	66	160	9
Scott Kazmir, TB	L	13	9	3.48	34	34	0	0	0	206.2	196	91	80	18	7	89	239	10
Mark Buehrle, Chi	L	10	9	3.63	30	30	3	1	0	201.0	208	86	81	22	5	45	115	1
Justin Verlander, Det	R	18	6	3.66	32	32	1	1	0	201.2	181	88	82	20	19	67	183	17
Gil Meche, KC	R	9	13	3.67	34	34	1	0	0	216.0	218	98	88	22	3	62	156	3
Jeremy Guthrie*, Bal	R	7	5	3.70	32	26	0	0	0	175.1	165	78	72	23	4	47	123	8
Chien-Ming Wang, NY	R	19	7	3.70	30	30	1	0	0	199.1	199	84	82	9	8	59	104	9
Roy Halladay, Tor	R	16	7	3.71	31	31	7	1	0	225.1	232	101	93	15	3	48	139	4

Note: Pitchers must have one inning pitched per their team's games played to qualify.

Wins

Beckett, Bos 20-7
Sabathia, Cle 19-7
Wang, NY 19-7
Carmona, Cle 19-8
Lackey, LA 19-9
Verlander, Det 18-6
Escobar, LA 18-7
Wakefield, Bos ... 17-12
Halladay, Tor 16-7
Batista, Sea 16-11

Appearances

Walker, Bal 81
Downs, Tor 81
Bradford, Bal 78
Vizcaino, NY 77
Gobble, KC 74
Neshek, Min 74
Guerrier, Min 73
Sherrill, Sea 73

Complete Games

Halladay, Tor 7
Sabathia, Cle 4
Escobar, LA 3
Weaver, Sea 3
Buehrle, Chi 3
Blanton, Oak 3
Ten tied with 2 each.

Shutouts

Byrd, Cle 2
Weaver, Sea 2
Lackey, LA 2
Contreras, Chi 2
Nineteen tied with 1 each.

Losses

Cabrera, Bal 9-18
Contreras, Chi 10-17
Jackson, TB 5-15
Washburn, Sea 10-15
Santana, LA 7-14
Millwood, Tex 10-14
Silva, Min 13-14
Seven tied with 13 each.

Innings

Sabathia, Cle 241.0
Blanton, Oak 230.0
Halladay, Tor 225.1
Lackey, LA 224.0
Haren, Oak 222.2
Santana, Min 219.0
Vazquez, Chi 216.2
Meche, KC 216.0
Pettite, NY 215.1
Carmona, Cle 215.0
Shields, TB 215.0

Saves

	SV	BS
Borowski, Cle .45		8
Rodriguez, LA ...40		6
Putz, Sea 40		2
Jenks, Chi 40		6
Jones, Det 38		6
Nathan, Min ...37		4
Papelbon, Bos ..37		3
Rivera, NY 30		4
Accardo, Tor ...30		5
Reyes, TB 26		4
Embree, Oak ...17		4
Soria*, KC 17		4

Walks

Cabrera, Bal 108
Gaudin, Oak 100
Kazmir, TB 89
Jackson, TB 88
Batista, Sea 85
Matsuzaka*, Bos ... 80
Trachsel, Bal 69
Pettite, NY 69
Millwood, Tex 67
Washburn, Sea 67
Verlander, Det 67

HRs Allowed

Santana, Min 33
Vazquez, Chi 29
Shields, TB 28
Danks*, Chi 28
Byrd, Cle 27
Marcum, Tor 27
Bonser, Min 27

Wild Pitches

Verlander, Det 17
Batista, Sea 15
McGowan, Tor 13
Bonderman, Det 12
Wakefield, Bos 10
Haren, Oak 10
Kazmir, TB 10
Tejeda, Tex 10

Hit Batters

Verlander, Det 19
Contreras, Chi 15
Cabrera, Bal 15
Matsuzaka*, Bos 13

Strikeouts

Kazmir, TB 239
Santana, Min 235
Bedard, Bal 221
Vazquez, Chi 213
Sabathia, Cle 209
Matsuzaka*, Bos ... 201
Beckett, Bos 194
Haren, Oak 192
Shields, TB 184
Verlander, Det 183

Opp. Batting Average

Bedard, Bal .... .212
Burnett, Tor .... .214
Santana, Min ...... .225
McGowan, Tor ..... .230
Verlander, Det ..... .233
Vazquez, Chi ...... .242
Beckett, Bos ...... .245
Matsuzaka*, Bos ... .246
Haren, Oak ...... .247
Shields, TB .... .247

WHIP
(Walks + Hits/IP)

Santana, Min 1.07
Bedard, Bal 1.09
Shields, TB 1.11
Vazquez, Chi 1.14
Sabathia, Cle 1.14
Beckett, Bos 1.14
Burnett, Tor 1.19
Haren, Oak 1.21
Guthrie*, Bal 1.21
Carmona, Cle 1.21

Fielding

Put Outs

Morneau, Min 1189
Konerko, Chi 1180
Garko, Cle 1073
Overbay, Tor 1060
Pena, TB 1054
Sexson, Sea....... 1000
Youkilis, Bos...... 995
Casey, Det....... 992
Kotchman, LA 978
Varitek, Bos 937

Assists

Hill, Tor 560
Ellis, Oak 499
Cano, NY 497
Roberts, Bal 457
Peralta, Cle 452
Young, Tex........ 446
Uribe, Chi 443
Pena, KC......... 438
Kinsler, Tex 436
Betancourt, Sea 435

OF Assists

Cuddyer, Min...... 19
Teahen, KC 17
Cabrera, NY 16
Young*, TB 16
Markakis, Bal...... 13
Rios, Tor 11
Upton, TB 11
Granderson, Det 10
Ibanez, Sea........ 10

Errors

Bartlett, Min....... 26
Guillen, Det........ 24
Betancourt, Sea 23
Pena, KC......... 23
Peralta, Cle 19
Young, Tex........ 19
Lugo, Bos 19
Jeter, NY 18
Inge, Det 18

Colorado Rockies
Matt Holliday
Avg., RBI, H, TB

Milwaukee Brewers
Prince Fielder
Home Runs

Philadelphia Phillies
Jimmy Rollins
Runs, Triples

San Diego Padres
Jake Peavy
ERA, Wins, K, WHIP

National League Leaders

(*) indicates rookie.

Batting

	Bat	Gm	AB	R	H	Avg	TB	2B	3B	HR	RBI	BB	SO	SB	Slg Pct	OBP
Matt Holliday, Col	R	158	636	120	216	**.340**	386	50	6	36	137	63	126	11	.607	.405
Chipper Jones, Atl	S	134	513	108	173	**.337**	310	42	4	29	102	82	75	5	.604	.425
Chase Utley, Phi.	L	132	530	104	176	**.332**	300	48	5	22	103	50	89	9	.566	.410
Edgar Renteria, St.L	R	124	494	87	164	**.332**	232	30	1	12	57	46	77	11	.470	.390
Hanley Ramirez, Fla	R	154	639	125	212	**.332**	359	48	6	29	81	52	95	51	.562	.386
Albert Pujols, St.L.	R	158	565	99	185	**.327**	321	38	1	32	103	99	58	2	.568	.429
David Wright, NY	R	160	604	113	196	**.325**	330	42	1	30	107	94	115	34	.546	.416
Miguel Cabrera, Fla	R	157	588	91	188	**.320**	332	38	2	34	119	79	127	2	.565	.401
Todd Helton, Col	L	154	557	86	178	**.320**	275	42	2	17	91	116	74	0	.494	.434
Dmitri Young, Wash.	S	136	460	57	147	**.320**	226	38	1	13	74	44	74	0	.491	.378
Derek Lee, Chi	R	150	567	91	180	**.317**	291	43	1	22	82	71	114	6	.513	.400
Aramis Ramirez, Chi	R	132	506	72	157	**.310**	278	35	4	26	101	43	66	0	.549	.366
Aaron Rowand, Phi	R	161	612	105	189	**.309**	315	45	0	27	89	47	119	6	.515	.374
Freddy Sanchez, Pit	R	147	602	77	183	**.304**	266	42	4	11	81	32	76	0	.442	.343
Carlos Lee, Hou	R	162	627	93	190	**.303**	331	43	1	32	119	53	63	10	.528	.354

Note: Batters must have 3.1 plate appearances per their team's games played to qualify.

Home Runs

Fielder, Mil	50
Howard, Phi	47
Dunn, Cin	40
Holliday, Col	36
Berkman, Hou	34
Cabrera, Fla	34
Braun*, Mil	34
Beltran, NY	33
Soriano, Chi	33
Three tied with 32 each.	

Runs Batted In

Holliday, Col	137
Howard, Phi	136
Lee, Hou	119
Cabrera, Fla	119
Fielder, Mil	119
Hawpe, Col	116
Beltran, NY	112
Atkins, Col	111
Wright, NY	107
Dunn, Cin	106

Hits

Holliday, Col	216
Rollins, Phi.	212
Ramirez, Fla	212
Pierre, LA	196
Wright, NY	196
Reyes, NY	191
Lee, Hou	190
Rowand, Phi	189
Cabrera, Fla	188
Francoeur, Atl	188

Stolen Bases

	SB	CS
Reyes, NY	78	21
Pierre, LA	64	15
Ramirez, Fla	51	14
Byrnes, Ari	50	7
Rollins, Phi	41	6
Victorino, Phi	37	4
Wright, NY	34	5
Taveras, Col	33	9

Triples

Rollins, Phi	20
Reyes, NY	12
Johnson, Atl	10
Roberts, SF	9
Hudson, Ari	9
Amezaga, Fla	9
Hart, Mil	9
Pence*, Hou	9

Doubles

Holliday, Col	50
Uggla, Fla	49
Utley, Phi	48
Ramirez, Fla	48
Gonzalez, SD	46
Rowand, Phi	45
Greene, SD	44

Runs

Rollins, Phi	139
Ramirez, Fla	125
Holliday, Col	120
Reyes, NY	119
Wright, NY	113
Uggla, Fla	113
Fielder, Mil	109
C. Jones, Atl	108

Total Bases

Holliday, Col	386
Rollins, Phi.	380
Ramirez, Fla	359
Fielder, Fla	354
Cabrera, Fla	332
Lee, Hou	331
Wright, NY	330
Soriano, Chi	324
Gonzalez, SD	324

On Base Pct.

Helton, Col	.434
Pujols, St.L.	.429
C. Jones, Atl	.425
Wright, NY	.416
Utley, Phi	.410
Holliday, Col	.405

Slugging Pct.

Fielder, Mil	.618
Holliday, Col	.607
C. Jones, Atl	.604
Howard, Phi	.584
Pujols, St.L.	.568
Utley, Phi	.566
Cabrera, Fla	.565

Walks

Bonds, SF	132
Helton, Col	116
Burrell, Phi.	114
Howard, Phi	107
Dunn, Cin	101
Pujols, St.L.	99

Strikeouts

Howard, Phi	199
Uggla, Fla	167
Dunn, Cin	165
Cameron, SD	160
Bay, Pit	141
Young, Ari	141

Pitching

	Arm	W	L	ERA	Gm	GS	CG	ShO	Sv	IP	H	R	ER	HR	HB	BB	SO	WP
Jake Peavy, SD	R	19	6	2.54	34	34	0	0	0	223.1	169	67	63	13	6	68	240	4
Brandon Webb, Ari	R	18	10	3.01	34	34	4	3	0	236.1	209	91	79	12	5	73	135	3
Brad Penny, LA	R	16	4	3.03	33	33	0	0	0	208.0	199	75	70	9	5	73	135	6
John Smoltz, Atl	R	14	8	3.11	32	32	0	0	0	205.2	196	78	71	18	4	47	197	8
Chris Young, SD	R	9	8	3.12	30	30	0	0	0	173.0	118	66	60	10	7	72	167	7
Roy Oswalt, Hou	R	14	7	3.18	33	32	1	0	0	212.0	221	80	75	14	7	60	154	1
Tim Hudson, Atl	R	16	10	3.33	34	34	1	1	0	224.1	221	87	83	10	8	53	132	5
Cole Hamels, Phi	L	15	5	3.39	28	28	2	0	0	183.1	163	72	69	25	3	43	177	5
Oliver Perez, NY	L	15	10	3.56	29	29	0	0	0	177.0	153	90	70	22	7	79	174	6
Matt Cain, SF	R	7	16	3.65	32	32	1	0	0	200.0	173	84	81	14	5	79	163	12
Adam Wainwright, St.L	R	14	12	3.70	32	32	1	0	0	202.0	212	93	83	13	9	70	136	6
Aaron Harang, Cin	R	16	6	3.73	34	34	2	1	0	231.2	213	100	96	28	8	52	218	12
Ian Snell, Pit	R	9	12	3.76	32	32	1	0	0	208.0	209	94	87	22	8	68	177	12
Ted Lilly, Chi	L	15	8	3.83	34	34	0	0	0	207.0	181	91	88	28	3	55	174	7
Tom Gorzelanny, Pit	L	14	10	3.88	32	32	1	1	0	201.2	214	90	87	18	11	68	135	5

Note: Pitchers must have one inning pitched per their team's games played to qualify.

Wins

Peavy, SD 19-6
Webb, Ari 18-10
Zambrano, Chi 18-13
Francis, Col. 17-9
Penny, LA 16-4
Harang, Cin 16-6
Hudson, Atl. 16-10
Hamels, Phi. 15-5
Lilly, Chi 15-8
Perez, NY 15-10
Maine, NY 15-10
Seven tied with 14 each.

Appearances

Rauch, Wash 88
Rivera, Wash 85
Beimel, LA 83
Broxton, LA 83
Heilman, NY 81
Bell, SD 81
Meredith, SD 80
Moylan*, Atl 80
Qualls, Hou 79
Three tied with 78 each.

Complete Games

Webb, Ari 4
Morris, SF-Pit 3
Lowe, LA 3
Seven tied with 2 each.

Shutouts

Webb, Ari 3
Thirteen tied with 1 each.

Losses

Wells, St.L 7-17
Cain, SF 7-16
Williams, Hou 8-15
Arroyo, Cin 9-15
Willis, Fla 10-15
Olsen, Fla 10-15
Maholm, Pit 10-15

Innings

Webb, Ari 236.1
Harang, Cin 231.2
Hudson, Atl 224.1
Peavy, SD 223.1
Zambrano, Chi 216.1
Francis, Col 215.1
Oswalt, Hou 212.0
Arroyo, Cin 210.2
Penny, LA 208.0
Snell, Pit 208.0

Saves

	SV	BS
Valverde, Ari . . .	.47	7
Cordero, Mil . . .	.44	7
Hoffman, SD . .	.42	7
Saito, LA	.39	4
Cordero, Wash . .	.37	9
Wagner, NY . . .	.34	5
Weathers, Cin . .	.33	6
Isringhausen, St.L .	.32	2
Gregg, Fla	.32	4
Dempster, Chi . .	.28	3
Myers, Phi	.21	3

Walks

Zambrano, Chi 101
Davis, Ari 95
Willis, Fla 87
Lowry, SF 87
Olsen, Fla 85
Zito, SF 83
Hernandez, Ari . . . 79
Perez, NY 79
Cain, SF 79

HR Allowed

Williams, Hou 35
Hernandez, Ari 34
James, Atl 32
Moyer, Phi 30
Eaton, Phi 30
Willis, Fla 29
Olsen, Fla 29

Wild Pitches

Harang, Cin 12
Snell, Pit 12
Cain, SF 12
Davis, Ari 10
Capuano, Mil 10
Lincecum*, SF 10

Hit Batters

Kim, Col-Fla-Ari . . . 16
Zambrano, Chi 14
Willis, Fla 14
Owings*, Ari 14
Four tied with 13 each.

Strikeouts

Peavy, SD 240
Harang, Cin 218
Smoltz, Atl. 197
Webb, Ari 194
Hill, Chi 183
Maine, NY 180
Zambrano, Chi 177
Snell, Pit 177
Hamels, Phi 177

Opp. Batting Average

Young, SD 192
Peavy, SD 208
Perez, NY 229
Zambrano, Chi 233
Cain, SF 235
Hill, Chi 235
Maine, NY 235
Lilly, Chi 236
Hamels, Phi 237
Webb, Ari 237

WHIP
(Walks + Hits/IP)

Peavy, SD 1.06
Young, SD 1.10
Hamels, Phi 1.12
Lilly, Chi 1.14
Harang, Cin 1.14
Smoltz, Atl 1.18
Webb, Ari 1.19
Hill, Chi 1.19
Hudson, Atl 1.22

Fielding

Put Outs

Gonzalez, SD 1470
Helton, Col 1448
Pujols, St.L 1325
LaRoche, Pit 1296
Howard, Phi 1191
Lee, Hou 1165
Fielder, Mil 1163
Delgado, NY 1133
Martin, LA 1065
Berkman, Hou 1015

Assists

Tulowitzki*, Col 561
Rollins, Phi 479
Greene, SD 461
Wilson, Pit 452
Reyes, NY 445
Vizquel, SF 444
Phillips, Cin 433
Furcal, LA 426
Drew, Ari 409
Uggla, Fla 402

OF Assists

Francouer, Atl 19
Soriano, Chi 19
Bay, Pit 13
Byrnes, Ari 12
Rowand, Phi 11
Ethier, LA 10
Victorino, Phi 10
Kearns, Wash 9
Werth, Phi 9
Willingham, Fla 9

Errors

Braun*, Mil 26
Ramirez, Fla 24
Zimmerman, Wash . . 23
Cabrera, Fla 23
Kouzmanoff*, SD . . . 22
Wright, NY 21
Eckstein, St.L 20
Lopez, Wash 20
Furcal, LA 19
Drew, Ari 17

Team Batting Statistics

American League

Team	Avg	AB	R	H	HR	RBI	SB
New York . . .	.290	5717	968	1656	201	929	123
Detroit.	.287	5757	887	1652	177	857	103
Seattle.	.287	5684	794	1629	153	754	81
Los Angeles . .	.284	5554	822	1578	123	776	139
Boston.	.279	5589	867	1561	166	829	96
Baltimore. . . .	.272	5631	756	1529	142	718	144
Cleveland . . .	.268	5604	811	1504	178	784	72
Tampa Bay . .	.268	5593	782	1500	187	750	131
Minnesota . . .	.264	5522	718	1460	118	671	112
Texas	.263	5555	816	1460	179	768	88
Kansas City . .	.261	5534	706	1447	102	660	78
Toronto	.259	5536	753	1434	165	719	57
Oakland	.256	5577	741	1430	171	711	52
Chicago	.246	5441	693	1341	190	667	78

National League

Team	Avg	AB	R	H	HR	RBI	SB
Colorado. . . .	.280	5691	860	1591	171	823	100
New York	.275	5605	804	1543	177	761	200
Los Angeles . .	.275	5614	735	1544	129	706	137
Atlanta	.275	5689	810	1562	176	781	64
Philadelphia . .	.274	5688	892	1558	213	850	138
St. Louis	.274	5529	725	1513	141	690	56
Chicago	.271	5643	752	1530	151	711	86
Florida	.267	5627	790	1504	201	749	105
Cincinnati . . .	.267	5607	783	1496	204	747	97
Pittsburgh . . .	.263	5569	724	1463	148	694	68
Milwaukee . . .	.262	5554	801	1455	231	774	96
Houston.	.260	5605	723	1457	167	700	65
Washington . . .	.256	5520	673	1415	123	646	69
San Francisco .	.254	5538	683	1407	131	641	119
San Diego. . . .	.251	5612	741	1408	171	704	55
Arizona.	.250	5398	712	1350	171	687	109

Team Pitching Statistics

American League

Team	ERA	W	Sv	CG	ShO	HR	BB	SO
Boston	3.87	96	45	5	13	151	482	1149
Toronto	4.00	83	44	11	9	157	479	1067
Cleveland . . .	4.05	96	49	9	9	146	410	1047
Minnesota . . .	4.15	79	38	5	8	185	420	1094
Los Angeles . .	4.23	94	43	5	9	151	477	1156
Oakland	4.28	76	36	4	9	138	530	1036
Kansas City . .	4.48	69	36	2	6	168	520	993
New York	4.49	94	34	1	5	150	578	1009
Detroit	4.57	88	44	1	9	174	566	1047
Seattle	4.73	88	43	6	12	147	546	1020
Texas	4.75	75	42	0	6	155	668	976
Chicago	4.77	72	42	9	9	174	499	1015
Baltimore	5.17	69	30	4	9	161	696	1087
Tampa Bay . .	5.53	66	28	2	2	199	568	1194

National League

Team	ERA	W	Sv	CG	ShO	HR	BB	SO
San Diego . . .	3.70	89	45	1	20	119	474	1136
Chicago	4.04	85	39	2	10	165	573	1211
Atlanta	4.11	84	36	1	6	172	537	1106
Arizona	4.13	90	51	7	12	169	546	1088
San Francisco .	4.19	71	37	5	10	133	593	1057
Los Angeles . .	4.20	82	43	4	6	146	518	1184
New York	4.26	88	39	2	10	165	570	1134
Colorado	4.32	90	39	4	7	164	504	967
Milwaukee . . .	4.42	83	49	3	6	161	507	1174
Washington . . .	4.58	73	46	0	6	187	580	931
St. Louis	4.65	78	34	2	8	168	509	945
Houston	4.68	73	38	2	6	206	510	1109
Philadelphia . .	4.73	89	42	5	5	198	558	1050
Pittsburgh	4.93	68	32	4	5	174	518	997
Cincinnati . . .	4.94	72	34	6	7	198	482	1068
Florida	4.94	71	40	0	4	176	661	1142

Team Fielding Statistics

American League

Team	Pct	TC	E	PO	A	DP	TP
Baltimore. . . .	.987	6085	79	4316	1690	155	0
Boston.	.986	5935	81	4316	1538	145	0
New York . . .	.985	6028	88	4352	1588	174	0
Oakland	.985	6121	90	4344	1687	153	0
Seattle.	.985	6049	90	4303	1656	167	0
Cleveland . . .	.985	6177	92	4388	1697	167	1
Minnesota . . .	.984	6016	95	4310	1611	151	0
Toronto	.984	6301	102	4346	1853	160	0
Detroit.	.984	6076	99	4342	1635	148	0
Los Angeles . .	.983	5956	101	4305	1550	154	0
Kansas City . .	.982	5971	106	4312	1553	160	0
Chicago	.982	6034	108	4322	1604	168	0
Tampa Bay . .	.980	5954	117	4289	1548	155	0
Texas	.980	6158	124	4290	1744	179	0

National League

Team	Pct	TC	E	PO	A	DP	TP
Colorado. . . .	.989	6326	68	4416	1842	180	1
Pittsburgh . . .	.986	6147	83	4343	1721	190	0
Philadelphia. .	.986	6187	89	4375	1723	162	2
San Francisco .	.986	6115	88	4361	1666	148	0
San Diego . . .	.985	6312	92	4454	1766	147	0
Chicago	.984	5969	94	4340	1535	134	0
Cincinnati . . .	.984	5961	95	4349	1517	155	0
Houston.	.983	6186	103	4394	1689	128	0
New York . . .	.983	5976	101	4357	1518	124	0
Atlanta	.983	6143	107	4369	1657	141	0
Arizona.	.983	6064	106	4323	1635	157	0
Washington . .	.982	6016	109	4340	1567	153	0
Milwaukee. . .	.982	5971	109	4333	1529	144	0
Los Angeles . .	.981	6115	114	4350	1651	160	0
St. Louis	.980	6100	121	4307	1672	155	0
Florida	.977	5978	137	4331	1510	159	0

Pct—Fielding Percentage; TC—Total Chances; E—Errors; PO—Put Outs; A—Assists; DP—Double Plays; TP—Triple Plays.

Barry Bonds: All-Time Home Run King

On August 7, 2007, controversial San Francisco Giants slugger Barry Bonds launched home run No. 756 to pass Hank Aaron and become Major League Baseball's all-time home run champ.

762 — By The Numbers

Home:	379
Away:	383
vs Righties:	535
vs Lefties:	227

Opponents (Top 5)

San Diego Padres	87
Washington Nationals (Expos)	65
Los Angeles Dodgers	64
Philadelphia Phillies	64
Cincinnati Reds	59

Pitchers (Top 5)

Greg Maddux	8
John Smoltz	8
Terry Mulholland	8
Curt Schilling	8
Chan Ho Park	8

Parks (Top 5)

AT&T Park (San Francisco)	160
3COM Park (San Francisco)	140
Three Rivers Stadium (Pittsburgh)	89
Qualcomm Stadium (San Diego)	39
Cinergy Field (Cincinnati)	31

By Month (Top 5)

August	148
July	127
May	126
September	119
April	117

By Inning (Top 5)

1st	133
3rd	102
4th	100
5th	85
6th	80

Milestone Home Runs

No.	Date	Pitcher	Opponent
1	6/4/86	Craig McMurtry	at Atlanta
100	7/12/90	Andy Benes	San Diego
200	7/8/93	Jose DeLeon	at Philadelphia
300	4/27/96	John Burkett	Florida
400	8/23/98	Kirt Ojala	Florida
500	4/17/01	Terry Adams	LA Dodgers
600	8/9/02	Kip Wells	Pittsburgh
660	4/12/04	Matt Kinney	Milwaukee
700	9/17/04	Jake Peavy	San Diego
715	5/28/06	ByungHyun Kim	Colorado
756	8/7/07	Mike Bacsik	Washington

ESPN SportsNation

The Nation Speaks...

Did you want Bonds to break the record?

58.5% —	No
41.5% —	Yes

Who was the greater player?

58.3% —	Hank Aaron
41.7% —	Barry Bonds

Who has the greatest chance of breaking Bonds' record? (w/HR totals after 2007)

75.8% —	Alex Rodriguez (518)
11.5% —	None
4.6% —	Albert Pujols (282)
3.4% —	Ryan Howard (129)
3.0% —	Manny Ramirez (490)
0.6% —	David Ortiz (266)
0.4% —	Miguel Cabrera (138)
0.3% —	Andruw Jones (368)
0.3% —	Adam Dunn (238)

Total Votes: 49,898

2007 All-Star Game

78th Baseball All-Star Game. **Date:** July 10 at AT&T Park, San Francisco, Calif.; **Managers:** Jim Leyland, Detroit (AL) and Tony La Russa, St. Louis (NL); **Ted Williams MVP Award:** Ichiro Suzuki (AL) 3-for-3 with the All-Star Game's first-ever inside-the-park home run. **Note:** The league that wins the All-Star Game also secures home-field advantage for the World Series.

American League

	AB	R	H	BI	BB	SO	Avg
Ichiro Suzuki, Sea, cf	3	1	3	2	0	0	1.000
Torii Hunter, Min, cf	2	0	0	0	0	0	.000
Derek Jeter, NY, ss	3	0	1	0	0	0	.333
Mike Lowell, Bos, 3b	1	1	1	0	0	0	1.000
David Ortiz, Bos, 1b	2	0	0	0	0	0	.000
Justin Morneau, Min, 1b	2	0	0	0	0	0	.000
Alex Rodriguez, NY, 3b	3	0	1	0	0	0	.333
Grady Sizemore, Cle, rf-cf	1	0	0	0	0	1	.000
Vladimir Guerrero, LA, rf	3	0	0	0	0	0	.000
Victor Martinez, Cle, ph	1	1	1	2	0	1	1.000
Alex Rios, Tor, rf	0	0	0	0	0	0	—
Magglio Ordonez, Det, lf	2	0	0	0	0	0	.000
Carl Crawford, TB, lf	2	1	1	1	0	0	.500
Ivan Rodriguez, Det, c	2	0	1	0	0	0	.500
Carlos Guillen, Det, ss	2	0	0	0	0	0	.000
Placido Polanco, Det, 2b	1	0	0	0	0	0	.000
Brian Roberts, Bal, 2b	2	1	0	0	0	1	.000
Dan Haren, Oak, p	0	0	0	0	0	0	—
Manny Ramirez, Bos, ph	1	0	0	0	0	0	.000
Jorge Posada, NY, ph-c	3	0	1	0	0	0	.333
TOTALS	36	5	10	5	1	1	.278

National League

	AB	R	H	BI	BB	SO	Avg
Jose Reyes, NY, ss	4	1	3	0	0	0	.750
J.J. Hardy, Mil, ss	0	0	0	0	1	0	—
Barry Bonds, SF, lf	2	0	0	0	0	0	.000
Derrek Lee, Chi, 1b	2	0	1	0	1	0	.500
Carlos Beltran, NY, cf	3	1	1	0	0	0	.333
Orlando Hudson, Ari, 2b	1	0	0	0	1	1	.000
Ken Griffey Jr., Cin, rf	2	0	1	2	0	1	.500
Aaron Rowand, Phi, cf	2	0	0	0	0	1	.000
David Wright, NY, 3b	3	0	1	0	0	0	.333
Freddy Sanchez, Pit, 3b	1	0	0	0	0	0	.000
Prince Fielder, Mil, 1b	1	0	0	0	1	0	.000
Matt Holliday, Col, ph-rf	2	0	0	0	0	1	.000
Russell Martin, LA, c	3	0	0	0	0	1	.000
Brian McCann, Atl, c	1	0	0	0	0	0	.000
Chase Utley, Phi, 2b	2	0	0	0	0	0	.000
Carlos Lee, Hou, ph	1	0	0	0	0	1	.000
Dmitri Young, Wash, ph	1	1	1	0	0	0	1.000
Jake Peavy, SD, p	0	0	0	0	0	0	—
Miguel Cabrera, Fla, ph	1	0	0	0	1	0	.000
Alfonso Soriano, Chi, lf	3	1	1	2	0	1	.333
TOTALS	35	4	9	4	4	9	.257

	1	2	3	4	5	6	7	8	9		R	H	E
American League	0	0	0	0	2	1	0	2	0	–	5	10	0
National League	1	0	0	0	0	1	0	0	2	–	4	9	1

E—Fielder (NL). **LOB**—American 5, National 9. **2B**—Posada (AL); Reyes (NL). **3B**—Beltran (NL). **HR**—Suzuki (AL, 5th inning off Young, 1 on), Crawford (AL, 6th inning off Cordero, 0 on), Martinez (AL, 8th inning off Wagner, 1 on); Soriano (NL, 9th inning off Putz, 1 on). **SB**—A. Rodriguez (AL); Reyes and D. Lee (NL). **SF**—Griffey (NL). **GIDP**—Jeter (AL). **DP**—National 1. **PB**—Posada (AL).

AL Pitching

	IP	H	R	ER	BB	SO
Dan Haren, Oak	2.0	2	1	1	1	2
Josh Beckett, Bos (W, 1-0)	2.0	1	0	0	0	0
C.C. Sabathia, Cle	1.0	1	0	0	0	0
Justin Verlander, Det	1.0	2	1	1	0	0
Johan Santana, Min	1.0	0	0	0	0	2
Jonathan Papelbon, Bos	1.0	1	0	0	0	2
J.J. Putz, Sea	0.2	2	2	2	1	1
Francisco Rodriguez, LA (S, 1)	0.1	0	0	0	2	0
TOTALS	9.0	9	4	4	4	9

NL Pitching

	IP	H	R	ER	BB	SO
Jake Peavy, SD	1.0	1	0	0	0	0
Brad Penny, LA	1.0	0	0	0	0	0
Ben Sheets, Mil	1.0	2	0	0	0	0
Cole Hamels, Phi	1.0	2	0	0	0	0
Chris Young, SD (L, 0-1)	1.0	1	2	2	1	0
Francisco Cordero, Mil	1.0	1	1	1	0	0
Takashi Saito, LA	1.0	0	0	0	0	0
Billy Wagner, NY	1.0	2	2	2	0	1
Trevor Hoffman, SD	1.0	1	0	0	0	0
TOTALS	9.0	10	5	5	1	1

Umpires—Bruce Froemming (plate); Charlie Reliford (1b); Mike Winters (2b); Kerwin Danley (3b); Ted Barrett (lf); Bill Miller (rf). **Attendance**—43,965 (41,777 capacity). **Time**—3:06. **TV Rating**—8.3/15 share (FOX).

Home Run Derby

Results of the 2007 All-Star Home Run Derby held at AT&T Park in San Francisco, Calif. on July 9. Contest includes four sluggers from the American League and four from the National League. Note that length of home runs listed below is in feet.

First Round

	HR	Long
Vladimir Guerrero, Los Angeles (AL)	5	463
Alex Rios, Toronto	5	435
Matt Holliday, Colorado	5	462
Albert Pujols, St. Louis	4*	432
Justin Morneau, Minnesota	4*	430
Prince Fielder, Milwaukee	3	455
Ryan Howard, Philadelphia	3	422
Magglio Ordonez, Detroit	2	422

(Top four advance to second round)

*Pujols won, 2-1, in a swingoff with Morneau.

Second Round

	2R	HR	Long
Alex Rios, Philadelphia	12	17	477
Vladimir Guerrero, LA (AL)	9	14	503
Albert Pujols, St. Louis	9	13	459
Matt Holliday, Colorado	8	13	475

HR from first round are carried over to second.
(Top two advance to Finals)

Finals

	HR	Long
Vladimir Guerrero, Los Angeles (AL)	3	380
Alex Rios, Toronto	2	425

AL Team by Team Statistics

At least 135 at bats or 40 innings pitched during the regular season, unless otherwise indicated. Players who competed for more than one AL team are listed with their final club. Players traded from the NL are listed with AL team only if they have 135 AB or 40 IP. Note that (*) indicates rookie and PTBN indicates player to be named.

Baltimore Orioles

Batting (135 AB)	Avg	AB	R	H	HR	RBI	SB
Nick Markakis	.300	637	97	191	23	112	18
Miguel Tejada	.296	514	72	152	18	81	2
Brian Roberts	.290	621	103	180	12	57	50
Aubrey Huff	.280	550	68	154	15	72	1
Melvin Mora	.274	467	67	128	14	58	9
Corey Patterson	.269	461	65	124	8	45	37
Ramon Hernandez	.258	364	40	94	9	62	1
Jay Payton	.256	434	48	111	7	58	5
Kevin Millar	.254	476	63	121	17	63	1
Jay Gibbons	.230	270	28	62	6	28	0
Paul Bako	.205	156	13	32	1	8	0

Traded: P Trachsel to ChC for IF Scott Moore and P Rocky Cherry (Aug. 31). **Signed:** P Cabrera (Aug. 21).

Pitching (40 IP)	ERA	W-L	Gm	IP	BB	SO
Erik Bedard	3.16	13-5	28	182.0	57	221
Jamie Walker	3.23	3-2	81	61.1	17	41
Chad Bradford	3.34	4-7	78	64.2	16	29
Jeremy Guthrie*	3.70	7-5	32	175.1	47	123
Chris Ray	4.43	5-6	43	42.2	18	44
Steve Trachsel	4.48	6-8	25	140.2	69	45
Daniel Cabrera	5.55	9-18	34	204.1	108	166
Rob Bell	5.94	4-3	30	53.0	24	28
Brian Burres*	5.95	6-8	37	121.0	66	96
Danys Baez	6.44	0-6	53	50.1	29	29
Fernando Cabrera	7.21	1-2	33	43.2	31	48

Saves: Ray (16); Walker (7); Baez (3); Bradford (2) Cabrera and Paul Shuey (1). **Complete games:** Bedard, Trachsel, D. Cabrera and Jon Leicester (1). **Shutouts:** Bedard (1).

Boston Red Sox

Batting (135 AB)	Avg	AB	R	H	HR	RBI	SB
David Ortiz	.332	549	116	182	35	117	3
Mike Lowell	.324	589	79	191	21	120	3
Dustin Pedroia*	.317	520	86	165	8	50	7
Manny Ramirez	.296	483	84	143	20	88	0
Kevin Youkilis	.288	528	85	152	16	83	4
J.D. Drew	.270	466	84	126	11	64	4
Coco Crisp	.268	526	85	141	6	60	28
Jason Varitek	.255	435	57	111	17	68	1
Alex Cora	.246	207	30	51	3	18	1
Royce Clayton	.246	195	24	48	1	12	2
Julio Lugo	.237	570	71	135	8	73	33
Eric Hinske	.204	186	25	38	6	21	3

Acquired: P Gagne and cash from Tex. for P Kason Gabbard, OF David Murphy and OF Engle Beltre (July 31). **Signed:** SS Clayton (Aug. 23).

Pitching (40 IP)	ERA	W-L	Gm	IP	BB	SO
Jonathan Papelbon	1.85	1-3	59	58.1	15	84
Manny Delcarmen	2.05	0-0	44	44.0	17	41
Hideki Okajima*	2.22	3-2	66	69.0	17	63
Javier Lopez	3.10	2-1	61	40.2	18	26
Josh Beckett	3.27	20-7	30	200.2	40	194
Mike Timlin	3.42	2-1	50	55.1	14	31
Eric Gagne	3.81	4-2	54	52.0	21	51
Kyle Snyder	3.81	2-3	46	54.1	32	41
Curt Schilling	3.87	9-8	24	151.0	23	101
Daisuke Matsuzaka*	4.40	15-12	32	204.2	80	201
Jon Lester	4.57	4-0	12	63.0	31	50
Tim Wakefield	4.76	17-12	31	189.0	64	110
Julian Tavarez	5.15	7-11	34	134.2	51	77

Saves: Papelbon (37); Gagne (16); Okajima (5); Delcarmen, Timlin and J.C. Romero (1). **Complete games:** Beckett, Schilling, Matsuzaka and Clay Buchholz (1). **Shutouts:** Schilling and Buchholz (1).

Chicago White Sox

Batting (186 AB)	Avg	AB	R	H	HR	RBI	SB
Rob Mackowiak	.278	237	34	66	6	36	3
Jim Thome	.275	432	79	119	35	96	0
Jerry Owens*	.267	356	44	95	1	17	32
A.J. Pierzynski	.263	472	54	124	14	50	1
Paul Konerko	.259	549	71	142	31	90	0
Jermaine Dye	.254	508	68	129	28	78	2
Tadahito Iguchi	.251	327	45	82	6	31	8
Darin Erstad	.248	310	33	77	4	32	7
Josh Fields*	.244	373	54	91	23	67	1
Scott Podsednik	.243	214	30	52	2	11	12
Juan Uribe	.234	513	55	120	20	68	1
Danny Richar*	.230	187	30	43	6	15	1
Andy Gonzalez*	.185	189	17	35	2	11	1

Traded: IF Iguchi to Phi. for P Michael Dubee (July 28); OF Mackowiak to SD for P Jon Link (July 31). **Signed:** P Myers (Aug. 19).

Pitching (45 IP)	ERA	W-L	Gm	IP	BB	SO
Bobby Jenks	2.77	3-5	66	65.0	13	56
Mark Buehrle	3.63	10-9	30	201.0	45	115
Javier Vazquez	3.74	15-8	32	216.2	50	213
Jon Garland	4.23	10-13	32	208.1	57	98
Matt Thornton	4.79	4-4	68	56.1	26	55
Mike Myers	4.80	4-0	72	54.1	23	27
Boone Logan	4.97	2-1	68	50.2	20	35
Gavin Floyd	5.27	1-5	16	70.0	19	49
John Danks*	5.50	6-13	26	139.0	54	109
Jose Contreras	5.57	10-17	32	189.0	62	113

Saves: Jenks (40); Thornton (2). **Complete games:** Buehrle (3); Vazquez, Garland and Contreras (2). **Shutouts:** Contreras (2); Buehrle and Garland (1).

Cleveland Indians

Batting (160 AB)	Avg	AB	R	H	HR	RBI	SB
Victor Martinez	.301	562	78	169	25	114	0
Chris Gomez	.297	222	21	66	1	21	1
Kenny Lofton	.296	490	86	145	7	38	23
Ryan Garko	.289	484	62	140	21	61	0
Grady Sizemore	.277	628	118	174	24	78	33
Casey Blake	.270	588	81	159	18	78	4
Jhonny Peralta	.270	574	87	155	21	72	4
Jason Michaels	.270	267	43	72	7	39	3
Travis Hafner	.266	545	80	145	24	100	1
Franklin Gutierrez	.266	271	41	72	13	36	8
Kelly Shoppach	.261	161	26	42	7	30	0
Trot Nixon	.251	307	30	77	3	31	0
Josh Barfield	.243	420	53	102	3	50	14
David Dellucci	.230	178	25	41	4	20	2

Acquired: OF Lofton from Tex. for C Max Ramirez (July 28). **Claimed:** IF Gomez off waivers from Bal. (Aug. 10).

Pitching (35 IP)	ERA	W-L	Gm	IP	BB	SO
Rafael Betancourt	1.47	5-1	68	79.1	9	80
Rafael Perez	1.78	1-2	44	60.2	15	62
Fausto Carmona	3.06	19-8	32	215.0	61	137
C.C. Sabathia	3.21	19-7	34	241.0	37	209
Jake Westbrook	4.32	6-9	25	152.0	55	93
Aaron Laffey*	4.56	4-2	9	49.1	12	25
Paul Byrd	4.59	15-8	31	192.1	28	88
Tom Mastny*	4.68	7-2	51	57.2	32	52
Joe Borowski	5.07	4-5	69	65.2	17	58
Cliff Lee	6.29	5-8	20	97.1	36	66
Jeremy Sowers	6.42	1-6	13	67.1	21	24

Saves: Borowski (45); Betancourt (3); Perez (1). **Complete games:** Sabathia (4); Carmona and Byrd (2); Lee (1). **Shutouts:** Byrd (2); Carmona and Sabathia (2).

Detroit Tigers

Batting (135 AB)	Avg	AB	R	H	HR	RBI	SB
Magglio Ordonez	.363	595	117	216	28	139	4
Placido Polanco	.341	587	105	200	9	67	7
Ryan Raburn*	.304	138	28	42	4	27	3
Curtis Granderson	.302	612	122	185	23	74	26
Carlos Guillen	.296	564	86	167	21	102	13
Sean Casey	.296	453	40	134	4	54	2
Ivan Rodriguez	.281	502	50	141	11	63	2
Omar Infante	.271	166	24	45	2	17	4
Gary Sheffield	.265	494	107	131	25	75	22
Mike Rabelo*	.256	168	14	43	1	18	0
Marcus Thames	.242	269	37	65	18	54	2
Brandon Inge	.236	508	64	120	14	71	9
Craig Monroe	.222	343	47	76	11	55	0

Traded: P Maroth to St.L for PTBN (June 23); OF Monroe and cash to ChC for PTBN (Aug. 23).

Pitching (40 IP)	ERA	W-L	Gm	IP	BB	SO
Bobby Seay	2.33	3-0	58	46.1	15	38
Zach Miner	3.02	3-4	34	53.2	22	34
Tim Byrdak	3.20	3-0	39	45.0	26	49
Justin Verlander	3.66	18-6	32	201.2	67	183
Todd Jones	4.26	1-4	61	61.1	23	33
Fernando Rodney	4.26	2-6	48	50.2	21	54
Kenny Rogers	4.43	3-4	11	63.0	25	36
Chad Durbin	4.72	8-7	36	127.2	49	66
Jason Grilli	4.74	5-3	57	79.2	32	62
Nate Robertson	4.76	9-13	30	177.2	63	119
Jeremy Bonderman	5.01	11-9	28	174.1	48	145
Mike Maroth	5.06	5-2	13	78.1	15	33
Andrew Miller*	5.63	5-5	13	64.0	39	56

Saves: Jones (38); Seay, Byrdak, Rodney, Durbin, Aquilino Lopez and Joel Zumaya (1). **Complete games:** Verlander (1). **Shutouts:** Verlander (1).

Kansas City Royals

Batting (140 AB)	Avg	AB	R	H	HR	RBI	SB
Joey Gathright	.307	228	28	70	0	19	9
Mark Grudzielanek	.302	453	70	137	6	51	1
Billy Butler*	.292	329	38	96	8	52	0
Ross Gload	.288	320	37	92	7	51	2
Mark Teahen	.285	544	78	155	7	60	13
Tony Pena Jr.	.267	509	58	136	2	47	5
Esteban German	.264	348	49	92	4	37	11
Mike Sweeney	.260	265	26	69	7	38	0
David DeJesus	.260	605	101	157	7	58	10
Emil Brown	.257	366	44	94	6	62	12
Alex Gordon*	.247	543	60	134	15	60	14
John Buck	.222	347	41	77	18	48	0
Ryan Shealy	.221	172	18	38	3	21	0
Jason LaRue	.148	169	14	25	4	13	1

Acquired: P Davies from Atl. for P Octavio Dotel (July 31).

Pitching (40 IP)	ERA	W-L	Gm	IP	BB	SO
David Riske	2.45	1-4	65	69.2	27	52
Joakim Soria*	2.48	2-3	62	69.0	19	75
Jimmy Gobble	3.02	4-1	74	53.2	23	50
Gil Meche	3.67	9-13	34	216.0	62	156
Zack Greinke	3.69	7-7	52	122.0	36	106
Joel Peralta	3.80	1-3	62	87.2	19	66
Brian Bannister*	3.87	12-9	27	165.0	44	77
Leo Nunez	3.92	2-4	13	43.2	10	37
John Bale	4.05	1-1	26	40.0	17	42
Brandon Duckworth	4.63	3-5	26	46.2	23	21
Odalis Perez	5.57	8-11	26	137.1	50	64
Jorge De La Rosa	5.82	8-12	26	130.0	53	82
Kyle Davies	6.66	3-7	11	50.0	26	40

Saves: Soria (17); Octavio Dotel (11); Riske (4); Gobble, Greinke, Peralta and Duckworth (1). **Complete games:** Meche and Bannister (1). **Shutouts:** none.

Los Angeles Angels

Batting (135 AB)	Avg	AB	R	H	HR	RBI	SB
Chone Figgins	.330	442	81	146	3	58	4
Vladimir Guerrero	.324	574	89	186	27	125	
Howie Kendrick	.322	338	55	109	5	39	
Orlando Cabrera	.301	638	101	192	8	86	2
Garret Anderson	.297	417	67	124	16	80	
Casey Kotchman	.296	443	64	131	11	68	
Reggie Willits*	.293	430	74	126	0	34	2
Maicer Izturis	.289	336	47	97	6	51	
Shea Hillenbrand	.254	197	19	50	3	22	
Gary Matthews Jr.	.252	516	79	130	18	72	1
Robb Quinlan	.247	178	21	44	3	21	
Mike Napoli	.247	219	40	54	10	34	
Erick Aybar	.237	194	18	46	1	19	
Jeff Mathis*	.211	171	24	36	4	23	

Waived: IF Hillenbrand on July 10.

Pitching (40 IP)	ERA	W-L	Gm	IP	BB	SO
Francisco Rodriguez	2.81	5-2	64	67.1	34	9
Justin Speier	2.88	2-3	51	50.0	12	4
John Lackey	3.01	19-9	33	224.0	52	17
Kelvim Escobar	3.40	18-7	30	195.2	66	16
Darren Oliver	3.78	3-1	61	64.1	23	5
Scot Shields	3.86	4-5	71	77.0	33	7
Jered Weaver	3.91	13-7	28	161.0	45	11
Dustin Moseley*	4.40	4-3	46	92.0	27	5
Joe Saunders	4.44	8-5	18	107.1	34	6
Chris Bootcheck*	4.77	3-3	51	77.1	24	5
Ervin Santana	5.76	7-14	28	150.0	58	12
Bartolo Colon	6.34	6-8	19	99.1	29	7

Saves: Rodriguez (40); Shields (2); Marc Gwyn (1). **Complete games:** Escobar (3); Lackey (2). **Shutouts:** Lackey (2); Escobar (1).

Minnesota Twins

Batting (135 AB)	Avg	AB	R	H	HR	RBI	SB
Luis Castillo	.304	349	54	106	0	18	
Mike Redmond	.294	272	23	80	1	38	
Joe Mauer	.293	406	62	119	7	60	
Torii Hunter	.287	600	94	172	28	107	1
Jason Tyner	.286	304	42	87	1	22	
Michael Cuddyer	.276	547	87	151	16	81	
Jason Kubel	.273	418	49	114	13	65	
Justin Morneau	.271	590	84	160	31	111	
Jason Bartlett	.265	510	75	135	5	43	2
Jeff Cirillo	.261	153	18	40	2	21	
Alexi Casilla*	.222	189	15	42	0	9	1
Luis Rodriguez	.219	155	18	34	2	12	
Nick Punto	.210	472	53	99	1	25	1

Traded: IF Castillo to NYM for C Drew Butera and C Dustin Martin (July 30); P Ortiz to Col. for IF Matt Mac (Aug. 15). **Waived:** IF Cirillo (Aug. 3).

Pitching (40 IP)	ERA	W-L	Gm	IP	BB	SO
Joe Nathan	1.88	4-2	68	71.2	19	7
Matt Guerrier	2.35	2-4	73	88.0	21	6
Pat Neshek	2.94	7-2	74	70.1	27	7
Johan Santana	3.33	15-13	33	219.0	52	23
Matt Garza*	3.69	5-7	16	83.0	32	6
Carlos Silva	4.19	13-14	33	202.0	36	8
Scott Baker	4.26	9-9	24	143.2	29	10
Kevin Slowey*	4.73	4-1	13	66.2	11	4
Boof Bonser	5.10	8-12	31	173.0	65	13
Juan Rincon	5.13	3-3	63	59.2	28	4
Ramon Ortiz	5.14	4-4	28	91.0	15	4

Saves: Nathan (37), Guerrier (1). **Complete games:** Silva and Baker (2); Santana (1). **Shutouts:** Santana, Silva and Baker (1).

New York Yankees

Batting (135 AB)	Avg	AB	R	H	HR	RBI	SB
Jorge Posada	.338	506	91	171	20	90	2
Derek Jeter	.322	639	102	206	12	73	15
Alex Rodriguez	.314	583	143	183	54	156	24
Robinson Cano	.306	617	93	189	19	97	4
Andy Phillips	.292	185	27	54	2	25	0
Hideki Matsui	.285	547	100	156	25	103	4
Bobby Abreu	.283	605	123	171	16	101	25
Doug Mientkiewicz	.277	166	26	46	5	24	0
Melky Cabrera	.273	545	66	149	8	73	13
Johnny Damon	.270	533	93	144	12	63	27
Jose Molina	.257	191	18	49	1	19	2
Jason Giambi	.236	254	31	60	14	39	1

Acquired: C Molina from LAA for P Jeff Kennard (July 22).
Traded: P Proctor to LAD for IF Wilson Betemit (July 31).

Pitching (40 IP)	ERA	W-L	Gm	IP	BB	SO
Mariano Rivera	3.15	3-4	67	71.1	12	74
Chien-Ming Wang	3.70	19-7	30	199.1	59	104
Scott Proctor	3.81	2-5	52	54.1	29	37
Andy Pettitte	4.05	15-9	36	215.1	69	141
Roger Clemens	4.18	6-6	18	99.0	31	68
Ron Villone	4.25	0-0	37	42.1	18	25
Luis Vizcaino	4.30	8-2	77	75.1	43	62
Phil Hughes*	4.46	5-3	13	72.2	29	58
Brian Bruney	4.68	3-2	58	50.0	37	39
Kyle Farnsworth	4.80	2-1	64	60.0	27	48
Mike Mussina	5.15	11-10	28	152.0	35	91
Kei Igawa*	6.25	2-3	14	67.2	37	53

Saves: Rivera (30); Jose Veras (2); Joba Chamberlain and Edwar Ramirez (1). **Complete games:** Wang (1). **Shutouts:** none.

Oakland Athletics

Batting (135 AB)	Avg	AB	R	H	HR	RBI	SB
Shannon Stewart	.290	576	79	167	12	48	11
Travis Buck*	.288	285	41	82	7	34	4
Jack Hannahan*	.278	144	16	40	3	24	1
Mark Ellis	.276	583	84	161	19	76	9
Mike Piazza	.275	309	33	85	8	44	0
Nick Swisher	.262	539	84	141	22	78	3
Marco Scutaro	.260	338	49	88	7	41	2
Jack Cust	.256	395	61	101	26	82	0
Kurt Suzuki	.249	213	27	53	7	39	0
Eric Chavez	.240	341	43	82	15	46	4
Dan Johnson	.236	416	53	98	18	62	0
Bobby Crosby	.226	349	40	79	8	31	10
Jason Kendall	.226	292	24	66	2	23	3
Mark Kotsay	.214	206	20	44	1	20	1

Claimed: P Lugo off waivers from TB (June 14). **Traded:** C Kendall and cash to ChC for C Rob Bowen and P Jerry Blevins (July 17).

Pitching (40 IP)	ERA	W-L	Gm	IP	BB	SO
Huston Street	2.88	5-2	48	50.0	12	63
Dan Haren	3.07	15-9	34	222.2	55	192
Joe Blanton	3.95	14-10	34	230.0	40	140
Alan Embree	3.97	1-2	68	68.0	19	51
Lenny DiNardo	4.11	8-10	35	131.1	50	59
Chad Gaudin	4.42	11-13	34	199.1	100	154
Santiago Casilla*	4.44	3-1	46	50.2	23	52
Andrew Brown*	4.54	3-3	33	41.2	17	43
Ruddy Lugo	5.40	6-0	38	48.1	37	34
Kiko Calero	5.75	1-5	46	40.2	21	31
Jay Marshall*	6.43	1-2	51	42.0	22	18
Dallas Braden*	6.72	1-8	20	72.1	26	55

Saves: Embree (17); Street (16); Casilla (2); Calero (1). **Complete games:** Blanton (3); Gaudin (1). **Shutouts:** Blanton (1).

Seattle Mariners

Batting (135 AB)	Avg	AB	R	H	HR	RBI	SB
Ichiro Suzuki	.351	678	111	238	6	68	37
Jose Vidro	.314	548	78	172	6	59	0
Raul Ibanez	.291	573	80	167	21	105	0
Jose Guillen	.290	593	84	172	23	99	5
Yuniesky Betancourt	.289	536	72	155	9	67	5
Kenji Johjima	.287	485	52	139	14	61	0
Willie Bloomquist	.277	173	28	48	2	13	7
Adrian Beltre	.276	595	87	164	26	99	14
Ben Broussard	.275	240	27	66	7	29	2
Jose Lopez	.252	524	58	132	11	62	2
Richie Sexson	.205	434	58	89	21	63	1

Acquired: P Parrish from Bal. for OF Sebastien Boucher (Aug. 10).

Pitching (40 IP)	ERA	W-L	Gm	IP	BB	SO
J.J. Putz	1.38	6-1	68	71.2	13	82
George Sherrill	2.36	2-0	73	45.2	17	56
Sean Green	3.84	5-2	64	68.0	34	53
Felix Hernandez	3.92	14-7	30	190.1	53	165
Brandon Morrow*	4.12	3-4	60	63.1	50	66
Miguel Batista	4.29	16-11	33	193.0	85	133
Jarrod Washburn	4.32	10-15	32	193.2	67	114
Eric O'Flaherty*	4.47	7-1	56	52.1	20	36
Cha Seung Baek	5.15	4-4	14	73.1	14	49
John Parrish	5.71	2-2	53	52.0	37	41
Jeff Weaver	6.20	7-13	27	146.2	35	80
Horacio Ramirez	7.16	8-7	20	98.0	42	40
Ryan Feierabend*	8.03	1-6	13	49.1	23	27

Saves: Putz (40); Sherrill (3). **Complete games:** Weaver (3); Hernandez, Washburn and Baek (1). **Shutouts:** Weaver (2); Hernandez and Washburn (1).

Tampa Bay Devil Rays

Batting (135 AB)	Avg	AB	R	H	HR	RBI	SB
Carl Crawford	.315	584	93	184	11	80	50
B.J. Upton	.300	474	86	142	24	82	22
Delmon Young*	.288	645	65	186	13	93	10
Brendan Harris	.286	521	72	149	12	59	4
Akinori Iwamura*	.285	491	82	140	7	34	12
Carlos Pena	.282	490	99	138	46	121	1
Ty Wigginton	.275	378	47	104	16	49	1
Josh Wilson*	.251	263	25	66	2	24	6
Jonny Gomes	.244	348	46	85	17	49	12
Greg Norton	.243	202	25	49	4	23	1
Dioner Navarro	.227	388	46	88	9	44	3
Rocco Baldelli	.204	137	16	28	5	12	4
Elijah Dukes*	.190	184	27	35	10	21	2

Claimed: IF Wilson off waivers from Wash. (May 10).
Traded: IF Wigginton to Hou. for P Dan Wheeler (July 29).

Pitching (40 IP)	ERA	W-L	Gm	IP	BB	SO
Scott Kazmir	3.48	13-9	34	206.2	89	239
James Shields	3.85	12-8	31	215.0	36	184
Gary Glover	4.89	6-5	67	77.1	27	51
Al Reyes	4.90	2-4	61	60.2	21	70
Edwin Jackson	5.76	5-15	32	161.0	88	128
Andy Sonnanstine*	5.85	6-10	22	130.2	26	97
Jason Hammel*	6.14	3-5	24	85.0	40	64
Brian Stokes*	7.07	2-7	59	62.1	25	35
Shawn Camp	7.20	0-3	50	40.0	18	36
J.P. Howell	7.59	1-6	10	51.0	21	49
Casey Fossum	7.70	5-8	40	76.0	27	53
Jae Seo	8.13	3-4	11	52.0	16	28

Saves: Reyes (26); Glover (2). **Complete games:** Shields and Jackson (1). **Shutouts:** Jackson (1).

Texas Rangers

Batting (135 AB)	Avg	AB	R	H	HR	RBI	SB
Michael Young	.315	639	80	201	9	94	13
Marlon Byrd	.307	414	60	127	10	70	5
Mark Teixeira	.297	286	48	85	13	49	0
Hank Blalock	.293	208	32	61	10	33	4
Ian Kinsler	.263	483	96	127	20	61	23
Frank Catalanotto	.260	331	52	86	11	44	2
Travis Metcalf*	.255	161	25	41	5	21	0
Sammy Sosa	.252	412	53	104	21	92	0
Jarrod Saltalamacchia*	.251	167	28	42	7	21	0
Jason Botts	.240	167	19	40	2	14	1
Nelson Cruz	.235	307	35	72	9	34	2
Brad Wilkerson	.234	338	54	79	20	62	4
Ramon Vazquez	.230	300	42	69	8	28	1
Gerald Laird	.224	407	48	91	9	47.	6
Jerry Hairston Jr.	.189	159	22	30	3	16	5

Acquired: C Saltalamacchia and 4 minor leaguers from Atl. for IF Teixeira and R Ron Mahay (July 31); P Gabbard, OF David Murphy and OF Engle Beltre from Bos. for P Eric Gagne and cash (July 31).

Pitching (50 IP)	ERA	W-L	Gm	IP	BB	SO
Joaquin Benoit	2.85	7-4	70	82.0	28	87
C.J. Wilson	3.03	2-1	66	68.1	33	63
Jamey Wright	3.62	4-5	20	77.0	41	39
Frank Francisco	4.55	1-1	59	59.1	38	49
Kason Gabbard*	4.65	6-1	15	81.1	41	55
Brandon McCarthy	4.87	5-10	23	101.2	48	59
Kevin Millwood	5.16	10-14	31	172.2	67	123
Willie Eyre	5.16	4-6	33	68.0	32	42
Mike Wood	5.33	3-2	21	50.2	15	25
Kameron Loe	5.36	6-11	28	136.0	56	78
John Rheinecker	5.36	4-3	23	50.1	28	40
Vicente Padilla	5.76	6-10	23	120.1	50	71
Robinson Tejeda	6.61	5-9	19	95.1	60	69

Saves: Wilson (12); Benoit (6); Akinori Otsuka (4); Littleton (2); Eyre (1). **Complete games:** Gabbard (1). **Shutouts:** Gabbard (1).

Toronto Blue Jays

Batting (100 AB)	Avg	AB	R	H	HR	RBI	SB
Alex Rios	.297	643	114	191	24	85	17
Aaron Hill	.291	608	87	177	17	78	
Matt Stairs	.289	357	58	103	21	64	
Frank Thomas	.277	531	63	147	26	95	
Troy Glaus	.262	385	60	101	20	62	
John McDonald	.251	327	32	82	1	31	7
Vernon Wells	.245	584	85	143	16	80	10
Gregg Zaun	.242	331	43	80	10	52	
Lyle Overbay	.240	425	49	102	10	44	2
Adam Lind*	.238	290	34	69	11	46	
Curtis Thigpen*	.238	101	13	24	0	11	
Reed Johnson	.236	275	31	65	2	14	
Jason Phillips	.208	144	11	30	1	12	

Signed: P Kennedy (Aug. 29).

Pitching (30 IP)	ERA	W-L	Gm	IP	BB	SO
Jeremy Accardo	2.14	4-4	64	67.1	24	5
Scott Downs	2.17	4-2	81	58.0	24	5
Casey Janssen	2.35	2-3	70	72.2	20	39
Brian Wolfe*	2.98	3-1	38	45.1	9	22
Brian Tallet	3.47	2-4	48	62.1	28	5
Roy Halladay	3.71	16-7	31	225.1	48	139
A.J. Burnett	3.75	10-8	25	165.2	66	176
Jesse Litsch*	3.81	7-9	20	111.0	36	5
Dustin McGowan	4.08	12-10	27	169.2	61	144
Shaun Marcum	4.13	12-6	38	159.0	49	122
Jason Frasor	4.58	1-5	51	57.0	23	5
Joe Kennedy	4.80	4-9	39	110.2	55	5
Josh Towers	5.38	5-10	25	107.0	22	76
Tomo Ohka	5.79	2-5	10	56.0	22	2

Saves: Accardo (30); Janssen (6); Frasor and B.J. Ryan (3); Downs and Marcum (1). **Complete games:** Halladay (7); Burnett and McGowan (2). **Shutouts:** Halladay and McGowan (1).

Home Attendance

Overall 2007 Major League Baseball regular season attendance (based on tickets sold) was 79,502,524, the highest total in history. It is the fourth consecutive season that the attendance record has been broken. The average per game crowd was 32,785. Numbers in parentheses indicate ranking in 2006. HD indicates home dates.

American League

		Attendance	HD	Average
1	New York (1)	4,271,083	81	52,729
2	Los Angeles (2)	3,365,632	81	41,551
3	Detroit (5)	3,047,133	81	37,619
4	Boston (4)	2,970,755	81	36,676
5	Chicago (3)	2,684,395	81	33,141
6	Seattle (6)	2,672,279	81	32,991
7	Toronto (8)	2,360,644	81	29,144
8	Texas (7)	2,353,862	79	29,796
9	Minnesota (9)	2,296,383	81	28,350
10	Cleveland (11)	2,275,912	80	28,449
11	Baltimore (10)	2,164,822	80	27,060
12	Oakland (12)	1,921,834	81	23,726
13	Kansas City (13)	1,616,867	81	19,961
14	Tampa Bay (14)	1,387,603	81	17,131
	TOTALS	35,389,204	1130	31,318

National League

		Attendance	HD	Average
1	Los Angeles (1)	3,857,036	81	47,618
2	New York (3)	3,853,937	81	47,579
3	St. Louis (2)	3,552,180	81	43,854
4	Chicago (5)	3,252,462	81	40,154
5	San Francisco (4)	3,223,215	81	39,793
6	Philadelphia (7)	3,108,325	81	38,374
7	Houston (6)	3,020,405	81	37,289
8	Milwaukee (10)	2,869,144	81	35,422
9	San Diego (8)	2,790,074	81	34,445
10	Atlanta (9)	2,745,207	81	33,891
11	Colorado (13)	2,376,250	82	28,979
12	Arizona (14)	2,325,233	81	28,707
13	Cincinnati (12)	2,058,593	81	25,415
14	Washington (11)	1,961,606	81	24,217
15	Pittsburgh (15)	1,749,142	79	22,141
16	Florida (16)	1,370,511	81	16,920
	TOTALS	44,113,320	1295	34,064

NL Team by Team Statistics

At least 135 at bats or 40 innings pitched during the regular season unless otherwise indicated. Players who competed for more than one NL team are listed with their final club. Players traded from the AL are listed with NL team only if they have 135 AB or 40 IP. Note that (*) indicates rookie and PTBN indicates player to be named.

Arizona Diamondbacks

Batting (135 AB)	Avg	AB	R	H	HR	RBI	SB
Orlando Hudson	.294	517	69	152	10	63	10
Eric Byrnes	.286	626	103	179	21	83	50
Conor Jackson	.284	415	56	118	15	60	2
Mark Reynolds*	.279	366	62	102	17	62	0
Chad Tracy	.264	227	30	60	7	35	0
Chris Snyder	.252	326	37	82	13	47	0
Tony Clark	.249	221	31	55	17	51	0
Stephen Drew	.238	543	60	129	12	60	9
Chris Young*	.237	569	85	135	32	68	27
Miguel Montero*	.224	214	30	48	10	37	0
Justin Upton*	.221	140	17	31	2	11	2
Alberto Callaspo*	.215	144	10	31	0	7	1
Carlos Quentin	.214	229	29	49	5	31	2

Signed: P Wickman (Sept. 7).

Pitching (40 IP)	ERA	W-L	Gm	IP	BB	SO
Jose Valverde	2.66	1-4	65	64.1	26	78
Brandon Lyon	2.68	6-4	73	74.0	22	40
Brandon Webb	3.01	18-10	34	236.1	72	194
Juan Cruz	3.10	6-1	53	61.0	32	87
Tony Pena	3.27	5-4	75	85.1	31	63
Bob Wickman	3.58	3-4	57	50.1	21	37
Randy Johnson	3.81	4-3	10	56.2	13	72
Doug Davis	4.25	13-12	33	192.2	95	144
Micah Owings*	4.30	8-8	29	152.2	50	106
Yusmeiro Petit	4.58	3-4	14	57.0	18	40
Livan Hernandez	4.93	11-11	33	204.1	79	90
Edgar Gonzalez	5.03	8-4	32	102.0	28	62
Dustin Nippert*	5.56	1-1	36	45.1	16	38

Saves: Valverde (27); Wickman (20); Lyon and Pena (2). **Complete games:** Webb (4); Owings (2); Hernandez (1). **Shutouts:** Webb (3); Owings (1).

Atlanta Braves

Batting (140 AB)	Avg	AB	R	H	HR	RBI	SB
Matt Diaz	.338	358	44	121	12	45	4
Chipper Jones	.337	513	108	173	29	102	5
Edgar Renteria	.332	494	87	164	12	57	11
Yunel Escobar*	.326	319	54	104	5	28	5
Mark Teixeira	.317	208	38	66	17	56	0
Jeff Francoeur	.293	642	84	188	19	105	5
J. Saltalamacchia*	.284	141	11	40	4	12	0
Kelly Johnson	.276	521	91	144	16	68	9
Willie Harris	.270	344	56	93	2	32	17
Brian McCann	.270	504	51	136	18	92	0
Andruw Jones	.222	572	83	127	26	94	5
Scott Thorman	.216	287	37	62	11	36	1

Traded: IF Teixeira and R Ron Mahay from Tex. for C Saltalamacchia and 4 minor leaguers (July 31); P Davies to KC for P Octavio Dotel (July 31).

Pitching (40 IP)	ERA	W-L	Gm	IP	BB	SO
Peter Moylan*	1.80	5-3	80	90.0	31	63
Rafael Soriano	3.00	3-3	71	72.0	15	70
John Smoltz	3.11	14-8	32	205.2	47	197
Tim Hudson	3.33	16-10	34	224.1	53	132
Chad Paronto	3.57	3-1	41	40.1	19	14
Chuck James	4.24	11-10	30	161.1	58	116
Oscar Villarreal	4.24	2-2	51	76.1	32	58
Tyler Yates	5.18	2-3	75	66.0	31	69
Buddy Carlyle	5.21	8-7	22	107.0	32	74
Kyle Davies	5.76	4-8	17	86.0	44	59
Jo-Jo Reyes*	6.22	2-2	11	50.2	30	27
Lance Cormier	7.09	2-6	10	45.2	22	27

Saves: Soriano (9); Yates and Mike Gonzalez (2); Moylan, Paronto and Villarreal (1). **Complete games:** Hudson (1). **Shutouts:** Hudson (1).

Chicago Cubs

Batting (135 AB)	Avg	AB	R	H	HR	RBI	SB
Derrek Lee	.317	567	91	180	22	82	6
Aramis Ramirez	.310	506	72	157	26	101	0
Alfonso Soriano	.299	579	97	173	33	70	19
Mark DeRosa	.293	502	64	147	10	72	1
Jacque Jones	.285	453	52	129	5	66	6
Cliff Floyd	.284	282	40	80	9	45	0
Matt Murton	.281	235	35	66	8	22	1
Mike Fontenot*	.278	234	32	65	3	29	5
Jason Kendall	.270	174	21	47	1	19	0
Ryan Theriot	.266	537	80	143	3	45	28
Angel Pagan	.264	148	21	39	4	21	4
Felix Pie*	.215	177	26	38	2	20	8

Acquired: C Kendall and cash from Oak. for C Rob Bowen and P Jerry Blevins (July 17).

Pitching (40 IP)	ERA	W-L	Gm	IP	BB	SO
Carlos Marmol	1.43	5-1	59	69.1	35	96
Bob Howry	3.32	6-7	78	81.1	19	72
Michael Wuertz	3.48	2-3	73	72.1	35	79
Ted Lilly	3.83	15-8	34	207.0	55	174
Sean Marshall	3.92	7-8	21	103.1	35	67
Rich Hill	3.92	11-8	32	195.0	63	183
Carlos Zambrano	3.95	18-13	34	216.1	101	177
Scott Eyre	4.13	2-1	55	52.1	35	45
Jason Marquis	4.60	12-9	34	191.2	76	109
Ryan Dempster	4.73	2-7	66	66.2	30	55

Saves: Dempster (28); Howry (8); Marmol, Will Ohman and Sean Gallagher (1). **Complete games:** Zambrano and Marquis (1). **Shutouts:** Marquis (1).

Cincinnati Reds

Batting (135 AB)	Avg	AB	R	H	HR	RBI	SB
Jeff Keppinger	.332	241	39	80	5	32	2
Norris Hopper*	.329	307	51	101	0	14	14
Scott Hatteberg	.310	361	50	112	10	47	0
Josh Hamilton*	.292	298	52	87	19	47	3
Edwin Encarnacion	.289	502	66	145	16	76	8
Brandon Phillips	.288	650	107	187	30	94	32
Ken Griffey Jr.	.277	528	78	146	30	93	6
Javier Valentin	.276	243	19	67	2	34	0
Alex Gonzalez	.272	393	55	107	16	55	0
Adam Dunn	.264	522	101	138	40	106	9
Ryan Freel	.245	277	44	68	3	16	15

Waived: P Santos (Aug. 21).

Pitching (40 IP)	ERA	W-L	Gm	IP	BB	SO
Jared Burton*	2.51	4-2	47	43.0	22	36
David Weathers	3.59	2-6	70	77.2	27	48
Aaron Harang	3.73	16-6	34	231.2	52	218
Bronson Arroyo	4.23	9-15	34	210.2	63	156
Jon Coutlangus*	4.39	4-2	64	41.0	27	38
Victor Santos	5.14	1-4	32	49.0	23	44
Bobby Livingston*	5.27	3-3	10	56.1	8	27
Matt Belisle	5.32	8-9	30	177.2	43	125
Homer Bailey*	5.76	4-2	9	45.1	28	28
Todd Coffey	5.82	2-1	58	51.0	19	43
Mike Stanton	5.93	1-3	69	57.2	18	40
Kirk Saarloos	7.17	1-5	34	42.2	19	27

Saves: Weathers (33); Bill Bray (1). **Complete games:** Harang (2); Arroyo and Belisle (1). **Shutouts:** Harang (1).

Colorado Rockies

Batting (135 AB)

	Avg	AB	R	H	HR	RBI	SB
Matt Holliday	.340	636	120	216	36	137	11
Willy Taveras	.320	372	64	119	2	24	33
Todd Helton	.320	557	86	178	17	91	0
Garrett Atkins	.301	605	83	182	25	111	3
Ryan Spilborghs	.299	264	40	79	11	51	4
Brad Hawpe	.291	516	80	150	29	116	0
Troy Tulowitzki*	.291	609	104	177	24	99	7
Kazuo Matsui	.288	410	84	118	4	37	32
Cory Sullivan	.286	140	19	40	2	14	2
Yorvit Torrealba	.255	396	47	101	8	47	2
Jamey Carroll	.225	227	45	51	2	22	6
Jeff Baker*	.222	144	17	32	4	12	0
Chris Iannetta*	.218	197	22	43	4	27	0

Acquired: P Julio from Fla. for P Byung-Hyun Kim (May 13).

Pitching (45 IP)

	ERA	W-L	Gm	IP	BB	SO
Manny Corpas	2.08	4-2	78	78.0	20	58
Matt Herges	2.96	5-1	35	48.2	15	30
Brian Fuentes	3.08	3-5	64	61.1	23	56
LaTroy Hawkins	3.42	2-5	62	55.1	16	29
Jeremy Affeldt	3.51	4-3	75	59.0	33	46
Aaron Cook	4.12	8-7	25	166.0	44	61
Jeff Francis	4.22	17-9	34	215.1	63	165
Taylor Buchholz	4.23	6-5	41	93.2	20	61
Ubaldo Jimenez*	4.28	4-4	15	82.0	37	68
Rodrigo Lopez	4.42	5-4	14	79.1	21	43
Jason Hirsh*	4.81	5-7	19	112.1	48	75
Josh Fogg	4.94	10-9	30	165.2	59	94
Jorge Julio	5.23	0-5	68	62.0	31	56

Saves: Fuentes (20); Corpas (19). **Complete games:** Cook (2), Francis and Hirsh (1). **Shutouts:** Francis (1).

Florida Marlins

Batting (135 AB)

	Avg	AB	R	H	HR	RBI	SB
Cody Ross	.335	173	35	58	12	39	2
Hanley Ramirez	.332	639	125	212	29	81	51
Miguel Cabrera	.320	588	91	188	34	119	2
Jeremy Hermida	.296	429	54	127	18	63	3
Aaron Boone	.286	189	27	54	5	28	2
Matt Treanor	.269	171	16	46	4	19	0
Mike Jacobs	.265	426	57	113	17	54	1
Josh Willingham	.265	521	75	138	21	89	8
Alfredo Amezaga	.263	400	46	105	2	30	13
Dan Uggla	.245	632	113	155	31	88	2
Todd Linden	.245	184	21	45	1	11	4
Miguel Olivo	.237	452	43	107	16	60	3
Alejandro De Aza*	.229	144	14	33	0	8	2
Joe Borchard	.196	179	20	35	4	19	4

Acquired: P Byung-Hyun Kim from Ari. for P Jorge Julio (May 13); P Benitez and cash from SF for P Randy Messenger (June 1). **Claimed:** OF Linden off waivers from SF (May 18).

Pitching (45 IP)

	ERA	W-L	Gm	IP	BB	SO
Lee Gardner	1.94	3-4	62	74.1	18	52
Matt Lindstrom*	3.09	3-4	71	67.0	21	62
Kevin Gregg	3.54	0-5	74	84.0	40	87
Justin Miller	3.65	5-0	62	61.2	24	74
Renyel Pinto	3.68	2-4	57	58.2	32	56
Taylor Tankersley	3.99	6-1	67	47.1	29	49
Sergio Mitre	4.65	5-8	27	149.0	41	80
Dontrelle Willis	5.17	10-15	35	205.1	87	146
Armando Benitez	5.36	2-8	55	50.1	29	57
Scott Olsen	5.81	10-15	33	176.2	85	133
Byung-Hyun Kim	6.08	10-8	28	118.1	68	107
Wes Obermueller	6.56	2-3	18	59.0	36	35
Rick VandenHurk*	6.83	4-6	18	81.2	48	82

Saves: Gregg (32); Benitez (9); Henry Owens (4); Gardner (2); Pinto and Tankersley (1). **Complete games:** none. **Shutouts:** none.

Houston Astros

Batting (135 AB)

	Avg	AB	R	H	HR	RBI	SB
Hunter Pence*	.322	456	57	147	17	69	1
Carlos Lee	.303	627	93	190	32	119	10
Mike Lamb	.289	311	45	90	11	40	4
Mark Loretta	.287	460	52	132	4	41	
Ty Wigginton	.284	169	24	48	6	18	
Lance Berkman	.278	561	95	156	34	102	2
Luke Scott	.255	369	49	94	18	64	2
Craig Biggio	.251	517	68	130	10	50	4
Eric Bruntlett	.246	138	16	34	0	14	6
Brad Ausmus	.235	349	38	82	3	25	6
Adam Everett	.232	220	18	51	2	15	4
Chris Burke	.229	319	39	73	6	28	5

Acquired: IF Wigginton from TB for P Wheeler (July 29).

Pitchers (40 IP)

	ERA	W-L	Gm	IP	BB	SO
Chad Qualls	3.05	6-5	79	82.2	25	78
Roy Oswalt	3.18	14-7	33	212.0	60	154
Brad Lidge	3.36	5-3	66	67.0	30	88
Brian Moehler	4.07	1-4	42	59.2	17	36
Wandy Rodriguez	4.58	9-13	31	182.2	62	158
Chris Sampson*	4.59	7-8	24	121.2	30	51
Trever Miller	4.86	0-0	76	46.1	23	46
Dan Wheeler	5.07	1-4	45	49.2	13	56
Dave Borowski	5.15	5-3	64	71.2	34	63
Woody Williams	5.27	8-15	33	188.0	53	101
Matt Albers*	5.86	4-11	31	110.2	50	71
Jason Jennings	6.45	2-9	19	99.0	34	71

Saves: Lidge (19); Wheeler (11); Qualls (5); Moehler, Miller and Borowski (1). **Complete games:** Oswalt and Rodriguez (1). **Shutouts:** Rodriguez (1).

Los Angeles Dodgers

Batting (135 AB)

	Avg	AB	R	H	HR	RBI	SB
Matt Kemp	.342	292	47	100	10	42	10
James Loney*	.331	344	41	114	15	67	0
Jeff Kent	.302	494	78	149	20	79	1
Juan Pierre	.293	668	96	196	0	41	64
Russell Martin	.293	540	87	158	19	87	21
Andre Ethier	.284	447	50	127	13	64	0
Nomar Garciaparra	.283	431	39	122	7	59	3
Luis Gonzalez	.278	464	70	129	15	68	6
Tony Abreu	.271	166	19	45	2	17	0
Rafael Furcal	.270	581	87	157	6	47	25
Wilson Betemit	.231	156	22	36	10	26	0

Signed: P Wells (Aug. 25). **Traded:** IF Betemit to NYY for P Scott Proctor (July 31).

Pitching (40 IP)

	ERA	W-L	Gm	IP	BB	SO
Takashi Saito	1.40	2-1	63	64.1	13	78
Jonathan Broxton	2.85	4-4	83	82.0	25	99
Brad Penny	3.03	16-4	33	208.0	73	135
Chad Billingsley	3.31	12-5	43	147.0	64	141
Rudy Seanez	3.79	6-3	73	76.0	27	73
Joe Beimel	3.88	4-2	83	67.1	24	39
Derek Lowe	3.88	12-14	33	199.1	59	147
Randy Wolf	4.73	9-6	18	102.2	39	94
Mark Hendrickson	5.21	4-8	39	122.2	29	92
David Wells	5.43	9-9	39	157.1	42	82

Saves: Saito (39); Broxton (2); Seanez and Beimel (1). **Complete games:** Lowe (3); Billingsley (1). **Shutouts:** none.

Milwaukee Brewers

Batting (135 AB)

	Avg	AB	R	H	HR	RBI	SB
Ryan Braun*	.324	451	91	146	34	97	15
Corey Hart	.295	505	86	149	24	81	23
Prince Fielder	.288	573	109	165	50	119	2
Johnny Estrada	.278	442	40	123	10	54	0
J.J. Hardy	.277	592	89	164	26	80	2
Kevin Mench	.267	288	39	77	8	37	3
Geoff Jenkins	.255	420	45	107	21	64	2
Bill Hall	.254	452	59	115	14	63	4
Tony Graffanino	.238	231	34	55	9	30	6
Damian Miller	.237	186	19	44	4	24	1
Gabe Gross	.235	183	28	43	7	24	3
Rickie Weeks	.235	409	87	96	16	36	25
Craig Counsell	.220	282	31	62	3	24	4

Acquired: P Linebrink from SD for 3 minor leaguers (July 26).

Pitching (40 IP)

	ERA	W-L	Gm	IP	BB	SO
Francisco Cordero	2.98	0-4	66	63.1	18	86
Brian Shouse	3.02	1-1	73	47.2	14	32
Yovani Gallardo*	3.67	9-5	20	110.1	37	101
Scott Linebrink	3.71	5-6	71	70.1	25	50
Ben Sheets	3.82	12-5	24	141.1	37	106
Carlos Villanueva	3.94	8-5	59	114.1	53	99
Matt Wise	4.19	3-2	56	53.2	17	43
Jeff Suppan	4.62	12-12	34	206.2	68	114
Derrick Turnbow	4.63	4-5	77	68.0	46	84
Chris Spurling	4.68	2-1	49	50.0	14	28
Claudio Vargas	5.09	11-6	29	134.1	54	107
Chris Capuano	5.10	5-12	29	150.0	54	132
Dave Bush	5.12	12-10	33	186.1	44	134

Saves: Cordero (44); Shouse, Linebrink, Villanueva, Wise, Turnbow and Vargas (1). **Complete games:** Sheets (2); Suppan (1). **Shutouts:** none.

New York Mets

Batting (135 AB)

	Avg	AB	R	H	HR	RBI	SB
Moises Alou	.341	328	51	112	13	49	3
David Wright	.325	604	113	196	30	107	34
Luis Castillo	.296	199	37	59	1	20	10
Ruben Gotay	.295	190	25	56	4	24	3
Shawn Green	.291	446	62	130	10	46	11
Endy Chavez	.287	150	20	43	1	17	5
Ramon Castro	.285	144	24	41	11	31	0
Jose Reyes	.280	681	119	191	12	57	78
Damion Easley	.280	193	24	54	10	26	0
Carlos Beltran	.276	554	93	153	33	112	23
Paul Lo Duca	.272	445	46	121	9	54	2
Lastings Milledge	.272	184	27	50	7	29	3
Carlos Delgado	.258	538	71	139	24	87	4
Jeff Conine	.254	256	25	65	6	37	4
Jose Valentin	.241	166	18	40	3	18	2

Acquired: IF Castillo from Min. for C Drew Butera and OF Dustin Martin (July 30); Of Conine from Cin. for IF Jose Castro and OF Sean Henry (Aug. 20).

Pitching (40 IP)

	ERA	W-L	Gm	IP	BB	SO
Billy Wagner	2.63	2-2	66	68.1	22	80
Aaron Heilman	3.03	7-7	81	86.0	20	63
Pedro Feliciano	3.09	2-2	78	64.0	31	61
Joe Smith*	3.45	3-2	54	44.1	21	45
Oliver Perez	3.56	15-10	29	177.0	79	174
Orlando Hernandez	3.72	9-5	27	147.2	64	128
John Maine	3.91	15-10	32	191.0	75	180
Tom Glavine	4.45	13-8	34	200.1	64	89
Jorge Sosa	4.47	9-8	42	112.2	41	69
Scott Schoeneweis	5.03	0-2	70	59.0	28	41
Aaron Sele	5.37	3-2	34	53.2	21	29
Mike Pelfrey*	5.57	3-8	15	72.2	39	45
Guillermo Mota	5.76	2-2	52	59.1	18	47

Saves: Wagner (34); Feliciano and Schoeneweis (2); Heilman (1). **Complete games:** Maine and Glavine (1). **Shutouts:** Maine and Glavine (1).

Philadelphia Phillies

Batting (135 AB)

	Avg	AB	R	H	HR	RBI	SB
Chase Utley	.332	530	104	176	22	103	9
Aaron Rowand	.309	612	105	189	27	89	6
Tadahito Iguchi	.304	138	22	42	3	12	6
Jayson Werth	.298	255	43	76	8	49	7
Jimmy Rollins	.296	716	139	212	30	94	41
Shane Victorino	.281	456	78	128	12	46	37
Greg Dobbs	.272	324	45	88	10	55	3
Ryan Howard	.268	529	94	142	47	136	1
Carlos Ruiz*	.259	374	42	97	6	54	6
Pat Burrell	.256	472	77	121	30	97	0
Wes Helms	.246	280	21	69	5	39	0
Abraham Nunez	.234	252	24	59	0	16	2

Acquired: IF Iguchi tfrom ChW for P Michael Dubee (July 28); P Lohse from Cin. for P Matt Maloney (July 30). **Claimed:** P Durbin from Bos. (Apr. 13).

Pitchers (40 IP)

	ERA	W-L	Gm	IP	BB	SO
Ryan Madson	3.05	2-2	38	56.0	23	43
Cole Hamels	3.39	15-5	28	183.1	43	177
Kyle Kendrick*	3.87	10-4	20	121.0	25	49
Brett Myers	4.33	5-7	51	68.2	27	83
Geoff Geary	4.41	3-2	57	67.1	25	38
Kyle Lohse	4.63	9-12	34	192.2	57	122
Tom Gordon	4.73	3-2	44	40.0	13	32
Jon Lieber	4.73	3-6	14	78.0	22	54
Jamie Moyer	5.01	14-12	33	199.1	66	133
Clay Condrey	5.04	5-0	39	50.0	16	27
Antonio Alfonseca	5.44	5-2	61	49.2	27	24
Freddy Garcia	5.90	1-5	11	58.0	19	50
J.D. Durbin*	6.06	6-5	19	65.1	37	40
Adam Eaton	6.29	10-10	30	161.2	71	97

Saves: Myers (21); Alfonseca (8); Gordon (6); Condrey (2); Madson, Durbin, Jose Mesa, John Ennis and Francisco Rosario (1). **Complete games:** Hamels and Lohse (2); Lieber, Moyer and Durbin (1). **Shutouts:** Lohse, Lieber and Durbin (1).

Pittsburgh Pirates

Batting (135 AB)

	Avg	AB	R	H	HR	RBI	SB
Freddy Sanchez	.304	602	77	183	11	81	0
Jack Wilson	.296	477	67	141	12	56	2
Xavier Nady	.278	431	55	120	20	72	3
Ryan Doumit	.274	252	33	69	9	32	1
Adam LaRoche	.272	563	71	153	21	88	1
Ronny Paulino	.263	457	56	120	11	55	2
Nate McLouth	.258	329	62	85	13	38	22
Cesar Izturis	.258	314	31	81	0	16	3
Jose Bautista	.254	532	75	135	15	63	6
Chris Duffy	.249	241	31	60	3	22	13
Jason Bay	.247	538	78	133	21	84	4
Jose Castillo	.244	221	18	54	0	24	0

Acquired: IF Izturis and cash from ChC for PTBN (July 20); P Morris from SF for OF Rajai Davis and PTBN (July 31).

Pitching (40 IP)

	ERA	W-L	Gm	IP	BB	SO
Matt Capps	2.28	4-7	76	79.0	16	64
Damaso Marte	2.38	2-0	65	45.1	18	51
Ian Snell	3.76	9-12	32	208.0	68	177
Tom Gorzelanny	3.88	14-10	32	201.2	68	135
Shawn Chacon	3.94	5-4	64	96.0	48	79
John Grabow	4.53	3-2	63	51.2	19	42
Matt Morris	4.89	10-11	32	198.2	61	102
Paul Maholm	5.02	10-15	29	177.2	49	105
Salomon Torres	5.47	2-4	56	52.2	17	45
Zach Duke	5.53	3-8	20	107.1	25	41
Shane Youman*	5.97	3-5	16	57.1	23	29
Tony Armas	6.03	4-5	31	97.0	38	73

Saves: Capps (18); Torres (12); Chacon and Grabow (1). **Complete games:** Morris (3); Maholm (2); Snell and Gorzelanny (1). **Shutouts:** Gorzelanny and Maholm (1).

St. Louis Cardinals

Batting (170 AB)	Avg	AB	R	H	HR	RBI	SB
Skip Schumaker	.333	177	19	59	2	19	1
Albert Pujols	.327	565	99	185	32	103	2
David Eckstein	.309	434	58	134	3	31	10
So Taguchi	.290	307	48	89	3	30	7
Aaron Miles	.290	414	55	120	2	32	2
Brendan Ryan*	.289	180	30	52	4	12	7
Rick Ankiel	.285	172	31	49	11	39	1
Juan Encarnacion	.283	283	43	80	9	47	2
Yadier Molina	.275	353	30	97	6	40	1
Scott Spiezio	.269	223	31	60	4	31	0
Ryan Ludwick	.267	303	42	81	14	52	4
Scott Rolen	.265	392	55	104	8	58	5
Chris Duncan	.259	375	51	97	21	70	2
Jim Edmonds	.252	365	39	92	12	53	0
Adam Kennedy	.219	279	27	61	3	18	6

Acquired: P Pineiro and cash from Bos. for PTBN (July 31). **Claimed:** P Wellemeyer off waivers from KC (May 15).

Pitching (40 IP)	ERA	W-L	Gm	IP	BB	SO
Troy Percival	1.80	3-0	34	40.0	10	36
Russ Springer	2.18	8-1	76	66.0	19	66
Jason Isringhausen	2.48	4-0	63	65.1	28	54
Ryan Franklin	3.04	4-4	69	80.0	11	44
Todd Wellemeyer	3.11	3-2	20	63.2	29	51
Adam Wainwright	3.70	14-12	32	202.0	70	136
Joel Pineiro	3.96	6-4	11	63.2	12	40
Randy Flores	4.25	3-0	70	55.0	15	47
Brad Thompson	4.73	8-6	44	129.1	40	53
Braden Looper	4.94	12-12	31	175.0	51	87
Kip Wells	5.70	7-17	34	162.2	78	122
Anthony Reyes	6.04	2-14	22	107.1	43	74
Kelvin Jimenez*	7.50	3-0	34	42.0	17	24

Saves: Isringhausen (32); Franklin and Flores (1). **Complete games:** Wainwright and Reyes (1). **Shutouts:** none.

San Diego Padres

Batting (140 AB)	Avg	AB	R	H	HR	RBI	SB
Josh Bard	.285	389	42	111	5	51	0
Adrian Gonzalez	.282	646	101	182	30	100	0
Kevin Kouzmanoff*	.275	484	57	133	18	74	1
Brian Giles	.271	483	72	131	13	51	4
Khalil Greene	.254	611	89	155	27	97	4
Geoff Blum	.252	330	34	83	5	33	0
Michael Barrett	.244	344	29	84	9	41	2
Scott Hairston	.243	263	37	64	11	36	2
Mike Cameron	.242	571	88	138	21	78	18
Jose Cruz Jr.	.234	256	37	60	6	21	6
Morgan Ensberg	.230	282	47	65	12	39	0
Marcus Giles	.229	420	52	96	4	39	10
Termel Sledge	.210	200	22	42	7	23	1

Acquired: C Barrett and cash from ChC for C Rob Bowen and OF Kyler Burke (June 21); OF Hairston from Ari. for P Leo Rosales (July 28); IF Ensberg and cash from Hou. for PTBN (July 31). **Signed:** P Tomko (Sept. 4).

Pitching (40 IP)	ERA	W-L	Gm	IP	BB	SO
Heath Bell	2.02	6-4	81	93.2	30	102
Jake Peavy	2.54	19-6	34	223.1	68	240
Justin Hampson*	2.70	2-3	39	53.1	16	34
Kevin Cameron*	2.79	2-0	48	58.0	36	50
Trevor Hoffman	2.98	4-5	61	57.1	15	44
Doug Brocail	3.05	5-1	67	76.2	24	43
Chris Young	3.12	9-8	30	173.0	72	167
Cla Meredith	3.50	5-6	80	79.2	17	59
Greg Maddux	4.14	14-11	34	198.0	25	104
Justin Germano*	4.46	7-10	26	133.1	40	78
Brett Tomko	5.55	4-12	40	131.1	48	105
Clay Hensley	6.84	2-3	13	50.0	32	30

Saves: Hoffman (42); Bell (2). **Complete games:** Maddux (1). **Shutouts:** none.

San Francisco Giants

Batting (135 AB)	Avg	AB	R	H	HR	RBI	SB
Randy Winn	.300	593	73	178	14	65	15
Fred Lewis*	.287	157	34	45	3	19	5
Dan Ortmeier*	.287	157	20	45	6	16	2
Rajai Davis*	.279	190	32	53	1	9	22
Barry Bonds	.276	340	75	94	28	66	5
Bengie Molina	.276	497	38	137	19	81	0
Kevin Frandsen	.269	264	26	71	5	31	4
Dave Roberts	.260	396	61	103	2	23	31
Ryan Klesko*	.260	362	51	94	6	44	5
Pedro Feliz	.253	557	61	141	20	72	2
Rich Aurilia	.252	329	40	83	5	33	0
Omar Vizquel	.246	513	54	126	4	51	14
Ray Durham	.218	464	56	101	11	71	10

Acquired: P Messenger from Fla. for P Armando Benitez and cash (June 1); OF Davis and PTBN from Pit. for P Matt Morris (July 31).

Pitching (40 IP)	ERA	W-L	Gm	IP	BB	SO
Brad Hennessey	3.42	4-5	69	68.1	23	40
Kevin Correia	3.45	4-7	59	101.2	40	80
Vinnie Chulk	3.57	5-4	57	53.0	14	41
Matt Cain	3.65	7-16	32	200.0	79	163
Noah Lowry	3.92	14-8	26	156.0	87	87
Tim Lincecum*	4.00	7-5	24	146.1	65	150
Randy Messenger	4.20	2-4	60	64.1	21	34
Patrick Misch*	4.24	0-4	18	40.1	12	26
Barry Zito	4.53	11-13	34	196.2	83	131
Steve Kline	4.70	1-2	68	46.0	18	17
Jack Taschner	5.40	3-1	63	50.0	29	51
Russ Ortiz	5.51	2-3	12	49.0	20	27
Jonathan Sanchez	5.88	1-5	33	52.0	28	69

Saves: Hennessey (19); Brian Wilson (6); Kline (2); Messenger (1). **Complete games:** Cain and Lowry (1). **Shutouts:** none.

Washington Nationals

Batting (135 AB)	Avg	AB	R	H	HR	RBI	SB
Cristian Guzman	.328	174	31	57	2	14	2
Dmitri Young	.320	460	57	147	13	74	0
Ronnie Belliard	.290	511	57	148	11	58	3
Ryan Church	.272	470	57	128	15	70	3
Ryan Zimmerman	.266	653	99	174	24	91	4
Austin Kearns	.266	587	84	156	16	74	2
Nook Logan	.265	325	39	86	0	21	23
Felipe Lopez	.245	603	70	148	9	50	24
Jesus Flores*	.244	180	21	44	4	25	0
Brian Schneider	.235	408	33	96	6	54	0
Robert Fick	.234	197	24	46	2	16	0
Ryan Langerhans	.227	210	27	35	6	23	3

Acquired: OF Langerhans from Oak. for OF Chris Snelling (May 3).

Pitching (45 IP)	ERA	W-L	Gm	IP	BB	SO
Chris Schroder*	3.18	2-3	37	45.1	15	43
Luis Ayala	3.19	2-2	44	42.1	12	28
Chad Cordero	3.36	3-3	76	75.0	29	62
Shawn Hill	3.42	4-5	16	97.1	25	65
Jon Rauch	3.61	8-4	88	87.1	21	71
Tim Redding	3.64	3-6	15	84.0	38	47
Saul Rivera	3.68	4-6	85	93.0	42	64
Jesus Colome	3.82	5-1	61	66.0	27	43
Jason Bergmann	4.45	6-6	21	115.1	42	86
Micah Bowie	4.55	4-3	30	57.1	27	42
Matt Chico*	4.63	7-9	31	167.0	74	94
Mike Bacsik	5.11	5-8	29	118.0	29	45
Joel Hanrahan*	6.00	5-3	12	51.0	38	43
Jason Simontacchi	6.37	6-7	13	70.2	23	42
Levale Speigner*	8.78	2-3	19	40.0	23	19

Saves: Cordero (37); Rauch (4); Rivera (3); Ayala and Colome (1). **Complete games:** none. **Shutouts:** none.

BASEBALL PLAYOFFS

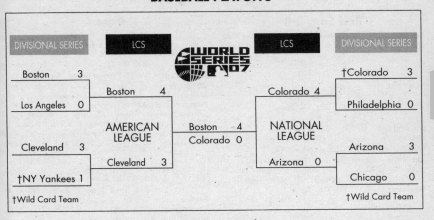

DIVISIONAL SERIES	LCS	WORLD SERIES '07	LCS	DIVISIONAL SERIES
Boston 3				†Colorado 3
	Boston 4		Colorado 4	
Los Angeles 0				Philadelphia 0
	AMERICAN LEAGUE	Boston 4 / Colorado 0	NATIONAL LEAGUE	
Cleveland 3				Arizona 3
	Cleveland 3		Arizona 0	
†NY Yankees 1				Chicago 0
†Wild Card Team				†Wild Card Team

DIVISIONAL SERIES SUMMARIES

American League

Indians, 3-1

Date	Winner	Home Field
Oct. 4	Indians, 12-3	at Cleveland
Oct. 5	Indians, 2-1 (11 inn.)	at Cleveland
Oct. 7	Yankees, 8-4	at New York
Oct. 8	Indians, 6-4	at New York

Game 1
Thursday, Oct. 4, at Cleveland

	1	2	3	4	5	6	7	8	9		R	H	E
New York	1	0	0	1	1	0	0	0	0	-	3	5	0
Cleveland	3	0	1	0	5	2	0	1	x	-	12	14	0

Win: Sabathia, Cle. (1-0). **Loss:** Wang, NY (0-1).
2B: New York—Abreu (1); Cleveland—Peralta (1), Martinez (1), Lofton (1). **HR:** New York—Damon (1, off Sabathia, 0 on), Cano (1, off Sabathia, 0 on); Cleveland—Cabrera (1, off Wang, 0 on), Martinez (1, off Wang, 1 on), Hafner (1, off Ohlendorf, 0 on), Garko (1, off Hughes, 0 on). **RBI:** New York—Damon (1), Cano (1), Abreu (1); Cleveland—Garko 2 (2), Lofton 4 (4), Cabrera (1), Martinez 2 (2), Blake 2 (2), Hafner (1). **SB:** Cleveland—Lofton (1). **CS:** New York—Cano (1); Cleveland—Sizemore (1).
Attendance: 44,608 (43,415). **Time:** 3:44.

Game 2
Friday, Oct. 5, at Cleveland

	1	2	3	4	5	6	7	8	9	10	11	R	H	E
New York	0	0	1	0	0	0	0	0	0	0	1	3	0
Cleveland	0	0	0	0	0	0	0	1	0	0	1	2	9	1

Win: Perez, Cle. (1-0). **Loss:** Vizcaino, NY (0-1).
2B: Cleveland—Michaels (1), Peralta (2). **3B:** Cleveland—Sizemore (1). **HR:** New York—Cabrera (1, off Carmona, 0 on). **RBI:** New York—Cabrera (1); Cleveland—Hafner (2). **SB:** New York—Abreu (1); Cleveland—Peralta (1). **CS:** Cleveland—Lofton (1). **E:** Cleveland—Cabrera (1).
Attendance: 44,732 (43,415). **Time:** 4:23.

Game 3
Sunday, Oct. 7, at New York

	1	2	3	4	5	6	7	8	9		R	H	E
Cleveland	1	1	1	0	0	0	0	1	0	-	4	9	1
New York	0	0	1	0	4	3	0	0	x	-	8	11	1

Win: Hughes, NY (1-0). **Loss:** Westbrook, Cle. (0-1).
2B: Cleveland—Peralta (3), Nixon (1); New York—Cano (1). **HR:** Cleveland—Nixon (1, off Clemens, 0 on); New York—Damon (2, off Westbrook, 2 on). **RBI:** Cleveland—Garko (3), Nixon 2 (2), Peralta (1); New York—Damon 4 (5), Cabrera (2), Cano (2). **SB:** Cleveland—Sizemore (1). **E:** Cleveland—Nixon (1); New York—Cano (1).
Attendance: 56,358 (56,937). **Time:** 3:38.

Game 4
Monday, Oct. 8, at New York

	1	2	3	4	5	6	7	8	9		R	H	E
Cleveland	2	2	0	2	0	0	0	0	0	-	6	13	0
New York	0	1	0	0	0	1	1	0	1	-	4	12	0

Win: Byrd, Cle. (1-0). **Loss:** Wang, NY (0-2). **Save:** Borowski, Cle. (1).
2B: Cleveland—Shoppach (1); New York—Posada (1). **HR:** Cleveland—Sizemore (1, off Wang, 0 on); New York—Cano (2, off Byrd, 0 on), Rodriguez (1, off Perez, 0 on), Abreu (1, off Borowski, 0 on). **RBI:** Cleveland—Sizemore (1), Peralta (2), Cabrera (2), Martinez 2 (4); New York—Jeter (1), Cano (3), Rodriguez (1), Abreu (2).
Attendance: 56,315 (56,937). **Time:** 4:03.

American League Divisional Series (Cont.)

Red Sox, 3-0

Date	Winner	Home Field
Oct. 3	Red Sox, 4-0	at Boston
Oct. 5	Red Sox, 6-3	at Boston
Oct. 7	Red Sox, 9-1	at Los Angeles

Game 1

Wednesday, Oct. 3, at Boston

	1 2 3	4 5 6	7 8 9	R	H	E
Los Angeles	0 0 0	0 0 0	0 0 0 -	0	4	0
Boston	1 0 3	0 0 0	0 0 x -	4	9	0

Win: Beckett, Bos. (1-0). **Loss:** Lackey, LA (0-1).
2B: Boston—Youkilis (1). **HR:** Boston—Youkilis (1, off Lackey, 0 on), Ortiz (1, off Lackey, 1 on). **RBI:** Boston—Youkilis (1), Ortiz 2 (2), Lowell (1). **CS:** Boston—Lugo (1).
Attendance: 37,597 (36,525). **Time:** 2:27.

Game 2

Friday, Oct. 5, at Boston

	1 2 3	4 5 6	7 8 9	R	H	E
Los Angeles	0 3 0	0 0 0	0 0 0 -	3	7	0
Boston	2 0 0	0 1 0	0 0 3 -	6	6	1

Win: Papelbon, Bos. (1-0). **Loss:** Speier, LA (0-1).
2B: Los Angeles—Figgins (1), Cabrera (1), Anderson (1); Boston—Pedroia (1). **HR:** Boston—Ramirez (1, off Rodriguez, 2 on). **RBI:** Los Angeles—Mathis (1), Figgins (1), Cabrera (1); Boston—Drew 2 (2), Lowell (2), Ramirez 3 (3). **SB:** Los Angeles—Izturis 2 (2), Kendrick 2 (2), Willits (1); Boston—Crisp (1). **E:** Boston—Lowell (1).
Attendance: 37,706 (36,525). **Time:** 4:05.

Game 3

Sunday, Oct. 7, at Anaheim

	1 2 3	4 5 6	7 8 9	R	H	E
Boston	0 0 0	2 0 0	0 7 0 -	9	10	0
Los Angeles	0 0 0	0 0 0	0 0 1 -	1	8	0

Win: Schilling, Bos. (1-0). **Loss:** Weaver, LA (0-1).
2B: Boston—Lowell 2 (2), Pedroia (2), Varitek (1); Los Angeles—Izturis 2 (2), Figgins (2). **HR:** Boston—Ortiz (2, off Weaver, 0 on), Ramirez (2, off Weaver, 0 on). **RBI:** Boston—Ortiz (3), Ramirez (4), Pedroia (1), Youkilis (2), Lowell (3), Drew (3), Varitek (1), Crisp 2 (2); Los Angeles—Kendrick (1). **SB:** Boston—Lugo (1).
Attendance: 45,262 (45,257). **Time:** 3:29.

National League

Diamondbacks, 3-0

Date	Winner	Home Field
Oct. 3	Diamondbacks, 3-1	at Arizona
Oct. 4	Diamondbacks, 8-4	at Arizona
Oct. 6	Diamondbacks, 5-1	at Chicago

Game 1

Wednesday, Oct. 3, at Arizona

	1 2 3	4 5 6	7 8 9	R	H	E
Chicago	0 0 0	0 0 1	0 0 0 -	1	4	0
Arizona	0 0 0	1 0 0	2 0 x -	3	6	1

Win: Webb, Ari. (1-0). **Loss:** Marmol, Chi. (0-1). **Save:** Valverde, Ari. (1).
2B: Chicago—Zambrano (1); Arizona—Ojeda (1). **HR:** Arizona—Drew (1, off Zambrano, 0 on), Reynolds (1, off Marmol, 0 on). **RBI:** Chicago—Theriot (1); Arizona—Drew (1), Reynolds (1), Jackson (1). **SB:** Arizona—Young (1). **E:** Arizona—Reynolds (1).
Attendance: 48,864 (48,785). **Time:** 2:33.

Game 2

Thursday, Oct. 4, at Arizona

	1 2 3	4 5 6	7 8 9	R	H	E
Chicago	0 0 0	0 0 1	0 0 0 -	1	4	0
Arizona	0 0 0	1 0 0	2 0 x -	3	6	1

Win: Davis, Ari. (1-0). **Loss:** Lilly, Chi. (0-1).
2B: Chicago—Ward (1). **3B:** Arizona—Byrnes (1), Drew (1). **HR:** Chicago—Soto (1, off Davis, 1 on); Arizona—Young (1, off Lilly, 2 on). **RBI:** Chicago—Soto 2 (2), Ward 2 (2); Arizona—Young 3 (3), Byrnes (1), Drew 2 (3), Ojeda (1), Davis (1). **E:** Arizona—Ojeda (1).
Attendance: 48,575 (48,785). **Time:** 3:44.

Game 3

Saturday, Oct. 6, at Chicago

	1 2 3	4 5 6	7 8 9	R	H	E
Arizona	2 0 0	1 0 1	0 0 1 -	5	10	1
Chicago	0 0 0	1 0 0	0 0 0 -	1	7	0

Win: Hernandez, Ari. (1-0). **Loss:** Hill, Chi. (0-1).
2B: Arizona—Drew (1), Jackson (1); Chicago—Jones (1). **HR:** Arizona—Young (2, off Hill, 0 on), Byrnes (1, off Marmol, 0 on), Drew (2, off Wood, 0 on). **RBI:** Arizona—Young (4), Upton (1), Byrnes 2 (3), Drew (4); Chicago—Kendall (1). **SB:** Arizona—Drew (1), Upton (1), Byrnes (1); Chicago—Theriot (1). **E:** Arizona—Drew (1).
Attendance: 42,157 (41,118). **Time:** 3:22.

Rockies, 3-0

Date	Winner	Home Field
Oct. 3	Rockies, 4-2	at Philadelphia
Oct. 4	Rockies, 10-5	at Philadelphia
Oct. 6	Rockies, 2-1	at Colorado

Game 1
Wednesday, Oct. 3, at Philadelphia

	1 2 3	4 5 6	7 8 9	R H E
Colorado	0 3 0	0 0 0	0 1 0 -	4 6 0
Philadelphia .	0 0 0	0 2 0	0 0 0 -	2 4 0

Win: Francis, Col. (1-0). **Loss:** Hamels, Phi. (0-1). **Save:** Corpas, Col. (1).

2B: Colorado—Atkins (1). **3B:** Colorado—Helton (1). **HR:** Colorado—Holliday (1, off Gordon, 0 on); Philadelphia—Rowand (1, off Francis, 0 on); Burrell (1, off Francis, 0 on). **RBI:** Colorado—Atkins (1), Torrealba (1), Tulowitzki (1), Holliday (1); Philadelphia—Rowand (1), Burrell (1). **SB:** Philadelphia—Ruiz (1).

Attendance: 45,655 (43,647). **Time:** 2:52.

Game 2
Thursday, Oct. 4, at Philadelphia

	1 2 3	4 5 6	7 8 9	R H E
Colorado	2 0 0	4 0 4	0 0 0 -10	12 1
Philadelphia .	1 2 0	0 0 1	1 0 0 - 5	9 0

Win: Fogg, Col. (1-0). **Loss:** Kendrick, Phi. (0-1). **Save:** Corpas, Col. (2).

2B: Colorado—Matsui (1), Atkins (1), Torrealba (1), Tulowitzki (1); Philadelphia—Ruiz (1). **3B:** Colorado—Matsui (1); Philadelphia—Rollins (1). **HR:** Colorado—Tulowitzki (1, off Kendrick, 0 on), Holliday (1, off Kendrick, 0 on), Matsui (1, off Lohse, 3 on); Philadelphia—Rollins (1, off Morales, 0 on); Howard (1, off Affeldt, 0 on). **RBI:** Colorado—Tulowitzki (2), Holliday 2 (3), Matsui 5 (5), Torrealba 2 (3); Philadelphia—Rollins 4 (4), Howard (1). **SB:** Philadelphia—Victorino (1). **E:** Colorado—Torrealba (1).

Attendance: 45,991 (43,647). **Time:** 3:32.

Game 3
Saturday, Oct. 6, at Colorado

	1 2 3	4 5 6	7 8 9	R H E
Philadelphia .	0 0 0	0 0 0	1 0 0 - 1	3 0
Colorado	0 0 0	0 1 0	0 1 x - 2	9 0

Win: Fuentes, Col. (1-0). **Loss:** Romero, Phi. (0-1). **Save:** Corpas, Col. (3).

3B: Colorado—Matsui (2). **HR:** Philadelphia—Victorino (1, off Jimenez, 0 on). **RBI:** Philadelphia—Victorino (1); Colorado—Matsui (6), Baker (1). **SB:** Philadelphia—Rollins (1). **CS:** Colorado—Tulowitzki (1).

Attendance: 50,724 (50,449). **Time:** 2:59.

AMERICAN LEAGUE CHAMPIONSHIP SERIES

Red Sox, 4-3

Date	Winner	Home Field
Oct. 12	Red Sox, 10-3	at Boston
Oct. 13	Indians, 13-6 (11 inn.)	at Boston
Oct. 15	Indians, 4-2	at Cleveland
Oct. 16	Indians, 7-3	at Cleveland
Oct. 18	Red Sox, 7-1	at Cleveland
Oct. 20	Red Sox, 12-2	at Boston
Oct. 21	Red Sox, 11-2	at Boston

Game 1
Friday, Oct. 12, at Boston

	1 2 3	4 5 6	7 8 9	R H E
Cleveland	1 0 0	0 0 1	0 1 0 - 3	8 0
Boston	1 0 4	0 3 2	0 0 x -10	12 0

Win: Beckett, Bos. (1-0). **Loss:** Sabathia, Cle. (0-1).

2B: Cleveland—Lofton 2 (2), Blake 2 (2); Boston—Lugo (1), Lowell (1), Varitek (1), Crisp (1), Ortiz (1). **HR:** Cleveland—Hafner (1, off Beckett, 0 on). **RBI:** Cleveland—Hafner (1), Cabrera 2 (2); Boston—Ramirez 3 (3), Lowell 3 (3), Varitek 2 (2), Kielty 2 (2).

Attendance: 36,986 (36,525). **Time:** 3:35.

ALCS Most Valuable Player
Josh Beckett, Boston, P

ERA	W-L	IP	H	R	BB	K
1.93	2-0	14.0	9	3	1	18

Game 2
Saturday, Oct. 13, at Boston

	1 2 3 4 5 6	7 8 9 10 11	R H E
Cleveland	1 0 0 3 1 1	0 0 0 0 7 -13	17 0
Boston ...	0 0 3 0 3 0	0 0 0 0 0 - 6	10 0

Win: Mastny, Cle. (1-0). **Loss:** Gagne, Bos. (0-1).

2B: Cleveland—Sizemore (1), Martinez (1), Peralta (1). **HR:** Cleveland—Peralta (1, off Schilling, 2 on), Sizemore (1, off Schilling, 0 on), Gutierrez (1, off Lester, 2 on); Boston—Ramirez (1, off Perez, 1 on), Lowell (1, off Perez, 0 on). **RBI:** Cleveland—Martinez (1), Peralta 4 (4), Sizemore (1), Gutierrez 4 (4), Nixon (1), Garko (1); Boston—Ramirez 3 (6), Lowell 3 (6). **SB:** Cleveland—Barfield (1); Boston—Crisp (1), Ellsbury (1).

Attendance: 37,051 (36,525). **Time:** 5:14.

Game 3
Monday, Oct. 15, at Cleveland

	1 2 3	4 5 6	7 8 9	R H E
Boston	0 0 0	0 0 0	2 0 0 - 2	7 0
Cleveland	0 2 0	0 2 0	0 0 x - 4	6 1

Win: Westbrook, Cle. (1-0). **Loss:** Matsuzaka, Bos. (0-1). **Save:** Borowski (1).

2B: Boston—Ortiz (2). **HR:** Boston—Varitek (1, off Westbrook, 1 on); Cleveland—Lofton (1, off Matsuzaka, 1 on); **RBI:** Boston—Varitek 2 (4); Cleveland—Lofton 2 (2), Cabrera (3), Hafner (2). **E:** Cleveland—Garko (1).

Attendance: 44,402 (43,415). **Time:** 3:28.

American League Championship Series (Cont.)

Game 4
Tuesday, Oct. 16, at Cleveland

	1 2 3	4 5 6	7 8 9	R H E
Boston	0 0 0	0 0 3	0 0 0	- 3 8 1
Cleveland ...	0 0 0	0 7 0	0 0 x	- 7 9 0

Win: Byrd, Cle. (1-0). **Loss:** Wakefield, Bos. (0-1).
2B: Cleveland—Peralta (2). **HR:** Boston—Youkilis (1, off Byrd, 0 on), Ortiz (1, off Byrd, 0 on), Ramirez (2, off Lewis, 0 on); Cleveland—Blake (1, off Wakefield, 0 on), Peralta (2, off Delcarmen, 2 on). **RBI:** Boston—Youkilis (1), Ortiz (1), Ramirez (7); Cleveland—Blake 2 (2), Cabrera (4), Martinez (2), Peralta 3 (7). **SB:** Cleveland—Sizemore (1), Lofton (1). **E:** Boston—Youkilis (1).
Attendance: 44,008 (43,415). **Time:** 3:12.

Game 5
Thursday, Oct. 18, at Cleveland

	1 2 3	4 5 6	7 8 9	R H E
Boston	1 0 1	0 0 0	2 3 0	- 7 12 1
Cleveland ...	1 0 0	0 0 0	0 0 0	- 1 6 1

2B: Boston—Ramirez (1), Pedroia (1), Drew (1); Cleveland—Sizemore (1), Garko (1). **3B:** Boston—Youkilis (1). **HR:** Boston—Youkilis (2, off Sabathia, 0 on). **RBI:** Boston—Youkilis 3 (4), Ramirez (8), Ortiz 2 (3). **E:** Boston—Beckett (1); Cleveland—Perez (1).
Attendance: 44,588 (43,415). **Time:** 3:46.

Game 6
Saturday, Oct. 20, at Boston

	1 2 3	4 5 6	7 8 9	R H E
Cleveland ...	0 0 1	0 0 0	1 0 0	- 2 6 1
Boston	4 0 6	0 0 0	0 2 x	- 12 13 0

Win: Schilling, Bos. (1-0). **Loss:** Carmona, Cle. (0-1).
2B: Boston—Pedroia (2), Lugo (2), Ortiz (3). **3B:** Cleveland—Garko (1). **HR:** Cleveland—Martinez (1, off Schilling, 0 on); Boston—Drew (1, off Carmona, 3 on). **RBI:** Cleveland—Martinez (3), Peralta (8); Boston—Drew 5 (5), Ellsbury (1), Lugo 2 (2), Youkilis (5), Ramirez (9), Lowell (7). **E:** Cleveland—Cabrera (1).
Attendance: 37,163 (36,525). **Time:** 3:09.

Game 7
Sunday, Oct. 21, at Boston

	1 2 3	4 5 6	7 8 9	R H E
Cleveland ...	0 0 0	1 1 0	0 0 0	- 2 10 1
Boston	1 1 1	0 0 0	2 6 x	- 11 15 1

Win: Matsuzaka, Bos. (1-0). **Loss:** Westbrook, Cle. (0-1). **Save:** Papelbon, Bos. (1).
2B: Cleveland—Hafner (1), Garko (2); Boston—Varitek (3), Youkilis (1), Lowell (2), Pedroia (3). **HR:** Boston—Pedroia (1, off Betancourt, 1 on); Youkilis (3, off Lewis, 1 on). **RBI:** Cleveland—Garko (2), Sizemore (2); Boston—Ramirez (10), Lowell (8), Pedroia 5 (5), Drew (5), Youkilis 2 (7). **E:** Cleveland—Blake (1); Boston—Lugo (1).
Attendance: 37,165 (36,525). **Time:** 3:33.

ALCS Composite Box Score

Boston Red Sox

Batting	LCS vs. Cleveland								Overall AL Playoffs							
	Avg	AB	R	H	HR	RBI	BB	SO	Avg	AB	R	H	HR	RBI	BB	SO
Kevin Youkilis	.500	28	10	14	3	7	5	3	.425	40	13	17	4	9	6	7
Manny Ramirez	.409	22	5	9	2	10	9	5	.400	30	8	12	4	14	14	7
Bobby Kielty	.400	5	1	2	0	2	1	2	.400	5	1	2	0	2	1	2
J.D. Drew	.360	25	5	9	1	6	1	2	.306	36	6	11	1	9	1	3
Dustin Pedroia	.345	29	8	10	1	5	3	5	.286	42	10	12	1	6	4	7
Mike Lowell	.333	27	3	9	1	8	2	3	.333	36	4	12	1	11	3	3
David Ortiz	.292	24	7	7	1	3	6	5	.387	31	12	12	3	6	12	6
Jason Varitek	.269	26	3	7	1	4	2	5	.243	37	4	9	1	5	2	9
Jacoby Ellsbury	.250	8	3	2	0	1	1	1	.222	9	4	2	0	1	1	1
Julio Lugo	.200	25	3	5	0	2	1	5	.229	35	5	8	0	2	2	9
Coco Crisp	.143	21	2	3	0	0	0	6	.161	31	2	5	0	1	2	9
Doug Mirabelli	.000	2	0	0	0	0	0	1	.000	2	0	0	0	0	0	1
Alex Cora	—	0	0	0	0	0	0	0	—	0	0	0	0	0	0	0
Eric Hinske	—	0	1	0	0	0	0	0	.000	1	1	0	0	0	0	0
TOTALS	.318	242	51	77	10	48	31	43	.304	335	70	102	15	67	47	65

Pitching	ERA	W-L	Sv	Gm	IP	H	BB	SO	ERA	W-L	Sv	Gm	IP	H	BB	SO
Mike Timlin	0.00	0-0	0	3	3.1	1	0	3	0.00	0-0	0	3	3.1	1	0	3
Jonathan Papelbon	0.00	0-0	1	3	5.0	3	2	3	0.00	1-0	1	4	6.1	3	4	4
Hideki Okajima	0.00	0-0	0	3	5.0	4	2	3	0.00	0-0	0	5	7.1	5	3	4
Josh Beckett	1.93	2-0	0	2	14.0	9	1	18	1.17	3-0	0	3	23.0	13	1	26
Jon Lester	4.91	0-0	0	2	3.2	3	1	5	4.91	0-0	0	2	3.2	3	1	5
Curt Schilling	5.40	1-0	0	2	11.2	15	0	8	3.38	2-0	0	3	18.2	21	1	12
Daisuke Matsuzaka	5.59	1-1	0	2	9.2	12	2	9	5.65	1-1	0	3	14.1	19	5	12
Eric Gagne	7.71	0-1	0	3	2.1	3	2	4	8.10	0-1	0	4	3.1	4	2	5
Tim Wakefield	9.64	0-1	0	1	4.2	5	2	7	9.64	0-1	0	1	4.2	5	2	7
Manny Delcarmen	16.20	0-0	0	3	1.2	4	2	3	9.00	0-0	0	4	3.0	4	2	3
Javier Lopez	18.00	0-0	0	3	2.0	3	2	0	15.43	0-0	0	4	2.1	3	2	0
TOTALS	4.57	4-3	1	7	63.0	62	16	63	3.60	7-3	1	10	90.0	81	23	83

Cleveland Indians

Batting		LCS vs. Boston								Overall AL Playoffs						
	Avg	AB	R	H	HR	RBI	BB	SO	Avg	AB	R	H	HR	RBI	BB	SO
Trot Nixon	.429	7	0	3	0	1	0	1	.455	11	1	5	1	3	0	2
Casey Blake	.346	26	4	9	1	2	1	7	.256	43	5	11	1	4	1	12
Kelly Shoppach	.333	3	0	1	0	0	0	2	.500	6	1	3	0	0	0	2
Victor Martinez	.296	27	4	8	1	3	3	5	.318	44	6	14	2	7	4	8
Ryan Garko	.292	24	4	7	0	2	0	5	.314	35	7	11	1	5	1	6
Jhonny Peralta	.259	27	4	7	2	8	1	8	.333	42	6	14	2	10	5	11
Asdrubal Cabrera	.241	29	2	7	0	4	1	8	.217	46	5	10	1	6	2	12
Kenny Lofton	.222	27	2	6	1	1	1	3	.279	43	4	12	1	6	3	4
Grady Sizemore	.222	27	6	6	1	2	4	5	.279	43	9	12	2	3	8	9
Franklin Gutierrez	.211	19	3	4	1	4	3	6	.207	29	5	6	1	4	5	11
Travis Hafner	.148	27	2	4	1	2	2	12	.186	43	6	8	2	4	7	15
Chris Gomez	.000	1	0	0	0	0	0	1	.000	1	0	0	0	0	0	1
Jason Michaels	—	0	1	0	0	0	0	0	1.000	1	1	1	0	0	0	0
Josh Barfield	—	0	0	0	0	0	0	0	—	0	0	0	0	0	0	0
TOTALS	.254	244	32	62	8	30	16	63	.276	387	56	107	14	52	36	93

Pitching																
	ERA	W-L	Sv	Gm	IP	H	BB	SO	ERA	W-L	Sv	Gm	IP	H	BB	SO
Aaron Fultz	—	0-0	0	1	0.0	0	2	0	0.00	0-0	0	2	1.0	2	3	1
Tom Mastny	0.00	1-0	0	3	4.2	2	2	3	0.00	1-0	0	3	4.2	2	2	3
Aaron Laffey	0.00	0-0	0	1	4.2	1	1	3	0.00	0-0	0	1	4.2	1	1	3
Jake Westbrook	3.55	1-1	0	2	12.2	16	4	7	5.60	1-2	0	3	17.2	25	4	8
Paul Byrd	3.60	1-0	0	1	5.0	6	0	4	3.60	2-0	0	2	10.0	14	2	6
Joe Borowski	4.50	0-0	1	4	4.0	6	3	1	4.50	0-0	2	6	6.0	7	5	2
Jensen Lewis	6.35	0-0	0	5	5.2	6	0	3	4.70	0-0	0	7	7.2	6	0	7
Rafael Betancourt	6.75	0-0	0	5	8.0	6	1	6	5.40	0-0	0	7	10.0	7	1	9
C.C. Sabathia	10.45	0-2	0	2	10.1	17	7	9	8.80	1-2	0	3	15.1	21	13	14
Fausto Carmona	16.50	0-1	0	2	6.0	10	9	7	7.20	0-1	0	3	15.0	13	11	12
Rafael Perez	45.00	0-0	0	3	1.0	7	2	0	7.71	1-0	0	6	7.0	10	3	6
TOTALS	6.82	3-4	1	7	62.0	77	31	43	5.55	6-5	2	11	99.0	108	45	71

Score by Innings

	1	2	3	4	5	6	7	8	9	10	11		R	H	E
Cleveland	3	3	0	4	11	2	1	1	0	0	7	–	32	62	4
Boston	7	1	15	0	6	5	6	11	0	0	0	–	51	77	3

NATIONAL LEAGUE CHAMPIONSHIP SERIES

Rockies, 4-0

Date	Winner	Home Field
Oct. 11	Rockies, 5-1	at Arizona
Oct. 12	Rockies, 3-2 (11 inn.)	at Arizona
Oct. 14	Rockies, 4-1	at Colorado
Oct. 15	Rockies, 6-4	at Colorado

Game 1
Thursday, Oct. 11, at Arizona

	1	2	3	4	5	6	7	8	9		R	H	E
Colorado	0	1	3	0	0	0	1	0	0	-	5	8	0
Arizona	1	0	0	0	0	0	0	0	0	-	1	9	1

Win: Francis, Col. (1-0). **Loss:** Webb, Ari. (0-1).
2B: Arizona—Byrnes (1), Snyder (1). **RBI:** Colorado—Matsui (1), Hawpe 2 (2); Arizona—Byrnes (1). **SB:** Colorado—Taveras (1), Matsui (1). **E:** Arizona—Jackson (1)
Attendance: 48,142 (48,785). **Time:** 3:12.

Game 2
Friday, Oct. 12, at Arizona

	1	2	3	4	5	6	7	8	9	10	11		R	H	E
Colorado	0	1	0	0	1	0	0	0	0	0	1	-	3	7	1
Arizona	0	0	1	0	0	0	0	0	1	0	0	-	2	9	1

Win: Corpas, Col. (1-0). **Loss:** Valverde, Ari. (0-1). **Save:** Speier, Col. (1).
2B: Colorado—Taveras (1); Arizona—Clark (1), Davis (1). **RBI:** Colorado—Torrealba (1), Helton (1), Taveras (1); Arizona—Young (1), Byrnes (2). **CS:** Arizona—Young (1). **E:** Colorado—Matsui (1); Arizona—Reynolds (1).
Attendance: 48,219 (48,785). **Time:** 4:26.

National League Championship Series (Cont.)

Game 3
Sunday, Oct. 14, at Colorado

```
            1 2 3  4 5 6  7 8 9    R  H  E
Arizona ....0 0 0  1 0 0  0 0 0 -  1  8  0
Colorado ...1 0 0  0 0 3  0 0 x -  4  9  6
```

Win: Fogg, Col. (1-0). **Loss:** Hernandez, Ari. (0.1). **Save:** Corpas, Col. (1).

2B: Colorado—Torrealba (1). **HR:** Arizona—Reynolds (1, off Fogg, 0 on); Colorado—Holliday (1, off Hernandez, 0 on), Torrealba (1, off Hernandez, 2 on). **RBI:** Arizona—Reynolds (1); Colorado—Holliday (1), Torrealba 3 (4). **Attendance:** 50,137 (50,449). **Time:** 3:04.

Game 4
Monday, Oct. 15, at Colorado

```
            1 2 3  4 5 6  7 8 9    R  H  E
Arizona ....0 0 1  0 0 0  0 3 0 -  4 10  1
Colorado ...0 0 0  6 0 0  0 0 x -  6  6  1
```

Win: Herges, Col. (1-0). **Loss:** Owings, Ari. (0.1). **Save:** Corpas, Col. (2).

2B: Arizona—Snyder (2), Upton (1), Young (1); Colorado—Smith (1). **3B:** Arizona—Upton (1). **HR:** Arizona—Snyder (1, off Fuentes, 2 on); Colorado—Holliday (2, off Owings, 2 on). **RBI:** Arizona—Jackson (1), Snyder 3 (3); Colorado—Smith 2 (2), Matsui (2), Holliday 3 (4). **CS:** Arizona—Young (2). **E:** Arizona—Jackson (2); Colorado—Hawkins (1). **Attendance:** 50,213 (50,449). **Time:** 3:17.

NLCS Most Valuable Player
Matt Holliday, Colorado, OF

AVG	AB	R	H	HR	RBI	BB
.333	15	3	5	2	4	1

NLCS Composite Box Score

Colorado Rockies

Batting	LCS vs. Arizona								Overall NL Playoffs							
	Avg	AB	R	H	HR	RBI	BB	SO	Avg	AB	R	H	HR	RBI	BB	SO
Jeff Baker	.500	2	0	1	0	0	0	1	.667	3	0	2	0	1	0	1
Ryan Spilborghs	.500	2	1	1	0	0	0	0	.300	10	3	3	0	3	3	3
Seth Smith	.500	2	1	1	0	2	0	0	.500	4	2	2	0	2	0	0
Matt Holliday	.333	15	3	5	2	4	1	6	.286	28	5	8	4	7	1	9
Brad Hawpe	.333	12	2	4	0	2	5	3	.304	23	3	7	0	2	7	8
Kazuo Matsui	.235	17	2	4	0	2	1	5	.310	29	4	9	1	8	3	7
Todd Helton	.214	14	3	3	0	1	2	4	.154	26	4	4	0	1	3	6
Yorvit Torrealba	.200	15	2	3	1	4	2	5	.320	25	5	8	1	7	4	5
Troy Tulowitzki	.188	16	1	3	0	0	1	5	.179	28	2	5	1	2	2	10
Willy Taveras	.167	18	3	3	0	1	2	5	.167	18	3	3	0	1	2	5
Garrett Atkins	.143	14	0	2	0	2	2	2	.185	27	3	5	0	1	2	3
Josh Fogg	.000	1	0	0	0	0	1	0	.000	2	0	0	0	0	1	0
Jamey Carroll	.000	1	0	0	0	0	0	1	.000	1	0	0	0	0	1	1
Cory Sullivan	.000	1	0	0	0	0	0	0	.333	3	0	1	0	0	0	0
Jeff Francis	.000	2	0	0	0	0	0	0	.000	4	0	0	0	0	0	0
Ubaldo Jimenez	.000	2	0	0	0	0	0	2	.000	3	0	0	0	0	0	2
Franklin Morales	.000	1	0	0	0	0	0	0	.000	2	0	0	0	0	0	1
LaTroy Hawkins	—	0	0	0	0	0	0	0	—	0	0	0	0	0	0	0
Matt Herges	—	0	0	0	0	0	0	0	—	0	0	0	0	0	0	0
Brian Fuentes	—	0	0	0	0	0	0	0	—	0	0	0	0	0	0	0
Jeremy Affeldt	—	0	0	0	0	0	0	0	—	0	0	0	0	0	0	0
Ryan Speier	—	0	0	0	0	0	0	0	—	0	0	0	0	0	0	0
Manny Corpas	—	0	0	0	0	0	0	0	—	0	0	0	0	0	0	0
TOTALS	.222	135	18	30	3	16	18	39	.242	236	34	57	7	32	29	61

Pitching	ERA	W-L	Sv	Gm	IP	H	BB	SO	ERA	W-L	Sv	Gm	IP	H	BB	SO
LaTroy Hawkins	0.00	0-0	0	2	2.0	1	0	1	0.00	0-0	0	3	3.0	1	1	1
Matt Herges	0.00	1-0	0	3	3.0	1	1	2	0.00	1-0	0	4	3.2	1	1	2
Jeremy Affeldt	0.00	0-0	0	2	1.1	0	0	2	3.86	0-0	0	3	2.1	1	0	2
Ryan Speier	0.00	0-0	0	1	1.0	0	1	0	0.00	0-0	0	2	2.1	1	0	1
Jeff Francis	1.35	1-0	0	1	6.2	7	1	4	2.13	2-0	0	2	12.2	11	3	12
Josh Fogg	1.50	1-0	0	1	6.0	7	1	3	1.13	2-0	0	2	8.0	8	1	4
Manny Corpas	1.69	1-0	2	4	5.1	3	1	3	1.04	1-0	5	7	8.2	5	0	6
Ubaldo Jimenez	1.80	0-0	0	1	5.0	5	4	6	1.59	0-0	0	2	11.1	8	8	11
Franklin Morales	2.25	0-0	0	1	4.0	5	1	2	5.14	0-0	0	2	7.0	8	3	5
Brian Fuentes	7.36	0-0	0	4	3.2	5	1	6	4.50	1-0	0	7	6.0	8	3	10
TOTALS	1.89	4-0	2	4	38.0	36	8	28	2.08	7-0	6	7	65.0	52	20	54

Arizona Diamondbacks

Batting

Batting	LCS vs. Colorado								Overall NL Playoffs							
	Avg	AB	R	H	HR	RBI	BB	SO	Avg	AB	R	H	HR	RBI	BB	SO
Doug Davis	1.000	1	1	1	0	0	0	0	.500	2	1	1	0	1	0	1
Livan Hernandez	.500	2	0	1	0	0	0	0	.400	5	0	2	0	0	0	1
Brandon Webb	.500	2	0	1	0	0	0	1	.250	4	0	1	0	0	0	3
Jeff Cirillo	.400	5	0	2	0	0	0	0	.333	6	0	2	0	0	0	0
Miguel Montero	.400	5	0	2	0	0	0	0	.286	7	1	2	0	0	1	0
Chris Snyder	.333	12	1	4	1	3	1	4	.263	19	3	5	1	3	2	6
Conor Jackson	.333	9	1	3	0	1	0	0	.235	17	1	4	0	2	0	3
Micah Owings	.333	3	1	1	0	0	0	1	.333	3	1	1	0	0	0	1
Stephen Drew	.294	17	2	5	0	0	1	2	.387	31	6	12	2	4	1	7
Chris Young	.286	14	1	4	0	1	4	5	.280	25	4	7	2	5	7	13
Tony Clark	.222	9	0	2	0	0	1	1	.133	15	0	2	0	0	1	3
Justin Upton	.222	9	0	2	0	0	0	3	.357	14	2	5	0	1	3	3
Eric Byrnes	.176	17	0	3	0	2	1	3	.207	29	1	6	1	5	2	7
Augie Ojeda	.167	12	0	2	0	0	0	2	.286	21	1	6	0	1	1	3
Jeff Salazar	.143	7	0	1	0	0	0	1	.100	10	0	1	0	0	1	3
Mark Reynolds	.125	16	1	2	1	1	0	5	.154	26	3	4	2	2	2	9
Alberto Callaspo	.000	2	0	0	0	0	0	0	.000	2	0	0	0	0	0	0
Brandon Lyon	—	0	0	0	0	0	0	0	—	0	0	0	0	0	0	0
Juan Cruz	—	0	0	0	0	0	0	0	—	0	0	0	0	0	0	0
Jose Valverde	—	0	0	0	0	0	0	0	—	0	0	0	0	0	0	0
Dustin Nippert	—	0	0	0	0	0	0	0	—	0	0	0	0	0	0	0
Tony Pena	—	0	0	0	0	0	0	0	—	0	0	0	0	0	0	0
Doug Slaten	—	0	0	0	0	0	0	0	—	0	0	0	0	0	0	0
TOTALS	.254	142	8	36	2	8	8	28	.258	236	24	61	8	24	21	63

Pitching

Pitching	ERA	W-L	Sv	Gm	IP	H	BB	SO	ERA	W-L	Sv	Gm	IP	H	BB	SO
Brandon Lyon	0.00	0-0	0	2	3.0	0	0	4	0.00	0-0	0	5	6.0	1	1	5
Juan Cruz	0.00	0-0	0	3	4.0	0	3	8	0.00	0-0	0	4	4.1	1	3	9
Dustin Nippert	0.00	0-0	0	2	2.1	1	0	2	0.00	0-0	0	2	2.1	1	0	2
Tony Pena	0.00	0-0	0	3	3.1	1	0	7	0.00	0-0	0	5	5.1	3	0	7
Doug Slaten	0.00	0-0	0	3	1.1	1	2	1	0.00	0-0	0	3	1.1	1	2	1
Doug Davis	1.80	0-0	0	1	5.0	5	4	5	4.22	1-0	0	2	10.2	10	8	13
Micah Owings	4.91	0-1	0	1	3.2	6	2	2	4.91	0-1	0	1	3.2	6	2	2
Jose Valverde	5.40	0-1	0	1	1.2	1	3	2	1.93	0-1	1	4	4.2	2	4	8
Brandon Webb	6.00	0-1	0	1	6.0	7	2	4	3.46	1-1	0	2	13.0	11	5	13
Livan Hernandez	6.35	0-1	0	1	5.2	8	2	4	3.86	1-1	0	2	11.2	13	7	6
TOTALS	3.00	0-4	0	4	36.0	30	18	39	2.57	3-4	1	7	63.0	49	32	66

Score by Innings

	1	2	3	4	5	6	7	8	9	10	11		R	H	E
Colorado	1	2	3	6	1	3	1	0	0	0	1	–	18	30	2
Arizona	1	0	2	1	0	0	0	3	1	0	0	–	8	36	3

WORLD SERIES

 vs.

Red Sox, 4-0

Date	Winner	Home Field
Oct. 24	Red Sox, 13-1	at Boston
Oct. 25	Red Sox, 2-1	at Boston
Oct. 27	Red Sox, 10-5	at Colorado
Oct. 28	Red Sox, 4-3	at Colorado

World Series (Cont.)

Game 1

Wednesday, Oct. 24, at Boston

Colorado	AB	R	H	RBI	Boston	AB	R	H	RBI
Taveras, cf	4	0	0	0	Pedroia, 2b	5	1	1	2
Matsui, 2b	4	0	1	0	Youkilis, 1b	5	3	2	1
Holliday, lf	4	0	0	0	Ortiz, dh	5	2	3	2
Helton, 1b	4	0	2	0	Hinske, ph-dh	1	0	0	0
Atkins, 3b	4	1	1	0	Ramirez, lf	4	3	3	2
Hawpe, rf	4	0	0	0	Crisp, cf	1	0	0	0
Tulowitzki, ss	3	0	2	1	Lowell, 3b	3	1	1	0
Torrealba, c	3	0	0	0	Varitek, c	4	1	2	2
Spilborghs, dh	2	0	0	0	Drew, rf	5	1	2	2
					Lugo, ss	4	0	3	1
					Cora, ss	0	0	0	0
					Ellsbury, cf-lf	4	1	0	1
Totals	**32**	**1**	**6**	**1**	**Totals**	**41**	**13**	**17**	**13**

```
                          R   H   E
Colorado ..... 010 000 000  —    1   6   0
Boston ....... 310 270 00x  —   13  17   0
```

2B: Colorado—Atkins (1), Tulowitzki 2 (2), Helton (1); Boston—Youkilis 2 (2), Drew (1), Ortiz 2 (2), Ramirez (1), Varitek (1), Lowell (1). **HR:** Boston—Pedroia (1, off Francis, 0 on). **BB:** Colorado—Spilborghs; Boston—Pedroia, Youkilis, Ramirez, Lowell 2, Varitek, Lugo, Ellsbury.

Colorado	IP	H	R	ER	BB	SO	P	ERA
Francis (L, 0-1)	4	10	6	6	3	3	103	13.50
Morales	2/3	6	7	7	1	0	35	94.50
Speier	0	0	0	0	3	0	16	0.00
Herges	1 1/3	0	0	0	1	1	25	0.00
Affeldt	1	1	0	0	0	0	11	0.00
Hawkins	1	0	0	0	0	2	7	0.00

Boston	IP	H	R	ER	BB	SO	P	ERA
Beckett (W, 1-0)	7	6	1	1	1	9	93	1.29
Timlin	1	0	0	0	0	2	15	0.00
Gagne	1	0	0	0	0	1	11	0.00

IBB: by Francis (Ramirez, Lowell). **Balk:** Morales.
Attendance: 36,733 (36,525). **Time:** 3:30.

Game 2

Thursday, Oct. 25, at Boston

Colorado	AB	R	H	RBI	Boston	AB	R	H	RBI
Taveras, cf	3	1	0	0	Pedroia, 2b	4	0	1	0
Matsui, 2b	4	0	0	0	Youkilis, 1b	3	0	0	0
Holliday, lf	4	0	4	0	Ortiz, dh	3	1	0	0
Helton, 1b	3	0	0	1	Ramirez, lf	4	1	0	0
Atkins, 3b	4	0	0	0	Lowell, 3b	3	1	1	1
Hawpe, rf	4	0	1	0	Drew, rf	2	0	2	0
Tulowitzki, ss	2	0	0	0	Varitek, c	3	0	0	1
Torrealba, c	2	0	0	0	Ellsbury, cf	3	0	1	0
Spilborghs, dh	3	0	0	0	Lugo, ss	3	0	0	0
Totals	**29**	**1**	**5**	**1**	**Totals**	**28**	**2**	**6**	**2**

```
                          R   H
Colorado ..... 100 000 000  —  1   5
Boston ....... 000 110 00x  —  2   6
```

E: Boston—Lowell (1). **2B:** Boston—Lowell (2). **SB:** Boston—Ellsbury (1). **Pick:** Colorado—Holliday (1). **BB:** Colorado—Helton, Tulowitzki; Boston—Pedroia, Youkilis 2, Ortiz, Lowell, Drew, Ellsbury. **S:** Boston—Lugo; Colorado—Torrealba. **SF:** Boston—Varitek.

Colorado	IP	H	R	ER	BB	SO	P	ERA
Jimenez (L, 0-1)	4 2/3	3	2	2	5	2	91	3.8
Affeldt	0	0	0	0	1	0	6	0.00
Herges	1	1	0	0	1	0	25	0.00
Fuentes	2	1	0	0	0	1	20	0.00
Corpas	1/3	1	0	0	0	0	7	0.00

Boston	IP	H	R	ER	BB	SO	P	ERA
Schilling (W, 1-0)	5 1/3	4	1	1	2	4	82	1.6
Okajima	2 1/3	0	0	0	0	4	28	0.00
Papelbon (S, 1)	1 1/3	1	0	0	0	2	16	0.00

HBP: by Jimenez (Drew); by Schilling (Taveras).
Attendance: 36,730 (36,525). **Time:** 3:39.

Game 3

Saturday, Oct. 27, at Colorado

Boston	AB	R	H	RBI	Colorado	AB	R	H	RBI
Ellsbury, cf-rf	5	2	4	2	Matsui, 2b	5	1	3	0
Pedroia, 2b	5	1	3	2	Tulowitzki, ss	4	1	1	0
Ortiz, 1b	4	1	1	1	Holliday, lf	5	1	1	3
Youkilis, 1b	1	0	0	0	Helton, 1b	4	1	1	0
Ramirez, lf	4	0	0	0	Atkins, 3b	2	1	0	0
Lowell, 3b	5	2	2	2	Hawpe, rf	5	0	2	1
Drew, rf	4	0	1	0	Torrealba, c	5	0	2	1
Cora, 2b	0	0	0	0	Sullivan, cf	2	0	0	0
Varitek, c	4	1	1	1	Spilbrghs, ph-cf	2	0	0	0
Lugo, ss	3	2	1	0	Fogg, p	1	0	0	0
Matsuzaka, p	3	0	1	2	Morales, p	1	0	0	0
Crisp, cf	1	1	1	0	Smith, ph	1	0	1	0
					Baker, ph	1	0	0	0
					Taveras, ph	1	0	0	0
Totals	**39**	**10**	**15**	**10**	**Totals**	**38**	**5**	**11**	**5**

```
                          R   H   E
Boston ....... 006 000 031  —  10  15   1
Colorado ..... 000 002 300  —   5  11   0
```

E: Boston—Lugo (1). **2B:** Boston—Lugo (1), Ellsbury 3 (3), Ortiz (3), Drew (2), Pedroia (1). **3B:** Colorado—Hawpe (1). **HR:** Colorado—Holliday (1, off Okajima, 2 on). **SB:** Boston—Lowell (1); Colorado—Matsui (1). **BB:** Boston—Ramirez, Lugo 2; Colorado—Tulowitzki, Helton, Atkins 2. **S:** Boston—Cora. **SF:** Boston—Varitek.

Boston	IP	H	R	ER	BB	SO	P	ERA
Matsuzaka (W, 1-0)	5 1/3	3	2	2	3	5	101	3.3
Lopez	0	2	0	0	0	0	6	0.00
Timlin	2/3	2	2	2	0	0	14	10.8
Okajima	1	2	1	0	0	2	29	2.7
Delcarmen	2/3	1	0	0	1	0	19	0.00
Papelbon (S, 2)	1 1/3	1	0	0	0	0	15	0.00

Colorado	IP	H	R	ER	BB	SO	P	ERA
Fogg (L, 0-1)	2 2/3	10	6	6	2	2	67	20.2
Morales	2 1/3	1	0	0	0	1	35	21.00
Affeldt	1	0	0	0	0	3	16	0.00
Herges	1	0	0	0	0	3	14	0.00
Fuentes	1	3	3	3	1	0	24	9.00
Hawkins	1	1	1	1	0	0	9	4.50

HBP: by Matsuzaka (Atkins). **IBB:** by Fogg (Ramirez).
Attendance: 49,983 (50,449). **Time:** 4:19.

Game 4
Sunday, Oct. 28, at Colorado

Boston	AB	R	H	RBI	Colorado	AB	R	H	RBI
Ellsbury, cf-lf	4	1	2	0	Matsui, 2b	4	0	1	0
Pedroia, 2b	4	0	0	0	Smith, ph	1	0	0	0
Ortiz, 1b	3	0	1	1	Tulowitzki, ss	4	0	0	0
Crisp, pr-cf	0	0	0	0	Holliday, lf	4	0	0	0
Ramirez, lf	4	0	0	0	Helton, 1b	4	1	2	0
Lowell, 3b	4	2	2	1	Atkins, 3b	3	1	1	2
Drew, rf	4	0	0	0	Spilborghs, cf	3	0	0	0
Varitek, c	4	0	2	1	Hawpe, rf	3	1	1	1
Lugo, ss	3	0	1	0	Torrealba, c	4	0	0	0
Lester, p	2	0	0	0	Cook, p	2	0	1	0
Kielty, ph	1	1	1	1	Sullivan, ph	1	0	1	0
					Carroll, 2b	1	0	0	0
Totals	**33**	**4**	**9**	**4**	**Totals**	**34**	**3**	**7**	**3**

```
                        R  H  E
Boston ...... 100  010  110  —   4  9  0
Colorado .... 000  000  120  —   3  7  0
```

2B: Boston—Ellsbury (4), Lowell (3); Colorado—Helton (2), Matsui (1). **HR:** Boston—Lowell (1, off Cook, 0 on), Kielty (1, off Fuentes, 0 on); Colorado—Hawpe (1, off Delcarmen, 0 on), Atkins (1, off Okajima, 1 on). **BB:** Boston—Ortiz; Colorado—Atkins, Spilborghs, Hawpe.

Boston	IP	H	R	ER	BB	SO	P	ERA
Lester (W, 1-0)	5⅔	3	0	0	3	3	92	0.00
Delcarmen	⅔	2	1	1	0	1	19	6.75
Timlin	⅔	0	0	0	0	2	11	7.71
Okajima	⅓	2	2	2	0	0	15	7.36
Papelbon (S, 3)	1⅔	0	0	0	0	1	23	0.00

Colorado	IP	H	R	ER	BB	SO	P	ERA
Cook (L, 0-1)	6	6	3	3	0	2	70	4.50
Affeldt	1	1	0	0	0	1	12	0.00
Fuentes	⅔	2	1	1	1	0	17	9.82
Corpas	1⅓	0	0	0	0	1	13	0.00

Attendance: 50,041 (50,449). **Time:** 3:35.

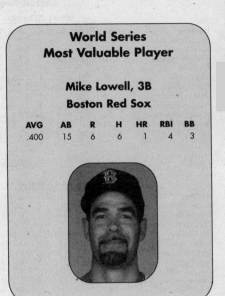

World Series Most Valuable Player

Mike Lowell, 3B
Boston Red Sox

AVG	AB	R	H	HR	RBI	BB
.400	15	6	6	1	4	3

World Series Composite Box Score

Boston Red Sox

	WS vs. Colorado							Overall Playoffs						
Batting	Avg	AB	R	H	HR	RBI	BB	SO	Avg	AB	R	H	HR	RBI	BB	SO
Bobby Kielty	1.000	1	1	1	1	1	0	0	.500	6	2	3	1	3	1	2
Coco Crisp	.500	2	1	1	0	0	0	0	.182	33	3	6	0	2	1	9
Jacoby Ellsbury	.438	16	4	7	0	3	2	2	.360	25	8	9	0	4	3	3
Mike Lowell	.400	15	6	6	1	4	3	1	.353	51	10	18	2	15	6	4
Julio Lugo	.385	13	2	5	0	1	3	0	.271	48	7	13	0	3	5	9
David Ortiz	.333	15	4	5	0	4	2	3	.370	46	16	17	3	10	14	9
Jason Varitek	.333	15	2	5	0	5	1	5	.269	52	6	14	1	10	3	14
J.D. Drew	.333	15	1	5	0	2	1	3	.314	51	7	16	1	11	2	6
Daisuke Matsuzaka	.333	3	0	1	0	2	0	1	.333	3	0	1	0	2	0	1
Dustin Pedroia	.278	18	2	5	1	4	2	0	.283	60	12	17	2	10	6	7
Manny Ramirez	.250	16	3	4	0	2	2	2	.348	46	11	16	4	16	16	9
Kevin Youkilis	.222	9	3	2	0	1	3	1	.388	49	16	19	4	10	9	8
Eric Hinske	.000	1	0	0	0	0	0	1	.000	2	1	0	0	0	0	2
Jon Lester	.000	2	0	0	0	0	0	1	.000	2	0	0	0	0	0	1
Doug Mirabelli	—	0	0	0	0	0	0	0	.000	2	0	0	0	0	0	1
Mike Timlin	—	0	0	0	0	0	0	0	—	0	0	0	0	0	0	0
Alex Cora	—	0	0	0	0	0	0	0	—	0	0	0	0	0	0	0
Javier Lopez	—	0	0	0	0	0	0	0	—	0	0	0	0	0	0	0
Manny Delcarmen	—	0	0	0	0	0	0	0	—	0	0	0	0	0	0	0
Jonathan Papelbon	—	0	0	0	0	0	0	0	—	0	0	0	0	0	0	0
Hideki Okajima	—	0	0	0	0	0	0	0	—	0	0	0	0	0	0	0
TOTALS	.333	141	29	47	3	29	19	20	.313	476	99	149	18	96	66	85

World Series Composite Box (Cont.)
Boston Red Sox (Cont.)

Pitching	WS vs. Colorado								Overall Playoffs							
	ERA	W-L	Sv	Gm	IP	H	BB	SO	ERA	W-L	Sv	Gm	IP	H	BB	SO
Eric Gagne	0.00	0-0	0	1	1.0	0	0	0	6.23	0-1	0	5	4.1	4	2	6
Javier Lopez	0.00	0-0	0	1	0.0	2	0	0	15.43	0-0	0	5	2.1	5	2	0
Jonathan Papelbon	0.00	0-0	3	3	4.1	2	0	3	0.00	1-0	4	7	10.2	5	4	7
Jon Lester	0.00	1-0	0	1	5.2	3	3	3	1.93	1-0	0	3	9.1	6	4	8
Josh Beckett	1.29	1-0	0	1	7.0	6	1	9	1.20	4-0	0	4	30.0	19	2	35
Curt Schilling	1.69	1-0	0	1	5.1	4	2	4	3.00	3-0	0	4	24.0	25	3	16
Daisuke Matsuzaka	3.38	1-0	0	1	5.1	3	3	5	5.03	2-1	0	4	19.2	22	8	17
Manny Delcarmen	6.75	0-0	0	1	1.1	3	1	1	8.31	0-0	0	6	4.1	7	3	5
Hideki Okajima	7.36	0-0	0	3	3.2	4	0	6	2.45	0-0	0	8	11.0	9	3	11
Mike Timlin	7.71	0-0	0	3	2.1	2	0	3	3.18	0-0	0	6	5.2	3	0	7
Tim Wakefield	—	0-0	0	0	0.0	0	0	0	9.64	0-1	0	1	4.2	5	2	7
TOTALS	2.50	4-0	3	4	36.0	29	10	36	3.29	11-3	4	14	126.0	110	33	119

Colorado Rockies

Batting	WS vs. Boston								Overall Playoffs							
	Avg	AB	R	H	HR	RBI	BB	SO	Avg	AB	R	H	HR	RBI	BB	SO
Aaron Cook	.500	2	0	1	0	0	0	0	.500	2	0	1	0	0	0	0
Seth Smith	.500	2	0	1	0	0	0	1	.500	6	2	3	0	2	0	1
Todd Helton	.333	15	2	5	0	1	2	3	.220	41	6	9	0	2	5	9
Cory Sullivan	.333	3	0	1	0	0	0	3	.333	6	0	2	0	0	0	1
Kazuo Matsui	.294	17	1	5	0	0	0	5	.304	46	5	14	1	8	3	12
Matt Holliday	.294	17	4	5	1	3	0	3	.289	45	4	13	5	10	1	12
Brad Hawpe	.250	16	1	4	1	2	1	8	.282	39	4	11	1	4	8	16
Troy Tulowitzki	.231	13	1	3	0	1	2	5	.195	41	3	8	1	3	4	15
Garrett Atkins	.154	13	3	2	1	2	0	3	.175	40	6	7	1	3	5	6
Yorvit Torrealba	.143	14	0	2	0	1	0	1	.256	39	5	10	1	8	4	6
Jamey Carroll	.000	1	0	0	0	0	0	0	.000	2	0	0	0	0	1	0
Jeff Baker	.000	1	0	0	0	0	0	0	.500	4	0	2	0	0	1	1
Franklin Morales	.000	1	0	0	0	0	0	1	.000	3	0	0	0	0	0	2
Willy Taveras	.000	8	1	0	0	0	0	0	.115	26	4	3	0	1	2	8
Ryan Spilborghs	.000	10	0	0	0	0	2	4	.150	20	1	3	0	5	5	7
Josh Fogg	—	0	0	0	0	0	0	0	.000	2	0	0	0	0	1	0
Jeff Francis	—	0	0	0	0	0	0	0	.000	4	0	0	0	0	0	1
Ubaldo Jimenez	—	0	0	0	0	0	0	0	.000	3	0	0	0	0	0	0
LaTroy Hawkins	—	0	0	0	0	0	0	0	—	0	0	0	0	0	0	0
Matt Herges	—	0	0	0	0	0	0	0	—	0	0	0	0	0	0	0
Brian Fuentes	—	0	0	0	0	0	0	0	—	0	0	0	0	0	0	0
Jermey Affeldt	—	0	0	0	0	0	0	0	—	0	0	0	0	0	0	0
Manny Corpas	—	0	0	0	0	0	0	0	—	0	0	0	0	0	0	0
Ryan Speier	—	0	0	0	0	0	0	0	—	0	0	0	0	0	0	0
TOTALS	.218	133	10	29	3	10	10	36	.233	369	44	86	10	42	39	97

Pitching	ERA	W-L	Sv	Gm	IP	H	BB	SO	ERA	W-L	Sv	Gm	IP	H	BB	SO
Matt Herges	0.00	0-0	0	3	3.1	1	2	4	0.00	1-0	0	7	7.0	2	3	6
Jeremy Affeldt	0.00	0-0	0	4	3.0	2	1	2	1.69	0-0	0	7	5.1	3	1	4
Ryan Speier	0.00	0-0	0	1	0.0	0	3	0	0.00	0-0	1	3	2.1	1	3	1
Manny Corpas	0.00	0-0	0	2	1.2	1	0	2	0.87	1-0	5	9	10.1	6	0	7
Ubaldo Jimenez	3.86	0-1	0	1	4.2	3	5	2	2.25	0-1	0	3	16.1	11	13	13
LaTroy Hawkins	4.50	0-0	0	2	2.0	1	0	2	1.80	0-0	0	5	5.0	2	1	3
Aaron Cook	4.50	0-1	0	1	6.0	6	0	2	4.50	0-1	0	1	6.0	6	0	2
Brian Fuentes	9.82	0-0	0	3	3.2	4	2	1	6.52	1-0	0	10	9.2	14	5	11
Jeff Francis	13.50	0-1	0	1	4.0	10	3	3	4.86	2-1	0	3	16.2	21	6	15
Josh Fogg	20.25	0-1	0	1	2.2	10	2	2	5.91	0-1	0	3	10.2	18	3	6
Franklin Morales	21.00	0-0	0	2	3.0	7	1	0	9.90	0-0	0	4	10.0	15	4	6
TOTALS	7.68	0-4	0	4	34.0	47	19	20	4.00	7-4	6	11	99.0	99	39	74

Score by Innings

	1	2	3	4	5	6	7	8	9		R	H	E
Colorado	1	1	0	0	0	2	4	2	0	–	10	29	0
Boston	4	1	6	3	9	0	1	4	1	–	29	47	2

E: Boston—Lowell, Drew. **2B:** Colorado—Helton 2, Tulowitzki 2, Matsui, Atkins; Boston—Ellsbury 4, Lowell 3, Ortiz 3, Drew 2, Youkilis 2, Pedroia, Ramirez, Varitek, Lugo. **3B:** Colorado—Hawpe. **HR:** Colorado—Holliday, Hawpe, Atkins; Boston—Kielty, Lowell, Pedroia. **SB:** Colorado—Matsui; Boston—Ellsbury, Lowell. **S:** Colorado—Torrealba; Boston—Lugo, Cora. **SF:** Boston—Varitek 2. **HBP:** by Jimemez (Drew), by Schilling (Taveras), by Matsuzaka (Atkins). **IBB:** by Francis (Lowell), by Fogg (Ramirez). **Balk:** Colorado—Morales. **DP:** Colorado—3; Boston—2. **LOB:** Colorado—28; Boston—34.

COLLEGE

Final *Baseball America* Top 25

Final 2007 Division I Top 25, voted on by the editors of *Baseball America* and released after the NCAA CollegeWorld Series. Given are final records (excluding ties) and winning percentage (including all postseason games); records in College World Series and team eliminated by (DNP indicates team did not play in tourney); head coach (career years and four-year college record including 2007 postseason); preseason ranking and rank before start of CWS.

	Record	Pct	CWS Recap	Head Coach	Preseason Rank	Rank before CWS
1 Oregon St.	48-18	.727	5-0	Pat Casey (13 yrs: 434-268-4)	16	16
2 North Carolina	57-16	.781	4-3 (Oregon St.)	Mike Fox (24 yrs: 938-317-5)	5	2
3 Rice	56-14	.800	2-2 (N. Carolina)	Wayne Graham (16 yrs: 740-284)	1	1
4 UC Irvine	47-17	.734	2-2 (Oregon St.)	Dave Serrano (3 yrs: 114-66-1)	NR	4
5 Arizona St.	49-15	.766	1-2 (UC Irvine)	Pat Murphy (20 yrs: 902-428-4)	20	3
6 Vanderbilt	54-13	.806		Tim Corbin (5 yrs: 198-108)	8	5
7 Louisville	47-24	.662	1-2 (N. Carolina)	Dan McDonnell (1 yr: 47-24)	NR	22
8 Mississippi St.	38-22	.633	0-2 (Louisville)	Ron Polk (34 yrs: 1351-669-2)	NR	19
9 CS-Fullerton	38-25	.603	0-2 (UC Irvine)	George Horton (11 yrs: 490-212-1)	14	25
10 South Carolina	46-20	.697		Ray Tanner (20 yrs: 895-393-3)	6	6
11 Texas	46-17	.730		Augie Garrido (39 yrs: 1629-755-8)	4	10
12 Texas A&M	48-20	.706		Rob Childress (2 yrs: 73-50-1)	NR	7
13 Wichita St.	53-21	.716		Gene Stephenson (30 yrs: 1605-533-3)	10	8
14 Florida St.	49-13	.790		Mike Martin (28 yrs: 1484-506-4)	18	11
15 Clemson	41-23	.640		Jack Leggett (28 yrs: 1026-572)	3	9
16 Virginia	45-16	.738		Brian O'Connor (4 yrs: 177-66)	9	12
17 Mississippi	40-25	.615		Mike Bianco (10 yrs: 382-228-1)	25	13
18 San Diego	43-18	.705		Rich Hill (18 yrs: 599-420-3)	NR	14
19 Michigan	42-19	.689		Rich Maloney (12 yrs: 447-256-1)	NR	15
20 Coastal Carolina	50-13	.794		Gary Gilmore (18 yrs: 717-357)	NR	17
21 Arkansas	43-21	.672		Dave Van Horn (14 yrs: 572-278)	7	18
22 UCLA	33-28	.541		John Savage (7 yrs: 169-178-1)	13	20
23 Oklahoma St.	42-21	.667		Frank Anderson (4 yrs: 154-91)	22	21
24 Missouri	42-18	.700		Tim Jamieson (13 yrs: 447-318-9)	NR	23
25 TCU	48-14	.774		Jim Schlossnagle (5 yrs: 214-100)	24	24

College World Series

CWS participants: Arizona St. (48-13); CS-Fullerton (38-23); Louisville (46-22); Mississippi St. (38-20); North Carolina (53-13); Oregon St. (43-18); Rice (54-12); UC Irvine (45-15).

Bracket One

June 15—Rice 15	Louisville 10
June 15—North Carolina 8	Mississippi St. 5
June 17—Louisville 12	Mississippi St. 4 (out)
June 17—Rice 14	North Carolina 4
June 19—North Carolina 3	Louisville 1 (out)
June 20—North Carolina 6	Rice 1
June 21—North Carolina 7	Rice 4 (out)

Bracket Two

June 16—Arizona St. 5	UC Irvine 4
June 16—Oregon St. 3	CS-Fullerton 2
June 18—UC Irvine 5 …13 inn	CS-Fullerton 4 (out)
June 18—Oregon St. 12	Arizona St. 6
June 19—UC Irvine 8 …10 inn	Arizona St. 7 (out)
June 20—Oregon St. 7	UC Irvine 1 (out)

Championship Series

June 23—Oregon St. 11	North Carolina 4
June 24—Oregon St. 9	North Carolina 3 (out)

Most Outstanding Player

Jorge Reyes, Oregon St., P

W-L	IP	H	ER	BB	K	ERA
2-0	12.1	11	4	3	6	2.92

All-Tournament Team

C–Mitch Canham, Oregon St.; **1B**–Dustin Ackley, North Carolina; **2B**–Joey Wong, Oregon St.; **3B**–Diego Seastrunk, Rice; **SS**–Darwin Barney, Oregon St.; **OF**–Bryan Petersen, UC Irvine; Tim Fedroff, North Carolina; Scott Santschi, Oregon St.; **DH**–Mike Lissman, Oregon St.; **P**–Jorge Reyes, Oregon St. and Andrew Carignan, North Carolina

Annual Awards

Chosen by *Baseball America, Collegiate Baseball*, National Collegiate Baseball Writers Association, American Baseball Coaches Association and USA Baseball.

Players of the Year

David Price, Vanderbilt, P . . . . .BA, ABCA, Dick Howser (NCBWA) & Golden Spikes (USA Baseball)

David Price, Vanderbilt, P . . . . .CB & Tony Thomas, Florida St., 2B

Coach of the Year

Dave Serrano, UC Irvine . . . . .BA
Pat Casey, Oregon St. . . . . .ABCA

Baseball America All-America Team

NCAA Division I All-Americans. Holdovers from 2006 First Team in **bold**.

First Team

Pos		Cl	Avg	HR	RBI
C	**Matt Wieters**, Georgia Tech	Jr.	.358	10	59
1B	Brett Wallace, Arizona St.	So.	.404	16	78
2B	Tony Thomas, Florida St.	Jr.	.430	11	43
3B	**Pedro Alvarez**, Vanderbilt	So.	.386	18	68
SS	Todd Frazier, Rutgers	Jr.	.377	22	65
OF	Kyle Russell, Texas	So.	.336	28	71
OF	**Kellen Kulbacki**, JMU	Jr.	.398	19	49
OF	Grant Desme, Cal Poly	Jr.	.405	15	53
DH	Matt LaPorta, Florida	Sr.	.402	20	52
UT	Joe Savery, Rice	Jr.	.356	6	60

Pos		Cl	W-L	Sv	ERA
SP	David Price, Vanderbilt	Jr.	11-1	0	2.63
SP	Jacob Thompson, Virginia	So.	11-0	0	1.50
SP	Adam Mills, Charlotte	Sr.	14-2	0	1.01
SP	Preston Guilmet, Arizona	So.	12-2	0	1.87
RP	Casey Weathers, Vanderbilt	Sr.	12-2	7	2.37

Second Team

Pos		Cl	Avg	HR	RBI
C	Buster Posey, Florida St.	So.	.382	3	65
1B	Yonder Alonso, Miami-FL	So.	.376	18	74
2B	Eric Sogard, Arizona St.	Jr.	.400	11	62
3B	Brandon Waring, Wofford	Jr.	.401	27	74
SS	Jaime Pedroza, UC Riverside	Jr.	.325	13	55
OF	Corey Brown, Oklahoma St.	Jr.	.335	22	71
OF	Dominic de la Osa, Vanderbilt	Jr.	.378	20	62
OF	Brian Rike, Louisiana Tech	Jr.	.346	20	66
DH	Blake Stouffer, Texas A&M	Sr.	.398	12	85
UT	Zach Putnam, Michigan	So.	.341	8	59

Pos		Cl	W-L	Sv	ERA
SP	Bryan Henry, Florida St.	Sr.	14-2	0	2.60
SP	Brian Matusz, San Diego	So.	10-3	0	2.85
SP	Nick Schmidt, Arkansas	Jr.	11-3	0	2.69
SP	James Simmons, UC Riverside	Jr.	11-3	0	2.40
RP	Pat Venditte, Creighton	Jr.	8-2	4	1.88

NCAA Division I Leaders

Batting

Average

(At least 100 AB & 2.5/Gm)	Cl	Gm	AB	H	Avg
Ryan Lavarnway, Yale	So.	43	150	70	.467
Greg Sexton, William & Mary	Sr.	54	209	95	.455
Ryne White, Purdue	So.	53	199	90	.452
John Koehnlein, Youngstown St.	So.	56	249	108	.434
Robbie Widlansky, Fla. Atlantic	Jr.	58	240	104	.433
Alex Gregory, Radford	So.	40	158	68	.430
Tony Thomas, Florida St.	Jr.	62	258	111	.430
Tim Binkoski, Quinnipiac	Sr.	48	191	81	.424
Ryan Curry, Bradley	Sr.	53	209	87	.416
Matt Prokopowicz, Hofstra	Fr.	54	197	82	.416

Home Runs (per game)

(At least 15 HR)	Cl	Gm	HR	Avg
Kyle Russell, Texas	So.	63	28	0.44
Brandon Waring, Wofford	Jr.	63	27	0.43
Steven Hill, Stephen F. Austin	Sr.	59	24	0.41
Jeff Cunningham, S. Alabama	Jr.	55	22	0.40
Matt LaPorta, Florida	Sr.	52	20	0.38
Scott Krieger, George Mason	So.	54	20	0.37
Brian Pellegrini, St. Bonaventure	Sr.	46	17	0.37
Kellen Kulbacki, James Madison	Jr.	53	19	0.36
Marcus Davis, Alcorn St.	Sr.	45	16	0.36
Corey Brown, Oklahoma St.	Jr.	63	22	0.35
Todd Frazier, Rutgers	Jr.	63	22	0.35

Runs Batted In (per game)

(At least 50 RBI)	Cl	Gm	RBI	Avg
Chris Campbell, Coll. of Charleston	Sr.	58	82	1.41
Marcus Davis, Alcorn St.	Sr.	45	62	1.38
Kenny Smith, Western Carolina	Sr.	62	84	1.35
Sean Coughlin, Kentucky	Sr.	54	73	1.35
Devin Thomas, Brown	Sr.	48	64	1.33
Tyler Mach, Oklahoma St.	Sr.	63	81	1.29
David Wood, Texas St.	Sr.	60	77	1.28
Brian Pellegrini, St. Bonaventure	Sr.	46	59	1.28
Ryan Lavarnway, Yale	So.	43	55	1.28
Blake Stouffer, Texas A&M	Jr.	67	85	1.27

Stolen Bases (per game)

(At least 25)	Cl	Gm	SB	CS	Avg
Tony Campana, Cincinnati	Jr.	56	60	14	1.07
Boomer Whiting, Louisville	Sr.	71	73	14	1.03
James Conrad, Lafayette	Sr.	52	49	6	0.94
Justin Kelly, Grambling	So.	41	33	5	0.80
Nate Parks, Virginia Tech	Sr.	54	39	9	0.72
Michael Richard, Prairie View	Sr.	59	42	8	0.71
Kyle Messineo, Monmouth	Sr.	60	42	4	0.70
Shawn Roof, Illinois	Sr.	58	40	8	0.69
Mark McLaughlin, Georgetown	Sr.	54	37	7	0.69
Marcus Davis, Alcorn St.	Sr.	46	29	4	0.64

Pitching

Earned Run Avg.

(At least 55 inn.)	Cl	Gm	IP	ERA
Adam Mills, Charlotte	Sr.	18	142.2	1.01
Chance Chapman, Oral Roberts	Jr.	22	94.0	1.34
Ryan Woods, Le Moyne	Sr.	30	60.1	1.34
Jay Monti, Sacred Heart	Jr.	12	80.1	1.34
Jacob Thompson, Virginia	So.	17	114.0	1.50
Luke Prihoda, Sam Houston St.	Sr.	35	72.2	1.61
Anthony Capra, Wichita St.	So.	24	76.2	1.76
Matthew Wilson, Bucknell	Jr.	9	60.2	1.78
Luke Pisker, VCU	Jr.	31	68.0	1.85
Preston Guilmet, Arizona	So.	18	135.0	1.87

Wins

	Cl	Gm	IP	W-L
Bryan Henry, Florida St.	Sr.	18	117.2	14-2
Adam Mills, Charlotte	Sr.	18	142.2	14-2
Mike Leake, Arizona St.	Fr.	25	127.0	13-2
Scott Gorgen, UC Irvine	So.	22	136.2	13-3
Josh Satow, Arizona St.	Jr.	20	133.2	13-3
Caleb Glafenhein, East Tenn. St.	Sr.	28	115.1	13-7
Nine tied with 12 wins each.				

Strikeouts (per 9 inn.)

(At least 55 inn.)	Cl	IP	SO	Avg
Josh Dew, Troy	Sr.	65.1	97	13.4
David Price, Vanderbilt	Jr.	133.1	194	13.1
Jess Todd, Arkansas	Jr.	93.1	128	12.3
Chance Chapman, Oral Roberts	Sr.	94.0	127	12.2
Mitch Harris, Navy	Jr.	88.1	119	12.1
Nich Conaway, Oklahoma	So.	63.1	85	12.1
Aaron Jenkins, UNI	Jr.	94.2	126	12.0
Brian Matusz, San Diego	So.	123.0	163	11.9
Danny Farquhar, La.-Lafayette	So.	87.2	115	11.8
Tim Murphy, UCLA	So.	76.0	96	11.4

Saves

	Cl	Gm	IP	Sv
Luke Prihoda, Sam Houston St.	Sr.	35	72.2	18
Andrew Carignan, North Carolina	Jr.	40	63.0	18
Paul Koss, USC	Sr.	29	29.0	16
Andy Masten, Creighton	Sr.	34	49.0	16
Kevin Crum, VMI	So.	24	34.0	14
Matt Shoemaker, Eastern Mich.	Jr.	25	34.0	14
Jordan Flasher, George Mason	So.	27	38.0	14
Ryan Woods, Le Moyne	Sr.	30	60.1	14
Brian Alas, Richmond	Jr.	36	66.0	14
Shane Matthews, East Carolina	Sr.	39	48.0	14
Randy Boone, Texas	Sr.	41	71.1	14

Other College World Series
Participants' final records in parentheses.

NCAA Div. II
at Montgomery, Ala. (May 25-June 1)

Participants: Angelo St. (51-20); Cal State-LA (48-14-1); Columbus St. (51-19); Franklin Pierce (49-11); Kutzown (49-7); Nebraska-Omaha (37-24); Southern Indiana (43-23); Tampa (53-10).

Championship: Tampa def. Columbus St., 7-2.

NCAA Div. III
at Appleton, Wis. (May 25-29)

Participants: Carthage (37-13); Cortland St. (42-7); Eastern Conn. St. (38-12); Chapman (41-8); Emory (43-10); Kean (43-8); Marietta (32-17); Wis.-Stevens Point (34-17).

Championship: Kean, NJ def. Emory, 5-4 (10 innings).

2007 MLB First-Year Player Draft

First round selections at the 43rd First-Year Player Draft held June 7-8, 2007 at Disney's Wide World of Sports complex in Orlando, Fla. Clubs select in reverse order of their standing from the preceding season. The Tampa Bay Devil Rays chose 19-year-old lefthanded pitcher David Price from Vanderbilt with the top overall pick.

First Round

No		Pos
1	Tampa Bay . . . . David Price, Vanderbilt	LHP
2	Kansas City . . . . . Mike Moustakas, Chatsworth (Calif) HS	SS
3	Chicago-NL . . . Josh Vitters, Cypress (Calif.) HS	3B
4	Pittsburgh . . . . Daniel Moskos, Clemson	LHP
5	Baltimore . . . . Matt Wieters, Georgia Tech	C
6	Washington . . . . . Ross Detwiler, Missouri St.	LHP
7	Milwaukee . . . . Matt LaPorta, Florida	1B
8	Colorado . . . . Casey Weathers, Vanderbilt	RHP
9	Arizona . . . . Jarrod Parker, Norwell HS, Ossian, Ind.	RHP
10	San Francisco . . . . . Madison Bumgarner, South Caldwell HS, Hudson, NC	LHP
11	Seattle . . . . Phillippe Aumont, Ecole secondaire du Versant Gatineau, Quebec	RHP
12	Florida Matt Dominguez, Chatsworth (Calif.) HS	3B
13	Cleveland . . . . Beau Mills, Lewis-Clark St.	3B
14	Atlanta . . . . Jason Heyward, Henry County HS, McDonough, Ga.	CF
15	Cincinnati . . . . Devin Mesoraco Punxsutawney (Pa.) HS	C

No		Pos
16	a-Toronto . . . . Kevin Ahrens, Memorial HS, Houston, Texas	3B
17	b-Texas . . . . Blake Beavan, Irving, Texas	RHP
18	St. Louis . . . . Peter Kozma, Owasso (Okla.) HS	SS
19	Philadelphia . . . . Joe Savery, Rice	LHP
20	c-Los Angeles . . . . Chris Withrow, Midland Christian HS, Odessa, Texas	RHP
21	Toronto . . . . J.P Arencibia, Tennessee	C
22	d-San Francisco . . . Tim Alderson, Horizon HS, Scottsdale, Ariz.	RHP
23	San Diego . . . . Nick Schmidt, Arkansas	LHP
24	e-Texas . . . . . . Michael Main, Deland (Fla.) HS	RHP
25	Chicago-AL . . . . . Aaron Poreda, San Francisco	LHP
26	Oakland . . . . . . James Simmons, UC Riverside	RHP
27	Detroit . . . . Rick Porcello, Seton Hall Prep, West Orange, NJ	RHP
28	Minnesota . . . . Ben Revere, Lexington (Ky.) Catholic HS	CF
29	f-San Francisco . . . . . Wendell Fairley, George County-Lucedale (Miss.) HS	RF
30	New York (AL) . . Andrew Brackman, N.C. State	RHP

a-from Tex. for Frank Catalanotto; **b-**from Hou. for Carlos Lee; **c-**from Bos. for Julio Lugo; **d-**from LAD for Jason Schmidt; **e-**from LAA for Gary Matthews Jr.; **f-**from NYM for Moises Alou.

Straight to the Majors
Since Major League baseball began its First-Year Player Draft in 1965, 20 selections have advanced directly to the major leagues without first playing in the minors

Draft		Pos	Team
1967	Mike Adamson, USC	P	Baltimore
1969	Steve Dunning, Stanford	P	Cleveland
1971	Pete Broberg, Dartmouth	P	Washington
	Rob Ellis, Michigan St.	OF	Milwaukee
	Burt Hooton, Texas	P	Chicago-NL
1972	Dave Roberts, Oregon	3B	San Diego
1973	Dick Ruthven, Fresno St.	P	Philadelphia
	David Clyde, Westchester HS (Tex.)	P	Texas
	Dave Winfield, Minnesota	OF	San Diego
	Eddie-Bane, Arizona St.	P	Minnesota

Draft		Pos	Team
1978	Tim Conroy, Gateway HS (Pa.)	P	Oakland
	Bob Horner, Arizona St.	3B	Atlanta
	Brian Milner, Southwest HS (Tex.)	C	Toronto
	Mike Morgan, Valley HS (Nev.)	P	Oakland
1985	Pete Incaviglia, Oklahoma St.	OF	Montreal
1988	Jim Abbott, Michigan	P	California
1989	John Olerud, Washington St.	1B	Toronto
1993	Darren Dreifort, Wichita St.	P	LA Dodgers
1995	Ariel Prieto, Fajardo U (Cuba)	P	Oakland
2000	Xavier Nady, California	3B	San Diego

Minor League Triple-A Final Standings

Playoff qualifiers (*) are noted.

International League

North Division

	W	L	Pct	GB
*Scranton/Wilkes-Barre (Yankees)	84	59	.587	—
Rochester (Twins)	77	67	.535	7½
Buffalo (Indians)	75	67	.528	8½
Pawtucket (Red Sox)	67	75	.472	16½
Syracuse (Blue Jays)	64	80	.444	20½
Ottawa (Phillies)	55	88	.385	29

South Division

	W	L	Pct	GB
*Durham (Devil Rays)	80	63	.559	—
*Richmond (Braves)	77	64	.546	2
Norfolk (Orioles)	69	74	.483	11
Charlotte (White Sox)	63	80	.441	17

West Division

	W	L	Pct	GB
*Toledo (Tigers)	82	61	.573	—
Louisville (Reds)	74	70	.514	8½
Indianapolis (Pirates)	70	73	.490	12
Columbus (Nationals)	64	80	.444	18½

Playoffs

First Round (Best-of-Five)

Richmond 3 . . . . Scranton-Wilkes Barre 1
Durham 3 . . . . Toledo 0

Championship (Best-of-Five)

Richmond vs. Durham

Sept. 11	Richmond, 4-2	at Durham
Sept. 12	Durham, 5-1	at Durham
Sept. 13	Durham, 3-2	at Richmond
Sept. 14	Richmond, 6-2	at Richmond
Sept. 15	Richmond, 7-2	at Richmond

Richmond wins Governors' Cup, 3-2

Pacific Coast League

American Conference

Northern Division

	W	L	Pct	GB
*Nashville (Brewers)	89	55	.618	—
Iowa (Cubs)	79	65	.549	10
Omaha (Royals)	73	71	.507	16
Memphis (Cardinals)	56	88	.389	33

Southern Division

	W	L	Pct	GB
*New Orleans (Mets)	75	69	.521	—
Albuquerque (Marlins)	72	70	.507	2
Oklahoma (Rangers)	71	72	.497	3½
Round Rock (Astros)	61	81	.430	13

Pacific Conference

Northern Division

	W	L	Pct	GB
*Salt Lake (Angels)	74	69	.517	—
Colorado Springs (Rockies)	69	75	.479	5½
Tacoma (Mariners)	68	76	.472	6½
Portland (Padres)	58	86	.403	16½

Southern Division

	W	L	Pct	GB
*Sacramento (A's)	84	60	.583	—
Fresno (Giants)	77	67	.535	7
Tucson (Diamondbacks)	75	67	.528	8
Las Vegas (Dodgers)	67	77	.465	17

Playoffs

Conference Finals (Best-of-Five)

Sacramento 3 . . . . Salt Lake 2
New Orleans 3 . . . . Nashville 1

Championship (Best-of-Five)

Sacramento vs. New Orleans

Sept. 11	Sacramento, 5-3	at New Orleans
Sept. 12	Sacramento, 3-2	at New Orleans
Sept. 14	Sacramento, 4-3	at Sacramento

Sacramento wins PCL Championship, 3-0

The 2007 Bricktown Showdown

On September 18, the Pacific Coast League champion Sacramento River Cats defeated the International League champion Richmond Braves, 7-1, in the winner-take-all Triple-A championship game at Oklahoma City's AT&T Bricktown Ballpark. Sacramento's Lou Merloni went 2-for-5 with a home run and 4 RBI to win the game's MVP award.

2007 International League All-Star Team

As selected by IL managers, coaches and media.

Pos	Name/Team
C	Jose Morales, Rochester
1B	Joey Votto, Louisville
2B	Martin Prado, Richmond
SS	Brian Bixler, Indianapolis
3B	Mike Hessman, Toledo
DH	Shelley Duncan, Scranton/Wilkes-Barre
OF	Ben Francisco, Buffalo
OF	Timo Perez, Toledo
OF	Justin Ruggiano, Durham
UT	Aaron Herr, Louisville
SP	Kevin Slowey, Rochester
REL	Cory Doyne, Norfolk

2007 Pacific Coast League All-Star Team

As selected by PCL managers and media representatives.

Pos	Name/Team
C	Geovany Soto, Iowa
1B	Joe Koshansky, Colorado Springs
2B	Eric Patterson, Iowa
SS	Robert Andino, Albuquerque
3B	Scott Seabol, Albuquerque
DH	Val Pascucci, Albuquerque
OF	Rick Ankiel, Memphis
OF	Adam Jones, Tacoma
OF	Delwyn Young, Las Vegas
RHP	R.A. Dickey, Nashville
LHP	Adam Pettyjohn, Nashville
REL	Ryan Speier, Colorado Springs

1876-2007
Through the Years

SPORTS ALMANAC

The World Series

The World Series began in 1903 when Pittsburgh of the older National League (founded in 1876) invited Boston of the American League (founded in 1901) to play a best-of-9 game series to determine which of the two league champions was the best. Boston was the surprise winner, 5 games to 3. The 1904 NL champion New York Giants refused to play Boston the following year, so there was no Series. Giants' owner John T. Brush and his manager John McGraw both despised AL president Ban Johnson and considered the junior circuit to be a minor league. By the following year, however, Brush and Johnson had smoothed out their differences and the Giants agreed to play Philadelphia in a best-of-7 game series. Since then the World Series has been a best-of-7 format, except from 1919-21 when it returned to best-of-9.

In the chart below, the National League teams are listed in CAPITAL letters. Also, each World Series champion's wins and losses are noted in parentheses after the Series score in games.

Multiple champions: New York Yankees (26); St. Louis Cardinals (10); Philadelphia-Oakland A's (9); Boston Red Sox (7); Brooklyn-Los Angeles Dodgers (6); Cincinnati Reds, New York-San Francisco Giants and Pittsburgh Pirates (5); Detroit Tigers (4); Baltimore Orioles, Boston-Milwaukee-Atlanta Braves, Chicago White Sox and Washington Senators-Minnesota Twins (3); Chicago Cubs, Cleveland Indians, Florida Marlins, New York Mets and Toronto Blue Jays (2).

Year	Winner	Manager	Series	Loser	Manager
1903	Boston Red Sox	Jimmy Collins	5-3 (LWLLWWWW)	PITTSBURGH	Fred Clarke
1904	Not held				
1905	NY GIANTS	John McGraw	4-1 (WLWWW)	Philadelphia A's	Connie Mack
1906	Chicago White Sox	Fielder Jones	4-2 (WLWLWW)	CHICAGO CUBS	Frank Chance
1907	CHICAGO CUBS	Frank Chance	4-0-1 (TWWWW)	Detroit	Hughie Jennings
1908	CHICAGO CUBS	Frank Chance	4-1 (WWLWW)	Detroit	Hughie Jennings
1909	PITTSBURGH	Fred Clarke	4-3 (WLWLWLW)	Detroit	Hughie Jennings
1910	Philadelphia A's	Connie Mack	4-1 (WWWLW)	CHICAGO CUBS	Frank Chance
1911	Philadelphia A's	Connie Mack	4-2 (WLWWLW)	NY GIANTS	John McGraw
1912	Boston Red Sox	Jake Stahl	4-3-1 (WTLWWLLW)	NY GIANTS	John McGraw
1913	Philadelphia A's	Connie Mack	4-1 (WLWWW)	NY GIANTS	John McGraw
1914	BOSTON BRAVES	George Stallings	4-0	Philadelphia A's	Connie Mack
1915	Boston Red Sox	Bill Carrigan	4-1 (LWWWW)	PHILA. PHILLIES	Pat Moran
1916	Boston Red Sox	Bill Carrigan	4-1 (WWLWW)	BROOKLYN	Wilbert Robinson
1917	Chicago White Sox	Pants Rowland	4-2 (WWLLWW)	NY GIANTS	John McGraw
1918	Boston Red Sox	Ed Barrow	4-2 (WLWLWW)	CHICAGO CUBS	Fred Mitchell
1919	CINCINNATI	Pat Moran	5-3 (WWLWWLLW)	Chicago White Sox	Kid Gleason
1920	Cleveland	Tris Speaker	5-2 (WWLWWW)	BROOKLYN	Wilbert Robinson
1921	NY GIANTS	John McGraw	5-3 (LLWWLWWW)	NY Yankees	Miller Huggins
1922	NY GIANTS	John McGraw	4-0-1 (WTWWW)	NY Yankees	Miller Huggins
1923	NY Yankees	Miller Huggins	4-2 (LWLWWW)	NY GIANTS	John McGraw
1924	Washington	Bucky Harris	4-3 (LWLWLWW)	NY GIANTS	John McGraw
1925	PITTSBURGH	Bill McKechnie	4-3 (LWLLWWW)	Washington	Bucky Harris
1926	ST.L. CARDINALS	Rogers Hornsby	4-3 (LWWLLWW)	NY Yankees	Miller Huggins
1927	NY Yankees	Miller Huggins	4-0	PITTSBURGH	Donie Bush
1928	NY Yankees	Miller Huggins	4-0	ST.L. CARDINALS	Bill McKechnie
1929	Philadelphia A's	Connie Mack	4-1 (WWLWW)	CHICAGO CUBS	Joe McCarthy
1930	Philadelphia A's	Connie Mack	4-2 (WWLLWW)	ST.L. CARDINALS	Gabby Street
1931	ST.L. CARDINALS	Gabby Street	4-3 (LWWLWLW)	Philadelphia A's	Connie Mack
1932	NY Yankees	Joe McCarthy	4-0	CHICAGO CUBS	Charlie Grimm
1933	NY GIANTS	Bill Terry	4-1 (WWLWW)	Washington	Joe Cronin
1934	ST.L. CARDINALS	Frankie Frisch	4-3 (WLWLLWW)	Detroit	Mickey Cochrane
1935	Detroit	Mickey Cochrane	4-2 (LWWWLW)	CHICAGO CUBS	Charlie Grimm
1936	NY Yankees	Joe McCarthy	4-2 (WLWWLW)	NY GIANTS	Bill Terry
1937	NY Yankees	Joe McCarthy	4-1 (WWWLW)	NY GIANTS	Bill Terry
1938	NY Yankees	Joe McCarthy	4-0	CHICAGO CUBS	Gabby Hartnett
1939	NY Yankees	Joe McCarthy	4-0	CINCINNATI	Bill McKechnie
1940	CINCINNATI	Bill McKechnie	4-3 (LWLWLWW)	Detroit	Del Baker
1941	NY Yankees	Joe McCarthy	4-1 (WLWWW)	BKLN. DODGERS	Leo Durocher
1942	ST.L. CARDINALS	Billy Southworth	4-1 (LWWWW)	NY Yankees	Joe McCarthy
1943	NY Yankees	Joe McCarthy	4-1 (WWLWW)	ST.L. CARDINALS	Billy Southworth
1944	ST.L. CARDINALS	Billy Southworth	4-2 (LWLWWW)	St. Louis Browns	Luke Sewell
1945	Detroit	Steve O'Neill	4-3 (LWWLWLW)	CHICAGO CUBS	Charlie Grimm

The World Series (Cont.)

Year	Winner	Manager	Series	Loser	Manager
1946	ST.L. CARDINALS	Eddie Dyer	4-3 (LWLWLWW)	Boston Red Sox	Joe Cronin
1947	NY Yankees	Bucky Harris	4-3 (WWLLWLW)	BKLN. DODGERS	Burt Shotton
1948	Cleveland	Lou Boudreau	4-2 (LWWWLW)	BOSTON BRAVES	Billy Southworth
1949	NY Yankees	Casey Stengel	4-1 (WLWWW)	BKLN. DODGERS	Burt Shotton
1950	NY Yankees	Casey Stengel	4-0	PHILA. PHILLIES	Eddie Sawyer
1951	NY Yankees	Casey Stengel	4-2 (LWLWWW)	NY GIANTS	Leo Durocher
1952	NY Yankees	Casey Stengel	4-3 (LWLWWLW)	BKLN. DODGERS	Charlie Dressen
1953	NY Yankees	Casey Stengel	4-2 (WWLLWW)	BKLN. DODGERS	Charlie Dressen
1954	NY GIANTS	Leo Durocher	4-0	Cleveland	Al Lopez
1955	BKLN. DODGERS	Walter Alston	4-3 (LLWWWLW)	NY Yankees	Casey Stengel
1956	NY Yankees	Casey Stengel	4-3 (LLWWWLW)	BKLN. DODGERS	Walter Alston
1957	MILW. BRAVES	Fred Haney	4-3 (LWLWLWW)	NY Yankees	Casey Stengel
1958	NY Yankees	Casey Stengel	4-3 (LLWLWWW)	MILW. BRAVES	Fred Haney
1959	LA DODGERS	Walter Alston	4-2 (LWWWLW)	Chicago White Sox	Al Lopez
1960	PITTSBURGH	Danny Murtaugh	4-3 (WLLWWLW)	NY Yankees	Casey Stengel
1961	NY Yankees	Ralph Houk	4-1 (WLWWW)	CINCINNATI	Fred Hutchinson
1962	NY Yankees	Ralph Houk	4-3 (WLWLWLW)	SF GIANTS	Alvin Dark
1963	LA DODGERS	Walter Alston	4-0	NY Yankees	Ralph Houk
1964	ST.L. CARDINALS	Johnny Keane	4-3 (WLLWLWW)	NY Yankees	Yogi Berra
1965	LA DODGERS	Walter Alston	4-3 (LLWWWLW)	Minnesota	Sam Mele
1966	Baltimore	Hank Bauer	4-0	LA DODGERS	Walter Alston
1967	ST.L. CARDINALS	Red Schoendienst	4-3 (WLWWWLLW)	Boston Red Sox	Dick Williams
1968	Detroit	Mayo Smith	4-3 (LWLWWWW)	ST.L. CARDINALS	Red Schoendienst
1969	NY METS	Gil Hodges	4-1 (LWWWW)	Baltimore	Earl Weaver
1970	Baltimore	Earl Weaver	4-1 (WWWLW)	CINCINNATI	Sparky Anderson
1971	PITTSBURGH	Danny Murtaugh	4-3 (LLWWWLW)	Baltimore	Earl Weaver
1972	Oakland A's	Dick Williams	4-3 (WWLWLLW)	CINCINNATI	Sparky Anderson
1973	Oakland A's	Dick Williams	4-3 (WLWLWLW)	NY METS	Yogi Berra
1974	Oakland A's	Alvin Dark	4-1 (WLWWW)	LA DODGERS	Walter Alston
1975	CINCINNATI	Sparky Anderson	4-3 (LWWLWLW)	Boston Red Sox	Darrell Johnson
1976	CINCINNATI	Sparky Anderson	4-0	NY Yankees	Billy Martin
1977	NY Yankees	Billy Martin	4-2 (WLWLWLW)	LA DODGERS	Tommy Lasorda
1978	NY Yankees	Bob Lemon	4-2 (LLWWWW)	LA DODGERS	Tommy Lasorda
1979	PITTSBURGH	Chuck Tanner	4-3 (LWLLWWW)	Baltimore	Earl Weaver
1980	PHILA. PHILLIES	Dallas Green	4-2 (WWLLWW)	Kansas City	Jim Frey
1981	LA DODGERS	Tommy Lasorda	4-2 (LLWWWW)	NY Yankees	Bob Lemon
1982	ST.L. CARDINALS	Whitey Herzog	4-3 (LWWLLWW)	Milwaukee Brewers	Harvey Kuenn
1983	Baltimore	Joe Altobelli	4-1 (LWWWW)	PHILA. PHILLIES	Paul Owens
1984	Detroit	Sparky Anderson	4-1 (WWWLW)	SAN DIEGO	Dick Williams
1985	Kansas City	Dick Howser	4-3 (LLWWLWW)	ST.L. CARDINALS	Whitey Herzog
1986	NY METS	Davey Johnson	4-3 (LLWWLWW)	Boston Red Sox	John McNamara
1987	Minnesota	Tom Kelly	4-3 (WWLLLWW)	ST.L. CARDINALS	Whitey Herzog
1988	LA DODGERS	Tommy Lasorda	4-1 (WWLWW)	Oakland A's	Tony La Russa
1989	Oakland A's	Tony La Russa	4-0	SF GIANTS	Roger Craig
1990	CINCINNATI	Lou Piniella	4-0	Oakland A's	Tony La Russa
1991	Minnesota	Tom Kelly	4-3 (WWLLLWW)	ATLANTA BRAVES	Bobby Cox
1992	Toronto	Cito Gaston	4-2 (LWWWLW)	ATLANTA BRAVES	Bobby Cox
1993	Toronto	Cito Gaston	4-2 (WLWLWW)	PHILA. PHILLIES	Jim Fregosi
1994	Not held				
1995	ATLANTA BRAVES	Bobby Cox	4-2 (WWLWLW)	Cleveland	Mike Hargrove
1996	NY Yankees	Joe Torre	4-2 (LLWWWW)	ATLANTA BRAVES	Bobby Cox
1997	FLORIDA	Jim Leyland	4-3 (WLWLWLW)	Cleveland	Mike Hargrove
1998	NY Yankees	Joe Torre	4-0	SAN DIEGO	Bruce Bochy
1999	NY Yankees	Joe Torre	4-0	ATLANTA BRAVES	Bobby Cox
2000	NY Yankees	Joe Torre	4-1 (WWLWW)	NY METS	Bobby Valentine
2001	ARIZONA	Bob Brenly	4-3 (WWLLLWW)	NY Yankees	Joe Torre
2002	Anaheim	Mike Scioscia	4-3 (LWWLLWW)	SF GIANTS	Dusty Baker
2003	FLORIDA	Jack McKeon	4-2 (WLLWWW)	NY Yankees	Joe Torre
2004	Boston	Terry Francona	4-0	ST. LOUIS	Tony La Russa
2005	Chicago White Sox	Ozzie Guillen	4-0	HOUSTON	Phil Garner
2006	ST. LOUIS	Tony La Russa	4-1 (WLWWW)	Detroit	Jim Leyland
2007	Boston	Terry Francona	4-0	COLORADO	Clint Hurdle

Most Valuable Players

urrently selected by media panel and World Series official scorers. Presented by *Sport* magazine from 1955-88 and by Major eague Baseball since 1989. Winner who did not play for World Series champions is in **bold** type.

Multiple winners: Bob Gibson, Reggie Jackson and Sandy Koufax (2).

ear	Year	Year
955 Johnny Podres, Bklyn, P	1974 Rollie Fingers, Oak., P	1991 Jack Morris, Min., P
956 Don Larsen, NY, P	1975 Pete Rose, Cin., 3B	1992 Pat Borders, Tor., C
957 Lew Burdette, Mil., P	1976 Johnny Bench, Cin., C	1993 Paul Molitor, Tor., DH/1B/3B
958 Bob Turley, NY, P	1977 Reggie Jackson, NY, OF	1994 Series not held.
959 Larry Sherry, LA, P.	1978 Bucky Dent, NY, SS	1995 Tom Glavine, Atl., P
	1979 Willie Stargell, Pit., 1B	1996 John Wetteland, NY, P
960 **Bobby Richardson**, NY, 2B		1997 Livan Hernandez, Fla., P
961 Whitey Ford, NY, P	1980 Mike Schmidt, Phi., 3B	1998 Scott Brosius, NY, 3B
962 Ralph Terry, NY, P	1981 Pedro Guerrero, LA, OF;	1999 Mariano Rivera, NY, P
963 Sandy Koufax, LA, P	Ron Cey, LA, 3B;	
964 Bob Gibson, St.L., P	& Steve Yeager, LA, C	2000 Derek Jeter, NY, SS
965 Sandy Koufax, LA, P	1982 Darrell Porter, St.L., C	2001 Curt Schilling, Ari., P
966 Frank Robinson, Bal., OF	1983 Rick Dempsey, Bal., C	& Randy Johnson, Ari., P
967 Bob Gibson, St.L., P	1984 Alan Trammell, Det., SS	2002 Troy Glaus, Ana., 3B
968 Mickey Lolich, Det., P	1985 Bret Saberhagen, KC, P	2003 Josh Beckett, Fla., P
969 Donn Clendenon, NY, 1B	1986 Ray Knight, NY, 3B	2004 Manny Ramirez, Bos., OF
	1987 Frank Viola, Min., P	2005 Jermaine Dye, Chi., OF
970 Brooks Robinson, Bal., 3B	1988 Orel Hershiser, LA, P	2006 David Eckstein, St.L, SS
971 Roberto Clemente, Pit., OF	1989 Dave Stewart, Oak., P	2007 Mike Lowell, Bos., 3B
972 Gene Tenace, Oak., C		
973 Reggie Jackson, Oak., OF	1990 Jose Rijo, Cin., P	

All-Time World Series Leaders

CAREER

World Series leaders through 2007. Years listed indicate number of World Series appearances.

Hitting

Games

	Yrs	Gm
Yogi Berra, NY Yankees	14	75
Mickey Mantle, NY Yankees	12	65
Elston Howard, NY Yankees—Boston	10	54
Hank Bauer, NY Yankees	9	53
Gil McDougald, NY Yankees	8	53

At Bats

	Yrs	AB
Yogi Berra, NY Yankees	14	259
Mickey Mantle, NY Yankees	12	230
Joe DiMaggio, NY Yankees	10	199
Frankie Frisch, NY Giants-St.L. Cards	8	197
Gil McDougald, NY Yankees	8	190

Batting Avg. (minimum 50 AB)

	AB	H	Avg
Pepper Martin, St.L. Cards	55	23	.418
Paul Molitor, Mil. Brewers-Tor. Blue Jays	55	23	.418
Lou Brock, St. Louis	87	34	.391
Marquis Grissom, Atl-Cle	77	30	.390
Thurman Munson, NY Yankees	67	25	.373
George Brett, Kansas City	51	19	.373
Hank Aaron, Milw. Braves	55	20	.364

Hits

	AB	H	Avg
Yogi Berra, NY Yankees	259	71	.274
Mickey Mantle, NY Yankees	230	59	.257
Frankie Frisch, NYG-St.L. Cards	197	58	.294
Joe DiMaggio, NY Yankees	199	54	.271
Hank Bauer, NY Yankees	188	46	.245
Pee Wee Reese, Brooklyn	169	46	.272

Runs

	Gm	R
Mickey Mantle, NY Yankees	65	42
Yogi Berra, NY Yankees	75	41
Babe Ruth, Boston Red Sox-NY Yankees	41	37
Lou Gehrig, NY Yankees	34	30
Joe DiMaggio, NY Yankees	51	27
Derek Jeter, NY Yankees	32	27

Home Runs

	AB	HR
Mickey Mantle, NY Yankees	230	18
Babe Ruth, Boston Red Sox-NY Yankees	129	15
Yogi Berra, NY Yankees	259	12
Duke Snider, Brooklyn-LA	133	11
Lou Gehrig, NY Yankees	119	10
Reggie Jackson, Oakland-NY Yankees	98	10

Runs Batted In

	Gm	RBI
Mickey Mantle, NY Yankees	65	40
Yogi Berra, NY Yankees	75	39
Lou Gehrig, NY Yankees	34	35
Babe Ruth, Boston Red Sox-NY Yankees	41	33
Joe DiMaggio, NY Yankees	51	30

Stolen Bases

	Gm	SB
Lou Brock, St. Louis	21	14
Eddie Collins, Phi. A's-Chisox	34	14
Frank Chance, Chi. Cubs	20	10
Davey Lopes, Los Angeles	23	10
Phil Rizzuto, NY Yankees	52	10

All-Time World Series Leaders (Cont.)

Total Bases

	Gm	TB
Mickey Mantle, NY Yankees	.65	123
Yogi Berra, NY Yankees	.75	117
Babe Ruth, Boston Red Sox-NY Yankees	.41	96
Lou Gehrig, NY Yankees	.34	87
Joe DiMaggio, NY Yankees	.51	84

Slugging Pct. (minimum 50 AB)

	AB	Pc
Reggie Jackson, Oakland-NY Yankees	.98	.75:
Babe Ruth, Boston Red Sox-NY Yankees	.129	.74.
Lou Gehrig, NY Yankees	.119	.73
Al Simmons, Phi. A's-Cincinnati	.73	.65!
Lou Brock, St. Louis	.87	.65!

Pitching

Games

	Yrs	Gm
Whitey Ford, NY Yankees	.11	22
Mike Stanton, Atlanta-NY Yankees	.6	20
Mariano Rivera, NY Yankees	.6	20
Rollie Fingers, Oakland	.3	16
Jeff Nelson, NY Yankees	.5	16
Allie Reynolds, NY Yankees	.6	15
Bob Turley, NY Yankees	.5	15

Shutouts

	GS	CG	Sh
Christy Mathewson, NY Giants	.11	10	
Three Finger Brown, Chi. Cubs	.7	5	
Whitey Ford, NY Yankees	.22	7	
Seven pitchers tied with 2 each.			

Wins

	Gm	W-L
Whitey Ford, NY Yankees	.22	10-8
Bob Gibson, St. Louis	.9	7-2
Allie Reynolds, NY Yankees	.15	7-2
Red Ruffing, NY Yankees	.10	7-2
Lefty Gomez, NY Yankees	.7	6-0
Chief Bender, Philadelphia A's	.10	6-4
Waite Hoyt, NY Yankees-Phi. A's	.12	6-4

Innings Pitched

	Gm	
Whitey Ford, NY Yankees	.22	146.
Christy Mathewson, NY Giants	.11	101.
Red Ruffing, NY Yankees	.10	85.
Chief Bender, Philadelphia A's	.10	85.
Waite Hoyt, NY Yankees-Phi. A's	.12	83.

ERA (minimum 25 IP)

	Gm	IP	ERA
Jack Billingham, Cincinnati	.7	25.1	0.36
Harry Brecheen, St. Louis	.7	32.2	0.83
Babe Ruth, Boston Red Sox	.3	31.0	0.87
Sherry Smith, Brooklyn	.3	30.1	0.89
Sandy Koufax, Los Angeles	.8	57.0	0.95

Complete Games

	GS	CG	W-
Christy Mathewson, NY Giants	.11	10	5-
Chief Bender, Philadelphia A's	.10	9	6-
Bob Gibson, St. Louis	.9	8	7-
Whitey Ford, NY Yankees	.22	7	10-
Red Ruffing, NY Yankees	.10	7	7-

Saves

	Gm	IP	Sv
Mariano Rivera, NY Yankees	.20	31.0	9
Rollie Fingers, Oakland	.16	33.1	6
Allie Reynolds, NY Yankees	.15	77.1	4
Johnny Murphy, NY Yankees	.8	16.1	4
John Wetteland, NY Yankees	.5	4.1	4
Robb Nen, Florida-SF	.7	7.2	4
Ten pitchers tied with 3 each.			

Strikeouts

	Gm	IP	SC
Whitey Ford, NY Yankees	.22	146.0	9.
Bob Gibson, St. Louis	.9	81.0	9
Allie Reynolds, NY Yankees	.15	77.1	6
Sandy Koufax, Los Angeles	.8	57.0	6
Red Ruffing, NY Yankees	.10	85.2	6

Losses

	Gm	W-l
Whitey Ford, NY Yankees	.22	10-
Christy Mathewson, NY Giants	.11	5-
Joe Bush, Phi. A's-Bosox-NY Yankees	.9	2-
Rube Marquard, NY Giants-Brooklyn	.11	2-
Eddie Plank, Philadelphia A's	.7	2-
Schoolboy Rowe, Detroit	.8	2-

World Series Appearances

In the 103 years that the World Series has been contested, American League teams have won 61 championships while National League teams have won 42. Note that the Brewers, now in the NL, were in the AL when they won their title. The following teams are ranked by number of appearances through the 2007 World Series; (*) indicates AL teams.

	App	W	L	Pct.	Last Series	Last Title
NY Yankees*	.39	26	13	.667	2003	2000
Bklyn/LA Dodgers	.18	6	12	.333	1988	1988
St.L. Cardinals	.17	10	7	.588	2006	2006
NY/SF Giants	.17	5	12	.294	2002	1954
Phi/KC/Oak.A's*	.14	9	5	.643	1990	1989
Boston Red Sox*	.11	7	4	.636	2007	2007
Detroit Tigers*	.10	4	6	.400	2006	1984
Chicago Cubs	.10	2	8	.200	1945	1908
Cincinnati Reds	.9	5	4	.556	1990	1990
Bos/Mil/Atl.Braves	.9	3	6	.333	1999	1995
Pittsburgh Pirates	.7	5	2	.714	1979	1979
St.L/Bal.Orioles*	.7	3	4	.429	1983	1983
Wash/Min.Twins*	.6	3	3	.500	1991	1991

	App	W	L	Pct.	Last Series	Last Title
Chi. White Sox*	.5	3	2	.600	2005	2005
Cle. Indians*	.5	2	3	.400	1997	1948
Phi. Phillies	.5	1	4	.200	1993	1980
NY Mets	.4	2	2	.500	2000	1986
Fla. Marlins	.2	2	0	1.000	2003	2003
Tor. Blue Jays*	.2	2	0	1.000	1993	1993
KC Royals*	.2	1	1	.500	1985	1985
SD Padres	.2	0	2	.000	1998	—
LA Angels of Anaheim*	1	1	0	1.000	2002	2002
Ari. Diamondbacks	.1	1	0	1.000	2001	2001
Colorado Rockies	.1	0	1	.000	2007	—
Sea/Mil.Brewers*	.1	0	1	.000	1982	—
Houston Astros	.1	0	1	.000	2005	—

League Championship Series

Division play came to the major leagues in 1969 when both the American and National Leagues expanded to 12 teams. With an East and West Division in each league, League Championship Series (LCS) became necessary to determine the NL and AL pennant winners. In 1994, teams were realigned into three divisions, the East, Central, and West with division winners and one wildcard team playing a best-of-5 League Divisional Series (see following pages for LDS results) to determine the LCS competitors.

In the tables below, the East Division champions are noted by the letter E, the Central division champions by C and the West Division champions by W. Wildcard winners are noted by WC. Also, each playoff winner's wins and losses are noted in parentheses after the series score. The LCS changed from best-of-5 to best-of-7 in 1985. Each league's LCS was canceled in 1994 due to the players' strike.

National League

Multiple champions: Atlanta, Cincinnati, LA Dodgers and St. Louis (5); NY Mets (4); Philadelphia (3); Florida, Pittsburgh, San Diego and San Francisco (2).

Year	Winner	Manager	Series	Loser	Manager
1969	E–New York	Gil Hodges	3-0	W–Atlanta	Lum Harris
1970	W–Cincinnati	Sparky Anderson	3-0	E–Pittsburgh	Danny Murtaugh
1971	E–Pittsburgh	Danny Murtaugh	3-1 (LWWW)	W–San Francisco	Charlie Fox
1972	W–Cincinnati	Sparky Anderson	3-2 (LWLWW)	E–Pittsburgh	Bill Virdon
1973	E–New York	Yogi Berra	3-2 (LWWLW)	W–Cincinnati	Sparky Anderson
1974	W–Los Angeles	Walter Alston	3-1 (WWLW)	E–Pittsburgh	Danny Murtaugh
1975	W–Cincinnati	Sparky Anderson	3-0	E–Pittsburgh	Danny Murtaugh
1976	W–Cincinnati	Sparky Anderson	3-0	E–Philadelphia	Danny Ozark
1977	W–Los Angeles	Tommy Lasorda	3-1 (LWWW)	E–Philadelphia	Danny Ozark
1978	W–Los Angeles	Tommy Lasorda	3-1 (WWLW)	E–Philadelphia	Danny Ozark
1979	E–Pittsburgh	Chuck Tanner	3-0	W–Cincinnati	John McNamara
1980	E–Philadelphia	Dallas Green	3-2 (WLLWW)	W–Houston	Bill Virdon
1981	W–Los Angeles	Tommy Lasorda	3-2 (WLLWW)	E–Montreal	Jim Fanning
1982	E–St. Louis	Whitey Herzog	3-0	W–Atlanta	Joe Torre
1983	E–Philadelphia	Paul Owens	3-1 (WLWW)	W–Los Angeles	Tommy Lasorda
1984	W–San Diego	Dick Williams	3-2 (LLWWW)	E–Chicago	Jim Frey
1985	E–St. Louis	Whitey Herzog	4-2 (LLWWWW)	W–Los Angeles	Tommy Lasorda
1986	E–New York	Davey Johnson	4-2 (LWWLWW)	W–Houston	Hal Lanier
1987	E–St. Louis	Whitey Herzog	4-3 (LWWLLWW)	W–San Francisco	Roger Craig
1988	W–Los Angeles	Tommy Lasorda	4-3 (LWLWWLW)	E–New York	Davey Johnson
1989	W–San Francisco	Roger Craig	4-1 (WLWWW)	E–Chicago	Don Zimmer
1990	W–Cincinnati	Lou Piniella	4-2 (LWWWLW)	E–Pittsburgh	Jim Leyland
1991	W–Atlanta	Bobby Cox	4-3 (LWWLLWW)	E–Pittsburgh	Jim Leyland
1992	W–Atlanta	Bobby Cox	4-3 (WWLWLLW)	E–Pittsburgh	Jim Leyland
1993	E–Philadelphia	Jim Fregosi	4-2 (WLLWWW)	W–Atlanta	Bobby Cox
1994	Not held				
1995	E–Atlanta	Bobby Cox	4-0	C–Cincinnati	Davey Johnson
1996	E–Atlanta	Bobby Cox	4-3 (WLLLWWW)	C–St. Louis	Tony La Russa
1997	WC–Florida	Jim Leyland	4-2 (WLWLWW)	E–Atlanta	Bobby Cox
1998	W–San Diego	Bruce Bochy	4-2 (WWLLW)	E–Atlanta	Bobby Cox
1999	E–Atlanta	Bobby Cox	4-2 (WWWLLW)	WC–New York	Bobby Valentine
2000	WC–New York	Bobby Valentine	4-1 (WWLWW)	C–St. Louis	Tony La Russa
2001	W–Arizona	Bob Brenly	4-1 (WLWW)	E–Atlanta	Bobby Cox
2002	WC–San Francisco	Dusty Baker	4-1 (WLWW)	C–St. Louis	Tony La Russa
2003	WC–Florida	Jack McKeon	4-3 (WLLLWWW)	C–Chicago	Dusty Baker
2004	C–St. Louis	Tony La Russa	4-3 (WWLLLWW)	WC–Houston	Phil Garner
2005	WC–Houston	Phil Garner	4-2 (LWWWLW)	C–St. Louis	Tony La Russa
2006	C–St. Louis	Tony La Russa	4-3 (LWWLWLW)	E–New York	Willie Randolph
2007	WC–Colorado	Clint Hurdle	4-0	W–Arizona	Bob Melvin

NLCS Most Valuable Players

Winners who did not play for NLCS champions are in **bold** type.

Multiple winner: Steve Garvey (2).

Year	Year	Year
1977 Dusty Baker, LA, OF	1988 Orel Hershiser, LA, P	1998 Sterling Hitchcock, SD, P
1978 Steve Garvey, LA, 1B	1989 Will Clark, SF, 1B	1999 Eddie Perez, Atl., C
1979 Willie Stargell, Pit., 1B	1990 Rob Dibble, Cin., P	2000 Mike Hampton, NY, P
1980 Manny Trillo, Phi., 2B	& Randy Myers, Cin., P	2001 Craig Counsell, Ari., 2B
1981 Burt Hooton, LA, P	1991 Steve Avery, Atl., P	2002 Benito Santiago, SF, C
1982 Darrell Porter, St.L., C	1992 John Smoltz, Atl., P	2003 Ivan Rodriguez, Fla., C
1983 Gary Matthews, Phi., OF	1993 Curt Schilling, Phi., P	2004 Albert Pujols, St.L, 1B
1984 Steve Garvey, SD, 1B	1994 LCS not held.	2005 Roy Oswalt, Hou., P
1985 Ozzie Smith, St.L., SS	1995 Mike Devereaux, Atl., OF	2006 Jeff Suppan, St.L, P
1986 **Mike Scott**, Hou., P	1996 Javy Lopez, Atl., C	2007 Matt Holliday, Col., OF
1987 **Jeff Leonard**, SF, OF	1997 Livan Hernandez, Fla., P	

League Championship Series (Cont.)
American League

Multiple champions: NY Yankees (10); Oakland (6); Baltimore (5); Boston (4); Cleveland, Detroit, Kansas City, Minnesota and Toronto (2).

Year	Winner	Manager	Series	Loser	Manager
1969	E–Baltimore	Earl Weaver	3-0	W–Minnesota	Billy Martin
1970	E–Baltimore	Earl Weaver	3-0	W–Minnesota	Bill Rigney
1971	E–Baltimore	Earl Weaver	3-0	W–Oakland	Dick Williams
1972	W–Oakland	Dick Williams	3-2 (WWLLW)	E–Detroit	Billy Martin
1973	W–Oakland	Dick Williams	3-2 (LWWLW)	E–Baltimore	Earl Weaver
1974	W–Oakland	Alvin Dark	3-1 (LWWW)	E–Baltimore	Earl Weaver
1975	E–Boston	Darrell Johnson	3-0	W–Oakland	Alvin Dark
1976	E–New York	Billy Martin	3-2 (WLWLW)	W–Kansas City	Whitey Herzog
1977	E–New York	Billy Martin	3-2 (LWLWW)	W–Kansas City	Whitey Herzog
1978	E–New York	Bob Lemon	3-1 (WLWW)	W–Kansas City	Whitey Herzog
1979	E–Baltimore	Earl Weaver	3-1 (WWLW)	W–California	Jim Fregosi
1980	W–Kansas City	Jim Frey	3-0	E–New York	Dick Howser
1981	E–New York	Bob Lemon	3-0	W–Oakland	Billy Martin
1982	E–Milwaukee	Harvey Kuenn	3-2 (LLWWW)	W–California	Gene Mauch
1983	E–Baltimore	Joe Altobelli	3-1 (LWWW)	W–Chicago	Tony La Russa
1984	E–Detroit	Sparky Anderson	3-0	W–Kansas City	Dick Howser
1985	W–Kansas City	Dick Howser	4-3 (LLWLWWW)	E–Toronto	Bobby Cox
1986	E–Boston	John McNamara	4-3 (WLLWWWW)	W–California	Gene Mauch
1987	W–Minnesota	Tom Kelly	4-1 (WWLWW)	E–Detroit	Sparky Anderson
1988	W–Oakland	Tony La Russa	4-0	E–Boston	Joe Morgan
1989	W–Oakland	Tony La Russa	4-1 (WWLWW)	E–Toronto	Cito Gaston
1990	W–Oakland	Tony La Russa	4-0	E–Boston	Joe Morgan
1991	W–Minnesota	Tom Kelly	4-1 (WLWLW)	E–Toronto	Cito Gaston
1992	E–Toronto	Cito Gaston	4-2 (LWWWLW)	W–Oakland	Tony La Russa
1993	E–Toronto	Cito Gaston	4-2 (WWLLWW)	W–Chicago	Gene Lamont
1994	Not held				
1995	C–Cleveland	Mike Hargrove	4-2 (LWLWWW)	W–Seattle	Lou Piniella
1996	E–New York	Joe Torre	4-1 (WLWWW)	WC–Baltimore	Davey Johnson
1997	C–Cleveland	Mike Hargrove	4-2 (LWWWLW)	E–Baltimore	Davey Johnson
1998	E–New York	Joe Torre	4-2 (WLWWLW)	C–Cleveland	Mike Hargrove
1999	E–New York	Joe Torre	4-1 (WWLWW)	WC–Boston	Jimy Williams
2000	E–New York	Joe Torre	4-2 (LWWWLW)	WC–Seattle	Lou Piniella
2001	E–New York	Joe Torre	4-1 (WLWWW)	W–Seattle	Lou Piniella
2002	WC–Anaheim	Mike Scioscia	4-1 (LWWWW)	C–Minnesota	Ron Gardenhire
2003	E–New York	Joe Torre	4-3 (LWLWWLW)	WC–Boston	Grady Little
2004	WC–Boston	Terry Francona	4-3 (LLLLWWWW)	E–New York	Joe Torre
2005	C–Chicago	Ozzie Guillen	4-1 (LWWWW)	W–Los Angeles	Mike Scioscia
2006	WC–Detroit	Jim Leyland	4-0	W–Oakland	Ken Macha
2007	E–Boston	Terry Francona	4-3 (WLLLWWW)	C–Cleveland	Eric Wedge

ALCS Most Valuable Players
Winner who did not play for ALCS champions is in **bold** type.
Multiple winner: Dave Stewart (2).

Year		Year		Year	
1980 Frank White, KC, 2B		1990 Dave Stewart, Oak., P		2000 Dave Justice, NY, OF	
1981 Graig Nettles, NY, 3B		1991 Kirby Puckett, Min., OF		2001 Andy Pettitte, NY, P	
1982 **Fred Lynn,** Cal., OF		1992 Roberto Alomar, Tor., 2B		2002 Adam Kennedy, Ana., 2B	
1983 Mike Boddicker, Bal., P		1993 Dave Stewart, Tor., P		2003 Mariano Rivera, NY, P	
1984 Kirk Gibson, Det., OF		1994 LCS not held.		2004 David Ortiz, Bos., DH	
1985 George Brett, KC, 3B		1995 Orel Hershiser, Cle., P		2005 Paul Konerko, Chi., 1B	
1986 Marty Barrett, Bos., 2B		1996 Bernie Williams, NY, OF		2006 Placido Polanco, Det., 2B	
1987 Gary Gaetti, Min., 3B		1997 Marquis Grissom, Cle., OF		2007 Josh Beckett, Bos., P	
1988 Dennis Eckersley, Oak., P		1998 David Wells, NY, P			
1989 Rickey Henderson, Oak., OF		1999 Orlando Hernandez, NY, P			

Walk-off HR to Win a Postseason Series

Year	Player	Team	Series, Game	Opponent	Final Score
2006	Magglio Ordonez	Detroit	ALCS, Game 4	Oakland	6-3
2005	Chris Burke	Houston	NLDS Game 4	Atlanta	7-6 (18 inn.)
2004	David Ortiz	Boston	ALDS Game 3	Anaheim	8-6 (10 inn.)
2003	Aaron Boone	NY Yankees	ALCS, Game 7	Boston	6-5 (11 inn.)
1999	Todd Pratt	NY Mets	NLDS Game 4	Arizona	4-3 (10 inn.)
1993	Joe Carter	Toronto	WS, Game 6	Philadelphia	8-6
1976	Chris Chambliss	NY Yankees	ALCS, Game 5	Kansas City	7-6
1960	Bill Mazeroski	Pittsburgh	WS, Game 7	NY Yankees	10-9

League Divisional Series

In 1994, leagues were realigned into three divisions, the East, Central, and West with division winners and one wildcard team playing a best-of-5 League Divisional Series to determine the LCS competitors. In the tables below, the East Division champions are noted by the letter E, the Central division champions by C and the West Division champions by W. Wildcard winners are noted by WC. Also, each playoff winner's wins and losses are noted in parentheses after the series score. Each league's LDS was cancelled in 1994 due to the players' strike.

National League

Multiple champions: Atlanta and St. Louis (6); NY Mets (3); Arizona, Florida and Houston (2).

Year	Winner	Manager	Series	Loser	Manager
1995	E–Atlanta	Bobby Cox	3-1 (WWLW)	WC–Colorado	Don Baylor
	C–Cincinnati	Davey Johnson	3-0	W–Los Angeles	Tommy Lasorda
1996	E–Atlanta	Bobby Cox	3-0	WC–Los Angeles	Bill Russell
	C–St. Louis	Tony La Russa	3-0	W–San Diego	Bruce Bochy
1997	E–Atlanta	Bobby Cox	3-0	C–Houston	Larry Dierker
	WC–Florida	Jim Leyland	3-0	W–San Francisco	Dusty Baker
1998	E–Atlanta	Bobby Cox	3-0	WC–Chicago	Jim Riggleman
	W–San Diego	Bruce Bochy	3-1 (WLWW)	C–Houston	Larry Dierker
1999	E–Atlanta	Bobby Cox	3-1 (LWWW)	C–Houston	Larry Dierker
	WC–New York	Bobby Valentine	3-1 (WLWW)	W–Arizona	Buck Showalter
2000	C–St. Louis	Tony La Russa	3-0	E–Atlanta	Bobby Cox
	WC–New York	Bobby Valentine	3-1 (LWWW)	W–San Francisco	Dusty Baker
2001	E–Atlanta	Bobby Cox	3-0	C–Houston	Larry Dierker
	W–Arizona	Bob Brenly	3-2 (WLWLW)	WC–St. Louis	Tony La Russa
2002	WC–San Francisco	Dusty Baker	3-2 (WLLWW)	E–Atlanta	Bobby Cox
	C–St. Louis	Tony La Russa	3-0	W–Arizona	Bob Brenly
2003	C–Chicago	Dusty Baker	3-2 (WLWLW)	E–Atlanta	Bobby Cox
	WC–Florida	Jack McKeon	3-1 (LWWW)	W–San Francisco	Felipe Alou
2004	C–St. Louis	Tony La Russa	3-1 (WWLW)	W–Los Angeles	Jim Tracy
	WC–Houston	Phil Garner	3-2 (WLWLW)	E–Atlanta	Bobby Cox
2005	C–St. Louis	Tony La Russa	3-0	W–San Diego	Bruce Bochy
	WC–Houston	Phil Garner	3-1 (WLWW)	E–Atlanta	Bobby Cox
2006	C–St. Louis	Tony La Russa	3-1 (WWLW)	W–San Diego	Bruce Bochy
	E–New York	Willie Randolph	3-0	WC–Los Angeles	Grady Little
2007	W–Arizona	Bob Melvin	3-0	C–Chicago	Lou Piniella
	WC–Colorado	Clint Hurdle	3-0	E–Philadelphia	Charlie Manuel

American League

Multiple champions: NY Yankees (7); Boston and Cleveland (4); Seattle (3); Anaheim-Los Angeles Angels, Baltimore (2).

Year	Winner	Manager	Series	Loser	Manager
1995	C–Cleveland	Mike Hargrove	3-0	E–Boston	Kevin Kennedy
	W–Seattle	Lou Piniella	3-2 (LLWWW)	WC–New York	Buck Showalter
1996	E–New York	Joe Torre	3-1 (LWWW)	W–Texas	Johnny Oates
	WC–Baltimore	Davey Johnson	3-1 (WWLW)	C–Cleveland	Mike Hargrove
1997	E–Baltimore	Davey Johnson	3-1 (LWWW)	W–Seattle	Lou Piniella
	C–Cleveland	Mike Hargrove	3-2 (LWLWW)	WC–New York	Joe Torre
1998	E–New York	Joe Torre	3-0	W–Texas	Johnny Oates
	C–Cleveland	Mike Hargrove	3-1 (LWWW)	WC–Boston	Jimy Williams
1999	E–New York	Joe Torre	3-0	W–Texas	Johnny Oates
	WC–Boston	Jimy Williams	3-2 (LLWWW)	C–Cleveland	Mike Hargrove
2000	E–New York	Joe Torre	3-2 (LWWLW)	W–Oakland	Art Howe
	WC–Seattle	Lou Piniella	3-0	C–Chicago	Jerry Manuel
2001	E–New York	Joe Torre	3-2 (LLWWW)	WC–Oakland	Art Howe
	W–Seattle	Lou Piniella	3-2 (LWLWW)	C–Cleveland	Charlie Manuel
2002	WC–Anaheim	Mike Scioscia	3-1 (WLWW)	E–New York	Joe Torre
	C–Minnesota	Ron Gardenhire	3-2 (WLLWW)	W–Oakland	Art Howe
2003	E–New York	Joe Torre	3-1 (LWWW)	C–Minnesota	Ron Gardenhire
	WC–Boston	Grady Little	3-2 (LLWWW)	W–Oakland	Ken Macha
2004	E–New York	Joe Torre	3-1 (LWWW)	C–Minnesota	Ron Gardenhire
	WC–Boston	Terry Francona	3-0	W–Anaheim	Mike Scioscia
2005	W–Los Angeles	Mike Scioscia	3-2 (LWLVW)	E–New York	Joe Torre
	C–Chicago	Ozzie Guillen	3-0	WC–Boston	Terry Francona
2006	W–Oakland	Ken Macha	3-0	C–Minnesota	Ron Gardenhire
	WC–Detroit	Jim Leyland	3-1 (LWWW)	E–New York	Joe Torre
2007	E–Boston	Terry Francona	3-0	W–Los Angeles	Mike Scioscia
	C–Cleveland	Eric Wedge	3-1 (WWLW)	E–New York	Joe Torre

Other Playoffs

Eleven times since 1946, playoffs have been necessary to decide league or division championships or wild card berths when two teams were tied at the end of the regular season. Additionally, in the strike year of 1981 there were playoffs between the first and second half-season champions in both leagues.

National League

Year	NL	W	L	Manager	Year	NL East	W	L	Manager
1946	Brooklyn	96	58	Leo Durocher	1981	(1st Half) Philadelphia	34	21	Dallas Green
	St. Louis	96	58	Eddie Dyer		(2nd Half) Montreal	30	23	Jim Fanning
	Playoff: (Best-of-3) St. Louis, 2-0					Playoff: (Best-of-5) Montreal, 3-2 (WWLLW)			

Year	NL	W	L	Manager	Year	NL West	W	L	Manager
1951	Brooklyn	96	58	Charlie Dressen	1981	(1st Half) Los Angeles	36	21	Tommy Lasorda
	New York	96	58	Leo Durocher		(2nd Half) Houston	33	20	Bill Virdon
	Playoff: (Best-of-3) New York, 2-1 (WLW)					Playoff: (Best-of-5) Los Angeles, 3-2 (LLWWW)			

Year	NL	W	L	Manager	Year	NL Wild Card	W	L	Manager
1959	Milwaukee	86	68	Fred Haney	1998	Chicago	89	73	Jim Riggleman
	Los Angeles	86	68	Walter Alston		San Francisco	89	73	Dusty Baker
	Playoff: (Best-of-3) Los Angeles, 2-0					Playoff: (1 game) Chicago, 5-3 (at Chicago)			

Year	NL	W	L	Manager	Year	NL Wild Card	W	L	Manager
1962	Los Angeles	101	61	Walter Alston	1999	Cincinnati	96	66	Jack McKeon
	San Francisco	101	61	Alvin Dark		New York	96	66	Bobby Valentine
	Playoff: (Best-of-3) San Francisco, 2-1 (WLW)					Playoff: (1 game) New York, 5-0 (at Cincinnati)			

Year	NL West	W	L	Manager	Year	NL Wild Card	W	L	Manager
1980	Houston	92	70	Bill Virdon	2007	Colorado	89	73	Clint Hurdle
	Los Angeles	92	70	Tommy Lasorda		San Diego	89	73	Bud Black
	Playoff: (1 game) Houston, 7-1 (at LA)					Playoff: (1 game) Colorado, 9-8 in 13 inn. (at Col.)			

American League

Year	AL	W	L	Manager	Year	AL West	W	L	Manager
1948	Boston	96	58	Joe McCarthy	1981	(1st Half) Oakland	37	23	Billy Martin
	Cleveland	96	58	Lou Boudreau		(2nd Half) Kan. City	30	23	Jim Frey
	Playoff: (1 game) Cleveland, 8-3 (at Boston)					Playoff: (Best-of-5), Oakland, 3-0			

Year	AL East	W	L	Manager	Year	AL West	W	L	Manager
1978	Boston	99	63	Don Zimmer	1995	Seattle	78	66	Lou Piniella
	New York	99	63	Bob Lemon		California	78	66	M. Lachemann
	Playoff: (1 game) New York, 5-4 (at Boston)					Playoff: (1 game) Seattle, 9-1 (at Seattle)			

Year	AL East	W	L	Manager
1981	(1st Half) N.Y.	34	22	Bob Lemon
	(2nd Half) Milw	31	22	Buck Rodgers
	Playoff: (Best-of-5) New York, 3-2 (WWLLW)			

Regular Season League & Division Winners

Regular season National and American League pennant winners from 1900-68, as well as West and East divisional champions from 1969-93. In 1994, both leagues went to three divisions, West, Central and East, and each league also sent a wild card (WC) team to the playoffs. Note that (*) indicates 1994 divisional champion is unofficial (due to the players' strike). Note that **GA** column indicates games ahead of the second place club.

National League

Year		W	L	Pct	GA	Year		W	L	Pct	GA
1900	Brooklyn	82	54	.603	4½	1921	New York	94	59	.614	4
1901	Pittsburgh	90	49	.647	7½	1922	New York	93	61	.604	7
1902	Pittsburgh	103	36	.741	27½	1923	New York	95	58	.621	4½
1903	Pittsburgh	91	49	.650	6½	1924	New York	93	60	.608	1½
1904	New York	106	47	.693	13	1925	Pittsburgh	95	58	.621	8½
1905	New York	105	48	.686	9	1926	St. Louis	89	65	.578	2
1906	Chicago	116	36	.763	20	1927	Pittsburgh	94	60	.610	1½
1907	Chicago	107	45	.704	17	1928	St. Louis	95	59	.617	2
1908	Chicago	99	55	.643	1	1929	Chicago	98	54	.645	10½
1909	Pittsburgh	110	42	.724	6½	1930	St. Louis	92	62	.597	2
1910	Chicago	104	50	.675	13	1931	St. Louis	101	53	.656	13
1911	New York	99	54	.647	7½	1932	Chicago	90	64	.584	4
1912	New York	103	48	.682	10	1933	New York	91	61	.599	5
1913	New York	101	51	.664	12½	1934	St. Louis	95	58	.621	2
1914	Boston	94	59	.614	10½	1935	Chicago	100	54	.649	4
1915	Philadelphia	90	62	.592	7	1936	New York	92	62	.597	5
1916	Brooklyn	94	60	.610	2½	1937	New York	95	57	.625	3
1917	New York	98	56	.636	10	1938	Chicago	89	63	.586	2
1918	Chicago	84	45	.651	10½	1939	Cincinnati	97	57	.630	4½
1919	Cincinnati	96	44	.686	9	1940	Cincinnati	100	53	.654	12
1920	Brooklyn	93	61	.604	7	1941	Brooklyn	100	54	.649	2½

Year		W	L	Pct	GA
1942	St. Louis	106	48	.688	2
1943	St. Louis	105	49	.682	18
1944	St. Louis	105	49	.682	14½
1945	Chicago	98	56	.636	3
1946	St. Louis†	98	58	.628	2
1947	Brooklyn	94	60	.610	5
1948	Boston	91	62	.595	6½
1949	Brooklyn	97	57	.630	1
1950	Philadelphia	91	63	.591	2
1951	New York†	98	59	.624	1
1952	Brooklyn	96	57	.627	4½
1953	Brooklyn	105	49	.682	13
1954	New York	97	57	.630	5
1955	Brooklyn	98	55	.641	13½
1956	Brooklyn	93	61	.604	1
1957	Milwaukee	95	59	.617	8
1958	Milwaukee	92	62	.597	8
1959	Los Angeles†	88	68	.564	2
1960	Pittsburgh	95	59	.617	7
1961	Cincinnati	93	61	.604	4
1962	San Francisco†	103	62	.624	1
1963	Los Angeles	99	63	.611	6
1964	St. Louis	93	69	.574	1
1965	Los Angeles	97	65	.599	2
1966	Los Angeles	95	67	.586	1½
1967	St. Louis	101	60	.627	10½
1968	St. Louis	97	65	.599	9
1969	West—Atlanta	93	69	.574	3
	East—N.Y. Mets	100	62	.617	8
1970	West—Cincinnati	102	60	.630	14½
	East—Pittsburgh	89	73	.549	5
1971	West—San Francisco	90	72	.556	1
	East—Pittsburgh	97	65	.599	7
1972	West—Cincinnati	95	59	.617	10½
	East—Pittsburgh	96	59	.619	11
1973	West—Cincinnati	99	63	.611	3½
	East—N.Y. Mets	82	79	.509	1½
1974	West—Los Angeles	102	60	.630	4
	East—Pittsburgh	88	74	.543	1½
1975	West—Cincinnati	108	54	.667	20
	East—Pittsburgh	92	69	.571	6½
1976	West—Cincinnati	102	60	.630	10
	East—Philadelphia	101	61	.623	9
1977	West—Los Angeles	98	64	.605	10
	East—Philadelphia	101	61	.623	5
1978	West—Los Angeles	95	67	.586	2½
	East—Philadelphia	90	72	.556	1½
1979	West—Cincinnati	90	71	.559	1½
	East—Pittsburgh	98	64	.605	2
1980	West—Houston†	93	70	.571	1
	East—Philadelphia	91	71	.562	1
1981	West—Los Angeles$	63	47	.573	—
	East—Montreal$	60	48	.556	—
1982	West—Atlanta	89	73	.549	1
	East—St. Louis	92	70	.568	3
1983	West—Los Angeles	91	71	.562	3
	East—Philadelphia	90	72	.556	6
1984	West—San Diego	92	70	.568	12
	East—Chicago	96	65	.596	6½
1985	West—Los Angeles	95	67	.586	5½
	East—St. Louis	101	61	.623	3
1986	West—Houston	96	66	.593	10
	East—N.Y. Mets	108	54	.667	21½
1987	West—San Francisco	90	72	.556	6
	East—St. Louis	95	67	.586	3
1988	West—Los Angeles	94	67	.584	7
	East—N.Y. Mets	100	60	.625	15
1989	West—San Francisco	92	70	.568	3
	East—Chicago	93	69	.574	6
1990	West—Cincinnati	91	71	.562	5
	East—Pittsburgh	95	67	.586	4
1991	West—Atlanta	94	68	.580	1
	East—Pittsburgh	98	64	.605	14
1992	West—Atlanta	98	64	.605	8
	East—Pittsburgh	96	66	.593	9
1993	West—Atlanta	104	58	.642	1
	East—Philadelphia	97	65	.599	3
1994	West—Los Angeles*	58	56	.509	3½
	Central—Cincinnati*	66	48	.579	½
	East—Montreal*	74	40	.649	6
1995	West—Los Angeles	78	66	.542	1
	Central—Cincinnati	85	59	.590	9
	East—Atlanta	90	54	.625	21
	WC—Colorado	77	67	.535	—
1996	West—San Diego	91	71	.562	1
	Central—St. Louis	88	74	.543	6
	East—Atlanta	96	66	.593	8
	WC—Los Angeles	90	72	.556	—
1997	West—San Francisco	90	72	.556	2
	Central—Houston	84	78	.519	5
	East—Atlanta	101	61	.623	9
	WC—Florida	92	70	.568	—
1998	West—San Diego	98	64	.605	9½
	Central—Houston	102	60	.630	12½
	East—Atlanta	106	56	.654	18
	WC—Chicago†	90	73	.552	—
1999	West—Arizona	100	62	.617	14
	Central—Houston	97	65	.599	1½
	East—Atlanta	103	59	.636	6½
	WC—N.Y. Mets†	97	66	.595	—
2000	West—San Francisco	97	65	.599	11
	Central—St. Louis	95	67	.586	10
	East—Atlanta	95	67	.586	1
	WC—N.Y. Mets	94	68	.580	—
2001	West—Arizona	92	70	.568	2
	Central—Houston@	93	69	.574	—
	East—Atlanta	88	74	.543	2
	WC—St. Louis	93	69	.574	—
2002	West—Arizona	98	64	.605	2½
	Central—St. Louis	97	65	.599	13
	East—Atlanta	101	59	.631	19
	WC—San Francisco	95	66	.590	—
2003	West—San Diego	100	61	.621	15½
	Central—Chicago	88	74	.543	1
	East—Atlanta	101	61	.623	10
	WC—Florida	91	71	.562	—
2004	West—Los Angeles	93	69	.574	2
	Central—St. Louis	105	57	.648	13
	East—Atlanta	96	66	.593	10
	WC—Houston	92	70	.568	—
2005	West—San Diego	82	80	.506	5
	Central—St. Louis	100	62	.617	11
	East—Atlanta	90	72	.556	2
	WC—Houston	89	73	.549	—
2006	West—San Diego@	88	74	.543	—
	Central—St. Louis	83	78	.516	1½
	East—N.Y. Mets	97	65	.599	12
	WC—Los Angeles	88	74	.543	—
2007	West—Arizona	90	72	.556	½
	Central—Chicago	85	77	.525	2
	East—Philadelphia	89	73	.549	1
	WC—Colorado†	90	73	.552	—

†**Regular season playoffs:** See "Other Playoffs" on page 102 for details.
$**Divisional playoffs:** See "Other Playoffs" on page 102 for details.
@In 2001, Houston (93-69) won the Central over St. Louis (93-69) due to a better head-to-head record. In 2006, San Diego (88-74) won the West over Los Angeles (88-74) due to a better head-to-head record.

Regular Season League & Division Winners (Cont.)
American League

Year	Team	W	L	Pct	GA	Year	Team	W	L	Pct	GA
1901	Chicago	83	53	.610	4	1967	Boston	92	70	.568	1
1902	Philadelphia	83	53	.610	5	1968	Detroit	103	59	.636	12
1903	Boston	91	47	.659	14½	1969	West—Minnesota	97	65	.599	9
1904	Boston	95	59	.617	1½		East—Baltimore	109	53	.673	19
1905	Philadelphia	92	56	.622	2	1970	West—Minnesota	98	64	.605	9
1906	Chicago	93	58	.616	3		East—Baltimore	108	54	.667	15
1907	Detroit	92	58	.613	1½	1971	West—Oakland	101	60	.627	16
1908	Detroit	90	63	.588	½		East—Baltimore	101	57	.639	12
1909	Detroit	98	54	.645	3½	1972	West—Oakland	93	62	.600	5½
1910	Philadelphia	102	48	.680	14½		East—Detroit	86	70	.551	½
1911	Philadelphia	101	50	.669	13½	1973	West—Oakland	94	68	.580	6
1912	Boston	105	47	.691	14		East—Baltimore	97	65	.599	8
1913	Philadelphia	96	57	.627	6½	1974	West—Oakland	90	72	.556	5
1914	Philadelphia	99	53	.651	8½		East—Baltimore	91	71	.562	2
1915	Boston	101	50	.669	2½	1975	West—Oakland	98	64	.605	7
1916	Boston	91	63	.591	2		East—Boston	95	65	.594	4½
1917	Chicago	100	54	.649	9	1976	West—KansasCity	90	72	.556	2½
1918	Boston	75	51	.595	2½		East—New York	97	62	.610	10½
1919	Chicago	88	52	.629	3½	1977	West—Kansas City	102	60	.630	8
1920	Cleveland	98	56	.636	2		East—New York	100	62	.617	2½
1921	New York	98	55	.641	4½	1978	West—Kansas City	92	70	.568	5
1922	New York	94	60	.610	1		East—New York†	100	63	.613	1
1923	New York	98	54	.645	16	1979	West—California	88	74	.543	3
1924	Washington	92	62	.597	2		East—Baltimore	102	57	.642	8
1925	Washington	96	55	.636	8½	1980	West—Kansas City	97	65	.599	14
1926	New York	91	63	.591	3		East—New York	103	59	.636	3
1927	New York	110	44	.714	19	1981	West—Oakland$	64	45	.587	—
1928	New York	101	53	.656	2½		East—New York$	59	48	.551	—
1929	Philadelphia	104	46	.693	18	1982	West—California	93	69	.574	3
1930	Philadelphia	102	52	.662	8		East—Milwaukee	95	67	.586	1
1931	Philadelphia	107	45	.704	13½	1983	West—Chicago	99	63	.611	20
1932	New York	107	47	.695	13		East—Baltimore	98	64	.605	6
1933	Washington	99	53	.651	7	1984	West—Kansas City	84	78	.519	3
1934	Detroit	101	53	.656	7		East—Detroit	104	58	.642	15
1935	Detroit	93	58	.616	3	1985	West—Kansas City	91	71	.562	1
1936	New York	102	51	.667	19½		East—Toronto	99	62	.615	2
1937	New York	102	52	.662	13	1986	West—California	92	70	.568	5
1938	New York	99	53	.651	9½		East—Boston	95	66	.590	5½
1939	New York	106	45	.702	17	1987	West—Minnesota	85	77	.525	2
1940	Detroit	90	64	.584	1		East—Detroit	98	64	.605	2
1941	New York	101	53	.656	17	1988	West—Oakland	104	58	.642	13
1942	New York	103	51	.669	9		East—Boston	89	73	.549	1
1943	New York	98	56	.636	13½	1989	West—Oakland	99	63	.611	7
1944	St. Louis	89	65	.578	1		East—Toronto	89	73	.549	2
1945	Detroit	88	65	.575	1½	1990	West—Oakland	103	59	.636	9
1946	Boston	104	50	.675	12		East—Boston	88	74	.543	2
1947	New York	97	57	.630	12	1991	West—Minnesota	95	67	.586	8
1948	Cleveland†	97	58	.626	1		East—Toronto	91	71	.562	7
1949	New York	97	57	.630	1	1992	West—Oakland	96	66	.593	6
1950	New York	98	56	.636	3		East—Toronto	96	66	.593	4
1951	New York	98	56	.636	5	1993	West—Chicago	94	68	.580	8
1952	New York	95	59	.617	2		East—Toronto	95	67	.586	7
1953	New York	99	52	.656	8½	1994	West—Texas*	52	62	.456	1
1954	Cleveland	111	43	.721	8		Central—Chicago*	67	46	.593	1
1955	New York	96	58	.623	3		East—New York*	70	43	.619	6½
1956	New York	97	57	.630	9	1995	West—Seattle†	79	66	.545	1
1957	New York	98	56	.636	8		Central—Cleveland	100	44	.694	30
1958	New York	92	62	.597	10		East—Boston	86	58	.597	7
1959	Chicago	94	60	.610	5		WC—New York	79	65	.549	—
1960	New York	97	57	.630	8	1996	West—Texas	90	72	.556	4½
1961	New York	109	53	.673	8		Central—Cleveland	99	62	.615	14½
1962	New York	96	66	.593	5		East—New York	92	70	.568	4
1963	New York	104	57	.646	10½		WC—Baltimore	88	74	.543	—
1964	New York	99	63	.611	1	1997	West—Seattle	90	72	.556	6
1965	Minnesota	102	60	.630	7		Central—Cleveland	86	75	.534	6
1966	Baltimore	97	63	.606	9		East—Baltimore	98	64	.605	2
							WC—New York	96	66	.593	—

Year		W	L	Pct	GA
1998	West—Texas	88	74	.543	3
	Central—Cleveland	89	73	.549	9
	East—New York	114	48	.704	22
	WC—Boston	92	70	.568	—
1999	West—Texas	95	67	.586	8
	Central—Cleveland	97	65	.599	21½
	East—New York	98	64	.605	4
	WC—Boston	94	68	.580	—
2000	West—Oakland	91	70	.565	½
	Central—Chicago	95	67	.586	5
	East—New York	87	74	.540	2½
	WC—Seattle	91	71	.562	—
2001	West—Seattle	116	46	.716	14
	Central—Cleveland	91	71	.562	6
	East—New York	95	65	.594	13½
	WC—Oakland	102	60	.630	—
2002	West—Oakland	103	59	.636	4
	Central—Minnesota	94	67	.584	13½
	East—New York	103	58	.640	10½
	WC—Anaheim	99	63	.611	—

Year		W	L	Pct	GA
2003	West—Oakland	96	66	.593	3
	Central—Minnesota	90	72	.556	4
	East—New York	101	61	.623	6
	WC—Boston	95	67	.586	—
2004	West—Anaheim	92	70	.568	1
	Central—Minnesota	92	70	.568	9
	East—New York	101	61	.623	3
	WC—Boston	98	64	.605	—
2005	West—Los Angeles	95	67	.586	7
	Central—Chicago	99	63	.611	6
	East—New York@	95	67	.586	—
	WC—Boston	95	67	.586	—
2006	West—Oakland	93	69	.574	4
	Central—Minnesota	96	66	.593	1
	East—New York	97	65	.599	10
	WC—Detroit	95	67	.586	—
2007	West—Los Angeles	94	68	.580	6
	Central—Cleveland	96	66	.593	8
	East—Boston	96	66	.593	2
	WC—New York	94	68	.580	—

†**Regular season playoffs:** See "Other Playoffs" on page 102 for details.
‡**Divisional playoffs:** See "Other Playoffs" on page 102 for details.
@In 2005, New York (95-67) won the East over Boston (95-67) due to a better head-to-head record.

The All-Star Game

Baseball's first All-Star Game was held on July 6, 1933, before 47,595 at Comiskey Park in Chicago. From that year on, the All-Star Game has matched the best players in the American League against the best in the National. From 1959-62, two All-Star Games were played. The only year an All-Star Game wasn't played was 1945, when World War II travel restrictions made it necessary to cancel the meeting. The NL leads the series, 40-36-2. In the chart below, the American League is listed in **bold** type.

Since 2002, the game's MVP award has been named the Ted Williams Award, after the Red Sox Hall of Famer. The actual trophy is the Arch Ward Trophy, named after the Chicago Tribune sports editor who founded the game in 1933. First given at the two All-Star Games in 1962, the name of the award was changed to the Commissioner's Trophy in 1970 and back to the Arch Ward Memorial Trophy in 1985.

Since 2003, the league that wins the All-Star Game receives home-field advantage in that season's World Series.

MVP Multiple winners: Gary Carter, Steve Garvey, Willie Mays and Cal Ripken Jr. (2).

Year	Host	AL Manager	NL Manager	MVP
1933	**American,** 4-2	Chicago (AL)	Connie Mack	John McGraw	No award
1934	**American,** 9-7	New York (NL)	Joe Cronin	Bill Terry	No award
1935	**American,** 4-1	Cleveland	Mickey Cochrane	Frankie Frisch	No award
1936	National, 4-3	Boston (NL)	Joe McCarthy	Charlie Grimm	No award
1937	**American,** 8-3	Washington	Joe McCarthy	Bill Terry	No award
1938	National, 4-1	Cincinnati	Joe McCarthy	Bill Terry	No award
1939	**American,** 3-1	New York (AL)	Joe McCarthy	Gabby Hartnett	No award
1940	National, 4-0	St. Louis (NL)	Joe Cronin	Bill McKechnie	No award
1941	**American,** 7-5	Detroit	Del Baker	Bill McKechnie	No award
1942	**American,** 3-1	New York (NL)	Joe McCarthy	Leo Durocher	No award
1943	**American,** 5-3	Philadelphia (AL)	Joe McCarthy	Billy Southworth	No award
1944	National, 7-1	Pittsburgh	Joe McCarthy	Billy Southworth	No award
1945	Not held				
1946	**American,** 12-0	Boston (AL)	Steve O'Neill	Charlie Grimm	No award
1947	**American,** 2-1	Chicago (NL)	Joe Cronin	Eddie Dyer	No award
1948	**American,** 5-2	St. Louis (AL)	Bucky Harris	Leo Durocher	No award
1949	**American,** 11-7	Brooklyn	Lou Boudreau	Billy Southworth	No award
1950	National, 4-3 (14)	Chicago (AL)	Casey Stengel	Burt Shotton	No award
1951	National, 8-3	Detroit	Casey Stengel	Eddie Sawyer	No award
1952	National, 3-2 (5, rain)	Philadelphia (NL)	Casey Stengel	Leo Durocher	No award
1953	National, 5-1	Cincinnati	Casey Stengel	Charlie Dressen	No award
1954	**American,** 11-9	Cleveland	Casey Stengel	Walter Alston	No award
1955	National, 6-5 (12)	Milwaukee	Al Lopez	Leo Durocher	No award
1956	National, 7-3	Washington	Casey Stengel	Walter Alston	No award
1957	**American,** 6-5	St. Louis	Casey Stengel	Walter Alston	No award
1958	**American,** 4-3	Baltimore	Casey Stengel	Fred Haney	No award
1959-a	National, 5-4	Pittsburgh	Casey Stengel	Fred Haney	No award
1959-b	**American,** 5-3	Los Angeles	Casey Stengel	Fred Haney	No award
1960-a	National, 5-3	Kansas City	Al Lopez	Walter Alston	No award
1960-b	National, 6-0	New York	Al Lopez	Walter Alston	No award
1961-a	National, 5-4 (10)	San Francisco	Paul Richards	Danny Murtaugh	No award
1961-b	TIE, 1-1 (9, rain)	Boston	Paul Richards	Danny Murtaugh	No award

The All-Star Game (Cont.)

Year	Host		AL Manager	NL Manager	MVP
1962-a	National, 3-1	Washington	Ralph Houk	Fred Hutchinson	Maury Wills, LA (NL), SS
1962-b	**American,** 9-4	Chicago (NL)	Ralph Houk	Fred Hutchinson	Leon Wagner, LA (AL), OF
1963	National, 5-3	Cleveland	Ralph Houk	Alvin Dark	Willie Mays, SF, OF
1964	National, 7-4	New York (NL)	Al Lopez	Walter Alston	Johnny Callison, Phi., OF
1965	National, 6-5	Minnesota	Al Lopez	Gene Mauch	Juan Marichal, SF, P
1966	National, 2-1 (10)	St. Louis	Sam Mele	Walter Alston	Brooks Robinson, Bal., 3B
1967	National, 2-1 (15)	California	Hank Bauer	Walter Alston	Tony Perez, Cin., 3B
1968	National, 1-0	Houston	Dick Williams	Red Schoendienst	Willie Mays, SF, OF
1969	National, 9-3	Washington	Mayo Smith	Red Schoendienst	Willie McCovey, SF, 1B
1970	National, 5-4 (12)	Cincinnati	Earl Weaver	Gil Hodges	Carl Yastrzemski, Bos., OF-1B
1971	**American,** 6-4	Detroit	Earl Weaver	Sparky Anderson	Frank Robinson, Bal., OF
1972	National, 4-3 (10)	Atlanta	Earl Weaver	Danny Murtaugh	Joe Morgan, Cin., 2B
1973	National, 7-1	Kansas	Dick Williams	Sparky Anderson	Bobby Bonds, SF, OF
1974	National, 7-2	Pittsburgh	Dick Williams	Yogi Berra	Steve Garvey, LA, 1B
1975	National, 6-3	Milwaukee	Alvin Dark	Walter Alston	Bill Madlock, Chi. (NL), 3B & Jon Matlack, NY (NL), P
1976	National, 7-1	Philadelphia	Darrell Johnson	Sparky Anderson	George Foster, Cin., OF
1977	National, 7-5	New York (AL)	Billy Martin	Sparky Anderson	Don Sutton, LA, P
1978	National, 7-3	San Diego	Billy Martin	Tommy Lasorda	Steve Garvey, LA, 1B
1979	National, 7-6	Seattle	Bob Lemon	Tommy Lasorda	Dave Parker, Pit., OF
1980	National, 4-2	Los Angeles	Earl Weaver	Chuck Tanner	Ken Griffey, Cin., OF
1981	National, 5-4	Cleveland	Jim Frey	Dallas Green	Gary Carter, Mon., C
1982	National, 4-1	Montreal	Billy Martin	Tommy Lasorda	Dave Concepcion, Cin., SS
1983	**American,** 13-3	Chicago (AL)	Harvey Kuenn	Whitey Herzog	Fred Lynn, Cal., OF
1984	National, 3-1	San Francisco	Joe Altobelli	Paul Owens	Gary Carter, Mon., C
1985	National, 6-1	Minnesota	Sparky Anderson	Dick Williams	LaMarr Hoyt, SD, P
1986	**American,** 3-2	Houston	Dick Howser	Whitey Herzog	Roger Clemens, Bos., P
1987	National, 2-0 (13)	Oakland	John McNamara	Davey Johnson	Tim Raines, Mon., OF
1988	**American,** 2-1	Cincinnati	Tom Kelly	Whitey Herzog	Terry Steinbach, Oak., C
1989	**American,** 5-3	California	Tony La Russa	Tommy Lasorda	Bo Jackson, KC, OF
1990	**American,** 2-0	Chicago (NL)	Tony La Russa	Roger Craig	Julio Franco, Tex., 2B
1991	**American,** 4-2	Toronto	Tony La Russa	Lou Piniella	Cal Ripken Jr., Bal., SS
1992	**American,** 13-6	San Diego	Tom Kelly	Bobby Cox	Ken Griffey Jr., Sea., OF
1993	**American,** 9-3	Baltimore	Cito Gaston	Bobby Cox	Kirby Puckett, Min., OF
1994	National, 8-7 (10)	Pittsburgh	Cito Gaston	Jim Fregosi	Fred McGriff, Atl., 1B
1995	National, 3-2	Texas	Buck Showalter	Felipe Alou	Jeff Conine, Fla., PH
1996	National, 6-0	Philadelphia	Mike Hargrove	Bobby Cox	Mike Piazza, LA, C
1997	**American,** 3-1	Cleveland	Joe Torre	Bobby Cox	Sandy Alomar Jr., Cle., C
1998	**American,** 13-8	Colorado	Mike Hargrove	Jim Leyland	Roberto Alomar, Bal., 2B
1999	**American,** 4-1	Boston	Joe Torre	Bruce Bochy	Pedro Martinez, Bos., P
2000	**American,** 6-3	Atlanta	Joe Torre	Bobby Cox	Derek Jeter, NY (AL), SS
2001	**American,** 4-1	Seattle	Joe Torre	Bobby Valentine	Cal Ripken Jr., Bal., SS-3B
2002	TIE, 7-7 (11 inn.) *	Milwaukee	Joe Torre	Bob Brenly	No award
2003	**American,** 7-6	Chicago (AL)	Mike Scioscia	Dusty Baker	Garret Anderson, Ana., OF
2004	**American,** 9-4	Houston	Joe Torre	Jack McKeon	Alfonso Soriano, Tex., 2B
2005	**American,** 7-5	Detroit	Terry Francona	Tony La Russa	Miguel Tejada, Bal., SS
2006	**American,** 3-2	Pittsburgh	Ozzie Guillen	Phil Garner	Michael Young, Tex., 2B
2007	**American,** 5-4	San Francisco	Jim Leyland	Tony La Russa	Ichiro Suzuki, Sea., OF

* Due to the depletion of both the AL and NL rosters, the 2002 game was called a tie after 11 innings.

Like Father, Like Son

Fifteen Father-Son combos have participated in the MLB All-Star Game. **Source:** MLB.com.

Family	Father	Son(s)
Alomar	Sandy Sr. (1970)	Sandy Jr. (1990, 91, 92, 96-98), Roberto (1990-2001)
Alou	Felipe (1962, 66, 68)	Moises (1994, 97, 98, 2001, 04, 05)
Bell	Gus (1953, 54, 56, 57)	Buddy (1973, 80, 81, 82, 84)
Bonds	Bobby (1971, 73, 75)	Barry (1990, 92-98, 2000, 01, 02, 03, 04)
Boone	Ray (1954, 56)	Bob (1976, 78, 79, 83)
	Bob (1976, 78, 79, 83)	Aaron (2003), Bret (1998, 2001, 03)
Coleman	Joe Sr. (1948)	Joe Jr. (1972)
Fielder	Cecil (1990, 91, 93)	Prince (2007)
Griffey	Ken Sr. (1976, 77, 80)	Ken Jr. (1990-99, 2000, 04)
Hegan	Jim (1947, 49-52)	Mike (1969)
Hundley	Randy (1969)	Todd (1996)
Law	Vern (1960)	Vance (1988)
Matthews	Gary Sr. (1979)	Gary Jr. (2006)

Major League Franchise Origins

Here is what the current 30 teams in Major League Baseball have to show for the years they have put in as members of the National League (NL) and American League (AL). Pennants and World Series championships are since 1901.

National League

	1st Year	Pennants & World Series	Franchise Stops
Arizona Diamondbacks	1998	1 NL (2001) 1 WS (2001)	• Phoenix (1998–)

Atlanta Braves	1876	9 NL (1914,48,57-58,91-92,95,96,99)
		3 WS (1914,57,95)
			• Boston (1876–1952)
			  Milwaukee (1953–65)
			  Atlanta (1966–)

Chicago Cubs	1876	10 NL (1906-08,10,18,29,32,35,38,45) 2 WS (1907-08)	• Chicago (1876–)
Cincinnati Reds	1876	9 NL (1919,39-40,61,70,72,75-76,90) 5 WS (1919,40,75-76,90)	• Cincinnati (1876–80) Cincinnati (1890–)
Colorado Rockies	1993	1 NL (2007)	• Denver (1993–)
Florida Marlins	1993	2 NL (1997, 2003) 2 WS (1997, 2003)	• Miami (1993–)
Houston Astros	1962	1 NL (2005)	• Houston (1962–)
Los Angeles Dodgers	1890	18 NL (1916,20,41,47,49,52-53,55-56, 59,63, 65-66,74,77-78, 81,88) 6 WS (1955,59,63,65,81,88)	• Brooklyn (1890-1957) Los Angeles (1958–)
Milwaukee Brewers	1969	1 AL (1982)	• Seattle (1969) Milwaukee (1970–)
New York Mets	1962	4 NL (1969,73,86,00) 2 WS (1969,86)	• New York (1962–)
Philadelphia Phillies	1883	5 NL (1915,50,80,83,93) 1 WS (1980)	• Philadelphia (1883–)
Pittsburgh Pirates	1887	7 NL (1903,09,25,27,60,71,79) 5 WS (1909,25,60,71,79)	• Pittsburgh (1887–)
St. Louis Cardinals	1892	17 NL (1926,28,30-31,34,42-44,46,64, 67-68,82,85,87,2004,06) 10 WS (1926,31,34,42,44,46,64,67,82,2006)	• St. Louis (1892–)
San Diego Padres	1969	2 NL (1984,98)	• San Diego (1969–)
San Francisco Giants	1883	17 NL (1905,11-13,17,21-24,33,36-37,51, 54,62,89,2002) 5 WS (1905,21-22,33,54)	• New York (1883–1957) San Francisco (1958–)
Washington Nationals	1969	None	• Montreal (1969–2004) Washington, DC (2005–)

American League

	1st Year	Pennants & World Series	Franchise Stops

Baltimore Orioles	1901	7 AL (1944,66,69-71,79,83)
		3 WS (1966,70,83)
			• Milwaukee (1901)
			  St. Louis (1902–53)
			  Baltimore (1954–)

Boston Red Sox	1901	11 AL (1903,12,15-16,18,46,67,75,86, 2004,07) 7 WS (1903,12,15-16,18,2004,07)	• Boston (1901–)
Chicago White Sox	1901	5 AL (1906,17,19,59,2005) 3 WS (1906,17,2005)	• Chicago (1901–)
Cleveland Indians	1901	5 AL (1920,48,54,95,97) 2 WS (1920,48)	• Cleveland (1901–)
Detroit Tigers	1901	10 AL (1907-09,34-35,40,45,68,84,2006) 4 WS (1935,45,68,84)	• Detroit (1901–)
Kansas City Royals	1969	2 AL (1980,85) 1 WS (1985)	• Kansas City (1969–)
Los Angeles Angels of Anaheim	1961	1 AL (2002) 1 WS (2002)	• Los Angeles (1961–65) Anaheim, CA (1966–)

Minnesota Twins	1901	6 AL (1924-25,33,65,87,91)
		3 WS (1924,87,91)
			• Washington, DC (1901–60)
			  Bloomington, MN (1961–81)
			  Minneapolis (1982–)

New York Yankees	1901	39 AL (1921-23,26-28,32,36-39,41-43,47, 49-53,55-58,60-64,76-78,81,96,98-01,03) 26 WS (1923,27-28,32,36-39,41,43,47, 49-53,56,58,61-62,77-78,96,98-00)	• Baltimore (1901–02) New York (1903–)

Oakland Athletics	1901	14 AL (1905,10-11,13-14,29-31,72-74,
		88-90)
		9 WS (1910-11,13,29-30,72-74,89)
			• Philadelphia (1901-54)
			  Kansas City (1955–67)
			  Oakland (1968–)

Seattle Mariners	1977	None	• Seattle (1977–)
Tampa Bay Devil Rays	1998	None	• Tampa Bay (1998–)
Texas Rangers	1961	None	• Washington, DC (1961–71) Arlington, TX (1972–)
Toronto Blue Jays	1977	2 AL (1992-93) 2 WS (1992-93)	• Toronto (1977–)

The Growth of Major League Baseball

The National League (founded in 1876) and the American League (founded in 1901) were both eight-team circuits at the turn of the century and remained that way until expansion finally came to Major League Baseball in the 1960s. The AL added two teams in 1961 and the NL did the same a year later. Both leagues went to 12 teams and split into two divisions in 1969. The AL then grew by two more teams to 14 in 1977, but the NL didn't follow suit until adding its 13th and 14th clubs in 1993. The NL added two teams (making it 16) in 1998 when the expansion Arizona Diamondbacks entered the league and the Milwaukee Brewers moved over from the AL. The Tampa Bay Devil Rays joined the AL in 1998, keeping the AL at 14 teams.

Expansion Timetable (Since 1901)

1961—Los Angeles Angels and Washington Senators (now Texas Rangers) join AL; **1962**—Houston Colt .45s (now Astros) and New York Mets join NL; **1969**—Kansas City Royals and Seattle Pilots (now Milwaukee Brewers) join AL, while Montreal Expos (now Washington Nationals) and San Diego Padres join NL; **1977**—Seattle Mariners and Toronto Blue Jays join AL; **1993**—Colorado Rockies and Florida Marlins join NL; **1998**—Arizona Diamondbacks join NL and Tampa Bay Devil Rays join AL.

City and Nickname Changes
National League

1953—Boston Braves move to Milwaukee; **1958**—Brooklyn Dodgers move to Los Angeles and New York Giants move to San Francisco; **1965**—Houston Colt .45s renamed Astros; **1966**—Milwaukee Braves move to Atlanta; **2004**—Montreal Expos move to Washington, D.C. and become Washington Nationals.

Other nicknames: Boston (Beaneaters and Doves through 1908; and Bees from 1936-40); **Brooklyn** (Superbas through 1926, then Robins from 1927-31; then Dodgers from 1932-57); **Cincinnati** (Red Legs from 1944-45, then Redlegs from 1954-60, then Reds since 1961); **Philadelphia** (Blue Jays from 1943-44).

American League

1902—Milwaukee Brewers move to St. Louis and become Browns; **1903**—Baltimore Orioles move to New York and become Highlanders; **1913**—NY Highlanders renamed Yankees; **1954**—St. Louis Browns move to Baltimore and become Orioles; **1955**—Philadelphia Athletics move to Kansas City; **1961**—Washington Senators move to Bloomington, Minn., and become Minnesota Twins; **1965**—LA Angels renamed California Angels; **1966**—California Angels move to Anaheim; **1968**—KC Athletics move to Oakland and become A's; **1970**—Seattle Pilots move to Milwaukee and become Brewers; **1972**—Washington Senators move to Arlington, Texas, and become Rangers; **1982**—Minnesota Twins move to Minneapolis; **1987**—Oakland A's renamed Athletics; **1997**—California Angels renamed Anaheim Angels; **2005**—Anaheim Angels renamed Los Angeles Angels of Anaheim.

Other nicknames: Boston (Pilgrims, Puritans, Plymouth Rocks and Somersets through 1906); **Cleveland** (Bronchos, Blues, Naps and Molly McGuires through 1914); **Washington** (Senators through 1904, then Nationals from 1905-44, then Senators again from 1945-60).

National League Pennant Winners from 1876-99

Founded in 1876, the National League played 24 seasons before the turn of the century and its eventual rivalry with the younger American League.

Multiple winners: Boston (8); Chicago (6); Baltimore (3); Brooklyn, New York and Providence (2).

Year		Year		Year		Year	
1876	Chicago	1882	Chicago	1888	New York	1894	Baltimore
1877	Boston	1883	Boston	1889	New York	1895	Baltimore
1878	Boston	1884	Providence	1890	Brooklyn	1896	Baltimore
1879	Providence	1885	Chicago	1891	Boston	1897	Boston
1880	Chicago	1886	Chicago	1892	Boston	1898	Boston
1881	Chicago	1887	Detroit	1893	Boston	1899	Brooklyn

Champions of Leagues That No Longer Exist

A Special Baseball Records Committee appointed by the commissioner found in 1968 that four extinct leagues qualified for major league status—the American Association (1882-91), the Union Association (1884), the Players' League (1890) and the Federal League (1914-15). The first years of the American League (1900) and Federal League (1913) were not recognized.

American Association

Year	Champion	Manager	Year	Champion	Manager	Year	Champion	Manager
1882	Cincinnati	Pop Snyder	1886	St. Louis	Charlie Comiskey	1890	Louisville	Jack Chapman
1883	Philadelphia	Lew Simmons	1887	St. Louis	Charlie Comiskey	1891	Boston	Arthur Irwin
1884	New York	Jim Mutrie	1888	St. Louis	Charlie Comiskey			
1885	St. Louis	Charlie Comiskey	1889	Brooklyn	Bill McGunnigle			

Union Association

Year	Champion	Manager
1884	St. Louis	Henry Lucas

Players' League

Year	Champion	Manager
1890	Boston	King Kelly

Federal League

Year	Champion	Manager
1914	Indianapolis	Bill Phillips
1915	Chicago	Joe Tinker

Annual Batting Leaders (since 1900)

Batting Average

National League

Multiple winners: Tony Gwynn and Honus Wagner (8); Rogers Hornsby and Stan Musial (7); Roberto Clemente and Bill Madlock (4); Pete Rose, Larry Walker and Paul Waner (3); Hank Aaron, Richie Ashburn, Barry Bonds, Jake Daubert, Tommy Davis, Ernie Lombardi, Willie McGee, Lefty O'Doul, Dave Parker and Edd Roush (2).

Year		Avg	Year		Avg	Year		Avg
1900	Honus Wagner, Pit	.381	1936	Paul Waner, Pit.	.373	1972	Billy Williams, Chi	.333
1901	Jesse Burkett, St.L	.382	1937	Joe Medwick, St.L	.374	1973	Pete Rose, Cin	.338
1902	Ginger Beaumont, Pit	.357	1938	Ernie Lombardi, Cin	.342	1974	Ralph Garr, Atl	.353
1903	Honus Wagner, Pit	.355	1939	Johnny Mize, St.L	.349	1975	Bill Madlock, Chi	.354
1904	Honus Wagner, Pit	.349	1940	Debs Garms, Pit	.355	1976	Bill Madlock, Chi	.339
1905	Cy Seymour, Cin	.377	1941	Pete Reiser, Bklyn	.343	1977	Dave Parker, Pit	.338
1906	George Stone, St.L	.339	1942	Ernie Lombardi, Bos	.330	1978	Dave Parker, Pit	.334
1907	Honus Wagner, Pit	.350	1943	Stan Musial, St.L	.357	1979	Keith Hernandez, St.L	.344
1908	Honus Wagner, Pit	.354	1944	Dixie Walker, Bklyn.	.357	1980	Bill Buckner, Chi	.324
1909	Honus Wagner, Pit	.339	1945	Phil Cavarretta, Chi.	.355	1981	Bill Madlock, Pit	.341
1910	Sherry Magee, Phi	.331	1946	Stan Musial, St.L	.365	1982	Al Oliver, Mon	.331
1911	Honus Wagner, Pit	.334	1947	Harry Walker, St.L-Phi	.363	1983	Bill Madlock, Pit	.323
1912	Heinie Zimmerman, Chi.	.372	1948	Stan Musial, St.L	.376	1984	Tony Gwynn, SD	.351
1913	Jake Daubert, Bklyn	.350	1949	Jackie Robinson, Bklyn	.342	1985	Willie McGee, St.L	.353
1914	Jake Daubert, Bklyn	.329	1950	Stan Musial, St.L	.346	1986	Tim Raines, Mon	.334
1915	Larry Doyle, NY	.320	1951	Stan Musial, St.L	.355	1987	Tony Gwynn, SD	.370
1916	Hal Chase, Cin	.339	1952	Stan Musial, St.L	.336	1988	Tony Gwynn, SD	.313
1917	Edd Roush, Cin	.341	1953	Carl Furillo, Bklyn	.344	1989	Tony Gwynn, SD	.336
1918	Zack Wheat, Bklyn	.335	1954	Willie Mays, NY.	.345	1990	Willie McGee, St.L	.335
1919	Edd Roush, Cin	.321	1955	Richie Ashburn, Phi	.338	1991	Terry Pendleton, Atl	.319
1920	Rogers Hornsby, St.L	.370	1956	Hank Aaron, Mil	.328	1992	Gary Sheffield, SD	.330
1921	Rogers Hornsby, St.L	.397	1957	Stan Musial, St.L	.351	1993	Andres Galarraga, Col	.370
1922	Rogers Hornsby, St.L	.401	1958	Richie Ashburn, Phi	.350	1994	Tony Gwynn, SD	.394
1923	Rogers Hornsby, St.L	.384	1959	Hank Aaron, Mil	.355	1995	Tony Gwynn, SD	.368
1924	Rogers Hornsby, St.L	.424	1960	Dick Groat, Pit	.325	1996	Tony Gwynn, SD	.353
1925	Rogers Hornsby, St.L	.403	1961	Roberto Clemente, Pit	.351	1997	Tony Gwynn, SD	.372
1926	Bubbles Hargrave, Cin	.353	1962	Tommy Davis, LA	.346	1998	Larry Walker, Col	.363
1927	Paul Waner, Pit	.380	1963	Tommy Davis, LA	.326	1999	Larry Walker, Col	.379
1928	Rogers Hornsby, Bos	.387	1964	Roberto Clemente, Pit	.339	2000	Todd Helton, Col	.372
1929	Lefty O'Doul, Phi	.398	1965	Roberto Clemente, Pit	.329	2001	Larry Walker, Col	.350
1930	Bill Terry, NY	.401	1966	Matty Alou, Pit	.342	2002	Barry Bonds, SF	.370
1931	Chick Hafey, St.L	.349	1967	Roberto Clemente, Pit	.357	2003	Albert Pujols, St.L	.359
1932	Lefty O'Doul, Bklyn	.368	1968	Pete Rose, Cin	.335	2004	Barry Bonds, SF	.362
1933	Chuck Klein, Phi	.368	1969	Pete Rose, Cin	.348	2005	Derrek Lee, Chi.	.335
1934	Paul Waner, Pit	.362	1970	Rico Carty, Atl	.366	2006	Freddy Sanchez, Pit.	.344
1935	Arky Vaughan, Pit	.385	1971	Joe Torre, St.L	.363	2007	Matt Holliday, Col.	.340

American League

Multiple winners: Ty Cobb (12); Rod Carew (7); Ted Williams (6); Wade Boggs (5); Harry Heilmann (4); George Brett, Nap Lajoie, Tony Oliva and Carl Yastrzemski (3); Luke Appling, Joe DiMaggio, Ferris Fain, Jimmie Foxx, Nomar Garciaparra, Edgar Martinez, Pete Runnels, Al Simmons, George Sisler, Ichiro Suzuki and Mickey Vernon (2).

Year		Avg	Year		Avg	Year		Avg
1901	Nap Lajoie, Phi.	.422	1926	Heinie Manush, Det	.378	1951	Ferris Fain, Phi	.344
1902	Ed Delahanty, Wash.	.376	1927	Harry Heilmann, Det	.398	1952	Ferris Fain, Phi	.327
1903	Nap Lajoie, Cle	.355	1928	Goose Goslin, Wash.	.379	1953	Mickey Vernon, Wash.	.337
1904	Nap Lajoie, Cle	.381	1929	Lew Fonseca, Cle	.369	1954	Bobby Avila, Clev.	.341
1905	Elmer Flick, Cle	.306	1930	Al Simmons, Phi	.381	1955	Al Kaline, Det.	.340
1906	George Stone, St.L	.358	1931	Al Simmons, Phi	.390	1956	Mickey Mantle, NY	.353
1907	Ty Cobb, Det	.350	1932	Dale Alexander, Det-Bos	.367	1957	Ted Williams, Bos	.388
1908	Ty Cobb, Det	.324	1933	Jimmie Foxx, Phi	.356	1958	Ted Williams, Bos	.328
1909	Ty Cobb, Det	.377	1934	Lou Gehrig, NY.	.363	1959	Harvey Kuenn, Det	.353
1910	Ty Cobb, Det	.383	1935	Buddy Myer, Wash.	.349	1960	Pete Runnels, Bos	.320
1911	Ty Cobb, Det	.420	1936	Luke Appling, Chi.	.388	1961	Norm Cash, Det	.361*
1912	Ty Cobb, Det	.409	1937	Charlie Gehringer, Det	.371	1962	Pete Runnels, Bos	.326
1913	Ty Cobb, Det	.390	1938	Jimmie Foxx, Bos.	.349	1963	Carl Yastrzemski, Bos.	.321
1914	Ty Cobb, Det	.368	1939	Joe DiMaggio, NY	.381	1964	Tony Oliva, Min	.323
1915	Ty Cobb, Det	.369	1940	Joe DiMaggio, NY	.352	1965	Tony Oliva, Min	.321
1916	Tris Speaker, Cle.	.386	1941	Ted Williams, Bos	.406	1966	Frank Robinson, Bal	.316
1917	Ty Cobb, Det	.383	1942	Ted Williams, Bos	.356	1967	Carl Yastrzemski, Bos.	.326
1918	Ty Cobb, Det	.382	1943	Luke Appling, Chi.	.328	1968	Carl Yastrzemski, Bos.	.301
1919	Ty Cobb, Det	.384	1944	Lou Boudreau, Clev.	.327	1969	Rod Carew, Min	.332
1920	George Sisler, St.L	.407	1945	Snuffy Stirnweiss, NY.	.309	1970	Alex Johnson, Cal.	.329
1921	Harry Heilmann, Det	.394	1946	Mickey Vernon, Wash.	.353	1971	Tony Oliva, Min	.337
1922	George Sisler, St.L	.420	1947	Ted Williams, Bos.	.343	1972	Rod Carew, Min	.318
1923	Harry Heilmann, Det	.403	1948	Ted Williams, Bos.	.369	1973	Rod Carew, Min	.350
1924	Babe Ruth, NY	.378	1949	George Kell, Det.	.343	1974	Rod Carew, Min	.364
1925	Harry Heilmann, Det	.393	1950	Billy Goodman, Bos	.354	1975	Rod Carew, Min	.359

Batting Average (Cont.)

Year		Avg	Year		Avg	Year		Avg
1976	George Brett, KC	.333	1987	Wade Boggs, Bos.	.363	1998	Bernie Williams, NY.	.339
1977	Rod Carew, Min	.388	1988	Wade Boggs, Bos.	.366	1999	Nomar Garciaparra, Bos.	.357
1978	Rod Carew, Min	.333	1989	Kirby Puckett, Min.	.339	2000	Nomar Garciaparra, Bos.	.372
1979	Fred Lynn, Bos	.333	1990	George Brett, KC	.329	2001	Ichiro Suzuki, Sea.	.350
1980	George Brett, KC	.390	1991	Julio Franco, Tex.	.341	2002	Manny Ramirez, Bos.	.349
1981	Carney Lansford, Bos.	.336	1992	Edgar Martinez, Sea.	.343	2003	Bill Mueller, Bos.	.326
1982	Willie Wilson, KC.	.332	1993	John Olerud, Tor.	.363	2004	Ichiro Suzuki, Sea.	.372
1983	Wade Boggs, Bos.	.361	1994	Paul O'Neill, NY	.359	2005	Michael Young, Tex.	.331
1984	Don Mattingly, NY	.343	1995	Edgar Martinez, Sea.	.356	2006	Joe Mauer, Min.	.347
1985	Wade Boggs, Bos.	.368	1996	Alex Rodriguez, Sea.	.358	2007	Magglio Ordonez, Det.	.363
1986	Wade Boggs, Bos.	.357	1997	Frank Thomas, Chi	.347			

*Norm Cash later admitted to using a corked bat the entire season. He played 16 other seasons and never hit better than .286.

Home Runs
National League

Multiple winners: Mike Schmidt (8); Ralph Kiner (7); Gavvy Cravath and Mel Ott (6); Hank Aaron, Chuck Klein, Willie Mays, Johnny Mize, Cy Williams and Hack Wilson (4); Willie McCovey (3); Ernie Banks, Johnny Bench, Barry Bonds, George Foster, Rogers Hornsby, Tim Jordan, Dave Kingman, Eddie Mathews, Mark McGwire, Dale Murphy, Bill Nicholson, Dave Robertson, Wildfire Schulte, Sammy Sosa and Willie Stargell (2).

Year		HR	Year		HR	Year		HR
1900	Herman Long, Bos	12	1935	Wally Berger, Bos	34	1972	Johnny Bench, Cin	40
1901	Sam Crawford, Cin	16	1936	Mel Ott, NY.	33	1973	Willie Stargell, Pit	44
1902	Tommy Leach, Pit	6	1937	Joe Medwick, St.L	31	1974	Mike Schmidt, Phi.	36
1903	Jimmy Sheckard, Bklyn	9		& Mel Ott, NY.	31	1975	Mike Schmidt, Phi.	38
1904	Harry Lumley, Bklyn	9	1938	Mel Ott, NY.	36	1976	Mike Schmidt, Phi.	38
1905	Fred Odwell, Cin	9	1939	Johnny Mize, St.L	28	1977	George Foster, Cin	52
1906	Tim Jordan, Bklyn	12	1940	Johnny Mize, St.L	43	1978	George Foster, Cin	40
1907	Dave Brain, Bos	10	1941	Dolph Camilli, Bklyn	34	1979	Dave Kingman, Chi	48
1908	Tim Jordan, Bklyn	12	1942	Mel Ott, NY.	30	1980	Mike Schmidt, Phi.	48
1909	Red Murray, NY	7	1943	Bill Nicholson, Chi	29	1981	Mike Schmidt, Phi.	31
1910	Fred Beck, Bos.	10	1944	Bill Nicholson, Chi	33	1982	Dave Kingman, NY.	37
	& Wildfire Schulte, Chi	10	1945	Tommy Holmes, Bos	28	1983	Mike Schmidt, Phi.	40
1911	Wildfire Schulte, Chi	21	1946	Ralph Kiner, Pit.	23	1984	Dale Murphy, Atl.	36
1912	Heinie Zimmerman, Chi.	14	1947	Ralph Kiner, Pit.	51		& Mike Schmidt, Phi.	36
1913	Gavvy Cravath, Phi.	19		& Johnny Mize, NY	51	1985	Dale Murphy, Atl.	37
1914	Gavvy Cravath, Phi.	19	1948	Ralph Kiner, Pit.	40	1986	Mike Schmidt, Phi.	37
1915	Gavvy Cravath, Phi.	24		& Johnny Mize, NY	40	1987	Andre Dawson, Chi	49
1916	Cy Williams, Phi	12	1949	Ralph Kiner, Pit.	54	1988	Darryl Strawberry, NY.	39
	& Dave Robertson, NY.	12	1950	Ralph Kiner, Pit.	47	1989	Kevin Mitchell, SF	47
1917	Gavvy Cravath, Phi.	12	1951	Ralph Kiner, Pit.	42	1990	Ryne Sandberg, Chi	40
	& Dave Robertson, NY.	12	1952	Ralph Kiner, Pit.	37	1991	Howard Johnson, NY.	38
1918	Gavvy Cravath, Phi.	8		& Hank Sauer, Chi	37	1992	Fred McGriff, SD	35
1919	Gavvy Cravath, Phi.	12	1953	Eddie Mathews, Mil	47	1993	Barry Bonds, SF	46
1920	Cy Williams, Phi.	15	1954	Ted Kluszewski, Cin	49	1994	Matt Williams, SF	43
1921	George Kelly, NY	23	1955	Willie Mays, NY.	51	1995	Dante Bichette, Col.	40
1922	Rogers Hornsby, St.L	42	1956	Duke Snider, Bklyn	43	1996	Andres Galarraga, Col	47
1923	Cy Williams, Phi.	41	1957	Hank Aaron, Mil	44	1997	Larry Walker, Col	49
1924	Jack Fournier, Bklyn	27	1958	Ernie Banks, Chi.	47	1998	Mark McGwire, St.L	70
1925	Rogers Hornsby, St.L	39	1959	Eddie Mathews, Mil	46	1999	Mark McGwire, St.L	65
1926	Hack Wilson, Chi	21	1960	Ernie Banks, Chi	41	2000	Sammy Sosa, Chi	50
1927	Cy Williams, Phi.	30	1961	Orlando Cepeda, SF.	46	2001	Barry Bonds, SF	73
	& Hack Wilson, Chi	30	1962	Willie Mays, SF	49	2002	Sammy Sosa, Chi	49
1928	Jim Bottomley, St.L	31	1963	Hank Aaron, Mil.	44	2003	Jim Thome, Phi	47
	& Hack Wilson, Chi	31		& Willie McCovey, SF	44	2004	Adrian Beltre, LA	48
1929	Chuck Klein, Phi	43	1964	Willie Mays, SF	47	2005	Andruw Jones, Atl.	51
1930	Hack Wilson, Chi	56	1965	Willie Mays, SF	52	2006	Ryan Howard, Phi.	58
1931	Chuck Klein, Phi	31	1966	Hank Aaron, Atl.	44	2007	Prince Fielder, Mil.	50
1932	Chuck Klein, Phi	38	1967	Hank Aaron, Atl	39			
	& Mel Ott, NY.	38	1968	Willie McCovey, SF	36			
1933	Chuck Klein, Phi	28	1969	Willie McCovey, SF	45			
1934	Rip Collins, St.L	35	1970	Johnny Bench, Cin	45			
	& Mel Ott, NY.	35	1971	Willie Stargell, Pit.	48			

Note: In 1997 Mark McGwire hit 58 home runs but hit 34 of them in the AL with Oakland before his trade to St. Louis.

American League

Multiple winners: Babe Ruth (12); Harmon Killebrew (6); Alex Rodriguez (5); Home Run Baker, Harry Davis, Jimmie Foxx, Hank Greenberg, Ken Griffey Jr., Reggie Jackson, Mickey Mantle and Ted Williams (3); Dick Allen, Tony Armas, Jose Canseco, Joe DiMaggio, Larry Doby, Cecil Fielder, Juan Gonzalez, Mark McGwire, Wally Pipp, Al Rosen and Gorman Thomas (2).

Year		HR	Year		HR	Year		HR
1901	Nap Lajoie, Phi	14	1905	Harry Davis, Phi.	8	1909	Ty Cobb, Det	9
1902	Socks Seybold, Phi	16	1906	Harry Davis, Phi	12	1910	Jake Stahl, Bos	10
1903	Buck Freeman, Bos	13	1907	Harry Davis, Phi	8	1911	Home Run Baker, Phi.	11
1904	Harry Davis, Phi	10	1908	Sam Crawford, Det.	7			

Year		HR	Year		HR	Year		HR
1912	Home Run Baker, Phi	10	1945	Vern Stephens, St.L	24	1979	Gorman Thomas, Mil	45
	& Tris Speaker, Bos.	10	1946	Hank Greenberg, Det.	44	1980	Reggie Jackson, NY	41
1913	Home Run Baker, Phi.	12	1947	Ted Williams, Bos	32		& Ben Oglivie, Mil	41
1914	Home Run Baker, Phi.	9	1948	Joe DiMaggio, NY	39	1981	Tony Armas, Oak	22
1915	Braggo Roth, Chi-Cle	7	1949	Ted Williams, Bos	43		Dwight Evans, Bos	22
1916	Wally Pipp, NY.	12	1950	Al Rosen, Cle.	37		Bobby Grich, Cal	22
1917	Wally Pipp, NY	9	1951	Gus Zernial, Chi-Phi	33		& Eddie Murray, Bal.	22
1918	Babe Ruth, Bos.	11	1952	Larry Doby, Cle.	32	1982	Reggie Jackson, Cal.	39
	& Tilly Walker, Phi	11	1953	Al Rosen, Cle.	43		& Gorman Thomas, Mil.	39
1919	Babe Ruth, Bos	29	1954	Larry Doby, Cle.	32	1983	Jim Rice, Bos	39
1920	Babe Ruth, NY	54	1955	Mickey Mantle, NY.	37	1984	Tony Armas, Bos	43
1921	Babe Ruth, NY	59	1956	Mickey Mantle, NY.	52	1985	Darrell Evans, Det.	40
1922	Ken Williams, St.L.	39	1957	Roy Sievers, Wash	42	1986	Jesse Barfield, Tor	40
1923	Babe Ruth, NY	41	1958	Mickey Mantle, NY.	42	1987	Mark McGwire, Oak	49
1924	Babe Ruth, NY	46	1959	Rocky Colavito, Cle	42	1988	Jose Canseco, Oak.	42
1925	Bob Meusel, NY	33		& Harmon Killebrew, Wash	42	1989	Fred McGriff, Tor	36
1926	Babe Ruth, NY	47	1960	Mickey Mantle, NY.	40	1990	Cecil Fielder, Det	51
1927	Babe Ruth, NY	60	1961	Roger Maris, NY.	61	1991	Jose Canseco, Oak.	44
1928	Babe Ruth, NY	54	1962	Harmon Killebrew, Min	48		& Cecil Fielder, Det.	44
1929	Babe Ruth, NY	46	1963	Harmon Killebrew, Min	45	1992	Juan Gonzalez, Tex.	43
1930	Babe Ruth, NY	49	1964	Harmon Killebrew, Min	49	1993	Juan Gonzalez, Tex.	46
1931	Lou Gehrig, NY.	46	1965	Tony Conigliaro, Bos	32	1994	Ken Griffey Jr., Sea.	40
	& Babe Ruth, NY	46	1966	Frank Robinson, Bal	49	1995	Albert Belle, Cle	50
1932	Jimmie Foxx, Phi	58	1967	Harmon Killebrew, Min	44	1996	Mark McGwire, Oak	52
1933	Jimmie Foxx, Phi.	48		& Carl Yastrzemski, Bos.	44	1997	Ken Griffey Jr., Sea.	56
1934	Lou Gehrig, NY.	49	1968	Frank Howard, Wash.	44	1998	Ken Griffey Jr., Sea.	56
1935	Jimmie Foxx, Phi.	36	1969	Harmon Killebrew, Min	49	1999	Ken Griffey Jr., Sea.	48
	& Hank Greenberg, Det.	36	1970	Frank Howard, Wash.	44	2000	Troy Glaus, Ana	47
1936	Lou Gehrig, NY.	49	1971	Bill Melton, Chi	33	2001	Alex Rodriguez, Tex	52
1937	Joe DiMaggio, NY	46	1972	Dick Allen, Chi	37	2002	Alex Rodriguez, Tex	57
1938	Hank Greenberg, Det.	58	1973	Reggie Jackson, Oak	32	2003	Alex Rodriguez, Tex	47
1939	Jimmie Foxx, Bos.	35	1974	Dick Allen, Chi	32	2004	Manny Ramirez, Bos.	43
1940	Hank Greenberg, Det.	41	1975	Reggie Jackson, Oak	36	2005	Alex Rodriguez, NY	48
1941	Ted Williams, Bos.	37		& George Scott, Mil	36	2006	David Ortiz, Bos.	54
1942	Ted Williams, Bos.	36	1976	Graig Nettles, NY	32	2007	Alex Rodriguez, NY	54
1943	Rudy York, Det.	34	1977	Jim Rice, Bos	39			
1944	Nick Etten, NY	22	1978	Jim Rice, Bos	46			

Runs Batted In
National League

Multiple winners: Hank Aaron, Rogers Hornsby, Sherry Magee, Mike Schmidt and Honus Wagner (4); Johnny Bench, George Foster, Joe Medwick, Johnny Mize and Heinie Zimmerman (3); Ernie Banks, Jim Bottomley, Orlando Cepeda, Gavvy Cravath, Andres Galarraga, George Kelly, Chuck Klein, Willie McCovey, Dale Murphy, Stan Musial, Bill Nicholson, Sammy Sosa and Hack Wilson (2).

Year		RBI	Year		RBI	Year		RBI
1900	Elmer Flick, Phi.	110	1926	Jim Bottomley, St.L	120	1954	Ted Kluszewski, Cin	141
1901	Honus Wagner, Pit	126	1927	Paul Waner, Pit.	131	1955	Duke Snider, Bklyn	136
1902	Honus Wagner, Pit	91	1928	Jim Bottomley, St.L.	136	1956	Stan Musial, St.L.	109
1903	Sam Mertes, NY.	104	1929	Hack Wilson, Chi.	159	1957	Hank Aaron, Mil	132
1904	Bill Dahlen, NY	80	1930	Hack Wilson, Chi.	191	1958	Ernie Banks, Chi.	129
1905	Cy Seymour, Cin	121	1931	Chuck Klein, Phi.	121	1959	Ernie Banks, Chi.	143
1906	Jim Nealon, Pit.	83	1932	Don Hurst, Phi.	143	1960	Hank Aaron, Mil	126
	& Harry Steinfeldt, Chi.	83	1933	Chuck Klein, Phi.	120	1961	Orlando Cepeda, SF.	142
1907	Sherry Magee, Phi	85	1934	Mel Ott, NY.	135	1962	Tommy Davis, LA	153
1908	Honus Wagner, Pit	109	1935	Wally Berger, Bos	130	1963	Hank Aaron, Mil	130
1909	Honus Wagner, Pit	100	1936	Joe Medwick, St.L.	138	1964	Ken Boyer, St.L.	119
1910	Sherry Magee, Phi	123	1937	Joe Medwick, St.L.	154	1965	Deron Johnson, Cin.	130
1911	Wildfire Schulte, Chi.	121	1938	Joe Medwick, St.L.	122	1966	Hank Aaron, Atl.	127
1912	Heinie Zimmerman, Chi.	103	1939	Frank McCormick, Cin	128	1967	Orlando Cepeda, St.L.	111
1913	Gavvy Cravath, Phi.	128	1940	Johnny Mize, St.L.	137	1968	Willie McCovey, SF	105
1914	Sherry Magee, Phi	103	1941	Dolph Camilli, Bklyn	120	1969	Willie McCovey, SF	126
1915	Gavvy Cravath, Phi.	115	1942	Johnny Mize, NY	110	1970	Johnny Bench, Cin	148
1916	Heinie Zimmerman, Chi-NY	83	1943	Bill Nicholson, Chi	128	1971	Joe Torre, St.L.	137
1917	Heinie Zimmerman, NY.	102	1944	Bill Nicholson, Chi	122	1972	Johnny Bench, Cin	125
1918	Sherry Magee, Cin.	76	1945	Dixie Walker, Bklyn.	124	1973	Willie Stargell, Pit.	119
1919	Hy Myers, Bklyn	73	1946	Enos Slaughter, St.L.	130	1974	Johnny Bench, Cin	129
1920	Rogers Hornsby, St.L.	94	1947	Johnny Mize, NY	138	1975	Greg Luzinski, Phi.	120
	& George Kelly, NY	94	1948	Stan Musial, St.L.	131	1976	George Foster, Cin.	121
1921	Rogers Hornsby, St.L.	126	1949	Ralph Kiner, Pit.	127	1977	George Foster, Cin.	149
1922	Rogers Hornsby, St.L.	152	1950	Del Ennis, Phi.	126	1978	George Foster, Cin.	120
1923	Irish Meusel, NY.	125	1951	Monte Irvin, NY	121	1979	Dave Winfield, SD	118
1924	George Kelly, NY.	136	1952	Hank Sauer, Chi.	121	1980	Mike Schmidt, Phi.	121
1925	Rogers Hornsby, St.L.	143	1953	Roy Campanella, Bklyn	142	1981	Mike Schmidt, Phi.	91

Runs Batted In (Cont.)

Year		RBI	Year		RBI	Year		RBI
1982	Dale Murphy, Atl	109	1990	Matt Williams, SF.	122	2000	Todd Helton, Col	147
	& Al Oliver, Mon	109	1991	Howard Johnson, NY	117	2001	Sammy Sosa, Chi.	160
1983	Dale Murphy, Atl	121	1992	Darren Daulton, Phi.	109	2002	Lance Berkman, Hou	128
1984	Gary Carter, Mon.	106	1993	Barry Bonds, SF	123	2003	Preston Wilson, Col	141
	& Mike Schmidt, Phi.	106	1994	Jeff Bagwell, Hou	116	2004	Vinny Castilla, Col	131
1985	Dave Parker, Cin	125	1995	Dante Bichette, Col	128	2005	Andruw Jones, Atl.	128
1986	Mike Schmidt, Phi.	119	1996	Andres Galarraga, Col.	150	2006	Ryan Howard, Phi.	149
1987	Andre Dawson, Chi	137	1997	Andres Galarraga, Col.	140	2007	Matt Holliday, Col	137
1988	Will Clark, SF	109	1998	Sammy Sosa, Chi.	158			
1989	Kevin Mitchell, SF.	125	1999	Mark McGwire, St.L.	147			

American League

Multiple winners: Babe Ruth (6); Lou Gehrig (5); Ty Cobb, Hank Greenberg and Ted Williams (4); Albert Belle, Sam Crawford, Cecil Fielder, Jimmie Foxx, Jackie Jensen, Harmon Killebrew, Vern Stephens and Bobby Veach (3); Home Run Baker, Cecil Cooper, Harry Davis, Joe DiMaggio, Buck Freeman, Nap Lajoie, Roger Maris, David Ortiz, Jim Rice, Alex Rodriguez, Al Rosen and Bobby Veach (2).

Year		RBI	Year		RBI	Year		RBI
1901	Nap Lajoie, Phi.	125	1937	Hank Greenberg, Det	183	1972	Dick Allen, Chi.	113
1902	Buck Freeman, Bos.	121	1938	Jimmie Foxx, Bos	175	1973	Reggie Jackson, Oak.	117
1903	Buck Freeman, Bos.	104	1939	Ted Williams, Bos.	145	1974	Jeff Burroughs, Tex	118
1904	Nap Lajoie, Cle	102	1940	Hank Greenberg, Det	150	1975	George Scott, Mil.	109
1905	Harry Davis, Phi	83	1941	Joe DiMaggio, NY.	125	1976	Lee May, Bal	109
1906	Harry Davis, Phi	96	1942	Ted Williams, Bos.	137	1977	Larry Hisle, Min	119
1907	Ty Cobb, Det.	116	1943	Rudy York, Det	118	1978	Jim Rice, Bos	139
1908	Ty Cobb, Det.	108	1944	Vern Stephens, St.L.	109	1979	Don Baylor, Cal	139
1909	Ty Cobb, Det.	107	1945	Nick Etten, NY	111	1980	Cecil Cooper, Mil.	122
1910	Sam Crawford, Det.	120	1946	Hank Greenberg, Det	127	1981	Eddie Murray, Bal.	78
1911	Ty Cobb, Det.	144	1947	Ted Williams, Bos.	114	1982	Hal McRae, KC.	133
1912	Home Run Baker, Phi.	133	1948	Joe DiMaggio, NY.	155	1983	Cecil Cooper, Mil.	126
1913	Home Run Baker, Phi.	126	1949	Ted Williams, Bos.	159		& Jim Rice, Bos.	126
1914	Sam Crawford, Det.	104		& Vern Stephens, Bos.	159	1984	Tony Armas, Bos.	123
1915	Sam Crawford, Det.	112	1950	Walt Dropo, Bos.	144	1985	Don Mattingly, NY	145
	& Bobby Veach, Det.	112		& Vern Stephens, Bos.	144	1986	Joe Carter, Cle.	121
1916	Del Pratt, St.L.	103	1951	Gus Zernial, Chi-Phi.	129	1987	George Bell, Tor.	134
1917	Bobby Veach, Det.	103	1952	Al Rosen, Cle.	105	1988	Jose Canseco, Oak.	124
1918	Bobby Veach, Det.	78	1953	Al Rosen, Cle.	145	1989	Ruben Sierra, Tex	119
1919	Babe Ruth, Bos.	114	1954	Larry Doby, Cle.	126	1990	Cecil Fielder, Det	132
1920	Babe Ruth, NY.	137	1955	Ray Boone, Det.	116	1991	Cecil Fielder, Det	133
1921	Babe Ruth, NY.	171		& Jackie Jensen, Bos.	116	1992	Cecil Fielder, Det	124
1922	Ken Williams, St.L.	155	1956	Mickey Mantle, NY.	130	1993	Albert Belle, Cle.	129
1923	Babe Ruth, NY.	131	1957	Roy Sievers, Wash	114	1994	Kirby Puckett, Min.	112
1924	Goose Goslin, Wash.	129	1958	Jackie Jensen, Bos.	122	1995	Albert Belle, Cle.	126
1925	Bob Meusel, NY.	138	1959	Jackie Jensen, Bos.	112		& Mo Vaughn, Bos.	126
1926	Babe Ruth, NY.	145	1960	Roger Maris, NY.	112	1996	Albert Belle, Cle.	148
1927	Lou Gehrig, NY.	175	1961	Roger Maris, NY.	142	1997	Ken Griffey Jr., Sea.	147
1928	Lou Gehrig, NY.	142	1962	Harmon Killebrew, Min.	126	1998	Juan Gonzalez, Tex.	157
	& Babe Ruth, NY.	142	1963	Dick Stuart, Bos.	118	1999	Manny Ramirez, Cle.	165
1929	Al Simmons, Phi.	157	1964	Brooks Robinson, Bal	118	2000	Edgar Martinez, Sea.	145
1930	Lou Gehrig, NY.	174	1965	Rocky Colavito, Cle.	108	2001	Bret Boone, Sea.	141
1931	Lou Gehrig, NY.	184	1966	Frank Robinson, Bal	122	2002	Alex Rodriguez, Tex.	142
1932	Jimmie Foxx, Phi.	169	1967	Carl Yastrzemski, Bos.	121	2003	Carlos Delgado, Tor	145
1933	Jimmie Foxx, Phi.	163	1968	Ken Harrelson, Bos.	109	2004	Miguel Tejada, Bal	150
1934	Lou Gehrig, NY.	165	1969	Harmon Killebrew, Min.	140	2005	David Ortiz, Bos.	148
1935	Hank Greenberg, Det	170	1970	Frank Howard, Wash.	126	2006	David Ortiz, Bos.	137
1936	Hal Trosky, Cle.	162	1971	Harmon Killebrew, Min.	119	2007	Alex Rodriguez, NY	156

Batting Triple Crown Winners

Players who led either league in Batting Average, Home Runs and Runs Batted In over a single season.

National League

	Year	Avg	HR	RBI
Paul Hines, Providence	1878	.358	4	50
Hugh Duffy, Boston	1894	.438	18	145
Heinie Zimmerman, Chicago	1912	.372	14	103
Rogers Hornsby, St. Louis	1922	.401	42	152
Rogers Hornsby, St. Louis	1925	.403	39	143
Chuck Klein, Philadelphia	1933	.368	28	120
Joe Medwick, St. Louis	1937	.374	31*	154

*Tied for league lead in HRs with Mel Ott, NY.

American League

	Year	Avg	HR	RBI
Nap Lajoie, Philadelphia	1901	.422	14	125
Ty Cobb, Detroit	1909	.377	9	115
Jimmie Foxx, Philadelphia	1933	.356	48	163
Lou Gehrig, New York	1934	.363	49	165
Ted Williams, Boston	1942	.356	36	137
Ted Williams, Boston	1947	.343	32	114
Mickey Mantle, New York	1956	.353	52	130
Frank Robinson, Baltimore	1966	.316	49	122
Carl Yastrzemski, Boston	1967	.326	44*	121

*Tied for league lead in HRs with Harmon Killebrew, Min.

Stolen Bases
National League

Multiple winners: Max Carey (10); Lou Brock (8); Vince Coleman and Maury Wills (6); Honus Wagner (5); Bob Bescher, Kiki Cuyler, Willie Mays and Tim Raines (4); Bill Bruton, Frankie Frisch, Pepper Martin, Jose Reyes and Tony Womack (3); George Burns, Luis Castillo, Frank Chance, Augie Galan, Marquis Grissom, Stan Hack, Sam Jethroe, Davey Lopes, Omar Moreno, Pete Reiser and Jackie Robinson (2).

Year		SB	Year		SB	Year		SB
1900	Patsy Donovan, St.L	45	1935	Augie Galan, Chi	22	1972	Lou Brock, St.L	63
	& George Van Haltren, NY.	45	1936	Pepper Martin, St.L	23	1973	Lou Brock, St.L	70
1901	Honus Wagner, Pit	49	1937	Augie Galan, Chi	23	1974	Lou Brock, St.L	118
1902	Honus Wagner, Pit	42	1938	Stan Hack, Chi	16	1975	Davey Lopes, LA	77
1903	Frank Chance, Chi	67	1939	Stan Hack, Chi	17	1976	Davey Lopes, LA	63
	& Jimmy Sheckard, Bklyn.	67		& Lee Handley, Pit	17	1977	Frank Taveras, Pit	70
1904	Honus Wagner, Pit	53	1940	Lonny Frey, Cin	22	1978	Omar Moreno, Pit	71
1905	Art Devlin, NY.	59	1941	Danny Murtaugh, Phi	18	1979	Omar Moreno, Pit	77
	& Billy Maloney, Chi	59	1942	Pete Reiser, Bklyn	20	1980	Ron LeFlore, Mon	97
1906	Frank Chance, Chi	57	1943	Arky Vaughan, Bklyn	20	1981	Tim Raines, Mon	71
1907	Honus Wagner, Pit	61	1944	Johnny Barrett, Pit	28	1982	Tim Raines, Mon	78
1908	Honus Wagner, Pit	53	1945	Red Schoendienst, St.L	26	1983	Tim Raines, Mon	90
1909	Bob Bescher, Cin	54	1946	Pete Reiser, Bklyn	34	1984	Tim Raines, Mon	75
1910	Bob Bescher, Cin	70	1947	Jackie Robinson, Bklyn	29	1985	Vince Coleman, St.L	110
1911	Bob Bescher, Cin	81	1948	Richie Ashburn, Phi	32	1986	Vince Coleman, St.L	107
1912	Bob Bescher, Cin	67	1949	Jackie Robinson, Bklyn	37	1987	Vince Coleman, St.L	109
1913	Max Carey, Pit	61	1950	Sam Jethroe, Bos.	35	1988	Vince Coleman, St.L	81
1914	George Burns, NY	62	1951	Sam Jethroe, Bos.	35	1989	Vince Coleman, St.L	65
1915	Max Carey, Pit	36	1952	Pee Wee Reese, Bklyn	30	1990	Vince Coleman, St.L	77
1916	Max Carey, Pit	63	1953	Bill Bruton, Mil.	26	1991	Marquis Grissom, Mon	76
1917	Max Carey, Pit	46	1954	Bill Bruton, Mil.	34	1992	Marquis Grissom, Mon	78
1918	Max Carey, Pit	58	1955	Bill Bruton, Mil.	25	1993	Chuck Carr, Fla.	58
1919	George Burns, NY	40	1956	Willie Mays, NY	40	1994	Craig Biggio, Hou	39
1920	Max Carey, Pit	52	1957	Willie Mays, NY	38	1995	Quilvio Veras, Fla	56
1921	Frankie Frisch, NY	49	1958	Willie Mays, SF	31	1996	Eric Young, Col	53
1922	Max Carey, Pit	51	1959	Willie Mays, SF	27	1997	Tony Womack, Pit	60
1923	Max Carey, Pit	51	1960	Maury Wills, LA	50	1998	Tony Womack, Pit	58
1924	Max Carey, Pit	49	1961	Maury Wills, LA	35	1999	Tony Womack, Ari	72
1925	Max Carey, Pit	46	1962	Maury Wills, LA	104	2000	Luis Castillo, Fla	62
1926	Kiki Cuyler, Pit.	35	1963	Maury Wills, LA	40	2001	Juan Pierre, Col.	46
1927	Frankie Frisch, St.L	48	1964	Maury Wills, LA	53		& Jimmy Rollins, Phi	46
1928	Kiki Cuyler, Chi.	37	1965	Maury Wills, LA	94	2002	Luis Castillo, Fla	48
1929	Kiki Cuyler, Chi.	43	1966	Lou Brock, St.L	74	2003	Juan Pierre, Fla.	65
1930	Kiki Cuyler, Chi.	37	1967	Lou Brock, St.L	52	2004	Scott Podsednik, Mil	70
1931	Frankie Frisch, St.L	28	1968	Lou Brock, St.L	62	2005	Jose Reyes, NY.	60
1932	Chuck Klein, Phi	20	1969	Lou Brock, St.L	53	2006	Jose Reyes, NY.	64
1933	Pepper Martin, St.L	26	1970	Bobby Tolan, Cin	57	2007	Jose Reyes, NY.	78
1934	Pepper Martin, St.L	23	1971	Lou Brock, St.L	64			

30 Homers & 30 Stolen Bases in One Season

National League	Year	Gm	HR	SB		Year	Gm	HR	SB
Willie Mays, NY Giants	1956	152	36	40	Jeff Bagwell, Houston	1999	162	42	30
Willie Mays, NY Giants	1957	152	35	38	Raul Mondesi, Los Angeles	1999	159	33	36
Hank Aaron, Milwaukee	1963	161	44	31	Preston Wilson, Florida	2000	161	31	36
Bobby Bonds, San Francisco	1969	158	32	45	Vladimir Guerrero, Montreal	2001	159	34	37
Bobby Bonds, San Francisco	1973	160	39	43	Bobby Abreu, Philadelphia	2001	162	31	36
Dale Murphy, Atlanta	1983	162	36	30	Vladimir Guerrero, Montreal	2002	161	39	40
Eric Davis, Cincinnati	1987	129	37	50	Bobby Abreu, Philadelphia	2004	159	30	40
Howard Johnson, NY Mets	1987	157	36	32	Alfonso Soriano, Washington	2006	159	46	41
Darryl Strawberry, NY Mets	1987	154	39	36	Brandon Phillips, Cincinnati	2007	158	30	32
Howard Johnson, NY Mets	1989	153	36	41	David Wright, NY Mets	2007	160	30	34
Ron Gant, Atlanta	1990	152	32	33	Jimmy Rollins, Philadelphia	2007	162	30	41
Barry Bonds, Pittsburgh	1990	151	33	52					
Ron Gant, Atlanta	1991	154	32	34	**American League**	**Year**	**Gm**	**HR**	**SB**
Howard Johnson, NY Mets	1991	156	38	30	Kenny Williams, St. Louis	1922	153	39	37
Barry Bonds, Pittsburgh	1992	140	34	39	Tommy Harper, Milwaukee	1970	154	31	38
Sammy Sosa, Chicago	1993	159	33	36	Bobby Bonds, New York	1975	145	32	30
Barry Bonds, San Francisco	1995	144	33	31	Bobby Bonds, California	1977	158	37	41
Sammy Sosa, Chicago	1995	144	36	34	Bobby Bonds, Chicago-Texas	1978	156	31	43
Barry Bonds, San Francisco	1996	158	42	40	Joe Carter, Cleveland	1987	149	32	31
Ellis Burks, Colorado	1996	156	40	32	Jose Canseco, Oakland	1988	158	42	40
Dante Bichette, Colorado	1996	159	31	31	Alex Rodriguez, Seattle	1998	161	42	46
Barry Larkin, Cincinnati	1996	152	33	36	Shawn Green, Toronto	1998	158	35	35
Larry Walker, Colorado	1997	153	49	33	Jose Cruz Jr., Toronto	2001	146	34	32
Barry Bonds, San Francisco	1997	159	40	37	Alfonso Soriano, New York	2002	156	39	41
Raul Mondesi, Los Angeles	1997	159	30	32	Alfonso Soriano, New York	2003	156	38	35
Jeff Bagwell, Houston	1997	162	43	31	Alfonso Soriano, Texas	2005	156	36	30

Note: In 2004, Carlos Beltran switched leagues mid-season. Combining his AL and NL totals, he hit 38 HR and stole 42 bases.

Stolen Bases (Cont.)
American League

Multiple winners: Rickey Henderson (12); Luis Aparicio (9); Bert Campaneris, George Case and Ty Cobb (6); Kenny Lofton (5); Ben Chapman, Eddie Collins, Carl Crawford and George Sisler (4); Bob Dillinger, Minnie Minoso and Bill Werber (3); Elmer Flick, Tommy Harper, Brian Hunter, Clyde Milan, Johnny Mostil, Bill North and Snuffy Stirnweiss (2).

Year		SB	Year		SB	Year		SB
1901	Frank Isbell, Chi	52	1937	Ben Chapman, Wash-Bos	35	1973	Tommy Harper, Bos	54
1902	Topsy Hartsel, Phi	47		& Bill Werber, Phi	35	1974	Bill North, Oak	54
1903	Harry Bay, Cle	45	1938	Frank Crosetti, NY	27	1975	Mickey Rivers, CA	70
1904	Elmer Flick, Cle	42	1939	George Case, Wash	51	1976	Bill North, Oak	75
1905	Danny Hoffman, Phi	46				1977	Freddie Patek, KC	53
1906	John Anderson, Wash	39	1940	George Case, Wash	35	1978	Ron LeFlore, Det	68
	& Elmer Flick, Cle	39	1941	George Case, Wash	33	1979	Willie Wilson, KC	83
1907	Ty Cobb, Det	49	1942	George Case, Wash	44			
1908	Patsy Dougherty, Chi	47	1943	George Case, Wash	61	1980	Rickey Henderson, Oak	100
1909	Ty Cobb, Det	76	1944	Snuffy Stirnweiss, NY	55	1981	Rickey Henderson, Oak	56
			1945	Snuffy Stirnweiss, NY	33	1982	Rickey Henderson, Oak	130
1910	Eddie Collins, Phi	81	1946	George Case, Cle	28	1983	Rickey Henderson, Oak	108
1911	Ty Cobb, Det	83	1947	Bob Dillinger, St.L	34	1984	Rickey Henderson, Oak	66
1912	Clyde Milan, Wash	88	1948	Bob Dillinger, St.L	28	1985	Rickey Henderson, NY	80
1913	Clyde Milan, Wash	75	1949	Bob Dillinger, St.L	20	1986	Rickey Henderson, NY	87
1914	Fritz Maisel, NY	74	1950	Dom DiMaggio, Bos	15	1987	Harold Reynolds, Sea	60
1915	Ty Cobb, Det	96	1951	Minnie Minoso, Cle-Chi	31	1988	Rickey Henderson, NY	93
1916	Ty Cobb, Det	68	1952	Minnie Minoso, Chi	22	1989	R. Henderson, NY-Oak	77
1917	Ty Cobb, Det	55	1953	Minnie Minoso, Chi	25			
1918	George Sisler, St.L	45	1954	Jackie Jensen, Bos	22	1990	Rickey Henderson, Oak	65
1919	Eddie Collins, Chi	33	1955	Jim Rivera, Chi	25	1991	Rickey Henderson, Oak	58
			1956	Luis Aparicio, Chi	21	1992	Kenny Lofton, Cle	66
1920	Sam Rice, Wash	63	1957	Luis Aparicio, Chi	28	1993	Kenny Lofton, Cle	70
1921	George Sisler, St.L	35	1958	Luis Aparicio, Chi	29	1994	Kenny Lofton, Cle	60
1922	George Sisler, St.L	51	1959	Luis Aparicio, Chi	56	1995	Kenny Lofton, Cle	54
1923	Eddie Collins, Chi	47	1960	Luis Aparicio, Chi	51	1996	Kenny Lofton, Cle	75
1924	Eddie Collins, Chi	42	1961	Luis Aparicio, Chi	53	1997	Brian Hunter, Det	74
1925	Johnny Mostil, Chi	43	1962	Luis Aparicio, Chi	31	1998	Rickey Henderson, Oak	66
1926	Johnny Mostil, Chi	35	1963	Luis Aparicio, Bal	40	1999	Brian Hunter, Det-Sea	44
1927	George Sisler, St.L	27	1964	Luis Aparicio, Bal	57			
1928	Buddy Myer, Bos	30	1965	Bert Campaneris, KC	51	2000	Johnny Damon, KC	46
1929	Charlie Gehringer, Det	28	1966	Bert Campaneris, KC	52	2001	Ichiro Suzuki, Sea	56
			1967	Bert Campaneris, KC	55	2002	Alfonso Soriano, NY	41
1930	Marty McManus, Det	23	1968	Bert Campaneris, Oak	62	2003	Carl Crawford, TB	55
1931	Ben Chapman, NY	61	1969	Tommy Harper, Sea	73	2004	Carl Crawford, TB	59
1932	Ben Chapman, NY	38	1970	Bert Campaneris, Oak	42	2005	Chone Figgins, LAA	62
1933	Ben Chapman, NY	27	1971	Amos Otis, KC	52	2006	Carl Crawford, TB	58
1934	Bill Werber, Bos	40	1972	Bert Campaneris, Oak	52	2007	Carl Crawford, TB	50
1935	Bill Werber, Bos	29					& Brian Roberts, Bal	50
1936	Lyn Lary, St.L	37						

Consecutive Game Streaks
(Regular season games through 2007)

Games Played

Gm		Dates of Streak
2632	Cal Ripken Jr., Bal	5/30/82 to 9/19/98
2130	Lou Gehrig, NY	6/1/25 to 4/30/39
1307	Everett Scott, Bos-NY	6/20/16 to 5/5/25
1207	Steve Garvey, LA-SD	9/3/75 to 7/29/83
1152	Miguel Tejada, Oak-Bal	6/1/00 to 6/21/07
1117	Billy Williams, Cubs	9/22/63 to 9/2/70
1103	Joe Sewell, Cle	9/13/22 to 4/30/30
895	Stan Musial, St.L	4/15/52 to 8/23/57
829	Eddie Yost, Wash	4/30/49 to 5/11/55
822	Gus Suhr, Pit	9/11/31 to 6/4/37
798	Nellie Fox, Chisox	8/8/55 to 9/3/60
745	Pete Rose, Cin-Phi	9/2/78 to 8/23/83
740	Dale Murphy, Atl	9/26/81 to 7/8/86
730	Richie Ashburn, Phi	6/7/50 to 4/13/55
717	Ernie Banks, Cubs	8/28/56 to 6/22/61
678	Pete Rose, Cin	9/28/73 to 5/7/78

Hitting

Gm		Year
Joe DiMaggio, New York (AL)	56	1941
Willie Keeler, Baltimore (NL)	44	1897
Pete Rose, Cincinnati (NL)	44	1978
Bill Dahlen, Chicago (NL)	42	1894
George Sisler, St. Louis (AL)	41	1922
Ty Cobb, Detroit (AL)	40	1911
Paul Molitor, Milwaukee (AL)	39	1987
Jimmy Rollins, Philadelphia (NL)	38	2005-06
Tommy Holmes, Boston (NL)	37	1945
Billy Hamilton, Philadelphia (NL)	36	1894
Fred Clarke, Louisville (NL)	35	1895
Ty Cobb, Detroit (AL)	35	1917
Luis Castillo, Florida (NL)	35	2002
Chase Utley, Philadelphia (NL)	35	2006
Ty Cobb, Detroit (AL)	34	1912
George Sisler, St. Louis (AL)	34	1925
George McQuinn, St. Louis (AL)	34	1938
Dom DiMaggio, Boston (AL)	34	1949
Benito Santiago, San Diego (NL)	34	1987

Note: Rollins had a 36-game streak at the end of 2005.

Annual Pitching Leaders (since 1900)

Winning Percentage

At least 15 wins, except in strike years of 1981 and 1994 (when the minimum was 10).

National League

Multiple winners: Ed Reulbach and Tom Seaver (3); Larry Benton, Harry Brecheen, Jack Chesbro, Paul Derringer, Freddie Fitzsimmons, Don Gullett, Claude Hendrix, Carl Hubbell, Randy Johnson, Sandy Koufax, Bill Lee, Greg Maddux, Christy Mathewson, Don Newcombe, Preacher Roe and John Smoltz (2).

Year		W-L	Pct	Year		W-L	Pct
1900	Jesse Tannehill, Pittsburgh	20-6	.769	1956	Don Newcombe, Brooklyn	27-7	.794
1901	Jack Chesbro, Pittsburgh	21-10	.677	1957	Bob Buhl, Milwaukee	18-7	.720
1902	Jack Chesbro, Pittsburgh	28-6	.824	1958	Warren Spahn, Milwaukee	22-11	.667
1903	Sam Leever, Pittsburgh	25-7	.781		& Lew Burdette, Milwaukee	20-10	.667
1904	Joe McGinnity, New York	35-8	.814	1959	Roy Face, Pittsburgh	18-1	.947
1905	Christy Mathewson, New York	31-8	.795				
1906	Ed Reulbach, Chicago	19-4	.826	1960	Ernie Broglio, St. Louis	21-9	.700
1907	Ed Reulbach, Chicago	17-4	.810	1961	Johnny Podres, Los Angeles	18-5	.783
1908	Ed Reulbach, Chicago	24-7	.774	1962	Bob Purkey, Cincinnati	23-5	.821
1909	Howie Camnitz, Pittsburgh	25-6	.806	1963	Ron Perranoski, Los Angeles	16-3	.842
	& Christy Mathewson, New York	25-6	.806	1964	Sandy Koufax, Los Angeles	19-5	.792
				1965	Sandy Koufax, Los Angeles	26-8	.765
1910	King Cole, Chicago	20-4	.833	1966	Juan Marichal, San Francisco	25-6	.806
1911	Rube Marquard, New York	24-7	.774	1967	Dick Hughes, St. Louis	16-6	.727
1912	Claude Hendrix, Pittsburgh	24-9	.727	1968	Steve Blass, Pittsburgh	18-6	.750
1913	Bert Humphries, Chicago	16-4	.800	1969	Tom Seaver, New York	25-7	.781
1914	Bill James, Boston	26-7	.788				
1915	Grover Alexander, Phila.	31-10	.756	1970	Bob Gibson, St. Louis	23-7	.767
1916	Tom Hughes, Boston	16-3	.842	1971	Don Gullett, Cincinnati	16-6	.727
1917	Ferdie Schupp, New York	21-7	.750	1972	Gary Nolan, Cincinnati	15-5	.750
1918	Claude Hendrix, Chicago	19-7	.731	1973	Tommy John, Los Angeles	16-7	.696
1919	Dutch Ruether, Cincinnati	19-6	.760	1974	Andy Messersmith, Los Angeles	20-6	.769
				1975	Don Gullett, Cincinnati	15-4	.789
1920	Burleigh Grimes, Brooklyn	23-11	.676	1976	Steve Carlton, Philadelphia	20-7	.741
1921	Bill Doak, St. Louis	15-6	.714	1977	John Candelaria, Pittsburgh	20-5	.800
1922	Pete Donohue, Cincinnati	18-9	.667	1978	Gaylord Perry, San Diego	21-6	.778
1923	Dolf Luque, Cincinnati	27-8	.771	1979	Tom Seaver, Cincinnati	16-6	.727
1924	Emil Yde, Pittsburgh	16-3	.842				
1925	Bill Sherdel, St. Louis	15-6	.714	1980	Jim Bibby, Pittsburgh	19-6	.760
1926	Ray Kremer, Pittsburgh	20-6	.769	1981	Tom Seaver, Cincinnati	14-2	.875
1927	Larry Benton, Boston-NY	17-7	.708	1982	Phil Niekro, Atlanta	17-4	.810
1928	Larry Benton, New York	25-9	.735	1983	John Denny, Philadelphia	19-6	.760
1929	Charlie Root, Chicago	19-6	.760	1984	Rick Sutcliffe, Chicago	16-1	.941
				1985	Orel Hershiser, Los Angeles	19-3	.864
1930	Freddie Fitzsimmons, NY	19-7	.731	1986	Bob Ojeda, New York	18-5	.783
1931	Paul Derringer, St. Louis	18-8	.692	1987	Dwight Gooden, New York	15-7	.682
1932	Lon Warneke, Chicago	22-6	.786	1988	David Cone, New York	20-3	.870
1933	Ben Cantwell, Boston	20-10	.667	1989	Mike Bielecki, Chicago	18-7	.720
1934	Dizzy Dean, St. Louis	30-7	.811				
1935	Bill Lee, Chicago	20-6	.769	1990	Doug Drabek, Pittsburgh	22-6	.786
1936	Carl Hubbell, New York	26-6	.813	1991	John Smiley, Pittsburgh	20-8	.714
1937	Carl Hubbell, New York	22-8	.733		& Jose Rijo, Cincinnati	15-6	.714
1938	Bill Lee, Chicago	22-9	.710	1992	Bob Tewksbury, St. Louis	16-5	.762
1939	Paul Derringer, Cincinnati	25-7	.781	1993	Mark Portugal, Houston	18-4	.818
				1994	Marvin Freeman, Colorado	10-2	.833
1940	Freddie Fitzsimmons, Bklyn	16-2	.889	1995	Greg Maddux, Atlanta	19-2	.905
1941	Elmer Riddle, Cincinnati	19-4	.826	1996	John Smoltz, Atlanta	24-8	.750
1942	Larry French, Brooklyn	15-4	.789	1997	Greg Maddux, Atlanta	19-4	.826
1943	Mort Cooper, St. Louis	21-8	.724	1998	John Smoltz, Atlanta	17-3	.850
1944	Ted Wilks, St. Louis	17-4	.810	1999	Mike Hampton, Houston	22-4	.846
1945	Harry Brecheen, St. Louis	14-4	.778				
1946	Murray Dickson, St. Louis	15-6	.714	2000	Randy Johnson, Arizona	19-7	.731
1947	Larry Jansen, New York	21-5	.808	2001	Curt Schilling, Arizona	22-6	.786
1948	Harry Brecheen, St. Louis	20-7	.741	2002	Randy Johnson, Arizona	24-5	.828
1949	Preacher Roe, Brooklyn	15-6	.714	2003	Jason Schmidt, San Francisco	17-5	.773
				2004	Roger Clemens, Houston	18-4	.818
1950	Sal Maglie, New York	18-4	.818	2005	Chris Carpenter, St. Louis	21-5	.808
1951	Preacher Roe, Brooklyn	22-3	.880	2006	Carlos Zambrano, Chicago	16-7	.696
1952	Hoyt Wilhelm, New York	15-3	.833	2007	Brad Penny, Los Angeles	16-4	.800
1953	Carl Erskine, Brooklyn	20-6	.769				
1954	Johnny Antonelli, New York	21-7	.750				
1955	Don Newcombe, Brooklyn	20-5	.800				

Note: In 1984, Sutcliffe was also 4-5 with Cleveland for a combined AL-NL record of 20-6 (.769).

Winning Percentage (Cont.)

American League

Multiple winners: Lefty Grove (5); Chief Bender, Roger Clemens and Whitey Ford (3); Johnny Allen, Eddie Cicotte, Mike Cuellar, Lefty Gomez, Ron Guidry, Roy Halladay, Catfish Hunter, Randy Johnson, Walter Johnson, Pedro Martinez, Jim Palmer, Pete Vuckovich and Smokey Joe Wood (2).

Year		W-L	Pct	Year		W-L	Pct
1901	Clark Griffith, Chicago	.24-7	.774	1958	Bob Turley, New York	.21-7	.750
1902	Bill Bernhard, Phila-Cleve	.18-5	.783	1959	Bob Shaw, Chicago	.18-6	.750
1903	Cy Young, Boston	.28-9	.757				
1904	Jack Chesbro, New York	.41-12	.774	1960	Jim Perry, Cleveland	.18-10	.643
1905	Andy Coakley, Philadelphia	.20-7	.741	1961	Whitey Ford, New York	.25-4	.862
1906	Eddie Plank, Philadelphia	.19-6	.760	1962	Ray Herbert, Chicago	.20-9	.690
1907	Wild Bill Donovan, Detroit	.25-4	.862	1963	Whitey Ford, New York	.24-7	.774
1908	Ed Walsh, Chicago	.40-15	.727	1964	Wally Bunker, Baltimore	.19-5	.792
1909	George Mullin, Detroit	.29-8	.784	1965	Mudcat Grant, Minnesota	.21-7	.750
				1966	Sonny Siebert, Cleveland	.16-8	.667
1910	Chief Bender, Philadelphia	.23-5	.821	1967	Joe Horlen, Chicago	.19-7	.731
1911	Chief Bender, Philadelphia	.17-5	.773	1968	Denny McLain, Detroit	.31-6	.838
1912	Smokey Joe Wood, Boston	.34-5	.872	1969	Jim Palmer, Baltimore	.16-4	.800
1913	Walter Johnson, Washington	.36-7	.837				
1914	Chief Bender, Philadelphia	.17-3	.850	1970	Mike Cuellar, Baltimore	.24-8	.750
1915	Smokey Joe Wood, Boston	.15-5	.750	1971	Dave McNally, Baltimore	.21-5	.808
1916	Eddie Cicotte, Chicago	.15-7	.682	1972	Catfish Hunter, Oakland	.21-7	.750
1917	Reb Russell, Chicago	.15-5	.750	1973	Catfish Hunter, Oakland	.21-5	.808
1918	Sad Sam Jones, Boston	.16-5	.762	1974	Mike Cuellar, Baltimore	.22-10	.688
1919	Eddie Cicotte, Chicago	.29-7	.806	1975	Mike Torrez, Baltimore	.20-9	.690
				1976	Bill Campbell, Minnesota	.17-5	.773
1920	Jim Bagby, Cleveland	.31-12	.721	1977	Paul Splittorff, Kansas City	.16-6	.727
1921	Carl Mays, New York	.27-9	.750	1978	Ron Guidry, New York	.25-3	.893
1922	Joe Bush, New York	.26-7	.788	1979	Mike Caldwell, Milwaukee	.16-6	.727
1923	Herb Pennock, New York	.19-6	.760				
1924	Walter Johnson, Washington	.23-7	.767	1980	Steve Stone, Baltimore	.25-7	.781
1925	Stan Coveleski, Washington	.20-5	.800	1981	Pete Vuckovich, Milwaukee	.14-4	.778
1926	George Uhle, Cleveland	.27-11	.711	1982	Pete Vuckovich, Milwaukee	.18-6	.750
1927	Waite Hoyt, New York	.22-7	.759		& Jim Palmer, Baltimore	.15-5	.750
1928	General Crowder, St. Louis	.21-5	.808	1983	Rich Dotson, Chicago	.22-7	.759
1929	Lefty Grove, Philadelphia	.20-6	.769	1984	Doyle Alexander, Toronto	.17-6	.739
				1985	Ron Guidry, New York	.22-6	.786
1930	Lefty Grove, Philadelphia	.28-5	.848	1986	Roger Clemens, Boston	.24-4	.857
1931	Lefty Grove, Philadelphia	.31-4	.886	1987	Roger Clemens, Boston	.20-9	.690
1932	Johnny Allen, New York	.17-4	.810	1988	Frank Viola, Minnesota	.24-7	.774
1933	Lefty Grove, Philadelphia	.24-8	.750	1989	Bret Saberhagen, Kansas City	.23-6	.793
1934	Lefty Gomez, New York	.26-5	.839				
1935	Eldon Auker, Detroit	.18-7	.720	1990	Bob Welch, Oakland	.27-6	.818
1936	Monte Pearson, New York	.19-7	.731	1991	Scott Erickson, Minnesota	.20-8	.714
1937	Johnny Allen, Cleveland	.15-1	.938	1992	Mike Mussina, Baltimore	.18-5	.783
1938	Red Ruffing, New York	.21-7	.750	1993	Jimmy Key, New York	.18-6	.750
1939	Lefty Grove, Boston	.15-4	.789	1994	Jason Bere, Chicago	.12-2	.857
				1995	Randy Johnson, Seattle	.18-2	.900
1940	Schoolboy Rowe, Detroit	.16-3	.842	1996	Charles Nagy, Cleveland	.17-5	.773
1941	Lefty Gomez, New York	.15-5	.750	1997	Randy Johnson, Seattle	.20-4	.833
1942	Ernie Bonham, New York	.21-5	.808	1998	David Wells, New York	.18-4	.818
1943	Spud Chandler, New York	.20-4	.833	1999	Pedro Martinez, Boston	.23-4	.852
1944	Tex Hughson, Boston	.18-5	.783				
1945	Hal Newhouser, Detroit	.25-9	.735	2000	Tim Hudson, Oakland	.20-6	.769
1946	Boo Ferriss, Boston	.25-6	.806	2001	Roger Clemens, New York	.20-3	.870
1947	Allie Reynolds, New York	.19-8	.704	2002	Pedro Martinez, Boston	.20-4	.833
1948	Jack Kramer, Boston	.18-5	.783	2003	Roy Halladay, Toronto	.22-7	.759
1949	Ellis Kinder, Boston	.23-6	.793	2004	Curt Schilling, Boston	.21-6	.778
				2005	Cliff Lee, Cleveland	.18-5	.783
1950	Vic Raschi, New York	.21-8	.724	2006	Roy Halladay, Toronto	.16-5	.762
1951	Bob Feller, Cleveland	.22-8	.733	2007	Justin Verlander, Detroit	.18-6	.750
1952	Bobby Shantz, Philadelphia	.24-7	.774				
1953	Ed Lopat, New York	.16-4	.800				
1954	Sandy Consuegra, Chicago	.16-3	.842				
1955	Tommy Byrne, New York	.16-5	.762				
1956	Whitey Ford, New York	.19-6	.760				
1957	Dick Donovan, Chicago	.16-6	.727				
	& Tom Sturdivant, New York	.16-6	.727				

Earned Run Average

...arned Run Averages were based on at least 10 complete games pitched (1900-49), at least 154 innings pitched (1950-...0), and at least 162 innings pitched since 1961 in the AL and 1962 in the NL. In the strike years of 1981, '94 and '95, ...ualifiers had to pitch at least as many innings as the total number of games their team played that season.

National League

Multiple winners: Grover Alexander, Sandy Koufax and Christy Mathewson (5); Greg Maddux (4); Carl Hubbell, Randy ...ohnson, Tom Seaver, Warren Spahn and Dazzy Vance (3); Kevin Brown, Bill Doak, Ray Kremer, Dolf Luque, Jake Peavy, ...Iowie Pollet, Nolan Ryan, Bill Walker and Bucky Walters (2).

Year		ERA	Year		ERA	Year		ERA
1900	Rube Waddell, Pit	2.37	1936	Carl Hubbell, NY	2.31	1972	Steve Carlton, Phi	1.97
1901	Jesse Tannehill, Pit	2.18	1937	Jim Turner, Bos	2.38	1973	Tom Seaver, NY	2.08
1902	Jack Taylor, Chi	1.33	1938	Bill Lee, Chi	2.66	1974	Buzz Capra, Atl	2.28
1903	Sam Leever, Pit	2.06	1939	Bucky Walters, Cin	2.29	1975	Randy Jones, SD	2.24
1904	Joe McGinnity, NY	1.61	1940	Bucky Walters, Cin	2.48	1976	John Denny, St.L	2.52
1905	Christy Mathewson, NY	1.27	1941	Elmer Riddle, Cin	2.24	1977	John Candelaria, Pit	2.34
1906	Three Finger Brown, Chi	1.04	1942	Mort Cooper, St.L	1.78	1978	Craig Swan, NY	2.43
1907	Jack Pfiester, Chi	1.15	1943	Howie Pollet, St.L	1.75	1979	J.R. Richard, Hou	2.71
1908	Christy Mathewson, NY	1.43	1944	Ed Heusser, Cin	2.38			
1909	Christy Mathewson, NY	1.14	1945	Hank Borowy, Chi	2.13	1980	Don Sutton, LA	2.21
1910	George McQuillan, Phi	1.60	1946	Howie Pollet, St.L	2.10	1981	Nolan Ryan, Hou	1.69
1911	Christy Mathewson, NY	1.99	1947	Warren Spahn, Bos	2.33	1982	Steve Rogers, Mon	2.40
1912	Jeff Tesreau, NY	1.96	1948	Harry Brecheen, St.L	2.24	1983	Atlee Hammaker, SF	2.25
1913	Christy Mathewson, NY	2.06	1949	Dave Koslo, NY	2.50	1984	Alejandro Peña, LA	2.48
1914	Bill Doak, St.L	1.72	1950	Jim Hearn, St.L-NY	2.49	1985	Dwight Gooden, NY	1.53
1915	Grover Alexander, Phi	1.22	1951	Chet Nichols, Bos	2.88	1986	Mike Scott, Hou	2.22
1916	Grover Alexander, Phi	1.55	1952	Hoyt Wilhelm, NY	2.43	1987	Nolan Ryan, Hou	2.76
1917	Grover Alexander, Phi	1.86	1953	Warren Spahn, Mil	2.10	1988	Joe Magrane, St.L	2.18
1918	Hippo Vaughn, Chi	1.74	1954	Johnny Antonelli, NY	2.30	1989	Scott Garrelts, SF	2.28
1919	Grover Alexander, Chi	1.72	1955	Bob Friend, Pit	2.83			
1920	Grover Alexander, Chi	1.91	1956	Lew Burdette, Mil	2.70	1990	Danny Darwin, Hou	2.21
1921	Bill Doak, St.L	2.59	1957	Johnny Podres, Bklyn	2.66	1991	Dennis Martinez, Mon	2.39
1922	Rosy Ryan, NY	3.01	1958	Stu Miller, SF	2.47	1992	Bill Swift, SF	2.08
1923	Dolf Luque, Cin	1.93	1959	Sam Jones, SF	2.83	1993	Greg Maddux, Atl	2.36
1924	Dazzy Vance, Bklyn	2.16	1960	Mike McCormick, SF	2.70	1994	Greg Maddux, Atl	1.56
1925	Dolf Luque, Cin	2.63	1961	Warren Spahn, Mil	3.02	1995	Greg Maddux, Atl	1.63
1926	Ray Kremer, Pit	2.61	1962	Sandy Koufax, LA	2.54	1996	Kevin Brown, Fla.	1.89
1927	Ray Kremer, Pit	2.47	1963	Sandy Koufax, LA	1.88	1997	Pedro Martinez, Mon	1.90
1928	Dazzy Vance, Bklyn	2.09	1964	Sandy Koufax, LA	1.74	1998	Greg Maddux, Atl	2.22
1929	Bill Walker, NY	3.09	1965	Sandy Koufax, LA	2.04	1999	Randy Johnson, Ari.	2.48
1930	Dazzy Vance, Bklyn	2.61	1966	Sandy Koufax, LA	1.73	2000	Kevin Brown, LA	2.58
1931	Bill Walker, NY	2.26	1967	Phil Niekro, Atl	1.87	2001	Randy Johnson, Ari.	2.49
1932	Lon Warneke, Chi	2.37	1968	Bob Gibson, St.L	1.12	2002	Randy Johnson, Ari.	2.32
1933	Carl Hubbell, NY	1.66	1969	Juan Marichal, SF	2.10	2003	Jason Schmidt, SF	2.34
1934	Carl Hubbell, NY	2.30	1970	Tom Seaver, NY	2.81	2004	Jake Peavy, SD	2.27
1935	Cy Blanton, Pit	2.58	1971	Tom Seaver, NY	1.76	2005	Roger Clemens, Hou	1.87
						2006	Roy Oswalt, Hou	2.98
						2007	Jake Peavy, SD	2.54

Note: In 1945, Borowy had a 3.13 ERA in 18 games with New York (AL) for a combined ERA of 2.65.

American League

Multiple winners: Lefty Grove (9); Roger Clemens (6); Walter Johnson (5); Pedro Martinez (4); Spud Chandler, Stan Coveleski, Red Faber, Whitey Ford, Lefty Gomez, Ron Guidry, Addie Joss, Hal Newhouser, Jim Palmer, Gary Peters, Johan Santana, Luis Tiant and Ed Walsh (2).

Year		ERA	Year		ERA	Year		ERA
1901	Cy Young, Bos	1.62	1918	Walter Johnson, Wash	1.27	1934	Lefty Gomez, NY	2.33
1902	Ed Siever, Det	1.91	1919	Walter Johnson, Wash	1.49	1935	Lefty Grove, Bos	2.70
1903	Earl Moore, Cle	1.77	1920	Bob Shawkey, NY	2.45	1936	Lefty Grove, Bos	2.81
1904	Addie Joss, Cle	1.59	1921	Red Faber, Chi	2.48	1937	Lefty Gomez, NY	2.33
1905	Rube Waddell, Phi	1.48	1922	Red Faber, Chi	2.80	1938	Lefty Grove, Bos	3.08
1906	Doc White, Chi	1.52	1923	Stan Coveleski, Cle	2.76	1939	Lefty Grove, Bos	2.54
1907	Ed Walsh, Chi	1.60	1924	Walter Johnson, Wash	2.72	1940	Ernie Bonham, NY	1.90
1908	Addie Joss, Cle	1.16	1925	Stan Coveleski, Wash	2.84	1941	Thornton Lee, Chi	2.37
1909	Harry Krause, Phi	1.39	1926	Lefty Grove, Phi	2.51	1942	Ted Lyons, Chi	2.10
1910	Ed Walsh, Chi	1.27	1927	Wilcy Moore, NY	2.28	1943	Spud Chandler, NY	1.64
1911	Vean Gregg, Cle	1.81	1928	Garland Braxton, Wash	2.51	1944	Dizzy Trout, Det.	2.12
1912	Walter Johnson, Wash	1.39	1929	Lefty Grove, Phi	2.81	1945	Hal Newhouser, Det	1.81
1913	Walter Johnson, Wash	1.09	1930	Lefty Grove, Phi.	2.54	1946	Hal Newhouser, Det	1.94
1914	Dutch Leonard, Bos	1.01	1931	Lefty Grove, Phi.	2.06	1947	Spud Chandler, NY	2.46
1915	Smokey Joe Wood, Bos	1.49	1932	Lefty Grove, Phi.	2.84	1948	Gene Bearden, Cle	2.43
1916	Babe Ruth, Bos	1.75	1933	Monte Pearson, Cle	2.33	1949	Mel Parnell, Bos	2.77
1917	Eddie Cicotte, Chi	1.53						

Earned Run Average (Cont.)

Year		ERA	Year		ERA	Year		ERA
1950	Early Wynn, Cle	3.20	1970	Diego Segui, Oak.	2.56	1990	Roger Clemens, Bos	1.93
1951	Saul Rogovin, Det-Chi	2.78	1971	Vida Blue, Oak	1.82	1991	Roger Clemens, Bos	2.62
1952	Allie Reynolds, NY	2.06	1972	Luis Tiant, Bos	1.91	1992	Roger Clemens, Bos	2.41
1953	Ed Lopat, NY	2.42	1973	Jim Palmer, Bal	2.40	1993	Kevin Appier, KC	2.56
1954	Mike Garcia, Cle	2.64	1974	Catfish Hunter, Oak	2.49	1994	Steve Ontiveros, Oak	2.65
1955	Billy Pierce, Chi	1.97	1975	Jim Palmer, Bal	2.09	1995	Randy Johnson, Sea	2.48
1956	Whitey Ford, NY	2.47	1976	Mark Fidrych, Det.	2.34	1996	Juan Guzman, Tor.	2.93
1957	Bobby Shantz, NY	2.45	1977	Frank Tanana, Cal	2.54	1997	Roger Clemens, Tor	2.05
1958	Whitey Ford, NY	2.01	1978	Ron Guidry, NY	1.74	1998	Roger Clemens, Tor	2.65
1959	Hoyt Wilhelm, Bal.	2.19	1979	Ron Guidry, NY	2.78	1999	Pedro Martinez, Bos	2.07
1960	Frank Baumann, Chi	2.67	1980	Rudy May, NY	2.47	2000	Pedro Martinez, Bos	1.74
1961	Dick Donovan, Wash	2.40	1981	Steve McCatty, Oak	2.32	2001	Freddy Garcia, Sea	3.05
1962	Hank Aguirre, Det.	2.21	1982	Rick Sutcliffe, Cle	2.96	2002	Pedro Martinez, Bos	2.26
1963	Gary Peters, Chi	2.33	1983	Rick Honeycutt, Tex	2.42	2003	Pedro Martinez, Bos	2.22
1964	Dean Chance, LA	1.65	1984	Mike Boddicker, Bal	2.79	2004	Johan Santana, Min	2.61
1965	Sam McDowell, Cle	2.18	1985	Dave Stieb, Tor	2.48	2005	Kevin Millwood, Cle	2.86
1966	Gary Peters, Chi	1.98	1986	Roger Clemens, Bos	2.48	2006	Johan Santana, Min	2.77
1967	Joe Horlen, Chi	2.06	1987	Jimmy Key, Tor	2.76	2007	John Lackey, LA	3.01
1968	Luis Tiant, Cle	1.60	1988	Allan Anderson, Min	2.45			
1969	Dick Bosman, Wash	2.19	1989	Bret Saberhagen, KC	2.16			

Strikeouts

National League

Multiple winners: Dazzy Vance (7); Grover Alexander (6); Steve Carlton, Randy Johnson, Christy Mathewson and Tom Seaver (5); Dizzy Dean, Sandy Koufax and Warren Spahn (4); Don Drysdale, Sam Jones and Warren Vander Meer (3); David Cone, Dwight Gooden, Bill Hallahan, Jake Peavy, J.R. Richard, Robin Roberts, Nolan Ryan, Curt Schilling, John Smoltz and Hippo Vaughn (2).

Year		SO	Year		SO	Year		SO
1900	Rube Waddell, Pit	130	1937	Carl Hubbell, NY	159	1972	Steve Carlton, Phi	310
1901	Noodles Hahn, Cin	239	1938	Clay Bryant, Chi	135	1973	Tom Seaver, NY	251
1902	Vic Willis, Bos	225	1939	Claude Passeau, Phi-Chi	137	1974	Steve Carlton, Phi	240
1903	Christy Mathewson, NY	267		& Bucky Walters, Cin	137	1975	Tom Seaver, NY	243
1904	Christy Mathewson, NY	212	1940	Kirby Higbe, Phi	137	1976	Tom Seaver, NY	235
1905	Christy Mathewson, NY	206	1941	John Vander Meer, Cin	202	1977	Phil Niekro, Atl	262
1906	Fred Beebe, Chi-St.L.	171	1942	John Vander Meer, Cin	186	1978	J.R. Richard, Hou	303
1907	Christy Mathewson, NY	178	1943	John Vander Meer, Cin	174	1979	J.R. Richard, Hou	313
1908	Christy Mathewson, NY	259	1944	Bill Voiselle, NY	161	1980	Steve Carlton, Phi	286
1909	Orval Overall, Chi	205	1945	Preacher Roe, Pit	148	1981	F. Valenzuela, LA	180
1910	Earl Moore, Phi	185	1946	Johnny Schmitz, Chi.	135	1982	Steve Carlton, Phi	286
1911	Rube Marquard, NY	237	1947	Ewell Blackwell, Cin.	193	1983	Steve Carlton, Phi	275
1912	Grover Alexander, Phi	195	1948	Harry Brecheen, St.L	149	1984	Dwight Gooden, NY	276
1913	Tom Seaton, Phi	168	1949	Warren Spahn, Bos	151	1985	Dwight Gooden, NY	268
1914	Grover Alexander, Phi	214	1950	Warren Spahn, Bos	191	1986	Mike Scott, Hou	306
1915	Grover Alexander, Phi	241	1951	Don Newcombe, Bklyn	164	1987	Nolan Ryan, Hou	270
1916	Grover Alexander, Phi	167		& Warren Spahn, Bos	164	1988	Nolan Ryan, Hou	228
1917	Grover Alexander, Phi	201	1952	Warren Spahn, Bos	183	1989	Jose DeLeon, St.L	201
1918	Hippo Vaughn, Chi	148	1953	Robin Roberts, Phi	198	1990	David Cone, NY	233
1919	Hippo Vaughn, Chi	141	1954	Robin Roberts, Phi	185	1991	David Cone, NY	241
1920	Grover Alexander, Chi	173	1955	Sam Jones, Chi	198	1992	John Smoltz, Atl.	215
1921	Burleigh Grimes, Bklyn	136	1956	Sam Jones, Chi	176	1993	Jose Rijo, Cin	227
1922	Dazzy Vance, Bklyn	134	1957	Jack Sanford, Phi	188	1994	Andy Benes, SD	189
1923	Dazzy Vance, Bklyn	197	1958	Sam Jones, St.L	225	1995	Hideo Nomo, LA	236
1924	Dazzy Vance, Bklyn	262	1959	Don Drysdale, LA	242	1996	John Smoltz, Atl	276
1925	Dazzy Vance, Bklyn	221	1960	Don Drysdale, LA	246	1997	Curt Schilling, Phi	319
1926	Dazzy Vance, Bklyn	140	1961	Sandy Koufax, LA	269	1998	Curt Schilling, Phi	300
1927	Dazzy Vance, Bklyn	184	1962	Don Drysdale, LA	232	1999	Randy Johnson, Ari	364
1928	Dazzy Vance, Bklyn	200	1963	Sandy Koufax, LA	306	2000	Randy Johnson, Ari	347
1929	Pat Malone, Chi	166	1964	Bob Veale, Pit	250	2001	Randy Johnson, Ari	372
1930	Bill Hallahan, St.L	177	1965	Sandy Koufax, LA	382	2002	Randy Johnson, Ari	334
1931	Bill Hallahan, St.L	159	1966	Sandy Koufax, LA	317	2003	Kerry Wood, Chi	266
1932	Dizzy Dean, St.L	191	1967	Jim Bunning, Phi	253	2004	Randy Johnson, Ari	290
1933	Dizzy Dean, St.L	199	1968	Bob Gibson, St.L	268	2005	Jake Peavy, SD	216
1934	Dizzy Dean, St.L	195	1969	Ferguson Jenkins, Chi	273	2006	Aaron Harang, Cin.	216
1935	Dizzy Dean, St.L	190	1970	Tom Seaver, NY	283	2007	Jake Peavy, SD	240
1936	Van Lingle Mungo, Bklyn	238	1971	Tom Seaver, NY	289			

Note: In 1998, Randy Johnson struck out 329 batters — 213 in the AL with Seattle, then 116 in the NL with Houston.

American League

Multiple winners: Walter Johnson (12); Nolan Ryan (9); Bob Feller and Lefty Grove (7); Rube Waddell (6); Roger Clemens and Sam McDowell (5); Randy Johnson (4); Lefty Gomez, Mark Langston, Pedro Martinez, Johan Santana and Camilo Pascual (3); Len Barker, Tommy Bridges, Jim Bunning, Hal Newhouser, Allie Reynolds, Herb Score, Ed Walsh and Early Wynn (2).

Year	SO	Year	SO	Year	SO
1901 Cy Young, Bos	158	1937 Lefty Gomez, NY	194	1972 Nolan Ryan, Cal	329
1902 Rube Waddell, Phi	210	1938 Bob Feller, Cle	240	1973 Nolan Ryan, Cal	383
1903 Rube Waddell, Phi	302	1939 Bob Feller, Cle	246	1974 Nolan Ryan, Cal	367
1904 Rube Waddell, Phi	349	1940 Bob Feller, Cle	261	1975 Frank Tanana, Cal	269
1905 Rube Waddell, Phi	287	1941 Bob Feller, Cle	260	1976 Nolan Ryan, Cal	327
1906 Rube Waddell, Phi	196	1942 Tex Hughson, Bos	113	1977 Nolan Ryan, Cal	341
1907 Rube Waddell, Phi	232	& Bobo Newsom, Wash	113	1978 Nolan Ryan, Cal	260
1908 Ed Walsh, Chi	269	1943 Allie Reynolds, Cle	151	1979 Nolan Ryan, Cal	223
1909 Frank Smith, Chi.	177	1944 Hal Newhouser, Det	187		
1910 Walter Johnson, Wash	313	1945 Hal Newhouser, Det	212	1980 Len Barker, Cle	187
1911 Ed Walsh, Chi	255	1946 Bob Feller, Cle	348	1981 Len Barker, Cle	127
1912 Walter Johnson, Wash	303	1947 Bob Feller, Cle	196	1982 Floyd Bannister, Sea	209
1913 Walter Johnson, Wash	243	1948 Bob Feller, Cle	164	1983 Jack Morris, Det	232
1914 Walter Johnson, Wash	225	1949 Virgil Trucks, Det	153	1984 Mark Langston, Sea	204
1915 Walter Johnson, Wash	203	1950 Bob Lemon, Cle	170	1985 Bert Blyleven, Cle-Min	206
1916 Walter Johnson, Wash	228	1951 Vic Raschi, NY	164	1986 Mark Langston, Sea	245
1917 Walter Johnson, Wash	188	1952 Allie Reynolds, NY	160	1987 Mark Langston, Sea	262
1918 Walter Johnson, Wash	162	1953 Billy Pierce, Chi	186	1988 Roger Clemens, Bos	291
1919 Walter Johnson, Wash	147	1954 Bob Turley, Bal	185	1989 Nolan Ryan, Tex	301
1920 Stan Coveleski, Cle	133	1955 Herb Score, Cle	245	1990 Nolan Ryan, Tex	232
1921 Walter Johnson, Wash	143	1956 Herb Score, Cle	263	1991 Roger Clemens, Bos	241
1922 Urban Shocker, St.L	149	1957 Early Wynn, Cle.	184	1992 Randy Johnson, Sea	241
1923 Walter Johnson, Wash	130	1958 Early Wynn, Chi.	179	1993 Randy Johnson, Sea	308
1924 Walter Johnson, Wash	158	1959 Jim Bunning, Det	201	1994 Randy Johnson, Sea	204
1925 Lefty Grove, Phi	116	1960 Jim Bunning, Det	201	1995 Randy Johnson, Sea	294
1926 Lefty Grove, Phi	194	1961 Camilo Pascual, Min	221	1996 Roger Clemens, Bos	257
1927 Lefty Grove, Phi	174	1962 Camilo Pascual, Min	206	1997 Roger Clemens, Tor	292
1928 Lefty Grove, Phi	183	1963 Camilo Pascual, Min	202	1998 Roger Clemens, Tor	271
1929 Lefty Grove, Phi	170	1964 Al Downing, NY	217	1999 Pedro Martinez, Bos	313
1930 Lefty Grove, Phi	209	1965 Sam McDowell, Cle	325	2000 Pedro Martinez, Bos	284
1931 Lefty Grove, Phi	175	1966 Sam McDowell, Cle	225	2001 Hideo Nomo, Bos	220
1932 Red Ruffing, NY	190	1967 Jim Lonborg, Bos	246	2002 Pedro Martinez, Bos	239
1933 Lefty Gomez, NY	163	1968 Sam McDowell, Cle	283	2003 Esteban Loaiza, Chi	207
1934 Lefty Gomez, NY	158	1969 Sam McDowell, Cle	279	2004 Johan Santana, Min	265
1935 Tommy Bridges, Det	163	1970 Sam McDowell, Cle	304	2005 Johan Santana, Min	238
1936 Tommy Bridges, Det	175	1971 Mickey Lolich, Det	308	2006 Johan Santana, Min	245
				2007 Scott Kazmir, TB	239

Pitching Triple Crown Winners

Pitchers who led either league in Earned Run Average, Wins and Strikeouts over a single season.

National League

	Year	ERA	W-L	SO
Tommy Bond, Bos	1877	2.11	40-17	170
Hoss Radbourn, Prov	1884	1.38	60-12	441
Tim Keefe, NY	1888	1.74	35-12	333
John Clarkson, Bos	1889	2.73	49-19	284
Amos Rusie, NY	1894	2.78	36-13	195
Christy Mathewson, NY	1905	1.27	31-8	206
Christy Mathewson, NY	1908	1.43	37-11	259
Grover Alexander, Phi	1915	1.22	31-10	241
Grover Alexander, Phi	1916	1.55	33-12	167
Grover Alexander, Phi	1917	1.86	30-13	201
Hippo Vaughn, Chi	1918	1.74	22-10	148
Grover Alexander, Chi	1920	1.91	27-14	173
Dazzy Vance, Bklyn	1924	2.16	28-6	262
Bucky Walters, Cin	1939	2.29	27-11	137
Sandy Koufax, LA	1963	1.88	25-5	306
Sandy Koufax, LA	1965	2.04	26-8	382
Sandy Koufax, LA	1966	1.73	27-9	317
Steve Carlton, Phi	1972	1.97	27-10	310
Dwight Gooden, NY	1985	1.53	24-4	268
Randy Johnson, Ari	2002	2.32	24-5	334
Jake Peavy, SD	2007	2.54	19-6	240

Ties: In 1894, Rusie tied for league lead in wins with Jouett Meekin, NY (36-10); in 1939, Walters tied for league lead in strikeouts with Claude Passeau, Phi-Chi; in 1963, Koufax tied for the league lead in wins with Juan Marichal, SF.

American League

	Year	ERA	W-L	SO
Cy Young, Bos	1901	1.62	33-10	158
Rube Waddell, Phi.	1905	1.48	26-11	287
Walter Johnson, Wash	1913	1.09	36-7	243
Walter Johnson, Wash	1918	1.27	23-13	162
Walter Johnson, Wash	1924	2.72	23-7	158
Lefty Grove, Phi	1930	2.54	28-5	209
Lefty Grove, Phi	1931	2.06	31-4	175
Lefty Gomez, NY	1934	2.33	26-5	158
Lefty Gomez, NY	1937	2.33	21-11	194
Hal Newhouser, Det	1945	1.81	25-9	212
Roger Clemens, Tor	1997	2.05	21-7	292
Roger Clemens, Tor	1998	2.65	20-6	271
Pedro Martinez, Bos	1999	2.07	23-4	313
Johan Santana, Min	2006	2.77	19-6	245

Ties: In 1998, Clemens tied for league lead in wins with David Cone, NY (20-7) and Rick Helling, Tex (20-7); in 2006, Santana tied for league lead in wins with Chien-Ming Wang, NY (19-6).

Saves

The "save" was created by Chicago baseball writer Jerome Holtzman in the 1960's and accepted as an official statistic by the Official Rules Committee of Major League Baseball in 1969. From 1969-72, a save was credited to a pitcher who finished a game his team won. From 1973-74, a save was credited to a pitcher who finished a game his team won with the tying or winning run on base or at bat. Since 1975 a pitcher has been credited with a save when he meets all three of the following conditions:

(1) He is the finishing pitcher in a game won by his club; (2) He is not the winning pitcher; (3) He qualifies under one of the following conditions: (a) He enters the game with a lead of no more than three runs and pitches for at least one inning; (b) He enters the game with the potential tying run either on base, or at bat, or on deck; (c) He pitches effectively for at least three innings.

National League

Multiple winners: Bruce Sutter (5); John Franco and Lee Smith (3); Rawly Eastwick, Rollie Fingers, Trevor Hoffman, Mike Marshall, Randy Myers and Todd Worrell (2).

Year		Svs	Year		Svs	Year		Svs
1969	Fred Gladding, Hou	29	1982	Bruce Sutter, St.L	36	1996	Jeff Brantley, Cin	44
1970	Wayne Granger, Cin	35	1983	Lee Smith, Chi	29		& Todd Worrell, LA	44
1971	Dave Giusti, Pit	30	1984	Bruce Sutter, St.L	45	1997	Jeff Shaw, Cin	42
1972	Clay Carroll, Cin.	37	1985	Jeff Reardon, Mon	41	1998	Trevor Hoffman, SD	53
1973	Mike Marshall, Mon.	31	1986	Todd Worrell, St.L	36	1999	Ugueth Urbina, Mon	41
1974	Mike Marshall, LA	21	1987	Steve Bedrosian, Phi.	40	2000	Antonio Alfonseca, Fla	45
1975	Rawly Eastwick, Cin	22	1988	John Franco, Cin	39	2001	Robb Nen, SF	45
	& Al Hrabosky, St.L	22	1989	Mark Davis, SD.	44	2002	John Smoltz, Atl	55
1976	Rawly Eastwick, Cin	26	1990	John Franco, NY	33	2003	Eric Gagne, LA	55
1977	Rollie Fingers, SD	35	1991	Lee Smith, St.L	47	2004	Armando Benitez, Fla	47
1978	Rollie Fingers, SD	37	1992	Lee Smith, St.L	43		& Jason Isringhausen, St.L	47
1979	Bruce Sutter, Chi	37	1993	Randy Myers, Chi	53	2005	Chad Cordero, Wash	47
1980	Bruce Sutter, Chi	28	1994	John Franco, NY	30	2006	Trevor Hoffman, SD	46
1981	Bruce Sutter, St.L	25	1995	Randy Myers, Chi	38	2007	Jose Valverde, Ari	47

American League

Multiple winners: Dan Quisenberry (5); Rich Gossage and Mariano Rivera (3); Dennis Eckersley, Sparky Lyle, Ron Perranoski and Francisco Rodriguez (2).

Year		Svs	Year		Svs	Year		Svs
1969	Ron Perranoski, Min	31	1983	Dan Quisenberry, KC	45	1997	Randy Myers, Bal	45
1970	Ron Perranoski, Min	34	1984	Dan Quisenberry, KC	44	1998	Tom Gordon, Bos	46
1971	Ken Sanders, Mil.	31	1985	Dan Quisenberry, KC	37	1999	Mariano Rivera, NY	45
1972	Sparky Lyle, NY.	35	1986	Dave Righetti, NY	46	2000	Todd Jones, Det.	42
1973	John Hiller, Det	38	1987	Tom Henke, Tor	34		& Derek Lowe, Bos	42
1974	Terry Forster, Chi	24	1988	Dennis Eckersley, Oak	45	2001	Mariano Rivera, NY.	50
1975	Rich Gossage, Chi	26	1989	Jeff Russell, Tex	38	2002	Eddie Guardado, Min	45
1976	Sparky Lyle, NY.	23	1990	Bobby Thigpen, Chi	57	2003	Keith Foulke, Oak	43
1977	Bill Campbell, Bos	31	1991	Bryan Harvey, Cal	46	2004	Mariano Rivera, NY.	53
1978	Rich Gossage, NY	27	1992	Dennis Eckersley, Oak	51	2005	Francisco Rodriguez, LA	45
1979	Mike Marshall, Min	32	1993	Jeff Montgomery, KC	45		& Bob Wickman, Cle	45
1980	Rich Gossage, NY	33		& Duane Ward, Tor	45	2006	Francisco Rodriguez, LA	47
	& Dan Quisenberry, KC	33	1994	Lee Smith, Bal	33	2007	Joe Borowski, Cle	45
1981	Rollie Fingers, Mil	28	1995	Jose Mesa, Cle	46			
1982	Dan Quisenberry, KC	35	1996	John Wetteland, NY	43			

Perfect Games

Eighteen pitchers have thrown perfect games (27 up, 27 down) in major league history. However, the game pitched by Ernie Shore is not considered to be official.

National League

	Game	Date	Score
Lee Richmond	Wor. vs Cle.	6/12/1880	1-0
Monte Ward	Prov. vs Buf.	6/17/1880	5-0
Jim Bunning	Phi. at NY	6/21/1964	6-0
Sandy Koufax	LA vs Chi.	9/9/1965	1-0
Tom Browning	Cin. vs LA	9/16/1988	1-0
Dennis Martinez	Mon. at LA	7/28/1991	2-0
Randy Johnson	Ari. at Atl.	5/18/2004	2-0

Note: Pittsburgh's Harvey Haddix pitched 12 perfect innings against the Milwaukee Braves on May 26, 1959 before losing, 1-0, in the 13th. Braves' lead-off batter Felix Mantilla reached on a throwing error by Pirates 3B Don Hoak, Eddie Mathews sacrificed Mantilla to 2nd, Hank Aaron was walked intentionally, and Joe Adcock hit a 3-run HR. Adcock, however, passed Aaron on the bases and was only credited with a 1-run double.

Note: Montreal's Pedro Martinez pitched nine perfect innings against the San Diego Padres on June 3, 1995 before surrendering a leadoff double to Bip Roberts in the 10th. He was then relieved by Mel Rojas, who finished the game, which Montreal won, 1-0.

American League

	Game	Date	Score
Cy Young	Bos. vs Phi.	5/5/1904	3-0
Addie Joss	Cle. vs Chi.	10/2/1908	1-0
Ernie Shore	Bos. vs Wash.	6/23/1917	4-0*
Charlie Robertson	Chi. at Det.	4/30/1922	2-0
Catfish Hunter	Oak. vs Min.	5/8/1968	4-0
Len Barker	Cle. vs Tor.	5/15/1981	3-0
Mike Witt	Cal. at Tex.	9/30/1984	1-0
Kenny Rogers	Tex. vs Cal.	7/28/1994	4-0
David Wells	NY vs Min.	5/17/1998	4-0
David Cone	NY vs Mon.	7/18/1999	6-0

*Babe Ruth started for Boston, walking Senators' lead-off batter Ray Morgan, then was thrown out of game by umpire Brick Owens for arguing the call. Shore came on in relief. Morgan was caught stealing and Shore retired the next 26 batters in a row. While technically not a perfect game— since he didn't start—Shore gets credit anyway.

World Series

Pitcher	Game	Date	Score
Don Larsen	NY vs Bklyn	10/8/1956	2-0

No-Hit Games

Nine innings or more, including perfect games, since 1876. Losing pitchers in **bold** type. **Multiple no-hitters:** Nolan Ryan (7); Sandy Koufax (4); Larry Corcoran, Bob Feller and Cy Young (3); Jim Bunning, Steve Busby, Carl Erskine, Bob Forsch, Pud Galvin, Ken Holtzman, Randy Johnson, Addie Joss, Hub (Dutch) Leonard, Jim Maloney, Christy Mathewson, Hideo Nomo, Allie Reynolds, Warren Spahn, Bill Stoneman, Virgil Trucks, Johnny Vander Meer and Don Wilson (2).

National League

Year	Date	Pitcher	Result
1876	7/15	George Bradley	St.L vs Har, 2-0
1880	6/12	Lee Richmond	Wor vs Cle, 1-0 (perfect game)
	6/17	Monte Ward	Prov vs Buf, 5-0 (perfect game)
	8/19	Larry Corcoran	Chi vs Bos, 6-0
	8/20	Pud Galvin	Buf at Wor, 1-0
1882	9/20	Larry Corcoran	Chi vs Wor, 5-0
1883	7/25	Old Hoss Radbourn	Prov at Cle, 8-0
	9/13	Hugh Daily	Cle at Phi, 1-0
1884	6/27	Larry Corcoran	Chi vs Prov, 6-0
	8/4	Pud Galvin	Buf at Det, 18-0
1885	7/27	John Clarkson	Chi vs Prov, 4-0
	8/29	Charlie Ferguson	Phi vs Prov, 1-0
1891	6/22	Tom Lovett	Bklyn vs NY, 4-0
	7/31	Amos Rusie	NY vs Bklyn, 6-0
1892	8/6	John Stivetts	Bos vs Bklyn, 11-0
	8/22	Ben Sanders	Lou vs Bal, 6-2
	10/15	Bumpus Jones	Cin vs Pit, 7-1 (1st major league game)
1893	8/16	Bill Hawke	Bal vs Wash, 5-0
1897	9/18	Cy Young	Cle vs Cin, 6-0
1898	4/22	Ted Breitenstein	Cin vs Pit, 11-0
	4/22	Jim Hughes	Bal vs Bos, 8-0
	7/8	Red Donahue	Phi vs Bos, 5-0
	8/21	Walter Thornton	Chi vs Bklyn, 2-0
1899	5/25	Deacon Phillippe	Lou vs NY, 7-0
1900	7/12	Noodles Hahn	Cin vs Phi, 4-0
1901	7/15	Christy Mathewson	NY at St.L, 5-0
1903	9/18	Chick Fraser	Phi at Chi, 10-0
1905	6/13	Christy Mathewson	NY at Chi, 1-0
1906	5/1	John Lush	Phi at Bklyn, 6-0
	7/20	Mal Eason	Bklyn at St.L, 2-0
1907	5/8	Frank Pfeffer	Bos vs Cin, 6-0
	9/20	Nick Maddox	Pit vs Bkn, 2-1
1908	7/4	Hooks Wiltse	NY vs Phi, 1-0 (10)
	9/5	Nap Rucker	Bklyn vs Bos, 6-0
1912	9/6	Jeff Tesreau	NY at Phi, 3-0
1914	9/9	George Davis	Bos vs Phi, 7-0
1915	4/15	Rube Marquard	NY vs Bklyn, 2-0
	8/31	Jimmy Lavender	Chi at N.Y, 2-0
1916	6/16	Tom Hughes	Bos vs. Pit, 2-0
1917	5/2	Fred Toney	Cin at Chi, 1-0 (10)
1919	5/11	Hod Eller	Cin at St.L, 6-0
1922	5/7	Jesse Barnes	NY vs Phi, 6-0
1924	7/17	Jesse Haines	St.L vs Bos, 5-0
1925	9/13	Dazzy Vance	Bklyn vs Phi, 10-1
1929	5/8	Carl Hubbell	NY vs Pit, 11-0
1934	9/21	Paul Dean	St.L at Bklyn, 3-0
1938	6/11	Johnny Vander Meer	Cin vs Bos, 3-0
	6/15	Johnny Vander Meer	Cin at Bklyn, 6-0 (consecutive starts)
1940	4/30	Tex Carleton	Bklyn at Cin, 3-0
1941	8/30	Lon Warneke	St.L at Cin, 2-0
1944	4/27	Jim Tobin	Bos vs Bklyn, 2-0
	5/15	Clyde Shoun	Cin vs Bos, 1-0
1946	4/23	Ed Head	Bklyn vs Bos, 5-0
1947	6/18	Ewell Blackwell	Cin vs Bos, 6-0
1948	9/9	Rex Barney	Bklyn at NY, 2-0
1950	8/11	Vern Bickford	Bos vs Bklyn, 7-0
1951	5/6	Cliff Chambers	Pit at Bos, 3-0
1952	6/19	Carl Erskine	Bklyn vs Chi, 5-0
1954	6/12	Jim Wilson	Mil vs Phi, 2-0
1955	5/12	Sam Jones	Chi vs Pit, 4-0
1956	5/12	Carl Erskine	Bklyn vs NY, 3-0
	9/25	Sal Maglie	Bklyn vs Phi, 5-0
1960	5/15	Don Cardwell	Chi vs St.L, 4-0
	8/18	Lew Burdette	Mil vs Phi, 1-0
	9/16	Warren Spahn	Mil vs Phi, 4-0
1961	4/28	Warren Spahn	Mil vs SF, 1-0

Year	Date	Pitcher	Result
1962	6/30	Sandy Koufax	LA vs NY, 5-0
1963	5/11	Sandy Koufax	LA vs SF, 8-0
	5/17	Don Nottebart	Hou vs Phi, 4-1
	6/15	Juan Marichal	SF vs Hou, 1-0
1964	4/23	**Ken Johnson**	Hou vs Cin, 0-1
	6/4	Sandy Koufax	LA at Phi, 3-0
	6/21	Jim Bunning	Phi at NY, 6-0 (perfect game)
1965	8/19	Jim Maloney	Cin at Chi, 1-0 (10)
	9/9	Sandy Koufax	LA vs Chi, 1-0 (perfect game)
1967	6/18	Don Wilson	Hou vs Atl, 2-0
1968	7/29	George Culver	Cin vs Phi, 6-1
	9/17	Gaylord Perry	SF vs St.L, 1-0
	9/18	Ray Washburn	St.L at SF, 2-0 (next day, same park)
1969	4/17	Bill Stoneman	Mon at Phi, 7-0
	4/30	Jim Maloney	Cin vs Hou, 10-0
	5/1	Don Wilson	Hou at Cin, 4-0
	8/19	Ken Holtzman	Chi vs Atl, 3-0
	9/20	Bob Moose	Pit at NY, 4-0
1970	6/12	Dock Ellis	Pit at SD, 2-0
	7/20	Bill Singer	LA vs Phi, 5-0
1971	6/3	Ken Holtzman	Chi at Cin, 1-0
	6/23	Rick Wise	Phi at Cin, 4-0
	8/14	Bob Gibson	St.L at Pit, 11-0
1972	4/16	Burt Hooton	Chi vs Phi, 4-0
	9/2	Milt Pappas	Chi vs SD, 8-0
	10/2	Bill Stoneman	Mon vs NY, 7-0
1973	8/5	Phil Niekro	Atl vs SD, 9-0
1975	8/24	Ed Halicki	SF vs NY, 6-0
1976	7/9	Larry Dierker	Hou vs Mon, 6-0
	8/9	John Candelaria	Pit vs LA, 2-0
	9/29	John Montefusco	SF vs Atl, 9-0
1978	4/16	Bob Forsch	St.L vs Phi, 5-0
	6/16	Tom Seaver	Cin vs St.L, 4-0
1979	4/7	Ken Forsch	Hou vs Atl, 6-0
1980	6/27	Jerry Reuss	LA at SF, 8-0
1981	5/10	Charlie Lea	Mon vs SF, 4-0
	9/26	Nolan Ryan	Hou vs LA, 5-0
1983	9/26	Bob Forsch	St.L vs Mon, 3-0
1986	9/25	Mike Scott	Hou vs SF, 2-0
1988	9/16	Tom Browning	Cin vs LA, 1-0 (perfect game)
1990	6/29	Fernando Valenzuela	LA vs St.L, 6-0
	8/15	Terry Mulholland	Phi vs SF, 6-0
1991	5/23	Tommy Greene	Phi at Mon, 2-0
	7/28	Dennis Martinez	Mon at LA, 2-0 (perfect game)
	9/11	Mercker (6), Wohlers (2) & Peña (1)	Atl vs SD, 1-0 (combined no-hitter)
1992	8/17	Kevin Gross	LA vs SF, 2-0
1993	9/8	Darryl Kile	Hou vs NY, 7-1
1994	4/8	Kent Mercker	Atl at LA, 6-0
1995	7/14	Ramon Martinez	LA vs Fla, 7-0
1996	5/11	Al Leiter	Fla vs Col, 11-0
	9/17	Hideo Nomo	LA at Col, 9-0
1997	6/10	Kevin Brown	Fla at SF, 9-0
	7/12	Francisco Cordova (9) Ricardo Rincon (1)	Pit vs. Hou, 3-0 (10 inn.) (combined no-hitter)
1999	6/25	Jose Jimenez	St.L at Ari, 1-0
2001	5/12	A.J. Burnett	Fla at SD, 3-0
	9/3	Bud Smith	St.L at SD, 4-0
2003	4/27	Kevin Millwood	Phi vs SF, 1-0
	6/11	Oswalt (1), Munro (2.2) Saarloos (1.1), Lidge (2), Dotel (1) & Wagner (1)	Hou at NY-AL, 8-0 (combined no-hitter)
2004	5/18	Randy Johnson	Ari at Atl, 2-0 (perfect game)
2006	9/6	Anibal Sanchez	Ari at Fla, 2-0

No-Hit Games (Cont.)
American League

Year	Date	Pitcher	Result	Year	Date	Pitcher	Result
1902	9/20	Jimmy Callahan	Chi vs Det, 3-0	1965	9/16	Dave Morehead	Bos vs Cle, 2-0
1904	5/5	Cy Young	Bos vs Phi, 3-0	1966	6/10	Sonny Siebert	Cle vs Wash, 2-0
			(perfect game)	1967	4/30	**Steve Barber** (8⅔)	Bal vs Det, 1-2
	8/17	Jesse Tannehill	Bos at Chi, 6-0			**& Stu Miller** (⅓)	(combined no-hitter)
1905	7/22	Weldon Henley	Phi at St. L, 6-0		8/25	Dean Chance	Min at Cle, 2-1
	9/6	Frank Smith	Chi at Det, 15-0		9/10	Joel Horlen	Chi vs Det, 6-0
	9/27	Bill Dinneen	Bos vs Chi, 2-0	1968	4/27	Tom Phoebus	Bal vs Bos, 6-0
1908	6/30	Cy Young	Bos at NY, 8-0		5/8	Catfish Hunter	Oak vs Min, 4-0
	9/18	Dusty Rhoades	Cle vs Bos, 2-1				(perfect game)
	9/20	Frank Smith	Chi vs Phi, 1-0	1969	8/13	Jim Palmer	Bal vs Oak, 8-0
	10/2	Addie Joss	Cle vs Chi, 1-0	1970	7/3	Clyde Wright	Cal vs Oak, 4-0
			(perfect game)		9/21	Vida Blue	Oak vs Min, 6-0
1910	4/20	Addie Joss	Cle at Chi, 1-0	1973	4/27	Steve Busby	KC at Det, 3-0
	5/12	Chief Bender	Phi vs Cle, 4-0		5/15	Nolan Ryan	Cal at KC, 3-0
1911	7/29	Smokey Joe Wood	Bos vs St. L, 5-0		7/15	Nolan Ryan	Cal at Det, 6-0
	8/27	Ed Walsh	Chi vs Bos, 5-0		7/30	Jim Bibby	Tex at Oak, 6-0
1912	7/4	George Mullin	Det vs St. L, 7-0	1974	6/19	Steve Busby	KC at Mil, 2-0
	8/30	Earl Hamilton	St. L at Det, 5-1		7/19	Dick Bosman	Cle vs Oak, 4-0
1914	5/31	Joe Benz	Chi vs Cle, 6-1		9/28	Nolan Ryan	Cal vs Min, 4-0
1916	6/16	Rube Foster	Bos vs NY, 2-0	1975	6/1	Nolan Ryan	Cal vs Bal, 1-0
	8/26	Joe Bush	Phi vs Cle, 5-0		9/28	Vida Blue (5),	Oak vs Cal, 5-0
	8/30	Hub (Dutch) Leonard	Bos vs St. L, 4-0			Glenn Abbott (1),	(combined no-hitter)
1917	4/14	Ed Cicotte	Chi at St. L, 11-0			Paul Lindblad (1),	
	4/24	George Mogridge	NY at Bos, 2-1			& Rollie Fingers (2)	
	5/5	Ernie Koob	St. L vs Chi, 1-0	1976	7/28	John Odom (5) &	Chi at Oak, 2-1
	5/6	Bob Groom	St. L vs Chi, 3-0			Francisco Barrios (4)	(combined no-hitter)
			(next day, same park)	1977	5/14	Jim Colborn	KC vs Tex, 6-0
	6/23	Babe Ruth (0)	Bos vs Wash, 4-0		5/30	Dennis Eckersley	Cle vs Cal, 1-0
		& Ernie Shore (9)	(combined no-hitter)		9/22	Bert Blyleven	Tex at Cal, 6-0
1918	6/3	Hub (Dutch) Leonard	Bos at Det, 5-0	1981	5/15	Len Barker	Cle vs Tor, 3-0
1919	9/10	Ray Caldwell	Cle at NY, 3-0				(perfect game)
1920	7/1	Walter Johnson	Wash at Bos, 1-0	1983	7/4	Dave Righetti	NY vs Bos, 4-0
1922	4/30	Charlie Robertson	Chi at Det, 2-0		9/29	Mike Warren	Oak vs Chi, 3-0
			(perfect game)	1984	4/7	Jack Morris	Det at Chi, 4-0
1923	9/4	Sam Jones	NY at Phi, 2-0		9/30	Mike Witt	Cal at Tex, 1-0
	9/7	Howard Ehmke	Bos at Phi, 4-0				(perfect game)
1926	8/21	Ted Lyons	Chi at Bos, 6-0	1986	9/19	Joe Cowley	Chi at Cal, 7-1
1931	4/29	Wes Ferrell	Cle vs St. L, 9-0	1987	4/15	Juan Nieves	Mil at Bal, 7-0
	8/8	Bob Burke	Wash vs Bos, 5-0	1990	4/11	Mark Langston (7)	Cal vs Sea, 1-0
1935	8/31	Vern Kennedy	Chi vs Cle, 5-0			& Mike Witt (2)	(combined no-hitter)
1937	6/1	Bill Dietrich	Chi vs St. L, 8-0		6/2	Randy Johnson	Sea vs Det, 2-0
1938	8/27	Monte Pearson	NY vs Cle, 13-0		6/11	Nolan Ryan	Tex at Oak, 5-0
1940	4/16	Bob Feller	Cle at Chi, 1-0		6/29	Dave Stewart	Oak at Tor, 5-0
			(Opening Day)		9/2	Dave Stieb	Tor at Cle, 3-0
1945	9/9	Dick Fowler	Phi vs St. L, 1-0	1991	5/1	Nolan Ryan	Tex vs Tor, 3-0
1946	4/30	Bob Feller	Cle at NY, 1-0		7/13	Bob Milacki (6),	Bal at Oak, 2-0
1947	7/10	Don Black	Cle vs Phi, 3-0			Mike Flanagan (1),	(combined no-hitter)
	9/3	Bill McCahan	Phi vs Wash, 3-0			Mark Williamson (1)	
1948	6/30	Bob Lemon	Cle at Det, 2-0			& Gregg Olson (1)	
1951	7/1	Bob Feller	Cle vs Det, 2-1		8/11	Wilson Alvarez	Chi at Bal, 7-0
	7/12	Allie Reynolds	NY at Cle, 1-0		8/26	Bret Saberhagen	KC vs Chi, 7-0
	9/28	Allie Reynolds	NY vs Bos, 8-0	1993	4/22	Chris Bosio	Sea vs Bos, 7-0
1952	5/15	Virgil Trucks	Det vs Wash, 1-0		9/4	Jim Abbott	NY vs Cle, 4-0
	8/25	Virgil Trucks	Det at NY, 1-0	1994	4/27	Scott Erickson	Min vs Mil, 6-0
1953	5/6	Bobo Holloman	St. L vs Phi, 6-0		7/28	Kenny Rogers	Tex vs Cal, 4-0
			(first major league start)				(perfect game)
1956	7/14	Mel Parnell	Bos vs Chi, 4-0	1996	5/14	Dwight Gooden	NY vs Sea, 2-0
	10/8	Don Larsen	NY vs Bklyn, 2-0	1998	5/17	David Wells	NY vs Min, 4-0
			(perfect W. Series game)				(perfect game)
1957	8/20	Bob Keegan	Chi vs Wash, 6-0	1999	7/18	David Cone	NY vs Mon, 6-0
1958	7/20	Jim Bunning	Det at Bos, 3-0				(perfect game)
	9/20	Hoyt Wilhelm	Bal vs NY, 1-0		9/11	Eric Milton	Min vs Ana, 7-0
1962	5/5	Bo Belinsky	LA vs Bal, 2-0	2001	4/4	Hideo Nomo	Bos at Bal, 3-0
	6/26	Earl Wilson	Bos vs LA, 2-0	2002	4/27	Derek Lowe	Bos vs TB, 10-0
	8/1	Bill Monbouquette	Bos at Chi, 1-0	2007	4/18	Mark Buehrle	Chi vs Tex, 6-0
	8/26	Jack Kralick	Min vs KC, 1-0		6/12	Justin Verlander	Det vs Mil, 4-0
					9/1	Clay Buchholz	Bos vs Bal, 10-0

All-Time Major League Leaders
Through the 2007 regular season.
CAREER
Players active in 2007 in **bold** type.
Batting
Note that (*) indicates left-handed hitter and (†) indicates switch-hitter.

Batting Average
(Minimum 3,000 AB)

		Yrs	AB	H	Avg
1	Ty Cobb*	24	11,434	4189	.366
2	Rogers Hornsby	23	8,173	2930	.358
3	Joe Jackson*	13	4,981	1772	.356
4	Ed Delahanty	16	7,505	2596	.346
5	Tris Speaker*	22	10,195	3514	.345
6	Ted Williams*	19	7,706	2654	.344
7	Billy Hamilton*	14	6,269	2159	.344
8	Dan Brouthers*	19	6,711	2296	.342
9	Babe Ruth*	22	8,399	2873	.342
10	Harry Heilmann	17	7,787	2660	.342
11	Pete Browning	13	4,820	1646	.341
12	Willie Keeler*	19	8,591	2932	.341
13	Bill Terry*	14	6,428	2193	.341
14	George Sisler*	15	8,267	2812	.340
15	Lou Gehrig*	17	8,001	2721	.340
16	Jesse Burkett*	16	8,421	2850	.338
17	Tony Gwynn*	20	9,288	3141	.338
18	Nap Lajoie	21	9,589	3242	.338
19	Riggs Stephenson	14	4,508	1515	.336
20	Al Simmons	20	8,759	2927	.334
21	**Ichiro Suzuki***	7	4,774	1592	.333
22	Paul Waner*	20	9,459	3152	.333
23	Eddie Collins*	25	9,949	3315	.333
24	**Todd Helton***	11	5,663	1878	.332
25	**Albert Pujols**	7	4,054	1344	.332

Hits

		Yrs	AB	H	Avg
1	Pete Rose†	24	14,053	**4256**	.303
2	Ty Cobb*	24	11,434	**4189**	.366
3	Hank Aaron	23	12,364	**3771**	.305
4	Stan Musial*	22	10,972	**3630**	.331
5	Tris Speaker*	22	10,195	**3514**	.345
6	Carl Yastrzemski*	23	11,988	**3419**	.285
7	Honus Wagner	21	10,430	**3415**	.327
8	Paul Molitor	21	10,835	**3319**	.306
9	Eddie Collins*	25	9,949	**3315**	.333
10	Willie Mays	22	10,881	**3283**	.302
11	Eddie Murray†	21	11,336	**3255**	.287
12	Nap Lajoie	21	9,589	**3242**	.338
13	Cal Ripken Jr	21	11,551	**3184**	.276
14	George Brett	21	10,349	**3154**	.305
15	Paul Waner*	20	9,459	**3152**	.333
16	Robin Yount	20	11,008	**3142**	.285
17	Tony Gwynn*	20	9,288	**3141**	.338
18	Dave Winfield	22	11,003	**3110**	.283
19	**Craig Biggio**	20	10,876	**3060**	.281
20	Rickey Henderson	25	10,961	**3055**	.279
21	Rod Carew*	19	9,315	**3053**	.328
22	Lou Brock*	19	10,332	**3023**	.293
23	Rafael Palmeiro*	20	10,472	**3020**	.288
24	Wade Boggs*	18	9,180	**3010**	.328
25	Al Kaline	22	10,116	**3007**	.297
26	Cap Anson	22	9,108	**3000**	.329
	Roberto Clemente	18	9,454	**3000**	.317

Players Active in 2007

		Yrs	AB	H	Avg
1	Ichiro Suzuki*	7	4,774	1592	.333
2	Todd Helton*	11	5,663	1878	.332
3	Albert Pujols	7	4,054	1344	.332
4	Vladimir Guerrero	12	6,076	1972	.325
5	Derek Jeter	13	7,429	2356	.317
6	Nomar Garciaparra	12	5,263	1659	.315
7	Manny Ramirez	15	7,058	2209	.313
8	Magglio Ordonez	11	5,300	1652	.312
9	Mike Piazza	16	6,911	2127	.308
10	Chipper Jones†	14	6,898	2117	.307

Players Active in 2007

		Yrs	AB	H	Avg
1	Craig Biggio	20	10,876	**3060**	.281
2	Barry Bonds*	22	9,847	**2935**	.298
3	Omar Vizquel†	19	9,479	**2598**	.274
4	Julio Franco	23	8,677	**2586**	.298
5	Ken Griffey Jr.*	19	8,826	**2558**	.290
6	Steve Finley*	19	9,397	**2548**	.271
7	Gary Sheffield	20	8,531	**2521**	.296
8	Luis Gonzalez*	18	8,816	**2502**	.284
9	Ivan Rodriguez	17	8,247	**2495**	.303
10	Kenny Lofton*	16	8,120	**2428**	.299

Games Played

1	Pete Rose	3562
2	Carl Yastrzemski	3308
3	Hank Aaron	3298
4	Rickey Henderson	3081
5	Ty Cobb	3035
6	Stan Musial	3026
	Eddie Murray	3026
8	Cal Ripken Jr.	3001
9	Willie Mays	2992
10	**Barry Bonds**	2986
11	Dave Winfield	2973
12	Rusty Staub	2951
13	Brooks Robinson	2896
14	Robin Yount	2856
15	**Craig Biggio**	2850
16	Al Kaline	2834
17	Rafael Palmeiro	2831
18	Harold Baines	2830
19	Eddie Collins	2826
20	Reggie Jackson	2820

At Bats

1	Pete Rose	14,053
2	Hank Aaron	12,364
3	Carl Yastrzemski	11,988
4	Cal Ripken Jr.	11,551
5	Ty Cobb	11,434
6	Eddie Murray	11,336
7	Robin Yount	11,008
8	Dave Winfield	11,003
9	Stan Musial	10,972
10	Rickey Henderson	10,961
11	Willie Mays	10,881
12	**Craig Biggio**	10,876
13	Paul Molitor	10,835
14	Brooks Robinson	10,654
15	Rafael Palmeiro	10,472
16	Honus Wagner	10,430
17	George Brett	10,349
18	Lou Brock	10,332
19	Luis Aparicio	10,230
20	Tris Speaker	10,195

Total Bases

1	Hank Aaron	6856
2	Stan Musial	6134
3	Willie Mays	6066
4	**Barry Bonds**	5976
5	Ty Cobb	5854
6	Babe Ruth	5793
7	Pete Rose	5752
8	Carl Yastrzemski	5539
9	Eddie Murray	5397
10	Rafael Palmeiro	5388
11	Frank Robinson	5373
12	Dave Winfield	5221
13	Cal Ripken Jr.	5168
14	Tris Speaker	5101
15	Lou Gehrig	5060
16	George Brett	5044
17	Mel Ott	5041
18	Jimmie Foxx	4956
19	Ted Williams	4884
	Ken Griffey Jr.	4884

Home Runs

		Yrs	AB	HR	AB/HR
1	**Barry Bonds***	22	9,847	**762**	12.9
2	Hank Aaron	23	12,364	**755**	16.4
3	Babe Ruth*	22	8,399	**714**	11.8
4	Willie Mays	22	10,881	**660**	16.5
5	**Sammy Sosa**	18	8,813	**609**	14.5
6	**Ken Griffey Jr.***	19	8,826	**593**	14.9
7	Frank Robinson	21	10,006	**586**	17.1
8	Mark McGwire	16	6,187	**583**	10.6
9	Harmon Killebrew	22	8,147	**573**	14.2
10	Rafael Palmeiro*	20	10,472	**569**	18.4
11	Reggie Jackson*	21	9,864	**563**	17.5
12	Mike Schmidt	18	8,352	**548**	15.2
13	Mickey Mantle†	18	8,102	**536**	15.1
14	Jimmie Foxx	20	8,134	**534**	15.2
15	Ted Williams*	19	7,706	**521**	14.8
	Willie McCovey*	22	8,197	**521**	15.7
17	**Alex Rodriguez**	14	7,350	**518**	14.2
18	**Frank Thomas**	18	7,953	**513**	15.5
19	Eddie Mathews*	17	8,537	**512**	16.7
	Ernie Banks	19	9,421	**512**	18.4
21	Mel Ott*	22	9,456	**511**	18.5
22	**Jim Thome***	17	6,841	**507**	13.5
23	Eddie Murray†	21	11,336	**504**	22.5
24	Lou Gehrig*	17	8,001	**493**	16.2
	Fred McGriff*	19	8,757	**493**	17.8

Runs Batted In

		Yrs	Gm	RBI	P/G
1	Hank Aaron	23	3298	**2297**	.70
2	Babe Ruth*	22	2503	**2213**	.88
3	**Barry Bonds***	22	2986	**1996**	.67
4	Lou Gehrig*	17	2164	**1995**	.92
5	Stan Musial*	22	3026	**1951**	.64
6	Ty Cobb*	24	3034	**1938**	.64
7	Jimmie Foxx	20	2317	**1922**	.83
8	Eddie Murray†	21	2980	**1917**	.64
9	Willie Mays	22	2992	**1903**	.64
10	Mel Ott*	22	2730	**1860**	.68
11	Carl Yastrzemski*	23	3308	**1844**	.56
12	Ted Williams*	19	2292	**1839**	.80
13	Rafael Palmeiro*	20	2831	**1835**	.65
14	Dave Winfield	22	2973	**1833**	.62
15	Al Simmons	20	2215	**1827**	.82
16	Frank Robinson	21	2808	**1812**	.65
17	Honus Wagner	21	2792	**1732**	.62
18	Cap Anson	27	2276	**1715**	.75
19	Reggie Jackson*	21	2820	**1702**	.60
20	**Ken Griffey Jr.***	19	2378	**1701**	.72
21	Cal Ripken Jr.	21	3001	**1695**	.56
22	**Frank Thomas**	18	2251	**1674**	.74
23	**Sammy Sosa**	18	2354	**1667**	.71
24	Tony Perez	23	2777	**1652**	.59
25	Ernie Banks	19	2528	**1636**	.65

Players Active in 2007

		Yrs	AB	HR	AB/HR
1	Barry Bonds*	22	9,847	**762**	12.9
2	Sammy Sosa	18	8,813	**609**	14.5
3	Ken Griffey Jr.*	19	8,826	**593**	14.9
4	Alex Rodriguez	14	7,350	**518**	14.2
5	Frank Thomas	18	7,953	**513**	15.5
6	Jim Thome*	17	6,841	**507**	13.5
7	Manny Ramirez	15	7,058	**490**	14.4
8	Gary Sheffield	20	8,531	**480**	17.8
9	Carlos Delgado*	15	6,591	**431**	15.3
10	Mike Piazza	16	6,911	**427**	16.2
11	Chipper Jones†	14	6,898	**386**	17.9
12	Andruw Jones	12	6,408	**368**	17.4
13	Vladimir Guerrero	12	6,076	**365**	16.6
	Jeff Kent	16	8,058	**365**	22.1
15	Jason Giambi*	13	5,874	**364**	16.1

Players Active in 2007

		Yrs	Gm	RBI	P/G
1	Barry Bonds*	22	2986	**1996**	.67
2	Ken Griffey Jr.*	19	2378	**1701**	.72
3	Frank Thomas	18	2251	**1674**	.74
4	Sammy Sosa	18	2354	**1667**	.71
5	Manny Ramirez	15	1950	**1604**	.82
6	Gary Sheffield	20	2362	**1576**	.67
7	Alex Rodriguez	14	1904	**1503**	.79
8	Jeff Kent	17	2177	**1459**	.67
9	Jim Thome*	17	2011	**1398**	.70
10	Luis Gonzalez*	18	2455	**1392**	.57
11	Carlos Delgado*	15	1850	**1374**	.74
12	Mike Piazza	16	1912	**1335**	.70
13	Chipper Jones†	14	1895	**1299**	.69
14	Moises Alou	16	1927	**1278**	.66
15	Garret Anderson*	14	1868	**1208**	.65

Runs

1	Rickey Henderson	2295
2	Ty Cobb	2246
3	**Barry Bonds**	2227
4	Babe Ruth	2174
	Hank Aaron	2174
6	Pete Rose	2165
7	Willie Mays	2062
8	Stan Musial	1949
9	Lou Gehrig	1888
10	Tris Speaker	1882
11	Mel Ott	1859
12	**Craig Biggio**	1844
13	Frank Robinson	1829
14	Eddie Collins	1821
15	Carl Yastrzemski	1816
16	Ted Williams	1798
17	Paul Molitor	1782
18	Charlie Gehringer	1774
19	Jimmie Foxx	1751
20	Honus Wagner	1736

Extra Base Hits

1	Hank Aaron	1477
2	**Barry Bonds**	1440
3	Stan Musial	1377
4	Babe Ruth	1356
5	Willie Mays	1323
6	Rafael Palmeiro	1192
7	Lou Gehrig	1190
8	Frank Robinson	1186
9	Carl Yastrzemski	1157
10	Ty Cobb	1136
11	Tris Speaker	1131
12	George Brett	1119
13	Ted Williams	1117
	Jimmie Foxx	1117
15	**Ken Griffey Jr.**	1103
16	Eddie Murray	1099
17	Dave Winfield	1093
18	Cal Ripken Jr.	1078
19	Reggie Jackson	1075
20	Mel Ott	1071

Slugging Percentage
(Minimum 3,000 AB)

1	Babe Ruth	.690
2	Ted Williams	.634
3	Lou Gehrig	.632
4	**Albert Pujols**	.620
5	Jimmie Foxx	.609
6	**Barry Bonds**	.607
7	Hank Greenberg	.605
8	**Manny Ramirez**	.593
9	Mark McGwire	.588
10	**Todd Helton**	.583
11	Joe DiMaggio	.579
12	**Vladimir Guerrero**	.579
13	**Alex Rodriguez**	.578
14	Rogers Hornsby	.577
15	**Jim Thome**	.565
16	Larry Walker	.565
17	Albert Belle	.564
18	Johnny Mize	.562
19	Juan Gonzalez	.561
20	**Frank Thomas**	.561

Stolen Bases

1. Rickey Henderson 1406
2. Lou Brock 938
3. Billy Hamilton 912
4. Ty Cobb 892
5. Tim Raines 808
6. Vince Coleman 752
7. Eddie Collins 745
8. Max Carey 738
9. Honus Wagner 722
10. Joe Morgan 689
11. Arlie Latham 679
12. Willie Wilson 668
13. Bert Campaneris 649
14. Tom Brown 627
15. **Kenny Lofton** 622
16. Otis Nixon 620
17. George Davis 616
18. Dummy Hoy 594
19. Maury Wills 586
20. George Van Haltren 583

Walks

1. **Barry Bonds** 2558
2. Rickey Henderson 2190
3. Babe Ruth 2062
4. Ted Williams 2019
5. Joe Morgan 1865
6. Carl Yastrzemski 1845
7. Mickey Mantle 1733
8. Mel Ott 1708
9. **Frank Thomas** 1628
10. Eddie Yost 1614
11. Darrell Evans 1605
12. Stan Musial 1599
13. Pete Rose 1566
14. Harmon Killebrew 1559
15. Lou Gehrig 1508
16. Mike Schmidt 1507
17. Eddie Collins 1499
18. Willie Mays 1464
19. **Jim Thome** 1459
20. Jimmie Foxx 1452

Strikeouts

1. Reggie Jackson 2597
2. **Sammy Sosa** 2306
3. **Jim Thome** 2043
4. Andres Galarraga 2003
5. Jose Canseco 1942
6. Willie Stargell 1936
7. Mike Schmidt 1883
8. Fred McGriff 1882
9. Tony Perez 1867
10. Dave Kingman 1816
11. Bobby Bonds 1757
12. **Craig Biggio** 1753
13. Dale Murphy 1748
14. Lou Brock 1730
15. Mickey Mantle 1710
16. Harmon Killebrew 1699
17. Chili Davis 1698
18. Dwight Evans 1697
19. Rickey Henderson 1694
20. Dave Winfield 1686

Pitching

Note that (*) indicates left-handed pitcher. Active pitching leaders are listed for wins and strikeouts.

Wins

		Yrs	GS	W	L	Pct
1	Cy Young	22	815	511	316	.618
2	Walter Johnson	21	666	417	279	.599
3	Christy Mathewson	17	551	373	188	.665
	Grover Alexander	20	598	373	208	.642
5	Pud Galvin	15	688	365	310	.541
6	Warren Spahn*	21	665	363	245	.597
	Kid Nichols	15	561	361	208	.634
8	**Roger Clemens**	23	707	354	184	.658
9	**Greg Maddux**	22	707	347	214	.619
10	Tim Keefe	14	594	342	225	.603
11	Steve Carlton*	24	709	329	244	.574
12	John Clarkson	12	518	328	178	.648
13	Eddie Plank*	17	529	326	194	.627
14	Don Sutton	23	756	324	256	.559
	Nolan Ryan	27	773	324	292	.526
16	Phil Niekro	24	716	318	274	.537
17	Gaylord Perry	22	690	314	265	.542
18	Tom Seaver	20	647	311	205	.603
19	Old Hoss Radbourn	12	503	309	195	.613
20	Mickey Welch	13	549	307	210	.594
21	**Tom Glavine***	21	669	303	199	.604
22	Lefty Grove*	17	456	300	141	.680
	Early Wynn	23	612	300	244	.551
24	Bobby Mathews	15	568	297	248	.545
25	Tommy John*	26	700	288	231	.555
26	Bert Blyleven	22	685	287	250	.534
27	Robin Roberts	19	609	286	245	.539
28	**Randy Johnson***	20	556	284	150	.654
	Tony Mullane	13	504	284	220	.563
	Ferguson Jenkins	19	594	284	226	.557

Strikeouts

		Yrs	IP	SO	P/9
1	Nolan Ryan	27	5386.0	5714	9.55
2	**Roger Clemens**	24	4916.2	4672	8.55
3	**Randy Johnson***	20	3855.1	4616	10.78
4	Steve Carlton*	24	5217.1	4136	7.13
5	Bert Blyleven	22	4970.0	3701	6.70
6	Tom Seaver	20	4782.2	3640	6.85
7	Don Sutton	23	5282.1	3574	6.09
8	Gaylord Perry	22	5350.1	3534	5.94
9	Walter Johnson	21	5914.1	3508	5.34
10	Phil Niekro	24	5404.1	3342	5.57
11	**Greg Maddux**	22	4814.1	3273	6.12
12	Ferguson Jenkins	19	4500.2	3192	6.38
13	Bob Gibson	17	3884.1	3117	7.22
14	**Curt Schilling**	20	3261.0	3116	8.60
15	**Pedro Martinez**	16	2673.2	3030	10.20
16	**John Smoltz**	20	3367.0	2975	7.95
17	Jim Bunning	17	3760.1	2855	6.83
18	Mickey Lolich*	16	3638.1	2832	7.01
19	Cy Young	22	7356.0	2803	3.43
20	Frank Tanana*	21	4186.2	2773	5.96
21	David Cone	17	2898.2	2668	8.28
22	**Mike Mussina**	17	3562.1	2663	7.13
23	Chuck Finley*	17	3197.1	2610	7.35
24	Warren Spahn*	21	5243.2	2583	4.43
25	Bob Feller	18	3827.0	2581	6.07
26	**Tom Glavine***	21	4350.0	2570	5.32
27	Tim Keefe	14	5049.2	2564	4.57
28	Jerry Koosman*	19	3839.1	2556	5.99
29	Christy Mathewson	17	4781.0	2502	4.71
30	Don Drysdale	14	3432.0	2486	6.52

Pitchers Active in 2007

		Yrs	GS	W	L	Pct
1	Roger Clemens	23	707	354	184	.658
2	Greg Maddux	22	707	347	214	.619
3	Tom Glavine*	21	669	303	199	.604
4	Randy Johnson*	20	556	284	150	.654
5	Mike Mussina	17	502	250	144	.635
6	David Wells*	21	489	239	157	.604
7	Jamie Moyer*	21	551	230	178	.564
8	Curt Schilling	20	436	216	146	.597
9	Kenny Rogers*	19	444	210	143	.595
10	Pedro Martinez	16	380	209	93	.692

Pitchers Active in 2007

		Yrs	IP	SO	P/9
1	Roger Clemens	24	4916.2	4672	8.55
2	Randy Johnson*	20	3855.1	4616	10.78
3	Greg Maddux	22	4814.1	3273	6.12
4	Curt Schilling	20	3261.0	3116	8.60
5	Pedro Martinez	16	2673.2	3030	10.20
6	John Smoltz	20	3367.0	2975	7.95
7	Mike Mussina	17	3562.1	2663	7.13
8	Tom Glavine*	21	4350.0	2570	5.32
9	David Wells*	21	3439.0	2201	5.76
10	Jamie Moyer*	21	3550.1	2125	5.39

Winning Pct.
(Minimum 100 wins)

		Yrs	W-L	Pct
1	Al Spalding	.7	252-65	.795
2	Spud Chandler	11	109-43	.717
3	**Pedro Martinez**	16	209-93	.692
4	Dave Foutz	11	147-66	.690
5	Whitey Ford*	16	236-106	.690
6	Bob Caruthers	9	218-99	.688
7	Don Gullett*	9	109-50	.686
8	Lefty Grove*	17	300-141	.680
9	**Roy Oswalt**	7	112-54	.675
10	Smokey Joe Wood	11	117-57	.672
11	**Roy Halladay**	10	111-55	.669
12	Vic Raschi	10	132-66	.667
13	Larry Corcoran	8	177-89	.665
14	Christy Mathewson	17	373-188	.665
15	Sam Leever	13	194-100	.660

Losses

		Yrs	GS	W	L	Pct
1	Cy Young	22	815	511	**316**	.618
2	Pud Galvin	15	688	365	**310**	.541
3	Nolan Ryan	27	773	324	**292**	.526
4	Walter Johnson	21	666	417	**279**	.599
5	Phil Niekro	24	716	318	**274**	.537
6	Gaylord Perry	22	690	314	**265**	.542
7	Don Sutton	23	756	324	**256**	.559
8	Jack Powell	16	516	245	**254**	.491
9	Eppa Rixey*	21	552	266	**251**	.515
10	Bert Blyleven	22	685	287	**250**	.534
11	Bobby Mathews	15	568	297	**248**	.545
12	Robin Roberts	19	609	286	**245**	.539
	Warren Spahn*	21	665	363	**245**	.597
14	Early Wynn	23	612	300	**244**	.551
	Steve Carlton*	24	709	329	**244**	.574

Appearances

1	Jesse Orosco	1252
2	**Mike Stanton**	1178
3	John Franco	1119
4	Dennis Eckersley	1071
5	Hoyt Wilhelm	1070
6	Dan Plesac	1064
7	Kent Tekulve	1050
8	Lee Smith	1022
	Jose Mesa	1022
10	**Mike Timlin**	1011
11	**Roberto Hernandez**	1010
12	Mike Jackson	1005
13	Rich Gossage	1002
14	Lindy McDaniel	987
15	Rollie Fingers	944

Innings Pitched

1	Cy Young	7356.0
2	Pud Galvin	6003.1
3	Walter Johnson	5914.1
4	Phil Niekro	5404.1
5	Nolan Ryan	5386.0
6	Gaylord Perry	5350.1
7	Don Sutton	5282.1
8	Warren Spahn	5243.2
9	Steve Carlton	5217.1
10	Grover Alexander	5190.0
11	Kid Nichols	5056.1
12	Tim Keefe	5049.2
13	Bert Blyleven	4970.0
14	Bobby Mathews	4956.0
15	**Roger Clemens**	4916.2

Earned Run Avg.
(Minimum 1500 IP)

1	Ed Walsh	1.82
2	Addie Joss	1.89
3	Al Spalding	2.04
4	Three Finger Brown	2.06
5	Monte Ward	2.10
6	Christy Mathewson	2.13
7	Rube Waddell	2.16
8	Walter Johnson	2.17
9	Orval Overall	2.23
10	Tommy Bond	2.25
11	Will White	2.28
12	Ed Reulbach	2.28
13	Jim Scott	2.30
14	Eddie Plank	2.35
15	Larry Corcoran	2.36

Shutouts

1	Walter Johnson	110
2	Grover Alexander	90
3	Christy Mathewson	79
4	Cy Young	76
5	Eddie Plank	69
6	Warren Spahn	63
7	Nolan Ryan	61
	Tom Seaver	61
9	Bert Blyleven	60
10	Don Sutton	58
11	Pud Galvin	57
	Ed Walsh	57
13	Bob Gibson	56
14	Three Finger Brown	55
	Steve Carlton	55

Walks Allowed

1	Nolan Ryan	2795
2	Steve Carlton	1833
3	Phil Niekro	1809
4	Early Wynn	1775
5	Bob Feller	1764
6	Bobo Newsom	1732
7	Amos Rusie	1704
8	Charlie Hough	1665
9	**Roger Clemens**	1580
10	Gus Weyhing	1566
11	Red Ruffing	1541
12	**Tom Glavine**	1463
13	Bump Hadley	1442
14	Warren Spahn	1434
15	Earl Whitehill	1431

HRs Allowed

1	Robin Roberts	505
2	Ferguson Jenkins	484
3	Phil Niekro	482
4	Don Sutton	472
5	Frank Tanana	448
6	**Jamie Moyer**	444
7	Warren Spahn	434
8	Bert Blyleven	430
9	Steve Carlton	414
10	**David Wells**	407
11	Gaylord Perry	399
12	Jim Kaat	395
13	Jack Morris	389
14	Charlie Hough	383
15	Tom Seaver	380

Saves

1	**Trevor Hoffman**	524
2	Lee Smith	478
3	**Mariano Rivera**	443
4	John Franco	424
5	Dennis Eckersley	390
6	Jeff Reardon	367
7	**Billy Wagner**	358
8	Randy Myers	347
9	Rollie Fingers	341
10	John Wetteland	330
11	**Roberto Hernandez**	326
12	**Troy Percival**	324
13	**Jose Mesa**	321
14	Rick Aguilera	318
15	Robb Nen	314
16	Tom Henke	311
17	Rich Gossage	310
18	Jeff Montgomery	304
19	Doug Jones	303
20	**Todd Jones**	301
21	Bruce Sutter	300
22	**Armando Benitez**	289
23	Rod Beck	286
24	**Jason Isringhausen**	281
25	**Bob Wickman**	267
26	Todd Worrell	256
27	Dave Righetti	252
28	Dan Quisenberry	244
29	Sparky Lyle	238
30	Ugueth Urbina	237

SINGLE SEASON
Through 2007 regular season.
Batting

Home Runs

		Year	Gm	AB	HR
1	Barry Bonds, SF	2001	153	476	73
2	Mark McGwire, St.L	1998	155	509	70
3	Sammy Sosa, Chi-NL	1998	159	643	66
4	Mark McGwire, St.L	1999	153	521	65
5	Sammy Sosa, Chi-NL	2001	160	577	64
6	Sammy Sosa, Chi-NL	1999	162	625	63
7	Roger Maris, NY-AL	1961	162	590	61
8	Babe Ruth, NY-AL	1927	151	540	60
9	Babe Ruth, NY-AL	1921	152	540	59
10	Mark McGwire, Oak-St.L	1997	156	540	58
	Hank Greenberg, Det	1938	155	556	58
	Ryan Howard, Phi	2006	159	581	58
	Jimmie Foxx, Phi-AL	1932	154	585	58
14	Alex Rodriguez, Tex	2002	162	624	57
	Luis Gonzalez, Ari	2001	162	609	57
16	Hack Wilson, Chi-NL	1930	155	585	56
	Ken Griffey Jr., Sea	1997	157	608	56
	Ken Griffey Jr., Sea	1998	161	633	56
19	Six tied with 54 each.				

Hits

		Year	AB	H	Avg
1	Ichiro Suzuki, Sea.	2004	704	262	.372
2	George Sisler, StL-AL	1920	631	257	.407
3	Bill Terry, NY-NL	1930	633	254	.401
	Lefty O'Doul, Phi-NL	1929	638	254	.398
5	Al Simmons, Phi-AL	1925	658	253	.384
6	Rogers Hornsby, StL-NL	1922	623	250	.401
	Chuck Klein, Phi-NL	1930	648	250	.386
8	Ty Cobb, Det	1911	591	248	.420
9	George Sisler, StL-AL	1922	586	246	.420
10	Ichiro Suzuki, Sea	2001	692	242	.350
11	Babe Herman, Bklyn	1930	614	241	.393
	Heinie Manush, StL-AL	1928	638	241	.378
13	Wade Boggs, Bos	1985	653	240	.368
	Darin Erstad, Ana	2000	676	240	.355
15	Rod Carew, Min	1977	616	239	.388
16	Don Mattingly, NY-AL	1986	677	238	.352
	Ichiro Suzuki, Sea	2007	678	238	.351
18	Harry Heilmann, Det	1921	602	237	.394
	Paul Waner, Pit	1927	623	237	.380
	Joe Medwick, StL-NL	1937	633	237	.374

Batting Average

From 1900-49

		Year	AB	H	Avg
1	Rogers Hornsby, StL-NL	1924	536	227	.424
2	Nap Lajoie, Phi-AL	1901	543	229	.422
3	George Sisler, StL-AL	1922	586	246	.420
4	Ty Cobb, Det	1911	591	248	.420
5	Ty Cobb, Det	1912	533	227	.410
6	Joe Jackson, Cle	1911	571	233	.408
7	George Sisler, StL-AL	1920	631	257	.407
8	Ted Williams, Bos-AL	1941	456	185	.406
9	Rogers Hornsby, StL-NL	1925	504	203	.403
10	Harry Heilmann, Det	1923	524	211	.403

Since 1950

		Year	AB	H	Avg
1	Tony Gwynn, SD	1994	419	175	.394
2	George Brett, KC	1980	449	175	.390
3	Ted Williams, Bos	1957	420	163	.388
4	Rod Carew, Min	1977	616	239	.388
5	Larry Walker, Col	1999	438	166	.379
6	Todd Helton, Col	2000	580	216	.372
7	Nomar Garciaparra, Bos	2000	529	197	.372
8	Ichiro Suzuki, Sea	2004	704	262	.372
9	Tony Gwynn, SD	1997	592	220	.372
10	Andres Galarraga, Col	1993	470	174	.370

Total Bases

From 1900-49

		Year	TB
1	Babe Ruth, New York-AL	1921	457
2	Rogers Hornsby, St. Louis-NL	1922	450
3	Lou Gehrig, New York-AL	1927	447
4	Chuck Klein, Philadelphia-NL	1930	445
5	Jimmie Foxx, Philadelphia-AL	1932	438
6	Stan Musial, St. Louis-NL	1948	429
7	Hack Wilson, Chicago-NL	1930	423
8	Chuck Klein, Philadelphia-NL	1932	420
9	Lou Gehrig, New York-AL	1930	419
10	Joe DiMaggio, New York-AL	1937	418

Since 1950

		Year	TB
1	Sammy Sosa, Chicago-NL	2001	425
2	Luis Gonzalez, Arizona	2001	419
3	Sammy Sosa, Chicago-NL	1998	416
4	Barry Bonds, San Francisco	2001	411
5	Larry Walker, Colorado	1997	409
6	Jim Rice, Boston	1978	406
7	Todd Helton, Colorado	2000	405
8	Todd Helton, Colorado	2001	402
9	Hank Aaron, Milwaukee	1959	400
10	Albert Belle, Chicago-AL	1998	399

Runs Batted In

From 1900-49

		Year	Avg	HR	RBI
1	Hack Wilson, Chi-NL	1930	.356	56	191
2	Lou Gehrig, NY-AL	1931	.341	46	184
3	Hank Greenberg, Det	1937	.337	40	183
4	Lou Gehrig, NY-AL	1927	.373	47	175
	Jimmie Foxx, Bos-AL	1938	.349	50	175
6	Lou Gehrig, NY-AL	1930	.379	41	174
7	Babe Ruth, NY-AL	1921	.378	59	171
8	Chuck Klein, Phi-NL	1930	.386	40	170
	Hank Greenberg, Det	1935	.328	36	170
10	Jimmie Foxx, Phi-AL	1932	.364	58	169

Since 1950

		Year	Avg	HR	RBI
1	Manny Ramirez, Cle	1999	.333	44	165
2	Sammy Sosa, Chi-NL	2001	.328	64	160
3	Sammy Sosa, Chi-NL	1998	.308	66	158
4	Juan Gonzalez, Tex	1998	.318	45	157
5	**Alex Rodriguez**, NY-AL	2007	.314	54	156
6	Tommy Davis, LA-NL	1962	.346	27	153
7	Albert Belle, Chi-AL	1998	.328	49	152
8	Andres Galarraga, Col	1996	.304	47	150
	Miguel Tejada, Bal	2004	.311	34	150
10	George Foster, Cin	1977	.320	52	149
	Ryan Howard, Phi	2006	.313	58*	149

Runs

		Year	Runs
1	Babe Ruth, New York-AL	1921	177
2	Lou Gehrig, New York-AL	1936	167
3	Babe Ruth, New York-AL	1928	163
	Lou Gehrig, New York-AL	1931	163
5	Babe Ruth, New York-AL	1920	158
	Babe Ruth, New York-AL	1927	158
	Chuck Klein, Philadelphia-NL	1930	158
8	Rogers Hornsby, Chicago-NL	1929	156
9	Kiki Cuyler, Chicago-NL	1930	155
10	Lefty O'Doul, Philadelphia-NL	1929	152
	Woody English, Chicago-NL	1930	152
	Al Simmons, Philadelphia-AL	1930	152
	Chuck Klein, Philadelphia-NL	1932	152
	Jeff Bagwell, Houston	2000	152
15	Babe Ruth, New York-AL	1923	151
	Jimmie Foxx, Philadelphia-AL	1932	151
	Joe DiMaggio, New York-AL	1937	151
18	Babe Ruth, New York-AL	1930	150
	Ted Williams, Boston-AL	1949	150
20	Lou Gehrig, New York-AL	1927	149
	Babe Ruth, New York-AL	1931	149

Walks

		Year	BB
1	Barry Bonds, San Francisco	2004	232
2	Barry Bonds, San Francisco	2002	198
3	Barry Bonds, San Francisco	2001	177
4	Babe Ruth, New York-AL	1923	170
5	Ted Williams, Boston-AL	1947	162
	Ted Williams, Boston-AL	1949	162
	Mark McGwire, St. Louis	1998	162
8	Ted Williams, Boston-AL	1946	156
9	Barry Bonds, San Francisco	1996	151
	Eddie Yost, Washington	1956	151

Extra Base Hits

		Year	EBH
1	Babe Ruth, New York-AL	1921	119
2	Lou Gehrig, New York-AL	1927	117
3	Chuck Klein, Philadelphia-NL	1930	107
	Barry Bonds, San Francisco	2001	107
5	Todd Helton, Colorado	2001	105
6	Chuck Klein, Philadelphia-NL	1932	103
	Hank Greenberg, Detroit	1937	103
	Stan Musial, St. Louis-NL	1948	103
	Albert Belle, Cleveland	1995	103
	Todd Helton, Colorado	2000	103
	Sammy Sosa, Chicago-NL	2001	103

Slugging Percentage
From 1900-49

		Year	Pct
1	Babe Ruth, New York-AL	1920	.847
2	Babe Ruth, New York-AL	1921	.846
3	Babe Ruth, New York-AL	1927	.772
4	Lou Gehrig, New York-AL	1927	.765
5	Babe Ruth, New York-AL	1923	.764
6	Rogers Hornsby, St. Louis-NL	1925	.756
7	Jimmie Foxx, Philadelphia-AL	1932	.749
8	Babe Ruth, New York-AL	1924	.739
9	Babe Ruth, New York-AL	1926	.737
10	Ted Williams, Boston-AL	1941	.735

Since 1950

		Year	Pct
1	Barry Bonds, San Francisco	2001	.863
2	Barry Bonds, San Francisco	2004	.812
3	Barry Bonds, San Francisco	2002	.799
4	Mark McGwire, St. Louis	1998	.752
5	Jeff Bagwell, Houston	1994	.750
6	Barry Bonds, San Francisco	2003	.749
	Sammy Sosa, Chicago-NL	2001	.737
8	Ted Williams, Boston	1957	.731
9	Mark McGwire, Oakland	1996	.730
10	Frank Thomas, Chicago-AL	1994	.729

Doubles

		Year	2B
1	Earl Webb, Boston-AL	1931	67
2	George Burns, Cleveland	1926	64
	Joe Medwick, St. Louis-NL	1936	64
4	Hank Greenberg, Detroit	1934	63
5	Paul Waner, Pittsburgh	1932	62
6	Charlie Gehringer, Detroit	1936	60
7	Tris Speaker, Cleveland	1923	59
	Chuck Klein, Philadelphia-NL	1930	59
	Todd Helton, Colorado	2000	59
10	Three tied with 57 each.		

Triples
From 1900-49

		Year	3B
1	Chief Wilson, Pittsburgh	1912	36
2	Joe Jackson, Cleveland	1912	26
3	Sam Crawford, Detroit	1914	26
4	Kiki Cuyler, Pittsburgh	1925	26
5	Three tied with 25 each.		

Since 1950

		Year	3B
1	**Curtis Granderson**, Detroit	2007	23
2	Willie Wilson, Kansas City	1985	21
	Lance Johnson, St. Louis-NL	1996	21
4	Willie Mays, New York-NL	1957	20
	George Brett, Kansas City	1979	20
	Cristian Guzman, Minnesota	2000	20
	Jimmy Rollins, Philadelphia	2007	20

Stolen Bases

		Year	SB
1	Rickey Henderson, Oakland	1982	130
2	Lou Brock, St. Louis	1974	118
3	Vince Coleman, St. Louis	1985	110
4	Vince Coleman, St. Louis	1987	109
5	Rickey Henderson, Oakland	1983	108
6	Vince Coleman, St. Louis	1986	107
7	Maury Wills, Los Angeles-NL	1962	104
8	Rickey Henderson, Oakland	1980	100
9	Ron LeFlore, Montreal	1980	97
10	Ty Cobb, Detroit	1915	96
	Omar Moreno, Pittsburgh	1980	96
12	Maury Wills, Los Angeles	1965	94
13	Rickey Henderson, New York-AL	1988	93
14	Tim Raines, Montreal	1983	90
15	Clyde Milan, Washington	1912	88

Strikeouts

		Year	SO
1	**Ryan Howard**, Philadelphia	2007	199
2	Adam Dunn, Cincinnati	2004	195
3	Adam Dunn, Cincinnati	2006	194
4	Bobby Bonds, San Francisco	1970	189
5	Jose Hernandez, Milwaukee	2002	188
6	Bobby Bonds, San Francisco	1969	187
	Preston Wilson, Florida	2000	187
8	Rob Deer, Milwaukee	1987	186
9	Pete Incaviglia, Texas	1986	185
	Jose Hernandez, Milwaukee	2001	185
	Jim Thome, Cleveland	2001	185

Pinch Hits
Career pinch hits in parentheses.

		Year	PH	
1	John Vander Wal, Colorado	1995	28	(129)
2	Lenny Harris, Col-Ari	1999	26	(212)
3	Jose Morales, Montreal	1976	25	(123)
4	Dave Philley, Baltimore	1961	24	(93)
	Vic Davalillo, St. Louis	1970	24	(95)
	Rusty Staub, New York-NL	1983	24	(100)
	Gerald Perry, St. Louis	1993	24	(95)

Pitching
Wins

From 1900-49

		Year	W	L	Pct
1	Jack Chesbro, NY-AL	1904	41	12	.774
2	Ed Walsh, Chi-AL	1908	40	15	.727
3	Christy Mathewson, NY-NL	1908	37	11	.771
4	Walter Johnson, Wash	1913	36	7	.837
5	Joe McGinnity, NY-NL	1904	35	8	.814
6	Smokey Joe Wood, Bos-AL	1912	34	5	.872
7	Cy Young, Bos-AL	1901	33	10	.767
	Grover Alexander, Phi-NL	1916	33	12	.733
	Christy Mathewson, NY-NL	1904	33	12	.733
10	Cy Young, Bos-AL	1902	32	11	.744

Since 1950

		Year	W	L	Pct
1	Denny McLain, Det	1968	31	6	.838
2	Robin Roberts, Phi-NL	1952	28	7	.800
3	Bob Welch, Oak	1990	27	6	.818
	Don Newcombe, Bkln	1956	27	7	.794
	Sandy Koufax, LA	1966	27	9	.750
	Steve Carlton, Phi	1972	27	10	.730
7	Sandy Koufax, LA	1965	26	8	.765
	Juan Marichal, SF	1968	26	9	.743

Note: 11 pitchers tied with 25 wins, including Marichal twice.

Earned Run Average

From 1900-49

		Year	ShO	ERA
1	Dutch Leonard, Bos-AL	1914	7	1.01
2	Three Finger Brown, Chi-NL	1906	10	1.04
3	Walter Johnson, Wash	1913	11	1.09
4	Christy Mathewson, NY-NL	1909	8	1.14
5	Jack Pfiester, Chi-NL	1907	3	1.15
6	Addie Joss, Cle	1908	9	1.16
7	Carl Lundgren, Chi-NL	1907	7	1.17
8	Grover Alexander, Phi-NL	1915	12	1.22
9	Cy Young, Bos-AL	1908	3	1.26
10	Three pitchers tied at 1.27			

Since 1950

		Year	ShO	ERA
1	Bob Gibson, St.L	1968	13	1.12
2	Dwight Gooden, NY-NL	1985	8	1.53
3	Greg Maddux, Atl	1994	3	1.56
4	Luis Tiant, Cle	1968	9	1.60
5	Greg Maddux, Atl	1995	3	1.63
6	Dean Chance, LA-AL	1964	11	1.65
7	Nolan Ryan, Cal	1981	3	1.69
8	Sandy Koufax, LA	1966	5	1.73
9	Sandy Koufax, LA	1964	7	1.74
10	Pedro Martinez, Bos	2000	4	1.74

Note: Koufax's ERA in 1964 was 1.735. Martinez' ERA in 2000 was 1.742. The Yankees' Ron Guidry narrowly missed the top 10 list with an ERA of 1.743 in 1978.

Winning Pct.

		Year	W-L	Pct
1	Roy Face, Pit	1959	18-1	.947
2	Rick Sutcliffe, Chi-NL*	1984	16-1	.941
3	Johnny Allen, Cle	1937	15-1	.938
4	Greg Maddux, Atl	1995	19-2	.904
5	Randy Johnson, Sea	1995	18-2	.900
6	Ron Guidry, NY-AL	1978	25-3	.893
7	Freddie Fitzsimmons, Bklyn	1940	16-2	.889
8	Lefty Grove, Phi-AL	1931	31-4	.886
9	Bob Stanley, Bos	1978	15-2	.882
10	Preacher Roe, Bklyn	1951	22-3	.880

*Sutcliffe began 1984 with Cleveland and was 4-5 before being traded to the Cubs; his overall winning pct. was .769 (20-6).

Strikeouts

		Year	SO	P/9
1	Nolan Ryan, Cal	1973	383	10.57
2	Sandy Koufax, LA	1965	382	10.24
3	Randy Johnson, Ari	2001	372	13.41
4	Nolan Ryan, Cal	1974	367	9.93
5	Randy Johnson, Ari	1999	364	12.06
6	Rube Waddell, Phi-AL	1904	349	8.20
7	Bob Feller, Cle	1946	348	8.43
8	Randy Johnson, Ari	2000	347	12.56
9	Nolan Ryan, Cal	1977	341	10.26
10	Randy Johnson, Ari	2002	334	11.56

Appearances

		Year	App	Sv
1	Mike Marshall, LA	1974	106	21
2	Kent Tekulve, Pit	1979	94	31
	Salomon Torres, Pit	2006	94	12
4	Mike Marshall, LA	1973	92	31
5	Kent Tekulve, Pit	1978	91	31
6	Wayne Granger, Cin	1969	90	27
	Mike Marshall, Min	1979	90	32
	Kent Tekulve, Phi	1987	90	3

Saves

		Year	App	Sv
1	Bobby Thigpen, Chi-AL	1990	77	57
2	John Smoltz, Atl	2002	75	55
	Eric Gagne, LA	2003	77	55
4	Randy Myers, Chi-NL	1993	73	53
	Trevor Hoffman, SD	1998	66	53
	Mariano Rivera, NY-AL	2004	74	53
7	Eric Gagne, LA	2002	77	52
8	Dennis Eckersley, Oak	1992	69	51
	Rod Beck, Chi-NL	1998	81	51
10	Mariano Rivera, NY-AL	2001	71	50

Innings Pitched (since 1920)

		Year	IP	W-L
1	Wilbur Wood, Chi-AL	1972	376.2	24-17
2	Mickey Lolich, Det	1971	376.0	25-14
3	Bob Feller, Cle	1946	371.1	26-15
4	Grover Alexander, Chi-NL	1920	363.1	27-14
5	Wilbur Wood, Chi-AL	1973	359.1	24-20

Shutouts

		Year	ShO	ERA
1	Grover Alexander, Phi-NL	1916	16	1.55
2	Jack Coombs, Phi-AL	1910	13	1.30
	Bob Gibson, St.L	1968	13	1.12
4	Christy Mathewson, NY-NL	1908	12	1.43
	Grover Alexander, Phi-NL	1915	12	1.22

Walks Allowed (since 1920)

		Year	BB	SO
1	Bob Feller, Cle	1938	208	240
2	Nolan Ryan, Cal	1977	204	341
3	Nolan Ryan, Cal	1974	202	367
4	Bob Feller, Cle	1941	194	260
5	Bobo Newsom, St.L-AL	1938	192	226

Home Runs Allowed

		Year	HRs
1	Bert Blyleven, Minnesota	1986	50
2	Jose Lima, Houston	2000	48
3	Robin Roberts, Philadelphia	1956	46
	Bert Blyleven, Minnesota	1987	46
5	Jamie Moyer, Seattle	2004	44

SINGLE GAME
Through 2007 regular season.

Batting

Home Runs

No		Date	Inn
4	Bobby Lowe, Boston-NL	5/30/1894	9
	Ed Delahanty, Philadelphia-NL	7/13/1896	9
	Lou Gehrig, New York-AL	6/3/1932	9
	Chuck Klein, Philadelphia-NL	7/10/1936	10
	Pat Seerey, Chicago-AL	7/18/1948	11
	Gil Hodges, Brooklyn	8/31/1950	9
	Joe Adcock, Milwaukee	7/31/1954	9
	Rocky Colavito, Cleveland	6/10/1959	9
	Willie Mays, San Francisco	4/30/1961	9
	Mike Schmidt, Philadelphia	4/17/1976	10
	Bob Horner, Atlanta	7/6/1986	9
	Mark Whiten, St. Louis	9/7/1993	9
	Mike Cameron, Seattle	5/2/2002	9
	Shawn Green, Los Angeles	5/23/2002	9
	Carlos Delgado, Toronto	9/25/2003	9

Runs

No		Date	Inn
7	Guy Hecker, Louisville	8/15/1886	9

Hits

No		Date	Inn
9	Johnny Burnett, Cleveland (9-for-11)	7/10/1932	18
7	Wilbert Robinson, Baltimore (7-for-7)	6/10/1892	9
	Rennie Stennett, Pittsburgh (7-for-7)	9/16/1975	9
	Cesar Gutierrez, Detroit (7-for-7)	6/21/1970	12
	Rocky Colavito, Detroit (7-for-10)	6/24/1962	22

Runs Batted In

No		Date	Inn
12	Jim Bottomley, St. Louis-NL	9/16/1924	9
	Mark Whiten, St. Louis	9/7/1993	9

Pitching

Strikeouts

No		Date	Inn
21	Tom Cheney, Washington	9/12/1962	16
20	Roger Clemens, Boston	4/29/1986	9
	Roger Clemens, Boston	9/18/1996	9
	Kerry Wood, Chicago-NL	5/6/1998	9
	Randy Johnson, Arizona	5/8/2001	9*

*Johnson struck out 20 in nine innings and was removed with the game tied, 1-1. Arizona beat Cincinnati, 4-3, in 11 innings.

Innings Pitched

No		Date
26	Leon Cadore, Brooklyn (tie, 1-1)	5/1/1920
	Joe Oeschger, Boston-NL (tie, 1-1)	5/1/1920

Unassisted Triple Plays

One of the rarest feats in baseball, the unassisted triple play has been accomplished only 13 times in major league history. Ironically, in what can only be described as a statistic anomaly, the trick was turned twice in two days in May of 1927.

Player, Position, Team	Date	Opponent
Paul Hines, OF, Providence	May 8, 1878	Boston-NL
Neal Ball, SS, Cleveland	July 19, 1909	Boston-AL
Bill Wambganss, 2B, Cleveland	Oct. 10, 1920	Brooklyn (World Series)
George Burns, 1B, Boston-AL	Sept. 14, 1923	Cleveland
Ernie Padgett, SS, Boston-NL	Oct. 6, 1923	Philadelphia
Glenn Wright, SS, Pittsburgh	May 7, 1925	St.Louis-NL
Jimmy Cooney, SS, Chicago-NL	May 30, 1927	Pittsburgh
Johnny Neun, 1B, Detroit	May 31, 1927	Cleveland
Ron Hansen, SS, Washington	July 30, 1968	Cleveland
Mickey Morandini, 2B, Philadelphia	Sept. 20, 1992	Pittsburgh
John Valentin, SS, Boston	July 8, 1994	Seattle
Randy Velarde, 2B, Oakland	May 29, 2000	NY Yankees
Rafael Furcal, SS, Atlanta	Aug. 10, 2003	St. Louis
Troy Tulowitzki, SS, Colorado	Apr. 29, 2007	Atlanta

Most Gold Gloves (by position)

Gold Gloves have been awarded since the 1957 season by Rawlings Sporting Goods to superior major league fielders at each position in both leagues. Voting has been conducted by a panel of sportswriters appointed by *The Sporting News* publisher J.G. Taylor Spink (1957), major league players (1958-1964) and managers and coaches (1965-present). Top 5 in each position are listed, through the 2006 season.

Pitchers	No	Catchers	No	First Basemen	No	Second Basemen	No
1 Jim Kaat	16	1 Ivan Rodriguez	12	1 Keith Hernandez	11	1 Roberto Alomar	10
Greg Maddux	16	2 Johnny Bench	10	2 Don Mattingly	9	2 Ryne Sandberg	9
3 Bob Gibson	9	3 Bob Boone	7	3 George Scott	8	3 Bill Mazeroski	8
4 Bobby Shantz	8	4 Jim Sundberg	6	4 Vic Power	7	Frank White	8
5 Mark Langston	7	5 Bill Freehan	5	Bill White	7	5 Joe Morgan	5
						Bobby Richardson	5

Third Basemen	No	Shortstops	No	Outfielders	No
1 Brooks Robinson	16	1 Ozzie Smith	13	1 Roberto Clemente	12
2 Mike Schmidt	10	2 Omar Vizquel	11	Willie Mays	12
3 Scott Rolen	7	3 Luis Aparicio	9	3 Ken Griffey Jr.	10
4 Three tied with 6 each.		4 Mark Belanger	8	Al Kaline	10
		5 Dave Concepcion	5	5 Andruw Jones	9

All-Time Winningest Managers

Top 20 Major League career victories through the 2007 season. Career, regular season and postseason (playoffs and World Series) records are noted along with AL and NL pennants and World Series titles won. Managers active during 2007 season in **bold** type.

		Yrs	Career W	L	Pct	Regular Season W	L	Pct	Postseason W	L	Pct	Titles
1	Connie Mack	53	**3755**	3967	.486	3731	3948	.486	24	19	.558	9 AL, 5 WS
2	John McGraw	33	**2866**	2012	.588	2840	1984	.589	26	28	.482	10 NL, 3 WS
3	**Tony La Russa**	29	**2434**	2118	.535	2375	2070	.534	59	48	.551	3 AL, 2 NL, 2 WS
4	**Bobby Cox**	26	**2321**	1830	.559	2255	1764	.561	66	66	.500	5 NL, 1 WS
5	Sparky Anderson	26	**2228**	1855	.547	2194	1834	.545	34	21	.618	4 NL, 1 AL, 3 WS
6	Bucky Harris	29	**2168**	2228	.493	2157	2218	.493	11	10	.524	3 AL, 2 WS
7	Joe McCarthy	24	**2155**	1346	.616	2125	1333	.615	30	13	.698	1 NL, 8 AL, 7 WS
8	**Joe Torre**	26	**2143**	1820	.541	2067	1770	.539	76	50	.603	6 AL, 4 WS
9	Walter Alston	23	**2063**	1634	.558	2040	1613	.558	23	21	.523	7 NL, 4 WS
10	Leo Durocher	24	**2015**	1717	.540	2008	1709	.540	7	8	.467	3 NL, 1 WS
11	Casey Stengel	25	**1942**	1868	.510	1905	1842	.508	37	26	.587	10 AL, 7 WS
12	Gene Mauch	26	**1907**	2044	.483	1902	2037	.483	5	7	.417	—None—
13	Bill McKechnie	25	**1904**	1737	.523	1896	1723	.524	8	14	.364	4 NL, 2 WS
14	Tommy Lasorda	21	**1630**	1469	.526	1599	1439	.526	31	30	.508	4 NL, 2 WS
15	**Lou Piniella**	20	**1627**	1521	.517	1604	1497	.517	23	24	.489	1 NL, 1 WS
	Ralph Houk	20	**1627**	1539	.514	1619	1531	.514	8	8	.500	3 AL, 3 WS
17	Fred Clarke	19	**1609**	1189	.575	1602	1181	.576	7	8	.467	4 NL, 1 WS
18	Dick Williams	21	**1592**	1474	.519	1571	1451	.520	21	23	.477	3 AL, 1 NL, 2 WS
19	Earl Weaver	17	**1506**	1080	.582	1480	1060	.583	26	20	.565	4 AL, 1 WS
20	Clark Griffith	20	**1491**	1367	.522	1491	1367	.522	0	0	.000	1 AL (1901)

Notes: John McGraw's postseason record also includes two World Series tie games (1912, '22).

Where They Managed

Alston—Brooklyn/Los Angeles NL (1954-76); **Anderson**—Cincinnati NL (1970-78), Detroit AL (1979-95); **Clarke**— Louisville NL (1897-99), Pittsburgh NL (1900-15); **Cox**—Atlanta (1978-81, 1990-), Toronto (1982-85); **Durocher**—Brooklyn NL (1939-46,48), New York NL (1948-55), Chicago NL (1966-72), Houston (1972-73); **Griffith**—Chicago NL (1901-02), New York AL (1903-08), Cincinnati NL (1909-11), Washington AL (1912-20); **Harris**—Washington AL (1924- 28,35-42,50-54), Detroit AL (1929-33,55-56), Boston AL (1934), Philadelphia NL (1943), New York AL (1947-48); **Houk**—New York AL (1961-63,66-73), Detroit AL (1974-78), Boston AL (1981-84); **La Russa**—Chicago AL (1979-86), Oakland (1986-95); St. Louis (1996-). **Lasorda**—Los Angeles NL (1976-96); **Mack**—Pittsburgh NL (1894-96), Philadelphia AL (1901-50). **Mauch**—Philadelphia NL (1960-68), Montreal NL (1969-75), Minnesota (1976-80), California AL (1981-82,85-87); **McCarthy**—Chicago NL (1926-30), New York AL (1931-46), Boston AL (1948-50); **McGraw**—Baltimore NL (1899), Baltimore AL (1901-02), New York NL (1902-32); **McKechnie**—Newark FL (1915), Pittsburgh NL (1922-26), St. Louis NL (1928-29), Boston NL (1930-37), Cincinnati NL (1938-46); **Piniella**—Cincinnati (1990-92), Seattle (1993-2002), Tampa Bay (2003-05), Chicago NL (2007-); **Stengel**—Brooklyn NL (1934-36), Boston NL (1938-43), New York AL (1949-60), New York NL (1962-65); **Torre**—New York NL (1977-81), Atlanta (1982-84), St. Louis (1990-95), New York AL (1996-2007); **Weaver**—Baltimore AL (1968-82,85-86); **Williams**—Boston AL (1967-69), Oakland AL (1971-73), California AL (1974-76), Montreal NL (1977-81), San Diego NL (1982-85), Seattle (1986-88).

Regular Season Winning Pct.

Minimum of 750 victories.

		Yrs	W	L	Pct	Pen
1	Joe McCarthy	24	2125	1333	**.615**	9
2	Charlie Comiskey	12	838	541	**.608**	4
3	Frank Selee	16	1284	862	**.598**	5
4	Billy Southworth	13	1044	704	**.597**	4
5	Frank Chance	11	946	648	**.593**	4
6	John McGraw	33	2840	1984	**.589**	10
7	Al Lopez	17	1410	1004	**.584**	2
8	Earl Weaver	17	1480	1060	**.583**	4
9	Cap Anson	20	1296	947	**.578**	5
10	Fred Clarke	19	1602	1181	**.576**	4
11	Davey Johnson	14	1148	888	**.564**	1
12	**Bobby Cox**	26	2255	1764	**.561**	5
13	Steve O'Neill	14	1040	821	**.559**	1
14	Walter Alston	23	2040	1613	**.558**	7
15	Bill Terry	10	823	661	**.555**	3
16	Miller Huggins	17	1413	1134	**.555**	6
17	Billy Martin	16	1253	1013	**.553**	2
18	Harry Wright	18	1000	825	**.548**	3
19	Charlie Grimm	19	1287	1067	**.547**	3
20	Sparky Anderson	26	2194	1834	**.545**	5

World Series Victories

		App	W	L	T	Pct	WS
1	Casey Stengel	10	**37**	26	0	.587	7
2	Joe McCarthy	9	**30**	13	0	.698	7
3	John McGraw	9	**26**	28	2	.482	3
4	Connie Mack	8	**24**	19	0	.558	5
5	**Joe Torre**	6	**21**	11	0	.656	4
6	Walter Alston	7	**20**	20	0	.500	4
7	Miller Huggins	6	**18**	15	1	.544	3
8	Sparky Anderson	5	**16**	12	0	.571	3
9	Tommy Lasorda	4	**12**	11	0	.522	2
	Dick Williams	4	**12**	14	0	.462	2
11	Frank Chance	4	**11**	9	1	.548	2
	Bucky Harris	3	**11**	10	0	.524	2
	Billy Southworth	4	**11**	11	0	.500	2
	Earl Weaver	4	**11**	13	0	.458	1
	Bobby Cox	5	**11**	18	0	.379	1
16	Whitey Herzog	3	**10**	11	0	.476	1
17	**Tony La Russa**	5	**9**	13	0	.409	2
18	Seven tied with eight wins each.						

Active Managers' Records

Regular season games only; through 2007 (updated as of Oct. 25).

National League

		Yrs	W	L	Pct
1	Tony La Russa, St.L.	29	**2375**	2070	.534
2	Bobby Cox, Atl.	26	**2255**	1764	.561
3	Lou Piniella, Chi	20	**1604**	1497	.517
4	Dusty Baker, Cin	14	**1162**	1041	.527
5	Bruce Bochy, SF	13	**1022**	1066	.489
6	Charlie Manuel, Phi	6	**482**	415	.537
7	Clint Hurdle, Col	6	**442**	509	.465
8	Bob Melvin, Ari	5	**399**	411	.493
9	Ned Yost, Mil	5	**374**	435	.462
10	Grady Little, LA	4	**358**	290	.552
11	Willie Randolph, NY	3	**268**	218	.551
12	Bud Black, SD	1	**89**	74	.546
13	Manny Acta, Wash.	1	**73**	89	.451
14	Fredi Gonzalez, Fla.	1	**71**	91	.438
15	Cecil Cooper, Hou. Pittsburgh	1	**15**	16	.484

American League

		Yrs	W	L	Pct
1	Jim Leyland, Det.	16	**1252**	1272	.496
2	Mike Scioscia, Ana.	8	**703**	593	.542
3	Terry Francona, Bos.	8	**660**	636	.509
4	Ron Gardenhire, Min.	6	**534**	437	.550
5	Eric Wedge, Cle.	5	**415**	396	.512
6	Ozzie Guillen, Chi	4	**344**	304	.531
7	John Gibbons, Tor.	4	**270**	266	.504
8	Joe Maddon, TB	4	**154**	221	.411
9	Bob Geren, Oak.	1	**76**	86	.469
10	Ron Washington, Tex.	1	**75**	87	.463
11	John McLaren, Sea	1	**43**	41	.512
12	Dave Tremblay, Bal.	1	**40**	53	.430
13	Trey Hillman, KC New York	0	**0**	0	.000

Annual Awards

MOST VALUABLE PLAYER

There have been three different Most Valuable Player awards in baseball since 1911—the Chalmers Award (1911-14), presented by the Detroit-based automobile company; the League Award (1922-29), presented by the National and American Leagues; and the Baseball Writers' Award (since 1931), presented by the Baseball Writers' Association of America. Statistics for winning players are provided below. Stats for winning pitchers before advent of Cy Young Award are in MVP Pitchers' Statistics table.

Multiple winners: NL—Barry Bonds (7); Roy Campanella, Stan Musial and Mike Schmidt (3); Ernie Banks, Johnny Bench, Rogers Hornsby, Carl Hubbell, Willie Mays, Joe Morgan and Dale Murphy (2). **AL**—Yogi Berra, Joe DiMaggio, Jimmie Foxx and Mickey Mantle (3); Mickey Cochrane, Lou Gehrig, Juan Gonzalez, Hank Greenberg, Walter Johnson, Roger Maris, Hal Newhouser, Cal Ripken Jr., Alex Rodriguez, Frank Thomas, Ted Williams and Robin Yount (2). **NL & AL**—Frank Robinson (2, one in each).

Chalmers Award

National League

Year		Pos	HR	RBI	Avg
1911	Wildfire Schulte, Chi	OF	21	121	.300
1912	Larry Doyle, NY	2B	10	90	.330
1913	Jake Daubert, Bklyn	1B	2	52	.350
1914	Johnny Evers, Bos	2B	1	40	.279

American League

Year		Pos	HR	RBI	Avg
1911	Ty Cobb, Det	OF	8	144	.420
1912	Tris Speaker, Bos	OF	10	98	.383
1913	Walter Johnson, Wash	P	—	—	—
1914	Eddie Collins, Phi	2B	2	85	.344

League Award

National League

Year		Pos	HR	RBI	Avg
1922	No selection				
1923	No selection				
1924	Dazzy Vance, Bklyn	P	—	—	—
1925	Rogers Hornsby, St.L	2B-Mgr	39	143	.403
1926	Bob O'Farrell, St.L	C	7	68	.293
1927	Paul Waner, Pit	OF	9	131	.380
1928	Jim Bottomley, St.L	1B	31	136	.325
1929	Rogers Hornsby, Chi	2B	39	149	.380

American League

Year		Pos	HR	RBI	Avg
1922	George Sisler, St.L	1B	8	105	.420
1923	Babe Ruth, NY	OF	41	131	.393
1924	Walter Johnson, Wash	P	—	—	—
1925	Roger Peckinpaugh, Wash	SS	4	64	.294
1926	George Burns, Cle	1B	4	114	.358
1927	Lou Gehrig, NY	1B	47	175	.373
1928	Mickey Cochrane, Phi	C	10	57	.293
1929	No selection				

Most Valuable Player

National League

Year		Pos	HR	RBI	Avg	Year		Pos	HR	RBI	Avg
1931	Frankie Frisch, St.L	2B	4	82	.311	1951	Roy Campanella, Bklyn	C	33	108	.325
1932	Chuck Klein, Phi	OF	38	137	.348	1952	Hank Sauer, Chi	OF	37	121	.270
1933	Carl Hubbell, NY	P	—	—	—	1953	Roy Campanella, Bklyn	C	41	142	.312
1934	Dizzy Dean, St.L	P	—	—	—	1954	Willie Mays, NY	OF	41	110	.345
1935	Gabby Hartnett, Chi	C	13	91	.344	1955	Roy Campanella, Bklyn	C	32	107	.318
1936	Carl Hubbell, NY	P	—	—	—	1956	Don Newcombe, Bklyn	P	—	—	—
1937	Joe Medwick, St.L	OF	31	154	.374	1957	Hank Aaron, Mil	OF	44	132	.322
1938	Ernie Lombardi, Cin	C	19	95	.342	1958	Ernie Banks, Chi	SS	47	129	.313
1939	Bucky Walters, Cin	P	—	—	—	1959	Ernie Banks, Chi	SS	45	143	.304
1940	Frank McCormick, Cin	1B	19	127	.309	1960	Dick Groat, Pit	SS	2	50	.325
1941	Dolf Camilli, Bklyn	1B	34	120	.285	1961	Frank Robinson, Cin	OF	37	124	.323
1942	Mort Cooper, St.L	P	—	—	—	1962	Maury Wills, LA	SS	6	48	.299
1943	Stan Musial, St.L	OF	13	81	.357	1963	Sandy Koufax, LA	P	—	—	—
1944	Marty Marion, St.L	SS	6	63	.267	1964	Ken Boyer, St.L	3B	24	119	.295
1945	Phil Cavarretta, Chi	1B	6	97	.355	1965	Willie Mays, SF	OF	52	112	.317
1946	Stan Musial, St.L	1B-OF	16	103	.365	1966	Roberto Clemente, Pit	OF	29	119	.317
1947	Bob Elliott, Bos	3B	22	113	.317	1967	Orlando Cepeda, St.L	1B	25	111	.325
1948	Stan Musial, St.L	OF	39	131	.376	1968	Bob Gibson, St.L	P	—	—	—
1949	Jackie Robinson, Bklyn	2B	16	124	.342	1969	Willie McCovey, SF	1B	45	126	.320
1950	Jim Konstanty, Phi	P	—	—	—						

Year		Pos	HR	RBI	Avg	Year		Pos	HR	RBI	Avg
1970	Johnny Bench, Cin	C	45	148	.293	1988	Kirk Gibson, LA	OF	25	76	.290
1971	Joe Torre, St.L	3B	24	137	.363	1989	Kevin Mitchell, SF	OF	47	125	.291
1972	Johnny Bench, Cin	C	40	125	.270	1990	Barry Bonds, Pit	OF	33	114	.301
1973	Pete Rose, Cin	OF	5	64	.338	1991	Terry Pendleton, Atl	3B	22	86	.319
1974	Steve Garvey, LA	1B	21	111	.312	1992	Barry Bonds, Pit	OF	34	103	.311
1975	Joe Morgan, Cin	2B	17	94	.327	1993	Barry Bonds, SF	OF	46	123	.336
1976	Joe Morgan, Cin	2B	27	111	.320	1994	Jeff Bagwell, Hou	1B	39	116	.368
1977	George Foster, Cin	OF	52	149	.320	1995	Barry Larkin, Cin	SS	15	66	.319
1978	Dave Parker, Pit	OF	30	117	.334	1996	Ken Caminiti, SD	3B	40	130	.326
1979	Keith Hernandez, St.L	1B	11	105	.344	1997	Larry Walker, Col	OF	49	130	.366
	Willie Stargell, Pit	1B	32	82	.281	1998	Sammy Sosa, Chi	OF	66	158	.308
1980	Mike Schmidt, Phi	3B	48	121	.286	1999	Chipper Jones, Atl	3B	45	110	.319
1981	Mike Schmidt, Phi	3B	31	91	.316	2000	Jeff Kent, SF	2B	33	125	.334
1982	Dale Murphy, Atl	OF	36	109	.281	2001	Barry Bonds, SF	OF	73	137	.328
1983	Dale Murphy, Atl	OF	36	121	.302	2002	Barry Bonds, SF	OF	46	110	.370
1984	Ryne Sandberg, Chi	2B	19	84	.314	2003	Barry Bonds, SF	OF	45	90	.341
1985	Willie McGee, St.L	OF	10	82	.353	2004	Barry Bonds, SF	OF	45	101	.362
1986	Mike Schmidt, Phi	3B	37	119	.290	2005	Albert Pujols, St.L	1B	41	117	.330
1987	Andre Dawson, Chi	OF	49	137	.287	2006	Ryan Howard, Phi	1B	58	149	.313

American League

Year		Pos	HR	RBI	Avg	Year		Pos	HR	RBI	Avg
1931	Lefty Grove, Phi	P	—	—	—	1969	Harmon Killebrew, Min	3B-1B	49	140	.276
1932	Jimmie Foxx, Phi	1B	58	169	.364	1970	Boog Powell, Bal	1B	35	114	.297
1933	Jimmie Foxx, Phi	1B	48	163	.356	1971	Vida Blue, Oak	P	—	—	—
1934	Mickey Cochrane, Det	C-Mgr	2	76	.320	1972	Dick Allen, Chi	1B	37	113	.308
1935	Hank Greenberg, Det	1B	36	170	.328	1973	Reggie Jackson, Oak	OF	32	117	.293
1936	Lou Gehrig, NY	1B	49	152	.354	1974	Jeff Burroughs, Tex	OF	25	118	.301
1937	Charlie Gehringer, Det	2B	14	96	.371	1975	Fred Lynn, Bos	OF	21	105	.331
1938	Jimmie Foxx, Bos	1B	50	175	.349	1976	Thurman Munson, NY	C	17	105	.302
1939	Joe DiMaggio, NY	OF	30	126	.381	1977	Rod Carew, Min	1B	14	100	.388
1940	Hank Greenberg, Det	OF	41	150	.340	1978	Jim Rice, Bos	OF-DH	46	139	.315
1941	Joe DiMaggio, NY	OF	30	125	.357	1979	Don Baylor, Cal	OF-DH	36	139	.296
1942	Joe Gordon, NY	2B	18	103	.322	1980	George Brett, KC	3B	24	118	.390
1943	Spud Chandler, NY	P	—	—	—	1981	Rollie Fingers, Mil	P	—	—	—
1944	Hal Hewhouser, Det	P	—	—	—	1982	Robin Yount, Mil	SS	29	114	.331
1945	Hal Newhouser, Det	P	—	—	—	1983	Cal Ripken Jr., Bal	SS	27	102	.318
1946	Ted Williams, Bos	OF	38	123	.342	1984	Willie Hernandez, Det	P	—	—	—
1947	Joe DiMaggio, NY	OF	20	97	.315	1985	Don Mattingly, NY	1B	35	145	.324
1948	Lou Boudreau, Cle	SS-Mgr	18	106	.355	1986	Roger Clemens, Bos	P	—	—	—
1949	Ted Williams, Bos	OF	43	159	.343	1987	George Bell, Tor	OF	47	134	.308
1950	Phil Rizzuto, NY	SS	7	66	.324	1988	Jose Canseco, Oak	OF	42	124	.307
1951	Yogi Berra, NY	C	27	88	.294	1989	Robin Yount, Mil	OF	21	103	.318
1952	Bobby Shantz, Phi	P	—	—	—	1990	Rickey Henderson, Oak	OF	28	61	.325
1953	Al Rosen, Cle	3B	43	145	.336	1991	Cal Ripken Jr., Bal	SS	34	114	.323
1954	Yogi Berra, NY	C	22	125	.307	1992	Dennis Eckersley, Oak	P	—	—	—
1955	Yogi Berra, NY	C	27	108	.272	1993	Frank Thomas, Chi	1B	41	128	.317
1956	Mickey Mantle, NY	OF	52	130	.353	1994	Frank Thomas, Chi	1B	38	101	.353
1957	Mickey Mantle, NY	OF	34	94	.365	1995	Mo Vaughn, Bos	1B	39	126	.300
1958	Jackie Jensen, Bos	OF	35	122	.286	1996	Juan Gonzalez, Tex	OF-DH	47	144	.314
1959	Nellie Fox, Chi	2B	2	70	.306	1997	Ken Griffey Jr., Sea	OF	56	147	.304
1960	Roger Maris, NY	OF	39	112	.283	1998	Juan Gonzalez, Tex	OF	45	157	.318
1961	Roger Maris, NY	OF	61	142	.269	1999	Ivan Rodriguez, Tex	C	35	113	.332
1962	Mickey Mantle, NY	OF	30	89	.321	2000	Jason Giambi, Oak	1B	43	137	.333
1963	Elston Howard, NY	C	28	85	.287	2001	Ichiro Suzuki, Sea	OF	8	69	.350
1964	Brooks Robinson, Bal	3B	28	118	.317	2002	Miguel Tejada, Oak	SS	34	131	.308
1965	Zoilo Versalles, Min	SS	19	77	.273	2003	Alex Rodriguez, Tex	SS	47	118	.298
1966	Frank Robinson, Bal	OF	49	122	.316	2004	Vladimir Guerrero, Ana	OF	39	126	.337
1967	Carl Yastrzemski, Bos	OF	44	121	.326	2005	Alex Rodriguez, NY	3B	48	130	.321
1968	Denny McLain, Det	P	—	—	—	2006	Justin Morneau, Min	1B	34	130	.321

MVP Pitchers' Statistics

Pitchers have been named Most Valuable Player on 23 occasions, 10 times in the NL and 13 in the AL. Four have been relief pitchers—Jim Konstanty, Rollie Fingers, Willie Hernandez and Dennis Eckersley. For statistics of MVP pitchers since 1956, see Cy Young Award tables on following page.

National League

Year		Gm	W-L	SV	ERA
1924	Dazzy Vance, Bklyn	.35	28-6	0	2.16
1933	Carl Hubbell, NY	.45	23-12	5	1.66
1934	Dizzy Dean, St.L	.50	30-7	7	2.66
1936	Carl Hubbell, NY	.42	26-6	3	2.31
1939	Bucky Walters, Cin	.39	27-11	0	2.29
1942	Mort Cooper, St.L	.37	22-7	0	1.78
1950	Jim Konstanty, Phi	.74	16-7	22	2.66

American League

Year		Gm	W-L	SV	ERA
1913	Walter Johnson, Wash	.47	36-7	2	1.09
1924	Walter Johnson, Wash	.38	23-7	0	2.72
1931	Lefty Grove, Phi	.41	31-4	5	2.06
1943	Spud Chandler, NY	.30	20-4	0	1.64
1944	Hal Hewhouser, Det	.47	29-9	2	2.22
1945	Hal Newhouser, Det	.40	25-9	2	1.81
1952	Bobby Shantz, Phi	.33	24-7	0	2.48

CY YOUNG AWARD

Voted on by the Baseball Writers Association of America. One award was presented from 1956-66, two since 1967. Pitchers who won the MVP and Cy Young awards in the same season are in **bold** type.

Multiple winners: NL—Steve Carlton, Greg Maddux and Randy Johnson (4); Sandy Koufax and Tom Seaver (3); Bob Gibson and Tom Glavine (2). **AL**—Roger Clemens (6); Jim Palmer (3); Pedro Martinez, Denny McLain and Johan Santana (2). **NL & AL**—Roger Clemens (7, six in AL, one in NL); Randy Johnson (5, four in NL, one in AL), Pedro Martinez (3, two in AL, one in NL) and Gaylord Perry (2, one in each).

NL and AL Combined

Year	National League	Gm	W-L	SV	ERA	Year	American League	Gm	W-L	SV	ERA
1956	**Don Newcombe**, Bklyn	38	27-7	0	3.06	1958	Bob Turley, NY	33	21-7	1	2.97
1957	Warren Spahn, Mil	39	21-11	3	2.69	1959	Early Wynn, Chi	37	22-10	0	3.17
1960	Vernon Law, Pit	35	20-9	0	3.08	1961	Whitey Ford, NY	39	25-4	0	3.21
1962	Don Drysdale, LA	43	25-9	1	2.83	1964	Dean Chance, LA	46	20-9	4	1.65
1963	**Sandy Koufax**, LA	40	25-5	0	1.88						
1965	Sandy Koufax, LA	43	26-8	2	2.04						
1966	Sandy Koufax, LA	41	27-9	0	1.73						

Separate League Awards

	National League					American League				
Year		Gm	W-L	SV	ERA	Year		Gm	W-L	SV	ERA
1967	Mike McCormick, SF	40	22-10	0	2.85	1967	Jim Lonborg, Bos	39	22-9	0	3.16
1968	**Bob Gibson**, St.L	34	22-9	0	1.12	1968	**Denny McLain**, Det	41	31-6	0	1.96
1969	Tom Seaver, NY	36	25-7	0	2.21	1969	Denny McLain, Det	42	24-9	0	2.80
1970	Bob Gibson, St.L	34	23-7	0	3.12		Mike Cuellar, Bal	39	23-11	0	2.38
1971	Ferguson Jenkins, Chi	39	24-13	0	2.77	1970	Jim Perry, Min	40	24-12	0	3.03
1972	Steve Carlton, Phi	41	27-10	0	1.97	1971	**Vida Blue**, Oak	39	24-8	0	1.82
1973	Tom Seaver, NY	36	19-10	0	2.08	1972	Gaylord Perry, Cle	41	24-16	1	1.92
1974	Mike Marshall, LA	106	15-12	21	2.42	1973	Jim Palmer, Bal	38	22-9	1	2.40
1975	Tom Seaver, NY	36	22-9	0	2.38	1974	Catfish Hunter, Oak	41	25-12	0	2.49
1976	Randy Jones, SD	40	22-14	0	2.74	1975	Jim Palmer, Bal	39	23-11	1	2.09
1977	Steve Carlton, Phi	36	23-10	0	2.64	1976	Jim Palmer, Bal	40	22-13	0	2.51
1978	Gaylord Perry, SD	37	21-6	0	2.72	1977	Sparky Lyle, NY	72	13-5	26	2.17
1979	Bruce Sutter, Chi	62	6-6	37	2.23	1978	Ron Guidry, NY	35	25-3	0	1.74
1980	Steve Carlton, Phi	38	24-9	0	2.34	1979	Mike Flanagan, Bal	39	23-9	0	3.08
1981	Fernando Valenzuela, LA	25	13-7	0	2.48	1980	Steve Stone, Bal	37	25-7	0	3.23
1982	Steve Carlton, Phi	38	23-11	0	3.10	1981	**Rollie Fingers**, Mil	47	6-3	28	1.04
1983	John Denny, Phi	36	19-6	0	2.37	1982	Pete Vuckovich, Mil	30	18-6	0	3.34
1984	Rick Sutcliffe, Chi	20*	16-1	0	2.69	1983	LaMarr Hoyt, Chi	36	24-10	0	3.66
1985	Dwight Gooden, NY	35	24-4	0	1.53	1984	**Willie Hernandez**, Det	80	9-3	32	1.92
1986	Mike Scott, Hou	37	18-10	0	2.22	1985	Bret Saberhagen, KC	32	20-6	0	2.87
1987	Steve Bedrosian, Phi	65	5-3	40	2.83	1986	**Roger Clemens**, Bos	33	24-4	0	2.48
1988	Orel Hershiser, LA	35	23-8	1	2.26	1987	Roger Clemens, Bos	36	20-9	0	2.97
1989	Mark Davis, SD	70	4-3	44	1.85	1988	Frank Viola, Min	35	24-7	0	2.64
1990	Doug Drabek, Pit	33	22-6	0	2.76	1989	Bret Saberhagen, KC	36	23-6	0	2.16
1991	Tom Glavine, Atl	34	20-11	0	2.55	1990	Bob Welch, Oak	35	27-6	0	2.95
1992	Greg Maddux, Chi	35	20-11	0	2.18	1991	Roger Clemens, Bos	35	18-10	0	2.62
1993	Greg Maddux, Atl	36	20-10	0	2.36	1992	**Dennis Eckersley**, Oak	69	7-1	51	1.91
1994	Greg Maddux, Atl	25	16-6	0	1.56	1993	Jack McDowell, Chi	34	22-10	0	3.37
1995	Greg Maddux, Atl	28	19-2	0	1.63	1994	David Cone, KC	23	16-5	0	2.94
1996	John Smoltz, Atl	35	24-8	0	2.94	1995	Randy Johnson, Sea	30	18-2	0	2.48
1997	Pedro Martinez, Mon	31	17-8	0	1.90	1996	Pat Hentgen, Tor	35	20-10	0	3.22
1998	Tom Glavine, Atl	33	20-6	0	2.47	1997	Roger Clemens, Tor	34	21-7	0	2.05
1999	Randy Johnson, Ari	35	17-9	0	2.48	1998	Roger Clemens, Tor	33	20-6	0	2.65
2000	Randy Johnson, Ari	35	19-7	0	2.64	1999	Pedro Martinez, Bos	31	23-4	0	2.07
2001	Randy Johnson, Ari	35	21-6	0	2.49	2000	Pedro Martinez, Bos	29	18-6	0	1.74
2002	Randy Johnson, Ari	35	24-5	0	2.32	2001	Roger Clemens, NY	33	20-3	0	3.51
2003	Eric Gagne, LA	77	2-3	55	1.20	2002	Barry Zito, Oak	35	23-5	0	2.75
2004	Roger Clemens, Hou	33	18-4	0	2.98	2003	Roy Halladay, Tor	36	22-7	0	3.25
2005	Chris Carpenter, St.L	33	21-5	0	2.83	2004	Johan Santana, Min	34	20-6	0	2.61
2006	Brandon Webb, Ari	33	16-8	0	3.10	2005	Bartolo Colon, LA	33	21-8	0	3.48
						2006	Johan Santana, Min	34	19-6	0	2.77

*NL games only, Sutcliffe pitched 15 games with Cleveland before being traded to the Cubs.

ROOKIE OF THE YEAR

Voted on by the Baseball Writers Assn. of America. One award was presented from 1947-48. Two awards (one for each league) have been presented since 1949. Winners who were also named MVP in the same season are in **bold** type.

NL and AL Combined

Year		Pos	Year		Pos
1947	Jackie Robinson, Brooklyn	1B	1948	Alvin Dark, Boston-NL	SS

National League

Year		Pos	Year		Pos	Year		Pos
1949	Don Newcombe, Bklyn	P	1951	Willie Mays, NY	OF	1953	Jim Gilliam, Bklyn	2B
1950	Sam Jethroe, Bos	OF	1952	Joe Black, Bklyn	P	1954	Wally Moon, St.L	OF

Year		Pos	Year		Pos	Year		Pos
1955	Bill Virdon, St.L	OF	1973	Gary Matthews, SF	OF	1989	Jerome Walton, Chi	OF
1956	Frank Robinson, Cin	OF	1974	Bake McBride, St.L	OF	1990	David Justice, Atl	OF
1957	Jack Sanford, Phi	P	1975	John Montefusco, SF	P	1991	Jeff Bagwell, Hou	1B
1958	Orlando Cepeda, SF	1B	1976	Butch Metzger, SD	P	1992	Eric Karros, LA	1B
1959	Willie McCovey, SF	1B		& Pat Zachry, Cin	P	1993	Mike Piazza, LA	C
1960	Frank Howard, LA	OF	1977	Andre Dawson, Mon	OF	1994	Raul Mondesi, LA	OF
1961	Billy Williams, Chi	OF	1978	Bob Horner, Atl	3B	1995	Hideo Nomo, LA	P
1962	Ken Hubbs, Chi	2B	1979	Rick Sutcliffe, LA	P	1996	Todd Hollandsworth, LA	OF
1963	Pete Rose, Cin	2B	1980	Steve Howe, LA	P	1997	Scott Rolen, Phi	3B
1964	Richie Allen, Phi	3B	1981	Fernando Valenzuela, LA	P	1998	Kerry Wood, Chi	P
1965	Jim Lefebvre, LA	2B	1982	Steve Sax, LA	2B	1999	Scott Williamson, Cin	P
1966	Tommy Helms, Cin	3B	1983	Darryl Strawberry, NY	OF	2000	Rafael Furcal, Atl	SS
1967	Tom Seaver, NY	P	1984	Dwight Gooden, NY	P	2001	Albert Pujols, St.L	OF-3B
1968	Johnny Bench, Cin	C	1985	Vince Coleman, St.L	OF	2002	Jason Jennings, Col	P
1969	Ted Sizemore, LA	2B	1986	Todd Worrell, St.L	P	2003	Dontrelle Willis, Fla	P
1970	Carl Morton, Mon	P	1987	Benito Santiago, SD	C	2004	Jason Bay, Pit	OF
1971	Earl Williams, Atl	C	1988	Chris Sabo, Cin	3B	2005	Ryan Howard, Phi	1B
1972	Jon Matlack, NY	P				2006	Hanley Ramirez, Fla	SS

American League

Year		Pos	Year		Pos	Year		Pos
1949	Roy Sievers, St.L	OF	1969	Lou Piniella, KC	OF	1987	Mark McGwire, Oak	1B
1950	Walt Dropo, Bos	1B	1970	Thurman Munson, NY	C	1988	Walt Weiss, Oak	SS
1951	Gil McDougald, NY	3B	1971	Chris Chambliss, Cle	1B	1989	Gregg Olson, Bal	P
1952	Harry Byrd, Phi	P	1972	Carlton Fisk, Bos	C	1990	Sandy Alomar Jr., Cle	C
1953	Harvey Kuenn, Det	SS	1973	Al Bumbry, Bal	OF	1991	Chuck Knoblauch, Min	2B
1954	Bob Grim, NY	P	1974	Mike Hargrove, Tex	1B	1992	Pat Listach, Mil	SS
1955	Herb Score, Cle	P	1975	**Fred Lynn**, Bos	OF	1993	Tim Salmon, Cal	OF
1956	Luis Aparicio, Chi	SS	1976	Mark Fidrych, Det	P	1994	Bob Hamelin, KC	DH
1957	Tony Kubek, NY	INF-OF	1977	Eddie Murray, Bal	DH-1B	1995	Marty Cordova, Min	OF
1958	Albie Pearson, Wash	OF	1978	Lou Whitaker, Det	2B	1996	Derek Jeter, NY	SS
1959	Bob Allison, Wash	OF	1979	John Castino, Min	3B	1997	Nomar Garciaparra, Bos	SS
1960	Ron Hansen, Bal	SS		& Alfredo Griffin, Tor	SS	1998	Ben Grieve, Oak	OF
1961	Don Schwall, Bos	P	1980	Joe Charboneau, Cle	OF-DH	1999	Carlos Beltran, KC	OF
1962	Tom Tresh, NY	SS-OF	1981	Dave Righetti, NY	P	2000	Kazuhiro Sasaki, Sea	P
1963	Gary Peters, Chi	P	1982	Cal Ripken Jr., Bal	SS-3B	2001	**Ichiro Suzuki**, Sea	OF
1964	Tony Oliva, Min	OF	1983	Ron Kittle, Chi	OF	2002	Eric Hinske, Tor	3B
1965	Curt Blefary, Bal	OF	1984	Alvin Davis, Sea	1B	2003	Angel Berroa, KC	SS
1966	Tommie Agee, Chi	OF	1985	Ozzie Guillen, Chi	SS	2004	Bobby Crosby, Oak	SS
1967	Rod Carew, Min	2B	1986	Jose Canseco, Oak	OF	2005	Huston Street, Oak	P
1968	Stan Bahnsen, NY	P				2006	Justin Verlander, Det	P

MANAGER OF THE YEAR

Voted on by the Baseball Writers Association of America. Two awards (one for each league) presented since 1983. Note that (*) indicates manager's team won division championship and (†) indicates unofficial division won in 1994.

Multiple winners: Bobby Cox and Tony La Russa (4); Dusty Baker and Jim Leyland (3); Sparky Anderson, Tommy Lasorda, Jack McKeon, Lou Piniella, Buck Showalter and Joe Torre (2).

National League

Year		Diff. from previous year		
1983	Tommy Lasorda, LA	88-74	to	91-71*
1984	Jim Frey, Chi	71-91	to	96-75*
1985	Whitey Herzog, St. L	84-78	to	101-61*
1986	Hal Lanier, Hou	83-79	to	96-66*
1987	Buck Rodgers, Mon	78-83	to	91-71
1988	Tommy Lasorda, LA	73-89	to	94-67*
1989	Don Zimmer, Chi	77-85	to	93-69*
1990	Jim Leyland, Pit	74-88	to	95-67*
1991	Bobby Cox, Atl	65-97	to	94-68*
1992	Jim Leyland, Pit	98-64*	to	96-66*
1993	Dusty Baker, SF	72-90	to	103-59
1994	Felipe Alou, Mon	94-68	to	74-40†
1995	Don Baylor, Col	53-64	to	77-67
1996	Bruce Bochy, SD	70-74	to	91-71*
1997	Dusty Baker, SF	68-94	to	90-72
1998	Larry Dierker, Hou	84-78	to	102-60*
1999	Jack McKeon, Cin	77-85	to	96-67
2000	Dusty Baker, SF	86-76	to	97-65*
2001	Larry Bowa, Phi	65-97	to	86-76
2002	Tony La Russa, St.L	93-69	to	97-65*
2003	Jack McKeon, Fla	79-83	to	91-71
2004	Bobby Cox	101-61	to	96-66*
2005	Bobby Cox	96-66*	to	90-72*
2006	Joe Girardi, Fla	83-79	to	78-84

American League

Year		Diff. from previous year		
1983	Tony La Russa, Chi	87-75	to	99-63*
1984	Sparky Anderson, Det	92-70	to	104-58*
1985	Bobby Cox, Tor	89-73	to	99-62*
1986	John McNamara, Bos	81-81	to	95-66*
1987	Sparky Anderson, Det	87-75	to	98-64*
1988	Tony La Russa, Oak	81-81	to	104-58*
1989	Frank Robinson, Bal	54-107	to	87-75
1990	Jeff Torborg, Chi	69-92	to	94-68
1991	Tom Kelly, Min	74-88	to	95-67*
1992	Tony La Russa, Oak	84-78	to	96-66*
1993	Gene Lamont, Chi	86-76	to	94-68*
1994	Buck Showalter, NY	88-74	to	70-43†
1995	Lou Piniella, Sea	49-63	to	79-66*
1996	Joe Torre, NY	79-65	to	92-70
	& Johnny Oates, Tex	74-70	to	90-72
1997	Davey Johnson, Bal	88-74	to	98-64
1998	Joe Torre, NY	96-66	to	114-48*
1999	Jimy Williams, Bos	92-70	to	94-68
2000	Jerry Manuel, Chi	75-86	to	95-67*
2001	Lou Piniella, Sea	91-71	to	116-46*
2002	Mike Scioscia, Ana	75-87	to	99-63
2003	Tony Pena, KC	62-100	to	83-79
2004	Buck Showalter, Tex	71-91	to	89-73
2005	Ozzie Guillen, Chi	83-79	to	99-63*
2006	Jim Leyland, Det	71-91	to	95-67

COLLEGE BASEBALL

College World Series

The NCAA Division I College World Series has been held in Kalamazoo, Mich. (1947-48), Wichita, Kan. (1949) and Omaha, Neb. (since 1950). Beginning in 2003, the championship series has been a best-of-three series.

Multiple winners: USC (12); Texas (6); Arizona St. and LSU (5); CS-Fullerton and Miami-FL (4); Arizona and Minnesota (3); California, Michigan, Oklahoma, Oregon St. and Stanford (2).

Year	Winner	Coach	Score	Runner-up
1947	California	Clint Evans	8-7	Yale
1948	USC	Sam Barry	9-2	Yale
1949	Texas	Bibb Falk	10-3	W. Forest
1950	Texas	Bibb Falk	3-0	Wash. St.
1951	Oklahoma	Jack Baer	3-2	Tennessee
1952	Holy Cross	Jack Barry	8-4	Missouri
1953	Michigan	Ray Fisher	7-5	Texas
1954	Missouri	Hi Simmons	4-1	Rollins
1955	Wake Forest	Taylor Sanford	7-6	W. Mich.
1956	Minnesota	Dick Siebert	12-1	Arizona
1957	California	Geo. Wolfman	1-0	Penn St.
1958	USC	Rod Dedeaux	8-7	Missouri
1959	Oklahoma St.	Toby Greene	5-3	Arizona
1960	Minnesota	Dick Siebert	2-1	USC
1961	USC	Rod Dedeaux	1-0	Okla. St.
1962	Michigan	Don Lund	5-4	S. Clara
1963	USC	Rod Dedeaux	5-2	Arizona
1964	Minnesota	Dick Siebert	5-1	Missouri
1965	Arizona St.	Bobby Winkles	2-1	Ohio St.
1966	Ohio St.	Marty Karow	8-2	Okla. St.
1967	Arizona St.	Bobby Winkles	11-2	Houston
1968	USC	Rod Dedeaux	4-3	So. Ill.
1969	Arizona St.	Bobby Winkles	10-1	Tulsa
1970	USC	Rod Dedeaux	2-1	Fla. St.
1971	USC	Rod Dedeaux	7-2	So. Ill.
1972	USC	Rod Dedeaux	1-0	Ariz. St.
1973	USC	Rod Dedeaux	4-3	Ariz. St.
1974	USC	Rod Dedeaux	7-3	Miami-FL
1975	Texas	Cliff Gustafson	5-1	S. Carolina
1976	Arizona	Jerry Kindall	7-1	E. Michigan
1977	Arizona St.	Jim Brock	2-1	S. Carolina
1978	USC	Rod Dedeaux	10-3	Ariz. St.
1979	CS-Fullerton	Augie Garrido	2-1	Arkansas
1980	Arizona	Jerry Kindall	5-3	Hawaii
1981	Arizona St.	Jim Brock	7-4	Okla. St.
1982	Miami-FL	Ron Fraser	9-3	Wichita St.
1983	Texas	Cliff Gustafson	4-3	Alabama
1984	CS-Fullerton	Augie Garrido	3-1	Texas
1985	Miami-FL	Ron Fraser	10-6	Texas
1986	Arizona	Jerry Kindall	10-2	Fla. St.
1987	Stanford	M. Marquess	9-5	Okla. St.
1988	Stanford	M. Marquess	9-4	Ariz. St.
1989	Wichita St.	G. Stephenson	5-3	Texas
1990	Georgia	Steve Webber	2-1	Okla. St.
1991	LSU	Skip Bertman	6-3	Wichita St.
1992	Pepperdine	Andy Lopez	3-2	CS-Fullerton
1993	LSU	Skip Bertman	8-0	Wichita St.
1994	Oklahoma	Larry Cochell	13-5	Ga. Tech
1995	CS-Fullerton	Augie Garrido	11-5	USC
1996	LSU	Skip Bertman	9-8	Miami-FL
1997	LSU	Skip Bertman	13-6	Alabama
1998	USC	Mike Gillespie	21-14	Arizona St.
1999	Miami-FL	Jim Morris	6-5	Fla. St.
2000	LSU	Skip Bertman	6-5	Stanford
2001	Miami-FL	Jim Morris	12-1	Stanford
2002	Texas	Augie Garrido	12-6	S. Carolina
2003	Rice	Wayne Graham	4-3 / 3-8 / 14-2	Stanford
2004	CS-Fullerton	George Horton	6-4 / 3-2	Texas
2005	Texas	Augie Garrido	4-2 / 6-2	Florida
2006	Oregon St.	Pat Casey	3-4 / 11-7 / 3-2	N. Carolina
2007	Oregon St.	Pat Casey	11-4 / 9-3	N. Carolina

Most Outstanding Player

The Most Outstanding Player has been selected every year of the College World Series since 1949. Winners who did not play for the CWS champion are listed in **bold** type. No player has won the award more than once.

Year		
1949 **Charles Teague,** W. Forest, 2B	1970 **Gene Ammann,** Fla. St., P	1991 Gary Hymel, LSU, C
1950 **Ray VanCleef,** Rutgers, CF	1971 **Jerry Tabb,** Tulsa, 1B	1992 **Phil Nevin,** CS-Fullerton, 3B
1951 **Sidney Hatfield,** Tenn., P-1B	1972 Russ McQueen, USC, P	1993 Todd Walker, LSU, 2B
1952 James O'Neill, Holy Cross, P	1973 **Dave Winfield,** Minn., P-OF	1994 Chip Glass, Oklahoma, OF
1953 **J.L. Smith,** Texas, P	1974 George Milke, USC, P	1995 Mark Kotsay, CS-Fullerton, OF
1954 **Tom Yewcic,** Mich. St., C	1975 Mickey Reichenbach, Texas, 1B	1996 **Pat Burrell,** Miami-FL, 3B
1955 **Tom Borland,** Okla. St., P	1976 Steve Powers, Arizona, P-DH	1997 Brandon Larson, LSU, SS
1956 Jerry Thomas, Minn., P	1977 Bob Horner, Ariz. St., 3B	1998 Wes Rachels, USC, 2B
1957 **Cal Emery,** Penn St., P-1B	1978 Rod Boxberger, USC, P	1999 **Marshall McDougall,** Fla. St., 2B
1958 Bill Thom, USC, P	1979 Tony Hudson, CS-Fullerton, P	
1959 Jim Dobson, Okla. St., 3B	1980 Terry Francona, Arizona, LF	2000 Trey Hodges, LSU, P
1960 John Erickson, Minn., 2B	1981 Stan Holmes, Ariz. St., LF	2001 Charlton Jimerson, Miami-FL, CF
1961 **Littleton Fowler,** Okla. St., P	1982 Dan Smith, Miami-FL, P	2002 Huston Street, Texas, P
1962 **Bob Garibaldi,** Santa Clara, P	1983 Calvin Schiraldi, Texas, P	2003 **John Hudgins,** Stanford, P
1963 Bud Hollowell, USC, C	1984 John Fishel, CS-Fullerton, LF	2004 Jason Windsor, CS-Fullerton, P
1964 **Joe Ferris,** Maine, P	1985 Greg Ellena, Miami-FL, LF	2005 David Maroul, Texas, 3B
1965 Sal Bando, Ariz. St., 3B	1986 Mike Senne, Arizona, DH	2006 Jonah Nickerson, Oregon St., P
1966 Steve Arlin, Ohio St., P	1987 Paul Carey, Stanford, RF	2007 Jorge Reyes, Oregon St., P
1967 Ron Davini, Ariz. St., C	1988 Lee Plemel, Stanford, P	
1968 Bill Seinsoth, USC, 1B	1989 Greg Brummett, Wich. St., P	
1969 John Dolinsek, Ariz. St., LF	1990 Mike Rebhan, Georgia, P	

Annual Awards
Golden Spikes Award

First presented in 1978 by USA Baseball, honoring the nation's best amateur player; sponsored by the Major League Baseball Players Association. Alex Fernandez, the 1990 winner, has been the only junior college player chosen.

Year		Year		Year	
1978	Bob Horner, Ariz. St, 2B	1988	Robin Ventura, Okla. St., 3B	1998	Pat Burrell, Miami-FL, 3B
1979	Tim Wallach, CS-Fullerton, 1B	1989	Ben McDonald, LSU, P	1999	Jason Jennings, Baylor, DH/P
1980	Terry Francona, Arizona, OF	1990	Alex Fernandez, Miami-Dade, P	2000	Kip Bouknight, South Carolina, P
1981	Mike Fuentes, Fla. St., OF	1991	Mike Kelly, Ariz. St., OF	2001	Mark Prior, USC, P
1982	Augie Schmidt, N. Orleans, SS	1992	Phil Nevin, CS-Fullerton, 3B	2002	Khalil Greene, Clemson, SS
1983	Dave Magadan, Alabama, 1B	1993	Darren Dreifort, Wichita St., P	2003	Rickie Weeks, Southern, 2B
1984	Oddibe McDowell, Ariz. St., OF	1994	Jason Varitek, Ga. Tech, C	2004	Jered Weaver, Long Beach St., P
1985	Will Clark, Miss. St., 1B	1995	Mark Kotsay, CS-Fullerton, OF	2005	Alex Gordon, Nebraska, IF
1986	Mike Loynd, Fla. St., P	1996	Travis Lee, San Diego St., 1B	2006	Tim Lincecum, Washington, P
1987	Jim Abbott, Michigan, P	1997	J.D. Drew, Florida St., OF	2007	David Price, Vanderbilt, P

Baseball America Player of the Year

Presented to the College Player of the Year since 1981 by *Baseball America.*

Year		Year		Year	
1981	Mike Sodders, Ariz. St., 3B	1990	Mike Kelly, Ariz. St., OF	1999	Jason Jennings, Baylor, DH/P
1982	Jeff Ledbetter, Fla. St., OF/P	1991	David McCarty, Stanford, 1B	2000	Mark Teixeira, Ga. Tech, 3B
1983	Dave Magadan, Alabama, 1B	1992	Phil Nevin, CS-Fullerton, 3B	2001	Mark Prior, USC, P
1984	Oddibe McDowell, Ariz. St., OF	1993	Brooks Kieschnick, Texas, DH/P	2002	Khalil Greene, Clemson, SS
1985	Pete Incaviglia, Okla. St., OF	1994	Jason Varitek, Ga. Tech, C	2003	Rickie Weeks, Southern, 2B
1986	Casey Close, Michigan, OF	1995	Todd Helton, Tenn., 1B/P	2004	Jered Weaver, Long Beach St., P
1987	Robin Ventura, Okla. St., 3B	1996	Kris Benson, Clemson, P	2005	Alex Gordon, Nebraska, IF
1988	John Olerud, Wash. St., 1B/P	1997	J.D. Drew, Florida St., OF	2006	Andrew Miller, N. Carolina, P
1989	Ben McDonald, LSU, P	1998	Jeff Austin, Stanford, P	2007	David Price, Vanderbilt, P

Dick Howser Trophy

Presented to the College Player of the Year since 1987, by the American Baseball Coaches Association (ABCA) from 1987-98 and the National Collegiate Baseball Writers Association (NCBWA) beginning in 1999. Founded and owned by the St. Petersburg (Fla.) Area Chamber of Commerce. Named after the late two-time All-America shortstop and college coach at Florida State. Howser was also a major league manager with Kansas City and the New York Yankees.

Multiple winner: Brooks Kieschnick (2).

Year		Year		Year	
1987	Mike Fiore, Miami-FL, OF	1994	Jason Varitek, Ga. Tech, C	2001	Mark Prior, USC, P
1988	Robin Ventura, Okla. St., 3B	1995	Todd Helton, Tenn., 1B/P	2002	Khalil Greene, Clemson, SS
1989	Scott Bryant, Texas, DH	1996	Kris Benson, Clemson, P	2003	Rickie Weeks, Southern, 2B
1990	Paul Ellis, UCLA, C	1997	J.D. Drew, Florida St., OF	2004	Jered Weaver, Long Beach St., P
1991	Bobby Jones, Fresno St., P	1998	Eddie Furniss, LSU, 1B	2005	Alex Gordon, Nebraska, IF
1992	Brooks Kieschnick, Texas, DH/P	1999	Jason Jennings, Baylor, DH/P	2006	Brad Lincoln, Houston, P/UT
1993	Brooks Kieschnick, Texas, DH/P	2000	Mark Teixeira, Ga. Tech, 3B	2007	David Price, Vanderbilt, P

Baseball America Coach of the Year

Presented to the College Coach of the Year since 1981 by *Baseball America.*

Multiple winners: Skip Bertman, Augie Garrido, Dave Snow and Gene Stephenson (2).

Year		Year		Year	
1981	Ron Fraser, Miami-FL	1990	Steve Webber, Georgia	2000	Ray Tanner, S. Carolina
1982	Gene Stephenson, Wichita St.	1991	Jim Hendry, Creighton	2001	Dave Van Horn, Nebraska
1983	Barry Shollenberger, Alabama	1992	Andy Lopez, Pepperdine	2002	Augie Garrido, Texas
1984	Augie Garrido, CS-Fullerton	1993	Gene Stephenson, Wichita St.	2003	George Horton, CS-Fullerton
1985	Ron Polk, Mississippi St.	1994	Jim Morris, Miami-FL	2004	Dave Perno, Georgia
1986	Skip Bertman, LSU	1995	Rod Delmonico, Tennessee	2005	Rick Jones, Tulane
	& Dave Snow, Loyola-CA	1996	Skip Bertman, LSU	2006	Pat Casey, Oregon St.
1987	Mark Marquess, Stanford	1997	Jim Wells, Alabama	2007	Dave Serrano, UC Irvine
1988	Jim Brock, Arizona St.	1998	Pat Murphy, Arizona St.		
1989	Dave Snow, Long Beach St.	1999	Wayne Graham, Rice		

All-Time Winningest Division I Coaches

Coaches active in 2007 are in **bold** type. Records given are for four-year colleges only. For winning percentage, a minimum 10 years in Division I is required.

Top 10 Winning Percentage

		Yrs	W	L	T	Pct
1	John Barry	.40	619	146	5	.807
2	Cliff Gustafson	.29	1427	373	2	.792
3	Harry Carlson	.17	143	41	0	.777
4	Bobby Winkles	.13	524	173	0	.752
5	**Gene Stephenson**	.30	1605	533	3	.750
6	**Mike Martin**	.28	1484	506	4	.745
7	Frank Sancet	.23	831	283	8	.744
8	Bob Wren	.23	464	160	4	.742
9	George Jacobs	.11	106	37	0	.741
10	Ron Fraser	.30	1267	440	9	.741

Top 10 Victories

		Yrs	W	L	T	Pct
1	**Augie Garrido**	.39	**1629**	755	8	.683
2	**Gene Stephenson**	.30	**1605**	533	3	.750
3	**Mike Martin**	.28	**1484**	506	4	.745
4	**Larry Hays**	.37	**1483**	830	3	.641
5	Chuck Hartman	.47	**1444**	816	8	.638
6	Cliff Gustafson	.29	**1427**	373	2	.792
7	**Ron Polk**	.34	**1351**	669	2	.669
8	Rod Dedeaux	.44	**1342**	597	16	.691
9	Larry Cochell	.39	**1330**	814	3	.620
10	Bob Bennett	.34	**1300**	757	8	.631

Other NCAA Champions

Division II

Multiple winners: Florida Southern (9); Tampa (5); Cal Poly Pomona (3); Central Missouri St., CS-Chico, CS-Northridge, Jacksonville St., Troy St., UC-Irvine and UC-Riverside (2).

Year		Year		Year		Year	
1968	Chapman, CA	1978	Florida Southern	1988	Florida Southern	1998	Tampa
1969	Illinois St.	1979	Valdosta St., GA	1989	Cal Poly SLO	1999	CS-Chico
1970	CS-Northridge	1980	Cal Poly Pomona	1990	Jacksonville St., AL	2000	Southeastern Okla.
1971	Florida Southern	1981	Florida Southern	1991	Jacksonville St., AL	2001	St. Mary's, TX
1972	Florida Southern	1982	UC-Riverside	1992	Tampa	2002	Columbus St., GA
1973	UC-Irvine	1983	Cal Poly Pomona	1993	Tampa	2003	Central Missouri St.
1974	UC-Irvine	1984	CS-Northridge	1994	Central Missouri St.	2004	Delta St., MS
1975	Florida Southern	1985	Florida Southern	1995	Florida Southern	2005	Florida Southern
1976	Cal Poly Pomona	1986	Troy St., AL	1996	Kennesaw St., GA	2006	Tampa
1977	UC-Riverside	1987	Troy St., AL	1997	CS-Chico	2007	Tampa

Division III

Multiple winners: Eastern Conn. St. and Marietta (4); Montclair St. (3); CS-Stanislaus, Glassboro St., Ithaca, NC-Wesleyan, Southern Maine and Wm. Paterson, NJ (2).

Year		Year		Year		Year	
1976	CS-Stanislaus	1984	Ramapo, NJ	1992	Wm. Paterson, NJ	2000	Montclair St., NJ
1977	CS-Stanislaus	1985	Wisconsin-Oshkosh	1993	Montclair St., NJ	2001	St. Thomas, MN
1978	Glassboro St., NJ	1986	Marietta, OH	1994	Wisconsin-Oshkosh	2002	Eastern Conn. St.
1979	Glassboro St., NJ	1987	Monclair St., NJ	1995	La Verne, CA	2003	Chapman, CA
1980	Ithaca, NY	1988	Ithaca, NY	1996	Wm. Paterson, NJ	2004	George Fox, OR
1981	Marietta, OH	1989	NC-Wesleyan	1997	Southern Maine	2005	Wis.-Whitewater
1982	Eastern Conn. St.	1990	Eastern Conn. St.	1998	Eastern Conn. St.	2006	Marietta, OH
1983	Marietta, OH	1991	Southern Maine	1999	NC-Wesleyan	2007	Kean, NJ

Major League Number One Draft Picks

The Major League First-Year Player Draft has been held every year since 1965. Clubs select in reverse order of their won-loss records from the previous regular season. Until 2005, the National League and American League teams alternated, with AL teams selecting first in odd years and NL teams going first in even years. Now, league affiliation does not come into play.

Year		Pos	Team	Year		Pos	Team
1965	Rick Monday	OF	Kansas City Athletics	1987	Ken Griffey Jr.	OF	Seattle Mariners
1966	Steve Chilcott	C	New York Mets	1988	Andy Benes	P	San Diego Padres
1967	Rom Blomberg	1B	New York Yankees	1989	Ben McDonald	P	Baltimore Orioles
1968	Tim Foli	IF	New York Mets	1990	Chipper Jones	SS	Atlanta Braves
1969	Jeff Burroughs	OF	Washington Senators	1991	Brien Taylor	P	New York Yankees
1970	Mike Ivie	C	San Diego Padres	1992	Phil Nevin	3B	Houston Astros
1971	Danny Goodwin	C	Chicago White Sox	1993	Alex Rodriguez	SS	Seattle Mariners
1972	Dave Roberts	IF	San Diego Padres	1994	Paul Wilson	P	New York Mets
1973	David Clyde	P	Texas Rangers	1995	Darin Erstad	OF/P	California Angels
1974	Bill Almon	IF	San Diego Padres	1996	Kris Benson	P	Pittsburgh Pirates
1975	Danny Goodwin	C	California Angels	1997	Matt Anderson	P	Detroit Tigers
1976	Floyd Bannister	P	Houston Astros	1998	Pat Burrell	3B	Philadelphia Phillies
1977	Harold Baines	OF	Chicago White Sox	1999	Josh Hamilton	OF	T.B. Devil Rays
1978	Bob Horner	3B	Atlanta Braves	2000	Adrian Gonzalez	1B	Florida Marlins
1979	Al Chambers	OF	Seattle Mariners	2001	Joe Mauer	C	Minnesota Twins
1980	Darryl Strawberry	OF	New York Mets	2002	Bryan Bullington	P	Pittsburgh Pirates
1981	Mike Moore	P	Seattle Mariners	2003	Delmon Young	OF	T.B. Devil Rays
1982	Shawon Dunston	SS	Chicago Cubs	2004	Matt Bush	SS	San Diego Padres
1983	Tim Belcher	P	Minnesota Twins	2005	Justin Upton	SS	Ariz. Diamondbacks
1984	Shawn Abner	OF	New York Mets	2006	Luke Hochevar	P	Kansas City Royals
1985	B.J. Surhoff	C	Milwaukee Brewers	2007	David Price	P	T.B. Devil Rays
1986	Jeff King	IF	Pittsburgh Pirates				

COLLEGE FOOTBALL

2006 / 2007 YEAR IN REVIEW

Urban Meyer brought some bite to the Gators and won a national title in just his second season at Florida.

GATOR RAID

The underdog Florida Gators ate up Heisman-winning quarterback Troy Smith and the powerhouse Ohio State Buckeyes.

IN A HALF HOUR, CAN EVERYTHING YOU THOUGHT YOU KNEW ABOUT AN UNDEFEATED, TOP-RATED TEAM BE SHATTERED?

Can a proven big game stud and Heisman trophy quarterback morph into a rattled, intimidated rookie? Can the swaggering winners of 19 straight so quickly seem disorganized and defeated?

Of course. This is the BCS Championship game, where experts' forecasts are usually cloudy and hindsight is crystal clear. Where seven weeks of hearing you won't win is proven and powerful motivation. Where what you thought you knew is wiped away and replaced by what you should have figured out all along.

Yes, on this night Florida was that good...that sharp...that creative... and that speedy. The underdog Gators reduced Ohio State to a ghost of itself. A proud, previously perfect team looked mentally whipped well before halftime.

No team has ever trailed a championship game after 16 seconds. Florida's response after Ted Ginn's blistering return of the opening kickoff was just the first clue to their readiness.

The brilliant offensive game plan was unleashed immediately—and the Gators' first 16 plays produced positive yards. In the weeks of preparation, Urban Meyer had to temper his urge to overdose on new wrinkles. Trusted offensive coordinator Dan Mullen kept things in check. Together, they mixed in just the perfect amount of trickery to fully baffle the Bucks.

In the first quarter, the Gators achieved a play-calling rhythm that was breathtaking. So was Chris Leak's execution. A confused defense is a passive, slow defense and Ohio State was playing this game in ankle weights and concrete galoshes. Florida's five-receiver sets created mismatches everywhere and

Chris Fowler is the host of ESPN's College GameDay

The **Florida Defense** really got to Ohio State's **Troy Smith,** who had the worst day of his stellar career as a Buckeye.

Leak found holes in the Bucks' zone all night.

Ohio State's offensive line looked like wounded water buffaloes, too, as Florida defensive ends Jarvis Moss and Derrick Harvey made cheetah-like rushes around the ends to pounce on poor Troy Smith.

Before kickoff, I had considered Smith one of the best big game quarterbacks in college history. Smith saved his worst performance for his last one—two turnovers and just four completions. Confronted with the Gators' speed, Smith looked like a plodder.

Sadly, the NFL draft stock of this classy guy evaporated in a couple of hours. It wasn't all Smith's fault. With Ginn lost to an ankle injury very early, Ohio State seemed to have no answers.

The stat sheet stunner was the Buckeyes' measly 82 yards of total offense!

I truly admire Meyer's boldness in his biggest game ever. At 42, he sits on the pinnacle of his profession. He molded a talented but fractured team inherited from Ron Zook into a football family that truly cares for each other.

It wasn't easy. After their lone loss at Auburn, the Gators turned on eachother in the locker room. There was hollering and finger pointing.

Meyer prevented his assistants from stopping this. He wanted all the

Oklahoma couldn't bring down Boise State's **Ian Johnson** when it counted at the Fiesta Bowl. It took a postgame proposal to his girlfriend to get him off his feet.

go 13-1, well they deserved it. Their schedule in the nation's toughest conference seemed too brutal to navigate.

The Gators' romp was not an endorsement for the existing BCS system. Without the gift of UCLA's surprising upset of #2 USC on the regular season's final weekend, Florida would not have been provided the opportunity to display its superiority. Plus, the January 8 game created a 50-day layoff for Ohio State, perhaps a factor in the Buckeyes' performance.

Turns out, the game most fans really wanted to see after the bowls was Florida vs. the Trojans, whose Rose Bowl humiliation of Michigan left me wondering how they'd blown the UCLA game.

Then again, I walked away from Glendale and the 2007 season wondering about a lot of things, including how another team in blue and orange that had used bold creativity to pull an upset on the same field a week earlier might have fared in a championship playoff.

Boise State's thrilling overtime Fiesta Bowl win over Oklahoma gave rise to among other things, an EA Sports commercial and a postgame marriage proposal.

Isn't the end of the season supposed to provide more clarity than questions? Oh wait, we are talking about college football.

built-up frustration to be vented, so that the team could move forward. It worked. Florida found unity and a renewed hunger the following week. At a crucial point in the season, Meyer showed the perfect coaching instinct. Without it, the Gators could have unraveled.

If the Gators needed more than a sliver of luck (a blocked field goal vs. South Carolina, self-destructing turnovers by LSU and Arkansas) to

LEE CORSO'S

10

Biggest Stories of the Year in **College Football**

10 Miami–Florida International Brawl.

It was a black eye in what was a disappointing season for the Miami Hurricanes. Following a Miami touchdown in which a personal foul was assessed, the Miami holder was basically attacked and what ensued was an ugly fight that resulted in 31 suspensions. Who knows what lasting effect it had on both teams' seasons? FIU suffered through a winless season and Miami had their worst season since probation. Both coaches would eventually lose their jobs at season's end.

09 Troy Smith.

He wasn't the biggest QB – or the fastest – but a 30-to-five touchdown to interception ratio, big play after big play and a perfect career record as a starter against the rival Wolverines helped make Troy Smith the sixth different Buckeye to capture the Heisman Trophy. Smith's career ended on a down note with a loss to Florida in the BCS championship game, but that should not diminish what Smith accomplished at Ohio State.

08 Fisher DeBerry retires.

The man who made Air Force the most successful military academy on the football field stepped aside after 23 seasons as a head coach. At any of the academies, you are judged by how you do against the others and Fisher DeBerry was an amazing 35-11 against Army and Navy and led the Falcons to 14 Commander-in-Chief trophies.

07 Notre Dame bowl losing streak.

Not only did Notre Dame's loss to LSU mark the second straight year (and the third time since 2001) that the Irish suffered a sound defeat in a BCS Bowl, it marked the NCAA-record ninth straight time the Irish lost their bowl game. Notre Dame hasn't won a bowl since the 1994 Cotton Bowl. Since then 87 teams have won a bowl game. Yo, Sweetheart!

06 Colt Brennan.

Brennan, a Colorado transfer, enjoyed one of the greatest seasons ever by a college quarterback, throwing for 5,549 yards and 58 touchdowns. By season's end, he broke or tied 18 NCAA records. The face of the Hawaii program made everyone in the Aloha State happy when he announced he would return for his senior season to try and top his remarkable 2006 accomplishments.

Lee Corso is the host of ESPN's College GameDay

05 **Bo Schembechler dies.** On the eve of the biggest Ohio State–Michigan game in years, legendary Michigan coach Bo Schembechler died at age 77. The Ohio native and Woody Hayes disciple helped take the rivalry to the next level in 1969 when he upset Hayes' Buckeyes. Bo won two Rose Bowls and never had a losing season as a head coach, but his presence off the field was what made him truly special.

04 **Rutgers rises.** If you would have told me five years ago that Rutgers would be undefeated and ranked in the top ten in November, I would have told you that you were crazy. But that's where we stood last year. Coach Greg Schiano and the Scarlet Knights were an OT loss at West Virginia away from playing in the BCS. Talk about a turnaround. Remember, Rutgers was 1-11 in 2002. Schiano's decision to stay at Rutgers was great news for Scarlet Knight fans everywhere.

03 **Boise State wins big.** After the national championship and BCS standings fallout, no story was more talked about nationally than Boise State's win over Oklahoma in the Fiesta Bowl to cap off an undefeated season. It wasn't just the win, it was how they won. Talk about a range of emotions. The interception, the comeback, the trick plays, the overtime and the marriage proposal. What a story.

02 **Who's No. 2?** For the fifth time in the BCS era, there was a major controversy as to who should be considered No. 2, Michigan or Florida. Michigan was No. 2 entering the final week of the season, but the Gators' win in the SEC title game was enough to get the pollsters to switch their votes, vaulting them into second. The pollsters ultimately decided they didn't want to see an Ohio State–Michigan rematch in the BCS title game and this controversy didn't end until...

01 **Florida wins national title, dominates Ohio State.** The Gators did what Michigan couldn't. Not only did they beat Ohio State, they dominated every facet of the game. The 41-14 rout ended all doubt as to who belonged in the big game. The Buckeyes had no answer for Florida's speed on defense and mustered just 82 total yards and eight first downs. Heisman winner Troy Smith was sacked five times, and hit just four of 14 passes for 35 yards.

DID YOU KNOW?

>> Of all the I-A programs in the country, it's **Boise State**, not Oklahoma, USC, Texas or Ohio State with the best win-loss record this decade. Entering the 2007 season, the Broncos' 76-13 (.854) record since 2000 was the best in the nation. Oklahoma was second (79-14, .850) but would have been first if they could have held on against Boise State in the 2007 Fiesta Bowl.

2006-2007 Season in Review

Final AP Top 25 Poll

oted on by panel of 65 sportswriters & broadcasters and released on Jan. 9, 2007, following the BCS Title Game: win-
ng team receives the Bear Bryant Trophy, given since 1983; first place votes in parentheses, records, total points (based
n 25 for 1st, 24 for 2nd, etc.) bowl game result, head coach and career record, preseason rank (released Aug. 21, 2006)
nd final regular season rank (released Dec. 3, 2006).

	Final Record	Points	Bowl Game	Head Coach	Aug. 21 Rank	Dec. 3 Rank
1 Florida (64)	13-1	1,624	won BCS	Urban Meyer (6 yrs: 61-12)	7	2
2 Ohio St.	12-1	1,492	lost BCS	Jim Tressel (21 yrs: 197-71-1)	1	1
3 LSU	11-2	1,452	won Sugar	Les Miles (6 yrs: 50-25)	8	4
4 USC	12-1	1,560	won Rose	Pete Carroll (6 yrs: 66-11)	6	8
5 Boise St. (1)	13-0	1,383	won Fiesta	Chris Petersen (1 yr: 13-0)	NR	9
6 Louisville	12-1	1,338	won Orange	Bobby Petrino (4 yrs: 41-9)	13	5
7 Wisconsin	12-1	1,288	won Capital One	Barry Alvarez (16 yrs: 118-73-4)	NR	6
8 Michigan	11-2	1,145	lost Rose	Lloyd Carr (12 yrs: 113-36)	14	3
9 Auburn	11-2	1,112	won Cotton	Tommy Tuberville (11 yrs: 85-47)	4	10
10 West Virginia	11-2	1,035	won Gator	Rich Rodriguez (13 yrs: 84-58-2)	5	13
11 Oklahoma	11-3	933	lost Fiesta	Bob Stoops (7 yrs: 86-19*)	10	7R
12 Rutgers	11-2	884	won Texas	Greg Schiano (6 yrs: 30-41)	NR	16
13 Texas	10-3	772	won Alamo	Mack Brown (23 yrs: 179-96-1)	3	18
14 California	10-3	697	won Holiday	Jeff Tedford (5 yrs: 43-20)	9	20
15 Arkansas	10-4	677	lost Capital One	Houston Nutt (14 yrs: 103-66)	NR	12
16 Brigham Young	11-2	673	won Las Vegas	Bronco Mendenhall (2 yrs: 17-8)	NR	19
17 Notre Dame	10-3	553	lost Sugar	Charlie Weis (2 yrs: 19-6)	2	11
18 Wake Forest	11-3	551	lost Orange	Jim Grobe (12 yrs: 70-68-1)	NR	15
19 Virginia Tech	10-3	407	lost Chick Fil-A	Frank Beamer (26 yrs: 198-105-4)	17	14
20 Boston College	10-3	353	won Meineke	Tom O'Brien (10 yrs: 76-45)	NR	23
21 Oregon St.	10-4	291	won Sun	Mike Riley (6 yrs: 38-34)	NR	24
22 TCU	11-2	279	won Poinsettia	Gary Patterson (7 yrs: 54-20)	22	25
23 Georgia	9-4	204	won Chick Fil-A	Mark Richt (6 yrs: 61-17)	15	NR
24 Penn St.	9-4	183	won Outback	Joe Paterno (41 yrs: 363-121-3)	19	NR
25 Tennessee	9-4	181	lost Outback	Philip Fulmer (15 yrs: 137-41)	23	17

Other teams receiving votes: 26. **Hawaii** (11-3, won Hawaii, 110 pts); 27. **Nebraska** (9-5, lost Cotton, 58 pts); 28.
Maryland (9-4, won Champs Sports, 24 pts); 29. **South Florida** (9-4, won Papajohns.com, 17 pts); 30. **Texas A&M** (9-
4, lost Holiday, 10 pts); 31. **Georgia Tech** (9-5, lost Gator, 8 pts); 32. **Kentucky** (8-5, won Music City), and **San Jose St.**
9-4, won New Mexico, 1 pt).
*The NCAA recently vacated Oklahoma's eight wins from the 2005 season. Bob Stoops' official career record is 78-19.

AP Preseason and Final Regular Season Polls

First place votes in parentheses.

Top 25
(Aug. 21, 2006)

		Pts
1	Ohio St. (35)	1,558
2	Notre Dame (10)	1,470
3	Texas (8)	1,411
4	Auburn (3)	1,395
5	West Virginia (6)	1,354
6	USC (3)	1,345
7	Florida	1,178
8	LSU	1,144
9	California	975
10	Oklahoma	960
11	Florida St.	949
12	Miami-FL	893
13	Louisville	844
14	Michigan	824
15	Georgia	743
16	Iowa	720
17	Virginia Tech	614
18	Clemson	479
19	Penn St.	386
20	Nebraska	332
21	Oregon	324
22	TCU	257
23	Tennessee	215
24	Arizona St.	182
25	Texas Tech	181

Top 25
(Dec. 3, 2006)

		Pts
1	Ohio St. (65)	1,625
2	Florida	1,529
3	Michigan	1,526
4	LSU	1,365
5	Louisville	1,333
6	Wisconsin	1,255
7	Oklahoma	1,232
8	USC	1,182
9	Boise St.	1,097
10	Auburn	1,020
11	Notre Dame	939
12	Arkansas	867
13	West Virginia	865
14	Virginia Tech	798
15	Wake Forest	766
16	Rutgers	631
17	Tennessee	576
18	Texas	564
19	Brigham Young	436
20	California	390
21	Texas A&M	379
22	Nebraska	193
23	Boston College	179
24	Oregon St.	112
25	TCU	80

2006-2007 Bowl Games

Listed by bowls matching highest-ranked teams as of final regular season AP poll (released Dec. 3, 2006). Attendanc
figures indicate tickets sold.

Bowl		Winner	Regular Season		Loser	Regular Season	Score	Date	Attendanc
BCS Title Game	#2	Florida	13-1	#1	Ohio St.	12-1	41-14	Jan. 8	74,628
Rose	#8	USC	11-2	#3	Michigan	11-2	32-18	Jan. 1	93,852
Sugar	#4	LSU	11-2	#11	Notre Dame	10-3	41-14	Jan. 3	77,781
Orange	#5	Louisville	12-1	#15	Wake Forest	11-3	24-13	Jan. 2	74,470
Capital One	#6	Wisconsin	12-1	#12	Arkansas	10-4	17-14	Jan. 1	60,774
Fiesta	#9	Boise St.	13-0	#7	Oklahoma	11-3	43-42 OT	Jan. 1	73,719
Cotton	#10	Auburn	11-2	#22	Nebraska	9-5	17-14	Jan. 1	66,777
Gator	#13	West Virginia	11-2		Georgia Tech	9-5	38-35	Jan. 1	67,714
Chick-fil-A		Georgia	9-4	#14	Virginia Tech	10-3	31-24	Dec. 30	75,406
Texas	#16	Rutgers	11-2		Kansas St.	7-6	37-10	Dec. 28	52,210
Outback		Penn St.	9-4	#17	Tennessee	9-4	20-10	Jan. 1	65,601
Alamo	#18	Texas	10-3		Iowa	6-7	26-24	Dec. 30	65,875
Las Vegas	#19	BYU	11-2		Oregon	7-6	38-8	Dec. 21	44,615
Holiday	#20	California	10-3	#21	Texas A&M	9-4	45-10	Dec. 28	62,395
Meineke Car Care	#23	Boston College	10-3		Navy	9-4	25-24	Dec. 30	52,303
Sun	#24	Oregon St.	10-4		Missouri	8-5	39-38	Dec. 29	48,732
Poinsettia	#25	TCU	11-2		Northern Illinois	7-6	37-7	Dec. 19	29,700
International		Cincinnati	8-5		West Michigan	8-5	27-24	Jan. 6	26,717
MPC Computers		Miami-FL	7-6		Nevada	8-5	21-20	Dec. 31	28,652
Champs Sports		Maryland	9-4		Purdue	8-6	24-7	Dec. 29	40,168
Emerald		Florida St.	7-6		UCLA	7-6	44-27	Dec. 27	40,331
Liberty		South Carolina	8-5		Houston	10-4	44-36	Dec. 29	56,103
Independence		Oklahoma St.	7-6		Alabama	6-7	34-31	Dec. 28	45,054
Music City		Kentucky	8-5		Clemson	8-5	28-20	Dec. 29	68,024
Insight		Texas Tech	8-5		Minnesota	6-7	44-41 OT	Dec. 29	48,391
Motor City		Central Michigan	10-4		Mid. Tenn St.	7-6	31-14	Dec. 26	54,113
Hawaii		Hawaii	11-3		Arizona St.	7-6	41-24	Dec. 24	40,623
Armed Forces		Utah	8-5		Tulsa	8-5	25-13	Dec. 23	32,412
Papajohns.com		South Florida	9-4		East Carolina	7-6	24-7	Dec. 23	32,023
GMAC		Southern Miss.	9-5		Ohio	9-5	28-7	Jan. 7	38,751
New Orleans		Troy	8-5		Rice	7-6	41-17	Dec. 22	24,791
New Mexico		San Jose St.	9-4		New Mexico	6-7	20-12	Dec. 23	34,111

2006 Final BCS Rankings

The Bowl Championship Series rankings were used for the first time during the 1998 season to determine BCS bowl match-ups
and revised slightly for the 1999, 2001, 2002, 2004 and 2005 seasons. The final rankings were released Dec. 3, 2006.

	Harris		Polls Pts	%	USA	Pts	%	A&H	RB	Computer Rankings CM	KM	JS	PW	% Avg	BCS Avg
1 Ohio St.	1	2824		.9996	1	1550	1.000	25	25	24	25	25	25	1.000 1	.9999
2 Florida	2	2670		.9451	2	1470	.9484	24	23	25	24	23	23	.940 t-2	.9445
3 Michigan	3	2632		.9317	3	1444	.9316	23	24	23	23	24	24	.940 t-2	.9344
4 LSU	4	2372		.8396	4	1299	.8381	22	17	19	21	21	21	.820 5	.8326
5 USC	7	2173		.7692	7	1173	.7568	20	18	22	22	22	22	.860 4	.7953
6 Louisville	5	2272		.8042	6	1223	.7890	21	22	21	17	13	20	.790 6	.7944
7 Wisconsin	6	2229		.7890	5	1263	.8148	11	21	16	13	18	17	.640 10	.7480
8 Boise St.	9	1950		.6903	9	1053	.6794	19	16	20	19	20	18	.760 7	.7099
9 Auburn	t-10	1725		.6106	10	1000	.6452	17	12	17	20	19	16	.690 8	.6486
10 Oklahoma	8	1977		.6998	8	1115	.7194	15	19	13	8	7	11	.470 16	.6297
11 Notre Dame	t-10	1725		.6106	11	923	.5955	18	15	18	15	17	19	.680 9	.6287
12 Arkansas	13	1483		.5250	13	798	.5148	10	9	10	18	16	15	.510 12	.5166
13 West Virginia	12	1485		.5257	12	800	.5161	14	13	15	11	8	10	.480 t-14	.5073
14 Wake Forest	14	1366		.4835	15	745	.4806	9	14	8	7	5	9	.330 18	.4314
15 Virginia Tech	15	1358		.4807	14	781	.5039	8	20	9	6	4	7	.300 19	.4282
16 Rutgers	16	1083		.3834	17	567	.3658	16	11	12	10	11	14	.480 t-14	.4097
17 Tennessee	18	940		.3327	18	500	.3226	13	10	11	14	14	12	.500 13	.3851
18 California	20	736		.2605	19	436	.2813	12	14	16	15	13		.540 11	.3606
19 Texas	17	952		.3370	16	582	.3755	6	4	6	0	0	5	.150 t-21	.2875
20 BYU	19	838		.2966	20	369	.2381	4	1	5	0	0	4	.090 23	.2082
21 Texas A&M	21	551		.1950	21	303	.1955	3	0	0	0	0	0	.050 t-24	.1468
22 Oregon St.	26	127		.0450	t-25	72	.0465	7	0	7	12	12	8	.340 17	.1438
23 Nebraska	22	352		.1246	22	242	.1561	0	0	0	0	0	0	.000 NR	.0936
24 Boston College	23	318		.1126	23	175	.1129	1	0	4	0	0	0	.040 NR	.0885
25 UCLA	33	10		.0035	NR	0	.0000	5	2	3	9	10	2	.190 20	.0645

Note: Team percentages are derived by dividing a team's actual voting points by a maximum 2850 possible points in the Harris Interactive Poll and 1550 in the *USA Today* Coaches Poll. Six computer rankings calculated in inverse points order (25 for #1, 24 for #2, etc.) are used to determine the overall computer component. The best and worst ranking for each team is dropped and the remaining four are added and divided by 100 (the maximum possible points) to produce a Computer Rankings Percentage. Each computer ranking accounts for schedule strength and home/away performance in its formula. The BCS Average is calculated by averaging the percent totals of the Harris, *USA Today* Coaches, and computer polls. *Computer Rankings*—A&H = Anderson & Hester, RB = Richard Billingsley, CM = Colley Matrix, KM = Kenneth Massey, JS = Jeff Sagarin, PW = Peter Wolfe, Avg. refers to the teams average position in the computer rankings.

BCS Championship Game

ndefeated Ohio State and one-loss Florida were ranked first and second, respectively, in the final Bowl Championship
eries standings (as well as the AP and *USA Today* Coaches polls) and met at University of Phoenix Stadium in the inau-
ural stand-alone BCS championship game to decide Div. 1 college football's national title. Opponents' records and AP
nk listed below are day of game. Final statistics listed below include the BCS title game.

Ohio State Buckeyes (12-1)

ate	AP Rank	Opponent	Result
ept. 2	#1	Northern Illinois (0-0)	W, 35-12
ept. 9	#1	at #2 Texas (1-0)	W, 24-7
ept. 16	#1	Cincinnati (1-1)	W, 37-7
ept. 23	#1	#24 Penn St. (2-1)	W, 28-6
ept. 30	#1	at #13 Iowa (4-0)	W, 38-17
ct. 7	#1	Bowling Green (3-2)	W, 35-7
ct. 14	#1	at Michigan St. (3-3)	W, 38-7
ct. 21	#1	at Indiana (4-3)	W, 44-3
ct. 28	#1	Minnesota (3-5)	W, 44-0
ov. 4	#1	at Illinois (2-7)	W, 17-10
ov. 11	#1	at Northwestern (3-7)	W, 54-10
ov. 18	#1	#2 Michigan (11-0)	W, 42-39
an. 8	#1	#2 Florida (12-0)†	L, 14-41

BCS Title Game at Glendale, Ariz.

Final Individual Statistics

Passing (5 Att)	Att	Cmp	Pct.	Yds	TD	Rate
roy Smith	311	203	65.3	2542	30	161.9
ustin Zwick	23	14	60.9	187	0	129.2

Interceptions: Smith 6.

op Receivers	No	Yds	Avg	Long	TD
ed Ginn Jr.	59	781	13.2	58	9
nthony Gonzalez	51	734	14.4	33	8
rian Robiskie	29	383	13.2	39	5
rian Hartline	17	256	15.1	32	2
ntonio Pittman	14	127	9.1	30	0
ory Nicol	13	151	11.6	38	3
oy Hall	13	147	11.3	27	2

op Rushers	Car	Yds	Avg	Long	TD
ntonio Pittman	242	1233	5.1	56	14
hris Wells	104	576	5.5	52	7
roy Smith	72	204	2.8	34	1
Maurice Wells	46	171	3.7	32	1

Most Touchdowns	TD	Run	Rec	Ret	Pts
ntonio Pittman	14	14	0	0	84
ed Ginn Jr.	11	0	9	2	66
nthony Gonzalez	8	0	8	0	48
hris Wells	7	7	0	0	42
rian Robiskie	5	0	5	0	30

2-Pt. Conversions: none.

Kicking	FG/Att	Lg	PAT/Att	Pts
aron Pettrey	8/11	51	55/58	79
yan Pretorius	1/2	52	2/2	8

Punting	No	Yds	Long	Blkd	Avg
.J. Trapasso	49	1990	60	0	40.6

Most Interceptions		Most Sacks	
ames Laurinaitis	5	Vernon Gholston	8.5
Malcolm Jenkins	4	Quinn Pitcock	8.0
randon Mitchell	2	James Laurinaitis	4.0
Marcus Freeman	2	Jay Richardson	4.0
ntonio Smith	2	Robert Rose	3.5

Florida Gators (13-1)

Date	AP Rank	Opponent	Result
Sept. 2	#7	Southern Miss (0-0)	W, 34-7
Sept. 9	#7	Central Florida (1-0)	W, 42-0
Sept. 16	#7	at #13 Tennessee (2-0)	W, 21-20
Sept. 23	#5	Kentucky (2-1)	W, 26-7
Sept. 30	#5	Alabama (3-1)	W, 28-13
Oct. 7	#5	#9 LSU (4-1)	W, 23-10
Oct. 14	#2	at #11 Auburn (6-0)	L, 17-27
Oct. 28	#9	Georgia* (5-3)	W, 21-14
Nov. 4	#7	at Vanderbilt (4-5)	W, 25-19
Nov. 11	#6	South Carolina (5-4)	W, 17-16
Nov. 18	#3	Western Carolina (2-8)	W, 62-0
Nov. 25	#4	at Florida St. (6-5)	W, 21-14
Dec. 2	#4	#8 Arkansas† (10-2)	W, 38-28
Jan. 8	#2	#1 Ohio St.‡ (12-0)	W, 41-14

*at Jacksonville
†SEC Championship at Atlanta, Ga.
‡BCS Title Game at Glendale, Ariz.

Final Individual Statistics

Passing (5 Att)	Att	Cmp	Pct.	Yds	TD	Rate
Chris Leak	365	232	63.6	2942	23	144.9
Tim Tebow	33	22	66.7	358	5	201.7

Interceptions: Leak 13, Tebow 1.

Top Receivers	No	Yds	Avg	Long	TD
Dallas Baker	60	920	15.3	33	10
Andre Caldwell	57	577	10.1	66	6
Jemalle Cornelius	34	523	15.4	34	3
Percy Harvin	34	427	12.6	58	2
Cornelius Ingram	30	380	12.7	38	1
Kestahn Moore	8	58	7.2	16	1

Top Rushers	Car	Yds	Avg	Long	TD
DeShawn Wynn	143	699	4.9	26	6
Tim Tebow	89	469	5.3	29	8
Percy Harvin	41	428	10.4	67	3
Kestahn Moore	54	282	5.2	28	2
Jarred Fayson	14	126	9.0	27	1
Andre Caldwell	21	102	4.9	27	1

Most Touchdowns	TD	Run	Rec	Ret	Pts
Dallas Baker	10	0	10	0	60
Tim Tebow	8	8	0	0	48
Andre Caldwell	7	1	6	0	42
DeShawn Wynn	6	0	6	0	36
Percy Harvin	5	3	2	0	30

2-Pt. Conversions: Casey (1).

Kicking	FG/Att	Lg	PAT/Att	Pts
Chris Hetland	6/15	42	43/45	61

Punting	No	Yds	Long	Blkd	Avg
Eric Wilbur	53	2244	64	1	42.3

Most Interceptions		Most Sacks	
Ryan Smith	8	Derrick Harvey	11.0
Reggie Nelson	6	Jarvis Moss	7.5
Reggie Lewis	4	Marcus Thomas	4.0
Tony Joiner	2	Brandon Siler	3.0
		Ray McDonald	3.0

BCS Title Game Box Score

Monday, Jan. 8, 2007 at University of Phoenix Stadium, Glendale, Ariz.

Florida 41, Ohio State 14

	1	2	3	4	F
#2 Florida (SEC)	14	20	0	7	41
#1 Ohio St. (Big Ten)	7	7	0	0	14

Favorite: Ohio St. by 7½   **Attendance:** 74,628
Field: Grass   **Weather:** roof closed
Time: 3:24   **TV Rating:** 17.3/27 (FOX)
Off. MVP: Chris Leak, Fla. **Def. MVP:** Derrick Harvey, Fl[

Scoring Summary

1st: 14:44; **OSU**—Ted Ginn Jr. 93-yd kickoff return (Aaron Pettrey kick).

10:31; **FLA**—Dallas Baker 14-yd pass from Chris Leak (Chris Hetland kick), 7 plays, 46 yards, 4:13.

05:51; **FLA**—Percy Harvin 4-yd run (Hetland kick), 7 plays, 80 yards, 1:53.

2nd: 14:56; **FLA**—DeShawn Wynn 2-yd run (Hetland kick), 10 plays, 71 yards, 2:53.

13:32; **OSU**—Antonio Pittman 18-yd run (Pettrey kick), 4 plays, 64 yards, 1:24.

06:00; **FLA**—Hetland kick 42-yd field goal, 9 plays, 32 yards, 3:04.

01:53; **FLA**—Hetland kick 40-yd field goal, 4 plays,4 yards, 1:44.

00:23; **FLA**—Andre Caldwell 1-yd pass from Tim Tebow (Hetland kick); 3 plays, 5 yards, 1:05.

4th: 10:20; **FLA**—Tebow 1-yd run (Hetland kick), 8 plays, 39 yards, 3:42.

Team Statistics

	FLA	OS
First downs	21	
Total Plays	80	3
Total Net Yards	370	8
Carries/yards (includ. sacks)	43/156	23/4
Passing yards	214	3
Completions/attempts	26/37	4/1
Had intercepted	0	
Fumbles/lost	0/0	1/
Penalties/yards	6/50	5/5
Punts/average	4/44.2	6/37.
3rd down conversions	10/19	1/
4th down conversions	2/3	0/
Red-Zone scores/chances	5/6	1/
Sacks by/yards	5/51	1/
Time of possession	40:48	19:1

Individual Statistics

Florida Gators

Passing	Att	Cmp	Int	Yds	TD	Sack
Chris Leak	36	25	0	213	1	1
Tim Tebow	1	1	0	1	1	0
TOTALS	37	26	0	214	2	1

Receivers	No	Yds	Avg	Long	TD
Percy Harvin	9	60	6.7	17	0
Jemalle Cornelius	5	50	10.0	19	0
Cornelius Ingram	4	58	14.5	20	0
Dallas Baker	4	23	5.8	14	1
Billy Latsko	2	17	8.5	11	0
Andre Caldwell	2	6	3.0	5	1
TOTALS	26	214	8.2	20	2

Rushers	Car	Yds	Avg	Long	TD
DeShawn Wynn	19	69	3.6	17	1
Tim Tebow	10	39	3.9	10	1
Percy Harvin	5	22	4.4	6	1
Chris Leak	3	7	2.3	14	0
Kestahn Moore	2	7	3.5	6	0
Team	1	-1	-1.0	0	0
TOTALS	43	156	3.6	17	3

Field Goals	20-29	30-39	40-49	50-59	Total
Chris Hetland	0-0	0-0	2-2	0-0	2-2

Punting	No	Yds	Long	Blkd	Avg
Eric Wilbur	4	177	59	0	44.2

Punt Returns	No	Yds	Long	Avg	TD
Brandon James	4	28	11	7.0	0

Kickoff Returns	No	Yds	Long	Avg	TD
Brandon James	1	33	33	33.0	0

Ohio State Buckeyes

Passing	Att	Cmp	Int	Yds	TD	Sack
Troy Smith	14	4	1	35	0	

Receivers	No	Yds	Avg	Long	T
Anthony Gonzalez	2	11	5.5	8	C
Brian Hartline	1	13	13.0	13	C
Antonio Pittman	1	11	11.0	11	C
TOTALS	4	35	8.8	13	C

Rushers	Car	Yds	Avg	Long	TD
Antonio Pittman	10	62	6.2	18	1
Chris Wells	2	9	4.5	7	0
Brian Hartline	1	5	5.0	5	C
Troy Smith	10	-29	-2.9	13	C
TOTALS	23	47	2.0	18	1

Field Goals	20-29	30-39	40-49	50-59	Total
none					

Punting	No	Yds	Long	Blkd	Avg
A.J. Trapasso	6	227	44	0	37.8

Punt Returns	No	Yds	Long	Avg	TD
Anthony Gonzalez	1	13	13	13.0	0

Kickoff Returns	No	Yds	Long	Avg	TD
Ted Ginn Jr.	1	93	93	93.0	1
Roy Hall	2	35	19	17.5	0
Maurice Wells	1	22	22	22.0	0
TOTALS	6	193	93	32.2	1

Heisman winner no advantage in national title game

Of the last six Heisman Trophy winners to play for a national championship in the same season, only one (USC's Matt Leinart in 2004) won the title game. Buckeye QB Troy Smith, the 2006 Heisman winner, had the worst game of his college career on the biggest stage at the BCS Title game, getting sacked five times and only completing four passes. Other Heisman winners have fared a bit better but the end result usually remains the same. USC's Reggie Bush (2005), Oklahoma's Jason White (2003), Nebraska's Eric Crouch (2000), and Florida State's Chris Weinke (2000) all came up empty in their national title hunt.

USA Today Coaches Poll

Voted on by panel of 63 Division I-A head coaches; winning team receives the Sears Trophy (originally the McDonald's Trophy, 1991-93); first place votes in parentheses with total points (based on 25 for 1st, 24 for 2nd, etc.). Released Jan. 8, 2007.

	Rec	Pts	Pvs		Rec	Pts	Pvs
1 Florida (63)	13-1	1575	2	14 California	10-3	716	19
2 Ohio St.	12-1	1435	1	15 BYU	11-2	615	20
3 LSU	11-2	1418	4	16 Arkansas	10-4	592	13
4 USC	11-2	1345	7	17 Wake Forest	11-3	535	15
5 Wisconsin	12-1	1328	5	18 Virginia Tech	10-3	494	14
6 Boise St.	13-0	1275	9	19 Notre Dame	10-3	485	11
7 Louisville	12-1	1270	6	20 Boston College	10-3	388	23
8 Auburn	11-2	1119	10	21 TCU	11-2	339	24
9 Michigan	11-2	1092	3	22 Oregon St.	10-4	206	25
10 West Virginia	11-2	1012	12	23 Tennessee	9-4	202	18
11 Oklahoma	11-3	849	8	24 Hawaii	11-3	152	NR
12 Rutgers	11-2	841	17	25 Penn St.	9-4	142	NR
13 Texas	10-3	791	16				

Other teams receiving votes: 26. Georgia (9-4, 133 points), 27. Nebraska (9-5, 43), 28. Texas A&M (9-4, 29), 29. Georgia Tech (9-5, 19), 30. South Carolina (8-5, 17), 31. Houston (10-4, 8), 32. Maryland (9-4, 7), 33. Texas Tech (8-5, 2), 34. Kentucky (8-5, 1).

AP Weekly Rankings

The Associated Press Top 25 college football polls on a weekly basis are listed below. The table starts with the preseason and progresses through the season.

	Pre	Sept 3	Sept 5	Sept 10	Sept 17	Sept 24	Oct 1	Oct 8	Oct 15	Oct 22	Oct 29	Nov 5	Nov 12	Nov 19	Nov 26	Dec 3	Jan 9
Ohio St.	1	1	1	1	1	1	1	1	1	1	1	1	1	1	1	1	2
Notre Dame	2	4	4	2	12	12	12	9	10	11	11	9	6	6	12	11	17
Texas	3	2	2	8	7	7	7	6	5	5	4	4	11	11	11	18	13
Auburn	4	4	4	3	2	2	2	11	8	7	6	5	15	14	11	10	9
West Virginia	5	6	6	5	4	4	4	5	4	4	3	10	8	7	15	13	10
USC	6	3	3	4	3	3	3	3	3	3	9	7	4	3	2	8	4
Florida	7	7	7	7	5	5	5	2	9	9	7	6	3	4	4	2	1
LSU	8	8	8	6	10	9	9	14	14	14	13	12	9	9	5	4	3
California	9	22	22	21	22	20	16	10	11	12	10	8	17	22	21	20	14
Oklahoma	10	15	15	15	17	16	14	23	20	19	18	17	16	13	8	7	11
Florida St.	11	9	9	9	18	19	17	-	-	-	-	-	-	-	-	-	-
Miami-FL	12	17	17	17	17	-	-	-	-	-	-	-	-	-	-	-	-
Louisville	13	13	13	12	8	8	8	7	6	6	5	3	10	8	6	5	6
Michigan	14	10	10	11	6	6	6	4	2	2	2	2	2	2	3	3	8
Georgia	15	12	12	10	9	10	10	16	-	-	-	-	-	-	-	-	23
Iowa	16	14	14	16	14	13	19	15	-	-	-	-	-	-	-	-	-
Virginia Tech	17	16	16	14	11	11	21	22	-	-	23	20	19	17	14	14	19
Clemson	18	18	18	-	19	18	15	12	12	10	19	-	25	24	-	-	-
Penn St.	19	19	19	25	24	-	-	-	-	-	-	-	-	-	-	-	24
Nebraska	20	21	21	19	23	21	22	21	17	20	-	-	24	23	19	22	-
Oregon	21	20	20	18	13	14	11	18	16	25	24	21	-	-	-	-	-
TCU	22	23	23	20	16	17	-	-	-	-	-	-	-	-	-	25	22
Tennessee	23	11	11	13	15	13	8	7	8	8	13	22	19	17	17	-	25
Arizona St.	24	25	25	22	20	-	-	-	-	-	-	-	-	-	-	-	-
Texas Tech	25	24	24	24	-	-	-	-	-	-	-	-	-	-	-	-	-
Boston College	-	-	-	23	20	-	25	-	22	18	16	22	20	18	25	23	20
Boise St.	-	-	-	-	-	25	22	20	18	15	14	14	13	12	10	9	5
Rutgers	-	-	-	-	-	23	24	24	19	16	15	15	7	15	13	16	12
Georgia Tech	-	-	-	-	24	18	13	21	20	19	18	16	23	-	-	-	-
Missouri	-	-	-	-	25	23	19	24	23	-	-	-	-	-	-	-	-
Arkansas	-	-	-	-	-	-	-	17	15	13	12	11	5	5	8	12	15
Wisconsin	-	-	-	-	-	-	-	25	21	17	16	12	10	7	6	6	7
Texas A&M	-	-	-	-	-	-	-	-	-	23	22	21	24	22	21	-	-
Wake Forest	-	-	-	-	-	-	-	-	25	24	22	18	14	20	16	15	18
Washington St.	-	-	-	-	-	-	-	-	-	-	25	-	-	-	-	-	-
Maryland	-	-	-	-	-	-	-	-	-	-	-	23	21	-	-	-	-
BYU	-	-	-	-	-	-	-	-	-	-	-	25	23	21	20	19	16
Hawaii	-	-	-	-	-	-	-	-	-	-	-	-	-	25	24	-	-
Oregon St.	-	-	-	-	-	-	-	-	-	-	-	-	-	-	-	24	21

NCAA Division I-A Final Standings

Standings based on conference games only; overall records include postseason games.

Atlantic Coast Conference

Atlantic	Conference				Overall			
	W	L	PF	PA	W	L	PF	PA
*Wake Forest 6		2	175	155	11	3	302	215
*Boston College ..5		3	189	133	10	3	338	204
*Maryland 5		3	171	198	9	4	284	284
*Clemson 5		3	209	136	8	5	425	210
*Florida St.......3		5	180	166	7	6	345	258
N.C. State 2		6	137	174	3	9	210	262

Coastal	Conference				Overall			
	W	L	PF	PA	W	L	PF	PA
*Georgia Tech ...7		1	213	155	9	5	349	257
*Virginia Tech ...6		2	186	93	10	3	336	143
Virginia 4		4	124	116	5	7	181	214
Miami-FL 3		5	127	127	7	6	255	201
North Carolina ..2		6	109	221	3	9	216	366
Duke 0		8	124	280	0	12	179	406

ACC championship game: Wake Forest 9, Georgia Tech 6 (Dec. 2, 2006).

***Bowls (4-4):** Florida St. (won Emerald); Clemson (lost Music City); Boston College (won Meineke); Maryland (won Champs Sports); Virginia Tech (lost Chick fil-A); Miami-FL (won MPC Computers); Georgia Tech (lost Gator); Wake Forest (lost Orange).

Big East Conference

	Conference				Overall			
	W	L	PF	PA	W	L	PF	PA
*Louisville 6		1	247	141	12	1	491	212
*West Virginia ...5		2	259	186	11	2	505	282
*Rutgers 5		2	182	146	11	2	387	186
*South Florida 4		3	145	133	9	4	299	220
*Cincinnati 4		3	152	141	8	5	274	255
Pittsburgh 2		5	172	207	6	6	381	274
Connecticut 1		6	140	238	4	8	257	324
Syracuse 1		6	81	186	4	8	209	295

***Bowls (5-0):** Cincinnati (won International); South Florida (won Papajohns.com); Rutgers (won Texas); West Virginia (won Gator); Louisville (won Orange).

Big Ten Conference

	Conference				Overall			
	W	L	PF	PA	W	L	PF	PA
*Ohio St.........8		0	305	92	12	1	450	166
*Wisconsin 7		1	245	116	12	1	380	157
*Michigan 7		1	213	104	11	2	380	207
*Penn St........5		3	135	117	9	4	290	187
*Purdue 5		3	165	179	8	6	364	374
*Minnesota 3		5	202	243	6	7	376	308
Indiana 3		5	179	302	5	7	277	394
*Iowa 2		6	174	192	6	7	310	269
Northwestern ...2		6	125	240	4	8	198	314
Michigan St. 1		7	148	241	4	8	302	341
Illinois 1		7	155	220	2	10	235	321

***Bowls (2-5):** Ohio St. (lost BCS Championship Game); Michigan (lost Rose); Wisconsin (won Capital One); Penn St. (won Outback); Iowa (lost Alamo); Purdue (lost Champs Sports); Minnesota (lost Insight).

I-A Independents

	W	L	PF	PA
*Notre Dame 10		3	403	310
*Navy 9		4	367	261
Army 3		9	232	335
Temple 1		11	131	496

***Bowls (0-2):** Notre Dame (lost Sugar); Navy (lost Meineke Car Care).

Big 12 Conference

North	Conference				Overall			
	W	L	PF	PA	W	L	PF	PA
*Nebraska 6		2	236	173	9	5	428	25
*Missouri 4		4	214	178	8	5	391	25
*Kansas St.......4		4	188	218	7	6	296	30
Kansas 3		5	234	225	6	6	348	30
Colorado 2		6	160	199	2	10	196	26
Iowa St.........1		7	120	262	4	8	226	36

South	Conference				Overall			
	W	L	PF	PA	W	L	PF	P
*Oklahoma 7		1	208	121	11	3	424	24
*Texas 6		2	270	173	10	3	467	23
*Texas A&M 5		3	193	174	9	4	362	26
*Texas Tech 4		4	240	235	8	5	422	32
*Oklahoma St....3		5	264	243	7	6	458	33
Baylor 3		5	194	320	4	8	283	39

Big 12 championship game: Oklahoma 21, Nebraska 7 (Dec. 2, 2006).

***Bowls (3-5):** Oklahoma (lost Fiesta); Nebraska (lost Cotton); Texas (won Alamo); Texas Tech (won Insight); Missouri (lost Sun); Texas A&M (lost Holiday); Kansas St. (lost Texas); Oklahoma St. (won Independence).

Conference USA

East	Conference				Overall			
	W	L	PF	PA	W	L	PF	P
*Southern Miss ..6		2	213	132	9	5	356	26
*East Carolina ...5		3	188	154	7	6	280	27
Marshall 4		4	233	222	5	7	311	35
UCF 3		5	173	211	4	8	232	34
UAB 2		6	177	220	3	9	225	29
Memphis 1		7	193	256	2	10	281	36

West	Conference				Overall			
	W	L	PF	PA	W	L	PF	P
*Houston 7		1	275	173	10	4	458	32
*Rice 6		2	255	244	7	6	350	43
*Tulsa 5		3	226	155	8	5	360	26
SMU 4		4	216	212	6	6	325	29
UTEP 3		5	202	246	5	7	328	37
Tulane 2		6	130	256	4	8	224	40

Conference USA championship game: Houston 34, Southern Miss 20 (Dec. 1, 2006).

***Bowls (1-4):** Rice (lost New Orleans); East Carolina (lost Papajohns.com); Tulsa (lost Armed Forces); Southern Miss (won GMAC); Houston (lost Liberty).

Mid-American Conference

East	Conference				Overall			
	W	L	PF	PA	W	L	PF	PA
*Ohio 7		1	197	119	9	5	276	25
Kent St.........5		3	172	140	6	6	214	24
Akron 3		5	153	187	5	7	236	27
Bowling Green ..3		5	166	214	4	8	234	34
Miami-OH 2		6	164	187	2	10	222	30
Buffalo 1		7	201	314	2	10	220	43

West	Conference				Overall			
	W	L	PF	PA	W	L	PF	P
*Central Michigan .7		1	235	145	10	4	416	3
*Western Michigan 6		2	177	148	8	5	299	25
*Northern Illinois ..5		3	207	144	7	6	331	27
Ball St.........5		3	225	184	5	7	326	30
Toledo 3		5	157	204	5	7	281	33
Eastern Michigan .1		7	106	174	1	11	167	32

MAC championship game: Central Michigan 31, Ohio 10 (Nov. 30, 2006).

***Bowls (1-3):** Ohio (lost GMAC); Western Michigan (lost International); Central Michigan (won Motor City); Northern Illinois (lost Poinsettia).

Mountain West Conference

	Conference				Overall			
	W	L	PF	PA	W	L	PF	PA
*BYU	8	0	317	113	11	2	478	191
*TCU	6	2	237	113	11	2	380	160
*Utah	5	3	232	171	8	5	363	258
Wyoming	5	3	164	187	6	6	258	264
New Mexico	4	4	189	207	6	7	284	312
Air Force	3	5	172	201	4	8	279	302
San Diego St.	3	5	119	230	3	9	170	325
Colorado State	1	7	113	196	2	8	202	263
UNLV	1	7	158	283	2	10	238	382

Bowls (3-1): BYU (won Las Vegas); TCU (won Poinsettia); Utah (won Armed Forces); New Mexico (won New Mexico).

Pacific-10 Conference

	Conference				Overall			
	W	L	PF	PA	W	L	PF	PA
*USC	7	2	242	131	11	2	396	197
*California	7	2	280	173	10	3	427	251
*Oregon St.	6	3	207	182	10	4	389	311
*UCLA	5	4	198	169	7	6	299	259
*Oregon	4	5	255	238	7	6	383	345
*Arizona St.	4	5	216	247	7	6	348	326
Washington St.	4	5	208	212	6	6	295	277
Arizona	4	5	152	167	6	6	199	235
Washington	3	6	186	225	5	7	262	311
Stanford	1	8	74	274	1	11	127	377

Bowls (3-3): USC (won Rose); Oregon (lost Las Vegas); UCLA (lost Emerald); California (won Holiday); Arizona St. (lost Hawaii); Oregon St. (won Sun).

Sun Belt Conference

	Conference				Overall			
	W	L	PF	PA	W	L	PF	PA
*Troy	6	1	177	136	8	5	296	289
*Middle Tenn.	6	1	204	92	7	6	296	302
Arkansas St.	4	3	126	143	6	6	182	289
Florida Atlantic	4	3	129	100	5	7	181	299
LA-Lafayette	3	4	126	151	6	6	248	296
LA-Monroe	3	4	162	113	4	8	262	267
North Texas	2	5	76	147	3	9	154	304
Florida Int'l	0	7	54	172	0	12	115	313

Bowls (1-1): Troy (won New Orleans); Middle Tenn. (lost Motor City).

Southeastern Conference

	Conference				Overall			
	W	L	PF	PA	W	L	PF	PA
*Florida	7	1	178	126	13	1	416	189
*Tennessee	5	3	212	172	9	4	362	254
*Kentucky	4	4	163	207	8	5	347	369
*Georgia	4	4	185	168	9	4	327	229
*South Carolina	3	5	147	146	8	5	346	243
Vanderbilt	1	7	131	206	4	8	264	284
Western	W	L	PF	PA	W	L	PF	PA
*Arkansas	7	1	221	134	10	4	404	256
*Auburn	6	2	162	133	11	2	322	181
*LSU	6	2	220	131	11	2	438	164
*Alabama	2	6	133	175	6	7	298	250
Mississippi	2	6	123	182	4	8	188	275
Mississippi St.	1	7	122	222	3	9	221	309

SEC championship game: Florida 38, Arkansas 28 (Dec. 2, 2006).

Bowls (6-3): Florida (won BCS Championship); LSU (won Sugar); Kentucky (won Music City); South Carolina (won Liberty); Georgia (won Chick-fil-A); Tennessee (lost Outback); Auburn (won Cotton); Arkansas (lost Capital One); Alabama (lost Independence).

Western Athletic Conference

	Conference				Overall			
	W	L	PF	PA	W	L	PF	PA
*Boise St.	8	0	333	160	13	0	516	229
*Hawaii	7	1	438	196	11	3	656	337
*San Jose St.	5	3	192	172	9	4	324	270
*Nevada	5	3	260	142	8	5	391	249
Fresno St.	4	4	203	214	4	8	276	339
Idaho	3	5	149	272	4	8	203	417
New Mexico St.	2	6	230	262	4	8	374	369
La. Tech	1	7	153	345	3	10	242	542
Utah St.	1	7	123	318	1	11	130	462

Bowls (3-1): Boise St. (won Fiesta); Hawaii (won Hawaii); Nevada (lost MPC Computers); San Jose St. (won New Mexico).

NCAA Division I-A Individual Leaders

Total Offense

		Rushing				Passing			Total Offense		
	Cl	Car	Gain	Loss	Net	Att	Yds	Plays	Yds	YdsPP	YdsPG
Colt Brennan, Hawaii	Jr.	86	504	138	366	559	5549	645	5915	9.17	422.5
Chase Holbrook, New Mexico St.	So.	80	153	231	-78	567	4619	647	4541	7.02	378.4
Graham Harrell, Texas Tech	So.	33	40	118	-78	616	4555	649	4477	6.90	344.4
John Beck, BYU	Sr.	50	123	131	-8	417	3885	467	3877	8.30	323.1
Chase Daniel, Missouri	So.	147	598	219	379	452	3527	599	3906	6.52	300.5
Jordan Palmer, UTEP	Sr.	47	100	186	-86	429	3595	476	3509	7.37	292.4
Curtis Painter, Purdue	So.	76	288	181	107	530	3985	606	4092	6.75	292.3
Kevin Kolb, Houston	Sr.	111	397	243	154	432	3809	543	3963	7.30	283.1
Brian Brohm, Louisville	Jr.	47	163	118	45	313	3049	360	3094	8.59	281.3
Shawn Bell, Baylor	Sr.	27	33	170	-137	383	2582	410	2445	5.96	271.7

All-Purpose Yards

	Cl	Gm	Rush	Rec	PR	KOR	Total Yds	YdsPG
Garrett Wolfe, Northern Illinois	Sr.	13	1928	249	0	0	2177	167.46
Steve Slaton, West Virginia	So.	13	1744	360	0	0	2104	161.85
Johnnie Lee Higgins Jr., UTEP	Jr.	12	-2	1319	281	275	1873	156.08
Chris Williams, New Mexico St.	So.	12	53	1415	92	301	1861	155.08
Ian Johnson, Boise St.	So.	12	1714	55	0	0	1769	147.42
Darren McFadden, Arkansas	So.	14	1647	149	0	262	2058	147.00
Patrick Jackson, Louisiana Tech	So.	12	854	181	0	702	1737	144.75
Curtis Brown, BYU	Sr.	13	1010	566	0	288	1864	143.38
Keenan Burton, Kentucky	Jr.	13	-7	1036	51	765	1845	141.92

Hawaii
Colt Brennan
Passing Efficiency

Northern Ill.
Garrett Wolfe
Rushing

Western Mich.
Ameer Ismail
Sacks

New Mexico St.
Chris Williams
Receptions

Passing Efficiency
(Minimum 15 attempts per game)

	Cl	Gm	Att	Cmp	Cmp Pct	Int	Int Pct	Yds	Yds/ Att	TD	TD Pct	Rating Points
Colt Brennan, Hawaii	Jr.	14	559	406	72.63	12	2.15	5549	9.93	58	10.38	186.0
John Beck, BYU	Sr.	12	417	289	69.30	8	1.92	3885	9.32	32	7.67	169.1
JaMarcus Russell, LSU	Jr.	13	342	232	67.84	8	2.34	3129	9.15	28	8.19	167.0
Tyler Palko, Pittsburgh	Sr.	12	322	220	68.32	9	2.80	2871	8.92	25	7.76	163.2
Kevin Kolb, Houston	Sr.	14	432	292	67.59	4	0.93	3809	8.82	30	6.94	162.7
Jared Zabransky, Boise St.. . . .	Sr.	13	288	191	66.32	8	2.78	2587	8.98	23	7.99	162.6
Troy Smith, Ohio St.	Sr.	13	311	203	65.27	6	1.93	2542	8.17	30	9.65	161.9
Colt McCoy, Texas	Fr.	13	318	217	68.24	7	2.20	2570	8.08	29	9.12	161.8
Brian Brohm, Louisville	Jr.	11	313	199	63.58	5	1.60	3049	9.74	16	5.11	159.1
Justin Willis, SMU	Fr.	11	270	182	67.41	6	2.22	2047	7.58	26	9.63	158.4
Adam Tafralis, San Jose St.. . .	Jr.	13	276	181	65.58	7	2.54	2284	8.28	21	7.61	155.1
Chase Holbrook, N. Mex. St. .	So.	12	567	397	70.02	9	1.59	4619	8.15	34	6.00	155.1
Andre Woodson, Kentucky . .	Jr.	13	419	264	63.01	7	1.67	3515	8.39	31	7.40	154.5
Erik Ainge, Tennessee	Jr.	12	348	233	66.95	9	2.59	2989	8.59	19	5.46	151.9
Jordan Palmer, UTEP	Sr.	12	429	282	65.73	14	3.26	3595	8.38	26	6.06	149.6

Rushing

	Cl	Car	Yds	TD	YdsPG
Garrett Wolfe, Northern Ill. . .	Sr.	309	1928	18	148.31
Ian Johnson, Boise St.	So.	276	1714	25	142.83
Ray Rice, Rutgers	So.	335	1794	20	138.00
Steve Slaton, West Virginia . .	So.	248	1744	16	134.15
Ahmad Bradshaw, Marshall . .	Jr.	249	1523	19	126.92
Dwayne Wright, Fresno St. .	Jr.	261	1462	11	121.83
Jon Cornish, Kansas	Sr.	250	1457	8	121.42
P.J. Hill, Wisconsin	Fr.	311	1569	15	120.69
Michael Hart, Michigan	Jr.	318	1562	14	120.15
Darren McFadden, Arkansas .	So.	284	1647	14	117.64
Damion Fletcher, So. Miss. . .	Fr.	276	1388	11	106.77
Tony Hunt, Penn St.	Sr.	277	1386	11	106.62

Games: All played 13, except Johnson, Bradshaw, Wright and Cornish (12), McFadden (14).

Field Goals

	Cl	FG/Att	Pct	P/Gm
Justin Medlock, UCLA	Sr.	28/32	.875	2.15
Jeremy Ito, Rutgers	Jr.	22/29	.759	1.69
Kevin Kelly, Penn St.	So.	22/34	.647	1.69
Sam Swank, Wake Forest . . .	So.	23/31	.742	1.64
Arthur Carmody, Louisville . .	Jr.	21/25	.840	1.62
Mason Crosby, Colorado . . .	Sr.	19/28	.679	1.58
Alexis Serna, Oregon St. . . .	Jr.	22/29	.759	1.57
Michael Torres, UCF	Jr.	17/24	.708	1.55
Dan Ennis, Maryland	Sr.	20/25	.800	1.54
Chris Nendick, Northern Ill. .	Jr.	20/27	.741	1.54
John Vaughn, Auburn	Jr.	20/24	.833	1.54

Games: All played 13, except Swank and Serna (14), Crosby (12), and Torres (11).

Receptions

	Cl	No	Yds	TD	P/Gm
Chris Williams, N. Mex. St. .	So.	92	1415	12	7.67
Ryne Robinson, Miami-OH . .	Sr.	91	1178	8	7.58
Mike Walker, UCF	Sr.	90	1178	7	7.50
Robert Johnson, Texas Tech .	Sr.	89	871	11	7.42
Jarett Dillard, Rice	So.	91	1247	21	7.00
Joel Filani, Texas Tech	Sr.	91	1300	13	7.00
Davone Bess, Hawaii	So.	96	1220	15	6.86
Earl Bennett, Vanderbilt . . .	So.	82	1146	6	6.83
Johnnie Lee Higgins Jr., UTEP .	Sr.	82	1319	13	6.83
Chandler Williams, Fla. Int'l. .	Sr.	67	664	1	6.70
Dorien Bryant, Purdue	Jr.	87	1068	5	6.21
Eric Deslauriers, E. Michigan	Sr.	74	898	5	6.17

Games: All played 12, except Dillard, Filani (13), Bess and Bryant (14), and Williams (10).

Interceptions

	Cl	No	Yds	TD	P/Gm
Stanley Franks, Idaho	Jr.	9	220	1	0.75
Dwight Lowery, San Jose St. .	Jr.	9	111	0	0.69
Daymeion Hughes, California .	Sr.	8	113	2	0.62
Agib Talib, Kansas	So.	6	82	0	0.60
John Talley, Duke	Jr.	7	150	1	0.58
Quintin Demps, UTEP	Jr.	7	61	0	0.58
Ryan Smith, Florida	Jr.	8	44	0	0.57
DeJuan Tribble, Boston Coll. .	Jr.	7	108	3	0.54
Eric Weddle, Utah	Sr.	7	80	2	0.54
Tony Taylor, Georgia	Sr.	7	97	1	0.54
Trae Williams, South Florida .	Jr.	7	80	0	0.54

Games: All played 13, except Franks, Talley and Demps (12), Talib (10) and Smith (14).

Scoring

Non-Kickers

	Cl	TD	Pts	P/Gm
an Johnson, Boise St.	So.	25	152	12.67
Ahmad Bradshaw, Marshall	Jr.	21	126	10.50
arett Dillard, Rice	So.	21	126	9.69
Ray Rice, Rutgers	So.	20	120	9.23
Patrick White, West Va.	So.	18	108	9.00
Garrett Wolfe, Northern Ill.	Sr.	19	116	8.92
orvorskie Lane, Texas A&M	So.	19	114	8.77
Branden Ore, Virginia Tech	So.	17	102	8.50
Steve Slaton, West Virginia	So.	18	108	8.31
Nate Ilaoa, Hawaii	Sr.	180	108	8.31

Games: All played 13, except Bradshaw, White and Ore (12).

Kickers

	FG/Att	PAT/Att	Pts	P/Gm
Arthur Carmody, Louisville	.21/25	60/60	123	9.46
Pat McAfee, West Virginia	.17/22	62/62	113	8.69
Justin Medlock, UCLA	.28/32	29/29	113	8.69
Jeremy Ito, Ruters	.22/29	41/42	107	8.23
Alex Trlica, Texas Tech	.15/21	51/51	96	8.00
Alexis Serna, Oregon St.	.22/29	45/45	111	7.93
A. Montgomery, Boise St.	.13/14	61/63	100	7.69
Jared McLaughlin, BYU	.14/18	58/62	100	7.69
Jeff Wolfert, Missouri	.18/20	45/45	99	7.62
Garrett Hartley, Oklahoma	.19/20	49/50	106	7.57

Games: All played 13, Trlica (12), Serna and Hartley (14).

Sacks

	Cl	No	Yds	P/Gm
Ameer Ismail, Western Mich.	Sr.	17	111	1.31
Abraham Wright, Colorado	Sr.	12	95	1.00
Jamaal Anderson, Arkansas	Jr.	13½	95	0.96
Gaines Adams, Clemson	Sr.	12½	79	0.96
Justin Hickman, UCLA	Sr.	12½	97	0.96
Bruce Davis, UCLA	Jr.	12½	75	0.96

Punting

(Minimum of 3.6 per game)

	Cl	No	Yds	Avg
Daniel Sepulveda, Baylor	Sr.	66	3068	46.48
Chris Miller, Ball St.	Jr.	57	2637	46.26
Kody Bliss, Auburn	Sr.	47	2149	45.72
Durant Brooks, Georgia Tech	Jr.	79	3596	45.52
Geoffrey Price, Notre Dame	Sr.	50	2272	45.44
Kip Facer, UNLV	Sr.	46	2078	45.17
Britton Colquitt, Tennessee	So.	46	2066	44.91
Matt Fodge, Oklahoma St.	So.	50	2244	44.88
Kyle Stringer, Boise St.	Sr.	47	2097	44.62
Justin Brantly, Texas A&M	So.	50	2215	44.30

Punt Returns

(Minimum of 1.2 per game)

	Cl	No	Yds	TD	Avg
DeSean Jackson, California	So.	25	455	4	18.20
Jeremy Trimble, Army	Jr.	18	325	2	18.06
Sammie Stroughter, Oregon St.	Jr.	30	470	3	15.67
Ean Randolph, South Florida	Sr.	25	370	1	14.80
Yamon Figurs, Kansas St.	Sr.	22	323	2	14.68
Mikey Henderson, Georgia	Jr.	25	367	2	14.68
Chris Garrett, Ohio	Fr.	26	378	1	14.54
Joe Chapple, Western Mich.	Sr.	16	230	0	14.38
DeAngelo Wilson, Nevada	So.	16	228	0	14.25
Derek Pegues, Miss. St.	So.	25	350	1	14.00

Kickoff Returns

(Minimum of 1.2 per game)

	Cl	No	Yds	TD	Avg
Marcus Thigpen, Indiana	So.	24	723	3	30.13
David Harvey, Akron	Sr.	17	510	0	30.00
Lionell Singleton, Fla. Int'l	Jr.	12	354	1	29.50
Darrell Blackman, N.C. State	Jr.	19	549	1	28.89
Damon Nickson, Mid. Tenn St.	Jr.	21	605	2	28.81
Jonathan Stewart, Oregon	So.	23	646	0	28.09
Jeff Smith, Boston College	Fr.	23	645	1	28.04
Brandon West, Western Mich.	Fr.	22	615	0	27.95
Lowell Robinson, Pittsburgh	Jr.	26	725	1	27.88
Kerry Franks, Texas A&M	Jr.	16	443	1	27.69

NCAA Division I-A Team Leaders

Scoring Offense

	Gm	Record	Pts	Avg
Hawaii	14	11-3	656	46.86
Boise St.	13	13-0	516	39.69
West Virginia	13	11-2	505	38.85
Louisville	13	12-1	491	37.77
BYU	13	11-2	478	36.77
Texas	13	10-3	467	35.92
Oklahoma St.	13	7-6	458	35.23
Ohio St.	13	12-1	450	34.62
LSU	13	11-2	438	33.69
Houston	14	10-4	462	33.00

Scoring Defense

	Gm	Record	Pts	Avg
Alabama	12	10-2	128	10.7
Virginia Tech	13	11-2	168	12.9
LSU	13	11-2	185	14.2
Miami-FL	12	9-3	171	14.3
Ohio St.	12	10-2	183	15.3
Auburn	12	9-3	186	15.5
Boston College	12	9-3	191	15.9
Georgia	13	10-3	213	16.4
Texas	13	13-0	213	16.4
Penn St.	12	11-1	204	17.0

Total Offense

	Gm	Plays	Yds	Avg	TD	YdsPG
Hawaii	14	913	7829	8.58	89	559.21
Louisville	13	867	6179	7.13	61	475.31
New Mexico St.	12	930	5702	6.13	53	475.17
BYU	13	889	6051	6.81	63	465.46
West Virginia	13	823	5998	7.29	65	461.38
Texas Tech	13	875	5822	6.65	54	447.85
Houston	14	935	6245	6.68	60	446.07
Missouri	13	922	5533	6.00	48	425.62
Oregon	13	958	5497	5.74	48	422.85
Boise St.	13	857	5468	6.38	68	420.62

Note: Touchdowns scored by rushing and passing only.

Total Defense

	Gm	Plays	Yds	Avg	TD	YdsPG
Virginia Tech	13	743	2853	3.84	14	219.46
TCU	13	753	3054	4.06	19	234.92
LSU	13	764	3156	4.13	20	242.77
Rutgers	13	759	3279	4.32	22	252.23
Wisconsin	13	753	3290	4.25	18	253.08
Florida	14	828	3576	4.32	23	255.43
Miami-FL	13	753	3322	4.41	22	255.54
Georgia	13	775	3357	4.33	28	258.23
Wyoming	12	723	3155	4.36	32	262.92
Michigan	13	789	3488	4.42	25	268.31

Note: Opponents' TDs scored by rushing and passing only.

Single Game Highs
INDIVIDUAL

Rushing Yards

Yds	
353	Garrett Wolfe, Northern Ill. vs. Ball St. (Sept. 30)
295	Dwayne Wright, Fresno St. vs. La. Tech. (Nov. 24)
263	Garrett Wolfe, Northern Ill. vs. Buffalo (Sept. 16)
261	Ahmad Bradshaw, Marshall vs. UTEP (Nov. 18)

Total Offense

Yds	
574	Colt Brennan, Hawaii vs. Arizona St. (Dec. 24)
518	Chase Holbrook, N. Mex. St. vs. La. Tech (Dec. 2)

Passing Yards

Yds	
559	Colt Brennan, Hawaii vs. Arizona St. (Dec. 24)
529	Chase Holbrook, N. Mex. St. vs. Boise St. (Oct. 15)
519	Graham Harrell, Texas Tech vs. Texas (Oct. 28)
514	Chase Holbrook, N. Mex. St. vs. La. Tech (Dec. 2)

Passes Completed

No	
50	Chase Holbrook, N. Mex. St. vs. Boise St. (Oct. 15)
48	Chase Holbrook, N. Mex. St. vs. UTEP (Sept. 30)

Receptions

No	
15	Robert Johnson, Texas Tech vs. SMU (Sept. 2)
14	Three tied.

Receiving Yards

Yds	
308	Jason Rivers, Hawaii vs. Arizona St. (Dec. 24)
300	Adarius Bowman, Okla. St. vs. Kansas (Oct. 14)
258	Steve Smith, USC vs. Oregon St. (Oct. 28)

Touchdowns

No	
5	Three tied.

TEAM

Total Offense Yards Gained

Yds	
682	Texas Tech vs. Baylor (Nov. 4)
680	Hawaii vs. Arizona St. (Dec. 24)

Total Defense Yards Allowed

Yds	
52	Arizona vs. Stanford (Oct. 14)
59	Florida vs. Western Carolina (Nov. 18)

Annual Awards

Players of the Year

Troy Smith, Ohio St. . . . . .AP, Camp, Heisman
Brady Quinn, Notre Dame, QB . . . . .Maxwell
Payton Award (I-AA) . . .Ricky Santos, New Hampshire, QB
Hill Trophy (Div. II) . . . .Danny Woodhead, Chadron St., RB
Gagliardi Trophy (Div. III) . . . . Josh Brehm, Alma, QB

Position Players of the Year

O'Brien Award (Quarterback) . . . . . . .Troy Smith, Ohio St.
Walker Award (Running Back) Darren McFadden, Arkansas
Biletnikoff Award (Receiver) .Calvin Johnson, Georgia Tech
Outland Trophy (Int. Lineman) . . . . Joe Thomas, Wisconsin
Lombardi Award (Lineman) . . .LaMarr Woodley, Michigan
Butkus Award (Linebacker) . . . .Patrick Willis, Mississippi
Thorpe Award (Def. Back) . . . . .Aaron Ross, Texas
Nagurski Award (Def. Player) . James Laurinaitis, Ohio St.
Bednarik Award (Def. Player) . . . .Paul Posluszny, Penn St.
Groza Award (Kicker) . . . . .Art Carmody, Louisville
Ray Guy Award (Punter) . . . . . .Daniel Sepulveda, Baylor
Mackey Award (Tight End) . . . . . .Matt Spaeth, Minnesota

Coaches of the Year

Greg Schiano, Rutgers . . . . .Camp, FWAA
Jim Grobe, Wake Forest . . . . AFCA, AP, Dodd

Heisman Trophy Vote

Presented since 1935 by the Downtown Athletic Club of New York City and named after former college coach and DAC athletic director John W. Heisman. Voting done by national media and former Heisman winners. Each ballot allows for three names (points based on 3 for 1st, 2 for 2nd and 1 for 3rd).

Top 10 Vote-Getters

	Pos	1st	2nd	3rd	Pts
Troy Smith, Ohio St.	QB	801	62	13	2540
Darren McFadden, Arkansas	RB	45	298	147	878
Brady Quinn, Notre Dame .	QB	13	276	191	782
Steve Slaton, West Va.	RB	6	51	94	214
Mike Hart, Michigan	RB	5	58	79	210
Colt Brennan, Hawaii	QB	6	44	96	202
Ray Rice, Rutgers	RB	2	16	44	79
Ian Johnson, Boise St.	RB	2	13	44	73
Dwayne Jarrett, USC	WR	1	11	22	47
Calvin Johnson, Ga. Tech . .WR		1	8	24	43

Consensus All-America Team

NCAA Division I-A players cited most frequently by the following selectors: AFCA, AP, and Walter Camp Foundation. (* indicates unanimous selection. Holdovers from the 2005 team is in **bold** type.

Offense

	Player	Class	Ht	Wt
WR	**Dwayne Jarrett**, USC	Jr.	6-5	210
WR	Calvin Johnson*, Georgia Tech . .	Jr.	6-5	235
TE	Zach Miller, Arizona St.	Jr.	6-5	260
OL	Jake Long, Michigan	Sr.	6-7	313
OL	Joe Thomas*, Wisconsin	Sr.	6-8	313
OL	Justin Blalock, Texas	Sr.	6-4	335
OL	Sam Baker, USC	Jr.	6-5	305
OL	Dan Mozes, West Virginia	Sr.	6-4	290
QB	Troy Smith*, Ohio St.	Sr.	6-1	215
RB	Darren McFadden*, Arkansas . .	So.	6-2	212
RB	Steve Slaton*, West Virginia . . .	So.	5-10	195
K	Justin Medlock, UCLA	Sr.	6-0	197

Defense

	Player	Class	Ht	Wt
DL	LaMarr Woodley*, Michigan	Sr.	6-2	269
DL	Gaines Adams*, Clemson	Sr.	6-5	265
DL	Quinn Pticock, Ohio St.	Sr.	6-3	29?
DL	Glenn Dorsey, LSU	Jr.	6-2	29?
LB	Patrick Willis, Mississippi	Sr.	6-2	24?
LB	**Paul Posluszny**, Penn St.	Sr.	6-2	23?
LB	James Laurinaitis, Ohio St.	So.	6-3	24?
DB	Leon Hall, Michigan	Sr.	5-11	19?
DB	Daymeion Hughes, California	Sr.	6-0	18?
DB	LaRon Landry, LSU	Sr.	6-2	20?
DB	Reggie Nelson, Florida	Jr.	6-1	17?
P	Daniel Sepulveda*, Baylor	Sr.	6-3	23?

Underclassmen who declared for the 2007 draft

39 players forfeited the remainder of their college eligibility and declared for the NFL draft in 2007. NFL teams drafted 26 underclassmen. Players listed in alphabetical order; first round selections in **bold** type.

	Pos	Drafted by	Overall Pick		Pos	Drafted by	Overall Pick
Jon Abbate, Wake Forest	LB	not drafted	—	**Robert Meachem**, Tenn.	WR	New Orleans	27
Jamaal Anderson, Arkansas	DE	Atlanta	8	Zach Miller, Arizona St.	TE	Oakland	38
Antwan Applewhite, S. Diego St	DE	not drafted	—	**Jarvis Moss**, Florida	DE	Denver	17
Jon Beason, Miami-FL	LB	Carolina	25	**Reggie Nelson**, Florida	S	Jacksonville	21
Ahmad Bradshaw, Marshall	RB	NY Giants	250	**Greg Olsen**, Miami-FL	TE	Chicago	31
Alan Branch, Michigan	DT	not drafted	—	**Adrian Peterson**, Oklahoma	RB	Minnesota	7
Michael Bush, Louisville	RB	Oakland	100	Antonio Pittman, Ohio St.	RB	New Orleans	107
Keenan Carter, Virginia	NT	not drafted	—	**Darrelle Revis**, Pittsburgh	CB	NY Jets	14
Stanley Doughty, So. Carolina	DT	not drafted	—	Sidney Rice, South Carolina	WR	Minnesota	44
C.J. Gaddis, Clemson	CB	Philadelphia	159	Gary Russell, Minnesota	RB	not drafted	—
Ted Ginn Jr., Ohio St.	WR	Miami	9	**JaMarcus Russell**, LSU	QB	Oakland	1
Anthony Gonzalez, Ohio St.	WR	Indianapolis	32	Brandon Siler, Florida	LB	San Diego	240
Chris Henry, Arizona	RB	Tennessee	50	Ryan Smith, Florida	CB	Tennessee	206
Jason Jack, Texas A&M	DE	not drafted	—	Brock Stratton, Texas Tech	LB	not drafted	—
Brandon Jackson, Nebraska	RB	not drafted	—	Ramonce Taylor, Texas	RB	not drafted	—
Dwayne Jarrett, USC	WR	Carolina	45	**Lawrence Timmons**, Fla. St.	LB	Pittsburgh	15
Calvin Johnson, Ga. Tech	WR	Detroit	2	Darius Walker, Notre Dame	RB	not drafted	—
Charles Johnson, Georgia	DE	Carolina	83	Danny Ware, Georgia	RB	not drafted	—
Rory Johnson, Mississippi	LB	not drafted	—	Eric Wright, UNLV	DB	Cleveland	53
Marshawn Lynch, California	RB	Buffalo	12				

NCAA Division I-AA Final Standings

Standings based on conference games only; overall records include postseason games.

Atlantic 10 Conference

	Conference				Overall			
North	W	L	PF	PA	W	L	PF	PA
*Massachusetts	8	0	222	89	13	2	413	200
*New Hampshire	5	3	249	212	9	4	459	312
Maine	5	3	141	76	6	5	217	144
Northeastern	4	4	166	215	5	6	200	290
Rhode Island	2	6	137	252	4	7	214	332
Hofstra	1	7	131	174	2	9	185	246

	Conference				Overall			
South	W	L	PF	PA	W	L	PF	PA
*James Madison	7	1	289	135	9	3	389	201
Villanova	5	3	176	187	6	5	247	273
Towson	4	4	172	215	7	4	236	237
Richmond	3	5	153	171	6	5	272	199
Delaware	3	5	239	255	6	6	289	285
William & Mary	1	7	143	237	3	8	209	283

*Playoffs (4-3): James Madison (0-1), New Hampshire (1-1), Massachusetts (3-1).

Big Sky Conference

	Conference				Overall			
	W	L	PF	PA	W	L	PF	PA
*Montana	8	0	264	140	12	2	385	225
*Montana St.	6	2	170	145	8	5	261	286
Portland St.	6	2	200	99	7	4	245	202
Northern Ariz.	5	3	291	202	6	5	378	296
Sacramento St.	4	4	142	196	4	7	168	288
Weber St.	3	5	171	205	4	7	201	265
Eastern Wash.	3	5	180	167	3	8	214	296
Idaho St.	1	7	173	237	2	9	255	373
Northern Colo†	0	8	80	280	1	10	129	373

*Playoffs (3-2): Montana (2-1), Montana St. (1-1).
†Northern Colorado was ineligible for the conference title.

Big South Conference

	Conference				Overall			
	W	L	PF	PA	W	L	PF	PA
Coastal Carolina	4	0	142	94	9	3	411	297
Charleston So.	2	2	92	101	4	2	300	199
Gardner-Webb	2	2	100	135	6	5	270	329
VMI	2	2	122	107	6	5	259	172
Liberty	0	4	112	131	1	10	199	433

Playoffs: No teams invited.

Gateway Football Conference

	Conference				Overall			
	W	L	PF	PA	W	L	PF	PA
*Youngstown St.	6	1	227	126	11	3	440	323
*Illinois St.	5	2	212	150	9	4	377	262
Northern Iowa	5	2	208	162	7	4	341	249
*Southern Ill.	4	3	218	162	9	4	448	256
Western Ky.	4	3	173	154	6	5	258	263
Western Ill.	2	5	192	209	5	6	333	277
Missouri St.	1	6	108	206	2	9	194	308
Indiana St.	1	6	126	295	1	10	236	493

*Playoffs (4-3): Youngstown St. (2-1), Illinois St. (1-1), Southern Ill. (1-1).

Great West Football Conference

	Conference				Overall			
	W	L	PF	PA	W	L	PF	PA
North Dakota St.	4	0	151	73	10	1	374	147
South Dakota St.	3	1	110	111	7	4	235	235
Cal Poly	2	2	83	111	4	8	248	162
UC Davis	1	3	89	80	6	5	309	227
Southern Utah	0	4	49	107	3	8	215	276

Playoffs: No teams invited.

Ivy League

	Conference				Overall			
	W	L	PF	PA	W	L	PF	PA
Princeton	6	1	166	129	9	1	233	179
Yale	6	1	177	111	8	2	257	208
Harvard	4	3	177	138	7	3	267	192
Pennsylvania	3	4	153	129	5	5	228	191
Cornell	3	4	123	162	5	5	189	217
Columbia	2	5	66	135	5	5	150	163
Brown	2	5	140	157	3	7	225	241
Dartmouth	2	5	105	146	2	8	147	254

Playoffs: League does not play postseason games.

NCAA Redubs I-A, I-AA

The NCAA announced in August 2006 it was redubbing Div. I-A and I-AA, NCAA Football Bowl Subdivision and NCAA Football Championship Subdivision, respectively.

COLLEGE FOOTBALL

NCAA Division I-AA Final Standings (Cont.)

Metro Atlantic Athletic Conference

	Conference				Overall			
	W	L	PF	PA	W	L	PF	PA
Duquesne	3	1	126	48	7	3	285	155
Marist	3	1	110	82	4	7	200	285
Iona	2	2	77	67	3	7	147	174
La Salle	1	3	44	135	3	7	140	255
St. Peter's	1	3	97	122	2	8	154	347

Playoffs: No teams invited.

Mid-Eastern Athletic Conference

	Conference				Overall			
	W	L	PF	PA	W	L	PF	PA
*Hampton	7	1	290	92	10	2	410	174
Delaware St.	6	2	207	141	8	3	335	192
S. Carolina St.	6	2	228	137	7	4	298	204
Florida A&M	5	3	213	233	7	4	273	327
Morgan St.	4	4	160	166	5	6	199	242
Howard	4	4	139	150	5	6	180	237
Bethune-Cookman	3	5	220	207	6	5	314	249
Norfolk St.	1	7	159	242	4	7	251	289
N. Carolina A&T	0	8	93	341	0	11	114	475

*Playoffs (0-1): Hampton (0-1).

Northeast Conference

	Conference				Overall			
	W	L	PF	PA	W	L	PF	PA
Monmouth (N.J.)	6	1	177	83	10	2	286	152
Robert Morris	5	2	157	99	7	4	234	161
Albany	5	2	162	85	7	4	224	143
Stony Brook	5	2	220	144	6	5	242	278
Central Conn. St.	4	3	210	134	8	3	363	192
St. Francis (Pa.)	2	5	130	267	3	8	227	398
Sacred Heart	1	6	108	207	2	9	189	300
Wagner	0	7	63	208	4	7	180	233

Gridiron Classic: San Diego (PFL) 27, Monmouth 7.
Playoffs: No teams invited.

Ohio Valley Conference

	Conference				Overall			
	W	L	PF	PA	W	L	PF	PA
*Eastern Illinois	7	1	197	100	8	5	297	275
*Tenn.-Martin	6	1	182	104	9	3	298	188
Tennessee St.	5	2	159	122	6	5	241	242
Jacksonville St.	5	3	256	131	6	5	285	193
Eastern Ky.	5	3	195	168	6	5	238	240
Tennessee Tech	4	4	159	191	4	7	192	296
SE Missouri St.	2	6	114	208	4	7	203	307
Samford	1	7	106	195	3	8	166	250
Murray St.	0	8	115	264	1	10	195	386

*Playoffs (0-2): Eastern Illinois (0-1), Tenn-Martin (0-1).

Patriot League

	Conference				Overall			
	W	L	PF	PA	W	L	PF	PA
*Lafayette	5	1	211	113	6	6	316	270
Lehigh	5	1	189	102	6	5	299	222
Holy Cross	4	2	161	129	7	4	275	235
Bucknell	3	3	78	134	6	5	222	268
Colgate	3	3	159	126	4	7	246	243
Fordham	1	5	103	193	3	8	158	289
Georgetown	0	6	81	185	2	9	164	287

*Playoffs (0-1): Lafayette (0-1)

Pioneer Football League

		Conference				Overall			
North	W	L	PF	PA	W	L	PF	PA
San Diego	7	0	349	87	11	1	514	155
Drake	6	1	186	103	9	2	303	168
Davidson	5	2	236	172	6	4	295	228
Jacksonville	4	3	173	192	4	6	206	323
Butler	2	5	82	210	3	8	156	331
Morehead St.	2	5	147	196	2	9	218	322
Dayton	1	6	166	194	4	6	250	259
Valparaiso	1	6	104	289	3	8	212	378

Gridiron Classic: San Diego 27, Monmouth (NEC) 7.
Playoffs: No teams invited.

Southern Conference

	Conference				Overall			
	W	L	PF	PA	W	L	PF	PA
*Appalachian St.	7	0	255	98	14	1	528	223
*Furman	6	1	172	130	8	4	295	255
Wofford	5	2	209	107	6	4	329	213
The Citadel	4	3	172	169	5	6	264	314
Elon	2	5	140	212	5	6	253	256
Ga. Southern	2	5	139	154	3	8	235	260
Chattanooga	2	5	125	223	3	8	201	304
W. Carolina	0	7	97	216	2	9	159	316

*Playoffs (4-1): Appalachian St. (4-0), Furman (0-1).

Southland Conference

	Conference				Overall			
	W	L	PF	PA	W	L	PF	PA
*McNeese St.	5	1	157	111	7	5	303	271
Sam Houston St.	4	2	155	126	6	5	263	285
Stephen F. Austin	4	2	129	88	4	7	204	232
Texas St.	3	3	135	119	5	6	244	248
Nicholls St.	2	4	65	117	4	7	189	228
Northwestern St.	2	4	109	120	4	7	187	249
SE Louisiana	1	5	104	173	2	9	181	351

*Playoffs (0-1): McNeese St. (0-1).

Southwestern Athletic Conference

		Conference				Overall			
Eastern	W	L	PF	PA	W	L	PF	PA
Alabama A&M	6	3	215	181	9	3	285	228
Jackson St.	5	4	238	222	6	5	312	273
Alcorn St.	5	4	233	230	6	5	262	260
Miss. Valley St.	5	4	178	186	6	5	199	245
Alabama St.	5	4	189	172	5	6	199	227

		Conference				Overall			
Western	W	L	PF	PA	W	L	PF	PA
Ark.-Pine Bluff	7	2	269	216	8	4	333	305
Southern	4	5	226	224	5	6	276	280
Grambling St.	3	6	247	212	3	8	295	281
Texas Southern	3	6	168	239	3	8	203	328
Prairie View A&M	2	7	119	200	3	7	156	200

SWAC Champ. Game: Ala. A&M 22, Ark-Pine Bluff 13
Playoffs: No teams invited.

NCAA I-AA Independents

	W	L	PF	PA
Central Arkansas	8	3	303	221
Winston-Salem	5	6	190	188
Austin Peay	3	8	245	271
Savannah St.	2	9	108	379

Playoffs: No teams invited.

NCAA Division I-AA Leaders
INDIVIDUAL
Passing Efficiency

	Cl	Gm	Att	Cmp	Cmp Pct	Int	Int Pct	Yds	Yds/ Att	TD	TD Pct	Rating Points
Josh Johnson, San Diego	Jr.	12	371	246	66.31	5	1.35	3320	8.95	34	9.16	169.0
Jason Murrietta, North Arizona .	Sr.	11	329	214	65.05	5	1.52	2827	8.59	34	10.33	168.3
Tyler Thigpen, Coastal Carolina	Sr.	12	339	217	64.01	11	3.24	3296	9.72	29	8.55	167.4
Chris Wallace, Ark-Pine Bluff . .	Sr.	12	210	129	61.43	9	4.29	2023	9.63	20	9.52	165.2
Justin Rascati, James Madison .	Sr.	12	231	153	66.23	6	2.60	2045	8.85	20	8.66	164.0
Liam Coen, Massachusetts	Jr.	15	334	217	64.97	10	2.99	3016	9.03	26	7.78	160.5
Nick Hill, Southern Ill.	Jr.	13	196	121	61.73	4	2.04	1721	8.78	15	7.65	156.7
Princeton Shepherd, Hampton .	Sr.	11	222	150	67.57	4	1.80	1750	7.88	17	7.66	155.5
Collin Drafts, Charleston So. . .	Sr.	11	319	223	69.91	14	4.39	2665	8.35	21	6.58	153.0
Ricky Santos, New Hampshire . .	Jr.	13	432	293	67.82	7	1.62	3125	7.23	29	6.71	147.5
Eric Sanders, Northern Iowa . .	Jr.	11	249	169	67.87	7	2.81	1934	7.77	15	6.02	147.4
Sean Schaefer, Towson	So.	10	380	260	68.42	9	2.37	3033	7.98	19	5.00	147.2
Scott Knapp, Duquesne	So.	10	351	209	59.54	13	3.70	2853	8.13	28	7.98	146.7

Total Offense

	Cl	Rush	Pass	Yds	YdsPG
Josh Johnson, San Diego . .	Jr.	720	3320	4040	336.7
Tyler Thigpen, Coastal Caro.	Sr.	656	3296	3952	329.3
Sean Schaefer, Towson	So.	-60	3033	2973	297.3
Collin Drafts, Charleston So.	Sr.	513	2665	3178	288.9
Scott Knapp, Duquesne	So.	-44	2853	2809	280.9
Ryan Alexander, Davidson .	Jr.	185	2581	2766	276.6
Jeff Terrell, Princeton	Sr.	272	2445	2717	271.7
Ricky Santos, N. Hampshire	Jr.	378	3125	3503	269.5
Jason Murrietta, No. Ariz. . .	Sr.	45	2827	2872	261.1
Dominic Randolph, Holy Cross	So.	89	2237	2326	258.4

Games: All played 10, except Johnson, Thigpen (12), Drafts, Murrietta (11), Randolph (9) and Santos (13).

Rushing

	Cl	Car	Yds	TD	YdsPG
Justise Hairston, C. Conn. St.	Sr.	277	1847	20	167.91
Marcus Mason, Y'gstown St.	Sr.	302	1847	23	153.92
Scott Phaydavong, Drake .	Jr.	277	1613	10	146.64
Arkee Whitlock, Southern Ill.	Sr.	317	1828	25	140.62
Mike McLeod, Yale	So.	297	1364	19	136.40
Pierre Rembert, Illinois St. . . .	Sr.	355	1743	16	134.08
D.D. Terry, Sam Houston St.	Sr.	215	1328	15	132.80
Steve Baylark, Massachusetts	Sr.	338	1960	15	130.67
Herb Donaldson, Western Ill.	So.	233	1417	18	128.82
Donald Chapman, Tenn-Martin	Jr.	269	1412	15	128.36

Games: All played 11, except Mason (12), Whitlock and Rembert (13), McLeod and Terry (10) and Baylark (15).

Field Goals

	Cl	FG/Att	Pct	P/Gm
Dan Carpenter, Montana . .	Jr.	24/30	.800	1.71
Rob Zarrilli, Hofstra	Jr.	18/21	.857	1.64
Robert Weeks, N'western St.	So.	18/24	.750	1.64
Brian Wingert, No. Iowa . . .	Sr.	17/23	.739	1.55
Blake Bercegeay, McNeese St.	Jr.	18/20	.900	1.50
Brett Bergstrom, E. Wash. . .	Sr.	15/18	.833	1.36
Andrew Paterini, Hampton .	Sr.	16/21	.762	1.33
Eric Azorr, Portland St.	Sr.	14/21	.667	1.27
Wesley Taylor, Florida A&M	Jr.	14/22	.636	1.27
Alan Kimball, Yale	Jr.	12/19	.632	1.20
Chris Lofrese, Iona	Jr.	12/14	.857	1.20

Games: All played 11, except Carpenter (14), Bercegeay and Paterini (12), Kimball and Lofrese (10).

Receptions

	Cl	No	Yds	TD	P/Gm
Maurice Price, Charleston So. . .	Jr.	103	985	10	9.36
Alex Watson, Northern Ariz. . .	Jr.	82	1017	15	7.45
Jaleel Kindell, St. Peter's	So.	74	855	3	7.40
David Ball, New Hampshire . .	Sr.	93	1114	13	7.15
Lou Russo, La Salle	Sr.	70	744	5	7.00
Lanis Frederick, Austin Peay . .	So.	77	1101	7	7.00
Terrell Hudgins, Elon	Fr.	69	1027	8	6.90
Michael Mayers, Elon	Jr.	73	866	3	6.64
Ryan Maher, Holy Cross	Jr.	69	797	6	6.27
Eric Weems, Bethune-Cookman	Sr.	69	918	9	6.27

Games: All played 11, except Kindell, Russo, and Hudgins (10) and Ball (13).

Interceptions

	Cl	No	Yds	TD	Int/Gm
Dre Dokes, Northern Iowa	Sr.	7	116	1	0.64
Brent Webber, Sacramento St.	Jr.	6	23	0	0.60
Chris Parsons, Northern Iowa .	Jr.	6	34	0	0.55
Dominique Rodgers, Tenn. St. .	Jr.	6	70	0	0.55
Jean-Pierre Marshall, Miss. Vall.	Jr.	6	2	0	0.55
Bobbie Williams, Bet-Cookman	Jr.	6	25	0	0.55
Andy Shalbrack, Columbia . .	Fr.	5	62	0	0.50
Steward Franks, Ark-Pine Bluff	So.	6	96	0	0.50
Frank Moore, Alabama A&M	So.	6	50	0	0.50

Games: All played 11, except Webber and Shalbrack (10), Franks and Moore (12).

Punt/Kickoff Leaders

Punting	Cl	No	Yds	Avg
Breck Ackley, Southern U.	Sr.	49	2228	45.47
David Simonhoff, SE Mo. St. . .	Jr.	59	2644	44.81
Benjamin Dato, Fordham	Jr.	58	2587	44.60

Punt Returns	Cl	No	Yds	TD	Avg
Derrick Harris, Sam Houston St.	Sr.	15	366	2	24.40
Nate Hughes, Alcorn St. . . .	Sr.	22	460	2	20.91
Eric Weems, Bet-Cookman . .	Sr.	19	331	1	17.42

Kickoff Returns	Cl	No	Yds	TD	Avg
Ulysses Banks, Ala. A&M .	Fr.	13	454	2	34.92
Kevin Teel, Hampton	So.	23	718	1	31.22
Dane Samuels, Iona	Jr.	16	439	0	27.44

NCAA Division I-AA Leaders (Cont.)

Scoring

(ranked by points per game)

Non-Kickers

	Cl	Gm	TD	XPt	Pts	P/Gm
Clifton Dawson, Harvard	Sr.	10	22	0	132	13.20
Kevin Richardson, App. St.	Jr.	15	31	0	186	12.40
Mike McLeod, Yale	So.	10	20	0	120	12.00
Jerome Felton, Furman	Jr.	12	23	0	140	11.67
Arkee Whitlock, Southern Ill.	Sr.	13	25	0	150	11.54
Marcus Mason, Y'gstown St.	Sr.	12	23	0	138	11.50
Justise Hairston, C. Conn. St.	Sr.	11	20	0	120	10.91
Herb Donaldson, Western Ill.	So.	11	18	0	108	9.82
Chris Fletcher, Austin Peay	Jr.	11	18	0	108	9.82
Willie Cashmore, Drake	Jr.	11	18	0	108	9.82

Kickers

	FG/Att	PAT/Att	Pts	P/Gm
Brian Wingert, No. Iowa	17/23	28/39	89	8.09
Dan Carpenter, Montana	24/30	41/44	113	8.07
Andrew Paterini, Hampton	16/21	48/52	96	8.00
Craig Coffin, Southern Ill.	15/16	55/55	100	7.69
Robbie Dehaze, No. Ariz.	13/17	43/44	82	7.45
Blake Bercegeay, McN'se St.	18/20	33/36	87	7.25
David Rabil, James Madison	11/13	50/51	83	6.92
Mike Troyan, Duquesne	10/17	31/33	61	6.78

Games: All played 12, except Wingert (11), Carpenter (14), Coffin (13) and Troyan (9).

TEAM

Scoring Offense

	Gm	Record	Pts	Avg
San Diego	12	11-1	514	42.83
New Hampshire	13	9-4	459	35.31
Appalachian St.	15	14-1	528	35.20
Southern Illinois	13	9-4	448	34.46
Northern Arizona	11	6-5	378	34.36
Coastal Carolina	12	9-3	411	34.25
Hampton	12	10-2	410	34.17
Central Conn. St.	12	9-3	363	33.00
James Madison	12	9-3	389	32.42
Youngstown St.	14	11-3	440	31.43
Northern Iowa	11	7-4	341	31.00
Delaware St.	11	8-3	335	30.45
Western Illinois	11	5-6	333	30.27
Wofford	11	7-4	329	29.91
Davidson	10	6-4	295	29.50

Scoring Defense

	Gm	Record	Pts	Avg
Monmouth	12	10-2	152	12.7
San Diego	12	11-1	155	12.9
Albany	11	7-4	143	13.0
Maine	11	6-5	144	13.1
Massachusetts	15	13-2	200	13.3
Hampton	12	10-2	174	14.5
Robert Morris	11	7-4	161	14.6
Cal Poly	11	7-4	162	14.7
Appalachian St.	15	14-1	223	14.9
Drake	11	9-2	.168	15.3
Duquesne	10	7-3	155	15.5
Liberty	11	6-5	172	15.6
Tenn-Martin	12	9-3	188	15.7
Montana	14	12-2	225	16.1
Columbia	10	5-5	163	16.3

Total Offense

	Record	Plays	Yds	Avg
San Diego	11-1	829	5931	494.25
Coastal Carolina	9-3	787	5617	468.08
Appalachian St.	14-1	1006	6265	417.67
Northern Iowa	7-4	698	4491	408.27
Drake	9-2	759	4459	405.36
Northern Arizona	6-5	730	4456	405.09
New Hampshire	9-4	930	5208	400.62
Illinois St.	9-4	871	5167	397.46
James Madison	9-3	730	4694	391.17
Central Conn. St.	8-3	694	4255	386.82
Holy Cross	7-4	765	4228	384.36
Massachusetts	13-2	898	5757	383.80
Davidson	6-4	689	3836	383.60
Youngstown St.	11-3	898	5343	381.64
Duquesne	7-3	641	3816	381.60

Total Defense

	Record	Plays	Yds	Avg
Robert Morris	7-4	650	2512	228.36
Maine	6-5	637	2529	229.91
Iona	3-7	574	2321	232.10
Albany	7-4	712	2649	240.82
Cal Poly	7-4	646	2731	248.27
Tenn-Martin	9-3	738	3066	255.50
Monmouth	10-2	699	3154	262.83
Prairie View	3-7	555	2660	266.00
Montana	12-2	863	3729	266.36
La Salle	3-7	547	2670	267.00
Richmond	6-5	660	2956	268.73
San Diego	11-1	710	3229	269.08
Mississippi Valley	6-5	624	2960	269.09
Jacksonville St.	6-5	668	2972	270.18
Hampton	10-2	755	3258	271.50

Home Attendance Leaders

	Gm	Total	Average
Montana	9	203,403	22,600
Delaware	7	152,773	21,825
Appalachian St.	9	184,911	20,546
Jackson St.	5	101,572	20,314
Yale	5	92,809	18,562
Southern U.	5	82,265	16,453
Florida A&M	4	63,663	15,916
Georgia Southern	7	109,281	15,612
Harvard	5	77,742	15,548
Youngstown St.	8	121,269	15,159

Division I-AA, II and III Awards

Players of the Year

NCAA I-AA	Ricky Santos, New Hampshire, QB
NCAA II	Danny Woodhead, Chardron St., RB
NCAA III	Josh Brehm, Alma, QB
NAIA	Brian Kurtz, Saint Francis-IN, LB

Coaches of the Year

AFCA	Jerry Moore, Appalachian St.

NCAA Playoffs

Division I-AA

First Round (Nov. 25)

at Massachusetts 35 . . . . .Lafayette 14
New Hampshire 41 . . . . .at Hampton 38
at Montana St. 31 . . . . .Furman 13
Illinois St. 24 . . . . .at Eastern Illinois 13
at Montana 31 . . . . .McNeese St. 6
at Southern Illinois 36 . . . . .Tennessee-Martin 30
at Appalachian St. 45 . . . . .Coastal Carolina 28
at Youngstown St. 35 . . . . .James Madison 31

Quarterfinals (Dec. 2)

at Massachusetts 24 . . . . .New Hampshire 17
at Montana 20 . . . . .Southern Illinois 3
at Appalachian St. 38 . . . . .Montana St. 17
at Youngstown St. 28 . . . . .Illinois St. 21

Semifinals (Dec. 8-9)

Massachusetts 19 . . . . .at Montana 17
at Appalachian St. 49 . . . . .Youngstown St. 24

Championship Game

Dec. 15 at Chattanooga, Tenn. (Att: 22,808)
Appalachian St. 28. . . . . .Massachusetts 17
(14-1)   (13-2)

Division II

First Round (Nov. 18)

South Dakota 31 . . . . .OT . . . . .at Northwood 28
at North Dakota 42 . . . . .Winona St. 0
Delta St. 17 . . . . .at Elizabeth City St. 10
at Newberry 34 . . . . .Albany St. (Ga.) 28
at Merrimack 28 . . . . .Southern Conn. St. 26
West Chester 31 . . . . .at Bryant 29
at Midwestern St. 28 . . . . .Mo. Western St. 26
at West Texas A&M 30 . . . . . .OT . . .Abilene Christian 27

Second Round (Nov. 25)

at Grand Valley St. 35 . . . . .South Dakota 17
North Dakota 38 . . . . .at Nebraska-Omaha 35
Delta St. 24 . . . . .at N.C. Central 17
at North Alabama 38 . . . . .Newberry 20
at Shepherd 31 .Merrimack 7
at Bloomsburg 21 . . . . .West Chester 20
at NW Missouri St. 27 . . . . .Midwestern St. 0
at Chadron St. 43 . . . . .West Texas A&M 17

Quarterfinals (Dec. 2)

at Grand Valley St. 30 . . . . .North Dakota 20
Delta St. 27 . . . . .at North Alabama 10
Bloomsburg 24 . . . . .at Shepherd 21
at NW Missouri St. 28 . . . . .Chadron St. 21

Semifinals (Dec. 10)

Grand Valley St. 49 . . . . .Delta St. 30
at NW Missouri St. 33 . . . . .Bloomsburg 3

Championship Game

Dec. 16 at Florence, Ala. (Att: 7,437)
Grand Valley St. 17 . . . . .NW Missouri St. 14
(15-0)   (14-1)

Division III

First Round (Nov. 18)

at Mount Union 49 . . . . .Hope 0
at Wheaton (Ill.) 42 . . . . .Mt. St. Joseph 28
North Central 35 . . . . .at Concordia 6
at Capital 32 . . . . .Wittenberg 14
at Wilkes 42 . . . . .Washington & Lee 0
at Rowan 20 . . . . .Hobart 18
at St. John Fisher 49 . . . . .Union 21
at Springfield 42 . . . . .Curry 14
at Wesley 49 . . . . .Dickinson 21
at Carnegie Mellon 21 . . . . .Millsaps 0
Washington & Jefferson 27 . . . .Chris. Newport 23
at Mary Hardin-Baylor 33 . . . . .Hardin-Simmons 0
at WI-Whitewater 59 . . . . .St. Norbert 17
at WI-La Crosse 28 . . . . .Bethel (Minn.) 21
at Whitworth 27 . . . . .Occidental 23
St. John's (Minn.) 21 . . . . .Central (Iowa) 13

Second Round (Nov. 25)

at Mount Union 35 . . . . .Wheaton 3
at Capital 41 . . . . .North Central 13
Rowan 21 .at Wilkes 14
St. John Fisher 27 . . . . .at Springfield 21
at Wesley 37 . . . . .Carnegie Mellon 0
at Mary Hardin-Baylor 30 . . . . . .Wash. & Jefferson 27
at WI-Whitewater 24 . . . . .WI-La Crosse 21
St. John's 21 . . . . .Whitworth 3

Quarterfinals (Dec. 2)

at Mount Union 17 . . . . .Capital 14
at St. John Fisher 31 . . . . .Rowan 0
at Wesley 34 . . . . .Mary Hardin-Baylor 20
at WI-Whitewater 17 . . . . .St. John's 14

Semifinals (Dec. 9)

at Mount Union 26 . . . . .St. John Fisher 14
at WI-Whitewater 44 . . . . .Wesley 7

Amos Alonzo Stagg Bowl

Dec. 17 at Salem, Va. (Att: 6,051)
Mount Union 35 . . . . .WI-Whitewater 16
(15-0)   (14-1)

NAIA Playoffs

Division I

First Round (Nov. 18)

St. Francis (Ind.) 42 . . . . .Walsh (Ohio) 3
Northwestern Iowa 17 . . . . . .Black Hills State (S.D.) 10
Saint Xavier (Ill.) 42 . . . . .Georgetown (Ky.) 28
Carroll (Mont.) 20 . . . . .Montana State Northern 7
Sioux Falls (S.D.) 48 . . . . .Jamestown (N.D.) 10
Morningside (Iowa) 38 . . .2OT .Saint Ambrose (Iowa) 31
Bethel (Tenn.) 35 . . . . .Friends (Kan.) 0
Missouri Valley 31 . . . . .Bethel (Kan.) 14

Quarterfinals (Nov. 25)

St. Francis 42 . . . . .Bethel 35
Sioux Falls 37 . . . . .Morningside 7
Saint Xavier 14 . . . . .Carroll 7
Missouri Valley 33 . . . . .Northwestern Iowa 26

Semifinals (Dec. 2)

St. Francis 49 . . . . .Saint Xavier (Ill.) 20
Sioux Falls 25 . . . . .Missouri Valley 18

Championship

Dec. 16 at Savannah, Tenn. (Att: 5,805)
Sioux Falls 23 . . . . .Saint Francis 19
(14-0)   (13-1)

1869-2007
Through the Years

SPORTS ALMANAC

National Champions

Over the last 132 years, there have been 25 major selectors of national champions by way of polls (11), mathematical rating systems (10) and historical research (4). The best-known and most widely circulated of these surveys, the Associated Press poll of sportswriters and broadcasters, first appeared during the 1936 season. Champions prior to 1936 have been determined by retro polls, ratings and historical research.

The Early Years (1869-1935)

National champions based on the Dickinson mathematical system (DS) and three historical retro polls taken by the College Football Researchers Association (CFRA), the National Championship Foundation (NCF) and the Helms Athletic Foundation (HF). The CFRA and NCF polls start in 1869, college football's inaugural year, while the Helms poll begins in 1883, the first season the game adopted a point system for scoring. Frank Dickinson, an economics professor at Illinois, introduced his system in 1926 and retro-picked winners in 1924 and '25. Bowl game results were counted in the Helms selections, but not in the other three.

Multiple champions: Yale (18); Princeton (17); Harvard (9); Michigan (7); Notre Dame and Penn (4); Alabama, California, Cornell, Illinois, Pittsburgh and USC (3); Georgia Tech, Minnesota and Penn St. (2).

Year		Record	Year		Record	Year		Record
1869	**Princeton**	.1-1-0	1880	**Yale** (CFRA)	.4-0-1	1891	**Yale**	.13-0-0
1870	**Princeton**	.1-0-0		**& Princeton** (NCF)	.4-0-1	1892	**Yale**	.13-0-0
1871	No games played		1881	**Yale**	.5-0-1	1893	**Princeton**	.11-0-0
1872	**Princeton**	.1-0-0	1882	**Yale**	.8-0-0	1894	**Yale**	.16-0-0
1873	**Princeton**	.1-0-0	1883	**Yale**	.8-0-0	1895	**Penn**	.14-0-0
1874	**Yale**	.3-0-0	1884	**Yale**	.8-0-1	1896	**Princeton** (CFRA)	.10-0-1
1875	**Princeton** (CFRA)	.2-0-0	1885	**Princeton**	.9-0-0		**& Lafayette** (NCF)	.11-0-1
	& Harvard (NCF)	.4-0-0	1886	**Yale**	.9-0-1	1897	**Penn**	.15-0-0
1876	**Yale**	.3-0-0	1887	**Yale**	.9-0-0	1898	**Harvard**	.11-0-0
1877	**Yale**	.3-0-1	1888	**Yale**	.13-0-0	1899	**Princeton** (CFRA)	.12-1-0
1878	**Princeton**	.6-0-0	1889	**Princeton**	.10-0-0		**& Harvard** (NCF, HF)	10-0-1
1879	**Princeton**	.4-0-1	1890	**Harvard**	.11-0-0			

Year		Record	Bowl Game	Head Coach	Outstanding Player
1900	**Yale**	.12-0-0	No bowl	Malcolm McBride	Perry Hale, HB
1901	**Harvard** (CFRA)	.12-0-0	No bowl	Bill Reid	Bob Kernan, HB
	& Michigan (NCF, HF)	.11-0-0	Won Rose	Hurry Up Yost	Neil Snow, E
1902	**Michigan**	.11-0-0	No bowl	Hurry Up Yost	Boss Weeks, QB
1903	**Princeton**	.11-0-0	No bowl	Art Hillebrand	John DeWitt, G
1904	**Penn** (CFRA, HF)	.12-0-0	No bowl	Carl Williams	Andy Smith, FB
	& Michigan (NCF)	.10-0-0	No bowl	Hurry Up Yost	Willie Heston, HB
1905	**Chicago**	.10-0-0	No bowl	Amos Alonzo Stagg	Walter Eckersall, QB
1906	**Princeton**	.9-0-1	No bowl	Bill Roper	Cap Wister, E
1907	**Yale**	.9-0-1	No bowl	Bill Knox	Tad Jones, HB
1908	**Penn** (CFRA, HF)	.11-0-1	No bowl	Sol Metzger	Hunter Scarlett, E
	& LSU (NCF)	.10-0-0	No bowl	Edgar Wingard	Doc Fenton, QB
1909	**Yale**	.12-1-0	No bowl	Howard Jones	Ted Coy, FB
1910	**Harvard** (CFRA, HF)	.8-0-1	No bowl	Percy Haughton	Percy Wendell, HB
	& Pittsburgh (NCF)	.9-0-0	No bowl	Joe Thompson	Ralph Galvin, C
1911	**Princeton** (CFRA, HF)	.8-0-2	No bowl	Bill Roper	Sam White, E
	& Penn St. (NCF)	.8-0-1	No bowl	Bill Hollenback	Dexter Very, E
1912	**Harvard** (CFRA, HF)	.9-0-0	No bowl	Percy Haughton	Charley Brickley, HB
	& Penn St. (NCF)	.8-0-0	No bowl	Bill Hollenback	Dexter Very, E
1913	**Harvard**	.9-0-0	No bowl	Percy Haughton	Eddie Mahan, FB
1914	**Army**	.9-0-0	No bowl	Charley Daly	John McEwan, C
1915	**Cornell**	.9-0-0	No bowl	Al Sharpe	Charley Barrett, QB
1916	**Pittsburgh**	.8-0-0	No bowl	Pop Warner	Bob Peck, C
1917	**Georgia Tech**	.9-0-0	No bowl	John Heisman	Ev Strupper, HB
1918	**Pittsburgh** (CFRA, HF)	.4-1-0	No bowl	Pop Warner	Tom Davies, HB
	& Michigan (NCF)	.5-0-0	No bowl	Hurry Up Yost	Frank Steketee, FB
1919	**Harvard**-tie (CFRA, HF)	.9-0-1	Won Rose	Bob Fisher	Eddie Casey, HB
	Illinois (CFRA-tie)	.6-1-0	No bowl	Bob Zuppke	Chuck Carney, E
	& Notre Dame (NCF)	.9-0-0	No bowl	Knute Rockne	George Gipp, HB
1920	**California**	.9-0-0	Won Rose	Andy Smith	Dan McMillan, T
1921	**California** (CFRA)	.9-0-1	Tied Rose	Andy Smith	Brick Muller, E
	& Cornell (NCF, HF)	.8-0-0	No bowl	Gil Dobie	Eddie Kaw, HB
1922	**Princeton** (CFRA)	.8-0-0	No bowl	Bill Roper	Herb Treat, T
	California (NCF)	.9-0-0	No bowl	Andy Smith	Brick Muller, E
	& Cornell (HF)	.8-0-0	No bowl	Gil Dobie	Eddie Kaw, HB

Year		Record	Bowl Game	Head Coach	Outstanding Player
1923	**Illinois** (CFRA, HF) 8-0-0		No bowl	Bob Zuppke	Red Grange, HB
	& Michigan (NCF) 8-0-0		No bowl	Hurry Up Yost	Jack Blott, C
1924	**Notre Dame** 10-0-0		Won Rose	Knute Rockne	"The Four Horsemen"*
1925	**Alabama** (CFRA, HF) 10-0-0		Won Rose	Wallace Wade	Johnny Mack Brown, HB
	& Dartmouth (DS) 8-0-0		No bowl	Jesse Hawley	Swede Oberlander, HB
1926	**Alabama** (CFRA, HF) 9-0-1		Tied Rose	Wallace Wade	Hoyt Winslett, E
	& Stanford (DS) 10-0-1		Tied Rose	Pop Warner	Ted Shipkey, E
1927	**Yale** (CFRA) 7-1-0		No bowl	Tad Jones	Bill Webster, G
	& Illinois (NCF, HF, DS) 7-0-1		No bowl	Bob Zuppke	Bob Reitsch, C
1928	**Georgia Tech** (CFRA, NCF, HF) . .10-0-0		Won Rose	Bill Alexander	Pete Pund, C
	& USC (DS) 9-0-1		No bowl	Howard Jones	Jesse Hibbs, T
1929	**Notre Dame** 9-0-0		No bowl	Knute Rockne	Frank Carideo, QB
1930	**Alabama** (CFRA) 10-0-0		Won Rose	Wallace Wade	Fred Sington, T
	& Notre Dame (NCF, HF, DS) . . .10-0-0		No bowl	Knute Rockne	Marchy Schwartz, HB
1931	**USC** 10-1-0		Won Rose	Howard Jones	John Baker, G
1932	**USC** (CFRA, NCF, HF) 10-0-0		Won Rose	Howard Jones	Ernie Smith, T
	& Michigan (DS) 8-0-0		No bowl	Harry Kipke	Harry Newman, QB
1933	**Michigan** 8-0-0		No bowl	Harry Kipke	Chuck Bernard, C
1934	**Minnesota** 8-0-0		No bowl	Bernie Bierman	Pug Lund, HB
1935	**Minnesota** (CFRA, NCF, HF) 8-0-0		No bowl	Bernie Bierman	Dick Smith, T
	& SMU (DS) 12-1-0		Lost Rose	Matty Bell	Bobby Wilson, HB

*Notre Dame's Four Horsemen were Harry Stuhldreher (QB), Jim Crowley (HB), Don Miller (HB-P) and Elmer Layden (FB).

The Media Poll Years (since 1936)

National champions according to seven media and coaches' polls: Associated Press (since 1936), United Press (1950-57), International News Service (1952-57), United Press International (1958-92), Football Writers Association of America (since 1954), National Football Foundation and Hall of Fame (since 1959) and USA Today/CNN (since 1991). In 1991, the American Football Coaches Association switched outlets for its poll from UPI to USA Today/CNN and then to USA Today/ESPN in 1997.

After 29 years of releasing its final Top 20 poll in early December, AP named its 1965 national champion following that season's bowl games. AP returned to a pre-bowls final vote in 1966 and '67, but has polled its writers and broadcasters after the bowl games since the 1968 season. The FWAA has selected its champion after the bowl games since the 1955 season, the NFF-Hall of Fame since 1971, UPI after 1974, USA Today/CNN 1991-96, and USA Today/ESPN since 1997.

The Associated Press changed the name of its national championship award from the AP trophy to the Bear Bryant Trophy after the legendary Alabama coach's death in 1983. The Football Writers' trophy is called the Grantland Rice Award (after the celebrated sportswriter) and the NFF-Hall of Fame trophy is called the MacArthur Bowl (in honor of Gen. Douglas MacArthur).

Multiple champions: Notre Dame (9); Alabama, Ohio St., Oklahoma and USC (7); Miami-FL and Nebraska (5); Minnesota (4); Michigan St. and Texas (3); Army, Florida, Florida St., Georgia Tech, LSU, Michigan, Penn St., Pittsburgh and Tennessee (2).

Year		Record	Bowl Game	Head Coach	Outstanding Player
1936	**Minnesota** 7-1-0		No bowl	Bernie Bierman	Ed Widseth, T
1937	**Pittsburgh** 9-0-1		No bowl	Jock Sutherland	Marshall Goldberg, HB
1938	**TCU** 11-0-0		Won Sugar	Dutch Meyer	Davey O'Brien, QB
1939	**Texas A&M** 11-0-0		Won Sugar	Homer Norton	John Kimbrough, FB
1940	**Minnesota** 8-0-0		No Bowl	Bernie Bierman	George Franck, HB
1941	**Minnesota** 8-0-0		No bowl	Bernie Bierman	Bruce Smith, HB
1942	**Ohio St.** 9-1-0		No bowl	Paul Brown	Gene Fekete, FB
1943	**Notre Dame** 9-1-0		No bowl	Frank Leahy	Angelo Bertelli, QB
1944	**Army** 9-0-0		No bowl	Red Blaik	Glenn Davis, HB
1945	**Army** 9-0-0		No bowl	Red Blaik	Doc Blanchard, FB
1946	**Notre Dame** 8-0-1		No bowl	Frank Leahy	Johnny Lujack, QB
1947	**Notre Dame** 9-0-0		No bowl	Frank Leahy	Johnny Lujack, QB
1948	**Michigan** 9-0-0		No bowl	Bennie Oosterbaan	Dick Rifenburg, E
1949	**Notre Dame** 10-0-0		No bowl	Frank Leahy	Leon Hart, E
1950	**Oklahoma** 10-1-0		Lost Sugar	Bud Wilkinson	Leon Heath, FB
1951	**Tennessee** 10-0-0		Lost Sugar	Bob Neyland	Hank Lauricella, TB
1952	**Michigan St.** (AP, UP) 9-0-0		No bowl	Biggie Munn	Don McAuliffe, HB
	& Georgia Tech (INS) 12-0-0		Won Sugar	Bobby Dodd	Hal Miller, T
1953	**Maryland** 10-1-0		Lost Orange	Jim Tatum	Bernie Faloney, QB
1954	**Ohio St.** (AP, INS) 10-0-0		Won Rose	Woody Hayes	Howard Cassady, HB
	& UCLA (UP, FW) 9-0-0		No bowl	Red Sanders	Jack Ellena, T
1955	**Oklahoma** 11-0-0		Won Orange	Bud Wilkinson	Jerry Tubbs, C
1956	**Oklahoma** 10-0-0		No bowl	Bud Wilkinson	Tommy McDonald, HB
1957	**Auburn** (AP) 10-0-0		No bowl	Shug Jordan	Jimmy Phillips, E
	& Ohio St. (UP, FW, INS) 9-1-0		Won Rose	Woody Hayes	Bob White, FB
1958	**LSU** (AP, UPI) 11-0-0		Won Sugar	Paul Dietzel	Billy Cannon, HB
	& Iowa (FW) 8-1-1		Won Rose	Forest Evashevski	Randy Duncan, QB
1959	**Syracuse** 11-0-0		Won Cotton	Ben Schwartzwalder	Ernie Davis, HB
1960	**Minnesota** (AP, UPI, NFF) 8-2-0		Lost Rose	Murray Warmath	Tom Brown, G
	& Mississippi (FW) 10-0-1		Won Sugar	Johnny Vaught	Jake Gibbs, QB
1961	**Alabama** (AP, UPI, NFF) 11-0-0		Won Sugar	Bear Bryant	Billy Neighbors, T
	& Ohio St. (FW) 8-0-1		No bowl	Woody Hayes	Bob Ferguson, HB
1962	**USC** 11-0-0		Won Rose	John McKay	Hal Bedsole, E

National Champions (Cont.)

Year		Record	Bowl Game	Head Coach	Outstanding Player
1963	**Texas**	11-0-0	Won Cotton	Darrell Royal	Scott Appleton, T1964
	Alabama (AP, UPI),	10-1-0	Lost Orange	Bear Bryant	Joe Namath, QB
	Arkansas (FW)	11-0-0	Won Cotton	Frank Broyles	Ronnie Caveness, LB
	& **Notre Dame** (NFF)	9-1-0	No bowl	Ara Parseghian	John Huarte, QB
1965	**Alabama** (AP, FW-tie)	9-1-1	Won Orange	Bear Bryant	Paul Crane, C
	& **Michigan St.** (UPI, NFF, FW-tie)	10-1-0	Lost Rose	Duffy Daugherty	George Webster, LB
1966	**Notre Dame** (AP, UPI, FW, NFF-tie)	9-0-1	No bowl	Ara Parseghian	Jim Lynch, LB
	& **Michigan St.** (NFF-tie)	9-0-1	No bowl	Duffy Daugherty	Bubba Smith, DE
1967	**USC**	10-1-0	Won Rose	John McKay	O.J. Simpson, HB
1968	**Ohio St.**	10-0-0	Won Rose	Woody Hayes	Rex Kern, QB
1969	**Texas**	11-0-0	Won Cotton	Darrell Royal	James Street, QB
1970	**Nebraska** (AP, FW)	11-0-1	Won Orange	Bob Devaney	Jerry Tagge, QB
	Texas (UPI, NFF-tie),	10-1-0	Lost Cotton	Darrell Royal	Steve Worster, RB
	& **Ohio St.** (NFF-tie)	9-1-0	Lost Rose	Woody Hayes	Jim Stillwagon, MG
1971	**Nebraska**	13-0-0	Won Orange	Bob Devaney	Johnny Rodgers, WR
1972	**USC**	12-0-0	Won Rose	John McKay	Charles Young, TE
1973	**Notre Dame** (AP, FW, NFF)	11-0-0	Won Sugar	Ara Parseghian	Mike Townsend, DB
	& **Alabama** (UPI)	11-1-0	Lost Sugar	Bear Bryant	Buddy Brown, OT
1974	**Oklahoma** (AP)	11-0-0	No bowl	Barry Switzer	Joe Washington, RB
	& **USC** (UPI, FW, NFF)	10-1-1	Won Rose	John McKay	Anthony Davis, RB
1975	**Oklahoma**	11-1-0	Won Orange	Barry Switzer	Lee Roy Selmon, DT
1976	**Pittsburgh**	12-0-0	Won Sugar	Johnny Majors	Tony Dorsett, RB
1977	**Notre Dame**	11-1-0	Won Cotton	Dan Devine	Ross Browner, DE
1978	**Alabama** (AP, FW, NFF)	11-1-0	Won Sugar	Bear Bryant	Marty Lyons, DT
	& **USC** (UPI)	12-1-0	Won Rose	John Robinson	Charles White, RB
1979	**Alabama**	12-0-0	Won Sugar	Bear Bryant	Jim Bunch, OT
1980	**Georgia**	12-0-0	Won Sugar	Vince Dooley	Herschel Walker, RB
1981	**Clemson**	12-0-0	Won Orange	Danny Ford	Jeff Davis, LB
1982	**Penn St.**	11-1-0	Won Sugar	Joe Paterno	Todd Blackledge, QB
1983	**Miami-FL**	11-1-0	Won Orange	H. Schnellenberger	Bernie Kosar, QB
1984	**BYU**	13-0-0	Won Holiday	LaVell Edwards	Robbie Bosco, QB
1985	**Oklahoma**	11-1-0	Won Orange	Barry Switzer	Brian Bosworth, LB
1986	**Penn St.**	12-0-0	Won Fiesta	Joe Paterno	D.J. Dozier, RB
1987	**Miami-FL**	12-0-0	Won Orange	Jimmy Johnson	Steve Walsh, QB
1988	**Notre Dame**	12-0-0	Won Fiesta	Lou Holtz	Tony Rice, QB
1989	**Miami-FL**	11-1-0	Won Sugar	Dennis Erickson	Craig Erickson, QB
1990	**Colorado** (AP, FW, NFF)	11-1-1	Won Orange	Bill McCartney	Eric Bieniemy, RB
	& **Georgia Tech** (UP)	11-0-1	Won Citrus	Bobby Ross	Shawn Jones, QB
1991	**Miami-FL** (AP)	12-0-0	Won Orange	Dennis Erickson	Gino Torretta, QB
	& **Washington** (USA, FW, NFF)	12-0-0	Won Rose	Don James	Steve Emtman, DT
1992	**Alabama**	13-0-0	Won Sugar	Gene Stallings	Eric Curry, DE
1993	**Florida St.**	12-1-0	Won Orange	Bobby Bowden	Charlie Ward, QB
1994	**Nebraska**	13-0-0	Won Orange	Tom Osborne	Zach Wiegert, OT
1995	**Nebraska**	12-0-0	Won Fiesta	Tom Osborne	Tommie Frazier, QB
1996	**Florida**	12-1*	Won Sugar	Steve Spurrier	Danny Wuerffel, QB
1997	**Michigan** (AP, FW, NFF)	12-0	Won Rose	Lloyd Carr	Charles Woodson, DB
	& **Nebraska** (ESPN/USA)	13-0	Won Orange	Tom Osborne	Ahman Green, RB
1998	**Tennessee**	13-0	Won Fiesta	Phillip Fulmer	Peerless Price, WR
1999	**Florida St.**	12-0	Won Sugar	Bobby Bowden	Peter Warrick, WR
2000	**Oklahoma**	13-0	Won Orange	Bob Stoops	Josh Heupel, QB
2001	**Miami-FL**	12-0	Won Rose	Larry Coker	Ken Dorsey, QB
2002	**Ohio St.**	14-0	Won Fiesta	Jim Tressel	Craig Krenzler, QB
2003	**USC** (AP)	12-1	Won Rose	Pete Carroll	Matt Leinart, QB
	& **LSU** (ESPN/USA)	13-1	Won Sugar	Nick Saban	Matt Mauck, QB
2004	**USC**	13-0	Won Orange	Pete Carroll	Matt Leinart, QB
2005	**Texas**	13-0	Won Rose	Mack Brown	Vince Young, QB
2006	**Florida**	13-1	Won BCS Game	Urban Meyer	Chris Leak, QB

*The NCAA instituted overtime for regular season games in 1996.

Number 1 vs. Number 2

Since the Associated Press writers poll started keeping track of such things in 1936, the No. 1 and No. 2 ranked teams in the country have met 35 times; 20 during the regular season and 15 in bowl games. Since the first showdown in 1943, the No. 1 team has beaten the No. 2 team 22 times, lost 11 and there have been two ties. Each showdown is listed below with the date, the match-up, each team's record going into the game, the final score, the stadium and site.

Date		Match-up		Stadium	Date		Match-up		Stadium
Oct. 9	#1	Notre Dame (2-0)	35	Michigan	Nov. 10	#1	Army (6-0)	48	Yankee
1943	#2	Michigan (3-0)	12	(Ann Arbor)	1945	#2	Notre Dame (5-0-1)	0	(New York)
Nov. 20	#1	Notre Dame (8-0)	14	Notre Dame	Dec. 1	#1	Army (8-0)	32	Municipal
1943	#2	Iowa Pre-Flight (8-0)	13	(South Bend)	1945	#2	Navy (7-0-1)	13	(Philadelphia)
Dec. 2	#1	Army (8-0)	23	Municipal	Nov. 9	#1	Army (7-0)	0	Yankee
1944	#2	Navy (6-2)	7	(Baltimore)	1946	#2	Notre Dame (5-0)	0	(New York)

Date		Match-up	Stadium
Jan. 1	#1	USC (10-0) 42	ROSE BOWL
1963	#2	Wisconsin (8-1) ...37	(Pasadena)
Oct. 12	#2	Texas (3-0) 28	Cotton Bowl
1963	#1	Oklahoma (2-0) ...7	(Dallas)
Jan. 1	#1	Texas (10-0) 28	COTTON BOWL
1964	#2	Navy (9-1) 6	(Dallas)
Nov. 19	#1	Notre Dame (8-0) .10	Spartan
1966	#2	Michigan St. (9-0) .10	(East Lansing)
Sept. 28	#1	Purdue (1-0) 37	Notre Dame
1968	#2	Notre Dame (1-0) ..22	(South Bend)
Jan. 1	#1	Ohio St. (9-0) 27	ROSE BOWL
1969	#2	USC (9-0-1) 16	(Pasadena)
Dec. 6	#1	Texas (9-0) 15	Razorback
1969	#2	Arkansas (9-0) 14	(Fayetteville)
Nov. 25	#1	Nebraska (10-0) ..35	Owen Field
1971	#2	Oklahoma (9-0) ...31	(Norman)
Jan. 1	#1	Nebraska (12-0) ..38	ORANGE BOWL
1972	#2	Alabama (11-0) 6	(Miami)
Jan. 1	#1	Alabama (10-1) ...14	SUGAR BOWL
1979	#1	Penn St. (11-0) 7	(New Orleans)
Sept. 26	#1	USC (2-0) 28	Coliseum
1981	#2	Oklahoma (1-0) ...24	(Los Angeles)
Jan. 1	#2	Penn St. (10-1) ...27	SUGAR BOWL
1983	#1	Georgia (11-0) 23	(New Orleans)
Oct. 19	#1	Iowa (5-0) 12	Kinnick
1985	#2	Michigan (5-0) 10	(Iowa City) ·
Sept. 27	#2	Miami-FL (3-0) ...28	Orange Bowl
1986	#1	Oklahoma (2-0) ...16	(Miami)
Jan. 2	#2	Penn St. (11-0) ...14	FIESTA BOWL
1987	#1	Miami-FL (11-0) ...10	(Tempe)
Nov. 21	#2	Oklahoma (10-0) ..17	Memorial
1987	#1	Nebraska (10-0) 7	(Lincoln)

Date		Match-up	Stadium
Jan. 1	#2	Miami-FL (11-0) 20	ORANGE BOWL
1988	#1	Oklahoma (11-0) ...14	(Miami)
Nov. 26	#1	Notre Dame (10-0) ..27	Coliseum
1988	#2	USC (10-0) 10	(Los Angeles)
Sept. 16	#1	Notre Dame (1-0) ...24	Michigan
1989	#2	Michigan (0-0) 19	(Ann Arbor)
Nov. 16	#2	Miami-FL (8-0) 17	Doak Campbell
1991	#1	Florida St. (10-0) ...16	(Tallahassee)
Jan. 1	#2	Alabama (12-0) 34	SUGAR BOWL
1993	#1	Miami-FL (11-0) ...13	(New Orleans)
Nov. 13	#2	Notre Dame (9-0) ...31	Notre Dame
1993	#1	Florida St. (9-0) 24	(South Bend)
Jan. 1	#1	Florida St. (11-1) ...18	ORANGE BOWL
1994	#2	Nebraska (11-0) 16	(Miami)
Jan. 2	#1	Nebraska (11-0) 62	FIESTA BOWL
1996	#2	Florida (12-0) 24	(Tempe)
Nov. 30	#2	Florida St. (10-0) ...24	Doak Campbell
1996	#1	Florida (10-1) 21	(Tallahassee)
Jan. 4	#1	Tennessee (12-0) ...23	FIESTA BOWL
1999	#2	Florida St. (11-1) ...16	(Tempe)
Jan. 4	#1	Florida St. (11-0) ...46	SUGAR BOWL
2000	#2	Virginia Tech (11-0) .29	(New Orleans)
Jan. 3	#2	Ohio St. (13-0) 31	FIESTA BOWL
2003	#1	Miami-FL (12-0) .2OT 24	(Tempe)
Jan. 4	#1	USC (12-0) 55	ORANGE BOWL
2005	#2	Oklahoma (12-0) ...19	(Miami)
Jan. 4	#1	Texas (12-0) 41	ROSE BOWL
2006	#2	USC (12-0) 38	(Pasadena)
Jan. 8	#2	Florida (12-1) 41	BCS Title Game
2007	#1	Ohio St. (12-0) 14	(Glendale)

Note: Bowl games are listed in CAPITAL letters.

Top 50 Rivalries

Top Division I-A and I-AA series records, including games through the 2006 season. All rivalries listed below are renewed annually with the following exception. **Nebraska-Oklahoma** now play only when matched up as part of the rotating Big 12 schedule.

RECENTLY DISCONTINUED SERIES: **Penn State vs Pitt** in 2001 after 96 games (Penn State ahead 50-42-4)

	Gm	Series Leader		Gm	Series Leader
Air Force-Army	41	Air Force (27-13-1)	**Michigan-Michigan St.**	99	Michigan (66-28-5)
Air Force-Navy	39	Air Force (25-14-0)	**Michigan-Notre Dame**	34	Michigan (19-14-1)
Alabama-Auburn	71	Alabama (38-32-1)	**Michigan-Ohio St.**	103	Michigan (57-40-6)
Alabama-Tennessee	89	Alabama (44-38-7)	**Minnesota-Wisconsin**	115	Minnesota (58-49-8)
Arizona-Arizona St.	80	Arizona (44-35-1)	**Mississippi-Miss. St.**	103	Ole Miss (59-38-6)
Army-Navy	107	Navy (51-49-7)	**Missouri-Kansas**	115	Tied (53-53-9)
Auburn-Georgia	110	Auburn (53-49-8)	**Nebraska-Oklahoma**	83	Oklahoma (42-38-3)
California-Stanford	109	Stanford (54-44-11)	**N. Mexico-N. Mexico St.**	96	New Mexico (63-28-5)
The Citadel-VMI	65	The Citadel (33-30-2)	**N. Carolina-N.C. State**	96	N. Carolina (63-27-6)
Clemson-S. Carolina	104	Clemson (63-37-4)	**Notre Dame-Purdue**	78	Notre Dame (52-24-2)
Colorado-Nebraska	65	Nebraska (46-17-2)	**Notre Dame-USC**	78	Notre Dame (42-31-5)
Colo. St.-Wyoming	96	Colorado St. (51-40-5)	**Oklahoma-Okla. St.**	101	Oklahoma (78-16-7)
Duke-N. Carolina	92	N. Carolina (53-36-4)*	**Oregon-Oregon St.**	110	Oregon (55-45-10)
Florida-Florida St.	51	Florida (30-19-2)	**Penn-Cornell**	113	Penn (65-43-5)
Florida-Georgia	85	Georgia (47-36-2)	**Pittsburgh-West Va**	99	Pitt (58-38-3)
Florida St.-Miami,FL	51	Miami (29-22-0)	**Princeton-Yale**	129	Yale (70-49-10)
Georgia-Georgia Tech	101	Georgia (58-38-5)*	**Purdue-Indiana**	109	Purdue (68-35-6)
Grambling-Southern	55	Southern (29-26-0)	**Richmond-Wm. & Mary**	116	Wm. & Mary (58-53-5)
Harvard-Yale	123	Yale (65-50-8)	**Tennessee-Vanderbilt**	98	Tennessee (68-27-5)
Iowa-Iowa St.	54	Iowa (36-18-0)	**Texas-Oklahoma**	101	Texas (58-38-5)
Kansas-Kansas St.	104	Kansas (63-36-5)	**Texas-Texas A&M**	113	Texas (73-35-5)
Kentucky-Tennessee	102	Tennessee (70-23-9)	**UCLA-USC**	76	USC (40-29-7)
Lafayette-Lehigh	142	Lafayette (75-62-5)	**Utah-BYU**	82	Utah (49-29-4)*
LSU-Mississippi	95	LSU (54-37-4)	**Utah-Utah St.**	104	Utah (71-29-4)
Miami,OH-Cincinnati	111	Miami (59-45-7)	**Washington-Wash. St.**	99	Washington (65-28-6)

*Disputed series records: UNC claims lead of 54-35-4; Georgia claims lead of 58-36-5; Utah claims lead of 52-32-4

Associated Press Final Polls

The Associated Press introduced its weekly college football poll of sportswriters (later, sportswriters and broadcasters) in 1936. The final AP poll was released at the end of the regular season until 1965, when bowl results were included for one year. After a two-year return to regular season games only, the final poll has come out after the bowls since 1968. Starting in 1989, the AP Poll has ranked 25 teams.

1936

Final poll released Nov. 30. Top 20 regular season results after that: **Dec. 5**–#8 Notre Dame tied USC, 13-13; #17 Tennessee tied Ole Miss, 0-0; #18 Arkansas over Texas, 6-0. **Dec. 12**–#16 TCU over #6 Santa Clara, 9-0.

	As of Nov. 30	Head Coach	After Bowls
1 Minnesota	.7-1-0	Bernie Bierman	same
2 LSU	.9-0-1	Bernie Moore	9-1-1
3 Pittsburgh	.7-1-1	Jock Sutherland	8-1-1
4 Alabama	.8-0-1	Frank Thomas	same
5 Washington	.7-1-1	Jimmy Phelan	7-2-1
6 Santa Clara	.7-0-0	Buck Shaw	8-1-0
7 Northwestern	.7-1-0	Pappy Waldorf	same
8 Notre Dame	.6-2-0	Elmer Layden	6-2-1
9 Nebraska	.7-2-0	Dana X. Bible	same
10 Penn	.7-1-0	Harvey Harman	same
11 Duke	.9-1-0	Wallace Wade	same
12 Yale	.7-1-0	Ducky Pond	same
13 Dartmouth	.7-1-1	Red Blaik	same
14 Duquesne	.7-2-0	John Smith	8-2-0
15 Fordham	.5-1-2	Jim Crowley	same
16 TCU	.7-2-2	Dutch Meyer	9-2-2
17 Tennessee	.6-2-1	Bob Neyland	6-2-2
18 Arkansas	.6-3-0	Fred Thomsen	7-3-0
Navy	.6-3-0	Tom Hamilton	same
20 Marquette	.7-1-0	Frank Murray	7-2-0

Key Bowl Games

Sugar–#6 Santa Clara over #2 LSU, 21-14; **Rose**–#3 Pitt over #5 Washington, 21-0; **Orange**–#14 Duquesne over Mississippi St., 13-12; **Cotton**–#16 TCU over #20 Marquette, 16-6.

1937

Final poll released Nov. 29. Top 20 regular season results after that: **Dec. 4**–#18 Rice over SMU, 15-7.

	As of Nov. 29	Head Coach	After Bowls
1 Pittsburgh	.9-0-1	Jock Sutherland	same
2 California	.9-0-1	Stub Allison	10-0-1
3 Fordham	.7-0-1	Jim Crowley	same
4 Alabama	.9-0-0	Frank Thomas	9-1-0
5 Minnesota	.6-2-0	Bernie Bierman	same
6 Villanova	.8-0-1	Clipper Smith	same
7 Dartmouth	.7-0-2	Red Blaik	same
8 LSU	.9-1-0	Bernie Moore	9-2-0
9 Notre Dame	.6-2-1	Elmer Layden	same
Santa Clara	.8-0-0	Buck Shaw	9-0-0
11 Nebraska	.6-1-2	Biff Jones	same
12 Yale	.6-1-1	Ducky Pond	same
13 Ohio St.	.6-2-0	Francis Schmidt	same
14 Holy Cross	.8-0-2	Eddie Anderson	same
Arkansas	.6-2-2	Fred Thomsen	same
16 TCU	.4-2-2	Dutch Meyer	same
17 Colorado	.8-0-0	Bunnie Oakes	8-1-0
18 Rice	.4-3-2	Jimmy Kitts	6-3-2
19 North Carolina	.7-1-1	Ray Wolf	same
20 Duke	.7-1-0	Wallace Wade	same

Key Bowl Games

Rose–#2 Cal over #4 Alabama, 13-0; **Sugar**–#9 Santa Clara over #8 LSU, 6-0; **Cotton**–#18 Rice over #17 Colorado, 28-14; **Orange**–Auburn over Michigan St., 6-0.

1938

Final poll released Dec. 5. Top 20 regular season results after that: **Dec. 26**–#14 Cal over Georgia Tech, 13-7.

	As of Dec. 5	Head Coach	After Bowls
1 TCU	.10-0-0	Dutch Meyer	11-0-0
2 Tennessee	.10-0-0	Bob Neyland	11-0-0
3 Duke	.9-0-0	Wallace Wade	9-1-0
4 Oklahoma	.10-0-0	Tom Stidham	10-1-0
5 Notre Dame	.8-1-0	Elmer Layden	same
6 Carnegie Tech	.7-1-0	Bill Kern	7-2-0
7 USC	.8-2-0	Howard Jones	9-2-0
8 Pittsburgh	.8-2-0	Jock Sutherland	same
9 Holy Cross	.8-1-0	Eddie Anderson	same
10 Minnesota	.6-2-0	Bernie Bierman	same
11 Texas Tech	.10-0-0	Pete Cawthon	10-1-0
12 Cornell	.5-1-1	Carl Snavely	same
13 Alabama	.7-1-1	Frank Thomas	same
14 California	.9-1-0	Stub Allison	10-1-0
15 Fordham	.6-1-2	Jim Crowley	same
16 Michigan	.6-1-1	Fritz Crisler	same
17 Northwestern	.4-2-2	Pappy Waldorf	same
18 Villanova	.8-0-1	Clipper Smith	same
19 Tulane	.7-2-1	Red Dawson	same
20 Dartmouth	.7-2-0	Red Blaik	same

Key Bowl Games

Sugar–#1 TCU over #6 Carnegie Tech, 15-7; **Orange**–#2 California over #4 Oklahoma, 17-0; **Rose**–#7 USC over #3 Duke, 7-3; **Cotton**–St. Mary's over #11 Texas Tech 20-13.

1939

Final poll released Dec. 11. Top 20 regular season results after that: None.

	As of Dec. 11	Head Coach	After Bowls
1 Texas A&M	.10-0-0	Homer Norton	11-0-0
2 Tennessee	.10-0-0	Bob Neyland	10-1-0
3 USC	.7-0-2	Howard Jones	8-0-2
4 Cornell	.8-0-0	Carl Snavely	same
5 Tulane	.8-0-1	Red Dawson	8-1-1
6 Missouri	.8-1-0	Don Faurot	8-2-0
7 UCLA	.6-0-4	Babe Horrell	same
8 Duke	.8-1-0	Wallace Wade	same
9 Iowa	.6-1-1	Eddie Anderson	same
10 Duquesne	.8-0-1	Buff Donelli	same
11 Boston College	.9-1-0	Frank Leahy	9-2-0
12 Clemson	.8-1-0	Jess Neely	9-1-0
13 Notre Dame	.7-2-0	Elmer Layden	same
14 Santa Clara	.5-1-3	Buck Shaw	same
15 Ohio St.	.6-2-0	Francis Schmidt	same
16 Georgia Tech	.7-2-0	Bill Alexander	8-2-0
17 Fordham	.6-2-0	Jim Crowley	same
18 Nebraska	.7-1-1	Biff Jones	same
19 Oklahoma	.6-2-1	Tom Stidham	same
20 Michigan	.6-2-0	Fritz Crisler	same

Key Bowl Games

Sugar–#1 Texas A&M over #5 Tulane, 14-13; **Rose**–#3 USC over #2 Tennessee, 14-0; **Orange**–#16 Georgia Tech over #6 Missouri, 21-7; **Cotton**–#12 Clemson over #11 Boston College, 6-3.

1940

Final poll released Dec. 2. Top 20 regular season results after that: **Dec. 7**–#16 SMU over Rice, 7-6.

		As of Dec. 2	Head Coach	After Bowls
1	Minnesota	8-0-0	Bernie Bierman	same
2	Stanford	9-0-0	Clark Shaughnessy	10-0-0
3	Michigan	7-1-0	Fritz Crisler	same
4	Tennessee	10-0-0	Bob Neyland	10-1-0
5	Boston College	10-0-0	Frank Leahy	11-0-0
6	Texas A&M	8-1-0	Homer Norton	9-1-0
7	Nebraska	8-1-0	Biff Jones	8-2-0
8	Northwestern	6-2-0	Pappy Waldorf	same
9	Mississippi St.	9-0-1	Allyn McKeen	10-0-1
10	Washington	7-2-0	Jimmy Phelan	same
11	Santa Clara	6-1-1	Buck Shaw	same
12	Fordham	7-1-0	Jim Crowley	7-2-0
13	Georgetown	8-1-0	Jack Hagerty	8-2-0
14	Penn	6-1-1	George Munger	same
15	Cornell	6-2-0	Carl Snavely	same
16	SMU	7-1-1	Matty Bell	8-1-1
17	Hardin-Simmons	9-0-0	Warren Woodson	same
18	Duke	7-2-0	Wallace Wade	same
19	Lafayette	9-0-0	Hooks Mylin	same
20	–			

Note: Only 19 teams ranked.

Key Bowl Games

Rose–#2 Stanford over #7 Nebraska, 21-13; **Sugar**– #5 Boston College over #4 Tennessee, 19-13; **Cotton**–#6 Texas A&M over #12 Fordham, 13-12; **Orange**–#9 Mississippi St. over #13 Georgetown, 14-7.

1941

Final poll released Dec. 1. Top 20 regular season results after that: **Dec. 6**–#4 Texas over Oregon, 71-7; #9 Texas A&M over #19 Washington St., 7-0; #16 Mississippi St. over San Francisco, 26-13.

		As of Dec. 1	Head Coach	After Bowls
1	Minnesota	8-0-0	Bernie Bierman	same
2	Duke	9-0-0	Wallace Wade	9-1-0
3	Notre Dame	8-0-1	Frank Leahy	same
4	Texas	7-1-1	Dana X. Bible	8-1-1
5	Michigan	6-1-1	Fritz Crisler	same
6	Fordham	7-1-0	Jim Crowley	8-1-0
7	Missouri	8-1-0	Don Faurot	8-2-0
8	Duquesne	8-0-0	Buff Donelli	same
9	Texas A&M	8-1-0	Homer Norton	9-2-0
10	Navy	7-1-1	Swede Larson	same
11	Northwestern	5-3-0	Pappy Waldorf	same
12	Oregon St.	7-2-0	Lon Stiner	8-2-0
13	Ohio St.	6-1-1	Paul Brown	same
14	Georgia	8-1-1	Wally Butts	9-1-1
15	Penn	7-1-1	George Munger	same
16	Mississippi St.	7-1-1	Allyn McKeen	8-1-1
17	Mississippi	6-2-1	Harry Mehre	same
18	Tennessee	8-2-0	John Barnhill	same
19	Washington St.	6-3-0	Babe Hollingbery	6-4-0
20	Alabama	8-2-0	Frank Thomas	9-2-0

Note: 1942 Rose Bowl moved to Durham, N.C., for one year after outbreak of World War II.

Key Bowl Games

Rose–#12 Oregon St. over #2 Duke, 20-16; **Sugar**–#6 Fordham over #7 Missouri, 2-0; **Cotton**–#20 Alabama over #9 Texas A&M, 29-21; **Orange**–#14 Georgia over TCU, 40-26.

1942

Final poll released Nov. 30. Top 20 regular season results after that: **Dec. 5**–#6 Notre Dame tied Great Lakes Naval Station, 13-13; #13 UCLA over Idaho, 40-13; #14 William & Mary over Oklahoma, 14-7; #17 Washington St. lost to Texas A&M, 21-0; #18 Mississippi St. over San Francisco, 19-7. **Dec. 12**–#13 UCLA over USC, 14-7.

		As of Nov. 30	Head Coach	After Bowls
1	Ohio St.	9-1-0	Paul Brown	same
2	Georgia	10-1-0	Wally Butts	11-1-0
3	Wisconsin	8-1-1	Harry Stuhldreher	same
4	Tulsa	10-0-0	Henry Frnka	10-1-0
5	Georgia Tech	9-1-0	Bill Alexander	9-2-0
6	Notre Dame	7-2-1	Frank Leahy	7-2-2
7	Tennessee	8-1-1	John Barnhill	9-1-1
8	Boston College	8-1-0	Denny Myers	8-2-0
9	Michigan	7-3-0	Fritz Crisler	same
10	Alabama	7-3-0	Frank Thomas	8-3-0
11	Texas	8-2-0	Dana X. Bible	9-2-0
12	Stanford	6-4-0	Marchy Schwartz	same
13	UCLA	5-3-0	Babe Horrell	7-4-0
14	William & Mary	8-1-1	Carl Voyles	9-1-1
15	Santa Clara	7-2-0	Buck Shaw	same
16	Auburn	6-4-1	Jack Meagher	same
17	Washington St.	6-1-2	Babe Hollingbery	6-2-2
18	Mississippi St.	7-2-0	Allyn McKeen	8-2-0
19	Minnesota	5-4-0	George Hauser	same
	Holy Cross	5-4-1	Ank Scanlon	same
	Penn St.	6-1-1	Bob Higgins	same

Key Bowl Games

Rose–#2 Georgia over #13 UCLA, 9-0; **Sugar**–#7 Tennessee over #4 Tulsa, 14-7; **Cotton**–#11 Texas over #5 Georgia Tech, 14-7; **Orange**–#10 Alabama over #8 Boston College, 37-21.

1943

Final poll released Nov. 29. Top 20 regular season results after that: **Dec. 11**–#10 March Field over #19 Pacific, 19-0.

		As of Nov. 29	Head Coach	After Bowls
1	Notre Dame	9-1-0	Frank Leahy	same
2	Iowa Pre-Flight	9-1-0	Don Faurot	same
3	Michigan	8-1-0	Fritz Crisler	same
4	Navy	8-1-0	Billick Whelchel	same
5	Purdue	9-0-0	Elmer Burnham	same
6	Great Lakes Naval Station	10-2-0	Tony Hinkle	same
7	Duke	8-1-0	Eddie Cameron	same
8	DelMonte Pre-Flight	7-1-0	Bill Kern	same
9	Northwestern	6-2-0	Pappy Waldorf	same
10	March Field	8-1-0	Paul Schissler	9-1-0
11	Army	7-2-1	Red Blaik	same
12	Washington	4-0-0	Ralph Welch	4-1-0
13	Georgia Tech	7-3-0	Bill Alexander	8-3-0
14	Texas	7-1-0	Dana X. Bible	7-1-1
15	Tulsa	6-0-1	Henry Frnka	6-1-1
16	Dartmouth	6-1-0	Earl Brown	same
17	Bainbridge Navy Training School	7-0-0	Joe Maniaci	same
18	Colorado College	7-0-0	Hal White	same
19	Pacific	7-1-0	Amos A. Stagg	7-2-0
20	Penn	6-2-1	George Munger	same

Key Bowl Games

Rose–USC over #12 Washington, 29-0; **Sugar**–#13 Georgia Tech over #15 Tulsa, 20-18; **Cotton**–#14 Texas tied Randolph Field, 7-7; **Orange**–LSU over Texas A&M, 19-14.

Associated Press Final Polls (Cont.)

1944

Final poll released Dec. 4. Top 20 regular season results after that: **Dec. 10**–#3 Randolph Field over #10 March Field, 20-7; #18 Fort Pierce over Kessler Field, 34-7; Morris Field over #20 Second Air Force, 14-7.

	As of Dec. 4	Head Coach	After Bowls
1 Army	.9-0-0	Red Blaik	same
2 Ohio St.	.9-0-0	Carroll Widdoes	same
3 Randolph Field	.10-0-0	Frank Tritico	12-0-0
4 Navy	.6-3-0	Oscar Hagberg	same
5 Bainbridge Navy Training School	.10-0-0	Joe Maniaci	same
6 Iowa Pre-Flight	.10-1-0	Jack Meagher	same
7 USC	.7-0-2	Jeff Cravath	8-0-2
8 Michigan	.8-2-0	Fritz Crisler	same
9 Notre Dame	.8-2-0	Ed McKeever	same
10 March Field	.7-0-2	Paul Schissler	7-1-2
11 Duke	.5-4-0	Eddie Cameron	6-4-0
12 Tennessee	.7-0-1	John Barnhill	7-1-1
13 Georgia Tech	.8-2-0	Bill Alexander	8-3-0
14 Norman Pre-Flight	.6-0-0	John Gregg	same
15 Illinois	.5-4-1	Ray Eliot	same
16 El Toro Marines	.8-1-0	Dick Hanley	same
17 Great Lakes Naval Station	.9-2-1	Paul Brown	same
18 Fort Pierce	.8-0-0	Hamp Pool	9-0-0
19 St. Mary's Pre-Flight	.9-1-0	Jules Sikes	same
20 Second Air Force	.10-2-1	Bill Reese	10-4-1

Key Bowl Games

Treasury–#3 Randolph Field over #20 Second Air Force, 13-6; **Rose**–#7 USC over #12 Tennessee, 25-0; **Sugar**–#11 Duke over Alabama, 29-26; **Orange**–Tulsa over #13 Georgia Tech, 26-12; **Cotton**–Oklahoma A&M over TCU, 34-0.

1945

Final poll released Dec. 3. Top 20 regular season results after that: None.

	As of Dec. 3	Head Coach	After Bowls
1 Army	.9-0-0	Red Blaik	same
2 Alabama	.9-0-0	Frank Thomas	10-0-0
3 Navy	.7-1-1	Oscar Hagberg	same
4 Indiana	.9-0-1	Bo McMillan	same
5 Oklahoma A&M	.8-0-0	Jim Lookabaugh	9-0-0
6 Michigan	.7-3-0	Fritz Crisler	same
7 St. Mary's-CA	.7-1-0	Jimmy Phelan	7-2-0
8 Penn	.6-2-0	George Munger	same
9 Notre Dame	.7-2-1	Hugh Devore	same
10 Texas	.9-1-0	Dana X. Bible	10-1-0
11 USC	.7-3-0	Jeff Cravath	7-4-0
12 Ohio St.	.7-2-0	Carroll Widdoes	same
13 Duke	.6-2-0	Eddie Cameron	same
14 Tennessee	.8-1-0	John Barnhill	same
15 LSU	.7-2-0	Bernie Moore	same
16 Holy Cross	.8-1-0	John DeGrosa	8-2-0
17 Tulsa	.8-2-0	Henry Frnka	8-3-0
18 Georgia	.8-2-0	Wally Butts	9-2-0
19 Wake Forest	.4-3-1	Peahead Walker	5-3-1
20 Columbia	.8-1-0	Lou Little	same

Key Bowl Games

Rose–#2 Alabama over #11 USC, 34-14; **Sugar**–#5 Oklahoma A&M over #7 St. Mary's, 33-13; **Cotton**–#10 Texas over Missouri, 40-27; **Orange**–Miami-FL over #16 Holy Cross, 13-6.

1946

Final poll released Dec. 2. Top 20 regular season results after that: None.

	As of Dec. 2	Head Coach	After Bowls
1 Notre Dame	.8-0-1	Frank Leahy	same
2 Army	.9-0-1	Red Blaik	same
3 Georgia	.10-0-0	Wally Butts	11-0-0
4 UCLA	.10-0-0	Bert LaBrucherie	10-1-0
5 Illinois	.7-2-0	Ray Eliot	8-2-0
6 Michigan	.6-2-1	Fritz Crisler	same
7 Tennessee	.9-1-0	Bob Neyland	9-2-0
8 LSU	.9-1-0	Bernie Moore	9-1-1
9 North Carolina	.8-1-1	Carl Snavely	8-2-1
10 Rice	.8-2-0	Jess Neely	9-2-0
11 Georgia Tech	.8-2-0	Bobby Dodd	9-2-0
12 Yale	.7-1-1	Howard Odell	same
13 Penn	.6-2-0	George Munger	same
14 Oklahoma	.7-3-0	Jim Tatum	8-3-0
15 Texas	.8-2-0	Dana X. Bible	same
16 Arkansas	.6-3-1	John Barnhill	6-3-2
17 Tulsa	.9-1-0	J.O. Brothers	same
18 N.C. State	.8-2-0	Beattie Feathers	8-3-0
19 Delaware	.9-0-0	Bill Murray	10-0-0
20 Indiana	.6-3-0	Bo McMillan	same

Key Bowl Games

Sugar–#3 Georgia over #9 N. Carolina, 20-10; **Rose**–#5 Illinois over #4 UCLA, 45-14; **Orange**–#10 Rice over #7 Tennessee, 8-0; **Cotton**–#8 LSU tied #16 Arkansas, 0-0.

1947

Final poll released Dec. 8. Top 20 regular season results after that: None.

	As of Dec. 8	Head Coach	After Bowls
1 Notre Dame	.9-0-0	Frank Leahy	same
2 Michigan	.9-0-0	Fritz Crisler	10-0-0
3 SMU	.9-0-1	Matty Bell	9-0-2
4 Penn St.	.9-0-0	Bob Higgins	9-0-1
5 Texas	.9-1-0	Blair Cherry	10-1-0
6 Alabama	.8-2-0	Red Drew	8-3-0
7 Penn	.7-0-1	George Munger	same
8 USC	.7-1-1	Jeff Cravath	7-2-1
9 North Carolina	.8-2-0	Carl Snavely	same
10 Georgia Tech	.9-1-0	Bobby Dodd	10-1-0
11 Army	.5-2-2	Red Blaik	same
12 Kansas	.8-0-2	George Sauer	8-1-2
13 Mississippi	.8-2-0	Johnny Vaught	9-2-0
14 William & Mary	.9-1-0	Rube McCray	9-2-0
15 California	.9-1-0	Pappy Waldorf	same
16 Oklahoma	.7-2-1	Bud Wilkinson	same
17 N.C. State	.5-3-1	Beattie Feathers	same
18 Rice	.6-3-1	Jess Neely	same
19 Duke	.4-3-2	Wallace Wade	same
20 Columbia	.7-2-0	Lou Little	same

Key Bowl Games

Rose–#2 Michigan over #8 USC, 49-0; **Cotton**–#3 SMU tied #4 Penn St., 13-13; **Sugar**–#5 Texas over #6 Alabama, 27-7; **Orange**–#10 Georgia Tech over #12 Kansas, 20-14.

Note: An unprecedented "Who's No. 1?" poll was conducted by AP after the Rose Bowl game, pitting Notre Dame against Michigan. The Wolverines won the vote, 226-119, but AP ruled that the Irish would be the No. 1 team of record.

1948

Final poll released Nov. 29. Top 20 regular season results after that: **Dec. 3**–#12 Vanderbilt over Miami-FL, 33-6. **Dec. 4**–#2 Notre Dame tied USC, 14-14; #11 Clemson over The Citadel, 20-0.

		As of Nov. 29	Head Coach	After Bowls
1	Michigan	9-0-0	Bennie Oosterbaan	same
2	Notre Dame	9-0-0	Frank Leahy	9-0-1
3	North Carolina	9-0-1	Carl Snavely	9-1-1
4	California	10-0-0	Pappy Waldorf	10-1-0
5	Oklahoma	9-1-0	Bud Wilkinson	10-1-0
6	Army	8-0-1	Red Blaik	same
7	Northwestern	7-2-0	Bob Voigts	8-2-0
8	Georgia	9-1-0	Wally Butts	9-2-0
9	Oregon	9-1-0	Jim Aiken	9-2-0
10	SMU	8-1-1	Matty Bell	9-1-1
11	Clemson	9-0-0	Frank Howard	11-0-0
12	Vanderbilt	7-2-1	Red Sanders	8-2-1
13	Tulane	9-1-0	Henry Frnka	same
14	Michigan St.	6-2-2	Biggie Munn	same
15	Mississippi	8-1-0	Johnny Vaught	same
16	Minnesota	7-2-0	Bernie Bierman	same
17	William & Mary	6-2-2	Rube McCray	7-2-2
18	Penn St.	7-1-1	Bob Higgins	same
19	Cornell	8-1-0	Lefty James	same
20	Wake Forest	6-3-0	Peahead Walker	6-4-0

Note: Big Nine "no-repeat" rule kept Michigan from Rose Bowl.

Key Bowl Games

Sugar–#5 Oklahoma over #3 North Carolina, 14-6; **Rose**–#7 Northwestern over #4 Cal, 20-14; **Orange**–Texas over #8 Georgia, 41-28; **Cotton**–#10 SMU over #9 Oregon, 21-13.

1949

Final poll released Nov. 28. Top 20 regular season results after that: **Dec. 2**–#14 Maryland over Miami-FL, 13-0. **Dec. 3**–#1 Notre Dame over SMU, 27-20; #10 Pacific over Hawaii, 75-0.

		As of Nov. 28	Head Coach	After Bowls
1	Notre Dame	9-0-0	Frank Leahy	10-0-0
2	Oklahoma	10-0-0	Bud Wilkinson	11-0-0
3	California	10-0-0	Pappy Waldorf	10-1-0
4	Army	9-0-0	Red Blaik	same
5	Rice	9-1-0	Jess Neely	10-1-0
6	Ohio St.	6-1-2	Wes Fesler	7-1-2
7	Michigan	6-2-1	Bennie Oosterbaan	same
8	Minnesota	7-2-0	Bernie Bierman	same
9	LSU	8-2-0	Gaynell Tinsley	8-3-0
10	Pacific	10-0-0	Larry Siemering	11-0-0
11	Kentucky	9-2-0	Bear Bryant	9-3-0
12	Cornell	8-1-0	Lefty James	same
13	Villanova	8-1-0	Jim Leonard	same
14	Maryland	7-1-0	Jim Tatum	9-1-0
15	Santa Clara	7-2-1	Len Casanova	8-2-1
16	North Carolina	7-3-0	Carl Snavely	7-4-0
17	Tennessee	7-2-1	Bob Neyland	same
18	Princeton	6-3-0	Charlie Caldwell	same
19	Michigan St.	6-3-0	Biggie Munn	same
20	Missouri	7-3-0	Don Faurot	7-4-0
	Baylor	8-2-0	Bob Woodruff	same

Key Bowl Games

Sugar–#2 Oklahoma over #9 LSU, 35-0; **Rose**–#6 Ohio St. over #3 Cal, 17-14; **Cotton**–#5 Rice over #16 North Carolina, 27-13; **Orange**–#15 Santa Clara over #11 Kentucky, 21-13.

1950

Final poll released Nov. 27. Top 20 regular season results after that: **Nov. 30**–#3 Texas over Texas A&M, 17-0. **Dec. 1**–#15 Miami-FL over Missouri, 27–9. **Dec. 2**–#1 Oklahoma over Okla. A&M, 41-14; Navy over #2 Army, 14-2; #4 Tennessee over Vanderbilt, 43-0; #16 Alabama over Auburn, 34-0; #19 Tulsa over Houston, 28-21; #20 Tulane tied LSU, 14-14. **Dec. 9**–#3 Texas over LSU, 21-6.

		As of Nov. 27	Head Coach	After Bowls
1	Oklahoma	9-0-0	Bud Wilkinson	10-1-0
2	Army	8-0-0	Red Blaik	8-1-0
3	Texas	7-1-0	Blair Cherry	9-2-0
4	Tennessee	9-1-0	Bob Neyland	11-1-0
5	California	9-0-1	Pappy Waldorf	9-1-1
6	Princeton	9-0-0	Charlie Caldwell	same
7	Kentucky	10-1-0	Bear Bryant	11-1-0
8	Michigan St.	8-1-0	Biggie Munn	same
9	Michigan	5-3-1	Bennie Oosterbaan	6-3-1
10	Clemson	8-0-1	Frank Howard	9-0-1
11	Washington	8-2-0	Howard Odell	same
12	Wyoming	9-0-0	Bowden Wyatt	10-0-0
13	Illinois	7-2-0	Ray Eliot	same
14	Ohio St.	6-3-0	Wes Fesler	same
15	Miami-FL	8-0-1	Andy Gustafson	9-1-1
16	Alabama	8-2-0	Red Drew	9-2-0
17	Nebraska	6-2-1	Bill Glassford	same
18	Wash. & Lee	8-2-0	George Barclay	8-3-0
19	Tulsa	8-1-1	J.O. Brothers	9-1-1
20	Tulane	6-2-0	Henry Frnka	6-2-1

Key Bowl Games

Sugar–#7 Kentucky over #1 Oklahoma, 13-7; **Cotton**–#4 Tennessee over #3 Texas, 20-14; **Rose**–#9 Michigan over #5 Cal, 14-6; **Orange**–#10 Clemson over #15 Miami-FL, 15-14.

1951

Final poll released Dec. 3. Top 20 regular season results after that: None.

		As of Dec. 3	Head Coach	After Bowls
1	Tennessee	10-0-0	Bob Neyland	10-1-0
2	Michigan St.	9-0-0	Biggie Munn	same
3	Maryland	9-0-0	Jim Tatum	10-0-0
4	Illinois	8-0-1	Ray Eliot	9-0-1
5	Georgia Tech	10-0-1	Bobby Dodd	11-0-1
6	Princeton	9-0-0	Charlie Caldwell	same
7	Stanford	9-1-0	Chuck Taylor	9-2-0
8	Wisconsin	7-1-1	Ivy Williamson	same
9	Baylor	8-1-1	George Sauer	8-2-1
10	Oklahoma	8-2-0	Bud Wilkinson	same
11	TCU	6-4-0	Dutch Meyer	6-5-0
12	California	8-2-0	Pappy Waldorf	same
13	Virginia	8-1-0	Art Guepe	same
14	San Francisco	9-0-0	Joe Kuharich	same
15	Kentucky	7-4-0	Bear Bryant	8-4-0
16	Boston Univ.	6-4-0	Buff Donelli	same
17	UCLA	5-3-1	Red Sanders	same
18	Washington St.	7-3-0	Forest Evashevski	same
19	Holy Cross	8-2-0	Eddie Anderson	same
20	Clemson	7-2-0	Frank Howard	7-3-0

Key Bowl Games

Sugar–#3 Maryland over #1 Tennessee, 28-13; **Rose**–#4 Illinois over #7 Stanford, 40-7; **Orange**–#5 Georgia Tech over #9 Baylor, 17-14; **Cotton**–#15 Kentucky over #11 TCU, 20-7.

Associated Press Final Polls (Cont.)

1952

Final poll released Dec. 1. Top 20 regular season results after that: **Dec. 6**–#15 Florida over #20 Kentucky, 27-20.

		As of Dec. 1	Head Coach	After Bowls
1	Michigan St.	.9-0-0	Biggie Munn	same
2	Georgia Tech	.11-0-0	Bobby Dodd	12-0-0
3	Notre Dame	.7-2-1	Frank Leahy	same
4	Oklahoma	.8-1-1	Bud Wilkinson	same
5	USC	.9-1-0	Jess Hill	10-1-0
6	UCLA	.8-1-0	Red Sanders	same
7	Mississippi	.8-0-2	Johnny Vaught	8-1-2
8	Tennessee	.8-1-1	Bob Neyland	8-2-1
9	Alabama	.9-2-0	Red Drew	10-2-0
10	Texas	.8-2-0	Ed Price	9-2-0
11	Wisconsin	.6-2-1	Ivy Williamson	6-3-1
12	Tulsa	.8-1-1	J.O. Brothers	8-2-1
13	Maryland	.7-2-0	Jim Tatum	same
14	Syracuse	.7-2-0	Ben Schwartzwalder	7-3-0
15	Florida	.6-3-0	Bob Woodruff	8-3-0
16	Duke	.8-2-0	Bill Murray	same
17	Ohio St.	.6-3-0	Woody Hayes	same
18	Purdue	.4-3-2	Stu Holcomb	same
19	Princeton	.8-1-0	Charlie Caldwell	same
20	Kentucky	.5-3-2	Bear Bryant	5-4-2

Note: Michigan St. would officially join Big Ten in 1953.

Key Bowl Games

Sugar–#2 Georgia Tech over #7 Ole Miss, 24-7; **Rose**–#5 USC over #11 Wisconsin, 7-0; **Cotton**–#10 Texas over #8 Tennessee, 16-0; **Orange**–#9 Alabama over #14 Syracuse, 61-6.

1953

Final poll released Nov. 30. Top 20 regular season results after that: **Dec. 5**–#2 Notre Dame over SMU, 40-14.

		As of Nov. 30	Head Coach	After Bowls
1	Maryland	.10-0-0	Jim Tatum	10-1-0
2	Notre Dame	.8-0-1	Frank Leahy	9-0-1
3	Michigan St.	.8-1-0	Biggie Munn	9-1-0
4	Oklahoma	.8-1-1	Bud Wilkinson	9-1-1
5	UCLA	.8-1-0	Red Sanders	8-2-0
6	Rice	.8-2-0	Jess Neely	9-2-0
7	Illinois	.7-1-1	Ray Eliot	same
8	Georgia Tech	.8-2-1	Bobby Dodd	9-2-1
9	Iowa	.5-3-1	Forest Evashevski	same
10	West Virginia	.8-1-0	Art Lewis	8-2-0
11	Texas	.7-3-0	Ed Price	same
12	Texas Tech	.10-1-0	DeWitt Weaver	11-1-0
13	Alabama	.6-2-3	Red Drew	6-3-3
14	Army	.7-1-1	Red Blaik	same
15	Wisconsin	.6-2-1	Ivy Williamson	same
16	Kentucky	.7-2-1	Bear Bryant	same
17	Auburn	.7-2-1	Shug Jordan	7-3-1
18	Duke	.7-2-1	Bill Murray	same
19	Stanford	.6-3-1	Chuck Taylor	same
20	Michigan	.6-3-0	Bennie Oosterbaan	same

Key Bowl Games

Orange–#4 Oklahoma over #1 Maryland, 7-0; **Rose**–#3 Michigan St. over #5 UCLA, 28-20; **Cotton**–#6 Rice over #13 Alabama, 28-6; **Sugar**–#8 Georgia Tech over #10 West Virginia, 42-19.

1954

Final poll released Nov. 29. Top 20 regular season results after that: **Dec. 4**–#4 Notre Dame over SMU, 26-14.

		As of Nov. 29	Head Coach	After Bowls
1	Ohio St.	.9-0-0	Woody Hayes	10-0-0
2	UCLA	.9-0-0	Red Sanders	same
3	Oklahoma	.10-0-0	Bud Wilkinson	same
4	Notre Dame	.8-1-0	Terry Brennan	9-1-0
5	Navy	.7-2-0	Eddie Erdelatz	8-2-0
6	Mississippi	.9-1-0	Johnny Vaught	9-2-0
7	Army	.7-2-0	Red Blaik	same
8	Maryland	.7-2-1	Jim Tatum	same
9	Wisconsin	.7-2-0	Ivy Williamson	same
10	Arkansas	.8-2-0	Bowden Wyatt	8-3-0
11	Miami-FL	.8-1-0	Andy Gustafson	same
12	West Virginia	.8-1-0	Art Lewis	same
13	Auburn	.7-3-0	Shug Jordan	8-3-0
14	Duke	.7-2-1	Bill Murray	8-2-1
15	Michigan	.6-3-0	Bennie Oosterbaan	same
16	Virginia Tech	.8-0-1	Frank Moseley	same
17	USC	.8-3-0	Jess Hill	8-4-0
18	Baylor	.7-3-0	George Sauer	7-4-0
19	Rice	.7-3-0	Jess Neely	same
20	Penn St.	.7-2-0	Rip Engle	same

Note: PCC and Big Seven "no-repeat" rules kept UCLA and Oklahoma from Rose and Orange bowls, respectively.

Key Bowl Games

Rose–#1 Ohio St. over #17 USC, 20-7; **Sugar**–#5 Navy over #6 Ole Miss, 21-0; **Cotton**–Georgia Tech over #10 Arkansas, 14-6; **Orange**–#14 Duke over Nebraska, 34-7.

1955

Final poll released Nov. 28. Top 20 regular season results after that: None.

		As of Nov. 28	Head Coach	After Bowls
1	Oklahoma	.10-0-0	Bud Wilkinson	11-0-0
2	Michigan St.	.8-1-0	Duffy Daugherty	9-1-0
3	Maryland	.10-0-0	Jim Tatum	10-1-0
4	UCLA	.9-1-0	Red Sanders	9-2-0
5	Ohio St.	.7-2-0	Woody Hayes	same
6	TCU	.9-1-0	Abe Martin	9-2-0
7	Georgia Tech	.8-1-1	Bobby Dodd	9-1-1
8	Auburn	.8-1-1	Shug Jordan	8-2-1
9	Notre Dame	.8-2-0	Terry Brennan	same
10	Mississippi	.9-1-0	Johnny Vaught	10-1-0
11	Pittsburgh	.7-3-0	John Michelosen	7-4-0
12	Michigan	.7-2-0	Bennie Oosterbaan	same
13	USC	.6-4-0	Jess Hill	same
14	Miami-FL	.6-3-0	Andy Gustafson	same
15	Miami-OH	.9-0-0	Ara Parseghian	same
16	Stanford	.6-3-1	Chuck Taylor	same
17	Texas A&M	.7-2-1	Bear Bryant	same
18	Navy	.6-2-1	Eddie Erdelatz	same
19	West Virginia	.8-2-0	Art Lewis	same
20	Army	.6-3-0	Red Blaik	same

Note: Big Ten "no-repeat" rule kept Ohio St. from Rose Bowl.

Key Bowl Games

Orange–#1 Oklahoma over #3 Maryland, 20-6; **Rose**–#2 Michigan St. over #4 UCLA, 17-14; **Cotton**–#10 Ole Miss over #6 TCU, 14-13; **Sugar**–#7 Georgia Tech over #11 Pitt, 7-0; **Gator**–Vanderbilt over #8 Auburn, 25-13.

1956

Final poll released Dec. 3. Top 20 regular season results after that: **Dec. 8**–#13 Pitt over #6 Miami-FL, 14-7.

		As of Dec. 3	Head Coach	After Bowls
1	Oklahoma	10-0-0	Bud Wilkinson	same
2	Tennessee	10-0-0	Bowden Wyatt	10-1-0
3	Iowa	8-1-0	Forest Evashevski	9-1-0
4	Georgia Tech	9-1-0	Bobby Dodd	10-1-0
5	Texas A&M	9-0-1	Bear Bryant	same
6	Miami-FL	8-0-1	Andy Gustafson	8-1-1
7	Michigan	7-2-0	Bennie Oosterbaan	same
8	Syracuse	7-1-0	Ben Schwartzwalder	7-2-0
9	Michigan St.	7-2-0	Duffy Daugherty	same
10	Oregon St.	7-2-1	Tommy Prothro	7-3-1
11	Baylor	8-2-0	Sam Boyd	9-2-0
12	Minnesota	6-1-2	Murray Warmath	same
13	Pittsburgh	6-2-1	John Michelosen	7-3-1
14	TCU	7-3-0	Abe Martin	8-3-0
15	Ohio St.	6-3-0	Woody Hayes	same
16	Navy	6-1-2	Eddie Erdelatz	same
17	G. Washington	7-1-1	Gene Sherman	8-1-1
18	USC	8-2-0	Jess Hill	same
19	Clemson	7-1-2	Frank Howard	7-2-2
20	Colorado	7-2-1	Dallas Ward	8-2-1

Note: Big Seven "no-repeat" rule kept Oklahoma from Orange Bowl and Texas A&M was on probation.

Key Bowl Games

Sugar–#11 Baylor over #2 Tennessee, 13-7; **Rose**–#3 Iowa over #10 Oregon St., 35-19; **Gator**–#4 Georgia Tech over #13 Pitt, 21-14; **Cotton**–#14 TCU over #8 Syracuse, 28-27; **Orange**–#20 Colorado over #19 Clemson, 27-21.

1957

Final poll released Dec. 2. Top 20 regular season results after that: **Dec. 7**–#10 Notre Dame over SMU, 54-21.

		As of Dec. 2	Head Coach	After Bowls
1	Auburn	10-0-0	Shug Jordan	same
2	Ohio St.	8-1-0	Woody Hayes	9-1-0
3	Michigan St.	8-1-0	Duffy Daugherty	same
4	Oklahoma	9-1-0	Bud Wilkinson	10-1-0
5	Navy	8-1-1	Eddie Erdelatz	9-1-1
6	Iowa	7-1-1	Forest Evashevski	same
7	Mississippi	8-1-1	Johnny Vaught	9-1-1
8	Rice	7-3-0	Jess Neely	7-4-0
9	Texas A&M	8-2-0	Bear Bryant	8-3-0
10	Notre Dame	6-3-0	Terry Brennan	7-3-0
11	Texas	6-3-1	Darrell Royal	6-4-1
12	Arizona St.	10-0-0	Dan Devine	same
13	Tennessee	7-3-0	Bowden Wyatt	8-3-0
14	Mississippi St.	6-2-1	Wade Walker	same
15	N.C. State	7-1-2	Earle Edwards	same
16	Duke	6-2-2	Bill Murray	6-3-2
17	Florida	6-2-1	Bob Woodruff	same
18	Army	7-2-0	Red Blaik	same
19	Wisconsin	6-3-0	Milt Bruhn	same
20	VMI	9-0-1	John McKenna	same

Note: Auburn on probation, ineligible for bowl game.

Key Bowl Games

Rose–#2 Ohio St. over Oregon, 10-7; **Orange**–#4 Oklahoma over #16 Duke, 48-21; **Cotton**–#5 Navy over #8 Rice, 20-7; **Sugar**–#7 Ole Miss over #11 Texas, 39-7; **Gator**–#13 Tennessee over #9 Texas A&M, 3-0.

1958

Final poll released Dec. 1. Top 20 regular season results after that: None.

		As of Dec. 1	Head Coach	After Bowls
1	LSU	10-0-0	Paul Dietzel	11-0-0
2	Iowa	7-1-1	Forest Evashevski	8-1-1
3	Army	8-0-1	Red Blaik	same
4	Auburn	9-0-1	Shug Jordan	same
5	Oklahoma	9-1-0	Bud Wilkinson	10-1-0
6	Air Force	9-0-1	Ben Martin	9-0-2
7	Wisconsin	7-1-1	Milt Bruhn	same
8	Ohio St.	6-1-2	Woody Hayes	same
9	Syracuse	8-1-0	Ben Schwartzwalder	8-2-0
10	TCU	8-2-0	Abe Martin	8-2-1
11	Mississippi	8-2-0	Johnny Vaught	9-2-0
12	Clemson	8-2-0	Frank Howard	8-3-0
13	Purdue	6-1-2	Jack Mollenkopf	same
14	Florida	6-3-1	Bob Woodruff	6-4-1
15	South Carolina	7-3-0	Warren Giese	same
16	California	7-3-0	Pete Elliott	7-4-0
17	Notre Dame	6-4-0	Terry Brennan	same
18	SMU	6-4-0	Bill Meek	same
19	Oklahoma St.	7-3-0	Cliff Speegle	8-3-0
20	Rutgers	8-1-0	John Stiegman	same

Key Bowl Games

Sugar–#1 LSU over #12 Clemson, 7-0; **Rose**–#2 Iowa over #16 Cal, 38-12; **Orange**–#5 Oklahoma over #9 Syracuse, 21-6; **Cotton**–#6 Air Force tied #10 TCU, 0-0.

1959

Final poll released Dec. 7. Top 20 regular season results after that: None.

		As of Dec. 7	Head Coach	After Bowls
1	Syracuse	10-0-0	Ben Schwartzwalder	11-0-0
2	Mississippi	9-1-0	Johnny Vaught	10-1-0
3	LSU	9-1-0	Paul Dietzel	9-2-0
4	Texas	9-1-0	Darrell Royal	9-2-0
5	Georgia	9-1-0	Wally Butts	10-1-0
6	Wisconsin	7-2-0	Milt Bruhn	7-3-0
7	TCU	8-2-0	Abe Martin	8-3-0
8	Washington	9-1-0	Jim Owens	10-1-0
9	Arkansas	8-2-0	Frank Broyles	9-2-0
10	Alabama	7-1-2	Bear Bryant	7-2-2
11	Clemson	8-2-0	Frank Howard	9-2-0
12	Penn St.	8-2-0	Rip Engle	9-2-0
13	Illinois	5-3-1	Ray Eliot	same
14	USC	8-2-0	Don Clark	same
15	Oklahoma	7-3-0	Bud Wilkinson	same
16	Wyoming	9-1-0	Bob Devaney	same
17	Notre Dame	5-5-0	Joe Kuharich	same
18	Missouri	6-4-0	Dan Devine	6-5-0
19	Florida	5-4-1	Bob Woodruff	same
20	Pittsburgh	6-4-0	John Michelosen	same

Note: Big Seven "no-repeat" rule kept Oklahoma from Orange Bowl.

Key Bowl Games

Cotton–#1 Syracuse over #4 Texas, 23-14; **Sugar**–#2 Ole Miss over #3 LSU, 21-0; **Orange**–#5 Georgia over #18 Missouri, 14-0; **Rose**–#8 Washington over #6 Wisconsin, 44-8; **Bluebonnet**–#11 Clemson over #7 TCU, 23-7; **Gator**–#9 Arkansas over Georgia Tech, 14-7; **Liberty**–#12 Penn St. over #10 Alabama, 7-0.

Associated Press Final Polls (Cont.)

1960

Final poll released Nov. 28. Top 20 regular season results after that: **Dec. 3**–UCLA over #10 Duke, 27-6.

		As of Nov. 28	Head Coach	After Bowls
1	Minnesota	.8-1-0	Murray Warmath	8-2-0
2	Mississippi	.9-0-1	Johnny Vaught	10-0-1
3	Iowa	.8-1-0	Forest Evashevski	same
4	Navy	.9-1-0	Wayne Hardin	9-2-0
5	Missouri	.9-1-0	Dan Devine	10-1-0
6	Washington	.9-1-0	Jim Owens	10-1-0
7	Arkansas	.8-2-0	Frank Broyles	8-3-0
8	Ohio St.	.7-2-0	Woody Hayes	same
9	Alabama	.8-1-1	Bear Bryant	8-1-2
10	Duke	.7-2-0	Bill Murray	8-3-0
11	Kansas	.7-2-1	Jack Mitchell	same
12	Baylor	.8-2-0	John Bridgers	8-3-0
13	Auburn	.8-2-0	Shug Jordan	same
14	Yale	.9-0-0	Jordan Olivar	same
15	Michigan St.	.6-2-1	Duffy Daugherty	same
16	Penn St.	.6-3-0	Rip Engle	7-3-0
17	New Mexico St.	10-0-0	Warren Woodson	11-0-0
18	Florida	.8-2-0	Ray Graves	9-2-0
19	Syracuse	.7-2-0	Ben Schwartzwalder	same
	Purdue	.4-4-1	Jack Mollenkopf	same

Key Bowl Games

Rose–#6 Washington over #1 Minnesota, 17-7; **Sugar**–#2 Ole Miss over Rice, 14-6; **Orange**–#5 Missouri over #4 Navy, 21-14; **Cotton**–#10 Duke over #7 Arkansas, 7-6; **Bluebonnet**–#9 Alabama tied Texas, 3-3.

1961

Final poll released Dec. 4. Top 20 regular season results after that: None.

		As of Dec. 4	Head Coach	After Bowls
1	Alabama	10-0-0	Bear Bryant	11-0-0
2	Ohio St.	.8-0-1	Woody Hayes	same
3	Texas	.9-1-0	Darrell Royal	10-1-0
4	LSU	.9-1-0	Paul Dietzel	10-1-0
5	Mississippi	.9-1-0	Johnny Vaught	9-2-0
6	Minnesota	.7-2-0	Murray Warmath	8-2-0
7	Colorado	.9-1-0	Sonny Grandelius	9-2-0
8	Michigan St.	.7-2-0	Duffy Daugherty	same
9	Arkansas	.8-2-0	Frank Broyles	8-3-0
10	Utah St.	.9-0-1	John Ralston	9-1-1
11	Missouri	.7-2-1	Dan Devine	same
12	Purdue	.6-3-0	Jack Mollenkopf	same
13	Georgia Tech	.7-3-0	Bobby Dodd	7-4-0
14	Syracuse	.7-3-0	Ben Schwartzwalder	8-3-0
15	Rutgers	.9-0-0	John Bateman	same
16	UCLA	.7-3-0	Bill Barnes	7-4-0
17	Rice	.7-3-0	Jess Neely	7-4-0
	Penn St.	.7-3-0	Rip Engle	8-3-0
	Arizona	.8-1-1	Jim LaRue	same
20	Duke	.7-3-0	Bill Murray	same

Note: Ohio St. faculty council turned down Rose Bowl invitation citing concern with OSU's overemphasis on sports.

Key Bowl Games

Sugar–#1 Alabama over #9 Arkansas, 10-3; **Cotton**–#3 Texas over #5 Ole Miss, 12-7; **Orange**–#4 LSU over #7 Colorado, 25-7; **Rose**–#6 Minnesota over #16 UCLA, 21-3; **Gotham**–Baylor over #10 Utah St., 24-9.

1962

Final poll released Dec. 3. Top 10 regular season results after that: None.

		As of Dec. 3	Head Coach	After Bowls
1	USC	10-0-0	John McKay	11-0-0
2	Wisconsin	.8-1-0	Milt Bruhn	8-2-0
3	Mississippi	.9-0-0	Johnny Vaught	10-0-0
4	Texas	.9-0-1	Darrell Royal	9-1-1
5	Alabama	.9-1-0	Bear Bryant	10-1-0
6	Arkansas	.9-1-0	Frank Broyles	9-2-0
7	LSU	.8-1-1	Charlie McClendon	9-1-1
8	Oklahoma	.8-2-0	Bud Wilkinson	8-3-0
9	Penn St.	.9-1-0	Rip Engle	9-2-0
10	Minnesota	.6-2-1	Murray Warmath	same

Key Bowl Games

Rose–#1 USC over #2 Wisconsin, 42-37; **Sugar**–#3 Ole Miss over #6 Arkansas, 17-13; **Cotton**–#7 LSU over #4 Texas, 13-0; **Orange**–#5 Alabama over #8 Oklahoma, 17-0; **Gator**–Florida over #9 Penn St., 17-7.

1963

Final poll released Dec. 9. Top 10 regular season results after that: **Dec. 14**–#8 Alabama over Miami-FL, 17-12.

		As of Dec. 9	Head Coach	After Bowls
1	Texas	10-0-0	Darrell Royal	11-0-0
2	Navy	.9-1-0	Wayne Hardin	9-2-0
3	Illinois	.7-1-1	Pete Elliott	8-1-1
4	Pittsburgh	.9-1-0	John Michelosen	same
5	Auburn	.9-1-0	Shug Jordan	9-2-0
6	Nebraska	.9-1-0	Bob Devaney	10-1-0
7	Mississippi	.7-0-2	Johnny Vaught	7-1-2
8	Alabama	.7-2-0	Bear Bryant	9-2-0
9	Michigan St.	.6-2-1	Duffy Daugherty	same
10	Oklahoma	.8-2-0	Bud Wilkinson	same

Key Bowl Games

Cotton–#1 Texas over #2 Navy, 28-6; **Rose**–#3 Illinois over Washington, 17-7; **Orange**–#6 Nebraska over #5 Auburn, 13-7; **Sugar**–#8 Alabama over #7 Ole Miss, 12-7.

1964

Final poll released Nov. 30. Top 10 regular season results after that: **Dec. 5**–Florida over #7 LSU, 20-6.

		As of Nov. 30	Head Coach	After Bowls
1	Alabama	10-0-0	Bear Bryant	10-1-0
2	Arkansas	10-0-0	Frank Broyles	11-0-0
3	Notre Dame	.9-1-0	Ara Parseghian	same
4	Michigan	.8-1-0	Bump Elliott	9-1-0
5	Texas	.9-1-0	Darrell Royal	10-1-0
6	Nebraska	.9-1-0	Bob Devaney	9-2-0
7	LSU	.7-1-1	Charlie McClendon	8-2-1
8	Oregon St.	.8-2-0	Tommy Prothro	8-3-0
9	Ohio St.	.7-2-0	Woody Hayes	same
10	USC	.7-3-0	John McKay	same

Key Bowl Games

Orange–#5 Texas over #1 Alabama, 21-17; **Cotton**–#2 Arkansas over #6 Nebraska, 10-7; **Rose**–#4 Michigan over #8 Oregon St., 34-7; **Sugar**–#7 LSU over Syracuse, 13-10.

1965

Final poll taken after bowl games for the first time.

		After Bowls	Head Coach	Regular Season
1	Alabama	9-1-1	Bear Bryant	8-1-1
2	Michigan St	10-1-0	Duffy Daugherty	10-0-0
3	Arkansas	10-1-0	Frank Broyles	10-0-0
4	UCLA	8-2-1	Tommy Prothro	7-1-1
5	Nebraska	10-1-0	Bob Devaney	10-0-0
6	Missouri	8-2-0	Dan Devine	7-2-1
7	Tennessee	8-1-2	Doug Dickey	6-1-2
8	LSU	8-3-0	Charlie McClendon	7-3-0
9	Notre Dame	7-2-1	Ara Parseghian	same
10	USC	7-2-1	John McKay	same

Key Bowl Games

Rankings below reflect final regular season poll, released Nov. 29. No bowls for then #8 USC or #9 Notre Dame. **Rose**–#5 UCLA over #1 Michigan St., 14-12; **Cotton**–LSU over #2 Arkansas, 14-7; **Orange**–#4 Alabama over #3 Nebraska, 39-28; **Sugar**–#6 Missouri over Florida, 20-18; **Bluebonnet**–#7 Tennessee over Tulsa, 27-6; **Gator**–Georgia Tech over #10 Texas Tech, 31-21.

1966

Final poll released Dec. 5, returning to pre-bowl status. Top 10 regular season results after that: None.

		As of Dec. 5	Head Coach	After Bowls
1	Notre Dame	9-0-1	Ara Parseghian	same
2	Michigan St	9-0-1	Duffy Daugherty	same
3	Alabama	10-0-0	Bear Bryant	11-0-0
4	Georgia	9-1-0	Vince Dooley	10-1-0
5	UCLA	9-1-0	Tommy Prothro	same
6	Nebraska	9-1-0	Bob Devaney	9-2-0
7	Purdue	8-2-0	Jack Mollenkopf	9-2-0
8	Georgia Tech	9-1-0	Bobby Dodd	9-2-0
9	Miami-FL	7-2-1	Charlie Tate	8-2-1
10	SMU	8-2-0	Hayden Fry	8-3-0

Key Bowl Games

Sugar–#3 Alabama over #6 Nebraska, 34-7; **Cotton**–#4 Georgia over #10 SMU, 24-9; **Rose**–#7 Purdue over USC, 14-13; **Orange**–Florida over #8 Georgia Tech, 27-12; **Liberty**–#9 Miami-FL over Virginia Tech, 14-7.

1967

Final poll released Nov. 27. Top 10 regular season results after that: **Dec. 2**–#2 Tennessee over Vanderbilt, 41-14; #3 Oklahoma over Oklahoma St., 38-14; #8 Alabama over Auburn, 7-3.

		As of Nov. 27	Head Coach	After Bowls
1	USC	9-1-0	John McKay	10-1-0
2	Tennessee	8-1-0	Doug Dickey	9-2-0
3	Oklahoma	8-1-0	Chuck Fairbanks	10-1-0
4	Indiana	9-1-0	John Pont	9-2-0
5	Notre Dame	8-2-0	Ara Parseghian	same
6	Wyoming	10-0-0	Lloyd Eaton	10-1-0
7	Oregon St.	7-2-1	Dee Andros	same
8	Alabama	7-1-1	Bear Bryant	8-2-1
9	Purdue	8-2-0	Jack Mollenkopf	same
10	Penn St.	8-2-0	Joe Paterno	8-2-1

Key Bowl Games

Rose–#1 USC over #4 Indiana, 14-3; **Orange**–#3 Oklahoma over #2 Tennessee, 26-24; **Sugar**–LSU over #6 Wyoming, 20-13; **Cotton**–Texas A&M over #8 Alabama, 20-16; **Gator**–#10 Penn St. tied Florida St. 17-17.

1968

Final poll taken after bowl games for first time since close of 1965 season.

		After Bowls	Head Coach	Regular Season
1	Ohio St.	10-0-0	Woody Hayes	9-0-0
2	Penn St.	11-0-0	Joe Paterno	10-0-0
3	Texas	9-1-1	Darrell Royal	8-1-1
4	USC	9-1-1	John McKay	9-0-1
5	Notre Dame	7-2-1	Ara Parseghian	same
6	Arkansas	10-1-0	Frank Broyles	9-1-0
7	Kansas	9-2-0	Pepper Rodgers	9-1-0
8	Georgia	8-1-2	Vince Dooley	8-0-2
9	Missouri	8-3-0	Dan Devine	7-3-0
10	Purdue	8-2-0	Jack Mollenkopf	same
11	Oklahoma	7-4-0	Chuck Fairbanks	7-3-0
12	Michigan	8-2-0	Bump Elliott	same
13	Tennessee	8-2-1	Doug Dickey	8-1-1
14	SMU	8-3-0	Hayden Fry	7-3-0
15	Oregon St.	7-3-0	Dee Andros	same
16	Auburn	7-4-0	Shug Jordan	6-4-0
17	Alabama	8-3-0	Bear Bryant	8-2-0
18	Houston	6-2-2	Bill Yeoman	same
19	LSU	8-3-0	Charlie McClendon	7-3-0
20	Ohio Univ.	10-1-0	Bill Hess	10-0-0

Key Bowl Games

Rankings below reflect final regular season poll, released Dec. 2. No bowls for then #7 Notre Dame and #11 Pudue. **Rose**–#1 Ohio St. over #2 USC, 27-16; **Orange**–#3 Penn St. over #6 Kansas, 15-14; **Sugar**–#9 Arkansas over #4 Georgia, 16-2; **Cotton**–#5 Texas over #8 Tennessee, 36-13; **Bluebonnet**–#20 SMU over #10 Oklahoma, 28-27; **Gator**–#16 Missouri over #12 Alabama, 35-10.

1969

Final poll taken after bowl games.

		After Bowls	Head Coach	Regular Season
1	Texas	11-0-0	Darrell Royal	10-0-0
2	Penn St	11-0-0	Joe Paterno	10-0-0
3	USC	10-0-1	John McKay	9-0-1
4	Ohio St.	8-1-0	Woody Hayes	same
5	Notre Dame	8-2-1	Ara Parseghian	8-1-1
6	Missouri	9-2-0	Dan Devine	9-1-0
7	Arkansas	9-2-0	Frank Broyles	9-1-0
8	Mississippi	8-3-0	Johnny Vaught	7-3-0
9	Michigan	8-3-0	Bo Schembechler	8-2-0
10	LSU	9-1-0	Charlie McClendon	same
11	Nebraska	9-2-0	Bob Devaney	8-2-0
12	Houston	9-2-0	Bill Yeoman	8-2-0
13	UCLA	8-1-1	Tommy Prothro	same
14	Florida	9-1-1	Ray Graves	8-1-1
15	Tennessee	9-2-0	Doug Dickey	9-1-0
16	Colorado	8-3-0	Eddie Crowder	7-3-0
17	West Virginia	10-1-0	Jim Carlen	9-1-0
18	Purdue	8-2-0	Jack Mollenkopf	same
19	Stanford	7-2-1	John Ralston	same
20	Auburn	8-3-0	Shug Jordan	8-2-0

Key Bowl Games

Rankings below reflect final regular season poll, released Dec. 8. No bowls for then #4 Ohio St., #8 LSU and #10 UCLA.

Cotton–#1 Texas over #9 Notre Dame, 21-17; **Orange**–#2 Penn St. over #6 Missouri, 10-3; **Sugar**–#13 Ole Miss over #3 Arkansas, 27-22; **Rose**–#5 USC over #7 Michigan, 10-3.

Associated Press Final Polls (Cont.)

1970

		After Bowls	Head Coach	Regular Season
1	Nebraska	11-0-1	Bob Devaney	10-0-1
2	Notre Dame	10-1-0	Ara Parseghian	9-0-1
3	Texas	10-1-0	Darrell Royal	10-0-0
4	Tennessee	11-1-0	Bill Battle	10-1-0
5	Ohio St.	9-1-0	Woody Hayes	9-0-0
6	Arizona St.	11-0-0	Frank Kush	10-0-0
7	LSU	9-3-0	Charlie McClendon	9-2-0
8	Stanford	9-3-0	John Ralston	8-3-0
9	Michigan	9-1-0	Bo Schembechler	same
10	Auburn	9-2-0	Shug Jordan	8-2-0
11	Arkansas	9-2-0	Frank Broyles	same
12	Toledo	12-0-0	Frank Lauterbur	11-0-0
13	Georgia Tech	9-3-0	Bud Carson	8-3-0
14	Dartmouth	9-0-0	Bob Blackman	same
15	USC	6-4-1	John McKay	same
16	Air Force	9-3-0	Ben Martin	9-2-0
17	Tulane	8-4-0	Jim Pittman	7-4-0
18	Penn St.	7-3-0	Joe Paterno	same
19	Houston	8-3-0	Bill Yeoman	same
20	Oklahoma	7-4-1	Chuck Fairbanks	7-4-0
	Mississippi	7-4-0	Johnny Vaught	7-3-0

Key Bowl Games

Rankings below reflect final regular season poll, released Dec. 7. No bowls for then #4 Arkansas and #7 Michigan.
Cotton–#6 Notre Dame over #1 Texas, 24-11; **Rose**–#12 Stanford over #2 Ohio St., 27-17; **Orange**–#3 Nebraska over #8 LSU, 17-12; **Sugar**–#5 Tennessee over #11 Air Force, 34-13; **Peach**–#9 Ariz. St. over N. Carolina, 48-26.

1971

		After Bowls	Head Coach	Regular Season
1	Nebraska	13-0-0	Bob Devaney	12-0-0
2	Oklahoma	11-1-0	Chuck Fairbanks	10-1-0
3	Colorado	10-2-0	Eddie Crowder	9-2-0
4	Alabama	11-1-0	Bear Bryant	11-0-0
5	Penn St.	11-1-0	Joe Paterno	10-1-0
6	Michigan	11-1-0	Bo Schembechler	11-0-0
7	Georgia	11-1-0	Vince Dooley	10-1-0
8	Arizona St.	11-1-0	Frank Kush	10-1-0
9	Tennessee	10-2-0	Bill Battle	9-2-0
10	Stanford	9-3-0	John Ralston	8-3-0
11	LSU	9-3-0	Charlie McClendon	8-3-0
12	Auburn	9-2-0	Shug Jordan	9-1-0
13	Notre Dame	8-2-0	Ara Parseghian	same
14	Toledo	12-0-0	John Murphy	11-0-0
15	Mississippi	10-2-0	Billy Kinard	9-2-0
16	Arkansas	8-3-1	Frank Broyles	8-2-1
17	Houston	9-3-0	Bill Yeoman	9-2-0
18	Texas	8-3-0	Darrell Royal	8-2-0
19	Washington	8-3-0	Jim Owens	same
20	USC	6-4-1	John McKay	same

Key Bowl Games

Rankings below reflect final regular season poll, released Dec. 6.
Orange–#1 Nebraska over #2 Alabama, 38-6; **Sugar**–#3 Oklahoma over #5 Auburn, 40-22; **Rose**–#16 Stanford over #4 Michigan, 13-12; **Gator**–#6 Georgia over N. Carolina, 7-3; **Bluebonnet**–#7 Colorado over #15 Houston, 29-17; **Fiesta**–#8 Ariz. St. over Florida St., 45-38; **Cotton**–#10 Penn St. over #12 Texas, 30-6.

1972

		After Bowls	Head Coach	Regular Season
1	USC	12-0-0	John McKay	11-0-0
2	Oklahoma	11-1-0	Chuck Fairbanks	10-1-0
3	Texas	10-1-0	Darrell Royal	9-1-0
4	Nebraska	9-2-1	Bob Devaney	8-2-1
5	Auburn	10-1-0	Shug Jordan	9-1-0
6	Michigan	10-1-0	Bo Schembechler	same
7	Alabama	10-2-0	Bear Bryant	10-1-0
8	Tennessee	10-2-0	Bill Battle	9-2-0
9	Ohio St.	9-2-0	Woody Hayes	9-1-0
10	Penn St.	10-2-0	Joe Paterno	10-1-0
11	LSU	9-2-1	Charlie McClendon	9-1-1
12	North Carolina	11-1-0	Bill Dooley	10-1-0
13	Arizona St.	10-2-0	Frank Kush	9-2-0
14	Notre Dame	8-3-0	Ara Parseghian	8-2-0
15	UCLA	8-3-0	Pepper Rodgers	same
16	Colorado	8-4-0	Eddie Crowder	8-3-0
17	N.C. State	8-3-1	Lou Holtz	7-3-1
18	Louisville	9-1-0	Lee Corso	same
19	Washington St.	7-4-0	Jim Sweeney	same
20	Georgia Tech	7-4-1	Bill Fulcher	6-4-1

Key Bowl Games

Rankings below reflect final regular season poll, released Dec. 4. No bowl for then #8 Michigan.
Rose–#1 USC over #3 Ohio St., 42-17; **Sugar**–#2 Oklahoma over #5 Penn St., 14-0; **Cotton**–#7 Texas over #4 Alabama, 17-13; **Orange**–#9 Nebraska over #12 Notre Dame, 40-6; **Gator**–#6 Auburn over #13 Colorado, 24-3; **Bluebonnet**–#11 Tennessee over #10 LSU, 24-17.

1973

		After Bowls	Head Coach	Regular Season
1	Notre Dame	11-0-0	Ara Parseghian	10-0-0
2	Ohio St.	10-0-1	Woody Hayes	9-0-1
3	Oklahoma	10-0-1	Barry Switzer	same
4	Alabama	11-1-0	Bear Bryant	11-0-0
5	Penn St.	12-0-0	Joe Paterno	11-0-0
6	Michigan	10-0-1	Bo Schembechler	same
7	Nebraska	9-2-1	Tom Osborne	8-2-1
8	USC	9-2-1	John McKay	9-1-1
9	Arizona St.	11-1-0	Frank Kush	10-1-0
	Houston	11-1-0	Bill Yeoman	10-1-0
11	Texas Tech	11-1-0	Jim Carlen	10-1-0
12	UCLA	9-2-0	Pepper Rodgers	same
13	LSU	9-3-0	Charlie McClendon	9-2-0
14	Texas	8-3-0	Darrell Royal	8-2-0
15	Miami-OH	11-0-0	Bill Mallory	10-0-0
16	N.C. State	9-3-0	Lou Holtz	8-3-0
17	Missouri	8-4-0	Al Onofrio	7-4-0
18	Kansas	7-4-1	Don Fambrough	7-3-1
19	Tennessee	8-4-0	Bill Battle	8-3-0
20	Maryland	8-4-0	Jerry Claiborne	8-3-0
	Tulane	9-3-0	Bennie Ellender	9-2-0

Key Bowl Games

Rankings below reflect final regular season poll, released Dec. 3. No bowls for then #2 Oklahoma (probation), #5 Michigan and #9 UCLA.
Sugar–#3 Notre Dame over #1 Alabama, 24-23; **Rose**–#4 Ohio St. over #7 USC, 42-21; **Orange**–#6 Penn St. over #13 LSU, 16-9; **Cotton**–#12 Nebraska over #8 Texas, 19-3; **Fiesta**–#10 Ariz. St. over Pitt, 28-7; **Bluebonnet**–#14 Houston over #17 Tulane, 47-7.

1974

		After Bowls	Head Coach	Regular Season
1	Oklahoma	11-0-0	Barry Switzer	same
2	USC	10-1-1	John McKay	9-1-1
3	Michigan	10-1-0	Bo Schembechler	same
4	Ohio St.	10-2-0	Woody Hayes	10-1-0
5	Alabama	11-1-0	Bear Bryant	11-0-0
6	Notre Dame	10-2-0	Ara Parseghian	9-2-0
7	Penn St.	10-2-0	Joe Paterno	9-2-0
8	Auburn	10-2-0	Shug Jordan	9-2-0
9	Nebraska	9-3-0	Tom Osborne	8-3-0
10	Miami-OH	10-0-1	Dick Crum	9-0-1
11	N.C. State	9-2-1	Lou Holtz	9-2-1
12	Michigan St.	7-3-1	Denny Stolz	same
13	Maryland	8-4-0	Jerry Claiborne	8-3-0
14	Baylor	8-4-0	Grant Teaff	8-3-0
15	Florida	8-4-0	Doug Dickey	8-3-0
16	Texas A&M	8-3-0	Emory Ballard	same
17	Mississippi St.	9-3-0	Bob Tyler	8-3-0
	Texas	8-4-0	Darrell Royal	8-3-0
19	Houston	8-3-1	Bill Yeoman	8-3-0
20	Tennessee	7-3-2	Bill Battle	6-3-2

Key Bowl Games

Rankings below reflect final regular season poll, released Dec. 2. No bowls for #1 Oklahoma (probation) and then #4 Michigan.

Orange—#9 Notre Dame over #2 Alabama, 13-11; **Rose**—#5 USC over #3 Ohio St., 18-17; **Gator**—#6 Auburn over #11 Texas, 27-3; **Cotton**—#7 Penn St. over #12 Baylor, 41-20; **Sugar**—#8 Nebraska over #18 Florida, 13-10; **Liberty**—Tennessee over #10 Maryland, 7-3.

1975

		After Bowls	Head Coach	Regular Season
1	Oklahoma	11-1-0	Barry Switzer	10-1-0
2	Arizona St.	12-0-0	Frank Kush	11-0-0
3	Alabama	11-1-0	Bear Bryant	10-1-0
4	Ohio St.	11-1-0	Woody Hayes	11-0-0
5	UCLA	9-2-1	Dick Vermeil	8-2-1
6	Texas	10-2-0	Darrell Royal	9-2-0
7	Arkansas	10-2-0	Frank Broyles	9-2-0
8	Michigan	8-2-2	Bo Schembechler	8-1-2
9	Nebraska	10-2-0	Tom Osborne	10-1-0
10	Penn St.	9-3-0	Joe Paterno	9-2-0
11	Texas A&M	10-2-0	Emory Ballard	10-1-0
12	Miami-OH	11-1-0	Dick Crum	10-1-0
13	Maryland	9-2-1	Jerry Claiborne	8-2-1
14	California	8-3-0	Mike White	same
15	Pittsburgh	8-4-0	Johnny Majors	7-4-0
16	Colorado	9-3-0	Bill Mallory	9-2-0
17	USC	8-4-0	John McKay	7-4-0
18	Arizona	9-2-0	Jim Young	same
19	Georgia	9-3-0	Vince Dooley	9-2-0
20	West Virginia	9-3-0	Bobby Bowden	8-3-0

Key Bowl Games

Rankings below reflect final regular season poll, released Dec. 1. Texas A&M was unbeaten and ranked 2nd in that poll, but lost to #18 Arkansas, 31-6, in its final regular season game on Dec.6.

Rose—#11 UCLA over #1 Ohio St., 23-10; **Liberty**—#17 USC over #2 Texas A&M, 20-0; **Orange**—#3 Oklahoma over #5 Michigan, 14-6; **Sugar**—#4 Alabama over #8 Penn St., 13-6; **Fiesta**—#7 Ariz. St. over #6 Nebraska, 17-14; **Bluebonnet**—#9 Texas over #10 Colorado, 38-21; **Cotton**—#18 Arkansas over #12 Georgia, 31-10.

1976

		After Bowls	Head Coach	Regular Season
1	Pittsburgh	12-0-0	Johnny Majors	11-0-0
2	USC	11-1-0	John Robinson	10-1-0
3	Michigan	10-2-0	Bo Schembechler	10-1-0
4	Houston	10-2-0	Bill Yeoman	9-2-0
5	Oklahoma	9-2-1	Barry Switzer	8-2-1
6	Ohio St.	9-2-1	Woody Hayes	8-2-1
7	Texas A&M	10-2-0	Emory Ballard	9-2-0
8	Maryland	11-1-0	Jerry Claiborne	11-0-0
9	Nebraska	9-3-1	Tom Osborne	8-3-1
10	Georgia	10-2-0	Vince Dooley	10-1-0
11	Alabama	9-3-0	Bear Bryant	8-3-0
12	Notre Dame	9-3-0	Dan Devine	8-3-0
13	Texas Tech	10-2-0	Steve Sloan	10-1-0
14	Oklahoma St.	9-3-0	Jim Stanley	8-3-0
15	UCLA	9-2-1	Terry Donahue	9-1-1
16	Colorado	8-4-0	Bill Mallory	8-3-0
17	Rutgers	11-0-0	Frank Burns	same
18	Kentucky	8-4-0	Fran Curci	7-4-0
19	Iowa St.	8-3-0	Earle Bruce	same
20	Mississippi St.	9-2-0	Bob Tyler	same

Key Bowl Games

Rankings below reflect final regular season poll, released Nov. 29. No bowl for then #20 Miss. St. (probation).

Sugar—#1 Pitt over #5 Georgia, 27-3; **Rose**—#3 USC over #2 Michigan, 14-6; **Cotton**—#6 Houston over #4 Maryland, 30-21; **Liberty**—#16 Alabama over #7 UCLA, 36-6; **Fiesta**—#8 Oklahoma over Wyoming, 41-7; **Bluebonnet**—#13 Nebraska over #9 Texas Tech, 27-24; **Sun**—#10 Texas A&M over Florida, 37-14; **Orange**—#11 Ohio St. over #12 Colorado, 27-10.

1977

		After Bowls	Head Coach	Regular Season
1	Notre Dame	11-1-0	Dan Devine	10-1-0
2	Alabama	11-1-0	Bear Bryant	10-1-0
3	Arkansas	11-1-0	Lou Holtz	10-1-0
4	Texas	11-1-0	Fred Akers	11-0-0
5	Penn St.	11-1-0	Joe Paterno	10-1-0
6	Kentucky	10-1-0	Fran Curci	same
7	Oklahoma	10-2-0	Barry Switzer	10-1-0
8	Pittsburgh	9-2-1	Jackie Sherrill	8-2-1
9	Michigan	10-2-0	Bo Schembechler	10-1-0
10	Washington	8-4-0	Don James	7-4-0
11	Ohio St.	9-3-0	Woody Hayes	9-2-0
12	Nebraska	9-3-0	Tom Osborne	8-3-0
13	USC	8-4-0	John Robinson	7-4-0
14	Florida St.	10-2-0	Bobby Bowden	9-2-0
15	Stanford	9-3-0	Bill Walsh	8-3-0
16	San Diego St.	10-1-0	Claude Gilbert	same
17	North Carolina	8-3-1	Bill Dooley	8-2-1
18	Arizona St.	9-3-0	Frank Kush	9-2-0
19	Clemson	8-3-1	Charley Pell	8-2-1
20	BYU	9-2-0	LaVell Edwards	same

Key Bowl Games

Rankings below reflect final regular season poll, released Nov. 28. No bowl for then #7 Kentucky (probation).

Cotton—#5 Notre Dame over #1 Texas, 38-10; **Orange**—#6 Arkansas over #2 Oklahoma, 31-6; **Sugar**—#3 Alabama over #9 Ohio St., 35-6; **Rose**—#13 Washington over #4 Michigan, 27-20; **Fiesta**—#8 Penn St. over #15 Ariz. St., 42-30; **Gator**—#10 Pitt over #11 Clemson, 34-3.

Associated Press Final Polls (Cont.)

1978

		After Bowls	Head Coach	Regular Season
1	Alabama	11-1-0	Bear Bryant	10-1-0
2	USC	12-1-0	John Robinson	11-1-0
3	Oklahoma	11-1-0	Barry Switzer	10-1-0
4	Penn St.	11-1-0	Joe Paterno	11-0-0
5	Michigan	10-2-0	Bo Schembechler	10-1-0
6	Clemson	11-1-0	Charley Pell	10-1-0
7	Notre Dame	9-3-0	Dan Devine	8-3-0
8	Nebraska	9-3-0	Tom Osborne	9-2-0
9	Texas	9-3-0	Fred Akers	8-3-0
10	Houston	9-3-0	Bill Yeoman	9-2-0
11	Arkansas	9-2-1	Lou Holtz	9-2-0
12	Michigan St.	8-3-0	Darryl Rogers	same
13	Purdue	9-2-1	Jim Young	8-2-1
14	UCLA	8-3-1	Terry Donahue	8-3-0
15	Missouri	8-4-0	Warren Powers	7-4-0
16	Georgia	9-2-1	Vince Dooley	9-1-0
17	Stanford	8-4-0	Bill Walsh	7-4-0
18	N.C. State	9-3-0	Bo Rein	8-3-0
19	Texas A&M	8-4-0	Emory Bellard (4-2) & Tom Wilson (4-2)	7-4-0
20	Maryland	9-3-0	Jerry Claiborne	9-2-0

Key Bowl Games

Rankings below reflect final regular season poll, released Dec. 4. No bowl for then #12 Michigan St. (probation).

Sugar–#2 Alabama over #1 Penn St., 14-7; **Rose**–#3 USC over #5 Michigan, 17-10; **Orange**–#4 Oklahoma over #6 Nebraska, 31-24; **Gator**–#7 Clemson over #20 Ohio St., 17-15; **Fiesta**–#8 Arkansas tied #15 UCLA, 10-10; **Cotton**–#10 Notre Dame over #9 Houston, 35-34.

1979

		After Bowls	Head Coach	Regular Season
1	Alabama	12-0-0	Bear Bryant	11-0-0
2	USC	11-0-1	John Robinson	10-0-1
3	Oklahoma	11-1-0	Barry Switzer	10-1-0
4	Ohio St.	11-1-0	Earle Bruce	11-0-0
5	Houston	11-1-0	Bill Yeoman	10-1-0
6	Florida St.	11-1-0	Bobby Bowden	11-0-0
7	Pittsburgh	11-1-0	Jackie Sherrill	10-1-0
8	Arkansas	10-2-0	Lou Holtz	10-1-0
9	Nebraska	10-2-0	Tom Osborne	10-1-0
10	Purdue	10-2-0	Jim Young	9-2-0
11	Washington	9-3-0	Don James	8-3-0
12	Texas	9-3-0	Fred Akers	9-2-0
13	BYU	11-1-0	LaVell Edwards	11-0-0
14	Baylor	8-4-0	Grant Teaff	7-4-0
15	North Carolina	8-3-1	Dick Crum	7-3-1
16	Auburn	8-3-0	Doug Barfield	same
17	Temple	10-2-0	Wayne Hardin	9-2-0
18	Michigan	8-4-0	Bo Schembechler	8-3-0
19	Indiana	8-4-0	Lee Corso	7-4-0
20	Penn St.	8-4-0	Joe Paterno	7-4-0

Key Bowl Games

Rankings below reflect final regular season poll, released Dec. 3. No bowl for then #17 Auburn (probation).

Sugar–#2 Alabama over #6 Arkansas, 24-9; **Rose**–#3 USC over #1 Ohio St., 17-16; **Orange**–#5 Oklahoma over #4 Florida St., 24-7; **Sun**–#13 Washington over #11 Texas, 14-7; **Cotton**–#8 Houston over #7 Nebraska, 17-14; **Fiesta**–#10 Pitt over Arizona, 16-10.

1980

		After Bowls	Head Coach	Regular Season
1	Georgia	12-0-0	Vince Dooley	11-0-0
2	Pittsburgh	11-1-0	Jackie Sherrill	10-1-0
3	Oklahoma	10-2-0	Barry Switzer	9-2-0
4	Michigan	10-2-0	Bo Schembechler	9-2-0
5	Florida St.	10-2-0	Bobby Bowden	10-1-0
6	Alabama	10-2-0	Bear Bryant	9-2-0
7	Nebraska	10-2-0	Tom Osborne	9-2-0
8	Penn St.	10-2-0	Joe Paterno	9-2-0
9	Notre Dame	9-2-1	Dan Devine	9-1-1
10	North Carolina	11-1-0	Dick Crum	10-1-0
11	USC	8-2-1	John Robinson	same
12	BYU	12-1-0	LaVell Edwards	11-1-0
13	UCLA	9-2-0	Terry Donahue	same
14	Baylor	10-2-0	Grant Teaff	10-1-0
15	Ohio St.	9-3-0	Earle Bruce	9-2-0
16	Washington	9-3-0	Don James	9-2-0
17	Purdue	9-3-0	Jim Young	8-3-0
18	Miami-FL	9-3-0	H. Schnellenberger	8-3-0
19	Mississippi St.	9-3-0	Emory Bellard	9-2-0
20	SMU	8-4-0	Ron Meyer	8-3-0

Key Bowl Games

Rankings below reflect final regular season poll, released Dec. 8.

Sugar–#1 Georgia over #7 Notre Dame, 17-10; **Orange**–#4 Oklahoma over #2 Florida St., 18-17; **Gator**–#3 Pitt over #18 S. Carolina, 37-9; **Rose**–#5 Michigan over #16 Washington, 23-6; **Cotton**–#9 Alabama over #6 Baylor, 30-2; **Sun**–#8 Nebraska over #17 Miss. St., 31-17; **Fiesta**–#10 Penn St. over #11 Ohio St., 31-19; **Bluebonnet**–#13 N. Carolina over Texas, 16-7.

1981

		After Bowls	Head Coach	Regular Season
1	Clemson	12-0-0	Danny Ford	11-0-0
2	Texas	10-1-1	Fred Akers	9-1-1
3	Penn St.	10-2-0	Joe Paterno	9-2-0
4	Pittsburgh	11-1-0	Jackie Sherrill	10-1-0
5	SMU	10-1-0	Ron Meyer	same
6	Georgia	10-2-0	Vince Dooley	10-1-0
7	Alabama	9-2-1	Bear Bryant	9-1-1
8	Miami-FL	9-2-0	H. Schnellenberger	same
9	North Carolina	10-2-0	Dick Crum	9-2-0
10	Washington	10-2-0	Don James	9-2-0
11	Nebraska	9-3-0	Tom Osborne	9-2-0
12	Michigan	9-3-0	Bo Schembechler	8-3-0
13	BYU	11-2-0	LaVell Edwards	10-2-0
14	USC	9-3-0	John Robinson	9-2-0
15	Ohio St.	9-3-0	Earle Bruce	8-3-0
16	Arizona St.	9-2-0	Darryl Rogers	same
17	West Virginia	9-3-0	Don Nehlen	8-3-0
18	Iowa	8-4-0	Hayden Fry	8-3-0
19	Missouri	8-4-0	Warren Powers	7-4-0
20	Oklahoma	7-4-1	Barry Switzer	6-4-1

Key Bowl Games

Rankings below reflect final regular season poll, released Nov. 30. No bowl for then #5 SMU (probation), #9 Miami-FL (probation), and #17 Ariz. St. (probation).

Orange–#1 Clemson over #4 Nebraska, 22-15; **Sugar**–#10 Pitt over #2 Georgia, 24-20; **Cotton**–#6 Texas over #3 Alabama, 14-12; **Fiesta**–#7 Penn St. over #8 USC, 26-10; **Gator**–#11 N. Carolina over Arkansas, 31-27; **Rose**–#12 Washington over #13 Iowa, 28-0.

1982

	After Bowls	Head Coach	Regular Season
1 Penn St.	11-1-0	Joe Paterno	10-1-0
2 SMU	11-0-1	Bobby Collins	10-0-1
3 Nebraska	12-1-0	Tom Osborne	11-1-0
4 Georgia	11-1-0	Vince Dooley	11-0-0
5 UCLA	10-1-1	Terry Donahue	9-1-1
6 Arizona St.	10-2-0	Darryl Rogers	9-2-0
7 Washington	10-2-0	Don James	9-2-0
8 Clemson	9-1-1	Danny Ford	same
9 Arkansas	9-2-1	Lou Holtz	8-2-1
10 Pittsburgh	9-3-0	Foge Fazio	9-2-0
11 LSU	8-3-1	Jerry Stovall	8-2-1
12 Ohio St.	9-3-0	Earle Bruce	8-3-0
13 Florida St.	9-3-0	Bobby Bowden	8-3-0
14 Auburn	9-3-0	Pat Dye	8-3-0
15 USC	8-3-0	John Robinson	same
16 Oklahoma	8-4-0	Barry Switzer	8-3-0
17 Texas	9-3-0	Fred Akers	9-2-0
18 North Carolina	8-4-0	Dick Crum	7-4-0
19 West Virginia	9-3-0	Don Nehlen	9-2-0
20 Maryland	8-4-0	Bobby Ross	8-3-0

Key Bowl Games

Rankings below reflect final regular season poll, released Dec. 6. No bowl for then #7 Clemson (probation) and #15 USC (probation).

Sugar–#2 Penn St. over #1 Georgia, 27-23; **Orange**–#3 Nebraska over #13 LSU, 21-20; **Cotton**–#4 SMU over #6 Pitt, 7-3; **Rose**–#5 UCLA over #19 Michigan, 24-14; **Aloha**–#9 Washington over #16 Maryland, 21-20; **Fiesta**–#11 Ariz. St. over #12 Oklahoma, 32-21; **Bluebonnet**–#14 Arkansas over Florida, 28-24.

1983

	After Bowls	Head Coach	Regular Season
1 Miami-FL	11-1-0	H. Schnellenberger	10-1-0
2 Nebraska	12-1-0	Tom Osborne	12-0-0
3 Auburn	11-1-0	Pat Dye	10-1-0
4 Georgia	10-1-1	Vince Dooley	9-1-1
5 Texas	11-1-0	Fred Akers	11-0-0
6 Florida	9-2-1	Charley Pell	8-2-1
7 BYU	11-1-0	LaVell Edwards	10-1-0
8 Michigan	9-3-0	Bo Schembechler	9-2-0
9 Ohio St.	9-3-0	Earle Bruce	8-3-0
10 Illinois	10-2-0	Mike White	10-1-0
11 Clemson	9-1-1	Danny Ford	same
12 SMU	10-2-0	Bobby Collins	10-1-0
13 Air Force	10-2-0	Ken Hatfield	9-2-0
14 Iowa	9-3-0	Hayden Fry	9-2-0
15 Alabama	8-4-0	Ray Perkins	7-4-0
16 West Virginia	9-3-0	Don Nehlen	8-3-0
17 UCLA	7-4-1	Terry Donahue	6-4-1
18 Pittsburgh	8-3-1	Foge Fazio	8-2-1
19 Boston College	9-3-0	Jack Bicknell	9-2-0
20 East Carolina	8-3-0	Ed Emory	same

Key Bowl Games

Rankings below reflect final regular season poll, released Dec. 5. No bowl for then #12 Clemson (probation).

Orange–#5 Miami-FL over #1 Nebraska, 31-30; **Cotton**–#7 Georgia over #2 Texas, 10-9; **Sugar**–#3 Auburn over #8 Michigan, 9-7; **Rose**–UCLA over #4 Illinois, 45-9; **Holiday**–#9 BYU over Missouri, 21-17; **Gator**–#11 Florida over #10 Iowa, 14-6; **Fiesta**–#14 Ohio St. over #15 Pitt, 28-23.

1984

	After Bowls	Head Coach	Regular Season
1 BYU	13-0-0	LaVell Edwards	12-0-0
2 Washington	11-1-0	Don James	10-1-0
3 Florida	9-1-1	Charley Pell (0-1-1) & Galen Hall (9-0)	same
4 Nebraska	10-2-0	Tom Osborne	9-2-0
5 Boston College	10-2-0	Jack Bicknell	9-2-0
6 Oklahoma	9-2-1	Barry Switzer	9-1-1
7 Oklahoma St.	10-2-0	Pat Jones	9-2-0
8 SMU	10-2-0	Bobby Collins	9-2-0
9 UCLA	9-3-0	Terry Donahue	8-3-0
10 USC	9-3-0	Ted Tollner	8-3-0
11 South Carolina	10-2-0	Joe Morrison	10-1-0
12 Maryland	9-3-0	Bobby Ross	8-3-0
13 Ohio St.	9-3-0	Earle Bruce	9-2-0
14 Auburn	9-4-0	Pat Dye	8-4-0
15 LSU	8-3-1	Bill Arnsparger	8-2-1
16 Iowa	8-4-1	Hayden Fry	7-4-1
17 Florida St.	7-3-2	Bobby Bowden	7-3-1
18 Miami-FL	8-5-0	Jimmy Johnson	8-4-0
19 Kentucky	9-3-0	Jerry Claiborne	8-3-0
20 Virginia	8-2-2	George Welsh	7-2-2

Key Bowl Games

Rankings below reflect final regular season poll, released Dec. 3. No bowl for then #3 Florida (probation).

Holiday–#1 BYU over Michigan, 24-17; **Orange**–#4 Washington over #2 Oklahoma, 28-17; **Sugar**–#5 Nebraska over #11 LSU, 28-10; **Rose**–#18 USC over #6 Ohio St., 20-17; **Gator**–#9 Okla. St. over #7 S. Carolina, 21-14; **Cotton**–#8 BC over Houston, 45-28; **Aloha**–#10 SMU over #17 Notre Dame, 27-20.

1985

	After Bowls	Head Coach	Regular Season
1 Oklahoma	11-1-0	Barry Switzer	10-1-0
2 Michigan	10-1-1	Bo Schembechler	9-1-1
3 Penn St.	11-1-0	Joe Paterno	11-0-0
4 Tennessee	9-1-2	Johnny Majors	8-1-2
5 Florida	9-1-1	Galen Hall	same
6 Texas A&M	10-2-0	Jackie Sherrill	9-2-0
7 UCLA	9-2-1	Terry Donahue	8-2-1
8 Air Force	12-1-0	Fisher DeBerry	11-1-0
9 Miami-FL	10-2-0	Jimmy Johnson	10-1-0
10 Iowa	10-2-0	Hayden Fry	10-1-0
11 Nebraska	9-3-0	Tom Osborne	9-2-0
12 Arkansas	10-2-0	Ken Hatfield	9-2-0
13 Alabama	9-2-1	Ray Perkins	8-2-1
14 Ohio St.	9-3-0	Earle Bruce	8-3-0
15 Florida St.	9-3-0	Bobby Bowden	8-3-0
16 BYU	11-3-0	LaVell Edwards	11-2-0
17 Baylor	9-3-0	Grant Teaff	8-3-0
18 Maryland	9-3-0	Bobby Ross	8-3-0
19 Georgia Tech	9-2-1	Bill Curry	8-2-1
20 LSU	9-2-1	Bill Arnsparger	9-1-1

Key Bowl Games

Rankings below reflect final regular season poll, released Dec. 9. No bowl for then #6 Florida (probation).

Orange–#3 Oklahoma over #1 Penn St., 25-10; **Sugar**–#8 Tennessee over #2 Miami-FL, 35-7; **Rose**–#13 UCLA over #4 Iowa, 45-28; **Fiesta**–#5 Michigan over #7 Nebraska, 27-23; **Bluebonnet**–#10 Air Force over Texas, 24-16; **Cotton**–#11 Texas A&M over #16 Auburn, 36-16.

Associated Press Final Polls (Cont.)

1986

		After Bowls	Head Coach	Regular Season
1	Penn St.	12-0-0	Joe Paterno	11-0-0
2	Miami-FL	11-1-0	Jimmy Johnson	11-0-0
3	Oklahoma	11-1-0	Barry Switzer	10-1-0
4	Arizona St.	10-1-1	John Cooper	9-1-1
5	Nebraska	10-2-0	Tom Osborne	9-2-0
6	Auburn	10-2-0	Pat Dye	9-2-0
7	Ohio St.	10-3-0	Earle Bruce	9-3-0
8	Michigan	11-2-0	Bo Schembechler	11-1-0
9	Alabama	10-3-0	Ray Perkins	9-3-0
10	LSU	9-3-0	Bill Arnsparger	9-2-0
11	Arizona	9-3-0	Larry Smith	8-3-0
12	Baylor	9-3-0	Grant Teaff	8-3-0
13	Texas A&M	9-3-0	Jackie Sherrill	9-2-0
14	UCLA	8-3-1	Terry Donahue	7-3-1
15	Arkansas	9-3-0	Ken Hatfield	9-2-0
16	Iowa	9-3-0	Hayden Fry	8-3-0
17	Clemson	8-2-2	Danny Ford	7-2-2
18	Washington	8-3-1	Don James	8-2-1
19	Boston College	9-3-0	Jack Bicknell	8-3-0
20	Virginia Tech	9-2-1	Bill Dooley	8-2-1

Key Bowl Games

Rankings below reflect final regular season poll, released Dec. 1.

Fiesta—#2 Penn St. over #1 Miami-FL, 14-10; **Orange**—#3 Oklahoma over #9 Arkansas, 42-8; **Rose**—#7 Ariz. St. over #4 Michigan, 22-15; **Sugar**—#6 Nebraska over #5 LSU, 30-15; **Cotton**—#11 Ohio St. over #8 Texas A&M, 28-12; **Citrus**—#10 Auburn over USC, 16-7; **Sun**—#13 Alabama over #12 Washington, 28-6.

1987

		After Bowls	Head Coach	Regular Season
1	Miami-FL	12-0-0	Jimmy Johnson	11-0-0
2	Florida St.	11-1-0	Bobby Bowden	10-1-0
3	Oklahoma	11-1-0	Barry Switzer	11-0-0
4	Syracuse	11-0-1	Dick MacPherson	11-0-0
5	LSU	10-1-1	Mike Archer	9-1-1
6	Nebraska	10-2-0	Tom Osborne	10-1-0
7	Auburn	9-1-2	Pat Dye	9-1-1
8	Michigan St.	9-2-1	George Perles	8-2-1
9	UCLA	10-2-0	Terry Donahue	9-2-0
10	Texas A&M	10-2-0	Jackie Sherrill	9-2-0
11	Oklahoma St.	10-2-0	Pat Jones	9-2-0
12	Clemson	10-2-0	Danny Ford	9-2-0
13	Georgia	9-3-0	Vince Dooley	8-3-0
14	Tennessee	10-2-1	Johnny Majors	9-2-1
15	South Carolina	8-4-0	Joe Morrison	8-3-0
16	Iowa	10-3-0	Hayden Fry	9-3-0
17	Notre Dame	8-4-0	Lou Holtz	8-3-0
18	USC	8-4-0	Larry Smith	8-3-0
19	Michigan	8-4-0	Bo Schembechler	7-4-0
20	Arizona St.	7-4-1	John Cooper	6-4-1

Key Bowl Games

Rankings below reflect final regular season poll, released Dec. 7.

Orange—#2 Miami-FL over #1 Oklahoma, 20-14; **Fiesta**—#3 Florida St. over #5 Nebraska, 31-28; **Sugar**—#4 Syracuse tied #6 Auburn, 16-16; **Gator**—#7 LSU over #9 S. Carolina, 30-13; **Rose**—#8 Mich. St. over #16 USC, 20-17; **Aloha**—#10 UCLA over Florida, 20-16; **Cotton**—#13 Texas A&M over #12 Notre Dame, 35-10.

1988

		After Bowls	Head Coach	Regular Season
1	Notre Dame	12-0-0	Lou Holtz	11-0-0
2	Miami-FL	11-1-0	Jimmy Johnson	10-1-0
3	Florida St.	11-1-0	Bobby Bowden	10-1-0
4	Michigan	9-2-1	Bo Schembechler	8-2-1
5	West Virginia	11-1-0	Don Nehlen	11-0-0
6	UCLA	10-2-0	Terry Donahue	9-2-0
7	USC	10-2-0	Larry Smith	10-1-0
8	Auburn	10-2-0	Pat Dye	10-1-0
9	Clemson	10-2-0	Danny Ford	9-2-0
10	Nebraska	11-2-0	Tom Osborne	11-1-0
11	Oklahoma St.	10-2-0	Pat Jones	9-2-0
12	Arkansas	10-2-0	Ken Hatfield	10-1-0
13	Syracuse	10-2-0	Dick MacPherson	9-2-0
14	Oklahoma	9-3-0	Barry Switzer	9-2-0
15	Georgia	9-3-0	Vince Dooley	8-3-0
16	Washington St.	9-3-0	Dennis Erickson	8-3-0
17	Alabama	9-3-0	Bill Curry	8-3-0
18	Houston	9-3-0	Jack Pardee	9-2-0
19	LSU	8-4-0	Mike Archer	8-3-0
20	Indiana	8-3-1	Bill Mallory	7-3-1

Key Bowl Games

Rankings below reflect final regular season poll, released Dec. 5.

Fiesta—#1 Notre Dame over #3 West Va., 34-21; **Orange**—#2 Miami-FL over #6 Nebraska, 23-3; **Sugar**—#4 Florida St. over #7 Auburn, 13-7; **Rose**—#11 Michigan over #5 USC, 22-14; **Cotton**—#9 UCLA over #8 Arkansas, 17-3; **Citrus**—#13 Clemson over #10 Oklahoma, 13-6.

1989

		After Bowls	Head Coach	Regular Season
1	Miami-FL	11-1-0	Dennis Erickson	10-1-0
2	Notre Dame	12-1-0	Lou Holtz	11-1-0
3	Florida St.	10-2-0	Bobby Bowden	9-2-0
4	Colorado	11-1-0	Bill McCartney	11-0-0
5	Tennessee	11-1-0	Johnny Majors	10-1-0
6	Auburn	10-2-0	Pat Dye	9-2-0
7	Michigan	10-2-0	Bo Schembechler	10-1-0
8	USC	9-2-1	Larry Smith	8-2-1
9	Alabama	10-2-0	Bill Curry	10-1-0
10	Illinois	10-2-0	John Mackovic	9-2-0
11	Nebraska	10-2-0	Tom Osborne	10-1-0
12	Clemson	10-2-0	Danny Ford	9-2-0
13	Arkansas	10-2-0	Ken Hatfield	10-1-0
14	Houston	9-2-0	Jack Pardee	same
15	Penn St.	8-3-1	Joe Paterno	7-3-1
16	Michigan St.	8-4-0	George Perles	7-4-0
17	Pittsburgh	8-3-1	Mike Gottfried (7-3-1) & Paul Hackett (1-0)	7-3-1
18	Virginia	10-3-0	George Welsh	10-2-0
19	Texas Tech	9-3-0	Spike Dykes	8-3-0
20	Texas A&M	8-4-0	R.C. Slocum	8-3-0
21	West Virginia	8-3-1	Don Nehlen	8-2-1
22	BYU	10-3-0	LaVell Edwards	10-2-0
23	Washington	8-4-0	Don James	7-4-0
24	Ohio St.	8-4-0	John Cooper	8-3-0
25	Arizona	8-4-0	Dick Tomey	7-4-0

Key Bowl Games

Rankings below reflect final regular season poll, released Dec. 11. No bowl for then #13 Houston (probation).

Orange—#4 Notre Dame over #1 Colorado, 21-6; **Sugar**—#6 Miami-FL over #7 Alabama, 33-25; **Rose**—#12 USC over #3 Michigan, 17-10; **Fiesta**—#5 Florida St. over #6 Nebraska, 41-17; **Cotton**—#8 Tennessee over #10 Arkansas, 31-27; **Hall of Fame**—#9 Auburn over #21 Ohio St., 31-14; **Citrus**—#11 Illinois over #15 Virginia, 31-21.

1990

		After Bowls	Head Coach	Regular Season
1	Colorado	11-1-1	Bill McCartney	10-1-1
2	Georgia Tech	11-0-1	Bobby Ross	10-0-1
3	Miami-FL	10-2-0	Dennis Erickson	9-2-0
4	Florida St.	10-2-0	Bobby Bowden	9-2-0
5	Washington	10-2-0	Don James	9-2-0
6	Notre Dame	9-3-0	Lou Holtz	9-2-0
7	Michigan	9-3-0	Gary Moeller	8-3-0
8	Tennessee	9-2-2	Johnny Majors	8-2-2
9	Clemson	10-2-0	Ken Hatfield	9-2-0
10	Houston	10-1-0	John Jenkins	same
11	Penn St.	9-3-0	Joe Paterno	9-2-0
12	Texas	10-2-0	David McWilliams	10-1-0
13	Florida	9-2-0	Steve Spurrier	same
14	Louisville	10-1-1	H. Schnellenberger	9-1-1
15	Texas A&M	9-3-1	R.C. Slocum	8-3-1
16	Michigan St.	8-3-1	George Perles	7-3-1
17	Oklahoma	8-3-0	Gary Gibbs	same
18	Iowa	8-4-0	Hayden Fry	8-3-0
19	Auburn	8-3-1	Pat Dye	7-3-1
20	USC	8-4-1	Larry Smith	8-3-1
21	Mississippi	9-3-0	Billy Brewer	9-2-0
22	BYU	10-3-0	LaVell Edwards	10-2-0
23	Virginia	8-4-0	George Welsh	8-3-0
24	Nebraska	9-3-0	Tom Osborne	9-2-0
25	Illinois	8-4-0	John Mackovic	8-3-0

Key Bowl Games

Rankings below reflect final regular season poll, released Dec. 3. No bowl for then #9 Houston (probation), #11 Florida (probation) and #20 Oklahoma (probation).
Orange—#1 Colorado over #5 Notre Dame, 10-9; **Citrus**—#2 Ga. Tech over #19 Nebraska, 45-21; **Cotton**—#4 Miami-FL over #3 Texas, 46-3; **Blockbuster**—#6 Florida St. over #7 Penn St., 24-17; **Rose**—#8 Washington over #17 Iowa, 46-34; **Sugar**—#10 Tennessee over Virginia, 23-22; **Gator**—#12 Michigan over #15 Ole Miss, 35-3.

1991

		After Bowls	Head Coach	Regular Season
1	Miami-FL	12-0-0	Dennis Erickson	11-0-0
2	Washington	12-0-0	Don James	11-0-0
3	Penn St.	11-2-0	Joe Paterno	10-2-0
4	Florida St.	11-2-0	Bobby Bowden	10-2-0
5	Alabama	11-1-0	Gene Stallings	10-1-0
6	Michigan	10-2-0	Gary Moeller	10-1-0
7	Florida	10-2-0	Steve Spurrier	10-1-0
8	California	10-2-0	Bruce Snyder	9-2-0
9	East Carolina	11-1-0	Bill Lewis	10-1-0
10	Iowa	10-1-1	Hayden Fry	10-1-0
11	Syracuse	10-2-0	Paul Pasqualoni	9-2-0
12	Texas A&M	10-2-0	R.C. Slocum	10-1-0
13	Notre Dame	10-3-0	Lou Holtz	9-3-0
14	Tennessee	9-3-0	Johnny Majors	9-2-0
15	Nebraska	9-2-1	Tom Osborne	9-1-1
16	Oklahoma	9-3-0	Gary Gibbs	8-3-0
17	Georgia	9-3-0	Ray Goff	8-3-0
18	Clemson	9-2-1	Ken Hatfield	9-1-1
19	UCLA	9-3-0	Terry Donahue	8-3-0
20	Colorado	8-3-1	Bill McCartney	8-2-1
21	Tulsa	10-2-0	David Rader	9-2-0
22	Stanford	8-4-0	Dennis Green	8-3-0
23	BYU	8-3-2	LaVell Edwards	8-3-1
24	N.C. State	9-3-0	Dick Sheridan	9-2-0
25	Air Force	10-3-0	Fisher DeBerry	9-3-0

Key Bowl Games

Rankings below reflect final regular season poll, taken Dec. 2. **Orange**—#1 Miami-FL over #11 Nebraska, 22-0; **Rose**—#2 Washington over #4 Michigan, 34-14; **Sugar**—#18 Notre Dame over #3 Florida, 39-28; **Cotton**—#5 Florida St. over #9 Texas A&M, 10-2; **Fiesta**—#6 Penn St. over #10 Tennessee, 42-17; **Holiday**—#7 Iowa tied BYU, 13-13; **Blockbuster**—#8 Alabama over #15 Colorado, 30-25; **Citrus**—#14 California over #13 Clemson, 37-13.

1992

		After Bowls	Head Coach	Regular Season
1	Alabama	13-0-0	Gene Stallings	12-0-0
2	Florida St.	11-1-0	Bobby Bowden	10-1-0
3	Miami-FL	11-1-0	Dennis Erickson	11-0-0
4	Notre Dame	10-1-1	Lou Holtz	9-1-1
5	Michigan	9-0-3	Gary Moeller	8-0-3
6	Syracuse	10-2-0	Paul Pasqualoni	9-2-0
7	Texas A&M	12-1-0	R.C. Slocum	12-0-0
8	Georgia	10-2-0	Ray Goff	9-2-0
9	Stanford	10-3-0	Bill Walsh	9-3-0
10	Florida	9-4-0	Steve Spurrier	8-4-0
11	Washington	9-3-0	Don James	9-2-0
12	Tennessee	9-3-0	Johnny Majors (5-3) & Phillip Fulmer (4-0)	8-3-0
13	Colorado	9-2-1	Bill McCartney	9-1-1
14	Nebraska	9-3-0	Tom Osborne	9-2-0
15	Washington St.	9-3-0	Mike Price	8-3-0
16	Mississippi	9-3-0	Billy Brewer	8-3-0
17	N.C. State	9-3-1	Dick Sheridan	9-2-1
18	Ohio St.	8-3-1	John Cooper	8-2-1
19	North Carolina	9-3-0	Mack Brown	8-3-0
20	Hawaii	11-2-0	Bob Wagner	10-2-0
21	Boston College	8-3-1	Tom Coughlin	8-2-1
22	Kansas	8-4-0	Glen Mason	7-4-0
23	Mississippi St.	7-5-0	Jackie Sherrill	7-4-0
24	Fresno St.	9-4-0	Jim Sweeney	9-3-0
25	Wake Forest	8-4-0	Bill Dooley	7-4-0

Key Bowl Games

Rankings below reflect final regular season poll, taken Dec. 5. **Sugar**—#2 Alabama over #1 Miami-FL, 34-13; **Orange**—#3 Florida St. over #11 Nebraska, 27-14; **Cotton**—#5 Notre Dame over #4 Texas A&M, 28-3; **Fiesta**—#6 Syracuse over #10 Colorado, 26-22; **Rose**—#7 Michigan over #9 Washington, 38-31; **Citrus**—#8 Georgia over #15 Ohio St., 21-14.

1993

		After Bowls	Head Coach	Regular Season
1	Florida St	12-1-0	Bobby Bowden	11-1-0
2	Notre Dame	11-1-0	Lou Holtz	10-1-0
3	Nebraska	11-1-0	Tom Osborne	11-0-0
4	Auburn	11-0-0	Terry Bowden	11-0-0
5	Florida	11-2-0	Steve Spurrier	10-2-0
6	Wisconsin	10-1-1	Barry Alvarez	9-1-1
7	West Virginia	11-1-0	Don Nehlen	11-0-0
8	Penn St	10-2-0	Joe Paterno	9-2-0
9	Texas A&M	10-2-0	R.C. Slocum	10-1-0
10	Arizona	10-2-0	Dick Tomey	9-2-0
11	Ohio St	10-1-1	John Cooper	9-1-1
12	Tennessee	9-2-1	Phillip Fulmer	9-1-1
13	Boston College	9-3-0	Tom Coughlin	8-3-0
14	Alabama	9-3-1	Gene Stallings	8-3-1
15	Miami-FL	9-3-0	Dennis Erickson	9-2-0
16	Colorado	8-3-1	Bill McCartney	7-3-1
17	Oklahoma	9-3-0	Gary Gibbs	8-3-0
18	UCLA	8-4-0	Terry Donahue	8-3-0
19	North Carolina	10-3-0	Mack Brown	10-2-0
20	Kansas St	9-2-1	Bill Snyder	8-2-1
21	Michigan	8-4-0	Gary Moeller	7-4-0
22	Va. Tech	9-3-0	Frank Beamer	9-2-0
23	Clemson	9-3-0	Ken Hatfield (8-3) & Tommy West (1-0)	8-3-0
24	Louisville	9-3-0	H. Schnellenberger	8-3-0
25	California	9-4-0	Keith Gilbertson	8-4-0

Key Bowl Games

Rankings below reflect final regular season poll, taken Dec. 5. No bowl for then #5 Auburn (probation). **Orange**—#1 Florida St. over #2 Nebraska, 18-16; **Sugar**—#8 Florida over #3 West Virginia, 41-7; **Cotton**—#4 Notre Dame over #7 Texas A&M, 24-21; **Citrus**—#13 Penn St. over #6 Tennessee, 31-13; **Rose**—#9 Wisconsin over #14 UCLA, 21-16; **Fiesta**—#16 Arizona over #10 Miami-FL, 29-0;

Associated Press Final Polls (Cont.)

1994

		After Bowls	Head Coach	Regular Season
1	Nebraska	13-0-0	Tom Osborne	12-0-0
2	Penn St	12-0-0	Joe Paterno	11-0-0
3	Colorado	11-1-0	Bill McCartney	10-1-0
4	Florida St	10-1-1	Bobby Bowden	9-1-1
5	Alabama	12-1-0	Gene Stallings	11-1-0
6	Miami-FL	10-2-0	Dennis Erickson	10-1-0
7	Florida	10-2-1	Steve Spurrier	10-1-1
8	Texas A&M	10-0-1	R.C. Slocum	same
9	Auburn	9-1-1	Terry Bowden	same
10	Utah	10-2-0	Ron McBride	9-2-0
11	Oregon	9-4-0	Rich Brooks	9-3-0
12	Michigan	8-4-0	Gary Moeller	7-4-0
13	USC	8-3-1	John Robinson	7-3-1
14	Ohio St	9-4-0	John Cooper	9-3-0
15	Virginia	9-3-0	George Welsh	8-3-0
16	Colorado St	10-2-0	Sonny Lubick	10-1-0
17	N.C. State	9-3-0	Mike O'Cain	8-3-0
18	BYU	10-3-0	LaVell Edwards	9-3-0
19	Kansas St	9-3-0	Bill Snyder	9-2-0
20	Arizona	8-4-0	Dick Tomey	8-3-0
21	Washington St	8-4-0	Mike Price	7-4-0
22	Tennessee	8-4-0	Phillip Fulmer	7-4-0
23	Boston College	7-4-1	Dan Henning	6-4-1
24	Mississippi St	8-4-0	Jackie Sherrill	8-3-0
25	Texas	8-4-0	John Mackovic	7-4-0

Key Bowl Games

Rankings below reflect final regular season poll, taken Dec. 4. No bowls for then #8 Texas A&M (probation) and #9 Auburn (probation). **Orange**–#1 Nebraska over #3 Miami-FL, 24-17; **Rose**–#2 Penn St. over #12 Oregon, 38-20; **Fiesta**–#4 Colorado over Notre Dame, 41-24; **Sugar**–#7 Florida St. over #5 Florida, 23-17; **Citrus**–#6 Alabama over #13 Ohio St., 24-17; **Freedom**–#14 Utah over #15 Arizona, 16-13.

1996

		After Bowls	Head Coach	Regular Season
1	Florida	12-1	Steve Spurrier	11-1
2	Ohio St.	11-1	John Cooper	10-1
3	Florida St	11-1	Bobby Bowden	11-0
4	Arizona St.	11-1	Bruce Snyder	11-0
5	BYU	14-1	LaVell Edwards	13-1
6	Nebraska	11-2	Tom Osborne	10-2
7	Penn St.	11-2	Joe Paterno	10-2
8	Colorado	10-2	Rick Neuheisel	9-2
9	Tennessee	10-2	Phillip Fulmer	9-2
10	North Carolina	10-2	Mack Brown	9-2
11	Alabama	10-3	Gene Stallings	9-3
12	LSU	10-2	Gerry DiNardo	9-2
13	Virginia Tech	10-2	Frank Beamer	10-1
14	Miami-FL	9-3	Butch Davis	8-3
15	Northwestern	9-3	Gary Barnett	9-2
16	Washington	9-3	Jim Lambright	9-2
17	Kansas St.	9-3	Bill Snyder	9-2
18	Iowa	9-3	Hayden Fry	8-3
19	Notre Dame	8-3	Lou Holtz	same
20	Michigan	8-4	Lloyd Carr	8-3
21	Syracuse	9-3	Paul Pasqualoni	8-3
22	Wyoming	10-2	Joe Tiller	same
23	Texas	8-5	John Mackovic	8-4
24	Auburn	8-4	Terry Bowden	7-4
25	Army	10-2	Bob Sutton	10-1

Key Bowl Games

Rankings below reflect final regular season poll, taken Dec. 8. No bowl for then #18 N. Dame and #22 Wyoming. **Sugar**–#3 Fla. over #1 Fla. St., 52-20; **Rose**–#4 Ohio St. over #2 Ariz. St., 20-17; **Fiesta**–#7 Penn St. over #20 Texas, 38-15; **Cotton**–#5 BYU over #14 Kansas St., 19-15; **Citrus**–#9 Tenn. over #11 Northwestern, 48-28; **Orange**–#6 Neb. over #10 Va. Tech, 41-21.

1995

		After Bowls	Head Coach	Regular Season
1	Nebraska	12-0-0	Tom Osborne	11-0-0
2	Florida	12-1-0	Steve Spurrier	12-0-0
3	Tennessee	11-1-0	Phillip Fulmer	10-1-0
4	Florida St	10-2-0	Bobby Bowden	9-2-0
5	Colorado	10-2-0	Rick Neuheisel	9-2-0
6	Ohio St	11-2-0	John Cooper	11-1-0
7	Kansas St	10-2-0	Bill Snyder	9-2-0
8	Northwestern	10-2-0	Gary Barnett	10-1-0
9	Kansas	10-2-0	Glen Mason	9-2-0
10	Virginia Tech	10-2-0	Frank Beamer	9-2-0
11	Notre Dame	9-3-0	Lou Holtz	9-2-0
12	USC	9-2-1	John Robinson	8-2-1
13	Penn St	9-3-0	Joe Paterno	8-3-0
14	Texas	10-2-1	John Mackovic	10-1-1
15	Texas A&M	9-3-0	R.C. Slocum	8-3-0
16	Virginia	9-4-0	George Welsh	8-4-0
17	Michigan	9-4-0	Lloyd Carr	9-3-0
18	Oregon	9-3-0	Mike Bellotti	9-2-0
19	Syracuse	9-3-0	Paul Pasqualoni	8-3-0
20	Miami-FL	8-3-0	Butch Davis	same
21	Alabama	8-3-0	Gene Stallings	same
22	Auburn	8-4-0	Terry Bowden	8-3-0
23	Texas Tech	9-3-0	Spike Dykes	8-3-0
24	Toledo	11-0-1	Gary Pinkel	10-0-1
25	Iowa	8-4-0	Hayden Fry	7-4-0

Key Bowl Games

Rankings below reflect final regular season poll, taken Dec. 3. No bowl for then #21 Ala. (probation) and #22 Miami-FL (probation). **Fiesta**–#1 Neb. over #2 Fla., 62-24; **Rose**–#17 USC over #3 Northwestern, 41-32; **Citrus**–#4† Tenn. over #4† Ohio St., 20-14; **Orange**–#8 Fla. St. over #6 N. Dame, 31-26; **Cotton**–#7 Colo. over #12 Oregon, 38-6; **Sugar**–#13 Va. Tech over #9 Texas, 28-10.

1997

		After Bowls	Head Coach	Regular Season
1	Michigan	12-0	Lloyd Carr	11-0
2	Nebraska	13-0	Tom Osborne	12-0
3	Florida St	11-1	Bobby Bowden	10-1
4	Florida	10-2	Steve Spurrier	9-2
5	UCLA	10-2	Bob Toledo	9-2
6	North Carolina	11-1	Mack Brown (10-1) & Carl Torbush	10-1 (1-0)
7	Tennessee	11-2	Phillip Fulmer	11-1
8	Kansas St	11-1	Bill Snyder	10-1
9	Washington St.	10-2	Mike Price	10-1
10	Georgia	10-2	Jim Donnan	9-2
11	Auburn	10-3	Terry Bowden	9-3
12	Ohio St.	10-3	John Cooper	10-2
13	LSU	9-3	Gerry DiNardo	8-3
14	Arizona St.	8-3	Bruce Snyder	7-3
15	Purdue	9-3	Joe Tiller	8-3
16	Penn St.	9-3	Joe Paterno	9-2
17	Colorado St.	11-2	Sonny Lubick	10-2
18	Washington	8-4	Jim Lambright	7-4
19	So. Mississippi	9-3	Jeff Bower	8-3
20	Texas A&M	9-4	R.C. Slocum	9-3
21	Syracuse	9-4	Paul Pasqualoni	9-3
22	Mississippi	8-4	Tommy Tuberville	7-4
23	Missouri	7-5	Larry Smith	6-5
24	Oklahoma St.	8-4	Bobby Simmons	8-3
25	Georgia Tech	7-5	George O'Leary	6-5

Key Bowl Games

Rankings below reflect final regular season poll, taken Dec. 7. **Rose**–#1 Michigan over #7 Washington St., 21-16; **Orange**–#2 Nebraska over #3 Tennessee, 42-17; **Sugar**–#4 Florida St. over #10 Ohio St., 31-14; **Gator**–#5 North Carolina over Virginia Tech, 42-3; **Cotton**–#6 UCLA over #19 Texas A&M, 29-23; **Citrus**–#8 Florida over #12 Penn St., 21-6; **Fiesta**–#9 Kansas St. over #14 Syracuse, 35-18.

1998

		After Bowls	Head Coach	Regular Season
1	Tennessee	13-0	Phillip Fulmer	12-0
2	Ohio St.	11-1	John Cooper	10-1
3	Florida St.	11-2	Bobby Bowden	11-1
4	Arizona	12-1	Dick Tomey	11-1
5	Florida	10-2	Steve Spurrier	9-2
6	Wisconsin	11-1	Barry Alvarez	10-1
7	Tulane	12-0	Tommy Bowden	11-0
8	UCLA	10-2	Bob Toledo	10-1
9	Georgia Tech	10-2	George O'Leary	9-2
10	Kansas St.	11-2	Bill Snyder	11-1
11	Texas A&M	11-3	R.C. Slocum	11-2
12	Michigan	10-3	Lloyd Carr	9-3
13	Air Force	12-1	Fisher DeBerry	11-1
14	Georgia	9-3	Jim Donnan	8-3
15	Texas	9-3	Mack Brown	8-3
16	Arkansas	9-3	Houston Nutt	9-2
17	Penn St.	9-3	Joe Paterno	8-3
18	Virginia	9-3	George Welsh	9-2
19	Nebraska	9-4	Frank Solich	9-3
20	Miami-FL	9-3	Butch Davis	8-3
21	Missouri	8-4	Larry Smith	7-4
22	Notre Dame	9-3	Bob Davie	9-2
23	Va. Tech	9-3	Frank Beamer	8-3
24	Purdue	9-4	Joe Tiller	8-4
25	Syracuse	8-4	Paul Pasqualoni	8-3

Key Bowl Games

Rankings below reflect final regular season poll, taken Dec. 6. **Fiesta**–#1 Tennessee over #2 Florida St., 23-16; **Sugar**–#3 Ohio St. over #8 Texas A&M, 24-14; **Orange**–#7 Florida over #18 Syracuse, 31-10; **Rose**–#9 Wisconsin over #6 UCLA, 38-31; **Holiday**–#5 Arizona over #14 Nebraska, 23-20; **Alamo**–Purdue over #4 Kansas St., 37-34.

1999

		After Bowls	Head Coach	Regular Season
1	Florida St.	12-0	Bobby Bowden	11-0
2	Va. Tech	11-1	Frank Beamer	11-0
3	Nebraska	12-1	Frank Solich	11-1
4	Wisconsin	10-2	Barry Alvarez	9-2
5	Michigan	10-2	Lloyd Carr	9-2
6	Kansas St.	11-1	Bill Snyder	10-1
7	Michigan St.	10-2	Nick Saban (9-2) & B. Williams (1-0)	9-2
8	Alabama	10-3	Mike DuBose	10-2
9	Tennessee	9-3	Phillip Fulmer	8-3
10	Marshall	13-0	Bob Pruett	12-0
11	Penn St.	10-3	Joe Paterno	9-3
12	Florida	9-4	Steve Spurrier	9-3
13	Mississippi St.	10-2	Jackie Sherrill	9-2
14	Southern Miss.	9-3	Jeff Bower	8-3
15	Miami-FL	9-4	Butch Davis	8-4
16	Georgia	8-4	Jim Donnan	7-4
17	Arkansas	8-4	Houston Nutt	7-4
18	Minnesota	8-4	Glen Mason	8-3
19	Oregon	9-3	Mike Bellotti	8-3
20	Georgia Tech	8-4	George O'Leary	8-3
21	Texas	9-5	Mack Brown	9-4
22	Mississippi	8-4	David Cutcliffe	7-4
23	Texas A&M	8-4	R.C. Slocum	8-3
24	Illinois	8-4	Ron Turner	7-4
25	Purdue	7-5	Joe Tiller	7-4

Key Bowl Games

Rankings below reflect final regular season poll, taken Dec. 5. **Sugar**–#1 Florida St. over #2 Va. Tech, 46-29; **Fiesta**–#3 Nebraska over #6 Tennessee, 31-21; **Rose**–#4 Wisconsin over #22 Stanford, 17-9; **Orange**–#8 Michigan over #5 Alabama, 35-34; **Holiday**–#7 Kansas St. over Washington, 24-20; **Citrus**–#9 Michigan St. over #10 Florida, 37-34.

2000

		After Bowls	Head Coach	Regular Season
1	Oklahoma	13-0	Bob Stoops	12-0
2	Miami-FL	11-1	Butch Davis	10-1
3	Washington	11-1	Rick Neuheisel	10-1
4	Oregon St.	11-1	Dennis Erickson	10-1
5	Florida St.	11-2	Bobby Bowden	11-1
6	Va. Tech	11-1	Frank Beamer	10-1
7	Oregon	10-2	Mike Bellotti	9-2
8	Nebraska	10-2	Frank Solich	9-2
9	Kansas St.	11-3	Bill Snyder	10-3
10	Florida	10-3	Steve Spurrier	10-2
11	Michigan	9-3	Lloyd Carr	8-3
12	Texas	9-3	Mack Brown	9-2
13	Purdue	8-4	Joe Tiller	8-3
14	Colorado St.	10-2	Sonny Lubick	9-2
15	Notre Dame	9-3	Bob Davie	9-2
16	Clemson	9-3	Tommy Bowden	9-2
17	Georgia Tech	9-3	George O'Leary	9-2
18	Auburn	9-4	Tommy Tuberville	9-3
19	South Carolina	8-4	Lou Holtz	7-4
20	Georgia	8-4	Jim Donnan	7-4
21	TCU	10-2	D. Franchione (10-1) & G. Patterson (0-1)	10-1
22	LSU	8-4	Nick Saban	7-4
23	Wisconsin	9-4	Barry Alvarez	8-4
24	Mississippi St.	8-4	Jackie Sherrill	7-4
25	Iowa St.	9-3	Dan McCarney	8-3

Key Bowl Games

Rankings below reflect final regular season poll, taken Dec. 4. **Orange**–#1 Oklahoma over #3 Florida St., 13-2; **Sugar**–#2 Miami-FL over #7 Florida, 37-20; **Rose**–#4 Washington over #14 Purdue, 34-24; **Fiesta**–#5 Oregon St. over #10 Notre Dame, 41-9; **Gator**–#6 Virginia Tech over #16 Clemson, 41-20; **Holiday**–#8 Oregon over #12 Texas, 35-30; **Alamo**–#9 Nebraska over #18 Northwestern, 66-17.

2001

		After Bowls	Head Coach	Regular Season
1	Miami-FL	12-0	Larry Coker	11-0
2	Oregon	11-1	Mike Bellotti	10-1
3	Florida	10-2	Steve Spurrier	9-2
4	Tennessee	11-2	Phillip Fulmer	10-2
5	Texas	11-2	Mack Brown	10-2
6	Oklahoma	11-2	Bob Stoops	10-2
7	LSU	10-3	Nick Saban	9-3
8	Nebraska	11-2	Frank Solich	11-1
9	Colorado	10-3	Gary Barnett	10-2
10	Washington St.	10-2	Mike Price	9-2
11	Maryland	10-2	Ralph Friedgen	10-1
12	Illinois	10-2	Ron Turner	10-1
13	South Carolina	9-3	Lou Holtz	8-3
14	Syracuse	10-3	Paul Pasqualoni	9-3
15	Florida St.	8-4	Bobby Bowden	7-4
16	Stanford	9-3	Tyrone Willingham	9-2
17	Louisville	11-2	John L. Smith	10-2
18	Va. Tech	8-4	Frank Beamer	8-3
19	Washington	8-4	Rick Neuheisel	8-3
20	Michigan	8-4	Lloyd Carr	8-3
21	Boston College	8-4	Tom O'Brien	7-4
22	Georgia	8-4	Mark Richt	8-3
23	Toledo	10-2	Tom Amstutz	9-2
24	Georgia Tech	8-5	George O'Leary (7-5) & Mac McWhorter (1-0)	7-5
25	BYU	12-2	Gary Crowton	12-1

Key Bowl Games

Rankings below reflect final regular season poll, taken Dec. 9. **Rose**–#1 Miami-FL over #4 Nebraska, 37-14; **Fiesta**–#2 Oregon over #3 Colorado, 38-16; **Orange**–#5 Florida over #6 Maryland, 56-23; **Sugar**–#12 LSU over #7 Illinois 47-34; **Citrus**–#8 Tennessee over #17 Michigan, 45-17; **Holiday**–#9 Texas over #21 Washington, 47-43; **Cotton**–#10 Oklahoma over Arkansas, 10-3;

Associated Press Final Polls (Cont.)

2002

		After Bowls	Head Coach	Regular Season
1	Ohio St.	14-0	Jim Tressel	13-0
2	Miami-FL	12-1	Larry Coker	12-0
3	Georgia	13-1	Mark Richt	12-1
4	USC	11-2	Pete Carroll	10-2
5	Oklahoma	12-2	Bob Stoops	11-2
6	Texas	11-2	Mack Brown	10-2
7	Kansas St.	11-2	Bill Snyder	10-2
8	Iowa	11-2	Kirk Ferentz	11-1
9	Michigan	10-3	Lloyd Carr	9-3
10	Washington St.	10-3	Mike Price	10-2
11	Alabama	10-3	Dennis Franchione	10-3
12	N.C. State	11-3	Chuck Amato	10-3
13	Maryland	11-3	Ralph Friedgen	10-3
14	Auburn	9-4	Tommy Tuberville	8-4
15	Boise St.	12-1	Dan Hawkins	11-1
16	Penn St.	9-4	Joe Paterno	9-2
17	Notre Dame	10-3	Tyrone Willingham	10-2
18	Va. Tech	10-4	Frank Beamer	9-4
19	Pittsburgh	9-4	Walt Harris	8-4
20	Colorado	9-5	Gary Barnett	9-4
21	Florida St.	9-5	Bobby Bowden	9-4
22	Virginia	9-5	Al Groh	8-5
23	TCU	10-2	Gary Patterson	9-2
24	Marshall	11-2	Bob Pruett	10-2
25	West Virginia	9-4	Rich Rodriguez	9-3

Key Bowl Games

Rankings below reflect final regular season poll, taken Dec. 8. No bowl for then #13 Alabama (probation).
Fiesta–#2 Ohio St. over #1 Miami-FL, 31-24 (2OT); **Orange**–#5 USC over #3 Iowa, 38-17; **Sugar**–#4 Georgia over #16 Florida St. 26-13; **Holiday**–#6 Kansas St. over Arizona St., 34-27; **Rose**–#8 Oklahoma over #7 Washington St., 34-14; **Cotton**–#9 Texas over LSU, 35-20; **Capital One**–#19 Auburn over #10 Penn St., 13-9;

2003

		After Bowls	Head Coach	Regular Season
1	USC	12-1	Pete Carroll	11-1
2	LSU	13-1	Nick Saban	12-1
3	Oklahoma	12-2	Bob Stoops	12-1
4	Ohio State	11-2	Jim Tressel	10-2
5	Miami-FL	11-2	Larry Coker	10-2
6	Michigan	11-2	Lloyd Carr	11-1
7	Georgia	11-3	Mark Richt	10-3
8	Iowa	10-3	Kirk Ferentz	9-3
9	Washington St.	10-3	Bill Doba	9-3
10	Miami-OH	13-1	Terry Hoeppner	12-1
11	Florida St.	10-3	Bobby Bowden	10-2
12	Texas	10-3	Mack Brown	10-2
13	Mississippi	10-3	David Cutcliffe	9-3
14	Kansas St.	11-4	Bill Snyder	11-3
15	Tennessee	10-3	Phillip Fulmer	10-2
16	Boise St.	13-1	Dan Hawkins	12-1
17	Maryland	10-3	Ralph Friedgen	9-3
18	Purdue	9-4	Joe Tiller	9-3
19	Nebraska	10-3	Frank Solich (9-3) & Bo Pelini (1-0)	9-3
20	Minnesota	10-3	Glen Mason	9-3
21	Utah	10-2	Urban Meyer	9-2
22	Clemson	9-4	Tommy Bowden	8-4
23	Bowling Green	11-3	Gregg Brandon	10-3
24	Florida	8-5	Ron Zook	8-4
25	TCU	11-2	Gary Patterson	11-1

Key Bowl Games

Rankings below reflect final regular season poll, taken Dec. 7. **Rose**–#1 USC over #4 Michigan, 28-14; **Sugar**–#2 LSU over #3 Oklahoma, 21-14; **Holiday**–#14 Washington St. over #5 Texas, 28-20; **Fiesta**–#6 Ohio St. over #10 Kansas St., 35-28; **Peach**–Clemson over #7 Tennessee, 27-14; **Orange**–#9 Miami-FL over #8 Florida St., 16-14.

2004

		After Bowls	Head Coach	Regular Season
1	USC	13-0	Pete Carroll	12-0
2	Auburn	13-0	Tommy Tuberville	12-0
3	Oklahoma	12-1	Bob Stoops	12-0
4	Utah	12-0	Urban Meyer	11-0
5	Texas	11-1	Mack Brown	10-1
6	Louisville	11-1	Bobby Petrino	10-1
7	Georgia	10-2	Mark Richt	9-2
8	Iowa	10-2	Kirk Ferentz	9-2
9	California	10-2	Jeff Tedford	10-1
10	Virginia Tech	10-3	Frank Beamer	12-1
11	Miami-FL	9-3	Larry Coker	8-3
12	Boise St.	11-1	Dan Hawkins	11-0
13	Tennessee	10-3	Philip Fullmer	9-3
14	Michigan	9-3	Lloyd Carr	8-3
15	Florida St.	9-3	Bobby Bowden	8-3
16	LSU	9-3	Nick Saban	9-2
17	Wisconsin	9-3	Barry Alvarez	9-2
18	Texas Tech	8-4	Mike Leach	7-4
19	Arizona St.	9-3	Dirk Koetter	8-3
20	Ohio St.	8-4	Jim Tressel	7-4
21	Boston College	9-3	Tom O'Brien	8-3
22	Fresno St.	9-3	Pat Hill	8-3
23	Virginia	8-4	Al Groh	8-3
24	Navy	10-2	Paul Johnson	9-2
25	Pittsburgh	8-4	Walt Harris	8-3

Key Bowl Games

Rankings below reflect final regular season poll, taken Dec. 5. **Orange**–#1 USC over #2 Oklahoma, 55-19; **Sugar**–#3 Auburn over #9 Virginia Tech, 16-13; **Holiday**–#23 Texas Tech over #4 California, 45-31; **Fiesta**–#5 Utah over #19 Pittsburgh, 35-7; **Rose**–#6 Texas over #13 Michigan, 38-37; **Liberty**–#7 Louisville over #10 Boise St., 44-40; **Outback**–#8 Georgia over #16 Wisconsin, 24-21.

2005

		After Bowls	Head Coach	Regular Season
1	Texas	13-0	Mack Brown	12-0
2	USC	12-1	Pete Carroll	12-0
3	Penn St.	11-1	Joe Paterno	10-1
4	Ohio St.	10-2	Jim Tressel	9-2
5	West Virginia	11-1	Rich Rodriguez	10-1
6	LSU	11-2	Les Miles	10-2
7	Virginia Tech	11-2	Frank Beamer	10-2
8	Alabama	10-2	Mike Shula	9-2
9	Notre Dame	9-3	Charlie Weis	9-2
10	Georgia	10-3	Mark Richt	9-3
11	TCU	11-1	Gary Patterson	10-1
12	Florida	9-3	Urban Meyer	8-3
	Oregon	10-2	Mike Bellotti	10-1
14	Auburn	9-3	Tommy Tuberville	9-2
15	Wisconsin	10-3	Barry Alvarez	9-3
16	UCLA	10-2	Karl Dorrell	9-2
17	Miami-FL	9-3	Larry Coker	9-2
18	Boston College	9-3	Tom O'Brien	8-3
19	Louisville	9-3	Bobby Petrino	9-2
20	Texas Tech	9-3	Mike Leach	9-2
21	Clemson	8-4	Tommy Bowden	7-4
22	Oklahoma	8-4	Bob Stoops	7-4
23	Florida St.	8-5	Bobby Bowden	8-4
24	Nebraska	8-4	Bill Callahan	7-4
25	California	8-4	Jeff Tedford	7-4

Key Bowl Games

Rankings below reflect final regular season poll, taken Dec. 6. **Rose**–#2 Texas over #1 USC over 41-38; **Orange**–#3 Penn St. over #22 Florida St., 26-23 3OT; **Fiesta**–#4 Ohio St. over #5 Notre Dame, 34-20; **Holiday**– Oklahoma over #6 Oregon, 17-14; **Capital One**–#21 Wisconsin over #7 Auburn, 24-10; **Sugar**–#11 West Virginia over #8 Georgia, 38-35; **Peach**–#10 LSU over #9 Miami-FL, 40-3.

2006

	After Bowls	Head Coach	Regular Season
1	Florida 13-1	Urban Meyer	12-1
2	Ohio St. 12-1	Jim Tressel	12-0
3	LSU 11-2	Les Miles	10-2
4	USC 12-1	Pete Carroll	11-1
5	Boise St. 13-0	Chris Petersen	12-0
6	Louisville 12-1	Bobby Petrino	11-1
7	Wisconsin 12-1	Barry Alvarez	11-1
8	Michigan 11-2	Lloyd Carr	11-1
9	Auburn 11-2	Tommy Tuberville	10-2
10	West Virginia 11-2	Rich Rodriguez	10-2
11	Oklahoma 11-3	Bob Stoops	11-2
12	Rutgers 11-2	Greg Schiano	10-2
13	Texas 10-3	Mack Brown	9-3
14	California 10-3	Jeff Tedford	9-3
15	Arkansas 10-4	Houston Nutt	10-3
16	Brigham Young . . .11-2	Bronco Mendenhall	10-2
17	Notre Dame 10-3	Charlie Weis	10-2
18	Wake Forest 11-3	Jim Grobe	11-2
19	Virginia Tech 10-3	Frank Beamer	10-2
20	Boston College . . .10-3	Tom O'Brien	9-3
21	Oregon St. 10-4	Mike Riley	9-4
22	TCU 11-2	Gary Patterson	10-2
23	Georgia 9-4	Mark Richt	8-4
24	Penn St. 9-4	Joe Paterno	8-4
25	Tennessee 9-4	Philip Fulmer	9-3

Key Bowl Games

Rankings below reflect final regular season poll, taken Dec. 3.
BCS–#2 Florida over #1 Ohio St. 41-14; **Sugar**–#4 LSU over #11 Notre Dame, 41-14; **Fiesta**–#9 Boise St. over #7 Oklahoma, 43-42 OT; **Orange**– #5 Louisville over #15 Wake Forest, 24-13; **Rose**–#8 USC over #3 Michigan, 32-18; **Capital One**– #6 Wisconsin over #12 Arkansas, 17-14.

All-Time AP Top 20

The composite AP Top 20 from the 1936 season through the 2006 season, based on the final rankings of each year. The final AP poll has been taken after the bowl games in 1965 and since 1968. Team point totals are based on 20 points for all 1st place finishes, 19 for each 2nd, etc. Also listed are the number of times each team has been named national champion by AP and times ranked in the final Top 10 and Top 20.

		Pts	No.1	Top 10	Top 20
1	Oklahoma	655	7	34	47
2	Notre Dame	652	8	35	48
3	Michigan	649	2	37	53
4	Ohio St	592	4	28	46
5	Alabama	587	6	32	44
6	Nebraska	548	4	29	42
7	USC	507	5	25	41
8	Texas	499	3	23	39
9	Tennessee	464	2	22	39
10	Penn St	426	2	22	37
11	Miami-FL	359	5	17	29
12	LSU	348	1	18	30
13	Florida St	336	2	16	23
14	Auburn	329	1	16	31
15	UCLA	327	0	16	30
16	Georgia	319	1	18	28
17	Florida	286	2	14	24
18	Arkansas	273	0	13	26
19	Michigan St	252	1	13	20
20	Washington	222	0	11	21

The Bowl Championship Series: a Convoluted History

Bowl Subdivision (formerly Division I-A) football remains the only NCAA sport on any level that does not have a sanctioned national champion. In an effort to clear up the confusion, the **Bowl Coalition** was formed in 1992. The 1992 Coalition, which lasted three seasons, consolidated the resources of four major bowls (Cotton, Fiesta, Orange, Sugar), the champions of five major conferences (ACC, Big East, Big Eight, SEC, SWC) and independent Notre Dame. It worked two out of three years with #1 vs. #2 showdowns in the 1993 Sugar Bowl (#2 Alabama over #1 Miami-FL) and 1994 Orange Bowl (#1 Florida St. over #2 Nebraska). The 1995 Orange Bowl settled for #1 Nebraska beating #3 Miami-FL because #2 Penn St., the Big Ten champion, was obligated to play in the Rose Bowl.

It was updated and redubbed the **Bowl Alliance** in 1995 in an attempt to keep the bowl system intact while forcing an annual championship game between the regular season's two top-ranked teams. The Bowl Alliance ended a three-year run after the 1997 season.

Organized in 1998, the **Bowl Championship Series** (BCS) was designed to finally guarantee that the teams ranked #1 and #2 will play each other in a "national title game" come January. The key difference from the 1992-97 Bowl Coalition/Bowl Alliance is that the BCS includes the Big Ten and Pac-10 champs. These teams were originally locked into playing in the Rose Bowl but were allowed, under the new system, to move to another bowl in order to create a match-up featuring the top two teams.

The bowls (Fiesta, Orange, Sugar) which made up the old Bowl Alliance kept their spots when the Rose Bowl joined this new four-bowl alliance. The Fiesta Bowl held the first national championship game under the BCS contract (Jan. 4, 1999 & Jan. 3, 2003), followed by the Sugar (Jan. 4, 2000 & Jan. 4, 2004) the Orange (Jan. 3, 2001 & Jan. 4, 2005) and the Rose Bowl (Jan. 3, 2002 & Jan. 4, 2006). The BCS, using a complex and frequently evolving rankings system, has successfully matched the top two teams in the country (according to the AP Poll) in six of the last nine years.

Oklahoma played Florida St. in the BCS title game on Jan. 3, 2001 despite the fact that Miami-FL was #2 in the AP poll. FSU was the second-ranked team in the BCS and therefore met Oklahoma, the top-ranked team, even though the Seminoles lost to Miami during the season. The following season, top-ranked Miami met BCS #2 Nebraska instead of Oregon, which was ranked second in both polls, at the Rose Bowl. Following the 2003 season, the final BCS matched the AP's #2 LSU (12-1) and #3 Oklahoma (12-1) in the Sugar Bowl while USC (11-1) sat atop the AP Poll but were third in the BCS rankings and met Michigan in the Rose Bowl. With LSU and USC won their bowls and the AP and Coaches polls split the national championship for the first time in the BCS era.

With the 2006-07 season, a separate BCS championship game was added following the four BCS bowls and two more at-large teams were added to the pool. The future schedule/locations for the BCS title game: Jan. 8, 2008 (New Orleans); Jan. 8, 2009 (Miami); Jan. 8, 2010 (Pasadena, Calif.).

Bowl Games

From Jan. 1, 1902 through Jan. 3, 2007. Please note that the Bowl selection process is now dominated by the Bowl Championship Series (which includes the Fiesta, Orange, Rose and Sugar bowls) and the following non-BCS bowls' so called "automatic berths" are contingent upon several factors, including the leftovers from the BCS, Notre Dame's record and the record of their designated choices.

Rose Bowl

City: Pasadena, Calif. **Stadium:** Rose Bowl. **Capacity:** 102,083. **Playing surface:** Grass. **First game:** Jan. 1, 1902.
Playing sites: Tournament Park (1902, 1916-22), Rose Bowl (1923-41 and since 1943) and Duke Stadium in Durham, N.C. (1942, due to wartime restrictions following Japan's attack at Pearl Harbor on Dec. 7, 1941). **Corporate sponsors:** AT&T (1998-2002), Sony Playstation 2 (2003) and Citi (2004).

Automatic berths: Pacific Coast Conference champion vs. opponent selected by PCC (1924-45 seasons); Big Ten champion vs. Pac-10 champion (1946-97); Bowl Championship Series: Big Ten champion vs. Pac-10 champion, if available (1998-2000, 2002-05 seasons) and #1 vs. #2 in Jan. 2002 and Jan. 2006.

Multiple wins: USC (22); Michigan (8); Washington (7); Ohio St. (6); Stanford and UCLA (5); Alabama (4); Illinois, Michigan St. and Wisconsin (3); California, Iowa and Texas (2).

Year		Year		Year	
1902*	Michigan 49, Stanford 0	1947	Illinois 45, UCLA 14	1979	USC 17, Michigan 10
1916	Washington St. 14, Brown 0	1948	Michigan 49, USC 0	1980	USC 17, Ohio St. 16
1917	Oregon 14, Penn 0	1949	Northwestern 20, California 14	1981	Michigan 23, Washington 6
1918	Mare Island 19, Camp Lewis 7	1950	Ohio St. 17, California 14	1982	Washington 28, Iowa 0
1919	Great Lakes 17, Mare Island 0	1951	Michigan 14, California 6	1983	UCLA 24, Michigan 14
1920	Harvard 7, Oregon 6	1952	Illinois 40, Stanford 7	1984	UCLA 45, Illinois 9
1921	California 28, Ohio St. 0	1953	USC 7, Wisconsin 0	1985	USC 20, Ohio St. 17
1922	0-0, California vs Wash. & Jeff.	1954	Michigan St. 28, UCLA 20	1986	UCLA 45, Iowa 28
1923	USC 14, Penn St. 3	1955	Ohio St. 20, USC 7	1987	Arizona St. 22, Michigan 15
1924	14-14, Navy vs Washington	1956	Michigan St. 17, UCLA 14	1988	Michigan St. 20, USC 17
1925	Notre Dame 27, Stanford 10	1957	Iowa 35, Oregon St. 19	1989	Michigan 22, USC 14
1926	Alabama 20, Washington 19	1958	Ohio St. 10, Oregon 7	1990	USC 17, Michigan 10
1927	7-7, Alabama vs Stanford	1959	Iowa 38, California 12	1991	Washington 46, Iowa 34
1928	Stanford 7, Pittsburgh 6	1960	Washington 44, Wisconsin 8	1992	Washington 34, Michigan 14
1929	Georgia Tech 8, California 7	1961	Washington 17, Minnesota 7	1993	Michigan 38, Washington 31
1930	USC 47, Pittsburgh 14	1962	Minnesota 21, UCLA 3	1994	Wisconsin 21, UCLA 16
1931	Alabama 24, Washington St. 0	1963	USC 42, Wisconsin 37	1995	Penn St. 38, Oregon 20
1932	USC 21, Tulane 12	1964	Illinois 17, Washington 7	1996	USC 41, Northwestern 32
1933	USC 35, Pittsburgh 0	1965	Michigan 34, Oregon St. 7	1997	Ohio St. 20, Arizona St. 17
1934	Columbia 7, Stanford 0	1966	UCLA 14, Michigan St. 12	1998	Michigan 21, Washington St. 16
1935	Alabama 29, Stanford 13	1967	Purdue 14, USC 13	1999	Wisconsin 38, UCLA 31
1936	Stanford 7, SMU 0	1968	USC 14, Indiana 3	2000	Wisconsin 17, Stanford 9
1937	Pittsburgh 21, Washington 0	1969	Ohio St. 27, USC 16	2001	Washington 34, Purdue 24
1938	California 13, Alabama 0	1970	USC 10, Michigan 3	2002	Miami-FL 37, Nebraska 14
1939	USC 7, Duke 3	1971	Stanford 27, Ohio St. 17	2003	Oklahoma 34, Washington St. 14
1940	USC 14, Tennessee 0	1972	Stanford 13, Michigan 12	2004	USC 28, Michigan 14
1941	Stanford 21, Nebraska 13	1973	USC 42, Ohio St. 17	2005	Texas 38, Michigan 37
1942	Oregon St. 20, Duke 16	1974	Ohio St. 42, USC 21	2006	Texas 41, USC 38
1943	Georgia 9, UCLA 0	1975	USC 18, Ohio St. 17	2007	USC 32, Michigan 18
1944	USC 29, Washington 0	1976	UCLA 23, Ohio St. 10		* January game since 1902.
1945	USC 25, Tennessee 0	1977	USC 14, Michigan 6		
1946	Alabama 34, USC 14	1978	Washington 27, Michigan 20		

Fiesta Bowl

City: Glendale, Ariz. **Stadium:** University of Phoenix. **Capacity:** 73,000. **Playing surface:** Grass. **First game:** Dec. 27, 1971. **Playing site:** Sun Devil Stadium (since 1971). **Corporate title sponsors:** Sunkist Citrus Growers (1986-91), IBM OS/2 (1993-95) and Frito-Lay Tostitos chips (since 1996).

Automatic berths: Western Athletic Conference champion vs. at-large opponent (1971-79 seasons); Two of first five picks from 8-team Bowl Coalition pool (1992-94). Bowl Alliance (#1 vs. #2 on Jan. 2, 1996; #3 vs. #5 on Jan. 1, 1997; and #4 vs. #6 on Dec. 31, 1997; Big 12 champion vs. next best team in pool (New Bowl Alliance 1995-1997 seasons); Bowl Championship Series: #1 vs. #2 on Jan. 4, 1999, Jan., 2003 and Jan. 2007 and Big 12 champion, if available, vs. at-large (1999-2001 and 2003-05 seasons).

Multiple wins: Penn St. (6); Arizona St. (5); Ohio St. (4); Florida St. and Nebraska (2).

Year		Year		Year	
1971†	Arizona St. 45, Florida St. 38	1985	UCLA 39, Miami-FL 37	1997†	Kansas St. 35, Syracuse 18
1972	Arizona St. 49, Missouri 35	1986	Michigan 27, Nebraska 23	1999	Tennessee 23, Florida St. 16
1973	Arizona St. 28, Pittsburgh 7	1987	Penn St. 14, Miami-FL 10	2000	Nebraska 31, Tennessee 21
1974	Oklahoma St. 16, BYU 6	1988	Florida St. 31, Nebraska 28	2001	Oregon St. 41, Notre Dame 9
1975	Arizona St. 17, Nebraska 14	1989	Notre Dame 34, West Va. 21	2002	Oregon 38, Colorado 16
1976	Oklahoma 41, Wyoming 7	1990	Florida St. 41, Nebraska 17	2003	Ohio St. 31, Miami-FL 24 (2OT)
1977	Penn St. 42, Arizona St. 30	1991	Louisville 34, Alabama 7	2004	Ohio St. 35, Kansas St. 28
1978	10-10, Arkansas vs UCLA	1992	Penn St. 42, Tennessee 17	2005	Utah 35, Pittsburgh 7
1979	Pittsburgh 16, Arizona 10	1993	Syracuse 26, Colorado 22	2006	Ohio St. 34, Notre Dame 20
1980	Penn St. 31, Ohio St. 19	1994	Arizona 29, Miami-FL 0	2007	Boise St. 43, Oklahoma 42 (OT)
1982*	Penn St. 26, USC 10	1995	Colorado 41, Notre Dame 24	†December game from 1971-80 and in
1983	Arizona St. 32, Oklahoma 21	1996	Nebraska 62, Florida 24	'97.
1984	Ohio St. 28, Pittsburgh 23	1997	Penn St. 38, Texas 15	*January game since 1982.

Sugar Bowl

City: Atlanta, Ga. **Stadium:** Georgia Dome. **Capacity:** 71,228. **Playing surface:** Turf. **First game:** Jan. 1, 1935.
Playing sites: Tulane Stadium (1935-74), Louisiana Superdome (1975-2005), Georgia Dome (2006). **Corporate title sponsors:** USF&G Financial Services (1987-95), Nokia (1995-2006) and Allstate (since 2006).

Automatic berths: SEC champion vs. at-large opponent (1976-91 seasons); SEC champion vs. one of first five picks from 8-team Bowl Coalition pool (1992-94 seasons); #4 vs. #6 on Dec. 31, 1995; #1 vs. #2 on Jan. 2, 1997; and #3 vs. #5 on Jan. 1, 1998; Bowl Championship Series: SEC champion, if available, vs. at-large (1998-99, 2000-02, 2004-05 seasons) and #1 vs. #2 on Jan. 4, 2000 and Jan. 2004.

Multiple wins: Alabama (8); LSU (6); Mississippi (5); Florida St., Georgia Tech, Oklahoma and Tennessee (4); Georgia and Nebraska (3); Auburn, Florida, Miami-FL, Notre Dame, Pittsburgh, Santa Clara and TCU (2).

Year		Year		Year	
1935*	Tulane 20, Temple 14	1961	Mississippi 14, Rice 6	1987	Nebraska 30, LSU 15
1936	TCU 3, LSU 2	1962	Alabama 10, Arkansas 3	1988	16-16, Syracuse vs Auburn
1937	Santa Clara 21, LSU 14	1963	Mississippi 17, Arkansas 13	1989	Florida St. 13, Auburn 7
1938	Santa Clara 6, LSU 0	1964	Alabama 12, Mississippi 7	1990	Miami-FL 33, Alabama 25
1939	TCU 15, Carnegie Tech 7	1965	LSU 13, Syracuse 10	1991	Tennessee 23, Virginia 22
1940	Texas A&M 14, Tulane 13	1966	Missouri 20, Florida 18	1992	Notre Dame 39, Florida 28
1941	Boston College 19, Tennessee 13	1967	Alabama 34, Nebraska 7	1993	Alabama 34, Miami-FL 13
1942	Fordham 2, Missouri 0	1968	LSU 20, Wyoming 13	1994	Florida 41, West Va. 7
1943	Tennessee 14, Tulsa 7	1969	Arkansas 16, Georgia 2	1995	Florida St. 23, Florida 17
1944	Georgia Tech 20, Tulsa 18	1970	Mississippi 27, Arkansas 22	1995†	Va. Tech 28, Texas 10
1945	Duke 29, Alabama 26	1971	Tennessee 34, Air Force 13	1997	Florida 52, Florida St. 20
1946	Okla. A&M 33, St. Mary's 13	1972	Oklahoma 40, Auburn 22	1998	Florida St. 31, Ohio St. 14
1947	Georgia 20, N. Carolina 10	1972†	Oklahoma 14, Penn St. 0	1999	Ohio St. 24, Texas A&M 14
1948	Texas 27, Alabama 7	1973	Notre Dame 24, Alabama 23	2000	Florida St. 46, Va. Tech 29
1949	Oklahoma 14, N. Carolina 6	1974	Nebraska 13, Florida 10	2001	Miami-FL 37, Florida 20
1950	Oklahoma 35, LSU 0	1975	Alabama 13, Penn St. 6	2002	LSU 47, Illinois 34
1951	Kentucky 13, Oklahoma 7	1977*	Pittsburgh 27, Georgia 3	2003	Georgia 26, Florida St. 13
1952	Maryland 28, Tennessee 13	1978	Alabama 35, Ohio St. 6	2004	LSU 21, Oklahoma 14
1953	Georgia Tech 24, Mississippi 7	1979	Alabama 14, Penn St. 7	2005	Auburn 16, Va. Tech 13
1954	Georgia Tech 42, West Va. 19	1980	Alabama 24, Arkansas 9	2006*	West Virginia 38, Georgia 35
1955	Navy 21, Mississippi 0	1981	Georgia 17, Notre Dame 10	2007	LSU 41, Notre Dame 14
1956	Georgia Tech 7, Pittsburgh 0	1982	Pittsburgh 24, Georgia 20		
1957	Baylor 13, Tennessee 7	1983	Penn St. 27, Georgia 23	* January game from 1935-72 and
1958	Mississippi 39, Texas 7	1984	Auburn 9, Michigan 7	since 1977 (except in 1995).
1959	LSU 7, Clemson 0	1985	Nebraska 28, LSU 10	† Game played on Dec. 31 from
1960	Mississippi 21, LSU 0	1986	Tennessee 35, Miami-FL 7	1972-75 and in 1995.

Orange Bowl

City: Miami, Fla. **Stadium:** Dolphin. **Capacity:** 74,916. **Playing surface:** Grass. **First game:** Jan. 1, 1935. **Playing sites:** Orange Bowl (1935-95); Dolphin Stadium (since 1996). Dolphin Stadium was originally named Joe Robbie Stadium then was named Pro Player Stadium (1996-2004). **Corporate title sponsor:** Federal Express (since 1989).

Automatic berths: Big 8 champion vs. Atlantic Coast Conference champion (1953-57 seasons); Big 8 champion vs. at-large opponent (1958-63 seasons and 1975-91 seasons); Big 8 champion vs. one of first five picks from 8-team Bowl Coalition pool (1992-94 seasons); #3 vs. #5 on Jan. 1, 1996; #4 vs. #6 on Dec. 31, 1996; and #1 vs. #2 on Jan. 2, 1998 (New Bowl Alliance 1995-97 seasons); Bowl Championship Series: Big East or ACC champion, if available, vs. at-large (1998-99, 2001-03, 2005 seasons) and #1 vs. #2 Jan. 3, 2001 and Jan. 2005.

Multiple wins: Oklahoma (12); Nebraska (8); Miami-FL (6); Alabama and Penn St. (4); Florida, Florida State and Georgia Tech (3); Clemson, Colorado, Georgia, LSU, Notre Dame, Texas and USC (2).

Year		Year		Year	
1935*	Bucknell 26, Miami-FL 0	1955	Duke 34, Nebraska 7	1975	Notre Dame 13, Alabama 11
1936	Catholic U. 20, Mississippi 19	1956	Oklahoma 20, Maryland 6	1976	Oklahoma 14, Michigan 6
1937	Duquesne 13, Mississippi St. 12	1957	Colorado 27, Clemson 21	1977	Ohio St. 27, Colorado 10
1938	Auburn 6, Michigan St. 0	1958	Oklahoma 48, Duke 21	1978	Arkansas 31, Oklahoma 6
1939	Tennessee 17, Oklahoma 0	1959	Oklahoma 21, Syracuse 6	1979	Oklahoma 31, Nebraska 24
1940	Georgia Tech 21, Missouri 7	1960	Georgia 14, Missouri 0	1980	Oklahoma 24, Florida St. 7
1941	Mississippi St. 14, Georgetown 7	1961	Missouri 21, Navy 14	1981	Oklahoma 18, Florida St. 17
1942	Georgia 40, TCU 26	1962	LSU 25, Colorado 7	1982	Clemson 22, Nebraska 15
1943	Alabama 37, Boston College 21	1963	Alabama 17, Oklahoma 0	1983	Nebraska 21, LSU 20
1944	LSU 19, Texas A&M 14	1964	Nebraska 13, Auburn 7	1984	Miami-FL 31, Nebraska 30
1945	Tulsa 26, Georgia Tech 12	1965†	Texas 21, Alabama 17	1985	Washington 28, Oklahoma 17
1946	Miami-FL 13, Holy Cross 6	1966	Alabama 39, Nebraska 28	1986	Oklahoma 25, Penn St. 10
1947	Rice 8, Tennessee 0	1967	Florida 27, Georgia Tech 12	1987	Oklahoma 42, Arkansas 8
1948	Georgia Tech 20, Kansas 14	1968	Oklahoma 26, Tennessee 24	1988	Miami-FL 20, Oklahoma 14
1949	Texas 41, Georgia 28	1969	Penn St. 15, Kansas 14	1989	Miami-FL 23, Nebraska 3
1950	Santa Clara 21, Kentucky 13	1970	Penn St. 10, Missouri 3	1990	Notre Dame, 21, Colorado 6
1951	Clemson 15, Miami-FL 14	1971	Nebraska 17, LSU 12	1991	Colorado 10, Notre Dame 9
1952	Georgia Tech 17, Baylor 14	1972	Nebraska 38, Alabama 6	1992	Miami-FL 22, Nebraska 0
1953	Alabama 61, Syracuse 6	1973	Nebraska 40, Notre Dame 6	1993	Florida St. 27, Nebraska 14
1954	Oklahoma 7, Maryland 0	1974	Penn St. 16, LSU 9	1994	Florida St. 18, Nebraska 16

Bowl Games (Cont.)
Orange Bowl (Cont.)

Year		Year		Year	
1995	Nebraska 24, Miami-FL 17	2001	Oklahoma 13, Florida St. 2	2007	Louisville 24, Wake Forest 13
1996	Florida St. 31, Notre Dame 26	2002	Florida 56, Maryland 23	* January game 1935-1996 and since	
1996**	Nebraska 41, Virginia Tech 21	2003	USC 38, Iowa 17	'98.	
1998*	Nebraska 42, Tennessee 17	2004	Miami-FL 16, Florida St. 14	** December game in 1996	
1999	Florida 31, Syracuse 10	2005	USC 55, Oklahoma 19	† Night game since 1965.	
2000	Michigan 35, Alabama 34	2006	Penn St. 26, Florida St. 23 3OT		

Cotton Bowl

City: Dallas, Tex. **Stadium:** Cotton Bowl. **Capacity:** 71,252. **Playing surface:** Grass. **First game:** Jan 1, 1937. **Playing sites:** Fair Park Stadium (1937) and Cotton Bowl (since 1938). **Corporate title sponsor:** Mobil Corporation (1988-95), AT&T Communications, previously Southwestern Bell and SBC Communications, (since 1997).

Automatic berths: SWC champion vs. at-large opponent (1941-91 seasons); SWC champion vs. one of first five picks from 8-team Bowl Coalition pool (1992-1994 seasons); second pick from Big 12 vs. first choice of WAC champion or second pick from Pac-10 (1995-97 seasons); Big 12 vs. SEC (since 1998).

Multiple wins: Texas (11); Notre Dame (5); Texas A&M (4); Alabama, Arkansas, Rice and Tennessee (3); Georgia, Houston, LSU, Mississippi, Penn St., SMU, TCU and UCLA (2).

Year		Year		Year	
1937*	TCU 16, Marquette 6	1962	Texas 12, Mississippi 7	1987	Ohio St. 28, Texas A&M 12
1938	Rice 28, Colorado 14	1963	LSU 13, Texas 0	1988	Texas A&M 35, Notre Dame 10
1939	St. Mary's 20, Texas Tech 13	1964	Texas 28, Navy 6	1989	UCLA 17, Arkansas 3
1940	Clemson 6, Boston College 3	1965	Arkansas 10, Nebraska 7	1990	Tennessee 31, Arkansas 27
1941	Texas A&M 13, Fordham 12	1966	LSU 14, Arkansas 7	1991	Miami-FL 46, Texas 3
1942	Alabama 29, Texas A&M 21	1966†	Georgia 24, SMU 9	1992	Florida St. 10, Texas A&M 2
1943	Texas 14, Georgia Tech 7	1968*	Texas A&M 20, Alabama 16	1993	Notre Dame 28, Texas A&M 3
1944	7-7, Texas vs Randolph Field	1969	Texas 36, Tennessee 13	1994	Notre Dame 24, Texas A&M 21
1945	Oklahoma A&M 34, TCU 0	1970	Texas 21, Notre Dame 17	1995	USC 55, Texas Tech 14
1946	Texas 40, Missouri 27	1971	Notre Dame 24, Texas 11	1996	Colorado 38, Oregon 6
1947	0-0, Arkansas vs LSU	1972	Penn St. 30, Texas 6	1997	BYU 19, Kansas St. 15
1948	13-13, SMU vs Penn St.	1973	Texas 17, Alabama 13	1998	UCLA 29, Texas A&M 23
1949	SMU 21, Oregon 13	1974	Nebraska 19, Texas 3	1999	Texas 38, Mississippi St. 11
1950	Rice 27, N. Carolina 13	1975	Penn St. 41, Baylor 20	2000	Arkansas 27, Texas 6
1951	Tennessee 20, Texas 14	1976	Arkansas 31, Georgia 10	2001	Kansas St. 35, Tennessee 21
1952	Kentucky 20, TCU 7	1977	Houston 30, Maryland 21	2002	Oklahoma 10, Arkansas 3
1953	Texas 16, Tennessee 0	1978	Notre Dame 38, Texas 10	2003	Texas 35, LSU 20
1954	Rice 28, Alabama 6	1979	Notre Dame 35, Houston 34	2004	Mississippi 31, Oklahoma St. 28
1955	Georgia Tech 14, Arkansas 6	1980	Houston 17, Nebraska 14	2005	Tennessee 38, Texas A&M 7
1956	Mississippi 14, TCU 13	1981	Alabama 30, Baylor 2	2006	Alabama 13, Texas Tech 10
1957	TCU 28, Syracuse 27	1982	Texas 14, Alabama 12	2007	Auburn 17, Nebraska 14
1958	Navy 20, Rice 7	1983	SMU 7, Pittsburgh 3	* January game from 1937-66 and	
1959	0-0, TCU vs Air Force	1984	Georgia 10, Texas 9	since 1968.	
1960	Syracuse 23, Texas 14	1985	Boston College 45, Houston 28	† Game played on Dec. 31, 1966.	
1961	Duke 7, Arkansas 6	1986	Texas A&M 36, Auburn 16		

Capital One Bowl

City: Orlando, Fla. **Stadium:** Florida Citrus Bowl. **Capacity:** 70,188. **Playing surface:** Grass. **First game:** Jan. 1, 1947. **Name change:** Tangerine Bowl (1947-82), Florida Citrus Bowl (1983-2002) and Capital One Bowl (since 2003). **Playing sites:** Tangerine Bowl (1947-72, 1974-82), Florida Field in Gainesville (1973), Orlando Stadium (1983-85) and Florida Citrus Bowl (since 1986). The Tangerine Bowl, Orlando Stadium and Florida Citrus Bowl are all the same stadium. **Corporate title sponsors:** Florida Department of Citrus (1983-2002), CompUSA (1992-99), Ourhouse.com (2000) and Capital One (since 2001).

Automatic berths: Championship game of Atlantic Coast Regional Conference (1964-67 seasons); Mid-American Conference champion vs. Southern Conference champion (1968-71 seasons); ACC champion vs. at-large opponent (1988-91 seasons); second pick from SEC, if available, vs. second pick from Big 10, if available (since 1992 season).

Multiple wins: Tennessee (4); Auburn, East Texas St., Miami-OH and Toledo (3); Catawba, Clemson, East Carolina, Florida, Georgia, Michigan and Wisconsin (2).

Year		Year		Year	
1947*	Catawba 31, Maryville 6	1958†	E. Texas St. 26, Mo. Valley 7	1970	Toledo 40, Wm. & Mary 12
1948	Catawba 7, Marshall 0	1960*	Mid. Tenn. 21, Presbyterian 12	1971	Toledo 28, Richmond 3
1949	21-21, Murray St. vs Sul Ross St.	1960†	Citadel 27, Tenn. Tech 0	1972	Tampa 21, Kent St. 18
1950	St. Vincent 7, Emory & Henry 6	1961	Lamar 21, Middle Tenn. 14	1973	Miami-OH 16, Florida 7
1951	M. Harvey 35, Emory & Henry 14	1962	Houston 49, Miami-OH 21	1974	Miami-OH 21, Georgia 10
1952	Stetson 35, Arkansas St. 20	1963	Western Ky. 27, Coast Guard 0	1975	Miami-OH 20, S. Carolina 7
1953	E. Texas St. 33, Tenn. Tech 0	1964	E. Carolina 14, Massachusetts 13	1976	Oklahoma 49, BYU 21
1954	7-7, E. Texas St. vs Arkansas St.	1965	E. Carolina 31, Maine 0	1977	Florida 40, Texas Tech 17
1955	Neb.-Omaha 7, Eastern Ky. 6	1966	Morgan St. 14, West Chester 6	1978	N.C. State 30, Pittsburgh 7
1956	6-6, Juniata vs Missouri Valley	1967	Tenn-Martin 25, West Chester 8	1979	LSU 34, Wake Forest 10
1957	W. Texas St. 20, So. Miss. 13	1968	Richmond 49, Ohio U. 42	1980	Florida 35, Maryland 20
1958	E. Texas St. 10, So. Miss. 9	1969	Toledo 56, Davidson 33	1981	Missouri 19, Southern Miss. 17

Year		Year		Year	
1982	Auburn 33, Boston College 26	1993	Georgia 21, Ohio St. 14	2003	Auburn 13, Penn St. 9
1983	Tennessee 30, Maryland 23	1994	Penn St. 31, Tennessee 13	2004	Georgia 34, Purdue 27 OT
1984	17-17, Florida St. vs Georgia	1995	Alabama 24, Ohio St. 17	2005	Iowa 30, LSU 25
1985	Ohio St. 10, BYU 7	1996	Tennessee 20, Ohio St. 14	2006	Wisconsin 24, Auburn 10
1987*	Auburn 16, USC 7	1997	Tennessee 48, Northwestern 28	2007	Wisconsin 17, Arkansas 14
1988	Clemson 35, Penn St. 10	1998	Florida 21, Penn St. 6	*January game from 1947-58, in
1989	Clemson 13, Oklahoma 6	1999	Michigan 45, Arkansas 31	1960 and since 1987.
1990	Illinois 31, Virginia 21	2000	Michigan St. 37, Florida 34	†December game in 1958, 1960-85.
1991	Georgia Tech 45, Nebraska 21	2001	Michigan 31, Auburn 28	
1992	California 37, Clemson 13	2002	Tennessee 45, Michigan 17	

Gator Bowl

City: Jacksonville, Fla. **Stadium:** Jacksonville Municipal. **Capacity:** 73,000. **Playing surface:** Grass. **First game:** Jan. 1, 1946. **Playing sites:** Gator Bowl (1946-93), Florida Field in Gainesville (1994) and Jacksonville Municipal Stadium (since 1995). Jacksonville Municipal Stadium was formerly named ALLTEL Stadium (1997-2006). **Corporate title sponsors:** Mazda Motors of America, Inc. (1986-91), Outback Steakhouse, Inc. (1992-94) and Toyota Motor Co. (since 1995).

Automatic berths: Third pick from SEC vs. sixth pick from 8-team Bowl Coalition pool (1992-94 seasons); second pick from ACC, if available, vs. second pick from Big East or Notre Dame, if available (since 1995 season).

Multiple wins: Florida (6); Florida St. and North Carolina (5); Auburn, Clemson (4); Georgia Tech, Maryland and Tennessee (3); Georgia, Miami-FL, Oklahoma, Pittsburgh, Texas Tech and Virginia Tech (2).

Year		Year		Year	
1946*	Wake Forest 26, S. Carolina 14	1968	Missouri 35, Alabama 10	1991†	Oklahoma 48, Virginia 14
1947	Oklahoma 34, N.C. State 13	1969	Florida 14, Tennessee 13	1992	Florida 27, N.C. State 10
1948	20-20, Maryland vs Georgia	1971*	Auburn 35, Mississippi 28	1993	Alabama 24, N. Carolina 10
1949	Clemson 24, Missouri 23	1971†	Georgia 7, N. Carolina 3	1994	Tennessee 45, Va. Tech 23
1950	Maryland 20, Missouri 7	1972	Auburn 24, Colorado 3	1996*	Syracuse 41, Clemson 0
1951	Wyoming 20, Wash. & Lee 7	1973	Texas Tech 28, Tennessee 19	1997	N. Carolina 20, West Va. 13
1952	Miami-FL 14, Clemson 0	1974	Auburn 27, Texas 3	1998	N. Carolina 42, Va. Tech 3
1953	Florida 14, Tulsa 13	1975	Maryland 13, Florida 0	1999	Ga. Tech 35, Notre Dame 28
1954	Texas Tech 35, Auburn 13	1976	Notre Dame 20, Penn St. 9	2000	Miami-FL 28, Ga. Tech 13
1954†	Auburn 33, Baylor 13	1977	Pittsburgh 34, Clemson 3	2001	Va. Tech 41, Clemson 20
1955	Vanderbilt 25, Auburn 13	1978	Clemson 17, Ohio St. 15	2002	Florida St. 30, Va. Tech 17
1956	Georgia Tech 21, Pittsburgh 14	1979	N. Carolina 17, Michigan 15	2003	N.C. State 28, Notre Dame 6
1957	Tennessee 3, Texas A&M 0	1980	Pittsburgh 37, S. Carolina 9	2004	Maryland 41, West Va. 7
1958	Mississippi 7, Florida 3	1981	N. Carolina 31, Arkansas 27	2005	Florida St. 30, West Va. 18
1960*	Arkansas 14, Georgia Tech 7	1982	Florida St. 31, West Va. 12	2006	Va. Tech 35, Louisville 24
1960†	Florida 13, Baylor 12	1983	Florida 14, Iowa 6	2007	West Virginia 38, Ga. Tech 35
1961	Penn St. 30, Georgia Tech 15	1984	Oklahoma St. 21, S. Carolina 14	* January game from 1946-54, 1960,
1962	Florida 17, Penn St. 7	1985	Florida St. 34, Oklahoma St. 23	1965, 1971, 1989, 1991 and since
1963	N. Carolina 35, Air Force 0	1986	Clemson 27, Stanford 21	1996.
1965*	Florida St. 36, Oklahoma 19	1987	LSU 30, S. Carolina 13	† December game from 1954-58, 1960-
1965†	Georgia Tech 31, Texas Tech 21	1989*	Georgia 34, Michigan St. 27	63, 1965-69, 1971-87, 1989 and
1966	Tennessee 18, Syracuse 12	1989†	Clemson 27, West Va. 7	1991-94.
1967	17-17, Florida St. vs Penn St.	1991*	Michigan 35, Mississippi 3	

Holiday Bowl

City: San Diego, Calif. **Stadium:** Qualcomm. **Capacity:** 71,000. **Playing surface:** Grass. **First game:** Dec. 22, 1978. **Playing site:** San Diego/Jack Murphy Stadium (since 1978). Name changed to Qualcomm Stadium in 1997. **Corporate title sponsors:** SeaWorld (1986-90), Thrifty Car Rental (1991-94), Chrysler-Plymouth Division of Chrysler Corp. (1995-97), U.S. Filter/Culligan Water Tech. (1998-2001) and Pacific Life Insurance Co. (since 2002).

Automatic berths: WAC champion vs. at-large opponent (1978-84, 1986-90 seasons); WAC champ vs. second pick from Big 10 (1991 season); WAC champ vs. third pick from Big 10 (1992-94 seasons); choice of WAC champion, if available, or second pick from Pac-10, if available vs. third pick from Big 12, if available (1995-99); second pick from Pac-10 vs. third pick from Big 12 (since 2000).

Multiple wins: BYU (4); Kansas St. (3) Iowa and Ohio St. (2).

Year		Year		Year	
1978†	Navy 23, BYU 16	1989	Penn St. 50, BYU 39	2000	Oregon 35, Texas 30
1979	Indiana 38, BYU 37	1990	Texas A&M 65, BYU 14	2001	Texas 47, Washington 43
1980	BYU 46, SMU 45	1991	13-13, Iowa vs BYU	2002	Kansas St. 34, Arizona St. 27
1981	BYU 38, Washington St. 36	1992	Hawaii 27, Illinois 17	2003	Washington St. 28, Texas 20
1982	Ohio St. 47, BYU 17	1993	Ohio St. 28, BYU 21	2004	Texas Tech 45, California 31
1983	BYU 21, Missouri 17	1994	Michigan 24, Colo. St. 14	2005	Oklahoma 17, Oregon 14
1984	BYU 24, Michigan 17	1995	Kansas St. 54, Colorado St. 21	2006	California 45, Texas A&M 10
1985	Arkansas 18, Arizona St. 17	1996	Colorado 33, Washington 21	
1986	Iowa 39, San Diego St. 38	1997	Colorado St. 35, Missouri 24	†December game since 1978.
1987	Iowa 20, Wyoming 19	1998	Arizona 23, Nebraska 20	
1988	Oklahoma St. 62, Wyoming 14	1999	Kansas St. 24, Washington 20	

Bowl Games (Cont.)
Chick-fil-A Bowl

City: Atlanta, Ga. **Stadium:** Georgia Dome. **Capacity:** 71,228. **Playing surface:** Turf. **First game:** Dec. 30, 1968. **Playing sites:** Grant Field (1968-70), Atlanta-Fulton County Stadium (1971-92) and Georgia Dome (since 1993). **Name change:** Peach Bowl (1968-2005), Chick-fil-A Bowl (since 2006); **Corporate title sponsor:** Chick-fil-A (since 1998).
   Automatic berths: Third pick from ACC vs. at-large opponent (1992 season); third pick from ACC vs. fourth pick from SEC (1993-94 seasons); third pick from ACC, if available, vs. fourth pick from SEC, if available (since 1995 season).
   Multiple wins: N.C. State (4); LSU, Georgia and West Virginia (3); Auburn, Miami-FL, North Carolina and Virginia (2).

Year		Year		Year	
1968†	LSU 31, Florida St. 27	1984	Virginia 27, Purdue 24	2000	LSU 28, Ga. Tech 14
1969	West Va. 14, S. Carolina 3	1985	Army 31, Illinois 29	2001	N. Carolina 16, Auburn 10
1970	Arizona St. 48, N. Carolina 26	1986	Va. Tech 25, N.C. State 24	2002	Maryland 30, Tennessee 3
1971	Mississippi 41, Georgia Tech 18	1988*	Tennessee 27, Indiana 22	2004*	Clemson 27, Tennessee 14
1972	N.C. State 49, West Va. 13	1988†	N.C. State 28, Iowa 23	2004†	Miami-FL 27, Florida 10
1973	Georgia 17, Maryland 16	1989	Syracuse 19, Georgia 18	2005	LSU 40, Miami-FL 3
1974	6-6, Vanderbilt vs Texas Tech	1990	Auburn 27, Indiana 23	2006	Georgia 31, Va. Tech 24
1975	West Va. 13, N.C. State 10	1992*	E. Carolina 37, N.C. State 34		
1976	Kentucky 21, N. Carolina 0	1993	N. Carolina 21, Miss. St. 17	†December game from 1968-79,	
1977	N.C. State 24, Iowa St. 14	1993†	Clemson 14, Kentucky 13	1981-86, 1988-90, 1993, 1995,	
1978	Purdue 41, Georgia Tech 21	1995*	N.C. State 28, Miss. St. 24	1996, 1998, 1999-2002 and 2004.	
1979	Baylor 24, Clemson 18	1995†	Virginia 34, Georgia 27	*January game in 1981, 1988, 1992-	
1981*	Miami-FL 20, Va. Tech 10	1996	LSU 10, Clemson 7	93, 1995 and 1998 and 2004.	
1981†	West Va. 26, Florida 6	1998*	Auburn 21, Clemson 17		
1982	Iowa 28, Tennessee 22	1998†	Georgia 35, Virginia 33		
1983	Florida St. 28, N. Carolina 3	1999	Mississippi St. 17, Clemson 7		

Sun Bowl

City: El Paso, Tex. **Stadium:** Sun Bowl. **Capacity:** 52,000. **Playing surface:** Turf. **First game:** Jan. 1, 1936. **Name changes:** Sun Bowl (1936-85), John Hancock Sun Bowl (1986-88), John Hancock Bowl (1989-93), Sun Bowl (1994) Norwest Sun Bowl (1996-98), Wells Fargo Sun Bowl (1999-2003), Vitalis Sun Bowl (2004-05) and Brut Sun Bowl (since 2006). **Playing sites:** Kidd Field (1936-62) and Sun Bowl (since 1963). **Corporate title sponsors:** John Hancock Financial Services (1986-93), Norwest Bank (1996-98), Wells Fargo (1999-2003), Helen of Troy Limited (since 2004).
   Automatic berths: Eighth pick from 8-team Bowl Coalition pool vs. at-large opponent (1992); Seventh and eighth picks from 8-team Bowl Coalition pool (1993-94 seasons); third pick from Pac-10, if available, vs. fifth pick from Big 10, if available (1995-2005); Pac-10 vs. Big 12/Big East/Notre Dame (2006-09).
   Multiple wins: Texas Western/UTEP (5); Alabama and Wyoming (3); Arizona St., Nebraska, New Mexico St., North Carolina, Oklahoma, Oregon, Pittsburgh, Southwestern, Stanford, Texas, UCLA, West Texas St. and West Virginia (2).

Year		Year		Year	
1936*	14-14, Hardin-Simmons vs New Mexico St.	1960	New Mexico St. 20, Utah St. 13	1987	Oklahoma St. 35, West Va. 33
1937	Hardin-Simmons 34, Texas Mines 6	1961	Villanova 17, Wichita St. 9	1988	Alabama 29, Army 28
1938	West Va. 7, Texas Tech 6	1962	West Texas 15, Ohio U. 14	1989	Pittsburgh 31, Texas A&M 28
1939	Utah 26, New Mexico 0	1963	Oregon 21, SMU 14	1990	Michigan St. 17, USC 16
1940	0-0, Catholic U. vs Arizona St.	1964	Georgia 7, Texas Tech 0	1991	UCLA 6, Illinois 3
1941	W. Reserve 26, Arizona St. 13	1965	Texas Western 13, TCU 12	1992	Baylor 20, Arizona 15
1942	Tulsa 6, Texas Tech 0	1966	Wyoming 28, Florida St. 20	1993	Oklahoma 41, Texas Tech 10
1943	Second Air Force 13, Hardin-Simmons 7	1967	UTEP 14, Mississippi 7	1994	Texas 35, N. Carolina 31
1944	Southwestern 7, New Mexico 0	1968	Auburn 34, Arizona 10	1995	Iowa 38, Washington 18
1945	Southwestern 35, U. of Mexico 0	1969	Nebraska 45, Georgia 6	1996	Stanford 38, Michigan St. 0
1946	New Mexico 34, Denver 24	1970	Georgia Tech 17, Texas Tech 9	1997	Arizona St. 17, Iowa 7
1947	Cincinnati 18, Va. Tech 6	1971	LSU 33, Iowa St. 15	1998	TCU 28, USC 19
1948	Miami-OH 13, Texas Tech 12	1972	N. Carolina 32, Texas Tech 28	1999	Oregon 24, Minnesota 20
1949	West Va. 21, Texas Mines 12	1973	Missouri 34, Auburn 17	2000	Wisconsin 21, UCLA 20
1950	Tex. Western 33, Georgetown 20	1974	Miss. St. 26, N. Carolina 24	2001	Washington St. 33, Purdue 27
1951	West Texas 14, Cincinnati 13	1975	Pittsburgh 33, Kansas 19	2002	Purdue 34, Washington 24
1952	Texas Tech 25, Pacific 14	1977*	Texas A&M 37, Florida 14	2003	Minnesota 31, Oregon 30
1953	Pacific 26, Southern Miss. 7	1977†	Stanford 24, LSU 14	2004	Arizona St. 27, Purdue 23
1954	Tex. Western 37, So. Miss. 14	1978	Texas 42, Maryland 0	2005	UCLA 50, Northwestern 38
1955	Tex. Western 47, Florida St. 20	1979	Washington 14, Texas 7	2006	Oregon St. 39, Missouri 38
1956	Wyoming 21, Texas Tech 14	1980	Nebraska 31, Miss. St. 17	*January game from 1936-58 and in	
1957	Geo. Wash. 13, Tex. Western 0	1981	Oklahoma 40, Houston 14	1977.	
1958*	Louisville 34, Drake 20	1982	N. Carolina 26, Texas 10	†December game from 1958-75 and	
1958†	Wyoming 14, Hardin-Simmons 6	1983	Alabama 28, SMU 7	since 1977.	
1959	New Mexico St. 28, N. Texas 8	1984	Maryland 28, Tennessee 27		
		1985	13-13, Georgia vs Arizona		
		1986	Alabama 28, Washington 6		

Outback Bowl

City: Tampa, Fla. **Stadium:** Raymond James. **Capacity:** 66,005. **Playing surface:** Grass. **First game:** Dec. 23, 1986. **Name change:** Hall of Fame Bowl (1986-95) and Outback Bowl (since 1995). **Playing sites:** Tampa/Houlihan's Stadium (1986-98) and Raymond James Stadium (since 1999). **Corporate title sponsor:** Outback Steakhouse, Inc. (since 1995).

Automatic berths: Fourth pick from ACC vs. third pick from Big 10 (1993-94 seasons); third pick from Big 10, if available, vs. third pick from SEC, if available (1995-99); fourth pick from Big 10 vs. third pick from SEC (2000 season).

Multiple wins: Georgia, Michigan and Penn St. (3); South Carolina and Syracuse (2).

Year		Year		Year	
1986†	Boston College 27, Georgia 24	1995	Wisconsin 34, Duke 20	2003	Michigan 38, Florida 30
1988*	Michigan 28, Alabama 24	1996	Penn St. 43, Auburn 14	2004	Iowa 37, Florida 17
1989	Syracuse 23, LSU 10	1997	Alabama 17, Michigan 14	2005	Georgia 24, Wisconsin 21
1990	Auburn 31, Ohio St. 14	1998	Georgia 33, Wisconsin 6	2006	Florida 31, Iowa 24
1991	Clemson 30, Illinois 0	1999	Penn St. 26, Kentucky 14	2007	Penn St. 20, Tennessee 10
1992	Syracuse 24, Ohio St. 17	2000	Georgia 28, Purdue 25 OT		
1993	Tennessee 38, Boston Col. 23	2001	S. Carolina 24, Ohio St. 7	†December game in 1986.	
1994	Michigan 42, N.C. State 7	2002	S. Carolina 31, Ohio St. 28	*January game since 1988.	

Liberty Bowl

City: Memphis, Tenn. **Stadium:** Liberty Bowl Memorial. **Capacity:** 62,338. **Playing surface:** Grass. **First game:** Dec. 19, 1959. **Playing sites:** Municipal Stadium in Philadelphia (1959-63), Convention Hall in Atlantic City, N.J. (1964), Memphis Memorial Stadium (1965-75) and Liberty Bowl Memorial Stadium (since 1976). Memphis Memorial Stadium renamed Liberty Bowl Memorial in 1976. **Corporate title sponsors:** St. Jude's Hospital (since 1993), AXA/Equitable (1997-2003), AutoZone (since 2004).

Automatic berths: Commander-in-Chief's Trophy winner (Army, Navy or Air Force) vs. at-large opponent (1989-92 seasons); none (1993 season); first pick from independent group of Cincinnati, East Carolina, Memphis, Southern Miss. and Tulane vs. at-large opponent (for 1994 and '95 seasons); Conference USA champion vs. fourth pick from the Big East (1996-97 seasons); Conference USA champion, if available, vs. fifth, sixth or seventh pick or at-large from SEC (1998-99 seasons); Mountain West champion vs. Conference USA champion, if available (2000-05); SEC vs. Conference USA champ (since 2006).

Multiple wins: Mississippi (4); Penn St. and Tennessee (3); Air Force, Alabama, Louisville, N.C. State, Southern Miss., Syracuse and Tulane (2).

Year		Year		Year	
1959†	Penn St. 7, Alabama 0	1976	Alabama 36, UCLA 6	1993	Louisville 18, Michigan St. 7
1960	Penn St. 41, Oregon 12	1977	Nebraska 21, N. Carolina 17	1994	Illinois 30, E. Carolina 0
1961	Syracuse 15, Miami-FL 14	1978	Missouri 20, LSU 15	1995	E. Carolina 19, Stanford 13
1962	Oregon St. 6, Villanova 0	1979	Penn St. 9, Tulane 6	1996	Syracuse 30, Houston 17
1963	Mississippi St. 16, N.C. State 12	1980	Purdue 28, Missouri 25	1997	Southern Miss. 41, Pittsburgh 7
1964	Utah 32, West Virginia 6	1981	Ohio St. 31, Navy 28	1998	Tulane 41, BYU 27
1965	Mississippi 13, Auburn 7	1982	Alabama 21, Illinois 15	1999	Southern Miss. 23, Colorado St. 17
1966	Miami-FL 14, Virginia Tech 7	1983	Notre Dame 19, Boston Col. 18	2000	Colorado St. 22, Louisville 17
1967	N.C. State 14, Georgia 7	1984	Auburn 21, Arkansas 15	2001	Louisville 28, BYU 10
1968	Mississippi 34, Virginia Tech 17	1985	Baylor 21, LSU 7	2002	TCU 17, Colorado St. 3
1969	Colorado 47, Alabama 33	1986	Tennessee 21, Minnesota 14	2003	Utah 17, Southern Miss. 0
1970	Tulane 17, Colorado 3	1987	Georgia 20, Arkansas 17	2004	Louisville 44, Boise St. 40
1971	Tennessee 14, Arkansas 13	1988	Indiana 34, S. Carolina 10	2005	Tulsa 31, Fresno St. 24
1972	Georgia Tech 31, Iowa St. 30	1989	Mississippi 42, Air Force 29	2006	South Carolina 44, Houston 36
1973	N.C. State 31, Kansas 18	1990	Air Force 23, Ohio St. 11	† December game since 1959.	
1974	Tennessee 7, Maryland 3	1991	Air Force 38, Mississippi St. 15		
1975	USC 20, Texas A&M 0	1992	Mississippi 13, Air Force 0		

Champs Sports Bowl

City: Orlando, Fla. **Stadium:** Florida Citrus Bowl. **Capacity:** 70,188. **Playing surface:** Grass. **First game:** Dec. 28, 1990. **Name change:** Blockbuster Bowl (1990-93), Carquest Bowl (1994-97), Micron PC Bowl (1998), Micron-PC.com Bowl (1999-2000), Visit Florida Tangerine Bowl (2001) and Mazda Tangerine Bowl (2002-03). The game was called the Sunshine Football Classic for a short time in the offseason after Carquest Auto Parts dropped its sponsorship and before Micron signed on. Also, this game should not be confused with the Tangerine Bowl that became the Citrus Bowl in 1982. **Playing sites:** Joe Robbie Stadium (1990-2000). Name changed to Pro Player Stadium in 1996; Florida Citrus Bowl (since 2001). ∂**Corporate title sponsors:** Blockbuster Video (1990-93), Carquest Auto Parts (1993-97), Micron Electronics (1998-2000), Mazda (2002-04) and Champs Sports (since 2005).

Automatic berths: Penn St. vs. seventh pick from 8-team Bowl Coalition pool (1992 season); third pick from Big East vs. fifth pick from SEC (1993-94 seasons); third pick from Big East vs. fifth pick from SEC (1995 season); third pick from Big East vs. fourth pick from ACC (1996-97 seasons); sixth pick from Big Ten, if available, vs. fourth pick from ACC, if available (1998-2000 seasons); fifth pick from ACC vs. fifth pick from Big East (2001-2005); ACC vs. Big Ten (since 2006).

Multiple wins: Georgia Tech, Miami-FL and N.C. State (2).

Year		Year		Year	
1990†	Florida St. 24, Penn St. 17	1997	Ga. Tech 35, W. Virginia 30	2004	Ga. Tech 51, Syracuse 14
1991	Alabama 30, Colorado 25	1998	Miami-FL 46, N.C. State 23	2005	Clemson 19, Colorado 10
1993*	Stanford 24, Penn St. 3	1999	Illinois 63, Virginia 21	2006	Maryland 24, Purdue 7
1994	Boston College 31, Virginia 13	2000	N.C. State 38, Minnesota 30	†December game from 1990-91 and	
1995	S. Carolina 24, West Va. 21	2001	Pittsburgh 34, N.C. State 19	since 1995.	
1995†	N. Carolina 20, Arkansas 10	2002	Texas Tech 55, Clemson 15	*January game 1993-95.	
1996	Miami-FL 31, Virginia 21	2003	N.C. State 56, Kansas 26		

Bowl Games (Cont.)

Insight Bowl

City: Tempe, Ariz. **Stadium:** Sun Devil. **Capacity:** 73,379. **Playing surface:** Grass. **First game:** Dec. 31, 1989. **Name changes:** Copper Bowl (1989-1996), Insight.com Bowl (1997-2001) and Insight Bowl (since 2002). **Playing sites:** Arizona Stadium (1989-2000), Chase Field, previously Bank One Ballpark (2000-05) and Sun Devil Stadium (2006–). **Corporate title sponsors:** Domino's Pizza (1990-91), Weiser Lock (1992-1996) and Insight Enterprises (since 1997).

Automatic berths: Third pick from WAC vs. at-large opponent (1992 season); third pick from WAC vs. fourth pick from Big Eight (1993-94 seasons); second pick from WAC vs. sixth pick from Big 12 (1995-97); third pick from Big East or Notre Dame, if available vs. fifth pick from Big 12, if available (1998-2001); third pick from Big East or Notre Dame, if available vs. fourth pick from Big East (2002); Big East vs. Pac-10 (2003-05); Big Ten vs. Big 12 (since 2006).

Multiple wins: Arizona and California (2).

Year		Year		Year	
1989†	Arizona 17, N.C. State 10	1996	Wisconsin 38, Utah 10	2003	California 52, Virginia Tech 49
1990	California 17, Wyoming 15	1997	Arizona 20, New Mexico 14	2004	Oregon St. 38, Notre Dame 21
1991	Indiana 24, Baylor 0	1998	Missouri 34, W. Virginia 31	2005	Arizona St. 45, Rutgers 40
1992	Washington St. 31, Utah 28	1999	Colorado 62, Boston College 28	2006	Texas Tech 44, Minnesota 41 OT
1993	Kansas St. 52, Wyoming 17	2000	Iowa St. 37, Pittsburgh 29		
1994	BYU 31, Oklahoma 6	2001	Syracuse 26, Kansas St. 3	†December game since 1989.	
1995	Texas Tech 55, Air Force 41	2002	Pittsburgh 38, Oregon St. 13		

Humanitarian Bowl

City: Boise, Idaho. **Stadium:** Bronco. **Capacity:** 30,000. **Playing surface:** Turf. **First game:** Dec. 29, 1997. **Name change:** Humanitarian Bowl (1997-98, 2004), Crucial.com Humanitarian Bowl (1999-2002), MPC Computers Bowl (2000-2006), Roady's Humanitarian Bowl (since 2007). **Corporate title sponsors:** World Sports Humanitarian Hall of Fame (1997-98), Crucial.com (1999-2002), MPC Computers (2004-06); Roady's Truck Stops (since 2007). **Automatic berths:** Big West champion, if available, vs. at-large (1997-2002) WAC vs. ACC (since 2004). **Multiple wins:** Boise St. (3).

Year		Year		Year	
1997†	Cincinnati 35, Utah St. 19	2001	Clemson 49, La. Tech 24	2005	Boston College 27, Boise St. 21
1998	Idaho 42, Southern Miss. 35	2002	Boise St. 34, Iowa St. 16	2006	Miami-FL 21, Nevada 20
1999	Boise St. 34, Louisville 31	2004*	Georgia Tech 52, Tulsa 10	†Dec. game 1997-2002 and since '04.	
2000	Boise St. 38, UTEP 23	2004†	Fresno St. 37, Virginia 34 OT	*January game in 2004	

Las Vegas Bowl

City: Las Vegas, Nev. **Stadium:** Sam Boyd. **Capacity:** 40,000. **Playing surface:** Turf. **First game:** Dec. 18, 1992. **Playing site:** Sam Boyd Stadium (since 1992). **Corporate title sponsors:** EA Sports (1999-2000) Sega Sports (2001-02). **Automatic berths:** Mid-American champion vs. Big West champion (1992-96 season); none (1997 season); second or third pick from WAC, if available vs. at-large (1998-2000), second pick from Mountain West vs. fifth pick from Pac-10 (since 2001). **Multiple wins:** Fresno St. (4); UNLV (3); Bowling Green, San Jose St., Toledo and Utah (2).

Year		Year		Year	
1981†	Toledo 27, San Jose St. 25	1991	Bowling Green 28, Fresno St. 21	2001	Utah 10, USC 6
1982	Fresno St. 29, Bowling Green 28	1992	Bowling Green 35, Nevada 34	2002	UCLA 27, New Mexico 13
1983	Northern Ill. 20, CS-Fullerton 13	1993	Utah St. 42, Ball St. 33	2003	Oregon St. 55, New Mexico 14
1984*	UNLV 30, Toledo 13	1994	UNLV 52, C. Michigan 24	2004	Wyoming 24, UCLA 21
1985	Fresno St. 51, Bowling Green 7	1995	Toledo 40, Nevada 37 (OT)	2005	California 35, BYU 28
1986	San Jose St. 37, Miami-OH 7	1996	Nevada 18, Ball St. 15	2006	BYU 38, Oregon 8
1987	E. Michigan 30, San Jose St. 27	1997	Oregon 41, Air Force 13	†December game since 1981.	
1988	Fresno St. 35, W. Michigan 30	1998	N. Carolina 20, San Diego St. 13	*Toledo later ruled winner of 1984	
1989	Fresno St. 27, Ball St. 6	1999	Utah 17, Fresno St. 16	game by forfeit because UNLV used	
1990	San Jose St. 48, C. Michigan 24	2000	UNLV 31, Arkansas 14	ineligible players.	

Note: The MAC and Big West champs met in a bowl game from 1981 to 1996, originally in Fresno at the California Bowl (1981-88, 1992) and California Raisin Bowl (1989-91). The results from 1981-91 are included above.

Independence Bowl

City: Shreveport, La. **Stadium:** Independence. **Capacity:** 50,832. **Playing surface:** Grass. **First game:** Dec. 13, 1976. **Playing site:** Independence Stadium (since 1976). **Corporate title sponsors:** Poulan/Weed Eater (1990-97), Sanford (1998-2000) and MainStay (since 2001). **Automatic berths:** Southland Conference champion vs. at-large opponent (1976-81 seasons); none (1982-95 seasons); fifth pick from SEC, if available, vs. at-large (1995-97 season); fifth, sixth or seventh pick from SEC, if available, vs. at-large (1998-99 season); sixth pick from Big 12 vs. SEC (since 2000 season).

Multiple wins: Mississippi (4); Air Force, LSU and Southern Miss (2).

Year		Year		Year	
1976†	McNeese St. 20, Tulsa 16	1987	Washington 24, Tulane 12	1998	Mississippi 35, Texas Tech 18
1977	La. Tech 24, Louisville 14	1988	Southern Miss 38, UTEP 18	1999	Mississippi 27, Oklahoma 25
1978	E. Carolina 35, La. Tech 13	1989	Oregon 27, Tulsa 24	2000	Mississippi St. 43, Texas A&M 41
1979	Syracuse 31, McNeese St. 7	1990	34-34, La. Tech vs Maryland	2001	Alabama 14, Iowa St. 13
1980	Southern Miss 16, McNeese St. 14	1991	Georgia 24, Arkansas 15	2002	Mississippi 27, Nebraska 23
1981	Texas A&M 33, Oklahoma St. 16	1992	Wake Forest 39, Oregon 35	2003	Arkansas 27, Missouri 14
1982	Wisconsin 14, Kansas St. 3	1993	Va. Tech 45, Indiana 20	2004	Iowa St. 17, Miami-OH 13
1983	Air Force 9, Mississippi 3	1994	Virginia 20, TCU 10	2005	Missouri 38, South Carolina 31
1984	Air Force 23, Va. Tech 7	1995	LSU 45, Michigan St. 26	2006	Oklahoma St. 34, Alabama 31
1985	Minnesota 20, Clemson 13	1996	Auburn 32, Army 29		
1986	Mississippi 20, Texas Tech 17	1997	LSU 27, Notre Dame 9	†December game since 1976.	

Alamo Bowl

City: San Antonio, Tex. **Stadium:** Alamodome. **Capacity:** 65,000. **Playing surface:** Turf. **First game:** Dec. 31, 1993.
Playing site: Alamodome (since 1993). **Corporate title sponsor:** Builders Square (1993-98), Sylvania (1999-2001) and Mastercard (2004).
Automatic berths: third pick from SWC vs. fourth pick from Pac-10 (1993-94 seasons); fourth pick from Big 10, if available vs. fourth pick from Big 12, if available (1995-99 seasons); fourth pick from Big 12 vs. third pick from Big 10 (2000 season).
Multiple wins: Nebraska (3), Iowa and Purdue (2).

Year		Year		Year	
1993†	California 37, Iowa 3	1998	Purdue 37, Kansas St. 34	2003	Nebraska 17, Michigan St. 3
1994	Washington St. 10, Baylor 3	1999	Penn St. 24, Texas A&M 0	2004	Ohio St. 33, Oklahoma St. 7
1995	Texas A&M 22, Michigan 20	2000	Nebraska 66, Northwestern 17	2005	Nebraska 32, Michigan 28
1996	Iowa 27, Texas Tech 0	2001	Iowa 19, Texas Tech 16	2006	Texas 26, Iowa 24
1997	Purdue 33, Oklahoma St. 20	2002	Wisconsin 31, Colorado 28 (OT)		†December game since 1993.

Motor City Bowl

City: Detroit, Mich. **Stadium:** Ford Field. **Capacity:** 65,000. **Playing surface:** Turf. **First game:** Dec. 26, 1997. **Playing site:** Pontiac Silverdome (1997-2001) and Ford Field (since 2002). **Corporate title sponsor:** Ford Division of Ford Motor Company (since 1997), Daimler Chrysler and General Motors (since 2002). **Automatic berths:** Mid-American champions vs at-large (1997-99 season); Mid-American champions vs. fourth pick from Conference USA (2000 season).
Multiple wins: Marshall (3).

Year		Year		Year	
1997†	Mississippi 34, Marshall 31	2001	Toledo 23, Cincinnati 16	2005	Memphis 38, Akron 31
1998	Marshall 48, Louisville 29	2002	Boston College 51, Toledo 25	2006	C. Mich. 31, Mid Tenn. St. 14
1999	Marshall 21, BYU 3	2003	Bowling Green 28, N'western 24		†December game since 1997.
2000	Marshall 25, Cincinnati 14	2004	Connecticut 39, Toledo 10		

Music City Bowl

City: Nashville, Tenn. **Stadium:** LP Field. **Capacity:** 67,000. **Playing surface:** Grass. **First game:** Dec. 29, 1998.
Playing sites: Vanderbilt Stadium (1998) and Adelphia Coliseum (since 1999). **Corporate title sponsors:** American General (1998), HomePoint.com (1999-2000) and Gaylord Hotels (since 2002). **Automatic berths:** sixth choice from the SEC, if available, vs. at-large (1998-99 season); fourth pick from Big East, if available vs. SEC (2000-01); Big Ten vs. SEC (2002-05); ACC vs. SEC (since 2006).
Multiple wins: Minnesota (2).

Year		Year		Year	
1998†	Va. Tech 38, Alabama 7	2002	Minnesota 29, Arkansas 14	2006	Kentucky 28, Clemson 20
1999	Syracuse 20, Kentucky 13	2003	Auburn 28, Wisconsin 14		†December game since 1998.
2000	West Va. 49, Mississippi 38	2004	Minnesota 20, Alabama 16		
2001	Boston College 20, Georgia 16	2005	Virginia 34, Minnesota 31		

GMAC Bowl

City: Mobile, Ala. **Stadium:** Ladd-Peebles. **Capacity:** 40,646. **Playing surface:** Grass. **First game:** Dec. 22, 1999.
Name change: Mobile Bowl (1999-2000), GMAC Bowl (since 2001). **Playing sites:** Ladd-Peebles Stadium (since 1999).
Corporate title sponsors: GMAC Financial Services (since 2001). **Automatic berths:** WAC champions (if team is from the east) or second pick from WAC vs. second pick from Conference USA, if available (2000), Mid-American vs. Conference USA (2001), Conference USA vs. Mid-American/WAC (2002-2006).
Multiple wins: Marshall and Southern Miss. (2).

Year		Year		Year	
1999†	TCU 28, E. Carolina 14	2002	Marshall 38, Louisville 15	2005	Toledo 45, UTEP 13
2000	So. Miss 28, TCU 21	2003	Miami-OH 49, Louisville 28	2006	So. Miss. 28, Ohio 7
2001	Marshall 64, E. Caro. 61 (2OT)	2004	Bowling Green 52, Memphis 35		†December game since 1999.

New Orleans Bowl

City: Lafayette, La. **Stadium:** Cajun Field. **Capacity:** 31,000. **Playing surface:** Grass. **First game:** Dec. 18, 2001.
Playing sites: Louisiana Superdome (2001-04), Cajun Field (2005). **Corporate title sponsors:** Wyndam Hotels (since 2004). **Automatic berths:** Sun Belt champion vs. Conference USA (since 2002).
Multiple wins: Southern Mississippi (2).

Year		Year		Year	
2001†	Colorado St. 45, North Texas 20	2003	Memphis 27, North Texas 17	2005	So. Miss. 31, Arkansas St. 19
2002	North Texas 24, Cincinnati 19	2004	So. Miss. 31, North Texas 10	2006	Troy 41, Rice 17
					†December game since 2001.

Emerald Bowl

City: San Francisco, Calif. **Stadium:** AT&T Park. **Capacity:** 37,000. **Playing surface:** Grass. **First game:** Dec. 31, 2002. **Name change:** Diamond Walnut San Francisco Bowl (2002-03), Emerald Bowl (since 2004). **Playing sites:** AT&T (formerly known as Pacific Bell then SBC) Park (since 2002). **Corporate title sponsors:** Diamond Walnut (2002-03), Emerald Nuts (since 2004). **Automatic berths:** Mountain West vs. Big East or Notre Dame (2002-03).

Year		Year		Year	
2002†	Virginia Tech 20, Air Force 13	2004	Navy 34, New Mexico 19	2006	Florida St. 44, UCLA 27
2003	Boston Col. 35, Colorado St. 21	2005	Utah 38, Georgia Tech 10		†December game since 2002.

Bowl Games (Cont.)
Meineke Car Care Bowl

City: Charlotte, N.C. **Stadium:** Bank of America. **Capacity:** 73,367. **Playing surface:** Grass. **First game:** Dec. 28, 2002. **Name change:** Continental Tire Bowl (2002-04), Meineke Car Care Bowl (starting in Dec. 2005). **Playing sites:** Bank of America (formerly known as Ericsson) Stadium (since 2002). **Corporate title sponsors:** Continental Tire North America (2002-04), Meineke Car Care (since 2005). **Automatic berths:** ACC vs. Big East or Notre Dame (since 2002). **Multiple wins:** Boston College and Virginia (2).

Year		Year		Year	
2002†	Virginia 48, West Va. 22	2004	Boston Col. 37, N. Carolina 24	2006	Boston Col. 25, Navy 24
2003	Virginia 23, Pittsburgh 16	2005	N.C. State 14, So. Florida 0		†December game since 2002.

Hawaii Bowl

City: Honolulu, Hi. **Stadium:** Aloha Bowl. **Capacity:** 50,000. **Playing surface:** Turf. **First game:** Dec. 25, 2002. **Playing sites:** Aloha Bowl (since 2002). **Corporate title sponsors:** ConAgra Foods (2002) and Sheraton Hotels & Resorts (since 2003). **Automatic berths:** Hawaii (if bowl eligible) otherwise another WAC school vs. Conference USA (since 2002). **Multiple wins:** Hawaii (3).

Year		Year		Year	
2002†	Tulane 36, Hawaii 28	2004	Hawaii 59, UAB 40	2006	Hawaii 41, Arizona St. 24
2003	Hawaii 54, Houston 48 (3OT)	2005	Nevada 49, C. Florida 48 OT		†December game since 2002.

Armed Forces Bowl

City: Fort Worth, Tex. **Stadium:** Amon Carter. **Capacity:** 46,000. **Playing surface:** Grass. **First game:** Dec. 23, 2003. **Playing sites:** Amon Carter Stadium (since 2003). **Corporate title sponsors:** PlainsCapital Corp. (2003-04) Bell Helicopter (since 2006) There was no title sponsor in 2005. **Name change:** Fort Worth Bowl (2003-2005), Bell Helicopter Armed Forces Bowl (since 2006); **Automatic berths:** Big 12 vs. Conference USA (2003-05), Mountain West vs. Conference USA (2006 and 2008), Pac-10 vs. Mountain West (2007 and 2009).

Year		Year			
2003†	Bosie St. 34, TCU 31	2005	Kansas 42, Houston 13		†December game since 2003.
2004	Cincinnati 32, Marshall 14	2006	Utah 25, Tulsa 13		

Poinsettia Bowl

City: San Diego, Calif. **Stadium:** Qualcomm Stadium. **Capacity:** 71,500. **Playing surface:** Grass. **First game:** Dec. 22, 2005. **Playing sites:** Qualcomm Stadium (since 2005). **Corporate title sponsors:** San Diego County Credit Union. (since 2005). **Automatic berths:** Mountain West vs. at-large (since 2005).

Year		Year			
2005†	Navy 51, Colorado St. 30	2006	TCU 37, No. Illinois 7		†December game since 2005.

Papajohns.com Bowl

City: Birmingham, Ala. **Stadium:** Legion Field. **Capacity:** 71,594. **Playing surface:** Grass. **First game:** Dec. 23, 2006. **Playing sites:** Legion Field (since 2006). **Corporate title sponsors:** Papajohns.com (since 2006). **Automatic berths:** Big East vs. Conference USA (since 2006).

Year			
2006†	So. Florida 24, E. Carolina 7		†December game since 2006.

New Mexico Bowl

City: Albuquerque, N.M. **Stadium:** University Stadium. **Capacity:** 37,000. **Playing surface:** Turf. **First game:** Dec. 23, 2006. **Playing sites:** University Stadium (since 2006). **Automatic berths:** Mountain West vs. WAC (since 2006).

Year			
2006†	San Jose St. 20, N. Mexico 12		†December game since 2006.

International Bowl

City: Toronto, Ontario. **Stadium:** Rogers Centre. **Capacity:** 53,506. **Playing surface:** Turf. **First game:** Jan. 6, 2007. **Playing sites:** Rogers Centre (since 2007). **Automatic berths:** Mid-American vs. Big East (since 2007).

Year			
2007†	Cincinnati 27, W. Michigan 24		†January game since 2007.

BCS Title Game

The BCS held the inaugural BCS Title game on Jan. 8, 2007

Year	
2007	Florida 41, Ohio St. 14

Division I-A Teams

Schools classified as Division I-A for at least 10 years; through 2006 season (including bowl games).

Top 25 Winning Percentage

		Yrs	Gm	W	L	T	Pct	Bowls App	Record	Bowl	2006 Season Record
1	Michigan	127	1178	860	282	36	.745	38	18-20-0	lost Rose	11-2
2	Notre Dame	118	1132	821	269	42	.744	28	13-15-0	lost Sugar	10-3
3	Texas	114	1156	810	313	33	.715	46	23-21-2	won Alamo	10-3
4	Oklahoma*	112	1113	768	292	53	.714	40	24-15-1	lost Fiesta	11-3
5	Ohio St.	117	1140	786	301	53	.713	38	18-20-0	lost BCS Title Game	12-1
6	Alabama*	112	1131	780	308	43	.709	54	30-21-3	lost Independence	6-7
7	Nebraska	117	1169	803	326	40	.704	44	22-22-0	lost Cotton	9-5
8	USC	114	1097	743	300	54	.702	45	29-16-0	won Rose	11-2
9	Tennessee*	110	1127	760	315	52	.697	46	24-22-0	lost Outback	9-4
10	Boise St.	39	459	317	140	2	.693	7	5-2-0	won Fiesta	13-0
11	Penn St.	120	1164	780	343	41	.688	39	25-12-2	won Orange	9-4
12	Florida St.*	60	671	443	211	17	.673	35	20-13-2	won Emerald	7-6
13	Georgia	113	1135	702	379	54	.642	42	23-16-3	won Chick-fil-A	9-4
14	LSU*	113	1103	680	376	47	.638	38	19-18-1	won Sugar	11-2
15	Miami-FL	80	848	532	297	19	.636	31	18-13-0	won MPC Computers	7-6
16	Miami-OH*	118	1047	641	362	44	.633	9	6-3-0	none	2-10
17	Auburn*	114	1098	667	384	47	.629	33	18-13-2	won Cotton	11-2
18	Washington*	117	1075	646	379	50	.624	29	14-14-1	none	5-7
19	Florida	100	1027	619	368	40	.622	34	15-19-0	won BCS Title Game	13-1
20	South Florida	10	113	70	43	0	.619	2	1-1-0	won Papajohns.com	9-4
21	Arizona St.	94	878	530	324	24	.617	23	12-10-1	lost Hawaii	7-6
22	Colorado*	117	1100	652	412	36	.609	27	12-15-0	none	2-10
23	Central Michigan	106	920	542	342	36	.609	3	1-2-0	won Motor City	10-4
24	Texas A&M	112	1115	648	419	48	.603	29	13-16-0	lost Holiday	9-4
25	UCLA	88	909	528	344	37	.601	28	13-14-1	lost Emerald	7-6

*Includes games forfeited following rulings by the NCAA Executive Council and/or the Committee on Infractions.

Top 50 Victories

		Wins			Wins			Wins
1	Michigan	.860	18	Washington	.646	35	Wisconsin	.587
2	Notre Dame	.821		Georgia Tech	.646	36	Maryland	.585
3	Texas	.810	20	Miami-OH	.641	37	Rutgers	.580
4	Nebraska	.803	21	Pittsburgh	.639	38	Missouri	.577
5	Ohio St	.786	22	Arkansas	.638	39	Utah	.572
6	Alabama	.780	23	Virginia Tech	.636	40	Purdue	.558
	Penn St	.780	24	Army	.631	41	Illinois	.549
8	Oklahoma	.768	25	Minnesota	.629	42	Iowa	.552
9	Tennessee	.760	26	North Carolina	.627	43	Kentucky	.545
10	USC	.743	27	Florida	.619	44	Stanford	.543
11	Georgia	.702	28	Clemson	.616	45	Vanderbilt	.542
12	LSU	.680		Navy	.616		Kansas	.542
13	Syracuse	.669	30	California	.598		Central Michigan	.542
14	Auburn	.667	31	Virginia	.597	48	Oregon	.539
15	West Virginia	.653	32	Mississippi	.594	49	Miami-FL	.532
16	Colorado	.652		Michigan St	.594	50	Arizona	.531
17	Texas A&M	.648	34	Boston College	.589			

Top 40 Bowl Appearances

		App	Record			App	Record			App	Record
1	Alabama	54	30-21-3	15	Florida	34	16-18-0	29	Pittsburgh	24	10-14-0
2	Tennessee	46	24-22-0	16	Auburn	33	18-13-2		Missouri	24	10-14-0
	Texas	46	23-21-2	17	Mississippi	31	19-12-0	31	N.C. State	23	12-10-1
4	USC	45	29-16-0		Miami-FL	31	18-13-0		Arizona St.	23	12-10-1
5	Nebraska	44	22-22-0	19	Texas Tech	30	9-20-1		TCU	23	9-13-1
6	Georgia	42	23-16-3	20	Washington	29	14-14-1	34	Syracuse	22	12-9-1
7	Oklahoma	40	24-15-1		Texas A&M	29	13-16-0		Iowa	22	11-10-1
8	Penn St	39	25-12-2		Clemson	29	15-14-0	36	Maryland	21	9-10-2
9	LSU	38	19-18-1	23	Notre Dame	28	13-15-0	37	Stanford	20	9-10-1
	Ohio St	38	18-20-0		UCLA	28	13-14-1	38	Oregon	19	7-12-0
	Michigan	38	18-20-0	25	Colorado	27	12-15-0		Virginia Tech	19	7-12-0
12	Arkansas	35	11-21-3	26	West Virginia	26	11-15-0	40	Boston College	18	12-6-0
	Georgia Tech	35	22-13-0	27	North Carolina	25	12-13-0		Wisconsin	18	10-8-0
	Florida St	35	20-13-2		BYU	25	8-16-1				

Major Conference Champions

Atlantic Coast Conference

Founded in 1953 when charter members all left Southern Conference to form ACC. **Charter members** (7): Clemson, Duke, Maryland, North Carolina, N.C. State, South Carolina and Wake Forest. **Admitted later** (6): Virginia in 1953 (began play in '54), Georgia Tech in 1979 (began play in '83), Florida St. in 1990 (began play in '92), Boston College, Virginia Tech and Miami-FL in 2003 (Virginia Tech and Miami began play in '04, Boston College in '05). **Withdrew later** (1): South Carolina in 1971 (became an independent after '70 season). **2007 playing membership** (12): ATLANTIC— Boston College, Clemson, Florida St., Maryland, N.C. State and Wake Forest; COASTAL—Duke, Georgia Tech, Miami-FL, North Carolina, Virginia and Virginia Tech.

Multiple titles: Clemson (13); Florida St. (12); Maryland (9); Duke and N.C. State (7); North Carolina (5); Georgia Tech, Virginia and Wake Forest (2).

Year		Year		Year		Year	
1953	Duke (4-0)	1965	Clemson (5-2)	1980	North Carolina (6-0)	1994	Florida St. (8-0)
	& Maryland (3-0)		& N.C. State (5-2)	1981	Clemson (6-0)	1995	Virginia (7-1)
1954	Duke (4-0)	1966	Clemson (6-1)	1982	Clemson (6-0)		& Florida St. (7-1)
1955	Maryland (4-0)	1967	Clemson (6-0)	1983	Clemson (7-0) †	1996	Florida St. (8-0)
	& Duke (4-0)	1968	N.C. State (6-1)		& Maryland (5-0)	1997	Florida St. (8-0)
1956	Clemson (4-0-1)	1969	South Carolina (6-0)	1984	Maryland (5-0)	1998	Florida St. (7-1)
1957	N.C. State (5-0-1)	1970	Wake Forest (5-1)	1985	Maryland (6-0)		& Georgia Tech (7-1)
1958	Clemson (5-1)	1971	North Carolina (6-0)	1986	Clemson (5-1-1)	1999	Florida St. (8-0)
1959	Clemson (6-1)	1972	North Carolina (6-0)	1987	Clemson (6-1)	2000	Florida St. (8-0)
1960	Duke (5-1)	1973	N.C. State (6-0)	1988	Clemson (6-1)	2001	Maryland (7-1)
1961	Duke (5-1)	1974	Maryland (6-0)	1989	Virginia (6-1)	2002	Florida St. (7-1)
1962	Duke (6-1)	1975	Maryland (5-0)		& Duke (6-1)	2003	Florida St. (7-1)
1963	North Carolina (6-1)	1976	Maryland (5-0)	1990	Georgia Tech (6-0-1)	2004	Virginia Tech (7-1)
	& N.C. State (6-1)	1977	North Carolina (5-0-1)	1991	Clemson (6-0-1)		
1964	N.C. State (5-2)	1978	Clemson (6-0)	1992	Florida St. (8-0)	†On probation, ineligible	
		1979	N.C. State (5-1)	1993	Florida St. (8-0)	for championship.	

ACC Championship Game

After expanding to 12 teams and splitting into two divisions in 2005, the ACC began staging a conference championship game between the two division winners on the first Saturday in December. The inaugural game was played at Alltel Stadium in Jacksonville, Fla. and the 2006 game was played there as well.

Year		Year	
2005	Florida St. 27, Va. Tech 22	2006	Wake Forest 9, Ga. Tech 6

Big East Conference

Founded in 1991 when charter members gave up independent football status to form Big East. **Charter members** (8): Boston College, Miami-FL, Pittsburgh, Rutgers, Syracuse, Temple, Virginia Tech and West Virginia. **Admitted later** (4): Connecticut (a charter member in all other sports) in 2004; Cincinnati, Louisville and South Florida in 2003 (to begin play in '05). **Withdrew later** (4): Boston College, Miami-FL and Virginia Tech in 2003 (Miami and Va. Tech joined ACC for 2004 season, Boston College joined ACC in 2005). Temple became an independent following 2004 season

2007 playing membership (8): Cincinnati, Connecticut, Louisville, Pittsburgh, Rutgers, South Florida, Syracuse and West Virginia. **Conference champion:** Member schools needed two years to adjust their regular season schedules in order to begin round-robin conference play in 1993. In the meantime, the 1991 and '92 Big East titles went to the highest-ranked member in the final regular season USA Today/CNN coaches' poll.

Multiple titles: Miami-FL (9); Syracuse (5); West Virginia (4); Virginia Tech (3).

Year		Year		Year		Year	
1991	Miami-FL (2-0, #1)	1996	Virginia Tech (6-1),	2000	Miami-FL (7-0)	2004	Boston College (4-2),
	& Syracuse (5-0, #16)		Miami-FL (6-1)	2001	Miami-FL (7-0)		Pittsburgh (4-2),
1992	Miami-FL (4-0, #1)		& Syracuse (6-1)	2002	Miami-FL (7-0)		Syracuse (4-2)
1993	West Virginia (7-0)	1997	Syracuse (6-1)	2003	Miami-FL (6-1)		& West Virginia (4-2)
1994	Miami-FL (7-0)	1998	Syracuse (6-1)		& West Virginia (6-1)	2005	West Virginia (7-0)
1995	Virginia Tech (6-1)	1999	Virginia Tech (7-0)			2006	Louisville (6-1)
	& Miami-FL (6-1)						

Big Ten Conference

Originally founded in 1895 as the Intercollegiate Conference of Faculty Representatives, better known as the Western Conference. **Charter members** (7): Chicago, Illinois, Michigan, Minnesota, Northwestern, Purdue and Wisconsin. **Admitted later** (5): Indiana and Iowa in 1899; Ohio St. in 1912; Michigan St. in 1950 (began play in '53); Penn St. in 1990 (began play in '93). **Withdrew later** (2): Michigan in 1907 (rejoined in '17); Chicago in 1940 (dropped football after '39 season). **Note:** Iowa belonged to both the Western and Missouri Valley conferences from 1907-10.

Unofficially called the **Big Ten** from 1912 until Chicago's withdrawal in 1939, then the **Big Nine** from 1940 until Michigan St. began conference play in 1953. Formally named the **Big Ten** in 1984 and has kept the name even after adding Penn St. as its 11th member in 1990.

2007 playing membership (11): Illinois, Indiana, Iowa, Michigan, Michigan St., Minnesota, Northwestern, Ohio St., Penn St., Purdue and Wisconsin.

Multiple titles: Michigan (42); Ohio St. (31); Minnesota (18); Illinois (15); Iowa and Wisconsin (11); Purdue and Northwestern (8); Chicago and Michigan St. (6); Indiana and Penn St. (2).

Year		Year		Year		Year	
1896	Wisconsin (2-0-1)	1901	Michigan (4-0)	1904	Minnesota (3-0)	1907	Chicago (4-0)
1897	Wisconsin (3-0)		& Wisconsin (2-0)		& Michigan (2-0)	1908	Chicago (5-0)
1898	Michigan (3-0)	1902	Michigan (5-0)	1905	Chicago (7-0)	1909	Minnesota (3-0)
1899	Chicago (4-0)	1903	Michigan (3-0-1),	1906	Wisconsin (3-0),	1910	Illinois (4-0)
1900	Iowa (3-0-1)		Minnesota (3-0-1)		Minnesota (2-0)		& Minnesota (2-0)
	& Minnesota (3-0-1)		& Northwestern (1-0-2)		& Michigan (1-0)	1911	Minnesota (3-0-1)

Year		Year		Year		Year	
1912	Wisconsin (6-0)	1935	Minnesota (5-0) & Ohio St. (5-0)	1964	Michigan (6-1)	1987	Michigan St. (7-0-1)
1913	Chicago (7-0)			1965	Michigan St. (7-0)	1988	Michigan (7-0-1)
1914	Illinois (6-0)	1936	Northwestern (6-0)	1966	Michigan St. (7-0)	1989	Michigan (8-0)
1915	Minnesota (3-0-1) & Illinois (3-0-2)	1937	Minnesota (5-0)	1967	Indiana (6-1), Purdue (6-1) & Minnesota (6-1)	1990	Iowa (6-2), Michigan (6-2), Michigan St. (6-2) & Illinois (6-2)
1916	Ohio St. (4-0)	1938	Minnesota (4-1)	1968	Ohio St. (7-0)		
1917	Ohio St. (4-0)	1939	Ohio St. (5-1)	1969	Ohio St. (6-1) & Michigan (6-1)	1991	Michigan (8-0)
1918	Illinois (4-0), Michigan (2-0) & Purdue (1-0)	1940	Minnesota (6-0)			1992	Michigan (6-0-2)
		1941	Minnesota (5-0)	1970	Ohio St. (7-0)	1993	Wisconsin (6-1-1) & Ohio St. (6-1-1)
1919	Illinois (6-1)	1942	Ohio St. (5-1)	1971	Michigan (8-0)		
1920	Ohio St. (5-0)	1943	Purdue (6-0) & Michigan (6-0)	1972	Ohio St. (7-1) & Michigan (7-1)	1994	Penn St. (8-0)
1921	Iowa (5-0)	1944	Ohio St. (6-0)	1973	Ohio St. (7-0-1) & Michigan (7-0-1)	1995	Northwestern (8-0)
1922	Iowa (5-0) & Michigan (4-0)	1945	Indiana (5-0-1)	1974	Ohio St. (7-1) & Michigan (7-1)	1996	Ohio St. (7-1) & Northwestern (7-1)
1923	Illinois (5-0) & Michigan (4-0)	1946	Illinois (6-1)	1975	Ohio St. (8-0)		
1924	Chicago (3-0-3)	1947	Michigan (6-0)	1976	Michigan (7-1) & Ohio St. (7-1)	1997	Michigan (8-0)
1925	Michigan (5-1)	1948	Michigan (6-0)	1977	Michigan (7-1) & Ohio St. (7-1)	1998	Ohio St. (7-1), Wisconsin (7-1) & Michigan (7-1)
1926	Michigan (5-0) & Northwestern (5-0)	1949	Ohio St. (4-1-1) & Michigan (4-1-1)	1978	Michigan (7-1) & Michigan St. (7-1)	1999	Wisconsin (7-1)
1927	Illinois (5-0) & Minnesota (3-0-1)	1950	Michigan (4-1-1)	1979	Ohio St. (8-0)	2000	Purdue (6-2), Michigan (6-2) & Northwestern (6-2)
1928	Illinois (4-1)	1951	Illinois (5-0-1)	1980	Michigan (8-0)		
1929	Purdue (5-0)	1952	Wisconsin (4-1-1) & Purdue (4-1-1)	1981	Iowa (6-2) & Ohio St. (6-2)	2001	Illinois (7-1)
1930	Michigan (5-0) & Northwestern (5-0)	1953	Michigan St. (5-1) & Illinois (5-1)	1982	Michigan (8-1)	2002	Ohio St. (8-0) & Iowa (8-0)
1931	Purdue (5-1), Michigan (5-1) & Northwestern (5-1)	1954	Ohio St. (7-0)	1983	Illinois (9-0)	2003	Michigan (7-1)
1932	Michigan (6-0) & Purdue (5-0-1)	1955	Ohio St. (6-0)	1984	Ohio St. (7-2)	2004	Iowa (7-1) & Michigan (7-1)
1933	Michigan (5-0-1) & Minnesota (2-0-4)	1956	Iowa (5-1)	1985	Iowa (7-1)	2005	Ohio St. (7-1) & Penn St. (7-1)
1934	Minnesota (5-0)	1957	Ohio St. (7-0)	1986	Michigan (7-1) & Ohio St. (7-1)	2006	Ohio St. (8-0)
		1958	Iowa (5-1)				
		1959	Wisconsin (5-2)				
		1960	Minnesota (5-1) & Iowa (5-1)				
		1961	Ohio St. (6-0)				
		1962	Wisconsin (6-1)				
		1963	Illinois (5-1-1)				

Big 12 Conference

Originally founded in 1996 by the former teams of the Big Eight and four schools from the Southwest Conference. The league stages a conference championship game between the two division winners on the first Saturday in December. **Playing sites:** Trans World Dome in St. Louis (1996, 1998), the Alamodome in San Antonio (1997, 1999), Arrowhead Stadium in Kansas City, Mo. (2000, 2003, 2004 and 2006), Texas Stadium in Irving, Texas (2001) and Reliant Stadium in Houston (2002, 2005). **2007 playing membership:** (12) NORTH—Colorado, Iowa St., Kansas, Kansas St., Missouri and Nebraska; SOUTH—Baylor, Oklahoma, Oklahoma St., Texas, Texas A&M and Texas Tech.

Multiple titles: Oklahoma (4), Nebraska and Texas (2).

Year		Year		Year	
1996	Texas 37, Nebraska 27	2000	Oklahoma 27, Kansas St. 24	2004	Oklahoma 42, Colorado 3
1997	Nebraska 54, Texas A&M 15	2001	Colorado 39, Texas 37	2005	Texas 70, Colorado 3
1998	Texas A&M 36, Kansas St. 33	2002	Oklahoma 29, Colorado 7	2006	Oklahoma 21, Nebraska 7
1999	Nebraska 22, Texas 6	2003	Kansas St. 35, Oklahoma 7		

Big West Conference (1969-2000)

Originally founded in 1969 as Pacific Coast Athletic Assn. **Charter members** (7): CS-Los Angeles, Fresno St., Long Beach St., Pacific, San Diego St., San Jose St. and UC-Santa Barbara. **Admitted later** (12): CS-Fullerton in 1974; Utah St. in 1977 (began play in '78); UNLV in 1982; New Mexico St. in 1983 (began play in '84); Nevada in 1991 (began play in '92); Arkansas St., Louisiana Tech, Northern Illinois and SW Louisiana in 1992 (all four began play in football only in '93); Boise St., Idaho and North Texas in 1994 (all three began play in '96); Arkansas St. rejoined in 1999 (in football only). **Withdrew later** (14): CS-Los Angeles and UC-Santa Barbara in 1972 (both dropped football after '71 season); San Diego St. in 1975 (became an independent after '75 season); Fresno St. in 1991 (left for WAC after '91 season); Long Beach St. in 1991 (dropped football after '91 season); CS-Fullerton in 1992 (dropped football after '92 season); San Jose St. and UNLV in 1994 (left for WAC after '95 season); Pacific in 1995 (dropped football after '95 season); Arkansas St., Louisiana Tech, Northern Illinois and SW Louisiana in 1995 (all four returned to independent football status after '95 season); Nevada in 2000 (left for WAC after '99 season). **Conference renamed** Big West in 1988.

Multiple titles: San Jose St. (8); Fresno St. (6); Nevada, San Diego St. and Utah St. (5); Long Beach St. (3); Boise St., CS-Fullerton and SW Louisiana (2).

Year		Year		Year		Year	
1969	San Diego St. (6-0)	1979	Utah St. (4-0-1)*	1991	Fresno St. (6-1) & San Jose St. (6-1)	1997	Utah St. (4-1) & Nevada (4-1)
1970	Long Beach St. (5-1) & San Diego St. (5-1)	1980	Long Beach St. (5-0)	1992	Nevada (5-1)	1998	Idaho (4-1)
		1981	San Jose St. (5-0)	1993	Utah St. (5-1) & SW Louisiana (5-1)	1999	Boise St. (5-1)
1971	Long Beach St. (5-1)	1982	Fresno St. (6-0)			2000	Boise St. (5-0)
1972	San Diego St. (4-0)	1983	CS-Fullerton (5-1)	1994	UNLV (5-1), Nevada (5-1), & SW Louisiana (5-1)		
1973	San Diego St. (3-0-1)	1984	CS-Fullerton (6-1)†			*San Jose St. (4-0-1) forfeited share of 1979 title for using ineligible player.	
1974	San Diego St. (4-0)	1985	Fresno St. (7-0)	1995	Nevada (6-0)		
1975	San Jose St. (5-0)	1986	San Jose St. (7-0)	1996	Nevada (5-1) & Utah St. (4-1)	†CS-Fullerton (7-0) forfeited title in 1984 for use of ineligible players.	
1976	San Jose St. (4-0)	1987	San Jose St. (7-0)				
1977	Fresno St. (4-0)	1988	Fresno St. (7-0)				
1978	San Jose St. (4-1) & Utah St. (4-1)	1989	Fresno St. (7-0)				
		1990	San Jose St. (7-0)				

Big Eight Conference (1907-1996)

Originally founded in 1907 as the Missouri Valley Intercollegiate Athletic Assn. **Charter members** (5): Iowa, Kansas, Missouri, Nebraska and Washington University of St. Louis. **Admitted later** (11): Drake and Iowa St. (then Ames College) in 1908; Kansas St. (then Kansas College of Applied Science and Agriculture) in 1913; Grinnell (Iowa) College in 1919; Oklahoma in 1920; Oklahoma A&M (now Oklahoma St.) in 1925; Colorado in 1947 (began play in '48).

Withdrew later (9): Iowa in 1911 (left for Big Ten after 1910 season), Colorado, Iowa St., Kansas, Kansas St. Missouri, Nebraska, Oklahoma and Oklahoma St. in 1996 (left for Big 12 after 1995 season); **Excluded later** (4): Drake, Grinnell, Oklahoma A&M and Washington-MO (left out when MVIAA cut membership to six teams in 1928).

Streamlined MVIAA unofficially called **Big Six** from 1928-47 with surviving members Iowa St., Kansas, Kansas St., Missouri, Nebraska and Oklahoma. Became the **Big Seven** after 1947 season when Colorado came over from the Skyline Conference, and then the **Big Eight** with the return of Oklahoma A&M in 1957. A&M, which resumed conference play in '60, became Oklahoma St. on July 10, 1957. The MVIAA was officially renamed the Big Eight in 1964. The league folded in 1996 when the existing members formed the newly created Big 12 along with four schools from the Southwest Conference.

Multiple titles: Nebraska (43); Oklahoma (34); Missouri (12); Colorado and Kansas (5); Iowa St. and Oklahoma St. (2).

Year		Year		Year		Year	
1907	Iowa (1-0) & Nebraska (1-0)	1928	Nebraska (4-0)	1952	Oklahoma (5-0-1)	1976	Colorado (5-2), Oklahoma (5-2) & Oklahoma St. (5-2)
1908	Kansas (4-0)	1929	Nebraska (3-0-2)	1953	Oklahoma (6-0)		
1909	Missouri (4-0-1)	1930	Kansas (4-1)	1954	Oklahoma (6-0)		
1910	Nebraska (2-0)	1931	Nebraska (5-0)	1955	Oklahoma (6-0)	1977	Oklahoma (7-0)
1911	Iowa St. (2-0-1) & Nebraska (2-0-1)	1932	Nebraska (5-0)	1956	Oklahoma (6-0)	1978	Nebraska (6-1) & Oklahoma (6-1)
1912	Iowa St. (2-0) & Nebraska (2-0)	1933	Nebraska (5-0)	1957	Oklahoma (6-0)		
		1934	Kansas St. (5-0)	1958	Oklahoma (6-0)	1979	Oklahoma (7-0)
1913	Missouri (4-0) & Nebraska (3-0)	1935	Nebraska (4-0-1)	1959	Oklahoma (5-1)	1980	Oklahoma (7-0)
		1936	Nebraska (5-0)	1960	Missouri (7-0)	1981	Nebraska (7-0)
1914	Nebraska (3-0)	1937	Nebraska (3-0-2)	1961	Colorado (7-0)	1982	Nebraska (7-0)
1915	Nebraska (4-0)	1938	Oklahoma (5-0)	1962	Oklahoma (7-0)	1983	Nebraska (7-0)
1916	Nebraska (3-1)	1939	Missouri (5-0)	1963	Nebraska (7-0)	1984	Oklahoma (6-1) & Nebraska (6-1)
1917	Nebraska (2-0)	1940	Nebraska (5-0)	1964	Nebraska (6-1)		
1918	Vacant (WW I)	1941	Missouri (5-0)	1965	Nebraska (7-0)	1985	Oklahoma (7-0)
1919	Missouri (4-0-1)	1942	Missouri (4-0-1)	1966	Nebraska (6-1)	1986	Oklahoma (7-0)
1920	Oklahoma (4-0-1)	1943	Oklahoma (4-0)	1967	Oklahoma (7-0)	1987	Oklahoma (7-0)
1921	Nebraska (3-0)	1944	Oklahoma (4-0-1)	1968	Kansas (6-1) & Oklahoma (6-1)	1988	Nebraska (7-0)
1922	Nebraska (5-0)	1945	Missouri (5-0)			1989	Colorado (7-0)
1923	Nebraska (3-0-2) & Kansas (3-0-3)	1946	Oklahoma (4-1) & Kansas (4-1)	1969	Missouri (6-1) & Nebraska (6-1)	1990	Colorado (7-0)
						1991	Nebraska (6-0-1) & Colorado (6-0-1)
1924	Missouri (5-1)	1947	Kansas (4-0-1) & Oklahoma (4-0-1)	1970	Nebraska (7-0)		
1925	Missouri (5-1)	1948	Oklahoma (5-0)	1971	Nebraska (7-0)	1992	Nebraska (6-1)
1926	Okla. A&M (3-0-1)	1949	Oklahoma (5-0)	1972	Nebraska (5-1-1)*	1993	Nebraska (7-0)
1927	Missouri (5-1)	1950	Oklahoma (6-0)	1973	Oklahoma (7-0)	1994	Nebraska (7-0)
		1951	Oklahoma (6-0)	1974	Oklahoma (7-0)	1995	Nebraska (7-0)
				1975	Nebraska (6-1) & Oklahoma (6-1)		

*Oklahoma (6-1) forfeited title in 1972 after a player was ruled ineligible.

Conference USA

Founded in 1994 by six independent football schools which began play as a conference in 1996. **Charter members** (6): Cincinnati, Houston, Louisville, Memphis, Southern Mississippi and Tulane. **Admitted later** (11): East Carolina in 1997, Army in 1998, Univ. of Alabama-Birmingham in 1999, Texas Christian Univ. in 2001, South Florida in 2003, Central Florida, Marshall, Rice, SMU, Tulsa and UTEP in 2005. **Withdrew later** (5): Cincinnati, Louisville and South Florida are set to leave for the Big East in 2005; Army is going back to independent and TCU is going to the Mountain West in 2005.

2007 playing members (12): EAST—Alabama-Birmingham, Central Florida, East Carolina, Marshall, Memphis and Southern Mississippi, WEST—Houston, Rice, SMU, Tulane, Tulsa and UTEP.

Multiple titles: Southern Mississippi (4), Louisville (3).

Year		Year		Year	
1996	Southern Mississippi (4-1) & Houston (4-1)	1999	Southern Mississippi (6-0)	2002	TCU (6-2) & Cincinnati (6-2)
1997	Southern Mississippi (6-0)	2000	Louisville (6-1)	2003	Southern Mississippi (8-0)
1998	Tulane (6-0)	2001	Louisville (6-1)	2004	Louisville (8-0)

Conference USA Championship Game

After expanding to 12 teams and splitting into two divisions in 2005, Conference USA began staging a conference championship game between the two division winners on the first Saturday in December. The inaugural game was held Dec. 3, 2005 at the Florida Citrus Bowl in Orlando, Fla. The 2006 game was held at Robertson Stadium in Houston.

Year	Year
2005 Tulsa 44, Central Florida 27	2006 Houston 34, Southern Miss. 20

Mid-American Conference

Founded in 1946. **Charter members** (6): Butler, Cincinnati, Miami-OH, Ohio University, Western Michigan and Western Reserve (Miami and WMU began play in '48). **Admitted later** (14): Kent St. (now Kent) and Toledo in 1951 (Toledo began play in '52); Bowling Green in 1952; Marshall in 1954; Central Michigan and Eastern Michigan in 1972 (CMU began play in '75 and EMU in '76); Ball St. and Northern Illinois in 1973 (both began play in '75); Akron in 1991 (began play in '92); Marshall and Northern Illinois in 1995 (both resumed play in '97); Buffalo in 1995 (resumed play in '99); Central Florida 2002; and Temple in 2007.

Withdrew later (6): Butler in 1950 (left for the Indiana Collegiate Conference); Cincinnati in 1953 (went independent); Western Reserve (now Case Western) in 1955 (left for President's Athletic Conference); Marshall in 1969 (went independent) and again in 2005 (left for Conference USA); Northern Illinois in 1986 (went independent); Central Florida in 2005 (left for Conference USA). **2007 playing membership** (13): EAST–Akron, Bowling Green, Buffalo, Kent St., Miami-OH, Ohio University and Temple; WEST–Ball St., Central Michigan, Eastern Michigan, Northern Illinois, Toledo and Western Michigan.

Multiple titles: Miami-OH (14); Bowling Green (10); Toledo (9); Ball St., Marshall and Ohio University (5); Central Michigan, Cincinnati (4); Western Michigan (2).

Year		Year		Year		Year	
1947	Cincinnati (3-1)	1959	Bowling Green (6-0)	1970	Toledo (5-0)	1984	Toledo (7-1-1)
1948	Miami-OH (4-0)	1960	Ohio Univ. (6-0)	1971	Toledo (5-0)	1985	Bowling Green (9-0)
1949	Cincinnati (4-0)	1961	Bowling Green (5-1)	1972	Kent St. (4-1)	1986	Miami-OH (6-2)
1950	Miami-OH (4-0)	1962	Bowling Green (5-0-1)	1973	Miami-OH (5-0)	1987	Eastern Mich. (7-1)
1951	Cincinnati (3-0)	1963	Ohio Univ. (5-1)	1974	Miami-OH (5-0)	1988	Western Mich. (7-1)
1952	Cincinnati (3-0)	1964	Bowling Green (5-1)	1975	Miami-OH (6-0)	1989	Ball St. (6-1-1)
1953	Ohio Univ. (5-0-1)	1965	Bowling Green (5-1)	1976	Ball St. (4-1)	1990	Central Mich. (7-1)
	& Miami-OH (3-0-1)		& Miami-OH (5-1)	1977	Miami-OH (5-0)		& Toledo (7-1)
1954	Miami-OH (4-0)	1966	Miami-OH (5-1)	1978	Ball St. (8-0)	1991	Bowling Green (8-0)
1955	Miami-OH (5-0)		& Western Mich. (5-1)	1979	Central Mich. (8-0-1)	1992	Bowling Green (8-0)
1956	Bowling Green (5-0-1)	1967	Toledo (5-1)	1980	Central Mich. (7-2)	1993	Ball St. (7-0-1)
	& Miami-OH (4-0-1)		& Ohio Univ. (5-1)	1981	Toledo (8-1)	1994	Central Mich. (8-1)
1957	Miami-OH (5-0)	1968	Ohio Univ. (6-0)	1982	Bowling Green (7-2)	1995	Toledo (7-0-1)
1958	Miami-OH (5-0)	1969	Toledo (5-0)	1983	Northern Ill. (8-1)	1996	Ball St. (7-1)

MAC Championship Game

After expanding to 12 teams and splitting into two divisions in 1997, the MAC began staging a conference championship game between the two division winners on the first Saturday in December. The game has been played at Marshall Stadium in Huntington, W.V. (1997-2000, 2002), Glass Bowl Stadium in Toledo, Ohio (2001), Doyt Perry Stadium in Bowling Green, Ohio (2003) and Ford Field in Detroit (2004-06).

Year		Year		Year	
1997	Marshall 34, Toledo 13	2001	Toledo 41, Marshall 36	2005	Akron 31, Northern Illinois 30
1998	Marshall 23, Toledo 17	2002	Marshall 49, Toledo 45	2006	C. Michigan 31, Ohio 10
1999	Marshall 34, W. Michigan 30	2003	Miami-OH 49, Bowl. Green 27		
2000	Marshall 19, W. Michigan 14	2004	Toledo 35, Miami-OH 27		

Mountain West Conference

Founded in 1999. **Charter members** (8): Air Force, Brigham Young, Colorado St., New Mexico, Nevada-Las Vegas, San Diego St., Utah and Wyoming. **Admitted later** (1): TCU (from Conference USA) in 2005.

2007 playing membership (9): Air Force, Brigham Young, Colorado St., New Mexico, Nevada-Las Vegas, San Diego St., TCU, Utah and Wyoming.

Multiple titles: BYU, Colorado St. and Utah (3).

Year		Year		Year		Year	
1999	BYU (5-2),	2000	Colorado St. (6-1)	2003	Utah (6-1)	2006	BYU (8-0)
	Colorado St. (5-2)	2001	BYU (7-0)	2004	Utah (7-0)		
	& Utah (5-2)	2002	Colorado St. (6-1)	2005	TCU (8-0)		

Pacific-10 Conference

Originally founded in 1915 as Pacific Coast Conference. **Charter members** (4): California, Oregon, Oregon St. and Washington. **Admitted later** (6): Washington St. in 1917; Stanford in 1918; Idaho and USC (Southern Cal) in 1922; Montana in 1924; and UCLA in 1928. **Withdrew later** (1): Montana in 1950 (left for the Mountain States Conf.).

The PCC dissolved in 1959 and the **AAWU** (Athletic Assn. of Western Universities) was founded. **Charter members** (5): California, Stanford, UCLA, USC and Washington. **Admitted later** (5):Washington St. in 1962; Oregon and Oregon St. in 1964; Arizona and Arizona St. in 1978. **Conference renamed** Pacific-8 in 1968 and Pacific-10 in 1978.

2007 playing membership (10): Arizona, Arizona St., California, Oregon, Oregon St., Stanford, UCLA, USC, Washington and Washington St.

Multiple titles: USC (36); UCLA (17); Washington (15); California (14); Stanford (12); Oregon (7); Oregon St. (5); Washington St. (4); Arizona St. (2).

Year		Year		Year		Year	
1916	Washington (3-0-1)	1933	Oregon (4-1)	1947	USC (6-0)	1962	USC (4-0)
1917	Washington St. (3-0)		& Stanford (4-1)	1948	California (6-0)	1963	Washington (4-1)
1918	California (3-0)	1934	Stanford (5-0)		& Oregon (6-0)	1964	Oregon St. (3-1)
1919	Oregon (2-1)	1935	California (4-1),	1949	California (7-0)		& USC (3-1)
	& Washington (2-1)		Stanford (4-1)	1950	California (5-0-1)	1965	UCLA (4-0)
1920	California (3-0)		& UCLA (4-1)	1951	Stanford (6-1)	1966	USC (4-1)
1921	California (5-0)	1936	Washington (6-0-1)	1952	USC (6-0)	1967	USC (6-1)
1922	California (3-0)	1937	California (6-0-1)	1953	UCLA (6-1)	1968	USC (6-0)
1923	California (5-0)	1938	USC (6-1)	1954	UCLA (6-0)	1969	USC (6-0)
1924	Stanford (3-0-1)		& California (6-1)	1955	UCLA (6-0)	1970	Stanford (6-1)
1925	Washington (5-0)	1939	USC (5-0-2)	1956	Oregon St. (6-1-1)	1971	Stanford (6-1)
1926	Stanford (4-0)		& UCLA (5-0-3)	1957	Oregon (6-2)	1972	USC (7-0)
1927	USC (4-0-1)	1940	Stanford (7-0)		& Oregon St. (6-2)	1973	USC (7-0)
	& Stanford (4-0-1)	1941	Oregon St. (7-2)	1958	California (6-1)	1974	USC (6-0-1)
1928	USC (4-0-1)	1942	UCLA (6-1)	1959	Washington (3-1),	1975	UCLA (6-1)
1929	USC (6-1)	1943	USC (4-0)		USC (3-1)		& California (6-1)
1930	Washington St. (6-0)	1944	USC (3-0-2)		& UCLA (3-1)	1976	USC (7-0)
1931	USC (7-0)	1945	USC (5-1)	1960	Washington (4-0)	1977	Washington (6-1)
1932	USC (6-0)	1946	UCLA (7-0)	1961	UCLA (3-1)	1978	USC (6-1)

Major Conference Champions (Cont.)
Pacific-10 Conference (Cont.)

Year		Year		Year		Year	
1979	USC (6-0-1)	1988	USC (8-0)	1995	USC (6-1-1)	2001	Oregon (7-1)
1980	Washington (6-1)	1989	USC (6-0-1)		& Washington (6-1-1)	2002	Washington St. (7-1)
1981	Washington (6-2)	1990	Washington (7-1)	1996	Arizona St. (8-0)		& USC (7-1)
1982	UCLA (5-1-1)	1991	Washington (8-0)	1997	Washington St. (7-1)	2003	USC (7-1)
1983	UCLA (6-1-1)	1992	Washington (6-2)		& UCLA (7-1)	2004	USC (8-0)
1984	USC (7-1)		& Stanford (6-2)	1998	UCLA (8-0)	2005	USC (8-0)
1985	UCLA (6-2)	1993	UCLA (6-2),	1999	Stanford (7-1)	2006	USC (7-2)
1986	Arizona St. (5-1-1)		Arizona (6-2)	2000	Washington (7-1),		& California (7-2)
1987	USC (7-1)		& USC (6-2)		Oregon St. (7-1)		
	& UCLA (7-1)	1994	Oregon (7-1)		& Oregon (7-1)		

Southwest Conference (1914-95)

Founded in 1914 as Southwest Intercollegiate Athletic Conference. **Charter members** (8): Arkansas, Baylor, Oklahoma, Oklahoma A&M (now Oklahoma St.), Rice, Southwestern, Texas and Texas A&M. **Admitted later** (5): SMU (Southern Methodist) in 1918; Phillips University in 1920; TCU (Texas Christian) in 1923; Texas Tech in 1956 (began play in '60); Houston in 1971 (began play in '76). **Withdrew later** (13): Southwestern in 1917 (went independent); Oklahoma in 1920 (left for Missouri Valley after '19 season); Phillips in 1921; Oklahoma A&M (now Oklahoma St.) in 1925 (left for Big Six); Arkansas in 1990 (left for SEC after '91 season); Baylor, Texas, Texas A&M and Texas Tech in 1994 (all four left for Big 12 after '95 season); Rice, SMU and TCU in 1994 (all three left for WAC after '95 season); Houston in 1994 (left for Conference USA after '95 season). Conference folded on June 30, 1996.

Multiple titles: Texas (25); Texas A&M (17); Arkansas (13); SMU (9); TCU (9); Rice (7); Baylor (5); Houston (4); Texas Tech (2).

Year		Year		Year		Year	
1914	No champion	1940	Texas A&M (5-1)	1961	Texas (6-1)	1981	SMU (7-1)
1915	Oklahoma (3-0)	1941	Texas A&M (5-1)		& Arkansas (6-1)	1982	SMU (7-0-1)
1916	No champion	1942	Texas (5-1)	1962	Texas (6-0-1)	1983	Texas (8-0)
1917	Texas A&M (2-0)	1943	Texas (5-0)	1963	Texas (7-0)	1984	SMU (6-2)
1918	No champion	1944	TCU (3-1-1)	1964	Arkansas (7-0)		& Houston (6-2)
1919	Texas A&M (4-0)	1945	Texas (5-1)	1965	Arkansas (7-0)	1985	Texas A&M (7-1)
1920	Texas (5-0)	1946	Rice (5-1)	1966	SMU (6-1)	1986	Texas A&M (7-1)
1921	Texas A&M (3-0-2)		& Arkansas (5-1)	1967	Texas A&M (6-1)	1987	Texas A&M (6-1)
1922	Baylor (5-0)	1947	SMU (5-0-1)	1968	Arkansas (6-1)	1988	Arkansas (7-0)
1923	SMU (5-0)	1948	SMU (5-0-1)		& Texas (6-1)	1989	Arkansas (7-1)
1924	Baylor (4-0-1)	1949	Rice (6-0)	1969	Texas (7-0)	1990	Texas (8-0)
1925	Texas A&M (4-1)	1950	Texas (6-0)	1970	Texas (7-0)	1991	Texas A&M (8-0)
1926	SMU (5-0)	1951	TCU (5-1)	1971	Texas (6-1)	1992	Texas A&M (7-0)
1927	Texas A&M (4-0-1)	1952	Texas (6-0)	1972	Texas (7-0)	1993	Texas A&M (7-0)
1928	Texas (5-1)	1953	Rice (5-1)	1973	Texas (7-0)	1994	Baylor, Rice, TCU,
1929	TCU (4-0-1)		& Texas (5-1)	1974	Baylor (6-1)		Texas and Texas Tech†
1930	Texas (4-1)	1954	Arkansas (5-1)	1975	Arkansas (6-1),		(4-3)
1931	SMU (5-0-1)	1955	TCU (5-1)		Texas (6-1)	1995	Texas (7-0)
1932	TCU (6-0)	1956	Texas A&M (6-0)		& Texas A&M (6-1)		
1933	Arkansas (4-1)*	1957	Rice (5-1)	1976	Houston (7-1)	*Arkansas (4-1) forced to
1934	Rice (5-1)	1958	TCU (5-1)		& Texas Tech (7-1)	vacate 1933 title for use of
1935	SMU (6-0)	1959	Texas (5-1),	1977	Texas (8-0)	ineligible player.
1936	Arkansas (5-1)		TCU (5-1)	1978	Houston (7-1)	†Texas A&M had the best
1937	Rice (4-1-1)		& Arkansas (5-1)	1979	Houston (7-1)	record (6-0-1) in 1994 but
1938	TCU (6-0)	1960	Arkansas (6-1)		& Arkansas (7-1)	was on probation and
1939	Texas A&M (6-0)			1980	Baylor (8-0)	therefore ineligible for the
						Southwest championship.

Southeastern Conference

Founded in 1933 when charter members all left Southern Conference to form SEC. **Charter members** (13): Alabama, Auburn, Florida, Georgia, Georgia Tech, Kentucky, LSU (Louisiana St.), Mississippi, Mississippi St., Sewanee, Tennessee, Tulane and Vanderbilt. **Admitted later** (2): Arkansas and South Carolina in 1990 (both began play in '92). **Withdrew later** (3): Sewanee in 1940; Georgia Tech in 1964; and Tulane in 1966.

2007 playing membership (12): Alabama, Arkansas, Auburn, Florida, Georgia, Kentucky, LSU, Mississippi, Mississippi St., South Carolina, Tennessee and Vanderbilt. **Note:** Conference title decided by championship game between Western and Eastern division winners since 1992.

Multiple titles: Alabama (21); Tennessee (13); Georgia (12); Florida (10); LSU (9); Auburn and Mississippi (6); Georgia Tech (5); Kentucky and Tulane (3).

Year		Year		Year		Year	
1933	Alabama (5-0-1)	1940	Tennessee (5-0)	1948	Georgia (6-0)	1957	Auburn (7-0)
1934	Tulane (8-0)	1941	Mississippi St. (4-0-1)	1949	Tulane (5-1)	1958	LSU (6-0)
	& Alabama (7-0)	1942	Georgia (6-1)	1950	Kentucky (5-1)	1959	Georgia (7-0)
1935	LSU (5-0)	1943	Georgia Tech (3-0)	1951	Georgia Tech (7-0)	1960	Mississippi (5-0-1)
1936	LSU (6-0)	1944	Georgia Tech (4-0)		& Tennessee (6-0)	1961	Alabama (7-0)
1937	Alabama (6-0)	1945	Alabama (6-0)	1952	Georgia Tech (6-0)		& LSU (6-0)
1938	Tennessee (7-0)	1946	Georgia (5-0)	1953	Alabama (4-0-3)	1962	Mississippi (6-0)
1939	Tennessee (6-0),		& Tennessee (5-0)	1954	Mississippi (5-1)	1963	Mississippi (5-0-1)
	Georgia Tech (6-0)	1947	Mississippi (6-1)	1955	Mississippi (5-1)	1964	Alabama (8-0)
	& Tulane (5-0)			1956	Tennessee (6-0)		

Year		Year		Year		Year	
1965	Alabama (6-1-1)	1974	Alabama (6-0)	1981	Georgia (6-0)	1988	Auburn (6-1)
1966	Alabama (6-0)	1975	Alabama (6-0)		& Alabama (6-0)		& LSU (6-1)
	& Georgia (6-0)	1976	Georgia (5-1)	1982	Georgia (6-0)	1989	Alabama (6-1),
1967	Tennessee (6-0)		& Kentucky (5-1)	1983	Auburn (6-0)		Tennessee (6-0)
1968	Georgia (5-0-1)	1977	Alabama (7-0)	1984	Florida (5-0-1)*		& Auburn (6-1)
1969	Tennessee (5-1)		& Kentucky (7-0)	1985	Florida (5-1)†	1990	Florida (6-1)†
1970	LSU (5-0)	1978	Alabama (6-0)		& Tennessee (5-1)		& Tennessee (5-1-1)
1971	Alabama (7-0)	1979	Alabama (6-0)	1986	LSU (5-1)	1991	Florida (7-0)
1972	Alabama (7-1)	1980	Georgia (6-0)	1987	Auburn (5-0-1)		*Title vacated.
1973	Alabama (8-0)						†On probation, ineligible
							for championship.

SEC Championship Game

Since expanding to 12 teams and splitting into two divisions in 1992, the SEC has staged a conference championship game between the two division winners on the first Saturday in December. The game has been played at Legion Field in Birmingham, Ala., (1992-93) and the Georgia Dome in Atlanta (since 1994). The divisions: EAST— Florida, Georgia, Kentucky, South Carolina, Tennessee and Vanderbilt; WEST— Alabama, Arkansas, Auburn, LSU, Mississippi and Mississippi St.

Year		Year		Year	
1992	Alabama 28, Florida 21	1997	Tennessee 30, Auburn 29	2002	Georgia 30, Arkansas 3
1993	Florida 28, Alabama 23	1998	Tennessee 24, Miss. St. 14	2003	LSU 34, Georgia 13
1994	Florida 24, Alabama 23	1999	Alabama 34, Florida 7	2004	Auburn 38, Tennessee 28
1995	Florida 34, Arkansas 3	2000	Florida 28, Auburn 6	2005	Georgia 34, LSU 14
1996	Florida 45, Alabama 30	2001	LSU 31, Tennessee 20	2006	Florida 38, Arkansas 28

Sun Belt Conference

Founded in 2001 when the Sun Belt Conference sponsored football for the first time. **Charter members** (7): Arkansas State, Idaho, Louisiana-Lafayette, Louisiana-Monroe, Middle Tennessee State, New Mexico State and North Texas. **Admitted later** (4): Utah St. in 2003, Troy St. (now Troy) in 2004, Florida Atlantic and Florida International in 2005. **Withdrew later** (3): Idaho, New Mexico St. and Utah St. in 2005 (left for WAC). **2007 playing membership** (8): Arkansas State, Florida Atlantic, Florida International, Louisiana-Lafayette, Louisiana-Monroe, Middle Tennessee, North Texas and Troy

Multiple titles: North Texas (4); Middle Tennessee St. (2)

Year		Year		Year	
2001	North Texas (5-1)	2004	North Texas (7-0)	2006	Troy (6-1)
	& Mid. Tenn. St. (5-1)	2005	Arkansas St. (5-2),		& Mid. Tenn. St. (6-1)
2002	North Texas (6-0)		LA-Lafayette (5-2),		
2003	North Texas (7-0)		LA-Monroe (5-2)		

Western Athletic Conference

Founded in 1962 when charter members left the Skyline and Border conferences to form theWAC. **Charter members** (6): Arizona and Arizona St. from Border; BYU (Brigham Young), New Mexico, Utah and Wyoming from Skyline. **Admitted later** (18): Colorado St. and UTEP (Texas-El Paso) in 1967 (both began play in '68); San Diego St. in 1978; Hawaii in 1979; Air Force in 1980; Fresno St. in 1991 (began play in '92); Rice, San Jose St., SMU , Tulsa and UNLV in 1994 (all began play in '96); Nevada in 2000; Boise St. and Louisiana Tech in 2001; Idaho, New Mexico St. and Utah St. in 2005. **Withdrew later** (13): Arizona and Arizona St. in 1978 (left for Pac-10 after '77 season); Air Force, BYU, Colorado St., New Mexico, San Diego St., UNLV, Utah and Wyoming (left to form Mountain West conference in '99); TCU in 2000 (left for Conference USA after 2000 season); Rice, SMU, Tulsa and UTEP in 2005 (left for Conference USA). **2007 playing membership** (9): Boise St., Fresno St., Hawaii, Idaho, Louisiana Tech, Nevada, New Mexico St., San Jose St., and Utah St.

Multiple titles: BYU (19); Arizona St. and Wyoming (7); Boise St. (5); Air Force, Fresno St., New Mexico and Colorado St. (3); Arizona, Hawaii, TCU and Utah (2).

Year		Year		Year		Year	
1962	New Mexico (2-1-1)	1974	BYU (6-0-1)	1986	San Diego St. (7-1)		BYU (6-2)
1963	New Mexico (3-1)	1975	Arizona St. (7-0)	1987	Wyoming (8-0)		& Utah (6-2)
1964	Utah (3-1),	1976	BYU (6-1)	1988	Wyoming (8-0)	1996-98	See below
	New Mexico (3-1)		& Wyoming (6-1)	1989	BYU (7-1)	1999	Fresno St. (5-2),
	& Arizona (3-1)	1977	Arizona St. (6-1)	1990	BYU (7-1)		Hawaii (7-2)
1965	BYU (4-1)		& BYU (6-1)	1991	BYU (7-0-1)		& TCU (7-2)
1966	Wyoming (5-0)	1978	BYU (5-1)	1992	Hawaii (6-2),	2000	TCU (7-1)
1967	Wyoming (5-0)	1979	BYU (7-0)		BYU (6-2)		& UTEP (7-1)
1968	Wyoming (6-1)	1980	BYU (6-1)		& Fresno St. (6-2)	2001	La. Tech (7-1)
1969	Arizona St. (6-1)	1981	BYU (7-1)	1993	BYU (6-2),	2002	Boise St. (8-0)
1970	Arizona St. (7-0)	1982	BYU (7-1)		Fresno St. (6-2)	2003	Boise St. (8-0)
1971	Arizona St. (7-0)	1983	BYU (7-0)		& Wyoming (6-2)	2004	Boise St. (8-0)
1972	Arizona St. (5-1)	1984	BYU (8-0)	1994	Colorado St. (7-1)	2005	Nevada (7-1)
1973	Arizona St. (6-1)	1985	Air Force (7-1)	1995	Colorado St. (6-2),		& Boise St. (7-1)
	& Arizona (6-1)		& BYU (7-1)		Air Force (6-2),	2006	Boise St. (8-0)

WAC Championship Game (1996-98)

In addition to expanding to 16 teams and splitting into two divisions in 1996, the WAC staged a conference championship game between the two division winners on the first Saturday in December at Sam Boyd Stadium in Las Vegas until eight teams split off and formed the Mountain West Conference in 1999. The divisions: PACIFIC—BYU, Fresno St., Hawaii, New Mexico, San Diego St., San Jose St., UTEP, Utah; MOUNTAIN—Air Force, Colorado St., Rice, SMU, TCU, Tulsa, UNLV, Wyoming.

Year		Year		Year	
1996	BYU 28, Wyoming 25 (OT)	1997	Colorado St. 41, New Mexico 13	1998	Air Force 20, BYU 13

Annual NCAA Division I-A Leaders

Note that Oklahoma A&M is now Oklahoma St. and Texas Mines is now UTEP.

Rushing

Individual championship decided on Rushing Yards (1937-69), and on Yards Per Game (since 1970).

Multiple winners: Troy Davis, Marshall Faulk, Art Luppino, Ed Marinaro, Rudy Mobley, Jim Pilot, O.J. Simpson, LaDa nian Tomlinson and Ricky Williams (2).

Year		Car	Yards	Year		Car	Yards	P/Gm
1937	Byron (Whizzer) White, Colorado	181	1121	1970	Ed Marinaro, Cornell	285	1425	158.3
1938	Len Eshmont, Fordham	132	831	1971	Ed Marinaro, Cornell	356	1881	209.0
1939	John Polanski, Wake Forest	137	882	1972	Pete VanValkenburg, BYU	232	1386	138.6
1940	Al Ghesquiere, Detroit	146	957	1973	Mark Kellar, Northern Ill	291	1719	156.3
1941	Frank Sinkwich, Georgia	209	1103	1974	Louie Giammona, Utah St.	329	1534	153.4
1942	Rudy Mobley, Hardin-Simmons	187	1281	1975	Ricky Bell, USC	357	1875	170.5
1943	Creighton Miller, Notre Dame	151	911	1976	Tony Dorsett, Pittsburgh	338	1948	177.1
1944	Red Williams, Minnesota	136	911	1977	Earl Campbell, Texas	267	1744	158.5
1945	Bob Fenimore, Oklahoma A&M	142	1048	1978	Billy Sims, Oklahoma	231	1762	160.2
1946	Rudy Mobley, Hardin-Simmons	227	1262	1979	Charles White, USC.	293	1803	180.3
1947	Wilton Davis, Hardin-Simmons	193	1173	1980	George Rogers, S. Carolina	297	1781	161.9
1948	Fred Wendt, Texas Mines	184	1570	1981	Marcus Allen, USC.	403	2342	212.9
1949	John Dottley, Ole Miss	208	1312	1982	Ernest Anderson, Okla. St.	353	1877	170.6
1950	Wilford White, Arizona St	199	1502	1983	Mike Rozier, Nebraska	275	2148	179.0
1951	Ollie Matson, San Francisco	245	1566	1984	Keith Byars, Ohio St.	313	1655	150.5
1952	Howie Waugh, Tulsa	164	1372	1985	Lorenzo White, Mich. St.	386	1908	173.5
1953	J.C. Caroline, Illinois	194	1256	1986	Paul Palmer, Temple	346	1866	169.6
1954	Art Luppino, Arizona	179	1359	1987	Ickey Woods, UNLV	259	1658	150.7
1955	Art Luppino, Arizona	209	1313	1988	Barry Sanders, Okla. St.	344	2628	238.9
1956	Jim Crawford, Wyoming	200	1104	1989	Anthony Thompson, Ind	358	1793	163.0
1957	Leon Burton, Arizona St	117	1126	1990	Gerald Hudson, Okla. St.	279	1642	149.3
1958	Dick Bass, Pacific	205	1361	1991	Marshall Faulk, S. Diego St.	201	1429	158.8
1959	Pervis Atkins, New Mexico St	130	971	1992	Marshall Faulk, S. Diego St.	265	1630	163.0
1960	Bob Gaiters, New Mexico St	197	1338	1993	LeShon Johnson, No. Ill.	327	1976	179.6
1961	Jim Pilot, New Mexico St	191	1278	1994	Rashaan Salaam, Colorado	298	2055	186.8
1962	Jim Pilot, New Mexico St	208	1247	1995	Troy Davis, Iowa St.	345	2010	182.7
1963	Dave Casinelli, Memphis St	219	1016	1996	Troy Davis, Iowa St.	402	2185	198.6
1964	Brian Piccolo, Wake Forest	252	1044	1997	Ricky Williams, Texas.	279	1893	172.1
1965	Mike Garrett, USC	267	1440	1998	Ricky Williams, Texas.	361	2124	193.1
1966	Ray McDonald, Idaho	259	1329	1999	LaDainian Tomlinson, TCU	268	1850	168.2
1967	O.J. Simpson, USC.	266	1415	2000	LaDainian Tomlinson, TCU	369	2158	196.2
1968	O.J. Simpson, USC.	355	1709	2001	Chance Kretschmer, Nevada	302	1732	157.5
1969	Steve Owens, Oklahoma	358	1523	2002	Larry Johnson, Penn St.	271	2087	160.5
				2003	Patrick Cobbs, No. Texas	307	1680	152.7
				2004	Jamario Thomas, No. Texas	285	1801	180.1
				2005	DeAngelo Williams, Memphis	310	1964	178.6
				2006	Garrett Wolfe, Northern Ill.	309	1928	148.3

All-Purpose Yardage

Multiple winners: Marcus Allen, Pervis Atkins, Ryan Benjamin, Troy Davis, Troy Edwards, Louie Giammona, Tom Harmo Art Luppino, Napolean McCallum, O.J. Simpson, Charles White and Gary Wood (2).

Year		Yards	P/Gm	Year		Yards	P/Gm
1937	Byron (Whizzer) White, Colorado	1970	246.3	1957	Overton Curtis, Utah St	1608	160.8
1938	Parker Hall, Ole Miss	1420	129.1	1958	Dick Bass, Pacific	1878	187.8
1939	Tom Harmon, Michigan.	1208	151.0	1959	Pervis Atkins, New Mexico St	1800	180.0
1940	Tom Harmon, Michigan.	1312	164.0	1960	Pervis Atkins, New Mexico St	1613	161.3
1941	Bill Dudley, Virginia	1674	186.0	1961	Jim Pilot, New Mexico St	1606	160.6
1942	Complete records not available			1962	Gary Wood, Cornell	1395	155.0
1943	Stan Koslowski, Holy Cross	1411	176.4	1963	Gary Wood, Cornell	1508	167.6
1944	Red Williams, Minnesota	1467	163.0	1964	Donny Anderson, Texas Tech	1710	171.0
1945	Bob Fenimore, Oklahoma A&M	1577	197.1	1965	Floyd Little, Syracuse	1990	199.0
1946	Rudy Mobley, Hardin-Simmons	1765	176.5	1966	Frank Quayle, Virginia	1616	161.6
1947	Wilton Davis, Hardin-Simmons	1798	179.8	1967	O.J. Simpson, USC	1700	188.9
1948	Lou Kusserow, Columbia	1737	193.0	1968	O.J. Simpson, USC.	1966	196.6
1949	Johnny Papit, Virginia	1611	179.0	1969	Lynn Moore, Army	1795	179.5
1950	Wilford White, Arizona St.	2065	206.5	1970	Don McCauley, North Carolina	2021	183.7
1951	Ollie Matson, San Francisco	2037	226.3	1971	Ed Marinaro, Cornell	1932	214.7
1952	Billy Vessels, Oklahoma	1512	151.2	1972	Howard Stevens, Louisville.	2132	213.2
1953	J.C. Caroline, Illinois	1470	163.3	1973	Willard Harrell, Pacific	1777	177.7
1954	Art Luppino, Arizona	2193	219.3	1974	Louie Giammona, Utah St	1984	198.4
1955	Tim Swink, TCU	1702	170.2	1975	Louie Giammona, Utah St	2045	185.9
	& Art Luppino, Arizona	1702	170.2	1976	Tony Dorsett, Pittsburgh	2021	183.7
1956	Jack Hill, Utah St	1691	169.1	1977	Earl Campbell, Texas	1855	168.6
				1978	Charles White, USC.	2096	174.7

Year		Yards	P/Gm	Year		Yards	P/Gm
1979	Charles White, USC	1941	194.1	1994	Rashaan Salaam, Colorado	2349	213.5
1980	Marcus Allen, USC	1794	179.4	1995	Troy Davis, Iowa St.	2466	224.2
1981	Marcus Allen, USC	2559	232.6	1996	Troy Davis, Iowa St.	2364	214.9
1982	Carl Monroe, Utah	2036	185.1	1997	Troy Edwards, La. Tech	2144	194.9
1983	Napoleon McCallum, Navy	2385	216.8	1998	Troy Edwards, La. Tech	2784	232.0
1984	Keith Byars, Ohio St	2284	207.6	1999	Trevor Insley, Nevada	2176	197.8
1985	Napoleon McCallum, Navy	2330	211.8	2000	Emmett White, Utah St.	2628	238.9
1986	Paul Palmer, Temple	2633	239.4	2001	Levron Williams, Indiana	2201	200.1
1987	Eric Wilkerson, Kent St.	2074	188.6	2002	Larry Johnson, Penn St.	2655	204.2
1988	Barry Sanders, Oklahoma St.	3250	295.5	2003	DeAngelo Williams, Memphis	2113	192.1
1989	Mike Pringle, CS-Fullerton	2690	244.6	2004	Darren Sproles, Kansas St.	2067	187.9
1990	Glyn Milburn, Stanford	2222	202.0	2005	Reggie Bush, USC	2890	222.3
1991	Ryan Benjamin, Pacific.	2995	249.6	2006	Garrett Wolfe, Northern Ill.	2177	167.5
1992	Ryan Benjamin, Pacific.	2597	236.1				
1993	LeShon Johnson, Northern Ill.	2082	189.3				

Total Offense

Individual championship decided on Total Yards (1937-69) and on Yards Per Game (since 1970).

Multiple winners: Tim Rattay (3); Colt Brennan, Johnny Bright, Bob Fenimore, Mike Maxwell and Jim McMahon (2).

Year		Plays	Yards	Year		Plays	Yards	P/Gm
1937	Byron (Whizzer) White, Colorado.	224	1596	1970	Pat Sullivan, Auburn.	333	2856	285.6
1938	Davey O'Brien, TCU	291	1847	1971	Gary Huff, Florida St.	386	2653	241.2
1939	Kenny Washington, UCLA	259	1370	1972	Don Strock, Va. Tech	480	3170	288.2
1940	Johnny Knolla, Creighton	298	1420	1973	Jesse Freitas, San Diego St.	410	2901	263.7
1941	Bud Schwenk, Washington-MO	354	1928	1974	Steve Joachim, Temple	331	2227	222.7
1942	Frank Sinkwich, Georgia.	341	2187	1975	Gene Swick, Toledo	490	2706	246.0
1943	Bob Hoernschemeyer, Indiana	355	1648	1976	Tommy Kramer, Rice	562	3272	297.5
1944	Bob Fenimore, Oklahoma A&M.	241	1758	1977	Doug Williams, Grambling	377	3229	293.5
1945	Bob Fenimore, Oklahoma A&M.	203	1641	1978	Mike Ford, SMU	459	2957	268.8
1946	Travis Tidwell, Auburn	339	1715	1979	Marc Wilson, BYU	488	3580	325.5
1947	Fred Enke, Arizona	329	1941	1980	Jim McMahon, BYU	540	4627	385.6
1948	Stan Heath, Nevada-Reno.	233	1992	1981	Jim McMahon, BYU	487	3458	345.8
1949	Johnny Bright, Drake	275	1950	1982	Todd Dillon, Long Beach St	585	3587	326.1
1950	Johnny Bright, Drake	320	2400	1983	Steve Young, BYU.	531	4346	395.1
1951	Dick Kazmaier, Princeton	272	1827	1984	Robbie Bosco, BYU	543	3932	327.7
1952	Ted Marchibroda, Detroit	305	1813	1985	Jim Everett, Purdue	518	3589	326.3
1953	Paul Larson, California.	262	1572	1986	Mike Perez, San Jose St.	425	2969	329.9
1954	George Shaw, Oregon	276	1536	1987	Todd Santos, San Diego St.	562	3688	307.3
1955	George Welsh, Navy.	203	1348	1988	Scott Mitchell, Utah	589	4299	390.8
1956	John Brodie, Stanford.	295	1642	1989	Andre Ware, Houston	628	4661	423.7
1957	Bob Newman, Washington St	263	1444	1990	David Klingler, Houston	704	5221	474.6
1958	Dick Bass, Pacific	218	1440	1991	Ty Detmer, BYU	478	4001	333.4
1959	Dick Norman, Stanford	319	2018	1992	Jimmy Klingler, Houston	544	3768	342.6
1960	Billy Kilmer, UCLA.	292	1889	1993	Chris Vargas, Nevada	535	4332	393.8
1961	Dave Hoppmann, Iowa St.	320	1638	1994	Mike Maxwell, Nevada	477	3498	318.0
1962	Terry Baker, Oregon St	318	2276	1995	Mike Maxwell, Nevada	443	3623	402.6
1963	George Mira, Miami-FL	394	2318	1996	Josh Wallwork, Wyoming	525	4209	350.8
1964	Jerry Rhome, Tulsa	470	3128	1997	Tim Rattay, La. Tech	541	3968	360.7
1965	Bill Anderson, Tulsa	580	3343	1998	Tim Rattay, La. Tech	602	4840	403.3
1966	Virgil Carter, BYU.	388	2545	1999	Tim Rattay, La. Tech	562	3810	381.0
1967	Sal Olivas, New Mexico St.	368	2184	2000	Drew Brees, Purdue	564	3939	358.1
1968	Greg Cook, Cincinnati	507	3210	2001	Rex Grossman, Florida	429	3904	354.9
1969	Dennis Shaw, San Diego St	388	3197	2002	Byron Leftwich, Marshall	528	4267	355.6
				2003	B.J. Symons, Texas Tech	798	5976	459.7
				2004	Sonny Cumbie, Texas Tech	694	4575	381.3
				2005	Colt Brennan, Hawaii	614	4455	371.3
				2006	Colt Brennan, Hawaii	645	5915	422.5

Sacks

Pass sacks have only been compiled by the NCAA since the 2000 season.

Year		Gms	Total	Year		Gms	Total
2000	Michael Josiah, Louisville	91	12½	2004	Jonathan Goddard, Marshall	12	16
2001	Dwight Freeney, Syracuse	12	17½	2005	Elvis Dumervil, Louisville	12	20
2002	Terrell Suggs, Arizona St.	14	24	2006	Ameer Ismail, Western Mich.	13	17
2003	Dave Ball, UCLA	13	16½				
	Kenechi Udeze, USC	13	16½				
	& D.D. Acholonu, Wash. St.	13	16½				

Annual NCAA Division I-A Leaders (Cont.)
Passing

Individual championship decided on Completions (1937-69), on Completions Per Game (1970-78) and on Passing Efficiency rating points (since 1979).

Multiple winners: Elvis Grbac, Don Heinrich, Jim McMahon, Davey O'Brien and Don Trull (2).

Year		Cmp	Pct	TD	Yds
1937	Davey O'Brien, TCU	.94	.402	–	969
1938	Davey O'Brien, TCU	.93	.557	–	1457
1939	Kay Eakin, Arkansas	.78	.404	–	962
1940	Billy Sewell, Wash. St	.86	.494	–	1023
1941	Bud Schwenk, Wash.-MO	.114	.487	–	1457
1942	Ray Evans, Kansas	.101	.505	–	1117
1943	Johnny Cook, Georgia	.73	.465	–	1007
1944	Paul Rickards, Pittsburgh	.84	.472	–	997
1945	Al Dekdebrun, Cornell	.90	.464	–	1227
1946	Travis Tidwell, Auburn	.79	.500	5	943
1947	Charlie Conerly, Ole Miss	.133	.571	18	1367
1948	Stan Heath, Nev-Reno	.126	.568	22	2005
1949	Adrian Burk, Baylor	.110	.576	14	1428
1950	Don Heinrich, Washington	.134	.606	14	1846
1951	Don Klosterman, Loyola-CA	.159	.505	9	1843
1952	Don Heinrich, Washington	.137	.507	13	1647
1953	Bob Garrett, Stanford	.118	.576	17	1637
1954	Paul Larson, California	.125	.641	10	1537
1955	George Welsh, Navy	.94	.627	8	1319
1956	John Brodie, Stanford	.139	.579	12	1633
1957	Ken Ford, H-Simmons	.115	.561	14	1254
1958	Buddy Humphrey, Baylor	.112	.574	7	1316
1959	Dick Norman, Stanford	.152	.578	11	1963
1960	Harold Stephens, H-Simm	.145	.566	3	1254
1961	Chon Gallegos, S. Jose St	.117	.594	14	1480
1962	Don Trull, Baylor	.125	.546	11	1627
1963	Don Trull, Baylor	.174	.565	12	2157
1964	Jerry Rhome, Tulsa	.224	.687	32	2870
1965	Bill Anderson, Tulsa	.296	.582	30	3464
1966	John Eckman, Wichita St	.195	.426	7	2339
1967	Terry Stone, N. Mexico	.160	.476	9	1946
1968	Chuck Hixson, SMU	.265	.566	21	3103
1969	John Reaves, Florida	.222	.561	24	2896

Year		Cmp	P/Gm	TD	Yds
1970	Sonny Sixkiller, Wash	.186	18.6	15	2303
1971	Brian Sipe, S. Diego St	.196	17.8	17	2532
1972	Don Strock, Va. Tech	.228	20.7	16	3243
1973	Jesse Freitas, S. Diego St.	.227	20.6	21	2993
1974	Steve Bartkowski, Cal	.182	16.5	12	2580
1975	Craig Penrose, S. Diego St	.199	18.0	15	2660
1976	Tommy Kramer, Rice	.269	24.5	21	3317
1977	Guy Benjamin, Stanford	.208	20.8	19	2521
1978	Steve Dils, Stanford	.247	22.5	22	2943

Year		Cmp	TD	Yds	Rating
1979	Turk Schonert, Stanford	.148	19	1922	163.0
1980	Jim McMahon, BYU	.284	47	4571	176.9
1981	Jim McMahon, BYU	.272	30	3555	155.0
1982	Tom Ramsey, UCLA	.191	21	2824	153.5
1983	Steve Young, BYU	.306	33	3902	168.5
1984	Doug Flutie, BC	.233	27	3454	152.9
1985	Jim Harbaugh, Michigan	.139	18	1913	163.7
1986	Vinny Testaverde, Miami-Fl	.175	26	2557	165.8
1987	Don McPherson, Syracuse	.129	22	2341	164.3
1988	Timm Rosenbach, Wash. St.	199	23	2791	162.0
1989	Ty Detmer, BYU	.265	32	4560	175.6
1990	Shawn Moore, Virginia	.144	21	2262	160.7
1991	Elvis Grbac, Michigan	.152	24	1955	169.0
1992	Elvis Grbac, Michigan	.112	15	1465	154.2
1993	Trent Dilfer, Fresno St.	.217	28	3276	173.1
1994	Kerry Collins, Penn St.	.176	21	2679	172.9
1995	Danny Wuerffel, Florida	.210	35	3266	178.4
1996	Steve Sarkisian, BYU	.278	33	4027	173.6
1997	Cade McNown, UCLA.	.173	22	2877	168.6
1998	Shaun King, Tulane	.223	36	3232	183.3
1999	Michael Vick, Va. Tech.	.90	12	1840	180.4
2000	Bart Hendricks, Boise St.	.210	35	3364	170.6
2001	Rex Grossman, Florida	.259	34	3896	170.8
2002	Brad Banks, Iowa	.170	26	2573	157.1
2003	Philip Rivers, N.C. State	.348	34	4491	170.5
2004	Stefan Lefors, Louisville	.189	20	2596	181.7
2005	Rudy Carpenter, Arizona St.	156	17	2273	175.0
2006	Colt Brennan, Hawaii	.406	58	5549	186.0

Receptions

Championship decided on Passes Caught (1937-69) and on Catches Per Game (since 1970). Touchdown totals unavailable in 1939 and 1941-45.

Multiple winners: Neil Armstrong, Hugh Campbell, Manny Hazard, Reid Moseley, Jason Phillips, Howard Twilley and Alex Van Dyke (2).

Year		No	TD	Yds
1937	Jim Benton, Arkansas	.47	7	754
1938	Sam Boyd, Baylor	.32	5	537
1939	Ken Kavanagh, LSU	.30	–	467
1940	Eddie Bryant, Virginia	.30	2	222
1941	Hank Stanton, Arizona	.50	–	820
1942	Bill Rogers, Texas A&M	.39	–.	432
1943	Neil Armstrong, Okla. A&M	.39	–	317
1944	Reid Moseley, Georgia	.32	–	506
1945	Reid Moseley, Georgia	.31	–	662
1946	Neil Armstrong, Okla. A&M	.32	1	479
1947	Barney Poole, Ole Miss	.52	8	513
1948	Red O'Quinn, Wake Forest	.39	7	605
1949	Art Weiner, N. Carolina	.52	7	762
1950	Gordon Cooper, Denver	.46	8	569
1951	Dewey McConnell, Wyoming	.47	9	725
1952	Ed Brown, Fordham	.57	6	774
1953	John Carson, Georgia	.45	4	663
1954	Jim Hanifan, California	.44	7	569
1955	Hank Burnine, Missouri	.44	2	594
1956	Art Powell, San Jose St	.40	5	583
1957	Stuart Vaughan, Utah	.53	5	756

Year		No	TD	Yds
1958	Dave Hibbert, Arizona	.61	4	606
1959	Chris Burford, Stanford	.61	6	756
1960	Hugh Campbell, Wash. St	.66	10	881
1961	Hugh Campbell, Wash. St	.53	5	723
1962	Vern Burke, Oregon St	.69	10	1007
1963	Lawrence Elkins, Baylor	.70	8	873
1964	Howard Twilley, Tulsa	.95	13	1178
1965	Howard Twilley, Tulsa	.134	16	1779
1966	Glenn Meltzer, Wichita St	.91	4	1115
1967	Bob Goodridge, Vanderbilt	.79	6	1114
1968	Ron Sellers, Florida St	.86	12	1496
1969	Jerry Hendren, Idaho	.95	12	1452

Year		No	P/Gm	TD	Yds
1970	Mike Mikolayunas, Davidson	87	8.7	8	1128
1971	Tom Reynolds, San Diego St	.67	6.7	7	1070
1972	Tom Forzani, Utah St	.85	7.7	8	1169
1973	Jay Miller, BYU	.100	9.1	8	1181
1974	D. McDonald, San Diego St	.86	7.8	7	1157
1975	Bob Farnham, Brown	.56	6.2	2	701
1976	Billy Ryckman, La. Tech	.77	7.0	10	1382
1977	W. Tolleson, W. Carolina	.73	6.6	7	1101

Year		No	P/Gm	TD	Yds
1978	Dave Petzke, Northern Ill	91	8.3	11	1217
1979	Rick Beasley, Appalach. St	74	6.7	12	1205
1980	Dave Young, Purdue	67	6.1	8	917
1981	Pete Harvey, N. Texas St	57	6.3	3	743
1982	Vincent White, Stanford.	68	6.8	8	677
1983	Keith Edwards, Vanderbilt	97	8.8	8	909
1984	David Williams, Illinois	101	9.2	8	1278
1985	Rodney Carter, Purdue	98	8.9	4	1099
1986	Mark Templeton, L. Beach St	99	9.0	2	688
1987	Jason Phillips, Houston	99	9.0	3	875
1988	Jason Phillips, Houston	108	9.8	15	1444
1989	Manny Hazard, Houston	142	12.9	22	1689
1990	Manny Hazard, Houston	78	7.8	9	946
1991	Fred Gilbert, Houston.	106	9.6	7	957
1992	Sherman Smith, Houston	103	9.4	6	923
1993	Chris Penn, Tulsa	105	9.6	12	1578
1994	Alex Van Dyke, Nevada	98	8.9	10	1246
1995	Alex Van Dyke, Nevada	129	11.7	16	1854
1996	Damond Wilkins, Nevada	114	10.4	4	1121
1997	Eugene Baker, Kent	103	9.4	18	1549
1998	Troy Edwards, La. Tech	140	11.7	27	1996
1999	Trevor Insley, Nevada	134	12.2	13	2060
2000	James Jordan, La. Tech	109	9.1	4	1003
2001	Kevin Curtis, Utah St.	100	9.1	10	1531
2002	Nate Burleson, Nevada	138	11.5	12	1629
2003	Lance Moore, Toledo	103	8.6	9	1194
2004	Dante Ridgeway, Ball St.	105	9.6	8	1399
2005	Greg Jennings, W. Mich.	98	8.9	14	1259
2006	Chris Williams, N. Mex. St.	92	7.7	12	1415

Scoring

Championship decided on Total Points (1937-69) and on Points Per Game (since 1970).

Multiple winners: Tom Harmon and Billy Sims (2).

Year		TD	XP	FG	Pts	P/Gm
1937	Byron (Whizzer) White, Colo	16	23	1	122	
1938	Parker Hall, Ole Miss	11	7	0	73	
1939	Tom Harmon, Michigan	14	15	1	102	
1940	Tom Harmon, Michigan	16	18	1	117	
1941	Bill Dudley, Virginia	18	23	1	134	
1942	Bob Steuber, Missouri.	18	13	0	121	
1943	Steve Van Buren, LSU	14	14	0	98	
1944	Glenn Davis, Army	20	0	0	120	
1945	Doc Blanchard, Army.	19	1	0	115	
1946	Gene Roberts, Tenn-Chatt.	18	9	0	117	
1947	Lou Gambino, Maryland	16	0	0	96	
1948	Fred Wendt, Texas Mines.	20	32	0	152	
1949	George Thomas, Oklahoma	19	3	0	117	
1950	Bobby Reynolds, Nebraska.	22	25	0	157	
1951	Ollie Matson, San Francisco	21	0	0	126	
1952	Jackie Parker, Miss. St.	16	24	0	120	
1953	Earl Lindley, Utah St.	13	3	0	81	
1954	Art Luppino, Arizona	24	22	0	166	
1955	Jim Swink, TCU	20	5	0	125	
1956	Clendon Thomas, Oklahoma	18	0	0	108	
1957	Leon Burton, Ariz. St.	16	0	0	96	
1958	Dick Bass, Pacific	18	8	0	116	
1959	Pervis Atkins, N. Mexico St.	17	5	0	107	
1960	Bob Gaiters, N. Mexico St.	23	7	0	145	
1961	Jim Pilot, N. Mexico St.	21	12	0	138	
1962	Jerry Logan, W. Texas St.	13	32	0	110	
1963	Cosmo Iacavazzi, Princeton	14	0	0	84	
	& Dave Casinelli, Memphis St.	14	0	0	84	
1964	Brian Piccolo, Wake Forest	17	9	0	111	
1965	Howard Twilley, Tulsa	16	31	0	127	
1966	Ken Hebert, Houston	11	41	2	113	
1967	Leroy Keyes, Purdue	19	0	0	114	
1968	Jim O'Brien, Cincinnati	12	31	13	142	
1969	Steve Owens, Oklahoma	23	0	0	138	
1970	Brian Bream, Air Force	20	0	0	120	12.0
	& Gary Kosins, Dayton	18	0	0	108	12.0
1971	Ed Marinaro, Cornell	24	4	0	148	16.4
1972	Harold Henson, Ohio St.	20	0	0	120	12.0
1973	Jim Jennings, Rutgers	21	2	0	128	11.6
1974	Bill Marek, Wisconsin	19	0	0	114	12.7
1975	Pete Johnson, Ohio St	25	0	0	150	13.6
1976	Tony Dorsett, Pitt	22	2	0	134	12.2
1977	Earl Campbell, Texas	19	0	0	114	10.4
1978	Billy Sims, Oklahoma	20	0	0	120	10.9
1979	Billy Sims, Oklahoma	22	0	0	132	12.0
1980	Sammy Winder, So. Miss	20	0	0	120	10.9
1981	Marcus Allen, USC	23	0	0	138	12.5
1982	Greg Allen, Fla. St	21	0	0	126	11.5
1983	Mike Rozier, Nebraska	29	0	0	174	14.5
1984	Keith Byars, Ohio St	24	0	0	144	13.1
1985	Bernard White, B. Green.	19	0	0	114	10.4
1986	Steve Bartalo, Colo. St	19	0	0	114	10.4
1987	Paul Hewitt, S. Diego St.	24	0	0	144	12.0
1988	Barry Sanders, Okla.St.	39	0	0	234	21.3
1989	Anthony Thompson, Ind	25	4	0	154	14.0
1990	Stacey Robinson, No. Ill.	19	6	0	120	10.9
1991	Marshall Faulk, S.D. St.	23	2	0	140	15.6
1992	Garrison Hearst, Georgia	21	0	0	126	11.5
1993	Bam Morris, Texas Tech	22	2	0	134	12.2
1994	Rashaan Salaam, Colo	24	0	0	144	13.1
1995	Eddie George, Ohio St.	24	0	0	144	12.0
1996	Corey Dillon, Washington	23	0	0	138	12.6
1997	Ricky Williams, Texas	25	2	0	152	13.8
1998	Troy Edwards, La. Tech	31	2	0	188	15.7
1999	Shaun Alexander, Alabama	24	0	0	144	13.1
2000	Lee Suggs, Va. Tech	28	0	0	168	15.3
2001	Luke Staley, BYU	28	2	0	170	15.5
2002	Brock Forsey, Boise St.	32	0	0	192	14.8
2003	Patrick Cobbs, No. Texas	21	0	0	126	11.5
2004	Tyler Jones, Boise St.	0	69	24	141	11.8
2005	Michael Bush, Louisville	24	0	0	144	14.4
2006	Ian Johnson, Boise St.	25	0	0	152	12.7

All-Time Best Records by a Starting Quarterback

(Minimum 25 starts) Source: NCAA Record Book

	Years	W-L-T	Win Pct.
Chuck Ealey, Toledo	1969-71	35-0-0	1.000
Jimmy Harris, Oklahoma	1954-56	25-0-0	1.000
Steve Davis, Oklahoma	1973-75	32-1-1	.956
Ken Dorsey, Miami-FL	1999-2002	38-2-0	.950
Matt Leinart, USC	2002-05	37-2-0	.949
Jerry Tagge, Nebraska	1969-71	24-1-1	.942

All-Time NCAA Division I-A Leaders

Through the 2006 regular season. The NCAA does not recognize active players among career Per Game leaders.

CAREER

Passing

(Minimum 500 Completions)

Passing Efficiency	Years	Rating
1 Ryan Dinwiddie, Boise St.	2000-03	168.9
2 Danny Wuerffel, Florida	1993-96	163.6
3 Omar Jacobs, Bowling Green	2003-05	163.5
4 Ty Detmer, BYU	1988-91	162.7
5 Steve Sarkisian, BYU	1995-96	162.0

Yards Gained	Years	Yards
1 Timmy Chang, Hawaii	2000-04	17,072
2 Ty Detmer, BYU	1988-91	15,031
3 Philip Rivers, N.C. State	2000-03	13,484
4 Kevin Kolb, Houston	2003-06	12,964
5 Tim Rattay, La. Tech	1997-99	12,746

Completions	Years	No
1 Timmy Chang, Hawaii	2000-04	1388
2 Kliff Kingsbury, Texas Tech	1999-02	1231
3 Philip Rivers, N.C. State	2000-03	1147
4 Luke McCown, La. Tech	2000-03	1063
5 Chris Redman, Louisville	1996-99	1031

Receptions

Catches	Years	No
1 Taylor Stubblefield, Purdue	2001-04	316
2 Josh Davis, Marshall	2001-04	306
3 Taurean Henderson, Texas Tech	2002-05	303
4 Arnold Jackson, Louisville	1997-00	300
5 Trevor Insley, Nevada	1996-99	298

Catches Per Game	Years	No	P/Gm
1 Manny Hazard, Houston	1989-90	220	10.5
2 Alex Van Dyke, Nevada	1994-95	227	10.3
3 Howard Twilley, Tulsa	1963-65	261	10.0
4 Jason Phillips, Houston	1987-88	207	9.4
5 Troy Edwards, La. Tech	1996-98	280	8.2

Yards Gained	Years	No	Yards
1 Trevor Insley, Nevada	1996-99	298	5005
2 Marcus Harris, Wyoming	1993-96	259	4518
3 Rashaun Woods, Oklahoma St.	2000-03	293	4412
4 Ryan Yarborough, Wyoming	1990-93	229	4357
5 Troy Edwards, La. Tech	1996-98	280	4352

Rushing

Yards Gained	Years	Yards
1 Ron Dayne, Wisconsin	1996-99	6397
2 Ricky Williams, Texas	1995-98	6279
3 Tony Dorsett, Pittsburgh	1973-76	6082
4 DeAngelo Williams, Memphis	2002-05	6026
5 Charles White, USC	1976-79	5598

Yards Per Game	Years	Yards	P/Gm
1 Ed Marinaro, Cornell	1969-71	4715	174.6
2 O.J. Simpson, USC	1967-68	3124	164.4
3 Herschel Walker, Georgia	1980-82	5259	159.4
4 Garrett Wolfe, No. Ill	2003-06	5164	156.5
5 LeShon Johnson, No. Ill.	1992-93	3314	150.6

Total Offense

Yards Gained	Years	Yards
1 Timmy Chang, Hawaii	2000-04	16,910
2 Ty Detmer, BYU	1988-91	14,665
3 Kevin Kolb, Houston	2003-06	13,715
4 Philip Rivers, N.C. State	2000-03	13,582
5 Brad Smith, Missouri	2002-05	13,088
6 Luke McCown, La. Tech	2000-03	12,731

Yards Per Game	Years	Yards	P/Gm
1 Tim Rattay, La. Tech	1997-99	12,689	382.4
2 Chris Vargas, Nevada	1992-93	6,417	320.9
3 Timmy Chang, Hawaii	2000-04	16,910	319.1
4 Ty Detmer, BYU	1988-91	14,665	318.8
5 Daunte Culpepper*, C. Fla.	1996-98	10,344	313.5

*Culpepper played I-AA with Central Florida in 1995.

All-Purpose Yardage

Yards Gained	Years	Yards
1 DeAngelo Williams, Memphis	2002-05	7573
2 Ricky Williams, Texas	1995-98	7206
3 Napoleon McCallum, Navy	1981-85	7172
4 Darrin Nelson, Stanford	1977-78, 80-81	6885
5 Kevin Faulk, LSU	1995-98	6833

Yards Per Game	Years	Yards	P/Gm
1 Ryan Benjamin, Pacific	1990-92	5706	237.8
2 Sheldon Canley, S. Jose St.	1988-90	5146	205.8
3 Howard Stevens, Louisville	1971-72	3873	193.7
4 O.J. Simpson, USC	1967-68	3666	192.9
5 Alex Van Dyke, Nevada	1994-95	4146	188.5

Miscellaneous

Punting Average*	Years	Avg
1 Shane Lechler, Texas A&M	1996-99	44.7
2 Bill Smith, Mississippi	1983-86	44.3
3 Jim Arnold, Vanderbilt	1979-82	43.9
4 Ralf Mojsiejenko, Michigan St.	1981-84	43.6
5 Jim Miller, Mississippi	1976-79	43.4

*Minimum 250 punts.

Punting Return Average*	Years	Avg
1 Jack Mitchell, Oklahoma	1946-48	23.6
2 Gene Gibson, Cincinnati	1949-50	20.5
3 Eddie Macon, Pacific	1949-51	18.9
4 Jackie Robinson, UCLA	1939-40	18.8
5 Dan Shelton, N. Illinois	2001-04	17.9

*Minimum 1.2 punt returns per game and 30 career returns.

Kickoff Return Average*	Years	Avg
1 Anthony Davis, USC	1972-74	35.1
2 Eric Booth, So. Miss.	1994-97	32.4
3 Overton Curtis, Utah St	1957-58	31.0
4 Fred Montgomery, New Mexico St.	1991-92	30.5
5 Altie Taylor, Utah St.	1966-68	29.3

*Minimum 1.2 kickoff returns per game and 30 career returns.

Interceptions	Years	No
1 Al Brosky, Illinois	1950-52	29
2 John Provost, Holy Cross	1972-74	27
Martin Bayless, Bowling Green	1980-83	27
4 Tom Curtis, Michigan	1967-69	25
Tony Thurman, Boston College	1981-84	25
Tracy Saul, Texas Tech.	1989-92	25

Blocked Kicks	Years	FG	XP	P	Tot
1 James Ferebee, N. Mexico St.	1978-81	8	6	5	19
2 Max McGeary, Baylor	1977-80	6	4	6	16
3 James King, C. Michigan	2001-04	1	2	10	13
4 Terrence Holt, N.C. State	1999-02	8	0	4	12
5 Matt Harding, Hawaii	1992-95	5	1	6	12

Note: The blocked kicks category is a combined total of blocked field goals (FG), extra points (XP) and punts (P).

Editor's Note: The keeping of complete defensive statistics, except for blocked kicks (see above), had been inconsistent until recently. As a result the NCAA only tracks most defensive stats back to 2000 and due to the lack of historical context, those records have been omitted here.

Scoring
Non-kickers

Points	Years	TD	Xpt	FG	Pts
1 Travis Prentice, Miami-OH	1996-99	78	0	0	468
2 Ricky Williams, Texas	1995-98	75	2	0	452
3 Taurean Henderson, Tex. Tech	2002-05	69	0	0	414
3 Brock Forsey, Boise St.	1999-02	68	0	0	408
4 Cedric Benson, Texas	2001-04	67	1	0	404

Points Per Game	Years	Pts	P/Gm
1 Marshall Faulk, S. Diego St.	1991-93	376	12.1
2 Ed Marinaro, Cornell	1969-71	318	11.8
3 Bill Burnett, Arkansas	1968-70	294	11.3
4 Steve Owens, Oklahoma	1967-69	336	11.2
5 Eddie Talboom, Wyoming	1948-50	303	10.8

Touchdowns Rushing	Years	No
1 Travis Prentice, Miami-OH	1996-99	73
2 Ricky Williams, Texas	1995-98	72
3 Anthony Thompson, Indiana	1986-89	64
Cedric Benson, Texas	2001-04	64
5 Ron Dayne, Wisconsin	1996-99	63

Touchdowns Passing	Years	No
1 Ty Detmer, BYU	1988-91	121
2 Timmy Chang, Hawaii	2000-04	117
3 Tim Rattay, La. Tech	1997-99	115
4 Danny Wuerffel, Florida	1993-96	114
5 Chad Pennington, Marshall	1997-99	100

Touchdowns Catches	Years	No
1 Troy Edwards, La. Tech	1996-98	50
2 Darius Watts, Marshall	2000-03	47
3 Aaron Turner, Pacific	1989-92	43
4 Ryan Yarborough, Wyoming	1990-93	42
Rashaun Woods, Oklahoma St.	2000-03	42

Kickers

Points	Years	FG	XP	Pts
1 Roman Anderson, Hou	1988-91	70	213	423
2 Billy Bennett, Georgia	2000-03	87	110	409
3 Carlos Huerta, Mia-FL	1988-91	73	178	397
4 Jason Elam, Hawaii	1988-89, 91-92	79	158	395
5 Nick Novak, Maryland	2001-04	80	153	393
Derek Schmidt, Florida St.	1984-87	73	174	393

Field Goals	Years	No
1 Billy Bennett, Georgia	2000-03	87
2 Jeff Jaeger, Washington	1983-86	80
Nick Novak, Maryland	2001-04	80
4 John Lee, UCLA	1982-85	79
Jason Elam, Hawaii	1988-89, 91-92	79

SINGLE SEASON

Note that starting with the 2002 season, postseason and bowl games are included in single season records.

Rushing

Yards Gained	Year	Gm	Car	Yards
Barry Sanders, Okla. St	1988	11	344	2628
Marcus Allen, USC	1981	11	403	2342
Troy Davis, Iowa St.	1996	11	402	2185
LaDainian Tomlinson, TCU	2000	11	369	2158
Mike Rozier, Nebraska	1983	12	275	2148

Yards Per Game	Year	Gm	Yards	P/Gm
Barry Sanders, Okla. St	1988	11	2628	238.9
Marcus Allen, USC	1981	11	2342	212.9
Ed Marinaro, Cornell	1971	9	1881	209.0
Troy Davis, Iowa St.	1996	11	2185	198.6
LaDainian Tomlinson, TCU	2000	11	2158	196.2

Passing
(Minimum 15 Attempts Per Game)

Passing Efficiency	Year	Rating
Colt Brennan, Hawaii	2006	186.0
Shaun King, Tulane	1998	183.3
Stefan Lefors, Louisville	2004	181.7
Michael Vick, Va. Tech	1999	180.4
Danny Wuerffel, Florida	1995	178.4

Yards Gained	Year	Yards
B.J. Symons, Texas Tech	2003	5833
Colt Brennan, Hawaii	2006	5549
Ty Detmer, BYU	1990	5188
David Klingler, Houston	1990	5140
Kliff Kingsbury, Texas Tech	2002	5017

Completions	Year	Att	No
Kliff Kingsbury, Texas Tech	2002	712	479
B.J. Symons, Texas Tech	2003	719	470
Colt Brennan, Hawaii	2006	559	406
Chase Holbrook, N. Mexico St.	2006	567	397
Tim Rattay, La. Tech	1998	559	380

Receptions

Catches	Year	Gm	No
Manny Hazard, Houston	1989	11	142
Troy Edwards, La. Tech	1998	12	140
Nate Burleson, Nevada	2002	12	138
Howard Twilley, Tulsa	1965	10	134
Trevor Insley, Nevada	1999	11	134

Catches Per Game	Year	No	P/Gm
Howard Twilley, Tulsa	1965	134	13.4
Manny Hazard, Houston	1989	142	12.9
Trevor Insley, Nevada	1999	134	12.2
Alex Van Dyke, Nevada	1995	129	11.7
Troy Edwards, La. Tech	1998	140	11.7

Yards Gained	Year	No	Yards
Trevor Insley, Nevada	1999	134	2060
Troy Edwards, La. Tech	1998	140	1996
Alex Van Dyke, Nevada	1995	129	1854
J.R. Tolver, San Diego St.	2002	128	1785
Howard Twilley, Tulsa	1965	134	1779
Josh Reed, LSU	2001	94	1740

Total Offense

Yards Gained	Year	Gm	Plays	Yards
B.J. Symons, Texas Tech	2003	13	798	5976
Colt Brennan, Hawaii	2006	14	645	5915
David Klingler, Houston	1990	11	704	5221
Ty Detmer, BYU	1990	12	635	5022
Kliff Kingsbury, Texas Tech	2002	14	814	4903

Yards Per Game	Year	Gm	Yards	P/Gm
David Klingler, Houston	1990	11	5221	474.6
B.J. Symons, Texas Tech	2003	13	5976	459.7
Andre Ware, Houston	1989	11	4661	423.7
Colt Brennan, Hawaii	2006	14	5915	422.5
Ty Detmer, BYU	1990	12	5022	418.5

All-Purpose Yardage

Yards Gained	Year	Yards
Barry Sanders, Okla. St	1988	3250
Ryan Benjamin, Pacific	1991	2995
Reggie Bush, USC	2005	2890
Troy Edwards, La. Tech	1998	2784
Darren Sproles, Kansas St.	2003	2735

Yards Per Game	Year	Yards	P/Gm
Barry Sanders, Okla. St	1988	3250	295.5
Ryan Benjamin, Pacific	1991	2995	249.6
Byron (Whizzer) White, Colo	1937	1970	246.3
Mike Pringle, CS-Fullerton	1989	2690	244.6
Paul Palmer, Temple	1986	2633	239.4

All-Time NCAA Division I-A Leaders (Cont.)
SINGLE SEASON
Scoring

Points	Year	TD	Xpt	FG	Pts
Barry Sanders, Okla. St	1988	39	0	0	234
Brock Forsey, Boise St.	2002	32	0	0	192
Troy Edwards, La. Tech	1998	31	2	0	188
Mike Rozier, Nebraska	1983	29	0	0	174
Lydell Mitchell, Penn St	1971	29	0	0	174

Points Per Game	Year	Pts	P/Gm
Barry Sanders, Okla. St	1988	234	21.3
Bobby Reynolds, Nebraska	1950	157	17.4
Art Luppino, Arizona	1954	166	16.6
Ed Marinaro, Cornell	1971	148	16.4
Lydell Mitchell, Penn St	1971	174	15.8

Touchdowns Rushing	Year	No
Barry Sanders, Okla. St	1988	37
Mike Rozier, Nebraska	1983	29
Willis McGahee, Miami-FL	2002	28
Ricky Williams, Texas	1998	27
Lee Suggs, Va. Tech	2000	27
Brock Forsey, Boise St.	2002	26

Touchdowns Passing	Year	No
Colt Brennan, Hawaii	2006	58
David Klingler, Houston	1990	54
B.J. Symons, Texas Tech	2003	52
Jim McMahon, BYU	1980	47
Andre Ware, Houston	1989	46
Tim Rattay, La. Tech	1998	46

Touchdown Catches	Year	No
Troy Edwards, La. Tech	1998	27
Randy Moss, Marshall	1997	25
Manny Hazard, Houston	1989	22
Larry Fitzgerald, Pittsburgh	2003	22
Jarett Dillard, Rice	2006	21

Field Goals	Year	No
Billy Bennett, Georgia	2003	31
John Lee, UCLA	1984	29
Paul Woodside, West Virginia	1982	28
Luis Zendejas, Arizona St	1983	28
Nick Browne, TCU	2003	28

Miscellaneous

Interceptions	Year	No
Al Worley, Washington	1968	14
George Shaw, Oregon	1951	13
Eight tied with 12 each.		

Punting Average*	Year	Avg
Chad Kessler, LSU	1997	50.3
Reggie Roby, Iowa	1981	49.8
Kirk Wilson, UCLA	1956	49.3
Todd Sauerbrun, West Virginia	1994	48.4
Travis Dorsch, Purdue	2001	48.4

*Qualifiers for championship.

Punt Return Average*	Year	Avg
Maurice Drew, UCLA	2005	28.5
Bill Blackstock, Tennessee	1951	25.9
Ted Ginn Jr., Ohio St.	2004	25.6
George Sims, Baylor	1948	25.0

*At least 1.2 punt returns per game.

Kickoff Return Average*	Year	Avg
Paul Allen, BYU	1961	40.1
Tremain Mack, Miami-FL	1996	39.5
Leeland McElroy, Texas A&M.	1993	39.3
Forrest Hall, San Francisco	1946	38.2

*At least 1.2 kickoff returns per game.

SINGLE GAME

Rushing

Yards Gained	Opponent	Year	Yds
LaDainian Tomlinson, TCU	UTEP	1999	406
Tony Sands, Kansas	Missouri	1991	396
Marshall Faulk, San Diego St	Pacific	1991	386
Troy Davis, Iowa St.	Missouri	1996	378
Anthony Thompson, Indiana	Wisconsin	1989	377
Robbie Mixon, C. Michigan	E. Michigan	2002	377

Passing

Yards Gained	Opponent	Year	Yds
David Klingler, Houston	Arizona St.	1990	716
Matt Vogler, TCU	Houston	1990	690
B.J. Symons, Texas Tech	Mississippi	2003	661
Cody Hodges, Texas Tech	Kansas St.	2005	643
Brian Lindgren, Idaho	Mid. Tenn. St.	2001	637

Completions	Opponent	Year	No
Drew Brees, Purdue	Wisconsin	1998	55
Rusty LaRue, Wake Forest	Duke	1995	55
Rusty LaRue, Wake Forest	N.C. St.	1995	50
Chase Holbrook, N. Mexico St.	Boise St.	2006	50

Four tied with 49 each (including twice by Kliff Kingsbury).

Total Offense

Yards Gained	Opponent	Year	Yds
David Klingler, Houston	Arizona St.	1990	732
Matt Vogler, TCU	Houston	1990	696
B.J. Symons, Texas Tech	Mississippi	2003	681
David Klingler, Houston	TCU	1990	625
Scott Mitchell, Utah	Air Force	1988	625

Receiving

Catches	Opponent	Year	No
Randy Gatewood, UNLV.	Idaho	1994	23
Jay Miller, BYU	New Mexico	1973	22
Troy Davis, La. Tech	Nebraska	1998	21
Chris Daniels, Purdue.	Mich. St.	1999	21
Two tied with 20 each.			

Yards Gained	Opponent	Year	Yds
Troy Edwards, La. Tech	Nebraska	1998	405
Randy Gatewood, UNLV.	Idaho	1994	363
Chuck Hughes, UTEP*	N. Texas St.	1965	349
Nate Burleson, Nevada	San Jose St.	2001	326
Rick Eber, Tulsa	Idaho St.	1967	322

*UTEP was Texas Western in 1965.

Scoring

Points	Opponent	Year	Pts
Howard Griffith, Illinois	So. Ill.	1990	48
Marshall Faulk, S. Diego St	Pacific	1991	44
Jim Brown, Syracuse	Colgate	1956	43
Showboat Boykin, Ole Miss	Miss. St.	1951	42
Fred Wendt, UTEP*	N. Mex. St.	1948	42
Rashaun Woods, Oklahoma St.	SMU	2003	42

*UTEP was Texas Mines in 1948.

Touchdowns Rushing	Opponent	Year	No
Howard Griffith, Illinois	So. Ill	1990	8
Showboat Boykin, Ole Miss	Miss. St.	1951	7

Note: Griffith's TD runs (5-51-7-41-5-18-5-3).

Touchdown Catches	Opponent	Year	No
Rashaun Woods, Oklahoma St.	SMU	2003	7
Tim Delaney, S. Diego St	N. Mex. St.	1969	6

Note: Woods's TD catches (2-10-34-32-25-5-11).

Touchdowns Passing	Opponent	Year	No
David Klingler, Houston	E.Wash.	1990	11
Dennis Shaw, San Diego St	N. Mex. St.	1969	9

Note: Klingler's TD passes (5-48-29-7-3-7-40-8-7-8-51).

Field Goals	Opponent	Year	No
Dale Klein, Nebraska	Missouri	1985	7
Mike Prindle, W. Michigan	Marshall	1984	7

Note: Klein's FGs (32-22-43-44-29-43-43); Prindle's FGs (32-44-42-23-48-41-27).

Extra Points (Kick)	Opponent	Year	No
Terry Leiweke, Houston	Tulsa	1968	13
Derek Mahoney, Fresno St	New Mexico	1991	13

Longest Plays (since 1941)

Rushing	Opponent	Year	Yds
Gale Sayers, Kansas	Nebraska	1963	99
Max Anderson, Ariz. St	Wyoming	1967	99
Ralph Thompson, W. Texas St	Wich. St.	1970	99
Kelsey Finch, Tennessee	Florida	1977	99
Eric Vann, Kansas	Oklahoma	1997	99

Eleven tied at 98 each.

Passing	Opponent	Year	Yds
Fred Owens to Jack Ford, Portland	St. Mary's	1947	99
Bo Burris to Warren McVea, Houston	Wash. St.	1966	99
Colin Clapton to Eddie Jenkins, Holy Cross	Boston U.	1970	99
Terry Peel to Robert Ford, Houston	Syracuse	1970	99
Terry Peel to Robert Ford, Houston	S. Diego St.	1972	99
Cris Collinsworth to Derrick Gaffney, Florida	Rice	1977	99
Scott Ankrom to James Maness, TCU	Rice	1984	99
Gino Torretta to Horace Copeland, Miami-FL	Ark.	1991	99

Passing (cont.)	Opponent	Year	Yds
John Paci to Thomas Lewis, Indiana	Penn St.	1993	99
Troy DeGar to Wes Caswell, Tulsa	Oklahoma	1996	99
Drew Brees to Vinny Sutherland, Purdue	N'western	1999	99
Dan Urban to Justin McCariens, N. Ill	Ball St.	2000	99
Jason Johnson to Brandon Marshall, Ariz.	Idaho	2001	99
Jim Sorgi to Lee Evans, Wisconsin	Akron	2003	99
Dondrial Pinkins to Troy Williamson, South Carolina	Virginia	2003	99

Field Goals	Opponent	Year	Yds
Steve Little, Arkansas	Texas	1977	67
Russell Erkleben, Texas	Rice	1977	67
Joe Williams, Wichita St	So. Ill.	1978	67
Tony Franklin, Tex. A&M	Baylor	1976	65
Martin Gramatica, Kan. St.	No. Ill.	1998	65

Note: Gramatica's FG is the only one listed above that was not off a tee and through the narrower (18'6") goal posts.

Longest Division I Streaks

Winning Streaks
(Including bowl games)

No		Seasons	Spoiler	Score
47	Oklahoma	1953-57	Notre Dame	7-0
39	Washington	1908-14	Oregon St.	0-0
37	Yale	1890-93	Princeton	6-0
37	Yale	1887-89	Princeton	10-0
35	Toledo	1969-71	Tampa	21-0
34	USC	2003-05	Texas	41-38*
34	Miami-FL	2000-02	Ohio St.	31-24*
34	Penn	1894-96	Lafayette	6-4
31	Oklahoma	1948-50	Kentucky	13-7*
31	Pittsburgh	1914-18	Cleve. Naval	10-9
31	Penn	1896-98	Harvard	10-0
30	Texas	1968-70	Notre Dame	24-11*
29	Miami-FL	1990-93	Alabama	34-13
29	Michigan	1901-03	Minnesota	6-6

*Texas beat USC in 2006 Rose Bowl; Ohio St. beat Miami in 2003 Fiesta Bowl in double overtime; Kentucky beat Oklahoma in 1951 Sugar Bowl and Notre Dame beat Texas in 1971 Cotton Bowl.

Unbeaten Streaks
(Including bowl games)

No	W-T		Seasons	Spoiler	Score
63	59-4	Washington	1907-17	California	27-0
56	55-1	Michigan	1901-05	Chicago	2-0
50	46-4	California	1920-25	Olympic Club	15-0
48	47-1	Oklahoma	1953-57	N. Dame	7-0
48	47-1	Yale	1885-89	Princeton	10-0
47	42-5	Yale	1879-85	Princeton	6-5
44	42-2	Yale	1894-96	Princeton	24-6
42	39-3	Yale	1904-08	Harvard	4-0
39	37-2	N. Dame	1946-50	Purdue	28-14

Losing Streaks

No		Seasons	Victim	Score
80	Prairie View	1989-98	Langston	14-12
44	Columbia	1983-88	Princeton	16-14
34	Northwestern	1979-82	No. Illinois	31-6
28	Virginia	1958-60	Wm. & Mary	21-6
28	Kansas St	1944-48	Arkansas St.	37-6

Note: Virginia ended its losing streak in the opening game of the 1961 season.

Annual Awards
Heisman Trophy

Originally presented in 1935 as the DAC Trophy by the Downtown Athletic Club of New York City to the best college football player east of the Mississippi. In 1936, players across the country were eligible and the award was renamed the Heisman Trophy following the death of former college coach and DAC athletic director John W. Heisman.

Multiple winner: Archie Griffin (2).

Winners in junior year (16): Doc Blanchard (1945), Reggie Bush (2005), Ty Detmer (1990); Archie Griffin (1974), Desmond Howard (1991), Vic Janowicz (1950), Matt Leinart (2004), Rashaan Salaam (1994), Barry Sanders (1988), Billy Sims (1978), Roger Staubach (1963), Doak Walker (1948), Herschel Walker (1982), Andre Ware (1989), Jason White (2003) and Charles Woodson (1997).

Winners on AP national champions (11): Angelo Bertelli (Notre Dame, 1943); Doc Blanchard (Army, 1945); Tony Dorsett (Pittsburgh, 1976); Leon Hart (Notre Dame, 1949); Matt Leinart (USC, 2004); Johnny Lujack (Notre Dame, 1947); Davey O'Brien (TCU, 1938); Bruce Smith (Minnesota, 1941); Charlie Ward (Florida St., 1993); Danny Wuerffel (Florida, 1996); Charles Woodson (Michigan, 1997).

Year		Points
1935	**Jay Berwanger,** Chicago, HB	.84
	2nd–Monk Meyer, Army, HB	.29
	3rd–Bill Shakespeare, Notre Dame, HB	.23
	4th–Pepper Constable, Princeton, FB	.20
1936	**Larry Kelley,** Yale, E	.219
	2nd–Sam Francis, Nebraska, FB	.47
	3rd–Ray Buivid, Marquette, HB	.43
	4th–Sammy Baugh, TCU, HB	.39
1937	**Clint Frank,** Yale, HB	.524
	2nd–Byron (Whizzer) White, Colo., HB	.264
	3rd–Marshall Goldberg, Pitt, HB	.211
	4th–Alex Wojciechowicz, Fordham, C	.85
1938	**Davey O'Brien,** TCU, QB	.519
	2nd–Marshall Goldberg, Pitt, HB	.294
	3rd–Sid Luckman, Columbia, HB	.154
	4th–Bob MacLeod, Dartmouth, HB	.78
1939	**Nile Kinnick,** Iowa, HB	.651
	2nd–Tom Harmon, Michigan, HB	.405
	3rd–Paul Christman, Missouri, QB	.391
	4th–George Cafego, Tennessee, QB	.296
1940	**Tom Harmon,** Michigan, HB	.1303
	2nd–John Kimbrough, Texas A&M, FB	.841
	3rd–George Franck, Minnesota, HB	.102
	4th–Frankie Albert, Stanford, QB	.90
1941	**Bruce Smith,** Minnesota, HB	.554
	2nd–Angelo Bertelli, Notre Dame, QB	.345
	3rd–Frankie Albert, Stanford, QB	.336
	4th–Frank Sinkwich, Georgia, HB	.249
1942	**Frank Sinkwich,** Georgia, TB	.1059
	2nd–Paul Governali, Columbia, QB	.218
	3rd–Clint Castleberry, Ga. Tech, HB	.99
	4th–Mike Holovak, Boston College, FB	.95
1943	**Angelo Bertelli,** Notre Dame, QB	.648
	2nd–Bob Odell, Penn, HB	.177
	3rd–Otto Graham, Northwestern, QB	.140
	4th–Creighton Miller, Notre Dame, HB	.134
1944	**Les Horvath,** Ohio St., TB-QB	.412
	2nd–Glenn Davis, Army, HB	.287
	3rd–Doc Blanchard, Army, FB	.237
	4th–Don Whitmire, Navy, T	.115
1945	**Doc Blanchard,** Army, FB	.860
	2nd–Glenn Davis, Army, HB	.638
	3rd–Bob Fenimore, Oklahoma A&M, HB	.187
	4th–Herman Wedemeyer, St. Mary's, HB	.152
1946	**Glenn Davis,** Army, HB	.792
	2nd–Charlie Trippi, Georgia, HB	.435
	3rd–Johnny Lujack, Notre Dame, QB	.379
	4th–Doc Blanchard, Army, FB	.267
1947	**Johnny Lujack,** Notre Dame, QB	.742
	2nd–Bob Chappuis, Michigan, HB	.555
	3rd–Doak Walker, SMU, HB	.196
	4th–Charlie Conerly, Mississippi, QB	.186
1948	**Doak Walker,** SMU, HB	.778
	2nd–Charlie Justice, N. Carolina, HB	.443
	3rd–Chuck Bednarik, Penn, C	.336
	4th–Jackie Jensen, California, HB	.143
1949	**Leon Hart,** Notre Dame, E	.995
	2nd–Charlie Justice, N. Carolina, HB	.272
	3rd–Doak Walker, SMU, HB	.229
	4th–Arnold Galiffa, Army, QB	.196

Year		Points
1950	**Vic Janowicz,** Ohio St., HB	.633
	2nd–Kyle Rote, SMU, HB	.280
	3rd–Reds Bagnell, Penn, HB	.231
	4th–Babe Parilli, Kentucky, QB	.214
1951	**Dick Kazmaier,** Princeton, TB	.1777
	2nd–Hank Lauricella, Tennessee, HB	.424
	3rd–Babe Parilli, Kentucky, QB	.344
	4th–Bill McColl, Stanford, E	.313
1952	**Billy Vessels,** Oklahoma, HB	.525
	2nd–Jack Scarbath, Maryland, QB	.367
	3rd–Paul Giel, Minnesota, HB	.329
	4th–Donn Moomaw, UCLA, C	.257
1953	**Johnny Lattner,** Notre Dame, HB	.1850
	2nd–Paul Giel, Minnesota, HB	.1794
	3rd–Paul Cameron, UCLA, HB	.444
	4th–Bernie Faloney, Maryland, QB	.258
1954	**Alan Ameche,** Wisconsin, FB	.1068
	2nd–Kurt Burris, Oklahoma, C	.838
	3rd–Howard Cassady, Ohio St., HB	.810
	4th–Ralph Guglielmi, Notre Dame, QB	.691
1955	**Howard Cassady,** Ohio St., HB	.2219
	2nd–Jim Swink, TCU, HB	.742
	3rd–George Welsh, Navy, QB	.383
	4th–Earl Morrall, Michigan St., QB	.323
1956	**Paul Hornung,** Notre Dame, QB	.1066
	2nd–Johnny Majors, Tennessee, HB	.994
	3rd–Tommy McDonald, Oklahoma, HB	.973
	4th–Jerry Tubbs, Oklahoma, C	.724
1957	**John David Crow,** Texas A&M, HB	.1183
	2nd–Alex Karras, Iowa, T	.693
	3rd–Walt Kowalczyk, Mich. St., HB	.630
	4th–Lou Michaels, Kentucky, T	.330
1958	**Pete Dawkins,** Army, HB	.1394
	2nd–Randy Duncan, Iowa, QB	.1021
	3rd–Billy Cannon, LSU, HB	.975
	4th–Bob White, Ohio St., FB	.365
1959	**Billy Cannon,** LSU, HB	.1929
	2nd–Richie Lucas, Penn St., QB	.613
	3rd–Don Meredith, SMU, QB	.286
	4th–Bill Burrell, Illinois, G	.196
1960	**Joe Bellino,** Navy, HB	.1793
	2nd–Tom Brown, Minnesota, G	.731
	3rd–Jake Gibbs, Mississippi, QB	.453
	4th–Ed Dyas, Auburn, HB	.319
1961	**Ernie Davis,** Syracuse, HB	.824
	2nd–Bob Ferguson, Ohio St., HB	.771
	3rd–Jimmy Saxton, Texas, HB	.551
	4th–Sandy Stephens, Minnesota, QB	.543
1962	**Terry Baker,** Oregon St., QB	.707
	2nd–Jerry Stovall, LSU, HB	.618
	3rd–Bobby Bell, Minnesota, T	.429
	4th–Lee Roy Jordan, Alabama, C	.321
1963	**Roger Staubach,** Navy, QB	.1860
	2nd–Billy Lothridge, Ga. Tech, QB	.504
	3rd–Sherman Lewis, Mich. St., HB	.369
	4th–Don Trull, Baylor, QB	.253
1964	**John Huarte,** Notre Dame, QB	.1026
	2nd–Jerry Rhome, Tulsa, QB	.952
	3rd–Dick Butkus, Illinois, C	.505
	4th–Bob Timberlake, Michigan, QB	.361

Year	Player	Points
1965	**Mike Garrett,** USC, HB	.926
	2nd–Howard Twilley, Tulsa, E	.528
	3rd–Jim Grabowski, Illinois, FB	.481
	4th–Donny Anderson, Texas Tech, HB	.408
1966	**Steve Spurrier,** Florida, QB	.1679
	2nd–Bob Griese, Purdue, QB	.816
	3rd–Nick Eddy, Notre Dame, HB	.456
	4th–Gary Beban, UCLA, QB	.318
1967	**Gary Beban,** UCLA, QB	.1968
	2nd–O.J. Simpson, USC, HB	.1722
	3rd–Leroy Keyes, Purdue, HB	.1366
	4th–Larry Csonka, Syracuse, FB	.136
1968	**O.J. Simpson,** USC, HB	.2853
	2nd–Leroy Keyes, Purdue, HB	.1103
	3rd–Terry Hanratty, Notre Dame, QB	.387
	4th–Ted Kwalick, Penn St., TE	.254
1969	**Steve Owens,** Oklahoma, HB	.1488
	2nd–Mike Phipps, Purdue, QB	.1344
	3rd–Rex Kern, Ohio St., QB	.856
	4th–Archie Manning, Mississippi, QB.	.582
1970	**Jim Plunkett,** Stanford, QB	.2229
	2nd–Joe Theismann, Notre Dame, QB	.1410
	3rd–Archie Manning, Mississippi, QB	.849
	4th–Steve Worster, Texas, RB	398
1971	**Pat Sullivan,** Auburn, QB	.1597
	2nd–Ed Marinaro, Cornell, RB.	.1445
	3rd–Greg Pruitt, Oklahoma, RB	.586
	4th–Johnny Musso, Alabama, RB	.365
1972	**Johnny Rodgers,** Nebraska, FL.	.1310
	2nd–Greg Pruitt, Oklahoma, RB.	.966
	3rd–Rich Glover, Nebraska, MG.	.652
	4th–Bert Jones, LSU, QB	.351
1973	**John Cappelletti,** Penn St., RB.	.1057
	2nd–John Hicks, Ohio St., OT	.524
	3rd–Roosevelt Leaks, Texas, RB	.482
	4th–David Jaynes, Kansas, QB.	.394
1974	**Archie Griffin,** Ohio St., RB	.1920
	2nd–Anthony Davis, USC, RB.	.819
	3rd–Joe Washington, Oklahoma, RB.	.661
	4th–Tom Clements, Notre Dame, QB.	.244
1975	**Archie Griffin,** Ohio St., RB	.1800
	2nd–Chuck Muncie, California, RB	.730
	3rd–Ricky Bell, USC, RB	.708
	4th–Tony Dorsett, Pitt, RB	.616
1976	**Tony Dorsett,** Pittsburgh, RB	.2357
	2nd–Ricky Bell, USC, RB	.1346
	3rd–Rob Lytle, Michigan, RB.	.413
	4th–Terry Miller, Oklahoma St., RB.	.197
1977	**Earl Campbell,** Texas, RB	.1547
	2nd–Terry Miller, Oklahoma St., RB.	.812
	3rd–Ken MacAfee, Notre Dame, TE	.343
	4th–Doug Williams, Grambling, QB.	.266
1978	**Billy Sims,** Oklahoma, RB	.827
	2nd–Chuck Fusina, Penn St., QB	.750
	3rd–Rick Leach, Michigan, QB.	.435
	4th–Charles White, USC, RB	.354
1979	**Charles White,** USC, RB	.1695
	2nd–Billy Sims, Oklahoma, RB	.773
	3rd–Marc Wilson, BYU, QB	.589
	4th–Art Schlichter, Ohio St., QB.	.251
1980	**George Rogers,** South Carolina, RB	.1128
	2nd–Hugh Green, Pittsburgh, DE	.861
	3rd–Herschel Walker, Georgia, RB	.683
	4th–Mark Herrmann, Purdue, QB.	.405
1981	**Marcus Allen,** USC, RB	.1797
	2nd–Herschel Walker, Georgia, RB	.1199
	3rd–Jim McMahon, BYU, QB	.706
	4th–Dan Marino, Pitt, QB	.256
1982	**Herschel Walker,** Georgia, RB	.1926
	2nd–John Elway, Stanford, QB	.1231
	3rd–Eric Dickerson, SMU, RB	.465
	4th–Anthony Carter, Michigan, WR	.142
1983	**Mike Rozier,** Nebraska, RB.	.1801
	2nd–Steve Young, BYU, QB	.1172
	3rd–Doug Flutie, Boston College, QB	.253
	4th–Turner Gill, Nebraska, QB.	.190

Year	Player	Points
1984	**Doug Flutie,** Boston College, QB	.2240
	2nd–Keith Byars, Ohio St., RB	.1251
	3rd–Robbie Bosco, BYU, QB	.443
	4th–Bernie Kosar, Miami-FL, QB.	.320
1985	**Bo Jackson,** Auburn, RB	.1509
	2nd–Chuck Long, Iowa, QB	.1464
	3rd–Robbie Bosco, BYU, QB	.459
	4th–Lorenzo White, Michigan St., RB	.391
1986	**Vinny Testaverde,** Miami-FL, QB	.2213
	2nd–Paul Palmer, Temple, RB	.672
	3rd–Jim Harbaugh, Michigan, QB.	.458
	4th–Brian Bosworth, Oklahoma, LB	.395
1987	**Tim Brown,** Notre Dame, WR.	.1442
	2nd–Don McPherson, Syracuse, QB	.831
	3rd–Gordie Lockbaum, Holy Cross, WR-DB.	.657
	4th–Lorenzo White, Michigan St., RB	.632
1988	**Barry Sanders,** Oklahoma St., RB	.1878
	2nd–Rodney Peete, USC, QB	.912
	3rd–Troy Aikman, UCLA, QB	.582
	4th–Steve Walsh, Miami-FL, QB.	.341
1989	**Andre Ware,** Houston, QB	.1073
	2nd–Anthony Thompson, Ind., RB	.1003
	3rd–Major Harris, West Va., QB	.709
	4th–Tony Rice, Notre Dame, QB	.523
1990	**Ty Detmer,** BYU, QB	.1482
	2nd–Rocket Ismail, Notre Dame, FL.	.1177
	3rd–Eric Bieniemy, Colorado, RB	.798
	4th–Shawn Moore, Virginia, QB	.465
1991	**Desmond Howard,** Michigan, WR	.2077
	2nd–Casey Weldon, Florida St., QB.	.503
	3rd–Ty Detmer, BYU, QB.	.445
	4th–Steve Emtman, Washington, DT	.357
1992	**Gino Torretta,** Miami-FL, QB	.1400
	2nd–Marshall Faulk, San Diego St., RB	.1080
	3rd–Garrison Hearst, Georgia, RB	.982
	4th–Marvin Jones, Florida St., LB	.392
1993	**Charlie Ward,** Florida St., QB	.2310
	2nd–Heath Shuler, Tennessee, QB	.688
	3rd–David Palmer, Alabama, RB	.292
	4th–Marshall Faulk, S. Diego St., RB	.250
1994	**Rashaan Salaam,** Colorado, RB	.1743
	2nd–Ki-Jana Carter, Penn St., RB	.901
	3rd–Steve McNair, Alcorn St., QB.	.655
	4th–Kerry Collins, Penn St., QB	.639
1995	**Eddie George,** Ohio St., RB	.1460
	2nd–Tommie Frazier, Nebraska, QB	.1196
	3rd–Danny Wuerffel, Florida, QB	.987
	4th–Darnell Autry, Northwestern, RB	.535
1996	**Danny Wuerffel,** Florida, QB	.1363
	2nd–Troy Davis, Iowa St., RB	.1174
	3rd–Jake Plummer, Arizona St., QB.	.685
	4th–Orlando Pace, Ohio St., OT	.599
1997	**Charles Woodson,** Michigan, DB-WR	.1815
	2nd–Peyton Manning, Tennessee, QB	.1543
	3rd–Ryan Leaf, Washington St., QB	.861
	4th–Randy Moss, Marshall, WR	.253
1998	**Ricky Williams,** Texas, RB	.2355
	2nd–Michael Bishop, Kansas St., QB	.792
	3rd–Cade McNown, UCLA, QB	.696
	4th–Tim Couch, Kentucky, QB.	.527
1999	**Ron Dayne,** Wisconsin, RB	.2042
	2nd–Joe Hamilton, Ga. Tech, QB	.994
	3rd–Michael Vick, Va. Tech, QB	.319
	4th–Drew Brees, Purdue, QB	.308
2000	**Chris Weinke,** Florida St., QB	.1628
	2nd–Josh Heupel, Oklahoma, QB	.1552
	3rd–Drew Brees, Purdue, QB	.619
	4th–LaDainian Tomlinson, TCU, RB	.566
2001	**Eric Crouch,** Nebraska, QB	.770
	2nd–Rex Grossman, Florida, QB	.708
	3rd–Ken Dorsey, Miami-FL, QB.	.638
	4th–Joey Harrington, Oregon, QB.	.364
2002	**Carson Palmer,** USC, QB.	.1328
	2nd–Brad Banks, Iowa, QB	.1095
	3rd–Larry Johnson, Penn St., RB	.726
	4th–Willis McGahee, Miami-FL, RB	.660

Annual Awards (Cont.)

2003	**Jason White**, Oklahoma, QB	1481	2005	**Reggie Bush**, USC, RB	2541
	2nd–Larry Fitzgerald, Pittsburgh, WR	1353		2nd–Vince Young, Texas, QB	1608
	3rd–Eli Manning, Mississippi, QB	710		3rd–Matt Leinart, USC, QB	797
	4th–Chris Perry, Michigan, RB	341		4th–Brady Quinn, Notre Dame, QB	191
2004	**Matt Leinart**, USC, QB	1325	2006	**Troy Smith**, Ohio St., QB	2540
	2nd–Adrian Peterson, Oklahoma, RB	997		2nd–Darren McFadden, Arkansas, RB	878
	3rd–Jason White, Oklahoma, QB	957		3rd–Brady Quinn, Notre Dame, QB	782
	4th–Alex Smith, Utah, QB	635		4th–Steve Slaton, West Virginia, RB	214

Maxwell Award

First presented in 1937 by the Maxwell Memorial Football Club of Philadelphia, the award is named after Robert (Tiny) Maxwell, a Philadelphia native who was a standout lineman at the University of Chicago at the turn of the century. Like the Heisman, the Maxwell is given to the outstanding college player in the nation. Both awards have gone to the same player in the same season 34 times. Those players are preceded by (#). Glenn Davis of Army and Doak Walker of SMU won both but in different years.

Multiple winner: Johnny Lattner (2).

Year		Year		Year	
1937	#Clint Frank, Yale, HB	1961	Bob Ferguson, Ohio St., HB	1985	Chuck Long, Iowa, QB
1938	#Davey O'Brien, TCU, QB	1962	#Terry Baker, Oregon St., QB	1986	#V. Testaverde, Miami-FL, QB
1939	#Nile Kinnick, Iowa, HB	1963	#Roger Staubach, Navy, QB	1987	Don McPherson, Syracuse, QB
1940	#Tom Harmon, Michigan, HB	1964	Glenn Ressler, Penn St., G	1988	#Barry Sanders, Okla. St., RB
1941	Bill Dudley, Virginia, HB	1965	Tommy Nobis, Texas, LB	1989	Anthony Thompson, Indiana, RB
1942	Paul Governali, Columbia, HB	1966	Jim Lynch, Notre Dame, LB	1990	#Ty Detmer, BYU, QB
1943	Bob Odell, Penn, HB	1967	#Gary Beban, UCLA, QB	1991	#Desmond Howard, Mich., WR
1944	Glenn Davis, Army, HB	1968	#O.J. Simpson, USC, HB	1992	#Gino Torretta, Miami-FL, QB
1945	#Doc Blanchard, Army, FB	1969	Mike Reid, Penn St., DT	1993	#Charlie Ward, Florida St., QB
1946	Charley Trippi, Georgia, HB	1970	#Jim Plunkett, Stanford, QB	1994	Kerry Collins, Penn St., QB
1947	Doak Walker, SMU, HB	1971	Ed Marinaro, Cornell, HB	1995	#Eddie George, Ohio St., RB
1948	Chuck Bednarik, Penn, C	1972	Brad Van Pelt, Michigan St., DB	1996	#Danny Wuerffel, Florida, QB
1949	#Leon Hart, Notre Dame, E	1973	#John Cappelletti, Penn St., RB	1997	Peyton Manning, Tennessee, QB
1950	Reds Bagnell, Penn, HB	1974	Steve Joachim, Temple, QB	1998	#Ricky Williams, Texas, RB
1951	#Dick Kazmaier, Princeton, TB	1975	#Archie Griffin, Ohio St., RB	1999	#Ron Dayne, Wisconsin, RB
1952	Johnny Lattner, Notre Dame, HB	1976	#Tony Dorsett, Pitt, RB	2000	Drew Brees, Purdue, QB
1953	#Johnny Lattner, N. Dame, HB	1977	Ross Browner, Notre Dame, DE	2001	Ken Dorsey, Miami-FL, QB
1954	Ron Beagle, Navy, E	1978	Chuck Fusina, Penn St., QB	2002	Larry Johnson, Penn St., RB
1955	#Howard Cassady, Ohio St., HB	1979	#Charles White, USC, RB	2003	Eli Manning, Mississippi, QB
1956	Tommy McDonald, Okla., HB	1980	Hugh Green, Pitt, DE	2004	Jason White, Oklahoma, QB
1957	Bob Reifsnyder, Navy, T	1981	#Marcus Allen, USC, RB	2005	Vince Young, Texas, QB
1958	#Pete Dawkins, Army, HB	1982	#Herschel Walker, Georgia, RB	2006	Brady Quinn, Notre Dame, QB
1959	Rich Lucas, Penn St., QB	1983	#Mike Rozier, Nebraska, RB		
1960	#Joe Bellino, Navy, HB	1984	#Doug Flutie, Boston Col., QB		

Outland Trophy

First presented in 1946 by the Football Writers Association of America, honoring the nation's outstanding interior lineman. The award is named after its benefactor, Dr. John H. Outland (Kansas, Class of 1898). Players listed in **bold** type helped lead their team to a national championship (according to AP).

Multiple winner: Dave Rimington (2). **Winners in junior year:** Ross Browner (1976), Steve Emtman (1991), Rien Long (2002), Orlando Pace (1996) and Rimington (1981).

Year		Year		Year	
1946	**George Connor,** N. Dame, T	1967	**Ron Yary,** USC, T	1988	Tracy Rocker, Auburn, DT
1947	Joe Steffy, Army, G	1968	Bill Stanfill, Georgia, T	1989	Mohammed Elewonibi, BYU, G
1948	Bill Fischer, Notre Dame, G	1969	Mike Reid, Penn St., DT	1990	Russell Maryland, Miami-FL, NT
1949	Ed Bagdon, Michigan St., G	1970	Jim Stillwagon, Ohio St., MG	1991	Steve Emtman, Washington, DT
1950	Bob Gain, Kentucky, T	1971	**Larry Jacobson,** Neb., DT	1992	Will Shields, Nebraska, G
1951	Jim Weatherall, Oklahoma, T	1972	Rich Glover, Nebraska, MG	1993	Rob Waldrop, Arizona, NG
1952	Dick Modzelewski, Maryland, T	1973	John Hicks, Ohio St., OT	1994	**Zach Wiegert,** Nebraska, OT
1953	J.D. Roberts, Oklahoma, G	1974	Randy White, Maryland, DT	1995	Jonathan Ogden, UCLA, OT
1954	Bill Brooks, Arkansas, G	1975	**Lee Roy Selmon,** Okla., DT	1996	Orlando Pace, Ohio St., OT
1955	Calvin Jones, Iowa, G	1976	Ross Browner, Notre Dame, DE	1997	Aaron Taylor, Nebraska, G
1956	Jim Parker, Ohio St., G	1977	Brad Shearer, Texas, DT	1998	Kris Farris, UCLA, OT
1957	Alex Karras, Iowa, T	1978	Greg Roberts, Oklahoma, G	1999	Chris Samuels, Alabama, OT
1958	Zeke Smith, Auburn, G	1979	Jim Richter, N.C. State, C	2000	John Henderson, Tennessee, DT
1959	Mike McGee, Duke, T	1980	Mark May, Pittsburgh, OT	2001	**Bryant McKinnie,** Miami-FL, OT
1960	**Tom Brown,** Minnesota, G	1981	Dave Rimington, Nebraska, C	2002	Rien Long, Washington St., DT
1961	Merlin Olsen, Utah St., T	1982	Dave Rimington, Nebraska, C	2003	Robert Gallery, Iowa, OT
1962	Bobby Bell, Minnesota, T	1983	Dean Steinkuhler, Nebraska, G	2004	Jammal Brown, Oklahoma, OT
1963	**Scott Appleton,** Texas, T	1984	Bruce Smith, Virginia Tech, DT	2005	Greg Eslinger, Minnesota, C
1964	Steve DeLong, Tennessee, T	1985	Mike Ruth, Boston College, NG	2006	Joe Thomas, Wisconsin, OT
1965	Tommy Nobis, Texas, G	1986	Jason Buck, BYU, DT		
1966	Loyd Phillips, Arkansas, T	1987	Chad Hennings, Air Force, DT		

Butkus Award

First presented in 1985 by the Downtown Athletic Club of Orlando, Fla., to honor the nation's outstanding linebacker. The award is named after Dick Butkus, two-time consensus All-America at Illinois and six-time All-Pro with the Chicago Bears.

Multiple winner: Brian Bosworth (2).

Year		Year		Year	
1985	Brian Bosworth, Oklahoma	1993	Trev Alberts, Nebraska	2001	Rocky Calmus, Oklahoma
1986	Brian Bosworth, Oklahoma	1994	Dana Howard, Illinois	2002	E.J. Henderson, Maryland
1987	Paul McGowan, Florida St.	1995	Kevin Hardy, Illinois	2003	Teddy Lehman, Oklahoma
1988	Derrick Thomas, Alabama	1996	Matt Russell, Colorado	2004	Derrick Johnson, Texas
1989	Percy Snow, Michigan St.	1997	Andy Katzenmoyer, Ohio St.	2005	Paul Posluszny, Penn St.
1990	Alfred Williams, Colorado	1998	Chris Claiborne, USC	2006	Patrick Willis, Mississippi
1991	Erick Anderson, Michigan	1999	LaVar Arrington, Penn St.		
1992	Marvin Jones, Florida St.	2000	Dan Morgan, Miami-FL		

Lombardi Award

First presented in 1970 by the Rotary Club of Houston, honoring the nation's best lineman. The award is named after pro football coach Vince Lombardi, who, as a guard, was a member of the famous "Seven Blocks of Granite" at Fordham in the 1930s. The Lombardi and Outland awards have gone to the same player in the same year ten times. Those players are preceded by (#). Ross Browner of Notre Dame won both, but in different years.

Multiple winner: Orlando Pace (2).

Year		Year		Year	
1970	#Jim Stillwagon, Ohio St., MG	1983	#Dean Steinkuhler, Neb., G	1996	#Orlando Pace, Ohio St., OT
1971	Walt Patulski, Notre Dame, DE	1984	Tony Degrate, Texas, DT	1997	Grant Wistrom, Nebraska, DE
1972	#Rich Glover, Nebraska, MG	1985	Tony Casillas, Oklahoma, NG	1998	Dat Nguyen, Tex. A&M, LB
1973	#John Hicks, Ohio St., OT	1986	Cornelius Bennett, Alabama, LB	1999	Corey Moore, Va. Tech, DE
1974	#Randy White, Maryland, DT	1987	Chris Spielman, Ohio St., LB	2000	Jamal Reynolds, Florida St., DE
1975	#Lee Roy Selmon, Okla., DT	1988	#Tracy Rocker, Auburn, DT	2001	Julius Peppers, N. Carolina, DE
1976	Wilson Whitley, Houston, DT	1989	Percy Snow, Michigan St., LB	2002	Terrell Suggs, Arizona St., DE
1977	Ross Browner, Notre Dame, DE	1990	Chris Zorich, Notre Dame, NT	2003	Tommie Harris, Oklahoma, DT
1978	Bruce Clark, Penn St., DT	1991	#Steve Emtman, Wash., DT	2004	David Pollack, Georgia, DE
1979	Brad Budde, USC, G	1992	Marvin Jones, Florida St., LB	2005	A.J. Hawk, Ohio St., LB
1980	Hugh Green, Pitt, DE	1993	Aaron Taylor, Notre Dame, OT	2006	LaMarr Woodley, Michigan, DE
1981	Kenneth Sims, Texas, DT	1994	Warren Sapp, Miami-FL, DT		
1982	#Dave Rimington, Neb., C	1995	Orlando Pace, Ohio St., OT		

O'Brien Quarterback Award

First presented in 1977 as the O'Brien Memorial Trophy, the award went to the outstanding player in the Southwest. In 1981, however, the Davey O'Brien Educational and Charitable Trust of Ft. Worth renamed the prize the O'Brien National Quarterback Award and now honors the nation's best quarterback. The award is named after 1938 Heisman Trophy-winning QB Davey O'Brien of Texas Christian.

Multiple winners: Ty Detmer, Mike Singletary, Jason White and Danny Wuerffel (2).

Memorial Trophy

Year		Year		Year	
1977	Earl Campbell, Texas, RB	1979	Mike Singletary, Baylor, LB	1980	Mike Singletary, Baylor, LB
1978	Billy Sims, Oklahoma, RB				

National QB Award

Year		Year		Year	
1981	Jim McMahon, BYU	1990	Ty Detmer, BYU	1999	Joe Hamilton, Ga. Tech
1982	Todd Blackledge, Penn St.	1991	Ty Detmer, BYU	2000	Chris Weinke, Florida St.
1983	Steve Young, BYU	1992	Gino Torretta, Miami-FL	2001	Eric Crouch, Nebraska
1984	Doug Flutie, Boston College	1993	Charlie Ward, Florida St.	2002	Brad Banks, Iowa
1985	Chuck Long, Iowa	1994	Kerry Collins, Penn St.	2003	Jason White, Oklahoma
1986	Vinny Testaverde, Miami, FL	1995	Danny Wuerffel, Florida	2004	Jason White, Oklahoma
1987	Don McPherson, Syracuse	1996	Danny Wuerffel, Florida	2005	Vince Young, Texas
1988	Troy Aikman, UCLA	1997	Peyton Manning, Tennessee	2006	Troy Smith, Ohio St.
1989	Andre Ware, Houston	1998	Michael Bishop, Kansas St.		

Thorpe Award

First presented in 1986 by the Jim Thorpe Athletic Club of Oklahoma City to honor the nation's outstanding defensive back. The award is named after Jim Thorpe–Olympic champion and two-time consensus All-America halfback at Carlisle.

Year		Year		Year	
1986	Thomas Everett, Baylor	1993	Antonio Langham, Alabama	2001	Roy Williams, Oklahoma
1987	Bennie Blades, Miami-FL	1994	Chris Hudson, Colorado	2002	Terence Newman, Kansas St.
	& Rickey Dixon, Oklahoma	1995	Greg Myers, Colorado St.	2003	Derrick Strait, Oklahoma
1988	Deion Sanders, Florida St.	1996	Lawrence Wright, Florida	2004	Carlos Rogers, Auburn
1989	Mike Carrier, USC	1997	Charles Woodson, Michigan	2005	Michael Huff, Texas
1990	Darryl Lewis, Arizona	1998	Antoine Winfield, Ohio St.	2006	Aaron Ross, Texas
1991	Terrell Buckley, Florida St.	1999	Tyrone Carter, Minnesota		
1992	Deon Figures, Colorado	2000	Jamar Fletcher, Wisconsin		

All-Time Winningest Division I-A Coaches

Minimum of 10 years in Division I-A through 2006 season. Regular season and bowl games included. Coaches active in 2006 in **bold** type.

Top 25 Winning Percentage

		Yrs	W	L	T	Pct
1	Knute Rockne	13	105	12	5	.881
2	Frank Leahy	13	107	13	9	.864
3	George Woodruff	12	142	25	2	.846
4	Barry Switzer	16	157	29	4	.837
5	Tom Osborne	25	255	49	3	.836
6	Percy Haughton	13	96	17	6	.832
7	Bob Neyland	21	173	31	12	.829
8	Hurry Up Yost	29	196	36	12	.828
9	Bud Wilkinson	17	145	29	4	.826
10	Jock Sutherland	20	144	28	14	.812
11	Bob Devaney	16	136	30	7	.806
12	Frank Thomas	19	141	33	9	.795
13	Henry Williams	23	141	34	12	.786
14	Gil Dobie	33	180	45	15	.781
15	Bear Bryant	38	323	85	17	.780
16	Fred Folsom	19	106	28	6	.779
17	Bo Schembechler	27	234	65	8	.775
18	**Phillip Fulmer**	15	137	41	0	.770
19	Fritz Crisler	18	116	32	9	.768
20	Charley Moran	18	122	33	12	.766
21	Wallace Wade	24	171	49	10	.765
22	**Bobby Bowden**	41	366	111	4	.765
23	Frank Kush	22	176	54	1	.764
24	Dan McGugin	30	197	55	19	.762
25	Jimmy Crowley	13	78	21	10	.761

Top 25 Victories

		Yrs	W	L	T	Pct
1	**Bobby Bowden**	41	366	111	4	.765
2	**Joe Paterno**	41	363	121	3	.748
3	Bear Bryant	38	323	85	17	.780
4	Pop Warner	44	319	106	32	.733
5	Amos Alonzo Stagg	57	314	199	35	.605
6	LaVell Edwards	29	257	101	3	.722
7	Tom Osborne	25	255	49	3	.836
8	Lou Holtz	33	249	132	7	.651
9	Woody Hayes	33	238	72	10	.759
10	Bo Schembechler	27	234	65	8	.775
11	Hayden Fry	37	232	178	10	.564
12	Jess Neely	40	207	176	19	.539
13	Warren Woodson	31	203	95	14	.673
14	Don Nehlen	30	202	128	8	.609
15	Vince Dooley	25	201	77	10	.715
	Eddie Anderson	39	201	128	15	.606
17	Jim Sweeney	32	200	154	4	.564
18	Dana X. Bible	33	198	72	23	.715
	Frank Beamer	26	198	105	4	.651
20	Dan McGugin	30	197	55	19	.762
21	Hurry Up Yost	29	196	36	12	.828
22	Howard Jones	29	194	64	21	.733
23	John Cooper	24	192	84	6	.691
24	Johnny Vaught	25	190	61	12	.745
25	George Welsh	28	189	132	4	.588

Note: John Gagliardi of Division III St. John's (Minn.) became the all-time leader in college football coaching wins in 2003 (passing Grambling's Eddie Robinson at 408 wins), and currently boasts a career record of 443-120-11 over 55 seasons at St. John's and three seasons at Montana's Carroll College.

Where They Coached

Anderson–Loras (1922-24), DePaul (1925-31), Holy Cross (1933-38), Iowa (1939-42), Holy Cross (1950-64); **Beamer**–Murray St. (1981-86), Virginia Tech (1987–); **Bible**–Mississippi College (1913-15), LSU (1916), Texas A&M (1917,1919-28), Nebraska (1929-36), Texas (1937-46); **Bowden**–Samford (1959-62), West Virginia (1970-75), Florida St. (1976–); **Bryant**–Maryland (1945), Kentucky (1946-53), Texas A&M (1954-57), Alabama (1958-82); **Cooper**–Tulsa (1977-84), Arizona St. (1985-87), Ohio St. (1988-2000); **Crisler**–Minnesota (1930-31), Princeton (1932-37), Michigan (1938-47); **Crowley**–Michigan St. (1929-32), Fordham (1933-41); **Devaney**–Wyoming (1957-61), Nebraska (1962-72); **Dobie**–North Dakota St. (1906-07), Washington (1908-16), Navy (1917-19), Cornell (1920-35), Boston College (1936-38); **V. Dooley**–Georgia (1964-88); **Edwards**–BYU (1972-2000); **Folsom**–Colorado (1895-99, 1901-02), Dartmouth (1903-06), Colorado (1908-15); **Fry**–SMU (1962-72), North Texas (1973-78), Iowa (1979-98); **Fulmer**–Tennessee (1992–).

Haughton–Cornell (1899-1900), Harvard (1908-16), Columbia (1923-24); **Hayes**–Denison (1946-48), Miami-OH (1949-50), Ohio St. (1951-78); **Holtz**–William & Mary (1969-71), N.C. State (1972-75), Arkansas (1977-83), Minnesota (1984-85), Notre Dame (1986-96), South Carolina (1999-2004); **Jones**–Syracuse (1908), Yale (1909), Ohio St. (1910), Yale (1913), Iowa (1916-23), Duke (1924), USC (1925-40); **Kush**–Arizona St. (1958-79); **Leahy**–Boston College (1939-40), Notre Dame (1941-43, 1946-53); **Moran**–Texas A&M (1909-14), Centre (1919-23), Bucknell (1924-26), Catawba (1930-33).

Neely–Rhodes (1924-27), Clemson (1931-39), Rice (1940-66); **Nehlen**–Bowling Green (1968-76), West Virginia (1980-2000); **Neyland**–Tennessee (1926-34, 1936-40, 1946-52); **Osborne**–Nebraska (1973-97); **Paterno**–Penn St. (1966–); **Rockne**–Notre Dame (1918-30); **Schembechler**–Miami-OH (1963-68), Michigan (1969-89); **Stagg**–Springfield College (1890-91), Chicago (1892-1932), Pacific (1933-46); **Sutherland**–Lafayette (1919-23), Pittsburgh (1924-38); **Sweeney**–Montana St. (1963-67), Washington St. (1968-75), Fresno St. (1976-96); **Switzer**–Oklahoma (1973-88).

Thomas–Chattanooga (1925-28), Alabama (1931-42, 1944-46); **Vaught**–Mississippi (1947-70); **Wade**–Alabama (1923-30), Duke (1931-41, 1946-50); **Warner**–Georgia (1895-96), Cornell (1897-98), Carlisle (1899-1903), Cornell (1904-06), Carlisle (1907-13), Pittsburgh (1915-23), Stanford (1924-32), Temple (1933-38); **Welsh**–Navy (1973-81), Virginia (1982-2000); **Wilkinson**–Oklahoma (1947-63); **Williams**–Army (1891), Minnesota (1900-21); **Woodruff**–Penn (1892-1901), Illinois (1903), Carlisle (1905); **Woodson**–Central Arkansas (1935-39), Hardin-Simmons (1941-42, 1946-51), Arizona (1952-56), New Mexico St. (1958-67), Trinity-TX (1972-73); **Yost**–Ohio Wesleyan (1897), Nebraska (1898), Kansas (1899), Stanford (1900), Michigan (1901-23, 1925-26).

All-Time Bowl Appearances

Coaches active in 2006 in **bold** type.

	App	W	L	T
1 **Joe Paterno**	.33	22	10	1
2 **Bobby Bowden**	.30	20	9	1
3 Bear Bryant	.29	15	12	2
4 Tom Osborne	.25	12	13	0
5 LaVell Edwards	.22	7	14	1
Lou Holtz	.22	12	8	2
7 Vince Dooley	.20	8	10	2
8 Johnny Vaught	.18	10	8	0
9 Hayden Fry	.17	7	9	1
Bo Schembechler	.17	5	12	0
11 Johnny Majors	.16	9	7	0
Darrell Royal	.16	8	7	1
13 Don James	.15	10	5	0
George Welsh	.15	5	10	0
Mack Brown	.15	9	6	0
16 Jackie Sherrill	.14	8	6	0
Steve Spurrier	.14	7	7	0
Phillip Fulmer	.14	7	7	0
Frank Beamer	.14	6	8	0
John Cooper	.14	5	9	0

Active Coaches' Victories

(Minimum 5 years in Division I-A.)

	Yrs	W	L	T	Pct
1 Bobby Bowden, Fla. St	.41	366	111	4	.765
2 Joe Paterno, Penn St	.41	363	121	3	.748
3 Frank Beamer, Va. Tech	.26	198	105	4	.651
4 Jim Tressel, Ohio St.	.21	197	71	2	.733
5 Chris Ault, Nevada	.22	185	78	1	.703
6 Dennis Franchione, Tex. A&M	23	180	96	2	.651
7 Mack Brown, Texas	.23	179	96	1	.650
8 Dick Tomey, San Jose St.	.26	170	122	7	.580
9 Steve Spurrier, So. Carolina	.17	157	50	2	.756
10 Mike Price, UTEP	.25	150	137	0	.523
11 Dennis Erickson, Ariz. St.	.18	148	65	1	.694
12 Phillip Fulmer, Tennessee	.15	137	41	0	.770
13 Howard Schnellenberger, FAU	22	133	114	3	.545
14 Larry Blakeney, Troy	.16	127	65	1	.661
15 Sonny Lubick, Colorado St.	.18	126.	84	0	.600
16 Mike Bellotti, Oregon	.17	118	73	2	.616
17 Joe Tiller, Purdue	.16	114	79	1	.593
18 Lloyd Carr, Michigan	.12	113	36	0	.758
19 Jeff Bower, So. Mississippi	.17	112	77	1	.592
20 Gary Pinkel, Missouri	.16	110	72	3	.603

AFCA Coach of the Year

First presented in 1935 by the American Football Coaches Association.

Multiple winners: Joe Paterno (5), Bear Bryant (3), John McKay and Darrell Royal (2).

Year

Year		Year		Year	
1935	Pappy Waldorf, Northwestern	1960	Murray Warmath, Minnesota	1983	Ken Hatfield, Air Force
1936	Dick Harlow, Harvard	1961	Bear Bryant, Alabama	1984	LaVell Edwards, BYU
1937	Hooks Mylin, Lafayette	1962	John McKay, USC	1985	Fisher DeBerry, Air Force
1938	Bill Kern, Carnegie Tech	1963	Darrell Royal, Texas	1986	Joe Paterno, Penn St.
1939	Eddie Anderson, Iowa	1964	Frank Broyles, Arkansas	1987	Dick MacPherson, Syracuse
1940	Clark Shaughnessy, Stanford		& Ara Parseghian, Notre Dame	1988	Don Nehlen, West Virginia
1941	Frank Leahy, Notre Dame	1965	Tommy Prothro, UCLA	1989	Bill McCartney, Colorado
1942	Bill Alexander, Georgia Tech	1966	Tom Cahill, Army	1990	Bobby Ross, Georgia Tech
1943	Amos Alonzo Stagg, Pacific	1967	John Pont, Indiana	1991	Bill Lewis, East Carolina
1944	Carroll Widdoes, Ohio St.	1968	Joe Paterno, Penn St.	1992	Gene Stallings, Alabama
1945	Bo McMillin, Indiana	1969	Bo Schembechler, Michigan	1993	Barry Alvarez, Wisconsin
1946	Red Blaik, Army	1970	Charlie McClendon, LSU	1994	Tom Osborne, Nebraska
1947	Fritz Crisler, Michigan		& Darrell Royal, Texas	1995	Gary Barnett, Northwestern
1948	Bennie Oosterbaan, Michigan	1971	Bear Bryant, Alabama	1996	Bruce Snyder, Arizona St.
1949	Bud Wilkinson, Oklahoma	1972	John McKay, USC	1997	Lloyd Carr, Michigan
1950	Charlie Caldwell, Princeton	1973	Bear Bryant, Alabama	1998	Phillip Fulmer, Tennessee
1951	Chuck Taylor, Stanford	1974	Grant Teaff, Baylor	1999	Frank Beamer, Va. Tech
1952	Biggie Munn, Michigan St.	1975	Frank Kush, Arizona St.	2000	Bob Stoops, Oklahoma
1953	Jim Tatum, Maryland	1976	Johnny Majors, Pittsburgh	2001	Ralph Friedgen, Maryland
1954	Red Sanders, UCLA	1977	Don James, Washington		& Larry Coker, Miami-FL
1955	Duffy Daugherty, Michigan St.	1978	Joe Paterno, Penn St.	2002	Jim Tressel, Ohio St.
1956	Bowden Wyatt, Tennessee	1979	Earle Bruce, Ohio St.	2003	Pete Carrol, USC
1957	Woody Hayes, Ohio St.	1980	Vince Dooley, Georgia	2004	Tommy Tuberville, Auburn
1958	Paul Dietzel, LSU	1981	Danny Ford, Clemson	2005	Joe Paterno, Penn St.
1959	Ben Schwartzwalder, Syracuse	1982	Joe Paterno, Penn St.	2006	Jim Grobe, Wake Forest

FWAA Coach of the Year

First presented in 1957 by the Football Writers Association of America. The FWAA and AFCA awards have both gone to the same coach in the same season 32 times. Those double winners are preceded by (#).

Multiple winners: Woody Hayes and Joe Paterno (3); Lou Holtz, Johnny Majors and John McKay (2).

Year		Year		Year	
1957	#Woody Hayes, Ohio St.	1970	Alex Agase, Northwestern	1983	Howard Schnellenberger, Miami-FL
1958	#Paul Dietzel, LSU	1971	Bob Devaney, Nebraska	1984	#LaVell Edwards, BYU
1959	#Ben Schwartzwalder, Syracuse	1972	#John McKay, USC	1985	#Fisher DeBerry, Air Force
1960	#Murray Warmath, Minnesota	1973	Johnny Majors, Pitt	1986	#Joe Paterno, Penn St.
1961	Darrell Royal, Texas	1974	#Grant Teaff, Baylor	1987	#Dick MacPherson, Syracuse
1962	#John McKay, USC	1975	Woody Hayes, Ohio St.	1988	Lou Holtz, Notre Dame
1963	#Darrell Royal, Texas	1976	#Johnny Majors, Pitt	1989	#Bill McCartney, Colorado
1964	#Ara Parseghian, Notre Dame	1977	Lou Holtz, Arkansas	1990	#Bobby Ross, Georgia Tech
1965	Duffy Daugherty, Michigan St.	1978	#Joe Paterno, Penn St.	1991	Don James, Washington
1966	#Tom Cahill, Army	1979	#Earle Bruce, Ohio St.	1992	#Gene Stallings, Alabama
1967	#John Pont, Indiana	1980	#Vince Dooley, Georgia	1993	Terry Bowden, Auburn
1968	Woody Hayes, Ohio St.	1981	#Danny Ford, Clemson	1994	Rich Brooks, Oregon
1969	#Bo Schembechler, Michigan	1982	#Joe Paterno, Penn St.	1995	#Gary Barnett, Northwestern

FWAA Coach of the Year (Cont.)

Year		Year		Year	
1996	#Bruce Snyder, Arizona St.	2000	#Bob Stoops, Oklahoma	2004	Urban Meyer, Utah
1997	Mike Price, Washington St.	2001	#Ralph Friedgen, Maryland	2005	Charlie Weis, Notre Dame
1998	#Phillip Fulmer, Tennessee	2002	#Jim Tressel, Ohio St.	2006	Greg Schiano, Rutgers
1999	#Frank Beamer, Va. Tech	2003	Nick Saban, LSU		

All-Time NCAA Division I-AA Leaders
CAREER

Total Offense

Yards Gained

		Years	Yards
1	Steve McNair, Alcorn St.	1991-94	16,823
2	Bruce Eugene, Grambling	2001-05	14,720
3	Marcus Brady, CS-Northridge	1998-01	13,095
4	Willie Totten, Miss. Valley	1982-85	13,007
5	Robert Kent, Jackson St.	2000-03	12,538

Yards per Game

		Years	Yards	P/Gm
1	Steve McNair, Alcorn St.	1991-94	16,823	400.5
2	Neil Lomax, Portland St.	1978-80	11,647	352.9
3	Aaron Flowers, CS-N'ridge	1996-97	6,754	337.7
4	David Macchi, Valparaiso	2002-03	7,628	331.7
5	Chris Sanders, Chattanooga	1999-00	7,247	329.4

Passing
(Minimum 300 Completions)

Passing Efficiency

		Years	Rating
1	Shawn Knight, William & Mary	1991-94	170.8
2	Erik Meyer, E. Washington	2002-05	166.5
3	Dave Dickenson, Montana	1992-95	166.3
4	Drew Miller, Montana	1999-00	160.5
5	Eric Rasmussen, San Diego	2001-03	160.1

Yards Gained

		Years	Yards
1	Steve McNair, Alcorn St.	1991-94	14,496
2	Bruce Eugene, Grambling	2002-05	12,820
3	Willie Totten, Miss. Valley	1982-85	12,711
4	Marcus Brady, CS-Northridge	1998-01	12,479
5	Jamie Martin, Weber St.	1989-92	12,207

Receiving

Catches

		Years	No
1	Jacquay Nunnally, Fla. A&M	1997-00	317
2	Stephen Campbell, Brown	1997-00	305
3	David Ball, New Hampshire	2003-06	304
4	Jerry Rice, Miss. Valley.	1981-84	301
5	Javarus Dudley, Fordham	2000-03	295

Yards Gained

		Years	No	Yards
1	Jerry Rice, Miss. Valley.	1981-84	301	4693
2	David Ball, New Hampshire	2003-06	304	4655
3	Jacquay Nunnally, Fla. A&M	1997-00	317	4239
4	Javarus Dudley, Fordham	2000-03	295	4197
5	Eric Kimble, E. Washington	2002-05	253	4140

All-Purpose Yardage

Yards per Game

		Years	Yards	P/Gm
1	B. Westbrook, Villanova	1997-98,00-01	9512	216.2
2	Jerry Azumah, N. Hampshire	1995-98	9376	204.3
3	Arnold Mickens, Butler	1994-95	3947	197.4
4	Tim Hall, Robert Morris	1994-95	3701	194.8
5	Reggie Greene, Siena	1994-97	6959	193.3

Rushing

Yards Gained

		Years	Yards
1	Adrian Peterson, Ga. So.	1998-01	6559
2	Charles Roberts, CS-Sac.	1997-00	6553
3	Jerry Azumah, N. Hampshire.	1995-98	6193
4	Matt Cannon, S. Utah	1997-00	5489
5	Reggie Greene, Siena	1994-97	5415

Yards per Game

		Years	Yards	P/Gm
1	Arnold Mickens, Butler	1994-95	3813	190.7
2	Adrian Peterson, Ga. So.	1998-01	6559	156.2
3	Aaron Stecker, W. Ill.	1997-98	3081	154.1
4	Tim Hall, Robert Morris	1994-95	2908	153.1
5	Jerry Azumah, N. Hampshire	1995-98	6193	151.0

Miscellaneous

Interceptions

		Years	No
1	Rashean Mathis, Bethune-Cookman	1999-02	31
2	Dave Murphy, Holy Cross	1986-89	28
	Leigh Bodde, Duquesne	1999-02	28
4	Cedric Walker, S.F. Austin	1990-93	25
5	Three tied at 24.		

Punting Average (min. 150 punts)

		Years	Avg
1	Mark Gould, Northern Ariz.	2000-03	44.8
2	Pumpy Tudors, Tenn.-Chatt.	1989-91	44.4
3	Case de Brujin, Idaho St.	1978-81	43.7
4	Mike Scifres, Western Illinois	1999-02	43.6
5	Terry Belden, Northern Ariz.	1990-93	43.4

Note: Northeastern's Tyler Grogan holds the 1-AA record for longest punt with a 93-yarder against Villanova in 2001.

Punt Return Average*

		Years	Avg
1	Terrence McGee, Northwesern St.	1999-02	17.4
2	Willie Ware, Miss. Valley	1982-85	16.4
3	Buck Phillips, Western Ill.	1994-95	16.4
4	Tim Egerton, Delaware St.	1986-89	16.1
5	Mark Orlando, Towson St.	1991-94	15.7

Kickoff Return Average*

		Years	Avg
1	Lamont Brightful, E. Wash.	1998-01	30.0
2	Troy Brown, Marshall	1991-92	29.7
3	Cedric Bowen, Ark-Pine Bluff	2001-04	29.6
4	Charles Swann, Indiana St.	1989-91	29.3
5	Craig Richardson, Eastern Wash.	1983-86	28.5

*(Minimum 1.2 returns per game)

Blocked Kicks

		Years	FG	XP	P	Tot
1	Leonard Smith, McNeese St.	1980-82	10	4	3	17
2	Trey Woods, Sam Houston St.	1992-95	2	2	8	12
3	Ryan Crawford, Davidson	1997-00	5	0	7	12
4	Mark Weivoda, Idaho St.	200-03	8	3	0	11
5	Bryan Cox, W. Illinois	1987-90	4	5	1	10

Note: The blocked kicks category is a combined total of blocked field goals (FG), extra points (XP) and punts (P).

Scoring
Non-Kickers

Points

		Years	TD	XP	Pts
1	B. Westbrook, Villanova	1997-98,00-01	89	10	544
2	Adrian Peterson, Ga. Southern	1998-01	87	2	524
3	Matt Cannon, S. Utah	1997-00	69	6	420
4	Jerry Azumah, New Hampshire.	1995-98	69	4	418
5	Clifton Dawson, Harvard	2003-06	66	1	398

Touchdowns Passing

		Years	No
1	Bruce Eugene, Grambling	2001-05	140
2	Willie Totten, Miss. Valley	1982-85	139
3	Steve McNair, Alcorn St.	1991-94	119
4	Marcus Brady, CS-Northridge	1998-01	109
4	Robert Kent, Jackson St.	2000-03	104

Touchdowns Rushing

		Years	No
1	Adrian Peterson, Ga. Southern	1998-01	84
2	Matt Cannon, S. Utah	1997-00	69
3	David Dinkins, Morehead St.	1997-00	63
4	Chaz Willaims, Ga. Southern	2001-04	62
5	Jerry Azumah, New Hampshire.	1995-98	60

Touchdown Catches

		Years	No
1	David Ball, New Hampshire	2003-06	58
2	Jerry Rice, Miss. Valley.	1981-84	50
3	Rennie Benn, Lehigh	1982-85	44
4	Dedric Ward, N. Iowa	1993-96	41
5	Rob Giancola, Valparaiso	2001-04	40

Kickers

Points		Years	FG	XP	Pts		Field Goals		Years	FG	Att
1	Chris Snyder, Montana	2000-03	70	182	394	1	Marty Zendejas, Nevada	1984-87	.72	90
2	Marty Zendejas, Nevada	1984-87	72	169	385	2	Kirk Roach, Western Carolina	1984-87	.71	102
3	Greg Kuehn, William & Mary	2002-05	59	166	343	3	Tony Zendejas, Nevada	1981-83	.70	86
4	Justin Langan, W. Illinois	2001-04	53	174	335		Chris Snyder, Montana	2000-03	.70	105
5	Dave Ettinger, Hofstra	1994-97	62	140	326	5	Scott Shields, Weber St.	1995-98	.67	90

Note: Chris Snyder's and Justin Langan's point totals each nclude one two-point conversion.

Note: South Florida's Bill Gramatica, Arkansas State's Scott Roper and Georgia Southern's Tim Foley share the 1-AA record for longest field goal at 63 yards.

Payton Award

First presented in 1987 by the Sports Network and Division I-AA sports information directors to honor the nation's outstanding Division I-AA player. The award is named after Walter Payton, the NFL's all-time leading rusher who was an All-America running back at Jackson St.

Year		Year		Year	
1987	Kenny Gamble, Colgate, RB	1995	Dave Dickenson, Montana, QB	2001	Brian Westbrook, Villanova, RB
1988	Dave Meggett, Towson St., RB	1996	Archie Amerson, N. Arizona, RB	2002	Tony Romo, Eastern Illinois, QB
1989	John Friesz, Idaho, QB	1997	Brian Finneran, Villanova, WR	2003	Jamaal Branch, Colgate, RB
1990	Walter Dean, Grambling, RB	1998	Jerry Azumah, N. Hampshire, RB	2004	Lang Campbell,
1991	Jamie Martin, Weber St., QB	1999	Adrian Peterson,		Wm & Mary, QB
1992	Michael Payton, Marshall, QB		Ga. Southern, RB	2005	Erik Meyer, E. Washington, QB
1993	Doug Nussmeier, Idaho, QB	2000	Louis Ivory, Furman, RB	2006	Ricky Santos, N. Hampshire, QB
1994	Steve McNair, Alcorn St., QB				

All-Time NCAA Division I-AA Winningest Programs

Includes record at a senior college only, minimum of 20 seasons of competition. Bowl and playoff games are included in the overall records but only 1-AA playoff games (since they began in 1978) are included in the W-L column under 1-AA playoffs.

Top 20 Winning Percentage

		Yrs	Gm	W	L	T	Pct.	1-AA Playoffs W-L	Titles
1	Georgia Southern	25	323	238	76	1	.738	38-11	6
2	Yale	134	1221	838	328	55	.709	0-0	0
3	Grambling St.	64	692	480	197	15	.704	9-7	0
4	Florida A&M	74	760	519	223	18	.695	5-6	1
5	Princeton	137	1173	772	351	50	.679	0-0	0
6	Tennessee St.	79	751	490	231	30	.672	2-5	0
7	Harvard	132	1202	781	371	50	.671	0-0	0
8	Pennsylvania	130	1273	786	445	42	.634	0-0	0
9	Southern	85	838	517	296	25	.632	0-0	0
10	Dayton	99	945	583	336	26	.631	0-0	0
11	Eastern Kentucky	82	823	506	290	27	.630	16-15	2
12	Jackson St.	61	633	390	230	13	.626	0-12	0
13	Appalachian St.	77	825	504	292	29	.628	16-12	2
14	Fordham	108	1206	725	428	53	.623	1-1	0
15	McNeese St.	56	612	373	225	14	.621	11-10	0
16	S. Carolina St.	79	745	447	271	27	.618	2-2	0
17	Dartmouth	125	1089	640	403	46	.609	0-0	0
18	Hofstra	66	648	387	250	11	.606	2-5	0
19	Delaware	116	1057	618	395	44	.6054	16-12	1
20	Western Kentucky	88	854	501	322	31	.6048	8-7	1

Top 50 Victories

		Wins			Wins			Wins
1	Yale	838		Furman	537	35	Western Ill.	468
2	Pennsylvania	786	19	Villanova	530	36	Chattanooga	467
3	Harvard	781	20	Massachusetts	522	37	Georgetown	459
4	Princeton	772	21	Florida A&M	519	38	Howard	458
5	Fordham	725	22	Butler	517		Texas St.-	458
6	Dartmouth	640		Southern	517	40	Richmond	455
7	Lafayette	626	24	William & Mary	512	41	VMI	452
8	Delaware	618		E. Kentucky	512	42	S. Carolina St.	447
9	Lehigh	615	26	Hampton	506		Eastern Ill.	447
10	Cornell	608	27	Appalachian St.	504	44	Elon	446
11	Dayton	583	28	W. Kentucky	501	45	Wofford	442
12	Colgate	571	29	Montana	491	46	The Citadel	440
	N. Iowa	571	30	Tennessee St.	490	47	Idaho St.	438
14	Holy Cross	569	31	New Hampshire	484	48	E. Washington	433
15	Brown	552	32	Northwestern St.	481	49	Murray St.	430
16	Bucknell	551	33	Grambling St.	480	50	Alabama St.	429
17	Drake	537	34	Maine	469			

Top 10 Playoff Game Appearances

Ranked by NCAA Division 1-AA playoff games played from 1978-2006. CH refers to championships won.

		Years	Games	Record	CH			Years	Games	Record	CH
1	Georgia Southern	16	48	38-10	6	6	Marshall*	8	29	23-6	2
2	Montana	17	39	24-15	2	7	Delaware	13	28	16-12	1
√3	Youngstown St.	11	32	25-7	4		Appalachian St.	14	28	16-12	2
4	Furman	15	31	17-14	1	9	Northern Iowa	12	27	15-12	0
	Eastern Ky.	17	31	16-15	2	10	McNeese St.	12	23	11-12	0

*Marshall moved up to I-A in 1997.

All-Time Winningest Division I-AA Coaches

Minimum of 10 years as a Division I-A and/or Division I-AA through 2006 season. Coaches active in 1-AA in 2006 in **bold** type. Active coaches and former 1-AA coaches who coached at only one school are listed with current/sole school.

Top 15 Winning Percentage

		Yrs	W	L	T	Pct
1	**Mike Kelly,** Dayton	26	235	53	1	.815
2	Greg Gattuso, Duquesne	12	97	32	0	.752
3	**Al Bagnoli,** Penn	25	190	63	0	.751
4	**Joe Taylor,** Hampton	24	193	73	4	.722
5	Chris Ault*, Nevada	16	138	53	1	.721
6	Tubby Raymond, Delaware	36	300	119	3	.714
7	Roy Kidd, Eastern Ky.	39	313	124	8	.712
8	W.C. Gorden, Jackson St.	19	119	47	5	.711
9	**Pete Richardson,** Southern	19	155	63	1	.710
10	Eddie Robinson, Grambling	55	408	165	15	.707
11	Jim Tressel*, Youngstown St.	15	135	57	2	.701
12	Billy Joe	31	237	108	4	.685
13	**Don Brown,** Massachusetts	10	78	37	0	.678
14	**Dick Biddle,** Colgate	11	88	42	0	.677
15	Mark Whipple	16	120	60	0	.667

Top 15 Victories

		Yrs	W	L	T	Pct
1	Eddie Robinson, Grambling	55	408	165	15	.707
2	Roy Kidd, Eastern Ky.	39	313	124	8	.712
3	Tubby Raymond, Delaware	36	300	119	3	.714
4	Billy Joe	31	237	108	4	.685
5	**Mike Kelly,** Dayton	26	235	53	1	.815
6	Ron Randleman	36	218	167	6	.565
7	Bill Hayes	27	196	103	2	.654
8	**Joe Taylor,** Hampton	24	193	73	4	.722
9	**Al Bagnoli,** Penn	25	190	63	0	.751
10	**Jerry Moore,** Appalachian St.	25	181	116	2	.609
11	Carmen Cozza, Yale	32	179	119	5	.599
	Walt Hameline, Wagner	26	179	93	2	.657
13	Jimmye Laycock, Wm. & Mary	27	178	127	2	.583
14	**Rob Ash,** Drake	27	176	99	5	.638
15	**Andy Talley,** Villanova	27	175	112	2	.609

*Chris Ault (Nevada) and Jim Tressel (Ohio St.) are still active in 1-A. Only their 1-AA numbers are included above.

Division I-AA Coach of the Year

First presented in 1983 by the American Football Coaches Association.

Multiple winners: Mark Duffner, Paul Johnson, Jerry Moore and Erk Russell (2).

Year		Year		Year	
1983	Rey Dempsey, Southern Ill.	1991	Mark Duffner, Holy Cross	1999	Paul Johnson, Ga. Southern
1984	Dave Arnold, Montana St.	1992	Charlie Taaffe, Citadel	2000	Paul Johnson, Ga. Southern
1985	Dick Sheridan, Furman	1993	Dan Allen, Boston Univ.	2001	Bobby Johnson, Furman
1986	Erk Russell, Ga. Southern	1994	Jim Tressel, Youngstown St.	2002	Jack Harbaugh, E. Kentucky
1987	Mark Duffner, Holy Cross	1995	Don Read, Montana	2003	Dick Biddle, Colgate
1988	Jimmy Satterfield, Furman	1996	Ray Tellier, Columbia	2004	Mickey Matthews, James Madison
1989	Erk Russell, Ga. Southern	1997	Andy Talley, Villanova	2005	Jerry Moore, Appalachian St.
1990	Tim Stowers, Ga. Southern	1998	Mark Whipple, Massachusetts	2006	Jerry Moore, Appalachian St

NCAA Playoffs

Division I-AA

Established in 1978 as a four-team playoff. Tournament field increased to eight teams in 1981, 12 teams in 1982 and 16 teams in 1986. Automatic berths are awarded to champions of the Big Sky, Gateway, Mid-Eastern Athletic, Ohio Valley, Patriot, Southern, Southland and Atlantic 10 conferences.

Multiple winners: Georgia Southern (6); Youngstown St. (4); Appalachian St., Eastern Kentucky, Marshall and Montana (2).

Year	Winner	Score	Loser	Year	Winner	Score	Loser
1978	Florida A&M	35-28	Massachusetts	1993	Youngstown St.	17-5	Marshall
1979	Eastern Kentucky	30-7	Lehigh, PA	1994	Youngstown St.	28-14	Boise St.
1980	Boise St., ID	31-29	Eastern Kentucky	1995	Montana	22-20	Marshall
1981	Idaho St.	34-23	Eastern Kentucky	1996	Marshall	49-29	Montana
1982	Eastern Kentucky	17-14	Delaware	1997	Youngstown St.	10-9	McNeese St.
1983	Southern Illinois	43-7	Western Carolina	1998	Massachusetts	55-43	Georgia Southern
1984	Montana St.	19-6	Louisiana Tech	1999	Georgia Southern	59-24	Youngstown St.
1985	Georgia Southern	44-42	Furman, SC	2000	Georgia Southern	27-25	Montana
1986	Georgia Southern	48-21	Arkansas St.	2001	Montana	13-6	Furman
1987	NE Louisiana	43-42	Marshall, WV	2002	Western Kentucky	34-14	McNeese St.
1988	Furman, SC	17-12	Georgia Southern	2003	Delaware	40-0	Colgate
1989	Georgia Southern	37-34	S.F. Austin St.	2004	James Madison	31-21	Montana
1990	Georgia Southern	36-13	Nevada-Reno	2005	Appalachian St.	21-16	Northern Iowa
1991	Youngstown St., OH	25-17	Marshall	2006	Appalachian St.	28-17	Massachusetts
1992	Marshall	31-28	Youngstown St.				

Division II

Established in 1973 as an eight-team playoff. Tournament field increased to 16 teams in 1988. From 1964-72, eight qualifying NCAA College Division member institutions competed in four regional bowl games, but there was no tournament and no national championship until 1973.

Multiple winners: North Dakota St. (5); Grand Valley St. (4); North Alabama (3); Northern Colorado, Northwest Missouri St., Southwest Texas St. and Troy St. (2).

Year	Winner	Score	Loser	Year	Winner	Score	Loser
1973	Louisiana Tech	34-0	Western Kentucky	1991	Pittsburg St., KS	23-6	Jacksonville St., AL
1974	Central Michigan	54-14	Delaware	1992	Jacksonville St., AL	17-13	Pittsburg St., KS
1975	Northern Michigan	16-14	Western Kentucky	1993	North Alabama	41-34	Indiana, PA
1976	Montana St.	24-13	Akron, OH	1994	North Alabama	16-10	Tex. A&M (Kings.)
1977	Lehigh, PA.	33-0	Jacksonville St., AL	1995	North Alabama	27-7	Pittsburg St., KS
1978	Eastern Illinois	10-9	Delaware	1996	Northern Colorado	23-14	Carson-Newman
1979	Delaware	38-21	Youngstown St., OH	1997	Northern Colorado	51-0	New Haven
1980	Cal Poly-SLO	21-13	Eastern Illinois	1998	NW Missouri St.	24-6	Carson-Newman
1981	SW Texas St.	42-13	North Dakota St.	1999	NW Missouri St.	58-52*	Carson-Newman
1982	SW Texas St.	34-9	UC-Davis	2000	Delta St., MS	63-34	Bloomsburg, PA
1983	North Dakota St.	41-21	Central St., OH	2001	North Dakota	17-14	Grand Valley St.
1984	Troy St., AL	18-17	North Dakota St.	2002	Grand Valley St., OH	31-24	Valdosta St., GA
1985	North Dakota St.	35-7	North Alabama	2003	Grand Valley St., OH	10-3	North Dakota
1986	North Dakota St.	27-7	South Dakota	2004	Valdosta St., GA	36-31	Pittsburg St., KS
1987	Troy St., AL	31-17	Portland St., OR	2005	Grand Valley St., OH	21-17	NW Missouri St.
1988	North Dakota St.	35-21	Portland St., OR	2006	Grand Valley St., OH	17-14	NW Missouri St.
1989	Mississippi Col.	3-0	Jacksonville St., AL		*Four overtimes		
1990	North Dakota St.	51-11	Indiana, PA				

Hill Trophy

First presented in 1986 by the Harlon Hill Awards Committee in Florence, Ala., to honor the nation's outstanding Division II player. The award is named after three-time NFL All-Pro Harlon Hill, who played college ball at North Alabama.

Multiple winners: Johnny Bailey (3), Dusty Bonner (2).

Year		Year		Year	
1986	Jeff Bentrim, N. Dakota St., QB	1994	Chris Hatcher, Valdosta St., QB	2002	Curt Anes, Grand Valley St., QB
1987	Johnny Bailey, Texas A&I, RB	1995	Ronald McKinnon, N. Ala., LB	2003	Will Hall, N. Alabama, QB
1988	Johnny Bailey, Texas A&I, RB	1996	Jarrett Anderson, Truman St., RB	2004	Chad Friehauf, Colo-Mines, QB
1989	Johnny Bailey, Texas A&I, RB	1997	Irv Sigler, Bloomsburg, RB	2005	Jimmy Terwilliger,
1990	Chris Simdorn, N. Dakota St., QB	1998	Brian Shay, Emporia St., RB		E. Stroudsburg, QB
1991	Ronnie West, Pittsburg St., WR	1999	Corte McGuffet, N. Colo., QB	2006	Danny Woodhead,
1992	Ronald Moore, Pittsburg St., RB	2000	Dusty Bonner, Valdosta St., QB		Chadron St., RB
1993	Roger Graham, New Haven, RB	2001	Dusty Bonner, Valdosta St., QB		

Division III

Established in 1973 as a four-team playoff. Tournament field increased to eight teams in 1975, 16 teams in 1985 and 28 teams in 1999. From 1969-72, four qualifying NCAA College Division member institutions competed in two regional bowl games, but there was no tournament and no national championship until 1973. (*) denotes overtime.

Multiple winners: Mt. Union (9); Augustana (4); Ithaca (3); Dayton, St. John's, Widener, WI-La Crosse and Wittenberg (2).

Year	Winner	Score	Loser	Year	Winner	Score	Loser
1973	Wittenberg, OH	41-0	Juniata, PA	1990	Allegheny, PA	21-14*	Lycoming, PA
1974	Central, IA	10-8	Ithaca, NY	1991	Ithaca, NY	34-20	Dayton, OH
1975	Wittenberg, OH	28-0	Ithaca, NY	1992	WI-La Crosse	16-12	Wash. & Jeff., PA
1976	St. John's, MN	31-28	Towson St., MD	1993	Mt. Union, OH	34-24	Rowan, NJ
1977	Widener, PA	39-36	Wabash, IN	1994	Albion, MI	38-15	Wash. & Jeff.
1978	Baldwin-Wallace	24-10	Wittenberg, OH	1995	WI-La Crosse	36-7	Rowan, NJ
1979	Ithaca, NY	14-10	Wittenberg, OH	1996	Mt. Union, OH	56-24	Rowan, NJ
1980	Dayton, OH	63-0	Ithaca, NY	1997	Mt. Union, OH	61-12	Lycoming
1981	Widener, PA	17-10	Dayton, OH	1998	Mt. Union, OH	44-24	Rowan, NJ
1982	West Georgia	14-0	Augustana, IL	1999	Pacific Lutheran	42-13	Rowan, NJ
1983	Augustana, IL	21-17	Union, NY	2000	Mt. Union, OH	10-7	St. John's, MN
1984	Augustana, IL	21-12	Central, IA	2001	Mt. Union, OH	30-27	Bridgewater, VA
1985	Augustana, IL	20-7	Ithaca	2002	Mt. Union, OH	48-7	Trinity, TX
1986	Augustana, IL	31-3	Salisbury St., MD	2003	St. John's, MN	24-6	Mt. Union, OH
1987	Wagner, NY	19-3	Dayton, OH	2004	Linfield	28-21	Mary Hardin-Baylor
1988	Ithaca, NY	39-24	Central, IA	2005	Mt. Union, OH	35-28	WI-Whitewater
1989	Dayton, OH	17-7	Union, NY	2006	Mt. Union, OH	35-16	WI-Whitewater

Gagliardi Trophy

First presented in 1993 by the St. John's (Minn.) University J-Club, to honor the nation's outstanding Division III player. The award is named after John Gagliardi, St. John's legendary head coach, one of only two (Eddie Robinson) coaches in college football history with 400 wins.

Year		Year		Year	
1993	Jim Ballard, Mt. Union, QB	1998	Scott Hvistendahl,	2002	Dan Pugh, Mt. Union, RB
1994	Carey Bender, Coe, RB		Augsburg, WR/P	2003	Blake Elliott, St. John's, WR
1995	Chris Palmer, St. John's, WR	1999	Danny Ragsdale, Redlands, QB	2004	Rocky Myers, Wesley, S
1996	Lon Erickson, Ill. Wesleyan, QB	2000	Chad Johnson, Pac. Luth., QB	2005	Brett Elliott, Linfield, QB
1997	Bill Borchert, Mt. Union, QB	2001	Chuck Moore, Mt. Union, RB	2006	Josh Brehm, Alma, QB

NAIA Playoffs

Division I

Established in 1956 as two-team playoff. Tournament field increased to four teams in 1958, eight teams in 1978 and 16 teams in 1987 before cutting back to eight teams in 1989. NAIA went back to a single division 16-team playoff in 1997. The title game has ended in a tie four times (1956, '64, '84 and '85). Note that Northeastern St., OK was called NE Oklahoma in 1958.

Multiple winners: Texas A&I (7); Carson-Newman (5); Carroll-MT (4); Central Arkansas and Central St-OH (3); Abilene Christian, Central St-OK, Elon, Georgetown-KY, Northeastern St-OK, Pittsburg St. and St. John's-MN (2).

Year	Winner	Score	Loser	Year	Winner	Score	Loser
1956	Montana St.	0-0	St. Joseph's, IN	1982	Central St., OK	14-11	Mesa, CO
1957	Pittsburg St., KS	27-26	Hillsdale, MI	1983	Car-Newman, TN	36-28	Mesa, CO
1958	NE Oklahoma	19-13	Northern Arizona	1984	Car-Newman, TN	19-19	Central Arkansas
1959	Texas A&I	20-7	Lenoir-Rhyne, NC	1985	Hillsdale, MI	10-10	Central Arkansas
1960	Lenoir-Rhyne, NC	15-14	Humboldt St., CA	1986	Car-Newman, TN	17-0	Cameron, OK
1961	Pittsburg St., KS	12-7	Linfield, OR	1987	Cameron, OK	30-2	Car-Newman, TN
1962	Central St., OK	28-13	Lenoir-Rhyne, NC	1988	Car-Newman, TN	56-21	Adams St., CO
1963	St. John's, MN	33-27	Prairie View A&M, TX	1989	Car-Newman, TN	34-20	Emporia St., KS
1964	Concordia, MN	7-7	Sam Houston St., TX	1990	Central St., OH	38-16	Mesa, CO
1965	St. John's, MN	33-0	Linfield, OR	1991	Central Arkansas	19-16	Central St., OH
1966	Waynesburg, PA	42-21	WI-Whitewater	1992	Central St., OH	19-16	Gardner-Webb, NC
1967	Fairmont St., WV	28-21	Eastern Wash.	1993	E. Central, OK	49-35	Glenville St., WV
1968	Troy St., AL	43-35	Texas A&I	1994	N'eastern St., OK	13-12	Ark-Pine Bluff
1969	Texas A&I	32-7	Concordia, MN	1995	Central St., OH	37-7	N'eastern St., OK
1970	Texas A&I	48-7	Wofford, SC	1996	SW Oklahoma St.	33-31	Montana Tech
1971	Livingston, AL	14-12	Arkansas Tech	1997	Findlay, OH	14-7	Willamette, OR
1972	East Texas St.	21-18	Car-Newman, TN	1998	Azusa Pacific, CA	17-14	Olivet Nazarene, IL
1973	Abilene Christian	42-14	Elon, NC	1999	NW Oklahoma St.	34-26	Georgetown, KY
1974	Texas A&I	34-23	Henderson St., AR	2000	Georgetown, KY	20-0	NW Oklahoma St.
1975	Texas A&I	37-0	Salem, WV	2001	Georgetown, KY	49-27	Sioux Falls, S.D.
1976	Texas A&I	26-0	Central Arkansas	2002	Carroll, MT	28-7	Georgetown, KY
1977	Abilene Christian	24-7	SW Oklahoma	2003	Carroll, MT	41-28	NW Oklahoma St.
1978	Angelo St., TX	34-14	Elon, NC	2004	Carroll, MT	15-13	St. Francis, IN
1979	Texas A&I	20-14	Central St., OK	2005	Carroll, MT	27-10	St. Francis, IN
1980	Elon, NC	17-10	NE Oklahoma	2006	Sioux Falls, SD	23-19	St. Francis, IN
1981	Elon, NC	3-0	Pittsburg St., KS				

Division II

Established in 1970 as four-team playoff. Tournament field increased to eight teams in 1978 and 16 teams in 1987. NAIA went back to a single division playoff in 1997. The title game has ended in a tie twice (1981 and '87).

Multiple winners: Westminster (6); Findlay, Linfield and Pacific Lutheran (3); Concordia-MN, Northwestern-IA and Texas Lutheran (2).

Year	Winner	Score	Loser	Year	Winner	Score	Loser
1970	Westminster, PA	21-16	Anderson, IN	1984	Linfield, OR	33-22	Northwestern, IA
1971	Calif. Lutheran	30-14	Westminster, PA	1985	WI-La Crosse	24-7	Pacific Lutheran
1972	Missouri Southern	21-14	Northwestern, IA	1986	Linfield, OR	17-0	Baker, KS
1973	Northwestern, IA	10-3	Glenville St., WV	1987	Pacific Lutheran	16-16	WI-Stevens Pt.*
1974	Texas Lutheran	42-0	Missouri Valley	1988	Westminster, PA	21-14	WI-La Crosse
1975	Texas Lutheran	34-8	Calif. Lutheran	1989	Westminster, PA	51-30	WI-La Crosse
1976	Westminster, PA	20-13	Redlands, CA	1990	Peru St., NE	17-7	Westminster, PA
1977	Westminster, PA	17-9	Calif. Lutheran	1991	Georgetown, KY	28-20	Pacific Lutheran
1978	Concordia, MN	7-0	Findlay, OH	1992	Findlay, OH	26-13	Linfield, OR
1979	Findlay, OH	51-6	Northwestern, IA	1993	Pacific Lutheran	50-20	Westminster, PA
1980	Pacific Lutheran	38-10	Wilmington, OH	1994	Westminster, PA	27-7	Pacific Lutheran
1981	Austin College, TX	24-24	Concordia, MN	1995	Findlay, OH	21-21	Central Wash.
1982	Linfield, OR	33-15	Wm. Jewell, MO	1996	Sioux Falls, S.D.	47-25	W. Washington
1983	Northwestern, IA	25-21	Pacific Lutheran				

*Wisconsin-Stevens Point forfeited its entire 1987 schedule due to its use of an ineligible player.

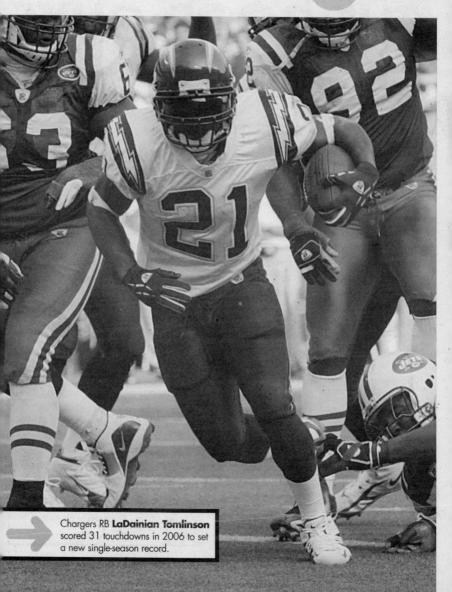

PRO
FOOTBALL

2006 / 2007 YEAR IN REVIEW

Chargers RB **LaDainian Tomlinson** scored 31 touchdowns in 2006 to set a new single-season record.

HERE'S TO
THE GOOD GUYS

Peyton Manning is brilliant as usual, but it's a surprisingly stout defense that helps the Colts to the title in Super Bowl XLI.

GOOD THINGS TRULY COME TO THOSE WHO WAIT.

The Indianapolis Colts — led by head coach Tony Dungy, quarterback Peyton Manning and team president Bill Polian — three of the best at their trade, at long last won it all.

The Colts started strong, slumped late, then got hot when it counted most, capping off a rollercoaster season with a 29-17 triumph over the Chicago Bears in soggy Super Bowl XLI at Miami's Dolphin Stadium. It was the franchise's first NFL championship since the then-Baltimore Colts edged the Dallas Cowboys in Super Bowl V at Miami's Orange Bowl 36 years earlier.

For the second consecutive year, the eventual Super Bowl champion bounced back from a season of enormous disappointment to capture the Vince Lombardi Trophy.

As they did when they opened 13-0 in 2005, the Colts got off to a magnificent start (9-0) but this time, would lose four of their last seven games. Relegated to taking the long way through the playoffs as a #3 seed,

Dungy's club — most notably a much-maligned defense — came through when it counted most, first stifling the Chiefs and Ravens in the playoffs. The Colts then fell behind their chief rival, the New England Patriots, 21-3, before Manning and company pulled off the greatest comeback in championship game annals to win, 38-34, en route to the win over the Bears two weeks later.

Hoisting the Lombardi Trophy provided a poignant and historic moment for Dungy, as he became the first African-American head coach to win a Super Bowl. It came against one-time assistant and close friend Lovie Smith, also an African-American head coach, making it the first time in history that such a matchup had occurred in the league's biggest game.

Of course, there was also plenty of history made throughout a memorable season. Smith's Bears were the talk of

 Chris Berman is the host of ESPN's *NFL Prime Time.*

AP/Wide World Photos

Colts quarterback **Peyton Manning** lifts the Vince Lombardi Trophy beside coach **Tony Dungy** and Dungy's wife, Lauren, following Super Bowl XLI.

the league during September, led by mercurial quarterback Rex Grossman, a fierce defense and rookie Devin Hester, who seemingly scored a touchdown every time he touched the football, setting a new single-season record with six return touchdowns, including a 108-yarder off a missed field goal. He capped off the season by doing what no player had done before — taking the opening kickoff in Super Bowl XLI the distance.

Perhaps no story in recent memory was more stirring than that of the New Orleans Saints, who gave a region battered by Hurricane Katrina just a year earlier a reason to rejoice. Jump-started by a rousing re-opening of the Superdome on Monday Night

Football, first-year head coach Sean Payton and quarterback Drew Brees were the ringleaders of an exciting offense. Meanwhile, a pair of rookies from opposite ends of the draft — running back Reggie Bush, the second overall pick, and wide receiver Marques Colston, taken 252nd out of 255 selections — were key contributors. It all added up to the franchise's first trip to the NFC Championship Game in its 40-year history.

One year after Seattle running back Shaun Alexander set a new league record with 28 touchdowns, Chargers' running back LaDainian Tomlinson set new single-season standards for reaching the end zone (31 touchdowns) and points scored (186)

D'oh. Despite this fumbled snap that ruined a bid for a game-winning field goal against Seattle, the future looks bright in Big D with **Tony Romo** at QB.

AP/Wide World Photos

ing champion Pittsburgh Steelers lost six of their first eight games as quarterback Ben Roethlisberger struggled, in what proved to be an 8-8 finish in Bill Cowher's 15th and final season as the team's head coach. The Seattle Seahawks became the first Super Bowl runner-up in six years to reach the postseason the following year, scratching and clawing their way to a 9-7 record and the NFC West title. They were ultimately knocked out of the NFC Divisional Playoffs in overtime at Chicago.

There were other great stories as well. Quarterback Donovan McNabb got off to a strong start but the Philadelphia Eagles' season appeared lost when he went down for the season in November. Enter veteran Jeff Garcia, who led the Birds to their fifth NFC East title in six seasons, highlighted by three straight divisional road wins in December.

There was a quarterback change for a different reason in Dallas as Tony Romo surprised many by jump-starting the Cowboys' offense and leading Bill Parcells' team to the playoffs. However, a postseason win at Seattle slipped though Romo's fingers when he mishandled the snap on a short game-winning field goal attempt.

In the end, though, 2006 was all about Manning, Dungy and the Colts, the ultimate example that good guys do indeed finish first.

for the team with the NFL's best record in 2006 (14-2). In the process, Tomlinson also reached 100 career touchdowns in a mere 89 career games — faster than any player in league history. Alas, Marty Schottenheimer's club ran into Tom Brady and those Patriots, who continued to show why they are the premiere organization in the league with their memorable 24-21 come-from-behind playoff win at San Diego.

Once again, it was also a season of disappointment for the previous Super Bowl participants. The defend-

A New Form of History

SO YOU THINK YOU KNOW THE NFL?

Last season, the Indianapolis Colts won Super Bowl XLI, the franchise's first NFL championship since the Baltimore Colts won Super Bowl V a mere 36 years earlier. It was a long time coming for one of the league's storied franchises.

But the victory was somewhat unexpected only because the 14-2 San Diego Chargers boasted the league's best record. Hence, it marked the eighth time in ten seasons that the team with the league's best record failed to win it all.

Unlike Major League Baseball, massive player movement remains a fairly new concept in the National Football League. The league's current form of free agency began with the 1993 season, and the NFL did not implement a salary cap until 1994.

What free agency has done for the NFL has made every team (yes, every team) a viable playoff contender at the beginning of the season, whether you believe it or not. Since the current playoff format began in 1990 (12 teams), the last time both top-seeded teams in their respective conferences made it to the Super Bowl was the 1993 season (the first year of free agency) when Dallas and Buffalo squared off in Super Bowl XXVIII in Atlanta.

While some franchises remain either consistently good or bad, every team has had its moments. Consider that the Houston Texans, who made their NFL debut in 2002, are the only team not to make the playoffs over that span.

But variety has now become the spice of life in terms of winning the Super Bowl and/or getting to the Big Game. During the first 27 years of the Super Bowl Era (1966-92) and prior to free agency, 19 different teams played in the Super Bowl, 14 of those clubs made two or more appearances, 12 teams won at least one title, and 13 different franchises lost at least one Super Bowl.

But over the last 14 seasons (1993-06), 20 different teams have played in the Super Bowl, and only six of those franchises have made more than one appearance. Also in that span, ten different clubs have walked away with at least one championship, while 14 different teams have lost the last 14 Super Bowls.

Last year's Super win by the Colts marked the fourth time in the last ten years that a team needed 20 games to capture the Lombardi Trophy, joining the Broncos (XXXII), Ravens (XXXV) and Steelers (XL) — who each made it to the postseason as a wild card entry.

So when you're preparing to make your playoff and Super Bowl picks in August, take a little extra time. Because the group you're selecting from may be bigger than you think.

 Russell Baxter is the NFL Research Coordinator for ESPN and appears regularly on *Mike & Mike in the Morning.*

THE TOP

10

Stories of the Year in Pro Football

10 Man-Genius
In between cold handshakes with Bill Belichick, first-year New York Jets head coach Eric Mangini rides a healthy Chad Pennington and leads his team to a 10-6 mark and a surprising playoff berth.

09 The Bears Are Who We THOUGHT They Were!
After the Bears' stunning 24-23 come-from-behind win over the Cardinals, Arizona coach Dennis Green delivers an emotional press conference, the likes of which hasn't been heard since Jim Mora's legendary "Playoffs?!?"

08 Eagles Fly
Backup Jeff Garcia steps in after Donovan McNabb goes down with a season-ending knee injury, and leads the Eagles to a 5-1 record and into the postseason.

07 Charge?
San Diego rolls to a 14-2 record, but lose their first playoff game, 24-21, to the Patriots.

06 Young Guns
An exciting crop of offensive rookies takes the league by storm as Reggie Bush, Vince Young, Joseph Addai, Laurence Maroney and Devin Hester all lead their teams to the playoffs, while Maurice Jones-Drew scores 16 touchdowns.

05 Da Bears
Amidst weekly calls for a quarterback change, a stellar defense carries the Bears to a 13-3 regular season record and their first Super Bowl appearance since 1986.

04 Comeback Kids
Down 21-6 at halftime, Peyton Manning leads a remarkable comeback, as the Indianapolis Colts get past their Achilles heel, the New England Patriots, 38-34, in the AFC Championship Game.

03 TD...LT
San Diego RB LaDainian Tomlinson scores 31 touchdowns, 28 on the ground, to set a new NFL single-season record.

02 Saints Are Coming
The New Orleans Saints return to the Superdome a year after Hurricane Katrina devastated the city, and go on to win the NFC South and advance to the NFC Championship Game.

01 Horse Power
Peyton Manning and Tony Dungy get their long-awaited championship with a 29-17 win over Chicago in Super Bowl XLI.

2006-2007
Season in Review

Final NFL Standings

Division champions (*) and wild card playoff qualifiers (†) are noted; division champions with two best records received first round byes. Number of seasons listed after each head coach refers to latest tenure with club through 2006 season.

American Football Conference

East Division

	W	L	T	PF	PA	vs Div	vs AFC
*New England	12	4	0	385	237	4-2	8-4
†NY Jets	10	6	0	316	295	4-2	7-5
Buffalo	7	9	0	300	311	3-3	5-7
Miami	6	10	0	260	283	1-5	3-9

2006 Head Coaches: NE—Bill Belichick (7th season); **NY**—Eric Mangini (1st); **Buf**—Dick Jauron (1st); **Mia**—Nick Saban (2nd).
2005 Standings: 1. New England (10-6); 2. Miami (9-7); 3. Buffalo (5-11); 4. NY Jets (4-12).

North Division

	W	L	T	PF	PA	vs Div	vs AFC
*Baltimore	13	3	0	353	201	5-1	10-2
Cincinnati	8	8	0	373	331	4-2	6-6
Pittsburgh	8	8	0	353	315	3-3	5-7
Cleveland	4	12	0	238	356	0-6	3-9

2006 Head Coaches: Bal—Brian Billick (8th season); **Cin**—Marvin Lewis (4th); **Pit**—Bill Cowher (15th); **Cle**—Romeo Crennel (2nd).
2005 Standings: 1. Cincinnati (11-5); 2. Pittsburgh (11-5); 3. Baltimore (6-10); 4. Cleveland (6-10).

South Division

	W	L	T	PF	PA	vs Div	vs AFC
*Indianapolis	12	4	0	427	360	3-3	9-3
Tennessee	8	8	0	324	400	4-2	5-7
Jacksonville	8	8	0	371	274	2-4	5-7
Houston	6	10	0	267	366	3-3	6-6

2006 Head Coaches: Ind—Tony Dungy (5th season); **Ten**—Jeff Fisher (13th); **Jax**—Jack Del Rio (4th); **Hou**—Gary Kubiak (1st).
2005 Standings: 1. Indianapolis (14-2); 2. Jacksonville (12-4); 3. Tennessee (4-12); 4. Houston (2-14).

West Division

	W	L	T	PF	PA	vs Div	vs AFC
*San Diego	14	2	0	492	303	5-1	10-2
†Kansas City	9	7	0	331	315	4-2	8-4
Denver	9	7	0	319	305	3-3	8-4
Oakland	2	14	0	168	332	0-6	1-11

2006 Head Coaches: SD—Marty Schottenheimer (5th season); **KC**—Herman Edwards (1st); **Den**—Mike Shanahan (12th); **Oak**—Art Shell (1st).
2005 Standings: 1. Denver (13-3); 2. Kansas City (10-6); 3. San Diego (9-7); 4. Oakland (4-12).
Note: Kansas City (9-7) won the wildcard berth over Denver (9-7) due to a better record within the division.

National Football Conference

East Division

	W	L	T	PF	PA	vs Div	vs NFC
*Philadelphia	10	6	0	398	328	5-1	9-3
†Dallas	9	7	0	425	350	2-4	6-6
†NY Giants	8	8	0	355	362	4-2	7-5
Washington	5	11	0	307	376	1-5	3-9

2006 Head Coaches: Phi—Andy Reid (7th season); **Dal**—Bill Parcells (4th); **NY**—Tom Coughlin (3rd); **Wash**—Joe Gibbs (3rd).
2005 Standings: 1. NY Giants (11-5); 2. Washington (10-6); 3. Dallas (9-7); 4. Philadelphia (6-10).
Note: NY Giants (8-8) won an NFC wild card berth over Carolina (8-8) and St. Louis (8-8) due to a better conference record, and over Green Bay (8-8) due to "strength of victory."

North Division

	W	L	T	PF	PA	vs Div	vs NFC
*Chicago	13	3	0	427	255	5-1	11-1
Green Bay	8	8	0	301	366	5-1	7-5
Minnesota	6	10	0	282	327	2-4	6-6
Detroit	3	13	0	305	398	0-6	2-10

2006 Head Coaches: Chi—Lovie Smith (3rd season); **GB**—Mike McCarthy (1st); **Min**—Brad Childress (1st); **Det**—Rod Marinelli (1st).
2005 Standings: 1. Chicago (11-5); 2. Minnesota (9-7); 3. Detroit (5-11); 4. Green Bay (4-12).

South Division

	W	L	T	PF	PA	vs Div	vs NFC
*New Orleans	10	6	0	413	322	4-2	9-3
Carolina	8	8	0	270	305	5-1	6-6
Atlanta	7	9	0	292	328	3-3	5-7
Tampa Bay	4	12	0	211	353	0-6	2-10

2006 Head Coaches: NO—Sean Payton (1st season); **Car**—John Fox (5th); **Atl**—Jim Mora Jr. (3rd); **TB**—Jon Gruden (5th).
2005 Standings: 1. Tampa Bay (11-5); 2. Carolina (11-5); 3. Atlanta (8-8); 4. New Orleans (3-13).

West Division

	W	L	T	PF	PA	vs Div	vs NFC
*Seattle	9	7	0	335	341	3-3	7-5
St. Louis	8	8	0	367	381	2-4	6-6
San Francisco	7	9	0	298	412	3-3	5-7
Arizona	5	11	0	314	389	4-2	5-7

2006 Head Coaches: Sea—Mike Holmgren (8th season); **St.L**—Scott Linehan (1st); **SF**—Mike Nolan (2nd); **Ariz**—Dennis Green (3rd).
2005 Standings: 1. Seattle (13-3); 2. St. Louis (6-10); 3. Arizona (5-11); 4. San Francisco (4-12).

NFL Regular Season Individual Leaders

(* indicates rookies)

Passing Efficiency

(Minimum of 224 attempts)

AFC	Att	Cmp	Cmp Pct	Yds	Yds/ Att	TD	Long	Int	Sack/Lost	Rating Points
Peyton Manning, Ind	557	362	65.0	4397	7.89	31	68-td	9	14/86	101.0
Damon Huard, KC	244	148	60.7	1878	7.70	11	78	1	16/106	98.0
Carson Palmer, Cin	520	324	62.3	4035	7.76	28	74-td	13	36/233	93.9
Philip Rivers, SD	460	284	61.7	3388	7.37	22	57-td	9	27/144	92.0
Tom Brady, NE	516	319	61.8	3529	6.84	24	62-td	12	26/175	87.9
J.P. Losman, Buf	429	268	62.5	3051	7.11	19	83-td	14	47/332	84.9
Chad Pennington, NYJ	485	313	64.5	3352	6.91	17	71-td	16	30/172	82.6
Steve McNair, Bal	468	295	63.0	3050	6.52	16	87-td	12	14/84	82.5
David Carr, Hou	442	302	68.3	2767	6.26	11	53	12	41/240	82.1
David Garrard, Jax	241	145	60.2	1735	7.20	10	49	9	20/119	80.5
Ben Roethlisberger, Pit	469	280	59.7	3513	7.49	18	67-td	23	46/280	75.4
Charlie Frye, Cle	392	252	64.1	2454	6.24	10	75	17	44/262	72.2
Jake Plummer, Den	317	175	55.2	1994	6.29	11	83-td	13	18/111	68.8
Joey Harrington, Mia	388	223	57.5	2236	5.76	12	48	15	15/116	68.2
Vince Young*, Ten	357	184	51.5	2199	6.16	12	53	13	25/129	66.7

NFC	Att	Cmp	Cmp Pct	Yds	Yds/ Att	TD	Long	Int	Sack/Lost	Rating Points
Drew Brees, NO	554	356	64.3	4418	7.97	26	86-td	11	18/105	96.2
Donovan McNabb, Phi	316	180	57.0	2647	8.38	18	87-td	6	21/140	95.5
Tony Romo, Dal	337	220	65.3	2903	8.61	19	56-td	13	21/124	95.1
Marc Bulger, St.L	588	370	62.9	4301	7.31	24	67-td	8	49/366	92.9
Mark Brunell, Wash	260	162	62.3	1789	6.88	8	74	4	12/92	86.5
Jake Delhomme, Car	431	263	61.0	2805	6.51	17	72-td	11	22/167	82.6
Jon Kitna, Det	596	372	62.4	4208	7.06	21	60-td	22	63/388	79.9
Eli Manning, NYG	522	301	57.7	3244	6.21	24	55-td	18	25/186	77.0
Matt Hasselbeck, Sea	371	210	56.6	2442	6.58	18	72-td	15	34/229	76.0
Michael Vick, Atl	388	204	52.6	2474	6.38	20	55	13	45/303	75.7
Alex Smith, SF	442	257	58.1	2890	6.54	16	75	16	35/202	74.8
Matt Leinart*, Ari	377	214	56.8	2547	6.76	11	58	12	21/158	74.0
Rex Grossman, Chi	480	262	54.6	3193	6.65	23	62	20	21/142	73.9
Brett Favre, GB	613	343	56.0	3885	6.34	18	82-td	18	21/134	72.7
Brad Johnson, Min	439	270	61.5	2750	6.26	9	46	15	29/200	72.0

Receptions

AFC	No	Yds	Avg	Long	TD
Andre Johnson, Hou	103	1147	11.1	53	5
Marvin Harrison, Ind	95	1366	14.4	68-td	12
Laveranues Coles, NYJ	91	1098	12.1	58-td	6
T.J. Houshmandzadeh, Cin	90	1081	12.0	40-td	9
Kellen Winslow, Cle	89	875	9.8	40	3
Chad Johnson, Cin	87	1369	15.7	74-td	7
Reggie Wayne, Ind	86	1310	15.2	51-td	9
Lee Evans, Buf	82	1292	15.8	83-td	8
Jerricho Cotchery, NYJ	82	961	11.7	71-td	6
Hines Ward, Pit	74	975	13.2	70-td	6
Tony Gonzalez, KC	73	900	12.3	57	5
Todd Heap, Bal	73	765	10.5	30	6
Antonio Gates, SD	71	924	13.0	57-td	9
Javon Walker, Den	69	1084	15.7	83-td	8

NFC	No	Yds	Avg	Long	TD
Mike Furrey, Det	98	1086	11.1	31	6
Torry Holt, St.L	93	1188	12.8	67-td	10
Donald Driver, GB	92	1295	14.1	82-td	8
Steven Jackson, St.L	90	806	9.0	64-td	3
Reggie Bush*, NO	88	742	8.4	74	2
Terrell Owens, Dal	85	1180	13.9	56-td	13
Anquan Boldin, Ari	83	1203	14.5	64	4
Steve Smith, Car	83	1166	14.0	72-td	8
Roy Williams, Det	82	1310	16.0	60-td	7
Brian Westbrook, Phi	77	699	9.1	52-td	4
Isaac Bruce, St.L	74	1098	14.8	45	3
Terry Glenn, Dal	70	1047	15.0	54	6
Marques Colston*, NO	70	1038	14.8	86-td	8
Keyshawn Johnson, Car	70	815	11.6	40	4

Rushing Yards

AFC	Att	Yds	Avg	Long	TD
LaDainian Tomlinson, SD	348	1815	5.2	85-td	28
Larry Johnson, KC	416	1789	4.3	47	17
Willie Parker, Pit	337	1494	4.4	76	13
Rudi Johnson, Cin	341	1309	3.8	22-td	12
Travis Henry, Ten	270	1211	4.5	70-td	7
Fred Taylor, Jax	231	1146	5.0	76	5
Jamal Lewis, Bal	314	1132	3.6	52	9
Joseph Addai*, Ind	226	1081	4.8	41	7
Tatum Bell, Den	233	1025	4.4	51	2
Ronnie Brown, Mia	241	1008	4.2	47	5
Willis McGahee, Buf	259	990	3.8	57-td	6
Maurice Jones-Drew*, Jax	166	941	5.7	74-td	13
Corey Dillon, NE	199	812	4.1	50	13
Reuben Droughns, Cle	220	758	3.4	22	4

NFC	Att	Yds	Avg	Long	TD
Frank Gore, SF	312	1695	5.4	72	8
Tiki Barber, NYG	327	1662	5.1	55-td	5
Steven Jackson, St.L	346	1528	4.4	59-td	13
Brian Westbrook, Phi	240	1217	5.1	71-td	7
Chester, Taylor, Min	303	1216	4.0	95-td	6
Thomas Jones, Chi	296	1210	4.1	30-td	6
Edgerrin James, Ari	337	1159	3.4	18	6
Ladell Betts, Wash	245	1154	4.7	26	4
Warrick Dunn, Atl	286	1140	4.0	90-td	4
Julius Jones, Dal	267	1084	4.1	77-td	4
Ahman Green, GB	266	1059	4.0	70-td	5
Deuce McAllister, NO	244	1057	4.3	57	10
Michael Vick, Atl	123	1039	8.4	51	2
DeShaun Foster, Car	227	897	4.0	43-td	3

Indianapolis Colts
Peyton Manning
Passing Efficiency

Houston Texans
Andre Johnson
Receptions

San Diego Chargers
LaDainian Tomlinson
Rushing, Scoring

Denver Broncos
Champ Bailey
Interceptions

All-Purpose Yardage

AFC	Rush	Rec	Ret	Total	NFC	Rush	Rec	Ret	Total
LaDainian Tomlinson, SD . .	1815	508	0	2323	Steven Jackson, St.L.	1528	806	0	2334
Maurice Jones-Drew*, Jax . .	941	436	873	2250	Frank Gore, SF	1695	485	0	2180
Larry Johnson, KC	1789	410	0	2199	Tiki Barber, NYG.	1662	465	0	2127
Wes Welker, Mia	0	687	1442	2129	Brian Westbrook, Phi	1217	699	39	1955
Chris Carr, Oak	0	0	2078	2078	Eddie Drummond, Det	4	10	1645	1659
Laurence Maroney*, NE . .	745	194	783	1722	Maurice Hicks, SF	82	137	1428	1647
Willie Parker, Pit	1494	222	0	1716	Ladell Betts, Wash	1154	445	27	1626
Bobby Wade, Ten	0	461	1221	1682	J.J. Arrington, Ari	19	58	1520	1597
Dante Hall, KC	11	204	1447	1662	Rock Cartwright, Wash	15	0	1541	1556
Joshua Cribbs, Cle	11	91	1545	1647	Reggie Bush*, NO	565	742	216	1523
Santonio Holmes*, Pit	13	824	700	1537	Michael Pittman, TB	245	405	867	1517
Michael Turner, SD	502	47	954	1503	Chester Taylor, Min	1216	288	0	1504
Terrence Wilkins, Ind	0	0	1465	1465	DeAngelo Williams, Car	501	313	623	1437
Rudi Johnson, Cin	1309	124	0	1433	Ahman Green, GB	1059	373	0	1432
Joseph Addai*, Ind	1081	325	0	1406	Edgerrin James, Ari	1159	217	0	1376

Ret column indicates all kickoff, punt, fumble and interception returns.

Scoring

Touchdowns

AFC	TD	Rush	Rec	Ret	Pts
LaDainian Tomlinson, SD . . .	31	28	3	0	186
Larry Johnson, KC	19	17	2	0	114
Maurice Jones-Drew*, Jax . .	16	13	2	1	96
Willie Parker, Pit	16	13	3	0	96
Corey Dillon, NE	13	13	0	0	78
Marvin Harrison, Ind	12	0	12	0	72
Rudi Johnson, Cin.	12	12	0	0	72
Reggie Wayne, Ind	9	0	9	0	56†
Antonio Gates, SD	9	0	9	0	54
Chris Henry, Cin	9	0	9	0	54
T.J. Houshmandzadeh, Cin . .	9	0	9	0	54
Jamal Lewis, Bal.	9	9	0	0	54
Javon Walker, Den	9	1	8	0	54

† Two-point conversions: Wayne (1).

NFC	TD	Rush	Rec	Ret	Pts
Marion Barber, Dal	16	14	2	0	96
Steven Jackson, St.L	16	13	3	0	96
Terrell Owens, Dal	13	0	13	0	80†
Deuce McAllister, NO.	11	10	0	1	66
Brian Westbrook, Phi	11	7	4	0	66
Plaxico Burress, NYG	10	0	10	0	60
Torry Holt, St.L	10	0	10	0	60
Darrell Jackson, Sea	10	0	10	0	60
Reggie Brown, Phi	9	1	8	0	54
Reggie Bush*, NO	9	6	2	1	54
Frank Gore, SF	9	8	1	0	54
Brandon Jacobs, NYG	9	9	0	0	54
Steve Smith, Car	9	1	8	0	54

† Two-point conversions: Owens (1).

Kickers

AFC	PAT	FG	Long	Pts
Nate Kaeding, SD	58/58	26/29	54	136
Matt Stover, Bal	37/37	28/30	52	121
Josh Scobee, Jax.	41/41	26/32	48	119
Jason Elam, Den	34/34	27/29	51	115
Shayne Graham, Cin	40/42	25/30	51	115
Adam Vinatieri, Ind	38/38	25/28	48	113
Lawrence Tynes, KC	35/36	24/31	53	107
Mike Nugent, NYJ	34/35	24/27	54	106
Stephen Gostkowski*, NE . .	43/44	20/26	52	103
Rian Lindell, Buf	33/33	23/25	53	102
Jeff Reed, Pit.	41/41	20/27	50	101
Olindo Mare, Mia	22/22	26/36	52	100
Rob Bironas, Ten.	32/32	22/28	60	98
Phil Dawson, Cle	25/25	21/29	51	88

NFC	PAT	FG	Long	Pts
Robbie Gould, Chi	47/47	32/36	49	143
Jeff Wilkins, St.L	35/35	32/37	53	131
Jason Hanson, Det	30/30	29/33	53	117
Joe Nedney, SF	29/29	29/35	51	116
Neil Rackers, Ari	32/32	28/37	50	116
John Carney, NO	46/47	23/25	51	115
Josh Brown, Sea	36/36	25/31	54	111
Dave Rayner, GB	31/32	26/35	54	109
Jay Feely, NYG	38/38	23/27	47	107
David Akers, Phi	48/48	18/23	47	102
John Kasay, Car	28/28	24/27	54	100
Ryan Longwell, Min	27/28	21/25	49	90
Morten Andersen, Atl	27/27	20/23	45	87
Matt Bryant, TB.	22/23	17/22	62	73

NFL Regular Season Individual Leaders (Cont.)

Sacks

AFC	No
Shawne Merriman, SD	17.0
Aaron Schobel, Buf	14.0
Jason Taylor, Mia	13.5
Trevor Pryce, Bal	13.0
Shaun Phillips, SD	11.5

NFC	No
Aaron Kampman, GB	15.5
Julius Peppers, Car	13.0
Leonard Little, St.L	13.0
Mark Anderson*, Chi	12.0
DeMarcus Ware, Dal	11.5

Interceptions

AFC	No	Yds	Long	TD
Champ Bailey, Den	10	162	70-td	1
Asante Samuel, NE	10	120	33	0
Rashean Mathis, Jax	8	146	55	0
Nnamdi Asomugha, Oak	8	59	24-td	1
Chris McAlister, Bal	6	121	60-td	2
Kevin Kaesviharn, Cin	6	24	22	0

NFC	No	Yds	Long	TD
Walt Harris, SF	8	84	42	1
Charles Woodson, GB	8	61	23-td	1
Lito Sheppard, Phi	6	157	102-td	1

Three tied with 5 int's each.

Punting

AFC	No	Yds	Lg	Avg	In20
Shane Lechler, Oak	77	3660	67	47.5	19
Kyle Larson, Cin	77	3428	67	44.5	26
Hunter Smith, Ind	47	2085	61	44.4	14
Dustin Colquitt, KC	71	3145	72	44.3	23
Ben Graham, NYJ	72	3182	69	44.2	26

NFC	No	Yds	Lg	Avg	In20
Mat McBriar, Dal	56	2697	75	48.2	22
Jason Baker, Car	98	4483	70	45.7	31
Ryan Plackemeier*, Sea	84	3778	72	45.0	25
Nick Harris, Det	66	2967	67	45.0	18
Scott Player, Ari	66	2965	58	44.9	18

Punt Returns
(Minimum of 20 returns)

AFC	No	Yds	Avg	Long	TD
Pacman Jones, Ten	34	440	12.9	90-td	3
Roscoe Parrish, Buf	32	364	11.4	82-td	1
Dennis Northcutt, Cle	28	312	11.1	81	0
Dexter Wynn, Phi-Hou	25	270	10.8	58	0
Kevin Faulk, NE	31	330	10.6	43	0

NFC	No	Yds	Avg	Long	TD
Devin Hester*, Chi	47	600	12.8	84-td	3
Eddie Drummond, Det	28	296	10.6	40	0
Troy Walters, Ari	24	250	10.4	37	0
Mewelde Moore, Min	36	365	10.1	71-td	1
Terence Newman, Dal	20	202	10.1	56-td	1

Kickoff Returns
(Minimum of 20 returns)

AFC	No	Yds	Avg	Long	TD
Justin Miller, NYJ	46	1304	28.3	103-td	2
Laurence Maroney*, NE	28	783	28.0	77	0
Maurice Jones-Drew*, Jax	31	860	27.7	93-td	1
Michael Turner, SD	36	954	26.5	58	0
Terrence McGee, Buf	52	1355	26.1	88	0

NFC	No	Yds	Avg	Long	TD
Devin Hester*, Chi	20	528	26.4	96-td	2
Tyson Thompson, Dal	21	546	26.0	41	0
Miles Austin*, Dal	29	753	26.0	37	0
Maurice Hicks, SF	57	1428	25.1	64	0
Nate Burleson, Sea	26	643	24.7	50	0

Single Game Highs

Passing Yards

AFC	Cmp/Att	Yds	TD
Carson Palmer, Cin vs SD (11/12)	31/42	440	3
Ben Roethlisberger, Pit vs Den (11/5)	38/54	433	4
Joey Harrington, Mia vs GB (10/22)	33/62	414	2
Peyton Manning, Ind vs Hou (9/17)	26/38	400	3
Steve McNair, Bal vs Ten (11/12)	29/47	373	3

NFC	Cmp/Att	Yds	TD
Drew Brees, NO vs Cin (11/19)	37/52	510	2
Chris Weinke, Car vs NYG (12/10)	34/61	423	1
Matt Leinart*, Ari vs Min (11/26)	31/51	405	1
Drew Brees, NO vs Pit (11/12)	31/47	398	1
Marc Bulger, St.L vs Wash (12/24, OT)	25/38	388	4

Rushing Yards

AFC	Car	Yds	TD
Willie Parker, Pit vs Cle (12/7)	32	223	1
Willie Parker, Pit vs NO (11/12)	22	213	2
LaDainian Tomlinson, SD vs KC (12/17)	25	199	2
LaDainian Tomlinson, SD vs St.L (10/29)	25	183	2
Two tied with 178 yards.			

NFC	Car	Yds	TD
Tiki Barber, NYG vs Wash (12/30)	23	234	3
Frank Gore, SF vs Sea (11/19)	24	212	0
Shawn Alexander, Sea vs GB (11/27)	40	201	0
Tiki Barber, NYG vs Atl (10/15)	26	185	0
Ladell Betts, Wash vs Phi (12/10)	33	171	0

Receiving Yards

AFC	Ct	Yds	TD
Lee Evans, Buf vs Hou (11/19)	11	265	2
Chad Johnson, Cin vs SD (11/12)	11	260	2
Chad Johnson, Cin vs NO (11/19)	6	190	3
Marvin Harrison, Ind vs Ten (12/3)	7	172	1
Hines Ward, Pit vs Atl (10/22, OT)	8	171	3

NFC	Ct	Yds	TD
Donald Driver, GB vs Min (11/12)	6	191	1
Steve Smith, Car vs Bal (10/15)	8	189	1
Hank Baskett*, Phi vs Atl (12/31)	7	177	1
Larry Fitzgerald, Ari vs Min (11/26)	11	172	0
Two tied with 169 yards.			

NFL Bests

Longest Field Goal
62 yds . . . . Matt Bryant, TB vs Phi (10/22)

Longest Run from Scrimmage
95 yds . . . . . . Chester Taylor, Min vs Sea (10/22) TD

Longest Pass Play
89 yds . . . . . . A.J Feeley to H. Baskett, Phi vs. Atl (12/31) TD

Longest Interception Return
102 yds . . . . Lito Sheppard, Phi vs Dal (10/8) TD

Longest Punt Return
90 yds . . . . by two players

Longest Kickoff Return
103 yds . . . . Justin Miller, NYJ vs Ind (10/1) TD

Note: On 11/12 Chicago's Devin Hester returned a missed FG 108 yards, tying the record for longest play in NFL history.

NFL Regular Season Team Leaders

Offense

AFC	Points For	Avg	Yardage (Avg/Gm) Rush	Pass	Total
Indianapolis	.427	26.7	110.1	269.3	379.4
San Diego	.492	30.8	161.1	203.9	365.0
Pittsburgh	.353	22.1	124.5	233.3	357.8
Cincinnati	.373	23.3	101.8	239.6	341.4
Jacksonville	.371	23.2	158.8	180.1	338.9
New England	.385	24.1	123.1	212.5	335.6
Kansas City	.331	20.7	133.9	187.5	321.4
Baltimore	.353	22.1	102.3	214.7	317.0
Miami	.260	16.3	104.6	205.4	310.0
Denver	.319	19.9	134.5	174.9	309.4
NY Jets	.316	19.8	108.6	197.1	305.7
Tennessee	.324	20.3	138.4	162.3	300.6
Houston	.267	16.7	105.4	173.6	279.1
Buffalo	.300	18.8	97.0	169.9	266.9
Cleveland	.238	14.9	83.4	181.1	264.6
Oakland	.168	10.6	94.9	151.3	246.2

NFC	Points For	Avg	Yardage (Avg/Gm) Rush	Pass	Total
New Orleans	.413	25.8	110.1	281.4	391.5
Philadelphia	.398	24.9	124.0	257.4	381.4
Dallas	.425	26.6	121.0	239.8	360.8
St. Louis	.367	22.9	112.8	247.6	360.4
Green Bay	.301	18.8	103.9	237.2	341.1
Atlanta	.292	18.3	183.7	148.2	331.9
Washington	.307	19.2	138.5	189.2	327.7
NY Giants	.355	22.2	134.8	191.1	325.9
Chicago	.427	26.7	119.9	205.1	324.9
Arizona	.314	19.6	83.6	228.9	312.5
Seattle	.335	20.9	120.2	190.9	311.1
Detroit	.305	19.1	70.6	238.8	309.3
Minnesota	.282	17.6	113.8	195.2	308.9
Carolina	.270	16.9	103.7	204.0	307.7
San Francisco	.298	18.6	135.8	168.0	303.8
Tampa Bay	.211	13.2	95.2	174.9	270.1

Defense

AFC	Points For	Avg	Yardage (Avg/Gm) Rush	Pass	Total
Baltimore	.201	12.6	75.9	188.2	264.1
Jacksonville	.274	17.1	91.3	192.4	283.6
Oakland	.332	20.8	134.0	150.8	284.8
Miami	.283	17.7	101.1	187.9	289.1
New England	.237	14.8	94.2	200.2	294.4
Pittsburgh	.315	19.7	88.3	212.1	300.3
San Diego	.303	18.9	100.8	200.8	301.6
Denver	.305	19.1	113.3	213.1	326.4
Kansas City	.315	19.7	120.5	208.4	328.9
Buffalo	.311	19.4	140.9	188.7	329.6
NY Jets	.295	18.4	130.3	201.4	331.6
Indianapolis	.360	22.5	173.0	159.3	332.3
Houston	.366	22.9	122.3	215.3	337.5
Cleveland	.356	22.3	142.2	202.6	344.8
Cincinnati	.331	20.7	116.4	238.6	355.1
Tennessee	.400	25.0	144.6	225.1	369.7

NFC	Points For	Avg	Yardage (Avg/Gm) Rush	Pass	Total
Chicago	.255	15.9	99.4	194.8	294.1
Carolina	.305	19.1	108.6	187.5	296.1
Minnesota	.327	20.4	61.6	238.6	300.2
New Orleans	.322	20.1	128.9	178.4	307.3
Green Bay	.366	22.9	114.1	206.8	320.9
Dallas	.350	21.9	103.7	219.1	322.8
Philadelphia	.328	20.5	136.4	191.7	328.1
Tampa Bay	.353	22.1	119.8	209.6	329.4
Seattle	.341	21.3	126.8	203.5	330.3
Atlanta	.328	20.5	103.6	229.3	332.8
St. Louis	.381	23.8	145.4	189.7	335.1
NY Giants	.362	22.6	114.4	228.1	342.4
San Francisco	.412	25.8	121.0	223.2	344.2
Detroit	.398	24.9	125.6	220.0	345.6
Arizona	.389	24.3	118.6	230.9	349.4
Washington	.376	23.5	137.3	218.2	355.5

Overall Club Rankings

Combined AFC and NFC rankings by yards gained on offense and yards given up on defense. Teams are ranked alphabetically, with AFC teams in *italics*. (†) indicates tied for position.

	Offense Rush	Pass	Rank	Defense Rush	Pass	Rank
Arizona	.30	10	18	16	30	29
Atlanta	.1	32	12	9	29	22
Baltimore	.25	11	17	2	6	1
Buffalo	.27	28	30	28	7	18
Carolina	.24	15	24	11	4	7
Chicago	.15	14	15	6	11	5
Cincinnati	.26	6	8	15	31†	30
Cleveland	.31	23	31	29	15	27
Dallas	.13	5	5	10	24	13
Denver	.8	25	21	12	21	14
Detroit	.32	7	22	21	25	28
Green Bay	.23	8	9	13	17	12
Houston	.21	27	28	20	22	24
Indianapolis	.18	2	3	32	2	21
Jacksonville	.3	24	10	4	10	2
Kansas City	.9	22	16	18	18	16
Miami	.22	13	20	8	5	4
Minnesota	.16	18	23	1	31†	8
New England	.12	12	11	5	12	6
New Orleans	.19	1	1	23	3	11
NY Giants	.7	19	14	14	28	25
NY Jets	.20	17	25	24	14	20
Oakland	.29	31	32	25	1	3
Philadelphia	.11	3	2	26	9	15
Pittsburgh	.10	9	7	3	20	9
St. Louis	.17	4	6	31	8	23
San Diego	.2	16	4	7	13	10
San Francisco	.6	29	26	19	26	26
Seattle	.14	20	19	22	16	19
Tampa Bay	.28	26	29	17	19	17
Tennessee	.5	31	27	30	27	32
Washington	.4	21	13	27	23	31

AFC Team by Team Results

(*) indicates overtime game.

Baltimore Ravens (13-3)

at Tampa Bay	W, 27-0
Oakland	W, 28-6
at Cleveland	W, 15-14
San Diego	W, 16-13
at Denver	L, 3-13
Carolina	L, 21-23
BYE	—
at New Orleans	W, 35-22
Cincinnati	W, 26-20
at Tennessee	W, 27-26
Atlanta	W, 24-10
Pittsburgh	W, 27-0
at Cincinnati	L, 7-13
at Kansas City	W, 20-10
Cleveland	W, 27-17
at Pittsburgh	W, 31-7
Buffalo	W, 19-7

Buffalo Bills (7-9)

at New England	L, 17-19
at Miami	W, 16-6
NY Jets	L, 20-28
Minnesota	W, 17-12
at Chicago	L, 7-40
at Detroit	L, 17-20
New England	L, 6-28
BYE	—
Green Bay	W, 24-10
at Indianapolis	L, 16-17
at Houston	W, 24-21
Jacksonville	W, 27-24
San Diego	L, 21-24
at NY Jets	W, 31-13
Miami	W, 21-0
Tennessee	L, 29-30
at Baltimore	L, 7-19

Cincinnati Bengals (8-8)

at Kansas City	W, 23-10
Cleveland	W, 34-17*
at Pittsburgh	W, 28-20
New England	L, 13-38
BYE	—
at Tampa Bay	L, 13-14
Carolina	W, 17-14
Atlanta	L, 27-29
at Baltimore	L, 20-26
San Diego	L, 41-49
at New Orleans	W, 31-16
at Cleveland	W, 30-0
Baltimore	W, 13-7
Oakland	W, 27-10
at Indianapolis	L, 16-34
at Denver	L, 23-24
Pittsburgh	L, 17-23*

Cleveland Browns (4-12)

New Orleans	L, 14-19
at Cincinnati	L, 17-34
Baltimore	L, 14-15
at Oakland	W, 24-21
at Carolina	L, 12-20
BYE	—
Denver	L, 7-17
NY Jets	W, 20-13
at San Diego	L, 25-32
at Atlanta	W, 17-13
Pittsburgh	L, 20-24
Cincinnati	L, 0-30
Kansas City	W, 31-28*
at Pittsburgh	L, 7-7
at Baltimore	L, 17-27
Tampa Bay	L, 7-22
at Houston	L, 6-14

Denver Broncos (9-7)

at St. Louis	L, 10-18
Kansas City	W, 9-6*
at New England	W, 17-7
BYE	—
Baltimore	W, 13-3
Oakland	W, 13-3
at Cleveland	W, 17-7
Indianapolis	L, 31-34
at Pittsburgh	W, 31-20
at Oakland	W, 17-13
San Diego	L, 27-35
at Kansas City	L, 10-19
Seattle	L, 20-23
at San Diego	L, 20-48
at Arizona	W, 37-20
Cincinnati	W, 24-23
San Francisco	L, 23-26*

Houston Texans (6-10)

Philadelphia	L, 10-24
at Indianapolis	L, 24-43
Washington	L, 15-31
Miami	W, 17-15
BYE	—
at Dallas	L, 6-34
Jacksonville	W, 27-7
at Tennessee	L, 22-28
at NY Giants	L, 10-14
at Jacksonville	W, 13-10
Buffalo	L, 21-24
at NY Jets	L, 11-26
at Oakland	W, 23-14
Tennessee	L, 20-26*
at New England	L, 7-40
Indianapolis	W, 27-24
Cleveland	W, 14-6

Indianapolis Colts (12-4)

at NY Giants	W, 26-21
Houston	W, 43-24
Jacksonville	W, 21-14
at NY Jets	W, 31-28
Tennessee	W, 14-13
BYE	—
Washington	W, 36-22
at Denver	W, 34-31
at New England	W, 27-20
Buffalo	W, 17-16
at Dallas	L, 14-21
Philadelphia	W, 45-21
at Tennessee	L, 17-20
at Jacksonville	L, 17-44
Cincinnati	W, 34-16
at Houston	L, 24-27
Miami	W, 27-22

Jacksonville Jaguars (8-8)

Dallas	W, 24-17
Pittsburgh	W, 9-0
at Indianapolis	L, 14-21
at Washington	L, 30-36*
NY Jets	W, 41-0
BYE	—
at Houston	L, 7-27
at Philadelphia	W, 13-6
Tennessee	W, 37-7
Houston	L, 10-13
NY Giants	W, 26-10
at Buffalo	L, 24-27
at Miami	W, 24-10
Indianapolis	W, 44-17
at Tennessee	L, 17-24
New England	L, 21-24
at Kansas City	L, 30-35

Kansas City Chiefs (9-7)

Cincinnati	L, 10-23
at Denver	L, 6-9*
BYE	—
San Francisco	W, 41-0
at Arizona	W, 23-20
at Pittsburgh	L, 7-45
San Diego	W, 30-27
Seattle	W, 35-28
at St. Louis	W, 31-17
at Miami	L, 10-13
Oakland	W, 17-13
Denver	W, 19-10
at Cleveland	L, 28-31*
Baltimore	L, 10-20
at San Diego	L, 9-20
at Oakland	W, 20-9
Jacksonville	W, 35-30

Miami Dolphins (6-10)

at Pittsburgh	L, 17-28
Buffalo	L, 6-16
Tennessee	W, 13-10
at Houston	L, 15-17
at New England	L, 10-20
at NY Jets	L, 17-20
Green Bay	L, 24-34
BYE	—
at Chicago	W, 31-13
Kansas City	W, 13-10
Minnesota	W, 24-20
at Detroit	W, 27-10
Jacksonville	L, 10-24
New England	W, 21-0
at Buffalo	L, 0-21
NY Jets	L, 10-13
at Indianapolis	L, 22-27

New England Patriots (12-4)

Buffalo	W, 19-17
at NY Jets	W, 24-17
Denver	L, 7-17
at Cincinnati	W, 38-13
Miami	W, 20-10
BYE	—
at Buffalo	W, 28-6
at Minnesota	W, 31-7
Indianapolis	L, 20-27
NY Jets	L, 14-17
at Green Bay	W, 35-0
Chicago	W, 17-13
Detroit	W, 28-21
at Miami	L, 0-21
Houston	W, 40-7
at Jacksonville	W, 24-21
at Tennessee	W, 40-23

New York Jets (10-6)

at Tennessee	W, 23-16
New England	L, 17-24
at Buffalo	W, 28-20
Indianapolis	L, 28-31
at Jacksonville	L, 0-41
Miami	W, 20-17
Detroit	W, 31-24
at Cleveland	L, 13-20
BYE	—
at New England	W, 17-14
Chicago	L, 0-10
Houston	W, 26-11
at Green Bay	W, 38-10
Buffalo	L, 13-31
at Minnesota	W, 26-13
at Miami	W, 13-10
Oakland	W, 23-3

Oakland Raiders (2-14)

San Diego	L, 0-27
at Baltimore	L, 6-28
BYE	—
Cleveland	L, 21-24
at San Francisco	L, 20-34
at Denver	L, 3-13
Arizona	W, 22-9
Pittsburgh	W, 20-13
at Seattle	L, 0-16
Denver	L, 13-17
at Kansas City	L, 13-17
at San Diego	L, 14-21
Houston	L, 14-23
at Cincinnati	L, 10-27
St. Louis	L, 0-20
Kansas City	L, 9-20
at NY Jets	L, 3-23

Pittsburgh Steelers (8-8)

Miami	W, 28-17
at Jacksonville	L, 0-9
Cincinnati	L, 20-28
BYE	—
at San Diego	L, 13-23
Kansas City	W, 45-7
at Atlanta	L, 38-41*
at Oakland	L, 13-20
Denver	L, 20-31
New Orleans	W, 38-31
at Cleveland	W, 24-20
at Baltimore	L, 0-27
Tampa Bay	W, 20-3
Cleveland	W, 27-7
at Carolina	W, 37-3
Baltimore	L, 7-31
at Cincinnati	W, 23-17*

San Diego Chargers (14-2)

at Oakland	W, 27-0
Tennessee	W, 40-7
BYE	—
at Baltimore	L, 13-16
Pittsburgh	W, 23-13
at San Francisco	W, 48-19
at Kansas City	L, 27-30
St. Louis	W, 38-24
Cleveland	W, 32-25
at Cincinnati	W, 49-41
at Denver	W, 35-27
Oakland	W, 21-14
at Buffalo	W, 24-21
Denver	W, 48-20
Kansas City	W, 20-9
at Seattle	W, 20-17
Arizona	W, 27-20

Tennessee Titans (8-8)

NY Jets	L, 16-23
at San Diego	L, 7-40
at Miami	L, 10-13
Dallas	L, 14-45
at Indianapolis	L, 13-14
at Washington	W, 25-22
BYE	—
Houston	W, 28-22
at Jacksonville	L, 7-37
Baltimore	L, 26-27
at Philadelphia	W, 31-13
NY Giants	W, 24-21
Indianapolis	W, 20-17
at Houston	W, 26-20*
Jacksonville	W, 24-17
at Buffalo	W, 30-29
New England	L, 23-40

NFC Team by Team Results
(*) indicates overtime game

Arizona Cardinals (5-11)

San Francisco	W, 34-27
at Seattle	L, 10-21
St. Louis	L, 14-16
at Atlanta	L, 10-32
Kansas City	L, 20-23
Chicago	L, 23-24
at Oakland	L, 9-22
at Green Bay	L, 14-31
BYE	—
Dallas	L, 10-27
Detroit	W, 17-10
at Minnesota	L, 26-31
at St. Louis	W, 34-20
Seattle	W, 27-21
Denver	L, 20-37
at San Francisco	W, 26-20
at San Diego	L, 20-27

Atlanta Falcons (7-9)

at Carolina	W, 20-6
Tampa Bay	W, 14-3
at New Orleans	L, 3-23
Arizona	W, 32-10
BYE	—
NY Giants	L, 14-27
Pittsburgh	W, 41-38*
at Cincinnati	W, 29-27
at Detroit	L, 14-30
Cleveland	L, 13-17
at Baltimore	L, 10-24
New Orleans	L, 13-31
at Washington	W, 24-14
at Tampa Bay	W, 17-6
Dallas	L, 28-38
Carolina	L, 3-10
at Philadelphia	L, 17-24

Carolina Panthers (8-8)

Atlanta	L, 6-20
at Minnesota	L, 13-16*
at Tampa Bay	W, 26-24
New Orleans	W, 21-18
Cleveland	W, 20-12
at Baltimore	W, 23-21
at Cincinnati	L, 14-17
Dallas	L, 14-35
BYE	—
Tampa Bay	W, 24-10
St. Louis	W, 15-0
at Washington	L, 13-17
at Philadelphia	L, 24-27
NY Giants	L, 13-27
Pittsburgh	L, 3-37
at Atlanta	W, 10-3
at New Orleans	W, 31-21

Chicago Bears (13-3)

at Green Bay	W, 26-0
Detroit	W, 34-7
at Minnesota	W, 19-16
Seattle	W, 37-6
Buffalo	W, 40-7
at Arizona	W, 24-23
BYE	—
San Francisco	W, 41-10
Miami	L, 13-31
at NY Giants	W, 38-20
at NY Jets	W, 10-0
at New England	L, 13-17
Minnesota	W, 23-13
at St. Louis	W, 42-27
Tampa Bay	W, 34-31
at Detroit	W, 26-21
Green Bay	L, 7-26

Dallas Cowboys (9-7)

at Jacksonville	L, 17-24
Washington	W, 27-10
BYE	—
at Tennessee	W, 45-14
at Philadelphia	L, 24-38
Houston	W, 34-6
NY Giants	L, 22-36
at Carolina	W, 35-14
at Washington	L, 19-22
at Arizona	W, 27-10
Indianapolis	W, 21-14
Tampa Bay	W, 38-10
at NY Giants	W, 23-20
New Orleans	L, 17-42
at Atlanta	W, 38-28
Philadelphia	L, 7-23
Detroit	L, 31-39

Detroit Lions (3-13)

Seattle	L, 6-9
at Chicago	L, 7-34
Green Bay	L, 24-31
at St. Louis	L, 34-41
at Minnesota	L, 17-26
Buffalo	W, 20-17
at NY Jets	L, 24-31
BYE	—
Atlanta	W, 30-14
San Francisco	L, 13-19
at Arizona	L, 10-17
Miami	L, 10-27
at New England	L, 21-28
Minnesota	L, 20-30
at Green Bay	L, 9-17
Chicago	L, 21-26
at Dallas	W, 39-31

Green Bay Packers (8-8)

Chicago	L, 0-26
New Orleans	L, 27-34
at Detroit	W, 31-24
at Philadelphia	L, 9-31
St. Louis	L, 20-23
BYE	—
at Miami	W, 34-24
Arizona	W, 31-14
at Buffalo	L, 10-24
at Minnesota	W, 23-17
New England	L, 0-35
at Seattle	L, 24-34
NY Jets	L, 10-38
at San Francisco	W, 30-19
Detroit	W, 17-9
Minnesota	W, 9-7
at Chicago	W, 26-7

Minnesota Vikings (6-10)

at Washington	W, 19-16
Carolina	W, 16-13*
Chicago	L, 16-19
at Buffalo	L, 12-17
Detroit	W, 26-17
BYE	—
at Seattle	W, 31-13
New England	L, 7-31
at San Francisco	L, 3-9
Green Bay	L, 17-23
at Miami	L, 20-24
Arizona	W, 31-26
at Chicago	L, 13-23
at Detroit	W, 30-20
NY Jets	L, 13-26
at Green Bay	L, 7-9
St. Louis	L, 21-41

NFC Team by Team Results (Cont.)

New Orleans Saints (10-6)

at Cleveland	W, 19-14
at Green Bay	W, 34-27
Atlanta	W, 23-3
at Carolina	L, 18-21
Tampa Bay	W, 24-21
Philadelphia	W, 27-24
BYE	—
Baltimore	L, 22-35
at Tampa Bay	W, 31-14
at Pittsburgh	L, 31-38
Cincinnati	L, 16-31
at Atlanta	W, 31-13
San Francisco	W, 34-10
at Dallas	W, 42-17
Washington	L, 10-16
at NY Giants	W, 30-7
Carolina	L, 31-31

New York Giants (8-8)

Indianapolis	L, 21-26
at Philadelphia	W, 30-24*
at Seattle	L, 30-42
BYE	—
Washington	W, 19-3
at Atlanta	W, 27-14
at Dallas	W, 36-22
Tampa Bay	W, 17-3
Houston	W, 14-10
Chicago	L, 20-38
at Jacksonville	L, 10-26
at Tennessee	L, 21-24
Dallas	L, 20-23
at Carolina	W, 27-13
Philadelphia	L, 22-36
New Orleans	L, 7-30
at Washington	W, 34-28

Philadelphia Eagles (10-6)

at Houston	W, 24-10
NY Giants	L, 24-30
at San Francisco	W, 38-24
BYE	—
Green Bay	W, 31-9
Dallas	W, 38-24
at New Orleans	L, 24-27
at Tampa Bay	L, 21-23
Jacksonville	L, 6-13
Washington	W, 27-3
Tennessee	L, 13-31
at Indianapolis	L, 21-45
Carolina	W, 27-24
at Washington	W, 21-19
at NY Giants	W, 36-22
at Dallas	W, 23-7
Atlanta	W, 24-17

St. Louis Rams (8-8)

Denver	W, 18-10
at San Francisco	L, 13-20
at Arizona	W, 16-14
Detroit	W, 41-34
at Green Bay	W, 23-20
Seattle	L, 28-30
BYE	—
at San Diego	L, 24-38
Kansas City	L, 17-31
at Seattle	L, 22-24
at Carolina	L, 0-15
San Francisco	W, 20-17
Arizona	L, 20-34
Chicago	L, 27-42
at Oakland	W, 20-0
Washington	W, 37-31*
at Minnesota	W, 41-21

San Francisco 49ers (7-9)

at Arizona	L, 27-34
St. Louis	W, 20-13
Philadelphia	L, 24-38
at Kansas City	L, 0-41
Oakland	W, 34-20
San Diego	L, 19-48
BYE	—
at Chicago	L, 10-41
Minnesota	W, 9-3
at Detroit	W, 19-13
Seattle	W, 20-14
at St. Louis	L, 17-20
at New Orleans	L, 10-34
Green Bay	L, 19-30
at Seattle	W, 24-14
Arizona	L, 20-26
at Denver	W, 26-23*

Seattle Seahawks (9-7)

at Detroit	W, 9-6
Arizona	W, 21-10
NY Giants	W, 42-30
at Chicago	L, 6-37
BYE	—
at St. Louis	W, 30-28
Minnesota	L, 13-31
at Kansas City	L, 28-35
Oakland	W, 16-0
St. Louis	W, 24-22
at San Francisco	L, 14-20
Green Bay	W, 34-24
at Denver	W, 23-20
at Arizona	L, 21-27
San Francisco	L, 14-24
San Diego	L, 17-20
at Tampa Bay	W, 23-7

Tampa Bay Buccaneers (4-12)

Baltimore	L, 0-27
at Atlanta	L, 3-14
Carolina	L, 24-26
BYE	—
at New Orleans	L, 21-24
Cincinnati	W, 14-13
Philadelphia	W, 23-21
at NY Giants	L, 3-17
New Orleans	L, 14-31
at Carolina	L, 10-24
Washington	W, 20-17
at Dallas	L, 10-38
at Pittsburgh	L, 3-20
Atlanta	L, 6-17
at Chicago	L, 31-34*
at Cleveland	W, 22-7
Seattle	L, 7-23

Washington Redskins (5-11)

Minnesota	L, 16-19
at Dallas	L, 10-27
at Houston	W, 31-15
Jacksonville	W, 36-30*
at NY Giants	L, 3-19
Tennessee	L, 22-25
at Indianapolis	L, 22-36
BYE	—
Dallas	W, 22-19
at Philadelphia	L, 3-27
at Tampa Bay	L, 17-20
Carolina	W, 17-13
Atlanta	L, 14-24
Philadelphia	L, 19-21
at New Orleans	W, 16-10
at St. Louis	L, 31-37*
NY Giants	L, 28-34

Takeaways/Giveaways

AFC	Takeaways Int	Fum	Total	Giveaways Int	Fum	Total	Net Diff	NFC	Takeaways Int	Fum	Total	Giveaways Int	Fum	Total	Net Diff
Baltimore	28	12	40	14	9	23	+17	St. Louis	17	15	32	8	10	18	+14
San Diego	16	12	28	9	6	15	+13	Chicago	24	20	44	22	14	36	+8
New England	22	13	35	12	15	27	+8	Atlanta	12	14	26	15	5	20	+6
Cincinnati	19	12	31	13	11	24	+7	Philadelphia	19	10	29	9	15	24	+5
Indianapolis	15	11	26	9	10	19	+7	Minnesota	21	15	36	20	12	32	+4
Kansas City	15	15	30	12	14	26	+4	Arizona	16	17	33	17	13	30	+3
Miami	8	19	27	19	6	25	+2	Dallas	18	13	31	21	9	30	+1
Tennessee	17	11	28	19	7	26	+2	Green Bay	23	10	33	18	15	33	0
Jacksonville	20	4	24	14	9	23	+1	NY Giants	17	11	28	18	10	28	0
Denver	17	13	30	18	12	30	0	New Orleans	11	8	19	13	10	23	-4
NY Jets	16	9	25	16	9	25	0	Carolina	14	8	22	17	10	27	-5
Houston	11	11	22	13	12	25	-3	San Francisco	14	13	27	16	16	32	-5
Buffalo	13	11	24	14	15	29	-5	Washington	6	6	12	10	7	17	-5
Pittsburgh	20	9	29	23	14	37	-8	Seattle	12	14	26	22	12	34	-8
Cleveland	18	9	27	25	17	42	-15	Detroit	12	18	30	22	17	39	-9
Oakland	18	5	23	24	22	46	-23	Tampa Bay	11	9	20	18	14	32	-12
TOTALS	273	176	449	254	188	442	+7	TOTALS	247	201	448	266	189	455	-7

AFC Team by Team Statistics

Players with more than one team during the regular season are listed with club they ended season with; (*) indicates rookies.

Baltimore Ravens

Passing (5 Att)	Att	Cmp	Pct	Yds	TD	Rate
Steve McNair	.467	295	63.0	3050	16	82.5
Kyle Boller	.55	33	60.0	485	5	104.0

Interceptions: McNair 12, Boller 2.

Top Receivers	No	Yds	Avg	Long	TD
Todd Heap	.73	765	10.5	30	6
Derrick Mason	.68	750	11.0	38	2
Mark Clayton	.67	939	14.0	87-td	5
Demetrius Williams*	.22	396	18.0	77-td	2
Musa Smith	.22	135	6.1	30	0
Ovie Mughelli	.21	182	8.7	30-td	2
Daniel Wilcox	.20	166	8.3	35	3

Top Rushers	Car	Yds	Avg	Long	TD
Jamal Lewis	.314	1132	3.6	52	9
Mike Anderson	.39	183	4.7	34-td	1
Musa Smith	.36	153	4.3	30	0
Ovie Mughelli	.12	50	4.2	12	0

Most Touchdowns	TD	Run	Rec	Ret	Pts
Jamal Lewis	.9	9	0	0	54
Todd Heap	.6	0	6	0	36
Mark Clayton	.5	0	5	0	30
Daniel Wilcox	.3	0	3	0	18

Four tied with 2 TD for 12 pts.

2-Pt. Conversions: (0-1).

Kicking	PAT/Att	FG/Att	Lg	Pts
Matt Stover	.37/37	28/30	52	121

Punts (10 or more)	No	Yds	Long	Avg	In20
Sam Koch*	.86	3695	61	43.0	30

Most Interceptions		Most Sacks	
Chris McAlister	.6	Trevor Pryce	.13.0

Buffalo Bills

Passing (5 Att)	Att	Cmp	Pct	Yds	TD	Rate
J.P. Losman	.429	268	62.5	3051	19	84.9

Interceptions: Losman 14.

Top Receivers	No	Yds	Avg	Long	TD
Lee Evans	.82	1292	15.8	83-td	8
Peerless Price	.49	402	8.2	25	3
Josh Reed	.34	410	12.1	52	2
Roscoe Parrish	.23	320	13.9	51-td	2
Robert Royal	.23	233	10.1	33-td	3
Anthony Thomas	.22	139	6.3	18	0
Willis McGahee	.18	156	8.7	56	0

Top Rushers	Car	Yds	Avg	Long	TD
Willis McGahee	.259	990	3.8	57-td	6
Anthony Thomas	.107	378	3.5	19	2
J.P. Losman	.38	140	3.7	15	1

Most Touchdowns	TD	Run	Rec	Ret	Pts
Lee Evans	.8	0	8	0	48
Willis McGahee	.6	0	0	0	36
Roscoe Parrish	.3	0	2	1	18
Peerless Price	.3	0	3	0	18
Robert Royal	.3	0	3	0	18

Three tied with 2 TD each for 12 pts.

2-Pt. Conversions: (0-0).

Kicking	PAT/Att	FG/Att	Lg	Pts
Rian Lindell	.33/33	23/25	53	102

Punts (10 or more)	No	Yds	Long	Avg	In20
Brian Moorman	.92	4012	66	43.6	33

Most Interceptions		Most Sacks	
London Fletcher-Baker	.4	Aaron Schobel	.14.0

Cincinnati Bengals

Passing (5 Att)	Att	Cmp	Pct	Yds	TD	Rate
Carson Palmer	.520	324	62.3	4035	28	93.9

Interceptions: Palmer 13.

Top Receivers	No	Yds	Avg	Long	TD
T.J. Houshmandzadeh	.90	1081	12.0	40-td	9
Chad Johnson	.87	1369	15.7	74-td	7
Chris Henry	.36	605	16.8	71	9
Kenny Watson	.23	213	9.3	46	0
Rudi Johnson	.23	124	5.4	18	0
Reggie Kelly	.21	254	12.1	32	1
Tony Stewart	.14	120	8.6	26	1

Top Rushers	Car	Yds	Avg	Long	TD
Rudi Johnson	.341	1309	3.8	22-td	12
Kenny Watson	.25	138	-5.5	18	1
Chris Perry	.10	57	5.7	18	0
Jeremi Johnson	.15	.56	3.7	15	1
Carson Palmer	.26	37	1.4	11	0

Most Touchdowns	TD	Run	Rec	Ret	Pts
Rudi Johnson	.12	12	0	0	72
Chris Henry	.9	0	9	0	54
T.J. Houshmandzadeh	.9	0	9	0	54
Chad Johnson	.7	0	7	0	42

Six tied with 1 TD for 6 pts.

2-Pt. Conversions: (0-1).

Kicking	PAT/Att	FG/Att	Lg	Pts
Shayne Graham	.40/42	25/30	51	115

Punts (10 or more)	No	Yds	Long	Avg	In20
Kyle Larson	.77	3428	67	44.5	26

Most Interceptions		Most Sacks	
Kevin Kaesviharn	.6	Robert Geathers	.10.5

Cleveland Browns

Passing (5 Att)	Att	Cmp	Pct	Yds	TD	Rate
Charlie Frye	.392	252	64.3	2454	10	72.2
Derek Anderson	.117	66	56.4	.793	5	63.1

Interceptions: Frye 17, Anderson 8.

Top Receivers	No	Yds	Avg	Long	TD
Kellen Winslow	.89	875	9.8	40	3
Braylon Edwards	.61	884	14.5	75	6
Joe Jurevicius	.40	495	12.4	52	3
Steve Heiden	.36	249	6.9	13	2
Reuben Droughns	.27	169	6.3	24	0
Dennis Northcutt	.22	228	10.4	43	0

Top Rushers	Car	Yds	Avg	Long	TD
Reuben Droughns	.220	758	3.4	22	4
Charlie Frye	.47	215	4.6	17	3
Jason Wright	.62	189	3.0	18	0
Jerome Harrison*	.20	60	3.0	15	0

Most Touchdowns	TD	Run	Rec	Ret	Pts
Braylon Edwards	.6	0	6	0	36
Reuben Droughns	.4	4	0	0	24
Charlie Frye	.3	3	0	0	18
Joe Jurevicius	.3	0	3	0	18
Kellen Winslow	.3	0	3	0	18

2-Pt. Conversions: (0-0).

Kicking	PAT/Att	FG/Att	Lg	Pts
Phil Dawson	.25/25	21/29	51	88

Punts (10 or more)	No	Yds	Long	Avg	In20
Dave Zastudil	.81	3563	61	44.0	28

Most Interceptions		Most Sacks	
Daven Holly	.5	Kamerion Wimbley	.11.0
Sean Jones	.5		

Denver Broncos

Passing (5 Att)	Att	Cmp	Pct	Yds	TD	Rate
Jake Plummer	.317	175	55.2	1994	11	68.8
Jay Cutler*	.137	81	59.1	1001	9	88.5

Interceptions: Plummer 13, Cutler 5.

Top Receivers	No	Yds	Avg	Long	TD
Javon Walker	.69	1084	15.7	83-td	8
Rod Smith	.52	512	9.8	20	3
Tatum Bell	.24	115	4.8	16	0
Brandon Marshall*	.20	309	15.5	71-td	2
Mike Bell*	.20	158	7.9	24	0
Tony Scheffler*	.18	286	15.9	29	4
Stephen Alexander	.18	160	8.9	24	2

Top Rushers	Car	Yds	Avg	Long	TD
Tatum Bell	.233	1025	4.4	51	2
Mike Bell*	.157	677	4.3	48	8
Javon Walker	.9	123	13.7	72-td	1
Jake Plummer	.36	112	3.1	19	1
Cecil Sapp	.10	80	8.0	28	0

Most Touchdowns	TD	Run	Rec	Ret	Pts
Javon Walker	9	1	8	0	54
Mike Bell*	8	8	0	0	48
Tony Scheffler*	4	0	4	0	24
Rod Smith	3	0	3	0	18

Three tied with 2 TD each for 12 pts.

2-Pt. Conversions: (0-0).

Kicking	PAT/Att	FG/Att	Lg	Pts
Jason Elam	.34/34	27/29	51	115

Punts (10 or more)	No	Yds	Long	Avg	In20
Paul Ernster	.80	3338	61	41.7	23

Most Interceptions		Most Sacks	
Champ Bailey	.10	Elvis Dumervil*	8.5

Houston Texans

Passing (5 Att)	Att	Cmp	Pct	Yds	TD	Rate
David Carr	.442	302	68.3	2767	11	81.2
Sage Rosenfels	.39	27	69.2	265	3	103.0

Interceptions: Carr 12, Rosenfels 1.

Top Receivers	No	Yds	Avg	Long	TD
Andre Johnson	.103	1147	11.1	53	5
Eric Moulds	.57	557	9.8	29	1
Owen Daniels*	.34	352	10.4	33-td	5
Wali Lundy*	.33	204	6.2	15	0
Jameel Cook	.18	107	5.9	15	0

Top Rushers	Car	Yds	Avg	Long	TD
Ron Dayne	.151	612	4.1	19	5
Wali Lundy*	.124	476	3.8	35	4
Samkon Gado	.56	210	3.8	34	1
GB	.2	-7	-3.5	-3	0
HOU	.54	217	4.0	34	1
David Carr	.53	195	3.7	16	2

Acquired: Gado from GB for RB Vernand Morency (Sept. 13).

Most Touchdowns	TD	Run	Rec	Ret	Pts
Ron Dayne	.5	5	0	0	32
Owen Daniels*	.5	0	5	0	30
Andre Johnson	.5	0	5	0	30
Wali Lundy*	.4	4	0	0	26

Two tied with 2 TD each for 12 pts.

2-Pt. Conversions: (2-3) Dayne, Lundy.

Kicking	PAT/Att	FG/Att	Lg	Pts
Kris Brown	.26/27	19/25	49	83

Punts (10 or more)	No	Yds	Long	Avg	In20
Chad Stanley	.76	3161	62	41.6	15

Most Interceptions		Most Sacks	
Dunta Robinson	.2	Jason Babin	5.0
Demarcus Faggins	.2		

Indianapolis Colts

Passing (5 Att)	Att	Cmp	Pct	Yds	TD	Rate
Peyton Manning	.557	362	65.0	4397	31	101.0

Interceptions: Manning 9.

Top Receivers	No	Yds	Avg	Long	TD
Marvin Harrison	.95	1366	14.4	68-td	12
Reggie Wayne	.86	1310	15.2	51-td	9
Joseph Addai*	.40	325	8.1	21-td	1
Ben Utecht	.37	377	10.2	26	0
Dominic Rhodes	.36	251	7.0	27	0
Dallas Clark	.30	367	12.2	40	4
Bryan Fletcher	.18	202	11.2	26	2

Top Rushers	Car	Yds	Avg	Long	TD
Joseph Addai*	.226	1081	4.8	41	7
Dominic Rhodes	.187	641	3.4	17	5
Peyton Manning	.23	36	1.6	12	4

Most Touchdowns	TD	Run	Rec	Ret	Pts
Marvin Harrison	.12	0	12	0	72
Reggie Wayne	.9	0	9	0	56
Joseph Addai*	.8	7	1	0	48
Dominic Rhodes	.5	5	0	0	30
Dallas Clark	.4	0	4	0	24
Peyton Manning	.4	4	0	0	24

2-Pt. Conversions: (1-2) Wayne.

Kicking	PAT/Att	FG/Att	Lg	Pts
Adam Vinatieri	.38/38	25/28	48	113

Signed: Martin Gramatica (Sept. 22, Oct. 8). **Released:** Gramatica (Oct. 4, Oct. 11, see Dallas).

Punts (10 or more)	No	Yds	Long	Avg	In20
Hunter Smith	.47	2085	61	44.4	14

Most Interceptions		Most Sacks	
Nick Harper	.3	Robert Mathis	9.5
Cato June	.3		

Jacksonville Jaguars

Passing (5 Att)	Att	Cmp	Pct	Yds	TD	Rate
David Garrard	.241	145	60.2	1735	10	80.5
Byron Leftwich	.183	108	59.0	1159	7	79.0
Quinn Gray	.22	13	59.1	166	0	82.8

Interceptions: Garrard 9; Leftwich 5.

Top Receivers	No	Yds	Avg	Long	TD
Reggie Williams	.52	616	11.8	48	4
Maurice Jones-Drew*	.46	436	9.5	51-td	2
Matt Jones	.41	643	15.7	49	4
George Wrighster	.39	353	9.1	23	3
Ernest Wilford	.36	524	14.6	41	2
Fred Taylor	.23	242	10.5	36	1

Top Rushers	Car	Yds	Avg	Long	TD
Fred Taylor	.231	1146	5.0	76	5
Maurice Jones-Drew*	166	941	5.7	74-td	13
David Garrard	.47	250	5.3	20	0
Alvin Pearman	.19	89	4.7	12	1

Most Touchdowns	TD	Run	Rec	Ret	Pts
Maurice Jones-Drew*	.16	13	2	1	96
Fred Taylor	.6	5	1	0	36
Matt Jones	.4	0	4	0	24
Reggie Williams	.4	0	4	0	24
George Wrighster	.3	0	3	0	18

2-Pt. Conversions: (0-1).

Kicking	PAT/Att	FG/Att	Lg	Pts
Josh Scobee	.41/41	26/32	48	119

Punts (10 or more)	No	Yds	Long	Avg	In20
Chris Hanson	.72	2920	58	40.6	20

Most Interceptions		Most Sacks	
Rashean Mathis	.8	Bobby McCray	10.0

Kansas City Chiefs

Passing (5 Att)	Att	Cmp	Pct	Yds	TD	Rate
Damon Huard	.244	148	60.7	1878	11	98.0
Trent Green	.198	121	61.1	1342	7	74.1
Brodie Croyle*	.7	3	42.9	23	0	11.9

Interceptions: Green 9, Croyle 2, Huard 1.

Top Receivers	No	Yds	Avg	Long	TD
Tony Gonzalez	.73	900	12.3	57	5
Eddie Kennison	.53	860	16.2	51	5
Samie Parker	.41	561	13.7	43	1
Larry Johnson	.41	410	10.0	78	2
Dante Hall	.26	204	7.8	19	2
Kris Wilson	.15	132	8.8	19	3

Top Rushers	Car	Yds	Avg	Long	TD
Larry Johnson	.416	1789	4.3	47	17
Michael Bennett	.36	200	5.6	41	0
Trent Green	.19	59	3.1	10	0
Dee Brown	.10	24	2.4	7	0

Most Touchdowns	TD	Run	Rec	Ret	Pts
Larry Johnson	.19	17	2	0	114
Tony Gonzalez	.5	0	5	0	32
Eddie Kennison	.5	0	5	0	30
Dante Hall	.3	0	2	1	18
Kris Wilson	.3	0	3	0	18

2-Pt. Conversions: (1-1) Gonzalez.

Kicking	PAT/Att	FG/Att	Lg	Pts
Lawrence Tynes	.35/36	24/31	53	107

Punts (10 or more)	No	Yds	Long	Avg	In20
Dustin Colquitt	.71	3145	72	44.3	23

Most Interceptions | | **Most Sacks** |
---|---|---|---
Ty Law | .4 | Tamba Hali* | .8.0

Miami Dolphins

Passing (5 Att)	Att	Cmp	Pct	Yds	TD	Rate
Joey Harrington	.388	223	57.5	2236	12	68.2
Daunte Culpepper	.134	81	60.4	929	2	77.0
Cleo Lemon	.68	38	55.9	412	2	77.6

Interceptions: Harrington 15, Culpepper 3, Lemon 1.

Top Receivers	No	Yds	Avg	Long	TD
Wes Welker	.67	687	10.3	38	1
Randy McMichael	.62	640	10.3	24	3
Chris Chambers	.59	677	11.5	46	4
Marty Booker	.55	747	13.6	52	6
Ronnie Brown	.33	276	8.4	24	0
Derek Hagan*	.21	221	10.5	24	1
Sammy Morris	.21	162	7.7	44	0

Top Rushers	Car	Yds	Avg	Long	TD
Ronnie Brown	.241	1008	4.2	47	5
Sammy Morris	.92	400	4.3	55	1
Chris Chambers	.8	95	11.9	39	0
Travis Minor	.19	74	3.9	9	0

Most Touchdowns	TD	Run	Rec	Ret	Pts
Marty Booker	.6	0	6	0	40
Ronnie Brown	.5	5	0	0	30
Chris Chambers	.4	0	4	0	24
Randy McMichael	.3	0	3	0	18
Jason Taylor	.2	0	0	2	12

2-Pt. Conversions: (0-1).

Kicking	PAT/Att	FG/Att	Lg	Pts
Olindo Mare	.22/22	26/36	53	100

Punts (10 or more)	No	Yds	Long	Avg	In20
Donnie Jones	.85	3640	64	42.8	28

Most Interceptions | | **Most Sacks** |
---|---|---|---
Jason Taylor | .2 | Jason Taylor | .13.5
Renaldo Hill | .2 | |

New England Patriots

Passing (5 Att)	Att	Cmp	Pct	Yds	TD	Rate
Tom Brady	.516	319	61.8	3529	24	87.9
Matt Cassel	.8	5	62.5	32	0	70.8

Interceptions: Brady 12.

Top Receivers	No	Yds	Avg	Long	TD
Reche Caldwell	.61	760	12.5	62-td	4
Ben Watson	.49	643	13.1	40	3
Troy Brown	.43	384	8.9	23	4
Kevin Faulk	.43	356	8.3	43-td	2
Laurence Maroney*	.22	194	8.8	31	1
Daniel Graham	.21	235	11.2	29	2

Released: Doug Gabriel on Dec. 12 (see Oak).

Top Rushers	Car	Yds	Avg	Long	TD
Corey Dillon	.199	812	4.1	50	13
Laurence Maroney*	.175	745	4.3	41	6
Kevin Faulk	.25	123	4.9	11-td	1
Heath Evans	.27	117	4.3	35	0
Tom Brady	.49	102	2.1	22	0

Most Touchdowns	TD	Run	Rec	Ret	Pts
Corey Dillon	.13	13	0	0	78
Laurence Maroney*	.7	6	1	0	42
Troy Brown	.4	0	4	0	26
Reche Caldwell	.4	0	4	0	26

Three tied with 3 TDs for 18 pts.

2-Pt. Conversions: (2-2) Brown, Caldwell.

Kicking	PAT/Att	FG/Att	Lg	Pts
Stephen Gostkowski*	.43/44	20/26	52	103

Punts (10 or more)	No	Yds	Long	Avg	In20
Josh Miller	.43	1848	62	43.0	12
Ken Walter	.16	591	47	36.9	5
Todd Sauerbrun	.10	408	58	40.8	2

Most Interceptions | | **Most Sacks** |
---|---|---|---
Asante Samuel | .10 | Rosevelt Colvin | .8.5

New York Jets

Passing (5 Att)	Att	Cmp	Pct	Yds	TD	Rate
Chad Pennington	.485	313	64.5	3352	17	82.6

Interceptions: Pennington 16.

Top Receivers	No	Yds	Avg	Long	TD
Laveranues Coles	.91	1098	12.1	58-td	6
Jerricho Cotchery	.82	961	11.7	71-td	6
Chris Baker	.31	300	9.7	28	4
Leon Washington*	.25	270	10.8	64	0
Justin McCareins	.23	347	15.1	50	1

Top Rushers	No	Yds	Avg	Long	TD
Leon Washington*	.151	650	4.3	23	4
Cedric Houston	.113	374	3.3	31	5
Kevan Barlow	.131	370	2.8	12	6
Chad Pennington	.35	109	3.1	15	0
Brad Smith*	.18	103	5.7	32	0

Most Touchdowns	TD	Run	Rec	Ret	Pts
Kevan Barlow	.6	6	0	0	36
Laveranues Coles	.6	0	6	0	36
Jerricho Cotchery	.6	0	6	0	36
Cedric Houston	.5	5	0	0	30
Chris Baker	.4	0	4	0	24
Leon Washington*	.4	4	0	0	24

2-Pt. Conversions: (0-0).

Kicking	PAT/Att	FG/Att	Lg	Pts
Mike Nugent*	.34/35	24/27	54	106

Punts (10 or more)	No	Yds	Long	Avg	In20
Ben Graham	.72	3182	69	44.2	26

Most Interceptions | | **Most Sacks** |
---|---|---|---
Kerry Rhodes | .4 | Bryan Thomas | .8.5
Andre Dyson | .4 | |

Oakland Raiders

Passing (5 Att)

	Att	Cmp	Pct	Yds	TD	Rate
Andrew Walter	...276	147	53.3	1677	3	55.8
Aaron Brooks	192	110	57.3	1105	3	61.7
Marques Tuiasosopo	..13	6	46.2	68	1	48.4

Interceptions: Walter 13, Brooks 8, Tuiasosopo 2.

Top Receivers

	No	Yds	Avg	Long	TD
Ronald Curry	62	727	11.7	39	1
Randy Moss	42	553	13.2	51	3
Doug Gabriel	30	428	14.3	45	3
NE	25	344	13.8	45	3
OAK	5	84	16.8	28	0
Randal Williams	28	293	10.5	28	0
Alvis Whitted	27	299	11.1	33	0

Claimed: Gabriel off waivers from NE (Dec. 13).

Top Rushers

	Car	Yds	Avg	Long	TD
Justin Fargas	178	659	3.7	48	1
LaMont Jordan	...114	434	3.8	59-td	2
Zack Crockett	39	163	4.2	17	0
Aaron Brooks	22	124	5.6	23	0

Most Touchdowns

	TD	Run	Rec	Ret	Pts
Doug Gabriel	3	0	3	0	18
NE	3	0	3	0	18
OAK	0	0	0	0	0
Randy Moss	3	0	3	0	18

Three tied with 2 TD each for 12 pts.

2-Pt. Conversions: (0-0).

Kicking

	PAT/Att	FG/Att	Lg	Pts
Sebastian Janikowski	....16/16	18/25	55	70

Punts (10 or more)

	No	Yds	Long	Avg	In20
Shane Lechler	77	3660	67	47.5	19

Most Interceptions	**Most Sacks**
Nnamdi Asomugha	...8	Derrick Burgess	.....11.0

Pittsburgh Steelers

Passing (5 Att)

	Att	Cmp	Pct	Yds	TD	Rate
Ben Roethlisberger	..469	280	59.7	3513	18	75.4
Charlie Batch	53	31	58.5	492	5	121.0

Interceptions: Roethlisberger 23.

Top Receivers

	No	Yds	Avg	Long	TD
Hines Ward	74	975	13.2	70-td	6
Santonio Holmes*	...49	824	16.8	67-td	2
Cedrick Wilson	37	504	13.6	38-td	1
Nate Washington	...35	624	17.8	49-td	4
Heath Miller	34	393	11.6	87-td	5
Willie Parker	31	222	7.2	25-td	3

Top Rushers

	Car	Yds	Avg	Long	TD
Willie Parker	337	1494	4.4	76	13
Najeh Davenport	...60	221	3.7	48	1
Ben Roethlisberger	..32	98	3.1	20	2
Verron Haynes	15	78	5.2	13	0

Most Touchdowns

	TD	Run	Rec	Ret	Pts
Willie Parker	16	13	3	0	96
Hines Ward	6	0	6	0	36
Heath Miller	5	0	5	0	30
Nate Washington	4	0	4	0	24
Santonio Holmes*	3	0	2	1	18

2-Pt. Conversions: (0-0).

Kicking

	PAT/Att	FG/Att	Lg	Pts
Jeff Reed	......41/41	20/27	50	101

Punts (10 or more)

	No	Yds	Long	Avg	In20
Chris Gardocki	65	2687	56	41.3	11

Most Interceptions	**Most Sacks**
Troy Polamalu	3	Joey Porter	.........7.0
Bryant McFadden	...3	

San Diego Chargers

Passing (5 Att)

	Att	Cmp	Pct	Yds	TD	Rate
Philip Rivers	460	284	61.7	3388	22	92.0

Interceptions: Rivers 9.

Top Receivers

	No	Yds	Avg	Long	TD
Antonio Gates	71	924	13.0	57-td	9
LaDainian Tomlinson	.56	508	9.1	51-td	3
Eric Parker	48	659	13.7	38	0
Keenan McCardell	...36	437	12.1	28	0
Vincent Jackson	27	453	16.8	55	6

Top Rushers

	No	Yds	Avg	Long	TD
LaDainian Tomlinson	..348	1815	5.2	85-td	28
Michael Turner	80	502	6.3	73	2
Lorenzo Neal	29	140	4.8	43	1
Philip Rivers	48	49	1.0	15	0

Most Touchdowns

	TD	Run	Rec	Ret	Pts
LaDainian Tomlinson	.31	28	3	0	186
Antonio Gates	9	0	9	0	54
Vincent Jackson	6	0	6	0	38
Malcom Floyd	3	0	3	0	18
Brandon Manumaleuna	.3	0	3	0	18
Michael Turner	2	2	0	0	12

2-Pt. Conversions: (1-1) Jackson.

Kicking

	PAT/Att	FG/Att	Lg	Pts
Nate Kaeding	.58/58	26/29	54	136

Punts (10 or more)

	No	Yds	Long	Avg	In20
Mike Scifres	69	2893	71	41.9	35

Most Interceptions	**Most Sacks**
Quentin Jammer	4	Shawne Merriman	...17.0

Tennessee Titans

Passing (5 Att)

	Att	Cmp	Pct	Yds	TD	Rate
Vince Young*	357	184	51.5	2199	12	66.7
Kerry Collins	90	42	46.7	549	1	42.3

Interceptions: Young 13, Collins 6.

Top Receivers

	No	Yds	Avg	Long	TD
Drew Bennett	46	737	16.0	39	3
Bobby Wade	33	461	14.0	25	2
Bo Scaife	29	370	12.8	34	2
Brandon Jones	27	384	14.2	53	4
Travis Henry	18	78	4.3	12	0
Ahmard Hall*	15	138	9.2	28	0
LenDale White*	14	60	4.3	13	0
Ben Troupe	13	150	11.5	32	2

Top Rushers

	Car	Yds	Avg	Long	TD
Travis Henry	270	1211	4.5	70-td	7
Vince Young*	83	552	6.7	39-td	7
LenDale White*	...61	244	4.0	26	0
Chris Brown	41	156	3.8	21	0

Most Touchdowns

	TD	Run	Rec	Ret	Pts
Travis Henry	7	7	0	0	44
Vince Young*	7	7	0	0	44
Pacman Jones	4	0	0	4	24
Brandon Jones	4	0	4	0	24
Drew Bennett	3	0	3	0	20
Bo Scaife	3	1	2	0	18

Two tied with 2 TDs for 12 pts.

2-Pt. Conversions: (0-1).

Kicking

	PAT/Att	FG/Att	Lg	Pts
Rob Bironas	.32/32	22/28	60	98

Punts (10 or more)

	No	Yds	Long	Avg	In20
Craig Hentrich	88	3760	73	42.7	32

Most Interceptions	**Most Sacks**
Chris Hope	5	Kyle Vanden Bosch	...6.5

NFC Team by Team Statistics

Players with more than one team during the regular season are listed with club they ended season with; (*) indicates rookies.

Arizona Cardinals

Passing (5 Att)

	Att	Cmp	Pct	Yds	TD	Rate
Matt Leinart*	377	214	56.8	2547	11	74.0
Kurt Warner	168	108	64.3	1377	6	89.3

Interceptions: Leinart 12, Warner 5.

Top Receivers

	No	Yds	Avg	Long	TD
Anquan Boldin	83	1203	14.5	64	4
Larry Fitzgerald	69	946	13.7	57	6
Bryant Johnson	40	740	18.5	58	4
Edgerrin James	38	217	5.7	14	0
Troy Walters	23	209	9.1	26	2
Obafemi Ayanbadejo	17	139	8.2	27	0

Top Rushers

	Car	Yds	Avg	Long	TD
Edgerrin James	337	1159	3.4	18	6
Matt Leinart*	22	49	2.2	14	2
Marcel Shipp	17	41	2.4	9-td	4
Obafemi Ayanbadejo	9	37	4.1	11	0

Most Touchdowns

	TD	Run	Rec	Ret	Pts
Larry Fitzgerald	6	0	6	0	36
Edgerrin James	6	6	0	0	36
Anquan Boldin	4	0	4	0	24
Bryant Johnson	4	0	4	0	24
Marcel Shipp	4	4	0	0	24

2-Pt. Conversions: (0-1).

Kicking

	PAT/Att	FG/Att	Lg	Pts
Neil Rackers	32/32	28/37	50	116

Punts (10 or more)

	No	Yds	Long	Avg	In20
Scott Player	66	2965	58	44.9	18

Most Interceptions — Adrian Wilson 4

Most Sacks — Chike Okeafor 8.5

Atlanta Falcons

Passing (5 Att)

	Att	Cmp	Pct	Yds	TD	Rate
Michael Vick	388	204	52.6	2474	20	75.7
Matt Schaub	27	18	66.7	208	1	71.2

Interceptions: Vick 13, Schaub 2.

Top Receivers

	No	Yds	Avg	Long	TD
Alge Crumpler	56	780	13.9	46	8
Michael Jenkins	39	436	11.2	34-td	7
Roddy White	30	506	16.9	55	0
Ashley Lelie	28	430	15.4	51	1
Justin Griffith	23	168	7.3	16	3
Warrick Dunn	22	170	7.7	18	1
Jerious Norwood*	12	102	8.5	32	0

Top Rushers

	Car	Yds	Avg	Long	TD
Warrick Dunn	286	1140	4.0	90-td	4
Michael Vick	123	1039	8.4	51	2
Jerious Norwood*	99	633	6.4	78-td	2
Justin Griffith	19	106	5.6	21-td	1

Most Touchdowns

	TD	Run	Rec	Ret	Pts
Alge Crumpler	8	0	8	0	48
Michael Jenkins	7	0	7	0	42
Warrick Dunn	5	4	1	0	30
Justin Griffith	4	1	3	0	24

2-Pt. Conversions: (0-1).

Kicking

	PAT/Att	FG/Att	Lg	Pts
Morten Andersen	27/27	20/23	45	87
Michael Koenen	4/4	3/9	51	13

Signed: Andersen on Sept. 20.

Punts (10 or more)

	No	Yds	Long	Avg	In20
Michael Koenen	76	3199	65	42.1	25

Most Interceptions — DeAngelo Hall 4

Most Sacks — Rod Coleman 6.0

Carolina Panthers

Passing (5 Att)

	Att	Cmp	Pct	Yds	TD	Rate
Jake Delhomme	431	263	61.0	2805	17	82.6
Chris Weinke	96	56	58.3	625	2	67.4
Brett Basanez*	11	6	54.5	56	0	30.9

Interceptions: Delhomme 11, Weinke 4, Basanez 1.

Top Receivers

	No	Yds	Avg	Long	TD
Steve Smith	83	1166	14.0	72-td	8
Keyshawn Johnson	70	815	11.6	40	4
DeAngelo Williams*	33	313	9.5	41	1
DeShaun Foster	32	159	5.0	14	0
Drew Carter	28	357	12.8	42-td	3
Kris Mangum	21	170	8.1	19	1

Top Rushers

	Car	Yds	Avg	Long	TD
DeShaun Foster	227	897	4.0	43-td	3
DeAngelo Williams*	121	501	4.1	31	1
Brad Hoover	22	73	3.3	17	1
Steve Smith	8	61	7.6	24	1

Most Touchdowns

	TD	Run	Rec	Ret	Pts
Steve Smith	9	1	8	0	54
Keyshawn Johnson	5	1	4	0	30
Drew Carter	3	0	3	0	18
DeShaun Foster	3	3	0	0	18

2-Pt. Conversions: (0-0).

Kicking

	PAT/Att	FG/Att	Lg	Pts
John Kasay	28/28	24/27	54	100

Punts (10 or more)

	No	Yds	Long	Avg	In20
Jason Baker	98	4483	70	45.7	31

Most Interceptions — Three tied with 3 each.

Most Sacks — Julius Peppers 13.0

Chicago Bears

Passing (5 Att)

	Att	Cmp	Pct	Yds	TD	Rate
Rex Grossman	480	262	54.6	3193	23	73.9
Brian Griese	32	18	56.3	220	1	62.0

Interceptions: Grossman 20, Griese 2.

Top Receivers

	No	Yds	Avg	Long	TD
Muhsin Muhammad	60	863	14.4	40	5
Bernard Berrian	51	775	15.2	62	6
Desmond Clark	45	626	13.9	33	6
Thomas Jones	36	154	4.3	21	0
Jason McKie	25	162	6.5	26	0
Rashied Davis	22	303	13.8	31	2

Top Rushers

	Car	Yds	Avg	Long	TD
Thomas Jones	296	1210	4.1	30-td	6
Cedric Benson	157	647	4.1	30	6
Adrian Peterson	10	41	4.1	11	2
Jason McKie	8	18	2.3	7	0

Most Touchdowns

	TD	Run	Rec	Ret	Pts
Cedric Benson	6	6	0	0	36
Bernard Berrian	6	0	6	0	36
Desmond Clark	6	0	6	0	36
Devin Hester*	6	0	0	6	36
Thomas Jones	6	6	0	0	36
Muhsin Muhammad	5	0	5	0	30

2-Pt. Conversions: (0-0).

Kicking

	PAT/Att	FG/Att	Lg	Pts
Robbie Gould	47/47	32/36	49	143

Punts (10 or more)

	No	Yds	Long	Avg	In20
Brad Maynard	77	3404	65	44.2	24

Most Interceptions — Ricky Manning ....5, Charles Tillman 5

Most Sacks — Mark Anderson* 12.0

Dallas Cowboys

Passing (5 Att)	Att	Cmp	Pct	Yds	TD	Rate
Tony Romo	.337	220	65.3	2903	19	95.1
Drew Bledsoe	.169	90	53.3	1164	7	69.2

Interceptions: Romo 13, Bledsoe 8.

Top Receivers	No	Yds	Avg	Long	TD
Terrell Owens	.85	1180	13.9	56-td	13
Terry Glenn	.70	1047	15.0	54	6
Jason Witten	.64	754	11.8	42	1
Patrick Crayton	.36	516	14.3	53-td	4
Marion Barber	.23	196	8.5	26	2

Top Rushers	Car	Yds	Avg	Long	TD
Julius Jones	.267	1084	4.1	77-td	4
Marion Barber	.135	654	4.8	25	14
Tony Romo	.34	102	3.0	16	0
Tyson Thompson	.13	30	2.3	7-td	1

Most Touchdowns	TD	Run	Rec	Ret	Pts
Marion Barber	.16	14	2	0	96
Terrell Owens	.13	0	13	0	80
Terry Glenn	.6	0	6	0	36
Patrick Crayton	.4	0	4	0	24
Julius Jones	.4	4	0	0	24

2-Pt. Conversions: (2-3) Owens, Romo.

Kicking	PAT/Att	FG/Att	Lg	Pts
Mike Vanderjagt	.33/33	13/18	50	72
Martin Gramatica	.23/23	7/9	48	44
IND	.9/9	1/1	20	12
DAL	.14/14	6/8	48	32

Signed: Gramatica (Nov. 27). **Released:** Vanderjagt (Nov. 27); Shaun Suisham (Oct. 12, see Wash.).

Punts (10 or more)	No	Yds	Long	Avg	In20
Mat McBriar	.56	2697	75	48.2	22

Most Interceptions		Most Sacks	
Roy Williams	.5	DeMarcus Ware	.11.0

Detroit Lions

Passing (5 Att)	Att	Cmp	Pct	Yds	TD	Rate
Jon Kitna	.596	372	62.4	4208	21	79.9

Interceptions: Kitna 22.

Top Receivers	No	Yds	Avg	Long	TD
Mike Furrey	.98	1086	11.1	31	6
Roy Williams	.82	1310	16.0	60-td	7
Kevin Jones	.61	520	8.5	26	2
Dan Campbell	.21	308	14.7	30	4
Arlen Harris	.18	132	7.3	20	0
Corey Bradford	.14	164	11.7	23	0

Top Rushers	Car	Yds	Avg	Long	TD
Kevin Jones	.181	689	3.8	52	6
Arlen Harris	.49	158	3.2	20	1
Jon Kitna	.34	156	4.6	18	2
Aveion Cason	.24	94	3.9	16	0

Most Touchdowns	TD	Run	Rec	Ret	Pts
Kevin Jones	.8	6	2	0	48
Roy Williams	.7	0	7	0	42
Mike Furrey	.6	0	6	0	36
Dan Campbell	.4	0	4	0	24
Jon Kitna	.2	2	0	0	12

2-Pt. Conversions: (0-1).

Kicking	PAT/Att	FG/Att	Lg	Pts
Jason Hanson	.30/30	29/33	53	117

Punts (10 or more)	No	Yds	Long	Avg	In20
Nick Harris	.66	2967	67	45.0	18

Most Interceptions		Most Sacks	
Jamar Fletcher	.3	Cory Redding	.8.0
Dre' Bly	.3		
Terrence Holt	.3		

Green Bay Packers

Passing (5 Att)	Att	Cmp	Pct	Yds	TD	Rate
Brett Favre	.613	343	56.0	3885	18	72.7
Aaron Rodgers	.15	6	40.0	46	0	48.2

Interceptions: Favre 18.

Top Receivers	No	Yds	Avg	Long	TD
Donald Driver	.92	1295	14.1	82-td	8
Ahman Green	.46	373	8.1	20	1
Greg Jennings*	.45	632	14.0	75-td	3
Noah Herron	.29	211	7.3	16	2
Bubba Franks	.25	232	9.3	19	0
Ruvell Martin*	.21	358	17.0	36-td	1
David Martin	.21	198	9.4	23	2

Top Rushers	Car	Yds	Avg	Long	TD
Ahman Green	.266	1059	4.0	70-td	5
Vernand Morency	.96	434	4.5	39	2
HOU	.5	13	2.6	12	0
GB	.91	421	4.6	39	2
Noah Herron	.37	150	4.1	19	1
Brett Favre	.23	29	1.3	14	1

Acquired: Morency from Hou. for RB Samkon Gado (Sept. 13).

Most Touchdowns	TD	Run	Rec	Ret	Pts
Donald Driver	.8	0	8	0	48
Ahman Green	.6	5	1	0	36
Noah Herron	.3	1	2	0	18
Greg Jennings*	.3	0	3	0	18

2-Pt. Conversions: (0-0).

Kicking	PAT/Att	FG/Att	Lg	Pts
Dave Rayner	.31/32	26/35	54	109

Punts (10 or more)	No	Yds	Long	Avg	In20
Jon Ryan	.84	3739	66	44.5	17

Most Interceptions		Most Sacks	
Charles Woodson	.8	Aaron Kampman	.15.5

Minnesota Vikings

Passing (5 Att)	Att	Cmp	Pct	Yds	TD	Rate
Brad Johnson	.439	270	61.5	2750	9	72.0
Tavaris Jackson*	.81	47	58.0	475	2	62.5
Brooks Bollinger	.13	7	72.2	146	0	72.2

Interceptions: Johnson 15, Jackson 4, Bollinger 1.

Top Receivers	No	Yds	Avg	Long	TD
Travis Taylor	.57	651	11.4	36	3
Mewelde Moore	.46	468	10.2	50	1
Jermaine Wiggins	.46	386	8.4	24	1
Chester Taylor	.42	288	6.9	24	0
Troy Williamson	.37	455	12.3	46	0
Marcus Robinson	.29	381	13.1	40-td	4
Billy McMullen	.23	307	13.3	40-td	2

Top Rushers	Car	Yds	Avg	Long	TD
Chester Taylor	.303	1216	4.0	95-td	6
Artose Pinner	.43	190	4.4	21	3
Mewelde Moore	.24	131	5.5	15	0
Ciatrick Fason	.18	99	5.5	15	1

Most Touchdowns	TD	Run	Rec	Ret	Pts
Chester Taylor	.6	6	0	0	36
Marcus Robinson	.4	0	4	0	24
Billy McMullen	.3	0	2	1	18
Artose Pinner	.3	3	0	0	18
Travis Taylor	.3	0	3	0	18

2-Pt. Conversions: (0-4).

Kicking	PAT/Att	FG/Att	Lg	Pts
Ryan Longwell	.27/28	21/25	49	90

Punts (10 or more)	No	Yds	Long	Avg	In20
Chris Kluwe	.93	3934	68	42.3	28

Most Interceptions		Most Sacks	
Three tied with 4 each.		Darrion Scott	.5.5

New Orleans Saints

Passing (5 Att)	Att	Cmp	Pct	Yds	TD	Rate
Drew Brees	554	356	64.3	4418	26	96.2
Jamie Martin	24	16	66.7	208	1	90.3

Interceptions: Brees 11, Martin 1.

Top Receivers	No	Yds	Avg	Long	TD
Reggie Bush*	88	742	8.4	74	2
Marques Colston*	70	1038	14.8	86-td	8
Joe Horn	37	679	18.4	72-td	4
Devery Henderson	32	745	23.3	76-td	5
Deuce McAllister	30	198	6.6	24	0
Terrance Copper	23	385	16.7	48-td	3
Aaron Stecker	19	190	10.0	48	1

Top Rushers	Car	Yds	Avg	Long	TD
Deuce McAllister	244	1057	4.3	57	10
Reggie Bush*	155	565	3.6	18	6
Mike Karney	11	33	3.0	8	1
Drew Brees	42	32	0.8	16	0

Most Touchdowns	TD	Run	Rec	Ret	Pts
Deuce McAllister	11	10	0	1	66
Reggie Bush*	9	6	2	1	54
Marques Colston*	8	0	8	0	48
Devery Henderson	6	1	5	0	36
Joe Horn	4	0	4	0	26

2-Pt. Conversions: (2-2) Horn, Billy Miller.

Kicking	PAT/Att	FG/Att	Lg	Pts
John Carney	46/47	23/25	51	115
Billy Cundiff	0/0	0/1	—	0

Signed: Cundiff on Nov. 25.

Punts (10 or more)	No	Yds	Long	Avg	In20
Steven Weatherford*	77	3369	59	43.8	19

Most Interceptions
Four tied with 2 each.

Most Sacks
Will Smith 10.5

New York Giants

Passing (5 Att)	Att	Cmp	Pct	Yds	TD	Rate
Eli Manning	522	301	57.7	3244	24	77.0

Interceptions: Manning 18.

Top Receivers	No	Yds	Avg	Long	TD
Jeremy Shockey	66	623	9.4	25	7
Plaxico Burress	63	988	15.7	55-td	10
Tiki Barber	58	465	8.0	28	0
Amani Toomer	32	360	11.3	44	3
Tim Carter	22	253	11.5	27	2
David Tyree	19	197	10.4	33	2
Visanthe Shiancoe	12	81	6.8	16	0

Top Rushers	Car	Yds	Avg	Long	TD
Tiki Barber	327	1662	5.1	55-td	5
Brandon Jacobs	96	423	4.4	16	9
Chad Morton	1	22	22.0	22	0
Eli Manning	25	21	0.8	9	0

Most Touchdowns	TD	Run	Rec	Ret	Pts
Plaxico Burress	10	0	10	0	60
Brandon Jacobs	9	9	0	0	54
Jeremy Shockey	7	0	7	0	42
Tiki Barber	5	5	0	0	30
Tim Carter	3	0	2	1	18
Amani Toomer	3	0	3	0	18

2-Pt. Conversions: (0-2).

Kicking	PAT/Att	FG/Att	Lg	Pts
Jay Feely	38/38	23/27	47	107

Punts (10 or more)	No	Yds	Long	Avg	In20
Jeff Feagles	77	3098	54	40.2	27

Most Interceptions
Seven tied with 2 each.

Most Sacks
Osi Umenyiora 6.0

Philadelphia Eagles

Passing (5 Att)	Att	Cmp	Pct	Yds	TD	Rate
Donovan McNabb	316	180	57.0	2647	18	95.5
Jeff Garcia	188	116	61.7	1309	10	95.8
A.J. Feeley	38	26	68.4	342	3	122.9

Interceptions: McNabb 6, Garcia 2.

Top Receivers	No	Yds	Avg	Long	TD
Brian Westbrook	77	699	9.1	52-td	4
L.J. Smith	50	611	12.2	65	5
Reggie Brown	46	816	17.7	60-td	8
Donte' Stallworth	38	725	19.1	84-td	5
Greg Lewis	24	348	14.5	45-td	2
Correll Buckhalter	24	256	10.7	55-td	1
Hank Baskett*	22	464	21.1	89-td	2

Top Rushers	Car	Yds	Avg	Long	TD
Brian Westbrook	240	1217	5.1	71-td	7
Correll Buckhalter	83	345	4.2	20	2
Donovan McNabb	32	212	6.6	37	3
Jeff Garcia	25	87	3.5	12	0
Ryan Moats	22	69	3.1	13	0

Most Touchdowns	TD	Run	Rec	Ret	Pts
Brian Westbrook	11	7	4	0	66
Reggie Brown	9	1	8	0	54
L.J. Smith	5	0	5	0	32
Donte' Stallworth	5	0	5	0	30
Correll Buckhalter	3	2	1	0	18
Donovan McNabb	3	3	0	0	18

Three tied with 2 TD each for 12 pts.

2-Pt. Conversions: (1-1) Smith.

Kicking	PAT/Att	FG/Att	Lg	Pts
David Akers	48/48	18/23	47	102

Punts (10 or more)	No	Yds	Long	Avg	In20
Dirk Johnson	78	3326	60	42.6	21

Most Interceptions
Lito Sheppard 6

Most Sacks
Trent Cole 8.0

St. Louis Rams

Passing (5 Att)	Att	Cmp	Pct	Yds	TD	Rate
Marc Bulger	588	370	62.9	4301	24	92.9

Interceptions: Bulger 8.

Top Receivers	No	Yds	Avg	Long	TD
Torry Holt	93	1188	12.8	67-td	10
Steven Jackson	90	806	9.0	64-td	3
Isaac Bruce	74	1098	14.8	45	3
Kevin Curtis	40	479	12.0	42	4
Joe Klopfenstein*	20	226	11.3	28	1
Tony Fisher	14	159	11.4	49	0
Shaun McDonald	13	136	10.5	28	1
Stephen Davis	12	90	7.5	18	1

Top Rushers	Car	Yds	Avg	Long	TD
Steven Jackson	346	1528	4.4	59-td	13
Stephen Davis	40	177	4.4	16	0
Marc Bulger	18	44	2.4	29	0

Most Touchdowns	TD	Run	Rec	Ret	Pts
Steven Jackson	16	13	3	0	96
Torry Holt	10	0	10	0	60
Kevin Curtis	4	0	4	0	24
Isaac Bruce	3	0	3	0	20

Six tied with 1 TD each for 6 points.

2-Pt. Conversions: (1-3) Bruce.

Kicking	PAT/Att	FG/Att	Lg	Pts
Jeff Wilkins	35/35	32/37	53	131

Punts (10 or more)	No	Yds	Long	Avg	In20
Matt Turk	72	3132	74	43.5	26

Most Interceptions
Four tied with 3 each.

Most Sacks
Leonard Little 13.0

San Francisco 49ers

Passing (5 Att)	Att	Cmp	Pct	Yds	TD	Rate
Alex Smith	.442	257	58.1	2890	16	74.8

Interceptions: Smith 16.

Top Receivers	No	Yds	Avg	Long	TD
Frank Gore	.61	485	8.0	39	1
Arnaz Battle	.59	686	11.6	56	3
Antonio Bryant	.40	733	18.3	72-td	3
Eric Johnson	.34	292	8.6	26	2
Vernon Davis*	.20	265	13.3	52-td	3
Maurice Hicks	.13	137	10.5	33-td	1

Top Rushers	Car	Yds	Avg	Long	TD
Frank Gore	.312	1695	5.4	72	8
Alex Smith	.44	147	3.3	22	2
Michael Robinson*	.38	116	3.1	33	2
Bryan Gilmore	.7	94	13.4	22	0
Maurice Hicks	.29	82	2.8	9	0

Most Touchdowns	TD	Run	Rec	Ret	Pts
Frank Gore	.9	8	1	0	54
Arnaz Battle	.3	0	3	0	18
Antonio Bryant	.3	0	3	0	18
Vernon Davis*	.3	0	3	0	18

Four tied with 2 TD for 12 pts.
2-Pt. Conversions: (0-1).

Kicking	PAT/Att	FG/Att	Lg	Pts
Joe Nedney	.29/29	29/35	51	116

Punts (10 or more)	No	Yds	Long	Avg	In20
Andy Lee	.81	3625	66	44.8	22

Most Interceptions		Most Sacks	
Walt Harris	.8	Brandon Moore	.6.5

Tampa Bay Buccaneers

Passing (5 Att)	Att	Cmp	Pct	Yds	TD	Rate
Bruce Gradkowski*	328	177	54.0	1661	9	65.9
Chris Simms	..106	58	54.7	585	1	46.3
Tim Rattay	..101	61	60.4	748	4	88.2

Interceptions: Gradkowski 9, Simms 7, Rattay 2.

Top Receivers	No	Yds	Avg	Long	TD
Joey Galloway	.62	1057	17.0	64-td	7
Michael Pittman	.47	405	8.6	25	0
Alex Smith	.35	250	7.1	27	3
Ike Hilliard	.34	339	10.0	44-td	2
Michael Clayton	.33	356	10.8	27	1
Cadillac Williams	.30	196	6.5	21	0

Top Rushers	Car	Yds	Avg	Long	TD
Cadillac Williams	.225	798	3.5	38	1
Michael Pittman	.50	245	4.9	32	1
Mike Alstott	.60	171	2.9	17	3
Bruce Gradkowski*	.41	161	3.9	14	0

Most Touchdowns	TD	Run	Rec	Ret	Pts
Joey Galloway	.7	0	7	0	42
Mike Alstott	.3	3	0	0	18
Alex Smith	.3	0	3	0	18
Ronde Barber	.2	0	0	2	12
Ike Hilliard	.2	0	2	0	12

2-Pt. Conversions: (0-0).

Kicking	PAT/Att	FG/Att	Lg	Pts
Matt Bryant	.22/23	17/22	62	73

Punts (10 or more)	No	Yds	Long	Avg	In20
Josh Bidwell	.93	4045	59	43.5	20

Most Interceptions	Most Sacks
Two tied with 3 each.	Three tied with 5 each.

Seattle Seahawks

Passing (5 Att)	Att	Cmp	Pct	Yds	TD	Rate
Matt Hasselbeck	..371	210	56.6	2442	18	76.0
Seneca Wallace	..141	82	58.2	927	8	76.2

Interceptions: Hasselbeck 15, Wallace 7.

Top Receivers	No	Yds	Avg	Long	TD
Darrell Jackson	..63	956	15.2	72-td	10
Deion Branch	..53	725	13.7	38-td	4
D.J. Hackett	..45	610	13.6	47	4
Mack Strong	..29	159	5.5	13	0
Bobby Engram	..24	290	12.1	54	1
Jerramy Stevens	..22	231	10.5	26	4
Nate Burleson	..18	192	10.7	36	2
Shaun Alexander	..12	48	4.0	14	0

Top Rushers	Car	Yds	Avg	Long	TD
Shaun Alexander	..252	896	3.6	33-td	7
Maurice Morris	..161	604	3.8	29	0
Mack Strong	..33	149	4.5	17	1
Seneca Wallace	..12	122	10.2	37	0
Matt Hasselbeck	..18	110	6.1	19	0

Most Touchdowns	TD	Run	Rec	Ret	Pts
Darrell Jackson	.10	0	10	0	60
Shaun Alexander	.7	7	0	0	42
Jerramy Stevens	.4	0	4	0	26
Deion Branch	.4	0	4	0	24
D.J. Hackett	.4	0	4	0	24
Nate Burleson	.3	0	2	1	18

2-Pt. Conversions: (1-1) Stevens.

Kicking	PAT/Att	FG/Att	Lg	Pts
Josh Brown	.36/36	25/31	54	111

Punts (10 or more)	No	Yds	Long	Avg	In20
Ryan Plackemeier	.84	3778	72	45.0	25

Most Interceptions		Most Sacks	
Ken Hamlin	.3	Julian Peterson	.10.0

Washington Redskins

Passing (5 Att)	Att	Cmp	Pct	Yds	TD	Rate
Mark Brunell	..260	162	62.3	1789	8	86.5
Jason Campbell	..207	110	53.1	1297	10	76.5

Interceptions: Campbell 6, Brunell 4.

Top Receivers	No	Yds	Avg	Long	TD
Chris Cooley	.57	734	12.9	66-td	6
Santana Moss	.55	790	14.4	68-td	6
Ladell Betts	.53	445	8.4	34	1
Antwaan Randle El	..32	351	11.0	34-td	3
Brandon Lloyd	.23	365	15.9	52	0

Top Rushers	Car	Yds	Avg	Long	TD
Ladell Betts	.245	1154	4.7	26	4
Clinton Portis	..127	523	4.1	38-td	7
T.J. Duckett	..38	132	3.5	19	2
Antwaan Randle El	..19	118	6.2	20	0

Most Touchdowns	TD	Run	Rec	Ret	Pts
Clinton Portis	.7	7	0	0	42
Chris Cooley	.6	0	6	0	38
Santana Moss	.6	0	6	0	38
Ladell Betts	.5	4	1	0	30
Antwaan Randle El	.4	0	3	1	24

2-Pt. Conversions: (2-2) Cooley, Moss.

Kicking	PAT/Att	FG/Att	Lg	Pts
Shaun Suisham	...14/14	9/11	52	41
DAL	..2/2	1/2	32	5
WASH	..12/12	8/9	52	36
John Hall	...9/9	9/11	46	36
Nick Novak	..10/10	5/10	47	25

Signed: Suisham (Nov. 28). Released: Novak (Dec. 4).

Punts (10 or more)	No	Yds	Long	Avg	In20
Derrick Frost	..81	3471	60	42.9	27

Most Interceptions		Most Sacks	
Six tied with 1 each.		Andre Carter	.6.0

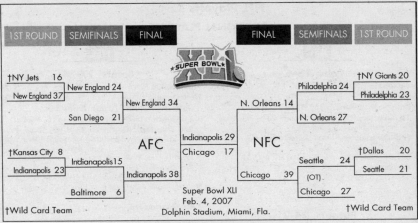

†NY Jets 16
New England 24
New England 37
New England 34
San Diego 21

AFC

†Kansas City 8
Indianapolis 15
Indianapolis 23
Indianapolis 38
Baltimore 6

Indianapolis 29
Chicago 17

★SUPER BOWL★ XLI

Super Bowl XLI
Feb. 4, 2007
Dolphin Stadium, Miami, Fla.

†Wild Card Team

N. Orleans 14
N. Orleans 27

NFC

Chicago 39
Seattle 24
(OT)
Chicago 27

†NY Giants 20
Philadelphia 24
Philadelphia 23

†Dallas 20
Seattle 21

†Wild Card Team

Playoff Game Summaries

Team records listed in parentheses indicate records before game.

WILD CARD ROUND

AFC

Colts, 23-8

Kansas City (9-7) 0   0   8   0—   **8**
Indianapolis (12-4) 6   3   7   7— **23**
Date—Jan. 6. **Att**—57,215. **Time**—2:42.
1st Quarter: IND—Adam Vinatieri 48-yd FG, 8:41; IND—Vinatieri 19-yd FG, 2:09.
2nd Quarter: IND—Vinatieri 50-yd FG, 0:00.
3rd Quarter: IND—Joseph Addai 6-yd run (Vinatieri kick), 4:14; KC—Tony Gonzalez 6-yd pass from Trent Green (Kris Wilson from Green pass), 0:08.
4th Quarter: IND—Reggie Wayne 5-yd pass from Peyton Manning (Vinatieri kick), 10:16.

Patriots, 37-16

NY Jets (10-6) 3   7   3   3— **16**
New England (12-4) 7   10   6   14— **37**
Date—Jan. 7. **Att**—68,756. **Time**—3:13.
1st Quarter: NE—Corey Dillon 11-yd run (Stephen Gostkowski kick), 11:53; NYJ—Mike Nugent 28-yd FG, 2:36.
2nd Quarter: NYJ—Jerricho Cotchery 77-yd pass from Chad Pennington (Nugent kick), 14:45; NE—Gostkowski 20-yd FG, 10:57; NE—Daniel Graham 1-yd pass from Tom Brady (Gostkowski kick), 0:11.
3rd Quarter: NYJ—Nugent 21-yd FG, 8:19; NE—Gostkowski 40-yd FG, 4:22; NE—Gostkowski 28-yd FG, 0:04.
4th Quarter: NYJ—Nugent 37-yd FG, 11:39; NE—Kevin Faulk 7-yd pass from Brady (Gostkowski kick), 5:16; NE—Asante Samuel 36-yd interception return (Gostkowski kick), 4:54.

NFC

Seahawks, 21-20

Dallas (9-7) 3   7   7   3— **20**
Seattle (9-7) 3   3   7   8— **21**
Date—Jan. 6. **Att**—68,058. **Time**—3:09.
1st Quarter: SEA—Josh Brown 23-yd FG, 11:13; DAL—Martin Gramatica 50-yd FG, 4:50.
2nd Quarter: SEA—Brown 30-yd FG, 8:23; DAL—Patrick Crayton 13-yd pass from Tony Romo (Gramatica kick), 0:11.
3rd Quarter: SEA—Jerramy Stevens 15-yd pass from Matt Hasselbeck (Brown kick), 6:08; DAL—Miles Austin 93-yd kickoff return (Gramatica kick). 5:57.
4th Quarter: DAL—Gramatica 29-yd FG, 10:15; SEA—Safety (ball through end zone), 6:32; SEA—Stevens 37-yd pass from Hasselbeck (pass failed), 4:24.

Eagles, 23-20

NY Giants (8-8) 7   3   0   10— **20**
Philadelphia (10-6) 0   17   3   3— **23**
Date—Jan. 7. **Att**—69,094. **Time**—3:16.
1st Quarter: NYG—Plaxico Burress 17-yd pass from Eli Manning (Jay Feely kick), 11:44.
2nd Quarter: PHI—Brian Westbrook 49-yd run (David Akers kick), 14:11; PHI—Akers 19-yd FG, 9:34; NYG—Feely 20-yd FG, 4:45; PHI—Donte' Stallworth 28-yd pass from Jeff Garcia (Akers kick), 1:01.
3rd Quarter: PHI—Akers 48-yd FG, 2:37.
4th Quarter: NYG—Feely 24-yd FG, 14:50; NYG—Burress 11-yd pass from Manning (Feely kick), 5:04; PHI—Akers 38-yd FG, 0:00.

NFL Playoffs (Cont.)
DIVISIONAL PLAYOFFS

AFC

Colts, 15-6

Indianapolis (13-4) 6   3   3   3—   **15**
Baltimore (13-3) 0   3   0   3—   **6**
    Date—Jan. 13. **Att**—71,162. **Time**—3:01.
    1st Quarter: IND—Adam Vinatieri 23-yd FG, 8:04; IND—Vinatieri 42-yd FG, 5:36.
    2nd Quarter: BAL—Matt Stover 40-yd FG, 14:56; IND—Vinatieri 51-yd FG, 3:15.
    3rd Quarter: IND—Vinatieri 48-yd FG, 10:57.
    4th Quarter: BAL—Stover 51-yd FG, 13:03; IND—Vinatieri 35-yd FG, 0:23.

Patriots, 24-21

New England (13-4) 3   7   3   11—   **24**
San Diego (14-2) 0   14   0   7—   **21**
    Date—Jan. 14. **Att**—68,810. **Time**—3:39.
    1st Quarter: NE—Stephen Gostkowski 50-yd FG, 0:40.
    2nd Quarter: SD—LaDainian Tomlinson 2-yd run (Nate Kaeding kick), 7:19; SD—Michael Turner 6-yd run (Kaeding kick), 2:04; NE—Jabar Gaffney 6-yd pass from Tom Brady (Gostkowski kick), 0:08.
    3rd Quarter: NE—Gostkowski 34-yd FG, 2:11.
    4th Quarter: SD—Tomlinson 3-yd run (Kaeding kick), 8:35; NE—Reche Caldwell 4-yd pass from Brady (Kevin Faulk run), 4:36; NE—Gostkowski 31-yd FG, 1:10.

NFC

Saints, 27-24

Philadelphia (11-6) 0   14   7   3—   **24**
New Orleans (10-6) 3   10   14   0—   **27**
    Date—Jan. 13. **Att**—70,001. **Time**—3:06.
    1st Quarter: NO—John Carney 33-yd FG, 9:24.
    2nd Quarter: NO—Carney 23-yd FG, 14:46; PHI—Donte' Stallworth 75-yd pass from Jeff Garcia (David Akers kick), 13:38; NO—Reggie Bush 4-yd run (Carney kick), 5:19; PHI—Brian Westbrook 1-yd run (Akers kick), 0:50.
    3rd Quarter: PHI—Westbrook 62-yd run (Akers kick), 13:25; NO—Deuce McAllister 5-yd run (Carney kick), 9:36; NO—McAllister 11-yd pass from Drew Brees (Carney kick), 1:05.
    4th Quarter: PHI—Akers 24-yd FG, 11:08.

Bears, 27-24 (OT)

Seattle (10-7) 0   14   10   0   0— **24**
Chicago (13-3) 7   14   0   3   3— **27**
    Date—Jan. 14. **Att**—62,184. **Time**—3:16.
    1st Quarter: CHI—Thomas Jones 9-yd run (Robbie Gould kick), 8:35.
    2nd Quarter: SEA—Nate Burleson 16-yd pass from Matt Hasselbeck (Josh Brown kick), 14:54; CHI—Bernard Berrian 68-yd pass from Rex Grossman (Gould kick), 14:36; SEA—Shaun Alexander 4-yd run (Brown kick), 2:29; CHI—Thomas Jones 7-yd run (Gould kick), 0:48.
    3rd Quarter: SEA—Brown 40-yd FG, 9:56; SEA—Alexander 13-yd run (Brown kick), 4:57.
    4th Quarter: CHI—Gould 41-yd FG, 4:24.
    Overtime: CHI—Gould 49-yd FG, 10:02.

CONFERENCE CHAMPIONSHIPS

AFC

Colts, 38-34

New England (14-4) 7   14   7   6—   **34**
Indianapolis (14-4) 3   3   15   17—   **38**
    Date—Jan. 21. **Att**—57,433. **Time**—3:34.
    1st Quarter: NE—Logan Mankins fumble recovery in endzone (Stephen Gostkowski kick), 7:24; IND—Adam Vinatieri 42-yd FG, 0:48.
    2nd Quarter: NE—Corey Dillon 7-yd run (Gostkowski kick), 10:18; NE—Asante Samuel 39-yd interception return (Gostkowski kick), 9:25; IND—Vinatieri 26-yd FG, 0:07.
    3rd Quarter: IND—Peyton Manning 1-yd run (Vinatieri kick), 8:13; IND—Dan Klecko 1-yd pass from Manning (Harrison pass from Manning), 4:00; NE—Jabar Gaffney 6-yd pass from Tom Brady (Gostkowski kick); 1:25.
    4th Quarter: IND—Jeff Saturday fumble recovery in end-zone (Vinatieri kick), 13:24; NE—Gostkowski 28-yd FG, 7:42; IND—Vinatieri 36-yd FG, 5:31; NE—Gostkowski 43-yd FG, 3:49; IND—Joseph Addai 3-yd run (Vinatieri kick), 1:00.

NFC

Bears, 39-14

New Orleans (11-6) 0   7   7   0—   **14**
Chicago (14-3) 3   13   2   21—   **39**
    Date—Jan. 21. **Att**—61,817. **Time**—3:10.
    1st Quarter: CHI—Robbie Gould 19-yd FG, 0:41.
    2nd Quarter: CHI—Gould 43-yd FG, 13:40; CHI—Gould 24-yd FG, 8:52; CHI—Thomas Jones 2-yd run (Gould kick), 1:56; NO—Marques Colston 13-yd pass from Drew Brees (Carney kick), 0:46.
    3rd Quarter: NO—Reggie Bush 88-yd run from Brees (Carney kick), 12:20; CHI—Safety (penalty on Brees in end-zone), 5:27.
    4th Quarter: CHI—Bernard Berrian 33-yd pass from Rex Grossman (Gould kick), 14:23; CHI—Cedric Benson 12-yd run (Gould kick), 11:37; CHI—Jones 15-yd run (Gould kick), 4:19.

Super Bowl XLI

Sunday, Feb. 4, 2007 at Dolphin Stadium in Miami, Florida

ndianapolis (15-4)	6	10	6	7—	**29**
Chicago (15-3)	14	0	3	0—	**17**

1st Quarter: CHI—Devin Hester 92-yd kickoff return (Robbie Gould kick), 14:46. **IND**—Reggie Wayne 53-yd pass from Peyton Manning (kick failed), 6:50. Drive: 80 yards in 9 plays. **CHI**—Muhsin Muhammad 4-yd pass from Rex Grossman (Gould kick), 4:34. Drive: 57 yards in 4 plays. Key play: Thomas Jones 52-yd run to IND 5.

2nd Quarter: IND—Adam Vinatieri 29-yd FG, 11:17. Drive: 47 yards in 8 plays. Key play: Marvin Harrison 15-yd pass from Manning to CHI 31. **IND**—Dominic Rhodes 1-yd run (Vinatieri kick), 6:09. Drive: 58 yards in 7 plays. Key play: Harrison 22-yd pass from Manning to CHI 36.

3rd Quarter: IND—Vinatieri 24-yd FG, 7:26. Drive: 56 yards in 13 plays. Key play: Joseph Addai 10-yd run to CHI 28. **IND**—Vinatieri 20-yd FG, 3:16. Drive: 62 yards in 6 plays. Key play: Rhodes 36-yd run to CHI 28. **CHI**—Gould 44-yd FG, 1:14. Drive: 14 yards in 6 plays. Key play: John Gilmore 9-yd kickoff return plus additional 15-yd Colts penalty for unnecessary roughness to IND 40.

4th Quarter: IND—Kelvin Hayden 56-yd interception return (Vinatieri kick), 11:44.

Favorite: Colts by 7   **Attendance:** 74,512
Field: Grass   **Time:** 3:31
Weather: Cloudy, rain   **TV Rating:** 42.6/64 share (CBS)

Most Valuable Player
Peyton Manning, Indianapolis, QB
25-38 for 247 yards, 1 TD, 1 int

Team Statistics

	Colts	Bears
First downs	24	11
Rushing	12	3
Passing	11	8
Penalty	1	0
3rd down efficiency	8/18	3/10
4th down efficiency	0/1	0/1
Total offense (net yards)	430	265
Plays	81	48
Average gain	5.3	5.5
Rushes/yards	42/191	19/111
Yards per rush	4.5	5.8
Passing yards (net)	239	154
Times sacked/yards lost	1/8	1/11
Passing yards (gross)	247	165
Completions/attempts	25/38	20/28
Yards per pass play	6.1	5.3
Times intercepted	1	2
Return yardage	225	147
Punt returns/yards	3/42	1/3
Kickoff returns/yards	4/89	6/138
Interceptions/yards	2/94	1/6
Fumbles/lost	2/2	4/3
Penalties/yards	6/40	4/35
Punts/average	4/40.5	5/45.2
Punts blocked	0	0
Field Goals made/attempted	3/4	1/1
Time of possession	38:04	21:56

Individual Statistics

Indianapolis Colts

Passing	Att	Cmp	Pct.	Yds	TD	Int	Rate
Peyton Manning	38	25	65.8	247	1	1	81.8

Receiving	No	Yds	Avg	Long	TD
Joseph Addai	10	66	6.6	12	0
Marvin Harrison	5	59	11.8	22	0
Dallas Clark	4	36	9.0	17	0
Reggie Wayne	2	61	30.5	53-td	1
Bryan Fletcher	2	9	4.5	6	0
Dominic Rhodes	1	8	8.0	8	0
Ben Utecht	1	8	8.0	8	0
TOTAL	25	247	9.9	53	1

Rushing	Car	Yds	Avg	Long	TD
Dominic Rhodes	21	113	5.4	36	1
Joseph Addai	19	77	4.1	14	0
Dallas Clark	1	1	1.0	1	0
Peyton Manning	1	0	0.0	0	0
TOTAL	42	191	4.5	36	1

Field Goals	20-29	30-39	40-49	50-59	Total
Adam Vinatieri	3-3	0-1	0-0	0-0	3-4

Punting	No	Yds	Avg	Long	In20	Blk
Hunter Smith	4	162	40.5	50	2	0

Punt Returns	Ret	Yds	Avg	Long	FC	TD
Terrence Wilkins	3	42	14.0	18	0	0

Kickoff Returns	Ret	Yds	Avg	Long	FC	TD
Terrence Wilkins	4	89	22.3	28	0	0

Interceptions	No	Yds	Avg	Long	TD
Kelvin Hayden	1	56	56.0	56-td	1
Bob Sanders	1	38	38.0	38	0

Sacks		Most Tackles (solo + asst)	
Anthony McFarland	1.0	Gary Brackett	8

Chicago Bears

Passing	Att	Cmp	Pct.	Yds	TD	Int	Rate
Rex Grossman	28	20	71.4	165	1	2	68.3

Receiving	No	Yds	Avg	Long	TD
Desmond Clark	6	64	10.7	18	0
Bernard Berrian	4	38	9.5	14	0
Thomas Jones	4	18	4.5	14	0
Muhsin Muhammad	3	35	11.7	22	1
Jason McKie	2	8	4.0	4	0
Rashied Davis	1	2	2.0	2	0
TOTAL	20	165	8.3	22	1

Rushing	Car	Yds	Avg	Long	TD
Thomas Jones	15	112	7.5	52	0
Rex Grossman	2	0	0.0	0	0
Cedric Benson	2	-1	-0.5	4	0
TOTAL	19	111	5.8	52	0

Field Goals	20-29	30-39	40-49	50-59	Total
Robbie Gould	0-0	0-0	1-1	0-0	1-1

Punting	No	Yds	Avg	Long	In20	Blk
Brad Maynard	5	226	45.2	58	0	0

Punt Returns	Ret	Yds	Avg	Long	FC	TD
Devin Hester	1	3	3.0	3	1	0

Kickoff Returns	Ret	Yds	Avg	Long	FC	TD
John Gilmore	2	12	6.0	9	0	0
Devin Hester	1	92	92.0	92-td	0	1
Rashied Davis	1	15	15.0	15	0	0
Adrian Peterson	1	10	10.0	10	0	0
Gabe Reid	1	9	9.0	9	0	0

Interceptions	No	Yds	Avg	Long	TD
Chris Harris	1	6	6.0	6	0

Sacks	Most Tackles (solo + asst)	
Two tied with 0.5 each.	Lance Briggs	13

Super Bowl Finalists' Playoff Statistics

Indianapolis Colts (4-0)

Passing (5 att)	Att	Cmp	Pct.	Yds	TD	Rating
Peyton Manning . . .153	97	63.4	1034	3	70.5

Interceptions: Manning 7.

Top Receivers	No	Yds	Avg	Long	TD
Joseph Addai. 22	118	5.4	16	0
Dallas Clark. 21	317	15.1	52	0
Reggie Wayne 17	216	12.7	53-td	2
Marvin Harrison 15	193	12.9	42	0
Dominic Rhodes 7	70	10.0	15	0

Top Rushers	Car	Yds	Avg	Long	TD
Dominic Rhodes 62	306	4.9	36	1
Joseph Addai. 76	294	3.9	14	2
Peyton Manning 8	3	0.4	7	1
Dallas Clark. 1	1	1.0	1	0

Most Touchdowns	TD	Run	Rec	Ret	Pts
Reggie Wayne 2	0	2	0	12
Joseph Addai 2	2	0	0	12

Five tied with 1 TD each for 6 pts.
2-Pt. Conversions: (1-1) Harrison.

Kicking	PAT/Att	FG/Att	Lg	Pts
Adam Vinatieri 7/7	14/15	51	49

Punts (5 or more)	No	Yds	Avg	Long	In20
Hunter Smith 14	629	44.9	58	4

Interceptions		Most Sacks	
Bob Sanders 2		Anthony McFarland . . .2.0
Antoine Bethea 2		Dwight Freeney 2.0
Three tied with 1 each.		Robert Mathis 1.5

Chicago Bears (2-1)

Passing (5 att)	Att	Cmp	Pct.	Yds	TD	Ratin
Rex Grossman 92	52	56.5	591	3	73.

Interceptions: Grossman 3.

Top Receivers	No	Yds	Avg	Long	T
Bernard Berrian 14	228	16.3	68-td
Desmond Clark 8	107	13.4	30
Muhsin Muhammad 7	93	13.3	22
Thomas Jones 6	24	4.0	14
Jason McKie 6	16	2.7	4

Top Rushers	Car	Yds	Avg	Long	T
Thomas Jones 55	301	5.5	52
Cedric Benson 38	104	2.7	12-td
Rashied Davis 2	25	12.5	16
Rex Grossman 4	-3	-0.8	0

Most Touchdowns	TD	Run	Rec	Ret	Pt
Thomas Jones 4	4	0	0	2
Bernard Berrian 2	0	2	0

Three tied with 1 TD each for 6 pts.
2-Pt. Conversions: (0-0).

Kicking	PAT/Att	FG/Att	Lg	Pt
Robbie Gould 9/9	6/6	49	2

Punts (5 or more)	No	Yds	Avg	Long	In2
Brad Maynard 18	800	44.4	66

Interceptions		Most Sacks	
Chris Harris 1		Adewale Ogunleye . . .2.
Ricky Manning 1		Tank Johnson . . . . . . .1.
Nathan Vasher 1		Mark Anderson . . . . . .1.

NFL Playoff Leaders

Passing Efficiency
(Minimum of 25 attempts)

	Gm	Att	Cmp	Cmp%	Yards	Avg Gain	TD	TD%	Int	Int%	Ratin
Tony Romo, Dal 1	29	17	58.6	189	6.52	1	3.4	0	0.0	89.
Drew Brees, NO 2	81	47	58.0	597	7.37	3	3.7	1	1.2	88.
Eli Manning, NYG 1	27	16	59.3	161	5.96	2	7.4	1	3.7	85.
Jeff Garcia, Phi 2	61	32	52.5	393	6.44	2	3.3	0	0.0	83.
Chad Pennington, NYJ 1	40	23	57.5	300	7.50	1	2.5	1	2.5	79.

Receptions

	No	Yds	Avg	Long	TD
Joseph Addai, Ind 22	118	5.4	16	0
Dallas Clark, Ind 21	317	15.1	52	0
Jabar Gaffney, NE 21	244	11.6	31	2
Reggie Wayne, Ind. 17	216	12.7	53-td	2
Reche Caldwell, NE 16	176	11.0	49	1

Kicking

	PAT	FG	Long	Pt
Adam Vinatieri, Ind 7/7	14/15	51	4
Stephen Gostkowski, NE . . .9/9	8/8	50	3
Robbie Gould, Chi 9/9	6/6	49	2
David Akers, Phi 5/5	4/4	48	1
Josh Brown, Sea 4/4	3/3	40	1

Rushing

	No	Yds	Avg	Long	TD
Dominic Rhodes, Ind 62	306	4.9	36	1
Thomas Jones, Chi 55	301	5.5	52	4
Joseph Addai, Ind 76	294	3.9	14	2
Brian Westbrook, Phi 33	257	7.8	62-td	3
Shaun Alexander, Sea 50	177	3.5	20	2

Interceptions

	No	Yds	Long	T
Asante Samuel, NE 2	75	39-td
Bob Sanders, Ind 2	55	38
Ty Law, KC 2	43	43
Antoine Bethea, Ind 2	16	16
Ed Reed, Bal 2	0	0

Touchdowns

	TD	Rush	Rec	Ret	Pts
Thomas Jones, Chi 4	4	0	0	24
Brian Westbrook, Phi 3	3	0	0	18

Thirteen tied with 2 TD each for 12 pts.

Sacks

Seven tied with 2.0 each.

NFL Pro Bowl

7th NFL Pro Bowl Game and 37th AFC-NFC contest (AFC leads,19-18). **Date:** Feb. 10, 2007 at Aloha Stadium in Honolulu. **Coaches:** Sean Payton, NO (NFC) and Bill Belichick, NE (AFC). **Most Valuable Player:** QB Carson Palmer, Cin. (8-17 for 190 yards and 2 TD). **Attendance:** 50,410. **TV Rating:** 5.1/10 (CBS). **Time:** 3:30.

NFC	0	14	0	14— **28**
AFC	0	14	7	10— **31**

2nd Quarter: NFC—Tiki Barber 1-yd run (Robbie Gould kick), 12:24; **AFC**—Reggie Wayne 72-yd pass from Carson Palmer (Nate Kaeding kick), 11:19; **AFC**—Adalius Thomas 0-yd fumble return (Kaeding kick), 7:42; **NFC**—Frank Gore 1-yd run (Gould kick), 4:09.

3rd Quarter: AFC—LaDainian Tomlinson 3-yd run (Kaeding kick), 9:36.

4th Quarter: AFC—Chad Johnson 42-yd pass from Palmer (Kaeding kick), 12:47; **NFC**—Steven Jackson 4-yd run (pass failed), 2:54; **NFC**—Anquan Boldin 47-yd pass from Tony Romo (Steve Smith pass from Romo), 1:48; **AFC**—Kaeding 21-yd FG, 0:00.

Individual Statistics

NFC

Passing	Att	Cmp	Pct.	Yds	TD	Int	Rate
Tony Romo	19	11	57.9	156	1	1	80.2
Marc Bulger	15	8	53.3	133	0	0	83.5
Drew Brees	7	2	28.6	23	0	0	40.8
Tiki Barber	1	0	0.0	0	0	1	0.0

Receiving Leaders	No	Yds	Avg	Long	TD
Anquan Boldin	5	86	17.2	47-td	1
Steve Smith	4	62	15.5	38	0
Roy Williams	3	58	19.3	26	0
Donald Driver	3	38	12.7	15	0
Alge Crumpler	2	50	25.0	35	0
Steven Jackson	2	10	5.0	9	0

Rushing Leaders	Car	Yds	Avg	Long	TD
Steven Jackson	7	26	3.7	11	1
Frank Gore	6	26	4.3	10	1
Tony Romo	2	7	3.5	7	0

Interceptions	No	Yds	Avg	Long	TD
Antonio Pierce	1	3	3.0	3	0

Sacks		Most Tackles	
Julius Peppers	1.0	DeAngelo Hall	7

AFC

Passing	Att	Cmp	Pct.	Yds	TD	Int	Rate
Carson Palmer	17	8	47.1	190	2	0	127.1
Peyton Manning	12	5	41.7	67	0	0	60.1
Vince Young	10	4	40.0	71	0	1	25.4

Receiving Leaders	No	Yds	Avg	Long	TD
Reggie Wayne	6	137	22.8	72-td	1
Andre Johnson	3	73	24.3	47	0
Chad Johnson	3	70	23.3	42-td	1
Tony Gonzalez	3	35	11.7	21	0
Antonio Gates	1	9	9.0	9	0
Larry Johnson	1	4	4.0	4	0

Rushing Leaders	Car	Yds	Avg	Long	TD
LaDainian Tomlinson	10	51	5.1	18	1
Larry Johnson	6	33	5.5	11	0
Willie Parker	8	19	2.4	7	0
Vince Young	3	15	5.0	13	0

Interceptions	No	Yds	Avg	Long	TD
Ed Reed	2	46	23.0	24	0

Sacks	Most Tackles	
Four tied with 1.0 each.	Aaron Schobel	6

2006 All-NFL Team

The 2006 All-NFL team combining the All-Pro selections of the Associated Press, The Sporting News (TSN) and the Pro Football Writers of America/Pro Football Weekly (PFWA). Holdovers from the 2005 All-NFL Team in **bold** type.

Offense

Pos		Selectors
WR—	Marvin Harrison, Indianapolis	AP, TSN, PFWA
WR—	**Chad Johnson**, Cincinnati	AP, TSN, PFWA
TE—	**Antonio Gates**, San Diego	AP, TSN, PFWA
T—	Jammal Brown, New Orleans	AP, PFWA
T—	**Willie Anderson**, Cincinnati	AP
T—	**Walter Jones**, Seattle	TSN, PFWA
T—	Jonathan Ogden, Baltimore	TSN
G—	Shawn Andrews, Philadelphia	AP, TSN
G—	**Alan Faneca**, Pittsburgh	AP, PFWA
G—	**Steve Hutchinson**, Minnesota	TSN, PFWA
C—	**Olin Kreutz**, Chicago	AP, TSN, PFWA
QB—	Drew Brees, New Orleans	AP, TSN, PFWA
RB—	**LaDainian Tomlinson**, SD	AP, TSN, PFWA
RB—	Larry Johnson, Kansas City	AP, TSN, PFWA
FB—	Lorenzo Neal, San Diego	AP

Defense

Pos		Selectors
DE—	Jason Taylor, Miami	AP, TSN, PFWA
DE—	Julius Peppers, Carolina	AP, TSN, PFWA
DT—	**Jamal Williams**, San Diego	AP, TSN, PFWA
DT—	Kevin Williams, Minnesota	AP, TSN, PFWA
LB—	**Shawne Merriman**, SD	AP, TSN, PFWA
LB—	Adalius Thomas, Baltimore	AP, PFWA
LB—	**Brian Urlacher**, Chicago	AP, TSN, PFWA
LB—	Zach Thomas, Miami	AP
LB—	**Lance Briggs**, Chicago	TSN
CB—	Rashean Mathis, Jacksonville	AP, TSN, PFWA
CB—	**Champ Bailey**, Denver	AP, TSN, PFWA
S—	Brian Dawkins, Philadelphia	AP
S—	Ed Reed, Baltimore	AP, TSN, PFWA
S—	Adrian Wilson, Arizona	TSN, PFWA

Specialists

Pos		Selectors
K—	Robbie Gould, Chicago	AP, TSN, PFWA
P—	**Brian Moorman**, Buffalo	AP, TSN, PFWA
ST—	Brendon Ayanbadejo, Chicago	PFWA

Pos		Selectors
KR—	Devin Hester, Chicago	AP
KR—	Justin Miller, NY Jets	TSN, PFWA
PR—	Devin Hester, Chicago	TSN, PFWA

Annual Awards

The NFL does not sanction any of the major postseason awards for players and coaches, but many are given out. Among the presenters for the 2006 regular season were AP, The Maxwell Football Club of Philadelphia (Bert Bell Award for player; Greasy Neale Award for coach), *The Sporting News* and the Pro Football Writers of America/*Pro Football Weekly*.

Most Valuable Player

LaDainian Tomlinson, San Diego, RB . AP, *TSN*, Bell, PFWA

Offensive Player of the Year

LaDainian Tomlinson, San Diego, RB . . . . .AP, PFWA

Defensive Player of the Year

Jason Taylor, Miami, DE . . . . .AP, PFWA

Comeback Player of the Year

Chad Pennington, NY Jets, QB . . . . .AP, PFWA

Rookies of the Year

NFL	Vince Young, Tennessee, QB	. . . .*TSN*
Offense	Vince Young, Tennessee, QB	. . . . . .AP, PFWA
Defense	DeMeco Ryans, Houston, LB	. . . . . . .AP, PFWA

Coach of the Year

Sean Payton, New Orleans . . . . . .AP, *TSN*, PFWA, Neale

2007 College Draft

First and second round selections at the 72nd annual NFL College Draft held April 28-29, 2007, at Radio City Music Hall in New York City. Twenty-two underclassmen were among the first 64 players chosen and are listed in capital LETTERS.

First Round

No	Team	Pos
1	Oakland . . . . .JAMARCUS RUSSELL, LSU	QB
2	Detroit . . . .CALVIN JOHNSON, Georgia Tech	WR
3	Cleveland . . . . .Joe Thomas, Wisconsin	T
4	Tampa Bay . . . . .Gaines Adams, Clemson	DE
5	Arizona . . . . .Levi Brown, Penn St.	T
6	Washington . . . . .LaRon Landry, LSU	DB
7	Minnesota . . .ADRIAN PETERSON, Oklahoma	RB
8	a-Atlanta . . . JAMAAL ANDERSON, Arkansas	DE
9	Miami . . . . .TED GINN, Ohio St.	WR
10	b-Houston . . . . .Amobi Okoye, Louisville	DT
11	San Francisco . . . . . .Patrick Willis, Mississippi	LB
12	Buffalo . . . . .MARSHAWN LYNCH, California	RB
13	St. Louis . . . . .Adam Carriker, Nebraska	DE
14	c-NY Jets . . . . .DARRELLE REVIS, Pittsburgh	DB
15	Pittsburgh . .LAWRENCE TIMMONS, Florida St.	LB
16	Green Bay . . . . .Justin Harrell, Tennessee	DT
17	d-Denver . . . . .JARVIS MOSS, Florida	DE
18	Cincinnati . . . . .Leon Hall, Michigan	DB
19	Tennessee . . . . .Michael Griffin, Texas	DB
20	NY Giants . . . . .Aaron Ross, Texas	DB
21	e-Jacksonville . . . .REGGIE NELSON, Florida	DB
22	f-Cleveland . . . . . .Brady Quinn, Notre Dame	QB
23	Kansas City . . . . .Dwayne Bowe, LSU	WR
24	g-New England . Brandon Meriweather, Miami-FL	DB
25	h-Carolina . . . . . .JON BEASON, Miami-FL	LB
26	i-Dallas . . . . .Anthony Spencer, Purdue	LB
27	New Orleans . .ROBERT MEACHEM, Tennessee	WR
28	j-San Francisco . . . .Joe Staley, Central Mich.	T
29	Baltimore . . . . .Ben Grubbs, Auburn	G
30	San Diego . . . . .Craig Davis, LSU	WR
31	Chicago . . . . .GREG OLSEN, Miami-FL	TE
32	Indianapolis . .ANTHONY GONZALEZ, Ohio St.	WR

Second Round

No	Team	Pos
33	k-Arizona . . . . . . .ALAN BRANCH, Michigan	DT
34	l-Buffalo . . . . .Paul Posluszny, Penn St.	LB
35	Tampa Bay . . . . .Arron Sears, Tennessee	G
36	m-Philadelphia . . . . .Kevin Kolb, Houston	QB
37	n-San Diego . . . . .Eric Weddle, Utah	DB
38	o-Oakland . . . . .ZACH MILLER, Arizona St.	TE
39	p-Atlanta . . . . .Justin Blalock, Texas	G
40	Miami . . . . . . .John Beck, Brigham Young	QB
41	q-Atlanta . . . .CHRIS HOUSTON, Arkansas	DB
42	r-Indianapolis . . . . .Tony Ugoh, Arkansas	T
43	s-Detroit . . . . .Drew Stanton, Michigan St.	QB
44	t-Minnesota . .SIDNEY RICE, South Carolina	WR
45	Carolina . . . . . . .DWAYNE JARRETT, USC	WR
46	Pittsburgh . . .LaMarr Woodley, Michigan	LB
47	u-NY Jets . . . . .David Harris, Michigan	LB
48	Jacksonville . . . . . . .Justin Durant, Hampton	LB
49	Cincinnati . . . . .Kenny Irons, Auburn	RB
50	Tennessee . . . .CHRIS HENRY, Arizona	RB
51	NY Giants . . . . .Steve Smith, USC	WR
52	St. Louis . . . . .Brian Leonard, Rutgers	RB
53	v-Cleveland . . . . .ERIC WRIGHT, UNLV	DB
54	Kansas City . . . . . . .Turk McBride, Tennessee	DE
55	Seattle . . . . .Josh Wilson, Maryland	DB
56	Denver . . . . .Tim Crowder, Texas	DE
57	Philadelphia . . . .Victor Abiamiri, Notre Dame	DE
58	w-Detroit . . . . .Ikaika Alama-Francis, Hawaii	DE
59	x-Carolina . . . . .Ryan Kalil, USC	C
60	y-Miami . . . . .Samson Satele, Hawaii	C
61	z-Detroit . . . . .Gerald Alexander, Boise St.	DB
62	aa-Chicago . . . . . . .Dan Bazuin, Central Mich.	DE
63	bb-Green Bay . .BRANDON JACKSON, Neb.	RB
64	cc-Tampa Bay . . . .Sabby Piscitelli, Oregon St.	DB

a-from Hou.; **b**-from Atl.; **c**-from Car.; **d**-from Jax.; **e**-from Den.; **f**-from Dal.; **g**-from Sea.; **h**-from NYJ; **i**-from Phi.; **j**-from NE; **k**-from Oak.; **l**-from Det.; **m**-from Cle. via Dal.; **n**-from Wash. via NYJ and Chi.; **o**-from Ari.; **p**-from Hou.; **q**-from Min.; **r**-from SF; **s**-from Buf.; **t**-from Atl.; **u**-from GB; **v**-from Dal.; **w**-from NO; **x**-from NYJ; **y**-from NE; **z**-from Bal.; **aa**-from SD; **bb**-from Chi. via NYJ; **cc**-from Ind.

2007 Draft By The Numbers

Through all seven rounds of the 2007 draft (255 players total).

By Position — Top 5		By School — Top 5		By Conference — Top 5	
1 Defensive Back 50		1 Florida 9		1 SEC 41	
2 Linebacker 35		2 Ohio St. 8		2 Big Ten 32	
3 Wide Receiver 34		3 Michigan 7		3 ACC 31	
4 Running Back 24		Notre Dame 7		4 Big 12 28	
5 Defensive End 22		Texas 7		Pacific-10 28	

Arena Football
Final 2007 Standings

Division champions (*) and playoff qualifiers (†) are noted; top six teams from each conference advance to the playoffs.

American Conference
Central Division

	W	L	T	Pct.	PF	PA
*Chicago	12	4	0	.750	869	719
†Kansas City	10	6	0	.625	840	776
†Colorado	8	8	0	.500	793	858
Nashville	7	9	0	.438	851	876
Grand Rapids	4	12	0	.250	835	1014

Western Division

	W	L	T	Pct.	PF	PA
*San Jose	13	3	0	.813	1012	761
†Los Angeles	9	7	0	.563	843	848
†Utah	8	8	0	.500	955	933
Arizona	4	12	0	.250	846	915
Las Vegas	2	14	0	.125	701	986

National Conference
Eastern Division

	W	L	T	Pct.	PF	PA
*Dallas	15	1	0	.938	1016	806
†Philadelphia	8	8	0	.500	900	835
†Columbus	7	9	0	.438	802	793
New York	5	11	0	.313	787	967

Southern Division

	W	L	T	Pct.	PF	PA
*Georgia	14	2	0	.875	1007	836
†Tampa Bay	9	7	0	.563	809	825
†Orlando	8	8	0	.500	814	766
New Orleans	5	11	0	.313	833	928
Austin	4	12	0	.250	879	950

Playoffs

Wild Card Round

American: Colorado 49 . . . . .at Kansas City 42
        at Los Angeles 64 . . . . .Utah 42
National: at Philadelphia 41 . . . . .Orlando 26
        Columbus 56 . . . . .at Tampa Bay 55

Division Round

American: at San Jose 76 . . . . .Colorado 67
        at Chicago 52 . . . . .Los Angeles 20
National: Columbus 66 . . . . .at Dallas 59
        at Georgia 65 . . . . .Philadelphia 39

Conference Championships

American: at San Jose 61 . . . . .Chicago 49
National: Columbus 66 . . . . .at Georgia 56

2007 All-Arena First Team

	Offense		Defense
QB	Chris Greisen, Geo	DL	Greg White, Orl
FB	Dan Alexander, Nash	DL	C. Weatherington, Dal
WR	Chris Jackson, Geo	DL	LaKendrick Jones, Clb
WR	Bobby Sippio, Chi	LB	Duke Pettijohn, Dal
WR	Siaha Burley, Utah	LB	DeJuan Alfonzo, Chi
OL	Phil Bogle, Phi	DB	Eddie Moten, Phi
OL	Devin Wyman, Dal	DB	Ahmad Hawkins, Nash
C	Kyle Moore-Brown, Col	DB	Clevan Thomas, SJ
K	Mark Lewis, Aus		

Annual Awards

Ironman of the Year . . . . .Will Pettis, Dallas, WR/DB
Offensive Player of the Year . . . . .Siaha Burley, Utah, WR
Defensive Player of the Year . . . .Greg White, Orlando, DL
Lineman of the Year . . . . .Greg White, Orlando, DL
Rookies of the Year . . .Charles Frederick, Kansas City, WR
                    & Brett Dietz, Tampa Bay, QB
Coach of the Year . . . . .Doug Plank, Georgia
Al Lucas Hero Award . . . . . . .John Dutton, Colorado, QB

ArenaBowl XXI

July 29, 2007 at New Orleans Arena, New Orleans, LA (Att: 17,056).
Offensive MVP: Mark Grieb, San Jose, QB; Defensive MVP: Omarr Smith, San Jose, DB

	1	2	3	4—	F
Columbus Destroyers (10-9)	7	7	13	6—	33
San Jose SaberCats (15-3)	14	14	7	21—	55

1st Quarter: SJ—Brian Johnson 4-yd run (A.J. Haglund kick), 11:47. **CLB**—Harold Wells 1-yd run (Peter Martinez kick), 6:55. **SJ**—James Roe 7-yd pass from Mark Grieb (Haglund kick), 3:50.

2nd Quarter: CLB—Jason Hilliard 1-yd pass from Matt Nagy (Martinez kick), 10:44. **SJ**—Trestin George 56-yd kickoff return (kick failed), 9:50. **SJ**—George Williams 1-yd pass from Grieb (Haglund kick), 3:17.

3rd Quarter: CLB—Cole Magner 3-yd pass from Nagy (Martinez kick), 8:44. **SJ**—Ben Nelson 4-yd pass from Grieb (Haglund kick), 3:44. **CLB**—Damien Groce 39-yd pass from Nagy (kick failed), 0:05.

4th Quarter: SJ—Phil Glover 1-yd run (Haglund kick), 11:07. **SJ**—Roe 20-yd pass from Grieb (Haglund kick), 6:51. **CLB**—David Saunders 8-yd pass from Nagy (pass failed), 1:29. **SJ**—Johnson 4-yd run (Haglund kick), 0:38.

Offensive Statistics

Passing: CLB—Matt Nagy 24-43, 201 yds, 4 TD, 2 Int. **SJ**—Mark Grieb 24-29, 218 yds, 4 TD, 0 Int.

Rushing: CLB—Damien Groce 4-7; Harold Wells 4-4, 1 TD; Matt Nagy 1-0. **SJ**—Brian Johnson 7-12, 2 TD's; Phil Glover 2-1, 1 TD.

Receiving: CLB—Damien Groce 10-99, 1 TD; Cole Magner 7-68, 1 TD; David Saunders 3-21, 1 TD; Josh Bush 2-7; Harold Wells 1-5; Jason Hilliard 1-1, 1 TD. **SJ**—Rodney Wright 10-94; James Roe 8-76, 2 TD's; Ben Nelson 5-47 1 TD; George Williams 1-1, 1 TD.

Arena Football (Cont.)
Regular Season Individual Leaders
Passing Yards

	Att	Cmp	Cmp Pct	Yds	Yds/ Att	TD	TD Pct	Int	Int Pct	Rating
Chris Greisen, Geo	530	392	74.0	4851	9.15	117	22.1	12	2.3	132.0
Clint Dolezel, Dal	533	375	70.4	4475	8.40	107	20.1	9	1.7	128.2
Mark Grieb, SJ	561	398	70.9	4605	8.21	100	17.8	13	2.3	125.
Joe Germaine, Utah	617	422	68.4	5005	8.11	107	17.3	12	1.9	124.4
Raymond Philyaw, KC	538	371	69.0	4338	8.06	85	15.8	11	2.0	124.1

Receptions

	No	Yards	Avg	TD
Siaha Burley, Utah	166	2129	12.8	49
Chris Jackson, Geo	145	1915	13.2	47
Derrick Lewis, Aus	139	1903	13.7	41
Troy Bergeron, Geo	132	1736	13.2	41
Damian Harrell, Col	132	1547	11.7	47

Rushing

	Car	Yards	Avg	TD
Dan Alexander, Nash	165	426	2.6	4
Adrian McPherson, GR	55	360	6.5	9
Josh White, Dal	93	278	3.0	10
Bo Kelly, Ari	81	222	2.7	13
Harold Wells, Clb	73	197	2.7	1

Touchdowns

	TD	Rus	Rec	Ret	Pts
Bobby Sippio, Chi	53	0	53	0	318
Chris Jackson, Geo	51	4	47	0	306
Siaha Burley, Utah	49	0	49	0	294
Damian Harrell, Col	47	0	47	0	282
Will Pettis, Dal	46	2	40	4	278

Kicking

	PAT	FG	Long	Pts
A.J. Haglund, SJ	128/138	10/18	39	158
Mark Lewis, Aus	110/118	15/25	33	155
Remy Hamilton, LA	101/114	16/30	36	149
Steve Videtich, Utah	113/127	10/19	32	143
Jason Bell, Col	90/105	17/28	38	141

Canadian Football League
Final 2006 Standings

Division champions (*) and playoff qualifiers (†) are noted. Wins are worth two points in the standings, ties are worth one point

East Division

	W	L	T	Pts	PF	PA
*Montreal	10	8	0	20	451	431
†Toronto	10	8	0	20	359	343
†Winnipeg	9	9	0	18	362	408
Hamilton	4	14	0	8	292	495

West Division

	W	L	T	Pts	PF	PA
*British Columbia	13	5	0	26	555	35
†Calgary	10	8	0	20	477	42
†Saskatchewan	9	9	0	18	465	43
Edmonton	7	11	0	14	399	46

Most Outstanding Awards

Player . . . . Geroy Simon, British Columbia, SB
Canadian . . . . Brent Johnson, British Columbia, DE
Lineman . . . . .Rob Murphy, British Columbia, OL
Defensive Player . . . .Brent Johnson, British Columbia, DE
Rookie . . . . .Aaron Hunt, British Columbia, DT
Special Teams . . . . .Sandro DeAngellis, Calgary, K
Coach (Annis Stukus award) . . . . . . .Wally Buono, B.C.
Tom Pate Award (Sportsmanship) . . . . .Mark Washington
British Columbia, DB

94th Grey Cup Championship
November 19, 2006
at Canad Inns Stadium in Winnipeg, Manitoba
(Att: 44,786)

British Columbia	9	10	0	6—	**25**
Montreal	0	3	9	2—	**14**

MVP: Dave Dickenson, British Columbia, QB
(18-29 for 184 yards, 6 rushes for 53 yards)

NFL Europa

Final 2007 Standings

	W	L	T	Pct.	PF	PA
*Hamburg	7	3	0	.700	231	176
*Frankfurt	7	3	0	.700	254	179
Cologne	6	4	0	.600	205	172
Rhein	4	6	0	.400	166	212
Amsterdam	4	6	0	.400	194	250
Berlin	2	8	0	.200	146	207

*The teams with the top two records after the regular season advance directly to the World Bowl.

World Bowl XV
June 23, 2007 at Commerzbank Arena,
Frankfurt, Germany (Att: 48,125)

Hamburg	13	10	7	7—	**37**
Frankfurt	0	14	14	0—	**28**

MVP: Casey Bramlet, Hamburg, QB
(20-27 for 347 yards and 4 TD)

Note: NFL Europa was discontinued following the 2007 season.

1920-2007
Through the Years

SPORTS ALMANAC

The Super Bowl

The first AFL-NFL World Championship Game, as it was originally called, was played seven months after the two leagues agreed to merge in June of 1966. It became the Super Bowl (complete with roman numerals) by the third game in 1969. The Super Bowl winner has been presented the Vince Lombardi Trophy since 1971. Lombardi, whose Green Bay teams won the first two title games, died in 1970. NFL champions (1966-69) and NFC champions (since 1970) are listed in CAPITAL letters.

Multiple winners: Dallas, Pittsburgh and San Francisco (5); Green Bay, New England, Oakland-LA Raiders and Washington (3); Baltimore-Indianapolis Colts, Denver, Miami and NY Giants (2).

Bowl	Date	Winner	Head Coach	Score	Loser	Head Coach	Site
I	1/15/67	GREEN BAY	Vince Lombardi	35-10	Kansas City	Hank Stram	Los Angeles
II	1/14/68	GREEN BAY	Vince Lombardi	33-14	Oakland	John Rauch	Miami
III	1/12/69	NY Jets	Weeb Ewbank	16- 7	BALT. COLTS	Don Shula	Miami
IV	1/11/70	Kansas City	Hank Stram	23- 7	MINNESOTA	Bud Grant	New Orleans
V	1/17/71	Balt. Colts	Don McCafferty	16-13	DALLAS	Tom Landry	Miami
VI	1/16/72	DALLAS	Tom Landry	24- 3	Miami	Don Shula	New Orleans
VII	1/14/73	Miami	Don Shula	14- 7	WASHINGTON	George Allen	Los Angeles
VIII	1/13/74	Miami	Don Shula	24- 7	MINNESOTA	Bud Grant	Houston
IX	1/12/75	Pittsburgh	Chuck Noll	16- 6	MINNESOTA	Bud Grant	New Orleans
X	1/18/76	Pittsburgh	Chuck Noll	21-17	DALLAS	Tom Landry	Miami
XI	1/ 9/77	Oakland	John Madden	32-14	MINNESOTA	Bud Grant	Pasadena
XII	1/15/78	DALLAS	Tom Landry	27-10	Denver	Red Miller	New Orleans
XIII	1/21/79	Pittsburgh	Chuck Noll	35-31	DALLAS	Tom Landry	Miami
XIV	1/20/80	Pittsburgh	Chuck Noll	31-19	LA RAMS	Ray Malavasi	Pasadena
XV	1/25/81	Oakland	Tom Flores	27-10	PHILADELPHIA	Dick Vermeil	New Orleans
XVI	1/24/82	SAN FRANCISCO	Bill Walsh	26-21	Cincinnati	Forrest Gregg	Pontiac, MI
XVII	1/30/83	WASHINGTON	Joe Gibbs	27-17	Miami	Don Shula	Pasadena
XVIII	1/22/84	LA Raiders	Tom Flores	38- 9	WASHINGTON	Joe Gibbs	Tampa
XIX	1/20/85	SAN FRANCISCO	Bill Walsh	38-16	Miami	Don Shula	Stanford
XX	1/26/86	CHICAGO	Mike Ditka	46-10	New England	Raymond Berry	New Orleans
XXI	1/25/87	NY GIANTS	Bill Parcells	39-20	Denver	Dan Reeves	Pasadena
XXII	1/31/88	WASHINGTON	Joe Gibbs	42-10	Denver	Dan Reeves	San Diego
XXIII	1/22/89	SAN FRANCISCO	Bill Walsh	20-16	Cincinnati	Sam Wyche	Miami
XXIV	1/28/90	SAN FRANCISCO	George Seifert	55-10	Denver	Dan Reeves	New Orleans
XXV	1/27/91	NY GIANTS	Bill Parcells	20-19	Buffalo	Marv Levy	Tampa
XXVI	1/26/92	WASHINGTON	Joe Gibbs	37-24	Buffalo	Marv Levy	Minneapolis
XXVII	1/31/93	DALLAS	Jimmy Johnson	52-17	Buffalo	Marv Levy	Pasadena
XXVIII	1/30/94	DALLAS	Jimmy Johnson	30-13	Buffalo	Marv Levy	Atlanta
XXIX	1/29/95	SAN FRANCISCO	George Seifert	49-26	San Diego	Bobby Ross	Miami
XXX	1/28/96	DALLAS	Barry Switzer	27-17	Pittsburgh	Bill Cowher	Tempe, AZ
XXXI	1/26/97	GREEN BAY	Mike Holmgren	35-21	New England	Bill Parcells	New Orleans
XXXII	1/25/98	Denver	Mike Shanahan	31-24	GREEN BAY	Mike Holmgren	San Diego
XXXIII	1/31/99	Denver	Mike Shanahan	34-19	ATLANTA	Dan Reeves	Miami
XXXIV	1/30/00	ST.L RAMS	Dick Vermeil	23-16	Tennessee	Jeff Fisher	Atlanta
XXXV	1/28/01	Balt. Ravens	Brian Billick	34- 7	NY GIANTS	Jim Fassel	Tampa
XXXVI	2/3/02	New England	Bill Belichick	20-17	ST.L RAMS	Mike Martz	New Orleans
XXXVII	1/26/03	TAMPA BAY	Jon Gruden	48-21	Oakland	Bill Callahan	San Diego
XXXVIII	2/1/04	New England	Bill Belichick	32-29	CAROLINA	John Fox	Houston
XXXIX	2/6/05	New England	Bill Belichick	24-21	PHILADELPHIA	Andy Reid	Jacksonville
XL	2/5/06	Pittsburgh	Bill Cowher	21-10	SEATTLE	Mike Holmgren	Detroit
XLI	2/4/07	Indianapolis	Tony Dungy	29-17	CHICAGO	Lovie Smith	Miami

Future Super Bowl Sites

Game	Date	Stadium	Location
Super Bowl XLII	February 3, 2008	University of Phoenix Stadium	Glendale, Arizona
Super Bowl XLIII	February 1, 2009	Raymond James Stadium	Tampa, Florida
Super Bowl XLIV	February 7, 2010	Dolphin Stadium	Miami, Florida
Super Bowl XLV	February 6, 2011	Dallas Cowboys new stadium	Arlington, Texas

Super Bowl Appearances

App		W	L	Pct	PF	PA	App		W	L	Pct	PF	PA
8	Dallas	.5	3	.625	221	132	3	LA/St.L Rams	.1	2	.333	59	67
6	Pittsburgh	.5	1	.833	141	110	2	Chicago	.1	1	.500	63	39
6	Denver	.2	4	.333	115	206	2	Kansas City	.1	1	.500	33	42
5	San Francisco	.5	0	1.000	188	89	2	Cincinnati	.0	2	.000	37	46
5	New England	.3	2	.600	107	148	2	Philadelphia	.0	2	.000	31	51
5	Oak./LA Raiders	.3	2	.600	132	114	1	Baltimore Ravens	.1	0	1.000	34	7
5	Washington	.3	2	.600	122	103	1	NY Jets	.1	0	1.000	16	7
5	Miami	.2	3	.400	74	103	1	Tampa Bay	.1	0	1.000	48	21
4	Green Bay	.3	1	.750	127	76	1	Atlanta	.0	1	.000	19	34
4	Buffalo	.0	4	.000	73	139	1	Carolina	.0	1	.000	29	32
4	Minnesota	.0	4	.000	34	95	1	San Diego	.0	1	.000	26	49
3	NY Giants	.2	1	.667	66	73	1	Seattle	.0	1	.000	10	21
3	Bal./Ind. Colts	.2	1	.667	52	46	1	Tennessee	.0	1	.000	16	23

Pete Rozelle Award (MVP)

The Most Valuable Player in the Super Bowl. Currently selected by a panel made up of national pro football writers and broadcasters chosen by the NFL (80 percent) and fans voting via the internet and text message (20 percent). Presented by *Spor* magazine from 1967-89 and by the NFL since 1990. Named after former NFL commissioner Pete Rozelle in 1990. Winner who did not play for Super Bowl champion is in **bold** type.

Multiple winners: Joe Montana (3); Terry Bradshaw, Tom Brady and Bart Starr (2).

Bowl		Bowl		Bowl	
I	Bart Starr, Green Bay, QB	XIV	Terry Bradshaw, Pittsburgh, QB	XXVIII	Emmitt Smith, Dallas, RB
II	Bart Starr, Green Bay, QB	XV	Jim Plunkett, Oakland, QB	XXIX	Steve Young, San Fran., QB
III	Joe Namath, NY Jets, QB	XVI	Joe Montana, San Francisco, QB	XXX	Larry Brown, Dallas, CB
IV	Len Dawson, Kansas City, QB	XVII	John Riggins, Washington, RB	XXXI	Desmond Howard, Gr. Bay, KR
V	Chuck Howley, Dallas, LB	XVIII	Marcus Allen, LA Raiders, RB	XXXII	Terrell Davis, Denver, RB
VI	Roger Staubach, Dallas, QB	XIX	Joe Montana, San Francisco, QB	XXXIII	John Elway, Denver, QB
VII	Jake Scott, Miami, S	XX	Richard Dent, Chicago, DE	XXXIV	Kurt Warner, St. Louis, QB
VIII	Larry Csonka, Miami, RB	XXI	Phil Simms, NY Giants, QB	XXXV	Ray Lewis, Baltimore, LB
IX	Franco Harris, Pittsburgh, RB	XXII	Doug Williams, Washington, QB	XXXVI	Tom Brady, New England, QB
X	Lynn Swann, Pittsburgh, WR	XXIII	Jerry Rice, San Francisco, WR	XXXVII	Dexter Jackson, Tampa Bay, S
XI	Fred Biletnikoff, Oakland, WR	XXIV	Joe Montana, San Francisco, QB	XXXVIII	Tom Brady, New England, QB
XII	Harvey Martin, Dallas, DE	XXV	Ottis Anderson, NY Giants, RB	XXXIX	Deion Branch, New England, WR
	& Randy White, Dallas, DT	XXVI	Mark Rypien, Washington, QB	XL	Hines Ward, Pittsburgh, WR
XIII	Terry Bradshaw, Pittsburgh, QB	XXVII	Troy Aikman, Dallas, QB	XLI	Peyton Manning, Ind., QB

Super Bowl MVP By Position

Position	No.	Position	No.	Position	No.
Quarterback	.21	Defensive End	.2	Cornerback	.1
Running Back	.7	Linebacker	.2	Defensive Tackle	.1
Wide Receiver	.5	Safety	.2	Kick Returner	.1

Five Super Bowl Wins
Dallas Cowboys

Year	Bowl	Head Coach	Quarterback	MVP	Opponent	Score	Site
1972	VI	Tom Landry	Roger Staubach	Staubach	Miami	24-3	New Orleans
1978	XII	Tom Landry	Roger Staubach	Martin/White	Denver	27-10	New Orleans
1993	XXVII	Jimmy Johnson	Troy Aikman	Aikman	Buffalo	52-17	Pasadena
1994	XXVIII	Jimmy Johnson	Troy Aikman	Emmitt Smith	Buffalo	30-13	Atlanta
1996	XXX	Barry Switzer	Troy Aikman	Larry Brown	Pittsburgh	27-17	Tempe

Pittsburgh Steelers

Year	Bowl	Head Coach	Quarterback	MVP	Opponent	Score	Site
1975	IX	Chuck Noll	Terry Bradshaw	Franco Harris	Minnesota	16-6	New Orleans
1976	X	Chuck Noll	Terry Bradshaw	Lynn Swann	Dallas	21-17	Miami
1979	XIII	Chuck Noll	Terry Bradshaw	Bradshaw	Dallas	35-31	Miami
1980	XIV	Chuck Noll	Terry Bradshaw	Bradshaw	LA Rams	31-19	Pasadena
2006	XL	Bill Cowher	Ben Roethlisberger	Hines Ward	Seattle	21-10	Detroit

San Francisco 49ers

Year	Bowl	Head Coach	Quarterback	MVP	Opponent	Score	Site
1982	XVI	Bill Walsh	Joe Montana	Montana	Cincinnati	26-21	Pontiac
1985	XIX	Bill Walsh	Joe Montana	Montana	Miami	38-16	Stanford
1989	XXIII	Bill Walsh	Joe Montana	Jerry Rice	Cincinnati	20-16	Miami
1990	XXIV	George Seifert	Joe Montana	Montana	Denver	55-10	New Orleans
1995	XXIX	George Seifert	Steve Young	Young	San Diego	49-26	Miami

All-Time Super Bowl Leaders

Through 2007; participants in Super Bowl XLI in **bold** type.

CAREER
Passing Efficiency

	(Minimum 25 passing attempts)	Gm	Att	Cmp	Cmp%	Yards	Avg Gain	TD	TD%	Int	Int%	Rating
1	Phil Simms, NYG	1	25	22	88.0	268	10.72	3	12.0	0	0.0	150.9
2	Steve Young, SF	2	39	26	66.7	345	8.85	6	15.4	0	0.0	134.1
3	Doug Williams, Wash.	1	29	18	62.1	340	11.72	4	13.8	1	3.4	128.1
4	Joe Montana, SF	4	122	83	68.0	1142	9.36	11	9.0	0	0.0	127.8
5	Jim Plunkett, Raiders	2	46	29	63.0	433	9.41	4	8.7	0	0.0	122.8
6	Jake Delhomme, Car.	1	33	16	48.5	323	9.79	3	9.1	0	0.0	113.6
7	Terry Bradshaw, Pit	4	84	49	58.3	932	11.10	9	10.7	4	4.8	112.8
8	Troy Aikman, Dal	3	80	56	70.0	689	8.61	5	6.3	1	1.3	111.9
9	Bart Starr, GB	2	47	29	61.7	452	9.62	3	6.4	1	2.1	106.0
10	Tom Brady, NE	3	108	71	65.7	735	6.81	6	5.6	1	0.9	99.9

Ratings based on performance standards established for completion percentage, average gain, touchdown percentage and interception percentage. Quarterbacks are allocated points according to how their statistics measure up to those standards.

Passing Yards

		Gm	Att	Cmp	Pct	Yds
1	Joe Montana, SF	4	122	83	68.0	1142
2	John Elway, Den	5	152	76	50.0	1128
3	Terry Bradshaw, Pit	4	84	49	58.3	932
4	Jim Kelly, Buf	4	145	81	55.9	829
5	Kurt Warner, St.L	2	89	52	58.4	779
6	Tom Brady, NE	3	108	71	65.7	735
7	Roger Staubach, Dal	4	98	61	62.2	734
8	Troy Aikman, Dal	3	80	56	70.0	689
9	Brett Favre, GB	2	69	39	56.5	502
10	Fran Tarkenton, Min	3	89	46	51.7	489

Receptions

		Gm	No	Yds	Avg	TD
1	Jerry Rice, SF-Oak	4	33	589	17.8	8
2	Andre Reed, Buf	4	27	323	12.0	0
3	Deion Branch, NE	2	21	276	13.1	1
4	Roger Craig, SF	3	20	212	10.6	2
	Thurman Thomas, Buf	4	20	144	7.2	0
6	Jay Novacek, Dal	3	17	148	8.7	2
7	Lynn Swann, Pit	4	16	364	22.8	3
	Michael Irvin, Dal	3	16	256	16.0	2
	Troy Brown, NE	3	16	182	11.4	0
10	Chuck Foreman, Min	3	15	139	9.3	0

Rushing

		Gm	Car	Yds	Avg	TD
1	Franco Harris, Pit	4	101	354	3.5	4
2	Larry Csonka, Mia	3	57	297	5.2	2
3	Emmitt Smith, Dal	3	70	289	4.1	5
4	Terrell Davis, Den	2	55	259	4.7	3
5	John Riggins, Wash	2	64	230	3.6	2
6	Timmy Smith, Wash	1	22	204	9.3	2
	Thurman Thomas, Buf	4	52	204	3.9	4
8	Roger Craig, SF	3	52	201	3.9	2
9	Marcus Allen, Raiders	1	20	191	9.5	2
10	Antowain Smith, NE	2	44	175	4.0	1

All-Purpose Yards

		Gm	Rush	Rec	Ret	Total
1	Jerry Rice, SF-Oak	4	15	589	0	604
2	Franco Harris, Pit	4	354	114	0	468
3	Roger Craig, SF	3	201	212	0	413
4	Lynn Swann, Pit	4	-7	364	34	391
5	Thurman Thomas, Buf	4	204	144	0	348

Interceptions

		Gm	No	Yds	TD
1	Larry Brown, Dal	3	3	77	0
	Chuck Howley, Dal	2	3	63	0
	Rod Martin, Raiders	2	3	44	0
4	Thirteen tied with 2 each.				

Scoring
Points

		Gm	TD	FG	PAT	Pts
1	Jerry Rice, SF-Oak	4	8	0	0	48
2	**Adam Vinatieri, NE-Ind**	5	0	7	13	34
3	Emmitt Smith, Dal	3	5	0	0	30
4	Roger Craig, SF	3	4	0	0	24
	Franco Harris, Pit	4	4	0	0	24
	Thurman Thomas, Buf	4	4	0	0	24
	John Elway, Den	5	4	0	0	24
8	Ray Wersching, SF	2	0	5	7	22
9	Don Chandler, GB	2	0	4	8	20
10	Six tied with 18 pts. each.					

Sacks

		Gm	No
1	Charles Haley, SF-Dal	5	4.5
2	Reggie White, GB	2	3.0
	Leonard Marshall, NYG	2	3.0
	Danny Stubbs, SF	2	3.0
	Mike Vrabel, NE	3	3.0
	Jeff Wright, Buf	4	3.0
	Tedy Bruschi, NE	4	3.0
	Willie McGinest, NE	4	3.0

Note: The NFL did not begin officially compiling sacks until 1982.

Touchdowns

		Gm	Rush	Rec	Ret	TD
1	Jerry Rice, SF-Oak	4	0	8	0	8
2	Emmitt Smith, Dal	3	5	0	0	5
3	Roger Craig, SF	3	2	2	0	4
	Franco Harris, Pit	4	4	0	0	4
	John Elway, Den	5	4	0	0	4
	Thurman Thomas, Buf	4	4	0	0	4
7	Six tied with 3 TD each.					

Punting

	(Minimum 10 Punts)	Gm	No	Yds	Avg.
1	Jerrel Wilson, KC	2	11	511	46.5
2	Tom Rouen, Den-Sea	3	11	482	43.8
3	Tom Tupa, NE-TB	2	12	516	43.0
	Kyle Richardson, Bal	1	10	430	43.0
5	Ray Guy, Raiders	3	14	587	41.9

All-Time Super Bowl Leaders (Cont.)

Punt Returns

(Minimum 4 Returns)	Gm	No	Yds	Avg.	TD
1 John Taylor, SF	3	6	94	15.7	0
2 Desmond Howard, GB	1	6	90	15.0	0
3 Dave Meggett, NYG-NE	2	6	67	11.2	0
4 Neal Colzie, Raiders	1	4	43	10.8	0
5 Dana McLemore, SF	1	5	51	10.2	0

Kickoff Returns

(Minimum 4 Returns)	Gm	No	Yds	Avg.	TD
1 Tim Dwight, Atl	1	5	210	42.0	1
2 Desmond Howard, GB	1	4	154	38.5	1
3 Fulton Walker, Mia	2	8	283	35.4	1
4 Andre Coleman, SD	1	8	242	30.3	1
5 Larry Anderson, Pit	2	8	207	25.9	0

SINGLE GAME
Passing

Yards Gained	Year	Att/Cmp	Yds
1 Kurt Warner, St.L vs Ten	2000	45/24	414
2 Kurt Warner, St.L vs NE	2002	44/28	365
3 Joe Montana, SF vs Cin	1989	36/23	357
Donovan McNabb, Phi vs NE	2005	51/30	357
5 Tom Brady, NE vs Car	2004	48/32	354

Touchdown Passes	Year	TD	Int
1 Steve Young, SF vs SD	1995	6	0
2 Joe Montana, SF vs Den	1990	5	0
3 Terry Bradshaw, Pit vs Dal	1979	4	1
Doug Williams, Wash vs Den	1988	4	1
Troy Aikman, Dal vs Buf	1993	4	0

Receiving

Catches	Year	No	Yds	TD
1 Dan Ross, Cin vs SF	1982	11	104	2
Jerry Rice, SF vs Cin	1989	11	215	1
Deion Branch, NE vs Phi	2005	11	133	0
4 Tony Nathan, Mia vs SF	1985	10	83	0
Jerry Rice, SF vs SD	1995	10	149	3
Andre Hastings, Pit vs Dal	1996	10	98	0
Deion Branch, NE vs Car	2004	10	143	1
Joseph Addai, Ind vs Chi	2007	10	66	0

Yards Gained	Year	No	Yds	TD
1 Jerry Rice, SF vs Cin	1989	11	215	1
2 Ricky Sanders, Wash vs Den	1988	9	193	2
3 Isaac Bruce, St.L vs Ten	2000	6	162	1
4 Lynn Swann, Pit vs Dal	1976	4	161	1
5 Andre Reed, Buf vs Dal	1993	8	152	0
Rod Smith, Den vs Atl	1999	5	152	1

Rushing

Yards Gained	Year	Car	Yds	TD
1 Timmy Smith, Wash vs Den	1988	22	204	2
2 Marcus Allen, Raiders vs Wash	1984	20	191	2
3 John Riggins, Wash vs Mia	1983	38	166	1
4 Franco Harris, Pit vs Min	1975	34	158	1
5 Terrell Davis, Den vs GB	1998	30	157	3

All-Purpose Yards

Yards Gained	Year	Run	Rec	Tot
1 Desmond Howard, GB vs NE	1997	0	0	244
2 Andre Coleman, SD vs SF	1995	0	0	242
3 Ricky Sanders, Wash vs Den	1988	193	-4	235
4 Antonio Freeman, GB vs Den	1998	0	126	230
5 Jerry Rice, SF vs Cin	1989	5	215	220

Return Yardage: Howard 244, Coleman 242, Sanders 46, Freeman 104.

Scoring

Points	Year	TD	FG	PAT	Pts
1 Roger Craig, SF vs Mia	1985	3	0	0	18
Jerry Rice, SF vs Den	1990	3	0	0	18
Jerry Rice, SF vs SD	1995	3	0	0	18
Ricky Watters, SF vs SD	1995	3	0	0	18
Terrell Davis, Den vs GB	1998	3	0	0	18

Touchdowns	Year	TD	Rush	Rec
1 Roger Craig, SF vs Mia	1985	3	1	2
Jerry Rice, SF vs Den	1990	3	0	3
Jerry Rice, SF vs SD	1995	3	0	3
Ricky Watters, SF vs SD	1995	3	1	2
Terrell Davis, Den vs GB	1998	3	3	0

Punt Returns

(Minimum 3 returns)	Year	No	Yds	Avg
1 John Taylor, SF vs Cin	1989	3	56	18.7
2 Desmond Howard, GB vs NE	1997	6	90	15.0
3 **Terrence Wilkins**, Ind vs Chi	2007	3	42	14.0
4 John Taylor, SF vs Den	1990	3	38	12.7
5 Kelvin Martin, Dal vs Buf	1993	3	35	11.7

Kickoff Returns

(Minimum 3 returns)	Year	No	Yds	Avg
1 Fulton Walker, Mia vs Wash	1983	4	190	47.5
2 Tim Dwight, Atl vs Den	1999	5	210	42.0
3 Desmond Howard, GB vs NE	1997	4	154	38.5
4 Larry Anderson, Pit vs Rams	1980	5	162	32.4
5 Rick Upchurch, Den vs Dal	1978	3	94	31.3

Punting

(Minimum 4 punts)	Year	No	Yds	Avg
1 Tom Rouen, Sea vs Pit	2006	6	301	50.2
2 Bryan Wagner, SD vs SF	1995	4	195	48.8
3 Chris Gardocki, Pit vs Sea	2006	6	292	48.7
4 Jerrel Wilson, KC vs Min	1970	4	194	48.5
5 Jim Miller, SF vs Cin	1982	4	185	46.3

Interceptions

	Year	No	Yds	TD
1 Rod Martin, Raiders vs Phi	1981	3	44	0

Eleven tied with 2 each.

*Kicker **Adam Vinatieri** played in his fifth Super Bowl in 2007, tying him with 12 other players for the second most in NFL history. Only one player has played in six Super Bowls — defensive lineman **Mike Lodish**, who lost four with the Bills (1991-94) before winning two with the Broncos (1998-99).*

Super Bowl Playoffs

The Super Bowl forced the NFL to set up pro football's first guaranteed multiple-game playoff format. Over the years, the NFL-AFL merger, the creation of two conferences comprised of four divisions each and the proliferation of wild card entries has seen the postseason field grow from four teams (1966), to six (1967-68), to eight (1969-77), to 10 (1978-81, 1983-89), to the present 12 (since1990). In 1968, there was a special playoff between Oakland and Kansas City which were both 12-2 and tied for first in the AFL's Western Division. In 1982, when a 57-day players' strike shortened the regular season to just nine games, playoff berths were extended to 16 teams (eight from each conference) and a 15-game tournament was played.

Note that in the following year-by-year summary, records of finalists include all games leading up to the Super Bowl; (*) indicates non-division winners or wild card teams.

1966 SEASON

AFL Playoffs

Championship . . . . .Kansas City 31, at Buffalo 7

NFL Playoffs

Championship . . . . .Green Bay 34, at Dallas 27

Super Bowl I
Jan. 15, 1967
Memorial Coliseum, Los Angeles
Favorite: Packers by 14—Attendance: 61,946

Kansas City (12-2-1) . . . . .0 10 0 0 —**10**
Green Bay (13-2) . . . . .7 7 14 7 —**35**
MVP: Green Bay QB Bart Starr (16 for 23, 250 yds, 2 TD)

1967 SEASON

AFL Playoffs

Championship . . . . .at Oakland 40, Houston 7

NFL Playoffs

Eastern Conference . . . . .at Dallas 52, Cleveland 14
Western Conference . . . . . . .at Green Bay 28, LA Rams 7
Championship . . . . .at Green Bay 21, Dallas 17

Super Bowl II
Jan. 14, 1968
Orange Bowl, Miami
Favorite: Packers by 13½—Attendance: 75,546

Green Bay (11-4-1) . . . . .3 13 10 7 —**33**
Oakland (14-1) . . . . .0 7 0 7 —**14**
MVP: Green Bay QB Bart Starr (13 for 24, 202 yds,1 TD)

1968 SEASON

AFL Playoffs

Western Div. Playoff . . . . . .at Oakland 41, Kansas City 6
AFL Championship . . . . .at NY Jets 27, Oakland 23

NFL Playoffs

Eastern Conference . . . . .at Cleveland 31, Dallas 20
Western Conference . . . . .at Baltimore 24, Minnesota 14
NFL Championship . . . . . . .Baltimore 34, at Cleveland 0

Super Bowl III
Jan. 12, 1969
Orange Bowl, Miami
Favorite: Colts by 18—Attendance: 75,389

NY Jets (12-3) . . . . .0 7 6 3 —**16**
Baltimore (15-1) . . . . .0 0 0 7 — **7**
MVP: NY Jets QB Joe Namath (17 for 28, 206 yds)

1969 SEASON

AFL Playoffs

Inter-Division . . . .*Kansas City 13, at NY Jets 6
at Oakland 56, *Houston 7
AFL Championship . . . . . . .Kansas City 17, at Oakland 7

NFL Playoffs

Eastern Conference . . . . .Cleveland 38, at Dallas 14
Western Conference . . . . . .at Minnesota 23, LA Rams 20
NFL Championship . . . . . .at Minnesota 27, Cleveland 7

Super Bowl IV
Jan. 11, 1970   Tulane Stadium, New Orleans
Favorite: Vikings by 12—Attendance: 80,562

Minnesota (14-2) . . . . .0 0 7 0 — **7**
Kansas City (13-3) . . . . .3 13 7 0 — **23**
MVP: KC QB Len Dawson (12 for 17, 142 yds, 1 TD, 1Int)

1970 SEASON

AFC Playoffs

First Round . . . . .at Baltimore 17, Cincinnati 0
at Oakland 21,*Miami 14
Championship . . . . .at Baltimore 27, Oakland 17

NFC Playoffs

First Round . . . . .at Dallas 5, *Detroit 0
San Francisco 17, at Minnesota 14
Championship . . . . .Dallas 17, at San Francisco 10

Super Bowl V
Jan. 17, 1971   Orange Bowl, Miami
Favorite: Cowboys by 2½—Attendance: 79,204

Baltimore (13-2-1) . . . . .0 6 0 10 — **16**
Dallas (12-4) . . . . .3 10 0 0 — **13**
MVP: Dallas LB Chuck Howley (2 interceptions for 22 yds)

1971 SEASON

AFC Playoffs

First Round . . . . .Miami 27, at Kansas City 24 (OT)
*Baltimore 20, at Cleveland 3
Championship . . . . .at Miami 21, Baltimore 0

NFC Playoffs

First Round . . . . .Dallas 20, at Minnesota 12
at San Francisco 24,*Washington 20
Championship . . . . .at Dallas 14, San Francisco 3

Super Bowl VI
Jan. 16, 1972   Tulane Stadium, New Orleans
Favorite: Cowboys by 6—Attendance: 81,023

Dallas (13-3) . . . . .3 7 7 7 — **24**
Miami (12-3-1) . . . . .0 3 0 0 — **3**
MVP: Dallas QB Roger Staubach (12 for 19, 119 yds, 2 TD)

1972 SEASON

AFC Playoffs

First Round . . . . .at Pittsburgh 13, Oakland 7
at Miami 20, *Cleveland 14
Championship . . . . .Miami 21, at Pittsburgh 17

NFC Playoffs

First Round . . . . *Dallas 30, at San Francisco 28
at Washington 16, Green Bay 3
Championship . . . . .at Washington 26, Dallas 3

Super Bowl VII

Jan. 14, 1973
Memorial Coliseum, Los Angeles
Favorite: Redskins by 1½—Attendance: 90,182

Miami (16-0)	.7	7	0	0 —	**14**
Washington (13-3)	.0	0	0	7 —	**7**

MVP: Miami safety Jake Scott (2 Interceptions for 63 yds)

1973 SEASON

AFC Playoffs

First Round . . . . .at Oakland 33, *Pittsburgh 14
at Miami 34, Cincinnati 16
Championship . . . . .at Miami 27, Oakland 10

NFC Playoffs

First Round . . . . .at Minnesota 27, *Washington 20
at Dallas 27, LA Rams 16
Championship . . . . .Minnesota 27, at Dallas 10

Super Bowl VIII

Jan. 13, 1974
Rice Stadium, Houston
Favorite: Dolphins by 6½—Attendance: 71,882

Minnesota (14-2)	.0	0	0	7 —	**7**
Miami (12-4)	.14	3	7	0 —	**24**

MVP: Miami FB Larry Csonka (33 carries, 145 yds, 2 TD)

1974 SEASON

AFC Playoffs

First Round . . . . .at Oakland 28, Miami 26
at Pittsburgh 32, *Buffalo 14
Championship . . . . .Pittsburgh 24, at Oakland 13

NFC Playoffs

First Round . . . . .at Minnesota 30, St. Louis 14
at LA Rams 19, *Washington 10
Championship . . . . .at Minnesota 14, LA Rams 10

Super Bowl IX

Jan. 12, 1975
Tulane Stadium, New Orleans
Favorite: Steelers by 3—Attendance: 80,997

Pittsburgh (12-3-1)	.0	2	7	7 —	**16**
Minnesota (12-4)	.0	0	0	6 —	**6**

MVP: Pittsburgh RB Franco Harris (34 carries, 158 yds, 1 TD)

1975 SEASON

AFC Playoffs

First Round . . . . .at Pittsburgh 28, Baltimore 10
at Oakland 31, *Cincinnati 28
Championship . . . . .at Pittsburgh 16, Oakland 10

NFC Playoffs

First Round . . . . .at LA Rams 35, St. Louis 23
*Dallas 17, at Minnesota 14
Championship . . . . .Dallas 37, at LA Rams 7

Super Bowl X

Jan. 18, 1976
Orange Bowl, Miami
Favorite: Steelers by 6½—Attendance: 80,187

Dallas (12-4)	.7	3	0	7 —	**17**
Pittsburgh (14-2)	.7	0	0	14 —	**21**

MVP: Pittsburgh WR Lynn Swann (4 catches, 161 yds, 1 TD)

1976 SEASON

AFC Playoffs

First Round . . . . .at Oakland 24, *New England 21
Pittsburgh 40, at Baltimore 14
Championship . . . . .at Oakland 24, Pittsburgh 7

NFC Playoffs

First Round . . . . .at Minnesota 35, *Washington 20
LA Rams 14, at Dallas 12
Championship . . . . .at Minnesota 24, LA Rams 13

Super Bowl XI

Jan. 9, 1977   Rose Bowl, Pasadena
Favorite: Raiders by 4½—Attendance: 103,438

Oakland (15-1)	.0	16	3	13 —	**32**
Minnesota (13-2-1)	.0	0	7	7 —	**14**

MVP: Oakland WR Fred Biletnikoff (4 catches, 79 yds)

1977 SEASON

AFC Playoffs

First Round . . . . .at Denver 34, Pittsburgh 21
*Oakland 37, at Baltimore 31 (OT)
Championship . . . . .at Denver 20, Oakland 17

NFC Playoffs

First Round . . . . .at Dallas 37, *Chicago 7
Minnesota 14, at LA Rams 7
Championship . . . . .at Dallas 23, Minnesota 6

Super Bowl XII

Jan. 15, 1978
Louisiana Superdome, New Orleans
Favorite: Cowboys by 6—Attendance: 75,583

Dallas (14-2)	.10	3	7	7 —	**27**
Denver (14-2)	.0	0	10	0 —	**10**

MVPs: Dallas DE Harvey Martin and DT Randy White (Cowboys' defense forced 8 turnovers)

Most Popular Playing Sites
Stadiums hosting more than one Super Bowl.

No		Years	No		Years
6	Superdome (N. Orleans)	1978, 81, 86, 90, 97, 2002	3	Tulane Stadium (N. Orleans)	1970, 72, 75
5	Orange Bowl (Miami)	1968-69, 71, 76, 79	3	Jack Murphy/Qualcomm Stadium (San Diego)	1988, 98, 2003
5	Rose Bowl (Pasadena)	1977, 80, 83, 87, 93	2	LA Memorial Coliseum	1967, 73
4	Joe Robbie/Pro Player/ Dolphin Stadium (Miami)	1989, 95, 99, 2007	2	Tampa Stadium	1984, 91
			2	Georgia Dome (Atlanta)	1994, 2000

1978 SEASON

AFC Playoffs

First Round ....*Houston 17, at *Miami 9
Second Round ....Houston 31, at New England 14
at Pittsburgh 33, Denver 10
Championship ....at Pittsburgh 34, Houston 5

NFC Playoffs

First Round ....at *Atlanta 14, *Philadelphia 13
Second Round ....at Dallas 27, Atlanta 20
at LA Rams 34, Minnesota 10
Championship ....Dallas 28, at LA Rams 0

Super Bowl XIII

Jan. 21, 1979   Orange Bowl, Miami
Favorite: Steelers by 4—Attendance: 79,484

Pittsburgh (16-2) 7   14   0 14 — **35**
Dallas (14-4) 7   7   3 14 — **31**
MVP: Pit. QB Terry Bradshaw (17 for 30, 318 yds, 4 TD)

1979 SEASON

AFC Playoffs

First Round ....at *Houston 13, *Denver 7
Second Round ....Houston 17, at San Diego 14
at Pittsburgh 34, Miami 14
Championship ....at Pittsburgh 27, Houston 13

NFC Playoffs

First Round ....at *Philadelphia 27, *Chicago 17
Second Round ....at Tampa Bay 24, Philadelphia 17
LA Rams 21, at Dallas 19
Championship ....LA Rams 9, at Tampa Bay 0

Super Bowl XIV

Jan. 20, 1980   Rose Bowl, Pasadena
Favorite: Steelers by 10½—Attendance: 103,985

LA Rams (11-7) 7   6   6 — **19**
Pittsburgh (14-4) 3   7   7 14 — **31**
MVP: Pit. QB Terry Bradshaw (14 for 21, 309 yds, 2 TD)

1980 SEASON

AFC Playoffs

First Round ....at *Oakland 27, *Houston 7
Second Round ....at San Diego 20, Buffalo 14
Oakland 14, at Cleveland 12
Championship ....Oakland 34, at San Diego 27

NFC Playoffs

First Round ....at *Dallas 34, *LA Rams 13
Second Round ....at Philadelphia 31, Minnesota 16
Dallas 30, at Atlanta 20
Championship ....at Philadelphia 20, Dallas 7

Super Bowl XV

Jan. 25, 1981   Louisiana Superdome, New Orleans
Favorite: Eagles by 3—Attendance: 76,135

Oakland (14-5) 14   0 10   3 — **27**
Philadelphia (14-4) 0   3   0   7 — **10**
MVP: Oakland QB Jim Plunkett (13 for 21, 261 yds, 3 TD)

1981 SEASON

AFC Playoffs

First Round ....*Buffalo 31, at *NY Jets 27
Second Round ....San Diego 41, at Miami 38 (OT)
at Cincinnati 28, Buffalo 21
Championship ....at Cincinnati 27, San Diego 7

NFC Playoffs

First Round ....*NY Giants 27, at *Philadelphia 21
Second Round ....at Dallas 38, Tampa Bay 0
at San Francisco 38, NY Giants 24
Championship ....at San Francisco 28, Dallas 27

Super Bowl XVI

Jan. 24, 1982
Pontiac Silverdome, Pontiac, Mich.
Favorite: Pick'em—Attendance: 81,270

San Francisco (15-3) ....7 13   0   6 — **26**
Cincinnati (14-4) 0   0   7 14 — **21**
MVP: San Francisco QB Joe Montana (14 for 22, 157 yds, 1 TD; 6 carries, 18 yds, 1 TD)

1982 SEASON

A 57-day players' strike shortened the regular season from 16 games to nine. The playoff format was changed to a 16-team tournament open to the top eight teams in each conference.

AFC Playoffs

First Round ....at LA Raiders 27, Cleveland 10
at Miami 28, New England 3
NY Jets 44, at Cincinnati 17
San Diego 31, at Pittsburgh 28
Second Round ....NY Jets 17, at LA Raiders 14
at Miami 34, San Diego 13
Championship ....at Miami 14, NY Jets 0

NFC Playoffs

First Round ....at Washington 31, Detroit 7
at Dallas 30, Tampa Bay 17
at Green Bay 41, St. Louis 16
at Minnesota 30, Atlanta 24
Second Round ....at Washington 21, Minnesota 7
at Dallas 37, Green Bay 26
Championship ....at Washington 31, Dallas 17

Super Bowl XVII

Jan. 30, 1983
Rose Bowl, Pasadena
Favorite: Dolphins by 3—Attendance: 103,667

Miami (10-2) ....7 10   0   0 — **17**
Washington (11-1) ....0 10   3 14 — **27**
MVP: Washington RB John Riggins (38 carries, 166 yds, 1 TD; 1 catch, 15 yds)

1983 SEASON

AFC Playoffs

First Round ....at *Seattle 31, *Denver 7
Second Round ....Seattle 27, at Miami 20
at LA Raiders 38, Pittsburgh 10
Championship ....at LA Raiders 30, Seattle 14

NFC Playoffs

First Round ....*LA Rams 24, at *Dallas 17
Second Round ....at San Francisco 24, Detroit 23
at Washington 51, LA Rams 7
Championship ......at Washington 24, San Francisco 21

Super Bowl XVIII

Jan. 22, 1984
Tampa Stadium, Tampa
Favorite: Redskins by 3—Attendance: 72,920

Washington (16-2) 0   3   6   0 — **9**
LA Raiders (14-4) ....7 14 14   3 — **38**
MVP: LA Raiders RB Marcus Allen (20 carries, 191 yds, 2 TD; 2 catches, 18 yds)

1984 SEASON

AFC Playoffs

First Round . . . . .at *Seattle 13, *LA Raiders 7
Second Round . . . . .at Miami 31, Seattle 10
Pittsburgh 24, at Denver 17
Championship . . . . .at Miami 45, Pittsburgh 28

NFC Playoffs

First Round . . . .*NY Giants 16, at *LA Rams 13
Second Round . . . . . . .at San Francisco 21, NY Giants 10
Chicago 23, at Washington 19
Championship . . . . .at San Francisco 23, Chicago 0

Super Bowl XIX

Jan. 20, 1985
Stanford Stadium, Stanford, Calif.
Favorite: 49ers by 3—Attendance: 84,059

Miami (16-2) . . . . .10　6　0　0　— **16**
San Francisco (17-1) . . . . .7　21　10　0 — **38**
MVP: San Francisco QB Joe Montana (24 for 35, 331 yds,
2 TD; 5 carries, 59 yards, 1 TD)

1985 SEASON

AFC Playoffs

First Round . . . .*New England 26, at *NY Jets 14
Second Round . . . . .at Miami 24, Cleveland 21
New England 27, at LA Raiders 20
Championship . . . . .New England 31, at Miami 14

NFC Playoffs

First Round . . . . . . .at *NY Giants 17, *San Francisco 3
Second Round . . . . .at LA Rams 20, Dallas 0
at Chicago 21, NY Giants 0
Championship . . . . .at Chicago 24, LA Rams 0

Super Bowl XX

Jan. 26, 1986
Louisiana Superdome, New Orleans
Favorite: Bears by 10—Attendance: 73,818

Chicago Bears (17-1) . . . . . . .13　10　21　2 — **46**
New England (14-5) . . . . .3　0　0　7 — **10**
MVP: Chicago DE Richard Dent (Bears defense: 7 sacks, 6
turnovers, 1 safety and gave up just 123 total yards)

1986 SEASON

AFC Playoffs

First Round . . . . .at *NY Jets 35, *Kansas City 15
Second Round . . . . . . .at Cleveland 23, NY Jets 20 (OT)
at Denver 22, New England 17
Championship . . . . .Denver 23, at Cleveland 20 (OT)

NFC Playoffs

First Round . . . . .at *Washington 19, *LA Rams 7
Second Round . . . . .Washington 27, at Chicago 13
at NY Giants 49, San Francisco 3
Championship . . . . .at NY Giants 17, Washington 0

Super Bowl XXI

Jan. 25, 1987
Rose Bowl, Pasadena
Favorite: Giants by 9½—Attendance: 101,063

Denver (13-5) . . . . .10　0　0　10 — **20**
NY Giants (16-2) . . . . .7　2　17　13 — **39**
MVP: NY Giants QB Phil Simms (22 for 25, 268 yds, 3 TD;
3 carries, 25 yds)

1987 SEASON

A 24-day players' strike shortened the regular season to
15 games with replacement teams playing for three weeks.

AFC Playoffs

First Round . . . . .at *Houston 23, *Seattle 20 (OT)
Second Round . . . . .at Cleveland 38, Indianapolis 21
at Denver 34, Houston 10
Championship . . . . .at Denver 38, Cleveland 33

NFC Playoffs

First Round . . . .*Minnesota 44, at *New Orleans 10
Second Round . . . . . . .Minnesota 36, at San Francisco 24
Washington 21, at Chicago 17
Championship . . . . .at Washington 17, Minnesota 10

Super Bowl XXII

Jan. 31, 1988
San Diego/Jack Murphy Stadium
Favorite: Broncos by 3½—Attendance: 73,302

Washington (13-4) . . . . .0　35　0　7 — **42**
Denver (12-4-1) . . . . .10　0　0　0 — **10**
MVP: Washington QB Doug Williams (18 for 29, 340 yds,
4 TD, 1 Int)

1988 SEASON

AFC Playoffs

First Round . . . .*Houston 24, at *Cleveland 23
Second Round . . . . .at Buffalo 17, Houston 10
at Cincinnati 21, Seattle 13
Championship . . . . .at Cincinnati 21, Buffalo 10

NFC Playoffs

First Round . . . . .at *Minnesota 28, *LA Rams 17
Second Round . . . . .at San Francisco 34, Minnesota 9
at Chicago 20, Philadelphia 12
Championship . . . . .San Francisco 28, at Chicago 3

Super Bowl XXIII

Jan. 22, 1989
Joe Robbie Stadium, Miami
Favorite: 49ers by 7—Attendance: 75,129

Cincinnati (14-4) . . . . .0　3　10　3 — **16**
San Francisco (12-6) . . . . .3　0　3　14 — **20**
MVP: San Francisco WR Jerry Rice (11 catches, 215 yds, 1
TD; 1 carry, 5 yds)

1989 SEASON

AFC Playoffs

First Round . . . .*Pittsburgh 26, at *Houston 23
Second Round . . . . .at Cleveland 34, Buffalo 30
at Denver 24, Pittsburgh 23
Championship . . . . .at Denver 37, Cleveland 21

NFC Playoffs

First Round . . . .*LA Rams 21, at *Philadelphia 7
Second Round . . . . .LA Rams 19, NY Giants 13 (OT)
at San Francisco 41, Minnesota 13
Championship . . . . .at San Francisco 30, LA Rams 3

Super Bowl XXIV

Jan. 28, 1990
Louisiana Superdome, New Orleans
Favorite: 49ers by 12½—Attendance: 72,919

San Francisco (17-2) . . . . .13　14　14　14 — **55**
Denver (13-6) . . . . .3　0　7　0 — **10**
MVP: San Francisco QB Joe Montana (22 for 29, 297 yds,
5 TD)

1990 SEASON

AFC Playoffs

First Round . . . . .at *Miami 17, *Kansas City 16
at Cincinnati 41, *Houston 14
Second Round . . . . .at Buffalo 44, Miami 34
at LA Raiders 20, Cincinnati 10
Championship . . . . .at Buffalo 51, LA Raiders 3

NFC Playoffs

First Round . . . .*Washington 20, at *Philadelphia 6
at Chicago 16, *New Orleans 6
Second Round . . . . . .at San Francisco 28, Washington 10
at NY Giants 31, Chicago 3
Championship . . . . . . .NY Giants 15, at San Francisco 13

Super Bowl XXV
Jan. 27, 1991
Tampa Stadium, Tampa
Favorite: Bills by 7—Attendance: 73,813

Buffalo (15-4)	3	9	0	7	**—19**
NY Giants (16-3)	3	7	7	3	**—20**

MVP: NY Giants RB Ottis Anderson (21 carries, 102 yds, 1 TD; 1 catch, 7 yds)

1991 SEASON

AFC Playoffs

First Round . . . . .at *Kansas City 10, *LA Raiders 6
at Houston 17, *NY Jets 10
Second Round . . . . .at Denver 26, Houston 24
at Buffalo 37, Kansas City 14
Championship . . . . .at Buffalo 10, Denver 7

NFC Playoffs

First Round . . . .*Atlanta 27, at New Orleans 20
*Dallas 17, at *Chicago 13
Second Round . . . . .at Washington 24, Atlanta 7
at Detroit 38, Dallas 6
Championship . . . . .at Washington 41, Detroit 10

Super Bowl XXVI
Jan. 26, 1992
Hubert Humphrey Metrodome, Minneapolis
Favorite: Redskins by 7—Attendance: 63,130

Washington (16-2)	0	17	14	6	**— 37**
Buffalo (15-3)	0	0	10	14	**— 24**

MVP: Washington QB Mark Rypien (18 for 33, 292 yds, 2 TD, 1 Int)

1992 SEASON

AFC Playoffs

First Round . . . . .at *Buffalo 41, *Houston 38 (OT)
at San Diego 17, *Kansas City 0
Second Round . . . . .Buffalo 24, at Pittsburgh 3
at Miami 31, San Diego 0
Championship . . . . .Buffalo 29, at Miami 10

NFC Playoffs

First Round . . . .*Washington 24, at Minnesota 7
*Philadelphia 36, at *New Orleans 20
Second Round . . . . . .at San Francisco 20, Washington 13
at Dallas 34, Philadelphia 10
Championship . . . . .Dallas 30, at San Francisco 20

Super Bowl XXVII
Jan. 31, 1993
Rose Bowl, Pasadena
Favorite: Cowboys by 7—Attendance: 98,374

Buffalo (14-5)	7	3	7	0	**— 17**
Dallas (15-3)	14	14	3	21	**— 52**

MVP: Dallas QB Troy Aikman (22 for 30, 273 yds, 4 TD)

1993 SEASON

AFC Playoffs

First Round . . . . . . .at Kansas City 27, *Pittsburgh 24 (OT)
at *LA Raiders 42, *Denver 24
Second Round . . . . .at Buffalo 29, LA Raiders 23
Kansas City 28, at Houston 20
Championship . . . . .at Buffalo 30, Kansas City 13

NFC Playoffs

First Round . . . .*Green Bay 28, at Detroit 24
at *NY Giants 17, *Minnesota 10
Second Round . . . . . .at San Francisco 44, NY Giants 3
at Dallas 27, Green Bay 17
Championship . . . . .at Dallas 38, San Francisco 21

Super Bowl XXVIII
Jan. 30, 1994
Georgia Dome, Atlanta
Favorite: Cowboys by 10½—Attendance: 72,817

Dallas (15-4)	6	0	14	10	**— 30**
Buffalo (14-5)	3	10	0	0	**— 13**

MVP: Dallas RB Emmitt Smith (30 carries, 132 yds, 2 TDs; 4 catches, 26 yds)

1994 SEASON

AFC Playoffs

First Round . . . . .at Miami 27, *Kansas City 17
at *Cleveland 20, *New England 13
Second Round . . . . .at Pittsburgh 29, Cleveland 9
at San Diego 22, Miami 21
Championship . . . . .San Diego 17, at Pittsburgh 13

NFC Playoffs

First Round . . . . .at *Green Bay 16, *Detroit 12
*Chicago 25, at Minnesota 18
Second Round . . . . .at San Francisco 44, Chicago 15
at Dallas 35, Green Bay 9
Championship . . . . .at San Francisco 38, Dallas 28

Super Bowl XXIX
Jan. 29, 1995
Joe Robbie Stadium, Miami
Favorite: 49ers by 18 —Attendance: 74,107

San Diego (13-5)	7	3	8	8	**—26**
San Francisco (15-3)	14	14	14	7	**—49**

MVP: San Francisco QB Steve Young (24 for 36, 325 yds, 6 TD)

1995 SEASON

AFC Playoffs

First Round . . . . .at Buffalo 37, *Miami 22
*Indianapolis 35, at *San Diego 20
Second Round . . . . .at Pittsburgh 40, Buffalo 21
Indianapolis 10, at Kansas City 7
Championship . . . . .at Pittsburgh 20, Indianapolis 16

NFC Playoffs

First Round . . . . .at *Philadelphia 58, *Detroit 37
at Green Bay 37, *Atlanta 20
Second Round . . . . .Green Bay 27, at San Francisco 17
at Dallas 30, Philadelphia 11
Championship . . . . .at Dallas 38, Green Bay 27

Super Bowl XXX
Jan. 28, 1996
Sun Devil Stadium, Tempe, Ariz.
Favorite: Cowboys by 13½—Attendance: 76,347

Dallas (14-4)	10	3	7	7	**— 27**
Pittsburgh (13-5)	0	7	0	10	**— 17**

MVP: Dallas CB Larry Brown (2 interceptions for 77 yds)

1996 SEASON

AFC Playoffs

First Round . . . .*Jacksonville 30, at *Buffalo 27
at Pittsburgh 42, *Indianapolis 14
Second Round . . . . Jacksonville 30, at Denver 27
at New England 28, Pittsburgh 3
Championship . . . . .at New England 20, Jacksonville 6

NFC Playoffs

First Round . . . . at Dallas 40, *Minnesota 15
at *San Francisco 14, *Philadelphia 0
Second Round . . . . . . at Green Bay 35, San Francisco 14
at Carolina 26, Dallas 17
Championship . . . . at Green Bay 30, Carolina 13

Super Bowl XXXI
Jan. 26, 1997
Louisiana Superdome, New Orleans
Favorite: Packers by 14—Attendance: 72,301

New England (13-5)	 14	0	7	0	**— 21**
Green Bay (15-3)	 10	17	8	0	**— 35**

MVP: Green Bay KR Desmond Howard (4 kickoff returns for 154 yds and 1 TD, also 6 punt returns for 90 yds)

1997 SEASON

AFC Playoffs

First Round . . . . .at *Denver 42, *Jacksonville 17
at New England 17, *Miami 3
Second Round . . . . .at Pittsburgh 7, New England 6
Denver 14, at Kansas City 10
Championship . . . . Denver 24, at Pittsburgh 21

NFC Playoffs

First Round . . . .*Minnesota 23, at NY Giants 22
at *Tampa Bay 20, *Detroit 10
Second Round . . . . . . at San Francisco 38, Minnesota 22
at Green Bay 21, Tampa Bay 7
Championship . . . . . . .Green Bay 23, at San Francisco 10

Super Bowl XXXII
Jan. 25, 1998
Qualcomm Stadium, San Diego
Favorite: Packers by 11½—Attendance: 68,912

Green Bay (15-3)	7	7	3	7	**—24**
Denver (15-4)	7	10	7	7	**—31**

MVP: Denver RB Terrell Davis (30 carries, 157 yds, 3 TD)

1998 SEASON

AFC Playoffs

First Round . . . . .at *Miami 24, *Buffalo 17
at Jacksonville 25, *New England 10
Second Round . . . . .at NY Jets 34, Jacksonville 24
at Denver 38, Miami 3
Championship . . . . at Denver 23, NY Jets 10

NFC Playoffs

First Round . . . . . . .at *San Francisco 30, *Green Bay 27
*Arizona 20, at Dallas 7
Second Round . . . . . . .at Atlanta 20, San Francisco 18
at Minnesota 41, Arizona 21
Championship . . . . .Atlanta 30, at Minnesota 27 (OT)

Super Bowl XXXIII
Jan. 31, 1999
Pro Player Stadium, Miami
Favorite: Broncos by 7½—Attendance: 74,803

Denver (16-2)	7	10	0	17	**— 34**
Atlanta (16-2)	3	3	0	13	**— 19**

MVP: Denver QB John Elway (18 for 29, 336 yds, 1 TD, 1 Int and 1 rushing TD)

1999 SEASON

AFC Playoffs

First Round . . . . .at *Tennessee 22, *Buffalo 16
*Miami 20, at Seattle 17
Second Round . . . . .at Jacksonville 62, Miami 7
Tennessee 19, at Indianapolis 16
Championship . . . . .Tennessee 33, at Jacksonville 14

NFC Playoffs

First Round . . . . .at Washington 27, *Detroit 13
at *Minnesota 27, *Dallas 10
Second Round . . . . . . .at Tampa Bay 14, Washington 13
at St. Louis 49, Minnesota 37
Championship . . . . .at St. Louis 11, Tampa Bay 6

Super Bowl XXXIV
Jan. 30, 2000
Georgia Dome, Atlanta
Favorite: Rams by 7—Attendance: 72,625

St. Louis (15-3)	3	6	7	7	**—23**
Tennessee (16-3)	0	0	6	10	**—16**

MVP: St. Louis QB Kurt Warner (24 for 45, 414 yds, 2 TD)

2000 SEASON

AFC Playoffs

First Round . . . . .at Miami 23, *Indianapolis 17 (OT)
at *Baltimore 21, *Denver 3
Second Round . . . . .at Oakland 27, Miami 0
Baltimore 24, at Tennessee 10
Championship . . . . .Baltimore 16, at Oakland 3

NFC Playoffs

First Round . . . . .at New Orleans 31, *St. Louis 28
at *Philadelphia 21, *Tampa Bay 3
Second Round . . . . . . .at Minnesota 34, New Orleans 16
at NY Giants 20, Philadelphia 10
Championship . . . . .at NY Giants 41, Minnesota 0

Super Bowl XXXV
Jan. 28, 2001
Raymond James Stadium, Tampa
Favorite: Ravens by 3—Attendance: 71,921

Baltimore (15-4)	7	3	14	10	**— 34**
NY Giants (14-4)	0	0	7	0	**— 7**

MVP: Baltimore LB Ray Lewis (5 tackles, 4 passes defended)

2001 SEASON

AFC Playoffs

First Round . . . . .at Oakland 38, *NY Jets 24
*Baltimore 20, at *Miami 3
Second Round . . . .at New England 16, Oakland 13 (OT)
at Pittsburgh 27, Baltimore 10
Championship . . . . New England 24, at Pittsburgh 17

NFC Playoffs

First Round . . . . .at Philadelphia 31, *Tampa Bay 9
at *Green Bay 25, *San Francisco 15
Second Round . . . . .Philadelphia 33, at Chicago 19
at St. Louis 45, Green Bay 17
Championship . . . . . . .at St. Louis 29, Philadelphia 24

Super Bowl XXXVI
Feb. 3, 2002
Louisiana Superdome, New Orleans
Favorite: Rams by 14—Attendance: 72,922

St. Louis (16-2)	3	0	0	14	**— 17**
New England (13-5)	0	14	3	3	**— 20**

MVP: New England QB Tom Brady (16 for 27, 145 yds, 1 TD)

2002 SEASON

AFC Playoffs

First Round ....at NY Jets 41, *Indianapolis 0
at Pittsburgh 36, *Cleveland 33
Second Round .....at Tennessee 34, Pittsburgh 31 (OT)
at Oakland 30, NY Jets 10
Championship ....at Oakland 41, Tennessee 24

NFC Playoffs

First Round ....*Atlanta 27, at Green Bay 7
at San Francisco 39, *NY Giants 38
Second Round ....at Philadelphia 20, Atlanta 6
at Tampa Bay 31, San Francisco 6
Championship ......Tampa Bay 27, at Philadelphia 10

Super Bowl XXXVII

Jan. 26, 2003
Qualcomm Stadium, San Diego
Favorite: Raiders by 3½—Attendance: 67,603

Oakland (13-5)	3	0	6	12—**21**
Tampa Bay (14-4)	3	17	14	14—**48**

MVP: Tampa Bay S Dexter Jackson (2 interceptions for 34 yards)

2003 SEASON

AFC Playoffs

First Round ....*Tennessee 20, at Baltimore 17
at Indianapolis 41, *Denver 10
Second Round ......at New England 17, Tennessee 14
Indianapolis 38, at Kansas City 31
Championship ....at New England 24, Indianapolis 14

NFC Playoffs

First Round ....at Carolina 29, *Dallas 10
at Green Bay 33, Seattle 27 (OT)
Second Round .....Carolina 29, at St. Louis 23 (2OT)
at Philadelphia 20, Green Bay 17 (OT)
Championship ......Carolina 14, at Philadelphia 3

Super Bowl XXXVIII

Feb. 1, 2004
Reliant Stadium, Houston
Favorite: Patriots by 7—Attendance: 71,525

Carolina (14-5)	0	0	10	19—**29**
New England (16-2)	0	14	0	18—**32**

MVP: New England QB Tom Brady (32 for 48, 354 yds, 3 TD, 1 Int)

2004 SEASON

AFC Playoffs

First Round ....*NY Jets 20, at San Diego 17 (OT)
at Indianapolis 49, *Denver 24
Second Round ......at Pittsburgh 20, NY Jets 17 (OT)
at New England 20, Indianapolis 3
Championship .....New England 41, at Pittsburgh 27

NFC Playoffs

First Round ....*St. Louis 27, at Seattle 20
*Minnesota 31, at Green Bay 17
Second Round ....at Atlanta 47, St. Louis 17
at Philadelphia 27, Minnesota 14
Championship ....at Philadelphia 27, Atlanta 10

Super Bowl XXXIX

Feb. 6, 2005
ALLTEL Stadium, Jacksonville
Favorite: Patriots by 7—Attendance: 78,125

New England (16-2)	0	7	7	10—**24**
Philadelphia (15-3)	0	7	7	7—**21**

MVP: New England WR Deion Branch (11 catches, 133 yds)

2005 SEASON

AFC Playoffs

First Round ....at New England 28, *Jacksonville 3
*Pittsburgh 31, at Cincinnati 17
Second Round ....at Denver 27, New England 13
Pittsburgh 21, at Indianapolis 18
Championship ....Pittsburgh 34, at Denver 17

NFC Playoffs

First Round ....*Washington 17, at Tampa Bay 10
*Carolina 23, at NY Giants 0
Second Round ....at Seattle 20, Washington 10
Carolina 29, at Chicago 21
Championship ....at Seattle 34, Carolina 14

Super Bowl XL

Feb. 5, 2006
Ford Field, Detroit
Favorite: Steelers by 3½—Attendance: 68,206

Seattle (15-3)	3	0	7	0—**10**
Pittsburgh (14-5)	0	7	7	7—**21**

MVP: Pittsburgh WR Hines Ward (5 catches, 123 yds, 1 TD)

2006 SEASON

AFC Playoffs

First Round ....at Indianapolis 23, *Kansas City 8
at New England 37, *NY Jets 16
Second Round ....Indianapolis 15, at Baltimore 6
New England 24, at San Diego 21
Championship ....at Indianapolis 38, New England 34

NFC Playoffs

First Round ....at Seattle 21, *Dallas 20
at Philadelphia 23, *NY Giants 20
Second Round .....at New Orleans 27, Philadelphia 24
at Chicago 27, Seattle 24 (OT)
Championship ......at Chicago 39, New Orleans 14

Super Bowl XLI

Feb. 4, 2007
Dolphin Stadium, Miami
Favorite: Colts by 7—Attendance: 74,512

Indianapolis (15-4)	6	10	6	7—**29**
Chicago (15-3)	14	0	3	0—**17**

MVP: Indianapolis QB Peyton Manning (25 for 38, 247 yds, 1 TD, 1 Int)

Super Bowl Champs That Didn't Make Playoffs The Following Year

Team	Bowl Won	Following Year (Record)
Green Bay	II	1968 (6-7-1)
Kansas City	IV	1970 (7-5-2)
Pittsburgh	XIV	1980 (9-7-0)
Oakland	XV	1981 (7-9-0)
San Francisco	XVI	1982 (3-6-0)*
NY Giants	XXI	1987 (6-9-0)*
Washington	XXII	1988 (7-9-0)
NY Giants	XXV	1991 (8-8-0)
Denver	XXXIII	1999 (6-10-0)
New England	XXXVI	2002 (9-7-0)
Tampa Bay	XXXVII	2003 (7-9-0)
Pittsburgh	XL	2006 (8-8-0)

*NFL players' strikes shortened the 1982 season from 16 games to nine and the 1987 season from 16 games to 15.

Before the Super Bowl

The first NFL champion was the Akron Pros in 1920, when the league was called the American Professional Football Association (APFA) and the title went to the team with the best regular season record. The APFA changed its name to the National Football League in 1922.

The first playoff game with the championship at stake came in 1932, when the Chicago Bears (6-1-6) and Portsmouth (Ohio) Spartans (6-1-4) ended the regular season tied for first place. The Bears won the subsequent playoff, 9-0. Due to a snowstorm and cold weather, the game was moved from Wrigley Field to an improvised 80-yard dirt field at Chicago Stadium, making it the first indoor title game as well.

The NFL Championship Game decided the league title until the NFL merged with the AFL and the first Super Bowl was played following the 1966 season.

NFL Champions, 1920-32

Winning player-coaches noted by position.

Multiple winners: Canton-Cleveland Bulldogs and Green Bay (3); Chicago Staleys/Bears (2).

Year	Champion	Head Coach	Year	Champion	Head Coach
1920	Akron Pros	Fritz Pollard, HB & Elgie Tobin, QB	1927	New York Giants	Earl Potteiger, QB
			1928	Providence Steam Roller	Jimmy Conzelman, HB
1921	Chicago Staleys	George Halas, E	1929	Green Bay Packers	Curly Lambeau, QB
1922	Canton Bulldogs	Guy Chamberlin, E	1930	Green Bay Packers	Curly Lambeau
1923	Canton Bulldogs	Guy Chamberlin, E	1931	Green Bay Packers	Curly Lambeau
1924	Cleveland Bulldogs	Guy Chamberlin, E	1932	Chicago Bears	Ralph Jones
1925	Chicago Cardinals	Norm Barry		(Bears beat Portsmouth-OH in playoff, 9-0)	
1926	Frankford Yellow Jackets	Guy Chamberlin, E			

NFL-NFC Championship Game

NFL Championship games from 1933-69 and NFC Championship games since the completion of the NFL-AFL merger following the 1969 season.

Multiple winners: Green Bay (10); Chicago Bears and Dallas (8); Washington (7); NY Giants (6); San Francisco, Cle-LA-St.L Rams and Philadelphia (5); Cleveland Browns, Detroit and Minnesota (4); Baltimore Colts (3).

Season	Winner	Head Coach	Score	Loser	Head Coach	Site
1933	Chicago Bears	George Halas	23-21	New York	Steve Owen	Chicago
1934	New York	Steve Owen	30-13	Chicago Bears	George Halas	New York
1935	Detroit	Potsy Clark	26-7	New York	Steve Owen	Detroit
1936	Green Bay	Curly Lambeau	21-6	Boston Redskins	Ray Flaherty	New York
1937	Washington Redskins	Ray Flaherty	28-21	Chicago Bears	George Halas	Chicago
1938	New York	Steve Owen	23-17	Green Bay	Curly Lambeau	New York
1939	Green Bay	Curly Lambeau	27-0	New York	Steve Owen	Milwaukee
1940	Chicago Bears	George Halas	73-0	Washington	Ray Flaherty	Washington
1941	Chicago Bears	George Halas	37-9	New York	Steve Owen	Chicago
1942	Washington	Ray Flaherty	14-6	Chicago Bears	Hunk Anderson & Luke Johnsos	Washington
1943	Chicago Bears	Hunk Anderson & Luke Johnsos	41-21	Washington	Arthur Bergman	Chicago
1944	Green Bay	Curly Lambeau	14-7	New York	Steve Owen	New York
1945	Cleveland Rams	Adam Walsh	15-14	Washington	Dudley DeGroot	Cleveland
1946	Chicago Bears	George Halas	24-14	New York	Steve Owen	New York
1947	Chicago Cardinals	Jimmy Conzelman	28-21	Philadelphia	Greasy Neale	Chicago
1948	Philadelphia	Greasy Neale	7-0	Chicago Cardinals	Jimmy Conzelman	Philadelphia
1949	Philadelphia	Greasy Neale	14-0	Los Angeles Rams	Clark Shaughnessy	Los Angeles
1950	Cleveland Browns	Paul Brown	30-28	Los Angeles	Joe Stydahar	Cleveland
1951	Los Angeles	Joe Stydahar	24-17	Cleveland	Paul Brown	Los Angeles
1952	Detroit	Buddy Parker	17-7	Cleveland	Paul Brown	Cleveland
1953	Detroit	Buddy Parker	17-16	Cleveland	Paul Brown	Detroit
1954	Cleveland	Paul Brown	56-10	Detroit	Buddy Parker	Cleveland
1955	Cleveland	Paul Brown	38-14	Los Angeles	Sid Gillman	Los Angeles
1956	New York	Jim Lee Howell	47-7	Chicago Bears	Paddy Driscoll	New York
1957	Detroit	George Wilson	59-14	Cleveland	Paul Brown	Detroit
1958	Balt. Colts	Weeb Ewbank	23-17*	New York	Jim Lee Howell	New York
1959	Balt. Colts	Weeb Ewbank	31-16	New York	Jim Lee Howell	Baltimore
1960	Philadelphia	Buck Shaw	17-13	Green Bay	Vince Lombardi	Philadelphia
1961	Green Bay	Vince Lombardi	37-0	New York	Allie Sherman	Green Bay
1962	Green Bay	Vince Lombardi	16-7	New York	Allie Sherman	New York
1963	Chicago	George Halas	14-10	New York	Allie Sherman	Chicago
1964	Cleveland	Blanton Collier	27-0	Balt. Colts	Don Shula	Cleveland
1965	Green Bay	Vince Lombardi	23-12	Cleveland	Blanton Collier	Green Bay
1966	Green Bay	Vince Lombardi	34-27	Dallas	Tom Landry	Dallas
1967	Green Bay	Vince Lombardi	21-17	Dallas	Tom Landry	Green Bay
1968	Balt. Colts	Don Shula	34-0	Cleveland	Blanton Collier	Cleveland
1969	Minnesota	Bud Grant	27-7	Cleveland	Blanton Collier	Minnesota

Season	Winner	Head Coach	Score	Loser	Head Coach	Site
1970	Dallas	Tom Landry	17-10	San Francisco	Dick Nolan	San Francisco
1971	Dallas	Tom Landry	14-3	SanFrancisco	Dick Nolan	Dallas
1972	Washington	George Allen	26-3	Dallas	Tom Landry	Washington
1973	Minnesota	Bud Grant	27-10	Dallas	Tom Landry	Dallas
1974	Minnesota	Bud Grant	14-10	Los Angeles	Chuck Knox	Minnesota
1975	Dallas	Tom Landry	37-7	Los Angeles	Chuck Knox	Los Angeles
1976	Minnesota	Bud Grant	24-13	Los Angeles	Chuck Knox	Minnesota
1977	Dallas	Tom Landry	23-6	Minnesota	Bud Grant	Dallas
1978	Dallas	Tom Landry	28-0	Los Angeles	Ray Malavasi	Los Angele
1979	Los Angeles	Ray Malavasi	9-0	Tampa Bay	John McKay	Tampa Bay
1980	Philadelphia	Dick Vermeil	20-7	Dallas	Tom Landry	Philadelphia
1981	San Francisco	Bill Walsh	28-27	Dallas	Tom Landry	San Francisco
1982	Washington	Joe Gibbs	31-17	Dallas	Tom Landry	Washington
1983	Washington	Joe Gibbs	24-21	San Francisco	Bill Walsh	Washington
1984	San Francisco	Bill Walsh	23-0	Chicago	Mike Ditka	San Francisco
1985	Chicago	Mike Ditka	24-0	Los Angeles	John Robinson	Chicago
1986	New York	Bill Parcells	17-0	Washington	Joe Gibbs	New York
1987	Washington	Joe Gibbs	17-10	Minnesota	Jerry Burns	Washington
1988	San Francisco	Bill Walsh	28-3	Chicago	Mike Ditka	Chicago
1989	San Francisco	George Seifert	30-3	Los Angeles	John Robinson	San Francisco
1990	New York	Bill Parcells	15-13	San Francisco	George Seifert	San Francisco
1991	Washington	Joe Gibbs	41-10	Detroit	Wayne Fontes	Washington
1992	Dallas	Jimmy Johnson	30-20	San Francisco	George Seifert	San Francisco
1993	Dallas	Jimmy Johnson	38-21	San Francisco	George Seifert	Dallas
1994	San Francisco	George Seifert	38-28	Dallas	Barry Switzer	San Francisco
1995	Dallas	Barry Switzer	38-27	Green Bay	Mike Holmgren	Dallas
1996	Green Bay	Mike Holmgren	30-13	Carolina	Dom Capers	Green Bay
1997	Green Bay	Mike Holmgren	23-10	San Francisco	Steve Mariucci	San Francisco
1998	Atlanta	Dan Reeves	30-27*	Minnesota	Dennis Green	Minnesota
1999	St. Louis	Dick Vermeil	11-6	Tampa Bay	Tony Dungy	St. Louis
2000	New York	Jim Fassel	41-0	Minnesota	Dennis Green	New York
2001	St. Louis	Mike Martz	29-24	Philadelphia	Andy Reid	St. Louis
2002	Tampa Bay	Jon Gruden	27-10	Philadelphia	Andy Reid	Philadelphia
2003	Carolina	John Fox	14-3	Philadelphia	Andy Reid	Philadelphia
2004	Philadelphia	Andy Reid	27-10	Atlanta	Jim Mora Jr.	Philadelphia
2005	Seattle	Mike Holmgren	34-14	Carolina	John Fox	Seattle
2006	Chicago	Lovie Smith	39-14	New Orleans	Sean Payton	Chicago

*Sudden death overtime

NFL-NFC Championship Game Appearances

App		W	L	Pct	PF	PA	App		W	L	Pct	PF	PA
17	NY Giants	6	11	.353	281	322	8	Minnesota	4	4	.500	135	151
16	Dallas Cowboys	8	8	.500	361	319	6	Detroit	4	2	.667	139	141
14	Chicago Bears	8	6	.571	325	259	4	Baltimore Colts	3	1	.750	88	60
14	Cle-LA-St.L Rams	5	9	.357	163	300	3	Tampa Bay	1	2	.333	33	30
13	Green Bay Packers	10	3	.769	303	177	3	Carolina	1	2	.333	41	67
12	Boston-Wash. Redskins	7	5	.583	222	255	2	Chicago Cardinals	1	1	.500	28	28
12	San Francisco	5	7	.417	245	222	2	Atlanta	1	1	.500	40	54
11	Cleveland Browns	4	7	.364	224	253	2	Seattle	1	0	1.000	34	14
9	Philadelphia	5	4	.556	143	128	1	New Orleans	0	1	.000	14	39

AFL-AFC Championship Game

AFL Championship games from 1960-69 and AFC Championship games since the completion of the NFL-AFL merger following the 1969 season.

Multiple winners: Buffalo, Denver and Pittsburgh (6); Miami, Oakland-LA Raiders and New England (5); Dallas Texans-KC Chiefs and Houston Oilers-Tennessee Titans (3); Cincinnati and San Diego (2).

Season	Winner	Head Coach	Score	Loser	Head Coach	Site
1960	Houston	Lou Rymkus	24-16	LA Chargers	Sid Gillman	Houston
1961	Houston	Wally Lemm	10-3	SD Chargers	Sid Gillman	San Diego
1962	Dallas	Hank Stram	20-17*	Houston	Pop Ivy	Houston
1963	San Diego	Sid Gillman	51-10	Boston Patriots	Mike Holovak	San Diego
1964	Buffalo	Lou Saban	20-7	SanDiego	Sid Gillman	Buffalo
1965	Buffalo	Lou Saban	23-0	San Diego	Sid Gillman	San Diego
1966	Kansas City	Hank Stram	31-7	Buffalo	Joe Collier	Buffalo
1967	Oakland	John Rauch	40-7	Houston	Wally Lemm	Oakland
1968	NY Jets	Weeb Ewbank	27-23	Oakland	John Rauch	New York
1969	Kansas City	Hank Stram	17-7	Oakland	John Madden	Oakland
1970	Balt. Colts	Don McCafferty	27-17	Oakland	John Madden	Baltimore
1971	Miami	Don Shula	21-0	Balt. Colts	Don McCafferty	Miami
1972	Miami	Don Shula	21-17	Pittsburgh	Chuck Noll	Pittsburgh
1973	Miami	Don Shula	27-10	Oakland	John Madden	Miami

AFL-AFC Championship Game (Cont.)

Season	Winner	Head Coach	Score	Loser	Head Coach	Site
1974	Pittsburgh	Chuck Noll	24-13	Oakland	John Madden	Oakland
1975	Pittsburgh	Chuck Noll	16-10	Oakland	John Madden	Pittsburgh
1976	Oakland	John Madden	24-7	Pittsburgh	Chuck Noll	Oakland
1977	Denver	Red Miller	20-17	Oakland	John Madden	Denver
1978	Pittsburgh	Chuck Noll	34-5	Houston	Bum Phillips	Pittsburgh
1979	Pittsburgh	Chuck Noll	27-13	Houston	Bum Phillips	Pittsburgh
1980	Oakland	Tom Flores	34-27	San Diego	Don Coryell	San Diego
1981	Cincinnati	Forrest Gregg	27-7	San Diego	Don Coryell	Cincinnati
1982	Miami	Don Shula	14-0	NY Jets	Walt Michaels	Miami
1983	LA Raiders	Tom Flores	30-14	Seattle	Chuck Knox	Los Angeles
1984	Miami	Don Shula	45-28	Pittsburgh	Chuck Noll	Miami
1985	New England	Raymond Berry	31-14	Miami	Don Shula	Miami
1986	Denver	Dan Reeves	23-20*	Cleveland	Marty Schottenheimer	Cleveland
1987	Denver	Dan Reeves	38-33	Cleveland	Marty Schottenheimer	Denver
1988	Cincinnati	Sam Wyche	21-10	Buffalo	Marv Levy	Cincinnati
1989	Denver	Dan Reeves	37-21	Cleveland	Bud Carson	Denver
1990	Buffalo	Marv Levy	51-3	LA Raiders	Art Shell	Buffalo
1991	Buffalo	Marv Levy	10-7	Denver	Dan Reeves	Buffalo
1992	Buffalo	Marv Levy	29-10	Miami	Don Shula	Miami
1993	Buffalo	Marv Levy	30-13	Kansas City	Marty Schottenheimer	Buffalo
1994	San Diego	Bobby Ross	17-13	Pittsburgh	Bill Cowher	Pittsburgh
1995	Pittsburgh	Bill Cowher	20-16	Indianapolis	Ted Marchibroda	Pittsburgh
1996	New England	Bill Parcells	20-6	Jacksonville	Tom Coughlin	New England
1997	Denver	Mike Shanahan	24-21	Pittsburgh	Bill Cowher	Pittsburgh
1998	Denver	Mike Shanahan	23-10	NY Jets	Bill Parcells	Denver
1999	Tennessee	Jeff Fisher	33-14	Jacksonville	Tom Coughlin	Jacksonville
2000	Balt. Ravens	Brian Billick	16-3	Oakland	Jon Gruden	Oakland
2001	New England	Bill Belichick	24-17	Pittsburgh	Bill Cowher	Pittsburgh
2002	Oakland	Bill Callahan	41-24	Tennessee	Jeff Fisher	Oakland
2003	New England	Bill Belichick	24-14	Indianapolis	Tony Dungy	New England
2004	New England	Bill Belichick	41-27	Pittsburgh	Bill Cowher	Pittsburgh
2005	Pittsburgh	Bill Cowher	34-17	Denver	Mike Shanahan	Denver
2006	Indianapolis	Tony Dungy	38-34	New England	Bill Belichick	Indianapolis

*Sudden death overtime

AFL-AFC Championship Game Appearances

App		W	L	Pct	PF	PA	App		W	L	Pct	PF	PA
14	Oakland-LA Raiders	5	9	.357	272	304	5	Baltimore-Indy Colts	2	3	.400	95	116
12	Pittsburgh	6	6	.500	258	229	4	Dallas Texans/KC Chiefs	3	1	.750	81	61
8	Buffalo	6	2	.750	180	92	3	NY Jets	1	2	.333	37	60
8	Denver	6	2	.750	189	166	3	Cleveland	0	3	.000	74	98
8	Houston Oilers/Ten. Titans	3	5	.375	133	195	2	Cincinnati	2	0	1.000	48	17
8	LA-San Diego Chargers	2	6	.250	128	161	2	Jacksonville	0	2	.000	20	53
7	Miami	5	2	.714	152	115	1	Baltimore Ravens	1	0	1.000	16	3
7	Boston-NE Patriots	5	2	.714	184	167	1	Seattle	0	1	.000	14	30

Overall Postseason Games

The postseason records of all NFL teams, ranked by number of playoff games participated in from 1933 through the 2006-07 postseason.

Gm		W	L	Pct	PF	PA	Gm		W	L	Pct	PF	PA
55	Dallas Cowboys	32	23	.582	1301	1029	31	Cleveland Browns	11	20	.355	629	728
46	Pittsburgh Steelers	28	18	.609	1066	928	29	Buffalo Bills	14	15	.483	681	658
43	Oakland-LA Raiders	25	18	.581	1028	797	21	Dallas Texans/KC Chiefs	8	13	.381	340	445
43	Cle-LA-St.L Rams	19	24	.442	770	944	20	LA-San Diego Chargers	7	13	.350	370	472
42	San Francisco 49ers	25	17	.595	1044	853	19	New York Jets	8	11	.421	388	389
42	Minnesota Vikings	18	24	.429	824	957	17	Detroit Lions	7	10	.412	365	404
39	Boston-Wash. Redskins	23	16	.590	805	672	15	Seattle Seahawks	6	9	.400	301	311
39	Miami Dolphins	20	19	.513	780	848	14	Atlanta Falcons	6	8	.429	298	331
39	New York Giants	16	23	.410	667	745	14	Tampa Bay Buccaneers	6	8	.429	216	255
38	Green Bay Packers	24	14	.632	888	723	13	Cincinnati Bengals	5	8	.385	263	288
33	Balt-Indianapolis Colts	17	16	.515	661	667	9	Carolina Panthers	6	3	.667	206	170
33	Chicago Bears	16	17	.485	702	681	9	Jacksonville Jaguars	4	5	.444	211	228
32	Denver Broncos	17	15	.531	694	794	8	Baltimore Ravens	5	3	.625	148	88
32	Philadelphia Eagles	17	17	.500	653	608	8	New Orleans Saints	2	6	.250	144	248
31	Boston-NE Patriots	19	12	.613	664	617	7	Chi-St.L-Ari. Cardinals	2	5	.286	122	182
31	Houston Oilers/Ten. Titans	14	17	.452	563	732							

NFL Divisional Champions

The NFL adopted divisional play for the first time in 1967, splitting both conferences into two four-team divisions—the Capitol and Century divisions in the East and the Central and Coastal divisions in the West. A merger with the AFL in 1970 increased NFL membership to 26 teams and made it necessary for realignment. Two 13-team conferences—the AFC and NFC—were formed by moving established NFL clubs in Baltimore, Cleveland and Pittsburgh to the AFC and rearranging both conferences into Eastern, Central and Western divisions. Expansion has since increased the league to 32 teams (beginning in 2002) with four NFC divisions and four AFC divisions, all with four teams each.

Division champions are listed below; teams that went on to win the Super Bowl are in **bold** type. Note that in the 1980 season, Oakland won the Super Bowl as a wild card team, as did Denver in 1997, Baltimore in 2000 and Pittsburgh in 2005; and in 1982, the players' strike shortened the regular season to nine games and eliminated divisional play for one season.

Multiple champions (since 1970): **AFC**–Pittsburgh (17); Miami and Oakland-LA Raiders (12); Baltimore-Indianapolis Colts, Denver (10); New England (9); Buffalo and San Diego (7); Cincinnati and Cleveland (6); Kansas City (5); Houston Oilers-Tennessee Titans (4); Baltimore Ravens, Jacksonville, NY Jets and Seattle (2). **NFC**–San Francisco (17); Dallas (15); Minnesota (14); LA-St. Louis Rams (11); Chicago (9); Green Bay and Philadelphia (7); NY Giants and Washington (6); Tampa Bay (5); Atlanta, Detroit, New Orleans and Seattle (3); Carolina and St. Louis Cardinals (2).

American Football League

Season	East	West
1966	Buffalo	Kansas City

Season	East	West
1967	Houston	Oakland
1968	**NY Jets**	Oakland
1969	NY Jets	Oakland

National Football League

Season	East	West
1966	Dallas	**Green Bay**

Season	Capitol	Century	Central	Coastal
1967	Dallas	Cleveland	**Green Bay**	LA Rams
1968	Dallas	Cleveland	Minnesota	Baltimore
1969	Dallas	Cleveland	Minnesota	LA Rams

Note: Kansas City, an AFL second-place team, won the Super Bowl in the 1969 season.

American Football Conference

Season	East	Central	West
1970	**Balt. Colts**	Cincinnati	Oakland
1971	Miami	Cleveland	Kansas City
1972	**Miami**	Pittsburgh	Oakland
1973	**Miami**	Cincinnati	Oakland
1974	Miami	**Pittsburgh**	Oakland
1975	Balt.Colts	**Pittsburgh**	Oakland
1976	Balt.Colts	Pittsburgh	**Oakland**
1977	Balt.Colts	Pittsburgh	Denver
1978	New England	**Pittsburgh**	Denver
1979	Miami	**Pittsburgh**	San Diego
1980	Buffalo	Cleveland	San Diego
1981	Miami	Cincinnati	San Diego
1982	—	—	—
1983	Miami	Pittsburgh	**LA Raiders**
1984	Miami	Pittsburgh	Denver
1985	Miami	Cleveland	LA Raiders
1986	New England	Cleveland	Denver
1987	Indianapolis	Cleveland	Denver
1988	Buffalo	Cincinnati	Seattle
1989	Buffalo	Cleveland	Denver
1990	Buffalo	Cincinnati	LA Raiders
1991	Buffalo	Houston	Denver
1992	Miami	Pittsburgh	San Diego
1993	Buffalo	Houston	Kansas City
1994	Miami	Pittsburgh	San Diego
1995	Buffalo	Pittsburgh	Kansas City
1996	New England	Pittsburgh	Denver
1997	New England	Pittsburgh	Kansas City
1998	NY Jets	Jacksonville	**Denver**
1999	Indianapolis	Jacksonville	Seattle
2000	Miami	Tennessee	Oakland
2001	**New England**	Pittsburgh	Oakland

National Football Conference

Season	East	Central	West
1970	Dallas	Minnesota	San Francisco
1971	**Dallas**	Minnesota	San Francisco
1972	Washington	Green Bay	San Francisco
1973	Dallas	Minnesota	LA Rams
1974	St. Louis	Minnesota	LA Rams
1975	St. Louis	Minnesota	LA Rams
1976	Dallas	Minnesota	LA Rams
1977	**Dallas**	Minnesota	LA Rams
1978	Dallas	Minnesota	LA Rams
1979	Dallas	Tampa Bay	LA Rams
1980	Philadelphia	Minnesota	Atlanta
1981	Dallas	Tampa Bay	**San Francisco**
1982	—	—	—
1983	Washington	Detroit	San Francisco
1984	Washington	Chicago	**San Francisco**
1985	Dallas	**Chicago**	LA Rams
1986	**NY Giants**	Chicago	San Francisco
1987	**Washington**	Chicago	San Francisco
1988	Philadelphia	Chicago	**San Francisco**
1989	NY Giants	Minnesota	**San Francisco**
1990	**NY Giants**	Chicago	San Francisco
1991	**Washington**	Detroit	New Orleans
1992	**Dallas**	Minnesota	San Francisco
1993	**Dallas**	Detroit	San Francisco
1994	Dallas	Minnesota	**San Francisco**
1995	**Dallas**	Green Bay	San Francisco
1996	Dallas	**Green Bay**	Carolina
1997	NY Giants	Green Bay	San Francisco
1998	Dallas	Minnesota	Atlanta
1999	Washington	Tampa Bay	**St. Louis**
2000	NY Giants	Minnesota	New Orleans
2001	Philadelphia	Chicago	St. Louis

Season	East	North	South	West
2002	NY Jets	Pittsburgh	Tennessee	Oakland
2003	**New Eng.**	Baltimore	Indianapolis	Kansas City
2004	**New Eng.**	Pittsburgh	Indianapolis	San Diego
2005	New Eng.	Cincinnati	Indianapolis	Denver
2006	New Eng.	Baltimore	**Indianap.**	San Diego

Season	East	North	South	West
2002	Philadelphia	Green Bay	**Tampa Bay**	San Fran.
2003	Philadelphia	Green Bay	Carolina	St. Louis
2004	Philadelphia	Green Bay	Atlanta	Seattle
2005	NY Giants	Chicago	Tampa Bay	Seattle
2006	Philadelphia	Chicago	New Orleans	Seattle

Champions of Leagues That No Longer Exist

No professional league in American sports has had to contend with more pretenders to the throne than the NFL. Eight times in nine decades, a rival league has risen up to challenge the NFL and seven of them went under in less than five seasons. Only the fourth American Football League (1960-69) succeeded, forcing the older league to sue for peace and a full partnership in 1966.

Of the seven leagues that didn't make it, only the All-America Football Conference (1946-49) lives on—the Cleveland Browns and San Francisco 49ers joined the NFL after the AAFC folded in 1949. The champions of leagues past are listed below.

American Football League I

Year		Head Coach
1926	Philadelphia Quakers (8-2)	Bob Folwell

Note: Philadelphia was challenged to a postseason game by the 7th place New York Giants (8-4-1) of the NFL. The Giants won, 31-0, in a snowstorm.

American Football League II

Year		Head Coach
1936	Boston Shamrocks (8-3)	George Kenneally
1937	Los Angeles Bulldogs (9-0)	Gus Henderson

Note: Boston was scheduled to play 2nd place Cleveland (5-2-2) in the '36 championship game, but the Shamrock players refused to participate because they were owed pay for past games.

American Football League III

Year		Head Coach
1940	Columbus Bullies (8-1-1)	Phil Bucklew
1941	Columbus Bullies (5-1-2)	Phil Bucklew

All-America Football Conference

Year	Winner	Head Coach	Score	Loser	Head Coach	Site
1946	Cleveland Browns	Paul Brown	14-9	NY Yankees	Ray Flaherty	Cleveland
1947	Cleveland Browns	Paul Brown	14-3	NY Yankees	Ray Flaherty	New York
1948	Cleveland Browns	Paul Brown	49-7	Buffalo Bills	Red Dawson	Cleveland
1949	Cleveland Browns	Paul Brown	21-7	S.F. 49ers	Buck Shaw	Cleveland

World Football League

Year	Winner	Head Coach	Score	Loser	Head Coach	Site
1974	Birmingham Americans	Jack Gotta	22-21	Florida Blazers	Jack Pardee	Birmingham

United States Football League

Year	Winner	Head Coach	Score	Loser	Head Coach	Site
1983	Michigan Panthers	Jim Stanley	24-22	Philadelphia Stars	Jim Mora	Denver
1984	Philadelphia Stars	Jim Mora	23-3	Arizona Wranglers	George Allen	Tampa
1985	Baltimore Stars	Jim Mora	28-24	Oakland Invaders	Charlie Sumner	E. Rutherford

XFL

Year	Winner	Head Coach	Score	Loser	Head Coach	Site
2001	Los Angeles Xtreme	Al Luginbill	38-6	San Fran. Demons	Jim Skipper	Los Angeles

---

Defunct Leagues

AFL I (1926): Boston Bulldogs, Brooklyn Horseman, Chicago Bulls, Cleveland Panthers, Los Angeles Wildcats, New York Yankees, Newark Bears, Philadelphia Quakers, Rock Island Independents.

AFL II (1936-37): Boston Shamrocks (1936-37); Brooklyn Tigers (1936); Cincinnati Bengals (1937); Cleveland Rams (1936); Los Angeles Bulldogs (1937); New York Yankees (1936-37); Pittsburgh Americans (1936-37); Rochester Tigers (1936-37).

AFL III (1940-41): Boston Bears (1940); Buffalo Indians (1940-41); Cincinnati Bengals (1940-41); Columbus Bullies (1940-41); Milwaukee Chiefs (1940-41); New York Yankees (1940) renamed Americans (1941).

AAFC (1946-49): Brooklyn Dodgers (1946-48) merged to become Brooklyn-New York Yankees (1949); Buffalo Bisons (1946) renamed Bills (1947-49); Chicago Rockets (1946-48) renamed Hornets (1949); Cleveland Browns (1946-49); Los Angeles Dons (1946-49); Miami Seahawks (1946) became Baltimore Colts (1947-49); New York Yankees (1946-48) merged to become Brooklyn-New York Yankees (1949); San Francisco 49ers (1946-49).

WFL (1974-75): Birmingham Americans (1974) renamed Vulcans (1975); Chicago Fire (1974) renamed Winds (1975); Detroit Wheels (1974); Florida Blazers (1974) became San Antonio Wings (1975); The Hawaiians (1974-75); Houston Texans (1974) became Shreveport (La.) Steamer (1974-75); Jacksonville Sharks (1974) renamed Express (1975); Memphis Southmen (1974) also known as Grizzlies (1975); New York Stars (1974) became Charlotte Hornets (1974-75); Philadelphia Bell (1974-75); Portland Storm (1974) renamed Thunder (1975); Southern California Sun (1974-75).

USFL (1983-85): Arizona Wranglers (1983-84) merged with Oklahoma to become Arizona Outlaws (1985); Birmingham Stallions (1983-85); Boston Breakers (1983) became New Orleans Breakers (1984) and then Portland Breakers (1985); Chicago Blitz (1983-84); Denver Gold (1983-85); Houston Gamblers (1984-85); Jacksonville Bulls (1984-85); Los Angeles Express (1983-85); Memphis Showboats (1984-85).
Michigan Panthers (1983-84) merged with Oakland (1985); New Jersey Generals (1983-85); Oakland Invaders (1983-85); Oklahoma Outlaws (1984) merged with Arizona to become Arizona Outlaws (1985); Philadelphia Stars (1983-84) became Baltimore Stars (1985); Pittsburgh Maulers (1984); San Antonio Gunslingers (1984-85); Tampa Bay Bandits (1983-85); Washington Federals (1983-84) became Orlando Renegades (1985).

XFL (2001): Birmingham Thunderbolts, Chicago Enforcers, Las Vegas Outlaws, Los Angeles Xtreme, Memphis Maniax, New York New Jersey Hitmen, Orlando Rage, San Francisco Demons.

NFL Pro Bowl

A postseason All-Star game between the new league champion and a team of professional all-stars was added to the NFL schedule in 1939. In the first game at Wrigley Field in Los Angeles, the NY Giants beat a team made up of players from NFL teams and two independent clubs in Los Angeles (the LA Bulldogs and Hollywood Stars). An all-NFL All-Star team provided the opposition over the next four seasons, but the game was cancelled in 1943.

The Pro Bowl was revived in 1951 as a contest between conference all-star teams: American vs National (1951-53), Eastern vs Western (1954-70), and AFC vs NFC (since 1971). The AFC leads the current series, 19-18.

The MVP trophy was named the Dan McGuire Award in 1984 after the late SF 49ers publicist and *Honolulu Advertiser* sports columnist.

Year	Winner	Score	Loser
1939	NY Giants	13-10	All-Stars
1940	Green Bay	16-7	All-Stars
1940	Chicago Bears	28-14	All-Stars
1942	Chicago Bears	35-24	All-Stars
1942	All-Stars	17-14	Washington
1943-50	No game		

Year	Winner	MVP
1951	American, 28-27	Otto Graham, Cle., QB
1952	National, 30-13	Dan Towler, LA Rams, HB
1953	National, 27-7	Don Doll, Det., DB
1954	East, 20-9	Chuck Bednarik, Phi., LB
1955	West, 26-19	Billy Wilson, SF, E
1956	East, 31-30	Ollie Matson, Cards, HB
1957	West, 19-10	Back—Bert Rechichar, Bal.
		Line—Ernie Stautner, Pit.
1958	West, 26-7	Back—Hugh McElhenny, SF
		Line—Gene Brito, Wash.
1959	East, 28-21	Back—Frank Gifford, NY
		Line—Doug Atkins, Chi.
1960	West, 38-21	Back—Johnny Unitas, Bal.
		Line—Big Daddy Lipscomb, Pit.
1961	West, 35-31	Back—Johnny Unitas, Bal.
		Line—Sam Huff, NY
1962	West, 31-30	Back—Jim Brown, Cle.
		Line—Henry Jordan, GB
1963	East, 30-20	Back—Jim Brown, Cle.
		Line—Big Daddy Lipscomb, Pit.
1964	West, 31-17	Back—Johnny Unitas, Bal.
		Line—Gino Marchetti, Bal.
1965	West, 34-14	Back—Fran Tarkenton, Min.
		Line—Terry Barr, Det.
1966	East, 36-7	Back—Jim Brown, Cle.
		Line—Dale Meinhart, St. L.
1967	East, 20-10	Back—Gale Sayers, Chi.
		Line—Floyd Peters, Phi.
1968	West, 38-20	Back—Gale Sayers, Chi.
		Line—Dave Robinson, GB
1969	West, 10-7	Back—Roman Gabriel, LA Rams
		Line—Merlin Olsen, LA Rams
1970	West, 16-13	Back—Gale Sayers, Chi.
		Line—George Andrie, Dal.

Year	Winner	MVP
1971	NFC, 27-6	Back—Mel Renfro, Dal.
		Line—Fred Carr, GB
1972	AFC, 26-13	Off—Jan Stenerud, KC
		Def—Willie Lanier, KC
1973	AFC, 33-28	O.J. Simpson, Buf., RB
1974	AFC, 15-13	Garo Yepremian, Mia., PK
1975	NFC, 17-10	James Harris, LA Rams, QB
1976	NFC, 23-20	Billy Johnson, Hou., KR
1977	AFC, 24-14	Mel Blount, Pit., CB
1978	NFC, 14-13	Walter Payton, Chi., RB
1979	NFC, 13-7	Ahmad Rashad, Min., WR
1980	NFC, 37-27	Chuck Muncie, NO, RB
1981	NFC, 21-7	Eddie Murray, Det., PK
1982	AFC, 16-13	Kellen Winslow, SD, WR
		& Lee Roy Selmon, TB, DE
1983	NFC, 20-19	Dan Fouts, SD, QB
		& John Jefferson, GB, WR
1984	NFC, 45-3	Joe Theismann, Wash., QB
1985	AFC, 22-14	Mark Gastineau, NYJ, DE
1986	NFC, 28-24	Phil Simms, NYG, QB
1987	AFC, 10-6	Reggie White, Phi., DE
1988	AFC, 15-6	Bruce Smith, Buf., DE
1989	NFC, 34-3	Randall Cunningham, Phi., QB
1990	NFC, 27-21	Jerry Gray, LA Rams, CB
1991	AFC, 23-21	Jim Kelly, Buf., QB
1992	NFC, 21-15	Michael Irvin, Dal., WR
1993	AFC, 23-20 (OT)	Steve Tasker, Buf., Sp. Teams
1994	NFC, 17-3	Andre Rison, Atl., WR
1995	AFC, 41-13	Marshall Faulk, Ind., RB
1996	NFC, 20-13	Jerry Rice, SF, WR
1997	AFC, 26-23 (OT)	Mark Brunell, Jax, QB
1998	AFC, 29-24	Warren Moon, Sea., QB
1999	AFC, 23-10	Ty Law, NE, CB
		& Keyshawn Johnson, NYJ, WR
2000	NFC, 51-31	Randy Moss, Min., WR
2001	AFC, 38-17	Rich Gannon, Oak., QB
2002	AFC, 38-30	Rich Gannon, Oak., QB
2003	AFC, 45-20	Ricky Williams, Mia., RB
2004	NFC, 55-52	Marc Bulger, St.L, QB
2005	AFC, 38-27	Peyton Manning, Ind., QB
2006	NFC, 23-17	Derrick Brooks, TB, LB
2007	AFC, 31-28	Carson Palmer, Cin., QB

Playing sites: Wrigley Field in Los Angeles (1939); Gilmore Stadium in Los Angeles (1940—both games); Polo Grounds in New York (Jan., 1942); Shibe Park in Philadelphia (Dec., 1942); Memorial Coliseum in Los Angeles (1951-72 and 1979); Texas Stadium in Irving, TX (1973); Arrowhead Stadium in Kansas City (1974); Orange Bowl in Miami (1975); Superdome in New Orleans (1976); Kingdome in Seattle (1977); Tampa Stadium in Tampa (1978) and Aloha Stadium in Honolulu (since 1980).

AFL All-Star Game

The AFL did not play an All-Star game after its first season in 1960 but did stage All-Star games from 1962-70. All-Star teams from the Eastern and Western divisions played each other every year except 1966 with the West winning the series, 6-2. In 1966, the league champion Buffalo Bills met an elite squad made up of the best players from the league's other eight clubs and lost, 30-19.

Year	Winner	MVP
1962	West, 47-27	Cotton Davidson, Oak., QB
1963	West, 21-14	Off—Curtis McClinton, Dal.
		Def—Earl Faison, SD
1964	West, 27-24	Off—Keith Lincoln, SD
		Def—Archie Matsos, Oak.
1965	West, 38-14	Off—Keith Lincoln, SD
		Def—Willie Brown, Den.
1966	All-Stars 30	Off—Joe Namath, NY
	Buffalo 19	Def—Frank Buncom, SD

Year	Winner	MVP
1967	East, 30-23	Off—Babe Parilli, Bos.
		Def—Verlon Biggs, NY
1968	East, 25-24	Off—Joe Namath, NY
		& Don Maynard, NY
		Def—Speedy Duncan, SD
1969	West, 38-25	Off—Len Dawson, KC
		Def—George Webster, Hou.
1970	West, 26-3	John Hadl, SD, QB

Playing sites: Balboa Stadium in San Diego (1962-64); Jeppesen Stadium in Houston (1965); Rice Stadium in Houston (1966); Oakland Coliseum (1967); Gator Bowl in Jacksonville (1968-69) and Astrodome in Houston (1970).

NFL Franchise Origins

Here is what the current 32 teams in the National Football League have to show for the years they have put in as members of the American Professional Football Association (APFA), the NFL, the All-America Football Conference (AAFC) and the American Football League (AFL). Years given for league titles indicate seasons championships were won.

American Football Conference

	First Season	League Titles	Franchise Stops
Baltimore Ravens	1996 (NFL)	1 Super Bowl (2000)	• Baltimore (1996—)
Buffalo Bills	1960 (AFL)	2 AFL (1964-65)	• Buffalo (1960-72)
			Orchard Park, NY (1973—)
Cincinnati Bengals	1968 (AFL)	None	• Cincinnati (1968—)
Cleveland Browns	1946 (AAFC)	4 AAFC (1946-49)	• Cleveland (1946-95, 99—)
		4 NFL (1950,54-55,64)	
Denver Broncos	1960 (AFL)	2 Super Bowls (1997-98)	• Denver (1960—)
Houston Texans	2002 (NFL)	None	• Houston (2002—)
Indianapolis Colts	1953 (NFL)	3 NFL (1958-59,68)	• Baltimore (1953-83)
		2 Super Bowls (1970, 2006)	Indianapolis (1984—)
Jacksonville Jaguars	1995 (NFL)	None	• Jacksonville, FL (1995—)
Kansas City Chiefs	1960 (AFL)	3 AFL (1962,66,69)	• Dallas (1960-62)
		1 Super Bowl (1969)	Kansas City (1963—)
Miami Dolphins	1966 (AFL)	2 Super Bowls (1972-73)	• Miami (1966—)
New England Patriots	1960 (AFL)	3 Super Bowls (2001,03-04)	• Boston (1960-70)
			Foxboro, MA (1971—)
New York Jets	1960 (AFL)	1 AFL (1968)	• New York (1960-83)
		1 Super Bowl (1968)	E. Rutherford, NJ (1984—)
Oakland Raiders	1960 (AFL)	1 AFL (1967)	• Oakland (1960-81, 1995—)
		3 Super Bowls (1976,80,83)	Los Angeles (1982-94)
Pittsburgh Steelers	1933 (NFL)	5 Super Bowls (1974-75,78-79, 2005)	• Pittsburgh (1933—)
San Diego Chargers	1960 (AFL)	1 AFL (1963)	• Los Angeles (1960)
			San Diego (1961—)
Tennessee Titans	1960 (AFL)	2 AFL (1960-61)	• Houston (1960-96)
			Memphis (1997)
			Nashville (1998—)

National Football Conference

	First Season	League Titles	Franchise Stops
Arizona Cardinals	1920 (APFA)	2 NFL (1925,47)	• Chicago (1920-59)
			St. Louis (1960-87)
			Tempe, AZ (1988-2005)
			Glendale, AZ (2006—)
Atlanta Falcons	1966 (NFL)	None	• Atlanta (1966—)
Carolina Panthers	1995 (NFL)	None	• Clemson, SC (1995)
			Charlotte, NC (1996—)
Chicago Bears	1920 (APFA)	8 NFL (1921, 32-33,40-41,43,46,63)	• Decatur, IL (1920)
		1 Super Bowl (1985)	Chicago (1921—)
Dallas Cowboys	1960 (NFL)	5 Super Bowls (1971,77,92-93,95)	• Dallas (1960-70)
			Irving, TX (1971—)
Detroit Lions	1930 (NFL)	4 NFL (1935,52-53,57)	• Portsmouth, OH (1930-33)
			Detroit (1934-74, 2002—)
			Pontiac, MI (1975-2001)
Green Bay Packers	1921 (APFA)	11 NFL (1929-31,36,39,44,61-62,65-67)	• Green Bay (1921—)
		3 Super Bowls (1966-67,96)	
Minnesota Vikings	1961 (NFL)	1 NFL (1969)	• Bloomington, MN (1961-81)
			Minneapolis, MN (1982—)
New Orleans Saints	1967 (NFL)	None	• New Orleans (1967—)
New York Giants	1925 (NFL)	4 NFL (1927,34,38,56)	• New York (1925-73,75)
		2 Super Bowls (1986,90)	New Haven, CT (1973-74)
			E. Rutherford, NJ (1976—)
Philadelphia Eagles	1933 (NFL)	3 NFL (1948-49,60)	• Philadelphia (1933—)
St. Louis Rams	1937 (NFL)	2 NFL (1945,51)	• Cleveland (1937-45)
		1 Super Bowl (1999)	Los Angeles (1946-79)
			Anaheim (1980-94)
			St. Louis (1995—)
San Francisco 49ers	1946 (AAFC)	5 Super Bowls (1981,84,88-89,94)	• San Francisco (1946—)
Seattle Seahawks	1976 (NFL)	None	• Seattle (1976—)
Tampa Bay Buccaneers	1976 (NFL)	1 Super Bowl (2002)	• Tampa, FL (1976—)
Washington Redskins	1932 (NFL)	2 NFL (1937,42)	• Boston (1932-36)
		3 Super Bowls (1982,87,91)	Washington, DC (1937-96)
			Raljon, MD (1997—)

The Growth of the NFL

Of the 14 franchises that comprised the American Professional Football Association in 1920, only two remain—the Arizona Cardinals (then the Chicago Cardinals) and the Chicago Bears (originally the Decatur-IL Staleys). Green Bay joined the APFC in 1921 and the league changed its name to the NFL in 1922. Since then, 54 NFL clubs have come and gone, six rival leagues have expired and two other leagues have been swallowed up.

The NFL merged with the **All-America Football Conference** (1946-49) following the 1949 season and adopted three of its seven clubs—the Baltimore Colts, Cleveland Browns and San Francisco 49ers. The four remaining AAFC teams—the Brooklyn/NY Yankees, Buffalo Bills, Chicago Hornets and Los Angeles Dons—did not survive. After the 1950 season, the financially troubled Colts were sold back to the NFL. The league folded the team and added its players to the 1951 college draft pool. A new Baltimore franchise, also named the Colts, joined the NFL in 1953.

The formation of the **American Football League** (1960-69) was announced in 1959 with ownership lined up in eight cities—Boston, Buffalo, Dallas, Denver, Houston, Los Angeles, Minneapolis and New York. Set to begin play in the autumn of 1960, the AFL was stunned early that year when Minneapolis withdrew to accept an offer to join the NFL as an expansion team in 1961. The new league responded by choosing Oakland to replace Minneapolis and inherit the departed team's draft picks. Since no AFL team actually played in Minneapolis, it is not considered the original home of the Oakland Raiders.

In 1966, the NFL and AFL agreed to a merger that resulted in the first Super Bowl (originally called the AFL-NFL World Championship Game) following the '66 league playoffs. In 1970, the now 10-member AFL officially joined the NFL, forming a 26-team league made up of two conferences of three divisions each. In 2002, the 32-team league was realigned into two conferences of four divisions each.

Expansion/Merger Timetable

For teams currently in NFL.

1921–Green Bay Packers; **1925**–New York Giants; **1930**–Portsmouth-OH Spartans (now Detroit Lions); **1932**–Boston Braves (now Washington Redskins); **1933**–Philadelphia Eagles and Pittsburgh Pirates (now Steelers); **1937**–Cleveland Rams (now St. Louis); **1950**–added AAFC's Cleveland Browns and San Francisco 49ers; **1953**–Baltimore Colts (now Indianapolis).

1960–Dallas Cowboys; **1961**–Minnesota Vikings; **1966**–Atlanta Falcons; **1967**–New Orleans Saints; **1970**–added AFL's Boston Patriots (now New England), Buffalo Bills, Cincinnati Bengals (1968 expansion team), Denver Broncos, Houston Oilers (now Tennessee Titans), Kansas City Chiefs, Miami Dolphins (1966 expansion team), New York Jets, Oakland Raiders and San Diego Chargers (the AFL-NFL merger divided the league into two 13-team conferences with old-line NFL clubs Baltimore, Cleveland and Pittsburgh moving to the AFC); **1976**–Seattle Seahawks and Tampa Bay Buccaneers (Seattle was originally in the NFC West and Tampa Bay in the AFC West, but were switched to AFC West and NFC Central, respectively, in 1977); **1995**–Carolina Panthers and Jacksonville Jaguars; **1996**—Cleveland Browns move to Baltimore and become Ravens. City of Cleveland retains rights to team name, colors and all memorabilia; **1999**–Cleveland Browns return to the NFL. **2002**–Houston Texans. Seattle moves back to the NFC West.

City and Nickname Changes

1921—Decatur Staleys move to Chicago; **1922**—Chicago Staleys renamed Bears; **1933**—Boston Braves renamed Redskins; **1937**—Boston Redskins move to Washington; **1934**—Portsmouth (Ohio) Spartans move to Detroit and become Lions; **1941**—Pittsburgh Pirates renamed Steelers; **1943**—Philadelphia and Pittsburgh merge for one season and become Phil-Pitt, or the "Steagles"; **1944**—Chicago Cardinals and Pittsburgh merge for one season and become Card-Pitt; **1946**—Cleveland Rams move to Los Angeles.

1960—Chicago Cardinals move to St. Louis; **1961**—Los Angeles Chargers (AFL) move to San Diego; **1963**—New York Titans (AFL) renamed Jets and Dallas Texans (AFL) move to Kansas City and become Chiefs; **1971**—Boston Patriots become New England Patriots; **1982**—Oakland Raiders move to Los Angeles; **1984**—Baltimore Colts move to Indianapolis; **1988**—St. Louis Cardinals move to Phoenix; **1994**—Phoenix Cardinals become Arizona Cardinals; **1995**—L.A. Rams move to St. Louis and L.A. Raiders move back to Oakland; **1996**—Cleveland Browns move to Baltimore and become Ravens. City of Cleveland retains rights to team name, colors and all memorabilia; **1997**—Houston Oilers move to Memphis and become Tennessee Oilers; **1998**—Tennessee Oilers move to Nashville; **1999**—Tennessee Oilers renamed Titans.

Defunct NFL Teams

Teams that once played in the APFA and NFL, but no longer exist.

Akron-OH–Pros (1920-25) and Indians (1926); **Baltimore**–Colts (1950); **Boston**–Bulldogs (1926) and Yanks (1944-48); **Brooklyn**–Lions (1926), Dodgers (1930-43) and Tigers (1944); **Buffalo**–All-Americans (1920-23), Bisons (1924-25), Rangers (1926), Bisons (1927,1929); **Canton-OH**–Bulldogs (1920-23,1925-26); **Chicago**–Tigers (1920); **Cincinnati**–Celts (1921) and Reds (1933-34); **Cleveland**–Tigers (1920), Indians (1921), Indians (1923), Bulldogs (1924-25,1927) and Indians (1931); **Columbus-OH**–Panhandles (1920-22) and Tigers (1923-26); **Dallas**–Texans (1952); **Dayton-OH**–Triangles (1920-29).

Detroit–Heralds (1920-21), Panthers (1925-26) and Wolverines (1928); **Duluth-MN**–Kelleys (1923-25) and Eskimos (1926-27); **Evansville-IN**–Crimson Giants (1921-22); **Frankford-PA**–Yellow Jackets (1924-31); **Hammond-IN**–Pros (1920-26); **Hartford**–Blues (1926); **Kansas City**–Blues (1924) and Cowboys (1925-26); **Kenosha-WI**–Maroons (1924); **Los Angeles**–Buccaneers (1926); **Louisville**–Brecks (1921-23) and Colonels (1926); **Marion-OH**–Oorang Indians (1922-23); **Milwaukee**–Badgers (1922-26); **Minneapolis**–Marines (1922-24) and Red Jackets (1929-30); **Muncie-IN**–Flyers (1920-21).

New York–Giants (1921), Yankees (1927-28), Bulldogs (1949) and Yankees (1950-51); **Newark-NJ**–Tornadoes (1930); **Orange-NJ**–Tornadoes (1929); **Pottsville-PA**–Maroons (1925-28); **Providence-RI**–Steam Roller (1925-31); **Racine-WI**–Legion (1922-24) and Tornadoes (1926); **Rochester-NY**–Jeffersons (1920-25); **Rock Island-IL**–Independents (1920-26); **Staten Island-NY**–Stapletons (1929-32); **St. Louis**–All-Stars (1923) and Gunners (1934); **Toledo-OH**–Maroons (1922-23); **Tonawanda-NY**–Kardex (1921), also called Lumbermen; **Washington**–Senators (1921).

Annual NFL Leaders

Individual leaders in NFL (1932-69), NFC (since 1970), AFL (1960-69) and AFC (since 1970).

Passing

Since 1932, the NFL has used several formulas to determine passing leadership, from Total Yards alone (1932-37), to the current rating system—adopted in 1973—that takes Completions, Completion Percentage, Yards Gained, TD Passes, Interceptions, Interception Percentage and other factors into account. The quarterbacks listed below all led the league according to the system in use at the time.

NFL-NFC

Multiple winners: Sammy Baugh and Steve Young (6); Joe Montana and Roger Staubach (5); Arnie Herber, Sonny Jurgensen, Bart Starr and Norm Van Brocklin (3); Daunte Culpepper, Ed Danowski, Otto Graham, Cecil Isbell, Milt Plum, Kurt Warner and Bob Waterfield (2).

Year		Att	Cmp	Yds	TD	Year		Att	Cmp	Yds	TD
1932	Arnie Herber, GB	101	37	639	9	1969	Sonny Jurgensen, Wash	442	274	3102	22
1933	Harry Newman, NY	136	53	973	11	1970	John Brodie, SF	378	223	2941	24
1934	Arnie Herber, GB	115	42	799	8	1971	Roger Staubach, Dal	211	126	1882	15
1935	Ed Danowski, NY	113	57	794	10	1972	Norm Snead, NY	325	196	2307	17
1936	Arnie Herber, GB	173	77	1239	11	1973	Roger Staubach, Dal	286	179	2428	23
1937	Sammy Baugh, Wash	171	81	1127	8	1974	Sonny Jurgensen, Wash	167	107	1185	11
1938	Ed Danowski, NY	129	70	848	7	1975	Fran Tarkenton, Min	425	273	2994	25
1939	Parker Hall, Cle. Rams	208	106	1227	9	1976	James Harris, LA	158	91	1460	8
1940	Sammy Baugh, Wash	177	111	1367	12	1977	Roger Staubach, Dal	361	210	2620	18
1941	Cecil Isbell, GB	206	117	1479	15	1978	Roger Staubach, Dal	413	231	3190	25
1942	Cecil Isbell, GB	268	146	2021	24	1979	Roger Staubach, Dal	461	267	3586	27
1943	Sammy Baugh, Wash	239	133	1754	23	1980	Ron Jaworski, Phi	451	257	3529	27
1944	Frank Filchock, Wash	147	84	1139	13	1981	Joe Montana, SF	488	311	3565	19
1945	Sammy Baugh, Wash	182	128	1669	11	1982	Joe Theismann, Wash	252	161	2033	13
	& Sid Luckman, Chi. Bears	217	117	1725	14	1983	Steve Bartkowski, Atl	432	274	3167	22
1946	Bob Waterfield, LA	251	127	1747	18	1984	Joe Montana, SF	432	279	3630	28
1947	Sammy Baugh, Wash	354	210	2938	25	1985	Joe Montana, SF	494	303	3653	27
1948	Tommy Thompson, Phi	246	141	1965	25	1986	Tommy Kramer, Min	372	208	3000	24
1949	Sammy Baugh, Wash	255	145	1903	18	1987	Joe Montana, SF	398	266	3054	31
1950	Norm Van Brocklin, LA	233	127	2061	18	1988	Wade Wilson, Min	332	204	2746	15
1951	Bob Waterfield, LA	176	88	1566	13	1989	Don Majkowski, GB	599	353	4318	27
1952	Norm Van Brocklin, LA	205	113	1736	14	1990	Joe Montana, SF	520	321	3944	26
1953	Otto Graham, Cle	258	167	2722	11	1991	Steve Young, SF	279	180	2517	17
1954	Norm Van Brocklin, LA	260	139	2637	13	1992	Steve Young, SF	402	268	3465	25
1955	Otto Graham, Cle	185	98	1721	15	1993	Steve Young, SF	462	314	4023	29
1956	Ed Brown, Chi. Bears	168	96	1667	11	1994	Steve Young, SF	461	324	3969	35
1957	Tommy O'Connell, Cle	110	63	1229	9	1995	Brett Favre, GB	570	359	4413	38
1958	Eddie LeBaron, Wash	145	79	1365	11	1996	Steve Young, SF	316	214	2410	14
1959	Charlie Conerly, NY	194	113	1706	14	1997	Steve Young, SF	356	241	3029	19
1960	Milt Plum, Cle	250	151	2297	21	1998	Randall Cunningham, Min	425	259	3704	34
1961	Milt Plum, Cle	302	177	2416	16	1999	Kurt Warner, St.L	499	325	4353	41
1962	Bart Starr, GB	285	178	2438	12	2000	Trent Green, St.L	240	145	2063	16
1963	Y.A. Tittle, NY	367	221	3145	36	2001	Kurt Warner, St.L	546	375	4830	36
1964	Bart Starr, GB	272	163	2144	15	2002	Brad Johnson, TB	451	281	3049	22
1965	Rudy Bukich, Chi	312	176	2641	20	2003	Daunte Culpepper, Min	454	295	3479	25
1966	Bart Starr, GB	251	156	2257	14	2004	Daunte Culpepper, Min	548	379	4717	39
1967	Sonny Jurgensen, Wash	508	288	3747	31	2005	Matt Hasselbeck, Sea	449	294	3459	24
1968	Earl Morrall, Bal	317	182	2909	26	2006	Drew Brees, NO	554	356	4418	26

AFL-AFC

Multiple winners: Dan Marino (5); Ken Anderson, Len Dawson and Peyton Manning (4); Bob Griese, Daryle Lamonica, Warren Moon and Ken Stabler (2).

Year		Att	Cmp	Yds	TD	Year		Att	Cmp	Yds	TD
1960	Jack Kemp, LA	406	211	3018	20	1984	Dan Marino, Mia	564	362	5084	48
1961	George Blanda, Hou	362	187	3330	36	1985	Ken O'Brien, NY	488	297	3888	25
1962	Len Dawson, Dal	310	189	2759	29	1986	Dan Marino, Mia	623	378	4746	44
1963	Tobin Rote, SD	286	170	2510	20	1987	Bernie Kosar, Cle	389	241	3033	22
1964	Len Dawson, KC	354	199	2879	30	1988	Boomer Esiason, Cin	388	223	3572	28
1965	John Hadl, SD	348	174	2798	20	1989	Dan Marino, Mia	550	308	3997	24
1966	Len Dawson, KC	284	159	2527	26	1990	Warren Moon, Hou	584	362	4689	33
1967	Daryle Lamonica, Oak	425	220	3228	30	1991	Jim Kelly, Buf	474	304	3844	33
1968	Len Dawson, KC	224	131	2109	17	1992	Warren Moon, Hou	346	224	2521	18
1969	Greg Cook, Cin	197	106	1854	15	1993	John Elway, Den	551	348	4030	25
1970	Daryle Lamonica, Oak	356	179	2516	22	1994	Dan Marino, Mia	615	385	4453	30
1971	Bob Griese, Mia	263	145	2089	19	1995	Jim Harbaugh, Ind	314	200	2575	17
1972	Earl Morrall, Mia	150	83	1360	11	1996	John Elway, Den	466	287	3328	26
1973	Ken Stabler, Oak	260	163	1997	14	1997	Mark Brunell, Jax	435	264	3281	18
1974	Ken Anderson, Cin	328	213	2667	18	1998	Vinny Testaverde, NYJ	421	259	3256	29
1975	Ken Anderson, Cin	377	228	3169	21	1999	Peyton Manning, Ind	533	331	4135	26
1976	Ken Stabler, Oak	291	194	2737	27	2000	Brian Griese, Den	336	216	2688	19
1977	Bob Griese, Mia	307	180	2252	22	2001	Rich Gannon, Oak	549	361	3828	27
1978	Terry Bradshaw, Pit	368	207	2915	28	2002	Chad Pennington, NYJ	399	275	3120	22
1979	Dan Fouts, SD	530	332	4082	24	2003	Steve McNair, Ten	400	250	3215	24
1980	Brian Sipe, Cle	554	337	4132	30	2004	Peyton Manning, Ind	497	336	4557	49
1981	Ken Anderson, Cin	479	300	3753	29	2005	Peyton Manning, Ind	453	305	3747	28
1982	Ken Anderson, Cin	309	218	2495	12	2006	Peyton Manning, Ind	557	362	4397	31
1983	Dan Marino, Mia	296	173	2210	20						

Receptions

NFL-NFC

Multiple winners: Don Hutson (8); Raymond Berry, Tom Fears, Pete Pihos, Jerry Rice, Sterling Sharpe and Billy Wilson (3); Dwight Clark, Torry Holt, Herman Moore, Muhsin Muhammad, Ahmad Rashad and Charley Taylor (2).

Year	Player	No	Yds	Avg	TD	Year	Player	No	Yds	Avg	TD
1932	Ray Flaherty, NY	21	350	16.7	3	1970	Dick Gordon, Chi	71	1026	14.5	13
1933	Shipwreck Kelly, Bklyn	22	246	11.2	3	1971	Bob Tucker, NY	59	791	13.4	4
1934	Joe Carter, Phi	16	238	14.9	4	1972	Harold Jackson, Phi	62	1048	16.9	4
	& Red Badgro, NY	16	206	12.9	1	1973	Harold Carmichael, Phi	67	1116	16.7	9
1935	Tod Goodwin, NY	26	432	16.6	4	1974	Charles Young, Phi	63	696	11.0	3
1936	Don Hutson, GB	34	536	15.8	8	1975	Chuck Foreman, Min	73	691	9.5	9
1937	Don Hutson, GB	41	552	13.5	7	1976	Drew Pearson, Dal	58	806	13.9	6
1938	Gaynell Tinsley, Chi. Cards	41	516	12.6	1	1977	Ahmad Rashad, Min	51	681	13.4	2
1939	Don Hutson, GB	34	846	24.9	6	1978	Rickey Young, Min	88	704	8.0	5
1940	Don Looney, Phi	58	707	12.2	4	1979	Ahmad Rashad, Min	80	1156	14.5	9
1941	Don Hutson, GB	58	739	12.7	10	1980	Earl Cooper, SF	83	567	6.8	4
1942	Don Hutson, GB	74	1211	16.4	17	1981	Dwight Clark, SF	85	1105	13.0	4
1943	Don Hutson, GB	47	776	16.5	11	1982	Dwight Clark, SF	60	913	12.2	5
1944	Don Hutson, GB	58	866	14.9	9	1983	Roy Green, St.L	78	1227	15.7	14
1945	Don Hutson, GB	47	834	17.7	9		Charlie Brown, Wash	78	1225	15.7	8
1946	Jim Benton, LA	63	981	15.6	6		& Earnest Gray, NY	78	1139	14.6	5
1947	Jim Keane, Chi. Bears	64	910	14.2	10	1984	Art Monk, Wash	106	1372	12.9	7
1948	Tom Fears, LA	51	698	13.7	4	1985	Roger Craig, SF	92	1016	11.0	6
1949	Tom Fears, LA	77	1013	13.2	9	1986	Jerry Rice, SF	86	1570	18.3	15
1950	Tom Fears, LA	84	1116	13.3	7	1987	J.T. Smith, St.L	91	1117	12.3	8
1951	Elroy Hirsch, LA	66	1495	22.7	17	1988	Henry Ellard, LA	86	1414	16.4	10
1952	Mac Speedie, Cle	62	911	14.7	5	1989	Sterling Sharpe, GB	90	1423	15.8	12
1953	Pete Pihos, Phi	63	1049	16.7	10	1990	Jerry Rice, SF	100	1502	15.0	13
1954	Pete Pihos, Phi	60	872	14.5	10	1991	Michael Irvin, Dal	93	1523	16.4	8
	& Billy Wilson, SF	60	830	13.8	5	1992	Sterling Sharpe, GB	108	1461	13.5	13
1955	Pete Pihos, Phi	62	864	13.9	7	1993	Sterling Sharpe, GB	112	1274	11.4	11
1956	Billy Wilson, SF	60	889	14.8	5	1994	Cris Carter, Min	122	1256	10.3	7
1957	Billy Wilson, SF	52	757	14.6	6	1995	Herman Moore, Det	123	1686	13.7	14
1958	Raymond Berry, Bal	56	794	14.2	9	1996	Jerry Rice, SF	108	1254	11.6	8
	& Pete Retzlaff, Phi	56	766	13.7	2	1997	Herman Moore, Det	104	1293	12.4	8
1959	Raymond Berry, Bal	66	959	14.5	14	1998	Frank Sanders, Ari	89	1145	12.9	3
1960	Raymond Berry, Bal	74	1298	17.5	10	1999	Muhsin Muhammad, Car	96	1253	13.1	8
1961	Red Phillips, LA	78	1092	14.0	5	2000	Muhsin Muhammad, Car	102	1183	11.6	6
1962	Bobby Mitchell, Wash	72	1384	19.2	11	2001	Keyshawn Johnson, TB	106	1266	11.9	1
1963	Bobby Joe Conrad, St.L	73	967	13.2	10	2002	Randy Moss, Min	106	1347	12.7	7
1964	Johnny Morris, Chi. Bears	93	1200	12.9	10	2003	Torry Holt, St.L	117	1696	14.5	12
1965	Dave Parks, SF	80	1344	16.8	12	2004	Joe Horn, NO	94	1399	14.9	11
1966	Charley Taylor, Wash	72	1119	15.5	12		& Torry Holt, St.L	94	1372	14.6	10
1967	Charley Taylor, Wash	70	990	14.1	9	2005	Steve Smith, Car	103	1563	15.2	12
1968	Clifton McNeil, SF	71	994	14.0	7		& Larry Fitzgerald, Ari	103	1409	13.7	10
1969	Dan Abramowicz, NO	73	1015	13.9	7	2006	Mike Furrey, Det	98	1086	11.1	6

AFL-AFC

Multiple winners: Lionel Taylor (5); Lance Alworth, Haywood Jeffires, Lydell Mitchell and Kellen Winslow (3); Fred Biletnikoff, Todd Christensen, Marvin Harrison, Carl Pickens and Al Toon (2).

Year	Player	No	Yds	Avg	TD	Year	Player	No	Yds	Avg	TD
1960	Lionel Taylor, Den	92	1235	13.4	12	1984	Ozzie Newsome, Cle	89	1001	11.2	5
1961	Lionel Taylor, Den	100	1176	11.8	4	1985	Lionel James, SD	86	1027	11.9	6
1962	Lionel Taylor, Den	77	908	11.8	4	1986	Todd Christensen, LA	95	1153	12.1	8
1963	Lionel Taylor, Den	78	1101	14.1	10	1987	Al Toon, NY	68	976	14.4	5
1964	Charley Hennigan, Hou	101	1546	15.3	8	1988	Al Toon, NY	93	1067	11.5	5
1965	Lionel Taylor, Den	85	1131	13.3	6	1989	Andre Reed, Buf	88	1312	14.9	9
1966	Lance Alworth, SD	73	1383	18.9	13	1990	Haywood Jeffires, Hou	74	1048	14.2	8
1967	George Sauer, NY	75	1189	15.9	6		& Drew Hill, Hou	74	1019	13.8	5
1968	Lance Alworth, SD	68	1312	19.3	10	1991	Haywood Jeffires, Hou	100	1181	11.8	7
1969	Lance Alworth, SD	64	1003	15.7	4	1992	Haywood Jeffires, Hou	90	913	10.1	9
1970	Marlin Briscoe, Buf	57	1036	18.2	8	1993	Reggie Langhorne, Ind	85	1038	12.2	3
1971	Fred Biletnikoff, Oak	61	929	15.2	9	1994	Ben Coates, NE	96	1174	12.2	7
1972	Fred Biletnikoff, Oak	58	802	13.8	7	1995	Carl Pickens, Cin	99	1234	12.5	17
1973	Fred Willis, Hou	57	371	6.5	1	1996	Carl Pickens, Cin	100	1180	11.8	12
1974	Lydell Mitchell, Bal	72	544	7.6	2	1997	Tim Brown, Oak	104	1408	13.5	5
1975	Reggie Rucker, Cle	60	770	12.8	3	1998	O.J. McDuffie, Mia	90	1050	11.7	7
	& Lydell Mitchell, Bal	60	544	9.1	4	1999	Jimmy Smith, Jax	116	1636	14.1	6
1976	MacArthur Lane, KC	66	686	10.4	1	2000	Marvin Harrison, Ind	102	1413	13.9	14
1977	Lydell Mitchell, Bal	71	620	8.7	4	2001	Rod Smith, Den	113	1343	11.9	11
1978	Steve Largent, Sea	71	1168	16.5	8	2002	Marvin Harrison, Ind	143	1722	12.0	11
1979	Joe Washington, Bal	82	750	9.1	3	2003	LaDainian Tomlinson, SD	100	725	7.3	4
1980	Kellen Winslow, SD	89	1290	14.5	9	2004	Tony Gonzalez, KC	102	1258	12.3	7
1981	Kellen Winslow, SD	88	1075	12.2	10	2005	Chad Johnson, Cin	97	1432	14.8	9
1982	Kellen Winslow, SD	54	721	13.4	6	2006	Andre Johnson, Hou	103	1147	11.1	5
1983	Todd Christensen, LA	92	1247	13.6	12						

Rushing

NFL-NFC

Multiple winners: Jim Brown (8); Walter Payton and Barry Sanders (5); Emmitt Smith and Steve Van Buren (4); Eric Dickerson (3); Shaun Alexander, Cliff Battles, John Brockington, Larry Brown, Bill Dudley, Leroy Kelly, Bill Paschal, Joe Perry, Gale Sayers, Stephen Davis and Whizzer White (2).

Year		Car	Yds	Avg	TD	Year		Car	Yds	Avg	TD
1932	Cliff Battles, Bos	148	576	3.9	3	1970	Larry Brown, Wash	237	1125	4.7	5
1933	Jim Musick, Bos	173	809	4.7	5	1971	John Brockington, GB	216	1105	5.1	4
1934	Beattie Feathers, Chi. Bears	119	1004	8.4	8	1972	Larry Brown, Wash	285	1216	4.3	8
1935	Doug Russell, Chi. Cards	140	499	3.6	0	1973	John Brockington, GB	265	1144	4.3	3
1936	Tuffy Leemans, NY	206	830	4.0	2	1974	Lawrence McCutcheon, LA	236	1109	4.7	3
1937	Cliff Battles, Wash	216	874	4.0	5	1975	Jim Otis, St.L	269	1076	4.0	5
1938	Whizzer White, Pit	152	567	3.7	4	1976	Walter Payton, Chi	311	1390	4.5	13
1939	Bill Osmanski, Chi. Bears	121	699	5.8	7	1977	Walter Payton, Chi	339	1852	5.5	14
1940	Whizzer White, Det	146	514	3.5	5	1978	Walter Payton, Chi	333	1395	4.2	11
1941	Pug Manders, Bklyn	111	486	4.4	5	1979	Walter Payton, Chi	369	1610	4.4	14
1942	Bill Dudley, Pit	162	696	4.3	5	1980	Walter Payton, Chi	317	1460	4.6	6
1943	Bill Paschal, NY	147	572	3.9	10	1981	George Rogers, NO	378	1674	4.4	13
1944	Bill Paschal, NY	196	737	3.8	9	1982	Tony Dorsett, Dal	177	745	4.2	5
1945	Steve Van Buren, Phi	143	832	5.8	15	1983	Eric Dickerson, LA	390	1808	4.6	18
1946	Bill Dudley, Pit	146	604	4.1	3	1984	Eric Dickerson, LA	379	2105	5.6	14
1947	Steve Van Buren, Phi	217	1008	4.6	13	1985	Gerald Riggs, Atl	397	1719	4.3	10
1948	Steve Van Buren, Phi	201	945	4.7	10	1986	Eric Dickerson, LA	404	1821	4.5	11
1949	Steve Van Buren, Phi	263	1146	4.4	11	1987	Charles White, LA	324	1374	4.2	11
1950	Marion Motley, Cle	140	810	5.8	3	1988	Herschel Walker, Dal	361	1514	4.2	5
1951	Eddie Price, NY Giants	271	971	3.6	7	1989	Barry Sanders, Det	280	1470	5.3	14
1952	Dan Towler, LA	156	894	5.7	10	1990	Barry Sanders, Det	255	1304	5.1	13
1953	Joe Perry, SF	192	1018	5.3	10	1991	Emmitt Smith, Dal	365	1563	4.3	12
1954	Joe Perry, SF	173	1049	6.1	8	1992	Emmitt Smith, Dal	373	1713	4.6	18
1955	Alan Ameche, Bal	213	961	4.5	9	1993	Emmitt Smith, Dal	283	1486	5.3	9
1956	Rick Casares, Chi. Bears	234	1126	4.8	12	1994	Barry Sanders, Det	331	1883	5.7	7
1957	Jim Brown, Cle	202	942	4.7	9	1995	Emmitt Smith, Dal	377	1773	4.7	25
1958	Jim Brown, Cle	257	1527	5.9	17	1996	Barry Sanders, Det	307	1553	5.1	11
1959	Jim Brown, Cle	290	1329	4.6	14	1997	Barry Sanders, Det	335	2053	6.1	11
1960	Jim Brown, Cle	215	1257	5.8	9	1998	Jamal Anderson, Atl	410	1846	4.5	14
1961	Jim Brown, Cle	305	1408	4.6	8	1999	Stephen Davis, Wash	290	1405	4.8	17
1962	Jim Taylor, GB	272	1474	5.4	19	2000	Robert Smith, Min	295	1521	5.2	7
1963	Jim Brown, Cle	291	1863	6.4	12	2001	Stephen Davis, Wash	356	1432	4.0	5
1964	Jim Brown, Cle	280	1446	5.2	7	2002	Deuce McAllister, NO	325	1388	4.3	13
1965	Jim Brown, Cle	289	1544	5.3	17	2003	Ahman Green, GB	355	1883	5.3	15
1966	Gale Sayers, Chi	229	1231	5.4	8	2004	Shaun Alexander, Sea	353	1696	4.8	16
1967	Leroy Kelly, Cle	235	1205	5.1	11	2005	Shaun Alexander, Sea	370	1880	5.1	27
1968	Leroy Kelly, Cle	248	1239	5.0	16	2006	Frank Gore, SF	312	1695	5.4	8
1969	Gale Sayers, Chi	236	1032	4.4	8						

AFL-AFC

Multiple winners: Earl Campbell and O.J. Simpson (4); Terrell Davis and Thurman Thomas (3); Eric Dickerson, Cookie Gilchrist, Edgerrin James, Floyd Little, Curtis Martin, Jim Nance and Curt Warner (2).

Year		Car	Yds	Avg	TD	Year		Car	Yds	Avg	TD
1960	Abner Haynes, Dal	157	875	5.6	9	1984	Earnest Jackson, SD	296	1179	4.0	8
1961	Billy Cannon, Hou	200	948	4.7	6	1985	Marcus Allen, LA	380	1759	4.6	11
1962	Cookie Gilchrist, Buf	214	1096	5.1	13	1986	Curt Warner, Sea	319	1481	4.6	13
1963	Clem Daniels, Oak	215	1099	5.1	3	1987	Eric Dickerson, Ind	223	1011	4.5	5
1964	Cookie Gilchrist, Buf	230	981	4.3	6	1988	Eric Dickerson, Ind	388	1659	4.3	14
1965	Paul Lowe, SD	222	1121	5.0	7	1989	Christian Okoye, KC	370	1480	4.0	12
1966	Jim Nance, Bos	299	1458	4.9	11	1990	Thurman Thomas, Buf	271	1297	4.8	11
1967	Jim Nance, Bos	269	1216	4.5	7	1991	Thurman Thomas, Buf	288	1407	4.9	7
1968	Paul Robinson, Cin	238	1023	4.3	8	1992	Barry Foster, Pit	390	1690	4.3	11
1969	Dickie Post, SD	182	873	4.8	6	1993	Thurman Thomas, Buf	355	1315	3.7	6
1970	Floyd Little, Den	209	901	4.3	3	1994	Chris Warren, Sea	333	1545	4.6	9
1971	Floyd Little, Den	284	1133	4.0	6	1995	Curtis Martin, NE	368	1487	4.0	14
1972	O.J. Simpson, Buf	292	1251	4.3	6	1996	Terrell Davis, Den	345	1538	4.5	13
1973	O.J. Simpson, Buf	332	2003	6.0	12	1997	Terrell Davis, Den	369	1750	4.7	15
1974	Otis Armstrong, Den	263	1407	5.3	9	1998	Terrell Davis, Den	392	2008	5.1	21
1975	O.J. Simpson, Buf	329	1817	5.5	16	1999	Edgerrin James, Ind	369	1553	4.2	13
1976	O.J. Simpson, Buf	290	1503	5.2	8	2000	Edgerrin James, Ind	387	1709	4.4	13
1977	Mark van Eeghen, Oak	324	1273	3.9	7	2001	Priest Holmes, KC	327	1555	4.8	8
1978	Earl Campbell, Hou	302	1450	4.8	13	2002	Ricky Williams, Mia	383	1853	4.8	16
1979	Earl Campbell, Hou	368	1697	4.6	19	2003	Jamal Lewis, Bal	387	2066	5.3	14
1980	Earl Campbell, Hou	373	1934	5.2	13	2004	Curtis Martin, NYJ	371	1697	4.6	12
1981	Earl Campbell, Hou	361	1376	3.8	10	2005	Larry Johnson, KC	336	1750	5.2	20
1982	Freeman McNeil, NY	151	786	5.2	6	2006	LaDainian Tomlinson, SD	348	1815	5.2	28
1983	Curt Warner, Sea	335	1449	4.3	13						

Note: Eric Dickerson was traded to Indianapolis from the NFC's LA Rams during the 1987 season. In three games with the Rams, he carried the ball 60 times for 277 yds, a 4.6 avg and 1 TD. His official AFC statistics above came in nine games with the Colts.

Scoring

NFL-NFC

Multiple winners: Don Hutson (5); Dutch Clark, Pat Harder, Paul Hornung, Chip Lohmiller and Mark Moseley (3); Kevin Butler, Mike Cofer, Fred Cox, Marshall Faulk, Jack Manders, Chester Marcol, Eddie Murray, Emmitt Smith, Gordy Soltau, Jeff Wilkins and Doak Walker (2).

Year		TD	FG	PAT	Pts	Year		TD	FG	PAT	Pts
1932	Dutch Clark, Portsmouth	6	3	10	55	1970	Fred Cox, Min	0	30	35	125
1933	Glenn Presnell, Portsmouth	6	6	10	64	1971	Curt Knight, Wash	0	29	27	114
	& Ken Strong, NY	6	5	13	64	1972	Chester Marcol, GB	0	33	29	128
1934	Jack Manders, Chi. Bears	3	10	31	79	1973	David Ray, LA	0	30	40	130
1935	Dutch Clark, Det	6	1	16	55	1974	Chester Marcol, GB	0	25	19	94
1936	Dutch Clark, Det	7	4	19	73	1975	Chuck Foreman, Min	22	0	0	132
1937	Jack Manders, Chi. Bears	5	8	15	69	1976	Mark Moseley, Wash	0	22	31	97
1938	Clarke Hinkle, GB	7	3	7	58	1977	Walter Payton, Chi	16	0	0	96
1939	Andy Farkas, Wash	11	0	2	68	1978	Frank Corral, LA	0	29	31	118
1940	Don Hutson, GB	7	0	15	57	1979	Mark Moseley, Wash	0	25	39	114
1941	Don Hutson, GB	12	1	20	95	1980	Eddie Murray, Det	0	27	35	116
1942	Don Hutson, GB	17	1	33	138	1981	Rafael Septien, Dal	0	27	40	121
1943	Don Hutson, GB	12	3	26	117		& Eddie Murray, Det	0	25	46	121
1944	Don Hutson, GB	9	0	31	85	1982	Wendell Tyler, LA	13	0	0	78
1945	Steve Van Buren, Phi	18	0	2	110	1983	Mark Moseley, Wash	0	33	62	161
1946	Ted Fritsch, GB	10	9	13	100	1984	Ray Wersching, SF	0	25	56	131
1947	Pat Harder, Chi. Cards	7	7	39	102	1985	Kevin Butler, Chi	0	31	51	144
1948	Pat Harder, Chi. Cards	7	7	53	110	1986	Kevin Butler, Chi	0	28	36	120
1949	Gene Roberts, NY Giants	17	0	0	102	1987	Jerry Rice, SF	23	0	0	138
	& Pat Harder, Chi. Cards	8	3	45	102	1988	Mike Cofer, SF	0	27	40	121
1950	Doak Walker, Det	11	8	38	128	1989	Mike Cofer, SF	0	29	49	136
1951	Elroy Hirsch, LA	17	0	0	102	1990	Chip Lohmiller, Wash	0	30	41	131
1952	Gordy Soltau, SF	7	6	34	94	1991	Chip Lohmiller, Wash	0	31	56	149
1953	Gordy Soltau, SF	6	10	48	114	1992	Chip Lohmiller, Wash	0	30	30	120
1954	Bobby Walston, Phi	11	4	36	114		& Morten Andersen, NO	0	29	33	120
1955	Doak Walker, Det	7	9	27	96	1993	Jason Hanson, Det	0	34	28	130
1956	Bobby Layne, Det	5	12	33	99	1994	Emmitt Smith, Dal	22	0	0	132
1957	Sam Baker, Wash	1	14	29	77		& Fuad Reveiz, Min	0	34	30	132
	& Lou Groza, Cle	0	15	32	77	1995	Emmitt Smith, Dal	25	0	0	150
1958	Jim Brown, Cle	18	0	0	108	1996	John Kasay, Car.	0	37	34	145
1959	Paul Hornung, GB	7	7	31	94	1997	Richie Cunningham, Dal	0	34	24	126
1960	Paul Hornung, GB	15	15	41	176	1998	Gary Anderson, Min	0	35	59	164
1961	Paul Hornung, GB	10	15	41	146	1999	Jeff Wilkins, St.L	0	20	64	124
1962	Jim Taylor, GB	19	0	0	114	2000	Marshall Faulk, St.L	26	0	4	160
1963	Don Chandler, NY	0	18	52	106	2001	Marshall Faulk, St.L	21	0	2	128
1964	Lenny Moore, Bal	20	0	0	120	2002	Jay Feely, Atl	0	32	42	138
1965	Gale Sayers, Chi	22	0	0	132	2003	Jeff Wilkins, St.L	0	39	46	163
1966	Bruce Gossett, LA	0	28	29	113	2004	David Akers, Phi	0	27	41	122
1967	Jim Bakken, St.L	0	27	36	117	2005	Shaun Alexander, Sea	28	0	0	168
1968	Leroy Kelly, Cle	20	0	0	120	2006	Robbie Gould, Chi	0	32	47	143
1969	Fred Cox, Min	0	26	43	121						

AFL-AFC

Multiple winners: Gino Cappelletti (5); Gary Anderson (3); Jim Breech, Roy Gerela, Priest Holmes, Gene Mingo, Nick Lowery, John Smith, Pete Stoyanovich, Jim Turner and Mike Vanderjagt (2).

Year		TD	FG	PAT	Pts	Year		TD	FG	PAT	Pts
1960	Gene Mingo, Den	6	18	33	123	1983	Gary Anderson, Pit	0	27	38	119
1961	Gino Cappelletti, Bos	8	17	48	147	1984	Gary Anderson, Pit	0	24	45	117
1962	Gene Mingo, Den	4	27	32	137	1985	Gary Anderson, Pit	0	33	40	139
1963	Gino Cappelletti, Bos	2	22	35	113	1986	Tony Franklin, NE	0	32	44	140
1964	Gino Cappelletti, Bos	7	25	36	155	1987	Jim Breech, Cin	0	24	25	97
1965	Gino Cappelletti, Bos	9	17	27	132	1988	Scott Norwood, Buf	0	32	33	129
1966	Gino Cappelletti, Bos	6	16	35	119	1989	David Treadwell, Den	0	27	39	120
1967	George Blanda, Oak	0	20	56	116	1990	Nick Lowery, KC	0	34	37	139
1968	Jim Turner, NY	0	34	43	145	1991	Pete Stoyanovich, Mia	0	31	28	121
1969	Jim Turner, NY	0	32	33	129	1992	Pete Stoyanovich, Mia	0	30	34	124
1970	Jan Stenerud, KC	0	30	26	116	1993	Jeff Jaeger, LA	0	35	27	132
1971	Garo Yepremian, Mia	0	28	33	117	1994	John Carney, SD	0	34	33	135
1972	Bobby Howfield, NY	0	27	40	121	1995	Norm Johnson, Pit	0	34	39	141
1973	Roy Gerela, Pit	0	29	36	123	1996	Cary Blanchard, Ind	0	36	27	135
1974	Roy Gerela, Pit	0	20	33	93	1997	Mike Hollis, Jax	0	31	41	134
1975	O.J. Simpson, Buf	23	0	0	138	1998	Steve Christie, Buf	0	33	41	140
1976	Toni Linhart, Bal	0	20	49	109	1999	Mike Vanderjagt, Ind	0	34	43	145
1977	Errol Mann, Oak	0	20	39	99	2000	Matt Stover, Bal	0	35	30	135
1978	Pat Leahy, NY	0	22	41	107	2001	Mike Vanderjagt, Ind	0	28	41	125
1979	John Smith, NE	0	23	46	115	2002	Priest Holmes, KC	24	0	0	144
1980	John Smith, NE	0	26	51	129	2003	Priest Holmes, KC	27	0	0	162
1981	Nick Lowery, KC	0	26	37	115	2004	Adam Vinatieri, NE	0	31	48	141
	& Jim Breech, Cin	0	22	49	115	2005	Shayne Graham, Cin	0	28	47	131
1982	Marcus Allen, LA	14	0	0	84	2006	LaDainian Tomlinson, SD	31	0	0	186

All-Time NFL Leaders
Through 2006 regular season.

CAREER
Players active in 2006 in **bold** type.

Passing Efficiency

Ratings based on performance standards established for completion percentage, average gain, touchdown percentage and interception percentage. Quarterbacks are allocated points according to how their statistics measure up to those standards. Minimum 1500 passing attempts.

		Yrs	Att	Cmp	Cmp%	Yards	Avg Gain	TD	TD%	Int	Int%	Rating
1	Steve Young	15	4149	2667	64.3	33,124	7.98	232	5.6	107	2.6	96.8
2	**Peyton Manning**	9	4890	3131	64.0	37,586	7.69	275	5.6	139	2.8	94.4
3	Kurt Warner	9	2508	1645	65.6	20,591	8.21	125	5.0	83	3.3	93.8
4	Joe Montana	15	5391	3409	63.2	40,551	7.52	273	5.1	139	2.6	92.3
5	**Marc Bulger**	5	2106	1357	64.4	16,233	7.71	95	4.5	59	2.8	91.3
6	**Daunte Culpepper**	8	2741	1759	64.2	21,091	7.69	137	5.0	89	3.2	90.8
7	**Chad Pennington**	7	1659	1080	65.1	11,973	7.22	72	4.3	46	2.8	89.3
8	**Tom Brady**	7	3064	1896	61.9	21,564	7.04	147	4.8	78	2.5	88.4
9	**Drew Brees**	6	2363	1481	62.7	16,766	7.10	106	4.5	64	2.7	87.5
10	**Trent Green**	9	3527	2143	60.8	26,963	7.64	157	4.5	101	2.9	87.5
11	**Jeff Garcia**	8	2973	1811	60.9	20,385	6.86	136	4.6	73	2.5	86.4
12	Dan Marino	17	8358	4967	59.4	61,361	7.34	420	5.0	252	3.0	86.4
13	**Donovan McNabb**	8	3259	1898	58.2	22,080	6.78	152	4.7	72	2.2	85.2
14	**Matt Hasselbeck**	8	2576	1552	60.3	18,367	7.13	114	4.4	72	2.8	85.1
15	**Brett Favre**	16	8223	5021	61.1	57,500	6.99	414	5.0	273	3.3	85.1
16	Rich Gannon	16	4206	2533	60.2	28,743	6.83	180	4.3	104	2.5	84.7
17	Brian Griese	9	2350	1481	63.0	16,564	7.05	104	4.4	80	3.4	84.5
18	Jim Kelly	11	4779	2874	60.1	35,467	7.42	237	5.0	175	3.7	84.4
19	**Mark Brunell**	13	4594	2738	59.6	31,826	6.93	182	4.0	106	2.3	84.2
20	**Jake Delhomme**	6	1936	1151	59.5	13,965	7.22	92	4.8	63	3.3	84.0
21	Roger Staubach	11	2958	1685	57.0	22,700	7.67	153	5.2	109	3.7	83.4
22	**Steve McNair**	12	4339	2600	59.9	30,191	6.96	172	4.0	115	2.7	83.2
23	**Brad Johnson**	13	4237	2620	61.8	28,548	6.74	164	3.9	117	2.8	83.1
24	Neil Lomax	8	3153	1817	57.6	22,771	7.22	136	4.3	90	2.9	82.7
25	Sonny Jurgensen	18	4262	2433	57.1	32,224	7.56	255	6.0	189	4.4	82.6

Note: The NFL does not recognize records from the All-American Football Conference (1946-49). If it did, **Otto Graham** would rank 11th (after Green) with the following stats: 10 Yrs; 2,626 Att; 1,464 Comp; 55.8 Comp Pct; 23,584 Yards; 8.98 Avg Gain; 174 TD; 6.6 TD Pct; 135 Int; 5.1 Int Pct; and 86.6 Rating Pts.

Touchdown Passes

		No
1	Dan Marino	420
2	**Brett Favre**	414
3	Fran Tarkenton	342
4	John Elway	300
5	Warren Moon	291
6	Johnny Unitas	290
7	**Peyton Manning**	275
8	Joe Montana	273
9	**Vinny Testaverde**	270
10	Dave Krieg	261
11	Sonny Jurgensen	255
12	Dan Fouts	254
13	**Drew Bledsoe**	251
14	Boomer Esiason	247
15	John Hadl	244
16	Len Dawson	239
17	Jim Kelly	237
18	George Blanda	236
19	Steve Young	232
20	Dan Brodie	214
21	Terry Bradshaw	212
	Y.A. Tittle	212
23	Jim Hart	209
24	Randall Cunningham	207
25	Jim Everett	203
26	Roman Gabriel	201
27	Phil Simms	199
28	Ken Anderson	197
29	Joe Ferguson	196
	Bobby Layne	196
	Norm Snead	196
	Steve DeBerg	196
33	Ken Stabler	194
34	Bob Griese	192
35	Sammy Baugh	187
36	Craig Morton	183
37	Steve Grogan	182
	Mark Brunell	182
39	Rich Gannon	180
40	Ron Jaworski	179
41	Babe Parilli	178
42	**Kerry Collins**	174
43	Charlie Conerly	173
	Joe Namath	173
	Norm Van Brocklin	173

Note: The NFL does not recognize records from the All-American Football Conference (1946-49). If it did, **Y.A. Tittle** would move up from 21st to 16th (after Hadl) with 242 TDs and **Otto Graham** would rank 42nd (tied with Collins) with 174 TDs.

Passes Intercepted

		No
1	George Blanda	277
2	**Brett Favre**	273
3	John Hadl	268
4	Fran Tarkenton	266
5	**Vinny Testaverde**	261
6	Norm Snead	257
7	Johnny Unitas	253
8	Dan Marino	252
9	Jim Hart	247
10	Bobby Layne	245
11	Dan Fouts	242
12	Warren Moon	233
13	John Elway	226
14	John Brodie	224
15	Ken Stabler	222
16	Y.A. Tittle	221
17	Joe Namath	220
	Babe Parilli	220
19	Terry Bradshaw	210
20	Joe Ferguson	209
21	Steve Grogan	208
22	**Drew Bledsoe**	206
23	Steve DeBerg	204
24	Sammy Baugh	203
25	Dave Krieg	199

Passing Yards

		Yrs	Att	Comp	Pct	Yards
1	Dan Marino	17	8358	4967	59.4	61,361
2	**Brett Favre**	16	8223	5021	61.1	57,500
3	John Elway	16	7250	4123	56.9	51,475
4	Warren Moon	17	6823	3988	58.5	49,325
5	Fran Tarkenton	18	6467	3686	57.0	47,003
6	**Vinny Testaverde**	20	6529	3693	56.6	45,281
7	**Drew Bledsoe**	14	6717	3839	57.2	44,611
8	Dan Fouts	15	5604	3297	58.8	43,040
9	Joe Montana	15	5391	3409	63.2	40,551
10	Johnny Unitas	18	5186	2830	54.6	40,239
11	Dave Krieg	19	5311	3105	58.5	38,147
12	Boomer Esiason	14	5205	2969	57.0	37,920
13	**Peyton Manning**	9	4890	3131	64.0	37,586
14	Jim Kelly	11	4779	2874	60.1	35,467
15	Jim Everett	12	4923	2841	57.7	34,837
16	Jim Hart	19	5076	2593	51.1	34,665
17	Steve DeBerg	17	5024	2874	57.2	34,241
18	**Kerry Collins**	12	5171	2868	55.5	34,186
19	John Hadl	16	4687	2363	50.4	33,503
20	Phil Simms	14	4647	2576	55.4	33,462
21	Steve Young	15	4149	2667	64.3	33,124
22	Troy Aikman	12	4715	2898	61.5	32,942
23	Ken Anderson	16	4475	2654	59.3	32,838
24	Sonny Jurgensen	18	4262	2433	57.1	32,224
25	**Mark Brunell**	13	4594	2738	59.6	31,826

Note: The NFL does not recognize records from the All-American Football Conference (1946-49). If it did, **Y.A. Tittle** would rank 22nd (after Young) with the following stats: 17 Yrs; 4,395 Att; 2,427 Comp; 55.2 Pct; and 33,070 Yards.

Receptions

		Yrs	No	Yards	Avg	TD
1	Jerry Rice	20	1549	22,895	14.8	197
2	Cris Carter	16	1101	13,899	12.6	130
3	Tim Brown	17	1094	14,934	13.7	100
4	**Marvin Harrison**	11	1022	13,697	13.4	122
5	Andre Reed	16	951	13,198	13.9	87
6	Art Monk	16	940	12,721	13.5	68
7	**Isaac Bruce**	13	887	13,376	15.1	80
8	Jimmy Smith	12	862	12,287	14.3	67
9	**Keenan McCardell**	15	861	11,117	12.9	62
10	Irving Fryar	17	851	12,785	15.0	84
11	**Rod Smith**	12	849	11,389	13.4	68
12	Larry Centers	14	827	6,797	8.2	28
13	Steve Largent	14	819	13,089	16.0	100
14	Shannon Sharpe	14	815	10,060	12.3	62
15	Henry Ellard	16	814	13,777	16.9	65
	Keyshawn Johnson	11	814	10,571	13.0	64
17	**Terrell Owens**	11	801	11,715	14.6	114
18	Marshall Faulk	12	767	6,875	9.0	36
19	James Lofton	16	764	14,004	18.3	75
20	Charlie Joiner	18	750	12,146	16.2	65
	Michael Irvin	12	750	11,904	15.9	65
22	Andre Rison	12	743	10,205	13.7	84
23	**Eric Moulds**	10	732	9,653	13.2	49
24	**Tony Gonzalez**	10	721	8,710	12.1	61
25	**Torry Holt**	8	712	10,675	15.0	64

Rushing Yards

		Yrs	Car	Yards	Avg	TD
1	Emmitt Smith	15	4409	18,355	4.2	164
2	Walter Payton	13	3838	16,726	4.4	110
3	Barry Sanders	10	3062	15,269	5.0	99
4	Curtis Martin	11	3518	14,101	4.0	90
5	Jerome Bettis	13	3479	13,662	3.9	91
6	Eric Dickerson	11	2996	13,259	4.4	90
7	Tony Dorsett	12	2936	12,739	4.3	77
8	Jim Brown	9	2359	12,312	5.2	106
9	Marshall Faulk	12	2836	12,279	4.3	100
10	Marcus Allen	16	3022	12,243	4.1	123
11	Franco Harris	13	2949	12,120	4.1	91
12	Thurman Thomas	13	2877	12,074	4.2	65
13	John Riggins	14	2916	11,352	3.9	104
14	**Corey Dillon**	10	2618	11,241	4.3	82
15	O.J. Simpson	11	2404	11,236	4.7	61
16	Ricky Watters	10	2622	10,643	4.1	78
17	**Tiki Barber**	10	2217	10,449	4.7	55
18	Eddie George	9	2865	10,441	3.6	68
19	**Edgerrin James**	8	2525	10,385	4.1	70
20	Ottis Anderson	14	2562	10,273	4.0	81
21	**Fred Taylor**	9	2062	9,513	4.6	56
22	**Warrick Dunn**	10	2256	9,461	4.2	43
23	Earl Campbell	8	2187	9,407	4.3	74
24	**LaDainian Tomlinson**	6	2050	9,176	4.5	100
25	**Shaun Alexander**	7	1969	8,713	4.4	96

Note: The NFL does not recognize records from the All-American Football Conference (1946-49). If it did, **Joe Perry** would rank 21st (after Anderson) with the following stats: 16 Yrs; 1,929 Att; 9,723 Yards; 5.0 Avg; and 71 TD.

All-Purpose Yards

		Rush	Rec	Ret	Total
1	Jerry Rice	645	22,895	6	23,546
2	Brian Mitchell	1,967	2,336	19,027	23,330
3	Walter Payton	16,726	4,538	539	21,803
4	Emmitt Smith	18,355	3,224	-15	21,564
5	Tim Brown	190	14,934	4,558	19,682
6	Marshall Faulk	12,279	6,875	36	19,190
7	Barry Sanders	15,269	2,921	118	18,308
8	Herschel Walker	8,225	4,859	5,084	18,168
9	Marcus Allen	12,243	5,411	-6	17,648
10	Curtis Martin	14,101	3,329	-9	17,421
11	**Tiki Barber**	10,449	5,183	1,727	17,359
12	Eric Metcalf	2,392	5,572	9,266	17,230
13	Thurman Thomas	12,074	4,458	0	16,532
14	Tony Dorsett	12,739	3,554	33	16,326
15	Henry Ellard	50	13,777	1,891	15,718
16	Irving Fryar	242	12,785	2,567	15,594
17	Jim Brown	12,312	2,499	648	15,459
18	Eric Dickerson	13,259	2,137	15	15,411
19	Jerome Bettis	13,662	1,449	2	15,113
20	Glyn Milburn	817	1,322	12,772	14,911
21	James Brooks	7,962	3,621	3,327	14,910
22	Ricky Watters	10,643	4,248	0	14,891
23	Franco Harris	12,120	2,287	215	14,622
24	O.J. Simpson	11,236	2,142	990	14,368
25	James Lofton	246	14,004	27	14,277

Years played: Allen (16), Barber (10), Bettis (12), Brooks (12), J. Brown (9), T. Brown (17), Dickerson (11), Dorsett (12), Ellard (16), Faulk (11), Fryar (17), Harris (13), Lofton (16), Martin (10), Metcalf (13), Milburn (9), Mitchell (14), Payton (13), Rice (20), Sanders (10), Simpson (11), Smith (15), Thomas (13), Walker (12) and Watters (10).

Scoring

Points

		Yrs	TD	FG	PAT	Total
1	**Morten Andersen**	24	0	540	825	2445
2	Gary Anderson	23	0	538	820	2434
3	George Blanda	26	9	335	943	2002
4	John Carney	19	0	413	510	1749
5	Norm Johnson	18	0	366	638	1736
6	Matt Stover	16	0	408	491	1715
7	Nick Lowery	18	0	383	562	1711
8	Jan Stenerud	19	0	373	580	1699
9	**Jason Elam**	14	0	368	568	1672
10	Eddie Murray	19	0	352	538	1594
11	Al Del Greco	17	0	347	543	1584
12	**Jason Hanson**	15	0	356	469	1537
13	Steve Christie	15	0	336	468	1476
14	Pat Leahy	18	0	304	558	1470
15	Jim Turner	16	1	304	521	1439
16	Matt Bahr	17	0	300	522	1422
17	**John Kasay**	15	0	334	403	1405
18	Mark Moseley	16	0	300	482	1382
19	Jim Bakken	17	0	282	534	1380
20	Fred Cox	15	0	282	519	1365
21	Lou Groza	17	1	234	641	1349
22	**Jeff Wilkins**	13	0	283	470	1319
23	**Adam Vinatieri**	11	0	288	408	1271†
24	Jerry Rice	20	208	0	0	1256†
25	Jim Breech	14	0	243	517	1246

†Vinatieri's total includes one 2-point conversion. Rice's total includes four 2-point conversions.

Note: The NFL does not recognize records from the All-American Football Conference (1946-49). If it did, **Lou Groza** would move up from 21st to 10th (after Elam) with the following stats: 21 Yrs; 1 TD; 264 FG, 810 PAT; 1,608 Pts.

Touchdowns

		Yrs	Rush	Rec	Ret	Total
1	Jerry Rice	20	10	197	1	208
2	Emmitt Smith	15	164	11	0	175
3	Marcus Allen	16	123	21	1	145
4	Marshall Faulk	12	100	36	0	136
5	Cris Carter	16	0	130	1	131
6	Jim Brown	9	106	20	0	126
7	Walter Payton	13	110	15	0	125
8	**Marvin Harrison**	11	0	122	0	122
9	John Riggins	14	104	12	0	116
	Terrell Owens	11	2	114	0	116
11	Lenny Moore	12	63	48	2	113
12	**LaDainian Tomlinson**	6	100	11	0	111
13	Barry Sanders	10	99	10	0	109
14	**Shaun Alexander**	7	96	11	0	107
15	Don Hutson	11	3	99	3	105
	Tim Brown	17	1	100	4	105
17	**Randy Moss**	9	0	101	1	102
18	Steve Largent	14	1	100	0	101
19	Franco Harris	13	91	9	0	100
	Curtis Martin	11	90	10	0	100
21	Eric Dickerson	11	90	6	0	96
22	Jerome Bettis	13	91	3	0	94
	Priest Holmes	9	86	8	0	94
24	Jim Taylor	10	83	10	0	93
25	Tony Dorsett	12	77	13	1	91
	Bobby Mitchell	11	18	65	8	91
	Ricky Watters	10	78	13	0	91

Interceptions

		Yrs	No	Yards	TD
1	Paul Krause	16	81	1185	3
2	Emlen Tunnell	14	79	1282	4
3	Rod Woodson	17	71	1483	12
4	Dick (Night Train) Lane	14	68	1207	5
5	Ken Riley	15	65	596	5

Sacks

		Yrs	No
1	Bruce Smith	19	200.0
2	Reggie White	15	198.0
3	Kevin Greene	15	160.0
4	Chris Doleman	15	150.5
5	Richard Dent	15	137.5
	John Randle	14	137.5

Note: The NFL did not begin officially compiling sacks until 1982. Deacon Jones, who played with the Rams, Chargers and Redskins from 1961-74, is often credited with 173.5 sacks. Jack Youngblood and Alan Page are unofficially credited with 150.5 and 148, respectively. Also, Lawrence Taylor has 142 career sacks if you count his rookie year of 1981, the year before sacks became an official stat.

Safeties

		Yrs	No
1	Ted Hendricks	15	4
	Doug English	10	4
3	Seventeen players tied with 3 each.		

Kickoff Returns

Minimum 75 returns.

		Yrs	No	Yards	Avg	TD
1	Gale Sayers	7	91	2781	30.6	6
2	Lynn Chandnois	7	92	2720	29.6	3
3	Abe Woodson	9	193	5538	28.7	5
4	Buddy Young	6	90	2514	27.9	2
5	Travis Williams	5	102	2801	27.5	6

Punting

Minimum 300 punts.

		Yrs	No	Yards	Avg
1	**Shane Lechler**	7	519	23,926	46.1
2	Sammy Baugh	16	338	15,245	45.1
3	Tommy Davis	11	511	22,833	44.7
4	Yale Lary	11	503	22,279	44.3
5	**Todd Sauerbrun**	12	842	37,008	44.0

Punt Returns

Minimum 75 returns.

		Yrs	No	Yards	Avg	TD
1	George McAfee	8	112	1431	12.8	2
2	Jack Christiansen	8	85	1084	12.8	8
3	Claude Gibson	5	110	1381	12.6	3
4	Bill Dudley	9	124	1515	12.2	3
5	Rick Upchurch	9	248	3008	12.1	8

Long-Playing Records

Seasons

		No
1	George Blanda, QB-K	26
2	**Morten Andersen**, K	24
3	Gary Anderson, K	23

Games

		No
1	**Morten Andersen**, K	368
2	Gary Anderson, K	353
3	George Blanda, QB-K	340

Consecutive Games

		No
1	**Jeff Feagles**, P	304
2	Jim Marshall, DE	282
3	Morten Andersen, K	248

SINGLE SEASON
Passing

Yards Gained	Year	Att	Cmp	Pct	Yds		Efficiency	Year	Att/Cmp	TD	Rtg
Dan Marino, Mia	1984	564	362	64.2	5084		Peyton Manning, Ind	2004	497/336	49	121.1
Kurt Warner, St.L	2001	546	375	68.7	4830		Steve Young, SF	1994	461/324	35	112.8
Dan Fouts, SD	1981	609	360	59.1	4802		Joe Montana, SF	1989	386/271	26	112.4
Dan Marino, Mia	1986	623	378	60.7	4746		Daunte Culpepper, Min	2004	548/379	39	110.9
Daunte Culpepper, Min	2004	548	379	69.2	4717		Milt Plum, Cle	1960	250/151	21	110.4
Dan Fouts, SD	1980	589	348	59.1	4715		Sammy Baugh, Wash	1945	182/128	11	109.9
Warren Moon, Hou	1991	655	404	61.7	4690		Kurt Warner, St.L	1999	499/325	41	109.2
Rich Gannon, Oak	2002	618	418	67.6	4689		Dan Marino, Mia	1984	564/362	48	108.9
Warren Moon, Hou	1990	584	362	62.0	4689		Sid Luckman, Chi. Bears	1943	202/110	28	107.5
Neil Lomax, St.L	1984	560	345	61.6	4614		Steve Young, SF	1992	402/268	25	107.0

Receptions

Catches	Year	No	Yds
Marvin Harrison, Ind	2002	143	1722
Herman Moore, Det	1995	123	1686
Jerry Rice, SF	1995	122	1848
Cris Carter, Min	1995	122	1371
Cris Carter, Min	1994	122	1256
Isaac Bruce, St.L	1995	119	1781
Torry Holt, St.L	2003	117	1696
Jimmy Smith, Jax	1999	116	1636
Marvin Harrison, Ind	1999	115	1663
Rod Smith, Den	2001	113	1343
Hines Ward, Pit	2002	112	1329
Jimmy Smith, Jax	2001	112	1373
Jerry Rice, SF	1994	112	1499
Sterling Sharpe, GB	1993	112	1274

Rushing

Yards Gained	Year	Car	Yds	Avg
Eric Dickerson, LA Rams	1984	379	2105	5.6
Jamal Lewis, Bal.	2003	387	2066	5.3
Barry Sanders, Det	1997	335	2053	6.1
Terrell Davis, Den	1998	392	2008	5.1
O.J. Simpson, Buf	1973	332	2003	6.0
Earl Campbell, Hou	1980	373	1934	5.2
Barry Sanders, Det	1994	331	1883	5.7
Ahman Green, GB	2003	355	1883	5.3
Shaun Alexander, Sea	2005	370	1880	5.1
Jim Brown, Cle	1963	291	1863	6.4
Tiki Barber, NYG	2005	357	1860	5.2
Ricky Williams, Mia	2002	383	1853	4.8
Walter Payton, Chi	1977	339	1852	5.5
Jamal Anderson, Atl	1998	410	1846	4.5

Scoring
Points

	Year	TD	PAT	FG	Pts
LaDainian Tomlinson, SD	2006	31	0	0	186
Paul Hornung, GB	1960	15	41	15	176
Shaun Alexander, Sea	2005	28	0	0	168
Gary Anderson, Min	1998	0	59	35	164
Jeff Wilkins, St.L	2003	0	46	39	163
Priest Holmes, KC	2003	27	0	0	162
Mark Moseley, Wash	1983	0	62	33	161
Marshall Faulk, St.L	2000	26	4	0	160
Mike Vanderjagt, Ind	2003	0	46	37	157
Gino Cappelletti, Bos	1964	7	38	25	155
Emmitt Smith, Dal	1995	25	0	0	150
Chip Lohmiller, Wash	1991	0	56	31	149

Touchdowns

	Year	Rush	Rec	Ret	Total
LaDainian Tomlinson, SD	2006	28	3	0	31
Shaun Alexander, Sea	2005	27	1	0	28
Priest Holmes, KC	2003	27	0	0	27
Marshall Faulk, St.L	2000	18	8	0	26
Emmitt Smith, Dal	1995	25	0	0	25
John Riggins, Wash	1983	24	0	0	24
Priest Holmes, KC	2002	21	3	0	24
Terrell Davis, Den	1998	21	2	0	23
O.J. Simpson, Buf	1975	16	7	0	23
Jerry Rice, SF	1987	1	22	0	23
Gale Sayers, Chi	1966	14	6	2	22
Chuck Foreman, Min	1975	13	9	0	22
Emmitt Smith, Dal	1994	21	1	0	22

Note: The NFL regular season schedule grew from 12 games (1947-60) to 14 (1961-77) to 16 (1978-present). The AFL regular season schedule was always 14 games (1960-69).

Touchdowns Passing

	Year	No
Peyton Manning, Indianapolis	2004	49
Dan Marino, Miami	1984	48
Dan Marino, Miami	1986	44
Kurt Warner, St. Louis	1999	41
Brett Favre, Green Bay	1996	39
Daunte Culpepper, Minnesota	2004	39
Brett Favre, Green Bay	1995	38
George Blanda, Houston	1961	36
Y.A. Tittle, NY Giants	1963	36
Steve Young, San Francisco	1998	36
Steve Beuerlein, Carolina	1999	36
Kurt Warner, St. Louis	2001	36
Brett Favre, Green Bay	1997	35
Steve Young, San Francisco	1994	35

Touchdowns Receiving

	Year	No
Jerry Rice, San Francisco	1987	22
Mark Clayton, Miami	1984	18
Sterling Sharpe, Green Bay	1994	18
Don Hutson, Green Bay	1942	17
Elroy (Crazylegs) Hirsch, LA Rams	1951	17
Bill Groman, Houston	1961	17
Jerry Rice, San Francisco	1989	17
Cris Carter, Minnesota	1995	17
Carl Pickens, Cincinnati	1995	17
Randy Moss, Minnesota	1998	17
Randy Moss, Minnesota	2003	17
Art Powell, Oakland	1963	16
Terrell Owens, SF	2001	16
Muhsin Muhammad, Carolina	2004	16

Touchdowns Rushing

	Year	No
LaDainian Tomlinson, San Diego	2006	28
Priest Holmes, Kansas City	2003	27
Shaun Alexander, Seattle	2005	27
Emmitt Smith, Dallas	1995	25
John Riggins, Washington	1983	24
Joe Morris, NY Giants	1985	21
Emmitt Smith, Dallas	1994	21
Terry Allen, Washington	1996	21
Terrell Davis, Denver	1998	21
Priest Holmes, Kansas City	2002	21
Larry Johnson, Kansas City	2005	20
Jim Taylor, Green Bay	1962	19
Earl Campbell, Houston	1979	19
Chuck Muncie, San Diego	1981	19

Field Goals

	Year	Att	No
Neil Rackers, Arizona	2005	42	40
Jeff Wilkins, St. Louis	2003	42	39
Olindo Mare, Miami	1999	46	39
Mike Vanderjagt, Indianapolis	2003	37	37
John Kasay, Carolina	1996	45	37
Cary Blanchard, Indianapolis	1996	40	36
Al Del Greco, Tennessee	1998	39	36
Ali Haji-Sheikh, NY Giants	1983	42	35
Jeff Jaeger, LA Raiders	1993	44	35
Gary Anderson, Minnesota	1998	35	35
Matt Stover, Baltimore	2000	39	35
Jay Feely, NY Giants	2005	42	35
Ten tied with 34 FG each.			

Interceptions

	Year	No
Dick (Night Train) Lane, Detroit	1952	14
Dan Sandifer, Washington	1948	13
Spec Sanders, NY Yanks	1950	13
Lester Hayes, Oakland	1980	13
Nine tied with 12 each.		

Punting

Qualifiers	Year	Avg
Sammy Baugh, Washington	1940	51.4
Yale Lary, Detroit	1963	48.9
Sammy Baugh, Washington	1941	48.7
Yale Lary, Detroit	1961	48.4
Sammy Baugh, Washington	1942	48.2

Kickoff Returns

	Year	Avg
Travis Williams, Green Bay	1967	41.1
Gale Sayers, Chicago Bears	1967	37.7
Ollie Matson, Chicago Cards	1958	35.5
Jim Duncan, Baltimore Colts	1970	35.4
Lynn Chandnois, Pittsburgh	1952	35.2

Punt Returns

	Year	Avg
Herb Rich, Baltimore	1950	23.0
Jack Christiansen, Detroit	1952	21.5
Dick Christy, NY Titans	1961	21.3
Bob Hayes, Dallas	1968	20.8
Claude Young, NY Yanks	1951	19.3

Sacks

	Year	No
Michael Strahan, NY Giants	2001	22.5
Mark Gastineau, NY Jets	1984	22
Reggie White, Philadelphia	1987	21

	Year	No
Chris Doleman, Minnesota	1989	21
Lawrence Taylor, NY Giants	1986	20.5
Derrick Thomas, Kansas City	1990	20

Note: The NFL did not begin officially compiling sacks until 1982. Cincinnati's Coy Bacon is widely, although not officially, credited with 26 sacks during the 1976 season.

SINGLE GAME

Passing

Yards Gained	Date	Yds
Norm Van Brocklin, LA vs NY Yanks	9/28/51	554
Warren Moon, Hou vs KC	12/16/90	527
Boomer Esiason, Ariz vs Wash.	11/10/96	522
Dan Marino, Mia vs NYJ	10/23/88	521
Phil Simms, NYG vs Cin	10/13/85	513

Completions	Date	No
Drew Bledsoe, NE vs Min	11/13/94	45
Rich Gannon, Oak vs Pit	9/15/02	43
Richard Todd, NYJ vs SF	9/21/80	42
Vinny Testaverde, NYJ vs Sea	12/6/98	42
Warren Moon, Hou vs Dal	11/10/91	41
Five tied with 40 each.		

Receiving

Catches	Date	No
Terrell Owens, SF vs Chi	12/17/00	20
Tom Fears, LA vs GB	12/3/50	18
Clark Gaines, NYJ vs SF	9/21/80	17
Four tied with 16 each.		

Yards Gained	Date	Yds
Flipper Anderson, LA Rams vs NO	11/26/89	336
Stephone Paige, KC vs SD	12/22/85	309
Jim Benton, Cle vs Det	11/22/45	303
Cloyce Box, Det vs Balt	12/3/50	302
Jimmy Smith, Jax vs Bal	9/10/00	291
Jerry Rice, SF vs Det	9/25/95	289

Rushing

Yards Gained	Date	Yds
Jamal Lewis, Bal vs Cle	9/14/03	295
Corey Dillon, Cin vs Den	10/22/00	278
Walter Payton, Chi vs Min	11/20/77	275
O.J. Simpson, Buf vs Det	11/25/76	273
Shaun Alexander, Sea vs Oak	11/11/01	266
Mike Anderson, Den vs NO	12/3/00	251
O.J. Simpson, Buf vs NE	9/16/73	250
Willie Ellison, LA Rams vs NO	12/5/71	247

All-Purpose Yards

	Date	Yds
Glyn Milburn, Den vs Sea	12/10/95	404
Billy Cannon, Hou vs NY Titans	12/10/61	373
Michael Lewis, NO vs Wash	10/13/02	356
Tyrone Hughes, NO vs LA Rams	10/23/94	347
Lionel James, SD vs Raiders	11/10/85	345
Timmy Brown, Phi vs St.L	12/16/62	341
Gale Sayers, Chi vs Min	12/18/66	339
Gale Sayers, Chi vs SF	12/12/65	336
Flipper Anderson, LA Rams vs NO	11/26/89	336

Scoring

Points

	Date	Pts
Ernie Nevers, Chi. Cards vs Chi. Bears	11/28/29	40
Dub Jones, Cle vs Chi. Bears	11/25/51	36
Gale Sayers, Chi vs SF	12/12/65	36
Paul Hornung, GB vs Bal	10/8/61	33
Bob Shaw, Chi. Cards vs Bal	10/2/50	30
Jim Brown, Cle vs Bal	11/1/59	30
Abner Haynes, Dal. Texans vs Oak	11/26/61	30
Billy Cannon, Hou vs NY Titans	12/10/61	30
Cookie Gilchrist, Buf vs NY Jets	12/8/63	30
Kellen Winslow, SD vs Oak	11/22/81	30
Jerry Rice, SF vs Atl	10/14/90	30
James Stewart, Jax vs Phi.	10/12/97	30
Shaun Alexander, Sea vs Min.	9/29/02	30
Clinton Portis, Den vs KC	12/7/03	30

Note: Nevers celebrated Thanksgiving, 1929, by scoring all of the Chicago Cardinals' points on six rushing TDs and four PATs. The Cards beat Red Grange and the Chicago Bears, 40-6.

Touchdowns Passing

	Date	No
Sid Luckman, Chi. Bears vs NYG	11/14/43	7
Adrian Burk, Phi vs Wash	10/17/54	7
George Blanda, Hou vs NY Titans	11/19/61	7
Y.A. Tittle, NYG vs Wash	10/28/62	7
Joe Kapp, Min vs Bal	9/28/69	7

Touchdowns Receiving

	Date	No
Bob Shaw, Chi. Cards vs Bal	10/2/50	5
Kellen Winslow, SD vs Oak	11/22/81	5
Jerry Rice, SF vs Atl	10/14/90	5

Touchdowns Rushing

	Date	No
Ernie Nevers, Chi. Cards vs Chi. Bears	11/28/29	6
Jim Brown, Cle vs Bal	11/1/59	5
Cookie Gilchrist, Buf vs NY Jets	12/8/63	5
James Stewart, Jax vs Phi.	10/12/97	5
Clinton Portis, Den vs KC	12/7/03	5

Field Goals

	Date	No
Jim Bakken, St.L vs Pit	9/24/67	7
Rich Karlis, Min vs LA Rams	11/5/89	7
Chris Boniol, Dal vs GB	11/18/96	7
Billy Cundiff, Dal vs NYG	9/15/03	7

Note: Bakken was 7-for-9, Cundiff was 7-for-8, Boniol and Karlis were 7-for-7.

Extra Point Kicks

	Date	No
Pat Harder, Cards vs NYG	10/17/48	9
Bob Waterfield, LA Rams vs Bal	10/22/50	9
Charlie Gogolak, Wash vs NYG	11/27/66	9

Interceptions

	No
By 18 players	4

Sacks

	Date	No
Derrick Thomas, KC vs Sea	11/11/90	7.0
Fred Dean, SF vs NO	11/13/83	6.0
Derrick Thomas, KC vs Oak	9/6/98	6.0
William Gay, Det vs TB	9/4/83	5.5

Longest Plays

Passing (all for TDs)

	Date	Yds
Frank Filchock to Andy Farkas, Wash vs Pit	10/15/39	99
George Izo to Bobby Mitchell, Wash vs Cle	9/15/63	99
Karl Sweetan to Pat Studstill, Det vs Bal	10/16/66	99
Sonny Jurgensen to Gerry Allen, Wash vs Chi	9/15/68	99
Jim Plunkett to Cliff Branch, LA Raiders vs Wash	10/2/83	99
Ron Jaworski to Mike Quick, Phi vs Atl	11/10/85	99
Stan Humphries to Tony Martin, SD vs Sea	9/18/94	99
Brett Favre to Robert Brooks, GB vs Chi	9/11/95	99
Trent Green to Marc Boerigter, KC vs SD	12/22/02	99
Jeff Garcia to Andre Davis, Cle vs Cin	10/17/04	99

Runs from Scrimmage (all for TDs)

	Date	Yds
Tony Dorsett, Dal vs Min	1/3/83	99
Ahman Green, GB vs Den	12/28/03	98
Andy Uram, GB vs Chi. Cards	10/8/39	97
Bob Gage, Pit vs Bears	12/4/49	97

Four players tied with 96-yd rushes.

Punts

	Date	Yds
Steve O'Neal, NYJ vs Den	9/21/69	98
Joe Lintzenich, Chi. Bears vs NYG	11/15/31	94
Shawn McCarthy, NE vs Buf	11/3/91	93

Field Goals

	Date	Yds
Tom Dempsey, NO vs Det	11/8/70	63
Jason Elam, Den vs Jax	10/25/98	63
Matt Bryant, TB vs Phi	10/22/06	62
Steve Cox, Cle vs Cin	10/21/84	60
Morten Andersen, NO vs Chi	10/27/91	60
Rob Bironas, Ten vs Ind	12/3/06	60

Four tied with 59-yard FGs.

Punt Returns (all for TDs)

	Date	Yds
Robert Bailey, Rams vs NO	10/23/94	103
Gil LeFebvre, Cin vs Bklyn	12/3/33	98
Charlie West, Min vs Wash	11/3/68	98
Dennis Morgan, Dal vs St.L	10/13/74	98
Terance Mathis, NYJ vs Dal	11/4/90	98
Greg Pruitt, LA Raiders vs Wash.	10/2/83	97

Kickoff Returns (all for TDs)

	Date	Yds
Al Carmichael, GB vs Chi. Bears	10/7/56	106
Noland Smith, KC vs Den	12/17/67	106
Roy Green, St.L vs Dal	10/21/79	106

Interception Returns (all for TDs)

	Date	Yds
Ed Reed, Bal vs Cle	11/17/04	106
James Willis (14 yds) lateral to Troy Vincent (90 yds), Phi vs Dal	11/3/96	104
Vencie Glenn, SD vs Den	11/29/87	103
Louis Oliver, Mia vs Buf	10/4/92	103

Seven players tied with 102-yd returns.

Note: Chicago's Nathan Vasher (11/13/05) and Devin Hester (11/12/06) each returned a missed FG 108 yards, the longest plays in NFL history.

Monday Night Football All-Time Leaders

The first episode of Monday Night Football aired on ABC on September 21, 1970 with the Cleveland Browns defeating the New York Jets, 31-21, at Municipal Stadium in Cleveland. The series continued on ABC for 36 seasons, until ESPN bought the rights to Monday Night games beginning with the 2006 season. Listed are all-time Monday Night Football records, through 2006 regular season.

Passing

Yards		**Touchdowns**		**300-yd Games**	
Dan Marino	9654	Dan Marino	74	Dan Marino	8
Brett Favre	7547	Brett Favre	55	Brett Favre	7
Joe Montana	5148	Steve Young	42	Joe Montana	6
John Elway	5012	Joe Montana	36	Randall Cunningham	6
Troy Aikman	4614	Jim Kelly	31	Steve Young	5
				Dan Fouts	5

Rushing

Yards		**Touchdowns**		**100-yd Games**	
Emmitt Smith	2434	Emmitt Smith	23	Emmitt Smith	12
Tony Dorsett	1897	Marcus Allen	17	Jerome Bettis	8
Thurman Thomas	1769	Eric Dickerson	14	Franco Harris	7
Marcus Allen	1486	John Riggins	13	Eric Dickerson	7
Franco Harris	1435	Chuck Muncie	10	Three tied with 6 games each.	
		Terrell Davis	10		

Receiving

Receptions		**Yards**		**Touchdowns**	
Jerry Rice	254	Jerry Rice	4029	Jerry Rice	34
Andre Reed	124	Andre Reed	1783	Terrell Owens	15
Cris Carter	123	Art Monk	1537	Mark Clayton	15
Tim Brown	121	Torry Holt	1518	Andre Reed	13
Art Monk	114	Michael Irvin	1512	Tony Hill	12

Interceptions		**Sacks**		**Coaching Wins**	
Everson Walls	11	Bruce Smith	24.5	Don Shula	31
Merton Hanks	9	Richard Dent	20.0	Tom Landry	19
Emmitt Thomas	8	Kevin Greene	18.0	George Seifert	18
Terrell Buckley	7	Reggie White	16.5	Bill Cowher	18
Michael Downs	7	Chris Doleman	16.5	Bill Parcells	15
Dick Anderson	7	Kabeer Gbaja-Biamila	16.5	Chuck Noll	15
				Tom Flores	15

In The Booth

A look at Monday Night Football announcers through the years.

Years	Announcer Combination	Years	Announcer Combination
1970	Keith Jackson, Howard Cosell, Don Meredith	1984	Frank Gifford, Don Meredith, O.J. Simpson
1971-73	Frank Gifford, Howard Cosell, Don Meredith	1985	Frank Gifford, O.J. Simpson, Joe Namath
1974	Frank Gifford, Howard Cosell, Alex Karras, Fred Williamson	1986	Al Michaels, Frank Gifford
		1987-97	Al Michaels, Frank Gifford, Dan Dierdorf
1975-76	Frank Gifford, Howard Cosell, Alex Karras	1998	Al Michaels, Dan Dierdorf, Boomer Esiason
1977-78	Frank Gifford, Howard Cosell, Don Meredith	1999	Al Michaels, Boomer Esiason
1979-82	Frank Gifford, Howard Cosell, Don Meredith, Fran Tarkenton	2000-01	Al Michaels, Dan Fouts, Dennis Miller
		2002-05	Al Michaels, John Madden
1983	Frank Gifford, Howard Cosell, Don Meredith, O.J. Simpson	2006	Mike Tirico, Joe Theisman, Tony Kornheiser
		2007	Mike Tirico, Ron Jaworski, Tony Kornheiser

Source: The ESPN Pro Football Encyclopedia and The NFL

Chicago College All-Star Game

On Aug. 31, 1934, a year after sponsoring Major League Baseball's first All-Star Game, *Chicago Tribune* sports editor Arch Ward presented the first Chicago College All-Star Game at Soldier Field. A crowd of 79,432 turned out to see an all-star team of graduated college seniors battle the 1933 NFL champion Chicago Bears to a scoreless tie. The preseason game was played at Soldier Field and pitted the College All-Stars against the defending NFL champions (1933-1966) or Super Bowl champions (1967-75) every year except 1935 until it was cancelled in 1977. The NFL champs won the series, 31-9-1.

Year

1934 Chi. Bears 0, All-Stars 0
1935 Chi. Bears 5, All-Stars 0
1936 Detroit 7, All-Stars 0
1937 All-Stars 6, Green Bay 0
1938 All-Stars 28, Washington 16
1939 NY Giants 9, All-Stars 0

1940 Green Bay 45, All-Stars 28
1941 Chi. Bears 37, All-Stars 13
1942 Chi. Bears 21, All-Stars 0
1943 All-Stars 27, Washington 7
1944 Chi. Bears 24, All-Stars 21
1945 Green Bay 19, All-Stars 7
1946 All-Stars 16, LA Rams 0
1947 All-Stars 16, Chi. Bears 0
1948 Chi. Cards 28, All-Stars 0

Year

1949 Philadelphia 38, All-Stars 0
1950 All-Stars 17, Philadelphia 7
1951 Cleveland 33, All-Stars 0
1952 LA Rams 10, All-Stars 7
1953 Detroit 24, All-Stars 10
1954 Detroit 31, All-Stars 6
1955 All-Stars 30, Cleveland 27
1956 Cleveland 26, All-Stars 0
1957 NY Giants 22, All-Stars 12
1958 All-Stars 35, Detroit 19
1959 Baltimore 29, All-Stars 0

1960 Baltimore 32, All-Stars 7
1961 Philadelphia 28, All-Stars 14
1962 Green Bay 42, All-Stars 20
1963 All-Stars 20, Green Bay 17

Year

1964 Chi. Bears 28, All-Stars 17
1965 Cleveland 24, All-Stars 16
1966 Green Bay 38, All-Stars 0
1967 Green Bay 27, All-Stars 0
1968 Green Bay 34, All-Stars 17
1969 NY Jets 26, All-Stars 24

1970 Kansas City 24, All-Stars 3
1971 Baltimore 24, All-Stars 17
1972 Dallas 20, All-Stars 7
1973 Miami 14, All-Stars 3
1974 No Game (NFLPA Strike)
1975 Pittsburgh 21, All-Stars 14
1976 Pittsburgh 24, All-Stars 0*

*Downpour flooded field, game called with 1:22 left in 3rd quarter.

Number One Draft Choices

In an effort to blunt the dominance of the Chicago Bears and New York Giants in the 1930s and distribute talent more even- ly throughout the league, the NFL established the college draft in 1936. The first player chosen in the first draft was Jay Berwanger, who was also college football's first Heisman Trophy winner. In all, 17 Heisman winners have also been the NFL's No. 1 choice. They are noted in **bold** type. The American Football League (formed in 1960) held its own draft for six years before agreeing to merge with the NFL and select players in a common draft starting in 1967.

Year Team

1936 Philadelphia — **Jay Berwanger**, HB, Chicago
1937 Philadelphia — Sam Francis, FB, Nebraska
1938 Cleveland Rams — Corbett Davis, FB, Indiana
1939 Chicago Cards — Ki Aldrich, C, TCU

1940 Chicago Cards — George Cafego, HB, Tennessee
1941 Chicago Bears — **Tom Harmon**, HB, Michigan
1942 Pittsburgh — Bill Dudley, HB, Virginia
1943 Detroit — **Frank Sinkwich**, HB, Georgia
1944 Boston Yanks — **Angelo Bertelli**, QB, N. Dame
1945 Chicago Cards — Charley Trippi, HB, Georgia
1946 Boston Yanks — Frank Dancewicz, QB, N. Dame
1947 Chicago Bears — Bob Fenimore, HB, Okla. A&M
1948 Washington — Harry Gilmer, QB, Alabama
1949 Philadelphia — Chuck Bednarik, C, Penn

1950 Detroit — **Leon Hart**, E, Notre Dame
1951 NY Giants — Kyle Rote, HB, SMU
1952 LA Rams — Bill Wade, QB, Vanderbilt
1953 San Francisco — Harry Babcock, E, Georgia
1954 Cleveland — Bobby Garrett, QB, Stanford
1955 Baltimore — George Shaw, QB, Oregon
1956 Pittsburgh — Gary Glick, DB, Colo. A&M
1957 Green Bay — **Paul Hornung**, QB, N. Dame
1958 Chicago Cards — King Hill, QB, Rice
1959 Green Bay — Randy Duncan, QB, Iowa

1960 NFL-LA Rams — **Billy Cannon**, HB, LSU
        AFL-No choice
1961 NFL-Minnesota — Tommy Mason, HB, Tulane
        AFL-Buffalo — Ken Rice, G, Auburn
1962 NFL-Washington — **Ernie Davis**, HB, Syracuse
        AFL-Oakland — Roman Gabriel, QB, N.C. State
1963 NFL-LA Rams — **Terry Baker**, QB, Oregon St.
        AFL-Kan.City — Buck Buchanan, DT, Grambling
1964 NFL-San Fran — Dave Parks, E, Texas Tech
        AFL-Boston — Jack Concannon, QB, Boston Col.
1965 NFL-NY Giants — Tucker Frederickson, FB, Auburn
        AFL-Houston — Lawrence Elkins, E, Baylor
1966 NFL-Atlanta — Tommy Nobis, LB, Texas
        AFL-Miami — Jim Grabowski, FB, Illinois
1967 Baltimore — Bubba Smith, DT, Michigan St.
1968 Minnesota — Ron Yary, T, USC

Year Team

1969 Buffalo — **O.J. Simpson**, RB, USC

1970 Pittsburgh — Terry Bradshaw, QB, La.Tech
1971 New England — **Jim Plunkett**, QB, Stanford
1972 Buffalo — Walt Patulski, DE, Notre Dame
1973 Houston — John Matuszak, DE, Tampa
1974 Dallas — Ed (Too Tall) Jones, DE, Tenn. St.
1975 Atlanta — Steve Bartkowski, QB, Calif.
1976 Tampa Bay — Lee Roy Selmon, DE, Oklahoma
1977 Tampa Bay — Ricky Bell, RB, USC
1978 Houston — **Earl Campbell**, RB, Texas
1979 Buffalo — Tom Cousineau, LB, Ohio St.

1980 Detroit — **Billy Sims**, RB, Oklahoma
1981 New Orleans — **George Rogers**, RB, S. Carolina
1982 New England — Kenneth Sims, DT, Texas
1983 Baltimore — John Elway, QB, Stanford
1984 New England — Irving Fryar, WR, Nebraska
1985 Buffalo — Bruce Smith, DE, Va. Tech
1986 Tampa Bay — **Bo Jackson**, RB, Auburn
1987 Tampa Bay — **V. Testaverde**, QB, Miami-FL
1988 Atlanta — Aundray Bruce, LB, Auburn
1989 Dallas — Troy Aikman, QB, UCLA

1990 Indianapolis — Jeff George, QB, Illinois
1991 Dallas — Russell Maryland, DT, Miami-FL
1992 Indianapolis — Steve Emtman, DT, Washington
1993 New England — Drew Bledsoe, QB, Washington St.
1994 Cincinnati — Dan Wilkinson, DT, Ohio St.
1995 Cincinnati — Ki-Jana Carter, RB, Penn St.
1996 NY Jets — Keyshawn Johnson, WR, USC
1997 St. Louis — Orlando Pace, OT, Ohio St.
1998 Indianapolis — Peyton Manning, QB, Tennessee
1999 Cleveland — Tim Couch, QB, Kentucky

2000 Cleveland — Courtney Brown, DE, Penn St.
2001 Atlanta — Michael Vick, QB, Va. Tech
2002 Houston — David Carr, QB, Fresno St.
2003 Cincinnati — **Carson Palmer**, QB, USC
2004 San Diego — Eli Manning, QB, Mississippi
2005 San Francisco — Alex Smith, QB, Utah
2006 Houston — Mario Williams, DE, NC State
2007 Oakland — JaMarcus Russell, QB, LSU

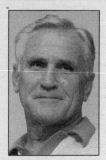   

AP/Wide World Photos	NFL Media	NFL Media	NFL Media
Don Shula	**Marv Levy**	**Bill Belichick**	**Tony Dungy**

All-Time Winningest NFL Coaches

NFL career victories through the 2006 season. Career, regular season and playoff records are noted along with NFL, AFL and Super Bowl titles won. Coaches active during 2006 season in **bold** type.

		Career					Regular Season				Playoffs			
		Yrs	W	L	T	Pct	W	L	T	Pct	W	L	Pct.	League Titles
1	Don Shula	33	**347**	173	6	.665	328	156	6	.676	19	17	.528	2 Super Bowls and 1 NFL
2	George Halas	40	**324**	151	31	.671	318	148	31	.671	6	3	.667	5 NFL
3	Tom Landry	29	**270**	178	6	.601	250	162	6	.605	20	16	.556	2 Super Bowls
4	Curly Lambeau	33	**229**	134	22	.623	226	132	22	.624	3	2	.600	6 NFL
5	Chuck Noll	23	**209**	156	1	.572	193	148	1	.566	16	8	.667	4 Super Bowls
6	M. Schottenheimer	21	**205**	139	1	.596	200	126	1	.613	5	13	.278	—None—
7	Dan Reeves	23	**201**	174	2	.536	190	165	2	.535	11	9	.550	—None—
8	Chuck Knox	22	**193**	158	1	.550	186	147	1	.558	7	11	.389	—None—
9	**Bill Parcells**	19	**183**	138	1	.570	172	130	1	.569	11	8	.579	2 Super Bowls
10	Paul Brown	21	**170**	108	6	.609	166	100	6	.621	4	8	.333	3 NFL
11	Bud Grant	18	**168**	108	5	.607	158	96	5	.620	10	12	.455	1 NFL
12	**Joe Gibbs**	15	**162**	93	0	.635	145	87	0	.625	17	6	.739	3 Super Bowls
13	**Bill Cowher**	15	**161**	99	1	.619	149	90	1	.598	12	9	.571	1 Super Bowl
14	**Mike Holmgren**	15	**159**	103	0	.607	147	93	0	.613	12	10	.545	1 Super Bowl
15	Marv Levy	17	**154**	120	0	.562	143	112	0	.561	11	8	.579	—None—
16	Steve Owen	23	**153**	108	17	.581	151	100	17	.595	2	8	.200	2 NFL
17	**Mike Shanahan**	14	**139**	86	0	.618	131	81	0	.618	8	5	.615	2 Super Bowls
18	Hank Stram	17	**136**	100	10	.573	131	97	10	.571	5	3	.625	1 Super Bowl and 3 AFL
19	Weeb Ewbank	20	**134**	130	7	.507	130	129	7	.502	4	1	.800	1 Super Bowl, 2 NFL, and 1 AFL
20	Mike Ditka	14	**127**	101	0	.557	121	95	0	.560	6	6	.500	1 Super Bowl
21	Dick Vermeil	15	**126**	114	0	.525	120	109	0	.524	6	5	.545	1 Super Bowl
22	Jim Mora	15	**125**	112	0	.527	125	106	0	.541	0	6	.000	—None—
23	George Seifert	11	**124**	67	0	.649	114	62	0	.648	10	5	.667	2 Super Bowls
	Bill Belichick	12	**124**	84	0	.596	111	81	0	.578	13	3	.813	3 Super Bowls
25	**Tony Dungy**	11	**123**	70	0	.637	114	62	0	.648	9	8	.529	1 Super Bowl
	Sid Gillman	18	**123**	104	7	.541	122	99	7	.550	1	5	.167	1 AFL

Notes: The NFL does not recognize records from the All-American Football Conference (1946-49). If it did, **Paul Brown** (52-4-3 in four AAFC seasons) would move up from 10th to 5th on the all-time list with the following career stats— 25 Yrs; 222 Wins; 112 Losses; 9 Ties; .660 Pct; 9-8 playoff record; and 4 AAFC titles.

The NFL also considers the Playoff Bowl or "Runner-up Bowl" (officially: the Bert Bell Benefit Bowl) as a postseason exhibition game. The Playoff Bowl was contested every year from 1960-69 in Miami between Eastern and Western Conference second place teams. While the games did not count, four of the coaches above went to the Playoff Bowl at least once and came away with the following records— Brown (0-1), Grant (0-1), Landry (1-2) and Shula (2-0).

Where They Coached

Belichick—Cleveland (1991-95), New England (2000—); **Brown**—Cleveland (1950-62), Cincinnati (1968-75); **Cowher**—Pittsburgh (1992-2006); **Ditka**— Chicago (1982-92), New Orleans (1997-99); **Dungy**— Tampa Bay (1996-2001), Indianapolis (2002—); **Ewbank**— Baltimore (1954-62), NY Jets (1963-73); **Gibbs**—Washington (1981-92, 2004—); **Gillman**—LA Rams (1955-59), LA-San Diego Chargers (1960-69), Houston (1973-74); **Grant**—Minnesota (1967-83,1985); **Halas**—Chicago Bears (1920-29,33-42,46-55,58-67); **Holmgren**—Green Bay (1992-98), Seattle (1999—); **Knox**— LA Rams (1973-77, 1992-94); Buffalo (1978-82), Seattle (1983-91); **Lambeau**— Green Bay (1921-49), Chicago Cards (1950-51), Washington (1952-53); **Landry**—Dallas (1960-88); **Levy**— Kansas City (1978-82), Buffalo (1986-97); **Mora**—New Orleans (1986-1995), Indianapolis (1998-2001); **Noll**—Pittsburgh (1969-91). **Owen**—NY Giants (1931-53); **Parcells**— NY Giants (1983-90), New England (1993-97), NY Jets (1997-99), Dallas (2003-06); **Reeves**— Denver (1981-92), NY Giants (1993-96), Atlanta (1997-2003); **Schottenheimer**— Cleveland (1984-88), Kansas City (1989-98), Washington (2001), San Diego (2002-06); **Seifert**—San Francisco (1989-96), Carolina (1999-2001); **Shanahan**—LA Raiders (1988-89), Denver (1995—); **Shula**—Baltimore (1963-69), Miami (1970-95); **Stram**—Dallas-Kansas City (1960-74), New Orleans (1976-77); **Vermeil**—Philadelphia (1976-82); St. Louis (1997-99); Kansas City (2001-05).

Top Winning Percentages

Minimum of 85 NFL victories, including playoffs.

		Yrs	W	L	T	Pct
1	Vince Lombardi	10	105	35	6	.740
2	John Madden	10	112	39	7	.731
3	George Allen	12	118	54	5	.681
4	George Halas	40	324	151	31	.671
5	Don Shula	33	347	173	6	.665
6	George Seifert	11	124	67	0	.649
7	**Tony Dungy**	11	123	70	0	.637
8	**Joe Gibbs**	15	162	93	0	.635
9	Curly Lambeau	33	229	134	22	.623
10	**Andy Reid**	8	88	54	0	.620
11	**Bill Cowher**	15	161	99	1	.619
12	**Mike Shanahan**	14	139	86	0	.618
13	Bill Walsh	10	102	63	1	.617
14	Paul Brown	21	170	108	6	.609
15	**Mike Holmgren**	15	159	103	0	.607
16	Bud Grant	18	168	108	5	.607
17	Tom Landry	29	270	178	6	.601
18	**Bill Belichick**	12	124	84	0	.596
19	**Marty Schottenheimer**	21	205	139	1	.596
20	Steve Owen	23	153	108	17	.581
21	Buddy Parker	15	107	76	9	.581
22	Hank Stram	17	136	100	10	.573
23	Chuck Noll	23	209	156	1	.572
24	**Bill Parcells**	19	183	138	1	.570
25	Jimmy Johnson	9	89	68	0	.567

Note: If AAFC records are included, **Paul Brown** moves from 14th to 6th with a percentage of .660 (25 yrs, 222-112-9) and **Buck Shaw** would be 12th at .619 (8 yrs, 91-55-5).

Active Coaches' Victories

Through 2006 season, including playoffs.

		Yrs	W	L	T	Pct
1	Joe Gibbs, Washington	15	**162**	93	0	.635
2	Mike Holmgren, Seattle	15	**159**	103	0	.607
3	Mike Shanahan, Denver	14	**139**	86	0	.618
4	Bill Belichick, New England	12	**124**	84	0	.596
5	Tony Dungy, Indianapolis	11	**123**	70	0	.637
6	Jeff Fisher, Tennessee	12	**110**	97	0	.531
7	Tom Coughlin, NY Giants	11	**97**	89	0	.522
8	Andy Reid, Philadelphia	8	**88**	54	0	.620
9	Jon Gruden, Tampa Bay	9	**82**	70	0	.539
10	Brian Billick, Baltimore	8	**80**	56	0	.588
11	Norv Turner, SD	9	**59**	83	1	.416
12	Herman Edwards, KC	6	**50**	52	0	.490
13	John Fox, Carolina	5	**49**	38	0	.563
14	Wade Phillips, Dallas	7	**48**	42	0	.533
15	Dick Jauron, Buffalo	7	**43**	59	0	.422
16	Marvin Lewis, Cincinnati	4	**35**	30	0	.538
17	Jack Del Rio, Jacksonville	4	**34**	31	0	.523
18	Lovie Smith, Chicago	3	**31**	21	0	.596
19	Sean Payton, New Orleans	1	**11**	7	0	.611
	Mike Nolan, San Fran.	2	**11**	21	0	.344
21	Eric Mangini, NY Jets	1	**10**	7	0	.588
	Romeo Crennel, Cleveland	2	**10**	22	0	.313
23	Scott Linehan, St. Louis	1	**8**	8	0	.500
	Mike McCarthy, Green Bay	1	**8**	8	0	.500
25	Brad Childress, Minnesota	1	**6**	10	0	.375
	Gary Kubiak, Houston	1	**6**	10	0	.375
27	Rod Marinelli, Detroit	1	**3**	13	0	.188
28	Cam Cameron, Miami	0	**0**	0	0	—
	Lane Kiffin, Oakland	0	**0**	0	0	—
	Bobby Petrino, Atlanta	0	**0**	0	0	—
	Mike Tomlin, Pittsburgh	0	**0**	0	0	—
	Ken Whisenhunt, Arizona	0	**0**	0	0	—

Annual Awards
Most Valuable Player

Currently, the NFL does not sanction an official MVP award. It awarded the Joe F. Carr Trophy (Carr was NFL president from 1921-39) to the league MVP from 1938 to 1946. Since then, four principal MVP awards have been given out throughout the years and are noted below: UPI (1953-69), AP (since 1957), the Maxwell Club of Philadelphia's Bert Bell Trophy (since 1959) and the Pro Football Writers Assn. (since 1976). UPI switched to AFC and NFC Player of the Year awards in 1970 and then discontinued its awards in 1997.

Multiple winners (more than one season): Jim Brown (4); Randall Cunningham, Brett Favre, Johnny Unitas and Y.A. Tittle (3); Earl Campbell, Marshall Faulk, Rich Gannon, Otto Graham, Don Hutson, Peyton Manning, Joe Montana, Walter Payton, Barry Sanders, Ken Stabler, Joe Theismann, Kurt Warner and Steve Young (2).

Year	Awards
1938 Mel Hein, NY Giants, C	Carr
1939 Parker Hall, Cleveland Rams, HB	Carr
1940 Ace Parker, Brooklyn, HB	Carr
1941 Don Hutson, Green Bay, E	Carr
1942 Don Hutson, Green Bay, E	Carr
1943 Sid Luckman, Chicago Bears, QB	Carr
1944 Frank Sinkwich, Detroit, HB	Carr
1945 Bob Waterfield, Cleveland Rams, QB	Carr
1946 Bill Dudley, Pittsburgh, HB	Carr
1947-52 No award	
1953 Otto Graham, Cleveland Browns, QB	UPI
1954 Joe Perry, San Francisco, FB	UPI
1955 Otto Graham, Cleveland, QB	UPI
1956 Frank Gifford, NY Giants, HB	UPI
1957 Y.A. Tittle, San Francisco, QB	UPI
& Jim Brown, Cleveland, FB	AP
1958 Jim Brown, Cleveland, FB	UPI
& Gino Marchetti, Baltimore, DE	AP
1959 Johnny Unitas, Baltimore, QB	UPI, Bell
& Charley Conerly, NY Giants, QB	AP
1960 Norm Van Brocklin, Phi., QB	UPI, AP (tie), Bell
& Joe Schmidt, Detroit, LB	AP (tie)
1961 Paul Hornung, Green Bay, HB	UPI, AP, Bell
1962 Y.A. Tittle, NY Giants, QB	UPI
Jim Taylor, Green Bay, FB	AP
& Andy Robustelli, NY Giants, DE	Bell
1963 Jim Brown, Cleveland, FB	UPI, Bell
& Y.A. Tittle, NY Giants, QB	AP

Year	Awards
1964 Johnny Unitas, Baltimore, QB	UPI, AP, Bell
1965 Jim Brown, Cleveland, FB	UPI, AP
& Pete Retzlaff, Philadelphia, TE	Bell
1966 Bart Starr, Green Bay, QB	UPI, AP
& Don Meredith, Dallas, QB	Bell
1967 Johnny Unitas, Baltimore, QB	UPI, AP, Bell
1968 Earl Morrall, Baltimore, QB	UPI, AP
& Leroy Kelly, Cleveland, RB	Bell
1969 Roman Gabriel, LA Rams, QB	UPI, AP, Bell
1970 John Brodie, San Francisco, QB	AP
& George Blanda, Oakland, QB-PK	Bell
1971 Alan Page, Minnesota, DT	AP
& Roger Staubach, Dallas, QB	Bell
1972 Larry Brown, Washington, RB	AP, Bell
1973 O.J. Simpson, Buffalo, RB	AP, Bell
1974 Ken Stabler, Oakland, QB	AP, Bell
& Merlin Olsen, LA Rams, DT	Bell
1975 Fran Tarkenton, Minnesota, QB	AP, Bell
1976 Bert Jones, Baltimore, QB	AP, PFWA
& Ken Stabler, Oakland, QB	Bell
1977 Walter Payton, Chicago, RB	AP, PFWA
& Bob Griese, Miami, QB	Bell
1978 Terry Bradshaw, Pittsburgh, QB	AP, Bell
& Earl Campbell, Houston, RB	PFWA
1979 Earl Campbell, Houston, RB	AP, Bell, PFWA
1980 Brian Sipe, Cleveland, QB	AP, PFWA
& Ron Jaworski, Philadelphia, QB	Bell
1981 Ken Anderson, Cincinnati, QB	AP, Bell, PFWA

Year	Awards
1982	Mark Moseley, Washington, PK . . . . .AP
	Joe Theismann, Washington, QB . . . . .Bell
	& Dan Fouts, San Diego, QB . . . . .PFWA
1983	Joe Theismann, Washington, QB . . . . . . .AP, PFWA
	& John Riggins, Washington, RB . . . . .Bell
1984	Dan Marino, Miami, QB . . . . . . .AP, Bell, PFWA
1985	Marcus Allen, LA Raiders, RB . . . . .AP, PFWA
	& Walter Payton, Chicago, RB . . . . .Bell
1986	Lawrence Taylor, NY Giants, LB . .AP, Bell, PFWA
1987	Jerry Rice, San Francisco, WR . . . . . . .Bell, PFWA
	& John Elway, Denver, QB . . . . .AP
1988	Boomer Esiason, Cincinnati, QB . . . .AP, PFWA &
	Randall Cunningham, Phila., QB . . . . .Bell
1989	Joe Montana, San Francisco, QB . . .AP, Bell, PFWA
1990	Randall Cunningham, Phila., QB . . . .Bell, PFWA
	& Joe Montana, San Francisco, QB . . . . .AP
1991	Thurman Thomas, Buffalo, RB . . . . . . .AP, PFWA
	& Barry Sanders, Detroit, RB . . . . .Bell
1992	Steve Young, San Francisco, QB . . .AP, Bell, PFWA
1993	Emmitt Smith, Dallas, RB . . . . .AP, Bell, PFWA

Year	Awards
1994	Steve Young, San Francisco, QB . . . AP, Bell, PFWA
1995	Brett Favre, Green Bay, QB . . . . .AP, Bell, PFWA
1996	Brett Favre, Green Bay, QB . . . . .AP, Bell, PFWA
1997	Barry Sanders, Detroit, RB . . . . .AP (tie), Bell, PFWA
	& Brett Favre, Green Bay, QB . . . . .AP (tie)
1998	Terrell Davis, Denver, RB . . . . .AP, PFWA
	& Randall Cunningham, Minnesota, QB . . . . . . .Bell
1999	Kurt Warner, St. Louis, QB . . . . .AP, Bell, PFWA
2000	Marshall Faulk, St. Louis, RB . . . . .AP, PFWA
	& Rich Gannon, Oakland, QB . . . . .Bell
2001	Kurt Warner, St. Louis, QB . . . . .AP
	& Marshall Faulk, St. Louis, RB . . . . . . .Bell, PFWA
2002	Rich Gannon, Oakland, QB . . . . . . .AP, Bell, PFWA
2003	Peyton Manning, Indianapolis, QB . . .AP (tie), Bell
	Steve McNair, Tennessee, QB . . . . .AP (tie)
	& Jamal Lewis, Baltimore, RB . . . . .PFWA
2004	Peyton Manning, Indianapolis, QB . . . .AP, Bell, PFWA
2005	Shaun Alexander, Seattle, RB . . . . . .AP, Bell, PFWA
2006	LaDainian Tomlinson, San Diego, RB . .AP, Bell, PFWA

AP Offensive Player of the Year

Selected by The Associated Press in balloting by a nationwide media panel. Given out since 1972. Rookie winners are in **bold** type.
Multiple winners: Earl Campbell and Marshall Faulk (3); Terrell Davis, Jerry Rice and Barry Sanders (2).

Year		Pos	Year		Pos	Year		Pos
1972	Larry Brown, Was	RB	1984	Dan Marino, Mia	QB	1996	Terrell Davis, Den	RB
1973	O.J. Simpson, Buf	RB	1985	Marcus Allen, Raiders	RB	1997	Barry Sanders, Det	RB
1974	Ken Stabler, Oak	QB	1986	Eric Dickerson, Rams	RB	1998	Terrell Davis, Den	RB
1975	Fran Tarkenton, Min	QB	1987	Jerry Rice, SF	WR	1999	Marshall Faulk, St.L	RB
1976	Bert Jones, Bal	QB	1988	Roger Craig, SF	RB	2000	Marshall Faulk, St.L	RB
1977	Walter Payton, Chi	RB	1989	Joe Montana, SF	QB	2001	Marshall Faulk, St.L	RB
1978	**Earl Campbell**, Hou	RB	1990	Warren Moon, Hou	QB	2002	Priest Holmes, KC	RB
1979	Earl Campbell, Hou	RB	1991	Thurman Thomas, Buf	RB	2003	Jamal Lewis, Bal	RB
1980	Earl Campbell, Hou	RB	1992	Steve Young, SF	QB	2004	Peyton Manning, Ind	QB
1981	Ken Anderson, Cin	QB	1993	Jerry Rice, SF	WR	2005	Shaun Alexander, Sea	RB
1982	Dan Fouts, SD	QB	1994	Barry Sanders, Det	RB	2006	LaDainian Tomlinson, SD	RB
1983	Joe Theismann, Was	QB	1995	Brett Favre, GB	QB			

AP Defensive Player of the Year

Selected by The Associated Press in balloting by a nationwide media panel. Given out since 1971. Rookie winners are in **bold** type.
Multiple winners: Lawrence Taylor (3); Joe Greene, Ray Lewis, Mike Singletary, Bruce Smith and Reggie White (2).

Year		Pos	Year		Pos	Year		Pos
1971	Alan Page, Min	DT	1983	Doug Betters, Mia	DE	1995	Bryce Paup, Buf	LB
1972	Joe Greene, Pit	DT	1984	Kenny Easley, Sea	S	1996	Bruce Smith, Buf	DE
1973	Dick Anderson, Mia	S	1985	Mike Singletary, Chi	LB	1997	Dana Stubblefield, SF	DT
1974	Joe Greene, Pit	DT	1986	Lawrence Taylor, NYG	LB	1998	Reggie White, GB	DE
1975	Mel Blount, Pit	CB	1987	Reggie White, Phi	DE	1999	Warren Sapp, TB	DT
1976	Jack Lambert, Pit	LB	1988	Mike Singletary, Chi	LB	2000	Ray Lewis, Bal	LB
1977	Harvey Martin, Dal	DE	1989	Keith Millard, Min	DT	2001	Michael Strahan, NYG	DE
1978	Randy Gradishar, Den	LB	1990	Bruce Smith, Buf	DE	2002	Derrick Brooks, TB	LB
1979	Lee Roy Selmon, TB	DE	1991	Pat Swilling, NO	LB	2003	Ray Lewis, Bal	LB
1980	Lester Hayes, Oak	CB	1992	Cortez Kennedy, Sea	DT	2004	Ed Reed, Bal	CB
1981	**Lawrence Taylor**, NYG	LB	1993	Rod Woodson, Pit	CB	2005	Brian Urlacher, Chi	LB
1982	Lawrence Taylor, NYG	LB	1994	Deion Sanders, SF	CB	2006	Jason Taylor, Mia	DE

UPI NFC Player of the Year

Given out by UPI from 1970-96. Offensive and defensive players honored since 1983. Rookie winners are in **bold** type.
Multiple winners: Eric Dickerson, Reggie White and Mike Singletary (3); Brett Favre, Charles Haley, Walter Payton, Lawrence Taylor and Steve Young (2).

Year		Pos	Year			Pos	Year			Pos
1970	John Brodie, SF	QB	1984	Off–	Eric Dickerson, Rams	RB	1991	Off–	Mark Rypien, Was	QB
1971	Alan Page, Min	DT		Def–	Mike Singletary, Chi	LB		Def–	Reggie White, Phi	DE
1972	Larry Brown, Was	RB	1985	Off–	Walter Payton, Chi	RB	1992	Off–	Steve Young, SF	QB
1973	John Hadl, Rams	QB		Def–	Mike Singletary, Chi	LB		Def–	Chris Doleman, Min	DE
1974	Jim Hart, St.L	QB	1986	Off–	Eric Dickerson, Rams	RB	1993	Off–	Emmitt Smith, Dal	RB
1975	Fran Tarkenton, Min	QB		Def–	Lawrence Taylor, NYG	LB		Def–	Eric Allen, Phi	CB
1976	Chuck Foreman, Min	RB	1987	Off–	Jerry Rice, SF	WR	1994	Off–	Steve Young, SF	QB
1977	Walter Payton, Chi	RB		Def–	Reggie White, Phi	DE		Def–	Charles Haley, Dal	DE
1978	Archie Manning, NO	QB	1988	Off–	Roger Craig, SF	RB	1995	Off–	Brett Favre, GB	QB
1979	Ottis Anderson, St.L	RB		Def–	Mike Singletary, Chi	LB		Def–	Reggie White, GB	DE
1980	Ron Jaworski, Phi	QB	1989	Off–	Joe Montana, SF	QB	1996	Off–	Brett Favre, GB	QB
1981	Tony Dorsett, Dal	RB		Def–	Keith Millard, Min	DT		Def–	Kevin Greene, Car	LB
1982	Mark Moseley, Was	PK	1990	Off–	Randall Cunningham, Phi	QB	1997	Award discontinued.		
1983	Off–Eric Dickerson, Rams	RB		Def–	Charles Haley, SF	LB				
	Def–Lawrence Taylor, NYG	LB								

UPI AFL-AFC Player of the Year

Presented by UPI to the top player in the AFL (1960-69) and AFC (1970-96). Offensive and defensive players have been honored since 1983. Rookie winners are in **bold** type.

Multiple winners: Bruce Smith (4); O.J. Simpson (3); Cornelius Bennett, George Blanda, John Elway, Dan Fouts, Daryle Lamonica, Dan Marino and Curt Warner (2).

Year	Pos	Year	Pos	Year	Pos
1960 **Abner Haynes**, Dal	HB	1978 **Earl Campbell**, Hou	RB	1989 Off–Christian Okoye, KC	RB
1961 George Blanda, Hou	QB	1979 Dan Fouts, SD	QB	Def–Michael Dean. Perry,Cle	NT
1962 Cookie Gilchrist, Buf	FB	1980 Brian Sipe, Cle	QB	1990 Off–Warren Moon, Hou	QB
1963 Lance Alworth, SD	FL	1981 Ken Anderson, Cin	QB	Def–Bruce Smith,Buf	DE
1964 Gino Cappelletti, Bos	FL-PK	1982 Dan Fouts, SD	QB	1991 Off–Thurman Thomas, Buf	RB
1965 Paul Lowe, SD	HB	1983 Off–**Curt Warner**, Sea	RB	Def–Cornelius Bennett, Buf	LB
1966 Jim Nance, Bos	FB	Def–Rod Martin, Raiders	LB	1992 Off–Barry Foster, Pit	RB
1967 Daryle Lamonica, Raiders	QB	1984 Off–Dan Marino, Mia	QB	Def–Junior Seau, SD	LB
1968 Joe Namath, NYJ	QB	Def–Mark Gastineau, NYJ	DE	1993 Off–John Elway, Den	QB
1969 Daryle Lamonica, Raiders	QB	1985 Off–Marcus Allen, Raiders	RB	Def–Rod Woodson, Pit	CB
1970 George Blanda, Raiders	QB-PK	Def–Andre Tippett, NE	LB	1994 Off–Dan Marino, Mia	QB
1971 Otis Taylor, KC	WR	1986 Off–Curt Warner, Sea	RB	Def–Greg Lloyd, Pit	LB
1972 O.J. Simpson, Buf	RB	Def–Rulon Jones, Den	DE	1995 Off–Jim Harbaugh, Ind	QB
1973 O.J. Simpson, Buf	RB	1987 Off–John Elway, Den	QB	Def–Bryce Paup, Buf	LB
1974 Ken Stabler, Raiders	QB	Def–Bruce Smith, Buf	DE	1996 Off–Terrell Davis, Den	RB
1975 O.J. Simpson, Buf	RB	1988 Off–Boomer Esiason, Cin	QB	Def–Bruce Smith, Buf	DE
1976 Bert Jones, Bal	QB	Def–Bruce Smith, Buf	DE	1997 Award discontinued.	
1977 Craig Morton, Den	QB	& Cornelius Bennett, Buf	LB		

UPI NFL-NFC Rookie of the Year

Presented by UPI to the top rookie in the NFL (1955-69) and NFC (1970-96). Players who were the overall first pick in the NFL draft are in **bold** type.

Year	Pos	Year	Pos	Year	Pos
1955 Alan Ameche, Bal	FB	1970 Bruce Taylor, SF	DB	1985 Jerry Rice, SF	WR
1956 Lenny Moore, Bal	HB	1971 John Brockington, GB	RB	1986 Reuben Mayes, NO	RB
1957 Jim Brown, Cle	FB	1972 Chester Marcol, GB	PK	1987 Robert Awalt, St.L	TE
1958 Jimmy Orr, Pit	FL	1973 Charle Young, Phi	TE	1988 Keith Jackson, Phi	TE
1959 Boyd Dowler, GB	FL	1974 John Hicks, NY	G	1989 Barry Sanders, Det	RB
1960 Gail Cogdill, Det	FL	1975 Mike Thomas, Wash	RB	1990 Mark Carrier, Chi	S
1961 Mike Ditka, Chi	TE	1976 Sammy White, Min	WR	1991 Lawrence Dawsey, TB	WR
1962 Ronnie Bull, Chi	FB	1977 Tony Dorsett, Dal	RB	1992 Robert Jones, Dal	LB
1963 Paul Flatley, Min	FL	1978 Bubba Baker, Det	DE	1993 Jerome Bettis, LA	RB
1964 Charley Taylor, Wash	HB	1979 Ottis Anderson, St.L	RB	1994 Bryant Young, SF	DT
1965 Gale Sayers, Chi	HB	1980 **Billy Sims**, Det	RB	1995 Rashaan Salaam, Chi	RB
1966 Johnny Roland, St.L	HB	1981 **George Rogers**, NO	RB	1996 Simeon Rice, Ari.	DE
1967 Mel Farr, Det	RB	1982 Jim McMahon, Chi	QB	1997 Award discontinued.	
1968 Earl McCullough, Det	FL	1983 Eric Dickerson, LA	RB		
1969 Calvin Hill, Dal	RB	1984 Paul McFadden, Phi	PK		

UPI AFL-AFC Rookie of the Year

Presented by UPI to the top rookie in the AFL (1960-69) and AFC (1970-96). Players who were the overall first pick in the AFL or NFL draft are in **bold** type.

Year	Pos	Year	Pos	Year	Pos
1960 Abner Haynes, Dal	HB	1973 Bobbie Clark, Cin	RB	1986 Leslie O'Neal, SD	DE
1961 Earl Faison, SD	DE	1974 Don Woods, SD	RB	1987 Shane Conlan, Buf	LB
1962 Curtis McClinton, Dal	FB	1975 Robert Brazile, Hou	LB	1988 John Stephens, NE	RB
1963 Billy Joe, Den	FB	1976 Mike Haynes, NE	DB	1989 Derrick Thomas, KC	LB
1964 Matt Snell, NY	FB	1977 A.J. Duhe, Mia	DE	1990 Richmond Webb, Mia	OT
1965 Joe Namath, NY	QB	1978 **Earl Campbell**, Hou	RB	1991 Mike Croel, Den	LB
1966 Bobby Burnett, Buf	HB	1979 Jerry Butler, Buf	WR	1992 Dale Carter, KC	CB
1967 George Webster, Hou	LB	1980 Joe Cribbs, Buf	RB	1993 Rick Mirer, Sea	QB
1968 Paul Robinson, Cin	RB	1981 Joe Delaney, KC	RB	1994 Marshall Faulk, Ind	RB
1969 Greg Cook, Cin	QB	1982 Marcus Allen, LA	RB	1995 Curtis Martin, NE	RB
1970 Dennis Shaw, Buf	QB	1983 Curt Warner, Sea	RB	1996 Terry Glenn, NE	WR
1971 **Jim Plunkett**, NE	QB	1984 Louis Lipps, Pit	WR	1997 Award discontinued.	
1972 Franco Harris, Pit	RB	1985 Kevin Mack, Cle	RB		

Annual Awards (Cont.)

AP Offensive Rookie of the Year

Selected by The Associated Press in balloting by a nationwide media panel. Given out since 1967.

Year	Pos	Year	Pos	Year	Pos
1967 Mel Farr, Det	RB	1981 George Rogers, NO	RB	1995 Curtis Martin, NE	RB
1968 Earl McCullouch, Det	OE	1982 Marcus Allen, Raiders	RB	1996 Eddie George, Hou	RB
1969 Calvin Hill, Dal	RB	1983 Eric Dickerson, Rams	RB	1997 Warrick Dunn, TB	RB
1970 Dennis Shaw, Buf	QB	1984 Louis Lipps, Pit	WR	1998 Randy Moss, Min	WR
1971 John Brockington, GB	RB	1985 Eddie Brown, Cin	WR	1999 Edgerrin James, Ind	RB
1972 Franco Harris, Pit	RB	1986 Reuben Mayes, NO	RB	2000 Mike Anderson, Den	RB
1973 Chuck Foreman, Min	RB	1987 Troy Stradford, Mia	RB	2001 Anthony Thomas, Chi	RB
1974 Don Woods, SD	RB	1988 John Stephens, NE	RB	2002 Clinton Portis, Den	RB
1975 Mike Thomas, Was	RB	1989 Barry Sanders, Det	RB	2003 Anquan Boldin, Ari	WR
1976 Sammy White, Min	WR	1990 Emmitt Smith, Dal	RB	2004 Ben Roethlisberger, Pit	QB
1977 Tony Dorsett, Dal	RB	1991 Leonard Russell, NE	RB	2005 Carnell Williams, TB	RB
1978 Earl Campbell, Hou	RB	1992 Carl Pickens, Cin	WR	2006 Vince Young, Ten	QB
1979 Ottis Anderson, St.L	RB	1993 Jerome Bettis, Rams	RB		
1980 Billy Sims, Det	RB	1994 Marshall Faulk, Ind	RB		

AP Defensive Rookie of the Year

Selected by The Associated Press in balloting by a nationwide media panel. Given out since 1967.

Year	Pos	Year	Pos	Year	Pos
1967 Lem Barney, Det	CB	1981 Lawrence Taylor, NYG	LB	1996 Simeon Rice, Ari	DE
1968 Claude Humphrey, Atl	DE	1982 Chip Banks, Cle	LB	1997 Peter Boulware, Bal	LB
1969 Joe Greene, Pit	DT	1983 Vernon Maxwell, Bal	LB	1998 Charles Woodson, Raiders	CB
1970 Bruce Taylor, SF	CB	1984 Bill Maas, KC	DT	1999 Jevon Kearse, Ten	DE
1971 Isiah Robertson, Rams	LB	1985 Duane Bickett, Ind	LB	2000 Brian Urlacher, Chi	LB
1972 Willie Buchanon, GB	CB	1986 Leslie O'Neal, SD	DE	2001 Kendrell Bell, Pit	LB
1973 Wally Chambers, Chi	DT	1987 Shane Conlan, Buf	LB	2002 Julius Peppers, Car	DE
1974 Jack Lambert, Pit	LB	1988 Erik McMillan, NYJ	S	2003 Terrell Suggs, Bal	LB
1975 Robert Brazile, Hou	LB	1989 Derrick Thomas, KC	LB	2004 Jonathan Vilma, NYJ	LB
1976 Mike Haynes, NE	CB	1990 Mark Carrier, Chi	S	2005 Shawne Merriman, SD	LB
1977 A.J. Duhe, Mia	DE	1991 Mike Croel, Den	LB	2006 DeMeco Ryans, Hou	LB
1978 Al Baker, Det	DE	1992 Dale Carter, KC	CB		
1979 Jim Haslett, Buf	LB	1993 Dana Stubblefield, SF	DT		
1980 Buddy Curry, Atl	LB	1994 Tim Bowens, Mia	DT		
& Al Richardson, Atl	LB	1995 Hugh Douglas, NYJ	DE		

Coach of the Year

Presented by UPI to the top coach in the AFL-NFL (1955-69) and AFC-NFC (1970-96). In 1997, the UPI awards were discontinued. Awards beginning in 1997 are the consensus selections from presenters such as AP, The Maxwell Football Club of Philadelphia, *The Sporting News* and the Pro Football Writers Association. Records indicate the team's change in record from the previous season.

Multiple winners: Dan Reeves (4); Paul Brown, Chuck Knox, Marty Schottenheimer and Don Shula (3); George Allen, Leeman Bennett, Mike Ditka, George Halas, Tom Landry, Marv Levy, Bill Parcells, Jack Pardee, Sam Rutigliano, Lou Saban, Allie Sherman, Dick Vermeil and Bill Walsh (2).

Year	Improvement	Year	Improvement
1955 NFL–Joe Kuharich, Washington	3-9 to 8-4	1969 NFL–Bud Grant, Minnesota	8-6 to 12-2
1956 NFL–Buddy Parker, Detroit	3-9 to 9-3	AFL–Paul Brown, Cincinnati	3-11 to 4-9-1
1957 NFL–Paul Brown, Cleveland	5-7 to 9-2-1	1970 NFC–Alex Webster, New York	6-8 to 9-5
1958 NFL–Weeb Ewbank, Baltimore	7-5 to 9-3	AFC–Paul Brown, Cincinnati	4-9-1 to 8-6
1959 NFL–Vince Lombardi, Green Bay	1-10-1 to 7-5	1971 NFC–George Allen, Washington	6-8 to 9-4-1
1960 NFL–Buck Shaw, Philadelphia	7-5 to 10-2	AFC–Don Shula, Miami	10-4 to 10-3-1
AFL–Lou Rymkus, Houston	10-4	1972 NFC–Dan Devine, Green Bay	4-8-2 to 10-4
1961 NFL–Allie Sherman, New York	6-4-2 to 10-3-1	AFC–Chuck Noll, Pittsburgh	6-8 to 11-3
AFL–Wally Lemm, Houston	10-4 to 10-3-1	1973 NFC–Chuck Knox, Los Angeles	6-7-1 to 12-2
1962 NFL–Allie Sherman, New York	10-3-1 to 12-2	AFC–John Ralston, Denver	5-9 to 7-5-2
AFL–Jack Faulkner, Denver	3-11 to 7-7	1974 NFC–Don Coryell, St. Louis	4-9-1 to 10-4
1963 NFL–George Halas, Chicago	9-5 to 11-1-2	AFC–Sid Gillman, Houston	1-13 to 7-7
AFL–Al Davis, Oakland	1-13 to 10-4	1975 NFC–Tom Landry, Dallas	8-6 to 10-4
1964 NFL–Don Shula, Baltimore	8-6 to 12-2	AFC–Ted Marchibroda, Baltimore	2-12 to 10-4
AFL–Lou Saban, Buffalo	7-6-1 to 12-2	1976 NFC–Jack Pardee, Chicago	4-10 to 7-7
1965 NFL–George Halas, Chicago	5-9 to 9-5	AFC–Chuck Fairbanks, New England	3-11 to 11-3
AFL–Lou Saban, Buffalo	12-2 to 10-3-1	1977 NFC–Leeman Bennett, Atlanta	4-10 to 7-7
1966 NFL–Tom Landry, Dallas	7-7 to 10-3-1	AFC–Red Miller, Denver	9-5 to 12-2
AFL–Mike Holovak, Boston	4-8-2 to 8-4-2	1978 NFC–Dick Vermeil, Philadelphia	5-9 to 9-7
1967 NFL–George Allen, Los Angeles	8-6 to 11-1-2	AFC–Walt Michaels, New York	3-11 to 8-8
AFL–John Rauch, Oakland	8-5-1 to 13-1	1979 NFC–Jack Pardee, Washington	8-8 to 10-6
1968 NFL–Don Shula, Baltimore	11-1-2 to 13-1	AFC–Sam Rutigliano, Cleveland	8-8 to 9-7
AFL–Hank Stram, Kansas City	9-5 to 12-2		

Year	Improvement
1980 NFC–Leeman Bennett, Atlanta	.6-10 to 12-4
AFC–Sam Rutigliano, Cleveland	.9-7 to 11-5
1981 NFC–Bill Walsh, San Francisco	.6-10 to 13-3
AFC–Forrest Gregg, Cincinnati	.6-10 to 12-4
1982 NFC–Joe Gibbs, Washington	.8-8 to 8-1
AFC–Tom Flores, Los Angeles	.7-9 to 8-1
1983 NFC–John Robinson, Los Angeles	.2-7 to 9-7
AFC–Chuck Knox, Seattle	.4-5 to 9-7
1984 NFC–Bill Walsh, San Francisco	.10-6 to 15-1
AFC–Chuck Knox, Seattle	.9-7 to 12-4
1985 NFC–Mike Ditka, Chicago	.10-6 to 15-1
AFC–Raymond Berry, New England	.9-7 to 11-5
1986 NFC–Bill Parcells, New York	.10-6 to 14-2
AFC–Marty Schottenheimer, Cleveland	.8-8 to 12-4
1987 NFC–Jim Mora, New Orleans	.7-9 to 12-3
AFC–Ron Meyer, Indianapolis	.3-13 to 9-6
1988 NFC–Mike Ditka, Chicago	.11-4 to 12-4
AFC–Marv Levy, Buffalo	.7-8 to 12-4
1989 NFC–Lindy Infante, Green Bay	.4-12 to 10-6
AFC–Dan Reeves, Denver	.8-8 to 11-5
1990 NFC–Jimmy Johnson, Dallas	.1-15 to 7-9
AFC–Art Shell, Los Angeles	.8-8 to 12-4
1991 NFC–Wayne Fontes, Detroit	.6-10 to 12-4
AFC–Dan Reeves, Denver	.5-11 to 12-4

Year	Improvement
1992 NFC–Dennis Green, Minnesota	.8-8 to 11-5
AFC–Bobby Ross, San Diego	.4-12 to 11-5
1993 NFC–Dan Reeves, New York	.6-10 to 11-5
AFC–Marv Levy, Buffalo	.11-5 to 12-4
1994 NFC–Dave Wannstedt, Chicago	.7-9 to 9-7
AFC–Bill Parcells, New England	.5-11 to 10-6
1995 NFC–Ray Rhodes, Philadelphia	.7-9 to 10-6
AFC–Marty Schottenheimer, Kansas City	9-7 to 13-3
1996 NFC–Dom Capers, Carolina	.7-9 to 12-4
AFC–Tom Coughlin, Jacksonville	.4-12 to 9-7
1997 NFL–Jim Fassel, NY Giants	.6-10 to 10-5-1
1998 NFL–Dan Reeves, Atlanta	.7-9 to 14-2
1999 NFL–Dick Vermeil, St. Louis	.4-12 to 13-3
2000 NFL–Jim Haslett, New Orleans	.3-13 to 10-6
2001 NFL–Dick Jauron, Chicago	.5-11 to 13-3
2002 NFL–Andy Reid, Philadelphia	.11-5 to 12-4
2003 NFL–Bill Belichick, New England	.9-7 to 14-2
2004 NFL–Marty Schottenheimer, San Diego	4-12 to 12-4
2005 NFL–Lovie Smith, Chicago	5-11 to 11-5
2006 NFL–Sean Payton, New Orleans	.3-13 to 10-6

ARENA FOOTBALL

The Arena Football League debuted in June of 1987 with four teams in Chicago, Denver, Pittsburgh and Washington D.C. Currently there are 19 teams in the league (including the New Orleans VooDoo, who returned in 2007 after a Hurricane Katrina-related absence in 2006), divided into two conferences and four divisions.

ArenaBowl

Multiple Winners: Tampa Bay (5); Detroit (4); San Jose (3); Arizona and Orlando (2).

Bowl	Year	Winner	Head Coach	Score	Loser	Head Coach	Site
I	1987	Denver	Tim Marcum	45-16	Pittsburgh	Joe Haering	Pittsburgh
II	1988	Detroit	Tim Marcum	24-13	Chicago	Perry Moss	Chicago
III	1989	Detroit	Tim Marcum	39-26	Pittsburgh	Joe Haering	Detroit
IV	1990	Detroit	Perry Moss	51-27	Dallas	Ernie Stautner	Detroit
V	1991	Tampa Bay	Fran Curci	48-42	Detroit	Tim Marcum	Detroit
VI	1992	Detroit	Tim Marcum	56-38	Orlando	Perry Moss	Orlando
VII	1993	Tampa Bay	Lary Kuharich	51-31	Detroit	Tim Marcum	Detroit
VIII	1994	Arizona	Danny White	36-31	Orlando	Perry Moss	Orlando
IX	1995	Tampa Bay	Tim Marcum	48-35	Orlando	Perry Moss	St. Petersburg
X	1996	Tampa Bay	Tim Marcum	42-38	Iowa	John Gregory	Des Moines
XI	1997	Arizona	Danny White	55-33	Iowa	John Gregory	Phoenix
XII	1998	Orlando	Jay Gruden	62-31	Tampa Bay	Tim Marcum	Tampa
XIII	1999	Albany	Mike Dailey	59-48	Orlando	Jay Gruden	Albany
XIV	2000	Orlando	Jay Gruden	41-38	Nashville	Pat Sperduto	Orlando
XV	2001	Grand Rapids	Michael Trigg	64-42	Nashville	Pat Sperduto	Grand Rapids
XVI	2002	San Jose	Darren Arbet	52-14	Arizona	Danny White	San Jose
XVII	2003	Tampa Bay	Tim Marcum	43-29	Arizona	Danny White	Tampa
XVIII	2004	San Jose	Darren Arbet	69-62	Arizona	Danny White	Phoenix
XIX	2005	Colorado	Mike Dailey	51-48	Georgia	Doug Plank	Las Vegas
XX	2006	Chicago	Mike Hohensee	69-61	Orlando	Jay Gruden	Las Vegas
XXI	2007	San Jose	Darren Arbet	55-33	Columbus	Doug Kay	New Orleans

ArenaBowl MVP

Multiple Winners: George LaFrance (3); Mark Grieb and Stevie Thomas (2).

Year	Year	Year
1987 Gary Mullen, Denver, WR	1996 Stevie Thomas, TB, WR/LB	2004 Off–Mark Grieb, San Jose, QB
1988 Steve Griffin, Detroit, WR/DB	1997 Donnie Davis, Arizona, QB	Def–Ricky Parker, Arizona, DS
1989 George LaFrance, Det., WR/DB	1998 Rick Hamilton, Orlando, FB/LB	2005 Off–Willis Marshall, Col., WR
1990 Art Schlichter, Detroit, QB	1999 Eddie Brown, Albany, OS	Def–Ahmad Hawkins, Col., DB
1991 Stevie Thomas, TB, WR/LB	2000 Connell Maynor, Orlando, QB	2006 Off–Matt D'Orazio, Chi. QB
1992 George LaFrance, Detroit, OS	2001 Terrill Shaw, Grand Rapids, OS	Def–Dennison Robinson, Chi., DB
1993 Jay Gruden, Tampa Bay, QB	2002 John Dutton, San Jose, QB	2007 Off–Mark Grieb, San Jose, QB
1994 Sherdrick Bonner, Arizona, QB	2003 Lawrence Samuels, TB, WR/LB	Def–Omarr Smith, San Jose, DB
1995 George LaFrance, Tampa Bay, OS		

Arena Football (Cont.)

Offensive Player Of The Year

Regular Season Offensive Player of the Year as voted on by AFL head coaches, fans, players and the Arena Football League Writers Association (AFLWA). The award was known as the Most Valuable Player Award from 1987-95.

Multiple Winners: Eddie Brown (3); Damian Harrell, George LaFrance and Barry Wagner (2).

Year	Year	Year
1987 Russell Hairston, Pittsburgh	1994 Eddie Brown, Albany	2001 Aaron Garcia, New York
1988 Ben Bennett, Chicago	1995 Barry Wagner, Orlando	2002 Mark Grieb, San Jose
1989 George LaFrance, Detroit	1996 Eddie Brown, Albany	2003 Chris Jackson, Los Angeles, WR
1990 Art Schlichter, Detroit	1997 Barry Wagner, Orlando	2004 Marcus Nash, Las Vegas
1991 George LaFrance, Detroit	1998 Calvin Schexnayder, Arizona	2005 Damian Harrell, Colorado
1992 Jay Gruden, Tampa Bay	1999 Eddie Brown, Albany	2006 Damian Harrell, Colorado
1993 Hunkie Cooper, Arizona	2000 Mike Horacek, Iowa	2007 Siaha Burley, Utah

Defensive Player Of The Year

Regular Season Offensive Player of the Year as voted on by AFL head coaches, fans, players and the Arena Football League Writers Association (AFLWA).

Multiple Winners: Kenny McEntyre (3); Clevan Thomas (2).

Year	Year	Year
1996 David McLeod, Albany	2000 Kenny McEntyre, Orlando	2004 Kenny McEntyre, Orlando
1997 Tracey Perkins, Tampa Bay	2001 Kenny McEntyre, Orlando	2005 Silas Demary, Los Angeles
1998 Johnnie Harris, Tamp Bay	2002 Clevan Thomas, San Jose	2006 Jerald Brown, Columbus
1999 James Baron, Nashville	2003 Clevan Thomas, San Jose	2007 Greg White, Orlando

---

Arena Football 101

The Field

- Indoor padded surface, 85 feet wide (size of an NHL rink) and 50 yards long with eight-yard end zones.
- Goal posts are nine feet wide with a crossbar height of 15 feet (NFL goal posts are 18 1/2 feet wide with the crossbar at 10 feet).
- The goal-side rebound nets are 30 feet wide by 32 feet high. The bottoms of the nets are eight feet above the ground.

The Ball

- Same size and weight as an NFL ball.

Cool Rules

- Punting is illegal. On fourth down, a team may go for a first down, touchdown or field goal.
- The receiving team may field any kickoff or missed field goal that rebounds off the net.
- A forward pass that rebounds off of the end zone net is a live ball and is in play until it touches the playing surface.
- One receiver may go in forward motion before the snap.
- Each team has eight players on the field at all times (as opposed to the NFL, which is 11 a side.
- Teams get three points for a field goal by placement...or four points for a field goal by drop kick.

Source: *Arena Football League*

CANADIAN FOOTBALL

The Grey Cup

Earl Grey, the Governor-General of Canada (1904-11), donated a trophy in 1909 for the Rugby Football Championship of Canada. The trophy, which later became known as the Grey Cup, was originally open to competition for teams registered with the Canada Rugby Union. Since 1954, the Cup has gone to the champion of the Canadian Football League (CFL).

Overall multiple winners: Toronto Argonauts (15); Edmonton Eskimos (13); Winnipeg Blue Bombers (9); Hamilton Tiger-Cats (8); Ottawa Rough Riders (7); B.C. Lions, Calgary Stampeders, Hamilton Tigers and Montreal Alouettes (5); University of Toronto (4); Queen's University (3); Ottawa Senators, Sarnia Imperials, Saskatchewan Roughriders and Toronto Balmy Beach (2).

CFL multiple winners (since 1954): Edmonton (13); Hamilton and Winnipeg (7); B.C. Lions, Ottawa and Toronto (5); Calgary and Montreal (4); Saskatchewan (2).

Year Cup Final	Year Cup Final
1909 Univ. of Toronto 26, Toronto Parkdale 6	1921 Toronto Argonauts 23, Edmonton Eskimos 0
1910 Univ. of Toronto 16, Hamilton Tigers 7	1922 Queens Univ. 13, Edmonton Elks 1
1911 Univ. of Toronto 14, Toronto Argonauts 7	1923 Queens Univ. 54, Regina Roughriders 0
1912 Hamilton Alerts 11, Toronto Argonauts 4	1924 Queens Univ. 11, Toronto Balmy Beach 3
1913 Hamilton Tigers 44, Toronto Parkdale 2	1925 Ottawa Senators 24, Winnipeg Tigers 1
1914 Toronto Argonauts 14, Univ. of Toronto 2	1926 Ottawa Senators 10, Univ. of Toronto 7
1915 Hamilton Tigers 13, Toronto Rowing 7	1927 Toronto Balmy Beach 9, Hamilton Tigers 6
1916-19 Not held (WWI)	1928 Hamilton Tigers 30, Regina Roughriders 0
	1929 Hamilton Tigers 14, Regina Roughriders 3
1920 Univ. of Toronto 16, Toronto Argonauts 3	

Year Cup Final
1930 Toronto Balmy Beach 11, Regina Roughriders 6
1931 Montreal AAA 22, Regina Roughriders 0
1932 Hamilton Tigers 25, Regina Roughriders 6
1933 Toronto Argonauts 4, Sarnia Imperials 3
1934 Sarnia Imperials 20, Regina Roughriders 12
1935 Winnipeg 'Pegs 18, Hamilton Tigers 12
1936 Sarnia Imperials 26, Ottawa Rough Riders 20
1937 Toronto Argonauts 4, Winnipeg Blue Bombers 3
1938 Toronto Argonauts 30, Winnipeg Blue Bombers 7
1939 Winnipeg Blue Bombers 8, Ottawa Rough Riders 7

1940 Gm 1: Ottawa Rough Riders 8, Toronto B-Beach 2
     Gm 2: Ottawa Rough Riders 12, Toronto B-Beach 5
1941 Winnipeg Blue Bombers 18, Ottawa Rough Riders 16

Year Cup Final
1942 Toronto RACF 8, Winnipeg RACF 5
1943 Hamilton Wildcats 23, Winnipeg RACF 14
1944 Montreal HMCS 7, Hamilton Wildcats 6
1945 Toronto Argonauts 35, Winnipeg Blue Bombers 0
1946 Toronto Argonauts 28, Winnipeg Blue Bombers 6
1947 Toronto Argonauts 10, Winnipeg Blue Bombers 9
1948 Calgary Stampeders 12, Ottawa Rough Riders 7
1949 Montreal Alouettes 28, Calgary Stampeders 15

1950 Toronto Argonauts 13, Winnipeg Blue Bombers 0
1951 Ottawa Rough Riders 21, Saskatch. Roughriders 14
1952 Toronto Argonauts 21, Edmonton Eskimos 11
1953 Hamilton Tiger-Cats 12, Winnipeg Blue Bombers 6

Year	Winner	Head Coach	Score	Loser	Head Coach	Site
1954	Edmonton	Frank (Pop) Ivy	26-25	Montreal	Doug Walker	Toronto
1955	Edmonton	Frank (Pop) Ivy	34-19	Montreal	Doug Walker	Vancouver
1956	Edmonton	Frank (Pop) Ivy	50-27	Montreal	Doug Walker	Toronto
1957	Hamilton	Jim Trimble	32-7	Winnipeg	Bud Grant	Toronto
1958	Winnipeg	Bud Grant	35-28	Hamilton	Jim Trimble	Vancouver
1959	Winnipeg	Bud Grant	21-7	Hamilton	Jim Trimble	Toronto
1960	Ottawa	Frank Clair	16-6	Edmonton	Eagle Keys	Vancouver
1961	Winnipeg	Bud Grant	21-14 (OT)	Hamilton	Jim Trimble	Toronto
1962	Winnipeg	Bud Grant	28-27*	Hamilton	Jim Trimble	Toronto
1963	Hamilton	Ralph Sazio	21-10	B.C. Lions	Dave Skrien	Vancouver
1964	B.C. Lions	Dave Skrien	34-24	Hamilton	Ralph Sazio	Toronto
1965	Hamilton	Ralph Sazio	22-16	Winnipeg	Bud Grant	Toronto
1966	Saskatchewan	Eagle Keys	29-14	Ottawa	Frank Clair	Vancouver
1967	Hamilton	Ralph Sazio	24-1	Saskatchewan	Eagle Keys	Ottawa
1968	Ottawa	Frank Clair	24-21	Calgary	Jerry Williams	Toronto
1969	Ottawa	Frank Clair	29-11	Saskatchewan	Eagle Keys	Montreal
1970	Montreal	Sam Etcheverry	23-10	Calgary	Jim Duncan	Toronto
1971	Calgary	Jim Duncan	14-11	Toronto	Leo Cahill	Vancouver
1972	Hamilton	Jerry Williams	13-10	Saskatchewan	Dave Skrien	Hamilton
1973	Ottawa	Jack Gotta	22-18	Edmonton	Ray Jauch	Toronto
1974	Montreal	Marv Levy	20-7	Edmonton	Ray Jauch	Vancouver
1975	Edmonton	Ray Jauch	9-8	Montreal	Marv Levy	Calgary
1976	Ottawa	George Brancato	23-20	Saskatchewan	John Payne	Toronto
1977	Montreal	Marv Levy	41-6	Edmonton	Hugh Campbell	Montreal
1978	Edmonton	Hugh Campbell	20-13	Montreal	Joe Scannella	Toronto
1979	Edmonton	Hugh Campbell	17-9	Montreal	Joe Scannella	Montreal
1980	Edmonton	Hugh Campbell	48-10	Hamilton	John Payne	Toronto
1981	Edmonton	Hugh Campbell	26-23	Ottawa	George Brancato	Montreal
1982	Edmonton	Hugh Campbell	32-16	Toronto	Bob O'Billovich	Toronto
1983	Toronto	Bob O'Billovich	18-17	B.C. Lions	Don Matthews	Vancouver
1984	Winnipeg	Cal Murphy	47-17	Hamilton	Al Bruno	Edmonton
1985	B.C. Lions	Don Matthews	37-24	Hamilton	Al Bruno	Montreal
1986	Hamilton	Al Bruno	39-15	Edmonton	Jack Parker	Vancouver
1987	Edmonton	Joe Faragalli	38-36	Toronto	Bob O'Billovich	Vancouver
1988	Winnipeg	Mike Riley	22-21	B.C. Lions	Larry Donovan	Ottawa
1989	Saskatchewan	John Gregory	43-40	Hamilton	Al Bruno	Toronto
1990	Winnipeg	Mike Riley	50-11	Edmonton	Joe Faragalli	Vancouver
1991	Toronto	Adam Rita	36-21	Calgary	Wally Buono	Winnipeg
1992	Calgary	Wally Buono	24-10	Winnipeg	Urban Bowman	Toronto
1993	Edmonton	Ron Lancaster	33-23	Winnipeg	Cal Murphy	Calgary
1994	B.C. Lions	Dave Ritchie	26-23	Baltimore	Don Matthews	Vancouver
1995	Baltimore	Don Matthews	37-20	Calgary	Wally Buono	Regina
1996	Toronto	Don Matthews	43-37	Edmonton	Ron Lancaster	Hamilton
1997	Toronto	Don Matthews	47-23	Saskatchewan	Jim Daley	Edmonton
1998	Calgary	Wally Buono	26-24	Hamilton	Ron Lancaster	Winnipeg
1999	Hamilton	Ron Lancaster	32-21	Calgary	Wally Buono	Vancouver
2000	B.C. Lions	Steve Buratto	28-26	Montreal	Charlie Taaffe	Calgary
2001	Calgary	Wally Buono	27-19	Winnipeg	Dave Ritchie	Montreal
2002	Montreal	Don Matthews	25-16	Edmonton	Tom Higgins	Edmonton
2003	Edmonton	Tom Higgins	34-22	Montreal	Don Matthews	Regina
2004	Toronto	Mike Clemons	27-19	B.C. Lions	Wally Buono	Ottawa
2005	Edmonton	Danny Maciocia	38-35 (OT)	Montreal	Don Matthews	Vancouver
2006	B.C. Lions	Wally Buono	25-14	Montreal	Jim Popp	Winnipeg

*Halted by fog in 4th quarter, final 9:29 played the following day.

CFL Most Outstanding Player

Regular season Player of the Year as selected by The Football Reporters of Canada since 1953.

Multiple winners: Doug Flutie (6); Russ Jackson and Jackie Parker (3); Dieter Brock, Ron Lancaster and Mike Pringle (2).

Year	Year	Year
1953 Billy Vessels, Edmonton, RB	1971 Don Jonas, Winnipeg, QB	1989 Tracy Ham, Edmonton, QB
1954 Sam Etcheverry, Montreal, QB	1972 Garney Henley, Hamilton, WR	1990 Mike Clemons, Toronto, RB
1955 Pat Abbruzzi, Montreal, RB	1973 Geo. McGowan, Edmonton, QB	1991 Doug Flutie, B.C. Lions, QB
1956 Hal Patterson, Montreal, E-DB	1974 Tom Wilkinson, Edmonton, QB	1992 Doug Flutie, Calgary, QB
1957 Jackie Parker, Edmonton, RB	1975 Willie Burden, Calgary, RB	1993 Doug Flutie, Calgary, QB
1958 Jackie Parker, Edmonton, QB	1976 Ron Lancaster, Saskatch., QB	1994 Doug Flutie, Calgary, QB
1959 Johnny Bright, Edmonton, RB	1977 Jimmy Edwards, Hamilton, RB	1995 Mike Pringle, Baltimore, RB
1960 Jackie Parker, Edmonton, QB	1978 Tony Gabriel, Ottawa, TE	1996 Doug Flutie, Toronto, QB
1961 Bernie Faloney, Hamilton, QB	1979 David Green, Montreal, RB	1997 Doug Flutie, Toronto, QB
1962 George Dixon, Montreal, RB	1980 Dieter Brock, Winnipeg, QB	1998 Mike Pringle, Montreal, RB
1963 Russ Jackson, Ottawa, QB	1981 Dieter Brock, Winnipeg, QB	1999 Danny McManus, Hamilton, QB
1964 Lovell Coleman, Calgary, RB	1982 Condredge Holloway, Tor., QB	2000 Dave Dickenson, Calgary, QB
1965 George Reed, Saskatchewan, RB	1983 Warren Moon, Edmonton, QB	2001 Khari Jones, Winnipeg, QB
1966 Russ Jackson, Ottawa, QB	1984 Willard Reaves, Winnipeg, RB	2002 Milt Stegall, Winnipeg, SB
1967 Peter Liske, Calgary, QB	1985 Merv Fernandez, B.C. Lions, WR	2003 Anthony Calvillo, Montreal, QB
1968 Bill Symons, Toronto, RB	1986 James Murphy, Winnipeg, WR	2004 Casey Printers, B.C. Lions, QB
1969 Russ Jackson, Ottawa, QB	1987 Tom Clements, Winnipeg, QB	2005 Ricky Ray, Edmonton, QB
1970 Ron Lancaster, Saskatch., QB	1988 David Williams, B.C. Lions, WR	2006 Geroy Simon, B.C. Lions, SB

Top 20 All-Time CFL Players

In 2006, *TSN* assembled an independent voting panel of 60 past and present CFL executives, players and media, who were asked to rank the top 50 players from a list of 185 nominees, in order, from the post-WWII history of the CFL. Listed below are the top 20.

1 **Doug Flutie**, QB, 1990-97	8 **Russ Jackson**, QB, 1958-69	15 **Milt Stegall**, WR, 1995–
2 **George Reed**, RB, 1963-75	9 **Wayne Harris Sr.**, LB, 1961-72	16 **Willie Pless**, LB, 1986-99
3 **Jackie Parker**, QB, 1954-68	10 **Allen Pitts**, WR, 1990-2000	17 **John Barrow**, DL/OL, 1957-70
4 **Mike Pringle**, RB, 1992-2004	11 **Dan Kepley**, LB, 1975-84	18 **Tony Gabriel**, WR, 1971-81
5 **Warren Moon**, QB, 1978-83	12 **John Helton**, DL, 1969-82	19 **Johnny Bright**, RB, 1952-64
6 **Garney Henley**, DB, 1960-75	13 **Hal Patterson**, WR/DB, 1954-67	20 **Brian Kelly**, WR, 1979-87
7 **Ron Lancaster**, QB, 1960-78	14 **Damon Allen**, QB, 1985–	

NFL EUROPA

The World League of American Football was formed in 1991 and consisted of three European teams (London, Barcelona and Frankfurt), and seven North American teams (New York/New Jersey, Orlando, Montreal, Raleigh-Durham, Birmingham, Sacramento and San Antonio). In the fall of 1992, the NFL and WLAF Board of Directors voted to restructure the league to include more European teams. Play was subsequently suspended. In 1993, NFL clubs approved a six-team European-only league to resume play in 1995. In January 1998, the name of the league was changed to NFL Europa. In August, 2007, the NFL discontinued NFL Europa, choosing instead to direct its focus on playing regular season NFL games overseas.

The World Bowl

Multiple Winners: Frankfurt (4); Berlin and Rhein (2).

Bowl	Year	Winner	Head Coach	Score	Loser	Head Coach	Site
I	1991	London	Larry Kennan	21-0	Barcelona	Jack Bicknell	London
II	1992	Sacramento	Kay Stephenson	21-17	Orlando	Galen Hall	Montreal
III	1995	Frankfurt	Ernie Stautner	26-22	Amsterdam	Al Luginbill	Amsterdam
IV	1996	Scotland	Jim Criner	32-27	Frankfurt	Ernie Stautner	Edinburgh, Scot.
V	1997	Barcelona	Jack Bicknell	38-24	Rhein	Galen Hall	Barcelona
VI	1998	Rhein	Galen Hall	34-10	Frankfurt	Dick Curl	Frankfurt
VII	1999	Frankfurt	Dick Curl	38-24	Barcelona	Jack Bicknell	Dusseldorf
VIII	2000	Rhein	Galen Hall	13-10	Scotland	Jim Criner	Frankfurt
IX	2001	Berlin	Peter Vaas	24-17	Barcelona	Jack Bicknell	Amsterdam
X	2002	Berlin	Peter Vaas	26-20	Rhein	Pete Kuharchek	Dusseldorf
XI	2003	Frankfurt	Doug Graber	35-16	Rhein	Pete Kuharchek	Glasgow
XII	2004	Berlin	Rick Lantz	30-24	Frankfurt	Mike Jones	Gelsenkirchen, Ger.
XIII	2005	Amsterdam	Bart Andrus	27-21	Berlin	Rick Lantz	Dusseldorf
XIV	2006	Frankfurt	Mike Jones	22-7	Amsterdam	Bart Andrus	Dusseldorf
XV	2007	Hamburg	Vince Martino	37-28	Frankfurt	Mike Jones	Frankfurt

World Bowl MVP

Year	Year	Year
1991 Dan Crossman, London, S	1998 Jim Arellanes, Rhein, QB	2003 Jonas Lewis, Frankfurt, RB
1992 Davis Archer, Sacramento, QB	1999 Andy McCullough, Frankfurt, WR	2004 Eric McCoo, Berlin, RB
1995 Paul Justin, Frankfurt, QB	2000 Aaron Stecker, Scotland, RB	2005 Kurt Kittner, Amsterdam, QB
1996 Yo Murphy, Scotland, WR	2001 Jonathan Quinn, Berlin, QB	2006 Butchie Wallace, Frankfurt, RB
1997 Jon Kitna, Barcelona, QB	2002 Dane Looker, Berlin, WR	2007 Casey Bramlet, Hamburg, QB

COLLEGE
BASKETBALL

2006 / 2007 YEAR IN REVIEW

Florida head coach **Billy Donovan** led his Gators to a second straight national title in 2007.

IT'S A GATOR NATION

Florida's starters spurn the NBA, coming back for another bite at the national title. They were not disappointed.

LET'S STEP BACK AND DIGEST WHAT OCCURRED IN COLLEGE BASKETBALL IN 2006-07.

It was, arguably, one of the most memorable seasons in recent memory, one that will be extremely hard to duplicate.

Think about this: in this age of rushing to the NBA as fast as you can, three likely first-round picks decided against bolting to the NBA after winning the NCAA title. In the previous year, Sean May, Marvin Williams and Raymond Felton talked a good game about staying at North Carolina. But the reality was, as soon as they won the title, they were gone, along with Rashad McCants.

So for Florida's Joakim Noah, Al Horford and Corey Brewer to all delay their NBA careers was simply from a time gone by. To be blunt players today don't think about the team as much as they do themselves. And often times, delayed gratification is a foreign concept.

But these three came back and joined teammates Taurean Green, Lee Humphrey and Chris Richard for another run at a title in 2007. It was almost more than any Gator fan could have hoped for.

That's why head coach Billy Donovan decided against signing a big-money extension at the time. He didn't want to insult the players who passed on millions while he was cashing on their success.

There have been other schools with legitimate shots at winning back-to-back titles since Duke did in 1991-92. Arkansas had the best opportunity, winning the title in 1994 and then getting to the title game in 1995 before losing to UCLA. Kentucky won in 1996, only to lose to one of Lute Olson's hardest-working, if not most talented, Arizona teams in 1997. In fact, Kentucky might have had a shot at a three-peat since it won again in 1998.

Florida's attempt to win back-to-back titles was the story from its trip to

 Andy Katz is a senior writer for ESPN.com

YOU AGAIN⁉⁉⁉ The **Florida Gators** starting five of (from left) Al Horford, Corey Brewer, Lee Humphrey (12), Joakim Noah and Taurean Green won their second straight national championship.

Canada on Labor Day weekend, through a showdown in Las Vegas against Kansas over Thanksgiving, to the countless attempts to rock this squad off its pillar in the SEC (see: Vanderbilt, Tennessee and LSU) to a run through the NCAAs in New Orleans, St. Louis and ultimately Atlanta.

Florida's crowning national championship, with wins over UCLA and Ohio State (after blitzing Ohio State right before Christmas in Gainesville) was one of the most impressive accomplishments this decade. Each of the Gators easily could have passed on this team thing, this college thing and chose to do something for themselves.

But they didn't.

They were unique, a blend of players from privileged backgrounds to simple folk from Tennessee to a fiery New Yorker as coach who was relentless in keeping this squad focused.

If this were the only story of 2006-07 then it still would have been a very good year.

Still, this was a season in which the NBA dictated that college basketball was going to have a shot with its top talent for at least a season by instituting a new draft rule that stated a player could only enter the draft if he were at least 19 years old and one year out of high school. That gave the college

Texas Tech coach **Bob Knight** put his name at the top of the list of college basketball's all-time winners with win 880 in 2007.

Conley Jr., gave the Buckeyes a freshmen-led squad that was at times as entertaining as the one Michigan had in the early 1990s, without the unnecessary sideshows.

Durant was simply sensational. From Rick Barnes' decision to bring Durant to the Big 12 media day, Texas had the best freshman check that, the best player in the country. Barnes was prophetic from the first day that Durant was going to be the best player in the country. Jim Boeheim made similar statements about Carmelo Anthony when he had him in Syracuse. And while neither coach has a perfect track record in the justifiable hype department, they have since earned the benefit of the doubt from here on out.

Durant's play, his dominance on the offensive end, his ability to hang defensively with his Stretch Armstrong like reach, made him the most anticipated performer of the season. He was the type of player that kept your TiVo busy. The Longhorns' triple-overtime loss to Oklahoma State was the best game of the season.

And, of course, the season can't be put into perspective without mentioning that Bob Knight became the all-time winningest coach in Division with his 880th win, over New Mexico on New Year's Day.

Knight's chase of the record was nearly Bondsian with hordes of media

game Greg Oden and Kevin Durant. Quite simply they would have been in the NBA, albeit not as highly touted or as refined, had the rule not been in place.

Oden got a late jump on the season because of offseason wrist surgery. But once he got settled, he was as dominant a big man as the college game has seen since Tim Duncan toiled for Wake Forest 10 years prior.

Oden's play in the final against Florida was downright scary, like the time he took Brewer down with him on Brewer's attempted dunk. Oden, and his high school teammate, Mike

Continued on page 292

DICK VITALE'S

Biggest Stories of the Year in **College Basketball**

10 **Winthrop scores one for the little guys** and wins its first tourney game by stunning Notre Dame, 74-64, in the first round of the NCAAs. The Big South gets the better of the Big East as the tiny 11-seed takes down a 6-seed from a true power conference.

09 **Tennessee's Pat Summitt** wins a sensational, scintillating seventh national title, leading the Lady Vols to yet another championship.

08 **Washington State stuns** Pac-10 with a solid season. The Cougars, picked ninth in the preseason, make a run at a Pac-10 title and fall just short of the Sweet 16 following their 2OT loss to Vanderbilt. Rookie head coach Tony Bennett, son of Dick, is rewarded with coach of the year honors and a big new contract.

Dick Vitale broadcasted ESPN's first college basketball game in 1979.

07 **Tubby Smith leaves Kentucky** for Minnesota after 10 years and a national title in Lexington. Texas A&M's Billy Gillispie takes over on the sidelines at historic Rupp Arena.

06 **The re-emergence of Georgetown as a Final Four program.** John Thompson III brings the Hoyas back to prominence and reminds everyone of the glory days that they enjoyed under his father in the 1980s.

05 **Billy D and The Three.** Donovan leaves for the NBA's Magic then changes his mind. Also, Florida's trio of Al Horford, Joakim Noah and Corey Brewer are all drafted in top 10. It's the first time a school has accomplished that feat.

04 **Super Frosh Greg Oden and Mike Conley Jr.** lead Ohio State to the national title game.

03 **The Ultimate Diaper Dandy!** Texas Kevin Durant becomes the first freshman to become the national player of the year.

02 **Bob Knight breaks** Dean Smith's all-time wins record. "The General" passes Smith on New Year's Day 2007 with win 880, a 70-68 victory over New Mexico.

01 **Florida wins back-to-back championships**, the first since Duke in 1991 and 1992.

⇒ *Continued from page 290*

following the legend in search of the elusive historic win. And once he got the record it was natural that Knight let his emotions flow a bit.

These were the headlines. But it would be a mistake to leave the scrapbook to the A-list performers.

Here are some subplots and things to remember from the past year:

• Butler shocked the country by winning the NIT Season Tip-Off.

• Boston College's Jared Dudley proved that not being the stereotypical athlete didn't matter. Dudley was as prolific in the stat box as any player in the ACC and deservedly won the conference Player of the Year Award.

• Virginia Commonwealth from the Colonial Athletic Association (remember George Mason?) stunned Duke in the first round of the NCAA Tournament.

• Southern Illinois once again proved it is one of the top programs—not just mid-major—but overall programs in the nation by reaching the Sweet 16.

Texas freshman **Kevin Durant** was easily the best player in the nation in 2006-07 and was rewarded thusly.

• Washington State had a hoops reviv unmatched in Pullman with nation coach of the year Tony Bennett leadin the Cougars to the NCAA's secor round and a second-place finish in th Pac-10.

>> Before Winthrop's win over Notre Dame in 2007, **the Big South had never won a first-round NCAA Tournament** game in 15 attempts. >> **Did you know** that leaves the Northeast as the only conference without a first-round tourney win (0-25).

2006-2007
Season in Review

Final Regular Season AP Men's Top 25 Poll
Taken **before** start of NCAA tournament.

The sportswriters & broadcasters poll: first place votes in parentheses; records through Monday, March 12, 2007; total points (based on 25 for 1st, 24 for 2nd, etc.); record in NCAA tourney and team lost to; head coach (career years and record including 2007 postseason), and preseason ranking. Teams in **bold** type went on to reach NCAA Final Four.

		Mar. 12 Record	Points	NCAA Recap	Head Coach	Preseason Rank
1	**Ohio St.** (70)	27-3	1798	5-1 (Florida)	Thad Matta (7 yrs: 183-53)	7
2	Kansas (2)	27-4	1706	3-1 (UCLA)	Bill Self (14 yrs: 312-134)	3
3	Wisconsin	27-4	1599	1-1 (UNLV)	Bo Ryan (23 yrs: 525-158)	9
4	**UCLA**	26-4	1583	4-1 (Florida)	Ben Howland (13 yrs: 259-140)	6
5	Memphis	27-3	1481	3-1 (Ohio St.)	John Calipari (15 yrs: 370-133)	14
6	**Florida**	26-5	1433	6-0	Billy Donovan (13 yrs: 296-123)	1
7	Texas A&M	25-5	1383	1-1 (Memphis)	Billy Gillispie (5 yrs: 100-58)	13
8	North Carolina	25-6	1331	-3-1 (Georgetown)	Roy Williams (19 yrs: 524-131)	2
9	**Georgetown**	23-6	1208	4-1 (Ohio St.)	John Thompson III (7 yrs: 140-72)	8
10	Nevada	27-3	1013	1-1 (Memphis)	Mark Fox (3 yrs: 80-17)	24
11	Washington St.	24-6	986	1-1 (Vanderbilt)	Tony Bennett (1 yr: 26-8)	-
12	Louisville	22-8	892	1-1 (Texas A&M)	Rick Pitino (21 yrs: 494-182)	-
13	Pittsburgh	25-6	882	2-1 (UCLA)	Jamie Dixon (4 yrs: 103-29)	4
14	Southern Illinois	27-6	878	2-1 (Kansas)	Chris Lowery (3 yrs: 78-26)	-
15	Texas	22-8	868	1-1 (USC)	Rick Barnes (20 yrs: 418-220)	21
16	Oregon	23-7	662	3-1 (Florida)	Ernie Kent (16 yrs: 283-200)	-
17	Maryland	24-7	639	1-1 (Butler)	Gary Williams (29 yrs: 585-328)	-
18	Marquette	23-8	536	0-1 (Michigan St.)	Tom Crean (8 yrs: 165-86)	16
19	Butler	27-5	517	2-1 (Florida)	Todd Lickliter (6 yrs: 131-61)	-
20	Notre Dame	23-6	442	0-1 (Winthrop)	Mike Brey (12 yrs: 241-130)	-
21	Duke	22-9	284	0-1 (VCU)	Mike Krzyzewski (32 yrs: 775-261)	12
22	Tennessee	22-9	243	2-1 (Ohio St.)	Bruce Pearl (15 yrs: 363-103)	25
23	Brigham Young	23-7	186	0-1 (Xavier)	Dave Rose (2 yrs: 45-18)	-
24	Winthrop	28-4	162	1-1 (Oregon)	Gregg Marshall (9 yrs: 194-83)	-
25	UNLV	28-6	125	2-1 (Oregon)	Lon Kruger (21 yrs: 382-267)	-

Others receiving votes: 26. **Vanderbilt** 124 points; 27. **Virginia** 104; 28. **Xavier** 68; 29. **Creighton** 53; 30. **Arizona** 42; 31. **USC** 25; 32. **Virginia Commonwealth** 21; 33. **Georgia Tech** 20; 34. **Indiana** 18; 35. **Air Force** 17; 36. **Virginia Tech** 16; 37. **Massachusetts** 11; 38. **Villanova** 9; 39. **Michigan St.** 8; 40. **Davidson** 6; 41. **Akron** and **Kansas St.** 4; 43. **Kentucky, Appalachian St., Fresno St., Syracuse** 3; 47. **Washington** 2, 48. **Texas A&M-Corpus Christi** and **Vermont** 1.

NCAA Men's Division I Tournament Seeds

	WEST		MIDWEST		SOUTH		EAST
1	Kansas (30-4)	1	Florida (29-5)	1	Ohio St. (30-3)	1	North Carolina (28-6)
2	UCLA (26-5)	2	Wisconsin (29-5)	2	Memphis (30-3)	2	Georgetown (26-6)
3	Pittsburgh (27-7)	3	Oregon (26-7)	3	Texas A&M (25-6)	3	Washington St. (25-7)
4	Southern Illinois (27-6)	4	Maryland (24-8)	4	Virginia (20-10)	4	Texas (24-9)
5	Virginia Tech (21-11)	5	Butler (27-6)	5	Tennessee (22-10)	5	USC (23-11)
6	Duke (22-10)	6	Notre Dame (24-6)	6	Louisville (23-9)	6	Vanderbilt (20-11)
7	Indiana (20-10)	7	UNLV (28-6)	7	Nevada (28-4)	7	Boston College (20-11)
8	Kentucky (21-11)	8	Arizona (20-10)	8	BYU (25-8)	8	Marquette (24-9)
9	Villanova (22-10)	9	Purdue (21-11)	9	Xavier (24-8)	9	Michigan St. (22-11)
10	Gonzaga (23-10)	10	Georgia Tech (20-11)	10	Creighton (22-10)	10	Texas Tech (21-12)
11	VCU (27-6)	11	Winthrop (28-4)	11	Stanford (18-12)	11	Geo. Washington (23-8)
12	Illinois (23-11)	12	Old Dominion (24-8)	12	Long Beach St. (24-7)	12	Arkansas (21-13)
13	Holy Cross (25-8)	13	Davidson (29-4)	13	Albany (23-9)	13	New Mexico St. (25-8)
14	Wright St. (23-9)	14	Miami-OH (18-14)	14	Pennsylvania (22-8)	14	Oral Roberts (23-10)
15	Weber St. (20-11)	15	Texas A&M-CC (26-6)	15	North Texas (23-10)	15	Belmont (23-9)
16	Niagara* (19-12)	16	Jackson St. (21-13)	16	Central Conn. St. (22-11)	16	Eastern Kentucky (21-11)

*Niagara defeated Florida A&M, 77-69, in the NCAA Tournament "opening-round" play-in game at Dayton, Ohio for a berth in the field of 64.

2007 NCAA Tournament Men's Division

	1st ROUND March 15-16
(1) Florida	112
(16) Jackson St.	69
(8) Arizona	63
(9) Purdue	72
(5) Butler	57
(12) Old Dom.	46
(4) Maryland	82
(13) Davidson	70
(6) Notre Dame	64
(11) Winthrop	74
(3) Oregon	58
(14) Miami-OH	56
(7) UNLV	67
(10) Ga. Tech	63
(2) Wisconsin	76
(15) Tex. A&M-CC	63

Midwest

	2nd ROUND March 17-18
Florida	74
Purdue	67
Butler	62
Maryland	59
Winthrop	61
Oregon	75
UNLV	74
Wisconsin	68

	Sweet 16 March 22-23
Florida	65
Butler	57
Oregon	76
UNLV	72

	Elite Eight March 24-25
Florida	85
Oregon	77

Florida 76

East

	1st ROUND March 15-16
(1) N. Carolina	77
(16) E. Kentucky	65
(8) Marquette	49
(9) Michigan St.	61
(5) USC	77
(12) Arkansas	60
(4) Texas	79
(13) N. Mex. St.	67
(6) Vanderbilt	77
(11) Geo. Wash.	44
(3) Washington St.	70
(14) Oral Roberts	54
(7) Boston Coll.	84
(10) Texas Tech	75
(2) Georgetown	80
(15) Belmont	55

	2nd ROUND March 17-18
N. Carolina	81
Michigan St.	67
USC	87
Texas	68
Vanderbilt	78
Washington St.	74
Boston Coll.	55
Georgetown	62

	Sweet 16 March 22-23
N. Carolina	74
USC	64
Vanderbilt	65
Georgetown	66

	Elite Eight March 24-25
N. Carolina	84
Georgetown	96

Georgetown 60

Florida 84
Ohio St. 75

West

	1st ROUND March 15-16
(1) Kansas	107
(16) Niagara	67
(8) Kentucky	67
(9) Villanova	58
(5) Va. Tech	54
(12) Illinois	52
(13) Holy Cross	51
(4) So. Illinois	61
(6) Duke	77
(11) VCU	79
(3) Pittsburgh	79
(14) Wright St.	58
(7) Indiana	70
(10) Gonzaga	57
(2) UCLA	70
(15) Weber St.	42

	2nd ROUND March 17-18
Kansas	88
Kentucky	76
Va. Tech	48
So. Illinois	63
VCU	—
Pittsburgh	84
Indiana	49
UCLA	54

	Sweet 16 March 22-23
Kansas	61
So. Illinois	58
Pittsburgh	84
UCLA	64

	Elite Eight March 24-25
Kansas	55
UCLA	68

UCLA 66

South

	1st ROUND March 15-16
(1) Ohio St.	78
(16) C. Conn. St.	57
(8) BYU	77
(9) Xavier	79
(5) Tennessee	121
(12) L. Beach St.	86
(4) Virginia	84
(13) Albany	57
(6) Louisville	78
(11) Stanford	58
(3) Texas A&M	68
(14) Penn	52
(7) Nevada	77
(10) Creighton	71
(2) Memphis	73
(15) N. Texas	58

	2nd ROUND March 17-18
Ohio St.	78
Xavier	71
Tennessee	77
Virginia	74
Louisville	69
Texas A&M	72
Nevada	62
Memphis	78

	Sweet 16 March 22-23
Ohio St.	85
Tennessee	84
Texas A&M	64
Memphis	65

	Elite Eight March 24-25
Ohio St.	92
Memphis	76

Ohio St. 67

Play-in Game to West (16) seed

Niagara 77
Florida A&M 69

NATIONAL CHAMPIONSHIP

Georgia Dome
Atlanta, Ga.
Monday, April 2, 2007

NCAA Men's Championship Game

69th NCAA Division I Championship Game. **Date:** Monday, April 2, at the Georgia Dome in Atlanta. **Coaches:** Billy Donovan of Florida and Thad Matta of Ohio St. **Favorite:** Florida by 4.5.
Attendance: 51,458; **Officials:** Karl Hess, Tony Greene and Edward Corbett. **TV Rating:** 12.1/20 share (CBS).

Florida 84

	Min	FG M-A	FT M-A	Pts	Reb O-T	A	PF
Corey Brewer	36	4-12	2-2	13	0-8	1	2
Joakim Noah	21	1-3	6-6	8	0-3	0	4
Al Horford	34	6-15	6-8	18	4-12	3	3
Taurean Green	38	4-6	5-5	16	0-3	6	0
Lee Humphrey	34	5-8	0-0	14	0-1	1	1
Walter Hodge	11	2-2	1-1	5	0-1	0	1
Chris Richard	20	3-5	2-3	8	5-8	0	5
Marreese Speights	6	1-2	0-0	2	1-2	0	3
TOTALS	200	26-53	22-25	84	10-38	11	19

Three-point FG: 10-18 (Brewer 3-8, Green 3-3. Humphrey 4-7); **Blocked Shots:** 3 (Brewer, Horford 2); **Turnovers:** 15 (Noah 2, Brewer, Horford 2, Green 6, Richard 3, Hodge); **Steals:** 5 (Brewer 3, Hodge, Noah); **Percentages:** 2-Pt FG (.457), 3-Pt FG (.556), Total FG (.491), Free Throws (.880).

Ohio St. 75

	Min	FG M-A	FT M-A	Pts	Reb O-T	A	PF
Ivan Harris	26	2-8	1-2	7	1-5	0	2
Greg Oden	38	10-15	5-8	25	4-12	1	4
Mike Conley Jr.	34	7-13	5-6	20	1-3	6	3
Ron Lewis	34	6-13	0-1	12	2-3	0	3
Jamar Butler	36	1-7	0-0	3	0-2	1	3
David Lighty	13	2-3	0-0	4	0-0	1	1
Daequan Cook	9	1-2	0-0	2	0-0	1	1
Matt Terwilliger	5	1-1	0-0	2	0-0	0	1
Othello Hunter	5	0-2	0-0	0	2-2	0	2
TOTALS	200	30-64	11-17	75	10-27	10	20

Three-point FGs: 4-23 (Butler 1-6, Cook 0-1. Conley Jr. 1-3, Harris 2-8, Lighty 0-1, Lewis 0-4); **Blocked Shots:** 4 (Oden 4); **Turnovers:** 7 (Butler, Conley Jr. 2, Hunter, Oden 2, Lewis); **Steals:** 11 (Butler 2, Cook, Conley Jr. 4, Harris, Lighty, Oden, Lewis). **Percentages:** 2-Pt FG (.634), 3-Pt FG (.174), Total FG (.469), Free Throws (.647).

Ohio St. (Big Ten)	29	46	—	**75**
Florida (SEC)	40	44	—	**84**

Final ESPN/USA Today Coaches' Poll

Taken **after** NCAA Tournament.
Voted on by a panel of 31 Division I head coaches following the NCAA tournament: first place votes in parentheses with total points (based on 25 for 1st, 24 for 2nd, etc.). Schools on major probation are ineligible to be ranked.

		W-L	Pts	Before NCAAs W-L	Rank
1	Florida (31)	36-5	775	29-5	3
2	Ohio St.	35-4	744	30-3	1
3	UCLA	30-6	699	26-5	6
4	Georgetown	30-7	694	26-6	8
5	Kansas	33-5	627	30-4	2
	North Carolina	31-7	627	28-6	4
7	Memphis	33-4	594	30-3	5
8	Oregon	29-8	531	26-7	12
9	Texas A&M	27-7	521	25-6	9
10	Pittsburgh	29-8	459	27-7	10
11	Southern Illinois	29-7	425	27-6	15
	Wisconsin	30-6	425	29-5	7
13	Butler	29-7	360	27-6	19
14	UNLV	30-7	309	28-6	18
15	USC	25-12	294	23-11	25
16	Texas	25-10	287	24-9	11
17	Washington St.	26-8	280	25-7	13
18	Tennessee	24-11	238	22-10	NR
19	Vanderbilt	22-12	234	20-11	NR
20	Louisville	24-10	222	23-9	16
21	Nevada	29-5	217	28-4	13
22	Winthrop	29-5	108	28-4	21
23	Maryland	25-9	72	24-8	22
24	Virginia	21-11	56	20-10	NR
25	Virginia Tech	22-12	54	21-11	NR

Others receiving votes: 26. **Xavier** (38 pts); 27. **Notre Dame** (37); 28. **Marquette** (28); 29. **VCU** (25); 30. **Creighton** (21); 31. **Michigan St.** (19); 32. **Boston College** (18); 33. **BYU** and **West Virginia** (10); 35. **Kentucky** (8); 36. **Davidson** (4); 37. **Clemson** (2); 38. **Akron**, **Duke** and **Indiana** (1).

THE FINAL FOUR

at the Georgia Dome in Atlanta.
(Mar. 31-Apr. 2, 2007).

Semifinal — Game One

East Regional champ Georgetown vs. South Regional champ Ohio State; Saturday, Mar. 31 (6:07 p.m. tipoff). **Coaches:** John Thompson III of Georgetown and Thad Matta of Ohio St. **Rating:** 8.4/18 (CBS).

Georgetown (Big East)	23	37	—	**60**
Ohio State (Big Ten)	27	40	—	**67**

High scorers— Roy Hibbert & Jonathan Wallace, Georgetown (19) and Mike Conley Jr., Ohio St. (15); **Att—** 51,458.

Semifinal — Game Two

West Regional champion UCLA vs. Midwest Regional champ Florida; Saturday, Mar. 31 (9:21 p.m. tipoff). **Coaches:** Ben Howland, UCLA and Billy Donovan, Florida. **Rating:** 8.9/17 (CBS).

UCLA (Pac-10)	23	43	—	**66**
Florida (SEC)	29	47	—	**76**

High scorers— Josh Shipp, UCLA (18) and Corey Brewer, Florida (17); **Att—** 51,458.

Most Outstanding Player

Corey Brewer, Florida junior forward.
SEMIFINAL—32 minutes, 19 points, 2 rebounds, 1 assist, 2 blocks; FINAL—36 minutes, 13 points, 8 rebounds, 1 assist, 3 steals, 1 block.

All-Final Four Team

Corey Brewer, junior forward/center Al Horford, senior guard Lee Humphrey of Florida, freshman center Greg Oden and freshman guard Mike Conley Jr. of Ohio State

NCAA Finalists' Tournament and Season Statistics

At least 10 games played during the overall season.

Florida (35-5)

	NCAA Tournament						Overall Season					
				—Per Game—						—Per Game—		
	Gm	FG %	TPts	Pts	Reb	Ast	Gm	FG %	TPts	Pts	Reb	Ast
Taurean Green	6	.377	84	14.0	2.8	4.5	40	.444	531	13.3	2.4	3.7
Corey Brewer	6	.448	95	15.8	5.5	2.2	37	.475	490	13.2	4.7	2.9
Al Horford	6	.605	81	13.5	11.3	2.2	38	.608	502	13.2	9.5	2.2
Joakim Noah	6	.571	69	11.5	9.7	1.5	40	.605	479	12.0	8.4	2.1
Lee Humphrey	6	.481	75	12.5	1.2	0.7	40	.475	412	10.3	1.3	1.3
Chris Richard	6	.846	54	9.0	4.7	0.5	40	.690	248	6.2	3.7	0.4
Walter Hodge	6	.429	10	1.7	0.7	1.2	40	.545	227	5.7	1.2	1.5
Marreese Speights	3	.615	20	6.7	2.7	0.0	33	.671	134	4.1	2.6	0.1
Dan Werner	5	.333	2	0.4	1.0	0.2	39	.306	70	1.8	1.3	0.8
Brandon Powell	1	.500	3	3.0	0.0	0.0	23	.611	36	1.6	0.4	0.3
Jonathan Mitchell	1	1.000	3	3.0	1.0	0.0	30	.415	41	1.4	1.2	0.4
Brett Swanson	1	—	0	0.0	0.0	1.0	17	.385	12	0.7	0.2	0.3
FLORIDA	6	.522	496	82.7	40.0	13.0	40	.526	3193	79.8	37.6	15.4
OPPONENTS	6	.426	411	68.5	25.0	11.3	40	.407	2504	62.6	29.1	10.8

Three-pointers: NCAA TOURNAMENT—Humphrey (23-49), Green (16-41), Brewer (12-32), Hodge (0-2), Mitchell (1-1) Powell (1-2), Werner (0-2), Team (53-129 for .411 pct.); OVERALL— Humphrey (113-246), Green (82-203), Brewer (40-119) Hodge (34-68), Werner (13-58), Powell (9-14), Mitchell (2-5), Swanson (2-7), Noah (1-1), Berry (l-2), Horford (0-3), Tyler (0-1), Team (297-727 for .409 pct.).

Ohio State (35-4)

	NCAA Tournament						Overall Season					
				—Per Game—						—Per Game—		
	Gm	FG %	TPts	Pts	Reb	Ast	Gm	FG %	TPts	Pts	Reb	Ast
Greg Oden	6	.621	97	16.2	9.2	0.5	32	.616	501	15.7	9.6	0.7
Ron Lewis	6	.466	108	18.0	4.7	0.8	39	.427	494	12.7	3.6	1.3
Mike Conley Jr.	6	.485	96	16.0	5.0	4.8	39	.518	441	11.3	3.4	6.1
Daequan Cook	6	.300	29	4.8	1.5	0.5	39	.445	382	9.8	4.3	1.0
Jamar Butler	6	.400	58	9.7	1.3	3.0	39	.394	331	8.5	2.1	3.0
Ivan Harris	6	.370	30	5.0	4.0	0.3	39	.432	298	7.6	3.3	0.8
Othello Hunter	6	.500	17	2.8	3.8	0.3	39	.560	223	5.7	4.5	0.2
David Lighty	6	.563	25	4.2	2.8	1.2	39	.374	143	3.7	2.3	1.0
Matt Terwilliger	6	.667	15	2.5	1.0	0.0	39	.451	85	2.2	1.8	0.2
Mark Titus	6	.000	0	0.0	0.0	0.0	14	.500	5	0.4	0.1	0.0
Danny Peters	6	.000	0	0.0	1.0	0.0	13	.200	2	0.2	0.1	0.0
OHIO ST	6	.476	475	79.2	35.3	11.5	39	.472	2905	74.5	35.6	14.9
OPPONENTS	6	.441	432	72.0	32.0	12.2	39	.404	2417	62.0	32.7	12.3

Three-pointers: NCAA TOURNAMENT— Butler (14-37), Lewis (12-33), Harris (7-16), Cook (4-15), Conley Jr. (3-12), Lighty (1-3), Terwilliger (0-1), Team (41-117 for .350 pct.); OVERALL— Butler (76-202), Lewis (64-186), Harris (58-148), Cook (54-130), Conley Jr. (21-69), Lighty (8-40), Terwilliger (3-12), Hunter (2-5), Titus (1-2), Team (287-794 for .361 pct.).

Florida's Schedule

Reg. Season
(26-5)

W	Samford	.79-54
W	North Florida	.86-40
W	Jacksonville	.90-61
W	Tenn-Chatt.	.93-44
W	Prairie View A&M	93-44
W	Western Ky	.101-68
L	Kansas	.80-82 OT
W	Southern	.83-27
L	at Florida St.	.66-70
W	Providence	.85-67
W	FAMU	.72-57
W	Stetson	.88-67
W	Ohio State	.86-60
W	UAB	.75-70
W	Liberty	.89-58
W	Georgia	.67-51
W	Arkansas	.79-72
W	at South Carolina	84-50
W	Mississippi	.79-70
W	at Mississippi St.	.70-67
W	at Auburn	.91-66
W	Vanderbilt	.74-64
W	Tennessee	.94-78
W	at Georgia	.71-61
W	at Kentucky	.64-61
W	at Alabama	.76-67
L	at Vanderbilt	.70-83
W	South Carolina	.63-49
L	at LSU	.56-66
L	at Tennessee	.76-86

SEC Tourney
(3-0)

W	Kentucky	.85-72
W	Georgia	.74-57
W	Mississippi	.80-59

NCAA Tourney
(6-0)

W	Jackson St.	.112-69
W	Purdue	.74-67
W	Butler	.65-57
W	Oregon	.85-77
W	UCLA	.76-66
W	Ohio St.	.84-75

Ohio State's Schedule

Reg. Season
(27-3)

W	VMI	.107-69
W	Loyola Chicago	.87-75
W	Kent St.	.81-59
W	Eastern Ky.	.74-45
W	San Francisco	.82-60
W	Youngstown St.	.91-57
L	at N. Carolina	.89-98
W	Valparaiso	.78-58
W	Cleveland St.	.78-57
W	Cincinnati	.72-50
W	Iowa St.	.75-56
L	at Florida	.60-86
W	Coppin St.	.91-54
W	Indiana	.74-67
L	at Wisconsin	.69-72
W	Tennessee	.68-66
W	Northwestern	.73-41
W	Iowa	.82-63
W	at Northwestern	.59-50
W	Michigan St.	.66-64
W	at Purdue	.78-60
W	at Michigan St.	.63-54
W	Michigan	.76-63
W	Purdue	.63-54
W	at Penn St.	.64-61
W	at Minnesota	.85-62
W	Penn St.	.68-64
W	Wisconsin	.49-41
W	at Michigan	.65-61

Big Ten Tourney
(3-0)

W	Michigan	.65-61
W	Purdue	.63-54
W	Wisconsin	.66-41

NCAA Tourney
(5-1)

W	Central Conn.	.78-57
W	Xavier	.78-71 OT
W	Tennessee	.85-84
W	Memphis	.92-76
W	Georgetown	.67-60
L	Florida	.75-84

Final NCAA Men's Division I Standings

Conference records include regular season games only. Overall records include all postseason tournament games.

America East Conference

Team	Conference			Overall		
	W	L	Pct	W	L	Pct
†Vermont	15	1	.938	25	8	.758
*Albany	13	3	.813	23	10	.697
Boston University	8	8	.500	12	18	.400
Maine	7	9	.438	12	18	.400
UMBC	7	9	.438	12	19	.387
Binghamton	6	10	.375	13	16	.448
Hartford	6	10	.375	13	18	.419
New Hampshire	6	10	.375	10	20	.333
Stony Brook	4	12	.250	9	20	.310

Conf. Tourney Final: Albany 60, Vermont 59.
*NCAA Tourney (0-1): Albany (0-1).
†NIT (0-1): Vermont (0-1)

Atlantic Coast Conference

Team	Conference			Overall		
	W	L	Pct	W	L	Pct
*North Carolina	11	5	.688	31	7	.816
*Virginia	11	5	.688	21	11	.656
*Maryland	10	6	.625	25	9	.735
*Virginia Tech	10	6	.625	22	12	.647
*Boston College	10	6	.625	21	12	.636
*Duke	8	8	.500	22	11	.667
*Georgia Tech	8	8	.500	20	12	.645
†Clemson	7	9	.438	25	11	.694
†Florida St	7	9	.438	22	13	.629
†N.C. State	5	11	.313	20	16	.556
Wake Forest	5	11	.313	15	16	.484
Miami-FL	4	12	.250	12	20	.375

Conf. Tourney Final: North Carolina 89, N.C. State 80.
*NCAA Tourney (7-7): North Carolina (3-1), Virginia (1-1), Maryland (1-1), Virginia Tech (1-1), Boston College (1-1), Duke (0-1), Georgia Tech (0-1).
†NIT (8-3): Clemson (4-1), Florida St. (2-1), N.C. State (2-1).

Atlantic 10 Conference

Team	Conference			Overall		
	W	L	Pct	W	L	Pct
*Xavier	13	3	.812	25	9	.735
†Massachusetts	13	3	.812	24	9	.727
*George Washington	11	5	.688	23	9	.719
Fordham	10	6	.625	18	12	.600
Rhode Island	10	6	.625	19	14	.576
St. Joseph's	9	7	.562	18	14	.562
Dayton	8	8	.500	19	12	.613
Saint Louis	8	8	.500	20	13	.606
Charlotte	7	9	.438	14	16	.467
Duquesne	6	10	.375	10	19	.345
Temple	6	10	.375	12	18	.400
Richmond	4	12	.250	8	22	.267
St. Bonaventure	4	12	.250	7	22	.241
La Salle	3	13	.188	10	20	.333

Conf. Tourney Final: Geo. Wash. 78, Rhode Island 69.
*NCAA Tourney (1-2): Xavier (1-1), George Wash. (0-1).
†NIT (1-1): Massachusetts (1-1).

2006-07 Conference Attendance Leaders				
	Teams	Games	Total	Avg
Big Ten	11	201	2,564,662	12,760
SEC	12	214	2,562,073	11,972
Big East	16	292	3,259,992	11,164
ACC	12	219	2,434,902	11,118
Big 12	12	211	2,261,697	10,719
Pac 10	10	176	1,500,188	8,524

Atlantic Sun Conference

Team	Conference			Overall		
	W	L	Pct	W	L	Pct
†East Tennese St.	16	2	.889	24	10	.706
*Belmont	14	4	.778	23	10	.697
Jacksonville	11	7	.611	15	14	.517
Lipscomb	11	7	.611	18	13	.581
Kennesaw St.	9	9	.500	14	18	.438
Mercer	8	10	.444	13	17	.433
Campbell	7	11	.389	14	17	.452
Gardner-Webb	7	11	.389	9	21	.300
Stetson	6	12	.333	11	20	.355
UNF	1	17	.056	3	26	.103

Conf. Tourney Final: Belmont 94, East Tenn. St. 67.
*NCAA Tourney (0-1): Belmont (0-1).
†NIT (0-1): East Tenn. St. (0-1).

Big East Conference

Team	Conference			Overall		
	W	L	Pct	W	L	Pct
*Georgetown	13	3	.812	30	7	.811
*Louisville	12	4	.750	24	10	.706
*Pittsburgh	12	4	.750	28	9	.757
*Notre Dame	11	5	.688	24	8	.750
†Syracuse	10	6	.625	24	11	.686
*Marquette	10	6	.625	24	10	.706
†West Virginia	9	7	.562	27	9	.750
†DePaul	9	7	.562	20	14	.588
*Villanova	9	7	.562	22	11	.667
†Providence	8	8	.500	18	13	.581
St. John's	7	9	.438	16	15	.516
Connecticut	6	10	.375	17	14	.548
Seton Hall	4	12	.250	13	16	.448
USF	3	13	.188	12	18	.400
Rutgers	3	13	.188	10	19	.345
Cincinnati	2	14	.125	11	19	.367

Conf. Tourney Final: Georgetown 65, Pittsburgh 42.
*NCAA Tourney (7-6): Georgetown (4-1), Pittsburgh (2-1), Louisville (1-1), Notre Dame (0-1), Marquette (0-1), Villanova (0-1).
†NIT (9-3): West Va. (5-0), DePaul (2-1), Syracuse (2-1), Providence (0-1).

Big Sky Conference

Team	Conference			Overall		
	W	L	Pct	W	L	Pct
*Weber St	11	5	.688	20	12	.625
Northern Arizona	11	5	.688	18	12	.600
Montana	10	6	.625	17	15	.531
Portland St.	9	7	.563	19	13	.594
Eastern Washington	8	8	.500	15	14	.517
Idaho St	8	8	.500	13	17	.433
Montana St	8	8	.500	11	19	.367
Sacramento St.	5	11	.313	10	19	.345
Northern Colorado	2	14	.125	4	24	.143

Conf. Tourney Final: Weber St. 88, Northern Ariz. 80.
*NCAA Tourney (0-1): Weber St. (0-1).

Big South Conference

Team	Conference			Overall		
	W	L	Pct	W	L	Pct
*Winthrop	14	0	1.000	29	5	.853
High Point	11	3	.786	22	10	.688
Liberty	8	6	.571	14	17	.452
Coastal Carolina	7	7	.500	15	15	.500
NC-Asheville	6	8	.429	12	19	.387
VMI	5	9	.357	14	19	.424
Radford	3	11	.214	8	22	.267
Charleston Southern	2	12	.143	8	22	.267

Conf. Tourney Final: Winthrop 84, VMI 81.
*NCAA Tourney (1-1): Winthrop (1-1).

Final NCAA Men's Division I Standings (Cont.)

Big Ten Conference

Team	Conference			Overall		
	W	L	Pct	W	L	Pct
*Ohio St	15	1	.938	35	4	.897
*Wisconsin	13	3	.812	30	6	.833
*Indiana	10	6	.625	21	11	.656
*Purdue	9	7	.562	22	12	.647
*Illinois	9	7	.562	23	12	.657
Iowa	9	7	.562	17	14	.548
*Michigan St	8	8	.500	23	12	.657
†Michigan	8	8	.500	22	13	.629
Minnesota	3	13	.188	9	22	.290
Northwestern	2	14	.125	13	18	.419
Penn St	2	14	.125	11	19	.367

Conf. Tourney Final: Iowa 67, Ohio St. 60.
NCAA Tourney (9-6): Ohio St. (5-1), Purdue (1-1), Indiana (1-1), Michigan St. (1-1), Wisconsin (1-1), Illinois (0-1).
†NIT (1-1): Michigan (1-1).

Big 12 Conference

Team	Conference			Overall		
	W	L	Pct	W	L	Pct
*Kansas	14	2	.875	33	5	.868
*Texas A&M	13	3	.813	27	7	.794
*Texas	12	4	.750	25	10	.714
†Kansas St	10	6	.625	23	12	.657
*Texas Tech	9	7	.563	21	13	.618
Missouri	7	9	.438	18	12	.600
†Oklahoma St.	6	10	.375	22	13	.629
Iowa St.	6	10	.375	15	16	.483
Oklahoma	6	10	.375	16	15	.516
Nebraska	6	10	.375	17	14	.548
Baylor	4	12	.250	15	16	.483
Colorado	3	13	.188	7	20	.259

Conf. Tourney Final: Kansas 88, Texas 84 OT.
NCAA Tourney (6-4): Kansas (3-1), Texas (1-1), Texas A&M (2-1), Texas Tech (0-1).
†NIT (1-2): Kansas St. (1-1), Oklahoma St. (0-1).

Big West Conference

Team	Conference			Overall		
	W	L	Pct	W	L	Pct
*Long Beach St	12	2	.857	24	8	.750
Cal St.-Fullerton	9	5	.643	20	10	.667
Cal Poly	9	5	.643	19	11	.633
UC-Santa Barbara	9	5	.643	18	11	.621
UC-Irvine	6	8	.429	15	18	.455
Cal St.-Northridge	5	9	.357	14	17	.452
Pacific	5	9	.357	12	19	.387
UC-Riverside	1	13	.071	7	24	.226

Conf. Tourney Final: Long Beach St. 94, Cal Poly 83.
NCAA Tourney (0-1): Long Beach St. (0-1).

Conference USA

Team	Conference			Overall		
	W	L	Pct	W	L	Pct
*Memphis	16	0	1.000	33	4	.892
UCF	11	5	.688	22	9	.710
Houston	10	6	.625	18	15	.545
Tulane	9	7	.563	17	13	.567
Tulsa	9	7	.563	20	11	.645
So. Mississippi	9	7	.563	20	11	.645
Rice	8	8	.500	16	16	.500
Marshall	7	9	.438	13	19	.406
Ala-Birmingham	7	9	.438	15	16	.484
UTEP	6	10	.375	14	17	.452
SMU	3	13	.188	14	17	.452
East Carolina	1	15	.063	6	24	.200

Conf. Tourney Final: Memphis 71, Houston 59.
NCAA Tourney (3-1): Memphis (3-1).

Colonial Athletic Association

Team	Conference			Overall		
	W	L	Pct	W	L	Pct
*Va. Commonwealth	16	2	.889	28	7	.800
*Old Dominion	15	3	.833	24	9	.727
†Hofstra	14	4	.778	22	10	.688
†Drexel	13	5	.722	23	9	.719
George Mason	9	9	.500	18	15	.545
Northeastern	9	9	.500	13	19	.406
William & Mary	8	10	.444	15	15	.500
Towson	8	10	.444	15	17	.469
Georgia St.	5	13	.278	11	20	.355
NC-Wilmington	4	14	.222	7	22	.241
James Madison	4	14	.222	7	23	.233
Delaware	3	15	.167	5	26	.161

Conf. Tourney Final: NC-Wilmington 78, Hofstra 67.
NCAA Tourney (1-2): VCU (1-1), Old Dominion (0-1).
†NIT (0-2): Drexel (0-1), Hofstra (0-1).

Horizon League

Team	Conference			Overall		
	W	L	Pct	W	L	Pct
*Butler	13	3	.813	29	7	.806
*Wright St	13	3	.813	23	10	.697
Loyola-IL	10	6	.625	21	11	.656
WI-Green Bay	7	9	.438	18	15	.545
Youngstown St.	7	9	.438	14	17	.452
Illinois-Chicago	7	9	.438	14	18	.438
WI-Milwaukee	6	10	.375	11	19	.367
Detroit	6	10	.375	9	22	.290
Cleveland St.	3	13	.188	10	21	.323

Conf. Tourney Final: Wright St. 60, Butler 55.
NCAA Tourney (2-2): Butler (2-1), Wright St. (0-1).

Ivy League

Team	Conference			Overall		
	W	L	Pct	W	L	Pct
*Pennsylvania	13	1	.929	22	9	.710
Yale	10	4	.714	14	13	.519
Cornell	9	5	.643	16	12	.571
Columbia	7	7	.500	16	12	.571
Brown	6	8	.429	11	18	.379
Harvard	5	9	.357	12	16	.429
Dartmouth	4	10	.286	9	18	.333
Princeton	2	12	.143	11	17	.393

Conf. Tourney Final: Ivy League has no tournament.
NCAA Tourney (0-1): Penn (0-1).

Metro Atlantic Athletic Conference

Team	Conference			Overall		
	W	L	Pct	W	L	Pct
*Marist	14	4	.778	25	9	.739
*Niagara	13	5	.722	23	12	.657
Siena	12	6	.667	20	12	.625
Loyola	12	6	.667	18	13	.581
Manhattan	10	8	.556	13	17	.433
Fairfield	10	8	.556	13	19	.406
Rider	9	9	.500	16	15	.516
Canisius	6	12	.333	12	19	.387
Saint Peter's	3	15	.167	5	25	.167
Iona	1	17	.056	2	28	.067

Conf. Tourney Final: Niagara 83, Siena 79.
NCAA Tourney (2-2): Marist (1-1), Niagara (1-1).

Mid-American Conference

East	Conference			Overall		
	W	L	Pct	W	L	Pct
Akron	13	3	.812	26	7	.788
Kent St.	12	4	.750	21	11	.656
*Miami-OH	10	6	.625	18	15	.545
Ohio	9	7	.562	19	13	.594
Buffalo	4	12	.250	12	19	.387
Bowling Green	3	13	.188	13	18	.419
West	W	L	Pct	W	L	Pct
†Toledo	14	2	.875	19	13	.594
Western Mich	9	7	.562	16	16	.500
Central Mich	7	9	.438	13	18	.419
Eastern Mich	6	10	.375	13	19	.406
Ball St.	5	11	.312	9	22	.290
N. Illinois	4	12	.250	7	23	.233

Conf. Tourney Final: Miami-OH 53, Akron 52.
*NCAA Tourney (0-1): Miami-OH (0-1).
†NIT (0-1): Toledo (0-1).

Mid-Continent Conference

Team	Conference			Overall		
	W	L	Pct	W	L	Pct
*Oral Roberts	12	2	.857	23	11	.676
Oakland	10	4	.714	19	14	.576
Valparaiso	9	5	.643	16	15	.516
IUPUI	7	7	.500	15	15	.500
Southern Utah	6	8	.429	16	14	.533
Missouri-KC	6	8	.429	12	20	.375
Western Illinois	3	11	.214	7	23	.233
Centenary	3	11	.214	10	21	.323

Conf. Tourney Final: Oral Roberts 71, Oakland 67.
*NCAA Tourney (0-1): Oral Roberts (0-1).
Note: The Mid-Continent Conference officially changed its name to The Summit League on June 1, 2007.

Mid-Eastern Athletic Conference

Team	Conference			Overall		
	W	L	Pct	W	L	Pct
†Delaware St.	16	2	.889	21	12	.636
*Florida A&M	12	6	.667	21	14	.600
Hampton	10	8	.556	15	16	.484
N. Carolina A&T	10	8	.556	15	17	.469
S.C. State	10	8	.556	13	17	.433
Morgan St.	10	8	.556	13	18	.419
Norfolk St.	10	8	.556	11	19	.367
Coppin St.	9	9	.500	12	20	.375
Bethune-Cookman	6	12	.333	9	21	.300
Howard	5	13	.278	9	22	.290
MD-Eastern Shore	1	17	.056	4	27	.129

Conf. Tourney Final: Florida A&M 58, Delaware St. 56.
*NCAA Tourney (0-1): Florida A&M (0-1).
†NIT (0-1): Delaware St. (0-1).

Missouri Valley Conference

Team	Conference			Overall		
	W	L	Pct	W	L	Pct
*Southern Illinois	15	3	.833	29	7	.806
*Creighton	13	5	.722	22	11	.667
†Missouri St.	12	6	.667	22	11	.667
†Bradley	10	8	.556	22	13	.629
Northern Iowa	9	9	.500	18	13	.581
Wichita St.	8	10	.444	17	14	.548
Drake	6	12	.333	17	15	.531
Illinois St.	6	12	.333	15	16	.484
Evansville	6	12	.333	14	17	.452
Indiana St.	5	13	.278	13	18	.419

Conf. Tourney Final: Creighton 67, So. Illinois 61.
*NCAA Tourney (2-2): Southern Illinois (2-1), Creighton (0-1).
†NIT (1-2): Bradley (1-1), Missouri St. (0-1).

Mountain West Conference

Team	Conference			Overall		
	W	L	Pct	W	L	Pct
*BYU	13	3	.812	25	9	.735
*UNLV	12	4	.750	30	7	.811
†Air Force	10	6	.625	26	9	.743
†San Diego St.	10	6	.625	22	11	.667
Wyoming	7	9	.438	17	15	.531
Colorado St.	6	10	.375	17	13	.567
Utah	6	10	.375	11	19	.367
New Mexico	4	12	.250	15	17	.469
TCU	4	12	.250	13	17	.433

Conf. Tourney Final: UNLV 78, BU 70.
*NCAA Tourney (2-2): UNLV (2-1), BYU (0-1).
†NIT (4-2): Air Force (3-1), San Diego St. (1-1).

Northeast Conference

Team	Conference			Overall		
	W	L	Pct	W	L	Pct
*Central Connecticut St.	16	2	.889	22	12	.647
Sacred Heart	12	6	.667	18	14	.562
Quinnipiac	11	7	.611	14	15	.483
Robert Morris	9	9	.500	17	11	.607
Fairleigh Dickinson	9	9	.500	14	16	.467
Mt. St. Mary's	9	9	.500	11	20	.355
Wagner	8	10	.444	11	19	.367
Monmouth	7	11	.389	12	18	.400
St. Francis-NY	7	11	.389	9	22	.290
LIU Brooklyn	6	12	.333	10	19	.345
St. Francis-PA	5	13	.278	8	21	.276

Conf. Tourney Final: C. Conn. St. 74, Sacred Heart 70.
*NCAA Tourney (0-1): C. Conn. St. (0-1).

Ohio Valley Conference

Team	Conference			Overall		
	W	L	Pct	W	L	Pct
†Austin Peay	16	4	.800	21	12	.636
*Eastern Kentucky	13	7	.650	21	12	.636
Tennessee Tech	13	7	.650	19	13	.594
Murray St	13	7	.650	16	14	.533
Samford	12	8	.600	16	16	.500
SE Missouri St	9	11	.450	11	20	.355
Morehead St	8	12	.400	12	18	.400
Tennessee St	8	12	.400	12	20	.375
Jacksonville St.	7	13	.350	9	21	.300
Eastern Illinois	6	14	.300	10	20	.333
Tennessee-Martin	5	15	.250	8	23	.258

Conf. Tourney Final: E. Kentucky 63, Austin Peay 62.
*NCAA Tourney (0-1): Eastern Kentucky (0-1).
†NIT (0-1): Austin Peay (0-1).

Pacific-10 Conference

Team	Conference			Overall		
	W	L	Pct	W	L	Pct
*UCLA	15	3	.833	30	6	.833
*Washington St	13	5	.722	26	8	.765
*Oregon	11	7	.611	29	8	.784
*USC	11	7	.611	25	12	.676
*Arizona	11	7	.611	20	11	.645
*Stanford	10	8	.556	18	13	.581
Washington	8	10	.444	19	13	.594
California	6	12	.333	16	17	.485
Oregon St	3	15	.167	11	21	.344
Arizona St	2	16	.111	8	22	.267

Conf. Tourney Final: Oregon 81, USC 57.
*NCAA Tourney (10-6): UCLA (4-1), Oregon (3-1), USC (2-1), Washington St. (1-1), Stanford (0-1), Arizona (0-1).

Final NCAA Men's Division I Standings (Cont.)

Patriot League

Team	Conference			Overall		
	W	L	Pct	W	L	Pct
*Holy Cross	13	1	.929	25	9	.735
Bucknell	13	1	.929	22	9	.710
Lehigh	7	7	.500	12	19	.387
American	7	7	.500	16	14	.533
Colgate	5	9	.357	10	19	.345
Army	4	10	.286	15	16	.484
Navy	4	10	.286	14	16	.467
Lafayette	3	11	.214	9	21	.300

Conf. Tourney Final: Holy Cross 74, Bucknell 66.
***NCAA Tourney (0-1):** Holy Cross (0-1).

Southeastern Conference

Eastern Div.	Conference			Overall		
	W	L	Pct	W	L	Pct
*Florida	13	3	.813	35	5	.875
*Vanderbilt	10	6	.625	22	12	.647
*Tennessee	10	6	.625	24	11	.686
*Kentucky	9	7	.563	22	12	.647
Georgia	8	8	.500	19	14	.576
South Carolina	4	12	.250	14	16	.467

Western Div.	Conference			Overall		
	W	L	Pct	W	L	Pct
†Mississippi St	8	8	.500	21	14	.600
†Mississippi	8	8	.500	21	13	.618
*Arkansas	7	9	.438	21	14	.600
Auburn	7	9	.438	17	15	.531
†Alabama	7	9	.438	20	12	.625
LSU	5	11	.313	17	15	.531

Conf. Tourney Final: Florida 77, Arkansas 56.
***NCAA Tourney (11-4):** Florida (6-0), Tennessee (2-1), Vanderbilt (2-1), Kentucky (1-1), Arkansas (0-1).
†NIT (4-3): Mississippi St. (3-1), Mississippi (1-1), Alabama (0-1).

Southern Conference

North Div.	Conference			Overall		
	W	L	Pct	W	L	Pct
†Appalachian St.	15	3	.833	25	8	.758
NC-Greensboro	12	6	.667	16	14	.533
W. Carolina	7	11	.389	11	20	.355
Chattanooga	6	12	.333	15	18	.455
Elon	5	13	.278	7	23	.233

South Div.	Conference			Overall		
	W	L	Pct	W	L	Pct
*Davidson	17	1	.944	29	5	.853
College of Charleston	13	5	.722	22	11	.667
Furman	8	10	.444	15	16	.484
Georgia Southern	7	11	.389	15	16	.484
Wofford	5	13	.278	10	20	.333
The Citadel	4	14	.222	7	23	.233

Conf. Tourney Final: Davidson 72, Col. of Charleston 65.
***NCAA Tourney (0-1):** Davidson (0-1).
†NIT (0-1): Appalachian St. (0-1).

Best in Show

Conferences with the most wins in the 2007 NCAA tournament. Number of tourney teams in parenthesis.

Conference	W-L	Pct.
SEC (5)	11-4	.733
Pac-10 (6)	10-6	.625
Big Ten (6)	9-6	.600
Big East (6)	7-6	.538
ACC (7)	7-7	.500
Big 12 (4)	6-4	.600

Southland Conference

East Div.	Conference			Overall		
	W	L	Pct	W	L	Pct
Northwestern St.	10	6	.625	17	15	.531
McNeese St.	9	7	.563	15	17	.469
SE Louisiana	8	8	.500	16	14	.533
Lamar	8	8	.500	15	17	.469
Nicholls St.	7	9	.438	8	22	.267
Central Arkansas	4	12	.250	10	20	.333

West Div.	Conference			Overall		
	W	L	Pct	W	L	Pct
*Texas A&M-Corpus Christi	14	2	.875	26	7	.788
Sam Houston St.	13	3	.813	21	10	.677
Stephen F. Austin	8	8	.500	15	14	.517
Texas-Arlington	8	8	.500	13	17	.433
Texas St.	4	12	.250	9	20	.310
Louisiana-Monroe	3	13	.188	7	22	.241

Conf. Tourney Final: Tex. A&M-CC 81, N'western 78.
***NCAA Tourney (0-1):** Texas A&M-CC (0-1).

Southwestern Athletic Conference

Team	Conference			Overall		
	W	L	Pct	W	L	Pct
Miss. Valley St	13	5	.722	18	16	.529
*Jackson St	12	6	.667	21	14	.600
Grambling St.	10	8	.556	12	14	.462
Alcorn St.	10	8	.556	11	19	.367
Texas Southern	9	9	.500	14	17	.452
Ark-Pine Bluff	9	9	.500	12	19	.387
Southern	9	9	.500	10	21	.323
Alabama St	8	10	.444	10	20	.333
Prairie View A&M	6	12	.333	8	22	.267
Alabama A&M	4	14	.222	10	20	.333

Conf. Tourney Final: Jackson St. 81, Miss. Valley St. 71
***NCAA Tourney (0-1):** Jackson St. (0-1).
†NIT (0-1): Mississippi Valley St. (0-1).

Sun Belt Conference

East Div.	Conference			Overall		
	W	L	Pct	W	L	Pct
†South Alabama	13	5	.722	20	12	.625
Western Kentucky	12	6	.667	22	11	.667
Florida Atlantic	10	8	.556	16	15	.516
Troy	8	10	.444	13	17	.433
Middle Tennessee	8	10	.444	15	17	.469
Florida International	7	11	.389	12	17	.414

West Div.	Conference			Overall		
	W	L	Pct	W	L	Pct
Arkansas St	11	7	.611	18	15	.545
Louisiana-Monroe	11	7	.611	18	15	.545
*North Texas	10	8	.556	23	11	.676
New Orleans	9	9	.500	14	17	.452
Arkansas-Little Rock	8	10	.444	13	17	.433
Louisiana-Lafayette	7	11	.389	9	21	.300
Denver	3	15	.167	4	25	.138

Conf. Tourney Final: North Texas 83, Arkansas St. 75.
***NCAA Tourney (0-1):** North Texas (0-1).
†NIT (0-1): South Alabama (0-1).

West Coast Conference

Team	Conference			Overall		
	W	L	Pct	W	L	Pct
*Gonzaga	11	3	.786	23	11	.676
Santa Clara	10	4	.714	21	10	.677
St. Mary's	8	6	.571	17	15	.531
San Francisco	8	6	.571	13	18	.453
San Diego	6	8	.429	18	14	.562
Loyola Marymount	5	9	.357	13	18	.419
Portland	4	10	.286	9	23	.281
Pepperdine	4	10	.286	8	23	.256

Conf. Tourney Final: Gonzaga 77, Santa Clara 68.
***NCAA Tourney (0-1):** Gonzaga (0-1).

Western Athletic Conference

Team	Conference		Pct	Overall		Pct
	W	L		W	L	
*Nevada	14	2	.875	29	5	.853
*New Mexico St.	11	5	.688	25	9	.735
†Fresno St.	10	6	.625	22	10	.688
†Utah St.	9	7	.563	23	12	.657
Hawaii	8	8	.500	18	13	.581
Boise St.	8	8	.500	17	14	.548
Louisiana Tech	7	9	.438	10	20	.333
San Jose St.	4	12	.250	5	25	.167
Idaho	1	15	.063	4	27	.129

Conf. Tourney Final: New Mexico St. 72, Utah St. 70.
*NCAA Tourney (1-2): Nevada (1-1), New Mexico St. (0-1)
†NIT (0-2): Fresno St. (0-1), Utah St. (0-1).

Division I Independents

Team	Overall		Pct
	W	L	
Utah Valley St.	22	7	.759
North Dakota St.	20	8	.714
Texas-Pan American	14	15	.483
IPFW	12	17	.414
Savannah St.	12	18	.400
Chicago St.	9	20	.310
Longwood	9	22	.290
South Dakota St.	6	24	.200
UC-Davis	5	23	.179
New Jersey Tech	5	24	.172

Annual Awards

Player of the Year

Kevin Durant, Texas, F . . . . .AP, Wooden, Naismith, Rupp, USBWA, NABC

Wooden Award Voting

Presented since 1977 by the Los Angeles Athletic Club and named after the former Purdue All-America and UCLA coach John Wooden. Voting done by panel of over 1,000 members of the national media; candidates must have a cumulative college grade point average of 2.0 (out of 4.0) and be making progress toward graduation.

		Cl	Pos	Pts
1	Kevin Durant, Texas	Fr.	F	4351
2	Greg Oden, Ohio St.	Fr.	C	2858
3	Alando Tucker, Wisconsin	Sr.	F	2779
4	Acie Law, Texas A&M	Sr.	G	2708
5	Tyler Hansbrough, North Carolina	So.	F	2142
6	Arron Afflalo, UCLA	Jr.	G	1891
7	Joakim Noah, Florida	Jr.	F/C	1741
8	Nick Fazekas, Nevada	Sr.	F	1409
9	Brandon Rush, Kansas	So.	G	837
10	Aaron Brooks, Oregon	Sr.	G	799

Defensive Player of the Year

Formerly the Henry Iba Award, for defensive skills, sportsmanship and dedication; first presented by the Rotary Club of River Oaks in Houston in 1987 and named after the late Oklahoma State and U.S. Olympic team coach. Voting done by the National Association of Basketball Coaches.

Greg Oden, Ohio St., C

Div. II and III Awards

Awarded by the National Association of Basketball Coaches.

Players of the Year
Div. II . . . . .John Smith, Winona St.
Div. III . . . . .Andrew Olson, Amherst & Ben Strong, Guilford

Coaches of the Year
Div. II . . . . .Ron Lievense, Barton College
Div. III . . . . .Dave Hixon, Amherst

Coaches of the Year

Tony Bennett, Washington St. . . . . . . .AP, USBWA, Naismith
Todd Lickliter, Butler . . . . .NABC

Consensus All-America Teams

The NCAA Division I players cited most frequently by the following All-America selectors: Associated Press, U.S. Basketball Writers, National Association of Basketball Coaches and Wooden Award Committee. (*) indicates unanimous first team selection. There were no holdovers from the 2005-06 first team.

First Team

	Class	Hgt	Pos
Kevin Durant, Texas	Fr.	6-9	F
Tyler Hansbrough, North Carolina	So.	6-9	F
Acie Law, Texas A&M	Sr.	6-3	G
Greg Oden, Ohio St.	Fr.	7-0	C
Alando Tucker, Wisconsin	Sr.	6-6	F

Second Team

	Class	Hgt	Pos
Arron Afflalo, UCLA	Jr.	6-5	G
Aaron Brooks, Oregon	Sr.	6-0	G
Nick Fazekas, Nevada	Sr.	6-11	F
Joakim Noah, Florida	Jr.	6-11	F/C
Jared Dudley, Boston College	Sr.	6-7	F

Third Team

	Class	Hgt	Pos
Jeff Green, Georgetown	Jr.	6-9	F
Brandon Rush, Kansas	So.	6-6	G
Al Horford, Florida	Jr.	6-10	F
Chris Lofton, Tennessee	Jr.	6-2	G
Aaron Gray, Pitt	Sr.	7-0	C

Also Mentioned: Sean Singletary, Virgina and Julian Wright, Kansas.

*Famous freshmen Kevin Durant and Greg Oden did not disappoint in their sole college seasons. Durant became the consensus national player of the Year, Oden led his team to the Final Four, and both were named to the AP All-America team as well, becoming only the third and fourth freshmen to earn that honor since they became eligible to play in 1972. **Did you know**, the only previous freshmen to be named to the team were Oklahoma's Wayman Tisdale in 1983 and LSU's Chris Jackson in 1989?*

NCAA Men's Division I Leaders

Includes games through NCAA and NIT tourneys.

INDIVIDUAL

Scoring

	Cl	Gm	FG%	3FG/Att	FT%	Reb	Ast	Stl	Blk	Pts	Avg	Hi
Reggie Williams, VMI	Jr.	33	.531	76/238	.659	263	146	55	10	928	28.1	45
Trey Johnson, Jackson St.	Sr.	35	.414	79/237	.743	158	90	32	3	947	27.1	49
Morris Almond, Rice	Sr.	32	.483	77/169	.846	210	37	38	24	844	26.4	44
Kevin Durant, Texas	Fr.	35	.473	82/203	.816	390	46	66	67	903	25.8	37
Gary Neal, Towson	Sr.	32	.446	93/278	.836	135	111	46	5	810	25.3	41
Bo McCalebb, New Orleans	Jr.	31	.478	26/78	.710	211	101	62	5	776	25.0	39
Rodney Stuckey, Eastern Wash.	So.	29	.453	43/161	.846	135	160	71	9	712	24.6	36
Gerald Brown, Loyola	Jr.	29	.441	58/169	.748	144	78	54	13	643	22.2	33
Stephen Curry, Davidson	Fr.	34	.463	122/299	.855	157	95	62	6	730	21.5	32
Jaycee Carroll, Utah St.	Jr.	35	.527	83/192	.888	220	62	31	7	746	21.3	44
Alex Harris, UC-Santa Barbara	Jr.	29	.476	71/155	.786	140	61	26	3	611	21.1	35
Adrian Banks, Arkansas St.	Jr.	33	.496	97/204	.732	144	63	29	3	695	21.1	33
Arizona Reid, High Point	Jr.	32	.509	20/58	.659	304	60	38	15	671	21.0	32
Kyle Hines, NC-Greensboro	Jr.	29	.555	1/6	.600	260	26	40	64	605	20.9	38
Chris Lofton, Tennessee	Jr.	31	.479	106/253	.811	95	54	45	4	645	20.8	35
Charron Fisher, Niagara	Jr.	27	.456	37/102	.768	205	26	23	13	555	20.6	33
Adam Haluska, Iowa	Sr.	31	.408	90/248	.870	144	80	42	8	637	20.5	36
Caleb Green, Oral Roberts	Sr.	34	.501	6/17	.760	302	84	45	12	698	20.5	32
Nick Fazekas, Nevada	Sr.	32	.568	28/65	.848	354	56	24	48	652	20.4	33
Larry Blair, Liberty	Sr.	31	.441	52/172	.847	130	102	58	6	631	20.4	40

Rebounding

	Cl	Gm	No	Avg
Rashad Jones-Jennings, Arkansas-LR	Sr.	30	392	13.1
Chris Holm, Vermont	Sr.	33	401	12.2
Kentrell Gransberry, So. Florida	Jr.	23	263	11.4
Kevin Durant, Texas	Fr.	35	390	11.1
Nick Fazekas, Nevada	Sr.	32	354	11.1
Obie Nwadike, C. Conn. St.	Sr.	31	331	10.7
Ryvon Covile, Detroit	Sr.	30	317	10.6
Glen Davis, LSU	Jr.	29	303	10.4
Jason Smith, Colorado St.	Jr.	30	304	10.1
Jason Thompson, Rider	Jr.	31	312	10.1
Christopher Moore, Texas Southern	Sr.	28	276	9.9
Lamar Sanders, Lamar	Jr.	32	315	9.8
Dominic McGuire, Fresno St.	Jr.	32	314	9.8
Clif Brown, Niagara	Sr.	33	321	9.7
Jeff Adrien, Connecticut	So.	31	301	9.7
Jon Brockman, Washington	So.	32	307	9.6
Greg Oden, Ohio St.	Fr.	32	306	9.6
Stephane Lasme, Massachusetts	Sr.	33	315	9.5
Arizona Reid, High Point	Jr.	32	304	9.5
Scott Cutley, CS-Fullerton	Jr.	26	247	9.5

Assists

	Cl	Gm	No	Avg
Jared Jordan, Marist	Sr.	33	286	8.7
Jason Richards, Davidson	Jr.	34	249	7.3
Mustafa Shakur, Arizona	Sr.	31	215	6.9
D.J. Augustin, Texas	Fr.	35	233	6.7
Eric Maynor, VCU	So.	35	224	6.4
Keenan Jones, Northwestern St.	Sr.	32	200	6.3
Mike Conley Jr., Ohio St.	Fr.	39	238	6.1
Dwayne Foreman, Ga. Southern	Jr.	29	176	6.1
Josh Wilson, Northern Ariz.	So.	30	181	6.0
Ishmael Smith, Wake Forest	Fr.	31	186	6.0
Trant Simpson, Alabama A&M	Jr.	28	167	6.0
Temi Soyebo, NC-Wilmington	Sr.	29	170	5.9
Kevin Kanaskie, Mid. Tenn. St.	So.	32	185	5.8
Brooks McKowen, UNI	Sr.	31	179	5.8
Charles Richardson Jr., Nebraska	Sr.	31	179	5.8
Javaris Crittenton, Ga. Tech	Fr.	32	184	5.8
Steve Barnes, Southern Utah	Sr.	30	172	5.7
Darren Collison, UCLA	So.	34	194	5.7
Ty Lawson, North Carolina	Fr.	38	213	5.6
Eugene Lawrence, St. John's	Jr.	31	173	5.6

Field Goal Percentage

Minimum 5 Field Goals made per game.

	Cl	Gm	FG	FGA	Pct
Mike Freeman, Hampton	Fr.	30	162	239	67.8
Roy Hibbert, Georgetown	Jr.	37	186	277	67.1
Florentino Valencia, Toledo	Sr.	32	164	246	66.7
Vladimir Kulijanin, NC-Wilm.	Jr.	29	165	249	66.3
Calvin Brown, Norfolk St.	Sr.	30	152	233	65.2
Brandan Wright, N. Carolina	Fr.	37	228	353	64.6
Herbert Hill, Providence	Sr.	31	240	375	64.0
Paul Butorac, Eastern Wash.	Sr.	28	158	247	64.0
Luke Nevill, Utah	So.	29	181	284	63.7
Ahmad Nivins, St. Joseph's	So.	31	176	279	63.1
Will Thomas, George Mason	Jr.	33	178	284	62.7
Jermaine Griffin, TX-Arlington	Jr.	29	161	257	62.6
Greg Oden, Ohio St.	Fr.	32	189	307	61.6
Stephane Lasme, Massachusetts	Sr.	33	165	270	61.1
Andrew Strait, Montana	Jr.	30	196	321	61.1

Free Throw Percentage

Minimum 2.5 Free Throws made per game.

	Cl	Gm	FT	FTA	Pct
Derek Raivio, Gonzaga	Sr.	34	148	154	96.1
A.J. Graves, Butler	Jr.	35	145	153	94.8
Blake Ahearn, Missouri St.	Sr.	33	111	120	92.5
Tristan Blackwood, C. Conn. St.	Jr.	34	97	105	92.4
David Kool, Western Mich.	Fr.	29	99	108	91.7
Mike Schachtner, WI-Green Bay	So.	33	104	114	91.2
Arvydas Eitutavicius, American	Jr.	30	95	105	90.5
Leemire Goldwire, Charlotte	Jr.	30	95	105	90.5
Sharaud Curry, Providence	So.	27	82	91	90.1
Brian Roberts, Dayton	Jr.	31	133	148	89.9
Jack McClinton, Miami-FL	So.	31	102	114	89.5
Jaycee Carroll, Utah St.	Jr.	35	151	170	88.8
Jim Goffredo, Harvard	Sr.	28	95	107	88.8
Josh Mayo, Ill-Chicago	So.	27	78	88	88.6
Solomon Bozeman, So. Florida	Fr.	30	130	147	88.4

Reggie Williams
VMI
Scoring

Jared Jordan
Marist
Assists

Rashad Jones-Jennings
Arkansas-Little Rock
Rebounds

Travis Holmes
VMI
Steals

3-Pt Field Goal Percentage
Minimum 2.5 Three-Point FGs made per game.

	Cl	Gm	FG	FGA	Pct
Josh Carter, Texas A&M	So.	34	86	172	50.0
Jeremy Crouch, Bradley	Jr.	27	83	166	50.0
Stephen Sir, No. Arizona	Sr.	30	124	253	49.0
Jimmy Baron, Rhode Island	So.	32	97	203	47.8
Josh Washington, Tex. A&M-CC	Sr.	32	90	189	47.6
Adrian Banks, Arkansas St.	Jr.	33	97	204	47.5
James Parlow, New Orleans	Jr.	27	85	180	47.2
Blake Ahearn, Missouri St.	Sr.	33	94	202	46.5
Chad Toppert, New Mexico	So.	32	85	183	46.4
Lee Humphrey, Florida	Sr.	40	113	246	45.9
Brian Roberts, Dayton	Jr.	31	82	179	45.8
Samuel Haanpaa, Valparaiso	Fr.	29	75	164	45.7

3-Pt Field Goals Per Game

	Cl	Gm	No	Avg
Stephen Sir, Northern Arizona	Sr.	30	124	4.1
Will Whittington, Marist	Sr.	34	137	4.0
Steve Rush, N.C. A&T	Jr.	30	115	3.8
Tristan Blackwood, C. Conn. St.	Jr.	34	122	3.6
Stephen Curry, Davidson	Fr.	34	122	3.6
Keddric Mays, Chattanooga	Sr.	33	118	3.6
Robert McKiver, Houston	Jr.	33	116	3.5
Daryl Cohen, SE Louisiana	Sr.	30	105	3.5
A.J. Abrams, Texas	So.	35	120	3.4
Chris Lofton, Tennessee	Jr.	31	106	3.4
Chavis Holmes, VMI	So.	32	108	3.4

Blocked Shots

	Cl	Gm	No	Avg
Mickell Gladness, Alabama A&M	Jr.	30	188	6.3
Stephane Lasme, Massacusetts	Sr.	33	168	5.1
Hasheem Thabeet, Connecticut	Fr.	31	118	3.8
McHugh Mattis, South Florida	Sr.	30	109	3.6
Dominic McGuire, Fresno St.	Jr.	32	114	3.6
Scott VanderMeer, Ill-Chicago	So.	32	111	3.5
Darryl Watkins, Syracuse	Sr.	33	112	3.4
Greg Oden, Ohio St.	Fr.	32	105	3.3
John Bunch, Monmouth	Sr.	29	95	3.3
Chaz Crawford, Drexel	Sr.	31	94	3.0
Joel Anthony, UNLV	Sr.	37	109	2.9
Herbert Hill, Providence	Sr.	31	91	2.9
Brandon Wallace, South Carolina	Sr.	30	86	2.9

Steals

	Cl	Gm	No	Avg
Travis Holmes, VMI	So.	33	111	3.4
Paul Gause, Seton Hall	So.	29	90	3.1
Ledell Eackles, Campbell	Sr.	31	94	3.0
Ibrahim Jaaber, Penn	Sr.	31	90	2.9
Chavis Holmes, VMI	So.	32	90	2.8
Torey Thomas, Holy Cross	Sr.	34	95	2.8
Jamon Gordon, Virginia Tech	Sr.	34	94	2.8
Tony Lee, Robert Morris	Jr.	28	77	2.8
Derek Johnson, Prairie View	So.	30	82	2.7
Jerel McNeal, Marquette	So.	29	76	2.6
Courtney Pigram, East Tenn. St.	So.	34	89	2.6

Single Game Highs

Points

No		Opponent	Date
49	Trey Johnson, Jackson St.	UTEP	Dec. 22
47	Bobby Brown, CS-Fullerton	Bet-Cookman	Dec. 16
45	Al Thornton, Florida St.	Miami-FL	Mar. 3
45	Reggie Williams, VMI	Va. Intermont	Nov. 15
44	Jaycee Carroll, Utah St.	N. Mex. St.	Feb. 5
44	Morris Almond, Rice	Vanderbilt	Jan. 2

Rebounds

No		Opponent	Date
25	Arizona Reid, High Point	VMI	Feb. 24
23	Kentrell Gransberry, So. Florda	DePaul	Mar. 3
23	Kevin Durant, Texas	Texas Tech	Jan. 31

Assists

No		Opponent	Date
19	Jason Richards, Davidson	Mt. St. Mary's	Dec. 15
16	Ryan Evanochko, WI-GB	Chicago St.	Dec. 12
16	Jason Richards, Davidson	Colby	Nov. 21

Blocks

No		Opponent	Date
16	Mickell Gladness, Ala. A&M	TX Southern	Feb. 24
13	Joel Anthony, UNLV	TCU	Feb. 7
13	Sean Williams, Boston Col.	Duquesne	Dec. 28

Steals

No		Opponent	Date
11	Travis Holmes, VMI	Bridgewater (Va.)	Jan. 18
10	Ledell Eackles, Campbell	NC-Pembroke	Nov. 11
9	Five tied.		

3-point FGs

No		Opponent	Date
12	Michael Jenkins, Winthrop	N. Greenville	Nov. 10
11	Eric Moore, Buffalo	Bowling Green	Jan. 7
11	Bobby Brown, CS-Fullerton	Bet-Cookman	Dec. 16

NCAA Men's Division I Leaders (Cont.)
TEAM

Scoring Offense

	Gm	W-L	Pts	Avg
VMI	33	14-19	3331	100.9
North Carolina	38	31-7	3258	85.7
Eastern Washington	29	15-14	2443	84.2
Northern Arizona	30	18-12	2490	83.0
CS-Fullerton	30	20-10	2462	82.1
Texas	35	25-10	2860	81.7
Davidson	34	29-5	2765	81.3
Notre Dame	32	24-8	2592	81.0
Tennessee	35	24-11	2831	80.9
Long Beach St.	32	24-8	2575	80.5

Field Goal Percentage Defense

	FG	FGA	Pct
Connecticut	.677	1824	37.1
Texas A&M	.672	1793	37.5
Syracuse	.834	2223	37.5
Kansas	.804	2136	37.6
Georgetown	.742	1935	38.3
Michigan St.	.671	1746	38.4
Fresno St.	.792	2058	38.5
Maryland	.823	2117	38.9
Tulsa	.649	1667	38.9
Alabama A&M	.707	1814	39.0

Scoring Defense

	Gm	W-L	Pts	Avg
Princeton	28	11-17	1493	53.3
Air Force	35	26-9	1960	56.0
Southern Ill.	36	29-7	2023	56.2
Illinois	35	23-12	1997	57.1
Butler	36	29-7	2056	57.1
Michigan St.	35	23-12	2001	57.2
Miami-OH	33	18-15	1895	57.4
Holy Cross	34	25-9	1954	57.5
Bucknell	31	22-9	1791	57.8
Wisconsin	36	30-6	2083	57.9

Rebound Margin

	Off	Def	Mar
Vermont	40.7	31.1	9.6
Washington	38.3	29.3	9.0
North Carolina	40.8	32.3	8.5
Florida	37.6	29.1	8.5
Massachusetts	40.4	32.8	7.7
Southern Miss.	38.6	31.4	7.2
Tulsa	39.7	32.5	7.2
Michigan St.	34.8	27.8	7.0
CS-Northridge	38.8	32.0	6.9
Kansas	39.7	33.0	6.7

Scoring Margin

	Off	Def	Mar
Florida	79.8	62.6	17.2
North Carolina	85.7	68.6	17.1
Kansas	78.4	61.7	16.7
Texas A&M	75.6	59.4	16.1
Memphis	78.9	63.1	15.8
Akron	75.3	61.0	14.3
Winthrop	74.9	61.4	13.4
Notre Dame	81.0	68.0	13.0
Air Force	69.0	56.0	13.0
Davidson	81.3	68.7	12.6

Free Throw Percentage

	FT	FTA	Pct
Villanova	.594	761	78.1
Utah St.	.492	631	78.0
California	.400	520	76.9
Oakland	.546	711	76.8
Oregon	.531	698	76.1
WI-Green Bay	.530	697	76.0
Butler	.553	728	76.0
Harvard	.497	655	75.9
Florida St.	.498	657	75.8
Robert Morris	.369	487	75.8

Won-Lost Percentage

	W	L	Pct
Ohio St.	35	4	89.7
Memphis	33	4	89.2
Florida	35	5	87.5
Kansas	33	5	86.8
UCLA	30	5	85.7
Davidson	29	5	85.3
Nevada	29	5	85.3
Winthrop	29	5	85.3
Wisconsin	29	5	85.3
North Carolina	31	7	81.6

3-point FG Percentage

	3PT	3PTA	Pct
Northern Arizona	.229	537	42.6
Texas A&M	.215	510	42.2
Bradley	.349	831	42.0
New Orleans	.225	542	41.5
Brigham Young	.256	617	41.5
Utah	.217	524	41.4
Hofstra	.256	621	41.2
Texas Tech	.208	505	41.2
Florida	.297	727	40.9
Nevada	.253	623	40.6

Field Goal Percentage

	FG	FGA	Pct
Florida	1125	2138	52.6
Texas A&M-Corpus Christi	.912	1747	52.2
Georgetown	.923	1826	50.5
North Carolina	1187	2379	49.9
Texas A&M	.908	1823	49.8
Eastern Washington	.846	1708	49.5
Northern Arizona	.873	1766	49.4
Kansas	1106	2241	49.4
N.C. State	.908	1849	49.1
Brigham Young	.972	1981	49.1

3-point FG Made Per Game

	Gm	No	Avg
VMI	33	442	13.4
West Virginia	36	371	10.3
Houston	33	330	10.0
Bradley	35	349	10.0
Wofford	30	297	9.9
Pepperdine	31	303	9.8
Davidson	34	328	9.6
Fresno St.	32	303	9.5
Oregon	37	350	9.5
New Mexico	32	299	9.3

Assists Per Game

	Gm	No	Avg
VMI	.33	681	20.6
Sam Houston St.	.31	596	19.2
North Carolina	.38	696	18.3
Northern Arizona	.30	544	18.1
Texas A&M-Corpus Christi	.33	595	18.0
Eastern Washington	.29	514	17.7
West Virginia	.36	633	17.6
Pittsburgh	.37	647	17.5
Hawaii	.31	539	17.4
Penn	.31	539	17.4

Blocks Per Game

	Gm	No	Avg
Connecticut	.31	264	8.5
Alabama A&M	.30	236	7.9
Massachusetts	.33	246	7.5
Syracuse	.35	250	7.1
Maryland	.34	233	6.9
Kansas	.38	246	6.5
Fresno St.	.32	206	6.4
Mississippi St.	.35	222	6.3
Arkansas	.35	221	6.3
Tulane	.30	188	6.3

Steals Per Game

	Gm	No	Avg
VMI	.33	490	14.8
Sacramento St.	.29	320	11.0
Seton Hall	.29	299	10.3
Northwestern St.	.32	326	10.2
Missouri	.30	302	10.1
East Tenn. St.	.34	338	9.9
Georgie Tech	.32	316	9.9
Campbell	.31	300	9.7
Tennessee	.35	336	9.6
Prairie View	.30	286	9.5

2006-07 NCAA Div. I Attendance Leaders

	Team (2005-06 rank)	Gms	Average
1	Kentucky (1)	.16	23,421
2	Syracuse (2)	.22	21,516
3	North Carolina (3)	.17	20,693
4	Tennessee (5)	.16	19,661
5	Louisville (4)	.20	18,488
6	Ohio St. (11)	.18	17,530
7	Wisconsin (7)	.19	17,190
8	Maryland (6)	.19	16,822
9	Arkansas (12)	.16	16,720
10	Illinois (9)	.17	16,618
11	Indiana (8)	.15	16,474
12	Kansas (10)	.18	16,300
13	Creighton (20)	.14	15,909
14	Marquette (18)	.20	15,345
15	Michigan St. (14)	.19	14,759
16	Memphis (13)	.19	14,527
17	Arizona (16)	.16	14,202
18	N.C. State (17)	.20	13,952
19	Virginia (66)	.17	13,521
20	Connecticut (19)	.20	13,012
21	Oklahoma St. (28)	.18	13,008
22	Texas (22)	.16	12,969
23	New Mexico (21)	.18	12,853
24	South Carolina (56)	.17	12,838
25	Iowa St. (26)	.17	12,489

Underclassmen in NBA Draft

Thirty-two collegiate players and six international players forfeited their college eligibility and declared for the 2007 NBA Draft which took place at Madison Square Garden in New York City on June 28.

Forty-six American and International players, who initially declared themselves eligible for the 2007 NBA Draft withdrew their names before the June 19 deadline. Under the new collective bargaining agreement signed following the 2005 NBA draft players from the United States will now have to wait one year after the date their high school class graduates. International players must turn 19 years old by the end of the calendar year. First round selections in **bold** type.

College Players	Cl	Drafted by	Overall Pick
Arron Afflalo, UCLA	Jr.	Detroit	27
Shagair Alleyne, Manhattan	Jr.	not drafted	–
Corey Brewer, Florida	Jr.	Minnesota	7
Dwight Brewington, Liberty	Jr.	not drafted	–
Wilson Chandler, DePaul	So.	New York	
Mike Conley Jr., Ohio St.	Fr.	Memphis	4
Daequan Cook, Ohio St.	Fr.	Philadelphia*	21
Javaris Crittenton, Ga. Tech	Fr.	LA Lakers	19
Jameson Curry, Oklahoma St.	Jr.	Chicago	51
Glen Davis, LSU	Jr.	Seattle**	35
Kevin Durant, Texas	Fr.	Seattle	2
Jeff Green, Georgetown	Jr.	Boston***	5
Taurean Green, Florida	Jr.	Portland	52
Spencer Hawes, Washington	Fr.	Sacramento	10
Al Horford, Florida	Jr.	Atlanta	3
Robert Earl Johnson, Clinton JC	Fr.	not drafted	–
Kellen Lee, Los Angeles CC	So.	not drafted	–
Dominic McGuire, Fresno St.	Jr.	Washington	47
Josh McRoberts, Duke	So.	Portland	37
Joakim Noah, Florida	Jr.	Chicago	9
Greg Oden, Ohio St.	Fr.	Portland	1
Kendaris Pelton, So. Miss.	Jr.	not drafted	–
Gabe Pruitt, USC	Jr.	Boston	32
Ramon Sessions, Nevada	Jr.	Milwaukee	56
Jason Smith, Colorado St.	Jr.	Miami†	20
Rodney Stuckey, E. Wash.	So.	Detroit	15
Marcus Williams, Arizona	Jr.	San Antonio	33
Sean Williams, Boston College	Jr.	New Jersey	17
Brandan Wright, Kansas	So.	Charlotte††	8
Julian Wright, Kansas	So.	New Orleans	13
Nick Young, USC	Jr.	Washington	16
Thaddeus Young, Ga. Tech	Fr.	Philadelphia	12

*traded to Miami
**traded to Boston   ***traded to Seattle
†traded to Philadelphia
††traded to Golden State

International Players	Hgt	Drafted by	Overall Pick
Ralfi Silva Ansaloni, Brazil	.7-0	not drafted	–
Stanko Barac, Bosnia	.7-2	Miami^	39
Marco Belinelli, Italy	.6-5	Golden St.	18
Kyrylo Fesenko, Ukraine	.7-0	Philadelphia	38
Petteri Koponen, Finland	.6-4	Philadelphia$	30
Yi Jianlian, China	.6-11	Milwaukee	6

^traded to Indiana
$traded to Portland

Other 2007 Men's Tournaments

NIT Tournament

The 70th annual National Invitation Tournament had a 32-team field, down from 40 teams in recent years. First three rounds played on home courts of higher seeded teams. Semifinal and Championship games played Mar 27-29 at Madison Square Garden in New York City.

1st Round

at Mississippi St. 82	....	Mississippi Valley St. 63
at Bradley 90	..........OT	......Providence 78
at Michigan 68	....	.......Utah St. 58
at Florida St. 77	....	.........Toledo 61
at West Virginia 74	....	...Delaware St. 50
at Massachusetts 89	.....OT	........Alabama 87
N.C. State 63	....	...at Drexel 56
Marist 67	....	at Oklahoma St. 64
at Air Force 75	....	.Austin Peay 51
at Georgia 88	....	.....Fresno St. 78
at DePaul 83	....	......Hofstra 71
at Kansas St. 59	....	......Vermont 57
at Clemson 64	....	.East Tenn. St. 57
at Mississippi 73	....	Appalachian St. 59
San Diego St. 74	....	.at Missouri 70
at Syracuse 79	....	South Alabama 73

2nd Round

at Mississippi St. 101	....	...Bradley 72
at Florida St. 87	....	.....Michigan 66
at West Virginia 90	....	Massachusetts 77
at N.C. State 69	....	......Marist 62
at Air Force 83	....	.......Georgia 52
DePaul 70	....	...at Kansas St. 65
at Clemson 89	....	....Mississippi 68
at Syracuse 80	....	...San Diego St. 64

Quarterfinals

at Mississippi St. 86	....	.Florida St. 71
at West Virginia 71	....	.N.C. State 66
at Air Force 52	....	......DePaul 51
at Clemson 74	....	......Syracuse 70

Semifinals

West Virginia 63	....	Mississippi St. 62
Clemson 68	....	....Air Force 67

Championship

West Virginia 78	....	...Clemson 73

Tournament MVPs

NIT

Frank Young
West Virginia senior forward

NCAA Division II

Anthony Atkinson
Barton senior guard

NCAA Division III

Andrew Olson
Amherst junior guard

NAIA Division I

Kameron Gray
Oklahoma City junior guard

NAIA Division II

Adam Hepker
MidAmerica Nazarene junior guard

NCAA Division II

The eight regional winners of the 64-team field: NORTH-EAST—Bentley (32-0); EAST—Barton (28-5); SOUTH ATLANTIC—Wingate (25-8); SOUTH—Montevallo (28-5); SOUTH CENTRAL—Central Missouri (30-3); GREAT LAKES—Grand Valley St. (29-4); NORTH CENTRAL—Winona St. (33-0); WEST—CS-San Bernadino (25-5).

The Elite Eight was played March 21-24, at Springfield, Massachusetts. There was no Third Place game.

Quarterfinals

Barton 83	.............OT	.....Grand Valley St. 81
CS-Bernadino 100	....	.....Wingate 73
Central Missouri 86	....	....Montevallo 69
Winona St. 64	....	........Bentley 51

Semifinals

Barton 80	....	....CS-San Bernardino 79
Winona St. 90	..........OT	...Central Missouri 85

Championship

Barton 77	....	.Winona St. 75

NCAA Division III

The four sectional winners of the 48-team field: Wooster (29-3), Virginia Wesleyan (27-4), Amherst (28-2), Washington-St. Louis (24-4).

The Final Four was played March 16-17, at Salem Civic Center in Salem, Va.

Semifinals

Virginia Wesleyan 67	....	Washington-St. Louis 65
Amherst 67	....	....Wooster 60

Championship

Amherst 80	....	..Va. Wesleyan 67

NAIA Division I

The quarterfinalists, in alphabetical order, after two rounds of the 32-team NAIA tournament: Azusa Pacific, Calif.; Concordia, Calif.; Crichton, Tenn.; Faulkner, Ala.; Northwestern Oklahoma; Oklahoma City; Robert Morris, Ill.; Union, Tenn.

All tournament games played, March 17-20, at the Municipal Auditorium, Kansas City, Mo. There was no Third Place game.

Quarterfinals: Robert Morris def. Crichton, 116-96; Concordia def. Union, 88-68; Oklahoma City def. Azusa Pacific, 84-68; Faulker def. NW Oklahoma St., 76-59.

Semifinals: Oklahoma City def. Faulkner, 76-61; Concordia def. Robert Morris, 124-119 (4 OT).

Championship: Oklahoma City def. Concordia, 79-71.

NAIA Division II

The quarterfinalists, in alphabetical order, after two rounds of the 32-team NAIA tournament: Cedarville Univ. (23-7); Cornerstone, Mich. (25-9); Indiana Wesleyan (30-4); Mayville St. (25-8); MidAmerica Nazarene (31-2); Northwest Univ., Wash. (26-8); Northwestern College, Iowa (25-8); College of the Ozarks (22-10).

All tournament games played, March 10-13, at Keeter Gymnasium in Point Lookout, Missouri. There was no Third Place game.

Quarterfinals: Northwest (Wash.) def. Cornerstone, 98-69; MidAmerica Nazarene def. Indiana Wesleyan, 77-68; Northwestern (Iowa) def. College of the Ozarks, 73-57; Mayville St. def. Cedarville, 82-81.

Semifinals: Mayville St. def. Northwest (Wash.), 74-65; MidAmerica Nazarene def. Northwestern (Iowa), 81-71.

Championship: MidAmerica Nazarene def. Mayville St., 78-60.

Final Regular Season AP Women's Top 25 Poll

Taken **before** start of NCAA tournament.

The sportswriters & broadcasters poll: first place votes in parentheses; records through Sunday, March 11, 2007; total points (based on 25 for 1st, 24 for 2nd, etc.); record in NCAA tourney and team lost to; head coach (career years and career record including 2007 postseason), and preseason ranking. Teams in **bold** type went on to reach the NCAA Final Four.

		Mar. 11 Record	Points	NCAA Recap	Head Coach	Preseason Rank
1	Duke (39)	30-1	1,225	2-1 (Rutgers)	Gail Goestenkors (15 yrs: 396-99)	6
2	Connecticut (7)	28-2	1,177	3-1 (LSU)	Geno Auriemma (22 yrs: 621-120)	8
3	**North Carolina** (4)	30-3	1,160	4-1 (Tennessee)	Sylvia Hatchell (32 yrs: 751-272)	2
4	**Tennessee**	28-3	1,110	6-0	Pat Summitt (33 yrs: 948-180)	5
5	Ohio St.	28-2	1,022	0-1 (Marist)	Jim Foster (29 yrs: 634-257)	7
6	Stanford	27-4	942	1-1 (FSU)	Tara VanDerveer (28 yrs: 689-184)	4
7	Maryland	27-5	936	1-1 (Mississippi)	Brenda Frese (8 yrs: 169-81)	1
8	Arizona St.	28-3	887	3-1 (Rutgers)	Charli Turner Thorne (14 yrs: 243-174)	13
9	Vanderbilt	27-5	849	1-1 (Bowling Green)	Melani Balcomb (15 yrs: 284-147)	16
10	**LSU**	26-7	785	4-1 (Rutgers)	Pokey Chatman (3 yrs: 90-14) & Bob Starkey (1 yr: 4-1)	10
11	Oklahoma	23-4	751	2-1 (Mississippi)	Sherri Coale (11 yrs: 232-118)	3
12	Purdue	27-5	640	3-1 (North Carolina)	Kristy Curry (8 yrs: 215-57)	11
13	Texas A&M	23-5	638	1-1 (G. Washington)	Gary Blair (22 yrs: 481-213)	14
14	Georgia	25-6	627	2-1 (Purdue)	Andy Landers (28 yrs: 684-215)	9
15	George Washington	26-3	611	2-1 (North Carolina)	Joe McKeown (21 yrs: 482-167)	-
16	Middle Tenn. St.	27-3	488	1-1 (Marist)	Rick Insell (2 yrs: 50-15)	-
17	N.C. State	23-9	429	2-1 (Connecticut)	Kay Yow (35 yrs: 718-330)	-
18	Baylor	24-6	425	1-1 (N.C. State)	Kim Mulkey (7 yrs: 183-53)	19
19	**Rutgers**	20-8	304	5-1 (Tennessee)	C. Vivian Stringer (36 yrs: 777-260)	-
20	Bowling Green	26-3	258	2-1 (Arizona)	Curt Miller (6 yrs: 124-60)	-
21	Marquette	25-5	238	1-1 (Oklahoma)	Terri Mitchell (11 yrs: 217-116)	-
22	Wisconsin-Green Bay	25-3	217	1-1 (Connecticut)	Kevin Borseth (20 yrs: 441-159)	-
23	Louisville	26-6	155	1-1 (Arizona St.)	Tom Collen (9 yrs: 217-70)	-
24	Michigan St.	23-8	152	1-1 (Rutgers)	Joanne P. McCallie (15 yrs: 316-148)	17
25	Montana	27-3	67	did not play	Robin Selvig (29 yrs: 672-192)	-

Others receiving votes: 26. California (57 points); 27. **Iowa St.** (34); 28. **Old Dominion** (28); 29. **Delaware** (8); 30. **James Madison** and **Pittsburgh** (7); 32. **Temple** (6); 33. **Xavier** (3); 34. **Mississippi** and **West Virginia** (2); 36. **Coppin St.**, **DePaul** and **Tulane** (1).

NCAA Women's Division I Tournament Seeds

	DALLAS		DAYTON		FRESNO		GREENSBORO
1	North Carolina (30-3)	1	Tennessee (28-3)	1	Connecticut (29-3)	1	Duke (30-1)
2	Purdue (28-5)	2	Maryland (27-5)	2	Stanford (28-4)	2	Vanderbilt (27-5)
3	Georgia (25-6)	3	Oklahoma (26-4)	3	LSU (26-7)	3	Arizona St. (28-4)
4	Texas A&M (24-6)	4	Ohio St. (28-3)	4	N.C. State (23-9)	4	Rutgers (22-8)
5	G. Washington (26-3)	5	Middle Tennessee (29-3)	5	Baylor (25-7)	5	Michigan St. (23-8)
6	Iowa St. (25-8)	6	Marquette (25-6)	6	Xavier (26-7)	6	Louisville (26-7)
7	Georgia Tech (20-11)	7	Mississippi (21-10)	7	Old Dominion (24-8)	7	Bowling Green (29-3)
8	California (23-8)	8	Pittsburgh (23-8)	8	New Mexico (24-8)	8	Temple (24-7)
9	Notre Dame (19-11)	9	James Madison (27-5)	9	Wisc-Green Bay (28-3)	9	Nebraska (22-9)
10	DePaul (19-12)	10	TCU (21-10)	10	Florida St. (22-9)	10	Oklahoma St. (20-10)
11	Washington (18-12)	11	LA-Lafayette (25-8)	11	West Virginia (20-10)	11	BYU (23-9)
12	Boise St. (24-8)	12	Gonzaga (24-9)	12	Chattanooga (25-7)	12	Delaware (26-5)
13	Texas-Arlington (24-8)	13	Marist (27-5)	13	Robert Morris (24-7)	13	East Carolina (19-13)
14	Belmont (25-6)	14	SE Missouri St. (24-7)	14	NC-Asheville (21-11)	14	UC-Riverside (21-10)
15	Oral Roberts (22-10)	15	Harvard (15-12)	15	Idaho St. (17-13)	15	Delaware St. (20-12)
16	Prairie View (19-13)	16	Drake (14-18)	16	UMBC (16-16)	16	Holy Cross (15-17)

2006-07 Most Improved Teams

Team	2005-06 W-L	2006-07 W-L	Improvement	Coach
Oklahoma St.	6-22	20-11	+12.5	Kurt Budke
Western Carolina	9-20	24-10	+12.5	Kellie Harper
Morgan St.	5-23	18-13	+11.5	Donald Beasley
San Diego	9-19	21-9	+11.0	Cindy Fisher
Seton Hall	6-21	19-12	+11.0	Phyllis Mangina
Jacksonville	10-18	21-9	+10.0	Jill Dunn
Mississippi St.	6-22	18-14	+10.0	Sharon Fanning
Niagara	4-25	14-16	+9.5	Bill Agronin
Prairie View	7-21	19-14	+9.5	Cynthia Cooper-Dyke

2007 NCAA Tournament Women's Division

1st ROUND March 17-18

(1) Connecticut 82
(16) MDBC 33
(8) New Mexico 52
(9) UW-GB 59
(12) Baylor 68
(12) Chattanooga 55
(4) N.C. State 84
(13) Rob. Morris 52
(11) Xavier 52
(11) West Va. 65
(3) LSU 77
(14) N.C.-Asheville 39
(7) ODU 75
(10) Florida St. 85
(2) Stanford 96
(15) Idaho St. 58

(1) Duke 81
(16) Holy Cross 44
(8) Temple 64
(9) Nebraska 61
(5) Michigan St. 69
(12) Delaware 58
(4) Rutgers 77
(13) ECU 34
(6) Louisville 80
(11) BYU 54
(3) Arizona St. 57
(14) Riverside 50
(7) Okla. St. 70
(10) Okla. St. 66
(2) Vanderbilt 62
(15) Delaware St. 47

2nd ROUND March 19-20

Connecticut 94
UW-GB 70
Baylor 72
N.C. State 78
West Va. 43
LSU 49
Florida St. 68
Stanford 61

Duke 62
Temple 52
Michigan St. 57
Rutgers 70
Louisville 58
Arizona St. 67
BGU 59
Vanderbilt 56

SWEET 16 March 24-25

Connecticut 78

N.C. State 71

LSU 55

Florida St. 43

Duke 52

Rutgers 53

Arizona St. 67

BGU 49

ELITE EIGHT March 26-27

Connecticut 50

Fresno

LSU 73

Rutgers 64

Greensboro

Arizona St. 45

FINAL FOUR April 1

LSU 35

Rutgers 59

NATIONAL CHAMPIONSHIP

Tennessee 59
Rutgers 46

Quicken Loans Arena
Cleveland, Ohio
Tuesday, April 3, 2007

FINAL FOUR April 1

No. Carolina 50

Tennessee 56

ELITE EIGHT March 26-27

No. Carolina 84

Dallas

Purdue 72

Tennessee 98

Dayton

Mississippi 62

SWEET 16 March 24-25

No. Carolina 70

Geo. Wash. 56

Georgia 65

Purdue 78

Tennessee 65

Marist 46

Oklahoma 82

Mississippi 90

2nd ROUND March 19-20

No. Carolina 60
Notre Dame 51
Geo. Wash. 59
Texas A&M 47
Iowa St. 56
Georgia 76
Ga. Tech 63
Purdue 76

Tennessee 68
Pittsburgh 54
Mid Tenn. 59
Marist 73
Marquette 47
Oklahoma 78
Mississippi 89
Maryland 78

1st ROUND March 17-18

(1) No. Carolina 95
(16) Prairie View 38
(8) Cal 59
(9) Notre Dame 62
(5) Geo. Wash. 76
(12) Boise St. 67
(4) Texas A&M 58
(13) UT-Arlington 50
(6) Iowa St. 79
(11) Washington 60
(3) Georgia 53
(14) Belmont 36
(7) Ga. Tech 55
(10) DePaul 54
(2) Purdue 63
(15) O. Roberts 42

(1) Tennessee 76
(16) Drake 37
(8) Pittsburgh 71
(9) J. Madison 61
(5) Mid Tenn. 85
(12) Gonzaga 46
(4) Marist 67
(13) Marquette 87
(11) LA-Lafayette 58
(3) Oklahoma 74
(14) SE Mo. St. 60
(10) Mississippi 88
(10) TCU 74
(2) Maryland 89
(15) Harvard 65

NCAA Championship Game

Apr. 3, 2007 at Quicken Loans Arena in Cleveland, Ohio

Rutgers 46

	Min	FG M-A	FT M-A	Pts	Reb O-T	A	PF
E. Carson	.40	4-11	0-3	8	1-6	1	4
H. Zurich	.23	2-6	0-0	4	0-1	0	3
K. Vaughn	.34	9-15	2-3	20	7-10	2	2
E. Prince	.26	0-0	2-4	2	1-3	2	4
M. Ajavon	.37	3-9	0-0	8	0-4	1	5
D. Jernigan	.1	0-0	0-0	0	0-0	0	0
K. Adams	.1	0-0	0-0	0	0-0	0	0
M. McCurdy	.17	1-3	0-0	2	0-1	0	3
J. Ray	.15	0-3	0-0	0	1-2	0	0
R. Junaid	.6	1-2	0-0	2	1-3	0	1
TOTALS	.200	20-49	4-10	11	30	6	22

Three-point FG: 2-10 (Carson 0-3, Ray 0-2, Ajavon 2-5); **Blocked Shots:** 3 (Vaughn, Zurich, Junaid); **Turnovers:** 17 (Vaughn 4, Carson 2, McCurdy 2, Ajavon 5); **Steals:** 6 (Vaughn 3, Zurich, McCurdy, Ajavon); **Percentages:** 3-Pt FG (.200); Total FG (.408); Free Throws (.400).

Tennessee 59

	Min	FG M-A	FT M-A	Pts	Reb O-T	A	PF
S. Spencer	.36	4-12	2-2	11	2-2	2	4
C. Parker	.39	5-15	7-10	17	2-7	3	2
N. Anosike	.34	2-9	0-5	4	10-16	2	2
S. Bobbitt	.32	4-9	1-2	13	2-3	0	1
A. Hornbuckle	.37	2-8	0-0	4	3-7	1	2
D. Redding	.1	0-0	0-0	0	0-0	0	0
A. Auguste	.15	3-5	4-4	10	4-5	1	1
A. Fuller	.6	0-0	0-0	0	0-0	0	0
TOTALS	.220	20-58	14-23	59	23-40	9	13

Three-point FG: 5-15 (Bobbitt 4-8, Hornbuckle 0-3, Spencer 1-4); **Blocked Shots:** 0; **Turnovers:** 12 (Bobbitt, Hornbuckle 7, Anosike, Fuller, Parker 2); **Steals:** 7 (Bobbitt 3, Hornbuckle 2, Anosike, Auguste); **Percentages:** 3-Pt FG (.333); Total FG (.345); Free Throws (.609).

	1	2	F
Rutgers (Big East)	18	28	— 46
Tennessee (SEC)	29	30	— 59

Technical Fouls: None. **Attendance:** 20,704. **Officials:** Lisa Mattingly, Michael Price, Tina Napier.

Final *ESPN/USA Today* Coaches' Poll

Taken **after** NCAA tournament.

Voted on by a panel of 31 women's coaches and media following the NCAA tournament: first place votes in parentheses.

	Pts		Pts
1 Tennessee (31)	.775	14 Maryland	.368
2 Rutgers	.727	15 Bowling Green	.306
3 North Carolina	.724	16 Stanford	.298
4 LSU	.678	17 Vanderbilt	.271
5 Connecticut	.630	18 Ohio St.	.201
6 Duke	.597	19 Florida St.	.198
7 Purdue	.569	20 Baylor	.189
8 Arizona St.	.549	21 Texas A&M	.181
9 Oklahoma	.474	22 Marist	.137
10 Mississippi	.434	23 Middle Tennessee	.104
11 G. Washington	.408	24 Louisville	.92
12 N.C. State	.404	25 Michigan St.	.79
13 Georgia	.387		

WOMEN'S FINAL FOUR

at Cleveland, Ohio (April 1-3).

Semifinals

Rutgers 59 . . . . .LSU 35
Tennessee 56 . . . . .North Carolina 50

Championship

Tennessee 59 . . . . .Rutgers 46

Final Records: Rutgers (27-10), North Carolina (34-4), Tennessee (35-3), LSU (30-8).

Most Outstanding Player: Candace Parker, Tennessee. SEMIFINAL—28 minutes, 14 points, 13 rebounds, 2 assists; FINAL—39 minutes, 17 points, 7 rebounds, 3 assists.

All-Tournament Team: Parker, Nicky Anosike and Shannon Bobbitt of Tennessee; Matee Ajavon and Kia Vaughn of Rutgers.

Annual Awards

Players of the Year

Candace Parker, Tenn...Wade, Wooden, Broderick, USBWA
Courtney Paris, Oklahoma . . . . .AP
Lindsey Harding, Duke . . . . .Naismith

Coaches of the Year

Gail Goestenkors, Duke . . . .AP, USBWA, Naismith, WBCA

Consensus All-America Team

The NCAA Division I players cited most frequently by the Associated Press, US Basketball Writers Association, the Women's Basketball Coaches Association and Wooden Committee. Holdovers from 2005-06 All-America first team are in **bold** type; (*) indicates unanimous first team selection.

First Team

	Class	Hgt	Pos
Candace Parker*, Tennessee	So.	6-4	F
Courtney Paris*, Oklahoma	So	6-4	C
Ivory Latta*, North Carolina	Sr.	5-6	G
Lindsey Harding*, Duke	Sr.	5-8	G
Jessica Davenport, Ohio St.	Sr.	6-5	C

Second Team

	Class	Hgt	Pos
Sylvia Fowles, LSU	Jr.	6-6	C
Crystal Langhorne, Maryland	Jr.	6-2	C/F
Candice Wiggins, Stanford	Jr.	5-11	G
Chrissy Givens, Middle Tennessee	Sr.	5-11	G
Angel McCoughtry, Louisville	So.	6-1	F

Players also named: Alison Bales, Duke; Armintie Price, Mississippi.

Other Women's Tournaments

WNIT (Mar. 31 at Laramie, Wyoming): Final— Wyoming def. Wisconsin, 72-56.

NCAA Division II (Mar. 24 at Kearney, Neb.): Southern Connecticut St. def. Florida Gulf Coast, 61-45.

NCAA Division III (Mar. 17 at Springfield, Mass.): DePauw def. Washington (Mo.), 55-52.

NAIA Division I (Mar. 20 at Jackson, Tenn.): Final— Lambuth (Tenn.) def. Cumberland (Tenn.), 63-50.

NAIA Division II (Mar. 13 at Sioux City, Iowa): Indiana Wesleyan def. Ozarks (Mo.), 48-34.

NCAA Women's Division I Leaders

Includes games through NCAA and WNIT tourneys.

INDIVIDUAL

Scoring

	Cl	Gm	Pts	Avg
Carrie Moore, Western Mich.	Sr.	32	813	25.4
Crystal Kelly, Western Ky.	Jr.	32	770	24.1
Courtney Paris, Oklahoma	So.	33	775	23.5
Chrissy Givens, Middle Tennessee	Sr.	34	768	22.6
Tye Jackson, Houston	Jr.	22	495	22.5
Alisha Dill, Coastal Carolina	Sr.	29	652	22.5
Natalie Doma, Idaho St.	Jr.	31	685	22.1
Carmen Guzman, UAB	Sr.	32	696	21.8
Joi Scott, Murray St.	Sr.	26	565	21.7
Angel McCoughtry, Louisville	So.	35	754	21.5
Adrianne Davie, Arkansas St.	Sr.	34	707	20.8
Alex Anderson, Chattanooga	Jr.	33	677	20.5
Traci Edwards, Wisc-Milwaukee	So.	30	615	20.5
Casey Nash, Oregon St.	Sr.	28	560	20.0
Jessica Davenport, Ohio St.	Sr.	32	639	20.0
Jolene Anderson, Wisconsin	Jr.	36	714	19.8
Tyresa Smith, Delaware	Sr.	32	632	19.8
Mandy Morales, Montana	So.	31	612	19.7
Jillian Robbins, Tulsa	Sr.	30	590	19.7
Amber Bland, N.C. A&T	So.	30	589	19.6

Assists

	Cl	Gm	No	Avg
Amanda Rego, San Diego	Jr.	30	230	7.7
Kristin Chaney, Southern Miss.	Sr.	30	210	7.0
Mandy Morales, Montana	So.	31	211	6.8
Andrea Benvenuto, James Madison	Sr.	33	223	6.8
Kelcey Roegiers-Jensen, Georgia St.	Sr.	30	197	6.6
Lyndsey Medders, Iowa St.	Sr.	33	216	6.5
Stephanie Raymond, Northern Ill.	Sr.	31	201	6.5
Mercedes Fox-Griffin, Oregon St.	So.	28	180	6.4
Ashley Langford, Tulane	So.	33	207	6.3
Sharnee Zoll, Virginia	Jr.	34	209	6.1
Tiera DeLaHoussaye, Western Mich.	So.	32	193	6.0
Brooke Wilhoit, East Tenn. St.	Sr.	32	189	5.9
Iva Ciglar, Florida International	So.	29	170	5.9
Johnell Burts, St. Peter's	Jr.	30	174	5.8
Noelle Quinn, UCLA	Sr.	32	184	5.8

Rebounding

	Cl	Gm	No	Avg
Lachelle Lyles, SE Missouri St.	Sr.	31	527	17.0
Courtney Paris, Oklahoma	So.	33	526	15.9
Alysha Clark, Belmont	So.	30	380	12.7
Sylvia Fowles, LSU	Jr.	38	477	12.6
Natalie Doma, Idaho St.	Jr.	31	372	12.0
Jillian Robbins, Tulsa	Sr.	30	349	11.6
Meredith Alexis, James Madison	Sr.	33	383	11.6
Stephanie Duda, UC-Irvine	Sr.	30	332	11.1
LaJoyce King, CS-Northridge	Sr.	26	284	10.9
Lauren Neaves, Rice	Sr.	29	315	10.9
Jackie McFarland, Colorado	Jr.	30	325	10.8
Sherell Neal, New Mexico St.	Jr.	31	335	10.8
Elisha Turek, Oral Roberts	Sr.	33	347	10.5
Khadijah Whittington, N.C. State	Jr.	35	366	10.5
Antionette Wells, Wichita St.	Sr.	28	291	10.4

Blocked Shots

	Cl	Gm	No	Avg
Alison Bales, Duke	Sr.	34	151	4.4
Allyssa DeHaan, Michigan St.	Fr.	33	145	4.4
Amber Harris, Xavier	Fr.	34	136	4.0
Courtney Paris, Oklahoma	So.	33	111	3.4
LaToya Pringle, North Carolina	Jr.	38	121	3.2

Steals

	Cl	Gm	No	Avg
Armintie Price, Mississippi	Sr.	35	131	3.7
Shannon Carlisle, Howard	Sr.	30	111	3.7
Whitney Tossie, Appalachian St.	Jr.	31	113	3.6
Amanda Pape, Sacred Heart	Sr.	32	107	3.3
Lele Hardy, Clemson	Fr.	30	98	3.3
Brittany Hollins, Georgia St.	So.	30	98	3.3
Jillian Robbins, Tulsa	Sr.	30	98	3.3

High-Point Games

Pts	Opponent	Date
47 Gabriela Marginean, Drexel	N'eastern	Feb. 22
43 Courtney Paris, Oklahoma	New Mexico	Dec. 30

TEAM

Scoring Offense

	Gm	W-L	Pts	Avg
North Carolina	38	34-4	3179	83.7
Maryland	34	28-6	2810	82.6
Idaho St.	31	17-14	2465	79.5
Middle Tennessee	34	30-4	2692	79.2
Mississippi	35	24-11	2718	77.7
Indiana St.	30	19-11	2329	77.6
Montana	31	27-4	2402	77.5
Connecticut	36	32-4	2781	77.3
Oklahoma	33	28-5	2529	76.6
Vanderbilt	34	28-6	2595	76.3
Wisconsin-Green Bay	33	29-4	2509	76.0
Duke	34	32-2	2568	75.5

Scoring Defense

	Gm	W-L	Pts	Avg
LSU	38	30-8	1863	49.0
Duke	34	32-2	1748	51.4
Arkansas-Little Rock	31	21-10	1633	52.7
Hartford	34	25-9	1809	53.2
Delaware St.	33	20-13	1758	53.3
Coppin St.	33	25-8	1766	53.5
Texas A&M	32	25-7	1715	53.6
Texas-Arlington	33	24-9	1779	53.9
Army	30	24-6	1618	53.9
Marist	35	29-6	1905	54.4
Rutgers	36	27-9	1960	54.4
Purdue	37	31-6	2021	54.6

Scoring Margin

	Off	Def	Mar
North Carolina	83.7	55.0	28.7
Duke	75.5	51.4	24.1
Connecticut	77.3	55.2	22.1
Maryland	82.6	61.3	21.3
Middle Tennessee	79.2	60.5	18.7
Tennessee	73.6	55.5	18.1
Bowling Green	74.4	57.2	17.2
LSU	65.9	49.0	16.9
Oklahoma	76.6	61.5	15.2

2006-07 NCAA Div. I Attendance Leaders

Team (2005-06)	Gms	Attendance	Average
1 Tennessee (1)	16	234,845	14,678
2 Connecticut (3)	22	237,642	10,802
3 Texas Tech (2)	14	149,351	10,668
4 Oklahoma (8)	12	125,247	10,437
5 New Mexico (4)	15	143,729	9,582

1901-2007
Through the Years

SPORTS ALMANAC

National Champions and NCAA Final Four

The Helms Foundation of Los Angeles, under the direction of founder Bill Schroeder, selected national college basketball champions from 1942-82 and researched retroactive picks from 1901-41. The first NIT tournament and then the NCAA tournament have settled the national championship since 1938, but there are four years (1939, '40, '44 and '54) where the Helms selections differ. In 1939, Helms picked undefeated LIU-Brooklyn (24-0), winners of the NIT. In 1940, Helms picked USC (20-3) although they were beaten by Kansas in the West Regionals of the NCAA tourney. In 1944, Helms picked unbeaten Army (15-0). Army did not lift its policy barring postseason play until the 1961 NIT. In 1954, Helms chose unbeaten Kentucky (25-0), even though Kentucky refused its NCAA bid after seniors Cliff Hagan, Frank Ramsey and Lou Tsioropoulos were declared ineligible.

Multiple champions (1901-37): Chicago, Columbia and Wisconsin (3); Kansas, Minnesota, Notre Dame, Penn, Pittsburgh, Syracuse and Yale (2).

Multiple champions (since 1938): UCLA (11); Kentucky (7); Indiana (5); North Carolina (4); Duke (3); Cincinnati, Connecticut, Florida, Kansas, Louisville, Michigan St., N.C. State, Oklahoma A&M (now Oklahoma St.) and San Francisco (2).

Year		Record	Head Coach	Outstanding Player
1901	Yale	10-4	No coach	G.M. Clark, F
1902	Minnesota	11-0	Louis Cooke	W.C. Deering, F
1903	Yale	15-1	W.H. Murphy	R.B. Hyatt,F
1904	Columbia	17-1	No coach	Harry Fisher, F
1905	Columbia	19-1	No coach	Harry Fisher, F
1906	Dartmouth	16-2	No coach	George Grebenstein, F
1907	Chicago	22-2	Joseph Raycroft	John Schommer, C
1908	Chicago	21-2	Joseph Raycroft	John Schommer, C
1909	Chicago	12-0	Joseph Raycroft	John Schommer, C
1910	Columbia	11-1	Harry Fisher	Ted Kiendl, F
1911	St. John's-NY	14-0	Claude Allen	John Keenan, F/C
1912	Wisconsin	15-0	Doc Meanwell	Otto Stangel, F
1913	Navy	9-0	Louis Wenzell	Laurence Wild, F
1914	Wisconsin	15-0	Doc Meanwell	Gene Van Gent, F
1915	Illinois	16-0	Ralph Jones	Ray Woods, G
1916	Wisconsin	20-1	Doc Meanwell	George Levis, F
1917	Washington St	25-1	Doc Bohler	Roy Bohler, G
1918	Syracuse	16-1	Edmund Dollard	Joe Schwarzer, G
1919	Minnesota	13-0	Louis Cooke	Arnold Oss, F
1920	Penn	22-1	Lon Jourdet	George Sweeney, F
1921	Penn	21-2	Edward McNichol	Danny McNichol, G
1922	Kansas	16-2	Phog Allen	Paul Endacott, G
1923	Kansas	17-1	Phog Allen	Paul Endacott, G
1924	North Carolina	25-0	Bo Shepard	Jack Cobb, F
1925	Princeton	21-2	Al Wittmer	Art Loeb, G
1926	Syracuse	19-1	Lew Andreas	Vic Hanson, F
1927	Notre Dame	19-1	George Keogan	John Nyikos, C
1928	Pittsburgh	21-0	Doc Carlson	Chuck Hyatt, F
1929	Montana St.	36-2	Schubert Dyche	John (Cat) Thompson, F
1930	Pittsburgh	23-2	Doc Carlson	Chuck Hyatt, F
1931	Northwestern	16-1	Dutch Lonborg	Joe Reiff, C
1932	Purdue	17-1	Piggy Lambert	John Wooden, G
1933	Kentucky	20-3	Adolph Rupp	Forest Sale, F
1934	Wyoming	26-3	Willard Witte	Les Witte, G
1935	NYU	19-1	Howard Cann	Sid Gross, F
1936	Notre Dame	22-2-1	George Keogan	John Moir, F
1937	Stanford	25-2	John Bunn	Hank Luisetti, F

Year		Record	Winner	Head Coach	Outstanding Player
1938	Temple	23-2	NIT	James Usilton	Meyer Bloom, G

Year	Champion	Runner-up	Score	Final Two	Third Place	
1939	Oregon	Ohio St.	46-33	@ Evanston, IL	Oklahoma	Villanova
1940	Indiana	Kansas	60-42	@ Kansas City	Duquesne	USC
1941	Wisconsin	Washington St.	39-34	@ Kansas City	Arkansas	Pittsburgh
1942	Stanford	Dartmouth	53-38	@ Kansas City	Colorado	Kentucky
1943	Wyoming	Georgetown	46-34	@ New York	DePaul	Texas
1944	Utah	Dartmouth	42-40 (OT)	@ New York	Iowa St.	Ohio St.
1945	Oklahoma A&M	NYU	49-45	@ New York	Arkansas	Ohio St.

NCAA Final Four (Cont.)

Year	Champion	Runner-up	Score	Final Two	Third Place	Fourth Place
1946	Oklahoma A&M	North Carolina	43-40	@ New York	Ohio St.	California
1947	Holy Cross	Oklahoma	58-47	@ New York	Texas	CCNY
1948	Kentucky	Baylor	58-42	@ New York	Holy Cross	Kansas St.
1949	Kentucky	Oklahoma A&M	46-36	@ Seattle	Illinois	Oregon St.
1950	CCNY	Bradley	71-68	@ New York	N.C. State	Baylor
1951	Kentucky	Kansas St.	68-58	@ Minneapolis	Illinois	Oklahoma A&M

Year	Champion	Runner-up	Score	Third Place	Fourth Place	Final Four
1952	Kansas	St. John's	80-63	Illinois	Santa Clara	@ Seattle
1953	Indiana	Kansas	69-68	Washington	LSU	@ Kansas City
1954	La Salle	Bradley	92-76	Penn St.	USC	@ Kansas City
1955	San Francisco	La Salle	77-63	Colorado	Iowa	@ Kansas City
1956	San Francisco	Iowa	83-71	Temple	SMU	@ Evanston, IL
1957	North Carolina	Kansas	54-53 (3OT)	San Francisco	Michigan St.	@ Kansas City
1958	Kentucky	Seattle	84-72	Temple	Kansas St.	@ Louisville
1959	California	West Virginia	71-70	Cincinnati	Louisville	@ Louisville
1960	Ohio St.	California	75-55	Cincinnati	NYU	@ San Francisco
1961	Cincinnati	Ohio St.	70-65 (OT)	St. Joseph's-PA	Utah	@ Kansas City
1962	Cincinnati	Ohio St.	71-59	Wake Forest	UCLA	@ Louisville
1963	Loyola-IL	Cincinnati	60-58 (OT)	Duke	Oregon St.	@ Louisville
1964	UCLA	Duke	98-83	Michigan	Kansas St.	@ Kansas City
1965	UCLA	Michigan	91-80	Princeton	Wichita St.	@ Portland, OR
1966	Texas Western	Kentucky	72-65	Duke	Utah	@ College Park, MD
1967	UCLA	Dayton	79-64	Houston	North Carolina	@ Louisville
1968	UCLA	North Carolina	78-55	Ohio St.	Houston	@ Los Angeles
1969	UCLA	Purdue	92-72	Drake	North Carolina	@ Louisville
1970	UCLA	Jacksonville	80-69	New Mexico St.	St. Bonaventure	@ College Park, MD
1971	UCLA	Villanova	68-62	Western Ky.	Kansas	@ Houston
1972	UCLA	Florida St.	81-76	North Carolina	Louisville	@ Los Angeles
1973	UCLA	Memphis St.	87-66	Indiana	Providence	@ St. Louis
1974	N.C. State	Marquette	76-64	UCLA	Kansas	@ Greensboro, NC
1975	UCLA	Kentucky	92-85	Louisville	Syracuse	@ San Diego
1976	Indiana	Michigan	86-68	UCLA	Rutgers	@ Philadelphia
1977	Marquette	North Carolina	67-59	UNLV	NC-Charlotte	@ Atlanta
1978	Kentucky	Duke	94-88	Arkansas	Notre Dame	@ St. Louis
1979	Michigan St.	Indiana St.	75-64	DePaul	Penn	@ Salt Lake City
1980	Louisville	UCLA	59-54	Purdue	Iowa	@ Indianapolis
1981	Indiana	North Carolina	63-50	Virginia	LSU	@ Philadelphia

Year	Champion	Runner-up	Score	Third Place	Final Four
1982	North Carolina	Georgetown	63-62	Houston	Louisville	@ New Orleans
1983	N.C. State	Houston	54-52	Georgia	Louisville	@ Albuquerque
1984	Georgetown	Houston	84-75	Kentucky	Virginia	@ Seattle
1985	Villanova	Georgetown	66-64	Memphis St.	St. John's	@ Lexington
1986	Louisville	Duke	72-69	Kansas	LSU	@ Dallas
1987	Indiana	Syracuse	74-73	Providence	UNLV	@ New Orleans
1988	Kansas	Oklahoma	83-79	Arizona	Duke	@ Kansas City
1989	Michigan	Seton Hall	80-79 (OT)	Duke	Illinois	@ Seattle
1990	UNLV	Duke	103-73	Arkansas	Georgia Tech	@ Denver
1991	Duke	Kansas	72-65	North Carolina	UNLV	@ Indianapolis
1992	Duke	Michigan	71-51	Cincinnati	Indiana	@ Minneapolis
1993	North Carolina	Michigan	77-71	Kansas	Kentucky	@ New Orleans
1994	Arkansas	Duke	76-72	Arizona	Florida	@ Charlotte
1995	UCLA	Arkansas	89-78	North Carolina	Oklahoma St.	@ Seattle
1996	Kentucky	Syracuse	76-67	UMass	Mississippi St.	@ E. Rutherford, NJ
1997	Arizona	Kentucky	84-79 (OT)	Minnesota	North Carolina	@ Indianapolis
1998	Kentucky	Utah	78-69	Stanford	North Carolina	@ San Antonio
1999	Connecticut	Duke	77-74	Michigan St.	Ohio St.	@ St. Petersburg, FL
2000	Michigan St.	Florida	89-76	Wisconsin	North Carolina	@ Indianapolis
2001	Duke	Arizona	82-72	Michigan St.	Maryland	@ Minneapolis
2002	Maryland	Indiana	64-52	Oklahoma	Kansas	@ Atlanta
2003	Syracuse	Kansas	81-78	Marquette	Texas	@ New Orleans
2004	Connecticut	Georgia Tech	82-73	Duke	Oklahoma St.	@ San Antonio
2005	North Carolina	Illinois	75-70	Michigan St.	Louisville	@ St. Louis
2006	Florida	UCLA	73-57	George Mason	LSU	@ Indianapolis
2007	Florida	Ohio St.	84-75	Georgetown	UCLA	@ Atlanta

Note: Six teams have had their standing in the Final Four vacated for using ineligible players: 1961–St. Joseph's-PA (3rd place); 1971–Villanova (Runner-up) and Western Kentucky (3rd); 1980–UCLA (Runner-up); 1985–Memphis St. (3rd); 1996–UMass (3rd).

Most Outstanding Player

A Most Outstanding Player has been selected every year of the NCAA tournament. Winners who did not play for the tournament champion are listed in **bold** type. The 1939 and 1951 winners are unofficial and not recognized by the NCAA. Statistics listed are for Final Four games only.

Multiple winners: Lew Alcindor (3); Alex Groza, Bob Kurland, Jerry Lucas and Bill Walton (2).

Year	Player	Gm	FGM	Pct	3PTM	3PTA	FTM	Pct	Reb	Ast	Blk	Stl	PPG
1939	**Jimmy Hull**, Ohio St.	2	15	—	—	—	10	.833	—	—	—	—	20.0
1940	Marv Huffman, Indiana	2	7	—	—	—	4	—	—	—	—	—	9.0
1941	John Kotz, Wisconsin	2	8	—	—	—	6	—	—	—	—	—	11.0
1942	Howie Dallmar, Stanford	2	8	—	—	—	4	.667	—	—	—	—	10.0
1943	Kenny Sailors, Wyoming	2	10	—	—	—	8	.727	—	—	—	—	14.0
1944	Arnie Ferrin, Utah	2	11	—	—	—	6	—	—	—	—	—	14.0
1945	Bob Kurland, Okla. A&M	2	16	—	—	—	5	—	—	—	—	—	18.5
1946	Bob Kurland, Okla. A&M	2	21	—	—	—	10	.667	—	—	—	—	26.0
1947	George Kaftan, Holy Cross	2	18	• —	—	—	12	.706	—	—	—	—	24.0
1948	Alex Groza, Kentucky	2	16	—	—	—	5	—	—	—	—	—	18.5
1949	Alex Groza, Kentucky	2	19	—	—	—	14	—	—	—	—	—	26.0
1950	Irwin Dambrot, CCNY	2	12	.429	—	—	4	.500	—	—	—	—	14.0
1951	Bill Spivey, Kentucky	2	20	.400	—	—	10	.625	37	—	—	—	25.0
1952	Clyde Lovellette, Kansas	2	24	—	—	—	18	—	—	—	—	—	33.0
1953	**B.H. Born**, Kansas	2	17	—	—	—	17	—	—	—	—	—	25.5
1954	Tom Gola, La Salle	2	12	—	—	—	14	—	—	—	—	—	19.0
1955	Bill Russell, San Francisco	2	19	—	—	—	9	—	—	—	—	—	23.5
1956	**Hal Lear**, Temple	2	32	—	—	—	16	—	—	—	—	—	40.0
1957	**Wilt Chamberlain**, Kansas	2	18	.514	—	—	19	.704	25	—	—	—	32.5
1958	**Elgin Baylor**, Seattle	2	18	.340	—	—	12	.750	41	—	—	—	24.0
1959	**Jerry West**, West Virginia	2	22	.667	—	—	22	.688	25	—	—	—	33.0
1960	Jerry Lucas, Ohio St.	2	16	.667	—	—	3	1.000	23	—	—	—	17.5
1961	**Jerry Lucas**, Ohio St.	2	20	.714	—	—	16	.941	25	—	—	—	28.0
1962	Paul Hogue, Cincinnati	2	23	.639	—	—	12	.632	38	—	—	—	29.0
1963	**Art Heyman**, Duke	2	18	.409	—	—	15	.682	19	—	—	—	25.5
1964	Walt Hazzard, UCLA	2	11	.550	—	—	8	.667	10	—	—	—	15.0
1965	**Bill Bradley**, Princeton	2	34	.630	—	—	19	.950	24	—	—	—	43.5
1966	**Jerry Chambers**, Utah	2	25	.532	—	—	20	.833	35	—	—	—	35.0
1967	Lew Alcindor, UCLA	2	14	.609	—	—	11	.458	38	—	—	—	19.5
1968	Lew Alcindor, UCLA	2	22	.629	—	—	9	.900	34	—	—	—	26.5
1969	Lew Alcindor, UCLA	2	23	.676	—	—	16	.640	41	—	—	—	31.0
1970	Sidney Wicks, UCLA	2	15	.714	—	—	9	.600	34	—	—	—	19.5
1971	**Howard Porter**, Villanova	2	20	.488	—	—	7	.778	24	—	—	—	23.5
1972	Bill Walton, UCLA	2	20	.690	—	—	17	.739	41	—	—	—	28.5
1973	Bill Walton, UCLA	2	28	.824	—	—	2	.400	30	—	—	—	29.0
1974	David Thompson, N.C. State	2	19	.514	—	—	11	.786	17	—	—	—	24.5
1975	Richard Washington, UCLA	2	23	.548	—	—	8	.727	20	—	—	—	27.0
1976	Kent Benson, Indiana	2	17	.500	—	—	7	.636	18	—	—	1	20.5
1977	Butch Lee, Marquette	2	11	.344	—	—	8	1.000	6	2	1	1	15.0
1978	Jack Givens, Kentucky	2	28	.651	—	—	8	.667	17	4	1	3	32.0
1979	Magic Johnson, Michigan St.	2	17	.680	—	—	19	.864	17	3	0	2	26.5
1980	Darrell Griffith, Louisville	2	23	.622	—	—	11	.688	7	15	0	2	28.5
1981	Isiah Thomas, Indiana	2	14	.560	—	—	9	.818	4	9	3	4	18.5
1982	James Worthy, N. Carolina	2	20	.741	—	—	2	.286	8	9	0	4	21.0
1983	**Akeem Olajuwon**, Houston	2	16	.552	—	—	9	.643	40	3	2	5	20.5
1984	Patrick Ewing, Georgetown	2	8	.571	—	—	2	1.000	18	1	15	1	9.0
1985	Ed Pinckney, Villanova	2	8	.571	—	—	12	.750	15	6	3	0	14.0
1986	Pervis Ellison, Louisville	2	15	.600	—	—	6	.750	24	2	3	1	18.0
1987	Keith Smart, Indiana	2	14	.636	0	1	7	.778	7	7	0	2	17.5
1988	Danny Manning, Kansas	2	25	.556	0	1	6	.667	17	4	8	9	28.0
1989	Glen Rice, Michigan	2	24	.490	7	16	4	1.000	16	1	0	3	29.5
1990	Anderson Hunt, UNLV	2	19	.613	9	16	2	.500	4	9	1	1	24.5
1991	Christian Laettner, Duke	2	12	.545	1	1	21	.913	17	2	1	2	23.0
1992	Bobby Hurley, Duke	2	10	.417	7	12	8	.800	3	11	0	3	17.5
1993	Donald Williams, N. Carolina	2	15	.652	10	14	10	1.000	4	1	0	2	25.0
1994	Corliss Williamson, Arkansas	2	21	.500	0	0	10	.714	21	8	3	4	26.0
1995	Ed O'Bannon, UCLA	2	16	.457	3	8	10	.769	25	3	1	7	22.5
1996	Tony Delk, Kentucky	2	15	.417	8	16	6	.546	9	2	3	2	22.0
1997	Miles Simon, Arizona	2	17	.459	3	10	17	.773	8	6	0	1	27.0
1998	Jeff Sheppard, Kentucky	2	16	.552	4	10	7	.778	10	7	0	4	21.5
1999	Richard Hamilton, Connecticut	2	20	.513	3	7	8	.727	12	4	1	2	25.5

Most Outstanding Player (Cont.)

Year		Gm	FGM	Pct	3PTM	3PTA	FTM	Pct	Reb	Ast	Blk	Stl	PPG
2000	Mateen Cleaves, Michigan St.	2	8	.444	3	4	10	.833	6	5	0	2	14.5
2001	Shane Battier, Duke	2	13	.464	5	12	12	.706	19	8	6	2	21.5
2002	Juan Dixon, Maryland	2	16	.593	7	15	12	.800	8	5	0	7	25.5
2003	Carmelo Anthony, Syracuse	2	19	.543	6	9	9	.818	24	8	0	4	26.5
2004	Emeka Okafor, Connecticut	2	17	.654	0	0	8	.533	22	2	4	1	21.0
2005	Sean May, North Carolina	2	19	.655	0	0	10	.714	17	5	2	1	24.0
2006	Joakim Noah, Florida	2	12	.600	0	1	4	1.000	17	5	10	2	14.0
2007	Corey Brewer, Florida	2	9	.474	7	13	7	.875	10	2	3	3	16.0

All-Time Seeds Records

All-time records of NCAA tournament seeds since tourney began seeding teams in 1979. Records are through the 2007 NCAA Tournament. Note that 1st refers to championships. 2nd refers to runners-up and FF refers to Final Four appearances not including 1st and 2nd place finishes.

Seed	W	L	Pct.	1st	2nd	FF
1	358	102	.778	15	11	21
2	261	110	.704	6	7	13
3	189	112	.628	4	5	5
4	161	115	.583	1	1	8
5	138	117	.541	0	2	3
6	151	114	.570	2	1	3
7	100	116	.463	0	0	1
8	86	115	.428	1	1	2
9	67	117	.364	0	0	1
10	76	116	.396	0	0	0
11	51	112	.313	0	0	2
12	47	112	.296	0	0	0
13	22	92	.193	0	0	0
14	17	92	.156	0	0	0
15	4	92	.043	0	0	0
16	0	92	.000	0	0	0

Note: Although a 16 seed has never won an NCAA tournament game (not including the recently added play-in round), four 15 seeds have pulled off the first round upset. They are, as follows: **2001**-Hampton over Iowa State, 58-57; **1997**-Coppin State over South Carolina, 78-65; **1993**-Santa Clara over Arizona, 64-61; **1991**-Richmond over Syracuse, 73-69. All four teams lost their second round games.

Fifteen 14 seeds have won first round games (most recently Northwestern St. in 2006). Two of those teams won their second-round game as well (Chattanooga in 1997 and Cleveland St. in 1986) before ultimately losing in the Sweet 16.

Teams in Both NCAA and NIT

Fourteen teams played in both the NCAA and NIT tournaments from 1940-52. Colorado (1940), Utah (1944), Kentucky (1949) and BYU (1951) won one of the titles, while CCNY won two in 1950, beating Bradley in both championship games.

Year		NIT	NCAA
1940	Colorado	**Won Final**	Lost 1st Rd
	Duquesne	Lost Final	Lost 2nd Rd
1944	Utah	Lost 1st Rd	**Won Final**
1949	Kentucky	Lost 2nd Rd	**Won Final**
1950	CCNY	**Won Final**	**Won Final**
	Bradley	Lost Final	Lost Final
1951	BYU	**Won Final**	Lost 2nd Rd
	St. John's	Lost 3rd Rd	Lost 2nd Rd
	N.C. State	Lost 2nd Rd	Lost 2nd Rd
	Arizona	Lost 2nd Rd	Lost 1st Rd
1952	St. John's	Lost 2nd Rd	Lost Final
	Dayton	Lost Final	Lost 1st Rd
	Duquesne	Lost 3rd Rd	Lost 2nd Rd

Seeds at the Final Four

NCAA champions in **bold** type.

Year	Seeds (Total)	Teams
1979	1,2,2,9 (14)	Indiana St., **Michigan St.,** DePaul, Pennsylvania
1980	2,5,6,8 (21)	**Louisville**, Iowa, Purdue, UCLA
1981	1,1,2,3 (7)	Virginia, LSU, No. Carolina, **Indiana**
1982	1,1,3,6 (11)	**North Carolina**, Georgetown, Louisville, Houston
1983	1,1,4,6 (12)	Houston, Louisville, Georgia, **N.C. State**
1984	1,1,2,7 (11)	Kentucky, **Georgetown**, Houston, Virginia
1985	1,1,2,8 (12)	St. John's, Georgetown, Memphis, **Villanova**
1986	1,1,2,11 (15)	Duke, Kansas, **Louisville**, LSU
1987	1,1,2,6 (10)	UNLV, **Indiana**, Syracuse, Providence
1988	1,1,2,6 (10)	Arizona, Oklahoma, Duke, **Kansas**
1989	1,2,3,3 (9)	Illinois, Duke, Seton Hall, **Michigan**
1990	1,3,4,4 (12)	**UNLV**, Duke, Georgia Tech, Arkansas
1991	1,1,2,3 (7)	UNLV, North Carolina, **Duke**, Kansas
1992	1,2,4,6 (13)	**Duke**, Indiana, Cincinnati, Michigan
1993	1,1,1,2 (5)	**No. Carolina**, Kentucky, Michigan, Kansas
1994	1,2,2,3 (8)	**Arkansas**, Arizona, Duke, Florida
1995	1,2,2,4 (9)	**UCLA**, Arkansas, North Carolina, Oklahoma St.
1996	1,1,4,5 (11)	**Kentucky**, Massachusetts, Syracuse, Mississippi St.
1997	1,1,1,4 (7)	Kentucky, North Carolina, Minnesota, **Arizona**
1998	1,2,3,3 (9)	North Carolina, **Kentucky**, Stanford, Utah
1999	1,1,1,4 (7)	**Connecticut**, Duke, Michigan St., Ohio St.
2000	1,5,8,8 (22)	**Michigan St.**, Florida, Wisconsin, North Carolina
2001	1,1,2,3 (7)	**Duke**, Michigan St., Arizona, Maryland
2002	1,1,2,5 (9)	**Maryland**, Kansas, Oklahoma, Indiana
2003	1,2,3,3 (9)	Texas, Kansas, **Syracuse**, Marquette
2004	1,2,2,3 (8)	Duke, **Connecticut**, Oklahoma St., Georgia Tech
2005	1,1,4,5 (11)	**North Carolina**, Illinois, Louisville, Michigan St.
2006	2,3,4,11 (20)	UCLA, **Florida**, LSU, George Mason
2007	1,1,2,2 (6)	**Florida**, Ohio St., UCLA, Georgetown

Note: teams were not seeded before 1979.

Most Number One Seeds, All-Time

No	Team	No	Team
11	North Carolina	5	Arizona
10	Duke	5	Georgetown
9	Kentucky	5	Oklahoma
7	Kansas	4	Three tied

NCAA Tournament Appearances

App		W-L	F4	Championships	App		W-L	F4	Championships
48	Kentucky	100-44	13	7 (1948-49, 51, 58, 78, 96, 98)	25	Texas	29-28	3	None
41	UCLA	94-34	17	11 (1964-65,67-73,75,95)	24	Ohio St.	43-23	10	1 (1960)
39	N. Carolina	92-37	16	4 (1957,82,93, 2005)	24	Cincinnati	40-23	6	2 (1961-62)
35	Kansas	71-35	11	2 (1952,88)	24	Oklahoma	31-24	4	None
34	Indiana	60-29	8	5 (1940,53,76,81,87)	24	Georgetown	44-23	5	1 (1984)
33	Louisville	54-34	8	2 (1980,86)	23	Princeton	13-27	1	None
31	Syracuse	48-31	4	1 (2003)	23	Pennsylvania	13-25	1	None
31	Duke	85-28	14	3 (1991-92, 2001)	22	Kansas St.	27-26	4	None
28	Notre Dame	29-32	1	None	22	DePaul	21-25	2	None
28	Arkansas	39-28	6	1 (1994)	22	Oklahoma St.	37-21	6	2 (1945-46)
28	Villanova	42-28	3	1 (1985)	22	Iowa	27-24	3	None
27	St. John's	27-29	2	None	22	N.C. State	32-21	3	2 (1974,83)
27	Connecticut	42-26	2	2 (1999, 2004)	22	BYU	11-25	0	None
27	Illinois	38-27	5	None	22	Maryland	36-21	2	1 (2002)
26	Utah	35-29	4	1 (1944)	21	Missouri	18-21	0	None
26	Arizona	41-25	4	1 (1997)	21	Purdue	27-20	2	None
25	Temple	31-25	2	None	21	Michigan St.	41-20	7	1 (1989)
25	Marquette	32-26	3	1 (1977)					

Note: Although all NCAA tournament appearances are included above, the NCAA has officially voided the records of Villanova (4-1) and Western Ky. (4-1) in 1971; UCLA (5-1) in 1980 and again (0-1) in 1999; Oregon St. (2-3) from 1980-82; DePaul (6-4) from 1986-89; N.C. State (0-2) from 1987-88; Kentucky (2-1) and Maryland (1-1) in 1988; Missouri (3-1) in 1994; Connecticut (2-1) and Purdue (1-1) in 1996; Arizona (0-1) in 1999.

All-Time NCAA Division I Tournament Leaders

Through 2007; minimum of six games; **Last** column indicates final year played.

CAREER

Scoring

Points

		Yrs	Last	Gm	Pts
1	Christian Laettner, Duke	4	1992	23	407
2	Elvin Hayes, Houston	3	1968	13	358
3	Danny Manning, Kansas	4	1988	16	328
4	Oscar Robertson, Cincinnati	3	1960	10	324
5	Glen Rice, Michigan	4	1989	13	308
6	Lew Alcindor, UCLA	3	1969	12	304
7	Bill Bradley, Princeton	3	1965	9	303
	Corliss Williamson, Arkansas	3	1995	15	303
9	Juan Dixon, Maryland	4	2002	16	294
10	Austin Carr, Notre Dame	3	1971	7	289

Average

		Yrs	Last	Pts	Avg
1	Austin Carr, Notre Dame	3	1971	289	41.3
2	Bill Bradley, Princeton	3	1965	303	33.7
3	Oscar Robertson, Cincinnati	3	1960	324	32.4
4	Jerry West, West Virginia	3	1960	275	30.6
5	Bob Pettit, LSU	2	1954	183	30.5
6	Dan Issel, Kentucky	3	1970	176	29.3
	Jim McDaniels, Western Ky	2	1971	176	29.3
8	Dwight Lamar, SW Louisiana	2	1973	176	29.2
9	Bo Kimble, Loyola-CA	3	1990	204	29.1
10	David Robinson, Navy	3	1987	200	28.6

Rebounds

Total

		Yrs	Last	Gm	No
1	Elvin Hayes, Houston	3	1968	13	222
2	Lew Alcindor, UCLA	3	1969	12	201
3	Jerry Lucas, Ohio St.	3	1962	12	197
4	Nick Collison, Kansas	4	2003	16	181
5	Bill Walton, UCLA	3	1974	12	176
6	Christian Laettner, Duke	4	1992	23	169
7	Tim Duncan, Wake Forest	4	1997	11	165
8	Paul Hogue, Cincinnati	3	1962	12	160
9	Sam Lacey, New Mexico St.	3	1970	11	157
10	Derrick Coleman, Syracuse	4	1990	14	155

Average

		Yrs	Last	Reb	Avg
1	Johnny Green, Michigan St.	2	1959	118	19.7
2	Artis Gilmore, Jacksonville	2	1971	115	19.2
3	Paul Silas, Creighton	3	1964	111	18.5
4	Len Chappell, Wake Forest	2	1962	137	17.1
5	Elvin Hayes, Houston	3	1968	222	17.1
6	Lew Alcindor, UCLA	3	1969	201	16.8
7	Jerry Lucas, Ohio St.	3	1962	197	16.4
8	Tim Duncan, Wake Forest	4	1997	165	15.0
9	Bill Walton, UCLA	3	1974	176	14.7
10	Sam Lacey, New Mexico St.	3	1970	157	14.3

3-Pt Field Goals

Total

		Yrs	Last	Gm	No
1	Lee Humphrey, Florida	4	2007	14	47
2	Bobby Hurley, Duke	4	1993	20	42
3	Tony Delk, Kentucky	4	1996	17	40
4	Jeff Fryer, Loyola-CA	3	1990	7	38
	Donald Williams, North Carolina	4	1995	15	38
	Juan Dixon, Maryland	4	2002	16	38

Assists

Total

		Yrs	Last	Gm	No
1	Bobby Hurley, Duke	4	1993	20	145
2	Ed Cota, N. Carolina	4	2000	16	118
3	Sherman Douglas, Syracuse	4	1989	14	106
4	Greg Anthony, UNLV	3	1991	15	100
	Aaron Miles, Kansas	3	2004	15	100

SINGLE TOURNAMENT

Scoring

Points

		Year	Gm	Pts
1	Glen Rice, Michigan	1989	6	184
2	Bill Bradley, Princeton	1965	5	177
3	Elvin Hayes, Houston	1968	5	167
4	Danny Manning, Kansas	1988	6	163
5	Hal Lear, Temple	1956	5	160
	Jerry West, West Virginia	1959	5	160

Average

		Year	Gm	Pts	Avg
1	Austin Carr, Notre Dame	1970	3	158	52.7
2	Austin Carr, Notre Dame	1971	3	125	41.7
3	Jerry Chambers, Utah	1966	4	143	35.8
	Bo Kimble, Loyola-CA	1990	4	143	35.8
5	Bill Bradley, Princeton	1965	5	177	35.4
6	Clyde Lovellette, Kansas	1952	4	141	35.3

Rebounds

	Total	Year	Gm	No	Avg
1	Elvin Hayes, Houston	1968	5	**97**	19.4
2	Artis Gilmore, Jacksonville	1970	5	**93**	18.6
3	Elgin Baylor, Seattle	1958	5	**91**	18.2
4	Sam Lacey, New Mexico St.	1970	5	**90**	18.0
5	Clarence Glover, Western Ky	1971	5	**89**	17.8
6	Len Chappell, Wake Forest	1962	5	**86**	17.2

Assists

	Total	Year	Gm	No	Avg
1	Mark Wade, UNLV	1987	5	**61**	12.2
2	Rumeal Robinson, Michigan	1989	6	**56**	9.3
3	T.J. Ford, Texas	2003	5	**51**	10.2
4	Sherman Douglas, Syracuse	1987	6	**49**	8.2
5	Bobby Hurley, Duke	1992	6	**47**	7.8
6	Lazarus Sims, Syracuse	1996	6	**46**	7.7

SINGLE GAME

Scoring

	Points	Year	Pts
1	Austin Carr, Notre Dame vs Ohio Univ	1970	61
2	Bill Bradley, Princeton vs Wichita St.	1965	58
3	Oscar Robertson, Cincinnati vs Arkansas	1958	56
4	Austin Carr, Notre Dame vs Kentucky	1970	52
	Austin Carr, Notre Dame vs TCU	1971	52
6	David Robinson, Navy vs Michigan	1987	50
7	Elvin Hayes, Houston vs Loyola-IL	1968	49
8	Hal Lear, Temple vs SMU	1956	48
9	Austin Carr, Notre Dame vs Houston	1971	47
10	Dave Corzine, DePaul vs Louisville	1978	46
11	Bob Houbregs, Washington vs Seattle	1953	45
	Austin Carr, Notre Dame vs Iowa	1970	45
	Bo Kimble, Loyola-CA vs New Mexico St.	1990	45
14	Seven players tied with 44 each.		

Rebounds

	Total	Year	No
1	Fred Cohen, Temple vs UConn	1956	34
2	Nate Thurmond, Bowl. Green vs Miss. St.	1963	31
3	Jerry Lucas, Ohio St. vs Kentucky	1961	30
4	Toby Kimball, UConn vs St. Joseph's-PA	1965	29
5	Elvin Hayes, Houston vs Pacific	1966	28
6	Four players tied with 27 each.		

Assists

	Total	Year	No
1	Mark Wade, UNLV vs Indiana	1987	18
2	Sam Crawford, N. Mexico St. vs Nebraska	1993	16
3	Kenny Patterson, DePaul vs Syracuse	1985	15
	Keith Smart, Indiana vs Auburn	1987	15
	Pepe Sanchez, Temple vs. Lafayette	2000	15

SINGLE FINAL FOUR GAME

Letters in the **Year** column indicate the following: C for Consolation Game, F for Final and S for Semifinal.

Scoring

	Points	Year	Pts
1	Bill Bradley, Princeton vs Wichita St	1965-C	58
2	Hal Lear, Temple vs SMU	1956-C	48
3	Bill Walton, UCLA vs Memphis St.	1973-F	44
4	Bob Houbregs, Washington vs LSU	1953-C	42
	Jack Egan, St. Joseph's-PA vs Utah	1961-C	42*
	Gail Goodrich, UCLA vs Michigan	1965-C	42
7	Jack Givens, Kentucky vs Duke	1978-F	41
8	Oscar Robertson, Cincinnati vs L'ville	1959-C	39
	Al Wood, N. Carolina vs Virginia	1981-S	39
10	Jerry West, West Va. vs Louisville	1959-S	38
	Jerry Chambers, Utah vs Texas Western	1966-S	38
	Freddie Banks, UNLV vs Indiana	1987-S	38
	*Four overtimes.		

3-Pt Field Goals

	Total	Year	No
1	Freddie Banks, UNLV vs. Indiana	1987-S	10
2	Four players tied with 7 each.		

Rebounds

	Total	Year	No
1	Bill Russell, San Francisco vs Iowa	1956-F	27
2	Elvin Hayes, Houston vs UCLA	1967-S	24
3	Bill Russell, San Francisco vs SMU	1956-S	23
4	Elgin Baylor, Seattle vs Kansas St.	1958-S	22
	Tom Sanders, NYU vs Ohio St.	1960-S	22
	Larry Kenon, Memphis vs Providence	1973-S	22
	Akeem Olajuwon, Houston vs Louisville	1983-S	22
8	Bill Spivey, Kentucky vs Kansas St.	1951-C	21
	Lew Alcindor, UCLA vs Drake	1969-C	21
	Artis Gilmore, Jacksonville vs St. Bonav.	1970-S	21
	Bill Walton, UCLA vs Louisville	1972-S	21
	Nick Collison, Kansas vs Syracuse	2003-C	21

Assists

	Total	Year	No
1	Mark Wade, UNLV vs Indiana	1987-S	18
2	T.J. Ford, Texas vs. Syracuse	2003-C	13
3	Rumeal Robinson, Michigan vs Illinois	1989-S	12
	Edgar Padilla, UMass vs. Ky.	1996-S	12
5	Michael Jackson, G'town vs St. John's	1985-S	11
	Milt Wagner, Louisville vs LSU	1986-S	11
	Rumeal Robinson, Mich. vs Seton Hall	1989-F	11*
	Steve Blake, Maryland vs. Kansas	2002-S	11
	*Overtime.		

Blocked Shots

	Total	Year	No
1	Danny Manning, Kansas vs Duke	1988-S	6
	Marcus Camby, UMass vs Kentucky	1996-S	6
	Joakim Noah, Florida vs UCLA	2006-C	6

Steals

	Total	Year	No
1	Tommy Amaker, Duke vs. Louisville	1986-C	7
	Mookie Blaylock, Oklahoma vs. Kansas	1988-C	7
3	Gilbert Arenas, Arizona vs Michigan St.	2001-S	6

Triple Doubles

	Total	Year	No
1	Oscar Robertson, Cincinnati vs. Louisville	1959-C	1
	Magic Johnson, Mich. St. vs. Penn	1979-S	1

Note: Robertson had 39 pts, 17 rebs and 10 asts; Johnson had 29 pts, 10 rebs, 10 asts

Most Popular Final Four Sites

The NCAA has staged its Men's Division I championship—the Final Two (1939-51) and Final Four (since 1952)—at 33 different arenas and indoor stadiums in 27 different cities. The following facilities have all hosted the event more than twice.

No	Arena	Years
9	Municipal Auditorium (KC)	1940-42, 53-55, 57, 61, 64
7	Madison Sq. Garden (NYC)	1943-48, 50
6	Freedom Hall (Louisville)	1958-59, 62-63, 67, 69
4	Superdome (New Orleans)	1982, 87, 93, 2003
	RCA Dome (Indianapolis)	1991, 97, 2000, 2006
3	Kingdome (Seattle)	1984, 89, 95

NIT Championship

The National Invitation Tournament began under the sponsorship of the Metropolitan New York Basketball Writers Association in 1938. The NIT is now administered by the Metropolitan Intercollegiate Basketball Association. All championship games have been played at Madison Square Garden. **Multiple winners:** St. John's (6); Bradley (4); Michigan (3); BYU, Dayton, Kentucky, LIU-Brooklyn, Minnesota, Providence, South Carolina, Temple, Tulsa, Virginia and Virginia Tech (2).

Year	Winner	Score	Loser	Year	Winner	Score	Loser
1938	Temple	60-36	Colorado	1973	Virginia Tech	92-91 (OT)	Notre Dame
1939	LIU-Brooklyn	44-32	Loyola-IL	1974	Purdue	97-81	Utah
1940	Colorado	51-40	Duquesne	1975	Princeton	80-69	Providence
1941	LIU-Brooklyn	56-42	Ohio Univ.	1976	Kentucky	71-67	NC-Charlotte
1942	West Virginia	47-45	Western Ky.	1977	St. Bonaventure	94-91	Houston
1943	St. John's	48-27	Toledo	1978	Texas	101-93	N.C. State
1944	St. John's	47-39	DePaul	1979	Indiana	53-52	Purdue
1945	DePaul	71-54	Bowling Green	1980	Virginia	58-55	Minnesota
1946	Kentucky	46-45	Rhode Island	1981	Tulsa	86-84 (OT)	Syracuse
1947	Utah	49-45	Kentucky	1982	Bradley	67-58	Purdue
1948	Saint Louis	65-52	NYU	1983	Fresno St.	69-60	DePaul
1949	San Francisco	48-47	Loyola-IL	1984	Michigan	83-63	Notre Dame
1950	CCNY	69-61	Bradley	1985	UCLA	65-62	Indiana
1951	BYU	62-43	Dayton	1986	Ohio St.	73-63	Wyoming
1952	La Salle	75-64	Dayton	1987	Southern Miss.	84-80	La Salle
1953	Seton Hall	58-46	St. John's	1988	Connecticut	72-67	Ohio St.
1954	Holy Cross	71-62	Duquesne	1989	St. John's	73-65	Saint Louis
1955	Duquesne	70-58	Dayton	1990	Vanderbilt	74-72	Saint Louis
1956	Louisville	93-80	Dayton	1991	Stanford	78-72	Oklahoma
1957	Bradley	84-83	Memphis St.	1992	Virginia	81-76 (OT)	Notre Dame
1958	Xavier-OH	78-74 (OT)	Dayton	1993	Minnesota	62-61	Georgetown
1959	St. John's	76-71 (OT)	Bradley	1994	Villanova	80-73	Vanderbilt
1960	Bradley	88-72	Providence	1995	Virginia Tech	65-64 (OT)	Marquette
1961	Providence	62-59	Saint Louis	1996	Nebraska	60-56	St. Joseph's
1962	Dayton	73-67	St. John's	1997	Michigan	82-72	Florida St.
1963	Providence	81-66	Canisius	1998	Minnesota	79-72	Penn St.
1964	Bradley	86-54	New Mexico	1999	California	61-60	Clemson
1965	St. John's	55-51	Villanova	2000	Wake Forest	71-61	Notre Dame
1966	BYU	97-84	NYU	2001	Tulsa	79-60	Alabama
1967	Southern Illinois	71-56	Marquette	2002	Memphis	72-62	South Carolina
1968	Dayton	61-48	Kansas	2003	St. John's	70-67	Georgetown
1969	Temple	89-76	Boston Coll.	2004	Michigan	62-55	Rutgers
1970	Marquette	65-53	St. John's	2005	South Carolina	60-57	St. Joseph's
1971	North Carolina	84-66	Georgia Tech	2006	South Carolina	76-64	Michigan
1972	Maryland	100-69	Niagara	2007	West Virginia	78-73	Clemson

Most Valuable Player

A Most Valuable Player has been selected every year of the NIT tournament. Winners who did not play for the tournament champion are listed in **bold** type. Note the all-time team listed below was selected by a media panel on Mar. 15, 1997.

Multiple winners: None. However, Tom Gola of La Salle is the only player to be named MVP in the NIT (1952) and Most Outstanding Player of the NCAA tournament (1954).

Year

1938 Don Shields, Temple
1939 **Bill Lloyd**, St. John's
1940 Bob Doll, Colorado
1941 **Frank Baumholtz**, Ohio U.
1942 Rudy Baric, West Virginia
1943 Harry Boykoff, St. John's
1944 Bill Kotsores, St. John's
1945 George Mikan, DePaul
1946 **Ernie Calverley**, Rhode Island
1947 Vern Gardner, Utah
1948 Ed Macauley, Saint Louis
1949 Don Lofgan, San Francisco
1950 Ed Warner, CCNY
1951 Roland Minson, BYU
1952 Tom Gola, La Salle
  & Norm Grekin, La Salle
1953 Walter Dukes, Seton Hall
1954 Togo Palazzi, Holy Cross
1955 **Maurice Stokes**, St. Francis-PA
1956 Charlie Tyra, Louisville
1957 **Win Wilfong**, Memphis St.
1958 Hank Stein, Xavier-OH
1959 Tony Jackson, St. John's
1960 **Lenny Wilkens**, Providence
1961 Vinny Ernst, Providence
1962 Bill Chmielewski, Dayton
1963 Ray Flynn, Providence

Year

1964 Lavern Tart, Bradley
1965 Ken McIntyre, St. John's
1966 **Bill Melchionni**, Villanova
1967 Walt Frazier, So. Illinois
1968 Don May, Dayton
1969 **Terry Driscoll,** Boston College
1970 Dean Meminger, Marquette
1971 Bill Chamberlain, N. Carolina
1972 Tom McMillen, Maryland
1973 **John Shumate**, Notre Dame
1974 **Mike Sojourner**, Utah
1975 **Ron Lee**, Oregon
1976 **Cedric Maxwell**, NC-Charlotte
1977 Greg Sanders, St. Bonaventure
1978 Ron Baxter, Texas
  & Jim Krivacs, Texas
1979 Clarence Carter, Indiana
  & Ray Tolbert, Indiana
1980 Ralph Sampson, Virginia
1981 Greg Stewart, Tulsa
1982 Mitchell Anderson, Bradley
1983 Ron Anderson, Fresno St.
1984 Tim McCormick, Michigan
1985 Reggie Miller, UCLA
1986 Brad Sellers, Ohio St.
1987 Randolph Keys, So. Miss.
1988 Phil Gamble, Connecticut

Year

1989 Jayson Williams, St. John's
1990 Scott Draud, Vanderbilt
1991 Adam Keefe, Stanford
1992 Bryant Stith, Virginia
1993 Voshon Lenard, Minnesota
1994 **Doremus Bennerman**, Siena
1995 Shawn Smith, Va. Tech
1996 Erick Strickland, Nebraska
1997 Robert Traylor, Michigan
1998 Kevin Clark, Minnesota
1999 Sean Lampley, California
2000 Robert O'Kelley, Wake Forest
2001 Marcus Hill, Tulsa
2002 Dajuan Wagner, Memphis
2003 Marcus Hatten, St. John's
2004 Daniel Horton, Michigan
2005 Carlos Powell, South Carolina
2006 Renaldo Balkman, South Carolina
2007 Frank Young, West Virginia

All-Time NIT Team

Walt Frazier, S. Illinois
George Mikan, DePaul
Tom Gola, La Salle
Maurice Stokes, St. Francis-PA
Ralph Beard, Kentucky

All-Time Winningest Division I Teams
Top 25 Winning Percentage

Division I schools with best winning percentages through 2006-07 season (including tournament games). Years in Division I only; minimum 20 years. NCAA tournament columns indicate years in tournament, record and number of championships.

		First Year	Yrs	Games	Won	Lost	Tied	Pct	NCAA Tourney Yrs	W-L	Titles
1	Kentucky	1903	104	2557	1948	608	1	.762	49	100-44	7
2	North Carolina	1911	97	2610	1914	696	0	.733	39	92-37	4
3	UNLV	1959	49	1420	1010	410	0	.711	15	32-14	1
4	Kansas	1899	109	2688	1906	782	0	.709	35	71-33	2
5	Duke	1906	102	2620	1818	802	0	.694	31	85-28	3
6	UCLA	1920	88	2324	1611	713	0	.693	41	94-34	11
7	Syracuse	1901	106	2486	1704	782	0	.685	31	48-31	1
8	Western Kentucky	1915	88	2312	1548	764	0	.670	19	15-20	0
9	St. John's	1908	100	2490	1659	831	0	.666	27	27-29	0
10	Utah	1909	99	2428	1595	833	0	.657	26	35-29	1
11	Illinois	1906	102	2393	1569	824	0	.656	26	38-27	0
12	Louisville	1912	93	2345	1529	816	0	.652	33	54-34	2
13	Missouri St.	1909	95	2267	1470	797	0	.648	6	3-6	0
14	Arizona	1905	102	2357	1528	829	1	.648	26	41-25	1
15	Indiana	1901	107	2486	1610	876	0	.648	34	60-29	5
16	Arkansas	1924	84	2244	1450	794	0	.646	28	39-28	1
17	Notre Dame	1898	102	2490	1605	885	1	.645	28	29-32	0
18	Pennsylvania	1897	107	2547	1634	913	2	.641	23	13-25	0
19	Temple	1895	111	2603	1668	935	0	.641	25	31-25	0
20	Villanova	1921	87	2282	1453	829	0	.637	28	42-28	1
21	Connecticut	1901	104	2269	1444	825	0	.636	27	42-26	2
22	Murray St.	1926	82	2141	1360	781	0	.635	13	1-13	0
23	DePaul	1924	84	2098	1332	766	0	.635	22	21-25	0
24	Weber St.	1963	45	1287	815	472	0	.633	14	6-15	0
25	Cincinnati	1902	106	2404	1522	882	0	.633	24	40-23	2

Top 35 All-Time Victories

Division I schools with most victories through 2006-07 (including postseason tournaments). Minimum 20 years in Division I.

		Wins			Wins			Wins			Wins
1	Kentucky	1948	10	Indiana	1610	19	Louisville	1529	28	Villanova	1453
2	North Carolina	1914	11	Notre Dame	1605	20	Arizona	1528	29	Arkansas	1450
3	Kansas	1906	12	Utah	1595	21	BYU	1526	30	Alabama	1447
4	Duke	1818	13	Oregon St.	1570	22	Cincinnati	1522	31	Oklahoma	1446
5	Syracuse	1704	14	Illinois	1569	23	Purdue	1513	32	Connecticut	1444
6	Temple	1668	15	Western Ky.	1548	24	N.C. State	1503	33	St. Joseph's	1439
7	St. John's	1659	16	Washington	1548	25	West Virginia	1501	34	Iowa	1438
8	Penn	1634	17	Princeton	1533	26	Bradley	1495	35	Oklahoma St.	1432
9	UCLA	1611	18	Texas	1532	27	Missouri St.	1470			

Top 25 Single-Season Victories

Division I schools with most victories in a season through 2006-07 (including postseason tournaments). NCAA champions in **bold** type.

	Year	W-L		Year	W-L
1 UNLV	1987	37-2	**UNLV**	1990	35-5
Duke	1999	37-2	Kentucky	1997	35-5
Illinois	2005	37-2	18 UNLV	1991	34-1
Duke	1986	37-3	**Connecticut**	1999	34-2
5 **Kentucky**	1948	36-3	Duke	1992	34-2
6 Massachusetts*	1996	35-2	**Kentucky**	1996	34-2
Georgetown	1985	35-3	Kansas	1997	34-2
Arizona	1988	35-3	Kentucky	1947	34-3
Duke	2001	35-4	**Georgetown**	1984	34-3
Kansas	1986	35-4	Arkansas	1991	34-4
Kansas	1998	35-4	**N. Carolina**	1993	34-4
Kentucky	1998	35-4	N. Carolina	1998	34-4
Oklahoma	1988	35-4			
Ohio St.	2007	35-4			
Florida	2007	35-5			

*NCAA later stripped Massachusetts of its four 1996 tournament victories after learning that center Marcus Camby accepted gifts from an agent.

Division I Winning Streaks
Full Season
(including tournaments)

No		Seasons	Broken by	Score
88	UCLA	1971-74	Notre Dame	71-70
60	San Francisco	1955-57	Illinois	62-33
47	UCLA	1966-68	Houston	71-69
45	UNLV	1990-91	Duke	79-77
44	Texas	1913-17	Rice	24-18
43	Seton Hall	1939-41	LIU-Bklyn	49-26
43	LIU-Brooklyn	1935-37	Stanford	45-31
41	UCLA	1968-69	USC	46-44
39	Marquette	1970-71	Ohio St.	60-59
37	Cincinnati	1962-63	Wichita St.	65-64
37	North Carolina	1957-58	West Virginia	75-64

Home Court

No		Seasons	Broken By	Score
129	Kentucky	1943-55	Georgia Tech	59-58
99	St. Bonaventure	1948-61	Detroit	77-70
98	UCLA	1970-76	Oregon	65-45
86	Cincinnati	1957-64	Kansas	51-47
81	Arizona	1945-51	Kansas St.	76-57
81	Marquette	1967-73	Notre Dame	71-69
80	Lamar	1978-84	Louisiana Tech	68-65

Associated Press Final Polls
Taken before NCAA, NIT and Collegiate Commissioner's Association (1974-75) tournaments.

The Associated Press introduced its weekly college basketball poll of sportswriters (later, sportswriters and broadcasters) during the 1948-49 season.

Since the NCAA Division I tournament has determined the national champion since 1939, the final AP poll ranks the nation's best teams through the regular season and conference tournaments.

Except for four seasons (see AP Post-Tournament Final Polls), the final AP poll has been released prior to the NCAA and NIT tournaments and has gone from a Top 10 (1949 and 1963-67) to a Top 20 (1950-62 and 1968-89) to a Top 25 (since 1990). Tournament champions are in **bold** type.

1949

		Before Tourns	Head Coach	Final Record
1	**Kentucky**	.29-1	Adolph Rupp	32-2
2	Oklahoma A&M	.21-4	Hank Iba	23-5
3	Saint Louis	.22-3	Eddie Hickey	22-4
4	Illinois	.19-3	Harry Combes	21-4
5	Western Ky.	.25-3	Ed Diddle	25-4
6	Minnesota	.18-3	Ozzie Cowles	same
7	Bradley	.25-6	Forddy Anderson	27-8
8	**San Francisco**	.21-5	Pete Newell	25-5
9	Tulane	.24-4	Cliff Wells	same
10	Bowling Green	.21-6	Harold Anderson	24-7

NCAA Final Four (at Edmundson Pavilion, Seattle): **Third Place**—Illinois 57, Oregon St. 53. **Championship**—Kentucky 46, Oklahoma A&M 36.

NIT Final Four (at Madison Square Garden): **Semifinals**—San Francisco 49, Bowling Green 39; Loyola-IL 55, Bradley 50. **Third Place**—Bowling Green 82, Bradley 77. **Championship**—San Francisco 48, Loyola-IL 47.

1950

		Before Tourns	Head Coach	Final Record
1	Bradley	.28-3	Forddy Anderson	32-5
2	Ohio St.	.21-3	Tippy Dye	22-4
3	Kentucky	.25-4	Adolph Rupp	25-5
4	Holy Cross	.27-2	Buster Sheary	27-4
5	N.C. State	.25-5	Everett Case	27-6
6	Duquesne	.22-5	Dudey Moore	23-6
7	UCLA	.24-5	John Wooden	24-7
8	Western Ky.	.24-5	Ed Diddle	25-6
9	St. John's	.23-4	Frank McGuire	24-5
10	La Salle	.20-3	Ken Loeffler	21-4
11	Villanova	.25-4	Al Severance	same
12	San Francisco	.19-6	Pete Newell	19-7
13	LIU-Brooklyn	.20-4	Clair Bee	20-5
14	Kansas St.	.17-7	Jack Gardner	same
15	Arizona	.26-4	Fred Enke	26-5
16	Wisconsin	.17-5	Bud Foster	same
17	San Jose St.	.21-7	Walter McPherson	same
18	Washington St.	.19-13	Jack Friel	same
19	Kansas	.14-11	Phog Allen	same
20	Indiana	.17-5	Branch McCracken	same

Note: Unranked CCNY, coached by Nat Holman, won both the NCAAs and NIT. The Beavers entered the postseason at 17-5 and had a final record of 24-5.

NCAA Final Four (at Madison Square Garden): **Third Place**—N. Carolina St. 53, Baylor 41. **Championship**—CCNY 71, Bradley 68.

NIT Final Four (at Madison Square Garden): **Semifinals**—Bradley 83, St. John's 72; CCNY 62, Duquesne 52. **Third Place**—St. John's 69, Duquesne 67 (OT). **Championship**—CCNY 69, Bradley 61.

1951

		Before Tourns	Head Coach	Final Record
1	**Kentucky**	.28-2	Adolph Rupp	32-2
2	Oklahoma A&M	.27-4	Hank Iba	29-6
3	Columbia	.22-0	Lou Rossini	22-1
4	Kansas St.	.22-3	Jack Gardner	25-4
5	Illinois	.19-4	Harry Combes	22-5
6	Bradley	.32-6	Forddy Anderson	same
7	Indiana	.19-3	Branch McCracken	same
8	N.C. State	.29-4	Everett Case	30-7
9	St. John's	.22-3	Frank McGuire	26-5
10	Saint Louis	.21-7	Eddie Hickey	22-8
11	BYU	.22-8	Stan Watts	26-10
12	Arizona	.24-4	Fred Enke	24-6
13	Dayton	.24-4	Tom Blackburn	27-5
14	Toledo	.23-8	Jerry Bush	same
15	Washington	.22-5	Tippy Dye	24-6
16	Murray St.	.21-6	Harlan Hodges	same
17	Cincinnati	.18-3	John Wiethe	18-4
18	Siena	.19-8	Dan Cunha	same
19	USC	.21-6	Forrest Twogood	same
20	Villanova	.25-6	Al Severance	25-7

NCAA Final Four (at Williams Arena, Minneapolis): **Third Place**—Illinois 61, Oklahoma St. 46. **Championship**—Kentucky 68, Kansas St. 58.

NIT Final Four (at Madison Sq. Garden): **Semifinals**—Dayton 69, St. John's 62 (OT); BYU 69, Seton Hall 59. **Third Place**—St. John's 70, Seton Hall 68 (2 OT). **Championship**—BYU 62, Dayton 43.

1952

		Before Tourns	Head Coach	Final Record
1	Kentucky	.28-2	Adolph Rupp	29-3
2	Illinois	.19-3	Harry Combes	22-4
3	Kansas St.	.19-5	Jack Gardner	same
4	Duquesne	.21-1	Dudey Moore	23-4
5	Saint Louis	.22-6	Eddie Hickey	23-8
6	Washington	.25-6	Tippy Dye	same
7	Iowa	.19-3	Bucky O'Connor	same
8	**Kansas**	.24-3	Phog Allen	28-3
9	West Virginia	.23-4	Red Brown	same
10	St. John's	.22-3	Frank McGuire	25-5
11	Dayton	.24-3	Tom Blackburn	28-5
12	Duke	.24-6	Harold Bradley	same
13	Holy Cross	.23-3	Buster Sheary	24-4
14	Seton Hall	.25-2	Honey Russell	25-3
15	St. Bonaventure	.19-5	Ed Melvin	21-6
16	Wyoming	.27-6	Everett Shelton	28-7
17	Louisville	.20-5	Peck Hickman	20-6
18	Seattle	.29-7	Al Brightman	29-8
19	UCLA	.19-10	John Wooden	19-12
20	SW Texas St.	.30-1	Milton Jowers	same

Note: Unranked La Salle, coached by Ken Loeffler, won the NIT. The Explorers entered the postseason at 21-7 and had a final record of 25-7.

NCAA Final Four (at Edmundson Pavillion, Seattle): **Semifinals**—St. John's 61, Illinois 59; Kansas 74, Santa Clara 59. **Third Place**—Illinois 67, Santa Clara 64. **Championship**—Kansas 80, St. John's 63.

NIT Final Four (at Madison Sq. Garden): **Semifinals**—La Salle 59, Duquesne 46; Dayton 69, St. Bonaventure 62. **Third Place**—St. Bonaventure 48, Duquesne 34. **Championship**—La Salle 75, Dayton 64.

Associated Press Final Polls (Cont.)

1953

		Before Tourns	Head Coach	Final Record
1	**Indiana**	.18-3	Branch McCracken	23-3
2	La Salle	.25-2	Ken Loeffler	25-3
3	**Seton Hall**	.28-2	Honey Russell	31-2
4	Washington	.27-2	Tippy Dye	30-3
5	LSU	.22-1	Harry Rabenhorst	24-3
6	Kansas	.16-5	Phog Allen	19-6
7	Oklahoma A&M	.22-6	Hank Iba	23-7
	Kansas St.	.17-4	Jack Gardner	same
9	Western Ky.	.25-5	Ed Diddle	25-6
10	Illinois	.18-4	Harry Combes	same
11	Oklahoma City	.18-4	Doyle Parrick	18-6
12	N.C. State	.26-6	Everett Case	same
13	Notre Dame	.17-4	John Jordan	19-5
14	Louisville	.21-5	Peck Hickman	22-6
	Seattle	.27-3	Al Brightman	29-4
16	Miami-OH	.17-5	Bill Rohr	17-6
17	Eastern Ky.	.16-8	Paul McBrayer	16-9
18	Duquesne	.18-7	Dudey Moore	21-8
	Navy	.16-4	Ben Carnevale	16-5
20	Holy Cross	.18-5	Buster Sheary	20-6

NCAA Final Four (at Municipal Auditorium, Kansas City): **Semifinals**—Indiana 80, LSU 67; Kansas 79, Washington 53. **Third Place**—Washington 88, LSU 69. **Championship**—Indiana 69, Kansas 68.
NIT Final Four (at Madison Sq. Garden): **Semifinals**—Seton Hall 74, Manhattan 56; St. John's 64, Duquesne 55. **Third Place**—Duquesne 81, Manhattan 67. **Championship**—Seton Hall 58, St. John's 46.

1955

		Before Tourns	Head Coach	Final Record
1	**San Francisco**	.23-1	Phil Woolpert	28-1
2	Kentucky	.22-2	Adolph Rupp	23-3
3	La Salle	.22-4	Ken Loeffler	26-5
4	N.C. State	.28-4	Everett Case	same
5	Iowa	.17-5	Bucky O'Connor	19-7
6	**Duquesne**	.19-4	Dudey Moore	22-4
7	Utah	.23-3	Jack Gardner	24-4
8	Marquette	.22-2	Jack Nagle	24-3
9	Dayton	.23-3	Tom Blackburn	25-4
10	Oregon St.	.21-7	Slats Gill	22-8
11	Minnesota	.15-7	Ozzie Cowles	same
12	Alabama	.19-5	Johnny Dee	same
13	UCLA	.21-5	John Wooden	same
14	G. Washington	.24-6	Bill Reinhart	same
15	Colorado	.16-5	Bebe Lee	19-6
16	Tulsa	.20-6	Clarence Iba	21-7
17	Vanderbilt	.16-6	Bob Polk	same
18	Illinois	.17-5	Harry Combes	same
19	West Virginia	.19-10	Fred Schaus	19-11
20	Saint Louis	.19-7	Eddie Hickey	20-8

NCAA Final Four (at Municipal Auditorium, Kansas City): **Semifinals**—La Salle 76, Iowa 73; San Francisco 62, Colorado 50. **Third Place**—Colorado 75, Iowa 74. **Championship**—San Francisco 77, La Salle 63.
NIT Final Four (at Madison Square Garden): **Semifinals**—Dayton 79, St. Francis-PA 73 (OT); Duquesne 65, Cincinnati 51. **Third Place**—Cincinnati 96, St. Francis-PA 91 (OT). **Championship**—Duquesne 70, Dayton 58.

1954

		Before Tourns	Head Coach	Final Record
1	Kentucky	.25-0	Adolph Rupp	same*
2	Indiana	.19-3	Branch McCracken	20-4
3	Duquesne	.24-2	Dudey Moore	26-3
4	Western Ky.	.28-1	Ed Diddle	29-3
5	Oklahoma A&M	.23-4	Hank Iba	24-5
6	Notre Dame	.20-2	John Jordan	22-3
7	Kansas	.16-5	Phog Allen	same
8	**Holy Cross**	.23-2	Buster Sheary	26-2
9	LSU	.21-3	Harry Rabenhorst	21-5
10	**La Salle**	.21-4	Ken Loeffler	26-4
11	Iowa	.17-5	Bucky O'Connor	same
12	Duke	.22-6	Harold Bradley	same
13	Colorado A&M	.22-5	Bill Strannigan	22-7
14	Illinois	.17-5	Harry Combes	same
15	Wichita	.27-3	Ralph Miller	27-4
16	Seattle	.26-1	Al Brightman	26-2
17	N.C. State	.26-6	Everett Case	28-7
18	Dayton	.24-6	Tom Blackburn	25-7
	Minnesota	.17-5	Ozzie Cowles	same
20	Oregon St.	.19-10	Slats Gill	same
	UCLA	.18-7	John Wooden	same
	USC	.17-12	Forrest Twogood	19-14

*Kentucky turned down invitation to NCAA tournament after NCAA declared seniors Cliff Hagan, Frank Ramsey and Lou Tsioropoulos ineligible for postseason play.
NCAA Final Four (at Municipal Auditorium, Kansas City): **Semifinals**—La Salle 69, Penn St. 54; Bradley 74, USC 72. **Third Place**—Penn St. 70, USC 61. **Championship**—La Salle 92, Bradley 76.
NIT Final Four (at Madison Square Garden): **Semifinals**—Duquesne 66, Niagara 51; Holy Cross 75, Western Ky. 69. **Third Place**—Niagara 71, Western Ky. 65. **Championship**—Holy Cross 71, Duquesne 62.

1956

		Before Tourns	Head Coach	Final Record
1	**San Francisco**	.25-0	Phil Woolpert	29-0
2	N.C. State	.24-3	Everett Case	24-4
3	Dayton	.23-3	Tom Blackburn	25-4
4	Iowa	.17-5	Bucky O'Connor	20-6
5	Alabama	.21-3	Johnny Dee	same
6	**Louisville**	.23-3	Peck Hickman	26-3
7	SMU	.22-2	Doc Hayes	25-4
8	UCLA	.21-5	John Wooden	22-6
9	Kentucky	.19-5	Adolph Rupp	20-6
10	Illinois	.18-4	Harry Combes	same
11	Oklahoma City	.18-6	Abe Lemons	20-7
12	Vanderbilt	.19-4	Bob Polk	same
13	North Carolina	.18-5	Frank McGuire	same
14	Holy Cross	.22-4	Roy Leenig	22-5
15	Temple	.23-3	Harry Litwack	27-4
16	Wake Forest	.19-9	Murray Greason	same
17	Duke	.19-7	Harold Bradley	same
18	Utah	.21-5	Jack Gardner	22-6
19	Oklahoma A&M	.18-8	Hank Iba	18-9
20	West Virginia	.21-8	Fred Schaus	21-9

NCAA Final Four (at McGaw Hall, Evanston, IL): **Semifinals**—Iowa 83, Temple 76; San Francisco 76, SMU 68. **Third Place**—Temple 90, SMU 81. **Championship**—San Francisco 83, Iowa 71.
NIT Final Four (at Madison Square Garden): **Semifinals**—Dayton 89, St. Francis-NY 58; Louisville 89, St. Joseph's-PA 79. **Third Place**—St. Joseph's-PA 93, St. Francis-NY 82. **Championship**—Louisville 93, Dayton 80.

1957

		Before Tourns	Head Coach	Final Record
1	N. Carolina	.27-0	Frank McGuire	32-0
2	Kansas	.21-2	Dick Harp	24-3
3	Kentucky	.22-4	Adolph Rupp	23-5
4	SMU	.21-3	Doc Hayes	22-4
5	Seattle	.24-2	John Castellani	24-3
6	Louisville	.21-5	Peck Hickman	same
7	West Va.	.25-4	Fred Schaus	25-5
8	Vanderbilt	.17-5	Bob Polk	same
9	Oklahoma City	.17-8	Abe Lemons	19-9
10	Saint Louis	.19-7	Eddie Hickey	19-9
11	Michigan St.	.14-8	Forddy Anderson	16-10
12	Memphis St.	.21-5	Bob Vanatta	24-6
13	California	.20-4	Pete Newell	21-5
14	UCLA	.22-4	John Wooden	same
15	Mississippi St.	.17-8	Babe McCarthy	same
16	Idaho St.	.24-2	John Grayson	25-4
17	Notre Dame	.18-7	John Jordan	20-8
18	Wake Forest	.19-9	Murray Greason	same
19	Canisius	.20-5	Joe Curran	22-6
20	Oklahoma A&M	.17-9	Hank Iba	same

Note: Unranked **Bradley**, coached by Chuck Osborn, won the NIT. The Braves entered the tourney at 19-7 and had a final record of 22-7.
NCAA Final Four (at Municipal Auditorium, Kansas City): **Semifinals**–North Carolina 74, Michigan St. 70 (3 OT); Kansas 80, San Francisco 56. **Third Place**–San Francisco 67, Michigan St. 60. **Championship**–North Carolina 54, Kansas 53 (3 OT).
NIT Final Four (at Madison Square Garden): **Semifinals**–Memphis St. 80, St. Bonaventure 78; Bradley 78, Temple 66. **Third Place**–Temple 67, St. Bonaventure 50. **Championship**–Bradley 84, Memphis St. 83.

1958

		Before Tourns	Head Coach	Final Record
1	West Virginia	.26-1	Fred Schaus	26-2
2	Cincinnati	.24-2	George Smith	25-3
3	Kansas St.	.20-3	Tex Winter	22-5
4	San Francisco	.24-1	Phil Woolpert	25-2
5	Temple	.24-2	Harry Litwack	27-3
6	Maryland	.20-6	Bud Millikan	22-7
7	Kansas	.18-5	Dick Harp	same
8	Notre Dame	.22-4	John Jordan	24-5
9	Kentucky	.19-6	Adolph Rupp	23-6
10	Duke	.18-7	Harold Bradley	same
11	Dayton	.23-3	Tom Blackburn	25-4
12	Indiana	.12-10	Branch McCracken	13-11
13	North Carolina	.19-7	Frank McGuire	same
14	Bradley	.20-6	Chuck Osborn	20-7
15	Mississippi St.	.20-5	Babe McCarthy	same
16	Auburn	.16-6	Joel Eaves	same
17	Michigan St.	.16-6	Forddy Anderson	same
18	Seattle	.20-6	John Castellani	24-7
19	Oklahoma St.	.19-7	Hank Iba	21-8
20	N.C. State	.18-6	Everett Case	same

Note: Unranked **Xavier-OH**, coached by Jim McCafferty, won the NIT. The Musketeers entered the tourney at 15-11 and had a final record of 19-11.
NCAA Final Four (at Freedom Hall, Louisville): **Semifinals**–Kentucky 61, Temple 60; Seattle 73, Kansas St. 51. **Third Place**–Temple 67, Kansas St. 57. **Championship**–Kentucky 84, Seattle 72.
NIT Final Four (at Madison Square Garden): **Semifinals**–Dayton 80, St. John's 56; Xavier-OH 72, St. Bonaventure 53. **Third Place**–St. Bonaventure 84, St. John's 69. **Championship**–Xavier-OH 78, Dayton 74 (OT).

1959

		Before Tourns	Head Coach	Final Record
1	Kansas St.	.24-1	Tex Winter	25-2
2	Kentucky	.23-2	Adolph Rupp	24-3
3	Mississippi St.	.24-1	Babe McCarthy	same*
4	Bradley	.23-3	Chuck Orsborn	25-4
5	Cincinnati	.23-3	George Smith	26-4
6	N.C. State	.22-4	Everett Case	same
7	Michigan St.	.18-3	Forddy Anderson	19-4
8	Auburn	.20-2	Joel Eaves	same
9	North Carolina	.20-4	Frank McGuire	20-5
10	West Virginia	.25-4	Fred Schaus	29-5
11	California	.21-4	Pete Newell	25-4
12	Saint Louis	.20-5	John Benington	20-6
13	Seattle	.23-6	Vince Cazzetta	same
14	St. Joseph's-PA	.22-3	Jack Ramsay	22-5
15	St. Mary's-CA	.18-5	Jim Weaver	19-6
16	TCU	.19-5	Buster Brannon	20-6
17	Oklahoma City	.20-6	Abe Lemons	20-7
18	Utah	.21-5	Jack Gardner	21-7
19	St. Bonaventure	.20-2	Eddie Donovan	20-3
20	Marquette	.22-4	Eddie Hickey	23-6

*Mississippi St. turned down invitation to NCAA tournament because it was an integrated event.
Note: Unranked **St. John's**, coached by Joe Lapchick, won the NIT. The Redmen entered the tourney at 16-6 and had a final record of 20-6.
NCAA Final Four (at Freedom Hall, Louisville): **Semifinals**–West Virginia 94, Louisville 79; California 64, Cincinnati 58. **Third Place**–Cincinnati 98, Louisville 85. **Championship**–California 71, West Virginia 70.
NIT Final Four (at Madison Square Garden): **Semifinals**–Bradley 59, NYU 57; St. John's 76, Providence 55. **Third Place**–NYU 71, Providence 57. **Championship**–St. John's 76, Bradley 71 (OT).

1960

		Before Tourns	Head Coach	Final Record
1	Cincinnati	.25-1	George Smith	28-2
2	California	.24-1	Pete Newell	28-2
3	Ohio St.	.21-3	Fred Taylor	25-3
4	Bradley	.24-2	Chuck Orsborn	27-2
5	West Virginia	.24-4	Fred Schaus	26-5
6	Utah	.24-2	Jack Gardner	26-3
7	Indiana	.20-4	Branch McCracken	same
8	Utah St.	.22-4	Cecil Baker	24-5
9	St. Bonaventure	.19-3	Eddie Donovan	21-5
10	Miami-FL	.23-3	Bruce Hale	23-4
11	Auburn	.19-3	Joel Eaves	same
12	NYU	.19-4	Lou Rossini	22-5
13	Georgia Tech	.21-5	Whack Hyder	22-6
14	Providence	.21-4	Joe Mullaney	24-5
15	Saint Louis	.19-7	John Benington	19-8
16	Holy Cross	.20-5	Roy Leenig	20-6
17	Villanova	.19-5	Al Severance	20-6
18	Duke	.15-10	Vic Bubas	17-11
19	Wake Forest	.21-7	Bones McKinney	same
20	St. John's	.17-7	Joe Lapchick	17-8

NCAA Final Four (at the Cow Palace, San Fran.): **Semifinals**–Ohio St. 76, NYU 54; California 77, Cincinnati 69. **Third Place**–Cincinnati 95, NYU 71. **Championship**–Ohio St. 75, California 55.
NIT Final Four (at Madison Square Garden): **Semifinals**–Bradley 82, St. Bonaventure 71; Providence 68, Utah St. 62. **Third Place**–Utah St. 99, St. Bonaventure 93. **Championship**–Bradley 88, Providence 72.

Associated Press Final Polls (Cont.)

1961

		Before Tourns	Head Coach	Final Record
1	Ohio St.	.24-0	Fred Taylor	27-1
2	**Cincinnati**	.23-3	Ed Jucker	27-3
3	St. Bonaventure	.22-3	Eddie Donovan	24-4
4	Kansas St.	.22-3	Tex Winter	23-4
5	North Carolina	.19-4	Frank McGuire	same
6	Bradley	.21-5	Chuck Orsborn	same
7	USC	.20-6	Forrest Twogood	21-8
8	Iowa	.18-6	S. Scheuerman	same
9	West Virginia	.23-4	George King	same
10	Duke	.22-6	Vic Bubas	same
11	Utah	.21-6	Jack Gardner	23-8
12	Texas Tech	.14-9	Polk Robison	15-10
13	Niagara	.16-4	Taps Gallagher	16-5
14	Memphis St.	.20-2	Bob Vanatta	20-3
15	Wake Forest	.17-10	Bones McKinney	19-11
16	St. John's	.20-4	Joe Lapchick	20-5
17	St. Joseph's-PA	.22-4	Jack Ramsay	25-5
18	Drake	.19-7	Maury John	same
19	Holy Cross	.19-4	Roy Leenig	22-5
20	Kentucky	.18-8	Adolph Rupp	19-9

Note: Unranked **Providence**, coached by Joe Mullaney, won the NIT. The Friars entered the tourney at 20-5 and had a final record of 24-5.

NCAA Final Four (at Municipal Auditorium, Kansas City): **Semifinals**—Ohio St. 95, St. Joseph's-PA 69; Cincinnati 82, Utah 67. **Third Place**—St. Joseph's-PA 127, Utah 120 (4 OT). **Championship**—Cincinnati 70, Ohio St. 65 (OT).

NIT Final Four (at Madison Square Garden) **Semifinals**—St. Louis 67, Dayton 60; Providence 90, Holy Cross 83 (OT). **Third Place**—Holy Cross 85, Dayton 67. **Championship**—Providence 62, St. Louis 59.

1962

		Before Tourns	Head Coach	Final Record
1	Ohio St.	.23-1	Fred Taylor	26-2
2	**Cincinnati**	.25-2	Ed Jucker	29-2
3	Kentucky	.22-2	Adolph Rupp	23-3
4	Mississippi St.	.19-6	Babe McCarthy	same
5	Bradley	.21-6	Chuck Orsborn	21-7
6	Kansas St.	.22-3	Tex Winter	same
7	Utah	.23-3	Jack Gardner	same
8	Bowling Green	.21-3	Harold Anderson	same
9	Colorado	.18-6	Sox Walseth	19-7
10	Duke	.20-5	Vic Bubas	same
11	Loyola-IL	.21-3	George Ireland	23-4
12	St. John's	.19-4	Joe Lapchick	21-5
13	Wake Forest	.18-8	Bones McKinney	22-9
14	Oregon St.	.22-4	Slats Gill	24-5
15	West Virginia	.24-5	George King	24-6
16	Arizona St.	.23-3	Ned Wulk	23-4
17	Duquesne	.20-5	Red Manning	22-7
18	Utah St.	.21-5	Ladell Andersen	22-7
19	UCLA	.16-9	John Wooden	18-11
20	Villanova	.19-6	Jack Kraft	21-7

Note: Unranked **Dayton**, coached by Tom Blackburn, won the NIT. The Flyers entered the tourney at 20-6 and had a final record of 24-6.

NCAA Final Four (at Freedom Hall, Louisville): **Semifinals**—Ohio St. 84, Wake Forest 68; Cincinnati 72, UCLA 70. **Third Place**—Wake Forest 82, UCLA 80. **Championship**—Cincinnati 71, Ohio St. 59.

NIT Final Four (at Madison Square Garden): **Semifinals**—Dayton 98, Loyola-IL 82; St. John's 76, Duquesne 65. **Third Place**—Loyola-IL 95, Duquesne 84. **Championship**—Dayton 73, St. John's 67.

1963

AP ranked only 10 teams from the 1962-63 season through 1967-68.

		Before Tourns	Head Coach	Final Record
1	Cincinnati	.23-1	Ed Jucker	26-2
2	Duke	.24-2	Vic Bubas	27-3
3	**Loyola-IL**	.24-2	George Ireland	29-2
4	Arizona St.	.24-2	Ned Wulk	26-3
5	Wichita	.19-7	Ralph Miller	19-8
6	Mississippi St.	.21-5	Babe McCarthy	22-6
7	Ohio St.	.20-4	Fred Taylor	same
8	Illinois	.19-5	Harry Combes	20-6
9	NYU	.17-3	Lou Rossini	18-5
10	Colorado	.18-6	Sox Walseth	19-7

Note: Unranked **Providence**, coached by Joe Mullaney, won the NIT. The Friars entered the tourney at 21-4 and had a final record of 24-4.

NCAA Final Four (at Freedom Hall, Louisville): **Semifinals**—Loyola-IL 94, Duke 75; Cincinnati 80, Oregon St. 46. **Third Place**—Duke 85, Oregon St. 63. **Championship**—Loyola-IL 60, Cincinnati 58 (OT).

NIT Final Four (at Madison Square Garden): **Semifinals**—Providence 70, Marquette 64; Canisius 61, Villanova 46. **Third Place**—Marquette 66, Villanova 58. **Championship**—Providence 81, Canisius 66.

1964

AP ranked only 10 teams from the 1962-63 season through 1967-68.

		Before Tourns	Head Coach	Final Record
1	**UCLA**	.26-0	John Wooden	30-0
2	Michigan	.20-4	Dave Strack	23-5
3	Duke	.23-4	Vic Bubas	26-5
4	Kentucky	.21-4	Adolph Rupp	21-6
5	Wichita St.	.22-5	Ralph Miller	23-6
6	Oregon St.	.25-3	Slats Gill	25-4
7	Villanova	.22-3	Jack Kraft	24-4
8	Loyola-IL	.20-5	George Ireland	22-6
9	DePaul	.21-3	Ray Meyer	21-4
10	Davidson	.22-4	Lefty Driesell	same

Note: Unranked **Bradley**, coached by Chuck Orsborn, won the NIT. The Braves entered the tourney at 20-6 and finished with a record of 23-6.

NCAA Final Four (at Municipal Auditorium, Kansas City): **Semifinals**—Duke 91, Michigan 80; UCLA 90, Kansas St. 84. **Third Place**—Michigan 100, Kansas St. 90. **Championship**—UCLA 98, Duke 83.

NIT Final Four (at Madison Square Garden): **Semifinals**—New Mexico 72, NYU 65; Bradley 67, Army 52. **Third Place**—Army 60, NYU 59. **Championship**—Bradley 86, New Mexico 54.

Undefeated National Champions

Seven NCAA seasons have ended with an undefeated national champion. UCLA has accomplished the feat four times.

Year		W-L
1956	San Francisco	.29-0
1957	North Carolina	.32-0
1964	UCLA	.30-0
1967	UCLA	.30-0
1972	UCLA	.30-0
1973	UCLA	.30-0
1976	Indiana	.32-0

1965

AP ranked only 10 teams from the 1962-63 season through 1967-68.

		Before Tours	Head Coach	Final Record
1	Michigan	21-3	Dave Strack	24-4
2	**UCLA**	24-2	John Wooden	28-2
3	St. Joseph's-PA	25-1	Jack Ramsay	26-3
4	Providence	22-1	Joe Mullaney	24-2
5	Vanderbilt	23-3	Roy Skinner	24-4
6	Davidson	24-2	Lefty Driesell	same
7	Minnesota	19-5	John Kundla	same
8	Villanova	21-4	Jack Kraft	23-5
9	BYU	21-5	Stan Watts	21-7
10	Duke	20-5	Vic Bubas	same

Note: Unranked **St. John's**, coached by Joe Lapchick, won the NIT. The Redmen entered the tourney at 17-8 and finished with a record of 21-8.
NCAA Final Four (at Memorial Coliseum, Portland, OR): **Semifinals**–Michigan 93, Princeton 76; UCLA 108, Wichita St. 89. **Third Place**–Princeton 118, Wichita St. 82. **Championship**–UCLA 91, Michigan 80.
NIT Final Four (at Madison Square Garden): **Semifinals**–Villanova 91, NYU 69; St. John's 67, Army 60. **Third Place**–Army 75, NYU 74. **Championship**– St. John's 55, Villanova 51.

1966

AP ranked only 10 teams from the 1962-63 season through 1967-68.

		Before Tours	Head Coach	Final Record
1	Kentucky	24-1	Adolph Rupp	27-2
2	Duke	23-3	Vic Bubas	26-4
3	**Texas Western**	23-1	Don Haskins	28-1
4	Kansas	22-3	Ted Owens	23-4
5	St. Joseph's-PA	22-4	Jack Ramsay	24-5
6	Loyola-IL	22-2	George Ireland	22-3
7	Cincinnati	21-5	Tay Baker	21-7
8	Vanderbilt	22-4	Roy Skinner	same
9	Michigan	17-7	Dave Strack	18-8
10	Western Ky.	23-2	Johnny Oldham	25-3

Note: Unranked **BYU**, coached by Stan Watts, won the NIT. The Cougars entered the tourney at 17-5 and had a final record of 20-5.
NCAA Final Four (at Cole Fieldhouse, College Park, MD): **Semifinals**–Kentucky 83, Duke 79; Texas Western 85, Utah 78. **Third Place**–Duke 79, Utah 77. **Championship**–Texas Western 72, Kentucky 65.
NIT Final Four (at Madison Square Garden): **Semifinals**–BYU 66, Army 60; NYU 69, Villanova 63. **Third Place**–Villanova 76, Army 65. **Championship**–BYU 97, NYU 84.

1967

AP ranked only 10 teams from the 1962-63 season through 1967-68.

		Before Tours	Head Coach	Final Record
1	**UCLA**	26-0	John Wooden	30-0
2	Louisville	23-3	Peck Hickman	23-5
3	Kansas	22-3	Ted Owens	23-4
4	North Carolina	24-4	Dean Smith	26-6
5	Princeton	23-2	B. van Breda Kolff	25-3
6	Western Ky.	23-2	Johnny Oldham	23-3
7	Houston	23-3	Guy Lewis	27-4
8	Tennessee	21-5	Ray Mears	21-7
9	Boston College	19-2	Bob Cousy	21-3
10	Texas Western	20-5	Don Haskins	22-6

Note: Unranked **Southern Illinois**, coached by Jack Hartman, won the NIT. The Salukis entered the tourney at 20-2 and had a final record of 24-2.
NCAA Final Four (at Freedom Hall, Louisville): **Semifinals**–Dayton 76, N. Carolina 62; UCLA 73, Houston 58. **Third Place**–Houston 84, N. Carolina 62. **Championship**–UCLA 79, Dayton 64.
NIT Final Four (at Madison Square Garden): **Semifinals**–Marquette 83, Marshall 78; Southern Ill. 79, Rutgers 70. **Third Place**–Rutgers 93, Marshall 76. **Championship**–Southern Ill. 71, Marquette 56.

1968

AP ranked only 10 teams from the 1962-63 season through 1967-68.

		Before Tours	Head Coach	Final Record
1	Houston	28-0	Guy Lewis	31-2
2	**UCLA**	25-1	John Wooden	29-1
3	St. Bonaventure	22-0	Larry Weise	23-2
4	North Carolina	25-3	Dean Smith	28-4
5	Kentucky	21-4	Adolph Rupp	22-5
6	New Mexico	23-3	Bob King	23-5
7	Columbia	21-4	Jack Rohan	23-5
8	Davidson	22-4	Lefty Driesell	24-5
9	Louisville	20-6	John Dromo	21-7
10	Duke	21-5	Vic Bubas	22-6

Note: Unranked **Dayton**, coached by Don Donoher, won the NIT. The Flyers entered the tourney at 17-9 and had a final record of 21-9.
NCAA Final Four (at the Sports Arena, Los Angeles): **Semifinals**–North Carolina 80, Ohio St. 66; UCLA 101, Houston 69. **Third Place**–Ohio St. 89, Houston 85. **Championship**–UCLA 78, North Carolina 55.
NIT Final Four (at Madison Square Garden): **Semifinals**–Dayton 76, Notre Dame 74 (OT); Kansas 58, St. Peter's 46. **Third Place**–Notre Dame 81, St.Peter's 78. **Championship**–Dayton 61, Kansas 48.

All-Time AP Top 20

The composite AP Top 20 from the 1948-49 season through 2006-07, based on the final regular season rankings of each year. The final AP poll has been taken before the NCAA and NIT tournaments each season since 1949 except in 1953 and '54 and again in 1974 and '75 when the final poll came out after the postseason. Team point totals are based on 20 points for all 1st place finishes, 19 for each 2nd, etc. Also listed are the number of times ranked No.1 by AP going into the tournaments, and times ranked in the pre-tournament Top 10 and Top 20.

		Pts	No.1	Top 10	Top 20			Pts	No.1	Top 10	Top 20
1	Kentucky	672	8	38	45	11	Ohio St	211	3	12	15
2	North Carolina	555	5	31	40	12	Michigan	200	2	10	15
3	Duke	482	7	27	36	13	Notre Dame	191	0	12	19
4	UCLA	480	7	24	37	14	Marquette	187	0	12	17
5	Kansas	397	1	20	31	15	N.C. State	182	1	9	17
6	Indiana	293	4	16	24	16	Syracuse	179	0	9	20
7	Louisville	266	0	12	25	17	UNLV	173	2	8	13
8	Cincinnati	259	2	13	19	18	Arkansas	166	0	9	15
9	Arizona	245	1	12	20	19	Maryland	164	0	8	18
10	Illinois	235	1	10	24	20	Oklahoma	157	1	7	13

Associated Press Final Polls (Cont.)

1969

		Before Tourns	Head Coach	Final Record
1	**UCLA**	25-1	John Wooden	29-1
2	La Salle	23-1	Tom Gola	same*
3	Santa Clara	26-1	Dick Garibaldi	27-2
4	North Carolina	25-3	Dean Smith	27-5
5	Davidson	24-2	Lefty Driesell	26-3
6	Purdue	20-4	George King	23-5
7	Kentucky	22-4	Adolph Rupp	23-5
8	St. John's	22-4	Lou Carnesecca	23-6
9	Duquesne	19-4	Red Manning	21-5
10	Villanova	21-4	Jack Kraft	21-5
11	Drake	23-4	Maury John	26-5
12	New Mexico St.	23-3	Lou Henson	24-5
13	South Carolina	20-6	Frank McGuire	21-7
14	Marquette	22-4	Al McGuire	24-5
15	Louisville	20-5	John Dromo	21-6
16	Boston College	21-3	Bob Cousy	24-4
17	Notre Dame	20-6	Johnny Dee	20-7
18	Colorado	20-6	Sox Walseth	21-7
19	Kansas	20-6	Ted Owens	20-7
20	Illinois	19-5	Harvey Schmidt	same

*On probation

Note: Unranked **Temple**, coached by Harry Litwack, won the NIT. The Owls entered the tourney at 18-8 and finished with a record of 22-8.

NCAA Final Four (at Freedom Hall, Louisville): **Semifinals**—Purdue 92, N. Carolina 65; UCLA 85, Drake 82. **Third Place**—Drake 104, N. Carolina 84. **Championship**—UCLA 92, Purdue 72.

NIT Final Four (at Madison Square Garden): **Semifinals**—Temple 63, Tennessee 58; Boston College 73, Army 61. **Third Place**—Tennessee 64, Army 52. **Championship**—Temple 89, Boston College 76.

1971

		Before Tourns	Head Coach	Final Record
1	**UCLA**	25-1	John Wooden	29-1
2	Marquette	26-0	Al McGuire	28-1
3	Penn	26-0	Dick Harter	28-1
4	Kansas	25-1	Ted Owens	27-3
5	USC	24-2	Bob Boyd	24-2
6	South Carolina	23-4	Frank McGuire	23-6
7	Western Ky.	20-5	John Oldham	24-6
8	Kentucky	22-4	Adolph Rupp	22-6
9	Fordham	25-1	Digger Phelps	26-3
10	Ohio St.	19-5	Fred Taylor	20-6
11	Jacksonville	22-3	Tom Wasdin	22-4
12	Notre Dame	19-7	Johnny Dee	20-9
13	**N. Carolina**	22-6	Dean Smith	26-6
14	Houston	20-6	Guy Lewis	22-7
15	Duquesne	21-3	Red Manning	21-4
16	Long Beach St.	21-4	Jerry Tarkanian	23-5
17	Tennessee	20-6	Ray Mears	21-7
18	Villanova	19-5	Jack Kraft	23-6
19	Drake	20-7	Maury John	21-8
20	BYU	18-9	Stan Watts	18-11

NCAA Final Four (at the Astrodome, Houston): **Semifinals**—Villanova 92, Western Ky. 89 (2 OT); UCLA 68, Kansas 60. **Third Place**—Western Ky. 77, Kansas 75. **Championship**—UCLA 68, Villanova 62.

NIT Final Four (at Madison Square Garden): **Semifinals**—N. Carolina 73, Duke 69; Ga.Tech 76, St. Bonaventure 71 (2 OT). **Third Place**—St. Bonaventure 92, Duke 88 (OT). **Championship**—N. Carolina 84, Ga. Tech 66.

1970

		Before Tourns	Head Coach	Final Record
1	Kentucky	25-1	Adolph Rupp	26-2
2	**UCLA**	24-2	John Wooden	28-2
3	St. Bonaventure	22-1	Larry Weise	25-3
4	Jacksonville	23-1	Joe Williams	27-2
5	New Mexico St.	23-2	Lou Henson	27-3
6	South Carolina	25-3	Frank McGuire	25-3
7	Iowa	19-4	Ralph Miller	20-5
8	**Marquette**	22-3	Al McGuire	26-3
9	Notre Dame	20-6	Johnny Dee	21-8
10	N.C. State	22-6	Norm Sloan	23-7
11	Florida St.	23-3	Hugh Durham	23-3
12	Houston	24-3	Guy Lewis	25-5
13	Penn	25-1	Dick Harter	25-2
14	Drake	21-6	Maury John	22-7
15	Davidson	22-4	Terry Holland	22-5
16	Utah St.	20-6	Ladell Andersen	22-7
17	Niagara	21-5	Frank Layden	22-7
18	Western Ky.	22-2	John Oldham	22-3
19	Long Beach St.	23-3	Jerry Tarkanian	24-5
20	USC	18-8	Bob Boyd	18-8

NCAA Final Four (at Cole Fieldhouse, College Park, MD): **Semifinals**—Jacksonville 91, St. Bonaventure 83; UCLA 93, New Mexico St. 77. **Third Place**—New Mexico St. 79, St. Bonaventure 73. **Championship**—UCLA 80, Jacksonville 69.

NIT Final Four (at Madison Square Garden): **Semifinals**—St. John's 60, Army 59; Marquette 101, LSU 79. **Third Place**—Army 75, LSU 68. **Championship**—Marquette 65, St. John's 53.

1972

		Before Tourns	Head Coach	Final Record
1	**UCLA**	26-0	John Wooden	30-0
2	North Carolina	23-4	Dean Smith	26-5
3	Penn	23-2	Chuck Daly	25-3
4	Louisville	23-4	Denny Crum	26-5
5	Long Beach St.	23-3	Jerry Tarkanian	25-4
6	South Carolina	22-4	Frank McGuire	24-5
7	Marquette	24-2	Al McGuire	25-4
8	SW Louisiana	23-3	Beryl Shipley	25-4
9	BYU	21-4	Stan Watts	21-5
10	Florida St.	23-5	Hugh Durham	27-6
11	Minnesota	17-6	Bill Musselman	18-7
12	Marshall	23-3	Carl Tacy	23-4
13	Memphis St.	21-6	Gene Bartow	21-7
14	**Maryland**	23-5	Lefty Driesell	27-5
15	Villanova	19-6	Jack Kraft	20-8
16	Oral Roberts	25-1	Ken Trickey	26-2
17	Indiana	17-7	Bob Knight	17-8
18	Kentucky	20-6	Adolph Rupp	21-7
19	Ohio St.	18-6	Fred Taylor	same
20	Virginia	21-6	Bill Gibson	21-7

NCAA Final Four (at the Sports Arena, Los Angeles): **Semifinals**—Florida St. 79, N. Carolina 75; UCLA 96, Louisville 77. **Third Place**—N. Carolina 105, Louisville 91. **Championship**—UCLA 81, Florida St. 76.

NIT Final Four (at Madison Square Garden): **Semifinals**—Maryland 91, Jacksonville 77; Niagara 69, St. John's 67. **Third Place**—Jacksonville 83, St. John's 80. **Championship**—Maryland 100, Niagara 69.

1973

		Before Tourns	Head Coach	Final Record
1	UCLA	26-0	John Wooden	30-0
2	N.C. State	27-0	Norm Sloan	same*
3	Long Beach St.	24-2	Jerry Tarkanian	26-3
4	Providence	24-2	Dave Gavitt	27-4
5	Marquette	23-3	Al McGuire	25-4
6	Indiana	19-5	Bob Knight	22-6
7	SW Louisiana	23-2	Beryl Shipley	24-5
8	Maryland	22-6	Lefty Driesell	23-7
9	Kansas St.	22-4	Jack Hartman	23-5
10	Minnesota	20-4	Bill Musselman	21-5
11	North Carolina	22-7	Dean Smith	25-8
12	Memphis St.	21-5	Gene Bartow	24-6
13	Houston	23-3	Guy Lewis	23-4
14	Syracuse	22-4	Roy Danforth	24-5
15	Missouri	21-5	Norm Stewart	21-6
16	Arizona St.	18-7	Ned Wulk	19-9
17	Kentucky	19-7	Joe B. Hall	20-8
18	Penn	20-5	Chuck Daly	21-7
19	Austin Peay	21-5	Lake Kelly	22-7
20	San Francisco	22-4	Bob Gaillard	23-5

*N.C. State was ineligible for NCAA tournament for using improper methods to recruit David Thompson.
Note: Unranked **Virginia Tech**, coached by Don DeVoe, won the NIT. The Hokies entered the tourney at 18-5 and finished with a record of 22-5.
NCAA Final Four (at The Arena, St. Louis): **Semifinals**—Memphis St. 98, Providence 85; UCLA 70, Indiana 59. **Third Place**—Indiana 97, Providence 79. **Championship**—UCLA 87, Memphis St. 66.
NIT Final Four (at Madison Square Garden): **Semifinals**—Va. Tech 74, Alabama 73; Notre Dame 78, N. Carolina 71. **Third Place**—N. Carolina 88, Alabama 69. **Championship**—Va. Tech 92, Notre Dame 91 (OT).

1975

		Before Tourns	Head Coach	Final Record
1	Indiana	29-0	Bob Knight	31-1
2	UCLA	23-3	John Wooden	28-3
3	Louisville	24-2	Denny Crum	28-3
4	Maryland	22-4	Lefty Driesell	24-5
5	Kentucky	22-4	Joe B. Hall	26-5
6	North Carolina	21-7	Dean Smith	23-8
7	Arizona St.	23-3	Ned Wulk	25-4
8	N.C. State	22-6	Norm Sloan	22-6
9	Notre Dame	18-8	Digger Phelps	19-10
10	Marquette	23-3	Al McGuire	23-4
11	Alabama	22-4	C.M. Newton	22-5
12	Cincinnati	21-5	Gale Catlett	23-6
13	Oregon St.	18-10	Ralph Miller	19-12
14	Drake	16-10	Bob Ortegel	19-10
15	Penn	23-4	Chuck Daly	23-5
16	UNLV	22-4	Jerry Tarkanian	24-5
17	Kansas St.	18-8	Jack Hartman	20-9
18	USC	18-7	Bob Boyd	18-8
19	Centenary	25-4	Larry Little	same
20	Syracuse	20-7	Roy Danforth	23-9

NCAA Final Four (at San Diego Sports Arena): **Semifinals**—Kentucky 95, Syracuse 79; UCLA 75, Louisville 74 (OT). **Third Place**—Louisville 96, Syracuse 88 (OT). **Championship**—UCLA 92, Kentucky 85.
NIT Championship (at Madison Sq. Garden): Princeton 80, Providence 69. No Top 20 teams played in NIT.
CCA Championship (at Freedom Hall, Louisville): Drake 83, Arizona 76. No.14 Drake and No.18 USC were only Top 20 teams in CCA.

1974

		Before Tourns	Head Coach	Final Record
1	N.C. State	26-1	Norm Sloan	30-1
2	UCLA	23-3	John Wooden	26-4
3	Notre Dame	24-2	Digger Phelps	26-3
4	Maryland	23-5	Lefty Driesell	same
5	Providence	26-3	Dave Gavitt	28-4
6	Vanderbilt	23-3	Roy Skinner	23-5
7	Marquette	22-4	Al McGuire	26-5
8	North Carolina	22-5	Dean Smith	22-6
9	Long Beach St.	24-2	Lute Olson	same
10	Indiana	20-5	Bob Knight	23-5
11	Alabama	22-4	C.M. Newton	same
12	Michigan	21-4	Johnny Orr	22-5
13	Pittsburgh	23-3	Buzz Ridl	25-4
14	Kansas	21-5	Ted Owens	23-7
15	USC	22-4	Bob Boyd	24-5
16	Louisville	21-6	Denny Crum	21-7
17	New Mexico	21-6	Norm Ellenberger	22-7
18	South Carolina	22-4	Frank McGuire	22-5
19	Creighton	22-6	Eddie Sutton	23-7
20	Dayton	19-7	Don Donoher	20-9

NCAA Final Four (at Greensboro, NC, Coliseum): **Semifinals**—N.C. State 80, UCLA 77 (2 OT); Marquette 64, Kansas 51. **Third Place**—UCLA 78, Kansas 61. **Championship**—N.C. State 76, Marquette 64.
NIT Final Four (at Madison Square Garden): **Semifinals**—Purdue 78, Jacksonville 63; Utah 117, Boston Col. 93. **Third Place**—Boston Col. 87, Jacksonville 77. **Championship**—Purdue 87, Utah 81.
CCA Final Four (at The Arena, St. Louis): **Semifinals**—Indiana 73, Toledo 72; USC 74, Bradley 73. **Championship**—Indiana 85, USC 60.

1976

		Before Tourns	Head Coach	Final Record
1	Indiana	27-0	Bob Knight	32-0
2	Marquette	25-1	Al McGuire	27-2
3	UNLV	28-1	Jerry Tarkanian	29-2
4	Rutgers	28-0	Tom Young	31-2
5	UCLA	24-3	Gene Bartow	28-4
6	Alabama	22-4	C.M. Newton	23-5
7	Notre Dame	22-5	Digger Phelps	23-6
8	North Carolina	25-3	Dean Smith	25-4
9	Michigan	21-6	Johnny Orr	25-7
10	Western Mich.	24-2	Eldon Miller	25-3
11	Maryland	22-6	Lefty Driesell	same
12	Cincinnati	25-5	Gale Catlett	25-6
13	Tennessee	21-5	Ray Mears	21-6
14	Missouri	24-4	Norm Stewart	26-5
15	Arizona	22-8	Fred Snowden	24-9
16	Texas Tech	24-5	Gerald Myers	25-6
17	DePaul	19-8	Ray Meyer	20-9
18	Virginia	18-11	Terry Holland	18-12
19	Centenary	22-5	Larry Little	same
20	Pepperdine	21-5	Gary Colson	22-6

NCAA Final Four (at the Spectrum, Phila.); **Semifinals**—Michigan 86, Rutgers 70; Indiana 65, UCLA 51. **Third Place**—UCLA 106, Rutgers 92. **Championship**—Indiana 86, Michigan 68.
NIT Championship (at Madison Square Garden): Kentucky 71, NC-Charlotte 67. No Top 20 teams played in NIT.

Associated Press Final Polls (Cont.)

1977

		Before Tourns	Head Coach	Final Record
1	Michigan	24-3	Johnny Orr	26-4
2	UCLA	24-3	Gene Bartow	25-4
3	Kentucky	24-3	Joe B. Hall	26-4
4	UNLV	25-2	Jerry Tarkanian	29-3
5	North Carolina	24-4	Dean Smith	28-5
6	Syracuse	25-3	Jim Boeheim	26-4
7	**Marquette**	20-7	Al McGuire	25-7
8	San Francisco	29-1	Bob Gaillard	29-2
9	Wake Forest	20-7	Carl Tacy	22-8
10	Notre Dame	21-6	Digger Phelps	22-7
11	Alabama	23-4	C.M. Newton	25-6
12	Detroit	24-3	Dick Vitale	25-4
13	Minnesota	24-3	Jim Dutcher	same*
14	Utah	22-6	Jerry Pimm	23-7
15	Tennessee	22-5	Ray Mears	22-6
16	Kansas St.	23-6	Jack Hartman	24-7
17	NC-Charlotte	25-3	Lee Rose	28-5
18	Arkansas	26-1	Eddie Sutton	26-2
19	Louisville	21-6	Denny Crum	21-7
20	VMI	25-3	Charlie Schmaus	26-4

*On probation

NCAA Final Four (at the Omni, Atlanta): **Semifinals**– Marquette 51, NC-Charlotte, 49; N. Carolina 84, UNLV 83. **Third Place**–UNLV 106, NC-Charlotte 94. **Championship**–Marquette 67, N. Carolina 59.

NIT Championship (at Madison Square Garden): St. Bonaventure 94, Houston 91. No.11 Alabama was only Top 20 team in NIT.

1979

		Before Tourns	Head Coach	Final Record
1	Indiana St.	29-0	Bill Hodges	33-1
2	UCLA	23-4	Gary Cunningham	25-5
3	**Michigan St.**	21-6	Jud Heathcote	26-6
4	Notre Dame	22-5	Digger Phelps	24-6
5	Arkansas	23-4	Eddie Sutton	25-5
6	DePaul	22-5	Ray Meyer	26-6
7	LSU	22-5	Dale Brown	23-6
8	Syracuse	25-3	Jim Boeheim	26-4
9	North Carolina	23-5	Dean Smith	23-6
10	Marquette	21-6	Hank Raymonds	22-7
11	Duke	22-7	Bill Foster	22-8
12	San Francisco	21-6	Dan Belluomini	22-7
13	Louisville	23-7	Denny Crum	24-8
14	Penn	21-5	Bob Weinhauer	25-7
15	Purdue	23-7	Lee Rose	27-8
16	Oklahoma	20-9	Dave Bliss	21-10
17	St. John's	18-10	Lou Carnesecca	21-11
18	Rutgers	21-8	Tom Young	22-9
19	Toledo	21-6	Bob Nichols	22-7
20	Iowa	20-7	Lute Olson	20-8

NCAA Final Four (at Special Events Center, Salt Lake City): **Semifinals**–Michigan St. 101, Penn 67; Indiana St. 76, DePaul 74; **Third Place**–DePaul 96, Penn 93; **Championship**–Michigan St. 75, Indiana St. 64.

NIT Championship (at Madison Square Garden): Indiana 53, Purdue 52. No. 15 Purdue was the only Top 20 team in NIT.

1978

		Before Tourns	Head Coach	Final Record
1	**Kentucky**	25-2	Joe B. Hall	30-2
2	UCLA	24-2	Gary Cunningham	25-3
3	DePaul	25-2	Ray Meyer	27-3
4	Michigan St.	23-4	Jud Heathcote	25-5
5	Arkansas	28-3	Eddie Sutton	32-3
6	Notre Dame	20-6	Digger Phelps	23-8
7	Duke	23-6	Bill Foster	27-7
8	Marquette	24-3	Hank Raymonds	24-4
9	Louisville	22-6	Denny Crum	23-7
10	Kansas	24-4	Ted Owens	24-5
11	San Francisco	22-5	Bob Gaillard	23-6
12	New Mexico	24-3	Norm Ellenberger	24-4
13	Indiana	20-7	Bob Knight	21-8
14	Utah	22-5	Jerry Pimm	23-6
15	Florida St.	23-5	Hugh Durham	23-6
16	North Carolina	23-7	Dean Smith	23-8
17	**Texas**	22-5	Abe Lemons	26-5
18	Detroit	24-3	Dave Gaines	25-4
19	Miami-OH	18-8	Darrell Hedric	19-9
20	Penn	19-7	Bob Weinhauer	20-8

NCAA Final Four (at the Checkerdome, St. Louis): **Semifinals**–Kentucky 64, Arkansas 59; Duke 90, Notre Dame 86. **Third Place**–Arkansas 71, Notre Dame 69. **Championship**–Kentucky 94, Duke 88.

NIT Championship (at Madison Square Garden): Texas 101, N.C. State 93. No. 17 Texas and No. 18 Detroit were only Top 20 teams in NIT.

1980

		Before Tourns	Head Coach	Final Record
1	DePaul	26-1	Ray Meyer	26-2
2	**Louisville**	28-3	Denny Crum	33-3
3	LSU	24-5	Dale Brown	26-6
4	Kentucky	28-5	Joe B. Hall	29-6
5	Oregon St.	26-3	Ralph Miller	26-4
6	Syracuse	25-3	Jim Boeheim	26-4
7	Indiana	20-7	Bob Knight	21-8
8	Maryland	23-6	Lefty Driesell	24-7
9	Notre Dame	20-7	Digger Phelps	20-8
10	Ohio St.	24-5	Eldon Miller	21-8
11	Georgetown	24-5	John Thompson	26-6
12	BYU	24-4	Frank Arnold	24-5
13	St. John's	24-4	Lou Carnesecca	24-5
14	Duke	22-8	Bill Foster	24-9
15	North Carolina	21-7	Dean Smith	21-8
16	Missouri	23-5	Norm Stewart	25-6
17	Weber St.	26-2	Neil McCarthy	26-3
18	Arizona St.	21-6	Ned Wulk	22-7
19	Iona	28-4	Jim Valvano	29-5
20	Purdue	19-9	Lee Rose	23-10

NCAA Final Four (at Market Square Arena, Indianapolis): **Semifinals**–Louisville 80, Iowa 72; UCLA 67, Purdue 62; **Championship**–Louisville 59, UCLA 54.

NIT Championship (at Madison Square Garden): Virginia 58, Minnesota 55. No Top 20 teams played in NIT.

1981

	Before Tourns	Head Coach	Final Record
1	DePaul 27-1	Ray Meyer	27-2
2	Oregon St. 26-1	Ralph Miller	26-2
3	Arizona St. 24-3	Ned Wulk	24-4
4	LSU 28-3	Dale Brown	31-5
5	Virginia 25-3	Terry Holland	29-4
6	North Carolina . .25-7	Dean Smith	29-8
7	Notre Dame 22-5	Digger Phelps	23-6
8	Kentucky 22-5	Joe B. Hall	22-6
9	**Indiana** 21-9	Bob Knight	26-9
10	UCLA 20-6	Larry Brown	20-7
11	Wake Forest . . .22-6	Carl Tacy	22-7
12	Louisville 21-8	Denny Crum	21-9
13	Iowa 21-6	Lute Olson	21-7
14	Utah 24-4	Jerry Pimm	25-5
15	Tennessee 20-7	Don DeVoe	21-8
16	BYU 22-6	Frank Arnold	25-7
17	Wyoming 23-5	Jim Brandenburg	24-6
18	Maryland 20-9	Lefty Driesell	21-10
19	Illinois 20-7	Lou Henson	21-8
20	Arkansas 22-7	Eddie Sutton	24-8

NCAA Final Four (at the Spectrum, Phila.): **Semifinals**–N. Carolina 78, Virginia 65; Indiana 67, LSU 49. **Third Place**–Virginia 78, LSU 74. **Championship**–Indiana 63, N. Carolina 50.
NIT Championship (at Madison Square Garden): Tulsa 86, Syracuse 84. No Top 20 teams played in NIT.

1982

	Before Tourns	Head Coach	Final Record
1	**N. Carolina** . . .27-2	Dean Smith	32-2
2	DePaul 26-1	Ray Meyer	26-2
3	Virginia 29-3	Terry Holland	30-4
4	Oregon St. 23-4	Ralph Miller	25-5
5	Missouri 26-3	Norm Stewart	27-4
6	Georgetown 26-6	John Thompson	30-7
7	Minnesota 22-5	Jim Dutcher	23-6
8	Idaho 26-2	Don Monson	27-3
9	Memphis St. 23-4	Dana Kirk	24-5
10	Tulsa 24-5	Nolan Richardson	24-6
11	Fresno St. 26-2	Boyd Grant	27-3
12	Arkansas 23-5	Eddie Sutton	23-6
13	Alabama 23-6	Wimp Sanderson	24-7
14	West Virginia . . .26-3	Gale Catlett	27-4
15	Kentucky 22-7	Joe B. Hall	22-8
16	Iowa 20-7	Lute Olson	21-8
17	Ala-Birmingham .23-5	Gene Bartow	25-6
18	Wake Forest 20-8	Carl Tacy	21-9
19	UCLA 21-6	Larry Farmer	21-6
20	Louisville 20-9	Denny Crum	23-10

NCAA Final Four (at the Superdome, New Orleans): **Semifinals**–N. Carolina 68, Houston 63; Georgetown 50, Louisville 46. **Championship**–N. Carolina 63, Georgetown 62.
NIT Championship (at Madison Square Garden): Bradley 67, Purdue 58. No Top 20 teams played in NIT.

1983

	Before Tourns	Head Coach	Final Record
1	Houston 27-2	Guy Lewis	31-3
2	Louisville 29-3	Denny Crum	32-4
3	St. John's 27-4	Lou Carnesecca	28-5
4	Virginia 27-4	Terry Holland	29-5
5	Indiana 23-5	Bob Knight	24-6
6	UNLV 28-2	Jerry Tarkanian	28-3
7	UCLA 23-5	Larry Farmer	23-6
8	North Carolina . .26-7	Dean Smith	28-8
9	Arkansas 25-3	Eddie Sutton	26-4
10	Missouri 26-7	Norm Stewart	26-8
11	Boston College . .24-6	Gary Williams	25-7
12	Kentucky 22-7	Joe B. Hall	23-8
13	Villanova 22-7	Rollie Massimino	24-8
14	Wichita St. 25-3	Gene Smithson	same*
15	Tenn-Chatt. 26-3	Murray Arnold	26-4
16	**N.C. State** 20-10	Jim Valvano	26-10
17	Memphis St. 22-7	Dana Kirk	23-8
18	Georgia 21-9	Hugh Durham	24-10
19	Oklahoma St. . . .24-6	Paul Hansen	24-7
20	Georgetown 21-9	John Thompson	22-10

*On probation

NCAA Final Four (at The Pit, Albuquerque, NM): **Semifinals**–N.C. State 67, Georgia 60; Houston 94, Louisville 81. **Championship**–N.C. State 54, Houston 52.
NIT Championship (at Madison Square Garden): Fresno St. 69, DePaul 60. No Top 20 teams played in NIT.

1984

	Before Tourns	Head Coach	Final Record
1	North Carolina . .27-2	Dean Smith	28-3
2	**Georgetown** 29-3	John Thompson	34-3
3	Kentucky 26-4	Joe B. Hall	29-5
4	DePaul 26-2	Ray Meyer	27-3
5	Houston 28-4	Guy Lewis	32-5
6	Illinois 24-4	Lou Henson	26-5
7	Oklahoma 29-4	Billy Tubbs	29-5
8	Arkansas 25-6	Eddie Sutton	25-7
9	UTEP 27-3	Don Haskins	27-4
10	Purdue 22-6	Gene Keady	22-7
11	Maryland 23-7	Lefty Driesell	24-8
12	Tulsa 27-3	Nolan Richardson	27-4
13	UNLV 27-5	Jerry Tarkanian	29-6
14	Duke 24-9	Mike Krzyzewski	24-10
15	Washington 22-6	Marv Harshman	24-7
16	Memphis St. 24-6	Dana Kirk	26-7
17	Oregon St. 22-6	Ralph Miller	22-7
18	Syracuse 22-8	Jim Boeheim	23-9
19	Wake Forest 21-8	Carl Tacy	23-9
20	Temple 25-4	John Chaney	26-5

NCAA Final Four (at the Kingdome, Seattle): **Semifinals**–Houston 49, Virginia 47 (OT); Georgetown 53, Kentucky 40. **Championship**–Georgetown 84, Houston 75.
NIT Championship (at Madison Square Garden): Michigan 83, Notre Dame 63. No Top 20 teams played in NIT.

Highest-Rated College Games on TV

The dozen highest-rated college basketball games seen on U.S. television have been NCAA tournament championship games, led by the 1979 Michigan State-Indiana State final that featured Magic Johnson and Larry Bird.

Listed below are the finalists (winning team first), date of game, TV network, and TV rating and audience share (according to Nielson Media Research).

	Date	Net	Rtg/Sh			Date	Net	Rtg/Sh
1	Michigan St.-Indiana St. . .3/26/79	NBC	24.1/38		7	N. Carolina-Georgetown .3/29/82	CBS	21.6/31
2	Villanova-Georgetown 4/1/85	CBS	23.3/33		8	UCLA-Kentucky 3/31/75	NBC	21.3/33
3	Duke-Michigan 4/6/92	CBS	22.7/35		9	Michigan-Seton Hall 4/3/89	CBS	21.3/33
4	N.C. State-Houston 4/4/83	CBS	22.3/32		10	Louisville-Duke 3/31/86	CBS	20.7/31
5	N. Carolina-Michigan 4/5/93	CBS	22.2/34		11	Indiana-N. Carolina 3/30/81	NBC	20.7/29
6	Arkansas-Duke 4/4/94	CBS	21.6/33		12	UCLA-Memphis St. 3/26/73	NBC	20.5/32

Associated Press Final Polls (Cont.)

1985

		Head Coach	Before Tourns	Final Record
1	Georgetown	John Thompson	30-2	35-3
2	Michigan	Bill Frieder	25-3	26-4
3	St. John's	Lou Carnesecca	27-3	31-4
4	Oklahoma	Billy Tubbs	28-5	31-6
5	Memphis St.	Dana Kirk	27-3	31-4
6	Georgia Tech	Bobby Cremins	24-7	27-8
7	North Carolina	Dean Smith	24-8	27-9
8	Louisiana Tech	Andy Russo	27-2	29-3
9	UNLV	Jerry Tarkanian	27-3	28-4
10	Duke	Mike Krzyzewski	22-7	23-8
11	VCU	J.D. Barnett	25-5	26-6
12	Illinois	Lou Henson	24-8	26-9
13	Kansas	Larry Brown	25-7	26-8
14	Loyola-IL	Gene Sullivan	25-5	27-6
15	Syracuse	Jim Boeheim	21-8	22-9
16	N.C. State	Jim Valvano	20-9	23-10
17	Texas Tech	Gerald Myers	23-7	23-8
18	Tulsa	Nolan Richardson	23-7	23-8
19	Georgia	Hugh Durham	21-8	22-9
20	LSU	Dale Brown	19-9	19-10

Note: Unranked **Villanova**, coached by Rollie Massimino, won the NCAAs. The Wildcats entered the tourney at 19-10 and had a final record of 25-10.

NCAA Final Four (at Rupp Arena, Lexington, KY): **Semifinals**– Georgetown 77, St. John's 59; Villanova 52, Memphis St. 45. **Championship**–Villanova 66, Georgetown 64.

NIT Championship (at Madison Square Garden): UCLA 65, Indiana 62. No Top 20 teams played in NIT.

1987

		Head Coach	Before Tourns	Final Record
1	UNLV	Jerry Tarkanian	33-1	37-2
2	North Carolina	Dean Smith	29-3	32-4
3	**Indiana**	Bob Knight	24-4	30-4
4	Georgetown	John Thompson	26-4	29-5
5	DePaul	Joey Meyer	26-2	28-3
6	Iowa	Tom Davis	27-4	30-5
7	Purdue	Gene Keady	24-4	25-5
8	Temple	John Chaney	31-3	32-4
9	Alabama	Wimp Sanderson	26-4	28-5
10	Syracuse	Jim Boeheim	26-6	31-7
11	Illinois	Lou Henson	23-7	23-8
12	Pittsburgh	Paul Evans	24-7	25-8
13	Clemson	Cliff Ellis	25-5	25-6
14	Missouri	Norm Stewart	24-9	24-10
15	UCLA	Walt Hazzard	24-6	25-7
16	New Orleans	Benny Dees	25-3	26-4
17	Duke	Mike Krzyzewski	22-8	24-9
18	Notre Dame	Digger Phelps	22-7	24-8
19	TCU	Jim Killingsworth	23-6	24-7
20	Kansas	Larry Brown	23-10	25-11

NCAA Final Four (at the Superdome, New Orleans): **Semifinals**–Syracuse 77, Providence 63; Indiana 97, UNLV 93. **Championship**–Indiana 74, Syracuse 73.

NIT Championship (at Madison Square Garden): Southern Miss. 84, La Salle 80. No Top 20 teams played in NIT.

1986

		Head Coach	Before Tourns	Final Record
1	Duke	Mike Krzyzewski	32-2	37-3
2	Kansas	Larry Brown	31-3	35-4
3	Kentucky	Eddie Sutton	29-3	32-4
4	St. John's	Lou Carnesecca	30-4	31-5
5	Michigan	Bill Frieder	27-4	28-5
6	Georgia Tech	Bobby Cremins	25-6	27-7
7	**Louisville**	Denny Crum	26-7	32-7
8	North Carolina	Dean Smith	26-5	28-6
9	Syracuse	Jim Boeheim	25-5	26-6
10	Notre Dame	Digger Phelps	23-5	23-6
11	UNLV	Jerry Tarkanian	31-4	33-5
12	Memphis St.	Dana Kirk	27-5	28-6
13	Georgetown	John Thompson	23-7	24-8
14	Bradley	Dick Versace	31-2	32-3
15	Oklahoma	Billy Tubbs	25-8	26-9
16	Indiana	Bob Knight	21-7	21-8
17	Navy	Paul Evans	27-4	30-5
18	Michigan St.	Jud Heathcote	21-7	23-8
19	Illinois	Lou Henson	21-9	22-10
20	UTEP	Don Haskins	27-5	27-6

NCAA Final Four (at Reunion Arena, Dallas): **Semifinals**–Duke 71, Kansas 67; Louisville 88, LSU 77. **Championship**–Louisville 72, Duke 69.

NIT Championship (at Madison Square Garden): Ohio St. 73, Wyoming 63. No Top 20 teams played in NIT.

1988

		Head Coach	Before Tourns	Final Record
1	Temple	John Chaney	29-1	32-2
2	Arizona	Lute Olson	31-2	35-3
3	Purdue	Gene Keady	27-3	29-4
4	Oklahoma	Billy Tubbs	30-3	35-4
5	Duke	Mike Krzyzewski	24-6	28-7
6	Kentucky	Eddie Sutton	25-5	27-6
7	North Carolina	Dean Smith	24-6	27-7
8	Pittsburgh	Paul Evans	23-6	24-7
9	Syracuse	Jim Boeheim	25-8	26-9
10	Michigan	Bill Frieder	24-7	26-8
11	Bradley	Stan Albeck	26-4	26-5
12	UNLV	Jerry Tarkanian	27-5	28-6
13	Wyoming	Benny Dees	26-5	26-6
14	N.C. State	Jim Valvano	24-7	24-8
15	Loyola-CA	Paul Westhead	27-3	28-4
16	Illinois	Lou Henson	22-9	23-10
17	Iowa	Tom Davis	22-9	24-10
18	Xavier-OH	Pete Gillen	26-3	26-4
19	BYU	Ladell Andersen	25-5	26-6
20	Kansas St.	Lon Kruger	22-8	25-9

Note: Unranked **Kansas**, coached by Larry Brown, won the NCAAs. The Jayhawks entered the tourney at 21-11 and had a final record of 27-11.

NCAA Final Four (at Kemper Arena, Kansas City): **Semifinals**–Kansas 66, Duke 59; Oklahoma 86, Arizona 78. **Championship**–Kansas 83, Oklahoma 79.

NIT Championship (at Madison Square Garden): Connecticut 72, Ohio St. 67. No Top 20 teams played in NIT.

1989

		Before Tourns	Head Coach	Final Record
1	Arizona	27-3	Lute Olson	29-4
2	Georgetown	26-4	John Thompson	29-5
3	Illinois	27-4	Lou Henson	31-5
4	Oklahoma	28-5	Billy Tubbs	30-6
5	North Carolina	27-7	Dean Smith	29-8
6	Missouri	27-7	Norm Stewart & Rich Daly*	29-8
7	Syracuse	27-7	Jim Boeheim	30-8
8	Indiana	25-7	Bob Knight	27-8
9	Duke	24-7	Mike Krzyzewski	28-8
10	**Michigan**	24-7	Bill Frieder (24-7) & Steve Fisher (6-0)	30-7
11	Seton Hall	26-6	P.J. Carlesimo	31-7
12	Louisville	22-8	Denny Crum	24-9
13	Stanford	26-6	Mike Montgomery	26-7
14	Iowa	22-9	Tom Davis	23-10
15	UNLV	26-7	Jerry Tarkanian	29-8
16	Florida St.	22-7	Pat Kennedy	22-8
17	West Virginia	25-4	Gale Catlett	26-5
18	Ball State	28-2	Rick Majerus	29-3
19	N.C. State	20-8	Jim Valvano	22-9
20	Alabama	23-7	Wimp Sanderson	23-8

NCAA Final Four (at The Kingdome, Seattle); **Semifinals**—Seton Hall 95, Duke 78; Michigan 83, Illinois 81. **Championship**—Michigan 80, Seton Hall 79 (OT). **NIT Championship** (at Madison Square Garden): St. John's 73, St. Louis 65. No Top 20 teams played in NIT. *Norm Stewart's assistant Rich Daly temporarily took over for his ailing boss (Daly coached the final 14 games of the season) but returned to his role as an assistant when Stewart recovered before the start of the following season.

1990

		Before Tourns	Head Coach	Final Record
1	Oklahoma	26-4	Billy Tubbs	27-5
2	**UNLV**	29-5	Jerry Tarkanian	35-5
3	Connecticut	28-5	Jim Calhoun	31-6
4	Michigan St.	26-5	Jud Heathcote	28-6
5	Kansas	29-4	Roy Williams	30-5
6	Syracuse	24-6	Jim Boeheim	26-7
7	Arkansas	26-4	Nolan Richardson	30-5
8	Georgetown	23-6	John Thompson	24-7
9	Georgia Tech	24-6	Bobby Cremins	28-7
10	Purdue	21-7	Gene Keady	22-8
11	Missouri	26-5	Norm Stewart	26-6
12	La Salle	29-1	Speedy Morris	30-2
13	Michigan	22-7	Steve Fisher	23-8
14	Arizona	24-6	Lute Olson	25-7
15	Duke	24-8	Mike Krzyzewski	29-9
16	Louisville	26-7	Denny Crum	27-8
17	Clemson	24-8	Cliff Ellis	26-9
18	Illinois	21-7	Lou Henson	21-8
19	LSU	22-8	Dale Brown	23-9
20	Minnesota	20-8	Clem Haskins	23-9
21	Loyola-CA	23-5	Paul Westhead	26-6
22	Oregon St.	22-6	Jim Anderson	22-7
23	Alabama	24-8	Wimp Sanderson	26-9
24	New Mexico St.	26-4	Neil McCarthy	26-5
25	Xavier-OH	26-4	Pete Gillen	28-5

NCAA Final Four (at McNichols Sports Arena, Denver): **Semifinals**—Duke 97, Arkansas 83; UNLV 90, Georgia Tech 81. **Championship**—UNLV 103, Duke 73. **NIT Championship** (at Madison Square Garden): Vanderbilt 74, St.Louis 72. No Top 25 teams played in NIT.

1991

		Before Tourns	Head Coach	Final Record
1	UNLV	30-0	Jerry Tarkanian	34-1
2	Arkansas	31-3	Nolan Richardson	34-4
3	Indiana	27-4	Bob Knight	29-5
4	North Carolina	25-5	Dean Smith	29-6
5	Ohio St.	25-3	Randy Ayers	27-4
6	**Duke**	26-7	Mike Krzyzewski	32-7
7	Syracuse	26-5	Jim Boeheim	26-6
8	Arizona	26-6	Lute Olson	28-7
9	Kentucky	22-6	Rick Pitino	same*
10	Utah	28-3	Rick Majerus	30-4
11	Nebraska	26-7	Danny Nee	26-8
12	Kansas	22-7	Roy Williams	27-8
13	Seton Hall	22-8	P.J. Carlesimo	25-9
14	Oklahoma St.	22-7	Eddie Sutton	24-8
15	New Mexico St.	23-5	Neil McCarthy	23-6
16	UCLA	23-8	Jim Harrick	23-9
17	E.Tennessee St.	28-4	Alan LaForce	28-5
18	Princeton	24-2	Pete Carril	24-3
19	Alabama	21-9	Wimp Sanderson	23-10
20	St. John's	20-8	Lou Carnesecca	23-9
21	Mississippi St.	20-8	Richard Williams	20-9
22	LSU	20-9	Dale Brown	20-10
23	Texas	22-8	Tom Penders	23-9
24	DePaul	20-8	Joey Meyer	20-9
25	Southern Miss.	21-7	M.K. Turk	21-8

*On probation

NCAA Final Four (at the Hoosier Dome, Indianapolis): **Semifinals**—Kansas 79, North Carolina 73; Duke 79, UNLV 77. **Championship**—Duke 72, Kansas 65. **NIT Championship** (at Madison Square Garden): Stanford 78, Oklahoma 72. No Top 25 teams played in NIT.

1992

		Before Tourns	Head Coach	Final Record
1	**Duke**	28-2	Mike Krzyzewski	34-2
2	Kansas	26-4	Roy Williams	27-5
3	Ohio St.	23-5	Randy Ayers	26-6
4	UCLA	25-4	Jim Harrick	28-5
5	Indiana	23-6	Bob Knight	27-7
6	Kentucky	26-6	Rick Pitino	29-7
7	UNLV	26-2	Jerry Tarkanian	same*
8	USC	23-5	George Raveling	24-6
9	Arkansas	25-7	Nolan Richardson	26-8
10	Arizona	24-6	Lute Olson	24-7
11	Oklahoma St.	26-7	Eddie Sutton	28-8
12	Cincinnati	25-4	Bob Huggins	29-5
13	Alabama	25-8	Wimp Sanderson	26-9
14	Michigan St.	21-7	Jud Heathcote	22-8
15	Michigan	20-8	Steve Fisher	25-9
16	Missouri	20-8	Norm Stewart	21-9
17	Massachusetts	28-4	John Calipari	30-5
18	North Carolina	21-9	Dean Smith	23-10
19	Seton Hall	21-8	P.J. Carlesimo	23-9
20	Florida St.	20-9	Pat Kennedy	22-10
21	Syracuse	21-9	Jim Boeheim	22-10
22	Georgetown	21-9	John Thompson	22-10
23	Oklahoma	21-8	Billy Tubbs	21-9
24	DePaul	20-8	Joey Meyer	20-9
25	LSU	20-9	Dale Brown	21-10

*On probation

NCAA Final Four (at the Metrodome, Minneapolis): **Semifinals**—Michigan 76, Cincinnati 72; Duke 81, Indiana 78. **Championship**—Duke 71, Michigan 51. **NIT Championship** (at Madison Square Garden): Virginia 81, Notre Dame 76 (OT). No Top 25 teams played in NIT.

Associated Press Final Polls (Cont.)

1993

		Before Tourns	Head Coach	Final Record
1	Indiana	28-3	Bob Knight	31-4
2	Kentucky	26-3	Rick Pitino	30-4
3	Michigan	26-4	Steve Fisher	31-5
4	**N. Carolina**	28-4	Dean Smith	34-4
5	Arizona	24-3	Lute Olson	24-4
6	Seton Hall	27-6	P.J. Carlesimo	28-7
7	Cincinnati	24-4	Bob Huggins	27-5
8	Vanderbilt	26-5	Eddie Fogler	28-6
9	Kansas	25-6	Roy Williams	29-7
10	Duke	23-7	Mike Krzyzewski	24-8
11	Florida St.	22-9	Pat Kennedy	25-10
12	Arkansas	20-8	Nolan Richardson	22-9
13	Iowa	22-8	Tom Davis	23-9
14	Massachusetts	23-6	John Calipari	24-7
15	Louisville	20-8	Denny Crum	22-9
16	Wake Forest	19-8	Dave Odom	21-9
17	New Orleans	26-3	Tim Floyd	26-4
18	Georgia Tech	19-10	Bobby Cremins	19-11
19	Utah	23-6	Rick Majerus	24-7
20	Western Ky.	24-5	Ralph Willard	26-6
21	New Mexico	24-6	Dave Bliss	24-7
22	Purdue	18-9	Gene Keady	18-10
23	Oklahoma St.	19-8	Eddie Sutton	20-9
24	New Mexico St.	25-7	Neil McCarthy	26-8
25	UNLV	21-7	Rollie Massimino	21-8

NCAA Final Four (at the Superdome, New Orleans): **Semifinals**–North Carolina 78, Kansas 68; Michigan 81, Kentucky 78 (OT). **Championship**–North Carolina 77, Michigan 71.

NIT Championship (at Madison Square Garden): Minnesota 62, Georgetown 61. No. 25 UNLV was the only Top 25 team that played in the NIT.

1994

		Before Tourns	Head Coach	Final Record
1	North Carolina	27-6	Dean Smith	28-7
2	**Arkansas**	25-3	Nolan Richardson	31-3
3	Purdue	26-4	Gene Keady	29-5
4	Connecticut	27-4	Jim Calhoun	29-5
5	Missouri	25-3	Norm Stewart	28-4
6	Duke	23-5	Mike Krzyzewski	28-6
7	Kentucky	26-6	Rick Pitino	27-7
8	Massachusetts	27-6	John Calipari	28-7
9	Arizona	25-5	Lute Olson	29-6
10	Louisville	26-5	Denny Crum	28-6
11	Michigan	21-7	Steve Fisher	24-8
12	Temple	22-7	John Chaney	23-8
13	Kansas	25-7	Roy Williams	27-8
14	Florida	25-7	Lon Kruger	29-8
15	Syracuse	21-6	Jim Boeheim	23-7
16	California	22-7	Todd Bozeman	22-8
17	UCLA	21-6	Jim Harrick	21-7
18	Indiana	19-8	Bob Knight	21-9
19	Oklahoma St.	23-9	Eddie Sutton	24-10
20	Texas	25-7	Tom Penders	26-8
21	Marquette	22-8	Kevin O'Neill	24-9
22	Nebraska	20-9	Danny Nee	20-10
23	Minnesota	20-11	Clem Haskins	21-12
24	Saint Louis	23-5	Charlie Spoonhour	23-6
25	Cincinnati	22-9	Bob Huggins	22-10

NCAA Final Four (at the Charlotte Coliseum): **Semifinals**–Arkansas 91, Arizona 82; Duke 70, Florida 65. **Championship**– Arkansas 76, Duke 72.

NIT Championship (at Madison Square Garden): Villanova 80, Vanderbilt 73. No top 25 teams played in NIT.

1995

		Before Tourns	Head Coach	Final Record
1	**UCLA**	25-2	Jim Harrick	31-2
2	Kentucky	25-4	Rick Pitino	28-5
3	Wake Forest	24-5	Dave Odom	26-6
4	North Carolina	24-5	Dean Smith	28-6
5	Kansas	23-5	Roy Williams	25-6
6	Arkansas	27-6	Nolan Richardson	32-7
7	Massachusetts	26-4	John Calipari	26-5
8	Connecticut	25-4	Jim Calhoun	28-5
9	Villanova	25-7	Steve Lappas	25-8
10	Maryland	24-7	Gary Williams	26-8
11	Michigan St.	22-5	Jud Heathcote	22-6
12	Purdue	24-6	Gene Keady	25-7
13	Virginia	22-8	Jeff Jones	25-9
14	Oklahoma St.	23-9	Eddie Sutton	27-10
15	Arizona	23-7	Lute Olson	23-8
16	Arizona St.	22-8	Bill Frieder	24-9
17	Oklahoma	23-8	Kelvin Sampson	23-9
18	Mississippi St.	20-7	Richard Williams	22-8
19	Utah	27-5	Rick Majerus	28-6
20	Alabama	22-9	David Hobbs	23-10
21	Western Ky.	26-3	Matt Kilcullen	27-4
22	Georgetown	19-9	John Thompson	21-10
23	Missouri	19-8	Norm Stewart	20-9
24	Iowa St.	22-10	Tim Floyd	23-11
25	Syracuse	19-9	Jim Boeheim	20-10

NCAA Final Four (at the Kingdome, Seattle): **Semifinals**– UCLA 74, Oklahoma St. 61; Arkansas 75, North Carolina 68. **Championship**– UCLA 89, Arkansas 78.

NIT Championship (at Madison Square Garden):Virginia Tech 65, Marquette 64 (OT). No top 25 teams played in NIT.

1996

		Before Tourns	Head Coach	Final Record
1	Massachusetts	31-1	John Calipari	35-2
2	**Kentucky**	28-2	Rick Pitino	34-2
3	Connecticut	30-2	Jim Calhoun	32-3
4	Georgetown	26-7	John Thompson	29-8
5	Kansas	26-4	Roy Williams	29-5
6	Purdue	25-5	Gene Keady	26-6
7	Cincinnati	25-4	Bob Huggins	28-5
8	Texas Tech	28-1	James Dickey	30-2
9	Wake Forest	23-5	Dave Odom	26-6
10	Villanova	25-6	Steve Lappas	26-7
11	Arizona	24-6	Lute Olson	26-7
12	Utah	25-6	Rick Majerus	27-7
13	Georgia Tech	22-11	Bobby Cremins	24-12
14	UCLA	23-7	Jim Harrick	23-8
15	Syracuse	24-8	Jim Boeheim	29-9
16	Memphis	22-7	Larry Finch	22-8
17	Iowa St.	23-8	Tim Floyd	24-9
18	Penn St.	21-6	Jerry Dunn	21-7
19	Mississippi St.	22-7	Richard Williams	26-8
20	Marquette	22-7	Mike Deane	23-8
21	Iowa	22-8	Tom Davis	23-9
22	Virginia Tech	22-5	Bill Foster	23-6
23	New Mexico	27-4	Dave Bliss	28-5
24	Louisville	20-11	Denny Crum	22-12
25	North Carolina	20-10	Dean Smith	21-11

NCAA Final Four (at the Meadowlands, E. Rutherford, N.J.): **Semifinals**– Kentucky 81, Massachusetts 74; Syracuse 77, Mississippi St. 69. **Championship**– Kentucky 76, Syracuse 67.

NIT Championship (at Madison Square Garden): Nebraska 60, St. Joseph's 56. No top 25 teams played in NIT.

1997

		Before Tourns	Head Coach	Final Record
1	Kansas	32-1	Roy Williams	34-2
2	Utah	26-3	Rick Majerus	29-4
3	Minnesota	27-3	Clem Haskins	31-4
4	North Carolina	24-6	Dean Smith	28-7
5	Kentucky	30-4	Rick Pitino	35-5
6	South Carolina	24-7	Eddie Fogler	24-8
7	UCLA	21-7	Steve Lavin	24-8
8	Duke	23-8	Mike Krzyzewski	24-9
9	Wake Forest	23-6	Dave Odom	24-7
10	Cincinnati	25-7	Bob Huggins	26-8
11	New Mexico	24-7	Dave Bliss	25-8
12	St. Joseph's	24-6	Phil Martelli	26-7
13	Xavier	22-5	Skip Prosser	23-6
14	Clemson	21-9	Rick Barnes	23-10
15	Arizona	19-9	Lute Olson	25-9
16	Charleston	28-2	John Kresse	29-3
17	Georgia	24-8	Tubby Smith	24-9
18	Iowa St.	20-8	Tim Floyd	22-9
19	Illinois	21-9	Lon Kruger	22-10
20	Villanova	23-9	Steve Lappas	24-10
21	Stanford	20-7	Mike Montgomery	22-8
22	Maryland	21-10	Gary Williams	21-11
23	Boston College	21-8	Jim O'Brien	22-9
24	Colorado	21-9	Ricardo Patton	22-10
25	Louisville	23-8	Denny Crum	26-9

NCAA Final Four (at the RCA Dome, Indianapolis): **Semifinals—** Kentucky 78, Minnesota 69; Arizona 66, North Carolina 58. **Championship—** Arizona 84, Kentucky 79 (OT).
NIT Championship (at Madison Square Garden): Michigan 82, Florida St. 72. No top 25 teams played in NIT.

1998

		Before Tourns	Head Coach	Final Record
1	North Carolina	30-3	Bill Guthridge	34-4
2	Kansas	34-3	Roy Williams	35-4
3	Duke	29-3	Mike Krzyzewski	32-4
4	Arizona	27-4	Lute Olson	30-5
5	Kentucky	29-4	Tubby Smith	35-4
6	Connecticut	29-4	Jim Calhoun	32-5
7	Utah	25-3	Rick Majerus	30-4
8	Princeton	26-1	Bill Carmody	27-2
9	Cincinnati	26-5	Bob Huggins	27-6
10	Stanford	26-4	Mike Montgomery	30-5
11	Purdue	26-7	Gene Keady	28-8
12	Michigan	24-8	Brian Ellerbe	25-9
13	Mississippi	22-6	Rob Evans	22-7
14	South Carolina	23-7	Eddie Fogler	23-8
15	TCU	27-5	Billy Tubbs	27-6
16	Michigan St.	20-7	Tom Izzo	22-8
17	Arkansas	23-8	Nolan Richardson	24-9
18	New Mexico	23-7	Dave Bliss	24-8
19	UCLA	22-8	Steve Lavin	24-9
20	Maryland	19-10	Gary Williams	21-11
21	Syracuse	24-8	Jim Boeheim	26-9
22	Illinois	22-9	Lon Kruger	23-10
23	Xavier	22-7	Skip Prosser	22-8
24	Temple	21-8	John Chaney	21-9
25	Murray St.	29-3	Mark Gottfried	29-4

NCAA Final Four (at the Alamodome, San Antonio): **Semifinals—** Kentucky 86, Stanford 85 (OT); Utah 65, North Carolina 59. **Championship—** Kentucky 78, Utah 69.
NIT Championship (at Madison Square Garden): Minnesota 79, Penn St. 72. No top 25 teams played in NIT.

1999

		Before Tourns	Head Coach	Final Record
1	Duke	32-1	Mike Krzyzewski	37-2
2	Michigan St.	29-4	Tom Izzo	33-5
3	Connecticut	28-2	Jim Calhoun	34-2
4	Auburn	27-3	Cliff Ellis	29-4
5	Maryland	26-5	Gary Williams	28-6
6	Utah	27-4	Rick Majerus	28-5
7	Stanford	25-6	Mike Montgomery	26-7
8	Kentucky	25-8	Tubby Smith	28-9
9	St. John's	25-8	Mike Jarvis	28-9
10	Miami-FL	22-6	Leonard Hamilton	23-7
11	Cincinnati	26-5	Bob Huggins	27-6
12	Arizona	22-6	Lute Olson	22-7
13	North Carolina	24-9	Bill Guthridge	24-10
14	Ohio St.	23-8	Jim O'Brien	27-9
15	UCLA	22-8	Steve Lavin	22-9
16	College of Charleston	28-2	John Kresse	28-3
17	Arkansas	22-10	Nolan Richardson	23-11
18	Wisconsin	22-9	Dick Bennett	22-10
19	Indiana	22-10	Bobby Knight	23-11
20	Tennessee	20-8	Jerry Green	21-9
21	Iowa	18-9	Tom Davis	20-10
22	Kansas	22-9	Roy Williams	23-10
23	Florida	20-8	Billy Donovan	22-9
24	NC-Charlotte	22-10	Bob Lutz	23-11
25	New Mexico	24-8	Dave Bliss	25-9

NCAA Final Four (at the Tropicana Field, St. Petersburg): **Semifinals—** Duke 68, Michigan St. 62; Connecticut 64, Ohio St. 58. **Championship—** Connecticut 77, Duke 74.
NIT Championship (at Madison Square Garden): California 61, Clemson 60. No top 25 teams played in NIT.

2000

		Before Tourns	Head Coach	Final Record
1	Duke	27-4	Mike Krzyzewski	29-5
2	Michigan St.	26-7	Tom Izzo	32-7
3	Stanford	26-3	Mike Montgomery	27-4
4	Arizona	26-6	Lute Olson	27-7
5	Temple	26-5	John Chaney	27-6
6	Iowa St.	29-4	Larry Eustachy	32-5
7	Cincinnati	28-3	Bob Huggins	29-4
8	Ohio St.	22-6	Jim O'Brien	23-7
9	St. John's	24-7	Mike Jarvis	25-8
10	LSU	26-5	John Brady	28-6
11	Tennessee	24-6	Jerry Green	26-7
12	Oklahoma	26-6	Kelvin Sampson	27-7
13	Florida	24-7	Billy Donovan	29-8
14	Oklahoma St.	24-6	Eddie Sutton	27-7
15	Texas	23-8	Rick Barnes	24-9
16	Syracuse	26-6	Jim Boeheim	26-6
17	Maryland	24-9	Gary Williams	25-10
18	Tulsa	29-4	Bill Self	32-5
19	Kentucky	22-9	Tubby Smith	23-10
20	Connecticut	24-9	Jim Calhoun	25-10
21	Illinois	21-9	Lon Kruger	22-10
22	Indiana	20-8	Bobby Knight	20-9
23	Miami-FL	21-10	Leonard Hamilton	23-11
24	Auburn	23-9	Cliff Ellis	24-10
25	Purdue	21-9	Gene Keady	24-10

NCAA Final Four (at the RCA Dome, Indianapolis): **Semifinals—** Michigan St. 53, Wisconsin 41; Florida 71, North Carolina 59. **Championship—** Michigan St. 89, Florida 76.
NIT Championship (at Madison Square Garden): Wake Forest 71, Notre Dame 61. No top 25 teams played in NIT.

Associated Press Final Polls (Cont.)

2001

		Before Tourns	Head Coach	Final Record
1	**Duke**	29-4	Mike Krzyzewski	35-4
2	Stanford	28-2	Mike Montgomery	31-3
3	Michigan St.	24-4	Tom Izzo	28-5
4	Illinois	24-7	Bill Self	27-8
5	Arizona	23-7	Lute Olson	28-8
6	North Carolina	25-6	Matt Doherty	26-7
7	Boston College	26-4	Al Skinner	27-5
8	Florida	23-6	Billy Donovan	24-7
9	Kentucky	22-9	Tubby Smith	24-10
10	Iowa St.	25-5	Larry Eustachy	25-6
11	Maryland	21-10	Gary Williams	25-11
12	Kansas	24-6	Roy Williams	26-7
13	Oklahoma	26-6	Kelvin Sampson	26-7
14	Mississippi	25-7	Rod Barnes	27-8
15	UCLA	21-8	Steve Lavin	23-9
16	Virginia	20-8	Pete Gillen	20-9
17	Syracuse	24-8	Jim Boeheim	25-9
18	Texas	25-8	Rick Barnes	25-9
19	Notre Dame	19-9	Mike Brey	20-10
20	Indiana	21-12	Mike Davis	21-13
21	Georgetown	23-7	Craig Esherick	25-8
22	St. Joseph's	25-6	Phil Martelli	26-7
23	Wake Forest	19-10	Dave Odom	19-11
24	Iowa	22-11	Steve Alford	23-12
25	Wisconsin	18-10	Dick Bennett (2-1) & Brad Soderberg (16-10)	18-11

NCAA Final Four (at the HHH Metrodome, Minneapolis): **Semifinals**–Duke 95, Maryland 84; Arizona 80, Michigan St. 61. **Championship**–Duke 82, Arizona 72.
NIT Championship (at Madison Square Garden): Tulsa 79, Alabama 60. No top 25 teams played in NIT.

2002

		Before Tourns	Head Coach	Final Record
1	Duke	29-3	Mike Krzyzewski	32-4
2	Kansas	29-3	Roy Williams	33-4
3	Oklahoma	27-4	Kelvin Sampson	31-5
4	**Maryland**	26-4	Gary Williams	32-4
5	Cincinnati	30-3	Bob Huggins	31-4
6	Gonzaga	29-3	Mark Few	29-4
7	Arizona	22-9	Lute Olson	24-10
8	Alabama	26-7	Mark Gottfried	27-8
9	Pittsburgh	27-5	Ben Howland	29-6
10	Connecticut	24-6	Jim Calhoun	27-7
11	Oregon	23-8	Ernie Kent	26-9
12	Marquette	26-6	Tom Crean	26-7
13	Illinois	24-8	Bill Self	26-9
14	Ohio St.	23-7	Jim O'Brien	24-8
15	Florida	22-8	Billy Donovan	22-9
16	Kentucky	20-9	Tubby Smith	22-10
17	Mississippi St.	26-7	Rick Stansbury	27-8
18	USC	22-9	Henry Bibby	22-10
19	Western Ky.	28-3	Dennis Felton	28-4
20	Oklahoma St.	23-8	Eddie Sutton	23-9
21	Miami-FL	24-7	Perry Clark	24-8
22	Xavier	25-5	Thad Matta	26-6
23	Georgia	21-9	Jim Harrick	22-10
24	Stanford	19-9	Mike Montgomery	20-10
25	Hawaii	27-5	Riley Wallace	27-6

NCAA Final Four (at the Georgia Dome, Atlanta): **Semifinals**–Maryland 97, Kansas 88; Indiana 73, Oklahoma 64. **Championship**–Maryland 64, Indiana 52.
NIT Championship (at Madison Square Garden): Memphis 72, South Carolina 62. No top 25 teams played in NIT.

2003

		Before Tourns	Head Coach	Final Record
1	Kentucky	29-3	Tubby Smith	32-4
2	Arizona	25-3	Lute Olson	28-4
3	Oklahoma	24-6	Kelvin Sampson	27-7
4	Pittsburgh	26-4	Ben Howland	28-5
5	Texas	22-6	Rick Barnes	26-7
6	Kansas	25-7	Roy Williams	30-8
7	Duke	24-6	Mike Krzyzewski	26-7
8	Wake Forest	24-5	Skip Prosser	25-6
9	Marquette	23-5	Tom Crean	27-6
10	Florida	24-7	Billy Donovan	25-8
11	Illinois	24-6	Bill Self	25-7
12	Xavier	25-5	Thad Matta	26-6
13	**Syracuse**	24-5	Jim Boeheim	30-5
14	Louisville	24-6	Rick Pitino	25-7
15	Creighton	29-4	Dana Altman	29-5
16	Dayton	25-5	Oliver Purnell	25-6
17	Maryland	19-9	Gary Williams	21-10
18	Stanford	23-8	Mike Montgomery	23-9
19	Memphis	23-6	John Calipari	23-7
20	Mississippi St.	21-9	Rick Stansbury	21-10
21	Wisconsin	22-7	Bo Ryan	24-8
22	Notre Dame	22-9	Mike Brey	24-10
23	Connecticut	21-9	Jim Calhoun	23-10
24	Missouri	21-10	Quin Snyder	22-11
25	Georgia	19-8	Jim Harrick	same*

*Georgia chose not to participate in any postseason tournaments due to an investigation into academic fraud.
NCAA Final Four (at the Superdome, New Orleans): **Semifinals**–Syracuse 95, Texas 84; Kansas 94, Marquette 61. **Championship**–Syracuse 81, Kansas 78.
NIT Championship (at Madison Square Garden): St. John's 70, Georgetown 67. No top 25 teams played in NIT.

2004

		Before Tourns	Head Coach	Final Record
1	Stanford	29-1	Mike Montgomery	30-2
2	Kentucky	26-4	Tubby Smith	27-5
3	Gonzaga	27-2	Mark Few	28-3
4	Oklahoma St.	27-3	Eddie Sutton	31-4
5	St. Joseph's	27-1	Phil Martelli	30-2
6	Duke	27-5	Mike Krzyzewski	31-6
7	Connecticut	27-6	Jim Calhoun	33-6
8	Mississippi St.	25-3	Rick Stansbury	26-4
9	Pittsburgh	29-4	Jamie Dixon	31-5
10	Wisconsin	23-6	Bo Ryan	25-7
11	Cincinnati	24-6	Bob Huggins	25-7
12	Texas	23-7	Rick Barnes	25-8
13	Illinois	24-6	Bruce Weber	26-7
14	Georgia Tech	23-9	Paul Hewitt	28-10
15	N.C. State	20-9	Herb Sendek	21-10
16	Kansas	21-8	Bill Self	24-9
17	Wake Forest	19-9	Skip Prosser	21-10
18	North Carolina	18-10	Roy Williams	19-11
19	Maryland	19-11	Gary Williams	20-12
20	Syracuse	21-7	Jim Boeheim	23-8
21	Providence	20-8	Tim Welsh	20-9
22	Arizona	20-9	Lute Olson	20-10
23	So. Illinois	25-4	Matt Painter	25-5
24	Memphis	21-7	John Calipari	22-8
25	Boston College	23-9	Al Skinner	24-10
	Utah St.	25-3	Stew Morrill	25-4

NCAA Final Four (at the Alamodome, San Antonio): **Semifinals**–Georgia Tech 67, Oklahoma St. 65; Connecticut 79, Duke 78. **Championship**–Connecticut 82, Georgia Tech 73.
NIT Championship (at Madison Square Garden): Michigan 62, Rutgers 55. No. 25 Utah St. was the only Top 25 team that played in the NIT.

2005

		Head Coach	Before Tourns	Final Record
1	Illinois	Bruce Weber	32-1	37-2
2	North Carolina	Roy Williams	27-4	33-4
3	Duke	Mike Krzyzewski	25-5	27-6
4	Louisville	Rick Pitino	29-4	33-5
5	Wake Forest	Skip Prosser	26-5	27-6
6	Oklahoma St.	Eddie Sutton	24-6	26-7
7	Kentucky	Tubby Smith	25-5	28-6
8	Washington	Lorenzo Romar	27-5	29-6
9	Arizona	Lute Olson	27-6	30-7
10	Gonzaga	Mark Few	25-4	26-5
11	Syracuse	Jim Boeheim	27-6	27-7
12	Kansas	Bill Self	23-6	23-7
13	Connecticut	Jim Calhoun	22-7	23-8
14	Boston College	Al Skinner	24-4	25-5
15	Michigan St.	Tom Izzo	22-6	26-7
16	Florida	Billy Donovan	23-7	24-8
17	Oklahoma	Kelvin Sampson	24-7	25-8
18	Utah	Ray Giacoletti	27-5	29-6
19	Villanova	Jay Wright	22-7	24-8
20	Wisconsin	Bo Ryan	22-8	25-9
21	Alabama	Mark Gottfried	24-7	24-8
22	Pacific	Bob Thomason	26-3	27-4
23	Cincinnati	Bob Huggins	24-7	25-8
24	Texas Tech	Bob Knight	20-10	22-11
25	Georgia Tech	Paul Hewitt	19-11	20-12

NCAA Final Four (at the Edward Jones Dome, St. Louis): **Semifinals**—Illinois 72, Louisville 57; North Carolina 87, Michigan St. 71. **Championship**—North Carolina 75, Illinois 70.

NIT Championship (at Madison Square Garden): South Carolina 60, St. Joseph's 57. No top 25 teams played in NIT.

2006

		Head Coach	Before Tourns	Final Record
1	Duke	Mike Krzyzewski	30-3	32-4
2	Connecticut	Jim Calhoun	27-3	30-4
3	Villanova	Jay Wright	25-4	28-5
4	Memphis	John Calipari	30-3	33-4
5	Gonzaga	Mark Few	27-3	29-4
6	Ohio St.	Thad Matta	25-5	26-6
7	Boston College	Al Skinner	26-7	28-8
	UCLA	Ben Howland	27-6	32-7
9	Texas	Rick Barnes	27-6	30-7
10	North Carolina	Roy Williams	27-4	33-4
11	Florida	Billy Donovan	23-7	24-8
12	Kansas	Bill Self	25-7	25-8
13	Illinois	Bruce Weber	25-6	26-7
14	Geo. Washington	Karl Hobbs	26-2	27-3
15	Iowa	Steve Alford	25-8	25-9
16	Pittsburgh	Jamie Dixon	24-7	25-8
17	Washington	Lorenzo Romar	24-6	26-7
18	Tennessee	Bruce Pearl	21-7	22-8
19	LSU	John Brady	23-8	27-9
20	Nevada	Mark Fox	27-5	27-6
21	Syracuse	Jim Boeheim	23-11	23-12
22	West Virginia	John Beilein	20-10	22-11
23	Georgetown	John Thompson III	21-9	23-10
24	Oklahoma	Kelvin Sampson	20-8	20-9
25	UAB	Mike Anderson	24-6	24-7

NCAA Final Four (at the RCA Dome, Indianapolis): **Semifinals**—Florida 73, George Mason 58; UCLA 59, LSU 45. **Championship**—Florida 73, UCLA 57.

NIT Championship (at Madison Square Garden): South Carolina 76, Michigan 64. No top 25 teams played in NIT.

2007

		Head Coach	Before Tourns	Final Record
1	Ohio St.	Thad Matta	27-3	35-4
2	Kansas	Bill Self	30-4	33-5
3	Wisconsin	Bo Ryan	29-5	30-6
4	UCLA	Ben Howland	26-5	30-6
5	Memphis	John Calipari	30-3	33-4
6	Florida	Billy Donovan	29-5	35-5
7	Texas A&M	Billy Gillispie	25-6	26-7
8	North Carolina	Roy Williams	28-6	31-7
9	Georgetown	John Thompson III	26-6	30-7
10	Nevada	Mark Fox	28-4	29-5
11	Washington St.	Tony Bennett	25-7	26-8
12	Louisville	Rick Pitino	23-9	24-10
13	Pittsburgh	Jamie Dixon	25-6	27-7
14	Southern Illinois	Chris Lowery	27-6	29-7
15	Texas	Rick Barnes	24-9	25-10
16	Oregon	Ernie Kent	26-7	29-8
17	Maryland	Gary Williams	24-8	25-9
18	Marquette	Tom Crean	24-9	24-10
19	Butler	Todd Lickliter	27-6	29-7
20	Notre Dame	Mike Brey	24-7	24-8
21	Duke	Mike Krzyzewski	22-10	22-11
22	Tennessee	Bruce Pearl	22-10	24-11
23	Brigham Young	Dave Rose	25-8	25-9
24	Winthrop	Gregg Marshall	28-4	29-5
25	UNLV	Lon Kruger	28-6	30-7

NCAA Final Four (at the Georgia Dome, Atlanta): **Semifinals**—Ohio St. 67, Georgetown 60; Florida 76, UCLA 66. **Championship**—Florida 84, Ohio St. 75.

NIT Championship (at Madison Square Garden): West Virginia 78, Clemson 73. No top 25 teams played in NIT

The Red Cross Benefit Games, 1943-45

For three seasons during World War II, the NCAA and NIT champions met in a benefit game at Madison Square Garden in New York to raise money for the Red Cross. The NCAA champs won all three games.

Year	Winner	Score	Loser
1943	Wyoming (NCAA)	52-47	St. John's (NIT)
1944	Utah (NCAA)	43-36	St. John's (NIT)
1945	Oklahoma A&M (NCAA)	52-44	DePaul (NIT)

Collegiate Commissioners Association Tournament

The Collegiate Commissioners Association staged an eight-team tournament for teams that didn't make the NCAA tournament in 1974 and '75.

Most Valuable Players: 1974–Kent Benson, Indiana; 1975–Bob Elliot, Arizona.

Year	Winner	Score	Loser	Site
1974	Indiana	85-60	USC	St. Louis
1975	Drake	83-76	Arizona	Louisville

Annual NCAA Division I Leaders
Scoring

The NCAA did not begin keeping individual scoring records until the 1947-48 season. All averages include postseason games where applicable.

Multiple winners: Pete Maravich and Oscar Robertson (3); Keydren Clark, Darrell Floyd, Charles Jones, Harry Kelly, Frank Selvy and Freeman Williams (2).

Year	Player	Gm	Pts	Avg
1948	Murray Wier, Iowa	19	399	21.0
1949	Tony Lavelli, Yale	30	671	22.4
1950	Paul Arizin, Villanova	29	735	25.3
1951	Bill Mlkvy, Temple	25	731	29.2
1952	Clyde Lovellette, Kansas	28	795	28.4
1953	Frank Selvy, Furman	25	738	29.5
1954	Frank Selvy, Furman	29	1209	41.7
1955	Darrell Floyd, Furman	25	897	35.9
1956	Darrell Floyd, Furman	28	946	33.8
1957	Grady Wallace, S. Carolina	29	906	31.2
1958	Oscar Robertson, Cincinnati	28	984	35.1
1959	Oscar Robertson, Cincinnati	30	978	32.6
1960	Oscar Robertson, Cincinnati	30	1011	33.7
1961	Frank Burgess, Gonzaga	26	842	32.4
1962	Billy McGill, Utah	26	1009	38.8
1963	Nick Werkman, Seton Hall	22	650	29.5
1964	Howie Komives, Bowling Green	23	844	36.7
1965	Rick Barry, Miami-FL	26	973	37.4
1966	Dave Schellhase, Purdue	24	781	32.5
1967	Jimmy Walker, Providence	28	851	30.4
1968	Pete Maravich, LSU	26	1138	43.8
1969	Pete Maravich, LSU	26	1148	44.2
1970	Pete Maravich, LSU	31	1381	44.5
1971	Johnny Neumann, Ole Miss	23	923	40.1
1972	Dwight Lamar, SW La	29	1054	36.3
1973	Bird Averitt, Pepperdine	25	848	33.9
1974	Larry Fogle, Canisius	25	835	33.4
1975	Bob McCurdy, Richmond	26	855	32.9
1976	Marshall Rodgers, Texas-Pan Am	25	919	36.8
1977	Freeman Williams, Portland St.	26	1010	38.8
1978	Freeman Williams, Portland St.	27	969	35.9
1979	Lawrence Butler, Idaho St	27	812	30.1
1980	Tony Murphy, Southern-BR	29	932	32.1
1981	Zam Fredrick, S. Carolina	27	781	28.9
1982	Harry Kelly, Texas Southern	29	862	29.7
1983	Harry Kelly, Texas Southern	29	835	28.8
1984	Joe Jakubick, Akron	27	814	30.1
1985	Xavier McDaniel, Wichita St	31	844	27.2
1986	Terrance Bailey, Wagner	29	854	29.4
1987	Kevin Houston, Army	29	953	32.9
1988	Hersey Hawkins, Bradley	31	1125	36.3
1989	Hank Gathers, Loyola-CA	31	1015	32.7
1990	Bo Kimble, Loyola-CA	32	1131	35.3
1991	Kevin Bradshaw, US Int'l	28	1054	37.6
1992	Brett Roberts, Morehead St	29	815	28.1
1993	Greg Guy, Texas-Pan Am	19	556	29.3
1994	Glenn Robinson, Purdue	34	1030	30.3
1995	Kurt Thomas, TCU	27	781	28.9
1996	Kevin Granger, Texas Southern	24	648	27.0
1997	Charles Jones, LIU-Brooklyn	30	903	30.1
1998	Charles Jones, LIU-Brooklyn	30	869	29.0
1999	Alvin Young, Niagara	29	728	25.1
2000	Courtney Alexander, Fresno St.	27	669	24.8
2001	Ronnie McCollum, Centenary	27	787	29.1
2002	Jason Conley, VMI	29	820	29.3
2003	Ruben Douglas, New Mexico	28	783	28.0
2004	Keydren Clark, St. Peter's	29	775	26.7
2005	Keydren Clark, St. Peter's	28	721	25.8
2006	Adam Morrison, Gonzaga	33	926	28.1
2007	Reggie Williams, VMI	33	928	28.1

Rebounds

The NCAA did not begin keeping individual rebounding records until the 1950-51 season. From 1956-62, the championship was decided on highest percentage of recoveries out of all rebounds made by both teams in all games. All averages include postseason games where applicable.

Multiple winners: Paul Millsap (3); Artis Gilmore, Jerry Lucas, Xavier McDaniel, Kermit Washington and Leroy Wright (2).

Year	Player	Gm	No	Avg
1951	Ernie Beck, Penn	27	556	20.6
1952	Bill Hannon, Army	17	355	20.9
1953	Ed Conlin, Fordham	26	612	23.5
1954	Art Quimby, Connecticut	26	588	22.6
1955	Charlie Slack, Marshall	21	538	25.6
1956	Joe Holup, G. Washington	26	604	25.6
1957	Elgin Baylor, Seattle	25	508	23.5
1958	Alex Ellis, Niagara	25	536	26.2
1959	Leroy Wright, Pacific	26	652	23.8
1960	Leroy Wright, Pacific	17	380	23.4
1961	Jerry Lucas, Ohio St.	27	470	19.8
1962	Jerry Lucas, Ohio St.	28	499	21.1
1963	Paul Silas, Creighton	27	557	20.6
1964	Bob Pelkington, Xavier-OH	26	567	21.8
1965	Toby Kimball, Connecticut	23	483	21.0
1966	Jim Ware, Oklahoma City	29	607	20.9
1967	Dick Cunningham, Murray St.	22	479	21.8
1968	Neal Walk, Florida	25	494	19.8
1969	Spencer Haywood, Detroit	22	472	21.5
1970	Artis Gilmore, Jacksonville	28	621	22.2
1971	Artis Gilmore, Jacksonville	26	603	23.2
1972	Kermit Washington, American	23	455	19.8
1973	Kermit Washington, American	25	439	20.0
1974	Marvin Barnes, Providence	32	597	18.7
1975	John Irving, Hofstra	21	323	15.4
1976	Sam Pellom, Buffalo	26	420	16.2
1977	Glenn Mosley, Seton Hall	29	473	16.3
1978	Ken Williams, N. Texas	28	411	14.7
1979	Monti Davis, Tennessee St.	26	421	16.2
1980	Larry Smith, Alcorn State	26	392	15.1
1981	Darryl Watson, Miss. Valley St.	27	379	14.0
1982	LaSalle Thompson, Texas	27	365	13.5
1983	Xavier McDaniel, Wichita St.	28	403	14.4
1984	Akeem Olajuwon, Houston	37	500	13.5
1985	Xavier McDaniel, Wichita St.	31	460	14.8
1986	David Robinson, Navy	35	455	13.0
1987	Jerome Lane, Pittsburgh	33	444	13.5
1988	Kenny Miller, Loyola-IL	29	395	13.6
1989	Hank Gathers, Loyola-CA	31	426	13.7
1990	Anthony Bonner, St. Louis	33	456	13.8
1991	Shaquille O'Neal, LSU	28	411	14.7
1992	Popeye Jones, Murray St.	30	431	14.4
1993	Warren Kidd, Mid. Tenn. St.	26	386	14.8
1994	Jerome Lambert, Baylor	24	355	14.8
1995	Kurt Thomas, TCU	27	393	14.6
1996	Marcus Mann, Miss. Valley St.	29	394	13.6
1997	Tim Duncan, Wake Forest	31	457	14.7
1998	Ryan Perryman, Dayton	33	412	12.5
1999	Ian McGinnis, Dartmouth	26	317	12.2
2000	Darren Phillip, Fairfield	29	405	14.0
2001	Chris Marcus, Western Ky.	31	374	12.1
2002	Jeremy Bishop, Quinnipiac	29	347	12.0
2003	Brandon Hunter, Ohio	30	378	12.6
2004	Paul Millsap, Louisiana Tech	30	374	12.5
2005	Paul Millsap, Louisiana Tech	29	360	12.4
2006	Paul Millsap, Louisiana Tech	33	438	13.3
2007	Rashad Jones-Jennings, Ark-LR	30	392	13.1

Assists

The NCAA did not begin keeping individual assist records until the 1983-84 season. All averages include postseason games where applicable.

Multiple winner: Avery Johnson and Jared Jordan (2).

Year		Gm	No	Avg
1984	Craig Lathen, IL-Chicago	.29	274	9.45
1985	Rob Weingard, Hofstra	.24	228	9.50
1986	Mark Jackson, St. John's	.36	328	9.11
1987	Avery Johnson, Southern-BR	.31	333	10.74
1988	Avery Johnson, Southern-BR	.30	399	13.30
1989	Glenn Williams, Holy Cross	.28	278	9.93
1990	Todd Lehmann, Drexel	.28	260	9.29
1991	Chris Corchiani, N.C. State	.31	299	9.65
1992	Van Usher, Tennessee Tech	.29	254	8.76
1993	Sam Crawford, N. Mexico St	.34	310	9.12
1994	Jason Kidd, California	.30	272	9.06
1995	Nelson Haggerty, Baylor	.28	284	10.14
1996	Raimonds Miglinieks, UC-Irvine	.27	230	8.52
1997	Kenny Mitchell, Dartmouth	.26	203	7.81
1998	Ahlon Lewis, Arizona St.	.32	294	9.19
1999	Doug Gottlieb, Oklahoma St.	.34	299	8.79
2000	Mark Dickel, UNLV	.31	280	9.03
2001	Markus Carr, CS-Northridge	.32	286	8.94
2002	T.J. Ford, Texas	.33	273	8.27
2003	Martell Bailey, Illinois-Chicago	.30	244	8.13
2004	Greg Day, Troy St.	.31	256	8.26
2005	Damitrius Coleman, Mercer	.28	224	8.00
	& Will Funn, Portland St.	.28	224	8.00
2006	Jared Jordan, Marist	.29	247	8.52
2007	Jared Jordan, Marist	.33	286	8.67

Blocked Shots

The NCAA did not begin keeping individual blocked shots records until the 1985-86 season. All averages include postseason games where applicable.

Multiple winners: Keith Closs, David Robinson and Tarvis Williams (2).

Year		Gm	No	Avg
1986	David Robinson, Navy	.35	207	5.91
1987	David Robinson, Navy	.32	144	4.50
1988	Rodney Blake, St. Joe's-PA	.29	116	4.00
1989	Alonzo Mourning, G'town	.34	169	4.97
1990	Kenny Green, Rhode Island	.26	124	4.77
1991	Shawn Bradley, BYU	.34	177	5.21
1992	Shaquille O'Neal, LSU	.30	157	5.23
1993	Theo Ratliff, Wyoming	.28	124	4.43
1994	Grady Livingston, Howard	.26	115	4.42
1995	Keith Closs, Cen. Conn. St.	.26	139	5.35
1996	Keith Closs, Cen. Conn. St.	.28	178	6.36
1997	Adonal Foyle, Colgate	.28	180	6.43
1998	Jerome James, Florida A&M	.27	125	4.63
1999	Tarvis Williams, Hampton	.27	135	5.00
2000	Ken Johnson, Ohio St.	.30	161	5.37
2001	Tarvis Williams, Hampton	.32	147	4.59
2002	Wojciech Myrda, La-Monroe	.32	172	5.38
2003	Emeka Okafor, Connecticut	.33	156	4.73
2004	Anwar Ferguson, Houston	.27	111	4.11
2005	Deng Gai, Fairfield	.30	165	5.50
2006	Shawn James, Northeastern	.30	196	6.53
2007	Mickell Gladness, Alabama A&M	.30	188	6.27

All-Time NCAA Division I Individual Leaders

Through 2006-07; includes regular season and tournament games; **Last** column indicates final year played.

CAREER

Scoring

	Points	Yrs	Last	Gm	Pts
1	Pete Maravich, LSU	.3	1970	83	3667
2	Freeman Williams, Port. St.	.4	1978	106	3249
3	Lionel Simmons, La Salle	.4	1990	131	3217
4	Alphonso Ford, Miss. Val. St.	.4	1993	109	3165
5	Harry Kelly, Texas Southern	.4	1983	110	3066
6	Hersey Hawkins, Bradley	.4	1988	125	3008
7	Oscar Robertson, Cincinnati	.3	1960	88	2973
8	Danny Manning, Kansas	.4	1988	147	2951
9	Alfredrick Hughes, Loyola-IL	.4	1985	120	2914
10	Elvin Hayes, Houston	.3	1968	93	2884
11	Larry Bird, Indiana St.	.3	1979	94	2850
12	Otis Birdsong, Houston	.4	1977	116	2832
13	Kevin Bradshaw, Beth-Cook/US Int'l	.4	1991	111	2804
14	Allan Houston, Tennessee	.4	1993	128	2801
15	J.J. Redick, Duke	.4	2006	139	2769
16	Hank Gathers, USC/Loyola-CA	.4	1990	117	2723
17	Reggie Lewis, Northeastern	.4	1987	122	2708
18	Daren Queenan, Lehigh	.4	1988	118	2703
19	Byron Larkin, Xavier-OH	.4	1988	121	2696
20	David Robinson, Navy	.4	1987	127	2669

	Average	Yrs	Last	Pts	Avg
1	Pete Maravich, LSU	.3	1970	3667	44.2
2	Austin Carr, Notre Dame	.3	1971	2560	34.6
3	Oscar Robertson, Cinn	.3	1960	2973	33.8
4	Calvin Murphy, Niagara	.3	1970	2548	33.1
5	Dwight Lamar, SW La	.2	1973	1862	32.7
6	Frank Selvy, Furman	.3	1954	2538	32.5
7	Rick Mount, Purdue	.3	1970	2323	32.3
8	Darrell Floyd, Furman	.3	1956	2281	32.1
9	Nick Werkman, Seton Hall	.3	1964	2273	32.0
10	Willie Humes, Idaho St.	.2	1971	1510	31.5
11	William Averitt, Pepperdine	.2	1973	1541	31.4
12	Elgin Baylor, Idaho/Seattle	.3	1958	2500	31.3
13	Elvin Hayes, Houston	.3	1968	2884	31.0
14	Freeman Williams, Port. St.	.4	1978	3249	30.7
15	Larry Bird, Indiana St.	.3	1979	2850	30.3
16	Bill Bradley, Princeton	.3	1965	2503	30.2
17	Rich Fuqua, Oral Roberts	.2	1973	1617	29.9
18	Wilt Chamberlain, Kansas	.2	1958	1433	29.9
19	Rick Barry, Miami-FL	.3	1965	2298	29.8
20	Doug Collins, Illinois St.	.3	1973	2240	29.1

	Field Goal Pct.	Yrs	Last	FG	FGA	Pct
1	Steve Johnson, Ore. St.	.4	1981	828	1222	.678
2	Michael Bradley, Kentucky/					
	Villanova	.3	2001	441	651	.677
3	Murray Brown, Fla. St.	.4	1980	566	847	.668
4	Lee Campbell, M.Tenn St./					
	SW Mo.St.	.3	1990	411	618	.665
5	Warren Kidd, M.Tenn.St.	.3	1993	496	747	.664
6	Todd MacCulloch, Wash.	.4	1999	702	1058	.664
7	Joe Senser, West Chester	.4	1979	476	719	.662
8	Kevin Magee, UC-Irvine	.2	1982	552	841	.656
9	Orlando Phillips, Pepperdine	2	1983	404	618	.654
10	Bill Walton, UCLA	.3	1974	747	1147	.651

Note: minimum 400 FGs made and an average of four per game.

	Free Throw Pct.	Yrs	Last	FT	FTA	Pct
1	Gary Buchanan, Villanova	.4	2003	324	355	.913
2	J.J. Redick, Duke	.4	2006	662	726	.912
3	Greg Starrick, Ky/So.Ill	.4	1972	341	375	.909
4	Jack Moore, Nebraska	.4	1982	446	495	.901
5	Steve Henson, Kansas St.	.4	1990	361	401	.900
6	Steve Alford, Indiana	.4	1987	535	596	.898
7	Bob Lloyd, Rutgers	.3	1967	543	605	.898
8	Jim Barton, Dartmouth	.4	1989	394	440	.895
9	Tommy Boyer, Arkansas	.3	1963	315	353	.892
10	Kyle Korver, Creighton	.4	2003	312	350	.891

Note: minimum 300 FTs made and an average of 2.5 per game.

All-Time NCAA Division I Individual Leaders (Cont.)
Rebounds

	Total (before 1973)	Yrs	Last	Gm	No
1	Tom Gola, La Salle	4	1955	118	2201
2	Joe Holup, G. Washington	4	1956	104	2030
3	Charlie Slack, Marshall	4	1956	88	1916
4	Ed Conlin, Fordham	4	1955	102	1884
5	Dickie Hemric, Wake Forest	4	1955	104	1802
6	Paul Silas, Creighton	3	1964	81	1751
7	Art Quimby, Connecticut	4	1955	80	1716
8	Jerry Harper, Alabama	4	1956	93	1688
9	Jeff Cohen, Wm. & Mary	4	1961	103	1679
10	Steve Hamilton, Morehead St.	4	1958	102	1675

	Total (since 1973)	Yrs	Last	Gm	No
1	Tim Duncan, Wake Forest	4	1997	128	1570
2	Derrick Coleman, Syracuse	4	1990	143	1537
3	Malik Rose, Drexel	4	1996	120	1514
4	Ralph Sampson, Virginia	4	1983	132	1511
5	Pete Padgett, Nevada-Reno	4	1976	104	1464
6	Lionel Simmons, La Salle	4	1990	131	1429
7	Anthony Bonner, St. Louis	4	1990	133	1424
8	Tyrone Hill, Xavier-OH	4	1990	126	1380
9	Popeye Jones, Murray St.	4	1992	123	1374
10	Michael Brooks, La Salle	4	1980	114	1372

	Average (before 1973)	Yrs	Last	Gm	Avg
1	Artis Gilmore, Jacksonville	2	1971	1224	22.7
2	Charlie Slack, Marshall	4	1956	1916	21.8
3	Paul Silas, Creighton	3	1964	1751	21.6
4	Leroy Wright, Pacific	3	1960	1442	21.5
5	Art Quimby, Connecticut	4	1955	1716	21.5

Note: minimum 800 rebounds.

	Average (since 1973)	Yrs	Last	Gm	Avg
1	Glenn Mosley, Seton Hall	4	1977	1263	15.2
2	Bill Campion, Manhattan	3	1975	1070	14.2
3	Pete Padgett, Nevada-Reno	4	1976	1464	14.1
4	Bob Warner, Maine	4	1976	1304	13.6
5	Shaquille O'Neal, LSU	3	1992	1217	13.5

Note: minimum 650 rebounds.

Assists

	Total	Yrs	Last	Gm	No
1	Bobby Hurley, Duke	4	1993	140	1076
2	Chris Corchiani, N.C. State	4	1991	124	1038
3	Ed Cota, N. Carolina	4	2000	138	1030
4	Keith Jennings, E. Tenn. St.	4	1991	127	983
5	Steve Blake, Maryland	4	2003	138	972
6	Sherman Douglas, Syracuse	4	1989	138	960
7	Tony Miller, Marquette	4	1995	123	956
8	Aaron Miles, Kansas	4	2005	138	954
9	Greg Anthony, Portland/UNLV	4	1991	138	950
10	Doug Gottlieb, ND/Okla St.	4	2000	124	947

	Average	Yrs	Last	No	Avg
1	Avery Johnson, Southern	2	1988	732	12.00
2	Sam Crawford, N. Mexico St.	2	1993	592	8.84
3	Mark Wade, Okla/UNLV	3	1987	693	8.77
4	Chris Corchiani, N.C. State	4	1991	1038	8.37
5	Taurence Chisholm, Delaware	4	1988	877	7.97
6	Van Usher, Tennessee Tech	3	1992	676	7.95
7	Anthony Manuel, Bradley	3	1989	855	7.92
8	Chico Fletcher, Ark. St.	4	2000	893	7.83
9	Gary Payton, Oregon St.	4	1990	938	7.82
10	Orlando Smart, San Francisco	4	1994	902	7.78

Note: minimum 550 assists.

Blocked Shots

	Average	Yrs	Last	No	Avg
1	Keith Closs, Cen. Conn. St.	2	1996	317	5.87
2	Adonal Foyle, Colgate	3	1997	492	5.66
3	David Robinson, Navy	2	1987	351	5.24
4	Wojciech Mydra, LA-Monroe	4	2002	535	4.65
5	Shaquille O'Neal, LSU	3	1992	412	4.58

Note: minimum 225 blocked shots.

Steals

	Average	Yrs	Last	No	Avg
1	Desmond Cambridge, Ala. A&M	3	2002	330	3.93
2	Mookie Blaylock, Oklahoma	2	1989	281	3.80
3	Ronn McMahon, Eastern Wash.	3	1990	225	3.52
4	Eric Murdock, Providence	4	1991	376	3.21
5	Van Usher, Tennessee Tech	3	1992	270	3.18

Note: minimum 225 steals.

3-PT Field Goals

	3-Pt Field Goals Made	Yrs	Last	Gm	3FG
1	J.J. Redick, Duke	4	2006	139	457
2	Curtis Staples, Virginia	4	1998	122	413
3	Keith Veney, Lamar/Marshall	4	1997	111	409
4	Doug Day, Radford	4	1993	117	401
5	Michael Watson, Missouri-KC	4	2004	117	391

	3-Pt Field Goals/Game	Yrs	Last	3FG	Avg
1	Timothy Pollard, Miss. Vall.	2	1989	256	4.57
2	Sydney Grider, LA-Lafayette	2	1990	253	4.36
3	Brian Merriweather, TX-Pan Am	3	2001	332	3.95
4	Josh Heard, Tenn. Tech	2	2000	210	3.82
5	Kareem Townes, La Salle	3	1995	300	3.70

	3-Pt Field Goal Pct.	Yrs	Last	3FG	Att	Pct
1	Tony Bennett, Wisc-GB	4	1992	290	584	.497
2	David Olson, Eastern Ill.	4	1992	262	562	.466
3	Ross Land, N. Arizona	4	2000	308	664	.464
4	Dan Dickau, Washington/ Gonzaga	4	2002	215	465	.462
5	Sean Jackson, Ohio/ Princeton	4	1992	243	528	.460

Note: minimum 200 3FGs made and an average of two per game.

SINGLE SEASON
Scoring

	Points	Year	Gm	Pts
1	Pete Maravich, LSU	1970	31	1381
2	Elvin Hayes, Houston	1968	33	1214
3	Frank Selvy, Furman	1954	29	1209
4	Pete Maravich, LSU	1969	26	1148
5	Pete Maravich, LSU	1968	26	1138
6	Bo Kimble, Loyola-CA	1990	32	1131
7	Hersey Hawkins, Bradley	1988	31	1125
8	Austin Carr, Notre Dame	1970	29	1106
9	Austin Carr, Notre Dame	1971	29	1101
10	Otis Birdsong, Houston	1977	36	1090

	Average	Year	Gm	Pts	Avg
1	Pete Maravich, LSU	1970	31	1381	44.5
2	Pete Maravich, LSU	1969	26	1148	44.2
3	Pete Maravich, LSU	1968	26	1138	43.8
4	Frank Selvy, Furman	1954	29	1209	41.7
5	Johnny Neumann, Ole Miss	1971	23	923	40.1
6	Freeman Williams, Port. St.	1977	26	1010	38.8
7	Billy McGill, Utah	1962	26	1009	38.8
8	Calvin Murphy, Niagara	1968	24	916	38.2
9	Austin Carr, Notre Dame	1970	29	1106	38.1
10	Austin Carr, Notre Dame	1971	29	1101	38.0

Field Goal Pct.

		Year	FG	FGA	Pct
1	Steve Johnson, Oregon St.	1981	235	315	.746
2	Dwayne Davis, Florida	1989	179	248	.722
3	Keith Walker, Utica	1985	154	216	.713
4	Steve Johnson, Oregon St.	1980	211	297	.710
5	Adam Mark, Belmont	2002	150	212	.708

Free Throw Pct.

		Year	FT	FTA	Pct
1	Blake Ahearn, SW Mo. St.	2004	117	120	.975
2	Derek Raivio, Gonzaga	2007	148	154	.961
3	Craig Collins, Penn St.	1985	94	98	.959
4	J.J. Redick, Duke	2004	143	150	.953
5	Rod Foster, UCLA	1982	95	100	.950

3-Pt Field Goal Pct.

		Year	3FG	Att	Pct
1	Glenn Tropf, Holy Cross	1988	52	82	.634
2	Sean Wightman, W. Mich	1992	48	76	.632
3	Keith Jennings, E. Tenn. St.	1991	84	142	.592
4	Dave Calloway, Monmouth	1989	48	82	.585
5	Steve Kerr, Arizona	1988	114	199	.573

Assists

	Average	Year	Gm	No	Avg
1	Avery Johnson, Southern-BR	1988	30	399	13.3
2	Anthony Manuel, Bradley	1988	31	373	12.0
3	Avery Johnson, Southern-BR	1987	31	333	10.7
4	Mark Wade, UNLV	1987	38	406	10.7
5	Nelson Haggerty, Baylor	1995	28	284	10.1
6	Glenn Williams, Holy Cross	1989	28	278	9.9
7	Chris Corchiani, N.C. State	1991	31	299	9.7
8	Tony Fairley, Charleston-So.	1987	28	270	9.6
9	Tyrone Bogues, Wake Forest	1987	29	276	9.5
10	Ron Weingard, Hofstra	1985	24	228	9.5

Rebounds

	Average (before 1973)	Year	Gm	No	Avg
1	Charlie Slack, Marshall	1955	21	538	25.6
2	Leroy Wright, Pacific	1959	26	652	25.1
3	Art Quimby, Connecticut	1955	25	611	24.4
4	Charlie Slack, Marshall	1956	22	520	23.6
5	Ed Conlin, Fordham	1953	26	612	23.5

	Average (since 1973)	Year	Gm	No	Avg
1	Kermit Washington, American	1973	25	511	20.4
2	Marvin Barnes, Providence	1973	30	571	19.0
3	Marvin Barnes, Providence	1974	32	597	18.7
4	Pete Padgett, Nevada	1973	26	462	17.8
5	Jim Bradley, Northern Ill	1973	24	426	17.8

Blocked Shots

	Average	Year	Gm	No	Avg
1	Shawn James, Northeastern	2006	30	196	6.53
2	Adonal Foyle, Colgate	1997	28	180	6.42
3	Keith Closs, Cen. Conn. St.	1996	28	178	6.36
4	Mickell Gladness, Ala. A&M	2007	30	188	6.27
5	David Robinson, Navy	1986	35	207	5.91

Steals

	Average	Year	Gm	No	Avg
1	Desmond Cambridge, Ala. A&M	2002	29	160	5.52
2	Darron Brittman, Chicago St.	1986	28	139	4.96
3	Aldwin Ware, Florida A&M	1988	29	142	4.90
4	John Linehan, Providence	2002	31	139	4.48
5	Ronn McMahon, East Wash	1990	29	130	4.48

SINGLE GAME

Scoring

	Points vs Div. I Team	Year	Pts
1	Kevin Bradshaw, US Int'l vs Loyola-CA	1991	72
2	Pete Maravich, LSU vs Alabama	1970	69
3	Calvin Murphy, Niagara vs Syracuse	1969	68
4	Jay Handlan, Wash. & Lee vs Furman	1951	66
	Pete Maravich, LSU vs Tulane	1969	66
	Anthony Roberts, Oral Rbts vs N.C. A&T	1977	66
7	Anthony Roberts, Oral Rbts vs Ore	1977	65
	Scott Haffner, Evansville vs Dayton	1989	65
9	Pete Maravich, LSU vs Kentucky	1970	64
10	Johnny Neumann, Ole Miss vs LSU	1971	63
	Hersey Hawkins, Bradley vs Detroit	1988	63

	Points vs Non-Div. I Team	Year	Pts
1	Frank Selvy, Furman vs Newberry	1954	100
2	Paul Arizin, Villanova vs Phi. NAMC	1949	85
3	Freeman Williams, Port. St. vs Rocky Mt	1978	81
4	Bill Mlkvy, Temple vs Wilkes	1951	73
5	Freeman Williams, Port. St. vs So. Ore	1977	71
6	Darrell Floyd, Furman vs Morehead St.	1955	67

Note: Bevo Francis of Division II Rio Grande (Ohio) scored an overall collegiate record 113 points against Hillsdale in 1954. He also scored 84 against Alliance and 82 against Bluffton that same season.

3-Pt Field Goals

		Year	No
1	Keith Veney, Marshall vs Morehead St.	1996	15
2	Dave Jamerson, Ohio U. vs Charleston	1989	14
	Askia Jones, Kansas St. vs Fresno St.	1994	14
	Ronald Blackshear, Marshall vs. Akron	2002	14
5	Gary Bossert, Niagara vs Siena	1987	12
	Darrin Fitzgerald, Butler vs Detroit	1987	12
	Al Dillard, Arkansas vs Delaware St.	1993	12
	Mitch Taylor, South-BR vs La. Christian	1995	12
	David McMahan, Winthrop vs C. Carolina	1996	12
	Clarence Gilbert, Missouri vs Colorado	2002	12
	Terrence Woods, Fla. A&M vs Coppin St.	2003	12
	Michael Jenkins, Winthrop vs. N.Greenville	2007	12

Assists

		Year	No
1	Tony Fairley, Baptist vs Armstrong St.	1987	22
	Avery Johnson, Southern-BR vs TX-South	1988	22
	Sherman Douglas, Syracuse vs Providence	1989	22
4	Mark Wade, UNLV vs Navy	1986	21
	Kelvin Scarborough, N. Mexico vs Hawaii	1987	21
	Anthony Manuel, Bradley vs UC-Irvine	1987	21
	Avery Johnson, Southern-BR vs Ala. St.	1988	21

Rebounds

	Total (before 1973)	Year	No
1	Bill Chambers, Wm. & Mary vs Virginia	1953	51
2	Charlie Slack, Marshall vs M. Harvey	1954	43
3	Tom Heinsohn, Holy Cross vs BC	1955	42
4	Art Quimby, UConn vs BU	1955	40
5	Three players tied with 39 each.		

	Total (since 1973)	Year	No
1	Larry Abney, Fresno St. vs SMU	2000	35
2	David Vaughn, Oral Roberts vs Brandeis	1973	34
3	Robert Parish, Centenary vs So. Miss	1973	33
4	Durand Macklin, LSU vs Tulane	1976	32
	Jervaughn Scales, South-BR vs Grambling	1994	32

Blocked Shots

		Year	No
1	Mickell Gladness, Ala. A&M vs. TX Southern	2007	16
2	David Robinson, Navy vs NC-Wilmington	1986	14
	Shawn Bradley, BYU vs Eastern Ky	1990	14
	Roy Rogers, Alabama vs Georgia	1996	14
	Loren Woods, Arizona vs Oregon	2000	14

Steals

		Year	No
1	Mookie Blaylock, Oklahoma vs Centenary	1987	13
	Mookie Blaylock, Oklahoma vs Loyola-CA	1988	13
3	Kenny Robertson, Cleve. St. vs Wagner	1988	12
	Terry Evans, Oklahoma vs Florida A&M	1993	12
	Richard Duncan, Mid. Tenn St. vs E. Ky.	1999	12
	Greedy Daniels, TCU vs Ark-Pine Bluff	2001	12
	Jehiel Lewis, Navy vs Bucknell	2002	12

Players of the Year and Top Draft Picks

Consensus College Players of the Year and first overall selections in NBA draft since the abolition of the NBA's territorial draft in 1966. Top draft picks who became Rookie of the Year are in **bold** type; (*) indicates top draft pick chosen as junior, (**) indicates top pick chosen as sophomore, (†) indicates top pick chosen as freshman, (‡) indicates top pick chosen as a high school senior. Only five players have been the unanimous college player of the year, the first overall pick in the NBA draft and then the NBA Rookie of the year.

Year	Player of the Year	Top Draft Pick	Year	Player of the Year	Top Draft Pick
1966	Cazzie Russell, Mich.	Cazzie Russell, NY	1989	Sean Elliott, Arizona	
1967	Lew Alcindor, UCLA	Jimmy Walker, Det.		& Danny Ferry, Duke	Pervis Ellison, Sac.
1968	Elvin Hayes, Houston	Elvin Hayes, SD	1990	Lionel Simmons, La Salle	**Derrick Coleman**, NJ
1969	Lew Alcindor, UCLA	**Lew Alcindor**, Mil.	1991	Larry Johnson, UNLV	
1970	Pete Maravich, LSU	Bob Lanier, Det.		& Shaquille O'Neal, LSU	**Larry Johnson**, Cha.
1971	Sidney Wicks, UCLA	Austin Carr, Cle.	1992	Christian Laettner, Duke	**Shaquille O'Neal**, Orl.*
1972	Bill Walton, UCLA	LaRue Martin, Por.	1993	Calbert Cheaney, Ind.	**Chris Webber**, Orl.**
1973	Bill Walton, UCLA	Doug Collins, Phi.	1994	Glenn Robinson, Purdue	Glenn Robinson, Mil.*
1974	Bill Walton, UCLA	Bill Walton, Por.	1995	Ed O'Bannon, UCLA	
1975	David Thompson, N.C. St.	David Thompson, Atl.		& Joe Smith, Maryland	Joe Smith, G. St.**
1976	Scott May, Indiana	John Lucas, Hou.	1996	Marcus Camby, UMass	**Allen Iverson**, Phi.**
1977	Marques Johnson, UCLA	Kent Benson, Ind.	1997	Tim Duncan, Wake Forest	**Tim Duncan**, SA
1978	Butch Lee, Marquette		1998	Antawn Jamison, N. Caro.	M. Olowokandi, LAC
	& Phil Ford, N. Caro.	Mychal Thompson, Por.	1999	Elton Brand, Duke	**Elton Brand**, Chi.**
1979	Larry Bird, Indiana St.	Magic Johnson, LAL**	2000	Kenyon Martin, Cincinnati	Kenyon Martin, NJ
1980	Mark Aguirre, DePaul	Joe Barry Carroll, G. St.	2001	Shane Battier, Duke	
1981	Ralph Sampson, Va.			& Jason Williams, Duke	Kwame Brown, Wash.‡
	& Danny Ainge, BYU	Mark Aguirre, Dal.	2002	Jason Williams, Duke	
1982	Ralph Sampson, Va.	James Worthy, LAL*		& Drew Gooden, Kansas	Yao Ming, Hou.
1983	Ralph Sampson, Va.	**Ralph Sampson**, Hou.	2003	T.J. Ford, Texas	
1984	Michael Jordan, N. Caro.	Akeem Olajuwon, Hou.		& David West, Xavier	**LeBron James**, Cle.‡
1985	Patrick Ewing, Georgetown		2004	Jameer Nelson, St. Joseph's	
	& Chris Mullin, St. John's	**Patrick Ewing**, NY		& Emeka Okafor, UConn	Dwight Howard, Orl.‡
1986	Walter Berry, St. John's	Brad Daugherty, Cle.	2005	Andrew Bogut, Utah	Andrew Bogut, Mil.**
1987	David Robinson, Navy	**David Robinson**, SA	2006	J.J. Redick, Duke	
1988	Hersey Hawkins, Bradley			& Adam Morrison, Gonz.	Andrea Bargnani, Tor.
	& Danny Manning, Kan.	Danny Manning, LAC	2007	Kevin Durant, Texas	Greg Oden, Ohio St.†

Annual Awards

UPI picked the first national Division I Player of the Year in 1955. Since then, the U.S. Basketball Writers Assn. (1959), the Associated Press Player of the Year (1961), the Atlanta Tip-Off Club (1969), the National Assn. of Basketball Coaches (1975) and the LA Athletic Club's John Wooden Award (1977) have joined in. UPI discontinued its award in 1997. Since 1977, the first year all the following awards were given out, the same player has won all of them in the same season 15 times: Marques Johnson in 1977, Larry Bird in 1979, Ralph Sampson in both 1982 and '83, Michael Jordan in 1984, David Robinson in 1987, Lionel Simmons in 1990, Calbert Cheaney in 1993, Glenn Robinson in 1994, Tim Duncan in 1997, Antawn Jamison in 1998, Elton Brand in 1999, Kenyon Martin in 2000, Andrew Bogut in 2005 and Kevin Durant in 2007.

Wooden Award

Voted on by a panel of coaches, sportswriters and broadcasters and first presented in 1977 by the Los Angeles Athletic Club in the name of former Purdue All-American and UCLA coach John Wooden. Unlike the other five player of the year awards, candidates for the Wooden must have a minimum grade point average of 2.00 (out of 4.00).

Multiple winner: Ralph Sampson (2).

Year		Year		Year	
1977	Marques Johnson, UCLA	1988	Danny Manning, Kansas	1999	Elton Brand, Duke
1978	Phil Ford, North Carolina	1989	Sean Elliott, Arizona	2000	Kenyon Martin, Cincinnati
1979	Larry Bird, Indiana St.	1990	Lionel Simmons, La Salle	2001	Shane Battier, Duke
1980	Darrell Griffith, Louisville	1991	Larry Johnson, UNLV	2002	Jason Williams, Duke
1981	Danny Ainge, BYU	1992	Christian Laettner, Duke	2003	T.J. Ford, Texas
1982	Ralph Sampson, Virginia	1993	Calbert Cheaney, Indiana	2004	Jameer Nelson, St. Joseph's
1983	Ralph Sampson, Virginia	1994	Glenn Robinson, Purdue	2005	Andrew Bogut, Utah
1984	Michael Jordan, N. Carolina	1995	Ed O'Bannon, UCLA	2006	J.J. Redick, Duke
1985	Chris Mullin, St. John's	1996	Marcus Camby, UMass	2007	Kevin Durant, Texas
1986	Walter Berry St. John's	1997	Tim Duncan, Wake Forest		
1987	David Robinson, Navy	1998	Antawn Jamison, N. Carolina		

United Press International

Voted on by a panel of UPI college basketball writers and first presented in 1955.

Multiple winners: Oscar Robertson, Ralph Sampson and Bill Walton (3); Lew Alcindor and Jerry Lucas (2).

Year		Year		Year	
1955	Tom Gola, La Salle	1962	Jerry Lucas, Ohio St.	1969	Lew Alcindor, UCLA
1956	Bill Russell, San Francisco	1963	Art Heyman, Duke	1970	Pete Maravich, LSU
1957	Chet Forte, Columbia	1964	Gary Bradds, Ohio St.	1971	Austin Carr, Notre Dame
1958	Oscar Robertson, Cincinnati	1965	Bill Bradley, Princeton	1972	Bill Walton, UCLA
1959	Oscar Robertson, Cincinnati	1966	Cazzie Russell, Michigan	1973	Bill Walton, UCLA
1960	Oscar Robertson, Cincinnati	1967	Lew Alcindor, UCLA	1974	Bill Walton, UCLA
1961	Jerry Lucas, Ohio St.	1968	Elvin Hayes, Houston	1975	David Thompson, N.C. State

Year		Year		Year	
1976	Scott May, Indiana	1984	Michael Jordan, N. Carolina	1992	Jim Jackson, Ohio St.
1977	Marques Johnson, UCLA	1985	Chris Mullin, St. John's	1993	Calbert Cheaney, Indiana
1978	Butch Lee, Marquette	1986	Walter Berry, St. John's	1994	Glenn Robinson, Purdue
1979	Larry Bird, Indiana St.	1987	David Robinson, Navy	1995	Joe Smith, Maryland
1980	Mark Aguirre, DePaul	1988	Hersey Hawkins, Bradley	1996	Ray Allen, UConn
1981	Ralph Sampson, Virginia	1989	Danny Ferry, Duke	1997	award discontinued
1982	Ralph Sampson, Virginia	1990	Lionel Simmons, La Salle		
1983	Ralph Sampson, Virginia	1991	Shaquille O'Neal, LSU		

U.S. Basketball Writers Association

Voted on by the USBWA and first presented in 1959.
Multiple winners: Ralph Sampson and Bill Walton (3); Lew Alcindor, Jerry Lucas and Oscar Robertson (2).

Year		Year		Year	
1959	Oscar Robertson, Cincinnati	1976	Adrian Dantley, Notre Dame	1993	Calbert Cheaney, Indiana
1960	Oscar Robertson, Cincinnati	1977	Marques Johnson, UCLA	1994	Glenn Robinson, Purdue
1961	Jerry Lucas, Ohio St.	1978	Phil Ford, North Carolina	1995	Ed O'Bannon, UCLA
1962	Jerry Lucas, Ohio St.	1979	Larry Bird, Indiana St.	1996	Marcus Camby, UMass
1963	Art Heyman, Duke	1980	Mark Aguirre, DePaul	1997	Tim Duncan, Wake Forest
1964	Walt Hazzard, UCLA	1981	Ralph Sampson, Virginia	1998	Antawn Jamison, N. Carolina
1965	Bill Bradley, Princeton	1982	Ralph Sampson, Virginia	1999	Elton Brand, Duke
1966	Cazzie Russell, Michigan	1983	Ralph Sampson, Virginia	2000	Kenyon Martin, Cincinnati
1967	Lew Alcindor, UCLA	1984	Michael Jordan, N. Carolina	2001	Shane Battier, Duke
1968	Elvin Hayes, Houston	1985	Chris Mullin, St. John's	2002	Jason Williams, Duke
1969	Lew Alcindor, UCLA	1986	Walter Berry, St. John's	2003	David West, Xavier
1970	Pete Maravich, LSU	1987	David Robinson, Navy	2004	Jameer Nelson, St. Joseph's
1971	Sidney Wicks, UCLA	1988	Hersey Hawkins, Bradley	2005	Andrew Bogut, Utah
1972	Bill Walton, UCLA	1989	Danny Ferry, Duke	2006	Adam Morrison, Gonzaga
1973	Bill Walton, UCLA	1990	Lionel Simmons, La Salle		& J.J. Redick, Duke
1974	Bill Walton, UCLA	1991	Larry Johnson, UNLV	2007	Kevin Durant, Texas
1975	David Thompson, N.C. State	1992	Christian Laettner, Duke		

Associated Press Player of the Year

Voted on by AP sportswriters and broadcasters.
Multiple winners: Ralph Sampson (3); Lew Alcindor, Jerry Lucas, David Thompson and Bill Walton (2).

Year		Year		Year	
1961	Jerry Lucas, Ohio St.	1977	Marques Johnson, UCLA	1993	Calbert Cheaney, Indiana
1962	Jerry Lucas, Ohio St.	1978	Butch Lee, Marquette	1994	Glenn Robinson, Purdue
1963	Art Heyman, Duke	1979	Larry Bird, Indiana St.	1995	Joe Smith, Maryland
1964	Gary Bradds, Ohio St.	1980	Mark Aguirre, DePaul	1996	Marcus Camby, UMass
1965	Bill Bradley, Princeton	1981	Ralph Sampson, Virginia	1997	Tim Duncan, Wake Forest
1966	Cazzie Russell, Michigan	1982	Ralph Sampson, Virginia	1998	Antawn Jamison, N. Carolina
1967	Lew Alcindor, UCLA	1983	Ralph Sampson, Virginia	1999	Elton Brand, Duke
1968	Elvin Hayes, Houston	1984	Michael Jordan, N. Carolina	2000	Kenyon Martin, Cincinnati
1969	Lew Alcindor, UCLA	1985	Patrick Ewing, Georgetown	2001	Shane Battier, Duke
1970	Pete Maravich, LSU	1986	Walter Berry, St. John's	2002	Jason Williams, Duke
1971	Austin Carr, Notre Dame	1987	David Robinson, Navy	2003	David West, Xavier
1972	Bill Walton, UCLA	1988	Hersey Hawkins, Bradley	2004	Jameer Nelson, St. Joseph's
1973	Bill Walton, UCLA	1989	Sean Elliott, Arizona	2005	Andrew Bogut, Utah
1974	David Thompson, N.C. State	1990	Lionel Simmons, La Salle	2006	J.J. Redick, Duke
1975	David Thompson, N.C. State	1991	Shaquille O'Neal, LSU	2007	Kevin Durant, Texas
1976	Scott May, Indiana	1992	Christian Laettner, Duke		

Naismith Award

Voted on by a panel of coaches, sportswriters and broadcasters and first presented in 1969 by the Atlanta Tip-Off Club in 1969 in the name of the inventor of basketball, Dr. James Naismith.
Multiple winners: Ralph Sampson and Bill Walton (3).

Year		Year		Year	
1969	Lew Alcindor, UCLA	1982	Ralph Sampson, Virginia	1995	Joe Smith, Maryland
1970	Pete Maravich, LSU	1983	Ralph Sampson, Virginia	1996	Marcus Camby, UMass
1971	Austin Carr, Notre Dame	1984	Michael Jordan, N. Carolina	1997	Tim Duncan, Wake Forest
1972	Bill Walton, UCLA	1985	Patrick Ewing, Georgetown	1998	Antawn Jamison, N. Carolina
1973	Bill Walton, UCLA	1986	Johnny Dawkins, Duke	1999	Elton Brand, Duke
1974	Bill Walton, UCLA	1987	David Robinson, Navy	2000	Kenyon Martin, Cincinnati
1975	David Thompson, N.C. State	1988	Danny Manning, Kansas	2001	Shane Battier, Duke
1976	Scott May, Indiana	1989	Danny Ferry, Duke	2002	Jason Williams, Duke
1977	Marques Johnson, UCLA	1990	Lionel Simmons, La Salle	2003	T.J. Ford, Texas
1978	Butch Lee, Marquette	1991	Larry Johnson, UNLV	2004	Jameer Nelson, St. Joseph's
1979	Larry Bird, Indiana St.	1992	Christian Laettner, Duke	2005	Andrew Bogut, Utah
1980	Mark Aguirre, DePaul	1993	Calbert Cheaney, Indiana	2006	J.J. Redick, Duke
1981	Ralph Sampson, Virginia	1994	Glenn Robinson, Purdue	2007	Kevin Durant, Texas

National Association of Basketball Coaches

Voted on by the National Assn. of Basketball Coaches and presented by the Eastman Kodak Co. from 1975-94.
Multiple winners: Ralph Sampson and Jason Williams (2).

Year		Year		Year	
1975	David Thompson, N.C. State	1987	David Robinson, Navy	1999	Elton Brand, Duke
1976	Scott May, Indiana	1988	Danny Manning, Kansas	2000	Kenyon Martin, Cincinnati
1977	Marques Johnson, UCLA	1989	Sean Elliott, Arizona	2001	Jason Williams, Duke
1978	Phil Ford, North Carolina	1990	Lionel Simmons, La Salle	2002	Jason Williams, Duke
1979	Larry Bird, Indiana St.	1991	Larry Johnson, UNLV		& Drew Gooden, Kansas
1980	Michael Brooks, La Salle	1992	Christian Laettner, Duke	2003	Nick Collison, Kansas
1981	Danny Ainge, BYU	1993	Calbert Cheaney, Indiana	2004	Jameer Nelson, St. Joseph's
1982	Ralph Sampson, Virginia	1994	Glenn Robinson, Purdue		& Emeka Okafor, Connecticut
1983	Ralph Sampson, Virginia	1995	Shawn Respert, Mich. St.	2005	Andrew Bogut, Utah
1984	Michael Jordan, N. Carolina	1996	Marcus Camby, UMass	2006	J.J. Redick, Duke
1985	Patrick Ewing, Georgetown	1997	Tim Duncan, Wake Forest		& Adam Morrison, Gonzaga
1986	Walter Berry, St. John's	1998	Antawn Jamison, N. Carolina	2007	Kevin Durant, Texas

All-Time Winningest Division I Coaches

Minimum of 10 seasons as Division I head coach; regular season and tournament games included; coaches active during 2006-07 in **bold** type.

Top 30 Winning Percentage

		Yrs	W	L	Pct
1	Clair Bee	21	412	87	.826
2	Adolph Rupp	41	876	190	.822
3	John Wooden	29	664	162	.804
4	**Roy Williams**	19	524	131	.800
5	John Kresse	23	560	143	.797
6	Jerry Tarkanian	31	729	201	.784
7	Francis Schmidt	17	258	72	.782
8	Dean Smith	36	879	254	.776
9	George Keogan	27	414	127	.765
10	Jack Ramsay	11	231	71	.765
11	Frank Keaney	28	401	124	.764
12	Vic Bubas	10	213	67	.761
13	Harry Fisher	16	189	60	.759
14	**Mike Krzyzewski**	32	775	261	.748
15	Fred Bennion	11	95	32	.748
16	Chick Davies	21	314	106	.748
17	Ray Mears	21	399	135	.747
18	Edward McNichol	10	186	63	.747
19	Rick Majerus	20	422	147	.742
20	Al McGuire	20	406	142	.741
21	**Jim Boeheim**	31	750	264	.740
22	Phog Allen	48	746	264	.739
23	Everett Case	19	377	134	.738
24	**Bob Huggins**	25	590	211	.737
25	**Lute Olson**	34	780	280	.736
26	Arthur Schabinger	19	245	88	.736
27	**John Calipari**	15	370	133	.736
28	G. Ott Romney	13	283	102	.735
29	Walter Meanwell	22	280	101	.735
30	**Rick Pitino**	21	494	182	.731

Top 30 Victories

		Yrs	W	L	Pct
1	**Bob Knight**	41	890	363	.710
2	Dean Smith	36	879	254	.776
3	Adolph Rupp	41	876	190	.822
4	Jim Phelan	49	830	524	.613
5	Eddie Sutton	36	798	315	.717
6	Lefty Driesell	41	786	394	.666
7	**Lute Olson**	34	780	280	.736
8	Lou Henson	41	779	408	.656
9	**Mike Krzyzewski**	32	775	261	.748
10	Hank Iba	41	767	338	.694
11	Ed Diddle	42	759	302	.715
12	**Jim Calhoun**	35	750	328	.696
	Jim Boeheim	31	750	264	.740
14	Phog Allen	48	746	264	.739
15	John Chaney	34	741	312	.704
16	Jerry Tarkanian	31	729	201	.784
17	Norm Stewart	38	728	374	.661
18	Ray Meyer	42	724	354	.672
19	Don Haskins	38	719	353	.671
20	Denny Crum	30	675	295	.696
21	John Wooden	29	664	162	.804
22	Ralph Miller	38	657	382	.632
23	Gene Bartow	34	647	353	.647
24	Billy Tubbs	31	641	340	.653
25	Marv Harshman	40	637	443	.590
26	Hugh Durham	37	633	429	.596
27	Cam Henderson	35	630	243	.722
28	Norm Sloan	37	624	393	.614
29	Slats Gill	36	599	392	.604
30	Tom Davis	32	598	355	.627

Note: Clarence (Bighouse) Gaines of Division II Winston-Salem St. (1947-93) retired after the 1992-93 season to finish his 47-year career ranked No. 3 on the all-time NCAA list of all coaches regardless of division. His record is 828-446 with a .650 winning percentage.

Where They Coached

Allen–Baker (1906-08), Kansas (1908-09), Haskell (1909), Central Mo. St. (1913-19), Kansas (1920-56); **Bartow**–Central Mo. St. (1962-64), Valparaiso (1965-70), Memphis St. (1971-74), Illinois (1975), UCLA (1976-77), UAB (1979-96); **Bennion**–BYU (1909-10), Utah (1911-14), Montana St. (1915-19); **Bee**–Rider (1929-31), LIU-Brooklyn (1932-45, 46-51); **Boeheim**–Syracuse (1977–); **Bubas**–Duke (1960-69); **Calhoun**–Northeastern (1973-86), Connecticut (1987–); **Calipari**–Massachusetts (1988-96), Memphis (2000–); **Case**–N.C. State (1947-64); **Chaney**–Cheyney St. (1973-82), Temple (1983-2006); **Crum**–Louisville (1972-01); **Davies**–Duquesne (1925-43, 47-48); **Davis**–Lafayette (1972-77), Boston College (1978-82), Stanford (1983-86), Iowa (1987-99), Drake (2004-07) **Diddle**–Western Ky. (1923-64); **Driesell**–Davidson (1961-69), Maryland (1970-86), Davis & Elkins (1923-35), Marshall (1936-55); **Durham**–Florida St. (1967-78), Georgia (1979-95), Jacksonville (1999-05); **Fisher**–Columbia (1907-16), Army (1922-23, 25). **Gill**–Oregon St. (1929-64); **Harshman**–Pacific Lutheran (1946-58), Wash. St. (1959-71), Washington (1972-85); **Haskins**–UTEP (1962-99); **Henderson**–Muskingum (1920-22), Davis & Elkins (1923-35), Marshall (1936-55); **Henson**–Hardin-Simmons (1963-66), N. Mexico St. (1967-75), Illinois (1976-96), N. Mexico St. (1997-05); **Huggins**–Walsh (1981-83), Akron (1985-89), Cincinnati (1990-05), Kansas St. (2006-07), West Virginia (2007–); **Iba**–NW Missouri St. (1930-33), Colorado (1934), Oklahoma St. (1935-70); **Keaney**–Rhode Island (1921-48); **Keogan**–St. Louis (1916), Allegheny (1919), Valparaiso (1920-21), Notre Dame (1924-43); **Knight**–Army (1966-71), Indiana (1972-00), Texas Tech (2001–); **Kresse**–Charleston (1979-2002);

Krzyzewski–Army (1976-80), Duke (1981–); **Majerus**–Marquette (1984-86), Ball St. (1988-89), Utah (1991-2003), St. Louis (2007–); **McGuire**–Belmont Abbey (1958-64), Marquette (1965-77); **Meanwell**– Wisconsin (1912-17, 21-34), Missouri (1918-20); **Mears**–Wittenberg (1957-62), Tennessee (1963-77); **Meyer**–DePaul (1943-84); **Miller**–Wichita St. (1952-64), Iowa (1965-70), Oregon St. (1971-89); **Olson**–Long Beach St. (1974), Iowa (1975-83), Arizona (1984–); **Phelan**–Mount St. Mary's (1955-2003); **Pitino**–Boston Univ. (1979-83), Providence (1986-87), Kentucky (1989-97), Louisville (2001–).

Ramsay–St. Joseph's-PA (1956-66); **Romney**–Montana St. (1923-28), BYU (1929-35); **Rupp**–Kentucky (1931-72); **Schabinger**–Ottawa (1917-20), Emportia St. (1921-22), Creighton (!923-35); **Schmidt**–Tulsa (1916-17, 19-22), Arkansas (1924-29), TCU (1930-34); **Sloan**–Presbyterian (1952-55), Citadel (1957-60), Florida (1961-66), N.C. State (1967-80), Florida (1981-89); **Smith**– North Carolina (1962-97); **Stewart**–No. Iowa (1962-67), Missouri (1968-99); **Sutton**–Creighton (1970-74), Arkansas (1975-85), Kentucky (1986-89), Oklahoma St. (1991-2006); **Tarkanian**–Long Beach St. (1969-73), UNLV (1974-92), Fresno St. (1995-2002); **Tubbs**–Southwestern (1971-73), Lamar (1976-80, 2003-06), Oklahoma (1981-94), TCU (1995-2002); **Williams**–Kansas (1989-2003), North Carolina (2003–); **Wooden**–Indiana St. (1947-48), UCLA (1949-75).

Most NCAA Tournaments

Through 2007; listed are number of appearances, overall tournament record, times reaching Final Four, and number of NCAA championships. (*) denotes that actual records are different from official NCAA records.

App		W-L	F4	Championships
28	**Lute Olson***	46-28	5	1 (1997)
27	Dean Smith	65-27	11	2 (1982, 93)
27	**Bob Knight**	44-23	5	3 (1976, 81, 87)
26	Eddie Sutton*	39-26	2	None
25	**Jim Boeheim**	40-24	3	1 (2003)
23	Denny Crum	42-23	6	2 (1980, 86)
23	**Mike Krzyzewski**	68-20	9	3 (1991-92, 2001)
20	Adolph Rupp	30-18	6	4 (1948-49, 51, 58)
20	John Thompson	34-19	3	1 (1984)
19	Lou Henson	19-20	2	None
19	**Jim Calhoun***	41-17	2	2 (1999, 2004)
18	**Roy Williams**	45-17	5	1 (2005)
18	Lou Carnesecca	17-20	1	None
18	Jerry Tarkanian	38-18	4	1 (1990)
18	Gene Keady*	19-18	0	None
17	John Chaney	23-17	0	None
16	John Wooden	47-10	12	10 (1964-65, 67-73, 75)
16	Norm Stewart*	12-16	0	None
16	Nolan Richardson	26-15	3	1 (1994)
16	Jim Harrick	18-15	1	1 (1995)
15	Digger Phelps	17-17	1	None
15	**Bob Huggins**	20-14	1	None
15	**Gary Williams**	27-14	2	1 (2002)
15	**Rick Barnes**	15-15	1	None
14	Don Haskins	14-13	1	1 (1966)
14	Guy Lewis	26-18	5	None

Active Coaches' Victories

Minimum five seasons in Division I.

		Yrs	W	L	Pct
1	Bob Knight, Texas Tech	.41	**890**	363	.710
2	Lute Olson, Arizona	.34	**780**	280	.736
3	Mike Krzyzewski, Duke	.32	**775**	261	.748
4	Jim Calhoun, UConn	.35	**750**	328	.696
	Jim Boeheim, Syracuse	.31	**750**	264	.740
6	Bob Huggins, Kansas St.	.25	**590**	211	.737
7	Gary Williams, Maryland	.29	**585**	328	.641
8	Tom Penders, Houston	.33	**584**	400	.593
9	Homer Drew, Valparaiso	.30	**571**	362	.612
10	Ben Braun, California	.30	**539**	373	.591
11	Cliff Ellis, Coastal Carolina	.29	**534**	337	.613
12	Larry Hunter, Western Carolina	.27	**533**	261	.673
13	Pat Douglass, UC-Irvine	.26	**529**	257	.673
14	Bo Ryan, Wisconsin	.23	**525**	158	.769
15	Roy Williams, North Carolina	.19	**524**	131	.800
16	Rick Byrd, Belmont	.26	**516**	294	.637
17	Rick Pitino, Louisville	.21	**494**	182	.731
18	Kelvin Sampson, Indiana	.24	**477**	267	.641
19	John Beilein, Michigan	.25	**476**	275	.634
	Bobby Cremins, C. of Charleston	26	**476**	321	.597
21	Pat Kennedy, Towson	.27	**448**	367	.550
22	Dave Bike, Sacred Heart	.29	**445**	401	.526
23	Stew Morrill, Utah St.	.21	**431**	213	.669
24	Rick Majerus, St. Louis	.20	**422**	147	.742
25	Don Maestri, Troy	.25	**442**	294	.601
26	Rick Barnes, Texas	.20	**418**	220	.655
27	L. Vann Pettaway, Ala. A&M	.21	**407**	214	.655
28	Mike Deane, Wagner	.23	**392**	285	.579
	Tom Green, Fairleigh Dickinson	.24	**392**	308	.560
30	Dave Odom, South Carolina	.21	**391**	261	.600

Annual Awards

UPI picked the first national Division I Coach of the Year in 1955. Since then, the U.S. Basketball Writers Assn. (1959), AP (1967), the National Assn. of Basketball Coaches (1969), and the Atlanta Tip-Off Club (1987) have joined in. Since 1987, the first year all five awards were given out, no coach has won all of them in the same season.

United Press International

Voted on by a panel of UPI college basketball writers and first presented in 1955.

Multiple winners: John Wooden (6); Bob Knight, Ray Meyer, Adolph Rupp, Norm Stewart, Fred Taylor and Phil Woolpert (2).

Year	Year	Year
1955 Phil Woolpert, San Francisco	1970 John Wooden, UCLA	1985 Lou Carnesecca, St. John's
1956 Phil Woolpert, San Francisco	1971 Al McGuire, Marquette	1986 Mike Krzyzewski, Duke
1957 Frank McGuire, North Carolina	1972 John Wooden, UCLA	1987 John Thompson, Georgetown
1958 Tex Winter, Kansas St.	1973 John Wooden, UCLA	1988 John Chaney, Temple
1959 Adolph Rupp, Kentucky	1974 Digger Phelps, Notre Dame	1989 Bob Knight, Indiana
1960 Pete Newell, California	1975 Bob Knight, Indiana	1990 Jim Calhoun, Connecticut
1961 Fred Taylor, Ohio St.	1976 Tom Young, Rutgers	1991 Rick Majerus, Utah
1962 Fred Taylor, Ohio St.	1977 Bob Gaillard, San Francisco	1992 Perry Clark, Tulane
1963 Ed Jucker, Cincinnati	1978 Eddie Sutton, Arkansas	1993 Eddie Fogler, Vanderbilt
1964 John Wooden, UCLA	1979 Bill Hodges, Indiana St.	1994 Norm Stewart, Missouri
1965 Dave Strack, Michigan	1980 Ray Meyer, DePaul	1995 Leonard Hamilton, Miami-FL
1966 Adolph Rupp, Kentucky	1981 Ralph Miller, Oregon St.	1996 Gene Keady, Purdue
1967 John Wooden, UCLA	1982 Norm Stewart, Missouri	1997 award discontinued
1968 Guy Lewis, Houston	1983 Jerry Tarkanian, UNLV	
1969 John Wooden, UCLA	1984 Ray Meyer, DePaul	

Annual Awards (Cont.)
U.S. Basketball Writers Association
Voted on by the USBWA and first presented in 1959.

Multiple winners: John Wooden (5); Bob Knight (3); Lou Carnesecca, John Chaney, Ray Meyer, Fred Taylor and Roy Williams (2).

Year	Year	Year
1959 Eddie Hickey, Marquette	1976 Bob Knight, Indiana	1993 Eddie Fogler, Vanderbilt
1960 Pete Newell, California	1977 Eddie Sutton, Arkansas	1994 Charlie Spoonhour, St. Louis
1961 Fred Taylor, Ohio St.	1978 Ray Meyer, DePaul	1995 Kelvin Sampson, Oklahoma
1962 Fred Taylor, Ohio St.	1979 Dean Smith, North Carolina	1996 Gene Keady, Purdue
1963 Ed Jucker, Cincinnati	1980 Ray Meyer, DePaul	1997 Clem Haskins, Minnesota
1964 John Wooden, UCLA	1981 Ralph Miller, Oregon St.	1998 Tom Izzo, Michigan St.
1965 Butch van Breda Kolff, Princeton	1982 John Thompson, Georgetown	1999 Cliff Ellis, Auburn
1966 Adolph Rupp, Kentucky	1983 Lou Carnesecca, St. John's	2000 Larry Eustachy, Iowa St.
1967 John Wooden, UCLA	1984 Gene Keady, Purdue	2001 Al Skinner, Boston College
1968 Guy Lewis, Houston	1985 Lou Carnesecca, St. John's	2002 Ben Howland, Pittsburgh
1969 Maury John, Drake	1986 Dick Versace, Bradley	2003 Tubby Smith, Kentucky
1970 John Wooden, UCLA	1987 John Chaney, Temple	2004 Phil Martelli, St. Joseph's
1971 Al McGuire, Marquette	1988 John Chaney, Temple	2005 Bruce Weber, Illinois
1972 John Wooden, UCLA	1989 Bob Knight, Indiana	2006 Roy Williams, North Carolina
1973 John Wooden, UCLA	1990 Roy Williams, Kansas	2007 Tony Bennett, Washington St.
1974 Norm Sloan, N.C. State	1991 Randy Ayers, Ohio St.	
1975 Bob Knight, Indiana	1992 Perry Clark, Tulane	

Associated Press
Voted on by AP sportswriters and broadcasters and first presented in 1967.

Multiple winners: John Wooden (5); Bob Knight (3); Guy Lewis, Ray Meyer, Ralph Miller, Eddie Sutton and Roy Williams (2).

Year	Year	Year
1967 John Wooden, UCLA	1981 Ralph Miller, Oregon St.	1995 Kelvin Sampson, Oklahoma
1968 Guy Lewis, Houston	1982 Ralph Miller, Oregon St.	1996 Gene Keady, Purdue
1969 John Wooden, UCLA	1983 Guy Lewis, Houston	1997 Clem Haskins, Minnesota
1970 John Wooden, UCLA	1984 Ray Meyer, DePaul	1998 Tom Izzo, Michigan St.
1971 Al McGuire, Marquette	1985 Bill Frieder, Michigan	1999 Cliff Ellis, Auburn
1972 John Wooden, UCLA	1986 Eddie Sutton, Kentucky	2000 Larry Eustachy, Iowa St.
1973 John Wooden, UCLA	1987 Tom Davis, Iowa	2001 Matt Doherty, North Carolina
1974 Norm Sloan, N.C. State	1988 John Chaney, Temple	2002 Ben Howland, Pittsburgh
1975 Bob Knight, Indiana	1989 Bob Knight, Indiana	2003 Tubby Smith, Kentucky
1976 Bob Knight, Indiana	1990 Jim Calhoun, Connecticut	2004 Phil Martelli, St. Joseph's
1977 Bob Gaillard, San Francisco	1991 Randy Ayers, Ohio St.	2005 Bruce Weber, Illinois
1978 Eddie Sutton, Arkansas	1992 Roy Williams, Kansas	2006 Roy Williams, North Carolina
1979 Bill Hodges, Indiana St.	1993 Eddie Fogler, Vanderbilt	2007 Tony Bennett, Washington St.
1980 Ray Meyer, DePaul	1994 Norm Stewart, Missouri	

National Association of Basketball Coaches
Voted on by NABC membership and first presented in 1969.

Multiple winners: John Wooden (3); Gene Keady and Mike Krzyzewski (2).

Year	Year	Year
1969 John Wooden, UCLA	1982 Don Monson, Idaho	1996 John Calipari, UMass
1970 John Wooden, UCLA	1983 Lou Carnesecca, St. John's	1997 Clem Haskins, Minnesota
1971 Jack Kraft, Villanova	1984 Marv Harshman, Washington	1998 Bill Guthridge, N. Carolina
1972 John Wooden, UCLA	1985 John Thompson, Georgetown	1999 Mike Krzyzewski, Duke
1973 Gene Bartow, Memphis St.	1986 Eddie Sutton, Kentucky	& Jim O'Brien, Ohio St.
1974 Al McGuire, Marquette	1987 Rick Pitino, Providence	2000 Gene Keady, Purdue
1975 Bob Knight, Indiana	1988 John Chaney, Temple	2001 Tom Izzo, Michigan St.
1976 Johnny Orr, Michigan	1989 P.J. Carlesimo, Seton Hall	2002 Kelvin Sampson, Oklahoma
1977 Dean Smith, North Carolina	1990 Jud Heathcote, Michigan St.	2003 Tubby Smith, Kentucky
1978 Bill Foster, Duke	1991 Mike Krzyzewski, Duke	2004 Phil Martelli, St. Joseph's
& Abe Lemons, Texas	1992 George Raveling, USC	& Mike Montgomery, Stanford
1979 Ray Meyer, DePaul	1993 Eddie Fogler, Vanderbilt	2005 Bruce Weber, Illinois
1980 Lute Olson, Iowa	1994 Nolan Richardson, Arkansas	2006 Jay Wright, Villanova
1981 Ralph Miller, Oregon St.	& Gene Keady, Purdue	2007 Todd Lickliter, Butler
& Jack Hartman, Kansas St.	1995 Jim Harrick, UCLA	

Naismith Award
Voted on by a panel of coaches, sportswriters and broadcasters and first presented by the Atlanta Tip-Off Club in 1987 in the name of the inventor of basketball, Dr. James Naismith.

Multiple winner: Mike Krzyzewski (3).

Year	Year	Year
1987 Bob Knight, Indiana	1994 Nolan Richardson, Arkansas	2001 Rod Barnes, Mississippi
1988 Larry Brown, Kansas	1995 Jim Harrick, UCLA	2002 Ben Howland, Pittsburgh
1989 Mike Krzyzewski, Duke	1996 John Calipari, UMass	2003 Tubby Smith, Kentucky
1990 Bobby Cremins, Georgia Tech	1997 Roy Williams, Kansas	2004 Phil Martelli, St. Joseph's
1991 Randy Ayers, Ohio St.	1998 Bill Guthridge, N. Carolina	2005 Bruce Weber, Illinois
1992 Mike Krzyzewski, Duke	1999 Mike Krzyzewski, Duke	2006 Jay Wright, Villanova
1993 Dean Smith, North Carolina	2000 Mike Montgomery, Stanford	2007 Tony Bennett, Washington St.

Player of the Year and NBA MVP

College Players of the Year who have gone on to win the NBA's Most Valuable Player award:

Bill Russell COLLEGE–San Francisco (1956); PROS–Boston Celtics (1958, 1961, 1962, 1963 and 1965).
Oscar Robertson COLLEGE–Cincinnati (1958, 1959 and 1960); PROS–Cincinnati Royals (1964).
Kareem Abdul-Jabbar COLLEGE–UCLA (1967 and 1969); PROS–Milwaukee Bucks (1971, 1972 and 1974) and LA Lakers (1976, 1977 and 1980).
Bill Walton COLLEGE–UCLA (1972, 1973 and 1974); PROS–Portland Trail Blazers (1978).
Larry Bird COLLEGE–Indiana St. (1979); PROS–Boston Celtics (1984, 1985, and 1986).
Michael Jordan COLLEGE–North Carolina (1984); PROS–Chicago Bulls (1988, 1991, 1992, 1996 and 1998).
David Robinson COLLEGE–Navy (1987); PROS–San Antonio Spurs (1995).
Shaquille O'Neal COLLEGE–LSU (1991); PROS–LA Lakers (2000).
Tim Duncan COLLEGE–Wake Forest (1997); PROS–San Antonio Spurs (2002, 2003).

Other Men's Champions

The NCAA has sanctioned national championship tournaments for Division II since 1957 and Division III since 1975. The NAIA sanctioned a single tournament from 1937-91, then split into two divisions in 1992.

NCAA Div. II Finals

Multiple winners: Kentucky Wesleyan (8); Evansville (5); CS-Bakersfield and Virginia Union (3); Metropolitan State, North Alabama (2).

Year	Winner	Score	Loser	Year	Winner	Score	Loser
1957	Wheaton, IL	89-65	Ky. Wesleyan	1983	Wright St., OH	92-73	Dist. of Columbia
1958	South Dakota	75-53	St. Michael's, VT	1984	Central Mo. St.	81-77	St. Augustine's, NC
1959	Evansville, IN	83-67	SW Missouri St.	1985	Jacksonville St.	74-73	South Dakota St.
1960	Evansville	90-69	Chapman, CA	1986	Sacred Heart, CT	93-87	SE Missouri St.
1961	Wittenberg, OH	42-38	SE Missouri St.	1987	Ky. Wesleyan	92-74	Gannon, PA
1962	Mt. St. Mary's, MD	58-57*	CS-Sacramento	1988	Lowell, MA	75-72	AK-Anchorage
1963	South Dakota St.	42-40	Wittenberg, OH	1989	N.C. Central	73-46	SE Missouri St.
1964	Evansville	72-59	Akron, OH	1990	Ky. Wesleyan	93-79	CS-Bakersfield
1965	Evansville	85-82*	Southern Illinois	1991	North Alabama	79-72	Bridgeport, CT
1966	Ky. Wesleyan	54-51	Southern Illinois	1992	Virginia Union	100-75	Bridgeport
1967	Winston-Salem, NC	77-74	SW Missouri St.	1993	CS-Bakersfield	85-72	Troy St., AL
1968	Ky. Wesleyan	63-52	Indiana St.	1994	CS-Bakersfield	92-86	Southern Ind.
1969	Ky. Wesleyan	75-71	SW Missouri St.	1995	Southern Indiana	71-63	UC-Riverside
1970	Phila. Textile	76-65	Tennessee St.	1996	Fort Hays St.	70-63	N. Kentucky
1971	Evansville	97-82	Old Dominion, VA	1997	CS-Bakersfield	57-56	N. Kentucky
1972	Roanoke, VA	84-72	Akron, OH	1998	UC-Davis	83-77	Ky. Wesleyan
1973	Ky. Wesleyan	78-76*	Tennessee St.	1999	Ky. Wesleyan	75-60	Metropolitan St.
1974	Morgan St., MD	67-52	SW Missouri St.	2000	Metropolitan St.	97-79	Ky. Wesleyan
1975	Old Dominion	76-74	New Orleans	2001	Ky. Wesleyan	72-63	Washburn, KS
1976	Puget Sound, WA	83-74	Tennessee-Chatt.	2002	Metropolitan St.	80-72	Ky. Wesleyan
1977	Tennessee-Chatt.	71-62	Randolph-Macon	2003	Northeastern St., OK	75-64	Ky. Wesleyan
1978	Cheyney, PA	47-40	WI-Green Bay	2004	Kennesaw St., GA	84-59	Southern Indiana
1979	North Alabama	64-50	WI-Green Bay	2005	Virginia Union	63-58	Bryant
1980	Virginia Union	80-74	New York Tech	2006	Winona St., MN	73-61	Virginia Union
1981	Florida Southern	73-68	Mt. St. Mary's, MD	2007	Barton	77-75	Winona St.
1982	Dist. of Columbia	73-63	Florida Southern		*Overtime		

NCAA Div. III Finals

Multiple winners: North Park (5); WI-Platteville (4); Calvin, Potsdam St., Scranton, WI-Stevens Point and WI-Whitewater (2).

Year	Winner	Score	Loser	Year	Winner	Score	Loser
1975	LeMoyne-Owen, TN	57-54	Glassboro St., NJ	1992	Calvin, MI	62-49	Rochester, NY
1976	Scranton, PA	60-57	Wittenberg, OH	1993	Ohio Northern	71-68	Augustana, IL
1977	Wittenberg, OH	79-66	Oneonta St., NY	1994	Lebanon Valley, PA	66-59*	NYU
1978	North Park, IL	69-57	Widener, PA	1995	WI-Platteville	69-55	Manchester, IN
1979	North Park, IL	66-62	Potsdam St., NY	1996	Rowan, NJ	100-93	Hope, MI
1980	North Park, IL	83-76	Upsala, NJ	1997	Illinois Wesleyan	89-86	Neb-Wesleyan
1981	Potsdam St., NY	67-65*	Augustana, IL	1998	WI-Platteville	69-56	Hope, MI
1982	Wabash, IN	83-62	Potsdam St., NY	1999	WI-Platteville	76-75**	Hampden-Sydney
1983	Scranton, PA	64-63	Wittenberg, OH	2000	Calvin, MI	79-74	WI-Eau Claire
1984	WI-Whitewater	103-86	Clark, MA	2001	Catholic, DC	76-62	Wm. Paterson
1985	North Park, IL	72-71	Potsdam St., NY	2002	Otterbein	102-83	Elizabethtown
1986	Potsdam St., NY	76-73	LeMoyne-Owen, TN	2003	Williams, MA	67-65	Gustavus Adolphus
1987	North Park, IL	106-100	Clark, MA	2004	WI-Stevens Point	84-82	Williams
1988	Ohio Wesleyan	92-70	Scranton, PA	2005	WI-Stevens Point	73-49	Rochester
1989	WI-Whitewater	94-86	Trenton St., NJ	2006	Virginia Wesleyan	59-56	Wittenberg
1990	Rochester, NY	43-42	DePauw, IN	2007	Amherst, MA	80-67	Virginia Wesleyan
1991	WI-Platteville	81-74	Franklin Marshall		*Overtime		
					**Double overtime		

NAIA Finals, 1937-91

Multiple winners: Grand Canyon, Hamline, Kentucky St. and Tennessee St. (3); Central Missouri, Central St., Fort Hays St. and SW Missouri St. (2).

Year	Winner	Score	Loser
1937	Central Missouri	35-24	Morningside, IA
1938	Central Missouri	45-30	Roanoke, VA
1939	Southwestern, KS	32-31	San Diego St.
1940	Tarkio, MO	52-31	San Diego St.
1941	San Diego St.	36-32	Murray St., KY
1942	Hamline, MN	33-31	SE Oklahoma
1943	SE Missouri St.	34-32	NW Missouri St.
1944	Not held		
1945	Loyola-LA	49-36	Pepperdine, CA
1946	Southern Illinois	49-40	Indiana St.
1947	Marshall, WV	73-59	Mankato St., MN
1948	Louisville, KY	82-70	Indiana St.
1949	Hamline, MN	57-46	Regis, CO
1950	Indiana St.	61-47	East Central, OK
1951	Hamline, MN	69-61	Millikin, IL
1952	SW Missouri St.	73-64	Murray St., KY
1953	SW Missouri St.	79-71	Hamline, MN
1954	St. Benedict's, KS	62-56	Western Illinois
1955	East Texas St.	71-54	SE Oklahoma
1956	McNeese St., LA	60-55	Texas Southern
1957	Tennessee St.	92-73	SE Oklahoma
1958	Tennessee St.	85-73	Western Illinois
1959	Tennessee St.	97-87	Pacific-Luth., WA
1960	SW Texas St.	66-44	Westminster, PA
1961	Grambling, LA	95-75	Georgetown, KY
1962	Prairie View, TX	62-53	Westminster, PA
1963	Pan American, TX	73-62	Western Carolina
1964	Rockhurst, MO	66-56	Pan American, TX
1965	Central St., OH	85-51	Oklahoma Baptist
1966	Oklahoma Baptist	88-59	Georgia Southern
1967	St. Benedict's, KS	71-65	Oklahoma Baptist
1968	Central St., OH	51-48	Fairmont St., WV
1969	Eastern N. Mex	99-76	MD-Eastern Shore
1970	Kentucky St.	79-71	Central Wash.
1971	Kentucky St.	102-82	Eastern Michigan
1972	Kentucky St.	71-62	WI-Eau Claire
1973	Guilford, NC	99-96	MD-Eastern Shore
1974	West Georgia	97-79	Alcorn St., MS
1975	Grand Canyon, AZ	65-54	M'western St., TX
1976	Coppin St., MD	96-91	Henderson St., AR
1977	Texas Southern	71-44	Campbell, NC
1978	Grand Canyon	79-75	Kearney St., NE
1979	Drury, MO	60-54	Henderson St., AR
1980	Cameron, OK	84-77	Alabama St.
1981	Beth. Nazarene, OK	86-85*	Al-Huntsville
1982	SC-Spartanburg	51-38	Biola, CA
1983	Charleston, SC	57-53	WV-Wesleyan
1984	Fort Hays St., KS	48-46*	WI-Stevens Pt.
1985	Fort Hays St.	82-80*	Wayland Bapt., TX
1986	David Lipscomb, TN	67-54	AR-Monticello
1987	Washburn, KS	79-77	West Virginia St.
1988	Grand Canyon	88-86*	Auburn-Montg, AL
1989	St. Mary's, TX	61-58	East Central, OK
1990	Birm-Southern, AL	88-80	WI-Eau Claire
1991	Oklahoma City	77-74	Central Arkansas

NAIA Div. I Finals

NAIA split tournament into two divisions in 1992.

Multiple winners: Life, GA and Oklahoma City (3).

Year	Winner	Score	Loser
1992	Oklahoma City	82-73*	Central Arkansas
1993	Hawaii Pacific	88-83	Okla. Baptist
1994	Oklahoma City	99-81	Life, GA
1995	Birm-Southern	92-76	Pfeiffer, NC
1996	Oklahoma City	86-80	Georgetown, KY
1997	Life, GA	73-64	Okla. Baptist
1998	Georgetown, KY	83-69	So. Nazarene
1999	Life, GA	63-60	Mobile, AL
2000	Life, GA	61-59	Georgetown, KY
2001	Faulkner, AL	63-59	Science & Arts, OK
2002	Science & Arts, OK	96-79	Okla. Baptist
2003	Concordia, CA	88-84*	Mountain St., WV
2004	Mountain St., WV	74-70	Concordia, CA
2005	John Brown	65-55	Azusa Pacific
2006	Texas Wesleyan	67-65	Oklahoma City
2007	Oklahoma City	79-71	Concordia

*Overtime

NAIA Div. II Finals

NAIA split tournament into two divisions in 1992.

Multiple winners: Bethel, IN (3), Northwestern, IA (2).

Year	Winner	Score	Loser
1992	Grace, IN	85-79*	Northwestern, IA
1993	Williamette, OR	63-56	Northern St., SD
1994	Eureka, IL	98-95*	Northern St.
1995	Bethel, IN	103-95*	NW Nazarene, ID
1996	Albertson, ID	81-72*	Whitworth, WA
1997	Bethel, IN	95-94	Siena Heights, MI
1998	Bethel, IN	89-87	Oregon Tech
1999	Cornerstone, MI	113-109	Bethel
2000	Embry-Riddle, FL	75-63	Ozarks, MO
2001	Northwestern, IA	82-78	MidAm. Nazarene, KS
2002	Evangel, MO	84-61	Robert Morris, IL
2003	Northwestern, IA	77-57	Bethany, KS
2004	Oregon Tech	81-72	Bellevue, NE
2005	Walsh, OH	81-70	Concordia, NE
2006	Ozarks, MO	74-56	Huntington, IN
2007	MidAm. Nazarene	78-60	Mayville St.

WOMEN

NCAA Final Four

Replaced the Association of Intercollegiate Athletics for Women (AIAW) tournament in 1982 as the official playoff for the national championship.

Multiple winners: Tennessee (7); Connecticut (5); Louisiana Tech, Stanford and USC (2)

Year	Champion	Head Coach	Score	Runner-up	—Third Place—	
1982	Louisiana Tech	Sonya Hogg	76-62	Cheyney	Maryland	Tennessee
1983	USC	Linda Sharp	69-67	Louisiana Tech	Georgia	Old Dominion
1984	USC	Linda Sharp	72-61	Tennessee	Cheyney	Louisiana Tech
1985	Old Dominion	Marianne Stanley	70-65	Georgia	NE Louisiana	Western Ky.
1986	Texas	Jody Conradt	97-81	USC	Tennessee	Western Ky.
1987	Tennessee	Pat Summitt	67-44	Louisiana Tech	Long Beach St.	Texas
1988	Louisiana Tech	Leon Barmore	56-54	Auburn	Long Beach St.	Tennessee
1989	Tennessee	Pat Summitt	76-60	Auburn	Louisiana Tech	Maryland
1990	Stanford	Tara VanDerveer	88-81	Auburn	Louisiana Tech	Virginia

Year	Champion	Head Coach	Score	Runner-up	—Third Place—	
1991	Tennessee	Pat Summitt	70-67 (OT)	Virginia	Connecticut	Stanford
1992	Stanford	Tara VanDerveer	78-62	Western Kentucky	SW Missouri St.	Virginia
1993	Texas Tech	Marsha Sharp	84-82	Ohio St.	Iowa	Vanderbilt
1994	N. Carolina	Sylvia Hatchell	60-59	Louisiana Tech	Alabama	Purdue
1995	Connecticut	Geno Auriemma	70-64	Tennessee	Georgia	Stanford
1996	Tennessee	Pat Summitt	83-65	Georgia	Connecticut	Stanford
1997	Tennessee	Pat Summitt	68-59	Old Dominion	Stanford	Notre Dame
1998	Tennessee	Pat Summitt	93-75	Louisiana Tech	Arkansas	N.C. State
1999	Purdue	Carolyn Peck	62-45	Duke	Louisiana Tech	Georgia
2000	Connecticut	Geno Auriemma	71-52	Tennessee	Penn St.	Rutgers
2001	Notre Dame	Muffet McGraw	68-66	Purdue	Connecticut	SW Missouri St.
2002	Connecticut	Geno Auriemma	82-70	Oklahoma	Tennessee	Duke
2003	Connecticut	Geno Auriemma	73-68	Tennessee	Texas	Duke
2004	Connecticut	Geno Auriemma	70-61	Tennessee	LSU	Minnesota
2005	Baylor	Kim Mulkey-Robertson	84-62	Michigan St.	LSU	Tennessee
2006	Maryland	Brenda Frese	78-75 (OT)	Duke	North Carolina	LSU
2007	Tennessee	Pat Summitt	59-46	Rutgers	LSU	North Carolina

Final Four sites: 1982 (Norfolk, Va.), **1983** (Norfolk, Va.), **1984** (Los Angeles), **1985** (Austin), **1986** (Lexington), **1987** (Austin), **1988** (Tacoma), **1989** (Tacoma), **1990** (Knoxville), **1991** (New Orleans), **1992** (Los Angeles), **1993** (Atlanta), **1994** (Richmond), **1995** (Minneapolis), **1996** (Charlotte), **1997** (Cincinnati), **1998** (Kansas City), **1999** (San Jose), **2000** (Philadelphia), **2001** (St. Louis), **2002** (San Antonio), **2003** (Atlanta), **2004** (New Orleans), **2005** (Indianapolis), **2006** (Boston), **2007** (Cleveland), **2008** (Tampa), **2009** (St. Louis), **2010** (San Antonio).

Most Outstanding Player

A Most Outstanding Player has been selected every year of the NCAA tournament. Winner who did not play for the tournament champion is listed in **bold**, type.

Multiple winners: Chamique Holdsclaw, Cheryl Miller and Diana Taurasi (2).

Year		Year		Year	
1982 Janice Lawrence, La. Tech		1991 **Dawn Staley**, Virginia		2000 Shea Ralph, Connecticut	
1983 Cheryl Miller, USC		1992 Molly Goodenbour, Stanford		2001 Ruth Riley, Notre Dame	
1984 Cheryl Miller, USC		1993 Sheryl Swoopes, Texas Tech		2002 Swin Cash, Connecticut	
1985 Tracy Claxton, Old Dominion		1994 Charlotte Smith, N. Carolina		2003 Diana Taurasi, Connecticut	
1986 Clarissa Davis, Texas		1995 Rebecca Lobo, Connecticut		2004 Diana Taurasi, Connecticut	
1987 Tonya Edwards, Tennessee		1996 Michelle Marciniak, Tennessee		2005 Sophia Young, Baylor	
1988 Erica Westbrooks, La. Tech		1997 Chamique Holdsclaw, Tenn.		2006 Laura Harper, Maryland	
1989 Bridgette Gordon, Tennessee		1998 Chamique Holdsclaw, Tenn.		2007 Candace Parker, Tennessee	
1990 Jennifer Azzi, Stanford		1999 Ukari Figgs, Purdue			

All-Time NCAA Division I Tournament Leaders

Through 2006-07; minimum of six games; **Last** column indicates final year played.

CAREER

Scoring

Total Points	Yrs	Last	Pts	Avg
1 Chamique Holdsclaw, Tennessee	4	1999	**479**	21.8
2 Diana Taurasi, Connecticut	4	2004	**430**	18.7
3 Bridgette Gordon, Tenn	4	1989	**388**	21.6
4 Seimone Augustus, LSU	4	2006	**372**	19.6
5 Alana Beard, Duke	4	2004	**352**	18.5
6 Cheryl Miller, USC	4	1986	**333**	20.8
7 Katie Douglas, Purdue	4	2001	**318**	14.4
8 Janice Lawrence, La. Tech	3	1984	**312**	22.3
9 Penny Toler, S. Diego St/L. Beach St	4	1989	**291**	22.4
10 Ruth Riley, Notre Dame	4	2001	**276**	19.7

Rebounds

Total Rebounds	Yrs	Last	No	Avg
1 Chamique Holdsclaw, Tennessee	4	1999	**196**	8.9
2 Cheryl Miller, USC	4	1986	**170**	10.6
3 Sheila Frost, Tennessee	4	1989	**162**	9.0
4 Val Whiting, Stanford	4	1993	**161**	10.1
5 Sylvia Fowles, LSU	3	active	**158**	8.8
6 Venus Lacy, La. Tech	3	1990	**148**	10.6
7 Bridgette Gordon, Tennessee	4	1989	**142**	7.9
Tamika Catchings, Tennessee	3	2000	**142**	7.9
9 Kirsten Cummings, Long Beach St.	4	1985	**136**	10.5
10 Gwen Jackson, Tennessee	4	2003	**133**	6.7

Assists

Total Assists	Yrs	Last	No	Avg
1 Temeka Johnson, LSU	4	2005	**136**	8.5
2 Teresa Witherspoon, La. Tech	4	1988	**127**	7.9
3 Diana Taurasi, Connecticut	4	2004	**106**	4.3

Steals

Total Steals	Yrs	Last	No	Avg
1 Ticha Penicheiro, Old Dominion	4	1998	**61**	4.7
2 Kelly Miller, Georgia	4	2001	**56**	4.7

SINGLE GAME

Scoring

	Year	Pts
1 Lorri Bauman, Drake vs Maryland	1982	50
2 Sheryl Swoopes, Texas Tech vs Ohio St	1993	47
3 Barbara Kennedy, Clemson vs Penn St	1982	43
4 Jackie Stiles, SW Mo. St. vs. Duke	2001	41
5 LaTaunya Pollard, L. Beach St. vs Howard	1982	40
Cindy Brown, L. Beach St. vs Ohio St	1987	40
Tamika Whitmore, Memphis vs. YSU	1998	40
Tara Mitchem, SW Mo. St. vs. Toledo	2001	40

Rebounds

	Year	No
1 Cheryl Taylor, Tenn. Tech vs Georgia	1985	23
Charlotte Smith, N. Car. vs La. Tech	1994	23
3 Daedra Charles, Tenn. vs SW Missouri	1991	22

Assists

	Year	No
1 Anne Troyan, Penn St. vs. N.C. State	1983	19
2 Tasha Pointer, Rutgers vs. S.F. Austin	2001	18
3 Three tied at 17 each.		

Associated Press Final Top 10 Polls

The Associated Press weekly women's college basketball poll was begun by Mel Greenberg of *The Philadelphia Inquirer* during the 1976-77 season. Although the poll was started as a Top 20 in 1977 and was expanded to a Top 25 in 1990, only the Top 10 from each poll are listed below due to space constraints. The Association of Intercollegiate Athletics for Women (AIAW) Tournament determined the Division I national champion from 1972-81. The NCAA began its women's Division I tournament in 1982. The final AP Polls were taken before the NCAA tournament. Eventual national champions are in **bold** type.

1977
1 **Delta St.**
2 Immaculata
3 St. Joseph's-PA
4 CS-Fullerton
5 Tennessee
6 Tennessee Tech
7 Wayland Baptist
8 Montclair St.
9 S.F. Austin St.
10 N.C. State

1978
1 Tennessee
2 Wayland Baptist
3 N.C. State
4 Montclair St.
5 **UCLA**
6 Maryland
7 Queens-NY
8 Valdosta St.
9 Delta St.
10 LSU

1979
1 **Old Dominion**
2 Louisiana Tech
3 Tennessee
4 Texas
5 S.F. Austin St.
6 UCLA
7 Rutgers
8 Maryland
9 Cheyney
10 Wayland Baptist

1980
1 **Old Dominion**
2 Tennessee
3 Louisiana Tech
4 South Carolina
5 S.F. Austin St.
6 Maryland
7 Texas
8 Rutgers
9 Long Beach St.
10 N.C. State

1981
1 **Louisiana Tech**
2 Tennessee
3 Old Dominion
4 USC
5 Cheyney
6 Long Beach St.
7 UCLA
8 Maryland
9 Rutgers
10 Kansas

1982
1 **Louisiana Tech**
2 Cheyney
3 Maryland
4 Tennessee
5 Texas
6 USC
7 Old Dominion
8 Rutgers
9 Long Beach St.
10 Penn St.

1983
1 USC
2 Louisiana Tech
3 Texas
4 Old Dominion
5 Cheyney
6 Long Beach St.
7 Maryland
8 Penn St.
9 Georgia
10 Tennessee

1984
1 Texas
2 Louisiana Tech
3 Georgia
4 Old Dominion
5 **USC**
6 Long Beach St.
7 Kansas St.
8 LSU
9 Cheyney
10 Mississippi

1985
1 Texas
2 NE Louisiana
3 Long Beach St.
4 Louisiana Tech
5 **Old Dominion**
6 Mississippi
7 Ohio St.
8 Georgia
9 Penn St.
10 Auburn

1986
1 **Texas**
2 Georgia
3 USC
4 Louisiana Tech
5 Western Ky.
6 Virginia
7 Auburn
8 Long Beach St.
9 LSU
10 Rutgers

1987
1 Texas
2 Auburn
3 Louisiana Tech
4 Long Beach St.
5 Rutgers
6 Georgia
7 **Tennessee**
8 Mississippi
9 Iowa
10 Ohio St.

1988
1 Tennessee
2 Iowa
3 Auburn
4 Texas
5 **Louisiana Tech**
6 Ohio St.
7 Long Beach St.
8 Rutgers
9 Maryland
10 Virginia

1989
1 **Tennessee**
2 Auburn
3 Louisiana Tech
4 Stanford
5 Maryland
6 Texas
7 Long Beach St.
8 Iowa
9 Colorado
10 Georgia

1990
1 Louisiana Tech
2 **Stanford**
3 Washington
4 Tennessee
5 UNLV
6 S.F. Austin St.
7 Georgia
8 Texas
9 Auburn
10 Iowa

1991
1 Penn St.
2 Virginia
3 Georgia
4 **Tennessee**
5 Purdue
6 Auburn
7 N.C. State
8 LSU
9 Arkansas
10 Western Ky.

1992
1 Virginia
2 Tennessee
3 **Stanford**
4 S.F. Austin St.
5 Mississippi
6 Miami-FL
7 Iowa
8 Maryland
9 Penn St.
10 SW Missouri St.

1993
1 Vanderbilt
2 Tennessee
3 Ohio St.
4 Iowa
5 **Texas Tech**
6 Stanford
7 Auburn
8 Penn St.
9 Virginia
10 Colorado

1994
1 Tennessee
2 Penn St.
3 Connecticut
4 **North Carolina**
5 Colorado
6 Louisiana Tech
7 USC
8 Purdue
9 Texas Tech
10 Virginia

1995
1 **Connecticut**
2 Colorado
3 Tennessee
4 Stanford
5 Texas Tech
6 Vanderbilt
7 Penn St.
8 Louisiana Tech
9 Western Ky.
10 Virginia

1996
1 Louisiana Tech
2 Connecticut
3 Stanford
4 **Tennessee**
5 Georgia
6 Old Dominion
7 Iowa
8 Penn St.
9 Texas Tech
10 Alabama

1997
1 Connecticut
2 Old Dominion
3 Stanford
4 North Carolina
5 Louisiana Tech
6 Georgia
7 Florida
8 Alabama
9 LSU
10 **Tennessee**

1998
1 **Tennessee**
2 Old Dominion
3 Connecticut
4 Louisiana Tech
5 Stanford
6 Texas Tech
7 North Carolina
8 Duke
9 Arizona
10 N.C. State

1999
1 **Purdue**
2 Tennessee
3 Louisiana Tech
4 Colorado St.
5 Old Dominion
6 Connecticut
7 Rutgers
8 Notre Dame
9 Texas Tech
10 Duke

2000
1 **Connecticut**
2 Tennessee
3 Louisiana Tech
4 Georgia
5 Notre Dame
6 Penn St.
7 Iowa St.
8 Rutgers
9 UC-Santa Barbara
10 Duke

2001
1 Connecticut
2 **Notre Dame**
3 Tennessee
4 Georgia
5 Duke
6 Louisiana Tech
7 Oklahoma
8 Iowa St.
9 Purdue
10 Vanderbilt

2002
1 **Connecticut**
2 Oklahoma
3 Duke
4 Vanderbilt
5 Stanford
6 Tennessee
7 Baylor
8 Louisiana Tech
9 Purdue
10 Iowa St.

2003
1 **Connecticut**
2 Duke
3 LSU
4 Tennessee
5 Texas
6 Louisiana Tech
7 Texas Tech
8 Kansas St.
9 Stanford
10 Purdue

2004
1 Duke
2 Tennessee
3 Purdue
4 Texas
5 Penn St.
6 **Connecticut**
7 Louisiana Tech
8 Kansas St.
9 Houston
10 Stanford

2005
1 Stanford
2 LSU
3 Tennessee
4 North Carolina
5 **Baylor**
6 Michigan St.
7 Duke
8 Ohio St.
9 Rutgers
10 Connecticut

2006
1 North Carolina
2 Ohio St.
3 **Maryland**
4 Duke
5 LSU
6 Tennessee
7 Oklahoma
8 Connecticut
9 Rutgers
10 Baylor

2007
1 Duke
2 Connecticut
3 North Carolina
4 **Tennessee**
5 Ohio St.
6 Stanford
7 Maryland
8 Arizona St.
9 Vanderbilt
10 LSU

All-Time AP Top 10

The composite AP Top 10 from the 1976-77 season through 2006-07, based on the final regular season rankings of each year. Team points are based on 10 points for all 1st place finishes, 9 for each 2nd, etc. Also listed are the number of times ranked No. 1 by AP going into the tournaments, and times ranked in the pre-tournament Top 10.

		Pts	No.1	Top 10			Pts	No.1	Top 10
1	Tennessee	218	5	29	6	Stanford	82	1	13
2	Louisiana Tech	173	4	24	7	Georgia	72	0	13
3	Connecticut	108	6	14	8	Duke	59	2	10
4	Texas	93	4	18	9	Penn St.	52	1	11
5	Old Dominion	81	2	11	10	Long Beach St.	45	0	10

All-Time Winningest Division I Teams

Division I schools with best winning percentages (with a minimum of 350 victories) and most victories through 2006-07 (including postseason tournaments). Although official NCAA women's basketball records didn't begin until the 1981-82 season, results from previous seasons are included below.

Top 15 Winning Percentage

		Yrs	W	L	Pct
1	Louisiana Tech	33	916	167	.846
2	Tennessee	62	1040	237	.814
3	Texas	33	821	272	.751
4	Old Dominion	38	841	282	.749
5	Montana	33	704	240	.746
6	Stephen F. Austin St.	38	794	296	.728
7	Stanford	33	716	268	.728
8	Utah	33	694	270	.720
9	Connecticut	33	713	282	.717
10	Rutgers	33	702	290	.708
11	Georgia	34	721	300	.706
12	Penn St.	43	739	313	.702
13	Wisconsin-Green Bay	34	695	296	.701
14	Texas Tech	32	719	315	.695
15	Auburn	36	710	313	.694

Top 15 Victories

		Yrs	W	L	Pct
1	Tennessee	62	1040	237	.814
2	Louisiana Tech	33	916	167	.846
3	Old Dominion	38	841	282	.749
4	Texas	33	821	272	.751
5	James Madison	85	799	478	.626
6	Stephen F. Austin St.	38	794	296	.728
7	Tennessee Tech	37	783	346	.694
8	Long Beach St.	45	767	372	.673
9	Ohio St.	42	753	382	.663
10	Western Kentucky	45	743	360	.674
11	Penn St.	43	739	313	.702
12	Richmond	87	737	510	.591
13	Kansas St.	39	721	431	.626
	Georgia	34	721	300	.706
15	Texas Tech	32	719	315	.695

Annual NCAA Division I Leaders

All averages include postseason games

Scoring

Multiple winners: Cindy Blodgett, Andrea Congreaves and Jackie Stiles (2).

Year		Gm	Pts	Avg
1982	Barbara Kennedy, Clemson	31	908	29.3
1983	LaTaunya Pollard, L. Beach St	31	907	29.3
1984	Deborah Temple, Delta St	28	873	31.2
1985	Anucha Browne, Northwestern	28	855	30.5
1986	Wanda Ford, Drake	30	919	30.6
1987	Tresa Spaulding, BYU	28	810	28.9
1988	LeChandra LeDay, Grambling	28	850	30.4
1989	Patricia Hoskins, Miss. Valley	27	908	33.6
1990	Kim Perrot, SW Louisiana	28	839	30.0
1991	Jan Jensen, Drake	30	888	29.6
1992	Andrea Congreaves, Mercer	28	925	33.0
1993	Andrea Congreaves, Mercer	26	805	31.0
1994	Kristy Ryan, CS-Sacramento	26	727	28.0
1995	Koko Lahanas, CS-Fullerton	29	778	26.8
1996	Cindy Blodgett, Maine	32	889	27.8
1997	Cindy Blodgett, Maine	30	810	27.0
1998	Allison Feaster, Harvard	28	797	28.5
1999	Tamika Whitmore, Memphis	32	843	26.3
2000	Jackie Stiles, SW Missouri St.	32	890	27.8
2001	Jackie Stiles, SW Missouri St.	35	1062	30.3
2002	Kelly Mazzante, Penn St.	35	872	24.9
2003	Chandi Jones, Houston	28	770	27.5
2004	Emily Faurholt, Idaho	29	737	25.4
2005	Tan White, Mississippi St.	29	681	23.5
2006	Seimone Augustus, LSU	35	795	22.7
2007	Carrie Moore, Western Mich.	32	813	25.4

Rebounds

Multiple winner: Patricia Hoskins (2).

Year		Gm	No	Avg
1982	Anne Donovan, Old Dominion	28	412	14.7
1983	Deborah Mitchell, Miss. Col	28	447	16.0
1984	Joy Kellog, Oklahoma City	23	373	16.2
1985	Rosina Pearson, Beth-Cookman	26	480	18.5
1986	Wanda Ford, Drake	30	506	16.9
1987	Patricia Hoskins, Miss. Valley St.	28	476	17.0
1988	Katie Beck, East Tenn. St.	25	441	17.6
1989	Patricia Hoskins, Miss. Valley St.	27	440	16.3
1990	Pam Hudson, Northwestern St	29	438	15.1
1991	Tarcha Hollis, Grambling	29	443	15.3
1992	Christy Greis, Evansville	28	383	13.7
1993	Ann Barry, Nevada	25	355	14.2
1994	DeShawne Blocker, E. Tenn. St.	26	450	17.3
1995	Tera Sheriff, Jackson St	29	401	13.8
1996	Dana Wynne, Seton Hall	29	372	12.8
1997	Etolia Mitchell, Georgia St.	25	330	13.2
1998	Alisha Hill, Howard	30	397	13.2
1999	Monica Logan, UMBC	27	364	13.5
2000	Malveata Johnson, N.C. A&T	27	363	13.4
2001	Andrea Gardner, Howard	31	439	14.2
2002	Mandi Carver, Idaho St.	27	336	12.4
2003	Jennifer Butler, Massachusetts	28	412	14.7
2004	Ashlee Kelly, Quinnipiac	29	392	13.5
2005	Sancho Lyttle, Houston	30	362	12.1
2006	Courtney Paris, Oklahoma	36	539	15.0
2007	Lachelle Lyles, SE Missouri St.	31	527	17.0

Note: Wanda Ford (1986) and Patricia Hoskins (1989) each led the country in scoring and rebounds in the same year.

All-Time NCAA Division I Individual Leaders

Through 2006-07; includes regular season and tournament games; Official NCAA women's basketball records began with 1981-82 season. Players who competed earlier than that are not included below; **Last** column indicates final year played.

CAREER

Scoring

Average

		Yrs	Last	Pts	Avg
1	Patricia Hoskins, Miss. Valley St.	.4	1989	3122	28.4
2	Sandra Hodge, New Orleans	. .4	1984	2860	26.7
3	Jackie Stiles, SW Mo. St.	4	2001	3206	26.1
4	Lorri Bauman, Drake	4	1984	3115	26.0
5	Andrea Congreaves, Mercer	. . .4	1993	2796	25.9
6	Cindy Blodgett, Maine	4	1998	3005	25.5
7	Valorie Whiteside, Aplach St.	4	1988	2944	25.4
8	Joyce Walker, LSU	4	1984	2906	24.8
9	Tarcha Hollis, Grambling	4	1991	2058	24.2
10	Korie Hlede, Duquesne	4	1998	2631	24.1

Rebounds

Average

		Yrs	Last	Reb	Avg
1	Wanda Ford, Drake	4	1986	1887	16.1
2	Patricia Hoskins, Miss. Valley St.	. . .4	1989	1662	15.1
3	Tarcha Hollis, Grambling	4	1991	1185	13.9
4	Katie Beck, East Tenn. St.	4	1988	1404	13.4
5	Marilyn Stephens, Temple	4	1984	1519	13.0
6	Natalie Williams, UCLA	4	1994	1137	12.8
7	Cheryl Taylor, Tenn. Tech	4	1987	1532	12.8
8	DeShawne Blocker, E. Tenn. St.	. .4	1995	1361	12.7
9	Olivia Bradley, West Virginia	4	1985	1484	12.7
10	Judy Mosley, Hawaii	4	1990	1441	12.6

SINGLE SEASON

Scoring

Average

		Year	Gm	Pts	Avg
1	Patricia Hoskins, Miss.Valley St.	1989	27	908	33.6
2	Andrea Congreaves, Mercer	. .1992	28	925	33.0
3	Deborah Temple, Delta St.	1984	28	873	31.2
4	Andrea Congreaves, Mercer	. .1993	26	805	31.0
5	Wanda Ford, Drake	. . . . .1986.	30	919	30.6
6	Anucha Browne, Northwestern	.1985	28	855	30.5
7	LeChandra LeDay, Grambling	. .1988	28	850	30.4
8	Jackie Stiles, SW Mo. St.	2001	35	1062	30.3
9	Kim Perrot, SW Louisiana	1990	28	841	30.0
10	Tina Hutchinson, San Diego St.	1984	30	898	29.9

SINGLE GAME

Scoring

			Year	Pts
1	Cindy Brown, Long Beach St. vs San José St.	.1987	60
2	Lorri Bauman, Drake vs SW Missouri St.	. . .1984	58
	Kim Perrot, SW La. vs SE La	. . . .	1990	58
4	Jackie Stiles, SW Mo. St. vs Evansville	2000	56
5	Patricia Stiles, Miss.Valley St. vs South-BR	.1989	55
	Patricia Hoskins, Miss.Valley St. vs Ala. St.	.1989	55

Rebounds (since 1982)

		Year	No
1	Deborah Temple, Delta St. vs UAB	1983	40
2	Rosina Pearson, Bet-Cookman vs Fla. Mem.	1984	37
3	Mauren Formico, Pepperdine vs. Loyola-CA	.1985	33

All-Time Winningest Division I Coaches

Minimum of 10 seasons as Division I head coach; regular season and tournament games included.

Top 10 Winning Percentage

		Yrs	W	L	Pct
1	Leon Barmore, La. Tech	20	576	87	.869
2	**Pat Summitt**, Tennessee	33	947	180	.840
3	**Geno Auriemma**, Connecticut	22	621	120	.838
4	**Gail Goestenkors**, Texas	15	396	99	.800
5	Bill Sheahan, Mt. St. Mary's	17	372	104	.782
6	**Robin Selvig**, Montana	29	672	192	.778
7	**Tara VanDerveer**, Stanford	. .28	689	184	.768
8	Marsha Sharp, Texas Tech	23	556	175	.761
9	**Andy Landers**, Georgia	28	684	215	.761
10	Jody Conradt, Texas	37	882	293	.751

Top 10 Victories

		Yrs	W	L	Pct
1	**Pat Summitt**, Tennessee	33	947	180	.840
2	Jody Conradt, Texas	37	882	293	.751
3	**C. Vivian Stringer**, Rutgers	.36	777	260	.749
4	**Sylvia Hatchell**, N. Carolina	.32	751	272	.734
5	Sue Gunter, LSU	34	708	308	.697
	Kay Yow, N.C. State	36	708	324	.686
7	**Tara VanDerveer**, Stanford	. .28	689	184	.768
8	**Andy Landers**, Georgia	28	684	215	.761
9	**Rene Portland**, Penn St.	30	681	249	.732
10	**Robin Selvig**, Montana	29	672	192	.778

Note: active coaches in **bold** type and listed with current teams. Retired coached listed with last team coached.

Annual Awards

The Broderick Award was first given out to the Women's Division I or Large School Player of the Year in 1977. Since then, the National Assn. for Girls and Women in Sports (1978), the Women's Basketball Coaches Assn. (1983), the Atlanta Tip-Off Club (1983) and the Associated Press (1995) have joined in.

Associated Press

Voted on by AP sportswriters and broadcasters and first presented in 1995.

Multiple winner: Seimone Augustus and Chamique Holdsclaw (2).

Year	Year	Year
1995 Rebecca Lobo, Connecticut	2000 Tamika Catchings, Tennessee	2004 Alana Beard, Duke
1996 Jennifer Rizzotti, Connecticut	2001 Ruth Riley, Notre Dame	2005 Seimone Augustus, LSU
1997 Kara Wolters, Connecticut	2002 Sue Bird, Connecticut	2006 Seimone Augustus, LSU
1998 Chamique Holdsclaw, Tennessee	2003 Diana Taurasi, Connecticut	2007 Courtney Paris, Oklahoma
1999 Chamique Holdsclaw, Tennessee		

Broderick Award

Voted on by a national panel of women's collegiate athletic directors and first presented by the late Thomas Broderick, an athletic outfitter, in 1977. Honda has presented the award since 1987. Basketball Player of the Year is one of 10 nominated for Collegiate Woman Athlete of the Year; (*) indicates player also won Athlete of the Year.

Multiple winners: Seimone Augustus, Chamique Holdsclaw, Nancy Lieberman, Cheryl Miller, Dawn Staley and Diana Taurasi (2).

Year	Year	Year
1977 Lucy Harris, Delta St.*	1980 Nancy Lieberman, Old Dominion*	1983 Anne Donovan, Old Dominion
1978 Ann Meyers, UCLA*	1981 Lynette Woodard, Kansas	1984 Cheryl Miller, USC*
1979 Nancy Lieberman, Old Dominion*	1982 Pam Kelly, La. Tech	1985 Cheryl Miller, USC

Year	Year	Year
1986 Kamie Ethridge, Texas*	1994 Lisa Leslie, USC	2001 Jackie Stiles, SW Missouri St.*
1987 Katrina McClain, Georgia	1995 Rebecca Lobo, Connecticut	2002 Sue Bird, Connecticut
1988 Teresa Weatherspoon, La. Tech*	1996 Jennifer Rizzotti, Connecticut	2003 Diana Taurasi, Connecticut
1989 Bridgette Gordon, Tennessee	1997 Chamique Holdsclaw, Tennessee	2004 Diana Taurasi, Connecticut
1990 Jennifer Azzi, Stanford	1998 Chamique Holdsclaw, Tennessee*	2005 Seimone Augustus, LSU
1991 Dawn Staley, Virginia	1999 Stephanie White-McCarty, Purdue	2006 Seimone Augustus, LSU
1992 Dawn Staley, Virginia	2000 Shea Ralph, Connecticut	2007 Candace Parker, Tennessee
1993 Sheryl Swoopes, Texas Tech		

Wade Trophy

Originally voted on by the National Assn. for Girls and Women in Sports (NAGWS) and awarded for academics and community service as well as player performance. First presented in 1978 in the name of former Delta St. coach Lily Margaret Wade. Since 2002, the trophy has been awarded to the Women's Basketball Coaches Association player of the year.

Multiple winner: Seimone Augustus and Nancy Lieberman (2).

Year	Year	Year
1978 Carol Blazejowski, Montclair St.	1988 Teresa Weatherspoon, La. Tech	1998 Ticha Penicheiro, Old Dominion
1979 Nancy Lieberman, Old Dominion	1989 Clarissa Davis, Texas	1999 Stephanie White-McCarty, Purdue
1980 Nancy Lieberman, Old Dominion	1990 Jennifer Azzi, Stanford	2000 Edwina Brown, Texas
1981 Lynette Woodard, Kansas	1991 Daedra Charles, Tennessee	2001 Jackie Stiles, SW Missouri St.
1982 Pam Kelly, La. Tech	1992 Susan Robinson, Penn St.	2002 Sue Bird, Connecticut
1983 LaTaunya Pollard, L. Beach St.	1993 Karen Jennings, Nebraska	2003 Diana Taurasi, Connecticut
1984 Janice Lawrence, La. Tech	1994 Carol Ann Shudlick, Minnesota	2004 Alana Beard, Duke
1985 Cheryl Miller, USC	1995 Rebecca Lobo, Connecticut	2005 Seimone Augustus, LSU
1986 Kamie Ethridge, Texas	1996 Jennifer Rizzotti, Connecticut	2006 Seimone Augustus, LSU
1987 Shelly Pennefather, Villanova	1997 DeLisha Milton, Florida	2007 Candace Parker, Tennessee

Naismith Trophy

Voted on by a panel of coaches, sportswriters and broadcasters and first presented in 1983 by the Atlanta Tip-Off Club in the name of the inventor of basketball, Dr. James Naismith.

Multiple winners: Cheryl Miller (3); Seimone Augustus, Clarissa Davis, Chamique Holdsclaw, Dawn Staley and Diana Taurasi (2).

Year	Year	Year
1983 Anne Donovan, Old Dominion	1992 Dawn Staley, Virginia	2000 Tamika Catchings, Tennessee
1984 Cheryl Miller, USC	1993 Sheryl Swoopes, Texas Tech	2001 Ruth Riley, Notre Dame
1985 Cheryl Miller, USC	1994 Lisa Leslie, USC	2002 Sue Bird, Connecticut
1986 Cheryl Miller, USC	1995 Rebecca Lobo, Connecticut	2003 Diana Taurasi, Connecticut
1987 Clarissa Davis, Texas	1996 Saudia Roundtree, Georgia	2004 Diana Taurasi, Connecticut
1988 Sue Wicks, Rutgers	1997 Kate Starbird, Stanford	2005 Seimone Augustus, LSU
1989 Clarissa Davis, Texas	1998 Chamique Holdsclaw, Tennessee	2006 Seimone Augustus, LSU
1990 Jennifer Azzi, Stanford	1999 Chamique Holdsclaw, Tennessee	2007 Candace Parker, Tennessee
1991 Dawn Staley, Virgina		

Women's Basketball Coaches Association

Voted on by the WBCA and first presented by Champion athletic outfitters in 1983. Merged with Wade Trophy in 2002.

Multiple winners: Chamique Holdsclaw, Cheryl Miller and Dawn Staley (2).

Year	Year	Year
1983 Anne Donovan, Old Dominion	1990 Venus Lacy, La. Tech	1996 Saudia Roundtree, Georgia
1984 Janice Lawrence, La. Tech	1991 Dawn Staley, Virginia	1997 Kate Starbird, Stanford
1985 Cheryl Miller, USC	1992 Dawn Staley, Virginia	1998 Chamique Holdsclaw, Tennessee
1986 Cheryl Miller, USC	1993 Sheryl Swoopes, Texas Tech	1999 Chamique Holdsclaw, Tennessee
1987 Katrina McClain, Georgia	1994 Lisa Leslie, USC	2000 Tamika Catchings, Tennessee
1988 Michelle Edwards, Iowa	1995 Rebecca Lobo, Connecticut	2001 Ruth Riley, Notre Dame
1989 Clarissa Davis, Texas		

Wooden Award

Voted on by a panel of coaches, sportswriters and broadcasters and first presented in 2004 by the Los Angeles Athletic Club in the name of former Purdue All-American and UCLA coach John Wooden. Unlike the other player of the year awards, candidates for the Wooden must have a minimum grade point average of 2.00 (out of 4.00).

Multiple winner: Seimone Augustus (2).

Year	Year	Year
2004 Alana Beard, Duke	2006 Seimone Augustus, LSU	2007 Candace Parker, Tennessee
2005 Seimone Augustus, LSU		

Coach of the Year Award

Voted on by the Women's Basketball Coaches Assn. and first presented by Converse athletic outfitters in 1983.

Multiple winners: Geno Auriemma and Pat Summitt (3); Jody Conradt, Gail Goestenkors, Rene Portland and Vivian Stringer (2).

Year	Year	Year
1983 Pat Summitt, Tennessee	1992 Ferne Labati, Miami-FL	2001 Muffet McGraw, Notre Dame
1984 Jody Conradt, Texas	1993 Vivian Stringer, Iowa	2002 Geno Auriemma, Connecticut
1985 Jim Foster, St. Joseph's-PA	1994 Marsha Sharp, Texas Tech	2003 Gail Goestenkors, Duke
1986 Jody Conradt, Texas	1995 Pat Summitt, Tennessee	2004 Rene Portland, Penn St.
1987 Theresa Grentz, Rutgers	1996 Leon Barmore, La. Tech	2005 Pokey Chatman, LSU
1988 Vivian Stringer, Iowa	1997 Geno Auriemma, Connecticut	2006 Sylvia Hatchell, N. Carolina
1989 Tara VanDerveer, Stanford	1998 Pat Summitt, Tennessee	2007 Gail Goestenkors, Duke
1990 Kay Yow, N.C. State	1999 Carolyn Peck, Purdue	
1991 Rene Portland, Penn St.	2000 Geno Auriemma, Connecticut	

Other Women's Champions

The NCAA has sanctioned national championship tournaments for Division II and Division III since 1982. The NAIA sanctioned a single tournament from 1981-91, then split in to two divisions in 1992. (*) denotes overtime

NCAA Div. II Finals

Multiple winners: North Dakota St. and Cal Poly Pomona (5); Delta St. and North Dakota (3).

Year	Winner	Score	Loser
1982	Cal Poly Pomona	93-74	Tuskegee, AL
1983	Virginia Union	73-60	Cal Poly Pomona
1984	Central Mo.St.	80-73	Virginia Union
1985	Cal Poly Pomona	80-69	Central Mo.St.
1986	Cal Poly Pomona	70-63	North Dakota St.
1987	New Haven, CT	77-75	Cal Poly Pomona
1988	Hampton, VA	65-48	West Texas St.
1989	Delta St., MS	88-58	Cal Poly Pomona
1990	Delta St., MS	77-43	Bentley, MA
1991	North Dakota St.	81-74	SE Missouri St.
1992	Delta St., MS	65-63	North Dakota St.
1993	North Dakota St.	95-63	Delta St.
1994	North Dakota St.	89-56	CS-San Bernardino
1995	North Dakota St.	98-85	Portland St.
1996	North Dakota St.	104-78	Shippensburg, PA
1997	North Dakota	94-78	S. Indiana
1998	North Dakota	92-76	Emporia St.
1999	North Dakota	80-63	Arkansas Tech
2000	Northern Kentucky	71-62	North Dakota St.
2001	Cal Poly Pomona	87-80*	North Dakota St.
2002	Cal Poly Pomona	74-62	SE Oklahoma St.
2003	South Dakota St.	65-60	Northern Kentucky
2004	California, PA	75-72	Drury
2005	Washburn	70-53	Seattle Pacific
2006	Grand Valley St.	58-52	AIC
2007	Southern Conn.	61-45	Florida Gulf Coast

NCAA Div. III Finals

Multiple winners: Washington (4); Capital, Elizabethtown, Hope and WI-Stevens Point (2).

Year	Winner	Score	Loser
1982	Elizabethtown, PA	67-66*	NC-Greensboro
1983	North Central, IL	83-71	Elizabethtown, PA
1984	Rust College, MS	51-49	Elizabethtown, PA
1985	Scranton, PA	68-59	New Rochelle, NY
1986	Salem St., MA	89-85	Bishop, TX
1987	WI-Stevens Pt.	81-74	Concordia, MN
1988	Concordia, MN	65-57	St. John Fisher, NY
1989	Elizabethtown, PA	66-65	CS-Stanislaus
1990	Hope, MI	65-63	St. John Fisher
1991	St. Thomas, MN	73-55	Muskingum, OH
1992	Alma, MI	79-75	Moravian, PA
1993	Central Iowa	71-63	Capital, OH
1994	Capital, OH	82-63	Washington, MO
1995	Capital, OH	59-55	WI-Oshkosh
1996	WI-Oshkosh	66-50	Mt. Union, OH
1997	NYU	72-70	WI-Eau Claire
1998	Washington, MO	77-69	So. Maine
1999	Washington, MO	74-65	Col.of St. Benedict, MN
2000	Washington, MO	79-33	So. Maine
2001	Washington, MO	67-45	Messiah, PA
2002	WI-Stevens Pt.	67-65	St. Lawrence, NY
2003	Trinity, TX	60-58	E. Connecticut St.
2004	Wilmington	59-53	Bowdoin
2005	Millikin	70-50	Randolph-Macon
2006	Hope, MI	69-56	Southern Maine
2007	DePauw	55-52	Washington, MO

NAIA Finals

Multiple winners: One tournament–SW Oklahoma (4); Div. I tourney–Southern Nazarene (6), Oklahoma City (4); Union (3); Arkansas Tech (2); Div. II tourney–Hastings (3); Morningside, Northern St. and Western Oregon (2).

Year	Winner	Score	Loser	Year	Winner	Score	Loser
1981	Kentucky St.	73-67	Texas Southern	1997	II– NW Nazarene	64-46	Black Hills St., SD
1982	SW Oklahoma	80-45	Mo. Southern	1998	I– Union, TN	73-70	So. Nazarene
1983	SW Oklahoma	80-68	AL-Huntsville		II– Walsh, OH	73-66	Mary Hardin-Baylor
1984	NC-Asheville	72-70*	Portland, OR	1999	I– Oklahoma City	72-55	Simon Fraser, B.C.
1985	SW Oklahoma	55-54	Saginaw Val., MI		II– Shawnee St., OH	80-65	St. Francis, IN
1986	Francis Marion, SC	75-65	Wayland Baptist, TX	2000	I– Oklahoma City	64-55	Simon Fraser, B.C.
1987	SW Oklahoma	60-58	North Georgia		II– Mary, N.D.	59-49	Northwestern, IA
1988	Oklahoma City	113-95	Claflin, SC	2001	I– Oklahoma City	69-52	Auburn Montgomery, AL
1989	So. Nazarene, OK	98-96	Claflin, SC		II– Northwestern, IA	77-50	Albertson, ID
1990	SW Oklahoma	82-75	AR-Monticello	2002	I– Oklahoma City	82-73	So. Nazarene
1991	Ft. Hays St., KS	57-53	SW Oklahoma		II–Hastings, NE	73-69	Cornerstone, MI
1992	I– Arkansas Tech	84-68	Wayland Baptist, TX	2003	I– So. Nazarene	71-70	Oklahoma City
	II– Northern St., SD	73-56	Tarleton St., TX		II– Hastings, NE	59-53	Dakota Wesleyan
1993	I– Arkansas Tech	76-75	Union, TN	2004	I– So. Nazarene	77-61	Oklahoma City
	II– No. Montana	71-68	Northern St., SD		II– Morningside	70-62	Mary, N.D.
1994	I– So. Nazarene	97-74	David Lipscomb, TN	2005	I– Union, TN	67-63	Oklahoma City
	II– Northern St., SD	48-45	Western Oregon		II– Morningside	75-65	Cedarville, OH
1995	I– So. Nazarene	78-77	SE Oklahoma	2006	I– Union, TN	79-62	Lubbock Christian
	II– Western Oregon	75-67	NW Nazarene, ID		II– Hastings, NE	58-39	Ozarks, MO
1996	I– So. Nazarene	80-79	SE Oklahoma	2007	I– Lambuth, TN	63-50	Cumberland, TN
	II– Western Oregon	80-77	Huron, SD		II– Indiana Wesleyan	48-34	Ozarks, MO
1997	I– So. Nazarene	78-73	Union, TN				

AIAW Finals

The Association of Intercollegiate Athletics for Women Large College tournament determined the women's national champion for 10 years until supplanted by the NCAA. In 1982, most Division I teams entered the first NCAA tournament rather than the last one staged by the AIAW.

Year	Winner	Score	Loser	Year	Winner	Score	Loser
1972	Immaculata, PA	52-48	West Chester, PA	1978	UCLA	90-74	Maryland
1973	Immaculata, PA	59-52	Queens College, NY	1979	Old Dominion	75-65	Louisiana Tech
1974	Immaculata, PA	68-53	Mississippi College	1980	Old Dominion	68-53	Tennessee
1975	Delta St., MS	90-81	Immaculata, PA	1981	Louisiana Tech	79-59	Tennessee
1976	Delta St., MS	69-64	Immaculata, PA	1982	Rutgers	83-77	Texas
1977	Delta St., MS	68-55	LSU				

PRO BASKETBALL

2006 / 2007 YEAR IN REVIEW

Tim Duncan was a factor in the Spurs' third title in five years but it was **Tony Parker** that earned the MVP.

OFFICIAL INQUIRIES

The Tim Donaghy affair cast a large shadow over the NBA and handed David Stern the biggest challenge of his long career.

DAVID STERN HAD JUST WATCHED one former No. 1 pick, Tim Duncan, lead the Spurs to their fourth championship against another former top pick, LeBron James, 22-year-old conqueror of the Eastern Conference. Now, the contented commissioner was eagerly awaiting the arrival of another top choice with title-type talent, be it Greg Oden or Kevin Durant.

Life was good for Stern.

But on June 20, everything changed. The league Stern had spent 23 years building into a global powerhouse was rocked to its core. Who would be drafted first no longer seemed so important. Who LeBron's Cavaliers added in the offseason really didn't matter. Arguments about whether or not the Spurs were a legitimate dynasty became irrelevant.

The National Basketball Association had a serious scandal on its hands.

Stern was informed by the FBI that it was investigating referee Tim Donaghy for betting on NBA games.

"This is the most serious situation and worst situation that I have ever experienced either as a fan of the NBA, a lawyer for the NBA or a commissioner of the NBA," Stern said a month later.

The FBI first caught wind of Donaghy's illegal actions when hearing his name mentioned on wiretaps during an investigation of the notorious Gambino crime family. It turned out that Donaghy, a 13-year veteran from Philadelphia, had compromised himself by racking up debts through gambling, which is a forbidden activity for NBA officials. League referees are allowed to do nothing more than go to the horseracing track in the offseason. Even setting foot in the gaming area of a casino is against the rules.

But court documents say the 40-year-old Donaghy began betting in 2003. In 2005, the NBA received

 Chris Broussard is a senior writer at *ESPN The Magazine*.

→ NBA Commissioner **David Stern** was forced to answer some tough questions in 2007 when referee **Tim Donaghy** (inset) was linked to gambling and organized crime.

tips that Donaghy was frequenting a casino in Atlantic City, but their investigation came up empty. In hindsight, however, there were warning signs that Donaghy might be a loose cannon. He was involved in a dispute with his neighbors so virulent that the NBA decided against having him referee the second round of the 2005 play-offs, warning him that if his volatile behavior continued they would take stronger measures.

Still, Donaghy continued to gamble and when he got into debt, he was pressured into giving professional gamblers inside information that would help them place more informed bets on NBA games. He told them what referees were scheduled to officiate certain games, which is information no one but the referees and their immediate family members are privy to. He told them how those referees officiated and interacted with certain players, which can affect the outcome of games. And he also reportedly began betting on games himself, including those he officiated.

It's even possible that the playoffs, and dare we say, the NBA championship were affected. Donaghy refereed Game 3 of the second-round Western Conference matchup between the San Antonio Spurs and the Phoenix Suns.

LeBron James had a monster year, taking his Cavs to the NBA Finals for the first time and helping get USA Basketball back on track just in time for the Summer Olympics in 2008.

diately known what games he bet on.

As horrific as the situation was for the NBA, league officials, coaches and players felt the damage would be controllable if Donaghy was "a rogue, isolated criminal," to use Stern's words.

That appears to be the case, but reports late in the summer stated that Donaghy would give information on 20 officials who took part in gambling that, while not illegal, nevertheless violated their NBA contracts.

As more and more information regarding the case leaked out over the summer, it overshadowed an offseason full of activity, whether it was the Kevin Garnett trade from Minnesota to Boston, Kobe Bryant's labor standoff with the Lakers, or Team USA's demolition of the field at the Tournament of the Americas.

For his part, Stern vowed to do everything in his power to regain the trust of NBA fans by instituting as secure a system as possible for monitoring officials in order to head off future trouble.

"We are going to make good on the covenant that we believe we have with our fans," Stern said. "And I pledge that my involvement will be as intense and complete as it can possibly be and what we do will be completely transparent."

The question is: will it be enough?

The game was notable because Suns star Amare Stoudemire played only 21 minutes due to foul trouble. Donaghy also made a blatantly late foul call on a missed layup by San Antonio's Manu Ginobili. The Spurs won, 108-101, and went on to upset the Suns in six games and win the NBA title.

Though Donaghy eventually pled guilty to providing inside information to gamblers, it was not imme-

CHRIS BROUSSARD'S

Biggest Stories of the Year in **Pro Basketball**

10 NO HEAT. Call it what you want: resting on their laurels; getting a big head; the injury bug blues; or the inevitable encounter with Father Time. Whatever the case, Shaquille O'Neal and the defending champion Miami Heat surrendered the throne immediately and without much of a fight. From the 42-point drubbing Chicago handed them on opening night, to the brutal shoulder injury that sidelined Dwyane Wade for a third of the season, to the four-game sweep the Bulls put on them in the first round of the playoffs, this season was as bad as the previous one was good.

09 KOBE ERUPTS. After three seasons of individual brilliance but Laker mediocrity sans Shaq, Kobe Bryant went ballistic. While LeBron James, Deron Williams and others were thriving in the playoff spotlight once reserved for Kobe, Bryant stole back the limelight by saying he wanted to be traded, then changing his mind, then changing his mind again – all in the same day! Weeks later, Bryant ripped teammate Andrew Bynum in an off-the-cuff spiel posted on YouTube.

08 END OF AN ERA. The good, bad and sometimes ugly Allen Iverson Era ended in Philadelphia when the Sixers traded the face of their franchise to Denver for Andre Miller, Joe Smith and two first-round draft picks. Before Iverson even reached the mountains, critics wondered whether he could play with Nuggets star Carmelo Anthony. Turns out the duo worked well together, with Iverson willingly playing second option to Anthony. Both averaged well over 20 points per game, but—as has typically been the case for both players—their playoff stay was brief.

07 THE SPIRIT OR THE LETTER? The Phoenix Suns had finally gotten over the hump, rallying to beat San Antonio at home to even their Western Conference semifinal series at 2-2. But when Amare Stoudemire and Boris Diaw instinctively left the bench after a late-game body check by Robert Horry sent Suns star Steve Nash flying, the Spurs had the edge again. Following the letter rather than the spirit of the law, the league suspended the two Suns for Game 5, leading Phoenix fans to cry foul. The Spurs won the series in six.

06 FROM PRINCE TO PAUPER. Dirk Nowitzki entered the rarified air of NBA MVPs after leading Dallas to a league-best 67 wins. But Nowitzki's glory was short-lived as he played poorly and even worse, tentatively, in the Mavericks' stunning first-round loss to eighth-seeded Golden State. Dirk was humiliated, and all the naysayers who've long labeled him as soft, timid and a playoff bust were vindicated.

05 NELLIE AND B-DIDDY. Nowitzki's nemesis was his onetime coach/discoverer Don Nelson. The renowned architect of basketball gimmickry used his intimate knowledge of Dirk's strengths and weaknesses to create the perfect game plan for his undersized Golden State Warriors. Baron Davis led Nellie's unorthodox, small ball attack with a Jordanesque performance that catapulted him into the class of Steve Nash and Jason Kidd.

04 FINALLY. After years of rumors and three years of downright futility, the Minnesota Timberwolves and Kevin Garnett finally parted ways in an offseason deal that sent the all-star power forward to the hallowed Boston Celtics. Garnett initially balked at going to Boston, but when the Celtics put star Ray Allen alongside star Paul Pierce, he excitedly went east to form arguably the league's top trio. Only one question remains: can KG and Co. resurrect one of the most storied franchises in sports?

03 A DYNASTY? They're not as exciting as Jordan's Bulls or the Showtime Lakers, but after winning their fourth title in nine years, can Tim Duncan's Spurs be denied dynasty status? After surviving the hard-hitting Western Conference, the Spurs bulldozed the Cavaliers in four straight as Tony Parker walked away with the MVP trophy.

02 THE KING AND HIS COURT. Just four years removed from high school, LeBron James took the Eastern Conference by storm, leading the young Cavaliers to their first-ever appearance in the NBA Finals. With a cast of role players by his side, he overwhelmed the star-studded Detroit Pistons, turning in one of the greatest playoff performances in memory by scoring 48 points, including Cleveland's last 25, in a double-overtime Game 5 victory in Detroit. But in the Finals, James learned he still has some work left to do before getting his crown.

01 TIM DONAGHY. Every other NBA storyline became secondary in July when news broke that the FBI was investigating whether veteran referee Tim Donaghy bet on league games. Three weeks later, Donaghy pleaded guilty to selling inside information to professional gamblers. Court documents charged that he bet on NBA games, including ones he officiated. The scandal rocked the league, placing the integrity of its games in question.

2006-2007
Season in Review

SPORTS ALMANAC

Final NBA Standings

Division champions (*) and playoff qualifiers (†) are noted. Number of seasons listed after each head coach refers to current tenure with club.

Western Conference

Northwest Div.	W	L	Pct	GB	Per Game For	Opp
*Utah	51	31	.622	–	101.5	98.6
†Denver	45	37	.549	6	105.4	103.7
Minnesota	32	50	.390	19	96.1	99.7
Portland	32	50	.390	19	94.1	98.4
Seattle	31	51	.378	20	99.1	102.0

Head Coaches: Utah—Jerry Sloan (19th season); **Den**—George Karl (3rd); **Min**—Dwane Casey (2nd, 20-20) was fired on Jan. 23, 2007 and replaced by assistant Randy Wittman (12-30); **Port**—Nate McMillan (2nd); **Sea**—Bob Hill (1st).

Pacific Div.	W	L	Pct	GB	Per Game For	Opp
*Phoenix	61	21	.744	–	110.2	102.9
†LA Lakers	42	40	.512	19	103.3	103.4
†Golden St.	42	40	.512	19	106.5	106.9
LA Clippers	40	42	.488	21	95.6	96.1
Sacramento	32	49	.390	28	101.3	103.1

Head Coaches: Pho—Mike D'Antoni (4th season); **LAL**—Phil Jackson (2nd); **G.St.**—Don Nelson (1st); **LAC**—Mike Dunleavy (4th); **Sac**—Eric Musselman (1st).

Southwest Div.	W	L	Pct	GB	Per Game For	Opp
*Dallas	67	15	.817	–	100.0	92.8
†San Antonio	58	24	.707	9	98.5	90.1
†Houston	52	30	.634	15	97.0	92.1
New Orleans/ Oklahoma City	39	43	.476	28	95.5	97.1
Memphis	22	60	.268	45	101.6	106.7

Head Coaches: Dal—Avery Johnson (3rd season); **SA**—Gregg Popovich (11th); **Hou**—Jeff Van Gundy (4th); **NO/OK**—Byron Scott (3rd); **Mem**—Mike Fratello (3rd, 6-24) was fired on Dec. 29, 2006 and replaced by player personnel director Tony Barone Sr. (16-19) on an interim basis.

Eastern Conference

Atlantic Div.	W	L	Pct	GB	Per Game For	Opp
*Toronto	47	35	.573	–	99.5	98.5
†New Jersey	41	41	.500	6	97.6	98.3
Philadelphia	35	47	.427	12	94.9	98.0
New York	33	49	.402	14	97.5	100.3
Boston	24	58	.293	23	95.8	99.2

Head Coaches: Tor—Sam Mitchell (3rd season); **NJ**—Lawrence Frank (4th); **Phi**—Maurice Cheeks (1st); **NY**—Isiah Thomas (1st); **Bos**—Doc Rivers (3rd).

Central Div.	W	L	Pct	GB	Per Game For	Opp
*Detroit	53	29	.646	–	96.0	91.8
†Cleveland	50	32	.610	3	96.8	92.9
†Chicago	49	33	.598	4	98.8	93.8
Indiana	35	47	.427	18	95.6	98.0
Milwaukee	28	54	.341	25	99.7	104.0

Head Coaches: Det—Flip Saunders (2nd season); **Cle**—Mike Brown (2nd); **Chi**—Scott Skiles (4th); **Ind**—Rick Carlisle (4th); **Mil**—Terry Stotts (2nd, 23-41) was fired on Mar. 14, 2007 and replaced by assistant Larry Krystkowiak (5-13).

Southeast Div.	W	L	Pct	GB	Per Game For	Opp
*Miami	44	38	.537	–	94.6	95.5
†Washington	41	41	.500	3	104.3	104.9
†Orlando	40	42	.488	4	94.8	94.0
Charlotte	33	49	.402	11	96.9	100.6
Atlanta	30	52	.366	14	93.7	98.4

Head Coaches: Mia—Pat Riley (2nd season); **Wash**—Eddie Jordan (4th); **Orl**—Stan Van Gundy (1st). **Cha**—Bernie Bickerstaff (3rd); **Atl**—Mike Woodson (3rd).

Overall Conference Standings

Sixteen teams—eight from each conference—qualify for the NBA Playoffs; (*) indicates division champions.

Western Conference

		W	L	Home	Away	Conf	Div
1	Dallas*	67	15	36-5	31-10	40-12	14-2
2	Phoenix*	61	21	33-8	28-13	36-16	11-5
3	San Antonio	58	24	31-10	27-14	38-14	10-6
4	Utah*	51	31	31-10	20-21	32-20	10-6
5	Houston	52	30	28-13	24-17	28-24	8-8
6	Denver	45	37	23-18	22-19	27-25	9-7
7	LA Lakers	42	40	25-16	17-24	28-24	10-6
8	Golden St.	42	40	30-11	12-29	28-24	6-10
	LA Clippers	40	42	25-16	15-26	23-29	8-8
	N.O./OK City	39	43	24-17	15-26	23-29	6-10
	Sacramento	33	49	20-21	13-28	18-34	5-11
	Portland	32	50	18-23	14-27	19-33	7-9
	Minnesota	32	50	20-21	12-29	18-34	6-10
	Seattle	31	51	20-21	11-30	18-34	8-8
	Memphis	22	60	14-27	8-33	14-38	2-14

Eastern Conference

		W	L	Home	Away	Conf	Div
1	Detroit*	53	29	26-15	27-14	36-16	9-7
2	Cleveland	50	32	30-11	20-21	31-21	9-7
3	Toronto*	47	35	30-11	17-24	33-9	11-5
4	Miami*	44	38	27-14	17-24	27-25	9-7
5	Chicago	49	33	33-10	18-23	36-16	12-4
6	New Jersey	41	41	24-17	17-24	31-21	10-6
7	Washington	41	41	25-16	15-26	27-25	8-8
8	Orlando	40	42	25-16	15-26	26-26	9-7
	Indiana	35	47	22-19	13-28	25-27	8-8
	Philadelphia	35	47	21-20	14-27	24-28	9-7
	Charlotte	33	49	20-21	13-28	24-28	9-7
	New York	33	49	19-22	14-27	22-30	3-13
	Atlanta	30	52	18-23	12-29	17-35	5-7
	Milwaukee	28	54	18-23	10-31	15-37	1-15
	Boston	24	58	12-29	12-29	16-36	7-9

2007 NBA All-Star Game
West, 153-132

56th NBA All-Star Game. **Date:** Feb. 18, at the Thomas and Mack Arena in Las Vegas; **Coaches:** Eddie Jordan, Washington (East) and Mike D'Antoni, Phoenix (West); **MVP:** Kobe Bryant, West (31 points, 6 assists, 6 steals, 5 assists); Starters chosen by fan vote, (Cleveland's LeBron James was the leading vote-getter, receiving 2,516,049 votes); bench chosen by conference coaches' vote.

Western Conference

Pos	Starters	Min	FG M-A	Pts	Reb	A
G	Kobe Bryant, LAL	28	13-24	31	5	6
G	Tracy McGrady, Hou	18	3-8	8	3	11
F	Kevin Garnett, Min	14	3-8	7	6	4
F	Dirk Nowitzki, Dal	16	4-9	9	5	2
C	Tim Duncan, SA	14	2-3	4	5	4
	Bench					
G	Carmelo Anthony, Den	25	10-15	20	9	1
G	Tony Parker, SA	24	4-7	8	2	10
F	Shawn Marion, Pho	22	9-15	18	8	4
G	Ray Allen, Sea	21	4-10	12	1	3
F	Amare Stoudamire, Pho	21	14-22	29	9	3
F	Josh Howard, Dal	20	1-3	3	4	3
C	Mehmet Okur, Utah	15	2-2	4	2	1
	TOTALS	240	69-126	153	59	52

Three-Point FG: 10-26 (Allen 4-7, Bryant 3-9, McGrady 2-5, Nowitzki 1-2, Marion 0-1, Stoudemire 0-1, Howard 0-1); **Free Throws:** 5-9 (Bryant 2-2, Garnett 1-2, Stoudemire 1-1, Howard 1-2, Okur 0-2); **Percentages:** FG (.548), Three-Pt. FG (.385), Free Throws (.556); **Turnovers:** 17 (Bryant 4, Parker 4, McGrady 3, Marion 2, Allen, Stoudemire, Howard, Garnett); **Steals:** 17 (Bryant 6, McGrady 2, Garnett 2, Marion 2, Duncan, Allen, Stoudemire, Anthony, Parker); **Blocked Shots:** 4 (Stoudemire 2, Duncan, Garnett); **Fouls:** 10 (Stoudemire 5, Anthony 2, Bryant, Duncan, Howard).

	1	2	3	4	F
East	31	28	29	44	132
West	39	40	40	34	153

Eastern Conference

Pos	Starters	Min	FG M-A	Pts	Reb	A
G	Gilbert Arenas, Wash.	20	3-8	8	1	4
G	Dwyane Wade, Mia	24	5-12	10	0	3
F	Chris Bosh, Tor	22	5-7	11	7	1
F	LeBron James, Cle	32	11-20	28	6	6
C	Shaquille O'Neal, Mia	17	5-13	10	6	1
	Bench					
F	Jermaine O'Neal, Ind	22	4-8	8	7	1
F	Dwight Howard, Orl	20	10-14	20	12	1
G	Joe Johnson, Atl	17	5-9	12	1	2
G	Chauncey Billups, Det	16	3-8	8	4	6
F	Vince Carter, NJ	16	3-7	7	1	2
F	Caron Butler, Wash	15	1-7	4	4	3
G	Richard Hamilton, Det	15	4-8	8	6	1
	TOTALS	240	59-121	132	55	29

Three-Point FG: 8-25 (James 4-8, Johnson 2-5, Arena 2-7, Billups 0-3, Carter 0-1, Hamilton 0-1); **Free Throws:** 6-13 (James 2-2, Billups 2-2, Bosh 1-2, Carter 1-2, Howard 0-5); **Percentages:** FG (.488), Three-Pt. FG (.320), Free Throws (.462); **Turnovers:** 20 (Wade 5, James 4, Howard 3, Hamilton 2, Arenas, S. O'Neal, J. O'Neal, Johnson, Carter, Butler); **Steals:** 10 (Wade 6, Arenas 2, James, Johnson); **Blocked Shots:** 4 (J. O'Neal 2, S. O'Neal, Howard); **Fouls:** 7 (Wade 2, S. O'Neal, J. O'Neal, Johnson, Carter, Hamilton).

Halftime— West, 79-59; **Third Quarter—** West, 119-88; **Technical Fouls—** none; **Officials—** #24 Mike Callahan, #33 Sean Corbin, #13 Monty McCutcheon; **Attendance—**15,694; **TV Rating—** 4.2 (TNT).

NBA 3-point Shootout

Six players are invited to compete in the annual three-point shooting contest held during All-Star Weekend, since 1986. Each shooter has 60 seconds to shoot the 25 balls in five racks outside the three-point line. Each ball is worth one point, except the last ball in each rack, which is worth two. Highest scores advance. First prize: $35,000.

First Round	Pts
Gilbert Arenas, Washington	23
Dirk Nowitzki, Dallas	20
Jason Kapono, Miami	19
Failed to advance	**Pts**
Mike Miller, Memphis	18
Damon Jones, Cleveland	15
Jason Terry, Dallas	10
Finals	**Pts**
Jason Kapono	24
Gilbert Arenas	17
Dirk Nowitzki	9

Slam Dunk Contest

The Dunk contest was held annually from 1984-97 before being replaced by the 2Ball competition. It made its return in 2000. The competitors are selected based on "the creativity and artistry they have displayed in dunking" over the course of the season. The dunks are judged by five judges on a scale from six to ten. The top two scorers from the first round advance to the final round and attempt two dunks. The combined score of the two dunks determines the winner. First prize: $35,000.

First Round	Pts
Gerald Green, Boston	95
Nate Robinson, New York	90
Failed to advance	**Pts**
Dwight Howard, Orlando	85
Tyrus Thomas, Chicago	80
Finals	**Score**
Gerald Green def. Nate Robinson	91-80

The 57th NBA All-Star Game will be played at **New Orleans Arena** on Feb. 17, 2008. The game will take place in the midst of a sporting renaissance for the city that was ravaged by floods in the aftermath of **Hurricane Katrina.** The NFL's **New Orleans Saints** advanced to the NFC Championship Game in 2007. Both the 2008 Sugar Bowl and the BCS National Championship game will take place the month before the NBA All-Star weekend.

Kobe Bryant
LA Lakers
Scoring

Kevin Garnett
Minnesota
Rebounding

Baron Davis
Golden State
Steals

Steve Nash
Phoenix
Assists

NBA Regular Season Individual Leaders

Scoring
(*indicates rookie)

	Gm	Min	FG	FG%	3pt/Att	FT	FT%	Reb	Ast	Stl	Blk	Pts	Avg	Hi
Kobe Bryant, LAL	77	3142	813	.463	137/398	667	.868	439	413	111	36	2430	**31.6**	65
Carmelo Anthony, Den	65	2481	691	.476	40/149	459	.808	392	249	77	22	1881	**28.9**	42
Gilbert Arenas, Wash	74	2105	647	.418	205/584	606	.844	338	443	139	13	2105	**28.4**	60
Dwyane Wade, Mia	51	1931	472	.491	21/79	432	.807	239	384	107	62	1397	**27.4**	41
LeBron James, Cle	78	3195	772	.476	99/310	489	.698	526	470	125	55	2132	**27.3**	41
Michael Redd, Mil	53	2036	477	.465	117/306	345	.829	196	124	63	9	1416	**26.7**	57
Ray Allen, Sea	55	2222	505	.438	165/443	279	.903	247	228	82	11	1454	**26.4**	54
Allen Iverson, Phi/Den	65	2764	581	.443	62/197	485	.795	193	468	123	13	1709	**26.3**	46
Vince Carter, NJ	82	3127	726	.454	156/437	462	.802	492	393	82	30	2070	**25.2**	46
Yao Ming, Hou	48	1624	423	5T6	0/2	356	.862	452	94	17	94	1202	**25.0**	39
Joe Johnson, Atl	57	2360	536	.471	119/312	235	.748	239	249	60	11	1426	**25.0**	39
Paul Pierce, Bos	47	1740	373	.439	107/275	320	.796	277	194	48	13	1173	**25.0**	39
Tracy McGrady, Hou	71	2540	638	.431	126/381	345	.707	378	458	92	36	1747	**24.6**	45
Dirk Nowitzki, Dal	78	2819	673	.502	72/173	498	.904	693	263	52	62	1916	**24.6**	43
Zach Randolph, Por	68	2426	600	.467	14/48	394	.819	688	147	53	15	1608	**23.6**	43
Chris Bosh, Tor	69	2655	543	.496	12/35	463	.785	741	175	39	90	1561	**22.6**	41
Kevin Garnett, Min	76	2999	638	.476	12/56	416	.835	975	313	89	126	1704	**22.4**	44
Rashard Lewis, Sea	60	2348	463	.461	151/387	265	.841	396	145	68	39	1342	**22.4**	36
Ben Gordon, Chi	82	2704	609	.455	155/375	380	.864	258	296	64	17	1753	**21.4**	48
Carlos Boozer, Utah	74	2564	647	.561	0/0	255	.685	867	221	70	21	1549	**20.9**	41
Pau Gasol, Mem	59	2133	462	.538	3/11	299	.748	581	201	29	126	1226	**20.8**	35
Elton Brand, LAC	80	3073	645	.533	1/1	351	.761	744	235	77	179	1642	**20.5**	37
Amare Stoudemire, Pho	82	2690	607	.575	0/3	457	.781	786	84	78	110	1671	**20.4**	43
Kevin Martin, Sac	80	2818	505	.473	127/333	481	.844	342	173	98	11	1618	**20.2**	40
Baron Davis, G. St.	63	2221	452	.439	85/280	275	.745	276	509	135	29	1264	**20.1**	38
Tim Duncan, SA	80	2727	618	.546	1/9	362	.637	845	273	66	190	1599	**20.0**	37
Antawn Jamison, Wash	70	2660	512	.450	138/379	226	.736	562	136	80	36	1388	**19.8**	48
Richard Hamilton, Det	75	2760	547	.468	44/129	347	.861	282	285	59	15	1485	**19.8**	51
Eddy Curry, NY	81	2850	585	.576	1/1	405	.615	571	68	34	40	1576	**19.5**	43
Jermaine O'Neal, Ind	69	2459	498	.436	0/7	343	.767	661	167	50	182	1339	**19.4**	39

Rebounds

	Gm	Off	Def	Tot	Avg
Kevin Garnett, Min	76	183	792	975	12.8
Tyson Chandler, Chi	73	320	584	904	12.4
Dwight Howard, Orl	82	283	725	1008	12.3
Carlos Boozer, Utah	74	235	632	867	11.7
Marcus Camby, Den	70	164	652	816	11.7
Emeka Okafor, Cha	67	258	499	757	11.3
Al Jefferson, Bos	69	237	519	756	11.0
Chris Bosh, Tor	69	186	555	741	10.7
Ben Wallace, Chi	77	303	518	821	10.7
Tim Duncan, SA	80	213	632	845	10.6
David Lee, NY	58	196	406	602	10.4
Zach Randolph, Por	68	199	489	688	10.1
Pau Gasol, Mem	59	149	432	581	9.8
Shawn Marion, Pho	80	172	613	785	9.8
Lamar Odom, LAL	56	102	445	547	9.8

Assists

	Gm	Ast	Avg
Steve Nash, Pho	76	884	11.6
Deron Williams, Utah	80	745	9.3
Jason Kidd, NJ	80	736	9.2
Chris Paul, NO/OK	64	569	8.9
Baron Davis, G.St.	63	509	8.1
T.J. Ford, Milw	75	595	7.9
Andre Miller, Den/Phi	80	625	7.8
Dwyane Wade, Mia	51	384	7.5
Allen Iverson, Phi/Den	65	468	7.2
Chauncey Billips, Det	70	502	7.2
Raymond Felton, Cha	78	545	7.0
Jamaal Tinsley, Ind	72	494	6.9
Brevin Knight, Cha	45	296	6.6
Tracy McGrady, Hou	71	458	6.5
Kirk Hinrich, Chi	80	500	6.2

Field Goal Pct.

	Gm	FG	Att	Pct
Mikki Moore, NJ	.79	308	506	.609
Dwight Howard, Orl	.82	526	873	.603
Andris Biedrins, G.St.	.82	348	581	.599
Eddy Curry, NY	.81	585	1016	.576
Amare Stoudemire, Pho	.82	607	1055	.575
Carlos Boozer, Utah	.74	647	1154	.561
Andrew Bogut, Milw	.66	348	629	.553
Ruben Patterson, Milw	.81	475	867	.548
Tim Duncan, SA	.80	618	1131	.546
Samuel Dalembert, Phi	.82	356	658	.541

Free Throw Pct.

	Gm	FT	Att	Pct
Kyle Korver, Phi	.74	191	209	.914
Matt Carroll, Cha	.72	188	208	.904
Dirk Nowtizki, Dal	.78	498	551	.904
Ray Allen, Sea	.55	279	309	.903
Steve Nash, Pho	.76	222	247	.899
Earl Boykins, Den/Milw	.66	220	245	.898
Tyronn Lue, Atl	.56	144	163	.883
Chauncey Billups, Det	.70	386	437	.883
Damien Wilkins, Sea	.82	150	170	.882
Sam Cassell, LAC	.58	160	182	.879

3-Point Field Goal Pct.

	Gm	3FG	Att	Pct
Jason Kapono, Mia	.67	108	210	.514
Steve Nash, Pho	.76	156	343	.455
Brent Barry, SA	.75	128	287	.446
Luther Head, Hou	.80	177	401	.441
Anthony Parker, Tor	.73	115	261	.441
Jason Terry, Dal	.81	162	370	.438
Leandro Barbosa, Pho	.80	190	438	.434
Al Harrington, Ind/G.St.	.78	127	293	.433
Kyle Korver, Phi	.74	132	307	.430
Eddie House, NJ	.56	75	175	.429
Bostjan Nachbar, NJ	.76	112	265	.423

High-Point Games

	Opp	Date	FG-FT—Pts
Kobe Bryant, LAL	vs. Port	3/16/07	23-11—65
Gilbert Arenas, Wash	vs. LAL	12/17/06	17-21—60
Kobe Bryant, LAL	vs. Mem	3/22/07	20-17—60
Kobe Bryant, LAL	vs. Cha	12/29/07	22-10—58
Michael Redd, Milw	vs. Utah	11/11/06	18-15—57
Ray Allen, Sea	vs. Utah	1/12/07	17-12—54
Gilbert Arenas, Wash	vs. Pho	12/22/07	21-6—54
Kobe Bryant, LAL	vs Hou	3/30/07	19-12—53
Kobe Bryant, LAL	vs Hou	12/15/07	17-14—53

Blocked Shots

	Gm	Blk	Avg
Marcus Camby, Den	.70	231	3.30
Josh Smith, Atl	.72	207	2.88
Jermaine O'Neal, Ind	.69	182	2.64
Emeka Okafor, Cha	.67	172	2.57
Tim Duncan, SA	.80	190	2.38
Alonzo Mourning, Mia	.77	178	2.31
Elton Brand, LA	.80	179	2.24
Pau Gasol, Mem	.59	126	2.14
Andrei Kirilenko, Utah	.70	144	2.06
Ben Wallace, Chi	.77	156	2.03

Steals

	Gm	Stl	Avg
Baron Davis, G. St.	.63	135	2.14
Ron Artest, Sac	.70	149	2.13
Caron Butler, Wash	.63	134	2.13
Andre Iguodala, Phi	.76	152	2.00
Gerald Wallace, Cha	.72	144	2.00
Shawn Marion, Pho	.80	156	1.95
Gilbert Arenas, Wash	.74	139	1.88
Monta Ellis, G. St.	.77	132	1.71
Rajon Rondo*, Bos	.78	128	1.64
Jamaal Tinsley, Ind	.72	117	1.63

Rookie Leaders

Scoring	Gm	FG	FT	Pts	Avg
Brandon Roy, Port	.57	349	202	955	16.8
Adam Morrison, Cha	.78	355	120	917	11.8
Andrea Bargnani, Tor	.65	267	117	751	11.6
Rudy Gay, Mem	.78	321	152	846	10.8
Randy Foye, Min	.82	300	164	832	10.1

Field Goal Pct.	Gm	FG	Att	Pct
Craig Smith, Min	.82	246	463	.531
Walter Hermann, Cha	.48	174	330	.527
Paul Millsap, Utah	.82	209	398	.525
LaMarcus Aldridge, Port	.63	241	479	.503
Rodney Carney, Phi	.67	182	392	.464

Rebounds	Gm	Off	Def	Tot	Avg
Sean Williams, Atl	.81	131	304	435	5.4
Paul Millsap, Utah	.82	183	240	423	5.2
Craig Smith, Min	.82	149	266	415	5.1
LaMarcus Aldridge	.63	144	168	312	5.0
Jorge Garbajosa, Tor	.67	48	282	330	4.9

Assists	Gm	No	Avg
Brandon Roy, Port	.57	230	4.0
Rajon Rondo, Bos	.78	297	3.8
Marcus Williams, NJ	.79	260	3.3
Sergio Rodriguez, Port	.67	218	3.3
Randy Foye, Min	.82	232	2.8

Personal Fouls

Andris Biedrins, G. St.	304
Amare Stoudemire, Pho	295
Nick Collison, Sea	289
Samuel Dalembert, Phi	287
Chuck Hayes, Hou	281
Kirk Hinrich, Chi	274
Jason Collins, NJ	279
Two players tied	269

Minutes

LeBron James, Cle	3195
Kobe Bryant, LAL	3142
Vince Carter, NJ	3127
Luol Deng, Chi	3074
Elton Brand, LAC	3073
Andre Iguodala, Phi	3062
Rafer Alston, Hou	3036
Dwight Howard, Orl	3025

Turnovers

Dwight Howard, Orl	317
Eddy Curry, NY	295
Steve Nash, Pho	287
Allen Iverson, Phi/Den	268
Andre Iguodala, Phi	261
Kobe Bryant, LAL	255
LeBron James, Cle	250
Ben Gordon, Chi	249

Triple Doubles

Jason Kidd, NJ	12
Kevin Garnett, Min	3
Andre Iguodala, Phi	3
Vince Carter, NJ	3
Twelve players tied	1

Double Doubles

Kevin Garnett, Minn	66
Dwight Howard, Orl	60
Carlos Boozer, Utah	53
Steve Nash, Pho	53
Amare Stoudemire, Pho	46
Tim Duncan, SA	45
Chris Bosh, Tor	42
Dirk Nowitzki, Dal	41

Technical Fouls

Rasheed Wallace, Det	21
Amare Stoudemire, Pho	15
Richard Hamilton, Det	15
Kobe Bryant, LAL	14
Gerald Wallace, Cha	13
Carmelo Anthony, Den	13
Stephen Jackson, Ind/G. St.	13
Kevin Garnett, Min	13

Team by Team Statistics

Players who competed for more than one team during the regular season are listed with their final club; (*) indicates rookies.

Atlanta Hawks

(min. 10 gms)	Gm	FG%	Tpts	PPG	RPG	APG
Joe Johnson	.57	.471	1426	25.0	4.2	4.4
Josh Smith	.72	.439	1178	16.4	86	3.3
Marvin Williams	.64	.433	839	13.1	5.3	1.9
Josh Childress	.55	.504	715	13.0	6.2	2.3
Zaza Pachulia	.72	.474	875	12.2	6.9	1.5
Tyronn Lue	.56	.416	636	11.4	1.9	3.6
Salim Stoudamire	.61	.416	471	7.7	1.2	1.1
Shelden Williams*	.81	.455	444	5.5	5.4	0.5
Anthony Johnson	.67	.414	355	5.3	1.5	3.0
Speedy Claxton	.42	.327	221	5.3	1.9	4.4
Solomon Jones*	.58	.508	189	3.3	2.3	0.2
Royal Ivey	.53	.448	157	3.0	1.0	0.8
Slava Medvedenko	.14	.414	42	3.0	1.0	0.1
Lorenzen Wright	.67	.448	173	2.6	3.2	0.6
Matt Freije	.19	.296	40	2.1	1.3	0.4
Esteban Batista	.13	.500	20	1.5	1.0	0.4
Cedric Bozeman	.23	.444	26	1.1	1.0	0.4

Triple Doubles: none. **3-pt FG leader:** Johnson (119).
Steals leader: Smith (101). **Blocks leader:** Smith (207).
Signed: F/C Medvedenko (Dec. 28); F Thompson (Jan. 6).
Acquired: Anthony Johnson from Dallas for 2007 second round pick.

Boston Celtics

(min. 10 gms)	Gm	FG%	Tpts	PPG	RPG	APG
Paul Pierce	.47	.439	1173	25.0	5.9	4.1
Al Jefferson	.69	.514	1107	16.0	11.0	1.3
Wally Szczerbiak	.32	.415	479	15.0	3.1	1.7
Delonte West	.36	.427	845	12.2	3.3	4.4
Ryan Gomes	.73	.467	881	12.1	5.6	1.6
Tony Allen	.33	.514	379	11.5	3.8	1.7
Gerald Green	.81	.419	843	10.4	2.6	1.0
Rajon Rondo*	.78	.418	501	6.4	3.7	3.8
Allan Ray*	.47	.386	290	6.2	1.5	0.9
Sebastian Telfair	.78	.371	479	6.1	1.4	2.8
Kendrick Perkins	.72	.491	324	4.5	5.2	1.3
Leon Powe*	.63	.446	264	4.2	3.4	0.2
Brian Scalabrine	.54	.403	216	4.0	1.9	1.1
Michael Olowokandi	.24	.413	40	1.7	2.0	0.2

Triple Doubles: Gomes (1). **3-pt FG leader:** Pierce (107). **Steals leaders:** Rondo (128). **Blocks leader:** Jefferson (106).

Charlotte Bobcats

	Gm	FG%	Tpts	PPG	RPG	APG
Gerald Wallace	.72	.502	1304	18.1	7.2	2.6
Emeka Okafor	.67	.532	963	14.4	11.3	1.2
Raymond Felton	.78	.384	1093	14.0	3.4	7.0
Matt Carroll	.72	.433	869	12.1	2.9	1.3
Sean May	.35	.500	416	11.9	6.7	1.9
Adam Morrison*	.78	.376	917	11.8	2.9	2.1
Walter Hermann*	.48	.527	442	9.2	2.9	0.5
Brevin Knight	.45	.419	408	9.1	2.6	6.6
Derek Anderson	.50	.429	399	8.0	2.3	2.7
Alan Anderson	.17	.457	98	5.8	1.9	1.2
Primoz Brezec	.58	.445	288	5.0	3.2	0.4
Jake Voskuhl	.73	.475	319	4.4	3.5	0.6
Jeff McInnis	.38	.392	165	4.3	1.6	3.3
Othella Harrington	.26	.446	67	2.6	1.5	0.2
Eric Williams	.21	.404	54	2.6	0.8	0.3
Ryan Hollins*	.27	.556	64	2.4	1.1	0.0

Triple Doubles: none. **3-pt FG leader:** Carroll (111). **Steals leaders:** Wallace (144). **Blocks leader:** Okafor (172).
Signed: G Derek Anderson (Nov. 28).
Acquired: G Jeff McInnis and cash from New Jersey for Bernard Robinson (Jan. 3); F Williams, a 2009 second round pick and cash from San Antonio for Melvin Ely. (Feb. 13).

Chicago Bulls

	Gm	FG%	Tpts	PPG	RPG	APG
Ben Gordon	.82	.455	1753	21.4	3.1	3.6
Luol Deng	.82	.517	1540	18.8	7.1	2.5
Kirk Hinrich	.80	.448	1327	16.6	3.4	6.3
Andres Nocioni	.53	.467	749	14.1	5.7	1.1
Chris Duhon	.78	.408	558	7.2	2.2	4.0
Ben Wallace	.77	.453	494	6.4	10.7	2.4
P.J. Brown	.72	.407	436	6.1	4.8	0.7
Tyrus Thomas*	.72	.475	374	5.2	3.7	0.6
Malik Allen	.60	.415	242	4.0	2.0	0.3
Thabo Sefolosha*	.71	.426	256	3.6	2.2	0.8
Michael Sweetney	.48	.433	153	3.2	2.5	0.6
Adrian Griffin	.54	.473	137	2.5	2.0	1.1
Viktor Khryapa	.33	.386	73	2.2	1.7	0.6
Andre Barrett	.6	.500	8	1.3	0.8	1.2

Triple Doubles: none. **3-pt FG leader:** Gordon (155). **Steals leader:** Wallace (111). **Blocks leader:** Wallace (156).

Cleveland Cavaliers

	Gm	FG%	Tpts	PPG	RPG	APG
LeBron James	.78	.476	2132	27.3	6.7	6.0
Larry Hughes	.70	.400	1045	14.9	3.8	3.7
Zydrunas Ilgauskas	.78	.485	925	11.9	7.7	1.6
Drew Gooden	.80	.473	885	11.1	8.5	1.1
Aleksandar Pavlovic	.67	.453	604	9.0	2.4	1.6
Donyell Marshall	.81	.424	566	7.0	4.0	0.6
Anderson Varejao	.81	.476	547	6.8	6.7	0.9
Damon Jones	.60	.386	393	6.6	1.1	1.6
Daniel Gibson*	.60	.276	276	4.6	1.5	1.2
Eric Snow	.82	.417	342	4.2	2.3	4.0
Shannon Brown*	.23	.378	73	3.2	0.9	0.4
Ira Newble	.15	.432	46	3.1	2.0	0.1
David Wesley	.35	.293	73	2.1	1.0	1.1
Scot Pollard	.24	.423	24	1.0	1.3	0.1
Dwayne Jones	.4	.000	3	0.8	0.5	0.0

Triple Doubles: James (1). **3-pt FG leader:** Jones (99). **Steals leader:** James (125). **Blocks leader:** Ilgauskas (98).

Dallas Mavericks

	Gm	FG%	Tpts	PPG	RPG	APG
Dirk Nowitzki	.78	.502	1916	24.6	8.9	3.4
Josh Howard	.70	.459	1321	18.9	6.8	1.8
Jason Terry	.81	.484	1350	16.7	2.9	5.2
Jerry Stackhouse	.67	.428	804	12.0	2.2	2.8
Devin Harris	.80	.492	813	10.2	2.5	3.7
Erick Dampier	.76	.626	537	7.1	7.4	0.6
Devean George	.60	.395	381	6.4	3.6	0.6
Greg Buckner	.76	.411	305	4.0	2.1	0.9
Austin Croshere	.61	.351	227	3.7	3.0	0.7
Jose Juan Barea*	.33	.359	78	2.4	1.6	0.2
Kevin Willis	.5	.385	12	2.4	1.6	0.2
Pops Mensah-Bonsu*	.12	.647	29	2.4	1.8	0.0
DeSagana Diop	.81	.470	190	2.3	5.4	0.4
Maurice Ager*	.32	.314	69	2.2	0.7	0.2
Didier Illunga-Mbenga	21	.313	17	0.8	0.5	0.3

Triple Doubles: none. **3-pt FG leader:** Terry (162). **Steals leader:** Harris (96). **Blocks leader:** Diop (113).

Denver Nuggets

	Gm	FG%	Tpts	PPG	RPG	APG
Carmelo Anthony . . .65		.476	1881	28.9	6.0	3.8
Allen Iverson 65		.442	1709	26.3	3.0	7.2
J.R. Smith 63		.441	819	13.0	2.3	1.4
Nene 64		.570	783	12.2	7.0	1.2
Marcus Camby 70		.473	785	11.2	11.7	3.2
Kenyon Martin 2		.500	19	9.5	10.0	0.5
Linas Kleiza 79		.422	598	7.6	3.4	0.6
Eduardo Najera 75		.576	497	6.6	4.1	0.9
Steve Blake 82		.411	528	6.4	2.1	5.0
Reggie Evans 66		.544	325	4.9	7.0	0.7
Yakhouba Diawara* . .64		.342	284	4.4	1.7	0.9
DerMarr Johnson . . .39		.325	135	3.5	1.5	0.4
Anthony Carter 2		.375	6	3.0	1.5	5.5
Jamal Sampson 22		.643	24	1.1	2.2	0.2

Triple Doubles: Anthony (1). **3-pt FG leader:** Smith (149). **Steals leader:** Iverson (123). **Blocks leader:** Camby (231).
Acquired: G Iverson and F Ivan McFarlin from Philadelphia for G Andre Miller, F Joe Smith and two first round picks. (Dec. 19); G Blake from Milwaukee for G Earl Boykins, G Julius Hodge and cash (Jan. 11).
Signed: G Carter (Apr. 13).

Detroit Pistons

	Gm	FG%	Tpts	PPG	RPG	APG
Richard Hamilton . . .75		.468	1485	19.8	3.8	3.8
Chauncey Billups . . .70		.427	1191	17.0	3.4	7.2
Tayshaun Prince 82		.460	1171	14.3	5.2	2.8
Rasheed Wallace . . .75		.423	926	12.3	7.2	1.7
Chris Webber 61		.452	684	11.2	7.2	3.1
Antonio McDyess . . .82		.526	664	8.1	6.0	0.9
Ronald Murray 69		.404	465	6.7	1.6	2.7
Amir Johnson 8		.545	47	5.9	4.6	0.4
Nazr Mohammed . . .51		.532	286	5.6	4.5	0.2
Carlos Delfino 82		.415	428	5.2	3.2	1.1
Jason Maxiell 67		.500	334	5.0	2.8	0.2
Lindsey Hunter 52		.385	256	4.9	0.9	1.8
Dale Davis 46		.446	83	1.8	3.0	0.3
Will Blalock* 14		.300	25	1.8	1.1	1.2
Ronald Dupree 19		.355	25	1.3	0.9	0.3

Triple Doubles: none. **3-pt FG leader:** Billups (109). **Steals leader:** Billups (84). **Blocks leader:** Wallace (118).
Signed: F/C Webber (Jan. 16).

Golden St. Warriors

	Gm	FG%	Tpts	PPG	RPG	APG
Baron Davis 63		.439	1264	20.1	4.4	8.1
Al Harrington 78		.457	1285	16.5	6.4	1.9
Monta Ellis 77		.475	1272	16.5	3.2	4.1
Stephen Jackson 75		.433	1161	15.5	3.0	3.8
Jason Richardson . . .51		.417	814	16.0	5.1	3.4
Mickael Pietrus 72		.488	801	11.1	4.5	0.9
Matt Barnes 76		.438	746	9.8	4.6	2.1
Andris Biedrins 82		.599	783	9.5	4.6	2.1
Kelenna Azubuike* . .41		.445	291	7.1	2.3	0.7
Sarunas Jasikevicius .63		.398	386	6.1	1.1	2.7
Anthony Roberson . .20		.423	111	5.6	1.1	0.5
Renaldo Major* 1		.200	5	5.0	2.0	0.0
Dajuan Wagner 1		1.000	4	4.0	0.0	1.0
Josh Powell 37		.462	116	3.1	2.4	0.6
Adonal Foyle 48		.565	107	2.2	2.6	0.4
Patrick O'Bryant* . . .16		.313	31	1.9	1.3	0.6

Triple Doubles: Davis (3). **3-pt FG leader:** Harrington (127). **Steals leader:** Davis (135). **Blocks leader:** Biedrins (136).
Signed: G Azubuike (Jan. 2); F Major (Jan. 17).
Acquired: F Harrington, G/F Jackson, G Jasikevicius and F Powell from Indiana for F Mike Dunleavy, F Troy Murphy, F Ike Diogu and G Keith McLeod (Jan. 17)

Houston Rockets

	Gm	FG%	Tpts	PPG	RPG	APG
Yao Ming 48		.516	1202	25.0	9.4	2.
Tracy McGrady 71		.431	1747	24.6	5.3	6.
Rafer Alston 82		.375	1088	13.3	3.4	5.
Luther Head 80		.437	872	10.9	3.2	2.
Shane Battier 82		.446	829	10.1	4.1	2.
Juwan Howard 80		.465	773	9.7	5.9	1.
Bonzi Wells 28		.411	217	7.8	4.3	1.
Chuck Hayes 78		.573	439	5.6	6.7	0.
Kirk Snyder 39		.452	192	4.9	2.1	1.
John Lucas III 47		.397	154	3.3	0.8	0.
Dikembe Mutombo . .75		.556	230	3.1	6.5	0.
Vassilis Spanoulis* . .31		.319	85	2.7	0.7	0.
Jake Tsakalidis 36		.403	84	2.3	2.9	0.
Steve Novak* 35		.360	51	1.5	0.7	0.

Triple Doubles: none. **3-pt FG leader:** Alston (192 **Steals leader:** Alston (129). **Blocks leader:** Ming (94).

Indiana Pacers

	Gm	FG%	Tpts	PPG	RPG	AP
Jermaine O'Neal . . .69		.436	1339	19.4	9.6	2.
Danny Granger 82		.459	1142	13.9	4.6	1.
Mike Dunleavy 82		.452	1049	12.8	5.3	2.
Jamaal Tinsley 72		.389	925	12.8	3.3	6.
Troy Murphy 68		.458	698	10.3	6.1	1.
Marquis Daniels 45		.459	320	7.1	1.8	1.
Ike Diogu 59		.477	366	6.2	3.4	0.
Darrell Armstrong . . .81		.414	457	5.6	1.7	2.
Keith McLeod 48		.388	231	4.8	0.9	1.
Jeff Foster 75		.469	322	4.3	8.1	0.
Shawne Williams* . . .46		.469	180	3.9	1.8	0.
David Harrison 24		.517	71	3.0	1.8	0.
Maceo Baston 47		.645	138	2.9	1.6	0.
Rawle Marshalll 40		.360	99	2.5	0.7	0.
Orien Greene 41		.371	63	1.5	1.1	0.

Triple Doubles: none. **3-pt FG leader:** Granger (110) **Steals leader:** Tinsley (117). **Blocks leader:** O'Ne (182).
Acquired: F Dunleavy, F Murphy, F Diogu, G McLeod fro Golden St. for F Al Harrington, G/F Stephen Jackson, Sarunas Jasikevicius and F Josh Powell (Jan. 17).

Los Angeles Clippers

	Gm	FG%	Tpts	PPG	RPG	AP
Elton Brand 80		.533	1642	20.5	9.3	2.
Corey Maggette 75		.454	1266	16.9	5.9	2.
Cuttino Mobley 78		.440	1077	13.8	3.4	2.
Sam Cassell 58		.418	714	12.3	2.9	4.
Tim Thomas 76		.414	836	11.0	5.0	2.
Chris Kaman 75		.451	754	10.1	7.8	1.
Shaun Livingston . . .54		.463	503	9.3	3.4	5.
Jason Hart 36		.446	249	6.9	2.7	2.
Quinton Ross 81		.467	424	5.2	2.3	1.
Daniel Ewing 61		.404	179	2.9	1.2	1.
Aaron Williams 38		.547	76	2.0	2.2	0.
Doug Christie 7		.294	13	1.9	1.6	1.
Paul Davis* 31		.423	51	1.6	1.4	0.
James Singleton 53		.366	85	1.6	2.0	0.
Yaroslav Korolev 10		.250	12	1.2	0.3	0.
Alvin Williams 2		.000	2	1.0	0.5	1.
Will Conroy* 7		.000	0	0.0	1.0	1.

Triple Doubles: none. **3-pt FG leader:** Thomas (136 **Steals leader:** Mobley (92). **Blocks leader:** Bra (179).
Signed: G Williams (Jan. 20); G Christie (Jan. 31); G C roy (Feb. 28); G Hart (Mar. 5).

Los Angeles Lakers

	Gm	FG%	Tpts	PPG	RPG	APG
Kobe Bryant	.77	.463	2430	31.6	5.7	5.4
Lamar Odom	.56	.468	890	15.9	9.8	4.8
Luke Walton	.60	.474	684	11.4	5.0	4.3
Smush Parker	.82	.436	907	11.1	2.5	2.8
Kwame Brown	.41	.591	345	8.4	6.0	1.8
Maurice Evans	.76	.432	638	8.4	2.9	1.0
Andrew Bynum	.82	.558	637	7.8	5.9	1.1
Brian Cook	.65	.453	450	6.9	3.3	1.0
Vladimir Radmanovic	55	.424	361	6.6	3.3	1.2
Ronny Turiaf	.72	.549	383	5.3	3.6	0.9
Jordan Farmar*	.72	.422	320	4.4	1.7	1.9
Sasha Vujacic	.73	.392	313	4.3	1.5	0.9
Shammond Williams	.30	.407	94	3.1	1.3	1.0
Aaron McKie	.10	.647	22	2.2	1.8	1.3

Triple Doubles: Odom (1). **3-pt FG leader:** Bryant (137). **Steals leader:** Parker (119). **Blocks leader:** Bynum (128).

Memphis Grizzlies

	Gm	FG%	Tpts	PPG	RPG	APG
Pau Gasol	.59	.538	1226	20.8	9.8	3.4
Mike Miller	.70	.460	1293	18.5	5.4	4.3
Chucky Atkins	.75	.434	988	13.2	1.9	4.6
Hakim Warrick	.82	.524	1045	12.7	5.1	0.9
Rudy Gay*	.78	.422	846	10.8	4.5	1.3
Stromile Swift	.54	.465	419	7.8	4.6	0.3
Tarence Kinsey*	.48	.457	369	7.7	2.0	0.9
Dahntay Jones	.78	.477	583	7.5	2.0	0.9
Damon Stoudamire	.62	.391	467	7.5	2.2	4.8
Kyle Lowry*	.10	.368	56	5.6	3.1	3.2
Lawrence Roberts	.54	.452	283	5.2	4.8	0.6
Junior Harrington	.29	.416	152	5.2	2.3	3.1
Brian Cardinal	.28	.494	127	4.5	2.1	1.1
Alexander Johnson*	.59	.538	260	4.4	3.1	0.3
Scott Padgett	.31	.286	46	1.5	1.7	0.3

Triple Doubles: Gasol (1). **3-pt FG leader:** Miller (202). **Steals leader:** Gay (71). **Blocks leader:** Gasol (126). **Signed:** G Harrington (Feb. 9). **Acquired:** F Padgett from Houston for C Jake Tsakalidis (Feb. 13).

Miami Heat

	Gm	FG%	Tpts	PPG	RPG	APG
Dwyane Wade	.51	.491	1397	27.4	4.7	7.5
Shaquille O'Neal	.40	.591	690	17.3	7.4	2.0
Jason Kapono	.67	.494	730	10.9	2.7	1.2
Jason Williams	.61	.413	664	10.9	2.3	5.3
Udonis Haslem	.79	.492	844	10.7	8.3	1.2
Alonzo Mourning	.77	.560	661	8.6	4.5	0.2
Antoine Walker	.78	.397	660	8.5	4.3	1.7
Eddie Jones	.64	.422	493	7.7	3.0	1.7
James Posey	.71	.431	550	7.7	5.0	1.3
Dorell Wright	.66	.445	393	6.0	4.1	1.4
Gary Payton	.68	.393	358	5.3	1.9	3.0
Robert Hite*	.12	.317	51	4.3	1.3	0.7
Michael Doleac	.56	.469	200	3.6	2.8	0.4
Chris Quinn*	.42	.366	141	3.4	0.7	1.5
Wayne Simien	.8	.391	23	2.9	1.4	0.5
Earl Barron	.28	.289	65	2.3	1.5	0.2

Triple Doubles: none. **3-pt FG leader:** Kapono (108). **Steals leader:** Wade (107). **Blocks leader:** Mourning (178). **Signed:** G Jones (Feb. 1).

Milwaukee Bucks

	Gm	FG%	Tpts	PPG	RPG	APG
Michael Redd	.53	.465	1416	26.7	3.7	2.3
Maurice Williams	.68	.446	1174	17.3	4.8	6.1
Ruben Patterson	.81	.548	1194	14.7	5.4	2.9
Earl Boykins	.66	.420	961	14.6	2.1	4.4
Charlie Bell	.82	.437	1110	13.5	2.9	3.0
Andrew Bogut	.66	.553	809	12.3	8.8	3.0
Charlie Villanueva	.39	.470	462	11.8	5.8	0.9
Ersan Ilyasova*	.66	.383	402	6.1	2.9	0.7
Dan Gadzuric	.54	.474	258	4.8	4.6	0.5
Brian Skinner	.67	.490	294	4.4	5.7	0.9
Lynn Greer*	.41	.433	167	4.1	0.7	1.3
David Noel*	.68	.367	184	2.7	1.8	1.0
Julius Hodge	.9	.500	15	1.7	0.9	1.3
Damir Markota	.30	.365	51	1.7	1.0	0.3
Jared Reiner	.27	.349	33	1.2	2.6	0.5
Chris McCray	.5	.000	0	0.0	0.0	0.0

Triple Doubles: Williams (1). **3-pt FG leader:** Bell (127). **Steals leader:** Patterson (110). **Blocks leader:** Skinner (64). **Acquired:** G Boykins, G/F Hodge and cash from Denver for G Steve Blake (Jan. 11). **Signed:** C Reiner (Feb. 8).

Minnesota Timberwolves

	Gm	FG%	Tpts	PPG	RPG	APG
Kevin Garnett	.76	.476	1704	22.4	12.8	4.1
Ricky Davis	.81	.465	1374	17.0	3.9	4.8
Mark Blount	.82	.509	1010	12.3	6.2	0.8
Randy Foye*	.82	.434	832	10.1	2.7	2.8
Mike James	.82	.422	828	10.1	2.0	3.6
Craig Smith*	.82	.531	608	7.4	5.1	0.6
Trenton Hassell	.76	.490	512	6.7	3.2	2.7
Troy Hudson	.34	.379	202	5.9	1.4	2.1
Marko Jaric	.70	.418	371	5.3	2.6	21
Rashad McCants	.37	.350	184	5.0	1.3	1.0
Bracey Wright	.19	.400	67	3.5	1.1	0.8
Justin Reed	.41	.374	106	2.6	1.1	0.4
Eddie Griffin	.13	.259	18	1.4	1.9	0.3
Mark Madsen	.56	.535	61	1.1	1.6	0.2

Triple Doubles: Garnett (3). **3-pt FG leader:** Davis (123). **Steals leader:** Garnett (89). **Blocks leader:** Garnett (126).

New Jersey Nets

	Gm	FG%	Tpts	PPG	RPG	APG
Vince Carter	.82	.454	2070	25.2	6.0	4.8
Nenad Krstic	.26	.526	426	16.4	6.8	1.8
Richard Jefferson	.55	.456	897	16.3	4.4	2.7
Jason Kidd	.80	.406	1041	13.0	8.2	9.2
Mikki Moore	.79	.609	776	9.8	5.1	0.9
Bostjan Nachbar	.76	.457	696	9.2	3.3	0.8
Eddie House	.56	.428	468	8.4	1.6	1.2
Marcus Williams*	.79	.395	534	6.8	2.1	3.3
Antoine Wright	.63	.438	283	4.5	2.8	0.9
Josh Boone*	.61	.579	254	4.2	2.9	0.2
Clifford Robinson	.50	.372	203	4.1	2.4	1.0
Hassan Adams*	.61	.556	174	2.9	1.3	0.2
Jason Collins	.80	.364	169	2.1	4.0	0.6
Bernard Robinson	.31	.306	61	2.0	1.5	0.6
Mile Ilic*	.5	.000	0	0.0	0.2	0.0

Triple Doubles: Kidd (12), Carter (2). **3-pt FG leader:** Carter (156). **Steals leader:** Kidd (127). **Blocks leaders:** Moore (60).

New Orleans/Oklahoma City Hornets

	Gm	FG%	Tpts	PPG	RPG	APG
David West	.52	.476	949	18.3	8.2	2.2
Peja Stojakovic	.13	.423	231	17.8	4.2	0.8
Chris Paul	.64	.437	1104	17.3	4.4	8.9
Desmond Mason	.75	.452	1028	13.7	4.6	1.5
Devin Brown	.58	.420	670	11.6	4.3	2.6
Bobby Jackson	.56	.394	592	10.6	3.2	2.5
Rasual Butler	.81	.398	818	10.1	3.2	0.8
Tyson Chandler	.73	.624	690	9.5	12.4	0.9
Jannero Pargo	.82	.409	751	9.2	2.2	2.5
Marc Jackson	.56	.410	408	7.3	3.4	1.0
Linton Johnson III	.54	.489	226	4.2	3.0	0.3
Hilton Armstrong*	.56	.544	176	3.1	2.7	0.2
Cedric Simmons*	.43	.417	176	2.9	2.5	0.3
Brandon Bass	.21	.341	42	2.0	2.0	0.1
Marcus Vinicius*	.13	.467	22	1.7	0.8	0.4

Triple Doubles: Paul (1). **3-pt FG leader:** Butler (134). **Steals leader:** Paul (118). **Blocks leader:** Chandler (129). **Signed:** G Brown (Dec. 22).

New York Knicks

	Gm	FG%	Tpts	PPG	RPG	APG
Eddy Curry	.81	.576	1576	19.5	7.0	0.8
Jamal Crawford	.59	.400	1039	17.6	3.2	4.4
Stephon Marbury	.74	.415	1210	16.4	2.9	5.4
Quentin Richardson	.49	.418	636	13.0	7.2	2.2
Steve Francis	.44	.408	497	11.3	3.6	3.9
David Lee	.58	.600	621	10.7	10.4	1.8
Nate Robinson	.64	.434	645	10.1	2.4	1.4
Channing Frye	.72	.433	684	9.5	5.5	0.9
Renaldo Balkman*	.68	.505	334	4.9	4.3	0.6
Mardy Collins*	.52	.382	235	4.5	2.0	1.6
Jared Jeffries	.55	.461	223	4.1	4.3	1.2
Malik Rose	.65	.398	192	3.0	2.7	1.0
Jerome James	.41	.418	76	1.9	1.6	0.1
Kelvin Cato	.18	.318	22	1.2	1.7	0.0
Randolph Morris*	.5	.167	4	0.8	1.8	0.2

Triple Doubles: none. **3-pt FG leader:** Marbury (123). **Steals leader:** Marbury (71). **Blocks leader:** Balkman (44).

Orlando Magic

	Gm	FG%	Tpts	PPG	RPG	APG
Dwight Howard	.82	.603	1443	17.6	12.3	1.9
Grant Hill	.65	.518	934	14.4	3.6	2.1
Hedo Turkoglu	.73	.419	970	13.3	4.0	3.2
Jameer Nelson	.77	.430	1000	13.0	3.1	4.3
Trevor Ariza	.57	.539	506	8.9	4.4	1.1
Darko Milicic	.80	.454	639	8.0	5.5	1.1
Keyon Dooling	.66	.410	521	7.9	1.3	1.7
Carlos Arroyo	.72	.425	552	7.7	1.9	2.8
Tony Battie	.66	.489	404	6.1	5.2	0.5
J.J. Redick*	.42	.410	252	6.0	1.2	0.9
Keith Bogans	.59	.404	298	5.1	1.6	1.0
Travis Diener	.26	.425	98	3.8	0.7	1.3
Pat Garrity	.33	.314	71	2.2	1.3	0.4
Bo Outlaw	.41	.667	81	2.0	2.6	0.4
James Augustine*	.2	.333	2	1.0	1.5	1.0

Triple Doubles: none. **3-pt FG leader:** Turkoglu (109). **Steals leader:** Nelson (73). **Blocks leader:** Howard (156).

NBA Points+Rebounds+Assists Leaders				
	PPG	RPG	APG	Avg
Kobe Bryant, LAL	31.6	5.7	5.4	42.6
LeBron James, Cle	27.3	6.7	6.0	40.1
Dwyane Wade, Mia	27.4	4.7	7.5	39.6
Kevin Garnett, Min	22.4	12.8	4.1	39.4
Gilbert Arenas, Wash	28.4	4.6	6.0	39.0
Carmelo Anthony, Den	28.9	6.0	3.8	38.8

Philadelphia 76ers

	Gm	FG%	Tpts	PPG	RPG	APG
Andre Iguodala	.76	.447	1386	18.2	5.7	5.7
Kyle Korver	.74	.440	1067	14.4	3.5	1.4
Andre Miller	.80	.466	1075	13.4	4.4	7.8
Willie Green	.74	.411	839	11.3	2.1	1.5
Samuel Dalembert	.82	.541	879	10.7	8.9	0.4
Joe Smith	.65	.449	553	8.5	6.2	0.8
Rodney Carney*	.67	.464	442	6.6	1.9	0.4
Steven Hunter	.70	.577	450	6.4	4.8	0.4
Shavlik Randolph	.13	.479	58	4.5	4.2	0.3
Louis Williams	.61	.441	262	4.3	1.1	1.8
Kevin Ollie	.53	.433	199	3.8	1.4	2.5
Alan Henderson	.38	.642	119	3.1	2.8	0.3
Bobby Jones*	.44	.462	110	2.5	1.3	0.4
Louis Amundson*	.11	.400	16	1.5	2.5	0.1
Ivan McFarlin	.11	.385	15	1.4	1.0	0.1
Steven Smith	.8	.250	5	0.6	0.8	0.1

Triple Doubles: Iguodala and Miller (1). **3-pt FG leader:** Korver (132). **Steals leader:** Iguodala (152). **Blocks leader:** Dalembert (159). **Acquired:** G Miller, F Smith and two first round pick from Denver for G Allen Iverson and F Ivan McFarlin (Dec. 19). **Signed:** F Amundson (Feb. 5).

Phoenix Suns

	Gm	FG%	Tpts	PPG	RPG	APG
Amare Stoudemire	.82	.575	1671	20.4	9.6	1.0
Steve Nash	.76	.532	1412	18.6	3.5	11.6
Leandro Barbosa	.80	.476	1444	18.1	2.7	4.0
Shawn Marion	.80	.524	1403	17.5	9.8	1.5
Raja Bell	.78	.432	1143	14.7	3.2	2.5
Boris Diaw	.73	.538	709	9.7	4.3	4.8
James Jones	.76	.368	485	6.4	2.3	0.6
Marcus Banks	.45	.429	221	4.9	0.8	1.1
Kurt Thomas	.67	.486	308	4.6	5.7	0.4
Jalen Rose	.29	.442	108	3.7	0.8	0.6
Pat Burke	.23	.354	60	2.6	2.0	0.2
Eric Piatkowski	.11	.360	27	2.5	0.8	0.4
Jumaine Jones	.18	.275	40	2.2	1.3	0.1
Sean Marks	.3	.333	6	2.0	1.0	0.0

Triple Doubles: Diaw (1). **3-pt FG leader:** Bell (205). **Steals leader:** Marion (156). **Blocks leader:** Marion (122).

Portland Trail Blazers

	Gm	FG%	Tpts	PPG	RPG	APG
Zach Randolph	.68	.467	1608	23.6	10.1	2.2
Brandon Roy*	.57	.456	955	16.8	4.4	4.0
Jarrett Jack	.79	.454	946	12.0	2.6	5.1
Travis Outlaw	.67	.434	645	9.6	3.2	0.4
LaMarcus Aldridge*	.63	.503	565	9.0	5.0	0.4
Ime Udoka	.75	.461	629	8.4	3.7	1.4
Martell Webster	.82	.396	574	7.0	2.9	0.4
Jamaal Magloire	.81	.504	529	6.5	6.1	0.4
Fred Jones	.63	.385	412	6.5	1.8	1.2
Raef LaFrentz	.27	.382	100	3.7	2.6	0.1
Sergio Rodriguez*	.67	.423	247	3.7	1.4	3.1
Dan Dickau	.50	.358	166	3.3	0.9	1.4
Stephen Graham	.14	.425	45	3.2	1.5	0.4
Joel Przybilla	.43	.474	84	2.0	3.9	0.4
Luke Schenscher	.11	.304	19	1.7	2.3	0.4
Jeremy Richardson	.6	.500	8	1.3	0.3	0.4

Triple Doubles: none. **3-pt FG leader:** Webster (91). **Steals leader:** Jack (86). **Blocks leader:** Outlaw (74).

Sacramento Kings

	Gm	FG%	Tpts	PPG	RPG	APG
Kevin Martin	.80	.473	1618	20.2	4.3	2.2
Ron Artest	.70	.440	1316	18.8	6.5	3.4
Mike Bibby	.82	.404	1403	17.1	3.2	4.7
Shareef Abdur-Rahim	.80	.474	793	9.9	5.0	1.4
Corliss Williamson	.68	.510	620	9.1	3.3	0.6
Brad Miller	.63	.453	568	9.0	6.4	3.6
John Salmons	.79	.456	671	8.5	3.3	3.2
Francisco Garcia	.79	.429	474	6.0	2.6	1.1
Kenny Thomas	.62	.482	331	5.3	6.1	1.2
Justin Williams*	.26	.614	131	5.0	4.4	0.1
Ronnie Price	.58	.390	192	3.3	1.2	0.8
Quincy Douby*	.42	.381	119	2.8	0.9	0.4
Maurice Taylor	.12	.286	24	2.0	2.3	0.4
Vitaly Potapenko	.3	.000	0	0.0	0.7	0.0

Triple Doubles: Miller and Salmons (1). **3-pt FG leader:** Bibby (173). **Steals leader:** Artest (149). **Blocks leaders:** Artest and Garcia (43).
Signed: F Williams (Jan. 14).

San Antonio Spurs

	Gm	FG%	Tpts	PPG	RPG	APG
Tim Duncan	.80	.546	1599	20.0	10.6	3.4
Tony Parker	.77	.520	1429	18.6	3.2	5.5
Manu Ginobili	.75	.464	1240	16.5	4.4	3.5
Michael Finley	.82	.412	740	9.0	2.7	1.3
Brent Barry	.75	.475	635	8.5	2.1	1.8
James White*	.6	.439	50	8.3	3.3	0.8
Bruce Bowen	.82	.405	510	6.2	2.7	1.4
Francisco Elson	.70	.511	350	5.0	4.8	0.8
Matt Bonner	.56	.447	275	4.9	2.8	0.4
Beno Udrih	.73	.369	340	4.7	1.1	1.7
Fabricio Oberto	.79	.562	349	4.4	4.7	0.9
Robery Horry	.68	.359	268	3.9	3.4	1.1
Jackie Butler	.11	.457	41	3.7	2.0	0.5
Melvin Ely	.30	.363	89	3.0	1.8	0.6
Jacque Vaughn	.64	.425	192	3.0	1.1	2.0

Triple Doubles: none. **3-pt FG leaders:** Ginobili and Barry (128).
Steals leader: Ginobili (109). **Blocks leader:** Duncan (190).
Signed: G/F White (Nov. 3).
Acquired: F/C Ely from Charlotte for F Eric Williams and a 2009 second round pick.

Seattle Supersonics

	Gm	FG%	Tpts	PPG	RPG	APG
Ray Allen	.55	.438	1454	26.4	4.5	4.1
Rashard Lewis	.60	.461	1342	22.4	6.6	2.4
Chris Wilcox	.82	.529	1106	13.5	7.7	1.0
Luke Ridnour	.71	.433	779	11.0	2.3	5.2
Nick Collison	.82	.500	790	9.6	8.1	1.0
Earl Watson	.77	.383	726	9.4	2.4	5.7
Damien Wilkins	.82	.435	724	8.8	2.8	1.9
Johan Petro	.81	.516	502	6.2	4.1	0.6
Mickael Gelabale*	.70	.462	321	4.6	2.5	0.8
Mike Wilks	.47	.468	170	3.6	1.1	1.7
Danny Fortson	.14	.500	40	2.9	3.1	0.1
Andre Brown*	.14	.568	93	2.4	1.9	0.1
Mouhamed Sene*	.28	.367	53	1.9	1.6	0.0
Desmon Farmer	.8	.333	13	1.6	0.1	1.1
Andreas Glyniadakis	.3	.471	17	1.3	0.6	0.1
Randy Livingston	.4	.000	0	0.0	0.3	1.0

Triple Doubles: none. **3-pt FG leader:** Allen (165). **Steals leader:** Watson (99). **Blocks leader:** Collison (66).
Signed: C Glyniadakis (Nov. 5); G Livingston (Apr. 11).

Toronto Raptors

	Gm	FG%	Tpts	PPG	RPG	APG
Chris Bosh	.69	.496	1561	22.6	10.7	2.5
T.J. Ford	.75	.436	1047	14.0	3.1	7.9
Anthony Parker	.73	.477	903	12.4	3.9	2.1
Andrea Bargnani*	.65	.427	751	11.6	3.9	0.8
Juan Dixon	.81	.425	778	9.6	2.0	1.5
Morris Peterson	.71	.429	634	8.9	3.3	0.7
Jose Calderon	.77	.521	668	8.7	1.7	5.0
Jorge Garbajosa*	.67	.420	567	8.5	4.9	1.9
Joey Graham	.79	.495	503	6.4	3.1	0.6
Rasho Nesterovic	.80	.546	494	6.2	4.5	0.9
Kris Humphries	.60	.470	227	3.8	3.1	0.3
Luke Jackson	.13	.442	48	3.7	0.8	1.0
Darrick Martin	.31	.351	94	3.0	0.4	1.4
Uros Slokar*	.20	.538	38	1.9	0.7	0.1
P.J. Tucker	.17	.500	30	1.8	1.4	0.2
Pape Sow	.7	.333	10	1.4	1.6	0.3

Triple Doubles: none. **3-pt FG leader:** Parker (115).
Steals leader: Ford (101). **Blocks leader:** Bosh (90).
Acquired: G Dixon from Portland for G/F Fred Jones (Feb. 21).
Signed: F Jackson (Mar. 25).

Utah Jazz

	Gm	FG%	Tpts	PPG	RPG	APG
Carlos Boozer	.74	.561	1549	20.9	11.7	3.0
Mehmet Okur	.80	.462	1405	17.6	7.2	2.0
Deron Williams	.80	.456	1297	16.2	3.3	9.3
Matt Harpring	.77	.491	894	11.6	4.6	1.3
Derek Fisher	.82	.382	826	10.1	1.8	3.3
Andrei Kirilenko	.70	.471	584	8.3	4.7	2.9
Gordan Giricek	.61	.462	475	7.8	2.1	1.0
Paul Millsap*	.82	.525	559	6.8	5.2	0.8
Ronnie Brewer*	.56	.528	260	4.6	1.3	0.4
C.J. Miles	.37	.345	101	2.7	0.9	0.7
Rafael Araujo	.28	.415	72	2.6	2.4	0.4
Jarron Collins	.82	.441	204	2.5	2.1	0.7
Dee Brown*	.49	.327	94	1.9	0.8	1.7
Roger Powell	.3	.000	2	0.7	1.0	0.0

Triple Doubles: none. **3-pt FG leader:** Okur (129).
Steals leader: Fisher (83). **Blocks leader:** Kirilenko (144).

Washington Wizards

	Gm	FG%	Tpts	PPG	RPG	APG
Gilbert Arenas	.74	.418	2105	28.4	4.6	6.0
Antawn Jamison	.70	.450	1388	19.8	8.0	1.9
Caron Butler	.63	.463	1203	19.1	7.4	3.7
DeShawn Stevenson	.82	.461	920	11.2	2.6	2.7
Darius Songaila	.37	.524	282	7.6	3.6	1.0
Jarvis Hayes	.81	.410	585	7.2	2.6	1.0
Antonio Daniels	.80	.442	571	7.1	1.9	3.6
Brendan Haywood	.77	.558	511	6.6	6.2	0.6
Etan Thomas	.65	.574	395	6.1	5.8	0.4
Andray Blatche	.56	.437	206	3.7	3.4	0.7
Roger Mason	.62	.330	165	2.7	0.7	0.6
Donell Taylor	.47	.400	126	2.7	1.1	1.0
Calvin Booth	.44	.470	69	1.6	1.8	0.4
Mike Hall*	.2	.250	2	1.0	1.0	0.5
James Lang	.11	.444	11	1.0	1.0	0.2
Michael Ruffin	.30	.278	17	0.6	2.1	0.2

Triple Doubles: none. **3-pt FG leader:** Arenas (205).
Steals leader: Arenas (139). **Blocks leader:** Thomas (89).
Signed: F Hall (Mar. 21).

NBA Regular Season Team Leaders

OFFENSE

WEST	Pts	Reb	Ast	FG%	3Pt%	FT%
			—Per Game—			
Phoenix	110.2	40.5	25.9	.494	.399	.808
Golden St.	106.5	41.4	23.8	.463	.356	.717
Denver	105.4	43.4	23.4	.465	.336	.746
LA Lakers	103.3	41.2	22.6	.466	.353	.747
Memphis	101.6	39.5	20.5	.465	.367	.761
Utah	101.5	42.5	24.7	.474	.335	.743
Sacramento	101.3	38.9	20.3	.450	.350	.765
Dallas	100.0	41.9	19.9	.467	.381	.805
Seattle	99.1	39.6	20.7	.460	.362	.791
San Antonio	98.5	40.7	22.1	.474	.381	.334
Houston	97.0	43.3	20.8	.445	.372	.753
Minnesota	96.1	40.2	22.5	.461	.353	.792
LA Clippers	95.6	41.1	21.5	.456	.348	.788
N.O./Okla. City	95.5	43.1	18.7	.445	.362	.740
Portland	94.1	39.3	18.5	.450	.346	.769

EAST	Pts	Reb	Ast	FG%	3Pt%	FT%
			—Per Game—			
Washington	104.3	41.2	20.2	.450	.348	.765
Milwaukee	99.7	39.2	21.6	.465	.356	.733
Toronto	99.5	39.5	22.2	.463	.363	.488
Chicago	98.8	43.7	22.3	.457	.388	.734
New Jersey	97.6	40.8	23.9	.457	.363	.727
New York	97.5	43.3	18.7	.457	.346	.715
Charlotte	96.9	39.8	22.4	.446	.357	.734
Cleveland	96.8	43.5	20.8	.447	.352	.696
Detroit	96.0	40.5	21.6	.454	.344	.774
Boston	95.8	40.4	19.9	.443	.367	.767
Indiana	95.6	41.8	20.5	.438	.346	.760
Philadelphia	94.9	39.7	20.4	.458	.345	.767
Orlando	94.8	40.7	18.6	.472	.356	.702
Miami	94.6	40.8	20.5	.464	.343	.690
Atlanta	93.7	40.1	19.2	.444	.319	.761

DEFENSE

WEST	Pts	Reb	Ast	FG%	3Pt%	FT%
			—Per Game—			
Golden State	106.9	46.4	24.7	.462	.366	.750
Memphis	106.7	42.0	25.1	.486	.389	.759
Denver	103.7	42.3	24.5	.460	.353	.739
LA Lakers	103.4	42.2	21.9	.461	.358	.760
Sacramento	103.1	43.4	22.4	.472	.365	.757
Phoenix	102.9	42.8	18.9	.457	.363	.767
Seattle	102.0	41.0	22.8	.476	.361	.751
Minnesota	99.7	41.4	21.7	.460	.348	.760
Utah	98.6	37.0	18.9	.455	.355	.767
Portland	98.2	39.0	20.8	.471	.361	.778
N.O./Okla. City	97.1	40.8	20.7	.457	.355	.759
LA Clippers	96.1	39.3	21.0	.452	.339	.748
Dallas	92.8	38.1	17.9	.447	.349	.746
Houston	92.1	40.8	19.4	.429	.351	.749
San Antonio	90.1	39.1	17.3	.443	.334	.740

EAST	Pts	Reb	Ast	FG%	3Pt%	FT%
			—Per Game—			
Washington	104.9	43.0	23.7	.473	.377	.777
Milwaukee	104.0	43.0	25.3	.480	.368	.742
Charlotte	100.6	42.6	20.9	.465	.363	.750
New York	100.3	38.8	21.3	.460	.376	.756
Boston	99.2	40.5	22.1	.468	.354	.747
Toronto	98.5	42.5	21.2	.463	.357	.754
Atlanta	98.4	40.5	21.1	.466	.376	.734
New Jersey	98.3	41.4	22.0	.450	.357	.762
Indiana	98.0	41.6	20.0	.457	.372	.753
Philadelphia	98.0	41.1	22.3	.463	.354	.754
Miami	95.5	41.3	20.2	.444	.355	.742
Orlando	94.0	40.7	19.6	.442	.353	.760
Chicago	93.7	40.9	20.4	.435	.349	.730
Cleveland	92.9	39.9	20.1	.448	.329	.734
Detroit	91.8	41.2	20.1	.445	.339	.740

Playoff Series Summaries

WESTERN CONFERENCE

FIRST ROUND (Best of 7)

(8) Golden St. Warriors 4, (1) Dallas Mavericks 2

Date	Winner	Home Court
Apr. 22	Warriors, 97-85	at Dallas
Apr. 25	Mavericks, 112-99	at Dallas
Apr. 27	Warriors, 109-91	at Golden St.
Apr. 29	Warriors, 103-99	at Golden St.
May 1	Mavericks, 118-112	at Dallas
May 3	Warriors, 111-86	at Golden St.

(2) Phoenix Suns 4, (7) LA Lakers 1

Date	Winner	Home Court
Apr. 22	Suns, 95-87	at Phoenix
Apr. 24	Suns, 126-98	at Phoenix
Apr. 26	Lakers, 95-89	at Los Angeles
Apr. 29	Suns, 113-100	at Los Angeles
May 2	Suns, 119-110	at Phoenix

(3) San Antonio Spurs 4, (6) Denver Nuggets 1

Date	Winner	Home Court
Apr. 22	Nuggets, 95-89	at San Antonio
Apr. 25	Spurs, 97-88	at San Antonio
Apr. 28	Spurs, 96-91	at Denver
Apr. 30	Spurs, 96-89	at Denver
May 2	Spurs, 93-78	at San Antonio

(4) Utah Jazz 4, (5) Houston Rockets 3

Date	Winner	Home Court
Apr. 21	Rockets, 84-75	at Utah
Apr. 23	Rockets, 98-90	at Utah
Apr. 26	Jazz, 81-67	at Houston
Apr. 28	Jazz, 98-85	at Houston
Apr. 30	Rockets, 96-92	at Utah
May 3	Jazz, 94-82	at Houston
May 5	Jazz, 103-99	at Utah

SEMIFINALS (Best of 7)

(4) Utah Jazz 4, (8) Golden State Warriors 1

Date	Winner	Home Court
May 7	Jazz, 116-112	at Utah
May 9	Jazz, 127-117 OT	at Utah
May 11	Warriors, 125-105	at Golden St.
May 13	Jazz, 115-101	at Golden St.
May 15	Jazz, 100-87	at Utah

(3) San Antonio Spurs 4, (2) Phoenix Suns 2

Date	Winner	Home Court
May 6	Spurs, 111-106	at Phoenix
May 8	Suns, 101-81	at Phoenix
May 12	Spurs, 108-101	at San Antonio
May 14	Suns, 104-98	at San Antonio
May 16	Spurs, 88-85	at Phoenix
May 18	Spurs, 114-106	at San Antonio

CHAMPIONSHIP (Best of 7)

(3) San Antonio 4, (3) Utah Jazz 1

Date	Winner	Home Court
May 20	Spurs, 108-100	at San Antonio
May 22	Spurs, 105-96	at San Antonio
May 26	Jazz, 109-83	at Utah
May 28	Spurs, 91-79	at Utah
May 30	Spurs, 109-84	at San Antonio

2007 NBA PLAYOFFS

| 1ST ROUND | SEMIFINALS | FINAL | | FINAL | SEMIFINALS | 1ST ROUND |

PLAYOFFS

(1) Dallas 2
(8) Golden State 4
　Golden State 1
(4) Utah 4
(5) Houston 3
　Utah 4
　Utah 1
　WESTERN
　CONFERENCE
(3) San Antonio 4
(6) Denver 1
　San Antonio 4
　San Antonio 4
(2) Phoenix 4
(7) LA Lakers 1
　Phoenix 2
　San Antonio 4
　Cleveland 0

　Detroit 2
　EASTERN
　CONFERENCE
　Cleveland 4

　Detroit 4
　Chicago 2
　New Jersey 2
　Cleveland 4

(1) Detroit 4
(8) Orlando 0
(4) Miami 0
(5) Chicago 4
(3) Toronto 2
(6) New Jersey 4
(2) Cleveland 4
(7) Washington 0

EASTERN CONFERENCE

FIRST ROUND (Best of 7)

(1) Detroit Pistons 4, (8) Orlando Magic 0

Date	Winner	Home Court
Apr. 21	Pistons, 100-92	at Detroit
Apr. 23	Pistons, 98-90	at Detroit
Apr. 26	Pistons, 93-77	at Orlando
Apr. 28	Pistons, 97-93	at Orlando

(2) Cleveland Cavaliers 4, (7) Wash. Wizards 0

Date	Winner	Home Court
Apr. 22	Cavaliers, 97-82	at Cleveland
Apr. 25	Cavaliers, 109-102	at Cleveland
Apr. 28	Cavaliers, 98-92	at Washington
Apr. 30	Cavaliers, 97-90	at Washington

(6) New Jersey Nets 4, (3) Toronto Raptors 2

Date	Winner	Home Court
Apr. 21	Nets, 96-91	at Toronto
Apr. 24	Raptors, 89-83	at Toronto
Apr. 27	Nets, 102-89	at New Jersey
Apr. 29	Nets, 102-81	at New Jersey
May 1	Raptors, 98-96	at Toronto
May 4	Nets, 98-97	at New Jersey

(5) Chicago Bulls 4, (4) Miami Heat 0

Date	Winner	Home Court
Apr. 21	Bulls, 96-91	at Miami
Apr. 24	Bulls, 107-89	at Miami
Apr. 27	Bulls, 104-96	at Chicago
Apr. 29	Bulls, 92-79	at Chicago

SEMIFINALS (Best of 7)

(1) Detroit Pistons 4, (5) Chicago Bulls 2

Date	Winner	Home Court
May 5	Pistons, 95-69	at Detroit
May 7	Pistons, 108-87	at Detroit
May 10	Pistons, 81-74	at Chicago
May 13	Bulls, 102-87	at Chicago
May 15	Bulls, 108-92	at Detroit
May 17	Pistons, 95-85	at Chicago

(2) Cleveland Cavaliers 4, (6) New Jersey Nets 2

Date	Winner	Home Court
May 6	Cavaliers, 81-77	at Cleveland
May 8	Cavaliers, 102-92	at Cleveland
May 12	Nets, 96-85	at New Jersey
May 14	Cavaliers, 87-85	at New Jersey
May 16	Nets, 83-72	at Cleveland
May 18	Cavaliers, 88-72	at New Jersey

CHAMPIONSHIP (Best of 7)

(2) Cleveland Cavaliers 4, (1) Detroit Pistons 2

Date	Winner	Home Court
May 21	Pistons, 79-76	at Detroit
May 24	Pistons, 79-76	at Detroit
May 27	Cavaliers, 88-82	at Cleveland
May 29	Cavaliers, 91-87	at Cleveland
May 31	Cavaliers, 109-107 2OT	at Detroit
June 2	Cavaliers, 98-82	at Cleveland

NBA FINALS (Best of 7)

	W-L	Avg.	Leading Scorer
Cleveland	0-4	80.5	L. James (22.0)
San Antonio	4-0	86.5	T. Parker (24.5)

Date	Winner	Home Court
June 7	Spurs, 85-76	at San Antonio
June 10	Spurs, 103-92	at San Antonio
June 12	Spurs, 75-72	at Cleveland
June 14	Spurs, 83-82	at Cleveland

Finals MVP

Tony Parker, San Antonio, G
24.5 ppg, 5.0 rpg, 3.3 apg

NBA Finalists' Composite Box Scores
Cleveland Cavaliers (12-8)

(3 Game Min.)	Gm	FG%	3PT-A	TPts	Pts	Reb	Ast	Gm	FG%	3PT-A	TPts	Pts	Reb	Ast
		Overall Playoffs			—Per Game—				Finals vs. San Antonio			—Per Game—		
LeBron James	20	.416	21-75	501	25.1	8.1	8.0	4	.356	4-20	88	22.0	7.0	6.8
Zydrunas Ilgauskas	20	.492	0-0	251	12.6	9.7	0.9	4	.351	0-0	31	7.8	10.3	0.5
Drew Gooden	20	.493	0-2	228	11.4	8.0	1.0	4	.500	0-1	51	12.8	8.3	0.3
Larry Hughes	18	.347	19-54	204	11.3	3.9	2.4	2	.100	0-2	2	1.0	2.5	1.0
Aleksandar Pavlovic	20	.381	20-58	183	9.2	2.6	1.6	4	.364	5-12	39	9.8	2.5	0.8
Daniel Gibson	20	.431	27-66	165	8.3	1.6	1.1	4	.439	6-19	43	10.8	1.8	2.5
Anderson Varejao	20	.511	0-4	119	6.0	6.0	0.6	4	.667	0-0	30	7.5	5.3	0.8
Donyell Marshalll	19	.333	14-45	67	3.5	2.2	0.3	4	.313	2-11	15	3.8	2.3	1.3
Damon Jones	11	.308	7-22	26	2.4	0.8	1.0	4	.455	5-9	18	4.5	1.3	1.0
Eric Snow	19	.316	12-38	32	1.7	1.5	1.5	4	.400	0-0	5	1.3	1.0	2.3
Ira Newble	6	.000	0-2	0	0.0	0.2	0.2	1	.000	0-1	0	0.0	1.0	0.0
CAVALIERS	20	.421	108-331	1776	88.8	43.3	17.5	4	.395	22-75	322	80.5	41.0	16.5
OPPONENTS	20	.425	117-353	1733	86.7	39.3	19.2	4	.444	29-78	346	86.5	43.8	16.8

San Antonio Spurs (16-4)

	Gm	FG%	3PT-A	TPts	Pts	Reb	Ast	Gm	FG%	3PT-A	TPts	Pts	Reb	Ast
		Overall Playoffs			—Per Game—				Finals vs. Cleveland			—Per Game—		
Tin Duncan	20	.521	0-0	444	22.2	11.5	3.3	4	.446	0-0	73	18.3	11.5	3.8
Tony Parker	20	.480	7-21	415	20.8	3.4	5.8	4	.568	4-7	98	24.5	5.0	3.3
Manu Ginobili	20	.401	38-99	333	16.7	5.5	3.7	4	.367	10-23	71	17.8	5.8	2.5
Michael Finley	20	.410	44-105	225	11.3	2.9	1.1	4	.261	1-12	15	3.8	2.0	0.8
Bruce Bowen	20	.395	33-74	130	6.5	4.1	1.3	4	.296	7-18	24	6.0	5.5	1.3
Fabricio Elson	20	.591	0-1	66	3.3	3.1	0.1	4	1.000	6-6	16	4.0	2.5	0.0
Brent Barry	19	.350	15-49	59	3.1	1.3	1.1	4	.364	4-10	12	3.0	1.5	0.5
Jacque Vaughn	20	.400	0-0	43	2.2	0.5	1.4	4	.571	0-0	8	2.0	1.3	1.0
Matt Bonner	9	.286	1-4	7	0.8	0.3	0.0	0	—	0-0	0	0.0	0.0	0.0
Beno Udrih	8	.000	0-2	2	0.3	0.1	0.1	2	—	0-0	0	0.0	0.0	0.0
SPURS	20	.459	151-393	1913	95.7	40.6	19.9	4	.444	29-78	346	86.5	43.8	16.8
OPPONENTS	20	.439	99-285	1834	91.7	40.7	18.5	4	.395	22-75	322	80.5	41.0	16.5

NBA Playoff Leaders

Scoring Average

	Gm	FG	FT	Pts	Avg
Kobe Bryant, LAL	5	60	34	164	32.8
Antawn Jamison, Wash	4	49	21	128	32.0
Carmelo Anthony, Den	5	47	31	134	26.8
Amare Stoudemire, Pho	10	91	70	253	25.3
Tracy McGrady, Hou	7	63	42	177	25.3
Baron Davis, G. St.	11	98	57	278	25.3
Yao Ming, Hou	7	55	66	176	25.1
LeBron James, Cle	20	166	148	501	25.0
Carlos Boozer, Utah	17	162	76	400	23.5
Dwyane Wade, Mia	4	36	22	94	23.5

Total Points

	Gm	FG	FT	Pts	Avg
LeBron James, Cle	20	166	148	**501**	25.0
Tim Duncan, SA	20	174	96	**444**	22.2
Tony Parker, SA	20	168	72	**415**	20.8
Carlos Boozer, Utah	17	162	76	**400**	23.5
Manu Ginobili, SA	20	99	97	**333**	16.6
Deron Williams, Utah	17	122	64	**327**	19.2

Rebounds

	Gm	Off	Def	Tot	Avg
Marcus Camby, Den	5	12	62	74	14.8
Dwight Howard, Orl	4	16	43	59	14.8
Lamar Odom, LAL	5	20	45	65	13.0
Carlos Boozer, Utah	17	54	153	207	12.2
Amare Stoudemire, Pho	10	30	91	121	12.1
Tim Duncan, SA	20	73	156	229	11.4

Assists

	Gm	No	Avg
Steve Nash, Pho	11	146	13.3
Antonio Daniels, Wash	4	47	11.8
Jason Kidd, NJ	12	131	10.9
Deron Williams, Utah	17	146	8.6
LeBron James, Cle	20	159	8.0
Kirk Hinrich, Chi	10	75	7.5

Final Playoff Standings
ranked by victories

	Gm	W	L	Pct	For	Opp
					Per Game	
San Antonio	20	16	4	.800	95.7	91.7
Cleveland	20	12	8	.600	88.8	86.7
Detroit	16	10	6	.625	91.4	88.4
Utah	17	9	8	.529	97.9	97.0
Chicago	10	6	4	.600	92.4	91.3
Phoenix	11	6	5	.545	104.1	99.1
New Jersey	12	6	6	.500	90.2	88.3
Golden St.	11	5	6	.455	106.6	104.9
Houston	7	3	4	.429	87.3	90.4
Toronto	6	2	4	.333	90.8	96.2
Dallas	6	2	4	.333	98.5	105.2
LA Lakers	5	1	4	.200	98.0	108.4
Denver	5	1	4	.200	88.2	94.2
Miami	4	0	4	.000	88.8	99.8
Washington	4	0	4	.000	91.5	100.3
Orlando	4	0	4	.000	88.0	97.0

Annual Awards

Most Valuable Player

The Maurice Podoloff Trophy; voting by 129-member panel of local and national pro basketball writers and broadcasters. Each ballot has five entries; points awarded on 10-7-5-3-1 basis.

	1st	2nd	3rd	4th	5th	Pts
Dirk Nowitzki, Dallas	83	39	7	-	-	1138
Steve Nash, Phoenix	44	74	11	-	-	1013
Kobe Bryant, LA Lakers	2	11	65	30	9	521
Tim Duncan, San Antonio	-	3	25	39	23	286
LeBron James, Cleveland	-	-	11	31	35	183
Tracy McGrady, Houston	-	2	6	16	18	110
Chris Bosh, Toronto	-	-	3	4	16	43
Gilbert Arenas, Washington	-	-	1	4	14	31
Kevin Garnett, Minnesota	-	-	2	1	7	7
Carlos Boozer, Utah	-	-	1	4	7	7
Chauncey Billups, Detroit	-	-	1	1	4	4
Dwyane Wade, Miami	-	-	-	3	3	3
Shaquille O'Neal, Miami	-	-	1	-	3	3

All-NBA Teams

Voting by a 129-member panel of local and national pro basketball writers and broadcasters. Each ballot has entries for three teams; points awarded on 5-3-1 basis. First Team repeaters from 2005-06 are in **bold** type.

Pos	First Team	1st	Pts
F	Tim Duncan, San Antonio	94	573
F	**Dirk Nowitzki**, Dallas	125	634
C	Amare Stoudemire, Phoenix	36	351
G	**Kobe Bryant**, LA Lakers	128	643
G	**Steve Nash**, Phoenix	129	645

Pos	Second Team	1st	Pts
F	LeBron James, Cleveland	64	494
F	Chris Bosh, Toronto	8	234
C	Yao Ming, Houston	38	333
G	Gilbert Arenas, Washington	0	295
G	Tracy McGrady, Houston	10	278

Pos	Third Team	1st	Pts
F	Carmelo Anthony, Denver	1	142
F	Kevin Garnett, Minnesota	5	225
C	Dwight Howard, Orlando	1	108
G	Dwyane Wade, Miami	1	241
G	Chauncey Billups, Detroit	0	86

Other players receiving votes (first team votes in parentheses): Carlos Boozer, Utah, 127; Shaquille O'Neal, Mia., 70 (3); Jason Kidd, N.J., 58; Marcus Camby, Den., 42 (2); Shawn Marion, Pho., 41; Allen Iverson, Den., 39; Tony Parker, S.A., 39; Vince Carter, N.J., 15; Deron Williams, Utah, 15; Josh Howard, Dal., 11; Elton Brand, LAC, 8; Mehmet Okur, Utah, 7; Baron Davis, G.St., 6; Michael Redd, Milw., 6; Ray Allen, Sea., 5; Richard Hamilton, Det., 4; Joe Johnson, Atl., 3; Ben Gordon, Chi., 3; Chris Paul, N.O./Okla. City, 3; Paul Pierce, Bos., 2; Ben Wallace, Chi., 2; Jason Terry, Dal., 2; Eddy Curry, N.Y., 2.

Rookie of the Year

The Eddie Gottlieb Trophy; voting by 128-member panel of local and national pro basketball writers and broadcasters. Each ballot has entries for three players; points awarded on 5-3-1 basis.

	1st	2nd	3rd	Pts
Brandon Roy, Portland	127	1	-	638
Andrea Bargnani, Toronto	1	77	28	264
Rudy Gay, Memphis	-	21	30	93
Adam Morrison, Charlotte	-	11	11	44
Randy Foye, Minnesota	-	7	16	37
LaMarcus Aldridge, Portland	-	5	3	18
Jorge Garbajosa, Toronto	-	2	11	17
Paul Millsap, Utah	-	1	16	19
Tyrus Thomas, Chicago	-	2	4	10
Walter Hermann, Charlotte	-	1	2	5
Craig Smith, Minnesota	-	-	4	4
Rajon Rondo, Boston	-	-	3	3

All-Defensive Teams

Voting by NBA head coaches. Each ballot has entries for two teams; two points given for 1st team, one for 2nd. Coaches cannot vote for own players. First Team repeaters from 2005-06 are in **bold** type.

Pos	First Team	1st	Pts
F	**Bruce Bowen**, San Antonio	19	42
F	Tim Duncan, San Antonio	16	36
C	Marcus Camby, Denver	11	34
G	**Kobe Bryant**, LA Lakers	14	32
G	Raja Bell, Phoenix	7	25

Pos	Second Team	1st	Pts
C	Ben Wallace, Chicago	12	33
G	Jason Kidd, New Jersey	8	23
F	Tayshaun Prince, Detroit	7	21
F	Kevin Garnett, Minnesota	8	20
G	Kirk Hinrich, Chicago	7	18

Other players receiving votes (first team votes in parentheses): Shane Battier, Hou., 17 (6); Shawn Marion, Pho., 15 (5); Chauncey Billups, Det. 13 (5); Ron Artest, Sac.12 (4); Gerald Wallace, Cha. 11 (2); Alonzo Mourning, Mia, 9 (4); Devin Harris, Dal., 8 (2); Tyson Chandler, N.O./Okla. City, 8 (2); Josh Howard, Dal., 7.

Coach of the Year

The Red Auerbach Trophy; voting by a 128-member panel of local and national pro basketball writers and broadcasters.

Top Vote-getters	1st	2nd	3rd	Pts
Sam Mitchell, Toronto	49	43	20	394
Jerry Sloan, Utah	39	28	22	301
Avery Johnson, Dallas	28	31	35	268
Jeff Van Gundy, Houston	10	19	27	134
Mike D'Antoni, Phoenix	2	3	3	22
Don Nelson, Golden St.	-	2	7	13
Scott Skiles, Chicago	-	1	9	12
Pat Riley, Miami	-	1	-	3
Gregg Popovich, San Antonio	-	-	2	2
George Karl, Denver	-	-	1	1
Flip Saunders, Detroit	-	-	1	1
Isiah Thomas, New York	-	-	1	1

All-Rookie Team

Voting by NBA's 30 head coaches, who cannot vote for players on their team. Each ballot has entries for two five-man teams, regardless of position; Coaches are not permitted to vote for players on their own team. two points given for 1st team, one for 2nd. First team votes in parentheses.

First Team	College	Pts
Brandon Roy, Portland (29)	Washington	58
Andrea Bargnani, Toronto (28)	none	57
Randy Foye, Minnesota (21)	Villanova	48
Rudy Gay, Memphis (12)	Connecticut	39
Jorge Garbajosa, Toronto (13)	none	37
LaMarcus Aldridge, Portland)14)	Texas	37

Second Team	College	Pts
Paul Millsap, Utah (10)	La. Tech	36
Adam Morrison, Charlotte (12)	Gonzaga	35
Tyrus Thomas, Chicago (5)	LSU	26
Craig Smith, Minnesota (1)	Boston College	21
Rajon Rondo, Boston (1)	Kentucky	10
Walter Hermann, Charlotte (1)	none	10
Marcus Williams, New Jersey (1)	Arizona	10

Executive of the Year

The Sporting News Executive of the Year Award; voting done by a 45-member panel of NBA executives.

	Votes
Bryan Colangelo, Toronto	20
Carroll Dawson, Houston	9

Note: seven other executives received votes.

Sixth-Man Award

Voted on by a 127-member panel of local and national pro basketball writers and broadcasters. Each ballot has entries for three players; points awarded on 5-3-1 basis.

Top Vote-getters	1st	2nd	3rd	Pts
Leandro Barbosa, Phoenix	101	24	1	578
Manu Ginobili, San Antonio	18	50	29	269
Jerry Stackhouse, Dallas	7	40	55	210
David Lee, New York	-	3	13	22
Kyle Korver, Philadelphia	1	2	8	19
Antonio McDyess, Detroit	-	2	9	7
Corey Maggette, L.A. Clippers	-	1	3	6
Luther Head, Houston	-	-	4	4
Chucky Atkins, Memphis	-	1	1	4
Matt Harpring, Utah	-	1	1	4

Most Improved Player Award

Voted on by a 129-member panel of local and national pro basketball writers and broadcasters. Each ballot has entries for three players; points awarded on 5-3-1 basis.

Top Vote-getters	1st	2nd	3rd	Pts
Monta Ellis, Golden St.	47	34	15	352
Kevin Martin, Sacramento	44	38	15	349
Deron Williams, Utah	13	6	18	101
Tyson Chandler, N.O./Okla. City	6	11	9	72
Andris Biedrins, Golden St.	8	4	12	64
Al Jefferson, Boston	2	13	13	62
Luol Deng, Chicago	2	7	13	44
Leandro Barbosa, Phoenix	3	3	-	24
Andre Iguodala, Philadelphia	1	2	3	14
David Lee, New York	-	3	3	12
Jason Kapono, Miami	-	1	7	10

Defensive Player of the Year Award

Voted on by a 130-member panel of local and national pro basketball writers and broadcasters.

Top Vote-getters	1st	2nd	3rd	Pts
Marcus Camby, Denver	70	23	12	431
Bruce Bowen, San Antonio	22	26	18	206
Tim Duncan, San Antonio	15	22	17	158
Shawn Marion, Phoenix	7	12	22	93
Shane Battier, Houston	7	11	18	86
Ben Wallace, Chicago	1	10	7	42
Gerald Wallace, Charlotte	3	3	3	27
Ron Artest, Sacramento	1	3	6	20
Tyson Chandler, N.O./Okla. City	-	5	-	15
Jermaine O'Neal, Ind	1	2	-	11

Sportsmanship Award

Each of the 30 NBA teams nominated a player from their roster "who best represents the ideals of sportsmanship on the court," then a panel of former players (Mike Bantom, Eddie Johnson, "Satch" Sanders, Kenny Smith and Steve Smith) selected the six divisional winners from the pool of nominees. The winner is chosen from the divisional winners in vote by current NBA players. The winner receives the Joe Dumars Trophy, named for the Pistons guard who won the inaugural sportsmanship award in 1996.

	1st	2nd	3rd	4th	5th	6th	Pts
Luol Deng, Chi	52	69	48	62	53	29	2027
Shane Battier, Hou.	65	58	59	38	36	57	2005
Derek Fisher, Utah	58	55	51	55	47	47	1953
Elton Brand, LAC	50	49	66	57	53	38	1935
Joe Johnson, Atl	47	45	43	52	64	62	1737
Anthony Parker, Tor	41	37	46	49	60	80	1611

2007 College Draft

First and second round picks at the 60th annual NBA Draft held June 28, 2007 held in New York City at the Theatre at Madison Square Garden. The order of the first 14 positions were determined by a Draft Lottery held May 22, in Secaucus, N.J. Positions 15 through 30 reflect regular season records in reverse order. Underclassmen are listed in CAPITAL letters.

First Round

	Team		Pos
1	Portland	GREG ODEN, Ohio St.	C
2	Seattle	KEVIN DURANT, Texas	F
3	Atlanta	AL HORFORD, Florida	F/C
4	Memphis	MIKE CONLEY JR., Ohio St.	G
5	Boston	JEFF GREEN, Georgetown	F
6	Milwaukee	Yi Jianlian, China	F
7	Minnesota	COREY BREWER, Florida	F
8	Charlotte	BRANDAN WRIGHT, No. Carolina	F
9	Chicago	JOAKIM NOAH, Florida	F/C
10	Sacramento	SPENCER HAWES, Washington	C
11	Atlanta	Acie Law IV, Texas A&M	G
12	Philadelphia	THADDEUS YOUNG, Ga. Tech	G
13	New Orleans	JULIAN WRIGHT, Kansas	F
14	L.A. Clippers	Al Thornton, Florida St.	F
15	Detroit	RODNEY STUCKEY, E. Wash.	G
16	Washington	NICK YOUNG, USC	G/F
17	New Jersey	SEAN WILLIAMS, Boston College	F/C
18	GoldenState	Marco Belinelli, Italy	G
19	L.A. Lakers	JAVARIS CRITTENTON, Ga. Tech	G
20	Miami	JASON SMITH, Colorado St.	F/C
21	Philadelphia	DAEQUAN COOK, Ohio St.	G
22	Charlotte	Jared Dudley, Boston College	F
23	New York	WILSON CHANDLER, DePaul	F
24	Phoenix	Rudy Fernandez, Spain	G
25	Utah	Morris Almond, Rice	G
26	Houston	Aaron Brooks, Oregon	G
27	Detroit	ARRON AFFLALO, UCLA	G
28	San Antonio	Tiago Splitter, Brazil	F
29	Phoenix	Alando Tucker, Wisconsin	F
30	Philadelphia	Petteri Koponen, Finland	G

Second Round

	Team		Pos
31	Seattle	Carl Landry, Purdue	F
32	Boston	GABE PRUITT, USC	G
33	San Antonio	MARCUS WILLIAMS, Arizona	F
34	Dallas	Nick Fazekas, Nevada	F
35	Seattle	GLEN DAVIS, LSU	F
36	Golden St.	Jermareo Davidson, Alabama	F
37	Portland	JOSH McROBERTS, Duke	F
38	Philadelphia	Kyrylo Fesenko, Ukraine	C
39	Miami	Stanko Barac, Bosnia	C
40	L.A. Lakers	Sun Yue, China	F
41	Minnesota	Chris Richard, Florida	F
42	Portland	Derrick Byars, Vanderbilt	G/F
43	NO/Okla. City	Adam Haluska, Iowa	G
44	Orlando	Reyshawn Terry, North Carolina	F
45	L.A. Clippers	Jared Jordan, Marist	G
46	Golden St.	Stephane Lasme, Massachusetts	F
47	Washington	DOMINIC MCGUIRE, Fresno St.	F
48	L.A. Lakers	Marc Gasol, Spain	C
49	Chicago	Aaron Gray, Pittsburgh	C
50	Dallas	Renaldas Seibutis, Lithuania	G
51	Chicago	JAMESON CURRY, Oklahoma St.	G
52	Portland	TAUREAN GREEN, Florida	G
53	Portland	Demetris Nichols, Syracuse	F
54	Houston	Brad Newley, Australia	G
55	Utah	Herbert Hill, Providence	F/C
56	Milwaukee	RAMON SESSIONS, Nevada	G
57	Detroit	Sammy Mejia, DePaul	G
58	San Antonio	Giorgios Printezis, Greece	F
59	Phoenix	D.J. Strawberry, Maryland	G
60	Dallas	Milovan Rakovic, Serbia	F

Continental Basketball Association
Final Standings

QW refers to quarters won. Teams get 3 points for a win, 1 point for each quarter won and ½ point for any quarters tied. The three highest quarter-point averages in each conference qualify for the playoffs. (*) denotes playoff qualifiers.

American Conference	W	L	Home	Away	QW	Pts	Avg
*Albany Patroons	30	18	17-7	13-11	107.5	197.5	4.1
Minot SkyRockets	31	17	17-7	14-10	102.5	195.5	4.1
Indiana Alley Cats	23	25	13-11	10-14	94.5	163.5	3.4
Pittsburgh Xplosion	10	38	6-18	4-20	81.5	108.5	2.3
National Conference	W	L	Home	Away	QW	Pts	Avg
*Yakama Sun Kings	35	13	21-3	14-10	125.0	230.0	4.8
Great Falls Explorers	24	24	15-9	9-15	90.0	162.0	3.4
Butte Daredevils	21	27	14-10	7-17	87.0	150.0	3.1
Utah Eagles	6	18	5-7	1-11	35.0	53.0	2.2

Note: The Utah Eagles franchise folded midway through the 2006-07 season with a 6-16 record. The CBA was able to reschedule all but two of their remaining games among the other teams in the league. Utah was forced to forfeit two games and ended their season with an official record of 6-18.

CBA Finals (best of five)

The CBA changed their playoff format for the 2006-07 when the league was unable to secure the necessary amount of home dates to accommodate the original number of playoff teams. It was decided that the two conference champions would meet in a best-of-five series to award the Jay Ramsdell Trophy.

Yakama vs. Albany

Mar. 27	Yakama 113	at Albany 99
Mar. 28	Yakama 92	at Albany 87
Mar. 30	at Yakama 120	Albany 90

Yakama wins series, 3 games to 0

Finals MVP: Eddy Barlow, Yakama

CBA Annual Awards

Most Valuable Player
Galen Young, Yakama

Newcomer of the Year
Shaun Fountain, Indiana

Rookie of the Year
Travis Garrison, Great Falls

Def. Player of the Year
Jamario Moon, Albany

Coach of the Year
Paul Woolpert, Yakama

CBA Regular Season Individual Leaders

Scoring

	Gm	Pts	Avg
Shaun Fountain, Indiana	47	1079	23.0
Carl Edwards, Indiana	39	862	22.1
Robert Griffin, Pittsburgh	42	868	20.7
Desmond Ferguson, Minot	44	905	20.6
Ralph Holmes, Yakama	38	748	19.7
Odell Bradley, Butte	46	868	18.9
Jamario Moon, Albany	44	829	18.8
Kwan Johnson, Albany	41	742	18.1

Assists

	Gm	Ast	Avg
Galen Young, Yakama	46	304	6.6
Shaun Fountain, Indiana	47	276	5.9
Malik Moore, Great Falls	47	265	5.6
Lewis Monroe, Pittsburgh	25	124	5.0
Jitim Young, Minot	47	210	4.5
Eddy Barlow, Yakama	45	200	4.4
Ronald Ross, Butte	48	181	3.8
Javon Harris, Great Falls	42	144	3.4

Rebounding

	Gm	Reb	Avg
Nick VanderLaan, Butte	47	550	11.7
Rocky Walls, Yakama	32	293	9.2
Chris Alexander, Yakama	43	346	8.0
Julius Nwosu, Utah	19	144	7.6
Jamario Moon, Albany	44	331	7.5
Ray Cunningham, Minot	47	348	7.4
Galen Young, Yakama	46	338	7.3
David Harrison, Minot	28	194	6.9

Steals

	Gm	Stl	Avg
Shaun Fountain, Indiana	47	118	2.5
Ronald Ross, Butte	48	114	2.4
Jamario Moon, Albany	44	86	2.0
Ralph Holmes, Yakama	38	69	1.8
Jamar Howard, Great Falls	48	83	1.7
Kwan Johnson, Albany	41	67	1.6
Jason Smith, Minot	30	46	1.5
Carl Edwards, Indiana	39	59	1.5

Field Goal Pct.

	FGM	FGA	Pct
Chris Alexander, Yakama	208	325	.640
Steve Castleberry, Minot	180	302	.596
Chris Sockwell, Albany	146	245	.596
Kevin Steenberg, Butte	47	79	.595
Marvin Phillips, Albany	183	316	.579
Greg Stevenson, Yakama	220	389	.566
Reggie Jessie, Albany	148	264	.561
Rocky Walls, Yakama	100	179	.559

Free Throw Pct.

	FTM	FTA	Pct
Harold Arceneaux, Great Falls	129	144	.896
Desmond Ferguson, Minot	115	130	.885
Robert Griffin, Pittsburgh	171	194	.881
David Bell, Butte	124	141	.879
Javon Harris, Great Falls	64	74	.865
Keith Salscheider, Great Falls	95	111	.856
Eric Walton, Indiana	40	47	.851
Shaun Fountain, Indiana	200	235	.851

National Basketball Association Development League

The newly redubbed D-League is a feeder league founded by the NBA in 2001. (*) denotes conference champion. (†) denotes playoff qualifier. Note that conference champions received a first round playoff bye.

2007 Final Standings

Eastern Conference	W	L	Pct	GB		Western Conference	W	L	Pct	GB
*Dakota Wizards	33	17	.660	—		*Idaho Stampede	33	17	.660	—
†Sioux Falls Skyforce	30	20	.600	3		†Colorado 14ers	28	22	.560	5
†Fort Worth Flyers	29	21	.580	4		†Albuquerque Thunderbirds	24	26	.480	9
Tulsa 66ers	21	29	.420	12		Anaheim Arsenal	23	27	.460	10
Austin Toros	21	29	.420	12		Los Angeles D-Fenders	23	27	.460	10
Arkansas RimRockers	16	34	.320	17		Bakersfield Jam	19	31	.380	14

Regular Season Individual Leaders

Scoring

	Gm	Pts	Avg
Roger Powell, Arkansas	28	624	22.3
Von Wafer, Colorado	42	883	21.0
Dijon Thompson, Albuquerque	31	643	20.7
Desmon Farmer, Tulsa	32	637	19.9
B.J. Elder, Austin	45	894	19.9
Clay Tucker, Arkansas	46	906	19.7
Jaward Williams, Anaheim	50	962	19.2
Kevinn Pinkney, Bakersfield	38	710	18.7
Denham Brown, Tulsa	42	782	18.6
Elton Brown, Colorado	50	920	18.4

Rebounds

	Gm	Reb	Avg
Pops Mensah-Bonsu, Fort Worth	26	271	10.4
Elton Brown, Colorado	50	482	9.6
Patrick O'Bryant, Bakersfield	25	241	9.6
Dijon Thompson, Albuquerque	31	272	8.8
Jared Reiner, Sioux Falls	28	241	8.6
Mike Hall, Tulsa	29	247	8.5

Assists

	Gm	Ast	Avg
Will Conroy, Tulsa	42	447	10.6
Randy Livingston, Idaho	46	488	10.6
Pooh Jeter, Colorado	50	355	7.1
Clay Tucker, Arkansas	46	252	5.5
Tony Bland, Albuquerque	42	223	5.3
Curtis Stinson, Fort Worth	28	147	5.3

Steals

	Gm	Stl	Avg
Clay Tucker, Arkansas	46	97	2.1
Dijon Thompson, Albuquerque	31	57	1.8
Frank Williams, Sioux Falls	44	78	1.8
Brandon Dean, Arkansas	46	80	1.7
Tony Bobbitt, Colorado	36	61	1.7
Randy Livingston, Idaho	46	75	1.6

Field Goal Pct.

	FG	FGA	Pct
Andre Brown, Sioux Falls	79	125	.632
Kevin Lude, Dakota	190	305	.623
Amir Johnson, Sioux Falls	157	252	.623
Mike Harris, Colorado	237	385	.616
Jeff Graves, Idaho	159	276	.576
Frans Steyn, Tulsa	114	201	.567

Blocks

	Gm	Blk	Avg
Julius Hodge, Albuquerque	22	166	7.6
Amir Johnson, Sioux Falls	22	69	3.1
Patrick O'Bryant, Bakersfield	25	72	2.9
Cezary Trybanski, Tulsa	47	120	2.6
Louis Amundson, Colorado	25	62	2.5
Andre Patterson, Los Angeles	50	81	1.6

Playoffs

Conference Semifinals

Eastern Conference

Apr. 17 at Sioux Falls, S.D.

	1	2	3	4	F
Fort Worth Flyers	25	30	33	27	105
Sioux Falls Skyforce	25	39	28	36	128

Western Conference

Apr. 18 at Broomfield, Colo.

	1	2	3	4	F
Albuquerque Thunderbirds	26	20	27	27	100
Colorado 14ers	31	36	36	27	130

Conference Finals

Eastern Conference

Apr. 20 at Bismarck, N.D.

	1	2	3	4	F
Sioux Falls Skyforce	29	34	24	26	113
Dakota Wizards	22	31	30	32	115

Western Conference

Apr. 20 at Boise, Idaho.

	1	2	3	4	OT	F
Colorado 14ers	24	17	25	13	15	94
Idaho Stampede	21	16	15	27	12	91

Final

Apr. 29 at Bismarck, N.D.   **Attendance: 5,224**

	1	2	3	4	OT	F
Colorado 14ers	33	23	24	29	12	121
Dakota Wizards	25	39	22	23	20	129

Annual Awards

Most Valuable Player . . . . . Randy Livingston, Idaho, G
Rookie of the Year . . . . Louis Amundson, Colorado, F
Defensive P.O.Y. . . . . Renaldo Major, Dakota, F
Coach of the Year . . . . Bryan Gates, Idaho
Sportmanship Award . . . . . . Roger Powell, Arkansas

All-NBDL First Team

There were no holdovers from 2005-06 first team.

Pos		Team
C	Elton Brown	Colorado
F	Louis Amundson	Colorado
F	Renaldo Major	Dakota
G	Von Wafer	Colorado
G	Randy Livingston	Idaho

All-NBDL Second Team

Pos		Team
F	Jawad Williams	Anaheim
F	Kevinn Pinkney	Bakersfield
F	Jeremy Richardson	Fort Worth
C	Jared Reiner	Sioux Falls
G	B.J. Elder	Austin
G	Will Conroy	Tulsa

2007 FIBA Americas Championships
Held Aug. 22–Sept. 2, 2007 at Las Vegas, Nevada.

Group Standings
Two points for a win and one for a loss; (*) indicated team advanced to semifinals.

Group X	W	L	For	Opp	Pts
*United States	7	0	791	541	14
*Argentina	6	1	626	530	13
*Brazil	4	3	606	590	11
*Puerto Rico	3	4	582	590	10
Canada	3	4	538	586	10
Uruguay	2	5	550	648	9
Mexico	2	5	636	703	9
Venezuela	1	6	522	663	8

Semifinals
Argentina 91 . . . . .Brazil 80
USA 135 . . . . .Puerto Rico 91

Bronze Medal
Puerto Rico 111 . . . . .Brazil 107

Gold Medal
USA 118 . . . . .Argentina 81

Tournament Individual Leaders

Scoring
	Gm	Pts	Avg
Leandrinho Barbosa	10	218	21.8
Carmelo Anthony, USA	9	191	21.2
Jason Edwin, Virgini Islands	4	84	21.0
Esteban Batista, Uruguay	8	166	20.8
Romel Beck, Mexico	7	142	20.3
Hector Romero, Venezuela	8	159	19.9
Luis Scola, Argentina	10	195	19.5

Rebounding
	Gm	Reb	Avg
Esteban Batista, Uruguay	8	99	12.4
Antonio Garcia, Panama	4	39	9.8
Angelo Reyes, Puerto Rico	10	95	9.5
Samuel Dalembert, Canada	8	75	9.4
Tiago Splitter, Brazil	10	80	8.0

Assists
	Gm	Ast	Avg
Pablo Prigioni, Argentina	10	63	6.3
LeBron James, USA	10	47	4.7
Carlos Arroyo, Puerto Rico	10	46	4.6
Valter Da Silva, Brazil	10	46	4.6
Jason Kidd, USA	10	46	4.6
Deron Williams, USA	10	46	4.6

Field Goal Pct.
	FG	FGA	Pct
LeBron James, USA	73	96	.760
Carmelo Anthony, USA	65	106	.613
Romel Beck, Mexico	53	90	.589
Jason Edwin, Virgin Islands	32	56	.751
Luis Scola, Argentina	73	131	.557
Kobe Bryant, USA	51	93	.548

Women's National Basketball Association
2007 WNBA Final Standings
Conference champions (*) and playoff qualifiers (†) are noted. GB refers to Games Behind leader.

Eastern Conference
	W	L	Pct	GB	Home	Road
*Detroit	24	10	.706	–	12-5	12-5
†Indiana	21	13	.618	3	12-5	9-8
†Connecticut	18	16	.529	6	8-9	10-7
†New York	16	18	.471	8	10-7	6-11
Washington	16	18	.471	8	8-9	8-9
Chicago	14	20	.412	10	6-11	8-9

2006 Standings: 1. Connecticut (26-8); 2. Detroit (23-11); 3. Indiana (21-13); 4. Washington (18-16); 5. New York (11-23); 6. Charlotte (11-23); 7. Chicago (5-29).

Western Conference
	W	L	Pct	GB	Home	Road
*Phoenix	23	11	.676	–	12-5	11-6
†San Antonio	20	14	.588	3	9-8	11-6
†Sacramento	19	15	.559	4	12-5	7-10
†Seattle	17	17	.500	6	12-5	5-12
Houston	13	21	.382	10	7-10	6-11
Minnesota	10	24	.294	13	7-10	3-14
Los Angeles	10	24	.294	13	5-12	5-12

2006 Standings: 1. Los Angeles (25-9); 2. Sacramento (21-13); 3. Houston (18-16); 4. Seattle (18-16); 5. Phoenix (18-16); 6. San Antonio (13-21); 7. Minnesota (10-24).

WNBA All-Star Game
Held July 15, 2007 at The Verizon Center, Washington, D.C. **Attendance:** 19,487

East 103, West 99

West
Pos		Min	FG M-A	Pts	Reb	A
G	Diana Taurasi, Pho	25	5-11	13	4	9
G	Becky Hammon, SA	23	3-9	13	3	6
F	Tina Thompson, Hou	26	7-13	19	6	3
F	Lauren Jackson, Sea	25	5-12	14	5	1
C	Yolanda Griffith, Sac	9	1-2	2	3	0
C	T. McWilliams-Franklin, LA	20	5-13	11	9	1
F	Seimone Augustus, Min	19	4-11	8	7	2
G	Cappie Pondexter, Pho	16	5-12	12	1	2
F	Penny Taylor, Pho	15	1-6	4	4	2
F	Sophia Young, SA	11	1-6	3	8	2
G	Kara Lawson, Sac	10	0-5	0	1	0

East
Pos		Min	FG M-A	Pts	Reb	A
G	Deanna Nolan, Det	23	5-16	11	4	2
G	Anna DeForge, Ind	13	1-5	2	0	1
F	Tamika Catchings, Ind	27	5-14	15	11	7
F	Cheryl Ford, Det	27	5-9	16	13	5
C	Kara Braxton, Det	12	2-7	4	4	0
C	Katie Douglas, Conn	23	6-8	18	2	1
F	Asjha Jones, Conn	18	5-5	10	7	2
G	Alana Beard, Wash	17	3-10	8	3	8
G	DeLisha Milton-Jones, Wash	17	4-9	11	5	2
F	Candice Dupree, Chi	14	4-5	8	4	0
C	Tammy Sutton-Brown, Ind	10	0-1	0	3	0

WNBA Regular Season Individual Leaders

Scoring

	Gm	Pts	Avg
Lauren Jackson, Seattle	31	739	23.8
Seimone Augustus, Minnesota	34	769	22.6
Diana Taurasi, Phoenix	32	613	19.2
Alana Beard, Washington	33	622	18.8
Becky Hammon, San Antonio	28	527	18.8
Tina Thompson, Hou	34	639	18.8

Field Goal Pct.

	FGM	FGA	Pct
Janel McCarville, New York	136	249	.546
Nakia Sanford, Washington	123	232	.530
Lauren Jackson, Seattle	258	497	.519

Steals

	Gm	Stl	Avg
Tamika Catchings, Indiana	21	66	3.14
Loree Moore, New York	34	75	2.21
Lindsay Whalen, Connecticut	34	73	2.15

Rebounds

	Gm	Reb	Avg
Lauren Jackson, Seattle	31	300	9.7
Rebekkah Brunson, Sacramento	33	295	8.9
Candice Dupree, Chicago	33	254	7.7
Nakia Sanford, Washington	34	242	7.1
Michelle Snow, Houston	34	230	6.8
Tina Thompson, Houston	34	229	6.7

Assists

	Gm	Ast	Avg
Becky Hammon, San Antonio	28	140	5.00
Lindsay Whalen, Connecticut	34	169	4.97
Sue Bird, Seattle	29	143	4.93

Blocks

	Gm	Blk	Avg
Margo Dydek, Connecticut	32	66	2.06
Lauren Jackson, Seattle	31	63	2.03
Ruth Riley, San Francisco	30	59	1.97

WNBA Playoffs

First Round (Best of 3)

Western Conference

(1) Phoenix vs. (4) Seattle

Aug. 24 Phoenix 101 . . . . .at Seattle 84
Aug. 26 at Phoenix 95 . . . . .Seattle 89
Phoenix wins series, 2-0

(2) San Antonio vs. (3) Sacramento

Aug. 23 at Sacramento 86 . . . . .San Antonio 65
Aug. 25 at San Antonio 86 . . . . .Sacramento 61
Aug. 27 at San Antonio 80 . . . . .Sacramento 78
San Antonio wins series, 2-1

Eastern Conference

(1) Detroit vs. (4) New York

Aug. 24 at New York 73 . . . . .Detroit 51
Aug. 26 at Detroit 76 . . . . .New York 73
Aug. 28 at Detroit 71 . . . . .New York 70
Detroit wins series, 2-1

(2) Indiana vs. (3) Connecticut

Aug. 23 at Connecticut 93 . . . . .Indiana 88
Aug. 25 at Indiana 78 . . . . .Connecticut 59
Aug. 27 at Indiana 93 . . . . .Connecticut 88
Indiana wins series, 2-1

Conference Finals (Best of 3)

Eastern

(1) Detroit vs. (2) Indiana

Aug. 31 at Indiana 75 . . . . .Detroit 65
Sept. 2 at Detroit 77 . . . . .Indiana 63
Sept. 3 at Detroit 81 . . . . .Indiana 65
Detroit wins series, 2-1

Western

(1) Phoenix vs. (2) San Antonio

Aug. 30 Phoenix 102 . . . . .at San Antonio 100
Sept. 1 at Phoenix 98 . . . . .San Antonio 92
Phoenix wins series, 2-0

WNBA Finals (Best of 5)

Detroit vs. Phoenix

Phoenix wins series, 3 games to 2

	W-L	Avg	Leading Scorer
Phoenix Mercury	3-3	93.2	Pondexter (22.0 ppg)
Detroit Shock	2-3	86.8	Nolan (17.4 ppg)

Date	Winner	Home Court
Sept. 5	Shock, 108-100	at Detroit
Sept. 8	Mercury, 98-70	at Detroit
Sept. 12	Shock, 88-83	at Phoenix
Sept. 14	Mercury, 77-76	at Phoenix
Sept. 16	Mercury, 108-92	at Detroit

Finals MVP: Cappie Pondexter, Phoenix, G (22.0 ppg, 3.2 rpg, 5.6 apg).

2007 WNBA Draft

First Round

Pick	Team	Player, College, Pos
1	Phoenix	Lindsey Harding, Duke, G
2	San Antonio	Jessica Davenport, Ohio St., C
3	Chicago	Armintie Price, Mississippi, G
4	Minnesota	Noelle Quinn, UCLA, G
5	New York	Tiffany Jackson, Texas, F
6	Washington	Bernice Mosby, Baylor, F
7	Seattle	Katie Gearlds, Purdue, G
8	Houston	Ashley Shields, SW Tenn. CC, G
9	Indiana	Alison Bales, Duke, C
10	Chicago	Carla Thomas, Vanderbilt, F
11	Detroit	Ivory Latta, North Carolina, G
12	Connecticut	Kamesha Hairston, Temple, G
13	Connecticut	Sandrine Gruda, France, C

Annual Awards

Most Valuable Player . . . .Lauren Jackson, Sea., F
Rookie of the Year . . . . . . .Armintie Price, Chi., G
Most Improved . . . . .Janel McCarville, Sea., C
Def. Player of the Year . . .Lauren Jackson, Sea., F
Sixth Woman . . . . .Plenette Pierson, Det., F
Coach of the Year . . . . .Dan Hughes, SA
Kim Perrot Sportsmanship Award . . . . .Tully Bevilaqua, Ind., G

All-WNBA First Team

Holdovers from 2005-06 team is in **bold** type.

Pos		Pts
C	**Lauren Jackson**, Seattle	243
G	Becky Hammon, San Antonio	217
F	**Diana Taurasi**, Phoenix	204
G	Deanna Nolan, Detroit	179
F	Penny Taylor, Phoenix	167

1938-2007
Through the Years

SPORTS ALMANAC

The NBA Finals

Although the National Basketball Association traces its first championship back to the 1946-47 season, the league was then called the Basketball Association of America (BAA). It did not become the NBA until after the 1948-49 season when the BAA and the National Basketball League (NBL) agreed to merge.

In the chart below, the Eastern finalists (representing the NBA Eastern Division from 1947-70, and the NBA Eastern Conference since 1971) are listed in CAPITAL letters. Also, each NBA champion's wins and losses are noted in parentheses after the series score.

Multiple winners: Boston (16); Minneapolis-LA Lakers (14); Chicago Bulls (6); San Antonio (4); Detroit, Phi-SF-Golden St. Warriors and Syracuse Nationals-Phi. 76ers (3); Houston and New York (2).

Year	Winner	Head Coach	Series		Loser	Head Coach
1947	PHILADELPHIA WARRIORS	Eddie Gottlieb	4-1	(WWWLW)	Chicago Stags	Harold Olsen
1948	Baltimore Bullets	Buddy Jeannette	4-2	(LWWWLW)	PHILA. WARRIORS	Eddie Gottlieb
1949	Minneapolis Lakers	John Kundla	4-2	(WWWLL)	WASH. CAPITOLS	Red Auerbach
1950	Minneapolis Lakers	John Kundla	4-2	(WWWLLW)	SYRACUSE	Al Cervi
1951	Rochester	Les Harrison	4-3	(WWWLLLW)	NEW YORK	Joe Lapchick
1952	Minneapolis Lakers	John Kundla	4-3	(WLWLWLW)	NEW YORK	Joe Lapchick
1953	Minneapolis Lakers	John Kundla	4-1	(LWWWW)	NEW YORK	Joe Lapchick
1954	Minneapolis Lakers	John Kundla	4-3	(WLWLWLW)	SYRACUSE	Al Cervi
1955	SYRACUSE	Al Cervi	4-3	(WWLLLWW)	Ft. Wayne Pistons	Charley Eckman
1956	PHILADELPHIA WARRIORS	George Senesky	4-1	(WLWWW)	Ft. Wayne Pistons	Charley Eckman
1957	BOSTON	Red Auerbach	4-3	(LWLWLWW)	St. Louis Hawks	Alex Hannum
1958	St. Louis Hawks	Alex Hannum	4-2	(WLWLWW)	BOSTON	Red Auerbach
1959	BOSTON	Red Auerbach	4-0		Mpls. Lakers	John Kundla
1960	BOSTON	Red Auerbach	4-3	(WLWLWLW)	St. Louis Hawks	Ed Macauley
1961	BOSTON	Red Auerbach	4-1	(WWLWW)	St. Louis Hawks	Paul Seymour
1962	BOSTON	Red Auerbach	4-3	(WLLWLWW)	LA Lakers	Fred Schaus
1963	BOSTON	Red Auerbach	4-2	(WWLWLW)	LA Lakers	Fred Schaus
1964	BOSTON	Red Auerbach	4-1	(WWLWW)	SF Warriors	Alex Hannum
1965	BOSTON	Red Auerbach	4-1	(WWLWW)	LA Lakers	Fred Schaus
1966	BOSTON	Red Auerbach	4-3	(LWWWLLW)	LA Lakers	Fred Schaus
1967	PHILADELPHIA 76ERS	Alex Hannum	4-2	(WWLWLW)	SF Warriors	Bill Sharman
1968	BOSTON	Bill Russell	4-2	(WLWLWW)	LA Lakers	B.van Breda Kolff
1969	BOSTON	Bill Russell	4-3	(LLWWLWW)	LA Lakers	B.van Breda Kolff
1970	NEW YORK	Red Holzman	4-3	(WLWLWLW)	LA Lakers	Joe Mullaney
1971	Milwaukee	Larry Costello	4-0		BALT. BULLETS	Gene Shue
1972	LA Lakers	Bill Sharman	4-1	(LWWWW)	NEW YORK	Red Holzman
1973	NEW YORK	Red Holzman	4-1	(LWWWW)	LA Lakers	Bill Sharman
1974	BOSTON	Tommy Heinsohn	4-3	(WLWLWLW)	Milwaukee	Larry Costello
1975	Golden St. Warriors	Al Attles	4-0		WASH. BULLETS	K.C. Jones
1976	BOSTON	Tommy Heinsohn	4-2	(WWLLWW)	Phoenix	John MacLeod
1977	Portland	Jack Ramsay	4-2	(LLWWWW)	PHILA. 76ERS	Gene Shue
1978	WASHINGTON BULLETS	Dick Motta	4-3	(LWLWLWW)	Seattle	Lenny Wilkens
1979	Seattle	Lenny Wilkens	4-1	(LWWWW)	WASH. BULLETS	Dick Motta
1980	LA Lakers	Paul Westhead	4-2	(WLWLWW)	PHILA. 76ERS	Billy Cunningham
1981	BOSTON	Bill Fitch	4-2	(WLWLWW)	Houston	Del Harris
1982	LA Lakers	Pat Riley	4-2	(WLWLWLW)	PHILA. 76ERS	Billy Cunningham
1983	PHILADELPHIA 76ERS	Billy Cunningham	4-0		LA Lakers	Pat Riley
1984	BOSTON	K.C. Jones	4-3	(LWWLWLW)	LA Lakers	Pat Riley
1985	LA Lakers	Pat Riley	4-2	(LWWWLW)	BOSTON	K.C. Jones
1986	BOSTON	K.C. Jones	4-2	(WWLWLW)	Houston	Bill Fitch
1987	LA Lakers	Pat Riley	4-2	(WWLWLW)	BOSTON	K.C. Jones
1988	LA Lakers	Pat Riley	4-3	(LWWLLWW)	DETROIT PISTONS	Chuck Daly
1989	DETROIT	Chuck Daly	4-0		LA Lakers	Pat Riley
1990	DETROIT	Chuck Daly	4-1	(WLWWW)	Portland	Rick Adelman
1991	CHICAGO	Phil Jackson	4-1	(LWWWW)	LA Lakers	Mike Dunleavy
1992	CHICAGO	Phil Jackson	4-2	(WLWLWW)	Portland	Rick Adelman
1993	CHICAGO	Phil Jackson	4-2	(WWLWLW)	Phoenix	Paul Westphal
1994	Houston	Rudy Tomjanovich	4-3	(WLWLLWW)	NEW YORK	Pat Riley
1995	Houston	Rudy Tomjanovich	4-0		ORLANDO	Brian Hill
1996	CHICAGO	Phil Jackson	4-2	(WWWLLW)	Seattle	George Karl
1997	CHICAGO	Phil Jackson	4-2	(WWLWLW)	Utah	Jerry Sloan
1998	CHICAGO	Phil Jackson	4-2	(LWWWLW)	Utah	Jerry Sloan

The NBA Finals (Cont.)

Year	Winner	Head Coach	Series	Loser	Head Coach
1999	San Antonio	Gregg Popovich	4-1 (WWLWW)	NEW YORK	Jeff Van Gundy
2000	LA Lakers	Phil Jackson	4-2 (WWLWLW)	INDIANA	Larry Bird
2001	LA Lakers	Phil Jackson	4-1 (LWWWW)	PHILA. 76ERS	Larry Brown
2002	LA Lakers	Phil Jackson	4-0	NEW JERSEY	Byron Scott
2003	San Antonio	Gregg Popovich	4-2 (WLWLWW)	NEW JERSEY	Byron Scott
2004	DETROIT	Larry Brown	4-1 (WLWWW)	LA Lakers	Phil Jackson
2005	San Antonio	Gregg Popovich	4-3 (WWLWLWW)	DETROIT	Larry Brown
2006	MIAMI	Pat Riley	4-2 (LLWWWW)	Dallas	Avery Johnson
2007	San Antonio	Gregg Popovich	4-0	Cleveland	Mike Brown

Note: Four finalists were led by player-coaches: **1948**—Buddy Jeannette (guard) of Baltimore; **1950**—Al Cervi (guard) of Syracuse; **1968**—Bill Russell (center) of Boston; **1969**—Bill Russell (center) of Boston.

Most Valuable Player

Winner who did not play for the NBA champion is in **bold** type.

Multiple winners: Michael Jordan (6); Tim Duncan, Magic Johnson and Shaquille O'Neal (3); Kareem Abdul-Jabbar, Larry Bird, Hakeem Olajuwon and Willis Reed (2).

Year		Year		Year	
1969	**Jerry West**, LA Lakers, G	1982	Magic Johnson, LA Lakers, G	1995	Hakeem Olajuwon, Houston, C
1970	Willis Reed, New York, C	1983	Moses Malone, Philadelphia, C	1996	Michael Jordan, Chicago, G
1971	Lew Alcindor, Milwaukee, C	1984	Larry Bird, Boston, F	1997	Michael Jordan, Chicago, G
1972	Wilt Chamberlain, LA Lakers, C	1985	K. Abdul-Jabbar, LA Lakers, C	1998	Michael Jordan, Chicago, G
1973	Willis Reed, New York, C	1986	Larry Bird, Boston, F	1999	Tim Duncan, San Antonio, F/C
1974	John Havlicek, Boston, F	1987	Magic Johnson, LA Lakers, G	2000	Shaquille O'Neal, LA Lakers, C
1975	Rick Barry, Golden State, F	1988	James Worthy, LA Lakers, F	2001	Shaquille O'Neal, LA Lakers, C
1976	Jo Jo White, Boston, G	1989	Joe Dumars, Detroit, G	2002	Shaquille O'Neal, LA Lakers, C
1977	Bill Walton, Portland, C	1990	Isiah Thomas, Detroit, G	2003	Tim Duncan, San Antonio, F/C
1978	Wes Unseld, Washington, C	1991	Michael Jordan, Chicago, G	2004	Chauncey Billups, Detroit, G
1979	Dennis Johnson, Seattle, G	1992	Michael Jordan, Chicago, G	2005	Tim Duncan, San Antonio, F/C
1980	Magic Johnson, LA Lakers, G/C	1993	Michael Jordan, Chicago, G	2006	Dwyane Wade, Miami, G
1981	Cedric Maxwell, Boston, F	1994	Hakeem Olajuwon, Houston, C	2007	Tony Parker, San Antonio, G

Note: Lew Alcindor changed his name to Kareem Abdul-Jabbar after the 1970-71 season.

All-Time NBA Playoff Leaders

CAREER

Years listed indicate number of playoff appearances. Players active in 2007 in **bold** type. DNP indicates player that was active in 2007 but did not participate in playoffs.

Points

		Yrs	Gm	Pts	Avg
1	Michael Jordan	13	179	**5987**	33.4
2	Kareem Abdul-Jabbar	18	237	**5762**	24.3
3	**Shaquille O'Neal**	14	198	**5045**	25.5
4	Karl Malone	19	193	**4761**	24.7
5	Jerry West	13	153	**4457**	29.1
6	Larry Bird	12	164	**3897**	23.8
7	John Havlicek	13	172	**3776**	22.0
8	Hakeem Olajuwon	15	145	**3755**	25.9
9	Magic Johnson	13	190	**3701**	19.5
10	Scottie Pippen	16	208	**3642**	17.5
11	Elgin Baylor	12	134	**3623**	27.0
12	Wilt Chamberlain	13	160	**3607**	22.5
13	**Tim Duncan**	9	138	**3282**	23.8
14	Kevin McHale	13	169	**3182**	18.8
15	Dennis Johnson	13	180	**3116**	17.3
16	Julius Erving	11	141	**3088**	21.9
17	**Kobe Bryant**	10	131	**3053**	23.3
18	James Worthy	9	143	**3022**	21.1
19	Reggie Miller	15	144	**2972**	20.6
20	Clyde Drexler	15	145	**2963**	20.4

Scoring Average

Minimum of 25 games or 700 points.

		Yrs	Gm	Pts	Avg
1	Michael Jordan	13	179	5987	33.4
2	**Allen Iverson**	7	67	2013	30.0
3	Jerry West	13	153	4457	29.1
4	**Tracy McGrady**	6	32	922	28.8
5	**LeBron James**	2	33	901	27.3
6	Elgin Baylor	12	134	3623	27.0
7	George Gervin	9	59	1592	27.0
8	Hakeem Olajuwon	15	145	3755	25.9
9	**Vince Carter**	6	42	1086	25.9
10	**Shaquille O'Neal**	14	198	5045	25.5
11	Bob Pettit	9	88	2240	25.5
12	Dominique Wilkins	10	56	1423	25.4
13	**Amare Stoudemire**	3	31	787	25.4
14	**Dwyane Wade**	4	54	1366	25.3
15	**Dirk Nowitzki**	9	82	2070	25.2
16	**Ray Allen**	4	37	920	24.9
17	Rick Barry	7	74	1833	24.8
18	Karl Malone	19	193	4761	24.7
19	**Paul Pierce** (DNP)	4	37	908	24.5
20	Bernard King	5	28	687	24.5

Field Goals

		Yrs	FG	Att	Pct
1	Kareem Abdul-Jabbar	18	**2356**	4422	.533
2	Michael Jordan	13	**2188**	4497	.487
3	**Shaquille O'Neal**	14	**1970**	3482	.566
4	Karl Malone	19	**1743**	3768	.463
5	Jerry West	13	**1622**	3460	.469
6	Hakeem Olajuwon	15	**1504**	2847	.528
7	Larry Bird	12	**1458**	3090	.472
8	John Havlicek	13	**1451**	3329	.436
9	Wilt Chamberlain	13	**1425**	2728	.522
10	Elgin Baylor	12	**1388**	3161	.439

Free Throws

		Yrs	FT	Att	Pct
1	Michael Jordan	13	**1463**	1766	.828
2	Karl Malone	19	**1269**	1725	.736
3	Jerry West	13	**1213**	1507	.805
4	**Shaquille O'Neal**	14	**1105**	2204	.501
5	Kareem Abdul-Jabbar	18	**1050**	1419	.740
6	Magic Johnson	13	**1040**	1241	.838
7	Larry Bird	12	**901**	1012	.891
8	John Havlicek	13	**874**	1046	.836
9	**Tim Duncan**	9	**855**	1227	.697
10	Elgin Baylor	12	**847**	1101	.769

Assists

		Yrs	Gm	No	Avg
1	Magic Johnson	13	190	**2346**	12.3
2	John Stockton	19	182	**1839**	10.1
3	Larry Bird	12	164	**1062**	6.5
4	Scottie Pippen	16	208	**1048**	5.0
5	Michael Jordan	13	179	**1022**	5.7

Rebounds

		Yrs	Gm	No	Avg
1	Bill Russell	13	165	**4104**	24.9
2	Wilt Chamberlain	13	160	**3913**	24.5
3	Kareem Abdul-Jabbar	18	237	**2481**	10.5
4	**Shaquille O'Neal**	14	198	**2401**	12.1
5	Karl Malone	19	193	**2062**	10.7

Steals

	No
Scottie Pippen	395
Michael Jordan	376
Magic Johnson	358
John Stockton	338
Larry Bird	296
Maurice Cheeks	295
Clyde Drexler	278

Blocks

	No
Hakeem Olajuwon	472
Shaquille O'Neal	433
K. Abdul-Jabbar	399
Tim Duncan	380
David Robinson	312
Patrick Ewing	303
Robert Parish	298

Games Played

	No		No
K. Abdul-Jabbar	237	Byron Scott	183
Robert Horry	229	John Stockton	182
Scottie Pippen	208	Dennis Johnson	180
Shaquille O'Neal	198	Michael Jordan	179
Danny Ainge	193	John Havlicek	172
Karl Malone	193	Horace Grant	170
Magic Johnson	190	Kevin McHale	169
Robert Parish	184	Dennis Rodman	169

SINGLE GAME

Points

	Date	FG-FT–Pts
Michael Jordan, Chi at Bos*	4/20/86	22-19–63
Elgin Baylor, LA at Bos	4/14/62	22-17–61
Wilt Chamberlain, Phi vs Syr	3/22/62	22-12–56
Michael Jordan, Chi at Mia	4/29/92	20-16–56
Charles Barkley, Pho vs G.St.	5/4/94	23-7–56
Rick Barry, SF vs Phi	4/18/67	22-11–55
Michael Jordan, Chi vs Cle	5/1/88	24-7–55
Michael Jordan, Chi vs Pho	4/16/93	21-13–55
Michael Jordan, Chi vs. Wash	4/27/97	22-10–55

*Double overtime.

Field Goals

	Date	FG	Att
Wilt Chamberlain, Phi vs Syr	3/14/60	24	42
John Havlicek, Bos vs Atl	4/1/73	24	36
Michael Jordan, Chi vs Cle	5/1/88	24	45
Eight tied with 22 each.			

Miscellaneous

3-Pt Field Goals

	Date	No
Rex Chapman, Pho at Sea	4/25/97	9
Dan Majerle, Pho vs Sea	6/1/93	8
Allen Iverson, Phi vs Tor	5/16/01	8
Nine tied with 7 each.		

Assists

	Date	No
Magic Johnson, LA vs Pho	5/15/84	24
John Stockton, Utah at LA Lakers	5/17/88	24
Magic Johnson, LA Lakers at Port	5/3/85	23
John Stockton, Utah vs Port	4/25/96	23
Doc Rivers, Atl vs Bos	5/16/88	22
Four tied with 21 each.		

Rebounds

	Date	No
Wilt Chamberlain, Phi vs Bos	4/5/67	41
Bill Russell, Bos vs Phi	3/23/58	40
Bill Russell, Bos vs St.L	3/29/60	40
Bill Russell, Bos vs LA*	4/18/62	40
Three tied with 39 each.		

*Overtime.

Appearances in NBA Finals

Standings of all NBA teams that have reached the NBA Finals since 1947.

App		Titles	Last Won
28	Minneapolis-LA Lakers	14	2002
19	Boston Celtics	16	1986
9	Syracuse Nats-Phila. 76ers	3	1983
8	New York Knicks	2	1973
7	Ft. Wayne-Detroit Pistons	3	2004
6	Chicago Bulls	6	1998
6	Phila-SF-Golden St. Warriors	3	1975
4	Houston Rockets	2	1995
4	St. Louis Hawks	1	1958
4	Baltimore-Washington Bullets	1	1978
4	San Antonio Spurs	4	2007
3	Portland Trail Blazers	1	1977
3	Seattle SuperSonics	1	1979
2	Milwaukee Bucks	1	1971
2	New Jersey Nets	0	—
2	Phoenix Suns	0	—
2	Utah Jazz	0	—
1	Baltimore Bullets	1	1948
1	Rochester Royals	1	1951
1	Miami Heat	1	2006
1	Cleveland Cavaliers	0	—
1	Chicago Stags	0	—
1	Orlando Magic	0	—
1	Washington Capitols	0	—
1	Indiana Pacers	0	—

Change of address: The St. Louis Hawks now play in Atlanta and the Rochester Royals are now the Sacramento Kings.
Teams now defunct: Baltimore Bullets (1947-55), Chicago Stags (1946-50) and Washington Capitols (1946-51).

NBA FINALS
Points

Series		Year	Pts
4-Gm	Shaquille O'Neal, LAL vs NJ	2002	145
5-Gm	Allen Iverson, Phi vs LAL	2001	178
6-Gm	Michael Jordan, Chi vs Pho	1993	246
7-Gm	Elgin Baylor, LA vs Bos	1962	284

Field Goals

Series		Year	No
4-Gm	Hakeem Olajuwon, Hou vs Orl	1995	56
5-Gm	Allen Iverson, Phi vs LAL	2001	66
6-Gm	Michael Jordan, Chi vs Pho	1993	101
7-Gm	Elgin Baylor, LA vs Bos	1962	101

Assists

Series		Year	No
4-Gm	Bob Cousy, Bos vs Mpls	1959	51
5-Gm	Magic Johnson, LAL vs Chi	1991	62
6-Gm	Magic Johnson, LAL vs Bos	1985	84
7-Gm	Magic Johnson, LA vs Bos	1984	95

Rebounds

Series		Year	No
4-Gm	Bill Russell, Bos vs Mpls	1959	118
5-Gm	Bill Russell, Bos vs St.L	1961	144
6-Gm	Wilt Chamberlain, Phi vs SF	1967	171
7-Gm	Bill Russell, Bos vs LA	1962	189

NBA All-Star Game

The NBA staged its first All-Star Game before 10,094 at Boston Garden on March 2, 1951. From that year on, the game has matched the best players in the East against the best in the West. Winning coaches are listed first. East leads series, 34-22.

Multiple MVP winners: Bob Pettit (4); Michael Jordan and Oscar Robertson (3); Kobe Bryant, Bob Cousy, Julius Erving, Allen Iverson, Magic Johnson, Karl Malone, Shaquille O'Neal and Isiah Thomas (2).

Year		Host	Coaches	Most Valuable Player
1951	East 111, West 94	Boston	Joe Lapchick, John Kundla	Ed Macauley, Boston
1952	East 108, West 91	Boston	Al Cervi, John Kundla	Paul Arizin, Philadelphia
1953	West 79, East 75	Ft. Wayne	John Kundla, Joe Lapchick	George Mikan, Minneapolis
1954	East 98, West 93 (OT)	New York	Joe Lapchick, John Kundla	Bob Cousy, Boston
1955	East 100, West 91	New York	Al Cervi, Charley Eckman	Bill Sharman, Boston
1956	West 108, East 94	Rochester	Charley Eckman, George Senesky	Bob Pettit, St. Louis
1957	East 109, West 97	Boston	Red Auerbach, Bobby Wanzer	Bob Cousy, Boston
1958	East 130, West 118	St. Louis	Red Auerbach, Alex Hannum	Bob Pettit, St. Louis
1959	West 124, East 108	Detroit	Ed Macauley, Red Auerbach	Bob Pettit, St. Louis & Elgin Baylor, Minneapolis
1960	East 125, West 115	Philadelphia	Red Auerbach, Ed Macauley	Wilt Chamberlain, Philadelphia
1961	West 153, East 131	Syracuse	Paul Seymour, Red Auerbach	Oscar Robertson, Cincinnati
1962	West 150, East 130	St. Louis	Fred Schaus, Red Auerbach	Bob Pettit, St. Louis
1963	East 115, West 108	Los Angeles	Red Auerbach, Fred Schaus	Bill Russell, Boston
1964	East 111, West 107	Boston	Red Auerbach, Fred Schaus	Oscar Robertson, Cincinnati
1965	East 124, West 123	St. Louis	Red Auerbach, Alex Hannum	Jerry Lucas, Cincinnati
1966	East 137, West 94	Cincinnati	Red Auerbach, Fred Schaus	Adrian Smith, Cincinnati
1967	West 135, East 120	San Francisco	Fred Schaus, Red Auerbach	Rick Barry, San Francisco
1968	East 144, West 124	New York	Alex Hannum, Bill Sharman	Hal Greer, Philadelphia
1969	East 123, West 112	Baltimore	Gene Shue, Richie Guerin	Oscar Robertson, Cincinnati
1970	East 142, West 135	Philadelphia	Red Holzman, Richie Guerin	Willis Reed, New York
1971	West 108, East 107	San Diego	Larry Costello, Red Holzman	Lenny Wilkens, Seattle
1972	West 112, East 110	Los Angeles	Bill Sharman, Tom Heinsohn	Jerry West, Los Angeles
1973	East 104, West 84	Chicago	Tom Heinsohn, Bill Sharman	Dave Cowens, Boston
1974	West 134, East 123	Seattle	Larry Costello, Tom Heinsohn	Bob Lanier, Detroit
1975	East 108, West 102	Phoenix	K.C. Jones, Al Attles	Walt Frazier, New York
1976	East 123, West 109	Philadelphia	Tom Heinsohn, Al Attles	Dave Bing, Washington
1977	West 125, East 124	Milwaukee	Larry Brown, Gene Shue	Julius Erving, Philadelphia
1978	East 133, West 125	Atlanta	Billy Cunningham, Jack Ramsay	Randy Smith, Buffalo
1979	West 134, East 129	Detroit	Lenny Wilkens, Dick Motta	David Thompson, Denver
1980	East 144, West 136 (OT)	Washington	Billy Cunningham, Lenny Wilkens	George Gervin, San Antonio
1981	East 123, West 120	Cleveland	Billy Cunningham, John MacLeod	Nate Archibald, Boston
1982	East 120, West 118	New Jersey	Bill Fitch, Pat Riley	Larry Bird, Boston
1983	East 132, West 123	Los Angeles	Billy Cunningham, Pat Riley	Julius Erving, Philadelphia
1984	East 154, West 145 (OT)	Denver	K.C. Jones, Frank Layden	Isiah Thomas, Detroit
1985	West 140, East 129	Indiana	Pat Riley, K.C. Jones	Ralph Sampson, Houston
1986	East 139, West 132	Dallas	K.C. Jones, Pat Riley	Isiah Thomas, Detroit
1987	West 154, East 149 (OT)	Seattle	Pat Riley, K.C. Jones	Tom Chambers, Seattle
1988	East 138, West 133	Chicago	Mike Fratello, Pat Riley	Michael Jordan, Chicago
1989	West 143, East 134	Houston	Pat Riley, Lenny Wilkens	Karl Malone, Utah
1990	East 130, West 113	Miami	Chuck Daly, Pat Riley	Magic Johnson, LA Lakers
1991	East 116, West 114	Charlotte	Chris Ford, Rick Adelman	Charles Barkley, Philadelphia
1992	West 153, East 113	Orlando	Don Nelson, Phil Jackson	Magic Johnson, LA Lakers
1993	West 135, East 132 (OT)	Salt Lake City	Paul Westphal, Pat Riley	Karl Malone, Utah & John Stockton, Utah
1994	East 127, West 118	Minneapolis	Lenny Wilkens, George Karl	Scottie Pippen, Chicago
1995	West 139, East 112	Phoenix	Paul Westphal, Brian Hill	Mitch Richmond, Sacramento
1996	East 129, West 118	San Antonio	Phil Jackson, George Karl	Michael Jordan, Chicago
1997	East 132, West 120	Cleveland	Doug Collins, Rudy Tomjanovich	Glen Rice, Charlotte
1998	East 135, West 114	New York	Larry Bird, George Karl	Michael Jordan, Chicago
1999	Not held—due to lockout			
2000	West 137, East 126	Oakland	Phil Jackson, Jeff Van Gundy	Tim Duncan, San Antonio & Shaquille O'Neal, LA Lakers
2001	East 111, West 110	Washington	Larry Brown, Rick Adelman	Allen Iverson, Philadelphia
2002	West 135, East 120	Philadelphia	Don Nelson, Byron Scott	Kobe Bryant, LA Lakers
2003	West 155, East 145 (2 OT)	Atlanta	Rick Adelman, Isiah Thomas	Kevin Garnett, Minnesota
2004	West 136, East 132	Los Angeles	Flip Saunders, Rick Carlisle	Shaquille O'Neal, LA Lakers
2005	East 125, West 115	Denver	Stan Van Gundy, Gregg Popovich	Allen Iverson, Philadelphia
2006	East 122, West 120	Houston	Flip Saunders, Avery Johnson	LeBron James, Cleveland
2007	West 153, East 132	Las Vegas	Mike D'Antoni, Eddie Jordan	Kobe Bryant, LA Lakers

NBA Franchise Origins

Here is what the current 30 teams in the National Basketball Association have to show for the years they have put in as members of the National Basketball League (NBL), Basketball Association of America (BAA), the NBA, and the American Basketball Association (ABA). League titles are noted by year won.

Western Conference

	First Season	League Titles	Franchise Stops
Dallas Mavericks	1980-81 (NBA)	None	•Dallas (1980–)
Denver Nuggets	1967-68 (ABA)	None	•Denver (1967–)
Golden St. Warriors	1946-47 (BAA)	1 BAA (1947)	•Philadelphia (1946-62)
		2 NBA (1956, 75)	San Francisco (1962-71)
			Oakland (1971–)
Houston Rockets	1967-68 (NBA)	2 NBA (1994-95)	•San Diego (1967-71)
			Houston (1971–)
Los Angeles Clippers	1970-71 (NBA)	None	•Buffalo (1970-78)
			San Diego (1978-84)
			Los Angeles (1984–)
Los Angeles Lakers	1947-48 (NBL)	1 NBL (1948)	•Minneapolis (1947-60)
		1 BAA (1949)	Los Angeles (1960-67)
		14 NBA (1950,52-54,72,	Inglewood, CA (1967-99)
		80,82,85,87-88,00-02)	Los Angeles (1999–)
Memphis Grizzlies	1995-96 (NBA)	None	•Vancouver (1995-01)
			Memphis, TN (2001–)
Minnesota Timberwolves	1989-90 (NBA)	None	•Minneapolis (1989–)
New Orleans Hornets	1988-89 (NBA)	None	•Charlotte (1988-2002)
			New Orleans (2002–)
			Oklahoma City (2005-07)
Phoenix Suns	1968-69 (NBA)	None	•Phoenix (1968–)
Portland Trail Blazers	1970-71 (NBA)	1 NBA (1977)	•Portland (1970–)
Sacramento Kings	1945-46 (NBL)	1 NBL (1946)	•Rochester, NY (1945-58)
		1 NBA (1951)	Cincinnati (1958-72)
			KC-Omaha (1972-75)
			Kansas City (1975-85)
			Sacramento (1985–)
San Antonio Spurs	1967-68 (ABA)	4 NBA (1999,2003,05,07)	•Dallas (1967-73)
			San Antonio (1973–)
Seattle SuperSonics	1967-68 (NBA)	1 NBA (1979)	•Seattle (1967–)
Utah Jazz	1974-75 (NBA)	None	•New Orleans (1974-79)
			Salt Lake City (1979–)

Eastern Conference

	First Season	League Titles	Franchise Stops
Atlanta Hawks	1946-47 (NBL)	1 NBA (1958)	•Tri-Cities (1946-51)
			Milwaukee (1951-55)
			St. Louis (1955-68)
			Atlanta (1968–)
Boston Celtics	1946-47 (BAA)	16 NBA (1957,59-66,68-69	•Boston (1946–)
		74,76,81,84,86)	
Charlotte Bobcats	2004-05 (NBA)	None	•Charlotte (2004–)
Chicago Bulls	1966-67 (NBA)	6 NBA (1991-93,96-98)	•Chicago (1966–)
Cleveland Cavaliers	1970-71 (NBA)	None	•Cleveland (1970-74)
			Richfield, OH (1974-94)
			Cleveland (1994–)
Detroit Pistons	1941-42 (NBL)	2 NBL (1944-45)	•Ft. Wayne, IN (1941-57)
		3 NBA (1989-90, 2004)	Detroit (1957-78)
			Pontiac, MI (1978-88)
			Auburn Hills, MI (1988–)
Indiana Pacers	1967-68 (ABA)	3 ABA (1970,72-73)	•Indianapolis (1967–)
Miami Heat	1988-89 (NBA)	1 NBA (2006)	•Miami (1988–)
Milwaukee Bucks	1968-69 (NBA)	1 NBA (1971)	•Milwaukee (1968–)
New Jersey Nets	1967-68 (ABA)	2 ABA (1974,76)	•Teaneck, NJ (1967-68)
			Commack, NY (1968-69)
			W. Hempstead, NY (1969-71)
			Uniondale, NY (1971-77)
			Piscataway, NJ (1977-81)
			E. Rutherford, NJ (1981–)
New York Knicks	1946-47 (BAA)	2 NBA (1970,73)	•New York (1946–)
Orlando Magic	1989-90 (NBA)	None	•Orlando, FL (1989–)
Philadelphia 76ers	1949-50 (NBA)	3 NBA (1955,67,83)	•Syracuse (1949-63)
			Philadelphia (1963–)
Toronto Raptors	1995-96 (NBA)	None	•Toronto (1995–)
Washington Wizards	1961-62 (NBA)	1 NBA (1978)	•Chicago (1961-63)
			Baltimore (1963-73)
			Landover, MD (1973–)

Note: The Tri-Cities Blackhawks represented Moline and Rock Island, Ill., and Davenport, Iowa.

The Growth of the NBA

Of the 11 franchises that comprised the Basketball Association of America (BAA) at the start of the 1946-47 season, only three remain—the Boston Celtics, New York Knickerbockers and Golden State Warriors (originally Philadelphia Warriors).

Just before the start of the 1948-49 season, four teams from the more established **National Basketball League** (NBL)—the Ft. Wayne Pistons (now Detroit), Indianapolis Jets, Minneapolis Lakers (now Los Angeles) and Rochester Royals (now Sacramento Kings)—joined the BAA.

A year later, the six remaining NBL franchises—Anderson (Ind.), Denver, Sheboygan (Wisc.), the Syracuse Nationals (now Philadelphia 76ers), Tri-Cities Blackhawks (now Atlanta Hawks) and Waterloo (Iowa)—joined along with the new Indianapolis Olympians and the BAA became the 17-team **National Basketball Association**.

The NBA was down to 10 teams by the 1950-51 season and slipped to eight by 1954-55 with Boston, New York, Philadelphia and Syracuse in the Eastern Division, and Ft. Wayne, Milwaukee (formerly Tri-Cities), Minneapolis and Rochester in the West.

By 1960, five of those surviving eight teams had moved to other cities but by the end of the decade the NBA was a 14-team league. It also had a rival, the **American Basketball Association**, which began play in 1967 with a red, white and blue ball, a three-point line and 11 teams. After a nine-year run, the ABA merged four clubs—the Denver Nuggets, Indiana Pacers, New York Nets and San Antonio Spurs—with the NBA following the 1975-76 season. The NBA adopted the three-point shot in 1979-80.

Expansion/Merger Timetable

For teams currently in NBA.

1948—Added NBL's Ft. Wayne Pistons (now Detroit), Minneapolis Lakers (now Los Angeles) and Rochester Royals (now Sacramento Kings); **1949**—Syracuse Nationals (now Philadelphia 76ers) and Tri-Cities Blackhawks (now Atlanta Hawks).

1961—Chicago Packers (now Washington Wizards); **1966**—Chicago Bulls; **1967**—San Diego Rockets (now Houston) and Seattle SuperSonics; **1968**—Milwaukee Bucks and Phoenix Suns.

1970—Buffalo Braves (now Los Angeles Clippers), Cleveland Cavaliers and Portland Trail Blazers; **1974**—New Orleans Jazz (now Utah); **1976**—added ABA's Denver Nuggets, Indiana Pacers, New York Nets (now New Jersey) and San Antonio Spurs.

1980—Dallas Mavericks; **1988**—Charlotte Hornets and Miami Heat; **1989**—Minnesota Timberwolves and Orlando Magic.

1995—Toronto Raptors and Vancouver Grizzlies (Now Memphis).

2004—Charlotte Bobcats.

City and Nickname Changes

1951—Tri-Cities Blackhawks, who divided home games between Moline and Rock Island, Ill., and Davenport, Iowa, move to Milwaukee and become the Hawks; **1955**—Milwaukee Hawks move to St. Louis; **1957**—Ft. Wayne Pistons move to Detroit, while Rochester Royals move to Cincinnati.

1960—Minneapolis Lakers move to Los Angeles; **1962**—Chicago Packers renamed Zephyrs, while Philadelphia Warriors move to San Francisco; **1963**—Chicago Zephyrs move to Baltimore and become Bullets, while Syracuse Nationals move to Philadelphia and become 76ers; **1968**—St. Louis Hawks move to Atlanta.

1971—San Diego Rockets move to Houston, while San Francisco Warriors move to Oakland and become Golden State Warriors; **1972**—Cincinnati Royals move to Midwest, divide home games between Kansas City, Mo., and Omaha, Neb., and become Kings; **1973**—Baltimore Bullets move to Landover, Md., outside Washington and become Capital Bullets; **1974**—Capital Bullets renamed Washington Bullets; **1975**—KC-Omaha Kings settle in Kansas City; **1977**—New York Nets move from Uniondale, N.Y., to Piscataway, N.J. (later East Rutherford) and become New Jersey Nets; **1978**—Buffalo Braves move to San Diego and become the Clippers; **1979**—New Orleans Jazz move to Salt Lake City and become Utah Jazz.

1984—San Diego Clippers move to Los Angeles; **1985**—Kansas City Kings move to Sacramento.

1997—Washington Bullets become Washington Wizards.

2001—Vancouver Grizzlies move to Memphis, Tenn.; **2002**—Charlotte Hornets move to New Orleans; **2005**—New Orleans Hornets become New Orleans/Oklahoma City Hornets and divide home games between New Orleans and Oklahoma City in aftermath of Hurricane Katrina; **2007**—Hornets move back to New Orleans full-time.

Defunct NBA Teams

Teams that once played in the BAA and NBA, but no longer exist.

Anderson (Ind.)—Packers (1949-50); **Baltimore**—Bullets (1947-55); **Chicago**—Stags (1946-50); **Cleveland**—Rebels (1946-47); **Denver**—Nuggets (1949-50); **Detroit**—Falcons (1946-47); **Indianapolis**—Jets (1948-49) and Olympians (1949-53); **Pittsburgh**—Ironmen (1946-47); **Providence**—Steamrollers (1946-49); **St. Louis**—Bombers (1946-50); **Sheboygan (Wisc.)**—Redskins (1949-50); **Toronto**—Huskies (1946-47); **Washington**—Capitols (1946-51); **Waterloo (Iowa)**—Hawks (1949-50).

ABA Teams (1967-76)

Anaheim—Amigos (1967-68, moved to LA); **Baltimore**—Claws (1975, never played); **Carolina**—Cougars (1969-74, moved to St. Louis); **Dallas**—Chaparrals (1967-73, called Texas Chaparrals in 1970-71, moved to San Antonio); **Denver**—Rockets (1967-76, renamed Nuggets in 1974-76); **Miami**—Floridians (1968-72, called simply Floridians from 1970-72).

Houston—Mavericks (1967-69, moved to North Carolina); **Indiana**—Pacers (1967-76); **Kentucky**—Colonels (1967-76); **Los Angeles**—Stars (1968-70, moved to Utah); **Memphis**—Pros (1970-75, renamed Tams in 1972 and Sounds in 1974, moved to Baltimore); **Minnesota**—Muskies (1967-68, moved to Miami) and Pipers (1968-69, moved back to Pittsburgh); **New Jersey**—Americans (1967-68, moved to New York).

New Orleans—Buccaneers (1967-70, moved to Memphis); **New York**—Nets (1968-76); **Oakland**—Oaks (1967-69, moved to Washington); **Pittsburgh**—Pipers (1967-68, moved to Minnesota), Pipers (1969-72, renamed Condors in 1970); **St. Louis**—Spirits of St. Louis (1974-76); **San Antonio**—Spurs (1973-76); **San Diego**—Conquistadors (1972-75, renamed Sails in 1975); **Utah**—Stars (1970-75); **Virginia**—Squires (1970-76); **Washington**—Caps (1969-70, moved to Virginia).

Annual NBA Leaders
Scoring

Decided by total points from 1947-69, and per game average since 1970. A lockout in 1999 shortened the regular season to 50 games.

Multiple winners: Michael Jordan (10); Wilt Chamberlain (7); George Gervin and Allen Iverson (4); Neil Johnston, Bob McAdoo and George Mikan (3); Kareem Abdul-Jabbar, Paul Arizin, Kobe Bryant, Adrian Dantley, Tracy McGrady, Shaquille O'Neal and Bob Pettit (2).

Year		Gm	Pts	Avg	Year		Gm	Pts	Avg
1947	Joe Fulks, Phi	.60	1389	23.2	1979	George Gervin, SA	.80	2365	29.6
1948	Max Zaslofsky, Chi	.48	1007	21.0	1980	George Gervin, SA	.78	2585	33.1
1949	George Mikan, Mpls	.60	1698	28.3	1981	Adrian Dantley, Utah	.80	2452	30.7
1950	George Mikan, Mpls	.68	1865	27.4	1982	George Gervin, SA	.79	2551	32.3
1951	George Mikan, Mpls	.68	1932	28.4	1983	Alex English, Den	.82	2326	28.4
1952	Paul Arizin, Phi	.66	1674	25.4	1984	Adrian Dantley, Utah	.79	2418	30.6
1953	Neil Johnston, Phi	.70	1564	22.3	1985	Bernard King, NY	.55	1809	32.9
1954	Neil Johnston, Phi	.72	1759	24.4	1986	Dominique Wilkins, Atl	.78	2366	30.3
1955	Neil Johnston, Phi	.72	1631	22.7	1987	Michael Jordan, Chi	.82	3041	37.1
1956	Bob Pettit, St.L	.72	1849	25.7	1988	Michael Jordan, Chi	.82	2868	35.0
1957	Paul Arizin, Phi	.71	1817	25.6	1989	Michael Jordan, Chi	.81	2633	32.5
1958	George Yardley, Det	.72	2001	27.8	1990	Michael Jordan, Chi	.82	2753	33.6
1959	Bob Pettit, St.L	.72	2105	29.2	1991	Michael Jordan, Chi	.82	2580	31.5
1960	Wilt Chamberlain, Phi	.72	2707	37.6	1992	Michael Jordan, Chi	.80	2404	30.1
1961	Wilt Chamberlain, Phi	.79	3033	38.4	1993	Michael Jordan, Chi	.78	2541	32.6
1962	Wilt Chamberlain, Phi	.80	4029	50.4	1994	David Robinson, SA	.80	2383	29.8
1963	Wilt Chamberlain, SF	.80	3586	44.8	1995	Shaquille O'Neal, Orl	.79	2315	29.3
1964	Wilt Chamberlain, SF	.80	2948	36.9	1996	Michael Jordan, Chi	.82	2491	30.4
1965	Wilt Chamberlain, SF-Phi	.73	2534	34.7	1997	Michael Jordan, Chi	.82	2431	29.7
1966	Wilt Chamberlain, Phi	.79	2649	33.5	1998	Michael Jordan, Chi	.82	2357	28.7
1967	Rick Barry, SF	.78	2775	35.6	1999	Allen Iverson, Phi	.48	1284	26.8
1968	Dave Bing, Det	.79	2142	27.1	2000	Shaquille O'Neal, LAL	.79	2344	29.7
1969	Elvin Hayes, SD	.82	2327	28.4	2001	Allen Iverson, Phi	.71	2207	31.1
1970	Jerry West, LA	.74	2309	31.2	2002	Allen Iverson, Phi	.60	1883	31.4
1971	Lew Alcindor, Mil	.82	2596	31.7	2003	Tracy McGrady, Orl	.75	2407	32.1
1972	Kareem Abdul-Jabbar, Mil	.81	2822	34.8	2004	Tracy McGrady, Orl	.67	1878	28.0
1973	Nate Archibald, KC-Omaha	.80	2719	34.0	2005	Allen Iverson, Phi	.75	2302	30.7
1974	Bob McAdoo, Buf	.74	2261	30.6	2006	Kobe Bryant, LAL	.80	2832	35.4
1975	Bob McAdoo, Buf	.82	2831	34.5	2007	Kobe Bryant, LAL	.77	2430	31.6
1976	Bob McAdoo, Buf	.78	2427	31.1					
1977	Pete Maravich, NO	.73	2273	31.1					
1978	George Gervin, SA	.82	2232	27.2					

Note: Lew Alcindor changed his name to Kareem Abdul-Jabbar after the 1970-71 season.

Rebounds

Decided by total rebounds from 1951-69 and per game average since 1970.

Multiple winners: Wilt Chamberlain (11); Dennis Rodman (7); Moses Malone (6); Kevin Garnett and Bill Russell (4); Elvin Hayes, Dikembe Mutombo, Hakeem Olajuwon and Ben Wallace (2).

Year		Gm	No	Avg	Year		Gm	No	Avg
1951	Dolph Schayes, Syr	.66	1080	16.4	1970	Elvin Hayes, SD	.82	1386	16.9
1952	Larry Foust, Ft. Wayne	.66	880	13.3	1971	Wilt Chamberlain, LA	.82	1493	18.2
	& Mel Hutchins, Mil	.66	880	13.3	1972	Wilt Chamberlain, LA	.82	1572	19.2
1953	George Mikan, Mpls	.70	1007	14.4	1973	Wilt Chamberlain, LA	.82	1526	18.6
1954	Harry Gallatin, NY	.72	1098	15.3	1974	Elvin Hayes, Cap*	.81	1463	18.1
1955	Neil Johnston, Phi	.72	1085	15.1	1975	Wes Unseld, Wash	.73	1077	14.8
1956	Bob Pettit, St.L	.72	1164	16.2	1976	Kareem Abdul-Jabbar, LA	.82	1383	16.9
1957	Maurice Stokes, Roch	.72	1256	17.4	1977	Bill Walton, Port	.65	934	14.4
1958	Bill Russell, Bos	.69	1564	22.7	1978	Len Robinson, NO	.82	1288	15.7
1959	Bill Russell, Bos	.70	1612	23.0	1979	Moses Malone, Hou	.82	1444	17.6
1960	Wilt Chamberlain, Phi	.72	1941	27.0	1980	Swen Nater, SD	.81	1216	15.0
1961	Wilt Chamberlain, Phi	.79	2149	27.2	1981	Moses Malone, Hou	.80	1180	14.8
1962	Wilt Chamberlain, Phi	.80	2052	25.7	1982	Moses Malone, Hou	.81	1188	14.7
1963	Wilt Chamberlain, SF	.80	1946	24.3	1983	Moses Malone, Phi	.78	1194	15.3
1964	Bill Russell, Bos	.78	1930	24.7	1984	Moses Malone, Phi	.71	950	13.4
1965	Bill Russell, Bos	.78	1878	24.1	1985	Moses Malone, Phi	.79	1031	13.1
1966	Wilt Chamberlain, Phi	.79	1943	24.6	1986	Bill Laimbeer, Det	.82	1075	13.1
1967	Wilt Chamberlain, Phi	.81	1957	24.2	1987	Charles Barkley, Phi	.68	994	14.6
1968	Wilt Chamberlain, Phi	.82	1952	23.8	1988	Michael Cage, LAC	.72	938	13.0
1969	Wilt Chamberlain, LA	.81	1712	21.1	1989	Hakeem Olajuwon, Hou	.82	1105	13.5

*The Baltimore Bullets moved to Landover, Md. in 1973-74 and became first the Capital Bullets, then the Washington Bullets in 1974-75.

Rebounds (Cont.)

Year		Gm	No	Avg	Year		Gm	No	Avg
1990	Hakeem Olajuwon, Hou	82	1149	14.0	1999	Chris Webber, Sac	42	545	13.0
1991	David Robinson, SA	82	1063	13.0	2000	Dikembe Mutombo, Atl	82	1157	14.1
1992	Dennis Rodman, Det	82	1530	18.7	2001	Dikembe Mutombo, Atl-Phi	75	1015	13.5
1993	Dennis Rodman, Det	62	1232	18.3	2002	Ben Wallace, Det	80	1039	13.0
1994	Dennis Rodman, SA	79	1132	17.3	2003	Ben Wallace, Det	73	1126	15.4
1995	Dennis Rodman, SA	49	823	16.8	2004	Kevin Garnett, Min	82	1139	13.9
1996	Dennis Rodman, Chi	64	952	14.9	2005	Kevin Garnett, Min	82	1108	13.5
1997	Dennis Rodman, Chi	55	883	16.1	2006	Kevin Garnett, Min	76	966	12.7
1998	Dennis Rodman, Chi	80	1201	15.0	2007	Kevin Garnett, Min	76	975	12.8

Assists

Decided by total assists from 1952-69 and per game average since 1970.

Multiple winners: John Stockton (9); Bob Cousy (8); Oscar Robertson (6); Jason Kidd (5); Magic Johnson and Kevin Porter (4); Steve Nash (3); Andy Phillip and Guy Rodgers (2).

Year		No	Year		No	Year		APG
1947	Ernie Calverley, Prov	202	1968	Wilt Chamberlain, Phi	702	1989	John Stockton, Utah	13.6
1948	Howie Dallmar, Phi	120	1969	Oscar Robertson, Cin	772	1990	John Stockton, Utah	14.5
1949	Bob Davies, Roch	321	1970	Lenny Wilkens, Sea	9.1	1991	John Stockton, Utah	14.2
1950	Dick McGuire, NY	386	1971	Norm Van Lier, Chi	10.1	1992	John Stockton, Utah	13.7
1951	Andy Phillip, Phi	414	1972	Jerry West, LA	9.7	1993	John Stockton, Utah	12.0
1952	Andy Phillip, Phi	539	1973	Nate Archibald, KC-O	11.4	1994	John Stockton, Utah	12.6
1953	Bob Cousy, Bos	547	1974	Ernie DiGregorio, Buf	8.2	1995	John Stockton, Utah	12.3
1954	Bob Cousy, Bos	518	1975	Kevin Porter, Wash	8.0	1996	John Stockton, Utah	11.2
1955	Bob Cousy, Bos	557	1976	Slick Watts, Sea	8.1	1997	Mark Jackson, Den-Ind	11.4
1956	Bob Cousy, Bos	642	1977	Don Buse, Ind	8.5	1998	Rod Strickland, Wash	10.5
1957	Bob Cousy, Bos	478	1978	Kevin Porter, Det-NJ	10.2	1999	Jason Kidd, Pho	10.8
1958	Bob Cousy, Bos	463	1979	Kevin Porter, Det	13.4	2000	Jason Kidd, Pho	10.1
1959	Bob Cousy, Bos	557	1980	M.R. Richardson, NY	10.1	2001	Jason Kidd, Pho	9.8
1960	Bob Cousy, Bos	715	1981	Kevin Porter, Wash	9.1	2002	Andre Miller, Cle	10.9
1961	Oscar Robertson, Cin	690	1982	Johnny Moore, SA	9.6	2003	Jason Kidd, NJ	8.9
1962	Oscar Robertson, Cin	899	1983	Magic Johnson, LA	10.5	2004	Jason Kidd, NJ	9.2
1963	Guy Rodgers, SF	825	1984	Magic Johnson, LA	13.1	2005	Steve Nash, Dal	11.5
1964	Oscar Robertson, Cin	868	1985	Isiah Thomas, Det	13.9	2006	Steve Nash, Pho	10.5
1965	Oscar Robertson, Cin	861	1986	Magic Johnson, LAL	12.6	2007	Steve Nash, Pho	11.6
1966	Oscar Robertson, Cin	847	1987	Magic Johnson, LA	12.2			
1967	Guy Rodgers, Chi	908	1988	John Stockton, Utah	13.8			

Field Goal Percentage

Multiple winners: Wilt Chamberlain and Shaquille O'Neal (9); Artis Gilmore (4); Neil Johnston (3); Bob Feerick, Johnny Green, Alex Groza, Cedric Maxwell, Kevin McHale, Gheorghe Muresan, Kenny Sears and Buck Williams (2).

Year		Pct	Year		Pct	Year		Pct
1947	Bob Feerick, Wash	.401	1968	Wilt Chamberlain, Phi	.595	1989	Dennis Rodman, Det	.595
1948	Bob Feerick, Wash	.340	1969	Wilt Chamberlain, LA	.583	1990	Mark West, Pho	.625
1949	Arnie Risen, Roch	.423	1970	Johnny Green, Cin	.559	1991	Buck Williams, Port	.602
1950	Alex Groza, Indpls	.478	1971	Johnny Green, Cin	.587	1992	Buck Williams, Port	.604
1951	Alex Groza, Indpls	.470	1972	Wilt Chamberlain, LA	.649	1993	Cedric Ceballos, Pho	.576
1952	Paul Arizin, Phi	.448	1973	Wilt Chamberlain, LA	.727	1994	Shaquille O'Neal, Orl	.599
1953	Neil Johnston, Phi	.452	1974	Bob McAdoo, Buf	.547	1995	Chris Gatling, G.St	.633
1954	Ed Macauley, Bos	.486	1975	Don Nelson, Bos	.539	1996	Gheorghe Muresan, Wash	.584
1955	Larry Foust, Ft.W	.487	1976	Wes Unseld, Wash	.561	1997	Gheorghe Muresan, Wash	.604
1956	Neil Johnston, Phi	.457	1977	K. Abdul-Jabbar, LA	.579	1998	Shaquille O'Neal, LAL	.584
1957	Neil Johnston, Phi	.447	1978	Bobby Jones, Den	.578	1999	Shaquille O'Neal, LAL	.576
1958	Jack Twyman, Cin	.452	1979	Cedric Maxwell, Bos	.584	2000	Shaquille O'Neal, LAL	.574
1959	Kenny Sears, NY	.490	1980	Cedric Maxwell, Bos	.609	2001	Shaquille O'Neal, LAL	.572
1960	Kenny Sears, NY	.477	1981	Artis Gilmore, Chi	.670	2002	Shaquille O'Neal, LAL	.579
1961	Wilt Chamberlain, Phi	.509	1982	Artis Gilmore, Chi	.652	2003	Eddy Curry, Chi	.585
1962	Walt Bellamy, Chi	.519	1983	Artis Gilmore, SA	.626	2004	Shaquille O'Neal, LAL	.584
1963	Wilt Chamberlain, SF	.528	1984	Artis Gilmore, SA	.631	2005	Shaquille O'Neal, Mia	.601
1964	Jerry Lucas, Cin	.527	1985	James Donaldson, LAC	.637	2006	Shaquille O'Neal, Mia	.600
1965	W. Chamberlain, SF-Phi	.510	1986	Steve Johnson, SA	.632	2007	Mikki Moore, NJ	.609
1966	Wilt Chamberlain, Phi	.540	1987	Kevin McHale, Bos	.604			
1967	Wilt Chamberlain, Phi	.683	1988	Kevin McHale, Bos	.604			

Free Throw Percentage

Multiple winners: Bill Sharman (7); Rick Barry (6); Reggie Miller (5); Larry Bird (4); Mark Price and Dolph Schayes (3); Mahmoud Abdul-Rauf, Larry Costello, Ernie DiGregorio, Bob Feerick, Kyle Macy, Calvin Murphy, Oscar Robertson and Larry Siegfried (2).

Year		Pct	Year		Pct	Year		Pct
1947	Fred Scolari, Wash	.811	1952	Bob Wanzer, Roch	.904	1957	Bill Sharman, Bos	.905
1948	Bob Feerick, Wash	.788	1953	Bill Sharman, Bos	.850	1958	Dolph Schayes, Syr	.904
1949	Bob Feerick, Wash	.859	1954	Bill Sharman, Bos	.844	1959	Bill Sharman, Bos	.932
1950	Max Zaslofsky, Chi	.843	1955	Bill Sharman, Bos	.897	1960	Dolph Schayes, Syr	.892
1951	Joe Fulks, Phi	.855	1956	Bill Sharman, Bos	.867	1961	Bill Sharman, Bos	.921

Free Throw Percentage (Cont.)

Year		Pct	Year		Pct	Year		Pct
1962	Dolph Schayes, Syr	.896	1978	Rick Barry, G.St.	.924	1994	M. Abdul-Rauf, Den	.956
1963	Larry Costello, Syr	.881	1979	Rick Barry, Hou	.947	1995	Spud Webb, Sac	.934
1964	Oscar Robertson, Cin	.853	1980	Rick Barry, Hou	.935	1996	M. Abdul-Rauf, Den	.930
1965	Larry Costello, Phi	.877	1981	Calvin Murphy, Hou	.958	1997	Mark Price, G.St.	.906
1966	Larry Siegfried, Bos	.881	1982	Kyle Macy, Pho	.899	1998	Chris Mullin, Ind	.939
1967	Adrian Smith, Cin	.903	1983	Calvin Murphy, Hou	.920	1999	Reggie Miller, Ind	.915
1968	Oscar Robertson, Cin	.873	1984	Larry Bird, Bos	.888	2000	Jeff Hornacek, Utah	.950
1969	Larry Siegfried, NY	.864	1985	Kyle Macy, Pho	.907	2001	Reggie Miller, Ind	.928
1970	Flynn Robinson, Mil	.898	1986	Larry Bird, Bos	.896	2002	Reggie Miller, Ind	.911
1971	Chet Walker, Chi	.859	1987	Larry Bird, Bos	.910	2003	Allan Houston, NY	.919
1972	Jack Marin, Bal	.894	1988	Jack Sikma, Mil	.922	2004	Predrag Stojakovic, Sac	.927
1973	Rick Barry, G.St.	.902	1989	Magic Johnson, LAL	.911	2005	Reggie Miller, Ind	.933
1974	Ernie DiGregorio, Buf	.902	1990	Larry Bird, Bos	.930	2006	Steve Nash, Pho	.921
1975	Rick Barry, G.St.	.904	1991	Reggie Miller, Ind	.918	2007	Kyle Korver, Phi	.914
1976	Rick Barry, G.St.	.923	1992	Mark Price, Cle	.947			
1977	Ernie DiGregorio, Buf	.945	1993	Mark Price, Cle	.948			

Three-Point Field Goal Percentage

Multiple winners: Craig Hodges, Steve Kerr (2)

Year		Pct	Year		Pct	Year		Pct
1980	Fred Brown, Sea	.443	1990	Steve Kerr, Cle	.507	2000	Hubert Davis, Dal	.491
1981	Brian Taylor, SD	.383	1991	Jim Les, Sac	.461	2001	Brent Barry, Sea	.476
1982	Campy Russell, NY	.439	1992	Dana Barros, Sea	.446	2002	Steve Smith, SA	.472
1983	Mike Dunleavy, SA	.345	1993	B.J. Armstrong, Chi	.453	2003	Bruce Bowen, SA	.441
1984	Darrell Griffith, Utah	.361	1994	Tracy Murray, Por	.459	2004	Anthony Peeler, Sac	.482
1985	Byron Scott, LAL	.433	1995	Steve Kerr, Chi	.524	2005	Fred Hoiberg, Min	.483
1986	Craig Hodges, Milw	.451	1996	Tim Legler, Wash	.522	2006	Richard Hamilton, Det	.458
1987	Kiki Vandeweghe, Por	.481	1997	Glen Rice, Cha	.470	2007	Jason Kapono, Mia	.514
1988	Craig Hodges, Milw-Pho	.491	1998	Dale Ellis, Sea	.464			
1989	Jon Sundvold, Mia	.522	1999	Dell Curry, Milw	.476			

Blocked Shots

Multiple winners: Kareem Abdul-Jabbar and Mark Eaton (4); Marcus Camby, George Johnson, Dikembe Mutombo, Hakeem Olajuwon and Theo Ratliff (3); Manute Bol and Alonzo Mourning (2).

Year		Gm	No	Avg
1974	Elmore Smith, LA	81	393	4.85
1975	Kareem Abdul-Jabbar, Mil	65	212	3.26
1976	Kareem Abdul-Jabbar, LA	82	338	4.12
1977	Bill Walton, Port	65	211	3.25
1978	George Johnson, NJ	81	274	3.38
1979	Kareem Abdul-Jabbar, LA	80	316	3.95
1980	Kareem Abdul-Jabbar, LA	82	280	3.41
1981	George Johnson, SA	82	278	3.39
1982	George Johnson, SA	75	234	3.12
1983	Tree Rollins, Atl	80	343	4.29
1984	Mark Eaton, Utah	82	351	4.28
1985	Mark Eaton, Utah	82	456	5.56
1986	Manute Bol, Wash	80	397	4.96
1987	Mark Eaton, Utah	79	321	4.06
1988	Mark Eaton, Utah	82	304	3.71
1989	Manute Bol, G.St.	80	345	4.31
1990	Akeem Olajuwon, Hou	82	376	4.59
1991	Hakeem Olajuwon, Hou	56	221	3.95
1992	David Robinson, SA	68	305	4.49
1993	Hakeem Olajuwon, Hou	82	342	4.17
1994	Dikembe Mutombo, Den	82	336	4.10
1995	Dikembe Mutombo, Den	82	321	3.91
1996	Dikembe Mutombo, Den	74	332	4.49
1997	Shawn Bradley, Dal-NJ	73	248	3.40
1998	Marcus Camby, Tor	63	230	3.65
1999	Alonzo Mourning, Mia	46	180	3.91
2000	Alonzo Mourning, Mia	79	294	3.72
2001	Theo Ratliff, Phi-Atl	50	187	3.74
2002	Ben Wallace, Det	80	278	3.48
2003	Theo Ratliff, Atl	81	262	3.23
2004	Theo Ratliff, Atl-Port	85	307	3.61
2005	Andrei Kirilenko, Utah	41	136	3.32
2006	Marcus Camby, Den	56	184	3.29
2007	Marcus Camby, Den	70	231	3.30

Steals

Multiple winners: Allen Iverson, Michael Jordan, Micheal Ray Richardson and Alvin Robertson (3); Mookie Blaylock, Baron Davis; Magic Johnson and John Stockton (2).

Year		Gm	No	Avg
1974	Larry Steele, Port	81	217	2.68
1975	Rick Barry, G.St.	80	228	2.85
1976	Slick Watts, Sea	82	261	3.18
1977	Don Buse, Ind	81	281	3.47
1978	Ron Lee, Pho	82	225	2.74
1979	M.L. Carr, Det	80	197	2.46
1980	Micheal Ray Richardson, NY	82	265	3.23
1981	Magic Johnson, LA	37	127	3.43
1982	Magic Johnson, LA	78	208	2.67
1983	Micheal Ray Richardson, G. ST-NJ	64	182	2.84
1984	Rickey Green, Utah	81	215	2.65
1985	Micheal Ray Richardson, NJ	82	243	2.96
1986	Alvin Robertson, SA	82	301	3.67
1987	Alvin Robertson, SA	81	260	3.21
1988	Michael Jordan, Chi	82	259	3.16
1989	John Stockton, Utah	82	263	3.21
1990	Michael Jordan, Chi	82	227	2.77
1991	Alvin Robertson, SA	81	246	3.04
1992	John Stockton, Utah	82	244	2.98
1993	Michael Jordan, Chi	78	221	2.83
1994	Nate McMillan, Sea	73	216	2.96
1995	Scottie Pippen, Chi	79	232	2.94
1996	Gary Payton, Sea	81	231	2.85
1997	Mookie Blaylock, Atl	78	212	2.72
1998	Mookie Blaylock, Atl.	70	183	2.61
1999	Kendall Gill, NJ	50	134	2.68
2000	Eddie Jones, Cha	72	192	2.67
2001	Allen Iverson, Phi.	71	178	2.51
2002	Allen Iverson, Phi.	60	168	2.80
2003	Allen Iverson, Phi	82	225	2.74
2004	Baron Davis, NO	67	158	2.36
2005	Larry Hughes, Wash	61	176	2.89
2006	Gerald Wallace, Cha	55	138	2.51
2007	Baron Davis, G. St.	63	135	2.14

Note: Akeem Olajuwon changed the spelling of his first name to Hakeem during the 1990-91 season.

All-Time NBA Regular Season Leaders
Through the 2006-07 regular season.
CAREER
Players active in 2006-07 in **bold** type.

Points

		Yrs	Gm	Pts	Avg
1	Kareem Abdul-Jabbar	20	1560	**38,387**	24.6
2	Karl Malone	19	1476	**36,928**	25.0
3	Michael Jordan	15	1072	**32,292**	30.1
4	Wilt Chamberlain	14	1045	**31,419**	30.1
5	Moses Malone	19	1329	**27,409**	20.6
6	Elvin Hayes	16	1303	**27,313**	21.0
7	Hakeem Olajuwon	18	1238	**26,946**	21.8
8	Oscar Robertson	14	1040	**26,710**	25.7
9	Dominique Wilkins	15	1074	**26,668**	24.8
10	John Havlicek	16	1270	**26,395**	20.8
11	Alex English	15	1193	**25,613**	21.5
12	**Shaquille O'Neal**	15	981	**25,454**	25.9
13	Reggie Miller	18	1389	**25,279**	18.2
14	Jerry West	14	932	**25,192**	27.0
15	Patrick Ewing	17	1183	**24,815**	21.0
16	Charles Barkley	16	1073	**23,757**	22.1
17	Robert Parish	21	1611	**23,334**	14.5
18	Adrian Dantley	15	955	**23,177**	24.3
19	Elgin Baylor	14	846	**23,149**	27.4
20	Clyde Drexler	15	1086	**22,195**	20.4
21	**Gary Payton**	17	1335	**21,813**	16.3
22	Larry Bird	13	897	**21,791**	24.3
23	Hal Greer	15	1122	**21,586**	19.2
24	Walt Bellamy	14	1043	**20,941**	20.1
25	Bob Pettit	11	792	**20,880**	26.4
26	**Allen Iverson**	11	747	**20,824**	27.9
26	David Robinson	14	987	**20,790**	21.1
27	George Gervin	10	791	**20,708**	26.2
28	Mitch Richmond	14	976	**20,497**	21.0
29	Tom Chambers	16	1107	**20,049**	18.1

Scoring Average
Minimum of 400 games or 10,000 points.

		Yrs	Gm	Pts	Avg
1	Michael Jordan	15	1072	32,292	30.1
2	Wilt Chamberlain	14	1045	31,419	30.1
3	**Allen Iverson**	11	747	20,824	27.9
4	Elgin Baylor	14	846	23,149	27.4
5	Jerry West	14	932	25,192	27.0
6	Bob Pettit	11	792	20,880	26.4
7	George Gervin	10	791	20,708	26.2
8	**Shaquille O'Neal**	15	981	25,454	25.9
9	Oscar Robertson	14	1040	26,710	25.7
10	Karl Malone	19	1476	36,928	25.0
11	Dominique Wilkins	15	1074	26,668	24.8
12	**Kobe Bryant**	11	784	19,296	24.6
13	Kareem Abdul-Jabbar	20	1560	38,387	24.6
14	Larry Bird	13	897	21,791	24.3
15	Adrian Dantley	15	955	23,177	24.3
16	Pete Maravich	10	658	15,948	24.2
17	**Vince Carter**	9	621	14,970	24.1
18	**Paul Pierce**	9	652	15,375	23.6
19	Rick Barry	10	794	18,395	23.2
20	**Gilbert Arenas**	6	418	9575	22.9
21	Paul Arizin	10	713	16,266	22.8
22	George Mikan	9	520	11,764	22.6
23	Bernard King	14	874	19,655	22.5
24	**Tracy McGrady**	10	683	15,317	22.4
25	**Dirk Nowitzki**	9	681	15,173	22.3
26	Charles Barkley	16	1073	23,757	22.1
27	David Thompson	8	509	11,264	22.1
27	Bob McAdoo	14	852	18,787	22.1
29	Julius Erving	11	836	18,364	22.0
30	**Tim Duncan**	10	746	16,288	21.8

Assists

		Yrs	Gm	No	Avg
1	John Stockton	19	1504	**15,806**	10.5
2	Mark Jackson	17	1296	**10,334**	8.0
3	Magic Johnson	13	906	**10,141**	11.2
4	Oscar Robertson	14	1040	**9,887**	9.5
5	Isiah Thomas	13	979	**9,061**	9.3
6	**Gary Payton**	17	1335	**8,966**	6.7
7	**Jason Kidd**	13	946	**8,691**	9.2
8	Rod Strickland	17	1094	**7,987**	7.3
9	Maurice Cheeks	15	1101	**7,392**	6.7
10	Lenny Wilkens	15	1077	**7,211**	6.7
11	Terry Porter	17	1274	**7,160**	5.6
12	Tim Hardaway	13	867	**7,095**	8.2

Rebounds

		Yrs	Gm	No	Avg
1	Wilt Chamberlain	14	1045	**23,924**	22.9
2	Bill Russell	13	963	**21,620**	22.5
3	Kareem Abdul-Jabbar	20	1560	**17,440**	11.2
4	Elvin Hayes	16	1303	**16,279**	12.5
5	Moses Malone	19	1329	**16,212**	12.2
6	Karl Malone	19	1476	**14,968**	10.1
7	Robert Parish	21	1611	**14,715**	9.1
8	Nate Thurmond	14	964	**14,464**	15.0
9	Walt Bellamy	14	1043	**14,241**	13.7
10	Wes Unseld	13	984	**13,769**	14.0
11	Hakeem Olajuwon	18	1238	**13,748**	11.1
12	Buck Williams	17	1307	**13,017**	10.0

Note: If rebounds accumulated in the ABA are included, consider the following totals: Moses Malone (17,834) and Artis Gilmore (16,330).

Steals

		Yrs	Gm	No
1	John Stockton	19	1504	3265
2	Michael Jordan	15	1072	2514
3	**Gary Payton**	17	1335	2445
4	Maurice Cheeks	15	1101	2310
5	Scottie Pippen	17	1178	2307

Note: Steals have only been an official stat since the 1973-74 season.

Blocked Shots

		Yrs	Gm	No
1	Hakeem Olajuwon	18	1238	3830
2	**Dikembe Mutombo**	16	1148	3230
3	Kareem Abdul-Jabbar	20	1560	3189
4	Mark Eaton	11	875	3064
5	David Robinson	14	987	2954

Note: Blocked shots have only been an official stat since the 1973-74 season. Also, note that if ABA records are included, consider the following block totals: Artis Gilmore (3,178).

Games Played

		Yrs	Career	Gm
1	Robert Parish	21	1976-97	1611
2	Kareem Abdul-Jabbar	20	1970-89	1560
3	John Stockton	19	1984-03	1504
4	Karl Malone	19	1985-04	1476
5	**Kevin Willis**	20	1985-05,07	1424

Note: If ABA records are included, consider the following game totals: Moses Malone (1,455).

Field Goals

		Yrs	FG	Att	Pct
1	Kareem Abdul-Jabbar	20	**15,837**	28,307	.559
2	Karl Malone	19	**13,528**	26,210	.516
3	Wilt Chamberlain	14	**12,681**	23,497	.540
4	Michael Jordan	15	**12,192**	24,537	.497
5	Elvin Hayes	16	**10,976**	24,272	.452
6	Hakeem Olajuwon	18	**10,749**	20,991	.512
7	Alex English	15	**10,659**	21,036	.507
8	John Havlicek	16	**10,513**	23,930	.439
9	**Shaquille O'Neal**	15	**10,091**	17,394	.580
10	Dominique Wilkins	15	**9,963**	21,589	.461
11	Patrick Ewing	17	**9,702**	19,241	.504
12	Robert Parish	21	**9,614**	17,914	.537

Note: If field goals made in the ABA are included, consider these NBA-ABA totals: Julius Erving (11,818), Dan Issel (10,431), George Gervin (10,368), Moses Malone (10,277) and Rick Barry (9,695).

Free Throws

		Yrs	FT	Att	Pct
1	Karl Malone	19	**9787**	13,188	.742
2	Moses Malone	19	**8531**	11,090	.769
3	Oscar Robertson	14	**7694**	9,185	.838
4	Michael Jordan	15	**7327**	8,772	.835
5	Jerry West	14	**7160**	8,801	.814
6	Dolph Schayes	16	**6979**	8,273	.844
7	Adrian Dantley	15	**6832**	8,351	.818
8	Kareem Abdul-Jabbar	20	**6712**	9,304	.721
9	Charles Barkley	16	**6349**	8,643	.734
10	Reggie Miller	18	**6237**	7,026	.888
11	Bob Pettit	11	**6182**	8,119	.761
12	Wilt Chamberlain	14	**6057**	11,862	.511

Note: If free throws made in the ABA are included, consider these totals: Moses Malone (9,018), Dan Issel (6,591), and Julius Erving (6,256).

Free Throw Percentage

		Yrs	FT	Att	Pct
1	Mark Price	12	2135	2362	.904
2	Rick Barry	10	3818	4243	.900
3	Steve Nash	11	1948	2173	.896
4	**Peja Stojakovic**	9	1895	2124	.892
5	Calvin Murphy	13	3445	3864	.892

Note: If ABA records are included, consider the following free throw percentage: Rick Barry (5713-6397 for .893)

3-Pt Field Goal Pct.

(minimum 250 3-pt FGs made)

		Yrs	Gm	Pct	3FGM
1	Steve Kerr	15	910	**.454**	726
2	Hubert Davis	12	685	**.441**	728
3	Drazen Petrovic	4	290	**.437**	255
4	Tim Legler	10	310	**.431**	260
5	**Steve Nash**	11	779	**.426**	1073

3-Pt Field Goals Made

		Yrs	Gm	Pct	3FGM
1	Reggie Miller	18	1389	.395	2560
2	**Ray Allen**	11	790	.397	1920
3	Dale Ellis	17	1209	.403	1719
4	Glen Rice	15	1000	.400	1559
5	Tim Hardaway	14	867	.355	1542

Minutes Played

		Gm	MPG	Min
1	Kareem Abdul-Jabbar	1560	36.8	57,446
2	Karl Malone	1476	37.2	54,852
3	Elvin Hayes	1303	38.4	50,000
4	Wilt Chamberlain	1045	45.8	47,859
5	John Stockton	1504	31.8	47,764

Triple-Doubles

		Yrs	Gm	No
1	Oscar Robertson	14	1040	181
2	Magic Johnson	13	906	138
3	**Jason Kidd**	13	946	87
4	Wilt Chamberlain	14	1045	78
5	Larry Bird	13	897	59

Note: The triple-double totals of Oscar Robertson and Wilt Chamberlain do not include games in which they may have recorded a triple-double with double-digit blocks and/or steals, since those stats have only be official since the 1973-74 season.

Personal Fouls

		Yrs	Gm	Fouls	DQ
1	Kareem Abdul-Jabbar	20	1560	**4657**	48
2	Karl Malone	19	1476	**4578**	28
3	Robert Parish	21	1611	**4443**	86
4	Charles Oakley	19	1282	**4421**	63
5	Hakeem Olajuwon	18	1238	**4383**	80

Note: If ABA records are included, consider the following personal foul totals: Artis Gilmore (4,529) and Caldwell Jones (4,436).

Disqualifications

		Yrs	Gm	No
1	Vern Mikkelsen	10	699	127
2	Walter Dukes	8	553	121
3	Shawn Kemp	14	1051	115
4	Charlie Share	8	555	105
5	Paul Arizin	10	713	101

NBA-ABA Top 20

Points

All-Time combined regular season scoring leaders, including ABA service (1968-76). NBA players with ABA experience are listed in CAPITAL letters. Players active during 2006-07 are in **bold** type.

		Yrs	Pts	Avg
1	Kareem Abdul-Jabbar	20	**38,387**	24.6
2	Karl Malone	19	**36,928**	25.0
3	Wilt Chamberlain	14	**31,419**	30.1
4	Michael Jordan	15	**32,292**	30.1
5	JULIUS ERVING	16	**30,026**	24.2
6	MOSES MALONE	21	**29,580**	20.3
7	DAN ISSEL	15	**27,482**	22.6
8	Elvin Hayes	16	**27,313**	21.0
9	Hakeem Olajuwon	18	**26,946**	21.8
10	Oscar Robertson	14	**26,710**	25.7
11	Dominique Wilkins	15	**26,668**	24.8
12	GEORGE GERVIN	14	**26,595**	25.1
13	John Havlicek	16	**26,395**	20.8
14	Alex English	15	**25,613**	21.5
15	**Shaquille O'Neal**	15	**25,454**	25.9
16	RICK BARRY	14	**25,279**	24.8
	Reggie Miller	18	**25,279**	18.2
18	Jerry West	14	**25,192**	27.0
19	ARTIS GILMORE	17	**24,941**	18.8
20	Patrick Ewing	17	**24,815**	21.0

ABA Totals: BARRY (4 yrs, 226 gm, 6884 pts, 30.5 avg); ERVING (5 yrs, 407 gm, 11,662 pts, 28.7 avg); GERVIN (4 yrs, 269 gm, 5887 pts, 21.9 avg); GILMORE (5 yrs, 420 gm, 9362 pts, 22.3 avg); ISSEL (6 yrs, 500 gm, 12,823 pts, 25.6 avg); MALONE (2 yrs, 126 gm, 2171 pts, 17.2 avg).

All-Time NBA Regular Season Leaders (Cont.)

SINGLE SEASON

Scoring Average

		Season	Avg
1	Wilt Chamberlain, Phi	1961-62	50.4
2	Wilt Chamberlain, SF	1962-63	44.8
3	Wilt Chamberlain, Phi	1960-61	38.4
4	Elgin Baylor, LA	1961-62	38.3
5	Wilt Chamberlain, Phi	1959-60	37.6
6	Michael Jordan, Chi	1986-87	37.1
7	Wilt Chamberlain, SF	1963-64	36.9
8	Rick Barry, SF	1966-67	35.6
9	Kobe Bryant, LAL	2005-06	35.4
10	Michael Jordan, Chi	1987-88	35.0

Field Goal Pct.

		Season	Pct
1	Wilt Chamberlain, LA	1972-73	.727
2	Wilt Chamberlain, SF	1966-67	.683
3	Artis Gilmore, Chi	1980-81	.670
4	Artis Gilmore, Chi	1981-82	.652
5	Wilt Chamberlain, LA	1971-72	.649

Free Throw Pct.

		Season	Pct
1	Calvin Murphy, Hou	1980-81	.958
2	Mahmoud Abdul-Rauf, Den.	1993-94	.956
3	Mark Price, Cle	1992-93	.948
4	Mark Price, Cle	1991-92	.947
	Rick Barry, Hou	1978-79	.947

3-Pt Field Goal Pct.

		Season	Pct
1	Steve Kerr, Chi	1994-95	.524
2	Jon Sundvold, Mia	1988-89	.522
3	Tim Legler, Wash	1995-96	.522
4	Steve Kerr, Chi	1995-96	.515
5	Jason Kapono, Mia	2006-07	.514

Personal Fouls

		Season	No
1	Darryl Dawkins, NJ	1983-84	386
2	Darryl Dawkins, NJ	1982-83	379

Assists

		Season	Avg
1	John Stockton, Utah	1989-90	14.5
2	John Stockton, Utah	1990-91	14.2
3	Isiah Thomas, Det	1984-85	13.9
4	John Stockton, Utah	1987-88	13.8
5	John Stockton, Utah	1991-92	13.7
6	John Stockton, Utah	1988-89	13.6
7	Kevin Porter, Det	1978-79	13.4
8	Magic Johnson, LAL	1983-84	13.1
9	Magic Johnson, LAL	1988-89	12.8
10	John Stockton, Utah	1993-94	12.6

Rebounds

		Season	Avg
1	Wilt Chamberlain, Phi	1960-61	27.2
2	Wilt Chamberlain, Phi	1959-60	27.0
3	Wilt Chamberlain, Phi	1961-62	25.7
4	Bill Russell, Bos	1963-64	24.7
5	Wilt Chamberlain, Phi	1965-66	24.6

Blocked Shots

		Season	Avg
1	Mark Eaton, Utah	1984-85	5.56
2	Manute Bol, Wash	1985-86	4.96
3	Elmore Smith, LA	1973-74	4.85
4	Mark Eaton, Utah	1985-86	4.61
5	Hakeem Olajuwon, Hou	1989-90	4.59

Steals

		Season	Avg
1	Alvin Robertson, SA	1985-86	3.67
2	Don Buse, Ind	1976-77	3.47
3	Magic Johnson, LAL	1980-81	3.43
4	Micheal Ray Richardson, NY	1979-80	3.23
5	Alvin Robertson, SA	1986-87	3.21

Turnovers

		Season	No
1	Artis Gilmore, Chi	1977-78	366
2	Kevin Porter, Det/NJ	1977-78	360

SINGLE GAME

Points

	Date	FG-FT	Pts
Wilt Chamberlain, Phi vs NY†	3/2/62	36-28–	100
Kobe Bryant, LAL vs. Tor	1/22/06	28-18–	81
Wilt Chamberlain, Phi vs LA***	12/8/61	31-16–	78
Wilt Chamberlain, Phi vs Chi	1/13/62	29-15–	73
Wilt Chamberlain, SF at NY	11/16/62	29-15–	73
David Thompson, Den at Det	4/9/78	28-17–	73
Wilt Chamberlain, SF at LA	11/3/62	29-14–	72
Elgin Baylor, LA at NY	11/15/60	28-15–	71
David Robinson, SA at LAC	4/24/94	26-18–	71
Wilt Chamberlain, SF at Syr	3/10/63	27-16–	70
Michael Jordan, Chi at Cle*	3/28/90	23-21–	69
Wilt Chamberlain, Phi at Chi	12/16/67	30-8–	68
Pete Maravich, NO vs NYK	2/25/77	26-16–	68
Wilt Chamberlain, Phi vs NY	3/9/61	27-13–	67
Wilt Chamberlain, Phi at St. L	2/17/62	26-15–	67
Wilt Chamberlain, Phi vs NY	2/25/62	25-17–	67
Wilt Chamberlain, SF vs LA	1/11/63	28-11–	67
Wilt Chamberlain, LA vs Pho	2/9/69	29-8–	66
Wilt Chamberlain, Phi at Cin	2/13/62	24-17–	65
Wilt Chamberlain, Phi at St. L	2/27/62	25-15–	65
Wilt Chamberlain, Phi vs LA	2/7/66	28-9–	65
Kobe Bryant, LAL vs Port	3/16/07	23-11–	65

*Overtime   ***Triple overtime.
†Game was played at Hershey, Penn.

Field Goals

	Date	FG	Att
Wilt Chamberlain, Phi vs NY	3/2/62	36	63
Wilt Chamberlain, Phi vs LA***	12/8/61	31	62
Wilt Chamberlain, Phi at Chi	12/16/67	30	30
Rick Barry, G.St. vs Port	2/26/74	30	45
Wilt Chamberlain made 29 four times.			

***Triple overtime.

Free Throws

	Date	FT	Att
Wilt Chamberlain, Phi vs NY	3/2/62	28	32
Adrian Dantley, Utah vs Hou	1/4/84	28	29
Adrian Dantley, Utah vs Den	11/25/83	27	31
Adrian Dantley, Utah vs Dal	10/31/80	26	29
Michael Jordan, Chi vs NJ	2/26/87	26	27

3-Pt Field Goals

	Date	No
Kobe Bryant, LAL vs Sea	1/7/03	12
Dennis Scott, Orl vs Atl	4/18/96	11
Ray Allen, Milw vs Char	4/14/02	10
Brian Shaw, Mia at Mil	4/8/93	10
Joe Dumars, Det vs Min	11/8/94	10
George McCloud, Dal vs Pho	12/16/95	10*
Many tied with 9 each		

* Overtime

Assists

	Date	No
Scott Skiles, Orl vs Den	12/30/90	30
Kevin Porter, NJ vs Hou	2/24/78	29
Bob Cousy, Bos vs Mpls	2/27/59	28
Guy Rodgers, SF vs St.L	3/14/63	28
John Stockton, Utah vs SA	1/15/91	28

Rebounds

	Date	No
Wilt Chamberlain, Phi vs Bos	11/24/60	55
Bill Russell, Bos vs Syr	2/5/60	51
Bill Russell, Bos vs Phi	11/16/57	49
Bill Russell, Bos vs Det	3/11/65	49
Wilt Chamberlain, Phi vs Syr	2/6/60	45
Wilt Chamberlain, Phi vs LA	1/21/61	45

Blocked Shots

	Date	No
Elmore Smith, LA vs Port	10/28/73	17
Manute Bol, Wash vs Atl	1/25/86	15
Manute Bol, Wash vs Ind	2/26/87	15
Shaquille O'Neal, Orl at NJ	11/20/93	15

Steals

	Date	No
Larry Kenon, San Antonio at KC	12/26/76	11
Kendall Gill, NJ vs Mia.	4/3/99	11

14 different players tied with 10 each, including Alvin Robertson, who had 10 steals in a game four times.

All-Time Winningest NBA Coaches

Top 25 NBA career victories through the 2006-07 season. Career, regular season and playoff records are noted along with NBA titles won. Coaches active during 2006-07 season in **bold** type.

		Career			Regular Season			Playoffs			
		Yrs	W	L	Pct	W	L	Pct	W	L	Pct	NBA Titles
1	Lenny Wilkens	32	1412	1253	.530	1332	1155	.536	80	98	.449	1 (1979)
2	**Pat Riley**	23	1366	738	.649	1195	627	.656	171	111	.606	5 (1982,85,87-88, 2006)
3	**Don Nelson**	28	1307	1011	.564	1232	880	.572	75	91	.452	None
4	**Jerry Sloan**	22	1122	777	.591	1035	689	.600	87	88	.497	None
5	Larry Brown	23	1110	889	.555	1010	800	.558	100	89	.529	1 (2004)
6	**Phil Jackson**	16	1098	470	.700	919	393	.700	179	77	.699	9 (1991-93,96-98,00-02)
7	Red Auerbach	20	1037	548	.654	938	479	.662	99	69	.589	9 (1957, 59-66)
8	Bill Fitch	25	999	1160	.463	944	1106	.460	55	54	.505	1 (1981)
9	Dick Motta	25	991	1087	.477	935	1017	.479	56	70	.444	1 (1978)
10	Jack Ramsay	21	908	841	.519	864	783	.525	44	58	.431	1 (1977)
11	Cotton Fitzsimmons	21	867	824	.513	832	775	.518	35	49	.417	None
12	**George Karl**	19	891	661	.574	829	582	.588	62	79	.440	None
13	Rick Adelman	16	822	581	.586	752	481	.610	70	68	.507	None
14	Gene Shue	22	814	908	.473	784	861	.477	30	47	.390	None
15	Red Holzman	18	754	652	.536	696	604	.535	58	48	.547	2 (1970, 73)
	John MacLeod	18	754	711	.515	707	657	.518	47	54	.465	None
17	Chuck Daly	14	713	488	.594	638	437	.593	75	51	.595	2 (1989-90)
18	**Mike Fratello**	17	687	590	.538	667	548	.549	20	42	.323	None
19	**Gregg Popovich**	11	668	327	.671	576	276	.676	92	51	.643	4 (1999, 2003, 05, 07)
20	Doug Moe	15	661	579	.533	628	529	.543	33	50	.398	None
21	K.C. Jones	10	603	309	.661	522	252	.674	81	57	.587	2 (1984,86)
22	Del Harris	14	594	507	.540	556	457	.549	38	50	.432	None
23	Al Attles	14	588	548	.518	557	518	.518	31	30	.508	1 (1975)
	Mike Dunleavy	14	588	590	.499	550	566	.493	38	33	.535	None
25	Rudy Tomjanovich	13	578	455	.560	527	416	.559	51	39	.567	2 (1994-95)

Note: The NBA does not recognize records from the National Basketball League (1937-49), the American Basketball League (1961-62) or the American Basketball Assn. (1968-76), so the following NBL, ABL and ABA overall coaching records are not included above: NBL—**John Kundla** (51-19 and a title in 1 year). ABA—**Larry Brown** (249-129 in 4 yrs), **Alex Hannum** (194-164 and one title in 4 yrs), **K.C. Jones** (30-58 in 1 yr); **Kevin Loughery** (189-95 and one title in 3 yrs).

Where They Coached

Adelman—Portland (1988-94), Golden State (1995-97), Sacramento (1998-06), Houston (2007-); **Attles**—Golden St. (1970-80,80-83); **Auerbach**—Washington (1946-49), Tri-Cities (1949-50), Boston (1950-66); **Brown**—Denver (1976-79), New Jersey (1981-83), San Antonio (1988-92), LA Clippers (1992-93), Indiana (1993-97), Philadelphia (1997-2003), Detroit (2003-05), New York (2005-06); **Daly**—Cleveland (1981-82), Detroit (1983-92), New Jersey (1992-94), Orlando (1997-99); **Dunleavy**—L.A. Lakers (1990-91), Milwaukee (1992-1995), Portland (1997-2000), L.A. Clippers (2003-); **Fitch**—Cleveland (1970-79), Boston (1979-83), Houston (1983-88), New Jersey (1989-92), LA Clippers (1994-98); **Fitzsimmons**—Phoenix (1970-72), Atlanta (1972-76), Buffalo (1977-78), Kansas City (1978-84), San Antonio (1984-86), Phoenix (1988-92, 95-96); **Fratello**—Atlanta (1980-90), Cleveland (1993-99), Memphis (2004-06).

Harris—Houston (1979-83), Milwaukee (1987-92), LA Lakers (1994-99); **Holzman**—Milwaukee-St. Louis Hawks (1954-57), NY Knicks (1968-77,78-82); **Jackson**—Chicago (1989-98), LA Lakers (1999-2004, 05-); **Jones**—Washington (1973-76), Boston (1983-88), Seattle (1990-92); **Karl**—Cleveland (1984-86), Seattle (1991-98), Milwaukee (1999-2003), Denver (2004-); **MacLeod**—Phoenix (1973-87), Dallas (1987-89), NY Knicks (1990-91); **Moe**—San Antonio (1976-80), Denver (1981-90), Philadelphia (1992-93).

Motta—Chicago (1968-76), Washington (1976-80), Dallas (1980-87), Sacramento (1990-91), Dallas (1994-96), Denver (1997); **Nelson**—Milwaukee (1976-87), Golden St. (1988-95, 2006—), New York (1995-96), Dallas (1997-2005); **Popovich**— San Antonio (1996—); **Ramsay**—Philadelphia (1968-72), Buffalo (1972-76), Portland (1976-86), Indiana (1986-89); **Riley**—LA Lakers (1981-90), New York (1991-95), Miami (1995-2003, 05-); **Shue**—Baltimore (1967-73), Philadelphia (1973-77), San Diego Clippers (1978-80), Washington (1980-86), LA Clippers (1987-89); **Sloan**—Chicago (1979-82), Utah (1988-); **Tomjanovich**—Houston (1991-2003), LA Lakers (2004-05); **Wilkens**—Seattle (1969-72), Portland (1974-76), Seattle (1977-85), Cleveland (1986-93), Atlanta (1993-2000), Toronto (2000-03), New York (2004-05).

All-Time Winningest NBA Coaches (Cont.)

Top Winning Percentages

Minimum of 350 victories, including playoffs; coaches active during 2006-07 season in **bold** type.

		Yrs	W	L	Pct
1	**Phil Jackson**	16	1098	470	**.700**
2	Billy Cunningham	8	520	235	**.689**
3	**Gregg Popovich**	11	668	327	**.671**
4	K.C. Jones	10	603	309	**.661**
5	Red Auerbach	20	1037	548	**.654**
6	**Pat Riley**	23	1366	738	**.649**
7	Tommy Heinsohn	9	474	296	**.616**
8	Chuck Daly	14	713	488	**.594**
9	Larry Costello	10	467	323	**.591**
10	**Jerry Sloan**	22	1122	777	**.591**
11	John Kundla	11	485	338	**.589**
12	Rick Adelman	16	822	581	**.586**
13	Bill Sharman	7	368	267	**.580**
14	**Phil "Flip" Saunders**	12	565	417	**.575**
15	**George Karl**	19	891	661	**.574**
16	Al Cervi	9	359	267	**.573**
17	**Jeff Van Gundy**	11	474	362	**.567**
18	**Don Nelson**	28	1307	1011	**.564**
19	Joe Lapchick	9	356	277	**.562**
20	Rudy Tomjanovich	13	578	455	**.560**
21	Larry Brown	23	1110	889	**.555**
22	Bill Russell	8	375	317	**.542**
23	Del Harris	14	594	507	**.540**
24	**Mike Fratello**	17	687	590	**.538**
25	Alex Hannum	12	518	446	**.537**
26	Red Holzman	18	754	652	**.536**
27	Doug Moe	15	661	579	**.533**
28	Lenny Wilkens	32	1412	1253	**.530**
29	Richie Guerin	8	353	325	**.521**
30	Jack Ramsay	21	908	841	**.519**

Active Coaches' Victories

Through 2006-07 season, including playoffs.

		Yrs	W	L	Pct
1	Pat Riley, Miami	23	**1366**	738	.649
2	Don Nelson, Golden St.	28	**1307**	1011	.564
3	Jerry Sloan, Utah	22	**1122**	777	.591
4	Phil Jackson, LA Lakers	16	**1098**	470	.700
5	George Karl, Denver	19	**891**	661	.574
6	Rick Adelman, Houston	16	**822**	581	.586
7	Gregg Popovich, San Antonio	11	**668**	327	.671
8	Mike Dunleavy, LA Clippers	14	**588**	590	.499
9	Flip Saunders, Detroit	12	**565**	417	.575
10	Scott Skiles, Chicago	7	**287**	255	.530
11	Doc Rivers, Boston	8	**281**	326	.463
12	Nate McMillan, Portland	7	**273**	302	.475
13	Byron Scott, New Orleans	8	**269**	305	.469
14	Maurice Cheeks, Philadelphia	6	**238**	237	.501
15	Mike D'Antoni, Phoenix	5	**237**	167	.587
16	Eddie Jordan, Washington	6	**192**	253	.431
17	Jim O'Brien, Indiana	5	**189**	158	.535
18	P.J. Carlesimo, Seattle	6	**183**	231	.442
19	Lawrence Frank, New Jersey	4	**175**	149	.540
20	Isiah Thomas, New York	3	**169**	174	.493
21	Avery Johnson, Dallas	3	**165**	59	.737
22	Stan Van Gundy, Orlando	3	**129**	84	.606
23	Mike Brown, Cleveland	2	**119**	78	.604
24	Sam Mitchell, Toronto	3	**109**	143	.433
25	Randy Wittman, Minnesota	3	**74**	132	.359
26	Mike Woodson, Atlanta	3	**69**	177	.280
27	Larry Krystkowiak, Milwaukee	1	**5**	13	.278
28	Marc Iavaroni, Memphis	0	**0**	0	—
	Reggie Theus, Sacramento	0	**0**	0	—
	Sam Vincent, Charlotte	0	**0**	0	—

Annual Awards
Most Valuable Player

The Maurice Podoloff Trophy for regular season MVP. Named after the first commissioner (then president) of the NBA. Winners first selected by the NBA players (1956-80) then a national panel of pro basketball writers and broadcasters (since 1981). Winners' scoring averages are provided; (*) indicates led league.

Multiple winners: Kareem Abdul-Jabbar (6); Michael Jordan and Bill Russell (5); Wilt Chamberlain (4); Larry Bird, Magic Johnson and Moses Malone (3); Tim Duncan, Karl Malone, Steve Nash and Bob Pettit (2).

Year		Avg
1956	Bob Pettit, St. Louis, F	25.7*
1957	Bob Cousy, Boston, G	20.6
1958	Bill Russell, Boston, C	16.6
1959	Bob Pettit, St. Louis, F	29.2*
1960	Wilt Chamberlain, Philadelphia, C	37.6*
1961	Bill Russell, Boston, C	16.9
1962	Bill Russell, Boston, C	18.9
1963	Bill Russell, Boston, C	16.8
1964	Oscar Robertson, Cincinnati, G	31.4
1965	Bill Russell, Boston, C	14.1
1966	Wilt Chamberlain, Philadelphia, C	33.5*
1967	Wilt Chamberlain, Philadelphia, C	24.1
1968	Wilt Chamberlain, Philadelphia, C	24.3
1969	Wes Unseld, Baltimore, C	13.8
1970	Willis Reed, New York, C	21.7
1971	Lew Alcindor, Milwaukee, C	31.7*
1972	Kareem Abdul-Jabbar, Milwaukee, C	34.8*
1973	Dave Cowens, Boston, C	20.5
1974	Kareem Abdul-Jabbar, Milwaukee, C	27.0
1975	Bob McAdoo, Buffalo, F	34.5*
1976	Kareem Abdul-Jabbar, LA, C	27.7
1977	Kareem Abdul-Jabbar, LA, C	26.2
1978	Bill Walton, Portland, C	18.9
1979	Moses Malone, Houston, C	24.8
1980	Kareem Abdul-Jabbar, LA, C	24.8
1981	Julius Erving, Philadelphia, F	24.6

Year		Avg
1982	Moses Malone, Houston, C	31.1
1983	Moses Malone, Philadelphia, C	24.5
1984	Larry Bird, Boston, F	24.2
1985	Larry Bird, Boston, F	28.7
1986	Larry Bird, Boston, F	25.8
1987	Magic Johnson, LAL, G	23.9
1988	Michael Jordan, Chicago, G	35.0*
1989	Magic Johnson, LAL, G	22.5
1990	Magic Johnson, LAL, G	22.3
1991	Michael Jordan, Chicago, G	31.5*
1992	Michael Jordan, Chicago, G	30.1*
1993	Charles Barkley, Phoenix, F	25.6
1994	Hakeem Olajuwon, Houston, C	27.3
1995	David Robinson, San Antonio, C	27.6
1996	Michael Jordan, Chicago, G	30.4*
1997	Karl Malone, Utah, F	27.4
1998	Michael Jordan, Chicago, G	28.7*
1999	Karl Malone, Utah, F	23.8
2000	Shaquille O'Neal, LAL, C	29.7*
2001	Allen Iverson, Philadelphia, G	31.1*
2002	Tim Duncan, San Antonio, F/C	25.5
2003	Tim Duncan, San Antonio, F/C	23.3
2004	Kevin Garnett, Minnesota, F	24.2
2005	Steve Nash, Phoenix, G	15.5
2006	Steve Nash, Phoenix, G	18.8
2007	Dirk Nowitzki, Dallas, F	24.6

Note: Lew Alcindor changed his name to Kareem Abdul-Jabbar after the 1970-71 season.

Rookie of the Year

The Eddie Gottlieb Trophy for outstanding rookie of the regular season. Named after the pro basketball pioneer and owner-coach of the first NBA champion Philadelphia Warriors. Winners selected by a national panel of pro basketball writers and broadcasters. Winners' scoring averages provided; (*) indicates led league; winners who were also named MVP are in **bold** type.

Year		Avg	Year		Avg
1953	Don Meineke, Ft. Wayne, F	10.8	1981	Darrell Griffith, Utah, G	20.6
1954	Ray Felix, Baltimore, C	17.6	1982	Buck Williams, New Jersey, F	15.5
1955	Bob Pettit, Milwaukee Hawks, F	20.4	1983	Terry Cummings, San Diego, F	23.7
1956	Maurice Stokes, Rochester, F/C	16.8	1984	Ralph Sampson, Houston, C	21.0
1957	Tommy Heinsohn, Boston, F	16.2	1985	Michael Jordan, Chicago, G	28.2
1958	Woody Sauldsberry, Philadelphia, F/C	12.8	1986	Patrick Ewing, New York, C	20.0
1959	Elgin Baylor, Minneapolis, F	24.9	1987	Chuck Person, Indiana, F	18.8
1960	**Wilt Chamberlain**, Philadelphia, C	37.6*	1988	Mark Jackson, New York, G	13.6
1961	Oscar Robertson, Cincinnati, G	30.5	1989	Mitch Richmond, Golden St., G	22.0
1962	Walt Bellamy, Chicago Packers, C	31.6	1990	David Robinson, San Antonio, C	24.3
1963	Terry Dischinger, Chicago Zephyrs, F	25.5	1991	Derrick Coleman, New Jersey, F	18.4
1964	Jerry Lucas, Cincinnati, F/C	17.7	1992	Larry Johnson, Charlotte, F	19.2
1965	Willis Reed, New York, C	19.5	1993	Shaquille O'Neal, Orlando,C	23.4
1966	Rick Barry, San Francisco, F	25.7	1994	Chris Webber, Golden St., F	17.5
1967	Dave Bing, Detroit, G	20.0	1995	Grant Hill, Detroit, F	19.9
1968	Earl Monroe, Baltimore, G	24.3		& Jason Kidd, Dallas, G	11.7
1969	**Wes Unseld**, Baltimore, C	13.8	1996	Damon Stoudamire, Toronto, G	19.0
1970	Lew Alcindor, Milwaukee Bucks, C	28.8	1997	Allen Iverson, Philadelphia, G	23.5
1971	Dave Cowens, Boston, C	17.0	1998	Tim Duncan, San Antonio, F/C	21.6
	& Geoff Petrie, Portland, G	24.8	1999	Vince Carter, Toronto, F	18.3
1972	Sidney Wicks, Portland, F	24.5	2000	Elton Brand, Chicago, F	20.1
1973	Bob McAdoo, Buffalo, C/F	18.0		& Steve Francis, Houston, G	18.0
1974	Ernie DiGregorio, Buffalo, G	15.2	2001	Mike Miller, Orlando, G/F	11.9
1975	Keith Wilkes, Golden St., F	14.2	2002	Pau Gasol, Memphis, F	17.6
1976	Alvan Adams, Phoenix, C	19.0	2003	Amare Stoudemire, Phoenix, F	13.5
1977	Adrian Dantley, Buffalo, F	20.3	2004	LeBron James, Cleveland, F	20.9
1978	Walter Davis, Phoenix, G	24.2	2005	Emeka Okafor, Charlotte, C	15.1
1979	Phil Ford, Kansas City, G	15.9	2006	Chris Paul, NO/Okla. City, G	16.1
1980	Larry Bird, Boston, F	21.3	2007	Brandon Roy, Portland, G	16.8

Note: The Chicago Packers changed their name to the Zephyrs after 1961-62 season. Also, Lew Alcindor changed his name to Kareem Abdul-Jabbar after the 1970-71 season.

Number One Draft Choices

Overall first choices in the NBA draft since the abolition of the territorial draft in 1966. Players who became Rookie of the Year are in **bold** type. The draft lottery began in 1985.

Year		Overall 1st Pick	Year		Overall 1st Pick
1966	New York	Cazzie Russell, Michigan	1987	San Antonio	**David Robinson**, Navy
1967	Detroit	Jimmy Walker, Providence	1988	LA Clippers	Danny Manning, Kansas
1968	San Diego	Elvin Hayes, Houston	1989	Sacramento	Pervis Ellison, Louisville
1969	Milwaukee	**Lew Alcindor**, UCLA	1990	New Jersey	**Derrick Coleman**, Syracuse
1970	Detroit	Bob Lanier, St. Bonaventure	1991	Charlotte	**Larry Johnson**, UNLV
1971	Cleveland	Austin Carr, Notre Dame	1992	Orlando	**Shaquille O'Neal**, LSU
1972	Portland	LaRue Martin, Loyola-Chicago	1993	Orlando	**Chris Webber**, Michigan
1973	Philadelphia	Doug Collins, Illinois St.	1994	Milwaukee	Glenn Robinson, Purdue
1974	Portland	Bill Walton, UCLA	1995	Golden St.	Joe Smith, Maryland
1975	Atlanta	David Thompson, N.C. State	1996	Philadelphia	**Allen Iverson**, Georgetown
1976	Houston	John Lucas, Maryland	1997	San Antonio	**Tim Duncan**, Wake Forest
1977	Milwaukee	Kent Benson, Indiana	1998	LA Clippers	Michael Olowokandi, Pacific
1978	Portland	Mychal Thompson, Minnesota	1999	Chicago	**Elton Brand**, Duke
1979	LA Lakers	Magic Johnson, Michigan St.	2000	New Jersey	Kenyon Martin, Cincinnati
1980	Golden St	Joe Barry Carroll, Purdue	2001	Washington	Kwame Brown, Glynn Acad.
1981	Dallas	Mark Aguirre, DePaul	2002	Houston	Yao Ming, China
1982	LA Lakers	James Worthy, N. Carolina	2003	Cleveland	**LeBron James**, St. Vincent/St. Mary
1983	Houston	**Ralph Sampson**, Virginia	2004	Orlando	Dwight Howard, SW Atlanta Christ.
1984	Houston	Akeem Olajuwon, Houston	2005	Milwaukee	Andrew Bogut, Utah
1985	New York	**Patrick Ewing**, Georgetown	2006	Toronto	Andrea Bargnani, Italy
1986	Cleveland	Brad Daugherty, N. Carolina	2007	Portland	Greg Oden, Ohio St.

Note: Lew Alcindor changed his name to Kareem Abdul-Jabbar after the 1970-71 season; Akeem Olajuwon changed his first name to Hakeem in 1991; in 1975 David Thompson signed with Denver of the ABA and did not play for Atlanta; David Robinson joined NBA for 1989-90 season after fulfilling military obligation.

Sixth Man Award

Awarded to the Best Player Off the Bench for the regular season. Winners selected by a national panel of pro basketball writers and broadcasters.

Multiple winners: Kevin McHale, Ricky Pierce and Detlef Schrempf (2).

Year		Year		Year	
1983	Bobby Jones, Phi., F	1992	Detlef Schrempf, Ind., F	2001	Aaron McKie, Phi., G
1984	Kevin McHale, Bos., F	1993	Cliff Robinson, Port., F	2002	Corliss Williamson, Det., F
1985	Kevin McHale, Bos., F	1994	Dell Curry, Char., G	2003	Bobby Jackson, Sac., G
1986	Bill Walton, Bos., F/C	1995	Anthony Mason, NY, F	2004	Antawn Jamison, Dal., F
1987	Ricky Pierce, Mil., G/F	1996	Toni Kukoc, Chi., F	2005	Ben Gordon, Chi., G
1988	Roy Tarpley, Dal., F	1997	John Starks, NY, G	2006	Mike Miller, Mem., G
1989	Eddie Johnson, Pho., F	1998	Danny Manning, Pho., F	2007	Leandro Barbosa, Pho., G
1990	Ricky Pierce, Mil., G/F	1999	Darrell Armstrong, Orl., G		
1991	Detlef Schrempf, Ind., F	2000	Rodney Rogers, Pho., F		

Defensive Player of the Year

Awarded to the Best Defensive Player for the regular season. Winners selected by a national panel of pro basketball writers and broadcasters.

Multiple winners: Dikembe Mutombo and Ben Wallace (4); Mark Eaton, Sidney Moncrief, Alonzo Mourning, Hakeem Olajuwon and Dennis Rodman (2).

Year		Year		Year	
1983	Sidney Moncrief, Mil., G	1992	David Robinson, SA, C	2000	Alonzo Mourning, Mia., C
1984	Sidney Moncrief, Mil., G	1993	Hakeem Olajuwon, Hou., C	2001	Dikembe Mutombo, Atl.-Phi., C
1985	Mark Eaton, Utah, C	1994	Hakeem Olajuwon, Hou., C	2002	Ben Wallace, Det., C/F
1986	Alvin Robertson, SA, G	1995	Dikembe Mutombo, Den., C	2003	Ben Wallace, Det., C/F
1987	Michael Cooper, LAL, F	1996	Gary Payton, Sea., G	2004	Ron Artest, Ind., F
1988	Michael Jordan, Chi., G	1997	Dikembe Mutombo, Atl., C	2005	Ben Wallace, Det., C/F
1989	Mark Eaton, Utah, C	1998	Dikembe Mutombo, Atl., C	2006	Ben Wallace, Det., C/F
1990	Dennis Rodman, Det., F	1999	Alonzo Mourning, Mia., C	2007	Marcus Camby, Den., C
1991	Dennis Rodman, Det., F				

Most Improved Player

Awarded to the Most Improved Player for the regular season. Winners selected by a national panel of pro basketball writers and broadcasters.

Year		Year		Year	
1986	Alvin Robertson, SA, G	1994	Don MacLean, Wash., F	2001	Tracy McGrady, Orl., F
1987	Dale Ellis, Sea., G	1995	Dana Barros, Phi., G	2002	Jermaine O'Neal, Ind., F
1988	Kevin Duckworth, Port., C	1996	Gheorghe Muresan, Wash., C	2003	Gilbert Arenas, G.St., G
1989	Kevin Johnson, Pho., G	1997	Isaac Austin, Miami, C	2004	Zach Randolph, Port., F
1990	Rony Seikaly, Mia., C	1998	Alan Henderson, Atl., F	2005	Bobby Simmons, LAC, F
1991	Scott Skiles, Orl., G	1999	Darrell Armstrong, Orl., G	2006	Boris Diaw, Pho., G
1992	Pervis Ellison, Wash., C	2000	Jalen Rose, Ind., G	2007	Monta Ellis, G. St., G
1993	Mahmoud Abdul-Rauf, Den., G				

Coach of the Year

The Red Auerbach Trophy for outstanding coach of the year. Renamed in 1967 for the former Boston coach who led the Celtics to nine NBA titles. Winners selected by a national panel of pro basketball writers and broadcasters. Previous season and winning season records are provided; (*) indicates division title.

Multiple winners: Don Nelson and Pat Riley (3); Hubie Brown, Bill Fitch, Cotton Fitzsimmons and Gene Shue (2).

Year		Improvement		Year		Improvement	
1963	Harry Gallatin, St. L	.29-51	to 48-32	1986	Mike Fratello, Atl	.34-48	to 50-32
1964	Alex Hannum, SF	.31-49	to 48-32*	1987	Mike Schuler, Port	.40-42	to 49-33
1965	Red Auerbach, Bos	.59-21*	to 61-18*	1988	Doug Moe, Den	.37-45	to 54-28*
1966	Dolph Schayes, Phi	.40-40	to 55-25*	1989	Cotton Fitzsimmons, Pho	.28-54	to 55-27
1967	Johnny Kerr, Chi	.Expan.	to 33-48	1990	Pat Riley, LA Lakers	.57-25*	to 63-19*
1968	Richie Guerin, St. L	.39-42	to 56-26*	1991	Don Chaney, Hou	.41-41	to 52-30
1969	Gene Shue, Balt	.36-46	to 57-25*	1992	Don Nelson, GS	.44-38	to 55-27
1970	Red Holzman, NY	.54-28	to 60-22*	1993	Pat Riley, NY	.51-31	to 60-22
1971	Dick Motta, Chi	.39-43	to 51-31	1994	Lenny Wilkens, Atl	.43-39	to 57-25*
1972	Bill Sharman, LA	.48-34*	to 69-13*	1995	Del Harris, LA Lakers	.33-49	to 48-34
1973	Tommy Heinsohn, Bos	.56-26*	to 68-14*	1996	Phil Jackson, Chi	.47-35	to 72-10*
1974	Ray Scott, Det	.40-42	to 52-30	1997	Pat Riley, Mia	.42-40	to 61-21
1975	Phil Johnson, KC-Omaha	.33-49	to 44-38	1998	Larry Bird, Ind	.39-43	to 58-24
1976	Bill Fitch, Cle	.40-42	to 49-33*	1999	Mike Dunleavy, Port.	.46-36	to 35-15*
1977	Tom Nissalke, Hou	.40-42	to 49-33*	2000	Doc Rivers, Orlando	.33-17	to 41-41
1978	Hubie Brown, Atl	.31-51	to 41-41	2001	Larry Brown, Phila.	.49-33	to 56-26*
1979	Cotton Fitzsimmons, KC	.31-51	to 48-34*	2002	Rick Carlisle, Det	.32-50	to 50-32
1980	Bill Fitch, Bos	.29-53	to 61-21*	2003	Gregg Popovich, SA	.58-24*	to 60-22*
1981	Jack McKinney, Ind	.37-45	to 44-38	2004	Hubie Brown, Mem.	.28-54	to 50-32
1982	Gene Shue, Wash	.39-43	to 43-39	2005	Mike D'Antoni, Pho	.29-53	to 62-30*
1983	Don Nelson, Mil	.55-27*	to 51-31*	2006	Avery Johnson, Dal	.58-24	to 60-22*
1984	Frank Layden, Utah	.30-52	to 45-37*	2007	Sam Mitchell, Tor	.27-55	to 47-35*
1985	Don Nelson, Mil	.50-32*	to 59-23*				

NBA's 50 Greatest Players

In October 1996, as part of its 50th anniversary celebration, the NBA named the 50 greatest players in league history. The voting was done by a league-approved panel of media, former players and coaches, current and former general managers and team executives. The players are listed alphabetically along with the dates of their professional careers and positions. Shaquille O'Neal, the only player active in 2005-06, is in **bold** type.

Player	Pos	Player	Pos	Player	Pos
Kareem Abdul-Jabbar, 1969-89	C	George Gervin, 1972-86	G	Robert Parish, 1976-97	C
Nate Archibald, 1970-84	G	Hal Greer, 1958-73	G	Bob Pettit, 1954-65	F/C
Paul Arizin, 1950-61	F/G	John Havlicek, 1962-78	F/G	Scottie Pippen, 1987-2005	F
Charles Barkley, 1984-00	F	Elvin Hayes, 1968-84	F/C	Willis Reed, 1964-74	C
Rick Barry, 1965-80	F	Magic Johnson, 1979-91, 96	G	Oscar Robertson, 1960-74	G
Elgin Baylor, 1958-72	F	Sam Jones, 1957-69	G	David Robinson, 1989-2003	C
Dave Bing, 1966-78	G	Michael Jordan, 1984-93,	G	Bill Russell, 1956-69	C
Larry Bird, 1979-92	F	95-98, 01-03		Dolph Schayes, 1948-64	F/C
Wilt Chamberlain, 1959-73	C	Jerry Lucas, 1963-74	F/C	Bill Sharman, 1950-61	G
Bob Cousy, 1950-63, 69-70	G	Karl Malone, 1985-2005	F	John Stockton, 1984-2003	G
Dave Cowens, 1970-80, 1982-83	C	Moses Malone, 1974-95	C	Isiah Thomas, 1981-94	G
Billy Cunningham, 1965-76	F	Pete Maravich, 1970-80	G	Nate Thurmond, 1963-77	C/F
Dave DeBusschere, 1962-74	F	Kevin McHale, 1980-93	F	Wes Unseld, 1968-81	C/F
Clyde Drexler, 1983-98	G	George Mikan, 1946-54, 55-56	C	Bill Walton, 1974-88	C
Julius Erving, 1971-87	F	Earl Monroe, 1967-80	G	Jerry West, 1960-74	G
Patrick Ewing, 1985-2002	C	Hakeem Olajuwon, 1984-2002	C	Lenny Wilkens, 1960-75	G
Walt Frazier, 1967-80	G	**Shaquille O'Neal**, 1992—	C	James Worthy, 1982-94	F

Note: Rick Barry, Billy Cunningham, Julius Erving, George Gervin and Moses Malone all played part of their pro careers in the ABA.

NBA's 10 Greatest Coaches

In December 1996, as part of its 50th anniversary celebration, the NBA named the 10 greatest coaches in league history. The voting was done by a league-approved panel of media. The coaches are listed alphabetically along with the dates of their professional coaching careers and overall records, including playoff games, and number of NBA titles won. Active coaches are in **bold** type.

Coach	W	L	Pct.	Titles	Coach	W	L	Pct.	Titles
Red Auerbach, 1946-66	1037	548	.654	9	John Kundla, 1947-59	485	338	.589	5
Chuck Daly, 1981-94, 97-99	.713	488	.594	2	**Don Nelson**, 1976-96,				
Bill Fitch, 1970-98	999	1160	.463		97-05, 06—	1307	1011	.564	0
Red Holzman, 1953-82	.754	652	.536	2	Jack Ramsay, 1968-89	.908	841	.519	1
Phil Jackson, 1989-98,					Pat Riley, 1981-2003, 05—	.1366	738	.649	5
99-04, 05—	1098	470	.700	9	Lenny Wilkens, 1969-2005	.1412	1253	.530	1
					TOTALS	10079	7499	.573	35

World Championships

The World Basketball Championships for men and women have been played regularly at four-year intervals (give or take a year) since 1970. The men's tournament began in 1950 and the women's in 1953. The Federation Internationale de Basketball Amateur (FIBA), which governs the World and Olympic tournaments, was founded in 1932. FIBA first allowed professional players from the NBA to participate in 1994. A team of collegians represented the USA in 1998.

Men

Multiple wins: Yugoslavia (5); Soviet Union and USA (3); Brazil (2).

Year			
1950	**Argentina**, United States, Chile
1954	**United States**, Brazil, Philippines
1959	**Brazil**, United States, Chile
1963	**Brazil**, Yugoslavia, Soviet Union
1967	**Soviet Union**, Yugoslavia, Brazil
1970	**Yugoslavia**, Brazil, Soviet Union
1974	**Soviet Union**, Yugoslavia, United States
1978	**Yugoslavia**, Soviet Union, Brazil
1982	**Soviet Union**, United States, Yugoslavia
1986	**United States**, Soviet Union, Yugoslavia
1990	**Yugoslavia**, Soviet Union, United States
1994	**United States**, Russia, Croatia
1998	**Yugoslavia**, Russia, United States
2002	**Yugoslavia**, Argentina, Germany
2006	**Spain**, Greece, United States
2010	at Turkey

Women

Multiple wins: USA (7); Soviet Union (6).

Year	
1953	**United States**, Chile, France
1957	**United States**, Soviet Union, Czechoslovakia
1959	**Soviet Union**, Bulgaria, Czechoslovakia
1964	**Soviet Union**, Czechoslovakia, Bulgaria
1967	**Soviet Union**, South Korea, Czechoslovakia
1971	**Soviet Union**, Czechoslovakia, Brazil
1975	**Soviet Union**, Japan, Czechoslovakia
1979	**United States**, South Korea, Canada
1983	**Soviet Union**, United States, China
1986	**United States**, Soviet Union, Canada
1990	**United States**, Yugoslavia, Cuba
1994	**Brazil**, China, United States
1998	**United States**, Russia, Australia
2002	**United States**, Russia, Australia
2006	**Australia**, Russia, United States
2010	TBD

American Basketball Association
ABA Finals

The original American Basketball Assn. began play in 1967-68 as a 10-team rival of the 21-year-old NBA. The ABA, which introduced the three-point basket, a multi-colored ball and the All-Star Game Slam Dunk Contest, lasted nine seasons before folding following the 1975-76 season. Four ABA teams—Denver, Indiana, New York and San Antonio—survived to enter the NBA in 1976-77. The NBA also adopted the three-point basket (in 1979-80) and the All-Star Game Slam Dunk Contest. The older league, however, refused to take in the ABA ball.

Multiple winners: Indiana (3); New York (2).

Year	Winner	Head Coach	Series	Loser	Head Coach
1968	Pittsburgh Pipers	Vince Cazzetta	4-3 (WLLWLWVW)	New Orleans Bucs	Babe McCarthy
1969	Oakland Oaks	Alex Hannum	4-1 (WLWVWW)	Indiana Pacers	Bob Leonard
1970	Indiana Pacers	Bob Leonard	4-2 (WWLWLW)	Los Angeles Stars	Bill Sharman
1971	Utah Stars	Bill Sharman	4-3 (WWLLWLW)	Kentucky Colonels	Frank Ramsey
1972	Indiana Pacers	Bob Leonard	4-2 (WLWLWW)	New York Nets	Lou Carnesecca
1973	Indiana Pacers	Bob Leonard	4-3 (WLLWWLW)	Kentucky Colonels	Joe Mullaney
1974	New York Nets	Kevin Loughery	4-1 (WWWLW)	Utah Stars	Joe Mullaney
1975	Kentucky Colonels	Hubie Brown	4-1 (WWWLW)	Indiana Pacers	Bob Leonard
1976	New York Nets	Kevin Loughery	4-2 (WLWWLW)	Denver Nuggets	Larry Brown

Most Valuable Player

Winners' scoring averages provided; (*) indicates led league.

Multiple winners: Julius Erving (3); Mel Daniels (2).

Year		Avg
1968	Connie Hawkins, Pittsburgh, C	.26.8*
1969	Mel Daniels, Indiana, C	.24.0
1970	Spencer Haywood, Denver, C	.30.0*
1971	Mel Daniels, Indiana, C	.21.0
1972	Artis Gilmore, Kentucky, C	.23.8
1973	Billy Cunningham, Carolina, F	.24.1
1974	Julius Erving, New York, F	.27.4*
1975	George McGinnis, Indiana, F	.29.8*
	& Julius Erving, New York, F	27.9
1976	Julius Erving, New York, F	.29.3*

Rookie of the Year

Winners' scoring averages provided; (*) indicates led league. Rookies who were also named Most Valuable Player are in **bold** type.

Year		Avg
1968	Mel Daniels, Minnesota, C	.22.2
1969	Warren Armstrong, Oakland, G	.21.5
1970	**Spencer Haywood**, Denver, C	.30.0*
1971	Dan Issel, Kentucky, C	.29.8*
	& Charlie Scott, Virginia, G	.27.1
1972	**Artis Gilmore**, Kentucky, C	.23.8
1973	Brian Taylor, New York, G	.15.3
1974	Swen Nater, Virginia-SA, C	.14.1
1975	Marvin Barnes, St. Louis, C	.24.0
1976	David Thompson, Denver, F	.26.0

Note: Warren Armstrong changed his name to Warren Jabali after the 1970-71 season.

Coach of the Year

Previous season and winning season records are provided; (*) indicates division title.

Multiple winner: Larry Brown (3).

Year		Improvement	
1968	Vince Cazzetta, Pittsburgh		54-24*
1969	Alex Hannum, Oakland	.22-56	to 60-18*
1970	Joe Belmont, Denver	.44-34	to 51-33*
	& Bill Sharman, LA Stars	.33-45	to 43-41
1971	Al Bianchi, Virginia	.44-40	to 55-29*
1972	Tom Nissalke, Dallas	.30-54	to 42-42
1973	Larry Brown, Carolina	.35-49	to 57-27*
1974	Babe McCarthy, Kentucky	.56-28	to 53-31
	& Joe Mullaney, Utah	.55-29*	to 51-33*
1975	Larry Brown, Denver	.37-47	to 65-19*
1976	Larry Brown, Denver	.65-19*	to 60-24*

Scoring Leaders

Scoring championship decided by per game point average every season.

Multiple winner: Julius Erving (3).

Year		Gm	Avg	Pts
1968	Connie Hawkins, Pittsburgh	.70	1875	26.8
1969	Rick Barry, Oakland	.35	1190	34.0
1970	Spencer Haywood, Denver	.84	2519	30.0
1971	Dan Issel, Kentucky	.83	2480	29.8
1972	Charlie Scott, Virginia	.73	2524	34.6
1973	Julius Erving, Virginia	.71	2268	31.9
1974	Julius Erving, New York	.84	2299	27.4
1975	George McGinnis, Indiana	.79	2353	29.8
1976	Julius Erving, New York	.84	2462	29.3

ABA All-Star Game

The ABA All-Star Game was an Eastern Division vs. Western Division contest from 1968-75. League membership had dropped to seven teams by 1976, the ABA's last season, so the team in first place at the break (Denver) played an All-Star team made up from the other six clubs.

Series: East won 5, West 3 and Denver 1.

Year	Result	Host	Coaches	Most Valuable Player
1968	East 126, West 120	Indiana	Jim Pollard, Babe McCarthy	Larry Brown, New Orleans
1969	West 133, East 127	Louisville	Alex Hannum, Gene Rhodes	John Beasley, Dallas
1970	West 128, East 98	Indiana	Babe McCarthy, Bob Leonard	Spencer Haywood, Denver
1971	East 126, West 122	Carolina	Al Bianchi, Bill Sharman	Mel Daniels, Indiana
1972	East 142, West 115	Louisville	Joe Mullaney, Ladell Andersen	Dan Issel, Kentucky
1973	West 123, East 111	Utah	Ladell Andersen, Larry Brown	Warren Jabali, Virginia
1974	East 128, West 112	Virginia	Babe McCarthy, Joe Mullaney	Artis Gilmore, Kentucky
1975	East 151, West 124	San Antonio	Kevin Loughery, Larry Brown	Freddie Lewis, St. Louis
1976	Denver 144, ABA 138	Denver	Larry Brown, Kevin Loughery	David Thompson, Denver

Continental Basketball Association

Originally named the Eastern Pennsylvania Basketball League when it formed on April 23, 1946, the league changed names several times before becoming known as the Eastern Basketball Association. In 1978, the EBA was redubbed the CBA. The CBA suspended operations following the 2000 season but reorganized for the 2001-02 season.

Multiple champions: Allentown and Wilkes-Barre (8); Yakima/Yakama (5); Scranton, Tampa Bay, and Williamsport (3); Albany, Dakota, La Crosse, Pottsville, Rochester, Sioux Falls and Wilmington (2).

League Champions

Year		Year		Year		Year	
1947	Wilkes-Barre Barons	1964	Camden Bullets	1979	Rochester Zeniths	1995	Yakima Sun Kings
1948	Reading Keys	1965	Allentown Jets	1980	Anchorage Northern	1996	Sioux Falls Skyforce
1949	Pottsville Packers	1966	Wilmington Blue		Knights	1997	Oklahoma City
1950	Williamsport Billies		Bombers	1981	Rochester Zeniths		Calvary
1951	Sunbury Mercuries	1967	Wilmington Blue	1982	Lancaster Lightning	1998	Quad City Thunder
1952	Pottsville Packers		Bombers	1983	Detroit Spirits	1999	Connecticut Pride
1953	Williamsport Billies	1968	Allentown Jets	1984	Albany Patroons	2000	Yakima Sun Kings
1954	Williamsport Billies	1969	Wilkes-Barre Barons	1985	Tampa Bay Thrillers	2001	suspended play
1955	Wilkes-Barre Barons	1970	Allentown Jets	1986	Tampa Bay Thrillers	2002	Dakota Wizards
1956	Wilkes-Barre Barons	1971	Scranton Apollos	1987	Rapid City Thrillers*	2003	Yakima Sun Kings
1957	Scranton Miners	1972	Allentown Jets	1988	Albany Patroons	2004	Dakota Wizards
1958	Wilkes-Barre Barons	1973	Wilkes-Barre Barons	1989	Tulsa Fast Breakers	2005	Sioux Falls Skyforce
1959	Wilkes-Barre Barons	1974	Hartford Capitols	1990	La Crosse Catbirds	2006	Yakama Sun Kings
1960	Easton Madisons	1975	Allentown Jets	1991	Wichita Falls Texans	2007	Yakama Sun Kings
1961	Baltimore Bullets	1976	Allentown Jets	1992	La Crosse Catbirds		
1962	Allentown Jets	1977	Scranton Apollos	1993	Omaha Racers		
1963	Allentown Jets	1978	Wilkes-Barre Barons	1994	Quad City Thunder		

*The Tampa Bay Thrillers moved to Rapid City, S.D. at the end of the 1987 regular season. The Yakima Sun Kings changed the spelling of their name to Yakama after they were purchased by the Yakama Indiana Nation in 2005.

National Basketball Association Development League

The D League was founded in 2001 as an eight-team player and coach development league owned and operated by the NBA. Until recently, the individual teams did not have a direct relationship with NBA clubs but occasionally players and coaches were called up to the NBA. The NBDL champion was determined in a best-of-three championship series for the first two seasons of the league before changing the format to a single-game playoff in 2004.

The league has expanded and contracted in the years since its founding and some franchises have relocated. In 2005, the league dropped the NBDL acronym and officially adopted the name D-League. Also. the NBA announced that each D-League team would now be officially affiliated with one or more NBA teams, making it more of a true minor league system, where players can be sent down to gain experience and called-up when the big league team has a need. In 2006, four teams (The Colorado 14ers, Dakota Wizards, Idaho Stampede and Sioux Falls Skyforce) withdrew from the CBA and ioined the D-League prior to the 2007 season.

League Champions

Multiple champions: Asheville (2).

Year	Champions	Head Coach	Score	Runners-up	Head Coach
2002	Greenville Groove	Milton Barnes	2-0	No. Charleston Lowgators	Alex English
2003	Mobile Revelers	Sam Vincent	2-1 (WLW)	Fayetteville Patriots	Jeff Capel
2004	Asheville Altitude	Joey Meyer	108-106 OT	Huntsville Flight	Ralph Lewis
2005	Asheville Altitude	Joey Meyer	90-67	Columbus Riverdragons	Jeff Malone
2006	Albuquerque Thunderbirds	Michael Cooper	119-108	Fort Worth Flyers	Sam Vincent
2007	Dakota Wizards	Dave Joerger	129-121	Colorado 14ers	Joe Wolf

Annual Awards

Most Valuable Player

Winner's scoring averages provided; (*) indicates led league.

Year		PPG
2002	Ansu Sesay, Greenville, F	16.5
2003	Devin Brown, Fayetteville, G	16.9
2004	Tierre Brown, Charleston, G	18.6
2005	Matt Carroll, Roanoke, G	20.1*
2006	Marcus Fizer, Austin, F	22.7
2007	Randy Livingston, Idaho, G	12.3

Rookie of the Year

Year	
2002	Fred House, N. Charleston
2003	Devin Brown, Fayetteville
2004	Desmond Penigar, Asheville
2005	James Thomas, Roanoke
2006	Will Bynum, Roanoke
2007	Louis Amundson, Colorado

Defensive Player of the Year

Year	
2002	Jeff Myers, Greenville
2003	Mikki Moore, Roanoke
2004	Karim Shabazz, Charleston
2005	Derrick Zimmerman, Columbus
2006	Derrick Zimmerman, Austin
2007	Renaldo Major, Dakota

Scoring Champion

Scoring championship decided by per game point average every season.

Year		PPG
2002	Isaac Fontaine, Mobile	17.4
2003	Nate Johnson, Columbus	19.5
2004	Desmond Penigar, Asheville	19.6
2005	Isiah Victor, Roanoke	19.5
2006	Bracey Wright, Florida	22.0
2007	Roger Powell, Arkansas	22.3

WOMEN
Women's National Basketball Association

The WNBA, owned and operated by the NBA, began play in 1997 as an eight-team summer league. The league added two teams prior to its second season (1998), then added two more teams before its third season in 1999. Four additional teams were added before the 2000 season, bringing the total number of teams to 16. Prior to the 2003 season two franchises were relocated and two were contracted and one franchise folded before the 2004 season. One team (Chicago Sky) was added for the 2006 season bringing the total back to 14. The WNBA champion was determined by a single-game playoff in the league's 1997 inaugural season, before going to a best-of-three championship series in 1998 and a best-of-five championship series starting in 2005. **Multiple winners:** Houston (4); Detroit and Los Angeles (2).

Year	Champions	Head Coach	Series	Runners-up	Head Coach
1997	Houston Comets	Van Chancellor	65-51	New York Liberty	Nancy Darsch
1998	Houston Comets	Van Chancellor	2-1 (LWW)	Phoenix Mercury	Cheryl Miller
1999	Houston Comets	Van Chancellor	2-1 (WLW)	New York Liberty	Richie Adubato
2000	Houston Comets	Van Chancellor	2-0	New York Liberty	Richie Adubato
2001	Los Angeles Sparks	Michael Cooper	2-0	Charlotte Sting	Anne Donovan
2002	Los Angeles Sparks	Michael Cooper	2-0	New York Liberty	Richie Adubato
2003	Detroit Shock	Bill Laimbeer	2-1 (LWW)	Los Angeles Sparks	Michael Cooper
2004	Seattle Storm	Anne Donovan	2-1 (LWW)	Connecticut Sun	Mike Thibault
2005	Sacramento Monarchs	John Whisenant	3-1 (WLWW)	Connecticut Sun	Mike Thibault
2006	Detroit Shock	Bill Laimbeer	3-2 (LWLWW)	Sacramento Monarchs	John Whisenant
2007	Phoenix Mercury	Paul Westhead	3-2 (LWLWW)	Dertoit Shock	Bill Laimbeer

Championship MVPs: 1997-Cynthia Cooper, Houston; 1998-Cynthia Cooper, Houston; 1999-Cynthia Cooper, Houston; 2000-Cynthia Cooper, Houston; 2001-Lisa Leslie, Los Angeles; 2002-Lisa Leslie, Los Angeles; 2003-Ruth Riley, Detroit; 2004-Betty Lennox, Seattle; 2005-Yolanda Griffith, Sacramento; 2006-Deanna Nolan, Detroit; 2007-Cappie Pondexter, Phoenix.

Annual Awards

Most Valuable Player

Winner's scoring averages provided; (*) indicates led league.
Multiple winners: Sheryl Swoopes and Lisa Leslie (3); Cynthia Cooper (2).

Year		Avg
1997	Cynthia Cooper, Houston	22.2*
1998	Cynthia Cooper, Houston	22.7*
1999	Yolanda Griffith, Sacramento	18.8
2000	Sheryl Swoopes, Houston	20.7*
2001	Lisa Leslie, Los Angeles	19.5
2002	Sheryl Swoopes, Houston	18.5
2003	Lauren Jackson, Seattle	21.2*
2004	Lisa Leslie, Los Angeles	17.6
2005	Sheryl Swoopes, Houston	18.6*
2006	Lisa Leslie, Los Angeles	20.0
2007	Lauren Jackson, Seattle	23.8*

Coach of the Year

Previous season and winning season's record are provided; (*) indicates division title.
Multiple winner: Van Chancellor (3).

Year		Improvement
1997	Van Chancellor, Houston	18-10*
1998	Van Chancellor, Houston	18-10 to 27-3*
1999	Van Chancellor, Houston	27-3 to 26-6*
2000	Michael Cooper, Los Angeles	20-12 to 28-4*
2001	Dan Hughes, Cleveland	17-15 to 22-10*
2002	Marianne Stanley, Washington	10-22 to 17-15
2003	Bill Laimbeer, Detroit	9-23 to 25-9*
2004	Suzie McConnell Serio, Minn.	18-16 to 18-16
2005	John Whisenant, Sacramento	18-16 to 25-9*
2006	Mike Thibault, Connecticut	26-8 to 26-8*
2007	Dan Hughes, San Antonio	13-21 to 20-14

Rookie of the Year

Year		Year	
1998	Tracy Reid, Cha	2003	Cheryl Ford, Det
1999	Chamique Holdsclaw, Wash	2004	Diana Taurasi, Pho
2000	Betty Lennox, Minn	2005	Temeka Johnson, Was
2001	Jackie Stiles, Port	2006	Seimone Augustus, Minn
2002	Tamika Catchings, Ind	2007	Armintie Price, Chi.

Defensive Player of the Year

Multiple winners: Sheryl Swoopes (3); Tamika Catchings and Teresa Weatherspoon (2).

Year		Year	
1997	T. Weatherspoon, NY	2003	Sheryl Swoopes, Hou
1998	T. Weatherspoon, NY	2004	Lisa Leslie, LA
1999	Yolanda Griffith, Sac	2005	Tamika Catchings, Ind
2000	Sheryl Swoopes, Hou	2006	Tamika Catchings, Ind
2001	Debbie Black, Mia	2007	Lauren Jackson, Sea.
2002	Sheryl Swoopes, Hou		

WNBA Number One Draft Picks

Year		Overall First Pick
1997	Utah Starzz	Dena Head
1998	Utah Starzz	Margo Dydek
1999	Washington Mystics	Chamique Holdsclaw
2000	Cleveland Rockers	Ann Wauters
2001	Seattle Storm	Lauren Jackson
2002	Seattle Storm	Sue Bird
2003	Cleveland Rockers	LaToya Thomas
2004	Phoenix Mercury	Diana Taurasi
2005	Charlotte Sting	Janel McCarville
2006	Minnesota Lynx	Seimone Augustus
2007	Phoenix Mercury	Lindsey Harding

American Basketball League (1997-98)
League Champions

Each ABL champion's wins and losses are noted in parentheses after the series score. Due largely to competition from the WNBA, the ABL folded before the 1999 season.

Year	Champions	Head Coach	Series	Runners-up	Head Coach
1997	Columbus Quest	Brian Agler	3-2 (WLLWW)	Richmond Rage	Lisa Boyer
1998	Columbus Quest	Brian Agler	3-2 (LLWWW)	Long Beach StingRays	Maura McHugh

Most Valuable Player

Year		PPG
1997	Nikki McCray, Columbus	19.9
1998	Natalie Williams, Portland	21.9

Coach of the Year

Year		Improvement
1997	Brian Agler, Columbus	31-9
1998	Lin Dunn, Portland	14-26 to 27-17

HOCKEY

2006 / 2007 YEAR IN REVIEW

In his second season, Pittsburgh's **Sidney Crosby** led the NHL with 120 points, then netted the Hart trophy as league MVP.

CALIFORNIA DREAMING

With a smothering defense led by Chris Pronger and Scott Niedermayer, the Anaheim Ducks took the Stanley Cup back to Cali.

WHEN BRIAN BURKE ARRIVED IN Anaheim to take the Ducks' general manager's position in 2005, the gruff but shrewd executive promised he would deliver an attacking, entertaining team that played on the edge.

He wasn't kidding.

Less than two years after accepting the job, Burke's tough and talented Ducks rolled over and through their four playoff opponents – losing just five games – en route to the franchise's first-ever championship.

In doing so, they became the first California-based team to win the Stanley Cup. That accomplishment, coaches will tell you, is quite significant considering the extra travel that West Coast teams must endure during a long NHL campaign. Those frequent trips cut into a player's rest and limit the team's practice time.

Burke's Ducks were a bit unique for another reason. They were the first team since the mid-1970s Flyers (you remember the Broad Street Bullies, right?) to win a Cup while leading the league in penalties. These belligerent Ducks – with big young kids like Ryan Getzlaf, Corey Perry and Dustin Penner – were eager to crash your crease and challenge you physically. They were the team envisioned by Burke and sternly directed by no-nonsense head coach Randy Carlyle.

Still, in the final analysis, these Ducks went the Stanley Cup distance because they possessed a pair of cornerstone defenders – Scott Niedermayer and Chris Pronger.

Niedermayer, a three-time Cup winner in New Jersey, came West via free agency in the summer of '05 to join his younger brother, Rob, with the Ducks. That acquisition was Burke's first major move to reshape the club. Clearly, Burke drew an inside straight in dealing with the ex-Devil star because he was the only GM who could reunite the Brothers Niedermayer. Once signed, Burke quickly slapped the captain's "C" on Scott's sweater and pointed the team in a different direction.

Less than a year later (in the summer of 2006), after Pronger had demanded a trade out of Edmonton, Burke quickly made a bold pitch to Oilers GM Kevin Lowe.

He offered a package of young players, prospects and draft picks for Pronger, a 6'6" defenseman with an intimidating presence to go along with excellent puck skills. Not wanting to endure a protracted battle with Pronger, Lowe accepted the deal.

 E.J. Hradek is a senior hockey writer for ESPN The Magazine.

Niedermayer!!! Anaheim captain **Scott**, right, had the rare honor of passing the Cup to his brother **Rob** after the Ducks' five-game Finals victory.

With the silky-smooth Niedermayer and hard-edged Pronger together on the same blue line, Burke figured opponents would have a very difficult time sustaining a forecheck against the Ducks. In simpler terms, with one of those guys on the ice for most of the game, he knew the puck wouldn't be spending too much time in the Ducks' defensive zone.

He also knew that his dynamic defensive duo could ignite the club's offense with their ability to skate or pass the puck quickly to forwards like Teemu Selanne or Andy McDonald, who, in their own right, could attack the opposing blue line with speed, creating turnovers and scoring chances deep in enemy territory.

The Ducks' new formula helped them to a terrific 12-0-4 start. They didn't suffer their first regulation loss until Nov. 10 and they took a 19-2-6 into the month of December. After Christmas, however, they were hit with a string of injuries that sidelined both of their star defenders, as well as goalies Jean-Sebastien Giguere and Ilya Bryzgalov.

The team staggered through January and February, going a pedestrian 9-10-4 in that two-month window. But as they got healthy in the closing weeks of the season, they began to right their listing ship. The Ducks finished the season with a six-game unbeaten streak and seemed ready for the playoff challenge.

In the first round, despite being without Giguere, the Ducks used their muscle to bounce the Minnesota Wild in five tight games. Then, in the second round, they dispatched Burke's former club, the Vancouver Canucks, also in a five-game series.

In the Western Conference final, however, they ran into a speed bump in red and white. The Detroit Red Wings, hardened by early-round wins over the Calgary Flames and San

AP/Wide World Photos

Islanders tough guy **Chris Simon** leveled Ranger Ryan Hollweg with a nasty two-handed swing to the face, earning him a 25-game suspension.

tie the game with just 47 seconds on the clock.

In overtime, an opportunistic Selanne pounced on a turnover by Wings defender Andreas Lilja and rifled a shot over a sliding Hasek to secure the critical win.

Back on home ice in Game 6, the Ducks built two three-goal leads, but still had to fight off a late Wings' rally to clinch the series. The victory set up a finals showdown with the Ottawa Senators, who were coached by former Ducks coach/GM Bryan Murray. The Senators had been equally impressive en route to the finals, winning each of their series in five games.

A nine-day layoff and the long trip to California seemed to take some of the starch out of the Senators, though. The Ducks took the rest of it. Anaheim won a pair of one-goal games on home ice to take a 2-0 series lead. In Game 3, the Senators grabbed a 5-3 win and Pronger again ran afoul of the league's lawmakers, earning another one-game suspension. The Ducks responded with a 3-2 win as defenseman Francois Beauchemin, another Burke acquisition, stepped up to fill the void.

With a 3-1 series lead, Ducks fans readied for a big celebration. And, they weren't disappointed. The Ducks rolled to an easy 6-2 victory to clinch the title in five games. Conn Smythe Trophy winner Scott Niedermayer accepted the Cup on behalf of his team, then immediately passed the trophy to his brother, who'd been denied that opportunity in two previous trips to the finals.

In just two years, Burke had assembled a champion in Southern California. He did it with some good fortune and a vision of how he wanted his team to play. With a Cup now on his resume, Burke won't be changing that vision anytime soon.

Jose Sharks, were ready for the battle. The clubs split the first four games; the Ducks winning Game 4 without Pronger, who served a one-game suspension for a nasty hit on Wings' forward Tomas Holmstrom.

In Game 5, down 1-0 in the final minute of regulation time, the Ducks found themselves on the power play. Sensing the desperation of the moment, Carlyle gave his team a two-man advantage when he pulled his goalie. The move paid off and the Ducks caught a break when a Scott Niedermayer shot deflected off the stick of defenseman Nicklas Lidstrom and fluttered over the shoulder of Wings' goalie Dominik Hasek to

E.J. HRADEK'S

10 ⬇

Biggest Stories of the
Year in **Hockey**

10 The Great Outdoors.
On Sept. 17, after several months of speculation, the league announces it is going back to its roots for a New Year's Day (2008) outdoor game between the Pittsburgh Penguins and Buffalo Sabres at Ralph Wilson Stadium in Buffalo. It will be the league's second outdoor game (2003 Edm. vs Mon). The idea seemed to be a hit with fans, who bought up the tickets in just 40 minutes.

09 London Nights.
The defending champion Anaheim Ducks and Los Angeles Kings open the 2007-08 regular season with a pair of games at the O2 Arena in London, England. The two-game series begins some debate about the future viability of having NHL franchises in Europe. The Ducks and Kings split the two games.

08 Law And Order.
The league continues its ongoing effort to police the game by issuing several suspensions for on-ice misconduct. In March, NHL VP of Hockey Operations Colin Campbell slapped a 25-game ban on New York Islanders forward Chris Simon for an ugly stick-swinging incident against the New York Rangers. In September, Campbell issued a 20-game suspension to Philadelphia Flyers rookie forward Steve Downie for a dangerous hit on Ottawa Senators winger Dean McAmmond.

07 Business As Usual.
In July, Edmonton Oilers General Manager Kevin Lowe irritates some of his peers around the league (particularly in Buffalo and Anaheim) by issuing big-money offer sheets to restricted free agents Thomas Vanek and Dustin Penner.

In the past, GMs rarely opted to raid another club's RFAs. The Sabres opt to match the offer and keep Vanek, while the Ducks decide to wave goodbye to Penner, accepting draft pick compensation. Lowe's moves may have signaled a change in the league's business practices.

06 The 600-Club.
New York Rangers teammates Jaromir Jagr and Brendan Shanahan, as well as Colorado Avalanche captain Joe Sakic, join an exclusive club during the 2006-07 season. The three superstars each crack the 600-goal mark. Including Jagr, Shanahan and Sakic, there are just 17 players in league history to reach that lofty number.

05 Class With Class.

With several of the game's icons first-time eligible for Hall of Fame induction, the 18-man selection committee had some tough choices. On June 28, after some deliberation, they elect a mega-class which includes Mark Messier, Ron Francis, Scott Stevens and Al MacInnis. The superstars are inducted in Toronto on Nov. 12.

04 L'Affair Saskin.

On May 10, the NHL Players' Association vote unanimously to fire Executive Director Ted Saskin with more than three years remaining on his contract. Saskin had been under increasing pressure since taking over for Bob Goodenow in 2005. The final decision came after the players learned that Saskin and Ken Kim, the NHLPA's head of business development, had monitored player e-mails through the union's web server.

03 America's Star.

On March 17, in a road game against the Nashville Predators, Dallas Stars center Mike Modano, 37, nets the 502nd and 503rd goals of his career to become the NHL's all-time leading goal-scorer among American-born players. Modano, a Michigan native, surpasses the mark set by Hall of Fame right wing Joe Mullen.

02 The Crosby Show, Episode II.

In his sophomore season, Pittsburgh Penguins center Sidney Crosby, 19, takes his game to another level. He leads the Pens to their first playoff appearance since 2001 (albeit a first-round loss to Ottawa) and racks up a league-high 120 points to become the youngest player in league history to win the Art Ross Trophy. On June 14, Crosby becomes the second youngest player to win the Hart Trophy as league Most Valuable Player. And, his peers vote him the league's outstanding player (Lester B. Pearson Award).

01 California Cup.

On June 6, the Anaheim Ducks clinch their first-ever Stanley Cup with a 6-2 victory over the Ottawa Senators in Game 5 of the final series. It marks the first time in league history the Cup is captured by a California club. Ducks defenseman Scott Niedermayer is awarded the Conn Smythe Trophy as playoff MVP. And, as team captain, he enjoys the rare opportunity of passing the Cup to his younger brother/teammate, Rob.

2006-2007
Season in Review

SPORTS ALMANAC

Final NHL Standings

Division champions (*) and playoff qualifiers (†) are noted. Teams get two points for a win and one point for an overtime loss (OL) and a shootout loss (SL). Number of seasons listed after each head coach refers to current tenure with club through 2006-07 season.

Western Conference

Central Division

	W	L	OL	SL	Pts	GF	GA
*Detroit	50	19	5	8	113	254	199
†Nashville	51	23	3	5	110	272	212
St. Louis	34	35	7	6	81	214	254
Columbus	33	42	2	5	73	201	249
Chicago	31	42	2	7	71	201	258

Head Coaches: Det—Mike Babcock (2nd season); **Nash**—Barry Trotz (8th); **St.L**—Mike Kitchen (3rd, 7-17-4) was fired on Dec. 11 and replaced by Andy Murray (27-18-9); **Clb**—Gerard Gallant (3rd, 5-9-1) was fired on Nov. 13 and replaced by asst. Gary Agnew (0-4-1), then Ken Hitchcock (28-29-5) on Nov. 23; **Chi**—Trent Yawney (2nd, 7-12-2) was fired on Nov. 27 and replaced by Denis Savard (24-30-7).

Northwest Division

	W	L	OL	SL	Pts	GF	GA
*Vancouver	49	26	3	4	105	222	201
†Minnesota	48	26	1	7	104	235	191
†Calgary	43	29	5	5	96	258	226
Colorado	44	31	3	4	95	272	251
Edmonton	32	43	4	3	71	195	248

Head Coaches: Van—Alain Vigneault (1st season); **Min**—Jacques Lemaire (6th); **Calg**—Jim Playfair (1st); **Col**—Joel Quenneville (2nd); **Edm**—Craig MacTavish (6th).

Pacific Division

	W	L	OL	SL	Pts	GF	GA
*Anaheim	48	20	4	10	110	258	208
†San Jose	51	26	3	2	107	258	199
†Dallas	50	25	3	4	107	226	197
Los Angeles	27	41	8	6	68	227	283
Phoenix	31	46	3	2	67	216	284

Head Coaches: Ana—Randy Carlyle (2nd season); **SJ**—Ron Wilson (4th); **Dal**—Dave Tippett (4th); **LA**—Marc Crawford (1st); **Pho**—Wayne Gretzky (2nd).

Eastern Conference

Northeast Division

	W	L	OL	SL	Pts	GF	GA
*Buffalo	53	22	3	4	113	308	242
†Ottawa	48	25	3	6	105	288	222
Toronto	40	31	4	7	91	258	269
Montreal	42	34	1	6	90	245	256
Boston	35	41	2	4	76	219	289

Head Coaches: Buf—Lindy Ruff (9th season); **Ott**—Bryan Murray (2nd); **Tor**—Paul Maurice (1st); **Mon**—Guy Carbonneau (1st); **Bos**—Dave Lewis (1st).

Atlantic Division

	W	L	OL	SL	Pts	GF	GA
*New Jersey	49	24	1	8	107	216	201
†Pittsburgh	47	24	5	6	105	277	246
†NY Rangers	42	30	5	5	94	242	216
†NY Islanders	40	30	7	5	92	248	240
Philadelphia	22	48	6	6	56	214	303

Head Coaches: NJ—Claude Julien (1st season, 47-24-8) was fired on April 2 and replaced by GM Lou Lamoriello (2-0-1); **Pit**—Michel Therrien (2nd); **NYR**—Tom Renney (3rd); **NYI**—Ted Nolan (1st); **Phi**—Ken Hitchcock (4th, 1-6-1) was fired on Oct. 22 and replaced by asst. John Stevens (21-42-11).

Southeast Division

	W	L	OL	SL	Pts	GF	GA
*Atlanta	43	28	7	4	97	246	245
†Tampa Bay	44	33	3	2	93	253	261
Carolina	40	34	3	5	88	241	253
Florida	35	31	8	8	86	247	257
Washington	28	40	3	11	70	235	286

Head Coaches: Atl—Bob Hartley (4th season); **TB**—John Tortorella (6th); **Car**—Peter Laviolette (3rd); **Fla**—Jacques Martin (2nd); **Wash**—Glen Hanlon (3rd).

Home & Away, Division Records

Sixteen teams—eight from each conference—qualify for the Stanley Cup Playoffs; (*) indicates division champions.

Western Conference

		Pts	Home	Away	Div
1	Detroit*	113	29-4-8	21-15-5	22-4-6
2	Anaheim*	110	26-6-9	22-14-5	19-8-5
3	Vancouver*	105	26-11-4	23-15-3	16-13-3
4	Nashville	110	28-8-5	23-15-3	21-8-3
5	San Jose	107	25-12-4	26-14-1	18-13-1
6	Dallas	107	28-11-2	22-14-5	24-7-1
7	Minnesota	104	29-7-5	19-19-3	18-8-6
8	Calgary	96	30-9-2	13-20-8	17-12-3
	Colorado	95	22-16-3	22-15-4	18-11-3
	St. Louis	81	18-19-4	16-16-9	12-16-4
	Columbus	73	18-19-4	15-23-3	11-17-4
	Edmonton	71	19-19-3	13-24-4	11-20-1
	Chicago	71	17-20-4	14-22-5	14-17-1
	Los Angeles	68	16-16-9	11-25-5	10-18-4
	Phoenix	67	18-20-3	13-26-2	9-18-5

Eastern Conference

		Pts	Home	Away	Div
1	Buffalo*	113	28-10-3	25-12-4	18-11-3
2	New Jersey*	107	25-10-6	24-14-3	23-6-3
3	Atlanta*	97	23-12-6	20-16-5	18-7-7
4	Ottawa	105	25-13-3	23-12-6	19-10-3
5	Pittsburgh	105	26-10-5	21-14-6	20-9-3
6	NY Rangers	94	21-15-5	21-15-5	15-12-5
7	Tampa Bay	93	22-18-1	22-15-4	19-11-2
8	NY Islanders	92	22-13-6	18-17-6	17-11-4
	Toronto	91	21-15-5	19-16-6	13-14-5
	Montreal	90	26-12-3	16-22-3	16-12-4
	Carolina	88	21-16-4	19-18-4	19-11-2
	Florida	86	22-15-6	12-19-10	13-14-5
	Boston	76	18-19-4	17-22-2	14-17-1
	Washington	70	17-17-7	11-23-7	11-15-6
	Philadelphia	56	10-24-7	12-24-5	5-20-7

Pittsburgh Penguins
Sidney Crosby
Scoring

Tampa Bay Lightning
Vincent Lecavalier
Goals

Anaheim Ducks
Scott Niedermayer
Defensemen Points

New Jersey Devils
Martin Brodeur
Wins, ShO, Min.

NHL Regular Season Individual Leaders

(*) indicates rookie eligible for Calder Trophy.

Scoring

	Pos	Gm	G	A	Pts	+/-	PM	PP	SH	GW	Shots	Pct
Sidney Crosby, Pittsburgh	C	79	36	84	**120**	10	60	13	0	4	250	14.4
Joe Thornton, San Jose	C	82	22	92	**114**	24	44	10	0	5	213	10.3
Vincent Lecavalier, Tampa Bay	C	82	52	56	**108**	2	44	16	5	7	339	15.3
Dany Heatley, Ottawa	R	82	50	55	**105**	31	74	17	3	10	310	16.1
Martin St. Louis, Tampa Bay	R	82	43	59	**102**	7	28	14	5	7	273	15.8
Marian Hossa, Atlanta	R	82	43	57	**100**	18	49	17	3	5	340	12.6
Joe Sakic, Colorado	C	82	36	64	**100**	2	46	16	0	4	258	14.0
Jaromir Jagr, NY Rangers	R	82	30	66	**96**	26	78	7	0	5	324	9.3
Marc Savard, Boston	C	82	22	74	**96**	-19	96	10	1	3	221	10.0
Daniel Briere, Buffalo	C	81	32	63	**95**	17	89	9	0	6	234	13.7
Teemu Selanne, Anaheim	R	82	48	46	**94**	26	82	25	0	10	257	18.7
Jarome Iginla, Calgary	R	70	39	55	**94**	12	40	13	1	7	264	14.8
Alexander Ovechkin, Washington	L	82	46	46	**92**	-19	52	16	0	8	392	11.7
Olli Jokinen, Florida	C	82	39	52	**91**	18	78	9	1	8	351	11.1
Jason Spezza, Ottawa	C	67	34	53	**87**	19	45	13	1	5	162	21.0
Daniel Alfredsson, Ottawa	R	77	29	58	**87**	42	42	7	2	7	240	12.1
Pavel Datsyuk, Detroit	C	79	27	60	**87**	36	20	5	2	5	207	13.0
Evgeni Malkin*, Pittsburgh	L	78	33	52	**85**	2	80	16	0	6	242	13.6
Thomas Vanek, Buffalo	L	82	43	41	**84**	47	40	15	0	5	237	18.1
Daniel Sedin, Vancouver	L	81	36	48	**84**	-19	36	16	0	8	236	15.3

Goals

Lecavalier, TB	52
Heatley, Ott	50
Selanne, Ana	48
Ovechkin, Wash	46
Hossa, Atl	43
St. Louis, TB	43
Vanek, Buf	43
Kovalchuk, Atl	42
Gagne, Phi	41
Blake, NYI	40
Iginla, Calg	39
Jokinen, Fla	39

Assists

Thornton, SJ	92
Crosby, Pit	84
Savard, Bos	74
H. Sedin, Van	71
Jagr, NYR	66
Sakic, Col	64
Briere, Buf	63
Datsyuk, Det	60
Tanguay, Calg	59
St. Louis, TB	59
Alfredsson, Ott	58
Two tied with 57.	

Defensemen Points

S. Niedermayer, Ana	69
Gonchar, Pit	67
Souray, Mon	64
Boyle, TB	63
Lidstrom, Det	62
Whitney, Pit	59
Pronger, Ana	59
Visnovsky, LA	58
Kaberle, Tor	58
McCabe, Tor	57
Two tied with 55.	

Rookie Points

Malkin, Pit	85
Stastny, Col	78
Kopitar, LA	61
Wolski, Col	50
Penner, Ana	45
Staal, Pit	42
Zajac, NJ	42
Carle, SJ	42
Radulov, Nash	37
Clowe, SJ	34
Latendresse, Mon	29
Kessel, Bos	29

Plus/Minus

Vanek, Buf	47
Alfredsson, Ott	42
Lidstrom, Det	40
Preissing, Ott	40
Roy, Pit	37
Volchenkov, Ott	37
Datsyuk, Det	36
Phillips, Ott	36
Malik, NYR	32

Game Winning Goals

Zetterberg, Det	10
Selanne, Ana	10
Heatley, Ott	10
Drury, Buf	9
Marleau, SJ	9
Michalek, SJ	9
Five tied with 8.	

Power Play Goals

Selanne, Ana	25
Souray, Mon	19
Kovalchuk, Atl	18
Drury, Buf	17
Semin, Wash	17
Hossa, Atl	17
Ryder, Mon	17
Heatley, Ott	17

Short-Handed Goals

Staal*, Pit	7
Draper, Det	5
St. Louis, TB	5
Lecavalier, TB	5
Five tied with 4.	

Shots

Ovechkin, Wash	.392
Jokinen, Fla	.351
Hossa, Atl	.340
Lecavalier, TB	.339
Kovalchuk, Atl	.336
Jagr, NYR	.324
Sundin, Tor	.321
Heatley, Ott	.310
Blake, NYI	.305
Rolston, Min	.305
Cammalleri, LA	.299

Shooting Pct.
(Min. 82 shots)

Staal*, Pit	.22.1
Spezza, Ott	.21.0
Tanguay, Calg	.20.6
Huselius, Calg	.19.7
Radulov*, Nash	.18.8
Selanne, Ana	.18.7
Drury, Buf	.18.6
Clark, Wash	.18.3
Vanek, Buf	.18.1
Sullivan, Nash	.18.0

Penalty Minutes

Eager*, Phi	.233
Gratton*, Pho	.188
Neil, Ott	.177
O'Brien*, Ana-TB	.176
Avery, LA-NYR	.174
Brashear, Wash	.156
Svitov, Clb	.145
Ivanans, LA	.140
Boynton, Pho	.138
Souray, Mon	.135
Bieksa, Van	.134

Minutes/Game
(Min. 50 Games)

Chara, Bos	.27:57
S. Niedermayer, Ana	27:30
Lidstrom, Det	.27:29
Pronger, Ana	.27:05
Boyle, TB	.27:03
McCabe, Tor	.26:49
Gonchar, Pit	.26:33
Bouwmeester, Fla	.26:08
Zubov, Dal	.25:56
Kaberle, Tor	.25:52

Goaltending
(Minimum 25 games)

	Gm	Min	GAA	Record	GA	Shots	Sv%	EN	Sho	G	A	Pts	PM
Niklas Backstrom, Minnesota	.41	2227	**1.97**	23-8-6	73	1028	.929	1	5	0	1	1	2
Dominik Hasek, Detroit	.56	3341	**2.05**	38-11-6	114	1309	.913	2	8	0	2	2	20
Martin Brodeur, New Jersey	.78	4697	**2.18**	48-23-7	171	2182	.922	5	12	0	1	1	12
Marty Turco, Dallas	.67	3764	**2.23**	38-20-5	140	1564	.910	5	6	0	4	4	18
Jean-Sebastien Giguere, Anaheim	.56	3245	**2.26**	36-10-8	122	1490	.918	1	4	0	2	2	0
Roberto Luongo, Vancouver	.76	4490	**2.28**	47-22-6	171	2169	.921	3	5	0	2	2	10
Evgeni Nabokov, San Jose	.50	2778	**2.29**	25-16-4	106	2778	.914	4	7	0	0	0	6
Henrik Lundqvist, NY Rangers	.70	4109	**2.34**	37-22-8	160	1927	.917	2	5	0	0	0	0
Vesa Toskala, San Jose	.38	2142	**2.35**	26-10-1	84	915	.908	3	4	0	3	3	0
Chris Mason, Nashville	.40	2342	**2.38**	24-11-4	93	1244	.925	5	5	0	1	1	4
Tomas Vokoun, Nashville	.44	2601	**2.40**	27-12-4	104	1299	.920	3	5	0	2	2	4
Miikka Kiprusoff, Calgary	.74	4419	**2.46**	40-24-9	181	2190	.917	6	7	0	0	0	2
Ilya Bryzgalov, Anaheim	.27	1509	**2.47**	10-8-6	62	668	.907	0	1	0	0	0	0
Ray Emery, Ottawa	.58	3351	**2.47**	33-16-6	138	1691	.918	3	5	0	1	1	30
Manny Fernandez, Minnesota	.44	2422	**2.55**	22-16-1	103	1158	.911	0	2	0	0	0	12

Wins

Brodeur, NJ	.48
Luongo, Van	.47
Kiprusoff, Calg	.40
Fleury, Pit	.40
Miller, Buf	.40
Turco, Dal	.38
Hasek, Det	.38
Raycroft, Tor	.37
Lundqvist, NYR	.37
Giguere, Ana	.36
Lehtonen, Atl	.34

Shutouts

Brodeur, NJ	.12
Hasek, Det	.8
Kiprusoff, Calg	.7
Nabokov, SJ	.7
Turco, Dal	.6
Nine tied with 5.	

Save Pct.

Backstrom, Min	.929
Mason, Nash	.925
Brodeur, NJ	.922
Luongo, Van	.921
Vokoun, Nash	.920
DiPietro, NYI	.919
Emery, Ott	.918
Giguere, Ana	.918
Kiprusoff, Calg	.917
Lundqvist, NYR	.917
Huet, Mon	.916

Minutes Played

Brodeur, NJ	.4697
Luongo, Dal	.4490
Kiprusoff, Calg	.4419
Lundqvist, NYR	.4109
Raycroft, Tor	.4108
Lehtonen, Atl	.3934
Roloson, Edm	.3932
Fleury, Pit	.3905
Turco, Dal	.3764
Miller, Buf	.3692
DiPietro, NYI	.3627

Power Play/Penalty Killing

Power play and penalty killing conversions. Power play: No—number of opportunities; GF—goals for; Pct—percentage. Penalty killing: No—number of times shorthanded; GA—goals against; Pct—percentage of penalties killed; SH—shorthanded goals for.

WESTERN	Power Play No	GF	Pct	Penalty Killing No	GA	Pct	SH
San Jose	.410	92	**22.4**	330	55	83.3	7
Anaheim	.398	89	**22.4**	410	61	85.1	4
Colorado	.374	79	**21.1**	353	70	80.2	7
Minnesota	.380	72	**18.9**	342	48	86.0	9
Dallas	.427	79	**18.5**	377	59	84.4	3
Los Angeles	.442	81	**18.3**	411	91	77.9	6
Calgary	.401	73	**18.2**	414	81	80.4	15
Nashville	.408	71	**17.4**	387	55	85.8	8
Vancouver	.407	70	**17.2**	436	57	86.9	5
Detroit	.398	68	**17.1**	408	63	84.6	12
Phoenix	.400	66	**16.5**	425	92	78.4	5
Columbus	.438	65	**14.8**	453	85	81.2	6
Edmonton	.373	53	**14.2**	382	59	84.6	6
St. Louis	.381	46	**12.1**	414	83	80.0	7
Chicago	.364	43	**11.8**	443	77	82.6	12

EASTERN	Power Play No	GF	Pct	Penalty Killing No	GA	Pct	SH
Montreal	.378	86	**22.8**	419	69	83.5	17
Pittsburgh	.463	94	**20.3**	419	75	82.1	14
NY Rangers	.406	75	**18.5**	400	65	83.8	11
Tampa Bay	.374	69	**18.4**	305	66	78.4	14
NY Islanders	.348	63	**18.1**	433	79	81.8	7
Florida	.337	61	**18.1**	443	78	82.4	5
Ottawa	.403	72	**17.9**	394	61	84.5	17
Toronto	.401	71	**17.7**	418	90	78.5	3
New Jersey	.367	65	**17.7**	271	40	85.2	4
Buffalo	.407	71	**17.4**	386	72	81.3	8
Boston	.412	71	**17.2**	442	81	81.7	8
Atlanta	.407	67	**16.5**	391	79	79.8	9
Washington	.408	67	**16.4**	414	82	80.2	12
Carolina	.447	67	**15.0**	395	61	84.6	12
Philadelphia	.376	53	**14.1**	420	65	84.5	15

Shootout Records

A shootout decides the game's winner if the score is still tied after a five-minute, four-on-four sudden death overtime. In the shootout, each team takes three shots. The team with the most goals after those three shots is the winner. If the score remains tied, the shootout goes to a sudden death format.

Of the 1230 NHL games played in 2006-07, 164 were decided via the shootout (13.33 percent). Players attempted 1215 shots and scored 398 goals (32.76 percent). The tables below show each team's record in shootouts, along with their goals (G) and shots (Sh) for and against. Teams are ranked by wins.

Western Conference

	GP	Record	For G	For Sh	Against G	Against Sh
Minnesota	17	10-7	27	62	25	67
Dallas	13	9-4	18	51	11	49
Nashville	11	6-5	14	34	13	37
St. Louis	12	6-6	14	36	14	37
Chicago	13	6-7	17	47	19	45
Phoenix	7	5-2	8	26	6	29
Colorado	9	5-4	12	33	11	33
Vancouver	9	5-4	15	37	12	35
Columbus	10	5-5	13	42	14	42
Los Angeles	10	4-6	18	46	19	45
Anaheim	14	4-10	14	55	19	52
Edmonton	6	3-3	6	22	8	24
Calgary	8	3-5	9	29	11	27
San Jose	4	2-2	7	12	13	46
Detroit	10	2-8	10	39	17	37

Eastern Conference

	GP	Record	For G	For Sh	Against G	Against Sh
Tampa Bay	12	10-2	16	53	6	53
Buffalo	14	10-4	17	47	9	46
Pittsburgh	16	10-6	17	47	12	44
New Jersey	18	10-8	25	62	23	66
Boston	13	9-4	18	54	13	57
NY Rangers	14	9-5	17	57	12	57
NY Islanders	13	8-5	16	58	13	58
Atlanta	11	7-4	15	29	10	30
Montreal	11	6-5	15	39	16	40
Toronto	11	4-7	14	44	16	43
Ottawa	8	2-6	9	31	11	29
Florida	10	2-8	9	38	15	35
Philadelphia	7	1-6	2	28	10	28
Washington	12	1-11	5	40	18	40
Carolina	5	0-5	1	17	8	17

Individual Shootout Leaders

Leading shootout scorers (ranked by goals) and goaltenders (ranked by wins) during the 2006-07 season.

Shooters

	Goals	Shots	Pct	GDG
Erik Christensen, Pit	8	14	57.1	3
Mikki Koivu, Min	8	15	53.3	4
Paul Kariya, Nash	7	11	63.6	1
Vyacheslav Kozlov, Atl	7	11	63.6	5
Brian Gionta, NJ	7	13	53.8	2
Zach Parise, NJ	7	14	50.0	2
Seven tied with 6 goals.				

Note: GDG denotes Game Deciding Goals

Goaltenders

	W-L	GA	Shots	SV%
Ryan Miller, Buf	10-4	9	46	.804
Martin Brodeur, NJ	10-6	20	60	.667
Marc-Andre Fleury, Pit	9-5	9	39	.769
Henrik Lundqvist, NYR	8-4	9	50	.820
Manny Fernandez, Min	7-1	9	32	.719
Kari Lehtonen, Atl	7-4	10	30	.667
Johan Holmqvist, TB	6-1	4	33	.879
Three tied with 5 wins.				

2007 NHL All-Star Game

55th NHL All-Star Game. **Date:** Jan. 24 at American Airlines Center in Dallas, Texas. **Coaches:** Lindy Ruff, Buffalo (Eastern) and Randy Carlyle, Anaheim (Western). Head coaches whose team had the best winning percentage in each conference on Jan. 5 (the half-way point of the season) were named all-star head coaches. **Attendance:** 18,532. **Time:** 2:32. **MVP:** Daniel Briere, Buffalo C (Eastern) — one goal, four assists.

Western 12, Eastern 9

	1	2	3	Final
Eastern Conference	3	3	3	— 9
Western Conference	3	6	3	— 12

1st Period: EAST—Briere (Heatley, Hossa), 3:38; WEST—Perreault (Rolston, Guerin), 5:08; WEST—Selanne (unassisted), 6:17; EAST—St. Louis (Lecavalier, Rafalski), 13:07; EAST—Staal (Williams, Blake), 13:43; WEST—Visnovsky (Sakic, Nash), 18:55.

2nd Period: WEST—Marleau (Cheechoo, Lidstrom), 2:41; EAST—Williams (Blake), 5:19; EAST—Chara (Briere, Rafalski), 6:29; WEST—Rolston (unassisted), 8:30; WEST—Nash (Sakic, Phaneuf), 10:40; WEST—Havlat (Sakic, Nash), 11:34; WEST—Perreault 2 (Guerin, Rolston), 12:47; EAST—Ovechkin (Briere, Souray), 13:32; WEST—Rolston 2 (Jovanovski), 18:58.

3rd Period: EAST—Heatley (Briere, Hossa), 2:01; WEST—Nash 2 (Sakic, Havlat), 7:12; EAST—Chara 2 (Hossa, Briere), 10:37; WEST—Havlat 2 (Smyth, Jovanovski), 19:00; EAST—Souray (Hossa, Heatley), 19:25; WEST—Phaneuf (Visnovsky), 19:48 (en).

Shots on Goal: Eastern—12-11-15—38; Western—12-16-11—39.

Power plays: none.

Goalies: Eastern—Miller (12 shots, 9 saves), Brodeur (16 shots, 10 saves), Huet (10 shots, 8 saves); Western—Luongo (12 shots, 9 saves), Kiprusoff (11 shots, 8 saves), Turco (15 shots, 12 saves).

Team by Team Statistics

High scorers and goaltenders with at least ten games played. Players who competed for more than one team during the regular season are listed with their final club; (*) indicates rookies eligible for Calder Trophy. Player positions are noted as follows: C—Center, L—Left wing, R—Right wing, D—Defenseman.

Anaheim Ducks

Top Scorers	Gm	G	A	Pts	+/-	PM	PP
Teemu Selanne, R	.82	48	46	94	26	82	25
Andy McDonald, C	.82	27	51	78	16	46	8
Scott Niedermayer, D	.79	15	54	69	6	86	9
Chris Kunitz, L	.81	25	35	60	23	81	11
Chris Pronger, D	.66	13	46	59	27	69	8
Ryan Getzlaf, C	.82	25	33	58	17	66	11
Dustin Penner*, R	.82	29	16	45	-2	58	9
Corey Perry, R	.82	17	27	44	12	55	4
Francois Beauchemin, D	71	7	21	28	7	49	2
Samuel Pahlsson, C	.82	8	18	26	-4	42	0
Todd Marchant, C	.56	8	15	23	7	44	0
Travis Moen, L	.82	11	10	21	-4	101	0
Sean O'Donnell, D	.79	2	15	17	9	92	0
Rob Niedermayer, C	.82	5	11	16	-8	77	0
Ric Jackman, D	.31	2	10	12	0	20	1
FLA	.7	1	0	1	-3	10	0
ANA	.24	1	10	11	3	10	1
Ryan Shannon, R	.53	2	9	11	-2	10	0
Shawn Thornton, L	.48	2	7	9	3	88	0
Joe DiPenta, D	.76	2	6	8	1	48	0

Acquired: D Jackman from Fla. for a cond'l '07 pick (Jan. 3).

Goalies (10 Gm)	Gm	Min	GAA	Record	SV%
Jean-Sebastien Giguere	.56	3245	2.26	36-10-8	.918
Ilja Bryzgalov	.27	1509	2.47	10-8-6	.907
ANAHEIM	.82	4987	2.67	43-27-12	.909

Shutouts: Giguere (4), Bryzgalov (1). **Assists:** Giguere (2). **PM:** none.

Atlanta Thrashers

Top Scorers	Gm	G	A	Pts	+/-	PM	PP
Marian Hossa, R	.82	43	57	100	18	49	17
Vyacheslav Kozlov, L	.81	28	52	80	9	36	8
Ilya Kovalchuk, L	.82	42	34	76	-2	66	18
Keith Tkachuk, L	.79	27	31	58	11	126	10
ST.L	.61	20	23	43	3	92	8
ATL	.18	7	8	15	8	34	2
Alexei Zhitnik, D	.79	7	31	38	1	92	3
NYI	.30	2	9	11	13	40	0
PHI	.31	3	10	13	-16	38	1
ATL	.18	2	12	14	4	14	2
Scott Mellanby, R	.69	12	24	36	-9	63	5
Eric Belanger, C	.80	17	18	35	-2	26	4
CAR	.56	8	12	20	-2	14	3
ATL	.24	9	6	15	0	12	1
Jonathan Sim, R	.77	17	12	29	-1	60	2
Bobby Holik, C	.82	11	18	29	-3	86	2
Greg de Vries, D	.82	3	21	24	-3	66	0
Steve Rucchin, C	.47	5	16	21	-4	14	1
Niclas Havelid, D	.77	3	18	21	-2	52	1
Pascal Dupuis, L	.71	14	5	19	-17	42	2
MIN	.48	10	3	13	-7	38	2
NYR	.6	1	0	1	-4	0	0
ATL	.17	3	2	5	-6	4	0

Acquired: C Belanger from Nash. for D Vitaly Vishnevski (Feb. 10); D Zhitnik from Phi. for D Braydon Coburn (Feb. 24); L Tkachuk from St.L for C Glen Metropolit, '07 1st-round and 3rd-round picks and an '08 2nd-round pick (Feb. 25); L Dupuis and an '07 3rd-round pick from NYR for F Alex Bourret (Feb. 27).

Goalies (10 Gm)	Gm	Min	GAA	Record	SV%
Kari Lehtonen	.68	3934	2.79	34-24-9	.912
Johan Hedberg	.21	1057	2.89	9-4-2	.898
ATLANTA	.82	5015	2.88	43-28-11	.907

Shutouts: Lehtonen (4). **Assists:** Garnett (2), Lehtonen and Hedberg (1). **PM:** Lehtonen and Hedberg (6).

Boston Bruins

Top Scorers	Gm	G	A	Pts	+/-	PM	PP
Marc Savard, C	.82	22	74	96	-19	96	10
Patrice Bergeron, C	.77	22	48	70	-28	26	14
Glen Murray, R	.59	28	17	45	-12	44	12
Marco Sturm, L	.76	27	17	44	-24	46	10
Zdeno Chara, D	.80	11	32	43	-21	100	9
Phil Kessel*, C	.70	11	18	29	-12	12	1
P.J. Axelsson, L	.55	11	16	27	-10	52	3
Dennis Wideman, D	.75	6	19	25	-10	71	4
ST.L	.55	5	17	22	-7	44	4
BOS	.20	1	2	3	-3	27	0
Brandon Bochenski, R	.41	13	11	24	1	16	3
CHI	.10	2	0	2	-2	2	0
BOS	.31	11	11	22	3	14	3
Chuck Kobasew, R	.50	5	14	19	1	62	2
CALG	.40	4	13	17	7	37	1
BOS	.10	1	1	2	-6	25	1
Shean Donovan, R	.76	6	11	17	-13	56	0
Mark Mowers, R	.78	5	12	17	-10	26	0

Acquired: R Bochenski from Chi. for F Kris Versteeg and a conditional pick (Feb. 4); R Kobasew and D Andrew Ference from Calg. for D Brad Stuart and C Wayne Primeau (Feb. 11); D Wideman from St.L for C Brad Boyes (Feb. 27). **Claimed:** G MacDonald off waivers from Det. (Feb. 24).

Goalies (10 Gm)	Gm	Min	GAA	Record	SV%
Joey MacDonald	.15	826	3.12	3-7-2	.894
DET	.8	468	3.46	1-5-1	.872
BOS	.7	358	2.68	2-2-1	.918
Tim Thomas	.66	3619	3.13	30-29-4	.905
Hannu Toivonen*	.18	894	4.23	3-9-1	.875
BOSTON	.82	4998	3.42	35-41-6	.896

Shutouts: Thomas (3). **Assists:** none. **PM:** Thomas (6), Toivonen (2).

Buffalo Sabres

Top Scorers	Gm	G	A	Pts	+/-	PM	PP
Daniel Briere, C	.81	32	63	95	17	89	9
Thomas Vanek, L	.82	43	41	84	47	40	15
Chris Drury, C	.77	37	32	69	1	30	17
Jason Pominville, R	.82	34	34	68	25	30	2
Derek Roy, R	.75	21	42	63	37	60	6
Maxim Afinogenov, R	.56	23	38	61	11	66	7
Dainius Zubrus, R	.79	24	36	60	-19	62	10
WASH	.60	20	32	52	-16	50	9
BUF	.19	4	4	8	-3	12	1
Jochen Hecht, L	.76	19	37	56	19	39	3
Brian Campbell, D	.82	6	42	48	28	35	1
Ales Kotalik, R	.66	16	22	38	-5	46	3
Dmitri Kalinin, D	.82	7	22	29	19	36	0
Teppo Numminen, D	.79	2	27	29	17	32	0
Drew Stafford*, R	.41	13	14	27	5	33	3
Nathan Paetsch*, D	.63	2	22	24	10	50	0
Paul Gaustad, C	.54	9	13	22	11	74	3
Jaroslav Spacek, D	.65	5	16	21	20	62	1
Toni Lydman, D	.67	2	17	19	10	55	0

Acquired: R Zubrus and D Timo Helbling from Wash. for C Jiri Novotny and an '07 1st-round pick (Feb. 27); G Conklin from Clb. for an '07 5th-round pick (Feb. 27).

Goalies (10 Gm)	Gm	Min	GAA	Record	Sv%
Ryan Miller	.63	3692	2.73	40-16-6	.911
Ty Conklin	.16	718	3.34	3-5-2	.879
CLB	.11	491	3.30	2-3-2	.871
BUF	.5	227	3.44	1-2-0	.892
BUFFALO	.82	4986	2.82	52-24-6	.906

Shutouts: Miller (2). **Assists:** Miller (2). **PM:** Miller and Conklin (2).

Calgary Flames

Top Scorers	Gm	G	A	Pts	+/-	PM	PP
Jarome Iginla, R	.70	39	55	94	12	40	13
Alex Tanguay, L	.81	22	59	81	12	44	5
Kristian Huselius, R	.81	34	43	77	21	26	14
Daymond Langkow, C	81	33	44	77	23	44	10
Dion Phaneuf, D	.79	17	33	50	10	98	13
Matthew Lombardi, C	.81	20	26	46	10	48	5
Roman Hamrlik, D	.75	7	31	38	22	88	1
Craig Conroy, C	.80	13	24	37	-3	56	4
LA	.52	5	11	16	-13	38	4
CALG	.28	8	13	21	10	18	0
Tony Amonte, R	.81	10	20	30	-4	40	1
Stephane Yelle, C	.56	10	14	24	5	32	1
Wayne Primeau, C	.78	10	12	22	-17	111	2
BOS	.51	7	8	15	-15	75	2
CALG	.27	3	4	7	-2	36	0
Brad Stuart, D	.75	7	15	22	-10	44	1
BOS	.48	7	10	17	-22	26	1
CALG	.27	0	5	5	12	18	0
Robyn Regehr, D	.78	2	19	21	27	75	0
David Moss*, L	.41	10	8	18	5	12	3
Mark Giordano*, D	.48	7	8	15	7	36	3
Marcus Nilson, L	.63	5	10	15	7	27	0
Byron Ritchie, C	.64	8	6	14	3	68	0
Jeff Friesen, L	.72	6	6	12	-2	34	0

Acquired: C Conroy from LA for C Jamie Lundmark, an '07 4th-round pick and an '08 2nd-round pick (Jan. 29); D Stuart and C Primeau from Bos. for R Chuck Kobasew and D Andrew Ference (Feb. 11).

Goalies (10 Gm)	Gm	Min	GAA	Record	SV%
Miikka Kiprusoff	.74	4419	2.46	40-24-9	.917
CALGARY	.82	4976	2.66	43-29-10	.912

Shutouts: Kiprusoff (7). **Assists:** none. **PM:** Jamie McLennan (16); Kiprusoff (2).

Carolina Hurricanes

Top Scorers	Gm	G	A	Pts	+/-	PM	PP
Ray Whitney, L	.81	32	51	83	-5	46	6
Rod Brind'Amour, C	.78	26	56	82	7	46	9
Eric Staal, C	.82	30	40	70	-6	68	12
Justin Williams, R	.82	33	34	67	-11	73	12
Erik Cole, L	.71	29	32	61	2	76	9
Scott Walker, R	.81	21	30	51	-10	45	6
Mike Commodore, D	.82	7	22	29	0	113	0
Anson Carter, R	.64	11	17	28	-4	18	4
CLB	.54	10	17	27	-1	16	3
CAR	.10	1	0	1	-3	2	1
Cory Stillman, L	.43	5	22	27	-8	24	1
Josef Vasicek, C	.63	6	16	22	-5	51	0
NASH	.38	4	9	13	1	29	0
CAR	.25	2	7	9	-6	22	0
Andrew Ladd, L	.65	11	10	21	1	46	2
Chad LaRose, R	.80	6	12	18	-2	10	0
David Tanabe, D	.60	5	12	17	5	44	2
Craig Adams, R	.82	7	7	14	-9	54	0
Andrew Hutchinson, D	41	3	11	14	0	30	2
Anton Babchuk, D	.52	2	12	14	-6	30	0
Glen Wesley, D	.68	1	12	13	11	56	0
Niclas Wallin, D	.67	2	8	10	-2	48	0
Bret Hedican, D	.50	0	10	10	-8	36	0

Three tied with 8 pts each.

Acquired: Vasicek from Nash. for C Eric Belanger (Feb. 9); R Carter from Clb. for an '08 5th-round pick (Feb. 23).

Goalies (10 Gm)	Gm	Min	GAA	Record	Sv%
John Grahame	.28	1515	2.85	10-13-2	.897
Cam Ward	.60	3422	2.93	30-21-6	.897
CAROLINA	.82	4962	3.00	40-34-8	.894

Shutouts: Ward (2). **Assists:** Grahame (3); Ward (1). **PM:** Ward (6), Grahame (2).

Chicago Blackhawks

Top Scorers	Gm	G	A	Pts	+/-	PM	PP
Martin Havlat, R	.56	25	32	57	15	28	5
Radim Vrbata, R	.77	14	27	41	-4	26	5
Jeffrey Hamilton, L	.70	18	21	39	-4	22	3
Tuomo Ruutu, C	.71	17	21	38	4	95	1
Patrick Sharp, R	.80	20	15	35	-15	74	5
Jason Williams, C	.78	15	17	32	1	44	5
DET	.58	11	15	26	7	24	3
CHI	.20	4	2	6	-6	20	2
Duncan Keith, D	.82	2	29	31	0	76	0
Denis Arkhipov, C	.79	10	17	27	-13	54	2
Martin Lapointe, R	.82	13	11	24	-14	98	5
Brent Seabrook, D	.81	4	20	24	-6	104	0
Nikita Alexeev, R	.78	12	11	23	7	12	2
TB	.63	10	11	21	10	12	2
CHI	.15	2	0	2	-3	0	0
Rene Bourque, L	.44	7	10	17	-4	38	2
Tony Salmelainen, L	.57	6	11	17	-3	26	0
Adrian Aucoin, D	.59	4	12	16	-22	50	2
Peter Bondra, R	.37	5	9	14	2	26	2
Mikael Holmqvist, C	.63	6	7	13	-5	31	1
James Wisniewski*, D	50	2	8	10	3	39	0
Michal Handzus, C	.8	3	5	8	4	6	1
Cam Barker*, D	.35	1	7	8	-12	44	1
Jim Vandermeer, D	.46	1	6	7	-3	53	0
Jassen Cullimore, D	.65	1	6	7	-6	64	0
Craig MacDonald, C	.25	3	2	5	-2	14	0
Martin St. Pierre*, C	.14	1	3	4	-3	8	1
Dustin Byfuglien*, D	...9	1	2	3	-2	10	0

Acquired: Williams from Det. in 3-team deal that sent D Lasse Kukkonen and an '07 3rd-round pick to Phi. and L Kyle Calder to Det. (Feb. 26); R Alexeev and an '07 6th-round pick from TB for L Karl Stewart (Feb. 27).

Goalies (10 Gm)	Gm	Min	GAA	Record	SV%
Nikolai Khabibulin	.60	3425	2.86	25-26-5	.902
Patrick Lalime	.12	645	3.07	4-6-1	.896
CHICAGO	.82	4996	3.01	31-42-9	.896

Shutouts: Khabibulin and Lalime (1). **Assists:** none. **PM:** Khabibulin (8).

Colorado Avalanche

Top Scorers	Gm	G	A	Pts	+/-	PM	PP
Joe Sakic, C	.82	36	64	100	2	46	16
Andrew Brunette, L	.82	27	56	83	-8	36	9
Paul Stastny*, C	.82	28	50	78	4	42	11
Milan Hejduk, R	.80	35	35	70	10	44	12
Wojtek Wolski*, L	.76	22	28	50	2	14	7
Tyler Arnason, C	.82	16	33	49	-8	26	1
John-Michael Liles, D	.71	14	30	44	0	24	8
Brett Clark, D	.82	10	29	39	5	50	4
Brett McLean, C	.78	15	20	35	8	36	0
Marek Svatos, R	.66	15	15	30	1	46	8
Ian Laperriere, R	.81	8	21	29	5	133	0
Brad Richardson, C	.73	14	8	22	4	28	0
Ken Klee, D	.81	3	16	19	18	68	0
Mark Rycroft, R	.66	6	6	12	-3	31	0
Ben Guite, C	.39	3	8	11	-4	16	0
Patrice Brisebois, D	.33	1	10	11	-5	22	1
Karlis Skrastins, D	.68	0	11	11	0	24	0
Ossi Vaananen, D	.74	2	6	8	6	69	0
Pierre Turgeon, C	.17	4	3	7	-1	10	1
Kurt Sauer, D	.48	0	6	6	-3	24	0
Jordan Leopold, D	.15	2	3	5	-4	14	1
Jeff Finger, D	.22	1	4	5	10	11	0

Goalies (10 Gm)	Gm	Min	GAA	Record	SV%
Peter Budaj	.57	3199	2.68	31-16-6	.905
Jose Theodore	.33	1748	3.26	13-15-1	.891
COLORADO	.82	4976	2.98	44-31-7	.896

Shutouts: Budaj (3). **Assists:** Budaj (2), Theodore (2). **PM:** Theodore (6).

Columbus Blue Jackets

Top Scorers	Gm	G	A	Pts	+/-	PM	PP
David Vyborny, R	.82	16	48	64	6	60	6
Rick Nash, L	.75	27	30	57	-8	73	9
Fredrik Modin, L	.79	22	20	42	-3	50	6
Sergei Fedorov, C	.73	18	24	42	-7	56	7
Jason Chimera, L	.82	15	21	36	2	91	2
Ron Hainsey, D	.80	9	25	34	-19	69	7
Nikolai Zherdev, R	.71	10	22	32	-19	26	3
Dan Fritsche, C	.59	12	15	27	3	35	5
Manny Malhotra, C	.82	9	16	25	-8	76	2
Anders Eriksson, D	.79	0	23	23	-12	46	0
Rostislav Klesla, D	.75	9	13	22	-13	105	2
Gilbert Brule*, C	.78	9	10	19	-21	28	3
Alexander Svitov, C	.76	7	11	18	-10	145	1
Adam Foote, D	.59	3	9	12	-17	71	2
Duvie Westcott, D	.23	4	6	10	-13	18	2
Aaron Johnson, D	.61	3	7	10	-9	38	0
Geoff Platt*, C	.26	4	5	9	1	10	0
Ole-Kristian Tollefsen*, D	70	2	3	5	2	123	1
Marc Methot*, D	.20	0	4	4	5	12	0
Bryan Berard, D	.11	0	3	3	-4	8	0

Claimed: Boucher off waivers from Chi. (Feb. 27).

Goalies (10 Gm)	Gm	Min	GAA	Record	SV%
Fredrik Norrena	.55	2952	2.78	24-23-3	.904
Pascal Leclaire	.24	1315	2.97	6-15-2	.897
Brian Boucher	.18	969	3.34	2-11-3	.882
CHI	.15	827	3.26	1-10-3	.884
CLB	.3	142	3.80	1-1-0	.866
COLUMBUS	.82	4983	2.94	33-42-7	.896

Shutouts: Norrena (3), Leclaire (1), Boucher (1, with Chi.).
Assists: none. **PM:** Norrena (6); Leclaire (2).

Dallas Stars

Top Scorers	Gm	G	A	Pts	+/-	PM	PP
Mike Ribeiro, C	.81	18	41	59	3	22	6
Ladislav Nagy, L	.80	12	43	55	-5	54	4
PHO	.55	8	33	41	-2	48	2
DAL	.25	4	10	14	-3	6	2
Sergei Zubov, D	.78	12	42	54	0	26	9
Philippe Boucher, D	.76	19	32	51	2	104	12
Jussi Jokinen, L	.82	14	34	48	8	18	6
Jere Lehtinen, R	.73	26	17	43	5	16	11
Mike Modano, C	.59	22	21	43	9	34	9
Brenden Morrow, L	.40	16	15	31	-2	33	8
Niklas Hagman, L	.82	17	12	29	3	34	2
Eric Lindros, C	.49	5	21	26	-1	70	1
Stu Barnes, C	.82	13	12	25	-2	40	1
Antti Miettinen, R	.74	11	14	25	-5	38	6
Jeff Halpern, C	.76	8	17	25	-7	78	1
Darryl Sydor, D	.74	5	16	21	-4	36	2
Loui Eriksson*, L	.59	6	13	19	-3	18	2
Stephane Robidas, D	.75	0	17	17	-1	86	0
Trevor Daley, D	.74	4	8	12	2	63	0
Patrik Stefan, C	.41	5	6	11	5	10	0
Mattias Norstrom, D	.76	2	9	11	-18	48	0
LA	.62	2	7	9	-20	40	0
DAL	.14	0	2	2	2	8	0
Matthew Barnaby, R	.39	1	6	7	5	127	0
Joel Lundqvist*, C	.36	3	3	6	-5	14	0

Acquired: L Nagy from Pho. for L Mathias Tjarnqvist and an '07 1st-round pick (Feb. 13); D Norstrom, R Konstantin Pushkarev and '07 3rd- and 4th-round picks from LA for D Jaroslav Modry, '07 2nd- and 3rd-round picks and an '08 1st-round pick (Feb. 27).

Goalies (10 Gm)	Gm	Min	GAA	Record	SV%
Mike Smith*	.23	1213	2.23	12-5-2	.912
Marty Turco	.67	3764	2.23	38-20-5	.910
DALLAS	.82	5009	2.31	50-25-7	.907

Shutouts: Turco (6), Smith (3). **Assists:** Turco (4). **PM:** Turco (18), Smith (2).

Detroit Red Wings

Top Scorers	Gm	G	A	Pts	+/-	PM	PP
Pavel Datsyuk, C	.79	27	60	87	36	20	5
Henrik Zetterberg, L	.63	33	35	68	26	36	11
Nicklas Lidstrom, D	.80	13	49	62	40	46	10
Tomas Holmstrom, L	.77	30	22	52	13	58	13
Robert Lang, C	.81	19	33	52	12	66	6
Mathieu Schneider, D	.68	11	41	52	12	66	2
Daniel Cleary, R	.71	20	20	40	6	24	6
Kyle Calder, L	.78	14	21	35	-25	58	3
PHI	.59	9	12	21	-31	36	2
DET	.19	5	9	14	6	22	1
Mikael Samuelsson, R	.53	14	20	34	1	28	6
Johan Franzen, C	.69	10	20	30	20	37	0
Kris Draper, C	.81	14	15	29	7	58	0
Jiri Hudler*, C	.76	15	10	25	16	36	3
Niklas Kronvall, D	.68	1	21	22	0	54	1
Brett Lebda*, D	.74	5	13	18	16	61	1
Valtteri Filppula*, C	.73	10	7	17	8	20	0
Danny Markov, D	.66	4	12	16	25	59	0
Kirk Maltby, L	.82	6	5	11	-9	50	0
Todd Bertuzzi, R	.15	3	8	11	-1	19	1
FLA	.7	1	6	7	-4	13	1
DET	.8	2	2	4	3	6	0
Chris Chelios, D	.71	0	11	11	11	34	0
Andreas Lilja, D	.57	0	5	5	6	54	0

Acquired: L Calder from Phi. in 3-team deal that sent D Lasse Kukkonen and an '07 3rd-round pick to Phi. and Jason Williams to Chi. (Feb. 26); R Bertuzzi from Fla. for F Shawn Matthias and 2 conditional draft picks (Feb. 27).

Goalies (10 Gm)	Gm	Min	GAA	Record	Sv%
Dominik Hasek	.56	3341	2.05	38-11-6	.913
Chris Osgood	.21	1161	2.38	11-3-6	.907
DETROIT	.82	4990	2.30	50-19-13	.905

Shutouts: Hasek (8). **Assists:** Hasek (2); Osgood (1). **PM:** Hasek (20); Osgood (6).

Edmonton Oilers

Top Scorers	Gm	G	A	Pts	+/-	PM	PP
Petr Sykora, R	.82	22	31	53	-20	40	6
Ales Hemsky, R	.64	13	40	53	-7	40	5
Shawn Horcoff, C	.80	16	35	51	-22	56	5
Jarret Stoll, C	.51	13	26	39	2	48	6
Raffi Torres, L	.82	15	19	34	-7	88	1
Joffrey Lupul, R	.81	16	12	28	-29	45	5
Fernando Pisani, R	.77	14	14	28	-1	40	2
Marty Reasoner, C	.72	6	14	20	-15	60	0
Steve Staios, D	.58	2	15	17	-5	97	0
Patrick Thoresen*, L	.68	4	12	16	-1	52	0
Toby Petersen, C	.64	6	9	15	-18	4	0
Daniel Tjarnqvist, D	.37	3	12	15	3	30	2
Petr Nedved, C	.40	2	10	12	-25	28	1
PHI	.21	1	6	7	-20	18	0
EDM	.19	1	4	5	-5	10	1
Marc-Antoine Pouliot*, C	46	4	7	11	-2	18	0
Jason Smith, D	.82	2	9	11	-13	103	0
Ladislav Smid*, D	.77	3	7	10	-16	37	0
Matt Greene, D	.78	1	9	10	-22	109	0
Brad Winchester*, L	.59	4	5	9	-10	86	0
Jan Hejda, D	.39	1	8	9	-6	20	0
Tom Gilbert*, D	.12	1	5	6	-1	0	0

Claimed: Nedved off waivers from Phi. (Jan. 2).

Goalies (10 Gm)	Gm	Min	GAA	Record	Sv%
Dwayne Roloson	.68	3932	2.75	27-34-6	.909
Jussi Markkanen	.22	992	3.15	5-9-1	.886
EDMONTON	.82	4958	2.96	32-43-7	.900

Shutouts: Roloson (4). **Assists:** Roloson (3). **PM:** Roloson (12).

Florida Panthers

Top Scorers	Gm	G	A	Pts	+/-	PM	PP
Olli Jokinen, C	.82	39	52	91	18	78	9
Nathan Horton, R	.82	31	31	62	15	61	7
Jozef Stumpel, C	.73	23	34	57	2	22	9
Stephen Weiss, C	.74	20	28	48	-1	28	10
Martin Gelinas, L	.82	14	30	44	7	36	7
Jay Bouwmeester, D	.82	12	30	42	23	66	3
Ville Peltonen, L	.72	17	20	37	7	28	4
Chris Gratton, C	.81	13	22	35	1	94	1
Ruslan Salei, D	.82	6	26	32	-13	102	2
Rostislav Olesz, L	.75	11	19	30	2	28	2
Mike Van Ryn, D	.78	4	25	29	-5	64	1
Juraj Kolnik, R	.64	11	14	25	2	18	0
Bryan Allen, D	.82	4	21	25	7	112	0
David Booth*, L	.48	3	7	10	0	12	0
Gregory Campbell, C	.79	6	3	9	-10	66	0
Steve Montador, D	.72	1	8	9	1	119	0
Joe Nieuwendyk, C	.15	5	3	8	-4	4	2
Alexei Semenov, D	.23	0	5	5	9	28	0
Noah Welch*, D	.24	2	1	3	4	24	0
PIT	.22	1	1	2	1	22	0
FLA	.2	1	0	1	3	2	0
Janis Sprukts*, C	.13	1	2	3	1	2	0
Branislav Mezei, D	.45	0	3	3	5	55	0

Acquired: D Welch from Pit for L Gary Roberts (Feb. 27).

Goalies (10 Gm)	Gm	Min	GAA	Record	Sv%
Ed Belfour	.58	3289	2.77	27-17-10	.902
Alex Auld	.27	1471	3.34	7-13-5	.888
FLORIDA	.82	4992	2.99	35-31-16	.896

Shutouts: Belfour and Auld (1). **Assists:** Belfour (2), Auld (1). **PM:** Belfour (10), Auld (2).

Los Angeles Kings

Top Scorers	Gm	G	A	Pts	+/-	PM	PP
Michael Cammalleri, C	81	34	46	80	5	48	16
Alexander Frolov, L	.82	35	36	71	-8	34	10
Anze Kopitar*, C	.72	20	41	61	-12	24	7
Lubomir Visnovsky, D	.69	18	40	58	1	26	8
Dustin Brown, R	.81	17	29	46	-21	54	13
Derek Armstrong, C	.67	11	33	44	13	62	3
Rob Blake, D	.72	14	20	34	-26	82	11
Jamie Heward, D	.71	6	18	24	2	47	3
WASH	.52	4	12	16	4	27	2
LA	.19	2	6	8	-2	20	1
Tom Kostopoulos, R	.76	7	15	22	-2	73	0
Brian Willsie, R	.81	11	10	21	-20	49	2
Patrick O'Sullivan*, C	44	5	14	19	-6	14	2
Jaroslav Modry, D	.76	1	17	18	11	54	0
DAL	.57	1	9	10	10	32	0
LA	.19	0	8	8	1	22	0
Scott Thornton, C	.58	7	6	13	-15	85	0
Jamie Lundmark, C	.68	7	6	13	-12	56	0
CALG	.39	0	4	4	-4	31	0
LA	.29	7	2	9	-8	25	0
Kevin Dallman, D	.53	1	9	10	-13	12	0
Mike Weaver, D	.39	3	6	9	4	16	1

Acquired: C Lundmark, an '07 4th-round pick and an '08 2nd-round pick from Calg. for C Craig Conroy (Jan. 29); D Heward from Wash. for a conditional '08 pick (Feb. 27); D Modry, '07 2nd- and 3rd-round picks and an '08 1st-round pick from Dal. for D Mattias Norstrom, R Konstantin Pushkarev and '07 3rd- and 4th-round picks (Feb. 27).

Goalies (10 Gm)	Gm	Min	GAA	Record	Sv%
Mathieu Garon	.32	1779	2.66	13-10-6	.907
Sean Burke	.23	1310	3.11	6-10-5	.901
Barry Brust*	.11	496	3.70	2-4-1	.878
Dan Cloutier	.24	1281	3.98	6-14-2	.860
LOS ANGELES	.82	4992	3.33	27-41-14	.886

Shutouts: Garon (2), Burke (1). **Assists:** Garon, Burke and Cloutier (1). **PM:** Cloutier (21), Garon (6), Burke (4).

Minnesota Wild

Top Scorers	Gm	G	A	Pts	+/-	PM	PP
Brian Rolston, C	.78	31	33	64	6	46	13
Pavol Demitra, R	.71	25	39	64	0	28	9
Marian Gaborik, R	.48	30	27	57	12	40	12
Pierre-Marc Bouchard, R	82	20	37	57	13	14	5
Mikko Koivu, C	.82	20	34	54	6	58	9
Todd White, C	.77	13	31	44	8	24	6
Mark Parrish, R	.76	19	20	39	9	18	5
Brent Burns, D	.77	7	18	25	16	26	3
Branko Radivojevic, R	.82	11	13	24	-9	21	4
Wes Walz, C	.62	9	15	24	3	30	0
Kurtis Foster, D	.57	3	20	23	-3	52	0
Kim Johnsson, D	.76	3	19	22	-4	64	3
Petteri Nummelin, D	.51	3	17	20	-15	22	0
Stephane Veilleux, L	.75	7	11	18	3	47	0
Dominic Moore, C	.69	8	9	17	4	56	0
PIT	.59	6	9	15	1	46	0
MIN	.10	2	0	2	3	10	0
Adam Hall, R	.72	6	11	17	-11	26	3
NYR	.49	4	8	12	-13	18	3
MIN	.23	2	3	5	2	8	0
Keith Carney, D	.80	4	13	17	22	58	0
Martin Skoula, D	.81	0	15	15	9	36	0
Nick Schultz, D	.82	2	10	12	0	42	0
Wyatt Smith, C	.61	3	3	6	-8	16	1

Acquired: R Hall from NYR for L Pascal Dupuis (Feb. 9); C Moore from Pit. for an '07 3rd-round pick (Feb. 27).

Goalies (10 Gm)	Gm	Min	GAA	Record	Sv%
Niklas Backstrom	.41	2227	1.97	23-8-6	.929
Manny Fernandez	.44	2422	2.55	22-16-1	.911
MINNESOTA	.82	5025	2.20	48-26-8	.922

Shutouts: Backstrom (5); Fernandez (2); Josh Harding (1). **Assists:** Backstrom (1). **PM:** Fernandez (12); Backstrom (2).

Montreal Canadiens

Top Scorers	Gm	G	A	Pts	+/-	PM	PP
Saku Koivu, C	.81	22	53	75	-21	74	11
Sheldon Souray, D	.81	26	38	64	-28	135	19
Michael Ryder, R	.82	30	28	58	-25	60	17
Andrei Markov, D	.77	6	43	49	2	56	5
Tomas Plekanec, C	.81	20	27	47	10	36	5
Alexei Kovalev, R	.73	18	29	47	-19	78	8
Chris Higgins, L	.61	22	16	38	-11	26	8
Mark Streit, D	.76	10	26	36	-5	14	2
Mike Johnson, R	.80	11	20	31	6	40	1
Guillaume Latendresse, L	80	16	13	29	-20	47	5
Sergei Samsonov, L	.63	9	17	26	-4	10	0
Radek Bonk, C	.74	13	10	23	0	54	1
Michael Komisarek, D	82	4	15	19	7	96	0
Alexander Perezhogin, R	61	6	9	15	11	48	1
Francis Bouillon, D	.62	3	11	14	-10	52	1
Maxim Lapierre*, C	.46	6	6	12	-7	24	0
Andrei Kostitsyn*, R	.22	1	10	11	3	6	0
Steve Begin, C	.52	5	5	10	-6	46	0
Mathieu Dandenault, D	68	2	6	8	-8	40	0
Josh Gorges, D	.54	1	3	4	-4	26	0
SJ	.47	1	3	4	-3	26	0
MON	.7	0	0	0	-1	0	0
Garth Murray, L	.43	2	1	3	-10	32	0
Janne Niinimaa, D	.41	0	3	3	-13	36	0

Acquired: D Gorges and an '07 1st-round pick from SJ for D Craig Rivet and an '08 5th-round pick (Feb. 25).

Goalies (10 Gm)	Gm	Min	GAA	Record	Sv%
Cristobal Huet	.42	2286	2.81	19-16-3	.916
Jaroslav Halak*	.16	912	2.89	10-6-0	.906
David Aebischer	.32	1760	3.17	13-12-3	.900
MONTREAL	.82	4987	3.02	42-34-6	.907

Shutouts: Huet and Halak (2). **Assists:** Huet and Halak (1). **PM:** Halak and Aebischer (2).

Nashville Predators

Top Scorers	Gm	G	A	Pts	+/-	PM	PP
Paul Kariya, L	.82	24	52	76	6	36	5
J.P. Dumont, R	.82	21	45	66	14	28	5
David Legwand, C	.78	27	36	63	23	44	3
Steve Sullivan, R	.57	22	38	60	16	20	6
Martin Erat, L	.68	16	41	57	13	50	5
Peter Forsberg, C	.57	13	42	55	7	88	6
PHI	.40	11	29	40	2	72	5
NASH	.17	2	13	15	5	16	1
Kimmo Timonen, D	.80	13	42	55	20	42	8
Jason Arnott, C	.68	27	27	54	15	48	12
Shea Weber, D	.79	17	23	40	13	60	6
Scott Hartnell, L	.64	22	17	39	19	96	10
Alexander Radulov*, R	64	18	19	37	19	26	5
Marek Zidlicky, D	.79	4	26	30	8	72	2
Vernon Fiddler, C	.72	11	15	26	11	40	0
Ryan Suter, D	.82	8	16	24	10	54	1
Dan Hamuis, D	.81	6	14	20	8	66	0
Scott Nichol, C	.59	7	6	13	7	79	1
Vitaly Vishnevski, D	.67	3	10	13	-4	41	0
ATL	.52	3	9	12	-5	31	0
NASH	..15	0	1	1	1	10	0
Jerred Smithson, C	.64	5	7	12	-8	42	1
Jordin Tootoo, R	.65	3	6	9	-11	116	0
Greg Zanon, D	..66	3	5	8	16	32	0
Ramzi Abid, L	.13	1	4	5	-3	13	0
Darcy Hordichuk, L	..53	1	3	4	-2	90	0
Mikko Lehtonen, D	..15	1	2	3	0	8	0

Acquired: D Vishnevski from Atl. for C Eric Belanger (Feb. 10); C Forsberg from Phi. for R Scottie Upshall, D Ryan Parent and '07 1st- and 3rd-round draft picks (Feb. 15).

Goalies (10 Gm)	Gm	Min	GAA	Record	Sv%
Chris Mason	.40	2342	2.38	24-11-4	.925
Tomas Vokoun	.44	2601	2.40	27-12-4	.920
NASHVILLE	.82	4989	2.49	51-23-8	.919

Shutouts: Vokoun and Mason (5); Vokoun and Mason also shared a shutout. **Assists:** Vokoun (2), Mason (1). **PM:** Vokoun and Mason (4).

New Jersey Devils

Top Scorers	Gm	G	A	Pts	+/-	PM	PP
Patrik Elias, L	.75	21	48	69	1	38	8
Zach Parise, L	.82	31	31	62	-3	30	9
Jamie Langenbrunner, R	.82	23	37	60	-9	64	12
Scott Gomez, C	.72	13	47	60	7	42	4
Brian Rafalski, D	.82	8	47	55	4	34	3
Brian Gionta, R	.62	25	20	45	-3	36	11
Travis Zajac*, C	.80	17	25	42	1	16	6
Sergei Brylin, L	.82	16	24	40	-5	35	8
John Madden, C	.74	12	20	32	-7	14	0
Jay Pandolfo, L	.82	13	14	27	-5	8	0
Paul Martin, D	.82	3	23	26	-9	18	1
Brad Lukowich, D	.75	4	8	12	1	36	0
John Oduya*, D	.76	2	9	11	-5	61	0
Erik Rasmussen, C	.71	3	7	10	-3	25	0
Michael Rupp, C	.76	6	3	9	-10	92	0
Jim Dowd, C	.66	4	4	8	-5	20	0
Colin White, D	.69	0	8	8	-8	69	0
Andy Greene*, D	..23	1	5	6	-1	6	1
David Clarkson*, R	.7	3	1	4	-1	6	2
Four tied with 1 pt. each.							

Goalies (10 Gm)	Gm	Min	GAA	Record	Sv%
Martin Brodeur	.78	4697	2.18	48-23-7	.922
Scott Clemmensen	..6	305	3.15	1-1-2	.889
NEW JERSEY	.82	5024	2.30	49-24-9	.917

Shutouts: Brodeur (12). **Assists:** Brodeur (1). **PM:** Brodeur (12).

New York Islanders

Top Scorers	Gm	G	A	Pts	+/-	PM	PP
Jason Blake, L	.82	40	29	69	1	34	14
Ryan Smyth, L	.71	36	32	68	2	52	15
EDM	.53	31	22	53	2	38	14
NYI	.18	5	10	15	0	14	1
Miroslav Satan, R	.81	27	32	59	-12	46	7
Mike Sillinger, C	.82	26	33	59	5	46	11
Viktor Kozlov, C	.81	25	26	51	12	28	5
Alexei Yashin, C	.58	18	32	50	6	44	5
Marc-Andre Bergeron, D	78	14	32	46	-4	38	10
EDM	.55	8	17	25	-9	28	6
NYI	..23	6	15	21	5	10	4
Tom Poti, D	.78	6	38	44	-1	74	6
Randy Robitaille, C	.78	11	29	40	-6	44	3
PHI	..28	5	12	17	-4	22	2
NYI	.50	6	17	23	-2	22	1
Trent Hunter, R	.77	20	15	35	5	22	5
Andy Hilbert, C	.81	8	20	28	10	34	0
Chris Simon, L	.67	10	17	27	17	75	2
Richard Park, C	.82	10	16	26	4	33	0
Sean Hill, D	.81	1	24	25	6	110	0
Arron Asham, R	.80	11	12	23	3	63	0
Richard Zednik, R	.42	7	14	21	-6	18	1
WASH	.32	6	12	18	-4	16	1
NYI	..10	1	2	3	-2	2	0
Radek Martinek, D	.43	2	15	17	19	40	0
Chris Campoli, D	.51	1	13	14	-3	23	0
Brendan Witt, D	..81	1	13	14	14	131	0

Acquired: C Robitaille and an '07 5th-round pick from Phi. for L Mike York (Dec. 21); D Bergeron from Edm. for D Denis Grebeshkov (Feb. 18); R Zednik from Wash. for an '07 2nd-round pick (Feb. 26); L Smyth from Edm. for C Robert Nilsson, C Ryan O'Marra and an '07 1st-round pick (Feb. 27).

Goalies (10 Gm)	15 Gm	Min	GAA	Record	Sv%
Rick DiPietro	.62	3627	2.58	32-19-9	.919
Mike Dunham	.19	979	3.74	4-10-3	.889
NY ISLANDERS	.82	5009	2.81	40-30-12	.912

Shutouts: DiPietro (5). **Assists:** DiPietro (2); Dunham (1). **PM:** DiPietro (24).

New York Rangers

Top Scorers	Gm	G	A	Pts	+/-	PM	PP
Jaromir Jagr, R	.82	30	66	96	26	78	7
Michael Nylander, C	.79	26	57	83	12	42	14
Martin Straka, L	.77	29	41	70	16	24	8
Brendan Shanahan, L	.67	29	33	62	2	47	14
Sean Avery, L	.84	18	30	48	1	174	2
LA	.55	10	18	28	-10	116	1
NYR	.29	8	12	20	11	58	1
Matt Cullen, C	.80	16	25	41	0	52	2
Petr Prucha, R	.79	22	18	40	-7	30	8
Michal Rozsival, D	.80	10	30	40	10	52	7
Karel Rachunek, D	.66	6	20	26	-9	38	4
Paul Mara, D	.78	5	18	23	-16	113	1
BOS	.59	3	15	18	-22	95	0
NYR	.19	2	3	5	6	18	1
Marek Malik, D	.69	2	19	21	32	70	0
Marcel Hossa, L	.64	10	8	18	-4	26	3
Fedor Tyutin, D	.66	2	12	14	-8	44	1
Blair Betts, C	.82	9	4	13	-4	24	1
Jed Ortmeyer, R	.41	2	9	11	7	22	0
Thomas Pock, D	.44	4	4	8	-4	16	0
Four tied with 6 pts. each.							

Acquired: L Avery from LA for R Jason Ward (Feb. 6); D Mara from Bos. for D Aaron Ward (Feb. 27).

Goalies (10 Gm)	Gm	Min	GAA	Record	SV%
Henrik Lundqvist	.70	4109	2.34	37-22-8	.917
Kevin Weekes	.14	761	3.39	4-6-2	.879
NY RANGERS	.82	5014	2.52	42-30-10	.909

Shutouts: Lundqvist (5). **Assists:** none. **PM:** none.

Ottawa Senators

Top Scorers	Gm	G	A	Pts	+/-	PM	PP
Dany Heatley, L	.82	50	55	105	31	74	17
Jason Spezza, C	.67	34	53	87	19	45	13
Daniel Alfredsson, R	.77	29	58	87	42	42	7
Mike Fisher, C	.68	22	26	48	15	41	7
Peter Schaefer, L	.77	12	34	46	7	32	5
Mike Comrie, R	.65	20	25	45	0	44	7
PHO	.24	7	13	20	1	20	4
OTT	.41	13	12	25	-1	24	3
Antoine Vermette, L	.77	19	20	39	-2	52	2
Chris Kelly, C	.82	15	23	38	28	40	1
Tom Preissing, D	.80	7	31	38	40	18	3
Joe Corvo, D	.76	8	29	37	8	42	3
Oleg Saprykin, L	.71	15	21	36	5	58	2
PHO	.59	14	20	34	8	54	2
OTT	.12	1	1	2	-3	4	0
Wade Redden, D	.64	7	29	36	1	50	4
Andrej Meszaros, D	.82	7	28	35	-15	102	0
Patrick Eaves, R	.73	14	18	32	1	36	3
Dean McAmmond, C	.81	14	15	29	11	28	0
Chris Neil, R	.82	12	16	28	6	177	3
Chris Phillips, D	.82	8	18	26	36	80	0
Christoph Schubert, D	.80	8	17	25	30	56	1
Anton Volchenkov, D	.78	1	18	19	37	67	0

Acquired: R Comrie from Pho. for C Alexei Kaigorodov (Jan. 3); L Saprykin and an '07 seventh-round pick from Pho. for an '08 2nd-round pick (Feb. 27).

Goalies (10 Gm)	Gm	Min	GAA	Record	Sv%
Ray Emery	.58	3351	2.47	33-16-6	.918
Martin Gerber	.29	1599	2.78	15-9-3	.906
OTTAWA	.82	4974	2.61	48-25-9	.913

Shutouts: Emery (5), Gerber (1). **Assists:** Emery (1). **PM:** Emery (30).

Philadelphia Flyers

Top Scorers	Gm	G	A	Pts	+/-	PM	PP
Simon Gagne, L	.76	41	27	68	2	30	13
Mike Knuble, R	.64	24	30	54	2	56	10
Joni Pitkanen, D	.77	4	39	43	-25	88	1
Jeff Carter, C	.62	14	23	37	-17	48	3
Mike Richards, C	.59	10	22	32	-12	52	1
Geoff Sanderson, L	.58	11	18	29	-16	44	3
R.J. Umberger, C	.81	16	12	28	-32	41	2
Randy Jones, D	.66	4	18	22	-14	38	0
Alexandre Picard*, D	.62	3	19	22	-19	17	1
Dimitry Afanasenkov, L	74	11	10	21	-25	20	0
TB	.33	3	3	6	-6	8	0
PHI	.41	8	7	15	-19	12	0
Mike York, L	.66	10	11	21	-18	22	2
NYI	.32	6	7	13	-9	14	2
PHI	.34	4	4	8	-9	8	0
Scottie Upshall, R	.32	8	8	16	3	26	1
NASH	.14	2	1	3	-1	18	0
PHI	.18	6	7	13	4	8	1

Acquired: L York from NYI for C Randy Robitaille and an '07 5th-round pick (Dec. 21); R Upshall, D Ryan Parent and '07 1st- and 3rd-round draft picks from Nash. for C Peter Forsberg (Feb. 15); G Biron from Buf. for an '07 2nd-round pick (Feb. 27). **Claimed:** L Afanasenkov off waivers from TB (Dec. 30).

Goalies (10 Gm)	Gm	Min	GAA	Record	Sv%
Martin Biron	.35	2001	3.03	18-12-3	.903
BUF	.19	1066	3.04	12-4-1	.899
PHI	.16	935	3.02	6-8-2	.908
Antero Niittymaki	.52	2943	3.38	9-29-9	.894
Robert Esche	.18	860	4.33	5-9-1	.872
PHILADELPHIA	.82	4978	3.58	22-48-12	.889

Shutouts: Esche (1). **Assists:** Esche (2). **PM:** Biron (25), Esche and Niittymaki (2).

Phoenix Coyotes

Top Scorers	Gm	G	A	Pts	+/-	PM	PP
Shane Doan, R	.73	27	28	55	-14	73	11
Owen Nolan, R	.76	16	24	40	-2	56	2
Steve Reinprecht, C	.49	9	24	33	-3	28	2
Ed Jovanovski, D	.54	11	18	29	-6	63	6
Jeremy Roenick, C	.70	11	17	28	-18	32	4
Zbynek Michalek, D	.82	4	24	28	-20	34	3
Keith Ballard, D	.69	5	22	27	-7	59	2
Derek Morris, D	.82	6	19	25	-18	115	2
Michael Zigomanis, C	75	14	9	23	-8	46	2
Niko Kapanen, C	.79	6	16	22	-23	28	2
ATL	.60	4	9	13	-12	20	1
PHO	.19	2	7	9	-11	8	1
Travis Roche, D	.50	6	13	19	2	22	2
Fredrik Sjostrom, R	.78	9	9	18	-11	48	2
Bill Thomas*, R	.24	8	6	14	-6	2	4
Mathias Tjarnqvist, L	.44	6	7	13	-5	6	0
DAL	.18	1	3	4	-3	4	0
PHO	.26	5	4	9	-2	2	0
Kevyn Adams, C	.68	3	9	12	-20	25	0
CAR	.35	2	2	4	-10	17	0
PHO	.33	1	7	8	-10	8	0

Acquired: C Adams from Car. for D Dennis Seidenberg (Jan. 8); L Tjarnqvist and an '07 1st-round pick from Dal. for L Ladislav Nagy (Feb. 13); **Claimed:** C Kapanen off waivers from Atl. (Feb. 27).

Goalies (10 Gm)	Gm	Min	GAA	Record	Sv%
Curtis Joseph	.55	2993	3.19	18-31-2	.893
Mikael Tellqvist	.31	1650	3.34	11-12-3	.885
TOR	.1	59	2.03	0-1-0	.895
PHO	.30	1591	3.39	11-11-3	.885
PHOENIX	.82	4970	3.40	31-46-5	.886

Shutouts: Joseph (4); Tellqvist (2). **Assists:** Tellqvist (1). **PM:** Joseph (10).

Pittsburgh Penguins

Top Scorers	Gm	G	A	Pts	+/-	PM	PP
Sidney Crosby, C	.79	36	84	120	10	60	13
Evgeni Malkin*, C	.78	33	52	85	2	80	16
Mark Recchi, R	.82	24	44	68	1	62	14
Sergei Gonchar, D	.82	13	54	67	-5	72	10
Ryan Whitney, D	.81	14	45	59	9	77	9
Michel Ouellet, R	.73	19	29	48	-3	30	11
Jordan Staal*, C	.81	29	13	42	16	24	4
Gary Roberts, L	.69	20	22	42	0	97	6
FLA	.50	13	16	29	5	71	-2
PIT	.19	7	6	13	-5	26	4
Colby Armstrong, R	.80	12	22	34	2	67	1
Erik Christensen, C	.61	18	15	33	-3	26	6
Ryan Malone, L	.64	16	15	31	4	71	1
Maxime Talbot, C	.75	13	11	24	-2	53	0
Georges Laraque, R	.73	5	19	24	4	70	1
PHO	.56	5	17	22	7	52	1
PIT	.17	0	2	2	-3	18	0
Jarkko Ruutu, L	.81	7	9	16	0	125	0
Nils Ekman, D	.34	6	9	15	-14	24	2
Josef Melichar, D	.70	1	11	12	1	44	0
Robert Scuderi, D	.78	1	10	11	3	28	0
Joel Kwiatkowski, D	.42	5	5	10	-6	20	1
FLA	.41	5	5	10	-5	20	1
PIT	.0	0	0	0	-1	0	0

Acquired: R Laraque from Pho. for F Daniel Carcillo and an '08 3rd-round pick (Feb. 27); L Roberts from Fla. for D Noah Welch (Feb. 27); D Kwiatkowski from Fla. for an '07 4th-round pick (Feb. 27).

Goalies (10 Gm)	Gm	Min	GAA	Record	Sv%
Jocelyn Thibault	.22	1101	2.83	7-8-2	.909
Marc-Andre Fleury	.67	3905	2.83	40-16-9	.906
PITTSBURGH	.82	5032	2.86	47-24-11	.905

Shutouts: Fleury (5); Thibault (1). **Assists:** Fleury (3). **PM:** Fleury (4).

St. Louis Blues

Top Scorers	Gm	G	A	Pts	+/-	PM	PP
Doug Weight, C	.82	16	43	59	10	56	5
Lee Stempniak, R	.82	27	25	52	-2	33	8
Petr Cajanek, C	.77	15	33	48	9	54	1
Brad Boyes, C	.81	17	29	46	-17	29	1
BOS	.62	13	21	34	-17	25	1
ST.L	.19	4	8	12	0	4	0
Radek Dvorak, R	.82	10	27	37	-6	48	1
Jay McClement, C	.81	8	28	36	3	55	0
Glen Metropolit, C	.77	14	19	33	9	34	5
ATL	.57	12	16	28	9	20	4
ST.L	.20	2	3	5	0	14	1
Martin Rucinsky, L	.52	12	21	33	-3	48	4
Eric Brewer, D	.82	6	23	29	-10	69	2
Barret Jackman, D	.70	3	24	27	20	82	1
David Backes*, C	.49	10	13	23	6	37	2
Jamal Mayers, R	.80	8	14	22	-19	89	0
Christian Backman, D	.61	7	11	18	13	36	1
Dallas Drake, R	.60	6	6	12	-14	38	0
Ryan Johnson, C	.59	7	4	11	-7	47	0
Dan Hinote, R	.41	5	5	10	-8	23	0
Bryce Salvador, D	.64	2	5	7	-5	55	0
Jeff Woywitka, D	.34	1	6	7	4	12	0

Acquired: C Metropolit, '07 1st-round and 3rd-round picks and an '08 2nd-round pick from Atl. for L Keith Tkachuk (Feb.25); C Boyes from Bos. for D Dennis Wideman (Feb. 27).

Goalies (10 Gm)	Gm	Min	GAA	Record	SV%
Manny Legace	.45	2522	2.59	23-15-5	.907
Jason Bacashihua*	.19	894	3.15	3-7-3	.896
Curtis Sanford	.31	1492	3.18	8-12-5	.888
ST. LOUIS	.82	5001	2.98	34-35-13	.895

Shutouts: Legace (5); Legace and Sanford also shared a shutout. **Assists:** none. **PM:** Legace and Bacashihua (2).

San Jose Sharks

Top Scorers	Gm	G	A	Pts	+/-	PM	PP
Joe Thornton, C	.82	22	92	114	24	44	10
Patrick Marleau, C	.77	32	46	78	9	33	14
Jonathan Cheechoo, R	76	37	32	69	11	69	15
Milan Michalek, R	.78	26	40	66	17	36	11
Bill Guerin, R	.77	36	20	56	10	66	9
ST.L	.61	28	19	47	8	52	7
SJ	.16	8	1	9	2	14	2
Matthew Carle*, D	.77	11	31	42	9	30	8
Ryane Clowe*, L	.58	16	18	34	4	78	4
Mike Grier, R	.81	16	17	33	-5	43	2
Christian Ehrhoff, D	.82	10	23	33	8	63	6
Steve Bernier, R	.62	15	16	31	5	39	5
Joe Pavelski*, C	.46	14	14	28	4	18	5
Marc-Edouard Vlasic*, D	81	3	23	26	13	18	2
Craig Rivet, D	.71	7	17	24	1	69	2
MON	.54	6	10	16	-7	57	2
SJ	.17	1	7	8	8	12	0
Scott Hannan, D	.79	4	20	24	1	38	0
Patrick Rissmiller, C	.79	7	15	22	1	22	1
Mark Bell, L	.71	11	10	21	-9	83	3
Curtis Brown, C	.78	8	12	20	-2	56	0
Kyle McLaren, D	.67	5	12	17	10	61	1
Marcel Goc, C	.78	5	8	13	-2	24	0
Mark Smith, C	.41	3	10	13	-4	42	2

Acquired: D Rivet and an '08 5th-round pick from Mon. for D Josh Gorges and an '07 1st-round pick (Feb. 25); R Guerin from St.L for L Ville Nieminen, F Jay Barriball and an '07 1st-round pick (Feb. 27).

Goalies (10 Gm)	Gm	Min	GAA	Record	Sv%
Evgeni Nabokov	.50	2778	2.29	25-16-4	.914
Vesa Toskala	.38	2142	2.35	26-10-1	.908
SAN JOSE	.82	4947	2.39	51-26-5	.908

Shutouts: Nabokov (7); Toskala (4). **Assists:** Toskala (3). **PM:** Nabokov (6).

Tampa Bay Lightning

Top Scorers	Gm	G	A	Pts	+/-	PM	PP
Vincent Lecavalier, C	.82	52	56	108	2	44	16
Martin St. Louis, R	.82	43	59	102	7	28	14
Brad Richards, C	.82	25	45	70	-19	23	12
Dan Boyle, D	.82	20	43	63	-5	62	10
Vaclav Prospal, L	.82	14	41	55	-24	36	2
Filip Kuba, D	.81	15	22	37	-9	36	5
Eric Perrin, C	.82	13	23	36	-7	30	2
Ruslan Fedotenko, R	.80	12	20	32	-3	52	2
Paul Ranger, D	.72	4	24	28	5	42	0
Ryan Craig, C	.72	14	13	27	-11	55	4
Jason Ward. R	.70	8	11	19	-15	40	0
NYR	.46	4	6	10	-3	26	0
LA	.7	0	1	1	-1	4	0
TB	.17	4	4	8	-11	10	0
Shane O'Brien*, D	.80	2	14	16	-3	176	1
ANA	.62	2	12	14	5	140	1
TB	.18	0	2	2	-8	36	0
Cory Sarich, D	.82	0	15	15	-6	70	0
Doug Janik, D	.75	2	9	11	-11	53	0
Nick Tarnasky*, C	.77	5	4	9	-6	80	0
Andreas Karlsson, C	.53	3	6	9	-4	12	0
Nolan Pratt, D	.81	1	7	8	0	44	0
Tim Taylor, C	.71	1	5	6	-5	16	0

Acquired: D O'Brien and an '08 3rd-round pick from Ana. for G Gerald Coleman and an '07 1st-round pick (Feb. 24); R Ward from LA for an '07 5th-round pick (Feb. 27).

Goalies (10 Gm)	Gm	Min	GAA	Record	SV%
Johan Holmqvist	.48	2548	2.85	27-15-3	.893
Marc Denis	.44	2353	3.19	17-18-2	.883
TAMPA BAY	.82	4995	3.11	44-33-5	.884

Shutouts: Holmqvist and Denis (1). **Assists:** Holmqvist (3). **PM:** Holmqvist (4); Denis (2).

Toronto Maple Leafs

Top Scorers	Gm	G	A	Pts	+/-	PM	PP
Mats Sundin, C	.75	27	49	76	-2	62	6
Tomas Kaberle, D	.74	11	47	58	3	20	2
Bryan McCabe, D	.82	15	42	57	3	115	11
Alexei Ponikarovsky, L	.71	21	24	45	8	63	6
Darcy Tucker, R	.56	24	19	43	-11	81	15
Jeff O'Neill, C	.74	20	22	42	1	54	6
Kyle Wellwood, C	.48	12	30	42	3	0	7
Matt Stajan, C	.82	10	29	39	3	44	1
Yanic Perreault, C	.66	21	17	38	-1	34	7
PHO	.49	19	14	33	-2	30	7
TOR	.17	2	3	5	1	4	0
Alex Steen, C	.82	15	20	35	5	26	4
Nik Antropov, C	.54	18	15	33	8	44	5
Bates Battaglia, L	.82	12	19	31	9	45	0
John Pohl, C	.74	13	16	29	-4	10	3
Chad Kilger, C	.82	14	14	28	-5	58	0
Ian White*, D	.76	3	23	26	8	40	1
Pavel Kubina, D	.61	7	14	21	7	48	4
Hal Gill, D	.82	6	14	20	11	91	0
Boyd Devereaux, C	.33	8	11	19	4	12	0
Carlo Colaiacovo*, D	48	8	9	17	6	20	0
Michael Peca, C	.35	4	11	15	2	60	0
Kris Newbury*, C	.15	2	2	4	4	26	0

Acquired: C Perreault from Pho. for D Brendan Bell and an '07 2nd-round pick (Feb. 27).

Goalies (10 Gm)	Gm	Min	GAA	Record	Sv%
Andrew Raycroft	.72	4108	2.99	37-25-9	.894
Jean-Sebastien Aubin	.20	804	3.43	3-5-2	.876
TORONTO	.82	4997	3.15	40-31-11	.888

Shutouts: Raycroft (2). **Assists:** Raycroft (1). **PM:** Raycroft (8).

Vancouver Canucks

Top Scorers	Gm	G	A	Pts	+/-	PM	PP
Daniel Sedin, L	.81	36	48	84	19	36	16
Henrik Sedin, C	.82	10	71	81	19	66	1
Markus Naslund, L	.82	24	36	60	3	54	9
Brendan Morrison, C	.82	20	31	51	-9	.60	4
Bryan Smolinski, C	.82	18	26	44	7	37	6
CHI	.62	14	23	37	10	29	4
VAN	.20	4	3	7	-3	8	2
Kevin Bieksa, D	.81	12	30	42	1	134	6
Taylor Pyatt, L	.76	23	14	37	5	42	9
Sami Salo, D	.67	14	23	37	21	26	5
Mattias Ohlund, D	.77	11	20	31	-3	80	6
Matt Cooke, L	.81	10	20	30	0	64	1
Brent Sopel, D	.64	5	23	28	2	24	2
LA	.44	4	19	23	2	14	2
VAN	.20	1	4	5	0	10	0
Trevor Linden, C	.80	12	13	25	-6	34	5
Jan Bulis, C	.79	12	11	23	-8	70	1
Ryan Kesler, C	.48	6	10	16	1	40	0
Lukas Krajicek, D	.78	3	13	16	-4	64	1
Jeff Cowan, L	.63	7	5	12	3	125	0
LA	.21	0	2	2	-1	32	0
VAN	.42	7	3	10	4	93	0

Acquired: C Smolinski from Chi. for an '07 2nd-round pick (Feb. 26); D Sopel from LA for an '07 or '08 2nd-round pick and '08 4th-round pick (Feb. 26). **Claimed:** L Cowan off waivers from LA (Dec. 30).

Goalies (10 Gm)	Gm	Min	GAA	Record	SV%
Roberto Luongo	.76	4490	2.29	47-22-6	.921
VANCOUVER	.82	5006	2.36	49-26-7	.918

Shutouts: Luongo (5). **Assists:** Luongo (2). **PM:** Luongo (10).

Washington Capitals

Top Scorers	Gm	G	A	Pts	+/-	PM	PP
Alexander Ovechkin, L	.82	46	46	92	-19	52	16
Alexander Semin, L	.77	38	35	73	-7	90	17
Chris Clark, R	.74	30	24	54	-10	66	9
Matt Pettinger, L	.64	16	16	32	-13	22	4
Boyd Gordon, C	.71	7	22	29	10	14	0
Brian Pothier, D	.72	3	25	28	-11	44	2
Kris Beech, C	.64	8	18	26	-11	46	3
Ben Clymer, R	.66	7	13	20	-17	44	0
Jiri Novotny*, C	.68	6	13	19	-4	28	0
BUF	.50	6	7	13	-2	26	0
WASH	.18	0	6	6	-2	2	0
Brooks Laich, C	.73	8	10	18	-2	29	2
Brian Sutherby, C	.69	7	10	17	-9	78	1
Steve Eminger, D	.68	1	16	17	-14	63	0
Matt Bradley, R	.57	4	9	13	-5	47	0
Donald Brashear, L	.77	4	9	13	1	156	0
Shaone Morrisonn, D	.78	3	10	13	3	106	0
Milan Jurcina, D	.70	4	8	12	0	44	0
BOS	.40	2	1	3	-5	20	0
WASH	.30	2	7	9	5	24	0
Mike Green*, D	.70	2	10	12	-10	36	0

Acquired: D Jurcina from Bos. for a conditional '08 pick (Feb. 1); C Jiri Novotny and an '07 1st-round pick from Buf. for R Dainius Zubrus and D Timo Helbling (Feb. 27).

Goalies (10 Gm)	Gm	Min	GAA	Record	Sv%
Olaf Kolzig	.54	3184	3.00	22-24-6	.910
Brent Johnson	.30	1644	3.61	6-15-7	.889
WASHINGTON	.82	4996	3.30	28-40-14	.899

Shutouts: Kolzig (1). **Assists:** Kolzig (3); Johnson (1). **PM:** Kolzig (10); Johnson (4).

2007 NHL Entry Draft

Top 50 selections at the 45th annual NHL Entry Draft held June 22-23, 2007, at Nationwide Arena in Columbus. First 30 picks are first-round selections, 31-50 are second round. The order of the first 14 positions were determined by a draft lottery of non-playoff teams held April 10 in New York City. Only the worst five teams from the 2006-07 regular season had the chance to win the first overall pick. No team could move up more than four spots in the draft order or drop more than one position. Positions 15 through 30 reflect regular season records in reverse order.

Top 50 Selections

	Team	Player, Last Team	Pos		Team	Player, Last Team	Pos
1	Chicago	Patrick Kane, London (OHL)	R	26	k-St. Louis	David Perron, Lewiston (QMJHL)	L
2	Philadelphia	James Van Riemsdyk, USA U-18	L	27	Detroit	Brendan Smith, St. Michaels (OPJRA)	D
3	Phoenix	Kyle Turris, Burnaby (BCHL)	C	28	l-San Jose	Nicholas Petrecki, Omaha (USHL)	D
4	Los Angeles	Thomas Hickey, Seattle (WHL)	D	29	Ottawa	James O'Brien, Minnesota (WCHA)	C
5	Washington	Karl Alzner, Calgary (WHL)	D	30	m-Phoenix	Nick Ross, Regina (WHL)	D
6	Edmonton	Sam Gagner, London (OHL)	C	31	n-Buffalo	T.J. Brennan, St. John's (QMJHL)	D
7	Columbus	Jakub Voracek, Halifax (QMJHL)	R	32	Phoenix	Brett MacLean, Oshawa (OHL)	L
8	Boston	Zach Hamill, Everett (WHL)	C	33	o-Vancouver	Taylor Ellington, Everett (WHL)	D
9	a-San Jose	Logan Couture, Ottawa (OHL)	C	34	Washington	Josh Godfrey, Sault Ste. Marie (OHL)	D
10	Florida	Keaton Ellerby, Kamloops (WHL)	D	35	p-Boston	Tommy Cross, Westminster (HS)	D
11	Carolina	Brandon Sutter, Red Deer (WHL)	C	36	q-Phoenix	Joel Gistedt, Frolunda (Swe)	G
12	Montreal	Ryan McDonagh, Cretin-Derham (HS)	D	37	Columbus	Stefan Legein, Mississauga (OHL)	R
13	b-St. Louis	Lars Eller, Frolunda Jr. (Swe)	C	38	r-Chicago	William Sweatt, Colorado Col. (WCHA)	L
14	Colorado	Kevin Shattenkirk, USA U-18	D	39	St. Louis	Simon Hjalmarsson, Frolunda Jr. (Swe)	R
15	c-Edmonton	Alex Plante, Calgary (WHL)	D	40	Florida	Michal Repik, Vancouver (WHL)	R
16	d-Minnesota	Colton Gillies, Saskatoon (WHL)	C	41	s-Philadelphia	Kevin Marshall, Lewiston (QMJHL)	D
17	NY Rangers	Alexei Cherepanov, Omsk (Rus)	R	42	t-Anaheim	Eric Tangradi, Belleville (OHL)	C
18	e-St. Louis	Ian Cole, USA U-18	D	43	Montreal	P.K. Subban, Belleville (OHL)	D
19	f-Anaheim	Logan MacMillan, Halifax (QMJHL)	C	44	u-St. Louis	Aaron Palushaj, Des Moines (USHL)	R
20	Pittsburgh	Angelo Esposito, Quebec (QMJHL)	C	45	Colorado	Colby Cohen, Lincoln (USHL)	D
21	g-Edmonton	Riley Nash, Salmon Arm (BCHL)	C	46	v-Washington	Ted Ruth, USA U-18	D
22	h-Montreal	Max Pacioretty, Sioux City (USHL)	L	47	Tampa Bay	Dana Tyrell, Prince George (WHL)	C
23	i-Nashville	Jonathon Blum, Vancouver (WHL)	D	48	NY Rangers	Antoine Lafleur, PEI (QMJHL)	G
24	j-Calgary	Mikael Backlund, Vasteras (Swe)	C	49	w-Colorado	Trevor Cann, Peterborough (OHL)	G
25	Vancouver	Patrick White, Tri-City (USHL)	C	50	x-Dallas	Nico Sacchetti, Virginia (HS)	C

Acquired picks: a—from St.L; **b**—from Tor; **c**—from NYI; **d**—from TB; **e**—from Calg; **f**—from Min; **g**—from Dal; **h**—from SJ; **i**—from Phi; **j**—from Atl; **k**—from NJ; **l**—from Buf; **m**—from Ana; **n**—from Phi; **o**—from LA; **p**—from Chi; **q**—from Edm; **r**—from Bos; **s**—from Car; **t**—from Min; **u**—from Tor; **v**—from NYI; **w**—from Calg; **x**—from Min.

Stanley Cup Playoffs

| QUARTERFINALS | SEMIFINALS | FINALS | | FINALS | SEMIFINALS | QUARTERFINALS |

(1) Detroit 4						(1) Buffalo 4
	Detroit 4			Buffalo 4		
(8) Calgary 2						(8) NY Islanders 1
		Detroit 2			Buffalo 4	
(4) Nashville 1						(3) Atlanta 0
	San Jose 2				NY Rangers 2	
(5) San Jose 4						(6) NY Rangers 4
		WESTERN CONFERENCE	Anaheim 4	EASTERN CONFERENCE		
(2) Anaheim 4			Ottawa 1			(2) New Jersey 4
	Anaheim 4				New Jersey 1	
(7) Minnesota 1						(7) Tampa Bay 2
		Anaheim 4		Ottawa 4		
(3) Vancouver 4						(4) Ottawa 4
	Vancouver 1				Ottawa 4	
(6) Dallas 3						(5) Pittsburgh 1

Stanley Cup Playoffs

Series Summaries

WESTERN CONFERENCE

FIRST ROUND (Best of 7)

	W-L	GF	Leading Scorers
Detroit	4-2	18	Lidstrom (2-6–8)
Calgary	2-4	10	Three tied with 4 pts.

Date	Winner	Home Ice
April 12	Red Wings, 4-1	at Detroit
April 15	Red Wings, 3-1	at Detroit
April 17	Flames, 3-2	at Calgary
April 19	Flames, 3-2	at Calgary
April 21	Red Wings, 5-1	at Detroit
April 22	Red Wings, 2-1 (2OT)	at Calgary

	W-L	GF	Leading Scorers
Anaheim	4-1	12	Pronger (2-4–6)
Minnesota	1-4	9	Demitra (1-3–4) & Gaborik (3-1–4)

Date	Winner	Home Ice
April 11	Ducks, 2-1	at Anaheim
April 13	Ducks, 3-2	at Anaheim
April 15	Ducks, 2-1	at Minnesota
April 17	Wild, 4-1	at Minnesota
April 19	Ducks, 4-1	at Anaheim

	W-L	GF	Leading Scorers
Vancouver	4-3	13	Linden (2-3–5) Pyatt (2-3–5)
Dallas	3-4	12	Barnes (1-3–4) & Zubov (0-4–4)

Date	Winner	Home Ice
April 11	Canucks, 5-4 (4OT)	at Vancouver
April 13	Stars, 2-0	at Vancouver
April 15	Canucks, 2-1 (OT)	at Dallas
April 17	Canucks, 2-1	at Dallas
April 19	Stars, 1-0 (OT)	at Vancouver
April 21	Stars, 2-0	at Dallas
April 23	Canucks, 4-1	at Vancouver

Shutouts: Turco, Dallas (3).

	W-L	GF	Leading Scorers
San Jose	4-1	16	Marleau (3-3–6) & Thornton (0-6–6)
Nashville	1-4	14	Dumont (4-2–6)

Date	Winner	Home Ice
April 11	Sharks, 5-4 (2OT)	at Nashville
April 13	Predators, 5-2	at Nashville
April 16	Sharks, 3-1	at San Jose
April 18	Sharks, 3-2	at San Jose
April 20	Sharks, 3-2	at Nashville

SEMIFINALS (Best of 7)

	W-L	GF	Leading Scorers
Detroit	4-2	13	Datsyuk (2-4–6)
San Jose	2-4	9	Thornton (1-4–5)

Date	Winner	Home Ice
April 26	Sharks, 2-0	at Detroit
April 28	Red Wings, 3-2	at Detroit
April 30	Sharks, 2-1	at San Jose
May 2	Red Wings, 3-2 (OT)	at San Jose
May 5	Red Wings, 4-1	at Detroit
May 7	Red Wings, 2-0	at San Jose

Shutouts: Nabokov, SJ; Hasek, Det.

	W-L	GF	Leading Scorers
Anaheim	4-1	14	Three tied with 5 pts.
Vancouver	1-4	8	Naslund (3-0–3) & Ohlund (0-3–3)

Date	Winner	Home Ice
April 25	Ducks, 5-1	at Anaheim
April 27	Canucks, 2-1 (2OT)	at Anaheim
April 29	Ducks, 3-2	at Vancouver
May 1	Ducks, 3-2 (OT)	at Vancouver
May 3	Ducks, 2-1 (2OT)	at Anaheim

CHAMPIONSHIP (Best of 7)

	W-L	GF	Leading Scorers
Anaheim	4-2	16	Selanne (2-4-6)
			& Getzlaf (2-4-6)
Detroit	2-4	17	Cleary (2-5-7)
			& Lidstrom (1-6-7)

Date	Winner	Home Ice
May 11	Red Wings, 2-1	at Detroit
May 13	Ducks, 4-3 (OT)	at Detroit
May 15	Red Wings, 5-0	at Anaheim
May 17	Ducks, 5-3	at Anaheim
May 20	Ducks, 2-1 (OT)	at Detroit
May 22	Ducks, 4-3	at Anaheim

Shutout: Hasek, Detroit.

EASTERN CONFERENCE

FIRST ROUND (Best of 7)

	W-L	GF	Leading Scorers
Buffalo	4-1	17	Three tied with 5 pts.
NY Islanders	1-4	11	Smyth (1-3-4)

Date	Winner	Home Ice
April 12	Sabres, 4-1	at Buffalo
April 14	Islanders, 3-2	at Buffalo
April 16	Sabres, 3-2	at NY Islanders
April 18	Sabres, 4-2	at NY Islanders
April 20	Sabres, 4-3	at Buffalo

	W-L	GF	Leading Scorers
NY Rangers	4-0	17	Nylander (4-4-8)
Atlanta	0-4	6	Tkachuk (1-2-3)
			& Dupuis (1-2-3)

Date	Winner	Home Ice
April 12	Rangers, 4-3	at Atlanta
April 14	Rangers, 2-1	at Atlanta
April 17	Rangers, 7-0	at New York
April 18	Rangers, 4-2	at New York

Shutout: Lundqvist, New York.

	W-L	GF	Leading Scorers
New Jersey	4-2	19	Gomez (2-7-9)
Tampa Bay	2-4	14	Richards (3-5-8)
			& St. Louis (3-5-8)

Date	Winner	Home Ice
April 12	Devils, 5-3	at New Jersey
April 14	Lightning, 3-2	at New Jersey
April 16	Lightning, 3-2	at Tampa Bay
April 18	Devils, 4-3 (OT)	at Tampa Bay
April 20	Devils, 3-0	at New Jersey
April 22	Devils, 3-2	at Tampa Bay

Shutout: Brodeur, New Jersey.

	W-L	GF	Leading Scorers
Ottawa	4-1	18	Alfredsson (3-3-6)
Pittsburgh	1-4	10	Crosby (3-2-5)

Date	Winner	Home Ice
April 11	Senators, 6-3	at Ottawa
April 14	Penguins, 4-3	at Ottawa
April 15	Senators, 4-2	at Pittsburgh
April 17	Senators, 2-1	at Pittsburgh
April 19	Senators, 3-0	at Ottawa

Shutout: Emery, Ottawa.

SEMIFINALS (Best of 7)

	W-L	GF	Leading Scorers
Buffalo	4-2	17	Briere (1-5-6)
NY Rangers	2-4	13	Straka (2-5-7)

Date	Winner	Home Ice
April 25	Sabres, 5-2	at Buffalo
April 27	Sabres, 3-2	at Buffalo
April 29	Rangers, 2-1 (2OT)	at New York
May 1	Rangers, 2-1	at New York
May 4	Sabres, 2-1 (OT)	at Buffalo
May 6	Sabres, 5-4	at New York

	W-L	GF	Leading Scorers
Ottawa	4-1	15	Heatley (3-7-10)
New Jersey	1-4	11	Gomez (2-3-5)

Date	Winner	Home Ice
April 26	Senators, 5-4	at New Jersey
April 28	Devils, 3-2 (2OT)	at New Jersey
April 30	Senators, 2-0	at Ottawa
May 2	Senators, 3-2	at Ottawa
May 5	Senators, 3-2	at New Jersey

Shutout: Emery, Ottawa.

CHAMPIONSHIP (Best of 7)

	W-L	GF	Leading Scorers
Ottawa	4-1	15	Spezza (2-6-8)
Buffalo	1-4	10	Three tied with 4 pts.

Date	Winner	Home Ice
May 10	Senators, 5-2	at Buffalo
May 12	Senators, 4-3 (2OT)	at Buffalo
May 14	Senators, 1-0	at Ottawa
May 16	Sabres, 3-2	at Ottawa
May 19	Senators, 3-2 (OT)	at Buffalo

Shutout: Emery, Ottawa.

STANLEY CUP FINALS (Best of 7)

	W-L	GF	Leading Scorers
Anaheim	4-1	16	McDonald (5-2-7)
Ottawa	1-4	11	Alfredsson (4-1-5)

Date	Winner	Home Ice
May 28	Ducks, 3-2	at Anaheim
May 30	Ducks, 1-0	at Anaheim
June 2	Senators, 5-3	at Ottawa
June 4	Ducks, 3-2	at Ottawa
June 6	Ducks, 6-2	at Anaheim

Shutouts: Giguere, Anaheim.

Stanley Cup Finals Box Scores

Game 1

Monday, May 28, at Anaheim

Ottawa 1 1 0	**— 2**
Anaheim 1 0 2	**—3**

1st Period: OTT—Fisher 4 (Meszaros, Comrie), 1:38 (pp); ANA—McDonald 6 (Selanne), 10:55.

2nd Period: OTT—Redden 3 (Alfredsson, Spezza), 4:36 (pp).

3rd Period: ANA—Getzlaf 6 (Perry, Jackman), 5:44; ANA—Moen 5 (R. Niedermayer, S. Niedermayer), 17:09.

Shots on Goal: Ottawa—3-10-7-20; Anaheim—7-10-14-32. **Power plays:** Ottawa 2-7; Anaheim 0-4. **Goalies:** Ottawa, Emery (32 shots, 29 saves); Anaheim, Giguere (20 shots, 18 saves). **Attendance:** 17,274.

Game 2

Wednesday, May 30, at Anaheim

Ottawa 0 0 0	**— 0**
Anaheim 0 0 1	**—1**

3rd Period: ANA—Pahlsson 3 (unassisted), 14:16.

Shots on Goal: Ottawa—7-4-5-16; Anaheim—12-14-5-31. **Power plays:** Ottawa 0-4; Anaheim 0-4. **Goalies:** Ottawa, Emery (31 shots, 30 saves); Anaheim, Giguere (16 shots, 16 saves). **Attendance:** 17,258.

Game 3

Saturday, June 2, at Ottawa

Anaheim 1 2 0	**— 3**
Ottawa 1 3 1	**—5**

1st Period: ANA—McDonald 7 (Selanne), 5:39 (pp); OTT—Neil 2 (Kelly, Meszaros), 16:10.

2nd Period: ANA—Perry 5 (Penner, Getzlaf), 5:20; OTT—Fisher 5 (Volchenkov), 5:47; ANA—Getzlaf 7 (Penner, Perry), 7:38; OTT—Alfredsson 11 (Redden, Corvo), 16:14 (pp); OTT—McAmmond 5 (Saprykin, Schubert), 18:34.

3rd Period: OTT—Volchenkov 2 (Vermette, Kelly), 8:22.

Shots on Goal: Anaheim—8-11-3-22; Ottawa—10-12-7-29. **Power plays:** Anaheim 1-3; Ottawa 1-7. **Goalies:** Anaheim, Giguere (29 shots, 24 saves); Ottawa, Emery (22 shots, 19 saves). **Attendance:** 20,500.

Game 4

Monday, June 4, at Ottawa

Anaheim 0 2 1	**— 3**
Ottawa 1 1 0	**—2**

1st Period: OTT—Alfredsson 12 (Schaefer, Fisher), 19:59 (pp).

2nd Period: ANA—McDonald 8 (Marchant, Perry), 10:06; ANA—McDonald 9 (R. Niedermayer, O'Donnell), 11:06; OTT—Heatley 7 (Eaves, Spezza), 18:00.

3rd Period: ANA—Penner 3 (Selanne, McDonald), 4:07.

Shots on Goal: Anaheim—2-13-6-21; Ottawa—13-4-6-23. **Power plays:** Anaheim 0-3; Ottawa 1-4. **Goalies:** Anaheim, Giguere (23 shots, 21 saves); Ottawa, Emery (21 shots, 18 saves). **Attendance:** 20,500.

Game 5

Wednesday, June 6, at Anaheim

Ottawa 0 2 0	**— 2**
Anaheim 2 2 2	**—6**

1st Period: ANA—McDonald 10 (Getzlaf, Pronger), 3:41 (pp); ANA—R. Niedermayer 5 (Perry), 17:41.

2nd Period: OTT—Alfredsson 13 (Schaefer, Fisher), 11:27; ANA—Moen 6 (unassisted), 15:44; OTT—Alfredsson 14 (unassisted), 17:38 (sh); ANA—Beauchemin 4 (McDonald), 18:28 (pp).

3rd Period: ANA—Moen 7 (S. Niedermayer, Pahlsson), 4:01; ANA—Perry 6 (unassisted), 17:00.

Shots on Goal: Ottawa—3-5-5-13; Anaheim—5-7-6-18. **Power plays:** Ottawa 0-3; Anaheim 2-6. **Goalies:** Ottawa, Emery (18 shots, 12 saves); Anaheim, Giguere (13 shots, 11 saves). **Attendance:** 17,372.

Stanley Cup Leaders

Scoring

(including all playoff games)

	Gm	G	A	Pts	+/-	PM	PP
Daniel Alfredsson, Ott	20	14	8	**22**	4	10	6
Dany Heatley, Ott	20	7	15	**22**	4	14	2
Jason Spezza, Ott	20	7	15	**22**	5	10	3
Nicklas Lidstrom, Det	18	4	14	**18**	0	6	4
Ryan Getzlaf, Ana	21	7	10	**17**	1	32	3
Pavel Datsyuk, Det	18	8	8	**16**	2	8	4
Corey Perry, Ana	21	6	9	**15**	5	37	1
Teemu Selanne, Ana	21	5	10	**15**	1	10	0
Daniel Briere, Buf	16	5	10	**15**	3	16	2
Chris Pronger, Ana	19	3	12	**15**	10	26	1

Goaltending

(Minimum 390 minutes)

	Gm	W-L	ShO	GAA	Sv%
Marty Turco, Dal	7	3-4	3	**1.30**	.952
Roberto Luongo, Van	12	5-7	0	**1.77**	.941
Dominik Hasek, Det	18	10-8	2	**1.79**	.923
J-S Giguere, Ana	18	13-4	1	**1.97**	.922
Henrik Lundqvist, NYR	10	6-4	1	**2.07**	.924

Final Stanley Cup Standings

				—Goals—		
	Gm	W	L	For	Opp	Dif
Anaheim	21	16	5	58	45	+13
Ottawa	20	13	7	59	47	+12
Detroit	18	10	8	48	35	+13
Buffalo	16	9	7	44	39	+5
NY Rangers	10	6	4	30	23	+7
San Jose	11	6	5	25	27	-2
New Jersey	11	5	6	30	29	+1
Vancouver	12	5	7	21	26	-5
Dallas	7	3	4	12	13	-1
Tampa Bay	6	2	4	14	19	-5
Calgary	6	2	4	10	18	-8
Nashville	5	1	4	14	16	-2
Minnesota	5	1	4	9	12	-3
NY Islanders	5	1	4	11	17	-6
Pittsburgh	5	1	4	10	18	-8
Atlanta	4	0	4	6	17	-11

Conn Smythe Trophy (Playoff MVP)
Scott Niedermayer, Anaheim, D
21 games, 3 goals, 8 assists, 11 points, plus 2.

Finalists' Composite Box Scores

Anaheim Ducks (16-5)

Top Scorers	Pos	Overall Playoffs								Finals vs Ottawa							
		Gm	G	A	Pts	+/-	PM	PP	S	Gm	G	A	Pts	+/-	PM	PP	S
Ryan Getzlaf	C	21	7	10	17	1	32	3	57	5	2	2	4	0	8	0	8
Corey Perry	R	21	6	9	15	5	37	1	58	5	2	4	6	3	10	0	11
Teemu Selanne	R	21	5	10	15	1	10	0	60	5	0	3	3	-1	2	0	8
Chris Pronger	D	19	3	12	15	10	26	1	58	4	0	1	1	4	4	0	6
Andy McDonald	C	21	10	4	14	6	10	5	64	5	5	2	7	3	4	2	10
Travis Moen	L	21	7	5	12	5	22	0	34	5	3	0	3	3	2	0	8
Samuel Pahlsson	C	21	3	9	12	10	20	0	30	5	1	1	2	4	8	0	11
Scott Niedermayer	D	21	3	8	11	2	26	1	42	5	0	2	2	1	6	0	3
Rob Niedermayer	C	21	5	5	10	9	39	0	42	5	1	2	3	4	0	0	15
Francois Beauchemin	D	20	4	4	8	2	16	4	58	5	1	0	1	-1	6	1	14
Dustin Penner*	R	21	3	5	8	4	2	0	37	5	1	2	3	2	2	0	11
Chris Kunitz	L	13	1	5	6	1	19	0	28	2	0	0	0	-1	0	0	1
Todd Marchant	C	11	0	3	3	-1	12	0	19	5	0	1	1	-1	0	0	9
Ric Jackman	D	7	1	1	2	2	2	1	2	4	0	1	1	2	2	0	0
Sean O'Donnell	D	21	0	2	2	8	10	0	13	5	0	1	1	4	2	0	2
Brad May	L	18	0	1	1	-1	28	0	14	5	0	0	0	1	4	0	2
Kent Huskins	D	21	0	1	1	4	11	0	5	5	0	0	0	2	0	0	1

Overtime goals—OVERALL (S. Niedermayer 2, Selanne, Moen); FINALS (none). **Shorthanded goals**—OVERALL (Getzlaf, R. Niedermayer); FINALS (none). **Power Play conversions**—OVERALL (16 for 105, 15.2%); FINALS (3 for 20, 15.0%).

Goaltending	Overall Playoffs							Finals vs Ottawa						
	Gm	Min	GAA	GA	SA	Sv%	W-L	Gm	Min	GAA	GA	SA	Sv%	W-L
Jean-Sebastien Giguere	18	1067	1.97	35	451	.922	13-4	5	298	2.21	11	101	.891	4-1
Ilja Bryzgalov	5	267	2.25	10	128	.922	3-1	0	0	—	0	0	—	0-0
TOTAL	21	1341	2.01	45	579	.922	16-5	5	300	2.20	11	101	.891	4-1

Empty Net Goals—OVERALL (none), FINALS (none). **Shutouts**—OVERALL (Giguere), FINALS (Giguere). **Assists**—OVERALL (none), FINALS (none). **Penalty Minutes**—OVERALL (none), FINALS (none).

Ottawa Senators (13-7)

Top Scorers	Pos	Overall Playoffs								Finals vs Anaheim							
		Gm	G	A	Pts	+/-	PM	PP	S	Gm	G	A	Pts	+/-	PM	PP	S
Daniel Alfredsson	R	20	14	8	22	4	10	6	66	5	4	1	5	-3	0	2	12
Dany Heatley	L	20	7	15	22	4	14	2	59	5	1	0	1	-3	2	0	9
Jason Spezza	C	20	7	15	22	5	10	3	49	5	0	2	2	-2	4	0	5
Mike Fisher	C	20	5	5	10	-2	24	2	54	5	2	2	4	-2	8	1	11
Wade Redden	D	20	3	7	10	6	10	3	23	5	1	1	2	-3	4	1	6
Joe Corvo	D	20	2	7	9	4	6	1	49	5	0	1	1	0	0	0	7
Dean McAmmond	L	18	5	3	8	5	11	0	15	3	1	0	1	0	0	0	3
Chris Kelly	C	20	3	4	7	-4	0	0	27	5	0	2	2	-2	0	0	2
Tom Preissing	D	20	2	5	7	3	10	1	21	5	0	0	0	-2	0	0	4
Andrej Meszaros	D	20	1	6	7	5	12	0	26	5	0	2	2	-2	2	0	4
Mike Comrie	R	20	2	4	6	-1	17	0	25	5	0	1	1	-3	2	0	3
Anton Volchenkov	D	20	2	4	6	-2	24	0	18	5	1	1	2	-4	6	0	7
Peter Schaefer	L	20	1	5	6	1	10	0	33	5	0	2	2	-2	4	0	4
Antoine Vermette	L	20	2	3	5	2	6	0	28	5	0	1	1	-1	0	0	6
Chris Neil	R	20	2	2	4	2	20	0	31	5	1	0	1	-1	6	0	5
Oleg Saprykin	L	15	1	1	2	0	4	0	19	4	0	1	1	1	0	0	3
Patrick Eaves	R	7	0	2	2	0	2	0	7	3	0	1	1	0	2	0	4
Ray Emery	G	20	0	2	2	0	0	0	0	5	0	0	0	0	0	0	0
Christoph Schubert	D	20	0	1	1	-5	22	0	16	5	0	1	1	-2	6	0	2
Chris Phillips	D	20	0	0	0	-2	24	0	7	5	0	0	0	-2	4	0	4

Overtime goals—OVERALL (Alfredsson, Corvo); FINALS (none). **Shorthanded goals**— OVERALL (Alfredsson, Fisher, McAmmond); FINALS (Alfredsson). **Power Play conversions**—OVERALL (18 for 95, 18.9%); FINALS (4 for 25, 16.0%).

Goaltending	Overall Playoffs							Finals vs Anaheim						
	Gm	Min	GAA	GA	SA	Sv%	W-L	Gm	Min	GAA	GA	SA	Sv%	W-L
Ray Emery	20	1249	2.26	47	505	.907	13-7	5	296	3.24	16	124	.871	1-4
TOTAL	20	1256	2.25	47	505	.907	13-7	5	300	3.20	16	124	.871	1-4

Empty Net Goals—OVERALL (none), FINALS (none). **Shutouts**—OVERALL (Emery 3), FINALS (none). **Assists**—OVERALL (Emery 2), FINALS (none). **Penalty Minutes**—OVERALL (none), FINALS (none).

Annual Awards

Voting for the Hart, Calder, Norris, Lady Byng, Selke, and Masterton Trophies is conducted after the regular season by the Professional Hockey Writers' Association. The Vezina Trophy is selected by the NHL general managers, while the Jack Adams Award is selected by NHL broadcasters. Points are awarded on 10–7–5–3–1 basis except for the Vezina Trophy and the Adams Award which are awarded 5–3–1.

Hart Trophy
For Most Valuable Player

	Pos	1st	2nd	3rd	4th	5th	Pts
Sidney Crosby, Pit	C	91	34	14	2	1—	1225
Roberto Luongo, Van	G	25	46	35	16	6—	801
Martin Brodeur, NJ	G	21	45	39	12	7—	763
Vincent Lecavalier, TB	C	5	6	22	48	16—	362
Joe Thornton, SJ	C	0	8	11	27	38—	230

Calder Trophy
For Rookie of the Year

	Pos	1st	2nd	3rd	4th	5th	Pts
Evgeni Malkin, Pit	C	120	21	2	0	0—	1357
Paul Stastny, Col	C	16	95	25	5	0—	965
Jordan Staal, Pit	C	6	14	52	45	12—	565
Anze Kopitar, LA	C	0	8	40	45	26—	417
Dustin Penner, Ana	R	0	2	6	11	30—	107

Norris Trophy
For Best Defenseman

	1st	2nd	3rd	4th	5th	Pts
Nicklas Lidstrom, Det	87	44	5	4	2—	1217
Scott Niedermayer, Ana	46	62	22	6	2—	1024
Chris Pronger, Ana	6	25	55	28	14—	608
Dan Boyle, TB	1	5	21	19	12—	219
Kimmo Timonen, Nash	0	2	9	24	13—	144

Vezina Trophy
For Outstanding Goaltender

	1st	2nd	3rd	Pts
Martin Brodeur, NJ	16	14	0—	122
Roberto Luongo, Van	14	15	1—	116
Miikka Kiprusoff, Calg	0	0	7—	7
Henrik Lundqvist, NYR	0	0	7—	7
Dominik Hasek, Det	0	0	5—	5

Lady Byng Trophy
For Sportsmanship and Gentlemanly Play

	Pos	1st	2nd	3rd	4th	5th	Pts
Pavel Datsyuk, Det	C	38	26	18	15	8—	705
Martin St. Louis, TB	R	26	19	19	6	7—	513
Joe Sakic, Col	C	17	17	7	9	3—	354
Jay Pandolfo, NJ	L	16	5	7	4	1—	243
Pierre-Marc Bouchard, Min	R	6	3	13	4	9—	167

Selke Trophy
For Best Defensive Forward

	Pos	1st	2nd	3rd	4th	5th	Pts
Rod Brind'Amour, Car	C	16	21	7	23	9—	420
Samuel Pahlsson, Ana	C	24	8	18	4	7—	405
Jay Pandolfo, NJ	L	16	10	10	7	10—	311
Chris Drury, Buf	C	18	6	9	10	3—	300
Mike Fisher, Ott	C	12	10	12	4	10—	272

Adams Award
For Coach of the Year

	1st	2nd	3rd	Pts
Alain Vigneault, Van	18	12	8—	134
Lindy Ruff, Buf	11	18	17—	126
Michel Therrien, Pit	11	10	6—	91
Barry Trotz, Nash	11	7	13—	89
Ted Nolan, NYI	5	5	7—	47

AP/Wide World Photos

Sidney Crosby took home the Hart, Lester B. Pearson and Art Ross Trophies at the 2007 NHL Awards Ceremony.

Other Awards

Lester B. Pearson Award (NHL Players Assn. MVP)—Sidney Crosby, Pit.

Jennings Trophy (goaltenders with a minimum of 25 games played for team with fewest goals against)—Niklas Backstrom and Manny Fernandez, Min.

Maurice "Rocket" Richard Trophy (regular season goal-scoring leader)—Vincent Lecavalier, TB

Art Ross Trophy (regular season points leader)—Sidney Crosby, Pit.

Masterton Trophy (perseverance, sportsmanship, and dedication to hockey)—Phil Kessel, Bos.

King Clancy Trophy (leadership and humanitarian contributions to community)—Saku Koivu, Mon.

Lester Patrick Trophy (outstanding service to hockey in the U.S.)—Steve Yzerman, Red Berenson, Reed Larson, Glen Sonmor and Marcel Dionne. (Awarded in 2006)

All-NHL Team
Voting by PHWA. Holdovers from 2005-06 first team in **bold**.

	First Team		Second Team
G	Martin Brodeur, NJ	G	Roberto Luongo, Van
D	**Scott Niedermayer**, Ana	D	Dan Boyle, TB
D	**Nicklas Lidstrom**, Det	D	Chris Pronger, Ana
C	Sidney Crosby, Pit	C	Vincent Lecavalier, TB
R	Dany Heatley, Ott	R	Martin St. Louis, TB
L	**Alex Ovechkin**, Wash	L	Thomas Vanek, Buf

All-Rookie Team
Voting by PHWA.

Pos		Pos	
G	Mike Smith, Dal	F	Evgeni Malkin, Pit
D	Matt Carle, SJ	F	Jordan Staal, Pit
D	Marc-Edouard Vlasic, SJ	F	Paul Stastny, Col

COLLEGE HOCKEY

NCAA Men's Division I

Final regular season standings; overall records, including all postseason tournament games, in parentheses.

Atlantic Hockey

	W	L	T	Pts	GF	GA
R.I.T. (21-11-2)	20	7	1	41	116	71
Sacred Heart (21-11-4)	17	7	4	38	91	74
Army (17-12-5)	15	8	5	35	82	69
Connecticut (16-18-2)	15	11	2	32	90	89
*Air Force (19-16-5)	13	10	5	31	94	70
Holy Cross (10-20-5)	9	14	5	23	87	94
Bentley (12-22-1)	11	17	0	22	75	101
Mercyhurst (9-20-6)	9	15	4	22	98	106
Canisius (9-23-3)	9	16	3	21	76	95
American Int'l (8-25-1)	7	20	1	15	68	108

Conf. Tourney Final: Air Force 6, Army 1.
*NCAA Tourney (0-1): Air Force (0-1).

Central Collegiate Hockey Assn.

	W	L	T	Pts	GF	GA
*Notre Dame (32-7-3)	21	4	3	45	90	51
*Michigan (26-14-1)	18	9	1	37	119	85
*Miami-OH (24-14-4)	16	8	4	36	93	70
*Michigan St. (26-13-3)	15	10	3	33	81	65
Nebraska-Omaha (18-16-8)	13	11	4	30	100	85
W. Michigan (18-18-1)	14	13	1	29	85	93
Ohio State (15-17-5)	12	12	4	28	89	86
Lake Superior (21-19-3)	11	14	3	25	65	74
Ferris St. (14-22-3)	10	16	2	22	70	92
N. Michigan (15-24-2)	10	17	1	21	66	80
Alaska-Fairbanks (11-22-6)	7	16	5	19	70	90
Bowling Green (7-29-2)	5	22	1	11	51	108

Conf. Tourney Final: Notre Dame 2, Michigan 1.
*NCAA Tourney (6-3): Notre Dame (1-1), Michigan (0-1), Miami-OH (1-1), Michigan St. (4-0).

College Hockey America

	W	L	T	Pts	GF	GA
Niagara (18-13-6)	9	5	6	24	70	62
Bemidji State (14-14-5)	9	6	5	23	56	54
Robert Morris (14-19-2)	9	10	1	19	67	72
Wayne State (12-21-2)	8	10	2	18	64	63
*Alab.-Huntsville (13-20-3)	7	11	2	16	63	69

Conf. Tourney Final: Alab.-Huntsville 5, Robert Morris 4 (OT).
*NCAA Tourney (0-1): Alab.-Huntsville (0-1).

ECAC Hockey League

	W	L	T	Pts	GF	GA
*St. Lawrence (23-14-2)	16	5	1	33	73	55
*Clarkson (25-9-5)	13	5	4	30	74	53
Dartmouth (18-12-3)	12	7	3	27	69	60
Cornell (14-13-4)	10	8	4	24	65	55
Quinnipiac (21-14-5)	10	8	4	24	74	63
Harvard (14-17-2)	10	10	2	22	67	65
Princeton (15-16-3)	10	10	2	22	69	63
Yale (11-17-3)	8	13	1	17	56	72
Colgate (15-21-4)	7	12	3	17	53	60
Rensselaer (10-21-8)	6	11	5	17	55	84
Brown (11-15-6)	6	12	4	16	65	69
Union (14-19-3)	7	14	1	15	54	74

Conf. Tourney Final: Clarkson 4, Quinnipiac 2.
*NCAA Tourney (0-2): St. Lawrence (0-1); Clarkson (0-1).

Hockey East Association

	W	L	T	Pts	GF	GA
*New Hampshire (26-11-2)	18	7	2	38	96	62
*Boston College (29-12-1)	18	8	1	37	89	65
*Boston University (20-10-9)	13	6	8	34	69	51
*UMass-Amherst (21-13-5)	15	9	3	33	71	63
*Maine (23-15-2)	14	12	1	29	80	69
Vermont (18-16-5)	12	10	5	29	55	56
Northeastern (13-18-5)	9	13	5	23	60	66
Providence (10-23-3)	9	15	3	21	66	71
UMass-Lowell (8-21-7)	7	16	4	18	51	76
Merrimack (3-27-4)	3	22	2	8	28	86

Conf. Tourney Final: B.C. 5, New Hampshire 2.
*NCAA Tourney (6-5): New Hampshire (0-1); Boston College (3-1), Boston University (0-1); UMass-Amherst (1-1); Maine (2-1).

Western Collegiate Hockey Assn.

	W	L	T	Pts	GF	GA
*Minnesota (31-10-3)	18	7	3	39	91	67
*St. Cloud St. (22-11-7)	14	7	7	35	89	70
*North Dakota (24-14-5)	13	10	5	31	93	75
Denver (21-15-4)	13	11	4	30	73	73
Colorado College (18-17-4)	13	12	3	29	79	74
Wisconsin (19-18-4)	12	13	3	27	59	53
Michigan Tech (18-17-5)	11	12	5	27	69	64
Minnesota St. (19-19-3)	10	13	5	25	81	99
Minnesota Duluth (13-21-5)	8	16	4	20	64	84
Alaska-Anchorage (13-21-3)	8	19	1	17	62	101

Conf. Tourney Final: Minnesota 3, North Dakota 2 (OT).
*NCAA Tourney (3-3): Minnesota (1-1), St. Cloud St. (0-1). North Dakota (2-1).

USCHO.com/CSTV
Division I Men's Poll

Compiled March 19, 2007, **before** the NCAA tournament. Voting panel consists of 28 Division I coaches and 12 writers from across the country. First place votes are in parentheses. Teams in **bold** type went on to reach the NCAA Frozen Four. Top-10 shown.

	League	W	L	T	Pts
1 Notre Dame (24)	CCHA	31	6	3	727
2 Minnesota (13)	WCHA	30	9	3	714
3 Clarkson	ECAC	25	8	5	637
4 **Boston College**	HEA	26	11	1	625
5 New Hampshire	HEA	26	10	2	581
6 **North Dakota**	WCHA	22	13	5	567
7 St. Cloud St.	WCHA	22	10	7	518
8 Michigan	CCHA	26	13	1	484
9 Boston University	HEA	20	9	9	465
10 **Michigan St.**	CCHA	22	13	3	399

Hobey Baker Award

For men's College Hockey Player of the Year. Voting is done by a 25-member panel of college hockey personnel, national media, and pro scouts, plus a one percent fan vote.

		Cl	Pos
Winner: Ryan Duncan, North Dakota		So.	F

NCAA Division I Tournament

Regional seeds in parentheses

East Regional

Held in Rochester, N.Y., March 23-24.

First Round

(4) UMass-Amherst 1 . . . . .OT . . . .(1) Clarkson 0
(3) Maine 4 . . . .(2) St. Cloud St. 1

Second Round

Maine 3 . . . . .UMass-Amherst 1

Northeast Regional

Held in Manchester, N.H., March 24-25.

First Round

(4) Miami-OH 2 . . . .(1) New Hampshire 1
(2) Boston College 4 . . . .(3) St. Lawrence 1

Second Round

Boston College 4 . . . . .Miami-OH 0

West Regional

Held in Denver, Colo., March 24-25.

First Round

(1) Minnesota 4 . . . .(4) Air Force 3
(3) North Dakota 8 . . . .(2) Michigan 5

Second Round

North Dakota 3 . . . . .OT . . . . .Minnesota 2

Midwest Regional

Held in Grand Rapids, Mich., March 23-24.

First Round

(1) Notre Dame 3 . . . . . .2OT . . . .(4) Alab.-Huntsville 2
(3) Michigan St. 5 . . . .(2) Boston University 1

Second Round

Michigan St. 2 . . . . .Notre Dame 1

The Frozen Four

Held at the Scottrade Center in St. Louis, Mo., April 5 and April 7. Single elimination; no consolation game.

Semifinals

Michigan St. 4 .Maine 2
Boston College 6 . . . . .North Dakota 4

Championship Game

Michigan St., 3-1

Michigan St. (CCHA)	. . . .	0	0	3	—3
Boston College (HEA)	. . . .	0	1	0	—1

2nd Period: BC—Boyle 19 (Bradford), 6:50 (pp).
3rd Period: MSU—Kennedy 18 (Abdelkader), 9:53 (pp); MSU—Abdelkader 15 (Kennedy, Howells), 19:41; MSU—Mueller 16 (McKenzie, Vukovic), 19:58 (en).

Shots on Goal: Michigan St.—6-12-11—29; Boston College—13-6-11—30. **Power plays:** Michigan St. 1-6; Boston College 1-4.

Goalies: Michigan St.—Lerg (30 shots, 29 saves); Boston College—Schneider (28 shots, 26 saves).

Attendance: 19,432. **Time:** 2:37.

Most Outstanding Player: Justin Abdelkader, Michigan St. sophomore forward.

All-Tournament Team: Abdelkader, goaltender Jeff Lerg, forward Tim Kennedy and defenseman Tyler Howells of Michigan St.; forwards Nathan Gerbe and Brian Boyle of Boston College.

Division I Leaders
Scoring

(Minimum 20 games)	Cl	Gm	G	A	Pts	Avg
T.J. Hensick, Michigan	Sr.	41	23	46	69	1.68
Eric Ehn, Air Force	Jr.	40	24	39	63	1.58
Kevin Porter, Michigan	Jr.	41	24	34	58	1.41
Jonathan Toews, N. Dakota	So.	34	18	28	46	1.35
James Sixsmith, Holy Cross	Sr.	35	17	30	47	1.34

Goaltending

(Minimum 15 games)	Cl	Record	Sv%	GAA
David Brown, Notre Dame	Sr.	30-6-3	.931	1.58
Joe Fallon, Vermont	Jr.	17-14-3	.920	1.86
Michael-Lee Teslak, Mich. Tech	So.	11-8-3	.916	2.00
John Curry, B.U.	Sr.	17-10-8	.928	2.01
Kevin Regan, UNH	Jr.	24-9-2	.935	2.06

Division III Championship

March 17-18 at Wessman Arena in Superior, Wis.

Semifinals

Oswego St. (N.Y.) 4 . . . . . .OT . . . . .St. Norbert (Wis.) 3
Middlebury (Vt.) 3 . . . . .Manhattanville (N.Y.) 2

Championship

Oswego St. 4 .Middlebury 3

Final records: Oswego St. (23-3-3); Middlebury (20-8-3); St. Norbert (25-4-2); Manhattanville (21-2-5).

Women's College Hockey

NCAA Division I Frozen Four

March 16 and 18 at Herb Brooks Arena in Lake Placid, N.Y.

Semifinals

Minnesota Duluth 4 . . . . . .2OT . . . . . . .Boston College 3
Wisconsin 4 . . . . .St. Lawrence 0

Championship

Wisconsin 4 . . . . .Minnesota Duluth 1

Final records: Wisconsin (36-1-4); Minnesota Duluth (24-11-4); St. Lawrence (29-8-3); Boston College (24-10-2).

All-Tournament Team: Forwards Sara Bauer (Most Outstanding) and Jinelle Zaugg, goaltender Jessie Vetter, defensemen Bobbi-Jo Slusar and Meagan Mikkelson of Wisconsin; forward Jessica Koizumi of Minnesota Duluth.

NCAA Division III Championship

March 16-17 at Stafford Arena in Plattsburgh, N.Y.

Semifinals

Middlebury (Vt.) 5 . . . . .Wis.-Stevens Point 1
Plattsburgh St. (NY) 3 . . . . .Amherst (Mass.) 2

Third Place

Wis.-Stevens Point 4 . . . . . .OT . . . . . .Amherst 3

Championship

Plattsburgh St. 2 . . . . .Middlebury 1

Final records: Plattsburgh St. (27-0-2); Middlebury (23-4-2); Wis.-Stevens Point (20-7-2); Amherst (20-7-3).

Patty Kazmaier Award

For women's College Hockey Player of the Year. Voting is done by a 13-member panel of national media, varsity coaches, and one USA Hockey member.

		Cl	Pos
Winner: Julie Chu, Harvard	. . . .	Sr.	F

MINOR LEAGUE HOCKEY

American Hockey League

Division champions (*) and playoff qualifiers (†) are noted. **OTL** denotes any game that was tied at the end of regulation and lost during a five-minute overtime period. If the game is tied after the overtime period, a shootout ensues with each team getting five attempts to score on a breakaway from the red line. Shootout Losses are listed as **SOL**. Teams are awarded two points for a win (regulation, overtime or shootout), one point for an OTL or SOL, and zero points for a regulation loss.

Eastern Conference

Atlantic Division

Team (Affiliate)	W	L	OTL	SOL	Pts
*Manchester (LA)	51	21	7	1	110
†Hartford (NYR)	47	29	3	1	98
†Providence (Bos)	44	30	2	4	94
†Worcester (SJ)	41	28	3	8	93
Lowell (NJ)	38	30	6	6	88
Portland (Ana)	37	31	3	9	86
Springfield (TB)	28	49	1	2	59

East Division

Team (Affiliate)	W	L	OTL	SOL	Pts
*Hershey (Wash)	51	17	6	6	114
†Wilkes-Barre/Scran. (Pit)	51	23	4	2	108
†Norfolk (Chi)	50	22	6	2	108
†Albany (Car/Col)	37	36	4	3	81
Bridgeport Sound (NYI)	36	37	1	6	79
Philadelphia (Phi)	31	41	2	6	70
Binghamton (Ott)	23	48	4	5	55

Western Conference

North Division

Team (Affiliate)	W	L	OTL	SOL	Pts
*Manitoba (Van)	45	23	7	5	102
†Rochester (Buf/Fla)	48	30	1	1	98
†Hamilton (Mon)	43	28	3	6	95
†Grand Rapids (Det)	37	32	6	5	85
Syracuse (Clb)	34	34	4	8	80
Toronto (Tor)	34	39	2	5	75

West Division

Team (Affiliate)	W	L	OTL	SOL	Pts
*Omaha Ak-Sar-Ben (Calg)	49	25	5	1	104
†Chicago (Atl)	46	25	3	6	101
†Milwaukee (Nash)	41	25	4	10	96
†Iowa (Dal)	42	34	3	1	88
Peoria (St.L)	37	33	2	8	84
San Antonio (Pho)	32	42	2	4	70
Houston (Min)	27	43	4	6	64

Scoring Leaders

	Gm	G	A	Pts	PM
Darren Haydar, Chi	73	41	81	**122**	55
Keith Aucoin, Alb	65	27	72	**99**	108
Martin St. Pierre, Nor	65	27	72	**99**	100
Brett Sterling, Chi	77	55	42	**97**	96
Corey Larose, Chi	63	22	61	**83**	75

Goaltending Leaders

(At least 1560 minutes)	GP	GAA	Sv%	Record
Jaroslav Halak, Ham	28	**2.00**	.932	16-11-0
Curtis McElhinney, Oma	57	**2.13**	.917	35-17-1
Drew MacIntyre, Man	41	**2.17**	.922	24-12-2

Calder Cup Finals

	W-L	GF	Leading Scorers
Hamilton	4-1	19	Jancevski (1-7–8)
Hershey	1-4	9	Klepis (5-0–5)

Date	Winner	Home Ice
June 1	Hamilton, 4-0	at Hershey
June 2	Hershey, 4-2	at Hershey
June 4	Hamilton, 5-2	at Hamilton
June 6	Hamilton, 6-2	at Hamilton
June 7	Hamilton, 2-1	at Hamilton

Playoff MVP: Carey Price, Hamilton, G

IIHF World Hockey Championships

Playoff Round results from the 2007 IIHF Men's and Women's World Hockey Championships.

MEN

Held April 27- May 13 in Moscow and Mytischi, Russia.

Quarterfinals

Russia 4		Czech Republic 0
Finland 5	2OT	United States 4
Canada 5		Switzerland 1
Sweden 7		Slovakia 4

Semifinals

Finland 2	OT	Russia 1
Canada 4		Sweden 1

Bronze Medal Game

Russia 3		Sweden 1

Gold Medal Game

Canada 4		Finland 2

All-Star Team (selected by media): **G**— Kari Lehtonen, Finland; **D**— Petteri Nummelin, Finland and Andrei Markov, Russia; **F**— Rick Nash, Canada (MVP), Alexei Morozov, Russia and Evgeni Malkin, Russia.

Scoring Leaders

	Gm	G	A	Pts
Johan Davidsson, Sweden	9	7	7	14
Alexei Morozov, Russia	7	8	5	13
Sergei Zinoviev, Russia	9	3	10	13
Matthew Lombardi, Canada	9	6	6	12
Danis Zaripov, Russia	9	3	9	12

Four tied with 11 points each.

WOMEN

Held April 3-10 in Winnipeg and Selkirk, Canada.

Bronze Medal Game

Sweden 1		Finland 0

Gold Medal Game

Canada 5		United States 1

All-Star Team (selected by media): **G**— Kim St. Pierre, Canada; **D**— Delaney Collins, Canada and Angela Ruggiero, USA; **F**— Natalie Darwitz, USA, Krissy Wendell, USA and Hayley Wickenheiser, Canada.

1893-2007
Through the Years

SPORTS ALMANAC

The Stanley Cup

The Stanley Cup was originally donated to the Canadian Amateur Hockey Association by Sir Frederick Arthur Stanley, Lord Stanley of Preston and 16th Earl of Derby, who had become interested in the sport while Governor General of Canada from 1888 to 1893. Stanley wanted the trophy to be a challenge cup, contested for each year by the best amateur hockey teams in Canada.

In 1893, the Cup was presented without a challenge to the AHA champion Montreal Amateur Athletic Association team. Every year since, however, there has been a playoff. In 1914, Cup trustees limited the field challenging for the trophy to the champion of the eastern professional National Hockey Association (NHA, organized in 1910) and the western professional Pacific Coast Hockey Association (PCHA, organized in 1912).

The NHA disbanded in 1917 and the National Hockey League (NHL) was formed. From 1918 to 1926, the NHL and PCHA champions played for the Cup with the Western Canada Hockey League (WCHL) champion joining in a three-way challenge in 1923 and '24. The PCHA disbanded in 1924, while the WCHL became the Western Hockey League (WHL) for the 1925-26 season and folded the following year. The NHL playoffs have decided the winner of the Stanley Cup ever since.

Champions, 1893-1917

Multiple winners: Montreal Victorias and Montreal Wanderers (4); Montreal Amateur Athletic Association and Ottawa Silver Seven (3); Montreal Shamrocks, Ottawa Senators, Quebec Bulldogs and Winnipeg Victorias (2).

Year		Year		Year	
1893	Montreal AAA	1901	Winnipeg Victorias	1909	Ottawa Senators
1894	Montreal AAA	1902	Montreal AAA	1910	Montreal Wanderers
1895	Montreal Victorias	1903	Ottawa Silver Seven	1911	Ottawa Senators
1896	(Feb.) Winnipeg Victorias	1904	Ottawa Silver Seven	1912	Quebec Bulldogs
	(Dec.) Montreal Victorias	1905	Ottawa Silver Seven	1913	Quebec Bulldogs
1897	Montreal Victorias	1906	Montreal Wanderers	1914	Toronto Blueshirts (NHA)
1898	Montreal Victorias	1907	(Jan.) Kenora Thistles	1915	Vancouver Millionaires (PCHA)
1899	Montreal Shamrocks		(Mar.) Montreal Wanderers	1916	Montreal Canadiens (NHA)
1900	Montreal Shamrocks	1908	Montreal Wanderers	1917	Seattle Metropolitans (PCHA)

Champions Since 1918

Multiple winners: Montreal Canadiens (23); Toronto Arenas-St. Pats-Maple Leafs (13); Detroit Red Wings (10); Boston Bruins and Edmonton Oilers (5); NY Islanders, NY Rangers and Ottawa Senators (4); Chicago Blackhawks and New Jersey Devils (3); Colorado Avalanche, Montreal Maroons, Philadelphia Flyers and Pittsburgh Penguins (2).

Year	Winner	Head Coach	Series	Loser	Head Coach
1918	Toronto Arenas	Dick Carroll	3-2 (WLWLW)	Vancouver (PCHA)	Frank Patrick
1919	No Decision*				
1920	Ottawa	Pete Green	3-2 (WWLLW)	Seattle (PCHA)	Pete Muldoon
1921	Ottawa	Pete Green	3-2 (LWWLW)	Vancouver (PCHA)	Frank Patrick
1922	Toronto St. Pats	Eddie Powers	3-2 (LWLWW)	Vancouver (PCHA)	Frank Patrick
1923	Ottawa	Pete Green	3-1 (WLWW)	Vancouver (PCHA)	Frank Patrick
			2-0	Edmonton (WCHL)	K.C. McKenzie
1924	Montreal	Leo Dandurand	2-0	Vancouver (PCHA)	Frank Patrick
			2-0	Calgary (WCHL)	Eddie Oatman
1925	Victoria (WCHL)	Lester Patrick	3-1 (WWLW)	Montreal	Leo Dandurand
1926	Montreal Maroons	Eddie Gerard	3-1 (WWLW)	Victoria (WHL)	Lester Patrick
1927	Ottawa	Dave Gill	2-0-2 (TWTW)	Boston	Art Ross
1928	NY Rangers	Lester Patrick	3-2 (LWLWW)	Montreal Maroons	Eddie Gerard
1929	Boston	Cy Denneny	2-0	NY Rangers	Lester Patrick
1930	Montreal	Cecil Hart	2-0	Boston	Art Ross
1931	Montreal	Cecil Hart	3-2 (WLLWW)	Chicago	Art Duncan
1932	Toronto	Dick Irvin	3-0	NY Rangers	Lester Patrick
1933	NY Rangers	Lester Patrick	3-1 (WWWL)	Toronto	Dick Irvin
1934	Chicago	Tommy Gorman	3-1 (WWLW)	Detroit	Jack Adams
1935	Montreal Maroons	Tommy Gorman	3-0	Toronto	Dick Irvin
1936	Detroit	Jack Adams	3-1 (WWWL)	Toronto	Dick Irvin
1937	Detroit	Jack Adams	3-2 (LWLWW)	NY Rangers	Lester Patrick
1938	Chicago	Bill Stewart	3-1 (WLWW)	Toronto	Dick Irvin
1939	Boston	Art Ross	4-1 (WLWWW)	Toronto	Dick Irvin

* The 1919 finals were cancelled after five games due to an influenza epidemic with Montreal and Seattle (PCHA) tied at 2-2-1.

The Stanley Cup (Cont.)

Year	Winner	Head Coach	Series	Loser	Head Coach
1940	NY Rangers	Frank Boucher	4-2 (WWLLWW)	Toronto	Dick Irvin
1941	Boston	Cooney Weiland	4-0	Detroit	Jack Adams
1942	Toronto	Hap Day	4-3 (LLLWWWW)	Detroit	Jack Adams
1943	Detroit	Ebbie Goodfellow	4-0	Boston	Art Ross
1944	Montreal	Dick Irvin	4-0	Chicago	Paul Thompson
1945	Toronto	Hap Day	4-3 (WWWLLLW)	Detroit	Jack Adams
1946	Montreal	Dick Irvin	4-1 (WWWLW)	Boston	Dit Clapper
1947	Toronto	Hap Day	4-2 (LWWWLW)	Montreal	Dick Irvin
1948	Toronto	Hap Day	4-0	Detroit	Tommy Ivan
1949	Toronto	Hap Day	4-0	Detroit	Tommy Ivan
1950	Detroit	Tommy Ivan	4-3 (WLWLLWW)	NY Rangers	Lynn Patrick
1951	Toronto	Joe Primeau	4-1 (WLWWW)	Montreal	Dick Irvin
1952	Detroit	Tommy Ivan	4-0	Montreal	Dick Irvin
1953	Montreal	Dick Irvin	4-1 (WLWWW)	Boston	Lynn Patrick
1954	Detroit	Tommy Ivan	4-3 (WLWWLLW)	Montreal	Dick Irvin
1955	Detroit	Jimmy Skinner	4-3 (WWLWWLW)	Montreal	Dick Irvin
1956	Montreal	Toe Blake	4-1 (WWWLW)	Detroit	Jimmy Skinner
1957	Montreal	Toe Blake	4-1 (WWWLW)	Boston	Milt Schmidt
1958	Montreal	Toe Blake	4-2 (WLWLWW)	Boston	Milt Schmidt
1959	Montreal	Toe Blake	4-1 (WWLWW)	Toronto	Punch Imlach
1960	Montreal	Toe Blake	4-0	Toronto	Punch Imlach
1961	Chicago	Rudy Pilous	4-2 (WWLLWW)	Detroit	Sid Abel
1962	Toronto	Punch Imlach	4-2 (WWLLWW)	Chicago	Rudy Pilous
1963	Toronto	Punch Imlach	4-1 (WWLWW)	Detroit	Sid Abel
1964	Toronto	Punch Imlach	4-3 (WLWLWLW)	Detroit	Sid Abel
1965	Montreal	Toe Blake	4-3 (WWLWLLW)	Chicago	Billy Reay
1966	Montreal	Toe Blake	4-2 (LLWWWW)	Detroit	Sid Abel
1967	Toronto	Punch Imlach	4-2 (LWWLWW)	Montreal	Toe Blake
1968	Montreal	Toe Blake	4-0	St. Louis	Scotty Bowman
1969	Montreal	Claude Ruel	4-0	St. Louis	Scotty Bowman
1970	Boston	Harry Sinden	4-0	St. Louis	Scotty Bowman
1971	Montreal	Al MacNeil	4-3 (LLWLWLWW)	Chicago	Billy Reay
1972	Boston	Tom Johnson	4-2 (WWWLWLW)	NY Rangers	Emile Francis
1973	Montreal	Scotty Bowman	4-2 (LWWWLW)	Chicago	Billy Reay
1974	Philadelphia	Fred Shero	4-2 (LWWWLW)	Boston	Bep Guidolin
1975	Philadelphia	Fred Shero	4-2 (WWLLWW)	Buffalo	Floyd Smith
1976	Montreal	Scotty Bowman	4-0	Philadelphia	Fred Shero
1977	Montreal	Scotty Bowman	4-0	Boston	Don Cherry
1978	Montreal	Scotty Bowman	4-2 (WWLLWW)	Boston	Don Cherry
1979	Montreal	Scotty Bowman	4-1 (LWWWW)	NY Rangers	Fred Shero
1980	NY Islanders	Al Arbour	4-2 (WLWLWW)	Philadelphia	Pat Quinn
1981	NY Islanders	Al Arbour	4-1 (WWWLW)	Minnesota	Glen Sonmor
1982	NY Islanders	Al Arbour	4-0	Vancouver	Roger Neilson
1983	NY Islanders	Al Arbour	4-0	Edmonton	Glen Sather
1984	Edmonton	Glen Sather	4-1 (WLWWW)	NY Islanders	Al Arbour
1985	Edmonton	Glen Sather	4-1 (LWWWW)	Philadelphia	Mike Keenan
1986	Montreal	Jean Perron	4-1 (LWWWW)	Calgary	Bob Johnson
1987	Edmonton	Glen Sather	4-3 (WWLWLLW)	Philadelphia	Mike Keenan
1988	Edmonton	Glen Sather	4-0	Boston	Terry O'Reilly
1989	Calgary	Terry Crisp	4-2 (WLLWWW)	Montreal	Pat Burns
1990	Edmonton	John Muckler	4-1 (WWLWW)	Boston	Mike Milbury
1991	Pittsburgh	Bob Johnson	4-2 (LWLWWW)	Minnesota	Bob Gainey
1992	Pittsburgh	Scotty Bowman	4-0	Chicago	Mike Keenan
1993	Montreal	Jacques Demers	4-1 (LWWWW)	Los Angeles	Barry Melrose
1994	NY Rangers	Mike Keenan	4-3 (LWWWLLW)	Vancouver	Pat Quinn
1995	New Jersey	Jacques Lemaire	4-0	Detroit	Scotty Bowman
1996	Colorado	Marc Crawford	4-0	Florida	Doug MacLean
1997	Detroit	Scotty Bowman	4-0	Philadelphia	Terry Murray
1998	Detroit	Scotty Bowman	4-0	Washington	Ron Wilson
1999	Dallas	Ken Hitchcock	4-2 (LWWLWW)	Buffalo	Lindy Ruff
2000	New Jersey	Larry Robinson	4-2 (WLWLWW)	Dallas	Ken Hitchcock
2001	Colorado	Bob Hartley	4-3 (WLWLLWW)	New Jersey	Larry Robinson
2002	Detroit	Scotty Bowman	4-1 (LWWWW)	Carolina	Paul Maurice
2003	New Jersey	Pat Burns	4-3 (WWWLLWW)	Anaheim	Mike Babcock
2004	Tampa Bay	John Tortorella	4-3 (LWLWLWW)	Calgary	Darryl Sutter
2005	Not held*				
2006	Carolina	Peter Laviolette	4-3 (WWWLWLLW)	Edmonton	Craig MacTavish
2007	Anaheim	Randy Carlyle	4-1 (WWLWW)	Ottawa	Bryan Murray

* The lack of a labor agreement between the owners and NHLPA and the ensuing owners' lockout, canceled the 2004-05 season.

M.J. O'Brien Trophy

Donated by Canadian mining magnate M.J. O'Brien, whose son Ambrose founded the National Hockey Association in 1910. Originally presented to the NHA champion until the league's demise in 1917, the trophy then passed to the NHL champion through 1927. It was awarded to the NHL's Canadian Division winner from 1927-38 and the Stanley Cup runner-up from 1939-50 before being retired in 1950.

NHA winners included the Montreal Wanderers (1910), original Ottawa Senators (1911 and '15), Quebec Bulldogs (1912 and '13), Toronto Blueshirts (1914) and Montreal Canadiens (1916 and '17).

Conn Smythe Trophy

The Most Valuable Player of the Stanley Cup Playoffs, as selected by the Pro Hockey Writers Association. Presented since 1965 by Maple Leaf Gardens Limited in the name of the former Toronto coach, GM and owner, Conn Smythe. Winners who did not play for the Cup champion are in **bold** type.

Multiple winners: Patrick Roy (3); Wayne Gretzky, Mario Lemieux, Bobby Orr and Bernie Parent (2).

Year		Year		Year	
1965	Jean Beliveau, Mon., C	1980	Bryan Trottier, NYI, C	1995	Claude Lemieux, NJ, RW
1966	**Roger Crozier**, Det., G	1981	Butch Goring, NYI, C	1996	Joe Sakic, Col., C
1967	Dave Keon, Tor., C	1982	Mike Bossy, NYI, RW	1997	Mike Vernon, Det., G
1968	**Glenn Hall**, St.L., G	1983	Billy Smith, NYI, G	1998	Steve Yzerman, Det., C
1969	Serge Savard, Mon., D	1984	Mark Messier, Edm., LW	1999	Joe Nieuwendyk, Dal., C
1970	Bobby Orr, Bos., D	1985	Wayne Gretzky, Edm., C	2000	Scott Stevens, NJ, D
1971	Ken Dryden, Mon., G	1986	Patrick Roy, Mon., G	2001	Patrick Roy, Col., G
1972	Bobby Orr, Bos., D	1987	**Ron Hextall**, Phi., G	2002	Nicklas Lidstrom, Det., D
1973	Yvan Cournoyer, Mon., RW	1988	Wayne Gretzky, Edm., C	2003	**J-S Giguere**, Ana., G
1974	Bernie Parent, Phi., G	1989	Al MacInnis, Calg., D	2004	Brad Richards, TB, C
1975	Bernie Parent, Phi., G	1990	Bill Ranford, Edm., G	2005	Not awarded
1976	**Reggie Leach**, Phi., RW	1991	Mario Lemieux, Pit., C	2006	Cam Ward, Car., G
1977	Guy Lafleur, Mon., RW	1992	Mario Lemieux, Pit., C	2007	Scott Niedermayer, Ana., D
1978	Larry Robinson, Mon., D	1993	Patrick Roy, Mon., G		
1979	Bob Gainey, Mon., LW	1994	Brian Leetch, NYR, D		

Note: Ken Dryden (1971), Patrick Roy (1986), Ron Hextall (1987) and Cam Ward (2006) are the only players to win as rookies.

All-Time Stanley Cup Playoff Leaders

CAREER

Stanley Cup Playoff leaders through 2007. Years listed indicate number of playoff appearances. Players active in 2006-07 are in **bold** type; (DNP) indicates player that was active in 2006-07 but did not participate in playoffs.

Scoring

Points

		Yrs	Gm	G	A	Pts
1	Wayne Gretzky	16	208	122	260	382
2	Mark Messier	17	236	109	186	295
3	Jari Kurri	14	200	106	127	233
4	Glenn Anderson	15	225	93	121	214
5	Paul Coffey	16	194	59	137	196
6	Brett Hull	19	202	103	87	190
7	Doug Gilmour	17	182	60	128	188
8	Steve Yzerman	20	196	70	115	185
9	Bryan Trottier	17	221	71	113	184
10	Ray Bourque	21	214	41	139	180
11	**Joe Sakic** (DNP)	12	162	82	96	178
12	Jean Beliveau	17	162	79	97	176
13	Denis Savard	16	169	66	109	175
14	Mario Lemieux	8	107	76	96	172
15	**Jaromir Jagr**	14	159	72	94	166
	Peter Forsberg	12	144	63	103	166
17	Denis Potvin	14	185	56	108	164
18	**Sergei Fedorov** (DNP)	13	162	50	113	163
19	Mike Bossy	10	129	85	75	160
	Gordie Howe	20	157*	68	92	160
	Bobby Smith	13	184	64	96	160
	Al MacInnis	19	177	39	121	160
23	Claude Lemieux	17	233	80	78	158
24	Adam Oates	15	163	42	114	156
25	Larry Murphy	20	215	37	115	152

Goals

		Yrs	Gm	G
1	Wayne Gretzky	16	208	122
2	Mark Messier	17	236	109
3	Jari Kurri	15	200	106
4	Brett Hull	19	202	103
5	Glenn Anderson	15	225	93
6	Mike Bossy	10	129	85
7	Maurice Richard	15	133	82
	Joe Sakic (DNP)	12	162	82
9	Claude Lemieux	17	233	80
10	Jean Beliveau	17	162	79

Assists

		Yrs	Gm	A
1	Wayne Gretzky	16	208	260
2	Mark Messier	17	236	186
3	Ray Bourque	21	214	139
4	Paul Coffey	16	194	137
5	Doug Gilmour	17	182	128
6	Jari Kurri	15	200	127
7	Glenn Anderson	15	225	121
	Al MacInnis	19	177	121
9	Larry Robinson	20	227	116
10	Steve Yzerman	20	196	115
	Larry Murphy	20	215	115

The Stanley Cup (Cont.)

Goaltending
Wins

		Gm	W-L	Pct	GAA
1	Patrick Roy	247	151-94	.616	2.30
2	**Martin Brodeur**	164	94-70	.573	1.93
3	Grant Fuhr	150	92-50	.648	2.92
4	Billy Smith	132	88-36	.710	2.73
	Ed Belfour (DNP)	161	88-68	.564	2.17
6	Ken Dryden	112	80-32	.714	2.40
7	Mike Vernon	138	77-56	.579	2.68
8	Jacques Plante	112	71-37	.657	2.17
9	Andy Moog	132	68-57	.544	3.04
10	**Dominik Hasek**	115	63-47	.573	1.99

Shutouts

		Gm	GAA	No
1	Patrick Roy	247	2.30	23
2	**Martin Brodeur**	164	1.93	22
3	**Curtis Joseph** (DNP)	131	2.44	16
4	Clint Benedict	48	1.80	15
	Jacques Plante	112	2.17	15

Appearances in Cup Finals
Standings of all teams that have reached the Stanley Cup championship round, since 1918.

App		Cups	Last Won
32	Montreal Canadiens	23 *	1993
22	Detroit Red Wings	10	2002
21	Toronto Maple Leafs	13 †	1967
17	Boston Bruins	5	1972
10	New York Rangers	4	1994
10	Chicago Blackhawks	3	1961
7	Edmonton Oilers	5	1990
7	Philadelphia Flyers	2	1975
5	New York Islanders	4	1983
5	Vancouver Millionaires (PCHA)	0	—
4	(original) Ottawa Senators	4	1927
4	Minnesota/Dallas (North) Stars	1	1999
4	New Jersey Devils	3	2003
3	Montreal Maroons	2	1935
3	Calgary Flames	1	1989
3	St. Louis Blues	0	—
2	Colorado Avalanche	2	2001
2	Pittsburgh Penguins	2	1992
2	Anaheim Ducks	1	2007
2	Carolina Hurricanes	1	2006
2	Victoria Cougars (WCHL-WHL)	1	1925
2	Buffalo Sabres	0	—
2	Seattle Metropolitans (PCHA)	0	—
2	Vancouver Canucks	0	—
1	Tampa Bay Lightning	1	2004
1	Calgary Tigers (WCHL)	0	—
1	Edmonton Eskimos (WCHL)	0	—
1	Florida Panthers	0	—
1	Los Angeles Kings	0	—
1	Ottawa Senators	0	—
1	Washington Capitals	0	—

*Les Canadiens also won the Cup in 1916 for a total of 24. Also, their final with Seattle in 1919 was cancelled due to an influenza epidemic that claimed the life of the Habs' Joe Hall.

†Toronto has won the Cup under three nicknames— Arenas (1918), St. Pats (1922) and Maple Leafs (1932,42,45,47-49,51,62-64,67).

Teams now defunct (7): Calgary Tigers, Edmonton Eskimos, Montreal Maroons, (original) Ottawa Senators, Seattle, Vancouver Millionaires and Victoria. Edmonton (1923) and Calgary (1924) represented the WCHL and later the WHL, while Vancouver (1918,1921-24) and Seattle (1919-20) played out of the PCHA.

Goals Against Average
Minimum of 50 games played

		Gm	Min	GA	GAA
1	**Martin Brodeur**	164	10,221	328	1.93
2	George Hainsworth	52	3486	112	1.93
3	Turk Broda	101	6389	211	1.98
4	**Dominik Hasek**	115	7112	236	1.99
5	Jacques Plante	112	6652	240	2.16
6	**Ed Belfour** (DNP)	161	9945	359	2.17
7	**Chris Osgood** (DNP)	87	5085	190	2.24
8	**N. Khabibulin** (DNP)	57	3464	131	2.27
9	Patrick Roy	247	15,209	584	2.30
10	Ken Dryden	112	6846	274	2.40

Note: Clint Benedict had an average of 1.80 but played in only 48 games.

Games Played
(Goalies only)

		Yrs	Gm
1	Patrick Roy, Mon-Col	17	247
2	**Martin Brodeur**, New Jersey	13	164
3	**Ed Belfour**, Chi-Dal-Tor (DNP)	13	161
4	Grant Fuhr, Edm-Buf-St.L	14	150
5	Mike Vernon, Calg-Det-SJ-Fla	14	138

Miscellaneous
Championships

		Yrs	Cups
1	Henri Richard, Montreal	18	11
2	Yvan Cournoyer, Montreal	15	10
	Jean Beliveau, Montreal	17	10
4	Claude Provost, Montreal	14	9
5	Jacques Lemaire, Montreal	11	8
	Maurice Richard, Montreal	15	8
	Red Kelly, Detroit-Toronto	19	8

Years in Playoffs

		Yrs	Gm
1	**Chris Chelios**, Mon-Chi-Det	22	246
	Ray Bourque, Boston-Colorado	21	214
3	Gordie Howe, Detroit-Hartford	20	157
	Larry Robinson, Montreal-Los Angeles	20	227
	Larry Murphy, LA-Wash-Min-Pit-Tor-Det	20	215
	Scott Stevens, Wash-St.L-NJ	20	233
	Steve Yzerman, Detroit	20	196

Games Played

		Yrs	Gm
1	Patrick Roy, Montreal-Colorado	17	247
2	**Chris Chelios**, Mon-Chi-Det	22	246
3	Mark Messier, Edm-NYR-Van	17	236
4	Claude Lemieux, Mon-NJ-Col-Pho-Dal	17	233
	Scott Stevens, Wash-St.L-NJ	20	233

Penalty Minutes

		Yrs	Gm	Min
1	Dale Hunter, Que-Wash-Col	18	186	729
2	Chris Nilan, Mon-NYR-Bos-Mon	12	111	541
3	Claude Lemieux, Mon-NJ-Col-Pho-Dal	17	233	529
4	Rick Tocchet, Phi-Pit-Bos-Pho	13	145	471
5	Willi Plett, Atl-Calg-Min-Bos	10	83	466

SINGLE SEASON

Points

		Year	Gm	G	A	Pts
1	Wayne Gretzky, Edm	1985	18	17	30	47
2	Mario Lemieux, Pit	1991	23	16	28	44
3	Wayne Gretzky, Edm	1988	19	12	31	43
4	Wayne Gretzky, LA	1993	24	15	25	40
5	Wayne Gretzky, Edm	1983	16	12	26	38
6	Paul Coffey, Edm	1985	18	12	25	37
7	Mike Bossy, NYI	1981	18	17	18	35
	Wayne Gretzky, Edm	1984	19	13	22	35
	Doug Gilmour, Tor	1993	21	10	25	35
10	Six tied with 34 each.					

Goals

		Year	Gm	No
1	Reggie Leach, Philadelphia	1976	16	19
	Jari Kurri, Edmonton	1985	18	19
3	Joe Sakic, Colorado	1996	22	18
4	Seven tied with 17 each, incl. 3 times by Mike Bossy.			

Assists

		Year	Gm	No
1	Wayne Gretzky, Edmonton	1988	19	31
2	Wayne Gretzky, Edmonton	1985	18	30
3	Wayne Gretzky, Edmonton	1987	21	29
4	Mario Lemieux, Pittsburgh	1991	23	29
5	Wayne Gretzky, Edmonton	1983	16	26

Goaltending

Wins

1 Sixteen tied with 16 each.

Shutouts

		Year	Gm	No
1	Martin Brodeur, New Jersey	2003	24	7
2	Dominik Hasek, Detroit	2002	23	6
3	J-S Giguere, Anaheim	2003	21	5
	Nikolai Khabibulin, Tampa Bay	2004	23	5
	Miikka Kiprusoff, Calgary	2004	26	5

Goals Against Average

	(Min. 8 games played)	Year	Gm	Min	GA	GAA
1	Terry Sawchuk, Det	1952	8	480	5	0.63
2	Clint Benedict, Mon-M	1928	9	555	8	0.89
3	Turk Broda, Tor	1951	9	509	9	1.06
4	Dave Kerr, NYR	1937	9	553	10	1.11
5	Jacques Plante, Mon	1960	8	489	11	1.35

Note: Average determined by games played through 1942-43 season and by minutes played since then.

SINGLE SERIES

Points

	Year	Rd	G-A—Pts
Rick Middleton, Bos vs Buf	1983	DF	5-14—19
Wayne Gretzky, Edm vs Chi	1985	CF	4-14—18
Mario Lemieux, Pit vs Wash	1992	DSF	7-10—17
Barry Pederson, Bos vs Buf	1983	DF	7-9—16
Doug Gilmour, Tor vs SJ	1994	CSF	3-13—16

Goals

	Year	Rd	No
Jari Kurri, Edm vs Chi	1985	CF	12
Newsy Lalonde, Mon vs Ott	1919	SF*	11
Tim Kerr, Phi vs Pit	1989	DF	10
Five tied with 9 each.			

*NHL final prior to Stanley Cup series with Seattle (PCHA).

Assists

	Year	Rd	No
Rick Middleton, Bos vs Buf	1983	DF	14
Wayne Gretzky, Edm vs Chi	1985	CF	14
Wayne Gretzky, Edm vs LA	1987	DSF	13
Doug Gilmour, Tor vs SJ	1994	CSF	13
Four tied with 11 each.			

SINGLE GAME

Points

	Date	G	A	Pts
Patrik Sundstrom, NJ vs Wash	4/22/88	3	5	8
Mario Lemieux, Pit vs Phi	4/25/89	5	3	8
Wayne Gretzky, Edm at Calg	4/17/83	4	3	7
Wayne Gretzky, Edm at Win	4/25/85	3	4	7
Wayne Gretzky, Edm vs LA	4/9/87	1	6	7

Goals

	Date	No
Newsy Lalonde, Mon vs Ott	3/1/19	5
Maurice Richard, Mon vs Tor	3/23/44	5
Darryl Sittler, Tor vs Phi	4/22/76	5
Reggie Leach, Phi vs Bos	5/6/76	5
Mario Lemieux, Pit vs Phi	4/25/89	5

Assists

	Date	No
Mikko Leinonen, NYR vs Phi	4/8/82	6
Wayne Gretzky, Edm vs LA	4/9/87	6
11 tied with 5 each.		

NHL All-Star Game

Three benefit NHL All-Star Games were staged in the 1930s for forward Ace Bailey and the families of Howie Morenz and Babe Siebert. Bailey, of Toronto, suffered a fractured skull on a career-ending check by Boston's Eddie Shore. Morenz, the Montreal Canadiens' legend, died of a heart attack at 35 after a severely broken leg ended his career. Siebert, who played with both Montreal teams, drowned at age 35.

The All-Star Game was revived at the start of the 1947-48 season as an annual exhibition match between the defending Stanley Cup champion and all-stars from the league's other five teams. The format has changed several times since then. The game was moved to midseason in 1966-67 and became an East vs. West contest in 1968-69. The Eastern (East, 1968-1974; Wales, 1975-93) Conference leads the series 19-9-1. From 1998-2002, the East-West format was abandoned for one pitting North America vs. the rest of the world (N. America leads that series 3-2). In 2003 the game returned to East vs. West. Since 2006, the game is no longer played during Olympic years.

Benefit Games

Date	Occasion		Host	Coaches
2/14/34	Ace Bailey Benefit	Toronto 7, All-Stars 3	Toronto	Dick Irvin, Lester Patrick
11/3/37	Howie Morenz Memorial	All-Stars 6, Montreals* 5	Montreal	Jack Adams, Cecil Hart
10/29/39	Babe Siebert Memorial	All-Stars 5, Canadiens 3	Montreal	Art Ross, Pit Lepine

*Combined squad of Montreal Canadiens and Montreal Maroons.

NHL All-Star Game (Cont.)

All-Star Games

Multiple MVP winners: Wayne Gretzky and Mario Lemieux (3); Bobby Hull and Frank Mahovlich (2).

Year		Host	Coaches	Most Valuable Player
1947	All-Stars 4, Toronto 3	Toronto	Dick Irvin, Hap Day	No award
1948	All-Stars 3, Toronto 1	Chicago	Tommy Ivan, Hap Day	No award
1949	All-Stars 3, Toronto 1	Toronto	Tommy Ivan, Hap Day	No award
1950	Detroit 7, All-Stars 1	Detroit	Tommy Ivan, Lynn Patrick	No award
1951	1st Team 2, 2nd Team 2	Toronto	Joe Primeau, Hap Day	No award
1952	1st Team 1, 2nd Team 1	Detroit	Tommy Ivan, Dick Irvin	No award
1953	All-Stars 3, Montreal 1	Montreal	Lynn Patrick, Dick Irvin	No award
1954	All-Stars 2, Detroit 2	Detroit	King Clancy, Jim Skinner	No award
1955	Detroit 3, All-Stars 1	Detroit	Jim Skinner, Dick Irvin	No award
1956	All-Stars 1, Montreal 1	Montreal	Jim Skinner, Toe Blake	No award
1957	All-Stars 5, Montreal 3	Montreal	Milt Schmidt, Toe Blake	No award
1958	Montreal 6, All-Stars 3	Montreal	Toe Blake, Milt Schmidt	No award
1959	Montreal 6, All-Stars 1	Montreal	Toe Blake, Punch Imlach	No award
1960	All-Stars 2, Montreal 1	Montreal	Punch Imlach, Toe Blake	No award
1961	All-Stars 3, Chicago 1	Chicago	Sid Abel, Rudy Pilous	No award
1962	Toronto 4, All-Stars 1	Toronto	Punch Imlach, Rudy Pilous	Eddie Shack, Tor., RW
1963	All-Stars 3, Toronto 3	Toronto	Sid Abel, Punch Imlach	Frank Mahovlich, Tor., LW
1964	All-Stars 3, Toronto 2	Toronto	Sid Abel, Punch Imlach	Jean Beliveau, Mon., C
1965	All-Stars 5, Montreal 2	Montreal	Billy Reay, Toe Blake	Gordie Howe, Det., RW
1966	No game (see below)			
1967	Montreal 3, All-Stars 0	Montreal	Toe Blake, Sid Abel	Henri Richard, Mon., C
1968	Toronto 4, All-Stars 3	Toronto	Punch Imlach, Toe Blake	Bruce Gamble, Tor., G
1969	West 3, East 3	Montreal	Scotty Bowman, Toe Blake	Frank Mahovlich, Det., LW
1970	East 4, West 1	St. Louis	Claude Ruel, Scotty Bowman	Bobby Hull, Chi., LW
1971	West 2, East 1	Boston	Scotty Bowman, Harry Sinden	Bobby Hull, Chi., LW
1972	East 3, West 2	Minnesota	Al MacNeil, Billy Reay	Bobby Orr, Bos., D
1973	East 5, West 4	NY Rangers	Tom Johnson, Billy Reay	Greg Polis, Pit., LW
1974	West 6, East 4	Chicago	Billy Reay, Scotty Bowman	Garry Unger, St.L., C
1975	Wales 7, Campbell 1	Montreal	Bep Guidolin, Fred Shero	Syl Apps Jr., Pit., C
1976	Wales 7, Campbell 5	Philadelphia	Floyd Smith, Fred Shero	Peter Mahovlich, Mon., C
1977	Wales 4, Campbell 3	Vancouver	Scotty Bowman, Fred Shero	Rick Martin, Buf., LW
1978	Wales 3, Campbell 2 (OT)	Buffalo	Scotty Bowman, Fred Shero	Billy Smith, NYI, G
1979	No game (see below)			
1980	Wales 6, Campbell 3	Detroit	Scotty Bowman, Al Arbour	Reggie Leach, Phi., RW
1981	Campbell 4, Wales 1	Los Angeles	Pat Quinn, Scotty Bowman	Mike Liut, St.L., G
1982	Wales 4, Campbell 2	Washington	Al Arbour, Glen Sonmor	Mike Bossy, NYI, RW
1983	Campbell 9, Wales 3	NY Islanders	Roger Neilson, Al Arbour	Wayne Gretzky, Edm., C
1984	Wales 7, Campbell 6	New Jersey	Al Arbour, Glen Sather	Don Maloney, NYR, LW
1985	Wales 6, Campbell 4	Calgary	Al Arbour, Glen Sather	Mario Lemieux, Pit., C
1986	Wales 4, Campbell 3 (OT)	Hartford	Mike Keenan, Glen Sather	Grant Fuhr, Edm., G
1987	No game (see below)			
1988	Wales 6, Campbell 5 (OT)	St. Louis	Mike Keenan, Glen Sather	Mario Lemieux, Pit., C
1989	Campbell 9, Wales 5	Edmonton	Glen Sather, Terry O'Reilly	Wayne Gretzky, LA, C
1990	Wales 12, Campbell 7	Pittsburgh	Pat Burns, Terry Crisp	Mario Lemieux, Pit., C
1991	Campbell 11, Wales 5	Chicago	John Muckler, Mike Milbury	Vincent Damphousse, Tor., LW
1992	Campbell 10, Wales 6	Philadelphia	Bob Gainey, Scotty Bowman	Brett Hull, St.L., RW
1993	Wales 16, Campbell 6	Montreal	Scotty Bowman, Mike Keenan	Mike Gartner, NYR, RW
1994	East 9, West 8	NY Rangers	Jacques Demers, Barry Melrose	Mike Richter, NYR, G
1995	No game (see below)			
1996	East 5, West 4	Boston	Doug MacLean, Scotty Bowman	Ray Bourque, Bos., D
1997	East 11, West 7	San Jose	Doug MacLean, Ken Hitchcock	Mark Recchi, Mon., RW
1998	North America 8, World 7	Vancouver	Jacques Lemaire, Ken Hitchcock	Teemu Selanne, Ana., RW
1999	North America 8, World 6	Tampa	Ken Hitchcock, Lindy Ruff	Wayne Gretzky, NYR, C
2000	World 6, North America 4	Toronto	Scotty Bowman, Pat Quinn	Pavel Bure, Fla., RW
2001	North America 14, World 12	Denver	Joel Quenneville, Jacques Martin	Bill Guerin, Bos., RW
2002	World 8, North America 5	Los Angeles	Scotty Bowman, Pat Quinn	Eric Daze, Chi., LW
2003	West 6, East 5 (OT)†	Florida	Marc Crawford, Jacques Martin	Dany Heatley, Atl., LW
2004	East 6, West 4	Minnesota	Pat Quinn, Dave Lewis	Joe Sakic, Col., C
2005	No game (see below)			
2006	No game (see below)			
2007	West 12, East 9	Dallas	Randy Carlyle, Lindy Ruff	Daniel Briere, Buf., C

†After a five-minute scoreless overtime, the game was settled by a shootout. The West outscored the East, 3-1.

No All-Star Game: in 1966 (moved from start of season to mid-season); in 1979 (replaced by Challenge Cup series with USSR); in 1987 (replaced by Rendez-Vous '87 series with USSR); in 1995 (canceled when NHL lockout shortened season to 48 games); in 2005 (NHL lockout canceled the entire season); in 2006 (game no longer played in Olympic years).

NHL Franchise Origins

Here is what the current 30 teams in the National Hockey League have to show for the years they have put in as members of the NHL, the early National Hockey Association (NHA) and the more recent World Hockey Association (WHA). League titles and Stanley Cup championships are noted by year won. The Stanley Cup has automatically gone to the NHL champion since the 1926-27 season. Following the 1992-93 season, the NHL renamed the Clarence Campbell Conference the Western Conference, while the Prince of Wales Conference became the Eastern Conference.

Western Conference

	First Season	League Titles	Franchise Stops
Anaheim Ducks	1993-94 (NHL)	1 Cup (2007)	•Anaheim, CA (1993—)
Calgary Flames	1972-73 (NHL)	1 Cup (1989)	•Atlanta (1972-80)
			Calgary (1980—)
Chicago Blackhawks	1926-27 (NHL)	3 Cups (1934,38,61)	•Chicago (1926—)
Colorado Avalanche	1972-73 (WHA)	1 WHA (1977)	•Quebec City (1972-95)
		2 Cups (1996, 2001)	Denver (1995—)
Columbus Blue Jackets	2000-01 (NHL)	None	•Columbus, OH (2000—)
Dallas Stars	1967-68 (NHL)	1 Cup (1999)	•Bloomington, MN (1967-93)
			Dallas (1993—)
Detroit Red Wings	1926-27 (NHL)	10 Cups (1936-37,43,50,52,54-	•Detroit (1926—)
		55,97,98, 2002)	
Edmonton Oilers	1972-73 (WHA)	5 Cups (1984-85,87-88,90)	•Edmonton (1972—)
Los Angeles Kings	1967-68 (NHL)	None	•Inglewood, CA (1967-99)
			Los Angeles (1999—)
Minnesota Wild	2000-01 (NHL)	None	•St. Paul, MN (2000—)
Nashville Predators	1998-99 (NHL)	None	•Nashville, TN (1998—)
Phoenix Coyotes	1972-73 (WHA)	3 WHA (1976, 78-79)	•Winnipeg (1972-96)
			Phoenix (1996—)
St. Louis Blues	1967-68 (NHL)	None	•St. Louis (1967—)
San Jose Sharks	1991-92 (NHL)	None	•San Francisco (1991-93)
			San Jose (1993—)
Vancouver Canucks	1970-71 (NHL)	None	•Vancouver (1970—)

Eastern Conference

	First Season	League Titles	Franchise Stops
Atlanta Thrashers	1999-00 (NHL)	None	•Atlanta (1999—)
Boston Bruins	1924-25 (NHL)	5 Cups (1929,39,41,70,72)	•Boston (1924—)
Buffalo Sabres	1970-71 (NHL)	None	•Buffalo (1970—)
Carolina Hurricanes	1972-73 (WHA)	1 WHA (1973)	•Boston (1972-74)
		1 Cup (2006)	W. Springfield, MA (1974-75)
			Hartford, CT (1975-78)
			Springfield, MA (1978-80)
			Hartford (1980-97)
			Greensboro, NC (1997-99)
			Raleigh, NC (1999—)
Florida Panthers	1993-94 (NHL)	None	•Miami (1993-98)
			Sunrise, FL (1998—)
Montreal Canadiens	1909-10 (NHA)	2 NHA (1916-17)	• •Montreal (1909—)
		2 NHL (1924-25)	
		24 Cups (1916,24,30-	
		31,44,46,53,56-60,65-66,68-	
		69,71,73,76-79,86,93)	
New Jersey Devils	1974-75 (NHL)	3 Cups (1995, 2000,03)	•Kansas City (1974-76)
			Denver (1976-82)
			E. Rutherford, NJ (1982—)
New York Islanders	1972-73 (NHL)	4 Cups (1980-83)	•Uniondale, NY (1972—)
New York Rangers	1926-27 (NHL)	4 Cups (1928,33,40,94)	•New York (1926—)
Ottawa Senators	1992-93 (NHL)	None	•Ottawa (1992-1996)
			Kanata, Ont. (1996—)
Philadelphia Flyers	1967-68 (NHL)	2 Cups (1974-75)	•Philadelphia (1967—)
Pittsburgh Penguins	1967-68 (NHL)	2 Cups (1991-92)	•Pittsburgh (1967—)
Tampa Bay Lightning	1992-93 (NHL)	1 Cup (2004)	•Tampa, FL (1992-93)
			St. Petersburg, FL (1993-96)
			Tampa, FL (1996—)
Toronto Maple Leafs	1916-17 (NHA)	2 NHL (1918,22)	•Toronto (1916—)
		13 Cups (1918,22,32,42,45,	
		47-49,51,62-64,67)	
Washington Capitals	1974-75 (NHL)	None	•Landover, MD (1974-97)
			Washington, D.C. (1997—)

Note: The Hartford Civic Center roof collapsed after a snowstorm in January 1978, forcing the Whalers to move their home games to Springfield, Mass., for two years.

The Growth of the NHL

Of the four franchises that comprised the National Hockey League (NHL) at the start of the 1917-18 season, only two remain—the Montreal Canadiens and the Toronto Maple Leafs (originally the Toronto Arenas). From 1919-26, eight new teams joined the league, but only four—the Boston Bruins, Chicago Blackhawks (originally Black Hawks), Detroit Red Wings (originally Cougars) and New York Rangers—survived.

It was 41 years before the NHL expanded again, doubling in size for the 1967-68 season with new teams in Bloomington (Minn.), Los Angeles, Oakland, Philadelphia, Pittsburgh and St. Louis. The league had 16 clubs by the start of the 1972-73 season, but it also had a rival in the **World Hockey Association,** which debuted that year with 12 teams.

The NHL added two more teams in 1974 and merged the struggling Cleveland Barons (originally the Oakland Seals) and Minnesota North Stars in 1978, before absorbing four WHA clubs—the Edmonton Oilers, Hartford Whalers, Quebec Nordiques and Winnipeg Jets—in time for the 1979-80 season. Seven expansion teams joined the league in the 1990s, with two more being added in 2000 to make it an even 30.

Expansion/Merger Timetable

For teams currently in NHL.

1919—Quebec Bulldogs finally take the ice after sitting out NHL's first two seasons; **1924**—Boston Bruins and Montreal Maroons; **1925**—New York Americans and Pittsburgh Pirates; **1926**—Chicago Black Hawks (now Blackhawks), Detroit Cougars (now Red Wings) and New York Rangers; **1932**—Ottawa Senators return after sitting out 1931-32 season.

1967—California-Oakland Seals (later Cleveland Barons), Los Angeles Kings, Minnesota North Stars, Philadelphia Flyers, Pittsburgh Penguins and St. Louis Blues.

1970—Buffalo Sabres and Vancouver Canucks; **1972**—Atlanta Flames (now Calgary) and New York Islanders; **1974**—Kansas City Scouts (now New Jersey Devils) and Washington Capitals; **1978**—Cleveland Barons merge with Minnesota North Stars (now Dallas Stars) and team remains in Minnesota; **1979**—added WHA's Edmonton Oilers, Hartford Whalers (now Carolina Hurricanes), Quebec Nordiques (now Colorado Avalanche) and Winnipeg Jets (now Phoenix Coyotes).

1991—San Jose Sharks; **1992**—Ottawa Senators and Tampa Bay Lightning; **1993**—Mighty Ducks of Anaheim and Florida Panthers; **1998**—Nashville Predators; **1999**—Atlanta Thrashers.

2000—Columbus Blue Jackets and Minnesota Wild.

City and Nickname Changes

1919—Toronto Arenas renamed St. Pats; **1920**—Quebec Bulldogs move to Hamilton and become Tigers (will fold in 1925); **1926**—Toronto St. Pats renamed Maple Leafs; **1929**—Detroit Cougars renamed Falcons.

1930—Pittsburgh Pirates move to Philadelphia and become Quakers (will fold in 1931); **1932**—Detroit Falcons renamed Red Wings; **1934**—Ottawa Senators move to St. Louis and become Eagles (will fold in 1935); **1941**—New York Americans renamed Brooklyn Americans (will fold in 1942).

1967—California Seals renamed Oakland Seals three months into first season; **1970**—Oakland Seals renamed California Golden Seals; **1975**—California Golden Seals renamed Seals; **1976**—California Seals move to Cleveland and become Barons, while Kansas City Scouts move to Denver and become Colorado Rockies; **1978**—Cleveland Barons merge with Minnesota North Stars and become Minnesota North Stars.

1980—Atlanta Flames move to Calgary; **1982**—Colorado Rockies move to East Rutherford, N.J., and become New Jersey Devils; **1986**—Chicago Black Hawks renamed Blackhawks; **1993**—Minnesota North Stars move to Dallas and become Stars. **1995**—Quebec Nordiques move to Denver and become Colorado Avalanche; **1996**—Winnipeg Jets move to Phoenix and become Coyotes; **1997**—Hartford Whalers move to Greensboro, N.C. and become Carolina Hurricanes; **1999**—Carolina Hurricanes move to Raleigh, N.C.; **2006**—Mighty Ducks of Anaheim renamed Anaheim Ducks.

Defunct NHL Teams

Teams that once played in the NHL, but no longer exist.

Brooklyn—Americans (1941-42, formerly NY Americans from 1925-41); **Cleveland**—Barons (1976-78, originally California-Oakland Seals from 1967-76); **Hamilton (Ont.)**—Tigers (1920-25, originally Quebec Bulldogs from 1919-20); **Montreal**—Maroons (1924-38) and Wanderers (1917-18); **New York**—Americans (1925-41, later Brooklyn Americans for 1941-42); **Oakland**—Seals (1967-76, also known as California Seals and Golden Seals and later Cleveland Barons from 1976-78); **Ottawa**—Senators (1917-31 and 1932-34, later St. Louis Eagles for 1934-35); **Philadelphia**—Quakers (1930-31), originally Pittsburgh Pirates from 1925-30); **Pittsburgh**—Pirates (1925-30, later Philadelphia Quakers for 1930-31); **Quebec**—Bulldogs (1919-20, later Hamilton Tigers from 1920-25); **St. Louis**—Eagles (1934-35), originally Ottawa Senators (1917-31 and 1932-34).

WHA Teams (1972-79)

Baltimore—Blades (1975); **Birmingham**—Bulls (1976-78); **Calgary**—Cowboys (1975-77); **Chicago**—Cougars (1972-75); **Cincinnati**—Stingers (1975-79); **Cleveland**—Crusaders (1972-76, moved to Minnesota); **Denver**—Spurs (1975-76, moved to Ottawa); **Edmonton**—Oilers (1972-79, originally called Alberta Oilers in 1972-73); **Houston**—Aeros (1972-78); **Indianapolis**—Racers (1974-78).

Los Angeles—Sharks (1972-74, moved to Michigan); **Michigan**—Stags (1974-75, moved to Baltimore); **Minnesota**—Fighting Saints (1972-76) and New Fighting Saints (1976-77); **New England**—Whalers (1972-79, played in Boston from 1972-74, West Springfield, MA from 1974-75, Hartford from 1975-78 and Springfield, MA in 1979); **New Jersey**—Knights (1973-74, moved to San Diego); **New York**—Raiders (1972-73, renamed Golden Blades in 1973, moved to New Jersey).

Ottawa—Nationals (1972-73, moved to Toronto) and Civics (1976); **Philadelphia**—Blazers (1972-73, moved to Vancouver); **Phoenix**—Roadrunners (1974-77); **Quebec**—Nordiques (1972-79); **San Diego**—Mariners (1974-77); **Toronto**—Toros (1973-76, moved to Birmingham, AL); **Vancouver**—Blazers (1973-75, moved to Calgary); **Winnipeg**—Jets (1972-79).

Annual NHL Leaders

Art Ross Trophy (Scoring)

Given to the player who leads the league in points scored and named after the former Boston Bruins general manager-coach. First presented in 1948, names of prior leading scorers have been added retroactively. A tie for the scoring championship is broken three ways: 1. total goals; 2. fewest games played; 3. first goal scored.

Multiple winners: Wayne Gretzky (10); Gordie Howe and Mario Lemieux (6); Phil Esposito and Jaromir Jagr (5); Stan Mikita (4); Bobby Hull and Guy Lafleur (3); Max Bentley, Charlie Conacher, Bill Cook, Babe Dye, Bernie Geoffrion, Elmer Lach, Newsy Lalonde, Joe Malone, Dickie Moore, Howie Morenz, Bobby Orr and Sweeney Schriner (2).

Year		Gm	G	A	Pts	Year		Gm	G	A	Pts
1918	Joe Malone, Mon	20	44	0	44	1963	Gordie Howe, Det	70	38	48	86
1919	Newsy Lalonde, Mon	17	23	9	32	1964	Stan Mikita, Chi	70	39	50	89
1920	Joe Malone, Que	24	39	6	45	1965	Stan Mikita, Chi	70	28	59	87
1921	Newsy Lalonde, Mon	24	33	8	41	1966	Bobby Hull, Chi	65	54	43	97
1922	Punch Broadbent, Ott	24	32	14	46	1967	Stan Mikita, Chi	70	35	62	97
1923	Babe Dye, Tor	22	26	11	37	1968	Stan Mikita, Chi	72	40	47	87
1924	Cy Denneny, Ott	21	22	1	23	1969	Phil Esposito, Bos	74	49	77	126
1925	Babe Dye, Tor	29	38	6	44	1970	Bobby Orr, Bos	76	33	87	120
1926	Nels Stewart, Maroons	36	34	8	42	1971	Phil Esposito, Bos	78	76	76	152
1927	Bill Cook, NYR	44	33	4	37	1972	Phil Esposito, Bos	76	66	67	133
1928	Howie Morenz, Mon	43	33	18	51	1973	Phil Esposito, Bos	78	55	75	130
1929	Ace Bailey, Tor	44	22	10	32	1974	Phil Esposito, Bos	78	68	77	145
1930	Cooney Weiland, Bos	44	43	30	73	1975	Bobby Orr, Bos	80	46	89	135
1931	Howie Morenz, Mon	39	28	23	51	1976	Guy Lafleur, Mon	80	56	69	125
1932	Busher Jackson, Tor	48	28	25	53	1977	Guy Lafleur, Mon	80	56	80	136
1933	Bill Cook, NYR	48	28	22	50	1978	Guy Lafleur, Mon	79	60	72	132
1934	Charlie Conacher, Tor	42	32	20	52	1979	Bryan Trottier, NYI	76	47	87	134
1935	Charlie Conacher, Tor	47	36	21	57	1980	Marcel Dionne, LA	80	53	84	137
1936	Sweeney Schriner, NYA	48	19	26	45	1981	Wayne Gretzky, Edm	80	55	109	164
1937	Sweeney Schriner, NYA	48	21	25	46	1982	Wayne Gretzky, Edm	80	92	120	212
1938	Gordie Drillon, Tor	48	26	26	52	1983	Wayne Gretzky, Edm	80	71	125	196
1939	Toe Blake, Mon	48	24	23	47	1984	Wayne Gretzky, Edm	74	87	118	205
1940	Milt Schmidt, Bos	48	22	30	52	1985	Wayne Gretzky, Edm	80	73	135	208
1941	Bill Cowley, Bos	46	17	45	62	1986	Wayne Gretzky, Edm	80	52	163	215
1942	Bryan Hextall, NYR	48	24	32	56	1987	Wayne Gretzky, Edm	79	62	121	183
1943	Doug Bentley, Chi	50	33	40	73	1988	Mario Lemieux, Pit	77	70	98	168
1944	Herbie Cain, Bos	48	36	46	82	1989	Mario Lemieux, Pit	76	85	114	199
1945	Elmer Lach, Mon	50	26	54	80	1990	Wayne Gretzky, LA	73	40	102	142
1946	Max Bentley, Chi	47	31	30	61	1991	Wayne Gretzky, LA	78	41	122	163
1947	Max Bentley, Chi	60	29	43	72	1992	Mario Lemieux, Pit	64	44	87	131
1948	Elmer Lach, Mon	60	30	31	61	1993	Mario Lemieux, Pit	60	69	91	160
1949	Roy Conacher, Chi	60	26	42	68	1994	Wayne Gretzky, LA	81	38	92	130
1950	Ted Lindsay, Det	69	23	55	78	1995	Jaromir Jagr, Pit	48	32	38	70
1951	Gordie Howe, Det	70	43	43	86	1996	Mario Lemieux, Pit	70	69	92	161
1952	Gordie Howe, Det	70	47	39	86	1997	Mario Lemieux, Pit	76	50	72	122
1953	Gordie Howe, Det	70	49	46	95	1998	Jaromir Jagr, Pit	77	35	67	102
1954	Gordie Howe, Det	70	33	48	81	1999	Jaromir Jagr, Pit	81	44	83	127
1955	Bernie Geoffrion, Mon	70	38	37	75	2000	Jaromir Jagr, Pit	63	42	54	96
1956	Jean Beliveau, Mon	70	47	41	88	2001	Jaromir Jagr, Pit	81	52	69	121
1957	Gordie Howe, Det	70	44	45	89	2002	Jarome Iginla, Calg	82	52	44	96
1958	Dickie Moore, Mon	70	36	48	84	2003	Peter Forsberg, Col	75	29	77	106
1959	Dickie Moore, Mon	70	41	55	96	2004	Martin St. Louis, TB	82	38	56	94
1960	Bobby Hull, Chi	70	39	42	81	2006	Joe Thornton, Bos-SJ	81	29	96	125
1961	Bernie Geoffrion, Mon	64	50	45	95	2007	Sidney Crosby, Pit	79	36	84	120
1962	Bobby Hull, Chi	70	50	34	84						

Note: The three times players have tied for total points in one season the player with more goals has won the trophy. In 1961-62, Hull outscored Andy Bathgate of NY Rangers, 50 goals to 28. In 1979-80, Dionne outscored Wayne Gretzky of Edmonton, 53-51. In 1995, Jagr outscored Eric Lindros of Philadelphia, 32-29.

Goals

Multiple winners: Bobby Hull (7); Phil Esposito (6); Charlie Conacher, Wayne Gretzky, Gordie Howe and Maurice Richard (5); Bill Cooke, Babe Dye, Brett Hull, Mario Lemieux, Pavel Bure and Teemu Selanne (3); Jean Beliveau, Doug Bentley, Peter Bondra, Mike Bossy, Bernie Geoffrion, Bryan Hextall, Jarome Iginla, Joe Malone and Nels Stewart (2).

Year		No	Year		No	Year		No
1918	Joe Malone, Mon	44	1927	Bill Cook, NYR	33	1936	Charlie Conacher, Tor	23
1919	Odie Cleghorn, Mon	23	1928	Howie Morenz, Mon	33		& Bill Thoms, Tor	23
	& Newsy Lalonde, Mon	23	1929	Ace Bailey, Tor	22	1937	Larry Aurie, Det	23
1920	Joe Malone, Que	39	1930	Cooney Weiland, Bos	43		& Nels Stewart, Bos-NYA	23
1921	Babe Dye, Ham-Tor	35	1931	Charlie Conacher, Tor	31	1938	Gordie Drillon, Tor	26
1922	Punch Broadbent, Ott	32	1932	Charlie Conacher, Tor	34	1939	Roy Conacher, Bos	26
1923	Babe Dye, Tor	26		& Bill Cook, NYR	34	1940	Bryan Hextall, NYR	24
1924	Cy Denneny, Ott	22	1933	Bill Cook, NYR	28	1941	Bryan Hextall, NYR	26
1925	Babe Dye, Tor	38	1934	Charlie Conacher, Tor	32	1942	Lynn Patrick, NYR	32
1926	Nels Stewart, Maroons	34	1935	Charlie Conacher, Tor	36	1943	Doug Bentley, Chi	33

Annual NHL Leaders (Cont.)

Year		No	Year		No	Year		No
1944	Doug Bentley, Chi	38	1966	Bobby Hull, Chi	54	1988	Mario Lemieux, Pit	70
1945	Maurice Richard, Mon	50	1967	Bobby Hull, Chi	52	1989	Mario Lemieux, Pit	85
1946	Gaye Stewart, Tor	37	1968	Bobby Hull, Chi	44			
1947	Maurice Richard, Mon	45	1969	Bobby Hull, Chi	58	1990	Brett Hull, St.L	72
1948	Ted Lindsay, Det	33				1991	Brett Hull, St.L	86
1949	Sid Abel, Det	28	1970	Phil Esposito, Bos	43	1992	Brett Hull, St.L	70
1950	Maurice Richard, Mon	43	1971	Phil Esposito, Bos	76	1993	Alexander Mogilny, Buf	76
1951	Gordie Howe, Det	43	1972	Phil Esposito, Bos	66		& Teemu Selanne, Win	76
1952	Gordie Howe, Det	47	1973	Phil Esposito, Bos	55	1994	Pavel Bure, Van	60
1953	Gordie Howe, Det	49	1974	Phil Esposito, Bos	68	1995	Peter Bondra, Wash	34
1954	Maurice Richard, Mon	37	1975	Phil Esposito, Bos	61	1996	Mario Lemieux, Pit	69
1955	Bernie Geoffrion, Mon	38	1976	Reggie Leach, Phi	61	1997	Keith Tkachuk, Pho	52
	& Maurice Richard, Mon	38	1977	Steve Shutt, Mon	60	1998	Teemu Selanne, Ana	52
1956	Jean Beliveau, Mon	47	1978	Guy Lafleur, Mon	60		& Peter Bondra, Wash	52
1957	Gordie Howe, Det	44	1979	Mike Bossy, NYI	69	1999	Teemu Selanne, Ana	47
1958	Dickie Moore, Mon	36						
1959	Jean Beliveau, Mon	45	1980	Danny Gare, Buf	56	2000	Pavel Bure, Fla	58
1960	Bronco Horvath, Bos	39		Charlie Simmer, LA	56	2001	Pavel Bure, Fla	59
	& Bobby Hull, Chi	39		& Blaine Stoughton, Hart	56	2002	Jarome Iginla, Calg	52
1961	Bernie Geoffrion, Mon	50	1981	Mike Bossy, NYI	68	2003	Milan Hejduk, Col	50
1962	Bobby Hull, Chi	50	1982	Wayne Gretzky, Edm	92	2004	Jarome Iginla, Calg	41
1963	Gordie Howe, Det	38	1983	Wayne Gretzky, Edm	71		Ilya Kovalchuk, Atl	41
1964	Bobby Hull, Chi	43	1984	Wayne Gretzky, Edm	87		& Rick Nash, Clb	41
1965	Norm Ullman, Tor	42	1985	Wayne Gretzky, Edm	73	2006	Jonathan Cheechoo, SJ	56
			1986	Jari Kurri, Edm	68	2007	Vincent Lecavalier, TB	52
			1987	Wayne Gretzky, Edm	62			

Assists

Multiple winners: Wayne Gretzky (16); Bobby Orr (5); Adam Oates, Frank Boucher, Bill Cowley, Phil Esposito, Gordie Howe, Jaromir Jagr, Elmer Lach, Mario Lemieux, Stan Mikita and Joe Primeau (3); Syl Apps, Andy Bathgate, Jean Beliveau, Doug Bentley, Art Chapman, Bobby Clarke, Ron Francis, Ted Lindsay, Bert Olmstead, Henri Richard, Joe Thornton and Bryan Trottier (2).

Year		No	Year		No	Year		No
1918	No official records kept.		1949	Doug Bentley, Chi	43	1979	Bryan Trottier, NYI	87
1919	Newsy Lalonde, Mon	9	1950	Ted Lindsay, Det	55	1980	Wayne Gretzky, Edm	86
1920	Corbett Denneny, Tor	12	1951	Gordie Howe, Det	43	1981	Wayne Gretzky, Edm	109
1921	Louis Berlinquette, Mon	9		& Teeder Kennedy, Tor	43	1982	Wayne Gretzky, Edm	120
	Harry Cameron, Tor	9	1952	Elmer Lach, Mon	50	1983	Wayne Gretzky, Edm	125
	& Joe Matte, Ham	9	1953	Gordie Howe, Det	46	1984	Wayne Gretzky, Edm	118
1922	Punch Broadbent, Ott	14	1954	Gordie Howe, Det	48	1985	Wayne Gretzky, Edm	135
	& Leo Reise, Ham	14	1955	Bert Olmstead, Mon	48	1986	Wayne Gretzky, Edm	163
1923	Ed Bouchard, Ham	12	1956	Bert Olmstead, Mon	56	1987	Wayne Gretzky, Edm	121
1924	King Clancy, Ott	8	1957	Ted Lindsay, Det	55	1988	Wayne Gretzky, Edm	109
1925	Cy Denneny, Ott	15	1958	Henri Richard, Mon	52	1989	Wayne Gretzky, LA	114
1926	Frank Nighbor, Ott	13	1959	Dickie Moore, Mon	55		& Mario Lemieux, Pit	114
1927	Dick Irvin, Chi	18	1960	Don McKenney, Bos	49	1990	Wayne Gretzky, LA	102
1928	Howie Morenz, Mon	18	1961	Jean Beliveau, Mon	58	1991	Wayne Gretzky, LA	122
1929	Frank Boucher, NYR	16	1962	Andy Bathgate, NYR	56	1992	Wayne Gretzky, LA	90
1930	Frank Boucher, NYR	36	1963	Henri Richard, Mon	50	1993	Adam Oates, Bos	97
1931	Joe Primeau, Tor	32	1964	Andy Bathgate, NYR-Tor	58	1994	Wayne Gretzky, LA	92
1932	Joe Primeau, Tor	37	1965	Stan Mikita, Chi	59	1995	Ron Francis, Pit	48
1933	Frank Boucher, NYR	28	1966	Jean Beliveau, Mon	48	1996	Ron Francis, Pit	92
1934	Joe Primeau, Tor	32		Stan Mikita, Chi	48		& Mario Lemieux, Pit	92
1935	Art Chapman, NYA	34		& Bobby Rousseau, Mon	48	1997	Mario Lemieux, Pit	72
1936	Art Chapman, NYA	28	1967	Stan Mikita, Chi	62		& Wayne Gretzky, NYR	72
1937	Syl Apps, Tor	29	1968	Phil Esposito, Bos	49	1998	Jaromir Jagr, Pit	67
1938	Syl Apps, Tor	29	1969	Phil Esposito, Bos	77		& Wayne Gretzky, NYR	67
1939	Bill Cowley, Bos	34	1970	Bobby Orr, Bos	87	1999	Jaromir Jagr, Pit	83
1940	Milt Schmidt, Bos	30	1971	Bobby Orr, Bos	102	2000	Mark Recchi, Phi	63
1941	Bill Cowley, Bos	45	1972	Bobby Orr, Bos	80	2001	Jaromir Jagr, Pit	69
1942	Phil Watson, NYR	37	1973	Phil Esposito, Bos	75		& Adam Oates, Wash	69
1943	Bill Cowley, Bos	45	1974	Bobby Orr, Bos	90	2002	Adam Oates, Wash-Phi	64
1944	Clint Smith, Chi	49	1975	Bobby Clarke, Phi	89	2003	Peter Forsberg, Col	77
1945	Elmer Lach, Mon	54		& Bobby Orr, Bos	89	2004	Scott Gomez, NJ	56
1946	Elmer Lach, Mon	34	1976	Bobby Clarke, Phi	89		& Martin St. Louis, TB	56
1947	Billy Taylor, Det	46	1977	Guy Lafleur, Mon	80	2006	Joe Thornton, Bos-SJ	96
1948	Doug Bentley, Chi	37	1978	Bryan Trottier, NYI	77	2007	Joe Thornton, SJ	92

Goals Against Average

Average determined by games played through 1942-43 season and by minutes played since then. Minimum of 15 games from 1917-18 season through 1925-26; minimum of 25 games since 1926-27 season. Not to be confused with the Vezina Trophy. Goaltenders who posted the season's lowest goals against average, but did not win the Vezina are in **bold** type.

Multiple winners: Jacques Plante (9); Clint Benedict and Bill Durnan (6); Johnny Bower, Ken Dryden and Tiny Thompson (4); Patrick Roy and Georges Vezina (3); Ed Belfour, Frankie Brimsek, Turk Broda, George Hainsworth, Dominik Hasek, Miikka Kiprusoff, Harry Lumley, Bernie Parent, Pete Peeters, Terry Sawchuk and Marty Turco (2).

Year	GAA	Year	GAA	Year	GAA
1918 Georges Vezina, Mon	3.82	1948 Turk Broda, Tor	2.38	1978 Ken Dryden, Mon	2.05
1919 Clint Benedict, Ott	2.94	1949 Bill Durnan, Mon	2.10	1979 Ken Dryden, Mon	2.30
1920 Clint Benedict, Ott	2.67	1950 Bill Durnan, Mon	2.20	1980 Bob Sauve, Buf	2.36
1921 Clint Benedict, Ott	3.13	1951 Al Rollins, Tor	1.77	1981 Richard Sevigny, Mon	2.40
1922 Clint Benedict, Ott	3.50	1952 Terry Sawchuk, Det	1.90	1982 **Denis Herron**, Mon	2.64
1923 Clint Benedict, Ott	2.25	1953 Terry Sawchuk, Det	1.90	1983 Pete Peeters, Bos	2.36
1924 Georges Vezina, Mon	2.00	1954 Harry Lumley, Tor	1.86	1984 **Pat Riggin**, Wash	2.66
1925 Georges Vezina, Mon	1.87	1955 **Harry Lumley**, Tor	1.94	1985 **Tom Barrasso**, Buf	2.66
1926 Alex Connell, Ott	1.17	1956 Jacques Plante, Mon	1.86	1986 **Bob Froese**, Phi	2.55
1927 **Clint Benedict**, Mon-M	1.51	1957 Jacques Plante, Mon	2.02	1987 **Brian Hayward**, Mon	2.81
1928 Geo. Hainsworth, Mon	1.09	1958 Jacques Plante, Mon	2.11	1988 **Pete Peeters**, Wash	2.78
1929 Geo. Hainsworth, Mon	0.98	1959 Jacques Plante, Mon	2.16	1989 Patrick Roy, Mon	2.47
1930 Tiny Thompson, Bos	2.23	1960 Jacques Plante, Mon	2.54	1990 **Mike Liut**, Hart-Wash	2.53
1931 Roy Worters, NYA	1.68	1961 Johnny Bower, Tor	2.50	1991 Ed Belfour, Chi	2.47
1932 Chuck Gardiner, Chi	1.92	1962 Jacques Plante, Mon	2.37	1992 Patrick Roy, Mon	2.36
1933 Tiny Thompson, Bos	1.83	1963 **Jacques Plante**, Mon	2.49	1993 **Felix Potvin**, Phi	2.50
1934 **Wilf Cude**, Det-Mon	1.57	1964 **Johnny Bower**, Tor	2.11	1994 Dominik Hasek, Buf	1.95
1935 Lorne Chabot, Chi	1.83	1965 Johnny Bower, Tor	2.38	1995 Dominik Hasek, Buf	2.11
1936 Tiny Thompson, Bos	1.71	1966 **Johnny Bower**, Tor	2.25	1996 **Ron Hextall**, Phi	2.17
1937 Norm Smith, Det	2.13	1967 Glenn Hall, Chi	2.38	1997 **Martin Brodeur**, NJ	1.88
1938 Tiny Thompson, Bos	1.85	1968 Gump Worsley, Mon	1.98	1998 **Ed Belfour**, Dal	1.88
1939 Frankie Brimsek, Bos	1.58	1969 **Jacques Plante**, St.L	1.96	1999 **Ron Tugnutt**, Ott	1.79
1940 Dave Kerr, NYR	1.60	1970 **Ernie Wakely**, St.L	2.11	2000 **Brian Boucher**, Phi	1.91
1941 Turk Broda, Tor	2.06	1971 **Jacques Plante**, Tor	1.88	2001 **Marty Turco**, Dal	1.90
1942 Frankie Brimsek, Bos	2.45	1972 Tony Esposito, Chi	1.77	2002 **Patrick Roy**, Col	1.94
1943 John Mowers, Det	2.47	1973 Ken Dryden, Mon	2.26	2003 **Marty Turco**, Dal	1.72
1944 Bill Durnan, Mon	2.18	1974 Bernie Parent, Phi	1.89	2004 **Miikka Kiprusoff**, Calg	1.69
1945 Bill Durnan, Mon	2.42	1975 Bernie Parent, Phi	2.03	2006 Miikka Kiprusoff, Calg	2.07
1946 Bill Durnan, Mon	2.60	1976 Ken Dryden, Mon	2.03	2007 **Niklas Backstrom**, Min	1.97
1947 Bill Durnan, Mon	2.30	1977 Bunny Larocque, Mon	2.09		

Penalty Minutes

Multiple winners: Red Horner (8); Gus Mortson and Dave Schultz (4); Bert Corbeau, Lou Fontinato and Tiger Williams (3); Sean Avery, Matthew Barnaby, Billy Boucher, Carl Brewer, Red Dutton, Pat Egan, Bill Ezinicki, Joe Hall, Tim Hunter, Keith Magnuson, Chris Nilan, Jimmy Orlando and Rob Ray (2).

Year	Min	Year	Min	Year	Min
1918 Joe Hall, Mon	60	1948 Bill Barilko, Tor	147	1978 Dave Schultz, LA-Pit	405
1919 Joe Hall, Mon	85	1949 Bill Ezinicki, Tor	145	1979 Tiger Williams, Tor	298
1920 Cully Wilson, Tor	79	1950 Bill Ezinicki, Tor	144	1980 Jimmy Mann, Win	287
1921 Bert Corbeau, Mon	86	1951 Gus Mortson, Tor	142	1981 Tiger Williams, Van	343
1922 Sprague Cleghorn, Mon	63	1952 Gus Kyle, Bos	127	1982 Paul Baxter, Pit	409
1923 Billy Boucher, Mon	52	1953 Maurice Richard, Mon	112	1983 Randy Holt, Wash	275
1924 Bert Corbeau, Tor	55	1954 Gus Mortson, Chi	132	1984 Chris Nilan, Mon	338
1925 Billy Boucher, Mon	92	1955 Fern Flaman, Bos	150	1985 Chris Nilan, Mon	358
1926 Bert Corbeau, Tor	121	1956 Lou Fontinato, NYR	202	1986 Joey Kocur, Det	377
1927 Nels Stewart, Mon-M	133	1957 Gus Mortson, Chi	147	1987 Tim Hunter, Calg	361
1928 Eddie Shore, Bos	165	1958 Lou Fontinato, NYR	152	1988 Bob Probert, Det	398
1929 Red Dutton, Mon-M	139	1959 Ted Lindsay, Chi	184	1989 Tim Hunter, Calg	375
1930 Joe Lamb, Ott	119	1960 Carl Brewer, Tor	150	1990 Basil McRae, Min	351
1931 Harvey Rockburn, Det	118	1961 Pierre Pilote, Chi	165	1991 Rob Ray, Buf	350
1932 Red Dutton, NYA	107	1962 Lou Fontinato, Mon	167	1992 Mike Peluso, Chi	408
1933 Red Horner, Tor	144	1963 Howie Young, Det	273	1993 Marty McSorley, LA	399
1934 Red Horner, Tor	146	1964 Vic Hadfield, NYR	151	1994 Tie Domi, Win	347
1935 Red Horner, Tor	125	1965 Carl Brewer, Tor	177	1995 Enrico Ciccone, TB	225
1936 Red Horner, Tor	167	1966 Reg Fleming, Bos-NYR	166	1996 Matthew Barnaby, Buf	335
1937 Red Horner, Tor	124	1967 John Ferguson, Mon	177	1997 Gino Odjick, Van	371
1938 Red Horner, Tor	82	1968 Barclay Plager, St.L	153	1998 Donald Brashear, Van	372
1939 Red Horner, Tor	85	1969 Forbes Kennedy, Phi-Tor	219	1999 Rob Ray, Buf	261
1940 Red Horner, Tor	87	1970 Keith Magnuson, Chi	213	2000 Denny Lambert, Atl	219
1941 Jimmy Orlando, Det	99	1971 Keith Magnuson, Chi	291	2001 Matthew Barnaby, Pit-TB	265
1942 Pat Egan, NYA	124	1972 Bryan Watson, Pit	212	2002 Peter Worrell, Fla	354
1943 Jimmy Orlando, Det	99	1973 Dave Schultz, Phi	259	2003 Jody Shelley, Clb	249
1944 Mike McMahon, Mon	98	1974 Dave Schultz, Phi	348	2004 Sean Avery, LA	261
1945 Pat Egan, Bos	86	1975 Dave Schultz, Phi	472	2006 Sean Avery, LA	257
1946 Jack Stewart, Det	73	1976 Steve Durbano, Pit-KC	370	2007 Ben Eager, Phi	233
1947 Gus Mortson, Tor	133	1977 Tiger Williams, Tor	338		

All-Time NHL Regular Season Leaders

Through 2007 regular season.

CAREER

Players active during 2007 season in **bold** type.

Points

		Yrs	Gm	G	A	Pts
1	Wayne Gretzky	20	1487	894	1963	2857
2	Mark Messier	25	1756	694	1193	1887
3	Gordie Howe	26	1767	801	1049	1850
4	Ron Francis	23	1731	549	1249	1798
5	Marcel Dionne	18	1348	731	1040	1771
6	Steve Yzerman	22	1514	692	1063	1755
7	Mario Lemieux	17	915	690	1033	1723
8	Phil Esposito	18	1282	717	873	1590
9	**Joe Sakic**	18	1319	610	979	1589
10	Ray Bourque	22	1612	410	1169	1579
11	Paul Coffey	21	1409	396	1135	1531
12	**Jaromir Jagr**	16	1191	621	907	1528
13	Stan Mikita	22	1394	541	926	1467
14	Bryan Trottier	18	1279	524	901	1425
15	Adam Oates	19	1337	341	1079	1420
16	Doug Gilmour	20	1474	450	964	1414
17	Dale Hawerchuk	16	1188	518	891	1409
18	Jari Kurri	17	1251	601	797	1398
19	Luc Robitaille	19	1431	668	726	1394
20	Brett Hull	20	1269	741	650	1391
21	John Bucyk	23	1540	556	813	1369
22	Guy Lafleur	17	1126	560	793	1353
23	Dave Andreychuk	23	1639	640	698	1338
	Denis Savard	17	1196	473	865	1338
25	Mike Gartner	19	1432	708	627	1335
26	**Mark Recchi**	18	1338	508	825	1333
27	Pierre Turgeon	19	1294	515	812	1327
28	Gilbert Perreault	17	1191	512	814	1326
29	**Brendan Shanahan**	19	1417	627	667	1294
30	Alex Delvecchio	24	1549	456	825	1281

Goals

		Yrs	Gm	No
1	Wayne Gretzky	20	1487	894
2	Gordie Howe	26	1767	801
3	Brett Hull	20	1269	741
4	Marcel Dionne	18	1348	731
5	Phil Esposito	18	1282	717
6	Mike Gartner	19	1432	708
7	Mark Messier	25	1756	694
8	Steve Yzerman	22	1514	692
9	Mario Lemieux	17	915	690
10	Luc Robitaille	19	1431	668
11	Dave Andreychuk	23	1639	640
12	**Brendan Shanahan**	19	1417	627
13	**Jaromir Jagr**	16	1191	621
14	Bobby Hull	16	1063	610
	Joe Sakic	18	1319	610
16	Dino Ciccarelli	19	1232	608
17	Jari Kurri	17	1251	601
18	Mike Bossy	10	752	573
19	**Joe Nieuwendyk**	20	1257	567
20	Guy Lafleur	17	1126	560
21	John Bucyk	23	1540	556
22	Ron Francis	23	1731	549
23	Michel Goulet	15	1089	548
24	Maurice Richard	18	978	544
25	Stan Mikita	22	1394	541
26	**Teemu Selanne**	14	1041	540
27	Frank Mahovlich	18	1181	533
28	Bryan Trottier	18	1279	524
29	**Mats Sundin**	16	1231	523
30	Pat Verbeek	20	1424	522

Assists

		Yrs	Gm	No
1	Wayne Gretzky	20	1487	1963
2	Ron Francis	23	1731	1249
3	Mark Messier	25	1756	1193
4	Ray Bourque	22	1612	1169
5	Paul Coffey	21	1409	1135
6	Adam Oates	19	1337	1079
7	Steve Yzerman	22	1514	1063
8	Gordie Howe	26	1767	1049
9	Marcel Dionne	18	1348	1040
10	Mario Lemieux	17	915	1033
11	**Joe Sakic**	18	1319	979
12	Doug Gilmour	20	1474	964
13	Al MacInnis	23	1416	934
14	Larry Murphy	21	1615	929
15	Stan Mikita	22	1394	926
16	**Jaromir Jagr**	16	1191	907
17	Bryan Trottier	18	1279	901
18	Phil Housley	21	1495	894
19	Dale Hawerchuk	16	1188	891
20	Phil Esposito	18	1281	873

Penalty Minutes

		Yrs	Gm	Min
1	Tiger Williams	14	962	3966
2	Dale Hunter	19	1407	3565
3	Tie Domi	16	1020	3515
4	Marty McSorley	17	961	3381
5	Bob Probert	16	935	3300
6	Rob Ray	15	900	3207
7	Craig Berube	17	1054	3149
8	Tim Hunter	16	815	3146
9	Chris Nilan	13	688	3043
10	Rick Tocchet	18	1144	2972
11	Pat Verbeek	20	1424	2905
12	**Chris Chelios**	23	1547	2837
13	Dave Manson	16	1103	2792
14	Scott Stevens	22	1635	2785
15	Willi Plett	12	834	2572

NHL-WHA Top 10

All-time regular season scoring leaders, including games played in World Hockey Association (1972-79). NHL players with WHA experience are listed in CAPITAL letters. Player active during 2007 is in **bold** type.

Points

		Yrs	G	A	Pts
1	WAYNE GRETZKY	21	940	2027	2967
2	GORDIE HOWE	32	975	1383	2358
3	MARK MESSIER	26	695	1203	1898
4	BOBBY HULL	23	913	895	1808
5	Ron Francis	23	549	1249	1798
6	Marcel Dionne	18	731	1040	1771
7	Steve Yzerman	22	692	1063	1755
8	Mario Lemieux	17	690	1033	1723
9	Phil Esposito	18	717	873	1590
10	**Joe Sakic**	18	610	979	1589

WHA Totals: GRETZKY (1 yr, 80 gm, 46-64—110); HOWE (6 yrs, 419 gm, 174-334—508); MESSIER (1 yr, 52 gm, 1-10—11); HULL (7 yrs, 411 gm, 303-335—638).

Years Played

		Yrs	Career	Gm
1	Gordie Howe	26	1946-71, 79-80	1767
2	Mark Messier	25	1979-2004	1756
3	Alex Delvecchio	24	1950-74	1549
	Tim Horton	24	1949-50, 51-74	1446
5	Ron Francis	23	1981-2004	1731
	Dave Andreychuk	23	1982-2006	1639
	Chris Chelios	23	1984–	1547
	John Bucyk	23	1955-78	1540
	Al MacInnis	23	1982-2004	1416
10	Scott Stevens	22	1982-2004	1635
	Ray Bourque	22	1979-2001	1612
	Steve Yzerman	22	1983-2006	1514
	Stan Mikita	22	1958-80	1394
	Doug Mohns	22	1953-75	1390
	Dean Prentice	22	1952-74	1378

Note: Combined NHL-WHA years played: Howe (32); Messier (26); Harry Howell (24); Bobby Hull (23); Norm Ullman, Eric Nesterenko, Frank Mahovlich and Dave Keon (22).

Games Played

		Yrs	Career	Gm
1	Gordie Howe	26	1946–71, 79–80	1767
2	Mark Messier	25	1979-2004	1756
3	Ron Francis	23	1981-2004	1731
4	Dave Andreychuk	23	1982-2006	1639
5	Scott Stevens	22	1982-2004	1635
6	Larry Murphy	21	1980-2001	1615
7	Ray Bourque	22	1979-2001	1612
8	Alex Delvecchio	24	1950–74	1549
9	**Chris Chelios**	23	1984–	1547
10	John Bucyk	23	1955–78	1540
11	Steve Yzerman	22	1983-2006	1514
12	Phil Housley	21	1982-2003	1495
13	Wayne Gretzky	20	1979-99	1487
14	Doug Gilmour	20	1983-2003	1474
15	Tim Horton	24	1949-50, 51-74	1446

Note: Combined NHL-WHA games played: Howe (2,186), Messier (1,808), Dave Keon (1,597), Harry Howell (1,581), Gretzky (1,567), Norm Ullman (1,554), Mike Gartner (1,510) and Bobby Hull (1,474).

Goaltending

Wins

		Yrs	Gm	W	L	T	Pct
1	Patrick Roy	19	1029	**551**	315	131	.618
2	**Martin Brodeur**	14	891	**494**	263	105	.653
3	**Ed Belfour**	18	963	**484**	320	111	.602
4	Terry Sawchuk	21	971	**447**	330	172	.562
5	**Curtis Joseph**	17	913	**446**	341	90	.567
6	Jacques Plante	18	837	**434**	247	146	.614
7	Tony Esposito	16	886	**423**	306	152	.566
8	Glenn Hall	18	906	**407**	326	163	.545
9	Grant Fuhr	19	868	**403**	295	114	.567
10	Mike Vernon	19	781	**385**	273	92	.575
11	John Vanbiesbrouck	20	882	**374**	346	119	.517
12	Andy Moog	18	713	**372**	209	88	.622
13	Tom Barrasso	19	777	**369**	277	86	.563
14	**Dominik Hasek**	15	694	**362**	213	82	.630
15	Rogie Vachon	16	795	**355**	291	127	.541
16	**Chris Osgood**	13	621	**336**	186	66	.644
17	Gump Worsley	21	861	**335**	352	150	.490
18	Harry Lumley	16	804	**330**	329	143	.501
19	**Sean Burke**	18	820	**324**	341	101	.487
20	Billy Smith	18	680	**305**	233	105	.556

Note: Beginning with the 2005-06 season, NHL ties were eliminated since shootouts decided games that were still tied after a five-minute overtime. Note that overtime losses and shootout losses are not included in the tables above or below.

Losses

		Yrs	Gm	W	L	T	Pct
1	Gump Worsley	21	861	335	**352**	150	.490
2	Gilles Meloche	18	788	270	**351**	131	.446
3	John Vanbiesbrouck	20	882	374	**346**	119	.517
4	**Sean Burke**	18	820	324	**341**	101	.487
	Curtis Joseph	17	913	446	**341**	90	.567

Shutouts

		Yrs	Games	No
1	Terry Sawchuk	21	971	103
2	George Hainsworth	11	465	94
3	**Martin Brodeur**	14	891	92
4	Glenn Hall	18	906	84
5	Jacques Plante	18	837	82
6	Alex Connell	12	417	81
	Tiny Thompson	12	553	81
8	Tony Esposito	16	886	76
	Ed Belfour	18	963	76
	Dominik Hasek	15	694	76

Goals Against Average

Minimum of 300 games played.

Before 1950

		Gm	Min	GA	GAA
1	George Hainsworth	465	29,415	937	1.91
2	Alex Connell	417	26,050	830	1.91
3	Chuck Gardiner	316	19,687	664	2.02
4	Lorne Chabot	411	25,307	860	2.04
5	Tiny Thompson	553	34,175	1183	2.08

Since 1950

		Gm	Min	GA	GAA
1	**Marty Turco**	320	18,021	635	2.11
2	**Martin Brodeur**	891	52,573	1931	2.20
3	**Dominik Hasek**	694	40,487	1488	2.21
4	Ken Dryden	397	23,352	870	2.24
5	Roman Turek	328	19,095	734	2.31
6	Jacques Plante	837	49,533	1965	2.38
7	**Evgeni Nabokov**	353	20,051	811	2.43
8	**Chris Osgood**	621	35,611	1455	2.45
9	**Jean-Sebastien Giguere**	353	20,353	840	2.48
10	Glen Hall	906	53,484	2222	2.49

NHL-WHA Top 10

All-time regular season wins leaders, including games played in World Hockey Association (1972-79). NHL goaltenders with WHA experience are listed in CAPITAL letters. Players active during 2007 are in bold type.

Wins

		Yrs	W	L	T	Pct
1	Patrick Roy	19	**551**	315	131	.618
2	**Martin Brodeur**	14	**494**	263	105	.653
3	**Ed Belfour**	18	**484**	320	111	.602
4	JACQUES PLANTE	19	**449**	261	147	.610
5	Terry Sawchuk	21	**447**	330	172	.562
6	**Curtis Joseph**	17	**446**	341	90	.567
7	Tony Esposito	16	**423**	306	152	.566
8	Glenn Hall	18	**407**	326	163	.545
9	Grant Fuhr	19	**403**	295	114	.567
10	Mike Vernon	19	**385**	273	92	.575

WHA Totals: PLANTE (1 yr, 31 gm, 15-14-1).

All-Time NHL Regular Season Leaders (Cont.)
SINGLE SEASON

Scoring
Points

		Season	G	A	Pts
1	Wayne Gretzky, Edm	1985-86	52	163	215
2	Wayne Gretzky, Edm	1981-82	92	120	212
3	Wayne Gretzky, Edm	1984-85	73	135	208
4	Wayne Gretzky, Edm	1983-84	87	118	205
5	Mario Lemieux, Pit	1988-89	85	114	199
6	Wayne Gretzky, Edm	1982-83	71	125	196
7	Wayne Gretzky, Edm	1986-87	62	121	183
8	Mario Lemieux, Pit	1987-88	70	98	168
	Wayne Gretzky, LA	1988-89	54	114	168
10	Wayne Gretzky, Edm	1980-81	55	109	164
11	Wayne Gretzky, LA	1990-91	41	122	163
12	Mario Lemieux, Pit	1995-96	69	92	161
13	Mario Lemieux, Pit	1992-93	69	91	160
14	Steve Yzerman, Det	1988-89	65	90	155
15	Phil Esposito, Bos	1970-71	76	76	152
16	Bernie Nicholls, LA	1988-89	70	80	150
17	Jaromir Jagr, Pit	1995-96	62	87	149
	Wayne Gretzky, Edm	1987-88	40	109	149
19	Pat LaFontaine, Buf.	1992-93	53	95	148
20	Mike Bossy, NYI	1981-82	64	83	147

WHA 150 points or more: 154—Marc Tardif, Que. (1977-78).

Goals

		Season	Gm	No
1	Wayne Gretzky, Edm	1981-82	80	92
2	Wayne Gretzky, Edm	1983-84	74	87
3	Brett Hull, St.L	1990-91	78	86
4	Mario Lemieux, Pit	1988-89	76	85
5	Alexander Mogilny, Buf.	1992-93	77	76
	Phil Esposito, Bos	1970-71	78	76
	Teemu Selanne, Win	1992-93	84	76
8	Wayne Gretzky, Edm	1984-85	80	73
9	Brett Hull, St.L	1989-90	80	72
10	Jari Kurri, Edm	1984-85	73	71
	Wayne Gretzky, Edm	1982-83	80	71
12	Brett Hull, St.L	1991-92	73	70
	Mario Lemieux, Pit	1987-88	77	70
	Bernie Nicholls, LA	1988-89	79	70
15	Mario Lemieux, Pit	1992-93	60	69
	Mario Lemieux, Pit	1995-96	70	69
	Mike Bossy, NYI	1978-79	80	69
18	Phil Esposito, Bos	1973-74	78	68
	Jari Kurri, Edm	1985-86	78	68
	Mike Bossy, NYI	1980-81	79	68

WHA 70 goals or more: 77—Bobby Hull, Win. (1974-75); 75—Real Cloutier, Que. (1978-79); 71—Marc Tardif, Que. (1975-76); 70—Anders Hedberg, Win. (1976-77).

Assists

		Season	Gm	No
1	Wayne Gretzky, Edm	1985-86	80	163
2	Wayne Gretzky, Edm	1984-85	80	135
3	Wayne Gretzky, Edm	1982-83	80	125
4	Wayne Gretzky, LA	1990-91	78	122
5	Wayne Gretzky, Edm	1986-87	79	121
6	Wayne Gretzky, Edm	1981-82	80	120
7	Wayne Gretzky, Edm	1983-84	74	118
8	Mario Lemieux, Pit	1988-89	76	114
	Wayne Gretzky, LA	1988-89	78	114
10	Wayne Gretzky, Edm	1987-88	64	109
	Wayne Gretzky, Edm	1980-81	80	109
12	Wayne Gretzky, LA	1989-90	73	102
	Bobby Orr, Bos	1970-71	78	102
14	Mario Lemieux, Pit	1987-88	77	98
15	Adam Oates, Bos	1992-93	84	97

WHA 95 assists or more: 106—Andre Lacroix, San Diego (1974-75).

Goaltending
Wins

		Season	Record
1	**Martin Brodeur**, NJ	2006-07	48-23-0
2	Bernie Parent, Phi	1973-74	47-13-12
	Roberto Luongo, Van	2006-07	47-22-0
4	Bernie Parent, Phi	1974-75	44-14-9
	Terry Sawchuk, Det	1950-51	44-13-13
	Terry Sawchuk, Det	1951-52	44-14-12
7	Martin Brodeur, NJ	1999-00	43-20-8
	Martin Brodeur, NJ	1997-98	43-17-8
	Martin Brodeur, NJ	2005-06	43-23-0
	Tom Barrasso, Pit	1992-93	43-14-5
	Ed Belfour, Chi	1990-91	43-19-7

Most WHA wins in one season: 44—Richard Brodeur, Que. (1975-76).

Losses

		Season	Record
1	Gary Smith, Cal	1970-71	19-48-4
2	Al Rollins, Chi.	1953-54	12-47-7
3	Peter Sidorkiewicz, Ott	1992-93	8-46-3
4	Harry Lumley, Chi	1951-52	17-44-9
5	Three tied with 41 losses each.		

Most WHA losses in one season: 36—Don McLeod, Van. (1974-75) and Andy Brown, Ind. (1974-75).

Shutouts

		Season	Gm	No
1	George Hainsworth, Mon . . .	1928-29	44	22
2	Alex Connell, Ott	1925-26	36	15
	Alex Connell, Ott	1927-28	44	15
	Hal Winkler, Bos	1927-28	44	15
	Tony Esposito, Chi	1969-70	63	15

Most WHA shutouts in one season: 5—Gerry Cheevers, Cle. (1972-73) and Joe Daly, Win. (1975-76).

Goals Against Average
Before 1950

		Season	Gm	GAA
1	George Hainsworth, Mon . . .	1928-29	44	0.98
2	George Hainsworth, Mon . . .	1927-28	44	1.09
3	Alex Connell, Ott	1925-26	36	1.17
4	Tiny Thompson, Bos	1928-29	44	1.18
5	Roy Worters, NY Americans .	1928-29	38	1.21

Since 1950

		Season	Gm	GAA
1	Miikka Kiprusoff, Calg	2003-04	38	1.69
2	Marty Turco, Dal	2002-03	55	1.72
3	Tony Esposito, Chi	1971-72	48	1.77
4	Al Rollins, Tor	1950-51	40	1.77
5	Ron Tugnutt, Ott	1998-99	43	1.79

Penalty Minutes

		Season	PM
1	Dave Schultz, Phi	1974-75	472
2	Paul Baxter, Pit.	1981-82	409
3	Mike Peluso, Chi	1991-92	408
4	Dave Schultz, LA-Pit	1977-78	405
5	Marty McSorley, LA	1992-93	399
6	Bob Probert, Det	1987-88	398
7	Basil McRae, Min.	1987-88	382
8	Joey Kocur, Det	1985-86	377
9	Tim Hunter, Calg	1988-89	375
10	Donald Brashear, Van.	1997-98	372

WHA 355 minutes or more: 365—Curt Brackenbury, Min-Que. (1975-76).

SINGLE GAME

Points

	Date	G-A—Pts
Darryl Sittler, Tor vs Bos	2/7/76	6-4—10
Maurice Richard, Mon vs Det	12/28/44	5-3— 8
Bert Olmstead, Mon vs Chi.	1/9/54	4-4— 8
Tom Bladon, Phi vs Cle.	12/11/77	4-4— 8
Bryan Trottier, NYI vs NYR	12/23/78	5-3— 8
Peter Stastny, Que at Wash.	2/22/81	4-4— 8
Anton Stastny, Que at Wash	2/22/81	3-5— 8
Wayne Gretzky, Edm vs NJ.	11/19/83	3-5— 8
Wayne Gretzky, Edm vs Min.	1/4/84	4-4— 8
Paul Coffey, Edm vs Det	3/14/86	2-6— 8
Mario Lemieux, Pit vs St.L.	10/15/88	2-6— 8
Bernie Nicholls, LA vs Tor	12/1/88	2-6— 8
Mario Lemieux, Pit vs NJ.	12/31/88	5-3— 8

Goals

	Date	No
Joe Malone, Que vs Tor	1/31/20	7
Newsy Lalonde, Mon vs Tor	1/10/20	6
Joe Malone, Que vs Ott	3/10/20	6
Corb Denneny, Tor vs Ham	1/26/21	6
Cy Denneny, Ott vs Ham	3/7/21	6
Syd Howe, Det vs NYR	2/3/44	6
Red Berenson, St.L at Phi	11/7/68	6
Darryl Sittler, Tor vs Bos	2/7/76	6

Assists

	Date	No
Billy Taylor, Det at Chi.	3/16/47	7
Wayne Gretzky, Edm vs Wash	2/15/80	7
Wayne Gretzky, Edm at Chi.	12/11/85	7
Wayne Gretzky, Edm vs Que	2/14/86	7
24 players tied with 6 each.		

Penalty Minutes

	Date	Min
Randy Holt, LA at Phi.	3/11/79	67
Brad Smith, Tor vs Det	11/15/86	57
Reed Low, St.L at Calg.	2/28/02	57
Frank Bathe, Phi vs LA	3/11/79	55
Reed Low, St.L at Det	12/31/02	53
Russ Anderson, Pit vs Edm	1/19/80	51

Penalties

	Date	No
Chris Nilan, Bos vs Har	3/31/91	10*
Nine tied with 9 each.		

* Nilan accumulated six minors, two majors, one 10-minute misconduct and one game misconduct.

All-Time Winningest NHL Coaches

Top 20 NHL career victories through the 2006-07 season. Career, regular season and playoff records are noted along with NHL titles won. Coaches active during 2006-07 season in **bold** type. In the following tables, overtime and shootout losses are considered losses.

		Career				Regular Season				Playoffs				
		Yrs	W	L	T	Pct	W	L	T	Pct	W	L	T	Pct	Stanley Cups
1	Scotty Bowman	30	**1467**	714	313	.651	1244	584	313	.654	223	130	0	.632	9 (1973, 76-79, 92, 97-98, 2002)
2	Al Arbour	22	**904**	663	248	.566	781	577	248	.564	123	86	0	.589	4 (1980-83)
3	Dick Irvin	26	**790**	609	228	.556	690	521	226	.559	100	88	2	.532	4 (1932,44,46,53)
4	Pat Quinn	19	**751**	596	154	.552	657	507	154	.557	94	89	0	.514	None
5	Mike Keenan	18	**675**	560	147	.542	584	491	147	.538	91	69	0	.569	1 (1994)
6	**Bryan Murray**	16	**665**	533	131	.550	613	477	131	.556	52	56	0	.443	None
7	Billy Reay	16	**599**	445	175	.563	542	385	175	.571	57	60	0	.487	None
8	Glen Sather	13	**586**	351	122	.611	497	314	121	.598	89	37	1	.705	4 (1984-85,87-88)
9	Toe Blake	13	**582**	292	159	.640	500	255	159	.634	82	37	0	.689	8 (1956-60,65-66,68)
10	Pat Burns	14	**579**	438	151	.560	501	367	151	.566	78	71	0	.523	1 (2003)
11	**Jacques Martin**	13	**517**	465	119	.524	479	418	119	.530	38	47	0	.447	None
12	**Jacques Lemaire**	13	**514**	435	124	.537	456	387	124	.536	58	48	0	.547	1 (1995)
13	Roger Neilson	17	**511**	436	159	.534	460	381	159	.540	51	55	0	.481	None
14	**Ron Wilson**	13	**510**	480	101	.514	469	439	101	.515	41	41	0	.500	None
15	Ken Hitchcock	11	**502**	346	88	.583	436	295	88	.586	66	51	0	.564	1 (1999)
16	**Marc Crawford**	12	**481**	404	103	.539	438	364	103	.541	43	40	0	.518	1 (1996)
17	Brian Sutter	13	**479**	477	140	.501	451	437	140	.507	28	40	0	.412	None
18	Jack Adams	21	**465**	442	162	.511	413	390	161	.512	52	52	1	.500	3 (1936-37, 43)
19	Jacques Demers	14	**464**	510	130	.479	409	467	130	.471	55	43	0	.561	1 (1993)
20	Darryl Sutter	11	**456**	404	101	.527	409	350	101	.534	47	54	0	.465	None

Where They Coached

Adams—Toronto (1922-23), Detroit (1927-47); **Arbour**—St. Louis (1970-73), NY Islanders (1973-86,88-94); **Blake**—Montreal (1955-68); **Bowman**—St. Louis (1967-71), Montreal (1971-79), Buffalo (1979-87), Pittsburgh (1991-93), Detroit (1993-2002); **Burns**—Montreal (1988-92), Toronto (1992-96), Boston (1997-2000), New Jersey (2002-05); **Crawford**—Quebec/Colorado (1994-98), Vancouver (98-2006), Los Angeles (2006–); **Demers**—Quebec (1979-80), St. Louis (1983-86), Detroit (1986-90), Montreal (1992-95), Tampa Bay (1997-99).

Hitchcock—Dallas (1996-2002), Philadelphia (2002-06), Columbus (2006–); **Irvin**—Chicago (1930-31,55-56), Toronto (1931-40), Montreal (1940-55); **Keenan**—Philadelphia (1984-88), Chicago (1988-92), NY Rangers (1993-94), St. Louis (1994-96), Vancouver (1997-99), Boston (2000-01), Florida (2001-03), Calgary (2007–); **Lemaire**—Montreal (1984-85), New Jersey (1993-98), Minnesota (2000–); **Martin**—St. Louis (1986-88), Ottawa (1995-2004), Florida (2004–); **Murray**—Washington (1982-90), Detroit (1990-93), Florida (1997-98), Anaheim (2001-02), Ottawa (2004-07).

Neilson—Toronto (1977-79), Buffalo (1979-81), Vancouver (1982-83), Los Angeles (1984), NY Rangers (1989-93), Florida (1993-95), Philadelphia (1998-2000), Ottawa (2002); **Quinn**—Philadelphia (1978-82), Los Angeles (1984-87), Vancouver (1990-94, 96), Toronto (1998-2006); **Reay**—Toronto (1957-59), Chicago (1963-77); **Sather**—Edmonton (1979-89, 93-94), NY Rangers (2003-04); **B. Sutter**—St. Louis (1988-92), Boston (1992-95), Calgary (1997-2000), Chicago (2001-05); **D. Sutter**—Chicago (1992-95), San Jose (1997-02), Calgary (2002-06); **Wilson**—Anaheim (1993-97), Washington (1997-2002), San Jose (2002–).

Top Winning Percentages

Minimum of 275 victories, including playoffs.

		Yrs	W	L	T	Pct.
1	Scotty Bowman	30	1467	714	313	.651
2	Toe Blake	13	582	292	159	.640
3	Glen Sather	13	586	351	122	.611
4	Fred Shero	10	451	272	119	.606
5	Don Cherry	6	281	177	77	.597
6	Tommy Ivan	9	324	205	111	.593
7	**Ken Hitchcock**	11	502	346	88	.583
8	Al Arbour	22	904	663	248	.566
9	**Joel Quenneville**	10	432	325	77	.564
10	Billy Reay	16	599	445	175	.563
11	Emile Francis	13	433	326	112	.561
12	**Bob Hartley**	8	378	289	61	.561
13	Pat Burns	14	579	438	151	.560
14	Hap Day	10	308	237	81	.557
15	Dick Irvin	26	790	609	228	.556
16	Lester Patrick	13	312	242	115	.552
17	Art Ross	18	393	310	95	.552
18	Pat Quinn	19	751	596	154	.552
19	**Bryan Murray**	16	665	533	131	.550
20	Bob Johnson	6	275	223	58	.547
21	Terry Murray	11	406	331	89	.545
22	**Lindy Ruff**	9	410	338	78	.544
23	Mike Keenan	18	675	560	147	.542
24	**Marc Crawford**	12	481	404	103	.539
25	**Jacques Lemaire**	13	514	435	124	.537
26	Roger Neilson	16	511	436	159	.534
27	Punch Imlach	15	439	384	148	.528
28	**Darryl Sutter**	11	456	404	101	.527
29	**Jacques Martin**	13	517	465	119	.524
30	Terry Crisp	9	310	286	78	.518

Active Coaches' Victories

Records through 2006-07 season, including playoffs.

		Yrs	W	L	T	Pct.
1	Mike Keenan, Calg.	18	675	560	147	.542
2	Jacques Martin, Fla.	13	517	465	119	.524
3	Jacques Lemaire, Min.	13	514	435	124	.537
4	Ron Wilson, SJ	13	510	480	101	.514
5	Ken Hitchcock, Clb.	11	502	346	88	.583
6	Marc Crawford, LA	12	481	404	103	.539
7	Joel Quenneville, Col	10	432	325	77	.564
8	Lindy Ruff, Buf.	9	410	338	78	.544
9	Bob Hartley, Atl.	8	378	289	61	.561
10	Paul Maurice, Tor.	10	325	367	99	.473
11	Barry Trotz, Nash.	8	287	325	60	.472
12	Andy Murray, St.L.	7	252	248	58	.504
13	Craig MacTavish, Edm.	6	241	240	47	.501
14	John Tortorella, TB	7	232	233	37	.499
15	Peter Laviolette, Car.	5	209	183	25	.531
16	Mike Babcock, Det.	4	204	150	19	.572
17	Dave Tippett, Dal.	4	201	128	28	.602
18	Alain Vigneault, Van.	5	167	168	35	.499
19	Michel Therrien, Pit.	5	145	172	23	.460
20	Tom Renney, NYR	5	136	154	9	.470
21	Claude Julien, Bos	4	123	116	11	.514
22	Ted Nolan, NYI	3	119	125	19	.489
23	Randy Carlyle, Ana.	2	116	85	0	.577
24	John Paddock, Ott.	4	111	146	37	.546
25	Glen Hanlon, Wash.	3	72	137	9	.351
26	Wayne Gretzky, Pho.	2	69	95	0	.421
27	Guy Carbonneau, Mon.	1	42	40	0	.512
28	Denis Savard, Chi.	1	24	37	0	.393
29	John Stevens, Phi	1	21	53	0	.284
30	Brent Sutter, NJ	0	0	0	0	.000

Annual Awards

Hart Memorial Trophy

Awarded to the player "adjudged to be the most valuable to his team" and named after Cecil Hart, the former manager-coach of the Montreal Canadiens. Winners selected by Pro Hockey Writers Assn. (PHWA). Winners' scoring statistics or goaltender W-L records and goals against average are provided; (*) indicates led or tied for league lead.

Multiple winners: Wayne Gretzky (9); Gordie Howe (6); Eddie Shore (4); Bobby Clarke, Mario Lemieux, Howie Morenz and Bobby Orr (3); Jean Beliveau, Bill Cowley, Phil Esposito, Dominik Hasek, Bobby Hull, Guy Lafleur, Mark Messier, Stan Mikita and Nels Stewart (2).

Year		G	A	Pts	Year		G	A	Pts
1924	Frank Nighbor, Ottawa, C	10	3	13	1952	Gordie Howe, Det., RW	47	39	86*
1925	Billy Burch, Hamilton, C	20	4	24	1953	Gordie Howe, Det., RW	49	46	95*
1926	Nels Stewart, Maroons, C	34	8	42*	1954	Al Rollins, Chi., G	12-47-7;		3.23
1927	Herb Gardiner, Mon., D	6	6	12	1955	Ted Kennedy, Tor., C	10	42	52
1928	Howie Morenz, Mon., C	33	18	51	1956	Jean Beliveau, Mon., C	47	41	88
1929	Roy Worters, NYA, G	16-13-9;		1.21	1957	Gordie Howe, Det.,RW	44	45	89*
1930	Nels Stewart, Maroons, C	39	16	55	1958	Gordie Howe, Det., RW	33	44	77
1931	Howie Morenz, Mon., C	28	23	51*	1959	Andy Bathgate, NYR, RW	40	48	88
1932	Howie Morenz, Mon., C	24	25	49	1960	Gordie Howe, Det., RW	28	45	73
1933	Eddie Shore, Bos., D	8	27	35	1961	Bernie Geoffrion, Mon., RW	50	45	95*
1934	Aurel Joliat, Mon., LW	22	15	37	1962	Jacques Plante, Mon., G	42-14-14;		2.37*
1935	Eddie Shore, Bos., D	7	26	33	1963	Gordie Howe, Det., RW	38	48	86*
1936	Eddie Shore, Bos., D	3	16	19	1964	Jean Beliveau, Mon., C	28	50	78
1937	Babe Siebert, Mon., D	8	20	28	1965	Bobby Hull, Chi., LW	39	32	71
1938	Eddie Shore, Bos., D	3	14	17	1966	Bobby Hull, Chi., LW	54	43	97*
1939	Toe Blake, Mon., LW	24	23	47*	1967	Stan Mikita, Chi., C	35	62	97*
1940	Ebbie Goodfellow, Det., D	11	17	28	1968	Stan Mikita, Chi., C	40	47	87*
1941	Bill Cowley, Bos., C	17	45	62*	1969	Phil Esposito, Bos., C	49	77	126*
1942	Tommy Anderson, NYA, D	12	29	41	1970	Bobby Orr, Bos., D	33	87	120*
1943	Bill Cowley, Bos., C	27	45	72	1971	Bobby Orr, Bos., D	37	102	139
1944	Babe Pratt, Tor., D	17	40	57	1972	Bobby Orr, Bos., D	37	80	117
1945	Elmer Lach, Mon., C	26	54	80*	1973	Bobby Clarke, Phi., C	37	67	104
1946	Max Bentley, Chi., C	31	30	61*	1974	Phil Esposito, Bos., C	68	77	145*
1947	Maurice Richard, Mon., RW	45	26	71	1975	Bobby Clarke, Phi., C	27	89	116
1948	Buddy O'Connor, NYR, C	24	36	60	1976	Bobby Clarke, Phi., C	30	89	119
1949	Sid Abel, Det., C	28	26	54	1977	Guy Lafleur, Mon., RW	56	80	136*
1950	Chuck Rayner, NYR, G	28-30-11;		2.62	1978	Guy Lafleur, Mon., RW	60	72	132*
1951	Milt Schmidt, Bos., C	22	39	61	1979	Bryan Trottier, NYI., C	47	87	134*

Year		G	A	Pts	Year		G	A	Pts
1980	Wayne Gretzky, Edm., C	51	86	137*	1994	Sergei Fedorov, Det., C	56	64	120
1981	Wayne Gretzky, Edm., C	55	109	164*	1995	Eric Lindros, Phi., C	29	41	70*
1982	Wayne Gretzky, Edm., C	92	120	212*	1996	Mario Lemieux, Pit., C	69	92	161*
1983	Wayne Gretzky, Edm., C	71	125	196*	1997	Dominik Hasek, Buf., G	37-20-10;		2.27
1984	Wayne Gretzky, Edm., C	87	118	205*	1998	Dominik Hasek, Buf., G	33-23-13;		2.09
1985	Wayne Gretzky, Edm., C	73	135	208*	1999	Jaromir Jagr, Pit., RW	44	83	127*
1986	Wayne Gretzky, Edm., C	52	163	215*	2000	Chris Pronger, St.L, D	14	48	62
1987	Wayne Gretzky, Edm., C	62	121	183*	2001	Joe Sakic, Col., C	54	64	118
1988	Mario Lemieux, Pit., C	70	98	168*	2002	Jose Theodore, Mon., G	30-24-10;		2.11
1989	Wayne Gretzky, LA, C	54	114	168	2003	Peter Forsberg, Col., C	29	77	106*
1990	Mark Messier, Edm., C	45	84	129	2004	Martin St. Louis, TB, RW	38	56	94*
1991	Brett Hull, St. L., RW	86	45	131	2006	Joe Thornton, Bos-SJ, C	29	96	125*
1992	Mark Messier, NYR, C	35	72	107	2007	Sidney Crosby, Pit., C	36	84	120*
1993	Mario Lemieux, Pit., C	69	91	160*					

Calder Memorial Trophy

Awarded to the most outstanding rookie of the year and named after Frank Calder, the late NHL president (1917-43). Since the 1990-91 season, all eligible candidates must not have attained their 26th birthday by Sept. 15 of their rookie year. Winners selected by PHWA. Winners' scoring statistics or goaltender W-L record & goals against average are provided.

Year		G	A	Pts	Year		G	A	Pts
1933	Carl Voss, NYR-Det., C	8	15	23	1970	Tony Esposito, Chi., G	38-17-8;		2.17
1934	Russ Blinco, Maroons, C	14	9	23	1971	Gilbert Perreault, Buf., C	38	34	72
1935	Sweeney Schriner, NYA, LW	18	22	40	1972	Ken Dryden, Mon., G	39-8-15;		2.24
1936	Mike Karakas, Chi., G	21-19-8;		1.92	1973	Steve Vickers, NYR, LW	30	23	53
1937	Syl Apps, Tor., C	16	29	45	1974	Denis Potvin, NYI, D	17	37	54
1938	Cully Dahlstrom, Chi., C	10	9	19	1975	Eric Vail, Atl., LW	39	21	60
1939	Frankie Brimsek, Bos., G	33-9-1;		1.58	1976	Bryan Trottier, NYI, C	32	63	95
1940	Kilby MacDonald, NYR, LW	15	13	28	1977	Willi Plett, Atl., RW	33	23	56
1941	John Quilty, Mon., C	18	16	34	1978	Mike Bossy, NYI, RW	53	38	91
1942	Knobby Warwick, NYR, RW	16	17	33	1979	Bobby Smith, Min., C	30	44	74
1943	Gaye Stewart, Tor., LW	24	23	47	1980	Ray Bourque, Bos., D	17	48	65
1944	Gus Bodnar, Tor., C	22	40	62	1981	Peter Stastny, Que., C	39	70	109
1945	Frank McCool, Tor., G	24-22-4;		3.22	1982	Dale Hawerchuk, Win., C	45	58	103
1946	Edgar Laprade, NYR, C	15	19	34	1983	Steve Larmer, Chi., RW	43	47	90
1947	Howie Meeker, Tor., RW	27	18	45	1984	Tom Barrasso, Buf., G	26-12-3;		2.84
1948	Jim McFadden, Det., C	24	24	48	1985	Mario Lemieux, Pit., C	43	57	100
1949	Penny Lund, NYR, RW	14	16	30	1986	Gary Suter, Calg., D	18	50	68
1950	Jack Gelineau, Bos., G	22-30-15;		3.28	1987	Luc Robitaille, LA, LW	45	39	84
1951	Terry Sawchuk, Det., G	44-13-13;		1.99	1988	Joe Nieuwendyk, Calg., C	51	41	92
1952	Bernie Geoffrion, Mon., RW	30	24	54	1989	Brian Leetch, NYR, D	23	48	71
1953	Gump Worsley, NYR, G	13-29-8;		3.06	1990	Sergei Makarov, Calg., RW	24	62	86
1954	Camille Henry, NYR, LW	24	15	39	1991	Ed Belfour, Chi., G	43-19-7;		2.47
1955	Ed Litzenberger, Mon-Chi., RW	23	28	51	1992	Pavel Bure, Van., RW	34	26	60
1956	Glenn Hall, Det., G	30-24-16;		2.11	1993	Teemu Selanne, Win., RW	76	56	132
1957	Larry Regan, Bos., RW	14	19	33	1994	Martin Brodeur, NJ, G	27-11-8;		2.40
1958	Frank Mahovlich, Tor., LW	20	16	36	1995	Peter Forsberg, Que., C	15	35	50
1959	Ralph Backstrom, Mon., C	18	22	40	1996	Daniel Alfredsson, Ott., RW	26	35	61
1960	Billy Hay, Chi., C	18	37	55	1997	Bryan Berard, NYI, D	8	40	48
1961	Dave Keon, Tor., C	20	25	45	1998	Sergei Samsonov, Bos., LW	22	25	47
1962	Bobby Rousseau, Mon., RW	21	24	45	1999	Chris Drury, Col., C	20	24	44
1963	Kent Douglas, Tor., D	7	15	22	2000	Scott Gomez, NJ, C	19	51	70
1964	Jacques Laperriere, Mon., D	2	28	30	2001	Evgeni Nabokov, SJ, G	32-21-7;		2.19
1965	Roger Crozier, Det., G	40-23-7;		2.42	2002	Dany Heatley, Atl., RW	26	41	67
1966	Brit Selby, Tor., LW	14	13	27	2003	Barret Jackman, St.L, D	3	16	19
1967	Bobby Orr, Bos., D	13	28	41	2004	Andrew Raycroft, Bos., G	29-18-9;		2.05
1968	Derek Sanderson, Bos., C	24	25	49	2006	Alexander Ovechkin, Wash., L.	52	54	106
1969	Danny Grant, Min., LW	34	31	65	2007	Evgeni Malkin, Pit., C	33	52	85

Vezina Trophy

From 1927-80, given to the principal goaltender(s) on the team allowing the fewest goals during the regular season. Trophy named after 1920's goalie Georges Vezina of the Montreal Canadiens, who died of tuberculosis in 1926. Since the 1980-81 season, the trophy has been awarded to the most outstanding goaltender of the year as selected by the league's general managers.

Multiple Winners: Jacques Plante (7, one of them shared); Bill Durnan and Dominik Hasek (6); Ken Dryden (5, three shared); Bunny Larocque (4, all shared); Terry Sawchuk (4, one shared); Tiny Thompson (4); Martin Brodeur (3); Tony Esposito (3, one shared); George Hainsworth (3); Glenn Hall (3, two shared); Patrick Roy (3); Ed Belfour (2); Johnny Bower (2, one shared); Frankie Brimsek (2); Turk Broda (2); Chuck Gardiner (2); Charlie Hodge (2, one shared); Bernie Parent (2, one shared); Gump Worsley (2, both shared).

Year		Record	GAA	Year		Record	GAA
1927	George Hainsworth, Mon	28-14-2	1.52	1931	Roy Worters, NYA	18-16-10	1.68
1928	George Hainsworth, Mon	26-11-7	1.09	1932	Chuck Gardiner, Chi	18-19-11	1.92
1929	George Hainsworth, Mon	22-7-15	0.98	1933	Tiny Thompson, Bos	25-15-8	1.83
1930	Tiny Thompson, Bos	38-5-1	2.23	1934	Chuck Gardiner, Chi	20-17-11	1.73

Annual Awards (Cont.)

Year		Record	GAA	Year		Record	GAA
1935	Lorne Chabot, Chi	26-17-5	1.83	1972	Tony Esposito, Chi	31-10-6	1.77
1936	Tiny Thompson, Bos	22-20-6	1.71		& Gary Smith, Chi	14-5-6	2.42
1937	Norm Smith, Det	25-14-9	2.13	1973	Ken Dryden, Mon	33-7-13	2.26
1938	Tiny Thompson, Bos	30-11-7	1.85	1974	(Tie) Bernie Parent, Phi	47-13-12	1.89
1939	Frankie Brimsek, Bos.	33-9-1	1.58		Tony Esposito, Chi	34-14-21	2.04
1940	Dave Kerr, NYR	27-11-10	1.60	1975	Bernie Parent, Phi.	44-14-10	2.03
1941	Turk Broda, Tor	28-14-6	2.06	1976	Ken Dryden, Mon	42-10-8	2.03
1942	Frankie Brimsek, Bos.	24-17-6	2.45	1977	Ken Dryden, Mon	41-6-8	2.14
1943	John Mowers, Det	25-14-11	2.47		& Bunny Larocque, Mon	19-2-4	2.09
1944	Bill Durnan, Mon	38-5-7	2.18	1978	Ken Dryden, Mon	37-7-7	2.05
1945	Bill Durnan, Mon	38-8-4	2.42		& Bunny Larocque, Mon.	22-3-4	2.67
1946	Bill Durnan, Mon	24-11-5	2.60	1979	Ken Dryden, Mon	30-10-7	2.30
1947	Bill Durnan, Mon	34-16-10	2.30		& Bunny Larocque, Mon.	22-7-4	2.84
1948	Turk Broda, Tor	32-15-13	2.38	1980	Bob Sauve, Buf	20-8-4	2.36
1949	Bill Durnan, Mon	28-23-9	2.10		& Don Edwards, Buf.	27-9-12	2.57
1950	Bill Durnan, Mon	26-21-17	2.20	1981	Richard Sevigny, Mon.	20-4-3	2.40
1951	Al Rollins, Tor.	27-5-8	1.77		Denis Herron, Mon.	6-9-6	3.50
1952	Terry Sawchuk, Det.	44-14-12	1.90		& Bunny Larocque, Mon.	16-9-3	3.03
1953	Terry Sawchuk, Det.	32-15-16	1.90	1982	Billy Smith, NYI	32-9-4	2.97
1954	Harry Lumley, Tor	32-24-13	1.86	1983	Pete Peeters, Bos	40-11-9	2.36
1955	Terry Sawchuk, Det.	40-17-11	1.96	1984	Tom Barrasso, Buf.	26-12-3	2.84
1956	Jacques Plante, Mon.	42-12-10	1.86	1985	Pelle Lindbergh, Phi	40-17-7	3.02
1957	Jacques Plante, Mon.	31-18-12	2.02	1986	John Vanbiesbrouck, NYR	31-21-5	3.32
1958	Jacques Plante, Mon.	34-14-8	2.11	1987	Ron Hextall, Phi	37-21-6	3.00
1959	Jacques Plante, Mon.	38-16-13	2.16	1988	Grant Fuhr, Edm.	40-24-9	3.43
1960	Jacques Plante, Mon.	40-17-12	2.54	1989	Patrick Roy, Mon	33-5-6	2.47
1961	Johnny Bower, Tor	33-15-10	2.50	1990	Patrick Roy, Mon	31-16-5	2.53
1962	Jacques Plante, Mon.	42-14-14	2.37	1991	Ed Belfour, Chi.	43-19-7	2.47
1963	Glenn Hall, Chi	30-20-16	2.55	1992	Patrick Roy, Mon.	36-22-8	2.36
1964	Charlie Hodge, Mon	33-18-11	2.26	1993	Ed Belfour, Chi.	41-18-11	2.59
1965	Johnny Bower, Tor	13-13-8	2.38	1994	Dominik Hasek, Buf	30-20-6	1.95
	& Terry Sawchuk, Tor	17-13-6	2.56	1995	Dominik Hasek, Buf	19-14-7	2.11
1966	Gump Worsley, Mon	29-14-6	2.36	1996	Jim Carey, Wash	35-24-9	2.26
	& Charlie Hodge, Mon.	12-7-2	2.58	1997	Dominik Hasek, Buf	37-20-10	2.27
1967	Glenn Hall, Chi	19-5-5	2.38	1998	Dominik Hasek, Buf	33-23-13	2.09
	& Denis Dejordy, Chi	22-12-7	2.46	1999	Dominik Hasek, Buf	30-18-14	1.87
1968	Gump Worsley, Mon	19-9-8	1.98	2000	Olaf Kolzig, Wash	41-20-11	2.24
	& Rogie Vachon, Mon	23-13-2	2.48	2001	Dominik Hasek, Buf	37-24-4	2.11
1969	Jacques Plante, St.L	18-12-6	1.96	2002	Jose Theodore, Mon.	30-24-10	2.11
	& Glenn Hall, St.L	19-12-8	2.17	2003	Martin Brodeur, NJ.	41-23-9	2.02
1970	Tony Esposito, Chi	38-17-8	2.17	2004	Martin Brodeur, NJ.	38-26-11	2.03
1971	Ed Giacomin, NYR.	27-10-7	2.16	2006	Miikka Kiprusoff, Calg	42-20-11	2.07
	& Gilles Villemure, NYR	22-8-4	2.30	2007	Martin Brodeur, NJ.	48-23-7	2.18

Lady Byng Memorial Trophy

Awarded to the player "adjudged to have exhibited the best type of sportsmanship and gentlemanly conduct combined with a high standard of playing ability" and named after Lady Evelyn Byng, the wife of former Canadian Governor General (1921-26) Baron Byng of Vimy. Winners selected by PHWA.

Multiple winners: Frank Boucher (7); Wayne Gretzky (5); Red Kelly (4); Bobby Bauer, Mike Bossy, Alex Delvecchio and Ron Francis (3); Johnny Bucyk, Pavel Datsyuk, Marcel Dionne, Paul Kariya, Dave Keon, Stan Mikita, Joey Mullen, Frank Nighbor, Jean Ratelle, Clint Smith and Sid Smith (2). **Note:** Bill Quackenbush and Red Kelly are the only defensemen to win the Lady Byng.

Year		Year		Year	
1925	Frank Nighbor, Ott., C	1944	Clint Smith, Chi., C	1963	Dave Keon, Tor., C
1926	Frank Nighbor, Ott., C	1945	Bill Mosienko, Chi., RW	1964	Ken Wharram, Chi., RW
1927	Billy Burch, NYA, C	1946	Toe Blake, Mon., LW	1965	Bobby Hull, Chi., LW
1928	Frank Boucher, NYR, C	1947	Bobby Bauer, Bos., RW	1966	Alex Delvecchio, Det., LW
1929	Frank Boucher, NYR, C	1948	Buddy O'Connor, NYR, C	1967	Stan Mikita, Chi., C
1930	Frank Boucher, NYR, C	1949	Bill Quackenbush, Det., D	1968	Stan Mikita, Chi., C
1931	Frank Boucher, NYR, C	1950	Edgar Laprade, NYR, C	1969	Alex Delvecchio, Det., LW
1932	Joe Primeau, Tor., C	1951	Red Kelly, Det., D	1970	Phil Goyette, St.L., C
1933	Frank Boucher, NYR, C	1952	Sid Smith, Tor., LW	1971	Johnny Bucyk, Bos., LW
1934	Frank Boucher, NYR, C	1953	Red Kelly, Det., D	1972	Jean Ratelle, NYR, C
1935	Frank Boucher, NYR, C	1954	Red Kelly, Det., D	1973	Gilbert Perreault, Buf., C
1936	Doc Romnes, Chi., F	1955	Sid Smith, Tor., LW	1974	Johnny Bucyk, Bos., LW
1937	Marty Barry, Det., C	1956	Earl Reibel, Det., C	1975	Marcel Dionne, Det., C
1938	Gordie Drillon, Tor., RW	1957	Andy Hebenton, NYR, RW	1976	Jean Ratelle, NY-Bos., C
1939	Clint Smith, NYR, C	1958	Camille Henry, NYR, LW	1977	Marcel Dionne, LA, C
1940	Bobby Bauer, Bos., RW	1959	Alex Delvecchio, Det., LW	1978	Butch Goring, LA, C
1941	Bobby Bauer, Bos., RW	1960	Don McKenney, Bos., C	1979	Bob MacMillan, Atl., RW
1942	Syl Apps, Tor., C	1961	Red Kelly, Tor., D	1980	Wayne Gretzky, Edm., C
1943	Max Bentley, Chi., C	1962	Dave Keon, Tor., C	1981	Rick Kehoe, Pit., RW

Year		Year		Year	
1982	Rick Middleton, Bos., RW	1991	Wayne Gretzky, LA, C	2000	Pavol Demitra, St.L, RW
1983	Mike Bossy, NYI, RW	1992	Wayne Gretzky, LA, C	2001	Joe Sakic, Col., C
1984	Mike Bossy, NYI, RW	1993	Pierre Turgeon, NYI, C	2002	Ron Francis, Car., C
1985	Jari Kurri, Edm., RW	1994	Wayne Gretzky, LA, C	2003	Alexander Mogilny, Tor., RW
1986	Mike Bossy, NYI, RW	1995	Ron Francis, Pit., C	2004	Brad Richards, TB, C
1987	Joey Mullen, Calg., RW	1996	Paul Kariya, Ana., LW	2006	Pavel Datsyuk, Det., C
1988	Mats Naslund, Mon., LW	1997	Paul Kariya, Ana., LW	2007	Pavel Datsyuk, Det., C
1989	Joey Mullen, Calg., RW	1998	Ron Francis, Pit., C		
1990	Brett Hull, St.L., RW	1999	Wayne Gretzky, NYR, C		

James Norris Memorial Trophy

Awarded to the most outstanding defenseman of the year and named after James Norris, the late Detroit Red Wings owner-president. Winners selected by PHWA.

Multiple winners: Bobby Orr (8); Doug Harvey (7); Ray Bourque and Nicklas Lidstrom (5); Chris Chelios, Paul Coffey, Pierre Pilote and Denis Potvin (3); Rod Langway, Brian Leetch and Larry Robinson (2).

Year		Year		Year	
1954	Red Kelly, Detroit	1972	Bobby Orr, Boston	1990	Ray Bourque, Boston
1955	Doug Harvey, Montreal	1973	Bobby Orr, Boston	1991	Ray Bourque, Boston
1956	Doug Harvey, Montreal	1974	Bobby Orr, Boston	1992	Brian Leetch, NY Rangers
1957	Doug Harvey, Montreal	1975	Bobby Orr, Boston	1993	Chris Chelios, Chicago
1958	Doug Harvey, Montreal	1976	Denis Potvin, NY Islanders	1994	Ray Bourque, Boston
1959	Tom Johnson, Montreal	1977	Larry Robinson, Montreal	1995	Paul Coffey, Detroit
1960	Doug Harvey, Montreal	1978	Denis Potvin, NY Islanders	1996	Chris Chelios, Chicago
1961	Doug Harvey, Montreal	1979	Denis Potvin, NY Islanders	1997	Brian Leetch, NY Rangers
1962	Doug Harvey, NY Rangers	1980	Larry Robinson, Montreal	1998	Rob Blake, Los Angeles
1963	Pierre Pilote, Chicago	1981	Randy Carlyle, Pittsburgh	1999	Al MacInnis, St. Louis
1964	Pierre Pilote, Chicago	1982	Doug Wilson, Chicago	2000	Chris Pronger, St. Louis
1965	Pierre Pilote, Chicago	1983	Rod Langway, Washington	2001	Nicklas Lidstrom, Detroit
1966	Jacques Laperriere, Montreal	1984	Rod Langway, Washington	2002	Nicklas Lidstrom, Detroit
1967	Harry Howell, NY Rangers	1985	Paul Coffey, Edmonton	2003	Nicklas Lidstrom, Detroit
1968	Bobby Orr, Boston	1986	Paul Coffey, Edmonton	2004	Scott Niedermayer, NJ
1969	Bobby Orr, Boston	1987	Ray Bourque, Boston	2006	Nicklas Lidstrom, Detroit
1970	Bobby Orr, Boston	1988	Ray Bourque, Boston	2007	Nicklas Lidstrom, Detroit
1971	Bobby Orr, Boston	1989	Chris Chelios, Montreal		

Frank Selke Trophy

Awarded to the outstanding defensive forward of the year and named after the late Montreal Canadiens general manager. Winners selected by the PHWA. **Multiple winners:** Bob Gainey (4); Guy Carbonneau and Jere Lehtinen (3); Rod Brind'Amour, Sergei Fedorov and Michael Peca (2).

Year		Year		Year	
1978	Bob Gainey, Mon., LW	1988	Guy Carbonneau, Mon., C	1998	Jere Lehtinen, Dal., RW
1979	Bob Gainey, Mon., LW	1989	Guy Carbonneau, Mon., C	1999	Jere Lehtinen, Dal., RW
1980	Bob Gainey, Mon., LW	1990	Rick Meagher, St.L., C	2000	Steve Yzerman, Det., C
1981	Bob Gainey, Mon., LW	1991	Dirk Graham, Chi., RW	2001	John Madden, NJ, LW
1982	Steve Kasper, Bos., C	1992	Guy Carbonneau, Mon., C	2002	Michael Peca, NYI, C
1983	Bobby Clarke, Phi., C	1993	Doug Gilmour, Tor., C	2003	Jere Lehtinen, Dal., RW
1984	Doug Jarvis, Wash., C	1994	Sergei Fedorov, Det., C	2004	Kris Draper, Det., C
1985	Craig Ramsay, Buf., LW	1995	Ron Francis, Pit., C	2006	Rod Brind'Amour, Car., C
1986	Troy Murray, Chi., C	1996	Sergei Fedorov, Det., C	2007	Rod Brind'Amour, Car., C
1987	Dave Poulin, Phi., C	1997	Michael Peca, Buf., C		

Jack Adams Award

Awarded to the coach "adjudged to have contributed the most to his team's success" and named after the late Detroit Red Wings coach and general manager. Winners selected by NHL Broadcasters' Assn.; (*) indicates division champion.

Multiple winners: Pat Burns (3); Scotty Bowman, Jacques Demers and Pat Quinn (2).

Year	Improvement		Year	Improvement	
1974	Fred Shero, Phi.	37-30-11 to 50-16-12*	1991	Brian Sutter, St.L	37-34-9 to 47-22-11
1975	Bob Pulford, LA.	41-14-23 to 37-35-8	1992	Pat Quinn, Van	28-43-9 to 42-26-12*
1976	Don Cherry, Bos	40-26-14 to 48-15-17*	1993	Pat Burns, Tor	30-43-7 to 44-29-11
1977	Scotty Bowman, Mon	58-11-11* to 60-8-12*	1994	Jacques Lemaire, NJ	40-37-7 to 47-25-12
1978	Bobby Kromm, Det	6-55-9 to 32-34-14	1995	Marc Crawford, Que	34-42-8 to 30-13-5*
1979	Al Arbour, NYI	48-17-15* to 51-15-14*	1996	Scotty Bowman, Det	33-11-4* to 62-13-7*
1980	Pat Quinn, Phi	40-25-15 to 48-12-20*	1997	Ted Nolan, Buf	33-42-7 to 40-30-12*
1981	Red Berenson, St.L	34-34-12 to 45-18-17*	1998	Pat Burns, Bos.	26-47-9 to 39-30-13
1982	Tom Watt, Win	9-57-14 to 33-33-14	1999	Jacques Martin, Ott	34-33-15 to 44-23-15*
1983	Orval Tessier, Chi	30-38-12 to 47-23-10	2000	Joel Quenneville, St.L.	37-32-13 to 51-20-11*
1984	Bryan Murray, Wash.	39-25-16 to 48-27-5	2001	Bill Barber, Phi	45-25-12 to 43-25-11-3
1985	Mike Keenan, Phi.	44-26-10 to 53-20-7*	2002	Bob Francis, Pho	35-27-17-3 to 40-27-9-6
1986	Glen Sather, Edm	49-20-11* to 56-17-7*	2003	Jacques Lemaire, Minn.	26-35-12-9 to 42-29-10-1
1987	Jacques Demers, Det	17-57-6 to 34-36-10	2004	John Tortorella, TB	36-25-16-5 to 46-22-8-6*
1988	Jacques Demers, Det	34-36-10 to 41-28-11*	2006	Lindy Ruff, Buf	37-34-7-4 to 52-24-1-5
1989	Pat Burns, Mon	45-22-13 to 53-18-9*	2007	Alain Vigneault, Van	42-32-4-4 to 49-26-3-4
1990	Bob Murdoch, Win	26-42-12 to 37-32-11			

Annual Awards (Cont.)
Lester B. Pearson Award

Awarded to the season's most outstanding player and named after the former diplomat, Nobel Peace Prize winner and Canadian prime minister. Winners selected by the NHL Players Association.

Multiple winners: Wayne Gretzky (5); Mario Lemieux (4); Jaromir Jagr and Guy Lafleur (3); Marcel Dionne, Phil Esposito, Dominik Hasek and Mark Messier (2).

Year		Year		Year	
1971	Phil Esposito, Bos., C	1983	Wayne Gretzky, Edm., C	1995	Eric Lindros, Phi., C
1972	Jean Ratelle, NYR, C	1984	Wayne Gretzky, Edm., C	1996	Mario Lemieux, Pit., C
1973	Bobby Clarke, Phi., C	1985	Wayne Gretzky, Edm., C	1997	Dominik Hasek, Buf., G
1974	Phil Esposito, Bos., C	1986	Mario Lemieux, Pit., C	1998	Dominik Hasek, Buf., G
1975	Bobby Orr, Bos., D	1987	Wayne Gretzky, Edm., C	1999	Jaromir Jagr, Pit., RW
1976	Guy Lafleur, Mon., RW	1988	Mario Lemieux, Pit., C	2000	Jaromir Jagr, Pit., RW
1977	Guy Lafleur, Mon., RW	1989	Steve Yzerman, Det., C	2001	Joe Sakic, Col., C
1978	Guy Lafleur, Mon., RW	1990	Mark Messier, Edm., C	2002	Jarome Iginla, Calg., RW
1979	Marcel Dionne, LA, C	1991	Brett Hull, St.L., RW	2003	Markus Naslund, Van., LW
1980	Marcel Dionne, LA, C	1992	Mark Messier, NYR, C	2004	Martin St. Louis, TB, RW
1981	Mike Liut, St.L., G	1993	Mario Lemieux, Pit., C	2006	Jaromir Jagr, NYR, RW
1982	Wayne Gretzky, Edm., C	1994	Sergei Fedorov, Det., C	2007	Sidney Crosby, Pit., C

King Clancy Memorial Trophy

Awarded to the player who "best exemplifies leadership on and off the ice and who has made a noteworthy humanitarian contribution to his community" and named after former player, coach, official and executive Frank "King" Clancy. Presented by the NHL's Board of Governors.

Year		Year		Year	
1988	Lanny McDonald, Calg., RW	1995	Joe Nieuwendyk, Calg., C	2001	Shjon Podein, Col., LW
1989	Bryan Trottier, NYI, C	1996	Kris King, Win., LW	2002	Ron Francis, Car., C
1990	Kevin Lowe, Edm., D	1997	Trevor Linden, Van., C	2003	Brendan Shanahan, Det., LW
1991	Dave Taylor, LA, RW	1998	Kelly Chase, St.L., RW	2004	Jarome Iginla, Calg., RW
1992	Ray Bourque, Bos., D	1999	Rob Ray, Buf., RW	2006	Olaf Kolzig, Wash., G
1993	Dave Poulin, Bos., C	2000	Curtis Joseph, Tor., G	2007	Saku Koivu, Mon., C
1994	Adam Graves, NYR, LW				

Bill Masterton Trophy

Awarded to the player who "best exemplifies the qualities of perseverance, sportsmanship and dedication to hockey" and named after the 29-year-old rookie center of the Minnesota North Stars who died of a head injury sustained in a 1968 NHL game. Presented by the PHWA.

Year		Year		Year	
1968	Claude Provost, Mon., RW	1981	Blake Dunlop, St.L., C	1994	Cam Neely, Bos., RW
1969	Ted Hampson, Oak., C	1982	Chico Resch, Colo., G	1995	Pat LaFontaine, Buf., C
1970	Pit Martin, Chi., C	1983	Lanny McDonald, Calg., RW	1996	Gary Roberts, Calg., LW
1971	Jean Ratelle, NYR, C	1984	Brad Park, Det., D	1997	Tony Granato, SJ, LW
1972	Bobby Clarke, Phi., C	1985	Anders Hedberg, NYR, RW	1998	Jamie McLennan, St.L, G
1973	Lowell MacDonald, Pit., RW	1986	Charlie Simmer, Bos., LW	1999	John Cullen, TB, C
1974	Henri Richard, Mon., C	1987	Doug Jarvis, Hart., C	2000	Ken Daneyko, NJ, D
1975	Don Luce, Buf., C	1988	Bob Bourne, LA, C	2001	Adam Graves, NYR, LW
1976	Rod Gilbert, NYR, RW	1989	Tim Kerr, Phi., C	2002	Saku Koivu, Mon., C
1977	Ed Westfall, NYI, RW	1990	Gord Kluzak, Bos., D	2003	Steve Yzerman, Det., C
1978	Butch Goring, LA, C	1991	Dave Taylor, LA, RW	2004	Bryan Berard, Chi., D
1979	Serge Savard, Mon., D	1992	Mark Fitzpatrick, NYI, G	2006	Teemu Selanne, Ana., R
1980	Al MacAdam, Min., RW	1993	Mario Lemieux, Pit., C	2007	Phil Kessel, Bos., C

Number One Draft Choices

Overall first choices in the NHL draft since the league staged its first universal amateur draft in 1969. Players are listed with team that selected them; those who became Rookie of the Year are in **bold** type.

Year		Year		Year	
1969	Rejean Houle, Mon., LW	1982	Gord Kluzak, Bos., D	1995	**Bryan Berard,** Ott., D
1970	**Gilbert Perreault,** Buf., C	1983	Brian Lawton, Min., C	1996	Chris Phillips, Ott., D
1971	Guy Lafleur, Mon., RW	1984	**Mario Lemieux,** Pit., C	1997	Joe Thornton, Bos., C
1972	Billy Harris, NYI, RW	1985	Wendel Clark, Tor., LW/D	1998	Vincent Lecavalier, TB, C
1973	**Denis Potvin,** NYI, D	1986	Joe Murphy, Det., C	1999	Patrik Stefan, Atl., C
1974	Greg Joly, Wash., D	1987	Pierre Turgeon, Buf., C	2000	Rick DiPietro, NYI, G
1975	Mel Bridgman, Phi., C	1988	Mike Modano, Min., C	2001	Ilya Kovalchuk, Atl., RW
1976	Rick Green, Wash., D	1989	Mats Sundin, Que., RW	2002	Rick Nash, Clb., LW
1977	Dale McCourt, Det., C	1990	Owen Nolan, Que., RW	2003	Marc-Andre Fleury, Pit., G
1978	**Bobby Smith,** Min., C	1991	Eric Lindros, Que., C	2004	**Alex Ovechkin,** Wash., LW
1979	Rob Ramage, Colo., D	1992	Roman Hamrlik, TB, D	2005	Sidney Crosby, Pit., C
1980	Doug Wickenheiser, Mon., C	1993	Alexandre Daigle, Ott., C	2006	Erik Johnson, St.L, D
1981	**Dale Hawerchuk,** Win., C	1994	Ed Jovanovski, Fla., D	2007	Patrick Kane, Chi., RW

World Hockey Association

WHA Finals

The World Hockey Association began play in 1972-73 as a 12-team rival of the 56-year-old NHL. The WHA played for the AVCO World Trophy in its seven playoff finals (Avco Financial Services underwrote the playoffs).

Multiple winners: Winnipeg (3); Houston (2).

Year	Winner	Head Coach	Series	Loser	Head Coach
1973	New England Whalers	Jack Kelley	4-1 (WWLWW)	Winnipeg Jets	Bobby Hull
1974	Houston Aeros	Bill Dineen	4-0	Chicago Cougars	Pat Stapleton
1975	Houston Aeros	Bill Dineen	4-0	Quebec Nordiques	Jean-Guy Gendron
1976	Winnipeg Jets	Bobby Kromm	4-0	Houston Aeros	Bill Dineen
1977	Quebec Nordiques	Marc Boileau	4-3 (LWLWWLW)	Winnipeg Jets	Bobby Kromm
1978	Winnipeg Jets	Larry Hillman	4-0	NE Whalers	Harry Neale
1979	Winnipeg Jets	Larry Hillman	4-2 (WWLWLW)	Edmonton Oilers	Glen Sather

Playoff MVPs—1973—No award; **1974**—No award; **1975**—Ron Grahame, Houston, G; **1976**—Ulf Nilsson, Winnipeg, C; **1977**—Serg Bernier, Quebec, C; **1978**—Bobby Guindon, Winnipeg, C; **1979**—Rich Preston, Winnipeg, RW.

Most Valuable Player

(Gordie Howe Trophy, 1976-79)

Year		G	A	Pts
1973	Bobby Hull, Win., LW	.51	52	103
1974	Gordie Howe, Hou., RW	.31	69	100
1975	Bobby Hull, Win., LW	.77	65	142
1976	Marc Tardif, Que., LW	.71	77	148
1977	Robbie Ftorek, Pho., C	.46	71	117
1978	Marc Tardif, Que., LW	.65	89	154
1979	Dave Dryden, Edm., G	.41-17-2;	2.89	

Scoring Leaders

Year		Gm	G	A	Pts
1973	Andre Lacroix, Phi	.78	50	74	124
1974	Mike Walton, Min	.78	57	60	117
1975	Andre Lacroix, S. Diego	.78	41	106	147
1976	Marc Tardif, Que	.81	71	77	148
1977	Real Cloutier, Que	.76	66	75	141
1978	Marc Tardif, Que	.78	65	89	154
1979	Real Cloutier, Que	.77	75	54	129

Note: In 1979, 18 year-old Rookie of the Year Wayne Gretzky finished third in scoring (46-64—110).

Rookie of the Year

Year		G	A	Pts
1973	Terry Caffery, N. Eng., C	.39	61	100
1974	Mark Howe, Hou., LW	.38	41	79
1975	Anders Hedberg, Win., RW	.53	47	100
1976	Mark Napier, Tor., RW	.43	50	93
1977	George Lyle, N. Eng., LW	.39	33	72
1978	Kent Nilsson, Win., C	.42	65	107
1979	Wayne Gretzky, Ind.-Edm., C	.46	64	110

Best Goaltender

Year		Record	GAA
1973	Gerry Cheevers, Cleveland	.32-20-0	2.84
1974	Don McLeod, Houston	.33-13-3	2.56
1975	Ron Grahame, Houston	.33-10-0	3.03
1976	Michel Dion, Indianapolis	.14-15-1	2.74
1977	Ron Grahame, Houston	.27-10-2	2.74
1978	Al Smith, New England	.30-20-3	3.22
1979	Dave Dryden, Edmonton	.41-17-2	2.89

Best Defenseman

Year	
1973	J.C. Tremblay, Quebec
1974	Pat Stapleton, Chicago
1975	J.C. Tremblay, Quebec
1976	Paul Shmyr, Cleveland
1977	Ron Plumb, Cincinnati
1978	Lars-Erik Sjoberg, Winnipeg
1979	Rick Ley, New England

Coach of the Year

Year			Improvement
1973	Jack Kelley, N. Eng		46-30-2*
1974	Billy Harris, Tor	.35-39-4	to	41-33-4
1975	Sandy Hucul, Pho	.Expan.	to	39-31-8
1976	Bobby Kromm, Win	.38-35-5	to	52-27-2*
1977	Bill Dineen, Hou	.53-27-0 *	to	50-24-6*
1978	Bill Dineen, Hou	.50-24-6 *	to	42-34-4
1979	John Brophy, Birm	.36-41-3	to	32-42-6

*Won Division.

WHA All-Star Game

The WHA All-Star Game was an Eastern Division vs Western Division contest from 1973-75. In 1976, the league's five Canadian-based teams played the nine teams in the US. Over the final three seasons—East played West in 1977; AVCO Cup champion Quebec played a WHA All-Star team in 1978; and in 1979, a full WHA All-Star team played a three-game series with Moscow Dynamo of the Soviet Union.

Year	Result	Host	Coaches	Most Valuable Player
1973	East 6, West 2	Quebec	Jack Kelley, Bobby Hull	Wayne Carleton, Ottawa
1974	East 8, West 4	St. Paul, MN	Jack Kelley, Bobby Hull	Mike Walton, Minnesota
1975	West 6, East 4	Edmonton	Bill Dineen, Ron Ryan	Rejean Houle, Quebec
1976	Canada 6, USA 1	Cleveland	Jean-Guy Gendron, Bill Dineen	Can—Real Cloutier, Que. USA—Paul Shmyr, Cleve.
1977	East 4, West 2	Hartford	Jacques Demers, Bobby Kromm	East—L. Levasseur, Min. West—W. Lindstrom, Win.
1978	Quebec 5, -WHA 4	Quebec	Marc Boileau, Bill Dineen	Quebec—Marc Tardif WHA—Mark Howe, NE
1979	WHA def. Moscow Dynamo 3 games to none (4-2, 4-2, 4-3)	Edmonton	Larry Hillman, P. Iburtovich	No awards

World Championship
Men

The World Hockey Championship tournament has been played regularly since 1930. The International Ice Hockey Federation (IIHF), which governs both the World and Winter Olympic tournaments, considers the Olympic champions from 1920-68 to also be the World champions. However the IIHF has not recognized an Olympic champion as World champion since 1968. The IIHF has sanctioned separate World Championships in Olympic years four times—in 1972, 1976, 1992 and 2002. The world championship is officially vacant for the three Olympic years from 1980-88.

Multiple winners: Canada (24); Soviet Union/Russia (23); Sweden (8); Czechoslovakia (6) Czech Republic (5), USA (2).

Year		Year		Year		Year	
1920	Canada	1952	Canada	1971	Soviet Union	1990	Soviet Union
1924	Canada	1953	Sweden	1972	Czechoslovakia	1991	Sweden
1928	Canada	1954	Soviet Union	1973	Soviet Union	1992	Sweden
1930	Canada	1955	Canada	1974	Soviet Union	1993	Russia
1931	Canada	1956	Soviet Union	1975	Soviet Union	1994	Canada
1932	Canada	1957	Sweden	1976	Czechoslovakia	1995	Finland
1933	United States	1958	Canada	1977	Czechoslovakia	1996	Czech Republic
1934	Canada	1959	Canada	1978	Soviet Union	1997	Canada
1935	Canada	1960	United States	1979	Soviet Union	1998	Sweden
1936	Great Britain	1961	Canada	1980	Not held	1999	Czech Republic
1937	Canada	1962	Sweden	1981	Soviet Union	2000	Czech Republic
1938	Canada	1963	Soviet Union	1982	Soviet Union	2001	Czech Republic
1939	Canada	1964	Soviet Union	1983	Soviet Union	2002	Slovakia
1940-46	Not held	1965	Soviet Union	1984	Not held	2003	Canada
1947	Czechoslovakia	1966	Soviet Union	1985	Czechoslovakia	2004	Canada
1948	Canada	1967	Soviet Union	1986	Soviet Union	2005	Czech Republic
1949	Czechoslovakia	1968	Soviet Union	1987	Sweden	2006	Sweden
1950	Canada	1969	Soviet Union	1988	Not held	2007	Canada
1951	Canada	1970	Soviet Union	1989	Soviet Union		

Women

The women's World Hockey Championship tournament is governed by the International Ice Hockey Federation (IIHF).

Multiple winner: Canada (9).

Year		Year		Year		Year		Year	
1990	Canada	1994	Canada	1999	Canada	2001	Canada	2005	United States
1992	Canada	1997	Canada	2000	Canada	2004	Canada	2007	Canada

Canada vs. USSR Summits

The first competition between the Soviet National Team and the NHL took place Sept. 2-28, 1972. A team of NHL All-Stars emerged as the winner of the heralded 8-game series, but just barely—winning with a record of 4-3-1 after trailing 1-3-1.

Two years later a WHA All-Star team played the Soviet Nationals and could win only one game and tie three others in eight contests. Two other Canada vs USSR series took place during NHL All-Star breaks: the three-game Challenge Cup at New York in 1979, and the two-game Rendez-Vous '87 in Quebec City in 1987.

The NHL All-Stars played the USSR in a three-game Challenge Cup series in 1979.

1972 Team Canada vs. USSR

NHL All-Stars vs Soviet National Team.

Date	City	Result	Goaltenders
9/2	Montreal	USSR, 7-3	Tretiak/Dryden
9/4	Toronto	Canada, 4-1	Esposito/Tretiak
9/6	Winnipeg	Tie, 4-4	Tretiak/Esposito
9/8	Vancouver	USSR, 5-3	Tretiak/Dryden
9/22	Moscow	USSR, 5-4	Tretiak/Esposito
9/24	Moscow	Canada, 3-2	Dryden/Tretiak
9/26	Moscow	Canada, 4-3	Esposito/Tretiak
9/28	Moscow	Canada, 6-5	Dryden/Tretiak

Standings

	W	L	T	Pts	GF	GA
Team Canada (NHL)	4	3	1	9	32	32
Soviet Union	3	4	1	7	32	32

Leading Scorers

1. Phil Esposito, Canada, (7-6—13); **2.** Aleksandr Yakushev, USSR (7-4—11); **3.** Paul Henderson, Canada (7-2—9); **4.** Boris Shadrin, USSR (3-5—8); **5.** Valeri Kharlamov, USSR (3-4—7) and Vladimir Petrov, USSR (3-4—7).

1974 Team Canada vs. USSR

WHA All-Stars vs Soviet National Team.

Date	City	Result	Goaltenders
9/17	Quebec City	Tie, 3-3	Tretiak/Cheevers
9/19	Toronto	Canada, 4-1	Cheevers/Tretiak
9/21	Winnipeg	USSR, 8-5	Tretiak/McLeod
9/23	Vancouver	Tie, 5-5	Tretiak/Cheevers
10/1	Moscow	USSR, 3-2	Tretiak/Cheevers
10/3	Moscow	USSR, 5-2	Tretiak/Cheevers
10/5	Moscow	Tie, 4-4	Cheevers/Tretiak
10/6	Moscow	USSR, 3-2	Sidelinkov/Cheevers

Standings

	W	L	T	Pts	GF	GA
Soviet Union	4	1	3	11	32	27
Team Canada (WHA)	1	4	3	5	27	32

Leading Scorers

1. Bobby Hull, Canada (7-2—9); **2.** Aleksandr Yakushev, USSR (6-2—8), Ralph Backstrom, Canada (4-4—8) and Valeri Kharlamov, USSR (2-6—8); **5.** Gordie Howe, Canada (3-4—7), Andre Lacroix, Canada (1-6—7) and Vladimir Petrov, USSR (1-6—7).

1979 Challenge Cup Series

NHL All-Stars vs Soviet National Team

Date	City	Result	Goaltenders
2/8	New York	NHL, 4-2	K. Dryden/Tretiak
2/10	New York	USSR, 5-4	Tretiak/K. Dryden
2/11	New York	USSR, 6-0	Myshkin/Cheevers

Rendez-Vous '87

NHL All-Stars vs Soviet National Team

Date	City	Result	Goaltenders
2/11	Quebec	NHL, 4-3	Fuhr/Belosheykhin
2/13	Quebec	USSR, 5-3	Belosheykhin/Fuhr

The Canada Cup

After organizing the historic 8-game Team Canada-Soviet Union series of 1972, NHL Players Association executive director Alan Eagleson and the NHL created the Canada Cup in 1976. For the first time, the best players from the world's six major hockey powers—Canada, Czechoslovakia, Finland, Russia, Sweden and the USA—competed together in one tournament.

1976
Round Robin Standings

	W	L	T	Pts	GF	GA
Canada	4	1	0	8	22	6
Czechoslovakia	3	1	1	7	19	9
Soviet Union	2	2	1	5	23	14
Sweden	2	2	1	5	16	18
United States	1	3	1	3	14	21
Finland	1	4	0	2	16	42

Finals (Best of 3)

Date	City	Score
9/13	Toronto	Canada 6, Czechoslovakia 0
9/15	Montreal	Canada 5, Czechoslovakia 4 (OT)

Note: Darryl Sittler scored the winning goal for Canada at 11:33 in overtime to clinch the Cup, 2 games to none.

Leading Scorers

1. Victor Hluktov, USSR (5-4—9), Bobby Orr, Canada (2-7—9) and Denis Potvin, Canada (1-8—9); **4.** Bobby Hull, Canada (5-3—8) and Milan Novy, Czechoslovakia (5-3—8).

Team MVPs

Canada—Rogie Vachon   Sweden—Borje Salming
Czech.—Milan Novy   USA—Robbie Ftorek
USSR—Alexandr Maltsev   Finland—Matti Hagman
Tournament MVP—Bobby Orr, Canada

1981
Round Robin Standings

	W	L	T	Pts	GF	GA
Canada	4	0	1	9	32	13
Soviet Union	3	1	1	7	20	13
Czechoslovakia	2	1	2	6	21	13
United States	2	2	1	5	17	19
Sweden	1	4	0	2	13	20
Finland	0	4	1	1	6	31

Semifinals

Date	City	Score
9/11	Ottawa	USSR 4, Czechoslovakia 1
9/11	Montreal	Canada 4, United States 1

Finals

Date	City	Score
9/13	Montreal	USSR 8, Canada 1

Leading Scorers

1. Wayne Gretzky, Canada (5-7—12); **2.** Mike Bossy, Canada (8-3—11), Bryan Trottier, Canada (3-8—11), Guy Lafleur, Canada (2-9—11), Alexei Kasatonov, USSR (1-10—11).

All-Star Team

Goal—Vladislav Tretiak, USSR; **Defense**—Arnold Kadlec, Czech. and Alexei Kasatonov, USSR; **Forwards**—Mike Bossy, Canada, Gil Perreault, Canada, and Sergei Shepelev, USSR. **Tournament MVP**—Tretiak.

1984
Round Robin Standings

	W	L	T	Pts	GF	GA
Soviet Union	5	0	0	10	22	7
United States	3	1	1	7	21	13
Sweden	3	2	0	6	15	16
Canada	2	2	1	5	23	18
West Germany	0	4	1	1	13	29
Czechoslovakia	0	4	1	1	10	21

Semifinals

Date	City	Score
9/12	Edmonton	Sweden 9, United States 2
9/15	Montreal	Canada 3, USSR 2 (OT)

Note: Mike Bossy scored the winning goal for Canada at 12:29 in overtime.

Finals (Best of 3)

Date	City	Score
9/16	Calgary	Canada 5, Sweden 2
9/18	Edmonton	Canada 6, Sweden 5

Leading Scorers

1. Wayne Gretzky, Canada (5-7—12); **2.** Michel Goulet, Canada (5-6—11), Kent Nilsson, Sweden (3-8—11), Paul Coffey, Canada (3-8—11); **5.** Hakan Loob, Sweden (6-4—10).

All-Star Team

Goal—Vladimir Myshkin, USSR; **Defense**—Paul Coffey, Canada and Rod Langway, USA; **Forwards**—Wayne Gretzky, Canada, John Tonelli, Canada, and Sergei Makarov, USSR. **Tournament MVP**—Tonelli.

1987
Round Robin Standings

	W	L	T	Pts	GF	GA
Canada	3	0	2	8	19	13
Soviet Union	3	1	1	7	22	13
Sweden	3	2	0	6	17	14
Czechoslovakia	2	2	1	5	12	15
United States	2	3	0	4	13	14
Finland	0	5	0	0	9	23

Semifinals

Date	City	Score
9/8	Hamilton	USSR 4, Sweden 2
9/9	Montreal	Canada 5, Czechoslovakia 3

Finals (Best of 3)

Date	City	Score
9/11	Montreal	USSR 6, Canada 5 (OT)
9/13	Hamilton	Canada 6, USSR 5 (2 OT)
9/15	Hamilton	Canada 6, USSR 5

Note: In Game 1, Alexander Semak of USSR scored at 5:33 in overtime. In Game 2, Mario Lemieux of Canada scored at 10:01 in the second overtime period. Lemieux also won Game 3 on a goal with 1:26 left in regulation time.

Leading Scorers

1. Wayne Gretzky, Canada (3-18—21); **2.** Mario Lemieux, Canada (11-7—18); **3.** Sergei Makarov, USSR (7-8—15); **4.** Vladimir Krutov, USSR (7-7—14); **5.** Viacheslav Bykov, USSR (2-7—9); **6.** Ray Bourque, Canada (2-6—8).

All-Star Team

Goal—Grant Fuhr, Canada; **Defense**—Ray Bourque, Canada and Viacheslav Fetisov, USSR; **Forwards**—Wayne Gretzky, Canada, Mario Lemieux, Canada, and Vladimir Krutov, USSR. **Tournament MVP**—Gretzky.

1991

Round Robin Standings

	W	L	T	Pts	GF	GA
Canada	3	0	2	8	21	11
United States	4	1	0	8	19	15
Finland	2	2	1	5	10	13
Sweden	2	3	0	4	13	17
Soviet Union	1	3	1	3	14	14
Czechoslovakia	1	4	0	2	11	18

Semifinals

Date	City	Score
9/11	Hamilton	United States 7, Finland 3
9/12	Toronto	Canada 4, Sweden 0

Finals (Best of 3)

Date	City	Score
9/14	Montreal	Canada 4, United States 1
9/16	Hamilton	Canada 4, United States 2

Leading Scorers

1. Wayne Gretzky, Canada (4-8—12); **2.** Steve Larmer, Canada (6-5—11); **3.** Brett Hull, USA (2-7—9); **4.** Mike Modano, USA (2-7—9); **5.** Mark Messier, Canada (2-6—8).

All-Star Team

Goal—Bill Ranford, Canada; **Defense**—Al MacInnis, Canada and Chris Chelios, USA; **Forwards**—Wayne Gretzky, Canada, Jeremy Roenick, USA and Mats Sundin, Sweden. **Tournament MVP**—Bill Ranford.

The World Cup

Formed jointly by the NHL and the NHL Players Association in cooperation with the International Ice Hockey Federation. The inaugural World Cup held games in nine different cities throughout North America and Europe, the most ever by a single international hockey tournament.

1996

Round Robin Standings

European Pool	W	L	T	Pts	GF	GA
Sweden	3	0	0	6	14	3
Finland	2	1	0	4	17	11
Germany	1	2	0	2	11	15
Czech Republic	0	3	0	0	4	17

North American Pool	W	L	T	Pts	GF	GA
United States	3	0	0	6	19	8
Canada	2	1	0	4	11	10
Russia	1	2	0	2	12	14
Slovakia	0	3	0	0	10	18

Semifinals

Date	City	Score
9/7	Philadelphia	Canada 3, Sweden 2 (OT)
9/8	Ottawa	United States 5, Russia 2

Finals (Best of 3)

Date	City	Score
9/10	Philadelphia	Canada 4, United States 3 (OT)
9/12	Montreal	United States 5, Canada 2
9/14	Montreal	United States 5, Canada 2

Leading Scorers

1. Brett Hull, USA (7-4—11); **2.** John LeClair, USA (6-4—10); **3.** Mats Sundin, Sweden (4-3—7); Wayne Gretzky, Canada (3-4—7); Doug Weight, USA (3-4—7); Paul Coffey, Canada (0-7—7); Brian Leetch, USA (0-7—7).

All-Tournament Team

Goal—Mike Richter, USA; **Defense**—Calle Johansson, Sweden and Chris Chelios, USA; **Forwards**—Brett Hull, USA; John LeClair, USA and Mats Sundin, Sweden. **Tournament MVP**—Mike Richter, USA.

2004

Round Robin Standings

European Pool	W	L	T	Pts	GF	GA
Finland	2	0	1	5	11	4
Sweden	2	0	1	5	13	9
Czech Republic	1	2	0	2	10	10
Germany	0	3	0	0	4	15

North American Pool	W	L	T	Pts	GF	GA
Canada	3	0	0	6	10	3
Russia	2	1	0	4	9	6
United States	1	2	0	2	5	6
Slovakia	0	3	0	0	4	13

Semifinals

Date	City	Score
9/10	St. Paul, Minn.	Finland 2, United States 1
9/11	Toronto	Canada 4, Czech Rep. 3 (OT)

Championship Game

Date	City	Score
9/14	Toronto	Canada 3, Finland 2

Leading Scorers

1. Fredrik Modin, Sweden (4-4—8); **2.** Vincent Lecavalier, Canada (2-5—7); **3.** Keith Tkachuk, USA (5-1—6); Joe Sakic, Canada (4-2—6); Martin Havlat, Czech Republic (3-3—6); Kimmo Timonen, Finland (1-5—6); Joe Thornton, Canada (1-5—6); Mike Modano, USA (0-6—6); Daniel Alfredsson, Sweden (0-6—6).

All-Tournament Team

Goal—Martin Brodeur, Canada; **Defense**—Kimmo Timonen, Finland and Adam Foote, Canada; **Forwards**—Vincent Lecavalier, Canada; Saku Koivu, Finland and Fredrik Modin, Sweden. **Tournament MVP**—Vincent Lecavalier, Canada.

Note: See Olympics chapter for all men's and women's Olympic hockey results.

U.S. DIVISION I COLLEGE HOCKEY

NCAA Men's Frozen Four

The NCAA Division I hockey tournament began in 1948 and was played at the Broadmoor Ice Palace in Colorado Springs from 1948-57. Since 1958, the tournament has moved around the country, stopping for consecutive years only at Boston Garden from 1972-74. Consolation games to determine third place were played from 1949-89 and discontinued in 1990.

Multiple winners: Michigan (9); North Dakota and Denver (7); Wisconsin (6); Minnesota (5); Boston University (4); Lake Superior St., Michigan St. and Michigan Tech (3); Boston College, Colorado College, Cornell, Maine and RPI (2).

Year	Champion	Head Coach	Score	Runner-up	Third Place		
1948	Michigan	Vic Heyliger	8-4	Dartmouth	Colorado College and Boston College		

Year	Champion	Head Coach	Score	Runner-up	Third Place	Score	Fourth Place
1949	Boston College	Snooks Kelley	4-3	Dartmouth	Michigan	10-4	Colorado Col.
1950	Colorado College	Cheddy Thompson	13-4	Boston Univ.	Michigan	10-6	Boston College
1951	Michigan	Vic Heyliger	7-1	Brown	Boston Univ.	7-4	Colorado College
1952	Michigan	Vic Heyliger	4-1	Colorado Col.	Yale	4-1	St. Lawrence
1953	Michigan	Vic Heyliger	7-3	Minnesota	RPI	6-3	Boston Univ.
1954	RPI	Ned Harkness	5-4 *	Minnesota	Michigan	7-2	Boston College
1955	Michigan	Vic Heyliger	5-3	Colorado Col.	Harvard	6-3	St. Lawrence
1956	Michigan	Vic Heyliger	7-5	Michigan Tech	St. Lawrence	6-2	Boston College
1957	Colorado College	Tom Bedecki	13-6	Michigan	Clarkson	2-1	Harvard
1958	Denver	Murray Armstrong	6-2	North Dakota	Clarkson	5-1	Harvard
1959	North Dakota	Bob May	4-3 *	Michigan St.	Boston College	7-6	St. Lawrence
1960	Denver	Murray Armstrong	5-3	Michigan St.	North Dakota	7-6	St. Lawrence
1961	Denver	Murray Armstrong	12-2	St. Lawrence	Minnesota	4-3	RPI
1962	Michigan Tech	John MacInnes	7-1	Clarkson	Michigan	5-1	St. Lawrence
1963	North Dakota	Barry Thorndycraft	6-5	Denver	Clarkson	5-3	Boston College
1964	Michigan	Allen Renfrew	6-3	Denver	RPI	2-1	Providence
1965	Michigan Tech	John MacInnes	8-2	Boston College	North Dakota	9-5	Brown
1966	Michigan St.	Amo Bessone	6-1	Clarkson	Denver	4-3	Boston Univ.
1967	Cornell	Ned Harkness	4-1	Boston Univ.	Michigan St.	6-1	North Dakota
1968	Denver	Murray Armstrong	4-0	North Dakota	Cornell	6-1	Boston College
1969	Denver	Murray Armstrong	4-3	Cornell	Harvard	6-5	Michigan Tech
1970	Cornell	Ned Harkness	6-4	Clarkson	Wisconsin	6-5	Michigan Tech
1971	Boston Univ.	Jack Kelley	4-2	Minnesota	Denver	1-0	Harvard
1972	Boston Univ.	Jack Kelley	4-0	Cornell	Wisconsin	5-2	Denver
1973	Wisconsin	Bob Johnson	4-2	Denver	Boston College	3-1	Cornell
1974	Minnesota	Herb Brooks	4-2	Michigan Tech	Boston Univ.	7-5	Harvard
1975	Michigan Tech	John MacInnes	6-1	Minnesota	Boston Univ.	10-5	Harvard
1976	Minnesota	Herb Brooks	6-4	Michigan Tech	Brown	8-7	Boston Univ.
1977	Wisconsin	Bob Johnson	6-5 *	Michigan	Boston Univ.	6-5	N. Hampshire
1978	Boston Univ.	Jack Parker	5-3	Boston College	Bowl. Green	4-3	Wisconsin
1979	Minnesota	Herb Brooks	4-3	North Dakota	Dartmouth	7-3	N. Hampshire
1980	North Dakota	Gino Gasparini	5-2	N. Michigan	Dartmouth	8-4	Cornell
1981	Wisconsin	Bob Johnson	6-3	Minnesota	Mich. Tech	5-2	N. Michigan
1982	North Dakota	Gino Gasparini	5-2	Wisconsin	Northeastern	10-4	N. Hampshire
1983	Wisconsin	Jeff Sauer	6-2	Harvard	Providence	4-3	Minnesota
1984	Bowling Green	Jerry York	5-4 *	Minn-Duluth	North Dakota	6-5	Michigan St.
1985	RPI	Mike Addesa	2-1	Providence	Minn. Duluth	7-6	Boston College
1986	Michigan St.	Ron Mason	6-5	Harvard	Minnesota	6-4	Denver
1987	North Dakota	Gino Gasparini	5-3	Michigan St.	Minnesota	6-3	Harvard
1988	Lake Superior St.	Frank Anzalone	4-3 *	St. Lawrence	Maine	5-2	Minnesota
1989	Harvard	Billy Cleary	4-3 *	Minnesota	Michigan St.	7-4	Maine

Year	Champion	Head Coach	Score	Runner-up	Third Place
1990	Wisconsin	Jeff Sauer	7-3	Colgate	Boston College and Boston Univ.
1991	Northern Michigan	Rick Comley	8-7 *	Boston Univ.	Maine and Clarkson
1992	Lake Superior St.	Jeff Jackson	5-3	Wisconsin	Michigan and Michigan St.
1993	Maine	Shawn Walsh	5-4	Lake Superior St.	Boston Univ. and Michigan
1994	Lake Superior St.	Jeff Jackson	9-1	Boston Univ.	Harvard and Minnesota
1995	Boston Univ.	Jack Parker	6-2	Maine	Michigan and Minnesota
1996	Michigan	Red Berenson	3-2 *	Colorado Col.	Vermont and Boston Univ.
1997	North Dakota	Dean Blais	6-4	Boston Univ.	Colorado College and Michigan
1998	Michigan	Red Berenson	3-2 *	Boston College	New Hampshire and Ohio St.
1999	Maine	Shawn Walsh	3-2 *	New Hampshire	Boston College and Michigan St.
2000	North Dakota	Dean Blais	4-2	Boston College	St. Lawrence and Maine
2001	Boston College	Jerry York	3-2 *	North Dakota	Michigan and Michigan St.
2002	Minnesota	Don Lucia	4-3 *	Maine	Michigan and New Hampshire
2003	Minnesota	Don Lucia	5-1	New Hampshire	Michigan and Cornell
2004	Denver	George Gwozdecky	1-0	Maine	Minnesota Duluth and Boston College
2005	Denver	George Gwozdecky	4-1	North Dakota	Colorado College and Minnesota
2006	Wisconsin	Mike Eaves	2-1	Boston College	North Dakota and Maine
2007	Michigan St.	Rick Comley	3-1	Boston College	North Dakota and Maine

*Championship game overtime goals: 1954—1:54; **1959**—4:22; **1977**—0: 23; **1984**—7:11 in 4th OT; **1988**—4:46; **1989**—4:16; **1991**—1:57 in 3rd OT; **1996**—3:35; **1998**—17:51; **1999**—10:50; **2001**—4:43; **2002**—16:58.

Note: Runners-up Denver (1973) and Wisconsin (1992) had participation voided by the NCAA for using ineligible players.

U.S. Division I College Hockey (Cont.)
Tournament Most Outstanding Player

The Most Outstanding Players of each NCAA Div. I tournament since 1948. Winners of the award who did not play for the tournament champion are in **bold** type. In 1960, three players, none on the winning team, shared the award.

Multiple winners: Lou Angotti and Marc Behrend (2).

Year	Year	Year
1948 **Joe Riley,** Dartmouth, F	1967 Walt Stanowski, Cornell, D	1988 Bruce Hoffort, Lk. Superior, G
1949 **Dick Desmond,** Dart., G	1968 Gerry Powers, Denver, G	1989 Ted Donato, Harvard, F
1950 **Ralph Bevins,** Boston U., G	1969 Keith Magnuson, Denver, D	1990 Chris Tancill, Wisconsin, F
1951 **Ed Whiston,** Brown, G	1970 Dan Lodboa, Cornell, D	1991 Scott Beattie, No. Mich., F
1952 **Ken Kinsley,** Colo. Col., G	1971 Dan Brady, Boston U., G	1992 Paul Constantin, Lk. Superior, F
1953 John Matchefts, Mich., F	1972 Tim Regan, Boston, U., G	1993 Jim Montgomery, Maine, F
1954 Abbie Moore, RPI, F	1973 Dean Talafous, Wisc., F	1994 Sean Tallaire, Lk. Superior, F
1955 **Phil Hilton,** Colo. Col., F	1974 Brad Shelstad, Minn., G	1995 Chris O'Sullivan, Boston U., F
1956 Lorne Howes, Mich., G	1975 Jim Warden, Mich. Tech, G	1996 Brendan Morrison, Michigan, F
1957 Bob McCusker, Colo. Col., F	1976 Tom Vannelli, Minn., F	1997 Matt Henderson, N. Dakota, F
1958 Murray Massier, Denver, F	1977 Julian Baretta, Wisc., G	1998 Marty Turco, Michigan, G
1959 Reg Morelli, N. Dakota, F	1978 Jack O'Callahan, Boston U., D	1999 Alfie Michaud, Maine, G
1960 **Lou Angotti,** Mich. Tech, F;	1979 Steve Janaszak, Minn., G	2000 Lee Goren, N. Dakota, F
Bob Marquis, Boston U., F;	1980 Doug Smail, N. Dakota, F	2001 Chuck Kobasew, Boston College, F
& **Barry Urbanski,** BU, G	1981 Marc Behrend, Wisc., G	2002 Grant Potulny, Minnesota, F
1961 Bill Masterton, Denver, F	1982 Phil Sykes, N. Dakota, F	2003 Thomas Vanek, Minnesota, F
1962 Lou Angotti, Mich. Tech, F	1983 Marc Behrend, Wisc., G	2004 Adam Berkhoel, Denver, G
1963 Al McLean, N. Dakota, F	1984 Gary Kruzich, Bowl. Green, G	2005 Peter Mannino, Denver, G
1964 Bob Gray, Michigan, G	1985 **Chris Terreri**, Prov., G	2006 Robbie Earl, Wisconsin, F
1965 Gary Milroy, Mich. Tech, F	1986 Mike Donnelly, Mich. St., F	2007 Justin Abdelkader, Michigan St., F
1966 Gaye Cooley, Mich. St., G	1987 Tony Hrkac, N. Dakota, F	

Hobey Baker Award

College hockey's Player of the Year award; voted on by a national panel of sportswriters, broadcasters, college coaches and pro scouts (plus a fan vote beginning in 2003). First presented in 1981 by the Decathlon Athletic Club of Bloomington, Minn., in the name of the Princeton collegiate hockey and football star who was killed in a plane crash.

Year	Year	Year
1981 Neal Broten, Minnesota, F	1990 Kip Miller, Michigan St., F	1999 Jason Krog, UNH, F
1982 George McPhee, Bowl. Green, F	1991 Dave Emma, Boston College, F	2000 Mike Mottau, Boston College, D
1983 Mark Fusco, Harvard, D	1992 Scott Pellerin, Maine, F	2001 Ryan Miller, Michigan St., G
1984 Tom Kurvers, Minn. Duluth, D	1993 Paul Kariya, Maine, F	2002 Jordan Leopold, Minnesota, D
1985 Bill Watson, Minn. Duluth, F	1994 Chris Marinucci, Minn. Duluth, F	2003 Peter Sejna, Colorado Coll., F
1986 Scott Fusco, Harvard, F	1995 Brian Holzinger, Bowl. Green, F	2004 Junior Lessard, Minn. Duluth, F
1987 Tony Hrkac, North Dakota, F	1996 Brian Bonin, Minnesota, F	2005 Marty Sertich, Colorado Coll., F
1988 Robb Stauber, Minnesota, G	1997 Brendan Morrison, Michigan, F	2006 Matt Carle, Denver, D
1989 Lane MacDonald, Harvard, F	1998 Chris Drury, Boston U., F	2007 Ryan Duncan, North Dakota, F

NCAA Women's Frozen Four

Women's college hockey was officially introduced as an NCAA Division I sport in 2000-01.

Multiple winner: Minnesota-Duluth (3); Minnesota and Wisconsin (2).

Year	Champion	Head Coach	Score	Runner-up	Third Place	Score	Fourth Place
2001	Minnesota Duluth	Shannon Miller	4-2	St. Lawrence	Harvard	3-2	Dartmouth
2002	Minnesota Duluth	Shannon Miller	3-2	Brown	(tie) Niagara and Minnesota, 2-2		
2003	Minnesota Duluth	Shannon Miller	4-3*	Harvard	Dartmouth	4-2	Minnesota
2004	Minnesota	Laura Halldorson	6-2	Harvard	St. Lawrence	2-1	Dartmouth
2005	Minnesota	Laura Halldorson	4-3	Harvard	St. Lawrence	5-1	Dartmouth
2006	Wisconsin	Mark Johnson	3-0	Minnesota	New Hampshire and St. Lawrence (no game)		
2007	Wisconsin	Mark Johnson	4-1	Minnesota Duluth	Boston College and St. Lawrence (no game)		

*Championship game overtime goal: 2003—4:19 in 2nd OT.

Patty Kazmaier Award

Awarded annually to the women's Division I player who displays the highest standards of personal and team excellence during the season; voted on by a 13-member panel of national media, college coaches and one USA Hockey member. First presented in 1998, in the name of the Princeton collegiate hockey and lacrosse star who died in 1990 of a rare blood disease.

Multiple winner: Jennifer Botterill (2).

Year	Year	Year
1998 Brandy Fisher, New Hampshire, F	2002 Brooke Whitney, Northeastern, F	2006 Sara Bauer, Wisconsin, F
1999 A.J. Mleczko, Harvard, F	2003 Jennifer Botterill, Harvard, F	2007 Julie Chu, Harvard, F
2000 Ali Brewer, Brown, G	2004 Angela Ruggiero, Harvard, D	
2001 Jennifer Botterill, Harvard, F	2005 Krissy Wendell, Minnesota, F	

FANTASY SPORTS

With a blend of speed and power, Marlins SS **Hanley Ramirez** could be a top-5 pick for years to come.

LIVING IN FANTASYLAND

Why the attraction to fantasy sports? Hey, we can't all be 6'4". And we can't all run a 4.3 40, but we can ALL shop for the groceries.

IT'S A RANDOM SUNDAY AFTERNOON IN MID-SEPTEMBER. Your favorite baseball team started playing at one o'clock. They are down, 4-2, in the ninth, needing the win to make the playoffs. If only the big free agent starting pitcher they signed this off-season had pitched better this year, or the new right fielder could have hit even fifteen homers or batted anywhere near .300, they wouldn't be in this spot.

You're frustrated, so you click over to find your football team already down, 10-0, in the first quarter. The starting running back has fumbled yet again and the defense couldn't stop your local Pop Warner team.

You curse the sports gods and swear you could do a better job of assembling a team than either GM. If only you had a chance to put your own team together, you know a championship would surely follow.

Welcome to the world of fantasy sports.

This immensely successful phenomenon is hardly just limited to football and baseball these days, though those are clearly the two most commonly heard around the water cooler.

There are leagues for hockey, basketball, golf, auto racing, bowling, bass fishing, the full array of college sports and just about anything else you can imagine (even political afficionados and entertainment junkies have caught on).

If you can watch it, root for it and dream of having the control yourself, you can find a league through which to live the dream. Select your own team. Set your own starting lineup. Watch your players rack up the points. Or not.

All the while doing your research and analysis to measure and project performance. Doing your homework and making the right selections and starting choices will take you to the promised land.

It's really that simple. Okay, winning a title really isn't all that easy, but even that emulates reality. Isn't that what we are all looking for?

Rams RB **Steven Jackson** high-steps into the endzone for one of his 16 TDs in 2006. His huge season made him a top-3 pick in most 2007 drafts.

So Why Is It Called "Rotisserie" Baseball?

As legend has it, publishing executive and Rotisserie Baseball founding father Dan Okrent typed out the preliminary rules in the late 70s and presented them to a group of friends and colleagues at Manhattan's **La Rotisserie Francaise** on East 52nd Street, between Lexington and Third (since shut down).

"An extremely undistinguished French restaurant," Okrent would later say.

Okrent, himself, can't confirm the exact dates (Dickson's Baseball Dictionary claims Rotisserie was born Nov. 17, 1979), but says the idea came to him during one of his many flights between Hartford, Connecticut and Austin, Texas in the fall of 1979 while employed as a publishing consultant for the *Texas Monthly*.

The original league consisted of 10 teams that included Okrent, Robert Sklar, Lee Eisenberg, Rob Fleder, Thomas Guinzberg, Cork Smith, Valerie Salembier, Peter Gethers, Bruce McCall, Michael Pollett and Glen Waggoner. Sadly, none made millions off their creation.

Sources: *New York Times, USA Today, ESPN The Magazine*

Place Your Bets

With total fantasy spending estimated at over $1 billion (that's billion with a "b"), it's no wonder Vegas is jumping on the bandwagon. Station Casinos Inc., said to be the fifth-largest sports book in the United States, now sets betting lines and takes wagers on select players' fantasy performances.

So, for example, bettors can plunk down 50 bucks if they think Peyton Manning will score over 20 fantasy points in a given week (based on six points per TD, 1 point for 30 yards passing, 1 point for 10 yards rushing or receiving). As expected, NFL execs are none too pleased. The real question is, what took so long?

Teach Your Children Well

Publisher Jossey-Bass has released a series of student workbooks and parent-teacher guides designed to help kids in fifth grade and higher learn mathematics through the use of fantasy sports. The books show kids how to form their own fantasy teams and hone their math skills by calculating points. Thus far, kids and parents can choose from fantasy football, baseball, soccer and basketball.

Source: www.fantasysportsmath.com

Fantasy Fast Facts

* 16 million adults played fantasy sports in 2006
* 92 percent are male, 77 percent are married
* Average player age is 36
* 86 percent own their own homes
* 71 percent have a bachelor's degree
* 59 percent make over $50,000 a year
* Avg. fantasy player owns two teams
* Players spend an average of $493.60 per year on fantasy sports
* $3 billion to $4 billion annual impact across the sports industry

Source:
Fantasy Sports Trade Association

What Are Players Playing?

Of the 16 million fantasy sports participants mentioned above, 80% play fantasy football. Listed are the most popular fantasy sports (figures are higher than 16 million and 100% because players play multiple sports):

1. Football   12.8 million (80%)
2. Baseball   4.8 million (30%)
3. Auto Racing   4.2 million (26%)
4. Basketball   3.2 million (20%)
5. Hockey   1.9 million (12%)
6. Golf   1.1 million (7%)

Fantasy Football Top Performers (1996-2006)

Time to relive all of your draft-day steals for the past 11 years. Listed are the top 20 fantasy football performers from 1996-2006. The scoring system used to devise the rankings is based on a combination of yardage accumulated and touchdowns scored/thrown. Note that TD shown below refer to passing touchdowns for quarterbacks, and total touchdowns for all others. (*) denotes rookie.

1996

Favre dominates in his only Super Bowl-winning season. Terry Allen explodes for 21 rushing touchdowns with the 'Skins.

Player	Pos	Key Statistics	Player	Pos	Key Statistics
1 Brett Favre, GB	QB	3899 passing yards, 39 TD	11 Emmitt Smith, Dal.	RB	1204 rushing yards, 15 TD
2 Vinny Testaverde, Bal.	QB	4177 passing yards, 33 TD	12 Barry Sanders, Det.	RB	1553 rushing yards, 10 TD
3 Terry Allen, Wash.	RB	1353 rushing yards, 21 TD	13 Jerome Bettis, Pit.	RB	1431 rushing yards, 11 TD
4 Terrell Davis, Den.	RB	1538 rushing yards, 15 TD	14 Michael Jackson, Bal.	WR	1201 receiving yards, 14 TD
5 Mark Brunell, Jax	QB	4367 passing yards, 19 TD	15 Tony Martin, SD	WR	1171 receiving yards, 14 TD
6 Ricky Watters, Phi.	RB	1411 rushing yards, 13 TD	16 Eddie George*, Hou.	RB	1368 rushing yards, 8 TD
7 John Elway, Den.	QB	3328 passing yards, 26 TD	17 Steve Young, SF	QB	2410 passing yards, 14 TD
8 Jeff Blake, Cin.	QB	3624 passing yards, 24 TD	18 Carl Pickens, Cin.	WR	1180 receiving yards, 12 TD
9 Curtis Martin, NE	RB	1152 rushing yards, 17 TD	19 Jeff Hostetler, Oak.	QB	2548 passing yards, 23 TD
10 Drew Bledsoe, NE	QB	4086 passing yards, 27 TD	20 Jerry Rice, SF	WR	1254 receiving yards, 9 TD

1997

Electrifying Lion Barry Sanders joins the 2000-yard club.

	Player	Pos	Key Statistics
1	Barry Sanders, Det.	RB	2053 rushing yards, 14 TD
2	Terrell Davis, Den.	RB	1750 rushing yards, 15 TD
3	Brett Favre, GB	QB	3867 passing yards, 35 TD
4	Kordell Stewart, Pit.	QB	21 passing TD, 11 rushing TD
5	Jeff George, Oak.	QB	3917 passing yards, 29 TD
6	Dorsey Levens, GB	RB	1435 rushing yards, 12 TD
7	John Elway, Den.	QB	3635 passing yards, 27 TD
8	Steve McNair, Ten.	QB	14 passing TD, 8 rushing TD
9	Drew Bledsoe, NE	QB	3706 passing yards, 28 TD
10	Steve Young, SF	QB	3029 passing yards, 19 TD
11	Mark Brunell, Jax	QB	3281 passing yards, 18 TD
12	Jerome Bettis, Pit.	RB	1665 rushing yards, 9 TD
13	Warren Moon, Sea.	QB	3678 passing yards, 25 TD
14	K. Abdul-Jabbar, Mia.	RB	892 rushing yards, 16 TD
15	N. Kaufman, Oak.	RB	1294 rushing yards, 9 TD
16	Rob Moore, Ari.	WR	1584 receiving yards, 8 TD
17	Corey Dillon*, Cin.	RB	1129 rushing yards, 10 TD
18	Antonio Freeman, GB	WR	1243 receiving yards, 12 TD
19	Marshall Faulk, Ind.	RB	1054 rushing yards, 8 TD
20	Brad Johnson, Min.	QB	3036 passing yards, 20 TD

1998

TD cracks 2000; welcome to the top-20 Moss and Owens.

	Player	Pos	Key Statistics
1	Terrell Davis, Den.	RB	2008 rushing yards, 21 TD
2	Steve Young, SF	QB	36 passing TD, 6 rushing TD
3	Jamal Anderson, Atl	RB	1846 rushing yards, 14 TD
4	R. Cunningham, Min	QB	3704 passing yards, 34 TD
5	Marshall Faulk, Ind.	RB	2227 all-purpose yards, 10 TD
6	Fred Taylor*, Jax	RB	1223 rushing yards, 17 TD
7	Brett Favre, GB	QB	4212 passing yards, 31 TD
8	Garrison Hearst, SF	RB	1570 rushing yards, 9 TD
9	Steve McNair, Ten	QB	3228 passing yards, 15 TD
10	Vinny Testaverde, NYJ	QB	3256 passing yards, 29 TD
11	Emmitt Smith, Dal.	RB	1332 rushing yards, 15 TD
12	Randy Moss*, Min.	WR	1313 receiving yards, 17 TD
13	Antonio Freeman, GB	WR	1424 receiving yards, 14 TD
14	Chris Chandler, Atl.	QB	3154 passing yards, 25 TD
15	Curtis Martin, NYJ	RB	1287 rushing yards, 9 TD
16	Trent Green, Wash.	QB	3441 passing yards, 23 TD
17	Ricky Watters, Sea.	RB	1239 rushing yards, 9 TD
18	Robert Edwards*, NE	RB	1115 rushing yards, 12 TD
19	Jake Plummer, Ari.	QB	3737 passing yards, 17 TD
20	Terrell Owens, SF	WR	1097 receiving yards, 15 TD

1999

Warner breaks out with the most surprising year in fantasy football history. Manning and Harrison join the party.

	Player	Pos	Key Statistics
1	Kurt Warner, St.L	QB	4353 passing yards, 41 TD
2	Marshall Faulk, St.L	RB	2429 all-purpose yards, 12 TD
3	Edgerrin James*, Ind.	RB	1553 rushing yards, 17 TD
4	Steve Beuerlein, Car.	QB	4436 passing yards, 36 TD
5	Rich Gannon, Oak.	QB	3840 passing yards, 24 TD
6	Peyton Manning, Ind.	QB	4135 passing yards, 26 TD
7	Stephen Davis, Wash.	RB	1405 rushing yards, 17 TD
8	Eddie George, Ten.	RB	1304 rushing yards, 13 TD
9	Marvin Harrison, Ind.	WR	1663 receiving yards, 12 TD
10	Brad Johnson, Wash.	QB	4005 passing yards, 24 TD
11	Emmitt Smith, Dal.	RB	1397 rushing yards, 13 TD
12	Randy Moss, Min.	WR	1413 receiving yards, 12 TD
13	Doug Flutie, Buf.	QB	3171 passing yards, 19 TD
14	Brett Favre, GB	QB	4091 passing yards, 22 TD

	Player	Pos	Key Statistics
15	Dorsey Levens, GB	RB	1034 rushing yards, 10 TD
16	Charlie Garner, SF	RB	1229 rushing yards, 6 TD
17	Cris Carter, Min.	WR	1241 receiving yards, 13 TD
18	Curtis Martin, NYJ	RB	1464 rushing yards, 5 TD
19	Steve McNair, Ten.	QB	12 passing TD, 8 rushing TD
20	Jimmy Smith, Jax	WR	1636 receiving yards, 6 TD

2000

Faulk scores 26 total touchdowns (18 rushing, 8 receiving) to break Emmitt Smith's former single-season record of 25.

	Player	Pos	Key Statistics
1	Marshall Faulk, St.L	RB	2207 all-purpose yards, 26 TD
2	D. Culpepper, Min.	QB	33 passing TD, 7 rushing TD
3	Jeff Garcia, SF	QB	4278 passing yards, 31 TD
4	Edgerrin James, Ind.	RB	1709 rushing yards, 18 TD
5	Peyton Manning, Ind.	QB	4413 passing yards, 33 TD
6	Rich Gannon, Oak.	QB	3430 passing yards, 28 TD
7	Eddie George, Ten.	RB	1509 rushing yards, 16 TD
8	D. McNabb, Phi.	QB	21 passing TD, 6 rushing TD
9	Elvis Grbac, KC	QB	4169 passing yards, 28 TD
10	Mike Anderson*, Den.	RB	1500 rushing yards, 15 TD
11	Robert Smith, Min.	RB	1521 rushing yards, 10 TD
12	Fred Taylor, Jax	RB	1399 rushing yards, 14 TD
13	Ahman Green, GB	RB	1175 rushing yards, 13 TD
14	Curtis Martin, NYJ	RB	1204 rushing yards, 11 TD
15	Ricky Watters, Sea.	RB	1242 rushing yards, 9 TD
16	Randy Moss, Min.	WR	1437 receiving yards, 15 TD
17	Charlie Garner, SF	RB	1142 rushing yards, 10 TD
18	Mark Brunell, Jax	QB	3640 passing yards, 20 TD
19	Lamar Smith, Mia.	RB	1139 rushing yards, 16 TD
20	Marvin Harrison, Ind.	WR	1413 receiving yards, 14 TD

2001

The Rams are at it again, at least until their meeting with the Pats in the Super Bowl; Priest Holmes has his bust-out season; how did Jay Fiedler get in there?

	Player	Pos	Key Statistics
1	Marshall Faulk, St.L	RB	2147 all-purpose yards, 21 TD
2	Kurt Warner, St.L	QB	4830 passing yards, 36 TD
3	Jeff Garcia, SF	QB	3538 passing yards, 32 TD
4	Priest Holmes, KC	RB	2169 all-purpose yards, 10 TD
5	Rich Gannon, Oak.	QB	3828 passing yards, 27 TD
6	Steve McNair, Ten.	QB	21 passing TD, 5 rushing TD
7	D. McNabb, Phi.	QB	3233 passing yards, 25 TD
8	Peyton Manning, Ind.	QB	4131 passing yards, 26 TD
9	Ahman Green, Gb	RB	1387 rushing yards, 11 TD
10	Brett Favre, GB	QB	3921 passing yards, 32 TD
11	Aaron Brooks, NO	QB	3832 passing yards, 26 TD
12	Shaun Alexander, Sea.	RB	1318 rushing yards, 16 TD
13	Curtis Martin, NYJ	RB	1513 rushing yards, 10 TD
14	Marvin Harrison, Ind.	WR	1524 receiving yards, 15 TD
15	Terrell Owens, SF	WR	1412 receiving yards, 16 TD
16	Kordell Stewart, Pit.	QB	14 passing TD, 5 rushing TD
17	Jay Fiedler, Mia.	QB	20 passing TD, 4 rushing TD
18	Corey Dillon, Cin.	RB	1315 rushing yards, 13 TD
19	L. Tomlinson*, SD	RB	1236 rushing yards, 10 TD
20	David Boston, Ari.	WR	1598 receiving yards, 8 TD

Fantasy Football Top Performers (Cont.)

2002

Priest Holmes solidifies himself as a top pick; Ricky Williams enjoys South Beach; Clinton Portis has a fine rookie season.

	Player	Pos	Key Statistics
1	Priest Holmes, KC	RB	2287 all-purpose yards, 24 TD
2	Ricky Williams, Mia.	RB	1853 rushing yards, 17 TD
3	L. Tomlinson, SD	RB	1683 rushing yards, 15 TD
4	Rich Gannon, Oak.	QB	4689 passing yards, 26 TD
5	Michael Vick, Atl.	QB	16 passing TD, 8 rushing TD
6	D. Culpepper, Min.	QB	18 passing TD, 10 rushing TD
7	Clinton Portis*, Den.	RB	1508 rushing yards, 17 TD
8	Shaun Alexander, Sea.	RB	1175 rushing yards, 18 TD
9	Deuce McAllister, NO	RB	1388 rushing yards, 16 TD
10	Peyton Manning, Ind.	QB	4200 passing yards, 27 TD
11	Charlie Garner, Oak.	RB	1903 all-purpose yards, 11 TD
12	Steve McNair, Ten.	QB	3387 passing yards, 22 TD
13	Trent Green, KC	QB	3690 passing yards, 26 TD
14	Drew Bledsoe, Buf.	QB	4359 passing yards, 24 TD
15	Tiki Barber, NYG	RB	1989 all-purpose yards, 11 TD
16	Aaron Brooks, NO	QB	3572 passing yards, 27 TD
17	Jeff Garcia, SF	QB	3344 passing yards, 21 TD
18	Tom Brady, NE	QB	3764 passing yards, 28 TD
19	Travis Henry, Buf.	RB	1438 rushing yards, 14 TD
20	Marvin Harrison, Ind,	WR	1722 receiving yards, 11 TD

2003

Holmes sets a new single-season touchdown record; Jamal Lewis misses the single-season rushing mark by 39 yards.

	Player	Pos	Key Statistics
1	Priest Holmes, KC	RB	2110 all-purpose yards, 27 TD
2	L. Tomlinson, SD	RB	2370 all-purpose yards, 17 TD
3	Ahman Green, GB	RB	1883 rushing yards, 20 TD
4	Jamal Lewis, Bal.	RB	2066 rushing yards, 14 TD
5	D. Culpepper, Min.	QB	3479 passing yards, 25 TD
6	Clinton Portis, Den.	RB	1591 rushing yards, 14 TD
7	Peyton Manning, Ind.	QB	4267 passing yards, 29 TD
8	Randy Moss, Min.	WR	1632 receiving yards, 17 TD
9	Shaun Alexander, Sea.	RB	1435 rushing yards, 16 TD
10	Deuce McAllister, NO	RB	1641 rushing yards, 8 TD
11	Trent Green, KC	QB	4039 passing yards, 24 TD
12	Matt Hasselbeck, Sea.	QB	3841 passing yards, 26 TD
13	Torry Holt, St.L	WR	1696 receiving yards, 12 TD
14	Steve McNair, Ten.	QB	24 passing TD, 4 rushing
15	Aaron Brooks, NO	QB	3546 passing yards, 24 TD
16	Fred Taylor, Jax	RB	1572 rushing yards, 7 TD
17	Jon Kitna, Cin.	QB	3591 passing yards, 26 TD
18	Jeff Garcia, SF	QB	18 passing TD, 7 rushing TD
19	Ricky Williams, Mia.	RB	1372 rushing yards, 10 TD
20	Brett Favre, GB	QB	3361 passing yards, 32 TD

2004

Manning breaks Marino's record for TD passes, still beaten out by Culpepper as the top fantasy scorer; Ricky Williams sticks it to keeper-league owners everywhere by retiring just before training camp.

	Player	Pos	Key Statistics
1	D. Culpepper, Min.	QB	4717 passing yards, 39 TD
2	Peyton Manning, Ind.	QB	4557 passing yards, 49 TD
3	Shaun Alexander, Sea.	RB	1696 rushing yards, 20 TD
4	Tiki Barber, NYG	RB	2096 all-purpose yards, 15 TD
5	D. McNabb, Phi.	QB	3875 passing yards, 31 TD
6	L. Tomlinson, SD	RB	1335 rushing yards, 18 TD
7	Curtis Martin, NYJ	RB	1697 rushing yards, 14 TD
8	Trent Green, KC	QB	4591 passing yards, 27 TD
9	Jake Plummer, Den	QB	4089 passing yards, 27 TD
10	Domanick Davis, Hou.	RB	1188 rushing yards, 14 TD

	Player	Pos	Key Statistics
11	Edgerrin James, Ind.	RB	1548 rushing yards, 9 TD
12	Brett Favre, GB	QB	4088 passing yards, 30 TD
13	Jake Delhomme, Car.	QB	3886 passing yards, 29 TD
14	Corey Dillon, NE	RB	1635 rushing yards, 13 TD
15	Aaron Brooks, NO	QB	21 passing TD, 4 rushing TD
16	Drew Brees, SD	QB	3159 passing yards, 27 TD
17	M. Muhammad, Car.	WR	1405 receiving yards, 16 TD
18	Marc Bulger, St.L	QB	3964 passing yards, 21 TD
19	Tom Brady, NE	QB	3692 passing yards, 28 TD
20	Michael Vick, Atl.	QB	2313 passing yards, 14 TD

2005

It's Shaun Alexander's turn to set a new single-season touchdown record (28); Larry Johnson takes advantage of the KC offensive line; Carson Palmer is the top-scoring fantasy quarterback of the year.

	Player	Pos	Key Statistics
1	Shaun Alexander, Sea.	RB	1880 rushing yards, 28 TD
2	Larry Johnson, KC	RB	1750 rushing yards, 21 TD
3	L. Tomlinson, SD	RB	1462 rushing yards, 20 TD
4	Tiki Barber, NYG	RB	2390 all-purpose yards, 11 TD
5	Edgerrin James, Ind.	RB	1506 rushing yards, 14 TD
6	Carson Palmer, Cin.	QB	3836 passing yards, 32 TD
7	Tom Brady, NE	QB	4110 passing yards, 26 TD
8	Peyton Manning, Ind.	QB	3747 passing yards, 28 TD
9	Clinton Portis, Wash.	RB	1516 rushing yards, 11 TD
10	Steve Smith, Car.	WR	1563 receiving yards, 13 TD
11	Matt Hasselbeck, Sea.	QB	3459 passing yards, 24 TD
12	Rudi Johnson, Cin.	RB	1458 rushing yards, 12 TD
13	Eli Manning, NYG	QB	3762 passing yards, 24 TD
14	LaMont Jordan, Oak.	RB	1025 rushing yards, 11 TD
15	Jake Plummer, Den.	QB	3366 passing yards, 18 TD
16	Michael Vick, Atl.	QB	15 passing TD, 6 rushing TD
17	Drew Brees, SD	QB	3576 passing yards, 24 TD
18	Trent Green, KC	QB	4014 passing yards, 17 TD
19	Kerry Collins, Oak.	QB	3759 passing yards, 20 TD
20	Drew Bledsoe, Dal.	QB	3639 passing yards, 23 TD

2006

Tomlinson has a season for the ages, smashing the single-season record for TD with 31; Manning continues to be his usual stellar self, leading the Colts to Super Bowl; Brees does his part to help the city of New Orleans recover.

	Player	Pos	Key Statistics
1	L. Tomlinson, SD	RB	2323 all-purpose yards, 31 TD
2	Peyton Manning, Ind.	QB	4397 passing yards, 31 TD
3	Larry Johnson, KC	RB	2199 all-purpose yards, 19 TD
4	Drew Brees, NO	QB	4418 passing yards, 26 TD
5	Steven Jackson, St.L	RB	2334 all-purpose yards, 16 TD
6	Jon Kitna, Det	QB	4208 passing yards, 21 TD
7	Michael Vick, Atl	QB	2272 pass/1039 rush yards
8	Carson Palmer, Cin	QB	4035 passing yards, 28 TD
9	Marc Bulger, St.L	QB	4301 passing yards, 24 TD
10	Tom Brady, NE	QB	3529 passing yards, 24 TD
11	Brett Favre, GB	QB	3885 passing yards, 18 TD
12	Frank Gore, SF	RB	2180 all-purpose yards, 9 TD
13	B. Roethlisberger, Pit.	QB	2513 passing yards, 18 TD
14	Willie Parker, Pit	RB	1494 rushing yards, 16 TD
15	M. Jones-Drew, Jax	RB	2250 all-purpose yards, 16 TD
16	Philip Rivers, SD	QB	3388 passing yards, 22 TD
17	Eli Manning, NYG	QB	3244 passing yards, 24 TD
18	Brian Westbrook, Phi	RB	1955 all-purpose yards, 11 TD
19	Tiki Barber, NYG	RB	2127 all-purpose yards, 5 TD
20	Marvin Harrison, Ind.	WR	1366 receiving yards, 12 TD

Fantasy Baseball Top Performers (1996-2007)

Listed are the top 10 fantasy baseball positional players and top five fantasy pitchers from 1996-2007. The rankings are based on a typical 5 x 5 scoring system, where the following stats are used: batting average, home runs, runs batted in, runs, stolen bases for hitters; and wins, saves, strikeouts, earned run average and WHIP (walks + hits per inning pitched) for pitchers. (*) denotes rookie.

1996

Coors Field provides three memorable performances, and who can forget the Brady Anderson 50-homer year?

Hitter	Pos	Avg	HR	RBI	SB	R
1 Ellis Burks, Col.	OF	.344	40	128	32	142
2 Barry Bonds, SF	OF	.308	42	129	40	122
3 Alex Rodriguez, Sea.	SS	.358	36	123	15	141
4 A. Galarraga, Col.	1B	.304	47	150	18	119
5 Ken Griffey Jr., Sea.	OF	.303	49	140	16	125
6 Albert Belle, Cle.	OF	.311	48	148	11	124
7 Brady Anderson, Bal.	OF	.297	50	110	21	117
8 Kenny Lofton, Cle.	OF	.317	14	67	75	132
9 Dante Bichette, Col.	OF	.313	31	141	31	114
10 Mo Vaughn, Bos.	1B	.326	44	143	2	118

Pitcher	Pos	W	Sv	ERA	WHIP	K
1 John Smoltz, Atl.	SP	24	0	2.94	1.00	276
2 Kevin Brown, Fla.	SP	17	0	1.89	0.94	159
3 Greg Maddux, Atl.	SP	15	0	2.72	1.03	172
4 Hideo Nomo, LA	SP	16	0	3.19	1.16	234
5 Trevor Hoffman, SD	RP	9	42	2.25	0.92	111

1997

Griffey's best season still not enough to win, while Rocket's first year in Canada takes pitching honors.

Hitter	Pos	Avg	HR	RBI	SB	R
1 Larry Walker, Col.	OF	.366	49	130	33	143
2 Ken Griffey Jr., Sea.	OF	.304	56	147	15	125
3 Jeff Bagwell, Hou.	1B	.286	43	135	31	109
4 A. Galarraga, Col.	1B	.318	41	140	15	120
5 Barry Bonds, SF	OF	.291	40	101	37	123
6 Mike Piazza, LA	C	.362	40	124	5	104
7 Craig Biggio, Hou.	2B	.309	22	81	47	146
8 M. McGwire, Oak.-St.L.	1B	.274	58	123	3	86
9 Frank Thomas, ChW	DH	.347	35	125	1	110
10 Raul Mondesi, LA	OF	.310	30	87	32	95

Pitcher	Pos	W	Sv	ERA	WHIP	K
1 Roger Clemens, Tor.	SP	21	0	2.05	1.03	292
2 Pedro Martinez, Mon.	SP	17	0	1.90	0.93	305
3 Randy Johnson, Sea.	SP	20	0	2.28	1.05	291
4 Curt Schilling, Phi.	SP	17	0	2.97	1.05	319
5 Greg Maddux, Atl.	SP	19	0	2.20	0.95	177

1998

The single-season homer mark gets broken by two hitters, but Sosa gets the nod with his stolen bases.

Hitter	Pos	Avg	HR	RBI	SB	R
1 Sammy Sosa, ChC	OF	.308	66	158	18	134
2 Alex Rodriguez, Sea.	SS	.310	42	124	46	123
3 Mark McGwire, St.L	1B	.299	70	147	1	130
4 Ken Griffey Jr., Sea.	OF	.284	56	146	20	120
5 Albert Belle, ChW	OF	.328	49	152	6	113
6 Vinny Castilla, Col.	3B	.319	46	144	5	108
7 Juan Gonzalez, Tex.	OF	.318	45	157	2	110
8 Barry Bonds, SF	OF	.303	37	122	28	120
9 Craig Biggio, Hou.	2B	.325	20	88	50	123
10 V. Guerrero, Mon.	OF	.324	38	109	11	108

Pitcher	Pos	W	Sv	ERA	WHIP	K
1 Greg Maddux, Atl.	SP	18	0	2.22	0.98	204
2 Roger Clemens, Tor.	SP	20	0	2.65	1.10	271
3 Kevin Brown, SD	SP	18	0	2.38	1.07	257
4 Pedro Martinez, Bos.	SP	19	0	2.89	1.09	251
5 Curt Schilling, Phi.	SP	15	0	3.25	1.11	300

1999

The power of power is evident as Bagwell's second 30-30 season gets trumped by Slammin' Sammy.

Hitter	Pos	Avg	HR	RBI	SB	R
1 Sammy Sosa, ChC	OF	.288	63	141	7	114
2 Jeff Bagwell, Hou.	1B	.304	42	126	30	143
3 Chipper Jones, Atl.	3B	.319	45	110	25	116
4 Mark McGwire, St.L.	1B	.278	65	147	0	118
5 Ken Griffey Jr., Sea.	OF	.285	48	134	24	123
6 Manny Ramirez, Cle.	OF	.333	44	165	2	131
7 Shawn Green, Tor.	OF	.309	42	123	20	134
8 Ivan Rodriguez, Tex.	C	.332	35	113	25	116
9 Larry Walker, Col.	OF	.379	37	115	11	108
10 Roberto Alomar, Cle.	2B	.323	24	120	37	138

Pitcher	Pos	W	Sv	ERA	WHIP	K
1 Pedro Martinez, Bos.	SP	23	0	2.07	0.92	313
2 Randy Johnson, Ari.	SP	17	0	2.48	1.02	364
3 Kevin Millwood, Atl.	SP	18	0	2.68	1.00	205
4 Kevin Brown, LA	SP	18	0	3.00	1.07	221
5 Billy Wagner, Hou.	SP	4	39	1.57	0.78	124

2000

Todd Helton enjoys his best season to keep Jeff Bagwell at No. 2, while Pedro edges the Big Unit for the second straight season.

Hitter	Pos	Avg	HR	RBI	SB	R
1 Todd Helton, Col.	1B	.372	42	147	5	138
2 Jeff Bagwell, Hou.	1B	.310	47	132	9	152
3 Sammy Sosa, Chc	OF	.320	50	138	7	106
4 V. Guerrero, Mon.	OF	.345	44	123	9	101
5 Alex Rodriguez, Sea.	SS	.316	41	132	15	134
6 Darin Erstad, Ana.	OF	.355	25	100	28	121
7 Richard Hidalgo, Hou.	OF	.314	44	122	13	118
8 Barry Bonds, SF	OF	.306	49	106	11	129
9 Carlos Delgado, Tor.	1B	.344	41	137	0	115
10 Frank Thomas, ChW	DH	.328	43	143	1	115

Pitcher	Pos	W	Sv	ERA	WHIP	K
1 Pedro Martinez, Bos.	SP	18	0	1.74	0.74	284
2 Randy Johnson, Ari.	SP	19	0	2.64	1.12	347
3 Kevin Brown, LA	SP	13	0	2.58	0.99	216
4 Greg Maddux, Atl.	SP	19	0	3.00	1.07	190
5 Robb Nen, SF	RP	4	41	1.50	0.85	92

2001

Bonds breaks HR record for his only time as fantasy's top hitter.

Hitter	Pos	Avg	HR	RBI	SB	R
1 Barry Bonds, SF	OF	.328	73	137	13	129
2 Sammy Sosa, ChC	OF	.328	64	160	0	146
3 Alex Rodriguez, Tex.	SS	.318	52	135	18	133
4 Luis Gonzalez, Ari.	OF	.325	57	142	1	128
5 Todd Helton, Col.	1B	.336	49	146	7	132
6 Shawn Green, LA	OF	.297	49	125	20	121
7 V. Guerrero, Mon.	OF	.307	34	108	37	107
8 Larry Walker, Col.	OF	.350	38	123	14	107
9 Ichiro Suzuki, Sea,	OF	.350	8	69	56	127
10 Bret Boone, Sea.	2B	.331	37	141	5	118

Pitcher	Pos	W	Sv	ERA	WHIP	K
1 Randy Johnson, Ari.	SP	21	0	2.49	1.01	372
2 Curt Schilling, Ari.	SP	22	0	2.98	1.08	293
3 Mike Mussina, NYY	SP	17	0	3.15	1.07	214
4 Greg Maddux, Atl.	SP	17	0	3.05	1.06	173
5 Javier Vazquez, Mon.	SP	16	0	3.42	1.08	208

Fantasy Baseball Top Performers (Cont.)

2002

One homer from 40-40, Vlad keeps A-Rod a runner up, while a pair of Arizona hurlers dominate the mound again.

Hitter	Pos	Avg	HR	RBI	SB	R
1 V. Guerrero, Mon.	OF	.336	39	111	40	106
2 Alex Rodriguez, Tex.	SS	.300	57	142	9	125
3 Alfonso Soriano, NYY	2B	.300	39	102	41	128
4 Barry Bonds, SF	OF	.370	46	110	9	117
5 Jim Thome, Cle.	1B	.304	52	118	1	101
6 M. Ordonez, ChW	OF	.320	38	135	7	116
7 Jason Giambi, NYY.	1B	.314	41	122	2	120
8 Sammy Sosa, ChC	OF	.288	49	108	2	122
9 Lance Berkman, Hou.	OF	.292	42	128	8	106
10 Miguel Tejada, Oak.	SS	.308	34	131	7	108

Pitcher	Pos	W	Sv	ERA	WHIP	K
1 Randy Johnson, Ari.	SP	24	0	2.32	1.03	334
2 Curt Schilling, Ari.	SP	23	0	3.23	0.97	316
3 Pedro Martinez, Bos.	SP	20	0	2.26	0.92	239
4 Eric Gagne, LA	RP	4	52	1.97	0.86	114
5 Barry Zito, Oak.	SP	23	0	2.75	1.13	182

2003

Welcome to the list, Albert. Two top-10 newcomers (Pujols and Schmidt) are tops for the year.

Hitter	Pos	Avg	HR	RBI	SB	R
1 Albert Pujols, St.L	1B	.359	43	124	5	137
2 Gary Sheffield, Atl.	OF	.330	39	132	18	126
3 Alez Rodriguez, Tex.	SS	.298	47	118	17	124
4 Alfonso Soriano, NYY	2B	.290	38	91	35	114
5 Todd Helton, Col.	1B	.358	33	117	0	135
6 Barry Bonds, SF	OF	.341	45	90	7	111
7 Carlos Beltran, KC	OF	.307	26	100	41	102
8 Carlos Delgado, Tor.	1B	.302	42	145	0	117
9 Manny Ramirez, Bos.	OF	.325	37	104	3	117
10 Bret Boone, Sea.	2B	.294	35	117	16	111

Pitcher	Pos	W	Sv	ERA	WHIP	K
1 Jason Schmidt, SF	SP	17	0	2.34	0.95	208
2 Eric Gagne, LA	RP	2	55	1.20	0.69	137
3 Mark Prior, ChC	SP	18	0	2.43	1.10	245
4 Roy Halladay, Tor.	SP	22	0	3.25	1.07	204
5 Esteban Loaiza, ChW	SP	21	0	2.90	1.11	207

2004

The Twins' Johan Santana finishes No. 1 among all players, a feat that will be duplicated the following two seasons.

Hitter	Pos	Avg	HR	RBI	SB	R
1 V. Guerrero, LAA	OF	.337	39	126	15	124
2 Albert Pujols, St.L	1B	.331	46	123	5	133
3 Adrian Beltre, LA	3B	.334	48	121	7	104
4 Barry Bonds, SF	OF	.362	45	101	6	129
5 C. Beltran, KC-Hou.	OF	.267	38	104	42	121
6 Bobby Abreu, Phi.	OF	.301	30	105	40	118
7 Alex Rodriguez, NYY	3B	.286	36	106	28	112
8 Manny Ramirez, Bos.	OF	.308	43	130	2	108
9 Miguel Tejada, Bal.	SS	.311	34	150	4	107
10 Ichiro Suzuki, Sea.	OF	.372	8	60	36	101

Pitcher	Pos	W	Sv	ERA	WHIP	K
1 Johan Santana, Min.	SP	20	0	2.61	0.92	265
2 Randy Johnson, Ari.	SP	16	0	2.60	0.90	290
3 Curt Schilling, Bos.	SP	21	0	3.26	1.06	203
4 Jason Schmidt, SF	SP	18	0	3.20	1.08	251
5 Roger Clemens, Hou.	SP	18	0	2.98	1.16	218

2005

A-Rod's third best season finally results in top fantasy hitter honors. Santana plays sweet music again.

Hitter	Pos	Avg	HR	RBI	SB	R
1 A. Rodriguez, NYY	3B	.321	48	130	21	124
2 Derrek Lee, ChC	1B	.335	46	107	15	120
3 Albert Pujols, St.L	1B	.330	41	117	16	129
4 David Ortiz, Bos.	DH	.300	47	148	1	119
5 Mark Texeira, Tex.	1B	.301	43	144	4	112
6 Manny Ramirez, Bos.	OF	.292	45	144	1	112
7 Jason Bay, Pit.	OF	.306	32	101	21	110
8 Andruw Jones, Atl.	OF	.263	51	128	5	95
9 Alfonso Soriano, Tex.	2B	.268	36	104	30	102
10 V. Guerrero, LAA	OF	.317	32	108	13	95

Pitcher	Pos	W	Sv	ERA	WHIP	K
1 Johan Santana, Min.	SP	16	0	2.87	0.97	238
2 Chris Carpenter, St.L	SP	21	0	2.83	1.06	213
3 Roger Clemens, Hou.	SP	13	0	1.87	1.01	185
4 Pedro Martinez, NYM	SP	15	0	2.82	0.95	208
5 Dontrelle Willis, Fla.	SP	22	0	2.63	1.13	170

2006

Pujols holds off the HR champ, SB leader and 40-40 entrant for his second fantasy hitting title.

Hitter	Pos	Avg	HR	RBI	SB	R
1 Albert Pujols, St.L	1B	.331	49	137	7	119
2 Ryan Howard, Phi.	1B	.313	58	149	0	104
3 Jose Reyes, NYM	SS	.300	19	81	64	122
4 A. Soriano, Wash.	OF	.277	46	95	41	119
5 David Ortiz, Bos.	DH	.287	54	137	1	115
6 Derek Jeter, NYY	SS	.343	14	97	34	118
7 Matt Holliday, Col.	OF	.326	34	114	10	119
8 Carlos Beltran, NYM	OF	.275	41	116	18	127
9 Chase Utley, Phi.	2B	.309	32	102	15	131
10 Lance Berkman, Hou.	OF	.315	45	136	3	95

Pitcher	Pos	W	Sv	ERA	WHIP	K
1 Johan Santana, Min.	SP	19	0	2.77	0.98	245
2 Chris Carpenter, St.L	SP	15	0	3.09	1.07	184
3 Brandon Webb, Ari.	SP	16	0	3.10	1.13	178
4 John Smoltz, Atl.	SP	16	0	3.49	1.19	211
5 Roy Oswalt, Hou.	SP	15	0	2.98	1.17	166

2007

After a relatively tough 2006, A-Rod puts up a monster season in his contract year. Han-Ram and Beckett have the Marlins-Red Sox trade working out well for both teams.

Hitter	Pos	Avg	HR	RBI	SB	R
1 A. Rodriguez, NYY	3B	.314	54	156	24	143
2 Hanley Ramirez, Fla.	SS	.332	29	81	51	125
3 Matt Holiday, Col.	OF	.340	36	137	11	120
4 M. Ordonez, Det.	OF	.363	28	139	4	117
5 David Wright, NYM	3B	.325	30	107	34	113
6 Jimmy Rollins, Phi	SS	.296	30	94	41	139
7 David Ortiz, Bos.	DH	.332	35	117	3	116
8 Prince Fielder, Mil.	1B	.288	50	119	2	109
9 Jose Reyes, NYM	SS	.280	12	57	78	119
10 Brandon Phillips, Cin.	2B	.288	30	94	32	107

Pitcher	Pos	W	Sv	ERA	WHIP	K
1 Jake Peavy, SD	SP	19	0	2.54	1.06	240
2 C.C. Sabathia, Cle.	SP	19	0	3.21	1.14	209
3 Johan Santana, Min.	SP	15	0	3.33	1.07	235
4 Josh Beckett, Bos.	SP	20	0	3.27	1.14	194
5 Brandon Webb, Ari.	SP	18	0	3.01	1.19	194

COLLEGE SPORTS

2006 / 2007 YEAR IN REVIEW

Heavyweight champ **Cole Konrad** led Minnesota to the 2007 NCAA Division I wrestling title.

A TRAGIC
RUSH TO ACCUSE

The tables are turned in the Duke lacrosse case as the three athletes are cleared...and the district attorney heads to jail.

IN THE END THERE WERE NO WINNERS.

Certainly not the three Duke lacrosse players — Collin Finnerty, Reade Seligmann and David Evans — who were accused, then indicted, on charges of rape, kidnapping and sexual offense. They were labeled, among other things, "a bunch of hooligans." Two were suspended from the university (Evans graduated a day before being indicted), and all three had their entire lives, and the lives of their families, turned completely upside down. In 2007, they were totally exonerated — proven innocent of all charges. But winners? No.

Certainly not Durham County District Attorney Mike Nifong, whose stubbornness and overall disregard for the truth caused him to force the issue despite a crumbling case that increasingly lacked any concrete evidence.

Certainly not the school and its president Richard Brodhead, who caved into peer pressure and barred Seligmann and Finnerty from class, and later admitted to showing a lack of public support to the three student athletes and their families.

Certainly not the nationally ranked lacrosse program, which had the rest of its season canceled, lost potential recruits, and was forced to say goodbye to head coach Mike Pressler, who resigned after a successful 16-year tenure marked by three ACC championships.

Certainly not the Durham community, where residents essentially split down racial lines – one side believing not enough was done, and the other believing too much was done. The cameras are gone, but damage was done. No winners here.

And certainly not the accuser, a North Carolina Central student and exotic dancer who claimed the players took her into a bathroom at an off-campus team party in March 2006, then physically beat her and raped her. According to North Carolina Attorney General Roy Cooper, she likely won't have charges brought against her for false accusations because she 'may actually believe' the many conflicting stories she told.

From left, **David Evans**, **Collin Finnerty**, and **Reade Seligmann** applaud during a news conference on April 11, 2007 after all charges against the three former Duke lacrosse players were dropped

From the outset, almost nothing involved with this case was handled properly. The media pounced and presumed guilt, the school (and many of its faculty) gave itself a black eye with its knee-jerk reaction, even the police admitted to and apologized for mistakes made in the lineup used to obtain the initial rape indictment.

But the person most embarrassed, most vilified, and perhaps most responsible for the proliferation of the case was Nifong. And when all was said and done, the players were free...and *he* was the one in jail. He resigned as district attorney in July, 2007. He was disgraced, disbarred for more than 20 violations of the state's rules of professional conduct, and ultimately, found guilty of contempt for lying to the court.

Superior Court Judge W. Osmond Smith III ruled that Nifong had provided defense attorneys with a knowingly incomplete DNA testing report, and then insisted that he provided all of the results. The data he conveniently left out contained test results showing that DNA of multiple men was found on the accuser's underwear and body. And none of the DNA belonged to any of the Duke lacrosse players. Eventually one of the defense attorneys discov-

AP/Wide World Photos

Former Durham County district attorney **Mike Nifong** is led into the Durham County Detention Center on Sept. 7, 2007. Nifong was sentenced to one day in jail after being charged with contempt of court in his handling of the Duke lacrosse case.

ered the missing information, buried in the nearly 2,000 pages of test data.

Nifong, in the midst of his election campaign for district attorney, was relentless in his verbal attacks on the players, announcing that he wouldn't allow Durham to become known for "a bunch of lacrosse players from Duke raping a black girl."

Many believed, and the state bar disciplinary committee ultimately agreed, that he was simply trying to manipulate the case to improve his chances at the ballot box.

In September he served his one-day sentence. Weeks later, President Brodhead publicly apologized on behalf of Duke for its lack of support. Seligmann and Finnerty were invited back to school, but declined, opting to attend Brown and Loyola, MD, respectively. At press time, the three players were seeking a $30 million settlement, as well as reforms in a legal process that had clearly wronged them. But even if they win, there will still be no winners.

Source: *Associated Press* reports

THE TOP
10
Stories of the Year in **College Sports**

10 UCLA Hits the Century Mark. UCLA's women's water polo team defeats Stanford, 5-4, to give the school its 100th overall championship, more than any school in any division (see page 477 for a rundown of the top 10). The school's first title was won by the men's tennis team in 1950.

09 Cardinal Rule...Again. Led by two team victories and 10 top-four finishes, the Stanford Cardinal continue their amazing run, winning their 13th consecutive Directors' Cup as the nation's top Division I athletics program. Grand Valley State and Williams won the Division II and II titles, respectively.

08 Back-To-Back Beavers. Oregon State beats North Carolina for the second straight year to become just the fifth school to win back-to-back Division I baseball titles. The Beavers lost one game to Virginia in regional play, then reeled off 10 straight victories en route to the title. And they did all of this after limping through a regular season in which they had a losing conference record.

07 Flame-throwing Phenoms Meet. While Tennessee's Monica Abbott will go down as arguably the best NCAA softball pitcher ever, Arizona's Taryne Mowatt wins their head-to-head duel, leading the Wildcats to their second straight title.

Abbott concludes a stellar college career in which she set NCAA all-division career records for wins, strikeouts, shutouts, appearances and games started, and threw 21 no-hitters and six perfect games. Mowatt throws every pitch for Arizona during its eight-game World Series title run, finishing the season at 42-12 with 522 strikeouts in 370 innings.

06 Fantastic Finish. In one of the most spectacular finishes in college water polo history, California's Jeff Tyrrell scores with no time left on the clock to give the Bears a 7-6 win over USC for their 12th national championship. The goal comes just two seconds after USC's Thomas Hale tied the game at six.

05 New Sheriff in Kentucky. After ten seasons that included a national title in his first, Tubby Smith resigns as head coach of the Kentucky men's basketball team to take the job at Minnesota. Texas A&M coach Billy Gillispie is chosen as Smith's successor.

04 **Pi-Nick-io!** After weeks of denials and statements such as, "I'm not going to be the Alabama coach," Nick Saban bolts the Miami Dolphins just two years into a five-year deal to become the Alabama football coach. While hoards of rabid Tide fans are overjoyed, fans of the Dolphins as well as Alabama's SEC rivals LSU (Saban's job from 2000-2004) are none too pleased.

03 **Coaching Legend Retires.** Hall of Fame women's basketball coach Jody Conradt leaves the game after 31 seasons behind the University of Texas bench, and 38 seasons as a head coach overall. She is one of just two coaches, male or female, to record 900 victories.

02 **Great Gators!** Florida becomes the first Division I school in NCAA history to hold both the men's football and basketball titles simultaneously. The Gators defeat Ohio State in the BCS Championship Game, 41-14, nine months after the school won its first hoops title. For good measure, Billy Donovan's squad added its second straight title three months later, also over the Buckeyes.

01 **Justice Served?** The tables are turned in the Duke lacrosse rape case as all charges are dropped against players David Evans, Reade Seligmann and Collin Finnerty...and district attorney Mike Nifong is subsequently disbarred, found guilty of contempt and sent to jail for a day.

The Most Common College Nicknames

	Name	Examples	No.		Name	Examples	No.		Name	Examples	No.
1	Eagles	B.C., Biola	64	9	Crusaders	Susquehanna	30	16	Hawks	Monmouth	18
2	Tigers	LSU, Occidental	46	10	Pioneers	Denver	27		Rams	Colorado St.	18
3	Bulldogs	Yale, The Citadel	40	11	Knights	Fair. Dickinson	24	18	Vikings	Cleveland St.	17
4	Lions	Columbia	37	12	Bears	Brown, Shaw	21	19	Golden		
5	Wildcats	Arizona	33		Falcons	Air Force	21		Eagles	Marquette	16
6	Warriors	Winona St.	32	14	Saints	Marymount	20		Spartans	Michigan St.	16
7	Cougars	Houston	31	15	Cardinals	Ball St.	19				
	Panthers	Pitt, York	31								

...And Some of the More Uncommon
(all nicknames below belong to just one school)

Auggies — Augsburg College
Banana Slugs — Cal-Santa Cruz
Battlin' Beavers — Blackburn Coll.
Bloodhounds — John Jay College of Criminal Justice
Blueboys — Illinois College
Chanticleers — Coastal Carolina
Eutectics — St. Louis College of Pharmacy

Fords — Haverford
Gorloks — Webster
Judges — Brandeis
Jumbos — Tufts
Nanooks — Alaska-Fairbanks
Otters — CS-Monterey Bay
Paladins — Furman
Pelicans — Spalding

Phantoms — East-West
Pilgrims — New England College
Profs — Rowan
Silverswords — Chaminade
Stormy Petrels — Oglethorpe
Violets — NYU
White Mules — Colby College

Sources:
Pete Fournier, *The Handbook of Mascots and Nicknames*
(via) *23 Ways To Get To First Base: The ESPN Uncyclopedia*

NCAA Schools & Champions

SPORTS ALMANAC

NCAA Football Bowl Subdivision Schools

(Formerly Division I-A)

2007 Season

Conferences and coaches as of Sept. 30, 2007.

Joined Mid-American in 2007: TEMPLE from I-A Independent (affiliate member in 2005 & 2006).
Joining Sun Belt in 2009: WESTERN KENTUCKY from FCS Gateway (affiliate member in 2007 & 2008).

	Nickname	Conference	Head Coach	Location	Colors
Air Force	Falcons	Mountain West	Troy Calhoun	Colo. Springs, CO	Blue/Silver
Akron	Zips	Mid-American	J.D. Brookhart	Akron, OH	Blue/Gold
Alabama	Crimson Tide	SEC-West	Nick Saban	Tuscaloosa, AL	Crimson/White
Arizona	Wildcats	Pac-10	Mike Stoops	Tucson, AZ	Cardinal/Navy
Arizona St.	Sun Devils	Pac-10	Dennis Erickson	Tempe, AZ	Maroon/Gold
Arkansas	Razorbacks	SEC-West	Houston Nutt	Fayetteville, AR	Cardinal/White
Arkansas St.	Indians	Sun Belt	Steve Roberts	State Univ., AR	Scarlet/Black
Army	Cadets, Black Knights	Independent	Stan Brock	West Point, NY	Black/Gold/Gray
Auburn	Tigers	SEC-West	Tommy Tuberville	Auburn, AL	Orange/Blue
Ball St.	Cardinals	Mid-American	Brady Hoke	Muncie, IN	Cardinal/White
Baylor	Bears	Big 12	Guy Morriss	Waco, TX	Green/Gold
Boise St.	Broncos	WAC	Chris Petersen	Boise, ID	Orange/Blue
Boston College	Eagles	ACC	Jeff Jagodzinski	Chestnut Hill, MA	Maroon/Gold
Bowling Green	Falcons	Mid-American	Gregg Brandon	Bowling Green, OH	Orange/Brown
Brigham Young	Cougars	Mountain West	Bronco Mendenhall	Provo, UT	Blue/White/Tan
Buffalo	Bulls	Mid-American	Turner Gill	Buffalo, NY	Royal Blue/White
California	Golden Bears	Pac-10	Jeff Tedford	Berkeley, CA	Blue/Gold
Central Florida	Golden Knights	USA	George O'Leary	Orlando, FL	Black/Gold
Central Michigan	Chippewas	Mid-American	Butch Jones	Mt. Pleasant, MI	Maroon/Gold
Cincinnati	Bearcats	Big East	Brian Kelly	Cincinnati, OH	Red/Black
Clemson	Tigers	ACC	Tommy Bowden	Clemson, SC	Purple/Orange
Colorado	Buffaloes	Big 12	Dan Hawkins	Boulder, CO	Silver/Gold/Black
Colorado St.	Rams	Mountain West	Sonny Lubick	Ft. Collins, CO	Green/Gold
Connecticut	Huskies	Big East	Randy Edsall	Storrs, CT	Blue/White
Duke	Blue Devils	ACC	Ted Roof	Durham, NC	Royal Blue/White
East Carolina	Pirates	USA	Skip Holtz	Greenville, NC	Purple/Gold
Eastern Michigan	Eagles	Mid-American	Jeff Genyk	Ypsilanti, MI	Green/White
Florida	Gators	SEC-East	Urban Meyer	Gainesville, FL	Orange/Blue
Florida Atlantic	Owls	Sun Belt	H. Schnellenberger	Boca Raton, FL	Blue/Red
Florida Int'l	Golden Panthers	Sun Belt	Mario Cristobal	Miami, FL	Blue/Gold
Florida St.	Seminoles	ACC	Bobby Bowden	Tallahassee, FL	Garnet/Gold
Fresno St.	Bulldogs	WAC	Pat Hill	Fresno, CA	Red/Blue
Georgia	Bulldogs	SEC-East	Mark Richt	Athens, GA	Red/Black
Georgia Tech	Yellow Jackets	ACC	Chan Gailey	Atlanta, GA	Old Gold/White
Hawaii	Warriors	WAC	June Jones	Honolulu, HI	Green/White
Houston	Cougars	USA	Art Briles	Houston, TX	Scarlet/White
Idaho	Vandals	WAC	Robb Akey	Moscow, ID	Silver/Gold
Illinois	Fighting Illini	Big Ten	Ron Zook	Champaign, IL	Orange/Blue
Indiana	Hoosiers	Big Ten	Bill Lynch	Bloomington, IN	Cream/Crimson
Iowa	Hawkeyes	Big Ten	Kirk Ferentz	Iowa City, IA	Old Gold/Black
Iowa St.	Cyclones	Big 12	Gene Chizik	Ames, IA	Cardinal/Gold
Kansas	Jayhawks	Big 12	Mark Mangino	Lawrence, KS	Crimson/Blue
Kansas St.	Wildcats	Big 12	Ron Prince	Manhattan, KS	Purple/White
Kent St.	Golden Flashes	Mid-American	Doug Martin	Kent, OH	Navy Blue/Gold
Kentucky	Wildcats	SEC-East	Rich Brooks	Lexington, KY	Blue/White
LSU	Fighting Tigers	SEC-West	Les Miles	Baton Rouge, LA	Purple/Gold
LA-Lafayette	Ragin' Cajuns	Sun Belt	Rickey Bustle	Lafayette, LA	Vermilion/White
LA-Monroe	Warhawks	Sun Belt	Charlie Weatherbie	Monroe, LA	Maroon/Gold
Louisiana Tech	Bulldogs	WAC	Derek Dooley	Ruston, LA	Red/Blue
Louisville	Cardinals	Big East	Steve Kragthorpe	Louisville, KY	Red/Black/White

	Nickname	Conference	Head Coach	Location	Colors
Marshall	Thundering Herd	USA	Mark Snyder	Huntington, WV	Green/White
Maryland	Terrapins, Terps	ACC	Ralph Friedgen	College Park, MD	Red/White/Black/Gold
Memphis	Tigers	USA	Tommy West	Memphis, TN	Blue/Gray
Miami-FL	Hurricanes	ACC	Randy Shannon	Coral Gables, FL	Orange/Grn./Wt.
Miami-OH	RedHawks	Mid-American	Shane Montgomery	Oxford, OH	Red/White
Michigan	Wolverines	Big Ten	Lloyd Carr	Ann Arbor, MI	Maize/Blue
Michigan St.	Spartans	Big Ten	Mark Dantonio	E. Lansing, MI	Green/White
Middle Tennessee	Blue Raiders	Sun Belt	Rick Stockstill	Murfreesboro, TN	Royal Blue/White
Minnesota	Golden Gophers	Big Ten	Tim Brewster	Minneapolis, MN	Maroon/Gold
Mississippi	Ole Miss, Rebels	SEC-West	Ed Orgeron	Oxford, MS	Cardinal/Navy Bl.
Mississippi St.	Bulldogs	SEC-West	Sylvester Croom	Starkville, MS	Maroon/White
Missouri	Tigers	Big 12	Gary Pinkel	Columbia, MO	Old Gold/Black
Navy	Midshipmen	Independent	Paul Johnson	Annapolis, MD	Navy Blue/Gold
Nebraska	Cornhuskers	Big 12	Bill Callahan	Lincoln, NE	Scarlet/Cream
Nevada	Wolf Pack	WAC	Chris Ault	Reno, NV	Silver/Blue
New Mexico	Lobos	Mountain West	Rocky Long	Albuquerque, NM	Cherry/Silver
New Mexico St.	Aggies	WAC	Hal Mumme	Las Cruces, NM	Crimson/White
North Carolina	Tar Heels	ACC	Butch Davis	Chapel Hill, NC	Carolina Blue/Wt.
North Carolina St.	Wolfpack	ACC	Tom O'Brien	Raleigh, NC	Red/White
North Texas	Mean Green	Sun Belt	Todd Dodge	Denton, TX	Green/White
Northern Illinois	Huskies	Mid-American	Joe Novak	DeKalb, IL	Cardinal/Black
Northwestern	Wildcats	Big Ten	Pat Fitzgerald	Evanston, IL	Purple/White
Notre Dame	Fighting Irish	Independent	Charlie Weis	Notre Dame, IN	Gold/Blue
Ohio University	Bobcats	Mid-American	Frank Solich	Athens, OH	Hunter Green/Wt.
Ohio St.	Buckeyes	Big Ten	Jim Tressel	Columbus, OH	Scarlet/Gray
Oklahoma	Sooners	Big 12	Bob Stoops	Norman, OK	Crimson/Cream
Oklahoma St.	Cowboys	Big 12	Mike Gundy	Stillwater, OK	Orange/Black
Oregon	Ducks	Pac-10	Mike Bellotti	Eugene, OR	Green/Yellow
Oregon St.	Beavers	Pac-10	Mike Riley	Corvallis, OR	Orange/Black
Penn St.	Nittany Lions	Big Ten	Joe Paterno	University Park, PA	Blue/White
Pittsburgh	Panthers	Big East	Dave Wannstedt	Pittsburgh, PA	Blue/Gold
Purdue	Boilermakers	Big Ten	Joe Tiller	W. Lafayette, IN	Old Gold/Black
Rice	Owls	USA	David Bailiff	Houston, TX	Blue/Gray
Rutgers	Scarlet Knights	Big East	Greg Schiano	New Brunswick, NJ	Scarlet
San Diego St.	Aztecs	Mountain West	Chuck Long	San Diego, CA	Scarlet/Black
San Jose St.	Spartans	WAC	Dick Tomey	San Jose, CA	Gold/White/Blue
South Carolina	Gamecocks	SEC-East	Steve Spurrier	Columbia, SC	Garnet/Black
South Florida	Bulls	Big East	Jim Leavitt	Tampa, FL	Green/Gold
SMU	Mustangs	USA	Phil Bennett	Dallas, TX	Red/Blue
Southern Miss.	Golden Eagles	USA	Jeff Bower	Hattiesburg, MS	Black/Gold
Stanford	Cardinal	Pac-10	Jim Harbaugh	Stanford, CA	Cardinal/White
Syracuse	Orange	Big East	Greg Robinson	Syracuse, NY	Orange
Temple	Owls	Mid-American	Al Golden	Philadelphia, PA	Cherry/White
Tennessee	Volunteers	SEC-East	Phillip Fulmer	Knoxville, TN	Orange/White
Texas	Longhorns	Big 12	Mack Brown	Austin, TX	Burnt Orange/Wt.
Texas A&M	Aggies	Big 12	Dennis Franchione	College Station, TX	Maroon/White
TCU	Horned Frogs	Mountain West	Gary Patterson	Ft. Worth, TX	Purple/White
Texas Tech	Red Raiders	Big 12	Mike Leach	Lubbock, TX	Scarlet/Black
Toledo	Rockets	Mid-American	Tom Amstutz	Toledo, OH	Blue/Gold
Troy	Trojans	Sun Belt	Larry Blakeney	Troy, AL	Cardinal/Slvr./Blk.
Tulane	Green Wave	USA	Bob Toledo	New Orleans, LA	Olive Grn./Sky Bl.
Tulsa	Golden Hurricane	USA	Todd Graham	Tulsa, OK	Blue/Gold/Crimson
UAB	Blazers	USA	Neil Callaway	Birmingham, AL	Green/Gold
UCLA	Bruins	Pac-10	Karl Dorrell	Los Angeles, CA	Blue/Gold
UNLV	Rebels	Mountain West	Mike Sanford	Las Vegas, NV	Scarlet/Gray
USC	Trojans	Pac-10	Pete Carroll	Los Angeles, CA	Cardinal/Gold
Utah	Utes	Mountain West	Kyle Whittingham	Salt Lake City, UT	Crimson/White
Utah St.	Aggies	WAC	Brent Guy	Logan, UT	Navy Blue/White
UTEP	Miners	USA	Mike Price	El Paso, TX	Orange/Blue/Silver
Vanderbilt	Commodores	SEC-East	Bobby Johnson	Nashville, TN	Black/Gold
Virginia	Cavaliers	ACC	Al Groh	Charlottesville, VA	Orange/Blue
Virginia Tech	Hokies, Gobblers	ACC	Frank Beamer	Blacksburg, VA	Orange/Maroon
Wake Forest	Demon Deacons	ACC	Jim Grobe	Winston-Salem, NC	Old Gold/Black
Washington	Huskies	Pac-10	Tyrone Willingham	Seattle, WA	Purple/Gold
Washington St.	Cougars	Pac-10	Bill Doba	Pullman, WA	Crimson/Gray
West Virginia	Mountaineers	Big East	Rich Rodriguez	Morgantown, WV	Old Gold/Blue
Western Kentucky	Hilltoppers	Independent	David Elson	Bowling Green, KY	Red/White
Western Michigan	Broncos	Mid-American	Bill Cubit	Kalamazoo, MI	Brown/Gold
Wisconsin	Badgers	Big Ten	Bret Bielema	Madison, WI	Cardinal/White
Wyoming	Cowboys	Mountain West	Joe Glenn	Laramie, WY	Brown/Gold

NCAA Football Championship Subdivision Schools

(Formerly Division I-AA)

2007 Season

Conferences and coaches as of Sept. 30, 2007.

Joining Big South in 2007: PRESBYTERIAN COLLEGE from Division II.
Joining Mid Eastern in 2007: WINSTON-SALEM ST. from Division II (2006 as an FCS Independent).
Joining Ohio Valley in 2007: AUSTIN PEAY ST. from Pioneer (2006 as an FCS Independent).
Joining Southland in 2007: CENTRAL ARKANSAS from Division II (2006 as an FCS Independent).
New Conference in 2007: Colonial Athletic Association (12 teams) — DELAWARE, HOFSTRA, JAMES MADISON, MAINE, MASSACHUSETTS, NEW HAMPSHIRE, NORTHEASTERN, RHODE ISLAND, RICHMOND, TOWSON, VILLANOVA and WILLIAM & MARY from Atlantic 10 (conference will no longer sponsor football).
Joining Football Championship Subdivision in 2007: NORTH CAROLINA CENTRAL from Division II.
Joining Big South in 2008: STONY BROOK from Northeast (2007 as an FCS Independent).
Joining Gateway in 2008: NORTH DAKOTA ST. and SOUTH DAKOTA ST. from Great West.
Joining Great West in 2008: NORTH DAKOTA and SOUTH DAKOTA from Division II.
Joining Southern in 2008: SAMFORD from Ohio Valley.
Joining Football Championship Subdivision in 2008: CAMPBELL (resurrecting its football program).
Joining Colonial Athletic Association in 2009: OLD DOMINION (resurrecting its football program).

	Nickname	Conference	Head Coach	Location	Colors
Alabama A&M	Bulldogs	SWAC	Anthony Jones	Huntsville, AL	Maroon/White
Alabama St.	Hornets	SWAC	Reggie Barlow	Montgomery, AL	Black/Gold
Albany	Great Danes	Northeast	Bob Ford	Albany, NY	Purple/Gold
Alcorn St.	Braves	SWAC	Johnny Thomas	Lorman, MS	Purple/Gold
Appalachian St.	Mountaineers	Southern	Jerry Moore	Boone, NC	Black/Gold
Ark.-Pine Bluff	Golden Lions	SWAC	Mo Forte	Pine Bluff, AR	Black/Gold
Austin Peay St.	Governors	Ohio Valley	Rick Christophel	Clarksville, TN	Red/White
Bethune-Cookman	Wildcats	Mid-Eastern	Alvin Wyatt	Daytona Beach, FL	Maroon/Gold
Brown	Bears	Ivy	Phil Estes	Providence, RI	Brown/Red/White
Bucknell	Bison	Patriot	Tim Landis	Lewisburg, PA	Orange/Blue
Butler	Bulldogs	Pioneer	Jeff Voris	Indianapolis, IN	Blue/White
Cal Poly	Mustangs	Great West	Rich Ellerson	San Luis Obispo, CA	Green/Gold
Central Arkansas	Bears	Southland	Clint Conque	Conway, AR	Purple/Gray
Central Conn. St.	Blue Devils	Northeast	Jeff McInerney	New Britain, CT	Blue/White
Charleston So.	Buccaneers	Big South	Jay Mills	Charleston, SC	Blue/Gold
Chattanooga	Mocs	Southern	Rodney Allison	Chattanooga, TN	Navy Blue/Old Gold
The Citadel	Bulldogs	Southern	Kevin Higgins	Charleston, SC	Blue/White
Coastal Carolina	Chanticleers	Big South	David Bennett	Conway, SC	Green/Bronze/Black
Colgate	Raiders	Patriot	Dick Biddle	Hamilton, NY	Maroon/White/Gray
Columbia	Lions	Ivy	Norries Wilson	New York, NY	Lt. Blue/White
Cornell	Big Red	Ivy	Jim Knowles	Ithaca, NY	Carnelian/White
Dartmouth	Big Green	Ivy	Buddy Teevens	Hanover, NH	Green/White
Davidson	Wildcats	Pioneer	Tripp Merritt	Davidson, NC	Red/Black
Dayton	Flyers	Pioneer	Mike Kelly	Dayton, OH	Red/Blue
Delaware	Blue Hens	Colonial	K.C. Keeler	Newark, DE	Blue/Gold
Delaware St.	Hornets	Mid-Eastern	Al Lavan	Dover, DE	Red/Blue
Drake	Bulldogs	Pioneer	Steve Loney	Des Moines, IA	Blue/White
Duquesne	Dukes	Metro Atlantic	Jerry Schmitt	Pittsburgh, PA	Red/Blue
Eastern Illinois	Panthers	Ohio Valley	Bob Spoo	Charleston, IL	Blue/Gray
Eastern Kentucky	Colonels	Ohio Valley	Danny Hope	Richmond, KY	Maroon/White
Eastern Washington	Eagles	Big Sky	Paul Wulff	Cheney, WA	Red/White
Elon	Phoenix	Southern	Pete Lembo	Elon, NC	Maroon/Gold
Florida A&M	Rattlers	Mid-Eastern	Rubin Carter	Tallahassee, FL	Orange/Green
Fordham	Rams	Patriot	Tom Masella	Bronx, NY	Maroon/White
Furman	Paladins	Southern	Bobby Lamb	Greenville, SC	Purple/White
Gardner-Webb	Bulldogs	Big South	Steve Patton	Boiling Springs, NC	Scarlet/Black
Georgetown	Hoyas	Patriot	Kevin Kelly	Washington, DC	Blue/Gray
Georgia Southern	Eagles	Southern	Chris Hatcher	Statesboro, GA	Blue/White
Grambling St.	Tigers	SWAC	Rod Broadway	Grambling, LA	Black/Gold
Hampton	Pirates	Mid-Eastern	Joe Taylor	Hampton, VA	Royal Blue/White
Harvard	Crimson	Ivy	Tim Murphy	Cambridge, MA	Crimson/Black/White
Hofstra	Pride	Colonial	Dave Cohen	Hempstead, NY	Gold/White/Blue
Holy Cross	Crusaders	Patriot	Tom Gilmore	Worcester, MA	Royal Purple
Howard	Bison	Mid-Eastern	Carey Bailey	Washington, DC	Blue/Wt./Red
Idaho St.	Bengals	Big Sky	John Zamberlin	Pocatello, ID	Orange/Black
Illinois St.	Redbirds	Gateway	Denver Johnson	Normal, IL	Red/White
Indiana St.	Sycamores	Gateway	Lou West	Terre Haute, IN	Royal Blue/White
Iona	Gaels	Metro Atlantic	Fred Mariani	New Rochelle, NY	Maroon/Gold
Jackson St.	Tigers	SWAC	Rick Comegy	Jackson, MS	Blue/White
Jacksonville	Dolphins	Pioneer	Kerwin Bell	Jacksonville, FL	Green/White
Jacksonville St.	Gamecocks	Ohio Valley	Jack Crowe	Jacksonville, AL	Red/White
James Madison	Dukes	Colonial	Mickey Matthews	Harrisonburg, VA	Purple/Gold

	Nickname	Conference	Head Coach	Location	Colors
Lafayette	Leopards	Patriot	Frank Tavani	Easton, PA	Maroon/White
La Salle	Explorers	Metro Atlantic	Tim Miller	Philadelphia, PA	Blue/Gold
Lehigh	Mountain Hawks	Patriot	Andy Coen	Bethlehem, PA	Brown/White
Liberty	Flames	Big South	Danny Rocco	Lynchburg, VA	Red/White/Blue
Maine	Black Bears	Colonial	Jack Cosgrove	Orono, ME	Blue/White
Marist	Red Foxes	Metro Atlantic	Jim Parady	Poughkeepsie, NY	Red/White
Massachusetts	Minutemen	Colonial	Don Brown	Amherst, MA	Maroon/White
McNeese St.	Cowboys	Southland	Matt Viator	Lake Charles, LA	Blue/Gold
Miss. Valley St.	Delta Devils	SWAC	Willie Totten	Itta Bena, MS	Green/White
Missouri St.	Bears	Gateway	Terry Allen	Springfield, MO	Maroon/White
Monmouth	Hawks	Northeast	Kevin Callahan	W. Long Branch, NJ	Royal Blue/White
Montana	Grizzlies	Big Sky	Bobby Hauck	Missoula, MT	Maroon/Silver
Montana St.	Bobcats	Big Sky	Rob Ash	Bozeman, MT	Blue/Gold
Morehead St.	Eagles	Pioneer	Matt Ballard	Morehead, KY	Blue/Gold
Morgan St.	Bears	Mid-Eastern	Donald Hill-Eley	Baltimore, MD	Blue/Orange
Murray St.	Racers	Ohio Valley	Matt Griffin	Murray, KY	Blue/Gold
New Hampshire	Wildcats	Colonial	Sean McDonnell	Durham, NH	Blue/White
Nicholls St.	Colonels	Southland	Jay Thomas	Thibodaux, LA	Red/Gray
Norfolk State	Spartans	Mid-Eastern	Pete Adrian	Norfolk, VA	Green/Gold
North Carolina A&T	Aggies	Mid-Eastern	Lee Fobbs	Greensboro, NC	Blue/Gold
NC Central	Eagles	Independent	Mose Rison	Durham, NC	Maroon/Gray
North Dakota St.	Bison	Great West	Craig Bohl	Fargo, ND	Green/Yellow
Northeastern	Huskies	Colonial	Rocky Hager	Boston, MA	Red/Black
Northern Arizona	Lumberjacks	Big Sky	Jerome Souers	Flagstaff, AZ	Blue/Gold
Northern Colorado	Bears	Big Sky	Scott Downing	Greeley, CO	Blue/Gold
Northern Iowa	Panthers	Gateway	Mark Farley	Cedar Falls, IA	Purple/Old Gold
Northwestern St.	Demons	Southland	Scott Stoker	Natchitoches, LA	Purple/White
Pennsylvania	Quakers	Ivy	Al Bagnoli	Philadelphia, PA	Red/Blue
Portland St.	Vikings	Big Sky	Jerry Glanville	Portland, OR	Green/White
Prairie View A&M	Panthers	SWAC	Henry Frazier	Prairie View, TX	Purple/Gold
Presbyterian	Blue Hose	Big South	Bobby Bentley	Clinton, SC	Garnet/Blue
Princeton	Tigers	Ivy	Roger Hughes	Princeton, NJ	Orange/Black
Rhode Island	Rams	Colonial	Tim Stowers	Kingston, RI	Light Blue/Navy/Wt.
Richmond	Spiders	Colonial	Dave Clawson	Richmond, VA	Red/Blue
Robert Morris	Colonials	Northeast	Joe Walton	Moon Township, PA	Blue/White
Sacramento St.	Hornets	Big Sky	Marshall Sperbeck	Sacramento, CA	Green/Gold
Sacred Heart	Pioneers	Northeast	Paul Gorham	Fairfield, CT	Scarlet/White
St. Francis-PA	Red Flash	Northeast	Dave Opfar	Loretto, PA	Red/White
Saint Peter's	Peacocks	Metro Atlantic	Chris Taylor	Jersey City, NJ	Blue/White
Sam Houston St.	Bearkats	Southland	Todd Whitten	Huntsville, TX	Orange/White
Samford	Bulldogs	Ohio Valley	Pat Sullivan	Birmingham, AL	Crimson/Blue
San Diego	Toreros	Pioneer	Ron Caragher	San Diego, CA	Lt. Blue/Navy
Savannah St.	Tigers	Independent	Theo Lemon	Savannah, GA	Orange/Blue
South Carolina St.	Bulldogs	Mid-Eastern	Oliver Pough	Orangeburg, SC	Garnet/Blue
South Dakota St.	Jackrabbits	Great West	John Stiegelmeier	Brookings, SD	Yellow/Blue
SE Missouri St.	Redhawks	Ohio Valley	Tony Samuel	Cape Girardeau, MO	Red/Black
Southeastern Louisiana	Lions	Southland	Mike Lucas	Hammond, LA	Green/Gold
Southern-BR	Jaguars	SWAC	Pete Richardson	Baton Rouge, LA	Blue/Gold
Southern Illinois	Salukis	Gateway	Jerry Kill	Cardondale, IL	Maroon/White
Southern Utah	Thunderbirds	Great West	Wes Meier	Cedar City, UT	Scarlet/White
Stephen F. Austin	Lumberjacks	Southland	J.C. Harper	Nacogdoches, TX	Purple/White
Stony Brook	Seawolves	Independent	Chuck Priore	Stony Brook, NY	Scarlet/Gray
Tennessee-Martin	Skyhawks	Ohio Valley	Jason Simpson	Martin, TN	Orange/White/Blue
Tennessee St.	Tigers	Ohio Valley	James Webster	Nashville, TN	Blue/White
Tennessee Tech	Golden Eagles	Ohio Valley	Watson Brown	Cookeville, TN	Purple/Gold
Texas Southern	Tigers	SWAC	Steve Wilson	Houston, TX	Maroon/Gray
Texas St.	Bobcats	Southland	Brad Wright	San Marcos, TX	Maroon/Gold
Towson	Tigers	Colonial	Gordy Combs	Towson, MD	Gold/White
UC-Davis	Aggies	Great West	Bob Biggs	Davis, CA	Yale Blue/Gold
Valparaiso	Crusaders	Pioneer	Stacy Adams	Valparaiso, IN	Brown/Gold
Villanova	Wildcats	Colonial	Andy Talley	Villanova, PA	Blue/White
VMI	Keydets	Big South	Jim Reid	Lexington, VA	Red/White/Yellow
Wagner	Seahawks	Northeast	Walt Hameline	Staten Island, NY	Green/White
Weber St.	Wildcats	Big Sky	Ron McBride	Ogden, UT	Royal Purple/White
Western Carolina	Catamounts	Southern	Kent Briggs	Cullowhee, NC	Purple/Gold
Western Illinois	Leathernecks	Gateway	Don Patterson	Macomb, IL	Purple/Gold
William & Mary	Tribe	Colonial	Jimmye Laycock	Williamsburg, VA	Green/Gold/Silver
Winston-Salem St.	Rams	Mid-Eastern	Kermit Blount	Winston-Salem, NC	Red/White
Wofford	Terriers	Southern	Mike Ayers	Spartanburg, SC	Old Gold/Black
Yale	Bulldogs, Elis	Ivy	Jack Siedlecki	New Haven, CT	Yale Blue/White
Youngstown St.	Penguins	Gateway	Jon Heacock	Youngstown, OH	Red/White

NCAA Division I Basketball Schools
2007-2008 Season
Conferences and coaches as of Sept. 30, 2007.

Conference Name Change: Mid-Continent Conference changed its name to The Summit League as of July 1, 2007.
Joining Atlantic Sun in 2007-08: FLORIDA GULF COAST and SOUTH CAROLINA UPSTATE from Division II.
Joining Big South in 2007-08: PRESBYTERIAN COLLEGE from Division II.
Joining Big West in 2007-08: UC-DAVIS from Independent.
Joining Horizon in 2007-08: VALPARAISO from The Summit League.
Joining Mid Eastern in 2007-08: WINSTON-SALEM ST. from Division II (2006-07 as an Independent).
Joining Southland in 2007-08: CENTRAL ARKANSAS from Division II (2006-07 as an Independent).
Joining The Summit League in 2007-08: IPFW, NORTH DAKOTA ST. and SOUTH DAKOTA ST. from Independent.
Joining Division I in 2007-08: CAL STATE BAKERSFIELD, NEW JERSEY INSTITUTE OF TECHNOLOGY and NORTH CAROLINA CENTRAL from Division II.
Joining Big South in 2008-09: GARDNER-WEBB from Atlantic Sun.
Leaving Big South in 2007-08: BIRMINGHAM SOUTHERN to Division III.
Joining Division I in 2008-09: NORTH DAKOTA from Division II.
Joining Southern in 2008-09: SAMFORD from Ohio Valley.

	Nickname	Conference	Head Coach	Location	Colors
Air Force	Falcons	Mountain West	Jeff Reynolds	Colo. Springs, CO	Blue/Silver
Akron	Zips	Mid-American	Keith Dambrot	Akron, OH	Blue/Gold
Alabama	Crimson Tide	SEC-West	Mark Gottfried	Tuscaloosa, AL	Crimson/White
Alabama A&M	Bulldogs	SWAC	Vann Pettaway	Huntsville, AL	Maroon/White
Alabama St.	Hornets	SWAC	Lewis Jackson	Montgomery, AL	Black/Gold
Albany	Great Danes	America East	Will Brown	Albany, NY	Purple/Gold
Alcorn St.	Braves	SWAC	Samuel West	Lorman, MS	Purple/Gold
American	Eagles	Patriot	Jeff Jones	Washington, DC	Red/Blue
Appalachian St.	Mountaineers	Southern	Houston Fancher	Boone, NC	Black/Gold
Arizona	Wildcats	Pac-10	Lute Olson	Tucson, AZ	Cardinal/Navy
Arizona St.	Sun Devils	Pac-10	Herb Sendek	Tempe, AZ	Maroon/Gold
Arkansas	Razorbacks	SEC-West	John Pelphrey	Fayetteville, AR	Cardinal/White
Ark.-Little Rock	Trojans	Sun Belt	Steve Shields	Little Rock, AR	Silver/Black/Maroon
Ark.-Pine Bluff	Golden Lions	SWAC	Van Holt	Pine Bluff, AR	Black/Gold
Arkansas St.	Indians	Sun Belt	Dickey Nutt	State Univ., AR	Scarlet/Black
Army	Black Knights	Patriot	Jim Crews	West Point, NY	Black/Gold/Gray
Auburn	Tigers	SEC-West	Jeff Lebo	Auburn, AL	Orange/Blue
Austin Peay St.	Governors	Ohio Valley	Dave Loos	Clarksville, TN	Red/White
Ball St.	Cardinals	Mid-American	Billy Taylor	Muncie, IN	Cardinal/White
Baylor	Bears	Big 12	Scott Drew	Waco, TX	Green/Gold
Belmont	Bruins	Atlantic Sun	Rick Byrd	Nashville, TN	Navy Blue/Red
Bethune-Cookman	Wildcats	Mid-Eastern	Clifford Reed	Daytona Beach, FL	Maroon/Gold
Binghamton	Bearcats	America East	Kevin Broadus	Binghamton, NY	Green/Black/White
Boise St.	Broncos	WAC	Greg Graham	Boise, ID	Orange/Blue
Boston College	Eagles	ACC	Al Skinner	Chestnut Hill, MA	Maroon/Gold
Boston University	Terriers	America East	Dennis Wolff	Boston, MA	Scarlet/White
Bowling Green	Falcons	Mid-American	Louis Orr	Bowling Green, OH	Orange/Brown
Bradley	Braves	Mo. Valley	Jim Les	Peoria, IL	Red/White
Brigham Young	Cougars	Mountain West	Dave Rose	Provo, UT	Blue/White/Tan
Brown	Bears	Ivy	Craig Robinson	Providence, RI	Brown/Cardinal/White
Bucknell	Bison	Patriot	Pat Flannery	Lewisburg, PA	Orange/Blue
Buffalo	Bulls	Mid-American	R. Witherspoon	Buffalo, NY	Royal Blue/White
Butler	Bulldogs	Horizon	Brad Stevens	Indianapolis, IN	Blue/White
California	Golden Bears	Pac-10	Ben Braun	Berkeley, CA	Blue/Gold
Cal Poly	Mustangs	Big West	Kevin Bromley	San Luis Obispo, CA	Green/Gold
CS-Bakersfield	Roadrunners	Independent	Keith Brown	Bakersfield, CA	Blue/Gold
CS-Fullerton	Titans	Big West	Bob Burton	Fullerton, CA	Blue/Orange/White
CS-Northridge	Matadors	Big West	Bobby Braswell	Northridge, CA	Red/White/Black
Campbell	Camels	Atlantic Sun	Robbie Laing	Buies Creek, NC	Orange/Black
Canisius	Golden Griffins	Metro Atlantic	Tom Parrotta	Buffalo, NY	Blue/Gold
Centenary	Gents, Gentlemen	Summit	Rob Flaska	Shreveport, LA	Maroon/White
Central Arkansas	Bears	Southland	Rand Chappell	Conway, AR	Purple/Gray
Central Conn. St.	Blue Devils	Northeast	Howie Dickenman	New Britain, CT	Blue/White
Central Florida	Golden Knights	USA	Kirk Speraw	Orlando, FL	Black/Gold
Central Michigan	Chippewas	Mid-American	Ernie Zeigler	Mt. Pleasant, MI	Maroon/Gold
Charleston So.	Buccaneers	Big South	Barclay Radebaugh	Charleston, SC	Blue/Gold
Charlotte	49ers	Atlantic 10	Bobby Lutz	Charlotte, NC	Green/White
Chattanooga	Mocs	Southern	John Shulman	Chattanooga, TN	Navy Blue/Old Gold
Chicago St.	Cougars	Independent	Benjy Taylor	Chicago, IL	Green/White
Cincinnati	Bearcats	Big East	Mick Cronin	Cincinnati, OH	Red/Black
The Citadel	Bulldogs	Southern	Ed Conroy	Charleston, SC	Blue/White
Clemson	Tigers	ACC	Oliver Purnell	Clemson, SC	Purple/Orange
Cleveland St.	Vikings	Horizon	Gary Waters	Cleveland, OH	Forest Green/White

	Nickname	Conference	Head Coach	Location	Colors
Coastal Carolina	Chanticleers	Big South	Cliff Ellis	Conway, SC	Green/Bronze/Black
Colgate	Raiders	Patriot	Emmett Davis	Hamilton, NY	Maroon/Gray/White
College of Charleston	Cougars	Southern	Bobby Cremins	Charleston, SC	Maroon/White
Colorado	Buffaloes	Big 12	Jeff Bzdelik	Boulder, CO	Silver/Gold/Black
Colorado St.	Rams	Mountain West	Tim Miles	Ft. Collins, CO	Green/Gold
Columbia	Lions	Ivy	Joseph Jones	New York, NY	Lt. Blue/White
Connecticut	Huskies	Big East	Jim Calhoun	Storrs, CT	Blue/White
Coppin St.	Eagles	Mid-Eastern	Ron Mitchell	Baltimore, MD	Royal Blue/Gold
Cornell	Big Red	Ivy	Steve Donahue	Ithaca, NY	Carnelian/White
Creighton	Bluejays	Mo. Valley	Dana Altman	Omaha, NE	Blue/White
Dartmouth	Big Green	Ivy	Terry Dunn	Hanover, NH	Green/White
Davidson	Wildcats	Southern	Bob McKillop	Davidson, NC	Red/Black
Dayton	Flyers	Atlantic 10	Brian Gregory	Dayton, OH	Red/Blue
Delaware	Fightin' Blue Hens	Colonial	Monte Ross	Newark, DE	Blue/Gold
Delaware St.	Hornets	Mid-Eastern	Greg Jackson	Dover, DE	Red/Columbia Blue
Denver	Pioneers	Sun Belt	Joe Scott	Denver, CO	Crimson/Gold
DePaul	Blue Demons	Big East	Jerry Wainwright	Chicago, IL	Scarlet/Blue
Detroit Mercy	Titans	Horizon	Perry Watson	Detroit, MI	Red/White/Blue
Drake	Bulldogs	Mo. Valley	Keno Davis	Des Moines, IA	Blue/White
Drexel	Dragons	Colonial	Bruiser Flint	Philadelphia, PA	Navy Blue/Gold
Duke	Blue Devils	ACC	Mike Krzyzewski	Durham, NC	Royal Blue/White
Duquesne	Dukes	Atlantic 10	Ron Everhart	Pittsburgh, PA	Red/Blue
East Carolina	Pirates	USA	Mack McCarthy	Greenville, NC	Purple/Gold
East Tenn. St.	Buccaneers	Atlantic Sun	Murry Bartow	Johnson City, TN	Blue/Gold
Eastern Illinois	Panthers	Ohio Valley	Mike Miller	Charleston, IL	Blue/Gray
Eastern Kentucky	Colonels	Ohio Valley	Jeff Neubauer	Richmond, KY	Maroon/White
Eastern Michigan	Eagles	Mid-American	Charles Ramsey	Ypsilanti, MI	Green/White
Eastern Washington	Eagles	Big Sky	Kirk Earlywine	Cheney, WA	Red/White
Elon	Phoenix	Southern	Ernie Nestor	Elon, NC	Maroon/Gold
Evansville	Aces	Mo. Valley	Marty Simmons	Evansville, IN	Purple/White
Fairfield	Stags	Metro Atlantic	Ed Cooley	Fairfield, CT	Cardinal Red
Fairleigh Dickinson	Knights	Northeast	Tom Green	Teaneck, NJ	Maroon/Blue
Florida	Gators	SEC-East	Billy Donovan	Gainesville, FL	Orange/Blue
Florida A&M	Rattlers	Mid-Eastern	Eugene Harris	Tallahassee, FL	Orange/Green
Florida Atlantic	Owls	Sun Belt	Rex Walters	Boca Raton, FL	Blue/Red
Florida Gulf Coast	Eagles	Atlantic Sun	Dave Balza	Fort Myers, FL	Kelly Green/Royal Blue
Florida Int'l	Golden Panthers	Sun Belt	Sergio Rouco	Miami, FL	Blue/Gold
Florida St.	Seminoles	ACC	Leonard Hamilton	Tallahassee, FL	Garnet/Gold
Fordham	Rams	Atlantic 10	Dereck Whittenburg	Bronx, NY	Maroon/White
Fresno St.	Bulldogs	WAC	Steve Cleveland	Fresno, CA	Red/Blue
Furman	Paladins	Southern	Jeff Jackson	Greenville, SC	Purple/White
Gardner-Webb	Bulldogs	Atlantic Sun	Rick Scruggs	Boiling Springs, NC	Scarlet/Black
George Mason	Patriots	Colonial	Jim Larranaga	Fairfax, VA	Green/Gold
George Washington	Colonials	Atlantic 10	Karl Hobbs	Washington, DC	Buff/Blue
Georgetown	Hoyas	Big East	John Thompson III	Washington, DC	Blue/Gray
Georgia	Bulldogs, 'Dawgs	SEC-East	Dennis Felton	Athens, GA	Red/Black
Georgia Southern	Eagles	Southern	Jeff Price	Statesboro, GA	Blue/White
Georgia St.	Panthers	Colonial	Rod Barnes	Atlanta, GA	Roy. Blue/White
Georgia Tech	Yellow Jackets	ACC	Paul Hewitt	Atlanta, GA	Old Gold/White
Gonzaga	Bulldogs, Zags	West Coast	Mark Few	Spokane, WA	Blue/White/Red
Grambling St.	Tigers	SWAC	Larry Wright	Grambling, LA	Black/Gold
Hampton	Pirates	Mid-Eastern	Kevin Nickelberry	Hampton, VA	Royal Blue/White
Hartford	Hawks	America East	Dan Leibovitz	W. Hartford, CT	Scarlet/White
Harvard	Crimson	Ivy	Tommy Amaker	Cambridge, MA	Crimson/Black/White
Hawaii	Rainbow Warriors	WAC	Bob Nash	Honolulu, HI	Green/White
High Point	Panthers	Big South	Bart Lundy	High Point, NC	Purple/White
Hofstra	Pride	Colonial	Tom Pecora	Hempstead, NY	Blue/Gold/White
Holy Cross	Crusaders	Patriot	Ralph Willard	Worcester, MA	Royal Purple
Houston	Cougars	USA	Tom Penders	Houston, TX	Scarlet/White
Howard	Bison	Mid-Eastern	Gil Jackson	Washington, DC	Blue/White/Red
Idaho	Vandals	WAC	George Pfeifer	Moscow, ID	Silver/Gold
Idaho St.	Bengals	Big Sky	Joe O'Brien	Pocatello, ID	Orange/Black
Illinois	Fighting Illini	Big Ten	Bruce Weber	Champaign, IL	Orange/Blue
Illinois-Chicago	Flames	Horizon	Jim Collins	Chicago, IL	Navy Blue/Red
Illinois St.	Redbirds	Mo. Valley	Tom Jankovich	Normal, IL	Red/White
Indiana	Hoosiers	Big Ten	Kelvin Sampson	Bloomington, IN	Cream/Crimson
IPFW	Mastodons	Summit	Dane Fife	Fort Wayne, IN	Royal Blue/White
IUPUI	Jaguars	Summit	Ron Hunter	Indianapolis, IN	Red/Gold
Indiana St.	Sycamores	Mo. Valley	Kevin McKenna	Terre Haute, IN	Blue/White
Iona	Gaels	Metro Atlantic	Kevin Willard	New Rochelle, NY	Maroon/Gold
Iowa	Hawkeyes	Big Ten	Todd Lickliter	Iowa City, IA	Old Gold/Black
Iowa St.	Cyclones	Big 12	Greg McDermott	Ames, IA	Cardinal/Gold

	Nickname	Conference	Head Coach	Location	Colors
Jackson St.	Tigers	SWAC	Tevester Anderson	Jackson, MS	Blue/White
Jacksonville	Dolphins	Atlantic Sun	Cliff Warren	Jacksonville, FL	Green/White
Jacksonville St.	Gamecocks	Ohio Valley	Mike LaPlante	Jacksonville, AL	Red/White
James Madison	Dukes	Colonial	Dean Keener	Harrisonburg, VA	Purple/Gold
Kansas	Jayhawks	Big 12	Bill Self	Lawrence, KS	Crimson/Blue
Kansas St.	Wildcats	Big 12	Frank Martin	Manhattan, KS	Purple/White
Kennesaw St.	Owls	Atlantic Sun	Tony Ingle	Kennesaw, GA	Black/Gold
Kent St.	Golden Flashes	Mid-American	Jim Christian	Kent, OH	Navy Blue/Gold
Kentucky	Wildcats	SEC-East	Billy Gillispie	Lexington, KY	Blue/White
La Salle	Explorers	Atlantic 10	John Giannini	Philadelphia, PA	Blue/Gold
Lafayette	Leopards	Patriot	Fran O'Hanlon	Easton, PA	Maroon/White
Lamar	Cardinals	Southland	Steve Roccaforte	Beaumont, TX	Red/White
Lehigh	Mountain Hawks	Patriot	Brett Reed	Bethlehem, PA	Brown/White
Liberty	Flames	Big South	Ritchie McKay	Lynchburg, VA	Red/White/Blue
Lipscomb	Bisons	Atlantic Sun	Scott Sanderson	Nashville, TN	Purple/Gold
Long Beach St.	49ers	Big West	Dan Monson	Long Beach, CA	Black/Gold
Long Island	Blackbirds	Northeast	Jim Ferry	Brooklyn, NY	Black/Silver/Blue
Longwood	Lancers	Independent	Mike Gillian	Farmville, VA	Blue/White
LSU	Fighting Tigers	SEC-West	John Brady	Baton Rouge, LA	Purple/Gold
LA-Lafayette	Ragin' Cajuns	Sun Belt	Robert Lee	Lafayette, LA	Vermilion/White
LA-Monroe	Warhawks	Sun Belt	Orlando Early	Monroe, LA	Maroon/Gold
Louisiana Tech	Bulldogs	WAC	Kerry Rupp	Ruston, LA	Red/Blue
Louisville	Cardinals	Big East	Rick Pitino	Louisville, KY	Red/Black/White
Loyola Chicago	Ramblers	Horizon	Jim Whitesell	Chicago, IL	Maroon/Gold
Loyola Maryland	Greyhounds	Metro Atlantic	Jimmy Patsos	Baltimore, MD	Green/Gray
Loyola Marymount	Lions	West Coast	Rodney Tention	Los Angeles, CA	Crimson/Blue
Maine	Black Bears	America East	Ted Woodward	Orono, ME	Blue/White
Manhattan	Jaspers	Metro Atlantic	Barry Rohrssen	Riverdale, NY	Kelly Green/White
Marist	Red Foxes	Metro Atlantic	Matt Brady	Poughkeepsie, NY	Red/White
Marquette	Golden Eagles	Big East	Tom Crean	Milwaukee, WI	Blue/Gold
Marshall	Thundering Herd	USA	Donnie Jones	Huntington, WV	Green/White
Maryland	Terrapins, Terps	ACC	Gary Williams	College Park, MD	Red/Wt./Black/Gold
MD-Balt. County	Retrievers	America East	Randy Monroe	Baltimore, MD	Black/Gold/Red
MD-Eastern Shore	Hawks	Mid-Eastern	Meredith Smith	Princess Anne, MD	Maroon/Gray
Massachusetts	Minutemen	Atlantic 10	Travis Ford	Amherst, MA	Maroon/White
McNeese St.	Cowboys	Southland	Dave Simmons	Lake Charles, LA	Blue/Gold
Memphis	Tigers	USA	John Calipari	Memphis, TN	Blue/Gray
Mercer	Bears	Atlantic Sun	Mark Slonaker	Macon, GA	Orange/Black
Miami-FL	Hurricanes	ACC	Frank Haith	Coral Gables, FL	Orange/Grn./White
Miami-OH	RedHawks	Mid-American	Charlie Coles	Oxford, OH	Red/White
Michigan	Wolverines	Big Ten	John Beilein	Ann Arbor, MI	Maize/Blue
Michigan St.	Spartans	Big Ten	Tom Izzo	East Lansing, MI	Green/White
Middle Tennessee	Blue Raiders	Sun Belt	Kermit Davis Jr.	Murfreesboro, TN	Royal Blue/White
Minnesota	Golden Gophers	Big Ten	Tubby Smith	Minneapolis, MN	Maroon/Gold
Mississippi	Ole Miss, Rebels	SEC-West	Andy Kennedy	Oxford, MS	Cardinal/Navy Blue
Mississippi St.	Bulldogs	SEC-West	Rick Stansbury	Starkville, MS	Maroon/White
Miss. Valley St.	Delta Devils	SWAC	James Green	Itta Bena, MS	Green/White
Missouri	Tigers	Big 12	Mike Anderson	Columbia, MO	Old Gold/Black
Missouri St.	Bears	Mo. Valley	Barry Hinson	Springfield, MO	Maroon/White
Missouri-KC	Kangaroos	Summit	Matt Brown	Kansas City, MO	Blue/Gold
Monmouth	Hawks	Northeast	Dave Calloway	W. Long Branch, NJ	Midnight Blue/White
Montana	Grizzlies	Big Sky	Wayne Tinkle	Missoula, MT	Copper/Silver/Gold
Montana St.	Bobcats	Big Sky	Brad Huse	Bozeman, MT	Blue/Gold
Morehead St.	Eagles	Ohio Valley	Donnie Tyndall	Morehead, KY	Blue/Gold
Morgan St.	Bears	Mid-Eastern	Todd Bozeman	Baltimore, MD	Blue/Orange
Mt. St. Mary's	Mountaineers	Northeast	Milan Brown	Emmitsburg, MD	Blue/White
Murray St.	Racers	Ohio Valley	Billy Kennedy	Murray, KY	Blue/Gold
Navy	Midshipmen	Patriot	Billy Lange	Annapolis, MD	Navy Blue/Gold
Nebraska	Cornhuskers	Big 12	Doc Sadler	Lincoln, NE	Scarlet/Cream
Nevada	Wolf Pack	WAC	Mark Fox	Reno, NV	Silver/Blue
New Hampshire	Wildcats	America East	Bill Herrion	Durham, NH	Blue/White
NJ Inst. of Tech.	Highlanders	Independent	Jim Casciano	Newark, NJ	Red/White
New Mexico	Lobos	Mountain West	Steve Alford	Albuquerque, NM	Cherry/Silver
New Mexico St.	Aggies	WAC	Marvin Menzies	Las Cruces, NM	Crimson/White
New Orleans	Privateers	Sun Belt	Joe Pasternack	New Orleans, LA	Royal Blue/Silver
Niagara	Purple Eagles	Metro Atlantic	Joe Mihalich	Lewiston, NY	Purple/White/Gold
Nicholls St.	Colonels	Southland	J.P. Piper	Thibodaux, LA	Red/Gray
Norfolk St.	Spartans	Mid-Eastern	Anthony Evans	Norfolk, VA	Green/Gold
North Carolina	Tar Heels	ACC	Roy Williams	Chapel Hill, NC	Carolina Blue/Wht.
North Carolina A&T	Aggies	Mid-Eastern	Jerry Eaves	Greensboro, NC	Blue/Gold
North Carolina St.	Wolfpack	ACC	Sidney Lowe	Raleigh, NC	Red/White
NC-Asheville	Bulldogs	Big South	Eddie Biedenbach	Asheville, NC	Royal Blue/White

	Nickname	Conference	Head Coach	Location	Colors
NC-Central	Eagles	Independent	Henry Dickerson	Durham, NC	Maroon/Gray
NC-Greensboro	Spartans	Southern	Mike Dement	Greensboro, NC	Gold/White/Navy
NC-Wilmington	Seahawks	Colonial	Benny Moss	Wilmington, NC	Green/Gold/Navy
North Dakota St.	Bison	Summit	Saul Phillips	Fargo, ND	Yellow/Green
North Florida	Ospreys	Atlantic Sun	Matt Kilcullen	Jacksonville, FL	Navy Blue/Gray
North Texas	Mean Green	Sun Belt	Johnny Jones	Denton, TX	Green/White
Northeastern	Huskies	Colonial	Bill Coen	Boston, MA	Red/Black
Northern Arizona	Lumberjacks	Big Sky	Mike Adras	Flagstaff, AZ	Blue/Gold
Northern Colorado	Bears	Big Sky	Tad Boyle	Greeley, CO	Blue/Gold
Northern Illinois	Huskies	Mid-American	Ricardo Patton	DeKalb, IL	Cardinal/Black
Northern Iowa	Panthers	Mo. Valley	Ben Jacobson	Cedar Falls, IA	Purple/Old Gold
Northwestern	Wildcats	Big Ten	Bill Carmody	Evanston, IL	Purple/White
Northwestern St.	Demons	Southland	Mike McConathy	Natchitoches, LA	Purple/Orange/Wt.
Notre Dame	Fighting Irish	Big East	Mike Brey	Notre Dame, IN	Gold/Blue
Oakland-MI	Golden Grizzlies	Summit	Greg Kampe	Rochester, MI	Black/Gold
Ohio University	Bobcats	Mid-American	Tim O'Shea	Athens, OH	Hunter Green/White
Ohio St.	Buckeyes	Big Ten	Thad Matta	Columbus, OH	Scarlet/Gray
Oklahoma	Sooners	Big 12	Jeff Capel	Norman, OK	Crimson/Cream
Oklahoma St.	Cowboys	Big 12	Sean Sutton	Stillwater, OK	Orange/Black
Old Dominion	Monarchs	Colonial	Blaine Taylor	Norfolk, VA	Slate Blue/Silver
Oral Roberts	Golden Eagles	Summit	Scott Sutton	Tulsa, OK	Navy Blue/White
Oregon	Ducks	Pac-10	Ernie Kent	Eugene, OR	Green/Yellow
Oregon St.	Beavers	Pac-10	Jay John	Corvallis, OR	Orange/Black
Pacific	Tigers	Big West	Bob Thomason	Stockton, CA	Orange/Black
Pennsylvania	Quakers	Ivy	Glen Miller	Philadelphia, PA	Red/Blue
Penn St.	Nittany Lions	Big Ten	Ed DeChellis	University Park, PA	Blue/White
Pepperdine	Waves	West Coast	Vance Walberg	Malibu, CA	Blue/Orange
Pittsburgh	Panthers	Big East	Jamie Dixon	Pittsburgh, PA	Gold/Blue
Portland	Pilots	West Coast	Eric Reveno	Portland, OR	Purple/White
Portland St.	Vikings	Big Sky	Ken Bone	Portland, OR	Green/White
Prairie View A&M	Panthers	SWAC	Byron Rimm II	Prairie View, TX	Purple/Gold
Presbyterian	Blue Hose	Big South	Gregg Nibert	Clinton, SC	Garnet/Blue
Princeton	Tigers	Ivy	Sydney Johnson	Princeton, NJ	Orange/Black
Providence	Friars	Big East	Tim Welsh	Providence, RI	Black/White
Purdue	Boilermakers	Big Ten	Matt Painter	W. Lafayette, IN	Old Gold/Black
Quinnipiac	Bobcats	Northeast	Tom Moore	Hamden, CT	Navy/Gold
Radford	Highlanders	Big South	Brad Greenberg	Radford, VA	Blue/Red/Green/Wt.
Rhode Island	Rams	Atlantic 10	Jim Baron	Kingston, RI	Lt. Blue/White/Navy
Rice	Owls	USA	Willis Wilson	Houston, TX	Blue/Gray
Richmond	Spiders	Atlantic 10	Chris Mooney	Richmond, VA	Red/Blue
Rider	Broncs	Metro Atlantic	Tommy Dempsey	Lawrenceville, NJ	Cranberry/White
Robert Morris	Colonials	Northeast	Mike Rice	Moon Township, PA	Blue/Red/White
Rutgers	Scarlet Knights	Big East	Fred Hill Jr.	New Brunswick, NJ	Scarlet
Sacramento St.	Hornets	Big Sky	Jerome Jenkins	Sacramento, CA	Green/Gold
Sacred Heart	Pioneers	Northeast	Dave Bike	Fairfield, CT	Scarlet/White
St. Bonaventure	Bonnies	Atlantic 10	Mark Schmidt	St. Bonaventure, NY	Brown/White
St. Francis-NY	Terriers	Northeast	Brian Nash	Brooklyn, NY	Red/Blue
St. Francis-PA	Red Flash	Northeast	Bobby Jones	Loretto, PA	Red/White
St. John's	Red Storm	Big East	Norm Roberts	Jamaica, NY	Red/White
Saint Joseph's	Hawks	Atlantic 10	Phil Martelli	Philadelphia, PA	Crimson/Gray
Saint Louis	Billikens	Atlantic 10	Rick Majerus	St. Louis, MO	Blue/White
Saint Mary's-CA	Gaels	West Coast	Randy Bennett	Moraga, CA	Red/Blue
Saint Peter's	Peacocks	Metro Atlantic	John Dunne	Jersey City, NJ	Blue/White
Sam Houston St.	Bearkats	Southland	Bob Marlin	Huntsville, TX	Orange/White
Samford	Bulldogs	Ohio Valley	Jimmy Tillette	Birmingham, AL	Red/Blue
San Diego	Toreros	West Coast	Bill Grier	San Diego, CA	Lt. Blue/Navy
San Diego St.	Aztecs	Mountain West	Steve Fisher	San Diego, CA	Scarlet/Black
San Francisco	Dons	West Coast	Jessie Evans	San Francisco, CA	Green/Gold
San Jose St.	Spartans	WAC	George Nessman	San Jose, CA	Gold/White/Blue
Santa Clara	Broncos	West Coast	Kerry Keating	Santa Clara, CA	Bronco Red/White
Savannah St.	Tigers	Independent	Horace Broadnax	Savannah, GA	Orange/Blue
Seton Hall	Pirates	Big East	Bobby Gonzalez	South Orange, NJ	Blue/White
Siena	Saints	Metro Atlantic	Fran McCaffery	Loudonville, NY	Green/Gold
South Alabama	Jaguars	Sun Belt	Ronnie Arrow	Mobile, AL	Red/White/Blue
South Carolina	Gamecocks	SEC-East	Dave Odom	Columbia, SC	Garnet/Black
South Carolina St.	Bulldogs	Mid-Eastern	Tim Carter	Orangeburg, SC	Garnet/Blue
South Carolina Upstate	Spartans	Atlantic Sun	Eddie Payne	Spartanburg, SC	Green/White/Black
South Dakota St.	Jackrabbits	Summit	Scott Nagy	Brookings, SD	Yellow/Blue
South Florida	Bulls	Big East	Stan Heath	Tampa, FL	Green/Gold
SE Missouri St.	Redhawks	Ohio Valley	Scott Edgar	Cape Girardeau, MO	Red/Black
Southeastern Louisiana	Lions	Southland	Jim Yarbrough Jr.	Hammond, LA	Green/Gold
Southern-BR	Jaguars	SWAC	Rob Spivery	Baton Rouge, LA	Blue/Gold

	Nickname	Conference	Head Coach	Location	Colors
Southern Illinois	Salukis	Mo. Valley	Chris Lowery	Carbondale, IL	Maroon/White
SMU	Mustangs	USA	Matt Doherty	Dallas, TX	Red/Blue
Southern Miss	Golden Eagles	USA	Larry Eustachy	Hattiesburg, MS	Black/Gold
Southern Utah	Thunderbirds	Summit	Roger Reid	Cedar City, UT	Scarlet/White
Stanford	Cardinal	Pac-10	Trent Johnson	Stanford, CA	Cardinal/White
S.F. Austin St.	Lumberjacks	Southland	Danny Kaspar	Nacogdoches, TX	Purple/White
Stetson	Hatters	Atlantic Sun	Derek Waugh	DeLand, FL	Green/White
Stony Brook	Seawolves	America East	Steve Pikiell	Stony Brook, NY	Scarlet/Gray
Syracuse	Orange	Big East	Jim Boeheim	Syracuse, NY	Orange
Temple	Owls	Atlantic 10	Fran Dunphy	Philadelphia, PA	Cherry/White
Tennessee	Volunteers	SEC-East	Bruce Pearl	Knoxville, TN	Orange/White
Tenn-Martin	Skyhawks	Ohio Valley	Bret Campbell	Martin, TN	Orange/Wt./Blue
Tennessee St.	Tigers	Ohio Valley	Cy Alexander	Nashville, TN	Blue/White
Tennessee Tech	Golden Eagles	Ohio Valley	Mike Sutton	Cookeville, TN	Purple/Gold
Texas	Longhorns	Big 12	Rick Barnes	Austin, TX	Burnt Orange/White
Texas A&M	Aggies	Big 12	Mark Turgeon	College Station, TX	Maroon/White
TX A&M Corpus-Christi	Islanders	Southland	Perry Clark	Corpus Christi, TX	Blue/Green/Silver
TCU	Horned Frogs	Mountain West	Neil Dougherty	Ft. Worth, TX	Purple/White
Texas Southern	Tigers	SWAC	Ronnie Courtney	Houston, TX	Maroon/Gray
Texas St.	Bobcats	Southland	Doug Davalos	San Marcos, TX	Maroon/Gold
Texas Tech	Red Raiders	Big 12	Bob Knight	Lubbock, TX	Scarlet/Black
TX-Arlington	Mavericks	Southland	Scott Cross	Arlington, TX	Royal Blue/White
TX-Pan American	Broncs	Independent	Tom Schuberth	Edinburg, TX	Green/White
TX-San Antonio	Roadrunners	Southland	Brooks Thompson	San Antonio, TX	Orange/Navy/White
Toledo	Rockets	Mid-American	Stan Joplin	Toledo, OH	Blue/Gold
Towson	Tigers	Colonial	Pat Kennedy	Towson, MD	Gold/White/Black
Troy	Trojans	Sun Belt	Don Maestri	Troy, AL	Cardinal/Silver/Black
Tulane	Green Wave	USA	Dave Dickerson	New Orleans, LA	Olive Grn./Sky Blue
Tulsa	Golden Hurricane	USA	Doug Wojcik	Tulsa, OK	Blue/Gold/Crimson
UAB	Blazers	USA	Mike Davis	Birmingham, AL	Green/Gold
UC-Irvine	Anteaters	Big West	Pat Douglass	Irvine, CA	Blue/Gold
UCLA	Bruins	Pac-10	Ben Howland	Los Angeles, CA	Blue/Gold
UC-Davis	Aggies	Big West	Gary Stewart	Davis, CA	Yale Blue/Gold
UC-Riverside	Highlanders	Big West	Jim Wooldridge	Riverside, CA	Blue/Gold
UC-Santa Barbara	Gauchos	Big West	Bob Williams	Santa Barbara, CA	Blue/Gold
UNLV	Runnin' Rebels	Mountain West	Lon Kruger	Las Vegas, NV	Scarlet/Gray
USC	Trojans	Pac-10	Tim Floyd	Los Angeles, CA	Cardinal/Gold
Utah	Utes, Runnin' Utes	Mountain West	Jim Boylen	Salt Lake City, UT	Crimson/White
Utah St.	Aggies	WAC	Stew Morrill	Logan, UT	Navy Blue/White
Utah Valley St.	Wolverines	Independent	Dick Hunsaker	Orem, UT	Green/Gold/White
UTEP	Miners	USA	Tony Barbee	El Paso, TX	Orange/Blue/Silver
Valparaiso	Crusaders	Horizon	Homer Drew	Valparaiso, IN	Brown/Gold
Vanderbilt	Commodores	SEC-East	Kevin Stallings	Nashville, TN	Black/Gold
Vermont	Catamounts	America East	Mike Lonergan	Burlington, VT	Green/Gold
Villanova	Wildcats	Big East	Jay Wright	Villanova, PA	Blue/White
Virginia	Cavaliers	ACC	Dave Leitao	Charlottesville, VA	Orange/Blue
VCU	Rams	Colonial	Anthony Grant	Richmond, VA	Black/Gold
VMI	Keydets	Big South	Duggar Baucom	Lexington, VA	Red/White/Yellow
Virginia Tech	Hokies, Gobblers	ACC	Seth Greenberg	Blacksburg, VA	Orange/Maroon
Wagner	Seahawks	Northeast	Mike Deane	Staten Island, NY	Green/White
Wake Forest	Demon Deacons	ACC	Dino Gaudio	Winston-Salem, NC	Old Gold/Black
Washington	Huskies	Pac-10	Lorenzo Romar	Seattle, WA	Purple/Gold
Washington St.	Cougars	Pac-10	Tony Bennett	Pullman, WA	Crimson/Gray
Weber St.	Wildcats	Big Sky	Randy Rahe	Ogden, UT	Purple/White
West Virginia	Mountaineers	Big East	Bob Huggins	Morgantown, WV	Old Gold/Blue
Western Carolina	Catamounts	Southern	Larry Hunter	Cullowhee, NC	Purple/Gold
Western Illinois	Leathernecks	Summit	Derek Thomas	Macomb, IL	Purple/Gold
Western Kentucky	Hilltoppers	Sun Belt	Darrin Horn	Bowling Green, KY	Red/White
Western Michigan	Broncos	Mid-American	Steve Hawkins	Kalamazoo, MI	Brown/Gold
Wichita St.	Shockers	Mo. Valley	Gregg Marshall	Wichita, KS	Yellow/Black
William & Mary	Tribe	Colonial	Tony Shaver	Williamsburg, VA	Green/Gold/Silver
Winston-Salem St.	Rams	Mid-Eastern	Bobby Collins	Winston-Salem, NC	Red/White
Winthrop	Eagles	Big South	Randy Peele	Rock Hill, SC	Garnet/Gold
Wisconsin	Badgers	Big Ten	Bo Ryan	Madison, WI	Cardinal/White
WI-Green Bay	Phoenix	Horizon	Tod Kowalczyk	Green Bay, WI	Green/White/Red
WI-Milwaukee	Panthers	Horizon	Rob Jeter	Milwaukee, WI	Black/Gold
Wofford	Terriers	Southern	Mike Young	Spartanburg, SC	Old Gold/Black
Wright St.	Raiders	Horizon	Brad Brownell	Dayton, OH	Green/Gold
Wyoming	Cowboys	Mountain West	Heath Schroyer	Laramie, WY	Brown/Gold
Xavier	Musketeers	Atlantic 10	Sean Miller	Cincinnati, OH	Blue/Gray/White
Yale	Bulldogs, Elis	Ivy	James Jones	New Haven, CT	Yale Blue/White
Youngstown St.	Penguins	Horizon	Jerry Slocum	Youngstown, OH	Red/White

Scouts Inc. Evaluations

Listed are the top recruiting prospects for the 2008 high school graduating class for boys basketball, and the 2007 and 2008 graduating classes for football, as graded by the members of ESPN's Scouts Inc.

The analysts and talent evaluators at Scouts Inc. watch games, break down film and use their extensive experience and contacts in their respective sports to provide the deepest and most detailed scouting reports available.

For expanded lists and in-depth information on each recruit, as well as expert analysis on professional basketball, football, baseball and more, go to the "Scouts" tab on ESPN.com.

Basketball Top 30 — High School Class of 2008

List is as of Sept. 30, 2007 and subject to change. *NCAA schools listed have been given only a verbal commitment at press time.

	Name	Hometown	Position	HT	WT	Rank	Grade	NCAA School*
1	Brandon Jennings	Mouth of Wilson, VA	PG	6-2	165	PG#1	92	Arizona
2	Tyreke Evans	Aston, PA	SG	6-5	195	SG#1	92	undeclared
3	Samardo Samuels	Newark, NJ	C	6-8	235	C#1	92	Louisville
4	Jrue Holiday	North Hollywood, CA	SG	6-3	180	SG#2	92	UCLA
5	Delvon Roe	Lakewood, OH	PF	6-8	220	PF#1	92	Michigan St.
6	Scotty Hopson	Hopkinsville, KY	SF	6-5	185	SF#1	92	Mississippi
7	Greg Monroe	Gretna, LA	PF	6-10	226	PF#2	92	undeclared
8	William Buford	Toledo, OH	SG	6-5	188	SG#3	91	Ohio St.
9	Demar Derozan	Compton, CA	SF	6-6	200	SF#2	91	USC
10	Tyler Zeller	Washington, IN	PF	6-11	215	PF#3	91	undeclared
11	Kemba Walker	Bronx, NY	PG	6-2	175	PG#2	91	Connecticut
12	B.J. Mullens	Canal Winchester, OH	C	7-0	260	C#2	91	Ohio St.
13	Emmanuel Negedu	Wolfeboro, NH	PF	6-7	230	PF#4	91	Arizona
14	JaMychal Green	Montgomery, AL	PF	6-8	225	PF#5	91	Alabama
15	Al-Faroug Aminu	Norcross, GA	SF	6-9	215	SF#3	91	Wake Forest
16	Elliott Williams	Memphis, TN	SG	6-4	180	SG#4	91	undeclared
17	Willie Warren	Mouth of Wilson, VA	SG	6-4	195	SG#5	91	undeclared
18	Luke Babitt	Reno, NV	PF	6-7	220	PF#6	91	Nevada
19	DeAndre Liggins	Henderson, NV	SF	6-6	200	SF#4	91	Kentucky
20	Devin Ebanks	Oakdale, CT	SF	6-8	185	SF#5	91	Indiana
21	Ed Davis	Richmond, VA	PF	6-8	215	PF#7	91	North Carolina
22	Malcolm Lee	Riverside, CA	PG	6-4	170	PG#3	91	UCLA
23	Howard Thompkins	Norcross, GA	PF	6-9	230	PF#8	91	Georgia
24	Iman Shumpert	Oak Park, IL	SG	6-4	185	SG#6	91	undeclared
25	Mike Rosario	Jersey City, NJ	SG	6-3	180	SG#7	91	Rutgers
26	Yancy Gates	Cincinnati, OH	PF	6-9	245	PF#9	90	Cincinnati
27	Kenneth Kadji	Bradenton, FL	C	6-10	240	C#3	90	Florida
28	Eloy Vargas	Ft. Lauderdale, FL	PF	6-10	215	PF#10	90	Florida
29	Chris Singleton	Canton, GA	PF	6-8	210	PF#11	90	undeclared
30	Romero Osby	Meridian, MS	PF	6-7	200	PF#12	90	Mississippi St.

Top 25 NCAA Football Recruiting Classes of 2007

Listed are the NCAA programs with the best recruiting classes from the pool of 2007 high school seniors, along with respective letter grades. These grades and rankings are purely subjective and were assigned by Tom Luginbill, the national director of recruiting for Scouts Inc.

	School		School		School		School
1	Florida	8	Auburn	15	Clemson	22	Nebraska
2	USC	9	Georgia	16	Miami-FL	23	Iowa
3	Texas	10	Illinois	17	Pittsburgh	24	Oregon
4	South Carolina	11	Georgia Tech	18	Alabama	25	Mississippi
5	Notre Dame	12	Michigan	19	Ohio State		
6	Tennessee	13	Virginia Tech	20	Penn State		
7	LSU	14	Texas A&M	21	North Carolina		

Football Top 30 — High School Class of 2007

	Name	Hometown	Position	HT	WT	Rank	Grade	NCAA School
1	Joe McKnight	River Ridge, LA	RB	6-0	190	RB#1	92	USC
2	Chris Galippo	Anaheim, CA	ILB	6-2	240	ILB#1	90	USC
3	Marc Tyler	Westlake Village, CA	RB	6-1	210	RB#2	90	USC
4	Eric Berry	Fairburn, GA	CB	5-11	195	CB#1	90	Tennessee
5	Martez Wilson	Chicago, IL	DE	6-4	230	DE#1	87	Illinois
6	Noel Devine	North Fort Myers, FL	RB	5-8	180	RB#3	87	West Virginia
7	Terrance Toliver	Hempstead, TX	WR	6-4	190	WR#1	86	LSU
8	J.B. Walton	Indian Head, MD	OG	6-3	275	OG#1	86	Penn State
9	Jimmy Clausen	Westlake Village, CA	QB	6-3	218	QB#1	86	Notre Dame
10	Michael McNeil	Mobile, AL	S	6-2	200	S#1	86	Auburn
11	Marvin Austin	Washington, DC	DT	6-2	290	DT#1	85	North Carolina
12	Golden Tate	Hendersonville, TN	WR	5-11	180	WR#2	85	Notre Dame
13	Ryan Mallett	Texarkana, TX	QB	6-6	230	QB#2	85	Michigan
14	Gary Gray	Columbia, SC	CB	5-11	170	CB#2	85	Notre Dame
15	Brian Maddox	Anderson, SC	RB	6-2	215	RB#4	85	South Carolina
16	Carlos Dunlap	North Charleston, SC	DE	6-6	250	DE#2	84	Florida
17	LeSean McCoy	Harrisburg, PA	RB	5-11	200	RB#5	84	Pittsburgh
19	Tyrod Taylor	Hampton, VA	QB	6-1	185	QB#3	84	Virginia Tech
20	Arrelious Benn	Washington, DC	WR	6-1	210	WR#3	84	Illinois
21	Marshall Jones	Westlake Village, CA	S	6-0	190	S#2	84	USC
22	Junior Hemingway	Conway, SC	WR	6-3	205	WR#4	84	Michigan
23	Allen Bailey	Darien, GA	DE	6-3	252	DE#3	84	Miami-FL
24	Tray Allen	Grand Prairie, TX	OT	6-4	300	OT#1	84	Texas
25	Greg Little	Durham, NC	WR	6-3	225	WR#5	84	North Carolina
26	Antwain Easterling	Miami, FL	RB	5-11	195	RB#6	84	Southern Miss
27	Christian Scott	Dallas, TX	S	6-0	188	S#3	84	Texas
28	John Brantley	Ocala, FL	QB	6-3	205	QB#4	84	Florida
29	Kerry Neal	Bunn, NC	DE	6-3	232	DE#4	84	Notre Dame
30	Israel Troupe	Tifton, GA	WR	6-1	215	WR#6	83	Georgia

Football Top 30 — High School Class of 2008

List is as of Sept. 30, 2007 and subject to change. *Note that 2008 National Signing Day is in February, so the NCAA schools listed have been given only a verbal commitment at press time.

	Name	Hometown	Position	HT	WT	Rank	Grade	NCAA School*
1	Julio Jones	Foley, AL	WR	6-4	215	WR#1	95	undeclared
2	Will Hill	West Orange, NJ	ATH	6-3	203	ATH#1	93	Florida
3	Terrelle Pryor	Jeannette, PA	ATH	6-6	220	ATH#2	93	undeclared
4	Jermie Calhoun	Van, TX	RB	6-0	210	RB#1	92	Oklahoma
5	A.J. Green	Ridgeville, SC	WR	6-4	184	WR#2	91	Georgia
6	Arthur Brown	Wichita, KS	ILB	6-1	210	ILB#1	90	undeclared
7	Darrell Scott	Moorpark, CA	RB	6-0	204	RB#2	89	undeclared
8	Patrick Johnson	Pembroke Pines, FL	CB	6-1	193	CB#1	89	Miami-FL
9	DaQuan Bowers	Bamberg, SC	DT	6-4	265	DT#1	88	Clemson
10	Blaine Gabbert	Ballwin, MO	QB	6-4	226	QB#1	88	Nebraska
11	Dee Finley	Auburn, AL	S	6-3	210	S#1	88	Florida
12	E.J. Manuel	Virginia Beach, VA	QB	6-4	201	QB#2	87	Florida St.
13	R.J. Washington	Keller, TX	DE	6-3	245	DE#1	87	Oklahoma
14	Dayne Crist	Canoga Park, CA	QB	6-5	228	QB#3	86	Notre Dame
15	Jamie Harper	Jacksonville, FL	RB	6-0	210	RB#3	86	undeclared
16	Brice Butler	Norcross, GA	WR	6-2	178	WR#3	86	USC
17	Chancey Aghayere	Garland, TX	DE	6-4	244	DE#2	85	undeclared
18	Deion Walker	Christchurch, VA	WR	6-4	185	WR#4	85	undeclared
19	Etienne Sabino	Miami, FL	ILB	6-3	228	ILB#2	85	undeclared
20	T.J. Bryant	Tallahassee, FL	CB	6-0	175	CB#2	84	undeclared
21	Burton Scott	Prichard, AL	ATH	5-11	194	ATH#3	84	Alabama
22	Tyler Love	Birmingham, AL	OT	6-7	280	OT#1	84	Alabama
23	Brandon Barnes	Bunn, NC	ATH	6-0	185	ATH#4	84	N.C. State
24	Joe Adams	Little Rock, AR	ATH	6-0	167	ATH#5	84	USC
25	Dan Buckner	Allen, TX	WR	6-4	209	WR#5	84	Texas
26	Jonathan Baldwin	Aliquippa, PA	TE	6-6	220	TE#1	83	undeclared
27	Ryan Williams	Manassas, VA	RB	5-10	192	RB#4	83	undeclared
28	Marcus Forston	Miami, FL	DT	6-2	286	DT#2	83	Miami-FL
29	Michael Brewster	Orlando, FL	OT	6-6	290	OT#2	83	Ohio St.
30	Brandon Harris	Miami, FL	CB	5-10	174	CB#3	83	undeclared

NCAA Coaching Changes

New head coaches were named at 24 Bowl Subdivision (formerly I-A) and 20 Championship Subdivision (formerly I-AA) football schools, while 60 Division 1 basketball schools changed head coaches during or after the 2006-07 season. Coaching changes listed below are as of September 30, 2007.

Football — Bowl Subdivision

	Old Coach	Record	Why Left?	New Coach	Old Job
Air Force	Fisher DeBerry	4-8	Retired	Troy Calhoun	Off. Coord., NFL Houston
Alabama	Mike Shula	6-7 †	Fired	Nick Saban	Coach, NFL Miami
Arizona St.	Dirk Koetter	7-6	Fired	Dennis Erickson	Coach, Idaho
Army	Bobby Ross	3-9	Retired	Stan Brock	Asst. Coach, Army
Boston College	Tom O'Brien	10-3 #	to N.C. State*	Jeff Jagodzinski	Off. Coord., NFL Green Bay
Central Michigan	Brian Kelly	10-4 $	to Cincinnati*	Butch Jones	Asst., West Virginia
Cincinnati	Mark Dantonio	8-5 +	to Michigan St.*	Brian Kelly	Coach, Central Michigan
Florida Int'l	Don Strock	0-12	Resigned	Mario Cristobal	Asst., Miami-FL
Idaho	Dennis Erickson	4-8	to Arizona St.*	Robb Akey	Def. Coord., Washington St.
Indiana	Terry Hoeppner	5-7	deceased@	Bill Lynch	Off. Coord., Indiana
Iowa St.	Dan McCarney	4-8	Resigned	Gene Chizik	Co-Def. Coord., Texas
Louisiana Tech	Jack Bicknell	3-10	Fired	Derek Dooley	Asst., NFL Miami
Louisville	Bobby Petrino	12-1	to NFL Atlanta*	Steve Kragthorpe	Coach, Tulsa
Miami-FL	Larry Coker	7-6	Fired	Randy Shannon	Def. Coord., Miami-FL
Michigan St.	John L. Smith	4-8	Fired	Mark Dantonio	Coach, Cincinnati
Minnesota	Glen Mason	6-7	Fired	Tim Brewster	Asst., NFL Denver
North Carolina	John Bunting	3-9	Fired	Butch Davis	Fmr. Coach, NFL Cleveland
North Carolina St.	Chuck Amato	3-9	Fired	Tom O'Brien	Coach, Boston College
North Texas	Darrell Dickey	3-9	Fired	Todd Dodge	Coach, Carroll Sr. HS (Tex.)
Rice	Todd Graham	7-6	to Tulsa*	David Bailiff	Coach, Texas St.
Stanford	Walt Harris	1-11	Fired	Jim Harbaugh	Coach, San Diego
Tulane	Chris Scelfo	4-8	Fired	Bob Toledo	Off. Coord., New Mexico
Tulsa	Steve Kragthorpe	8-5	to Louisville*	Todd Graham	Coach, Rice
UAB	Watson Brown	3-9	to Tennessee Tech*	Neil Callaway	Off. Coord., Georgia

* as head coach   ** as assistant coach

† Shula (6-6) was fired on Nov. 28 and replaced for the Independence Bowl by defensive coordinator Joe Kines (0-1).

O'Brien (9-3) accepted the N.C. State job on Dec. 8. Defensive coordinator Frank Spaziani (1-0) coached the team in the Meineke Car Care Bowl.

$ Kelly (9-4) accepted the Cincinnati job on Dec. 3. Assistant coach Jeff Quinn (1-0) coached the team in the Motor City Bowl.

+ Dantonio (7-5) accepted the Michigan St. job on Nov. 27. New coach Brian Kelly (1-0) coached the team in the International Bowl.

@ Hoeppner died of complications from a brain tumor on June 19 at the age of 59.

Football — Championship Subdivision

	Old Coach	Record	Why Left?	New Coach	Old Job
Alabama St.	Charles Coe	5-6	to NFL Oakland**	Reggie Barlow	Asst., Alabama St.
Austin Peay St.	Carroll McCray	3-8	to Furman**	Rick Christophel	Asst., UAB
Drake	Rob Ash	9-2	to Montana St.*	Steve Loney	Asst., NFL Arizona
Georgia Southern	Brian VanGorder	3-8	to NFL Atlanta**	Chris Hatcher	Coach, Valdosta St.
Grambling	Melvin Spears	3-8	Fired	Rod Broadway	Coach, N.C. Central
Howard	Rayford Petty	5-6	Fired	Carey Bailey	Asst., Minnesota
Idaho St.	Larry Lewis	2-9	Fired	John Zamberlin	Coach, Central Wash.
Jacksonville	Steve Gilbert	4-6	Fired	Kerwin Bell	Coach, Trinity Cath. HS (Fla)
McNeese St.	Tommy Tate	7-5 †	Resigned	Matt Viator	Off. Coord., McNeese St.
Montana St.	Mike Kramer	8-5	Fired	Rob Ash	Coach, Drake
Old Dominion	none	@	—	Bobby Wilder	Asst., Maine
Portland St.	Tim Walsh	7-4	to Army**	Jerry Glanville	Def. Coord., Hawaii
Presbyterian	Tommy Spangler	7-4	to Louisiana Tech**	Bobby Bentley	Coach, Byrnes HS (S.C.)
Sacramento St.	Steve Mooshagian	4-7	Fired	Marshall Sperbeck	Coach, Foothill College
Samford	Bill Gray	3-8	Fired	Pat Sullivan	Asst., UAB
San Diego	Jim Harbaugh	11-1	to Stanford*	Ron Caragher	Asst., Kentucky
Southeastern La.	Dennis Roland	2-9 #	Health reasons	Mike Lucas	Def. Coord., SLU
Stephen F. Austin	Robert McFarland	4-7	to Iowa St.**	J.C. Harper	Def. Coord., S. F. Austin
Tennessee Tech	Mike Hennigan	4-7 +	Health reasons	Watson Brown	Coach, UAB
Texas St.	David Bailiff	5-6	to Rice*	Brad Wright	Asst., Texas St.

* as head coach   ** as assistant coach

† Tate (1-3) resigned on Oct. 4 and was replaced by offensive coordinator Matt Viator (6-2), initially on an interim basis, then on a permanent basis on Nov. 13.

Roland (2-6) took a medical leave of absence on Oct. 24 and was replaced by defensive coordinator Mike Lucas (0-3), initially on an interim basis, then on a permanent basis on Dec. 14.

+ Hennigan resigned before the season and was replaced on an interim basis by Doug Malone.

@ Old Dominion is resurrecting its football program in 2009.

Division I Basketball

	Old Coach	Record	Why Left?	New Coach	Old Job
Air Force	Jeff Bzdelik	26-9	to Colorado*	Jeff Reynolds	Asst., Air Force
Arkansas	Stan Heath	21-14	Fired	John Pelphrey	Coach, South Alabama
Ball State	Ronny Thompson	9-22	Resigned	Billy Taylor	Coach, Lehigh
Binghamton	Al Walker	13-16	Fired	Kevin Broadus	Asst., Georgetown
Bowling Green	Dan Dakich	13-18	Resigned	Louis Orr	Fmr. Coach, Seton Hall
Butler	Todd Lickliter	29-7	to Iowa*	Brad Stevens	Asst., Butler
Chicago St.	Kevin Jones	9-20	Fired	Benjy Taylor	Asst., Tulane
Coastal Carolina	Buzz Peterson	15-15	to NBA Charlotte†	Cliff Ellis	Fmr. Coach, Auburn
Colorado	Ricardo Patton	7-20	Resigned	Jeff Bzdelik	Coach, Air Force
Colorado St.	Dale Layer	17-13	Fired	Tim Miles	Coach, North Dakota St.
Denver	Terry Carroll	4-25	Fired	Joe Scott	Coach, Princeton
Drake	Tom Davis	17-15	Retired	Keno Davis	Asst., Drake
East Carolina	Ricky Stokes	6-24	Reassigned	Mack McCarthy	Asst., East Carolina
Eastern Wash.	Mike Burns	15-14	Fired	Kirk Earlywine	Asst., NC-Wilmington
Evansville	Steve Merfeld	14-17	Resigned	Marty Simmons	Coach, SIU-Edwardsville
Florida A&M	Mike Gillespie	21-14	Fired	Eugene Harris	Asst., Georgia St.
Georgia St.	Michael Perry	11-20	Fired	Rod Barnes	Asst., Oklahoma
Harvard	Frank Sullivan	12-16	Fired	Tommy Amaker	Coach, Michigan
Hawaii	Riley Wallace	18-13	Retired	Bob Nash	Asst., Hawaii
Illinois St.	Porter Moser	15-16	Fired	Tim Jankovich	Asst., Kansas
Indiana St.	Royce Waltman	13-18	Fired	Kevin McKenna	Asst., Creighton
Iona	Jeff Ruland	2-28	Fired	Kevin Willard	Asst., Louisville
Iowa	Steve Alford	17-14	to New Mexico*	Todd Lickliter	Coach, Butler
Kansas St.	Bob Huggins	23-12	to West Virginia	Frank Martin	Asst., Kansas St.
Kentucky	Tubby Smith	22-12	to Minnesota*	Billy Gillispie	Coach, Texas A&M
Lehigh	Billy Taylor	12-19	to Ball St.*	Brett Reed	Asst., Lehigh
Liberty	Randy Dunton	14-17	Fired	Ritchie McKay	Coach, New Mexico
Long Beach St.	Larry Reynolds	24-8	Fired	Dan Monson	Coach, Minnesota
Louisiana Tech	Keith Richard	10-20	Fired	Kerry Rupp	Asst., UAB
Marshall	Ron Jirsa	13-19	Fired	Donnie Jones	Asst., Florida
MD-Eastern Shore	Larry Lessett	4-27	Resigned	Meredith Smith	Asst., Md-Eastern Shore
Michigan	Tommy Amaker	22-13	Fired	John Beilein	Coach, West Virginia
Minnesota	Dan Monson	9-22@	Resigned	Tubby Smith	Coach, Kentucky
Missouri-KC	Rich Zvosec	12-20	Fired	Matt Brown	Asst., West Virginia
New Mexico	Ritchie McKay	15-17	Fired	Steve Alford	Coach, Iowa
New Mexico St.	Reggie Theus	25-9	to NBA Sacramento*	Marvin Menzies	Asst., Louisville
New Orleans	Buzz Williams	14-17	to Marquette**	Joe Pasternack	Asst., California
Norfolk St.	Dwight Freeman	11-19	Reassigned	Anthony Evans	Asst., Norfolk St.
North Dakota St.	Tim Miles	20-8	to Colorado St.*	Saul Phillips	Asst., North Dakota St.
Northern Illinois	Rob Judson	7-23	Fired	Ricardo Patton	Coach, Colorado
Princeton	Joe Scott	11-17	to Denver*	Sydney Johnson	Asst., Georgetown
Quinnipiac	Joe DeSantis	14-15	Fired	Tom Moore	Asst., Connecticut
Radford	Byron Samuels	8-22	Resigned	Brad Greenberg	Asst., Virginia Tech
Robert Morris	Mark Schmidt	17-11	to St. Bonaventure*	Mike Rice	Asst., Pittsburgh
Saint Louis	Brad Soderberg	20-13	Fired	Rick Majerus	ESPN analyst
San Diego	Brad Holland	18-14	Fired	Bill Grier	Asst., Gonzaga
Santa Clara	Dick Davey	21-10	Retired	Kerry Keating	Asst., UCLA
South Alabama	John Pelphrey	20-12	to Arkansas*	Ronnie Arrow	Coach, Texas A&M C.C.
South Carolina St.	Jamal Brown	13-17	Fired	Tim Carter	Asst., Florida St.
South Florida	Robert McCullom	12-18	Fired	Stan Heath	Coach, Arkansas
Southern Utah	Bill Evans	16-14	Fired	Roger Reid	Coach, Snow College
St. Bonaventure	Anthony Solomon	7-22	Fired	Mark Schmidt	Coach, Robert Morris
Texas A&M	Billy Gillispie	27-7	to Kentucky*	Mark Turgeon	Coach, Wichita St.
Texas A&M C.C.	Ronnie Arrow	26-8	to South Alabama*	Perry Clark	TV analyst
UC-Riverside	David Spencer	7-24#	Resigned	Jim Wooldridge	Fmr. coach, Kansas St.
Utah	Ray Giacoletti	11-19	Resigned	Jim Boylen	Asst., Michigan St.
Wake Forest	Skip Prosser	15-16	Deceased+	Dino Gaudio	Asst., Wake Forest
West Virginia	John Beilein	27-9	to Michigan*	Bob Huggins	Coach, Kansas St.
Wichita St.	Mark Turgeon	17-14	to Texas A&M*	Gregg Marshall	Coach, Winthrop
Winthrop	Gregg Marshall	29-5	to Wichita St.*	Randy Peele	Asst., Winthrop
Wyoming	Steve McClain	17-15	Fired	Heath Schroyer	Asst., Fresno St.

* as head coach   ** as assistant coach   † as director of player personnel

@ Monson (2-5) resigned on Nov. 30 and was replaced by asst. coach Jim Molinari (7-17) on an interim basis.

\# Spencer took a medical leave of absence on Nov. 3 (before the start of the season) and was replaced by asst. coach Vonn Webb. Spencer officially resigned after the season on March 13.

\+ Prosser died of an apparent heart attack on July 26 at the age of 56.

2006-07 Directors' Cup

Sponsored by the United States Sports Academy (USSA). Developed as a joint effort between the National Association of Collegiate Directors of Athletics (NACDA) and USA Today. Introduced in 1993-94 to honor the nation's best overall NCAA Division I athletic department (combining men's and women's sports). Winners in NCAA Division II and III and NAIA were named for the first time following the 1995-96 season.

Standings are computed by NACDA with points awarded for each Div. I school's finish in 20 sports (top 10 scoring sports for both men and women). Div. II schools are awarded points in 14 sports (top 7 scoring sports for both men and women). Div III schools are awarded points in 18 sports (top 9 scoring sports for both men and women). NAIA schools are awarded points in 12 sports (top 6 scoring sports for both men and women). National champions in each sport earn 100 points, while 2nd through 64th-place finishers earn decreasing points depending on the size of the tournament field. Division I-A football points are based on the final *USA Today* Coaches' Top 25 poll, as well as non-Top 25 bowl participants. Listed below are team conferences (for Div. I only), combined Final Four finishes (1st through 4th place) for men's and women's programs, overall points in **bold** type, and the previous year's ranking (for Div. I only).

Multiple winners: Stanford (13); Williams, MA (11); Simon Fraser, BC and UC-Davis (6); Grand Valley St., MI (4); Azusa Pacific, CA (3); Lindenwood, MO (2).

Division I

		Conf	1-2-3-4	Pts	05-06 Rank			Conf	1-2-3-4	Pts	05-06 Rank
1	Stanford	Pac-10	2-3-2-3	**1429.00**	1	14	Ohio St.	Big Ten	0-2-1-0	**927.50**	12
2	UCLA	Pac-10	1-2-4-1	**1257.00**	2	15	Florida St.	ACC	1-1-1-0	**924.25**	17
3	North Carolina	ACC	1-1-1-0	**1161.33**	4	16	Wisconsin	Big Ten	2-1-0-1	**913.25**	22
4	Michigan	Big Ten	0-0-2-1	**1135.25**	24	17	LSU	SEC	0-3-2-0	**888.00**	20
5	USC	Pac-10	0-1-1-2	**1103.50**	10	18	Texas A&M	Big 12	0-0-0-1	**881.00**	23
6	Florida	SEC	2-0-1-1	**1064.25**	5	19	Auburn	SEC	2-0-1-0	**866.25**	25
7	Tennessee	SEC	0-1-1-1	**1045.75**	14	20	Minnesota	Big Ten	1-0-0-0	**862.75**	16
8	Texas	Big 12	0-0-1-0	**1037.25**	3	21	Penn St.	Big Ten	2-0-1-0	**848.83**	15
9	California	Pac-10	1-0-2-0	**1030.00**	7	22	Notre Dame	Big East	0-1-0-1	**789.50**	6
10	Arizona St.	Pac-10	2-0-0-0	**1005.00**	13	23	Wake Forest	ACC	0-1-0-0	**708.50**	44
11	Duke	ACC	1-1-2-0	**988.25**	8	24	Arizona	Pac-10	1-1-1-0	**703.33**	11
12	Georgia	SEC	2-1-0-1	**971.00**	9	25	Oklahoma	Big 12	0-1-0-0	**702.75**	37
13	Virginia	ACC	0-2-2-0	**945.00**	26						

Division II

		1-2-3-4	Pts			1-2-3-4	Pts
1	Grand Valley St., MI	1-1-2-0	**995.75**	14	West Florida	0-1-2-0	**495.50**
2	UC San Diego	0-1-4-0	**802.00**	15	Western St., CO	0-1-1-0	**491.25**
3	Abilene Christian, TX	2-2-0-1	**761.75**	16	Truman St., MO	0-1-0-0	**472.50**
4	Minnesota St.-Mankato	0-0-1-0	**642.25**	17	Cal State-Chico	0-0-0-1	**470.00**
5	North Dakota	0-1-1-0	**635.00**	18	Indianapolis	0-0-0-0	**464.50**
6	Central Missouri	0-0-1-0	**628.75**	19	Tampa, FL	2-0-1-0	**459.00**
7	Nebraska-Omaha	0-0-1-0	**624.50**	20	Lock Haven, PA	0-1-1-0	**457.00**
8	Adams St., CO	1-1-0-1	**589.00**	21	Cal State-Los Angeles	0-0-1-1	**453.00**
9	Drury, MO	2-0-0-1	**556.00**	22	Nebraska-Kearney	0-1-0-0	**452.75**
10	Florida Southern	1-0-1-1	**554.00**	23	UMass-Lowell	0-0-1-0	**439.25**
11	Southern Ill. Edwardsville	1-0-0-0	**546.50**	24	North Carolina Central	0-0-1-0	**430.50**
12	West Chester, PA	0-1-1-1	**504.50**	25	Wayne St., MI	0-0-1-0	**430.00**
13	Ashland, OH	0-0-0-1	**504.00**				

Division III

		1-2-3-4	Pts			1-2-3-4	Pts
1	Williams, MA	2-0-1-1	**1137.50**	14	New York	0-1-2-0	**578.00**
2	Middlebury, VT	1-2-2-0	**1064.50**	15	DePauw, IN	1-1-0-0	**547.00**
3	Cortland St., NY	0-2-0-2	**892.75**	16	Tufts, MA	0-0-0-0	**545.25**
4	Amherst, MA	1-3-0-2	**887.25**	17	Luther, IA	0-0-0-1	**526.00**
5	Washington, MO	0-3-1-1	**845.00**	18	Wisconsin Eau Claire	0-0-2-0	**525.00**
6	New Jersey	0-1-0-0	**793.00**	19	Keene St., NH	0-0-0-0	**501.50**
7	Wisconsin-La Crosse	1-1-1-1	**718.75**	20	Hope, MI	0-0-0-0	**501.00**
8	Calvin MI	1-1-1-1	**713.00**	21	Ithaca, NY	0-0-0-0	**495.75**
9	Emory, GA	0-2-2-0	**694.50**	22	St. John's, MN	1-0-0-1	**467.00**
10	Johns Hopkins	1-0-0-0	**686.25**	23	Messiah, PA	1-1-1-0	**466.50**
11	Gustavus Adolphus, MN	0-0-2-0	**633.50**	24	Wartburg, IA	0-1-0-0	**454.25**
12	Wisconsin Oshkosh	1-0-1-0	**601.00**	25	UC Santa Cruz	1-0-0-0	**445.50**
13	Wisconsin Stevens Point	0-0-2-0	**598.00**				

NAIA

	1-2-3-4	Pts		1-2-3-4	Pts
1 Azusa Pacific, CA	2-3-2-1	**978.25**	14 Savannah Art & Design, GA	0-0-2-0	**539.00**
2 Lindenwood, MO	1-1-0-1	**796.25**	15 California Baptist	2-0-2-0	**531.50**
3 Concordia, CA	0-2-2-0	**740.00**	16 Lee, TN	0-0-0-0	**523.00**
4 Cedarville, OH	0-2-1-0	**698.50**	17 Point Loma Nazarene, CA	0-1-0-0	**517.75**
5 Oklahoma Baptist	2-1-1-1	**639.50**	18 Concordia, OR	0-0-1-0	**495.00**
6 Lindsey Wilson, KY	1-1-1-0	**630.50**	19 Morningside, IA	0-0-0-0	**492.00**
7 Simon Fraser, BC	1-1-1-2	**614.00**	20 Northwestern, IA	0-0-1-0	**490.00**
8 Dickinson St., ND	0-1-2-0	**579.50**	21 Cumberlands, KY	0-0-0-0	**485.00**
9 MidAmerica Nazarene, KS	1-0-1-0	**573.75**	22 Hastings, NE	0-0-0-0	**479.25**
10 McKendree, IL	0-0-0-1	**570.00**	23 Southern Nazarene, OK	0-0-0-0	**459.50**
11 Olivet Nazarene, IL	0-0-0-0	**565.25**	24 Vanguard, CA	0-0-1-0	**455.50**
12 Oklahoma City	4-0-0-0	**557.00**	25 Indiana Wesleyan	1-0-0-0	**449.50**
13 Embry Riddle, FL	0-0-1-1	**555.50**			

NCAA Division I Schools on Probation

As of Sept. 30, 2007, there were 24 Division I member institutions serving NCAA probations.

School	Sport	Yrs	Penalty To End	School	Sport	Yrs	Penalty To End
Weber St.	Numerous	2	1/18/08	Louisiana-Lafayette	Football	2	4/18/09
Texas St.-San Marcos	Numerous	3	3/9/08		M Basketball	2	4/18/09
Georgia	M Basketball	4	4/16/08	West Virginia	M Soccer	2	5/1/09
Stony Brook	Numerous	3	4/20/08	Nicholls St.	M Basketball	4	5/9/09
St. John's	M Basketball	2	5/10/08		Football	4	5/9/09
Oklahoma	M Basketball	2	5/24/08	Temple	M Tennis	2	5/9/09
	M & W Gymnastics	2	5/24/08	Savannah St.	Football	3	5/18/09
Florida International	Football	3	5/20/08	Colorado	Football	2	6/20/09
South Carolina	Football	3	6/6/08	Alcorn St.	W Basketball	3	6/28/09
Mississippi St.	Football	4	6/11/08	Purdue	W Basketball	2	8/21/09
Iowa	M Swimming	2	11/1/08	Kansas	Football	3	10/11/09
McNeese St.	Football	2	2/7/09		M Basketball	3	10/11/09
	M & W X Country	2	2/7/09	Florida A&M	Numerous	4	1/31/10
	M & W Indoor	2	2/7/09	Fresno St.	M Basketball	4	4/25/10
	M & W Outdoor	2	2/7/09	Oklahoma	Football	2	5/23/10
Ohio St.	M & W Basketball	3	3/9/09	Baylor	M Basketball	5	6/22/10
	Football	3	3/9/09		Football	5	6/22/10

Remaining postseason and TV sanctions

2007-2008 postseason bans: None.
2007-2008 television bans: None.

NCAA Graduation Rates Set All-Time High

The following table compares graduation rates of NCAA Division I student athletes with the entire student body in those schools. **Years** given denote the year in which students entered college. **Rates** are based on students who enrolled as freshmen, received an athletics scholarship and graduated in six years or less. All figures are percentages.

Source: NCAA Graduation Rates Report, 2006.

	1994	**1995**	**1996**	**1997**	**1998**	**1999**
All Student Athletes	58	60	62	62	62	63
Entire Student Body	56	58	59	60	60	61
Male Student Athletes	51	54	55	55	55	56
Male Student Body	54	56	56	57	57	58
Female Student Athletes	69	69	70	70	71	71
Female Student Body	59	61	62	63	63	64
Div. I-A Football Players	51	53	54	57	54	54
Male Basketball Players	40	43	44	44	43	46
Female Basketball Players	65	65	66	64	63	64

2006-07 NCAA Team Champions

The NCAA administers 88 championships in 23 sports (not including Division I-A football). In 2006-07, 76 different schools won titles and 13 won multiple titles (including I-A football champ Florida).

Multiple winners: Two—ABILENE CHRISTIAN (Div. II men's cross country and men's outdoor track); ARIZONA ST. (Div. I women's indoor and outdoor track); AUBURN (Div. I men's and women's swimming & diving); DRURY, MO (Div. II men's and women's swimming & diving); FLORIDA (Div. I-A Football and Div. I men's basketball); GEORGIA (Div. I men's tennis and National div. women's gymnastics); KENYON, OH (Div. III men's and women's swimming & diving); PENN ST. (Nat'l Division combined fencing and men's gymnastics); ST. AUGUSTINE'S, NC (Div. II men's and women's indoor track); STANFORD (Div. I women's cross country and men's golf); TAMPA (Div. II baseball and women's volleyball); WILLIAMS, MA (Div. III women's indoor track and rowing); WISCONSIN (Div. I women's ice hockey and men's indoor track).

Overall titles in parentheses; (*) indicates defending champions.

FALL

Cross Country
Men

Div.	Winner		Runner-Up	Score
I	Colorado	(3)	Wisconsin*	94-142
II	Abilene Christian	(1)	Adams St., CO	65-82
III	Calvin, MI	(4)	NYU	37-92

Women

Div.	Winner		Runner-Up	Score
I	Stanford*	(4)	Colorado	195-223
II	Adams St., CO*	(12)	Western St., CO	94-101
III	Middlebury, VT	(4)	Amherst, MA	144-145

Field Hockey

Div.	Winner		Runner-Up	Score
I	Maryland*	(5)	Wake Forest	1-0
II	Bloomsburg, PA	(13)	Bentley, MA	1-0
III	Ursinus	(1)	Messiah, PA	3-2

Football

Div.	Winner		Runner-Up	Score
I-A	Florida	(2)	Ohio St.	41-14
I-AA	Appalachian St.*	(2)	UMass	28-17
II	Grand Valley St.*	(4)	Northwest Mo. St.	17-14
III	Mount Union, OH*	(9)	Wis.-Whitewater	35-16

Note: There is no official Div. I-A playoff. Florida defeated Ohio St. in the BCS Championship Game.

Soccer
Men

Div.	Winner		Runner-Up	Score
I	UC Santa Barbara	(1)	UCLA	2-1
II	Dowling, NY	(1)	Fort Lewis, CO*	1-0
III	Messiah, PA*	(5)	Wheaton, IL	3-0

Women

Div.	Winner		Runner-Up	Score
I	North Carolina	(18)	Notre Dame	2-1
II	Metro St., CO	(2)	Grand Valley St.	1-0 (OT)
III	Wheaton, IL	(2)	New Jersey	2-0

Volleyball
Women

Div.	Winner		Runner-Up	Score
I	Nebraska	(3)	Stanford	3-1
II	Tampa	(1)	North Alabama	3-1
III	Juniata, PA	(2)	Washington, MI	3-2

Water Polo
Men

Div.	Winner		Runner-Up	Score
National	California	(12)	USC*	7-6

WINTER

Basketball
Men

Div.	Winner		Runner-Up	Score
I	Florida*	(2)	Ohio St.	84-75
II	Barton, NC	(1)	Winona St., MN*	77-75
III	Amherst, MA	(1)	Virginia Wesleyan*	80-67

Women

Div.	Winner		Runner-Up	Score
I	Tennessee	(7)	Rutgers	59-46
II	Southern Conn. St.	(1)	Florida Gulf Coast	61-45
III	DePauw, IN	(2)	Washington, MO	55-52

Bowling
Women

Div.	Winner		Runner-Up	Score
Nat'l	Vanderbilt	(1)	MD-Eastern Shore	4-3

Fencing

Div.	Winner		Runner-Up	Score
Combined	Penn St.	(10)	St. John's	194-176

Gymnastics

Div.	Winner		Runner-Up	Margin
Men	Penn St.	(12)	Oklahoma	by .800
Women	Georgia*	(8)	Utah	by .600

Ice Hockey
Men

Div.	Winner		Runner-Up	Score
I	Michigan St.	(3)	Boston College	3-1
III	Oswego St., NY	(1)	Middlebury, VT	4-3 (OT)

Women

Div.	Winner		Runner-Up	Score
I	Wisconsin*	(2)	Minnesota Duluth	4-1
III	Plattsburgh St., NY	(1)	Middlebury, VT*	2-1

Rifle

Div.	Winner		Runner-Up	Score
Combined	AK-Fairbanks*	(9)	Army	4662-4644

Skiing

Div.	Winner		Runner-Up	Score
Combined	Dartmouth	(3)	Denver	698-648

Swimming & Diving
Men

Div.	Winner		Runner-Up	Score
I	Auburn*	(7)	Stanford	566-397
II	Drury, MO*	(5)	North Dakota	665.5-485
III	Kenyon, OH*	(28)	Denison, OH	570-351

Women

Div.	Winner		Runner-Up	Score
I	Auburn*	(5)	Arizona	535-477
II	Drury, MO*	(5)	Truman St., MO*	646.5-518
III	Kenyon, OH	(21)	Amherst, MA	538-320

Indoor Track
Men

Div.	Winner		Runner-Up	Score
I	Wisconsin	(1)	Florida St.	40-35
II	St. Augustine's, NC*	(10)	Abilene Christian	88-48.5
III	Lincoln, PA	(6)	Wis.-La Crosse*	59-48

Women

Div.	Winner		Runner-Up	Score
I	Arizona St.	(1)	LSU	38-33
II	St. Augustine's, NC	(6)	Lincoln, MO*	105-64
III	Williams, MA	(1)	City College of NY	42-35

Wrestling
Men

Div.	Winner		Runner-Up	Score
I	Minnesota	(3)	Iowa St.	98-88.5
II	Central Oklahoma	(7)	Neb.-Kearney	124.5-108.5
III	Augsburg, MN	(10)	Wartburg, IA*	135.5-99.5

SPRING
Baseball

Div.	Winner		Runner-Up	Score
I	Oregon St.*	(2)	North Carolina	11-4, 9-3
II	Tampa*	(5)	Columbus St., GA	7-2
III	Kean, NJ	(1)	Emory, GA	5-4 (10 inn.)

Note: The Division I Championship Series is best-of-three.

Golf
Men

Div.	Winner		Runner-Up	Score
I	Stanford	(8)	Georgia	1109-1121
II	Barry, FL	(1)	SC-Upstate	1186-1187
III	St. John's, MN	(7)	La Verne, CA	1204-1216

Women

Div.	Winner		Runner-Up	Score
I	Duke*	(5)	Purdue	1170-1185
II	Florida Southern	(4)	Rollins, FL*	1188-1198
III	Methodist, NC*	(11)	DePauw, IN	1215-1303

Lacrosse
Men

Div.	Winner		Runner-Up	Score
I	Johns Hopkins	(9)	Duke	12-11
II	Le Moyne, NY*	(3)	Mercyhurst, PA	6-5
III	Salisbury, MD	(6)	Cortland, NY*	15-9

Women

Div.	Winner		Runner-Up	Score
I	Northwestern*	(3)	Virginia	15-13
II	C.W. Post, NY	(2)	West Chester, PA	15-7
III	Franklin & Marshall	(1)	Salisbury, MD	11-8

Rowing
Women

Div.	Winner		Runner-Up	Score
I	Brown	(5)	Virginia	58-54
II	Western Washington*	(3)	UC-San Diego	20-15
III	Williams, MA*	(3)	Trinity, CT	18-16

Softball

Div.	Winner		Runner-Up	Score
I	Arizona*	(8)	Tennessee	0-3, 1-0, 5-0
II	SIU-Edwardsville	(1)	Lock Haven, PA*	3-2 (12 inn.)
III	Linfield, OR	(1)	Washington, MO	10-2

Note: The Division I Championship Series is best-of-three.

Tennis
Men

Div.	Winner		Runner-Up	Score
I	Georgia	(5)	Illinois	4-0
II	Lynn, FL	(1)	Valdosta St., GA*	5-1
III	UC Santa Cruz	(6)	Emory, GA	5-1

Women

Div.	Winner		Runner-Up	Score
I	Georgia Tech	(1)	UCLA	4-2
II	BYU-Hawaii*	(7)	West Florida	5-0
III	Washington & Lee, VA	(1)	Amherst, MA	5-2

Outdoor Track
Men

Div.	Winner		Runner-Up	Score
I	Florida St.*	(2)	LSU	54-48
II	Abilene Christian*	(17)	St Augustine's, NC	105.5-73
III	Wis.-La Crosse*	(11)	Cortland, NY	99-34

Women

Div.	Winner		Runner-Up	Score
I	Arizona St.	(1)	LSU	60-53
II	Lincoln, MO*	(5)	Abilene Christian	82.5-69
III	Wis-Oshkosh*	(8)	Calvin, MI	57-44.5

Volleyball
Men

Div.	Winner		Runner-Up	Score
National	UC Irvine	(1)	IPFW	3-1

Water Polo
Women

Div.	Winner		Runner-Up	Score
National	UCLA*	(5)	Stanford	5-4

All-Time Team Champions
Division I - Top Ten

Combined NCAA Division I men's, women's and coed team champions through spring 2007.

	School	Men's	Women's	Coed	Total
1	UCLA	70	30	0	**100**
2	Stanford	58	36	0	**94**
3	USC	73	11	0	**84**
4	Oklahoma St.	48	0	0	**48**
5	Arkansas	43	0	0	**43**
6	LSU	16	24	0	**40**
7	Texas	17	22	0	**39**
8	Michigan	30	2	0	**32**
	North Carolina	9	23	0	**32**
	Penn State	18	4	10	**32**

Note: Totals above do not reflect Division I-A football championships, which are not conducted by the NCAA. Coed championships include rifle, skiing and fencing (since 1990).

Source: NCAA

Georgia
Courtney Kupets
Gymnastics

Denver
Adam Cole
Skiing

Minnesota
Cole Konrad
Wrestling

Georgia
Kara Lynn Joyce
Swimming

2006-07 Division I Individual Champions
Repeat champions in **bold** type.

FALL

Cross Country

Men (10,000 meters)	**Time**
1 Josh Rohatinsky, Brigham Young	30:44.9
2 Neftalem Araia, Stanford	30:52.6
3 Jess Baumgartner, Southern Utah	30:53.2

Women (6,000 meters)	**Time**
1 Sally Kipyego, Texas Tech	20:11.1
2 Jenny Barringer, Colorado	20:37.9
3 Lindsay Donaldson, Yale	20:42.7

WINTER

Fencing
Men

Event		Score
Foil	Andras Horanyi, Ohio St.	13-12
Epee	Slava Zingerman, Wayne St.	15-13
Sabre	Timothy Hagamen, Harvard	15-14

Women

Event		Score
Foil	Doris Willette, Penn St.	15-10
Epee	Anna Garina, Wayne St.	15-13
Sabre	Daria Schneider, Columbia	15-11

Gymnastics
Men

Event		Points
All-Around	Taqiy Abdullah-Simmons, Oklahoma	55.750
Floor Exercise	**Jonathan Horton**, Oklahoma	9.650
Pommel Horse	**Tim McNeil**, California	9.650
Rings	Alex Schorsch, Stanford	9.750
Vault	Pejman Ebrahimi, Ohio St.	9.300
	& David Sender, Stanford (tie)	9.300
Parallel Bars	Tim McNeil, California	9.725
High Bar	Jonathan Horton, Oklahoma	9.675

Women

Event		Points
All-Around	**Courtney Kupets**, Georgia	39.750
Vault	Courtney Kupets, Georgia	9.9188
Uneven Bars	Terin Humphrey, Alabama	9.9500
Balance Beam	Ashley Postell, Utah	9.9375
Floor Exercise	Morgan Dennis, Alabama	9.9625

Rifle
Combined
Number in parentheses denotes inner tens.

Smallbore

		Points
1	Josh Albright, Navy	679.5
2	Kirsten Weiss, Nebraska	678.4
3	Joseph Hall, Jacksonville St.	677.9

Air Rifle

		Points
1	Michael Dickinson, Jacksonville St.	692.2
2	Matthias Dierolf, AK-Fairbanks	691.4
3	Christopher Abalo, Army	691.2

Skiing
Men

Event		Time
Slalom	Adam Cole, Denver	1:43.36
Giant Slalom	Adam Cole, Denver	2:20.42
10-k Freestyle	Rene Reisshauer, Denver	24:52.2
20-k Classic	Snorri Einarsson, Utah	55:06.0

Women

Event		Time
Slalom	Malin Hemmingsson, New Mexico	1:45.77
Giant Slalom	Sarah Schaedler, Western St.	2:30.47
5-k Freestyle	Lindsey Williams, N. Michigan	13:50.4
15-k Classic	Lindsey Weier, N. Michigan	47:21.0

Wrestling

Wgt	Champion	Runner-Up
125	Paul Donahoe, Nebraska	S. Hazewinkel, Okla.
133	**Matt Valenti**, Penn	C. Scott, Okla. St.
141	Derek Moore, UC Davis	R. Lang, Northwestern
149	Gregor Gillespie, Edinboro	J. Churella, Mich.
157	Trent Paulson, Iowa St.	C. Henning, Wisconsin
165	Mark Perry, Iowa	J. Hendricks, Okla. St.
174	**Ben Askren**, Missouri	K. Gavin, Pittsburgh
184	Jake Herbert, Northwestern	J. Varner, Iowa St.
197	Joshua Glenn, American	K. Backes, Iowa St.
285	**Cole Konrad**, Minn.	A. Anspach, Penn. St.

Florida St.
Walter Dix
Track & Field

Auburn
Kerron Stewart
Track & Field

USC
Jamie Lovemark
Golf

Miami-FL
Audra Cohen
Tennis

Swimming & Diving
(*) indicates meet record.

Men

Event (yards)		Time
50 free	Cesar Cielo, Auburn	18.69*
100 free	Cesar Cielo, Auburn	41.17*
200 free	Darian Townsend, Arizona	1:33.29
500 free	Larsen Jensen, USC	4:09.80
1650 free	Larsen Jensen, USC	14:26.70
100 back	Albert Subirats, Arizona	44.83
200 back	Matt Grevers, Northwestern	1:38.71
100 breast	Mike Alexandrov, Northwestern	51.56*
200 breast	Vlad Polyakov, Alabama	1:52.71
100 butterfly	Albert Subirats, Arizona	44.57*
200 butterfly	Patrick O'Neil, Arizona	1:42.98
200 IM	Adam Ritter, Arizona	1:41.72
400 IM	Alex Vanderkaay, Michigan	3:40.89
200 free relay	**Auburn**	1:14.71*
400 free relay	Auburn	2:46.56*
800 free relay	**Arizona**	6:14.14*
200 medley relay	Auburn	1:23.37*
400 medley relay	Northwestern	3:04.40*

Diving		Points
1-meter	Terry Horner, Florida St.	399.35
3-meter	Steven Segerlin, Auburn	415.80
Platform	**Steven Segerlin**, Auburn	414.90

Women

Event (yards)		Time
50 free	**Kara Lynn Joyce**, Georgia	21.71
100 free	**Kara Lynn Joyce**, Georgia	47.24
200 free	Lacey Nymeyer, Arizona	1:43.49
500 free	Adrienne Binder, Auburn	4:36.96
1650 free	**Hayley Peirsol**, Auburn	15:45.92
100 back	**Rachel Goh**, Auburn	51.97
200 back	Gemma Spofforth, Florida	1:52.96
100 breast	**Jessica Hardy**, California	59.43
200 breast	Rebecca Soni, USC	2:08.23
100 butterfly	Dana Vollmer, California	50.69
200 butterfly	Elaine Breeden, Stanford	1:53.02*
200 IM	**Whitney Myers**, Arizona	1:54.89
400 IM	Ava Ohlgren, Arizona	4:04.08
200 free relay	**Arizona**	1:27.23
400 free relay	California	3:12.13*
800 free relay	California	7:00.89*
200 medley relay	Arizona	1:36.09*
400 medley relay	California	3:30.18*

Diving		Points
1-meter	Cassidy Krug, Stanford	361.55
3-meter	Cassidy Krug, Stanford	420.90
Platform	Jessica Livingston, Texas	357.85

Indoor Track
(*) indicates meet record.

Men

Event		Time
60 meters	Travis Padgett, Clemson	6.56
200 meters	**Walter Dix**, Florida St.	20.32
400 meters	Ricardo Chambers, Florida St.	45.65
800 meters	Ryan Brown, Washington	1:48.40
Mile	Leonel Manzano, Texas	3:59.90
3000 meters	Lopez Lomong, Northern Ariz.	7:49.74
5000 meters	Chris Solinsky, Wisconsin	13:38.61
60-m hurdles	Jeff Porter, Michigan	7.64
4x400-m relay	Baylor	3:04.24
Distance medley relay	Stanford	9:33.64

Event		Hgt/Dist
High Jump	Donald Thomas, Auburn	7-7¾
Pole Vault	Brad Gebauer, McNeese St.	18-0½
Long Jump	Tone Belt, Louisville	26-1¾
Triple Jump	Andre Black, Louisville	53-5½
Shot Put	Noah Bryant, USC	67-5¼
35-lb Throw	Egor Agafonov, Kansas	77-5¼
Heptathlon	**Donovan Kilmartin**, Texas	5998 pts.

Women

Event		Time
60 meters	Kerron Stewart, Auburn	7.15
200 meters	Kerron Stewart, Auburn	22.58
400 meters	Natasha Hastings, S. Carolina	50.80
800 meters	Alysia Johnson, California	2:03.47
Mile	Shannon Rowbury, Duke	4:42.17
3000 meters	Sally Kipyego, Texas Tech	9:02.05
5000 meters	Sally Kipyego, Texas Tech	15:27.42
60-m hurdles	Shantia Moss, Georgia Tech	7.98
4x400-m relay	South Carolina	3:29.57
Distance medley relay	**North Carolina**	10:59.46

Event		Hgt/Dist
High Jump	Patty Sylvester, Georgia	6-2¼
Pole Vault	Elouise Rudy, Montana St.	14-1¼
Long Jump	Rhonda Watkins, UCLA	21-6¾
Triple Jump	Erica McLain, Stanford	45-7¾
Shot Put	Sarah Stevens, Arizona St.	59-7
20-lb Throw	Brittany Riley, Southern Illinois	83-10¼
Pentathlon	**Jacquelyn Johnson**, Ariz. St.	4393 pts.

SPRING
Golf
Men

			Total
1	Jamie Lovemark, USC	72-71-64-64	—271
2	Kyle Stanley, Clemson	70-69-65-69	—273
3	Rob Grube, Stanford	64-71-69-70	—274

Golf (cont.)
Women

		Total
1	Stacy Lewis, Arkansas	71-71-74-66—282
2	Christel Boeljon, Purdue	72-69-69-76—286
	Paola Moreno, USC	73-72-70-71—286

Tennis
Men

Singles— Somdev Devvarman (Virginia) def. John Isner (Georgia), 7-6(7), 4-6, 7-6(2).

Doubles— Marco Born & Andreas Siljestrom (Middle Tennessee St.) def. Kevin Anderson & Ryan Rowe (Illinois), 4-6, 8-6, 7-4.

Women

Singles— Audra Cohen (Miami-FL) def. Lindsey Nelson (USC), 7-5, 6-2.

Doubles— Sara Anundsen & Jenna Long (North Carolina) def. Megan Moulton-Levy & Katarina Zoricic (William & Mary), 1-6, 6-2, 6-2.

Outdoor Track
(*) indicates meet record
Men

Event		Time
100 meters	Walter Dix, Florida St.	9.93
200 meters	**Walter Dix**, Florida St.	20.32
400 meters	Ricardo Chambers, Florida St.	44.66
800 meters	Andrew Ellerton, Michigan	1:47.48
1500 meters	Lopez Lomong, N. Arizona	3:37.07
5000 meters	**Chris Solinsky**, Wisconsin	13:35.12
10,000 meters	Shadrack Songok, Tex. A&M CC	28:55.83
110-m hurdles	Tyron Akins, Auburn	13.42
400-m hurdles	Isa Phillips, LSU	48.51
3000-m steeple	Barnabas Kirui, Mississippi	8:20.36
4x100-m relay	Florida St.	38.60
4x400-m relay	Baylor	3:00.04

Event		Hgt/Dist
High Jump	Scott Sellers, Kansas St.	7-7¼
Pole Vault	**Thomas Skipper**, Oregon	18-0½
Long Jump	Dashalle Andrews, CS-Northridge	25-2½
Triple Jump	Ray Taylor, Cornell	53-8½
Shot Put	Noah Bryant, USC	65-9
Discus	Niklas Arrhenius, BYU	206-2
Javelin	Justin Ryncavage, North Carolina	241-5
Hammer	Jake Dunkleberger, Auburn	235-9
Decathlon	**Jake Arnold**, Arizona	8215 pts.

Women

Event		Time
100 meters	Sherry Fletcher, LSU	11.20
200 meters	Kerron Stewart, Auburn	22.42
400 meters	Natasha Hastings, S. Carolina	50.15
800 meters	Alysia Johnson, California	1:59.29
1500 meters	Brie Felnagle, North Carolina	4:09.93
5000 meters	Michelle Sikes, Wake Forest	15:16.76*
10,000 meters	Sally Kipyego, Texas Tech	32:55.71
100-m hurdles	Tiffany Ofili, Michigan	12.80
400-m hurdles	Nicole Leach, UCLA	54.32
3000-m steeple	Anna Willard, Michigan	9:38.08*
4x100-m relay	Texas A&M	43.05
4x400-m relay	**LSU**	3:28.07

Event		Hgt/Dist
High Jump	**Destinee Hooker**, Texas	6-3½
Pole Vault	April Kubishta, Arizona St.	13-11¼
Long Jump	Rhonda Watkins, UCLA	22-10
Triple Jump	Yvette Lewis, Hampton	45-0½
Shot Put	Jessica Pressley, California	59-0¾
Discus	Kelechi Anyanwu, California	188-11
Javelin	Lindsey Blaine, Purdue	182-3
Hammer	**Jenny Dahlgren**, Georgia	232-0
Heptathlon	**Jacquelyn Johnson**, Ariz. St.	5984 pts.

Championships Most Outstanding Players
Men

Baseball	Jorge Reyes, Oregon St.
Basketball	Corey Brewer, Florida
Cross Country	Josh Rohatinsky, Brigham Young*
Golf	Jamie Lovemark, USC*
Gymnastics	Taqiy Abdullah-Simmons, Oklahoma*
Ice Hockey	Justin Abdelkader, Michigan St.
Lacrosse	Jesse Schwartzman, Johns Hopkins
Soccer: Offense	Nick Perera, UC Santa Barbara
Soccer: Defense	Andy Iro, UC Santa Barbara
Swimming	Cesar Cielo, Auburn†
& Diving	Steven Segerlin, Auburn†
Tennis	Somdev Devvarman, Virginia*
Track: Indoor	Chris Solinsky, Wisconsin†
Track: Outdoor	Walter Dix, Florida St.†
Volleyball	Matt Webber, UC Irvine
Water Polo	Mark Sheredy, California
Wrestling	Derek Moore, UC Davis

Women

Basketball	Candace Parker, Tennessee
Bowling	Josie Earnest, Vanderbilt
Cross Country	Sally Kipyego, Texas Tech*
Golf	Stacy Lewis, Arkansas*
Gymnastics	Courtney Kupets, Georgia*
Ice Hockey	Sara Bauer, Wisconsin
Lacrosse	Hilary Bowen, Northwestern
Soccer: Offense	Heather O'Reilly, North Carolina
Soccer: Defense	Robin Gayle, North Carolina
Softball	Taryne Mowatt, Arizona
Swimming	Kara Lynn Joyce, Georgia†
& Diving	Cassidy Krug, Stanford†
Tennis	Audra Cohen, Miami-FL*
Track: Indoor	Kerron Stewart, Auburn†
Track: Outdoor	Sherry Fletcher, LSU†
Volleyball	Sarah Pavan, Nebraska
Water Polo	Kelly Rulon, UCLA

(*) indicates won individual or all-around NCAA championship; There were no official Outstanding Players in fencing, field hockey, I-AA football, rifle, rowing and skiing. (†) Outstanding players in Swimming & Diving and Indoor and Outdoor Track are the individuals earning the most points in the Championships.

2006-07 NAIA Team Champions
Total NAIA titles in that sport in parentheses.

FALL

Cross Country: MEN'S–Virginia Intermont (3); WOMEN'S–Simon Fraser, BC (9). **Football:** MEN'S– Sioux Falls, SD (2). **Soccer:** MEN'S–Graceland, IA (1); WOMEN'S–Lindsey Wilson, KY (2). **Volleyball:** WOMENS–National American, SD (2).

WINTER

Basketball: MEN'S–Division I: Oklahoma City (5) and Division II: MidAmerica Nazarene, KS (1); WOMEN'S–Division I: Lambuth, TN (1) and Division II: Indiana Wesleyan (1). **Swimming & Diving:** MEN'S–California Baptist (2); WOMEN'S– California Baptist (3). **Indoor Track:** MEN'S–Azusa Pacific, CA (5); WOMEN'S–Oklahoma Baptist (2). **Wrestling:** MEN'S–Lindenwood, MO (3).

SPRING

Baseball: MEN'S–Lewis-Clark St., ID (15). **Golf:** MEN'S–Oklahoma City (6); WOMEN'S–Oklahoma City (3). **Softball:** WOMEN'S–Oklahoma City (8). **Tennis:** MEN'S–Auburn-Montgomery (7); WOMEN'S–Auburn-Montgomery (8). **Outdoor Track:** MEN'S–Oklahoma Baptist (2); WOMEN'S–Azusa Pacific, CA (3).

Annual NCAA Division I Team Champions

Men's and women's NCAA Division I team champions from bowling to wrestling. Also see team champions for baseball, basketball, football, golf, ice hockey, soccer and tennis in the appropriate chapters throughout the almanac. See pages 478-480 for the list of 2006-07 individual champions.

BOWLING

Women

Vanderbilt won its first national title in any sport in school history by defeating Maryland-Eastern Shore, 4 games to 3 in the best-of-seven championship series. The Commodores took charge in the last five frames of the deciding game seven and went on to win, 198-150. Freshman Josie Earnest, the tournament's most valuable player, came through with two clutch strikes in the 10th frame to clinch the victory. *(Apopka, FL; April 12-14, 2007.)*

Multiple winner: Nebraska (2).

Year	Year	Year	Year
2004 Nebraska	2005 Nebraska	2006 Fairleigh Dickinson	2007 Vanderbilt

CROSS COUNTRY

Men

Colorado placed three runners in the top 15 and eased to its third national cross country championship in the last six years. Brent Vaughn (8th), Stephen Pifer (10th) and Erik Heinonen (15th) paced the Buffs while James Strang (27th) and Billy Nelson (34th) rounded out the scoring. Colorado finished with 94 points to easily outdistance defending champion Wisconsin (142) and third place Iona (172). *(Terre Haute, IN; Nov. 20, 2006.)*

Multiple winners: Arkansas (11); Michigan St. (8); UTEP (7); Oregon, Stanford, Villanova and Wisconsin (4); Colorado, Drake, Indiana and Penn St. (3); Iowa St., San Jose St. and Western Michigan (2).

Year	Year	Year	Year	Year
1938 Indiana	1951 Syracuse	1965 Western Mich.	1979 UTEP	1993 Arkansas
1939 Michigan St.	1952 Michigan St.	1966 Villanova	1980 UTEP	1994 Iowa St.
1940 Indiana	1953 Kansas	1967 Villanova	1981 UTEP	1995 Arkansas
1941 Rhode Island	1954 Oklahoma St.	1968 Villanova	1982 Wisconsin	1996 Stanford
1942 Indiana	1955 Michigan St.	1969 UTEP	1983 Vacated	1997 Stanford
& Penn St.	1956 Michigan St.	1970 Villanova	1984 Arkansas	1998 Arkansas
1943 Not held	1957 Notre Dame	1971 Oregon	1985 Wisconsin	1999 Arkansas
1944 Drake	1958 Michigan St.	1972 Tennessee	1986 Arkansas	2000 Arkansas
1945 Drake	1959 Michigan St.	1973 Oregon	1987 Arkansas	2001 Colorado
1946 Drake	1960 Houston	1974 Oregon	1988 Wisconsin	2002 Stanford
1947 Penn St.	1961 Oregon St.	1975 UTEP	1989 Iowa St.	2003 Stanford
1948 Michigan St.	1962 San Jose St.	1976 UTEP	1990 Arkansas	2004 Colorado
1949 Michigan St.	1963 San Jose St.	1977 Oregon	1991 Arkansas	2005 Wisconsin
1950 Penn St.	1964 Western Mich.	1978 UTEP	1992 Arkansas	2006 Colorado

Women

Junior Arianna Lambie finished in fourth overall to carry Stanford to its second consecutive NCAA Division I women's cross country title and fourth overall. The Cardinal finished with 195 points to better runner-up Colorado (223) and third place Michigan (233). Texas Tech sophomore Sally Kipyego (20:11.1) was the individual race winner. *(Terre Haute, IN; Nov. 20, 2006.)*

Multiple winners: Villanova (7); BYU and Stanford (4); Colorado, Oregon, Virginia and Wisconsin (2).

Year	Year	Year	Year	Year
1981 Virginia	1987 Oregon	1993 Villanova	1999 BYU	2005 Stanford
1982 Virginia	1988 Kentucky	1994 Villanova	2000 Colorado	2006 Stanford
1983 Oregon	1989 Villanova	1995 Providence	2001 BYU	
1984 Wisconsin	1990 Villanova	1996 Stanford	2002 BYU	
1985 Wisconsin	1991 Villanova	1997 BYU	2003 Stanford	
1986 Texas	1992 Villanova	1998 Villanova	2004 Colorado	

FENCING

Men & Women

Doris Willette took the gold in the women's foil competition to lead Penn St. to its 10th national fencing championship and first since 2002. The Nittany Lions recorded 194 total bout wins to better runner-up St. John's (176). Of those 194 wins, 105 came from the Penn St. women and 24 came from Willette, who lost just once during the tournament. Teammate Caitlin Thompson placed second in the women's sabre, losing to Columbia's Daria Schneider. *(Madison, NJ; Mar. 12-25, 2007.)*

Multiple winners: Penn St. (10); Notre Dame (3); Columbia/Barnard (2). **Note:** Prior to 1990, men and women held separate championships. Men's multiple winners included: NYU (12); Columbia (11); Wayne St. (7); Navy, Notre Dame and Penn (3); Illinois (2). Women's multiple winners included: Wayne St. (3); Yale (2).

Year	Year	Year	Year
1990 Penn St.	1995 Penn St.	2000 Penn St.	2005 Notre Dame
1991 Penn St.	1996 Penn St.	2001 St. John's	2006 Harvard
1992 Columbia/Barnard	1997 Penn St.	2002 Penn St.	2007 Penn St.
1993 Columbia/Barnard	1998 Penn St.	2003 Notre Dame	
1994 Notre Dame	1999 Penn St.	2004 Ohio St.	

Annual NCAA Division I Team Champions (Cont.)

FIELD HOCKEY

Women

Senior Emily Trycinski scored an unassisted goal with five minutes remaining in the first half to lead Maryland to a 1-0 win over Wake Forest and its second straight Division I national field hockey title. Maryland's stifling defense allowed just four shots en route the victory. They finished the season at 23-2, while Wake Forest fell to 22-2(Winston-Salem, NC; Nov. 19, 2006.)

Multiple winners: Old Dominion (9); Maryland (5); North Carolina (4); Wake Forest (3); Connecticut (2).

Year	Year	Year	Year	Year
1981 Connecticut	1987 Maryland	1993 Maryland	1999 Maryland	2005 Maryland
1982 Old Dominion	1988 Old Dominion	1994 J. Madison	2000 Old Dominion	2006 Maryland
1983 Old Dominion	1989 North Carolina	1995 North Carolina	2001 Michigan	
1984 Old Dominion	1990 Old Dominion	1996 North Carolina	2002 Wake Forest	
1985 Connecticut	1991 Old Dominion	1997 North Carolina	2003 Wake Forest	
1986 Iowa	1992 Old Dominion	1998 Old Dominion	2004 Wake Forest	

GYMNASTICS

Men

Buoyed by stellar performances in the rings and pommel horse, Penn St. won its record 12th national gymnastics title and third in the last eight years. Penn St. was trailing defending champ Oklahoma entering the final rings rotation, but none of the six Nittany Lions scored below 9.2 to push them to the win, 221-220.2. (University Park, PA; Apr. 12-14, 2007.)

Multiple winners: Penn St. (12); Illinois (9); Nebraska (8); Oklahoma (7); California and So. Illinois (4); Iowa St., Michigan, Ohio St. and Stanford (3); Florida St and UCLA (2).

Year	Year	Year	Year	Year
1938 Chicago	1957 Penn St.	1970 Michigan	1983 Nebraska	1998 California
1939 Illinois	1958 Michigan St.	& Michigan (T)	1984 UCLA	1999 Michigan
1940 Illinois	& Illinois	1971 Iowa St.	1985 Ohio St.	2000 Penn St.
1941 Illinois	1959 Penn St.	1972 So. Illinois	1986 Arizona St.	2001 Ohio St.
1942 Illinois	1960 Penn St.	1973 Iowa St.	1987 UCLA	2002 Oklahoma
1943-47 Not held	1961 Penn St.	1974 Iowa St.	1988 Nebraska	2003 Oklahoma
1948 Penn St.	1962 USC	1975 California	1989 Illinois	2004 Penn St.
1949 Temple	1963 Michigan	1976 Penn St.	1990 Nebraska	2005 Oklahoma
1950 Illinois	1964 So. Illinois	1977 Indiana St.	1991 Oklahoma	2006 Oklahoma
1951 Florida St.	1965 Penn St.	& Oklahoma	1992 Stanford	2007 Penn St.
1952 Florida St.	1966 So. Illinois	1978 Oklahoma	1993 Stanford	
1953 Penn St.	1967 So. Illinois	1979 Nebraska	1994 Stanford	(T) indicates won tram-
1954 Penn St.	1968 California	1980 Nebraska	1995 Stanford	poline competition
1955 Illinois	1969 Iowa	1981 Nebraska	1996 Ohio St.	(1969-70).
1956 Illinois	& Michigan (T)	1982 Nebraska	1997 California	

Women

Courtney Kupets won her second consecutive individual all-around title and led Georgia to its third straight team title and eighth overall. Georgia (31-2-1) amassed 197.850 points, ahead of runner-up Utah (197.250) and third-place Florida (197.225). Since 1982, only four schools have won the title. (Salt Lake City, UT; Apr. 26-28, 2007.)

Multiple winners: Utah (9); Georgia (8); UCLA (5); Alabama (4).

Year	Year	Year	Year	Year
1982 Utah	1988 Alabama	1994 Utah	2000 UCLA	2006 Georgia
1983 Utah	1989 Georgia	1995 Utah	2001 UCLA	2007 Georgia
1984 Utah	1990 Utah	1996 Alabama	2002 Alabama	
1985 Utah	1991 Alabama	1997 UCLA	2003 UCLA	
1986 Utah	1992 Utah	1998 Georgia	2004 UCLA	
1987 Georgia	1993 Georgia	1999 Georgia	2005 Georgia	

LACROSSE

Men

Junior Kevin Huntley scored the game-winning goal with 3:25 left to give Johns Hopkins a tough 12-11 win over Duke in the Division I lacrosse title game. The game was iced when goalie and tournament MVP Jesse Schwartzman booted away Duke midfielder Brad Ross's shot with 10 seconds left. (Philadelphia, PA; May 29, 2006.)

Multiple winners: Johns Hopkins (9); Syracuse (8); Princeton (6); North Carolina and Virginia (4); Cornell (3); Maryland (2).

Year	Year	Year	Year	Year
1971 Cornell	1979 Johns Hopkins	1987 Johns Hopkins	1995 Syracuse	2003 Virginia
1972 Virginia	1980 Johns Hopkins	1988 Syracuse	1996 Princeton	2004 Syracuse
1973 Maryland	1981 North Carolina	1989 Syracuse	1997 Princeton	2005 Johns Hopkins
1974 Johns Hopkins	1982 North Carolina	1990 Syracuse*	1998 Princeton	2006 Virginia
1975 Maryland	1983 Syracuse	1991 North Carolina	1999 Virginia	2007 Johns Hopkins
1976 Cornell	1984 Johns Hopkins	1992 Princeton	2000 Syracuse	
1977 Cornell	1985 Johns Hopkins	1993 Syracuse	2001 Princeton	
1978 Johns Hopkins	1986 North Carolina	1994 Princeton	2002 Syracuse	

*Title was later vacated due to action by the NCAA Committee on Infractions.

Women

Hilary Bowen netted five goals to lead top-ranked Northwestern to a 15-13 win over Virginia for its third Division I women's lacrosse title. Katrina Dowd added three goals for the Wildcats, while Meredith Frank and Aly Josephs scored two each. Northwestern jumped out to an 11-5 first-half lead, but Virginia closed to within one at 14-13 until Dowd gave Northwestern an insurance goal minutes later. The Wildcats finished the season at 21-1, while the Cavaliers dropped to 19-4. *(Philadelphia, PA; May 27, 2007.)*

Multiple winners: Maryland (9); Northwestern, Princeton and Virginia (3); Penn St. and Temple (2).

Year	Year	Year	Year	Year
1982 Massachusetts	1988 Temple	1994 Princeton	2000 Maryland	2006 Northwestern
1983 Delaware	1989 Penn St.	1995 Maryland	2001 Maryland	2007 Northwestern
1984 Temple	1990 Harvard	1996 Maryland	2002 Princeton	
1985 New Hampshire	1991 Virginia	1997 Maryland	2003 Princeton	
1986 Maryland	1992 Maryland	1998 Maryland	2004 Virginia	
1987 Penn St.	1993 Virginia	1999 Maryland	2005 Northwestern	

RIFLE

Men & Women

In front of its hometown crowd, Alaska-Fairbanks powered to an 18-point victory for its second straight NCAA national rifle title and eighth in the last nine years. Behind a second-place finish from Matthias Dierolf in the air rifle, the Nanooks amassed 4,662 points to beat runner-up Army (4,644) and third-place Jacksonville St. (4,639). *(Fairbanks, AK; Mar. 9-10, 2007.)*

Multiple winners: West Virginia (13); Alaska-Fairbanks (9); Tennessee Tech (3); Murray St. (2).

Year	Year	Year	Year	Year
1980 Tenn. Tech	1986 West Virginia	1992 West Virginia	1998 West Virginia	2004 AK-Fairbanks
1981 Tenn. Tech	1987 Murray St.	1993 West Virginia	1999 AK-Fairbanks	2005 Army
1982 Tenn. Tech	1988 West Virginia	1994 AK-Fairbanks	2000 AK-Fairbanks	2006 AK-Fairbanks
1983 West Virginia	1989 West Virginia	1995 West Virginia	2001 AK-Fairbanks	2007 AK-Fairbanks
1984 West Virginia	1990 West Virginia	1996 West Virginia	2002 AK-Fairbanks	
1985 Murray St.	1991 West Virginia	1997 West Virginia	2003 AK-Fairbanks	

ROWING

Intercollegiate Rowing Association Regatta
VARSITY EIGHTS
Men

The Washington crew crossed the finish line in 5:33.16, finishing five seats ahead of Harvard and Stanford for its first IRA Varsity Eights title since 1997. Washington ended their season undefeated *(Cooper River, Camden, NJ; May 31-June 2, 2007.)*

The IRA was formed in 1895 by several Northeastern colleges after Harvard and Yale quit the Rowing Association (established in 1871) to stage an annual race of their own. Since then the IRA Regatta has been contested over courses of varying lengths in Poughkeepsie, N.Y., Marietta, Ohio, Syracuse, N.Y. and Camden, N.J.

Distances: 4 miles (1895-97,1899-1916,1925-41); 3 miles (1898,1921-24,1947-49,1952-63,1965-67); 2 miles (1920,1950-51); 2000 meters (1964, since 1968).

Multiple winners: Cornell (24); California (15); Navy (13); Washington (12); Penn (9); Brown and Wisconsin (7); Syracuse (6); Columbia (4); Harvard and Princeton (3); Northeastern (2).

Year	Year	Year	Year	Year
1895 Columbia	1917-19 Not held	1941 Washington	1967 Penn	1989 Penn
1896 Cornell	1920 Syracuse	1942-46 Not held	1968 Penn	1990 Wisconsin
1897 Cornell	1921 Navy	1947 Navy	1969 Penn	1991 Northeastern
1898 Penn	1922 Navy	1948 Washington	1970 Washington	1992 Dartmouth,
1899 Penn	1923 Washington	1949 California	1971 Cornell	Navy & Penn†
1900 Penn	1924 Washington	1950 Washington	1972 Penn	1993 Brown
1901 Cornell	1925 Navy	1951 Wisconsin	1973 Wisconsin	1994 Brown
1902 Cornell	1926 Washington	1952 Navy	1974 Wisconsin	1995 Brown
1903 Cornell	1927 Columbia	1953 Navy	1975 Wisconsin	1996 Princeton
1904 Syracuse	1928 California	1954 Navy*	1976 California	1997 Washington
1905 Cornell	1929 Columbia	1955 Cornell	1977 Cornell	1998 Princeton
1906 Cornell	1930 Cornell	1956 Cornell	1978 Syracuse	1999 California
1907 Cornell	1931 Navy	1957 Cornell	1979 Brown	2000 California
1908 Syracuse	1932 California	1958 Cornell	1980 Navy	2001 California
1909 Cornell	1933 Not held	1959 Wisconsin	1981 Cornell	2002 California
1910 Cornell	1934 California	1960 California	1982 Cornell	2003 Harvard
1911 Cornell	1935 California	1961 California	1983 Brown	2004 Harvard
1912 Cornell	1936 Washington	1962 Cornell	1984 Navy	2005 Harvard
1913 Syracuse	1937 Washington	1963 Cornell	1985 Princeton	2006 California
1914 Columbia	1938 Navy	1964 California	1986 Brown	2007 Washington
1915 Cornell	1939 California	1965 Navy	1987 Brown	
1916 Syracuse	1940 Washington	1966 Wisconsin	1988 Northeastern	

*In 1954, Navy was disqualified because of an ineligible coxswain; no trophies were given.
†First dead heat in history of IRA Regatta.

Annual NCAA Division I Team Champions (Cont.)

NCAA Rowing Championships

Women

Brown won its fifth NCAA national rowing title, becoming the second team to win the championship without winning a race. The Bears placed fourth in the Varsity Eights, second in the Fours and third in the Second Eights. Yale led wire-to-wire in the Varsity Eights to beat runner-up Ohio State by three seats. The Bulldogs finished in 6:37.08 to capture their first win in NCAA Championships history. Brown finished with 58 points overall to top runner-up Virginia (54) and third-place Ohio St. (52). (*Oak Ridge, TN; May 25-27, 2007.*)

Multiple winners: Brown (5); Washington (3); California (2).

Year	Overall winner	Varsity Eights	Year	Overall winner	Varsity Eights
1997	Washington	Washington	2003	Harvard	Harvard
1998	Washington	Washington	2004	Brown	Brown
1999	Brown	Brown	2005	California	California
2000	Brown	Brown	2006	California	Princeton
2001	Washington	Washington	2007	Brown	Yale
2002	Brown	Washington			

National Rowing Championship
VARSITY EIGHTS
Men

National championship raced annually from 1982-96 in Bantam, Ohio over a 2,000-meter course on Lake Harsha. Winner received the Herschede Cup. Regatta discontinued in 1997.

Multiple winners: Harvard (6); Brown (3); Wisconsin (2).

Year	Champion	Time	Runner-up	Time	Year	Champion	Time	Runner-up	Time
1982	Yale	5:50.8	Cornell	5:54.15	1990	Wisconsin	5:52.5	Harvard	5:56.84
1983	Harvard	5:59.6	Washington	6:00.0	1991	Penn	5:58.21	Northeastern	5:58.48
1984	Washington	5:51.1	Yale	5:55.6	1992	Harvard	5:33.97	Dartmouth	5:34.28
1985	Harvard	5:44.4	Princeton	5:44.87	1993	Brown	5:54.15	Penn	5:56.98
1986	Wisconsin	5:57.8	Brown	5:59.9	1994	Brown	5:24.52	Harvard	5:25.83
1987	Harvard	5:35.17	Brown	5:35.63	1995	Brown	5:23.40	Princeton	5:25.83
1988	Harvard	5:35.98	Northeastern	5:37.07	1996	Princeton	5:57.47	Penn	6:03.28
1989	Harvard	5:36.6	Washington	5:38.93	1997	discontinued			

Women

National championship held over various distances at 10 different venues from 1979-96. Distances– 1000 meters (1979-81); 1500 meters (1982-83); 1000 meters (1984); 1750 meters (1985); 2000 meters (1986-88, 1991-96); 1852 meters (1989-90). Winner received the Ferguson Bowl. Regatta discontinued in 1997.

Multiple winners: Washington (7); Princeton (4); Boston University (2).

Year	Champion	Time	Runner-up	Time	Year	Champion	Time	Runner-up	Time
1979	Yale	3:06	California	3:08.6	1988	Washington	6:41.0	Yale	6:42.37
1980	California	3:05.4	Oregon St.	3:05.8	1989	Cornell	5:34.9	Wisconsin	5:37.5
1981	Washington	3:20.6	Yale	3:22.9	1990	Boston Univ.	7:03.2	Cornell	7:06.21
1982	Washington	4:56.4	Wisconsin	4:59.83	1991	Boston Univ.	6:28.79	Cornell	6:32.79
1983	Washington	4:57.5	Dartmouth	5:03.02	1992	Princeton	6:40.75	Washington	6:43.86
1984	Washington	3:29.48	Radcliffe	3:31.08	1993	Princeton	6:11.38	Yale	6:14.46
1985	Washington	5:28.4	Wisconsin	5:32.0	1994	Princeton	6:11.98	Washington	6:12.69
1986	Wisconsin	6:53.28	Radcliffe	6:53.34	1995	Brown	6:45.7	Princeton	6:49.3
1987	Washington	6:33.8	Yale	6:37.4	1996	discontinued			

SKIING
Men & Women

Dartmouth used a balanced attack to win its third NCAA skiing national title and first in over 30 years. The Big Green were led by former individual titlist David Chodounsky who placed second in the men's slalom, and Evan Weiss who placed second in the men's Giant Slalom. Denver's Adam Cole was the winner of each of those races. (*Bartlett, NH; March 7-10, 2007.*)

Multiple winners: Denver (18); Colorado (16); Utah (10); Vermont (5); Dartmouth (3); Wyoming (2).

Year	Year	Year	Year	Year
1954 Denver	1965 Denver	1976 Colorado	1986 Utah	1997 Utah
1955 Denver	1966 Denver	& Dartmouth	1987 Utah	1998 Colorado
1956 Denver	1967 Denver	1977 Colorado	1988 Utah	1999 Colorado
1957 Denver	1968 Wyoming	1978 Colorado	1989 Vermont	2000 Denver
1958 Dartmouth	1969 Denver	1979 Colorado	1990 Vermont	2001 Denver
1959 Colorado	1970 Denver	1980 Vermont	1991 Colorado	2002 Denver
1960 Colorado	1971 Denver	1981 Utah	1992 Vermont	2003 Utah
1961 Denver	1972 Colorado	1982 Colorado	1993 Utah	2004 New Mexico
1962 Denver	1973 Colorado	1983 Utah	1994 Vermont	2005 Denver
1963 Denver	1974 Colorado	1984 Utah	1995 Colorado	2006 Colorado
1964 Denver	1975 Colorado	1985 Wyoming	1996 Utah	2007 Dartmouth

SOFTBALL
Women

Ace pitcher Taryne Mowatt tossed yet another shutout to lead Arizona to a 5-0 win over Tennessee and its eighth overall national softball title. The Wildcats had to battle out of the losers bracket to advance to the World Series final round vs. the Volunteers. They finished out the season at 50-14-1, while Tennessee fell to 63-8. Mowatt was selected the tournament's most outstanding player, throwing every pitch for the Wildcats during their eight-game World Series run and improving her overall record to 42-12 with 522 strikeouts in 370 innings. (*Oklahoma City, OK; May 30-June 6, 2007.*)

Multiple winners: UCLA (10); Arizona (8); Texas A&M (2).

Year	Year	Year	Year	Year
1982 UCLA	1988 UCLA	1994 Arizona	2000 Oklahoma	2006 Arizona
1983 Texas A&M	1989 UCLA	1995 UCLA*	2001 Arizona	2007 Arizona
1984 UCLA	1990 UCLA	1996 Arizona	2002 California	
1985 UCLA	1991 Arizona	1997 Arizona	2003 UCLA	
1986 CS-Fullerton	1992 UCLA	1998 Fresno St.	2004 UCLA	
1987 Texas A&M	1993 Arizona	1999 UCLA	2005 Michigan	

*Title was later vacated due to action by the NCAA Committee on Infractions.

SWIMMING & DIVING

Men

Auburn set five NCAA records and cruised to its fifth consecutive Division I swimming and diving title and seventh overall. The Tigers recorded 566 points to easily outdistance runner-up Stanford (397) and third-place Arizona (371). Swimmer of the Year Cesar Cielo won the 50- and 100-freestyle events to pace the Tigers, while Diver of the Year Steven Segerlin grabbed titles in two of the three diving events (3-meter and platform). Auburn also took three of the meet's four relay events, all in meet record time. USC's Larsen Jensen was a double winner in the 500- and 1650-freestyle. (*Minneapolis, MN; Mar. 15-17, 2007.*)

Multiple winners: Michigan and Ohio St. (11); Texas and USC (9); Stanford (8); Auburn (7); Indiana (6); Yale (4); California and Florida (2).

Year	Year	Year	Year	Year
1937 Michigan	1952 Ohio St.	1967 Stanford	1982 UCLA	1997 Auburn
1938 Michigan	1953 Yale	1968 Indiana	1983 Florida	1998 Stanford
1939 Michigan	1954 Ohio St.	1969 Indiana	1984 Florida	1999 Auburn
1940 Michigan	1955 Ohio St.	1970 Indiana	1985 Stanford	2000 Texas
1941 Michigan	1956 Ohio St.	1971 Indiana	1986 Stanford	2001 Texas
1942 Yale	1957 Michigan	1972 Indiana	1987 Stanford	2002 Texas
1943 Ohio St.	1958 Michigan	1973 Indiana	1988 Texas	2003 Auburn
1944 Yale	1959 Michigan	1974 USC	1989 Texas	2004 Auburn
1945 Ohio St.	1960 USC	1975 USC	1990 Texas	2005 Auburn
1946 Ohio St.	1961 Michigan	1976 USC	1991 Texas	2006 Auburn
1947 Ohio St.	1962 Ohio St.	1977 USC	1992 Stanford	2007 Auburn
1948 Michigan	1963 USC	1978 Tennessee	1993 Stanford	
1949 Ohio St.	1964 USC	1979 California	1994 Stanford	
1950 Ohio St.	1965 USC	1980 California	1995 Michigan	
1951 Yale	1966 USC	1981 Texas	1996 Texas	

Women

Auburn successfully defended its title at the Division I Women's Swimming and Diving Championships, making up a 35-point deficit heading into the final day for its fifth overall national title. The Tigers amassed 535 points to best runner-up Arizona (477) and third-place California (372.5). Hayley Peirsol and Adrienne Binder were pivotal in the comeback with a win and runner-up finish, respectively, in the 1650-freestyle. The Tigers also received wins from Binder in the 500-freestyle, Rachel Goh in the 100-backstroke and Ava Ohlgren in the 400 IM. (*Minneapolis, MN; Mar. 8-10, 2007.*)

Multiple winners: Stanford (8); Texas (7); Auburn (5); Georgia (4).

Year	Year	Year	Year	Year
1982 Florida	1988 Texas	1994 Stanford	2000 Georgia	2006 Auburn
1983 Stanford	1989 Stanford	1995 Stanford	2001 Georgia	2007 Auburn
1984 Texas	1990 Texas	1996 Stanford	2002 Auburn	
1985 Texas	1991 Texas	1997 USC	2003 Auburn	
1986 Texas	1992 Stanford	1998 Stanford	2004 Auburn	
1987 Texas	1993 Stanford	1999 Georgia	2005 Georgia	

The Harvard-Yale Regatta

Yale's Varsity Eights crew came from behind in the race's final strokes to nip Harvard by just 0.5 seconds at the 142nd running of the Harvard/Yale Regatta held June 8-9, 2007. It was Yale's first win over Harvard since 1999 and third in the last 23 years. The margin of victory was the closest since Yale's 0.2-second victory in 1914. Yale was also took in the Second Varsity race, while Harvard's freshman squad was victorious to prevent the sweep. The Harvard/Yale Regatta is the nation's oldest intercollegiate sporting event. Harvard holds an 88-54 series edge.

Annual NCAA Division I Team Champions (Cont.)

INDOOR TRACK

Men

Distance ace Chris Solinsky won the 5,000 meters and placed second in the 3,000 to lead Wisconsin to its first NCAA indoor track and field national championship. The Badgers totaled 40 points to outpace runner-up Florida State (35) and become the first Big Ten school in history to win the NCAA indoor title. Senior Joe Detmer placed fifth in the heptathlon for Wisconsin, setting a world record in the heptathlon 1,000 meters (2:29.42) along the way. Texas' Donovan Kilmartin won the event for his third national title in four years. Florida State sprinter Walter Dix won his second straight 200 meters but slipped in the 60-meter event, placing last and all but solidifying Wisconsin's victory over the Seminoles. (*Fayetteville, AR; Mar. 9-10, 2007.*)

Multiple winners: Arkansas (19); UTEP (7); Kansas and Villanova (3); LSU and USC (2).

Year	Year	Year	Year	Year
1965 Missouri	1974 UTEP	1983 SMU	1992 Arkansas	2001 LSU
1966 Kansas	1975 UTEP	1984 Arkansas	1993 Arkansas	2002 Tennessee
1967 USC	1976 UTEP	1985 Arkansas	1994 Arkansas	2003 Arkansas
1968 Villanova	1977 Washington St.	1986 Arkansas	1995 Arkansas	2004 LSU
1969 Kansas	1978 UTEP	1987 Arkansas	1996 George Mason	2005 Arkansas
1970 Kansas	1979 Villanova	1988 Arkansas	1997 Arkansas	2006 Arkansas
1971 Villanova	1980 UTEP	1989 Arkansas	1998 Arkansas	2007 Wisconsin
1972 USC	1981 UTEP	1990 Arkansas	1999 Arkansas	
1973 Manhattan	1982 UTEP	1991 Arkansas	2000 Arkansas	

Women

Jacquelyn Johnson repeated as champion in the pentathlon, Sarah Stevens grabbed the title in the shot put and their Arizona State squad powered to its first title at the NCAA Women's Division I Indoor Track & Field Championships. The Sun Devils accumulated 38 points to claim the crown over LSU (33), Tennessee (30) and Georgia (28). Arizona State's Amy Hastings finished sixth in the 3,000-meter event, then the Sun Devils (2nd) bettered Tennessee (3rd) in the 4x400-meter relay to clinch the title. Auburn sprinter Kerron Stewart (60 and 200 meters) and Texas Tech distance runner Sally Kipyego (3,000 and 5,000 meters) were the meet's only double individual champions (*Fayetteville, AR; Mar. 9-10, 2007.*)

Multiple winners: LSU (11); Texas (6); Nebraska and UCLA (2).

Year	Year	Year	Year	Year
1983 Nebraska	1988 Texas	1993 LSU	1998 Texas	2003 LSU
1984 Nebraska	1989 LSU	1994 LSU	1999 Texas	2004 LSU
1985 Florida St.	1990 Texas	1995 LSU	2000 UCLA	2005 Tennessee
1986 Texas	1991 LSU	1996 LSU	2001 UCLA	2006 Texas
1987 LSU	1992 Florida	1997 LSU	2002 LSU	2007 Arizona St.

OUTDOOR TRACK

Men

Florida State dominated the sprints en route to its second consecutive Division I outdoor track and field title. Walter Dix took the 100-meter event in 9.93 and grabbed his second consecutive title in the 200 meters with a time of 20.32. Teammate Ricardo Chambers finished just four one-hundredths of a second in front of USC's Lionel Larry to take the gold in 44.66. The Seminoles finished with 54 points to finish ahead of LSU (48), Auburn (34) and Tennessee (31). Wisconsin's Chris Solinsky successfully defended his title in the 5,000 meters, while Oregon's Thomas Skipper and Arizona's Jake Arnold were repeat winners in the pole vault and decathlon, respectively. (*Sacramento, CA; June 6-9, 2007.*)

Multiple winners: USC (26); Arkansas (12); UCLA (8); UTEP (6); Illinois and Oregon (5); LSU and Stanford (4); Kansas and Tennessee (3); Florida St. and SMU (2).

Year	Year	Year	Year	Year
1921 Illinois	1939 USC	1957 Villanova	1974 Tennessee	1992 Arkansas
1922 California	1940 USC	1958 USC	1975 UTEP	1993 Arkansas
1923 Michigan	1941 USC	1959 Kansas	1976 USC	1994 Arkansas
1924 Not held	1942 USC		1977 Arizona St.	1995 Arkansas
1925 Stanford*	1943 USC	1960 Kansas	1978 UCLA & UTEP	1996 Arkansas
1926 USC*	1944 Illinois	1961 USC	1979 UTEP	1997 Arkansas
1927 Illinois*	1945 Navy	1962 Oregon		1998 Arkansas
1928 Stanford	1946 Illinois	1963 USC	1980 UTEP	1999 Arkansas
1929 Ohio St.	1947 Illinois	1964 Oregon	1981 UTEP	
	1948 Minnesota	1965 Oregon & USC	1982 UTEP	2000 Stanford
1930 USC	1949 USC	1966 UCLA	1983 SMU	2001 Tennessee
1931 USC		1967 USC	1984 Oregon	2002 LSU
1932 Indiana	1950 USC	1968 USC	1985 Arkansas	2003 Arkansas
1933 LSU	1951 USC	1969 San Jose St.	1986 SMU	2004 Arkansas
1934 Stanford	1952 USC	1970 BYU, Kansas	1987 UCLA	2005 Arkansas
1935 USC	1953 USC	& Oregon	1988 UCLA	2006 Florida St.
1936 USC	1954 USC	1971 UCLA	1989 LSU	2007 Florida St.
1937 USC	1955 USC	1972 UCLA		
1938 USC	1956 UCLA	1973 UCLA	1990 LSU	
			1991 Tennessee	

(*) indicates unofficial championship.

Arizona State's **Jacquelyn Johnson** clears the bar at 5 feet, 10 inches during the heptathlon high jump at the NCAA Division I Track and Field Championships.

Women

Led by Jessica Pressley's winning heave of 59-0¾ in the shot put, Arizona St. captured its first title at the NCAA Women's Division I Outdoor Track & Field Championships. The Sun Devils scored 60 points to beat runner-up LSU (53) and third-place Michigan (36) and became the 13th team in NCAA women's history to win both the indoor and outdoor team titles in the same year. Jacquelyn Johnson repeated as heptathlon national champ and April Kubishta won the pole vault to account for Arizona State's other individual victories. (*Sacramento, CA; June 6-9, 2007.*)

Multiple winners: LSU (13); Texas (4); UCLA (3).

Year	Year	Year	Year	Year
1982 UCLA	1988 LSU	1994 LSU	2000 LSU	2006 Auburn
1983 UCLA	1989 LSU	1995 LSU	2001 USC	2007 Arizona St.
1984 Florida St.	1990 LSU	1996 LSU	2002 South Carolina	
1985 Oregon	1991 LSU	1997 LSU	2003 LSU	
1986 Texas	1992 LSU	1998 Texas	2004 UCLA	
1987 LSU	1993 LSU	1999 Texas	2005 Texas	

VOLLEYBALL

Men

Matt Webber pounded 22 kills and Brian Thornton dished out 59 assists to lead UC Irvine to a victory over IPFW and its first NCAA national volleyball title. The Anteaters took the title in four games, 30-20, 24-30, 30-23, 30-28. Webber hit .457 and was awarded the Most Valuable Player award, while teammate Jayson Jablonsky added 18 kills. C.J. Macias led the Mastodons with 21 kills. The Anteaters finished the season at 29-5, more wins than any team in the country. IPFW ended their year at 23-8. (*Columbus, OH; May 5, 2007.*)

Multiple winners: UCLA (19); Pepperdine (5); USC (4); BYU (3).

Year	Year	Year	Year	Year
1970 UCLA	1978 Pepperdine	1986 Pepperdine	1994 Penn St.	2002 Hawaii†
1971 UCLA	1979 UCLA	1987 UCLA	1995 UCLA	2003 Lewis, IL*
1972 UCLA	1980 USC	1988 USC	1996 UCLA	2004 BYU
1973 San Diego St.	1981 UCLA	1989 UCLA	1997 Stanford	2005 Pepperdine
1974 UCLA	1982 UCLA	1990 USC	1998 UCLA	2006 UCLA
1975 UCLA	1983 UCLA	1991 Long Beach St.	1999 BYU	2007 UC Irvine
1976 UCLA	1984 UCLA	1992 Pepperdine	2000 UCLA	
1977 USC	1985 Pepperdine	1993 UCLA	2001 BYU	

†Title was later vacated due to action by the NCAA Committee on Infractions.
*Division II

Annual NCAA Division I Team Champions (Cont.)
Women

Top-seed Nebraska (33-1) came from behind to defeat second-seeded Stanford, 27-20, 30-26, 30-28, 30-27, for its third NCAA Division I women's volleyball championship and first in six years. Tournament Most Outstanding Player Sarah Pavan paced the Husker attack with 22 kills, Jordan Larson added 19, and Rachel Holloway handed out 58 assists. Tracy Stalls was stellar at the net, recording seven blocks. Erin Waller led Stanford (30-4) with 18 kills. (*Omaha, NE; Dec. 16 2006.*)

Multiple winners: Stanford (6); Hawaii, Long Beach St., Nebraska, UCLA and USC (3); Pacific (2).

Year	Year	Year	Year	Year
1981 USC	1987 Hawaii	1993 Long Beach St.	1999 Penn St.	2005 Washington
1982 Hawaii	1988 Texas	1994 Stanford	2000 Nebraska	2006 Nebraska
1983 Hawaii	1989 Long Beach St.	1995 Nebraska	2001 Stanford	
1984 UCLA	1990 UCLA	1996 Stanford	2002 USC	
1985 Pacific	1991 UCLA	1997 Stanford	2003 USC	
1986 Pacific	1992 Stanford	1998 Long Beach St.	2004 Stanford	

WATER POLO
Men

In one of the most spectacular finishes in college water polo history, California's Jeff Tyrrell scored with no time left on the clock to give the Bears a 7-6 win over USC for their 12th national championship. The goal came just two seconds after USC tied the game at six on a goal from Thomas Hale. Cal goalie Mark Sheredy made multiple impressive saves, including one on a penalty shot by Hale with 6:10 remaining, and was awarded MVP honors. (*Los Angeles, CA; Dec. 3, 2006.*)

Multiple winners: California (12); Stanford (10); UCLA (8); UC-Irvine and USC (3).

Year	Year	Year	Year	Year
1969 UCLA	1977 California	1985 Stanford	1993 Stanford	2001 Stanford
1970 UC-Irvine	1978 Stanford	1986 Stanford	1994 Stanford	2002 Stanford
1971 UCLA	1979 UC-S. Barbara	1987 California	1995 UCLA	2003 USC
1972 UCLA	1980 Stanford	1988 California	1996 UCLA	2004 UCLA
1973 California	1981 Stanford	1989 UC-Irvine	1997 Pepperdine	2005 USC
1974 California	1982 UC-Irvine	1990 California	1998 USC	2006 California
1975 California	1983 California	1991 California	1999 UCLA	
1976 Stanford	1984 California	1992 California	2000 UCLA	

Women

UCLA jumped out to a 3-1 halftime lead and held on to defeat Stanford, 5-4, for its third consecutive women's water polo title and fifth overall. The Bruins closed out the year at 28-2 and have won 90 of 96 games over the past three years. Courtney Mathewson netted three goals for UCLA and Jillian Kraus added two, but it was four-time champion Kelly Rulon who took home MVP honors. Lauren Silver led Stanford with three goals. (*Los Alamitos, CA; May 13, 2007.*)

Multiple winner: UCLA (5).

Year	Year	Year	Year	Year
2001 UCLA	2003 UCLA	2005 UCLA	2006 UCLA	2007 UCLA
2002 Stanford	2004 USC			

WRESTLING
Men

Heavyweight Cole Konrad pinned Penn State's Aaron Anspach to lead Minnesota to its third NCAA Division I wrestling championship in the last seven years. The Golden Gophers amassed a total of 98 points to cruise to the championship ahead of runner-up Iowa St. (88½). Konrad repeated his title, becoming the fourth two-time national champion in school history. Penn's Matt Valenti and Missouri's Ben Askren also successfully defended their titles. (*Auburn Hills, MI; Mar. 15-17, 2007.*)

Multiple winners: Oklahoma St. (34); Iowa (20); Iowa St. (8); Oklahoma (7); Minnesota (3).

Year	Year	Year	Year	Year
1928 Okla. A&M*	1943-45 Not held	1961 Okla. St.	1977 Iowa St.	1993 Iowa
1929 Okla. A&M	1946 Okla. A&M	1962 Okla. St.	1978 Iowa	1994 Okla. St.
1930 Okla. A&M	1947 Cornell Col.	1963 Oklahoma	1979 Iowa	1995 Iowa
1931 Okla. A&M*	1948 Okla. A&M	1964 Okla. St.	1980 Iowa	1996 Iowa
1932 Indiana*	1949 Okla. A&M	1965 Iowa St.	1981 Iowa	1997 Iowa
1933 Okla. A&M* & Iowa St.*	1950 Northern Iowa	1966 Okla. St.	1982 Iowa	1998 Iowa
	1951 Oklahoma	1967 Michigan St.	1983 Iowa	1999 Iowa
1934 Okla. A&M	1952 Oklahoma	1968 Okla. St.	1984 Iowa	2000 Iowa
1935 Okla. A&M	1953 Penn St.	1969 Iowa St.	1985 Iowa	2001 Minnesota
1936 Oklahoma	1954 Okla. A&M	1970 Iowa St.	1986 Iowa	2002 Minnesota
1937 Okla. A&M	1955 Okla. A&M	1971 Okla. St.	1987 Iowa St.	2003 Okla. St.
1938 Okla. A&M	1956 Okla. A&M	1972 Iowa St.	1988 Arizona St.	2004 Okla. St.
1939 Okla. A&M	1957 Oklahoma	1973 Iowa St.	1989 Okla. St.	2005 Okla. St.
1940 Okla. A&M	1958 Okla. St.	1974 Oklahoma	1990 Okla. St.	2006 Okla. St.
1941 Okla. A&M	1959 Okla. St.	1975 Iowa	1991 Iowa	2007 Minnesota
1942 Okla. A&M	1960 Oklahoma	1976 Iowa	1992 Iowa	

(*) indicates unofficial champions. **Note:** Oklahoma A&M became Oklahoma St. in 1958.

HALLS of FAME & AWARDS

Tony Gwynn and Cal Ripken Jr. were voted into the Baseball Hall of Fame in 2007. Mark McGwire was not.

BASEBALL

National Baseball Hall of Fame & Museum

Established in 1935 by Major League Baseball to celebrate the game's 100th anniversary. **Address:** 25 Main Street, Cooperstown, NY 13326. **Telephone:** (607) 547-7200. **Web:** www.baseballhalloffame.org

Eligibility: In August 2001, the Hall of Fame announced changes in the way players are elected via the Veterans Committee. The voting done by Baseball Writers' Association of America remains unchanged. Nominated players must have played at least parts of 10 seasons in the major leagues and be retired for at least five. Certain nominated players not elected by the writers can become eligible via the Veterans Committee. The new Veterans Committee will be comprised of all living Hall of Famers as well as all living winners of the Ford Frick and J.G. Taylor Spink Awards and three members of the old 15-member Veterans Committee with unexpired terms. There was no Veterans Committee vote in 2002. Beginning in 2003 the new Veterans Committee votes every two years on former players and every four years on managers, umpires and executives. Previously, the committee voted annually.

Also, the eligibility of all players that had been dropped from the ballots for not receiving five percent of the vote was restored and those players can now be immediately considered by the new Veterans Committee. The players on baseball's ineligible list are still excluded from consideration. Pete Rose is the only living ex-player on that list.
Class of 2007 (2): BBWAA vote— **Cal Ripken Jr.**, Baltimore Orioles (1981-2001); **Tony Gwynn**, San Diego Padres (1982-2001).

2007 Top vote-getters (545 BBWAA ballots cast, 409 needed to elect, 28 to remain on ballot): 1. **Cal Ripken Jr.** (537), 2. **Tony Gwynn** (532), 3. **Rich Gossage** (388), 4. **Jim Rice** (346); 5. **Andre Dawson** (309), 6. **Bert Blyleven** (260), 7. **Lee Smith** (217), 8. **Jack Morris** (202), 9. **Mark McGwire** (128); 10. **Tommy John** (125), 11. **Steve Garvey** (115), 12. **Dave Concepcion** (74); 13. **Alan Trammell** (73), 14. **Dave Parker** (62), 15. **Don Mattingly** (54), 16. **Dale Murphy** (50), 17. **Harold Baines** (29), 18. **Orel Hershiser** (24).

Elected first year on ballot (43): Hank Aaron, Ernie Banks, Johnny Bench, Wade Boggs, George Brett, Lou Brock, Rod Carew, Steve Carlton, Ty Cobb, Dennis Eckersley, Bob Feller, Bob Gibson, Tony Gwynn, Reggie Jackson, Walter Johnson, Al Kaline, Sandy Koufax, Mickey Mantle, Christy Mathewson, Willie Mays, Willie McCovey, Paul Molitor, Joe Morgan, Eddie Murray, Stan Musial, Jim Palmer, Kirby Puckett, Cal Ripken Jr., Brooks Robinson, Frank Robinson, Jackie Robinson, Babe Ruth, Nolan Ryan, Mike Schmidt, Tom Seaver, Ozzie Smith, Warren Spahn, Willie Stargell, Honus Wagner, Ted Williams, Dave Winfield, Carl Yastrzemski and Robin Yount.

Members are listed with years of induction; (+) indicates deceased members.

Catchers

Bench, Johnny 1989	+ Cochrane, Mickey 1947	+ Hartnett, Gabby 1955
Berra, Yogi 1972	+ Dickey, Bill 1954	+ Lombardi, Ernie 1986
+ Bresnahan, Roger 1945	+ Ewing, Buck 1939	+ Schalk, Ray 1955
+ Campanella, Roy 1969	+ Ferrell, Rick 1984	
Carter, Gary 2003	Fisk, Carlton 2000	

1st Basemen

+ Anson, Cap 1939	+ Connor, Roger 1976	McCovey, Willie 1986
+ Beckley, Jake 1971	+ Foxx, Jimmie 1951	+ Mize, Johnny 1981
+ Bottomley, Jim 1974	+ Gehrig, Lou 1939	Murray, Eddie 2003
+ Brouthers, Dan 1945	+ Greenberg, Hank 1956	Perez, Tony 2000
Cepeda, Orlando 1999	+ Kelly, George 1973	+. Sisler, George 1939
+ Chance, Frank 1946	Killebrew, Harmon 1984	+ Terry, Bill 1954

2nd Basemen

Carew, Rod 1991	+ Herman, Billy 1975	+ Robinson, Jackie 1962
+ Collins, Eddie 1939	+ Hornsby, Rogers 1942	Sandberg, Ryne 2005
Doerr, Bobby 1986	+ Lajoie, Nap 1937	Schoendienst, Red 1989
+ Evers, Johnny 1946	+ Lazzeri, Tony 1991	
+ Fox, Nellie 1997	Mazeroski, Bill 2001	**Designated Hitters**
+ Frisch, Frankie 1947	+ McPhee, Bid 2000	Molitor, Paul 2004
+ Gehringer, Charlie 1949	Morgan, Joe 1990	

Shortstops

Aparicio, Luis 1984	+ Jackson, Travis 1982	Smith, Ozzie 2002
+ Appling, Luke 1964	+ Jennings, Hugh 1945	+ Tinker, Joe 1946
+ Bancroft, Dave 1971	+ Maranville, Rabbit 1954	+ Vaughan, Arky 1985
Banks, Ernie 1977	+ Reese, Pee Wee 1984	+ Wagner, Honus 1936
+ Boudreau, Lou 1970	Ripken Jr., Cal 2007	+ Wallace, Bobby 1953
+ Cronin, Joe 1956	+ Rizzuto, Phil 1994	+ Ward, Monte 1964
+ Davis, George 1998	+ Sewell, Joe 1977	Yount, Robin 1999

3rd Basemen

+ Baker, Frank 1955	Kell, George 1983	Schmidt, Mike 1995
Boggs, Wade 2005	+ Lindstrom, Fred 1976	+ Traynor, Pie 1948
Brett, George 1999	+ Mathews, Eddie 1978	
+ Collins, Jimmy 1945	Robinson, Brooks 1983	

Center Fielders

+ Ashburn, Richie 1995	+ Doby, Larry 1998	+ Roush, Edd 1962
+ Averill, Earl 1975	+ Duffy, Hugh 1945	Snider, Duke 1980
+ Carey, Max 1961	+ Hamilton, Billy 1961	+ Speaker, Tris 1937
+ Cobb, Ty 1936	+ Mantle, Mickey 1974	~ Waner, Lloyd 1967
+ Combs, Earle 1970	Mays, Willie 1979	+ Wilson, Hack 1979
+ DiMaggio, Joe 1955	+ Puckett, Kirby 2001	

Left Fielders

Brock, Lou 1985	+ Kelley, Joe 1971	+ Simmons, Al 1953
+ Burkett, Jesse 1946	Kiner, Ralph 1975	+ Stargell, Willie 1988
+ Clarke, Fred 1945	+ Manush, Heinie 1964	+ Wheat, Zack 1959
+ Delahanty, Ed 1945	+ Medwick, Joe 1968	Williams, Billy 1987
+ Goslin, Goose 1968	Musial, Stan 1969	+ Williams, Ted 1966
+ Hafey, Chick 1971	+ O'Rourke, Jim 1945	Yastrzemski, Carl 1989

Right Fielders

Aaron, Hank 1982	Jackson, Reggie 1993	Robinson, Frank 1982
+ Clemente, Roberto 1973	Kaline, Al 1980	+ Ruth, Babe 1936
+ Crawford, Sam 1957	+ Keeler, Willie 1939	+ Slaughter, Enos 1985
+ Cuyler, Kiki 1968	+ Kelly, King 1945	+ Thompson, Sam 1974
+ Flick, Elmer 1963	+ Klein, Chuck 1980	+ Waner, Paul 1952
Gwynn, Tony 2007	+ McCarthy, Tommy 1946	Winfield, Dave 2001
+ Heilmann, Harry 1952	+ Ott, Mel 1951	+ Youngs, Ross 1972
+ Hooper, Harry 1971	+ Rice, Sam 1963	

Major League Baseball's All-Time Team — 1969 and 1997

The Baseball Writers' Association of America originally selected an all-time team as part of major league baseball's 100th anniversary, announcing the outcome of its vote on July 21, 1969. Vote totals were not released. Another vote was released when a panel of 36 BWAA members picked an all-time team for the *Classic Sports Network* just before the 1997 All-Star Game. This time vote totals were given, the single outfield category was divided into three (left, center and right) and two recently popularized positions—the designated hitter and relief pitcher—were added. In the most recent vote two points were awarded for first-place votes and one point for second place. Point totals follow the names with the number of first-place votes in parentheses. All-time team members are listed in **bold** type

1969 Vote

C   **Mickey Cochrane**, Bill Dickey, Roy Campanella
1B **Lou Gehrig**, George Sisler, Stan Musial
2B **Rogers Hornsby**, Charlie Gehringer, Eddie Collins
SS **Honus Wagner**, Joe Cronin, Ernie Banks
3B **Pie Traynor**, Brooks Robinson, Jackie Robinson
OF **Babe Ruth, Ty Cobb, Joe DiMaggio**, Ted
    Williams, Tris Speaker, Willie Mays

RHP **Walter Johnson**, Christy Mathewson, Cy Young
LHP **Lefty Grove**, Sandy Koufax, Carl Hubbell
Mgr. **John McGraw**, Casey Stengel, Joe McCarthy

1969 Vote All-Time Outstanding Player: **Ruth**, Cobb, Wagner, DiMaggio

1997 Vote

C   **Johnny Bench** (24) 52; Yogi Berra (4) 22; Roy Campanella (4) 17; Mickey Cochrane (1) 5; Bill Dickey (1) 4; Gabby Hartnett (1) 3; Carlton Fisk 2.
1B **Lou Gehrig** (31) 661/2; Jimmie Foxx (3) 19; George Sisler (2) 8; Willie McCovey 6; Hank Greenberg 21/2; Stan Musial, Eddie Murray, Mark McGwire and Frank Thomas 1.
2B **Rogers Hornsby** (17) 44; Joe Morgan (6) 23; Jackie Robinson (6) 15; Charley Gehringer (4) and Napoleon Lajoie (3) 11; Eddie Collins (1) 3; Rod Carew 2; Ryne Sandberg 1.
SS **Honus Wagner** (23) 55; Cal Ripken Jr. (6) 24; Ozzie Smith (5) 16; Ernie Banks (1) 8; Lou Boudreau and Luke Appling 1.
3B **Mike Schmidt** (21) 50; Brooks Robinson (13) 37; Eddie Mathews (3), George Brett (1) 8; Pie Traynor 3; Pete Rose (1) 2; Frank Baker, Al Rosen and Wade Boggs 1.
LF **Ted Williams** (32) 68; Stan Musial (4) 36; Pete Rose, Ralph Kiner, Rickey Henderson and Barry Bonds 1.
CF **Willie Mays** (25) 57; Ty Cobb (7) 22; Joe DiMaggio (3) 17; Mickey Mantle (1) 10; Tris Speaker 2.
RF **Babe Ruth** (31) 67; Hank Aaron (5) 36; Frank Robinson 2; Al Kaline, Roberto Clemente and Tony Gwynn 1.

DH **Paul Molitor** (22) 48; Harold Baines (3) 12; Don Baylor (1) 10; Edgar Martinez (2) 9; Ty Cobb (2) 6; Hal McRae (1) 5; Mickey Mantle (1) and Dave Parker (1) 3; Joe DiMaggio (1) 2; Lee May, Frank Robinson and Tony Oliva 1.
RHP **Walter Johnson** (9) 30, Cy Young (12) 25; Christy Mathewson (5) 18; Bob Feller (4) 10; Bob Gibson (2) 9; Nolan Ryan (2) 7; Tom Seaver (1) 3; Greg Maddux (1), Grover Cleveland Alexander and Juan Marichal 2.
LHP **Sandy Koufax** (11) 32; Warren Spahn (11) 28; Lefty Grove (8) 25; Steve Carlton (4) 12; Carl Hubbell 6; Whitey Ford (1) 3; Eddie Plank (1) 2.
RP **Dennis Eckersley** (16) 40; Rollie Fingers (9) 29; Lee Smith (4) 13; Hoyt Wilhelm (3) 10; Rich Gossage (3) 9; Bruce Sutter (1) 6, Dan Quisenberry 1.
Mgr. **Casey Stengel** (6) 22, Joe McCarthy (6) 18; Connie Mack (7) 17; John McGraw (6) 16; Sparky Anderson (3) 11; Leo Durocher (2) 6; Dick Williams (1) 4; Billy Martin (1) 3; Al Lopez (1), Ned Hanlon (1), Whitey Herzog (1), Earl Weaver and Bobby Cox 2; Tony La Russa 1.

Baseball (Cont.)

Pitchers

+ Alexander, Grover 1938
+ Bender, Chief 1953
+ Brown, Mordecai 1949
  Bunning, Jim 1996
  Carlton, Steve 1994
+ Chesbro, Jack 1946
+ Clarkson, John 1963
+ Coveleski, Stan 1969
+ Dean, Dizzy 1953
+ Drysdale, Don 1984
  Eckersley, Dennis 2004
+ Faber, Red 1964
  Feller, Bob 1962
  Fingers, Rollie 1992
  Ford, Whitey 1974
+ Galvin, Pud 1965
  Gibson, Bob 1981
+ Gomez, Lefty 1972
+ Grimes, Burleigh 1964
+ Grove, Lefty 1947
+ Haines, Jess 1970

+ Hoyt, Waite 1969
+ Hubbell, Carl 1947
+ Hunter, Catfish 1987
  Jenkins, Ferguson 1991
+ Johnson, Walter 1936
+ Joss, Addie 1978
+ Keefe, Tim 1964
  Koufax, Sandy 1972
+ Lemon, Bob 1976
+ Lyons, Ted 1955
  Marichal, Juan 1983
+ Marquard, Rube 1971
+ Mathewson, Christy 1936
+ McGinnity, Joe 1946
  Niekro, Phil 1997
+ Newhouser, Hal 1992
+ Nichols, Kid 1949
  Palmer, Jim 1990
  Pennock, Herb 1948
  Perry, Gaylord 1991
+ Plank, Eddie 1946

+ Radbourne, Old Hoss 1939
+ Rixey, Eppa 1963
  Roberts, Robin 1976
+ Ruffing, Red 1967
+ Rusie, Amos 1977
  Ryan, Nolan 1999
  Seaver, Tom 1992
+ Spahn, Warren 1973
  Sutter, Bruce 2006
  Sutton, Don 1998
+ Vance, Dazzy 1955
+ Waddell, Rube 1946
+ Walsh, Ed 1946
+ Welch, Mickey 1973
+ Wilhelm, Hoyt 1985
+ Willis, Vic 1995
+ Wynn, Early 1972
+ Young, Cy 1937

Managers

+ Alston, Walter 1983
  Anderson, Sparky 2000
+ Durocher, Leo 1994
+ Hanlon, Ned 1996
+ Harris, Bucky 1975
+ Huggins, Miller 1964

  Lasorda, Tommy 1997
  Lopez, Al 1977
+ Mack, Connie 1937
+ McCarthy, Joe 1957
+ McGraw, John 1937
+ McKechnie, Bill 1962

+ Robinson, Wilbert 1945
+ Selee, Frank 1999
+ Stengel, Casey 1966
  Weaver, Earl 1996

Umpires

+ Barlick, Al 1989
+ Chylak, Nestor 1999
+ Conlan, Jocko 1974

+ Connolly, Tom 1953
+ Evans, Billy 1973
+ Hubbard, Cal 1976

+ Klem, Bill 1953
+ McGowan, Bill 1992

From Negro Leagues

+ Bell, Cool Papa (OF) 1974
+ Brown, Ray (P) 2006
+ Brown, Willard (OF) 2006
+ Cooper, Andy (P) 2006
+ Charleston, Oscar (1B-OF) . .1976
+ Dandridge, Ray (3B) 1987
+ Day, Leon (P-OF-2B) 1995
+ Dihigo, Martin (P-OF) 1977
+ Foster, Rube (P-Mgr) 1981
+ Foster, Willie (P) 1996

+ Gibson, Josh (C) 1972
+ Grant, Frank (2B) 2006
+ Hill, Pete (OF) 2006
  Irvin, Monte (OF) 1973
+ Johnson, Judy (3B) 1975
+ Leonard, Buck (1B) 1972
+ Lloyd, Pop (SS) 1977
+ Mackey, Biz (C) 2006
+ Mendez, Jose (P) 2006
+ Paige, Satchel (P) 1971

+ Rogan, Wilber (P) 1998
+ Santop, Luis (C) 2006
+ Smith, Hilton 2001
+ Stearnes, Turkey (OF) 2000
+ Suttles, Mule (1B) 2006
+ Taylor, Ben (1B) 2006
+ Torriente, Cristobal (OF) . . .2006
+ Wells, Willie (SS) 1997
+ Williams, Joe (P) 1999
+ Wilson, Jud (3B) 2006

Pioneers and Executives

+ Barrow, Ed 1953
+ Bulkeley, Morgan 1937
+ Cartwright, Alexander 1938
+ Chadwick, Henry 1938
+ Chandler, Happy 1982
+ Comiskey, Charles 1939
+ Cummings, Candy 1939
+ Frick, Ford 1970
+ Giles, Warren 1979
+ Griffith, Clark 1946

+ Harridge, Will 1972
+ Hulbert, William 1995
+ Johnson, Ban 1937
+ Landis, Kenesaw 1944
+ MacPhail, Larry 1978
  MacPhail, Lee 1998
+ Manley, Effa 2006
+ Pompez, Alex 2006
+ Posey, Cumberland 2006
+ Rickey, Branch 1967

+ Spalding, Al 1939
+ White, Sol 2006
+ Veeck, Bill 1991
+ Weiss, George 1971
+ Wilkinson, J.L. 2006
+ Wright, George 1937
+ Wright, Harry 1953
+ Yawkey, Tom 1980

BASKETBALL

Naismith Memorial Basketball Hall of Fame

Established in 1949 by the National Association of Basketball Coaches in memory of the sport's inventor, Dr. James Naismith. Original Hall opened in 1968 and a renovated version of the Hall opened in 1985. A completely new building opened Sept. 28, 2002. **Address:** 1000 West Columbus Avenue, Springfield, MA 01105. **Telephone:** (413) 781-6500. **Web:** www.hoophall.com.

Eligibility: Nominated players and referees must be retired for five years, coaches must have coached 25 years or be retired for five, and contributors must have already completed their noteworthy service to the game. Voting done by 24-member honors committee made up of media representatives, Hall of Fame members and trustees. Any nominee not elected after five years becomes eligible for consideration by the Veterans' Committee after a five-year wait.

Class of 2007 (7): COACHES—**Van Chancellor, Pedro Ferrandiz, Phil Jackson, Mirko Novosel, Roy Williams**; TEAM—**Texas Western**; REFEREE—**Marvin "Mendy" Rudolph**.

2007 finalists (nominated but not elected): PLAYERS—Adrian Dantley, Richie Guerin and Chris Mullin. COACHES—Bob Hurley Sr., Eddie Sutton and Harley Redin. CONTRIBUTOR—Bill Davidson and Dick Vitale.

Note: John Wooden, Lenny Wilkens and **Bill Sharman** are the only members to be inducted as both a player and a coach.

Members are listed with years of induction; (+) indicates deceased members.

Men

Abdul-Jabbar, Kareem	1995	Goodrich, Gail	1996
Archibald, Nate	1991	Greer, Hal	1981
+ Arizin, Paul	1977	+ Gruenig, Robert	1963
Barkley, Charles	2006	Hagan, Cliff	1977
+ Barlow, Thomas (Babe)	1980	+ Hanson, Victor	1960
Barry, Rick	1987	Havlicek, John	1983
Baylor, Elgin	1976	Hawkins, Connie	1992
+ Beckman, John	1972	Hayes, Elvin	1990
Bellamy, Walt	1993	Haynes, Marques	1998
Belov, Sergei	1992	Heinsohn, Tom	1986
Bing, Dave	1990	+ Holman, Nat	1964
Bird, Larry	1998	Houbregs, Bob	1987
+ Borgmann, Bennie	1961	Howell, Bailey	1997
Bradley, Bill	1982	+ Hyatt, Chuck	1959
+ Brennan, Joe	1974	Issel, Dan	1993
Cervi, Al	1984	+ Jeannette, Buddy	1994
+ Chamberlain, Wilt	1978	+ Johnson, Bill (Skinny)	1976
+ Cooper, Charles (Tarzan)	1976	Johnson, Earvin (Magic)	2002
+ Cosic, Kresimir	1996	+ Johnston, Neil	1990
Cousy, Bob	1970	Jones, K. C	1989
Cowens, Dave	1991	Jones, Sam	1983
Cunningham, Billy	1986	+ Krause, Edward (Moose)	1975
+ Davies, Bob	1969	Kurland, Bob	1961
+ DeBernardi, Forrest	1961	Lanier, Bob	1992
+ DeBusschere, Dave	1982	+ Lapchick, Joe	1966
+ Dehnert, Dutch	1968	Lovellette, Clyde	1988
Drexler, Clyde	2004	Lucas, Jerry	1979
Dumars, Joe	2006	Luisetti, Hank	1959
+ Endacott, Paul	1971	Macauley, Ed	1960
English, Alex	1997	Malone, Moses	2001
Erving, Julius (Dr. J)	1993	+ Maravich, Pete	1987
+ Foster, Bud	1964	Martin, Slater	1981
Frazier, Walt	1987	McAdoo, Bob	2000
+ Friedman, Marty	1971	+ McCracken, Branch	1960
+ Fulks, Joe	1977	+ McCracken, Jack	1962
+ Gale, Laddie	1976	+ McDermott, Bobby	1988
Gallatin, Harry	1991	McGuire, Dick	1993
+ Gates, William (Pop)	1989	McHale, Kevin	1999
Gervin, George	1996	+ Mikan, George	1959
Gola, Tom	1975	Mikkelsen, Vern	1995

Monroe, Earl	1990
Murphy, Calvin	1993
+ Murphy, Charles (Stretch)	1960
+ Page, Harlan (Pat)	1962
Parish, Robert	2003
+ Petrovic, Drazen	2002
Pettit, Bob	1970
+ Phillip, Andy	1961
+ Pollard, Jim	1977
Ramsey, Frank	1981
Reed, Willis	1981
Risen, Arnie	1998
Robertson, Oscar	1979
+ Roosma, John	1961
Russell, Bill	1974
+ Russell, John (Honey)	1964
Schayes, Dolph	1972
+ Schmidt, Ernest J	1973
+ Schommer, John	1959
+ Sedran, Barney	1962
Sharman, Bill	1975
+ Steinmetz, Christian	1961
Thomas, Isiah	2000
Thompson, David	1996
+ Thompson, John (Cat)	1962
Thurmond, Nate	1984
Twyman, Jack	1982
Unseld, Wes	1988
+ Vandivier, Robert (Fuzzy)	1974
+ Wachter, Ed	1961
Walton, Bill	1993
Wanzer, Bobby	1987
West, Jerry	1979
Wilkens, Lenny	1989
Wilkins, Dominique	2006
Wooden, John	1960
Worthy, James	2003
+ Yardley, George	1996

Women

Blazejowski, Carol	1994	Marcari, Hortencia	2005
Crawford, Joan	1997	Meyers, Ann	1993
Curry, Denise	1997	Miller, Cheryl	1995
Donovan, Anne	1995	Semenova, Uljana	1993
Harris-Stewart, Lucia	1992	White, Nera	1992
Lieberman, Nancy	1996	Woodard, Lynette	2004

Teams

Buffalo Germans	1961
First Team	1959
Harlem Globetrotters	2002
New York Renaissance	1963
Original Celtics	1959
Texas Western (1966)	2007

Referees

+ Enright, Jim	1978
+ Hepbron, George	1960
+ Hoyt, George	1961
+ Kennedy, Pat	1959
+ Leith, Lloyd	1982

+ Mihalik, Red	1986
+ Nucatola, John	1977
+ Quigley, Ernest (Quig)	1961
+ Rudolph, Marvin (Mendy)	2007
+ Shirley, J. Dallas	1979

+ Strom, Earl	1995
+ Tobey, Dave	1961
+ Walsh, David	1961

Coaches

+ Allen, Forrest (Phog)	1959
+ Anderson, Harold (Andy)	1984
+ Auerbach, Red	1968
Auriemma, Geno	2006
Barmore, Leon	2003
+ Barry, Sam	1978
+ Blood, Ernest (Prof)	1960
Boeheim, Jim	2005
Brown, Larry	2002
Calhoun, Jim	2005
+ Cann, Howard	1967
+ Carlson, Henry (Doc)	1959
Carnesecca, Lou	1992
Carnevale, Ben	1969
Carril, Pete	1997
+ Case, Everett	1981
Chancellor, Van	2007
Chaney, John	2001
Conradt, Jody	1998
Crum, Denny	1994
Daly, Chuck	1994
+ Dean, Everett	1966
+ Diaz-Miguel, Antonio	1997
+ Diddle, Ed	1971
+ Drake, Bruce	1972
Ferrandiz, Pedro	2007
Gaines, Clarence (Bighouse)	1981

+ Gardner, Jack	1983
+ Gill, Amory (Slats)	1967
+ Gomelsky, Aleksandr	1995
+ Gunter, Sue	2005
+ Hannum, Alex	1998
Harshman, Marv	1984
Haskins, Don	1997
+ Hickey, Eddie	1978
+ Hobson, Howard (Hobby)	1965
+ Holzman, Red	1986
+ Iba, Hank	1968
Jackson, Phil	2007
+ Julian, Alvin (Doggie)	1967
+ Keaney, Frank	1960
+ Keogan, George	1961
Knight, Bob	1991
Krzyzewski, Mike	2001
Kundla, John	1995
+ Lambert, Ward (Piggy)	1960
+ Litwack, Harry	1975
+ Loeffler, Ken	1964
+ Lonborg, Dutch	1972
+ McCutchan, Arad	1980
+ McGuire, Al	1992
+ McGuire, Frank	1976
+ McLendon, John	1978
+ Meanwell, Walter (Doc)	1959

Meyer, Ray	1978
+ Miller, Ralph	1988
Moore, Billie	1999
Newell, Pete	1978
+ Nikolic, Aleksandar	1998
Novosel, Mirko	2007
Olson, Lute	2002
Ramsay, Jack	1992
Rubini, Cesare	1994
+ Rupp, Adolph	1968
+ Sachs, Leonard	1961
Sharman, Bill	2004
+ Shelton, Everett	1979
Smith, Dean	1982
Summitt, Pat	2000
+ Taylor, Fred	1986
Thompson, John	1999
+ Wade, Margaret	1984
Watts, Stan	1985
Wilkens, Lenny	1998
Williams, Roy	2007
Wooden, John	1972
+ Woolpert, Phil	1992
Wootten, Morgan	2000
Yow, Kay	2002

Contributors

+ Abbott, Senda Berenson	1984
+ Bee, Clair	1967
+ Biasone, Danny	2000
Brown, Hubie	2005
+ Brown, Walter A	1965
+ Bunn, John	1964
Colangelo, Jerry	2004
+ Douglas, Bob	1971
+ Duer, Al	1981
Embry, Wayne	1999
+ Fagan, Clifford B	1983
+ Fisher, Harry	1973
+ Fleisher, Larry	1991
Gavitt, Dave	2006
+ Gottlieb, Eddie	1971
+ Gulick, Luther	1959
+ Harrison, Les	1979

+ Hearn, Francis (Chick)	2003
+ Hepp, Ferenc	1980
+ Hickox, Ed	1959
+ Hinkle, Tony	1965
+ Irish, Ned	1964
+ Jones, R. William	1964
+ Kennedy, Walter	1980
Lemon, Meadowlark	2003
+ Liston, Emil (Liz)	1974
+ Mokray, Bill	1965
+ Morgan, Ralph	1959
+ Morgenweck, Frank (Pop)	1962
+ Naismith, James	1959
Newton, Charles M.	2000
+ O'Brien, John J. (Jack)	1961
+ O'Brien, Larry	1991
+ Olsen, Harold G	1959

+ Podoloff, Maurice	1973
+ Porter, Henry (H.V.)	1960
+ Reid, William A	1963
+ Ripley, Elmer	1972
+ St. John, Lynn W	1962
+ Saperstein, Abe	1970
+ Schabinger, Arthur	1961
+ Stagg, Amos Alonzo	1959
Stankovic, Boris	1991
+ Steitz, Ed	1983
+ Taylor, Chuck	1968
+ Teague, Bertha	1984
+ Tower, Oswald	1959
+ Trester, Arthur (A.L.)	1961
+ Wells, Cliff	1971
+ Wilke, Lou	1982
+ Zollner, Fred	1999

National Collegiate Basketball Hall of Fame

Established in 2006 by the National Association of Basketball Coaches. The five inaugural honorees inducted into the new college basketball hall of fame in November 2006 represent each of the three categories that will be recognized every year—coach, player and contributor. They are part of a founding class of over 100 individuals who are already members of the Naismith Basketball Hall of Fame with roots in college basketball and will automatically be included in the National Collegiate Basketball Hall of Fame located in Kansas City, Mo.

Class of 2007 (12): PLAYERS—**Kareem Abdul-Jabbar**, UCLA; **Dick Groat**, Duke; **Dick Barnett**, Tenn. St.; **Austin Carr**, Notre Dame; COACHES—**Forrest "Phog" Allen**, John McLendon, Adolph Rupp, Henry Iba, **Norm Stewart**, **Guy Lewis**, **Charles "Lefty" Driesell**; CONTRIBUTOR—**Vic Bubas**.

Players

Abdul-Jabbar, Kareem	2007
Barnett, Dick	2007
Carr, Austin	2007
Groat, Dick	2007
Robertson, Oscar	2006
Russell, Bill	2006

Coaches

Allen, Forrest (Phog)	2007
Driesell, Charles (Lefty)	2007
Iba, Henry	2007
McLendon, John	2007
Rupp, Adolph	2007
Smith, Dean	2006

Stewart, Norm	2007
Wooden, John	2006

Contributors

Bubas, Vic	2007
Naismith, Dr. James	2006

BOWLING

International Bowling Hall of Fame & Museum

The National Bowling Hall is one museum with separate wings for honorees of the American Bowling Congress (ABC), Professional Bowlers' Association (PBA), Women's International Bowling Congress (WIBC) and Professional Women Bowlers Association (PWBA). In 2005 the ABC and WIBC merged, becoming the United States Bowling Congress. The museum merged the respective wings and the USBC will induct those who would have previously been honored by the ABC and WIBC. **Address:** 111 Stadium Plaza, St. Louis, MO 63102. **Telephone:** (314) 231-6340. **Web:** www.bowlingmuseum.com

Professional Bowlers Association

Established in 1975. **Eligibility:** The criteria was revamped in 2002. Nominees must now be retired from full-time competition on the PBA Tour for a minimum of at least five years, or reached the age of 50, and must have won a minimum of 10 PBA Tour titles or two major titles. Those inducted under the meritorious service category have been omitted due to space constraints.

Members are listed with years of induction; (+) indicates deceased members.

Performance

+	Allen, Bill	1983	+	Fazio, Buzz	1976	Roth, Mark	1987
+	Anthony, Earl	1986		Ferraro, Dave	1997	Salvino, Carmen	1975
	Aulby, Mike	1996	+	Godman, Jim	1987	Semiz, Teata	1998
	Berardi, Joe	1990		Hardwick, Billy	1977	Smith, Harry	1975
	Bluth, Ray	1975		Holman, Marshall	1990	Soutar, Dave	1979
	Bohn, Parker III	2000		Hudson, Tommy	1989	Stefanich, Jim	1980
	Buckley, Roy	1992		Husted, Dave	1996	Voss, Brian	1994
	Burton, Nelson Jr	1979		Johnson, Don	1977	Webb, Wayne	1993
	Carter, Don	1975		Laub, Larry	1985	+ Weber, Dick	1975
	Colwell, Paul	1991		Monacelli, Amleto	1997	Weber, Pete	1998
	Cook, Steve	1993		Ozio, David	1995	+ Welu, Billy	1975
	Davis, Dave	1978		Pappas, George	1986	Williams, Mark	1999
	Dickinson, Gary	1988		Petraglia, John	1982	Williams, Walter Ray Jr.	1995
	Durbin, Mike	1984		Ritger, Dick	1978	Zahn, Wayne	1981

Veterans

	Allison, Glenn	1984	+	Joseph, Joe	1985	Schlegel, Ernie	1997
	Asher, Barry	1988		Limongello, Mike	1994	+ St. John, Jim	1989
	Baker, Tom	1999		Marzich, Andy	1990	Strampe, Bob	1987
	Foremsky, Skee	1992		McCune, Don	1991		
	Guenther, Johnny	1986		McGrath, Mike	1988		

United States Bowling Congress

Established in 2005 with the merger of the American Bowling Congress and Women's International Bowling Congress. **Class of 2007:** PERFORMANCE— Gordon Vadakin; MERITORIUS SERVICE— Connie Marchione

Performance		Meritorious Service	
Fehr, Nancy	2006	Deken, Fran	2006
Pollard, Rick	2006	Marchione, Connie	2007
Pollard, Ron	2006	Sommer Jr., John	2006
Vadakin, Gordon	2007		

American Bowling Congress

Established in 1941 and open to professional and amateur bowlers, now part of the USBC Hall of Fame. **Eligibility:** Nominated bowlers must have competed in at least 20 years of ABC tournaments.

Members are listed with years of induction; (+) indicates deceased members.

Performance

	Allison, Glenn	1979	+	Brosius, Eddie	1976	+ Crimmins, Johnny	1962
+	Anthony, Earl	1986	+	Bujack, Fred	1967	Davis, Dave	1990
	Asher, Barry	1998		Bunetta, Bill	1968	+ Daw, Charlie	1941
+	Asplund, Harold	1978		Burton, Nelson Jr	1981	+ Day, Ned	1952
	Aulby, Mike	2001	+	Burton, Nelson Sr	1964	Dickinson, Gary	1992
	Baer, Gordy	1987	+	Campi, Lou	1968	Duke, Norm	2002
	Beach, Bill	1991	+	Carlson, Adolph	1941	+ Easter, Sarge	1963
+	Benkovic, Frank	1958		Carter, Don	1970	Ellis, Don	1981
	Berlin, Mike	1994	+	Caruana, Frank	1977	+ Falcaro, Joe	1968
+	Billick, George	1982	+	Cassio, Marty	1972	+ Faragalli, Lindy	1968
+	Blouin, Jimmy	1953	+	Castellano, Graz	1976	+ Fazio, Buzz	1963
	Bluth, Ray	1973		Chamberlain, Bob	2005	Fehr, Steve	1993
+	Bodis, Joe	1941	+	Clause, Frank	1980	+ Gersonde, Russ	1968
+	Bomar, Buddy	1966		Cohn, Alfred	1985	+ Gibson, Therm	1965
	Bower, Gary	2001		Colwell, Paul	1999	+ Godman, Jim	1987
+	Brandt, Allie	1960		Couture, Pete	2004	Goike, Robert	1996

Bowling (Cont.)

+ Golembiewski, Billy 1979
Griffo, Greg 1995
Guenther, Johnny 1988
Hanson, Bob 2004
Hardwick, Billy 1985
Hart, Bob 1994
+ Hennessey, Tom 1976
Hoover, Dick 1974
Horn, Bud 1992
Howard, George 1986
Jackson, Eddie 1988
+ Jackson, Lowell 2003
+ Johnson, Don 1982
Johnson, Earl 1987
+ Joseph, Joe 1969
+ Jouglard, Lee 1979
+ Kartheiser, Frank 1967
+ Kawolics, Ed 1968
+ Kissoff, Joe 1976
+ Klares, John 1982
+ Knox, Billy 1954
+ Koster, John 1941
+ Krems, Eddie 1973
Kristof, Joe 1968
+ Krumske, Paul 1968
+ Lange, Herb 1941
+ Lauman, Hank 1976
Lewis, Mark 2004
Lillard, Bill 1972
Lindemann, Tony 1979
+ Lindsey, Mort 1941

+ Lippe, Harry 1989
Lubanski, Ed 1971
+ Lucci, Vince Sr 1978
+ Marino, Hank 1941
+ Martino, John 1969
Marzich, Andy 1993
McGrath, Mike 1993
+ McMahon, Junie 1967
+ Meisel, Darold 1998
+ Mercurio, Skang 1967
+ Meyers, Norm 1984
+ Nagy, Steve 1963
+ Norris, Joe 1954
+ O'Donnell, Chuck 1968
Pappas, George 1989
+ Patterson, Pat 1974
+ Powell, John (Junior) ..2000
Ritger, Dick 1984
+ Rogoznica, Andy 1993
Salvino, Carmen 1979
Savoy, Todd 2005
Schissler, Les 1991
Schlegel, Ernie 1997
Schroeder, Jim 1990
+ Schwoegler, Connie 1968
Scudder, Don 1999
Semiz, Teata 1991
+ Sielaff, Lou 1968
+ Sinke, Joe 1977
+ Sixty, Billy 1961
Smith, Harry 1978

+ Smith, Jimmy 1941
Soutar, Dave 1985
+ Sparando, Tony 1968
Spigner, Bill 2001
+ Spinella, Barney 1968
+ Steers, Harry 1941
Stefanich, Jim 1983
+ Stein, Otto Jr 1971
Stoudt, Bud 1991
Strampe, Bob 1977
+ Thoma, Sykes 1971
Toft, Rod 1991
+ Totsky, Mike 1996
Tountas, Pete 1989
Tucker, Bill 1988
Tuttle, Tommy 1995
+ Varipapa, Andy 1957
+ Ward, Walter 1959
+ Weber, Dick 1970
Weber, Pete 2002
+ Welu, Billy 1975
Wilcox, John 1999
Williams, Walter Ray Jr. ...2005
+ Wilman, Joe 1951
+ Wolf, Phil 1961
Wonders, Rich 1990
+ Young, George 1959
Zahn, Wayne 1980
Zikes, Les 1983
+ Zunker, Gil 1941

Pioneers

+ Allen, Lafayette Jr. 1994
+ Briell, Frank 1996
+ Carow, Rev. Charles 1995
+ Celestine, Sydney 1993
+ Curtis, Thomas 1993
+ de Freitas, Eric 1994

+ Hall, William Sr. 1994
Hirashima, Hiroto 1995
+ Karpf, Samuel 1993
+ Moore, Henry 1996
+ Pasdeloup, Frank 1993
+ Rhodman, Bill 1997

+ Satow, Masao 1994
+ Schutte, Louis 1993
Shimada, Fuzzy 1997
+ Stein, Louis 1997
+ Thompson, William V. ..1993
+ Timm, Dr. Henry 1993

Meritorious Service

+ Allen, Harold 1966
Archibald, John 1996
+ Baker, Frank 1975
+ Baumgarten, Elmer 1963
+ Bellisimo, Lou 1986
+ Bensinger, Bob 1969
Borden, Fred 2002
+ Chase, LeRoy 1972
+ Coker, John 1980
+ Collier, Chuck 1963
+ Cruchon, Steve 1983
+ Ditzen, Walt 1973
+ Dobs, Darold 1999
+ Doehrman, Bill 1968
+ Elias, Eddie 1985
Esposito, Frank 1997
Evans, Dick 1992

+ Franklin, Bill 1992
+ Hagerty, Jack 1963
+ Hattstrom, H.A. (Doc) ..1980
+ Hermann, Cornelius 1968
+ Howley, Pete 1941
James, Steve 2005
Jensen, Mark 2002
Jowdy, John 2001
+ Kennedy, Bob 1981
+ Langtry, Abe 1963
+ Levine, Sam 1971
+ Luby, David 1969
Luby, Mort Jr.. 1988
+ Luby, Mort Sr. 1974
Matzelle, Al 1995
+ McCullough, Howard ...1971
Mormando, Nick 2003

+ Patterson, Morehead ...1985
+ Petersen, Louie 1963
Pezzano, Chuck 1982
Picchietti, Remo 1993
Pluckhahn, Bruce 1989
+ Raymer, Milt 1972
+ Reed, Elmer 1978
Reichert, Jack 1998
Rudo, Milt 1984
Schenkel, Chris 1988
Skelton, Max 2002
+ Sweeney, Dennis 1974
Tessman, Roger 1994
+ Thum, Joe 1980
Weinstein, Sam 1970
+ Whitney, Eli 1975
+ Wolf, Fred 1976

Women's International Bowling Congress

Established in 1953. **Eligibility:** Performance nominees must have won at least one WIBC Championship Tournament title, a WIBC Queens tournament title or an international competition title and have bowled in at least 15 national WIBC Championship Tournaments (unless injury or illness cut career short).

Members are listed with years of induction; (+) indicates deceased members.

Performance

Abel, Joy 1984
Adamek, Donna 1996
Ann, Patty 1995
Bolt, Mae 1978
Bouvia, Gloria 1987
Boxberger, Loa 1984

Buckner, Pam 1990
+ Burling, Catherine 1958
+ Burns, Nina 1977
Cantaline, Anita 1979
Carter, LaVerne 1977
Carter, Paula 1994

Coburn, Doris 1976
Coburn-Carroll, Cindy ...1998
Costello, Pat 1986
Costello, Patty 1989
Daniels, Cheryl 2002
Dryer, Pat 1978

Duggan, Anne Marie 2005
Duval, Helen 1970
+ Fellmeth, Catherine 1970
Fiebig, Cora 2004
Fothergill, Dotty 1980
+ Fulton, Louise 2001
+ Fritz, Deane 1966
Garms, Shirley 1971
Gianulias, Nikki 1997
+ Gloor, Olga 1976
Gonzalez, Ashie 1998
Graham, Linda 1992
Graham, Mary Lou 1989
+ Greenwald, Goldie 1953
Grinfelds, Vesma 1991
+ Harman, Janet 1985
+ Hartrick, Stella 1972
+ Hatch, Grayce 1953
Havlish, Jean 1987
+ Hoffman, Martha 1979
Holm, Joan 1974
+ Humphreys, Birdie 1979
Ignizio, Millie Martorella . .1975
Jacobson, D.D 1981
+ Jaeger, Emma 1953

Johnson, Tish 2002
Kelly, Annese 1985
Kelly, Linda 2003
+ Knechtges, Doris 1983
Kuczynski, Betty 1981
Ladewig, Marion 1964
+ Matthews, Merle 1974
+ McCutcheon, Floretta 1956
Merrick, Marge 1980
+ Mikiel, Val 1979
Miller-Mackey, Dana 2000
Miller, Carol 1997
+ Miller, Dorothy 1954
Mivelaz, Betty 1991
Mohacsi, Mary 1994
Morris, Betty 1983
Naccarato, Jeanne 1999
Nichols, Lorrie Koch 1989
Norman, Carol 2001
Norman, Edie Jo 1993
Norton, Virginia 1988
Notaro, Phyllis 1979
Ortner, Bev 1972
+ Powers, Connie 1973
Reichley, Susie 2000

Rickard, Robbie 1994
+ Robinson, Leona 1969
Romeo, Robin 1995
+ Rump, Anita 1962
+ Ruschmeyer, Addie 1961
+ Ryan, Esther 1963
+ Sablatnik, Ethel 1979
Sandelin, Lucy 1999
+ Schulte, Myrtle 1965
+ Shablis, Helen 1977
Sill, Aleta 1996
+ Simon, Violet (Billy) 1960
+ Small, Tess 1971
+ Smith, Grace 1968
Soutar, Judy 1976
+ Stockdale, Louise 1953
Toepfer, Elvira 1976
+ Twyford, Sally 1964
Wagner, Lisa 2000
+ Warmbier, Marie 1953
Wene-Martin, Sylvia 1966
Wilkinson, Dorothy 1990
+ Winandy, Cecelia 1975
Zimmerman, Donna 1982

Meritorious Service

+ Baetz, Helen 1977
+ Baker, Helen 1989
+ Banker, Gladys 1994
+ Bayley, Clover 1992
Bennie, Bernice 2003
+ Berger, Winifred 1976
+ Bohlen, Philena 1955
Borschuk, Lo 1988
+ Botkin, Freda 1986
Broyles, Sylvia 2005
+ Chapman, Emily 1957
Chapman, Nancy 2002
+ Crowe, Alberta 1982
Deitch, Joyce 2003
+ Dornblaser, Gertrude 1979
Duffy, Agnes 1987
Finke, Gertrude 1990
+ Fisk, Rae 1983

+ Haas, Dorothy 1977
Hagin, Elaine 2000
+ Herold, Mitzi 1998
+ Higley, Margaret 1969
+ Hochstadter, Bee 1967
+ Kay, Nora 1964
Keller, Pearl 1999
+ Kelly, Ellen 1979
Kelone, Theresa 1978
+ Knepprath, Jeannette 1963
+ Lasher, Iolia 1967
+ Marrs, Mabel 1979
+ McBride, Bertha 1968
McLeary, Hazel 2000
+ Menne, Catherine 1979
Mitchell, Flora 1996
Morton, Clara 2001
+ Mraz, Jo 1959

O'Connor, Billie 1992
+ Phaler, Emma 1965
+ Porter, Cora 1986
+ Quin, Zoe 1979
+ Rishling, Gertrude 1972
Robinson, Jeanette 2000
Rowe, Dorothy 2004
Simone, Anne 1991
Sloan, Catherine 1985
+ Speck, Berdie 1966
Spitalnick, Mildred 1994
+ Spring, Alma 1979
+ Switzer, Pearl 1973
+ Todd, Trudy 1993
+ Veatch, Georgia 1974
+ White, Mildred 1975
+ Wood, Ann 1970

Professional Women Bowlers Hall of Fame

Established in 1995 by the Ladies Pro Bowlers Tour. The LPBT has since been renamed the Professional Women Bowlers Association and the PWBA Hall of Fame has since been folded into the International Bowling Hall of Fame. The PWBA has not inducted any new members since 2003.

Eligibility: Nominees in performance category must have at least five titles from organizations including All-Star, World Invitational, LPBT, WPBA, PWBA, TPA and LPBA.

Members are listed with year of induction; (+) indicates deceased member.

Performance

Adamek, Donna 1995
Coburn-Carroll, Cindy 1997
Costello, Pat 1997
Costello, Patty 1995
Duggan, Anne Marie 2003
Fothergill, Dotty 1995
Gianulias, Nikki 1996

Grinfelds, Vesma 1997
Johnson, Tish 1998
Ladewig, Marion 1995
Martorella, Millie 1995
Miller-Mackie, Dana 2002
Morris, Betty 1995
Naccarato, Jeanne 2002

Nichols, Lorrie 1996
Norton, Virginia 2003
Romeo, Robin 1996
Sill, Aleta 1998
Wagner, Lisa 1996

Pioneers

Able, Joy 1998
Boxberger, Loa 1997
Carter, LaVerne 1995

Coburn, Doris 1996
Duval, Helen 1995
Garms, Shirley 1995

Ortner, Bev 1998
Soutar, Judy 1997
Zimmerman, Donna 1996

Builders

+ Buehler, Janet 1996
Keller, Pearl 1997

Robinson, Jeanette 1996
Sommer Jr., John 1997

+ Veatch, Georgia 1995

BOXING
International Boxing Hall of Fame

Established in 1984 and opened in 1989. **Address:** 1 Hall of Fame Drive, Canastota, NY 13032. **Telephone:** (315) 697-7095. **Web:** www.ibhof.com.

Eligibility: All nominees must be retired for five years. Voting done by 142-member panel made up of Boxing Writers' Association members and world-wide boxing historians.

Class of 2007 (13): MODERN ERA—**Roberto Duran, Ricardo Lopez** and **Pernell Whitaker.** OLD TIMERS—**George Godfrey, Pedro Montanez** and **Kid Norfolk.** PIONEER—**Young Barney Aaron** and **Dick Curtis;** NON-PARTICIPANTS—**Cuco Conde, Amilar Brusa, Jose Sulaiman** and **LeRoy Neiman.** OBSERVERS—**TAD Dorgan.**

Members are listed with year of induction; (+) indicates deceased member.

Modern Era

	Ali, Muhammad	1990		Giardello, Joey	1993
+	Angott, Sammy	1998		Gomez, Wilfredo	1995
+	Apostoli, Fred	2003		Gonzalez, Humberto	2006
	Arguello, Alexis	1992	+	Graham, Billy	1992
+	Armstrong, Henry	1990	+	Graziano, Rocky	1991
	Basilio, Carmen	1990		Griffith, Emile	1990
	Benitez, Wilfredo	1996		Hagler, Marvelous Marvin	1993
	Benvenuti, Nino	1992		Harada, Masahiko (Fighting)	1995
+	Berg, Jackie (Kid)	1994		Jack, Beau	1991
	Bivins, Jimmy	1999	+	Jenkins, Lew	1999
+	Brown, Joe	1996		Jofre, Eder	1992
	Buchanan, Ken	2000		Johansson, Ingemar	2002
+	Burley, Charley	1992		Johnson, Harold	1993
	Canto, Miguel	1998		Laguna, Ismael	2001
	Carbajal, Michael	2006		LaMotta, Jake	1990
+	Carter, Jimmy	2000		Leonard, Sugar Ray	1997
+	Cerdan, Marcel	1991	+	Liston, Sonny	1991
	Cervantes, Antonio	1998	+	Locche, Nicolino	2003
	Chacon, Bobby	2005		Loi, Duilio	2005
	Chandler, Jeff	2000		Lopez, Ricardo	2007
+	Charles, Ezzard	1990	+	Louis, Joe	1990
	Cokes, Curtis	2003	+	Marciano, Rocky	1990
+	Conn, Billy	1990	+	Maxim, Joey	1994
	Cuevas, Pipino	2002		McCallum, Mike	2003
	Duran, Roberto	2007		McGuigan, Barry	2005
+	Elorde, Gabriel (Flash)	1993		Montgomery, Bob	1995
	Fenech, Jeff	2002	+	Monzon, Carlos	1990
	Foreman, George	2003	+	Moore, Archie	1990
	Foster, Bob	1990		Muhammad, Matthew Saad	1998
	Frazier, Joe	1990		Napoles, Jose	1990
	Fullmer, Gene	1991		Nelson, Azumah	2004
	Galaxy, Khaosai	1999		Norris, Terry	2005
+	Galindez, Victor	2002		Norton, Ken	1992
	Gavilan, Kid	1990		Olivares, Ruben	1991

+	Olson, Carl (Bobo)	2000
	Ortiz, Carlos	1991
+	Ortiz, Manuel	1996
	Palomino, Carlos	2004
	Papp, Laszlo	2001
+	Pastrano, Willie	2001
	Patterson, Floyd	1991
	Pedroza, Eusebio	1999
	Pep, Willie	1990
+	Perez, Pascual	1995
	Pryor, Aaron	1996
	Qawi, Dwight Muhammad	2004
	Ramos, Ultiminio	2001
+	Robinson, Sugar Ray	1990
+	Rodriguez, Luis	1997
+	Rosario, Edwin	2006
+	Saddler, Sandy	1990
+	Saldivar, Vicente	1999
+	Sanchez, Salvador	1991
+	Schmeling, Max	1992
	Spinks, Michael	1994
+	Tiger, Dick	1991
	Torres, Jose	1997
+	Turpin, Randy	2001
+	Walcott, Jersey Joe	1990
	Whitaker, Pernell	2007
+	Williams, Ike	1990
+	Wright, Chalky	1997
+	Zale, Tony	1991
	Zaragoza, Daniel	2004
	Zarate, Carlos	1994
+	Zivic, Fritzie	1993

Old-Timers

+	Ambers, Lou	1992	+	Delaney, Jack	1996
+	Arizmendi, Baby	2004	+	Dempsey, Jack	1990
+	Attell, Abe	1990	+	Dempsey, Jack (Nonpareil)	1992
+	Baer, Max	1995	+	Dillon, Jack	1995
+	Barry, Jimmy	2000	+	Dixon, George	1990
+	Bass, Benny	2002	+	Driscoll, Jim	1990
+	Battalino, Battling	2003	+	Dundee, Johnny	1991
+	Berlenbach, Paul	2001	+	Escobar, Sixto	2002
+	Braddock, Jim	2001	+	Fields, Jackie	2004
+	Britton, Jack	1990	+	Fitzsimmons, Bob	1990
+	Brouillard, Lou	2006	+	Flowers, Theodore (Tiger)	1993
+	Brown, Aaron (Dixie Kid)	2002	+	Gans, Joe	1990
+	Brown, Panama Al	1992	+	Genaro, Frankie	1998
+	Burns, Tommy	1996	+	Gibbons, Mike	1992
+	Canzoneri, Tony	1990	+	Gibbons, Tommy	1993
+	Carpentier, Georges	1991	+	Godfrey, George	2007
+	Chocolate, Kid	1991	+	Greb, Harry	1990
+	Choynski, Joe	1998	+	Griffo, Young	1991
+	Corbett, James J.	1990	+	Harris, Harry	2002
+	Corbett III, Young	2004	+	Herman, Pete	1997
+	Coulon, Johnny	1999	+	Jackson, Peter	1990
+	Criqui, Eugene	2005	+	Jeanette, Joe	1997
+	Darcy, Les	1993	+	Jeffries, James J	1990

+	Johnson, Jack	1990
+	Kaplan, Louis (Kid)	2003
+	Ketchel, Stanley	1990
+	Kilbane, Johnny	1995
+	LaBarba, Fidel	1996
+	Langford, Sam	1990
+	Lavigne, George (Kid)	1998
+	Leonard, Benny	1990
+	Levinsky, Battling	2000
+	Lewis, John Henry	1994
+	Lewis, Ted (Kid)	1992
+	Loughran, Tommy	1991
+	Lynch, Benny	1998
+	Lynch, Joe	2005
+	Mandell, Sammy	1998
+	McAuliffe, Jack	1995
+	McCoy, Charles (Kid)	1991
+	McFarland, Packey	1992
+	McGovern, Terry	1990
+	McLarnin, Jimmy	1991
+	McVey, Sam	1999
+	Miller, Freddie	1997
+	Mitchell, Charley	2002

+ Montanez, Pedro 2007
+ Moran, Owen 2002
+ Nelson, Battling 1992
+ Norfolk, Kid 2007
+ O'Brien, Philadelphia Jack .1994
+ Papke, Billy 2001
+ Petrolle, Billy 2000
+ Ritchie, Willie 2004
+ Rosenbloom, Maxie 1993
+ Ross, Barney 1990
+ Ryan, Tommy 1991

+ Sharkey, Jack 1994
+ Sharkey, Tom 2003
+ Slattery, Jimmy 2006
+ Steele, Freddie 1999
+ Stribling, Young 1996
+ Taylor, Charles (Bud) 2005
+ Tendler, Lew 1999
+ Thil, Marcel 2005
+ Tunney, Gene 1990
+ Villa, Pancho 1994
+ Walcott, Joe (Barbados) . . .1991

+ Walker, Mickey 1990
+ Welsh, Freddie 1997
+ Wilde, Jimmy 1990
+ Willard, Jess 2003
+ Williams, Kid 1996
+ Wills, Harry 1992
+ Wolgast, Ad 2000
+ Wolgast, Midget 2001
+ Yarosz, Teddy 2006

Pioneers

+ Aaron, Barney 2001
+ Aaron, Young Barney 2007
+ Baldwin, Caleb 2003
+ Belcher, Jem 1992
+ Brain, Ben 1994
+ Broughton, Jack 1990
+ Burke, James (Deaf) 1992
+ Carney, Jem . . . . , ...2006
+ Chambers, Arthur 2000
+ Cribb, Tom 1991
+ Curtis, Dick 2007
+ Donovan, Prof. Mike 1998

+ Duffy, Paddy 1994
+ Goss, Joe 2003
+ Edwards, Billy 2004
+ Figg, James 1992
+ Heenan, John C. 2002
+ Jackson, Gentleman John . .1992
+ Johnson, Tom 1995
+ King, Tom 1992
+ Langham, Nat 1992
+ Mace, Jem 1990
+ Mendoza, Daniel 1990
+ Molineaux, Tom 1997

+ Morrissey, John 1996
+ Pearce, Henry 1993
+ Randall, Jack 2005
+ Richmond, Bill 1999
+ Sam, Dutch 1997
+ Sam, Young Dutch 2002
+ Sayers, Tom 1990
+ Spring, Tom 1992
+ Sullivan, John L 1990
+ Thompson, William 1991
+ Ward, Jem 1995

Non-Participants

+ Andrews, Thomas S 1992
+ Arcel, Ray 1991
  Arum, Bob 1999
  Astaire, Jarvis 2006
+ Ballarati, Giuseppe 1999
  Benton, George 2001
+ Bimstein, Whitey 2006
+ Blackburn, Jack 1992
+ Brady, William A. 1998
+ Branchini, Umberto 2004
  Brenner, Teddy 1993
  Brusa, Amilcar 2007
+ Cayton, Bill 2005
+ Chambers, John Graham . .1990
  Chargin, Don 2001
  Christodolou, Stanley 2004
  Clancy, Gil 1993
+ Coffroth, James W. 1991
+ Cohen, Irving 2002
+ Conde, Cuco 2007
+ D'Amato, Cus. 1995
  Dickson, Jeff 2000
+ Donovan, Arthur 1993
  Duff, Mickey 1999
  Dundee, Angelo 1992

+ Dundee, Chris 1994
+ Dunphy, Don 1993
+ Duva, Dan 2003
  Duva, Lou 1998
+ Eaton, Aileen 2002
+ Egan, Pierce 1991
+ Fleischer, Nat 1990
+ Fox, Richard K. 1997
+ Fragetta, Dewey 2003
  Fraser, Don 2005
+ Futch, Eddie 1994
+ Goldman, Charley 1992
+ Goldstein, Ruby 1994
  Goodman, Murray 1999
+ Humphreys, Joe 1997
+ Ichinose, Sam 2001
+ Jacobs, Jimmy 1993
+ Jacobs, Mike 1990
+ Johnston, Jimmy 1999
+ Kearns, Jack (Doc) 1990
  King, Don 1997
  Lectoure, Tito 2000
+ Liebling, A.J 1992
+ Lonsdale, Lord 1990
+ Markson, Harry 1992

  Mercante, Arthur 1995
+ Morgan, Dan 2000
+ Muldoon, William 1996
  Neiman, LeRoy 2007
  Odd, Gilbert 1995
+ O'Rourke, Tom 1999
+ Parker, Dan 1996
+ Parnassus, George 1991
  Peltz, J. Russell 2004
+ Queensberry, Marquis of . .1990
+ Rickard, Tex 1990
+ Rudd, Irving 1999
+ Sabbatini, Rodolfo 2006
+ Sarreal Lope 2005
+ Siler, George 1995
+ Silverman, Sam 2002
+ Solomons, Jack 1995
  Steward, Emanuel 1996
  Sulaiman, Jose 2007
+ Taub, Sam 1994
+ Taylor, Herman 1998
+ Viscusi, Lou 2004
+ Walker, James J. (Jimmy) . .1992
+ Weill, Al 2003

Observers

+ Bromberg, Lester 2001
+ Cannon, Jimmy 2002
+ Citro, Ralph 2001
+ Dorgan, TAD 2007
  Fiske, Jack 2003
  Gallo, Bill 2001

  Gutteridge, Reg 2002
  Heinz, W.C. 2004
+ Jones, Jersey 2005
  Kaplan, Hank 2006
+ Mullan, Harry 2005
+ Nagler, Barney 2004

+ Runyon, Damon 2002
  Schulberg, Budd 2003
  Sugar, Bert 2005
+ Weston, Stanley 2006

FOOTBALL

College Football Hall of Fame

Established in 1955 by the National Football Foundation. **Address:** 111 South St. Joseph St., South Bend, IN 46601. **Telephone:** (574) 235-9999. **Web:** www.collegefootball.org

Eligibility: Nominated players must be out of college 10 years and a first team All-America pick by a major selector during their careers; coaches must be retired three years or active and over 75 years old. Voting done by 12-member panel of athletic directors, conference and bowl officials and media representatives. The first year representatives from NCAA Div. I-AA, II, and III, and the NAIA were eligible for induction was 1996.

Class of 2007 (20): LARGE COLLEGE—C **Tom Brahaney**, Oklahoma (1970-72); DB **Dave Brown**, Michigan (1972-74); LB **Jeff Davis**, Clemson (1978-81); QB **Doug Flutie**, Boston College (1981-84); DB **Johnnie Johnson**, Texas (1976-79); QB **Rex Kern**, Ohio St., (1968-70); RB/WR **Ahmad Rashad**, Oregon (1969-71); RB **Anthony Thompson**, Indiana (1986-89); DT **Wilson Whitley**, Houston (1973-76); LB **Reggie Williams**, Dartmouth (1973-75); LB **Richard Wood**, USC (1972-74); DT **Chris Zorich**, Notre Dame (1988-90); COACHES—**Herb Deromedi**, Central Michigan (1978-93); **Joe Paterno**, Penn St. (1966—). SMALL COLLEGE—QB **Tracy Ham**, Georgia Southern (1983-86); HB **Joe Kendall**, Kentucky St. (1933-36); LB **Frank Sheptock**, Bloomsburg (1982-85); LB **Jessie Tuggle**, Valdosta St. (1983-86)) SMALL COLLEGE COACHES—**Jim Christopherson**, Concordia-MN (1969-2000); **Billy Joe**, Cheyney St., Central St., Florida A&M (1972-2004).

Note: Bobby Dodd and **Amos Alonzo Stagg** are the only members to be honored as both players and coaches.

Players are listed with *final year they played* in college and coaches are listed with year of induction; (+) indicates deceased members.

Players

+ Abell, Earl-Colgate 1915	Bennett, Cornelius-Alabama 1986	Cappelletti, John-Penn St . . .1973
Agase, Alex-Purdue/Ill 1946	+ Berry, Charlie-Lafayette 1924	+ Carideo, Frank-N.Dame 1930
+ Agganis, Harry-Boston U . .1952	+ Bertelli, Angelo-N.Dame . . .1943	+ Carney, Charles-Illinois 1921
Albert, Frank-Stanford 1941	+ Berwanger, Jay-Chicago 1935	Caroline, J.C.-Illinois 1954
+ Aldrich, Ki-TCU 1938	+ Bettencourt, L.-St.Mary's . . .1927	Carpenter, Bill-Army 1959
+ Aldrich, Malcolm-Yale 1921	Biletnikoff, Fred-Fla.St. 1964	+ Carpenter, Hunter-NC/
+ Alexander, Joe-Syracuse . . .1920	Blades, Benny-Miami,FL 1987	Va. Tech 1905
Allen, Marcus-USC 1981	Blanchard, Doc-Army 1946	Carroll, Chas.-Washington . .1928
Alworth, Lance-Arkansas . . .1961	+ Blozis, Al-Georgetown 1941	Carter, Anthony-Michigan . .1982
+ Ameche, Alan-Wisconsin . . .1954	Bock, Ed-Iowa St 1938	Casanova, Tommy-LSU 1971
+ Ames, Knowlton-Princeton . .1889	Bomar, Lynn-Vanderbilt 1924	+ Casey, Edward-Harvard 1919
+ Amling, Warren-Ohio St 1946	+ Bomeisler, Bo-Yale 1912	Casillas, Tony-Oklahoma . . .1985
Anderson, Bob P.-Army 1959	Booth, Albie-Yale 1931	Cassady, Howard-Ohio St . . .1955
Anderson, Bobby-Colorado .1969	+ Borries, Fred-Navy 1934	+ Chamberlin, Guy-Neb.Wes./
Anderson, Dick-Colorado . . .1967	+ Bosley, Bruce-West Va 1955	Nebraska 1915
Anderson, Donny-Tex.Tech . .1965	Bosseler, Don-Miami,FL 1956	Chapman, Sam-California . . .1937
+ Anderson, Hunk-N.Dame . . .1921	Bottari, Vic-California 1938	Chappuis, Bob-Michigan . . .1947
Arnett, Jon-USC 1956	Bowden, Murry-Dartmouth . .1970	+ Christman, Paul-Missouri . . .1940
Atkins, Doug-Tennessee 1952	+ Boynton, Ben-Williams 1920	+ Clark, Dutch-Colo. Col. 1929
Babich, Bob-Miami-OH 1968	Brahaney, Tom-Oklahoma . .1972	Cleary, Paul-USC 1947
+ Bacon, Everett-Wesleyan . . .1912	+ Brewer, Charles-Harvard . . .1895	+ Clevenger, Zora-Indiana 1903
+ Bagnell, Reds-Penn 1950	+ Bright, Johnny-Drake 1951	Cloud, Jack-Wm. & Mary . . .1949
+ Baker, Hobey-Princeton 1913	Brodie, John-Stanford 1956	+ Cochran, Gary-Princeton . . .1897
+ Baker, John-USC 1931	+ Brooke, George-Penn 1895	+ Cody, Josh-Vanderbilt 1919
+ Baker, Moon-N'western 1926	Brosky, Al-Illinois 1952	Coleman, Don-Mich.St 1951
Baker, Terry-Oregon St 1962	Brown, Bob-Nebraska 1963	+ Conerly, Charlie-Miss 1947
+ Ballin, Harold-Princeton 1914	+ Brown, Dave-Michigan 1974	Connor, George-HC/ND . . .1947
+ Banker, Bill-Tulane 1929	Brown, Geo/Navy/S.Diego St .1947	+ Corbin, William-Yale 1888
Banonis, Vince-Detroit 1941	+ Brown, Gordon-Yale 1900	Corbus, William-Stanford . . .1933
+ Barnes, Stan-California 1921	Brown, Jim-Syracuse 1956	Covert, Jimbo-Pittsburgh . . .1983
+ Barrett, Charles-Cornell 1915	+ Brown, John, Jr.-Navy 1913	+ Cowan, Hector-Princeton . . .1889
+ Baston, Bert-Minnesota 1916	+ Brown, Johnny Mack-Ala . .1925	+ Coy, Edward (Ted)-Yale 1909
+ Battles, Cliff-WV Wesleyan .1931	+ Brown, Tay-USC 1932	+ Crawford, Fred-Duke 1933
Baugh, Sammy-TCU 1936	Brown, Tom-Minnesota 1960	Crow, John David-Tex.A&M .1957
Baughan, Maxie-Ga.Tech . . .1959	Browner, Ross-Notre Dame . .1977	+ Crowley, Jim-Notre Dame . . .1924
+ Bausch, James-Wichita/	Budde, Brad-USC 1979	Csonka, Larry-Syracuse 1967
Kansas 1930	+ Bunker, Paul-Army 1902	Curtis, Tom-Michigan 1969
Beagle, Ron-Navy 1955	Burford, Chris-Stanford 1959	+ Cutter, Slade-Navy 1934
Beasley, Terry-Auburn 1971	+ Burris, Kurt-Oklahoma 1954	+ Czarobski, Ziggie-N.Dame .1947
Beban, Gary-UCLA 1967	Burton, Ron-N'western 1959	Dale, Carroll-Va.Tech 1959
Bechtol, Hub-Tex.Tech/Texas 1946	Butkus, Dick-Illinois 1964	+ Dalrymple, Gerald-Tulane . . .1931
+ Beck, Ray-Ga. Tech 1951	Butler, Kevin-Georgia 1984	+ Dalton, John-Navy 1911
+ Beckett, John-Oregon 1916	+ Butler, Robert-Wisconsin . . .1913	+ Daly, Chas.-Harvard/Army .1902
Bednarik, Chuck-Penn 1948	+ Cafego, George-Tenn 1939	Daniell, Averell-Pitt 1936
Behm, Forrest-Nebraska 1940	+ Cagle, Red-SWLa/Army 1929	+ Daniell, James-Ohio St 1941
Bell, Bobby-Minnesota 1962	+ Cain, John-Alabama 1932	+ Davies, Tom-Pittsburgh 1921
Bell, Ricky-USC 1976	Cameron, Ed-Wash.& Lee . .1924	Davis, Anthony-USC 1974
Bellino, Joe-Navy 1960	+ Campbell, David-Harvard . .1901	+ Davis, Ernie-Syracuse 1961
Below, Marty-Wisconsin 1923	Campbell, Earl-Texas 1977	+ Davis, Glenn-Army 1946
+ Benbrook, Al-Michigan 1910	+ Cannon, Jack-N.Dame 1929	Davis, Jeff-Clemson 1981

Davis, Robert-Ga.Tech 1947
Dawkins, Pete-Army 1958
DeLong, Steve-Tennessee ...1964
+ DeRogatis, Al-Duke 1948
+ DesJardien, Paul-Chicago ..1914
+ Devine, Aubrey-Iowa 1921
+ DeWitt, John-Princeton 1903
Dial, Buddy-Rice 1958
Dicus, Chuck-Arkansas 1970
Dierdorf, Dan-Michigan 1970
Ditka, Mike-Pittsburgh 1960
Dobbs, Glenn-Tulsa 1942
+ Dodd, Bobby-Tennessee ...1930
Donan, Holland-Princeton ..1950
+ Donchess, Joseph-Pitt 1929
Dorney, Keith-Penn St. 1978
Dorsett, Tony-Pitt 1976
+ Dougherty, Nathan-Tenn ...1909
+ Dove, Bob-Notre Dame 1942
Drahos, Nick-Cornell 1940
+ Driscoll, Paddy-N'western ..1917
+ Drury, Morley-USC 1927
Duden, Dick-Navy 1945
Dudley, Bill-Virginia 1941
Duncan, Randy-Iowa 1958
Easley, Kenny-UCLA 1980
+ Eckersall, Walter-Chicago ..1906
+ Edwards, Turk-Wash.St 1931
+ Edwards, Wm.-Princeton ...1899
+ Eichenlaub, Ray-N.Dame ..1914
Eisenhauer, Steve-Navy ...1953
Elkins, Larry-Baylor 1964
Eller, Carl-Minnesota 1963
Elliott, Bump-Mich/Purdue .1947
Elliott, Pete-Michigan 1948
Elmendorf, Dave-Tex. A&M .1970
Elway, John-Stanford 1982
Emanuel, Frank-Tennessee .1965
Emtman, Steve-Washington .1991
+ Evans, Ray-Kansas 1947
Everett, Thomas-Baylor 1986
+ Exendine, Albert-Carlisle ..1907
Falaschi, Nello-S.Clara 1936
Fears, Tom-S.Clara/UCLA ..1947
+ Feathers, Beattie-Tenn 1933
Fenimore, Bob-Okla.St 1946
+ Fenton, Doc-Mansfield/LSU .1909
Ferguson, Bob-Ohio St. 1961
+ Ferraro, John-USC 1947
Fesler, Wes-Ohio St 1930
+ Fincher, Bill-Ga.Tech 1920
Fischer, Bill-Notre Dame ...1948
+ Fish, Hamilton-Harvard 1909
+ Fisher, Robert-Harvard 1911
+ Flowers, Buck-Davidson/
  Ga.Tech..............1920
Flowers, Charlie-Ole Miss. ..1959
Flutie, Doug-Boston College .1984
+ Fortmann Danny-Colgate ..1935
Fralic, Bill-Pittsburgh 1984
+ Francis, Sam-Nebraska 1936
Franck, George-Minnesota ..1940
Franco, Ed-Fordham 1937
+ Frank, Clint-Yale 1937
Franz, Rodney-California ..1949
Fredrickson, Tucker-Auburn .1964
+ Friedman, Benny-Michigan .1926
Gabriel, Roman-N.C. State .1961
Gain, Bob-Kentucky 1950
+ Galiffa, Arnold-Army 1949
+ Gallarneau, Hugh-Stanford .1940
+ Garbisch, Edgar-W.& J./Army .1924
Garrett, Mike-USC 1965

+ Gelbert, Charles-Penn 1896
+ Geyer, Forest-Oklahoma ...1915
Gibbs, Jake-Miss 1960
+ Giel, Paul-Minnesota 1953
Gifford, Frank-USC 1951
Gilbert, Chris-Texas 1968
+ Gilbert, Walter-Auburn 1936
Gilmer, Harry-Alabama ...1947
+ Gipp, George-N.Dame 1920
+ Gladchuk, Chet-Boston Col .1940
Glass, Bill-Baylor 1956
Glover, Rich-Nebraska 1972
+ Goldberg, Marshall-Pitt ...1938
Goodreault, Gene-BC 1940
+ Gordon, Walter-Calif 1918
+ Governali, Paul-Columbia ..1942
Grabowski, Jim-Illinois 1965
Gradishar, Randy-Ohio St. ..1973
Graham, Otto-N'western ...1943
+ Grange, Red-Illinois 1925
+ Grayson, Bobby-Stanford ..1935
Green, Hugh-Pitt 1980
+ Green, Jack-Tulane/Army ..1945
Green, Tim-Syracuse 1985
Greene, Joe-N.Texas St 1968
Griese, Bob-Purdue 1966
Griffin, Archie-Ohio St 1975
Groom, Jerry-Notre Dame ..1950
+ Gulick, Merle-Toledo/Hobart .1929
Guglielmi, Ralph-N.Dame ..1954
Guy, Ray-SMU 1972
+ Guyon, Joe-Carlisle/Ga.Tech .1918
Hadl, John-Kansas 1961
+ Hale, Edwin-Miss.College ..1921
Hall, Parker-Miss 1938
Ham, Jack-Penn St 1970
+ Hamilton, Bob-Stanford ...1935
+ Hamilton, Tom-Navy 1926
Hannah, John-Alabama ...1972
+ Hanson, Vic-Syracuse 1926
+ Harder, Pat-Wisconsin 1942
+ Hardwick, Tack-Harvard ...1914
+ Hare, T.Truxton-Penn 1900
+ Harley, Chick-Ohio St 1919
+ Harmon, Tom-Michigan ...1940
+ Harpster, Howard-Carnegie .1928
Harris, Wayne-Arkansas ...1960
+ Hart, Edward-Princeton ...1911
+ Hart, Leon-Notre Dame ...1949
Hartman, Bill-Georgia 1937
Haynes, Michael-Arizona St .1975
+ Hazel, Homer-Rutgers 1924
Hazeltine, Matt-Calif 1954
+ Healey, Ed-H. Cross/Dart. ..1916
+ Heffelfinger, Pudge-Yale ...1891
+ Hein, Mel-Washington St ...1930
+ Heinrich, Don-Washington ..1952
Hendricks, Ted-Miami,FL ...1968
Hennings, Chad-Air Force ..1987
+ Henry, Pete-Wash&Jeff 1919
+ Herschberger, C.-Chicago ..1898
+ Herwig, Robert-Calif 1937
+ Heston, Willie-SJ St./Mich ..1904
+ Hickman, Herman-Tenn ...1931
+ Hickok, William-Yale 1894
Hicks, John-Ohio State 1973
Hill, Dan-Duke 1938
+ Hillebrand, Art-Princeton ..1899
+ Hinkey, Frank-Yale 1894
Hinkle, Carl-Vanderbilt 1937
+ Hinkle, Clarke-Bucknell ...1931
Hirsch, Elroy-Wisc./Mich ..1943
+ Hitchcock, James-Auburn ..1932

Hoage, Terry-Georgia 1983
Hoffmann, Frank-N.Dame ..1931
+ Hogan, James J.-Yale 1904
+ Holland, Brud-Cornell 1938
+ Holleder, Don-Army 1955
+ Hollenback, Bill-Penn 1908
Holovak, Mike-Boston Col ..1942
Holub, E.J.-Texas Tech 1960
Hornung, Paul-N.Dame ...1956
+ Horrell, Edwin-California ..1924
+ Horvath, Les-Ohio St 1944
Houston, Jim-Ohio St. 1959
+ Howe, Arthur-Yale 1911
+ Howell, Dixie-Alabama 1934
Huarte, John-Notre Dame ..1964
+ Hubbard, Cal-Centenary/
  Geneva..............1926
+ Hubbard, John-Amherst ...1906
+ Hubert, Pooley-Ala. 1925
Huff, Sam-West Virginia ...1955
Humble, Weldon-SWLa/Rice 1946
Hunley, Ricky-Arizona 1983
+ Hunt, Joe-Texas A&M 1927
Huntington, Ellery-Colgate .1913
+ Hutson, Don-Alabama 1934
Iacavazzi, Cosmo-Princeton .1964
+ Ingram, Jonas-Navy 1906
+ Isbell, Cecil-Purdue 1937
+ Jablonsky, J.-Army/Wash-MO 1933
Jackson, Bo-Auburn 1985
Jackson, Keith-Oklahoma ..1987
+ Janowicz, Vic-Ohio St 1951
Jefferson, John-Arizona St. ..1977
+ Jenkins, Darold-Missouri ..1941
+ Jensen, Jackie-California ..1948
+ Joesting, Herbert-Minn 1927
Johnson, Bob-Tennessee ...1967
Johnson, Johnnie-Texas ...1979
+ Johnson, Jimmie-Carlisle/
  Northwestern..........1905
Johnson, Ron-Michigan ...1968
+ Jones, Calvin-Iowa 1955
+ Jones, Gomer-Ohio St 1935
Jones, Stan-Maryland 1953
Jordan, Lee Roy-Alabama ..1962
+ Juhan, Frank-U.of South ...1910
Justice, Charlie-N.Car 1949
+ Kaer, Mort-USC 1926
Kapp, Joe-California 1958
Karras, Alex-Iowa 1957
+ Kavanaugh, Ken-LSU 1939
+ Kaw, Edgar-Cornell 1922
Kazmaier, Dick-Princeton ..1951
+ Keck, Stan-Princeton 1921
Kell, Chip-Tennessee 1970
+ Kelley, Larry-Yale 1936
+ Kelly, Wild Bill-Montana ...1926
Kenna, Doug-Army 1944
Kern, Rex-Ohio St. 1970
+ Kerr, George-Boston Col ...1940
+ Ketcham, Henry-Yale 1913
Keyes, Leroy-Purdue 1968
+ Killinger, Glenn-Penn St ...1921
Kilmer, Billy-UCLA 1960
+ Kilpatrick, John-Yale 1910
Kimbrough, John-Tex A&M .1940
+ Kinard, Bruiser-Mississippi .1937
Kinard, Terry-Clemson 1982
Kiner, Steve-Tennessee 1969
+ King, Phil-Princeton 1893
+ Kinnick, Nile-Iowa 1939
+ Kipke, Harry-Michigan 1923
+ Kitzmiller, John-Oregon ...1930

College Football Hall of Fame (Cont.)

+ Koch, Barton-Baylor 1930
+ Koppisch, Walt-Columbia . . .1924
  Kramer, Ron-Michigan 1956
  Kroll, Alex-Yale/Rutgers 1961
  Krueger, Charlie-Tex. A&M . .1957
  Kutner, Malcolm-Texas 1941
  Kwalick, Ted-Penn St 1968
+ Lach, Steve-Duke 1941
+ Lane, Myles-Dartmouth 1927
  Lattner, Johnny-N.Dame 1953
  Lauricella, Hank-Tenn 1951
+ Lautenschlaeger, Les-Tulane . .1925
+ Layden, Elmer-N.Dame 1924
+ Layne, Bobby-Texas 1947
+ Lea, Langdon-Princeton 1895
  Leaks, Roosevelt-Texas 1974
  LeBaron, Eddie-Pacific 1949
+ Leech, James-VMI 1920
+ Lester, Darrell-TCU 1935
  Levias, Jerry-SMU 1968
  Lewis, D.D.-Mississippi State .1967
  Lilly, Bob-TCU 1960
  Little, Floyd-Syracuse 1966
+ Lio, Augie-Georgetown 1940
+ Locke, Gordon-Iowa 1922
+ Long, Chuck-Iowa 1985
  Long, Mel-Toledo 1971
+ Loria, Frank-Virginia Tech 1967
  Lott, Ronnie-USC 1980
+ Lourie, Don-Princeton 1921
  Lucas, Richie-Penn St 1959
+ Luckman, Sid-Columbia 1938
  Lujack, Johnny-N.Dame 1947
+ Lund, Pug-Minnesota 1934
  Lynch, Jim-Notre Dame 1966
  MacAfee, Ken Jr.-N. Dame .1977
+ Macomber, Bart-Illinois 1916
+ MacLeod, Robert-Dart. 1938
  Maegle, Dick-Rice 1954
+ Mahan, Eddie-Harvard 1915
  Majors, John-Tennessee 1956
+ Mallory, William-Yale 1923
  Mancha, Vaughn-Ala 1947
  Mandich, Joe-Michigan 1969
+ Mann, Gerald-SMU 1927
  Manning, Archie-Miss 1970
  Manske, Edgar-N'western . . .1933
+ Marinaro, Ed-Cornell 1971
  Marino, Dan-Pittsburgh 1982
+ Markov, Vic-Washington 1937
+ Marshall, Bobby-Minn 1906
  Martin, Jim-Notre Dame 1949
  Matson, Ollie-San Fran 1951
  Matthews, Ray-TCU 1927
+ Maulbetsch, John-Adrian/
  Mich 1916
+ Mauthe, Pete-Penn St 1912
+ Maxwell,Robert-Chicago/
  Swarthmore 1905
  May, Mark-Pittsburgh 1980
  McAfee, George-Duke 1939
  McCallum, Napoleon-Navy .1985
  McCauley, Donald-N. Carolina 1970
+ McClung, Lee-Yale 1891
  McColl, Bill-Stanford 1951
+ McCormick, Jim-Princeton . . .1907
  McDonald, Tommy-Okla 1956
+ McDowall, Jack-N.C.State . . .1927
  McElhenny, Hugh-Wash 1951
+ McEver, Gene-Tennessee 1931
+ McEwan, John-Army 1916

+ McFadden, Banks-Clemson .1939
  McFadin, Bud-Texas 1950
  McGee, Mike-Duke 1959
+ McGinley, Edward-Penn 1924
+ McGovern, John-Minn 1910
  McGraw, Thurman-Colo.St .1949
+ McKeever, Mike-USC 1960
  McKenzie, Reggie-Michigan .1971
+ McLaren, George-Pitt 1918
  McMahon, Jim-BYU 1981
+ McMillan, Dan-USC/Calif . .1921
+ McMillin, Bo-Centre 1921
  McWhorter, Bob-Georgia . . .1913
+ Mercer, LeRoy-Penn 1912
  Meredith, Don-SMU 1959
  Merritt, Frank-Army 1943
+ Metzger, Bert-N.Dame 1930
+ Meylan, Wayne-Nebraska . . .1967
  Michaels, Lou-Kentucky 1957
  Michels, John-Tennessee . . .1952
+ Mickal, Abe-LSU 1935
+ Miller, Creighton-N.Dame . . .1943
+ Miller, Don-Notre Dame 1924
+ Miller, Eugene-Penn St 1913
+ Miller, Fred-Notre Dame 1928
  Miller, Rip-Notre Dame 1924
  Millner, Wayne-N.Dame 1935
+ Milstead, C.A.-Wabash/Yale .1923
+ Minds, John-Penn 1897
+ Minisi, Skip-Penn/Navy 1947
  Mitchell, Lydell-Penn St. 1971
  Modzelewski, Dick-Md. 1952
+ Moffat, Alex-Princeton 1883
+ Molinski, Ed-Tenn 1940
+ Montgomery, Cliff-Columbia .1933
  Moomaw, Donn-UCLA 1952
+ Morley, William-Columbia . .1901
  Morris, George-Ga.Tech 1952
  Morris, Larry-Ga.Tech 1954
+ Morton, Bill-Dartmouth 1931
  Morton, Craig-California 1964
+ Moscrip, Monk-Stanford 1935
+ Muller, Brick-California 1922
  Musso, Johnny-Alabama . . .1971
+ Nagurski, Bronko-Minn 1929
  Neighbors, Billy-Alabama . . .1961
+ Nevers, Ernie-Stanford 1925
+ Newell, Marshall-Harvard . . .1893
+ Newman, Harry-Michigan . .1932
  Newsome, Ozzie-Alabama .1977
  Nielson, Gifford-BYU 1977
  Nobis, Tommy-Texas 1965
  Nomellini, Leo-Minnesota . .1949
+ Oberlander, Andrew-Dart . . .1925
+ O'Brien, Davey-TCU 1938
  Odell, Bob-Penn 1943
+ O'Dea, Pat-Wisconsin 1899
+ O'Hearn, Jack-Cornell 1914
  Olds, Robin-Army 1942
+ Oliphant, Elmer-Army/Pur . .1917
  Olsen, Merlin-Utah St 1961
  Onkotz, Dennis-Penn St. 1969
+ Oosterbaan, Bennie-Mich . . .1927
  O'Rourke, Charles-BC 1940
+ Orsi, John-Colgate 1931
+ Osgood, Win-Cornell/Penn .1894
  Osmanski, Bill-Holy Cross . .1938
+ Outland, John-Penn. 1899
+ Owen, George-Harvard 1922
  Owens, Jim-Oklahoma 1949
  Owens, Steve-Oklahoma . . .1969

  Page, Alan-Notre Dame 1966
  Palumbo, Joe-Virginia 1951
  Pardee, Jack-Texas A&M . . .1956
  Parilli, Babe-Kentucky 1951
  Parker, Ace-Duke 1936
  Parker, Jackie-Miss.St 1953
+ Parker, Jim-Ohio St 1956
+ Pazzetti, Vince-Wesleyan/
  Lehigh 1912
+ Peabody, Chub-Harvard 1941
+ Peck, Robert-Pittsburgh 1916
  Pellegrini, Bob-Maryland 1955
+ Pennock, Stan-Harvard 1914
  Pfann, George-Cornell 1923
+ Phillips, H.D.-Sewanee 1905
  Phillips, Loyd-Arkansas 1966
  Phipps, Mike-Purdue 1969
  Pihos, Pete-Indiana 1946
  Pingel, John-Michigan St . . .1938
+ Pinckert, Erny-USC 1931
  Plunkett, Jim-Stanford 1970
+ Poe, Arthur-Princeton 1899
+ Pollard, Fritz-Brown 1916
+ Poole, B.-Miss/NC/Army . . .1948
  Powell, Marvin-USC 1976
  Pregulman, Merv-Michigan .1943
+ Price, Eddie-Tulane 1949
  Pritchard, Ron-Arizona St. . . .1968
  Pruitt, Greg-Oklahoma 1972
+ Pund, Peter-Georgia Tech . . .1928
+ Ramsey, G.-Wm&Mary 1942
  Rashad, Ahmad-Oregon . . .1971
  Rauch, John-Georgia 1948
  Redman, Rick-Wash 1964
+ Reeds, Claude-Oklahoma . .1913
  Reid, Mike-Penn St 1969
  Reid, Steve-Northwestern . . .1936
+ Reid, William-Harvard 1899
  Reifsnyder, Bob-Navy 1958
  Renfro, Mel-Oregon 1963
+ Rentner, Pug-N'western 1932
  Ressler, Glenn-Penn St. 1964
+ Reynolds, Bob-Stanford 1935
+ Reynolds, Bobby-Nebraska . .1952
  Rhino, Randy-Georgia Tech .1974
  Rhome, Jerry-SMU/Tulsa . . .1964
  Richter, Les-California 1951
  Richter, Pat-Wisconsin 1962
+ Riley, Jack-Northwestern 1931
  Rimington, Dave-Nebraska .1982
+ Rinehart, Chas.-Lafayette . . .1897
  Ritcher, Jim-NC St. 1979
  Roberts, J. D.-Oklahoma . . .1953
+ Robeson, Paul-Rutgers 1918
  Robinson, Dave-Penn St. . . .1962
  Robinson, Jerry-UCLA 1978
  Rocker, Tracy-Auburn 1988
+ Rodgers, Ira-West Va 1919
  Rodgers, Johnny-Nebraska .1972
+ Rogers, Ed-Carlisle/Minn . . .1903
  Rogers, George-S. Carolina .1980
  Roland, Johnny-Missouri . . .1965
  Romig, Joe-Colorado 1961
+ Rosenberg, Aaron-USC 1933
+ Rote, Kyle-SMU 1950
+ Routt, Joe-Texas A&M 1937
  Rozier, Mike-Nebraska 1983
+ Salmon, Red-Notre Dame . .1903
  Sanders, Barry-Okla. St. 1988
  Sarkisian, Alex-Northwestern 1948
+ Sauer, George-Nebraska . . .1933

College Football Hall of Fame (Cont.)

+ Daugherty, Duffy 1984
+ Devaney, Bob 1981
+ Devine, Dan 1985
  Deromedi, Herb 2007
  Dickey, Doug 2003
+ Dobie, Gil 1951
+ Dodd, Bobby 1993
  Donahue, Tom 2000
+ Donohue, Michael 1951
  Dooley, Vince 1994
+ Dorais, Gus 1954
  Dye, Pat 2005
+ Edwards, Bill 1986
  Edwards, LaVell 2004
+ Engle, Rip 1973
  Evashevski, Forest 2000
  Faurot, Don 1961
  Fry, Hayden 2003
+ Gaither, Jake 1973
  Gillman, Sid 1989
+ Godfrey, Ernest 1972
  Graves, Ray 1990
+ Gustafson, Andy 1985
+ Hall, Edward 1951
+ Harding, Jack 1980
+ Harlow, Richard 1954
+ Harman, Harvey 1981
+ Harper, Jesse 1971
+ Haughton, Percy 1951
+ Hayes, Woody 1983
+ Heisman, John W 1954
+ Higgins, Robert 1954
+ Hollingbery, Babe 1979
+ Howard, Frank 1989
+ Ingram, Bill 1973
  James, Don 1997
+ Jennings, Morley 1973
+ Jones, Biff 1954
+ Jones, Howard 1951
+ Jones, Tad 1958

+ Jordan, Lloyd 1978
+ Jordan, Ralph (Shug) 1982
+ Kerr, Andy 1951
  Kush, Frank 1995
+ Leahy, Frank 1970
+ Little, George 1955
+ Little, Lou 1960
+ Madigan, Slip 1974
  Maurer, Dave 1991
+ McClendon, Charley 1986
+ McCracken, Herb 1973
+ McGugin, Dan 1951
+ McKay, John 1988
+ McKeen, Allyn 1991
+ McLaughry, Tuss 1962
+ Merritt, John 1994
+ Meyer, Dutch 1956
+ Mollenkopf, Jack 1988
+ Moore, Bernie 1954
+ Moore, Scrappy 1980
+ Morrison, Ray 1954
+ Munger, George 1976
+ Munn, Clarence (Biggie) . . .1959
+ Murray, Bill 1974
+ Murray, Frank 1983
+ Mylin, Ed (Hooks) 1974
+ Neale, Earle (Greasy) 1967
+ Neely, Jess 1971
  Nehlen, Don 2005
+ Nelson, David 1987
+ Neyland, Robert 1956
+ Norton, Homer 1971
+ O'Neill, Frank (Buck) 1951
+ Osborne, Tom 1998
+ Owen, Bennie 1951
  Parseghian, Ara 1980
  Paterno, Joe 2007
+ Perry, Doyt 1988
+ Phelan, Jimmy 1973

+ Prothro, Tommy 1991
  Ralston, John 1992
+ Robinson, E.N. 1955
+ Rockne, Knute 1951
+ Romney, Dick 1954
+ Roper, Bill 1951
  Royal, Darrell 1983
+ Sanders, Henry (Red) 1996
+ Sanford, George 1971
  Schembechler, Bo 1993
+ Schmidt, Francis 1971
+ Schwartzwalder, Ben 1982
+ Shaughnessy, Clark 1968
+ Shaw, Buck 1972
+ Smith, Andy 1951
+ Snavely, Carl 1965
+ Stagg, Amos Alonzo 1951
+ Sutherland, Jock 1951
  Switzer, Barry 2001
+ Tatum, Jim 1984
  Teaff, Grant 2001
+ Thomas, Frank 1951
+ Vann, Thad 1987
  Vaught, Johnny 1979
+ Wade, Wallace 1955
+ Waldorf, Lynn (Pappy) 1966
+ Warner, Glenn (Pop) 1951
  Welsh, George 2004
+ Wieman, E.E. (Tad) 1956
+ Wilce, John 1954
+ Wilkinson, Bud 1969
+ Williams, Henry 1951
+ Woodruff, George 1963
+ Woodson, Warren 1989
+ Wyatt, Bowden 1997
  Yeoman, Bill 2001
+ Yost, Fielding (Hurry Up) . . .1951
  Young, Jim 1999
+ Zuppke, Bob 1951

Small College
Players

  Bailey, Johnny-Texas A&I . . .1989
  Barber, Mike-Marshall 1988
  Baumgartner, Kirk-
    WI-Stevens Point 1989
  Bentrim, Jeff-N.Dakota St. . . .1986
+ Blazine, Tony-Ill Wesleyan . .1934
  Bork, George-N. Illinois 1963
  Bradshaw, Terry-La. Tech . . .1969
  Bruner, Teel-Centre KY 1985
+ Buchanon, Buck-Grambling .1962
  Calip, Brad-E. Central 1984
  Carson, Harry, S.C. State . . .1975
  Cason, Rod, Angelo St. 1971
  Cichy, Joe-N.Dakota St. 1970
  Cooper, Bill-Muskinghum . . .1960
  Crawford, Brad-Franklin 1977
  Davis, Harold-Wesminster . . .1956
  Deery, Tom-Widener 1981
+ Delaney, Joe-N'western St. . .1980
  Dement, Kenneth-SE Mo St. .1954
  Den Herder, Vern-Central IA .1970
  Dent, Kevin-Jackson St. 1988
  Dryer, Fred-San Diego St. . . .1968
  Dudek, Joe-Plymouth St. 1985
  Floyd, George-E. Kentucky . .1981

  Friesz, John-Idaho 1989
  Galimore, Willie-Fla. A&M . . .1956
  Gamble, Kenny-Colgate 1987
  Green, Charlie-Wittenberg . . .1964
  Green, Darrell-Texas A&I 1982
  Grinnell, Williams-Tufts 1934
  Ham, Tracy-Ga. Southern . . .1986
  Haslett, Jim-Indiana, PA 1978
  Hawkins, Frank-Nevada 1980
  Henley, Garney-Huron 1959
  Holt, Pierce-Angelo St. 1987
+ Hunt, Jackie-Marshall 1941
  Johnson, Billy-Widener 1973
  Johnson, Gary-Grambling . . .1974
  Kendall, Joe-Kentucky St. . . .1936
  Lanier, Willie-Morgan St. . . .1966
  LeClair, Jim-North Dakota . . .1971
  Lewis, Leo-Lincoln 1954
  Lockbaum, Gordie-Holy Cross 1987
  Lomax, Neil-Portland 1980
  Mallett, Ronnie-C. Arkansas .1981
  McGriff, Tyrone-Jackson St. .1974
  Montgomery, Wilbert-
    Abilene Christian 1976
  Nix, Dwayne-Texas A&I 1968

  O'Brien, Ken-UC Davis 1982
+ Payton, Walter-Jackson St. . . .1974
  Pugh, Larrry-Westminster 1964
  Reasons, Gary-N'western St. 1983
  Redell, Bill-Occidental 1963
  Reppert, Scott-Lawrence 1982
  Rice, Jerry-Miss. Valley St. . .1984
  Richardson, Willie-Jackson St. 1962
  Ritchie, Richard-Texas A&I . .1976
+ Roberts, Calvin-
    Gustavus Adolphus 1952
+ Ross, Dan-Northeastern 1978
  Scott, Freddie-Amherst 1973
  Shell, Donnie-S.C. State 1973
  Sheplock, Frank-Bloomsburg .1985
+ Stevenson, Ben-Tuskegee . . .1930
  Stromberg, Bill-Johns Hopkins 1981
  Taylor, Bruce-Boston U. 1969
  Thomsen, Lynn-Augustana . .1986
  Totten, Willie-Miss. Valley St. 1985
  Trautman, Randy-Boise St. . .1964
  Tuggle, Jessie-Valdosta 1986
  Williams, Doug-Grambling . . .1977
  Youngblood, Jim-Tenn. Tech .1972
  Younger, Paul-Grambling . . .1948

Coaches

  Ault, Chris 2002
  Beck, Tom 2004

+ Burry, Harold 1996
  Butterfield, Jim 1997

  Casem, Marino 2003
  Christopherson, Jim 2007

Small College Coaches (Cont.)

Fusco, Joe 2001
Harring, Roger 2005
Hoerneman, Paul 1997
Huerta, Marcelino 2002
Joe, Billy 2007
Keade, Bob 1998
Kidd, Roy 2003
Klausing, Chuck 1998
Martinelli, Fred 1993

Mudra, Darrell 2000
+ Mumford, Ace 2001
Nicks, Billy 1999
Raymond, Tubby 2003
Reade, Bob 1998
Robinson, Eddie G. 1997
+ Richard, Charlie 2004
Rutschman, Ad 1998

+ Schipper, Ron 2000
Sherman, Edgar 1996
Sochor, James 1999
+ Steinke, Gilbert 1996
Strahm, Dick 2004
+ Tressel, Lee 1996
Waters, Frank 2000
Westering, Frosty 2005

Pro Football Hall of Fame

Established in 1963 by National Football League to commemorate the sport's professional origins. **Address:** 2121 George Halas Drive NW, Canton, OH 44708. **Telephone:** (330) 456-8207. **Web:** www.profootballhof.com

Eligibility: Nominated players must be retired five years, coaches must be retired, and contributors can still be active. Voting done by 39-member panel made up of media representatives from all 31 NFL cities (two from New York), one PFWA representative and six selectors-at-large.

Class of 2007 (6): PLAYERS—G **Gene Hickerson**, Cleveland Browns (1958-1973); WR **Michael Irvin**, Dallas Cowboys (1988-99); OL **Bruce Matthews**, Houston Oilers, Tennessee Oilers/Titans (1983-2001); TE **Charlie Sanders**, Detroit Lions (1968-77); RB **Thurman Thomas**, Buffalo Bills (1988-99), Miami Dolphins (2000); CB **Roger Wehrli**, St. Louis Cardinals (1969-82).

Quarterbacks

Aikman, Troy 2006
Baugh, Sammy 1963
Blanda, George (also PK) . .1981
Bradshaw, Terry 1989
+ Clark, Dutch 1963
+ Conzelman, Jimmy 1964
Dawson, Len 1987
+ Driscoll, Paddy 1965
Elway, John 2004
Fouts, Dan 1993
+ Friedman, Benny 2005

+ Graham, Otto 1965
Griese, Bob 1990
+ Herber, Arnie 1966
Jurgensen, Sonny 1983
Kelly, Jim 2002
+ Layne, Bobby 1967
+ Luckman, Sid 1965
Marino, Dan 2005
Montana, Joe 2000
Moon, Warren 2006

Namath, Joe 1985
Parker, Clarence (Ace) 1972
Starr, Bart 1977
Staubach, Roger 1985
Tarkenton, Fran 1986
Tittle, Y.A 1971
+ Unitas, Johnny 1979
+ Van Brocklin, Norm 1971
+ Waterfield, Bob 1965
Young, Steve 2005

Running Backs

Allen, Marcus 2003
+ Battles, Cliff 1968
Brown, Jim 1971
Campbell, Earl 1991
Canadeo, Tony 1974
Csonka, Larry 1987
Dickerson, Eric 1999
Dorsett, Tony 1994
Dudley, Bill 1966
Gifford, Frank 1977
+ Grange, Red 1963
+ Guyon, Joe 1966
Harris, Franco 1990
+ Hinkle, Clarke 1964

Hornung, Paul 1986
Johnson, John Henry 1987
Kelly, Leroy 1994
+ Leemans, Tuffy 1978
Matson, Ollie 1972
McAfee, George 1966
McElhenny, Hugh 1970
+ McNally, Johnny (Blood) . . .1963
Moore, Lenny 1975
+ Motley, Marion 1968
+ Nagurski, Bronko 1963
+ Nevers, Ernie 1963
+ Payton, Walter 1993

Perry, Joe 1969
+ Pollard, Fritz 2005
Riggins, John 1992
Sanders, Barry 2004
Sayers, Gale 1977
Simpson, O.J. 1985
+ Strong, Ken 1967
Taylor, Jim 1976
Thomas, Thurman 2007
+ Thorpe, Jim 1963
Trippi, Charley 1968
Van Buren, Steve 1965
+ Walker, Doak 1986

Ends & Wide Receivers

Alworth, Lance 1978
+ Badgro, Red 1981
Berry, Raymond 1973
Biletnikoff, Fred 1988
Casper, Dave 2002
+ Chamberlin, Guy 1965
Ditka, Mike 1988
+ Fears, Tom 1970
+ Hewitt, Bill 1971
Hirsch, Elroy (Crazylegs) . . .1968

+ Hutson, Don 1963
Irvin, Michael 2007
Joiner, Charlie 1996
Largent, Steve 1995
Lavelli, Dante 1975
Lofton, James 2003
Mackey, John 1992
Maynard, Don 1987
McDonald, Tommy 1998
+ Millner, Wayne 1968

Mitchell, Bobby 1983
Newsome, Ozzie 1999
Pihos, Pete 1970
Sanders, Charlie 2007
Smith, Jackie 1994
Stallworth, John 2002
Swann, Lynn 2001
Taylor, Charley 1984
Warfield, Paul 1983
Winslow, Kellen 1995

Offensive Linemen

Bednarik, Chuck (C-LB) 1967
Brown, Bob (T) 2004
Brown, Roosevelt (T) 1975
DeLamielleure, Joe (G) 2003
Dierdorf, Dan (T) 1996
Gatski, Frank (C) 1985
Gregg, Forrest (T-G) 1977
+ Groza, Lou (T-PK) 1974
Hannah, John (G) 1991
Hickerson, Gene (G) 2007
Jones, Stan (T-G-DT) 1991

Langer, Jim (C) 1987
Little, Larry (G) 1993
Mack, Tom (G) 1999
Matthews, Bruce (G-T-C) . . .2007
McCormack, Mike (T) 1984
Mix, Ron (T-G) 1979
Munchak, Mike (G) 2001
Munoz, Anthony (T) 1998
+ Musso, George (T-G) 1982
Otto, Jim (C) 1980
Parker, Jim (G) 1973

Ringo, Jim (C) 1981
St. Clair, Bob (T) 1990
Shaw, Billy (G) 1999
Shell, Art (T) 1989
Slater, Jackie (T) 2001
Stephenson, Dwight (C) 1998
Upshaw, Gene (G) 1987
Yary, Ron (T) 2001
+ Webster, Mike (C) 1997
Wright, Rayfield (T) 2006

Linemen (pre-World War II)

+ Edwards, Turk (T) 1969
+ Fortmann, Dan (G) 1985
+ Healey, Ed (T) 1964
+ Hein, Mel (C) 1963
+ Henry, Pete (T) 1963

+ Hubbard, Cal (T) 1963
+ Kiesling, Walt (G) 1966
+ Kinard, Bruiser (T) 1971
+ Lyman, Link (T) 1964
+ Michalske, Mike (G) 1964

+ Musso, George (T-G) 1982
+ Stydahar, Joe (T) 1967
+ Trafton, George (C) 1964
+ Turner, Bulldog (C) 1966
+ Wojciechowicz, Alex (C) . .1968

Defensive Linemen

Atkins, Doug 1982
Bethea, Elvin 2003
+ Buchanan, Buck 1990
Creekmur, Lou 1996
Davis, Willie 1981
Donovan, Art 1968
Eller, Carl 2004
+ Ford, Len 1976
Greene, Joe 1987

Hampton, Dan 2002
Jones, Deacon 1980
+ Jordan, Henry 1995
Lilly, Bob 1980
Long, Howie 2000
Marchetti, Gino 1972
+ Nomellini, Leo 1969
Olsen, Merlin 1982
Page, Alan 1988

Robustelli, Andy 1971
Selmon, Lee Roy 1995
Stautner, Ernie 1969
+ Weinmeister, Arnie 1984
White, Randy 1994
+ White, Reggie 2006
Willis, Bill 1977
Youngblood, Jack 2001

Linebackers

Bell, Bobby 1983
Buoniconti, Nick 2001
Butkus, Dick 1979
Carson, Harry 2006
Connor, George (DT-OT) . . .1975
+ George, Bill 1974

Ham, Jack 1988
Hendricks, Ted 1990
Huff, Sam 1982
Lambert, Jack 1990
Lanier, Willie 1986
+ Nitschke, Ray 1978

Schmidt, Joe 1973
Singletary, Mike 1998
Taylor, Lawrence 1999
Wilcox, Dave 2000

Defensive Backs

Adderley, Herb 1980
Barney, Lem 1992
Blount, Mel 1989
Brown, Willie 1984
+ Christiansen, Jack 1970
Haynes, Michael 1997
Houston, Ken 1986

Johnson, Jimmy 1994
Krause, Paul 1998
+ Lane, Dick (Night Train) . . .1974
Lary, Yale 1979
Lott, Ronnie 2000
Renfro, Mel 1996
+ Tunnell, Emlen 1967

Wehrli, Roger 2007
Wilson, Larry 1978
Wood, Willie 1989

Placekicker

Stenerud, Jan 1991

Coaches

+ Allen, George 2002
+ Brown, Paul 1967
+ Ewbank, Weeb 1978
+ Flaherty, Ray 1976
Gibbs, Joe 1996
Gillman, Sid 1983
Grant, Bud 1994

+ Halas, George 1963
+ Lambeau, Curly 1963
+ Landry, Tom 1990
Levy, Marv 2001
+ Lombardi, Vince 1971
Madden, John 2006
+ Neale, Earle (Greasy) 1969

Noll, Chuck 1993
+ Owen, Steve 1966
Shula, Don 1997
Stram, Hank 2003
+ Walsh, Bill 1993

Contributors

+ Bell, Bert 1963
+ Bidwill, Charles 1967
+ Carr, Joe 1963
Davis, Al 1992
+ Finks, Jim 1995
+ Halas, George 1963

+ Hunt, Lamar 1972
+ Mara, Tim 1963
+ Mara, Wellington 1997
+ Marshall, George 1963
+ Ray, Hugh (Shorty) 1966
+ Reeves, Dan 1967

+ Rooney, Art 1964
Rooney, Dan 2000
+ Rozelle, Pete 1985
Schramm, Tex 1991

NFL's All-Time Team

Selected by the Pro Football Hall of Fame voters and released Aug. 1, 2000 as part of the NFL Century celebration.

Offense

Wide Receivers: Don Hutson and Jerry Rice
Tight End: John Mackey
Tackles: Roosevelt Brown and Anthony Munoz
Guards: John Hannah and Jim Parker
Center: Mike Webster
Quarterback: Johnny Unitas
Running Backs: Jim Brown and Walter Payton

Defense

Ends: Deacon Jones and Reggie White
Tackles: Joe Greene and Bob Lilly
Linebackers: Dick Butkus, Jack Ham
and Lawrence Taylor
Cornerbacks: Mel Blount
and Dick (Night Train) Lane
Safeties: Ronnie Lott and Larry Wilson

Specialists

Placekicker: Jan Stenerud
Punter: Ray Guy
Kick Returner: Gale Sayers

Punt Returner: Deion Sanders
Special Teams: Steve Tasker

GOLF

World Golf Hall of Fame

The World Golf Hall of Fame opened its doors in 1998 at the World Golf Village outside of Jacksonville, Fla. **Address:** One World Golf Place, St. Augustine, FL 32092. **Telephone:** (904) 940-4000. **Web:** www.wghof.com/hof/hof.php **Eligibility:** Professionals have three avenues into the WGHF. A PGA Tour player qualifies for the ballot if he has at least 10 victories in approved tournaments, or at least two victories among The Players Championship, Masters, U.S. Open, British Open and PGA Championship, is at least 40 years old and has been a member of the Tour for 10 years. A senior PGA Tour player qualifies if he has been a Senior Tour member for five years and has 20 wins between the PGA Tour and Senior Tour or five wins among the PGA majors, the Players Championship and the senior majors (U.S. Senior Open, Tradition, PGA Seniors' Championship and Senior Players Championship). Final selections for both Veteran's (for players who played bulk of their career before 1974) and Lifetime Achievement Categories are made by the Executive Committee of the World Golf Hall of Fame, which includes leaders from the major golf organizations.

Any player qualifying for the LPGA Hall automatically qualifies for the WGHF. Until 1999, nominees must have had played 10 years on the LPGA tour and won 30 official events, including two major championships; 35 official events and one major; or 40 official events and no majors. The eligibility requirements were loosened somewhat in 1999. The new guidelines are based on a system which awards two points for winning a major and one point for winning other tournaments, the Vare trophy (for lowest scoring average) and the player of the year award. Players must win at least one major, Vare trophy, or player of the year award and accumulate a total of 27 points to be inducted. For players not eligible for either the PGA Tour or the LPGA Hall of Fame, a body of more than 300 international golf writers and historians will vote each year.

Members are listed with year of induction; (+) indicates deceased members.

Class of 2007 (6): MEN—**Hubert Green**, **Kel Nagle** and **Curtis Strange**. WOMEN—**Se Ri Pak**; LIFETIME ACHIEVEMENT—**Joe Carr** and **Charles Blair Macdonald**.

Men

+ Anderson, Willie 1975	Green, Hubert 2007	Norman, Greg 2001
Aoki, Isao 2004	+ Guldahl, Ralph 1981	+ Ouimet, Francis 1974
+ Armour, Tommy 1976	+ Hagen, Walter 1974	Palmer, Arnold 1974
+ Ball, John, Jr 1977	+ Hilton, Harold 1978	+ Park, Willie Sr. 2005
Ballesteros, Seve 1999	+ Hogan, Ben 1974	+ Picard, Henry 2006
+ Barnes, Jim 1989	Irwin, Hale 1992	Player, Gary 1974
Beman, Deane 2000	Jacklin, Tony 2002	Price, Nick 2003
Bolt, Tommy 2002	Jacobs, John 2000	+ Robertson, Allan 2001
Bonallack, Sir Michael . . .2000	+ Jones, Bobby 1974	+ Runyan, Paul 1990
+ Boros, Julius 1982	Kite, Tom 2004	+ Sarazen, Gene 1974
+ Braid, James 1976	Langer, Bernhard 2002	Sifford, Charlie 2004
Burke, Jack Jr. 2000	+ Little, Lawson 1980	Singh, Vijay 2006
Casper, Billy 1978	Littler, Gene 1990	+ Smith, Horton 1990
Coles, Neil 2000	+ Locke, Bobby 1977	+ Snead, Sam 1974
+ Cooper, Lighthorse Harry . .1992	+ Mangrum, Lloyd 1998	+ Stewart, Payne 2001
+ Cotton, Sir Henry 1980	+ Middlecoff, Cary 1986	Strange, Curtis 2007
Crenshaw, Ben 2002	Miller, Johnny 1996	+ Taylor, John H 1975
+ Demaret, Jimmy 1983	+ Morris, Tom Jr 1975	Thomson, Peter 1988
De Vicenzo, Roberto 1989	+ Morris, Tom Sr 1976	+ Travers, Jerry 1976
+ Diegel, Leo 2003	+ Nagle, Kel 2007	+ Travis, Walter 1979
+ Evans, Chick 1975	+ Nelson, Byron 1974	Trevino, Lee 1981
Faldo, Nick 1997	Nelson, Larry 2006	+ Vardon, Harry 1974
Floyd, Ray 1989	Nicklaus, Jack 1974	Watson, Tom 1988

Women

Alcott, Amy 1999	Inkster, Julie 2000	Smith, Marilynn 2006
+ Berg, Patty 1974	Jameson, Betty 1951	Sorenstam, Annika 2003
Bradley, Pat 1986	King, Betsy 1995	Streit, Marlene Stewart 2004
Carner, JoAnne 1985	Lopez, Nancy 1989	Suggs, Louise 1979
Caponi, Donna 2001	Mann, Carol 1977	+ Vare, Glenna Collett 1975
Daniel, Beth 1999	Okamoto, Ayako 2005	Webb, Karrie 2005
Hagge, Marlene 2002	Pak, Se Ri 2007	+ Wethered, Joyce 1975
Haynie, Sandra 1977	Rankin, Judy 2000	Whitworth, Kathy 1982
Higuchi, Chako 2003	Rawls, Betsy 1987	Wright, Mickey 1976
+ Howe, Dorothy C.H 1978	Sheehan, Patty 1993	+ Zaharias, Babe Didrikson . .1974

Lifetime Achievement

Bell, Judy 2001	+ Graffis, Herb 1977	+ Penick, Harvey 2002
Campbell, William 1990	+ Harlow, Robert 1988	+ Roberts, Clifford 1978
+ Carr, Joe 2007	+ Hope, Bob 1983	Rodriguez, Chi Chi 1992
+ Corcoran, Fred 1975	+ Jones, Robert Trent 1987	+ Ross, Donald 1977
+ Crosby, Bing 1978	+ Macdonald, Charles Blair . .2007	+ Solheim, Karsten 2001
+ Darwin, Bernard 2005	+ MacKenzie, Alister 2005	+ Shore, Dinah 1994
+ Dey, Joe 1975	+ McCormack, Mark 2006	+ Tufts, Richard 1992

HOCKEY

Hockey Hall of Fame

Established in 1945 by the National Hockey League and opened in 1961. **Address:** BCE Place, 30 Yonge Street, Toronto, Ontario, M5E 1X8. **Telephone:** (416) 360-7735. **Web:** www.hhof.com

Eligibility: Nominated players and referees must be retired three years. However that waiting period has now been waived 10 times. Players that have had the waiting period waived are indicated with an asterisk. Voting done by 18-member panel made up of pro and amateur hockey personalities and media representatives. A 15-member Veterans Committee that selected older players was eliminated in 2000.

Class of 2007 (5): PLAYERS—F **Ron Francis**, Hartford Whalers (1981-1991), Pittsburgh Penguins (1991-1998), Carolina Hurricanes (1998-2004); D **Al MacInnis**, Calgary Flames (1981-94), St. Louis Blues (1994-2004); F **Mark Messier**, Indianapolis Racers (1978), Cincinnati Stingers (1978-79), Edmonton Oilers (1979-1991), New York Rangers (1991-97, 2000-04), Vancouver Canucks (1997-2000); D **Scott Stevens**, Washington Capitals (1982-90), St. Louis Blues (1990-91), New Jersey Devils (1991-2004). BUILDER—**Jim Gregory**, executive.

Members are listed with year of induction; (+) indicates deceased members.

Forwards

+ Abel, Sid 1969	+ Gardner, Jimmy 1962	Mullen, Joe 2000
+ Adams, Jack 1959	Gartner, Mike 2001	Neely, Cam 2005
+ Apps, Syl 1961	+ Geoffrion, Bernie 1972	+ Nighbor, Frank 1947
Armstrong, George 1975	Gerard, Eddie 1945	+ Noble, Reg 1962
+ Bailey, Ace 1975	Gilbert, Rod 1982	+ O'Connor, Buddy 1988
+ Bain, Dan 1945	Gillies, Clark 2002	+ Oliver, Harry 1967
+ Baker, Hobey 1945	+ Gilmour, Billy 1962	Olmstead, Bert 1985
Barber, Bill 1990	Goulet, Michel 1998	+ Patrick, Lynn 1980
+ Barry, Marty 1965	Gretzky, Wayne* 1999	Perreault, Gilbert 1990
Bathgate, Andy 1978	+ Griffis, Si 1950	+ Phillips, Tom 1945
+ Bauer, Bobby 1996	Hawerchuk, Dale 2001	+ Primeau, Joe 1963
Beliveau, Jean* 1972	+ Hay, George 1958	Pulford, Bob 1991
+ Bentley, Doug 1964	+ Hextall, Bryan 1969	+ Rankin, Frank 1961
+ Bentley, Max 1966	+ Hooper, Tom 1962	Ratelle, Jean 1985
+ Blake, Toe 1966	+ Howe, Gordie* 1972	Richard, Henri 1979
Bossy, Mike 1991	+ Howe, Syd 1965	+ Richard, Maurice (Rocket)* .1961
+ Boucher, Frank 1958	Hull, Bobby 1983	+ Richardson, George 1950
+ Bowie, Dubbie 1945	+ Hyland, Harry 1962	+ Roberts, Gordie 1971
+ Broadbent, Punch 1962	+ Irvin, Dick 1958	+ Russel, Blair 1965
Bucyk, John (Chief) 1981	+ Jackson, Busher 1971	+ Russell, Ernie 1965
+ Burch, Billy 1974	+ Joliat, Aurel 1947	+ Ruttan, Jack 1962
Clarke, Bobby 1987	+ Keats, Duke 1958	Savard, Denis 2000
+ Colville, Neil 1967	Kennedy, Ted (Teeder) . . .1966	+ Scanlan, Fred 1965
+ Conacher, Charlie 1961	Keon, Dave 1986	Schmidt, Milt 1961
Conacher, Roy 1998	+ Kharlamov, Valeri 2005	+ Schriner, Sweeney 1962
+ Cook, Bill 1952	Kurri, Jari 2001	+ Seibert, Oliver 1961
+ Cook, Bun 1995	Lach, Elmer 1966	Shutt, Steve 1993
Cournoyer, Yvan 1982	Lafleur, Guy 1988	+ Siebert, Babe 1964
+ Cowley, Bill 1968	LaFontaine, Pat 2003	Sittler, Darryl 1989
+ Crawford, Rusty 1962	+ Lalonde, Newsy 1950	+ Smith, Alf 1962
+ Darragh, Jack 1962	Laprade, Edgar 1993	Smith, Clint 1991
+ Davidson, Scotty 1950	Lemaire, Jacques 1984	+ Smith, Hooley 1972
+ Day, Hap 1961	Lemieux, Mario* 1997	+ Smith, Tommy 1973
Delvecchio, Alex 1977	+ Lewis, Herbie 1989	+ Stanley, Barney 1962
+ Denneny, Cy 1959	Lindsay, Ted* 1966	Stastny, Peter 1998
Dionne, Marcel 1992	+ MacKay, Mickey 1952	+ Stewart, Nels 1962
+ Drillon, Gordie 1975	Mahovlich, Frank 1981	+ Stuart, Bruce 1961
+ Drinkwater, Graham 1950	+ Malone, Joe 1950	+ Taylor, Fred (Cyclone) 1947
Duff, Dick 2006	+ Marshall, Jack 1965	+ Trihey, Harry 1950
Dumart, Woody 1992	+ Maxwell, Fred 1962	Trottier, Bryan 1997
+ Dunderdale, Tommy 1974	McDonald, Lanny 1992	Ullman, Norm 1982
+ Dye, Babe 1970	+ McGee, Frank 1945	+ Walker, Jack 1960
Esposito, Phil 1984	+ McGimsie, Billy 1962	+ Walsh, Marty 1962
+ Farrell, Arthur 1965	Messier, Mark 2007	+ Watson, Harry (Whipper) . .1994
Federko, Bernie 2002	Mikita, Stan 1983	+ Watson, Harry (Moose) . . .1962
+ Foyston, Frank 1958	Moore, Dickie 1974	+ Weiland, Cooney 1971
Francis, Ron 2007	+ Morenz, Howie 1945	+ Westwick, Harry (Rat) 1962
+ Frederickson, Frank 1958	+ Mosienko, Bill 1965	+ Whitcroft, Fred 1962
Gainey, Bob 1992		

Referees & Linesmen

Armstrong, Neil 1991	+ Hayes, George 1988	+ Smeaton, J. Cooper 1961
Ashley, John 1981	+ Hewitson, Bobby 1963	Storey, Red 1967
Chadwick, Bill 1964	+ Ion, Mickey 1961	Udvari, Frank 1973
D'Amico, John 1993	Pavelich, Matt 1987	van Hellemond, Andy 1999
+ Elliott, Chaucer 1961	+ Rodden, Mike 1962	

Goaltenders

+ Benedict, Clint 1965
Bower, Johnny 1976
+ Brimsek, Frankie 1966
+ Broda, Turk 1967
Cheevers, Gerry 1985
+ Connell, Alex 1958
Dryden, Ken 1983
+ Durnan, Bill 1964
Esposito, Tony 1988
Fuhr, Grant 2003
+ Gardiner, Chuck 1945

Giacomin, Eddie 1987
+ Hainsworth, George 1961
Hall, Glenn 1975
+ Hern, Riley 1962
+ Holmes, Hap 1972
+ Hutton, J.B. (Bouse) 1962
+ Lehman, Hughie 1958
+ LeSueur, Percy 1961
+ Lumley, Harry 1980
+ Moran, Paddy 1958
Parent, Bernie 1984

+ Plante, Jacques 1978
+ Rayner, Chuck 1973
Roy, Patrick 2006
+ Sawchuk, Terry* 1971
Smith, Billy 1993
+ Thompson, Tiny 1959
Tretiak, Vladislav 1989
+ Vezina, Georges 1945
+ Worsley, Gump 1980
+ Worters, Roy 1969

Defensemen

Boivin, Leo 1986
+ Boon, Dickie 1952
Bouchard, Butch 1966
+ Boucher, George 1960
Bourque, Ray 2004
+ Cameron, Harry 1962
+ Clancy, King 1958
+ Clapper, Dit* 1947
+ Cleghorn, Sprague 1958
Coffey, Paul 2004
+ Conacher, Lionel 1994
+ Coulter, Art 1974
+ Dutton, Red 1958
Fetisov, Viacheslav 2001
Flaman, Fernie 1990
Gadsby, Bill 1970
+ Gardiner, Herb 1958
+ Goheen, F.X. (Moose) 1952
+ Goodfellow, Ebbie 1963
+ Grant, Mike 1950
+ Green, Wilf (Shorty) 1962

+ Hall, Joe 1961
+ Harvey, Doug 1973
Horner, Red 1965
+ Horton, Tim 1977
Howell, Harry 1979
+ Johnson, Ching 1958
+ Johnson, Ernie 1952
Johnson, Tom 1970
Kelly, Red* 1969
Langway, Rod 2002
Laperriere, Jacques 1987
Lapointe, Guy 1993
+ Laviolette, Jack 1962
MacInnis, Al 2007
+ Mantha, Sylvio 1960
+ McNamara, George 1958
Murphy, Larry 2004
Orr, Bobby* 1979
Park, Brad 1988
+ Patrick, Lester 1947
Pilote, Pierre 1975

+ Pitre, Didier 1962
Potvin, Denis 1991
+ Pratt, Babe 1966
Pronovost, Marcel 1978
+ Pulford, Harvey 1945
+ Quackenbush, Bill 1976
Reardon, Kenny 1966
Robinson, Larry 1995
+ Ross, Art 1945
Salming, Borje 1996
Savard, Serge 1986
+ Seibert, Earl 1963
+ Shore, Eddie 1947
+ Simpson, Joe 1962
Stanley, Allan 1981
Stevens, Scott 2007
+ Stewart, Jack 1964
+ Stuart, Hod 1945
+ Wilson, Gordon (Phat) 1962

Builders

+ Adams, Charles 1960
+ Adams, Weston W. Sr 1972
+ Ahearn, Frank 1962
+ Ahearne, J.F. (Bunny) 1977
+ Allan, Sir Montagu 1945
Allen, Keith 1992
Arbour, Al 1996
+ Ballard, Harold 1977
+ Bauer, Fr. David 1989
+ Bickell, J.P. 1978
Bowman, Scotty 1991
+ Brooks, Herb 2006
+ Brown, George 1961
+ Brown, Walter 1962
+ Buckland, Frank 1975
Bush, Walter 2000
Butterfield, Jack 1980
+ Calder, Frank 1945
+ Campbell, Angus 1964
+ Campbell, Clarence 1966
+ Cattarinich, Joseph 1977
Costello, Murray 2005
+ Dandurand, Leo 1963
+ Dilio, Frank 1964
+ Dudley, George 1958
+ Dunn, James 1968
Fletcher, Cliff 2004
Francis, Emile 1982
+ Gibson, Jack 1976
+ Gorman, Tommy 1963
Gregory, Jim 2007
+ Griffiths, Frank A. 1993

+ Hanley, Bill 1986
+ Hay, Charles 1984
+ Hendy, Jim 1968
+ Hewitt, Foster 1965
+ Hewitt, W.A. 1945
Hotchkiss, Harley 2006
+ Hume, Fred 1962
Ilitch, Mike 2003
+ Imlach, Punch 1984
+ Ivan, Tommy 1964
+ Jennings, Bill 1975
+ Johnson, Bob 1992
+ Juckes, Gordon 1979
+ Kilpatrick, John 1960
Kilrea, Brian 2003
+ Knox, Seymour III 1993
+ Leader, Al 1969
+ LeBel, Bob 1970
+ Lockhart, Tom 1965
+ Loicq, Paul 1961
+ Mariucci, John 1985
Mathers, Frank 1992
+ McLaughlin, Frederic 1963
+ Milford, Jake 1984
+ Molson, Hartland 1973
Morrison, Ian (Scotty) 1999
+ Murray, Athol (Pere) 1998
+ Nelson, Francis 1945
+ Neilson, Roger 2002
+ Norris, Bruce 1969
+ Norris, James D 1962
+ Norris, James Sr 1958

+ Northey, William 1945
+ O'Brien, J.A 1962
O'Neill, Brian 1994
Page, Fred 1993
Patrick, Craig 2001
+ Patrick, Frank 1958
+ Pickard, Allan 1958
+ Pilous, Rudy 1985
Poile, Bud 1990
Pollock, Sam 1978
+ Raymond, Donat 1958
+ Robertson, John Ross 1945
+ Robinson, Claude 1945
+ Ross, Philip 1976
+ Sabetzki, Gunther 1995
Sather, Glen 1997
+ Selke, Frank 1960
Sinden, Harry 1983
+ Smith, Frank 1962
+ Smythe, Conn 1958
Snider, Ed 1988
+ Stanley, Lord of Preston 1945
+ Sutherland, James 1945
Tarasov, Anatoli 1974
Torrey, Bill 1995
+ Turner, Lloyd 1958
+ Tutt, William Thayer 1978
+ Voss, Carl 1974
+ Waghorne, Fred 1961
+ Wirtz, Arthur 1971
+ Wirtz, Bill 1976
Ziegler, John 1987

Note: Alan Eagleson was inducted into the Hockey Hall of Fame in 1989 but resigned in 1998 after being found guilty of fraud.

U.S. Hockey Hall of Fame

Established in 1968 by the Eveleth (Minn.) Civic Association Project H Committee and opened in 1973. **Address:** 801 Hat Trick Ave., P.O. Box 657, Eveleth, MN 55734. **Telephone:** (218) 744-5167. **Web:** www.ushockeyhall.com

Eligibility: Nominated players and referees must be American-born and retired five years; coaches must be American-born and must have coached predominantly American teams. Voting done by 12-member panel made up of Hall of Fame members and U.S. hockey officials.

Class of 2007 (3): PLAYERS—**Milton "Curly" Brink, Gary Gambucci** and **Mike Milbury.**

Members are listed with year of induction; (+) indicates deceased members.

Players

+ Abel, Clarence (Taffy) 1973	Fusco, Mark 2002	Mayasich, John 1976
+ Baker, Hobey 1973	Fusco, Scott 2002	McCartan, Jack 1983
Bartholome, Earl 1977	Gambucci, Gary 2007	Milbury, Mike 2007
+ Bessone, Peter 1978	+ Garrison, John 1974	Moe, Bill 1974
Blake, Bob 1985	Garrity, Jack 1986	Morrow, Ken 1995
Boucha, Henry 1995	+ Goheen, Frank (Moose) . . .1973	+ Moseley, Fred 1975
+ Brimsek, Frankie 1973	Grant, Wally 1994	Mullen, Joe 1998
+ Brink, Milton (Curly) 2007	+ Harding, Austie 1975	+ Murray, Hugh (Muzz) Sr . . .1987
Broten, Neal 2000	Housley, Phil 2004	+ Nelson, Hub 1978
Cavanagh, Joe 1994	Howe, Mark 2003	+ Nyrop, William D. 1997
+ Chaisson, Ray 1974	Iglehart, Stewart 1975	Olson, Eddie 1977
Chase, John 1973	Ikola, Willard 1990	+ Owen, George 1973
Christian, Bill 1984	Johnson, Mark 2004	+ Palmer, Winthrop 1973
Christian, Dave 2001	Johnson, Paul 2001	Paradise, Bob 1989
Christian, Roger 1989	Johnson, Virgil 1974	+ Purpur, Clifford (Fido) 1974
Christiansen, Keith 2005	+ Karakas, Mike 1973	Ramsey, Mike 2001
Cleary, Bill 1976	Kirrane, Jack 1987	Riley, Bill 1977
Cleary, Bob 1981	LaFontaine, Pat 2003	Riley, Joe 2002
+ Conroy, Tony 1975	Lane, Myles 1973	+ Roberts, Maurice 2005
Coppo, Paul 2004	Langevin, Dave 1993	+ Romnes, Elwin (Doc) 1973
Curran, Mike 1998	Langway, Rod 1999	+ Rondeau, Dick 1985
+ Dahlstrom, Carl (Cully) 1973	Larson, Reed 1996	Sheehy, Timothy 1997
+ Desjardins, Vic 1974	+ Linder, Joe 1975	Watson, Gordie 1999
Desmond, Richard 1988	+ LoPresti, Sam 1973	+ Williams, Tom 1981
+ Dill, Bob 1979	MacDonald, Lane 2005	Williamson, Murray 2005
Dougherty, Richard 2003	+ Mariucci, John 1973	+ Winters, Frank (Coddy) 1973
+ Everett, Doug 1974	+ Matchefts, John 1991	+ Yackel, Ken 1986
Ftorek, Robbie 1991	+ Mather, Bruce 1998	

Coaches

+ Almquist, Oscar 1983	Heyliger, Vic 1974	Pleban, Connie 1990
Bessone, Amo 1992	+ Holt Jr., Charles E. 1997	Ramsay, Mike 2001
+ Brooks, Herb 1990	Ikola, Willard 1990	Riley, Jack 1979
Ceglarski, Len 1992	+ Jeremiah, Eddie 1973	+ Ross, Larry 1988
+ Cunniff, John 2003	+ Johnson, Bob 1991	+ Thompson, Cliff 1973
+ Fullerton, James 1992	Johnson, Paul 2001	+ Stewart, Bill 1982
Gambucci, Sergio 1996	Kelley, Jack 1993	Watson, Sid 1999
+ Gordon, Malcolm 1973	+ Kelly, John (Snooks) 1974	+ Winsor, Ralph 1973
Harkness, Ned 1994	Nanne, Lou 1998	Woog, Doug 2002

Referee   Contributor

Chadwick, Bill 1974   + Schulz, Charles M. 1993

Administrators

+ Brown, George 1973	+ Jennings, Bill 1981	Ridder, Bob 1976
+ Brown, Walter 1973	+ Kahler, Nick 1980	Trumble, Hal 1970
Bush, Walter 1980	+ Lockhart, Tom 1973	+ Tutt, Thayer 1973
+ Clark, Don 1978	Marvin, Cal 1982	+ Wirtz, Bill 1967
Claypool, Jim 1995	Palazzari, Doug 2000	+ Wright, Lyle 1973
+ Gibson, J.L. (Doc) 1973	Patrick, Craig 1996	
Ilitch, Mike 2004	Pleau, Larry 2000	

Members of Both Hockey and U.S. Hockey Halls of Fame

Players	Coaches		Builders
Hobey Baker	Bob Johnson	George Brown	Bill Jennings
Frankie Brimsek	Herb Brooks	Walter Brown	Tom Lockhart
Frank (Moose) Goheen		Walter Bush	Craig Patrick
Rod Langway	**Referee**	Doc Gibson	Thayer Tutt
Pat LaFontaine	Bill Chadwick	Mike Ilitch	Bill Wirtz
John Mariucci			
Joe Mullen			

HORSE RACING

National Museum of Racing and Hall of Fame

Established in 1950 by the Saratoga Springs Racing Association and opened in 1955. **Address:** National Museum of Racing and Hall of Fame, 191 Union Ave., Saratoga Springs, NY 12866. **Telephone:** (518) 584-0400. **Web:** www.racingmuseum.org

Eligibility: Nominated horses must be retired five years; jockeys must be active at least 15 years; trainers must be active at least 25 years. Voting done by 125-member panel of horse racing media.

Class of 2007 (8): JOCKEYS—**Jose Santos** and **John Sellers**. TRAINERS—**Henry Forrest, Frank McCabe** and **John Veitch**. HORSES—**Mom's Command, Silver Charm** and **Swoon's Son**.

Members are listed with year of induction; (+) indicates deceased member.

Jockeys

+ Adams, Frank (Dooley)* . . .1970
+ Adams, John 1965
+ Aitcheson, Joe Jr.* 1978
+ Arcaro, Eddie 1958
  Atkinson, Ted 1957
  Baeza, Braulio 1976
  Bailey, Jerry 1995
+ Barbee, George 1996
+ Bassett, Carroll* 1972
  Baze, Russell 1999
+ Blum, Walter 1987
  Boland, Bill 2006
+ Bostwick, George H.* 1968
+ Boulmetis, Sam 1973
+ Brooks, Steve 1963
  Brumfield, Don 1996
+ Burns, Tommy 1983
+ Butwell, Jimmy 1984
+ Byers, J.D. (Dolly) 1967
  Cauthen, Steve . . . . : . .1994
+ Coltiletti, Frank 1970
  Cordero, Angel Jr. 1988
+ Crawford, Robert (Specs)* . .1973
  Day, Pat 1991
  Delahoussaye, Eddie 1993
  Desormeaux, Kent 2004
+ Ensor, Lavelle (Buddy) 1962
+ Fator, Laverne 1955
  Fires, Earlie 2001
  Fishback, Jerry* 1992

+ Garner, Andrew (Mack) 1969
+ Garrison, Snapper 1955
+ Gomez, Avelino 1982
+ Griffin, Henry 1956
+ Guerin, Eric 1972
  Hartack, Bill 1959
  Hawley, Sandy 1992
+ Johnson, Albert 1971
+ Knapp, Willie 1969
  Krone, Julie 2000
+ Kummer, Clarence 1972
+ Kurtsinger, Charley 1967
+ Loftus, Johnny 1959
  Longden, Johnny 1958
  Maher, Danny 1955
+ McAtee, Linus 1956
  McCarron, Chris 1989
+ McCreary, Conn 1975
+ McKinney, Rigan 1968
+ McLaughlin, James . . : 1955
+ Miller, Walter 1955
+ Murphy, Isaac 1955
+ Neves, Ralph 1960
+ Notter, Joe 1963
+ O'Connor, Winnie 1956
+ Odom, George 1955
+ O'Neill, Frank 1956
+ Parke, Ivan 1978
+ Patrick, Gil 1970
  Pincay, Laffit Jr. 1975

+ Purdy, Sam 1970
+ Reiff, John 1956
+ Robertson, Alfred 1971
  Rotz, John L. 1983
+ Sande, Earl 1955
  Santos, Jose 2007
  Sellers, John 2007
+ Shilling, Carroll 1970
+ Shoemaker, Bill 1958
+ Simms, Willie 1977
+ Sloan, Todhunter 1955
  Smith, Mike 2003
+ Smithwick, A. Patrick* 1973
  Stevens, Gary 1997
+ Stout, James 1968
+ Taral, Fred 1955
+ Tuckerman, Bayard Jr.* 1973
  Turcotte, Ron 1979
+ Turner, Nash 1955
  Ussery, Robert 1980
  Vasquez, Jacinto 1998
  Velasquez, Jorge 1990
+ Walsh, Thomas* 2005
+ Westrope, Jack 2002
+ Woolf, George 1955
+ Workman, Raymond 1956
  Ycaza, Manuel 1977

*Steeplechase jockey

Trainers

+ Barrera, Laz 1979
+ Bedwell, H. Guy 1971
+ Brown, Edward D. 1984
  Burch, Elliot 1980
+ Burch, Preston M. 1963
+ Burch, W.P. 1955
+ Burlew, Fred 1973
+ Childs, Frank E. . . : 1968
+ Clark, Henry 1982
+ Cocks, W. Burling 1985
  Conway, James P. 1996
  Croll, Jimmy 1994
  Delp, Bud 2002
  Drysdale, Neil 2000
+ Duke, William 1956
+ Feustel, Louis 1964
+ Fitzsimmons, J. (Sunny Jim) .1958
+ Forrest, Henry 2007
  Frankel, Bobby 1995
+ Gaver, John M. 1966
  Hanford, Carl 2006
+ Healey, Thomas 1955
+ Hildreth, Samuel 1955
+ Hine, Hubert (Sonny) 2003
+ Hirsch, Max 1959

+ Hirsch, W.J. (Buddy) 1982
+ Hitchcock, Thomas Sr. 1973
+ Hughes, Hollie 1973
+ Hyland, John 1956
+ Jacobs, Hirsch 1958
  Jerkens, H. Allen 1975
  Johnson, Philip 1997
+ Johnson, William R. 1986
+ Jolley, LeRoy 1987
+ Jones, Ben A. 1958
+ Jones, H.A. (Jimmy) 1959
+ Joyner, Andrew 1955
  Kelly, Tom 1993
+ Laurin, Lucien 1977
+ Lewis, J. Howard 1969
  Lukas, D. Wayne 1999
+ Luro, Horatio 1980
  Mandella, Richard 2001
+ Madden, John 1983
+ Maloney, Jim 1989
  Martin, Frank (Pancho) 1981
  McAnally, Ron 1990
+ McCabe, Frank 2007
+ McDaniel, Henry 1956
  McGaughey, Shug 2004

+ Miller, MacKenzie 1987
+ Molter, William, Jr. 1960
  Mott, Bill 1998
+ Mulholland, Winbert 1967
+ Neloy, Eddie 1983
  Nerud, John 1972
+ Parke, Burley 1986
+ Penna, Angel Sr. 1988
+ Pincus, Jacob 1988
+ Rogers, John 1955
+ Rowe, James Sr. 1955
  Schulhofer, Scotty 1992
  Sheppard, Jonathan 1990
+ Smith, Robert A. 1976
  Smith, Tom 2001
+ Smithwick, Mike 1976
+ Stephens, Woody 1976
  Tenny, Mesh 1991
+ Thompson, H.J. 1969
+ Trotsek, Harry 1984
  Van Berg, Jack 1985
+ Van Berg, Marion 1970
  Veitch, John 2007
+ Veitch, Sylvester 1977
+ Walden, Robert 1970

Horse Racing (Cont.)

Trainers (Cont.)

Walsh, Michael 1997	Whiteley, Frank Jr. 1978	Winfrey, W.C. (Bill) 1971
+ Ward, Sherrill 1978	+ Whittingham, Charlie 1974	Zito, Nick 2005
Watters, Sidney Jr. 2005	+ Williamson, Ansel 1998	

Horses
Year foaled in parentheses.

A.P. Indy (1989) 2000	+ Elkridge (1938) 1966	+ Noor (1945) 2002
+ Ack Ack (1966) 1986	+ Emperor of Norfolk (1885) .1988	+ Northern Dancer (1961) . . .1976
Affectionately (1960) 1989	+ Equipoise (1928) 1957	+ Oedipus (1941) 1978
+ Affirmed (1975) 1980	+ Exceller (1973) 1999	+ Old Rosebud (1911) 1968
All-Along (1979) 1990	+ Exterminator (1915) 1957	+ Omaha (1932) 1965
+ Alsab (1939) 1976	+ Fairmount (1921) 1985	+ Pan Zareta (1910) 1972
+ Alydar (1975) 1989	+ Fair Play (1905) 1956	+ Parole (1873) 1984
Alysheba (1984) 1993	+ Firenze (1885) 1981	Personal Ensign (1984) . . .1993
+ American Eclipse (1814) . .1970	Flatterer (1979) 1994	Paseana (1987) 2001
+ Armed (1941) 1963	Flawlessly (1989) 2004	+ Peter Pan (1904) 1956
+ Artful (1902) 1956	+ Foolish Pleasure (1972) . . .1995	Precisionist (1983) 2003
+ Arts and Letters (1966) . . .1994	+ Forego (1971) 1979	Princess Rooney (1980) . . .1991
+ Assault (1943) 1964	+ Fort Marcy (1964) 1998	+ Real Delight (1949) 1987
+ Battleship (1927) 1969	+ Gallant Bloom (1966) 1977	+ Regret (1912) 1957
+ Bayakoa (1984) 1998	+ Gallant Fox (1927) 1957	+ Reigh Count (1925) 1978
+ Bed O'Roses (1947) 1976	+ Gallant Man (1954) 1987	Riva Ridge (1969) 1998
+ Beldame (1901) 1956	+ Gallorette (1942) 1962	+ Roamer (1911) 1981
+ Ben Brush (1893) 1955	+ Gamely (1964) 1980	+ Roseben (1901) 1956
+ Bewitch (1945) 1977	Genuine Risk (1977) 1986	+ Round Table (1954) 1972
+ Bimelech (1937) 1990	+ Good and Plenty (1900) . . .1956	+ Ruffian (1972) 1976
+ Black Gold (1919) 1989	+ Go For Wand (1987) 1996	+ Ruthless (1864) 1975
+ Black Helen (1932) 1991	+ Granville (1933) 1997	+ Salvator (1886) 1955
+ Blue Larkspur (1926) 1957	+ Grey Lag (1918) 1957	+ Sarazen (1921) 1957
+ Bold 'n Determined (1977) .1997	+ Gun Bow (1960) 1999	+ Seabiscuit (1933) 1958
+ Bold Ruler (1954) 1973	+ Hamburg (1895) 1986	+ Searching (1952) 1978
+ Bon Nouvel (1960) 1976	+ Hanover (1884) 1955	+ Seattle Slew (1974) 1981
+ Boston (1833) 1955	+ Henry of Navarre (1891) . .1985	Secretariat (1970) 1974
+ Broomstick (1901) 1956	+ Hill Prince (1947) 1991	Serena's Song (1992) 2002
+ Buckpasser (1963) 1970	+ Hindoo (1878) 1955	+ Shuvee (1966) 1975
+ Busher (1942) 1964	Holy Bull (1991) 2001	Silver Charm (1995) 2007
+ Bushranger (1930) 1967	+ Imp (1894) 1965	+ Silver Spoon (1956) 1978
+ Cafe Prince (1970) 1985	+ Jay Trump (1957) 1971	+ Sir Archy (1805) 1955
+ Carry Back (1958) 1975	John Henry (1975) 1990	+ Sir Barton (1916) 1957
+ Cavalcade (1931) 1993	+ Johnstown (1936) 1992	Skip Away (1993) 2004
+ Challendon (1936) 1977	+ Jolly Roger (1922) 1965	Slew o' Gold (1980) 1992
+ Chris Evert (1971) 1988	+ Kingston (1884) 1955	+ Stymie (1941) 1975
+ Cicada (1959) 1967	+ Kelso (1957) 1967	+ Sun Beau (1925) 1996
Cigar (1990) 2002	+ Kentucky (1861) 1983	+ Sunday Silence (1986) 1996
+ Citation (1945) 1959	Lady's Secret (1982) 1992	+ Susan's Girl (1969) 1976
+ Coaltown (1945) 1983	+ La Prevoyante (1970) 1995	+ Swaps (1952) 1966
+ Colin (1905) 1956	+ L'Escargot (1963) 1977	+ Swoon's Sun (1952) 2007
+ Commando (1898) 1956	+ Lexington (1850) 1955	+ Sword Dancer (1956) 1977
Cougar II (1969) 2006	Lonesome Glory (1989) . . .2005	+ Sysonby (1902) 1956
+ Count Fleet (1940) 1961	+ Longfellow (1867) 1971	+ Ta Wee (1966) 1994
+ Crusader (1923) 1995	+ Luke Blackburn (1877) 1956	+ Tim Tam (1955) 1985
+ Dahlia (1971) 1981	+ Majestic Prince (1966) 1988	+ Tom Fool (1949) 1960
+ Damascus (1964) 1974	+ Man o' War (1917) 1957	+ Top Flight (1929) 1966
Dance Smartly (1989) 2003	+ Maskette (1906) 2001	+ Tosmah (1961) 1984
+ Dark Mirage (1965) 1974	Miesque (1984) 1999	+ Twenty Grand (1928) 1957
+ Davona Dale (1976) 1985	+ Miss Woodford (1880) 1967	+ Twilight Tear (1941) 1963
+ Desert Vixen (1970) 1979	Mom's Command (1983) . .2007	+ War Admiral (1934) 1958
+ Devil Diver (1939) 1980	+ Myrtlewood (1933) 1979	+ Whirlaway (1938) 1959
+ Discovery (1931) 1969	+ Nashua (1952) 1965	+ Whisk Broom II (1907) 1979
+ Domino (1891) 1955	+ Native Dancer (1950) 1963	Winning Colors (1985) 2000
+ Dr. Fager (1964) 1971	+ Native Diver (1959) 1978	Zaccio (1976) 1990
Easy Goer (1986) 1997	+ Needles (1953) 2000	+ Zev (1920) 1983
+ Eight 30 (1936) 1994	+ Neji (1950) 1959	

Exemplars of Racing

+ Hanes, John W 1982	+ Mellon, Paul 1989	Widener, George D 1971
+ Jeffords, Walter M 1973		

MEDIA

National Sportscasters and Sportswriters Hall of Fame

Established in 1959 by the National Sportscasters and Sportswriters Association. **Address:** 322 East Innes St., Salisbury, NC 28144. **Telephone:** (704) 633-4275. **Web:** www.nssahalloffame.com. **Eligibility:** Nominees must be active for at least 25 years. Voting done by NSSA membership and other media representatives.

Class of 2007 (2): **Dave Kindred** and **Vern Lundquist**.

Members are listed with year of induction; (+) indicates deceased members.

Sportscasters

+ Allen, Mel	1972	+ Gowdy, Curt	1981	+ Murphy, Bob	2002

+ Allen, Mel 1972
+ Barber, Walter (Red) 1973
Brennaman, Marty 2005
+ Brickhouse, Jack 1983
+ Buck, Jack 1990
+ Caray, Harry 1989
+ Cosell, Howard 1993
+ Dean, Dizzy 1976
+ Dunphy, Don 1986
+ Elson, Bob 1995
Enberg, Dick 1996
Garagiola, Joe 2004
+ Glickman, Marty 1992

+ Gowdy, Curt 1981
Harwell, Ernie 1989
+ Hearn, Chick 1997
+ Hodges, Russ 1975
+ Hoyt, Waite 1987
+ Husing, Ted 1963
Jackson, Keith 1995
Lundquist, Vern 2007
+ McCarthy, Clem 1970
McKay, Jim 1987
+ McNamee, Graham 1964
Michaels, Al 1998
Miller, Jon 1999

+ Murphy, Bob 2002
+ Nelson, Lindsey 1979
+ Prince, Bob 1986
+ Rizzuto, Phil 2006
+ Schenkel, Chris 1981
+ Scott, Ray 1982
Scully, Vin 1991
Simpson, Jim 2000
+ Stern, Bill 1974
Summerall, Pat 1994
Whitaker, Jack 2001
Wolff, Bob 2003

Sportswriters

Anderson, Dave 1990
Bisher, Furman 1989
Broeg, Bob 1997
+ Burick, Si 1985
+ Cannon, Jimmy 1986
+ Carmichael, John P. 1994
Collins, Bud 2002
+ Connor, Dick 1992
+ Considine, Bob 1980
+ Daley, Arthur 1976
Deford, Frank 1998
Durslag, Mel 1995
+ Gould, Alan 1990
+ Graham, Frank Sr. 1995

+ Grimsley, Will 1987
Heinz, W.C. 2001
Holtzman, Jerome 2004
Izenberg, Jerry 2000
Jenkins, Dan 1996
Jenkins, Sally 2005
+ Kieran, John 1971
Kindred, Dave 2007
+ Lardner, Ring 1967
+ McDonough, Will 2003
McGeehan, W.O. 2006
+ Murphy, Jack 1988
+ Murray, Jim 1978
Olderman, Murray 1993

+ Parker, Dan 1975
Pope, Edwin 1994
+ Povich, Shirley 1984
+ Rice, Grantland 1962
+ Runyon, Damon 1964
Russell, Fred 1988
Sherrod, Blackie 1991
+ Smith, Walter (Red) 1977
+ Spink, J.G. Taylor 1969
+ Steadman, John 1999
Vecsey, George 2001
+ Ward, Arch 1973
+ Woodward, Stanley 1974

MOTORSPORTS

Motorsports Hall of Fame of America

Established in 1989. **Mailing Address:** P.O. Box 194, Novi, MI 48376. **Telephone:** (248) 349-7223. **Web:** www.mshf.com. **Eligibility:** Nominees must be retired at least three years or engaged in their area of motorsports for at least 20 years. Areas include: open wheel, stock car, dragster, sports car, motorcycle, off road, power boat, air racing, land speed records, historic and at-large.

Class of 2007 (9): DRIVERS—**Bill Elliott, Leo Mehl, Jim Rathmann, Ronnie Sox, Buddy Martin, John Fitch, Bubba Shobert**. CONTRIBUTORS—**Jim McGee** and **Leo Mehl**.

Members are listed with year of induction; (+) indicates deceased members.

Drivers

Allison, Bobby 1992
Amato, Joe 2004
Andretti, Mario 1990
Arfons, Art 1991
+ Baker, Buck 1998
+ Baker, Cannonball 1989
+ Bettenhausen, Tony 1997
Brabham, Geoff 2004
Breedlove, Craig 1993
Bryan, Jimmy 1999
+ Campbell, Sir Malcolm 1994
+ Cantrell, Bill 1992
Chenoweth, Dean 1991
+ Chevrolet, Gaston 2002
Chrisman, Art 1997
+ Clark, Jim 1990
+ Cook, Betty 1996
+ Cooper, Earl 2001
Cunningham, Briggs 1997
+ Davis, Jim 1997
D'Eath, Tom 2000

DeCoster, Roger 1994
+ DePalma, Ralph 1992
+ DePaolo, Peter 1995
+ Donahue, Mark 1990
+ Earnhardt, Dale 2002
Elliott, Bill 2007
Fittipaldi, Emerson 2001
Flock, Tim 1999
Follmer, George 1999
Forbes-Robinson, Elliott . . .2006
Foster, Danny 2005
Foyt, A.J. 1989
Garlits, Don 1989
Glidden, Bob 1994
+ Gregg, Peter 2000
Gurney, Dan 1991
Hanauer, Chip 1995
Hannah, Bob 2000
Hanks, Sam 2000
+ Harroun, Ray 2000
Hart, C.J. 1999

Haywood, Hurley 2005
Hill, Eddie 2002
Hill, Phil 1989
+ Hinnershitz, Tommy 2003
+ Holbert, Al 1993
+ Horn, Ted 1993
+ Hulme, Denis 1998
Ivo, Tommy 2005
Jarrett, Ned 1997
Jenkins, Bill (Grumpy) 1996
Johncock, Gordon 2002
Johnson, Junior 1991
Jones, Parnelli 1992
Kalitta, Connie 1992
Karamesines, Chris 2006
Kenyon, Mel 2003
+ Kurtis, Frank 1999
Lawson, Eddie 2002
Leonard, Joe 1991
+ Lockhart, Frank 1999
Lorenzen, Fred 2001

Motorsports (Cont.)

+ McLaren, Bruce 1995
Mann, Dick 1993
Mansell, Nigel 2006
Markle, Bart 1999
Martin, Buddy 2007
+ Mays, Rex 1995
McEwen, Tom 2001
McGriff, Hershel 2006
Mears, Rick 1998
+ Meyer, Louis 1993
+ Miles, Ken 2001
+ Milton, Tommy 1998
Muldowney, Shirley ...1990
+ Muncy, Bill 1989
+ Murphy, Jimmy 1998
+ Musson, Ron 1993
Nickelson, Don 1998
Nixon, Gary 2003
+ Nordskog, Bob 1997
+ Oldfield, Barney 1989

+ Agajanian, J.C 1992
Bignotti, George 1993
+ Black, Keith 1995
Bondurant, Bob 2003
+ Brawner, Clint 1998
Carnegie, Tom 2006
Chapman, Colin 1997
+ Chevrolet, Louis 1995
+ Donovan, Ed 2003
Duesenberg, Fred 1997
Economaki, Chris 1994
+ Ford, Henry 1996

Ongais, Danny 2000
Parks, Wally 1993
Parsons, Benny 2005
+ Parsons, Johnnie 2004
Pearson, David 1993
+ Petrali, Joe 1992
+ Petty, Lee 1996
Petty, Richard 1989
Prudhomme, Don 1991
Rahal, Bobby 2004
Rathman, Jim 2007
Resweber, Carroll 1998
Redman, Brian 2002
+ Revson, Peter 1996
+ Roberts, Fireball ...1995
Roberts, Kenny 1990
Rutherford, Johnny ...1996
+ Ruttman, Troy 2005
Seebold, Bill 1999

Contributors

+ France, Bill Jr. 2004
+ France, Bill Sr. 1990
Glick, Shav 2004
Granatelli, Andy 2001
Hall, Jim 1994
+ Holman, John 2005
+ Hulman, Tony 1991
+ Jones, Ted 2003
+ Kiekhaefer, Carl 1998
Little, Bernie 1994
McGee, Jim 2007
Mehl, Leo 2007

+ Shaw, Wilbur 1991
Shobert, Bubba 2007
Slovak, Mira 2001
Smith, Malcolm 1996
Sneva, Tom 2005
Sox, Ronnie 2007
Spencer, Freddie 2001
Springsteen, Jay 2005
+ Thompson, Mickey 1990
+ Turner, Curtis 2006
Unser, Al 1991
Unser, Bobby 1994
Vesco, Don 2004
+ Vukovich, Bill Sr ...1992
Waltrip, Darrell 2003
Ward, Jeff 2006
Ward, Rodger 1995
+ Wood, Gar 1990
Yarborough, Cale 1994

+ Miller, Harry 1999
+ Moody, Ralph 2005
+ Offenhauser, Fred ...2002
Penske, Roger 1995
+ Rickenbacker, Eddie .1994
+ Rose, Mauri 1996
Shelby, Carroll 1992
Simpson, Bill 2003
Watson, A.J. 1996
Wood, Glen 2000
Wood, Leonard 2000
+ Yunick, Smokey 2000

International Motorsports Hall of Fame

Established in 1990 by the International Motorsports Hall of Fame Commission. **Mailing Address:** P.O. Box 1018, Talladega, AL 35161. **Telephone:** (256) 362-5002. **Web:** www.motorsportshalloffame.com.

Eligibility: Nominees must be retired from their specialty in motorsports for five years. Voting done by 150-member panel made up of the world-wide auto racing media. Members are listed with year of induction; (+) indicates deceased members.

Class of 2007 (5): DRIVERS—**Junie Donlavey** (stock cars), **Ray Hendrick** (stock cars), **Jack Ingram** (stock cars), **Warren Johnson** (drag racing), **Wayne Rainey** (motorcycles); CONTRIBUTORS—**Bruton Smith**.

Drivers

Allison, Bobby 1993
Amato, Joe 2005
Andretti, Mario 2000
+ Ascari, Alberto 1992
+ Baker, Buck 1990
Bonnett, Neil 2001
+ Bettenhausen, Tony ..1991
Brabham, Jack 1990
Bryan, Jimmy 2001
+ Campbell, Sir Malcolm 1990
+ Caracciola, Rudolph .1998
+ Clark, Jim 1990
+ DePalma, Ralph 1991
+ Donahue, Mark 1990
Donlavey, Junie 2007
+ Earnhardt, Dale 2006
Evans, Richie 1996
+ Fangio, Juan Manuel .1990
Farmer, Charles 2004
Fittipaldi, Emerson ..2003
+ Flock, Tim 1991
Foyt, A.J. 2000
Gant, Harry 2006
Glidden, Bob 2005
+ Gregg, Peter 1992
Gurney, Dan 1990
Guthrie, Janet 2006
Hailwood, Mike 2001
+ Haley, Donald 1996

Hanauer, Chip 2005
+ Hendrick, Ray 2007
+ Hill, Graham 1990
Hill, Phil 1991
+ Holbert, Al 1993
Hulme, Denis 2002
Ickx, Jacky 2002
Ingram, Jack 2007
+ Isaac, Bobby 1996
Jarrett, Ned 1991
Johncock, Gordon 1999
Johnson, Junior 1990
Johnson, Warren 2007
Jones, Parnelli 1990
Kenyon, Mel 2003
+ Kulwicki, Alan 2002
Lauda, Niki 1993
Lorenzen, Fred 1991
+ Lund, Tiny 1994
Mansell, Chip 2005
+ Mays, Rex 1993
+ McLaren, Bruce 1991
+ Meyer, Louis 1992
Moss, Stirling 1990
Muldowney, Shirley ...2004
+ Muncy, Bill 2004
+ Nuvolari, Tazio 1998
+ Oldfield, Barney 1990
Parsons, Benny 1994

Pearson, David 1993
+ Petty, Lee 1990
Piquet, Nelson 2000
Prodhomme, Don 2000
Prost, Alain 1999
Rahal, Bobby 2004
Rainey, Wayne 2007
+ Richmond, Tim 2002
+ Roberts, Fireball ...1990
Roberts, Kenny 1992
Rose, Mauri 1994
Rutherford, Johnny ...1996
Scott, Wendell 1999
+ Senna, Ayrton 2000
+ Shaw, Wilbur 1991
Smith, Louise 1999
Stewart, Jackie 1990
Surtees, John 1996
+ Thomas, Herb 1994
+ Turner, Curtis 1992
Unser, Al Sr. 1998
Unser, Bobby 1990
+ Vukovich, Bill 1991
Waltrip, Darrell 2005
Ward Rodger 1992
+ Weatherly, Joe 1994
Wood, Glen 2002
Yarborough, Cale 1993

Contributors

Bignotti, George 1993
Breedlove, Craig 2000
+ Bugatti, Ettore 2002
+ Chapman, Colin 1994
+ Chevrolet, Louis 1992
+ Cunningham, Briggs 2003
+ Ferrari, Enzo 1994
+ Ford, Henry 1993
Fox, Ray 2003
+ France, Bill Jr. 2004

+ France, Bill Sr 1990
Granatelli, Andy 1992
+ Hulman, Tony 1990
Hyde, Harry 1999
Marcum, John 1994
+ Matthews, Banjo 1998
Moody, Ralph 1994
+ Offenhauser, Fred 2001
Parks, Wally 1992
Penske, Roger 1998

+ Porsche, Ferdinand 1996
+ Rickenbacker, Eddie 1992
Roush, Jack 2006
Shelby, Carroll 1991
Smith, Bruton 2007
+ Thompson, Mickey 1990
Watson, A.J. 2003
Wheeler, H.A. (Humpy) ...2006
+ Yunick, Smokey 1990

OLYMPICS

U.S. Olympic Hall of Fame

Established in 1983 by the United States Olympic Committee. **Mailing Address:** U.S. Olympic Committee, 1750 East Boulder Street, Colorado Springs, CO 80909. Plans for a permanent museum site have been suspended due to lack of funding. **Telephone:** (719) 866-4529. **Web:** www.usoc.org

Eligibility: Nominated athletes must be four years removed from their last Olympic competition. Voting for membership in the Hall was suspended in 1993 but resumed in 2004. Voting from 1983-92 was done by National Sportscasters and Sportswriters Association, Hall of Fame members and the USOC board members of directors. Beginning in 2004 the voting weight was divided among U.S. Olympians, select U.S. Olympic family/media and fans.

Class of 2006: ATHLETES—**Evelyn Ashford** (track & field), **Rowdy Gaines** (swimming), **Bob Hayes** (track & field), **Shannon Miller** (gymnastics), **Kristi Yamaguchi** (figure skating), **Diana Golden-Brosnihan** (paralympian), COACH—**Herb Brooks**. VETERAN—**Jack Shea**. SPECIAL CONTRIBUTOR— **Dick Ebersol**.

Members are listed with year of induction; (+) indicates deceased members.

Teams

1956 Basketball Dick Boushka, Carl Cain, Chuck Darling, Bill Evans, Gib Ford, Burdy Haldorson, Bill Hougland, Bob Jeangerard, K.C. Jones, Bill Russell, Ron Tomsic, +Jim Walsh and coach +Gerald Tucker.

1960 Basketball Jay Arnette, Walt Bellamy, Bob Boozer, Terry Dischinger, Burdy Haldorson, Darrall Imhoff, Allen Kelley, +Lester Lane, Jerry Lucas, Oscar Robertson, Adrian Smith, Jerry West and coach Pete Newell.

1964 Basketball Jim Barnes, Bill Bradley, Larry Brown, Joe Caldwell, Mel Counts, Richard Davies, Walt Hazzard, Luke Jackson, John McCaffrey, Jeff Mullins, Jerry Shipp, George Wilson and coach +Hank Iba.

1960 Ice Hockey Billy Christian, Roger Christian, Billy Cleary, Bob Cleary, Gene Grazia, Paul Johnson, Jack Kirrane, John Mayasich, Jack McCartan, Bob McKay, Dick Meredith, Weldon Olson, Ed Owen, Rod Paavola, Larry Palmer, Dick Rodenheiser, +Tom Williams and coach Jack Riley.

1980 Ice Hockey Bill Baker, Neal Broten, Dave Christian, Steve Christoff, Jim Craig, Mike Eruzione, John Harrington, Steve Janaszak, Mark Johnson, Ken Morrow, Rob McClanahan, Jack O'Callahan, Mark Pavelich, Mike Ramsey, Buzz Schneider, Dave Silk, Eric Strobel, Bob Suter, Phil Verchota, Mark Wells and coach +Herb Brooks.

1996 Women's Soccer Michelle Akers, Brandi Chastain, Amanda Cromwell, Joy Fawcett, Julie Foudy, Carin Gabarra, Mia Hamm, Mary Harvey, Kristine Lilly, Shannon MacMillan, Tiffeny Milbrett, Carla Overbeck, Cindy Parlow, Tiffany Roberts, Briana Scurry, Thori Staples Bryan, Tisha Venturini, Saskia Webber, Staci Wilson and coach Tony DiCicco

Alpine Skiing

Mahre, Phil 1992

Bobsled

+ Eagan, Eddie (see Boxing) .1983

Boxing

Clay, Cassius 1983
+ Eagan, Eddie (see Bobsled) .1983
Foreman, George 1990
Frazier, Joe 1989
Leonard, Sugar Ray 1985
Patterson, Floyd 1987

Coaches

+ Brooks, Herb 2006

Cycling

Carpenter-Phinney, Connie .1992

Diving

King, Miki 1992
Lee, Sammy 1990
Louganis, Greg 1985
McCormick, Pat 1985

Figure Skating

Albright, Tenley 1988
Button, Dick 1983
Fleming, Peggy 1983
Hamill, Dorothy 1991
Hamilton, Scott 1990
Yamaguchi, Kristi 2006

Gymnastics

Conner, Bart 1991
Retton, Mary Lou 1985
Miller, Shannon 2006
Vidmar, Peter 1991

Paralympian

Golden-Brosnihan, Diana ..2006

Rowing

+ Kelly, Jack Sr. 1990

Speed Skating

Blair, Bonnie 2004
Heiden, Eric 1983
Jansen, Dan 2004

Veterans

+ Shea, Jack 2006

Wrestling

Gable, Dan 1985

Swimming

Babashoff, Shirley 1987
Biondi, Matt 2004
Caulkins, Tracy 1990
+ Daniels, Charles 1988
de Varona, Donna 1987
Evans, Janet 2004
Gaines, Rowdy 2006
+ Kahanamoku, Duke 1984
+ Madison, Helene 1992
Meyer, Debbie 1986
Naber, John 1984
Schollander, Don 1983
Spitz, Mark 1983
+ Weissmuller, Johnny 1983

Weight Lifting

+ Davis, John 1989
Kono, Tommy 1990

Contributors

+ Arledge, Roone 1989
+ Brundage, Avery 1983
+ Bushnell, Asa 1990
Ebersol, Dick 2006
Greenspan, Bud 2004
Hull, Col. Don 1992
+ Iba, Hank 1985

+ Kane, Robert 1986
+ Kelly, Jack Jr. 1992
McKay, Jim 1988
Miller, Don 1984
+ Simon, William 1991
Walker, LeRoy 1987

U.S. Olympic Hall of Fame (Cont.)
Track & Field

Ashford, Evelyn	2006	Hayes, Bob	2006	+ Oerter, Al	1983
Beamon, Bob	1983	Jenner, Bruce	1986	+ Owens, Jesse	1983
Boston, Ralph	1985	Johnson, Rafer	1983	+ Paddock, Charley	1991
+ Calhoun, Lee	1991	+ Joyner, Florence Griffith	2004	Richards, Bob	1983
Campbell, Milt	1992	Joyner-Kersee, Jackie	2004	+ Rudolph, Wilma	1983
Coachman, Alice	2004	+ Kraenzlein, Alvin	1985	+ Sheppard, Mel	1989
+ Davenport, Willie	1991	Lewis, Carl	1985	Shorter, Frank	1984
Davis, Glenn	1986	Mathias, Bob	1983	+ Thorpe, Jim	1983
+ Didrikson, Babe	1983	Mills, Billy	1984	Toomey, Bill	1984
Dillard, Harrison	1983	Morrow, Bobby	1989	Tyus, Wyomia	1985
Evans, Lee	1989	Moses, Edwin	1985	Whitfield, Mal	1988
+ Ewry, Ray	1983	O'Brien, Parry	1984	+ Wykoff, Frank	1984
Fosbury, Dick	1992				

SOCCER
National Soccer Hall of Fame

Established in 1950 by the Philadelphia Oldtimers Association. First exhibit unveiled in Oneonta, NY in 1982. Moved into new Hall of Fame building in the summer of 1999. **Address:** 18 Stadium Circle, Oneonta, NY 13820. **Telephone:** (607) 432-3351. **Web:** www.soccerhall.org

Eligibility: Players must have been retired as a player for at least three years, but for no more than 10 years He or she must have played at least 20 full international games for the United States. He or she must have played at least five seasons in an American first-division professional league (NASL or MLS), and won the league championship, won the U.S. Open Cup or been a league all-star at least once. Other categories include Veterans (included under Players) and Builders. Voting done by a committee made up of Hall of Famers, U.S. Soccer officials and members of the national media.

Class of 2007 (4): **Mia Hamm, Julie Foudy, Alan Rothenberg** and **Bobby Smith.**

Members are listed with home state and year of induction; (+) indicates deceased members.

Players

Akers, Michelle	2004	+ Fricker, Werner	1992	Nanoski, Jukey	1993
Alberto, Carlos	2003	+ Fryer, William J.	1951	Nelson, Johnny	2005
Annis, Robert	1976	Gabarra, Carin	2000	Nilsen, Werner	2005
+ Auld, Andrew	1986	Gaetjens, Joe	1976	+ Ntsoelengoe, Ace (S.Afr.)	2003
Bachmeier, Adolph	2002	+ Gallagher, James	1986	+ O'Brien, Shamus	1990
Bahr, Walter	1976	Gard, Gino	1976	Olaff, Gene	1971
Balboa, Marcelo	2005	+ Gentle, James	1986	+ Oliver, Arnie	1968
+ Barr, George	1983	Getzinger, Rudy	1991	Oliver, Len	1996
+ Beardsworth, Fred	1965	+ Glover, Teddy	1965	Overbeck, Carla	2006
Beckenbauer, Franz (Ger)	1998	+ Gonsalves, Billy	1950	Pariani, Gino	1976
Bernabei, Ray	1978	Gormley, Bob	1989	+ Patenaude, Bert	1971
Bogicevic, Vladislav (Yug)	2002	+ Govier, Sheldon	1950	Pel|fe (Brazil)	1993
+ Bookie, Michael	1986	Granitza, Karl-Heinz (Ger)	2003	Ramos, Tab	2005
Borghi, Frank	1976	Gryzik, Joe	1973	+ Ratican, Harry	1950
+ Boulos, Frenchy	1980	Hamm, Mia	2007	+ Renzulli, Pete	1951
+ Brittan, Harold	1951	+ Harker, Al	1979	+ Roe, Jimmy	1997
Brown, David	1951	Harkes, John	2005	Roth, Werner	1989
Brown, George	1995	Heinrichs, April	1998	Roy, Willy	1989
+ Brown, James	1986	Higgins, Shannon	2002	+ Ryan, Hun	1958
Caligiuri, Paul	2004	Howard, Ted	2003	Salcedo Frabie	2005
+ Carenza, Joe	1982	Hynes, John	1977	Schaller, Willy	1995
+ Caraffi, Ralph	1959	+ Japp, John	1953	Slone, Philip	1986
Chacurian, Chico	1992	Keough, Harry	1976	Smith, Bobby	2007
+ Chesney, Stan	1966	Kropfelder, Nicholas	1996	+ Souza, Ed	1976
Child, Paul (Eng)	2003	+ Kunter, Rudy	1963	Souza, Clarkie	1976
Chinaglia, Giorgio (Italy)	2000	Lalas, Alexi	2006	+ Spalding, Dick	1951
Clavijo, Fernando	2005	Lang, Millard	1950	Stark, Archie	1950
+ Colombo, Charlie	1976	Lenarduzzi, Bob (Can)	2003	+ Swords, Thomas	1951
Coombes, Geoff	1976	+ Looby, Bill	2001	+ Tintle, Joseph	1952
Craddock Jr., Robert	1976	+ Maca, Joe	1976	+ Tracey, Ralph	1986
Danilo, Paul	1997	Mausser, Arnie	2003	Trost, Al	2006
Davis, Rick	2001	McBride, Pat	1994	+ Vaughn, Frank	1986
+ Dick, Walter	1989	+ McGhee, Bart	1986	+ Wallace, Frank	1976
Diorio, Nick	1974	+ McGuire, John	1951	Weir, Alex	1975
+ Donelli, Buff	1954	McIlveney, Eddie	1976	Willey, Alan (Eng)	2003
+ Douglas, Jimmy	1953	McLaughlin, Bennie	1977	Wilson, Bruce (Can)	2003
+ Duggan, Thomas	1951	+ Mieth, Werner	1974	+ Wilson, Peter	1950
+ Dunn, James	1974	+ Millar, Robert	1950	Wolanin, Adam	1976
Ely, Alexander	1997	Monsen, Lloyd	1994	+ Wood, Alex	1986
+ Ferguson, John	1950	Moore, Johnny	1997	Wynalda, Eric	2004
Fleming, Tom (Whitey)	2005	Moorehouse, George	1986	Zerhusen, Al	1978
+ Florie, Thomas	1986	+ Morrison, Robert	1951		
Foudy, Julie	2007	Murphy, Edward	1998		

Builders

Abronzino, Umberto 1971
Aimi, Milton 1991
+ Alonso, Julie 1972
+ Andersen, William 1956
Anschutz, Philip 2006
+ Ardizzone, John 1971
+ Armstrong, James 1952
+ Barriskill, Joe 1953
Berling, Clay 1995
+ Best, John O. 1982
+ Booth, Joseph 1952
+ Boxer, Matt 1961
Bradley, Gordon (Eng) ...1996
+ Briggs, Lawrence E. 1978
+ Brock, John 1950
+ Brown, Andrew M. 1950
+ Cahill, Thomas W 1950
+ Chyzowych, Walter 1997
+ Coll, John 1986
Collins, Peter 1998
+ Collins, George M. 1951
+ Commander, Colin 1967
+ Cordery, Ted 1975
+ Craddock, Robert 1959
+ Craggs, Edmund 1969
Craggs, George 1981
+ Cummings, Wilfred R. ...1953
+ Delach, Joseph 1973
DeLuca, Enzo 1979
+ Donaghy, Edward J. 1951
+ Donnelly, George 1989
+ Dresmich, John W. 1968
+ Duff, Duncan 1972
+ Edwards, Gene 1985
+ Epperleim, Rudy 1951
+ Ertegun, Ahmet 2003
Ertegun, Nesuhi 2003
+ Fairfield, Harry 1951
Feibusch, Ernst 1984
+ Fernley, John A. 1951
+ Ferro, Charles 1958
+ Fishwick, George E. 1974
+ Flamhaft, Jack 1964
+ Fleming, Harry G. 1967
+ Foulds, Pal 1953
+ Foulds, Sam 1969
+ Fowler, Dan 1970

+ Fowler, Peg 1979
+ Garcia, Pete 1964
+ Giesler, Walter 1962
+ Gould, David L. 1953
+ Greer, Don 1985
+ Guelker, Bob 1980
Guennel, Joe 1980
+ Healey, George 1951
Heilpern, Herb 1988
+ Hemmings, William 1961
Hermann, Robert 2001
+ Hudson, Maurice 1966
+ Hunt, Lamar ....1982.
+ Iglehart, Alfredda 1951
+ Jeffrey, William 1951
+ Johnston, Jack 1952
+ Kabanica, Mike 1987
Kehoe, Bob 1990
+ Kelly, Frank 1994
+ Kempton, George 1950
+ Klein, Paul 1953
Kleinaitis, Al 1995
+ Kozma, Oscar 1964
+ Kracher, Frank 1983
Kraft, Granny 1984
+ Kraus, Harry 1963
+ Lamm, Kurt 1979
Larson, Bert 1988
+ Lewis, H. Edgar 1950
Lombardo, Joe 1984
Long, Denny 1993
+ MacEwan, John J. 1953
+ Magnozzi, Enzo 1977
+ Maher, Jack 1970
+ Manning, Dr. Randolf ..1950
+ Marre, John 1953
+ McClay, Allan 1971
+ McGrath, Frank 1978
+ McGuire, Jimmy 1951
+ McSkimming, Dent 1951
Merovich, Pete 1971
Miller, Al 1995
+ Miller, Milton 1971
+ Mills, Jimmy 1954
+ Moore, James F. 1971
+ Morrissette, Bill 1967
+ Netto, Fred 1958

Newman, Ron 1992
+ Niotis, D.J. 1963
+ Palmer, William 1952
+ Pearson, Eddie 1990
+ Peel, Peter 1951
+ Peters, Wally 1967
Phillipson, Don 1987
+ Piscopo, Giorgio 1978
+ Pomeroy, Edgar 1955
+ Ramsden, Arnold 1957
+ Reese, Doc 1957
Ringsdorf, Gene 1979
Robbie, Elizabeth 2003
+ Robbie, Joe 2003
Ross, Steve 2003
Rothenberg, Alan 2007
+ Rottenberg, Jack 1971
+ Sager, Tom 1968
Saunders, Harry 1981
Schellscheidt, Mannie ..1990
+ Schillinger, Emil 1960
+ Schroeder, Elmer 1951
+ Schwarz, Erno 1951
+ Shields, Fred 1968
+ Single, Erwin 1981
+ Smith, Alfred 1951
Smith, Patrick 1998
Spath, Reinhold 1997
+ Steelink, Nicolaas 1971
Steinbrecher, Hank 2005
Stern, Lee 2003
+ Steur, August 1969
+ Stewart, Douglas 1950
+ Stone, Robert T 1971
Toye, Clive 2003
+ Triner, Joseph 1951
+ Walder, Jimmy 1971
+ Washauer, Adolph 1977
+ Webb, Tom 1987
+ Weston, Victor 1956
+ Woods, John W. 1952
Woosnam, Phil 1997
Yeagley, Jerry 1989
+ Young, John 1958
+ Zampini, Dan 1963

SWIMMING

International Swimming Hall of Fame

Established in 1965 by the U.S. College Coaches' Swim Forum. **Address:** One Hall of Fame Drive, Ft. Lauderdale, FL 33316. **Telephone:** (954) 462-6536. **Web:** www.ishof.org.

Categories for induction are: swimming, diving, water polo, synchronized swimming, coaching, pioneers and contributors. Coaches and contributors are not included in the following list. Only U.S. men and women listed below.

Class of 2007 (1): U.S. WOMEN—**Amy Van Dyken.**

Members are listed with year of induction; (+) indicates deceased members.

U.S. Men

+ Anderson, Miller 1967
Barrowman, Mike 1997
Berkoff, David 2005
Biondi, Matt 1997
+ Boggs, Phil 1985
Bottom, Joe 2006
Breen, George 1975
+ Browning, Skippy 1975
Bruner, Mike 1988
Burton, Mike 1977
+ Cann, Tedford 1967
Carey, Rick 1993

Clark, Earl 1972
Clark, Steve 1966
+ Cleveland, Dick 1991
Clotworthy, Robert 1980
+ Crabbe, Buster 1965
+ Daniels, Charlie 1965
Degener, Dick 1971
DeMont, Rick 1990
Dempsey, Frank 1996
+ Desjardins, Pete 1966
Dolan, Tom 2006
Dysdale, Taylor 1994

Edgar, David 1996
+ Faricy, John 1990
+ Farrell, Jeff 1968
+ Fick, Peter 1978
+ Flanagan, Ralph 1978
Ford, Alan 1966
Furniss, Bruce 1987
Gaines, Rowdy 1995
Garton, Tim 1997
+ Glancy, Harrison 1990
Goodell, Brian 1986
+ Goodwin, Budd 1971

U.S. Women

TENNIS
International Tennis Hall of Fame

Originally the National Tennis Hall of Fame. Established in 1953 by James Van Alen and sanctioned by the U.S. Tennis Association in 1954. Renamed the International Tennis Hall of Fame in 1976. **Address:** 194 Bellevue Ave., Newport, RI 02840. **Telephone:** (401) 849-3990. **Web:** www.tennisfame.com

Eligibility: Nominated players must be five years removed from being a "significant factor" in competitive tennis. Voting done by members of the international tennis media. Due to space constraints only players are listed below.

Class of 2007 (3): **Pete Sampras, Arantxa Sanchez-Vicario** and **Sven Davidson**.

Members are listed with year of induction; (+) indicates deceased members.

Men

+ Adee, George 1964
+ Alexander, Fred 1961
+ Allison, Wilmer 1963
+ Alonso, Manuel 1977
  Anderson, Malcolm 2000
+ Ashe, Arthur 1985
+ Austin, Bunny 1997
  Becker, Boris 2003
+ Behr, Karl 1969
  Borg, Bjorn 1987
+ Borotra, Jean 1976
+ Bromwich, John 1984
+ Brookes, Norman 1977
+ Brugnon, Jacques 1976
+ Budge, Don 1964
+ Campbell, Oliver 1955
+ Chace, Malcolm 1961
+ Clark, Clarence 1983
+ Clark, Joseph 1955
+ Clothier, William 1956
+ Cochet, Henri 1976
  Connors, Jimmy 1998
  Cooper, Ashley 1991
  Courier, Jim 2005
+ Crawford, Jack 1979
+ David, Herman 1998
  Davidson, Sven 2007
+ Doeg, John 1962
+ Doherty, Lawrence 1980
+ Doherty, Reginald 1980
+ Drobny, Jaroslav 1983
+ Dwight, James 1955
  Edberg, Stefan 2004
  Emerson, Roy 1982
+ Etchebaster, Pierre 1978
  Falkenburg, Bob 1974
  Fraser, Neale 1984
+ Garland, Chuck 1969
+ Gonzales, Pancho 1968

+ Grant, Bryan (Bitsy) 1972
+ Griffin, Clarence 1970
+ Hackett, Harold 1961
  Hewitt, Bob 1992
+ Hoad, Lew 1980
+ Hovey, Fred 1974
+ Hunt, Joe 1966
+ Hunter, Frank 1961
+ Johnston, Bill 1958
+ Jones, Perry 1970
  Kelleher, Robert 2000
  Kodes, Jan 1990
  Kramer, Jack 1968
+ Lacoste, Rene 1976
+ Larned, William 1956
  Larsen, Art 1969
  Laver, Rod 1981
  Lendl, Ivan 2001
+ Lott, George 1964
  Mako, Gene 1973
  McEnroe, John 1999
  McGregor, Ken 1999
+ McKinley, Chuck 1986
+ McLoughlin, Maurice 1957
  McMillan, Frew 1992
+ McNeill, Don 1965
  Mulloy, Gardnar 1972
+ Murray, Lindley 1958
+ Myrick, Julian 1963
  Nastase, Ilie 1991
  Newcombe, John 1986
+ Nielsen, Arthur 1971
  Noah, Yannick 2005
  Olmedo, Alex 1987
+ Osuna, Rafael 1979
+ Parker, Frank 1966
+ Patterson, Gerald 1989
  Patty, Budge 1977
+ Perry, Fred 1975

+ Pettitt, Tom 1982
  Pietrangeli, Nicola 1986
+ Quist, Adrian 1984
  Rafter, Patrick 2006
  Ralston, Dennis 1987
+ Renshaw, Ernest 1983
+ Renshaw, William 1983
+ Richards, Vincent 1961
+ Riggs, Bobby 1967
  Roche, Tony 1986
  Rose, Mervyn 2001
  Rosewall, Ken 1980
  Sampras, Pete . . . . . . : . . . 2007
  Santana, Manuel 1984
  Savitt, Dick 1976
  Schroeder, Ted 1966
+ Sears, Richard 1955
  Sedgman, Frank 1979
  Segura, Pancho 1984
  Seixas, Vic 1971
+ Shields, Frank 1964
+ Slocum, Henry 1955
  Smith, Stan 1987
  Stolle, Fred 1985
+ Talbert, Bill 1967
+ Tilden, Bill 1959
  Trabert, Tony 1970
+ Van Ryn, John 1963
  Vilas, Guillermo 1991
+ Vines, Ellsworth 1962
+ von Cramm, Gottfried 1977
+ Ward, Holcombe 1956
+ Washburn, Watson 1965
+ Whitman, Malcolm 1955
  Wilander, Mats 2002
+ Wilding, Anthony 1978
+ Williams, Richard 2nd 1957
  Wood, Sidney 1964
+ Wrenn, Robert 1955

Women

+ Atkinson, Juliette 1974
  Austin, Tracy 1992
+ Barger-Wallach, Maud . . . 1958
  Betz Addie, Pauline 1965
+ Bjurstedt Mallory, Molla . . 1958
  Bowrey, Lesley Turner 1997
  Brough Clapp, Louise 1967
+ Browne, Mary 1957
  Bueno, Maria 1978
+ Cahill, Mabel 1976
  Casals, Rosie 1996
  Cheney, Dorothy (Dodo) . . 2004
+ Connolly Brinker, Maureen . 1968
+ Dod, Charlotte (Lottie) . . . 1983
+ Douglass Chambers, Dorothy 1981
  Dürr, Françoise 2003
  Evert, Chris 1995
  Fry Irvin, Shirley 1970
+ Gibson, Althea 1971

  Goolagong Cawley, Evonne 1988
  Graf, Steffi 2004
+ Hansell, Ellen 1965
  Hard, Darlene 1973
  Hart, Doris 1969
  Haydon Jones, Ann 1985
  Heldman, Gladys 1979
+ Hotchkiss Wightman, Hazel 1957
+ Jacobs, Helen Hull 1962
  King, Billie Jean 1987
+ Lenglen, Suzanne 1978
  Mandlikova, Hana 1994
+ Marble, Alice 1964
+ McKane Godfree, Kitty . . . 1978
+ Moore, Elisabeth 1971
  Mortimer Barrett, Angela . . 1993
  Novotna, Jana 2005
  Navratilova, Martina 2000
+ Nuthall Shoemaker, Betty . 1977

  Osborne duPont, Margaret . 1967
+ Palfrey Danzig, Sarah 1963
  Richey, Nancy 2003
+ Roosevelt, Ellen 1975
+ Round Little, Dorothy 1986
+ Ryan, Elizabeth 1972
  Sabatini, Gabriela 2006
  Sanchez-Vicario, Arantxa . . 2007
+ Sears, Eleanora 1968
  Shriver, Pam 2002
  Smith Court, Margaret 1979
+ Sutton Bundy, May 1956
+ Townsend Toulmin, Bertha . 1974
  Wade, Virginia 1989
+ Wagner, Marie 1969
+ Wills Moody Roark, Helen . 1959

TRACK & FIELD

National Track & Field Hall of Fame

Established in 1974 by the The Athletics Congress (now USA Track & Field). **Address:** 216 Fort Washington Ave., New York, NY 10032. **Telephone:** (212) 923-1803, ext. 10. **Web:** www.usatf.com/HallOfFame/TF/

Eligibility: Nominated athletes must be retired three years and coaches must have coached at least 20 years if retired or 35 years if still coaching. Voting done by 800-member panel made up of Hall of Fame and USA Track & Field officials, Hall of Fame members, current U.S. champions and members of the Track & Field Writers of America. Due to space contraints, the coaches and contributors are not listed below.

Class of 2006 (7): MEN—**Rex Cawley** (hurdles), **Ben Eastman** (middle distances), **Matt McGrath** (thrower), **Bill Nieder** (Thrower), **Dan O'Brien** (decathlete), **Kevin Young** (hurdles). WOMEN—**Lynn Jennings** (long distances).

Members are listed with year of induction; (+) indicates deceased members.

Men

+ Albritton, Dave	1980	James, Larry	2003
Ashenfelter, Horace	1975	Jenkins, Charlie	1992
Banks, Willie	1999	Jenner, Bruce	1980
+ Bausch, James	1979	+ Johnson, Cornelius	1994
Beamon, Bob	1977	Johnson, Michael	2004
Beatty, Jim	1990	Johnson, Rafer	1974
Bell, Earl	2002	Jones, Hayes	1976
Bell, Greg	1988	+ Kelley, John A.	1980
+ Boeckmann, Dee	1976	Kingdom, Roger	2005
Boston, Ralph	1974	+ Kiviat, Abel	1985
+ Borican, Jonn	2000	+ Kraenzlein, Alvin	1974
Bragg, Don	1996	Laird, Ron	1986
+ Calhoun, Lee	1974	Larrabee, Mike	2003
Campbell, Milt	1989	+ Lash, Don	1995
Carlos, John	2003	+ Laskau, Henry	1997
Carr, Henry	1997	Lewis, Carl	2001
Cawley, Rex	2006	Lindgren, Gerry	2004
+ Clark, Ellery	1991	Liquori, Marty	1995
Conley, Mike	2004	Long, Dr. Dallas	1996
Connolly, Harold	1984	Marsh, Henry	2001
Courtney, Tom	1978	+ Mathias, Bob	1974
+ Cunningham, Glenn	1974	Matson, Randy	1984
+ Curtis, William	1979	McCluskey, Joe	1996
+ Davenport, Willie	1982	+ McGrath, Matt	2006
Davis, Glenn	1974	+ Meadows, Earle	1996
Davis, Harold	1974	+ Meredith, Ted	1982
Davis, Jack	2004	+ Metcalfe, Ralph	1975
Davis, Otis	2004	+ Milburn, Rod	1993
Dillard, Harrison	1974	Mills, Billy	1976
Dumas, Charles	1990	Moore, Charles	1999
+ Eastman, Ben	2006	Moore, Tom	1988
Evans, Lee	1983	Morrow, Bobby	1975
+ Ewell, Barney	1986	Mortensen, Jess	1992
+ Ewry, Ray	1974	Moses, Edwin	1994
+ Flanagan, John	1975	+ Myers, Lawrence	1974
Fosbury, Dick	1981	Myricks, Larry	2001
Foster, Greg	1998	Nehemiah, Renaldo	1997
Fuchs, Jim	2005	Nieder, Bill	2006
+ Gordien, Fortune	1979	O'Brien, Dan	2006
Greene, Charles	1992	O'Brien, Parry	1974
+ Hahn, Archie	1983	+ Oerter, Al	1974
+ Hardin, Glenn	1978	+ Osborn, Harold	1974
+ Hayes, Bob	1976	+ Owens, Jesse	1974
Held, Bud	1987	+ Paddock, Charlie	1976
Hines, Jim	1979	Patton, Mel	1985
+ Houser, Bud	1979	+ Peacock, Eulace	1987
+ Hubbard, DeHart	1979	Penel, John	2004

Powell, Mike	2005
+ Prefontaine, Steve	1976
Prinstein, Meyer	2000
+ Ray, Joie	1976
+ Rice, Greg	1977
Richards, Rev. Bob	1975
Robinson, Arnie	2000
Rodgers, Bill	1999
+ Rose, Ralph	1976
Ryun, Jim	1980
Salazar, Alberto	2001
Santee, Wes	2005
+ Scholz, Jackson	1977
Schul, Bob	1991
Scott, Steve	2002
Seagren, Bob	1986
+ Sheppard, Mel	1976
+ Sheridan, Martin	1988
Shorter, Frank	1989
Silvester, Jay	1998
Sime, Dave	1981
+ Simpson, Robert	1974
Smith, Tommie	1978
+ Stanfield, Andy	1977
Steers, Les	1974
Stones, Dwight	1998
+ Taylor, Frederick Morgan	2000
+ Tewksbury, Dr. Walter	1996
Thomas, John	1985
+ Thomson, Earl	1977
+ Thorpe, Jim	1975
+ Tolan, Eddie	1982
Toomey, Bill	1975
+ Towns, Forrest (Spec)	1976
+ Warmerdam, Cornelius	1974
Whitfield, Mal	1974
Wilkins, Mac	1993
+ Williams, Archie	1992
Wohlhuter, Rick	1990
Wolcott, Fred	2005
Woodruff, John	1978
Wottle, Dave	1982
+ Wykoff, Frank	1977
Young, George	1981
Young, Kevin	2006
Young, Larry	2002

Women

Ashford, Evelyn	1997	Heritage, Doris Brown	1990
Brisco, Valerie	1995	+ Jackson, Nell	1989
Brown, Earlene	2005	Jennings, Lynn	2006
Cheeseborough, Chandra	2000	Joyner-Kersee, Jackie	2004
Coachman, Alice	1975	Larrieu Smith, Francie	1998
+ Copeland, Lillian	1994	Manning-Mims, Madeline	1984
+ Didrikson, Babe	1974	McDaniel, Mildred	1983
+ Faggs, Mae	1976	McGuire, Edith	1979
Ferrell, Barbara	1988	Ritter, Louise	1995
+ Griffith Joyner, Florence	1995	+ Robinson, Betty	1977
+ Hall Adams, Evelyne	1988	+ Rudolph, Wilma	1974

Samuelson, Joan	2004
Schmidt, Kate	1994
Seidler, Maren	2000
+ Shiley Newhouse, Jean	1993
Slaney, Mary	2003
+ Stephens, Helen	1975
Torrence, Gwen	2002
Tyus, Wyomia	1980
+ Walsh, Stella	1975
Watson, Martha	1987
White, Willye	1981

WOMEN

International Women's Sports Hall of Fame

stablished in 1980 by the Women's Sports Foundation. **Address:** Women's Sports Foundation, Eisenhower Park, East Meadow, NY 11554. **Telephone:** (516) 542-4700.

Eligibility: Nominees' achievements and commitment to the development of women's sports must be internationally recognized. Athletes are elected in two categories—Pioneer (before 1960) and Contemporary (since 1960). Members are divided below by sport for the sake of easy reference; (*) indicates member inducted in Pioneer category. Coaching nominees must have coached at least 10 years. Members are listed with year of induction; (+) indicates deceased members.

Class of 2006 (4): CONTEMPORARY—**Shane Gould** (swimming); **Nawal El Moutawakel** (track & field); **Diana Nyad** (swimming); COACH—**C. Vivian Stringer** (basketball).

Alpine Skiing

Cranz, Christl* 1991
Golden Brosnihan, Diana . .1997
Lawrence, Andrea Mead* . .1983
Moser-Proell, Annemarie . . .1982

Auto Racing

Guthrie, Janet 1980

Aviation

Coleman, Bessie* 1992
Earhart, Amelia* 1980
Marvingt, Marie* 1987

Badminton

Hashman, Judy Devlin* . . .1995

Baseball

Stone, Toni* 1993

Basketball

Meyers, Ann 1985
Miller, Cheryl 1991
Stewart, Lusia Harris 2005

Bowling

Ladewig, Marion* 1984

Cycling

Carpenter Phinney, Connie .1990

Diving

Gao, Min 2003
King, Micki 1983
McCormick, Pat* 1984
Riggin, Aileen* 1988

Equestrian

Hartel, Lis 1994

Fencing

Schacherer-Elek, Ilona* . . .1989

Figure Skating

Albright, Tenley* 1983
Blanchard, Theresa Weld* .1989
Fleming, Peggy 1981
Heiss Jenkins, Carol* 1992
Henie, Sonja* 1982
Protopopov, Ludmila 1992
Rodnina, Irena 1988
Scott-King, Barbara Ann* . .1997
Torvill, Jayne 2002
Witt, Katarina* 2005

Golf

Berg, Patty* 1980
Carner, JoAnne 1987
Haynie, Sandra 1999
Hicks, Betty* 1995
Jameson, Betty* 1999
Mann, Carol 1982
Rawls, Betsy* 1986
+ Sears, Eleanora 1984
Suggs, Louise* 1987
+ Vare, Glenna Collett* 1981
Whitworth, Kathy 1984
Wright, Mickey 1981
+ Zaharias, Babe Didrikson* . .1980

Gymnastics

Caslavska, Vera 1991
Comaneci, Nadia 1990
Korbut, Olga 1982
Latynina, Larysa* 1985
Retton, Mary Lou 1993
Tourischeva, Lyudmila 1987

Orienteering

Kringstad, Annichen 1995

Shooting

Murdock, Margaret 1988

Softball

Joyce, Joan 1989

Speed Skating

+ Klein Outland, Kit* 1993
Young, Sheila 1981

Squash

McKay, Heather* 2003

Swimming

Caulkins, Tracy 1986
+ Chadwick, Florence* 1996
Curtis Cuneo, Ann* 1985
de Varona, Donna 1983
Ederle, Gertrude* 1980
Fraser, Dawn 1985
Gould, Shane 2006
Hogshead-Makar, Nancy . .2004
Holm, Eleanor* 1980
Meagher, Mary T. 1993
Meyer-Reyes, Debbie 1987
Nyad, Diana 2006
Ruiz-Confronto, Tracie 2001

Tennis

Bueno, Maria Esther 2004
+ Connolly, Maureen* 1987
+ Dod, Charlotte (Lottie)* 1986
Evert, Chris 1981
+ Gibson, Althea* 1980
Goolagong Cawley, Evonne 1989
+ Hotchkiss Wightman, Hazel*1986
King, Billie Jean 1980
+ Lenglen, Suzanne* 1984
Navratilova, Martina 1984
Osbourne du Pont,Margaret*1998
+ Sears, Eleanora* 1984
Smith Court, Margaret 1986

Track & Field

Ashford, Evelyn 1997
Blankers-Koen, Fanny* 1982
Brisco, Valerie 2002
Cheng, Chi 1994
Coachman Davis, Alice* . . .1991
Cuthbert, Betty* 2002
+ Faggs Star, Aeriwentha Mae* 1996
+ Griffith Joyner, Florence . . .1998
Joyner-Kersee, Jackie 2003
Manning Mims, Madeline . .1987
Moutawakel, Nawal El 2006
Nelson, Marjorie Jackson* .2001
+ Rudolph, Wilma 1980
Samuelson, Joan Benoit . . .1999
+ Stephens, Helen* 1983
Strickland de la Hunty, Shirley*1998
Szewinska, Irena 1992
Tyus, Wyomia 1981
Waitz, Grete 1995
White, Willye 1988
+ Zaharias, Babe Didrikson* .1980

Volleyball

+ Hyman, Flo 1986

Water Skiing

McGuire, Willa Worthington* 1990

Coaches

+ Applebee, Constance 1991
Backus, Sharron 1993
Carver, Chris 2001
Conradt, Judy 1995
Emery, Gail 1997
Franke, Nikki 2002
Green, Tina Sloan 1999
Grossfeld, Muriel 1991
Holum, Diana 1996
Jacket, Barbara 1995
+ Jackson, Nell 1990
Kanakogi, Rusty 1994
Kearney, Beverly 2004
Stringer, C. Vivian 2006
Summitt, Pat Head 1990
VanDerveer, Tara 1998
Vollstedt, Linda 2003
+ Wade, Margaret 1992
Wright, Marjorie 2005

Women inducted in multiple categories

Babe Didrikson Zaharias is inducted for both golf and track and field; **Charlotte "Lottie" Dod** is inducted for tennis, as well as archery and golf; **Marie Marvingt** is inducted for aviation, as well as mountaineering; **Eleanora Sears** is inducted for golf, as well as polo and squash.

RETIRED NUMBERS

Major League Baseball

The New York Yankees have retired the most uniform numbers (14) in the major leagues; followed by the Brooklyn/Los Angeles Dodgers (10), the St. Louis Cardinals (9), the Chicago White Sox, the Pittsburgh Pirates and New York/San Francisco Giants (8). **Jackie Robinson** had his #42 retired by Major League Baseball in 1997. Players who were already wearing the number were allowed to continue to do so. Los Angeles had already retired Robinson's number so he's only listed with the Dodgers below. **Nolan Ryan** has had his number retired by three teams—#34 by Texas and Houston and #30 by California (now Los Angeles Angels of Anaheim). Six players and a manager have had their numbers retired by two teams: **Hank Aaron**—#44 by the Boston/Milwaukee/Atlanta Braves and the Milwaukee Brewers; **Rod Carew**—#29 by Minnesota and California (now Anaheim); **Rollie Fingers**—#34 by Milwaukee and Oakland; **Carlton Fisk**—#27 by Boston and #72 by the Chicago White Sox; **Reggie Jackson**— #9 by the Oakland Athletics and #44 by the New York Yankees; **Frank Robinson**—#20 by Cincinnati and Baltimore; **Casey Stengel**—#37 by the New York Yankees and New York Mets.
    Number retired in 2007 (3): PITTSBURGH PIRATES—#11 worn by **Paul Waner** (1926-40 with Pirates); CINCINNATI REDS—#13 worn by **Dave Concepcion** (1970-88); HOUSTON ASTROS—#5 worn by **Jeff Bagwell** (1991-2006).

American League

Two AL teams—the Seattle Mariners and the Toronto Blue Jays—have not retired any numbers. The Blue Jays have a "level of excellence" which includes Joe Carter (#29), Tony Fernandez (#1), Dave Stieb (#11), George Bell (#37), and Cito Gaston (#43). All numbers have been used in recent years, however.

Baltimore Orioles
4 Earl Weaver
5 Brooks Robinson
8 Cal Ripken Jr.
20 Frank Robinson
22 Jim Palmer
33 Eddie Murray

Boston Red Sox
1 Bobby Doerr
4 Joe Cronin
8 Carl Yastrzemski
9 Ted Williams
27 Carlton Fisk

Chicago White Sox
2 Nellie Fox
3 Harold Baines
4 Luke Appling
9 Minnie Minoso
11 Luis Aparicio
16 Ted Lyons
19 Billy Pierce
72 Carlton Fisk

Cleveland Indians
3 Earl Averill
5 Lou Boudreau
14 Larry Doby
18 Mel Harder
19 Bob Feller
21 Bob Lemon
455 Fans (# of consecutive sellouts)

Detroit Tigers
2 Charlie Gehringer
5 Hank Greenberg
6 Al Kaline
16 Hal Newhouser
23 Willie Horton

Kansas City Royals
5 George Brett
10 Dick Howser
20 Frank White

LA Angels of Anaheim
11 Jim Fregosi
26 Gene Autry
29 Rod Carew
30 Nolan Ryan
50 Jimmie Reese

Minnesota Twins
3 Harmon Killebrew
6 Tony Oliva
14 Kent Hrbek
29 Rod Carew
34 Kirby Puckett

Oakland Athletics
9 Reggie Jackson
27 Catfish Hunter
34 Rollie Fingers
43 Dennis Eckersley

New York Yankees
1 Billy Martin
3 Babe Ruth
4 Lou Gehrig
5 Joe DiMaggio
7 Mickey Mantle
8 Yogi Berra & Bill Dickey
9 Roger Maris
10 Phil Rizzuto
15 Thurman Munson
16 Whitey Ford
23 Don Mattingly
32 Elston Howard
37 Casey Stengel
44 Reggie Jackson
49 Ron Guidry

Tampa Bay Devil Rays
12 Wade Boggs

Texas Rangers
26 Johnny Oates
34 Nolan Ryan

National League

Three NL teams—the Arizona Diamondbacks, Colorado Rockies and Washington Nationals—have not retired any numbers. San Francisco has honored former NY Giants Christy Mathewson and John McGraw even though they played before numbers were worn. As did the Philadelphia Phillies for Grover Cleveland Alexander and Chuck Klein. The Montreal Expos had retired #8 for Gary Carter, #10 for Rusty Staub and Andre Dawson but Washington has used those numbers.

Atlanta Braves
3 Dale Murphy
21 Warren Spahn
35 Phil Niekro
41 Eddie Mathews
44 Hank Aaron

Chicago Cubs
10 Ron Santo
14 Ernie Banks
23 Ryne Sandberg
26 Billy Williams

Cincinnati Reds
1 Fred Hutchinson
5 Johnny Bench
8 Joe Morgan
10 Sparky Anderson
13 Dave Concepcion
18 Ted Kluszewski
20 Frank Robinson
24 Tony Perez

Florida Marlins
5 Carl Barger

Houston Astros
5 Jeff Bagwell
24 Jimmy Wynn
25 Jose Cruz
32 Jim Umbricht
33 Mike Scott
34 Nolan Ryan
40 Don Wilson
49 Larry Dierker

Los Angeles Dodgers
1 Pee Wee Reese
2 Tommy Lasorda
4 Duke Snider
19 Jim Gilliam
20 Don Sutton
24 Walter Alston
32 Sandy Koufax
39 Roy Campanella
42 Jackie Robinson
53 Don Drysdale

Milwaukee Brewers
4 Paul Molitor
19 Robin Yount
34 Rollie Fingers
44 Hank Aaron

New York Mets
14 Gil Hodges
37 Casey Stengel
41 Tom Seaver

Philadelphia Phillies
1 Richie Ashburn
14 Jim Bunning
20 Mike Schmidt
32 Steve Carlton
36 Robin Roberts

Pittsburgh Pirates
1 Billy Meyer
4 Ralph Kiner
8 Willie Stargell
9 Bill Mazeroski
11 Paul Waner
20 Pie Traynor
21 Roberto Clemente
33 Honus Wagner
40 Danny Murtaugh

San Diego Padres
6 Steve Garvey
19 Tony Gwynn
31 Dave Winfield
35 Randy Jones

San Francisco Giants
3 Bill Terry
4 Mel Ott
11 Carl Hubbell
24 Willie Mays
27 Juan Marichal
30 Orlando Cepeda
36 Gaylord Perry
44 Willie McCovey

St. Louis Cardinals
1 Ozzie Smith
2 Red Schoendienst
6 Stan Musial
9 Enos Slaughter
14 Ken Boyer
17 Dizzy Dean
20 Lou Brock
42 Bruce Sutter
45 Bob Gibson
85 August (Gussie) Busch (age)

National Basketball Association

Boston has retired the most numbers (21) in the NBA, followed by Portland (9); the Rochester/Cincinnati Royals/K.C./Sacramento Kings, Syracuse Nats/Philadelphia 76ers and New York Knicks (8); Detroit, Los Angeles Lakers, Milwaukee and Phoenix Suns have (6); Cleveland and New Jersey have (7). **Wilt Chamberlain** is the only player to have his number retired by three teams: #13 by the LA Lakers, Golden State and Philadelphia; Nine players have had their numbers retired by two teams: **Kareem Abdul-Jabbar**—#33 by LA Lakers and Milwaukee; **Charles Barkley**—#34 by Philadelphia and Phoenix; **Clyde Drexler**—#22 by Houston and Portland; **Julius Erving**—#6 by Philadelphia and #32 by New Jersey; **Michael Jordan**—#23 by Chicago and Miami (in his honor); **Bob Lanier**—#16 by Detroit and Milwaukee; **Pete Maravich**—#7 by Utah and New Orleans; **Oscar Robertson**—#1 by Milwaukee and #14 by Sacramento; **Nate Thurmond**—#42 by Cleveland and Golden State. Miami retired #23 for **Michael Jordan** eventhough he never played for the team.

Numbers retired in 2006-07 (3): PORTLAND—#14 worn by **Lionel Hollins** (1975-80 with Blazers); SEATTLE—#24 worn by **Spencer Haywood** (1971-75 with SuperSonics); UTAH—#4 worn by **Adrian Dantley** (1979-86 with Jazz).

Eastern Conference

Two Eastern teams—the Charlotte Bobcats and Toronto Raptors—have not retired any numbers.

Atlanta Hawks
9	Bob Pettit
17	Ted Turner
21	Dominique Wilkins
23	Lou Hudson
40	Jason Collier

Chicago Bulls
4	Jerry Sloan
10	Bob Love
23	Michael Jordan
33	Scottie Pippen

Cleveland Cavaliers
7	Bingo Smith
22	Larry Nance
25	Mark Price
34	Austin Carr
42	Nate Thurmond
43	Brad Daugherty

Detroit Pistons
2	Chuck Daly
4	Joe Dumars
11	Isiah Thomas
15	Vinnie Johnson
16	Bob Lanier
21	Dave Bing
40	Bill Laimbeer

Boston Celtics
1	Walter A. Brown
2	Red Auerbach
3	Dennis Johnson
6	Bill Russell
10	Jo Jo White
14	Bob Cousy
15	Tom Heinsohn
16	Tom (Satch) Sanders
17	John Havlicek
18	Dave Cowens
19	Don Nelson
21	Bill Sharman
22	Ed Macauley
23	Frank Ramsey
24	Sam Jones
25	K.C. Jones
31	Cedric Maxwell
32	Kevin McHale
33	Larry Bird
35	Reggie Lewis
00	Robert Parish
Loscy	Jim Loscutoff (#18)
Radio mic	Johnny Most

Indiana Pacers
30	George McGinnis
31	Reggie Miller
34	Mel Daniels
35	Roger Brown
529	Bob "Slick" Leonard

Miami Heat
23	Michael Jordan

Milwaukee Bucks
1	Oscar Robertson
2	Junior Bridgeman
4	Sidney Moncrief
14	Jon McGlocklin
16	Bob Lanier
32	Brian Winters
33	Kareem Abdul-Jabbar

New York Knicks
10	Walt Frazier
12	Dick Barnett
15	Dick McGuire & Earl Monroe
19	Willis Reed
22	Dave DeBusschere
24	Bill Bradley
33	Patrick Ewing
613	Red Holzman

New Jersey Nets
3	Drazen Petrovic
4	Wendell Ladner
23	John Williamson
25	Bill Melchionni
32	Julius Erving
52	Buck Williams

Orlando Magic
6	Fans ("Sixth Man")

Philadelphia 76ers
2	Moses Malone
6	Julius Erving
10	Maurice Cheeks
13	Wilt Chamberlain
15	Hal Greer
24	Bobby Jones
32	Billy Cunningham
34	Charles Barkley
P.A. mic	Dave Zinkoff

Washington Wizards
11	Elvin Hayes
25	Gus Johnson
41	Wes Unseld

Western Conference

Two Western teams—the Los Angeles Clippers and Memphis Grizzlies—have not retired any numbers.

Dallas Mavericks
15	Brad Davis
22	Rolando Blackman

Denver Nuggets
2	Alex English
33	David Thompson
40	Byron Beck
44	Dan Issel
432	Doug Moe

Golden St. Warriors
13	Wilt Chamberlain
14	Tom Meschery
16	Al Attles
24	Rick Barry
42	Nate Thurmond

Houston Rockets
22	Clyde Drexler
23	Calvin Murphy
24	Moses Malone
34	Hakeem Olajuwon
45	Rudy Tomjanovich

Los Angeles Lakers
13	Wilt Chamberlain
22	Elgin Baylor
25	Gail Goodrich
32	Magic Johnson
33	Kareem Abdul-Jabbar
42	James Worthy
44	Jerry West
Radio mic	Chick Hearn

Minn. Timberwolves
2	Malik Sealy

New Orleans Hornets
7	Pete Maravich
13	Bobby Phills

Phoenix Suns
5	Dick Van Arsdale
6	Walter Davis
7	Kevin Johnson
9	Dan Majerle
24	Tom Chambers
33	Alvan Adams
34	Charles Barkley
42	Connie Hawkins
44	Paul Westphal
832	Cotton Fitzsimmons

Portland Trail Blazers
1	Larry Weinberg
13	Dave Twardzik
14	Lionel Hollins
15	Larry Steele
20	Maurice Lucas
22	Clyde Drexler
32	Bill Walton
36	Lloyd Neal
45	Geoff Petrie
77	Jack Ramsay

Sacramento Kings
1	Nate Archibald
2	Mitch Richmond
6	Fans ("Sixth Man")
11	Bob Davies
12	Maurice Stokes
14	Oscar Robertson
27	Jack Twyman
44	Sam Lacey

San Antonio Spurs
13	James Silas
32	Sean Elliott
44	George Gervin
50	David Robinson
00	Johnny Moore

Seattle SuperSonics
1	Gus Williams
10	Nate McMillan
19	Lenny Wilkens
24	Spencer Haywood
32	Fred Brown
43	Jack Sikma
Radio mic	Bob Blackburn

Utah Jazz
1	Frank Layden
4	Adrian Dantley
7	Pete Maravich
12	John Stockton
14	Jeff Hornacek
32	Karl Malone
35	Darrell Griffith
53	Mark Eaton

Retired Numbers (Cont.)
National Football League

The Chicago Bears have retired the most uniform numbers (13) in the NFL; followed by the New York Giants (11); the Dallas Texans/Kansas City Chiefs, Boston-New England Patriots and San Francisco (8); the Baltimore-Indianapolis Colts (7); Detroit and Philadelphia (6); Cleveland (5). No player has ever had his number retired by more than one NFL team.

Number retired in 2007: None.

AFC

Four AFC teams—the Baltimore Ravens, Houston Texans, Jacksonville Jaguars and Oakland Raiders—have not retired any numbers.

Buffalo Bills
- 12 Jim Kelly

Cincinnati Bengals
- 54 Bob Johnson

Cleveland Browns
- 14 Otto Graham
- 32 Jim Brown
- 45 Ernie Davis
- 46 Don Fleming
- 76 Lou Groza

Denver Broncos
- 7 John Elway
- 18 Frank Tripucka
- 44 Floyd Little

Indianapolis Colts
- 19 Johnny Unitas
- 22 Buddy Young
- 24 Lenny Moore
- 70 Art Donovan
- 77 Jim Parker
- 82 Raymond Berry
- 89 Gino Marchetti

Kansas City Chiefs
- 3 Jan Stenerud
- 16 Len Dawson
- 28 Abner Haynes
- 33 Stone Johnson
- 36 Mack Lee Hill
- 63 Willie Lanier
- 78 Bobby Bell
- 86 Buck Buchanan

Miami Dolphins
- 12 Bob Griese
- 13 Dan Marino
- 39 Larry Csonka

New England Patriots
- 20 Gino Cappelletti
- 40 Mike Haynes
- 56 Andre Tippett
- 57 Steve Nelson
- 73 John Hannah
- 78 Bruce Armstrong
- 79 Jim Lee Hunt
- 89 Bob Dee

New York Jets
- 12 Joe Namath
- 13 Don Maynard
- 73 Joe Klecko

Pittsburgh Steelers
- 70 Ernie Stautner

San Diego Chargers
- 14 Dan Fouts
- 19 Lance Alworth

Tennessee Titans
- 34 Earl Campbell
- 43 Jim Norton
- 63 Mike Munchak
- 65 Elvin Bethea
- 74 Bruce Matthews

NFC

Dallas is the only NFC team that hasn't officially retired any numbers. The Falcons haven't issued uniform #10 (Steve Bartkowski) and #78 (Mike Kenn) since those players retired. The Cowboys have a "Ring of Honor" at Texas Stadium that includes 15 players, one coach and one president/GM—Troy Aikman, Tony Dorsett, Cliff Harris, Bob Hayes, Chuck Howley, Michael Irvin, Lee Roy Jordan, Tom Landry, Bob Lilly, Don Meredith, Don Perkins, Mel Renfro, Tex Schramm, Emmitt Smith, Roger Staubach, Randy White and Rayfield Wright.

Arizona Cardinals
- 8 Larry Wilson
- 40 Pat Tillman
- 77 Stan Mauldin
- 88 J.V. Cain
- 99 Marshall Goldberg

Atlanta Falcons
- 31 William Andrews
- 57 Jeff Van Note
- 60 Tommy Nobis

Carolina Panthers
- 51 Sam Mills

Chicago Bears
- 3 Bronko Nagurski
- 5 George McAfee
- 7 George Halas
- 28 Willie Galimore
- 34 Walter Payton
- 40 Gale Sayers
- 41 Brian Piccolo
- 42 Sid Luckman
- 51 Dick Butkus
- 56 Bill Hewitt
- 61 Bill George
- 66 Bulldog Turner
- 77 Red Grange

Detroit Lions
- 7 Dutch Clark
- 22 Bobby Layne
- 37 Doak Walker
- 56 Joe Schmidt
- 85 Chuck Hughes
- 88 Charlie Sanders

Green Bay Packers
- 3 Tony Canadeo
- 14 Don Hutson
- 15 Bart Starr
- 66 Ray Nitschke
- 92 Reggie White

Minnesota Vikings
- 10 Fran Tarkenton
- 53 Mick Tingelhoff
- 70 Jim Marshall
- 77 Korey Stringer
- 80 Cris Carter
- 88 Alan Page

New Orleans Saints
- 31 Jim Taylor
- 81 Doug Atkins

New York Giants
- 1 Ray Flaherty
- 4 Tuffy Leemans
- 7 Mel Hein
- 11 Phil Simms
- 14 Y.A. Tittle
- 16 Frank Gifford
- 32 Al Blozis
- 40 Joe Morrison
- 42 Charlie Conerly
- 50 Ken Strong
- 56 Lawrence Taylor

Philadelphia Eagles
- 15 Steve Van Buren
- 40 Tom Brookshier
- 44 Pete Retzlaff
- 60 Chuck Bednarik
- 70 Al Wistert
- 92 Reggie White
- 99 Jerome Brown

St. Louis Rams
- 7 Bob Waterfield
- 29 Eric Dickerson
- 74 Merlin Olsen
- 78 Jackie Slater
- 85 Jack Youngblood

San Francisco 49ers
- 12 John Brodie
- 16 Joe Montana
- 34 Joe Perry
- 37 Jimmy Johnson
- 39 Hugh McElhenny
- 42 Ronnie Lott
- 70 Charlie Krueger
- 73 Leo Nomellini
- 79 Bob St. Clair
- 87 Dwight Clark

Seattle Seahawks
- 12 Fans ("12th Man")
- 80 Steve Largent

Tampa Bay Buccaneers
- 63 Lee Roy Selmon

Washington Redskins
- 33 Sammy Baugh

National Hockey League

The Montreal Canadiens have retired the most uniform numbers (13) in the NHL; followed by Boston (10); Detroit and N.Y. Islanders (6); Chicago (5). Following his retirement in 1999, the NHL announced that the league would retire **Wayne Gretzky**'s #99. Four other players have had their numbers retired by two teams: **Gordie Howe**—#9 by Detroit and Hartford; **Bobby Hull**—#9 by Chicago and Winnipeg (now Phoenix); **Ray Bourque**—#77 by Boston and Colorado; **Mark Messier**—#11 by Edmonton and NY Rangers.

Numbers retired in 2006-07 (2): DETROIT—#19 worn by **Steve Yzerman** (1983-2006 with Red Wings); EDMONTON—#11 worn by **Mark Messier** (1979-91 with Oilers). Montreal announced plans to retire Larry Robinson's #19 and Bob Gainey's #23 and the New York Rangers announced plans to retire Brian Leetch's #2 during the 2007-08 season.

Eastern Conference

Five Eastern teams—the Atlanta Thrashers, Carolina Hurricanes, Florida Panthers, New Jersey Devils and Tampa Bay Lightning—have not retired any numbers. The Hartford Whalers had retired three numbers: #2 Rick Ley, #9 Gordie Howe and #19 John McKenzie.

Boston Bruins
2 Eddie Shore
3 Lionel Hitchman
4 Bobby Orr
5 Dit Clapper
7 Phil Esposito
8 Cam Neely
9 John Bucyk
15 Milt Schmidt
24 Terry O'Reilly
77 Ray Bourque

Buffalo Sabres
2 Tim Horton
7 Rick Martin
11 Gilbert Perreault
14 Rene Robert

Montreal Canadiens
1 Jacques Plante
2 Doug Harvey
4 Jean Beliveau
5 Bernard Geoffrion
7 Howie Morenz
9 Maurice Richard
10 Guy Lafleur
12 Dickie Moore
  Yvan Cournoyer
16 Henri Richard
18 Serge Savard
19 Larry Robinson (2008)
23 Bob Gainey (2008)
29 Ken Dryden

New York Islanders
5 Denis Potvin
9 Clark Gillies
19 Bryan Trottier
22 Mike Bossy
23 Bob Nystrom
31 Billy Smith

New York Rangers
1 Eddie Giacomin
2 Brian Leetch (2008)
7 Rod Gilbert
11 Mark Messier
35 Mike Richter

Ottawa Senators
8 Frank Finnigan

Philadelphia Flyers
1 Bernie Parent
4 Barry Ashbee
7 Bill Barber
16 Bobby Clarke

Pittsburgh Penguins
21 Michel Briere
66 Mario Lemieux

Toronto Maple Leafs
5 Bill Barilko
6 Ace Bailey

Washington Capitals
5 Rod Langway
7 Yvon Labre
32 Dale Hunter

Western Conference

Four Western teams—the Columbus Blue Jackets, Mighty Ducks of Anaheim, Nashville Predators and San Jose Sharks—have not retired any numbers. Note, the Quebec Nordiques retired the numbers of J.C. Tremblay (3), Marc Tardif (8) and Michel Goulet (16) but these numbers have been worn since the team moved to Colorado. Detroit has not officially retired the numbers of Larry Aurie (6) and Vladimir Konstantinov (16) but has kept them "out of circulation." Similarly, St. Louis has not officially retired the number of Doug Wickenheiser (14) but has kept it out of circulation since his death in 1999.

Calgary Flames
9 Lanny McDonald

Chicago Blackhawks
1 Glenn Hall
9 Bobby Hull
18 Denis Savard
21 Stan Mikita
35 Tony Esposito

Colorado Avalanche
33 Patrick Roy
77 Ray Bourque

Dallas Stars
7 Neal Broten
8 Bill Goldsworthy
19 Bill Masterton

Detroit Red Wings
1 Terry Sawchuk
7 Ted Lindsay
9 Gordie Howe
10 Alex Delvecchio
12 Sid Abel
19 Steve Yzerman

Edmonton Oilers
3 Al Hamilton
7 Paul Coffey
11 Mark Messier
17 Jari Kurri
31 Grant Fuhr
99 Wayne Gretzky

Los Angeles Kings
16 Marcel Dionne
18 Dave Taylor
30 Rogie Vachon
99 Wayne Gretzky

Minnesota Wild
1 Fans

Phoenix Coyotes
9 Bobby Hull
25 Thomas Steen

St. Louis Blues
3 Bob Gassoff
8 Barclay Plager
11 Brian Sutter
24 Bernie Federko

Vancouver Canucks
12 Stan Smyl

AWARDS

Associated Press Athletes of the Year

Selected annually by AP newspaper sports editors since 1931.

Male

The top 5 vote-getters: 1. **Tiger Woods**, golf, 260 points; 2. **LaDainian Tomlinson**, football, 230; 3. **Roger Federer**, tennis, 110; 4. **Dwyane Wade**, basketball, 40; 5. **Albert Pujols**, baseball and **Ryan Howard**, baseball, 20.

Multiple winners: Lance Armstrong and Tiger Woods (4); Michael Jordan (3); Don Budge, Sandy Koufax, Carl Lewis, Joe Montana and Byron Nelson (2).

Year		Year		Year	
1931	**Pepper Martin**, baseball	1941	**Joe DiMaggio**, baseball	1951	**Dick Kazmaier**, col. football
1932	**Gene Sarazen**, golf	1942	**Frank Sinkwich**, col. football	1952	**Bob Mathias**, track
1933	**Carl Hubbell**, baseball	1943	**Gunder Haegg**, track	1953	**Ben Hogan**, golf
1934	**Dizzy Dean**, baseball	1944	**Byron Nelson**, golf	1954	**Willie Mays**, baseball
1935	**Joe Louis**, boxing	1945	**Byron Nelson**, golf	1955	**Hopalong Cassady**, col. football
1936	**Jesse Owens**, track	1946	**Glenn Davis**, college football	1956	**Mickey Mantle**, baseball
1937	**Don Budge**, tennis	1947	**Johnny Lujack**, col. football	1957	**Ted Williams**, baseball
1938	**Don Budge**, tennis	1948	**Lou Boudreau**, baseball	1958	**Herb Elliott**, track
1939	**Nile Kinnick**, college football	1949	**Leon Hart**, college football	1959	**Ingemar Johansson**, boxing
1940	**Tom Harmon**, college football	1950	**Jim Konstanty**, baseball		

Awards (Cont.)

Year		Year		Year	
1960	**Rafer Johnson**, track	1976	**Bruce Jenner**, track	1992	**Michael Jordan**, pro basketball
1961	**Roger Maris**, baseball	1977	**Steve Cauthen**, horse racing	1993	**Michael Jordan**, pro basketball
1962	**Maury Wills**, baseball	1978	**Ron Guidry**, baseball	1994	**George Foreman**, boxing
1963	**Sandy Koufax**, baseball	1979	**Willie Stargell**, baseball	1995	**Cal Ripken Jr.**, baseball
1964	**Don Schollander**, swimming	1980	**U.S. Olympic hockey team**	1996	**Michael Johnson**, track
1965	**Sandy Koufax**, baseball	1981	**John McEnroe**, tennis	1997	**Tiger Woods**, golf
1966	**Frank Robinson**, baseball	1982	**Wayne Gretzky**, hockey	1998	**Mark McGwire**, baseball
1967	**Carl Yastrzemski**, baseball	1983	**Carl Lewis**, track	1999	**Tiger Woods**, golf
1968	**Denny McLain**, baseball	1984	**Carl Lewis**, track	2000	**Tiger Woods**, golf
1969	**Tom Seaver**, baseball	1985	**Dwight Gooden**, baseball	2001	**Barry Bonds**, baseball
1970	**George Blanda**, pro football	1986	**Larry Bird**, pro basketball	2002	**Lance Armstrong**, cycling
1971	**Lee Trevino**, golf	1987	**Ben Johnson**, track	2003	**Lance Armstrong**, cycling
1972	**Mark Spitz**, swimming	1988	**Orel Hershiser**, baseball	2004	**Lance Armstrong**, cycling
1973	**O.J. Simpson**, pro football	1989	**Joe Montana**, pro football	2005	**Lance Armstrong**, cycling
1974	**Muhammad Ali**, boxing	1990	**Joe Montana**, pro football	2006	**Tiger Woods**, golf
1975	**Fred Lynn**, baseball	1991	**Michael Jordan**, pro basketball		

Female

The top 5 vote-getters: 1. **Lorena Ochoa**, golf, 220 points; 2. **Amelie Mauresmo**, tennis, 110 ; 3. **Maria Sharapova**, tennis and **Lisa Leslie**, basketball, 60; 5. **Justin Henin-Hardenne**, tennis and **Hannah Teter**, snowboarding, 50.

Multiple winners: Babe Didrikson Zaharias (6); Chris Evert (4); Patty Berg, Maureen Connolly and Annika Sorenstam (3); Tracy Austin, Althea Gibson, Billie Jean King, Nancy Lopez, Alice Marble, Martina Navratilova, Wilma Rudolph, Monica Seles, Kathy Whitworth and Mickey Wright (2).

Year		Year		Year	
1931	**Helene Madison**, swimming	1957	**Althea Gibson**, tennis	1983	**Martina Navratilova**, tennis
1932	**Babe Didrikson**, track	1958	**Althea Gibson**, tennis	1984	**Mary Lou Retton**, gymnastics
1933	**Helen Jacobs**, tennis	1959	**Maria Bueno**, tennis	1985	**Nancy Lopez**, golf
1934	**Virginia Van Wie**, golf	1960	**Wilma Rudolph**, track	1986	**Martina Navratilova**, tennis
1935	**Helen Wills Moody**, tennis	1961	**Wilma Rudolph**, track	1987	**Jackie Joyner-Kersee**, track
1936	**Helen Stephens**, track	1962	**Dawn Fraser**, swimming	1988	**Florence Griffith Joyner**, track
1937	**Katherine Rawls**, swimming	1963	**Mickey Wright**, golf	1989	**Steffi Graf**, tennis
1938	**Patty Berg**, golf	1964	**Mickey Wright**, golf	1990	**Beth Daniel**, golf
1939	**Alice Marble**, tennis	1965	**Kathy Whitworth**, golf	1991	**Monica Seles**, tennis
1940	**Alice Marble**, tennis	1966	**Kathy Whitworth**, golf	1992	**Monica Seles**, tennis
1941	**Betty Hicks Newell**, golf	1967	**Billie Jean King**, tennis	1993	**Sheryl Swoopes**, basketball
1942	**Gloria Callen**, swimming	1968	**Peggy Fleming**, skating	1994	**Bonnie Blair**, speed skating
1943	**Patty Berg**, golf	1969	**Debbie Meyer**, swimming	1995	**Rebecca Lobo**, col. basketball
1944	**Ann Curtis**, swimming	1970	**Chi Cheng**, track	1996	**Amy Van Dyken**, swimming
1945	**Babe Didrikson Zaharias**, golf	1971	**Evonne Goolagong**, tennis	1997	**Martina Hingis**, tennis
1946	**Babe Didrikson Zaharias**, golf	1972	**Olga Korbut**, gymnastics	1998	**Se Ri Pak**, golf
1947	**Babe Didrikson Zaharias**, golf	1973	**Billie Jean King**, tennis	1999	**U.S. Soccer Team**
1948	**Fanny Blankers-Koen**, track	1974	**Chris Evert**, tennis	2000	**Marion Jones**, track
1949	**Marlene Bauer**, golf	1975	**Chris Evert**, tennis	2001	**Jennifer Capriati**, tennis
1950	**Babe Didrikson Zaharias**, golf	1976	**Nadia Comaneci**, gymnastics	2002	**Serena Williams**, tennis
1951	**Maureen Connolly**, tennis	1977	**Chris Evert**, tennis	2003	**Annika Sorenstam**, golf
1952	**Maureen Connolly**, tennis	1978	**Nancy Lopez**, golf	2004	**Annika Sorenstam**, golf
1953	**Maureen Connolly**, tennis	1979	**Tracy Austin**, tennis	2005	**Annika Sorenstam**, golf
1954	**Babe Didrikson Zaharias**, golf	1980	**Chris Evert Lloyd**, tennis	2006	**Lorena Ochoa**, golf
1955	**Patty Berg**, golf	1981	**Tracy Austin**, tennis		
1956	**Pat McCormick**, diving	1982	**Mary Decker Tabb**, track		

USOC Sportsman & Sportswoman of the Year

To the outstanding overall male and female athletes from within the U.S. Olympic Committee member organizations. Winners are chosen from nominees of the national governing bodies for Olympic and Pan American Games and affiliated organizations. Voting is done by members of the national media, USOC board of directors and Athletes' Advisory Council.

Sportsman

Multiple winners: Lance Armstrong (4); Eric Heiden and Michael Johnson (3); Matt Biondi and Greg Louganis (2).

Year		Year		Year	
1974	**Jim Bolding**, track	1985	**Willie Banks**, track	1996	**Michael Johnson**, track
1975	**Clint Jackson**, boxing	1986	**Matt Biondi**, swimming	1997	**Pete Sampras**, tennis
1976	**John Naber**, swimming	1987	**Greg Louganis**, diving	1998	**Jonny Moseley**, skiing
1977	**Eric Heiden**, speed skating	1988	**Matt Biondi**, swimming	1999	**Lance Armstrong**, cycling
1978	**Bruce Davidson**, equestrian	1989	**Roger Kingdom**, track	2000	**Rulon Gardner**, wrestling
1979	**Eric Heiden**, speed skating	1990	**John Smith**, wrestling	2001	**Lance Armstrong**, cycling
1980	**Eric Heiden**, speed skating	1991	**Carl Lewis**, track	2002	**Lance Armstrong**, cycling
1981	**Scott Hamilton**, fig. skating	1992	**Pablo Morales**, swimming	2003	**Lance Armstrong**, cycling
1982	**Greg Louganis**, diving	1993	**Michael Johnson**, track	2004	**Michael Phelps**, swimming
1983	**Rick McKinney**, archery	1994	**Dan Jansen**, speed skating	2005	**Hunter Kemper**, triathlon
1984	**Edwin Moses**, track	1995	**Michael Johnson**, track	2006	**Joey Cheek**, speedskating

Sportswoman

Multiple winners: Bonnie Blair, Tracy Caulkins, Jackie Joyner-Kersee, Picabo Street and Sheila Young Ochowicz (2).

Year		Year		Year	
1974	**Shirley Babashoff**, swimming	1985	**Mary Decker Slaney**, track	1997	**Tara Lipinski,** figure skating
1975	**Kathy Heddy**, swimming	1986	**Jackie Joyner-Kersee**, track	1998	**Picabo Street**, skiing
1976	**Sheila Young**, speedskating	1987	**Jackie Joyner-Kersee**, track	1999	**Jenny Thompson**, swimming
1977	**Linda Fratianne**, fig. skating	1988	**Florence Griffith Joyner**, track	2000	**Marion Jones**, track
1978	**Tracy Caulkins**, swimming	1989	**Janet Evans**, swimming	2001	**Jennifer Capriati**, tennis
1979	**Sippy Woodhead**, swimming	1990	**Lynn Jennings**, track	2002	**Sarah Hughes**, figure skating
1980	**Beth Heiden**, speed skating	1991	**Kim Zmeskal**, gymnastics	2003	**Michelle Kwan**, figure skating
1981	**Sheila Ochowicz**, speed skating & cycling	1992	**Bonnie Blair**, speed skating	2004	**Carly Patterson**, gymnastics
1982	**Melanie Smith**, equestrian	1993	**Gail Devers**, track	2005	**Katie Hoff**, swimming
1983	**Tamara McKinney**, skiing	1994	**Bonnie Blair**, speed skating	2006	**Hannah Teter**, snowboarding
1984	**Tracy Caulkins**, swimming	1995	**Picabo Street**, skiing		
		1996	**Amy Van Dyken**, swimming		

UPI International Athletes of the Year

Selected annually by United Press International's European newspaper sports editors from 1974-95.

Male

Multiple winners: Sebastian Coe, Alberto Juantorena and Carl Lewis (2).

Year		Year		Year	
1974	**Muhammad Ali**, boxing	1982	**Daley Thompson**, track	1990	**Stefan Edberg**, tennis
1975	**Joao Oliveira**, track	1983	**Carl Lewis**, track	1991	**Sergei Bubka**, track
1976	**Alberto Juantorena**, track	1984	**Carl Lewis**, track	1992	**Kevin Young**, track
1977	**Alberto Juantorena**, track	1985	**Steve Cram**, track	1993	**Miguel Indurain**, cycling
1978	**Henry Rono**, track	1986	**Diego Maradona**, soccer	1994	**Johann Olav Koss**, speed skating
1979	**Sebastian Coe**, track	1987	**Ben Johnson**, track	1995	**Jonathan Edwards**, track
1980	**Eric Heiden**, speed skating	1988	**Matt Biondi**, swimming	1996	discontinued
1981	**Sebastian Coe**, track	1989	**Boris Becker**, tennis		

Female

Multiple winners: Nadia Comaneci, Steffi Graf, Marita Koch and Monica Seles (2).

Year		Year		Year	
1974	**Irena Szewinska**, track	1982	**Marita Koch**, track	1990	**Merlene Ottey**, track
1975	**Nadia Comaneci**, gymnastics	1983	**Jarmila Kratochvilova**, track	1991	**Monica Seles**, tennis
1976	**Nadia Comaneci**, gymnastics	1984	**Martina Navratilova**, tennis	1992	**Monica Seles**, tennis
1977	**Rosie Ackermann**, track	1985	**Mary Decker Slaney**, track	1993	**Wang Junxia**, track
1978	**Tracy Caulkins**, swimming	1986	**Heike Drechsler**, track	1994	**Le Jingyi**, swimming
1979	**Marita Koch**, track	1987	**Steffi Graf**, tennis	1995	**Gwen Torrence**, track
1980	**Hanni Wenzel**, alpine skiing	1988	**Florence Griffith Joyner**, track	1996	discontinued
1981	**Chris Evert Lloyd**, tennis	1989	**Steffi Graf**, tennis		

Honda-Broderick Cup

To the outstanding collegiate woman athlete of the year in NCAA competition. Winner is chosen from nominees in each of the NCAA's 10 competitive sports. Final voting is done by member athletic directors. Award is named after founder and sportswear manufacturer Thomas Broderick.

Multiple winner: Tracy Caulkins (2).

Year			Year		
1977	**Lucy Harris**, Delta St	basketball	1992	**Missy Marlowe**, Utah	gymnastics
1978	**Ann Meyers**, UCLA	basketball	1993	**Lisa Fernandez**, UCLA	softball
1979	**Nancy Lieberman**, Old Dominion	basketball	1994	**Mia Hamm**, North Carolina	soccer
1980	**Julie Shea**, N.C. State	track & field	1995	**Rebecca Lobo**, UConn	basketball
1981	**Jill Sterkel**, Texas	swimming	1996	**Jennifer Rizzotti**, UConn	basketball
1982	**Tracy Caulkins**, Florida	swimming	1997	**Cindy Daws**, Notre Dame	soccer
1983	**Deitre Collins**, Hawaii	volleyball	1998	**Chamique Holdsclaw**, Tennessee	basketball
1984	**Tracy Caulkins**, Florida & **Cheryl Miller**, USC	swimming basketball	1999	**Misty May**, Long Beach St.	volleyball
1985	**Jackie Joyner**, UCLA	track & field	2000	**Cristina Teuscher**, Columbia	swimming
1986	**Kamie Ethridge**, Texas	basketball	2001	**Jackie Stiles**, SW Missouri St.	basketball
1987	**Mary T. Meagher**, California	swimming	2002	**Angela Williams**, USC	track
1988	**Teresa Weatherspoon**, La. Tech	basketball	2003	**Natasha Watley**, UCLA	softball
1989	**Vicki Huber**, Villanova	track	2004	**Tara Kirk**, Stanford	swimming
1990	**Suzy Favor**, Wisconsin	track	2005	**Ogonna Nnamani**, Stanford	volleyball
1991	**Dawn Staley**, Virginia	basketball	2006	**Christine Sinclair**, Portland	soccer
			2007	**Sarah Pavan**, Nebraska	volleyball

Awards (Cont.)

Flo Hyman Award

Presented annually since 1987 by the Women's Sports Foundation for "exemplifying dignity, spirit and commitment to excellence" and named in honor of the late captain of the 1984 U.S. Women's Volleyball team. Voting by WSF members.

Year		Year		Year	
1987	**Martina Navratilova**, tennis	1993	**Lynette Woodard**, basketball	1999	**Bonnie Blair**, speed skating
1988	**Jackie Joyner-Kersee**, track	1994	**Patty Sheehan**, golf	2000	**Monica Seles**, tennis
1989	**Evelyn Ashford**, track	1995	**Mary Lou Retton**, gymnastics	2001	**Lisa Leslie**, basketball
1990	**Chris Evert**, tennis	1996	**Donna de Varona**, swimming	2002	**Dot Richardson**, softball
1991	**Diana Golden**, skiing	1997	**Billie Jean King**, tennis	2003	**Nawal El Moutawakel**, track
1992	**Nancy Lopez**, golf	1998	**Nadia Comaneci**, gymnastics	2004	**Kristi Yamaguchi**, fig. skating

James E. Sullivan Memorial Award

Presented annually by the Amateur Athletic Union since 1930. The Sullivan Award is named after the former AAU president and given to the athlete who, "by his or her performance, example and influence as an amateur, has done the most during the year to advance the cause of sportsmanship."

Teeanager **Jessica Long** won the 77th Sullivan Award. The 15-year-old swimmer won nine gold medals at the International Paralympic Committee Swimming World Championships held in Durban, South Africa. Long beat out an impressive list of finalists including Brady Quinn, Michael Phelps, Hannah Teter, Chris Leak, Joakim Noah and Candace Parker.

Year		Year		Year	
1930	**Bobby Jones**, golf	1957	**Bobby Morrow**, track	1983	**Edwin Moses**, track
1931	**Barney Berlinger**, track	1958	**Glenn Davis**, track	1984	**Greg Louganis**, diving
1932	**Jim Bausch**, track	1959	**Parry O'Brien**, track	1985	**Joan B. Samuelson**, track
1933	**Glenn Cunningham**, track	1960	**Rafer Johnson**, track	1986	**Jackie Joyner-Kersee**, track
1934	**Bill Bonthron**, track	1961	**Wilma Rudolph**, track	1987	**Jim Abbott**, baseball
1935	**Lawson Little**, golf	1962	**Jim Beatty**, track	1988	**Florence Griffith Joyner**, track
1936	**Glenn Morris**, track	1963	**John Pennel**, track	1989	**Janet Evans**, swimming
1937	**Don Budge**, tennis	1964	**Don Schollander**, swimming	1990	**John Smith**, wrestling
1938	**Don Lash**, track	1965	**Bill Bradley**, basketball	1991	**Mike Powell**, track
1939	**Joe Burk**, rowing	1966	**Jim Ryun**, track	1992	**Bonnie Blair**, speed skating
1940	**Greg Rice**, track	1967	**Randy Matson**, track	1993	**Charlie Ward**, football
1941	**Leslie MacMitchell**, track	1968	**Debbie Meyer**, swimming	1994	**Dan Jansen**, speed skating
1942	**Cornelius Warmerdam**, track	1969	**Bill Toomey**, track	1995	**Bruce Baumgartner**, wrestling
1943	**Gilbert Dodds**, track	1970	**John Kinsella**, swimming	1996	**Michael Johnson**, track
1944	**Ann Curtis**, swimming	1971	**Mark Spitz**, swimming	1997	**Peyton Manning**, football
1945	**Doc Blanchard**, football	1972	**Frank Shorter**, track	1998	**Chamique Holdsclaw**,
1946	**Arnold Tucker**, football	1973	**Bill Walton**, basketball		basketball
1947	**John B. Kelly, Jr.**, rowing	1974	**Rich Wohlhuter**, track	1999	**Coco and Kelly Miller**,
1948	**Bob Mathias**, track	1975	**Tim Shaw**, swimming		basketball
1949	**Dick Button**, skating	1976	**Bruce Jenner**, track	2000	**Rulon Gardner**, wrestling
1950	**Fred Wilt**, track	1977	**John Naber**, swimming	2001	**Michelle Kwan**, figure skating
1951	**Bob Richards**, track	1978	**Tracy Caulkins**, swimming	2002	**Sarah Hughes**, figure skating
1952	**Horace Ashenfelter**, track	1979	**Kurt Thomas**, gymnastics	2003	**Michael Phelps**, swimming
1953	**Sammy Lee**, diving	1980	**Eric Heiden**, speed skating	2004	**Paul Hamm**, gymnastics
1954	**Mal Whitfield**, track	1981	**Carl Lewis**, track	2005	**J.J. Redick**, basketball
1955	**Harrison Dillard**, track	1982	**Mary Decker**, track	2006	**Jessica Long**, paralympic
1956	**Pat McCormick**, diving				swimmer

ESPY Awards

The ESPY Awards, which represent the convergence of the sports and entertainment communities, were created by ESPN in 1993 and are given for Excellence in Sports Performance Yearly in more than 30 categories. Until 2004, ESPYs were awarded by a panel of sports executives, journalists and retired athletes whose decisions are based on the performances of the nominees during the year preceding the awards ceremony. Currently, online balloting is used. Note that not all categories are listed below.

Breakthrough Athlete

Year		Year	
1993	Gary Sheffield, San Diego Padres	2001	Daunte Culpepper, Minnesota Vikings
1994	Mike Piazza, Los Angeles Dodgers	2002	Tom Brady, New England Patriots
1995	Jeff Bagwell, Houston Astros	2003	Alfonso Soriano, New York Yankees
1996	Hideo Nomo, Los Angeles Dodgers	2004	LeBron James, Cleveland Cavaliers
1997	Tiger Woods, golf	2005	Dwyane Wade, Miami Heat
1998	Nomar Garciaparra, Boston Red Sox	2006	Chris Paul, New Orleans Hornets
1999	Randy Moss, Minnesota Vikings	2007	Devin Hester, Chicago Bears
2000	Kurt Warner, St. Louis Rams		

Outstanding Performance Under Pressure

Year		Year	
1993	Christian Laettner, Duke	1997	Kerri Strug, Olympic gymnast
1994	Joe Carter, Toronto Blue Jays	1998	Terrell Davis, Denver Broncos
1995	Mark Messier, New York Rangers	1999	Mark O'Meara, golf
1996	Martin Brodeur, New Jersey Devils		

Best Coach/Manager

Year	
1993	Jimmy Johnson, Dallas Cowboys
1994	Jimmy Johnson, Dallas Cowboys
1995	George Siefert, San Francisco 49ers
1996	Gary Barnett, Northwestern
1997	Joe Torre, New York Yankees
1998	Jim Leyland, Florida Marlins
1999	Joe Torre, New York Yankees
2000	Joe Torre, New York Yankees
2001	Joe Torre, New York Yankees
2002	Phil Jackson, Los Angeles Lakers
2003	Jon Gruden, Tampa Bay Buccaneers
2004	Larry Brown, Detroit Pistons
2005	Bill Belichick, New England Patriots
2006	Bill Cowher, Pittsburgh Steelers
2007	Tony Dungy, Indianapolis Colts

Best Comeback Athlete

Year	
1993	Dave Winfield, Toronto Blue Jays
1994	Mario Lemieux, Pittsburgh Penguins
1995	Dan Marino, Miami Dolphins
1996	Michael Jordan, Chicago Bulls
1997	Evander Holyfield, boxer
1998	Roger Clemens, Toronto Blue Jays
1999	Eric Davis, Baltimore Orioles
2000	Lance Armstrong, cycling
2001	Andres Galarraga, baseball
2002	Jennifer Capriati, tennis
2003	Tommy Maddox, Pittsburgh Steelers
2004	Bethany Hamilton, surfing
2005	Mark Fields, Carolina Panthers
2006	Tedy Bruschi, New England Patriots

Best Female Athlete

Year		Year	
1993	Monica Seles, tennis	2001	Marion Jones, track
1994	Julie Krone, jockey	2002	V. Williams, tennis
1995	Bonnie Blair, speed skater	2003	S. Williams, tennis
1996	Rebecca Lobo, basketball	2004	Diana Taurasi, basketball
1997	Amy Van Dyken, swimming	2005	Annika Sorenstam, golf
1998	Mia Hamm, soccer	2006	Annika Sorenstam, golf
1999	C. Holdsclaw, college basketball	2007	Taryne Mowatt, softball
2000	Mia Hamm, soccer		

Best Male Athlete

Year	
1993	Michael Jordan, Chicago Bulls
1994	Barry Bonds, San Francisco Giants
1995	Steve Young, San Francisco 49ers
1996	Cal Ripken, Baltimore Orioles
1997	Michael Johnson, Olympic sprinter
1998	Tiger Woods, golf
1999	Mark McGwire, St. Louis Cardinals
2000	Tiger Woods, golf
2001	Tiger Woods, golf
2002	Tiger Woods, golf
2003	Lance Armstrong, cycling
2004	Lance Armstrong, cycling
2005	Lance Armstrong, cycling
2006	Lance Armstrong, cycling
2007	LaDainian Tomlinson, San Diego Chargers

Best Team

Year		Year	
1993	Dallas Cowboys	2001	NY Yankees & Oklahoma football
1994	Toronto Blue Jays	2002	Los Angeles Lakers
1995	New York Rangers	2003	Anaheim Angels
1996	UConn women's basketball	2004	Detroit Pistons
1997	New York Yankees	2005	Boston Red Sox
1998	Denver Broncos	2006	Pittsburgh Steelers
1999	New York Yankees	2007	Indianapolis Colts
2000	U.S. Women's World Cup Team		

Best Baseball Player

Year		Year	
1993	Dennis Eckersley, Oak	2001	Pedro Martinez, Bos.
1994	Barry Bonds, S.F.	2002	Barry Bonds, S.F.
1995	Jeff Bagwell, Hou.	2003	Barry Bonds, S.F.
1996	Greg Maddux, Atl.	2004	Barry Bonds, S.F.
1997	Ken Caminiti, S.D.	2005	Albert Pujols, St. L.
1998	Larry Walker, Colo.	2006	Albert Pujols, St. L.
1999	Mark McGwire, St.l	2007	Derek Jeter, N.Y.
2000	Pedro Martinez, Bos.		

Best NFL Player

Year		Year	
1993	Emmitt Smith, Dal.	2002	Marshall Faulk, St. L
1994	Emmitt Smith, Dal.	2003	Michael Vick, Atl.
1995	Barry Sanders, Det.	2004	Peyton Manning, Ind
1996	Brett Favre, G.B.	2005	Peyton Manning, Ind
1997	Brett Favre, G.B.	2006	Shaun Alexander, Sea
1998	Barry Sanders, Det.		
1999	Terrell Davis, Den.	2007	LaDainian Tomlinson, S.D.
2000	Kurt Warner, St. L		
2001	Marshall Faulk, St. L		

Best NBA Player

Year		Year	
1993	Michael Jordan, Chi.	2001	Shaquille O'Neal, LAL
1994	Charles Barkley, Pho.		
1995	Hakeem Olajuwon, Hou.	2002	Shaquille O'Neal, LAL
1996	Hakeem Olajuwon, Hou.	2003	Tim Duncan, S.A.
		2004	Kevin Garnett, Min.
1997	Michael Jordan, Chi.	2005	Steve Nash, Pho.
1998	Michael Jordan, Chi.	2006	Dwyane Wade, Mia.
1999	Michael Jordan, Chi.	2007	LeBron James, Cle.
2000	Tim Duncan, S.A.		

Best WNBA Player

Year		Year	
1998	Cynthia Cooper, Hou.	2002	Lisa Leslie, L.A.
		2003	Lisa Leslie, L.A.
1999	Cynthia Cooper, Hou.	2004	Lauren Jackson, Sea.
		2005	Lauren Jackson, Sea.
2000	Cynthia Cooper, Hou.	2006	Sheryl Swoopes, Hou.
2001	Sheryl Swoopes, Hou.	2007	Lisa Leslie, L.A.

Best NHL Player

Year		Year	
1993	Mario Lemieux, Pit.	2001	Chris Pronger, St. L
1994	Mario Lemieux, Pit.	2002	Jarome Iginla, Cal.
1995	Mark Messier, NYR	2003	Jean-Sebastien Giguere, Ana.
1996	Eric Lindros, Phi.		
1997	Joe Sakic, Col.	2004	Jarome Iginla, Cal.
1998	Mario Lemieux, Pit.	2005	not awarded
1999	Dominik Hasek, Buf.	2006	Jaromir Jagr, NYR
2000	Dominik Hasek, Buf.	2007	Sidney Crosby, Pit.

Outstanding College Football Performer of the Year

Year	
1993	Garrison Hearst, Georgia
1994	Charlie Ward, Florida State
1995	Rashaan Salaam, Colorado
1996	Eddie George, Ohio State
1997	Danny Wuerffel, Florida
1998	Peyton Manning, Tennessee
1999	Ricky Williams, Texas
2000	Michael Vick, Virginia Tech
2001	Chris Weinke, Florida State

Outstanding Men's College Basketball Performer of the Year

Year		Year	
1993	Christian Laettner, Duke	1998	Keith Van Horn, Utah
1994	Bobby Hurley, Duke	1999	Antawn Jamison, N. Carolina
1995	Grant Hill, Duke		
1996	Ed O'Bannon, UCLA	2000	Elton Brand, Duke
1997	Tim Duncan, Wake Forest	2001	Kenyon Martin, Cincinnati

Outstanding Women's College Basketball Performer of the Year

Year	
1993	Dawn Staley, Virginia
1994	Sheryl Swoopes, Texas Tech
1995	Charlotte Smith, North Carolina
1996	Rebecca Lobo, Connecticut
1997	Saudia Roundtree, Georgia
1998	Chamique Holdsclaw, Tennessee
1999	Chamique Holdsclaw, Tennessee
2000	Chamique Holdsclaw, Tennessee
2001	Tamika Catchings, Tennessee

Best Men's Tennis Player

Year		Year	
1993	Jim Courier	2001	Pete Sampras
1994	Pete Sampras	2002	Lleyton Hewitt
1995	Pete Sampras	2003	Andre Agassi
1996	Pete Sampras	2004	Andy Roddick
1997	Pete Sampras	2005	Roger Federer
1998	Pete Sampras	2006	Roger Federer
1999	Pete Sampras	2007	Roger Federer
2000	Andre Agassi		

Best Women's Tennis Player

Year		Year	
1993	Monica Seles	2001	Venus Williams
1994	Steffi Graf	2002	Venus Williams
1995	A. Sanchez Vicario	2002	Venus Williams
1996	Steffi Graf	2003	Serena Williams
1997	Steffi Graf	2004	Serena Williams
1998	Martina Hingis	2005	Maria Sharapova
1999	Lindsay Davenport	2006	Venus Williams
2000	Lindsay Davenport	2007	Maria Sharapova

Best Men's Golfer

Year		Year	
1993	Fred Couples	1999	Mark O'Meara
1994	Nick Price	2000	Tiger Woods
1995	Nick Price	2001	Tiger Woods
1996	Corey Pavin	2002	Tiger Woods
1997	Tom Lehman	2003	Tiger Woods
1998	Tiger Woods	2004	Phil Mickelson

Best Women's Golfer

Year		Year	
1993	Dottie Mochrie	1999	Annika Sorenstam
1994	Betsy King	2000	Julie Inkster
1995	Laura Davies	2001	Karrie Webb
1996	Annika Sorenstam	2002	Annika Sorenstam
1997	Karrie Webb	2003	Annika Sorenstam
1998	Annika Sorenstam	2004	Annika Sorenstam

Best Golfer

Year		Year	
2004	Tiger Woods	2006	Tiger Woods
2005	Tiger Woods	2007	Tiger Woods

Best Jockey

Year		Year	
1994	Mike Smith	2001	Kent Desormeaux
1995	Chris McCarron	2002	Victor Espinoza
1996	Jerry Bailey	2003	Jose Santos
1997	Jerry Bailey	2004	Stewart Elliot
1998	Gary Stevens	2005	Jeremy Rose
1999	Kent Desormeaux	2006	Edgar Prado
2000	Chris Antley	2007	Calvin Borel

Best Bowler

Year		Year	
1995	Norm Duke	2002	Pete Weber
1996	Mike Aulby	2003	Walter Ray Williams
1997	Bob Learn Jr.	2004	Pete Weber
1998	Walter Ray Williams	2005	Walter Ray Williams
1999	Walter Ray Williams	2006	Walter Ray Williams
2000	Parker Bohn III	2007	Norm Duke
2001	Walter Ray Williams		

Best Men's Track Athlete

Year		Year	
1993	Kevin Young	2000	Michael Johnson
1994	Michael Johnson	2001	Maurice Greene
1995	Dennis Mitchell	2002	Maurice Greene
1996	Michael Johnson	2003	Tim Montgomery
1997	Michael Johnson	2004	Tom Pappas
1998	Wilson Kipketer	2005	not awarded
1999	Maurice Greene	2006	Justin Gatlin

Best Women's Track Athlete

Year		Year	
1993	Evelyn Ashford	2000	Marion Jones
1994	Gail Devers	2001	Marion Jones
1995	Gwen Torrence	2002	Marion Jones
1996	Kim Batten	2003	Gail Devers
1997	Marie-Jose Perec	2004	Gail Devers
1998	Marion Jones	2005	not awarded
1999	Marion Jones	2006	Allyson Felix

Best Track and Field Athlete

Year	
2007	Jeremy Wariner

All-Time ESPYs Hosts

Year		Year	
1993	Dennis Miller	2003	Jamie Foxx
1994	Dennis Miller	2004	Jamie Foxx
1995	John Goodman	2005	Matthew Perry
1996	Tony Danza	2006	Lance Armstrong
1997	Jeff Foxworthy	2007	LeBron James & Jimmy Kimmel
1998	Norm Macdonald		
1999	Samuel L. Jackson		
2000	Jimmy Smits		
2001	Samuel L. Jackson		
2002	Samuel L. Jackson		

Best U.S. Olympian

Year	
2006	Shaun White, snowboarding

Best Driver

Year		Year	
1993	Nigel Mansell	2001	Bobby Labonte
1994	Nigel Mansell	2002	Michael Schumacher
1995	Al Unser Jr.	2003	Tony Stewart
1996	Jeff Gordon	2004	Dale Earnhardt Jr.
1997	Jimmy Vasser	2005	Michael Schumacher
1998	Jeff Gordon	2006	Tony Stewart
1999	Jeff Gordon	2007	Jeff Gordon
2000	Dale Jarrett		

Game of the Year

Year	
1996	AFC championship between Colts and Steelers
1997	Rose Bowl, Ohio State edges Arizona St.
1998	Super Bowl XXXII, Broncos over Packers
1999-2001	not awarded
2002	World Series Game 7, Diamondbacks-Yankees
2003	Fiesta Bowl, Ohio State beat Miami-FL in OT
2004	Super Bowl XXXVIII, Patriots over Panthers
2005	ALCS Game 5, Red Sox beat Yankees
2006	Rose Bowl, Texas beat USC
2007	Fiesta Bowl, Boise State beat Oklahoma

Best Play

Year	
2002	Derek Jeter's throw in World Series Game 3.
2003	LSU's Hail Mary TD.
2004	New Orleans Saints' lateral
2005	Blake Hoffarber's last second 3-pointer from flat on his back.
2006	Tyrone Prothro's behind-the-back catch
2007	Boise State's Fiesta Bowl Statue of Liberty play

Best Boxer

Year		Year	
1993	Riddick Bowe	2001	Felix Trinidad
1994	Evander Holyfield	2002	Lennox Lewis
1995	George Foreman	2003	Roy Jones Jr.
1996	Roy Jones Jr.	2004	Antonio Tarver
1997	Evander Holyfield	2005	Bernard Hopkins
1998	Evander Holyfield	2006	Oscar De La Hoya
1999	Oscar De La Hoya	2007	Floyd Mayweather
2000	Roy Jones Jr.		

Best Male College Athlete

Year	
2002	Cael Sanderson, Iowa St. wrestling
2003	Carmelo Anthony, Syracuse basketball
2004	Emeka Okafor, UConn basketball
2005	Matt Leinart, USC football
2006	Reggie Bush, USC football
2007	Kevin Durant, Texas basketball

Best Female College Athlete

Year	
2002	Sue Bird, UConn basketball
2003	Diana Taurasi, UConn basketball
2004	Diana Taurasi, UConn basketball
2005	Cat Osterman, Texas softball
2006	Cat Osterman, Texas softball
2007	Taryne Mowatt, Arizona softball

Best Male Soccer Player

Year		Year	
2002	Landon Donovan	2004	David Beckham
2003	Ronaldo		

Best Female Soccer Player

Year		Year	
2002	Tiffeny Milbrett	2004	Mia Hamm
2003	Katia		

Best Soccer Player

Year		Year	
2005	Mia Hamm, USA	2006	Ronaldinho, Brazil

Best MLS Player

Year		Year	
2006	Landon Donovan, LA	2007	Landon Donovan, LA

Best Outdoors Athlete

Year		Year	
2002	Kevin VanDam, fishing	2005	J.R. Salzman, lumberjack
2003	Jay Yelas, fishing		
2004	Tina Bosworth, log rolling		

Best Action Sports Athlete

Year		Year	
2002	Kelly Clark, snowboarding	2003	Shaun White, snowboarding

Best Male Action Sports Athlete

Year		Year	
2004	Ryan Nyquist, bike	2007	Travis Pastrana, motocross
2005	Dave Mirra, bike		
2006	Shaun White, snowboarding		

Best Female Action Sports Athlete

Year		Year	
2004	Dallas Friday, wakeboarding	2006	Hannah Teter, snowboarding
2005	Sofia Mulanovich, surfing	2007	Sarah Burke, skiing

Best Male Athlete with a Disability

Year		Year	
2005	Marlon Shirley, track	2007	Casey Tubbs, track
2006	Bobby Martin, football		

Best Female Athlete with a Disability

Year	
2005	Erin Popovich, swimming
2006	Sarah Reinertsen, triathon
2007	Jessica Long, swimming

Best Sports Movie

Year		Year	
2002	The Rookie	2005	Friday Night Lights
2003	Bend it like Beckham	2006	Glory Road
2004	Miracle	2007	Talladega Nights

Best Record-Breaking Performance

Year	
2001	Pete Sampras, Grand Slam singles titles
2002	Tiger Woods, four straight Majors
2003	Emmitt Smith, NFL rushing record
2004	Eric Gagne, baseball consecutive saves
2005	Peyton Manning, NFL single-season TD passes
2006	Shaun Alexander, NFL single-season TDs scored
2007	LaDainian Tomlinson, NFL single-season TDs scored

Best Upset

Year	
2004	Pistons over Lakers in NBA Finals
2005	#14 Bucknell over #3 Kansas in NCAA tournament
2006	not awarded
2007	Warriors over Mavericks in NBA Playoffs

Best Moment

Year	
2006	Jason McElwaine, Greece-Athena HS basketball
2007	Saints return home, beat Falcons on MNF

Arthur Ashe Award for Courage

Presented since 1993 on the annual ESPN "ESPYs" telecast. Given to a member of the sports community who has exemplifie the same courage, spirit and determination to help others despite personal hardship that characterized Arthur Ashe, the la tennis champion and humanitarian. Voting done by select 26-member committee of media and sports personalities.

Year	Year	Year
1993 **Jim Valvano**, basketball	2000 **Dave Sanders**, Columbine	2004 **George Weah**, soccer
1994 **Steve Palermo**, baseball	H.S. coach	2005 **Emmanuel Ofosu Yeboah**
1995 **Howard Cosell**, TV & radio	2001 **Cathy Freeman**, track	**Jim MacLaren**, disabled ath-
1996 **Loretta Clairborne**, special	2002 **Todd Beamer, Mark Bing-**	letes
olympics	**ham, Tom Burnett & Jere-**	2006 **Afghanistan female soccer**
1997 **Muhammad Ali**, boxing	**my Glick**, Flight 93	2007 **Trevor Ringland & David**
1998 **Dean Smith**, college basketball	2003 **Pat Tillman**, football	**Cullen**, Peace Players Interna-
1999 **Billie Jean King**, tennis	**& Kevin Tillman**, baseball	tional

The Hickok Belt

Officially known as the S. Rae Hickok Professional Athlete of the Year Award and presented by the Kickik Manufacturing Co. Arlington, Texas, from 1950-76. The trophy was a large belt of gold, diamonds and other jewels, reportedly worth $30,000 1976, the last year it was handed out. Voting was done by 270 newspaper sports editors from around the country.

Multiple winner: Sandy Koufax (2).

Year	Year	Year
1950 **Phil Rizzuto**, baseball	1960 **Arnold Palmer**, golf	1970 **Brooks Robinson**, baseball
1951 **Allie Reynolds**, baseball	1961 **Roger Maris**, baseball	1971 **Lee Trevino**, golf
1952 **Rocky Marciano**, boxing	1962 **Maury Wills**, baseball	1972 **Steve Carlton**, baseball
1953 **Ben Hogan**, golf	1963 **Sandy Koufax**, baseball	1973 **O.J. Simpson**, football
1954 **Willie Mays**, baseball	1964 **Jim Brown**, football	1974 **Muhammad Ali**, boxing
1955 **Otto Graham**, football	1965 **Sandy Koufax**, baseball	1975 **Pete Rose**, baseball
1956 **Mickey Mantle**, baseball	1966 **Frank Robinson**, baseball	1976 **Ken Stabler**, football
1957 **Carmen Basilio**, boxing	1967 **Carl Yastrzemski**, baseball	1977 Discontinued
1958 **Bob Turley**, baseball	1968 **Joe Namath**, football	
1959 **Ingemar Johansson**, boxing	1969 **Tom Seaver**, baseball	

Presidential Medal of Freedom

Since President John F. Kennedy established the Medal of Freedom as America's highest civilian honor in 1963, only 17 spor figures have won the award. Note that (*) indicates the presentation was made posthumously.

Year		President	Year		President
1963	**Bob Kiphuth**, swimming	Kennedy	2002	**Hank Aaron**, baseball	G.W. Bush
1976	**Jesse Owens**, track & field	Ford	2003	**John Wooden**, basketball	G.W. Bush
1977	**Joe DiMaggio**, baseball	Ford	2003	**Roberto Clemente***, baseball	G.W. Bush
1983	**Paul (Bear) Bryant***, football	Reagan	2004	**Arnold Palmer**, golf	G.W. Bush
1984	**Jackie Robinson***, baseball	Reagan	2005	**Muhammad Ali**, boxing	G.W. Bush
1986	**Earl (Red) Blaik**, football	Reagan	2005	**Jack Nicklaus**, golf	G.W. Bush
1991	**Ted Williams**, baseball	G. Bush	2005	**Frank Robinson**, baseball	G.W. Bush
1992	**Richard Petty**, auto racing	G. Bush	2006	**John "Buck" O'Neill***, baseball	G.W. Bush
1993	**Arthur Ashe***, tennis	Clinton			

Congressional Gold Medal

Since the American Revolution, the U.S. Congress has commissioned gold medals as its highest expression of national appr ciation for distinguished achievements and contributions. The medals are produced by the U.S. Mint. Each medal honors a pa ticular individual, institution or event. Only five sports figure have won the award but note that track legend **Wilma Rudolp** and golfer **Arnold Palmer** have been nominated for, but not yet awarded, the Congressional gold medal.

Year	Year
1973 **Roberto Clemente**, baseball	2005 **Jackie Robinson**, baseball
1982 **Joe Louis**, boxing	2007 **Byron Nelson**, golf
1988 **Jesse Owens**, track & field	

Time Person of the Year

Since Charles Lindbergh was named *Time* magazine's first Man of the Year for 1927, two individuals with significant sports credentials have won the honor.

Year
1984 **Peter Ueberroth**, president of the Los Angeles Olympic Organizing Committee.
1991 **Ted Turner**, owner-president of Turner Broadcasting System, founder of CNN cable news network, owner of the Atlanta Braves (NL) and Atlanta Hawks (NBA), and former winning America's Cup skipper.

TROPHY CASE

From the first organized track meet at Olympia in 776 B.C., to the Turin Winter Olympics over 2,700 years later, championships have been officially recognized with prizes that are symbolically rich and eagerly pursued. Here are 15 of the most coveted trophies in America.

(Illustrations by Lynn Mercer Michaud)

America's Cup

First presented by England's Royal Yacht Squadron to the winner of an invitational race around the Isle of Wight on Aug. 22, 1851 . . . originally called the Hundred Guinea Cup . . . renamed after the U.S. boat America, winner of the first race . . . made of sterling silver and designed by London jewelers R. & G. Garrard . . . measures 2 feet, 3 inches high and weighs 16 lbs . . . originally cost 100 guineas ($500), now valued at $250,000 . . . bell-shaped base added in 1958 . . . challenged for every three to four years . . . trophy held by yacht club sponsoring winning boat . . . Cup was badly damaged when a Maori protester repeatedly smashed it with a sledgehammer on March 14, 1997. It was sent back to the original maker and fully restored.

Vince Lombardi Trophy

First presented at the AFL-NFL World Championship Game (now Super Bowl) on Jan. 15, 1967 . . . originally called the World Championship Game Trophy . . . renamed in 1971 in honor of former Green Bay Packers GM-coach and two-time Super Bowl winner Vince Lombardi, who died in 1970 as coach of Washington . . . made of sterling silver and designed by Tiffany & Co. of New York . . . measures 21 inches high and weighs 7 lbs (football depicted is regulation size) . . . valued at $12,500 . . . competed for annually . . . winning team keeps trophy.

Olympic Gold Medal

First presented by International Olympic Committee in 1908 (until then winners received silver medals) . . . second and third place finishers also got medals of silver and bronze for first time in 1908 . . . each medal must be at least 2.4 inches in diameter and 0.12 inches thick . . . the gold medal is actually made of silver, but must be gilded with at least 6 grams (0.21 ounces) of pure gold . . . the medals for the 1996 Atlanta Games were designed by Malcolm Grear Designers and produced by Reed & Barton of Taunton, Mass . . . 604 gold, 604 silver and 630 bronze medals were made . . . competed for every two years as Winter and Summer Games alternate . . . winners keep medals.

Awards (Cont.)

Stanley Cup

Donated by Lord Stanley of Preston, the Governor General of Canada and first presented in 1893 . . . original cup was made of sterling silver by an unknown London silversmith and measured 7 inches high with an 11½-inch diameter . . . in order to accommodate all the rosters of winning teams, the cup now measures 35½ inches high with a base 54 inches around and weighs 32 lbs . . . in order to add new names each year, bands on the trophy are often retired and displayed at the Hall of Fame . . . originally bought for 10 guineas ($48.67), it is now insured for $75,000 . . . actual cup retired to Hall of Fame and replaced in 1970 . . . presented to NHL playoff champion since 1918 . . . trophy loaned to winning team for one year.

World Cup

First presented by the Federation Internationale de Football Association (FIFA) . . . originally called the World Cup Trophy . . . renamed the Jules Rimet Cup (after the then FIFA president) in 1946, but retired by Brazil after that country's third title in 1970 . . . new World Cup trophy created in 1974 . . . designed by Italian sculptor Silvio Gazzaniga and made of solid 18 carat gold with two malachite rings inlaid at the base . . . measures 14.2 inches high and weighs 11 lbs . . . insured for $200,000 (U.S.) . . . competed for every four years . . . winning team gets gold-plated replica.

Commissioner's Trophy

First presented by the Commissioner of baseball to the winner of the 1967 World Series . . . also known as the World Championship Trophy . . . made of brass and gold plate with an ebony base and a baseball in the center made of pewter with a silver finish . . . designed by Balfour & Co. of Attleboro, Mass . . . 30 pennants represent 14 AL and 16 NL teams . . . measures 30 inches high and 36 inches around at the base and weighs 30 lbs . . . valued at $15,000 . . . competed for annually . . . winning team keeps trophy.

Larry O'Brien Trophy

First presented in 1978 to winner of NBA Finals . . . originally called the Walter A. Brown Trophy after the league pioneer and Boston Celtics owner (an earlier NBA championship bowl was also named after Brown) . . . renamed in 1984 in honor of outgoing commissioner O'Brien, who served from 1975-84 . . . made of sterling silver with 24 carat gold overlay and designed by Tiffany & Co. of New York . . . measures 2 feet high and weighs 14½ lbs (basketball depicted is regulation size) . . . valued at $13,500 . . . competed for annually . . . winning team keeps trophy.

Heisman Trophy

First presented in 1935 to the best college football player east of the Mississippi by the Downtown Athletic Club of New York . . . players across the entire country eligible since 1936 . . . originally called the DAC Trophy . . . renamed in 1936 following the death of DAC athletic director and former college coach John W. Heisman . . . made of bronze and designed by New York sculptor Frank Eliscu, it measures 13½ in. high, 6½ in. wide and 14 in. long at the base and weighs 25 lbs . . . valued at $2,000 . . . voting done by national media and former Heisman winners . . . trophy sponsor American Suzuki announced plans for limited fan voting starting in 1999 . . . awarded annually . . . winner keeps trophy.

James E. Sullivan Memorial Award

First presented by the Amateur Athletic Union (AAU) in 1930 as a gold medal and given to the nation's outstanding amateur athlete . . . trophy given since 1933 . . . named after the amateur sports movement pioneer, who was a founder and past president of AAU and the director of the 1904 Olympic Games in St. Louis . . . made of bronze with a marble base, it measures 17½ in. high and 11 in. wide at the base and weighs 13½ lbs . . . valued at $2,500 . . . voting done by AAU and USOC officials, former winners and selected media . . . awarded annually . . . winner keeps trophy.

Ryder Cup

Donated in 1927 by English seed merchant Samuel Ryder, who offered the gold cup for a biennial match between teams of golfing pros from Great Britain and the United States . . . the format changed in 1977 to include the best players on the European PGA Tour . . . made of 14 carat gold on a wood base and designed by Mappin and Webb of London . . . the golfer depicted on the top of the trophy is Ryder's friend and teaching pro Abe Mitchell . . . the cup measures 16 in. high and weighs 4 lbs . . . insured for $50,000 . . . competed for every two years at alternating European and U.S. sites . . . the cup is held by the PGA headquarters of the winning side.

Davis Cup

Donated by American college student and U.S. doubles champion Dwight F. Davis in 1900 and presented by the International Tennis Federation (ITF) to the winner of the annual 16-team men's competition . . . officially called the International Lawn Tennis Challenge Trophy . . . made of sterling silver and designed by Shreve, Crump and Low of Boston, the cup has a matching tray (added in 1921) and a very heavy two-tiered base containing rosters of past winning teams . . . it stands 34½ in. high and 108 in. around at the base and weighs 400 lbs . . . insured for $150,000 . . . competed for annually . . . trophy loaned to winning country for one year.

Borg-Warner Trophy

First presented by the Borg-Warner Automotive Co. of Chicago in 1936 to the winner of the Indianapolis 500 . . . replaced the Wheeler-Schebler Trophy which went to the 400-mile leader from 1911-32 . . . made of sterling silver with bas-relief sculptured heads of each winning driver and a gold bas-relief head of Tony Hulman, the owner of the Indy Speedway from 1945-77 . . . designed by Robert J. Hill and made by Gorham, Inc. of Rhode Island . . . measures 51½ in. high and weighs over 80 lbs . . . new base added in 1988 and the entire trophy restored in 1991 . . . competed for annually . . . insured for $1 million . . . trophy stays at Speedway Hall of Fame . . . winner gets a 14-in. high replica valued at $30,000.

NCAA Championship Trophy

First presented in 1952 by the NCAA to all 1st, 2nd and 3rd place teams in sports with sanctioned tournaments . . . 1st place teams receive gold-plated awards, 2nd place award is silver-plated and 3rd is bronze . . . replaced silver cup given to championship teams from 1939-51 . . . made of walnut, the trophy stands 24¾ in. high, 14⅛ in. wide and 4½ in. deep at the base and weighs 15 lbs . . . designed by Medallic Art Co. of Danbury, Conn. and made by House of Usher of Kansas City since 1990 . . . valued at $500 . . . competed for annually . . . winning teams keep trophies.

World Championship Belt

First presented in 1921 by the World Boxing Association, one of the three organizations (the World Boxing Council and International Boxing Federation are the others) generally accepted as sanctioning legitimate world championship fights . . . belt weighs 8 lbs. and is made of hand tanned leather . . . the outsized buckle measures 10½ in. high and 8 in. wide, is made of pewter with 24 carat gold plate and contains crystal and semi-precious stones . . . side panels of polished brass are for engraving title bout results . . . currently made by Champbelts by Ronn Scala in Pittsburgh . . . champions keep belts even if they lose their title.

World Championship Ring

Rings decorated with gems and engraving date back to ancient Egypt where the wealthy wore heavy gold and silver rings to indicate social status . . . championship rings in sports serve much the same purpose, indicating the wearer is a champion . . . As an example, the Dallas Cowboys' ring for winning Superbowl XXX on Jan. 28, 1996 was designed by Diamond Cutters International of Houston . . . each ring is made of 14 carat yellow gold, weighs 48-51 penny weights and features five trimmed marquis diamonds interlocking in the shape of the Cowboys' star logo as well as five more marquis diamonds (for the team's five Super Bowl wins) on a bed of 51 smaller diamonds . . . rings were appraised at over $30,000 each.

Boston Celtics' **Bill Russell** (6) and Philadelphia 76ers' **Wilt Chamberlain** (13) reach for a rebound at Boston Garden on Jan. 15, 1967.

Sports Personalities

Nine hundred sixty-five entries dating back to the 19th century. Entries updated through Oct. 1, 2007.

Hank Aaron (b. Feb. 5, 1934): Baseball OF; led NL in HRs and RBI 4 times each and batting twice with Milwaukee and Atlanta Braves; MVP in 1957; played in 24 All-Star Games; was all-time leader in HRs (755) until being passed by Barry Bonds in 2007; all-time leader in RBI (2,297), total bases (6,856), 3rd in hits (3,771); won 3 Gold Gloves.

Kareem Abdul-Jabbar (b. Lew Alcindor, Apr. 16, 1947): Basketball C; led UCLA to 3 NCAA titles (1967-69); Final 4 MOP 3 times; Player of Year twice; led Milwaukee (1) and LA Lakers (5) to 6 NBA titles; playoff MVP twice (1971,85), regular season MVP 6 times (1971-72,74,76-77,80); retired in 1989 after 20 seasons as all-time leader in over 20 categories.

Andre Agassi (b. Apr. 29, 1970): Tennis; 60 career tournament wins including the career grand slam; Wimbledon (1992), U.S. Open (1994,99), Australian Open (1995,2000,01,03), French Open (1999); helped U.S. win 2 Davis Cup finals (1990,92); regained the world No. 1 ranking in 1999 for the first time since 1996; retired after 2006 U.S. Open; married to former tennis star Steffi Graf.

Troy Aikman (b. Nov. 21, 1966): Football QB; consensus All-America at UCLA (1988); 1st overall pick in 1989 NFL Draft (by Dallas); led Cowboys to 3 Super Bowl titles (1992,93,95 seasons); MVP of Super Bowl XXVII; inducted into Pro Football HOF in 2006.

Marv Albert (b. June 12, 1941): Radio-TV; NBC announcer and radio broadcaster for the New York Knicks, Rangers and Giants who pleaded guilty to a misdemeanor assault charge amid embarrassing allegations of his sex life. Rehired to MSG and Turner networks in 1998 and NBC in '99.

Tenley Albright (b. July 18, 1935): Figure skater; 2-time world champion (1953,55); won Olympic silver (1952) and gold (1956) medals; became a surgeon.

Amy Alcott (b. Feb. 22, 1956): Golfer; 29 career wins, including five majors; inducted into World Golf Hall of Fame in 1999.

Grover Cleveland (Pete) Alexander (b. Feb. 26, 1887, d. Nov. 4, 1950): Baseball RHP; won 20 or more games 9 times; 373 career wins and 90 shutouts.

Muhammad Ali (b. Cassius Clay, Jan. 17, 1942): Boxer; 1960 Olympic light heavyweight champion; 3-time world heavyweight champ (1964-67, 1974-78,1978-79); defeated Sonny Liston (1964), George Foreman (1974) and Leon Spinks (1978) for title; fought Joe Frazier in 3 memorable bouts (1971-75), winning twice; adopted Black Muslim faith in 1964 and changed name; stripped of title in 1967 after conviction for refusing induction into U.S. Army; verdict reversed by Supreme Court in 1971; career record of 56-5 with 37 KOs and 19 successful title defenses; lit the flaming cauldron to signal the beginning of the 1996 Summer Olympics in Atlanta.

Forrest (Phog) Allen (b. Nov. 18, 1885, d. Sept. 16, 1974): Basketball; college coach 48 years; directed Kansas to NCAA title (1952); 746 wins.

Bobby Allison (b. Dec. 3, 1937): Auto racer; 3-time winner of Daytona 500 (1978,82,88); NASCAR national champ in 1983; father of Davey.

Davey Allison (b. Feb. 25, 1961, d. July 13, 1993): Auto racer; stock car Rookie of Year (1987); winner of 19 NASCAR races, including 1992 Daytona 500; killed at age 32 in helicopter accident at Talladega Superspeedway; son of Bobby.

Roberto Alomar (b. Feb. 5, 1968): Baseball; 10-time Gold Glove second baseman; MVP of 1992 ALCS; became known well beyond baseball for spitting in the face of umpire John Hirschbeck.

Walter Alston (b. Dec. 1, 1911, d. Oct. 1, 1984): Baseball; managed Brooklyn-LA Dodgers 23 years, won 7 pennants and 4 World Series (1955,59,63,65); retired after 1976 season with 2,063 wins (2,040 regular season and 23 postseason).

Morten Andersen (b. Aug 19, 1960): Football P; all-time leading scorer in NFL history; played in mor games than anyone in NFL history (368 entering 200 season); signed by Falcons in Sept. 2007 – at age 4.

Gary Anderson (b. July 16, 1959): Football P 2nd leading scorer in NFL history; had perfect regul season in 1998 (59/59 PAT, 35/35 FG); led AFC i scoring 3 times and NFC once.

Sparky Anderson (b. Feb. 22, 1934): Basebal one of two managers (La Russa) to win World Serie in each league—Cincinnati in NL (1975-76) and Detro in AL (1984); 5th-ranked skipper on career list wit 2,228 wins (2,194 regular season and 34 postsea son; inducted into the Baseball Hall of Fame in 200(

Mario Andretti (b. Feb. 28, 1940): Auto race 4-time USAC-CART national champion (1965 66,69,84); only driver to win Daytona 500 (1967 Indy 500 (1969) and Formula One world title (1978 Indy 500 Rookie of Year (1965); retired after 199 racing season ranked 1st in poles (67) and starts (40? and 2nd in wins (52) on all-time CART list; father o Michael and Jeff, uncle of John, grandfather of Marco

Michael Andretti (b. Oct. 5, 1962): Auto race 1991 CART national champion with single-seaso record 8 wins; Indy 500 Rookie of Year (1984); le IndyCar in career wins; tried Formula One try in 1993; returne to IndyCar in 1994; son of Mario, father of Marco

Earl Anthony (b. Apr. 27, 1938, d. Aug. 14 2001): Bowler; 6-time PBA Bowler of Year; 41 caree titles; first to earn $100,000 in 1 season (1975); firs to earn $1 million in career; won 10 Majors (2 Tou nament of Champions, 6 PBA National Championship and 2 ABC Masters).

Said Aouita (b. Nov. 2, 1959): Moroccan runne won gold (5000m) and bronze (800m) in 198 Olympics; won 5000m at 1987 World Championships formerly held 2 world records recognized by IAAF– 2000m and 5000m.

Luis Aparicio (b. Apr. 29, 1934): Baseball SS retired as all-time leader in most games, assists an double plays by shortstop; led AL in stolen bases times (1956-64); 506 career steals.

Al Arbour (b. Nov. 1, 1932): Hockey; coache NY Islanders to 4 straight Stanley Cup titles (1980-83) retired after 1993-94 season; 2nd on all-time caree list with 904 wins (781 regular season and 123 pos season); inducted to Hockey Hall of Fame in 1996.

Eddie Arcaro (b. Feb. 19, 1916, d. Nov. 14 1997): Jockey; 2-time Triple Crown winner (Whirlawa in 1941, Citation in '48); he won Kentucky Derby times, Preakness and Belmont 6 times each.

Roone Arledge (b. July 8, 1931, d. Dec. 5 2002): Sports TV pioneer; innovator of live events anthology shows, Olympic coverage, "Monday Nigh Football" and "Wide World of Sports"; ran ABC Sport from 1968-86; ran ABC News from 1977-98.

Henry Armstrong (b. Dec. 12, 1912, d. Oc 22, 1988): Boxer; held feather-, light- and welterweigh titles simultaneously in 1938; pro record 152-21-8 wit 100 KOs.

Lance Armstrong (b. Sept. 18, 1971): Cyclist Texan who made cycling history becoming the first 6 time, then 7-time winner of the Tour de France (1999 2005); returned from treatment for testicular cancer to become the world's top cyclist; 4-time AP Mal Athlete of the Year.

Arthur Ashe (b. July 10, 1943, d. Feb. 6, 1993 Tennis; first black man to win U.S. Championship (1968 and Wimbledon (1975); 1st U.S. player to earn $100,000 in 1 year (1970); won Davis Cup as playe (1968-70) and captain (1981-82); wrote black sport history, *Hard Road to Glory*; announced in 1992 tha he was infected with AIDS virus from a blood transfu sion during 1983 heart surgery; in 1997, the new hom for the U.S. Open was named Arthur Ashe Stadium.

velyn Ashford (b. Apr. 15, 1957): Track & Field; nner of 4 Olympic gold medals—100m in 1984, d 4x100m in 1984, '88 and '92; also won silver dal in 100m in '88; member of 5 U.S. Olympic ms (1976-92); Inducted into Track and Field and men's Sports Halls of Fame in 1997.

ed Auerbach (b. Sept. 20, 1917, d. Oct. 28, 06): Basketball; retired as winningest all-time coach gular season and playoffs) in NBA history (now]; won 1,037 times in 20 years; as coach-GM, led ston to a record 9 NBA titles, including 8 in a row 259-66); also coached defunct Washington Capitols 246-49); NBA Coach of the Year award named after n; retired as Celtics coach in 1966 and as GM in ?; club president from 1970 to 1997 and then again ginning in 2001.

racy Austin (b. Dec. 12, 1962): Tennis; youngest yer to win U.S. Open (age 16 in 1979); won 2nd 5. Open in '81; named AP Female Athlete of Year ce before she was 20; recurring neck and back uries shortened career after 1983; youngest player er inducted into Tennis Hall of Fame (age 29 in 1992).

Paul Azinger (b. Jan. 6, 1960): Golf; PGA Player Year (1987); 12 career wins, including '93 PGA ampionship; missed most of '94 season overcoming lymphoma (a form of cancer) in right shoulder ade; member of 4 U.S. Ryder Cup teams 289,91,93,2002).

Bob Baffert (b. Jan. 13, 1953): Horse racing; ime Eclipse Award winner as outstanding trainer 997-99); trained 3 Kentucky Derby winners 997,98,02), 4 Preakness winners (1997,98,01,02) d 1 Belmont Stakes winner (2001); 4-time leading nual money leader for trainers (1998-01).

Donovan Bailey (b. Dec. 16, 1967): Track; naican-born Canadian sprinter who set world record the 100m (9.84) in gold medal-winning performance 1996 Olympics which stood until '99; set indoor cord in 50m (5.56) in 1996; member of Canadian 100 relay that won gold in 1996 Olympics.

Oksana Baiul (b. Feb. 26, 1977): Ukrainian fig-skater; 1993 world champion at age 15; edged incy Kerrigan by a 5-4 judges' vote for 1994 ympic gold medal.

Hobey Baker (b. Jan. 15, 1892, d. Dec. 21, 18): Football and hockey star at Princeton (1911-); member of college football and pro hockey Halls Fame; college hockey Player of Year award named him; killed in plane crash.

Seve Ballesteros (b. Apr. 9, 1957): Spanish golfer; s won British Open 3 times (1979,84,88) and Mas-s twice (1980,83); 3-time European Golfer of Year 986,88,91); led Europe to 5 Ryder Cup titles 285,87,89,95,97).

Ernie Banks (b. Jan. 31, 1931): Baseball SS-1B; d NL in home runs and RBI twice each; 2-time MVP 258-59) with Chicago Cubs; 512 career HRs.

Roger Bannister (b. Mar. 23, 1929): British run-r; first to run mile in less than 4 minutes (3:59.4 May 6, 1954).

Walter (Red) Barber (b. Feb. 17, 1908, d. Oct. , 1992): Radio-TV; renowned baseball play-by-play oadcaster for Cincinnati, Brooklyn and N.Y. Yankees m 1934-66; won Peabody Award for radio com-ntary in 1991.

Charles Barkley (b. Feb. 20, 1963): Basketball 5-time All-NBA 1st team with Philadelphia and oenix; U.S. Olympic Dream Team member in '92; 3A regular season MVP in 1993; currently a bas-ball announcer for TNT; inducted into Basketball Hall Fame in 2006.

Rick Barry (b. Mar. 28, 1944): Basketball F; only yer to lead both NBA and ABA in scoring; 5-time -NBA 1st team; Finals MVP with Golden St. in 1975. rfected the underhand foul shot.

Sammy Baugh (b. Mar. 17, 1914): Football QB-P; led Washington to NFL titles in 1937 (his rookie ar) and '42; led league in passing 6 times, punt-g 4 times and interceptions once.

Elgin Baylor (b. Sept. 16, 1934): Basketball F; Most Outstanding Player of Final Four in 1958; led Minneapolis-LA Lakers to 8 NBA Finals; 10-time All-NBA 1st team (1959-65,67-69); LA Clippers' Vice President of Basketball Operations.

Bob Beamon (b. Aug. 29, 1946): Track & Field; won 1968 Olympic gold medal in long jump with world record (29-ft, 2½in.) that shattered old mark by nearly 2 feet; record finally broken by 2 inches in 1991 by Mike Powell.

Franz Beckenbauer (b. Sept. 11, 1945): Soccer; captain of West German World Cup champions in 1974 then coached West Germany to World Cup title in 1990; invented sweeper position; played in U.S. for NY Cosmos (1977-80,83).

David Beckham (b. May 2, 1975): Soccer; Eng-lish star perhaps known more for his good looks, his 1999 marriage to former Spice Girl, Victoria Adams (Posh Spice), and his trademark free kick; captain of the English national team from 2000-2006; scored goals in 3 different World Cups (1998,2002,2006); played for Manchester United (1993-95, 1995-2003) then Real Madrid (2003-07) before coming to Amer-ica in 2007 to join the MLS' Los Angeles Galaxy.

Boris Becker (b. Nov. 22, 1967): German tennis player; 3-time Wimbledon champ (1985-86,89); youngest male (17) to win Wimbledon; led country to 1st Davis Cup win in 1988; has also won U.S. (1989) and Australian (1991,96) Opens.

Chuck Bednarik (b. May 1, 1925): Football C-LB; 2-time All-America at Penn and 7-time All-Pro with NFL Eagles as both center (1950) and linebacker (1951-56); missed only 3 games in 14 seasons; led Eagles to 1960 NFL title as a 35-year-old two-way player.

Clair Bee (b. Mar. 2, 1896, d. May 20, 1983): Basketball coach who led LIU to 2 undefeated sea-sons (1936,39) and 2 NIT titles (1939,41); his teams won 95 percent of their games between 1931-51, including 43 in a row from 1935-37; coached NBA Baltimore Bullets from 1952-54, but was only 34-116; contributions to game include 1-3-1 zone defense, 3-second rule and NBA 24-second clock.

Bill Belichick (b. Apr. 16, 1952): Football; long-time assistant to Bill Parcells who became head coach of N.E. Patriots in 2000 and went on to win 3 Super Bowls; gained unwanted attention in Sept. 2007 after a Patriots cameraman was found to have videotaped the NY Jets sidelines in an attempt to steal signals; 124 wins entering 2007 (13-3 postseason).

Jean Beliveau (b. Aug. 31, 1931): Hockey C; led Montreal to 10 Stanley Cups in 17 playoffs; play-off MVP (1965); 2-time regular season MVP (1956,64).

Bert Bell (b. Feb. 25, 1895, d. Oct. 11, 1959): Football; team owner and 2nd NFL commissioner (1946-59); proposed college draft in 1935 and instituted TV blackout rule.

James (Cool Papa) Bell (b. May 17, 1903, d. Mar. 8, 1991): Baseball; member of the Negro Leagues; widely considered the fastest player ever to play baseball; also coached for the Kansas City Mon-archs, teaching such players as Jackie Robinson; mem-ber of the National Baseball Hall of Fame.

Deane Beman (b. Apr. 22, 1938): Golf; 1st com-missioner of PGA Tour (1974-94); introduced "stadium golf" and created The Players Championship; as play-er, won U.S. Amateur twice and British Amateur once; inducted into the World Golf Hall of Fame in 2000.

Johnny Bench (b. Dec. 7, 1947): Baseball C; led NL in HRs twice and RBI 3 times; 2-time regular sea-son MVP (1970,72) with Cincinnati, World Series MVP in 1976; 389 career HRs.

Patty Berg (b. Feb. 13, 1918, d. Sept. 10, 2006): Golfer; 60 career pro wins, including 15 majors; 3-time AP Female Athlete of Year (1938,43,55).

Chris Berman (b. May 10, 1955): Radio-TV; 6-time National Sportscaster of Year famous for his nicknames and jovial studio anchoring on ESPN; play-by-play man first year Brown University football team won the Ivy League (1976).

Yogi Berra (b. May 12, 1925): Baseball C; played on 10 World Series winners with NY Yankees; holds WS records for games played (75), at bats (259) and hits (71); 3-time All MVP (1951,54-55); managed both Yankees (1964) and NY Mets (1973) to pennants.

Jay Berwanger (b. Mar. 19, 1914, d. June 26, 2002): Football HB; Univ. of Chicago star; won 1st Heisman Trophy in 1935; top selection in the 1st-ever NFL Draft (1936).

Gary Bettman (b. June 2, 1952): Hockey; former NBA executive, who was named first commissioner of NHL on Dec. 11, 1992; took office on Feb. 1, 1993; commissioner during NHL lockout of 2004-05.

Abebe Bikila (b. Aug. 7, 1932, d. Oct. 25, 1973): Ethiopian runner; 1st to win consecutive Olympic marathons (1960,64).

Matt Biondi (b. Oct. 8, 1965): Swimmer; won 7 medals in 1988 Olympics, including 5 gold (2 individual, 3 relay); won a total of 11 medals (8 gold, 2 silver and a bronze) in 3 Olympics (1984,88,92).

Larry Bird (b. Dec. 7, 1956): Basketball F; college Player of Year (1979) at Indiana St.; 1980 NBA Rookie of Year; 9-time All-NBA 1st team; 3-time regular season MVP (1984-86); led Boston to 3 NBA titles (1981,84, 86); 2-time Finals MVP (1984,86); U.S. Olympic Dream Team member in '92; inducted into Hall of Fame in 1998; in 1997, named coach of Indiana Pacers and won Coach of the Year honors in first season; led the Pacers to the NBA Finals in 2000 but lost in 6 games to the Lakers and retired; named president of basketball operations of Pacers in 2003.

The Black Sox: Eight Chicago White Sox players who were banned from baseball for life in 1921 for allegedly throwing the 1919 World Series— RHP Eddie Cicotte (1884-1969), OF Happy Felsch (1891-1964), 1B Chick Gandil (1887-1970), OF Shoeless Joe Jackson (1889-1951), INF Fred McMullin (1891-1952), SS Swede Risberg (1894-1975), 3B-SS Buck Weaver (1890-1956), and LHP Lefty Williams (1893-1959).

Earl (Red) Blaik (b. Feb. 15, 1897, d. May 6, 1989): Football; coached Army to consecutive national titles in 1944-45; 166 career wins and 3 Heisman winners (Blanchard, Davis, Dawkins).

Bonnie Blair (b. Mar. 18, 1964): Speed skater; only American woman to win 5 Olympic gold medals in Winter Games; won 500-meters in 1988, then 500-meters and 1,000-m in both 1992 and '94; added 1,000-m bronze in 1988; Sullivan Award winner (1992); retired on 31st birthday as reigning world sprint champ.

Hector (Toe) Blake (b. Aug. 21, 1912, d. May 17, 1995): Hockey LW; led Montreal to 2 Stanley Cups as a player and 8 more as coach; 1939 NHL MVP.

Felix (Doc) Blanchard (b. Dec. 11, 1924): Football FB; 3-time All-America; led Army to national titles in 1944-45; Glenn Davis' running mate; won Heisman Trophy and Sullivan Award in 1945.

George Blanda (b. Sept. 17, 1927): Football QB-PK; was pro football's all-time leading scorer (2,002 points) until 2000 when he was finally passed by kicker Gary Anderson; led Houston to 2 AFL titles (1960-61); played 26 pro seasons; retired at age 48.

Fanny Blankers-Koen (b. Apr. 26, 1918, d. Jan. 25, 2004): Dutch sprinter; 30-year-old mother of two, who won 4 gold medals (100m, 200m, 800m hurdles and 4x100m relay) at 1948 Olympics.

Drew Bledsoe (b. Feb. 14, 1972): Football QB; 1st overall pick in 1993 NFL draft (N.E. Patriots); one of only 10 QBs in NFL history with 40,000 career passing yards; played with Buffalo (2002-04) then Dallas (2005-06); announced retirement in April, 2007.

Jim Boeheim (b. Nov. 17, 1944): Basketball; long-time coach at Syracuse; won 1st NCAA title in 2003; one of 19 Div. I coaches with 700 career victories.

Wade Boggs (b. June 15, 1958): Baseball 3B; 5 AL batting titles (1983,85-88) with Boston Red Sox; 11-time All-Star; two Gold Gloves; later played with NY Yankees and Tampa Bay; retired in 1999 with 3,010 hits (3,000th hit was a HR); inducted into Hall of Fame in 2005.

Barry Bonds (b. July 24, 1964): Baseball OF; MLB all-time and single-season home run leader; broke Hank Aaron's career record with his 756th HR on Aug. 7, 2007 — a shot to right-center off Washington lefty Mike Bacsik; set MLB single-season HR record in 2001 with 73; 7-time NL MVP, 2 with Pittsburgh (1990,92) and 5 with San Francisco (1993,2001-04); one of only 3 men with 40 HRs and 40 SBs in same season (1996); holds major league record for single season (2004) and career walks; hit .370 in 2002 at age 38; finished 2007 season with 762 HR; polarizing and controversial, he is viewed by many as a poster child for baseball's steroid problems; son of Bobby.

Bjorn Borg (b. June 6, 1956): Swedish tennis player; 2-time Player of Year (1979-80); won 6 French Opens and 5 straight Wimbledons (1976-80); led Sweden to 1st Davis Cup win in 1975; retired in 1983 at age 26; attempted unsuccessful comeback in 1991.

Mike Bossy (b. Jan. 22, 1957): Hockey RW; led NY Isles to 4 Stanley Cups; playoff MVP in 1982; 50 goals or more 9 straight years; 573 career goals.

Ralph Boston (b. May 9, 1939): Track & Field; medaled in 3 consecutive Olympic long jumps— gold (1960), silver (1964), bronze (1968).

Ray Bourque (b. Dec. 28, 1960): Hockey; 12-time All-NHL 1st team; won 5 Norris Trophies (1987-88,1990-91,94) with Boston; '96 All-Star Game MVP; all-time leader for points and assists by a defenseman; won 2001 Stanley Cup with Colorado then retired; elected to Hall of Fame in 2004.

Bobby Bowden (b. Nov. 8, 1929): Football; coached Florida St. to 2 national titles (1993,99); entered 2007 season as all-time wins leader in college football history with 366 victories including 20-9-1 bowl record in 41 years as coach at Samford, West Va. and FSU; father of Clemson head coach Tommy and former Auburn coach Terry.

Riddick Bowe (b. Aug. 10, 1967): Boxer; former undisputed heavyweight champ who fought career-defining trilogy with Evander Holyfield (1992-1995); won 1st meeting by decision, lost rematch in "Fan Man Fight," won last Holyfield fight by 8th-round KO.

Scotty Bowman (b. Sept. 18, 1933): Hockey coach; all-time winningest NHL coach in both regular season (1,244) and playoffs (223) over 30 seasons; coached a record nine Stanley Cup winners with Montreal (1973,76-79), Pittsburgh (1992) and Detroit (1997,98,2002); retired after 2001-02 season.

Jack Brabham (b. Apr. 2, 1926): Australian auto racer; 3-time Formula One champion (1959-60,66); 14 career wins; member of the Hall of Fame.

James J. Braddock (b. June 7, 1905, d. Nov. 29, 1974): Boxer; journeyman who won heavyweight belt in 10-1 upset of hard-hitting Max Baer in 1935.

Bill Bradley (b. July 28, 1943): Basketball F; 3-time All-America at Princeton; Player of the Year and Final 4 MOP in 1965; captain of gold medal-winning 1964 Olympic team; Sullivan Award winner (1965); led NY Knicks to 2 NBA titles (1970,73); U.S. Senator (D, N.J.) 1979-95; ran for President in 2000.

Pat Bradley (b. Mar. 24, 1951): Golfer; 2-time LPGA Player of Year (1986,91); won career LPGA grand slam, including 3 du Maurier Classics; inducted into the LPGA Hall of Fame on Jan. 18, 1992; among all-time LPGA money leaders and tournament winners (31); captained the 2000 U.S. Solheim Cup team.

Terry Bradshaw (b. Sept. 2, 1948): Football QB; led Pittsburgh to 4 Super Bowl titles (1975-76,79-80); 2-time Super Bowl MVP (1979-80) and regular season MVP in 1978; Fox TV studio analyst.

Tom Brady (b. Aug. 3, 1977): Football QB; 6th round draft pick (Michigan) who became 3-time Super Bowl winner with N.E. Patriots, 2-time Super Bowl MVP.

George Brett (b. May 15, 1953): Baseball 3B-1B; AL batting champion in 3 different decades (1976,80,90); MVP in 1980; led KC to World Series title in 1985; retired after 1993 season with 3,154 hits and .305 average; inducted into Hall of Fame in 1999.

Valerie Brisco-Hooks (b. July 6, 1960): Track & field; won three gold medals at the 1984 Olympics 00 meters, 400 meters and 4x100 relay); first athlete to ever win the 200 and 400 in the same Olympics.

Lou Brock (b. June 18, 1939): Baseball OF; former -time SB leader (938); led NL in SBs 8 times; led St. uis to 2 WS titles (1964,67); 3,023 career hits.

Herb Brooks (b. Aug. 5, 1937, d. Aug. 11, 003): Hockey; former U.S. Olympic player (1964,68) no coached 1980 "Miracle on Ice" team to gold edal and 2002 U.S. team to silver medal; coached innesota to 3 NCAA titles (1974,76,78); also ached 4 NHL teams.

Jim Brown (b. Feb. 17, 1936): Football FB; All-nerica at Syracuse (1956) and NFL Rookie of Year 957); led NFL in rushing 8 times; 8-time All-Pro 957-61,63-65); 3-time MVP (1958,63,65) with Cleve-nd; ran for 12,312 yards and scored 126 touch-owns in just 9 seasons; first player to reach the 100-uchdown milestone; member of pro and college otball halls of fame.

Larry Brown (b. Sept. 14, 1940): Basketball; ayed in ACC, AAU, 1964 Olympics and ABA; 3-e assist leader (1968-70) and 3-time Coach of Year 973,75-76) in ABA; coached ABA's Carolina and enver and NBA's Denver, N.J., San Antonio, LA Clip-rs, Indiana, Philadelphia, Detroit and N.Y. Knicks, inning the 2004 NBA title with Pistons; also coached CLA to NCAA Final (1980), Kansas to NCAA title 988) and the USA men's basketball team to a dis-pointing bronze medal in Athens in 2004.

Mordecai (Three-Finger) Brown (b. Oct. 18, 876, d. Feb. 14, 1948): Baseball; nickname derived om injury in a childhood accident that left him with ree digits on right hand; injury gave him a particu-rly nasty curve ball; won the decisive game of the e 1907 World Series as a Chicago Cub; in 1908, st pitcher to record 4 consecutive shutouts and fin-hed at 29-9; career record of 239-130 with lifetime A of 2.06; member of Hall of Fame.

Paul Brown (b. Sept. 7, 1908, d. Aug. 5, 1991): otball innovator; coached Ohio St. to national title 1942; in pros, directed Cleveland Browns to 4 aight AAFC titles (1946-49) and 3 NFL titles (1950,54-5); formed Cincinnati Bengals as head coach and rt owner in 1968 (reached playoffs in '70).

Valery Brumel (b. Apr. 14, 1942, d. Jan. 26, 003): Soviet high jumper; dominated event from 1961-4; broke world record 5 times; won silver in 1960 lympics and gold in 1964; highest jump was 7-5¾.

Avery Brundage (b. Sept. 28, 1887, d. May 5, 975): Amateur sports czar for over 40 years as pres-ent of AAU (1928-35), U.S. Olympic Committee 929-53) and Int'l Olympic Committee (1952-72).

Kobe Bryant (b. Aug. 23, 1978): Basketball; G/F r the LA Lakers; graduated from Lower Merion (Penn.) S and made the jump directly to the NBA; youngest ayer (18 yrs., 2 mos., 11 days) ever to appear in n NBA game; youngest all-star in NBA history; won consecutive titles with the Lakers (2000,01,02); accused rape in 2003 but charges were dropped in 2004.

Paul (Bear) Bryant (b. Sept. 11, 1913, d. Jan. 6, 1983): Football; coached at 4 colleges over 38 ears; directed Alabama to 6 national titles (1961,64-5,73,78-79); retired as the winningest coach of all-ne (323-85-17 record) finally passed by Joe Pater-o in 2001; 15 bowl wins, including 8 Sugar Bowls.

Sergey Bubka (b. Dec. 4, 1963): Ukrainian pole aulter; 1st man to clear 20 feet both indoors and out 991); holder of indoor (20-2) and outdoor (20-1¾) orld records; 6-time world champion (1983, 87, 91, 3, 95, 97); won Olympic gold medal in 1988, but iled to clear any height in 1992 Games.

Buck Buchanan (b. Sept. 10, 1940, d. July 16, 992): Football DT; played both ways in college at rambling; first pick in the first AFL draft by the Chiefs s Texans; missed one game in 13 seasons; star of C Chiefs team that won Super Bowl IV; later coached aints and Browns; member of Pro Football HOF.

Jack Buck (b. Aug. 21, 1924, d. June 18, 2002): Radio-TV; broadcast baseball games for St. Louis Cardinals from 1954-2001; CBS Radio voice for Monday Night Football (1978-96) and announcer for 1st televised AFL game in 1960; recipient of Baseball Hall of Fame's Ford Frick Award (1987) and Football Hall of Fame's Pete Rozelle Award (1996); received the Purple Heart in WWII; father of sportscaster Joe.

Don Budge (b. June 13, 1915, d. Jan. 26, 2000): Tennis; in 1938 became 1st player to win the Grand Slam— the French, Wimbledon, U.S. and Australian titles in 1 year; led U.S. to 2 Davis Cups (1937-38); turned pro in late '38.

Maria Bueno (b. Oct. 11, 1939): Brazilian tennis player; won 4 U.S. Championships (1959,63-64,66) and 3 Wimbledons (1959-60,64).

Leroy Burrell (b. Feb. 21, 1967): Track & Field; set former world record of 9.85 in 100 meters, July 6, 1994; previously held record (9.90) in 1991; member of 4 world record-breaking 4x100m relay teams.

Susan Butcher (b. Dec. 26, 1954, d. Aug. 5, 2006): Sled Dog racer; 4-time winner of Iditarod Trail race (1986-88,90).

Dick Butkus (b. Dec. 9, 1942): Football LB; 2-time All-America at Illinois (1963-64); All-Pro 7 of 9 NFL seasons with Chicago Bears; worked with XFL in 2001.

Dick Button (b. July 18, 1929): Figure skater; 5-time world champion (1948-52); 2-time Olympic champ (1948,52); Sullivan Award winner (1949); won Emmy Award as Best Analyst for 1980-81 TV season.

Walter Byers (b. Mar. 13, 1922): College athletics; 1st executive director of NCAA, serving from 1951-88.

Frank Calder (b. Nov. 17, 1877, d. Feb. 4, 1943): Hockey; 1st NHL president (1917-43); guided league through its formative years; NHL's Rookie of the Year award named after him.

Jim Calhoun (b. May 10, 1942): Basketball; has coached UConn to 2 NCAA titles (1999, 2004); inducted into Basketball Hall of Fame in 2005.

Lee Calhoun (b. Feb. 23, 1933, d. June 22, 1989): Track & Field; won consecutive Olympic gold medals in the 110m hurdles (1956,60).

Walter Camp (b. Apr. 7, 1859, d. Mar. 14, 1925): Football coach and innovator; established scrim-mage line, center snap, downs, 11 players per side; selected 1st team All-America team (1889).

Roy Campanella (b. Nov. 19, 1921, d. June 26, 1993): Baseball C; 3-time NL MVP (1951,53,55); led Brooklyn to 5 pennants and 1st World Series title (1955); career tragically cut short when he was paralyzed in a 1958 car crash.

Clarence Campbell (b. July 9, 1905, d. June 24, 1984): Hockey; 3rd NHL president (1946-77), league tripled in size from 6 to 18 teams during his tenure.

Earl Campbell (b. Mar. 29, 1955): Football RB; won Heisman Trophy in 1977; led NFL in rushing 3 times; 3-time All-Pro; 2-time MVP (1978-79) at Houston.

John Campbell (b. Apr. 8, 1955): Harness racing; 6-time winner of Hambletonian (1987,88,90,95,98, 2006); 3-time Driver of Year; first driver to go over $100 million in career winnings.

Milt Campbell (b. Dec. 9, 1933): Track & Field; won silver medal in 1952 Olympic decathlon and gold medal in '56.

Jimmy Cannon (b. 1910, d. Dec. 5, 1973): Tough, opinionated New York sportswriter and essayist who viewed sports as an extension of show business; protégé of Damon Runyon; covered World War II for Stars & Stripes.

Jose Canseco (b. July 2, 1964): Baseball OF/DH; 1986 AL ROY and 1988 MVP with the Oakland A's; became the 1st player in MLB history with 40 HRs and 40 steals in a season (1988); retired in 2003 with 462 career HRs; admitted steroid use in 2005 book.

Tony Canzoneri (b. Nov. 6, 1908, d. Dec. 9, 1959): Boxer; 2-time world lightweight champion (1930-33,35-36); pro record 141-24-10 with 44 KOs.

AP/Wide World Photos

Babe Ruth pats **Ty Cobb** on the head after a charity golf match on June 27, 1941. Each was a member of baseball's inaugural Hall of Fame class in 1936.

Jennifer Capriati (b. Mar. 29, 1976): Tennis; youngest Grand Slam semifinalist ever (age 14 in 1990 French Open); surprise gold medalist at 1992 Olympics; left Tour from 1994-96 due to personal problems; waged successful comeback, winning French Open (2001) and 2 Australian Opens (2001,02).

Harry Caray (b. Mar. 1, 1917, d. Feb. 18, 1998): Radio-TV; baseball play-by-play broadcaster for St. Louis Cardinals, Oakland, Chicago White Sox and Cubs 1945-98; father of sportscaster Skip and grandfather of sportscaster Chip.

Rod Carew (b. Oct. 1, 1945): Baseball 2B-1B; led AL in batting 7 times (1969,72-75,77-78) with Minnesota; MVP in 1977; had 3,053 career hits.

Steve Carlton (b. Dec. 22, 1944): Baseball LHP; won 20 or more games 6 times; 4-time Cy Young winner (1972,77,80,82) with Philadelphia; 329-244 career record; 4,136 career Ks.

JoAnne Carner (b. Apr. 4, 1939): Golfer; 5-time U.S. Amateur champion; 2-time U.S. Open champ; 3-time LPGA Player of Year (1974,81-82); 43 career wins.

Cris Carter (b. Nov. 25, 1965): Football; WR with Philadelphia (1987-89), Minnesota (1990-2001) and Miami (2002); twice caught 122 passes in a season (1994, '95), the first time establishing an NFL record for catches in a season that was beaten a year later; 2nd player to reach 1000 career catches.

Don Carter (b. July 29, 1926): Bowler; 6-time Bowler of Year (1953-54,57-58,60,62); voted Greatest of All-Time in 1970.

Joe Carter (b. Mar. 7, 1960): Baseball OF; 3-time All-America at Wichita St. (1979-81); won 1993 World Series for Toronto with 3-run HR in bottom of the 9th of Game 6.

Alexander Cartwright (b. Apr. 17, 1820, d. July 12, 1892): Baseball; engineer and draftsman who spread gospel of baseball from New York City to California gold fields; widely regarded as the father of modern game; his guidelines included setting 3 strikes for an out and 3 outs for each half inning.

Billy Casper (b. June 24, 1931): Golfer; 2-time PGA Player of Year (1966,70); has won U.S. Open (1959,66), Masters (1970), U.S. Senior Open (1983); compiled 51 PGA Tour wins and 9 on Senior Tour.

Tracy Caulkins (b. Jan. 11, 1963): Swimmer; wc 3 gold medals (2 individual) at 1984 Olympics; s 5 world records and won 48 U.S. national titles fro 1978-84; Sullivan Award winner (1978); 2-time Hond Broderick Cup winner (1982,84).

Steve Cauthen (b. May 1, 1960): Jockey; becam youngest jockey (18) to win the Triple Crown wi Affirmed in 1978; won a record $6.1 million in 197 winning the Eclipse Award as the nation's top rid and the award for AP male athlete of the year.

Evonne Goolagong Cawley (b. July 31, 1951 Australian tennis player; won Australian Open 4 time Wimbledon twice (1971,80), French once (1971).

Florence Chadwick (b. Nov. 9, 1917, d. Ma 15, 1995): Dominant distance swimmer of 1950s; s English Channel records from France to England (195C and England to France (1951 and '55).

Wilt Chamberlain (b. Aug. 21, 1936, d. Oc 12, 1999): Basketball C; consensus All-America 1957 and '58 at Kansas; Final Four MOP in 195; led NBA in scoring 7 times and rebounding 11 time 7-time All-NBA first team; 4-time MVP (1960,66-68) Philadelphia; scored 100 points vs. NY Knicks in He shey, Pa., Mar. 2, 1962; led 76ers (1967) and L Lakers (1972) to NBA titles; Finals MVP in 1972.

A.B. (Happy) Chandler (b. July 14, 1898, June 15, 1991): Baseball; former Kentucky governe and U.S. Senator who succeeded Judge Landis as con missioner in 1945; backed Branch Rickey's move 1947 to make Jackie Robinson 1st black player major leagues; deemed too pro-player and ousted k owners in 1951.

Michael Chang (b. Feb. 22, 1972): Tennis; wc the 1989 French Open, becoming the youngest men champion of a grand slam event (17 years, 3 months. went 11 consecutive years (1988-98) with at least on title; finished in top 10 in the ATP year-end rankin from 1992-97 (career high no. 2 in 1996).

Julio Cesar Chavez (b. July 12, 1962): Mexica boxer; world jr. welterweight champ (1989-94); als held titles as jr. lightweight (1984-87) and lightweig (1987-89); won over 100 bouts; 90-bout unbeate streak ended 1/29/94 when Frankie Randall won tit on split decision; Chavez won title back 4 month later.

Linford Christie (b. Apr. 2, 1960): British sprinter; won 100-meter gold medals at both 1992 Olympics (9.96) and '93 World Championships (9.87).

Jim Clark (b. Mar. 14, 1936, d. Apr. 7, 1968): Scottish auto racer; 2-time Formula One world champion (1963,65); won Indy 500 in 1965; killed in car crash.

Bobby Clarke (b. Aug. 13, 1949): Hockey C; led Philadelphia Flyers to consecutive Stanley Cups in 1974-75; 3-time regular season MVP (1973,75-76); currently Flyers Senior Vice President.

Ron Clarke (b. Feb. 21, 1937): Australian runner; from 1963-70 set 17 world records in races from 2 miles to 20,000m; never won Olympic gold medal.

Roger Clemens (b. Aug. 4, 1962): Baseball RHP; twice fanned MLB record 20 batters in 9-inning game (April 29, 1986 & Sept. 18, 1996); won a record 7 Cy Young Awards with Boston (1986-87,91), Toronto (1997,98), N.Y. Yankees (2001) and Houston (2004); AL MVP in 1986; won 2 World Series with N.Y. (1999-2000); got 300th win in 2003; led majors in ERA in 2005 at age 43; 2nd to Nolan Ryan in career K's.

Roberto Clemente (b. Aug. 18, 1934, d. Dec. 31, 1972): Baseball OF; hit over .300 13 times with Pittsburgh; led NL in batting 4 times; World Series MVP in 1971; regular season MVP in 1966; had 3,000 career hits; killed in plane crash; MLB Man of the Year award is named for him.

Alice Coachman (b. Nov. 9, 1923): Track & Field; became the first black woman to win an Olympic gold medal with her win in the high jump in 1948 (London); broke the high school and college high jump records despite not wearing any shoes; member of the National Track & Field Hall of Fame.

Ty Cobb (b. Dec. 18, 1886, d. July 17, 1961): Baseball OF; all-time highest career batting average (.367); hit over .400 3 times; led AL in batting 12 times and stolen bases 6 times with Detroit; MVP in 1911; had 4,191 career hits, 2,245 career runs and 892 steals; played 24 years (22 with Detroit, 2 with Philadelphia); nicknamed "The Georgia Peach"; part of Baseball Hall of Fame's inaugural class.

Mickey Cochrane (b. Apr. 6, 1903, d. June 28, 1962): Baseball C; led Philadelphia A's (1929-30) and Detroit (1935) to 3 World Series titles; 2-time AL MVP (1928,34).

Sebastian Coe (b. Sept. 29, 1956): British runner; won gold medal in 1500m and silver medal in 800m at both 1980 and '84 Olympics; long-time world record holder in 800m and 1000m; elected to Parliament as Conservative in 1992.

Paul Coffey (b. June 1, 1961): Hockey D; 3-time Norris Trophy winner; member of 4 Stanley Cup champions at Edmonton (1984-85,87) and Pittsburgh (1991); ranks 10th on NHL all-time scoring list; elected to Hall of Fame in 2004.

Rocky Colavito (b. August 10, 1933): Baseball OF; six-time all-star who hit 374 HRs over his 14-year career; hugely popular in Cleveland where he played from 1955-59 and then 1965-67; led the league in HRs in 1959 with 42 and RBI in 1965 with 108; hit four consecutive HRs in one game.

Eddie Collins (b. May 2, 1887, d. Mar. 25, 1951): Baseball 2B; led Philadelphia A's (1910-11) and Chicago White Sox (1917) to 3 World Series titles; AL MVP in 1914; had 3,311 career hits and 743 stolen bases.

Nadia Comaneci (b. Nov. 12, 1961): Romanian gymnast; first to record perfect 10 in Olympics; won 3 individual golds at 1976 Olympics and 2 more in '80.

Lionel Conacher (b. May 24, 1901, d. May 26, 1954): Canada's greatest all-around athlete; NHL hockey (2 Stanley Cups), CFL football (1 Grey Cup), minor league baseball, soccer, lacrosse, track, amateur boxing champion; member of Parliament (1949-54).

Tony Conigliaro (b. Jan. 7, 1945, d. Feb. 24, 1990): Baseball OF; youngest (20 years old) to lead the AL in HRs (32 in 1965); hit in the face with a fastball in 1967; came back to hit 36 HRs in 1970 with Red Sox, but was never the same.

Gene Conley (b. Nov. 10, 1930): Baseball and Basketball; played for World Series and NBA champions with Milwaukee Braves (1957) and Boston Celtics (1959-61); losing pitcher in 1954 All-Star Game and winning pitcher in 1955 Game; 91-96 record in 11 seasons.

Billy Conn (b. Oct. 8, 1917, d. May 29, 1993): Boxer; Pittsburgh native and world light heavyweight champion from 1939-41; nearly upset heavyweight champ Joe Louis in 1941 title bout, but was knocked out in 13th round; pro record 63-11-1 with 14 KOs.

Dennis Conner (b. Sept. 16, 1942): Sailing; 3-time America's Cup-winning skipper aboard *Freedom* (1980), *Stars & Stripes* (1987) and the *Stars & Stripes* catamaran (1988); only American skipper to lose Cup, first in 1983 when *Australia II* beat *Liberty* and again in '95 when New Zealand's *Black Magic* swept Conner and his *Stars & Stripes* crew aboard the borrowed *Young America*.

Maureen Connolly (b. Sept. 17, 1934, d. June 21, 1969): Tennis; 1st woman to win Grand Slam (in 1953 at age 18); horse riding accident ended her career in '54 at age 19; won 3 Wimbledons (1952-54), 3 U.S. Opens (1951-53), 2 French Opens (1953-54) and 1 Australian Open (1953); 3-time AP Female Athlete of Year (1951-53).

Jimmy Connors (b. Sept. 2, 1952): Tennis; No.1 player 5 times (1974-78); won 5 U.S. Opens, 2 Wimbledons and 1 Australian; rose from No. 936 at the close of 1990 to U.S. Open semifinals in 1991 at age 39; NCAA singles champ (1971); all-time leader in pro singles titles (109) and matches won at U.S. Open (98) and Wimbledon (84).

Jack Kent Cooke (b. Oct. 25, 1912, d. April 6, 1997): Football; sole owner of NFL Washington Redskins from 1985-97; teams won 2 Super Bowls (1988,92); also owned NBA Lakers and NHL Kings in LA; built LA Forum for $12 million in 1967.

Cynthia Cooper (b. April 14, 1963): Women's basketball G; won two NCAA basketball titles at USC (1983-84); won gold medal with U.S. team in 1988; 2-time WNBA MVP and 4-time league champion with Houston Comets; coach of WNBA's Phoenix Mercury 2001-02; coach of Prairie View A&M since 2005.

Angel Cordero Jr. (b. Nov. 8, 1942): Jockey; retired third on all-time list with 7,057 wins in 38,646 starts; won Kentucky Derby 3 times (1974,76,85), Preakness twice and Belmont once; 2-time Eclipse Award winner (1982-83).

Howard Cosell (b. Mar. 25, 1920, d. Apr. 23, 1995): Radio-TV; former ABC commentator on *Monday Night Football* and *Wide World of Sports*, who energized TV sports journalism with abrasive "tell it like it is" style.

Bob Costas (b. Mar. 22, 1952): Radio-TV; NBC broadcaster who has been anchor for NBA, NFL and Olympics as well as baseball play-by-play man; 15-time Emmy winner as studio host/play-by-play and 8-time National Sportscaster of Year.

James (Doc) Counsilman (b. Dec. 28, 1920, d. Jan. 4, 2004): Swimming; coached Indiana men's swim team to 6 NCAA championships (1968-73); coached the 1964 and '76 U.S. men's Olympic teams that won a combined 21 of 24 gold medals; in 1979 became oldest person (59) to swim English Channel; retired in 1990 with dual meet record of 287-36-1.

Fred Couples (b. Oct. 3, 1959): Golfer; 2-time PGA Tour Player of the Year (1991,92); 15 Tour victories, including 1992 Masters.

Jim Courier (b. Aug. 17, 1970): Tennis; No. 1 player in world in 1992, won 2 Australian Opens (1992-93) and 2 French Opens (1991-92); played on 1992 Davis Cup winner; Nick Bollettieri Academy classmate of Andre Agassi; entered Hall of Fame in 2005.

Margaret Smith Court (b. July 16, 1942): Australian tennis player; won Grand Slam in both singles (1970) and mixed doubles (1963 with Ken Fletcher); record 24 Grand Slam singles titles—11 Australian, 5 U.S., 5 French and 3 Wimbledon.

Bob Cousy (b. Aug. 9, 1928): Basketball G; led NBA in assists 8 times; 10-time All-NBA 1st team; 1957 MVP; led Boston to 6 NBA titles (1957,59-63); elected to Hall of Fame in 1970, one of NBA's 50 Greatest Players.

Buster Crabbe (b. Feb. 7, 1908, d. Apr. 23, 1983): Swimmer; 2-time Olympic freestyle medalist with bronze in 1928 (1500m) and gold in '32 (400m); became movie star and King of Serials as Flash Gordon and Buck Rogers.

Ben Crenshaw (b. Jan. 11, 1952): Golfer; co-NCAA champion with Tom Kite in 1972; battled Graves' disease in mid-1980s; 19 career Tour victories; won Masters for second time in 1995 and dedicated it to 90-year-old mentor Harvey Penick, who had died a week earlier; captain of 1999 Ryder Cup team.

Joe Cronin (b. Oct. 12, 1906, d. Sept. 7, 1984): Baseball SS; hit over .300 and drove in over 100 runs 8 times each; player-manager in Washington and Boston (1933-47); AL president (1959-73).

Larry Csonka (b. Dec. 25, 1946): Football RB; powerful runner and blocker who gained 8,081 yards in 11 seasons in the AFL and NFL; won two consecutive Super Bowls with the Miami Dolphins (1973-74) and was named MVP in the latter, rushing for 145 yards and two TDs; member of the College and Pro Football Halls of Fame; rescued from storm-tossed vessel by Coast Guard in Bering Sea in 2005.

Mark Cuban (b. July 31, 1958): Basketball; enthusiastic, outspoken owner of the Dallas Mavericks; co-creator of Broadcast.com, which he sold to Yahoo! in 1999 for roughly $5 billion in Yahoo! stock; purchased the Mavericks in 2000 for $280 million; has spent slightly less than that in fines to the NBA for, among other things, criticizing officials and getting involved in on-court fracases.

Ann Curtis (b. Mar. 6, 1926): Swimming; won two gold medals and one silver in 1948 Olympics; set four world and 18 U.S. records during career; first woman and swimmer to win Sullivan Award (1944).

Betty Cuthbert (b. Apr. 20, 1938): Australian runner; won gold medals in 100 and 200 meters and 4x100m relay at 1956 Olympics; also won 400m gold at 1964 Olympics.

Bjorn Dählie (b. June 19, 1967): Norwegian cross-country skier; winner of a record eight gold and 12 overall Winter Olympic medals from 1992-98.

Chuck Daly (b. July 20, 1930): Basketball; coached Detroit to two NBA titles (1989-90); also coached NBA "Dream Team" to gold medal in 1992 Olympics; retired in 1994 but returned in 1997 to coach Orlando Magic for two seasons.

John Daly (b. Apr. 28, 1966): Golfer; big hitter who was surprise winner of 1991 PGA Championship as unknown 25-year old; battled through personal troubles in 1994 to return in '95 and win 2nd major at British Open, beating Italy's Costantino Rocca in 4-hole playoff; won first PGA Tour event in nine years at 2004 Buick Invitational; has admitted to accumulating somewhere in the range of $50-60 million in gambling losses.

Johnny Damon (b. Nov. 5, 1973): Baseball CF; long-haired lead-off man for the 2004 World Series champion Boston Red Sox; became a short-haired lead-off man when he was signed by NY Yankees in 2006.

Stanley Dancer (b. July 25, 1927, d. Sept. 8, 2005): Harness racing; winner of 4 Hambletonians; trainer-driver of Triple Crown winners in trotting (Nevele Pride in 1968 and Super Bowl in '72) and pacing (Most Happy Fella in 1970).

Beth Daniel (b. Oct. 14, 1956): Golfer; 33 career wins, including 1 major; inducted into World Golf Hall of Fame in 1999.

Alvin Dark (b. Jan. 7, 1922): Baseball IF and MGR; hit .322 to win the NL Rookie of the Year award in 1948 with the Boston Braves; won 994 games as a manager and led the Oakland A's to a World Series win in 1974.

Tamas Darnyi (b. June 3, 1967): Hungarian swimmer; 2-time double gold medal winner in 200m and 400m individual medley at 1988 and '92 Olympics; also won both events in 1986 and '91 world championships; set world records in both at '91 worlds; 1st swimmer to break 2 minutes in 200m IM (1:59:36).

Lindsay Davenport (b. June 8, 1976): Tennis player; became first American female ranked No. 1 in the world (1998) since Chris Evert in 1985; won U.S. Open (1998), Wimbledon (1999) and Australian Open (2000); won Olympic gold medal in 1996.

Al Davis (b. July 4, 1929): Football; GM-coach of Oakland 1963-66; helped force AFL-NFL merger as AFL commissioner in 1966; returned to Oakland as managing general partner and directed club to 3 Super Bowl wins (1977,81,84); defied fellow NFL owners and moved Raiders to LA in 1982; turned down owners' 1995 offer to build him a new stadium in LA and moved back to Oakland instead.

Dwight Davis (b. July 5, 1879, d. Nov. 28, 1945): Tennis; donor of Davis Cup; played for winning U.S. team in 1st two Cup finals (1900,02); won U.S. and Wimbledon doubles titles in 1901; Secretary of War (1925-29) under President Coolidge.

Ernie Davis (b. Dec. 14, 1939, d. May 18, 1963): Football; star running back at Syracuse University; first black player to win the Heisman Trophy in 1961; drafted by the Washington Redskins and traded to Cleveland but died the following year of leukemia before playing a pro game.

Glenn Davis (b. Dec. 26, 1924, d. Mar. 9, 2005): Football HB; 3-time All-America; led Army to national titles in 1944-45; Doc Blanchard's running mate; won Heisman Trophy in 1946.

John Davis (b. Jan. 12, 1921, d. July 13, 1984): Weightlifting; 6-time world champion; 2-time Olympic super-heavyweight champ (1948,52); undefeated from 1938-53.

Terrell Davis (b. Oct. 28, 1972): Football RB; 1998 NFL MVP, rushing for a league-leading 2,008 yards (4th all-time); played for two Super Bowl winners in Denver (XXXII and XXXIII), earning MVP honors in the former with Super Bowl-record 3 rushing touchdownss.

Pat Day (b. Oct. 13, 1953): Jockey; four-time Eclipse award winner (1984,86,87,91); became all-time leader in earnings in 2002; 4th all-time with 8,803 career victories; won Kentucky Derby (1992), five Preaknesses (1985,90,94-96) and three Belmonts (1989,94,2000); inducted into Hall of Fame in 1991; retired in 2005.

Ron Dayne (b. Mar. 14, 1978): Football RB; NCAA Div. I-A all-time leading rusher, gaining 6,397 yards at Wisconsin (1996-99); 1999 Heisman Trophy winner; selected in 1st round (11th overall) of 2000 NFL draft by NY Giants.

Dizzy Dean (b. Jan. 16 1911, d. July 17, 1974): Baseball RHP; led NL in strikeouts and complete games four times; last NL pitcher to win 30 games (30-7 in 1934); MVP in 1934 with St. Louis; 150-83 all-time record.

Dave DeBusschere (b. Oct. 16, 1940, d. May, 14, 2003): Basketball F; youngest coach in NBA history (24 in 1964); player-coach of Detroit Pistons (1964-67); played in 8 All-Star games; won 2 NBA titles as player with NY Knicks (1970, 73); ABA commissioner (1975-76); also pitched 2 seasons for Chicago White Sox (1962-63) with 3-4 record.

Pierre de Coubertin (b. Jan. 1, 1863, d. Sept. 2, 1937): French educator; father of the Modern Olympic Games; IOC president from 1896-1925.

Brian Deegan (b. May 9, 1975): Freestyle Motocross Rider; early pioneer of FMX, winner of 10 combined X Games medals, first rider to land a 360 in competition, WFA Series champ (1999), L.A. Coliseum Supercross winner (1999–125cc), experienced numerous life-threatening crashes, featured in over 20 motocross videos.

Anita DeFrantz (b. Oct. 4, 1952): Olympics; attorney who became the International Olympic Committee's first female vice president in 1997; first woman to represent U.S. on IOC (elected in 1986); member of USOC Executive Committee; member of bronze medal U.S. women's eight-oared shell at Montreal in 1976.

Oscar De La Hoya (b. Feb. 4, 1973): Boxer; 1992 Olympic gold medallist (lightweight); has held world titles in 4 weight classes; was unbeaten until losing WBC Welterweight belt to Felix Trinidad in a majority decision in 1999; later moved to jr. middleweight and won WBA and WBC belts; TKO'd by Bernard Hopkins in their undisputed middleweight title fight in 2004; defeated Ricardo Mayorga in 2005 for WBC Super Welterweight title, then lost title to Floyd Mayweather Jr. in a split decision in May 2007.

Cedric Dempsey (b. Apr. 14, 1932): College sports; succeeded Dick Schultz as NCAA executive director (title later changed to president) in 1993 and served until the end of 2002; former athletic director at Pacific (1967-79), San Diego St. (1979), Houston (1979-82) and Arizona (1983-93).

Jack Dempsey (b. June 24, 1895, d. May 31, 1983): Boxer; world heavyweight champion from 1919-26; lost title to Gene Tunney, then lost "Long Count" rematch in 1927 when he floored Tunney in 7th round but failed to retreat to neutral corner; pro record 64-6-9 with 49 KOs.

Bob Devaney (b. April 13, 1915, d. May 9, 1997): Football; head coach at Wyoming from 1957-1961; from 1962 to 1972 built Nebraska into a college football power; won 2 consecutive national titles in 1970-71; later served as Nebraska's A.D.

Donna de Varona (b. Apr. 26, 1947): Swimming; won gold medals in 400 IM and 400 freestyle relay at 1964 Olympics; set 18 world records during career; co-founder of Women's Sports Foundation in 1974.

Gail Devers (b. Nov. 19, 1966): Track & Field; won Olympic gold medal in 100 meters in 1992 and '96; world champion in 100 meters (1993) and 100-meter hurdles (1993,95,99); overcame thyroid disorder (Graves' disease) that sidelined her in 1989-90 and nearly resulted in having both feet amputated.

Eric Dickerson (b. Sept. 2, 1960): Football RB; led NFL in rushing 4 times (1983-84,86,88); ran for single-season record 2,105 yards in 1984; NFC Rookie of Year in 1983; All-Pro 5 times; traded from LA Rams to Indianapolis (Oct. 31, 1987) in 3-team, 10-player deal (including draft picks); 6th on all-time career rushing list with 13,259 yards in 11 seasons.

Harrison Dillard (b. July 8, 1923): Track & Field; only man to win Olympic gold medals in both sprints (100m in 1948) and hurdles (110m in 1952).

Joe DiMaggio (b. Nov. 25, 1914, d. Mar. 8, 1999): Baseball OF; hit safely in 56 straight games (1941); led AL in batting, HRs and RBI twice each; 3-time MVP (1939,41,47); hit .325 with 361 HRs over 13 seasons; led NY Yankees to 10 World Series titles.

Marcel Dionne (b. Aug. 3, 1951): Hockey C; fifth on NHL's all-time points list (1,771) and fourth on goals list (731) through 2007; tied Wayne Gretzky for the league lead in points (137) in 1980; scored 50 goals in a season 6 times; member of the Hockey HOF.

Mike Ditka (b. Oct. 18, 1939): Football; All-America at Pitt (1960); NFL Rookie of Year (1961); 5-time Pro Bowl tight end for Chicago Bears; returned to Chicago as head coach in 1982 and won Super Bowl XX in 1986; left Bears in 1992 and worked as a broadcaster at NBC for four years; coached the New Orleans Saints from 1997-99; compiled 127-101-0 record in 14 seasons; currently an analyst on ESPN.

Larry Doby (b. Dec. 13, 1924, d. June 18, 2003): Baseball OF; first black player in the AL; joined the Cleveland Indians in July 1947, three months after Jackie Robinson entered the Majors with the NL's Brooklyn Dodgers; an all-star centerfielder from 1949-55; managed the Chicago White Sox in 1978, becoming the second black major league manager; inducted into the Hall of Fame in 1998.

Charlotte (Lottie) Dod (b. Sept. 24, 1871, d. June 27, 1960): British athlete; 5-time Wimbledon singles champion (1887-88,91-93); youngest player ever to win Wimbledon (15 in 1887); archery silver medalist at 1908 Olympics; member of national field hockey team in 1899; 1904 British Amateur golf champ.

Tim Donaghy (b. Jan. 7, 1967): Basketball; NBA referee from 1994-2007; rocked the NBA in 2007 when he plead guilty to betting on games, including some he officiated, and providing inside information to other bettors.

Tony Dorsett (b. Apr. 7, 1954): Football RB; won Heisman Trophy leading Pitt to national title in 1976; 3rd all-time in NCAA Div. I-A rushing with 6,082 yards; led Dallas to Super Bowl title as NFC Rookie of Year (1977); NFC Player of Year (1981); rushed for 12,739 yards in 12 years.

James (Buster) Douglas (b. Apr. 7, 1960): Boxer; 42-1 shot who knocked out undefeated Mike Tyson in 10th round on Feb. 10, 1990 to win heavyweight title in Tokyo; 8½ months later, lost only title defense to Evander Holyfield by KO in 3rd round.

Vicki Manalo Draves (b. Dec. 31, 1924): Diver; First woman in olympic history to win gold medals in both platform diving and springboard diving; inducted into Int'l Swimming Hall of Fame in 1969.

The Dream Team Head coach Chuck Daly's "Best Ever" 12-man NBA All-Star squad that headlined the 1992 Summer Olympics in Barcelona and easily won the basketball gold medal; co-captained by Larry Bird and Magic Johnson, with veterans Charles Barkley, Clyde Drexler, Patrick Ewing, Michael Jordan, Karl Malone, Chris Mullin, Scottie Pippen, David Robinson, John Stockton and Duke's Christian Laettner.

Heike Drechsler (b. Dec. 16, 1964): German long jumper and sprinter; East German before reunification in 1991; set world long jump record (24-2¼) in 1988; won long jump gold medals at 1992 Olympics and 1983 and '93 World Championships.

Ken Dryden (b. Aug. 8, 1947): Hockey G; led Montreal to 6 Stanley Cup titles; playoff MVP as rookie in 1971; won or shared 5 Vezina trophies; 2.24 career GAA; Canadian politician, lawyer and businessman.

Don Drysdale (b. July 23, 1936, d. July 3, 1993): Baseball RHP; led NL in strikeouts 3 times and games started 4 straight years; pitched record 6 shutouts in a row in 1968; won Cy Young (1962); had 209-166 record and hit 29 HRs in 14 years.

Charley Dumas (b. Feb. 12, 1937): U.S. high jumper; first man to clear 7 feet (7-0½) on June 29, 1956; won gold medal at 1956 Olympics.

Tim Duncan (b. Apr. 25, 1976): Basketball C/F; drafted first overall by San Antonio in 1997 NBA Draft; 7-footer who dominates on offense and defense; has won 4 NBA titles (1999, 2003, 2005, 2007) earning Finals MVP honors each time; 2-time NBA MVP (2002-03); 1997 College Player of the Year at Wake Forest; 1998 NBA Rookie of the Year.

Margaret Osborne du Pont (b. Mar. 4, 1918): Tennis; won 5 French, 7 Wimbledon and an unprecedented 25 U.S. national titles in singles, doubles and mixed doubles from 1941-62.

Roberto Duran (b. June 16, 1951): Panamanian boxer; one of only 6 fighters to hold 4 different world titles— lightweight (1972-79), welterweight (1980), junior middleweight (1983) and middleweight (1989-90); lost famous "No Mas" welterweight title bout when he quit in 8th round against Sugar Ray Leonard (1980); retired in 2002 at age 50 (104-16, 69 KOs).

Tony Dungy (b. Oct. 6, 1955): Football; Coach of Tampa Bay Buccaneers from 1996-2001 and current coach of Indianapolis Colts since 2002; became first black head coach in NFL history to win a Super Bowl with the Colts' victory over the Bears in 2007; also won Super Bowl as a player with Steelers (1978).

Leo Durocher (b. July 27, 1905, d. Oct. 7, 1991): Baseball; managed in NL 24 years; won 2,015 games, including postseason; 3 pennants with Brooklyn (1941) and NY Giants (1951,54); won World Series in 1954.

Eddie Eagan (b. Apr. 26, 1898, d. June 14, 1967): Only athlete to win gold medals in both Summer and Winter Olympics (Boxing–1920, Bobsled–1932).

Alan Eagleson (b. Apr. 24, 1933): Hockey; Toronto lawyer, agent and 1st executive director of NHL Players Assn. (1967-90); midwifed Team Canada vs. Soviet series (1972) and Canada Cup; charged with racketeering and defrauding NHLPA in indictment handed down by U.S. grand jury in 1994; was sentenced to 18 months in jail in Jan. 1998 after pleading guilty but only served 6 months; resigned from Hall of Fame in 1998.

Dale Earnhardt (b. Apr. 29, 1951, d. Feb. 18, 2001): Auto racer; 7-time NASCAR national champion (1980,86-87,90-91,93-94); Rookie of Year in 1979; was all-time NASCAR money leader with over $34 million won and 76 career wins when he died; finally won Daytona 500 in 1998 on 20th attempt; died in last lap crash at the 2001 Daytona 500.

James Easton (b. July 26, 1935): Olympics; archer and sporting goods manufacturer (Easton softball bats); one of 4 American delegates to the International Olympic Committee; president of International Archery Federation (FITA); member of LA Olympic Organizing Committee in 1984.

Dennis Eckersley (b. Oct. 3, 1954): Baseball P; began his career as a starter in 1975 with Cleveland; no-hit Angels in 1977; won 20 games in 1978 with Boston; moved to the bullpen after 12 seasons as a starter and became one of the best closers of all-time with Oakland; won 1992 AL Cy Young and MVP.

Stefan Edberg (b. Jan. 19, 1966): Swedish tennis player; 2-time No.1 player (1990-91); 2-time winner of Australian Open (1985,87), Wimbledon (1988,90) and U.S. Open (1991-92).

Gertrude Ederle (b. Oct. 23, 1906, d. Nov. 30, 2003): Swimmer; 1st woman to swim English Channel, breaking men's record by 2 hours in 1926; won 3 medals in 1924 Olympics.

Krisztina Egerszegi (b. Aug. 16, 1974): Hungarian swimmer; 3-time gold medal winner (100m and 200m backstroke and 400m IM) at 1992 Olympics; also won a gold (200m back) and silver (100m back) at 1988 Games; youngest (14) ever to win swimming gold. Won fifth gold medal (200m back) at '96 Games.

Lee Elder (b. July 14, 1934): Golf; in 1975, became the first black golfer to play in the Masters Tournament; also played in the 1977 Masters; member of the 1979 U.S. Ryder Cup team; played in South Africa's first integrated tournament in 1972.

Todd Eldredge (b. Aug. 28, 1971): Figure Skater; 6-time U.S. champion (1990,91,95,97,98,2002); 1996 World Champion; won U.S. titles at all three levels (novice, junior and senior); most decorated American figure skater without an Olympic medal.

Bill Elliott (b. Oct. 8, 1955): Auto racer; 2-time winner of Daytona 500 (1985,87); NASCAR national champ in 1988; 44 career NASCAR wins.

Herb Elliott (b. Feb. 25, 1938): Australian runner; undefeated from 1958-60; ran 17 sub-4:00 miles; 3 world records; won gold medal in 1500 meters at 1960 Olympics; retired at age 22.

Ernie Els (b. Oct. 17, 1969): Golfer; sweet swinging South African; 1994 PGA Tour Rookie of the Year and European Golfer of the Year; 2-time U.S. Open winner (1994,97); won 3rd major in 2002 British Open playoff; 15 PGA Tour wins.

John Elway (b. June 28, 1960): Football QB; All-American at Stanford; #1 overall pick in the famous quarterback draft of 1983; known for his last-minute, game-winning scoring drives; led Broncos to 3 Super Bowl losses before back-to-back wins in Super Bowl XXXII and XXXIII; 1987 NFL MVP; 4-time Pro Bowler; one of only three quarterbacks (Marino & Favre) to throw for over 50,000 yards.

Roy Emerson (b. Nov. 3, 1936): Australian tennis player; won 12 majors in singles— 6 Australian, 2 French, 2 Wimbledon and 2 U.S. from 1961-67.

Kornelia Ender (b. Oct. 25, 1958): East German swimmer; 1st woman to win 4 gold medals at one Olympics (1976), all in world-record time.

Julius Erving (b. Feb. 22, 1950): Basketball F; "Dr. J"; changed game in the ABA, then NBA with his "above-the-rim" style of play; in ABA (1971-76): 3-time MVP, 3-time playoff MVP, led NY Nets to 2 titles (1974,76); in NBA (1976-87): 5-time All-NBA 1st team, MVP in 1981, led Philadelphia 76ers to 1983 NBA title.

Phil Esposito (b. Feb. 20, 1942): Hockey C; 1st NHL player to score 100 points in a season (126 in 1969); 6-time All-NHL 1st team with Boston (1969-74); 2-time MVP (1969,74); 5-time scoring champ; star of 1972 Canada-Soviet series; former president-GM of Tampa Bay Lightning.

Janet Evans (b. Aug. 28, 1971): Swimmer; won 3 individual gold medals (400m & 800m freestyle, 400m IM) at 1988 Olympics; 1989 Sullivan Award winner; won 1 gold (800m) and 1 silver (400m) at 1992 Olympics.

Lee Evans (b. Feb. 25, 1947): Track & Field; dominant quarter-miler in world from 1966-72; world record in 400m set at 1968 Olympics stood 20 years.

Chris Evert (b. Dec. 21, 1954): Tennis; No. 1 player in world 5 times (1975-77,80-81); won at least 1 Grand Slam singles title every year from 1974-86; 18 majors in all— 7 French, 6 U.S., 3 Wimbledon and 2 Australian; retired after 1989 season with 154 singles titles and $8,896,195 in career earnings.

Weeb Ewbank (b. May 6, 1907, d. Nov. 18, 1998): Football; only coach to win NFL and AFL titles; led Baltimore to 2 NFL titles (1958-59) and NY Jets to Super Bowl III win.

Patrick Ewing (b. Aug. 5, 1962): Basketball C; 3-time All-America; led Georgetown to 3 NCAA Finals and 1984 title; Final 4 MOP in '84; 1986 NBA Rookie of Year with New York; All-NBA (1990); on U.S. Olympic gold medal-winning teams in 1984 and '92; named one of the NBA's 50 Greatest Players.

Ray Ewry (b. Oct. 14, 1873, d. Sept. 29, 1937): Track & Field; won 10 gold medals (although 2 are not recognized by IOC) over 4 consecutive Olympics (1900,04,06,08); all events he won (Standing HJ, LJ and TJ) were discontinued in 1912.

Nick Faldo (b. July 18, 1957): British golfer; 3-time winner of British Open (1987,90,92) and Masters (1989, 90, 96); 3-time European Golfer of Year (1989-90,92); PGA Player of Year in 1990.

Juan Manuel Fangio (b. June 24, 1911, d. July 17, 1995): Argentine auto racer; 5-time F1 world champ (1951,54-57); 24 career wins, retired in 1958.

Marshall Faulk (b. Feb. 26, 1973): Football RB; 3-time consensus All-America at San Diego St.; 2-time NCAA Div. I-A rushing leader (1991-92); 2nd overall pick (Indianapolis) of the 1994 NFL draft; traded to St.L Rams in 1999; NFL MVP in 2000 (AP/PFWA) and 2001 (Bell/PFWA); set NFL single season record with 26 TDs in 2000 (since broken).

Brett Favre (b. Oct. 10, 1969): Football; Strong-armed Southern Miss. QB drafted in 1991 in the 2nd round (33rd overall) by Atlanta; traded to Green Bay in 1992; 3-time league MVP (1995-97); 8-time Pro Bowl QB; led Packers to Super Bowl victory in 1997; became NFL all-time leader in TD passes in 2007; holds NFL quarterback record for consecutive games started with over 200...and counting.

Sergei Fedorov (b. Dec. 13, 1969): Hockey C; first Russian to win NHL Hart Trophy as 1993-94 regular season MVP; 5-time All-Star and 3-time Stanley Cup winner (1997,98,2002) with Detroit.

Roger Federer (b. Aug. 8, 1984): Tennis; top-ranked men's tennis player since October, 2004, the longest streak as the ATP's #1 player in history; winner of 12 Grand Slam events (tied with Roy Emerson and behind only Pete Sampras' 14): Australian Open (2004,06,07), Wimbledon (2003-07); U.S. Open (2004-07); recorded a 55-match win streak in North America; 3-time ATP Player of the Year (2004-06).

Donald Fehr (b. July 18, 1948): Baseball labor leader; protégé of Marvin Miller; executive director and general counsel of Major League Players Assn. since 1983; led players in 1994 "salary cap" strike that lasted eight months and resulted in first cancellation of World Series since 1904.

Bob Feller (b. Nov. 3, 1918): Baseball RHP; Hall of Fame fire-baller who led AL in strikeouts 7 times and wins 6 times with Cleveland Indians; threw 3 no-hitters and major league record 12 one-hitters; 266-162 record; amassed 2,581 Ks despite missing four seasons to military service during WWII.

Tom Ferguson (b. Dec. 20, 1950): Rodeo; 6-time All-Around champion (1974-79); 1st cowboy to win $100,000 in one season (1978); 1st to win $1 million in career (1986).

Herve Filion (b. Feb. 1, 1940): Harness racing; 10-time Driver of Year; first driver to win over 15,000 races.

Rollie Fingers (b. Aug. 25, 1946): Baseball RHP; mustachioed relief ace with 341 career saves; won AL MVP and Cy Young awards in 1981 with Milwaukee; World Series MVP in 1974 with Oakland; elected to Hall of Fame in 1992.

Charles O. Finley (b. Feb. 22, 1918, d. Feb. 19, 1997): Baseball owner; moved KC A's to Oakland in 1968; won 3 straight World Series from 1972-74; also owned teams in NHL and ABA.

Bobby Fischer (b. Mar. 9, 1943): Chess; at 15, became youngest international grandmaster in chess history; only American to hold world championship (1972-75); was stripped of title in 1975 after refusing to defend against Anatoly Karpov and became recluse; re-emerged to defeat old foe and former world champion Boris Spassky in 1992.

Carlton Fisk (b. Dec. 26, 1947): Baseball C; holds all-time major league record for games caught (2,226); also held HR record for catchers (351) until 2004 (Mike Piazza); AL Rookie of Year (1972) and 10-time All-Star; hit epic, 12th-inning Game 6 homer for Boston Red Sox in 1975 World Series; elected to the Hall of Fame in 2000.

Emerson Fittipaldi (b. Dec. 12, 1946): Brazilian auto racer; 2-time Formula One world champion (1972,74); 2-time winner of Indy 500 (1989,93); won overall IndyCar title in 1989.

Bob Fitzsimmons (b. May 26, 1863, d. Oct. 22, 1917): British boxer; held 3 world titles— middleweight (1881-97), heavyweight (1897-99) and light heavyweight (1903-05); pro record 40-11 with 32 KOs.

James (Sunny Jim) Fitzsimmons (b. July 23, 1874, d. Mar. 11, 1966): Horse racing; trained horses that won over 2,275 races, including 2 Triple Crown winners—Gallant Fox in 1930 and Omaha in '35.

Jim Fixx (b. Apr. 23, 1932, d. July 20, 1984): Running; author who popularized the sport of running; his 1977 bestseller The Complete Book of Running, is credited with helping start America's fitness revolution; ironically died of a heart attack while running.

Larry Fleisher (b. Sept. 26, 1930, d. May 4, 1989): Basketball; led NBA players union from 1961-89; increased average yearly salary from $9,400 in 1967 to $600,000 without a strike.

Peggy Fleming (b. July 27, 1948): Figure skating; 3-time world champion (1966-68); won Olympic gold medal in 1968.

Curt Flood (b. Jan. 18, 1938, d. Jan. 20, 1997): Baseball OF; played 15 years (1956-69,71) mainly with St. Louis; hit over .300 6 times with 7 Gold Gloves; refused trade to Phillies in 1969; lost challenge to baseball's reserve clause in Supreme Court in 1972 but his case helped bring free agency to MLB.

Ray Floyd (b. Sept. 14, 1942): Golfer; has 22 PGA victories in 4 decades; joined Senior PGA Tour in 1992 and has 14 Senior wins; has won Masters (1976), U.S. Open (1986), PGA twice (1969,82) and PGA Seniors Championship (1995); first player to win on PGA and Senior tours in same year (1992); member of 8 Ryder Cup teams and captain in 1989.

Doug Flutie (b. Oct. 23, 1962): Football QB; Boston College QB who threw famous 48-yard "Hail Mary" to defeat Miami on Nov. 23, 1984; 1984 Heisman Trophy winner; played in USFL, NFL and CFL; 6-time CFL MVP; led Calgary (1992) and Toronto (1996-97) to Grey Cup titles; on Jan. 1, 2007, recorded the NFL's first drop-kick since 1941; retired from football after the 2005 season (with New England).

Whitey Ford (b. Oct. 21, 1928): Baseball LHP; all-time leader in World Series wins (10); led AL in wins 3 times; won Cy Young and World Series MVP in 1961 with NY Yankees; 236-106 record.

George Foreman (b. Jan. 10, 1949): Boxer; Olympic heavyweight champ (1968); world heavyweight champ (1973-74, 94-95); lost title to Muhammad Ali (KO-8th) in '74; recaptured it on Nov. 5, 1994 at age 45 with a 10-round KO of WBA/IBF champ Michael Moorer, becoming the oldest man to win heavyweight crown; named AP Male Athlete of Year 20 years after losing title to Ali; stripped of WBA title in 1995 after declining to fight No. 1 contender; successfully defended title at age 46 against 26-year-old Axel Schulz in controversial maj. decision; gave up IBF title after refusing rematch with Schulz.

Dick Fosbury (b. Mar. 6, 1947): Track & Field; revolutionized high jump with back-first "Fosbury Flop"; won gold medal at 1968 Olympics.

Greg Foster (b. Aug. 4, 1958): Track & Field; 3-time winner of World Championship in 110-m hurdles (1983,87,91); won silver in 1984 Olympics; world indoor champion in 1991.

The Four Horsemen Senior backfield that led Notre Dame to national collegiate football championship in 1924; put together as sophomores by Irish coach Knute Rockne; immortalized by sportswriter Grantland Rice, whose report of the Oct. 19, 1924, Notre Dame-Army game began: "Outlined against a blue, gray October sky the Four Horsemen rode again..."; HB Jim Crowley (b. Sept. 10, 1902, d. Jan. 15, 1986), FB Elmer Layden (b. May 4, 1903, d. June 30, 1973), HB Don Miller (b. May 30, 1902, d. July 28, 1979) and QB Harry Stuhldreher (b. Oct. 14, 1901, d. Jan. 26, 1965).

The Four Musketeers French quartet that dominated men's tennis in 1920s and '30s, winning 8 straight French singles titles (1925-32), 6 Wimbledons in a row (1924-29) and 6 consecutive Davis Cups (1927-32)— Jean Borotra (b. Aug. 13, 1898, d. July 17, 1994), Jacques Brugnon (b. May 11, 1895, d. Mar. 20, 1978), Henri Cochet (b. Dec. 14, 1901, d. Apr. 1, 1987), Rene Lacoste (b. July 2, 1905, d. Oct. 13, 1996).

Nellie Fox (b. Dec. 25, 1927, d. Dec. 1, 1975): Baseball 2B; batted .306 in 1959 to win the AL MVP award with the pennant-winning Chicago White Sox; led the league in fielding percentage six times, hits four times and triples once; ended his 19-year career with 2,663 hits, 1,279 runs and .288 average.

Jimmie Foxx (b. Oct. 22, 1907, d. July 21, 1967): Baseball 1B; led AL in home runs 4 times and batting average twice; won Triple Crown in 1933; 3-time MVP (1932-33,38) with Philadelphia and Boston; hit 30 HRs or more 12 years in a row; 534 career HRs.

A.J. Foyt (b. Jan. 16, 1935): Auto racer; 7-time USAC-CART national champion (1960-61,63-64, 67,75,79); 4-time Indy 500 winner (1961,64, 67,77); only driver in history to win Indy 500, Daytona 500 (1972) and 24 Hours of LeMans (1967 with Dan Gurney); retired in 1993 as all-time CART wins leader with 67.

Bill France Sr. (b. Sept. 26, 1909, d. June 7, 1992): Stock car pioneer and promoter; founded NASCAR in 1948; guided race circuit through formative years; built both Daytona (Fla.) Int'l Speedway and Talladega (Ala.) Superspeedway.

Dawn Fraser (b. Sept. 4, 1937): Australian swimmer; won gold medals in 100m freestyle at 3 consecutive Olympics (1956,60,64).

Joe Frazier (b. Jan. 12, 1944): Boxer; 1964 Olympic heavyweight champion; world heavyweight champ (1970-73); decisioned former champ Muhammad Ali in March 1971 in one of the most anticipated prizefights in history, fought Ali twice more, losing both times including the "Thrilla in Manila" in 1975; pro record 32-4-1 with 27 KOs.

Walt Frazier (b. March 29, 1945): Basketball G; won the NBA championship twice (1970 and 73) with the New York Knicks; stole spotlight from teammate Willis Reed in Game 7 of 1970 Finals vs. the Lakers with 36 points, 19 assists and 5 steals; averaged 18.9 PPG and 6.1 APG over his career; four-time all-NBA and a member of the Hall of Fame; nicknamed "Clyde" after well-dressed gangster Clyde Barrow.

Cathy Freeman (b. Feb. 16, 1973): Track & Field; Australian Aborigine who lit the cauldron at the start of the 2000 Olympic Games in Sydney and later won gold in the 400-meters on her home soil; 2-time world champion in the 400-meters (1997,99).

Ford Frick (b. Dec. 19, 1894, d. Apr. 8, 1978): Baseball; sportswriter and radio announcer who served as NL president (1934-51) and commissioner (1951-65); convinced record-keepers to list Roger Maris' and Babe Ruth's season records separately; major leagues moved to West Coast and expanded from 16 to 20 teams during his tenure.

Frankie Frisch (b. Sept. 9, 1898, d. Mar. 12, 1973): Baseball 2B; played on 8 NL pennant winners in 19 years with NY and St. Louis; hit .300 or better 11 years in a row (1921-31); MVP in 1931; player-manager from 1933-37.

Dan Gable (b. Oct. 25, 1948): Wrestling; career wrestling record of 118-1 (Larry Owings beat him in his final collegiate match) at Iowa St., where he was a 2-time NCAA champ (1968,69) and tourney MVP in 1969 (137 lbs); won gold medal (149 lbs) at 1972 Olympics; coached Iowa to 9 straight NCAA titles (1978-86) and 15 overall in 21 years.

Eddie Gaedel (b. June 8, 1925, d. June 18, 1961): Baseball PH; St. Louis Browns' 3-foot-7 player whose career lasted one at bat (he walked) on Aug 19, 1951; hired as a publicity stunt by owner Bill Veeck.

Clarence (Big House) Gaines (b. May 21, 1924): Basketball; retired as coach of Div. II Winston-Salem in 1993 with 828-447 record in 47 years.

Alonzo (Jake) Gaither (b. Apr. 11, 1903, d. Feb. 18, 1994): Football; head coach at Florida A&M for 25 years; led Rattlers to 6 national black college titles; retired after 1969 season with record of 203-36-4 and a winning percentage of .844; coined phrase, "I like my boys agile, mobile and hostile."

Rulon Gardner (b. Aug. 16, 1971): Olympic wrestler; surprise winner of the super heavyweight Greco-Roman gold medal at the 2000 Sydney Games; beat unbeatable Russian legend Alexandre Kareline, 1-0; won 2000 Sullivan Award and USOC Sportsman of the Year Award; lost a toe to frostbite in 2002 but still took bronze medal in Athens (2004).

Cito Gaston (b. Mar. 17, 1944): Baseball; managed Toronto to consecutive World Series titles (1992-93); first black manager to win Series.

Justin Gatlin (b. Feb. 10, 1982): American sprinter; won 100m gold medal and 200m bronze at 2004 Summer Olympics in Athens; won 100m and 200m dashes at 2005 World Outdoor Championships; tied 100-m record (9.77) in May 2006; currently serving an 8-year ban for a 2nd positive drug test (under appeal).

Lou Gehrig (b. June 19, 1903, d. June 2, 1941): Baseball 1B; played in 2,130 consecutive games from 1925-39 a major league record until Cal Ripken Jr. surpassed it in 1995; led AL in RBI 5 times and HRs 3 times; drove in 100 runs or more 13 years in a row; 2-time MVP (1927,36); hit .340 with 493 HRs over 17 seasons; led NY Yankees to 6 World Series titles; died at age 37 of Amyotrophic Lateral Sclerosis (ALS), a rare and incurable disease of the nervous system now better known as Lou Gehrig's disease.

Bernie Geoffrion (b. Feb. 14, 1931, d. Mar. 11, 2006): Hockey RW; credited with popularizing the slap shot, earning his nickname "Boom Boom"; scored 30 goals in 1952 to win the NHL's Calder Trophy (Rookie of the Year Award); won the MVP award (Hart) in 1955; became the second player in history to score 50 goals in one season; led the league in points in 1955 and 61; won 6 Stanley Cups with Montreal; member of the Hockey Hall of Fame.

George Gervin (b. April 27, 1952): Basketball G/F; joined the ABA in 1972 and came to the NBA with San Antonio in 1976; a five-time NBA all-star; led the league in scoring four times; scored 26,595 points with an average of 25.1 per game; known as the "Iceman" because of his cool style; elected to the Hall of Fame in 1996.

A. Bartlett Giamatti (b. Apr. 14, 1938, d. Sept. 1, 1989): Scholar and seventh commissioner of baseball; banned Pete Rose for life for betting on Major League games and associating with known gamblers; also served as the president of Yale (1978-86) and the National League (1986-89); father of character actor Paul.

Joe Gibbs (b. Nov. 25, 1940): Football; coached Washington to 3 Super Bowl titles in 12 seasons before retiring in 1993; owner of NASCAR racing team that won 1993 Daytona 500 and 2000 Winston Cup title; lured out of retirement to coach Redskins in 2004; began 2007 season with 162 wins, 12th on the all-time list.

Althea Gibson (b. Aug. 25, 1927, d. Sept. 28, 2003): Tennis; won both Wimbledon and U.S. championships in 1957 and '58; 1st African-American to play in either tourney and 1st to win each title.

Bob Gibson (b. Nov. 9, 1935): Baseball RHP; won 20 or more games 5 times; won 2 NL Cy Youngs (1968,70); MVP in 1968; led St. Louis to 2 World Series titles (1964,67); his ERA of 1.12 in 1968 is the lowest for a starter since 1914; 251-174 record.

Josh Gibson (b. Dec. 21, 1911, d. Jan. 20, 1947): Baseball C; the "Babe Ruth of the Negro Leagues"; Satchel Paige's battery mate with Pittsburgh Crawfords. The Negro Leagues did not keep accurate records but Gibson hit 84 home runs in one season and his Baseball Hall of Fame plaque says he hit "almost 800" home runs in his 17-year career.

Kirk Gibson (b. May 28, 1957): Baseball OF; All-America flanker at Mich. St. in 1978; chose baseball career and was AL playoff MVP with Detroit in 1984 and NL regular season MVP with Los Angeles in 1988; hit famous pinch-hit home run against Oakland's Dennis Eckersley in Game 1 of the 1988 World Series to vault the Dodgers to the title.

Frank Gifford (b. Aug. 16, 1930): Football HB; 4-time all-Pro (1955-57,59); NFL MVP in 1956; led NY Giants to 3 NFL title games; longtime TV sportscaster, beginning career in 1958 while still a player; scandal struck the married Gifford after he was videotaped in a compromising position with a former stewardess in 1997.

Sid Gillman (b. Oct. 26, 1911, d. Jan. 3, 2003): Football innovator; coach elected to both College and Pro Football Halls of Fame; led college teams at Miami-OH and Cincinnati to combined 81-19-2 record from 1944-54; coached LA Rams (1955-59) in NFL, then led LA-San Diego Chargers to 5 Western titles and 1 league championship in first six years of AFL.

George Gipp (b. Feb. 18, 1895, d. Dec. 14, 1920): Football HB; died of throat infection 2 weeks before he made All-America at Notre Dame; rushed for 2,341 yards, scored 156 points and averaged 38 yards a punt in 4 years (1917-20); inspiration for Knute Rockne's "Win one for the Gipper" speech.

Marc Girardelli (b. July 18, 1963): Luxembourg Alpine skier; Austrian native who refused to join Austrian Ski Federation because he wanted to be coached by his father; won unprecedented 5th overall World Cup title in 1993; winless at Olympics, although he won 2 silver medals in 1992.

Tom Glavine (b. Mar. 26, 1966): Baseball LHP; led the majors in wins from 1991-95 with 91; NL Cy Young winner in 1991 and '98; eight-time All-Star; World Series MVP with Atlanta in 1995; defeated the Cubs on Aug. 5, 2007 to become the 23rd pitcher in MLB history to record 300 wins.

Tom Gola (b. Jan. 13, 1933): Basketball F; 4-time All-America and 1955 Player of Year at La Salle; MOP in 1952 NIT and '54 NCAA Final 4, leading Explorers to both titles; won NBA title as rookie with Philadelphia Warriors in 1956; 4-time NBA All-Star.

Marshall Goldberg (b. Oct. 24, 1917, d. Apr. 3, 2006): Football HB; 2-time consensus All-America at Pittsburgh (1937-38); led Pitt to national championship in 1937; played with NFL champion Chicago Cardinals 10 years later.

Lefty Gomez (b. Nov. 26, 1908, d. Feb. 17, 1989): Baseball LHP; 4-time 20-game winner with NY Yankees; holds World Series record for most wins (6) without a defeat; pitched on 5 world championship clubs in 1930s.

Pancho Gonzales (b. May 9, 1928, d. July 3, 1995): Tennis; won consecutive U.S. Championships in 1948-49 before turning pro at 21; dominated pro tour from 1950-61; in 1969 at age 41, played longest Wimbledon match ever (5:12), beating Charlie Pasarell 22-24,1-6,16-14,6-3,11-9.

Bob Goodenow (b. Oct. 29, 1952): Hockey; succeeded Alan Eagleson as executive director of NHL Players Association in 1990; led players on 10-day strike in 1992, during 103-day owners' lockout in 1994-95 and lockout in 2004; resigned in 2005.

Roger Goodell (b. Feb. 19, 1959): Football; former NFL intern who rose quickly through the ranks and was elected to succeed Paul Tagliabue as the Commissioner of the league on Aug. 8, 2006; joined the NFL as an intern in 1981 after graduating from Washington & Jefferson College; also worked in P.R. for the N.Y. Jets, as assistant to AFC president Lamar Hunt, and in many positions for Tagliabue including Executive V.P. and COO from 2001-06.

Gail Goodrich (b. April 23, 1943): Basketball G; starred at UCLA and won two national championships in 1964 and 1965 under legendary coach John Wooden's tutelage; won the NBA championship with the L.A. Lakers in 1972 and led the team in scoring (25.9 ppg); averaged 18.6 ppg over his 14-year career.

Jeff Gordon (b. Aug. 4, 1971): Auto racer; 1993 NASCAR Rookie of Year; 4-time Winston Cup champion (1995,97,98,2001); won inaugural Brickyard 400 in 1994; became youngest winner (25) of the Daytona 500 in 1997, won Daytona 500 again in 1999 and 2005; in 1998 he tied Richard Petty for the modern-era record for wins in a single season with 13; NASCAR's all-time leading money winner; has 79 Winston/Nextel Cup wins as of Sept. 2007.

Rich (Goose) Gossage (b. July 5, 1951): Baseball RHP; Nine-time All-Star (1975-78, 80-82, 84-85); intimidating relief pitcher; Fireman of the Year in 1975 with White Sox and 1978 with Yankees; led AL in saves with 26 (1975), 27 (1978); 1,002 career appearances; 310 saves.

Shane Gould (b. Nov. 23, 1956): Australian swimmer; set world records in 5 different women's freestyle events between July 1971 and Jan. 1972; won 3 gold medals, a silver and bronze in 1972 Olympics then retired at age 16.

Alf Goullet (b. Apr. 5, 1891, d. Mar. 11, 1995): Cycling; Australian who gained fame and fortune early in century as premier performer on U.S. 6-day bike race circuit; won 8 annual races at Madison Square Garden with 6 different partners from 1913-23.

Curt Gowdy (b. July 31, 1919, d. Feb. 20, 2006): Radio/TV; former radio voice of NY Yankees and then Boston Red Sox from 1949-66; TV play-by-play man for AFL, NFL and major league baseball; has broadcast World Series, All-Star Games, Rose Bowls, Super Bowls, Olympics and NCAA Final Fours for 3 networks; hosted "The American Sportsman."

Steffi Graf (b. June 14, 1969): German tennis player; won Grand Slam and Olympic gold medal in 1988 at age 19; won three of four majors in 1993, '95 and '96; won 22 Grand Slam singles titles— 7 at Wimbledon, 6 French, 5 U.S. and 4 Australian Opens, retired in 1999 as 3rd all-time with 107 career singles titles and as all-time tour leader in career earnings with over $21 million in prize money; married to fellow tennis great Andre Agassi.

Otto Graham (b. Dec. 6, 1921, d. Dec. 17, 2003): Football QB and basketball All-America at Northwestern; in pro ball, led Cleveland Browns to 7 league titles in 10 years, winning 4 AAFC championships (1946-49) and 3 NFL (1950,54-55); 5-time All-Pro; 2-time NFL MVP (1953,55).

Cammi Granato (b. Mar. 25, 1971): Hockey; American women's hockey pioneer; captain of U.S. team that won gold at the inaugural Olympic women's hockey competition in 1998 at Nagano; sister of NHL veteran Tony.

Red Grange (b. June 13, 1903, d. Jan. 28, 1991): Football HB; 3-time All-America at Illinois who brought 1st huge crowds to pro football when he signed with Chicago Bears in 1925; formed 1st AFL with manager-promoter C.C. Pyle in 1926, but league folded and he returned to Bears.

Bud Grant (b. May 20, 1927): Football and Basketball; only coach to win 100 games in both CFL and NFL and only member of both CFL and U.S. Pro Football Halls of Fame; led Winnipeg to 4 Grey Cup titles (1958-59,61-62) in 6 appearances, but his Minnesota Vikings lost all 4 Super Bowl attempts in 1970s; accumulated 122 CFL wins and 168 NFL wins; also All-Big Ten at Minnesota in both football and basketball in late 1940s; a 3-time CFL All-Star offensive end; also member of 1950 NBA champion Minneapolis Lakers.

Rocky Graziano (b. June 7, 1922, d. May 22, 1990): Boxer; world middleweight champion (1946-47); fought Tony Zale for title 3 times in 21 months, losing twice; pro record 67-10-6 with 52 KOs; movie "Somebody Up There Likes Me" based on his life.

Hank Greenberg (b. Jan. 1, 1911, d. Sept. 4, 1986): Baseball 1B/LF; slugging right-hander who led AL in HRs and RBI 4 times each; 2-time MVP (1935, 40) with Detroit; 331 career HRs, including 58 in 1938; elected to Hall of Fame in 1956.

Joe Greene (b. Sept. 24, 1946): Football DT; 5-time All-Pro (1972-74,77,79); led Pittsburgh to 4 Super Bowl titles in 1970s; nicknamed "Mean Joe."

Maurice Greene (b. July 23, 1974): Track & Field; world 100m champion in 1997, 99 and 2001 and 200m champion in 1999; former world record holder (9.79) in the 100m; won the gold medal in the 100m and 4x100m at the 2000 Sydney Olympics; took 100m bronze at 2004 Athens Olympics.

Bud Greenspan (b. Sept. 18, 1926): Filmmaker specializing in the Olympic Games; has won Emmy awards for 22-part "The Olympiad" (1976-77) and historical vignettes for ABC-TV's coverage of 1980 Winter Games; won 1994 Emmy award for edited special on Lillehammer Winter Olympics; won The Peabody Award in 1996 for his outstanding service in chronicling the Olympic Games.

Wayne Gretzky (b. Jan. 26, 1961): Hockey C; 10-time NHL scoring champion; 9-time regular season MVP (1979-87,89) and 9-time All-NHL first team; scored 200 points or more in a season 4 times; led Edmonton to 4 Stanley Cups (1984-85,87-88); 2-time playoff MVP (1985,88); traded to LA Kings (Aug. 9, 1988); broke Gordie Howe's all-time NHL goal scoring record of 801 on Mar. 23, 1994; all-time NHL leader in points (2857), goals (894) and assists (1963); also all-time Stanley Cup leader in points, goals and assists; spent the end of the 1996 season with the St. Louis Blues and then signed a free agent contract with the New York Rangers; retired in 1999 at age 38 with 61 NHL scoring records in 20 seasons; became part-owner of NHL's Coyotes in 2000 and stepped behind the bench as Coyotes head coach in 2005.

Bob Griese (b. Feb. 3, 1945): Football QB; 2-time All-Pro (1971,77); led Miami to undefeated season (17-0) in 1972 and consecutive Super Bowl titles (1973-74); father of Brian.

Ken Griffey Jr. (b. Nov. 21, 1969): Baseball OF; overall 1st pick of 1987 draft by Seattle; 10-time Gold Glove winner; 13-time All-Star; 1997 AL MVP; MVP of 1992 All-Star game at age 23; hit home runs in 8 consecutive games in 1993; son of Ken Sr. and in 1990 they became the first father-son combination to appear in the same major league lineup; traded to the Cincinnati Reds before the 2000 season; hit 30 homers in 2007 to reach 593 for his career.

Archie Griffin (b. Aug. 21, 1954): Football RB; only college player to win two Heisman Trophies (1974-75); rushed for 5,177 yards in career at Ohio St. and played in four straight Super Bowls; drafted by Cincinnati Bengals and played 8 years in NFL.

Emile Griffith (b. Feb. 3, 1938): Boxer; world welterweight champion (1961,62-63,63-65); world middleweight champ (1966-67,67-68); pro record 85-24-2 with 23 KOs.

Dick Groat (b. Nov. 4, 1930): Basketball G and Baseball SS; 2-time basketball All-America at Duke and college Player of Year in 1951; won NL MVP award as shortstop with Pittsburgh in 1960; won World Series with Pirates (1960) and St. Louis (1964).

Lefty Grove (b. Mar. 6, 1900, d. May 23, 1975): Baseball LHP; won 20 or more games 8 times; led AL in ERA 9 times and strikeouts 7 times; 31-4 record and MVP in 1931 with Philadelphia; 300-141 record; real name: Robert Moses Grove.

Lou Groza (b. Jan. 25, 1924, d. Nov. 29, 2000): Football T-PK; 6-time All-Pro; played in 13 championship games for Cleveland from 1946-67; kicked winning field goal in 1950 NFL title game; 1,608 career points (1,349 in NFL).

Janet Guthrie (b. Mar. 7, 1938): Auto racer; in 1977, became 1st woman to race in Indianapolis 500; placed 9th at Indy in 1978.

Tony Gwynn (b. May 9, 1960): Baseball OF; 8-time NL batting champion (1984,87-89,94-97) with San Diego; 15-time All-Star; got 3,000th career hit Aug. 6, 1999 at Montreal; played basketball at San Diego St. leaving as school's all-time assist leader; drafted in 10th round of 1981 NBA draft by then San Diego Clippers; retired with 3,141 career hits; inducted into the Baseball Hall of Fame in 2007.

Harvey Haddix (b. Sept. 18, 1925, d. Jan. 9, 1994): Baseball LHP; pitched 12 perfect innings for Pittsburgh, but lost to Milwaukee in the 13th, 1-0 (May 26, 1959); won Game 7 of 1960 World Series.

Walter Hagen (b. Dec. 21, 1892, d. Oct. 5, 1969): Pro golf pioneer; won 2 U.S. Opens (1914,19), 4 British Opens (1922,24,28-29), 5 PGA Championships (1921,24-27) and 5 Western Opens; 44 career PGA wins; 6-time U.S. Ryder Cup captain.

Marvin Hagler (b. May 23, 1954): Boxer; hard-punching world middleweight champion from 1980-87; enjoyed his nickname "Marvelous Marvin" so much he had his name legally changed; pro record of 62-3-2 with 52 KOs; retired after suffering 1987 upset loss to Sugar Ray Leonard.

Mika Hakkinen (b. Sept. 28, 1968): Finnish auto racer; won two consecutive Formula One world drivers championships in 1998 and '99; recorded eight wins in '98 and five in '99; 20 career F1 wins.

George Halas (b. Feb. 2, 1895, d. Oct. 31, 1983): Football pioneer; MVP in 1919 Rose Bowl; player-coach-owner of Chicago Bears from 1920-83; signed Red Grange in 1925; coached Bears for 40 seasons and won 8 NFL titles (1921,32-33,40-41,43,46,63); 2nd on all-time career list with 324 wins; elected to NFL Hall of Fame in 1963.

Dorothy Hamill (b. July 26, 1956): Figure skater; won Olympic gold medal and world championship in 1976; Ice Capades headliner from 1977-84; bought the financially-strapped Ice Capades in 1993 and sold it several years later.

Scott Hamilton (b. Aug. 28, 1958): Figure skater; 4-time world champion (1981-84); won gold medal at 1984 Olympics.

Mia Hamm (b. Mar. 17, 1972): Soccer F; all-time leading international scorer with 158 goals; member of three U.S. Olympic team (1996,2000,04), and four U.S. World Cup teams (1991,95,99,2003); made the U.S. National Team at 15; a three-time collegiate All-American; led UNC to four national titles (1989,90, 92,93); Two-time FIFA Women's World Player of the Year (2001-02); inducted into National Hall of Fame in 2007; married to baseball's Nomar Garciaparra.

Tonya Harding (b. Nov. 12, 1970): Figure skater; 1991 and 1994 U.S. women's champion; involved in plot hatched by ex-husband Jeff Gillooly to injure rival Nancy Kerrigan and keep her off Olympic team; won '94 U.S. title in Kerrigan's absence; denied any role in assault and sued USOC to keep her spot in Olympics; finished 8th at Lillehammer (Kerrigan recovered and won silver medal); pleaded guilty on Mar. 16 to conspiracy to hinder investigation; stripped of 1994 title by U.S. Figure Skating Association.

Tom Harmon (b. Sept. 28, 1919, d. Mar. 17, 1990): Football HB; 2-time All-America at Michigan; won Heisman Trophy in 1940; played with AFL NY Americans in 1941 and NFL LA Rams (1946-47);World War II fighter pilot who won Silver Star and Purple Heart; became radio-TV commentator.

Franco Harris (b. Mar. 7, 1950): Football RB; ran for over 1,000 yards in a season 8 times; rushed for 12,120 yards in 13 years; led Pittsburgh to 4 Super Bowl titles.

Leon Hart (b. Nov. 2, 1928, d. Sept. 24, 2002): Football E; only player to win 3 national championships in college and 3 more in the NFL; won his titles at Notre Dame (1946-47,49) and with Detroit Lions (1952-53,57); 3-time All-America and last lineman to win Heisman Trophy (1949); All-Pro on both offense and defense in 1951.

Bill Hartack (b. Dec. 9, 1932): Jockey; won Kentucky Derby 5 times (1957,60,62,64,69), Preakness 3 times (1956,64,69), and the Belmont once (1960).

Doug Harvey (b. Dec. 19, 1924, d. Dec. 26, 1989): Hockey D; 10-time All-NHL 1st team; won Norris Trophy 7 times (1955-58,60-62); led Montreal to 6 Stanley Cups.

Dominik Hasek (b. Jan. 29, 1965): Czech hockey goaltender; 2-time NHL MVP (1997,98) with Buffalo; 6-time Vezina Trophy winner (1994,95,97,98,99, 2001); led Czech Republic to Olympic gold medal in 1998 at Nagano; won Stanley Cup with Detroit in 2002.

Billy Haughton (b. Nov. 2, 1923, d. July 15, 1986): Harness racing; 4-time winner of Hambletonian; trainer-driver of one Pacing Triple Crown winner (1968); 4,910 career wins.

João Havelange (b. May 8, 1916): Soccer; Brazilian-born president of Federation Internationale de Football Assoc. (FIFA) 1974-98; also member of International Olympic Committee.

John Havlicek (b. Apr. 8, 1940): Basketball F; played in three NCAA Finals at Ohio St. (1960-62); led Boston to eight NBA titles (1963-66,68-69,74,76); Finals MVP in 1974; four-time All-NBA 1st team; #17 retired by the Celtics.

Tony Hawk (b. May 12, 1968): Skateboarder; winner of 16 X Games medals; top-ranked ranked vert skater for 12 consecutive years; in 1999, became the first person to land the 900; credited with inventing nearly 100 tricks; creator, Tony Hawk's Pro Skater best-selling video game franchise ($1billion+ in sales), autobiography appeared on *The New York Times* bestseller list (2000).

Bob Hayes (b. Dec. 20, 1942, d. Sept. 18, 2002): Track & Field and Football; won gold medal in 100m at 1964 Olympics; all-pro SE for Dallas in 1966; won Super Bowl with Cowboys in 1972; convicted of drug trafficking in 1979 and served 18 months of a 5-year sentence.

Elvin Hayes (b. Nov. 17, 1945): Basketball C; Known as "the Big E"; Overall number one pick of the 1968 NBA draft; three-time All-NBA first team (1975,77,79); 1978 Finals MVP; 12-time NBA all-star (1969-80); named to NBA's 50 Greatest Players; amassed 27,313 points and 16,279 rebounds; member of basketball Hall of Fame.

Woody Hayes (b. Feb. 14, 1913, d. Mar. 12, 1987): Football; coached Ohio St. to 6 national titles (1954,57,61,68,70) and 4 Rose Bowl victories; 238 career wins in 28 seasons at Denison, Miami-OH and OSU; his coaching career ended abruptly in 1978 after he attacked an opposing player on the sidelines after an interception.

Thomas Hearns (b. Oct. 18, 1958): Boxer; held world titles as welterweight, junior middleweight, middleweight and light heavyweight; four career losses came against Ray Leonard, Marvin Hagler and twice to Iran Barkley; pro record of 60-4-1, 46 KOs.

Eric Heiden (b. June 14, 1958): Speed skater; 3-time overall world champion (1977-79); won all 5 men's speed skating gold medals at 1980 Olympics, setting records in each; Sullivan Award winner (1980).

Mel Hein (b. Aug. 22, 1909, d. Jan. 31, 1992): Football; NFL All-Pro 8 straight years (1933-40); MVP in 1938 with Giants; didn't miss a game in 15 years.

John W. Heisman (b. Oct. 23, 1869, d. Oct. 3, 1936): Football; coached at 9 colleges from 1892-1927; won 185 games; Director of Athletics at Downtown Athletic Club in NYC (1928-36); DAC named Heisman Trophy after him.

Carol Heiss (b. Jan. 20, 1940): Figure skater; 5-time world champion (1956-60); won Olympic silver medal in 1956 and gold in '60; married 1956 men's gold medalist Hayes Jenkins.

Rickey Henderson (b. Dec. 25, 1958): Baseball OF; AL playoff MVP (1989) and AL regular season MVP (1990); set single-season base stealing record of 130 in 1982; led AL in steals a record 12 times; broke Lou Brock's all-time record of 938 on May 1, 1991; holds all-time MLB records in runs (2295), stolen bases (1406), and HRs as leadoff batter (81).

Sonja Henie (b. Apr. 8, 1912, d. Oct. 12, 1969): Norwegian figure skater; 10-time world champion (1927-36); won 3 consecutive Olympic gold medals (1928,32,36); became movie star.

Foster Hewitt (b. Nov. 21, 1902, d. Apr. 21, 1985): Radio-TV; Canada's premier hockey play-by-play broadcaster from 1923-81; coined phrase, "He shoots, he scores!"

Damon Hill (b. Sept. 17, 1960): British auto racer; 1996 Formula 1 champion; 22 F1 wins places him 10th all-time; retired following 1999 season; son of Graham.

Graham Hill (b. Feb. 15, 1929, d. Nov. 29, 1975): British auto racer; 2-time Formula One world champion (1962,68); won Indy 500 in 1966; killed in plane crash; father of Damon.

Phil Hill (b. Apr. 20, 1927): Auto racer; first U.S. driver to win Formula One championship (1961); 3 career wins (1958-64).

Sir Edmund Hillary (b. July 20, 1919): New Zealand mountaineer; On May 29, 1953, along with Sherpa Tenzing Norgay, Hillary became the first to reach summit of Mt. Everest, the world's highest peak.

Martina Hingis (b. Sept. 30, 1980): Swiss tennis player; in March 1997 at 16 years, 6 months, she became the youngest No. 1 ranked player since the ranking system began in 1975; won Wimbledon (1997), U.S. Open (1997) and 3 Australian Opens (1997,98,99); first woman to surpass the $3 million mark in earnings for one season (1997).

Max Hirsch (b. July 30, 1880, d. Apr. 3, 1969): Horse racing; trained 1,933 winners from 1908-68; won Triple Crown with Assault in 1946.

Tommy Hitchcock (b. Feb. 11, 1900, d. Apr. 19, 1944): Polo; world class player at 20; achieved 10-goal rating 18 times from 1922-40.

Lew Hoad (b. Nov. 23, 1934, d. July 3, 1994): Australian tennis player; 2-time Wimbledon winner (1956-57); won Australian, French and Wimbledon titles in 1956, but missed capturing Grand Slam at Forest Hills when beaten by Ken Rosewall in 4-set final.

Gil Hodges (b. Apr. 4, 1924, d. Apr. 2, 1972): Baseball 1B-Manager; tied Major League record with four home runs in one game on Aug 31, 1950; won three Gold Gloves (1957-59); drove in 100 runs in seven consecutive seasons (1949-55); hit 370 home runs and 1,274 RBIs lifetime; won 660 games as a manager (Senators and Mets).

Mat Hoffman (b. Jan. 9, 1972): BMX; youngest pro in BMX history at age 16, world record holder for High Air on a BMX Bike (26.5 feet out of a 24-foot quarterpipe in 2001); invented over 100 staple BMX tricks; started the Bike Stunt Series (1992-televised by ESPN starting in 1995); founded the Hoffman Sports Association (1999 – governing body for major BMX events today).

Trevor Hoffman (b. Oct. 13, 1967): Baseball RHP; 2-time NL saves leader (1998, 2006); earned his 479th save on Sept, 24, 2006 to pass Lee Smith as the all-time major league leader; finished 2007 with 524; recorded eight 40-save seasons and one 50-save season (53 in 1998).

Ben Hogan (b. Aug. 13, 1912, d. July 25, 1997): Golfer; 4-time PGA Player of Year; one of only five players to win all four Grand Slam titles (others are Nicklaus, Player, Sarazen and Woods); won 4 U.S. Opens, 2 Masters, 2 PGAs and 1 British Open between 1946-53; nearly killed in Feb. 2, 1949 car accident, but came back to win 1950 U.S. Open just 16 months later; one of only two players (Woods) to win three of the four current majors in one year when he won Masters, U.S. Open and British Open in 1953 at age 41; third on all-time list with 64 career wins.

Chamique Holdsclaw (b. Aug. 9, 1977): Basketball F; 2-time national player of the year, leading Tennessee to 3 straight national championships (1996-98); 1998 Sullivan Award winner; top selection by the Washington Mystics in the 1999 WNBA draft; 1999 WNBA Rookie of the Year.

Eleanor Holm (b. Dec. 6, 1913, d. Jan. 31, 2004): Swimmer; won gold medal in 100m backstroke at 1932 Olympics; thrown off '36 U.S. team for drinking champagne in public and shooting craps on boat to Germany.

Nat Holman (b. Oct. 18, 1896, d. Feb. 12, 1995): Basketball pioneer; played with Original Celtics (1920-28); coached CCNY to both NCAA and NIT titles in 1950 (a year later, several of his players were caught up in a point-shaving scandal); 423 career wins.

Larry Holmes (b. Nov. 3, 1949): Boxer; heavyweight champion (WBC or IBF) from 1978-85; beat Gerry Cooney on a 13th-round TKO in their 1982 mega-fight; successfully defended title 20 times before losing to Michael Spinks; returned from first retirement in 1988 and was KO'd in 4th by champ Mike Tyson; launched second comeback in 1991; fought and lost title bids against Evander Holyfield in '92 and Oliver McCall in '95; pro record of 69-6 and 44 KOs.

Lou Holtz (b. Jan. 6, 1937): Football; coached Notre Dame to national title in 1988; 2-time Coach of Year (1977,88); also coached NFL's NY Jets for 13 games (3-10) in 1976.

Evander Holyfield (b. Oct. 19, 1962): Boxer; only man to win (and lose) world heavyweight title 4 times; Wore belt off and on from 1990-2001; defeated former champ Mike Tyson in 1996 to win WBA belt; in 1997 rematch, Tyson was DQ'd for twice biting his ear; former undisputed cruiserweight world (1987-88) champ before moving to heavyweight; returned to ring in Aug. 2006 with a 2nd-round TKO of Jeremy Bates.

Red Holzman (b. Aug. 10, 1920, d. Nov. 13, 1998): Basketball; played for NBL and NBA champions at Rochester (1946,51); coached NY Knicks to 2 NBA titles (1970,73); Coach of Year (1970); 754 career NBA wins.

Bernard Hopkins (b. Jan. 15, 1965): Boxer; became first undisputed world middleweight champion since Marvin Hagler when he upset undefeated Felix Trinidad with a 12th-round TKO in 2001 to unify belts; defended title for a division-record 20 times before finally losing belts on a split decision to Jermain Taylor in 2005; won decision over Antonio Tarver in June, 2006, then retired; promptly unretired in 2007 with a unanimous decision over Winky Wright; 48-4-1 (32 KOs).

Rogers Hornsby (b. Apr. 27, 1896, d. Jan. 5, 1963): Baseball 2B; hit .400 3 times, including .424 in 1924; led NL in batting 7 times; 2-time MVP (1925,29); career BA of .358 over 23 years is highest in NL.

Paul Hornung (b. Dec. 23, 1935): Football HB-PK; only Heisman Trophy winner to play for losing team (2-8 Notre Dame in 1956); 3-time NFL scoring leader (1959-61) at Green Bay; 176 points in 1960, an all-time record; MVP in 1961; suspended by NFL for 1963 season for betting on his own team.

Gordie Howe (b. Mar. 31, 1928): Hockey RW; played 32 seasons in NHL and WHA from 1946-80; led NHL in scoring 6 times; All-NHL 1st team 12 times; MVP 6 times in NHL (1952-53,57-58,60,63) with Detroit and once in WHA (1974) with Houston; ranks 2nd on all-time NHL list in goals (801) & 3rd in points (1,850); played with sons Mark and Marty at Houston (1973-77) and New England-Hartford (1977-80).

Cal Hubbard (b. Oct. 31, 1900, d. Oct. 17, 1977): Member of college football, pro football and baseball halls of fame; 9 years in NFL; 4-time All-Pro at end and tackle; AL umpire (1936-51).

William DeHart Hubbard (b. Nov. 25, 1903, d. June 23, 1976): Track & Field; won the long jump at the 1924 Olympics, becoming the first black athlete to win an Olympic gold medal in an individual event; set the long jump world record in 1925 (25-10¾) and tied the 100-yd dash record (9.6) in 1926.

Carl Hubbell (b. June 22, 1903, d. Nov. 21, 1988): Baseball LHP; led NL in wins and ERA 3 times each; 2-time MVP (1933,36) with NY Giants; fanned Ruth, Gehrig, Foxx, Simmons and Cronin in succession in 1934 All-Star Game; 253-154 career record.

Sam Huff (b. Oct. 4, 1934): Football LB; glamorized NFL's middle linebacker position with NY Giants from 1956-63; subject of "The Violent World of Sam Huff" TV special in 1961; helped club win 6 division titles and a national championship (1956).

Miller Huggins (b. Mar. 27, 1878, d. Sept. 25, 1929): Baseball; managed NY Yankees from 1918 until his death late in '29 season; led Yanks to 6 pennants and 3 World Series titles from 1921-28.

Bobby Hull (b. Jan. 3, 1939): Hockey LW; led NHL in scoring 3 times; 2-time MVP (1965-66) with Chicago; All-NHL first team 10 times; jumped to WHA in 1972, 2-time MVP there (1973,75) with Winnipeg; scored 913 goals in both leagues; father of Brett.

Brett Hull (b. Aug. 9, 1964): Hockey RW; NHL MVP in 1991 with St. Louis; holds single season RW scoring record with 86 goals; he and father Bobby have both won Hart (MVP), Lady Byng (sportsmanship) and All-Star Game MVP trophies; won 2 Stanley Cups.

Lamar Hunt (b. Aug. 2, 1932, d. Dec. 13, 2006): Football/Soccer; Founder of the Kansas City Chiefs (formerly Dallas Texans); instrumental in forming the AFL in 1959 and merging the league with NFL in 1966; elected to the Pro Football HOF in 1972; AFC Championship trophy bear his name; investor/operator in MLS; also member of National Soccer HOF.

Jim (Catfish) Hunter (b. Apr. 8, 1946, d. Sept. 9, 1999): Baseball RHP; won 20 games or more 5 times (1971-75); played on 5 World Series winners with Oakland and NY Yankees; threw perfect game in 1968; won AL Cy Young Award in 1974; 224-166 career record.

Ibrahim Hussein (b. June 3, 1958): Kenyan distance runner; 3-time winner of Boston Marathon (1988,91-92) and 1st African runner to win in Boston; won New York Marathon in 1987.

Don Hutson (b. Jan. 31, 1913, d. June 24, 1997): Football E-PK; led NFL in receptions 8 times and interceptions once; 9-time All-Pro (1936,38-45) for Green Bay; 99 career TD catches.

Flo Hyman (b. July 31, 1954, d. Jan. 24, 1986): Volleyball; 3-time All-America spiker at Houston and captain of 1984 U.S. Women's Olympic team; died of heart attack caused by Marfan Syndrome during a match in Japan in 1986; namesake of award given out annually by the Women's Sports Foundation.

Hank Iba (b. Aug. 6, 1904, d. Jan. 15, 1993): Basketball; coached Oklahoma A&M to 2 straight NCAA titles (1945-46); 767 career wins in 41 years; coached U.S. Olympic team to 2 gold medals (1964,68), but lost to Soviets in controversial '72 final.

Punch Imlach (b. Mar. 15, 1918, d. Dec. 1, 1987): Hockey; directed Toronto to 4 Stanley Cups (1962-64,67) in 11 seasons as GM-coach.

Miguel Induráin (b. July 16, 1964): Spanish cyclist; won 5 straight Tour de Frances (1991-95), won gold in time trial at '96 Olympics; retired in 1997.

Juli Inkster (b. June 24, 1960): Golfer; 31 career LPGA victories; winner of 7 major LPGA tournaments and 3 consecutive U.S. Women's Amateur tournaments (1980-82); inducted into the World Golf Hall of Fame in 2000; LPGA Rookie of the Year in 1984.

Hale Irwin (b. June 3, 1945): Golfer; oldest player ever to win U.S. Open (45 in 1990); NCAA champion in 1967; 20 PGA victories, including 3 U.S. Opens (1974,79,90); 5-time Ryder Cup team member; joined Senior PGA Tour in 1995 and has already won 45 titles.

Allen Iverson (b. June 7, 1975): Basketball G; former Georgetown Hoya chosen first overall by the Philadelphia 76ers in the 1996 NBA Draft; NBA Rookie of the Year (1997); 3-time NBA scoring leader (2001-02,05) and steals leader (2001-02); voted regular season MVP in 2001 and led 76ers to NBA Finals; traded to Denver Nuggets in December 2006.

Bo Jackson (b. Nov. 30, 1962): Baseball OF and Football RB; won Heisman Trophy in 1985 and MVP of baseball All-Star Game in 1989; starter for both baseball's KC Royals and NFL's LA Raiders in 1988 and '89; severely injured left hip Jan. 13, 1991, in NFL playoffs; waived by Royals but signed by Chicago White Sox in 1991; missed entire 1992 season recovering from hip surgery; played for White Sox in 1993 and California in '94 before retiring.

Joe Jackson (b. July 16, 1889, d. Dec. 5, 1951): Baseball OF; hit .300 or better 11 times; nicknamed "Shoeless Joe"; career average of .356, third highest all-time; was placed on MLB's ineligible list in 1921 following the Black Sox scandal in which he and 7 teammates were accused of fixing 1919 World Series.

Phil Jackson (b. Sept. 17, 1945): Basketball; NBA champion as reserve forward with New York in 1973 (injured when Knicks won in '70); coached Chicago to six NBA titles in eight years (1991-93, 96-98); coach of the year in 1996 and 97; returned to coach the LA Lakers in 1999 and won 3 more titles (2000,01,02); all-time leader in winning pct. for NBA coaches with 350 or more wins; left Lakers after 2004 Finals loss to Detroit but returned after one season; all-time NBA leader in playoff wins (179).

Reggie Jackson (b. May 18, 1946): Baseball OF; led AL in HRs 4 times; MVP in 1973; played on 5 World Series winners with Oakland and NY Yankees; 1977 Series MVP with 5 HRs; 563 career HRs; all-time strikeout leader (2,597); member of the Hall of Fame.

Dr. Robert Jackson (b. Aug. 6, 1932): Surgeon; revolutionized sports medicine by popularizing the use of arthroscopic surgery to treat injuries; learned technique from Japanese physician that allowed athletes to return quickly from potentially career-ending injuries.

Helen Jacobs (b. Aug. 6, 1908, d. June 2, 1997): Tennis; 4-time winner of U.S. Championship (1932-35); Wimbledon winner in 1936; lost 4 Wimbledon finals to arch-rival Helen Wills Moody.

Jaromir Jagr (b. Feb. 15, 1972): Czech Hockey RW; fifth overall pick by Pittsburgh (1990); NHL All-Rookie team (1991); NHL MVP (1999); Won Art Ross Trophy (1995,98,99,00,01); 7-time All-NHL First Team; NHL single season record for most points by a right wing (149); NHL single season record for most assists by a RW (87).

LeBron James (b. Dec. 30, 1984): Basketball; mega-hyped top overall pick in 2003 NBA Draft (Cleveland) straight out of high school; youngest-ever NBA Rookie of the Year (2004); led Cavs to Finals in 2007 (loss to Spurs); scored 48 points (including team's final 25) in a win over Pistons in 2007 conference finals.

Dan Jansen (b. June 17, 1965): Speed skater; fell in 500m and 1,000m in 1988 Olympics just after sister Jane's death; placed 4th in 500m and didn't attempt 1,000m in 1992; fell in 500m at '94 Games, but finally won an Olympic medal with world record (1:12.43) effort in 1,000m.

Dale Jarrett (b. Nov. 26, 1956): Auto racer; 1999 Winston Cup champion; 3-time Daytona 500 champion (1993,96,2000); son of driver Ned Jarrett.

James J. Jeffries (b. Apr. 15, 1875, d. Mar. 3, 1953): Boxer; world heavyweight champion (1899-1905); retired undefeated but came back to fight Jack Johnson in 1910 and lost (KO, 15th).

David Jenkins (b. June 29, 1936): Figure skater; brother of Hayes; 3-time world champion (1957-59); won gold medal at 1960 Olympics.

Hayes Jenkins (b. Mar. 23, 1933): Figure skater; 4-time world champion (1953-56); won gold medal at 1956 Olympics; married 1960 women's gold medalist Carol Heiss.

Bruce Jenner (b. Oct. 28, 1949): Track & Field; won gold medal in 1976 Olympic decathlon.

Jackie Jensen (b. Mar. 9, 1927, d. July 14, 1982): Football RB and Baseball OF; All-America at Cal in 1948; AL MVP with Boston Red Sox in 1958.

Derek Jeter (b. June 26, 1974): Baseball SS; 1st-round draft choice (6th overall) of the N.Y. Yankees in 1992; became Yankees' everyday starting shortstop in 1996 and the team hasn't missed the postseason since; won 4 World Series championships in his first 5 seasons (1996, 98-2000); MVP of the 2000 All-Star Game and World Series; named captain of the Yankees in 2003; all-time postseason hits leader.

Ben Johnson (b. Dec. 30, 1961): Canadian sprinter; set 100m world record (9.83) at 1987 World Championships; won 100m at 1988 Olympics, but flunked drug test and forfeited gold medal; 1987 world record revoked in '89 for admitted steroid use; returned drug-free in 1991, but performed poorly; banned for life by IAAF in 1993 for testing positive again.

Bob Johnson (b. Mar. 4, 1931, d. Nov. 26, 1991): Hockey; coached Pittsburgh Penguins to 1st Stanley Cup title in 1991; led Wisconsin to 3 NCAA titles (1973,77,81); also coached 1976 U.S. Olympic team and NHL Calgary Flames (1982-87).

Earvin (Magic) Johnson (b. Aug. 14, 1959): Basketball G; led Michigan St. to NCAA title in 1979 and was Final 4 MOP; All-NBA 1st team 9 times; 3-time MVP (1987,89-90); led LA Lakers to 5 NBA titles; 3-time Finals MVP (1980, 82, 87); 3rd all-time in NBA assists with 10,141; retired on Nov. 7, 1991 after announcing he was HIV-positive; returned to score 25 points in 1992 NBA All-Star Game; U.S. Olympic Dream Team co-captain; announced NBA comeback then retired again before start of 1992-93 season; named head coach of Lakers on Mar. 23, 1994, but finished season at 5-11 and quit; later became minority owner of team; came back a final time and played 32 games during 1995-96 season.

Jack Johnson (b. Mar. 31, 1878, d. June 10, 1946): Boxer; controversial heavyweight champion (1908-15) and 1st black to hold title; defeated Tommy-Burns for crown at age 30; fled to Europe in 1913 after Mann Act conviction; lost title to Jess Willard in Havana, but claimed to have taken a dive; pro record 78-8-12 with 45 KOs.

Jimmy Johnson (b. July 16, 1943): Football; All-SWC defensive lineman on Arkansas' 1964 national championship team; coached U. of Miami-FL to national title in 1987; college record of 81-34-3 in 10 years; hired by old pal Jerry Jones to succeed Tom Landry in 1989; went 1-15 in '89, then led Cowboys to consecutive Super Bowl victories (1993-94); quit in 1994 after feuding with Jones; replaced Don Shula as Miami Dolphins head coach from 1996-99.

Judy Johnson (b. Oct. 26, 1899, d. June 13, 1989): Baseball IF; one of the great stars of the Negro Leagues; a terrific fielding third baseman who regularly batted over .300; when baseball integrated Johnson's playing days were over but he coached and scouted for the Philadelphia Athletics, Boston Braves and Philadelphia Phillies; member of Hall of Fame.

Junior Johnson (b. June 28, 1931): Auto Racing; won Daytona 500 in 1960; also won 13 NASCAR races in 1965, including the Rebel 300 at Darlington; retired from racing to become a highly successful car owner; his first driver was Bobby Allison.

Michael Johnson (b. Sep 13, 1967): Track & Field; Shattered world record in 200m (19.32) and set Olympic record in 400m (43.49) to become first man to win the gold in both races in the same Olympic Games at Atlanta in 1996; two-time world champion in 200 (1991,95) and four-time world champ in 400 (1993,95,97,99); set world record in 400m (43.18) at '99 world championships in Seville; won the 400 in Sydney in 2000 to become the only man to win the event in two consecutive Olympics; retired in 2001.

Rafer Johnson (b. Aug. 18, 1935): Track & Field; won silver medal in 1956 Olympic decathlon and gold medal in 1960.

Randy Johnson (b. Sept. 10, 1963): Baseball LHP; 6'10" flamethrower; struck out over 300 batters 6 times (1993,98,99,00,01,02); led AL in Ks 4 times (1992-95) and NL 5 times (1999-2002,04); struck out 20 batters in a game (5/8/01); 5-time Cy Young Award winner with Seattle and Arizona (AL-1995, NL-1999-2002); won 3 games and co-MVP honors (Curt Schilling) in 2001 World Series; became oldest in baseball history to pitch a perfect game at age 40; pitched for N.Y. Yankees 2005-06, Arizona in 2007.

Walter Johnson (b. Nov. 6, 1887, d. Dec. 10, 1946): Baseball RHP; nicknamed "Big Train" Johnson had an overpowering fastball; won 20 games or more 10 straight years; led AL in ERA 5 times, wins 6 times and strikeouts 12 times; twice MVP (1913, 24) with Washington Senators; all-time leader in shutouts (110) and 2nd in wins (417); part of the Hall of Fame's inaugural class of 1936

Ben A. Jones (b. Dec. 31, 1882, d. June 13, 1961): Horse racing; Calumet Farm trainer (1939-47); saddled 6 Kentucky Derby champions, including 2 Triple Crown winners—Whirlaway in 1941 and Citation in '48.

Bobby Jones (b. Mar. 17, 1902, d. Dec. 18, 1971): Won U.S. and British Opens plus U.S. and British Amateurs in 1930 to become golf's only Grand Slam winner ever; between 1922-30, he won 4 U.S. Opens, 5 U.S. Amateurs, 3 British Opens, and 1 British Amateur for 13 Major titles in all, a record that stood until Jack Nicklaus broke it; played in 6 Walker Cups; designed Augusta National (with Alister Mackenzie) and founded Masters tournament in 1934.

Deacon Jones (b. Dec. 9, 1938): Football DE; 5-time All-Pro (1965-69) with LA Rams; unofficially 3rd all-time in NFL sacks with 173½ in 14 years; inducted into Pro Football Hall of Fame in 1980.

Jerry Jones (b. Oct. 13, 1942): Football; owner-GM of Dallas Cowboys; maverick who bought declining team (3-13) and Texas Stadium for $140 million in 1989; hired pal Jimmy Johnson to replace legendary coach Tom Landry; their partnership led to 2 Super Bowl titles (1993-94); when feud developed, he fired Johnson and hired Barry Switzer and won Super Bowl in 1996; hired Bill Parcells as head coach in 2003, then Wade Phillips in 2007.

Marion Jones (b. Oct. 12, 1975): Track & Field; American sprinter who won 3 golds (100m, 200m, 4x100m) at 2000 Sydney Olympics; 5-time world champion: 100m (1997,99), 200m (2001), 4x100m (1997, 2001); voted Women's Athlete of the Year by *Track & Field News* in 1997,98 and 2000; 1999 Jesse Owens Award winner; 2000 AP and USOC Female Athlete of the Year.

Roy Jones Jr. (b. Jan. 16, 1969): Boxing; robbed of gold medal at 1988 Olympics on a scoring error; still voted Outstanding Boxer of the Games; won IBF middleweight crown, beating Bernard Hopkins in 1993; moved up to super middleweight and won IBF title from James Toney in 1994; moved up to light heavyweight, winning WBC (1997), WBA (1998) and IBF titles (1999); made temporary move to heavyweight in 2003 and decisioned John Ruiz for WBA belt; lost WBC light heavyweight belt to Antonio Tarver in a 2nd round KO in 2004; knocked out in comeback fight with Glen Johnson in 2004; fought Tarver for a 3rd time in 2005.

Michael Jordan (b. Feb. 17, 1963): Basketball G; College Player of Year with North Carolina in 1984; NBA Rookie of the Year (1985); led NBA in scoring 7 years in a row (1987-93) and also 1996-98; 10-time All-NBA 1st team; 5-time regular season MVP (1988,91-92,96,98) and 6-time MVP of NBA Finals (1991-93,96-98); 3-time AP Male Athlete of Year; led U.S. Olympic team to gold in 1984 and '92; stunned sports world when he retired at age 30 on Oct. 6, 1993; signed as OF with Chi. White Sox and spent summer of '94 in AA with Birmingham; struggled with .204 average; made one of the most anticipated comebacks in sports history when he returned to the Bulls lineup on Mar. 19, 1995 but Bulls were eliminated by Orlando in 2nd round of playoffs later that season; led Bulls to NBA titles for the next 3 years for 6 titles in all (1991-93,96-98); retired in 1999; became pres. of Wash. Wizards before unretiring again in 2001 and returning to play with Wizards for 2 seasons; became part-owner of the Charlotte Bobcats in June, 2006.

Florence Griffith Joyner (b. Dec. 21, 1959, d. Sept. 21, 1998): Track & Field; set world records in 100 and 200m in 1988; won 3 gold medals at '88 Olympics (100m, 200m, 4x100m relay); Sullivan Award winner (1988); retired in 1989; named as co-chairperson of President's Council on Physical Fitness and Sports in 1993; sister-in-law of Jackie Joyner-Kersee; died of suffocation during an epileptic seizure in 1998.

Jackie Joyner-Kersee (b. Mar. 3, 1962): Track & Field; 2-time world champion in both long jump (1987,91) and heptathlon (1987,93); won heptathlon gold medals at 1988 and '92 Olympics and LJ gold at '88 Games; also won Olympic silver (1984) in heptathlon and bronze (1992,96) in LJ; Sullivan Award winner (1986); only woman to receive *The Sporting News* Man of Year award.

Alberto Juantorena (b. Nov. 21, 1950): Cuban runner; won 400m and 800m golds at 1976 Olympics.

Sonny Jurgensen (b. Aug. 23, 1934): Football QB; played 18 seasons with Philadelphia and Washington; led NFL in passing twice (1967,69); All-Pro in 1961; 255 career TD passes.

Duke Kahanamoku (b. Aug. 24, 1890, d. Jan. 22, 1968): Swimmer; won 3 gold medals and 2 silver over 3 Olympics (1912,20,24); also surfing pioneer.

Al Kaline (b. Dec. 19, 1934): Baseball; youngest player (at age 20) to win batting title (led AL with .340 in 1955); had 3,007 hits, 399 HRs in 22 years with Detroit.

Paul Kariya (b. Oct. 16, 1974): Hockey LW; first-ever selection of Anaheim (4th overall in 1993); led Maine to an NCAA Div. I national title in 1993; won Hobey Baker Award in 1993 as a freshman.

Anatoly Karpov (b. May 23, 1951): Chess; Soviet world champion from 1975-85; regained International Chess Federation (FIDE) championship in 1993 when countryman Garry Kasparov was stripped of title after forming new Professional Chess Association; held FIDE title until 1999.

Garry Kasparov (b. Apr. 13, 1963): Chess; Azerbaijani who became youngest player (22 years, 210 days) ever to win world championship as Soviet in 1985; defeated countryman Anatoly Karpov for title; split with International Chess Federation (FIDE) to form Professional Chess Association (PCA) in 1993; stripped of FIDE title in '93 but successfully defended PCA title against Briton Nigel Short; beat IBM supercomputer "Deep Blue" 4 games to 2 in 1996 much-publicized match in New York; lost rematch to computer in 1997; finally lost world title to Vladimir Kramnik in 2000.

Mike Keenan (b. Oct. 21, 1949): Hockey; coach who finally led NY Rangers to Stanley Cup title in 1994 after 53 unsuccessful years; ranks 5th all-time on NHL coaching wins list; hired as coach of Calgary Flames in 2007.

Kipchoge (Kip) Keino (b. Jan. 17, 1940): Kenyan runner; policeman who beat USA's Jim Ryun to win 1,500m gold medal at 1968 Olympics; won again in steeplechase at 1972 Summer Games; his success spawned long line of distance champions from Kenya.

Johnny A. Kelley (b. Sept. 6, 1907, d. Oct. 7, 2004): Distance runner; ran in his 61st and final Boston Marathon at age 84 in 1992, finishing in 5:58:36; won Boston twice (1935,45) and was 2nd seven times.

Jim Kelly (b. Feb. 14, 1960): Football QB; led Buffalo to four straight Super Bowls, and is only QB to lose four times; named to AFC Pro Bowl team 5 times; inducted into Pro Football Hall of Fame in 2002.

Leroy Kelly (b. May 20, 1942): Football; replaced Jim Brown in the Cleveland Browns backfield; in 1967, he led the NFL in rushing yards (1,205), rushing average (5.1 per carry) and rushing touchdowns (11).

Walter Kennedy (b. June 8, 1912, d. June 26, 1977): Basketball; 2nd NBA commissioner (1963-75); league doubled in size to 18 teams during his tenure.

Nancy Kerrigan (b. Oct. 13, 1969): Figure skating; 1993 U.S. women's champion and Olympic medalist in 1992 (bronze) and '94 (silver); victim of Jan. 6, 1994 assault at U.S. nationals in Detroit when Shane Stant clubbed her right knee with a baton after a practice session; conspiracy hatched by Jeff Gillooly, ex-husband of rival Tonya Harding; though unable to compete in nationals, she recovered and was granted berth on Olympic team; finished 2nd in Lillehammer to Oksana Baiul of Ukraine by a 5-4 judges' vote.

Billy Kidd (b. Apr. 13, 1943): Skiing; the first great Amercian male Alpine skier; first American male to win an Olympic medal when he won a silver in the slalom and a bronze in the Alpine combined in 1964; competed respectably with the great Jean-Claude Killy; won the world Alpine combined event in 1970, which was the first world championship for an American male.

Harmon Killebrew (b. June 29, 1936): Baseball 3B-1B; led AL in HRs 6 times and RBI 3 times; MVP in 1969 with Minnesota; 573 career HRs.

Jean-Claude Killy (b. Aug. 30, 1943): French alpine skier; 2-time World Cup champion (1967-68); won 3 gold medals at 1968 Olympics in Grenoble; co-president of 1992 Winter Games in Albertville; president of coordination commission for 2006 Turin Games.

Ralph Kiner (b. Oct. 27, 1922): Baseball OF; led NL in home runs 7 straight years (1946-52) with Pittsburgh; 369 career HRs and 1,015 RBI in 10 seasons; long-time NY Mets announcer.

Betsy King (b. Aug. 13, 1955): Golfer; 2-time LPGA Player of Year (1984,89); 3-time winner of Dinah Shore (1987,90,97) and 2-time winner of U.S. Open (1989,90); 34 overall Tour wins; 1st player in LPGA history to break $5 million mark in career earnings; member of LPGA Hall of Fame.

Billie Jean King (b. Nov. 22, 1943): Tennis; women's rights pioneer; Wimbledon singles champ 6 times; U.S. champ 4 times; first woman athlete to earn $100,000 in one year (1971); beat 55-year-old Bobby Riggs 6-4,6-3,6-3, in "Battle of the Sexes" to win $100,000 at Astrodome in 1973; founded the Women's Sports Foundation in 1974; captained the U.S. Olympic team in 1996 and 2000.

Don King (b. Aug. 20, 1931): Boxing promoter; first major black promoter who has controlled heavyweight title off and on since 1978; first big promotion was Muhammad Ali's fight against George Foreman in 1974; former numbers operator who served 4 years for manslaughter (1967-70); acquitted of tax evasion and fraud in 1985; also promoted Larry Holmes, Mike Tyson, Evander Holyfield, Roberto Duran and Julio Cesar Chavez among others; has been accused of bilking his fighters out of money; famous for his gravity-defying hairstyle and his catchphrase "Only in America!".

Karch Kiraly (b. Nov. 3, 1960): Volleyball; USA's preeminent volleyball player; led UCLA to three NCAA championships (1979,81,82); played on US national teams that won Olympic gold medals in 1984 and '88, world championships in '82 and '86; won the inaugural gold medal for Olympic beach volleyball with Kent Steffes in 1996.

Tom Kite (b. Dec. 9, 1949): Golfer; co-NCAA champion with Ben Crenshaw (1972); PGA Rookie of Year (1973); PGA Player of Year (1989); finally won 1st major with victory in 1992 U.S. Open at Pebble Beach; captain of 1997 US Ryder Cup team; 19 career PGA wins, plus wins on the Champions tour since 2000 (currently has 9 wins).

Gene Klein (b. Jan. 29, 1921, d. Mar. 12, 1990): Horseman; won 3 Eclipse awards as top owner (1985-87); his filly Winning Colors won 1988 Kentucky Derby; also owned San Diego Chargers football team (1966-84).

Bob Knight (b. Oct. 25, 1940): Basketball; all-time NCAA Div. I coaching leader with 890 wins in 41 years; coached Indiana to 3 NCAA titles (1976,81,87); 3-time Coach of Year (1975-76,89); coached 1984 U.S. Olympic team to gold medal; his volatile temper finally cost him when he was fired from Indiana in Sept. 2000 after a string of unacceptable incidents that included choking one of his players; returned to coaching with Texas Tech in 2001.

Phil Knight (b. Feb. 24, 1938): Founder and chairman of Nike, Inc., the multi-billion dollar shoe and fitness company founded in 1972 and based in Beaverton, Ore.; named "The Most Powerful Man in Sports" by *The Sporting News* in 1992.

Bill Koch (b. June 7, 1955): Cross country skiing; first highly accomplished American male in his sport; first American male to win a cross country Olympic medal when he took home a silver in the 30-kilometer race in 1976; in 1982, he was the first American male to win the Nordic World Cup.

Tommy Kono (b. June 27, 1930): weight lifter; won 2 olympic gold medals for U.S. (1952,56) and 1 silver (1960); all 3 medals were in different weight classes; set world records in four different classes; inducted into U.S. Olympic Hall of Fame in 1990.

Olga Korbut (b. May 16, 1955): Soviet gymnast; became the media darling of the 1972 Olympics in Munich by winning 3 gold medals (balance beam, floor exercise and team all-around); came back in the 1976 Olympics in Montreal and was a part of the USSR's gold medal winning all-around team; first to perform back somersault on balance beam; was inducted into the International Women's Sports Hall of Fame in 1982, the first gymnast to be inducted.

Johann Olav Koss (b. Oct. 29, 1968): Norwegian speed skater; won three gold medals at 1994 Olympics in Lillehammer with world records in the 1,500m, 5,000m and 10,000m; also won 1,500m gold and 10,000m silver in 1992 Games; retired shortly after '94 Olympics.

Sandy Koufax (b. Dec. 30, 1935): Baseball LHP; led NL in strikeouts 4 times and ERA 5 straight years; won 3 Cy Young Awards (1963,65,66) with LA Dodgers; MVP in 1963; 2-time World Series MVP (1963, 65); threw perfect game against Chicago Cubs (1-0, Sept. 9, 1965) and had 3 other no-hitters, 40 shutouts and 137 complete games in a career that ended prematurely due to an arm injury.

Alvin Kraenzlein (b. Dec. 12, 1876, d. Jan. 6, 1928): Track & Field; won 4 individual gold medals in 1900 Olympics (60m, long jump and the 110m and 200m hurdles).

Jack Kramer (b. Aug. 1, 1921): Tennis; Wimbledon singles champ 1947; U.S. champ 1946-47; promoter and Open pioneer.

Lenny Krayzelburg (b. Sept. 28, 1975): Swimmer; born in Ukraine but became American citizen in 1995; won gold for U.S. in the 100m and 200m backstrokes at the 2000 Sydney Games; was also part of U.S. team that set a world record in the 4x100m medley relay in Sydney.

Ingrid Kristiansen (b. Mar. 21, 1956): Norwegian runner; 2-time Boston Marathon winner (1986,89); won New York City Marathon in 1989; former world record holder in the marathon.

Julie Krone (b. July 24, 1963): Jockey; only woman to ride winner in a Triple Crown race when she took 1993 Belmont Stakes aboard Colonial Affair; retired in 1999 as all-time winningest female jockey with over 3,000 wins; became the first female jockey named to hall of fame in 2000; came out of retirement in 2002, winning 2003 Breeders Cup race aboard Halfbridled.

Mike Krzyzewski (b. Feb. 13, 1947): Basketball; has coached Duke to 10 Final Four appearances and 3 NCAA titles (1991-92,2001); has coached at Army (1976-80) and Duke (1981–); inducted into Hall of Fame in 2001.

Bowie Kuhn (b. Oct. 28, 1926, d. March 15, 2007): Baseball Commissioner; Elected commissioner on Feb. 4, 1969 and served until Sept. 30, 1984; kept Willie Mays and Mickey Mantle out of baseball for their employment with casinos; handed down one-year suspensions of several players for drug involvement; nixed Charlie Finley's sale of three players for $3.5 million; baseball enjoyed unprecedented attendance and television contracts during his reign.

Alan Kulwicki (b. Dec. 14, 1954, d. Apr. 1, 1993): Auto racer; 1992 NASCAR national champion; 1st college grad and Northerner to win title; NASCAR Rookie of Year in 1986; famous for driving car backwards on victory lap; killed at age 38 in plane crash near Bristol, Tenn.

Michelle Kwan (b. July 7, 1980): Figure Skater; 1998 Olympic silver medalist at Nagano and 2002 bronze medalist at Salt Lake City; 9-time U.S. Champion (1996,98-05) and 5-time World Champ (1996,98,00,01,03); holds U.S. record with 8 career overall medals at the World Championships (5 gold, 3 silver); was U.S. alternate to the Olympics in 1994 as a 13-year-old.

Tony La Russa (b. Oct. 4, 1944): Baseball; former manager of the White Sox and A's and now current manager of the St. Louis Cardinals (since 1996); led A's (1989) and Cardinals (2006) to titles—just the 2nd manager to accomplish that feat in MLB history.

Marion Ladewig (b. Oct. 30, 1914): Bowler; named Woman Bowler of the Year 9 times (1950-54,57-59,63).

Guy Lafleur (b. Sept. 20, 1951): Hockey RW; led NHL in scoring 3 times (1976-78); 2-time MVP (1977-78), played for 5 Stanley Cup winners in Montreal; playoff MVP in 1977; returned to NHL as player in 1988 after election to Hall of Fame; retired again in 1991 with 560 goals and 1,353 points.

Napoleon (Nap) Lajoie (b. Sept. 5, 1874, d. Feb. 7, 1959): Baseball 2B; led AL in batting 3 times (1901,03-04); batted .422 in 1901; hit .339 for career with 3,251 hits.

Jack Lambert (b. July 8, 1952): Football LB; 6-time All-Pro (1975-76,79-82); led Pittsburgh to 4 Super Bowl titles.

Floyd Landis (b. Oct. 14, 1975): Cycling; surprising winner of the 2006 Tour de France; it was later revealed that 2 of his' urine samples taken during the race tested positive for high testosterone levels; arbitration panel ruled against him in Sept. 2007, thus formally stripping him of his title.

Kenesaw Mountain Landis (b. Nov. 20, 1866, d. Nov. 25, 1944): U.S. District Court judge who became first baseball commissioner (1920-44); banned eight Chicago "Black Sox" from baseball for life for throwing 1919 World Series.

Tom Landry (b. Sept. 11, 1924, d. Feb. 12, 2000): Football; All-Pro DB for NY Giants (1954); coached Dallas for 29 years (1960-88); won 2 Super Bowls (1972,78); 3rd on NFL all-time list with 270 wins.

Steve Largent (b. Sept. 28, 1954): Football WR; retired in 1989 after 14 years in Seattle with then NFL records in passes caught (819) and TD passes caught (100); elected to U.S. House of Representatives (R, Okla.) in 1994 and Pro Football Hall of Fame in '95; ran for governor of Oklahoma in 2002 but suffered a narrow defeat.

Don Larsen (b. Aug. 7, 1929): Baseball RHP; NY Yankees hurler who pitched the only perfect game in World Series history—a 2-0 victory over Brooklyn in Game 5 of the 1956 Series; Series MVP that year.

Tommy Lasorda (b. Sept. 22, 1927): Baseball; managed LA Dodgers to 2 World Series titles (1981,88) in 4 appearances; retired as manager during 1996 season with 1,599 regular-season wins in 21 years; named interim GM of Dodgers in 1998; member of Baseball Hall of Fame; managed gold-medal winning U.S. Olympic team in 2000 at Sydney.

Larissa Latynina (b. Dec. 27, 1934): Soviet gymnast; won total of 18 medals, (9 gold) in 3 Olympics (1956,60,64).

Nikki Lauda (b. Feb. 22, 1949): Austrian auto racer; 3-time world Formula One champion (1975, 77,84); 25 career wins from 1971-85.

Rod Laver (b. Aug. 9, 1938): Australian tennis player; undersized but big-hitting left-hander is only player to win Grand Slam twice (1962,69); Wimbledon champion 4 times; 1st to earn $1 million in career prize money, won 11 Grand Slam and 47 professional singles titles.

Bobby Layne (b. Dec. 19, 1926, d. Dec. 1, 1986): Football QB; college star at Texas; master of 2-minute offense; led Detroit to 4 divisional titles and 3 NFL championships in 1950s.

Frank Leahy (b. Aug. 27, 1908, d. June 21, 1973): Football; coached Notre Dame to four national titles (1943,46-47,49); career record of 107-13-9 for a winning pct. of .864.

Sammy Lee (b. Aug. 1, 1920): Diving; won Olympic gold medals for U.S. in the platform diving event in 1948 and 1952, the first male diver in history to win 2 golds in that event; Sullivan Award winner (1953); former Dr. in U.S. Army; trained Greg Louganis.

Brian Leetch (b. Mar. 3, 1968): Hockey D; NHL Rookie of Year in 1989; won Norris Trophy as top defenseman in 1992; Conn Smythe Trophy winner as playoffs' MVP in 1994 when he helped lead NY Rangers to 1st Stanley Cup title in 54 years.

Jacques Lemaire (b. Sept. 7, 1945): Hockey C; member of 8 Stanley Cup champions in Montreal; scored 366 goals in 12 seasons; coached Canadiens (1983-85) and NJ Devils (1993-98), won 1995 Stanley Cup with New Jersey; returned to coaching with the expansion Minnesota Wild in 2000.

Mario Lemieux (b. Oct. 5, 1965): Hockey C; 6-time NHL scoring leader (1988-89,92-93,96-97); Rookie of Year (1985); 4-time All-NHL 1st team (1988-89,93,96); 3-time regular season MVP (1988,93,96); 3-time All-Star Game MVP; led Pittsburgh to consecutive Stanley Cup titles (1991 and '92) and was playoff MVP both years; won 1993 scoring title despite missing 24 games to undergo radiation treatments for Hodgkin's disease; missed 62 games during 1993-94 season and entire 1994-95 season due to back injuries and fatigue; returned in 1995-96 to lead NHL in scoring and win the MVP trophy; retired after 1996-97 season and inducted into the Hall of Fame; headed group of investors that bought bankrupt Penguins in 1999; made surprising return to the ice in 2001 as owner-player with Penguins; retired again in 2006.

Greg LeMond (b. June 26, 1961): American cyclist; 3-time Tour de France winner (1986,89-90); only non-European to win the event until Lance Armstrong in 1999; retired in Dec. 1994 after being diagnosed with a rare muscular disease known as mitochondrial myopathy.

Ivan Lendl (b. Mar. 7, 1960): Czech tennis player; No. 1 player in world 4 times (1985-87,89); won both French and U.S. Opens 3 times and Australian twice; owns 94 career tournament wins.

Suzanne Lenglen (b. May 24, 1899, d. July 4, 1938): French tennis player; dominated women's tennis from 1919-26; won both Wimbledon and French singles titles 6 times.

Sugar Ray Leonard (b. May 17, 1956): Boxer; light welterweight Olympic champ (1976); won world welterweight title in 1979 and 4 more titles; in 1987 he upset Marvin Hagler for the middleweight crown; retired and unretired several times, before ending his career for good in 1997 with record of 36-3-1 and 25 KOs following a TKO loss to Hector Camacho.

Walter (Buck) Leonard (b. Sept. 8, 1907, d. Nov. 27, 1997): Baseball 1B; won Negro League championship nine years in a row with the Homestead Grays; hit .391 in 1948 to lead the league; usually batted cleanup behind Josh Gibson; retired at the age of 48; member of the National Baseball Hall of Fame.

Lisa Leslie (b. July 7, 1972): Basketball C; 2-time WNBA Finals MVP (2001-02) with the champion Los Angeles Sparks; 3-time regular season MVP (2001,2004,2006); 3-time WNBA All-Star Game MVP (1999,2001-02); 3-time Olympic gold medalist (1996,2000,2004); consensus National Player of the Year at USC (1994).

Marv Levy (b. Aug. 3, 1928): Football; coached Buffalo to four consecutive Super Bowls, but is one of two coaches who are 0-4 (Bud Grant is the other); won 50 games and two CFL Grey Cups with Montreal (1974,77); returned to Bills as GM in 2006.

Bill Lewis (b. Nov. 30, 1868, d. Jan. 1, 1949): Football; college star at Amherst College and then Harvard; first black player to be selected as an All-American (1892-93); also the first black admitted to the American Bar Association (1911); was U.S. Assistant Attorney General.

Carl Lewis (b. July 1, 1961): Track & Field; won 9 Olympic gold medals; 4 in 1984 (100m, 200m, 4x100m, LJ), 2 in '88 (100m, LJ), 2 in '92 (4x100m, LJ) and 1 in '96 (LJ); has record 8 World Championship titles and 9 medals in all; Sullivan Award winner (1981); two-time AP Athlete of the Year (1983-84); in 1991, set world record in 100m with a 9.86 (since broken).

Lennox Lewis (b. Sept. 2, 1965): British boxer; won 1988 Olympic super heavyweight gold medal for Canada; was awarded WBC heavyweight belt when Riddick Bowe tossed it in a London trash can in 1993; lost title in a 2nd round TKO loss to Oliver McCall; won rematch 3 years later when McCall suffered emotional breakdown in the ring; unified titles in his rematch with Evander Holyfield in Nov. 1999; lost belts in upset loss to Hasim Rahman in April 2001 but took them back 7 months later; recorded 8th-round KO of Mike Tyson in June 2002.

Nancy Lieberman (b. July 1, 1958): Basketball; 3-time All-America and 2-time Player of Year (1979-80); led Old Dominion to consecutive AIAW titles in 1979 and '80; played in defunct WPBL and WABA and became 1st woman to play in men's pro league (USBL) in 1986; played in the inaugural season of the WNBA for the Phoenix Mercury and served as coach/GM of Detroit Shock (1998-2000).

Eric Lindros (b. Feb. 28, 1973): Hockey C; No. 1 pick in 1991 NHL draft by Quebec but sat out 1991-92 season rather than play for Nordiques; traded to Philadelphia in 1992 for 6 players, 2 No. 1 picks and $15 million; elected Flyers captain at age 22; won Hart Trophy as NHL MVP in 1995; 6-time NHL all-star; suffered series of concussions since 1999.

Tara Lipinski (b. June 10, 1982): Figure Skater; won the 1998 women's figure skating gold medal at the Olympics in Nagano, becoming the youngest in history (15 yrs., 7 mos.) to do so; she and Michelle Kwan gave the U.S. its first 1-2 finish in that event since 1956; 1997 U.S. and World champion; turned pro in April 1998.

Sonny Liston (b. May 8, 1932, d. Dec. 30, 1970): Boxer; heavyweight champion (1962-64), who knocked out Floyd Patterson twice in the first round, then lost title to Muhammad Ali (then Cassius Clay) in 1964; pro record of 50-4 with 39 KOs.

Vince Lombardi (b. June 11, 1913, d. Sept. 3, 1970): Football; coached Green Bay to five NFL titles; won first two Super Bowls (1967-68); died as NFL's alltime winningest coach with percentage of .740 (105-35-6); Super Bowl trophy named in his honor.

Johnny Longden (b. Feb. 14, 1907, d. Feb. 14, 2003): Jockey; first to win 6,000 races; rode Count Fleet to Triple Crown in 1943.

Jeannie Longo (b. Oct. 31, 1958): French cyclist; 12-time world cycling champion and 1996 olympic road race gold medallist.

Nancy Lopez (b. Jan. 6, 1957): Golfer; 4-time LPGA Player of the Year (1978-79,85,88); Rookie of Year (1977); 3-time winner of LPGA Championship; reached Hall of Fame by age 30 with 35 victories; 48 career wins.

Donna Lopiano (b. Sept. 11, 1946): Former basketball and softball star who was women's athletic director at Texas for 18 years before leaving to become executive director of Women's Sports Foundation in 1992; resigned from that position in 2007.

Greg Louganis (b. Jan. 29, 1960): U.S. diver; widely considered the greatest diver in history; won platform and springboard gold medals at both 1984 and '88 Olympics; also won a silver medal at the 1976 Olympics at the age of 16; won five world championships and 47 U.S. National Diving titles; revealed on Feb. 22, 1995 that he has AIDS.

Joe Louis (b. May 13, 1914, d. Apr. 12, 1981): Boxer; world heavyweight champion from June 22, 1937 to Mar. 1, 1949; his reign of 11 years, 8 months longest in division history; successfully defended title 25 times; retired in 1949, but returned to lose title shot against successor Ezzard Charles in 1950 and then to Rocky Marciano in '51; pro record of 63-3 with 49 KOs.

Sid Luckman (b. Nov. 21, 1916, d. July 5, 1998): Football QB; 6-time All-Pro; led Chicago Bears to 4 NFL titles (1940-41,43,46); MVP in 1943.

Hank Luisetti (b. June 16, 1916, d. Dec. 17, 2002): Basketball F; 3-time All-America at Stanford (1936-38); revolutionized game with one-handed shot.

Johnny Lujack (b. Jan. 4, 1925): Football QB; led Notre Dame to three national titles (1943,46-47); won Heisman Trophy in 1947.

Darrell Wayne Lukas (b. Sept. 2, 1935): Horse racing; 4-time Eclipse-winning trainer who saddled Horses of Year Lady's Secret in 1988 and Criminal Type in 1990; first trainer to earn over $100 million in purses; led nation in earnings 14 times since 1983; Grindstone's Kentucky Derby win in 1996 gave him six Triple Crown wins in a row; has won Preakness 5 times, Kentucky Derby 4 times and Belmont 4 times; his most recent Triple Crown victory came in the 2000 Belmont with Commendable; leads all Breeders' Cup trainers with 16 victories.

Gen. Douglas MacArthur (b. Jan. 26, 1880, d. Apr. 5, 1964): Controversial U.S. general of World War II and Korea; president of U.S. Olympic Committee (1927-28); college football devotee, National Football Foundation MacArthur Bowl named after him.

Connie Mack (b. Dec. 22, 1862, d. Feb. 8, 1956): Baseball owner; managed Philadelphia A's until he was 87 (1901-50); all-time major league wins leader with 3,755, including World Series; won 9 AL pennants and 5 World Series (1910-11,13,29-30); also finished last 17 times.

Andy MacPhail (b. Apr. 5, 1953): Baseball; Former Chicago Cubs president/CEO who was GM of 2 World Series champions in Minnesota (1987,91); won first title at age 34; son of Lee, grandson of Larry.

Larry MacPhail (b. Feb. 3, 1890, d. Oct. 1, 1975): Baseball exec. and innovator; introduced major leagues to night games at Cincinnati (May 24, 1935); won pennant in Brooklyn (1941) and World Series with NY Yankees (1947); father of Lee, grandfather of Andy.

Lee MacPhail (b. Oct. 25, 1917): Baseball; AL president (1974-83); president of owners' Player Relations Committee (1984-85); also GM of Baltimore (1959-65) and NY Yankees (1967-74); son of Larry and father of Andy.

Wendy Macpherson (b. Jan. 28, 1968): Bowling; voted Bowler of the Decade for the 1990s; Major titles include the 1986 BPAA U.S. Open, 1988, 2000 and 2003 WIBC Queens and 1999 Sam's Town Invitational; annual PWBA money winner 4 times.

John Madden (b. Apr. 10, 1936): Football and Radio-TV; won 112 games and a Super Bowl (1976 season) as coach of Oakland Raiders; has won 15 Emmy Awards since 1982 as NFL analyst; signed 4-year, $32 million deal with Fox in 1994— a richer contract than any NFL player at the time; joined Al Michaels in ABC's Monday Night Football booth in 2002 after 21 seasons alongside Pat Summerall; joined NBC for Sunday Night Football beginning in 2006.

Greg Maddux (b. Apr. 14, 1966): Baseball RHP; won unprecedented 4 straight NL Cy Young Awards with Cubs (1992) and Atlanta (1993-95); has led NL in ERA four times (1993-95,98); won 15th gold glove in 2005; only pitcher to win at least 15 games in 17 straight seasons (1988-2004); got his 300th win in 2004 (347 through 2007).

Larry Mahan (b. Nov. 21, 1943): Rodeo; 6-time All-Around world champion cowboy (1966-70,73).

Phil Mahre (b. May 10, 1957): Alpine skier; 3-time World Cup overall champ (1981-83); finished 1-2 with twin brother Steve in 1984 Olympic slalom.

Karl Malone (b. July 24, 1963): Basketball F; 11-time All-NBA 1st team (1989-99) with Utah; 2-time NBA MVP (1997,99); all-time NBA leader in free throws made (9,787), 2nd in career points (36,928) and field goals made (13,528); member of the 1992 and '96 Olympic gold medal teams; named one of the NBA's 50 greatest players.

Moses Malone (b. Mar. 23, 1955): Basketball C; signed with Utah of ABA out of high school at age 19; led NBA in rebounding 6 times; 4-time All-NBA 1st team; 3-time NBA MVP (1979,82-83); Finals MVP with Philadelphia in 1983; played 21 pro seasons.

Peyton Manning (b. Mar. 24, 1976): Football QB; graduated from Tennessee in 1998 and became the top overall pick by the Indianapolis Colts in the 1998 draft; 2-time Associated Press NFL MVP (2003-04); led AFC in passing efficiency 4 times (1998,2004-06); entered 2007 with 275 touchdown passes, 7th on the all-time list; threw an NFL record 49 TD passes in 2004, breaking Dan Marino's record of 48; led Colts to long-awaited Super Bowl title in 2007 (XLI); son of Archie, brother of Eli.

Nigel Mansell (b. Aug. 8, 1953): British auto racer; won 1992 Formula One driving championship with record 9 victories and 14 poles; quit Grand Prix circuit to race Indy cars in 1993; 1st rookie to win IndyCar title; 3rd driver to win IndyCar and F1 titles; returned to F1 after 1994 IndyCar season and won '94 Australian Grand Prix; left F1 again on May 23, 1995 with 31 wins and 32 poles in 15 years.

Mickey Mantle (b. Oct. 20, 1931, d. Aug. 13, 1995): Baseball CF; led AL in home runs 4 times; won Triple Crown in 1956; hit 52 HRs in 1956 and 54 in '61; 3-time MVP (1956-57,62); hit 536 career HRs; played in 12 World Series with NY Yankees and won 7 times; all-time World Series leader in HRs (18), RBI (40), runs (42) and strikeouts (54); inducted into Baseball Hall of Fame in 1974.

Diego Maradona (b. Oct. 30, 1960): Soccer F; captain and MVP of 1986 World Cup champion Argentina; also led national team to 1990 World Cup final; consensus Player of Decade in 1980s; led Napoli to 2 Italian League titles (1987,90) and UEFA Cup (1989); tested positive for cocaine and suspended 15 months by FIFA in 1991; returned to World Cup as Argentine captain in 1994, but was kicked out after two games when test found 5 banned substances in his urine.

Pete Maravich (b. June 27, 1947, d. Jan. 5, 1988): Basketball; NCAA scoring leader 3 times at LSU (1968-70); averaged NCAA-record 44.2 points a game over career; Player of Year in 1970; NBA scoring champ in '77 with New Orleans.

Alice Marble (b. Sept. 28, 1913, d. Dec. 13, 1990): Tennis; 4-time U.S. champion (1936,38-40); won Wimbledon in 1939; swept U.S. singles, doubles and mixed doubles from 1938-40.

Gino Marchetti (b. Jan. 2, 1927): Football DE; 8-time NFL All-Pro (1957-64) with Baltimore Colts.

Rocky Marciano (b. Sept. 1, 1923, d. Aug. 31, 1969): Boxer; heavyweight champion (1952-56); only heavyweight champ in history to retire undefeated; pro record of 49-0 with 43 KOs; killed in plane crash.

Juan Marichal (b. Oct. 20, 1938): Baseball RHP; won 21 or more games 6 times for S.F. Giants from 1963-69; ended 16-year career at 243-142.

Dan Marino (b. Sept. 15, 1961): Football QB; 2nd all-time (to Favre) in career NFL TD passes (420), attempts (8,358) and completions (4,967); leader in passing yards (61,361); 4-time leading passer in AFC (1983-84,86,89); set NFL single-season records for TD passes (48) and passing yards (5,084) in 1984 (TD passes since broken by P. Manning with 49 in 2004).

Roger Maris (b. Sept. 10, 1934, d. Dec. 14, 1985): Baseball OF; broke Babe Ruth's season HR record with 61 in 1961 and held record until 1998 (Mark McGwire); 2-time AL MVP (1960-61) with NY Yankees; 275 HRs in 12 years.

Jim Marshall (b. Dec. 30, 1937): Football; long-time Vikings DE and NFL ironman; played in 282 consecutive games (1960-1979); also famous for picking up a fumble and running 66 yards the wrong way into the opponent's (49ers) endzone.

Billy Martin (b. May 16, 1928, d. Dec. 25, 1989): Baseball; 5-time manager of NY Yankees; won 2 pennants and 1 World Series (1977); also managed Minnesota, Detroit, Texas and Oakland; played on 5 Yankee world champions in 1950s.

Pedro Martinez (b. Oct. 25, 1971): Baseball RHP; won 1997 NL Cy Young award with Montreal; traded to Boston Red Sox in Nov. 1997; 2-time AL Cy Young Award winner with Boston (1999,2000); signed with NY Mets in 2005.

Eddie Mathews (b. Oct. 13, 1931, d. Feb. 18, 2001): Baseball 3B; led NL in HRs twice (1953,59); hit 30 or more HRs 9 straight years; 512 career HRs.

Christy Mathewson (b. Aug. 12, 1880, d. Oct. 7, 1925): Baseball RHP; won 22 or more games 12 straight years (1903-14); 373 career wins; pitched 3 shutouts in 1905 World Series.

Bob Mathias (b. Nov. 17, 1930, d. Sept. 2, 2006): Track & Field; youngest winner of decathlon with gold medal in 1948 Olympics at age 17; first to repeat as decathlon champ in 1952; Sullivan Award winner (1948); 4-term member of U.S. Congress (R, Calif.) from 1967-74.

Ollie Matson (b. May 1, 1930): Football HB; All-America at San Francisco (1951); bronze medal winner in 400m at 1952 Olympics; 4-time All-Pro for NFL Chicago Cardinals (1954-57); traded to LA Rams for 9 players in 1959; accounted for 12,884 all-purpose yards and scored 73 TDs in 14 seasons.

Don Mattingly (b. Apr. 20, 1961): Baseball 1B; AL MVP (1985); won AL batting title in 1984 (.343); led majors with 145 RBI in 1985; led AL with 238 hits (Yankee record) and 53 doubles in 1986; won 9 Gold Glove Awards at 1B (1985-89, 91-94).

Willie Mays (b. May 6, 1931): Baseball OF; nick-named the "Say Hey Kid"; led NL in HRs and stolen bases 4 times each; 2-time MVP (1954,65) with NY-SF Giants; Hall of Famer who played in 24 All-Star Games, earning MVP honors twice (1963,68); 12-time Gold Glove winner; 660 HRs, 1,903 RBI and 3,283 hits in career.

Bill Mazeroski (b. Sept. 5, 1936): Baseball 2B; career .260 hitter who won the 1960 World Series for Pittsburgh with a lead-off HR in the bottom of the 9th inning of Game 7; the pitcher was Ralph Terry of the NY Yankees, the count was 1-0 and the score was tied 9-9; also a sure-fielder, Maz won 8 Gold Gloves in 17 seasons.

Bob McAdoo (b. Sept. 25, 1951): Basketball F/C; 1972 *Sporting News* First Team All-American; NBA Rookie of the Year (1973); NBA MVP (1975); All-NBA First Team (1975); Led NBA in scoring three consecutive years (1974-76); 5-time All-Star (1974-78); two championships with LA Lakers (1982,85).

Joe McCarthy (b. Apr. 21, 1887, d. Jan. 13, 1978): Baseball; first manager to win pennants in both leagues (Chicago Cubs in 1929 and NY Yankees in 1932); greatest success came with Yankees when he won seven pennants and six World Series championships from 1936 to 1943; first manager to win four World Series in a row (1936-39); finished his career with the Boston Red Sox (1948-50); lifetime record of 2125-1333; member of Baseball Hall of Fame.

Pat McCormick (b. May 12, 1930): U.S. diver; won women's platform and springboard gold medals in both 1952 and '56 Olympics.

Willie McCovey (b. Jan. 10, 1938): Baseball 1B; led NL in HRs 3 times and RBI twice; MVP in 1969 with SF; 521 career HRs; "McCovey Cove," the bay outside the rightfield fence at San Francisco's AT&T Park is named for him.

John McEnroe (b. Feb. 16, 1959): Tennis; No.1 player in the world 4 times (1981-84); 4-time U.S. Open champ (1979-81,84); 3-time Wimbledon champ (1981,83-84); played on 5 Davis Cup winners (1978,79,81,82,92); won NCAA singles title (1978); finished career with 77 singles championships, 77 more in men's doubles (including 9 Grand Slam titles), and U.S. Davis Cup records for years played (13) and singles matches won (41).

John McGraw (b. Apr. 7, 1873, d. Feb. 25, 1934): Baseball; managed NY Giants to 9 NL pennants between 1905-24; won 3 World Series (1905,21-22); 2nd on all-time career list with 2,866 wins in 33 seasons (2,840 regular season and 26 World Series).

Frank McGuire (b. Nov. 8, 1916, d. Oct. 11, 1994): Basketball; winner of 731 games as high school, college and pro coach; won at least 100 games at 3 colleges— St. John's (103), North Carolina (164) and South Carolina (283); won 550 games in 30 college seasons; 1957 UNC team went 32-0 and beat Kansas 54-53 in triple OT to win NCAA title; coached NBA Philadelphia Warriors to 49-31 record in 1961-62, but refused to move with team to San Francisco.

Mark McGwire (b. Oct. 1, 1963): Baseball 1B; Member of 1984 U.S. Olympic baseball team; won AL Rookie of the Year and hit rookie-record 49 HRs in 1987; shattered Roger Maris' season home run record (61) in 1998 with St. Louis (70); followed that with 65 HRs in 1999; retired in 2001 with 583 HR; took a tremendous media hit and became a target for steroid accusations after he stood up in Congress in 2005 and refused to "talk about the past."

Jim McKay (b. Sept. 24, 1921): Radio-TV; host and commentator of ABC's Olympic coverage and "Wide World of Sports" show since 1961; 12-time Emmy winner; also given Peabody Award in 1988 and Life Achievement Emmy in 1990; became part owner of Baltimore Orioles in 1993.

Tamara McKinney (b. Oct. 16, 1962): Skiing; first American woman to win overall Alpine World Cup championship (1983); won World Cup slalom (1984) and giant slalom titles twice (1981,83).

Denny McLain (b. Mar. 29, 1944): Baseball RHP; last pitcher to win 30 games (1968); 2-time Cy Young winner (1968-69) with Detroit; convicted of racketeering, extortion and drug possession in 1985, served 29 months of 25-year jail term, sentence overturned when court ruled he had not received a fair trial; he has faced subsequent legal troubles.

Rick Mears (b. Dec. 3, 1951): Auto racer; 3-time CART national champ (1979,81-82); 4-time winner of Indy 500 (1979,84,88,91) and only driver to win 6 Indy 500 poles; Indy 500 Rookie of Year (1978); retired in 1992 with 29 CART wins and 40 poles.

Mark Messier (b. Jan. 18, 1961): Hockey C; 2-time NHL MVP with Edmonton (1990) and NY Rangers (1992); captain of 1994 Rangers team that won 1st Stanley Cup since 1940; ranks 2nd in all-time play-off points, goals and assists; 2nd in all-time regular season points list (1,887); retired in 2005.

Mike Metzger (b. Nov. 19, 1975): Freestyle Motocross Rider; AMA National mini-bike champion (1990), credited as "The Godfather" of FMX for his early creative influences and trick inventions; first to land back-to-back backflips in competition (2002 X Games), winner of five X Games medals.

Debbie Meyer (b. Aug. 14, 1952): Swimmer; 1st swimmer to win 3 individual golds at 1 Olympics (1968).

Ann Meyers (b. Mar. 26, 1955): Basketball G; in 1974, became first high schooler to play for U.S. national team; 4-time All-American at UCLA (1976-79); member of 1976 U.S. Olympic team; Broderick Award and Cup winner (1978); Signed $50,000 no cut contract with NBA's Indiana Pacers (1980); married Dodger great Don Drysdale.

George Mikan (b. June 18, 1924, d. June 2, 2005): Basketball C; 3-time All-America (1944-46); led DePaul to NIT title (1945); led Minneapolis Lakers to 5 NBA titles in 6 years (1949-54); first commissioner of ABA (1967-69).

Stan Mikita (b. May 20, 1940): Hockey C; led NHL in scoring 4 times; won both MVP and Lady Byng awards in 1967 and '68 with Chicago.

Bode Miller (b. Oct. 12, 1977): Alpine Skier; won 2 silver medals at 2002 Winter Games; 2 golds, 1 silver at 2003 World Championships; 2nd overall in 2003 World Cup standings; 2004 Giant Slalom World Cup champion; 2005 Overall World Cup champ; came up empty at Turin Games in 2006; 2007 Super G World Cup champ.

Cheryl Miller (b. Jan. 3, 1964): Basketball; 3-time College Player of Year (1984-86); led USC to NCAA title and U.S. to Olympic gold medal in 1984; coached USC to 44-14 record in 2 years; coached WNBA's Phoenix Mercury for 4 years; sister of NBA's Reggie.

Del Miller (b. July 5, 1913, d. Aug. 19, 1996): Harness racing; driver, trainer, owner, breeder, seller and track owner; drove to 2,441 wins from 1929-90.

Marvin Miller (b. Apr. 14, 1917): Baseball labor leader; executive director of Players' Assn. from 1966-82; increased average salary from $19,000 to over $240,000; led 13-day strike in 1972 and 50-day walkout in '81.

Shannon Miller (b. Mar. 10, 1977): Gymnast; won 5 medals in 1992 Olympics and 2 golds in '96 Games; All-Around world champion in 1993 and '94.

Billy Mills (b. June 30, 1938): Track & Field; Native American who was upset winner of 10,000m gold medal at 1964 Olympics.

Bora Milutinovic (b. Sept. 7, 1944): Soccer; Serbian who coached U.S. national team from 1991-95; led Mexico (1986), Costa Rica ('90), USA ('94) and Nigeria ('98) into the 2nd round of the World Cup; coached China in 2002 Cup but was ousted in the first round.

Dave Mirra (b. Apr. 4, 1974): BMX; medaled in every summer X Games since 1995; has 20 X Games medals (14 gold); first to do a double backflip on a BMX bike; nicknamed "Miracle Boy" after his brush with death when he was hit by a drunk driver (1994).

Tommy Moe (b. Feb. 17, 1970): Alpine skier; won Downhill gold and Super-G silver at 1994 Winter Olympics; 1st U.S. man to win 2 Olympic alpine medals in one year.

Paul Molitor (b. Aug. 22, 1956): Baseball DH-1B; All-America SS at Minnesota in 1976; spent 15 years with Milwaukee, then 3 each with Toronto and Minnesota; led Blue Jays to 2nd straight World Series title as MVP (1993); hit .418 in 2 Series appearances (1982,93); holds World Series game record with 5 hits.

Joe Montana (b. June 11, 1956): Football QB; led Notre Dame to national title in 1977; led San Francisco to 4 Super Bowl titles in 1980s; only 3-time Super Bowl MVP; 2-time NFL MVP (1989-90); led NFL in passing 5 times; traded to K.C. in 1993; ranks 4th all-time in passing efficiency (92.3); 273 career TD passes and 40,551 passing yards; inducted into Pro Football Hall of Fame in 2000.

Helen Wills Moody (b. Oct. 6, 1905, d. Jan. 1, 1998): Tennis; won 8 Wimbledon singles titles, 7 U.S. and 4 French from 1923-38.

Warren Moon (b. Nov. 18, 1956): Football QB; MVP of 1978 Rose Bowl with Washington; MVP of CFL with Edmonton in 1983; led Eskimos to 5 consecutive Grey Cup titles (1978-82) and was playoff MVP twice (1980,82); entered NFL in 1984 and played for 4 different teams; picked for 9 Pro Bowls; inducted into Pro Football Hall of Fame in 2006.

Archie Moore (b. Dec. 13, 1913, d. Dec. 9, 1998): Boxer; world light heavyweight champion (1952-60); pro record 199-26-8 with a record 145 KOs.

Noureddine Morceli (b. Feb. 28, 1970): Algerian runner; 3-time world champion at 1,500 meters (1991,93,95) and 1996 Olympic gold medal winner; former holder of world records in several middle distance events.

Howie Morenz (b. June 21, 1902, d. Mar. 8, 1937): Hockey C; 3-time NHL MVP (1928,31,32); led Montreal Canadiens to 3 Stanley Cups; voted Outstanding Player of the Half-Century in 1950.

Joe Morgan (b. Sept. 19, 1943): Baseball 2B; regular-season MVP both years he led Cincinnati to World Series titles (1975-76); 1,865 career walks; led NL in walks 4 times; ESPN baseball announcer.

Bobby Morrow (b. Oct. 15, 1935): Track & Field; won 3 gold medals at 1956 Olympics (100m, 200m and 4x400m relay).

Willie Mosconi (b. June 27, 1913, d. Sept. 12, 1993): Pocket Billiards; 14-time world champ (1941-57).

Annemarie Moser-Pröll (b. Mar. 27, 1953): Austrian alpine skier; won World Cup overall title 6 times (1971-75,79); all-time women's World Cup leader in career wins with 61; won Downhill in 1980 Olympics.

Edwin Moses (b. Aug. 31, 1955): Track & Field; won 400m hurdles at 1976 and '84 Olympics, bronze medal in '88; also winner of 122 consecutive races from 1977-87.

Stirling Moss (b. Sept. 17, 1929): Auto racer; won 194 of 466 career races and 16 Formula One events, but was never world champion.

Marion Motley (b. June 5, 1920, d. June 27, 1999): Football FB/LB; hard-charging runner who was all-time leading AAFC rusher; ran for over 4,700 yards and 31 TDs for Cleveland Browns (1946-53), leading the NFL in 1950; first black member of the Pro Football Hall of Fame.

Shirley Muldowney (b. June 19, 1940): Drag Racer; "Cha Cha"; women's racing pioneer; 3-time Winston drag racing Top Fuel champion (1977,80,82); recorded 18 career NHRA National Event victories.

Anthony Munoz (b. Aug. 19, 1958): Football OT; drafted 3rd overall in 1980 out of USC; 11-time All-Pro with Cincinnati; member of NFL 75th Anniv. All-Team; elected to Hall of Fame in 1998.

Calvin Murphy (b. May 9, 1948): Basketball G; NBA All-Rookie team (1971); holds NBA single season free throw percentage (.958); has all-time career free throw pct. of .892; elected to Basketball Hall of Fame in 1992; only 5'9" and 165 pounds.

Dale Murphy (b. Mar. 12, 1956): Baseball OF; led NL in HRs and RBI twice; 2-time MVP (1982-83) with Atlanta; also played with Philadelphia and Colorado; retired in 1993 with 398 HRs.

Jack Murphy (b. Feb. 5, 1923, d. Sept. 24, 1980): Sports editor and columnist of *The San Diego Union* from 1951-80; instrumental in bringing AFL Chargers south from LA in 1961, landing Padres as NL expansion team in '69, and lobbying for San Diego stadium that would later bear his name.

Eddie Murray (b. Feb. 24, 1956): Baseball 1B-DH; AL Rookie of Year in 1977; became 20th player in history, but only 2nd switch hitter (after Pete Rose) to get 3,000 hits; one of only 4 men (Aaron, Mays and Palmeiro) with 500 HRs and 3,000 hits.

Jim Murray (b. Dec. 29, 1919, d. Aug. 16, 1998): Sports columnist for *LA Times* 1961-98; 14-time Sportswriter of the Year; won Pulitzer Prize for commentary in 1990.

Ty Murray (b. Oct. 11, 1969): Rodeo cowboy; 7-time All-Around world champion (1989-94,98); Rookie of Year in 1988; youngest (age 20) to win All-Around title; set single season earnings mark with $297,896 in 1993; career hampered by injury.

Stan Musial (b. Nov. 21, 1920): Baseball OF-1B; led NL in batting 7 times and RBI 2 times; 3-time MVP (1943,46,48) with St. Louis; played in 24 All-Star Games; had 3,630 career hits (4th all-time) and .331 average.

John Naber (b. Jan. 20, 1956): Swimmer; won 4 gold medals and a silver in 1976 Olympics.

Bronko Nagurski (b. Nov. 3, 1908, d. Jan. 7, 1990): Football FB-T; All-America at Minnesota (1929); All-Pro with Chicago Bears (1932-34); charter member of college and pro Halls of Fame.

James Naismith (b. Nov. 6, 1861, d. Nov. 28, 1939): Canadian physical education instructor who invented basketball in 1891 at the YMCA Training School (now Springfield College) in Springfield, Mass.

Joe Namath (b. May 31, 1943): Football QB; signed for unheard-of $400,000 as rookie with AFL's NY Jets in 1965; 2-time All-AFL (1968-69) and All-NFL (1972); led Jets to Super Bowl upset as MVP in '69 after making brash prediction of victory.

Ilie Nastase (b. July 19, 1946): Romanian tennis player; No.1 in the world twice (1972-73); won U.S. (1972) and French (1973) Opens; has since entered Romanian politics.

Martina Navratilova (b. Oct. 18, 1956): Tennis player; No.1 player in the world 7 times (1978-79,82-86); won her record 9th Wimbledon singles title in 1990; also won 4 U.S. Opens, 3 Australian and 2 French; in all, won 18 Grand Slam singles titles, 41 Grand Slam doubles titles; all-time leader among men and women in singles titles (167); 3rd all-time on women's career money list with over $21 million; inducted into Int'l Tennis Hall of Fame in 2000; retired in 2006 after winning U.S. Open mixed doubles title.

Cosmas Ndeti (b. Nov. 24, 1971): Kenyan distance runner; winner of three consecutive Boston Marathons (1993-95); set course record in 1994 — 2:07:15 (since broken in 2006).

Earle (Greasy) Neale (b. Nov. 5, 1891, d. Nov. 2, 1973): Baseball and Football; hit .357 for Cincinnati in 1919 World Series; also played with pre-NFL Canton Bulldogs; later coached Philadelphia Eagles to 2 NFL titles (1948-49).

Primo Nebiolo (b. July 14, 1923, d. Nov. 7, 1999): Italian president of International Amateur Athletic Federation (IAAF) since 1981; also an at-large member of International Olympic Committee; regarded as dictatorial, but credited with elevating track & field to world class financial status.

Byron Nelson (b. Feb. 4, 1912, d. Sept. 26, 2006): Golfer; 2-time winner of both Masters (1937,42) and PGA (1940,45); also U.S. Open champion in 1939; won 19 tournaments in 1945, including 11 in a row; also set all-time PGA stroke average with 68.33 strokes per round over 120 rounds in '45.

Lindsey Nelson (b. May 25, 1919, d. June 10, 1995): Radio-TV; all-purpose play-by-play broadcaster for CBS, NBC and others; 4-time Sportscaster of the Year (1959-62); voice of Cotton Bowl for 25 years and NY Mets from 1962-78; given Life Achievement Emmy Award in 1991.

Ernie Nevers (b. June 11, 1903, d. May 3, 1976): Football FB; earned 11 letters in four sports at Stanford; played pro football, baseball and basketball; scored 40 points for Chicago Cardinals in one NFL game (1929).

Paula Newby-Fraser (b. June 2, 1962): Zimbabwean triathlete; 8-time winner of Ironman Triathlon in Hawaii; established women's record of 8:55:28 in 1992.

John Newcombe (b. May 23, 1944): Australian tennis player; No.1 player in world 3 times (1967,70-71); won Wimbledon 3 times and U.S. and Australian championships twice each.

Pete Newell (b. Aug. 31, 1915): Basketball; coached at Univ. of San Francisco, Michigan St. and the Univ. of California; first coach to win NIT (San Francisco-1949), NCAA (California-1959) and Olympic gold medal (1960); later served as the general manager of the San Diego Rockets and LA Lakers in the NBA; member of Basketball Hall of Fame.

Jack Nicklaus (b. Jan. 21, 1940): Golfer; all-time leader in major tournament wins with 18— 6 Masters, 5 PGAs, 4 U.S. Opens and 3 British Opens; oldest player to win Masters (46 in 1986); PGA Player of Year 5 times (1967,72-73,75-76); named Golfer of the Century by PGA in 1988; 6-time Ryder Cup player and 2-time captain (1983,87); won NCAA title (1961) and 2 U.S. Amateurs (1959,61); 73 PGA Tour wins (2nd to Sam Snead's 82); fourth win in Tradition in 1996 gave him 8 majors on Senior PGA Tour; nicknamed "the Golden Bear."

Chuck Noll (b. Jan. 5, 1932): Football; coached Pittsburgh to 4 Super Bowl titles (1975-76,79-80); retired after 1991 season with 209 career wins (including playoffs) in 23 years.

Greg Norman (b. Feb. 10, 1955): Australian golfer; 73 tournament wins worldwide including 20 PGA Tour victories; 2-time British Open winner (1986,93); lost Masters by a stroke in both 1986 (to Jack Nicklaus) and '87 (to Larry Mize in sudden death); 1995 PGA Tour Player of the Year.

James D. Norris (b. Nov. 6, 1906, d. Feb. 25, 1966): Boxing promoter and NHL owner; president of International Boxing Club from 1949 until U.S. Supreme Court ordered its break-up (for anti-trust violations) in 1958; only NHL owner to win Stanley Cups in two cities: Detroit (1936-37,43) and Chicago (1961).

Paavo Nurmi (b. June 13, 1897, d. Oct. 2, 1973): Finnish runner; won 9 gold medals (6 individual) in 1920, '24 and '28 Olympics; from 1921-31 broke 23 world outdoor records in events ranging from 1,500 to 20,000 meters.

Dan O'Brien (b. July 18, 1966): Track & Field; Olympic decathlon gold medalist (1996); set former world record in decathlon (8,891 pts) in 1992, after shockingly failing to qualify for event at U.S. Olympic Trials; three-time gold medalist at World Championships (1991,93,95).

Larry O'Brien (b. July 7, 1917, d. Sept. 27, 1990): Basketball; former U.S. Postmaster General and 3rd NBA commissioner (1975-84), league absorbed 4 ABA teams and created salary cap during his term in office.

Parry O'Brien (b. Jan. 28, 1932): Track & Field; in 4 consecutive Olympics, won two gold medals, a silver and placed 4th in the shot put (1952-64).

Al Oerter (b. Sept. 19, 1936, d. Oct. 1, 2007): Track & Field; won 4 discus gold medals in consecutive Olympics from 1956-68.

Sadaharu Oh (b. May 20, 1940): Baseball 1B; led Japan League in HRs 15 times; 9-time MVP for Tokyo Giants; all-time Japan League HR leader with 868 in 22 years.

Hakeem Olajuwon (b. Jan. 21, 1963): Basketball C; Nigerian native who was All-America in 1984 and Final Four MOP in 1983 for Houston; overall 1st pick by Houston Rockets in 1984 NBA draft; led Rockets to back-to-back NBA titles (1994-95); regular season MVP (1994) and 2-time Finals MVP ('94-95); 6-time All-NBA 1st team (1987-89,93-95); all-time NBA blocks leader.

Jose Maria Olazabal (b. Feb. 5, 1966): Spanish golfer; has 28 worldwide victories including 2 Masters (1994,99); played on 6 European Ryder Cup teams.

Barney Oldfield (b. Jan. 29, 1878, d. Oct. 4, 1946): Auto racing pioneer; drove cars built by Henry Ford; first man to drive car a mile per minute (1903).

Walter O'Malley (b. Oct. 9, 1903, d. Aug. 9, 1979): Baseball owner; moved Brooklyn Dodgers to Los Angeles after 1957 season; won 4 World Series (1955,59,63,65).

Shaquille O'Neal (b. Mar. 6, 1972): Basketball C; 2-time All-America at LSU (1991-92); overall 1st pick (as a junior) by Orlando in 1992 NBA draft; Rookie of Year in 1993; 2-time NBA scoring leader (1995,2000); regular season MVP (2000) and 3-time NBA Finals MVP (2000,01,02); named one of the NBA's 50 Greatest Players; traded to Miami in 2004 and won a title with the Heat in 2006.

Bobby Orr (b. Mar. 20, 1948): Hockey D; league's only 8-time Norris Trophy winner as best defenseman (1968-75); credited with revolutionizing the position; 3-time Hart Trophy winner as NHL regular season MVP (1970-72); led NHL in scoring twice and assists 5 times; All-NHL 1st team 8 times; playoff MVP twice (1970,72) with Boston; career cut short due to a series of knee injuries.

Tom Osborne (b. Feb. 23, 1937): Football; Nebraska head coach from 1973-97; retired with career record of 255-49-3 and winning percentage of .836; won national championships in 1994 and '95 and shared national title with Michigan in '97; elected to U.S. Congress (R., Neb.) in 2000.

Mel Ott (b. Mar. 2, 1909, d. Nov. 21, 1958): Baseball OF; joined NY Giants at age 16; led NL in HRs 6 times; had 511 HRs and 1,860 RBI in 22 years.

Kristin Otto (b. Feb. 7, 1966): East German swimmer; 1st woman to win 6 gold medals (4 individual) at one Olympics (1988).

Francis Ouimet (b. May 8, 1893, d. Sept. 3, 1967): Golfer; won 1913 U.S. Open as 20-year-old amateur playing on Brookline, Mass. course where he used to caddie; won U.S. Amateur twice; 8-time Walker Cup player.

Jesse Owens (b. Sept. 12, 1913, d. Mar. 31, 1980): Track & Field; set 4 world records in one afternoon competing for Ohio State at the Big Ten Championships (May 25, 1935); a year later, he soundly debunked Adolf Hitler's "master race" claims, winning 4 gold medals (100m, 200m, 4x100m relay and long jump) at 1936 Summer Olympics in Berlin.

Alan Page (b. Aug. 7, 1945): Football DE; All-America at Notre Dame in 1966 and member of two national championship teams; 6-time NFL All-Pro and 1971 Player of Year with Minnesota Vikings; later a lawyer who was elected to Minnesota Supreme Court in 1992.

Satchel Paige (b. July 7, 1906, d. June 6, 1982): Baseball RHP; pitched 55 career no-hitters over 20 seasons in Negro Leagues; entered major leagues with Cleveland in 1948 at age 42; had 28-31 record in 5 years; returned to AL at age 59 to start 1 game for Kansas City in 1965 (went 3 innings, gave up a hit and got a strikeout); elected to Baseball Hall of Fame in 1971.

Se Ri Pak (b. Sept. 28, 1977): Golfer; won two Majors as an LPGA rookie in 1998 (LPGA Championship and U.S. Open); youngest player to win the U.S. Open (20); her win at the 2006 LPGA Championship gave her a total of 5 majors.

Arnold Palmer (b. Sept. 10, 1929): Golfer; winner of 4 Masters, 2 British Opens and a U.S. Open; 2-time PGA Player of Year (1960,62); 1st player to earn over $1 million in career (1968); annual PGA Tour money leader award named after him; 62 wins on PGA Tour and 10 more on Champions Tour; made 48 consecutive Masters starts.

Jim Palmer (b. Oct. 15, 1945): Baseball RHP; 3-time Cy Young Award winner (1973,75-76); won 20 or more games 8 times with Baltimore; elected to the Baseball Hall of Fame in 1990.

Bill Parcells (b. Aug. 22, 1941): Football; coached NY Giants to 2 Super Bowl titles (1987,91); retired after 1990 season then returned in 1993 as coach of New England; took hapless Pats from 2-14 in 1992 to Super Bowl (loss to Green Bay); coached the Jets for 3 seasons (1997-99), turning them from 1-15 doormat to AFC East champ in 2 years; retired again in 2000; returned to coach the Dallas Cowboys from 2003-07.

Jack Pardee (b. Apr. 19, 1936): Football; All-America LB at Texas A&M; All-Pro with LA Rams (1963) and Washington (1971); 2-time NFL Coach of Year (1976,79); won 87 games in 11 seasons; only man hired as head coach in NFL, WFL, USFL and CFL.

Bernie Parent (b. Apr. 3, 1945): Hockey G; led Philadelphia Flyers to 2 Stanley Cups as playoff MVP (1974,75); 2-time Vezina Trophy winner; posted 55 career shutouts and 2.55 GAA in 13 seasons.

Joe Paterno (b. Dec. 21, 1926): Football; passed Bear Bryant in 2001 as all-time wins leader in college football (since passed by Bobby Bowden); has coached Penn St. to 363-121-3 record, 22-10-1 bowl record and 2 national titles (1982,86) in 41 years; also had three unbeaten teams that didn't finish No. 1; 4-time Coach of Year (1968,78,82,86).

Craig Patrick (b. May 20, 1946): Hockey; 3rd generation Patrick to have name inscribed on Stanley Cup; GM of 2-time Cup champion Pittsburgh Penguins (1991-92); also captain of 1969 NCAA champion at Denver; assistant coach-GM of 1980 gold medal-winning U.S. Olympic team; grandson of Lester.

Lester Patrick (b. Dec. 30, 1883, d. June 1, 1960): Hockey; pro hockey pioneer as player, coach and general manager for 43 years; led NY Rangers to Stanley Cups as coach (1928,33) and GM (1940); grandfather of Craig.

Carly Patterson (b. Feb. 4, 1988): American gymnast; Olympic all-around champ at Athens in 2004.

Floyd Patterson (b. Jan. 4, 1935, d. May 11, 2006): Boxer; Olympic middleweight champ in 1952; world heavyweight champ (1956-59,60-62); 1st to regain heavyweight crown; fought Ingemar Johansson 3 times in 22 months from 1959-61, won last 2; pro record 55-8-1 (40 KOs).

Walter Payton (b. July 25, 1954, d. Nov. 1, 1999): Football RB; formerly NFL's all-time leading rusher with 16,726 yards (1984-2002, passed by Emmitt Smith); scored 125 career TDs; All-Pro 7 times with Chicago; led NFC in rushing 5 times (1976-80); league MVP in 1977 (AP & PFWA) and 1985 (Bell); won ring with Bears in Super Bowl XX; known as superb runner, receiver and blocker; nicknamed "Sweetness".

Calvin Peete (b. July 18, 1943): Golf; began playing golf at age 23; over $2 million in career earnings; selected to 2 U.S. Ryder Cup teams (1983,85).

Pelé (b. Oct. 23, 1940): Brazilian soccer F; given name— Edson Arantes do Nascimento; led Brazil to 3 World Cup titles (1958,62,70); came to U.S. in 1975 to play for NY Cosmos in NASL; scored 1,281 goals in 22 years including 12 goals in the World Cup; served as Brazil's minister of sport (1990-98); named IOC Athlete of the Century and FIFA's co-Player of the Century (along with Diego Maradona).

Roger Penske (b. Feb. 20, 1937): Auto racing; national sports car driving champion (1964); established racing team in 1961; co-founder of CART; Penske Racing has won 14 Indianapolis 500s and 11 CART points titles; announced move to IRL for 2002 season; won IRL points title with Sam Hornish Jr. in 2006.

Willie Pep (b. Sept. 19, 1922): Boxer; 2-time world featherweight champion (1942-48,49-50); pro record 230-11-1 with 65 KOs.

Marie-Jose Perec (b. May 9, 1968): Track & Field; French sprinter who became 2nd woman to win the 200m and 400m events in the same Olympics (1996); also won the 400 in 1992 Games.

Fred Perry (b. May 18, 1909, d. Feb. 2, 1995): British tennis player; 3-time Wimbledon champ (1934-36); first player to win all four Grand Slam singles titles, though not in same year; last native to win All-England men's title.

Gaylord Perry (b. Sept. 15, 1938): Baseball RHP; one of only four pitchers to win the Cy Young Award in both leagues; retired in 1983 with 314-265 record and 3,534 K over 22 years with 8 teams; brother Jim won 215 games for family total of 529.

Bob Pettit (b. Dec. 12, 1932): Basketball F; All-NBA 1st team 10 times (1955-64); 2-time MVP (1956,59) with St. Louis Hawks; first player to score 20,000 points.

Richard Petty (b. July 2, 1937): Auto racer; 7-time winner of Daytona 500; 7-time NASCAR national champ (1964,67,71-72,74-75,79); first stock car driver to win $1 million in career; all-time NASCAR leader in races won (200), poles (126) and wins in a single season (27 in 1967); son of Lee (55 race wins), father of Kyle (8 career wins), grandfather of Adam; nicknamed "The King".

Michael Phelps (b. June 30, 1985): American swimmer who attempted to break Mark Spitz's Olympic record of 7 gold medals in 2004 but "settled" for 6 golds and two bronzes in Athens; did however win 7 golds at the 2007 World Championships in Melbourne.

Mike Piazza (b. Sept. 4, 1968): Baseball C; slugger who broke Carlton Fisk's MLB record for HRs by a catcher in 2004 with his 352nd; 11-time All-Star.

Laffit Pincay Jr. (b. Dec. 29, 1946): Jockey; 5-time Eclipse Award winner (1971,73-74,79,85); winner of 3 Belmonts and 1 Kentucky Derby (aboard Swale in 1984); retired as all-time winningest jockey with 9,530 career wins (passed in 2006, Baze).

Scottie Pippen (b. Sept. 25, 1965): Basketball F; started on 6 NBA champions with Chicago (1991-93, 96-98); 3-time All-NBA first team (1994-96). Voted one of NBA's 50 Greatest Players.

Nelson Piquet (b. Aug. 17, 1952): Brazilian auto racer; 3-time Formula One world champion (1981,83, 87); left circuit in 1991 with 23 career wins.

Rick Pitino (b. Sept. 18, 1952): Basketball coach; won 1996 NCAA title at Kentucky; coach and president of NBA's Celtics (1997-2001); returned to college with Louisville and in 2005 became 1st to take 3 schools to the Final Four (Providence, Ky., Louisville).

Jacques Plante (b. Jan. 17, 1929, d. Feb. 27, 1986): Hockey G; led Montreal to 6 Stanley Cups (1953,56-60); won 7 Vezina Trophies; MVP in 1962; first goalie to regularly wear a mask; posted 82 shutouts with 2.38 GAA.

Gary Player (b. Nov. 1, 1936): South African golfer; 3-time winner of Masters (1961,74,78) and British Open (1959,68,74); one of only 5 players to win career Grand Slam (Hogan, Nicklaus, Sarazen and Woods); also won 2 PGAs, a U.S. Open and 2 U.S. Senior Opens.

Jim Plunkett (b. Dec. 5, 1947): Football QB; Heisman Trophy winner (Stanford) in 1970; AFL Rookie of the Year in 1971; led Oakland-LA Raiders to Super Bowl wins in 1981 and '84; MVP in '81.

Maurice Podoloff (b. Aug. 18, 1890, d. Nov. 24, 1985): Basketball; engineered merger of Basketball Assn. of America and National Basketball League into NBA in 1949; NBA commissioner (1949-63); league MVP trophy named after him.

Fritz Pollard (b. Jan. 27, 1894, d. May 11, 1986): Football; 1st black All-America RB (1916 at Brown); 1st black to play in Rose Bowl; 7-year NFL pro (1920-26); 1st black NFL coach at Milwaukee and Hammond, Ind.

Sam Pollock (b. Dec. 15, 1925): Hockey GM; managed NHL Montreal Canadiens to 9 Stanley Cups in 14 years (1965-78).

Denis Potvin (b. Oct. 29, 1953): Hockey D; won Norris Trophy 3 times (1976,78-79); 5-time All-NHL 1st-team; led NY Islanders to 4 Stanley Cups.

Asafa Powell (b. Nov. 11, 1982): Track & Field; Jamaican sprinter who broke world record in 100m with a 9.77 on June 14, 2005; ran 9.77 two more times, then in Sept. 2007, shattered his own mark by running a 9.74 at the Rieti Grand Prix in Italy (mark still pending).

Mike Powell (b. Nov. 10, 1963): Track & Field; broke Bob Beamon's 23-year-old long jump world record by 2 inches with leap of 29-ft., 4½ in. at the 1991 World Championships; Sullivan Award winner (1991); won long jump silver medals in 1988 and '92 Olympics; repeated as world champ in 1993.

Steve Prefontaine (b. Jan. 25, 1951, d. May 30, 1975): Track & Field; All-America distance runner at Oregon; first athlete to win same event at NCAA championships 4 straight years (5,000 meters from 1970-73); finished 4th in 5,000 at 1972 Munich Olympics; first athlete to endorse Nike running shoes; killed in a one-car accident.

Nick Price (b. Jan. 28, 1957): Zimbabwean golfer; PGA Tour Player of Year in 1993 and '94; won PGA Championship in 1992 and '94, British Open in 1994.

Alain Prost (b. Feb. 24, 1955): French auto racer; 4-time Formula One world champion (1985-86,89,93); retired after '93 season as all-time F1 wins leader with 51 (passed by Michael Schumacher in 2001).

Kirby Puckett (b. Mar. 14, 1961, d. Mar. 6, 2006): Baseball OF; led Minnesota Twins to World Series titles in 1987 and '91; retired in 1996 due to an eye ailment with a batting title (1989), 2,304 hits and a .318 career average in 12 seasons; elected to Hall of Fame in 2001.

C.C. Pyle (b. 1882, d. Feb. 3, 1939): Promoter; known as "Cash and Carry"; hyped Red Grange's pro football debut by arranging 1925 barnstorming tour with Chicago Bears; had Grange bolt NFL for new AFL in 1926 (AFL folded in '27); also staged two transcontinental footraces (1928-29), known as "Bunion Derbies."

Bobby Rahal (b. Jan. 10, 1953): Auto racer; 3-time PPG Cup champ (1986,87,92); 24 career Indy-Car wins, including 1986 Indy 500; current IRL team owner with TV's David Letterman; acted as interim president-CEO of CART in 2000.

Jack Ramsay (b. Feb. 21, 1925): Basketball; coach who won 239 college games with St. Joe's-PA in 11 seasons and 906 NBA games (including playoffs) with 4 teams over 21 years; led Portland to 1977 NBA title; placed 3rd in 1961 Final Four (later vacated).

Bill Rasmussen (b. Oct. 15, 1932): Radio-TV; unemployed radio broadcaster who founded ESPN, the nation's first 24-hour all-sports cable-TV network, in 1978; bought out by Getty Oil in 1981.

Willis Reed (b. June 25, 1942): Basketball C; led NY Knicks to NBA titles in 1970 and '73, Finals MVP both years; 1970 regular season MVP. Voted one of NBA's 50 Greatest Players; fought off serious injury and limped onto court just prior to Game 7 of the 1970 Finals, his dramatic entrance helped inspire his team to victory over Wilt Chamberlain's Lakers.

Pee Wee Reese (b. July 23, 1918, d. Aug. 14, 1999): Baseball SS; member of Brooklyn/Los Angeles Dodgers from 1940-58; led NL in runs scored (132) in 1949 and stolen bases (30) in 1952; hit over .300 in a season once (.309 in 1954); led the NL in putouts four times; real name was Harold H. Reese.

Mary Lou Retton (b. Jan. 24, 1968): Gymnast; won gold medal in women's All-Around at the 1984 Olympics; also won 2 silvers and 2 bronzes.

Grantland Rice (b. Nov. 1, 1880, d. July 13, 1954): First celebrated American sportswriter; chronicled the Golden Age of Sport in 1920s; immortalized Notre Dame's "Four Horsemen."

Jerry Rice (b. Oct. 13, 1962): Football WR; 2-time Div. I-AA All-America at Mississippi Valley St. (1983-84); won 3 Super Bowls with San Francisco (1989,90,95); 10-time All-Pro; regular season MVP in 1987 and Super Bowl MVP in 1989; all-time NFL leader in touchdowns (208), receptions (1549) and receiving yards (22,895); retired in 2005 after a 20-year NFL career.

Henri Richard (b. Feb. 29, 1936): Hockey C; leap year baby who played on more Stanley Cup championship teams (11) than anybody else; at 5-foot-7, known as the "Pocket Rocket"; brother of Maurice.

Maurice Richard (b. Aug. 4, 1921, d. May 27, 2000): Hockey RW; the "Rocket"; 8-time NHL 1st team All-Star; MVP in 1947; 1st to score 50 goals in one season (1944-45); 544 career goals; played on 8 Stanley Cup winners in Montreal.

Bob Richards (b. Feb. 2, 1926): Track & Field; pole vaulter, ordained minister and original *Wheaties* pitchman, remains only 2-time Olympic pole vault champ (1952,56).

Tex Rickard (b. Jan. 2, 1870, d. Jan. 6, 1929): Promoter who handled boxing's first $1 million gate (Dempsey vs. Carpentier in 1921); built Madison Square Garden in 1925; founded NY Rangers as Garden tenant in 1926 and named NHL team after himself (Tex's Rangers); also built Boston Garden in 1928.

Eddie Rickenbacker (b. Oct. 8, 1890, d. July 23, 1973): Mechanic and auto racer; became America's top flying ace (22 kills) in World War I; owned Indianapolis Speedway (1927-45) and ran Eastern Air Lines (1938-59).

Branch Rickey (b. Dec. 20, 1881, d. Dec. 9, 1965): Baseball innovator; revolutionized game with creation of modern farm system while GM of St. Louis Cardinals (1917-42); integrated major leagues in 1947 as president-GM of Brooklyn Dodgers when he brought up Jackie Robinson (whom he had signed on Oct. 23, 1945); later GM of Pittsburgh Pirates.

Leni Riefenstahl (b. Aug. 22, 1902, d. Sept. 8, 2003): German filmmaker of 1930s; directed classic sports documentary "Olympia" on 1936 Berlin Summer Olympics; infamous, however, for also making 1934 Hitler propaganda film "Triumph of the Will."

Roy Riegels (b. Apr. 4, 1908, d. Mar. 26, 1993): Football; California center who picked up fumble in 2nd quarter of 1929 Rose Bowl and raced 70 yards in the wrong direction to set up a 2-point safety in 8-7 loss to Georgia Tech.

Bobby Riggs (b. Feb. 25, 1918, d. Oct. 25, 1995): Tennis; won Wimbledon (1939) and U.S. title twice (1939,41); legendary hustler who made his biggest score in 1973 as 55-year-old male chauvinist challenging the best women players; beat No. 1 Margaret Smith Court 6-2,6-1, but was thrashed by No. 2 Billie Jean King, 6-4,6-3,6-3 in nationally televised "Battle of the Sexes" on Sept. 20, before 30,492 at the Astrodome.

Pat Riley (b. Mar. 20, 1945): Basketball; coached LA Lakers to 4 of their 5 NBA titles in 1980s (1982,85,87-88); coached New York Knicks from 1991-95, then signed with Miami Heat as coach, team president and part-owner; coached Heat to NBA title in 2006; 3-time Coach of Year (1990,93,97); 2nd on list of all-time coaching victories behind Lenny Wilkens.

Cal Ripken Jr. (b. Aug. 24, 1960): Baseball SS; broke Lou Gehrig's major league Iron Man record of 2,130 consecutive games played on Sept. 6, 1995; record streak began on May 30, 1982 and ended Sept. 19, 1998 after 2,632 games; 2-time AL MVP (1983,91) for Baltimore; AL Rookie of Year (1982); AL starter in All-Star Game from 1984-2001; 2-time All-Star Game MVP (1991,2001); holds record for career HR by a shortstop; inducted into HOF in 2007.

Phil Rizzuto (b. Sept. 25, 1918, d. Aug. 13, 2007): Baseball SS; nicknamed "the Scooter"; AL MVP with the Yankees in 1950; 5-time All-Star; retired in 1956 and became Yankees radio and television announcer; elected to the Hall of Fame in 1994.

Oscar Robertson (b. Nov. 24, 1938): Basketball G; 3-time College Player of Year (1958-60) at Cincinnati; led 1960 U.S. Olympic team to gold medal; NBA Rookie of Year (1961); 9-time All-NBA 1st team; MVP in 1964 with Cincinnati Royals; NBA champion in 1971 with Milwaukee Bucks; 6-time annual NBA assist leader; 4th in career assists with 9,887; 8th in career points with 26,710.

Paul Robeson (b. Apr. 8, 1898, d. Jan. 23, 1976): Black 4-sport star and 2-time football All-America (1917-18) at Rutgers; 3-year NFL pro; also scholar, lawyer, singer, actor and political activist; long-tainted by Communist sympathies, he was finally inducted into College Football Hall of Fame in 1995.

Brooks Robinson (b. May 18, 1937): Baseball 3B; led AL in fielding 12 times from 1960-72 with Baltimore; AL MVP in 1964; World Series MVP in 1970; 16 Gold Gloves; entered Hall of Fame in 1983.

David Robinson (b. Aug. 6, 1965): Basketball C; 1987 College Player of Year at Navy; overall 1st pick by San Antonio in 1987 NBA draft; served in military (1987-89); NBA Rookie of Year (1990) and MVP (1995); 2-time All-NBA 1st team (1991,92); led NBA in scoring in 1994; member of 1988, '92 and '96 U.S. Olympic teams; won 2 NBA titles (1999, 2003).

Eddie Robinson (b. Feb. 13, 1919, d. Apr. 3, 2007): Football; head coach at Div. I-AA Grambling from 1941-97; retired as winningest coach in college history (408-165-15), since passed by St. John's-Minn. (Div. III) coach John Gagliardi; led Tigers to 8 national black college titles.

Frank Robinson (b. Aug. 31, 1935): Baseball OF; won MVP in NL (1961) and AL (1966); Triple Crown winner and World Series MVP in 1966 with Baltimore; 6th on all-time home run list with 586; 1st black manager in major leagues with Cleveland in 1975; has also managed in San Francisco, Baltimore and Montreal/Washington; served as the league's VP of on-field operations (2000-01).

Jackie Robinson (b. Jan. 31, 1919, d. Oct. 24, 1972): Baseball 1B-2B-3B; 4-sport athlete at UCLA (baseball, basketball, football and track); hit .387 with Kansas City Monarchs of Negro Leagues in 1945; signed by Brooklyn Dodgers' Branch Rickey on Oct. 23, 1945. Played in minors (Montreal) in 1946 and broke Major League Baseball's color line in 1947; Rookie of Year in 1947 and NL's MVP in 1949; hit .311 over 10 seasons. His #42 was retired by Major League Baseball in 1997.

Sugar Ray Robinson (b. May 3, 1921, d. Apr. 12, 1989): Boxer; arguably the greatest pound-for-pound prizefighter of all-time; world welterweight champion (1946-51); 5-time middleweight champ; retired at age 45 with pro record of 174-19-6 (109 KOs).

Knute Rockne (b. Mar. 4, 1888, d. Mar. 31, 1931): Football; coached Notre Dame to 3 consensus national titles (1924,29,30), highest winning percentage in college history (.881) with record of 105-12-5 over 13 seasons; killed in plane crash.

Bill Rodgers (b. Dec. 23, 1947): Distance runner; won Boston and New York City marathons 4 times each from 1975-80.

Dennis Rodman (b. May 13, 1961): Basketball F; superb rebounder and defender; known for dyeing his hair and getting suspended; in 1997, he was suspended for 11 games for kicking a cameraman; led NBA in rebounding 7 straight years (1992-98); won 5 NBA titles with Detroit (1989,90) and Chicago (1996-98); 2-time defensive player of the year (1990-91).

Irina Rodnina (b. Sept. 12, 1949): Soviet figure skater; won 10 world championships and 3 Olympic gold medals in pairs competition from 1969-80.

Alex Rodriguez (b. July 27, 1975): Baseball 3B; led AL in hitting (.358) his first full season in the majors (1996); in 1998 became third player ever with 40 HRs and 40 steals in one season; signed a 10-year, $252m deal (the biggest in U.S. sports history) with Texas in 2000, won AL MVP in 2003; was traded to NY Yankees in 2004 and won AL MVP in 2005.

Juan (Chi Chi) Rodriguez (b. Oct. 23, 1935): Golfer; popular player with 8 PGA Tour victories and 22 Senior Tour wins; 1973 U.S. Ryder Cup Team.

Ronaldo (b. Sept. 22, 1976): Brazilian soccer F; named to the Brazilian National Team when he was 17; 3-time FIFA World Player of the Year (1996,97,2002); European Player of the Year in 1997 and 2002; named 1998 World Cup MVP; led Brazil to World Cup title in 2002, scoring 8 times including both of Brazil's goals in its win over Germany in the final; all-time leading scorer in World Cup history with 15 in 4 World Cups.

Art Rooney (b. Jan. 27, 1901, d. Aug. 25, 1988): Race track legend and pro football pioneer; bought Pittsburgh Steelers franchise in 1933 for $2,500; finally won NFL title with 1st of 4 Super Bowls in 1974 season.

Theodore Roosevelt (b. Oct. 27, 1858, d. Jan. 6, 1919): 26th President of the U.S.; physical fitness buff who boxed as undergraduate at Harvard; credited with presidential assist in forming of Intercollegiate Athletic Assn. (now NCAA) in 1905-06.

Mauri Rose (b. May 26, 1906, d. Jan. 1, 1981): Auto racer; 3-time winner of Indy 500 (1941,47-48).

Murray Rose (b. Jan. 6, 1939): Australian swimmer; won 3 gold medals at 1956 Olympics; added a gold, silver and bronze in 1960.

Pete Rose (b. Apr. 14, 1941): Baseball OF-IF; all-time hits leader with 4,256 and games leader with 3562; led NL in batting 3 times; regular-season MVP in 1973; World Series MVP in 1975; had 44-game hitting streak in '78; managed Cincinnati (1984-89); banned for life in 1989 for conduct detrimental to baseball (betting on baseball); convicted of tax evasion in 1990 and sentenced to 5 months in prison.

Ken Rosewall (b. Nov. 2, 1934): Tennis; won French and Australian singles titles at age 18; U.S. champ twice, but never won Wimbledon.

Mark Roth (b. Apr. 10, 1951): Bowler; 4-time PBA Player of Year (1977-79,84); has 34 tournament wins and over $1.6 million in career earnings.

Alan Rothenberg (b. Apr. 10, 1939): Soccer; president of U.S. Soccer 1990-98; surprised European skeptics by directing hugely successful 1994 World Cup tournament; successfully got oft-delayed outdoor Major League Soccer off ground in 1996.

Chad Rowan (Akebono) (b. May 8, 1969): Sumo Wrestling; 6-foot-9, 510-pound naturalized Japanese citizen born in Hawaii; first foreign grand champion in sumo wrestling's 2,000-year history.

Patrick Roy (b. Oct. 5, 1965): Hockey G; led Montreal to 2 Stanley Cup titles (1986,93) and won 3rd and 4th Cups with Colorado (1996,2001); 3-time playoff MVP (as rookie in 1986,93,2001); won Vezina Trophy 3 times (1989-90,92); led NHL in goals against average 3 times (1989,92,2002); all-time leader in career regular season wins (551) and playoff wins (151).

Pete Rozelle (b. Mar. 1, 1926, d. December 6, 1996): Football; NFL Commissioner from 1960-89; presided over growth of league from 12 to 28 teams, merger with AFL, creation of Super Bowl and advent of huge TV rights fees.

Wilma Rudolph (b. June 23, 1940, d. Nov. 12, 1994): Track & Field; won 3 gold medals (100m, 200m and 4x100m relay) at 1960 Olympics; also won relay silver in '56 Games at age 16; 2-time AP Athlete of Year (1960-61) and Sullivan Award winner in 1961; suffered from polio and wore leg braces until she was 9.

John Ruiz (b. Jan. 4, 1972): Boxer; defeated Evander Holyfield by decision in 2001 for the WBA heavyweight title; the first-ever Hispanic heavyweight champ; lost belt to Roy Jones Jr. on unanimous dec. in 2003.

Damon Runyon (b. Oct. 4, 1884, d. Dec. 10, 1946): Kansas native who gained fame as New York journalist, sports columnist and short-story writer; best known for 1932 story collection, "Guys and Dolls."

Adolph Rupp (b. Sept. 2, 1901, d. Dec. 10, 1977): Basketball; 2nd in all-time college coaching wins with 876; led Kentucky to 4 NCAA championships (1948-49,51,58) and 1 NIT title (1946).

Bill Russell (b. Feb. 12, 1934): Basketball C; won titles in college (with San Francisco in 1955,56), Olympics (1956) and pros; 5-time NBA MVP (1958,61,62,63,65); led Boston Celtics to an amazing 11 titles from 1957-69; 4-time NBA rebound leader (1958-59,64-65); 2nd on all-time rebound list with 21,620; became first black NBA (and major professional sports) head coach in 1966.

Babe Ruth (b. Feb. 6, 1895, d. Aug. 16, 1948): Baseball LHP-OF; two-time 20-game winner with Boston Red Sox (1916-17); had a 94-46 record with a 2.28 ERA, while he was 3-0 in the World Series with an ERA of 0.87; sold to New York Yankees for $100,000 in 1920; AL MVP in 1923; led AL in slugging average 13 times, HRs 12 times, RBI 6 times and batting once (.378 in 1924); hit 60 HRs in 1927 and at least 54 3 other times; ended career with Boston Braves in 1935 with 714 HRs, 2,211 RBI, 2,062 walks and a batting average of .342; remains all-time leader in slugging percentage (.690); member of the Hall of Fame's inaugural class of 1936.

Johnny Rutherford (b. Mar. 12, 1938): Auto racer; 3-time winner of Indy 500 (1974,76,80); CART national champion in 1980.

Nolan Ryan (b. Jan. 31, 1947): Baseball RHP; recorded 7 no-hitters against Kansas City and Detroit (1973), Minnesota (1974), Baltimore (1975), LA Dodgers (1981), Oakland A's (1990) and Toronto (1991 at age 44); 2-time 20-game winner (1973-74); 2-time NL leader in ERA (1981,87); led AL in strikeouts 9 times and NL twice in 27 years; retired after 1993 season with 324 wins, 292 losses and all-time records for strikeouts (5,714) and walks (2,795); number retired by three teams (California, Houston, Texas).

Samuel Ryder (b. Mar. 24, 1858, d. Jan. 2, 1936): Golf; English seed merchant who donated the Ryder Cup in 1927 for competition between pro golfers from Great Britain and the U.S.; made his fortune by coming up with idea of selling seeds in small packages.

Toni Sailer (b. Nov. 17, 1935): Austrian skier; 1st to win 3 alpine gold medals in Winter Olympics— taking downhill, slalom and giant slalom events in 1956.

Alberto Salazar (b. Aug. 7, 1958): Track and Field; broke 12-year-old record at New York Marathon in 1981 and broke Boston Marathon record in 1982; won three straight NY Marathons (1980-82).

Juan Antonio Samaranch (b. July 17, 1920): president of International Olympic Committee (1980-2001); the native of Barcelona was re-elected in 1996 after IOC's move in '95 to bump membership age limit to 80; replaced by Belgian Jacques Rogge.

Pete Sampras (b. Aug. 12, 1971): Tennis; No.1 in world (1993-98); youngest ever U.S. Open men's champ (19 years, 28 days) in 1990; his win at 2002 U.S. Open was record 14th grand slam singles title; won 2 Australian Opens (1994,97), 7 Wimbledons (1993-95, 1997-2000) and 5 U.S. Opens (1990,93, 95-96,2002); career money leader on ATP Tour.

Joan Benoit Samuelson (b. May 16, 1957): Distance runner; won Boston Marathon twice (1979,83); won first women's Olympic marathon in 1984 Games; Sullivan Award recipient in 1985.

Arantxa Sanchez-Vicario (b. Dec. 18, 1971): Spanish tennis player; won 29 singles titles including 3 French Opens (1989,94,98) and 1 U.S. Open (1994); 6 doubles and 4 mixed doubles grand slam titles.

Earl Sande (b. Nov. 13, 1898, d. Aug. 19, 1968): Jockey; rode Gallant Fox to Triple Crown in 1930; won 5 Belmonts and 3 Kentucky Derbies.

Barry Sanders (b. July 16, 1968): Football RB; won 1988 Heisman Trophy as junior at Oklahoma St.; all-time NCAA single season leader in rushing (2,628 yards), scoring (234 points) and TDs (39); 4-time NFL rushing leader with Detroit Lions (1990,94,96,97); NFC Rookie of Year (1988); 2-time NFL Player of Year (1991,97); NFC MVP (1994); rushed for 2,053 yards in 1997; No. 3 all-time rusher (15,269 yds); retired prior to 1999 season; inducted into Pro Football hall of Fame in 2004.

Deion Sanders (b. Aug. 9, 1967): Baseball OF and Football DB-KR-WR; 2-time All-America at Florida St. in football (1987-88); 7-time NFL All-Pro CB with Atlanta, San Fran. and Dallas (1991-94,96-98); led majors in triples (14) with Braves in 1992 and hit .533 in World Series that year; played on 2 Super Bowl winners (SF in XXIX, and Dallas in XXX); first 2-way starter in NFL since 1962 (Chuck Bednarik); only athlete to play in both World Series and Super Bowl.

Cael Sanderson (b. June 20, 1979): Wrestling; first 4-time undefeated NCAA college wrestling champion (1999-2002); went 159-0 during 4-year career at Iowa State; 4-time NCAA Most Outstanding Wrestler; won gold medal at Athens Games in 2004.

Abe Saperstein (b. July 4, 1901, d. Mar. 15, 1966): Basketball; founded all-black, Harlem Globetrotters barnstorming team in 1927; coached sharpshooting comedians to 1940 world pro title in Chicago and established troupe as game's foremost goodwill ambassadors; also served as 1st commissioner of American Basketball League (1961-62).

Gene Sarazen (b. Feb. 27, 1902, d. May 13, 1999): Golfer; one of only five players to win all four Grand Slam titles (others are Hogan, Nicklaus, Player and Woods); won Masters, British Open, 2 U.S. Opens and 3 PGA titles between 1922-35; invented sand wedge in 1930.

Glen Sather (b. Sept. 2, 1943): Hockey; GM-coach of 4 Stanley Cup winners in Edmonton (1984-85,87-88) and GM-only for another in 1990; ranks 8th on all-time NHL coaching list with 586 wins (including playoffs); entered Hockey Hall of Fame in 1997; named President-GM of NY Rangers in 2000.

Terry Sawchuk (b. Dec. 28, 1929, d. May 31, 1970): Hockey G; recorded 103 shutouts in 21 NHL seasons; 4-time Vezina Trophy winner; played on 4 Stanley Cup winners at Detroit and Toronto; posted career 2.52 GAA.

Gale Sayers (b. May 30, 1943): Football HB; 2-time All-America at Kansas; NFL Rookie of Year (1965) and 5-time All-Pro with Chicago; scored then-record 22 TDs in rookie year; led league in rushing twice (1966,69).

Chris Schenkel (b. Aug. 21, 1923, d. Sept. 11, 2005): Radio-TV; 4-time Sportscaster of Year; easygoing baritone who covered basketball, bowling, football, golf and the Olympics for ABC and CBS; host of ABC's Pro Bowlers Tour for 33 years; received lifetime achievement Emmy Award in 1992.

Vitaly Scherbo (b. Jan. 13, 1972): Russian gymnast; winner of unprecedented 6 gold medals in gymnastics, including men's All-Around, for Unified Team in 1992 Olympics; also won 3 bronze in '96 Games.

Curt Schilling (b. Nov. 14, 1966): Baseball RHP; led majors in strikeouts twice (1997-98) with Philadelphia; 3-time 20-game winner with Arizona (2001-02,04); shared 2001 World Series MVP award with teammate Randy Johnson; traded to Boston and helped Red Sox end 86-year championship drought in 2004.

Mike Schmidt (b. Sept. 27, 1949): Baseball 3B; led NL in HRs 8 times; 3-time MVP (1980,81,86) with Philadelphia; 548 career HRs and 10 Gold Gloves; inducted into Hall of Fame in 1995.

Don Schollander (b. Apr. 30, 1946): Swimming; won 4 gold medals at 1964 Olympics, plus one gold and one silver in 1968; won Sullivan Award in 1964.

Dick Schultz (b. Sept. 5, 1929): Reform-minded executive director of NCAA from 1988-93; announced resignation on May 11, 1993 in wake of special investigator's report citing Univ. of Virginia with improper student-athlete loan program during Schultz's tenure as athletic director (1981-87); executive director of the USOC 1995-2000.

Michael Schumacher (b. Jan. 3, 1969): German auto racer; Formula One's all-time win leader with 84 grand prix victories (and counting); 7-time world champion (1994-95,2000-04); broke his own F1 single-season record with 13 wins in 2004; announced retirement at the end of the 2006 F1 season.

Bob Seagren (b. Oct. 17, 1946): Track & Field; won gold medal in pole vault at 1968 Olympics; broke world outdoor record 5 times.

Tom Seaver (b. Nov. 17, 1944): Baseball RHP; won 3 Cy Young Awards (1969,73,75); led NL in K 5 times (1970,71,73,75,76); pitched no-hitter in 1978 for Cin.; had 311 wins, 3,640 strikeouts and 2.86 ERA over 20 years.

Peter Seitz (b. May 17, 1905, d. Oct. 17, 1983): Baseball arbitrator; ruled on Dec. 23, 1975 that players who perform for one season without a signed contract can become free agents; decision ushered in big money era for players.

Monica Seles (b. Dec. 2, 1973): Tennis; No. 1 in the world in 1991 and '92 after winning Australian, French and U.S. Opens both years; won 4 Australian, 3 French and 2 US Opens; winner of 30 singles titles in just 5 years before she was stabbed in the back by Steffi Graf fan Gunter Parche on Apr. 30, 1993 during match in Hamburg, Germany; spent remainder of 1993, all of '94 and most of '95 recovering; returned to tennis with win at the 1995 Canadian Open; won 1996 Australian Open; winner of 53 WTA tournaments.

Bud Selig (b. July 30, 1934): Baseball; Milwaukee car dealer who bought AL Seattle Pilots for $10.8 million in 1970 and moved team to Midwest; as de facto commissioner, he presided over 232-day players' strike that resulted in cancellation of World Series for first time since 1904; officially elected baseball's ninth commissioner on July 9, 1998; has overseen many changes in MLB including interleague play, wild card playoffs, and new steroid testing policy.

Frank Selke (b. May 7, 1893, d. July 3, 1985): Hockey; GM of 6 Stanley Cup champions in Montreal (1953,56-60); the annual NHL trophy for best defensive forward bears his name.

Ayrton Senna (b. Mar. 21, 1960, d. May 1, 1994): Brazilian auto racer; 3-time Formula One champion (1988,90-91); died as all-time F1 leader in poles (65) and 2nd in wins (41, currently in 3rd); killed in crash at Imola, Italy during '94 San Marino GP.

Wilbur Shaw (b. Oct. 13, 1902, d. Oct. 30, 1954): Auto racer; 3-time winner and 3-time runner-up of Indy 500 from 1933-1940.

Patty Sheehan (b. Oct. 27, 1956): Golfer; LPGA Player of Year in 1983; clinched entry into LPGA Hall of Fame with her 30th career win in 1993; her 6 major titles include 3 LPGA Champ. (1983-84,93), 2 U.S. Opens (1992,94) 1 Dinah Shore (1996).

Bill Shoemaker (b. Aug. 19, 1931, d. Oct. 12, 2003): Jockey; ranks 3rd all-time in career wins with 8,833; 3-time Eclipse Award winner as jockey (1981) and special award recipient (1976,81); won 5 Belmonts, 4 Kentucky Derbys and 2 Preaknesses; oldest jockey to win Kentucky Derby (age 54, aboard Ferdinand in 1986); retired in 1990 to become trainer; paralyzed in 1991 auto accident but continued to train horses.

Eddie Shore (b. Nov. 25, 1902, d. Mar. 16, 1985): Hockey D; only NHL defenseman to win Hart Trophy as MVP 4 times (1933,35-36,38); led Boston Bruins to Stanley Cup titles in 1929 and '39; had 105 goals and 1,047 penalty minutes in 14 seasons.

Frank Shorter (b. Oct. 31, 1947): Track & Field; won gold medal in marathon at 1972 Olympics, 1st American to win in 64 years.

Don Shula (b. Jan. 4, 1930): Football; retired after 1995 season with an NFL-record 347 career wins (including playoffs) and a winning percentage of .665; took six teams to Super Bowl and won twice with Miami (VII, VIII); 4-time Coach of Year, twice with Baltimore (1964,68) and twice with Miami (1970-71); coached 1972 Dolphins to 17-0 record, the only undefeated team in NFL history.

Charlie Sifford (b. June 2, 1922): Golf; won the Hartford Open in 1967 with a final-round 64, becoming the first black player to win a PGA event; amassed over $1 million in career earnings; published his autobiography "Just Let Me Play" in 1992.

Al Simmons (b. May 22, 1902, d. May 26, 1956): Baseball OF; led AL in batting twice (1930-31) with Philadelphia A's and knocked in 100 runs or more 11 straight years (1924-34).

O.J. Simpson (b. July 9, 1947): Football RB; won Heisman Trophy in 1968 at USC; ran for 2,003 yards in NFL in 1973; All-Pro 5 times; MVP in 1973; rushed for 11,236 career yards; TV analyst and actor after career ended; arrested June 17, 1994 as suspect in double murder of ex-wife Nicole Brown Simpson and her friend Ronald Goldman; acquitted on Oct. 3, 1995 by a Los Angeles jury in criminal trial but forced to make financial reparations after losing wrongful death suit; made headlines once again in Sept. 2007 after being arrested for robbery and assault for reportedly storming into a Las Vegas hotel room and demanding sports memorabilia that he claimed belonged to him.

Vijay Singh (b. Feb. 22, 1963): Fijian golfer; temporarily dethroned Tiger Woods as world's top-ranked player in 2004; has 31 career PGA Tour wins including 1998 and 2004 PGA championships and 2000 Masters; 2003-04 PGA Tour money leader.

George Sisler (b. Mar. 24, 1893, d. Mar. 26, 1973): Baseball 1B; hit over .400 twice (1920,22) and batted over .300 in 13 of his 15 seasons; his MLB record of 257 hits (1920) was finally broken by Seattle's Ichiro Suzuki (262) in 2004; played most of his career with the St. Louis Browns; inducted into Baseball Hall of Fame in 1939.

Mary Decker Slaney (b. Aug. 4, 1958): U.S. middle distance runner; has held 7 separate American track & field records from the 800 to 10,000 meters; won both 1,500 and 3,000 meters at 1983 World Championships in Helsinki, but no Olympic medals.

Kelly Slater (b. Feb. 11, 1972): Surfer; 7-time world champion; member of the Surfers' Hall of Fame; started the new school movement of surfing; holds records for being the youngest (1992) and oldest (2005) world champion; earned the only perfect two-wave score at a WCT event, ties for most WCT event wins in a tour season, and in number of career WCT event wins, highest money-earner in the history of the ASP (Association of Surfing Professionals).

Raisa Smetanina (b. Feb. 29, 1952): Russian Nordic skier; all-time leading female Winter Olympics medalist with 10 cross country medals (4 gold, 5 silver and a bronze) in 5 appearances (1976,80,84, 88,92) for USSR and Unified Team.

Billy Smith (b. Dec. 12, 1950): Hockey G; led NY Islanders to 4 consecutive Stanley Cups (1980-83); won Vezina Trophy in 1982; Stanley Cup MVP in 1983.

Dean Smith (b. Feb. 28, 1931): Basketball; No. 2 on all-time NCAA coaches victory list (879 wins, previous leader until he was passed in 2007 by Bobby Knight); led North Carolina to 25 NCAA tournaments in 34 years, reaching Final Four 10 times and winning championship twice (1982,93); coached U.S. Olympic team to gold medal in 1976.

Emmitt Smith (b. May 15, 1969): Football RB; NFL's all-time leading rusher (18,355 yards); also holds all-time record for rushing TDs (164); 4-time NFL rushing leader (1991-93,95); recorded 11 straight 1,000-yard seasons (1991-2001) with Dallas Cowboys; regular season and Super Bowl MVP in 1993; played on three Super Bowl champions (1993,94,96); retired in 2005 after 15 seasons.

John Smith (b. Aug. 9, 1965): Wrestler; 2-time NCAA champion for Oklahoma St. at 134 lbs (1987-88) and Most Outstanding Wrestler of '88 championships; 3-time world champion; gold medal winner at 1988 and '92 Olympics at 137 lbs; won Sullivan Award (1990); coached Oklahoma St. to 1994 NCAA title and brother Pat was Most Outstanding Wrestler.

Lee Smith (b. Dec. 4, 1957): Baseball RHP; 3-time NL saves leader (1983,91-92); retired as all-time saves leader with 478 (since passed by T. Hoffman); 10 seasons with 30+ saves, 3 times saved over 40.

Ozzie Smith (b. Dec. 26, 1954): Baseball SS; won 13 straight Gold Gloves (1980-92); played in 12 straight All-Star Games (1981-92); MVP of 1985 NL playoffs; all-time MLB assist leader (8,375); inducted into Baseball Hall of Fame in 2002.

Walter (Red) Smith (b. Sept. 25, 1905, d. Jan. 15, 1982): Sportswriter for newspapers in Philadelphia and New York from 1936-82; won Pulitzer Prize for commentary in 1976.

Conn Smythe (b. Feb. 1, 1895, d. Nov. 18, 1980): Hockey pioneer; built Maple Leaf Gardens in 1931; managed Toronto to 7 Stanley Cups.

Sam Snead (b. May 27, 1912, d. May 23, 2002): Golfer; won both Masters and PGA 3 times and British Open once; runner-up in U.S. Open 4 times; PGA Player of Year in 1949; oldest player (52 years, 10 months) to win PGA event with Greater Greensboro Open title in 1965; all-time PGA Tour career victory leader with 82.

Peter Snell (b. Dec. 17, 1938): Track & Field; New Zealander who won gold medal in 800m at 1960 Olympics, then won both the 800m and 1,500m at 1964 Games.

Duke Snider (b. Sept. 19, 1926): Baseball OF; hit 40 or more home runs five straight seasons (1953-57); led the league in runs scored 1953-55; played in six World Series with the Dodgers and batted .286 with 11 home runs; nicknamed "Duke of Flatbush"; in 18 seasons hit 407 home runs, scored 1,259 runs and had 1,333 RBI.

Annika Sorenstam (b. Oct. 9, 1970): Swedish golfer; has won 10 women's majors; 8-time Rolex Player of the Year (1995,97-98, 2001-05); shot an LPGA-record 59 in round 2 of the 2001 Standard Register Ping; LPGA all-time leading money winner; in 2003 she became first woman in 58 years to play on men's PGA Tour (via a sponsor's exemption); shot 71-74 but missed the cut at the Colonial by 4 strokes.

Sammy Sosa (b. Nov. 12, 1968): Baseball OF; slugging Chicago Cub who surpassed Roger Maris' season home run record (61), just after Mark McGwire did in 1998 and finished the year with 66; followed that up with seasons of 63, 50 and 64 HRs; 1998 NL MVP; 7-time All-Star; 609 career homers.

Javier Sotomayor (b. Oct. 13, 1967): Cuban high jumper; first man to clear 8 feet (8-0) on July 29, 1989; won gold medal at 1992 Olympics with jump of only 7-ft, 8-in.; broke world record with leap of 8-0½ in 1993; had a controversial drug suspension reduced, which allowed him to participate in 2000 Olympics; won the silver medal in Sydney with a leap of 7-7¼.

Warren Spahn (b. Apr. 23, 1921, d. Nov. 23, 2003): Baseball LHP; led NL in wins 8 times; won 20 or more games 13 times; Cy Young winner in 1957; most career wins (363) by a lefthander.

Tris Speaker (b. Apr. 4, 1888, d. Dec. 8, 1958): Baseball OF; all-time leader in outfield assists (449) and doubles (792); had .344 career BA and 3,515 hits.

J.G. Taylor Spink (b. Nov. 6, 1888, d. Dec. 7, 1962): Publisher of The Sporting News from 1914-62; BBWAA annual meritorious service award named after him.

Leon Spinks (b. July 11, 1953): Boxing; won heavyweight crown in split decision over Muhammad Ali in Feb. 1978; Ali regained title seven months later; won gold medal in light heavyweight division at 1976 Olympics; brother Michael won the heavyweight title in 1983; were the only brothers to hold world titles; known more for frequent traffic violations and lavish lifestyle than bouts late in career; filed for bankruptcy in 1986.

Mark Spitz (b. Feb. 10, 1950): American swimmer; set 23 world and 35 U.S. records; won all-time record 7 gold medals (4 individual, 3 relay) in 1972 Olympics; also won 4 medals (2 gold, a silver and a bronze) in 1968 Games for a total of 11; comeback attempt at age 41 foundered in 1991.

Latrell Sprewell (b. Sept. 8, 1970): Basketball G; former NBA All-Star who made headlines in 1997 for attacking Golden State Warriors head coach P.J. Carlesimo during a practice.

Lyn St. James (b. Mar. 13, 1947): Auto racer; one of just 4 women to qualify for the Indianapolis 500; best finish in the race came in 1992 when she came in 11th and won Indianapolis 500 Rookie of the Year.

Amos Alonzo Stagg (b. Aug. 16, 1862, d. Mar. 17, 1965): Football innovator; coached at U. of Chicago for 41 seasons and College of the Pacific for 14 more; 314-199-35 record; elected to both college football and basketball Halls of Fame.

Willie Stargell (b. Mar. 6, 1940, d. Apr. 9, 2001): Baseball OF-1B; "Pops"; led NL in home runs twice (1971,73); 475 career HRs; NL co-MVP and World Series MVP in 1979.

Bart Starr (b. Jan. 9, 1934): Football QB; led Green Bay to 5 NFL titles and 2 Super Bowl wins from 1961-67; regular season MVP in 1966; MVP of Super Bowls I and II.

Roger Staubach (b. Feb. 5, 1942): Football QB; Heisman Trophy winner as Navy junior in 1963; led Dallas to 2 Super Bowl titles (1972,78) and was Super Bowl MVP in 1972; 5-time leading passer in NFC (1971,73,77-79).

George Steinbrenner (b. July 4, 1930): Baseball; principal owner of NY Yankees since 1973; teams have won 10 pennants and 6 World Series (1977-78,96,98,99,00); ordered by commissioner Fay Vincent in 1990 to surrender control of club for dealings with small-time gambler; reinstated in 1993; demanding and highly successful, he once claimed, "Winning is the most important thing in my life, after breathing."

Casey Stengel (b. July 30, 1890, d. Sept. 29, 1975): Baseball; player for 14 years and manager for 25; outfielder and lifetime .284 hitter with 5 clubs (1912-25); guided NY Yankees to 10 AL pennants and 7 World Series titles from 1949-60; 1st NY Mets skipper from 1962-65.

Ingemar Stenmark (b. Mar. 18, 1956): Swedish alpine skier; 3-time World Cup overall champ (1976-78); posted 86 World Cup wins in 16 years; won 2 gold medals at 1980 Olympics.

Helen Stephens (b. Feb. 3, 1918, d. Jan. 17, 1994): Track & Field; set 3 world records in 100-yard dash and 4 more in 100 meters in 1935-36; won gold medals in 100 meters and 4x100-meter relay in 1936 Olympics; retired in 1937.

Woody Stephens (b. Sept. 1, 1913, d. Aug. 22, 1998): Horse racing; trainer who saddled an unprecedented 5 straight winners in Belmont Stakes (1982-86); also had two Kentucky Derby winners (1974,84) and one Preakness winner (1952); trained 1982 Horse of Year Conquistador Cielo; won Eclipse award as nation's top trainer in 1983.

David Stern (b. Sept. 22, 1942): Basketball; marketing expert and NBA commissioner since 1984; took office the year Michael Jordan turned pro; league has grown from 23 teams to 30 during his watch and opened offices worldwide; oversaw launch of WNBA in 1997.

Teófilo Stevenson (b. Mar. 29, 1952): Cuban boxer; won 3 consecutive gold medals as Olympic heavyweight (1972,76,80); was denied a chance to win a fourth when Cuba boycotted 1984 Los Angeles Games; did not turn pro.

Jackie Stewart (b. June 11, 1939): Auto racer; won 27 Formula One races and 3 world driving titles from 1969-73.

John Stockton (b. Mar 26, 1962): Basketball G; all-time NBA leader in every major assist category, including most in a season (1,164) and most in a career (15,806); also the NBA's all-time leader in steals (3,265); All-NBA team in '94 and '95; member of 1992 and '96 US Olympic basketball teams; 10-time All-Star; played 19 seasons with Utah Jazz—18 of them with Karl Malone—perfecting the pick and roll.

Curtis Strange (b. Jan. 30, 1955): Golfer; won consecutive U.S. Open titles (1988-89); 3-time leading money winner on PGA Tour (1985,87-88); first PGA player to win $1 million in one year (1988); captain of the 2002 U.S. Ryder Cup team.

Picabo Street (b. Apr. 3, 1971): Skiing; 2-time Olympic medalist, gold (Super G in 1998) and silver (downhill in 1994); her 1995 World Cup downhill series title first-ever by U.S. woman, she repeated the feat in 1996.

Kerri Strug (b. Nov. 10, 1977): Gymnastics; delivered the most dramatic moment of the 1996 Summer Olympics when she completed a vault (9.712) after spraining her ankle; the second vault helped assure the first all-around gold medal for a US Women's gymnastics team.

Louise Suggs (b. Sept. 7, 1923): Golfer; won 11 majors and 58 LPGA events overall from 1949-62; founder and charter member of the LPGA; first woman elected to LPGA Hall of Fame (1951).

James E. Sullivan (b. Nov. 18, 1862, d. Sept. 16, 1914): Track & Field; pioneer who founded Amateur Athletic Union (AAU) in 1888; director of St. Louis Olympic Games in 1904; AAU's annual Sullivan Award for performance and sportsmanship named after him.

John L. Sullivan (b. Oct. 15, 1858, d. Feb. 2, 1918): Boxer; nicknamed "The Boston Strong Boy"; world heavyweight champion (1882-92); last of bareknuckle champions, beating Jake Kilrain after 75 rounds in 1889; was knocked out by "Gentleman" Jim Corbett in the 21st round in 1892, never fought again.

Pat Summitt (b. June 14, 1952): Basketball; women's basketball coach at Tennessee (1974—); entered 2007-08 season as all-time leader in career victories with 947; coached 1984 US women's basketball team to its first Olympic gold medal; has coached Lady Vols to 7 national championships (1987, 89,91,96,97,98,2007); her Lady Vols have made 10 of the last 13 Final Fours.

Don Sutton (b. April 2, 1945): Baseball RHP; won 324 games and tossed 58 shutouts in his 23-year career; recorded NL record five career 1-hitters; played with Dodgers, Astros, Brewers, Athletics, Angels and was a 4-time All-Star; elected to Hall of Fame in 1998.

Ichiro Suzuki (b. Oct. 22, 1973): Baseball OF; became the 2nd player (Fred Lynn) to win AL Rookie of the Year and MVP in same year (2001); 1st Japanese-born position player to play in MLB; won 7 consecutive Japanese batting titles (1994-2000) and has won two more in AL with Seattle (2001,04); broke George Sisler's 84-year-old hits record with 262 in 2004; MVP of 2007 All-Star Game (hit inside-the-park HR); has 200+ hits in each of his 7 MLB seasons.

Lynn Swann (b. Mar. 7, 1952): Football WR; played nine seasons with Pittsburgh (1974-82); appeared in four Super Bowls and had 16 catches for 364 yards and three TDs; named MVP of Super Bowl X for 4 catch, 161 yard, 1 TD performance.

Barry Switzer (b. Oct. 5, 1937): Football; coached Oklahoma to 3 national titles (1974-75,85); all-time winning percentage of .837 (157-29-4); resigned in 1989 after OU was slapped with 3-year NCAA probation; hired as Dallas Cowboys head coach in 1994 and led team to victory in Super Bowl XXX in 1996.

Sheryl Swoopes (b. Mar. 25, 1971): Basketball; forward for WNBA's Houston Comets; 4-time WNBA regular season MVP (2000,02,03,05); 3-time Olympic gold medalist (1996,2000,2004); led Texas Tech to Div. I NCAA championship in 1993; consensus National Player of the Year in 1993.

Paul Tagliabue (b. Nov. 24, 1940): Football; NFL attorney who was elected league's 4th commissioner in 1989 and served until his retirement in 2006; ushered in salary cap in 1994; the league expanded from 28 teams to 32 in his tenure.

Anatoli Tarasov (b. 1918, d. June 23, 1995): Hockey; coached Soviet Union to 9 straight world championships and 3 Olympic gold medals (1964, 68,72).

Jerry Tarkanian (b. Aug. 30, 1930): Basketball; amassed 778 wins in 31 years at Long Beach St., UNLV and Fresno St.; led UNLV to 4 Final Fours and 1 national title (1990); fought battle with NCAA over purity of UNLV program; quit as coach after going 26-2 in 1991-92; fired after 20 games (9-11) as coach of NBA San Antonio Spurs in 1992.

Fran Tarkenton (b. Feb. 3, 1940): Football QB; scrambling two-time NFL All-Pro (1973,75); 1975 Player of the Year; threw for 47,003 yards and 342 TDs (both former NFL records) in 18 seasons with Vikings and N.Y. Giants; selected to 9 Pro Bowls; inducted into Pro Football Hall of Fame in 1986.

Chuck Taylor (b. June 24, 1901, d. June 23, 1969): Converse traveling salesman whose name came to grace the classic, high-top canvas basketball sneakers known as "Chucks"; over 750 million pairs have been sold since 1917; he also ran clinics worldwide and edited Converse Basketball Yearbook (1922-68).

Lawrence Taylor (b. Feb. 4, 1959): Football LB; All-America at North Carolina (1980); only defensive player in NFL history to be consensus Player of Year (1986); led N.Y. Giants to Super Bowl titles in 1986 and '90 seasons; played in 10 Pro Bowls (1981-90); retired after 1993 season with 132½ sacks; had several drug-related arrests in retirement; inducted into Hall of Fame in 1999.

Marshall (Major) Taylor (b. Nov. 26, 1878, d. June 21, 1932): Cyclist; Considered one of the first African-American sports heroes; held 7 world cycling records at the turn of the century, racing mostly in Europe, Australia and New Zealand after being barred from many events in the U.S. due to racial prejudices; won the world one-mile championship in 1899.

Gustavo Thoeni (b. Feb. 28, 1951): Italian alpine skier; 4-time World Cup overall champion (1971-73,75); won giant slalom at 1972 Olympics.

Isiah Thomas (b. Apr. 30, 1961): Basketball; led Indiana to NCAA title as sophomore and Final 4 MOP in 1981; consensus All-America guard in '81; led Detroit to 2 NBA titles (1989,1990); NBA Finals MVP in 1990; 3-time All-NBA 1st team (1984-86); elected to Hall of Fame in 2000; currently president and head coach of the N.Y. Knicks.

Thurman Thomas (b. May 16, 1966): Football RB; 3-time AFC rushing leader (1990-91,93); 2-time All-Pro (1990-91); 1991 NFL Player of Year; led Buffalo to 4 straight Super Bowls (1991-94).

Daley Thompson (b. July 30, 1958): British Track & Field; won consecutive gold medals in decathlon at 1980 and '84 Olympics.

Jenny Thompson (b. Feb. 26, 1973): American swimmer; 8-time Olympic gold medalist (all in relays) and winner of 12 Olympic medals overall, more than any other American; competed in 5 Olympic Games (1988,92,96,2000,04).

John Thompson (b. Sept. 2, 1941): Basketball; coached centers Patrick Ewing, Alonzo Mourning and Dikembe Mutombo at Georgetown; reached NCAA tourney final 3 out of 4 years with Ewing, winning title in 1984; also led Hoyas to 6 Big East tourney titles; coached 1988 U.S. Olympic team to bronze medal; retired abruptly during 1999 season with 27-year mark of 596-239.

Bobby Thomson (b. Oct. 25, 1923): Baseball OF; career .270 hitter who won the 1951 NL pennant for the NY Giants with a 1-out, 3-run HR in the bottom of the 9th inning of Game 3 of a best-of-3 playoff with Brooklyn; the pitcher was Ralph Branca, the count was 0-1 and the Dodgers were ahead 4-2; the Giants had trailed Brooklyn by 13½ games on Aug. 11.

Ian Thorpe (b. Oct. 13, 1982): Australian swimmer; 5-time gold medalist; won 400m free at Sydney Olympics (breaking his own world record) and silver in 200m free; won gold and broke the world record in the 4x100m and 4x200 free relays; won 200m free and 400m Olympic gold at Athens in 2004; 2002 Jesse Owens Award winner.

Jim Thorpe (b. May 28, 1887, d. Mar. 28, 1953): Native American multi-sport superstar; 2-time All-America halfback at Carlisle; won both pentathlon and decathlon gold medals at 1912 Olympics; stripped of medals a month later for playing semi-pro baseball prior to Games (medals restored in 1982); played major league baseball (1913-19) and pro football (1920-26,28); became first president of NFL (then known as the APFA) in 1920; chosen "Athlete of the Half Century" by AP in 1950.

Bill Tilden (b. Feb. 10, 1893, d. June 5, 1953): Tennis; won 7 U.S. and 3 Wimbledon titles in 1920s; led U.S. to 7 straight Davis Cup victories (1920-26).

Tinker to Evers to Chance Chicago Cubs double play combination from 1903-10; immortalized in poem by New York sportswriter Franklin P. Adams—SS Joe Tinker (1880-1948), 2B Johnny Evers (1883-1947) and 1B Frank Chance (1877-1924); all 3 managed the Cubs and made the Hall of Fame.

Y.A. Tittle (b. Oct. 24, 1926): Football QB; Yelberton Abraham Tittle played 17 years in AAFC and NFL; All-Pro 4 times; league MVP with San Francisco (1957) and NY Giants (1962, 63); passed for 28,339 career yards.

Alberto Tomba (b. Dec. 19, 1966): Italian alpine skier; winner of 5 Olympic medals (3 gold, 2 silver); became 1st alpine skier to win gold medals in 2 consecutive Winter Games when he won the slalom and giant slalom in 1988 then repeated in the GS in '92.

Dara Torres (b. April 15, 1967): Swimmer; her 9 career Olympic medals (4G, 1S, 4B) are the 2nd-most for an American woman.

Vladislav Tretiak (b. Apr. 25, 1952): Hockey G; led USSR to Olympic gold medals in 1972 and '76; starred for Soviets against Team Canada in 1972, and again in 2 Canada Cups (1976,81).

Lee Trevino (b. Dec. 1, 1939): Golfer; 2-time winner of 3 majors—U.S. Open (1968, 71), British Open (1971-72) and PGA (1974,84); PGA Tour Player of the Year (1971) and 3 times with Seniors (1990,92,94); 29 PGA Tour and 29 Champions Tour wins.

Felix Trinidad (b. Jan. 10, 1973): Puerto Rican boxer; former WBC/IBF welterweight champion; won WBC belt with a maj. dec. over Oscar De La Hoya in 1999; stepped up to jr. middleweight and won the WBA title from David Reid in 2000; moved to middleweight and suffered a 12th-round TKO to Bernard Hopkins in 2001 then retired; KO'd Ricardo Mayorga in 2004 comeback fight; lost to Winky Wright in 2005.

Bryan Trottier (b. July 17, 1956): Hockey C; led NY Islanders to 4 straight Stanley Cups (1980-83); Rookie of Year (1976); scoring champion (134 points) and regular season MVP in 1979; playoff MVP (1980); added 5th and 6th Cups with Pittsburgh in 1991 and '92; entered Hockey Hall of Fame in 1997.

Gene Tunney (b. May 25, 1897, d. Nov. 7, 1978): Boxer; world heavyweight champion from 1926-28; beat 31-year-old champ Jack Dempsey in unanimous 10 round decision in 1926; beat him again in famous "long count" rematch in '27; quit while still champion in 1928 with 65-1-1 record and 47 KOs.

Ted Turner (b. Nov. 19, 1938): Sportsman and TV mogul; skippered *Courageous* to America's Cup win in 1977; one-time owner of MLB Braves, NBA Hawks and NHL Thrashers; founder of CNN, TNT and TBS; founder of Goodwill Games; 1991 *Time* Man of Year.

Mike Tyson (b. June 30, 1966): Boxer; youngest (19) heavyweight champion ever (WBC in 1986); undisputed champ from 1987 until upset loss to 42-1 shot Buster Douglas on Feb. 10, 1990, in Tokyo; found guilty on Feb. 10, 1992, of raping 18-year-old Miss Black America contestant Desiree Washington in Indianapolis on July 19, 1991; sentenced to 6-year prison term; released May 9, 1995 after serving 3 years; reclaimed WBC and WBA belts with wins over Frank Bruno and Bruce Seldon in 1996; lost WBA title to Evander Holyfield in 1996; bit Holyfield's ear twice during their 1997 WBA title rematch; KO'd in 8th round by Lennox Lewis in 2002; 50-6 with 44 KO.

Wyomia Tyus (b. Aug. 29, 1945): Track & Field; 1st woman to win consecutive Olympic gold medals in 100m (1964-68).

Peter Ueberroth (b. Sept. 2, 1937): Organizer of 1984 Summer Olympics in LA; 1984 *Time* Man of Year; baseball commissioner from 1984-89; headed Rebuild Los Angeles for one year after 1992 riots; currently chairman of USOC.

Johnny Unitas (b. May 7, 1933, d. Sept. 11, 2002): Football QB; Big-game field general who led Baltimore Colts to 2 NFL titles (1958-59) and a Super Bowl win (1971); All-Pro 5 times; 3-time MVP (1959,64,67); selected to 10 Pro Bowls; passed for 40,239 career yards and 290 TDs.

Al Unser Jr. (b. Apr. 19, 1962): Auto racer; 2-time CART-IndyCar champion (1990,94); 2-time Indy 500 winer (1992,94), giving Unser family 9 overall titles at the Brickyard; retired in 2004 with 31 CART wins in 19 years; left CART for Indy Racing League in 2000; son of Al and nephew of Bobby.

Al Unser Sr. (b. May 29, 1939): Auto racer; 3-time USAC-CART national champion (1970,83,85); 4-time winner of Indy 500 (1970-71,78,87); retired in 1994 with 39 wins; younger brother of Bobby and father of Al Jr.

Bobby Unser (b. Feb. 20, 1934): Auto racer; 2-time USAC-CART national champion (1968,74); 3-time winner of Indy 500 (1968,75,81); retired after 1981 season; recorded 35 career wins.

Gene Upshaw (b. Aug. 15, 1945): Football G; 2-time All-AFL and 3-time All-NFL selection with Oakland; helped lead Raiders to 2 Super Bowl titles in 1976 and '80 seasons; executive director of NFL Players Assn. since 1987; agreed to application of salary cap in 1994.

Jim Valvano (b. Mar. 10, 1946, d. Apr. 28, 1993): Basketball; coach at N.C. State whose team upset Houston to win national title in 1983; in 19 seasons as a coach appeared in 8 NCAA tournaments; twice voted ACC Coach of the Year; career record 346-212; AD at N.C. State (1986-89) when a recruiting and admissions scandal forced him out of the job; worked as a broadcaster for ESPN and ABC; died after a year-long battle with cancer; The V Foundation for cancer research is named for him.

Norm Van Brocklin (b. Mar. 15, 1926, d. May 2, 1983): Football QB-P; led NFL in passing 3 times and punting twice; led LA Rams (1951) and Philadelphia (1960) to NFL titles; MVP in 1960.

Amy Van Dyken (b. Feb. 17, 1973): Swimming; first American woman to win four gold medals in one Olympics (1996); also won gold at Sydney in 2000.

Johnny Vander Meer (b. Nov. 2, 1914, d. Oct. 6, 1997): Baseball LHP; only major leaguer to pitch consecutive no-hitters (June 11 & 15, 1938).

Harold S. Vanderbilt (b. July 6, 1884, d. July 4, 1970): Sportsman; successfully defended America's Cup 3 times (1930, 34,37); also invented contract bridge in 1926.

Glenna Collett Vare (b. June 20, 1903, d. Feb. 10, 1989): Golfer; won record 6 U.S. Women's Amateur titles from 1922-35; "the female Bobby Jones."

Andy Varipapa (b. Mar. 31, 1891, d. Aug. 25, 1984): Bowler; trick-shot artist; won consecutive All-Star match game titles (1947-48) at age 55 and 56.

Bill Veeck (b. Feb. 9, 1914, d. Jan. 2, 1986): Maverick baseball executive; owned AL teams in Cleveland, St. Louis and Chicago from 1946-80; introduced ballpark giveaways, exploding scoreboards, Wrigley Field's ivy-covered walls and midget Eddie Gaedel; won World Series with Indians (1948) and pennant with White Sox (1959).

Michael Vick (b. June 26, 1980): Football QB; 1st overall pick in 2001 NFL draft out of Virginia Tech; led Atlanta Falcons to NFC Championship Game in 2004; in 2006 became the first QB to rush for over 1,000 yards in single season; became well-known outside of sports world in 2007 after pleading guilty to financing and operating an interstate dogfighting ring.

Jacques Villeneuve (b. Apr. 9, 1971): Canadian auto racer; won Indy 500 and IndyCar driving championship in 1995; jumped to Formula One racing in 1996 and won the F1 title in 1997.

Fay Vincent (b. May 29, 1938): Baseball; became 8th commissioner after death of A. Bartlett Giamatti in 1989; presided over World Series earthquake, owners' lockout and banishment of NY Yankees owner George Steinbrenner in his first year on the job; contentious relationship with owners resulted in his resignation on Sept. 7, 1992, four days after 18-9 "no confidence" vote.

Lasse Viren (b. July 22, 1949): Finnish runner; won gold medals at 5,000 and 10,000 meters in 1972 Munich Olympics; repeated 5,000/10,000 double in 1976 Games and added a fifth place finish in the marathon.

Dick Vitale (b. June 9, 1939): Broadcaster; Radio and television commentator for ESPN and ABC Sports known for his enthusiastic, almost spastic style; had successful college and pro basketball coaching career with the University of Detroit (1973-77) and the Detroit Pistons (1978-79).

Lanny Wadkins (b. Dec. 5, 1949): Golfer; member of 8 U.S. Ryder Cup teams (captain in 1995); won 1977 PGA Championship; 21 PGA Tour wins.

Honus Wagner (b. Feb. 24, 1874, d. Dec. 6, 1955): Baseball SS; hit .300 for 17 consecutive seasons (1897-1913) with Louisville and Pittsburgh; led NL in batting 8 times; ended career with 3,430 career hits, a .329 average and 722 stolen bases.

Grete Waitz (b. Oct. 1, 1953): Norwegian runner; 9-time winner of New York City Marathon from 1978-88; won silver medal at 1984 Olympics.

Jersey Joe Walcott (b. Jan. 31, 1914, d. Feb. 27, 1994): Boxer; oldest heavyweight (37) to win the championship until George Foreman surpassed him in 1994; lost four championship bouts before knocking out Ezzard Charles in the seventh round in 1951; lost the title the following year to Rocky Marciano; pro career record of 50-17-1 with 30 KOs; later became sheriff of Camden County, NJ.

Doak Walker (b. Jan. 1, 1927, d. Sept. 27, 1998): Football HB; won Heisman Trophy as SMU junior in 1948; led Detroit to 2 NFL titles (1952-53); All-Pro 4 times in 6 years.

Herschel Walker (b. Mar. 3, 1962): Football RB; led Georgia to national title as freshman in 1980; won Heisman in 1982 then jumped to upstart USFL in '83; signed by Dallas Cowboys after USFL folded; led NFL in rushing in 1988; traded to Minnesota in 1989 for 5 players and 6 draft picks.

Rusty Wallace (b. Aug. 14, 1956): Auto racing; NASCAR Winston Cup champ in 1989 and runner-up in 1980, 1988 and 1993; recorded 55 victories and won over $40 million in earnings in more than 25 years of racing; currently a racing analyst for ESPN.

Bill Walsh (b. Nov. 30, 1931, d. July 30, 2007): Football; Hall of Fame coach and GM of 3 Super Bowl winners with San Francisco (1982,85,89); retired after 1989 Super Bowl; returned to college coaching in 1992 for his second stint at Stanford; retired again after 1994 season; returned as 49er GM from 1999-2001; known as "The Genius"; devised what would later become known as the West Coast offense; created the Minority Coaching Fellowship in 1987.

Bill Walton (b. Nov. 5, 1952): Basketball C; 3-time College Player of Year (1972-74); led UCLA to 2 national titles (1972-73); led Portland to NBA title as MVP in 1977; regular season MVP in 1978; won 1986 NBA title with Boston.

Darrell Waltrip (b. Feb. 5, 1947): Auto racing; 3-time NASCAR Winston Cup champion (1981,82,85); 84 career Winston Cup wins and 59 poles.

Arch Ward (b. Dec. 27, 1896, d. July 9, 1955): Promoter and sports editor of *Chicago Tribune* from 1930-55; founder of baseball All-Star Game (1933), Chicago College All-Star Football Game (1934) and the All-America Football Conference (1946-49).

Charlie Ward (b. Oct. 12, 1970): Football QB and Basketball G; 1993 Heisman winner with national champion Florida St.; won Sullivan Award (1993); 3-year starter for FSU basketball team; 1st round pick of NY Knicks in 1994 NBA draft.

Glenn (Pop) Warner (b. Apr. 5, 1871, d. Sept. 7, 1954): Football innovator; coached at 7 colleges over 49 years; 319 career wins, 4th all-time; produced 47 All-Americas, including Jim Thorpe and Ernie Nevers.

Kurt Warner (b. June 22, 1971): Football QB; former Arena leaguer who led the St. Louis Rams to 2000 Super Bowl win; threw for a record 414 yards and was Super Bowl MVP; 2-time NFL MVP (1999,2001).

Tom Watson (b. Sept. 4, 1949): Golfer; 6-time PGA Player of the Year (1977-80,82,84); has won 5 British Opens, 2 Masters and a U.S. Open; 4-time Ryder Cup member and captain of 1993 team; 39 PGA tour wins; 10 Champions tour wins.

Danny Way (b. Apr. 15, 1974): Skateboarder; conceived the Megaramp (2002) and brought the Big Air event to the X Games (2004); set world records for longest distance jumped (79 feet—2004), height out of a ramp (23.5 feet— 2003), and highest bomb drop (28 feet—2006, from the guitar outside the Hard Rock Hotel in Las Vegas); first person to jump over the Great Wall of China without motorized aid (2005), two-time Thrasher Magazine Skater of the Year (1991, 2004).

Earl Weaver (b. Aug. 14, 1930): Baseball; managed the Baltimore Orioles to 6 Eastern Division titles, four AL pennants and a World Series victory in 1970; was ejected 91 times and suspended four times for outbursts against umpires; record of 1,480-1,060 from 1968-82 and 1985-86.

Alan Webb (b. Jan. 13, 1983): Track; in 2001, he ran a mile in 3:53.43 to break Jim Ryun's 36-year-old national high school record; ran 3:46.91 in July, 2007 to set a new American record (pending).

Karrie Webb (b. Dec. 21, 1974): Australian golfer; youngest woman (26) to win career Grand Slam; her win in the 2002 British Open made her the first player to win the "Super Grand Slam" (5 different majors) and gave her 6 major titles; won the 2006 Kraft Nabisco Championship to make it 7 majors; 2-time Rolex Player of the Year (1999-2000); entered Hall of Fame in 2005.

Dick Weber (b. Dec. 23, 1929, d. Feb. 13, 2005): Bowler; 3-time PBA Bowler of the Year (1961,63,65); won 30 PBA titles in 4 decades; father of Pete.

Pete Weber (b. Aug. 21, 1962): Bowler; 2nd on all-time PBA money list; 1990 PBA Rookie of the Year; inducted into PBA Hall of Fame (1998); winner of 34 PBA titles; son of Dick.

Johnny Weissmuller (b. June 2, 1904, d. Jan. 20 1984): American swimmer; won 3 gold medals (100m free, 400m free, 4x200m free) at 1924 Olympics and 2 more at 1928 Games (100m free and 4x200m free); set 51 world records; became Hollywood's most famous Tarzan.

Jerry West (b. May 28, 1938): Basketball G; 2-time All-America and NCAA Final 4 MOP (1959) at West Virginia; led 1960 U.S. Olympic team to gold medal; 10-time All-NBA 1st-team; NBA finals MVP (1969); led LA Lakers to NBA title once as player (1972) and then 6 more times (1980,82,85,87,88,00) as an executive in various positions with the club; hired as President of Basketball Ops. by Memphis Grizzlies in 2002; his silhouette serves as the NBA's logo.

Pernell Whitaker (b. Jan. 2, 1964): Boxer; won Olympic gold medal as lightweight in 1984; won 4 world championships as lightweight, jr. welterweight, welterweight and jr. middleweight; outfought but failed to beat Julio Cesar Chavez when 1993 welterweight title defense ended in controversial draw; pro record of 41-3-1 (17 KOs); nicknamed "Sweet Pea".

Bill White (b. Jan. 28, 1934): Baseball; former NL president and highest ranking black executive in sports from 1989-94; as 1st baseman, won 7 Gold Gloves and hit .286 with 202 HRs in 13 seasons.

Byron (Whizzer) White (b. June 8, 1917, d. Apr. 15, 2002): Football; All-America HB at Colorado (1937); signed with Pittsburgh in 1938 for the then largest contract in pro history ($15,800); took Rhodes Scholarship in 1939; returned to NFL in 1940 to lead league in rushing and retired in 1941; named to U.S. Supreme Court by President Kennedy in 1962 and stepped down in 1993.

Reggie White (b. Dec. 19, 1961, d. Dec. 26, 2004): Football DE; nicknamed the "Minister of Defense"; consensus All-America in 1983 at Tennessee; 7-time All-NFL (1986-92) with Philadelphia; won Super Bowl with Green Bay in 1997; 2nd all-time in career NFL sacks (198).

Shaun White (b. Sept. 3, 1986): Snowboarder/Skateboarder; first athlete to compete in both Winter and Summer X Games; winner of 12 combined X Games medals (10 snowboarding, 2 skateboarding); won an Olympic gold medal in 2006 for Halfpipe; nicknamed "The Flying Tomato."

Kathy Whitworth (b. Sept. 27, 1939): Golf; 7-time LPGA Player of the Year (1966-69,71-73); won 6 majors; 88 tour wins, most on LPGA or PGA tour.

Hoyt Wilhelm (b. July 26, 1923, d. Aug. 23, 2002): Baseball RHP; Knuckleballer who is 1st in games won in relief (123); career ERA of 2.52, 227 saves and 651 games finished; 1st reliever inducted into Hall of Fame (1985); threw no-hitter vs. NY Yankees (1958); hit lone HR of career in first major league at bat (1952); won Purple Heart at Battle of the Bulge.

Lenny Wilkens (b. Oct. 28, 1937): Basketball; NBA's all-time winningest coach; MVP of 1960 NIT as Providence guard; played 15 years in NBA, including 4 as player-coach; 9-time All-Star and MVP of 1971 game; coached Seattle to 1979 NBA title; Coach of Year in 1994 with Atlanta; career record of 1412-1253 including playoffs with 7 NBA teams; coached USA basketball team to gold medal in 1996; member of the basketball hall of fame as player and coach.

Dominique Wilkins (b. Jan. 12, 1960): Basketball F; prolific scorer and ferocious dunker who led NBA in scoring (30.3 ppg) in 1986 with Atlanta; All-NBA 1st team in 1986; 2-time NBA slam dunk champion; nicknamed "The Human Highlight Film"; inducted into Basketball Hall of Fame in 2006.

Bud Wilkinson (b. Apr. 23, 1916, d. Feb. 9, 1994): Football; played on 1936 national championship team at Minnesota; coached Oklahoma to 3 national titles (1950, 55, 56); won 4 Orange and 2 Sugar Bowls; teams had winning streaks of 47 (1953-57) and 31 (1948-50); retired after 1963 season with 145-29-4 record in 17 years; also coached St. Louis of NFL to 9-20 record from 1978-79.

Ricky Williams (b. May 21, 1977): Football RB; became all-time NCAA Div. I-A leader in rushing yards (6,279) and TDs (75) at Texas but has been passed in both categories; 1998 Heisman Trophy winner; 5th overall in 1999 NFL draft by Saints; traded to Miami in 2002; stunned teammates when he retired suddenly just prior to 2004 season; returned in 2005; suspended from the NFL for 2006; instead played in CFL.

Serena Williams (b. Sept. 26, 1981): Tennis; first African-American woman to win a Grand Slam title since Althea Gibson in 1958 by winning the 1999 U.S. Open; has 8 career Grand Slam titles: 2 Wimbledons (2002-03), French Open (2002), 2 U.S. Opens (1999,02) and 3 Australian Opens (2003,05,07); has won career doubles Grand Slam with Venus.

Ted Williams (b. Aug. 30, 1918, d. July 5, 2002): Baseball OF; led AL in batting 6 times, and HRs and RBI 4 times each; won Triple Crown twice (1942,47); 2-time MVP (1946,49); last player to bat .400 when he hit .406 in 1941; Marine Corps combat pilot who missed 3 full seasons during WWII (1943-45) and most of two others (1952-53) during Korean War; hit .344 lifetime with 521 HRs in 19 years with Boston Red Sox; also known as avid fisherman; furor erupted following his death when plans to keep his body frozen at a cryogenic lab were made public.

Venus Williams (b. June 17, 1980): Tennis; won 4 Wimbledon (2000,01,05,07) and 2 U.S. Open (2000-01) singles titles; 2000 Olympic singles and doubles gold medalist; recorded fastest serve in main-draw match history with 128 mph blast in 2007; won career doubles grand slam with Serena.

Walter Ray Williams Jr. (b. Oct. 6, 1959): Bowling and Horseshoes; 6-time PBA Bowler of Year (1986,93,96,97,98,2003); all-time leading money winner on the PBA Tour; has 42 all-time record PBA titles; also won 6 World Horseshoe Pitching titles.

Hack Wilson (b. Apr. 26, 1900, d. Nov. 23, 1948): Baseball; as a Chicago Cub, he produced one of baseball's most outstanding seasons in 1930 with 56 home runs, .356 batting average, 105 walks and, most amazingly, a major league record 191 RBIs that still stands; finished career with 244 HRs, 1,062 RBIs.

Dave Winfield (b. Oct. 3, 1951): Baseball OF-DH; selected in 4 major sports league drafts in 1973—NFL, NBA, ABA, and MLB; chose baseball and played in 12 All-Star Games over 22-year career; won World Series with Toronto in 1992; career 3,110 hits and 465 HRs; inducted into Baseball Hall of Fame in 2001.

Katarina Witt (b. Dec. 3, 1965): East German figure skater; 4-time world champion (1984-85,87-88); won consecutive Olympic gold medals (1984,88).

John Wooden (b. Oct. 14, 1910): Basketball; College Player of Year at Purdue in 1932; coached UCLA to 88 straight wins (1971-74), 10 national titles (1964-65,67-73,75); inducted into the Hall of Fame as both player and coach; career college coaching record of 664-162 over 29 years.

Tiger Woods (b. Dec. 30, 1975): Golfer; 3-time winner of U.S. Amateur (1994-96); won 6 events and broke the single season money record in his 1st full season on PGA Tour; won 1997 Masters by a record 18-under par and 13 strokes; won 2nd major at 1999 PGA Championship; in 2000 won the U.S. Open at Pebble Beach by a record 15 strokes, the British Open by 8 strokes and the PGA Championship in a playoff; held all 4 Major titles simultaneously with his win at 2001 Masters; has since won 7 more majors for a total of 13: 2 Masters (2002,05); 2 British Opens (2005-06), 2 PGA Championships (2006-07) and the 2002 U.S. Open; all-time PGA Tour money leader with over $76 million; 1 of only 5 players to win all 4 Grand Slam titles (others are Hogan, Nicklaus, Player and Sarazen); winner of PGA Tour's first FedEx Cup in 2007; 8-time PGA Tour Player of the Year.

Mickey Wright (b. Feb. 14, 1935): Golfer; won 3 of 4 majors (LPGA, U.S. Open, Titleholders) in 1961; 4-time winner of both U.S. Open and LPGA titles; 82 career wins including 13 majors.

Early Wynn (b. Jan. 6, 1920, d. Mar. 4, 1999): Baseball RHP; won 20 games 5 times; Cy Young winner in 1959; 300-244 record in 23 years.

Kristi Yamaguchi (b. July 12, 1971): Figure Skating; 1991 world champion; won the national, world and Olympic titles in 1992, then turned professional.

Cale Yarborough (b. Mar. 27, 1940): Auto racer; 3-time NASCAR national champion (1976-78); 4-time winner of Daytona 500 (1968,77,83-84); 83 career NASCAR wins.

Carl Yastrzemski (b. Aug. 22, 1939): Baseball OF; led AL in batting 3 times; won Triple Crown and MVP in 1967; had 3,419 hits and 452 HRs in 23 years with Boston Red Sox; member of Hall of Fame.

Cy Young (b. Mar. 29, 1867, d. Nov. 4, 1955): Baseball RHP; all-time leader in wins (511), losses (313), complete games (751) and innings pitched (7,356); had career 2.63 ERA in 22 years (1890-1911); 30-game winner 5 times and 20-game winner 11 other times; threw three no-hitters and a perfect game (1904); annual AL and NL pitching awards named after him.

Dick Young (b. Oct. 17, 1917, d. Aug. 31, 1987): Confrontational sportswriter for 44 years with NY tabloids; as baseball beat writer and columnist, he led change from flowery prose to hard-nosed reporting.

Sheila Young (b. Oct. 14, 1950): Speed skater and cyclist; 1st U.S. athlete to win 3 medals at Winter Olympics (1976); won speed skating overall and sprint cycling world titles in 1976.

Steve Young (b. Oct. 11, 1961): Football QB; All-America at BYU (1983); NFL Player of Year (1992) with SF 49ers; only QB to lead NFL in passer rating 4 straight years (1991-94); rating of 112.8 in 1994 is highest ever; threw record 6 TD passes in MVP performance in Super Bowl XXIX; retired with NFL records for highest passer rating (96.8) and completion pct. (64.4); 232 career TD passes and 33,124 yards.

Robin Yount (b. Sept. 16, 1955): Baseball SS-OF; AL MVP at 2 positions—as SS in 1982 and OF in '89; retired after 1993 season with 3,142 hits, 251 HRs and a major-league-record 123 sacrifice flies after 20 seasons with Brewers; inducted into Hall of Fame in 1999.

Steve Yzerman (b. May 9, 1965): Hockey C; Captained the Detroit Red Wings to 3 Stanley Cup wins (1997-98,2002); won the Conn Smythe Trophy as the playoff MVP in 1998; one of only 14 NHL players to score more than 600 goals; retired after 2005-06 with 692 goals and 1,755 career points.

Mario Zagalo (b. Aug. 9, 1931): Soccer; Brazilian forward who is one of only two men (Franz Beckenbauer is the other) to serve as both captain (1962) and coach (1970,94) of World Cup champion.

Babe Didrikson Zaharias (b. June 26, 1911, d. Sept. 27, 1956): All-around athlete who was chosen AP Female Athlete of Year 6 times from 1932-54; won 2 gold medals (javelin and 80-meter hurdles) and a silver (high jump) at 1932 Olympics; played baseball and acquired the nickname "Babe" for her tape measure home runs; real first name was Mildred; took up golf in 1935 and went on to win 55 pro and amateur events; won 10 majors, including 3 U.S. Opens (1948,50,54); helped found LPGA in 1949; chosen female "Athlete of the Half Century" by AP in 1950; when asked if there was anything she didn't play, she replied, "Yeah, dolls."

Tony Zale (b. May 29, 1913, d. March 20, 1997): Boxer; 2-time world middleweight champion (1941-47,48); fought Rocky Graziano for title 3 times in 21 months in 1947-48, winning twice; pro record 67-18-2 with 44 KOs.

Frank Zamboni (b. Jan. 16, 1901, d. July 27, 1988): Mechanic, ice salesman and skating rink owner in Paramount, Calif.; invented ice-resurfacing machine in 1949; now there are few skating rinks without one as thousands have been sold in over 35 countries.

Emil Zatopek (b. Sept. 19, 1922, d. Nov. 22, 2000): Czech distance runner; winner of 1948 Olympic gold medal at 10,000 meters; 4 years later, won unprecedented Olympic triple crown (5,000 meters, 10,000 meters and marathon) at 1952 Games in Helsinki.

Zinedine Zidane (b. June 23, 1972): French soccer player; 3-time FIFA World Player of the Year (1998, 2000, 2003); led host nation France to 1998 World Cup title, scoring twice in final against Brazil; a record $64m transfer fee sent the midfielder from Juventus to Real Madrid in 2001; led France to the World Cup final in 2006 (loss to Italy in penalty kicks); won Golden Ball as the tournament's most outstanding player, despite being given a red card in the 110th minute of the final for his notorious headbutt into the chest of Italy's Marco Materazzi.

John Ziegler (b. Feb. 9, 1934): Hockey; NHL president from 1977-92; negotiated settlement with rival WHA in 1979 that led to inviting four WHA teams (Edmonton, Hartford, Quebec and Winnipeg) to join NHL; stepped down June 12, 1992, 2 months after settling 10-day players' strike.

Pirmin Zurbriggen (b. Feb. 4, 1963): Swiss alpine skier; 4-time World Cup overall champ (1984,87-88,90) and 3-time runner-up; 40 World Cup wins in 10 years; won gold and bronze medals at 1988 Olympics.

Minority Firsts

Jackie Robinson's breaking of the baseball color barrier took on mythic status, but many other athletes of color entered their chosen sport or won major championships with decidedly less fanfare. This list attempts to chronicle their successes. Official sources were used where available; some entries are based on published reports at the time or anecdotal information.

African-American

Auto Racing

NASCAR driver: Charlie Scott, Daytona Beach, Fla., 1956
NASCAR winner: Wendell Scott, Jacksonville, Fla., 1963

Baseball

MLB player: Jackie Robinson, Brooklyn Dodgers, 1947
MLB coach: Buck O'Neil, Chicago Cubs, 1962
MLB manager: Frank Robinson, Cleveland Indians, 1975
Hall of Fame: Jackie Robinson, 1962

Boxing

Heavyweight champion: Jack Johnson, 1908

College Football

Player, major college: George Jewett, Michigan, 1890
Head coach, Div. I-A: Willie Jeffries, Wichita State, 1979
Heisman Trophy: Ernie Davis, Syracuse, 1961
Hall of Fame: Fritz Pollard, 1954

Golf

PGA Tour: Charlie Sifford, 1961
PGA winner: Peter Brown, Waco Open, 1964
Major winner: Tiger Woods, Masters, 1997
World Hall of Fame: Charlie Sifford, 2004
LPGA Tour: Althea Gibson, 1963

NBA

Player: Earl Lloyd, Washington Capitols, 1950
Coach: Bill Russell, Boston Celtics, 1968
Hall of Fame: Bill Russell, Boston Celtics, 1975

NFL

Player, pre-merger: Charles Follis, Shelby Athletic Club, 1902
QB: Willie Thrower, Chicago Bears, 1953
Head coach, pre-merger: Fritz Pollard, Akron Pros, 1921
Hall of Fame: Emlen Tunnell, New York Giants, 1967

NHL

Player: Willie O'Ree, Boston Bruins, 1958 (Canadian); Val James, Buffalo Sabres, 1982 (American)
Coach: Dirk Graham, Chicago Blackhawks, 1998 (Canadian)
Hall of Fame: Grant Fuhr (Canadian), Edmonton Oilers, 2003

Olympics

Summer Games
Gold medalist (men): DeHart Hubbard, long jump, 1924
Gold medalist (women): Alice Coachman, high jump, 1948
Winter Games
Gold medalist (men): Shani Davis, speedskating, 2006
Gold medalist (women): Vonetta Flowers, bobsled, 2002

Tennis

Grand Slam event: Althea Gibson, French Open, 1956; Arthur Ashe, U.S. Open, 1968
Hall of Fame: Althea Gibson, 1971; Arthur Ashe, 1985

Hispanic

Auto Racing

NASCAR driver: Frank Mundy, Strictly Stock Race #1 at Charlotte (N.C.) Speedway, 1949

Baseball

Player: Esteban Bellán, Troy, N.Y. Haymakers, 1871
Manager: Mike Gonzalez, St. Louis Cardinals, 1940
Hall of Fame: Roberto Clemente, 1973

Boxing

Heavyweight champion: John Ruiz, WBA, 2001

College Football

QB, starting, major college: Tom Flores, Pacific; Joe Kapp, California, 1956
Heisman Trophy: Jim Plunkett, Stanford, 1970
Head coach, major coll.: Marcelino Huerta, Wichita St., 1962

Golf

PGA Tour winner: Chi Chi Rodriguez, Denver Open, 1963
LPGA Tour winner: Fay Crocker, Serbin Open (Miami), 1955

NBA

Player: Butch Lee, Atlanta Hawks, 1979
Coach: Dick Versace, Indiana Pacers, 1989

NFL

Player: Lou Molinet, Frankford Yellowjackets, 1927
Quarterback: Tom Flores, Oakland Raiders (AFL), 1960
Head coach: Tom Fears, New Orleans Saints, 1967

NHL

Player: Bill Guerin, New Jersey Devils, 1991

Olympics

Summer Games
Medalist (men): Miguel Capriles, fencing, bronze, 1932
Winter Games
Gold medalist (men): Derek Parra, speedskating, 2006
Medalist (women): Jennifer Rodriguez, speedskating, bronze, 2002

Tennis

Grand Slam event: Pancho Gonzalez, U.S. Champ's, 1948

Asian

Auto Racing

NASCAR driver: George Tet, Grand National race #21, Charlotte (N.C.) Motor Speedway, 1960

Baseball

Player: Masanori Murakami, San Francisco Giants, 1964 (Japanese); Ryan Kurosaki, St. Louis Cardinals, 1975 (Japanese-American)

College Football

QB, starting: Roman Gabriel, NC State, 1959

Golf

PGA Tour winner: Isao Aoki, Hawaiian Open, 1983
LPGA Major winner: Chako Higuchi, LPGA Champ., 1977

NBA

Player: Wataru Misaka, New York Knicks, 1947

NFL

Player: Walter Achiu, Dayton Triangles, 1927
QB: Roman Gabriel, Los Angeles Rams, 1962

NHL

Player: Larry Kwong, New York Rangers, 1948 (Canadian)

Olympics

Summer Games
Gold medalist (men): Sammy Lee, diving, 1948
Gold medalist (women): Victoria Manalo Draves, diving, 1948
Winter Games
Gold medalist (men): Apolo Anton Ohno, short-track speed skating, 2002
Gold medalist (women): Kristi Yamaguchi, figure skating, 1992

Tennis

Grand Slam event: Michael Chang, French Open, 1988

BALLPARKS & ARENAS

The 2008 Summer Olympics will take flight at Beijing's **Olympic National Stadium**, nicknamed the Bird's Nest.

Coming Attractions

SPORTS ALMANAC

2007

NHL HOCKEY

New Jersey (East): The Prudential Center (Prudential Financial is the title sponsor), a new 17,625-seat arena in Newark for the New Jersey Devils, was scheduled to open Oct. 25, 2007 with a concert by Bon Jovi. Prudential purchased the naming rights for "The Rock" at a cost of $105.3 million over 20 years; Groundbreaking took place on Oct. 3, 2005. The arena site is located in downtown Newark near Penn Station; estimated cost: $375 million of which the city will contribute $210 million. The arena will include 68 luxury suites.

2008

BASEBALL

Washington (NL): The Nationals broke ground on a new ballpark on May 4, 2006. The stadium, to be built largely with public funds and with a so-called environmentally friendly "Green" design, will be owned by the D.C. Sports & Entertainment Commission. The site of the new ballpark is located along the Anacostia River at South Capitol and M Streets. The exterior design includes a lot of glass, similar to the new Washington Convention Center. Included in the ballpark's 41,222-seat capacity are approximately 22,000 seats in the lower bowl, 12,100 in the upper seating bowl, from where fans can see the U.S. Capitol building, 2,500 club seats and 1,112 suite seats. The project, whose budget is currently set at $611 million, will include a 4,500 square foot high-definition scoreboard. The home opener is scheduled for April 2008.

NFL FOOTBALL

Indianapolis (AFC): Construction on Lucas Oil Stadium, the new home for the Colts, is well underway. Lucas Oil bought the stadium naming rights for 20 years for $121.5 million. The new glass and brick stadium, designed by HKS, Inc. will seat 63,000 (expandable to 70,000) and cost about $675 million. Lucas Oil Stadium will feature a retractable-roof and FieldTurf surface. It will be located in the parking lot across South Street from the RCA Dome, which will continue to serve as the Colts' home until the new stadium is completed. The RCA Dome will then be demolished. The opening is scheduled to be in time for the 2008 season.

2009

BASEBALL

New York (AL): The Yankees broke ground on the new Yankee Stadium on Aug. 16, 2006 to be located on the sites of Macombs Dam and Mullaly Parks. The plan also calls for a new waterfront park and esplanade along the Harlem River, major infrastructure improvements, and the construction of more than 5,000 new parking spaces. The Yankees agreed to privately finance the new $800 million facility with the city chipping in $135 million to replace parkland (and make the necessary infrastructure improvements) and the State on the hook for $70 million for the construction of new parking facilities. The new retro-styled

park will have 53,000 seats, fewer than "The House that Ruth Built" but it will have a lot more luxury suites. The Yankees hired HOK Sport as their architect and the stadium is set to open in April 2009.

New York (NL): Citi Field (Citigroup Inc. will pay $400 million over 20 years for the naming rights) will seat approximately 45,000 (with 54 luxury suites) and feature natural grass. Although the park will be located in Willets Point, Queens between Shea Stadium and 126th Street it will be designed to evoke memories of Brooklyn's beloved but long lost Ebbets Field. The asymmetrical outfield walls and generous dimensions (LF—335'; LC—379'; CF—408'; RC—383'; RF—330') should make for a traditional pitcher's park. The estimated cost of the ballpark and infrastructure improvements is $610 million. The Mets are expected to cover $420 million of the total. The deal includes a 40-year lease that will keep the Mets in New York until at least 2049. Construction is scheduled to be completed by April 2009.

NBA BASKETBALL

New Jersey (East): The Barclays Center (Barclays Bank PLC is paying $400 million over 20 years for the naming rights) will be located in Brooklyn's Prospect Heights as part of Atlantic Yards, a $4.2 billion office, residential and shopping complex. The 19,000-seat, Frank Gehry-designed arena is aiming to be open for business for the 2009-10 season. The Nets recently made arrangements to the stay at Continental Airlines Arena in the Meadowlands through at least the 2008-09 season, with a team option to extend their lease through the 2012-13 season should the project hit construction delays. The team is likely to be redubbed the Brooklyn Nets.

NFL FOOTBALL

Dallas (NFC): Construction on a new publicly funded stadium for the Cowboys in Arlington, Texas is underway. The 80,000-seat stadium will be located south of the Tom Landry Freeway, next door to the Texas Rangers' Ballpark. Designed by HKS, Inc., the distinctive hole in the roof from Texas Stadium will be replicated with a retractable-roof; The stadium will be expandable to hold close to 100,000 fans and cost an estimated $1 billion. The stadium will also feature an enormous 60-yard long videoboard. Adjacent to the new stadium will be a 1.2 million-square-foot shopping area called Glorypark. Construction will be partially funded by the sale of personal seat licenses. The home opener is set for the fall of 2009 and the NFL has awarded the stadium Super Bowl XLV (Feb. 6, 2011).

2010

BASEBALL

Minnesota (AL): The Twins' broke ground on their new ballpark Aug. 30, 2007. The open-air, natural grass park will seat 42,000 including 72 suites and 4,000 club seats. It will be located behind the Target Center, which is located at the convergence of I-394 and I-94. The preliminary field dimensions are as follows: LF—339'; LC—377'; CF—404'; RC—367'; RF—328'. Estimated cost of the project is $522 million; The home opener is scheduled for 2010.

AP/Wide World Photos

"The House that Ruth Built" will be replaced by a new house in 2009. Originally built in 1923, **Yankee Stadium**, the third oldest ballpark in the majors, will be torn down upon the completion of a new ballpark (left) in the Bronx.

NFL FOOTBALL

New York (AFC/NFC): Ground was officially broken on a new stadium that will be shared by the New York Jets and New York Giants on Sept. 5, 2007; The new 82,500-seat stadium will be located in the Meadowlands adjacent to the existing Giants Stadium. The stadium will include 9,200 club seats and 200 luxury suites. Design plans include ways to customize the theme of the stadium including a distinctive lighting system that will illuminate the stadium and will switch colors (green for the Jets, blue for the Giants) depending on who is playing. The price tag for the privately financed stadium is $1.3 billion. Construction is scheduled for completion in 2010.

NBA BASKETBALL

Orlando (East): Construction on the new Orlando Events Center (title sponsor pending), the future home of the Magic, is almost underway. The 20,000-seat arena will be located at the southwest corner of Church Street and Hughey Avenue, with construction starting in early 2008. The total cost of the project is $480 million and earliest opening would be 2010.

NHL HOCKEY

Pittsburgh (East): The Penguins signed a long term lease on their new, yet-to-be-built arena in Pittsburgh in September 2007, officially ending threats to relocate the franchise to Kansas City, Las Vegas or Houston. The $290 million Uptown arena will serve as the Pens' new home until at least 2040. The arena will be designed by famed stadium architects HOK Sport and will seat an estimated 18,000; Groundbreaking at the site bordering Centre Avenue, Washington Place and Fifth Avenue is set for the spring of 2008 and the earliest home opener would be 2010.

2011

BASEBALL

Oakland (AL): The Oakland A's announced plans for the new Cisco Field (Cisco Systems is the title sponsor) to be located west of Interstate 880 in Fremont, Calif. about 20 miles south of McAfee Coliseum where they will continue to play through at least 2010. The park will seat approximately 32,000, feature a natural grass field and cost an estimated $450 million. The projected opening is for the 2011 season.

Other Ballparks & Stadia in the Works

The **Florida Marlins** may finally have the funding and political will to realize their decade-old dream of a new ballpark in South Florida. The *Miami Herald* reported in September 2007 that the decision by the University of Miami to abandon plans to stay at a renovated **Orange Bowl** and instead move their home field to Dolphin Stadium, starting in 2008, has freed up $85 million. The money was originally slated for rehabbing the Orange Bowl but could be reappropriated to help pay for a new park for the Marlins. The current lease that the Marlins hold at Dolphin Stadium will expire in 2010. An exact site has yet to be determined, with city and county officials seemingly in favor of imploding the Orange Bowl and using that site, while the team has stated it prefers a downtown location for their proposed retractable-roof ballpark.

The **Kansas City Royals** have announced plans for a **major renovation to Kauffman Stadium**. The project, which will occur in several stages over the next few years is expected to be complete by 2010. The improvements will include altering the layout of the bullpens, new, wider fan concourses, a high-def scoreboard, an outdoor plaza and new premium seating areas and luxury suites. The total price tag is expected to be $250 million.

Aborting plans for a stadium at Candlestick Point due to a myriad of issues including financing, site approval and public access, the **San Francisco 49ers** announced preliminary plans to build a new stadium 45 miles south of the city in Santa Clara, Calif., where the team's headquarters and training facility currently reside. Many issues still need to be resolved and the earliest opening for a new stadium would be 2012.

The **Minnesota Vikings** have hired ROMA Design Group, builders of San Francisco's AT&T Park to design a new downtown, retractable-roof stadium for the team. The team's lease at the Metrodome expires after the 2011 season.

The **San Diego Chargers** have stepped up efforts to leave Qualcomm Stadium and recently announced interest in moving south of the city to **Chula Vista** where two suitable sites were identified.

Home, Sweet Home

The home fields, home courts and home ice of the AL, NL, NBA, NFL, NHL, NCAA Division I-A college football and Division I basketball. Also included are MLS stadiums, Formula One, Champ Car, Indy Racing League and NASCAR auto racing tracks.

Attendance figures for the 2006 NFL regular season and the 2006-07 NBA and NHL regular seasons are provided. See Baseball chapter for 2007 AL and NL attendance figures.

MAJOR LEAGUE BASEBALL

American League

		Built	Capacity	LF	LCF	CF	RCF	RF	Field
Baltimore Orioles	**Oriole Park at Camden Yards**	1992	**48,190**	337	376	406	391	320	Grass
Boston Red Sox	**Fenway Park**	1912	**38,805**	310	379	390*	380	302	Grass
Chicago White Sox	**U.S. Cellular Field**	1991	**41,000**	330	377	400	372	335	Grass
Cleveland Indians	**Jacobs Field**	1994	**43,068**	325	370	405	375	325	Grass
Detroit Tigers	**Comerica Park**	2000	**40,120**	345	395	420	365	330	Grass
Kansas City Royals	**Kauffman Stadium**	1973	**40,793**	330	375	400	375	330	Grass
Los Angeles Angels of Anaheim	**Angel Stadium of Anaheim**	1966	**45,030**	365	387	400	370	365	Grass
Minnesota Twins	**Hubert H. Humphrey Metrodome**	1982	**48,678**	343	385	408	367	327	Turf
New York Yankees	**Yankee Stadium**	1923	**57,478**	318	399	408	385	314	Grass
Oakland Athletics	**McAfee Coliseum**	1966	**34,007†**	330	367	400	367	330	Grass
Seattle Mariners	**SAFECO Field**	1999	**47,116**	331	390	405	387	327	Grass
Tampa Bay Devil Rays	**Tropicana Field**	1990	**43,761**	315	370	404	370	322	Turf
Texas Rangers	**Rangers Ballpark in Arlington**	1994	**49,115**	332	390	400	381	325	Grass
Toronto Blue Jays	**Rogers Centre**	1989	**50,516**	328	375	400	375	328	Turf

*The straightaway center-field fence at Fenway Park is 390 feet from home plate but the deepest part of center-field, a.k.a. "the Triangle," is 420 feet away. The left-field fence, known as "the Green Monster," is 37 feet tall. Two hundred and seventy seats were added to the top of the wall in 2003 replacing the 23-foot screen that previously topped the Monster.

†The Oakland A's have closed off the upper deck of McAfee Coliseum and covered the seats with a tarp. The stadium could accomodate 43,662 fans if the upper tier was reopened.

National League

		Built	Capacity	LF	LCF	CF	RCF	RF	Field
Arizona Diamondbacks	**Chase Field**	1998	**49,033**	330	376	407	376	334	Grass
Atlanta Braves	**Turner Field**	1996	**50,091**	335	380	401	390	330	Grass
Chicago Cubs	**Wrigley Field**	1914	**39,111**	355	368	400	368	353	Grass
Cincinnati Reds	**Great American Ball Park**	2003	**42,059**	328	379	404	370	325	Grass
Colorado Rockies	**Coors Field**	1995	**50,449**	347	390	415	375	350	Grass
Florida Marlins	**Dolphin Stadium**	1987	**36,331**	330	385	434	385	345	Grass
Houston Astros	**Minute Maid Park**	2000	**40,950**	315	362	436	373	326	Grass
Los Angeles Dodgers	**Dodger Stadium**	1962	**56,000**	330	385	395	385	330	Grass
Milwaukee Brewers	**Miller Park**	2001	**42,400**	340	374	400	378	345	Grass
New York Mets	**Shea Stadium**	1964	**56,749**	338	378	410	378	338	Grass
Philadelphia Phillies	**Citizens Bank Park**	2004	**43,000**	329	369	401*	369	330	Grass
Pittsburgh Pirates	**PNC Park**	2001	**37,898**	326	368	399*	375	324	Grass
St. Louis Cardinals	**Busch Stadium**	2006	**46,000**	336	390	400	390	335	Grass
San Diego Padres	**PETCO Park**	2004	**46,000**	334	367	396*	387	322	Grass
San Francisco Giants	**AT&T Park**	2000	**41,467**	339	364	399	421	309	Grass
Washington Nationals	**Nationals Park**	2008	**41,222**	337	377	409	377	335	Grass

*The deepest part of PNC Park is 410 feet between straightaway center and left-center. The deepest part of Citizens Bank Park is 409 feet in part of left-center. The deepest part of PETCO Park is 411 feet in part of right-center.

Rank by Capacity

AL

New York	57,478
Toronto	50,516
Texas	49,115
Minnesota	48,678
Baltimore	48,190
Seattle	47,116
Los Angeles	45,030
Tampa Bay	43,761
Cleveland	43,068
Chicago	41,000
Kansas City	40,793
Detroit	40,120
Boston	38,805
Oakland	34,007

NL

New York	56,749
Los Angeles	56,000
Colorado	50,449
Atlanta	50,091
Arizona	49,033
St. Louis	46,000
San Diego	46,000
Philadelphia	43,000
Milwaukee	42,400
Cincinnati	42,059
San Francisco	41,467
Washington	41,222
Houston	40,950
Chicago	39,111
Pittsburgh	37,898
Florida	36,331

Rank by Age

AL

Boston	1912
New York	1923
Los Angeles	1966
Oakland	1966
Kansas City	1973
Minnesota	1982
Toronto	1989
Tampa Bay	1990
Chicago	1991
Baltimore	1992
Cleveland	1994
Texas	1994
Seattle	1999
Detroit	2000

Note: New York's Yankee Stadium (AL) was rebuilt in 1976.

NL

Chicago	1914
Los Angeles	1962
New York	1964
Florida	1987
Atlanta	1993
Colorado	1995
Arizona	1998
Houston	2000
San Francisco	2000
Milwaukee	2001
Pittsburgh	2001
Cincinnati	2003
Philadelphia	2004
San Diego	2004
St. Louis	2006
Washington	2008

Home Fields

Listed below are the principal home fields used through the years by current American and National League teams. The NL became a major league in 1876, the AL in 1901.

The capacity figures in the right-hand column indicate the largest seating capacity of the ballpark while the club played there. Capacity figures before 1915 (and the introduction of concrete grandstands) are sketchy at best and have been left blank.

American League

Baltimore Orioles

1901	Lloyd Street Grounds (Milwaukee)	—
1902–53	Sportsman's Park II (St. Louis)	30,500
1954–91	Memorial Stadium (Baltimore)	53,371
1992–	Oriole Park at Camden Yards	48,190

Boston Red Sox

1901–11	Huntington Ave. Grounds	—
1912–	Fenway Park	38,805
	(1934 capacity—27,000)	

Chicago White Sox

1901–10	Southside Park	—
1910–90	Comiskey Park I	43,931
1991–	U.S. Cellular Field	41,000
	(2003 capacity—46,943)	

Cleveland Indians

1901–09	League Park I	—
1910–46	League Park II	21,414
1932–93	Cleveland Stadium	74,483
1994–	Jacobs Field	43,068

Detroit Tigers

1901–11	Bennett Park	—
1912–99	Tiger Stadium	46,945
2000–	Comerica Park	40,120
	(1912 capacity—23,000)	

Kansas City Royals

1969–72	Municipal Stadium	35,020
1973–	Kauffman Stadium	40,793
	(1973 capacity—40,762)	

Los Angeles Angels of Anaheim

1961	Wrigley Field (Los Angeles)	20,457
1962-65	Dodger Stadium	56,000
1966–	Angel Stadium of Anaheim	45,030
	(1966 capacity—43,250)	

Minnesota Twins

1901-02	American League Park (Washington, DC)	—
1903-60	Griffith Stadium	27,410
1960-81	Metropolitan Stadium (Bloomington, MN)	45,919
1982–	HHH Metrodome (Minneapolis)	48,678
	(1982 capacity—54,000)	

New York Yankees

1901–02	Oriole Park (Baltimore)	—
1903–12	Hilltop Park (New York)	—
1913–22	Polo Grounds II	38,000
1923–73	Yankee Stadium I	67,224
1974–75	Shea Stadium	55,101
1976–	Yankee Stadium II	57,478
	(1976 capacity—57,145)	

Oakland Athletics

1901–08	Columbia Park (Philadelphia)	—
1909–54	Shibe Park	33,608
1955–67	Municipal Stadium (Kansas City)	35,020
1968–	McAfee Coliseum	43,662
	(1968 capacity—48,621)	

Seattle Mariners

| 1977–99 | The Kingdome | 59,166 |
| 1999– | SAFECO Field | 47,116 |

Tampa Bay Devil Rays

| 1990– | Tropicana Field | 43,761 |

Texas Rangers

1961	Griffith Stadium (Washington, DC)	27,410
1962–71	RFK Stadium	45,016
1972–93	Arlington Stadium (Texas)	43,521
1994–	Rangers Ballpark in Arlington	49,115

Toronto Blue Jays

1977–89	Exhibition Stadium	43,737
1989–	Rogers Centre	50,516
	(1989 capacity—49,500)	

Ballpark Name Changes: ANAHEIM—**Angel Stadium of Anaheim**, originally Anaheim Stadium (1966-98), then Edison International Field of Anaheim (1998-2003); CHICAGO—**Comiskey Park I** originally White Sox Park (1910-12), then Comiskey Park in 1913, then White Sox Park again in 1962, then Comiskey Park again in 1976; **U.S. Cellular Field** originally Comiskey Park (1991-2002); CLEVELAND—**League Park** renamed Dunn Field in 1920, then League Park again in 1928; **Cleveland Stadium** originally Municipal Stadium (1932-74); DETROIT—**Tiger Stadium** originally Navin Field (1912-37), then Briggs Stadium (1938-60); KANSAS CITY—**Kauffman Stadium** originally Royals Stadium (1973-93); LOS ANGELES—**Dodger Stadium** referred to as Chavez Revine by AL while Angels played there (1962-65); OAKLAND—**McAfee Coliseum** originally Oakland Alameda Coliseum (1968-98), then Network Associates Coliseum (1998-2004); PHILADELPHIA—**Shibe Park** renamed Connie Mack Stadium in 1953; ST. LOUIS—**Sportsman's Park** renamed Busch Stadium in 1953; WASHINGTON—**Griffith Stadium** originally National Park (1892-1920), **RFK Stadium** originally D.C. Stadium (1961-68); TEXAS—**Rangers Ballpark in Arlington** originally The Ballpark in Arlington (1994-2004), then Ameriquest Field in Arlington (2004-07); TORONTO—**Rogers Centre** originally Skydome (1989-2005).

National League

Arizona Diamondbacks

| 1998– | Chase Field | 49,033 |

Atlanta Braves

1876–94	South End Grounds I (Boston)	—
1894–1914	South End Grounds II	—
1915–52	Braves Field	40,000
1953–65	County Stadium (Milwaukee)	43,394
1966–96	Atlanta-Fulton County Stadium	52,769
	(1966 capacity—50,000)	
1997–	Turner Field	50,091

Chicago Cubs

1876–77	State Street Grounds	—
1878–84	Lakefront Park	—
1885–91	West Side Park	—
1891–93	Brotherhood Park	—
1893–1915	West Side Grounds	—
1916–	Wrigley Field	39,111
	(1916 capacity—16,000)	

Cincinnati Reds

1876–79	Avenue Grounds	—
1880	Bank Street Grounds	—
1890–1901	Redland Field I	—
1902–11	Palace of the Fans	—
1912–70	Crosley Field	29,603
1970–2002	Cinergy Field	40,007
	(1970 capacity—52,000)	
2003–	Great American Ball Park	42,059

Major League Baseball (Cont.)

Colorado Rockies
1993–94	Mile High Stadium (Denver)	.76,100
1995–	Coors Field	.50,449

Florida Marlins
1993–	Dolphin Stadium (Miami)	.36,331
	(1993 capacity—47,662)	

Houston Astros
1962–64	Colt Stadium	.32,601
1965–99	The Astrodome	.54,370
	(1965 capacity—45,011)	
2000–	Minute Maid Park	.40,950

Los Angeles Dodgers
1890	Washington Park I (Brooklyn)	—
1891–97	Eastern Park	—
1898–1912	Washington Park II	—
1913–55	Ebbets Field	.31,497
1956–57	Ebbets Field	.31,497
	& Roosevelt Stadium (Jersey City)	.24,167
1958–61	Memorial Coliseum (Los Angeles)	.93,600
1962–	Dodger Stadium	.56,000

Milwaukee Brewers
1969	Sick's Stadium (Seattle)	.59,166
1970–	County Stadium (Milwaukee)	.53,192
2000	(1970 capacity—46,620)	
2001–	Miller Park	.42,400

New York Mets
1962–63	Polo Grounds	.55,987
1964–	Shea Stadium	.56,749
	(1964 capacity—55,101)	

Philadelphia Phillies
1883–86	Recreation Park	—
1887–94	Huntingdon Ave. Grounds	—
1895–1938	Baker Bowl	.18,800
1938–70	Shibe Park	.33,608

Philadelphia Phillies (Cont.)
1971–2003	Veterans Stadium	.62,418
2004–	Citizens Bank Park	.43,000

Pittsburgh Pirates
1887–90	Recreation Park	—
1891–1909	Exposition Park	—
1909–70	Forbes Field	.35,000
1970–2000	Three Rivers Stadium	.47,687
	(1970 capacity—50,235)	
2001–	PNC Park	.37,898

St. Louis Cardinals
1876–77	Sportsman's Park I	—
1885–86	Vandeventer Lot	—
1892–1920	Robison Field	.18,000
1920–66	Sportsman's Park II	.30,500
1966–2005	Busch Stadium	.49,814
2006–	Busch Stadium II	.46,000

San Diego Padres
1969–2003	Qualcomm Stadium	.66,083
2004–	PETCO Park	.46,000

San Francisco Giants
1876	Union Grounds (Brooklyn)	—
1883–88	Polo Grounds I (New York)	—
1889–90	Manhattan Field	—
1891–1957	Polo Grounds II	.55,987
1958–59	Seals Stadium (San Francisco)	.22,900
1960–99	3Com Park	.63,000
	(1960 capacity—42,553)	
2000–	AT&T Park	.41,467

Washington Nationals
1969–76	Jarry Park (Montreal)	.28,000
1977–2002	Olympic Stadium	.46,500
2003–04	Olympic Stadium	.46,500
	& Hiram Bithon Stadium (San Juan)	.18,000
2005–07	RFK Stadium (Washington D.C.)	.45,250
2008–	Nationals Ballpark	.41,222

Ballpark Name Changes: ARIZONA—**Chase Field** originally named Bank One Ballpark (1998-2005); ATLANTA—**Atlanta-Fulton County Stadium** originally Atlanta Stadium (1966-74), **Turner Field** originally Centennial Olympic Stadium (1996); CHICAGO—**Wrigley Field** originally Weeghman Park (1914-17), then Cubs Park (1918-25); CINCINNATI—**Redland Field** originally League Park (1890-93), **Crosley Field** originally Redland Field II (1912-33) and **Cinergy Field** originally Riverfront Stadium (1970-96); FLORIDA—**Dolphin Stadium** originally Joe Robbie Stadium (1987-96), then Pro Player Stadium (1997-2004), then Dolphins Stadium (2004-06); HOUSTON—**Astrodome** originally Harris County Domed Stadium before it opened in 1965; **Enron Field** renamed Astros Field briefly and then Minute Maid Park in 2002; PHILADELPHIA—**Baker Field** originally Philadelphia Park (1895-1912), **Shibe Park** renamed Connie Mack Stadium in 1953; ST. LOUIS—**Robison Field** originally Vandeventer Lot, then League Park, then Cardinal Park all before becoming Robison Field in 1901, **Sportsman's Park** renamed Busch Stadium in 1953, and **Busch Stadium** originally Busch Memorial Stadium (1966-82); SAN DIEGO—**Qualcomm Stadium** originally San Diego Stadium (1967-81) and San Diego/Jack Murphy Stadium (1982-96); SAN FRANCISCO—**3Com Park** originally Candlestick Park (1960-95), **AT&T Park** originally Pacific Bell Park (2000-03), then SBC Park (2003-06).

NATIONAL BASKETBALL ASSOCIATION

Western Conference

		Location	Built	Capacity
Dallas Mavericks	**American Airlines Center**	Dallas, Texas	2001	**19,200**
Denver Nuggets	**Pepsi Center**	Denver, Colo.	1999	**19,099**
Golden State Warriors	**Oracle Arena**	Oakland, Calif.	1997	**19,596**
Houston Rockets	**Toyota Center**	Houston, Texas	2003	**18,300**
Los Angeles Clippers	**Staples Center**	Los Angeles, Calif.	1999	**18,694**
Los Angeles Lakers	**Staples Center**	Los Angeles, Calif.	1999	**18,997**
Memphis Grizzlies	**FedEx Forum**	Memphis, Tenn.	2004	**18,400**
Minnesota Timberwolves	**Target Center**	Minneapolis, Minn.	1990	**19,006**
New Orleans Hornets	**New Orleans Arena**	New Orleans, La.	1999	**18,500**
Phoenix Suns	**U.S. Airways Center**	Phoenix, Ariz.	1992	**19,023**
Portland Trail Blazers	**Rose Garden**	Portland, Ore.	1995	**19,980**
Sacramento Kings	**ARCO Arena**	Sacramento, Calif.	1988	**17,317**
San Antonio Spurs	**AT&T Center**	San Antonio, Texas	2002	**18,500**
Seattle SuperSonics	**KeyArena at Seattle Center**	Seattle, Wash.	1962	**17,072**
Utah Jazz	**EnergySolutions Arena**	Salt Lake City, Utah	1991	**19,911**

Notes: Seattle's KeyArena was originally the Seattle Center Coliseum before being rebuilt in 1995; The Staples Center has different listed capacities for Clippers games and Lakers games because of different floor seating arrangements.

Eastern Conference

		Location	Built	Capacity
Atlanta Hawks	**Philips Arena**	Atlanta, Ga.	1999	**19,445**
Boston Celtics	**TD Banknorth Garden**	Boston, Mass.	1995	**18,624**
Charlotte Bobcats	**Charlotte Bobcats Arena**	Charlotte, N.C.	2005	**18,500**
Chicago Bulls	**United Center**	Chicago, Ill.	1994	**21,711**
Cleveland Cavaliers	**The Quicken Loans Arena**	Cleveland, Ohio	1994	**20,562**
Detroit Pistons	**The Palace of Auburn Hills**	Auburn Hills, Mich.	1988	**22,076**
Indiana Pacers	**Conseco Fieldhouse**	Indianapolis, Ind.	1999	**18,345**
Miami Heat	**AmericanAirlines Arena**	Miami, Fla.	1999	**16,500**
Milwaukee Bucks	**Bradley Center**	Milwaukee, Wisc.	1988	**18,717**
New Jersey Nets	**Continental Airlines Arena**	E. Rutherford, N.J.	1981	**20,049**
New York Knicks	**Madison Square Garden**	New York, N.Y.	1968	**19,763**
Orlando Magic	**Amway Arena**	Orlando, Fla.	1989	**17,248**
Philadelphia 76ers	**Wachovia Center**	Philadelphia, Penn.	1996	**20,444**
Toronto Raptors	**Air Canada Centre**	Toronto, Ont.	1999	**19,800**
Washington Wizards	**Verizon Center**	Washington, D.C.	1997	**20,674**

Rank by Capacity

Western		Eastern	
Portland	19,980	Detroit	22,076
Utah	19,911	Chicago	21,711
New Orleans	19,675	Washington	20,674
Golden State	19,596	Cleveland	20,562
Dallas	19,200	Philadelphia	20,444
Denver	19,099	New Jersey	20,049
Phoenix	19,023	Toronto	19,800
Minnesota	19,006	New York	19,763
LA Lakers	18,997	Atlanta	19,445
LA Clippers	18,694	Milwaukee	18,717
San Antonio	18,500	Boston	18,624
Memphis	18,400	Charlotte	18,500
Houston	18,300	Indiana	18,345
Sacramento	17,317	Orlando	17,248
Seattle	17,072	Miami	16,500

Rank by Age

Western		Eastern	
Seattle	1962	New York	1968
Sacramento	1988	New Jersey	1981
Minnesota	1990	Detroit	1988
Utah	1991	Milwaukee	1988
Phoenix	1992	Orlando	1989
Portland	1995	Chicago	1994
Golden St.	1997	Cleveland	1994
Denver	1999	Boston	1995
LA Clippers	1999	Philadelphia	1996
LA Lakers	1999	Washington	1997
Dallas	2001	Toronto	1999
San Antonio	2002	Atlanta	1999
New Orleans	2002	Indiana	1999
Houston	2003	Miami	1999
Memphis	2004	Charlotte	2005

Note: The Seattle Center Coliseum was rebuilt and renamed KeyArena in 1995.

2006-07 NBA Attendance

Official overall attendance in the NBA for the 2006-07 season was 21,841,480 for an average per game crowd of 17,757 over 1,230 games. Teams in each conference are ranked by attendance over 41 home games based on total tickets distributed. Rank column refers to rank in entire league. Numbers in parentheses indicate conference rank in 2005-06.

Western Conference

		Attendance	Rank	Average
1	Dallas (1)	834,411	3	20,351
2	Utah (4)	802,294	6	19,568
3	LA Lakers (2)	778,415	7	18,985
4	San Antonio (3)	764,823	9	18,654
5	Phoenix (7)	755,302	10	18,422
6	LA Clippers (8)	755,261	11	18,421
7	Golden St. (5)	742,267	14	18,104
8	New Orleans (6)	731,065	15	17,830
9	Sacramento (9)	709,817	16	17,312
10	Denver (10)	706,437	17	17,230
11	Houston (14)	678,262	21	16,542
12	Portland (15)	670,778	22	16,360
13	Seattle (11)	654,163	25	15,955
14	Minnesota (12)	655,947	24	15,998
15	Memphis (13)	600,836	30	14,654
	TOTAL	10,840,078	—	17,626

Eastern Conference

		Attendance	Rank	Average
1	Chicago (2)	908,600	1	22,160
2	Detroit (1)	905,116	2	22,076
3	Cleveland (4)	837,883	3	20,436
4	Miami (3)	808,741	5	19,725
5	New York (5)	770,617	8	18,795
6	Washington (6)	753,283	12	18,372
7	Toronto (7)	748,603	13	18,258
8	Orlando (14)	700,887	18	17,094
9	New Jersey (9)	693,955	19	16,926
10	Boston (8)	690,576	20	16,843
11	Milwaukee (10)	663,629	23	16,186
12	Atlanta (15)	639,375	26	15,594
13	Charlotte (12)	637,520	27	15,549
14	Indiana (13)	629,750	28	15,359
15	Philadelphia (11)	615,480	29	15,011
	TOTAL	11,040,015	—	17,893

Home Courts

Listed below are the principal home courts used through the years by current NBA teams. The largest capacity of each arena is noted in the right-hand column. ABA arenas (1967-76) are included for Denver, Indiana, New Jersey and San Antonio.

Western Conference

Dallas Mavericks
1980–2000	Reunion Arena	.18,187
2001–	American Airlines Center	.19,200

Denver Nuggets
1967–75	Auditorium Arena	.6,841
1975–99	McNichols Sports Arena	.17,171
	(1975 capacity—16,700)	
1999–	Pepsi Center	.19,099

Golden State Warriors
1946–52	Philadelphia Arena	.7,777
1952–62	Convention Hall (Philadelphia)	.9,200
	& Philadelphia Arena	.7,777
1962–64	Cow Palace (San Francisco)	.13,862
1964–66	Civic Auditorium	.7,500
	& (USF Memorial Gym)	.6,000
1966–67	Cow Palace, Civic Auditorium	
	& Oakland Coliseum Arena	.15,000
1967–71	Cow Palace	.14,500
1971–96	Oakland Coliseum Arena	.15,025
	(1971 capacity—12,905)	
1996–97	San Jose Arena	.18,500
1997–	Oracle Arena	.19,596

Houston Rockets
1967–71	San Diego Sports Arena	.14,000
1971–72	Hofheinz Pavilion (Houston)	.10,218
1972–73	Hofheinz Pavilion	.10,218
	& HemisFair Arena (San Antonio)	.10,446
1973–75	Hofheinz Pavilion	.10,218
1975–2002	Compaq Center	.16,285
2003–	Toyota Center	.18,300

Los Angeles Clippers
1970–78	Memorial Auditorium (Buffalo)	.17,300
1978–84	San Diego Sports Arena	.12,167
1985–94	Los Angeles Sports Arena	.16,005
1994–99	Los Angeles Sports Arena	.16,021
	& Arrowhead Pond	.18,211
1999–	Staples Center	.18,694

Los Angeles Lakers
1948–60	Minneapolis Auditorium	.10,000
1960–67	Los Angeles Sports Arena	.14,781
1967–99	Great Western Forum (Inglewood, CA)	.17,505
	(1967 capacity—17,086)	
1999–	Staples Center	.18,997

Memphis Grizzlies
1995–2001	General Motors Place (Vancouver)	.19,193
2001–03	The Pyramid (Memphis, TN)	.19,342
2004–	FedEx Forum	.18,400

Minnesota Timberwolves
1989–90	Hubert H. Humphrey Metrodome	.23,000
1990–	Target Center	.19,006

New Orleans Hornets
1988–2002	Charlotte Coliseum	.19,925
	(1988 capacity—23,500)	

New Orleans (Cont.)
2002-05	New Orleans Arena	.18,500
2005-06	Ford Center (Oklahoma City)	.19,675
	& Maravich Center (Baton Rouge)	.14,164
2007–	New Orleans Arena	.18,500

Phoenix Suns
1968–92	Arizona Veterans' Memorial Coliseum	14,487
1992–	U.S. Airways Center	.19,023

Portland Trail Blazers
1970–95	Memorial Coliseum	.12,888
1995–	Rose Garden	.19,980
	(1995 capacity—21,538)	

Sacramento Kings
1948–55	Edgarton Park Arena (Rochester, NY)	.5,000
1955–58	Rochester War Memorial	.10,000
1958–72	Cincinnati Gardens	.11,438
1972–74	Municipal Auditorium (Kansas City)	.9,929
	& Omaha (NE) Civic Auditorium	.9,136
1974–78	Kemper Arena (Kansas City)	.16,785
	& Omaha Civic Auditorium	.9,136
1978–85	Kemper Arena	.16,886
1985–88	ARCO Arena I	.10,333
1988–	ARCO Arena II	.17,317
	(1988 capacity—16,517)	

San Antonio Spurs
1967–70	Memorial Auditorium (Dallas)	.8,088
	& Moody Coliseum (Dallas)	.8,500
1970–71	Moody Coliseum	.8,500
	Tarrant County	
	Convention Center (Ft. Worth)	.13,500
	& Municipal Coliseum (Lubbock)	.10,400
1971–73	Moody Coliseum	.9,500
	& Memorial Auditorium	.8,088
1973–93	HemisFair Arena (San Antonio)	.16,057
1993–2002	The Alamodome	.20,557
2002–	AT&T Center	.18,500

Seattle SuperSonics
1967–78	Seattle Center Coliseum	.14,098
1978–85	Kingdome	.40,192
1985–94	Seattle Center Coliseum	.14,252
1994–95	Tacoma Dome	.19,000
1995–	KeyArena at Seattle Center	.17,072

Utah Jazz
1974–75	Municipal Auditorium (New Orleans)	.7,853
	& Louisiana Superdome	.47,284
1975–79	Superdome	.47,284
1979–83	Salt Palace (Salt Lake City)	.12,519
1983–84	Salt Palace	.12,519
	& Thomas & Mack Center (Las Vegas)	.18,500
1984–91	Salt Palace	.12,616
1991–	EnergySolutions Arena	.19,911

Note: The Sacramento (then Kansas City) Kings played 30 home games at Kansas City Municipal Auditorium during the 1979-80 season after the Kemper Auditorium roof collapsed during a severe rain and wind storm on June 4, 1979.

Eastern Conference

Atlanta Hawks
1949–51	Wharton Field House (Moline, IL)	.6,000
1951–55	Milwaukee Arena	.11,000
1955–68	Kiel Auditorium (St. Louis)	.10,000
1968–72	Alexander Mem. Coliseum (Atlanta)	.7,166
1972–96	The Omni	.16,378
1997–99	Georgia Dome	.21,570
	& Alexander Mem. Coliseum	.9,300
1999–	Philips Arena	.19,445

Boston Celtics
1946–95	Boston Garden	.14,890
1995–	TD Banknorth Garden	.18,624

Note: From 1975-95 the Celtics played some regular season games at the Hartford Civic Center (15,418).

Charlotte Bobcats
2004-05	Charlotte Coliseum	.19,925
2005–	Charlotte Bobcats Arena	.18,500

Chicago Bulls
1966–67	Chicago Amphitheater	.11,002
1967–94	Chicago Stadium	.18,676
1994–	United Center	.21,711

Cleveland Cavaliers
1970–74	Cleveland Arena	.11,000
1974–94	The Coliseum (Richfield, OH)	.20,273
1994–	The Quicken Loans Arena	.20,562

Detroit Pistons

1948–52	North Side H.S. Gym (Ft. Wayne, IN)	3,800
1952–57	Memorial Coliseum (Ft. Wayne)	9,306
1957–61	Olympia Stadium (Detroit)	14,000
1961–78	Cobo Arena	11,147
1978–88	Silverdome (Pontiac, MI)	22,366
1988–	The Palace of Auburn Hills	22,076

Indiana Pacers

1967–74	State Fairgrounds (Indianapolis)	9,479
1974–99	Market Square Arena	16,530
	(1974 capacity—17,287)	
1999–	Conseco Fieldhouse	18,345

Miami Heat

1988–99	Miami Arena	15,200
2000–	AmericanAirlines Arena	16,500

Milwaukee Bucks

1968–88	Milwaukee Arena (The Mecca)	11,052
1988–	Bradley Center	18,717

New Jersey Nets

1967–68	Teaneck (NJ) Armory	3,500
1968–69	Long Island Arena (Commack, NY)	6,500
1969–71	Island Garden (W. Hempstead, NY)	5,200
1971–77	Nassau Coliseum (Uniondale, NY)	15,500
1977–81	Rutgers Ath. Center (Piscataway, NJ)	9,050
1981–	Continental Airlines Arena (E. Ruth., NJ)	20,049

New York Knicks

1946–68	Madison Sq. Garden III (50th St.)	18,496
1968–	Madison Sq. Garden IV (33rd St.)	19,763
	(1968 capacity—19,694)	

Orlando Magic

1989–	Amway Arena	17,248

Philadelphia 76ers

1949–51	State Fair Coliseum (Syracuse, NY)	7,500
1951–63	Onondaga County (NY) War Memorial	8,000
1963–67	Convention Hall (Philadelphia)	12,000
	& Philadelphia Arena	7,777
1967–96	CoreStates Spectrum	18,136
1996–	Wachovia Center	20,444

Toronto Raptors

1995–99	SkyDome	20,125
1999–	Air Canada Centre	19,800

Washington Wizards

1961–62	Chicago Amphitheater	11,000
1962–63	Chicago Coliseum	7,100
1963–73	Baltimore Civic Center	12,289
1973–97	USAir Arena (Landover, MD)	18,756
1997–	Verizon Center	20,674

Note: From 1988-96 the Wizards (then Bullets) played four regular season games at Baltimore Arena (12,756).

Building Name Changes: BOSTON—**TD Banknorth Garden** originally FleetCenter (1995-2005); CLEVELAND—**The Quicken Loans Arena** originally Gund Arena (1994-2005); GOLDEN ST—**Oracle Arena** originally The Arena in Oakland (1997-2007); HOUSTON—**Compaq Center** originally The Summit (1975-97); NEW JERSEY—**Continental Airlines Arena** originally Byrne Meadowlands Arena (1981-96); ORLANDO—**Amway Arena** originally Orlando Arena (1989-99) then TD Waterhouse Centre (1999-2007); PHILADELPHIA—**Wachovia Center** originally the CoreStates Center (1996-98), then the First Union Center (1998-2003) and **CoreStates Spectrum** originally The Spectrum (1967-94); PHOENIX—U.S. Airways Center originally AmericaWest Arena (1992-2007); SAN ANTONIO—**AT&T Center** originally SBC Center (2002-07); UTAH—**EnergySolutions Arena** originally Delta Center (1991-2007); WASHINGTON—**USAir Arena** originally Capital Centre (1973-93); **Verizon Center** originally MCI Center (1997-2006).

NATIONAL FOOTBALL LEAGUE

American Football Conference

		Location	Built	Capacity	Field
Baltimore Ravens	**M&T Bank Stadium**	Baltimore, Md.	1998	**69,084**	Grass
Buffalo Bills	**Ralph Wilson Stadium**	Orchard Park, N.Y.	1973	**73,967**	Turf
Cincinnati Bengals	**Paul Brown Stadium**	Cincinnati, Ohio	2000	**65,352**	Grass
Cleveland Browns	**Cleveland Browns Stadium**	Cleveland, Ohio	1999	**73,200**	Grass
Denver Broncos	**INVESCO Field at Mile High**	Denver, Colo.	2001	**76,125**	Grass
Houston Texans	**Reliant Stadium**	Houston, Tex.	2002	**69,500**	Grass
Indianapolis Colts	**RCA Dome**	Indianapolis, Ind.	1984	**56,127**	Turf
Jacksonville Jaguars	**Jacksonville Municipal Stadium**	Jacksonville, Fla.	1995	**67,164**	Grass
Kansas City Chiefs	**Arrowhead Stadium**	Kansas City, Mo.	1972	**79,451**	Grass
Miami Dolphins	**Dolphin Stadium**	Miami, Fla.	1987	**75,540**	Grass
New England Patriots	**Gillette Stadium**	Foxboro, Mass.	2002	**68,000**	Turf
New York Jets	**Giants Stadium**	E. Rutherford, N.J.	1976	**80,062**	Grass
Oakland Raiders	**McAfee Coliseum**	Oakland, Calif.	1966	**63,132**	Grass
Pittsburgh Steelers	**Heinz Field**	Pittsburgh, Pa.	2001	**64,450**	Grass
San Diego Chargers	**Qualcomm Stadium**	San Diego, Calif.	1967	**71,294**	Grass
Tennessee Titans	**LP Field**	Nashville, Tenn.	1999	**68,798**	Grass

National Football Conference

		Location	Built	Capacity	Field
Arizona Cardinals	**University of Phoenix Stadium**	Glendale, Ariz.	2006	**63,500**	Grass
Atlanta Falcons	**Georgia Dome**	Atlanta, Ga.	1992	**71,228**	Turf
Carolina Panthers	**Bank of America Stadium**	Charlotte, N.C.	1996	**73,500**	Grass
Chicago Bears	**Soldier Field**	Chicago, Ill.	1924	**63,000**	Grass
Dallas Cowboys	**Texas Stadium**	Irving, Texas	1971	**65,639**	Turf
Detroit Lions	**Ford Field**	Detroit, Mich.	2002	**65,000**	Turf
Green Bay Packers	**Lambeau Field**	Green Bay, Wis.	1957	**72,515**	Grass
Minnesota Vikings	**Hubert H. Humphrey Metrodome**	Minneapolis, Minn.	1982	**64,121**	Turf
New Orleans Saints	**Louisiana Superdome**	New Orleans, La.	1975	**69,703**	Turf
New York Giants	**Giants Stadium**	E. Rutherford, N.J.	1976	**80,062**	Grass
Philadelphia Eagles	**Lincoln Financial Field**	Philadelphia, Pa.	2003	**68,532**	Grass
St. Louis Rams	**Edward Jones Dome**	St. Louis, Mo.	1995	**66,000**	Turf
San Francisco 49ers	**Monster Park**	San Francisco, Calif.	1960	**69,400**	Grass
Seattle Seahawks	**Qwest Field**	Seattle, Wash.	2002	**67,000**	Grass
Tampa Bay Buccaneers	**Raymond James Stadium**	Tampa, Fla.	1998	**65,657**	Grass
Washington Redskins	**FedEx Field**	Raljon, Md.	1997	**86,484**	Grass

National Football League (Cont.)

Rank by Capacity

AFC		NFC	
NY Jets	.80,062	Washington	.86,484
Kansas City	.79,451	NY Giants	.80,062
Denver	.76,125	Carolina	.73,500
Miami	.75,540	Green Bay	.72,515
Buffalo	.73,967	Atlanta	.71,228
Cleveland	.73,200	New Orleans	.69,703
San Diego	.71,294	San Francisco	.69,400
Houston	.69,500	Philadelphia	.68,532
Baltimore	.69,084	Seattle	.67,000
Tennessee	.68,798	St. Louis	.66,000
New England	.68,000	Tampa Bay	.65,657
Jacksonville	.67,164	Dallas	.65,639
Cincinnati	.65,352	Detroit	.65,000
Pittsburgh	.64,450	Minnesota	.64,121
Oakland	.63,132	Arizona	.63,500
Indianapolis	.56,127	Chicago	.63,000

Rank by Age

AFC		NFC	
Oakland	.1966	Chicago	.1924
San Diego	.1967	Green Bay	.1957
Kansas City	.1972	San Francisco	.1960
Buffalo	.1973	Dallas	.1971
NY Jets	.1976	New Orleans	.1975
Indianapolis	.1984	NY Giants	.1976
Miami	.1987	Minnesota	.1982
Jacksonville	.1995	Atlanta	.1992
Baltimore	.1998	St. Louis	.1995
Cleveland	.1999	Carolina	.1996
Tennessee	.1999	Washington	.1997
Cincinnati	.2000	Tampa Bay	.1998
Denver	.2001	Seattle	.2002
Pittsburgh	.2001	Detroit	.2002
New England	.2002	Philadelphia	.2003
Houston	.2002	Arizona	.2006

Notes: Chicago's Soldier Field was rebuilt and Green Bay's Lambeau Field was renovated in 2003.

2006 NFL Attendance

Overall paid attendance in the NFL for the 2006 season was 17,606,077 for an average per game crowd of 68,774 over 256 games. Teams in each conference are ranked by attendance over eight home games. Rank column indicates rank in entire league. Numbers in parentheses indicate conference rank in 2005.

AFC

		Attendance	Rank	Average
1	Kansas City (1)	.623,275	3	77,909
2	N.Y. Jets (2)	.618,575	4	77,321
3	Denver (3)	.610,782	5	76,347
4	Miami (5)	.585,973	7	73,246
5	Cleveland (4)	.578,672	8	72,334
6	Baltimore (7)	.566,547	9	70,818
7	Houston (8)	.561,469	12	70,183
8	Tennessee (9)	.553,144	14	69,143
9	New England (10)	.550,048	16	68,756
10	Buffalo (6)	.541,169	19	67,646
11	Jacksonville (13)	.534,866	20	66,858
12	San Diego (11)	.531,031	21	66,378
13	Cincinnati (12)	.527,870	22	65,983
14	Pittsburgh (14)	.499,461	28	62,432
15	Oakland (16)	.467,964	31	58,495
16	Indianapolis (15)	.457,154	32	57,144
	TOTAL	.8,808,000	—	68,813

NFC

		Attendance	Rank	Average
1	Washington (1)	.701,049	1	87,631
2	NY Giants (2)	.628,910	2	78,613
3	Carolina (3)	.588,543	6	73,567
4	Atlanta (4)	.563,462	11	70,432
5	Green Bay (5)	.565,749	10	70,718
6	Philadelphia (6)	.553,794	13	69,224
7	New Orleans (15)	.550,470	15	68,808
8	San Francisco (9)	.545,207	17	68,150
9	Seattle (7)	.543,820	18	67,977
10	Tampa Bay (10)	.524,661	23	65,582
11	St. Louis (8)	.522,610	24	65,326
12	Minnesota (11)	.509,743	25	63,717
13	Arizona (16)	.508,829	26	63,603
14	Dallas (12)	.506,308	27	63,288
15	Chicago (13)	.497,786	29	62,223
16	Detroit (14)	.487,116	30	60,889
	TOTAL	.8,798,077	—	68,735

Home Fields

Listed below are the principal home fields used through the years by current NFL teams. The largest capacity of each stadium is noted in the right-hand column. All-America Football Conference stadiums (1946-49) are included for Cleveland and San Francisco.

AFC

Baltimore Ravens

1996–97	Memorial Stadium	.65,000
1998–	M&T Bank Stadium	.69,084

Buffalo Bills

1960–72	War Memorial Stadium	.45,748
1973–	Ralph Wilson Stadium (Orchard Park, NY)	.73,967
	(1973 capacity—80,020)	

Cincinnati Bengals

1968–69	Nippert Stadium (Univ. of Cincinnati)	.26,500
1970–99	Cinergy Field	.60,389
	(1970 capacity—56,200)	
2000–	Paul Brown Stadium	.65,352

Cleveland Browns

1946–95	Cleveland Stadium	.78,512
	(1946 capacity—85,703)	
1999–	Cleveland Browns Stadium	.73,200

Denver Broncos

1960–2000	Mile High Stadium	.76,123
	(1960 capacity—34,000)	
2001–	INVESCO Field at Mile High	.76,125

Houston Texans

2002–	Reliant Stadium	.69,500

Indianapolis Colts

1953–83	Memorial Stadium (Baltimore)	.60,020
1984–	RCA Dome (Indianapolis)	.56,127
	(1984 capacity—60,127)	

Jacksonville Jaguars

1995–	Jacksonville Municipal Stadium	.67,164
	(1995 capacity—73,000)	

Kansas City Chiefs

1960–62	Cotton Bowl (Dallas)	.72,000
1963–71	Municipal Stadium (Kansas City)	.47,000
1972–	Arrowhead Stadium	.79,451
	(1972 capacity—78,097)	

Miami Dolphins

1966–86	Orange Bowl	.75,206
1987–	Dolphin Stadium	.75,540

New England Patriots

1960–62	Nickerson Field (Boston Univ.)	.17,369
1963–68	Fenway Park	.33,379
1969	Alumni Stadium (Boston College)	.26,000
1970	Harvard Stadium	.37,300
1971-2001	Foxboro Stadium	.60,292
	(1971 capacity—61,114)	
2002–	Gillette Stadium (Foxboro, Mass.)	.68,000

New York Jets

1960–63	Polo Grounds	.55,987
1964–83	Shea Stadium	.60,372
1984–	Giants Stadium (E. Rutherford, NJ)	.80,062

Oakland Raiders

1960	Kesar Stadium (San Francisco)	.59,636
1961	Candlestick Park	.42,500
1962–65	Frank Youell Field (Oakland)	.20,000
1966–81	Oakland-Alameda County Coliseum	.54,587
1982–94	Memorial Coliseum (Los Angeles)	.67,800
1995–	McAfee Coliseum	.63,132

Pittsburgh Steelers

1933–57	Forbes Field	.35,000
1958–63	Forbes Field	.35,000
	& Pitt Stadium	.54,500
1964–69	Pitt Stadium	.54,500
1970–	Three Rivers Stadium	.59,600
2000	(1970 capacity—49,000)	
2001–	Heinz Field	.64,450

San Diego Chargers

1960	Memorial Coliseum (Los Angeles)	.92,604
1961–66	Balboa Stadium (San Diego)	.34,000
1967–	Qualcomm Stadium	.71,294
	(1967 capacity—54,000)	

Tennessee Titans

1960–64	Jeppesen Stadium (Houston)	.23,500
1965–67	Rice Stadium (Rice Univ.)	.70,000
1968–96	Astrodome	.59,969
1997	Liberty Bowl (Memphis)	.62,380
1998	Vanderbilt Stadium (Nashville)	.41,600
1999–	LP Field (Nashville)	.68,798

Stadium Name Changes: BALTIMORE—**M&T Bank Stadium** was originally named Ravens Stadium (1998-99) then was renamed PSInet Stadium (1999-2002) and renamed Ravens Stadium (2002-03); BUFFALO—**Ralph Wilson Stadium** originally Rich Stadium (1973-99); CINCINNATI—Cinergy Field originally Riverfront Stadium (1970-96); CLEVELAND—Cleveland Stadium originally Municipal Stadium (1932-74); DENVER—**Mile High Stadium** originally Bears Stadium (1948-66); INDIANAPOLIS—**RCA Dome** originally Hoosier Dome (1984-94); JACKSONVILLE—**Jacksonville Municipal Stadium** (1995-97, 2007—) was formerly named ALLTEL Stadium (1997-2007); MIAMI—**Dolphin Stadium** originally Joe Robbie Stadium (1987-96), then Pro Player Stadium (1996-2005); NEW ENGLAND—Foxboro Stadium originally Schaefer Stadium (1971-82), then Sullivan Stadium (1983-89); **Gillette Stadium** originally CMGI Field; OAKLAND—**McAfee Coliseum** originally Oakland Alameda Coliseum (1995-99), Network Associates Coliseum (1999-2004); SAN DIEGO—**Qualcomm Stadium** originally San Diego Stadium (1967-81) then San Diego/Jack Murphy Stadium (1981-96); TENNESSEE—**LP Field** originally Adelphia Coliseum (1999-2001), then The Coliseum (2001-06).

NFC

Arizona Cardinals

1920–21	Normal Field (Chicago)	.7,500
1922–25	Comiskey Park	.28,000
1926–28	Normal Field	.7,500
1929–59	Comiskey Park	.52,000
1960–65	Busch Stadium (St. Louis)	.34,000
1966–87	Busch Memorial Stadium	.54,392
1988–05	Sun Devil Stadium (Tempe, AZ)	.73,273
2006–	Univ. of Phoenix Stadium (Glendale)	.63,500

Atlanta Falcons

1966-91	Atlanta-Fulton County Stadium	.59,643
1992–	Georgia Dome	.71,228

Carolina Panthers

1995	Memorial Stadium (Clemson, SC)	.81,473
1996–	Bank of America Stadium	.73,500

Chicago Bears

1920	Staley Field (Decatur, IL)	—
1921–70	Wrigley Field (Chicago)	.37,741
1971–2001	Soldier Field	.66,944
	(1971 capacity—55,049)	
2002	Memorial Stadium (Champaign, IL)	.69,249
2003–	Soldier Field	.63,000

Dallas Cowboys

1960–70	Cotton Bowl	.72,132
1971–	Texas Stadium (Irving, TX)	.65,639
	(1971 capacity—65,101)	

Detroit Lions

1930–33	Spartan Stadium (Portsmouth, OH)	.8,200
1934–37	Univ. of Detroit Stadium	.25,000
1938–74	Tiger Stadium	.54,468
1975-2001	Pontiac Silverdome	.80,311
	(1975 capacity—80,638)	
2002–	Ford Field	.65,000

Green Bay Packers

1921–22	Hagemeister Brewery Park	—
1923–24	Bellevue Park	—
1925–56	City Stadium I	.24,800
1957–	Lambeau Field	.72,515
	(1957 capacity—32,150)	
	(2002 capacity—62,500)	

Note: The Packers played games in Milwaukee from 1933-94: at Borchert Field, State Fair Park and Marquette Stadium (1933-52), and County Stadium (1953-94).

Minnesota Vikings

1961–81	Metropolitan Stadium (Bloomington)	.48,446
1982–	HHH Metrodome (Minneapolis)	.64,121
	(1982 capacity—62,220)	

New Orleans Saints

1967–74	Tulane Stadium	.80,997
1975–2004	Louisiana Superdome	.69,703
	(1975 capacity—74,472)	
2005	Tiger Stadium (Baton Rouge)	.91,644
	& Alamodome (San Antonio)	.65,000
2006–	Louisiana Superdome	.69,703

Note: The Saints were unable to play at the Louisiana Superdome in the wake of Hurricane Katrina and played four home games at LSU's Tiger Stadium and three at the Alamodome in San Antonio in 2005.

New York Giants

1925–55	Polo Grounds II	.55,200
1956–73	Yankee Stadium I	.63,800
1973–74	Yale Bowl (New Haven, CT)	.70,896
1975	Shea Stadium	.60,372
1976–	Giants Stadium (E. Rutherford, NJ)	.80,062
	(1976 capacity—76,800)	

National Football League (Cont.)

Philadelphia Eagles

1933–35	Baker Bowl	18,800
1936–39	Municipal Stadium	73,702
1940	Shibe Park	33,608
1941	Municipal Stadium	73,702
1942	Shibe Park	33,608
1943	Forbes Field (Pittsburgh)	34,528
1944–57	Shibe Park	33,608
1958–70	Franklin Field (Univ. of Penn.)	60,546
1971–2002	Veterans Stadium	65,352
2003–	Lincoln Financial Field	68,532

St. Louis Rams

1937–42	Municipal Stadium (Cleveland)	85,703
1937	League Park (Cleveland)	—
1938	Shaw Stadium (Cleveland)	—
1937	League Park	—
1943	Suspended operations for one year.	
1944–45	Municipal Stadium	85,703
1946–79	Memorial Coliseum (Los Angeles)	92,604
1980–94	Anaheim Stadium	69,008
1995	Busch Stadium	60,000
1995–	Edward Jones Dome	66,000

San Francisco 49ers

1946–70	Kezar Stadium	59,636
1971–	Monster Park	69,400
	(1971 capacity—61,246)	

Seattle Seahawks

1976–94	Kingdome	66,000
1994	Kingdome	66,400
	& Husky Stadium	72,500
1995–99	Kingdome	66,400
2000-01	Husky Stadium	72,500
2002–	Qwest Field	67,000

Tampa Bay Buccaneers

1976–97	Houlihan's Stadium	74,300
1998–	Raymond James Stadium	65,657

Washington Redskins

1932	Braves Field (Boston)	40,000
1933–36	Fenway Park	27,000
1937–60	Griffith Stadium (Washington, DC)	35,000
1961–97	RFK Stadium	56,454
1997–	FedEx Field (Raljon, MD)	86,484

Stadium Name Changes: ATLANTA—**Atlanta-Fulton County Stadium** originally Atlanta Stadium (1966-74); CAROLINA—**Bank of America Stadium** originally Ericsson Stadium (1996-2004); CHICAGO—**Wrigley Field** originally Cubs Park (1916-25); DETROIT—**Tiger Stadium** originally Navin Field (1912-37), then Briggs Stadium (1938-60), also, **Pontiac Silverdome** originally Pontiac Metropolitan Stadium (1975); GREEN BAY—**Lambeau Field** originally City Stadium II (1957-64); PHILADELPHIA—**Shibe Park** renamed Connie Mack Stadium in 1953; ST. LOUIS—**Busch Memorial Stadium** renamed Busch Stadium in 1983, **Edward Jones Dome** originally Trans World Dome (1995-99), then The Dome at America's Center (2000-01); SAN FRANCISCO—**Monster Park** originally Candlestick Park (1960-94), then 3Com Park (1995-2001) and again Candlestick Park (2001-04); SEATTLE—**Qwest Field** originally Seahawks Stadium (2002-04); TAMPA BAY—**Raymond James Stadium** originally Tampa Stadium (1976-96), then **Houlihan's Stadium** (1996-98); WASHINGTON—**RFK Stadium** originally D.C. Stadium (1961-68), also, **FedEx Field** originally Jack Kent Cooke Stadium (1997-99).

NATIONAL HOCKEY LEAGUE

Western Conference

		Location	Built	Capacity
Anaheim Ducks	**Honda Center**	Anaheim, Calif.	1993	**17,174**
Calgary Flames	**Pengrowth Saddledome**	Calgary, Alb.	1983	**17,135**
Chicago Blackhawks	**United Center**	Chicago, Ill.	1994	**20,500**
Colorado Avalanche	**Pepsi Center**	Denver, Colo.	1999	**18,007**
Columbus Blue Jackets	**Nationwide Arena**	Columbus, Ohio	2000	**18,136**
Dallas Stars	**American Airlines Center**	Dallas, Texas	2001	**18,532**
Detroit Red Wings	**Joe Louis Arena**	Detroit, Mich.	1979	**20,058**
Edmonton Oilers	**Rexall Place**	Edmonton, Alb.	1974	**16,839**
Los Angeles Kings	**Staples Center**	Los Angeles, Calif.	1999	**18,118**
Minnesota Wild	**Xcel Energy Center**	St. Paul, Minn.	2000	**18,064**
Nashville Predators	**Sommet Center**	Nashville, Tenn.	1996	**17,113**
Phoenix Coyotes	**Jobing.com Arena**	Glendale, Ariz.	2003	**17,799**
St. Louis Blues	**Scottrade Center**	St. Louis, Mo.	1994	**19,022**
San Jose Sharks	**HP Pavilion at San Jose**	San Jose, Calif.	1993	**17,496**
Vancouver Canucks	**General Motors Place**	Vancouver, B.C.	1995	**18,422**

Eastern Conference

		Location	Built	Capacity
Atlanta Thrashers	**Philips Arena**	Atlanta, Ga.	1999	**18,545**
Boston Bruins	**TD Banknorth Garden**	Boston, Mass.	1995	**17,565**
Buffalo Sabres	**HSBC Arena**	Buffalo, N.Y.	1996	**18,690**
Carolina Hurricanes	**RBC Center**	Raleigh, N.C.	1999	**18,730**
Florida Panthers	**BankAtlantic Center**	Sunrise, Fla.	1998	**19,250**
Montreal Canadiens	**Bell Centre**	Montreal, Que.	1996	**21,273**
New Jersey Devils	**Prudential Center**	Newark, N.J.	2007	**17,625**
New York Islanders	**Nassau Veterans' Mem. Coliseum**	Uniondale, N.Y.	1972	**16,234**
New York Rangers	**Madison Square Garden**	New York, N.Y.	1968	**18,200**
Ottawa Senators	**Scotiabank Place**	Kanata, Ont.	1996	**19,311**
Philadelphia Flyers	**Wachovia Center**	Philadelphia, Penn.	1996	**18,523**
Pittsburgh Penguins	**Mellon Arena**	Pittsburgh, Penn.	1961	**16,958**
Tampa Bay Lightning	**St. Pete Times Forum**	Tampa Bay, Fla.	1996	**19,758**
Toronto Maple Leafs	**Air Canada Centre**	Toronto, Ont.	1999	**18,819**
Washington Capitals	**Verizon Center**	Washington, D.C.	1997	**18,672**

Rank by Capacity

Western		Eastern	
Chicago	.20,500	Montreal	.21,273
Detroit	.20,058	Tampa Bay	.19,758
St. Louis	.19,022	Florida	.19,250
Dallas	.18,532	Toronto	.18,819
Vancouver	.18,422	Carolina	.18,730
Columbus	.18,136	Buffalo	.18,690
Los Angeles	.18,118	Washington	.18,672
Minnesota	.18,064	Atlanta	.18,545
Colorado	.18,007	Philadelphia	.18,523
Phoenix	.17,799	Ottawa	.18,500
San Jose	.17,496	NY Rangers	.18,200
Anaheim	.17,174	New Jersey	.17,625
Calgary	.17,135	Boston	.17,565
Nashville	.17,113	Pittsburgh	.16,958
Edmonton	.16,839	NY Islanders	.16,234

Rank by Age

Western		Eastern	
Edmonton	.1974	Pittsburgh	.1961
Detroit	.1979	NY Rangers	.1968
Calgary	.1983	NY Islanders	.1972
Anaheim	.1993	Boston	.1995
San Jose	.1993	Montreal	.1996
Chicago	.1994	Ottawa	.1996
St. Louis	.1994	Buffalo	.1996
Nashville	.1994	Philadelphia	.1996
Vancouver	.1995	Tampa Bay	.1996
Colorado	.1999	Washington	.1997
Los Angeles	.1999	Florida	.1998
Columbus	.2000	Toronto	.1999
Minnesota	.2000	Carolina	.1999
Dallas	.2001	Atlanta	.1999
Phoenix	.2003	New Jersey	.2007

2006-07 NHL Attendance

Official overall paid attendance for the 2006-07 season according to the NHL accounting office was 20,857,288 (paid tickets) for an average per game crowd of 16,957 over 1,230 games. Teams in each conference are ranked by attendance over 41 home games. Rank column refers to rank in entire league. Numbers in parentheses indicate conference rank in 2005-06.

Western Conference

		Attendance	Rank	Average
1	Detroit (1)	.822,706	2	20,066
2	Calgary (2)	.790,849	6	19,289
3	Vancouver (3)	.763,830	9	18,630
4	Minnesota (4)	.757,280	10	18,470
5	Dallas (7)	.734,508	12	17,914
6	Colorado (5)	.722,127	13	17,612
7	San Jose (9)	.714,316	14	17,422
9	Los Angeles (6)	.691,229	16	16,859
10	Edmonton (8)	.690,399	17	16,839
11	Columbus (10)	.672,443	19	16,401
11	Anaheim (12)	.670,916	20	16,363
12	Nashville (13)	.625,649	23	15,259
13	Phoenix (11)	.614,519	24	14,988
14	Chicago (15)	.521,809	29	12,727
15	St. Louis (14)	.513,345	30	12,520
	TOTAL	.10,305,925	—	16,758

Eastern Conference

		Attendance	Rank	Average
1	Montreal (1)	.872,193	1	21,273
2	Tampa Bay (5)	.814,944	3	19,876
3	Toronto (2)	.798,981	4	19,487
4	Ottawa (6)	.794,271	5	19,372
5	Philadelphia (3)	.790,591	7	19,282
6	Buffalo (8)	.766,290	8	18,690
7	NY Rangers (4)	.746,200	11	18,200
8	Carolina (14)	.712,861	15	17,386
9	Pittsburgh (15)	.673,395	18	16,424
10	Atlanta (10)	.665,417	21	16,229
11	Florida (7)	.630,183	22	15,370
12	Boston (9)	.605,352	25	14,764
13	New Jersey (11)	.581,225	26	14,176
14	Washington (12)	.571,129	27	13,929
15	NY Islanders (13)	.528,331	28	12,886
	TOTAL	.10,551,363	—	17,157

Home Ice

Listed below are the principal home buildings used through the years by current NHL teams. The largest capacity of each arena is noted in the right hand column. World Hockey Association arenas (1972-79) are included for Edmonton, Hartford (now Carolina), Quebec (now Colorado) and Winnipeg (now Phoenix).

Western Conference

Anaheim Ducks

1993–	Honda Center	.17,174

Calgary Flames

1972–80	The Omni (Atlanta)	.15,278
1980–83	Calgary Corral	.7,424
1983–	Pengrowth Saddledome	.17,135
	(1983 capacity—16,674)	

Chicago Blackhawks

1926–29	Chicago Coliseum	.5,000
1929–94	Chicago Stadium	.17,317
1994–	United Center	.20,500

Colorado Avalanche

1972–95	Le Colisee de Quebec	.15,399
1995–99	McNichols Arena (Denver)	.16,061
1999–	Pepsi Center	.18,007

Columbus Blue Jackets

2000–	Nationwide Arena	.18,136

Dallas Stars

1967–93	Met Center (Bloomington, MN)	.15,174
1993–2000	Reunion Arena (Dallas)	.17,001
2001–	American Airlines Center	.18,532

Detroit Red Wings

1926–27	Border Cities Arena (Windsor, Ont.)	.3,200
1927–79	Olympia Stadium (Detroit)	.16,700
1979–	Joe Louis Arena	.20,058

Edmonton Oilers

1972–74	Edmonton Gardens	.7,200
1974–	Rexall Place	.16,839
	(1974 capacity—15,513)	

Los Angeles Kings

1967–99	Great Western Forum (Inglewood)	.16,005
	(1967 capacity—15,651)	
1999–	Staples Center	.18,118

Note: The Kings played 17 games at Long Beach Sports Arena and LA Sports Arena at the start of the 1967-68 season.

Minnesota Wild

2000–	Xcel Energy Center (St. Paul)	.18,064

Nashville Predators

1998–	Sommet Center	.17,113

National Hockey League (Cont.)

Phoenix Coyotes

1972–96	Winnipeg Arena (1972 capacity—10,177)	15,393
1996–2002	America West (Phoenix)	16,210
2003–	Jobing.com Arena (Glendale, Ariz.)	17,799

St. Louis Blues

1967–94	St. Louis Arena	17,188
1994–	Scottrade Center	19,022

San Jose Sharks

1991–93	Cow Palace (Daly City, CA)	11,100
1993–	HP Pavilion at San Jose	17,496

Vancouver Canucks

1970–95	Pacific Coliseum	16,150
1995–	General Motors Place	18,422

Building Name Changes: ANAHEIM—**Honda Center** originally Arrowhead Pond (1993-2006); CALGARY—**Pengrowth Saddledome** formerly named Canadian Airlines Saddledome (1996-2000) which was originally Olympic Saddledome (1983-95); DALLAS—**Met Center** in Minneapolis originally Metropolitan Sports Center (1967-82); EDMONTON—**Rexall Place** was formerly named Skyreach Centre (1999-2004) which was formerly named Edmonton Coliseum (1995-99) which was originally Northlands Coliseum (1974-94); LOS ANGELES—**Great Western Forum** originally The Forum (1967-88); NASHVILLE—**Sommet Center** originally Nashville Arena (1994-99), then Gaylord Entertainment Center (1999-2007); PHOENIX—**Jobing.com Arena** originally Glendale Arena (2003-07); ST. LOUIS—**Scottrade Center** originally Kiel Center (1994-2000) then Savvis Center (2000-06), **St. Louis Arena** renamed The Checkerdome in 1977, then St. Louis Arena again in 1982; SAN JOSE—**HP Pavilion at San Jose** originally San Jose Arena (1993-2000), then Compaq Center at San Jose (2000-03).

Eastern Conference

Atlanta Thrashers

1999–	Philips Arena	18,545

Boston Bruins

1924–28	Boston Arena	6,200
1928–95	Boston Garden	14,448
1995–	TD Banknorth Garden	17,565

Buffalo Sabres

1970–96	Memorial Auditorium (The Aud) (1970 capacity—10,429)	16,284
1996–	HSBC Arena	18,690

Carolina Hurricanes

1972–73	Boston Garden	14,442
1973–74	Boston Garden (regular season)	14,442
	West Springfield (MA) Big E (playoffs)	5,513
1974–75	West Springfield Big E	5,513
	& Hartford (CT) Civic Center	10,507
1975–77	Hartford Civic Center	10,507
1977–78	Hartford Civic Center	10,507
	& Springfield (MA) Civic Center	7,725
1978–79	Springfield Civic Center	7,725
1979–80	Springfield Civic Center	7,725
	& Hartford Civic Center II	14,250
1980–97	Hartford Civic Center II	15,635
1997–99	Greensboro Coliseum	21,500
1999–	RBC Center	18,730

Note: The Hartford Civic Center roof caved in January 1978, forcing the Whalers to move their home games to Springfield, MA for two years.

Florida Panthers

1993–98	Miami Arena	14,703
1998–	BankAtlantic Center	19,250

Montreal Canadiens

1910–21	Jubilee Arena	3,200
1913–18	Montreal Arena (Westmount)	6,000
1918–26	Mount Royal Arena	6,750
1926–68	Montreal Forum I	15,500
1968–96	Montreal Forum II	17,959
1996–	Bell Centre	21,273

New Jersey Devils

1974–76	Kemper Arena (Kansas City)	16,300
1976–82	McNichols Arena (Denver)	15,900
1982-2006	Continental Airlines Arena (1982 capacity—19,023)	19,040
2007–	Prudential Center	17,625

New York Islanders

1972–	Nassau Veterans' Mem. Coliseum (1972 capacity—14,500)	16,234

New York Rangers

1925–68	Madison Square Garden III	15,925
1968–	Madison Square Garden IV (1968 capacity—17,250)	18,200

Ottawa Senators

1992–96	Ottawa Civic Center	10,755
1996–	Scotiabank Place (Kanata) (1996 capacity—18,500)	19,311

Philadelphia Flyers

1967–96	CoreStates Spectrum (1967 capacity—14,558)	17,380
1996–	Wachovia Center	18,523

Pittsburgh Penguins

1967–	Mellon Arena (1967 capacity—12,508)	16,958

Tampa Bay Lightning

1992–93	Expo Hall (Tampa)	10,500
1993–96	ThunderDome (St. Petersburg)	26,000
1996–	St. Pete Times Forum	19,758

Toronto Maple Leafs

1917–31	Mutual Street Arena	8,000
1931–99	Maple Leaf Gardens (1931 capacity—13,542)	15,746
1999–	Air Canada Centre	18,819

Washington Capitals

1974–97	USAir Arena (Landover, MD)	18,130
1997–	Verizon Center	18,672

Building Name Changes: BOSTON—**TD Banknorth Garden** originally FleetCenter (1995-2005); BUFFALO—**HSBC Arena** originally Marine Midland Arena (1996-99); CALGARY—**Pengrowth Saddledome** originally Canadian Airlines Arena (1983-2000); CAROLINA—**RBC Center** originally Raleigh Entertainment and Sports Arena (1999-2002); DALLAS—**American Airlines Center** originally Reunion Arena (1993-2000); FLORIDA—**BankAtlantic Center** formerly named Office Depot Center (2002-05) and originally National Car Rental Center (1998-2002); MONTREAL—**Bell Centre** originally Molson Centre (1996-2002); NEW JERSEY—**Continental Airlines Arena** originally Meadowlands Arena (1982-96); OTTAWA—**Scotiabank Place** originally Corel Center (1996-2006); PHILADELPHIA—**Wachovia Center** originally the CoreStates Center (1996-98), then First Union Center (1998-2003) and **CoreStates Spectrum** originally The Spectrum (1967-94); PITTSBURGH—**Mellon Arena** originally Civic Arena (1967-2000); TAMPA BAY—**St. Pete Times Forum** originally Ice Palace (1996-2002); WASHINGTON—**USAir Arena** originally Capital Centre (1974-93); **Verizon Center** originally MCI Center (1997-2006).

AUTO RACING

Formula One, NASCAR Winston Cup, Champ Car and Indy Racing League (IRL) racing circuits. Qualifying records accurate as of Sept. 30, 2007. Capacity figures for NASCAR, Champ Car and IRL tracks are approximate and pertain to grandstand seating only. Standing room and hillside terrain seating featured at most road courses are not included.

Champ Car World Series

	Location	Miles	Qual.mph record	Set by	Seats
TT Circuit Assen	Assen, Holland	2.83*	129.347	Sebastien Bourdais (2007)	
Burke Lakefront Airport	Cleveland, Ohio	2.106**	134.705	A.J. Allmendinger (2006)	50,000
Exhibition Place	Toronto, Ont.	1.755**	110.565	Gil de Ferran (1999)	60,000
Rexall Speedway	Edmonton, Alb.	1.973**	121.617	Will Power (2007)	70,000
Mont-Tremblant	Mont-Tremblant, Que.	2.65	187.602	Will Power (2007)	
Laguna Seca	Monterey, Calif.	2.238*	122.295	Sebastien Bourdais (2007)^	
Las Vegas Motor Speedway	Las Vegas, Nev.	1.500	113.154	Will Power (2007)	126,000
Long Beach	Long Beach, Calif.	1.968**	105.924	Sebastien Bourdais (2006)	63,000
Autódromo Hermanos Rodríguez	Mexico City, Mexico	2.786*	116.733	Sebastien Bourdais (2004)	
Portland International Raceway	Portland, Ore.	1.964*	122.768	Helio Castroneves (2000)	50,000
Reliant Park	Houston, Tex.	1.69**	105.545	Will Power (2007)	
Road America	Elkhart Lake, Wisc.	4.048*	145.924	Dario Franchitti (2000)	10,000
Gold Coast-Surfers Paradise	Queensland, Australia	2.795**	111.547	Cristiano da Matta (2002)	55,000
Heusden-Zolder	Zolder, Belgium	2.622*	123.195	Sebastien Bourdais (2007)	

*Road courses (not ovals). **Temporary street circuits. ^set during a test session.

IndyCar Series

	Location	Miles	Qual.mph Record	Set by	Seats
The Raceway at Belle Isle	Detroit, Mich.	2.096**	102.299	Tony Kanaan (2007)	30,000
Chicagoland Speedway	Joliet, Ill.	1.5	223.159	Richie Hearn (2003)	75,000
Homestead-Miami Speedway	Homestead, Fla.	1.5	218.539	Sam Hornish Jr. (2006)	65,000
Indianapolis Motor Speedway	Indianapolis, Ind.	2.5	237.498	Arie Luyendyk (1996)*	250,000
Infineon Raceway	Sonoma, Calif.	2.26*	108.248	Ryan Briscoe (2005)	102,000
Iowa Speedway	Newton, Iowa	0.875	182.360	Scott Dixon (2007)	30,000
Kansas Speedway	Kansas City, Kan.	1.5	218.085	Scott Dixon (2003)	75,000
Kentucky Speedway	Sparta, Ky.	1.5	219.191	Scott Goodyear (2000)	70,000
Michigan Intl. Speedway	Brooklyn, Mich.	2.0	222.458	Tomas Scheckter (2003)	136;373
Mid-Ohio Sports Car Course	Lexington, Ohio	2.258*	120.473	Scott Dixon (2007)	
The Milwaukee Mile	West Allis, Wisc.	1.032	172.477	Helio Castroneves (2006)	45,000
Nashville Superspeedway	Nashville, Tenn.	1.33	206.211	Scott Dixon (2003)	50,000
Grand Prix of St. Petersburg	St. Petersburg, Fla.	1.8**	105.202	Tony Kanaan (2007)	
Richmond International Raceway	Richmond, Va.	0.75	171.202	Helio Castroneves (2004)	107,097
Texas Motor Speedway	Fort Worth, Texas	1.5	225.979	Billy Boat (1998)	154,861
Twin Ring Motegi	Motegi, Japan	1.549	206.996	Scott Dixon (2003)	50,000
Watkins Glen International	Watkins Glen, N.Y.	3.4	135.449	Scott Dixon (2007)	35,000

*Road course. **Temporary street circuit. †Indicates world closed-course record for auto racing.

Sprint Cup

	Location	Miles	Qual.mph Record	Set by	Seats
Atlanta Motor Speedway	Hampton, Ga.	1.54	197.478	Geoff Bodine (1997)	125,000
Bristol Motor Speedway	Bristol, Tenn.	0.533	128.709	Ryan Newman (2003)	147,000
California Speedway	Fontana, Calif.	2.0	188.245	Kyle Busch (2005)	92,000
Chicagoland Speedway	Joliet, Ill.	1.5	188.147	Jimmie Johnson (2005)	75,000
Darlington International Raceway	Darlington, S.C.	1.366	173.797	Ward Burton (1996)	65,000
Daytona International Speedway	Daytona Beach, Fla.	2.5	210.364	Bill Elliott (1987)	168,000
Dover International Speedway	Dover, Del.	1.0	161.522	Jeremy Mayfield (2004)	140,000
Homestead-Miami Speedway	Homestead, Fla.	1.5	181.111	Jamie McMurray (2003)	72,000
Indianapolis Motor Speedway	Indianapolis, Ind.	2.5	186.293	Casey Mears (2004)	250,000
Infineon Raceway	Sonoma, Calif.	1.99*	94.325	Jeff Gordon (2005)	42,500
Kansas Speedway	Kansas City, Kan.	1.5	180.856	Matt Kenseth (2005)	75,000
Las Vegas Motor Speedway	Las Vegas, Nev.	1.5	184.856	Kasey Kahne (2007)	126,000
Lowe's Motor Speedway	Concord, N.C.	1.5	193.216	Elliot Sadler (2005)	167,000
Martinsville Speedway	Martinsville, Va.	0.526	98.084	Tony Stewart (2005)	91,000
Michigan Intl. Speedway	Brooklyn, Mich.	2.0	194.232	Ryan Newman (2005)	136,384
New Hampshire Int'l Speedway	Loudon, N.H.	1.058	133.357	Ryan Newman (2003)	91,000
Phoenix International Raceway	Phoenix, Ariz.	1.0	135.854	Ryan Newman (2004)	76,812
Pocono Raceway	Long Pond, Penn.	2.5	172.533	Kasey Kahne (2004)	77,000
Richmond International Raceway	Richmond, Va.	0.75	129.983	Brian Vickers (2004)	107,097
Talladega Superspeedway	Talladega, Ala.	2.66	212.809	Bill Elliott (1987)†	143,000
Texas Motor Speedway	Ft. Worth, Texas	1.5	196.235	Brian Vickers (2006)	154,861
Watkins Glen International	Watkins Glen, N.Y.	2.45*	124.580	Jeff Gordon (2003)	41,000

*Road courses (not ovals).

Formula One

Race track capacity figures unavailable.

Grand Prix		Miles	Qual.mph Record	Set by
Australian	Albert Park (Melbourne)	3.295	140.537	Michael Schumacher (2004)
Bahrain	Bahrain International (Sakhir)	3.366	134.432	Michael Schumacher (2004)
Belgian	Spa-Francorchamps	4.333	143.418	Mika Hakkinen (1998)
Brazilian	Interlagos (Sao Paulo)	2.684	193.747	Rubens Barrichello (2003)
British	Silverstone (Towcester)	3.194	148.043	Nigel Mansell (1992)
Canadian	Circuit Gilles Villeneuve (Montreal)	2.747	133.941	Juan Montoya (2002)
China	Shanghai International	3.387	129.867	Rubens Barrichello (2004)
European	Nürburgring (Nürburg, Germany)	2.822	135.959	Michael Schumacher (2001)
French	Magny Cours (Nevers)	2.641	159.757	Juan Montoya (2002)
Hungarian	Hungaroring (Budapest)	2.468	122.410	Michael Schumacher (2005)
Italian	Autodromo Nazionale di Monza (Milan)	3.585	161.460	Juan Pablo Montoya (2002)
Japanese	Fuji Speedway (Oyama)	2.835	n/a	Lewis Hamilton (2007)
Malaysian	Sepang (Kuala Lumpur)	3.444	133.220	Michael Schumacher (2004)
Monaco	Monte Carlo (Monaco)	2.082	141.595	Rubens Barrichello (2002)
Spanish	Catalunya (Barcelona)	2.937	140.935	Michael Schumacher (2004)
Turkish	Otodrom (Istanbul)	3.293	137.323	Kimi Raikkonen (2005)
United States	Indianapolis Motor Speedway	2.606	133.595	Rubens Barrichello (2004)

SOCCER

World's Premier Soccer Stadiums

(Listed alphabetically by city)

Stadium	Location	Seats	Stadium	Location	Seats
New Olympic	Athens, Greece	72,000	Old Trafford	Manchester, England	67,650
Eden Park	Auckland, New Zealand	50,000	Estadio Azteca	Mexico City, Mexico	106,000
Nou Camp	Barcelona, Spain	98,000	Meazza (San Siro)	Milan, Italy	85,700
Beijing National	Beijing, China	91,000	Centenario	Montevideo, Uruguay	76,609
Olympiastadion	Berlin, Germany	76,243	Luzhniki Stadion	Moscow, Russia	80,840
Népstadion	Budapest, Hungary	65,000	Olympiastadion	Munich, Germany	63,000
Antonio Liberti	Buenos Aires, Argentina	76,689	San Paolo	Naples, Italy	78,210
National	Cairo, Egypt	90,000	Stade de France	Paris, France	80,000
Salt Lake	Calcutta, India	120,000	Rungnado (May Day)	Pyongyang, N. Korea	150,000
Millennium	Cardiff, Wales	72,500	Maracana	Rio de Janeiro, Brazil	70,000
Westfalenstadion	Dortmund, Germany	68,600	King Fahd II	Riyadh, Saudi Arabia	79,000
Lansdowne Road	Dublin, Ireland	50,000	Olimpico	Rome, Italy	82,307
Veltins Arena	Gelsenkirchen, Germany	53,951	Nacional	Santiago, Chile	77,000
Celtic Park	Glasgow, Scotland	60,506	Morumbi	Sao Paulo, Brazil	80,000
Hampden Park	Glasgow, Scotland	52,670	Chasmil	Seoul, S. Korea	100,000
Guangdong	Guanzhou, China	80,000	Soccer City	Soweto, South Africa	104,000
FNB Stadium	Johannesburg, S. Africa	94,700	Stadium Australia	Sydney, Australia	80,000
Olympic Stadium	Kiev, Ukraine	83,160	Azadi	Tehran, Iran	100,000
new Estadio da Luz	Lisbon, Portugal	65,000	Delle Alpi	Turin, Italy	69,041
Wembley Stadium	Londo, England	90,000	Ernst Happel	Vienna, Austria	47,500
Santiago Bernabeu	Madrid, Spain	106,500	International	Yokohama, Japan	70,574

Major League Soccer

The 13-team MLS is the only U.S. Division I professional outdoor league sanctioned by FIFA and U.S. Soccer. Note that some capacity figures are approximate given the adjustments of football stadium seating to soccer.

Western Conference

	Stadium	Built	Seats	Field
CD Chivas USA	Home Depot Center	2003	27,000	Grass
Colorado Rapids	Dick's Sporting Goods Park	2007	18,458	Grass
FC Dallas	Pizza Hut Park	2005	21,193	Grass
Houston Dynamo	Robertson	1942	32,000	Grass
L.A. Galaxy	Home Depot Center	2003	27,000	Grass
Real Salt Lake	Real Salt Lake	2008	20,000	Grass

Eastern Conference

	Stadium	Built	Seats	Field
Chicago Fire	Toyota Park	2006	21,210	Grass
Columbus Crew	Columbus Crew	1999	22,555	Grass
D.C. United	RFK	1961	26,169	Grass
Kansas City Wizards	Arrowhead	1972	20,571	Grass
N.E. Revolution	Gillette	2002	21,000	Grass
Red Bull New York	Red Bull Park	2008	25,000	Grass
Toronto FC	BMO Field	2007	20,000	Turf

Horse Racing

Triple Crown race tracks

Race	Racetrack	Seats	Infield
Kentucky Derby	Churchill Downs	48,500	65,000
Preakness Stakes	Pimlico Race Course	13,047	60,000
Belmont Stakes	Belmont Park	32,941	N/A

Record crowds: Kentucky Derby—163,628 (1974); Preakness—112,668 (2004); Belmont—120,139 (2004).
Note: Belmont Park does not open infield for Belmont Stakes.

Tennis

Grand Slam center courts

Event	Main Stadium	Seats
Australian Open	Melbourne Park	15,021
French Open	Stade Roland Garros	16,300
Wimbledon	Centre Court	13,813
U.S. Open	Arthur Ashe Stadium	22,547

COLLEGE BASKETBALL

The 50 Largest Arenas

The 50 largest arenas in Division I for the 2006-07 NCAA regular season. Note that (*) indicates part-time home court.

	Seats	Home Team
1 Carrier Dome	33,000	Syracuse
2 Thompson-Boling Arena	24,535	Tennessee
3 Rupp Arena	23,500	Kentucky
4 Marriott Center	22,700	BYU
5 Dean Smith Center	21,750	N. Carolina
6 Verizon Center	20,674	Georgetown*
7 Scottrade Center	20,000	Saint Louis
8 RBC Center	19,722	N.C. State
9 Value City Arena	19,500	Ohio St.
10 Bud Walton Arena	19,200	Arkansas
11 Wachovia Center	19,010	Villanova*
12 Freedom Hall	18,865	Louisville
13 Kemper Arena	18,646	UMKC*
14 Bradley Center	18,717	Marquette
15 Thomas & Mack Center	18,500	UNLV
16 Madison Square Garden	18,470	St. John's*
17 FedEx Forum	18,400	Memphis
18 University Arena (The Pit)	18,018	New Mexico
19 Prudential Center	18,000	Seton Hall
20 Comcast Center	17,950	Maryland
21 Colonial Center	17,600	South Carolina
22 Qwest Center Omaha	17,560	Creighton
23 Allstate Arena	17,500	DePaul
24 Assembly Hall	17,456	Indiana
25 Herb Kohl Center	17,142	Wisconsin

	Seats	Home Team
26 Frank Erwin Center	16,755	Texas
27 Assembly Hall	16,450	Illinois
28 Allen Fieldhouse	16,300	Kansas
29 Hartford Civic Center	16,294	UConn*
30 Save Mart Center	16,116	Fresno St.
31 JVM Arena	16,000	Jacksonville
32 Carver-Hawkeye Arena	15,500	Iowa
Times Union Center	15,500	Siena
34 Bryce Jordan Center	15,261	Penn St.
35 John Paul Jones Arena	15,219	Virginia
36 United Spirit Arena	15,098	Texas Tech
37 Breslin Events Center	15,085	Michigan St.
38 Mizzou Arena	15,061	Missouri
39 Coleman Coliseum	15,043	Alabama
40 Arena-Auditorium	15,028	Wyoming
41 Huntsman Center	15,000	Utah
42 LJVM Coliseum	14,665	Wake Forest & Winston-Salem*
43 Williams Arena	14,625	Minnesota
44 McKale Center	14,545	Arizona
45 Maravich Assembly Ctr	14,236	LSU
46 Wells Fargo Arena	14,198	Arizona St.
47 Memorial Gym	14,168	Vanderbilt
48 Mackey Arena	14,123	Purdue
49 James H. Hilton Coliseum	14,092	Iowa St.
50 WVU Coliseum	14,000	West Virginia

Division I Conference Home Courts

NCAA Division I conferences for the 2006-07 season. Teams with home games in more than one arena are noted.

America East

	Home Floor	Seats
Albany	SEFCU Arena	4,538
Binghamton	Events Center	5,142
Boston University	Case Gym	1,800
	& Agganis Arena	5,687
Hartford	Reich Family Pavilion	3,977
Maine	Alfond Arena	5,712
MD-Balt. County	RAC Arena	4,024
New Hampshire	Lundholm Gym	3,500
Stony Brook	SB Sports Complex	4,103
Vermont	Patrick Gym	3,266

Atlantic Coast

	Home Floor	Seats
Boston College	Silvio O. Conte Forum	8,606
Clemson	Littlejohn Coliseum	9,749
Duke	Cameron Indoor Stadium	9,314
Florida St.	Donald L. Tucker Center	12,200
Georgia Tech	Alexander Memorial Coliseum	9,191
Maryland	Comcast Center	17,950
Miami-FL	BankUnited Center	7,000
North Carolina	Dean Smith Center	21,750
N.C. State	RBC Center	19,722
Virginia	John Paul Jones Arena	15,219
Virginia Tech	Cassell Coliseum	10,052
Wake Forest	LJVM Coliseum	14,665

Atlantic Sun

	Home Floor	Seats
Belmont	Curb Event Center	5,000
Campbell	Carter Gym	1,050
East Tennessee St.	Memorial Center	12,000
Florida Gulf Coast	Alico Arena	4,000
Gardner-Webb	Paul Porter Arena	5,000
Jacksonville	JVM Arena	16,000
Kennesaw St.	KSU Convocation Center	4,500
Lipscomb	Allen Arena	5,028
Mercer	University Center	3,200
North Florida	UNF Arena	5,800
Stetson	Edmunds Center	5,000
So. Carolina-Upstate	G.B. Hodge Center	1,535

Men's Basketball Attendance Leaders

Schools ranked by average attendance for 2006-07 season.

	Gm	Attendance	Average
1 Kentucky	16	374,737	23,421
2 Syracuse	22	473,353	21,516
3 North Carolina	17	351,785	20,693
4 Tennessee	16	314,571	19,661
5 Louisville	20	369,763	18,488
6 Ohio St.	18	315,539	17,530
7 Wisconsin	19	326,610	17,190

College Basketball (Cont.)

Atlantic 10

	Home Floor	Seats
Charlotte	Halton Arena	9,105
Dayton	U. of Dayton Arena	13,266
Duquesne	Palumbo Center	6,200
Fordham	Rose Hill Gym	3,470
George Washington	Smith Center	5,000
La Salle	Tom Gola Arena	4,000
Massachusetts	Mullins Center	9,493
Rhode Island	Ryan Center	7,657
Richmond	Robins Center	9,071
St. Bonaventure	Reilly Center	6,000
Saint Louis	Scottrade Center	20,000
St. Joseph's	Alumni Mem. Fieldhouse	3,200
Temple	Liacouras Center	10,206
Xavier-OH	Cintas Center	10,250

Big East

	Home Floor	Seats
Cincinnati	Fifth Third Arena	13,176
Connecticut	Gampel Pavilion	10,167
	& Hartford Civic Center	16,294
DePaul	Allstate Arena	17,500
Georgetown	Verizon Center	20,674
Louisville	Freedom Hall	18,865
Marquette	Bradley Center	18,717
Notre Dame	Joyce Center	11,418
Pittsburgh	Petersen Event Center	12,500
Providence	Dunkin Donuts Center	12,993
Rutgers	Louis Brown Athletic Center (The RAC)	9,000
St. John's	Carnesecca Arena	6,008
	& Madison Square Garden	18,470
Seton Hall	Prudential Center	18,000
South Florida	Sun Dome	10,411
Syracuse	Carrier Dome	33,000
Villanova	The Pavilion	6,500
	& Wachovia Center	19,010
West Virginia	WVU Coliseum	14,000

Big Sky

	Home Floor	Seats
Eastern Wash	Reese Court	6,000
Idaho St.	Holt Arena	8,000
Montana	Dahlberg Arena	7,321
Montana St.	Worthington Arena	7,250
Northern Arizona	Walkup Skydome	7,000
Northern Colorado	Butler-Hancock Sports Pavilion	4,500
Portland St.	Stott Center	1,500
Sacramento St.	Hornets Nest	1,200
Weber St.	Dee Events Center	12,000

Big South

	Home Floor	Seats
Birmingham-Southern	Bill Battle Coliseum	2,000
Charleston Southern	CSU Fieldhouse	1,500
Coastal Carolina	Kimbel Arena	1,037
High Point	Millis Center	2,565
Liberty	Vines Center	9,000
NC-Asheville	Justice Center	1,100
	& Asheville Civic Center	6,000
Radford	Dedmon Center	5,000
VMI	Cameron Hall	5,800
Winthrop	Winthrop Coliseum	6,100

Longest Home Court Win Streaks

Wins	Team	Seasons	Ended By
129	Kentucky	1943-55	Ga. Tech, 59-58
99	St. Bonaventure	1948-61	Niagara, 87-77
98	UCLA	1970-76	Oregon, 65-45
86	Cincinnati	1957-64	Bradley, 87-77
81	Arizona	1945-51	Kansas St., 76-57
81	Marquette	1967-73	N. Dame, 71-69

Big Ten

	Home Floor	Seats
Illinois	Assembly Hall	16,450
Indiana	Assembly Hall	17,456
Iowa	Carver-Hawkeye Arena	15,500
Michigan	Crisler Arena	13,751
Michigan St.	Breslin Events Center	15,085
Minnesota	Williams Arena	14,625
Northwestern	Welsh-Ryan Arena	8,117
Ohio St.	Value City Arena	19,500
Penn St.	Bryce Jordan Center	15,261
Purdue	Mackey Arena	14,123
Wisconsin	Kohl Center	17,142

Big 12

	Home Floor	Seats
Baylor	Ferrell Center	10,284
Colorado	Coors Events Conference Ctr.	11,064
Iowa St.	Hilton Coliseum	14,092
Kansas	Allen Fieldhouse	16,300
Kansas St.	Bramlage Coliseum	13,595
Missouri	Mizzou Arena	15,061
Nebraska	Devaney Sports Center	13,500
Oklahoma	Lloyd Noble Center	12,000
Oklahoma St.	Gallagher-Iba Arena	13,611
Texas	Erwin Center	16,755
Texas A&M	Reed Arena	12,500
Texas Tech	United Spirit Arena	15,098

Big West

	Home Floor	Seats
Cal Poly	Mott Gym	3,032
CS-Fullerton	Titan Gym	4,000
CS-Northridge	The Matadome	1,600
Long Beach St.	The Walter Pyramid	5,000
Pacific	Alex G. Spanos Center	6,150
UC-Davis	The Pavilion	7,200
UC-Irvine	Bren Events Center	5,000
UC-Riverside	Student Rec. Center	3,168
UC-Santa Barbara	The Thunderdome	6,000

Colonial Athletic Association

	Home Floor	Seats
Delaware	Bob Carpenter Center	5,000
Drexel	Daskalakis Athletic Center	2,300
George Mason	Patriot Center	10,000
Georgia St.	GSU Sports Arena	4,500
Hofstra	Hofstra Arena	5,124
James Madison	JMU Convocation Center	7,156
Northeastern	Solomon Court	1,500
	& Matthews Arena	6,000
NC-Wilmington	Trask Coliseum	6,100
Old Dominion	Ted Constant Convocation Ctr.	8,650
Towson	Towson Center	5,000
VCU	Siegel Center	7,500
William & Mary	Kaplan Arena	8,600

Conference USA

	Home Floor	Seats
UAB	Bartow Arena	8,508
Central Fla.	UCF Convocation Center	10,000
East Carolina	Williams Arena at Minges Coliseum	8,000
Houston	Hofheinz Pavilion	8,479
Marshall	Cam Henderson Center	9,043
Memphis	FedEx Forum	18,400
Rice	Autry Court	5,000
SMU	Moody Coliseum	8,998
Southern Miss	Reed Green Coliseum	8,095
Tulane	Fogelman Arena	3,600
Tulsa	Reynolds Center	8,355
UTEP	Haskins Center	12,000

Horizon League

	Home Floor	Seats
Butler	Hinkle Fieldhouse	11,043
Cleveland St.	Wolstein Center	13,610
Detroit Mercy	Calihan Hall	8,837
IL-Chicago	UIC Pavilion	8,000
Loyola-IL	Gentile Center	5,200
Valparaiso	Athletics-Recreation Center	5,000
WI-Green Bay	Resch Center	10,400
WI-Milwaukee	U.S. Cellular Arena	10,783
Wright St.	Nutter Center	10,632
Youngstown St.	Beeghly Center	6,500

Ivy League

	Home Floor	Seats
Brown	Pizzitola Sports Center	2,800
Columbia	Levien Gymnasium	3,408
Cornell	Newman Arena	4,473
Dartmouth	Leede Arena	2,100
Harvard	Lavietes Pavilion	2,195
Penn	The Palestra	8,700
Princeton	Jadwin Gymnasium	6,854
Yale	Payne Whitney Gym	3,100

Metro Atlantic Athletic

	Home Floor	Seats
Canisius	Koessler Athletic Center	2,176
Fairfield	Arena at Harbor Yard	9,000
Iona	Hynes Athletic Center	2,611
Loyola-MD	Reitz Arena	3,000
Manhattan	Draddy Gymnasium	3,000
Marist	McCann Field House	3,944
Niagara	Gallagher Center	2,400
Rider	Alumni Gymnasium	1,650
St. Peter's	Yanitelli Center	3,200
Siena	Times Union Center	15,500

Mid-American

	Home Floor	Seats
Akron	JAR Arena	5,942
Ball St.	John E. Worthen Arena	11,500
Bowling Green	Anderson Arena	5,000
Buffalo	Alumni Arena	6,100
Central Mich.	Rose Arena	5,200
Eastern Mich.	Convocation Center	8,824
Kent St.	MAC Center	6,327
Miami-OH	Millett Hall	9,200
Northern Illinois	Convocation Center	9,100
Ohio Univ.	Convocation Center	13,000
Toledo	Savage Hall	9,000
Western Mich.	University Arena	5,421

Mid-Eastern Athletic

	Home Floor	Seats
Bethune-Cookman	Moore Gym	3,000
Coppin St.	Coppin Center	1,720
Delaware St.	Memorial Hall	3,000
Florida A&M	Gaither Gym	3,365
Hampton	Hampton Convocation Center	7,500
Howard	Burr Gym	2,200
MD-East.Shore	W.P. Hytche Center	5,500
Morgan St.	Hill Fieldhouse	4,500
Norfolk St.	Echols Hall	7,600
N. Carolina A&T	Corbett Sports Center	6,700
South Carolina St.	SHM Center	3,200
Winston-Salem St.	LJVM Coliseum Annex	4,000

Missouri Valley

	Home Floor	Seats
Bradley	Carver Arena	11,300
Creighton	Qwest Center Omaha	17,560
Drake	Knapp Center	7,002
Evansville	Roberts Stadium	11,600
Illinois St.	Redbird Arena	10,200
Indiana St.	Hulman Center	10,200
Missouri St.	Hammons Student Center	8,846
Northern Iowa	McLeod Center	7,018
Southern Ill.	SIU Arena	10,000
Wichita St.	Charles Koch Arena	10,400

Mountain West

	Home Floor	Seats
Air Force	Clune Arena	6,002
BYU	Marriott Center	22,700
Colorado St.	Moby Arena	8,745
UNLV	Thomas & Mack Center	18,500
New Mexico	The Pit	18,018
San Diego St.	Cox Arena at the Aztec Bowl	12,414
TCU	Daniel-Meyer Coliseum	7,201
Utah	Jon M. Huntsman Center	15,000
Wyoming	Arena-Auditorium	15,028

Northeast

	Home Floor	Seats
Central Conn. St.	Detrick Gym	3,200
Farleigh Dickinson	Rothman Center	5,000
LIU-Brooklyn	ARW Center	3,000
Monmouth	Boylan Gym	2,500
Mt. St. Mary's	Knott Arena	3,121
Quinnipiac	TD Banknorth Sports Center	3,570
Robert Morris	Sewall Center	3,056
Sacred Heart	Pitt Center	2,100
St. Francis-NY	Pope Center	1,200
St. Francis-PA	DeGol Arena	3,500
Wagner	Spiro Sports Center	2,100

Ohio Valley

	Home Floor	Seats
Austin Peay	Dunn Center	9,000
Eastern Illinois	Lantz Arena	5,300
Eastern Ky.	McBrayer Arena	6,500
Jacksonville St.	Mathews Coliseum	5,500
Morehead St.	Johnson Arena	6,500
Murray St.	Regional Special Events Ctr.	8,602
Samford	Corts Arena	5,000
SE Missouri St.	Show Me Center	7,000
Tennessee-Martin	Skyhawk Arena	6,700
Tennessee St.	Gentry Complex	10,500
Tennessee Tech	Eblen Center	10,152

Pacific-10

	Home Floor	Seats
Arizona	McKale Center	14,545
Arizona St.	Wells Fargo Arena	14,198
California	Haas Pavillion	11,877
Oregon	McArthur Court	9,087
Oregon St.	Gill Coliseum	10,400
Stanford	Maples Pavilion	7,391
UCLA	Pauley Pavilion	12,819
USC	Galen Center	10,258
Washington	Bank of America Arena	10,000
Washington St.	Friel Court	11,566

Future NCAA Final Four Sites

Men				Women			
Year	Arena	Seats	Location	Year	Arena	Seats	Location
2008	Alamodome	36,500	San Antonio	2008	St. Pete Times Forum	19,758	Tampa
2009	Ford Field	65,000	Detroit	2009	Edward Jones Dome	66,000	St. Louis
2010	Lucas Oil Stadium	63,000	Indianapolis	2010	Alamodome	36,500	San Antonio
2011	Reliant Stadium	69,500	Houston	2011	Lucas Oil Stadium	63,000	Indianapolis

College Basketball (Cont.)

Patriot League

	Home Floor	Seats
American	Bender Arena	4,500
Army	Christl Arena	5,043
Bucknell	Gary A. Sojka Pavilion	4,000
Colgate	Cotterell Court	3,000
Holy Cross	Hart Recreation Center	3,600
Lafayette	Kirby Sports Center	3,500
Lehigh	Stabler Arena	5,600
Navy	Alumni Hall	5,710

Southeastern

Eastern	Home Floor	Seats
Florida	O'Connell Center	12,000
Georgia	Stegeman Coliseum	10,523
Kentucky	Rupp Arena	23,500
South Carolina	Colonial Center	17,600
Tennessee	Thompson-Boling Arena	24,535
Vanderbilt	Memorial Gymnasium	14,168
Western	**Home Floor**	**Seats**
Alabama	Coleman Coliseum	15,043
Arkansas	Bud Walton Arena	19,200
Auburn	Beard-Eaves-Memorial Coliseum	10,500
LSU	Maravich Assembly Center	14,164
Mississippi	Tad Smith Coliseum	8,700
Mississippi St.	Humphrey Coliseum	10,500

Southern

	Home Floor	Seats
Appalachian St.	Seby Jones Arena	8,325
Chattanooga	McKenzie Arena	11,218
The Citadel	McAlister Field House	6,200
Coll. of Charleston	John Kresse Arena	5,000
Davidson	Belk Arena	5,700
Elon	Koury Center	2,000
Furman	Timmons Arena	5,000
Ga. Southern	Hanner Fieldhouse	5,500
NC-Greensboro	Fleming Gymnasium	2,320
W. Carolina	Ramsey Center	7,286
Wofford	Johnson Arena	3,500

Southland

	Home Floor	Seats
Central Arkansas	Farris Center	5,500
Lamar	Montagne Center	10,080
McNeese St.	Burton Coliseum	8,000
Nicholls St.	Stopher Gym	3,800
Northwestern St.	Prather Coliseum	4,300
Sam Houston St.	Johnson Coliseum	6,172
SE Louisiana	University Center	7,500
S.F. Austin St.	W.R. Johnson Coliseum	7,200
Texas A&M-Corpus Christi	American Bank Center	8,156
TX-Arlington	Texas Hall	4,200
TX-San Antonio	Convocation Center	5,100
Texas St.	Strahan Coliseum	7,200

Southwestern Athletic

	Home Floor	Seats
Alabama A&M	Elmore Gymnasium	6,000
Alabama St.	Joe Reed Acadome	8,000
Alcorn St.	Whitney Complex	7,000
Arkansas-Pine Bluff	K.L. Johnson Complex	4,500
Grambling St.	Health & P.E. Building	7,500
	& Memorial Gym	2,200
Jackson St.	Williams Center	8,000
Miss.Valley St.	Harrison HPER Athletic Complex	6,000
Prairie View A&M	William Nicks Building	5,520
Southern-BR	Clark Activity Center	7,500
TX Southern	Health & P.E. Building	8,100

The Summit League

	Home Floor	Seats
Centenary	Gold Dome	3,000
IUPUI	IUPUI Gym	2,000
IPFW	Memorial Coliseum	11,500
	& Hilliard Gates Sports Center	2,700
Missouri-KC	Municipal Auditorium	9,827
	& Kemper Arena	18,646
North Dakota St.	Bison Sports Arena	6,000
Oakland	Athletics Center O'Rena	4,005
Oral Roberts	Mabee Center	10,575
South Dakota St.	Frost Arena	8,500
Southern Utah	Centrum	5,300
Western Ill.	Western Hall	5,139

Sun Belt

	Home Floor	Seats
Arkansas-Little Rock	Stephens Center	5,600
Arkansas St	Convocation Center	10,563
Denver	Magness Arena	7,200
Fla. Atlantic	FAU Gym	5,000
Florida International	Pharmed Arena	5,000
LA-Lafayette	The Cajundome	11,550
LA-Monroe	Fant-Ewing Coliseum	7,085
Middle Tennessee	Murphy Center	11,520
New Orleans	Human Performance Center	1,200
	& Lakefront Arena	8,933
North Texas	The Super Pit	10,032
South Alabama	Mitchell Center	10,000
Troy	Trojan Arena	4,000
Western Ky.	E.A. Diddle Arena	7,326

West Coast

	Home Floor	Seats
Gonzaga	McCarthey Athletic Center	6,000
Loyola Marymount	Gersten Pavilion	4,156
Pepperdine	Firestone Fieldhouse	3,104
Portland	Chiles Center	5,000
St. Mary's-CA	McKeon Pavilion	3,500
San Diego	Jenny Craig Pavilion	5,100
San Francisco	War Memorial Gym	5,300
Santa Clara	Leavey Center	5,000

Western Athletic

	Home Floor	Seats
Boise St.	Taco Bell Arena	12,380
Fresno St.	Save Mart Center	16,116
Hawaii	Stan Sheriff Center	10,300
Idaho	Cowan Spectrum	7,000
Louisiana Tech	Thomas Assembly Center	8,000
Nevada	Lawlor Events Center	11,200
New Mexico St.	Pan American Center	13,071
San Jose St.	The Event Center	5,000
Utah St.	Dee Glen Smith Spectrum	10,270

Independents

	Home Floor	Seats
Chicago St.	Jones Convocation Center	7,000
IPFW	Allen County Memorial	11,500
Longwood	Henry I. Willet Jr. Hall	2,522
Savannah St.	Tiger Arena	6,000
Texas-Pan Am	UTPA Fieldhouse	4,000
Utah Valley St.	McKay Center	8,500
UC Davis	The Pavilion	7,580
N.J.I.T	Fleisher Athletic Center	1,500
Winston-Salem	LJVM Coliseum Annex,	4,200
	C.E. Gaines Center	3,200
	& Lawrence Joel Coliseum	14,665

COLLEGE FOOTBALL

The 40 Largest I-A Stadiums

The 40 largest stadiums in NCAA Division I-A college football (officially Football Bowl Subdivision) heading into the 2007 season. Note that (*) indicates stadium not on campus.

		Location	Seats	Home Team	Conference	Built	Field
1	Michigan Stadium	Ann Arbor, Mich.	107,501	Michigan	Big Ten	1927	Turf
2	Beaver Stadium	University Park, Penn.	107,282	Penn St.	Big Ten	1960	Grass
3	Neyland Stadium	Knoxville, Tenn.	104,079	Tennessee	SEC-East	1921	Grass
4	Ohio Stadium	Columbus, Ohio	101,568	Ohio St.	Big Ten	1922	Grass
5	Sanford Stadium	Athens, Ga.	92,746	Georgia	SEC-East	1929	Grass
6	LA Memorial Coliseum*	Los Angeles, Calif.	92,516	USC	Pac-10	1923	Grass
7	Tiger Stadium	Baton Rouge, La.	92,400	LSU	SEC-West	1924	Grass
8	Bryant-Denny Stadium	Tuscaloosa, Ala.	92,158	Alabama	SEC-West	1929	Grass
9	Rose Bowl*	Pasadena, Calif.	91,500	UCLA	Pac-10	1922	Grass
10	Griffin Stadium at Florida Field	Gainesville, Fla.	88,548	Florida	SEC-East	1929	Grass
11	Jordan-Hare Stadium	Auburn, Ala.	87,451	Auburn	SEC-West	1939	Grass
12	Memorial Stadium	Lincoln, Neb.	85,157	Nebraska	Big 12-North	1923	Turf
13	Royal-Texas Memorial Stadium	Austin, Texas	85,123	Texas	Big 12-South	1924	Grass
14	Kyle Field	College Station, Texas	82,600	Texas A&M	Big 12-South	1925	Grass
15	Doak Campbell Stadium	Tallahasse, Fla.	82,300	Florida St.	ACC	1950	Grass
16	Gaylord Family-Oklahoma Memorial Stadium	Norman, Okla.	82,112	Oklahoma	Big 12-South	1924	Grass
17	Memorial Stadium	Clemson, S.C.	81,474	Clemson	ACC	1942	Grass
18	Notre Dame Stadium	Notre Dame, Ind.	80,795	Notre Dame	Independent	1930	Grass
19	Camp Randall Stadium	Madison, Wis.	80,321	Wisconsin	Big Ten	1917	Turf
20	Williams-Brice Stadium	Columbia, S.C.	80,250	South Carolina	SEC-East	1934	Grass
21	Razorback Stadium	Fayetteville, Ark.	80,000	Arkansas	SEC-West	1938	Grass
22	Spartan Stadium	East Lansing, Mich.	75,005	Michigan St.	Big Ten	1957	Turf
23	Sun Devil Stadium	Tempe, Ariz.	73,379	Arizona St.	Pac-10	1959	Grass
24	Memorial Stadium	Berkeley, Calif.	73,347	California	Pac-10	1923	Turf
25	Husky Stadium	Seattle, Wash.	72,500	Washington	Pac-10	1920	Turf
26	Orange Bowl*	Miami, Fla.	72,319	Miami-FL & FIU	ACC	1935	Grass
27	Legion Field*	Birmingham, Ala.	71,594	UAB	USA	1927	Grass
28	Qualcomm Stadium	San Diego, Calif.	71,295	San Diego St.	Mountain West	1967	Grass
29	Kinnick Stadium	Iowa City, Iowa	70,585	Iowa	Big Ten	1929	Grass
30	Citrus Bowl*	Orlando, Fla.	70,188	Central Florida	USA	1936	Grass
31	Rice Stadium	Houston, Texas	70,000	Rice	USA	1950	Turf
32	Louisiana Superdome*	New Orleans, La.	69,767	Tulane	USA	1975	Turf
33	Memorial Stadium	Champaign, Ill.	69,249	Illinois	Big Ten	1923	Turf
34	Lincoln Financial Field*	Philadelphia, Penn.	68,532	Temple	Mid-American	2003	Grass
35	Memorial Stadium	Columbia, Mo.	68,349	Missouri	Big 12-North	1926	Turf
36	Commonwealth	Lexington, Ky.	67,606	Kentucky	SEC-East	1973	Grass
37	Lane Stadium	Blacksburg, Va.	66,233	Va. Tech	ACC	1965	Grass
38	Raymond James Stadium*	Tampa, Fla.	65,657	South Florida	Big East	1998	Grass
39	LaVell Edwards Stadium	Provo, Utah	65,524	BYU	Mountain West	1964	Grass
40	Heinz Field*	Pittsburgh, Penn.	64,450	Pittsburgh	Big East	2001	Grass

Note: The capacities for several stadiums including the Rose Bowl, Louisiana Superdome and Sun Devil Stadium are often listed differently for other events, such as bowl games, which they host.

2007 Conference Home Fields

NCAA Division I-A (FBS) conference by conference listing includes member teams heading into the 2007 season. Note that (*) indicates stadium is not on campus. For the purposes of this list anything other than natural grass is called turf.

Atlantic Coast

Atlantic	Stadium	Built	Seats	Field
Boston College	Alumni	1957	44,500	Turf
Clemson	Memorial	1942	81,474	Grass
Florida St.	Doak Campbell	1950	82,300	Grass
Maryland	Byrd	1950	51,500	Grass
N.C. State	Carter-Finley	1966	60,000	Grass
Wake Forest	BB&T Field	1968	31,500	Turf

Coastal	Stadium	Built	Seats	Field
Duke	Wallace Wade	1929	33,941	Grass
Georgia Tech	Bobby Dodd	1913	55,000	Grass
Miami-FL	Orange Bowl*	1935	72,319	Grass
No. Carolina	Kenan Memorial	1927	60,000	Grass
Virginia	Scott	1931	61,500	Grass
Virginia Tech	Lane	1965	66,233	Grass

Big East

	Stadium	Built	Seats	Field
Cincinnati	Nippert	1924	35,000	Turf
Connecticut	Rentschler Field*	2003	40,000	Grass
Louisville	Papa John's Cardinal	1998	42,000	Turf
Pittsburgh	Heinz Field*	2001	64,450	Grass
Rutgers	Rutgers	1994	41,500	Grass
South Florida	Raymond James*	1988	65,657	Grass
Syracuse	Carrier Dome	1980	51,000	Turf
West Virginia	Mountaineer Field	1980	60,000	Turf

Independents

	Stadium	Built	Seats	Field
Army	Michie	1924	39,929	Turf
Navy	Navy-Marine Corps Memorial	1959	30,000	Turf
Notre Dame	Notre Dame	1930	80,795	Grass
Western Ky.	Houchens Industries –L.T. Smith	1968	22,000	Turf

College Football (Cont.)

Big Ten

	Stadium	Built	Seats	Field
Illinois	Memorial	1923	69,249	Turf
Indiana	Memorial	1960	52,354	Turf
Iowa	Kinnick	1929	70,585	Grass
Michigan	Michigan	1927	107,501	Turf
Michigan St.	Spartan	1957	75,005	Grass
Minnesota	HHH Metrodome*	1982	64,172	Turf
Northwestern	Ryan Field	1926	49,256	Grass
Ohio St.	Ohio	1922	101,568	Grass
Penn St.	Beaver	1960	107,282	Grass
Purdue	Ross-Ade	1924	62,500	Grass
Wisconsin	Camp Randall	1917	80,320	Turf

Big 12

North	Stadium	Built	Seats	Field
Colorado	Folsom Field	1924	53,750	Turf
Iowa St.	Jack Trice Field	1975	55,000	Grass
Kansas	Memorial	1921	50,071	Turf
Kansas St.	Snyder Family	1968	52,000	Turf
Missouri	Memorial	1926	68,349	Turf
Nebraska	Memorial	1923	85,157	Grass
South	**Stadium**	**Built**	**Seats**	**Field**
Baylor	Floyd Casey	1950	50,000	Grass
Oklahoma	Gaylord Family-Oklahoma Memorial	1924	82,112	Grass
Oklahoma St.	Boone Pickens	1920	44,700†	Turf
Texas	Royal-Memorial	1924	85,123	Grass
Texas A&M	Kyle Field	1925	82,600	Grass
Texas Tech	Jones AT&T	1947	53,702	Turf

†The capacity of Boone Pickens Stadium has been temporarily downsized until renovations to expand the stadium are completed.
Note: The annual Oklahoma-Texas game has been played at the Cotton Bowl (capacity 68,252) in Dallas since 1937.

Conference USA

East	Stadium	Built	Seats	Field
UAB	Legion Field	1927	71,594	Grass
C. Florida	Bright House Networks	2007	45,031	Grass
E. Carolina	Dowdy-Ficklen	1963	43,000	Grass
Marshall	Joan C. Edwards	1991	38,019	Turf
Memphis	Liberty Bowl*	1965	62,380	Grass
Southern Miss	M.M. Roberts	1976	33,000	Grass
West	**Stadium**	**Built**	**Seats**	**Field**
Houston	Robertson	1942	32,000	Grass
Rice	Rice	1950	70,000	Turf
SMU	Gerald J. Ford Stadium	2000	32,000	Grass
Tulane	Superdome*	1975	69,767	Turf
Tulsa	Skelly	1930	35,542	Turf
UTEP	Sun Bowl*	1963	51,500	Turf

Mid-American

	Stadium	Built	Seats	Field
Akron	Rubber Bowl*	1940	35,202	Turf
Ball St.	Scheumann	1967	25,400	Grass
Bowling Green	Doyt Perry	1966	28,599	Grass
Buffalo	U. at Buffalo	1993	29,013	Turf
Central Mich.	Kelly/Shorts	1972	30,199	Turf
Eastern Mich.	Rynearson	1969	30,200	Turf
Kent	Dix	1969	29,287	Turf
Miami-OH	Fred Yager	1983	24,286	Turf
Northern Ill.	Huskie	1965	31,000	Turf
Ohio Univ.	Peden	1929	24,000	Turf
Temple	Lincoln Financial Field*	2003	68,532	Grass
Toledo	Glass Bowl	1937	26,248	Turf
Western Mich.	Waldo	1939	30,200	Turf

Mountain West

	Stadium	Built	Seats	Field
Air Force	Falcon	1962	52,480	Turf
BYU	LaVell Edwards	1964	65,524	Grass
Colorado St.	Hughes	1968	34,000	Turf
New Mexico	University	1960	38,634	Grass
San Diego St.	Qualcomm*	1967	71,295	Grass
TCU	Amon G. Carter	1929	46,083	Grass
UNLV	Sam Boyd*	1971	36,800	Grass
Utah	Rice-Eccles	1927	45,017	Turf
Wyoming	War Memorial	1950	32,580	Turf

Pacific-10

	Stadium	Built	Seats	Field
Arizona	Arizona	1928	57,803	Grass
Arizona St.	Sun Devil	1958	73,379	Grass
California	Memorial	1923	73,347	Turf
Oregon	Autzen	1967	53,800	Turf
Oregon St.	Reser	1953	45,674	Turf
Stanford	Stanford	1921	50,000	Grass
UCLA	Rose Bowl*	1922	92,542	Grass
USC	LA Memorial Coliseum*	1923	92,516	Grass
Washington	Husky	1920	72,500	Turf
Washington St.	Martin	1972	37,600	Turf

Southeastern

East	Stadium	Built	Seats	Field
Florida	Florida Field	1929	88,548	Grass
Georgia	Sanford	1929	92,746	Grass
Kentucky	Commonwealth	1973	67,530	Grass
South Carolina	Williams-Brice	1934	80,250	Grass
Tennessee	Neyland	1921	104,079	Grass
Vanderbilt	Vanderbilt	1981	39,790	Grass
West	**Stadium**	**Built**	**Seats**	**Field**
Alabama	Bryant-Denny	1929	92,158	Grass
Arkansas	Razorback & War Memorial*	1938 1948	80,000 53,727	Grass Grass
Auburn	Jordan-Hare	1939	87,451	Grass
LSU	Tiger	1924	92,400	Grass
Mississippi	Vaught-Hemingway	1915	60,580	Grass
Miss. St.	Davis Wade	1915	55,082	Grass

Note: EAST—Vanderbilt Stadium was rebuilt in 1981.

Sun Belt

	Stadium	Built	Seats	Field
Arkansas St.	Indian	1974	33,410	Turf
Florida Atlantic	Lockhart	1959	20,450	Grass
Florida International	FIU† & Orange Bowl	1995 1935	23,500 72,319	Turf Grass
LA-Lafayette	Cajun Field	1971	31,000	Grass
LA-Monroe	Malone	1978	30,427	Grass
Mid. Tenn. St.	Johnny 'Red' Floyd	1933	30,788	Turf
North Texas	Fouts Field	1952	30,500	Turf
Troy	Movie Gallery Veterans	1950	30,000	Turf

†Florida International will play the 2007 season at the Orange Bowl while FIU Stadium is being renovated.

Western Athletic

	Stadium	Built	Seats	Field
Boise St.	Bronco	1970	30,000	Turf
Fresno St.	Bulldog	1980	41,031	Grass
Hawaii	Aloha*	1975	50,000	Turf
Idaho	Kibbie Dome	1975	16,000	Turf
Louisiana Tech	Joe Aillet	1968	30,600	Grass
Nevada	Mackay	1967	31,900	Grass
New Mexico St.	Aggie Memorial	1978	30,343	Grass
San Jose St.	Spartan	1933	30,456	Grass
Utah St.	Romney	1968	30,257	Grass

NFL commissioner **Roger Goodell** had his hands full in 2007 with a number of high profile disciplinary issues.

BAD BUSINESS

Scandals rocked the sports world in 2007, as athletes...and even coaches and execs...made headlines for all the wrong reasons.

DOG FIGHTING AND DIRTY REFS. STEROIDS AND SEXUAL HARASSMENT.

There's no getting around it: Off the field, 2007 was one of the worst sports years ever. Bad news was on the back page nearly every week.

Here are the stories that made the biggest waves in 2007:

10 **Bad Boys.**
On October 2nd, Isiah Thomas and Madison Square Garden were found liable for sexually harassing former Knicks Executive Vice President Anucha Browne Sanders. After a three-week trial that portrayed the Garden behind the scenes as an out-of-control frathouse, a New York jury ordered MSG and James Dolan, CEO of its parent company Cablevision, to pay Sanders $11.6 million.

09 **Long Way To Go.**
The percentage of black players in Major League Baseball declined to its lowest level since the days of legal segregation, prompting concern as baseball celebrated the 60th anniversary of Jackie Robinson's debut in April. The reasons for the long-term decline seem primarily financial: no inexpensive way for kids to play baseball between Little League and high school; full college scholarships for athletes in revenue sports, but not many for baseball; MLB teams that invest far more in developing Latin American talent than U.S. players.

08 **High Tech Hockey.**
The NHL went interactive and digital in 2007, signing deals with more than a dozen websites and software platforms, often arriving ahead of any other sports leagues. NHL games, recent as well as classic, are now on Google Video, highlights are on YouTube, and clips are on iTunes. You can even make the NHL one of your MySpace friends.

Peter Keating writes "The Biz" column for *ESPN The Magazine* and is the author of "Dingers! A Short History of the Long Ball."

AP/Wide World Photos

In October, a jury found Knicks coach/executive **Isiah Thomas** guilty of sexual harassment against former team executive Anucha Browne Sanders.

07 Financial Knockout.

Floyd Mayweather's split-decision victory over Oscar De La Hoya in their junior middleweight title bout on May 5th was the most lucrative boxing match of all time. Top-level stars with contrasting personalities plus creative and relentless marketing led to staggering numbers: 2.15 million pay-per-view buys, $120 million in PPV revenue, and $19 million at the gate — all records.

De La Hoya has become the biggest PPV attraction ever, helping to generate $612 million in revenues across 18 PPV events over his career.

06 Coming To America.

David Beckham announced on January 11th that he would be coming to America in 2007 to play for the Los Angeles Galaxy. Beckham could net $250 million over the next five years in salary, endorsements and a share of Galaxy ticket revenues and jersey sales. The deal is a crucial part of MLS' bid to attract top-level talent across the pond. The league has never paid market value to star players, let alone shared profits with them. Beckham debuted in an exhibition match on July 21st (for more, see the Soccer Essay on page 723).

05 Concussion Dangers.

Concussions and pro football stayed in the headlines all year. Researchers examining the brains of former NFLers Andre Waters (who committed suicide in November 2006) and Justin Strzelczyk (who died in a car wreck in September 2004) found irreversible brain damage from multiple blows to the head.

Elliot Pellman, the controversial head of the NFL's concussions committee, resigned in February, dogged by an ESPN investigation into his tactics and research methods. Former NFL players seeking disability benefits focused on the brain trauma they had suffered during their careers. The league has responded by instituting new guidelines to prevent concussions, including not allowing players who are knocked unconscious to return to games, setting up a confidential hotline for players to discuss any instance in which they're forced to play or practice against medical advice, and launching long-overdue research into the long-term effects of concussions.

04 Broadcasting Blunder.

On April 4, longtime radio host Don Imus referred to the Rutgers women's basketball team as "nappy-headed hos" and "rough girls."

One of Imus' sidekicks, Bernard McGuirk, responded by comparing the Rutgers-Tennessee contest for the NCAA championship to "the Jigaboos vs. the Wannabes," referring to the Spike Lee movie *School Daze*. The comments triggered a firestorm of protests and national debates over race and speech, and eight days later, CBS Radio canceled *Imus in the Morning*, which had been nationally syndicated since 1993 and on the air since 1979.

03 Dope!

A disgraced Marion Jones admitted on October 5 that she had lied to federal investigators when she denied using performance-enhancing drugs. Caught up in a check-fraud scheme, Jones reversed four years of denials and copped to taking "the clear," a designer steroid made by BALCO and provided to her by her ex-coach, Trevor Graham.

Jones has announced her retirement and has given back the five medals she won at the Sydney Olympics in 2000 (for more, see the International Sports Essay on page 617).

02 Personal Foul.

On August 15, Tim Donaghy admitted in federal court that he had given inside information about NBA games to gamblers while working as a referee during the 2006-07 season. Donaghy reportedly received $30,000 for his tips; prosecutors have also alleged that he bet on games himself.

An ashen David Stern called the Donaghy case the "worst situation that I have ever experienced" as commissioner of the NBA. (for more, see the Pro Basketball Essay on page 351).

 Longtime radio personality **Don Imus** faced the music in 2007 for insensitive comments he made about the Rutgers women's basketball team. Here he faces Rev. Al Sharpton.

01 New Sheriff In Town.

The top business story of the year was the barrage of negative headlines to hit the once teflon-coated NFL...and more specifically, how its new leader responded to each. Roger Goodell, in just his first year as NFL commissioner, established himself as the most powerful person in sports by cracking down on a bevy of bad citizens.

In April, Goodell announced a new personal conduct policy for the league and suspended Adam "Pacman" Jones for the entire 2007 season for a number of off-field incidents, most notably his alleged involvement in a shooting at a Las Vegas strip club that left a man paralyzed.

In August, Goodell suspended Michael Vick indefinitely, after he pleaded guilty to participating in a dog fighting ring in Virginia. Vick faces prison time and his return to the NFL is uncertain.

And in September, Goodell fined Bill Belichick $500,000 and the Patriots $250,000, and penalized the team at least one 2008 draft pick for violating league rules after a Patriots videographer is caught taping the Jets sidelines in an effort to steal defensive signals.

Each of these decisions had its critics. But the bottom line is that all the embarrassments (and a supine NFLPA) gave Goodell the chance to solidify his command. And that's what he's done.

Honorable Mention Stories

* **The Starbury**, the $14.98 basketball shoe marketed by Stephon Marbury, won Footwear News' "Launch of the Year" award, the Oscar of the shoe industry, in December 2006. Starbury shoes and apparel sold so well in 2007 that the brand line expanded from 50 to more than 200 products, all for under $15.

* Two major new **steroid investigations** hit headlines in 2007. In February, federal and state narcotics agents raided Signature Pharmacy, an Orlando company that sent human growth hormone and other performance-enhancing drugs to athletes. In the months that followed, media reports linked six MLB players (including comeback star Rick Ankiel) and Patriots safety Rodney Harrison (whom the NFL suspended for four games) with shipments from Signature.

Meanwhile, in April, Kirk Radomski, a former clubhouse employee of the Mets, pleaded guilty to providing anabolics and other drugs to "dozens of current and former players, and associates, on teams throughout Major League Baseball." Radomski is now reportedly cooperating with MLB's Mitchell Commission.

* **Dale Earnhardt, Jr.** announced in May that he would be leaving Dale Earnhardt, Inc., the company his father founded and his stepmother now runs. The following month, he inked a five-year deal with Hendrick Motorsports.

* In March, the **Ultimate Fighting Championship** reported record pay-per-view revenues of $223 million in 2006, demonstrating mixed martial arts' continued climb into the mainstream of sports business.

* In September, fashion designer Mark Ecko won an online auction for Barry Bonds' record-breaking **756th home run ball**, paying $752,467. Ecko then left the fate of the ball up to an Internet vote; fans chose to brand it with an asterisk (see page 605 for vote totals). The Baseball Hall of Fame typically does not accept defaced property, but said it would take the ball.

* With LeBron James leading his team into the NBA Finals, Cavaliers attendance hit a club record 20,436 fans per game. Wins, TV ratings, website hits, and playoff revenues have all zoomed since **King James** arrived in Cleveland, leading ESPN The Magazine to name him literally the most valuable player in sports.

* Following a 36-year run on ABC, **Monday Night Football** moved to ESPN in the fall of 2006, and became the most-watched series in cable television history, averaging a 9.9 rating.

* The Red Sox won the rights to negotiate with **Daisuke Matsuzaka** by paying a posting fee of $51.1 million to the Seibu Lions, by far the most ever for a Japanese player. The following month, Boston signed Matsuzaka to a six-year, $52-million contract. Matsuzaka went 15-12 with a 4.40 ERA in 2007.

2006-07 Top 50 Network TV Sports Events

Final 2006-07 network television ratings for the top nationally telecast sports events, according to Nielsen Media Research. Covers period from Sept. 1, 2006 through Aug. 31, 2007. Events are listed with ratings points and audience share; each ratings point represents 1,114,000 households and shares indicate percentage of TV sets in use.

Multiple entries: SPORTS—NFL Football (43); Major League Baseball (4); NCAA Football (3). NETWORKS—FOX (22); CBS (16); NBC (11); ABC (2).

		Date	Net	Rtg/Sh
1	**Super Bowl XLI** (Colts vs Bears) 2/4/07		CBS	42.0/64
2	**AFC Championship Game** (Patriots at Colts) 1/21/07		CBS	26.1/38
3	**NFC Championship Game** (Saints at Bears) 1/21/07		FOX	24.9/44
4	**AFC Div. Playoff Game** (Patriots at Chargers) 1/14/07		CBS	20.4/35
5	**NFC Div. Playoff Game** (Seahawks at Bears) 1/14/07		FOX	19.7/39
6	**NFC Wild Card Game** (Giants at Eagles) 1/7/07		FOX	18.0/31
7	**NFL Regular Season Late Game** (Various teams) 12/3/06		FOX	17.6/32
8	**Tostitos BCS Championship Game** (Florida vs Ohio St.) . . .1/8/07		FOX	17.3/27
9	**AFC Div. Playoff Game** (Colts at Ravens) 1/13/07		CBS	16.3/32
10	**NFC Wild Card Game** (Cowboys at Seahawks) . .1/6/07		NBC	16.2/27
11	**NFC Div. Playoff Game** (Eagles at Saints) 1/13/07		FOX	16.1/27
12	**AFC Wild Card Game** (Jets at Patriots) 1/7/07		CBS	16.0/33
13	**NFL Regular Season Late Game** (Various teams) 11/26/06		FOX	15.3/28
14	**NFL Regular Season Late Game** (Various teams) 11/19/06		CBS	14.6/27
15	**NFL Regular Season Late Game** (Various teams) 9/10/06		FOX	14.2/28
	NFL Sunday Night Football (Colts at Giants) 9/10/06		NBC	14.2/23
17	**NFL Sunday Night Football** (Colts at Patriots) 11/5/06		NBC	13.9/22
18	**Rose Bowl** (USC vs Michigan) 1/1/07		ABC	13.8/23
	NFL Regular Season Late Game (Various teams) 10/8/06		FOX	13.8/28
20	**NFL Regular Season Late Game** (Various teams) 10/29/06		CBS	13.7/26
21	**NFL Regular Season Late Game** (Various teams) 11/12/06		FOX	13.5/25
22	**NFL Regular Season Late Game** (Various teams) 12/17/06		FOX	13.4/25
23	**NFL Regular Season Late Game** (Various teams) 10/22/06		FOX	13.0/25
	NFL Regular Season Late Game (Various teams) 11/5/06		CBS	13.0/24
25	**NCAA Regular Season Game** (Michigan at Ohio St.) . .11/18/06		ABC	12.9/28
26	**NFL Sunday Night Football** (Saints at Cowboys) . .12/10/06		NBC	12.7/20
27	**AFC Wild Card Game** (Chiefs at Colts) 1/6/07		NBC	12.6/26
	NFL Thursday Night Opening Game (Dolphins at Steelers) . . .9/7/06		NBC	12.6/21
29	**NFL Regular Season Late Game** (Various teams) 12/10/06		CBS	12.5/24
	NFL Regular Season Late Game (Various teams) 10/15/06		CBS	12.5/25
31	**NFL Regular Season Late Game** (Various teams) 10/1/06		CBS	12.3/25
	NFL Sunday Night Football (Bears at Giants) 11/12/06		NBC	12.3/19

		Date	Net	Rtg/Sh
33	**NFL Regular Season Late Game** (Various teams) 9/24/06		FOX	12.2/25
34	**NCAA Men's Basketball Championship Game** (Florida vs Ohio St.) 4/2/07		CBS	12.1/20
	NFL Regular Season Late Game (Various teams) 12/24/06		CBS	12.1/29
36	**NFL Christmas Day Game** (Eagles at Cowboys) . . .12/25/06		NBC	12.0/29
	NFL Thanksgiving Day Late Game (Bucs at Cowboys) . . .11/23/06		FOX	12.0/31
38	**NFL Sunday Night Football** (Redskins at Cowboys) . .9/17/06		NBC	11.9/19
39	**NFL Regular Season Early Game** (Various teams) 9/17/06		FOX	11.5/26
	MLB World Series—Game 2 (Cardinals at Tigers) . .10/22/06		FOX	11.5/18
41	**NFL Regular Season Early Game** (Various teams) 11/12/06		CBS	11.4/24
42	**NFL Thanksgiving Day Early Game** (Dolphins at Lions) 11/23/06		CBS	11.2/29
43	**NFL Sunday Night Football** (Cowboys at Panthers) .10/29/06		NBC	11.1/18
44	**NFL Regular Season Early Game** (Various teams) 10/29/06		FOX	11.0/24
45	**NFL Sunday Night Football** (Seahawks at Bears) 10/1/06		NBC	10.8/17
	MLB NLCS—Game 7 (Cardinals at Mets) . . .10/19/06		FOX	10.8/18
47	**NFL Regular Season Late Game** (Various teams) 12/31/06		FOX	10.7/21
48	**NFL Regular Season Late Game** (Various teams) 9/17/06		CBS	10.6/21
49	**MLB World Series—Game 4** (Tigers at Cardinals) . . .10/26/06		FOX	10.4/18
50	**MLB World Series—Game 5** (Tigers at Cardinals) . . .10/27/06		FOX	10.3/18
	NFL Regular Season Early Game (Various teams) 12/10/06		FOX	10.3/22

Other top non-NFL TV sports events

		Date	Net	Rtg/Sh
52	**MLB World Series—Game 3** (Tigers at Cardinals) . . .10/24/06		FOX	10.2/17
53	**Daytona 500** (Kevin Harvick wins) 2/18/07		FOX	10.0/20
68	**Sugar Bowl** (LSU vs Notre Dame) 1/3/07		FOX	9.2/16
70	**The Masters—Sunday** (Zach Johnson wins) 4/8/07		CBS	9.0/22
72	**NCAA Men's Basketball Semifinal Game** (Florida vs UCLA) 3/31/07		CBS	8.9/17
76	**Kentucky Derby** (Street Sense wins) 5/5/07		NBC	8.7/21
79	**NCAA Men's Basketball Semifinal Game** (Ohio St. vs Georgetown) 3/31/07		CBS	8.4/18
	Fiesta Bowl (Boise St. vs Oklahoma) . . .1/1/07		FOX	8.4/15
82	**MLB All-Star Game** (AL wins, 5-4) 7/10/07		FOX	8.3/15
88	**MLB NLCS—Game 6** (Cardinals at Mets) 10/18/06		FOX	8.0/13

All-Time Top-Rated TV Programs

NFL Football dominates television's All-Time Top-Rated 50 Programs with 22 Super Bowls and the 1981 NFC Championship Game making the list. Rankings based on surveys taken from January 1961 through August 31, 2006; include only sponsored programs seen on individual networks; and programs under 30 minutes scheduled duration are excluded. Programs are listed with ratings points, audience share and number of households watching, according to Nielsen Media Research.

Multiple entries: The Super Bowl (22); "Roots" (7); "The Beverly Hillbillies" and "The Thorn Birds" (3); "The Bob Hope Christmas Show," "The Ed Sullivan Show," "Gone With The Wind" and 1994 Winter Olympics (2).

	Program	Episode/Game	Net	Date	Rating	Share	Households
1	M*A*S*H (series)	Final episode	CBS	2/28/83	**60.2**	77	50,150,000
2	Dallas (series)	"Who Shot J.R.?"	CBS	11/21/80	**53.3**	76	41,470,000
3	Roots (mini-series)	Part 8	ABC	1/30/77	**51.1**	71	36,380,000
4	**Super Bowl XVI**	49ers 26, Bengals 21	CBS	1/24/82	**49.1**	73	40,020,000
5	**Super Bowl XVII**	Redskins 27, Dolphins 17	NBC	1/30/83	**48.6**	69	40,480,000
6	**XVII Winter Olympics**	Women's Figure Skating	CBS	2/23/94	**48.5**	64	45,690,000
7	**Super Bowl XX**	Bears 46, Patriots 10	NBC	1/26/86	**48.3**	70	41,490,000
8	Gone With the Wind (movie)	Part 1	NBC	11/7/76	**47.7**	65	33,960,000
9	Gone With the Wind (movie)	Part 2	NBC	11/8/76	**47.4**	64	33,750,000
10	**Super Bowl XII**	Cowboys 27, Broncos 10	CBS	1/15/78	**47.2**	67	34,410,000
11	**Super Bowl XIII**	Steelers 35, Cowboys 31	NBC	1/21/79	**47.1**	74	35,090,000
12	Bob Hope Special	Christmas Show	NBC	1/15/70	**46.6**	64	27,260,000
13	**Super Bowl XVIII**	Raiders 38, Redskins 9	CBS	1/22/84	**46.4**	71	38,800,000
	Super Bowl XIX	49ers 38, Dolphins 16	ABC	1/20/85	**46.4**	63	39,390,000
15	**Super Bowl XIV**	Steelers 31, Rams 19	CBS	1/20/80	**46.3**	67	35,330,000
16	**Super Bowl XXX**	Cowboys 27, Steelers 17	NBC	1/28/96	**46.0**	68	44,114,400
	ABC Theater (special)	"The Day After"	ABC	11/20/83	**46.0**	62	38,550,000
18	Roots (mini-series)	Part 6	ABC	1/28/77	**45.9**	66	32,680,000
	The Fugitive (series)	Final episode	ABC	8/29/67	**45.9**	72	25,700,000
20	**Super Bowl XXI**	Giants 39, Broncos 20	CBS	1/25/87	**45.8**	66	40,030,000
21	Roots (mini-series)	Part 5	ABC	1/27/77	**45.7**	71	32,540,000
22	**Super Bowl XXVIII**	Cowboys 30, Bills 13	NBC	1/30/94	**45.5**	66	42,860,000
	Cheers (series)	Final episode	NBC	5/20/93	**45.5**	64	42,360,500
24	The Ed Sullivan Show	Beatles' 1st appearance	CBS	2/9/64	**45.3**	60	23,240,000
25	**Super Bowl XXVII**	Cowboys 52, Bills 17	NBC	1/31/93	**45.1**	66	41,988,100
26	Bob Hope Special	Christmas Show	NBC	1/14/71	**45.0**	61	27,050,000
27	Roots (mini-series)	Part 3	ABC	1/25/77	**44.8**	68	31,900,000
28	**Super Bowl XXXII**	Broncos 31, Packers 24	NBC	1/25/98	**44.5**	67	43,630,000
29	**Super Bowl XI**	Raiders 32, Vikings 14	NBC	1/9/77	**44.4**	73	31,610,000
	Super Bowl XV	Raiders 27, Eagles 10	NBC	1/25/81	**44.4**	63	34,540,000
31	**Super Bowl VI**	Cowboys 24, Dolphins 3	CBS	1/16/72	**44.2**	74	27,450,000
32	**XVII Winter Olympics**	Women's Figure Skating	CBS	2/25/94	**44.1**	64	41,540,000
	Roots (mini-series)	Part 2	ABC	1/24/77	**44.1**	62	31,400,000
34	The Beverly Hillbillies (series)	Regular episode	CBS	1/8/64	**44.0**	65	22,570,000
35	Roots (mini-series)	Part 4	ABC	1/26/77	**43.8**	66	31,190,000
	The Ed Sullivan Show	Beatles' 2nd appearance	CBS	2/16/64	**43.8**	60	22,445,000
37	**Super Bowl XXIII**	49ers 20, Bengals 16	NBC	1/22/89	**43.5**	68	39,320,000
38	The Academy Awards	John Wayne wins Oscar	ABC	4/7/70	**43.4**	78	25,390,000
39	**Super Bowl XXXI**	Packers 35, Patriots 21	FOX	1/26/97	**43.3**	65	42,000,000
	Super Bowl XXXIV	Rams 23, Titans 16	ABC	1/30/00	**43.3**	63	43,618,000
41	The Thorn Birds (mini-series)	Part 3	ABC	3/29/83	**43.2**	62	35,990,000
42	The Thorn Birds (mini-series)	Part 4	ABC	3/30/83	**43.1**	62	35,900,000
43	**NFC Championship Game**	49ers 28, Cowboys 27	CBS	1/10/82	**42.9**	62	34,940,000
44	The Beverly Hillbillies (series)	Regular episode	CBS	1/15/64	**42.8**	62	21,960,000
45	**Super Bowl VII**	Dolphins 14, Redskins 7	NBC	1/14/73	**42.7**	72	27,670,000
46	The Thorn Birds (mini-series)	Part 2	ABC	3/28/83	**42.5**	59	35,400,000
47	**Super Bowl IX**	Steelers 16, Vikings 6	NBC	1/12/75	**42.4**	72	29,040,000
	The Beverly Hillbillies (series)	Regular episode	CBS	2/26/64	**42.4**	60	21,750,000
49	**Super Bowl X**	Steelers 21, Cowboys 17	CBS	1/18/76	**42.3**	78	29,440,000
	ABC Sunday Night Movie	"Airport"	ABC	11/11/73	**42.3**	63	28,000,000
	ABC Sunday Night Movie	"Love Story"	ABC	10/1/72	**42.3**	62	27,410,000
	Cinderella	Musical special	CBS	2/22/65	**42.3**	59	22,250,000
	Roots (mini-series)	Part 7	ABC	1/29/77	**42.3**	65	30,120,000

All-Time Top-Rated Cable TV Sports Events

All-time cable television for sports events, according to ESPN, Turner Sports research and *The Sports Business Daily.* Covers period from Sept. 1, 1980 through Aug. 31, 2007.

NFL Telecasts

		Date	Net	Rtg
1	Chicago at Minnesota	12/6/87	ESPN	17.6
2	Detroit at Miami	12/25/94	ESPN	15.1
3	Chicago at Minnesota	12/3/89	ESPN	14.7
4	Cleveland at San Fran	11/29/87	ESPN	14.2
5	Pittsburgh at Houston	12/30/90	ESPN	13.8

Non-NFL Telecasts

		Date	Net	Rtg
1	MLB: Chicago (NL)-St. Louis	9/7/98	ESPN	9.5
2	NBA: Detroit-Boston	6/1/88	TBS	8.8
3	NBA: Chicago-Detroit	5/31/89	TBS	8.2
4	NBA: Detroit-Boston	5/26/88	TBS	8.1
5	MLB: Giants-Chicago (NL)	9/28/98	ESPN	8.0

Screen Gems

The Top-Grossing Sports Movies of All Time

Movie (Year)	Domestic Revenue
1 The Waterboy (1998)	$161,491,646
2 The Longest Yard (2005)	158,119,460
3 Jerry Maguire (1996)	153,952,592
4 Talladega Nights: The Ballad of Ricky Bobby (2006)	148,213,375
5 Rocky IV (1985)	127,873,716
6 Rocky III (1982)	125,049,125
7 Seabiscuit (2003)	120,277,854
8 Rocky (1976)	117,235,147
9 Remember the Titans (2000)	115,654,751
10 The Karate Kid, Part II (1986)	115,103,979
11 Dodgeball: A True Underdog Story (2004)	$114,326,736
12 A League of Their Own (1992)	107,928,762
13 Million Dollar Baby (2004)	100,492,203
14 The Karate Kid (1984)	90,815,558
15 Space Jam (1996)	90,418,342
16 Rocky II (1979)	85,182,160
17 Days of Thunder (1990)	82,670,733
18 Nacho Libre (2006)	80,197,993
19 White Men Can't Jump (1992)	76,253,806
20 The Rookie (2002)	75,600,072

Source: boxofficemojo.com

Oscar Might

Sports Movies Nominated For Best Picture

Movie	Sport	Year
The Champ	Boxing	1931
Here Comes Mr. Jordan	Boxing	1941
The Pride of the Yankees	Baseball	1942
The Hustler	Billiards	1961
Rocky	Boxing	1976*
Heaven Can Wait	Football	1978
Breaking Away	Cycling	1979
Raging Bull	Boxing	1980
Chariots of Fire	Track	1981*
Field of Dreams	Baseball	1989
Jerry Maguire	Football	1996
Seabiscuit	Horse Racing	2003
Million Dollar Baby	Boxing	2004

* won Academy Award

Visionary Moments

Sports Television Firsts

The first sporting event ever televised in the United States was a baseball game between Columbia University and Princeton University on May 17, 1939. Here are some other firsts in televised sports:

BOXING

Max Baer vs Lou Nova, Yankee Stadium; June 1, 1939

TENNIS

Eastern Grass Court championship matches; Westchester (New York) Country Club, August 9, 1939

FOOTBALL

Fordham University vs Waynesburg College; New York City, September 30, 1939

HOCKEY

New York Rangers vs Montreal Canadiens; Madison Square Garden, February 28, 1940

BASKETBALL

Fordham University vs University of Pittsburgh; Madison Square Garden, February 28, 1940

TRACK & FIELD

AAAA Track & Field Championships; Madison Square Garden, March 2, 1940

OLYMPICS

Winter Games, Squaw Valley (California), February 18, 1960

Information on this page was excerpted from
23 Ways To Get To First Base:
The ESPN Uncyclopedia

Drama Kings

Actors Who Were Athletes

Known now mostly for their film and TV roles, these thespians were serious athletes in a previous life:

Randall "Tex" Cobb (Fletch Lives, Raising Arizona)
Heavyweight boxer, 1977-93

Chuck Connors (The Rifleman)
Celtics forward, 1946-48; Cubs 1st base, 1951

Mark Harmon (St. Elsewhere, NCIS)
UCLA quarterback, 1972-73

Burt Reynolds (The Longest Yard, Deliverance)
Florida St. running back, 1954

Bob Uecker (Major League, Mr. Belvedere)
Braves, Cardinals, Phillies catcher, 1962-67

Carl Weathers (Rocky I-IV, Predator, Happy Gilmore)
Raiders linebacker, 1970-71

Alex Karras (Webster, Blazing Saddles)
Lions defensive tackle, 1958-62, 1964-70

ESPN The Magazine's Ultimate Standings
Fan Satisfaction Rankings

ESPN The Magazine, in conjunction with *SportsNation*, surveyed over 80,000 fans in order to rank the current 122 major men's professional sports franchises (MLB, NFL, NBA, NHL). The following eight criteria were used:

Bang for the Buck: Revenues directly from fans divided by wins in the past three years; **Fan Relations**: Ease of access to players, coaches and management; **Ownership**: Honesty; loyalty to players and city; **Affordability**: Price of tickets, parking and concessions; **Stadium Experience**: Friendliness of environment, quality of game-day promotions; **Players**: Effort on the field, likability off it; **Coach/Manager**: Strong on-field leadership; **Title Track**: Titles already won or expected soon.

Note that no NHL teams were ranked in 2005 and 2006 due to the 2004-05 lockout.

Team	2004	2005	2006	2007
Buffalo Sabres	63	—	—	1
San Antonio Spurs	1	2	1	2
Dallas Mavericks	2	13	15	3
Indianapolis Colts	40	3	4	4
Detroit Pistons	4	1	2	5
Anaheim Ducks	37	—	—	6
Los Angeles Angels	6	5	5	7
Nashville Predators	56	—	—	8
Pittsburgh Steelers	16	9	3	9
Carolina Hurricanes	65	—	—	10
Phoenix Suns	55	21	20	11
Detroit Tigers	113	53	76	12
Seattle Seahawks	54	59	24	13
Minnesota Twins	51	29	38	14
Atlanta Braves	33	16	9	15
Milwaukee Brewers	112	45	17	16
Tampa Bay Lightning	27	—	—	17
Detroit Red Wings	15	—	—	18
St. Louis Cardinals	18	11	7	19
Dallas Stars	43	—	—	20
Miami Heat	79	18	23	21
San Jose Sharks	83	—	—	22
Green Bay Packers	3	8	30	23
Denver Broncos	19	26	14	24
Jacksonville Jaguars	75	28	16	25
Utah Jazz	26	20	35	26
Houston Rockets	53	56	21	27
Chicago White Sox	99	70	13	28
Minnesota Wild	11	—	—	29
Houston Astros	71	27	11	30
New England Patriots	13	4	10	31
Baltimore Ravens	22	22	54	32
Cleveland Indians	87	42	25	33
Ottawa Senators	10	—	—	34
Pittsburgh Penguins	91	—	—	35
Cleveland Cavaliers	82	34	46	36
Carolina Panthers	42	12	8	37
Calgary Flames	52	—	—	38
Chicago Bulls	93	74	44	39
Colorado Avalanche	12	—	—	40
Toronto Blue Jays	47	67	47	41
New Orleans Saints	78	87	91	42
Arizona Diamondbacks	9	32	51	43
New Orleans Hornets	30	83	55	44
Toronto Raptors	50	75	84	45
Edmonton Oilers	8	—	—	46
Washington Wizards	105	62	59	47
New York Yankees	28	17	28	48
Philadelphia Eagles	23	6	18	49
Chicago Bears	103	69	43	50
Denver Nuggets	68	48	29	51
Oakland Athletics	66	38	42	52
Texas Rangers	76	31	41	53
New Jersey Devils	44	—	—	54
Atlanta Thrashers	59	—	—	55
Buffalo Bills	96	15	31	56
Cincinnati Reds	101	54	60	57
Orlando Magic	108	44	77	58
San Diego Chargers	118	37	45	59
Los Angeles Dodgers	64	52	82	60
New York Mets	111	86	67	61
Tennessee Titans	7	19	34	62
St. Louis Blues	21	—	—	63
San Diego Padres	62	47	49	64
Washington Capitals	109	—	—	65
Kansas City Chiefs	5	24	26	66
Los Angeles Lakers	31	49	61	67
Kansas City Royals	25	58	74	68
Philadelphia Phillies	58	78	83	69
Montreal Canadiens	73	—	—	70
Phoenix Coyotes	69	—	—	71
Tampa Bay Buccaneers	32	36	22	72
Miami Dolphins	57	55	36	73
Vancouver Canucks	20	—	—	74
Pittsburgh Pirates	102	64	68	75
Columbus Blue Jackets	49	—	—	76
Los Angeles Clippers	86	65	78	77
Washington Nationals	97	68	64	78
New York Jets	81	41	63	79
Charlotte Bobcats	—	—	—	80
St. Louis Rams	34	66	50	81
Dallas Cowboys	36	39	27	82
New York Rangers	114	—	—	83
Florida Marlins	24	25	53	84
Colorado Rockies	100	85	75	85
Tampa Bay Devil Rays	77	73	85	86
New York Islanders	85	—	—	87
Boston Red Sox	95	46	62	88
Golden State Warriors	94	80	58	89
Seattle Mariners	67	61	72	90
San Francisco Giants	39	35	56	91
Portland Trail Blazers	115	79	89	92
Houston Texans	—	—	79	93
Milwaukee Bucks	46	51	52	94
Memphis Grizzlies	38	30	32	95
Philadelphia Flyers	41	—	—	96
Arizona Cardinals	119	82	86	97
Chicago Cubs	45	57	73	98
Toronto Maple Leafs	88	—	—	99
San Francisco 49ers	72	89	81	100
New York Giants	90	71	33	101
Cincinnati Bengals	74	43	19	102
Los Angeles Kings	48	—	—	103
New Jersey Nets	80	76	65	104
Baltimore Orioles	84	50	80	105
Atlanta Falcons	70	7	6	106
Florida Panthers	98	—	—	107
Washington Redskins	92	60	37	108
Minnesota Timberwolves	29	14	39	109
Sacramento Kings	14	23	40	110
Seattle SuperSonics	60	33	57	111
Boston Celtics	61	63	70	112
Atlanta Hawks	117	88	87	113
Indiana Pacers	17	10	12	114
Philadelphia 76ers	35	40	48	115
Cleveland Browns	110	90	66	116
Boston Bruins	89	—	—	117
Chicago Blackhawks	120	—	—	118
Minnesota Vikings	106	81	90	119
New York Knicks	116	77	88	120
Oakland Raiders	104	84	71	121
Detroit Lions	107	72	69	122

Costliest Collectibles

Listed are the most expensive pieces of sports memorabilia ever sold, according to the following auction houses and other sources: Lelands, Guernsey's, Sotheby's, Christie's, Gotta Have It! Collectibles, Grey Flannel Auctions, Mastro Auctions and Hunt Auctions. Figures are as of Sept. 30, 2007. (*) indicates estimated amount paid.

	Item	Sold For
1	Mark McGwire 70th HR ball, 1998 HR chase (purchased by Todd McFarlane)	$3,005,000
2	Honus Wagner 1909 American Tobacco Co. "Gretzky" T206 PSA-8 baseball card (sale 2007)	2,800,000
3	Honus Wagner 1909 American Tobacco Co. "Gretzky" T206 PSA-8 baseball card (sale 2007)	2,350,000
4	Honus Wagner 1909 American Tobacco Co. "Gretzky" T206 PSA-8 baseball card (sale 2000)	1,265,000
	Babe Ruth bat, first HR in Yankee Stadium	1,265,000
6	Babe Ruth sale contract (Red Sox to Yankees)	996,000
7	Babe Ruth 1933 inaugural All-Star Game HR ball	805,000
8	Barry Bonds 700th HR ball	804,129
9	SGC co. 1914 Cracker Jack complete baseball card set	800,000
10	Babe Ruth 1934 Tour of Japan Game Worn Uniform	787,859
11	Barry Bonds record-breaking 756th home run ball	752,467
12	Hank Aaron 755th home run ball	650,000
12	Honus Wagner 1909 American Tobacco Co. "Gretzky" T206 PSA-8 baseball card (sale 1996)	640,500
13	Barry Bonds 73rd HR (purchased by Todd McFarlane)	517,500
14	Honus Wagner 1909 American Tobacco Co. "Gretzky" T206 PSA-8 baseball card (sale 1995)	500,000*
15	1921 Bath Ruth bat used in hitting record setting 59th HR	483,000
16	1869 Cincinnati Red Stockings Trophy Ball Collection (17)	473,383
17	Honus Wagner American Tobacco Co. "Frank Nagy" T206 GAI 3.5 baseball card	456,057
18	Honus Wagner 1909 American Tobacco Co. T206 "Gretzky" PSA-8 baseball card (sale 1991)	451,000
	(purchased by Wayne Gretzky and then-owner of L.A. Kings Bruce McNall)	
19	1941 Bruce Smith (Minnesota RB) Heisman Trophy	395,240
20	Lou Gehrig's last game-used 1939 baseball glove	387,500
21	Joe DiMaggio's 1941 bat used during 56-game hitting streak	345,596
	(purchased by Hillerich & Bradsby, authenticity of streak-bat since called into question)	
22	Ty Cobb's 1928 signed Philadelphia A's jersey	332,500
23	Mickey Mantle's 1956 American League MVP Award	319,250
24	Mickey Mantle's 1956 Batting Champion of the Year Silver Bat Award	313,500
25	Lou Gehrig's signed 1927 Yankees road jersey	305,000
26	Roger Maris 1961 New York Yankees Home Pinstripe Jersey	302,106
27	Mickey Mantle's 1962 American League MVP Award	290,500
28	Jim Thorpe's 1916-1917 football jersey	284,350

Note: Barry Bonds' record-tying 755th HR ball was sold in 2007 for $186,750.

The Vote for 756!

Fashion designer and entrepeneur Marc Ecko acquired Barry Bonds' record-breaking 756th home run ball at auction for $752,467. Then he left the ball's fate up to the public, by putting it to a vote on www.vote756.com. Voter choices and totals are noted below. Voting ended at 11:59 pm on Sept. 24, 2007. Over 10 million votes were cast.

34%	**Bestow it:**	The ball that broke Hank Aaron's career home run record belongs in the hall of fame.
47%	**Brand it:**	Place an asterisk on the ball, adding a permanent footnote to the record. Then send it to Cooperstown.
19%	**Banish it:**	Put the ball on a rocket ship and launch it into orbit, a moon shot for the ages. Out of sight, out of mind.

Teams Bought in 2007

Major league clubs acquiring new majority owners from Oct. 1, 2006 through Sept. 30, 2007.

Major League Baseball

Atlanta Braves: On May 16, MLB owners unanimously approved the sale of the Braves from Time Warner to cable operator Liberty Media Corporation in a complicated franchise-for-stock transaction. Liberty reportedly paid an estimated 68.5 million shares of Time Warner stock in return for the Braves, a number of craft magazines and $960 million. The Braves are valued at an estimated $450 million.

NHL Hockey

Tampa Bay Lightning: On August 7, Absolute Hockey Enterprises executed a purchase and sale agreement with Palace Sports & Entertainment (PS&E) to include the Lightning, the team's lease agreement with Hillsborough County — owners of the St. Pete Times Forum, and two pieces of adjacent land. Absolute Hockey includes former NHL coach Doug MacLean, real estate developer Jeff Sherrin, TV producer Oren Koules and Tampa attorney Steve Burton. Financial terms of the deal were not disclosed. The ownership transfer is subject to approval by the NHL Board of Governors.

Also of Note:

Kansas City Chiefs (NFL): Following the death of Chiefs founder, owner and NFL pioneer Lamar Hunt in December 2006, the Chiefs were inherited evenly by Hunt's daughter and three sons. However, Clark Hunt is the only one who assumed an active role in running the team.

Team Payrolls

Team payrolls for active players during the 2006-07 season for the NBA and NHL, the 2006 season for the NFL and the 2007 season (as of opening day) for Major League Baseball. Figures are in millions of dollars. **Note:** The NFL, NHL and NBA use a salary cap to limit payrolls. The NFL's cap was $102 million in 2006, the NHL's cap was $44 million in 2006-07, and the NBA's cap was $53.135 million, though teams can circumvent the cap via bonuses and other exceptions. Note, however, that the totals listed below reflect actual player salaries, not salary cap numbers. **Sources**: USA Today, NHLPA, NFLPA and AP.

	NBA		MLB		NHL		NFL	
1	Phoenix	$82.4	1 NY Yankees	$195.2	1 New Jersey	$49.6	1 Indianapolis	$131.2
2	New York	81.7	2 Boston	143.1	2 Calgary	45.8	2 Minnesota	125.0
3	Miami	78.2	3 NY Mets	116.1	3 NY Rangers	45.1	3 Dallas	113.6
4	Detroit	75.5	4 Chi. White Sox	109.3	4 Dallas	43.9	4 Cincinnati	113.0
5	Minnesota	66.7	5 LA Angels	109.3	5 San Jose	43.9	5 Baltimore	111.6
6	San Antonio	65.6	6 LA Dodgers	108.7	6 Philadelphia	43.7	6 Washington	110.3
7	Denver	65.0	7 Seattle	106.5	7 Boston	43.7	7 Houston	108.7
8	Dallas	64.8	8 Chi. Cubs	99.9	8 Ottawa	43.6	8 NY Giants	108.2
9	Portland	64.8	9 Detroit	95.2	9 Montreal	43.6	9 Seattle	107.4
10	New Jersey	63.8	10 Baltimore	95.1	10 Toronto	43.3	10 Carolina	106.6
11	Cleveland	63.0	11 San Francisco	90.5	11 Nashville	43.0	11 Arizona	105.5
12	Houston	62.6	12 St. Louis	90.3	12 Vancouver	42.9	12 New England	105.1
13	LA Lakers	62.3	13 Atlanta	89.5	13 Edmonton	42.3	13 Atlanta	105.1
14	Golden State	62.1	14 Philadelphia	89.4	14 Tampa Bay	41.9	14 Philadelphia	104.8
15	Washington	61.9	15 Houston	87.8	15 Los Angeles	40.7	15 St. Louis	104.7
16	Indiana	61.5	16 Oakland	79.9	16 Anaheim	40.5	16 Detroit	101.0
17	Sacramento	61.1	17 Toronto	79.9	17 Buffalo	40.0	17 San Diego	99.8
18	Orlando	60.5	18 Milwaukee	72.0	18 Detroit	39.9	18 Green Bay	98.6
19	Utah	60.3	19 Minnesota	71.4	19 Minnesota	39.5	19 Jacksonville	97.7
20	LA Clippers	58.2	20 Cincinnati	69.7	20 Carolina	39.0	20 Miami	97.7
21	Seattle	56.7	21 Texas	68.8	21 Chicago	38.5	21 San Francisco	95.1
22	Chicago	54.7	22 Kansas City	67.4	22 Colorado	38.0	22 Denver	94.4
23	Milwaukee	54.6	23 Cleveland	61.3	23 NY Islanders	37.8	23 Pittsburgh	94.0
24	Boston	53.6	24 San Diego	58.2	24 Atlanta	37.6	24 Chicago	91.6
25	New Orleans	53.2	25 Colorado	54.4	25 Florida	37.6	25 New Orleans	91.0
26	Atlanta	47.8	26 Arizona	52.1	26 Phoenix	37.0	26 Tennessee	89.8
27	Memphis	47.1	27 Pittsburgh	38.6	27 Columbus	36.9	27 Cleveland	89.2
28	Philadelphia	44.4	28 Washington	37.3	28 St. Louis	33.7	28 NY Jets	86.1
29	Toronto	42.2	29 Florida	30.5	29 Washington	29.7	29 Kansas City	81.7
30	Charlotte	42.0	30 Tampa Bay	24.1	30 Pittsburgh	26.3	30 Buffalo	80.9
							31 Tampa Bay	78.8
							32 Oakland	71.8

Top 10 Salaries In Each Sport

The top 10 highest paid athletes in the NBA and NHL (2006-07 season), Major League Baseball (2007 - opening day) and the NFL (2006). Figures are in millions of dollars. Note that NFL figures include signing bonuses. **Sources**: USA Today, Street & Smith's SportsBusiness Journal, NHLPA and AP.

NFL

		Position	Team	Salary
1	Richard Seymour	Def. Lineman	New Eng.	$24.691
2	Drew Brees	Quarterback	New Orl.	22.000
3	Bryant McKinnie	Off. Lineman	Minnesota	17.500
4	Steve Hutchinson	Off. Lineman	Minnesota	16.588
5	Jeff Backus	Off. Lineman	Detroit	16.252
6	Tom Brady	Quarterback	New Eng.	16.005
7	Carson Palmer	Quarterback	Cincinnati	15.750
8	John Abraham	Def. Lineman	Atlanta	15.503
9	Shaun Alexander	Running Back	Seattle	15.125
10	Reggie Wayne	Receiver	Indianapolis	15.100
	League Avg			1.400

MLB

		Position	Team	Salary
1	Jason Giambi	First Base	NY Yankees	$23.429
2	Alex Rodriguez	Third Base	NY Yankees	22.709
3	Derek Jeter	Shortstop	NY Yankees	21.600
4	Manny Ramirez	Left Field	Boston	17.016
5	Todd Helton	First Base	Colorado	16.600
6	Bartolo Colon	Pitcher	LA Angels	16.000
	Andy Pettitte	Pitcher	NY Yankees	16.000
8	Jason Schmidt	Pitcher	LA Dodgers	15.704
9	Barry Bonds	Left Field	San Fran.	15.534
10	Richie Sexson	First Base	Seattle	15.500
	League Avg			2.699

NBA

		Position	Team	Salary
1	Kevin Garnett	Forward	Minnesota	$21.000
2	Shaquille O'Neal	Center	Miami	20.000
3	Jalen Rose	Guard	Phoenix	18.442
4	Jason Kidd	Guard	New Jersey	18.084
	Jermaine O'Neal	Forward	Indiana	18.084
6	Chris Webber	Forward	Detroit	18.007
7	Kobe Bryant	Guard	LA Lakers	17.719
8	Tim Duncan	Center	San Antonio	17.430
9	Allen Iverson	Guard	Denver	17.184
	Stephon Marbury	Guard	New York	17.184
	League Avg			5.215

NHL

		Position	Team	Salary
1	Jaromir Jagr	Right Wing	NY Rangers	$8.360
2	Brad Richards	Center	Tampa Bay	7.800
3	Nicklas Lidstrom	Defense	Detroit	7.600
	Mats Sundin	Center	Toronto	7.600
	Alexei Yashin	Center	NY Islanders	7.600
6	Zdeno Chara	Defense	Boston	7.500
	Patrik Elias	Center	New Jersey	7.500
8	Vincent Lecavalier	Center	Tampa Bay	7.167
9	Bryan McCabe	Defense	Toronto	7.150
10	Two players tied			7.000
	League Avg			1.460

Collective Bargaining Agreements

Listed are highlights from the collective bargaining agreements (CBAs) of the four major sports leagues.

Sources: League CBAs, league players' associations, *USA Today*

Expiration: Current agreement expires December 11, 2011.

Salary cap: None, though it does tax teams whose payrolls exceed agreed-upon limits, which vary from year to year.

Maximum player salary: None.

Minimum player salary: $380,000 (2007).

Free Agency: A player can become eligible for free agency after six years of MLB service.

Revenue Sharing: Each team contributes 31% of its Net Local Revenue into a pool, which is then divided equally among all teams.

Luxury Tax: Referred to by MLB as the "Competitive Balance Tax." In 2007 the tax threshold was $148 million. The amount of tax is charged on the difference between the threshold and the team's payroll and depends upon how many consecutive years the team has exceeded the tax threshold.

Steroid Policy (through 2008): 50-game suspension for first offense, 100 games for second offense, lifetime ban for third offense. At least one regular season test.

Expiration: Current agreement is valid through the 2010-11 season, with a league option for an additional season.

Salary cap: In 2007-08, the cap is set at $55.63 million, while the minimum (75% of max.) is $41.72 million. The NBA operates under a soft salary cap and contains exceptions that allow teams to exceed the cap. For example, the Larry Bird exception allows a team to exceed the salary cap to re-sign its own free agents up to the players' maximum salary.

Maximum player salary: Depends on the number of years played, but rookie maximum in 2007-08 is $13.041 million and the maximun for a veteran with more than ten years played is $18.258 million (without bonuses).

Minimum player salary: Depends on the number of years played, but rookie minimum in 2007-08 is $427,163 and the minimum for a veteran with more than ten years played is $1.22 million.

Steroid Policy: 10-game suspension for first offense, 25 games for second, one year for third and a lifetime ban for a fourth. Up to four random tests per season.

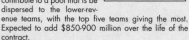

Expiration: Agreement signed in March, 2006 is valid through 2011 season.

Salary cap: $109 million for 2007. Future years are to be determined by league revenues.

Revenue Sharing: Top 15 revenue-generating teams contribute to a pool that is be dispersed to the lower-revenue teams, with the top five teams giving the most. Expected to add $850-900 million over the life of the contract.

Rookies: Players drafted in the first round of the draft can sign contracts longer than five years. Those drafted in rounds 2-7 can sign only four-year deals, preventing teams from locking up players who prove to be worth more than their initial contract allows.

Franchise Players: Teams can no longer protect a player with the "franchise" tag for more than two years. "Franchise" becomes a "transition" player in the third year of his contract, so it's easier for him to leave.

Steroid Policy: Four-game suspension for first offense, eight games for second offense, one-year ban for third offense. Players subject to at least one test per season.

Expiration: Agreement is valid until Sept. 15, 2011. However, the NHLPA has the option to terminate it on Sept. 15, 2009 or extend it to 2012.

Salary cap: In 2006-07, the cap was set at $44 million, while the minimum was set at $28 million. In 2007-08, those figures were upped to $50.3 million (maximum) and $34.3 million (minimum).

Maximum player salary: Players can earn no more than 20 percent of the salary cap (or $10.06 million in 2007-08).

Minimum player salary: $450,000 for 2005-06 and 2006-07, $475,000 in 2007-09 and $500,000 for 2009-11.

Revenue Sharing: All clubs are eligible for revenue sharing that are ranked in the bottom half (bottom 15) in league revenue and those that operate in cities with a demographic of 2.5 million or fewer TV households.

Steroid Policy: 20-game suspension for first offense, 60 games for second offense, lifetime ban for third offense. Players subject to up to two tests per season.

Highest and Lowest Ticket Prices

The most expensive and least expensive average ticket prices for NFL, MLB, NBA and NHL franchises. Average ticket prices for each league are as follows: **NFL** $62.38, **MLB** $22.69, **NBA** $56.13 and **NHL** $43.13.

Source: *Team Marketing Report*

NFL

	Highest	Venue	Avg. Price
1	New England	Gillette Stadium	$90.89
2	Washington	FedEx Field	79.13
3	Chicago	Soldier Field	77.78
4	NY Giants	Giants Stadium	76.59
5	NY Jets	Giants Stadium	74.98

	Lowest	Venue	Avg. Price
1	Buffalo	Ralph Wilson Stadium	$41.29
2	Jacksonville	Jacksonville Mun. Stadium	45.08
3	Tennessee	LP Field	47.82
4	Cleveland	Cleveland Browns Stadium	48.79
5	Seattle	Qwest Field	50.46

MLB

	Highest	Venue	Avg. Price
1	Boston	Fenway Park	$47.71
2	Chicago Cubs	Wrigley Field	34.30
3	NY Yankees	Yankee Stadium	29.01
4	Chi. White Sox	U.S. Cellular Field	28.78
5	St. Louis	Busch Stadium	28.43

	Lowest	Venue	Avg. Price
1	Arizona	Chase Field	$13.79
2	Texas	Ameriquest Field	14.19
3	Kansas City	Kauffman Stadium	14.48
4	Colorado	Coors Field	16.50
5	Florida	Dolphin Stadium	16.57

NBA

	Highest	Venue	Avg. Price
1	LA Lakers	Staples Center	$79.21
2	New York	Madison Sq. Garden	70.51
3	Sacramento	ARCO Arena	59.80
4	Boston	TD Banknorth Garden	55.93
5	Houston	Toyota Center	55.59

	Lowest	Venue	Avg. Price
1	Golden St.	Oracle Arena	$27.69
2	New Orleans	New Orleans Arena	31.00
3	Seattle	KeyArena	34.01
4	Denver	Pepsi Center	35.50
5	Charlotte	Charlotte Coliseum	36.61

NHL

	Highest	Venue	Avg. Price
1	Vancouver	General Motors Place	$58.96
2	Montreal	Bell Centre	56.82
3	Boston	TD Banknorth Garden	56.44
4	Philadelphia	Wachovia Center	55.66
5	New Jersey	Continental Airlines Arena	54.67

	Lowest	Venue	Avg. Price
1	Phoenix	Glendale Arena	$25.41
2	St. Louis	Scottrade Center	28.23
3	Buffalo	HSBC Arena	30.07
4	Anaheim	Honda Center	30.32
5	San Jose	HP Pavilion	33.00

Commissioners and Presidents

Chief Executives of Established Major Sports Organizations since 1876. (*) indicates died in office.

Major League Baseball

Commissioner	Tenure
Kenesaw Mountain Landis*	1920–44
Albert (Happy) Chandler	1945–51
Ford Frick	1951–65
William Eckert	1965–68
Bowie Kuhn	1969–84
Peter Ueberroth	1984–89
A. Bartlett Giamatti*	1989
Fay Vincent†	1989–92
Bud Selig†	1998–

†Served as interim commissioner from 1992-98.

National League

President	Tenure
Morgan G. Bulkeley	1876
William A. Hulbert*	1877–82
A.G. Mills	1883–84
Nicholas Young	1885–1902
Henry Pulliam*	1903–09
Thomas J. Lynch	1910–13
John K. Tener	1914–18
John A. Heydler	1918–34
Ford Frick	1935–51
Warren Giles	1951–69
Charles (Chub) Feeney	1970–86
A. Bartlett Giamatti	1987–89
Bill White	1989–94
Leonard Coleman	1994–99

Note: League president jobs were eliminated after the 1999 season.

American League

President	Tenure
Bancroft (Ban) Johnson	1901–27
Ernest Barnard*	1927–31
William Harridge	1931–59
Joe Cronin	1959–73
Lee McPhail	1974–83
Bobby Brown	1984–94
Gene Budig	1994–99

Note: League president jobs were eliminated after the 1999 season.

NBA

Commissioner	Tenure
Maurice Podoloff	1949–63
Walter Kennedy	1963–75
Larry O'Brien	1975–84
David Stern	1984–

NFL

President	Tenure
Jim Thorpe	1920
Joe Carr	1921–39
Carl Storck	1939–41

Commissioner	
Elmer Layden	1941–46
Bert Bell*	1946–59
Austin Gunsel	1959–60
Pete Rozelle	1960–89
Paul Tagliabue	1989-2006
Roger Goodell	2006–

NHL

President	Tenure
Frank Calder*	1917–43
Red Dutton	1943–46
Clarence Campbell	1946–77
John Ziegler	1977–92
Gil Stein	1992–93

Commissioner	
Gary Bettman	1993–

NCAA

President	Tenure
Walter Byers	1951–88
Dick Schultz	1988–93
Cedric Dempsey	1993–2002
Myles Brand	2003–

Note: Office was known as Executive Director until 1998.

IOC

President	Tenure
Demetrius Vikelas, Greece	1894–96
Baron Pierre de Coubertin, France	1896–1925
Count Henri de Baillet-Latour, Belgium	1925–42
Vacant	1942–46
J. Sigfried Edstrom, Sweden	1946–52
Avery Brundage, USA	1952–72
Lord Michael Killanin, Ireland	1972–80
Juan Antonio Samaranch, Spain	1980–2001
Jacques Rogge, Belgium	2001–

Pro Stadium Naming Rights

Names like Dodger Stadium, Fenway Park and Lambeau Field are a dying breed, as owners continue to sell their venues' naming rights to the highest bidder. Listed are the most lucrative sponsorship deals to date, ranked by the total amount over the life of the contract. Totals are in millions. As of Sept. 30, 2007. **Source:** *Street & Smith's SportsBusiness Journal* research.

	Facility	Sponsor	Home Teams	Price	Years	Avg/Yr	Expires
1	Citi Field#, Queens	Citigroup	Mets	$400.0†	20	$20.00	2028
	Barclays Center#, Brooklyn	Barclays	Nets	400.0†	20	20.00	2028
3	Reliant Stadium, Houston	Reliant Energy	Texans	300.0	30	10.00	2032
4	FedEx Field, Raljon, MD	Federal Express	Redskins	205.0	27	7.60	2025
5	American Airlines Center, Dallas	American Airlines	Mavericks, Stars	195.0	30	6.50	2030
6	Philips Arena, Atlanta	Royal Philips Electron.	Hawks, Thrashers	185.0	20	9.25	2019
7	Minute Maid Park, Houston	Minute Maid	Astros	170.0	28	6.07	2029
8	U. of Phoenix Stadium, Glendale	University of Phoenix	Cardinals	154.5	20	7.73	2025
9	Bank of America Stadium, Charlotte	Bank of America	Car. Panthers	140.0	20	7.00	2023
10	Lincoln Financial Field, Phila.	Lincoln Financial Group	Eagles	139.6	20	6.98	2022
11	Nationwide Arena, Columbus	Nationwide Insurance	Blue Jackets	135.0		indefinitely	
12	Lucas Oil Stadium*, Indianapolis	Lucas Oil Products	Colts	121.5	20	6.08	2028
13	Invesco Field at Mile High, Denver	Invesco Funds	Broncos	120.0	20	6.00	2021
	TD Banknorth Garden, Boston	TD Banknorth	Bruins, Celtics	120.0	20	6.00	2025
	Cisco Field@, Fremont	Cisco Systems	A's	120.0	30	4.00	2040
16	Staples Center, Los Angeles	Staples	Lakers, Clippers, LA Kings	116.0	20	5.80	2019
17	Prudential Center, Newark	Prudential	Devils	105.3	20	5.27	2026
18	Citizens Bank Park, Philadelphia	Citizens Bank	Phillies	95.0	25	3.80	2029
	Toyota Center, Houston	Toyota	Rockets	95.0	20	4.75	2022
20	FedEx Forum, Memphis	Federal Express	Grizzlies	90.0	23	3.91	2026
	Gillette Stadium, Foxborough, MA	Gillette	Patriots	90.0	15	6.00	2016
22	Gaylord Ent. Center, Memphis	Gaylord Entertainment	Predators	80.0	20	4.00	2018
	RBC Center, Raleigh	RBC Centura Banks	Hurricanes	80.0	20	4.00	2022
24	Qwest Field, Seattle	Qwest Communications	Seahawks	75.0	15	5.00	2018
	Great American Ball Park, Cincinnati	Great American Ins.	Reds	75.0	30	2.50	2032
	M&T Bank Stadium, Baltimore	M&T Bank	Ravens	75.0	15	5.00	2017
	Xcel Energy Center, St. Paul	Xcel Energy	Wild	75.0	25	3.00	2024

† estimated.　　*scheduled to open in 2008.　　#scheduled to open in 2009.　　@scheduled to open in 2011.

Television Rights

Major sports and their television deals as of Sept. 30, 2007.

League	Network	Yrs (Ends)	Amount
NFL	ESPN (MNF)	8 (2013)	$8.8 billion
	NBC (Sun. nights)	6 (2011)	3.6 billion
	FOX (Sundays)	6 (2011)	4.4 billion
	CBS (Sundays)	6 (2011)	3.7 billion
	DirecTV (Sundays)	5 (2010)	3.5 billion
NBA	ABC/ESPN	6 (2008)*	$2.4 billion
	TNT	6 (2008)*	2.2 billion
MLB	ESPN	8 (2013)	2.368 billion
	FOX	7 (2013)	undisclosed
	TBS	7 (2013)	undisclosed

League	Network	Yrs (Ends)	Amount
NHL	NBC	2 (2008)	— †
	Versus	2 (2008)	$135 million
NCAA Men's Hoops Tournament	CBS	11 (2013)	$6 billion
NCAA Women's Hoops Tournament	ESPN	11 (2013)	$200 million@
NCAA Football BCS	ABC	8 (2014)	$300 million%
	FOX	6 (2010)	320 million%
NASCAR	FOX, TNT ABC, ESPN, SPEED	8 (2014)	$4.48 billion
Olympics	NBC	13 (2008)	$3.5 billion #
	NBC	9 (2012)	2.2 billion #
PGA Tour	CBS, NBC	6 (2012)	undisclosed
	The Golf Channel	15 (2021)	undisclosed

Super Bowl TV Rights

2007	CBS	2009	NBC	2011	FOX
2008	FOX	2010	CBS	2012	NBC

* In June, 2007, the NBA extended its deals with ESPN/ABC and TNT for an additional eight years through 2016. While the deal is said to be worth a total of $7.4 billion ($930 million per year), the breakdown has not yet been disclosed.

† NBC and the NHL agreed to a deal whereby the two entities share advertising revenues. NBC paid no rights fees.

@ Also included are all rights to the College World Series and various other NCAA championships.

% ABC and the Rose Bowl agreed to an eight-year deal (2007-2014) to include eight Rose Bowls and two other BCS title games. FOX and the BCS inked a deal worth an estimated $320 million which gives them rights to the Fiesta, Orange and Sugar bowls from 2007-10 and the BCS National Championship Game from 2007-09.

NBC paid approximately $3.5 billion for exclusive rights to the 1996 Summer Games (Atlanta), the 2000 Summer Games (Sydney), the 2002 Winter Games (Salt Lake City), the 2004 Summer Games (Athens), the 2006 Winter Games (Turin) and the 2008 Summer Games (Beijing). In July 2003, NBC announced a deal worth $2.2 billion which also gave them rights to the 2010 Winter Games (Vancouver) and the 2012 Summer Games (London).

Note: The NFL and NBA also have league-owned channels. The NFL Network shows preseason games, as well as an eight-game regular season package. NBA TV will offer 96 NBA regular season games during the 2007-08 season.

AWARDS

The Peabody Award

Presented annually since 1940 for outstanding achievement in radio and television broadcasting. Named after Georgia banker and philanthropist George Foster Peabody, the awards are administered by the Henry W. Grady College of Journalism and Mass Communication at the University of Georgia.

Television

Year

1960 **CBS** for coverage of 1960 Winter and Summer Olympic Games

1966 ABC's **"Wide World of Sports"** (for Outstanding Achievement in Promotion of International Understanding).

1968 **ABC Sports** coverage of both the 1968 Winter and Summer Olympic Games.

1972 **ABC Sports** coverage of the 1972 Summer Olympics in Munich.

1973 **Joe Garagiola** of NBC Sports (for "The Baseball World of Joe Garagiola").

1976 **ABC Sports** coverage of both the 1976 Winter and Summer Olympic Games.

1984 **Roone Arledge**, president of ABC News & Sports (for significant contributions to news and sports programming).

1986 **WFAA-TV**, Dallas for its investigation of the Southern Methodist University football program.

1988 **Jim McKay** of ABC Sports (for pioneering efforts and career accomplishments in the world of TV sports).

1991 **CBS Sports** coverage of the 1991 Masters golf tournament
    & **HBO Sports** and **Black Canyon Productions** for the baseball special "When It Was A Game."

1995 **Kartemquin Educational Films** and **KTCA-TV** in St. Paul, MN, presented on PBS for "Hoop Dreams"
    & **Turner Original Productions** for the baseball special "Hank Aaron: Chasing the Dream."

1996 **HBO Sports** for its documentary "The Journey of the African-American Athlete"
    & **Bud Greenspan**, a personal award for excellence in chronicling the Olympic Games.

1997 **HBO Pictures** and **The Thomas Carter Company** for the original movie "Don King: Only in America."

1998 **KTVX-TV**, Salt Lake City for its investigation into the policies and practices of the IOC during the Olympic bribery scandal & **HBO Sports** for its ongoing series of sports documentaries.

1999 **WCPO-TV**, Cincinnati for its investigation of fraud and misrepresentation in the construction of new sports stadiums, **HBO Sports** for its documentary "Dare to Compete: The Struggle of Women in Sports," and its documentary "Fists of Freedom: The Story of the '68 Summer Games" & **ESPN** for its "SportsCentury" series.

2000 **HBO Sports** for its documentary "Ali-Frazier 1: One Nation...Divisible."

2001 **The Ciesla Foundation** and **Cinemax** for the documentary "The Life and Times of Hank Greenberg."

2002 **ESPN** for "The Complete Angler," its documentary celebrating nature, art and fly-fishing.

2005 **Showtime** and **Red Rock Entertainment** for the original movie "Edge of America," about an African-American teacher who agrees to coach the girls basketball team at an American Indian-reservation school in Utah.

2006 **CBS News** for its "60 Minutes" segment on the allegations of rape against Duke University lacrosse players and its role in stopping a prosecutorial rush to judgment, **HBO Sports** for its sports biography, "Billie Jean King: Portrait of a Pioneer," & **NBC Universal Television Studio** in association with **Imagine Entertainment** and **Film 44** for its dramatic series, "Friday Night Lights," based around high-school football in a Texas town.

Radio

Year

1974 **WSB** radio in Atlanta for "Henry Aaron: A Man with a Mission."

1991 **Red Barber** of National Public Radio (for his six decades as a broadcaster and his 10 years as a commentator on NPR's "Morning Edition").

National Emmy Awards
Sports Programming

Presented by the Academy of Television Arts and Sciences since 1948. Eligibility period covered the calendar year from 1948-57 and since 1988. Note that due to space constraints, not every award is listed below.

Multiple major award winners: ABC "Wide World of Sports" (20), ESPN "SportsCenter," NFL Films Football coverage and HBO "Real Sports with Bryant Gumbel" (15); NBC Olympics coverage (11); CBS NFL Football coverage (10); ABC Olympics coverage, ABC "Monday Night Football" and and FOX MLB coverage (9); ESPN "Outside the Lines" (8); ESPN "GameDay/ Sunday NFL Countdown and CBS NCAA Basketball coverage (6); CBS "NFL Today" (5); ESPN "SportsCentury" series and NBC Ironman Triathlon coverage (4); ABC "The American Sportsman," ABC Indianapolis 500 coverage, CBS Golf coverage, CBS Tour de France coverage, FOX "NFL Sunday," HBO "Inside the NFL" and The NBA on TNT (3); ABC Kentucky Derby coverage, ABC "Sportsbeat," Bud Greenspan Olympic specials, CBS Olympics coverage, ESPN "Speedworld," ESPN Sunday Night Football, ESPN Wimbledon coverage, MTV Sports series, The NBA on NBC and NBC World Series coverage (2).

1949
Coverage—"Wrestling" (KTLA, Los Angeles)

1950
Program—"Rams Football" (KNBH-TV, Los Angeles)

1954
Program—"Gillette Cavalcade of Sports" (NBC)

1965-66
Programs—"Wide World of Sports" (ABC), "Shell's Wonderful World of Golf" (NBC) and "CBS Golf Classic" (CBS)

1966-67
Program—"Wide World of Sports" (ABC)

1967-68
Program—"Wide World of Sports" (ABC)

1968-69

Program—"1968 Summer Olympics" (ABC)

1969-70

Programs—"NFL Football" (CBS) and "Wide World of Sports" (ABC)

1970-71

Program—"Wide World of Sports" (ABC)

1971-72

Program—"Wide World of Sports" (ABC)

1972-73

News Special—"Coverage of Munich Olympic Tragedy" (ABC)
Sports Programs—"1972 Summer Olympics" (ABC) and "Wide World of Sports" (ABC)

1973-74

Program—"Wide World of Sports" (ABC)

1974-75

Non-Edited Program— "Jimmy Connors vs. Rod Laver Tennis Challenge" (CBS)
Edited Program— "Wide World of Sports" (ABC)

1975-76

Live Special—"1975 World Series: Cincinnati vs. Boston" (NBC)
Live Series—"NFL Monday Night Football" (ABC)
Edited Specials—"1976 Winter Olympics" (ABC) and "Triumph and Tragedy: The Olympic Experience" (ABC)
Edited Series—"Wide World of Sports" (ABC)

1976-77

Live Special—"1976 Summer Olympics" (ABC)
Live Series—"The NFL Today/NFL Football" (CBS)
Edited Special—"1976 Summer Olympics Preview" (ABC)
Edited Series—"The Olympiad" (PBS)

1977-78

Live Special—"Muhammad Ali vs. Leon Spinks Heavyweight Championship Fight" (CBS)
Live Series—"The NFL Today/NFL Football" (CBS)
Edited Special—"The Impossible Dream: Ballooning Across the Atlantic" (CBS)
Edited Series—"The Way It Was" (PBS)

1978-79

Live Special—"Super Bowl XIII: Pittsburgh vs Dallas" (NBC)
Live Series—"NFL Monday Night Football" (ABC)
Edited Special—"Spirit of '78: The Flight of Double Eagle II" (ABC)
Edited Series—"The American Sportsman" (ABC)

1979-80

Live Special—"1980 Winter Olympics" (ABC)
Live Series—"NCAA College Football" (ABC)
Edited Special—"Gossamer Albatross: Flight of Imagination" (CBS)
Edited Series—"NFL Game of the Week" (NFL Films)

1980-81

Live Special—"1981 Kentucky Derby" (ABC)
Live Series—"PGA Golf Tour" (CBS)
Edited Special—"Wide World of Sports 20th Anniversary Show" (ABC)
Edited Series—"The American Sportsman" (ABC)

1981-82

Live Special—"1982 NCAA Basketball Final: North Carolina vs Georgetown" (CBS)
Live Series—"NFL Football" (CBS)
Edited Special—"1982 Indianapolis 500" (ABC)
Edited Series—"Wide World of Sports" (ABC)

1982-83

Live Special—"1982 World Series: St. Louis vs Milwaukee" (NBC)
Live Series—"NFL Football" (CBS)
Edited Special—"Wimbledon '83" (NBC)
Edited Series—"Wide World of Sports" (ABC)
Journalism—"ABC Sportsbeat" (ABC)

1983-84

No awards given

1984-85

Live Special—"1984 Summer Olympics" (ABC)
Live Series—No award given
Edited Special—"Road to the Super Bowl '85" (NFL Films)
Edited Series—"The American Sportsman" (ABC)
Journalism—"ABC Sportsbeat" (ABC), "CBS Sports Sunday" (CBS), Dick Schaap features (ABC) and 1984 Summer Olympic features (ABC)

1985-86

No awards given

1986-87

Live Special—"1987 Daytona 500" (CBS)
Live Series—"NFL Football" (CBS)
Edited Special—"Wide World of Sports 25th Anniversary Special" (ABC)
Edited Series—"Wide World of Sports" (ABC)

1987-88

Live Special—"1987 Kentucky Derby" (ABC)
Live Series—"NFL Monday Night Football" (ABC)
Edited Special—"Paris-Roubaix Bike Race" (CBS)
Edited Series—"Wide World of Sports" (ABC)

1988

Live Special—"1988 Summer Olympics" (NBC)
Live Series—"1988 NCAA Basketball" (CBS)
Edited Special—"Road to the Super Bowl '88" (NFL Films)
Edited Series—"Wide World of Sports" (ABC)
Studio Show—"NFL GameDay" (ESPN)
Journalism—1988 Summer Olympic reporting (NBC)

1989

Live Special—"1989 Indianapolis 500" (ABC)
Live Series—"NFL Monday Night Football" (ABC)
Edited Special—"Trans-Antarctical The International Expedition" (ABC)
Edited Series—"This is the NFL" (NFL Films)
Studio Show—"NFL Today" (CBS)
Journalism—1989 World Series Game 3 earthquake coverage (ABC)

National Emmy Awards (Cont.)

1990

Live Special—"1990 Indianapolis 500" (ABC)
Live Series—"1990 NCAA Basketball Tournament" (CBS)
Edited Special—"Road to Super Bowl XXIV" (NFL Films)
Edited Series—"Wide World of Sports" (ABC)
Studio Show—"SportsCenter" (ESPN)
Journalism—"Outside the Lines: The Autograph Game" (ESPN)

1991

Live Special—"1991 NBA Finals: Chicago vs LA Lakers" (NBC)
Live Series—"1991 NCAA Basketball Tournament" (CBS)
Edited Special—"Wide World of Sports 30th Anniversary Special" (ABC)
Edited Series—"This is the NFL" (NFL Films)
Studio Show—"NFL GameDay" (ESPN) and "NFL Live" (NBC)
Journalism—"Outside the Lines: Steroids–Whatever It Takes" (ESPN)

1992

Live Special—"1992 Breeders' Cup" (NBC)
Live Series—"1992 NCAA Basketball Tournament" (CBS)
Edited Special—"1992 Summer Olympics" (NBC)
Edited Series—"MTV Sports" (MTV)
Studio Show—"The NFL Today" (CBS)
Journalism—"Outside the Lines: Portraits in Black and White" (ESPN)

1993

Live Special—"1993 World Series" (CBS)
Live Series—"Monday Night Football" (ABC)
Edited Special—"Road to the Super Bowl" (NFL Films)
Edited Series—"This is the NFL" (NFL Films)
Studio Show—"The NFL Today" (CBS)
Journalism (TIE)—"Outside the Lines: Mitch Ivey Feature" (ESPN) and "SportsCenter: University of Houston Football" (ESPN).
Feature—"Arthur Ashe: His Life, His Legacy" (NBC).

1994

Live Special—"NHL Stanley Cup Finals" (ESPN)
Live Series—"Monday Night Football" (ABC)
Edited Special—"Lillehammer '94: 16 Days of Glory" (Disney/Cappy Productions)
Edited Series—"MTV Sports" (MTV)
Studio Show—"NFL GameDay" (ESPN)
Journalism—"1994 Winter Olympic Games: Mossad feature" (CBS)
Feature (TIE)—"Heroes of Telemark" on Winter Olympic Games (CBS); and "SportsCenter: Vanderbilt running back Brad Gaines" (ESPN).

> #### "Baseball" Wins Prime Time Emmy
> Ken Burns's miniseries "Baseball" won the 1994 Emmy Award for Outstanding Informational Series. The nine-part documentary aired from Sept. 18-28, 1994 and ran more than 18 hours, drawing the largest audience in PBS history.

1995

Live Special—"Cal Ripken 2131" (ESPN)
Live Series—"ESPN Speedworld" (ESPN)
Edited Special (quick turn-around)—"Outside the Lines: Playball–Opening Day in America" (ESPN)
Edited Special (long turn-around)—"Lillehammer, an Olympic Diary" (CBS)
Edited Series—"NFL Films Presents" (NFL Films)
Studio Show (TIE)—"NFL GameDay" (ESPN) and "FOX NFL Sunday"(FOX)
Journalism—"Real Sports with Bryant Gumbel: Broken Promises" (HBO)
Feature (TIE)—"SportsCenter: Jerry Quarry" (ESPN) and "Real Sports with Bryant Gumbel: Coach" (HBO).

1996

Live Special—"1996 World Series" (FOX)
Live Series—"ESPN Speedworld" (ESPN)
Edited Special—"Football America" (TNT/NFL Films)
Edited Series—"NFL Films Presents" (NFL Films)
Live Event Turnaround—"The Centennial Olympic Games" (NBC)
Studio Show—"SportsCenter" (ESPN)
Journalism—"Outside the Lines: AIDS in Sports" (ESPN)
Feature—"Real Sports with Bryant Gumbel: 1966 Texas Western NCAA Champs" (HBO).

1997

Live Special—"The NBA Finals" (NBC)
Live Series—"NFL Monday Night Football" (ABC)
Edited Special—"Ironman Triathlon World Championship" (NBC/World Triathlon Corporation)
Edited Series—"NFL Films Presents" (NFL Films)
Live Event Turnaround—"Outside The Lines: Inside The Kentucky Derby" (ESPN)
Studio Show—"FOX NFL Sunday" (FOX)
Journalism—"Real Sports with Bryant Gumbel: Pros and Cons" (HBO)
Feature—"NFL Films Presents: Eddie George" (NFL Films).

1998

Live Special—"McGwire's 62nd Home Run Game" (FOX)
Live Series—"NBC Golf Tour" (NBC)
Edited Special—"A Cinderella Season: The Lady Vols Fight Back" (HBO)
Edited Series—"Real Sports with Bryant Gumbel" (HBO)
Live Event Turnaround—"Wimbledon '98" (NBC)
Studio Show—"FOX NFL Sunday" (FOX)
Journalism (TIE)—"Real Sports with Bryant Gumbel: Winning At All Costs" (HBO) and "Real Sports with Bryant Gumbel: Diamond Bucks" (HBO)
Feature—"NFL Films Presents: Steve Mariucci" (ESPN2 and NFL Films).

1999

Live Special—"2000 MLB All-Star Game" (FOX)
Live Series—"MLB Regular Season" (FOX)
Edited Special—"Ironman Triathlon World Championship" (NBC)
Edited Series—"SportsCentury: 50 Greatest Athletes" (ESPN)
Live Event Turnaround—"The World Track & Field Championships" (NBC)
Studio Show—"MLB Pre-Game Show" (FOX)
Journalism—"Real Sports with Bryant Gumbel: Fake Golf Clubs" (HBO)
Feature—"NFL Films Presents: Lt. Kalsu" (ESPN2)

2000

Live Special—"2000 World Series" (FOX)
Live Series—"NFL Sunday Night Football" (ESPN)
Edited Special—"Hoops and Hoosiers: The Story of the Final Four 2000" (CBS)
Edited Series—"SportsCentury: The Top 50 & Beyond" (ESPN)
Live Event Turnaround—"The Games of the XXVII Olympiad" (NBC)
Studio Show—"FOX NFL Sunday" (FOX)
Journalism—"Real Sports with Bryant Gumbel: Dominican Free-For-All" (HBO)
Feature—"The Games of the XXVII Olympiad" (NBC)

2001

Live Special—"2001 World Series" (FOX)
Live Series—"NASCAR on FOX" (FOX)
Edited Special—"ABC's Wide World of Sports 40th Anniversary Special" (ABC)
Edited Series—"SportsCentury" (ESPN Classic)
Live Event Turnaround—"Tour de France" (CBS)
Studio Show—Weekly—"Sunday NFL Countdown" (ESPN)
Studio Show—Daily—"Inside the NBA" (TNT/TBS)
Journalism—"Real Sports with Bryant Gumbel: Amare Stoudemire" (HBO)
Feature—"NFL Films Presents: Gerry Faust—The Golden Dream" (ESPN2)
Documentary—"Do You Believe in Miracles? The Story of the 1980 U.S. Hockey Team" (HBO)

2002

Live Special—"XIX Olympic Winter Games" (NBC)
Live Series—"The NBA on NBC" (NBC)
Edited Special—"America's Heroes: The Bravest vs. The Finest" (NBC)
Edited Series—"Real Sports with Bryant Gumbel" (HBO)
Live Event Turnaround—"Tour de France" (CBS)
Studio Show—Weekly—"Inside the NFL" (HBO & NFL Films)
Studio Show—Daily—"Baseball Tonight" (ESPN)
Journalism—"Outside the Lines, Weekly: Eligibility for Sale" (ESPN) and "Outside the Lines, Weekly: Iraqi Atletes, Tales of Torture" (ESPN)
Long Feature—"SportsCenter: Flight 93" (ESPN)
Short Feature—"SportsCenter: Chris Paul" (ESPN), "XIX Olympic Winter Games: Bill Johnson" (NBC) and "XIX Olympic Winter Games: The Sheas" (NBC)
Documentary—"Our Greatest Hopes, Our Worst Fears: The Tragedy of the Munich Games" (ABC)

2003

Live Special— "MLB on FOX: Post Season" (FOX)
Live Series— "ESPN NFL Sunday Night Football" (ESPN)
Edited Special— "Ironman Triathlon World Championship" (NBC/World Triathlon Corporation)
Edited Series/Anthology—Legendary Nights" (HBO)
Live Event Turnaround—"Tour de France" (CBS)
Studio Show—Weekly—"Sunday NFL Countdown" (ESPN)
Studio Show—Daily—"SportsCenter" (ESPN)
Journalism—"Real Sports with Bryant Gumbel: Marcus Dixon" (HBO)
Editing—"Jim McKay — My World in My Words " (HBO)
The Dick Schaap Outstanding Writing Award— "Wimbledon — Where is Wimbledon?" (ESPN)
Long Feature—"NFL Films Presents on The NFL Network: Big Charlie's" (NFL Network/NFL Films) and "Real Sports with Bryant Gumbel: Alex Zanardi" (HBO)
Short Feature—"SportsCenter: Picking Up Butch" (ESPN)
Documentary—"The Curse of the Bambino" (HBO/Black Canyon Productions/Clear Channel Entertainment Television)

2004

Live Special—"The Masters" (CBS)
Live Series—"ABC's NFL Monday Night Football" (ABC)
Edited Special—"Ironman Triathlon World Championship" (NBC/Ironman Productions)
Edited Series/Anthology—"Real Sports with Bryant Gumbel" (HBO)
Live Event Turnaround—"The Games of the XXVIII Olympiad" (NBC)
Studio Show—Weekly—"Inside the NFL" (HBO)
Studio Show—Daily—"SportsCenter" (ESPN)
Journalism—"Real Sports with Bryant Gumbel: Sport of Sheikhs" (HBO)
Editing (TIE)—"NFL Films Presents on NFL Network: Michael Zagaris" (NFL Network/NFL Films) and "Wimbledon on NBC: Patrick Stewart Tease and Closing Thoughts" (NBC)
The Dick Schaap Outstanding Writing Award— "Wimbledon on ESPN2—Wimbledon Reflections" (ESPN2)
Long Feature—"SportsCenter: Ben Comen" (ESPN)
Short Feature—"The Super Bowl Today: NFL Quarterbacks" (CBS)
Documentary—"The Games of the XXVIII Olympiad: Stylianos Kryiakides, The Journey of a Warrior" (NBC)

2005

Live Special—"134th British Open Championship" (TNT)
Live Series—"NASCAR on FOX" (FOX)
Edited Special—"CostasNOW: David Robinson—A Man In Full" (HBO)
Edited Series/Anthology—"SportsCentury" (ESPN Classic)
Live Event Turnaround—"Best of Winter X Games Nine" (ABC & ESPN Productions)
Studio Show—Weekly—"Inside the NFL" (HBO)
Studio Show—Daily—"Inside the NBA, Playoffs" (TNT)
Journalism—"Real Sports with Bryant Gumbel: Soccer Racism" (HBO)
Editing—"PGA Tour Sunday: Kevin Hall" (USA & PGA Tour Productions)
The Dick Schaap Outstanding Writing Award— "SportsCenter: Finding Bobby Fischer" (Jeremy Schaap, ESPN)
Long Feature—"Real Sports with Bryant Gumbel: The Hoyts" (HBO)
Short Feature—"Timeless: Lama Kunga" (ESPN2 & Red Line Films)
Documentary—"Rhythym in the Rope" (ESPN2)

2006

Live Special— "MLB on FOX: Post Season" (FOX)
Live Series— "NASCAR on TNT & NBC" (TNT/NBC)
Edited Special— "2006 Ford Ironman World Championships" (NBC/Ironman Productions)
Edited Series/Anthology— "Real Sports with Bryant Gumbel" (HBO)
Live Event Turnaround— "Beyond the Wheel" (NASCAR Images/Speed)
Studio Show—Weekly— "Sunday NFL Countdown" (ESPN)
Studio Show—Daily— "Inside the NBA – Playoffs" (TNT)
Journalism— "Real Sports with Bryant Gumbel: Uninsured" (HBO)
Editing—"NBA on TNT" (TNT)
The Dick Schaap Outstanding Writing Award— "One of a Kind: The Rise and Fall of Stu Ungar" (ESPN/Red Line Films)
Long Feature— "SportsCenter: Travis Roy" (ESPN)
Short Feature— "NCAA Men's Basketball Tournament" (CBS)
Documentary— "One of a Kind: The Rise and Fall of Stu Ungar" (ESPN/Red Line Films)

Sportscasters of the Year
National Emmy Awards

An Emmy Award for Sportscasters was first introduced in 1968 and given for Outstanding Host/Commentator for the 1967-68 TV season. Two awards, one for Outstanding Host or Play-by-Play and the other for Outstanding Analyst, were first presented in 1981 for the 1980-81 season. Three awards, for Outstanding Studio Host, Play-by-Play and Studio Analyst, have been given since the 1993 season, and one more, Sports Event Analyst, was added in 1997.

Multiple winners: Bob Costas and John Madden (15); Jim McKay (9); Cris Collinsworth (8); Joe Buck (6); Al Michaels (5); Dick Enberg (4); Keith Jackson and Tim McCarver (3); Terry Bradshaw, James Brown, Ernie Johnson and Joe Morgan (2). Note that Jim McKay has won a total of 12 Emmy awards: eight for Host/Commentator, one for Host/Play-by-Play, two for Sports Writing and one for News Commentary.

Season	Host/Commentator	Season	Host/Play-by-Play	Season	Analyst
1967-68	Jim McKay, ABC	1980-81	Dick Enberg, NBC	1980-81	Dick Button, ABC
1968-69	No award	1981-82	Jim McKay, ABC	1981-82	John Madden, CBS
1969-70	No award	1982-83	Dick Enberg, NBC	1982-83	John Madden, CBS
1970-71	Jim McKay, ABC	1983-84	No award	1983-84	No award
	& Don Meredith, ABC	1984-85	George Michael, NBC	1984-85	No award
1971-72	No award	1985-86	No award	1985-86	No award
1972-73	Jim McKay, ABC	1986-87	Al Michaels, ABC	1986-87	John Madden, CBS
1973-74	Jim McKay, ABC	1987-88	Bob Costas, NBC	1987-88	John Madden, CBS
1974-75	Jim McKay, ABC	1988	Bob Costas, NBC	1988	John Madden, CBS
1975-76	Jim McKay, ABC	1989	Al Michaels, ABC	1989	John Madden, CBS
1976-77	Frank Gifford, ABC	1990	Dick Enberg, NBC	1990	John Madden, CBS
1977-78	Jack Whitaker, CBS	1991	Bob Costas, NBC	1991	John Madden, CBS
1978-79	Jim McKay, ABC	1992	Bob Costas, NBC	1992	John Madden, CBS
1979-80	Jim McKay, ABC				

Studio Host

Year		Year		Year	
1993	Bob Costas, NBC	1998	James Brown, FOX	2002	Bob Costas, HBO/NBC
1994	Bob Costas, NBC	1999	James Brown, FOX	2003	Bob Costas, HBO/NBC
1995	Bob Costas, NBC	2000	Bob Costas, NBC	2004	Bob Costas, HBO/NBC
1996	Bob Costas, NBC	2001	Bob Costas, HBO &	2005	Bob Costas, HBO/NBC
1997	Dan Patrick, ESPN		Ernie Johnson, TNT/TBS	2006	Ernie Johnson, TNT

Play-by-Play

Year		Year		Year	
1993	Dick Enberg, NBC	1998	Keith Jackson, ABC	2003	Joe Buck, FOX
1994	Keith Jackson, ABC	1999	Joe Buck, FOX	2004	Joe Buck, FOX
1995	Al Michaels, ABC	2000	Al Michaels, ABC	2005	Joe Buck, FOX
1996	Keith Jackson, ABC	2001	Joe Buck, FOX	2006	Al Michaels, ABC/NBC
1997	Bob Costas, NBC	2002	Joe Buck, FOX		

Studio Analyst

Year		Year		Year	
1993	Billy Packer, CBS	1998	Cris Collinsworth, HBO/FOX	2003	Cris Collinsworth, HBO
1994	John Madden, FOX	1999	Terry Bradshaw, FOX	2004	Cris Collinsworth, HBO
1995	John Madden, FOX	2000	Steve Lyons, FOX	2005	Cris Collinsworth, HBO
1996	Howie Long, FOX	2001	Terry Bradshaw, FOX	2006	Cris Collinsworth, HBO/NBC
1997	Cris Collinsworth, HBO/NBC	2002	Cris Collinsworth, HBO		

Sports Events Analyst

Year		Year		Year	
1997	Joe Morgan, ESPN	2001	Tim McCarver, FOX	2005	John Madden, ABC
1998	John Madden, FOX	2002	Tim McCarver, FOX	2006	Cris Collinsworth, NFL Network
1999	John Madden, FOX	2003	John Madden, ABC		
2000	Tim McCarver, FOX	2004	Joe Morgan, ESPN		

Lifetime Achievement Emmy Award

Year		Year		Year		Year	
1989	Jim McKay	1994	Howard Cosell	1999	Jack Buck	2004	Chet Simmons
1990	Lindsey Nelson	1995	Vin Scully	2000	Dick Enberg	2005	Bud Greenspan
1991	Curt Gowdy	1996	Frank Gifford	2001	Herb Granath	2006	Don Ohlmeyer
1992	Chris Schenkel	1997	Jim Simpson	2002	Roone Arledge*		
1993	Pat Summerall	1998	Keith Jackson	2003	Ed and Steve Sabol		

*Arledge is the only recipient of two Lifetime Achievement Emmy Awards. In addition to sports, he won the lifetime award for "News and Documentary" in 2002.

National Sportscasters and Sportswriters Assn. Award

Sportscaster of the Year presented annually since 1959 by the National Sportcasters and Sportswriters Association, based in Salisbury, N.C. Voting is done by NSSA members and selected national media.

Multiple winners: Bob Costas (8); Chris Berman (6) Keith Jackson (5); Joe Buck, Lindsey Nelson and Chris Schenkel (4); Dick Enberg, Al Michaels and Vin Scully (3); Curt Gowdy, Jim Nantz and Ray Scott (2).

Year		Year		Year		Year	
1959	Lindsey Nelson	1972	Keith Jackson	1984	John Madden	1997	Bob Costas
1960	Lindsey Nelson	1973	Keith Jackson	1985	Bob Costas	1998	Jim Nantz
1961	Lindsey Nelson	1974	Keith Jackson	1986	Al Michaels	1999	Dan Patrick
1962	Lindsey Nelson	1975	Keith Jackson	1987	Bob Costas	2000	Bob Costas
1963	Chris Schenkel	1976	Keith Jackson	1988	Bob Costas	2001	Chris Berman
1964	Chris Schenkel	1977	Pat Summerall	1989	Chris Berman	2002	Joe Buck
1965	Vin Scully	1978	Vin Scully	1990	Chris Berman	2003	Joe Buck
1966	Curt Gowdy	1979	Dick Enberg	1991	Bob Costas	2004	Joe Buck
1967	Chris Schenkel	1980	Dick Enberg	1992	Bob Costas	2005	Jim Nantz
1968	Ray Scott		& Al Michaels	1993	Chris Berman	2006	Joe Buck
1969	Curt Gowdy	1981	Dick Enberg	1994	Chris Berman		
1970	Chris Schenkel	1982	Vin Scully	1995	Bob Costas		
1971	Ray Scott	1983	Al Michaels	1996	Chris Berman		

The Pulitzer Prize

The Pulitzer Prizes for journalism, letters, drama and music have been presented annually since 1917 in the name of Joseph Pulitzer (1847-1911), the publisher of the *New York World*. Prizes are awarded by the president of Columbia University on the recommendation of a board of review. Sixteen Pulitzers have been awarded for newspaper sports reporting, sports commentary and sports photography.

News Coverage

1935 **Bill Taylor,** *NY Herald Tribune,* for his reporting on the 1934 America's Cup yacht races.

Special Citation

1952 **Max Kase,** *NY Journal-American,* for his reporting on the 1951 college basketball point-shaving scandal.

Meritorious Public Service

1954 **Newsday** (Garden City, N.Y.) for its expose of New York State's race track scandals and labor racketeering.

General Reporting

1956 **Arthur Daley,** *NY Times,* for his 1955 columns.

Investigative Reporting

1981 **Clark Hallas** & **Robert Lowe,** *(Tucson) Arizona Daily Star,* for their 1980 investigation of the University of Arizona athletic department.

1986 **Jeffrey Marx** & **Michael York,** Lexington (Ky.) *Herald-Leader,* for their 1985 investigation of the basketball program at the University of Kentucky and other major colleges.

Photography

1949 **Nat Fein,** *NY Herald Tribune,* for his photo, "Babe Ruth Bows Out."

1952 **John Robinson** & **Don Ultang,** *Des Moines* (Iowa) *Register and Tribune,* for their sequence of six pictures of the 1951 Drake-Oklahoma A&M football game, in which Drake's Johnny Bright had his jaw broken.

Specialized Reporting

1985 **Randall Savage** & **Jackie Crosby,** Macon (Ga.) *Telegraph and News,* for their 1984 investigation of athletics and academics at the University of Georgia and Georgia Tech.

Beat Reporting

2000 **George Dohrmann,** St. Paul (Min.) *Pioneer Press,* for his investigation that revealed academic fraud in the men's basketball program at the University of Minnesota.

Feature Writing

1997 **Lisa Pollak,** *Baltimore Sun,* for her story about baseball umpire John Hirschbeck dealing with the death of one son and the illness of another from the same disease.

Commentary

1976 **Red Smith,** *NY Times,* for his 1975 columns.

1981 **Dave Anderson,** *NY Times,* for his 1980 columns.

1990 **Jim Murray,** *LA Times,* for his 1989 columns.

Photography

1985 **The Photography Staff** of the *Orange County* (Calif.) *Register,* for their coverage of the 1984 Summer Olympics in Los Angeles.

1993 **William Snyder** & **Ken Geiger,** *The Dallas Morning News,* for their coverage of the 1992 Summer Olympics in Barcelona, Spain.

Red Smith Award

Presented annually by the Associated Press Sports Editors (APSE) to a person who has made "major contributions to sports journalism" and named in honor of the late newspaper columnist for the *New York Herald-Tribune* and *New York Times.*

Year		Year		Year	
1981	Red Smith, *NY Times*	1990	Dave Smith, *Dallas Morning News*	2000	Jerry Izenberg, *Newark Star Ledger*
1982	Jim Murray, *LA Times*	1991	Dave Kindred, *Nat'l Sports Daily*	2001	John Steadman, *Baltimore Sun*
1983	Shirley Povich, *Washington Post*	1992	Ed Storin, *Miami Herald*	2002	Dick Schaap, *ESPN*
1984	Fred Russell, *Nashville Banner*	1993	Tom McEwen, *Tampa Tribune*		*"The Sports Reporters"*
1985	Blackie Sherrod, *Dallas Morning News*	1994	Dave Anderson, *NY Times*	2003	George Solomon, *Washington Post*
		1995	Richard Sandler, *Newsday*	2004	Jimmy Cannon, NYC columnist
1986	Si Burick, *Dayton Daily News*	1996	Bill Dwyre, *LA Times*	2005	Mary Garber, *Winston-Salem Journal*
1987	Will Grimsley, AP	1997	Jerome Holtzman, *Chicago Tribune*		
1988	Furman Bisher, *Atlanta Journal*	1998	Sam Lacy, *Baltimore Afro-American*	2006	Joe McGuff, *Kansas City Star*
1989	Edwin Pope, *Miami Herald*	1999	Bud Collins, *Boston Globe*	2007	Van McKenzie, *Orlando Sentinel*

Sportswriter of the Year
NSSA Award

Presented annually since 1959 by the National Sportscasters and Sportswriters Association, based in Salisbury, N.C. Voting is done by NSSA members and selected national media.

Multiple winners: Jim Murray (14); Rick Reilly (11); Frank Deford (6); Red Smith (5); Will Grimsley (4); Peter Gammons (3).

Year		Year		Year	
1959	Red Smith, *NY Herald-Tribune*	1976	Jim Murray, *LA Times*	1993	Peter Gammons, *Boston Globe*
1960	Red Smith, *NY Herald-Tribune*	1977	Jim Murray, *LA Times*	1994	Rick Reilly, *Sports III.*
1961	Red Smith, *NY Herald-Tribune*	1978	Will Grimsley, *AP*	1995	Rick Reilly, *Sports III.*
1962	Red Smith, *NY Herald-Tribune*	1979	Jim Murray, *LA Times*	1996	Rick Reilly, *Sports III.*
1963	Arthur Daley, *NY Times*	1980	Will Grimsley, *AP*	1997	Dave Kindred, *The Sporting*
1964	Jim Murray, *LA Times*	1981	Will Grimsley, *AP*		*News*
1965	Red Smith, *NY Herald-Tribune*	1982	Frank Deford, *Sports III.*	1998	Mitch Albom, *Detroit Free Press*
1966	Jim Murray, *LA Times*	1983	Will Grimsley, *AP*	1999	Rick Reilly, *Sports III.*
1967	Jim Murray, *LA Times*	1984	Frank Deford, *Sports III.*	2000	Bob Ryan, *Boston Globe*
1968	Jim Murray, *LA Times*	1985	Frank Deford, *Sports III.*	2001	Rick Reilly, *Sports III.*
1969	Jim Murray, *LA Times*	1986	Frank Deford, *Sports III.*	2002	Rick Reilly, *Sports III.*
1970	Jim Murray, *LA Times*	1987	Frank Deford, *Sports III.*	2003	Rick Reilly, *Sports III.*
1971	Jim Murray, *LA Times*	1988	Frank Deford, *Sports III.*	2004	Rick Reilly, *Sports III.*
1972	Jim Murray, *LA Times*	1989	Peter Gammons, *Sports III.*	2005	Steve Rushin, *Sports III.*
1973	Jim Murray, *LA Times*	1990	Peter Gammons, *Boston Globe*	2006	Rick Reilly, *Sports III.*
1974	Jim Murray, *LA Times*	1991	Rick Reilly, *Sports III.*		
1975	Jim Murray, *LA Times*	1992	Rick Reilly, *Sports III.*		

Best Newspaper Sports Sections of 2006

Winners of the annual Associated Press Sports Editors contest for best daily and Sunday sports sections. Awards are divided into different categories, based on circulation figures. Selections are made by a committee of APSE members.

Circulation Over 250,000

Top 10 Daily		Top 10 Sunday	
Atlanta Journal-Constitution	*New York Times*	*Atlanta Journal-Constitution*	*Kansas City Star*
Dallas Morning News	*Orlando Sentinel*	*Boston Globe*	*Los Angeles Times*
Fort Worth Star-Telegram	*South Florida Sun-Sentinel*	*Chicago Sun-Times*	*Miami Herald*
Kansas City Star	*USA Today*	*Dallas Morning News*	*Minneapolis Star-Tribune*
Los Angeles Times	*Washington Post*	*Houston Chronicle*	*Orlando Sentinel*

Circulation 100,000-250,000

Top 10 Daily		Top 10 Sunday	
Charlotte Observer	*Pittsburgh Post-Gazette*	*Charlotte Observer*	*Raleigh News & Observer*
Columbus Dispatch	*Raleigh News & Observer*	*The State*	*St. Paul Pioneer Press*
Detroit News	*Riverside Press-Enterprise*	*(Columbia, SC)*	*San Antonio Express-News*
Hartford Courant	*St. Paul Pioneer Press*	*Hartford Courant*	*Seattle Times*
Palm Beach Post	*Seattle Times*	*Palm Beach Post*	*Tampa Tribune*
		Pittsburgh Post-Gazette	

Best Sportswriting of 2006

Winners of the annual Associated Press Sports Editors Contest for best sportswriting in 2006. Eventual winners were chosen from five finalists in each writing division. Selections are made by a committee of APSE members. Note the investigative writing division included all circulation categories.

Circulation over 250,000

Column:	Bill Plaschke, *Los Angeles Times*	**Explanatory:**	Eric Sharp, *Detroit Free Press*
Feature:	Mike Wise, *Washington Post*	**Project:**	Jodi Upton, Steve Wieberg, Michael
Breaking News:	Juliet Macur, *New York Times*		McCarthy, Steve Berkowitz and Kelly
Game story:	Kevin Manahan, *Newark Star-Ledger*		Whiteside, *USA Today*

Circulation 100,000-250,000

Column:	Geoff Calkins, *Memphis Commercial Appeal*	**Game story:**	Sam Weinman, *Westchester Journal News*
		Explanatory:	David Poole, *Charlotte Observer*
Feature:	Carlos Frias, *Palm Beach Post*	**Project:**	Greg Bishop, *Seattle Times*
Breaking News:	Jeff Darlington, *Palm Beach Post*		

All Categories

Investigative: Scott M. Reid, Robert Kuwada and Tony Saavedra, *Orange County Register*

INTERNATIONAL SPORTS

2006 / 2007 YEAR IN REVIEW

Disgraced champion **Marion Jones** wasn't smiling in 2007 when she handed back her Olympic medals.

SHAMED NAMES

While one confessed and the other maintained his innocence, both Marion Jones and Floyd Landis paid big prices in 2007.

TRUST NO ONE.

That was the lesson we learned in 2007 when we thought it couldn't get much worse in the world of sports.

Things were certainly easier when we could laugh at the old joke about the East German swimmers' manly appearance. But the joke isn't as funny when it's on us.

Now, no one would confuse American sprinter Marion Jones with a man. Her grace and feminine beauty were obvious to anyone who saw her compete at the 2000 Summer Olympics. And while her performance was certainly wondrous, for most observers it didn't quite reach the threshold of implausibility.

Now we know it's no wonder that no one could keep up with Jones in Sydney.

In a sad and humiliating end to such a legendary athletic career, the American hero came clean in October and admitted to taking the now infamous "clear" in the months leading up to and following the Sydney Games.

The banned performance-enhancing substance that Jones and others caught in the BALCO quicksand have taken may be the only thing transparent in the cloudy world of sports cheaters these days.

In a dust storm of alibis, excuses, cries of conspiracies and pleaded ignorance, universal skepticism is the only shelter.

Do you believe in miracles? No.

What tremendous performances in recent years are beyond reproach?

Certainly not Floyd Landis and his incredible comeback at the 2006 Tour de France. You may recall that Landis was practically left for dead in the late stages of the Tour when he climbed out of the grave and pulled the seemingly impossible comeback. His win, along with Lance Armstrong's dominant run, gave the United States it's eighth straight Tour de France title.

Landis was officially stripped of his title in 2007 when a three-man panel voted 2-1 to uphold the results of the French laboratory that decided he

Gerry Brown is Co-Editor of the ESPN Sports Almanac

AP/Wide World Photos

American track and field legend **Marion Jones** revealed that her unbelievable performance at the 2000 Summer Olympics was just that...not to be believed.

used a synthetic testosterone to achieve greatness.

Landis does retain one final shot at appeal to the Court of Arbirtration for Sport, pinning his hopes that it will find that his testers were careless enough in their handling of his specimen that a false positive result is a reasonable possibility.

And while rumors have dogged Armstrong and his so-called "too good to be true" accomplishments, he has been considered largely untainted in the eyes of the majority of fans and media.

Who wants to be a sports fan in a world where the whole legitimacy of world records and championships is questionable?

Can you imagine if fans thought baseball's all-time home run king or the Super Bowl champions cheated their ways into the record books? Or if it came out that a referee was on the take from gamblers to influence the outcome of games?

Oh. Wait. Nevermind.

Still, even in the total absence of real evidence any eye-popping accomplishments will be automatically accompanied by raised eyebrows for the foreseeable future.

But rewind the mental TiVo seven years to Sydney, Australia. Marion Jones and her mega-hyped bid for five gold medals were on sports pages everywhere.

She fell short and ended up with three gold (100, 200 and 4x400 relay) and two bronze (long jump and

American swimmming star
Michael Phelps continued to
rule the pool in 2007.

and American swimmer Michael Phelps and his attempt to make history in the global spotlight of Beijing. If he, as anticipated, destroys the competition, much like he did this year at the swimming world championships in Melbourne, Australia will the whispers commence?

Will he get the benefit of the doubt? Maybe. And he probably should when you take a close look at the other side of the coin.

Phelps (and Armstrong for that matter) has never tested positive for anything. And even the panel that voted to make Floyd Landis the first man in the 104-year history of the Tour de France to lose his title for doping took to task the French lab that performed the test for sloppy work.

By nearly all accounts the science of the testers is already well behind the science of the cheaters. When the testers are not procedurally rigorous, especially when the potential consequences of a positive test are so life-changing, it's horribly irresponsible at best and criminally negligent at worst.

Although it was seven years too late, Marion Jones did the honorable thing and handed back her Olympic medals from Sydney so that they can be awarded to the legitimate winners.

Not so fast.

Who finished second to Jones in the 100 meters in Sydney and is therefore in line to inherit the gold medal?

4x100 relay), nevertheless becoming the first female athlete to win five medals in a single Olympics.

Did many fans really think she was juicing?

Well, the signs were there.

In the midst of the Games it came to light that her husband at the time, Olympic shot putter C.J. Hunter had tested positive for steroids and faced a two-year ban. In a tearful press conference both Hunter and Jones denied knowing how it all could have happened.

Now fast forward to next summer

None other than Greek sprinter Katerina Thanou.

The same Katerina Thanou who was caught up in a drug scandal of her own when she missed a test on the eve of the 2004 Games in Athens, reportedly staged a motorcycle accident to serve as an alibi, then ultimately pulled out of the competition.

In the world of drug testing, a missed test is the same as a positive test, and she was suspended for two years.

Despite all that, assuming the International Olympic Committee vacates Jones' results, they will be forced into the awkward position of awarding Thanou, another cheater, the gold.

Other athletes that didn't get their moment in the spotlight thanks to Jones' ill-gotten gains may get the medals they've deserved all this time. But there is no getting back the glory they should have received Down Under in 2000.

Also some of the hidden victims of Jones' mea culpa are her own relay teammates. Jearl Miles-Clark, Monique Hennagan, Tasha Colander-Richardson and Andrea Anderson all won golds as part of the 4x400 meter relay squad in 2000. Chryste Gaines, Torri Edwards, Nanceen Perry and Passion Richardson were on the bronze medal-winning 4x100-meter relay team with Jones.

While both Edwards and Gaines have served doping bans since the 2000 Olympics it's a possibility, if not a certainty that the others were completely innocent bystanders that must face the likelihood of losing their medals because of all this.

The United States Olympic Committee has apologized for the entire affair and has promised to bring a clean team to Beijing in 2008.

These days, that'd be a miracle.

Biggest Stories of the Year in **International Sports**

10 Streak Struck. Kenenisa Bekele's amazing five-year win streak at the World Cross Country Championships ends. The 24-year-old Ethiopian dropped out on the last lap of the 12-kilometer men's race held in Mombasa, Kenya. Eritrean Zersenay Tadesse beat the competition and the 90-degree temps to win in 35:50.

09 18-year-old beats 19-year-old. Kate Ziegler smashes the 19-year old world record in the women's 1500-meter freestyle by nearly 10 seconds. Janet Evans set the previous mark in 1988 before Ziegler was born. Despite the amazing record-breaking performance in what Evans herself called "one of the greatest swims ever" Ziegler will not be the favorite in the women's 1500-meter freestyle at next year's Summer Games, because it's not an Olympic event.

08 24-year-old beats 25-year-old. Former High school phenom Alan Webb sets a new American record in the mile with a 3:46.91, besting the 25-year-old mark of 3:47.69 set by Steve Scott in 1982, the year before Webb's birth.

07 New Marathon Man. Under ideal conditions at the Berlin Marathon Ethiopia's Haile Gebrselassie, 34, runs a 2:04:26 and breaks the world marathon record held by his friend and rival Paul Tergat by 29 seconds.

06 Still World's Fastest Man. Two weeks after finishing a disappointing third at the track and field world championships in Osaka, Jamaican sprinter Asafa Powell finds a small bit of consolation when he breaks his own 100-meter world record by 0.03 seconds with a 9.74 in Rieti, Italy.

05 Gay Duo. American sprinter Tyson Gay pulls off the rare sprint double at the world track and field championships in Osaka, Japan winning gold in both the 100- and 200-meter dashes. Gay becomes just the third man in history to accomplish this rare feat following in the footsteps of Maurice Greene in 1999 and Justin Gatlin in 2005.

04 Floyd Destroyed. American cyclist Floyd Landis is officially stripped of his 2006 Tour de France title when a panel of arbitrators votes to reaffirm the positive test results that showed he used synthetic testosterone to fuel his improbable comeback victory in the late stages of the event.

03 Flat Tires. Spain's Alberto Contador beats a drug-depleted peleton to win the 2007 Tour de France. Contador seemed locked into second place until pack leader Michael Rasmussen of Denmark was ousted from competition with just five days to go in the month-long race for missing drug tests. The increasingly tainted race was already without Landis, the defending champion, and it lost, among many others, pre-race favorite Alexandre Vinokourov of Kazakhstan and Cristian Moreni of Italy when they failed doping tests of their own.

02 Pool Shark. Michael Phelps, 21, continues to eat up the competition and wins a meet record seven gold medals at the world swimming championships in Melbourne, Australia. Phelps breaks five world records along the way and looks well positioned to take another shot at Mark Spitz's record of seven Olympic golds next year in Beijing.

01 Say it ain't so, Jones. The American hero of the 2000 Summer Games in Sydney pleads guilty to lying to federal authorities investigating the BALCO case and comes clean, admitting to using "the clear" during her record-setting Olympic performance in 2000 in Sydney, Australia. Jones handed over the three gold and two bronze medals she won and made a tearful apology to her family, friends and fans.

2006-2007
Season in Review

SPORTS ALMANAC

TRACK & FIELD

2007 IAAF World Championships

The 11th IAAF World Championships in Athletics held in Osaka, Japan, Aug. 25 through Sept. 2, 2007. Note that (CR) indicates championship meet record.

Final Medal Leaders

		G	S	B	Total			G	S	B	Total
1	United States	14	4	8	26	5	Germany	2	2	3	7
2	Russia	4	9	3	16	6	Great Britain & N.I.	1	1	3	5
3	Kenya	5	3	5	13	7	Ethiopia	3	1	0	4
4	Jamaica	1	6	3	10	8	Eight countries tied with 3 medals each.				

MEN

Event		Time	
100 meters	Tyson Gay, USA	9.85	
200 meters	Tyson Gay, USA	19.76	CR
400 meters	Jeremy Wariner, USA	43.45	
800 meters	Alfred Kirwa Yego, KEN	1:47.09	
1500 meters	Bernard Lagat, USA	3:34.77	
5000 meters	Bernard Lagat, USA	13:45.87	
10,000 meters	Kenenisa Bekele, ETH	27:05.90	
Marathon	Luke Kibet, KEN	2:15:59	
4x100m relay	USA (Patton, Spearmon, Gay, Dixon)	37.78	
4x400m relay	USA (Merritt, Taylor, Williamson, Wariner)	2:55.56	
110m hurdles	Xiang Liu, CHN	12.95	
400m hurdles	Kerron Clement, USA	47.61	
3000m steeple	Brimin Kiprop Kipruto, KEN	8:13.82	
20k walk	Jefferson Perez, ECU	1:22:20	
50k walk	Nathan Deakes, AUS	3:43:53	
1500m wheelchair	Kurt Fearnley, AUS	3:26.30	

Event		Hgt/Dist
High Jump	Donald Thomas, BAH	7-8½
Pole Vault	Brad Walker, USA	19-2¾
Long Jump	Irving Saladino, PAN	28-1½
Triple Jump	Nelson Evora, POR	58-2½
Shot Put	Reese Hoffa, USA	72-3¾
Discus	Gerd Kanter, EST	226-2
Hammer	Ivan Tikhon, BLR	274-4
Javelin	Tero Pitkamaki, FIN	296-4
Decathlon	Roman Sebrle, CZR	8676 pts

WOMEN

Event		Time	
100 meters	Veronica Campbell, JAM	11.01	
200 meters	Allyson Felix, USA	21.81	
400 meters	Christine Ohuruogu, GBR	49.61	
800 meters	Janeth Jepkosgei, KEN	1:56.04	
1500 meters	Maryam Yusuf Jamal, BRN	3:58.75	
5000 meters	Meseret Defar, ETH	14:57.91	
10,000 meters	Tirunesh Dibaba, ETH	31:55.41	
Marathon	Catherine Ndereba, KEN	2:30:37	
4x100m relay	USA (Williams, Felix, Barber, Edwards)	41.98	
4x400m relay	USA (Trotter, Felix, Wineberg, Richards)	3:18.55	
100m hurdles	Michelle Perry, USA	12.46	
400m hurdles	Jana Rawlinson, AUS	53.31	
3000m steeple	Yekaterina Volkova, RUS	9:06.57	CR
20k walk	Olga Kaniskina, RUS	1:30:09	
1500m wheelchair	Chantal Petitclerc, CAN	3:37.10	

Event		Hgt/Dist
High Jump	Blanka Vlasic, CRO	6-8½
Pole Vault	Yelena Isinbayeva, RUS	15-9
Long Jump	Tatyana Lebedeva, RUS	23-0¾
Triple Jump	Yargelis Savigne, CUB	50-1½
Shot Put	Valerie Vili, NZ	67-4¾
Discus	Franka Dietzsch, GER	218-6
Hammer	Betty Heidler, GER	245-3
Javelin	Barbora Spotakova, CZR	220-0
Heptathlon	Carolina Kluft, SWE	7032 pts

World Outdoor Records Set in 2007

World outdoor records set or equaled between Sept. 29, 2006 and Sept. 30, 2007; (p) indicates record is pending ratification by the IAAF.

MEN

Event	Name	Record	Old Mark	Former Holder
100 meters	**Asafa Powell**, JAM	9.74	9.77	Asafa Powell, JAM (2006)
20,000 meters	**Haile Gebrselassie**, ETH	56:26.0	56:55.6	Arturo Barrios, MEX (1991)
20km walk	**Vladimir Kanaykin**, RUS	1:17:16p	1:17:21	Jefferson Perez, ECU (2003)
50 km walk	**Nathan Deakes**, AUS	3:35:47	3:36:03	Robert Korzienowski, POL (2003)
Marathon	**Haile Gebrselassie**, ETH	2:04:26p	2:04:55	Paul Tergat, KEN (2003)

WOMEN

Event	Name	Record	Old Mark	Former Holder
5,000 meters	**Meseret Defar**, ETH	14:16.63	14:24.53	Meseret Defar, ETH (2006)
Hammer	**Tatyana Lysenko**, RUS	257-11 p	255-3	Tatyana Lysenko, RUS (2006)

World, Olympic and American Records
As of Sept. 30, 2007

World outdoor records officially recognized by the International Amateur Athletics Federation (IAAF); (p) indicates record is pending ratification. Note that marathon records are not officially recognized by the IAAF.

MEN
Running

Event		Time		Date Set	Location
100 meters:	**World**	9.74	**Asafa Powell**, Jamaica	Sept. 9, 2007	Rieti, ITA
	Olympic	9.84	Donovan Bailey, Canada	July 27, 1996	Atlanta
	American	9.79	Maurice Greene	June 16, 1999	Athens
200 meters:	**World**	19.32	**Michael Johnson**, USA	Aug. 1, 1996	Atlanta
	Olympic	19.32	Johnson (same as World)	—	
	American	19.32	Johnson (same as World)	—	
400 meters:	**World**	43.18	**Michael Johnson**, USA	Aug. 26, 1999	Seville
	Olympic	43.49	Michael Johnson, USA	July 29, 1996	Atlanta
	American	43.18	Johnson (same as World)	—	
800 meters:	**World**	1:41.11	**Wilson Kipketer**, Denmark	Aug. 24, 1997	Cologne
	Olympic	1:42.58	Vebjoern Rodal, Norway	July 31, 1996	Atlanta
	American	1:42.60	Johnny Gray	Aug. 28, 1985	Koblenz, W. Ger.
1000 meters:	**World**	2:11.96	**Noah Ngeny**, Kenya	Sept. 5, 1999	Rieti, ITA
	Olympic		Not an event	—	
	American	2:13.9	Rick Wohlhuter	July 30, 1974	Oslo
1500 meters:	**World**	3:26.00	**Hicham El Guerrouj**, Morocco	July 14, 1998	Rome
	Olympic	3:32.07	Noah Ngeny, Kenya	Sept. 29, 2000	Sydney
	American	3:29.30	Bernard Lagat	Aug. 28, 2005	Rieti, ITA
Mile:	**World**	3:43.13	**Hicham El Guerrouj**, Morocco	July 7, 1999	Rome
	Olympic		Not an event	—	
	American	3:46.91p	Alan Webb	July 21, 2007	Brasschaa, BEL
2000 meters:	**World**	4:44.79	**Hicham El Guerrouj**, Morocco	Sept. 7, 1999	Berlin
	Olympic		Not an event	—	
	American	4:52.44	Jim Spivey	Sept. 15, 1987	Lausanne, SWI
3000 meters:	**World**	7:20.67	**Daniel Komen**, Kenya	Sept. 1, 1996	Rieti, ITA
	Olympic		Not an event	—	
	American	7:30.84	Bob Kennedy	Aug. 8, 1998	Monte Carlo
5000 meters:	**World**	12:37.35	**Kenenisa Bekele**, Ethiopia	May 31, 2004	Hengelo, NED
	Olympic	13:05.59	Said Aouita, Morocco	Aug. 11, 1984	Los Angeles
	American	12:58.21	Bob Kennedy	Aug. 14, 1996	Zurich
10,000 meters:	**World**	26:17.53	**Kenenisa Bekele**, Ethiopia	Aug. 26, 2005	Brussels
	Olympic	27:05.10	Kenenisa Bekele, Ethiopia	Aug. 20, 2004	Athens
	American	27:13.98	Meb Keflezighi	May 4, 2001	Stanford, Calif.
20,000 meters:	**World**	56:26.0	**Haile Gebrselassie**, Ethiopia	June 27, 2007	Ostrava, CZR
	Olympic		Not an event	—	
	American	58:15.0	Bill Rodgers	Aug. 9, 1977	Boston
Marathon:	**World**	2:04:26p	**Haile Gebrselassie**, Ethiopia	Sept. 30, 2007	Berlin
	Olympic	2:09:21	Carlos Lopes, Portugal	Aug. 12, 1984	Los Angeles
	American	2:05:38	Khalid Khannouchi	Apr. 14, 2002	London

Relays

Event		Time		Date Set	Location
4 x 100m:	**World**	37.40	USA (Marsh, Burrell, Mitchell, C. Lewis)	Aug. 8, 1992	Barcelona
		37.40	USA (Drummond, Cason, Mitchell, Burrell)	Aug. 21, 1993	Stuttgart
	Olympic	37.40	USA (same as World - 1992)	—	
	American	37.40	USA (same as World)	—	
4 x 200m:	**World**	1:18.68	USA (Marsh, Burrell, Heard, C. Lewis)	Apr. 17, 1994	Walnut, Calif.
	Olympic		Not an event	—	
	American	1:18.68	USA (same as World)	—	
4 x 400m:	**World**	2:54.20	USA (Young, Pettigrew, Washington, Johnson)	July 22, 1998	Uniondale, N.Y.
	Olympic	2:55.74	USA (Valmon, Watts, Johnson, S. Lewis)	Aug. 8, 1992	Barcelona
	American	2:54.20	USA (same as World)	—	
4 x 800m:	**World**	7:02.43	Kenya (Mutua, Yiampoy, Kombich, Bungei)	Aug. 25, 2006	Brussels
	Olympic		Not an event	—	
	American	7:02.82	USA (Harris, Robinson, Burley, Krummenacker)	Aug. 25, 2006	Brussels
4 x 1500m:	**World**	14:38.8	West Germany (Wessinghage, Hudak, Lederer, Fleschen)	Aug. 17, 1977	Cologne
	Olympic		Not an event	—	
	American	14:46.3	USA (Aldredge, Clifford, Harbour, Duits)	June 24, 1979	Bourges, FRA

Steeplechase

Event		Time		Date Set	Location
3000 meters:	**World**	....7:53.63	**Saif Saaeed Shaheen**, Qatar	Sept. 3, 2004	Brussels
	Olympic	...8:05.51	Julius Kariuki, Kenya	Sept. 30, 1988	Seoul
	American	..8:08.82	Daniel Lincoln	July 14, 2006	Rome

Note: A men's steeplechase course consists of 28 hurdles (3 feet high) and seven water jumps (12 feet long).

Hurdles

Event		Time		Date Set	Location
110 meters:	**World**	......12.88	**Xiang Liu**, China	July 11, 2006	Lausanne
	Olympic	.....12.91	Xiang Liu, China	Aug. 27, 2004	Athens
	American	....12.90	Dominique Arnold	July 11, 2006	Lausanne
400 meters:	**World**	......46.78	**Kevin Young**, USA	Aug. 6, 1992	Barcelona
	Olympic	.....46.78	Young (same as World)	—	—
	American	....46.78	Young (same as World)	—	—

Note: The 10 hurdles at 110 meters are 3 feet, 6 inches high and those at 400 meters are 3 feet.

Walking

Event		Time		Date Set	Location
20 km:	**World**	...1:17:16	**Vladimir Kanaykin**, Russia	Sept. 29, 2007	Saransk, RUS
	Olympic	...1:18:59	Robert Korzeniowski, Poland	Sept. 22, 2000	Sydney
	American	..1:23:40	Tim Seaman	Aug. 19, 2000	San Diego
50 km:	**World**	...3:35:47	**Nathan Deakes**, Australia	Dec. 2, 2006	Geelong, AUS
	Olympic	...3:38:29	Vyacheslav Ivanenko, USSR	Sept. 30, 1988	Seoul
	American	..3:48:04	Curt Clausen	May 2, 1999	Deauville, FRA

Field Events

Event		Mark		Date Set	Location
High Jump:	**World**	......8-0½	**Javier Sotomayor**, Cuba	July 27, 1993	Salamanca, SPA
	Olympic	7-10	Charles Austin, USA	July 28, 1996	Atlanta
	American	....7-10½	Charles Austin	Aug. 7, 1991	Zurich
Pole Vault:	**World**	.....20-1¾	**Sergey Bubka**, Ukraine	July 31, 1994	Sestriere, ITA
	Olympic	....19-6¼	Tim Mack, USA	Aug. 27, 2004	Athens
	American	....19-9¼	Jeff Hartwig	June 14, 2000	Jonesboro, Ark.
Long Jump:	**World**	.....29-4½	**Mike Powell**, USA	Aug. 30, 1991	Tokyo
	Olympic	....29-2½	Bob Beamon, USA	Oct. 18, 1968	Mexico City
	American	....29-4½	Powell (same as World)	—	—
Triple Jump:	**World**	.....60- 0¼	**Jonathan Edwards**, GBR	Aug. 7, 1995	Göteborg, SWE
	Olympic	....59-4¼	Kenny Harrison, USA	July 27, 1996	Atlanta
	American	....59-4¼	Kenny Harrison (same as Olympic)	—	—
Shot Put:	**World**	....75-10¼	**Randy Barnes**, USA	May 20, 1990	Los Angeles
	Olympic	...73- 8¾	Ulf Timmermann, East Germany	Sept. 23, 1988	Seoul
	American	...75-10¼	Barnes (same as World)	—	—
Discus:	**World**	243-0	**Jurgen Schult**, East Germany	June 6, 1986	Neubrandenburg
	Olympic	...229-3½	Virgilijus Alekna, Lithuania	Aug. 23, 2004	Athens
	American	...237-4	Ben Plucknett	July 7, 1981	Stockholm
Javelin:	**World**	323-1	**Jan Zelezny**, Czech Republic	May 25, 1996	Jena, GER
	Olympic	...295-10	Jan Zelezny, Czech Republic	Sept. 23, 2000	Sydney
	American	...299-6 p	Breaux Greer	June 21, 2007	Indianapolis
Hammer:	**World**	284-7	**Yuriy Sedykh**, USSR	Aug. 30, 1986	Stuttgart
	Olympic	...278-2	Sergey Litvinov, USSR	Sept. 26, 1988	Seoul
	American	...270-9	Lance Deal	Sept. 7, 1996	Milan

Note: The international weights for men—**Shot** (16 lbs); **Discus** (4 lbs/6.55 oz); **Javelin** (minimum 1 lb/12¼ oz.); **Hammer** (16 lbs).

Decathlon

Event		Points		Date Set	Location
Ten Events:	**World**	9026	**Roman Sebrle**, Czech Republic	May 26-27, 2001	Gotzis, AUT
	Olympic	8893	Roman Sebrle, Czech Republic	Aug. 23-24, 2004	Athens
	American	8891	Dan O'Brien	Sept. 4-5, 1992	Talence, FRA

Note: Sebrle's WR times and distances, in order over two days—**100m** (10.64); **LJ** (26-7¼); **Shot** (50-3½); **HJ** (6-11½); **400m** (47.79); **110m H** (13.92); **Discus** (157-3); **PV** (15-9); **Jav** (230-2); **1500m** (4:21.98).

World, Olympic and American Outdoor Records (Cont.)

WOMEN
Running

Event		Time		Date Set	Location
100 meters:	**World**	10.49	**Florence Griffith Joyner**, USA	July 16, 1988	Indianapolis
	Olympic	10.62	Florence Griffith Joyner, USA	Sept. 24, 1988	Seoul
	American	10.49	Griffith Joyner (same as World)	—	—
200 meters:	**World**	21.34	**Florence Griffith Joyner**, USA	Sept. 29, 1988	Seoul
	Olympic	21.34	Griffith Joyner (same as World)	—	—
	American	21.34	Griffith Joyner (same as World)	—	—
400 meters:	**World**	47.60	**Marita Koch**, East Germany	Oct. 6, 1985	Canberra, AUS
	Olympic	48.25	Marie-Jose Perec, France	July 29, 1996	Atlanta
	American	48.70	Sanya Richards	Sept. 16, 2006	Athens
800 meters:	**World**	1:53.28	**Jarmila Kratochvilova**, Czech.	July 26, 1983	Munich
	Olympic	1:53.42	Nadezhda Olizarenko, USSR	July 27, 1980	Moscow
	American	1:56.40	Jearl Miles-Clark	Aug. 11, 1999	Zurich
1000 meters:	**World**	2:28.98	**Svetlana Masterkova**, Russia	Aug. 23, 1996	Brussels
	Olympic		Not an event	—	—
	American	2:31.80	Regina Jacobs	July 3, 1999	Brunswick, Me.
1500 meters:	**World**	3:50.46	**Qu Yunxia**, China	Sept. 11, 1993	Beijing
	Olympic	3:53.96	Paula Ivan, Romania	Oct. 1, 1988	Seoul
	American	3:57.12	Mary Slaney	July 26, 1983	Stockholm
Mile:	**World**	4:12.56	**Svetlana Masterkova**, Russia	Aug. 14, 1996	Zurich
	Olympic		Not an event	—	—
	American	4:16.71	Mary Slaney	Aug. 21, 1985	Zurich
2000 meters:	**World**	5:25.36	**Sonia O'Sullivan**, Ireland	July 8, 1994	Edinburgh
	Olympic		Not an event	—	—
	American	5:32.7	Mary Slaney	Aug. 3, 1984	Eugene, Ore.
3000 meters:	**World**	8:06.11	**Wang Junxia**, China	Sept. 13, 1993	Beijing
	Olympic	8:26.53	Tatyana Samolenko, USSR	Sept. 25, 1988	Seoul
	American	8:25.83	Mary Slaney	Sept. 7, 1985	Rome
5000 meters:	**World**	14:16.63	**Meseret Defar**, Ethiopia	June 15, 2007	Oslo
	Olympic	14:40.79	Gabriela Szabo, Romania	Sept. 25, 2000	Sydney
	American	14:44.80p	Shalane Flanagan	April 13, 2007	Sacramento
10,000 meters:	**World**	29:31.78	**Wang Junxia**, China	Sept. 8, 1993	Beijing
	Olympic	30:17.49	Derartu Tulu, Ethiopia	Sept. 30, 2000	Sydney
	American	30:50.32p	Deena Kastor	May 3, 2002	Stanford, Calif.
Marathon:	**World**	2:15:25	**Paula Radcliffe**, Great Britain	Apr. 13, 2003	London
	Olympic	2:23:14	Naoko Takahashi, Japan	Sept. 24, 2000	Sydney
	American	2:19:36	Deena Kastor	Apr. 23, 2006	London

Relays

Event		Time		Date Set	Location
4 x 100m:	**World**	41.37	**East Germany** (Gladisch, Rieger, Auerswald, Gohr)	Oct. 6, 1985	Canberra, AUS
	Olympic	41.60	East Germany (Muller, Wockel, Auerswald, Gohr)	Aug. 1, 1980	Moscow
	American	41.47	USA (Gaines, Jones, Miller, Devers)	Aug. 9, 1997	Athens
4 x 200m:	**World**	1:27.46	**USA** (Jenkins, Colander-Richardson, Perry, Jones)	Apr. 29, 2000	Philadelphia
	Olympic		Not an event	—	—
	American	1:27.46	USA (same as World)	—	—
4 x 400m:	**World**	3:15.17	**USSR** (Ledovskaya, Nazarova, Pinigina, Bryzgina)	Oct. 1, 1988	Seoul
	Olympic	3:15.17	USSR (same as World)	—	—
	American	3:15.51	USA (Howard, Dixon, Brisco, Griffith Joyner)	Oct. 1, 1988	Seoul
4 x 800m:	**World**	7:50.17	**USSR** (Olizarenko, Gurina, Borisova, Podyalovskaya)	Aug. 5, 1984	Moscow
	Olympic		Not an event	—	—
	American	8:17.09	Athletics West (Addison, Arbogast, Decker Slaney, Mullen)	Apr. 24, 1983	Walnut, Calif.

Hurdles

Event		Time		Date Set	Location
100 meters:	**World**	12.21	**Yordanka Donkova**, Bulgaria	Aug. 20, 1988	Stara Zagora, BUL
	Olympic	12.37	Joanna Hayes, USA	Aug. 24, 2004	Athens
	American	12.33	Gail Devers	July 23, 2000	Sacramento

400 meters:	**World** 52.34	**Yuliya Pechenkina**, Russia	Aug. 8, 2003	Tula, RUS
	Olympic 52.77	Fani Halkia, Greece -	Aug. 22, 2004	Athens
	American. 52.61	Kim Batten	Aug. 11, 1995	Göteborg, SWE

Note: The 10 hurdles at 110 meters are 3 feet, 6 inches high and those at 400 meters are 3 feet.

Walking

Event	Time		Date Set	Location
20 km:	**World** 1:25:41	**Olimpiada Ivanova**, Russia	Aug. 7, 2005	Helsinki
	Olympic 1:29:05	Wang Liping, China	Sept. 28, 2000	Sydney
	American 1:31:51	Michelle Rohl	May 13, 2000	Kenosha, Wis.

Steeplechase

Event	Time		Date Set	Location
3000 meters:	**World** 9:01.59	**Gulnara Samitova**, Russia	July 4, 2004	Heraklion, GRE
	Olympic	Will debut in Beijing (2008)		
	American . . . 9:28.75p	Lisa Galaviz	July 28, 2007	Heusden-Zolder, BEL

Note: A women's steeplechase course consists of 28 hurdles (30 inches high) and seven water jumps (10 feet long).

Field Events

Event	Mark		Date Set	Location
High Jump:	**World** 6-10¼	**Stefka Kostadinova,** Bulgaria	Aug. 30, 1987	Rome
	Olympic 6-9	Yelena Slesarenko, Russia	Aug. 28, 2004	Athens
	American. 6-8	Louise Ritter	July 8, 1988	Austin, Texas
	6-8	Louise Ritter	Sept. 30, 1988	Seoul
Pole Vault:	**World** 16-5¼	**Yelena Isinbayeva**, Russia	Aug. 12, 2005	Helsinki
	Olympic 16-1¼	Yelena Isinbayeva, Russia	Aug. 24, 2004	Athens
	American . . . . 16-0 p	Jenn Stuczynski	June 2, 2007	New York
Long Jump:	**World** 24-8¼	**Galina Chistyakova**, USSR	June 11, 1988	Leningrad
	Olympic 24-3¼	Jackie Joyner-Kersee, USA	Sept. 29, 1988	Seoul
	American 24-7	Jackie Joyner-Kersee	May 22, 1994	New York
Triple Jump:	**World** 50-10¼	**Inessa Kravets**, Ukraine	Aug. 10, 1995	Göteborg, SWE
	Olympic 50-3½	Inessa Krävets, Ukraine	July 31, 1996	Atlanta
	American 47-5	Tiombe Hurd	July 11, 2004	Sacramento, Calif.
Shot Put:	**World** 74-3	**Natalya Lisovskaya**, USSR	June 7, 1987	Moscow
	Olympic 73-6¼	Ilona Slupianek, E. Germany	July 24, 1980	Moscow
	American 66-2½	Ramona Pagel	June 25, 1988	San Diego
Discus:	**World** 252-0	**Gabriele Reinsch**, E. Germany	July 9, 1988	Neubrandenburg
	Olympic 237-2½	Martina Hellmann, E. Germany	Sept. 29, 1988	Seoul
	American 227-10	Suzy Powell	Apr. 27, 2002	La Jolla, Calif.
Javelin:	**World** 235-3	**Osleidys Menendez**, Cuba	Aug. 14, 2005	Helsinki
	Olympic 234-8	Osleidys Menendez, Cuba	Aug. 27, 2004	Athens
	American . . . . 210-7 p	Kim Kreiner	May 17, 2007	Fortaleza, BRA
Hammer:	**World** . . . . 257-11 p	**Tatyana Lysenko**, Russia	May 26, 2007	Sochi, RUS
	Olympic . . : 246-1	Olga Kuzenkova, Russia	Aug. 25, 2004	Athens
	American . . . 242-4	Erin Gilreath	June 25, 2005	Carson, Calif.

Note: The international weights for women—**Shot** (8 lbs/13 oz); **Discus** (2 lbs/3.27 oz); **Javelin** (minimum 1 lb/5.16 oz); **Hammer** (8 lbs/13 oz).

Heptathlon

	Points		Date Set	Location
Seven Events:	**World** 7291	**Jackie Joyner-Kersee**, USA	Sept. 23-24, 1988	Seoul
	Olympic 7291	Joyner-Kersee (same as World)	—	—
	American 7291	Joyner-Kersee (same as World)	—	—

Note: Joyner-Kersee's WR times and distances, in order over two days—**100m H** (12.69); **HJ** (61¼); **Shot** (51-10); **200m** (22.56); **LJ** (2310¼); **Jav** (149-10); **800m** (2:08.51).

World Indoor Records Set in 2007

World indoor records set or equaled between Sept. 29, 2006 and Sept. 28, 2007. (p) indicates pending ratification.

MEN

No world records set.

WOMEN

Event	Name	Record	Old Mark	Former Holder
3000 meters	**Liliya Shobukhova**, RUS	8:23.72p	8:27.86	Liliya Shobukhova, RUS (2006)
5000 meters	**Tirunesh Dibaba**, ETH	14:27.42	14:32.93	Tirunesh Dibaba, ETH (2005)
4 x 800m relay	**Russia**	8:18.54p	8:18.71	Russia (1994)
Pole Vault	**Yelena Isinbayeva**, RUS	16-2p	16-1¾	Yelena Isinbayeva, RUS (2006)

World and American Indoor Records
As of Sept. 30, 2007

World indoor records officially recognized by the International Amateur Athletics Federation (IAAF); (p) indicates record is pending ratification by the IAAF; (a) indicates record was set at an altitude over 1000 meters.

MEN
Running

Event		Time		Date Set	Location
50 meters:	**World**	.5.56a	**Donovan Bailey**, Canada	Feb. 9, 1996	Reno, Nev.
		5.56	**Maurice Greene**, USA	Feb. 13, 1999	Los Angeles
	American	.5.56	Greene (same as World)	Feb. 13, 1999	Los Angeles
60 meters:	**World**	.6.39	**Maurice Greene**, USA	Feb. 3, 1998	Madrid
		6.39	**Maurice Greene**, USA	Mar. 3, 2001	Atlanta
	American	.6.39	Greene (same as World)	—	
200 meters:	**World**	.19.92	**Frankie Fredericks**, Namibia	Feb. 18, 1996	Lievin, FRA
	American	.20.10	Wallace Spearmon	Mar. 11, 2005	Fayetteville, Ark.
400 meters:	**World**	.44.57	**Kerron Clement**, USA	Mar. 12, 2005	Fayetteville, Ark.
	American	.44.57	Clement (same as World)	—	
800 meters:	**World**	.1:42.67	**Wilson Kipketer**, Denmark	Mar. 9, 1997	Paris
	American	.1:45.00	Johnny Gray	Mar. 8, 1992	Sindelfingen, GER
1000 meters:	**World**	.2:14.96	**Wilson Kipketer**, Denmark	Feb. 20, 2000	Birmingham, ENG
	American	.2:17.86	David Krummenacker	Jan. 27, 2002	Boston
1500 meters:	**World**	.3:31.18	**Hicham El Guerrouj**, Morocco	Feb. 2, 1997	Stuttgart
	American	.3:33.34	Bernard Lagat	Feb. 11, 2005	Fayetteville, Ark.
Mile:	**World**	.3:48.45	**Hicham El Guerrouj**, Morocco	Feb. 12, 1997	Ghent, BEL
	American	.3:49.89	Bernard Lagat	Feb. 11, 2005	Fayetteville, Ark.
3000 meters:	**World**	.7:24.90	**Daniel Komen**, Kenya	Feb. 6, 1998	Budapest
	American	.7:32.43	Bernard Lagat	Feb. 17, 2007	Birmingham, ENG
5000 meters:	**World**	.12:49.60	**Kenenisa Bekele**, Ethiopia	Feb. 20, 2004	Birmingham, ENG
	American	.13:20.55	Doug Padilla	Feb. 12, 1982	New York

Note: The Mile run is 1,609.344 meters.

Hurdles

Event		Time		Date Set	Location
50 meters:	**World**	.6.25	**Mark McKoy**, Canada	Mar. 5, 1986	Kobe, JPN
	American	.6.35	Greg Foster	Jan. 27, 1985	Rosemont, Ill.
		6.35	Greg Foster	Jan. 31, 1987	Ottawa
60 meters:	**World**	.7.30	**Colin Jackson**, Great Britain	Mar. 6, 1994	Sindelfingen, GER
	American	.7.36	Greg Foster	Jan. 16, 1987	Los Angeles
		7.36	Allen Johnson	March 6, 2004	Budapest

Note: The hurdles for both distances are 3 feet, 6 inches high. There are four hurdles in the 50 meters and five in the 60.

Walking

Event		Time		Date Set	Location
5000 meters:	**World**	.18:07.08	**Mikhail Shchennikov**, Russia	Feb. 14, 1995	Moscow
	American	.19:15.88	Tim Seaman	Feb. 25, 2006	Boston

Relays

Event		Time		Date Set	Location
4 x 200 meters:	**World**	.1:22.11	**Great Britain**	Mar. 3, 1991	Glasgow
	American	.1:22.71	National Team	Mar. 3, 1991	Glasgow
4 x 400 meters:	**World**	.3:02.83	**United States**	Mar. 7, 1999	Maebashi, JPN
	American	.3:02.83	National Team (same as World)	Mar. 7, 1999	Maebashi, JPN
4 x 800 meters:	**World**	.7:13.94	**United States**	Feb. 6, 2000	Boston
	American	.7:13.94	Global Athletics (same as World)	Feb. 6, 2000	Boston

Field Events

Event		Mark		Date Set	Location
High Jump:	**World**	.7-11½	**Javier Sotomayor**, Cuba	Mar. 4, 1989	Budapest
	American	.7-10½	Hollis Conway	Mar. 10, 1991	Seville
Pole Vault:	**World**	.20-2	**Sergey Bubka**, Ukraine	Feb. 21, 1993	Donyetsk, UKR
	American	.19-9p	Jeff Hartwig	Mar. 10, 2002	Sindelfingen, GER
Long Jump:	**World**	.28-10¼	**Carl Lewis**, USA	Jan. 27, 1984	New York
	American	.28-10¼	Lewis (same as World)	—	
Triple Jump:	**World**	.58-6	**Aliecer Urrutia**, Cuba	Mar. 1, 1997	Sindelfingen, GER
		58-6	**Christian Olsson**, Sweden	Mar. 7, 2004	Budapest
	American	.58-3¼	Mike Conley	Feb. 27, 1987	New York
Shot Put:	**World**	.74-4¼	**Randy Barnes**, USA	Jan. 20, 1989	Los Angeles
	American	.74-4¼	Barnes (same as World)	—	

Note: The international shot put weight for men is 16 lbs.

Heptathlon

	Points		Date Set	Location
Seven Events:	**World** 6476	**Dan O'Brien**, USA	Mar. 13-14, 1993	Toronto
	American 6476	O'Brien (same as World)	—	—

Note: O'Brien's WR times and distances, in order over two days—**60m** (6.67); **LJ** (25-8¾); **SP** (52-6¾); **HJ** (6-11¾); **60m H** (7.85); **PV** (17-0¾); **1000m** (2:57.96).

WOMEN
Running

Event	Time		Date Set	Location
50 meters:	**World** 5.96	**Irina Privalova**, Russia	Feb. 9, 1995	Madrid
	American 6.02	Gail Devers	Feb. 21, 1999	Lievin, FRA
60 meters:	**World** 6.92	**Irina Privalova**, Russia	Feb. 11, 1993	Madrid
	6.92	**Irina Privalova**, Russia	Feb. 9, 1995	Madrid
	American 6.95	Gail Devers	Mar. 12, 1993	Toronto
	6.95	Marion Jones	Mar. 7, 1998	Maebashi, JPN
200 meters:	**World** 21.87	**Merlene Ottey**, Jamaica	Feb. 13, 1993	Lievin, FRA
	American 22.18	Michelle Collins	Mar. 15, 2003	Birmingham, ENG
400 meters:	**World** 49.59	**Jarmila Kratochvilova**, Czech.	Mar. 7, 1982	Milan
	American 50.64	Diane Dixon	Mar. 10, 1991	Seville
800 meters:	**World** 1:55.82	**Jolanda Ceplak**, Slovenia	Mar. 3, 2002	Vienna
	American . .1:58.71	Nicole Teter	Mar. 2, 2002	New York
1000 meters:	**World** . . .2:30.94	**Maria Mutola**, Mozambique	Feb. 25, 1999	Stockholm
	American . .2:34.19	Jennifer Toomey	Feb. 20, 2004	Birmingham, ENG
1500 meters:	**World** . . .3:58.28	**Yelena Soboleva**, Russia	Feb. 18, 2006	Moscow
	American . .3:59.98	Regina Jacobs	Feb. 1, 2003	Boston
Mile:	**World** 4:17.14	**Doina Melinte**, Romania	Feb. 9, 1990	E. Rutherford, N.J.
	American 4:20.5	Mary Slaney	Feb. 19, 1982	San Diego
3000 meters:	**World** . . .8:23.72p	**Meseret Defar**, Ethiopia	Feb. 3, 2007	Stuttgart
	American . .8:33.25p	Shalane Flanagan	Jan. 27, 2007	Boston
5000 meters:	**World** . . .14:27.42	**Tirunesh Dibaba**, Ethiopia	Jan. 27, 2007	Boston
	American . .15:07.44	Marla Runyan	Feb. 18, 2001	New York City

Note: The Mile run is 1,609.344 meters.

Hurdles

Event	Time		Date Set	Location
50 meters:	**World** 6.58	**Cornelia Oschkenat**, E. Ger.	Feb. 20, 1988	East Berlin
	American 6.67a	Jackie Joyner-Kersee	Feb. 10, 1995	Reno, Nev.
60 meters:	**World** 7.69	**Ludmila Engquist**, USSR	Feb. 4, 1990	Chelyabinsk, USSR
	American 7.74	Gail Devers	Mar. 1, 2003	Boston

Note: The hurdles for both distances are 2 feet, 9 inches high. There are four hurdles in the 50 meters and five in the 60.

Walking

Event	Time		Date Set	Location
3000 meters:	**World** . . .11:40.33	**Claudia Stef**, Romania	Jan. 30, 1999	Bucharest
	American . .12:20.79	Debbi Lawrence	Mar. 12, 1993	Toronto

Relays

Event	Time		Date Set	Location
4 x 200 meters:	**World** 1:32.41	**Russia**	Jan. 29, 2005	Glasgow
	American 1:33.24	National Team	Feb. 12, 1994	Glasgow
4 x 400 meters:	**World** 3:23.37	**Russia**	Jan. 28, 2006	Glasgow
	American . 3:27.59	National Team	Mar. 7, 1999	Maebashi, JPN
4 x 800 meters:	**World** 8:18.54p	**Russia**	Feb. 11, 2007	Volgograd, RUS
	American . . . 8:25.5	Villanova	Feb. 7, 1987	Gainesville, Fla.

Field Events

Event	Mark		Date Set	Location
High Jump:	**World** 6-9¾	**Kajsa Bergqvist**, Sweden	Feb. 4, 2006	Arnstadt, GER
	American 6-7	Tisha Waller	Feb. 28, 1998	Atlanta
Pole Vault:	**World** . . . . 16-2 p	**Yelena Isinbayeva**, Russia	Feb. 10, 2007	Donetsk, UKR
	American 15-9¼	Stacy Dragila, USA	Mar. 6, 2004	Budapest
Long Jump:	**World** 24-2¼	**Heike Drechsler**, E. Germany	Feb. 13, 1988	Vienna
	American 23-4¾	Jackie Joyner-Kersee	Mar. 5, 1994	Atlanta
Triple Jump:	**World** 50-4¾	**Tatyana Lebedeva**, Russia	Mar. 6, 2004	Budapest
	American 46-8¼	Sheila Hudson	Mar. 4, 1995	Atlanta
Shot Put:	**World** 73-10	**Helena Fibingerova**, Czech.	Feb. 19, 1977	Jablonec, CZE
	American . . 65-0¾	Ramona Pagel	Feb. 20, 1987	Inglewood, Calif.

Note: The international shotput weight for women is 8 lbs. and 13 oz.

Pentathlon

	Points		Date Set	Location
Five Events:	**World** 4991	**Irina Byelova**, Russia	Feb. 14-15, 1992	Berlin
	American 4753	DeDee Nathan	Mar. 4-5, 1999	Maebashi, JPN

Note: Byelova's WR times and distances, in order over two days—**60m H** (8.22); **HJ** (6-4); **SP** (43-5¾); **LJ** (21-1¾); **800m** (2:10.26).

SWIMMING

2007 FINA World Championships

The 12th FINA World Championships in swimming, diving, synchronized swimming and water polo held in Melbourne, Australia, March 17-April 1, 2007. Note that (WR) indicates world record, (CR) indicates championship meet record and (=CR) indicates the championship meet record was tied.

Final Medal Leaders — Swimming Top 10

		G	S	B	Total			G	S	B	Total
1	United States	18	13	4	35	6	Germany	2	4	4	10
2	Australia	7	6	9	22	7	France	3	2	2	7
3	Russia	11	4	6	21		Italy	1	2	4	7
4	China	9	5	2	16	9	Spain	0	4	2	6
5	Japan	1	3	8	12	10	Canada	1	3	1	5

MEN

Event		Time	
50m free	Benjamin Wildman-Tobriner, USA	21.88	
100m free	Filippo Magnini, ITA	48.43	
200m free	Michael Phelps, USA	1:43.86	WR
400m free	Tae Hwan Park, KOR	3:44.30	
800m free	Oussama Mellouli, TUN	7:46.95	
1500m free	Mateusz Sawrymowicz, POL	14:45.94	
50m back	Gerhard Zandberg, RSA	24.98	
100m back	Aaron Peirsol, USA	52.98	WR
200m back	Ryan Lochte, USA	1:54.32	WR
50m breast	Oleg Lisogor, UKR	27.66	
100m breast	Brendan Hansen, USA	59.80	
200m breast	Kosuke Kitajima, JPN	2:09.80	
50m fly	Roland Schoeman, RSA	23.18	
100m fly	Michael Phelps, USA	50.77	
200m fly	Michael Phelps, USA	1:52.09	WR
200m I.M.	Michael Phelps, USA	1:54.98	WR
400m I.M.	Michael Phelps, USA	4:06.22	WR

Men's Relays

Event		Time	
4x100m free	USA (Phelps, Walker, Jones, Lezak)	3:12.72	CR
4x200m free	USA (Phelps, Lochte, Keller, Vanderkaay)	7:03.24	WR
4x100m medley	Australia (Welsh, Rickard, Lauterstein, Sullivan)	3:34.93	

Men's Open Water

Event		Time
5km	Thomas Lurz, GER	56:49.6
10km	Vladimir Dyatchin, RUS	1:55:32.52
25km	Yury Kudinov, RUS	5:16:45.55

WOMEN

Event		Time	
50m free	Lisbeth Lenton, AUS	24.53	
100m free	Lisbeth Lenton, AUS	53.40	=CR
200m free	Laure Manaudou, FRA	1:55.52	WR
400m free	Laure Manaudou, FRA	4:02.61	CR
800m free	Kate Ziegler, USA	8:18.52	CR
1500m free	Kate Ziegler, USA	15:53.05	CR
50m back	Leila Vaziri, USA	28.16	WR
100m back	Natalie Coughlin, USA	59.44	WR
200m back	Margaret Hoelzer, USA	2:07.16	CR
50m breast	Jessica Hardy, USA	30.63	
100m breast	Leisel Jones, AUS	1:05.72	CR
200m breast	Leisel Jones, AUS	2:21.84	
50m fly	Therese Alshammar, SWE	25.91	
100m fly	Lisbeth Lenton, AUS	57.15	CR
200m fly	Jessicah Schipper, AUS	2:06.39	
200m I.M.	Katie Hoff, USA	2:10.13	CR
400m I.M.	Katie Hoff, USA	4:32.89	WR

Women's Relays

Event		Time	
4x100m free	Australia (Lenton, Schlanger, Reese, Henry)	3:35.48	CR
4x200m free	USA (Coughlin, Vollmer, Nymeyer, Hoff)	7:50.09	WR
4x100m medley	Australia (Seebohm, Jones, Schipper, Lenton)	3:55.74	WR

Women's Open Water

Event		Time
5km	Larisa Ilchenko, RUS	1:00:41.3
10km	Larisa Ilchenko, RUS	2:03:57.9
25km	Britta Kamrau-Corestein, GER	5:37:11.66

Diving

MEN

Event		Points
1m springboard	Luo Yutong, CHN	477.40
3m springboard	Qin Kai, CHN	545.35
10m platform	Gleb Galperin, RUS	554.70
3m springboard (synchronized)	Qin Kai & Wang Feng, CHN	458.76
10m platform (synchronized)	Huo Liang & Lin Yue, CHN	489.48

WOMEN

Event		Points
1m springboard	He Zi, CHN	316.65
3m springboard	Guo Jingjing, CHN	381.75
10m platform	Wang Xin, CHN	432.85
3m springboard (synchronized)	Wu Minxia & Guo Jingjing, CHN	355.80
10m platform (synchronized)	Jia Tong & Chen Ruolin, CHN	361.32

Synchronized Swimming
Championships Trophy

	Country	Points
1	Russia	334
2	Japan	290
3	Spain	288
4	USA	238
5	China	186

Water Polo
Men's Final

Croatia	1	3	1	2	1	1	—	9
Hungary	2	1	3	1	1	0	—	8

Women's Final

Australia	1	0	3	1	—	5
United States	0	1	4	1	—	6

World, Olympic and American Records

As of September 28, 2007

World long course records officially recognized by the Federation Internationale de Natation Amateur (FINA). Note that (p) indi-cates preliminary heat; (r) relay lead-off split; and (s) indicates split time. Note that (*) denotes that a record is awaiting ratification.

MEN

Freestyle

Distance	Time		Date Set	Location
50 meters:	**World** 21.64	**Aleksandr Popov**, Russia	June 16, 2000	Moscow
	Olympic 21.91	Aleksandr Popov, Unified Team	July 30, 1992	Barcelona
	American 21.76	Gary Hall Jr.	Aug. 15, 2000	Indianapolis
100 meters:	**World** 47.84p	**P. van den Hoogenband**, NED	Sept. 19, 2000	Sydney
	Olympic 47.84p	P. van den Hoogenband, NED (same as World)	—	—
	American 48.17p	Jason Lezak	July 10, 2004	Long Beach, Calif.
200 meters:	**World** 1:43.86	**Michael Phelps**, USA	Mar. 26, 2007	Melbourne
	Olympic . . . 1:44.71	Ian Thorpe, Australia	Aug. 16, 2004	Athens
	American . . 1:43.86	Phelps (same as World)	—	—
400 meters:	**World** . . . 3:40.08	**Ian Thorpe**, Australia	July 30, 2002	Manchester, GBR
	Olympic . . . 3:40.59	Ian Thorpe, Australia	Sept. 16, 2000	Sydney
	American . . 3:44.11	Klete Keller	Aug. 14, 2004	Athens
800 meters:	**World** 7:38.65	**Grant Hackett**, Australia	July 27, 2005	Montreal
	Olympic	Not an event	—	—
	American . . 7:45.63	Larsen Jensen	July 27, 2005	Montreal
1500 meters:	**World** . . 14:34.56	**Grant Hackett**, Australia	July 29, 2001	Fukuoka, JPN
	Olympic . . 14:43.40	Grant Hackett, Australia	Aug. 21, 2004	Athens
	American . 14:45.29	Larsen Jensen	Aug. 21, 2004	Athens

Backstroke

Distance	Time		Date Set	Location
50 meters:	**World** 24.80	**Thomas Rupprath**, Germany	July 27, 2003	Barcelona
	Olympic	Not an event	—	—
	American 24.84	Randall Bal	Aug. 2, 2007	Paris
100 meters:	**World** 52.98	**Aaron Peirsol**, USA	Mar. 26, 2007	Melbourne
	Olympic 53.45r	Aaron Peirsol, USA	Aug. 21, 2004	Athens
	American 52.98	Peirsol (same as World)	—	—
200 meters:	**World** 1:54.32	**Ryan Lochte**, USA	Mar. 29, 2007	Melbourne
	Olympic . . . 1:54.95	Aaron Peirsol, USA	Aug. 19, 2004	Athens
	American . . 1:54.32	Lochte (same as World)	—	—

Breaststroke

Distance	Time		Date Set	Location
50 meters:	**World** 27.18	**Oleg Lisogor**, Ukraine	Aug. 1, 2002	Berlin
	Olympic	Not an event	—	—
	American 27.39	Ed Moses	Mar. 31, 2001	Austin, Texas
100 meters:	**World** 59.13	**Brendan Hansen**, USA	Aug. 1, 2006	Irvine, Calif.
	Olympic . . . 1:00.01p	Brendan Hansen, USA	Aug. 14, 2004	Athens
	American 59.13	Hansen (same as World)	—	—
200 meters:	**World** 2:08.50	**Brendan Hansen**, USA	Aug. 20, 2006	Victoria, B.C.
	Olympic . . . 2:09.44	Kosuke Kitajima, Japan	Aug. 18, 2004	Athens
	American . . 2:08.50	Hansen (same as World)	—	—

Butterfly

Distance	Time		Date Set	Location
50 meters:	**World** 22.96	**Roland Schoeman**, South Africa	July 25, 2005	Montreal
	Olympic	Not an event	—	—
	American 23.12	Ian Crocker	July 25, 2005	Montreal
100 meters:	**World** 50.40	**Ian Crocker**, USA	July 30, 2005	Montreal
	Olympic 51.25	Michael Phelps, USA	Aug. 20, 2004	Athens
	American 50.40	Crocker (same as World)	—	—
200 meters:	**World** 1:52.09	**Michael Phelps**, USA	Mar. 27, 2007	Melbourne
	Olympic . . . 1:54.04	Michael Phelps, USA	Aug. 17, 2004	Athens
	American . . 1:52.09	Phelps (same as World)	—	—

Individual Medley

Distance	Time		Date Set	Location
200 meters:	**World** 1:54.98	**Michael Phelps**, USA	Mar. 28, 2007	Melbourne
	Olympic . . . 1:57.14	Michael Phelps, USA	Aug. 19, 2004	Athens
	American . . 1:54.98	Phelps (same as World)	—	—
400 meters:	**World** 4:06.22	**Michael Phelps**, USA	Apr. 1, 2007	Melbourne
	Olympic . . . 4:08.26	Phelps (same as World)	—	—
	American . . 4:06.22	Phelps (same as World)	—	—

Swimming (Cont.)
Relays

Distance		Time		Date Set	Location
4x100m free:	**World**	.... 3:12.46	**USA** (Phelps, Walker, Jones, Lezak)	Aug. 19, 2006	Victoria, B.C.
	Olympic	... 3:13.17	South Africa (Schoeman, Ferns, Townsend, Neethling)	Aug. 15, 2004	Athens
	American	.. 3:12.46	USA (same as World)	—	—
4x200m free:	**World**	.... 7:03.24	**USA** (Phelps, Lochte, Keller, Vanderkaay)	Mar. 30, 2007	Melbourne
	Olympic	... 7:07.05	Australia (Thorpe, Klim, Pearson, Kirby)	Sept. 19, 2000	Sydney
	American	. 7:03.24	USA (same as World)	—	—
4x100m medley:	**World**	3:30.68	**USA** (Peirsol, Hansen, Crocker, Lezak)	Aug. 21, 2004	Athens
	Olympic	... 3:30.68	USA (same as World)	—	—
	American	.. 3:30.68	USA (same as World)	—	—

WOMEN
Freestyle

Distance		Time		Date Set	Location
50 meters:	**World**	.... 24.13p	**Inge de Bruijn**, Netherlands	Sept. 22, 2000	Sydney
	Olympic	.... 24.13p	de Bruijn (same as World)	—	—
	American	.. 24.53	Dara Torres	Aug. 4, 2007	Indianapolis
100 meters:	**World**	.... 53.30	**Britta Steffen**, Germany	Aug. 2, 2006	Budapest
	Olympic	.... 53.52p	Jodie Henry, Australia	Aug. 18, 2004	Athens
	American	.. 53.40	Natalie Coughlin	Mar. 29, 2007	Melbourne
200 meters:	**World**	.. 1:55.52	**Laure Manaudou**, France	Mar. 27, 2007	Melbourne
	Olympic	... 1:57.65	Heike Friedrich, E. Germany	Sept. 21, 1988	Seoul
	American	.. 1:56.43	Natalie Coughlin	Mar. 27, 2007	Melbourne
400 meters:	**World**	.. 4:02.13	**Laure Manaudou**, France	Aug. 6, 2006	Budapest
	Olympic	... 4:03.85	Janet Evans, USA	Sept. 22, 1988	Seoul
	American	.. 4:03.85	Evans (same as Olympics)	—	—
800 meters:	**World**	... 8:16.22	**Janet Evans**, USA	Aug. 20, 1989	Tokyo
	Olympic	... 8:19.67	Brooke Bennett, USA	Sept. 22, 2000	Sydney
	American	.. 8:16.22	Evans (same as World)	—	—
1500 meters:	**World**	... 15:42.54	**Kate Ziegler**, USA	June 17, 2007	Mission Viejo, CA
	Olympic	....	Not an event	—	—
	American	. 15:42.54	Ziegler (same as World)	—	—

Backstroke

Distance		Time		Date Set	Location
50 meters:	**World**	.... 28.16	**Leila Vaziri**, USA	Mar. 28, 2007	Melbourne
	Olympic	....	Not an event	—	—
	American	..28.16	Vaziri (same as World)	—	—
100 meters:	**World**	.... 59.44	**Natalie Coughlin**, USA	Mar. 26, 2007	Melbourne
	Olympic	.... 59.68r	Natalie Coughlin, USA	Aug. 21, 2004	Athens
	American	.. 59.44	Coughlin (same as World)	—	—
200 meters:	**World**	. 2:06.62	**Krisztina Egerszegi**, Hungary	Aug. 25, 1991	Athens
	Olympic	... 2:07.06	Krisztina Egerszegi, Hungary	July 31, 1992	Barcelona
	American	.. 2:08.53	Natalie Coughlin	Aug. 16, 2002	Ft. Lauderdale, Fla.

Breaststroke

Distance		Time		Date Set	Location
50 meters:	**World**	.... 30.31	**Jade Edmistone**, Australia	Jan. 30, 2006	Melbourne, AUS
	Olympic	....	Not an event	—	—
	American	.. 30.85	Jessica Hardy	July 31, 2005	Montreal
100 meters:	**World**	.... 1:05.09	**Leisel Jones**, AUS	Mar. 20, 2006	Melbourne, AUS
	Olympic	... 1:06.64	Luo Xuejuan, China	Aug. 16, 2004	Athens
	American	.. 1:06.20p	Jessica Hardy	July 26, 2005	Montreal
200 meters:	**World**	..2:20.54	**Leisel Jones**, AUS	Feb. 1, 2006	Melbourne, AUS
	Olympic	... 2:23.37	Amanda Beard, USA	Aug. 19, 2004	Athens
	American	.. 2:22.44	Amanda Beard	July 12, 2004	Long Beach, Calif.

Butterfly

Distance		Time		Date Set	Location
50 meters:	**World**	25.46	**Therese Alshammar**, Sweden	June 13, 2007	Barcelona
	Olympic		Not an event	—	
	American	26.00	Jenny Thompson	July 26, 2003	Barcelona
100 meters:	**World**	56.61	**Inge de Bruijn**, Netherlands	Sept. 17, 2000	Sydney
	Olympic	56.61	de Bruijn (same as World)	—	
	American	57.34	Natalie Coughlin	Mar. 25, 2007	Melbourne
200 meters:	**World**	2:05.40	**Jessicah Schipper**, Australia	Aug. 17, 2006	Victoria, B.C.
	Olympic	2:05.88	Misty Hyman, USA	Sept. 20, 2000	Sydney
	American	2:05.88	Hyman (same as Olympic)	—	

Individual Medley

Distance		Time		Date Set	Location
200 meters:	**World**	2:09.72	**Wu Yanyan**, China	Oct. 17, 1997	Shanghai
	Olympic	2:10.68	Yana Klochkova, Ukraine	Sept. 19, 2000	Sydney
	American	2:10.05	Katie Hoff	Aug. 1, 2006	Irvine, Calif.
400 meters:	**World**	4:32.89	**Katie Hoff**, USA	Apr. 1, 2007	Melbourne
	Olympic	4:33.59	Yana Klochkova, UKR	Sept. 16, 2000	Sydney
	American	4:32.89	Hoff (same as World)	—	

Relays

Distance		Time		Date Set	Location
4x100m free:	**World**	3:35.22	**Germany** (Dallman, Goetz, Steffen, Liebs)	July 31, 2006	Budapest
	Olympic	3:35.94	Australia (Mills, Lenton, Thomas, Henry)	Aug. 14, 2004	Athens
	American	3:35.68	USA (Coughlin, Nymeyer, Weir, Joyce)	Mar. 25, 2007	Melbourne
4x200m free:	**World**	7:50.09	**USA** (Coughlin, Vollmer, Nymeyer, Hoff)	Mar. 29, 2007	Melbourne
	Olympic	7:53.42	USA (Coughlin, Piper, Vollmer, Sandeno)	Aug. 18, 2004	Athens
	American	7:50.09	USA (same as World)	—	
4x100m medley:	**World**	3:55.74	**Australia** (Seebohm, Jones, Schipper, Lenton)	Mar. 31, 2007	Melbourne
	Olympic	3:57.32	Australia (Rooney, Jones, Thomas, Henry)	Aug. 21, 2004	Athens
	American	3:58.30	USA (Bedford, Quann, Thompson, Torres)	Sept. 23, 2000	Sydney

World Swimming Records Set in 2007

World long course records set or equaled between Sept. 29, 2006 and Sept. 28, 2007; (*) indicates record is awaiting ratification. (r) indicates relay leadoff split.

MEN

Event	Name	Record	Old Mark	Former Holder
200m freestyle	**Michael Phelps**, USA	1:43.86	1:44.06	Ian Thorpe, AUS (2001)
100m backstroke (1)	**Michael Phelps**, USA	53.01	53.17	Aaron Peirsol, USA (2005)
100m backstroke (2)	**Aaron Peirsol**, USA	52.98	53.01	Michael Phelps, USA (2007)
200m backstroke	**Ryan Lochte**, USA	1:54.32	1:54.66	Aaron Peirsol, USA (2005)
200m butterfly	**Michael Phelps**, USA	1:52.09	1:53.93	Michael Phelps, USA (2003)
200m I.M.	**Michael Phelps**, USA	1:54.98	1:55.94	Michael Phelps, USA (2003)
400m I.M.	**Michael Phelps**, USA	4:06.22	4:08.26	Michael Phelps, USA (2004)
4x200m freestyle relay	**USA** (Phelps, Lochte, Keller, Vanderkaay)	7:03.24	7:04.66	Australia (2001)

WOMEN

Event	Name	Record	Old Mark	Former Holder
200m freestyle (1)	**Frederica Pellegrini**, ITA	1:56.47	1:56.64	Franziska van Almsick, GER (2002)
200m freestyle (2)	**Laure Manaudou**, FRA	1:55.52	1:56.47	Frederica Pellegrini, ITA (2007)
50m backstroke	**Leila Vaziri**, USA	28.16	28.19	Janine Pietsch, GER (2005) & A. Herasimenia, BLR (2006)
100m backstroke	**Natalie Coughlin**, USA	59.44	59.58	Natalie Coughlin, USA (2002)
50m butterfly	**Therese Alshammar**, SWE	25.46	25.57	Anna-Karin Kammerling, SWE ('02)
400m I.M.	**Katie Hoff**, USA	4:32.89	4:33.59	Yana Klochkova, UKR (2000)
4x200m freestyle relay	**USA** (Coughlin, Vollmer, Nymeyer, Hoff)	7:50.09	7:50.82	Germany (2006)
4x100m medley relay	**Australia** (Seebohm, Jones, Schipper, Lenton)	3:55.74	3:56.30	Australia (2006)

WINTER SPORTS

Alpine Skiing
World Cup Champions
Top Five Standings
MEN

Overall 1. Aksel Lund Svindal, NOR (1268 pts); 2. Benjamin Raich, AUT (1255); 3. Didier Cuche, SUI (1098); 4. Bode Miller, USA (882); 5. Mario Matt, AUT (744).

Downhill 1. Didier Cuche, SUI (652 pts); 2. Marco Buechel, LIE (471); 3. Erik Guay, CAN (393); 4. Peter Fill, ITA (382); 5. Michael Walchhofer, AUT (370). *Best USA*—Bode Miller (8th, 318 pts).

Slalom 1. Benjamin Raich, AUT (605 pts); 2. Mario Matt, AUT (600); 3. Jens Byggmark, SWE (410); 4. Markus Larsson, SWE (340); 5.Manfred Moelgg, ITA (334). *Best USA*—Ted Ligety (15th, 170 pts).

Giant Slalom 1. Aksel Lund Svindal, NOR (416 pts); 2. Massimiliano Blardone, ITA (380); 3. Benjamin Raich, AUT (319); 4. Kalle Palander, FIN (299); 5. Francois Bourque, CAN (249). *Best USA*—Bode Miller (6th, 232 pts).

Super G 1. Bode Miller, USA (304 pts); 2. Didier Cuche, SUI (208); 3. John Kucera, CAN (194); 4. Mario Scheiber, AUT (190); 5. Aksel Lund Svindal, NOR (181).

Combined 1. Aksel Lund Svindal, NOR (232 pts); 2. Marc Berthod, SUI (202); 3. Ivica Kostelic, CRO (200); 4. Silvan Zurbriggen, SUI (169); 5. Benjamin Raich, AUT (166). *Best USA*—Ted Ligety (t-11th, 102 pts).

Nation's Cup Champion: Austria

WOMEN

Overall 1. Nicole Hosp, AUT (1572 pts); 2. Marlies Schild, AUT (1482); 3. Julia Mancuso, USA (1356); 4. Renate Goetschl, AUT (1300); 5. Anja Paerson, SWE (885).

Downhill 1. Renate Goetschl, AUT (705 pts); 2. Julia Mancuso, USA (536); 3. Lindsey Kildow, USA (390); 4. Anja Paerson, SWE (293); 5. Ingrid Jacquemod, FRA (264).

Slalom 1. Marlies Schild, AUT (760 pts); 2. Nicole Hosp, AUT (418); 3. Sarka Zahrobska, CZE (405); 4. Therese Borssen, SWE (389); 5. Veronika Zuzulova, SVK (344). *Best USA*—Resi Stiegler (17th, 141 pts).

Giant Slalom 1. Nicole Hosp, AUT (490 pts); 2. Tanja Poutiainen, FIN (419); 3. Michaela Kirchgasser, AUT (357); 4. Julia Mancuso, USA (275); 5. Kathrin Hoelzl, GER (228).

Super G 1. Renate Goetschl, AUT (540 pts); 2. Nicole Hosp AUT (352); 3. Lindsey Kildow, USA (310); 4. Julia Mancuso, USA (273); 5. Alexander Meissnitzer, AUT (207).

Combined 1. Marlies Schild, AUT (220 pts); 2. Julia Mancuso, USA (195); 3. Nicole Hosp, AUT (190); 4. Michaela Kirchgasser, AUT (152); 5. Resi Stiegler, USA (119).

Nation's Cup Champion: Austria

2007 Alpine World Championships
at Are, Sweden (Feb. 6-18)
MEN

Downhill	Aksel Lund Svindal, Norway
Slalom	Mario Matt, Austria
Giant Slalom	Aksel Lund Svindal, Norway
Super G	Patrick Staudacher, Italy
Combined	Daniel Albrecht, Switzerland

WOMEN

Downhill	Anja Paerson, Sweden
Slalom	Sarka Zahrobska, Czech Republic
Giant Slalom	Nicole Hosp, Austria
Super G	Anja Paerson, Sweden
Combined	Anja Paerson, Sweden
Nations (men & women combined)	Austria

Freestyle Skiing
World Cup Champions
MEN

Overall	Dale Begg-Smith, Australia
Aerials	Steve Omischl, Canada
Dual Moguls	Dale Begg-Smith, Australia
Moguls	Dale Begg-Smith, Australia
Ski Cross	Audun Groenvold, Norway
Halfpipe	Kalle Leinonen, Finland

WOMEN

Overall	Jennifer Heil, Canada
Aerials	Jacqui Cooper, Australia
Dual Moguls	Jennifer Heil, Canada
Moguls	Jennifer Heil, Canada
Ski Cross	Ophelie David, France
Halfpipe	Jessica Cumming, United States

2007 Freestyle World Championships
at Madonna di Campiglio, Italy (March 6-10)
MEN

Aerials	Han Xiaopeng, China
Moguls	Pierre-Alexandre Rousseau, Canada
Dual Moguls	Dale Begg-Smith, Australia
Ski Cross	Tomas Kraus, Czech Republic

WOMEN

Aerials	Li Nina, China
Moguls	Kristi Richards, Canada
Dual Moguls	Jennifer Heil, Canada
Ski Cross	Ophelie David, France

Snowboarding
World Cup Champions
MEN

Overall	Simon Schoch, Switzerland
Halfpipe	Ryoh Aono, Japan
Parallel Slalom	Simon Schoch, Switzerland
Snowboardcross	Drew Neilson, Canada
Big Air	Peetu Piiroinen, Finland

WOMEN

Overall	Doresia Krings, Austria
Halfpipe	Manuela Laura Pesko, Switzerland
Parallel Slalom	Doresia Krings, Austria
Snowboardcross	Lindsey Jacobellis, United States

2007 World Snowboarding Championships
at Arosa, Switzerland (Jan. 13-20)
MEN

Halfpipe	Mathieu Crepel, France
Parallel Slalom	Simon Schoch, Switzerland
Parallel Giant Slalom	Rok Flander, Slovenia
Snowboardcross	Xavier Delerue, France
Big Air	Mathieu Crepel, France

WOMEN

Halfpipe	Manuela Laura Pesko, Switzerland
Parallel Slalom	Heidi Neururer, Austria
Parallel Giant Slalom	Ekaterina Tudigescheva, Russia
Snowboardcross	Lindsey Jacobellis, United States

Nordic Skiing
World Cup Champions
MEN

Cross Country - Overall . . . . . .Tobias Angerer, Germany
Cross Country - Distance . . . . . .Tobias Angerer, Germany
Cross Country - Sprint . . . Jens Arne Svartedal, Norway

Nordic Combined - Overall . . . .Hannu Manninen, Finland
Nordic Combined - Sprint . . Jason Lamy Chappuis, France
Nordic Combined - Grand Prix . .Hannu Manninen, Finland

Ski Jumping - Overall . . . . .Adam Malysz, Poland
Ski Jumping - Four Hills . . . . .Anders Jacobsen, Norway
Ski Jumping - Nordic Tourn. . . . . . . .Adam Malysz, Poland

WOMEN

Cross Country - Overall . . . . .Virpi Kuitunen, Finland
Cross Country - Distance . . . . .Virpi Kuitunen, Finland
Cross Country - Sprint . . . . .Virpi Kuitunen, Finland

2007 Nordic World Championships
at Sapporo, Japan (Feb. 22-Mar. 4)
MEN

Sprint . . . . .Jens Arne Svartedal, Norway
15-k Freestyle . . . . .Lars Berger, Norway
50-k Classic . . . . .Odd-Bjoern Hjelmeset, Norway
Pursuit (15-kClassic+15k Free) . .Axel Teichmann, Germany
4x10-k Relay . . . . .Norway
Team Sprint . . . . .Italy

Nordic Combined - Indiv. . . . .Ronny Ackermann, Germany
Nordic Combined - Sprint . . . . .Hannu Manninen, Finland
Nordic Combined - Team . . . . .Finland

Ski Jumping - K90m . . . .-. . .Adam Malysz, Poland
Ski Jumping - K120m . . . . . .Simon Ammann, Switzerland
Ski Jumping - K120m Team . . . . .Austria

WOMEN

Sprint . . . . .Astrid Jacobsen, Norway
10-k Freestyle . . . .Katerina Neumannova, Czech Republic
30-k Classic . . . . .Virpi Kuitunen, Finland
Pursuit (7.5-k Classic+7.5k Free) . . .Olga Savialova, Russia
4x5-k Relay . . . . .Finland
Team Sprint . . . . .Finland

Speed Skating
World Cup Champions
MEN

100 meters . . . . .Yuya Oikawa, Japan
500 meters . . . . .Tucker Fredricks, United States
1000 meters . . . . .Erben Wennemars, Netherlands
1500 meters . . . . .Erben Wennemars, Netherlands
5000/10,000 meters . . . . .Sven Kramer, Netherlands

WOMEN

100 meters . . . . Jenny Wolf, Germany
500 meters . . . . Jenny Wolf, Germany
1000 meters . . . . .Chiara Simionato, Italy
1500 meters . . . . .Ireen Wust, Netherlands
3000/5000 meters . . .Martina Sablikova, Czech Republic

2007 World Allround Championships
at Heerenveen, Netherlands (Feb. 9-11)
MEN

500 meters . . . . .Erben Wennemars, Netherlands
1500 meters . . . . .Erben Wennemars, Netherlands
5000 meters . . . . .Sven Kramer, Netherlands
10,000 meters . . . . .Sven Kramer, Netherlands
All-Around . . . . .Sven Kramer, Netherlands

WOMEN

500 meters . . . . .Anni Friesinger, Germany
1500 meters . . . . .Ireen Wust, Netherlands
3000 meters . . . . .Ireen Wust, Netherlands
5000 meters . . . . .Martina Sablikova, Czech Republic
All-Around . . . . .Ireen Wust, Netherlands

2007 World Short Track Championships
at Milan, Italy (Mar. 9-11)
MEN

500 meters . . . . .Charles Hamelin, Canada
1000 meters . . . . .Ahn Hyun-Soo, Korea
1500 meters . . . . .Apolo Anton Ohno, United States
3000 meters . . . . .Song Kyung-Taek, Korea
5000 meter relay . . . . .Korea
All-Around .Ahn Hyun-Soo, Korea

WOMEN

500 meters . . . . .Kalyna Roberge, Canada
1000 meters .Jin Sun-Yu, Korea
1500 meters . . . . .Jung Eun-Ju, Korea
3000 meters .Jin Sun-Yu, Korea
3000 meter relay . . . . .Korea
All-Around .Jin Sun-Yu, Korea

Figure Skating

World Championships
at Tokyo, Japan (March 19-25)

Men's —1. Brian Joubert, France; 2. Daisuke Takahashi, Japan; 3. Stephane Lambiel, Switzerland; 4. Tomas Verner, Czech Republic; 5. Evan Lysacek, USA.

Women's —1. Miki Ando, Japan; 2. Mao Asada, Japan; 3. Kim Yu-Na, Korea; 4. Kimmie Meissner, USA; 5. Yukari Nakano, Japan.

Pairs —1. Shen Xue & Zhao Hongbo, China; 2. Pang Qing & Tong Jian, China; 3. Aliona Savchenko & Robin Szolkowy, Germany; 4. Tatiana Volosozhar & Stanislav Morozov, Ukraine; 5. Zhang Dan & Zhang Hao, China.

Ice Dance —1. Albena Denkova & Maxim Staviski, Bulgaria; 2. Marie-France Dubreuil & Patrice Lauzon, Canada; 3. Tanith Belbin & Benjamin Agosto, USA; 4. Isabelle Delobel & Olivier Schoenfelder, France; 5. Oksana Domnina & Maxim Shabalin, Russia.

U.S. Championships
at Spokane, Washington (Jan. 21-28)

Men's . . . . .Evan Lysacek
Women's .Kimmie Meissner
Pairs . . . . .Brooke Castile
                                              & Benjamin Okolski
Ice Dance . . . . .Tanith Belbin
                                              & Benjamin Agosto

European Championships
at Warsaw, Poland (Jan. 23-28)

Men's . . . . .Brian Joubert, France
Women's . . . . .Carolina Kostner, Italy
Pairs . . . . .Aliona Savchenko
                                        & Robin Szolkowy, Germany
Ice Dance . . . . .Isabelle Delobel
                                        & Olivier Schoenfelder, France

SUMMER SPORTS

Cycling
2007 Tour de France

The 94th Tour de France (July 7-29) ran 20 stages, covering 3,550 kilometers (2,204 miles) starting in London, passing through Belgium, winding through the French countryside, and finishing in Paris on the Avenue des Champs-Elysees.

In a scene that has become commonplace over the past several years, doping accusations, police raids, positive drug tests and rider disqualifications rocked cycling's biggest event in 2007. Spain's Alberto Contador, riding for the American Discovery Channel team, seemed as though he was headed for the race's runner-up position until five days before the finish, when then-leader Michael Rasmussen of Denmark was ousted from the race after his Rabobank team accused him of lying and missing drug tests before the start of the race. Contador held on during the final few stages, finishing in 91:00:26, just 23 seconds ahead of runner-up Cadel Evans. The 24-year-old Contador, who had brain surgery in 2004 after a career- and life-threatening crash, became the Tour's youngest winner since 1997.

	Team	Behind		Team	Behind
1 Alberto Contador, ESP	Discovery Chan	—	6 Alejandro Valverde, ESP	Caisse d'Epargne	11:37
2 Cadel Evans, AUS	Predictor-Lotto	0:23	7 Kim Kirchen, LUX	T-Mobile	12:18
3 Levi Leipheimer, USA	Discovery Chan	0:31	8 Yaroslav Popovych, UKR	Discovery Chan	12:25
4 Carlos Sastre, ESP	CSC	7:08	9 Mikel Astarloza, ESP	Euskaltel	14:14
5 Haimar Zubeldia, ESP	Euskaltel	8:17	10 Oscar Pereiro, ESP	Caisse d'Epargne	14:25

Other Worldwide Champions

2007 Major UCI (Union Cycliste Internationale) Road results through Sept. 17. Note that in some instances, the date shown below is the final day of that particular race.

MEN

Race	Winner	Race	Winner
Jan. 21: Tour Down Under (AUS)	Martin Elmiger, SWI	Apr. 15: Paris-Roubaix (FRA)	Stuart O'Grady, AUS
Feb. 11: Tour de Langwaki (MAS)	Anthony Charteau, FRA	Apr. 22: Amstel Gold Race (NED)	S. Schumacher, GER
Feb. 18: Mediterranean Tour (FRA)	Ivan Gutierrez, ESP	Apr. 25: Fleche Wallonne (BEL)	Davide Rebellin, ITA
Feb. 22: Ruta del Sol (ESP)	Oscar Freire, ESP	Apr. 29: Liege-Bastogne-Liege (BEL)	Danilo Di Luca, ITA
Mar. 3: Tour of Valencia (ESP)	Alejandro Valverde, ESP	May 6: Tour de Romandie (SWI)	Thomas Dekker, NED
Mar. 3: Omloop Het Volk (BEL)	Filippo Pozzato, ITA	May 13: Four Days of Dunkirk (FRA)	M. Ladagnous, FRA
Mar. 18: Paris-Nice (FRA)	Alberto Contador, ESP	May 27: Tour of Catalunya (ESP)	Vladimir Karpets, RUS
Mar. 20: Tirreno-Adriatico (ITA)	Andreas Kloden, GER	June 3: Giro d'Italia (ITA)	Danilo Di Luca, ITA
Mar. 24: Milan-San Remo (ITA)	Oscar Freire, ESP	June 17: Dauphine Libere (FRA)	Christophe Moreau, FRA
Apr. 1: Criterium Int'l (FRA)	Jens Voigt, GER	June 24: Tour of Switzerland (SWI)	Vladimir Karpets, RUS
Apr. 8: Tour de Flanders (BEL)	Alessandro Ballan, ITA	Aug. 4: San Sebastian Classic (ESP)	L. Bertagnolli, ITA
Apr. 11: Gent-Wevelgem (BEL)	Marcus Burghardt, GER	Aug. 18: Tour of Germany (GER)	Jens Voigt, GER
Apr. 14: Tour of the Basque Country (ESP)	Juan Jose Cobo, ESP	Aug. 19: Vattenfall Cyclassics (GER)	Alessandro Ballan, ITA
		Sept. 23: Tour of Spain (ESP)	Denis Menchov, RUS

WOMEN

Race	Winner	Race	Winner
Mar. 1: Geelong Women's Tour (AUS)	Nicole Cooke, GBR	May 27: Tour de L'Aude (FRA)	Susanne Ljungskog, SWE
Mar. 11: Tour of New Zealand (NZ)	Judith Arndt, GER	June 2: Montreal World Cup (CAN)	Fabiana Luperini, ITA
Apr. 8: Tour de Flanders (BEL)	Nicole Cooke, GBR	July 15: Giro d'Italia Femminile (ITA)	Edita Pucinskaite, LTU
Apr. 14: Ronde van Drenthe (NED)	Adrie Visser, NED	Aug. 5: Vagarda Open (SWE)	Chantal Beltman, NED
Apr. 25: Fleche Wallonne (BEL)	Marianne Vos, NED	Sept. 1: GP of Plouay (FRA)	Noemi Cantele, ITA
May 13: Tour de Berne (SWI)	Edita Pucinskaite, LTU	Sept. 17: Tour of Nuremberg (GER)	Marianne Vos, NED

Gymnastics
2007 World Championships

The 40th Artistic Gymnastics World Championships held September 1-9, 2007 at the Hanns-Martin-Schleyer-Halle in Stuttgart, Germany.

MEN		WOMEN	
All-Around	Wei Yang, China	All-Around	Shawn Johnson, United States
High Bar	Fabian Hambüchen, Germany	Vault	Fei Cheng, China
Parallel Bars	Kim Dae-Eun, Korea & Mitja Petkovsek, Slovenia	Uneven Bars	Ksenia Semenova, Russia
Vault	Leszek Blanik, Poland	Balance Beam	Anastasia Liukin, United States
Pommel Horse	Qin Xiao, China	Floor Exercise	Shawn Johnson, United States
Rings	Yibing Chen, China	Team	United States
Floor Exercise	Diego Hypolito, Brazil		
Team	China		

Marathons
2007 Boston Marathon

The 111th edition of the Boston Marathon was held Monday, April 16, 2007 and run, as always, from Hopkinton through Ashland, Framingham, Natick, Wellesley, Newton and Brookline to Boston, Mass. Kenya's Robert Kipkoech Cheruiyot made it two consecutive wins at Boston and three in the past five years with a 20-second victory over countryman James Kwambai. While runners were "lucky" enough to not have to run through the snowstorm that had been predicted for race day, they did have to fight through near-50-mph winds and heavy rains during the early stages of the race. Due in large part to the nasty weather, the winning time was nearly seven minutes slower than the course record Cheruiyot had set a year earlier.

In the women's division, 33-year-old Russian Lidiya Grigoryeva shrugged off the conditions, made her move with just about two miles to go and held on to win in 2:29:18, beating runner-up Jelena Prokopcuka of Latvia by 40 seconds. "During my training in Russia, the weather conditions were very similar," she said. **Distance:** 26.2 miles.

	MEN	Time
1	Robert Kipkoech Cheruiyot, Kenya	2:14:13
2	James Kwambai, Kenya	2:14:33
3	Stephen Kiogora, Kenya	2:14:47
4	James Koskei, Kenya	2:15:05
5	Teferi Wodajo, Ethiopia	2:15:06

Best USA: 8th—Peter Gilmore, California, 2:16:41

	WOMEN	Time
1	Lidiya Grigoryeva, Russia	2:29:18
2	Jelena Prokopcuka, Latvia	2:29:58
3	Madai Perez, Mexico	2:30:16
4	Rita Jeptoo, Kenya	2:33:08
5	Deena Kastor, United States	2:35:09

	WHEELCHAIR	Time
1	Masazumi Soejima, Japan	1:29:16
2	Krige Schabort, South Africa	1:36:27
3	Ernst Van Dyk, South Africa	1:37:10

	WHEELCHAIR	Time
1	Wakako Tsuchida, Japan	1:53:30
2	Amanda McGrory, United States	1:58:01
3	Sandra Graf, Switzerland	2:02:30

World Marathon Majors

On January 23, 2006, the Boston, London, Berlin, Chicago and New York City marathons collectively launched the World Marathon Majors – a new series offering a $1 million prize purse to be split equally between the top male and female marathoners in the world. The inaugural 2006-2007 series launched at the Boston Marathon on April 17, 2006 and will conclude at the New York City Marathon on November 4, 2007.

Other 2007 Winners

Osaka
Jan. 28	Women	Yumiko Hara, JPN	2:23:48
	(No men's division)		

Tokyo
Feb. 18	Men	Daniel Njenga, KEN	2:09:45
	(No women's division)		

Los Angeles
Mar. 4	Men	Fred Mogaka, KEN	2:17:14
	Women	Ramilia Burangolova, RUS	2:37:54

Rome
Mar. 18	Men	Chelimo Kemboi, KEN	2:09:36
	Women	Souad Ait Salem, ALG	2:25:07

Paris
Apr. 15	Men	Mubarak Shami, QAT	2:07:19
	Women	Tafa Magarsa, ETH	2:25:07

Rotterdam
Apr. 15	Men	Joshua Chelanga, KEN	2:08:21
	Women	Hiromi Ominami, JPN	2:26:37

London
Apr. 22	Men	Martin Lel, KEN	2:07:41
	Women	Zhou Chunxiu, CHN	2:20:38

Berlin
Sept. 30	Men	Haile Gebrselassie, ETH	2:04:26*
	Women	Gete Wami, ETH	2:23:17
			World Record*

Late 2006

Chicago
Oct. 22	Men	Robert K. Cheruiyot, KEN	2:07:35
	Women	Berhane Adere, ETH	2:20:42

New York City
Nov. 5	Men	M. Gomes dos Santos, BRA	2:09:58
	Women	Jelena Prokopcuka, LAT	2:25:05

Tokyo Women's
Nov. 19	Women	Reiko Tosa, JPN	2:26:15

Fukuoka
Dec. 3	Men	Haile Gebrselassie, ETH	2:06:52
	(No women's division)		

2007 IAAF World Cross Country Championships
The 35th IAAF World Cross Country Championships held in Mombasa, Kenya (March 24).

MEN		
12 km	1. Zersenay Tadesse, Eritrea	35:50
(7.45 mi)	2. Moses Mosop, Kenya	36:13
	3. Bernard Kiprop Kipyego, Kenya	36:37
	Best USA—Michael Spence, 56th	39:32

WOMEN		
8 km	1. Lornah Kiplagat, Netherlands	26:23
(4.97 mi)	2. Tirunesh Dibaba, Ethiopia	26:47
	3. Meselech Melkamu, Ethiopia	26:48
	Best USA—Catherine Ferrell, 30th	29:34

1882-2007
Through the Years

SPORTS ALMANAC

TRACK & FIELD

IAAF World Championships

While the Summer Olympics have served as the unofficial world outdoor championships for track and field throughout the centuries, a separate World Championship meet was started in 1983 by the International Amateur Athletic Federation (IAAF). The meet was held every four years from 1983-91, but began an every-other-year cycle in 1993. Sites include Helsinki (1983, 2005), Rome (1987), Tokyo (1991), Stuttgart (1993), Göteborg, Sweden (1995), Athens (1997), Seville, Spain (1999), Edmonton (2001), Paris (2003) and Osaka, Japan (2007). Looking forward, the Championships will be held in Berlin (2009), Daegu, South Korea (2011) and Moscow (2013). Note that (WR) indicates world record and (CR) indicates championship meet record. (W) indicates wind-aided.

MEN

Most gold medals (at least three, including relays): Michael Johnson (9); Carl Lewis (8); Sergey Bubka (6); Maurice Greene and Lars Riedel (5); Hicham El Guerrouj, Haile Gebrselassie, Allen Johnson, Ivan Pedroso, Antonio Pettigrew, Calvin Smith and Jeremy Wariner (4); Donovan Bailey, Kenenisa Bekele, Tomas Dvorak, Greg Foster, Tyson Gay, John Godina, Werner Gunthor, Wilson Kipketer, Moses Kiptanui, Robert Korzeniowski, Dennis Mitchell, Noureddine Morceli, Dan O'Brien, Jefferson Perez, Butch Reynolds, Ivan Tikhon and Jan Zelezny (3).

100 Meters

Year		Time	
1983	Carl Lewis, USA	10.07	
1987	Carl Lewis, USA	9.93*	
1991	Carl Lewis, USA	9.86	**WR**
1993	Linford Christie, GBR	9.87	
1995	Donovan Bailey, CAN	9.97	
1997	Maurice Greene, USA	9.86	
1999	Maurice Greene, USA	9.80	**CR**
2001	Maurice Greene, USA	9.82	
2003	Kim Collins, SKN	10.07	
2005	Justin Gatlin, USA	9.88	
2007	Tyson Gay, USA	9.85	

*Original winner Ben Johnson, CAN, was stripped of his medal.

200 Meters

Year		Time	
1983	Calvin Smith, USA	20.14	
1987	Calvin Smith, USA	20.16	
1991	Michael Johnson, USA	20.01	
1993	Frank Fredericks, NAM	19.85	
1995	Michael Johnson, USA	19.79	
1997	Ato Boldon, USA	20.04	
1999	Maurice Greene, USA	19.90	
2001	Konstantinos Kenteris, GRE	20.04	
2003	John Capel, USA	20.30	
2005	Justin Gatlin, USA	20.04	
2007	Tyson Gay, USA	19.76	**CR**

400 Meters

Year		Time	
1983	Bert Cameron, JAM	45.05	
1987	Thomas Schonlebe, E. Ger	44.33	
1991	Antonio Pettigrew, USA	44.57	
1993	Michael Johnson, USA	43.65	
1995	Michael Johnson, USA	43.39	
1997	Michael Johnson, USA	44.12	
1999	Michael Johnson, USA	43.18	**WR**
2001	Avard Moncur, BAH	44.64	
2003	Jerome Young, USA	44.50	
2005	Jeremy Wariner, USA	43.93	
2007	Jeremy Wariner, USA	43.45	

800 Meters

Year		Time	
1983	Willi Wülbeck, W. Ger	1:43.65	
1987	Billy Konchellah, KEN	1:43.06	**CR**
1991	Billy Konchellah, KEN	1:43.99	
1993	Paul Ruto, KEN	1:44.71	
1995	Wilson Kipketer, DEN	1:45.08	
1997	Wilson Kipketer, DEN	1:43.38	
1999	Wilson Kipketer, DEN	1:43.30	
2001	Andre Bucher, SWI	1:43.70	
2003	Djabir Said-Guerni, ALG	1:44.81	
2005	Rashid Ramzi, BRN	1:44.24	
2007	Alfred Kirwa Yego, KEN	1:47.09	

1500 Meters

Year		Time	
1983	Steve Cram, GBR	3:41.59	
1987	Abdi Bile, SOM	3:36.80	
1991	Noureddine Morceli, ALG	3:32.84	
1993	Noureddine Morceli, ALG	3:34.24	
1995	Noureddine Morceli, ALG	3:33.73	
1997	Hicham El Guerrouj, MOR	3:35.83	
1999	Hicham El Guerrouj, MOR	3:27.65	**CR**
2001	Hicham El Guerrouj, MOR	3:30.68	
2003	Hicham El Guerrouj, MOR	3:31.77	
2005	Rashid Ramzi, BRN	3:37.88	
2007	Bernard Lagat, USA	3:34.77	

5000 Meters

Year		Time	
1983	Eammon Coghlan, IRL	13:28.53	
1987	Said Aouita, MOR	13:26.44	
1991	Yobes Ondieki, KEN	13:14.45	
1993	Ismael Kirui, KEN	13:02.75	
1995	Ismael Kirui, KEN	13:16.77	
1997	Daniel Komen, KEN	13:07.38	
1999	Salah Hissou, MOR	12:58.13	
2001	Richard Limo, KEN	13:00.77	
2003	Eliud Kipchoge, KEN	12:52.79	**CR**
2005	Benjamin Limo, KEN	13:32.55	
2007	Bernard Lagat, USA	13:45.87	

10,000 Meters

Year		Time	
1983	Alberto Cova, ITA	28:01.04	
1987	Paul Kipkoech, KEN	27:38.63	
1991	Moses Tanui, KEN	27:38.74	
1993	Haile Gebrselassie, ETH	27:46.02	
1995	Haile Gebrselassie, ETH	27:12.95	
1997	Haile Gebrselassie, ETH	27:24.58	
1999	Haile Gebrselassie, ETH	27:57.27	
2001	Charles Kamathi, KEN	27:53.25	
2003	Kenenisa Bekele, ETH	26:49.57	CR
2005	Kenenisa Bekele, ETH	27:08.33	
2007	Kenenisa Bekele, ETH	27:05.90	

Marathon

Year		Time	
1983	Rob de Castella, AUS	2:10:03	
1987	Douglas Wakiihuri, KEN	2:11:48	
1991	Hiromi Taniguchi, JPN	2:14:57	
1993	Mark Plaatjes, USA	2:13:57	
1995	Martin Fíz, SPA	2:11:41	
1997	Abel Anton, SPA	2:13:16	
1999	Abel Anton, SPA	2:13:36	
2001	Gezahegne Abera, ETH	2:12:42	
2003	Jaouad Gharib, MOR	2:08:31	CR
2005	Jaouad Gharib, MOR	2:10:10	
2007	Luke Kibet, KEN	2:15:59	

110-Meter Hurdles

Year		Time	
1983	Greg Foster, USA	13.42	
1987	Greg Foster, USA	13.21	
1991	Greg Foster, USA	13.06	
1993	Colin Jackson, GBR	12.91	WR
1995	Allen Johnson, USA	13.00	
1997	Allen Johnson, USA	12.93	
1999	Colin Jackson, GBR	13.04	
2001	Allen Johnson, USA	13.04	
2003	Allen Johnson, USA	13.12	
2005	Ladji Doucoure, FRA	13.07	
2007	Xiang Liu, CHN	12.95	

400-Meter Hurdles

Year		Time	
1983	Edwin Moses, USA	47.50	
1987	Edwin Moses, USA	47.46	
1991	Samuel Matete, ZAM	47.64	
1993	Kevin Young, USA	47.18	CR
1995	Derrick Adkins, USA	47.98	
1997	Stephane Diagana, FRA	47.70	
1999	Fabrizio Mori, ITA	47.72	
2001	Felix Sanchez, DOM	47.49	
2003	Felix Sanchez, DOM	47.25	
2005	Bershawn Jackson, USA	47.30	
2007	Kerron Clement, USA	47.61	

3000-Meter Steeplechase

Year		Time	
1983	Patriz Ilg, W. Ger	8:15.06	
1987	Francesco Panetta, ITA	8:08.57	
1991	Moses Kiptanui, KEN	8:12.59	
1993	Moses Kiptanui, KEN	8:06.36	
1995	Moses Kiptanui, KEN	8:04.16	CR
1997	Wilson B. Kipketer, KEN	8:05.84	
1999	Christopher Koskei, KEN	8:11.76	
2001	Reuben Kosgei, KEN	8:15.16	
2003	Saif Saaeed Shaheen, QAT	8:04.39	
2005	Saif Saaeed Shaheen, QAT	8:13.31	
2007	Brimin Kiprop Kipruto, KEN	8:13.82	

4 x 100-Meter Relay

Year		Time	
1983	United States	37.86	WR
1987	United States	37.90	
1991	United States	37.50	WR
1993	United States	37.48	CR
1995	Canada	38.31	
1997	Canada	37.86	
1999	United States	37.59	
2001	United States	37.96	
2003	United States	38.06	
2005	France	38.08	
2007	United States	37.78	

4 x 400-Meter Relay

Year		Time	
1983	Soviet Union	3:00.79	
1987	United States	2:57.29	
1991	Great Britain	2:57.53	
1993	United States	2:54.29	WR
1995	United States	2:57.32	
1997	United States	2:56.47	
1999	United States	2:56.45	
2001	United States	2:57.54	
2003	France	2:58.88*	
2005	United States	2:56.91	
2007	United States	2:55.56	

*The United States was stripped of its 2003 gold after lead runner Calvin Harrison's second doping violation.

20-Kilometer Walk

Year		Time	
1983	Ernesto Canto, MEX	1:20:49	
1987	Maurizio Damilano, ITA	1:20:45	
1991	Maurizio Damilano, ITA	1:19:37	
1993	Valentin Massana, SPA	1:22:31	
1995	Michele Didoni, ITA	1:19:59	
1997	Daniel Garcia, MEX	1:21:43	
1999	Ilya Markov, RUS	1:23:34	
2001	Roman Rasskazov, RUS	1:20:31	
2003	Jefferson Perez, ECU	1:17:21	WR
2005	Jefferson Perez, ECU	1:18:35	
2007	Jefferson Perez, ECU	1:22:20	

50-Kilometer Walk

Year		Time	
1983	Ronald Weigel, E. Ger	3:43:08	
1987	Hartwig Gauder, E. Ger	3:40:53	
1991	Aleksandr Potashov, USSR	3:53:09	
1993	Jesus Angel Garcia, SPA	3:41:41	
1995	Valentin Kononen, FIN	3:43:42	
1997	Robert Korzeniowski, POL	3:44:46	
1999	Ivano Brugnetti, ITA	3:47:54*	
2001	Robert Korzeniowski, POL	3:42:08	
2003	Robert Korzeniowski, POL	3:36:03	WR
2005	Sergey Kirdyapkin, RUS	3:38:08	
2007	Nathan Deakes, AUS	3:43:53	

* Original winner German Skurygin, RUS, was stripped of his 1999 title after testing positive for a banned substance.

High Jump

Year		Height	
1983	Gennedy Avdeyenko, USSR	7-7¼	
1987	Patrik Sjoberg, SWE	7-9¾	
1991	Charles Austin, USA	7-9¾	
1993	Javier Sotomayor, CUB	7-10½	CR
1995	Troy Kemp, BAH	7-9¼	
1997	Javier Sotomayor, CUB	7-9¼	
1999	Vyacheslav Voronin, RUS	7-9¼	
2001	Martin Buss, GER	7-8¾	
2003	Jacques Freitag, RSA	7-8½	
2005	Yuriy Krymarenko, UKR	7-7¼	
2007	Donald Thomas, BAH	7-8½	

Pole Vault

Year		Height	
1983	Sergey Bubka, USSR	18- 8¼	
1987	Sergey Bubka, USSR	19- 2¼	
1991	Sergey Bubka, USSR	19- 6¼	
1993	Sergey Bubka, UKR	19- 8¼	
1995	Sergey Bubka, UKR	19- 5	
1997	Sergey Bubka, UKR	19- 8½	
1999	Maksim Tarasov, RUS	19- 9	
2001	Dmitri Markov, AUS	19-10¼	CR
2003	Giuseppe Gibilisco, ITA	19- 4¼	
2005	Rens Blom, NED	19- 0½	
2007	Brad Walker, USA	19- 2¾	

Long Jump

Year		Distance	
1983	Carl Lewis, USA	28- 0¾	
1987	Carl Lewis, USA	28- 0¼	
1991	Mike Powell, USA	29- 4½	WR
1993	Mike Powell, USA	28- 2¼	
1995	Ivan Pedroso, CUB	28- 6½	
1997	Ivan Pedroso, CUB	27- 7½	
1999	Ivan Pedroso, CUB	28- 1	
2001	Ivan Pedroso, CUB	27- 6¾	
2003	Dwight Phillips, USA	27- 3¾	
2005	Dwight Phillips, USA	28- 2¾	
2007	Irving Saladino, PAN	28- 1¾	

Triple Jump

Year		Distance	
1983	Zdzislaw Hoffmann, POL	57- 2	
1987	Khristo Markov, BUL	58- 9	
1991	Kenny Harrison, USA	58- 4	
1993	Mike Conley, USA	58- 7¼	
1995	Jonathan Edwards, GBR	60- 0¼	WR
1997	Yoelvis Quesada, CUB	58- 6¾	
1999	Charles Michael Friedek, GER	57- 8½	
2001	Jonathan Edwards, GBR	58- 9½	
2003	Christian Olsson, SWE	58- 1¾	
2005	Walter Davis, USA	57- 7¾	
2007	Nelson Evora, POR	58- 2½	

Shot Put

Year		Distance	
1983	Edward Sarul, POL	70- 2¼	
1987	Werner Günthör SWI	72-11¼	CR
1991	Werner Günthör, SWI	71- 1¼	
1993	Werner Günthör, SWI	72- 1	
1995	John Godina, USA	70- 5¼	
1997	John Godina, USA	70- 4¼	
1999	C.J. Hunter, USA	71- 6	
2001	John Godina, USA	71- 9	
2003	Andrei Mikhnevich, BLR	71- 2	
2005	Adam Nelson, USA	71- 3½	
2007	Reese Hoffa, USA	72- 3¾	

Discus

Year		Distance	
1983	Imrich Bugar, CZE	222- 2	
1987	Jurgen Schult, E. Ger	225- 6	
1991	Lars Riedel, GER	217- 2	
1993	Lars Riedel, GER	222- 2	
1995	Lars Riedel, GER	225- 7	
1997	Lars Riedel, GER	224-10	
1999	Anthony Washington, USA	226- 7	
2001	Lars Riedel, GER	228- 9	
2003	Virgilijus Alekena, LIT	228- 7	
2005	Virgilijus Alekena, LIT	230- 2	CR
2007	Gerd Kanter, EST	226- 2	

Hammer Throw

Year		Distance	
1983	Sergey Litvinov, USSR	271- 3	
1987	Sergey Litvinov, USSR	272- 6	
1991	Yuri Sedykh, USSR	268- 0	
1993	Andrey Abduvaliyev, TAJ	267-10	
1995	Andrey Abduvaliyev, TAJ	267- 7	
1997	Heinz Weis, GER	268- 4	
1999	Karsten Kobs, GER	263- 3	
2001	Szymon Ziolkowski, POL	273- 7	
2003	Ivan Tikhon, BLR	272- 5	
2005	Ivan Tikhon, BLR	275- 2	CR
2007	Ivan Tikhon, BLR	274- 4	

Javelin

Year		Distance	
1983	Detlef Michel, E. Ger	293-7	
1987	Seppo Raty, FIN	274-1	
1991	Kimmo Kinnunen, FIN	297-11	
1993	Jan Zelezny, CZR	282-1	
1995	Jan Zelezny, CZR	293-11	
1997	Marius Corbett, S. Afr.	290-0	
1999	Aki Parviainen, FIN	293-8	
2001	Jan Zelezny, CZR	304- 5	CR
2003	Sergey Makarov, RUS	280- 3	
2005	Andrus Varnik, EST	286- 0	
2007	Tero Pitkamaki, FIN	296- 4	

Decathlon

Year		Points	
1983	Daley Thompson, GBR	8714	
1987	Torsten Voss, E. Ger	8680	
1991	Dan O'Brien, USA	8812	
1993	Dan O'Brien, USA	8817	
1995	Dan O'Brien, USA	8695	
1997	Tomas Dvorak, CZR	8837	
1999	Tomas Dvorak, CZR	8744	
2001	Tomas Dvorak, CZR	8902	CR
2003	Tom Pappas, USA	8750	
2005	Bryan Clay, USA	8732	
2007	Roman Sebrle, CZR	8676	

WOMEN

Multiple gold medals (at least 3, including relays): Gail Devers (5); Jearl Miles Clark, Tirunesh Dibaba, Allyson Felix, Jackie Joyner-Kersee and Marion Jones (4); Franka Dietzsch, Tatyana Samolenko Dorovskikh, Silke Gladisch, Marita Koch, Carolina Kluft, Astrid Kumbernuss, Tatyana Lebedeva, Maria Mutola, Merlene Ottey, Gabriela Szabo, Gwen Torrence and Lauryn Williams (3).

100 Meters

Year		Time	
1983	Marlies Gohr, E. Ger	10.97	
1987	Silke Gladisch, E. Ger	10.90	
1991	Katrin Krabbe, GER	10.99	
1993	Gail Devers, USA	10.81	
1995	Gwen Torrence, USA	10.85	
1997	Marion Jones, USA	10.83	
1999	Marion Jones, USA	10.70	CR
2001	Zhanna Pintusevich-Block, UKR	10.82	
2003	Torri Edwards, USA	10.93*	
2005	Lauryn Williams, USA	10.93	
2007	Veronica Campbell, JAM	11.01	

*Original winner Kelli White, USA, was stripped of her medal.

200 Meters

Year		Time	
1983	Marita Koch, E. Ger	22.13	
1987	Silke Gladisch, E. Ger	21.74	CR
1991	Katrin Krabbe, GER	22.09	
1993	Merlene Ottey, JAM	21.98	
1995	Merlene Ottey, JAM	22.12	
1997	Zhanna Pintusevich, UKR	22.32	
1999	Inger Miller, USA	21.77	
2001	Marion Jones, USA	22.39	
2003	Anastasiya Kapachinskaya, RUS	22.38*	
2005	Allyson Felix, USA	22.16	
2007	Allyson Felix, USA	21.81	

*Original winner Kelli White, USA, was stripped of her medal.

400 Meters

Year		Time	
1983	Jarmila Kratochvilova, CZE	.47.99	WR
1987	Olga Bryzgina, USSR	.49.38	
1991	Marie-José Pérec, FRA	.49.13	
1993	Jearl Miles, USA	.49.82	
1995	Marie-José Pérec, FRA	.49.28	
1997	Cathy Freeman, AUS	.49.77	
1999	Cathy Freeman, AUS	.49.67	
2001	Amy Mbacke Thiam, SEN	.49.86	
2003	Ana Guevara, MEX	.48.89	
2005	Tonique Williams-Darling, BAH	.49.55	
2007	Christine Ohuruogu, GBR	.49.61	

800 Meters

Year		Time	
1983	Jarmila Kratochvilova, CZE	1:54.68	CR
1987	Sigrun Wodars, E. Ger	1:55.26	
1991	Lilia Nurutdinova, USSR	1:57.50	
1993	Maria Mutola, MOZ	1:55.43	
1995	Ana Quirot, CUB	1:56.11	
1997	Ana Quirot, CUB	1:57.14	
1999	Ludmila Formanova, CZR	1:56.68	
2001	Maria Mutola, MOZ	1:57.17	
2003	Maria Mutola, MOZ	1:59.89	
2005	Zulia Calatayud, CUB	1:58.82	
2007	Janeth Jepkosgei, KEN	1:56.04	

1500 Meters

Year		Time	
1983	Mary Decker, USA	4:00.90	
1987	Tatiana Samolenko, USSR	3:58.56	
1991	Hassiba Boulmerka, ALG	4:02.21	
1993	Liu Dong, CHN	4:00.50	
1995	Hassiba Boulmerka, ALG	4:02.42	
1997	Carla Sacramento, POR	4:04.24	
1999	Svetlana Masterkova, RUS	3:59.53	
2001	Gabriela Szabo, ROM	4:00.57	
2003	Tatyana Tomashova, RUS	3:58.52	CR
2005	Tatyana Tomashova, RUS	4:00.35	
2007	Maryam Yusuf Jamal, BRN	3:58.75	

5000 Meters
Held as 3000-meter race from 1983-93

Year		Time	
1983	Mary Decker, USA	8:34.62	
1987	Tatyana Samolenko, USSR	8:38.73	
1991	T. Samolenko Dorovskikh, USSR	8:35.82	
1993	Qu Yunxia, CHN	8:28.71	
1995	Sonia O'Sullivan, IRL	14:46.47	
1997	Gabriela Szabo, ROM	14:57.68	
1999	Gabriela Szabo, ROM	14:41.82	
2001	Olga Yegorova, RUS	15:03.39	
2003	Tirunesh Dibaba, ETH	14:51.72	
2005	Tirunesh Dibaba, ETH	14:38.59	CR
2007	Meseret Defar, ETH	14:57.91	

10,000 Meters

Year		Time	
1983	Not held		
1987	Ingrid Kristiansen, NOR	31:05.85	
1991	Liz McColgan, GBR	31:14.31	
1993	Wang Junxia, CHN	30:49.30	
1995	Fernanda Ribeiro, POR	31:04.99	
1997	Sally Barsosio, KEN	31:32.92	
1999	Gete Wami, ETH	30:24.56	
2001	Derartu Tulu, ETH	31:48.81	
2003	Berhane Adere, ETH	30:04.18	CR
2005	Tirunesh Dibaba, ETH	30:24.02	
2007	Tirunesh Dibaba, ETH	31:55.41	

3000-Meter Steeplechase

Year		Time	
2005	Docus Inzikuru, UGA	9:18.24	
2007	Yekaterina Volkova, RUS	9:06.57	CR

Marathon

Year		Time	
1983	Grete Waitz, NOR	2:28:09	
1987	Rose Mota, POR	2:25:17	
1991	Wanda Panfil, POL	2:29:53	
1993	Junko Asari, JPN	2:30:03	
1995	Manuela Machado, POR	2:25:39	
1997	Hiromi Suzuki, JPN	2:29:48	
1999	Jong Song-Ok, N. Kor	2:26:59	
2001	Lidia Simon, ROM	2:26:01	
2003	Catherine Ndereba, KEN	2:23:55	
2005	Paula Radcliffe, GBR	2:20:57	CR
2007	Catherine Ndereba, KEN	2:30:37	

100-Meter Hurdles

Year		Time	
1983	Bettine Jahn, E. Ger	12.35ᵂ	
1987	Ginka Zagorcheva, BUL	12.34	CR
1991	Lyudmila Narozhilenko, USSR	12.59	
1993	Gail Devers, USA	12.46	
1995	Gail Devers, USA	12.68	
1997	Ludmila Enquist, SWE	12.50	
1999	Gail Devers, USA	12.37	
2001	Anjanette Kirkland, USA	12.42	
2003	Perdita Felicien, CAN	12.53	
2005	Michelle Perry, USA	12.66	
2007	Michelle Perry, USA	12.46	

400-Meter Hurdles

Year		Time	
1983	Yekaterina Fesenko, USSR	.54.14	
1987	Sabine Busch, E. Ger	.53.62	
1991	Tatiana Ledovskaya, USSR	.53.11	
1993	Sally Gunnell, GBR	.52.74	WR
1995	Kim Batten, USA	.52.61	WR
1997	Nezha Bidouane, MOR	.52.97	
1999	Daima Pernia, CUB	.52.89	
2001	Nezha Bidouane, MOR	.53.34	
2003	Jana Pittman, AUS	.53.22	
2005	Yuliya Pechonkina, RUS	.52.90	
2007	Jana Rawlinson, AUS	.53.31	

4 x 100-Meter Relay

Year		Time	
1983	East Germany	.41.76	
1987	United States	.41.58	
1991	Jamaica	.41.94	
1993	Russia	.41.49	
1995	United States	.42.12	
1997	United States	.41.47	CR
1999	Bahamas	.41.92	
2001	Germany	.42.32*	
2003	France	.41.78	
2005	United States	.41.78	
2007	United States	.41.98	

*The United States was stripped of its 2001 gold after lead runner Kelli White tested positive for a stimulant.

4 x 400-Meter Relay

Year		Time	
1983	East Germany	3:19.73	
1987	East Germany	3:18.63	
1991	Soviet Union	3:18.43	
1993	United States	3:16.71	CR
1995	United States	3:22.39	
1997	Germany	3:20.92	
1999	Russia	3:21.98	
2001	Jamaica	3:20.65	
2003	United States	3:22.63	
2005	Russia	3:20.95	
2007	United States	3:18.55	

20-Kilometer Walk

Held as 10-Kilometer race from 1987-97

Year		Time	
1983	Not held		
1987	Irina Strakhova, USSR	.44:12	
1991	Alina Ivanova, USSR	.42:57	
1993	Sari Essayah, FIN	.42:59	
1995	Irina Stankina, RUS	.42:13	
1997	Anna Sidoti, ITA	.42:55	
1999	Hongyu Liu, CHN	1:30:50	
2001	Olimpiada Ivanova, RUS	1:27:48	
2003	Yelena Nikolayeva, RUS	1:26:52	
2005	Olimpiada Ivanova, RUS	1:25:41	**WR**
2007	Olga Kaniskina, RUS	1:30:09	

High Jump

Year		Height	
1983	Tamara Bykova, USSR	.6- 7	
1987	Stefka Kostadinova, BUL	.6-10¼	**WR**
1991	Heike Henkel, GER	.6- 8¾	
1993	Ioamnet Quintero, CUB	.6- 6¼	
1995	Stefka Kostadinova, BUL	.6- 7	
1997	Hanne Haugland, NOR	.6- 6¼	
1999	Inga Babakova, UKR	.6- 6¼	
2001	Hestrie Cloete, RSA	.6- 6¾	
2003	Hestrie Cloete, RSA	.6- 9	
2005	Kajsa Bergqvist, SWE	.6- 7½	
2007	Blanka Vlasic, CRO	.6- 8½	

Pole Vault

Year		Height	
1999	Stacy Dragila, USA	.15- 1	
2001	Stacy Dragila, USA	.15- 7	
2003	Svetlana Feofanova, RUS	.15- 7	
2005	Yelena Isinbayeva, RUS	16- 5¼	**WR**
2007	Yelena Isinbayeva, RUS	.15- 9	

Long Jump

Year		Distance	
1983	Heike Daute, E. Ger	23-10¼ʷ	
1987	Jackie Joyner-Kersee, USA	24- 1¾	**CR**
1991	Jackie Joyner-Kersee, USA	24- 0¼	
1993	Heike Drechsler, GER	23- 4	
1995	Fiona May, ITA	22-10¾ʷ	
1997	Lyudmila Galkina, RUS	23- 1¾	
1999	Niurka Montalvo, SPA	23- 2	
2001	Fiona May, ITA	23- 0½	
2003	Eunice Barber, FRA	22-11¼	
2005	Tianna Madison, USA	22- 7¼	
2007	Tatyana Lebedeva, RUS	23- 0¾	

Triple Jump

Year		Distance	
1993	Ana Biryukova, RUS	46- 6¼	
1995	Inessa Kravets, UKR	50- 10¾	**WR**
1997	Sarka Kasparkova, CZR	49- 10½	
1999	Paraskevi Tsiamita, GRE	48- 10	
2001	Tatyana Lebedeva, RUS	50- 0½	
2003	Tatyana Lebedeva, RUS	49- 9¾	
2005	Trecia Smith, JAM	49- 7	
2007	Yargelis Savigne, CUB	50- 1½	

Shot Put

Year		Distance	
1983	Helena Fibingerova, CZE	.69- 0	
1987	Natalia Lisovskaya, USSR	.69- 8	**CR**
1991	Huang Zhihong, CHN	.68- 4	
1993	Huang Zhihong, CHN	.67- 6	
1995	Astrid Kumbernuss, GER	.69- 7½	
1997	Astrid Kumbernuss, GER	.67- 11½	
1999	Astrid Kumbernuss, GER	.65- 1½	
2001	Yanina Korolchik, BLR	.67- 7½	
2003	Svetlana Krivelyova, RUS	.67- 8¼	
2005	Nadezhda Ostapchuk, BLR	.67- 3½	
2007	Valerie Vili, NZ	.67- 4¾	

Discus

Year		Distance	
1983	Martina Opitz, E. Ger	.226- 2	
1987	Martina Opitz Hellmann, E. Ger	.235- 0	**CR**
1991	Tsvetanka Khristova, BUL	.233- 0	
1993	Olga Burova, RUS	.221- 1	
1995	Ellina Zvereva, BLR	.225- 2	
1997	Beatrice Faumuina, NZE	.219- 3	
1999	Franka Dietzsch, GER	.223- 6	
2001	Natalya Sadova, RUS	.224-11	
2003	Irina Yatchenko, BLR	.220-10	
2005	Franka Dietzsch, GER	.218- 4	
2007	Franka Dietzsch, GER	.218- 6	

Hammer Throw

Year		Distance	
1999	Mihaela Melinte, ROM	.246-8¾	**CR**
2001	Yipsi Moreno, CUB	.231- 9	
2003	Yipsi Moreno, CUB	.240- 7	
2005	Olga Kuzenkova, RUS	.246- 5	
2007	Betty Heidler, GER	.245- 3	

Javelin

Year		Distance	
1983	Tiina Lillak, FIN	.232- 4	
1987	Fatima Whitbread, GBR	.251- 5	**CR**
1991	Xu Demei, CHN	.225- 8	
1993	Trine Hattestad, NOR	.227- 0	
1995	Natalya Shikolenko, BLR	.221- 8	
1997	Trine Hattestad, NOR	.225-8	
1999	Mirela Manjani-Tzelili, GRE	.220- 1	
2001	Osleidys Menendez, CUB	.228- 1	
2003	Mirela Manjani, GRE	.218- 3	
2005	Osleidys Menendez, CUB	.235- 3	**WR**
2007	Barbora Spotakova, CZR	.220- 0	

Heptathlon

Year		Points	
1983	Ramona Neubert, E. Ger	6770	
1987	Jackie Joyner-Kersee, USA	7128	**CR**
1991	Sabine Braun, GER	6672	
1993	Jackie Joyner-Kersee, USA	6837	
1995	Ghada Shouaa, SYR	6651	
1997	Sabine Braun, GER	6739	
1999	Eunice Barber, FRA	6861	
2001	Yelena Prokhorova, RUS	6694	
2003	Carolina Kluft, SWE	7001	
2005	Carolina Kluft, SWE	6887	
2007	Carolina Kluft, SWE	7032	

World Cross Country Championships
MEN

Multiple winners: Kenenisa Bekele, John Ngugi and Paul Tergat (5); Carlos Lopes (3); Mohammed Mourhit, Khalid Skah, William Sigei, John Treacy and Craig Virgin (2).

Year		Year		Year	
1973	Pekka Paivarinta, Finland	1978	John Treacy, Ireland	1983	Bekele Debele, Ethiopia
1974	Eric DeBeck, Belgium	1979	John Treacy, Ireland	1984	Carlos Lopes, Portugal
1975	Ian Stewart, Scotland	1980	Craig Virgin, USA	1985	Carlos Lopes, Portugal
1976	Carlos Lopes, Portugal	1981	Craig Virgin, USA	1986	John Ngugi, Kenya
1977	Leon Schots, Belgium	1982	Mohammed Kedir, Ethiopia	1987	John Ngugi, Kenya

Year		Year		Year	
1988	John Ngugi, Kenya	1995	Paul Tergat, Kenya	2002	Kenenisa Bekele, Ethiopia
1989	John Ngugi, Kenya	1996	Paul Tergat, Kenya	2003	Kenenisa Bekele, Ethiopia
1990	Khalid Skah, Morocco	1997	Paul Tergat, Kenya	2004	Kenenisa Bekele, Ethiopia
1991	Khalid Skah, Morocco	1998	Paul Tergat, Kenya	2005	Kenenisa Bekele, Ethiopia
1992	John Ngugi, Kenya	1999	Paul Tergat, Kenya	2006	Kenenisa Bekele, Ethiopia
1993	William Sigei, Kenya	2000	Mohammed Mourhit, Belgium	2007	Zersenay Tadesse, Eritrea
1994	William Sigei, Kenya	2001	Mohammed Mourhit, Belgium		

WOMEN

Multiple winners: Grete Waitz (5); Lynn Jennings and Derartu Tulu (3); Zola Budd, Paola Cacchi, Tirunesh Dibaba, Maricica Puica, Paula Radcliffe, Annette Sergent, Carmen Valero and Gete Wami (2).

Year		Year		Year	
1973	Paola Cacchi, Italy	1985	Zola Budd, England	1997	Derartu Tulu, Ethiopia
1974	Paola Cacchi, Italy	1986	Zola Budd, England	1998	Sonia O'Sullivan, Ireland
1975	Julie Brown, USA	1987	Annette Sergent, France	1999	Gete Wami, Ethiopia
1976	Carmen Valero, Spain	1988	Ingrid Kristiansen, Norway	2000	Derartu Tulu, Ethiopia
1977	Carmen Valero, Spain	1989	Annette Sergent, France	2001	Paula Radcliffe, Gr. Britain
1978	Grete Waitz, Norway	1990	Lynn Jennings, USA	2002	Paula Radcliffe, Gr. Britain
1979	Grete Waitz, Norway	1991	Lynn Jennings, USA	2003	Werknesh Kidane, Ethiopia
1980	Grete Waitz, Norway	1992	Lynn Jennings, USA	2004	Benita Johnson, Australia
1981	Grete Waitz, Norway	1993	Albertina Dias, Portugal	2005	Tirunesh Dibaba, Ethiopia
1982	Maricica Puica, Romania	1994	Helen Chepngeno, Kenya	2006	Tirunesh Dibaba, Ethiopia
1983	Grete Waitz, Norway	1995	Derartu Tulu, Ethiopia	2007	Lornah Kiplagat, Netherlands
1984	Maricica Puica, Romania	1996	Gete Wami, Ethiopia		

Marathons

Boston

America's oldest regularly contested foot race, the Boston Marathon is held on Patriots' Day every April. It has been run at four different distances: 24 miles, 1232 yards (1897-1923); 26 miles, 209 yards (1924-26); 26 miles, 385 yards (1927-52, since 1957); 25 miles, 958 yards (1953-56).

MEN

Multiple winners: Clarence DeMar (7); Gerard Cote and Bill Rodgers (4); Robert Kipkoech Cheruiyot, Ibrahim Hussein, Cosmas Ndeti, Eino Oksanen and Leslie Pawson (3); Tarzan Brown, Jim Caffrey, John A. Kelley, John Miles, Toshihiko Seko, Geoff Smith, Moses Tanui and Aurele Vandendriessche (2).

Year		Time	Year		Time
1897	John McDermott, New York	2:55:10	1931	James Henigan, Massachusetts	2:46:45
1898	Ronald McDonald, Massachusetts	2:42:00	1932	Paul deBruyn, Germany	2:33:36
1899	Lawrence Brignolia, Massachusetts	2:54:38	1933	Leslie Pawson, Rhode Island	2:31:01
1900	Jim Caffrey, Canada	2:39:44	1934	Dave Komonen, Canada	2:32:53
1901	Jim Caffrey, Canada	2:29:23	1935	John A. Kelley, Massachusetts	2:32:07
1902	Sam Mellor, New York	2:43:12	1936	Ellison (Tarzan) Brown, Rhode Island	2:33:40
1903	J.C. Lorden, Massachusetts	2:41:29	1937	Walter Young, Canada	2:33:20
1904	Mike Spring, New York	2:38:04	1938	Leslie Pawson, Rhode Island	2:35:34
1905	Fred Lorz, New York	2:38:25	1939	Ellison (Tarzan) Brown, Rhode Island	2:28:51
1906	Tim Ford, Massachusetts	2:45:45	1940	Gerard Cote, Canada	2:28:28
1907	Tom Longboat, Canada	2:24:24	1941	Leslie Pawson, Rhode Island	2:30:38
1908	Tom Morrissey, New York	2:25:43	1942	Joe Smith, Massachusetts	2:26:51
1909	Henri Renaud, New Hampshire	2:53:36	1943	Gerard Cote, Canada	2:28:25
1910	Fred Cameron, Nova Scotia	2:28:52	1944	Gerard Cote, Canada	2:31:50
1911	Clarence DeMar, Massachusetts	2:21:39	1945	John A. Kelley, Massachusetts	2:30:40
1912	Mike Ryan, Illinois	2:21:18	1946	Stylianos Kyriakides, Greece	2:29:27
1913	Fritz Carlson, Minnesota	2:25:14	1947	Yun Bok Suh, Korea	2:25:39
1914	James Duffy, Canada	2:25:01	1948	Gerard Cote, Canada	2:31:02
1915	Edouard Fabre, Canada	2:31:41	1949	Karle Leandersson, Sweden	2:31:50
1916	Arthur Roth, Massachusetts	2:27:16	1950	Kee Yonh Ham, Korea	2:32:39
1917	Bill Kennedy, New York	2:28:37	1951	Shigeki Tanaka, Japan	2:27:45
1918	World War relay race		1952	Doroteo Flores, Guatemala	2:31:53
1919	Carl Linder, Massachusetts	2:29:13	1953	Keizo Yamada, Japan	2:18:51
1920	Peter Trivoulidas, New York	2:29:31	1954	Veiko Karvonen, Finland	2:20:39
1921	Frank Zuna, New Jersey	2:18:57	1955	Hideo Hamamura, Japan	2:18:22
1922	Clarence DeMar, Massachusetts	2:18:10	1956	Antti Viskari, Finland	2:14:14
1923	Clarence DeMar, Massachusetts	2:23:37	1957	John J. Kelley, Connecticut	2:20:05
1924	Clarence DeMar, Massachusetts	2:29:40	1958	Franjo Mihalic, Yugoslavia	2:25:54
1925	Charles Mellor, Illinois	2:33:00	1959	Eino Oksanen, Finland	2:22:42
1926	John Miles, Nova Scotia	2:25:40	1960	Paavo Kotila, Finland	2:20:54
1927	Clarence DeMar, Massachusetts	2:40:22	1961	Eino Oksanen, Finland	2:23:39
1928	Clarence DeMar, Massachusetts	2:37:07	1962	Eino Oksanen, Finland	2:23:48
1929	John Miles, Nova Scotia	2:33:08	1963	Aurele Vandendriessche, Belgium	2:18:58
1930	Clarence DeMar, Massachusetts	2:34:48	1964	Aurele Vandendriessche, Belgium	2:19:59

Boston Marathon (Cont.)

Year		Time	Year		Time
1965	Morio Shigematsu, Japan	2:16:33	1987	Toshihiko Seko, Japan	2:11:50
1966	Kenji Kimihara, Japan	2:17:11	1988	Ibrahim Hussein, Kenya	2:08:43
1967	David McKenzie, New Zealand	2:15:45	1989	Abebe Mekonnen, Ethiopia	2:09:06
1968	Amby Burfoot, Connecticut	2:22:17	1990	Gelindo Bordin, Italy	2:08:19
1969	Yoshiaki Unetani, Japan	2:13:49	1991	Ibrahim Hussein, Kenya	2:11:06
			1992	Ibrahim Hussein, Kenya	2:08:14
1970	Ron Hill, England	2:10:30	1993	Cosmas Ndeti, Kenya	2:09:33
1971	Alvaro Mejia, Colombia	2:18:45	1994	Cosmas Ndeti, Kenya	2:07:15
1972	Olavi Suomalainen, Finland	2:15:39	1995	Cosmas Ndeti, Kenya	2:09:22
1973	Jon Anderson, Oregon	2:16:03	1996	Moses Tanui, Kenya	2:09:16
1974	Neil Cusack, Ireland	2:13:39	1997	Lameck Aguta, Kenya	2:10:34
1975	Bill Rodgers, Massachusetts	2:09:55	1998	Moses Tanui, Kenya	2:07:34
1976	Jack Fultz, Pennsylvania	2:20:19	1999	Joseph Chebet, Kenya	2:09:52
1977	Jerome Drayton, Canada	2:14:46			
1978	Bill Rodgers, Massachusetts	2:10:13	2000	Elijah Lagat, Kenya	2:09:47
1979	Bill Rodgers, Massachusetts	2:09:27	2001	Lee Bong-Ju, South Korea	2:09:43
			2002	Rodgers Rop, Kenya	2:09:02
1980	Bill Rodgers, Massachusetts	2:12:11	2003	Robert Kipkoech Cheruiyot, Kenya	2:10:11
1981	Toshihiko Seko, Japan	2:09:26	2004	Timothy Cherigat, Kenya	2:10:37
1982	Alberto Salazar, Oregon	2:08:52	2005	Hailu Negussie, Ethiopia	2:11:45
1983	Greg Meyer, New Jersey	2:09:00	2006	Robert Kipkoech Cheruiyot, Kenya	2:07:14*
1984	Geoff Smith, England	2:10:34	2007	Robert Kipkoech Cheruiyot, Kenya	2:14:13
1985	Geoff Smith, England	2:14:05	*Course record.		
1986	Rob de Castella, Australia	2:07:51			

WOMEN

Multiple winners: Catherine Ndereba (4); Rosa Mota, Uta Pippig and Fatuma Roba (3); Joan Benoit, Miki Gorman, Ingrid Kristiansen and Olga Markova (2).

Year		Time	Year		Time
1972	Nina Kuscsik, New York	3:08:58	1991	Wanda Panfil, Poland	2:24:18
1973	Jacqueline Hansen, California	3:05:59	1992	Olga Markova, CIS	2:23:43
1974	Miki Gorman, California	2:47:11	1993	Olga Markova, Russia	2:25:27
1975	Liane Winter, West Germany	2:42:24	1994	Uta Pippig, Germany	2:21:45
1976	Kim Merritt, Wisconsin	2:47:10	1995	Uta Pippig, Germany	2:25:11
1977	Miki Gorman, California	2:48:33	1996	Uta Pippig, Germany	2:27:12
1978	Gayle Barron, Georgia	2:44:52	1997	Fatuma Roba, Ethiopia	2:26:23
1979	Joan Benoit, Maine	2:35:15	1998	Fatuma Roba, Ethiopia	2:23:21
			1999	Fatuma Roba, Ethiopia	2:23:25
1980	Jacqueline Gareau, Canada	2:34:28			
1981	Allison Roe, New Zealand	2:26:46	2000	Catherine Ndereba, Kenya	2:26:11
1982	Charlotte Teske, West Germany	2:29:33	2001	Catherine Ndereba, Kenya	2:23:53
1983	Joan Benoit, Maine	2:22:43	2002	Margaret Okayo, Kenya	2:20:43*
1984	Lorraine Moller, New Zealand	2:29:28	2003	Svetlana Zakharova, Russia	2:25:20
1985	Lisa Larsen Weidenbach, Mass	2:34:06	2004	Catherine Ndereba, Kenya	2:24:27
1986	Ingrid Kristiansen, Norway	2:24:55	2005	Catherine Ndereba, Kenya	2:25:13
1987	Rosa Mota, Portugal	2:25:21	2006	Rita Jeptoo, Kenya	2:23:38
1988	Rosa Mota, Portugal	2:24:30	2007	Lidiya Grigoryeva, Russia	2:29:18
1989	Ingrid Kristiansen, Norway	2:24:33	*Course record.		
1990	Rosa Mota, Portugal	2:25:23			

New York City

Started in 1970, the New York City Marathon is run in the fall, usually on the first Sunday in November. The route winds through all of the city's five boroughs and finishes in Central Park.

MEN

Multiple winners: Bill Rodgers (4); Alberto Salazar (3); Tom Fleming, John Kagwe, Orlando Pizzolato and German Silva (2).

Year		Time	Year		Time	Year		Time
1970	Gary Muhrcke, USA	2:31:38	1983	Rod Dixon, NZE	2:08:59	1996	Giacomo Leone, ITA	2:09:54
1971	Norman Higgins, USA	2:22:54	1984	Orlando Pizzolato, ITA	2:14:53	1997	John Kagwe, KEN	2:08:12
1972	Sheldon Karlin, USA	2:27:52	1985	Orlando Pizzolato, ITA	2:11:34	1998	John Kagwe, KEN	2:08:45
1973	Tom Fleming, USA	2:21:54	1986	Gianni Poli, ITA	2:11:06	1999	Joseph Chebet, KEN	2:09:14
1974	Norbert Sander, USA	2:26:30	1987	Ibrahim Hussein, KEN	2:11:01			
1975	Tom Fleming, USA	2:19:27	1988	Steve Jones, WAL	2:08:20	2000	Abdelkhader El Mouaziz, MOR	2:10:08
1976	Bill Rodgers, USA	2:10:09	1989	Juma Ikangaa, TAN	2:08:01	2001	Tesfaye Jifar, ETH	2:07:43*
1977	Bill Rodgers, USA	2:11:28	1990	Douglas Wakiihuri, KEN	2:12:39	2002	Rodgers Rop, KEN	2:08:07
1978	Bill Rodgers, USA	2:12:12	1991	Salvador Garcia, MEX	2:09:28	2003	Martin Lel, KEN	2:10:30
1979	Bill Rodgers, USA	2:11:42	1992	Willie Mtolo, S. Afr.	2:09:29	2004	Hendrik Ramaala, RSA	2:09:28
			1993	Andres Espinosa, MEX	2:10:04	2005	Paul Tergat, KEN	2:09:30
1980	Alberto Salazar, USA	2:09:41	1994	German Silva, MEX	2:11:21	2006	M. Gomes dos Santos, BRA	2:09:58
1981	Alberto Salazar, USA	2:08:13	1995	German Silva, MEX	2:11:00	*Course record.		
1982	Alberto Salazar, USA	2:09:29						

WOMEN

Multiple winners: Grete Waitz (9); Miki Gorman, Nina Kuscsik, Tegla Loroupe, Margaret Okayo and Jelena Prokopcuka (2).

Year		Time	Year		Time	Year		Time
1970	No Finisher		1983	Grete Waitz, NOR	2:27:00	1996	Anuta Catuna, ROM	2:28:18
1971	Beth Bonner, USA	2:55:22	1984	Grete Waitz, NOR	2:29:30	1997	F. Rochat-Moser, SWI	2:28:43
1972	Nina Kuscsik, USA	3:08:41	1985	Grete Waitz, NOR	2:28:34	1998	Franca Fiacconi, ITA	2:25:17
1973	Nina Kuscsik, USA	2:57:07	1986	Grete Waitz, NOR	2:28:06	1999	Adriana Fernandez, MEX	2:25:06
1974	Katherine Switzer, USA	3:07:29	1987	Priscilla Welch, GBR	2:30:17	2000	Ludmila Petrova, RUS	2:25:45
1975	Kim Merritt, USA	2:46:14	1988	Grete Waitz, NOR	2:28:07	2001	Margaret Okayo, KEN	2:24:21
1976	Miki Gorman, USA	2:39:11	1989	Ingrid Kristiansen, NOR	2:25:30	2002	Joyce Chepchumba, KEN	2:25:56
1977	Miki Gorman, USA	2:43:10	1990	Wanda Panfil, POL	2:30:45	2003	Margaret Okayo, KEN	2:22:31*
1978	Grete Waitz, NOR	2:32:30	1991	Liz McColgan, GBR	2:27:23	2004	Paula Radcliffe, GBR	2:23:10
1979	Grete Waitz, NOR	2:27:33	1992	Lisa Ondieki, AUS	2:24:40	2005	Jelena Prokopcuka, LAT	2:24:41
1980	Grete Waitz, NOR	2:25:41	1993	Uta Pippig, GER	2:26:24	2006	Jelena Prokopcuka, LAT	2:25:05
1981	Allison Roe, NZE	2:25:29	1994	Tegla Loroupe, KEN	2:27:37	*Course record.		
1982	Grete Waitz, NOR	2:27:14	1995	Tegla Loroupe, KEN	2:28:06			

Annual Awards

Track & Field News Athletes of the Year

Voted on by an international panel of track and field experts and presented since 1959 for men and 1974 for women.

MEN

Multiple winners: Hicham El Guerrouj and Carl Lewis (3); Kenenisa Bekele, Sergey Bubka, Sebastian Coe, Haile Gebrselassie, Michael Johnson, Alberto Juantorena, Noureddine Morceli, Jim Ryun and Peter Snell (2).

Year		Event	Year		Event
1959	Martin Lauer, W. Germany	110H/Decathlon	1983	Carl Lewis, USA	100/200/Long Jump
1960	Rafer Johnson, USA	Decathlon	1984	Carl Lewis, USA	100/200/Long Jump
1961	Ralph Boston, USA	Long Jump/110 Hurdles	1985	Said Aouita, Morocco	1500/5000
1962	Peter Snell, New Zealand	800/1500	1986	Yuri Sedykh, USSR	Hammer Throw
1963	C.K. Yang, Taiwan	Decathlon/Pole Vault	1987	Ben Johnson, Canada	100
1964	Peter Snell, New Zealand	800/1500	1988	Sergey Bubka, USSR	Pole Vault
1965	Ron Clarke, Australia	5000/10,000	1989	Roger Kingdom, USA	110 Hurdles
1966	Jim Ryun, USA	800/1500	1990	Michael Johnson, USA	200/400
1967	Jim Ryun, USA	1500	1991	Sergey Bubka, USSR	Pole Vault
1968	Bob Beamon, USA	Long Jump	1992	Kevin Young, USA	400 Hurdles
1969	Bill Toomey, USA	Decathlon	1993	Noureddine Morceli, Algeria	Mile/1500/3000
1970	Randy Matson, USA	Shot Put	1994	Noureddine Morceli, Algeria	Mile/1500/3000
1971	Rod Milburn, USA	110 Hurdles	1995	Haile Gebrselassie, Ethiopia	5000/10,000
1972	Lasse Viren, Finland	5000/10,000	1996	Michael Johnson, USA	200/400
1973	Ben Jipcho, Kenya	1500/5000/Steeplechase	1997	Wilson Kipketer, Denmark	800
1974	Rick Wohlhuter, USA	800/1500	1998	Haile Gebrselassie, Ethiopia	3000/5000/10,000
1975	John Walker, New Zealand	800/1500	1999	Hicham El Guerrouj, Morocco	Mile/1500
1976	Alberto Juantorena, Cuba	400/800	2000	Virgilijus Alekna, Lithuania	Discus
1977	Alberto Juantorena, Cuba	400/800	2001	Hicham El Guerrouj, Morocco	Mile/1500
1978	Henry Rono, Kenya	5000/10,000/Steeplechase	2002	Hicham El Guerrouj, Morocco	Mile/1500
1979	Sebastian Coe, Great Britain	800/1500	2003	Felix Sanchez, Dominican Republic	400 Hurdles
1980	Edwin Moses, USA	400 Hurdles	2004	Kenenisa Bekele, Ethiopia	5000/10,000
1981	Sebastian Coe, Great Britain	800/1500	2005	Kenenisa Bekele, Ethiopia	5000/10,000
1982	Carl Lewis, USA	100/200/Long Jump	2006	Asafa Powell, Jamaica	100

WOMEN

Multiple winners: Marita Koch (4); Marion Jones and Jackie Joyner-Kersee (3); Evelyn Ashford and Yelena Isinbayeva (2).

Year		Event	Year		Event
1974	Irena Szewinska, Poland	100/200/400	1991	Heike Henkel, Germany	High Jump
1975	Faina Melnik, USSR	Shot Put/Discus	1992	Heike Drechsler, Germany	Long Jump
1976	Tatiana Kazankina, USSR	800/1500	1993	Wang Junxia, China	1500/3000/10,000
1977	Rosemarie Ackermann, E. Germany	High Jump	1994	Jackie Joyner-Kersee, USA	100H/Heptathlon
1978	Marita Koch, E. Germany	100/200/400	1995	Sonia O'Sullivan, Ireland	1500/3000/5000
1979	Marita Koch, E. Germany	100/200/400	1996	Svetlana Masterkova, Russia	800/1500
1980	Ilona Briesenick, E. Germany	Shot Put	1997	Marion Jones, USA	100/200
1981	Evelyn Ashford, USA	100/200	1998	Marion Jones, USA	100/200/LJ
1982	Marita Koch, E. Germany	100/200/400	1999	Gabriela Szabo, Romania	3000/5000
1983	Jarmila Kratochvilova, Czech	200/400/800	2000	Marion Jones, USA	100/200/LJ
1984	Evelyn Ashford, USA	100	2001	Stacy Dragila, USA	Pole Vault
1985	Marita Koch, E. Germany	100/200/400	2002	Paula Radcliffe, Gr. Britain	3000/5000/10k/Mar
1986	Jackie Joyner-Kersee, USA	Heptathlon/Long Jump	2003	Maria Mutola, Mozambique	800
1987	Jackie Joyner-Kersee, USA	100H/Heptathlon/LJ	2004	Yelena Isinbayeva, Russia	Pole Vault
1988	Florence Griffith Joyner, USA	100/200	2005	Yelena Isinbayeva, Russia	Pole Vault
1989	Ana Quirot, Cuba	400/800	2006	Sanya Richards, USA	200/400
1990	Merlene Ottey, Jamaica	100/200			

SWIMMING & DIVING
FINA World Championships

While the Summer Olympics have served as the unofficial world championships for swimming and diving throughout the centuries, a separate World Championship meet was started in 1973 by the Federation Internationale de Natation Amateur (FINA). The meet has varied between being held every two years, every three years or every four years. Currently it is held every two years. Sites have been Belgrade (1973); Cali, COL (1975); West Berlin (1978); Guayaquil, ECU (1982); Madrid (1986); Perth (1991 & 98), Rome (1994), Fukuoka, JPN (2001), Barcelona (2003), Montreal (2005) and Melbourne (2007). Looking forward, the Championships will be held in Rome (2009) and Shanghai (2011).

MEN

Most gold medals (including relays): Michael Phelps (15); Ian Thorpe (11); Grant Hackett (10); Aaron Peirsol (8); Jim Montgomery (7); Matt Biondi, Michael Klim and Aleksandr Popov (6); Rowdy Gaines, Brendan Hansen and Matt Welsh (5); Joe Bottom, Ian Crocker, Tamas Darnyi, Michael Gross, Tom Jager, Jason Lezak, David McCagg, Vladimir Salnikov and Tim Shaw (4); Billy Forrester, Andras Hargitay, Kosuke Kitajima, Ryan Lochte, Roland Matthes, John Murphy, Jeff Rouse, Norbert Rozsa and David Wilkie (3).

50-Meter Freestyle

Year		Time	
1973-82 Not held			
1986	Tom Jager, USA	22.49	
1991	Tom Jager, USA	22.16	
1994	Aleksandr Popov, RUS	22.17	
1998	Bill Pilczuk, USA	22.29	
2001	Anthony Ervin, USA	22.09	
2003	Aleksandr Popov, RUS	21.92	
2005	Roland Schoeman, RSA	21.69	CR
2007	Benjamin Wildman-Tobriner, USA	21.88	

100-Meter Freestyle

Year		Time	
1973	Jim Montgomery, USA	51.70	
1975	Tim Shaw, USA	51.25	
1978	David McCagg, USA	50.24	
1982	Jorg Woithe, E. Ger	50.18	
1986	Matt Biondi, USA	48.94	
1991	Matt Biondi, USA	49.18	
1994	Aleksandr Popov, RUS	49.12	
1998	Aleksandr Popov, RUS	48.93	
2001	Anthony Ervin, USA	48.33	
2003	Aleksandr Popov, RUS	48.42	
2005	Filippo Magnini, ITA	48.12	CR
2007	Filippo Magnini, ITA	48.43	

200-Meter Freestyle

Year		Time	
1973	Jim Montgomery, USA	1:53.02	
1975	Tim Shaw, USA	1:52.04	
1978	Billy Forrester, USA	1:51.02	
1982	Michael Gross, W. Ger	1:49.84	
1986	Michael Gross, W. Ger	1:47.92	
1991	Giorgio Lamberti, ITA	1:47.27	
1994	Antti Kasvio, FIN	1:47.32	
1998	Michael Klim, AUS	1:47.41	
2001	Ian Thorpe, AUS	1:44.06	WR
2003	Ian Thorpe, AUS	1:45.14	
2005	Michael Phelps, USA	1:45.20	
2007	Michael Phelps, USA	1:43.86	WR

400-Meter Freestyle

Year		Time	
1973	Rick DeMont, USA	3:58.18	
1975	Tim Shaw, USA	3:54.88	
1978	Vladimir Salnikov, USSR	3:51.94	
1982	Vladimir Salnikov, USSR	3:51.30	
1986	Rainer Henkel, W. Ger	3:50.05	
1991	Jorg Hoffman, GER	3:48.04	
1994	Kieren Perkins, AUS	3:43.80	
1998	Ian Thorpe, AUS	3:46.29	
2001	Ian Thorpe, AUS	3:40.17	WR
2003	Ian Thorpe, AUS	3:42.58	
2005	Grant Hackett, AUS	3:42.91	
2007	Tae Hwan Park, KOR	3:44.30	

800-Meter Freestyle

Year		Time	
1973-98 Not held			
2001	Ian Thorpe, AUS	7:39.16	
2003	Grant Hackett, AUS	7:43.82	
2005	Grant Hackett, AUS	7:38.65	WR
2007	Oussama Mellouli, TUN	7:46.95	

1500-Meter Freestyle

Year		Time	
1973	Stephen Holland, AUS	15:31.85	
1975	Tim Shaw, USA	15:28.92	
1978	Vladimir Salnikov, USSR	15:03.99	
1982	Vladimir Salnikov, USSR	15:01.77	
1986	Rainer Henkel, W. Ger	15:05.31	
1991	Jorg Hoffman, GER	14:50.36	
1994	Kieren Perkins, AUS	14:50.52	
1998	Grant Hackett, AUS	14:51.70	
2001	Grant Hackett, AUS	14:34.56	WR
2003	Grant Hackett, AUS	14:43.14	
2005	Grant Hackett, AUS	14:42.58	
2007	Mateusz Sawrymowicz, POL	14:45.94	

50-Meter Backstroke

Year		Time	
1973-98 Not held			
2001	Randall Bal, USA	25.34	
2003	Thomas Rupprath, GER	24.80	WR
2005	Aristeidis Grigoriadis, GRE	24.95	
2007	Gerhard Zandberg, RSA	24.98	

100-Meter Backstroke

Year		Time	
1973	Roland Matthes, E. Ger	57.47	
1975	Roland Matthes, E. Ger	58.15	
1978	Bob Jackson, USA	56.36	
1982	Dirk Richter, E. Ger	55.95	
1986	Igor Polianski, USSR	55.58	
1991	Jeff Rouse, USA	55.23	
1994	Martin Lopez-Zubero, SPA	55.17	
1998	Lenny Krayzelburg, USA	55.00	
2001	Matt Welsh, AUS	54.31	
2003	Aaron Peirsol, USA	53.61	
2005	Aaron Peirsol, USA	53.62	
2007	Aaron Peirsol, USA	52.98	WR

200-Meter Backstroke

Year		Time	
1973	Roland Matthes, E. Ger	2:01.87	
1975	Zoltan Varraszto, HUN	2:05.05	
1978	Jesse Vassallo, USA	2:02.16	
1982	Rick Carey, USA	2:00.82	
1986	Igor Polianski, USSR	1:58.78	
1991	Martin Zubero, SPA	1:59.52	
1994	Vladimir Selkov, RUS	1:57.42	
1998	Lenny Krayzelburg, USA	1:58.84	
2001	Aaron Peirsol, USA	1:57.13	
2003	Aaron Peirsol, USA	1:55.92	
2005	Aaron Peirsol, USA	1:54.66	
2007	Ryan Lochte, USA	1:54.32	WR

50-Meter Breaststroke

Year		Time
1973-98	Not held	
2001	Oleg Lisogor, UKR	.27.52
2003	James Gibson, GBR	.27.56
2005	Mark Warnecke, GER	.27.63
2007	Oleg Lisogor, UKR	.27.66

100-Meter Breaststroke

Year		Time	
1973	John Hencken, USA	1:04.02	
1975	David Wilkie, GBR	1:04.26	
1978	Walter Kusch, W. Ger	1:03.56	
1982	Steve Lundquist, USA	1:02.75	
1986	Victor Davis, CAN	1:02.71	
1991	Norbert Rozsa, HUN	1:01.45	
1994	Norbert Rozsa, HUN	1:01.24	
1998	Frederik deBurghgraeve, BEL	1:01.34	
2001	Roman Sloudnov, RUS	1:00.16	
2003	Kosuke Kitajima, JPN	.59.78	
2005	Brendan Hansen, USA	.59.37	CR
2007	Brendan Hansen, USA	.59.80	

200-Meter Breaststroke

Year		Time	
1973	David Wilkie, GBR	2:19.28	
1975	David Wilkie, GBR	2:18.23	
1978	Nick Nevid, USA	2:18.37	
1982	Victor Davis, CAN	2:14.77	
1986	Jozsef Szabo, HUN	2:14.27	
1991	Mike Barrowman, USA	2:11.23	
1994	Norbert Rozsa, HUN	2:12.81	
1998	Kurt Grote, USA	2:13.40	
2001	Brendan Hansen, USA	2:10.69	
2003	Kosuke Kitajima, JPN	2:09.42	WR
2005	Brendan Hansen, USA	2:09.85	
2007	Kosuke Kitajima, JPN	2:09.80	

50-Meter Butterfly

Year		Time	
1973-98	Not held		
2001	Geoff Huegill, AUS	.23.50	
2003	Matt Welsh, AUS	.23.43	
2005	Roland Schoeman, RSA	.22.96	WR
2007	Roland Schoeman, RSA	.23.18	

100-Meter Butterfly

Year		Time	
1973	Bruce Robertson, CAN	.55.69	
1975	Greg Jagenburg, USA	.55.63	
1978	Joe Bottom, USA	.54.30	
1982	Matt Gribble, USA	.53.88	
1986	Pablo Morales, USA	.53.54	
1991	Anthony Nesty, SUR	.53.29	
1994	Rafal Szukala, POL	.53.51	
1998	Michael Klim, AUS	.52.25	
2001	Lars Frolander, SWE	.52.10	
2003	Ian Crocker, USA	.50.98	
2005	Ian Crocker, USA	.50.40	WR
2007	Michael Phelps, USA	.50.77	

200-Meter Butterfly

Year		Time	
1973	Robin Backhaus, USA	2:03.32	
1975	Billy Forrester, USA	2:01.95	
1978	Mike Bruner, USA	1:59.38	
1982	Michael Gross, W. Ger	1:58.85	
1986	Michael Gross, W. Ger	1:56.53	
1991	Melvin Stewart, USA	1:55.69	WR
1994	Denis Pankratov, RUS	1:56.54	
1998	Denys Sylantyev, UKR	1:56.61	
2001	Michael Phelps, USA	1:54.58	WR
2003	Michael Phelps, USA	1:54.35	
2005	Pawel Korzeniowski, POL	1:55.02	
2007	Michael Phelps, USA	1:52.09	

200-Meter Individual Medley

Year		Time	
1973	Gunnar Larsson, SWE	2:08.36	
1975	Andras Hargitay, HUN	2:07.72	
1978	Graham Smith, CAN	2:03.65	
1982	Alexander Sidorenko, USSR	2:03.30	
1986	Tamás Darnyi, HUN	2:01.57	
1991	Tamás Darnyi, HUN	1:59.36	
1994	Janis Sievinen, FIN	1:58.16	
1998	Marcel Wouda, NET	2:01.18	
2001	Massimiliano Rosolino, ITA	1:59.71	
2003	Michael Phelps, USA	1:56.04	WR
2005	Michael Phelps, USA	1:56.68	
2007	Michael Phelps, USA	1:54.98	WR

400-Meter Individual Medley

Year		Time	
1973	Andras Hargitay, HUN	4:31.11	
1975	Andras Hargitay, HUN	4:32.57	
1978	Jesse Vassallo, USA	4:20.05	
1982	Ricardo Prado, BRA	4:19.78	
1986	Tamás Darnyi, HUN	4:18.98	
1991	Tamás Darnyi, HUN	4:12.36	
1994	Tom Dolan, USA	4:12.30	
1998	Tom Dolan, USA	4:14.95	
2001	Alessio Boggiatto, ITA	4:13.15	
2003	Michael Phelps, USA	4:09.09	WR
2005	Laszlo Cseh, HUN	4:09.63	
2007	Michael Phelps, USA	4:06.22	WR

4 x 100-Meter Freestyle Relay

Year		Time	
1973	United States	3:27.18	
1975	United States	3:24.85	
1978	United States	3:19.74	
1982	United States	3:19.26	
1986	United States	3:19.98	
1991	United States	3:17.15	
1994	United States	3:16.90	
1998	United States	3:16.69	
2001	Australia	3:14.10	
2003	Russia	3:14.06	
2005	United States	3:13.77	
2007	United States	3:12.72	CR

4 x 200-Meter Freestyle Relay

Year		Time	
1973	United States	7:33.22	
1975	West Germany	7:39.44	
1978	United States	7:20.82	
1982	United States	7:21.09	
1986	East Germany	7:15.91	
1991	Germany	7:13.50	
1994	Sweden	7:17.34	
1998	Australia	7:12.48	
2001	Australia	7:04.66	WR
2003	Australia	7:08.58	
2005	United States	7:06.58	
2007	United States	7:03.24	WR

4 x 100-Meter Medley Relay

Year		Time	
1973	United States	3:49.49	
1975	United States	3:49.00	
1978	United States	3:44.63	
1982	United States	3:40.84	
1986	United States	3:41.25	
1991	United States	3:39.66	
1994	United States	3:37.74	
1998	Australia	3:37.98	
2001	Australia	3:35.35	
2003	United States	3:31.54	WR
2005	United States	3:31.85	
2007	Australia	3:34.93	

WOMEN

Most gold medals (including relays): Kornelia Ender and Lisbeth Lenton (8); Leisel Jones and Kristin Otto (7); Katie Hoff and Jenny Thompson (6); Natalie Coughlin, Inge De Bruijn, Hannah Stockbauer and Luo Xuejuan (5); Tracy Caulkins, Heike Friedrich, Le Jingyi, Jana Klochkova, Rosemarie Kother, Ulrike Richter and Kate Ziegler (4).

50-Meter Freestyle

Year		Time	
1973-82	Not held		
1986	Tamara Costache, ROM	.25.28	
1991	Zhuang Yong, CHN	.25.47	
1994	Le Jingyi, CHN	.24.51	WR
1998	Amy Van Dyken, USA	.25.15	
2001	Inge de Bruijn, NED	.24.47	
2003	Inge de Bruijn, NED	.24.47	
2005	Lisbeth Lenton, AUS	.24.59	
2007	Lisbeth Lenton, AUS	.24.53	

100-Meter Freestyle

Year		Time	
1973	Kornelia Ender, E. Ger	.57.54	
1975	Kornelia Ender, E. Ger	.56.50	
1978	Barbara Krause, E. Ger	.55.68	
1982	Birgit Meineke, E. Ger	.55.79	
1986	Kristin Otto, E. Ger	.55.05	
1991	Nicole Haislett, USA	.55.17	
1994	Le Jingyi, CHN	.54.01	WR
1998	Jenny Thompson, USA	.54.95	
2001	Inge de Bruijn, NED	.54.18	
2003	Hanna-Maria Seppala, FIN	.54.37	
2005	Jodie Henry, AUS	.54.18	
2007	Lisbeth Lenton, AUS	.53.40	CR

200-Meter Freestyle

Year		Time	
1973	Keena Rothhammer, USA	.2:04.99	
1975	Shirley Babashoff, USA	.2:02.50	
1978	Cynthia Woodhead, USA	.1:58.53	
1982	Annemarie Verstappen, NED	.1:59.53	
1986	Heike Friedrich, E. Ger	.1:58.26	
1991	Hayley Lewis, AUS	.2:00.48	
1994	Franziska Van Almsick, GER	.1:56.78	WR
1998	Claudia Poll, CRC	.1:58.90	
2001	Giaan Rooney, AUS	.1:58.57	
2003	Alena Popchenko, BLR	.1:58.32	
2005	Solenne Figues, FRA	.1:58.60	
2007	Laure Manaudou, FRA	.1:55.52	WR

400-Meter Freestyle

Year		Time	
1973	Heather Greenwood, USA	.4:20.28	
1975	Shirley Babashoff, USA	.4:22.70	
1978	Tracey Wickham, AUS	.4:06.28	WR
1982	Carmela Schmidt. E. Ger	.4:08.98	
1986	Heike Friedrich, E. Ger	.4:07.45	
1991	Janet Evans, USA	.4:08.63	
1994	Yang Aihua, CHN	.4:09.64	
1998	Yan Chen, CHN	.4:06.72	
2001	Yana Klochkova, UKR	.4:07.30	
2003	Hannah Stockbauer, GER	.4:06.75	
2005	Laure Manaudou, FRA	.4:06.44	
2007	Laure Manaudou, FRA	.4:02.61	CR

800-Meter Freestyle

Year		Time	
1973	Novella Calligaris, ITA	.8:52.97	
1975	Jenny Turrall, AUS	.8:44.75	
1978	Tracey Wickham, AUS	.8:25.94	
1982	Kim Linehan, USA	.8:27.48	
1986	Astrid Strauss, E. Ger	.8:28.24	
1991	Janet Evans, USA	.8:24.05	
1994	Janet Evans, USA	.8:29.85	
1998	Brooke Bennett, USA	.8:28.71	
2001	Hannah Stockbauer, GER	.8:24.66	
2003	Hannah Stockbauer, GER	.8:23.66	CR
2005	Kate Ziegler, USA	.8:25.31	
2007	Kate Ziegler, USA	.8:18.52	CR

1500-Meter Freestyle

Year		Time	
1973-98	Not held		
2001	Hannah Stockbauer, GER	.16:01.02	
2003	Hannah Stockbauer, GER	.16:00.18	CR
2005	Kate Ziegler, USA	.16:00.41	
2007	Kate Ziegler, USA	.15:53.05	CR

50-Meter Backstroke

Year		Time	
1973-98	Not held		
2001	Haley Cope, USA	.28.51	
2003	Nina Zhivanevskaya, ESP	.28.48	CR
2005	Giaan Rooney, AUS	.28.63	
2007	Leila Vaziri, USA	.28.16	WR

100-Meter Backstroke

Year		Time	
1973	Ulrike Richter, E. Ger	.1:05.42	
1975	Ulrike Richter, E. Ger	.1:03.30	
1978	Linda Jezek, USA	.1:02.55	
1982	Kristin Otto, E. Ger	.1:01.30	
1986	Betsy Mitchell, USA	.1:01.74	
1991	Krisztina Egerszegi, HUN	.1:01.78	
1994	He Cihong, CHN	.1:00.57	
1998	Lea Maurer, USA	.1:01.16	
2001	Natalie Coughlin, USA	.1:00.37	
2003	Antje Buschschulte, GER	.1:00.50	
2005	Kirsty Coventry, ZIM	.1:00.24	
2007	Natalie Coughlin, USA	.59.44	WR

200-Meter Backstroke

Year		Time	
1973	Melissa Belote, USA	.2:20.52	
1975	Birgit Treiber, E. Ger	.2:15.46	
1978	Linda Jezek, USA	.2:11.93	
1982	Cornelia Sirch, E. Ger	.2:09.91	
1986	Cornelia Sirch, E. Ger	.2:11.37	
1991	Krisztina Egerszegi, HUN	.2:09.15	
1994	He Cihong, CHN	.2:07.40	CR
1998	Roxana Maracineanu, FRA	.2:11.26	
2001	Diana Iuliana Mocanu, ROM	.2:09.94	
2003	Katy Sexton, GBR	.2:08.74	
2005	Kirsty Coventry, ZIM	.2:08.52	
2007	Margaret Hoelzer, USA	.2:07.16	CR

50-Meter Breaststroke

Year		Time	
1973-82	Not held		
2001	Luo Xuejuan, CHN	.30.84	
2003	Luo Xuejuan, CHN	.30.67	
2005	Jade Edmistone, AUS	.30.45	WR
2007	Jessica Hardy, USA	.30.63	

100-Meter Breaststroke

Year		Time	
1973	Renate Vogel, E. Ger	.1:13.74	
1975	Hannalore Anke, E. Ger	.1:12.72	
1978	Julia Bogdanova, USSR	.1:10.31	
1982	Ute Geweniger, E. Ger	.1:09.14	
1986	Sylvia Gerasch, E. Ger	.1:08.11	
1991	Linley Frame, AUS	.1:08.81	
1994	Samantha Riley, AUS	.1:07.69	
1998	Kristy Kowal, USA	.1:08.42	
2001	Luo Xuejuan, CHN	.1:07.18	
2003	Luo Xuejuan, CHN	.1:06.80	
2005	Leisel Jones, AUS	.1:06.25	
2007	Leisel Jones, AUS	.1:05.72	CR

200-Meter Breaststroke

Year		Time
1973	Renate Vogel, E. Ger	2:40.01
1975	Hannalore Anke, E. Ger	2:37.25
1978	Lina Kachushite, USSR	2:31.42
1982	Svetlana Varganova, USSR	2:28.82
1986	Silke Hoerner, E. Ger	2:27.40
1991	Elena Volkova, USSR	2:29.53
1994	Samantha Riley, AUS	2:26.87
1998	Agnes Kovacs, HUN	2:25.45
2001	Agnes Kovacs, HUN	2:24.90
2003	Amanda Beard, USA	2:22.99
2005	Leisel Jones, AUS	2:21.72	WR
2007	Leisel Jones, AUS	2:21.84

50-Meter Butterfly

Year		Time	
1973-98 Not held			
2001	Inge de Bruijn, NED	25.90	
2003	Inge de Bruijn, NED	25.84	CR
2005	Danni Miatke, AUS	26.11	
2007	Therese Alshammar, SWE	25.91	

100-Meter Butterfly

Year		Time	
1973	Kornelia Ender, E. Ger	1:02.53	
1975	Kornelia Ender, E. Ger	1:01.24	
1978	Joan Pennington, USA	1:00.20	
1982	Mary T. Meagher, USA	59.41	
1986	Kornelia Gressler, E. Ger	59.51	
1991	Qian Hong, CHN	59.68	
1994	Liu Limin, CHN	58.98	
1998	Jenny Thompson, USA	58.46	
2001	Petria Thomas, AUS	58.27	
2003	Jenny Thompson, USA	57.96	
2005	Jessicah Schipper, AUS	57.23	CR
2007	Lisbeth Lenton, AUS	57.15	WR

200-Meter Butterfly

Year		Time	
1973	Rosemarie Kother, E. Ger	2:13.76	
1975	Rosemarie Kother, E. Ger	2:15.92	
1978	Tracy Caulkins, USA	2:09.78	
1982	Ines Geissler, E. Ger	2:08.66	
1986	Mary T. Meagher, USA	2:08.41	
1991	Summer Sanders, USA	2:09.24	
1994	Liu Limin, CHN	2:07.25	
1998	Susie O'Neill, AUS	2:07.93	
2001	Petria Thomas, AUS	2:06.73	
2003	Otylia Jedrzejczak, POL	2:07.56	
2005	Otylia Jedrzejczak, POL	2:05.61	WR
2007	Jessicah Schipper, AUS	2:06.39	

200-Meter Individual Medley

Year		Time	
1973	Andre Huebner, E. Ger	2:20.51	
1975	Kathy Heddy, USA	2:19.80	
1978	Tracy Caulkins, USA	2:19.80	
1982	Petra Schneider, E. Ger	2:11.79	
1986	Kristin Otto, E. Ger	2:15.56	
1991	Lin Li, CHN	2:13.40	
1994	Lu Bin, CHN	2:12.34	
1998	Yanyan Wu, CHN	2:10.88	
2001	Maggie Bowen, USA	2:11.93	
2003	Yana Klochkova, UKR	2:10.75	
2005	Katie Hoff, USA	2:10.41	WR
2007	Katie Hoff, USA	2:10.13	CR

400-Meter Individual Medley

Year		Time
1973	Gudrun Wegner, E. Ger	4:57.71
1975	Ulrike Tauber, E. Ger	4:52.76
1978	Tracy Caulkins, USA	4:40.83
1982	Petra Schneider, E. Ger	4:36.10
1986	Kathleen Nord, E. Ger	4:43.75
1991	Lin Li, CHN	4:41.45

1994	Dai Guohong, CHN	4:39.14	
1998	Yan Chen, CHN	4:36.66	
2001	Yana Klochkova, UKR	4:36.98	
2003	Yana Klochkova, UKR	4:36.74	
2005	Katie Hoff, USA	4:36.07	CR
2007	Katie Hoff, USA	4:32.89	CR

4 x 100-Meter Freestyle Relay

Year		Time	
1973	East Germany	3:52.45	
1975	East Germany	3:49.37	
1978	United States	3:43.43	
1982	East Germany	3:43.97	
1986	East Germany	3:40.57	
1991	United States	3:43.26	
1994	China	3:37.91	
1998	United States	3:42.11	
2001	Germany	3:39.58	
2003	United States	3:38.09	
2005	Australia	3:37.32	CR
2007	Australia	3:35.48	CR

4 x 200-Meter Freestyle Relay

Year		Time	
1973-82 Not held			
1986	East Germany	7:59.33	
1991	Germany	8:02.56	
1994	China	7:57.96	
1998	Germany	8:01.46	
2001	Great Britain	7:58.69	
2003	United States	7:55.70	
2005	United States	7:53.70	CR
2007	United States	7:50.09	WR

4 x 100-Meter Medley Relay

Year		Time	
1973	East Germany	4:16.84	
1975	East Germany	4:14.74	
1978	United States	4:08.21	
1982	East Germany	4:05.80	
1986	East Germany	4:04.82	
1991	United States	4:06.51	
1994	China	4:01.67	
1998	United States	4:01.93	
2001	Australia	4:01.50	
2003	China	3:59.89	
2005	Australia	3:57.47	CR
2007	Australia	3:55.74	WR

Diving

Most Gold Medals: MEN–Greg Louganis and Dmitri Sautin (5); Phil Boggs, Alexandre Despatie and Wang Feng (3). WOMEN–Guo Jingjing (8); Irina Kalinina, Gao Min and Wu Minxia (3).

MEN

1-Meter Springboard

Year		Pts
1973-86 Not Held		
1991	Edwin Jongejans, NED	588.51
1994	Evan Stewart, ZIM	382.14
1998	Yu Zhuocheng, CHN	417.54
2001	Wang Feng, CHN	444.03
2003	Xu Xiang, CHN	431.94
2005	Alexandre Despatie, CAN	489.69
2007	Luo Yutong, CHN	477.40

3-Meter Springboard

Year		Pts
1973	Phil Boggs, USA	618.57
1975	Phil Boggs, USA	597.12
1978	Phil Boggs, USA	913.95
1982	Greg Louganis, USA	752.67
1986	Greg Louganis, USA	750.06
1991	Kent Ferguson, USA	650.25

3-Meter Springboard (Cont.)

Year		Pts
1994	Yu Zhuocheng, CHN	.655.44
1998	Dmitri Sautin, RUS	.746.79
2001	Dmitri Sautin, RUS	.725.82
2003	Alexander Dobroskok, RUS	.788.37
2005	Alexandre Despatie, CAN	.813.60
2007	Qin Kai, CHN	.545.35

Platform

Year		Pts
1973	Klaus Dibiasi, ITA	.559.53
1975	Klaus Dibiasi, ITA	.547.98
1978	Greg Louganis, USA	.844.11
1982	Greg Louganis, USA	.634.26
1986	Greg Louganis, USA	.668.58
1991	Sun Shuwei, CHN	.626.79
1994	Dmitri Sautin, RUS	.634.71
1998	Dmitri Sautin, RUS	.750.99
2001	Tian Liang, CHN	.688.77
2003	Alexandre Despatie, CAN	.716.91
2005	Hu Jia, CHN	.698.01
2007	Gleb Galperin, RUS	.544.70

3-Meter Synchronized

Year		Pts
1973-98	Not held	
2001	Peng Bo & Wang Kenan, CHN	.342.63
2003	A. Dobroskok & D. Sautin, RUS	.369.18
2005	He Chong & Wang Feng, CHN	.384.42
2007	Qin Kai & Wang Feng, CHN	.458.76

10-Meter Synchronized

Year		Pts
1973-98	Not held	
2001	Tian Liang & Hu Jia, CHN	.361.41
2003	M. Helm & R. Newbery, AUS	.384.60
2005	D. Dobrosok & G. Galperin, RUS	.392.88
2007	Huo Liang & Lin Yue, CHN	.489.48

WOMEN

1-Meter Springboard

Year		Pts
1973-86	Not held	
1991	Gao Min, CHN	.478.26
1994	Chen Lixia, CHN	.279.30
1998	Irina Lashko, RUS	.296.07
2001	Blythe Hartley, CAN	.300.81
2003	Irina Lashko, AUS	.299.97
2005	Blythe Hartley, CAN	.325.65
2007	He Zi, CHN	.316.65

3-Meter Springboard

Year		Pts
1973	Christa Koehler, E. Ger	.442.17
1975	Irina Kalinina, USSR	.489.81
1978	Irina Kalinina, USSR	.691.43
1982	Megan Neyer, USA	.501.03
1986	Gao Min, CHN	.582.90
1991	Gao Min, CHN	.539.01
1994	Tan Shuping, CHN	.548.49
1998	Yulia Pakhalina, RUS	.544.52
2001	Guo Jingjing, CHN	.596.67
2003	Guo Jingjing, CHN	.617.94
2005	Guo Jingjing, CHN	.645.54
2007	Guo Jingjing, CHN	.381.75

Platform

Year		Pts
1973	Ulrike Knape, SWE	.406.77
1975	Janet Ely, USA	.403.89
1978	Irina Kalinina, USSR	.412.71
1982	Wendy Wyland, USA	.438.79
1986	Chen Lin, CHN	.449.67
1991	Fu Mingxia, CHN	.426.51
1994	Fu Mingxia, CHN	.434.04
1998	Olena Zhupyna	.550.41
2001	Xu Mian, CHN	.532.65
2003	Emilie Heymans, CAN	.597.45
2005	Laura Wilkinson, USA	.564.87
2007	Wang Xin, CHN	.432.85

3-Meter Synchronized

Year		Pts
1973-98	Not held	
2001	Wu Minxia & Guo Jingjing, CHN	.347.31
2003	Wu Minxia & Guo Jingjing, CHN	.357.30
2005	Li Ting & Guo Jingjing, CHN	.351.60
2007	Wu Minxia & Guo Jingjing, CHN	.355.80

10-Meter Synchronized

Year		Pts
1973-98	Not held	
2001	Duan Qing & Sang Xue, CHN	.329.94
2003	Lao Lishi & Li Ting, CHN	.344.58
2005	Jia Tong & Yuan Pei Lin, CHN	.344.58
2007	Jia Tong & Chen Ruolin, CHN	.361.32

ALPINE SKIING

World Cup Overall Champions

World Cup Overall Champions (downhill and slalom events combined) since the tour was organized in 1967.

MEN

Multiple winners: Marc Girardelli (5); Hermann Maier, Gustavo Thoeni and Pirmin Zurbriggen (4); Phil Mahre and Ingemar Stenmark (3); Stephan Eberharter, Jean-Claude Killy, Lasse Kjus and Karl Schranz (2).

Year		Year		Year	
1967	Jean-Claude Killy, France	1981	Phil Mahre, USA	1995	Alberto Tomba, Italy
1968	Jean-Claude Killy, France	1982	Phil Mahre, USA	1996	Lasse Kjus, Norway
1969	Karl Schranz, Austria	1983	Phil Mahre, USA	1997	Luc Alphand, France
1970	Karl Schranz, Austria	1984	Pirmin Zurbriggen, Switzerland	1998	Hermann Maier, Austria
1971	Gustavo Thoeni, Italy	1985	Marc Girardelli, Luxembourg	1999	Lasse Kjus, Norway
1972	Gustavo Thoeni, Italy	1986	Marc Girardelli, Luxembourg	2000	Hermann Maier, Austria
1973	Gustavo Thoeni, Italy	1987	Pirmin Zurbriggen, Switzerland	2001	Hermann Maier, Austria
1974	Piero Gros, Italy	1988	Pirmin Zurbriggen, Switzerland	2002	Stephan Eberharter, Austria
1975	Gustavo Thoeni, Italy	1989	Marc Girardelli, Luxembourg	2003	Stephan Eberharter, Austria
1976	Ingemar Stenmark, Sweden	1990	Pirmin Zurbriggen, Switzerland	2004	Hermann Maier, Austria
1977	Ingemar Stenmark, Sweden	1991	Marc Girardelli, Luxembourg	2005	Bode Miller, USA
1978	Ingemar Stenmark, Sweden	1992	Paul Accola, Switzerland	2006	Benjamin Raich, Austria
1979	Peter Luescher, Switzerland	1993	Marc Girardelli, Luxembourg	2007	Aksel Lund Svindal, Norway
1980	Andreas Wenzel, Liechtenstein	1994	Kjetil Andre Aamodt, Norway		

WOMEN

Multiple winners: Annemarie Moser-Pröll (6); Janica Kostelic, Petra Kronberger and Vreni Schneider (3); Michela Figini, Nancy Greene, Erika Hess, Anja Paerson, Katja Seizinger, Maria Walliser and Hanni Wenzel (2).

Year		Year		Year	
1967	Nancy Greene, Canada	1981	Marie-Therese Nadig, SWI	1995	Vreni Schneider, Switzerland
1968	Nancy Greene, Canada	1982	Erika Hess, Switzerland	1996	Katja Seizinger, Germany
1969	Gertrud Gabi, Austria	1983	Tamara McKinney, USA	1997	Pernilla Wiberg, Sweden
1970	Michele Jacot, France	1984	Erika Hess, Switzerland	1998	Katja Seizinger, Germany
1971	Annemarie Pröll, Austria	1985	Michela Figini, Switzerland	1999	Alexandra Meissnitzer, Austria
1972	Annemarie Pröll, Austria	1986	Maria Walliser, Switzerland	2000	Renate Goetschl, Austria
1973	Annemarie Pröll, Austria	1987	Maria Walliser, Switzerland	2001	Janica Kostelic, Croatia
1974	Annemarie Pröll, Austria	1988	Michela Figini, Switzerland	2002	Michaela Dorfmeister, Austria
1975	Annemarie Moser-Pröll, Austria	1989	Vreni Schneider, Switzerland	2003	Janica Kostelic, Croatia
1976	Rosi Mittermaier, W. Germany	1990	Petra Kronberger, Austria	2004	Anja Paerson, Sweden
1977	Lise-Marie Morerod, Switzerland	1991	Petra Kronberger, Austria	2005	Anja Paerson, Sweden
1978	Hanni Wenzel, Liechtenstein	1992	Petra Kronberger, Austria	2006	Janica Kostelic, Croatia
1979	Annemarie Moser-Pröll, Austria	1993	Anita Wachter, Austria	2007	Nicole Hosp, Austria
1980	Hanni Wenzel, Liechtenstein	1994	Vreni Schneider, Switzerland		

World Cup Event Champions

World Cup Champions in each individual event since the tour was organized in 1967.

MEN

Downhill

Multiple winners: Franz Klammer (5); Luc Alphand, Stephan Eberharter, Franz Heinzer and Peter Muller (3); Roland Collumbin, Marc Girardelli, Helmut Hoflehner, Hermann Maier, Bernard Russi, Karl Schranz, Michael Walchhofer and Pirmin Zurbriggen (2).

Year		Year		Year	
1967	Jean-Claude Killy, France	1981	Harti Weirather, Austria	1995	Luc Alphand, France
1968	Gerhard Nenning, Austria	1982	Steve Podborski, Canada	1996	Luc Alphand, France
1969	Karl Schranz, Austria		Peter Muller, Switzerland	1997	Luc Alphand, France
1970	Karl Schranz, Austria	1983	Franz Klammer, Austria	1998	Andreas Schiffer, Austria
	Karl Cordin, Austria	1984	Urs Raber, Switzerland	1999	Lasse Kjus, Norway
1971	Bernard Russi, Switzerland	1985	Helmut Hoflehner, Austria	2000	Hermann Maier, Austria
1972	Bernard Russi, Switzerland	1986	Peter Wirnsberger, Austria	2001	Hermann Maier, Austria
1973	Roland Collumbin, Switzerland	1987	Pirmin Zurbriggen, Switzerland	2002	Stephan Eberharter, Austria
1974	Roland Collumbin, Switzerland	1988	Pirmin Zurbriggen, Switzerland	2003	Stephan Eberharter, Austria
1975	Franz Klammer, Austria	1989	Marc Girardelli, Luxembourg	2004	Stephan Eberharter, Austria
1976	Franz Klammer, Austria	1990	Helmut Hoflehner, Austria	2005	Michael Walchhofer, Austria
1977	Franz Klammer, Austria	1991	Franz Heinzer, Switzerland	2006	Michael Walchhofer, Austria
1978	Franz Klammer, Austria	1992	Franz Heinzer, Switzerland	2007	Didier Cuche, Switzerland
1979	Peter Muller, Switzerland	1993	Franz Heinzer, Switzerland		
1980	Peter Muller, Switzerland	1994	Marc Girardelli, Luxembourg		

Slalom

Multiple winners: Ingemar Stenmark (8); Alberto Tomba (4); Jean-Noel Augert, Marc Girardelli and Benjamin Raich (3); Armin Bittner, Thomas Sykora and Gustavo Thoeni (2).

Year		Year		Year	
1967	Jean-Claude Killy, France	1980	Ingemar Stenmark, Sweden	1994	Alberto Tomba, Italy
1968	Domeng Giovanoli, Switzerland	1981	Ingemar Stenmark, Sweden	1995	Alberto Tomba, Italy
1969	Jean-Noel Augert, France	1982	Phil Mahre, USA	1996	Sebastien Amiez, France
1970	Patrick Russel, France	1983	Ingemar Stenmark, Sweden	1997	Thomas Sykora, Austria
	Alain Penz, France	1984	Marc Girardelli, Luxembourg	1998	Thomas Sykora, Austria
1971	Jean-Noel Augert, France	1985	Marc Girardelli, Luxembourg	1999	Thomas Stangassinger, Austria
1972	Jean-Noel Augert, France	1986	Rok Petrovic, Yugoslavia	2000	Kjetil Andre Aamodt, Norway
1973	Gustavo Thoeni, Italy	1987	Bojan Krizaj, Yugoslavia	2001	Benjamin Raich, Austria
1974	Gustavo Thoeni, Italy	1988	Alberto Tomba, Italy	2002	Ivica Kostelic, Croatia
1975	Ingemar Stenmark, Sweden	1989	Armin Bittner, West Germany	2003	Kalle Palander, Finland
1976	Ingemar Stenmark, Sweden	1990	Armin Bittner, West Germany	2004	Rainer Schoenfelder, Austria
1977	Ingemar Stenmark, Sweden	1991	Marc Girardelli, Luxembourg	2005	Benjamin Raich, Austria
1978	Ingemar Stenmark, Sweden	1992	Alberto Tomba, Italy	2006	Giorgio Rocca, Italy
1979	Ingemar Stenmark, Sweden	1993	Tomas Fogdof, Sweden	2007	Benjamin Raich, Austria

Giant Slalom

Multiple winners: Ingemar Stenmark (8); Michael von Gruenigen and Alberto Tomba (4); Hermann Maier and Pirmin Zurbriggen (3); Joel Gaspoz, Jean-Claude Killy, Phil Mahre, Benjamin Raich and Gustavo Thoeni (2).

Year		Year		Year	
1967	Jean-Claude Killy, France	1976	Ingemar Stenmark, Sweden	1984	Ingemar Stenmark, Sweden
1968	Jean-Claude Killy, France	1977	Heini Hemmi, Switzerland		Pirmin Zurbriggen, Switzerland
1969	Karl Schranz, Austria		Ingemar Stenmark, Sweden	1985	Marc Girardelli, Luxembourg
1970	Gustavo Thoeni, Italy	1978	Ingemar Stenmark, Sweden	1986	Joel Gaspoz, Switzerland
1971	Patrick Russel, France	1979	Ingemar Stenmark, Sweden	1987	Joel Gaspoz, Switzerland
1972	Gustavo Thoeni, Italy	1980	Ingemar Stenmark, Sweden		Pirmin Zurbriggen, Switzerland
1973	Hans Hinterseer, Austria	1981	Ingemar Stenmark, Sweden	1988	Alberto Tomba, Italy
1974	Piero Gros, Italy	1982	Phil Mahre, USA	1989	Pirmin Zurbriggen, Switzerland
1975	Ingemar Stenmark, Sweden	1983	Phil Mahre, USA		

Giant Slalom (Cont.)

Year		Year		Year	
1990	Ole-Cristian Furuseth, Norway	1996	Michael von Gruenigen, SWI	2003	Michael von Gruenigen, SWI
	Gunther Mader, Austria	1997	Michael von Gruenigen, SWI	2004	Bode Miller, USA
1991	Alberto Tomba, Italy	1998	Hermann Maier, Austria	2005	Benjamin Raich, Austria
1992	Alberto Tomba, Italy	1999	Michael von Gruenigen, SWI	2006	Benjamin Raich, Austria
1993	Kjetil Andre Aamodt, Norway	2000	Hermann Maier, Austria	2007	Aksel Lund Svindal, Norway
1994	Christian Mayer, Austria	2001	Hermann Maier, Austria		
1995	Alberto Tomba, Italy	2002	Frederic Covili, France		

Super G

Multiple winners: Hermann Maier (5); Pirmin Zurbriggen (4); Stephan Eberharter and Bode Miller (2).

Year		Year		Year	
1986	Markus Wasmeier, W. Ger.	1994	Jan Einar Thorsen, Norway	2002	Stephan Eberharter, Austria
1987	Pirmin Zurbriggen, Switzerland	1995	Peter Runggaldier, Italy	2003	Stephan Eberharter, Austria
1988	Pirmin Zurbriggen, Switzerland	1996	Atle Skaardal, Norway	2004	Hermann Maier, Austria
1989	Pirmin Zurbriggen, Switzerland	1997	Luc Alphand, France	2005	Bode Miller, USA
1990	Pirmin Zurbriggen, Switzerland	1998	Hermann Maier, Austria	2006	Aksel Lund Svindal, Norway
1991	Franz Heinzer, Switzerland	1999	Hermann Maier, Austria	2007	Bode Miller, USA
1992	Paul Accola, Switzerland	2000	Hermann Maier, Austria		
1993	Kjetil Andre Aamodt, Norway	2001	Hermann Maier, Austria		

Combined

Multiple winners: Marc Girardelli and Andreas Wenzel (4); Kjetil Andre Aamodt and Phil Mahre (3); Bode Miller, Benjamin Raich and Pirmin Zurbriggen (2).

Year		Year		Year	
1979	Andreas Wenzel, Liechtenstein	1988	Hubert Strolz, Austria	1997-99	Not awarded
1980	Andreas Wenzel, Liechtenstein	1989	Marc Girardelli, Luxembourg	2000	Kjetil Andre Aamodt, Norway
1981	Phil Mahre, USA	1990	Pirmin Zurbriggen, Switzerland	2001	Lasse Kjus, Norway
1982	Phil Mahre, USA	1991	Marc Girardelli, Luxembourg	2002	Kjetil Andre Aamodt, Norway
1983	Phil Mahre, USA	1992	Paul Accola, Switzerland	2003	Bode Miller, USA
1984	Andreas Wenzel, Liechtenstein	1993	Marc Girardelli, Luxembourg	2004	Bode Miller, USA
1985	Andreas Wenzel, Liechtenstein	1994	Kjetil Andre Aamodt, Norway	2005	Benjamin Raich, Austria
1986	Markus Wasmeier, W. Ger	1995	Marc Girardelli, Luxembourg	2006	Benjamin Raich, Austria
1987	Pirmin Zurbriggen, Switzerland	1996	Gunther Mader, Austria	2007	Aksel Lund Svindal, Norway

WOMEN

Downhill

Multiple winners: Annemarie Moser-Pröll (7), Renate Goetschl (5); Michela Figini and Katja Seizinger (4); Michaela Dorfmeister, Isolde Kostner, Isabelle Mir, Marie-Therese Nadig, Picabo Street, Bridgitte Totschnig-Habersatter and Maria Walliser (2).

Year		Year		Year	
1967	Marielle Goitschel, France	1980	Marie-Therese Nadig, SWI	1994	Katja Seizinger, Germany
1968	Isabelle Mir, France	1981	Marie-Therese Nadig, SWI	1995	Picabo Street, USA
	Olga Pall, Austria	1982	Marie-Cecile Gros-Gaudenier, FRA	1996	Picabo Street, USA
1969	Wiltrud Drexel, Austria	1983	Doris De Agostini, Switzerland	1997	Renate Goetschl, Austria
1970	Isabelle Mir, France	1984	Maria Walliser, Switzerland	1998	Katja Seizinger, Germany
1971	Annemarie Pröll, Austria	1985	Michela Figini, Switzerland	1999	Renate Goetschl, Austria
1972	Annemarie Pröll, Austria	1986	Maria Walliser, Switzerland	2000	Regina Haeusl, Germany
1973	Annemarie Pröll, Austria	1987	Michela Figini, Switzerland	2001	Isolde Kostner, Italy
1974	Annemarie Pröll, Austria	1988	Michela Figini, Switzerland	2002	Isolde Kostner, Italy
1975	Annemarie Moser-Pröll, Austria	1989	Michela Figini, Switzerland	2003	Michaela Dorfmeister, Austria
1976	Bridgitte Totschnig-Habersatter, AUT	1990	Katrin Gutensohn-Knopf, GER	2004	Renate Goetschl, Austria
1977	Bridgitte Totschnig-Habersatter, AUT	1991	Chantal Bournissen, SWI	2005	Renate Goetschl, Austria
1978	Annemarie Moser-Pröll, Austria	1992	Katja Seizinger, Germany	2006	Michaela Dorfmeister, Austria
1979	Annemarie Moser-Pröll, Austria	1993	Katja Seizinger, Germany	2007	Renate Goetschl, Austria

Slalom

Multiple winners: Vreni Schneider (6); Erika Hess (5); Janica Kostelic (3); Marielle Goitschel, Britt Lafforgue, Lisa-Marie Morerod and Roswitha Steiner (2).

Year		Year		Year	
1967	Marielle Goitschel, France	1982	Erika Hess, Switzerland	1995	Vreni Schneider, Switzerland
1968	Marielle Goitschel, France	1983	Erika Hess, Switzerland	1996	Elfi Eder, Austria
1969	Gertrud Gabl, Austria	1984	Tamara McKinney, USA	1997	Pernilla Wiberg, Sweden
1970	Ingrid Lafforgue, France	1985	Erika Hess, Switzerland	1998	Ylva Nowen, Sweden
1971	Britt Lafforgue, France	1986	Roswitha Steiner, Austria	1999	Sabine Egger, Austria
1972	Britt Lafforgue, France		Erika Hess, Switzerland	2000	Spela Pretnar, Slovenia
1973	Patricia Emonet, France	1987	Corrine Schmidhauser,	2001	Janica Kostelic, Croatia
1974	Christa Zechmeister, W. Germany		Switzerland	2002	Laure Pequegnot, France
1975	Lisa-Marie Morerod, Switzerland	1988	Roswitha Steiner, Austria	2003	Janica Kostelic, Croatia
1976	Rosi Mittermaier, W. Germany	1989	Vreni Schneider, Switzerland	2004	Anja Paerson, Sweden
1977	Lisa-Marie Morerod, Switzerland	1990	Vreni Schneider, Switzerland	2005	Tanja Poutiainen, Finland
1978	Hanni Wenzel, Liechtenstein	1991	Petra Kronberger, Austria	2006	Janica Kostelic, Croatia
1979	Regina Sackl, Austria	1992	Vreni Schneider, Switzerland	2007	Marlies Schild, Austria
1980	Perrine Pelene, France	1993	Vreni Schneider, Switzerland		
1981	Erika Hess, Switzerland	1994	Vreni Schneider, Switzerland		

Giant Slalom

Multiple winners: Vreni Schneider (5); Lisa-Marie Morerod, Annemarie Moser-Pröll and Anja Paerson (3); Martina Ertl, Nancy Greene, Carole Merle, Sonja Nef, Anita Wachter and Hanni Wenzel (2).

Year		Year		Year	
1967	Nancy Greene, Canada	1981	Marie-Therese Nadig, SWI	1994	Anita Wachter, Austria
1968	Nancy Greene, Canada	1982	Irene Epple, West Germany	1995	Vreni Schneider, Switzerland
1969	Marilyn Cochran, USA	1983	Tamara McKinney, USA	1996	Martina Ertl, Germany
1970	Michele Jacot, France	1984	Erika Hess, Switzerland	1997	Deborah Compagnoni, Italy
	Francoise Macchi, France	1985	Maria Keihl, West Germany	1998	Martina Ertl, Germany
1971	Annemarie Pröll, Austria		Michela Figini, Switzerland	1999	Alexandra Meissnitzer, Austria
1972	Annemarie Pröll, Austria	1986	Vreni Schneider, Switzerland	2000	Michaela Dorfmeister, Austria
1973	Monika Kaserer, Austria	1987	Vreni Schneider, Switzerland	2001	Sonja Nef, Switzerland
1974	Hanni Wenzel, Liechtenstein		Maria Walliser, Switzerland	2002	Sonja Nef, Switzerland
1975	Annemarie Moser-Pröll, Austria	1988	Mateja Svet, Yugoslavia	2003	Anja Paerson, Sweden
1976	Lisa-Marie Morerod, SWI	1989	Vreni Schneider, Switzerland	2004	Anja Paerson, Sweden
1977	Lisa-Marie Morerod, SWI	1990	Anita Wachter, Austria	2005	Tanja Poutiainen, Finland
1978	Lisa-Marie Morerod, SWI	1991	Vreni Schneider, Switzerland	2006	Anja Paerson, Sweden
1979	Christa Kinshofer, W. Ger.	1992	Carole Merle, France	2007	Nicole Hosp, Austria
1980	Hanni Wenzel, Liechtenstein	1993	Carole Merle, France		

Super G

Multiple winners: Katja Seizinger (5); Carole Merle (4); Renate Goetschl (3); Michaela Dorfmeister and Hilde Gerg (2).

Year		Year		Year	
1986	Maria Kiehl, West Germany	1994	Katja Seizinger, Germany	2002	Hilde Gerg, Germany
1987	Maria Walliser, Switzerland	1995	Katja Seizinger, Germany	2003	Carole Montillet, France
1988	Michela Figini, Switzerland	1996	Katja Seizinger, Germany	2004	Renate Goetschl, Austria
1989	Carole Merle, France	1997	Hilde Gerg, Germany	2005	Michaela Dorfmeister, Austria
1990	Carole Merle, France	1998	Katja Seizinger, Germany	2006	Michaela Dorfmeister, Austria
1991	Carole Merle, France	1999	Alexandra Meissnitzer, Austria	2007	Renate Goetschl, Austria
1992	Carole Merle, France	2000	Renate Goetschl, Austria		
1993	Katja Seizinger, Germany	2001	Regine Cavagnoud, France		

Combined

Multiple winners: Brigitte Oertli (5); Janica Kostelic (4); Anita Wachter and Hanni Wenzel (3); Sabine Ginther, Renate Goetschl and Pernilla Wiberg (2).

Year		Year		Year	
1979	Annemarie Moser-Pröll, Austria	1987	Brigitte Oertli, Switzerland	1996	Anita Wachter, Austria
	Hanni Wenzel, Liechtenstein	1988	Brigitte Oertli, Switzerland	1997–99	Not Awarded
1980	Hanni Wenzel, Liechtenstein	1989	Brigitte Oertli, Switzerland	2000	Renate Goetschl, Austria
1981	Maria-Therese Nadig, Switzerland	1989	Brigitte Oertli, Switzerland	2001	Janica Kostelic, Croatia
	Switzerland	1990	Anita Wachter, Austria	2002	Renate Goetschl, Austria
1982	Irene Epple, West Germany	1991	Sabine Ginther, Austria	2003	Janica Kostelic, Croatia
1983	Hanni Wenzel, Liechtenstein	1992	Sabine Ginther, Austria	2004	Not Awarded
1984	Erika Hess, Switzerland	1993	Anita Wachter, Austria	2005	Janica Kostelic, Croatia
1985	Brigitte Oertli, Switzerland	1994	Pernilla Wiberg, Sweden	2006	Janica Kostelic, Croatia
1986	Maria Walliser, Switzerland	1995	Pernilla Wiberg, Sweden	2007	Marlies Schild, Austria

FIGURE SKATING

World Champions

Skaters who won World and Olympic championships in the same year are listed in **bold** type.

MEN

Multiple winners: Ulrich Salchow (10); Karl Schafer (7); Dick Button (5); Willy Bockl, Kurt Browning, Scott Hamilton and Hayes Jenkins and Alexei Yagudin (4); Emmerich Danzer, Gillis Grafstrom, Gustav Hugel, David Jenkins, Fritz Kachler, Ondrej Nepela, Evgeni Plushenko and Elvis Stojko (3); Brian Boitano, Gilbert Fuchs, Jan Hoffmann, Felix Kaspar, Vladimir Kovalev, Stephane Lambiel and Tim Wood (2).

Year		Year		Year	
1896	Gilbert Fuchs, Germany	1907	Ulrich Salchow, Sweden	1924	**Gillis Grafstrom,** Sweden
1897	Gustav Hugel, Austria	1908	**Ulrich Salchow**, Sweden	1925	Willy Bockl, Austria
1898	Henning Grenander, Sweden	1909	Ulrich Salchow, Sweden	1926	Willy Bockl, Austria
1899	Gustav Hugel, Austria	1910	Ulrich Salchow, Sweden	1927	Willy Bockl, Austria
1900	Gustav Hugel, Austria	1911	Ulrich Salchow, Sweden	1928	Willy Bockl, Austria
1901	Ulrich Salchow, Sweden	1912	Fritz Kachler, Austria	1929	Gillis Grafstrom, Sweden
1902	Ulrich Salchow, Sweden	1913	Fritz Kachler, Austria		
1903	Ulrich Salchow, Sweden	1914	Gosta Sandhal, Sweden	1930	Karl Schafer, Austria
1904	Ulrich Salchow, Sweden	1915-21	Not held	1931	Karl Schafer, Austria
1905	Ulrich Salchow, Sweden	1922	Gillis Grafstrom, Sweden	1932	**Karl Schafer**, Austria
1906	Gilbert Fuchs, Germany	1923	Fritz Kachler, Austria	1933	Karl Schafer, Austria
				1934	Karl Schafer, Austria

Figure Skating (Cont.)

Year		Year		Year	
1935	Karl Schafer, Austria	1965	Alain Calmat, France	1990	Kurt Browning, Canada
1936	**Karl Schafer**, Austria	1966	Emmerich Danzer, Austria	1991	Kurt Browning, Canada
1937	Felix Kaspar, Austria	1967	Emmerich Danzer, Austria	1992	**Viktor Petrenko**, CIS
1938	Felix Kaspar, Austria	1968	Emmerich Danzer, Austria	1993	Kurt Browning, Canada
1939	Graham Sharp, Britain	1969	Tim Wood, USA	1994	Elvis Stojko, Canada
1940-46	Not held			1995	Elvis Stojko, Canada
1947	Hans Gerschwiler, Switzerland	1970	Tim Wood, USA	1996	Todd Eldredge, USA
1948	**Dick Button**, USA	1971	Ondrej Nepela, Czechoslovakia	1997	Elvis Stojko, Canada
1949	Dick Button, USA	1972	**Ondrej Nepela**, Czechoslovakia	1998	Alexei Yagudin, Russia
		1973	Ondrej Nepela, Czechoslovakia	1999	Alexei Yagudin, Russia
1950	Dick Button, USA	1974	Jan Hoffmann, E. Germany		
1951	Dick Button, USA	1975	Sergie Volkov, USSR	2000	Alexei Yagudin, Russia
1952	**Dick Button**, USA	1976	**John Curry**, Britain	2001	Evgeni Plushenko, Russia
1953	Hayes Jenkins, USA	1977	Vladimir Kovalev, USSR	2002	**Alexei Yagudin**, Russia
1954	Hayes Jenkins, USA	1978	Charles Tickner, USA	2003	Evgeni Plushenko, Russia
1955	Hayes Jenkins, USA	1979	Vladimir Kovalev, USSR	2004	Evgeni Plushenko, Russia
1956	**Hayes Jenkins**, USA			2005	Stephane Lambiel, Switzerland
1957	David Jenkins, USA	1980	Jan Hoffmann, E. Germany	2006	Stephane Lambiel, Switzerland
1958	David Jenkins, USA	1981	Scott Hamilton, USA	2007	Brian Joubert, France
1959	David Jenkins, USA	1982	Scott Hamilton, USA		
		1983	Scott Hamilton, USA		
1960	Alan Giletti, France	1984	**Scott Hamilton**, USA		
1961	Not held	1985	Alexander Fadeev, USSR		
1962	Donald Jackson, Canada	1986	Brian Boitano, USA		
1963	Donald McPherson, Canada	1987	Brian Orser, Canada		
1964	**Manfred Schnelldorfer**, W. Germany	1988	**Brian Boitano**, USA		
		1989	Kurt Browning, Canada		

WOMEN

Multiple winners: Sonja Henie (10); Carol Heiss, Michelle Kwan and Herma Planck Szabo (5); Lily Kronberger and Katarina Witt (4); Sjoukje Dijkstra, Peggy Fleming and Meray Horvath (3); Tenley Albright, Linda Fratianne, Anett Poetzsch, Beatrix Schuba, Barbara Ann Scott, Gabriele Seyfert, Irina Slutskaya, Megan Taylor, Alena Vrzanova and Kristi Yamaguchi (2).

Year		Year		Year	
1906	Madge Syers, Britain	1949	Alena Vrzanova, Czechoslovakia	1980	**Anett Poetzsch**, E. Germany
1907	Madge Syers, Britain	1950	Alena Vrzanova, Czechoslovakia	1981	Denise Biellmann, Switzerland
1908	Lily Kronberger, Hungary	1951	Jeannette Altwegg, Britain	1982	Elaine Zayak, USA
1909	Lily Kronberger, Hungary	1952	Jacqueline Du Bief, France	1983	Rosalyn Sumners, USA
1910	Lily Kronberger, Hungary	1953	Tenley Albright, USA	1984	**Katarina Witt**, E. Germany
1911	Lily Kronberger, Hungary	1954	Gundi Busch, W. Germany	1985	Katarina Witt, E. Germany
1912	Meray Horvath, Hungary	1955	Tenley Albright, USA	1986	Debi Thomas, USA
1913	Meray Horvath, Hungary	1956	Carol Heiss, USA	1987	Katarina Witt, E. Germany
1914	Meray Horvath, Hungary	1957	Carol Heiss, USA	1988	**Katarina Witt**, E. Germany
1915-21	Not held	1958	Carol Heiss, USA	1989	Midori Ito, Japan
		1959	Carol Heiss, USA		
1922	Herma Planck-Szabo, Austria	1960	**Carol Heiss**, USA	1990	Jill Trenary, USA
1923	Herma Planck-Szabo, Austria	1961	Not held	1991	Kristi Yamaguchi, USA
1924	**Herma Planck-Szabo**, AUT	1962	Sjoukje Dijkstra, Netherlands	1992	**Kristi Yamaguchi**, USA
1925	Herma Planck-Szabo, Austria	1963	Sjoukje Dijkstra, Netherlands	1993	Oksana Baiul, Ukraine
1926	Herma Planck-Szabo, Austria	1964	**Sjoukje Dijkstra**, Netherlands	1994	Yuka Sato, Japan
1927	Sonja Henie, Norway	1965	Petra Burka, Canada	1995	Lu Chen, China
1928	**Sonja Henie**, Norway	1966	Peggy Fleming, USA	1996	Michelle Kwan, USA
1929	Sonja Henie, Norway	1967	Peggy Fleming, USA	1997	Tara Lipinski, USA
1930	Sonja Henie, Norway	1968	**Peggy Fleming**, USA	1998	Michelle Kwan, USA
1931	Sonja Henie, Norway	1969	Gabriele Seyfert, E. Germany	1999	Maria Butyrskaya, Russia
1932	**Sonja Henie**, Norway	1970	Gabriele Seyfert, E. Germany	2000	Michelle Kwan, USA
1933	Sonja Henie, Norway	1971	Beatrix Schuba, Austria	2001	Michelle Kwan, USA
1934	Sonja Henie, Norway	1972	**Beatrix Schuba**, Austria	2002	Irina Slutskaya, Russia
1935	Sonja Henie, Norway	1973	Karen Magnussen, Canada	2003	Michelle Kwan, USA
1936	**Sonja Henie**, Norway	1974	Christine Errath, E. Germany	2004	Shizuka Arakawa, Japan
1937	Cecilia Colledge, Britain	1975	Dianne DeLeeuw, Netherlands	2005	Irina Slutskaya, Russia
1938	Megan Taylor, Britain	1976	**Dorothy Hamill**, USA	2006	Kimmie Meissner, USA
1939	Megan Taylor, Britain	1977	Linda Fratianne, USA	2007	Miki Ando, Japan
		1978	Anett Poetzsch, E. Germany		
1940-46	Not held	1979	Linda Fratianne, USA		
1947	Barbara Ann Scott, Canada				
1948	**Barbara Ann Scott**, Canada				

U.S. Champions

Skaters who won U.S., World and Olympic championships in same year are in **bold** type.

MEN

Multiple winners: Dick Button and Roger Turner (7); Todd Eldredge (6); Sherwin Badger and Robin Lee (5); Brian Boitano, Scott Hamilton, David Jenkins, Hayes Jenkins and Charles Tickner (4); Gordon McKellen, Nathaniel Niles, Johnny Weir, Michael Weiss and Tim Wood (3); Scott Allen, Christopher Bowman, Scott Davis, Eugene Turner and Gary Visconti (2).

Year		Year		Year		Year	
1914	Norman Scott	1940	Eugene Turner	1965	Gary Visconti	1989	Christopher Bowman
1915-17	Not held	1941	Eugene Turner	1966	Scott Allen	1990	Todd Eldredge
1918	Nathaniel Niles	1942	Robert Specht	1967	Gary Visconti	1991	Todd Eldredge
1919	Not held	1943	Arthur Vaughn	1968	Tim Wood	1992	Christopher Bowman
1920	Sherwin Badger	1944-45	Not held	1969	Tim Wood	1993	Scott Davis
1921	Sherwin Badger	1946	Dick Button			1994	Scott Davis
1922	Sherwin Badger	1947	Dick Button	1970	Tim Wood	1995	Todd Eldredge
1923	Sherwin Badger	1948	**Dick Button**	1971	John (Misha) Petkevich	1996	Rudy Galindo
1924	Sherwin Badger	1949	Dick Button	1972	Ken Shelley	1997	Todd Eldredge
1925	Nathaniel Niles	1950	Dick Button	1973	Gordon McKellen	1998	Todd Eldredge
1926	Chris Christenson	1951	Dick Button	1974	Gordon McKellen	1999	Michael Weiss
1927	Nathaniel Niles	1952	**Dick Button**	1975	Gordon McKellen	2000	Michael Weiss
1928	Roger Turner	1953	Hayes Jenkins	1976	Terry Kubicka	2001	Tim Goebel
1929	Roger Turner	1954	Hayes Jenkins	1977	Charles Tickner	2002	Todd Eldredge
1930	Roger Turner	1955	Hayes Jenkins	1978	Charles Tickner	2003	Michael Weiss
1931	Roger Turner	1956	**Hayes Jenkins**	1979	Charles Tickner	2004	Johnny Weir
1932	Roger Turner	1957	David Jenkins	1980	Charles Tickner	2005	Johnny Weir
1933	Roger Turner	1958	David Jenkins	1981	Scott Hamilton	2006	Johnny Weir
1934	Roger Turner	1959	David Jenkins	1982	Scott Hamilton	2007	Evan Lysacek
1935	Robin Lee	1960	David Jenkins	1983	Scott Hamilton		
1936	Robin Lee	1961	Bradley Lord	1984	**Scott Hamilton**		
1937	Robin Lee	1962	Monty Hoyt	1985	Brian Boitano		
1938	Robin Lee	1963	Thomas Litz	1986	Brian Boitano		
1939	Robin Lee	1964	Scott Allen	1987	Brian Boitano		
				1988	**Brian Boitano**		

WOMEN

Multiple winners: Michelle Kwan and Maribel Vinson (9); Theresa Weld Blanchard and Gretchen Merrill (6); Tenley Albright, Peggy Fleming and Janet Lynn (5); Linda Fratianne and Carol Heiss (4); Dorothy Hamill, Beatrix Loughran, Rosalyn Summers, Joan Tozzer and Jill Trenary (3); Yvonne Sherman and Debi Thomas (2).

Year		Year		Year		Year	
1914	Theresa Weld	1940	Joan Tozzer	1964	Peggy Fleming	1988	Debi Thomas
1915-17	Not held	1941	Jane Vaughn	1965	Peggy Fleming	1989	Jill Trenary
1918	Rosemary Beresford	1942	Jane Sullivan	1966	Peggy Fleming	1990	Jill Trenary
1919	Not held	1943	Gretchen Merrill	1967	Peggy Fleming	1991	Tonya Harding
1920	Theresa Weld	1944	Gretchen Merrill	1968	**Peggy Fleming**	1992	**Kristi Yamaguchi**
1921	Theresa Blanchard	1945	Gretchen Merrill	1969	Janet Lynn	1993	Nancy Kerrigan
1922	Theresa Blanchard	1946	Gretchen Merrill	1970	Janet Lynn	1994	vacated*
1923	Theresa Blanchard	1947	Gretchen Merrill	1971	Janet Lynn	1995	Nicole Bobek
1924	Theresa Blanchard	1948	Gretchen Merrill	1972	Janet Lynn	1996	Michelle Kwan
1925	Beatrix Loughran	1949	Yvonne Sherman	1973	Janet Lynn	1997	Tara Lipinski
1926	Beatrix Loughran	1950	Yvonne Sherman	1974	Dorothy Hamill	1998	Michelle Kwan
1927	Beatrix Loughran	1951	Sonya Klopfer	1975	Dorothy Hamill	1999	Michelle Kwan
1928	Maribel Vinson	1952	Tenley Albright	1976	**Dorothy Hamill**	2000	Michelle Kwan
1929	Maribel Vinson	1953	Tenley Albright	1977	Linda Fratianne	2001	Michelle Kwan
1930	Maribel Vinson	1954	Tenley Albright	1978	Linda Fratianne	2002	Michelle Kwan
1931	Maribel Vinson	1955	Tenley Albright	1979	Linda Fratianne	2003	Michelle Kwan
1932	Maribel Vinson	1956	Tenley Albright	1980	Linda Fratianne	2004	Michelle Kwan
1933	Maribel Vinson	1957	Carol Heiss	1981	Elaine Zayak	2005	Michelle Kwan
1934	Suzanne Davis	1958	Carol Heiss	1982	Rosalyn Sumners	2006	Sasha Cohen
1935	Maribel Vinson	1959	Carol Heiss	1983	Rosalyn Sumners	2007	Kimmie Meissner
1936	Maribel Vinson	1960	**Carol Heiss**	1984	Rosalyn Sumners		
1937	Maribel Vinson	1961	Laurence Owen	1985	Tiffany Chin		
1938	Joan Tozzer	1962	Barbara Pursley	1986	Debi Thomas		
1939	Joan Tozzer	1963	Lorraine Hanlon	1987	Jill Trenary		

* Tonya Harding was stripped of the 1994 women's title and banned from membership in the U.S. Figure Skating Assn. for life on June 30, 1994 for violating the USFSA Code of Ethics after she pleaded guilty to a charge of conspiracy to hinder the prosecution related to the Jan. 6, 1994 attack on Nancy Kerrigan.

TOUR DE FRANCE

The world's premier cycling event, the Tour de France is staged throughout the country (sometimes passing through neighboring countries) over four weeks. The 1946 Tour, however, the first after World War II, was only a five-day race.

Multiple winners: Lance Armstrong (7); Jacques Anquetil, Bernard Hinault, Miguel Induráin and Eddy Merckx (5); Louison Bobet, Greg LeMond and Philippe Thys (3); Gino Bartali Ottavio Bottecchia, Fausto Coppi, Laurent Fignon, Nicholas Frantz, Firmin Lambot, André Leducq, Sylvere Maes, Antonin Magne, Lucien Petit-Breton and Bernard Thevenet (2).

Year		Time (hrs:min:sec)
1903	Maurice Garin, France	94:33:14
1904	Henri Cornet, France	96:05:55
1905	Louis Trousselier, France	112:18:09
1906	René Pottier, France	185:47:26
1907	Lucien Petit-Breton, France	156:22:30
1908	Lucien Petit-Breton, France	156:09:31
1909	Francois Faber, Luxembourg	156:55:10
1910	Octave Lapize, France	163:52:38
1911	Gustave Garrigou, France	195:35:25
1912	Odile Defraye, Belgium	184:50:00
1913	Philippe Thys, Belgium	197:54:00
1914	Philippe Thys, Belgium	200:28:49
1915-18	Not held	
1919	Firmin Lambot, Belgium	231:07:15
1920	Philippe Thys, Belgium	228:36:13
1921	Léon Scieur, Belgium	221:50:00
1922	Firmin Lambot, Belgium	222:08:06
1923	Henri Pelissier, France	222:15:30
1924	Ottavio Bottecchia, Italy	226:18:21
1925	Ottavio Bottecchia, Italy	219:10:13
1926	Lucien Buysse, Belgium	238:44:25
1927	Nicholas Frantz, Luxembourg	198:16:42
1928	Nicholas Frantz, Luxembourg	192:48:58
1929	Maurice Dewaele, Belgium	186:39:16
1930	André Leducq, France	172:12:10
1931	Antonin Magne, France	177:10:03
1932	André Leducq, France	154:11:49
1933	Georges Speicher, France	147:51:37
1934	Antonin Magne, France	147:03:58
1935	Romain Maes, Belgium	141:32:00
1936	Sylvere Maes, Belgium	142:47:32
1937	Roger Lapebie, France	138:58:31
1938	Gino Bartali, Italy	148:29:12
1939	Sylvere Maes, Belgium	132:03:17
1940-45	Not held	
1946	Jean Lazarides, France	44:31:42
1947	Jean Robic, France	148:11:25
1948	Gino Bartali, Italy	147:10:36
1949	Fausto Coppi, Italy	149:40:49
1950	Ferdinand Kubler, Switzerland	145:36:56
1951	Hugo Koblet, Switzerland	142:20:14
1952	Fausto Coppi, Italy	151:57:20
1953	Louison Bobet, France	129:23:25
1954	Louison Bobet, France	140:06:50
1955	Louison Bobet, France	130:29:26
1956	Roger Walkowiak, France	124:01:16
1957	Jacques Anquetil, France	135:44:42
1958	Charly Gaul, Luxembourg	116:59:05
1959	Federico Bahamontes, Spain	113:50:54
1960	Gastone Nencini, Italy	112:08:42
1961	Jacques Anquetil, France	122:01:33
1962	Jacques Anquetil, France	114:31:54
1963	Jacques Anquetil, France	113:30:05
1964	Jacques Anquetil, France	127:09:44
1965	Felice Gimondi, Italy	116:42:06
1966	Lucien Aimar, France	117:34:21
1967	Roger Pingeon, France	136:53:50
1968	Jan Janssen, Netherlands	133:49:42
1969	Eddy Merckx, Belgium	116:16:02
1970	Eddy Merckx, Belgium	119:31:48
1971	Eddy Merckx, Belgium	96:45:14
1972	Eddy Merckx, Belgium	108:17:18

Year		Time (hrs:min:sec)
1973	Luis Ocana, Spain	122:25:34
1974	Eddy Merckx, Belgium	116:16:58
1975	Bernard Thevenet, France	114:35:31
1976	Lucien van Impe, Belgium	116:22:23
1977	Bernard Thevenet, France	115:38:30
1978	Bernard Hinault, France	108:18:00
1979	Bernard Hinault, France	103:06:50
1980	Joop Zoetemelk, Netherlands	109:19:14
1981	Bernard Hinault, France	96:19:38
1982	Bernard Hinault, France	92:08:46
1983	Laurent Fignon, France	105:07:52
1984	Laurent Fignon, France	112:03:40
1985	Bernard Hinault, France	113:24:23
1986	Greg LeMond, USA	110:35:19
1987	Stephen Roche, Ireland	115:27:42
1988	Pedro Delgado, Spain	84:27:53
1989	Greg LeMond, USA	87:38:35
1990	Greg LeMond, USA	90:43:20
1991	Miguel Induráin, Spain	101:01:20
1992	Miguel Induráin, Spain	100:49:30
1993	Miguel Induráin, Spain	95:57:09
1994	Miguel Induráin, Spain	103:38:38
1995	Miguel Induráin, Spain	92:44:59
1996	Bjarne Riis, Denmark	95:57:16
1997	Jan Ullrich, Germany	100:30:35
1998	Marco Pantani, Italy	92:49:46
1999	Lance Armstrong, USA	91:32:16
2000	Lance Armstrong, USA	92:33:08
2001	Lance Armstrong, USA	86:17:28
2002	Lance Armstrong, USA	82:05:12
2003	Lance Armstrong, USA	83:41:12
2004	Lance Armstrong, USA	83:36:02
2005	Lance Armstrong, USA	86:15:02
2006	Oscar Pereiro, Spain	89:40:27
2007	Alberto Contador, Spain	91:00:26

Note: On September 20, 2007, an arbitration panel ruled against American Floyd Landis' appeal of a positive doping test result, thus formally stripping him of his 2006 Tour de France title and awarding runner-up Pereiro the official victory.

Tour de France Dress Code

Yellow Jersey
Leader in the overall standings

Green Jersey
Leader in the points standings

Red Polka-Dot Jersey
King of the Mountains (best climber)

White Jersey
Highest-ranking rider under the age of 25

Yellow Helmet
Entire team that is leading in the standings

Red Number
Most aggressive rider in each stage

Note: Riders leading in more than one category wear only the highest-ranking jersey, in this order: yellow, green, red polka-dot, white.

Source:
23 Ways To Get To First Base: The ESPN Uncyclopedia

OLYMPIC
GAMES

Six-time gold medalist **Michael Phelps** poses with the Fuwa, mascots for the 2008 Summer Games in Beijing.

1924-2004
Through the Years

SPORTS ALMANAC

Modern Olympic Games

The original Olympic Games were celebrated as a religious festival from 776 B.C. until 393 A.D., when Roman emperor Theodosius I banned all pagan festivals (the Olympics celebrated the Greek god Zeus). On June 23, 1894, French educator Baron Pierre de Coubertin, speaking at the Sorbonne in Paris to a gathering of international sports leaders, proposed that the ancient games be revived on an international scale. The idea was enthusiastically received and the Modern Olympics were born. The first Olympics were held two years later in Athens, where 245 athletes from 14 nations competed in the ancient Panathenaic stadium to large and ardent crowds. Americans captured nine out of 12 track and field events, but Greece won the most medals with 47.

The Summer Olympics

Year	No	Location	Dates	Nations	Most medals	USA medals	
1896	I	Athens, GRE	Apr. 6-15	14	Greece (10-19-18—47)	11- 6- 2— 19	(2nd)
1900	II	Paris, FRA	May 20-Oct. 28	26	France (26-37-32—95)	18-14-15— 47	(2nd)
1904	III	St. Louis, USA.	July 1-Nov. 23	13	USA (78-84-82—244)	78-84-82—244	(1st)
1906-a	—	Athens, GRE	Apr. 22-May 2	20	France (15-9-16—40)	12-6- 6— 24	(3rd)
1908	IV	London, GBR	Apr. 27-Oct. 31	22	Britain (54-46-38—138)	23-12-12— 47	(2nd)
1912	V	Stockholm, SWE	May 5-July 22	28	Sweden (23-24-17—64)	25-18-20— 63	(2nd)
1916	VI	Berlin, GER	Cancelled (WWI)				
1920	VII	Antwerp, BEL	Apr. 20-Sept. 12	29	USA (41-27-27—95)	41-27-27— 95	(1st)
1924	VIII	Paris, FRA	May 4-July 27	44	USA (45-27-27—99)	45-27-27— 99	(1st)
1928	IX	Amsterdam, NED	May 17-Aug. 12	46	USA (22-18-16—56)	22-18-16— 56	(1st)
1932	X	Los Angeles, USA.	July 30-Aug. 14	37	USA (41-32-30—103)	41-32-30—103	(1st)
1936	XI	Berlin, GER	Aug. 1-16	49	Germany (33-26-30—89)	24-20-12— 56	(2nd)
1940-b	XII	Tokyo, JPN	Cancelled (WWII)				
1944	XIII	London, GBR	Cancelled (WWII)				
1948	XIV	London, GBR	July 29-Aug. 14	59	USA (38-27-19—84)	38-27-19— 84	(1st)
1952-cd	XV	Helsinki, FIN	July 19-Aug. 3	69	USA (40-19-17—76)	40-19-17— 76	(1st)
1956-e	XVI	Melbourne, AUS	Nov. 22-Dec. 8	72	USSR (37-29-32—98)	32-25-17— 74	(2nd)
1960	XVII	Rome, ITA	Aug. 25-Sept. 11	83	USSR (43-29-31—103)	34-21-16— 71	(2nd)
1964	XVIII	Tokyo, JPN	Oct. 10-24	93	USSR (30-31-35—96)	36-26-28— 90	(2nd)
1968-f	XIX	Mexico City, MEX	Oct. 12-27	112	USA (45-28-34—107)	45-28-34—107	(1st)
1972	XX	Munich, W. GER	Aug. 26-Sept. 10	121	USSR (50-27-22—99)	33-31-30— 94	(2nd)
1976-g	XXI	Montreal, CAN	July 17-Aug. 1	92	USSR (49-41-35—125)	34-35-25— 94	(3rd)
1980-h	XXII	Moscow, USSR	July 19-Aug. 3	80	USSR (80-69-46—195)	Boycotted games	
1984-i	XXIII	Los Angeles, USA	July 28-Aug. 12	140	USA (83-61-30—174)	83-61-30—174	(1st)
1988	XXIV	Seoul, S. KOR	Sept. 17-Oct. 2	159	USSR (55-31-46—132)	36-31-27— 94	(3rd)
1992-j	XXV	Barcelona, SPA	July 25-Aug. 9	169	UT (45-38-29—112)	37-34-37—108	(2nd)
1996	XXVI	Atlanta, USA	July 20-Aug. 4	197	USA (44-32-25—101)	44-32-25—101	(1st)
2000	XXVII	Sydney, AUS	Sept. 15-Oct. 1	199	USA (40-24-33—97)	40-24-33— 97	(1st)
2004	XXVIII	Athens, GRE	Aug. 13-29	202	USA (35-39-29—103)	35-39-29—103	(1st)
2008	XXIX	Beijing, CHN	Aug. 8-24				
2012	XXX	London, ENG	July 27-Aug. 12				

a—The 1906 Intercalated Games in Athens are considered unofficial by the IOC because they did not take place in the four-year cycle established in 1896. However, most record books include these interim games with the others.

b—The 1940 Summer Games are originally scheduled for Tokyo, but Japan resigns as host after the outbreak of the Sino-Japanese War in 1937. Helsinki is the next choice, but the IOC cancels the Games after Soviet troops invade Finland in 1939.

c—Germany and Japan are allowed to rejoin the Olympic community for the first Summer Games since 1936. Though a divided country, the Germans send a joint East-West team until 1964.

d—The Soviet Union (USSR) participates in its first Olympics, Winter or Summer, since the Russian revolution in 1917 and takes home the second most medals (22-30-19—71).

e—Due to Australian quarantine laws, the equestrian events for the 1956 Games are held in Stockholm, June 10-17.

f—East Germany and West Germany send separate teams for the first time and will continue to do so through 1988.

g—The 1976 Games are boycotted by 32 nations, most of them from black Africa, because the IOC will not ban New Zealand. Earlier that year, a rugby team from New Zealand had toured racially segregated South Africa.

h—The 1980 Games are boycotted by 64 nations, led by the USA, to protest the Soviet invasion of Afghanistan on Dec. 27, 1979.

i—The 1984 Games are boycotted by 14 Eastern Bloc nations, led by the USSR, to protest America's overcommercialization of the Games, inadequate security and an anti-Soviet attitude by the U.S. government. Most believe, however, the communist walkout is simply revenge for 1980.

j—Germany sends a single team after East and West German reunification in 1990 and the USSR competes as the Unified Team after the breakup of the Soviet Union in 1991.

1896

Athens

The ruins of ancient Olympia were excavated by the German archaeologist Ernst Curtius from 1875-81.

Among the remains uncovered was the ancient stadium where the original Olympic Games were celebrated from 776 B.C. to 393 A.D., when Roman emperor Theodosius I banned all pagan festivals.

Athletics played an important role in the religious festivals of the ancient Greeks, who believed competitive sports pleased the spirits of the dead. The festivals honoring gods like Zeus were undertaken by many Greek tribes and cities and usually held every four years.

During the first 13 Olympiads (an Olympiad is an interval of four years between celebrations of the Olympic Games), the only contested event was a foot race of 200 yards. Longer races were gradually introduced and by 708 B.C., field events like the discus, javelin throw and the long jump were part of the program. Wrestling and boxing followed and in 640 B.C., four-horse chariot races became a fixture at the Games.

During the so-called Golden Age of Greece, which most historians maintain lasted from 477 to 431 B.C., Olympia was considered holy ground. Victorious athletes gave public thanks to the gods and were revered as heroes. Three-time winners had statues erected in their likeness and received various gifts and honors, including exemption from taxation.

Eventually, however, winning and the rewards that went with victory corrupted the original purpose of the Ancient Games. Idealistic amateurs gave way to skilled foreign athletes who were granted the citizenship needed to compete and were paid handsomely by rich Greek gamblers.

There is evidence to suggest that the Games continued until the temples of Olympia were physically demolished in 426 A.D. by a Roman army sent by Theodosius II. Over the next 15 centuries, earthquakes and floods buried the site, until its discovery in 1875.

On June 23, 1894, French educator Baron Pierre de Coubertin, speaking at the Sorbonne in Paris to a gathering of international sports leaders from nine nations— including the United States and Russia— proposed that the ancient Games be revived on an international scale. The idea was enthusiastically received and the Modern Olympics, as we know them, were born.

The first Olympiad was celebrated two years later in Athens, where an estimated 245 athletes (all men) from 14 nations competed in the ancient Panathenaic stadium before large and ardent crowds.

Americans won nine of the 12 track and field events, but Greece won the most medals with 47. The highlight was the victory by native peasant Spiridon Louis in the first marathon race, which was run over the same course covered by the Greek hero Pheidippides after the battle of Marathon in 490 B.C.

Top 10 Standings

National medal standings are not recognized by the IOC. The unofficial point totals are based on 3 points for a gold medal, 2 for a silver and 1 for a bronze.

		Gold	Silver	Bronze	Total	Pts
1	Greece	10	19	18	47	86
2	USA	11	6	2	19	47
3	Germany	7	5	3	15	34
4	France	5	4	2	11	25
5	Great Britain	3	3	1	7	16
6	Denmark	1	2	4	7	11
	Hungary	2	1	3	6	11
8	Austria	2	0	3	5	9
9	Switzerland	1	2	0	3	7
10	Australia	2	0	0	2	6

Leading Medal Winners

Number of individual medals won on the left; gold, silver and bronze breakdown to the right.

No		Sport	G-S-B
6	Hermann Weingärtner, GER	Gymnastics	3-2-1
4	Karl Schuman, GER	Gymnastics & Wrestling	4-0-0
4	Alfred Flatow, GER	Gymnastics	3-1-0
4	Bob Garrett, USA	Track/Field	2-1-1
4	Viggo Jensen, DEN	Shooting & Weightlifting	1-2-1
3	Paul Masson, FRA	Cycling	3-0-0
3	Teddy Flack, AUS	Track/Field & Tennis	2-0-1
3	Jules Zutter, SWI	Gymnastics	1-2-0
3	James Connolly, USA	Track/Field	1-1-1
3	Leon Flameng, FRA	Cycling	1-1-1
3	Adolf Schmal, AUT	Cycling	1-0-2
3	Efstathios Choraphas, GRE	Swimming	0-1-2
3	Holger Nielsen, DEN	Shooting	0-1-2

1900

Paris

The success of the revived Olympics moved Greece to declare itself the rightful host of all future Games, but de Coubertin and the International Olympic Committee were determined to move the athletic feast around. In France, however, the Games were overshadowed by the brand new Eiffel Tower and all but ignored by the organizers of the 1900 Paris Exposition.

Despite their sideshow status, the Games attracted 1,225 athletes from 26 nations and enjoyed more publicity, if not bigger crowds, than in Athens.

University of Pennsylvania roommates Alvin Kraenzlein, Irving Baxter and John Tewksbury and Purdue grad Ray Ewry dominated the 23 track and field events, winning 11 and taking five seconds and a third. Kraenzlein remains the only track and fielder to win four individual titles in one year.

Women were invited to compete for the first time and Britain's Charlotte Cooper won the singles and mixed doubles in tennis.

No gold medals were given out in Paris. Winners received silver medals with bronze for second place.

Top 10 Standings

National team medal standings are not recognized by the IOC. The unofficial point totals are based on 3 points for a gold medal, 2 for a silver and 1 for a bronze.

		Gold	Silver	Bronze	Total	Pts
1	France	26	37	32	95	184
2	USA	18	14	15	47	97
3	Great Britain	16	6	8	30	68
4	Belgium	6	5	5	16	33
5	Switzerland	6	1	1	8	21
6	Germany	3	2	2	7	15
7	Denmark	1	3	2	6	11
	Hungary	1	3	2	6	11
9	Australia	2	0	4	6	10
	Holland	1	2	3	6	10

Leading Medal Winners

Number of individual medals won on the left; gold, silver and bronze breakdown to the right.

MEN

No		Sport	G-S-B
5	Irving Baxter, USA	Track/Field	2-3-0
5	John W. Tewksbury, USA	Track/Field	2-2-1
4	Alvin Kraenzlein, USA	Track/Field	4-0-0
4	Konrad Stäheli, SWI	Shooting	3-0-1
4	Achille Paroche, FRA	Shooting	1-2-1
4	Stan Rowley, AUS	Track/Field	1-0-3
4	Ole Östmo, NOR	Shooting	0-2-2
3	Ray Ewry, USA	Track/Field	3-0-0
3	Charles Bennett, AUS	Track/Field	2-1-0
3	Emil Kellenberger, SWI	Shooting	2-1-0
3	Laurie Doherty, GBR	Tennis	2-0-1
3	Reggie Doherty, GBR	Tennis	2-0-1
3	E. Michelet, FRA	Yachting	1-0-2
3	F. Michelet, FRA	Yachting	1-0-2
3	Anders Nielsen, DEN	Shooting	0-3-0
3	Zoltán Halmay, HUN	Swimming	0-2-1
3	Léon Moreaux, FRA	Shooting	0-2-1

WOMEN

No		Sport	G-S-B
2	Charlotte Cooper, GBR	Tennis	2-0-0
2	Marion Jones, USA	Tennis	0-0-2

1904

St. Louis

Originally scheduled for Chicago, the Games were moved to St. Louis and held in conjunction with the centennial celebration of the Louisiana Purchase.

The program included more sports than in Paris, but with only 13 nations sending athletes, the first Olympics to be staged in the United States had a decidedly All-American flavor—over 500 of the 687 competitors were Americans. Little wonder the home team won 80 percent of the medals.

The rout was nearly total in track and field where the U.S.–led by triple-winners Ray Ewry, Archie Hahn, Jim Lightbody and Harry Hillman–took 23 of 25 gold medals and swept 20 events.

The marathon, which was run over dusty roads in brutally hot weather, was the most bizarre event of the Games. Thomas Hicks of the U.S. won, but only after his handlers fed him painkillers during the race. And an impostor nearly stole the victory when Fred Lorz, who dropped out after nine miles, was seen trotting back to the finish line to retrieve his clothes. Amused that officials thought he had won the race, Lorz played along until he was found out shortly after the medal ceremony. Banned for life by the AAU, Lorz was reinstated a year later and won the 1905 Boston Marathon.

Top 10 Standings

National medal standings are not recognized by the IOC. The unofficial point totals are based on 3 points for a gold medal, 2 for a silver and 1 for a bronze.

		Gold	Silver	Bronze	Total	Pts
1	USA	78	84	82	244	484
2	Germany	4	4	4	12	24
3	Canada	4	1	1	6	15
4	Hungary	2	1	1	4	9
	Cuba	3	0	0	3	9
6	Austria	1	1	1	3	6
	Britain/Ireland	1	1	1	3	6
8	Greece	1	0	1	2	4
	Switzerland	1	0	1	2	4
10	Cuba/USA	1	0	0	1	3

Leading Medal Winners

Number of individual medals won on the left; gold, silver and bronze breakdown to the right.

MEN

No		Sport	G-S-B
6	Anton Heida, USA	Gymnastics	5-1-0
6	George Eyser, USA	Gymnastics	3-2-1
6	Burton Downing, USA	Cycling	2-3-1
5	Marcus Hurley, USA	Cycling	4-0-1
5	Charles Daniels, USA	Swimming	3-1-1
5	Albertson Van Zo Post, USA	Fencing	2-1-2
5	William Merz, USA	Gymnastics	0-1-4
4	Jim Lightbody, USA	Track/Field	3-1-0
4	Francis Gailey, USA	Swimming	0-3-1
4	Teddy Billington, USA	Cycling	0-1-3
4	Frank Kungler, USA	Weightlifting, Wrestling & Tug of War	0-1-3
3	Ray Ewry, USA	Track/Field	3-0-0
3	Ramón Fonst, CUB	Fencing	3-0-0
3	Archie Hahn, USA	Track/Field	3-0-0
3	Harry Hillman, USA	Track/Field	3-0-0
3	Julius Lenhart, AUT	Gymnastics	2-1-0
3	George Bryant, USA	Archery	2-0-1
3	Emil Rausch, GER	Swimming	2-0-1
3	Robert Williams, USA	Archery	1-2-0
3	Ralph Rose, USA	Track/Field	1-1-1
3	William Thompson, USA	Archery	1-0-2
3	Charles Tatham, USA	Fencing	0-2-1
3	William Hogenson, USA	Track/Field	0-1-2
3	Emil Voigt, USA	Gymnastics	0-1-2

WOMEN

No		Sport	G-S-B
2	Lida Howell, USA	Archery	2-0-0
2	Emma Cooke, USA	Archery	0-2-0
2	Jessie Pollack, USA	Archery	0-0-2

1906

Athens

After disappointing receptions in Paris and St. Louis, the Olympic movement returned to Athens for the Intercalated Games of 1906.

The mutual desire of Greece and Baron de Coubertin to recapture the spirit of the 1896 Games led to an understanding that the Greeks would host an interim games every four years between Olympics.

Nearly 900 athletes from 20 countries came to Athens, including, for the first time, an official American team picked by the USOC.

As usual, the U.S. dominated track and field, taking 11 of 21 events, including double wins by Martin Sheridan (shot put and freestyle discus), Ray Ewry (standing high and long jumps) and Paul Pilgrim (400 and 800 meters). The previously unknown Pilgrim had been an 11th-hour addition to the team.

Verner Järvinen, the first Finn to compete in the Olympics, won the Greek-style discus throw and placed second in the freestyle discus. He returned home a national hero and inspired Finland to become a future Olympic power.

The Intercalated Games were cancelled due to political unrest in 1910 and never reappeared. Medals won are considered unofficial by the IOC.

Top 10 Standings

National medal standings are not recognized by the IOC. The unofficial point totals are based on 3 points for a gold medal, 2 for a silver and 1 for a bronze.

		Gold	Silver	Bronze	Total	Pts
1	France	15	9	16	40	79
2	Greece	8	13	12	33	62
3	USA	12	6	6	24	54
4	Great Britain	8	11	5	24	51
5	Italy	7	6	3	16	36
6	Switzerland	5	6	4	15	31
7	Germany	4	6	5	15	29
8	Sweden	2	5	7	14	23
9	Hungary	2	5	3	10	19
10	Austria	3	3	2	8	17
	Norway	4	2	1	7	17

Leading Medal Winners

Number of individual medals won on the left; gold, silver and bronze breakdown to the right.

MEN

No		Sport	G-S-B
6	Louis Richardet, SWI	Shooting	4-2-0
5	Martin Sheridan, USA	Track/Field	2-3-0
5	Konrad Stäheli, SWI	Shooting	2-2-1
5	Léon Moreaux, FRA	Shooting	2-1-2
5	Jean Reich, SWI	Shooting	1-1-3
4	Gudbrand Skatteboe, NOR	Shooting	3-1-0
4	Gustav Casmir, GER	Fencing	2-2-0
4	Eric Lemming, SWE	Track/Field & Tug of War	1-0-3
3	Francesco Verri, ITA	Cycling	3-0-0
3	Enrico Bruna, ITA	Rowing	3-0-0
3	Georgio Cesana, ITA	Rowing	3-0-0
3	Max Decugis, FRA	Tennis	3-0-0
3	Emilio Fontanella, ITA	Rowing	3-0-0
3	Georges Dillon-Cavanaugh, FRA	Fencing	2-1-0
3	Henry Taylor, GBR	Swimming	1-1-1
3	Fernand Vast, FRA	Cycling	1-0-2
3	Raoul de Boigne, FRA	Shooting	0-1-2
3	John Jarvis, GBR	Swimming	0-1-2

WOMEN

No		Sport	G-S-B
2	Sophia Marinou, GRE	Tennis	0-2-0

1908

London

The fourth Olympic Games were certainly the wettest and probably the most contentious in history.

Held at a new 68,000-seat stadium in the Shepherds Bush section of London, the 1908 Games were played out under continually rainy skies and suffered from endless arguments between British officials and many of the other countries involved—especially the United States.

"The Battle of Shepherds Bush" began almost immediately, when the U.S. delegation noticed that there was no American flag among the national flags decorating the stadium for the opening ceremonies. U.S. flag bearer and discus champion Martin Sheridan responded by refusing to dip the Stars and Stripes when he passed King Edward VII's box in the parade of athletes. "This flag dips to no earthly king," Sheridan said. And it hasn't since.

The Americans, at least, got to march with their flag. Finland, then ruled by Russia, could not. Informed they would have to use a Russian flag, the furious Finns elected to march with no flag at all.

Once again the marathon proved to be the Games' most memorable event. Laid out over a 26-mile, 365-yard course that stretched from Windsor Castle to the royal box at Shepherds Bush, the race ended in controversy when leader Dorando Pietri of Italy staggered into the packed stadium, took a wrong turn, collapsed, was helped up by doctors, wobbled and fell three more times before being half-carried across the finish line by race officials. Caught up in the drama of Pietri's agony, the cheering crowd hardly noticed that he was declared the winner just as second place runner, Johnny Hayes of the U.S., entered the stadium.

Pietri was later disqualified in favor of Hayes, but only after British and U.S. officials argued for an hour and fights had broken out in the stands.

Top 10 Standings

National medal standings are not recognized by the IOC. The unofficial point totals are based on 3 points for a gold medal, 2 for a silver and 1 for a bronze

		Gold	Silver	Bronze	Total	Pts
1	Great Britain	54	46	38	138	292

2	USA	23	12	12	47	105
3	Sweden	8	6	11	25	47
4	France	5	5	9	19	34
5	Canada	3	3	10	16	25
6	Germany	3	5	5	13	24
7	Hungary	3	4	2	9	19
8	Norway	2	3	3	8	15
	Belgium	1	5	2	8	15
10	Italy	2	2	0	4	10

Leading Medal Winners

Number of individual medals won on the left; gold, silver and bronze breakdown to the right.

MEN

No		Sport	G-S-B
3	Mel Sheppard, USA	Track/Field	3-0-0
3	Henry Taylor, GBR	Swimming	3-0-0
3	Benjamin Jones, GBR	Cycling	2-1-0
3	Martin Sheridan, USA	Track/Field	2-0-1
3	Oscar Swahn, SWE	Shooting	2-0-1
3	Josiah Ritchie, GBR	Tennis	1-1-1
3	Ted Ranken, GBR	Shooting	0-3-0

WOMEN

No		Sport	G-S-B
2	Madge Syers, GBR	Figure Skating	1-0-1

Note: Figure Skating was part of the Summer Olympics in 1908 and '20.

1912
Stockholm

The belligerence of 1908 was replaced with benevolence four years later, as Sweden provided a well-organized and pleasant haven for the troubled Games.

And then there were Jim Thorpe and Hannes Kolehmainen.

Thorpe, a 24-year-old American Indian who was a two-time consensus All-America football player at Carlisle (Pa.) Institute, won the two most demanding events in track and field—the pentathlon and decathlon. And he did it with ease. "You sir," said the Swedes' King Gustav V at the medal ceremony, "are the greatest athlete in the world." To which Thorpe is said to have replied, "Thanks, King."

Kolehmainen, a 22-year-old Finnish vegetarian, ran away with three distance events being run for the first time—the 5,000 and 10,000-meter races and the 12,000-meter cross-country run. He also picked up a silver medal in the 12,000-meter team race.

Ralph Craig of the U.S. was the only other winner of two individual track gold medals, taking both the 100 and 200-meter runs. The 100 final had seven false starts, one with Craig sprinting the entire distance before being called back.

Although Thorpe returned to the U.S. a hero, a year later it was learned that he had played semi-pro baseball for $25 a week in 1909 and 1910. The IOC, with the full support of the American Olympic Committee, stripped him of his medals

and erased his records.

The medals and records were restored in 1982—29 years after Thorpe's death.

Top 10 Standings

National medal standings are not recognized by the IOC. The unofficial point totals are based on 3 points for a gold medal, 2 for a silver and 1 for a bronze.

		Gold	Silver	Bronze	Total	Pts
1	Sweden	23	24	17	64	134
2	USA	25	18	20	63	131
3	Great Britain	10	15	16	41	76
4	Finland	9	8	9	26	52
5	Germany	5	13	7	25	48
6	France	7	4	3	14	32
7	Denmark	1	6	5	12	20
8	Norway	3	2	5	10	18
9	Canada	3	2	3	8	16
	Hungary	3	2	3	8	16
	South Africa	4	2	0	6	16

Leading Medal Winners

Number of individual medals won on the left; gold, silver and bronze breakdown to the right.

MEN

No		Sport	G-S-B
6	Louis Richardet, SWI	Shooting	4-2-0
5	Wilhelm Carlberg, SWE	Shooting	3-2-0
4	Hannes Kolehmainen, FIN	Track/Field	3-1-0
4	Eric Carlberg, SWE	Shooting	2-2-0
4	Johan von Holst, SWE	Shooting	2-1-1
4	Carl Osburn, USA	Shooting	1-2-1
3	Alfred Lane, USA	Shooting	3-0-0
3	Åke Lundeberg, SWE	Shooting	2-1-0
3	Frederick Hird, USA	Shooting	2-0-1
3	Jean Cariou, FRA	Equestrian	1-1-1
3	Charles Dixon, GBR	Tennis	1-1-1
3	Harold Hardwick, AUS	Swimming	1-0-2
3	Jack Hatfield, GBR	Swimming	0-2-1
3	Charles Stewart, GBR	Shooting	0-0-3

WOMEN

No		Sport	G-S-B
2	Edith Hannam, GBR	Tennis	2-0-0
2	Jennie Fletcher, GBR	Swimming	1-0-1
2	Sigrid Fick, SWE	Tennis	0-1-1

1920
Antwerp

The Olympic quadrennial, scheduled for Berlin in 1916, was interrupted by World War I—the so-called "War to End All Wars," which had involved 28 countries and killed nearly 10 million troops in four years.

The four-year cycle of Olympiads–Berlin would have been the sixth—is still counted, however, even though the Games were not played.

Less than two years after the armistice, the Olympics resumed in Belgium, a symbolic and austere choice considering it had been occupied for four years by enemy forces. Still, 29 countries (one more than participated in the war) sent a record 2,600 athletes to the Games. Germany and Austria, the defeated enemies of Belgium and the Allies, were not invited.

The United States turned in the best overall team performance, winning 41 gold medals, but the talk of the Games was 23-year-old distance runner Paavo Nurmi of Finland. Nurmi won the 10,000-meter run and 8,000-meter cross-country, took a third gold in the team cross-country and silver in the 5,000-meter run. In all, Finland won nine track and field gold medals to break the U.S. dominance in the sport.

Elsewhere, Albert Hill of Britain made his Olympic debut at age 36 and won both the 800 and 1,500-meter runs. World record holder Charley Paddock of the U.S. won the 100 meters, but was upset in the 200 by teammate Allen Woodring, who was a last-minute addition to the team. And in swimming, the U.S. won 11 of 15 events, led by triple gold medalists Norman Ross and Ethelda Bleibtrey, defending men's 100-meter freestyle champion Duke Kahanamoku and 14-year-old springboard diving champion Aileen Riggin.

The Antwerp Games were also noteworthy for the introduction of the Olympic oath—uttered for the first time by Belgium fencer Victor Bion—and the Olympic flag, with its five multicolored, intersecting rings.

Top 10 Standings

National medal standings are not recognized by the IOC. The unofficial point totals are based on 3 points for a gold medal, 2 for a silver and 1 for a bronze.

		Gold	Silver	Bronze	Total	Pts
1	USA	41	27	27	95	204
2	Sweden	19	20	25	64	122
3	Great Britain	14	15	13	42	85
4	France	9	19	13	41	78
5	Finland	15	10	9	34	74
	Belgium	13	11	11	35	72
7	Norway	13	9	9	31	66
8	Italy	13	5	5	23	54
9	Denmark	3	9	1	13	28
10	Holland	4	2	5	11	21

Leading Medal Winners

Number of individual medals won on the left; gold, silver and bronze breakdown to the right.

MEN

No		Sport	G-S-B
7	Willis Lee, USA	Shooting	5-1-1
7	Lloyd Spooner, USA	Shooting	4-1-2
6	Hubert van Innis, BEL	Archery	4-2-0
6	Carl Osburn, USA	Shooting	4-1-1
5	Nedo Nadi, ITA	Fencing	5-0-0
5	Otto Olsen, NOR	Shooting	3-2-0
5	Larry Nuesslein, USA	Shooting	2-1-2
5	Julien Brulé, FRA	Archery	1-3-1
4	Dennis Fenton, USA	Shooting	3-0-1
4	Aldo Nadi, ITA	Fencing	3-1-0
4	Paavo Nurmi, FIN	Track/Field	3-1-0
4	Harold Natvig, NOR	Shooting	2-1-1
4	Östen Östensen, NOR	Shooting	0-2-2
4	Erik Backman, SWE	Track/Field	0-1-3
4	Fritz Kuchen, SWI	Shooting	0-0-4
3	Norman Ross, USA	Swimming	3-0-0
3	Albert Hill, GBR	Track/Field	2-1-0
3	Morris Kirksey, USA	Track/Field & Rugby	2-1-0
3	Charley Paddock, USA	Track/Field	2-1-0
3	Bevil Rudd, S. Afr.	Track/Field	1-0-2
3	Ettore Caffaratti, ITA	Equestrian	0-1-2

Fourteen shooters tied with 3 each.

WOMEN

No		Sport	G-S-B
3	Ethelda Bleibtrey, USA	Swimming	3-0-0
3	Suzanne Lenglen, FRA	Tennis	2-0-1
3	Kitty McKane, GBR	Tennis	1-1-1
3	Frances Schroth, USA	Swimming	1-0-2
2	Irene Guest, USA	Swimming	1-1-0
2	Margaret Woodbridge, USA	Swimming	1-1-0
2	Dorothy Holman, GBR	Tennis	0-2-0

1924

Paris

Paavo Nurmi may have been the talk of Antwerp in 1920, but he was the sensation of Paris four years later.

It wasn't just that the "Flying Finn" won five gold medals, it was the way he did it. Running with a stopwatch on his wrist, Peerless Paavo captured the 1,500 and 5,000-meter finals within an hour of each other and set Olympic records in both. Two days later, he blew away the field in the 10,000-meter cross-country run where the heat and an unusually difficult course combined to knock out 23 of 38 starters (Finland also won the team gold in the event). And finally, the next day he led the Finns to victory in the 3,000-meter team race. His performance overshadowed the four gold medals of teammate Ville Ritola.

The gold medals won by British runners Harold Abrahams in the 100 meters and Eric Liddell in the 400 were chronicled in the 1981 Academy Award-winning film "Chariots of Fire." The movie, however, was not based on fact. Liddell, a devout Christian, knew months in advance that the preliminary for the 100 (his best event) was on a Sunday, so he had plenty of time to change plans and train for the 400. Also, he and Abrahams never competed against each other in real life.

Speaking of the movies, Johnny Weissmuller of the U.S. won three swimming gold medals in the 100 and 400-meter freestyles and the 4x200 freestyle relay. He would later become Hollywood's most famous Tarzan.

Top 10 Standings

National medal standings are not recognized by the IOC. The unofficial point totals are based on 3 points for a gold medal, 2 for a silver and 1 for a bronze.

		Gold	Silver	Bronze	Total	Pts
1	USA	45	27	27	99	216
2	France	13	15	10	38	79
3	Finland	14	13	10	37	78
4	Great Britain	9	13	12	34	65
5	Sweden	4	13	12	29	50
6	Switzerland	7	8	10	25	47
7	Italy	8	3	5	16	35
8	Belgium	3	7	3	13	26
9	Norway	5	2	3	10	22
10	Holland	4	1	5	10	19

Leading Medal Winners

Number of individual medals won on the left; gold, silver and bronze breakdown to the right.

MEN

No		Sport	G-S-B
6	Ville Ritola, FIN	Track/Field	4-2-0
5	Paavo Nurmi, FIN	Track/Field	5-0-0
5	Roger Ducret, FRA	Fencing	3-2-0
4	Johnny Weissmuller, USA	Swimming & Water Polo	3-0-1

No		Sport	G-S-B
3	Ole Lilloe-Olsen, NOR	Shooting	2-1-0
3	Vincent Richards, USA	Tennis	2-1-0
3	Albert Séquin, FRA	Gymnastics	1-2-0
3	Boy Charlton, AUS	Swimming	1-1-1
3	August Güttinger, SWI	Gymnastics	1-0-2
3	Robert Prazák, CZE	Gymnastics	0-3-0
3	Arne Borg, SWE	Swimming	0-2-1
3	Jean Gutweniger, SWI	Gymnastics	0-2-1
3	Henri Hoevenaers, BEL	Cycling	0-2-1

WOMEN

No		Sport	G-S-B
3	Gertrude Ederle, USA	Swimming	1-0-2
2	Ethel Lackie, USA	Swimming	2-0-0
2	Hazel Wightman, USA	Tennis	2-0-0
2	Helen Wills, USA	Tennis	2-0-0
2	Betty Becker, USA	Diving	1-1-0
2	Mariechen Wehselau, USA	Swimming	1-1-0
2	Kitty McKane, GBR	Tennis	0-1-1
2	Aileen Riggin, USA	Swimming & Diving	0-1-1

1928

Amsterdam

"We are here to represent the greatest country on earth. We did not come here to lose gracefully. We came here to win—and win decisively."

So ordered American Olympic Committee president Gen. Douglas MacArthur before the start of the 1928 Games. His athletes would deliver, easily winning the unofficial national standings for the third Olympiad in a row.

The U.S. men won eight gold medals in track and field, but were victorious in only one individual running race (Ray Barbuti in the 400 meters). In the sprints, Canada's Percy Williams became the first non-American to win both the 100 and 200. Finland claimed four running titles, including Paavo Nurmi's victory in the 10,000 meters—his ninth overall gold medal in three Olympic Games. Teammate and arch-rival Ville Ritola placed second in the 10,000 and outran Nurmi in the 5,000.

These Games marked Germany's return to the Olympic fold after serving a 10-year probation for its "aggressiveness" in World War I. It was also the first Olympics that women were

allowed to participate in track and field (despite objections from Pope Pius IX). And in swimming, the U.S. got double gold performances from Martha Norelius, Albina Osipowich and Johnny Weissmuller, as well as diver Pete Desjardins.

Top 10 Standings

National medal standings are not recognized by the IOC. The unofficial point totals are based on 3 points for a gold medal, 2 for a silver and 1 for a bronze.

		Gold	Silver	Bronze	Total	Pts
1	USA	22	18	16	56	118
2	Germany	10	7	14	31	58
3	Finland	8	8	9	25	49
4	Sweden	7	6	12	25	45
5	France	6	10	5	21	43
6	Holland	6	9	4	19	40
7	Italy	7	5	7	19	38
8	Great Britain	3	10	7	20	36
9	Switzerland	7	4	4	15	33
10	Canada	4	4	7	15	27

Leading Medal Winners

Number of individual medals won on the left; gold, silver and bronze breakdown to the right.

MEN

No		Sport	G-S-B
4	Georges Miez, SWI	Gymnastics	3-1-0
4	Hermann Hänggi, SWI	Gymnastics	2-1-1
3	Lucien Gaudin, FRA	Fencing	2-1-0
3	Eugen Mack, SWI	Gymnastics	2-0-1
3	Paavo Nurmi, FIN	Track/Field	1-2-0
3	Ladislav Vácha, CZE	Gymnastics	1-2-0
3	Leon Stukelj, YUG	Gymnastics	1-0-2
3	Emanuel Löffler, CZE	Gymnastics	0-2-1

WOMEN

No		Sport	G-S-B
3	Joyce Cooper, GBR	Swimming	0-1-2
2	Martha Norelius, USA	Swimming	2-0-0
2	Albina Osipowich, USA	Swimming	2-0-0
2	Maria Braun, NED	Swimming	1-1-0
2	Eleanor Garatti, USA	Swimming	1-1-0
2	Betty Robinson, USA	Track/Field	1-1-0
2	Fanny Rosenfeld, CAN	Track/Field	1-1-0
2	Ethel Smith, CAN	Track/Field	1-0-1
2	Ellen King, GBR	Swimming	0-2-0
2	Georgia Coleman, USA	Diving	0-1-1

1932

Los Angeles

Despite a world-wide economic depression and predictions that the 1932 Summer Olympics were doomed to failure, 37 countries sent over 1,300 athletes to southern California and the Games were a huge success.

Energized by perfect weather and the buoyant atmosphere of the first Olympic Village, the com petition was fierce. Sixteen world and Olympic records fell in men's track and field alone.

In women's track, 21-year-old Babe Didrikson, who had set world records in the 80-meter hurdles, javelin and high jump at the AAU Olympic Trials three weeks before, came to L.A. and announced, "I am out to beat everybody in sight." She almost did toowinning the hurdles and javelin, but taking second in the high jump (despite tying teammate Jean Shiley for first) when her jumping style was ruled illegal.

Didrikson's heroics, along with American Eddie Tolan's double in the 100 and 200 meters and Italian Luigi Beccali's upset victory in the 1,500, were among the Games' highlights, but they didn't quite make up for the absence of Finland's famed distance runner Paavo Nurmi.

Just before the Games, the IOC said that Nurmi would not be allowed to participate in his fourth Olympics because he had received excessive expense money on a trip to Germany in 1929. The ruling came as no surprise in the track world where it was said, "Nurmi has the lowest heartbeat and the highest asking price of any athlete in the world."

The Japanese men and American women dominated in swimming, each winning five of six events. Helene Madison of the U.S. won two races and anchored the winning relay team.

Top 10 Standings

National medal standings are not recognized by the IOC. The unofficial point totals are based on 3 points for a gold medal, 2 for a silver and 1 for a bronze.

		Gold	Silver	Bronze	Total	Pts
1	USA	41	32	30	103	217
2	Italy	12	12	12	36	72
3	Sweden	9	5	9	23	46
4	France	10	5	4	19	44
5	Finland	5	8	12	25	43
6	Germany	3	12	5	20	38
7	Japan	7	7	4	18	39
8	Great Britain	4	7	5	16	31
	Hungary	6	4	5	15	31
10	Canada	2	5	8	15	24

Leading Medal Winners

Number of individual medals won on the left; gold, silver and bronze breakdown to the right.

MEN

No		Sport	G-S-B
4	István Pelle, HUN	Gymnastics	2-2-0
4	Giulio Gaudini, ITA	Fencing	0-3-1
4	Heikki Savolainen, FIN	Gymnastics	0-1-3
4	Romeo Neri, ITA	Gymnastics	3-0-0
3	Alex Wilson, CAN	Track/Field	0-1-2
3	Philip Edwards, CAN	Track/Field	0-0-3

WOMEN

No		Sport	G-S-B
3	Helene Madison, USA	Swimming	3-0-0
3	Babe Didrikson, USA	Track/Field	2-1-0
2	Georgia Coleman, USA	Diving	1-1-0
2	Eleanor Garatti, USA	Swimming	1-0-1
2	Willy den Ouden, HOL	Swimming	0-2-0
2	Valerie Davies, GBR	Swimming	0-0-2

1936

Berlin

At the Big Ten Track and Field Championships of 1935, Ohio State's Jesse Owens equaled or set world records in four events: the 100 and 220-yard dashes, 200-yard low hurdles and the long jump. He was also credited with world marks in the 200-meter run and 200-meter hurdles. That's six world records in one afternoon, and he did it all in 45 minutes!

The following year, he swept the 100 and 200 meters and long jump at the Olympic Trials and headed for Germany favored to win all three.

In Berlin, dictator Adolf Hitler and his Nazi followers felt sure that the Olympics would be the ideal venue to demonstrate Germany's oft-stated racial superiority. He directed that $25 million be spent on the finest facilities, the cleanest streets and the temporary withdrawal of all outward signs of the state-run anti-Jewish campaign. By the time over 4,000 athletes from 49 countries arrived for the Games, the stage was set.

Then Owens, a black sharecropper's son from Alabama, stole the show—winning his three individual events and adding a fourth gold medal in the 4x100-meter relay. The fact that four other American blacks also won did little to please Herr Hitler, but the applause from the German crowds, especially for Owens, was thunderous. As it was for New Zealander Jack Lovelock's thrilling win over Glenn Cunningham and defending champ Luigi Beccali in the 1,500 meters.

Germany won only five combined gold medals in men's and women's track and field, but saved face for the "master race" in the overall medal count with an 89-56 margin over the United States.

The top female performers in Berlin were 17-year-old Dutch swimmer Rie Mastenbroek, who won three gold medals, and 18-year-old American runner Helen Stephens, who captured the 100 meters and anchored the winning 4x100-meter relay.

Basketball also made its debut as a medal sport and was played outdoors. The U.S. men easily won the first gold medal championship game with a 19-8 victory over Canada in the rain.

Top 10 Standings

National medal standings are not recognized by the IOC. The unofficial point totals are based on 3 points for a gold medal, 2 for a silver and 1 for a bronze.

		Gold	Silver	Bronze	Total	Pts
1	Germany	33	26	30	89	181
2	USA	24	20	12	56	124
3	Italy	8	9	5	22	47
4	Finland	7	6	6	19	39
	France	7	6	6	19	39
6	Sweden	6	5	9	20	37
	Hungary	10	1	5	16	37

No					
8	Japan 6	4	8	18	34
9	Holland 6	4	7	17	33
10	Great Britain 4	7	3	14	29

Leading Medal Winners

Number of individual medals won on the left; gold, silver and bronze breakdown to the right.

MEN

No		Sport	G-S-B
6	Konrad Frey, GER . . . . .Gymnastics		3-1-2
5	Alfred Schwarzmann, GER . . . .Gymnastics		3-0-2
5	Eugen Mack, SWI . . . . .Gymnastics		0-4-1
4	Jesse Owens, USA . . . . .Track/Field		4-0-0
3	Robert Charpentier, FRA . . . . . . .Cycling		3-0-0
3	Guy Lapébie, FRA . . . . .Cycling		2-1-0
3	Jack Medica, USA . . . . .Swimming		1-2-0
3	Matthias Volz, GER . . . . .Gymnastics		1-0-2

WOMEN

No		Sport	G-S-B
4	Rie Mastenbroek, NED . . . . . .Swimming		3-1-0
2	Helen Stephens, USA . . . . . . .Track/Field		2-0-0
2	Dorothy Poynton Hill, USA . . . . . . .Diving		1-0-1
2	Gisela Arendt, GER . . . . .Swimming		0-1-1

1948

London

The Summer Olympics were scheduled for Tokyo in 1940, but by mid-1938, Japan was at war with China and withdrew as host. The IOC immediately transferred the Games to Helsinki and the Finns eagerly began preparations only to be invaded by the Soviet Union in 1939.

By then, of course, Germany had marched into Poland and World War II was on. The Japanese attacked Pearl Harbor two years later, and the bombs didn't stop falling until 1945. Against this backdrop of global conflict, the Olympic Games were cancelled again in 1940 and '44. Many of the participants in the 1936 Games died in the war.

Eager to come back after two dormant Olympiads, the IOC offered the 1948 Games to London. Much of the British capital had been reduced to rubble in the blitz, but the offer was accepted and the Games went on—successfully, without frills, and without invitations extended to Germany and Japan. The Soviet Union was invited, but chose not to show.

The United States reclaimed its place at the top of the overall medal standings, but the primary individual stars were a 30-year-old Dutch mother of two and a 17-year-old kid from California.

Fanny Blankers-Koen duplicated Jesse Owens' track and field grand slam of 12 years

before by winning the 100-meter and 200-meter runs, the 80-meter hurdles, and anchoring the women's 4x100-meter relay.

And Bob Mathias, just two months after graduating from Tulare High School, won the gold medal in the decathlon, an event he had taken up for the first time earlier in the year.

Top 10 Standings

National medal standings are not recognized by the IOC. The unofficial point totals are based on 3 points for a gold medal, 2 for a silver and 1 for a bronze.

		Gold	Silver	Bronze	Total	Pts
1	USA 38		27	19	84	187
2	Sweden 16		11	17	44	87
3	Italy 8		12	9	29	57
4	France 10		6	13	29	55
5	Hungary 10		5	12	27	52
6	Great Britain 3		14	6	23	43
	Finland 8		7	5	20	43
8	Switzerland 5		10	5	20	40
9	Denmark 5		7	8	20	37
10	Holland 5		2	9	16	28
	Turkey 6		4	2	12	28

Leading Medal Winners

Number of individual medals won on the left; gold, silver and bronze breakdown to the right.

MEN

No		Sport	G-S-B
5	Veikko Huhtanen, FIN . . . . . . .Gymnastics		3-1-1
4	Paavo Aaltonen, FIN . . . . .Gymnastics		3-0-1
3	Jimmy McLane, USA . . . . .Swimming		2-1-0
3	Humberto Mariles, MEX . . . . . .Equestrian		2-0-1
3	Mal Whitfield, USA . . . . .Track/Field		2-0-1
3	Barney Ewell, USA . . . . .Track/Field		1-2-0
3	Michael Reusch, SWI . . . . .Gymnastics		1-2-0
3	Josef Stalder, SWI . . . . .Gymnastics		1-1-1
3	Ferenc Pataki, HUN . . . . .Gymnastics		1-0-2
3	Walter Lehmann, SWI . . . . . . .Gymnastics		0-3-0
3	Edoardo Mangiarotti, ITA . . . . . . .Fencing		0-2-1
3	János Mogyorósi, HUN . . . . . .Gymnastics		0-1-2

WOMEN

No		Sport	G-S-B
4	Fanny Blankers-Koen, NED . . . .Track/Field		4-0-0
3	Ann Curtis, USA . . . . .Swimming		2-1-0
3	Micheline Ostermeyer, FRA . . . .Track/Field		2-0-1
3	Karen-Margrete Harup, DEN . . .Swimming		1-2-0
3	Shirley Strickland, AUS . . . . . . .Track/Field		0-1-2

1952

Helsinki

The Soviet Union returned to the Olympic fold in 1952 after a 40-year absence, a period of time that included a revolution and two world wars. Ironically, the Soviets chose to make their comeback in Finland, a country they had invaded twice during World War II.

This time it was the United States that was surprised by the Soviets, and the USA had to scramble on the last day of competition to hold off the USSR's assault on first place in the overall standings. It was the beginning of an all-consuming 36-year Cold War rivalry.

Despite the Soviets' impressive debut, it was a Communist from another Iron Curtain country who turned in the most memorable individual performance of the Games. Emil Zátopek of Czechoslovakia, the 10,000-meter champion in London, not only repeated at 10,000 meters, but also won at 5,000 and in the marathon—an event he had never run before. He also set Olympic records in each race and topped it off by watching his wife Dana Zátopková win the women's javelin.

Zátopek's unique triple was wildly applauded by the distance-minded Finns, but their greatest outburst came in the opening ceremonies when legendary countryman Paavo Nurmi, now 56, ran into the stadium with the Olympic torch and handed it off to another native legend Hannes Kolehmainen, now 62, who lit the flame to start the Games.

Also, Harrison Dillard of the U.S. won the 110-meter hurdles. In 1948, Dillard, the world's best hurdler, failed to qualify for the hurdles and won the 100-meter dash instead.

Top 10 Standings

National medal standings are not recognized by the IOC. The unofficial point totals are based on 3 points for a gold medal, 2 for a silver and 1 for a bronze.

		Gold	Silver	Bronze	Total	Pts
1	USA	40	19	17	76	175
2	USSR	21	30	18	69	141
3	Hungary	16	10	16	42	84
4	Sweden	12	13	10	35	72
5	Italy	8	9	4	21	46
6	Finland	6	3	13	22	37
7	France	6	6	6	18	36
8	Germany	0	7	17	24	31
9	Czechoslovakia	7	3	3	13	30
10	Australia	6	2	3	11	25

Leading Medal Winners

Number of individual medals won on the left; gold, silver and bronze breakdown to the right.

MEN

No		Sport	G-S-B
6	Viktor Chukarin, USSR	Gymnastics	4-2-0
4	Edoardo Mangiarotti, ITA	Fencing	2-2-0
4	Grant Shaginyan, USSR	Gymnastics	2-2-0
4	Josef Stalder, SWI	Gymnastics	0-2-2
3	Emil Zátopek, CZE	Track/Field	3-0-0
3	Ford Konno, USA	Swimming	2-1-0
3	Herb McKenley, JAM	Track/Field	1-2-0
3	Hans Eugster, SWI	Gymnastics	1-1-1

WOMEN

No		Sport	G-S-B
7	Maria Gorokhovskaya, USSR	Gymnastics	2-5-0
6	Margit Korondi, HUN	Gymnastics	1-1-4
4	Nina Bocharova, USSR	Gymnastics	2-2-0
4	Ágnes Keleti, HUN	Gymnastics	1-1-2
3	Yekaterina Kalinchuk, USSR	Gymnastics	2-1-0
3	Éva Novák, USA	Swimming	1-2-0
3	Galina Minaicheva, USSR	Gymnastics	1-1-1
3	Aleksandra Chudina, USSR	Track/Field	0-2-1

1956
Melbourne

Armed conflicts in Egypt and Hungary threatened to disrupt the 1956 Games, which were scheduled to begin on Nov. 22 (during the summer Down Under).

In July, Egypt seized the Suez Canal from British and French control. In October, Britain and France invaded Egypt in an attempt to retake the canal. Then in November, Soviet tanks rolled into Hungary to crush an anti-Communist revolt.

The only direct bearing these events had in Melbourne came when the Soviet water polo team met the Hungarians in the semifinals. Hungary won 4-0, but the match turned ugly after a Hungarian player was pulled bleeding from the pool with a deep gash over his eye from a Soviet head butt. A brawl quickly ensued involving both players and spectators and the police had to step in to prevent a riot.

Otherwise, the Soviets outmedaled the U.S. for the first time, cleaning up in gymnastics and winning their first track and field titles when Vladimir Kuts ran off with the 5,000 and 10,000 meters.

The American men won 15 track and field titles, including three golds for sprinter Bobby Morrow and Al Oerter's first victory in the discus.

Harold Connolly of the U.S. won the hammer throw and the heart of the women's discus champion, Olga Fikotová of Czechoslovakia. Their romance captured the imagination of the world and three months after the Games they were married.

Emil Zátopek, the Czech hero of Helsinki, returned to defend his marathon title but came in sixth. Winner Alain Mimoun of France had finished second to Zátopek three times in previous Olympic races.

Top 10 Standings

National medal standings are not recognized by the IOC. The unofficial point totals are based on 3 points for a gold medal, 2 for a silver and 1 for a bronze.

		Gold	Silver	Bronze	Total	Pts
1	USSR	37	29	32	98	201
2	USA	32	25	17	74	163
3	Australia	13	8	14	35	69
4	Hungary	9	10	7	26	54
5	Germany	6	13	7	26	51
6	Italy	8	8	9	25	49
7	Great Britain	6	7	11	24	43
8	Sweden	8	5	6	19	40
9	Japan	4	10	5	19	37
10	Romania	5	3	5	13	26
	France	4	4	6	14	26

Leading Medal Winners

Number of individual medals won on the left; gold, silver and bronze breakdown to the right.

MEN

No		Sport	G-S-B
5	Viktor Chukarin, USSR	Gymnastics	3-1-1
5	Takashi Ono, JPN	Gymnastics	1-3-1
4	Valentin Muratov, USSR	Gymnastics	3-1-0
4	Yuriy Titov, USSR	Gymnastics	1-1-2
4	Masao Takemoto, JPN	Gymnastics	0-1-3
3	Bobby Morrow, USA	Track/Field	3-0-0
3	Murray Rose, AUS	Swimming	3-0-0
3	Edoardo Mangiarotti, ITA	Fencing	2-0-1
3	Thane Baker, USA	Track/Field	1-1-1
3	Masami Kubota, JPN	Gymnastics	0-2-1
3	George Breen, USA	Swimming	0-1-2

WOMEN

No		Sport	G-S-B
6	Agnes Keleti, HUN	Gymnastics	4-2-0
6	Larissa Latynina, USSR	Gymnastics	4-1-1
4	Tamara Manina, USSR	Gymnastics	1-2-1
4	Sofiya Muratova, USSR	Gymnastics	1-0-3
3	Betty Cuthbert, AUS	Track/Field	3-0-0
3	Lorraine Crapp, AUS	Swimming	2-1-0
3	Dawn Fraser, AUS	Swimming	2-1-0
3	Olga Tass, HUN	Gymnastics	1-1-1

1960

Rome

Free of political entanglements, save the ruling that Nationalist China had to compete as Formosa, the 1960 Games attracted a record 5,348 athletes from 83 countries. More importantly, it was the first Summer Games covered by U.S. television. CBS bought the rights for $394,000.

Rome was a coming-out party for 18-year-old Louisville boxer Cassius Clay. The brash but engaging Clay, who would later change his name to Muhammad Ali and hold the world heavyweight title three times, won the Olympic light heavyweight crown, pummeling Polish opponent Zbigniew Pietry-skowsky in the final. Clay was so proud of his gold medal that he didn't take it off for two days.

Sprinter Wilma Rudolph and swimmer Chris von Saltza each won three gold medals for the U.S. Rudolph, who was one of her father's 22 children and who couldn't walk without braces until she was nine, struck gold at 100 and 200 meters and anchored the winning 400-meter relay team. Von Saltza won the 400-meter freestyle, placed second in the 100-free and anchored the winning 4x100-free and medley relays.

The U.S. men won nine track and field titles, including repeat gold medals for Lee Calhoun, Glenn Davis and Al Oerter. Rafer Johnson and

C.K. Yang of Formosa, college teammates at UCLA, finished 1-2 in the decathlon.

Among the other stars in Rome were barefoot Ethiopian marathoner Abebe Bikila, Australia's Herb Elliott in the 1,500 meters, Soviet gymnasts Boris Shakhlin and Larissa Latynina.

Finally, the greatest amateur basketball team ever assembled represented the U.S. and won easily. The 12-man roster included Oscar Robertson, Jerry West, Jerry Lucas, Walt Bellamy and Terry Dischinger—four of whom would become NBA Rookies of the Year from 1961-64.

Top 10 Standings

National medal standings are not recognized by the IOC. The unofficial point totals are based on 3 points for a gold medal, 2 for a silver and 1 for a bronze.

		Gold	Silver	Bronze	Total	Pts
1	USSR	43	29	31	103	218
2	USA	34	21	16	71	160
3	Germany	12	19	11	42	85
4	Italy	13	10	13	36	72
5	Australia	8	8	6	22	46
6	Hungary	6	8	7	21	41
7	Poland	4	6	11	21	35
8	Japan	4	7	7	18	33
9	Great Britain	2	6	12	20	30
10	Turkey	7	2	0	9	25

Leading Medal Winners

Number of individual medals won on the left; gold, silver and bronze breakdown to the right.

MEN

No		Sport	G-S-B
7	Boris Shakhlin, USSR	Gymnastics	4-2-1
6	Takashi Ono, JPN	Gymnastics	3-1-2
3	Murray Rose, AUS	Swimming	1-1-1
3	John Konraads, AUS	Swimming	1-0-2
3	Yuri Titov, USSR	Gymnastics	0-2-1

WOMEN

No		Sport	G-S-B
5	Larissa Latynina, USSR	Gymnastics	3-2-1
4	Chris von Saltza, USA	Swimming	3-1-0
4	Polina Astakhova, USSR	Gymnastics	2-1-1
4	Sofia Muratova, USSR	Gymnastics	1-2-1
3	Wilma Rudolph, USA	Track/Field	3-0-0
3	Dawn Fraser, AUS	Swimming	1-2-0
3	Tamara Lyukhina, USSR	Gymnastics	1-0-2

1964

Tokyo

Twenty-six years after Japan's wartime government forced the Japanese Olympic Committee to resign as hosts of the 1940 Summer Games, Tokyo welcomed the world to the first Asian Olympics. The new Japan spared no expense—a staggering $3 billion was spent to rebuild the city—and was rewarded with a record-breaking fortnight.

Twelve world and six Olympic records fell in swimming alone, with Americans accounting for 13. Eighteen-year-old Don Schollander led the way, winning two individual and two relay gold medals to become the first swimmer to win four events in one Games. Sharon Stouder collected three golds and a silver for the U.S. women, but the most remarkable performance of all belonged to Australian Dawn Fraser, who won the 100-meter freestyle for the third straight Olympics.

In track and field, Al Oerter of the U.S. won the discus for the third straight time. His record toss was one of 25 world and Olympic marks broken. Another fell when Billy Mills of the U.S. electrified the Games by coming from behind for an upset win in the 10,000 meters. New Zealander Peter Snell, the defending 800-meter champion, won both the 800 and 1,500 (last done in 1920).

Sprinter Bob Hayes of the U.S. equaled the world record of 10 seconds flat in the 100 meters, but stunned the crowd with a sub-nine second, come-from-behind anchor leg to lead the U.S. to set a world record in the 4x100 meters.

Abebe Bikila of Ethiopia became the first runner to win consecutive marathons. The remarkable Betty Cuthbert of Australia, who won three sprint gold medals in Melbourne, came back eight years later at age 26 to win the 400. And Soviet gymnast Larissa Latynina won six medals for the second Olympics in a row.

Top 10 Standings

National medal standings are not recognized by the IOC. The unofficial point totals are based on 3 points for a gold medal, 2 for a silver and 1 for a bronze.

		Gold	Silver	Bronze	Total	Pts
1	USA	36	26	28	90	188
2	USSR	30	31	35	96	187
3	Germany	10	22	18	50	92
4	Japan	16	5	8	29	66
5	Italy	10	10	7	27	57
6	Hungary	10	7	5	22	49
7	Poland	7	6	10	23	43
8	Great Britain	4	12	2	18	38
9	Australia	6	2	10	18	32
10	Czechoslovakia	5	6	3	14	30

Leading Medal Winners

Number of individual medals won on the left; gold, silver and bronze breakdown to the right.

MEN

No		Sport	G-S-B
4	Don Schollander, USA	Swimming	4-0-0
4	Yukio Endo, JPN	Gymnastics	3-1-0
4	Shuji Tsurumi, JPN	Gymnastics	1-3-0
4	Boris Shakhlin, USSR	Gymnastics	1-2-1
4	Viktor Lisitsky, USSR	Gymnastics	0-4-0
4	Hans-Joachim Klein, GER	Swimming	0-3-1
3	Steve Clark, USA	Swimming	3-0-0
3	Franco Menichelli, ITA	Gymnastics	1-1-1
3	Frank Wiegard, GER	Swimming	0-3-0

WOMEN

No		Sport	G-S-B
6	Larissa Latynina, USSR	Gymnastics	2-2-2
4	Vera Cáslavská, CZE	Gymnastics	3-1-0
4	Polina Astakhova, USSR	Gymnastics	2-1-1
4	Sharon Stouder, USA	Swimming	3-1-0
4	Kathy Ellis, USA	Swimming	2-0-2
3	Irena Kirszenstein, POL	Track/Field	1-2-0
3	Ada Kok, NED	Swimming	1-2-0
3	Edith Maguire, USA	Track/Field	1-2-0
3	Mary Rand, GBR	Track/Field	1-1-1

1968

Mexico City

The Games of the Nineteenth Olympiad were the highest and most controversial ever held.

Staged at 7,349 feet above sea level where the thin air was a major concern to many competing countries, the Mexico City Olympics were another chapter in a year buffeted by the Vietnam War, the assassinations of Martin Luther King and Robert Kennedy, the Democratic Convention in Chicago, and the Soviet invasion of Czechoslovakia.

Ten days before the Olympics were scheduled to open on Oct. 12, over 30 Mexico City university students were killed by army troops when a campus protest turned into a riot. Still, the Games began on time and were free of discord until black Americans Tommie Smith and John Carlos, who finished 1-3 in the 200-meter run, bowed their heads and gave the Black Power salute during the national anthem as a protest against racism in the U.S.

They were immediately thrown off the team by the USOC.

The thin air helped shatter records in every men's and women's race up to 1,500 meters and may have played a role in U.S. long jumper Bob Beamon's incredible gold medal leap of 29 feet, 2½ inches –beating the existing world mark by nearly two feet.

Other outstanding American performances included Al Oerter's record fourth consecutive discus title, Debbie Meyer's three individual swimming gold medals, the innovative Dick Fosbury winning the high jump with his backwards "flop" and Wyomia Tyus becoming the first woman to win back-to-back golds in the 100 meters.

Top 10 Standings

National medal standings are not recognized by the IOC. The unofficial point totals are based on 3 points for a gold medal, 2 for a silver and 1 for a bronze.

		Gold	Silver	Bronze	Total	Pts
1	USA	45	28	34	107	225
2	USSR	29	32	30	91	181
3	Hungary	10	10	12	32	62
4	Japan	11	7	7	25	54
5	E. Germany	9	9	7	25	52
6	W. Germany	5	10	10	25	45
7	Australia	5	7	5	17	34
8	France	7	3	5	15	32
9	Poland	5	2	11	18	30
10	Czechoslovakia	7	2	4	13	29
	Romania	4	6	5	15	29

Leading Medal Winners

Number of individual medals won on the left; gold, silver and bronze breakdown to the right.

MEN

No		Sport	G-S-B
7	Mikhail Voronin, USSR	Gymnastics	2-4-1
6	Akinori Nakayama, JPN	Gymnastics	4-1-1
4	Charles Hickcox, USA	Swimming	3-1-0
4	Sawao Kato, JPN	Gymnastics	3-0-1
4	Mark Spitz, USA	Swimming	2-1-1
4	Mike Wenden, AUS	Swimming	2-1-1
3	Roland Matthes, E. Ger	Swimming	2-1-0
3	Ken Walsh, USA	Swimming	2-1-0
3	Pierre Trentin, FRA	Cycling	2-0-1
3	Vladimir Kosinski, USSR	Swimming	0-2-1
3	Leonid Ilyichev, USSR	Swimming	0-1-2

WOMEN

No		Sport	G-S-B
6	Vera Cáslavská, CZE	Gymnastics	4-2-0
4	Sue Pedersen, USA	Swimming	2-2-0
4	Natalya Kuchinskaya, USSR	Gymnastics	2-0-2
4	Jan Henne, USA	Swimming	2-1-1
4	Zinaida Voronina, USSR	Gymnastics	1-1-2
3	Debbie Meyer, USA	Swimming	3-0-0
3	Kaye Hall, USA	Swimming	2-0-1
3	Larissa Petrik, USSR	Gymnastics	2-0-1
3	Ellie Daniel, USA	Swimming	1-1-1
3	Linda Gustavson, USA	Swimming	1-1-1
3	Elaine Tanner, CAN	Swimming	0-2-1

1972

Munich

On Sept. 5, with six days left in the Games, eight Arab commandos slipped into the Olympic Village, killed two Israeli team members and seized nine others as hostages. Early the next morning, all nine were killed in a shootout between the terrorists and West German police at a military airport.

The tragedy stunned the world and stopped the XXth Olympiad in its tracks. But after suspending competition for 24 hours and holding a memorial service attended by 80,000 at the main stadium, 84-year-old outgoing IOC president Avery Brundage and his committee ordered "the Games must go on."

They went on without 22-year-old swimmer Mark Spitz, who had set an Olympic gold medal record by winning four individual and three relay events, all in world record times. Spitz, an American Jew, was an inviting target for further terrorism and agreed with West German officials when they advised him to leave the country.

The pall that fell over Munich quieted an otherwise boisterous Games in which American swimmer Rick DeMont was stripped of a gold medal for taking asthma medication and track medalists Vince Matthews and Wayne Collett of the U.S. were banned for life for fooling around on the victory stand during the American national anthem.

The United States also lost an Olympic basketball game for the first time ever (they were 62-0) when the Soviets were given three chances to convert a last-second inbound pass and finally won, 51-50. The U.S. refused the silver medal.

Munich was also where 17-year-old Soviet gymnast Olga Korbut and 16-year-old swimmer Shane Gould of Australia won three gold medals each and Britain's 33-year-old Mary Peters won the pentathlon.

Top 10 Standings

National medal standings are not recognized by the IOC. The unofficial point totals are based on 3 points for a gold medal, 2 for a silver and 1 for a bronze.

		Gold	Silver	Bronze	Total	Pts
1	USSR	50	27	22	99	226
2	USA	33	31	30	94	191
3	E. Germany	20	23	23	66	129
4	W. Germany	13	11	16	40	77
5	Japan	13	8	8	29	63
6	Hungary	6	13	16	35	60
7	Bulgaria	6	10	5	21	43
8	Australia	8	7	2	17	40
	Poland	7	5	9	21	40
10	Italy	5	3	10	18	31
	Great Britain	4	5	9	18	31

Leading Medal Winners

Number of individual medals won on the left; gold, silver and bronze breakdown to the right.

MEN

No		Sport	G-S-B
7	Mark Spitz, USA	Swimming	7-0-0
5	Sawao Kato, JPN	Gymnastics	3-2-0
4	Jerry Heidenreich, USA	Swimming	2-1-1
4	Roland Matthes, E. Ger	Swimming	2-1-1
4	Akinori Nakayama, JPN	Gymnastics	2-1-1
4	Shigeru Kasamatsu, JPN	Gymnastics	1-1-2
4	Eizo Kenmotsu, JPN	Gymnastics	1-1-2
3	Valery Borsov, USSR	Track/Field	2-1-0
3	Mitsuo Tsukahara, JPN	Gymnastics	2-0-1
3	Steve Genter, USA	Swimming	1-2-0
3	Viktor Klimenko, USSR	Gymnastics	1-2-0
3	Mike Stamm, USA	Swimming	1-2-0
3	Vladimir Bure, USSR	Swimming	0-1-2

WOMEN

No		Sport	G-S-B
5	Shane Gould, AUS	Swimming	3-1-1
5	Karin Janz, E. Ger	Gymnastics	2-2-1
4	Olga Korbut, USSR	Gymnastics	3-1-0
4	Lyudmila Tourischeva, USSR	Gymnastics	2-1-1
4	Tamara Lazakovitch, USSR	Gymnastics	1-1-2

CANADA 1976

1976

Montreal

In 1970, when Montreal was named to host the Summer Olympics '76, organizers estimated it would cost $310 million to stage the Games. However, due to political corruption, mismanagement, labor disputes, inflation and a $100 million outlay for security to prevent another Munich, the final bill came to more than $1.5 billion.

Then, right before the Games were scheduled to open in July, 32 nations, most of them from black Africa, walked out when the IOC refused to ban New Zealand because its national rugby team was touring racially segregated South Africa. Taiwan also withdrew when Communist China pressured trading partner Canada to deny the Taiwanese the right to compete as the Republic of China.

When the Games finally got started they were quickly stolen by 14-year-old Romanian gymnast Nadia Comaneci, who scored seven perfect 10s on her way to three gold medals.

East Germany's Kornelia Ender did Comaneci one better, winning four times as the GDR captured 11 of 13 events in women's swimming. John Naber (4 gold) and the U.S. men did the East German women one better when they won 12 of 13 gold medals in swimming.

In track and field, Cuba's Alberto Juantorena won the 400 and 800-meter runs, and Finland's Lasse Viren took the 5,000 and 10,000. Viren missed a third gold when he placed fifth in the marathon.

Four Americans who became household names during the Games were decathlon winner Bruce Jenner and three future world boxing champions—Ray Leonard and the Spinks brothers, Michael and Leon.

Top 10 Standings

National medal standings are not recognized by the IOC. The unofficial point totals are based on 3 points for a gold medal, 2 for a silver and 1 for a bronze.

		Gold	Silver	Bronze	Total	Pts
1	USSR	49	41	35	125	264
2	USA	34	35	25	94	197
3	E. Germany	40	25	25	90	195
4	W. Germany	10	12	17	39	71
5	Japan	9	6	10	25	49
6	Poland	7	6	13	26	46
7	Romania	4	9	14	27	44
8	Bulgaria	6	9	7	22	43
9	Cuba	6	4	3	13	29
10	Hungary	4	5	13	22	35

Leading Medal Winners

Number of individual medals won on the left; gold, silver and bronze breakdown to the right.

MEN

No		Sport	G-S-B
7	Nikolai Andrianov, USSR	Gymnastics	4-2-1
5	John Naber, USA	Swimming	4-1-0
5	Mitsuo Tsukahara, JPN	Gymnastics	2-1-2
4	Jim Montgomery, USA	Swimming	3-0-1
3	John Hencken, USA	Swimming	2-1-0
3	Sawao Kato, JPN	Gymnastics	2-1-0
3	Eizo Kenmotsu, JPN	Gymnastics	1-2-0
3	Rüdiger Helm, E. Ger	Canoeing	1-0-2

WOMEN

No		Sport	G-S-B
5	Kornelia Ender, E. Ger	Swimming	4-1-0
5	Nadia Comaneci, ROM	Gymnastics	3-1-1
5	Shirley Babashoff, USA	Swimming	1-4-0
4	Nelli Kim, USSR	Gymnastics	3-1-0
4	Andrea Pollack, E. Ger	Swimming	2-2-0

4	Lyudmila Tourischeva, USSR	Gymnastics	1-2-1
3	Ulrike Richter, E. Ger	Swimming	3-0-0
3	Annagret Richter, W. Ger	Track/Field	1-2-0
3	Renate Stecher, E. Ger	Track/Field	1-1-1
3	Teodora Ungureanu, ROM	Gymnastics	0-2-1

1980

Moscow

Four years after 32 nations walked out of the Montreal Games, twice that many chose to stay away from Moscow– many in support of an American-led boycott to protest the December 1979, Soviet invasion of Afghanistan.

Unable to persuade the IOC to cancel or move the Summer Games, U.S. President Jimmy Carter pressured the USOC to officially withdraw in April. Many western governments, like West Germany and Japan, followed suit and withheld their athletes. But others, like Britain and France, while supporting the boycott, allowed their Olympic committees to participate if they wished

The first Games to be held in a Communist country opened in July with 8 nations competing and were dominated by the USSR and East Germany. They were also plagued by charges of rigged judging and poor sportsmanship by Moscow fans who, without the Americans around, booed the Poles and East Germans unmercifully.

While Soviet gymnast Aleksandr Dityatin became the first athlete to win eight medals in one year, the belle of Montreal, Nadia Comaneci of Romania, returned to win two more gold medals and Cuban heavyweight Teofilo Stevenson became the first boxer to win three golds in the same weight division.

In track and field, Miruts Yifter of Ethiopia won at 5,000 and 10,000 meters, but the most thrilling moment of the Games came in the last lap of the 1,500 meters where Sebastian Coe of Great Britain outran countryman Steve Ovett and Jurgen Straub of East Germany for the gold.

Top 10 Standings

National medal standings are not recognized by the IOC. The unofficial point totals are based on 3 points for a gold medal, 2 for a silver and 1 for a bronze.

		Gold	Silver	Bronze	Total	Pts
1	USSR	80	69	46	195	424
2	E. Germany	47	37	42	126	257
3	Bulgaria	8	16	17	41	73
4	Hungary	7	10	15	32	56
5	Poland	3	14	15	32	52
6	Cuba	8	7	5	20	43
	Romania	6	6	13	25	43
8	Great Britain	5	7	9	21	38
9	Italy	8	3	4	15	34
10	France	6	5	3	14	31

Leading Medal Winners

Number of individual medals won on the left; gold, silver and bronze breakdown to the right.

MEN

No		Sport	G-S-B
8	Aleksandr Dityatin, USSR . . . . .Gymnastics		3-4-1
5	Nikolai Andrianov, USSR . . . . . .Gymnastics		2-2-1
4	Roland Brückner, E. Ger . . . . . .Gymnastics		1-1-2
3	Vladimir Parfenovich, USSR . . . .Canoeing		3-0-0
3	Vladimir Salnikov, USSR . . . . . . .Swimming		3-0-0
3	Sergei Kopliakov, USSR . . . . . . .Swimming		2-1-0
3	Aleksandr Tkachyov, USSR . . . .Gymnastics		2-1-0
3	Andrei Krylov, USSR . . . . .Swimming		1-2-0
3	Arsen Miskarov, USSR . . . . .Swimming		0-2-1

WOMEN

No		Sport	G-S-B
5	Ines Diers, E. Ger . . . . .Swimming		2-2-1
4	Caren Metschuck, E. Ger . . . . . .Swimming		3-1-0
4	Nadia Comaneci, ROM . . . . . .Gymnastics		2-2-0
4	Natalya Shaposhnikova, USSR .Gymnastics		2-0-2
4	Maxi Gnauck, E. Ger . . . . .Gymnastics		1-1-2
3	Barbara Krause, E. Ger . . . . . . .Swimming		3-0-0
3	Rica Reinisch, E. Ger . . . . .Swimming		3-0-0
3	Yelena Davydova, USSR . . . . . .Gymnastics		2-1-0
3	Steffi Kraker, E. Ger . . . . .Gymnastics		0-1-2
3	Melita Ruhn, ROM . . . . .Gymnastics		0-1-2

1984

Los Angeles

For the third consecutive Olympiad, a boycott prevented all member nations from attending the Summer Games. This time, the Soviet Union and 13 Communist allies stayed home in an obvious payback for the West's snub of Moscow in 1980. Romania was the only Warsaw Pact country to come to L.A.

While a record 140 nations did show up, the level of competition was hardly what it might have been had the Soviets and East Germans made the trip. As a result, the United States won a record 83 gold medals in the most lopsided Summer Games since St. Louis 80 years before.

The American gold rush was led by 23-year-old Carl Lewis, who duplicated Jesse Owens' 1936 track and field grand slam by winning the 100 and 200 meters and the long jump, and anchoring the 4x100 meter relay. Teammate Valerie Brisco-Hooks won three times, taking the 200, 400 and 4x100 relay.

Sebastian Coe of Britain became the first repeat winner of the 1,500 meters since Jim Lightbody of the U.S. in 1906. Other repeaters were Briton Daley Thompson in the decathlon

and U.S. hurdler Edwin Moses, who won in 1976 but was not allowed to defend his title in '80.

Romanian gymnast Ecaterina Szabó matched Lewis' four gold medals and added a silver, but the darling of the Games was little (4-foot-8¾), 16-year-old Mary Lou Retton, who won the women's All-Around with a pair of 10s in her last two events.

The L.A. Olympics were the first privately financed Games ever and made an unheard of profit of $215 million. *Time* magazine was so impressed it named organizing president Peter Ueberroth its Man of the Year.

Top 10 Standings

National medal standings are not recognized by the IOC. The unofficial point totals are based on 3 points for a gold medal, 2 for a silver and 1 for a bronze.

		Gold	Silver	Bronze	Total	Pts
1	USA 83		61	30	174	401
2	W. Germany 17		19	23	59	112
3	Romania 20		16	17	53	109
4	Canada 10		18	16	44	82
5	China 15		8	9	32	70
6	Italy 14		6	12	32	66
7	Japan 10		8	14	32	60
8	Great Britain 5		11	21	37	58
9	France 5		7	16	28	45
10	Australia 4		8	12	24	40

Leading Medal Winners

Number of individual medals won on the left; gold, silver and bronze breakdown to the right.

MEN

No		Sport	G-S-B
6	Li Ning, CHN . . . . .Gymnastics		3-2-1
5	Koji Gushiken, JPN . . . . .Gymnastics		2-1-2
4	Carl Lewis, USA . . . . .Track/Field		4-0-0
4	Mike Heath, USA . . . . .Swimming		3-1-0
4	Michael Gross, W. Ger . . . . . . .Swimming		2-2-0
4	Mitch Gaylord, USA . . . . .Gymnastics		1-1-2
3	Rick Carey, USA . . . . .Swimming		3-0-0
3	Ian Ferguson, NZE . . . . .Canoeing		3-0-0
3	Rowdy Gaines, USA . . . . .Swimming		3-0-0
3	Peter Vidmar, USA . . . . .Gymnastics		2-1-0
3	Victor Davis, CAN . . . . .Swimming		1-2-0
3	Pablo Morales, USA . . . . .Swimming		1-2-0
3	Lou Yun, CHN . . . . .Gymnastics		1-2-0
3	Shinji Morisue, JPN . . . . .Gymnastics		1-1-1
3	Lars-Erik Moberg, SWE . . . . . . .Canoeing		0-3-0
3	Mark Stockwell, AUS . . . . .Swimming		0-2-1

WOMEN

No		Sport	G-S-B
5	Ecaterina Szabó, ROM . . . . . .Gymnastics		4-1-0
5	Mary Lou Retton, USA . . . . . .Gymnastics		1-2-2
4	Nancy Hogshead, USA . . . . . .Swimming		3-1-0
3	Valerie Brisco-Hooks, USA . . . .Track/Field		3-0-0
3	Tracy Caulkins, USA . . . . .Swimming		3-0-0
3	Mary T. Meagher, USA . . . . . . .Swimming		3-0-0
3	Agneta Andersson, SWE . . . . .Canoeing		2-1-0
3	Chandra Cheeseborough, USA .Track/Field		2-1-0
3	Simona Pauca, ROM . . . . .Gymnastics		2-0-1
3	Julie McNamara, USA . . . . . . .Gymnastics		1-2-0
3	Anne Ottenbrite, CAN . . . . . . .Swimming		1-1-1
3	Karin Seick, W. Ger . . . . .Swimming		0-1-2
3	Annemarie Verstappen, NED . . .Swimming		0-1-2

SÉOUL 1988

1988

Seoul

For the first time since Munich in 1972, there was no organized boycott of the Summer Olympics. Cuba and Ethiopia stayed away in support of North Korea (the IOC turned down the North Koreans' demand to co-host the Games, so they refused to participate), but that was about it.

More countries (159) sent more athletes (9,465) to South Korea than to any previous Olympics. There were also more security personnel (100,000) than ever before given Seoul's proximity (30 miles) to the North and the possibility of student demonstrations for reunification.

Ten days into the Games, Canadian Ben Johnson beat defending champion Carl Lewis in the 100-meter dash with a world record time of 9.79. Two days later, however, Johnson was stripped of his gold medal and sent packing by the IOC when his post-race drug test indicated steroid use.

Lewis, who finished second in the 100, was named the winner. He also repeated in the long jump, was second in the 200 and did not run the 4x100-relay. Teammate Florence Griffith Joyner claimed four medals—gold in the 100, 200 and 4x100-meter relay, and silver in the 4x400 relay. Her sister-in-law, Jackie Joyner-Kersee, won the long jump and heptathlon.

The most gold medals were won by swimmers—Kristin Otto of East Germany (6) and American Matt Biondi (5). Otherwise, Steffi Graf added an Olympic gold medal to her Grand Slam sweep in tennis, Greg Louganis won both men's diving events for the second straight time, and the U.S. men's basketball team had to settle for third place after losing to the gold medal-winning Soviets, 82-76, in the semifinals.

Top 10 Standings

National medal standings are not recognized by the IOC. The unofficial point totals are based on 3 points for a gold medal, 2 for a silver and 1 for a bronze.

		Gold	Silver	Bronze	Total	Pts
1	USSR	55	31	46	132	273
2	E. Germany	37	35	30	102	211
3	USA	36	31	27	94	197
4	W. Germany	11	14	15	40	76
5	Bulgaria	10	12	13	35	67
	South Korea	12	10	11	33	67
7	Hungary	11	6	6	23	51
8	China	5	11	12	28	49
	Romania	7	11	6	24	49
10	Great Britain	5	10	9	24	44

Leading Medal Winners

Number of individual medals won on the left; gold, silver and bronze breakdown to the right.

MEN

No		Sport	G-S-B
7	Matt Biondi, USA	Swimming	5-1-1
5	Vladimir Artemov, USSR	Gymnastics	4-1-0
4	Dmitri Bilozerchev, USSR	Gymnastics	3-0-1
4	Valeri Lyukin, USSR	Gymnastics	2-2-0
3	Chris Jacobs, USA	Swimming	2-1-0
3	Carl Lewis, USA	Track/Field	2-1-0
3	Holger Behrendt, E. Ger	Gymnastics	1-1-1
3	Uwe Dassler, E. Ger	Swimming	1-1-1
3	Paul McDonald, NZE	Canoeing	1-1-1
3	Igor Polianski, USSR	Swimming	1-0-2
3	Gennadi Prigoda, USSR	Swimming	0-1-2
3	Sven Tippelt, E. Ger	Gymnastics	0-1-2

WOMEN

No		Sport	G-S-B
6	Kristin Otto, E. Ger	Swimming	6-0-0
6	Daniela Silivas, ROM	Gymnastics	3-2-1
4	Florence Griffith Joyner, USA	Track/Field	3-1-0
4	Svetlana Boguinskaya, USSR	Gymnastics	2-1-1
4	Elena Shushunova, USSR	Gymnastics	2-1-1
3	Janet Evans, USA	Swimming	3-0-0
3	Silke Hörner, E. Ger	Swimming	2-0-1
3	Daniela Hunger, E. Ger	Swimming	2-0-1
3	Katrin Meissner, E. Ger	Swimming	2-0-1
3	Birgit Schmidt, E. Ger	Canoeing	2-1-0
3	Birte Weigang, E. Ger	Swimming	1-2-0
3	Vania Guecheva, BUL	Canoeing	1-1-1
3	Gabriela Potorac, ROM	Gymnastics	0-2-1
3	Heike Drechsler, E. Ger	Track/Field	0-1-2

Barcelona'92

1992

Barcelona

The year IOC president Juan Antonio Samaranch brought the Olympics to his native Spain marked the first renewal of the Summer Games since the fall of communism in Eastern Europe and the reunification of Germany in 1990.

A record 10,563 athletes from 172 nations gathered without a single country boycotting the Games. Both Cuba and North Korea returned after 12 years and South Africa was welcomed back after 32, following the national government's denunciation of apartheid racial policies.

While Germany competed under one flag for the first time since 1964, 12 nations from the former Soviet Union joined forces one last time as the Unified Team.

This was also the year the IOC threw open the gates to professional athletes after 96 years of high-minded opposition. Basketball was the chief beneficiary as America's popular "Dream Team" of NBA All-Stars easily won the gold.

Carl Lewis earned his seventh and eighth career gold medals with a third consecutive Olympic win in the long jump, and an anchor-leg performance on the American 4x100-meter relay team that helped establish a world record. Gail Devers of the U.S., whose feet had nearly been amputated by doctors in 1990 as a result of radiation treatment for Graves' disease, won the women's 100 meters.

Other track and field athletes stumbled, however. After Olympic favorite and world champion Dan O'Brien failed to even make the U.S. team, Dave Johnson, the new favorite, settled for the bronze. Ukrainian pole vaulter Sergey Bubka, who had dominated the sport for the past decade, was the heavy favorite, but he failed to clear any height.

China's Fu Mingxia, 13, won the women's platform diving gold, becoming the second-youngest person to win an individual gold medal. In gymnastics, Vitaly Scherbo of Belarus, competing for the Unified Team, won six golds. Cuba made its Olympic return rewarding, capturing seven boxing golds as well as the gold in baseball.

Top 10 Standings

National medal standings are not recognized by the IOC. The unofficial point totals are based on 3 points for a gold medal, 2 for a silver and 1 for a bronze.

		Gold	Silver	Bronze	Total	Pts
1	Unified Team	45	38	29	112	240
2	United States	37	34	37	108	216
3	Germany	33	21	28	82	169
4	China	16	22	16	54	108
5	Cuba	14	6	11	31	65
6	Hungary	11	12	7	30	64
7	South Korea	12	5	12	29	58
8	Spain	13	7	2	22	55
9	France	8	5	16	29	50
	Australia	7	9	11	27	50

Leading Medal Winners
MEN

No		Sport	G-S-B
6	Vitaly Scherbo, UT	Gymnastics	6-0-0
5	Grigory Misiutin, UT	Gymnastics	1-4-0
4	Aleksandr Popov, UT	Gymnastics	2-2-0
3	Yevgeny Sadovyi, UT	Swimming	3-0-0
3	Matt Biondi, USA	Swimming	2-1-0
3	Jon Olsen, USA	Swimming	2-0-1
3	Mel Stewart, USA	Swimming	2-0-1
3	Vladimir Pychnenko, UT	Swimming	1-2-0
3	Li Xiaosahuang, CHN	Gymnastics	1-1-1
3	Li Jing, CHN	Gymnastics	0-3-0
3	Anders Holmertz, SWE	Swimming	0-2-1
3	Andreas Wecker, GER	Gymnastics	0-1-2

WOMEN

No		Sports	G-S-B
5	Shannon Miller, USA	Gymnastics	0-2-3
4	Tatiana Gutsu, UT	Gymnastics	2-1-1
4	Lavinia Milosovici, ROM	Gymnastics	2-1-1
4	Summer Sanders, USA	Swimming	2-1-1
4	Franziska van Almsick, GER	Swimming	0-2-2
3	Krisztina Egerszegi, HUN	Swimming	3-0-0
3	Nicole Haislett, USA	Swimming	3-0-0
3	Crissy Ahmann-Leighton, USA	Swimming	2-1-0
3	Jenny Thompson, USA	Swimming	2-1-0
3	Gwen Torrence, USA	Track/Field	2-1-0
3	Tatyana Lysenko, UT	Gymnastics	2-0-1
3	Lin Li, CHN	Swimming	1-2-0
3	Dagmar Hase, GER	Swimming	1-2-0
3	Zhuang Yong, CHN	Swimming	1-2-0
3	Rita Koban, HUN	Kayaking	1-1-1
3	Anita Hall, USA	Swimming	1-1-1
3	Daniela Hunger, GER	Swimming	0-1-2

1996
Atlanta

Atlanta 1996

The Atlanta Games were certainly the largest (a record 197 nations competed), most logistically complicated Olympics to date and perhaps the most hyped and overcommercialized as well. Despite all the troubles that organizers faced, from computer scoring snafus and transportation problems to a horrific terrorist attack, these Olympics had some of the best stories ever.

The Games began so joyously with Muhammad Ali, the world's best-known sports figure now stricken by illness, igniting the Olympic cauldron.

Sadly, just eight days later horror was the prevailing mood after a terrorist's bomb ripped apart a peaceful Friday evening in Centennial Olympic Park. In the explosion, one women was killed, 111 were injured and the entire world was reminded of the terror and tragedy of Munich in 1972.

As they did in '72, the Games would go on. In track and field, Michael Johnson delivered on his much-anticipated, yet still startling, double in the 200 and 400 meters. One thing that many didn't foresee is that he would be matched by France's Marie-Jose Perec, who converted her own 200-400 double, albeit with much less attention. Carl Lewis pulled out one last bit of magic to win the long jump for the ninth gold medal of his amazing Olympic career. Donovan Bailey set a world record in the 100 and led Canada to a win over a faltering U.S. team in the 4x100 relay.

The U.S. women's gymnastics squad took the team gold after Kerri Strug hobbled up and completed her final gutsy vault in the Games' most compelling moment. Swimmer Amy Van Dyken became the first American woman to win four golds in a single Games. Ireland's Michelle Smith won three golds (and a bronze) of her own, but her victories were somewhat tainted by controversy surrounding unproven charges of drug use.

The USA faired well in team sports also. The men's basketball "Dream Team" was back and, predictably, stomped the competition on its way back to the winners' podium. Also the U.S. women won gold at the Olympic debut of two sports—softball and soccer.

Top 10 Standings

National medal standings are not recognized by the IOC. The unofficial point totals are based on 3 points for a gold medal, 2 for a silver and 1 for a bronze.

		Gold	Silver	Bronze	Total	Pts
1	United States	44	32	25	101	221
2	Russia	26	21	16	63	136
3	Germany	20	18	27	65	123
4	China	16	22	12	50	104
5	France	15	7	15	37	74
6	Italy	13	10	12	35	71
7	Australia	9	9	23	41	68
8	South Korea	7	15	5	27	56
9	Cuba	9	8	8	25	51
10	Ukraine	9	2	12	23	43

Leading Medal Winners

Number of individual medals won on the left; gold, silver and bronze breakdown to the right.

MEN

No		Sport	G-S-B
6	Alexei Nemov, RUS	Gymnastics	2-1-3
4	Gary Hall Jr., USA	Swimming	2-2-0
4	Aleksandr Popov, RUS	Swimming	2-2-0
3	Josh Davis, USA	Swimming	3-0-0
3	Denis Pankratov, RUS	Swimming	2-1-0
3	Daniel Kowalski, AUS	Swimming	0-1-2
3	Vitaly Scherbo, BEL	Gymnastics	0-0-3

WOMEN

No		Sport	G-S-B
4	Amy Van Dyken, USA	Swimming	4-0-0
4	Michelle Smith, IRL	Swimming	3-0-1
4	Angel Martino, USA	Swimming	2-0-2
4	Simona Amanar, ROM	Gymnastics	1-1-2
4	Dagmar Hase, GER	Swimming	0-3-1
4	Gina Gogean, ROM	Gymnastics	0-1-3
3	Jenny Thompson, USA	Swimming	3-0-0
3	Lilia Podkopayeva, UKR	Gymnastics	2-1-0
3	Amanda Beard, USA	Swimming	1-2-0
3	Le Jingyi, CHN	Swimming	1-2-0
3	Wendy Hedgepeth, USA	Swimming	1-2-0
3	Susan O'Neill, AUS	Swimming	1-1-1
3	Merlene Ottey, JAM	Track & Field	0-2-1
3	Franziska van Almsick, GER	Swimming	0-2-1
3	Sandra Volker, GER	Swimming	0-1-2

2000

Sydney

Billed as the Games of the New Millennium, the Sydney Summer Olympics were the largest in history—with 10,651 athletes competing but were praised for their superb organization.

Aussie sprinter Cathy Freeman lit the Olympic torch then warmed the hearts of a nation and a people with her performance in the 400 meters, becoming the first Australian aborigine to win Olympic gold.

Local boy Ian Thorpe also wowed the home crowds with an eye-popping performance in the pool, winning three gold medals and two sil-

vers. The 17-year-old "Thorpedo" broke his own world record in the 400-meter freestyle and just an hour later, in front of 17,500 screaming fans, he anchored the Aussie 4x100 meter freestyle relay team. Thorpe came from behind to edge American anchor Gary Hall Jr. in a thrilling finish.

Germany's Birgit Fischer earned two gold medals in Kayak, becoming the first woman in any sport to win medals 20 years apart. Ryoko Tamura lost in the final in both Barcelona and Atlanta, but came back to win the gold medal for Japan in the extra lightweight division of women's judo. Great Britain's Steve Redgrave became the first rower to win gold medals at five consecutive Olympics.

American sprinter Marion Jones made a highly publicized play to become the first track and field athlete to win five gold medals in a single games. Jones was golden in the 100 meters, 200 meters and 4x400 meter relay, but "fell short" of complete success, taking bronze in the long jump and 4x100 meter relay. Jones was still the first female to win five track and field medals at a single games.

Another American came out of obscurity to win a gold medal. In one of the biggest upsets in Olympic history, Greco-Roman wrestler Rulon Gardner shocked the world by beating the previously unbeatable Alexandre Kareline of Russia in the super heavyweight gold medal match.

The United States also took gold with a surprising run in baseball and a bounce-back victory in softball after losing three straight games before the medal round.

Top 10 Standings

National medal standings are not recognized by the IOC. The unofficial point totals are based on 3 points for a gold medal, 2 for a silver and 1 for a bronze.

		Gold	Silver	Bronze	Total	Pts
1	United States	40	24	33	97	201
2	Russia	32	28	28	88	180
3	China	28	16	15	59	131
4	Australia	16	25	17	58	115
5	Germany	13	17	26	56	99
6	France	13	14	11	38	78
7	Italy	13	8	13	34	68
8	Cuba	11	11	7	29	62
9	Great Britain	11	10	7	28	60
10	Netherlands	12	9	4	25	58

Leading Medal Winners

Number of individual medals won on the left; gold, silver and bronze breakdown to the right.

MEN

No		Sport	G-S-B
6	Alexei Nemov, RUS	Gymnastics	2-1-3
5	Ian Thorpe, Aus	Swimming	3-2-0
4	Michael Klim, Aus	Swimming	2-2-0
4	Gary Hall Jr., USA	Swimming	2-1-1
4	P. van den Hoogenband, NED	Swimming	2-0-2
4	Dmitri Sautin, RUS	Diving	1-1-2
3	Lenny Krayzelburg, USA	Swimming	3-0-0
3	Florian Rousseau, FRA	Cycling	2-1-0
3	Massimiliano Rosolino, ITA	Swimming	1-1-1
3	Matthew Welsh, AUS	Swimming	0-2-1

WOMEN

No		Sport	G-S-B
5	Marion Jones, USA	Track & Field	3-0-2
5	Dara Torres, USA	Swimming	2-0-3
4	Inge de Bruijn, NED	Swimming	3-1-0
4	Leontien Zijlaard, NED	Cycling	3-1-0
4	Jenny Thompson, USA	Swimming	3-0-1
4	Susie O'Neill, AUS	Swimming	1-3-0
3	Yana Klochkova, UKR	Swimming	2-1-0
3	Elena Zamolodtchikova, RUS	Gymnastics	2-1-0
3	Simona Amanar, ROM	Gymnastics	2-0-1
3	Svetlana Khorkina, RUS	Gymnastics	1-2-0
3	Liu Xuan, CHN	Gymnastics	1-0-2
3	Therese Alshammer, SWE	Swimming	0-2-1
3	Ekaterina Lobazniouk, RUS	Gymnastics	0-2-1
3	Petria Thomas, AUS	Swimming	0-2-1

ATHENS 2004

2004

Athens

The Summer Games returned home to its birthplace in 2004. The ancient home of what has evolved from a simple series of footraces and wrestling matches nearly a thousand years before the birth of Christ is now a truly global phenomenon with 10,625 athletes from 202 nations competing in more than 300 events.

Despite fears of unfinished venues, terrorist attacks and day-long traffic snarls, the Games were a roaring success in almost every regard. The Greek organizers made a point of incorporating historic sites into the 2004 Games. The Olympic archery competition was held at Panathinaiko Stadium, which hosted the first modern Olympics in 1896. The white marble temple of sport also served as the finish line for the Olympic marathon which started in—where else?—Marathon. That city, according to legend, was the staring point for Pheidippides, the Greek soldier who completed the world's first marathon in 490 B.C. when he was hastened on foot roughly 26 miles to inform Athens of their victory over the Persians.

American swimmer Michael Phelps won eight medals, including six golds, falling just short of his mega-hyped goal of surpassing Mark Spitz's record of seven golds in a single games. Another American swimmer Jenny Thompson became the most decorated U.S. Olympian, winning her 12th medal as a member of the 400-meter medley relay.

Carly Patterson became the first American gymnast to win all-around gold since Mary Lou Retton twenty years previous. Paul Hamm

became the first American man to ever win the men's all-around but was forced to go to court to keep his gold when a scoring mistake was discovered that might have affected the outcome.

In track and field, America was once again out in front, sweeping the medal podium in both then men's 200 and 400 meters. But in the women's 400-meter hurdles, surprise winner Fani Halkia delighted the home crowd and did a barefoot victory lap to cries of "Hell-as! Hell-as!"

One less successful American entrant was the men's basketball team, which was forced to settle for bronze despite a roster laden with NBA stars.

Finally, more widespread and thorough drug testing beared more rotten fruit. It was technically the dirtiest games on records as a record 24 athletes tested positive for performance-enhancing drugs including three medallists who were stripped of their medals during the games.

Top 10 Standings

National medal standings are not recognized by the IOC. The unofficial point totals are based on 3 points for a gold medal, 2 for a silver and 1 for a bronze.

		Gold	Silver	Bronze	Total	Pts
1	United States	35	39	29	103	212
2	Russia	27	27	38	92	173
3	China	32	17	14	63	144
4	Australia	17	16	16	49	99
5	Germany	14	16	18	48	92
6	Japan	16	9	12	37	78
7	France	11	9	13	33	64
8	Italy	10	11	11	32	63
9	South Korea	9	12	9	30	60
10	Great Britain	9	9	12	30	57

Leading Medal Winners

Number of individual medals won on the left; gold, silver and bronze breakdown to the right.

MEN

No		Sport	G-S-B
8*	Michael Phelps, USA	Swimming	6-0-2
3	Ian Thorpe, AUS	Swimming	2-1-1
3	Aaron Peirsol, USA	Swimming	3-0-0
3	Kosuke Kitajima, JPN	Swimming	2-1-0
3	Grant Hackett, AUS	Swimming	1-2-0
3	Paul Hamm, USA	Gymnastics	1-2-0
3	Brendan Hansen, USA	Swimming	1-1-1
3	Ian Crocker, USA	Swimming	1-1-1
3	Justin Gatlin, USA	Track and Field	1-1-1
3	Roland Mark Schoeman, RSA	Swimming	1-1-1
3	Bradley Wiggins, GBR	Cycling	1-1-1
3	Marian Dragulescu, ROM	Gymnastics	0-1-2

WOMEN

No		Sport	G-S-B
5	Natalie Coughlin, USA	Swimming	2-2-1
4	Petria Thomas, AUS	Swimming	3-1-0
4	Inge de Bruijn, NED	Swimming	1-1-2
3	Jodie Henry, AUS	Swimming	3-0-0
3	Catalina Ponor, ROM	Gymnastics	3-0-0
3	Veronica Campbell, JAM	Track and Field	2-0-1
3	Amanda Beard, USA	Swimming	1-2-0
3	Otylia Jedrzejczak, POL	Swimming	1-2-0
3	Carly Patterson, USA	Gymnastics	1-2-0
3	Kirsty Coventry, ZIM	Swimming	1-1-1
3	Leisel Jones, AUS	Swimming	1-1-1
3	Laure Manaudou, FRA	Swimming	1-1-1
3	Kaitlin Sandeno, USA	Swimming	1-1-1

BEIJING 2008
WHAT 2 WATCH 4

With almost a year until the torch will be lit at the Bird's Nest, the nickname for Beijing's striking (read: odd-looking) new Olympic stadium, and the start of competition at The Games of the XXIXth Olympiad on Aug. 8, 2008, it's a tricky proposition to attempt to accurately forecast possible outcomes. Still, let's snap the fortune cookie and look into the future.

First off, there will be a few new events to look for in 2008. The International Olympic Committee had **gender equity** on their minds and has added about 80 females with additional numbers of teams in the women's soccer, handball and field hockey competitions.

In a direct attempt to reach out to a younger audience, **BMX biking** will make it's debut at Beijing. BMX races will be held on dirt courses that include jumps, banked corners and other obstacles. You could very well see skateboarding in future Olympics. No joke.

Also, it will likely be the final chance to see Olympic baseball and softball, which have both been dropped from the program in London in 2012. USA Baseball, which failed to even qualify a team for Athens in 2004, should contend for a medal, just don't expect to see America's top major league stars. The Summer Games take place smack in the middle of the MLB season.

All told, there will be 302 medal events in Beijing, one more than at the 2004 Athens Games.

Along with BMX, another interesting new event will be a 10-kilometer "marathon" open-water swim for men and women.

Here's a rundown of some of the names that will make the biggest impacts in 2008...

Expect to hear the name **Michael Phelps** a few times next summer. He may already be recognized as the greatest swimmer of all-time but he wants to cement that legacy by eclipsing the legendary accomplishments of Mark Spitz, who won seven golds in 1972. You may remember Phelps from Athens in 2004, where he won six golds and two bronze and made one of the classier moves of the games when he stepped out of the spotlight, giving teammate Ian Crocker a chance to swim in the final of the 400-meter medley relay. The team won gold and Phelps, who swam for the team in the prelims got a gold for essentially taking a break.

Now four years older and wiser—a DUI charge will make you grow up quickly—and seemingly more dominant than ever (witness the seven golds and five world records he set at the swimming world championships in 2007), Phelps will renew his Spitz-ian quest.

Some other American swimmers will be looking to make a big splash. None bigger than **Dara Torres** who, after a six-year layoff, will be attempting to compete in her fifth(!) games. The new mother, who will be 41 years old by next summer, is attempting to become the **oldest swimmer to ever compete** at an Olympics. Initially she hoped to make the team as a member of a relay squad but her swimming has been so surprising that if she stays on track she could be a legitimate threat to add to her nine career Olympic medals.

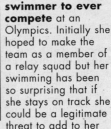

The Bird's Nest

Torres, who competed in her first Olympics in 1984, well before many of her competitors were born, eats organic food, practices yoga, and has a full-time staff of experts including two physical therapists, two masseurs, a nanny, and three coaches.

BEIJING 2008

"Her comeback is just mind-boggling," Torres's coach Michael Lohberg told *The Washington Post.*

"I don't think people can actually comprehend what's happening here. It hasn't happened before and it probably won't happen again. A 40-year-old who hasn't been swimming for years should never go this fast."

Speaking of speed, perhaps the fastest man on the planet right now is American sprinter **Tyson Gay**. He is headed for another showdown with 100-meter world record holder **Asafa Powell** of Jamaica. Gay came from behind to beat Powell heads up in the 100 meters at the 2007 world track and field championships in Osaka, Japan.

Jingjing the Panda

Gay also won the 200 meters in Osaka, becoming just the third man in history to pull off the feat in the world championships. The last man to win gold in the 100 and 200 meters in the same Olympics was **Carl Lewis** in 1984. Gay will make a serious run at matching Lewis.

Another showdown on the track should occur between American women **Allyson Felix** and **Sanya Richards**. Felix won the 200 in Osaka by a wide margin and won two more golds on relay squads, running an amazing 48-flat split in the 4x400 meter relay. Richards has stated she is going to make a play for the 200-400 double but Felix will be a significant hurdle, especially in the 200.

Richards has dealt with an illness during the past year and her star is not as bright as it was in 2006. Still she has a

Allyson Felix

chance to rival Felix as the golden girl of the American team in 2008.

Another American with high hopes will be gymnast **Nastia Liukin**. The 18-year-old certainly has the genetics. Her father Valeri won four medals (two gold, two silver) for the Soviet Union at the 1988 Seoul Games.

Liukun finished in fifth place in the all-around at the 2007 world championships in Stuttgart, Germany slipping on the balance beam to spoil her chances at the podium. Ironically, she later took the individual gold in the beam and should be America's best hope for multiple medals in women's gymnastics.

The **official mascots** of the Games are the "Five Friendlies"—**Beibei** the Fish, **Jingjing** the Panda, **Huanhuan** the Olympic Flame, **Yingting** the Tibetan Antelope and **Nini** the Swallow.

The Beijing area has already started to undergo a massive scrubbing for its international showcasing. During the Games, in an effort to minimize Beijing's **notorious traffic and air pollution**, the city will reportedly ban at least a third of its 3.3 million vehicles during the 17-day Olympics and shutter most local factories and dirt-spewing coal mines.

Finally, there will be teams from 205 nations competing in Beijing, up from the 202 that went to Athens. During the opening ceremonies be on the lookout for first-timers Montenegro, The Marshall Islands and Tuvalo.

Now, let the games begin.

Event-by-Event

Gold medal winners from 1896-2004 in the following events: Baseball, Basketball, Boxing, Diving, Field Hockey, Gymnastics, Soccer, Softball, Swimming, Tennis and Track & Field.

BASEBALL

Multiple gold medals: Cuba (3).

Year		Year	
1992	**Cuba**, Taiwan, Japan	2000	**United States**, Cuba, South Korea
1996	**Cuba**, Japan, United States	2004	**Cuba**, Australia, Japan

U.S. Medal-Winning Baseball Teams

1996 (bronze medal): P–Kris Benson, R.A. Dickey, Seth Greisinger, Billy Koch, Braden Looper, Jim Parque and Jeff Weaver; C–A.J. Hinch, Matt LeCroy and Brian Lloyd; INF–Troy Glaus, Kip Harkrider, Travis Lee, Warren Morris, Augie Ojeda and Jason Williams; OF–Chad Allen, Chad Green, Jacque Jones and Mark Kotsay; Manager–Skip Bertman. Final: Cuba over Japan, 13-9

2000 (gold medal): P–Kurt Ainsworth, Ryan Franklin, Chris George, Shane Heams, Rick Krivda, Roy Oswalt, Jon Rauch, Bobby Seay, Ben Sheets, Todd Williams and Tim Young; C–Pat Borders, Marcus Jensen and Mike Kinkade; INF–Brent Abernathy, Sean Burroughs, John Cotton, Gookie Dawkins, Adam Everett and Doug Mientkiewicz; OF–Mike Neill, Anthony Sanders, Brad Wilkerson and Ernie Young; Manager–Tommy Lasorda. Final: USA over Cuba, 4-0.

BASKETBALL

MEN

Multiple gold medals: USA (12), USSR (2).

Year		Year	
1936	**United States**, Canada, Mexico	1976	**United States**, Yugoslavia, Soviet Union
1948	**United States**, France, Brazil	1980	**Yugoslavia**, Italy, Soviet Union
1952	**United States**, Soviet Union, Uruguay	1984	**United States**, Spain, Yugoslavia
1956	**United States**, Soviet Union, Uruguay	1988	**Soviet Union**, Yugoslavia, United States
1960	**United States**, Soviet Union, Brazil	1992	**United States**, Croatia, Lithuania
1964	**United States**, Soviet Union, Brazil	1996	**United States**, Yugoslavia, Lithuania
1968	**United States**, Yugoslavia, Soviet Union	2000	**United States**, France, Lithuania
1972	**Soviet Union**, United States, Cuba	2004	**Argentina**, Italy, United States

U.S. Medal-Winning Men's Basketball Teams

1936 (gold medal): Sam Balter, Ralph Bishop, Joe Fortenberry, Tex Gibbons, Francis Johnson, Carl Knowles, Frank Lubin, Art Mollner, Don Piper, Jack Ragland, Carl Shy, Willard Schmidt, Duane Swanson and William Wheatley. Coach–Jim Needles; Assistant–Gene Johnson. Final: USA over Canada, 19-8.

1948 (gold medal): Cliff Barker, Don Barksdale, Ralph Beard, Louis Beck, Vince Boryla, Gordon Carpenter, Alex Groza, Wallace Jones, Bob Kurland, Ray Lumpp, R.C. Pitts, Jesse Renick, Robert (Jackie) Robinson and Ken Rollins. Coach–Omar Browning; Assistant–Adolph Rupp. Final: USA over France, 65-21.

1952 (gold medal): Ron Bontemps, Mark Freiberger, Wayne Glasgow, Charlie Hoag, Bill Hougland, John Keller, Dean Kelley, Bob Kenney, Bob Kurland, Bill Lienhard, Clyde Lovellette, Frank McCabe, Dan Pippin and Howie Williams. Coach–Warren Womble; Assistant–Forrest (Phog) Allen. Final: USA over USSR, 36-25.

1956 (gold medal): Dick Boushka, Carl Cain, Chuck Darling, Bill Evans, Gib Ford, Burdy Haldorson, Bill Hougland, Bob Jeangerard, K.C. Jones, Bill Russell, Ron Tomsic and Jim Walsh. Coach–Gerald Tucker; Assistant–Bruce Drake. Final: USA over USSR, 89-55.

1960 (gold medal): Jay Arnette, Walt Bellamy, Bob Boozer, Terry Dischinger, Jerry Lucas, Oscar Robertson, Adrian Smith, Burdy Haldorson, Darrall Imhoff, Allen Kelley, Lester Lane and Jerry West. Coach–Pete Newell; Assistant–Warren Womble. Final round: USA defeated USSR (81-57), Italy (112-81) and Brazil (90-63) in round robin.

1964 (gold medal): Jim (Bad News) Barnes, Bill Bradley, Larry Brown, Joe Caldwell, Mel Counts, Dick Davies, Walt Hazzard, Lucious Jackson, Pete McCaffrey, Jeff Mullins, Jerry Shipp and George Wilson. Final: USA over USSR, 73-59.

1964 (gold medal): Jim (Bad News) Barnes, Bill Bradley, Larry Brown, Joe Caldwell, Mel Counts, Dick Davies, Walt Hazzard, Lucious Jackson, Pete McCaffrey, Jeff Mullins, Jerry Shipp and George Wilson. Coach–Hank Iba; Assistant–Henry Vaughn. Final: USA over USSR, 73-59.

1968 (gold medal): Mike Barrett, John Clawson, Don Dee, Cal Fowler, Spencer Haywood, Bill Hosket, Jim King, Glynn Saulters, Charlie Scott, Mike Silliman, Ken Spain, and Jo Jo White. Coach–Hank Iba; Assistant–Henry Vaughn. Final: USA over Yugoslavia, 65-50.

1972 (silver medal refused): Mike Bantom, Jim Brewer, Tom Burleson, Doug Collins, Kenny Davis, Jim Forbes, Tom Henderson, Bobby Jones, Dwight Jones, Kevin Joyce, Tom McMillen and Ed Ratleff. Coach–Hank Iba; Assistants– John Bach and Don Haskins. Final: USSR over USA, 51-50.

1976 (gold medal): Tate Armstrong, Quinn Buckner, Kenny Carr, Adrian Dantley, Walter Davis, Phil Ford, Ernie Grunfeld, Phil Hubbard, Mitch Kupchak, Tommy LaGarde, Scott May and Steve Sheppard. Coach–Dean Smith; Assistants–Bill Guthridge and John Thompson. Final: USA over Yugoslavia, 95-74.

1980 (no medal): USA boycotted Moscow Games. Final: Yugoslavia over Italy, 86-77.

1984 (gold medal): Steve Alford, Patrick Ewing, Vern Fleming, Michael Jordan, Joe Kleine, Jon Koncak, Chris Mullin, Sam Perkins, Alvin Robertson, Wayman Tisdale, Jeff Turner and Leon Wood. Coach–Bobby Knight; Assistants– Don Donoher and George Raveling. Final: USA over Spain, 96-65.

1988 (bronze medal): Stacey Augmon, Willie Anderson, Bimbo Coles, Jeff Grayer, Hersey Hawkins, Dan Majerle, Danny Manning, Mitch Richmond, J.R. Reid, David Robinson, Charles D. Smith and Charles E. Smith. Coach–John Thompson; Assistants–George Raveling and Mary Fenlon. Final: USSR over Yugoslavia, 76-63.

1992 (gold medal): Charles Barkley, Larry Bird, Clyde Drexler, Patrick Ewing, Magic Johnson, Michael Jordan, Christian Laettner, Karl Malone, Chris Mullin, Scottie Pippen, David Robinson and John Stockton. Coach–Chuck Daly; Assistants–Lenny Wilkens, Mike Krzyzewski and P.J. Carlesimo. Final: USA over Croatia, 117-85.

1996 (gold medal): Charles Barkley, Anfernee Hardaway, Grant Hill, Karl Malone, Reggie Miller, Hakeem Olajuwon, Shaquille O'Neal, Gary Payton, Scottie Pippen, David Robinson and John Stockton. Coach–Lenny Wilkens; Assistants–Bobby Cremins, Clem Haskins and Jerry Sloan. Final: USA over Yugoslavia, 95-69.

2000 (gold medal): Shareef Abdur-Rahim, Ray Allen, Vin Baker, Vince Carter, Kevin Garnett, Tim Hardaway, Allan Houston, Jason Kidd, Antonio McDyess, Alonzo Mourning, Gary Payton and Steve Smith. Coach–Rudy Tomjanovich; Assistants–Larry Brown, Gene Keady and Tubby Smith. Final: USA over France, 85-75.

Basketball (Cont.)

2004 (bronze medal): Carmelo Anthony, Carlos Boozer, Tim Duncan, Allen Iverson, LeBron James, Richard Jefferson, Stephon Marbury, Shawn Marion, Lamar Odom, Emeka Okafor, Amare Stoudemire, Dwyane Wade. Coach—Larry Brown; Assistants—Gregg Popovich, Roy Williams, Oliver Purnell, Dr. Sheldon Burns. Final—USA over Lithuania, 104-96.

WOMEN

Multiple gold medals: USA (4), USSR/UT (3).

Year		Year	
1976	**Soviet Union**, United States, Bulgaria	1992	**Unified Team**, China, United States
1980	**Soviet Union**, Bulgaria, Yugoslavia	1996	**United States**, Brazil, Australia
1984	**United States**, South Korea, China	2000	**United States**, Australia, Brazil
1988	**United States**, Yugoslavia, Soviet Union	2004	**United States**, Australia, Russia

U.S. Gold Medal-Winning Women's Basketball Teams

1984 (gold medal): Cathy Boswell, Denise Curry, Anne Donovan, Teresa Edwards, Lea Henry, Janice Lawrence, Pamela McGee, Carol Menken-Schaudt, Cheryl Miller, Kim Mulkey, Cindy Noble and Lynette Woodard. Coach–Pat Summitt; Assistant–Kay Yow. Final: USA over South Korea, 85-55.

1988 (gold medal): Cindy Brown, Vicky Bullett, Cynthia Cooper, Anne Donovan, Teresa Edwards, Kamie Ethridge, Jennifer Gillom, Bridgette Gordon, Andrea Lloyd, Katrina McClain, Suzie McConnell and Teresa Weatherspoon. Coach–Kay Yow; Assistants–Sylvia Hatchell and Susan Yow. Final: USA over Yugoslavia, 77-70.

1996 (gold medal): Jennifer Azzi, Ruthie Bolton, Teresa Edwards, Venus Lacy, Lisa Leslie, Rebecca Lobo, Katrina McClain, Nikki McCray, Carla McGee, Dawn Staley, Katy Steding and Sheryl Swoopes. Coach—Tara VanDerveer; Assistants–Ceal Barry, Nancy Darsch and Marian Washington. Final: USA over Brazil, 111-87.

2000 (gold medal): Ruthie Bolton-Holyfield, Teresa Edwards, Yolanda Griffith, Chamique Holdsclaw, Lisa Leslie, Nikki McCray, DeLisha Milton, Katie Smith, Dawn Staley, Sheryl Swoopes, Natalie Williams and Kara Wolters. Coach—Nell Fortner; Assistants–Geno Auriemma and Peggie Gillom. Final: USA over Australia, 76-54.

2004 (gold medal): Sue Bird, Swin Cash, Tamika Catchings, Yolanda Griffith, Shannon Johnson, Lisa Leslie, Ruth Riley, Katie Smith, Dawn Staley, Sheryl Swoopes, Diana Taurasi, Tina Thompson. Coach—Van Chancellor; Assistants—Anne Donovan, Gail Goestenkors, C. Vivian Stringer. Final: USA over Australia, 74-63.

BOXING

Multiple gold medals: László Papp, Felix Savon and Teófilo Stevenson (3); Ariel Hernandez, Angel Herrera, Mario Kindelan, Oliver Kirk, Jerzy Kulej, Boris Lagutin, Harry Mallin, Guillermo Rigondeaux, Oleg Saitov and Hector Vinent (2). All fighters won titles in consecutive Olympics, except Kirk, who won both the bantamweight and featherweight titles in 1904 (he only had to fight once in each division).

Light Flyweight (106 lbs)

Year		Final Match	Year		Final Match
1968	Francisco Rodriguez, VEN	Decision, 3-2	1988	Ivailo Hristov, BUL	Decision, 5-0
1972	György Gedó, HUN	Decision, 5-0	1992	Rogelio Marcelo, CUB	Decision, 24-10
1976	Jorge Hernandez, CUB	Decision, 4-1	1996	Daniel Petrov Bojilov, BUL	Decision, 19-6
1980	Shamil Sabyrov, USSR	Decision, 3-2	2000	Brahim Asloum, FRA	Decision, 23-10
1984	Paul Gonzales, USA	Default	2004	Yan Bhartelemy, CUB	Decision, 21-16

Flyweight (112 lbs)

Year		Final Match	Year		Final Match
1904	George Finnegan, USA	Stopped, 1st	1968	Ricardo Delgado, MEX	Decision, 5-0
1920	Frank Di Gennara, USA	Decision	1972	Georgi Kostadinov, BUL	Decision, 5-0
1924	Fidel LaBarba, USA	Decision	1976	Leo Randolph, USA	Decision, 3-2
1928	Antal Kocsis, HUN	Decision	1980	Peter Lessov, BUL	Stopped, 2nd
1932	István Énekes, HUN	Decision	1984	Steve McCrory, USA	Decision, 4-1
1936	Willi Kaiser, GER	Decision	1988	Kim Kwang-Sun, S. Kor	Decision, 4-1
1948	Pascual Perez, ARG	Decision	1992	Su Choi-Chol, N. Kor	Decision, 12-2
1952	Nate Brooks, USA	Decision, 3-0	1996	Maikro Romero, CUB	Decision, 12-11
1956	Terence Spinks, GBR	Decision	2000	Wijan Ponlid, THA	Decision, 19-12
1960	Gyula Török, HUN	Decision, 3-2	2004	Yuriorkis Gamboa, CUB	Decision, 38-23
1964	Fernando Atzori, ITA	Decision, 4-1			

Bantamweight (119 lbs)

Year		Final Match	Year		Final Match
1904	Oliver Kirk, USA	Stopped, 3rd	1964	Takao Sakurai, JPN	Stopped, 2nd
1908	Henry Thomas, GBR	Decision	1968	Valery Sokolov, USSR	Stopped, 2nd
1920	Clarence Walker, RSA	Decision	1972	Orlando Martinez, CUB	Decision, 5-0
1924	William Smith, RSA	Decision	1976	Gu Yong-Ju, N. Kor	Decision, 5-0
1928	Vittorio Tamagnini, ITA	Decision	1980	Juan Hernandez, CUB	Decision, 5-0
1932	Horace Gwynne, CAN	Decision	1984	Maurizio Stecca, ITA	Decision, 4-1
1936	Ulderico Sergo, ITA	Decision	1988	Kennedy McKinney, USA	Decision, 5-0
1948	Tibor Csik, HUN	Decision	1992	Joel Casamayor, CUB	Decision, 14-8
1952	Pentti Hämäläinen, FIN	Decision, 2-1	1996	Istvan Kovacs, HUN	Decision, 14-7
1956	Wolfgang Behrendt, GER	Decision	2000	Guillermo Rigondeaux, CUB	Decision, 18-12
1960	Oleg Grigoryev, USSR	Decision	2004	Guillermo Rigondeaux, CUB	Decision, 22-13

Featherweight (125 lbs)

Year		Final Match	Year		Final Match
1904	Oliver Kirk, USA	Decision	1964	Stanislav Stepashkin, USSR	Decision, 3-2
1908	Richard Gunn, GBR	Decision	1968	Antonio Roldan, MEX	Won on Disq.
1920	Paul Fritsch, FRA	Decision	1972	Boris Kousnetsov, USSR	Decision, 3-2
1924	John Fields, USA	Decision	1976	Angel Herrera, CUB	KO, 2nd
1928	Lambertus van Klaveren, NED	Decision	1980	Rudi Fink, E. Ger	Decision, 4-1
1932	Carmelo Robledo, ARG	Decision	1984	Meldrick Taylor, USA	Decision, 5-0
1936	Oscar Casanovas, ARG	Decision	1988	Giovanni Parisi, ITA	Stopped, 1st
1948	Ernesto Formenti, ITA	Decision	1992	Andreas Tews, GER	Decision, 16-7
1952	Jan Zachara, CZE	Decision, 2-1	1996	Somluck Kamsing, THA	Decision, 8-5
1956	Vladimir Safronov, USSR	Decision	2000	Bekzat Sattarkhanov, KAZ	Decision, 22-14
1960	Francesco Musso, ITA	Decision, 4-1	2004	Alexei Tichtchenko, RUS	Decision, 39-17

Lightweight (132 lbs)

Year		Final Match	Year		Final Match
1904	Harry Spanger, USA	Decision	1964	József Grudzien, POL	Decision
1908	Frederick Grace, GBR	Decision	1968	Ronnie Harris, USA	Decision, 5-0
1920	Samuel Mosberg, USA	Decision	1972	Jan Szczepanski, POL	Decision, 5-0
1924	Hans Nielsen, DEN	Decision	1976	Howard Davis, USA	Decision, 5-0
1928	Carlo Orlandi, ITA	Decision	1980	Angel Herrera, CUB	Stopped, 3rd
1932	Lawrence Stevens, S. Afr	Decision	1984	Pernell Whitaker, USA	Foe quit, 2nd
1936	Imre Harangi, HUN	Decision	1988	Andreas Zuelow, E. Ger	Decision, 5-0
1948	Gerald Dreyer, S. Afr	Decision	1992	Oscar De La Hoya, USA	Decision, 7-2
1952	Aureliano Bolognesi, ITA	Decision, 2-1	1996	Hocine Soltani, ALG	Tiebreak, 3-3
1956	Richard McTaggart, GBR	Decision	2000	Mario Kindelan, CUB	Decision, 14-4
1960	Kazimierz Pazdzior, POL	Decision, 4-1	2004	Mario Kindelan, CUB	Decision, 30-22

Light Welterweight (141 lbs)

Year		Final Match	Year		Final Match
1952	Charles Adkins, USA	Decision, 2-1	1980	Patrizio Oliva, ITA	Decision, 4-1
1956	Vladimir Yengibaryan, USSR	Decision	1984	Jerry Page, USA	Decision, 5-0
1960	Bohumil Nemecek, CZE	Decision, 5-0	1988	Vyacheslav Yanovsky, USSR	Decision, 11-1
1964	Jerzy Kulej, POL	Decision, 5-0	1992	Hector Vinent, CUB	Decision, 11-1
1968	Jerzy Kulej, POL	Decision, 3-2	1996	Hector Vinent, CUB	Decision, 20-13
1972	Ray Seales, USA	Decision, 3-2	2000	Mahamadkadyz Abdullaev, UZB	Decision, 27-20
1976	Ray Leonard, USA	Decision, 5-0	2004	Manus Boonjumnong, THA	Decision, 17-11

Welterweight (152 lbs)

Year		Final Match	Year		Final Match
1904	Albert Young, USA	Decision	1968	Manfred Wolke, E. Ger	Decision, 4-1
1920	Bert Schneider, CAN	Decision	1972	Emilio Correa, CUB	Decision, 5-0
1924	Jean Delarge, BEL	Decision	1976	Jochen Bachfeld, E. Ger	Decision, 3-2
1928	Edward Morgan, NZE	Decision	1980	Andrés Aldama, CUB	Decision, 4-1
1932	Edward Flynn, USA	Decision	1984	Mark Breland, USA	Decision, 5-0
1936	Sten Suvio, FIN	Decision	1988	Robert Wangila, KEN	KO, 2nd
1948	Julius Torma, CZE	Decision	1992	Michael Carruth, IRE	Decision, 13-10
1952	Zygmunt Chychla, POL	Decision, 3-0	1996	Oleg Saitov, RUS	Decision, 14-9
1956	Nicolae Linca, ROM	Decision, 3-2	2000	Oleg Saitov, RUS	Decision, 24-16
1960	Nino Benvenuti, ITA	Decision, 4-1	2004	Bakhtiyar Artayev, KAZ	Decision, 36-26
1964	Marian Kasprzyk, POL	Decision, 4-1			

Light Middleweight (156 lbs)

Year		Final Match	Year		Final Match
1952	László Papp, HUN	Decision, 3-0	1980	Armando Martinez, CUB	Decision, 4-1
1956	László Papp, HUN	Decision	1984	Frank Tate, USA	Decision, 5-0
1960	Skeeter McClure, USA	Decision, 4-1	1988	Park Si-Hun, S. Kor	Decision, 3-2
1964	Boris Lagutin, USSR	Decision, 4-1	1992	Juan Lemus, CUB	Decision, 6-1
1968	Boris Lagutin, USSR	Decision, 5-0	1996	David Reid, USA	KO, 3rd
1972	Dieter Kottysch, W. Ger	Decision, 3-2	2000	Yermakhan Ibraimov, KAZ	Decision, 25-23
1976	Jerzy Rybicki, POL	Decision, 5-0	2004	weight class eliminated.	

Middleweight (165 lbs)

Year		Final Match	Year		Final Match
1904	Charles Mayer, USA	Stopped, 3rd	1964	Valery Popenchenko, USSR	Stopped, 1st
1908	John Douglas, GBR	Decision	1968	Christopher Finnegan, GBR	Decision, 3-2
1920	Harry Mallin, GBR	Decision	1972	Vyacheslav Lemechev, USSR	KO, 1st
1924	Harry Mallin, GBR	Decision	1976	Michael Spinks, USA	Stopped, 3rd
1928	Piero Toscani, ITA	Decision	1980	José Gomez, CUB	Decision, 4-1
1932	Carmen Barth, USA	Decision	1984	Shin Joon-Sup, S. Kor	Decision, 3-2
1936	Jean Despeaux, FRA	Decision	1988	Henry Maske, E. Ger	Decision, 5-0
1948	László Papp, HUN	Decision	1992	Ariel Hernandez, CUB	Decision, 12-7
1952	Floyd Patterson, USA	KO, 1st	1996	Ariel Hernandez, CUB	Decision, 11-3
1956	Gennady Schatkov, USSR	KO, 1st	2000	Jorge Gutierrez, CUB	Decision, 17-15
1960	Eddie Crook, USA	Decision, 3-2	2004	Gaydarbek Gaydarbekov, RUS	Decision, 28-18

Boxing (Cont.)

Light Heavyweight (178 lbs)

Year		Final Match	Year		Final Match
1920	Eddie Eagan, USA	Decision	1968	Dan Poznjak, USSR	Default
1924	Harry Mitchell, GBR	Decision	1972	Mate Parlov, YUG	Stopped, 2nd
1928	Victor Avendaño, ARG	Decision	1976	Leon Spinks, USA	Stopped, 3rd
1932	David Carstens, S. Afr	Decision	1980	Slobodan Kacar, YUG	Decision, 4-1
1936	Roger Michelot, FRA	Decision	1984	Anton Josipovic, YUG	Default
1948	George Hunter, S. Afr	Decision	1988	Andrew Maynard, USA	Decision, 5-0
1952	Norvel Lee, USA	Decision, 3-0	1992	Torsten May, GER	Decision, 8-3
1956	Jim Boyd, USA	Decision	1996	Vasilii Jirov, KAZ	Decision, 17-4
1960	Cassius Clay, USA	Decision, 5-0	2000	Alexander Lebziak, RUS	Decision, 20-6
1964	Cosimo Pinto, ITA	Decision, 3-2	2004	Andre Ward, USA	Decision, 20-13

Note: Cassius Clay changed his name to Muhammad Ali after winning the world heavyweight championship in 1964.

Heavyweight (201 lbs)

Year		Final Match	Year		Final Match
1984	Henry Tillman, USA	Decision, 5-0	1996	Felix Savon, CUB	Decision, 20-2
1988	Ray Mercer, USA	KO, 1st	2000	Felix Savon, CUB	Decision, 21-13
1992	Felix Savon, CUB	Decision, 14-1	2004	Odlanier Solis, CUB	Decision, 22-13

Super Heavyweight (Unlimited)

Year		Final Match	Year		Final Match
1904	Samuel Berger, USA	Decision	1964	Joe Frazier, USA	Decision, 3-2
1908	Albert Oldham, GBR	KO, 1st	1968	George Foreman, USA	Stopped, 2nd
1920	Ronald Rawson, GBR	Decision	1972	Teófilo Stevenson, CUB	Default
1924	Otto von Porat, NOR	Decision	1976	Teófilo Stevenson, CUB	KO, 3rd
1928	Arturo Rodriguez Jurado, ARG	Stopped, 1st	1980	Teófilo Stevenson, CUB	Decision, 4-1
1932	Santiago Lovell, ARG	Decision	1984	Tyrell Biggs, USA	Decision, 4-1
1936	Herbert Runge, GER	Decision	1988	Lennox Lewis, CAN	Stopped, 2nd
1948	Rafael Iglesias, ARG	KO, 2nd	1992	Roberto Balado, CUB	Decision, 13-2
1952	Ed Sanders, USA	Won on Disq.*	1996	Vladimir Klichko, UKR	Decision, 7-3
1956	Pete Rademacher, USA	Stopped, 1st	2000	Audley Harrison, GBR	Decision, 30-16
1960	Franco De Piccoli, ITA	KO, 1st	2004	Alexander Povetkin, RUS	walkover†

*Sanders' opponent, Ingemar Johansson, was disqualified in 2nd round for not trying.
†Povetkin was awarded the gold when his opponet Mohamed Aly failed a pre-fight physical due to a shoulder injury.
Note: Super Heavyweight was called heavyweight through 1980.

DIVING

MEN

Multiple gold medals: Greg Louganis (4); Klaus Dibiasi and Xiong Ni (3); Pete Desjardins, Sammy Lee, Tian Liang, Bob Webster and Albert White (2).

Springboard

Year		Points	Year		Points
1908	Albert Zürner, GER	85.5	1964	Ken Sitzberger, USA	159.90
1912	Paul Günther, GER	79.23	1968	Bernie Wrightson, USA	170.15
1920	Louis Kuehn, USA	675.4	1972	Vladimir Vasin, USSR	594.09
1924	Albert White, USA	696.4	1976	Phil Boggs, USA	619.05
1928	Pete Desjardins, USA	185.04	1980	Aleksandr Portnov, USSR	905.03
1932	Michael Galitzen, USA	161.38	1984	Greg Louganis, USA	754.41
1936	Richard Degener, USA	163.57	1988	Greg Louganis, USA	730.80
1948	Bruce Harlan, USA	163.64	1992	Mark Lenzi, USA	676.53
1952	David Browning, USA	205.29	1996	Xiong Ni, CHN	701.46
1956	Bob Clotworthy, USA	159.56	2000	Xiong Ni, CHN	708.72
1960	Gary Tobian, USA	170.00	2004	Peng Bo, CHN	787.38

Platform

Year		Points	Year		Points
1904	George Sheldon, USA	12.66	1960	Bob Webster, USA	165.56
1906	Gottlob Walz, GER	156.0	1964	Bob Webster, USA	148.58
1908	Hjalmar Johansson, SWE	83.75	1968	Klaus Dibiasi, ITA	164.18
1912	Erik Adlerz, SWE	73.94	1972	Klaus Dibiasi, ITA	504.12
1920	Clarence Pinkston, USA	100.67	1976	Klaus Dibiasi, ITA	600.51
1924	Albert White, USA	97.46	1980	Falk Hoffmann, E. Ger	835.65
1928	Pete Desjardins, USA	98.74	1984	Greg Louganis, USA	710.91
1932	Harold Smith, USA	124.80	1988	Greg Louganis, USA	638.61
1936	Marshall Wayne, USA	113.58	1992	Sun Shuwei, CHN	677.31
1948	Sammy Lee, USA	130.05	1996	Dmitri Sautin, RUS	692.34
1952	Sammy Lee, USA	156.28	2000	Tian Liang, CHN	724.53
1956	Joaquin Capilla, MEX	152.44	2004	Hu Jia, CHN	748.08

Synchronized Platform

Year		Points	Year		Points
2000	Igor Louckachine & Dmitri Sautin, RUS	365.04	2004	Tian Liang & Yang Jinghui, CHN	383.88

Synchronized Springboard

Year		Points	Year		Points
2000	Xiao Hailiang & Xiong Ni, CHN	365.58	2004	Nikolaos Siranidis & Thomas Bimis, GRE	353.34

WOMEN

Multiple gold medals: Pat McCormick and Fu Mingxia (4); Ingrid Engel-Krämer (3); Vicki Draves, Dorothy Poynton Hill, Guo Jingjing and Gao Min (2).

Springboard

Year		Points	Year		Points
1920	Aileen Riggin, USA	539.9	1968	Sue Gossick, USA	150.77
1924	Elizabeth Becker, USA	474.5	1972	Micki King, USA	450.03
1928	Helen Meany, USA	78.62	1976	Jennifer Chandler, USA	506.19
1932	Georgia Coleman, USA	87.52	1980	Irina Kalinina, USSR	725.91
1936	Marjorie Gestring, USA	89.27	1984	Sylvie Bernier, CAN	530.70
1948	Vicki Draves, USA	108.74	1988	Gao Min, CHN	580.23
1952	Pat McCormick, USA	147.30	1992	Gao Min, CHN	572.40
1956	Pat McCormick, USA	142.36	1996	Fu Mingxia, CHN	547.68
1960	Ingrid Krämer, GER	155.81	2000	Fu Mingxia, CHN	609.42
1964	Ingrid Engel-Krämer, GER	145.00	2004	Guo Jingjing, CHN	633.15

Platform

Year		Points	Year		Points
1912	Greta Johansson, SWE	39.9	1968	Milena Duchková, CZE	109.59
1920	Stefani Fryland-Clausen, DEN	34.6	1972	Ulrika Knape, SWE	390.00
1924	Caroline Smith, USA	33.2	1976	Elena Vaytsekhovskaya, USSR	406.59
1928	Elizabeth Becker Pinkston, USA	31.6	1980	Martina Jäschke, E. Ger	596.25
1932	Dorothy Poynton, USA	40.26	1984	Zhou Jihong, CHN	435.51
1936	Dorothy Poynton Hill, USA	33.93	1988	Xu Yanmei, CHN	445.20
1948	Vicki Draves, USA	68.87	1992	Fu Mingxia, CHN	461.43
1952	Pat McCormick, USA	79.37	1996	Fu Mingxia, CHN	521.58
1956	Pat McCormick, USA	84.85	2000	Laura Wilkinson, USA	543.75
1960	Ingrid Krämer, GER	91.28	2004	Chantelle Newberry, AUS	590.31
1964	Lesley Bush, USA	99.80			

Synchronized Platform

Year		Points	Year		Points
2000	Li Na & Sang Xue, CHN	345.12	2004	Lao Lishi & Li Ting, CHN	53.40

Synchronized Springboard

Year		Points	Year		Points
2000	Vera Ilyina & Yulia Pakhalina, RUS	332.64	2004	Wu Minxia & Guo Jingjing, CHN	336.90

FIELD HOCKEY

MEN

Multiple gold medals: India (8); Great Britain and Pakistan (3); West Germany/Germany and Netherlands (2).

Year		Year	
1908	**Great Britain**, Ireland, Scotland	1968	**Pakistan**, Australia, India
1920	**Great Britain**, Denmark, Belgium	1972	**West Germany**, Pakistan, India
1928	**India**, Netherlands, Germany	1976	**New Zealand**, Australia, Pakistan
1932	**India**, Japan, United States	1980	**India**, Spain, Soviet Union
1936	**India**, Germany, Netherlands	1984	**Pakistan**, West Germany, Great Britain
1948	**India**, Great Britain, Netherlands	1988	**Great Britain**, West Germany, Netherlands
1952	**India**, Netherlands, Great Britain	1992	**Germany**, Australia, Pakistan
1956	**India**, Pakistan, Germany	1996	**Netherlands**, Spain, Australia
1960	**Pakistan**, India, Spain	2000	**Netherlands**, South Korea, Australia
1964	**India**, Pakistan, Australia	2004	**Australia**, Netherlands, Germany

WOMEN

Multiple gold medals: Australia (3).

Year		Year	
1980	**Zimbabwe**, Czechoslovakia, Soviet Union	1996	**Australia**, South Korea, Netherlands
1984	**Netherlands**, West Germany, United States	2000	**Australia**, Argentina, Netherlands
1988	**Australia**, South Korea, Netherlands	2004	**Germany**, Netherlands, Argentina
1992	**Spain**, Germany, Great Britain		

GYMNASTICS

MEN

At least 4 gold medals (including team events): Sawao Kato (8); Nikolai Andrianov, Viktor Chukarin and Boris Shakhlin (7); Akinori Nakayama and Vitaly Scherbo (6); Yukio Endo, Anton Heida, Mitsuo Tsukahara and Takashi Ono (5); Vladimir Artemov, Georges Miez, Valentin Muratov and Alexei Nemov (4).

All-Around

Year		Points	Year		Points
1900	Gustave Sandras, FRA	302	1960	Boris Shakhlin, USSR	115.95
1904	Julius Lenhart, AUT	69.80	1964	Yukio Endo, JPN	115.95
1906	Pierre Payssé, FRA	97.0	1968	Sawao Kato, JPN	115.9
1908	Alberto Braglia, ITA	317.0	1972	Sawao Kato, JPN	114.650
1912	Alberto Braglia, ITA	135.0	1976	Nikolai Andrianov, USSR	116.65
1920	Giorgio Zampori, ITA	88.35	1980	Aleksandr Dityatin, USSR	118.65
1924	Leon Stukelj, YUG	110.340	1984	Koji Gushiken, JPN	118.7
1928	Georges Miez, SWI	247.500	1988	Vladimir Artemov, USSR	119.125
1932	Romeo Neri, ITA	140.625	1992	Vitaly Scherbo, UT	59.025
1936	Alfred Schwarzmann, GER	113.100	1996	Li Xiaosahuang, CHN	58.423
1948	Veikko Huhtanen, FIN	229.7	2000	Alexei Nemov, RUS	58.474
1952	Viktor Chukarin, USSR	115.7	2004	Paul Hamm, USA*	57.823
1956	Viktor Chukarin, USSR	114.25			

*Paul Hamm won the all-around gold but following the event it was discovered that a scoring error made by the judges in Athens and bronze medallist Yang Tae Young of South Korea was shorted a tenth of a point in the start value of his parallel bar routine. That difference could have given the South Korean the gold medal. The matter eventually ended when the Court of the Arbitration for Sport decided the result would stand and Hamm would keep his gold.

High Bar

Year		Points	Year		Points
1896	Hermann Weingärtner, GER	–	1968	(TIE) Akinori Nakayama, JPN	19.55
1904	(TIE) Anton Heida, USA	40		& Mikhail Voronin, USSR	19.55
	& Edward Hennig, USA	40	1972	Mitsuo Tsukahara, JPN	19.725
1924	Leon Stukelj, YUG	19.73	1976	Mitsuo Tsukahara, JPN	19.675
1928	Georges Miez, SWI	19.17	1980	Stoyan Deltchev, BUL	19.825
1932	Dallas Bixler, USA	18.33	1984	Shinji Morisue, JPN	20.00
1936	Aleksanteri Saarvala, FIN	19.367	1988	(TIE) Vladimir Artemov, USSR	19.900
1948	Josef Stalder, SWI	19.85		& Valeri Lyukin, USSR	19.900
1952	Jack Günthard, SWI	19.55	1992	Trent Dimas, USA	9.875
1956	Takashi Ono, JPN	19.60	1996	Andreas Wecker, GER	9.850
1960	Takashi Ono, JPN	19.60	2000	Alexei Nemov, RUS	9.787
1964	Boris Shakhlin, USSR	19.625	2004	Igor Cassina, ITA	9.812

Parallel Bars

Year		Points	Year		Points
1896	Alfred Flatow, GER	–	1968	Akinori Nakayama, JPN	19.475
1904	George Eyser, USA	44	1972	Sawao Kato, JPN	19.475
1924	August Güttinger, SWI	21.63	1976	Sawao Kato, JPN	19.675
1928	Ladislav Vácha, CZE	18.83	1980	Aleksandr Tkachyov, USSR	19.775
1932	Romeo Neri, ITA	18.97	1984	Bart Conner, USA	19.95
1936	Konrad Frey, GER	19.067	1988	Vladimir Artemov, USSR	19.925
1948	Michael Reusch, SWI	19.75	1992	Vitaly Scherbo, UT	9.900
1952	Hans Eugster, SWI	19.65	1996	Rustam Sharipov, UKR	9.837
1956	Viktor Chukarin, USSR	19.20	2000	Li Xiaopeng, CHN	9.825
1960	Boris Shakhlin, USSR	19.40	2004	Valeri Goncharov, UKR	9.787
1964	Yukio Endo, JPN	19.675			

Vault

Year		Points	Year		Points
1896	Karl Schumann, GER	–	1964	Haruhiro Yamashita, JPN	19.60
1904	(TIE) George Eyser, USA	36	1968	Mikhail Voronin, USSR	19.00
	& Anton Heida, USA	36	1972	Klaus Köste, E. Ger	18.85
1924	Frank Kriz, USA	9.98	1976	Nikolai Andrianov, USSR	19.45
1928	Eugen Mack, SWI	9.58	1980	Nikolai Andrianov, USSR	19.825
1932	Savino Guglielmetti, ITA	18.03	1984	Lou Yun, CHN	19.95
1936	Alfred Schwarzmann, GER	19.20	1988	Lou Yun, CHN	19.875
1948	Paavo Aaltonen, FIN	19.55	1992	Vitaly Scherbo, UT	9.856
1952	Viktor Chukarin, USSR	19.20	1996	Alexei Nemov, RUS	9.787
1956	(TIE) Helmut Bantz, GER	18.85	2000	Gervasio Deferr, SPA	9.712
	& Valentin Muratov, USSR	18.85	2004	Gervasio Deferr, SPA	9.737
1960	(TIE) Takashi Ono, JPN	19.35			
	& Boris Shakhlin, USSR	19.35			

Pommel Horse

Year		Points	Year		Points
1896	Louis Zutter, SWI	.–	1968	Miroslav Cerar, YUG	.19.325
1904	Anton Heida, USA	.42	1972	Viktor Klimenko, SOV	.19.125
1924	Josef Wilhelm, SWI	.21.23	1976	Zoltán Magyar, HUN	.19.70
1928	Hermann Hänggi, SWI	.19.75	1980	Zoltán Magyar, HUN	.19.925
1932	Istvän Pelle, HUN	.19.07	1984	(TIE) Li Ning, CHN	.19.95
1936	Konrad Frey, GER	.19.333		& Peter Vidmar, USA	.19.95
1948	(TIE) Paavo Aaltonen, FIN	.19.35	1988	(TIE) Dmitri Bilozerchev, USSR,	.19.95
	Veikko Huhtanen, FIN	.19.35		Zsolt Borkai, HUN	.19.95
	& Heikki Savolainen, FIN	.19.35		& Lyubomir Geraskov, BUL	.19.95
1952	Viktor Chukarin, USSR	.19.50	1992	(TIE) Pae Gil-Su, N. Kor	.9.925
1956	Boris Shakhlin, USSR	.19.25		& Vitaly Scherbo, UT	.9.925
1960	(TIE) Eugen Ekman, FIN	.19.375	1996	Li Donghua, SWI	.9.875
	& Boris Shakhlin, USSR	.19.375	2000	Marius Urzica, ROM	.9.862
1964	Miroslav Cerar, YUG	.19.525	2004	Teng Haibin, CHN	.9.837

Rings

Year		Points	Year		Points
1896	Ioannis Mitropoulos, GRE	.–	1972	Akinori Nakayama, JPN	.19.35
1904	Hermann Glass, USA	.45	1976	Nikolai Andrianov, USSR	.19.65
1924	Francesco Martino, ITA	.21.553	1980	Aleksandr Dityatin, USSR	.19.875
1928	Leon Stukelj, YUG	.19.25	1984	(TIE) Koji Gushiken, JPN	.19.85
1932	George Gulack, USA	.18.97		& Li Ning, CHN	.19.85
1936	Alois Hudec, CZE	.19.433	1988	(TIE) Holger Behrendt, E. Ger	.19.925
1948	Karl Frei, SWI	.19.80		& Dmitri Bilozerchev, USSR	.19.925
1952	Grant Shaginyan, USSR	.19.75	1992	Vitaly Scherbo, UT	.9.937
1956	Albert Azaryan, USSR	.19.35	1996	Yuri Chechi, ITA	.9.887
1960	Albert Azaryan, USSR	.19.725	2000	Szilveszter Csollany, HUN	.9.850
1964	Takuji Haytta, JPN	.19.475	2004	Dimonsthenis Tampakos, GRE	.9.862
1968	Akinori Nakayama, JPN	.19.45			

Floor Exercise

Year		Points	Year		Points
1932	Istvan Pelle, HUN	.9.60	1976	Nikolai Andrianov, USSR	.19.45
1936	Georges Miez, SWI	.18.666	1980	Roland Brückner, E. Ger	.19.75
1948	Ferenc Pataki, HUN	.19.35	1984	Li Ning, CHN	.19.925
1952	William Thoresson, SWE	.19.25	1988	Sergei Kharkov, USSR	.19.925
1956	Valentin Muratov, USSR	.19.20	1992	Li Xiaosahuang, CHN	.9.925
1960	Nobuyuki Aihara, JPN	.19.45	1996	Ioannis Melissanidis, GRE	.9.850
1964	Franco Menichelli, ITA	.19.45	2000	Igors Vihrovs, LAT	.9.812
1968	Sawao Kato, JPN	.19.475	2004	Kyle Shewfelt, CAN	.9.787
1972	Nikolai Andrianov, USSR	.19.175			

Team Combined Exercises

Year		Points	Year		Points
1904	United States	.374.43	1960	Japan	.575.20
1906	Norway	.19.00	1964	Japan	.577.95
1908	Sweden	.438	1968	Japan	.575.90
1912	Italy	.265.75	1972	Japan	.571.25
1920	Italy	.359.855	1976	Japan	.576.85
1924	Italy	.839.058	1980	Soviet Union	.598.60
1928	Switzerland	.1718.625	1984	United States	.591.40
1932	Italy	.541.850	1988	Soviet Union	.593.35
1936	Germany	.657.430	1992	Unified Team	.585.45
1948	Finland	.1358.30	1996	Russia	.576.778
1952	Soviet Union	.574.40	2000	China	.231.919
1956	Soviet Union	.568.25	2004	Japan	.173.821

WOMEN

At least 4 gold medals (including team events): Larissa Latynina (9); Vera Cáslavská (7); Polina Astakhova, Nadia Comaneci, Agnes Keleti and Nelli Kim (5); Olga Korbut, Ecaterina Szabó and Lyudmila Tourischeva (4).

All-Around

Year		Points	Year		Points
1952	Maria Gorokhovskaya, USSR	76.78	1980	Yelena Davydova, USSR	79.15
1956	Larissa Latynina, USSR	74.933	1984	Mary Lou Retton, USA	79.175
1960	Larissa Latynina, USSR	77.031	1988	Yelena Shushunova, USSR	79.662
1964	Vera Cáslavská, CZE	77.564	1992	Tatiana Gutsu, UT	39.737
1968	Vera Cáslavská, CZE	78.25	1996	Lilia Podkopayeva, UKR	39.255
1972	Lyudmila Tourischeva, USSR	77.025	2000	Simona Amanar, ROM*	38.642
1976	Nadia Comaneci, ROM	79.275	2004	Carly Patterson, USA	38.387

*Amanar finished second to **Andreea Raducan**, Romania, who was disqualified for testing positive for pseudo-ephedrine, a drug banned by the IOC and found in Nurofen—an over-the-counter medicine she purportedly took to treat a cold.

Vault

Year		Points	Year		Points
1952	Yekaterina Kalinchuk, USSR	19.20	1984	Ecaterina Szabó, ROM	19.875
1956	Larissa Latynina, USSR	18.833	1988	Svetlana Boginskaya, USSR	19.905
1960	Margarita Nikolayeva, USSR	19.316	1992	(TIE) Henrietta Onodi, HUN	9.925
1964	Vera Cáslavská, CZE	19.483		& Lavinia Milosovici, ROM	9.925
1968	Vera Cáslavská, CZE	19.775	1996	Simona Amanar, ROM	9.775
1972	Karin Janz, E. Ger	19.525	2000	Elena Zamolodtchikova, RUS	9.731
1976	Nelli Kim, USSR	19.80	2004	Monica Rosu, ROM	9.656
1980	Natalia Shaposhnikova, USSR	19.725			

Uneven Bars

Year		Points	Year		Points
1952	Margit Korondi, HUN	19.40	1984	(TIE) Julianne McNamara, USA	19.95
1956	Agnes Keleti, HUN	18.966		& Ma Yanhong, CHN	19.95
1960	Polina Astakhova, USSR	19.616	1988	Daniela Silivas, ROM	20.00
1964	Polina Astakhova, USSR	19.332	1992	Lu Li, CHN	10.00
1968	Vera Cáslavská, CZE	19.65	1996	Svetlana Khorkina, RUS	9.850
1972	Karin Janz, E. Ger	19.675	2000	Svetlana Khorkina, RUS	9.862
1976	Nadia Comaneci, ROM	20.00	2004	Emilie Lepennec, FRA	9.687
1980	Maxi Gnauck, E. Ger	19.875			

Balance Beam

Year		Points	Year		Points
1952	Nina Bocharova, USSR	19.22	1984	(TIE) Simona Pauca, ROM	19.80
1956	Agnes Keleti, HUN	18.80		& Ecaterina Szabó, ROM	19.80
1960	Eva Bosakova, CZE	19.283	1988	Daniela Silivas, ROM	19.924
1964	Vera Cáslavská, CZE	19.449	1992	Tatiana Lyssenko, UT	9.975
1968	Natalya Kuchinskaya, USSR	19.65	1996	Shannon Miller, USA	9.862
1972	Olga Korbut, USSR	19.40	2000	Liu Xuan, CHN	9.825
1976	Nadia Comaneci, ROM	19.95	2004	Catalina Ponor, ROM	9.787
1980	Nadia Comaneci, ROM	19.80			

Floor Exercise

Year		Points	Year		Points
1952	Agnes Keleti, HUN	19.36	1980	(TIE) Nadia Comaneci, ROM	19.875
1956	(TIE) Agnes Keleti, HUN	18.733		& Nelli Kim, USSR	19.875
	& Larissa Latynina, USSR	18.733	1984	Ecaterina Szabó, ROM	19.975
1960	Larissa Latynina, USSR	19.583	1988	Daniela Silivas, ROM	19.937
1964	Larissa Latynina, USSR	19.599	1992	Lavinia Milosovici, ROM	10.000
1968	(TIE) Vera Cáslavská, CZE	19.675	1996	Lilia Podkopayeva, UKR	9.887
	& Larissa Petrik, USSR	19.675	2000	Elena Zamolodtchikova, RUS	9.850
1972	Olga Korbut, USSR	19.575	2004	Catalina Ponor, ROM	9.750
1976	Nelli Kim, USSR	19.85			

Team Combined Exercises

Year		Points	Year		Points
1928	Netherlands	316.75	1976	Soviet Union	466.00
1936	Germany	506.50	1980	Soviet Union	394.90
1948	Czechoslovakia	445.45	1984	Romania	392.02
1952	Soviet Union	527.03	1988	Soviet Union	395.475
1956	Soviet Union	444.800	1992	Unified Team	395.666
1960	Soviet Union	382.320	1996	United States	389.225
1964	Soviet Union	280.890	2000	Romania	154.608
1968	Soviet Union	382.85	2004	Romania	114.283
1972	Soviet Union	380.50			

SOCCER

MEN

Multiple gold medals: Great Britain and Hungary (3); Uruguay and USSR (2).

Year		Year	
1900	**Great Britain**, France, Belgium	1960	**Yugoslavia**, Denmark, Hungary
1904	**Canada**, USA I, USA II	1964	**Hungary**, Czechoslovakia, Germany
1906	**Denmark**, Smyrna (Int'l entry), Greece	1968	**Hungary**, Bulgaria, Japan
1908	**Great Britain**, Denmark, Netherlands	1972	**Poland**, Hungary, East Germany & Soviet Union
1912	**Great Britain**, Denmark, Netherlands	1976	**East Germany**, Poland, Soviet Union
1920	**Belgium**, Spain, Netherlands	1980	**Czechoslovakia**, East Germany, Soviet Union
1924	**Uruguay**, Switzerland, Sweden	1984	**France**, Brazil, Yugoslavia
1928	**Uruguay**, Argentina, Italy	1988	**Soviet Union**, Brazil, West Germany
1936	**Italy**, Austria, Norway	1992	**Spain**, Poland, Ghana
1948	**Sweden**, Yugoslavia, Denmark	1996	**Nigeria**, Argentina, Brazil
1952	**Hungary**, Yugoslavia, Sweden	2000	**Cameroon**, Spain, Chile
1956	**Soviet Union**, Yugoslavia, Bulgaria	2004	**Argentina**, Paraguay, Italy

WOMEN

Multiple gold medals: United States (2).

Year		Year	
1996	**United States**, China, Norway	2004	**United States**, Brazil, Germany
2000	**Norway**, United States, Germany		

SOFTBALL

Multiple gold medals: United States (3).

Year		Year	
1996	**United States**, China, Australia	2004	**United States**, Australia, Japan
2000	**United States**, Japan, Australia		

U.S. Medal-Winning Softball Teams

1996 (gold medal): P–Lisa Fernandez, Michele Granger, Lori Harrigan and Michele Smith; C–Gillian Boxx and Shelly Stokes; INF–Sheila Cornell, Kim Maher, Leah O'Brien, Dot Richardson, Julie Smith and Dani Tyler; OF–Laura Berg, Dionna Harris; Manager–Ralph Raymond. Final: USA over China, 3-1.

2000 (gold medal): P–Lisa Fernandez, Lori Harrigan, Danielle Henderson, Michele Smith and Christa Williams; C–Stacey Nuveman and Michelle Venturella; INF–Jennifer Brundage, Crystl Bustos, Sheila Douty, Jennifer McFalls and Dot Richardson; OF–Christie Ambrosi, Laura Berg, Leah O'Brien-Amico; Manager–Ralph Raymond. Final: USA over Japan, 2-1.

2004 (gold medal): P–Lisa Fernandez, Jennie Finch, Lori Harrigan and Catherine Osterman; C–Stacey Nuveman and Jenny Topping; INF–Crystl Bustos, Jaime Clark, Lovieanne Jung and Natasha Watley; OF–Laura Berg, Nicole Giordano, Kelly Kretschman, Jessica Mendoza and Leah O'Brien-Amico; UT–Tairia Flowers, Amanda Freed and Lauren Lappin ; Manager–Mike Candrea. Final: USA over Australia, 5-1.

SWIMMING

World and Olympic records below that appear to be broken or equaled by winning times in subsequent years, but are not so indicated, were all broken in preliminary heats leading up to the finals. Some events were not held at every Olympics.

MEN

At least 4 gold medals (including relays): Mark Spitz (9); Matt Biondi (8); Gary Hall Jr. and Michael Phelps (6); Charles Daniels, Tom Jager, Don Schollander, Ian Thorpe and Johnny Weissmuller (5); Tamás Darnyi, Roland Matthes, John Naber, Aleksandr Popov, Murray Rose, Vladimir Salnikov and Henry Taylor (4).

50-meter Freestyle

Year	Time		Year	Time	
1904	Zoltán Halmay, HUN (50 yds)	28.0	1996	Aleksandr Popov, RUS	22.13
1906-84 Not held			2000	(TIE) Anthony Ervin, USA	21.98
1988	Matt Biondi, USA	22.14 **WR**		& Gary Hall Jr., USA	21.98
1992	Aleksandr Popov, UT	21.91 **OR**	2004	Gary Hall Jr., USA	21.93

100-meter Freestyle

Year	Time		Year	Time	
1896	Alfréd Hajós, HUN	1:22.2 **OR**	1960	John Devitt, AUS	55.2 **OR**
1904	Zoltán Halmay, HUN (100 yds)	1:02.8	1964	Don Schollander, USA	53.4 **OR**
1906	Charles Daniels, USA	1:13.4	1968	Michael Wenden, AUS	52.2 **WR**
1908	Charles Daniels, USA	1:05.6 **WR**	1972	Mark Spitz, USA	51.22 **WR**
1912	Duke Kahanamoku, USA	1:03.4	1976	Jim Montgomery, USA	49.99
1920	Duke Kahanamoku, USA	1:00.4 **WR**	1980	Jorg Woithe, E. Ger	50.40
1924	Johnny Weissmuller, USA	59.0 **OR**	1984	Rowdy Gaines, USA	49.80 **OR**
1928	Johnny Weissmuller, USA	58.6 **OR**	1988	Matt Biondi, USA	48.63 **OR**
1932	Yasuji Miyazaki, JPN	58.2	1992	Aleksandr Popov, UT	49.02
1936	Ferenc Csik, HUN	57.6	1996	Aleksandr Popov, RUS	48.74
1948	Wally Ris, USA	57.3 **OR**	2000	Pieter van den Hoogenband, NED	48.30
1952	Clarke Scholes, USA	57.4	2004	Pieter van den Hoogenband, NED	48.17
1956	Jon Henricks, AUS	55.4 **OR**			

Swimming (Cont.)

200-meter Freestyle

Year		Time		Year		Time	
1900	Frederick Lane, AUS (220 yds)	2:25.2	OR	1984	Michael Gross, W. Ger	1:47.44	WR
1904	Charles Daniels, USA (220 yds)	2:44.2		1988	Duncan Armstrong, AUS	1:47.25	WR
1968	Michael Wenden, AUS	1:55.2		1992	Yevgeny Sadovyi, UT	1:46.70	OR
1972	Mark Spitz, USA	1:52.78	WR	1996	Danyon Loader, NZE	1:47.63	
1976	Bruce Furniss, USA	1:50.29	WR	2000	Pieter van den Hoogenband, NED	1:45.35	OR
1980	Sergei Kopliakov, USSR	1:49.81	OR	2004	Ian Thorpe, AUS	1:44.71	OR

400-meter Freestyle

Year		Time		Year		Time	
1896	Paul Neumann, AUT (550m)	8:12.6		1960	Murray Rose, AUS	4:18.3	OR
1904	Charles Daniels, USA (440 yds)	6:16.2		1964	Don Schollander, USA	4:12.2	WR
1906	Otto Scheff, AUT	6:23.8		1968	Mike Burton, USA	4:09.0	OR
1908	Henry Taylor, GBR	5:36.8		1972	Bradford Cooper, AUS*	4:00.27	WR
1912	George Hodgson, CAN	5:24.4		1976	Brian Goodell, USA	3:51.93	WR
1920	Norman Ross, USA	5:26.8		1980	Vladimir Salnikov, USSR	3:51.31	OR
1924	Johnny Weissmuller, USA	5:04.2	OR	1984	George DiCarlo, USA	3:51.23	OR
1928	Alberto Zorilla, ARG	5:01.6	OR	1988	Uwe Dassler, E. Ger	3:46.95	WR
1932	Buster Crabbe, USA	4:48.4	OR	1992	Yevgeny Sadovyi, UT	3:45.00	WR
1936	Jack Medica, USA	4:44.5	OR	1996	Danyon Loader, NZE	3:47.97	
1948	Bill Smith, USA	4:41.0	OR	2000	Ian Thorpe, AUS	3:40.59	WR
1952	Jean Boiteux, FRA	4:30.7	OR	2004	Ian Thorpe, AUS	3:43.10	
1956	Murray Rose, AUS	4:27.3	OR				

*Cooper finished second to Rick DeMont of the U.S., who was disqualified when he flunked the post-race drug test (his asthma medication was on the IOC's banned list).

1500-meter Freestyle

Year		Time		Year		Time	
1896	Alfréd Hajós, HUN (1200m)	18:22.2	OR	1956	Murray Rose, AUS	17:58.9	
1900	John Arthur Jarvis, GBR (1000m)	13:40.2		1960	Jon Konrads, AUS	17:19.6	OR
1904	Emil Rausch, GER (1 mile)	27:18.2		1964	Robert Windle, AUS	17:01.7	OR
1906	Henry Taylor, GBR (1 mile)	28:28.0		1968	Mike Burton, USA	16:38.9	OR
1908	Henry Taylor, GBR	22:48.4	WR	1972	Mike Burton, USA	15:52.58	WR
1912	George Hodgson, CAN	22:00.0	WR	1976	Brian Goodell, USA	15:02.40	WR
1920	Norman Ross, USA	22:23.2		1980	Vladimir Salnikov, USSR	14:58.27	WR
1924	Andrew (Boy) Charlton, AUS	20:06.6	WR	1984	Mike O'Brien, USA	15:05.20	
1928	Arne Borge, SWE	19:51.8	OR	1988	Vladimir Salnikov, USSR	15:00.40	
1932	Kusuo Kitamura, JPN	19:12.4	OR	1992	Kieren Perkins, AUS	14:43.48	WR
1936	Noboru Terada, JPN	19:13.7		1996	Kieren Perkins, AUS	14:56.40	
1948	James McLane, USA	19:18.5		2000	Grant Hackett, AUS	14:48.33	
1952	Ford Konno, USA	18:30.3	OR	2004	Grant Hackett, AUS	14:43.40	OR

100-meter Backstroke

Year		Time		Year		Time	
1904	Walter Brack, GER (100 yds)	1:16.8		1960	David Theile, AUS	1:01.9	OR
1908	Arno Bieberstein, GER	1:24.6	WR	1968	Roland Matthes, E. Ger	58.7	OR
1912	Harry Hebner, USA	1:21.2		1972	Roland Matthes, E. Ger	56.58	OR
1920	Warren Kealoha, USA	1:15.2		1976	John Naber, USA	55.49	WR
1924	Warren Kealoha, USA	1:13.2	OR	1980	Bengt Baron, SWE	56.33	
1928	George Kojac, USA	1:08.2	WR	1984	Rick Carey, USA	55.79	
1932	Masaji Kiyokawa, JPN	1:08.6		1988	Daichi Suzuki, JPN	55.05	
1936	Adolf Kiefer, USA	1:05.9	OR	1992	Mark Tewksbury, CAN	53.98	OR
1948	Allen Stack, USA	1:06.4		1996	Jeff Rouse, USA	54.10	
1952	Yoshinobu Oyakawa, USA	1:05.4	OR	2000	Lenny Krayzelburg, USA	53.72	OR
1956	David Theile, AUS	1:02.2	OR	2004	Aaron Peirsol, USA	54.06	

200-meter Backstroke

Year		Time		Year		Time	
1900	Ernst Hoppenberg, GER	2:47.0		1984	Rick Carey, USA	2:00.23	
1964	Jed Graef, USA	2:10.3	WR	1988	Igor Poliansky, USSR	1:59.37	
1968	Roland Matthes, E. Ger	2:09.6	OR	1992	Martin Lopez-Zubero, SPA	1:58.47	OR
1972	Roland Matthes, E. Ger	2:02.82	=WR	1996	Brad Bridgewater, USA	1:58.54	
1976	John Naber, USA	1:59.19	WR	2000	Lenny Krayzelburg, USA	1:56.76	OR
1980	Sándor Wládar, HUN	2:01.93		2004	Aaron Peirsol, USA	1:54.95	OR

100-meter Breaststroke

Year		Time		Year		Time	
1968	Don McKenzie, USA	1:07.7	OR	1988	Adrian Moorhouse, GBR	1:02.04	
1972	Nobutaka Taguchi, JPN	1:04.94	WR	1992	Nelson Diebel, USA	1:01.50	OR
1976	John Hencken, USA	1:03.11	WR	1996	Fred deBurghgraeve, BEL	1:00.60	
1980	Duncan Goodhew, GBR	1:03.44		2000	Domenico Fioravanti, ITA	1:00.46	OR
1984	Steve Lundquist, USA	1:01.65	WR	2004	Kosuke Kitajima, JPN	1:00.08	

200-meter Breaststroke

Year		Time		Year		Time	
1908	Frederick Holman, GBR	3:09.2	WR	1964	Ian O'Brien, AUS	2:27.8	WR
1912	Walter Bathe, GER	3:01.8	OR	1968	Felipe Muñoz, MEX	2:28.7	
1920	Hakan Malmroth, SWE	3:04.4		1972	John Hencken, USA	2:21.55	WR
1924	Robert Skelton, USA	2:56.6		1976	David Wilkie, GBR.	2:15.11	WR
1928	Yoshiyuki Tsuruta, JPN	2:48.8	OR	1980	Robertas Zhulpa, USSR	2:15.85	
1932	Yoshiyuki Tsuruta, JPN	2:45.4		1984	Victor Davis, CAN	2:13.34	WR
1936	Tetsuo Hamuro, JPN	2:41.5	OR	1988	József Szabó, HUN	2:13.52	
1948	Joseph Verdeur, USA	2:39.3	OR	1992	Mike Barrowman, USA	2:10.16	WR
1952	John Davies, AUS	2:34.4	OR	1996	Norbert Rozsa, HUN	2:12.57	
1956	Masaru Furukawa, JPN	2:34.7*	OR	2000	Domenico Fioravanti, ITA	2:10.87	
1960	Bill Mulliken, USA	2:37.4		2004	Kosuke Kitajima, JPN	2:09.44	OR

*In 1956, the butterfly stroke and breaststroke were separated into two different events.

100-meter Butterfly

Year		Time		Year		Time	
1968	Doug Russell, USA	55.9	OR	1988	Anthony Nesty, SUR	53.0	OR
1972	Mark Spitz, USA	54.27	WR	1992	Pablo Morales, USA	53.32	
1976	Matt Vogel, USA	54.35		1996	Dennis Pankratov, RUS	52.27	
1980	Pär Arvidsson, SWE	54.92		2000	Lars Frolander, SWE	52.00	
1984	Michael Gross, W. Ger	53.08	WR	2004	Michael Phelps, USA	51.25	OR

200-meter Butterfly

Year		Time		Year		Time	
1956	Bill Yorzyk, USA	2:19.3	OR	1980	Sergei Fesenko, USSR	1:59.76	
1960	Mike Troy, USA	2:12.8	WR	1984	Jon Sieben, AUS	1:57.04	WR
1964	Kevin Berry, AUS	2:06.6	WR	1988	Michael Gross, W. Ger	1:56.94	OR
1968	Carl Robie, USA	2:08.7		1992	Melvin Stewart, USA	1:56.26	OR
1972	Mark Spitz, USA	2:00.70	WR	1996	Dennis Pankratov, RUS	1:56.51	
1976	Mike Bruner, USA	1:59.23	WR	2000	Tom Malchow, USA	1:55.35	OR
				2004	Michael Phelps, USA	1:54.04	OR

200-meter Individual Medley

Year		Time		Year		Time	
1968	Charles Hickcox, USA	2:12.0	OR	1992	Tamás Darnyi, HUN	2:00.76	
1972	Gunnar Larsson, SWE	2:07.17	WR	1996	Attila Czene, HUN	1:59.91	
1984	Alex Baumann, CAN	2:01.42	WR	2000	Massimiliano Rosolino, ITA	1:58.98	OR
1988	Tamás Darnyi, HUN	2:00.17	WR	2004	Michael Phelps, USA	1:57.14	OR

400-meter Individual Medley

Year		Time		Year		Time	
1964	Richard Roth, USA	4:45.4	WR	1988	Tamás Darnyi, HUN	4:14.75	WR
1968	Charles Hickcox, USA	4:48.4		1992	Tamás Darnyi, HUN	4:14.23	OR
1972	Gunnar Larsson, SWE	4:31.98	OR	1996	Tom Dolan, USA	4:14.90	
1976	Rod Strachan, USA	4:23.68	WR	2000	Tom Dolan, USA	4:11.76	WR
1980	Aleksandr Sidorenko, USSR	4:22.89	OR	2004	Michael Phelps, USA	4:08.26	WR
1984	Alex Baumann, CAN	4:17.41	WR				

4x100-meter Freestyle Relay

Year		Time		Year		Time	
1964	United States	3:32.2	WR	1988	United States	3:16.53	WR
1968	United States	3:31.7	WR	1992	United States	3:16.74	
1972	United States	3:26.42	WR	1996	United States	3:15.41	
1976-80	Not held			2000	Australia	3:13.67	WR
1984	United States	3:19.03	WR	2004	South Africa	3:13.17	WR

4x200-meter Freestyle Relay

Year		Time		Year		Time	
1906	Hungary (x250m)	16:52.4		1960	United States	8:10.2	WR
1908	Great Britain	10:55.6	WR	1964	United States	7:52.1	WR
1912	Australia/New Zealand	10:11.6	WR	1968	United States	7:52.33	
1920	United States	10:04.4	WR	1972	United States	7:35.78	WR
1924	United States	9:53.4	WR	1976	United States	7:23.22	
1928	United States	9:36.2	WR	1980	Soviet Union	7:23.50	
1932	Japan	8:58.4	WR	1984	United States	7:15.69	WR
1936	Japan	8:51.5	WR	1988	United States	7:12.51	WR
1948	United States	8:46.0	WR	1992	Unified Team	7:11.95	WR
1952	United States	8:31.1	OR	1996	United States	7:14.84	
1956	Australia	8:23.6	WR	2000	Australia	7:07.05	WR
				2004	United States	7:07.33	

Swimming (Cont.)

4x100-meter Medley Relay

Year		Time		Year		Time	
1960	United States	4:05.4	WR	1984	United States	3:39.30	WR
1964	United States	3:58.4	WR	1988	United States	3:36.93	WR
1968	United States	3:54.9	WR	1992	United States	3:36.93	=WR
1972	United States	3:48.16	WR	1996	United States	3:34.84	
1976	United States	3:42.22	WR	2000	United States	3:33.73	WR
1980	Australia	3:45.70		2004	United States	3:30.68	WR

WOMEN

At least 4 gold medals (including relays): Jenny Thompson (8); Kristin Otto and Amy Van Dyken (6); Krisztina Egerszegi (5), Kornelia Ender, Janet Evans, Dawn Fraser and Dara Torres (4).

50-meter Freestyle

Year		Time		Year		Time
1988	Kristin Otto, E. Ger	25.49	OR	2000	Inge de Bruijn, NED	24.32
1992	Yang Wenyi, CHN	24.79	WR	2004	Inge de Bruijn, NED	24.58
1996	Amy Van Dyken, USA	24.87				

100-meter Freestyle

Year		Time		Year		Time	
1912	Fanny Durack, AUS	1:22.2		1968	Jan Henne, USA	1:00.0	
1920	Ethelda Bleibtrey, USA	1:13.6	WR	1972	Sandra Neilson, USA	58.59	OR
1924	Ethel Lackie, USA	1:12.4		1976	Kornelia Ender, E. Ger	55.65	WR
1928	Albina Osipowich, USA	1:11.0	OR	1980	Barbara Krause, E. Ger	54.79	WR
1932	Helene Madison, USA	1:06.8	OR	1984	(TIE) Nancy Hogshead, USA	55.92	
1936	Rie Mastenbroek, NED	1:05.9	OR		& Carrie Steinseifer, USA	55.92	
1948	Greta Andersen, DEN	1:06.3		1988	Kristin Otto, E. Ger	54.93	
1952	Katalin Szöke, HUN	1:06.8		1992	Zhuang Yong, CHN	54.65	OR
1956	Dawn Fraser, AUS	1:02.0	WR	1996	Le Jingyi, CHN	54.50	
1960	Dawn Fraser, AUS	1:01.2	OR	2000	Inge de Bruijn, NED	53.83	
1964	Dawn Fraser, AUS	59.5	OR	2004	Jodie Henry, AUS	53.84	

200-meter Freestyle

Year		Time		Year		Time	
1968	Debbie Meyer, USA	2:10.5	OR	1988	Heike Friedrich, E. Ger	1:57.65	OR
1972	Shane Gould, AUS	2:03.56	WR	1992	Nicole Haislett, USA	1:57.90	
1976	Kornelia Ender, E. Ger	1:59.26	WR	1996	Claudia Poll, CRC	1:58.16	
1980	Barbara Krause, E. Ger	1:58.33	OR	2000	Susie O'Neill, AUS	1:58.24	
1984	Mary Wayte, USA	1:59.23		2004	Camelia Potec, ROM	1:58.03	

400-meter Freestyle

Year		Time		Year		Time	
1920	Ethelda Bleibtrey, USA (300m)	4:34.0	WR	1968	Debbie Meyer, USA	4:31.8	OR
1924	Martha Norelius, USA	6:02.2	OR	1972	Shane Gould, AUS	4:19.44	WR
1928	Martha Norelius, USA	5:42.8	OR	1976	Petra Thümer, E. Ger	4:09.89	WR
1932	Helene Madison, USA	5:28.5	OR	1980	Ines Diers, E. Ger	4:08.76	OR
1936	Rie Mastenbroek, NED	5:26.4	OR	1984	Tiffany Cohen, USA	4:07.10	OR
1948	Ann Curtis, USA	5:17.8	OR	1988	Janet Evans, USA	4:03.85	WR
1952	Valéria Gyenge, HUN	5:12.1	OR	1992	Dagmar Hase, GER	4:07.18	
1956	Lorraine Crapp, AUS	4:54.6	OR	1996	Michelle Smith, IRE	4:07.25	
1960	Chris von Saltza, USA	4:50.6	OR	2000	Brooke Bennett, USA	4:05.80	
1964	Ginny Duenkel, USA	4:43.3	OR	2004	Laure Manaudou, FRA	4:05.34	

800-meter Freestyle

Year		Time		Year		Time	
1968	Debbie Meyer, USA	9:24.0	OR	1988	Janet Evans, USA	8:20.20	OR
1972	Keena Rothhammer, USA	8:53.68	WR	1992	Janet Evans, USA	8:25.52	
1976	Petra Thümer, E. Ger	8:37.14	WR	1996	Brooke Bennett, USA	8:27.89	
1980	Michelle Ford, AUS	8:28.90	OR	2000	Brooke Bennett, USA	8:19.67	OR
1984	Tiffany Cohen, USA	8:24.95	OR	2004	Ai Shibata, JPN	8:24.54	

100-meter Backstroke

Year		Time		Year		Time	
1924	Sybil Bauer, USA	1:23.2	OR	1972	Melissa Belote, USA	1:05.78	OR
1928	Maria Braun, NED	1:22.0		1976	Ulrike Richter, E. Ger	1:01.83	OR
1932	Eleanor Holm, USA	1:19.4		1980	Rica Reinisch, E. Ger	1:00.86	WR
1936	Dina Senff, NED	1:18.9		1984	Theresa Andrews, USA	1:02.55	
1948	Karen-Margrete Harup, DEN	1:14.4	OR	1988	Kristin Otto, E. Ger	1:00.89	
1952	Joan Harrison, S. Afr.	1:14.3		1992	Krisztina Egerszegi, HUN	1:00.68	OR
1956	Judy Grinham, GBR	1:12.9	OR	1996	Beth Botsford, USA	1:01.19	
1960	Lynn Burke, USA	1:09.3	OR	2000	Diana Mocanu, ROM	1:00.21	OR
1964	Cathy Ferguson, USA	1:07.7	WR	2004	Natalie Coughlin, USA	1:03.37	
1968	Kaye Hall, USA	1:06.2	WR				

200-meter Backstroke

Year		Time		Year		Time	
1968	Pokey Watson, USA	2:24.8		1988	Krisztina Egerszegi, HUN	2:09.29	OR
1972	Melissa Belote, USA	2:19.19	WR	1992	Krisztina Egerszegi, HUN	2:07.06	OR
1976	Ulrike Richter, E. Ger	2:13.43	OR	1996	Krisztina Egerszegi, HUN	2:07.83	
1980	Rica Reinisch, E. Ger	2:11.77	WR	2000	Diana Mocanu, ROM	2:08.16	
1984	Jolanda de Rover, NED	2:12.38		2004	Kirsty Coventry, ZIM	2:09.19	

100-meter Breaststroke

Year		Time		Year		Time	
1968	Djurdjica Bjedov, YUG	1:15.8		1988	Tania Dangalakova, BUL	1:07.95	OR
1972	Cathy Carr, USA	1:13.58	WR	1992	Yelena Rudkovskaya, UT	1:08.00	
1976	Hannelore Anke, E. Ger	1:11.16		1996	Penny Heyns, RSA.	1:07.73	
1980	Ute Geweniger, E. Ger	1:10.22		2000	Megan Quann, USA	1:07.05	
1984	Petra van Staveren, NED	1:09.88	OR	2004	Luo Xuejuan, CHN	1:06.64	OR

200-meter Breaststroke

Year		Time		Year		Time	
1924	Lucy Morton, GBR	3:33.2	OR	1972	Beverley Whitfield, AUS	2:41.71	OR
1928	Hilde Schrader, GER	3:12.6		1976	Marina Koshevaya, USSR	2:33.35	WR
1932	Clare Dennis, AUS	3:06.3	OR	1980	Lina Kaciusyte, USSR	2:29.54	OR
1936	Hideko Maehata, JPN	3:03.6		1984	Anne Ottenbrite, CAN	2:30.38	
1948	Petronella van Vliet, NED	2:57.2		1988	Silke Hörner, E. Ger	2:26.71	WR
1952	éva Székely, HUN	2:51.7	OR	1992	Kyoko Iwasaki, JPN	2:26.65	OR
1956	Ursula Happe, GER	2:53.1	OR	1996	Penny Heyns, RSA	2:25.41	
1960	Anita Lonsbrough, GBR	2:49.5	WR	2000	Agnes Kovacs, HUN	2:24.35	
1964	Galina Prozumenshikova, USSR	2:46.4	OR	2004	Amanda Beard, USA	2:23.37	OR
1968	Sharon Wichman, USA	2:44.4	OR				

100-meter Butterfly

Year		Time		Year		Time	
1956	Shelley Mann, USA	1:11.0	OR	1984	Mary T. Meagher, USA	.59.26	
1960	Carolyn Schuler, USA	1:09.5	OR	1988	Kristin Otto, E. Ger	.59.00	OR
1964	Sharon Stouder, USA	1:04.7	WR	1992	Qian Hong, CHN	.58.62	OR
1968	Lynn McClements, AUS	1:05.5		1996	Amy Van Dyken, USA	.59.13	
1972	Mayumi Aoki, JPN	1:03.34	WR	2000	Inge de Bruijn, NED	.56.61	WR
1976	Kornelia Ender, E. Ger	1:00.13	=WR	2004	Petria Thomas, AUS	.57.72	
1980	Caren Metschuck, E. Ger	1:00.42					

200-meter Butterfly

Year		Time		Year		Time	
1968	Ada Kok, NED	2:24.7	OR	1988	Kathleen Nord, E. Ger	2:09.51	
1972	Karen Moe, USA	2:15.57	WR	1992	Summer Sanders, USA	2:08.67	
1976	Andrea Pollack, E. Ger	2:11.41	OR	1996	Susie O'Neill, AUS	2:07.76	
1980	Ines Geissler, E. Ger	2:10.44	WR	2000	Misty Hyman, USA	2:05.88	OR
1984	Mary T. Meagher, USA	2:06.90	OR	2004	Otylia Jedrzejczak, POL	2:06.05	

200-meter Individual Medley

Year		Time		Year		Time	
1968	Claudia Kolb, USA	2:24.7	OR	1992	Lin Li, CHN	2:11.65	WR
1972	Shane Gould, AUS	2:23.07	WR	1996	Michelle Smith, IRE	2:13.93	
1984	Tracy Caulkins, USA	2:12.64	OR	2000	Yana Klochkova, UKR	2:10.68	OR
1988	Daniela Hunger, E. Ger	2:12.59	OR	2004	Yana Klochkova, UKR	2:11.14	

400-meter Individual Medley

Year		Time		Year		Time	
1964	Donna de Varona, USA	5:18.7	OR	1988	Janet Evans, USA	4:37.76	
1968	Claudia Kolb, USA	5:08.5	OR	1992	Krisztina Egerszegi, HUN	4:36.54	
1972	Gail Neall, AUS	5:02.97	WR	1996	Michelle Smith, IRE	4:39.18	
1976	Ulrike Tauber, E. Ger	4:42.77	WR	2000	Yana Klochkova, UKR	4:33.59	WR
1980	Petra Schneider, E. Ger	4:36.29	WR	2004	Yana Klochkova, UKR	4:34.83	
1984	Tracy Caulkins, USA	4:39.24					

4x100-meter Freestyle Relay

Year		Time		Year		Time	
1912	Great Britain	5:52.8	WR	1968	United States	4:02.5	OR
1920	United States	5:11.6	WR	1972	United States	3:55.19	WR
1924	United States	4:58.8	WR	1976	United States	3:44.82	WR
1928	United States	4:47.6	WR	1980	East Germany	3:42.71	WR
1932	United States	4:38.0	WR	1984	United States	3:43.43	
1936	Netherlands	4:36.0	OR	1988	East Germany	3:40.63	OR
1948	United States	4:29.2	OR	1992	United States	3:39.46	WR
1952	Hungary	4:24.4	WR	1996	United States	3:39.29	
1956	Australia	4:17.1	WR	2000	United States	3:36.61	WR
1960	United States	4:08.9	WR	2004	Australia	3:35.94	WR
1964	United States	4:03.8	WR				

Swimming (Cont.)

4x200-meter Freestyle Relay

Year		Time	Year		Time
1996	United States	7:59.87	2004	United States	7:53.42 **WR**
2000	United States	7:57.80 **OR**			

4x100-meter Medley Relay

Year		Time	Year		Time
1960	United States	4:41.1 **WR**	1984	United States	4:08.34
1964	United States	4:33.9 **WR**	1988	East Germany	4:03.74 **OR**
1968	United States	4:28.3 **OR**	1992	United States	4:02.54 **WR**
1972	United States	4:20.75 **WR**	1996	United States	4:02.88
1976	East Germany	4:07.95 **WR**	2000	United States	3:58.30 **WR**
1980	East Germany	4:06.67 **WR**	2004	Australia	3:57.32 **WR**

New Open Water Swim

A new swimming event will make its debut at Beijing in 2008. It is a 10-kilometer open water swim for men and women. The event, by far the longest in Olympic swimming history, will take place in the coastal city of Qingdao. But it won't be the first time that Olympic swimming has taken place outside a pool. The swim events in the 1896 Athens Games were held in the Aegean Sea's Bay of Zea, and in 1900 they were were held in the Seine River in Paris.

TENNIS

MEN

Multiple gold medals (including men's doubles): John Boland, Max Decugis, Laurie Doherty, Reggie Doherty, Arthur Gore, Andre Grobert, Nicolas Massu, Vincent Richards, Charles Winslow and Beals Wright (2).

Singles

Year		
1896	John Boland	Great Britain/Ireland
1900	Laurie Doherty,	Great Britain
1904	Beals Wright	United States
1906	Max Decugis	France
1908	Josiah Ritchie	Great Britain
	(Indoor) Arthur Gore	Great Britain
1912	Charles Winslow	South Africa
	(Indoor) André Gobert	France

Year		
1920	Louis Raymond	South Africa
1924	Vincent Richards	United States
1928-84	Not held	
1988	Miloslav Mecir	Czechoslovakia
1992	Marc Rosset	Switzerland
1996	Andre Agassi	United States
2000	Yevgeny Kafelnikov	Russia
2004	Nicolas Massu	Chile

Doubles

Year	
1896	John Boland, IRE & Fritz Traun, GER
1900	Laurie and Reggie Doherty, GBR
1904	Edgar Leonard & Beals Wright, USA
1906	Max Decugis & Maurice Germot, FRA
1908	George Hillyard & Reggie Doherty, GBR
	(Indoor) Arthur Gore & Herbert Barrett, GBR
1912	Charles Winslow & Harold Kitson, S. Afr.
	(Indoor) Andre Gobert & Maurice Germot, FRA

Year	
1920	Noel Turnbull & Max Woosnam, GBR
1924	Vincent Richards & Frank Hunter, USA
1928-84	Not held
1988	Ken Flach & Robert Seguso, USA
1992	Boris Becker & Michael Stich, GER
1996	Todd Woodbridge & Mark Woodforde, AUS
2000	Sebastien Lareau & Daniel Nestor, CAN
2004	Fernando Gonzalez & Nicolas Massu, CHI

WOMEN

Multiple gold medals (including women's doubles): Helen Wills, Gigi Fernandez, Mary Joe Fernandez and Venus Williams (2).

Singles

Year		
1900	Charlotte Cooper	Great Britain
1906	Esmee Simiriotou	Greece
1908	Dorothea Chambers	Great Britain
	(Indoor) Gwen Eastlake-Smith	Great Britain
1912	Marguerite Broquedis	France
	(Indoor) Edith Hannam	Great Britain
1920	Suzanne Lenglen	France

Year		
1924	Helen Wills	United States
1928-84	Not held	
1988	Steffi Graf	West Germany
1992	Jennifer Capriati	United States
1996	Lindsay Davenport	United States
2000	Venus Williams	United States
2004	Justine Henin-Hardenne	Belgium

Doubles

Year	
1920	Winifred McNair & Kitty McKane, GBR
1924	Hazel Wightman & Helen Wills, USA
1928-84	Not held
1988	Pam Shriver & Zina Garrison, USA

Year	
1992	Gigi Fernandez & Mary Joe Fernandez, USA
1996	Gigi Fernandez & Mary Joe Fernandez, USA
2000	Serena Williams & Venus Williams, USA
2004	Li Ting & Sun Tian Tian, CHN

TRACK & FIELD

World and Olympic records below that appear to be broken or equaled by winning times, heights and distances in subsequent years, but are not so indicated, were all broken in preliminary races and field events leading up to the finals.

MEN

At least 4 gold medals (including relays and discontinued events): Ray Ewry (10); Carl Lewis and Paavo Nurmi (9); Ville Ritola and Martin Sheridan (5); Harrison Dillard, Archie Hahn, Michael Johnson, Hannes Kolehmainen, Alvin Kraenzlein, Eric Lemming, Jim Lightbody, Al Oerter, Jesse Owens, Meyer Prinstein, Mel Sheppard, Lasse Viren and Emil Zátopek (4). Note that all of Ewry's gold medals came before 1912, in the Standing High Jump, Standing Long Jump and Standing Triple Jump.

100 meters

Year		Time		Year		Time	
1896	Tom Burke, USA	12.0		1960	Armin Hary, GER	10.2	OR
1900	Frank Jarvis, USA	11.0		1964	Bob Hayes, USA	10.0	=WR
1904	Archie Hahn, USA	11.0		1968	Jim Hines, USA	9.95	WR
1906	Archie Hahn, USA	11.2		1972	Valery Borzov, USSR	10.14	
1908	Reggie Walker, S. Afr.	10.8	=OR	1976	Hasely Crawford, TRI	10.06	
1912	Ralph Craig, USA	10.8		1980	Allan Wells, GBR	10.25	
1920	Charley Paddock, USA	10.8		1984	Carl Lewis, USA	9.99	
1924	Harold Abrahams, GBR	10.6	=OR	1988	Carl Lewis, USA*	9.92	WR
1928	Percy Williams, CAN	10.8		1992	Linford Christie, GBR	9.96	
1932	Eddie Tolan, USA	10.3	OR	1996	Donovan Bailey, CAN	9.84	WR
1936	Jesse Owens, USA	10.3w		2000	Maurice Greene, USA	9.87	
1948	Harrison Dillard, USA	10.3	=OR	2004	Justin Gatlin, USA	9.85	
1952	Lindy Remigino, USA	10.4					
1956	Bobby Morrow, USA	10.5					

windicates wind-aided.

*Lewis finished second to Ben Johnson of Canada, who set a world record of 9.79 seconds. Two days later, Johnson was stripped of his gold medal and his record when he tested positive for steroid use in a post-race drug test.

200 meters

Year		Time		Year		Time	
1900	Walter Tewksbury, USA	22.2		1960	Livio Berruti, ITA	20.5	=WR
1904	Archie Hahn, USA	21.6	OR	1964	Henry Carr, USA	20.3	OR
1908	Bobby Kerr, CAN	22.6		1968	Tommie Smith, USA	19.83	WR
1912	Ralph Craig, USA	21.7		1972	Valery Borzov, USSR	20.00	
1920	Allen Woodring, USA	22.0		1976	Donald Quarrie, JAM	20.23	
1924	Jackson Scholz, USA	21.6		1980	Pietro Mennea, ITA	20.19	
1928	Percy Williams, CAN	21.8		1984	Carl Lewis, USA	19.80	OR
1932	Eddie Tolan, USA	21.2	OR	1988	Joe DeLoach, USA	19.75	OR
1936	Jesse Owens, USA	20.7	OR	1992	Mike Marsh, USA	20.01	
1948	Mel Patton, USA	21.1		1996	Michael Johnson, USA	19.32	WR
1952	Andy Stanfield, USA	20.7		2000	Konstantinos Kenteris, GRE	20.09	
1956	Bobby Morrow, USA	20.6	OR	2004	Shawn Crawford, USA	19.79	

400 meters

Year		Time		Year		Time	
1896	Tom Burke, USA	54.2		1956	Charley Jenkins, USA	46.7	
1900	Maxey Long, USA	49.4	OR	1960	Otis Davis, USA	44.9	WR
1904	Harry Hillman, USA	49.2	OR	1964	Mike Larrabee, USA	45.1	
1906	Paul Pilgrim, USA	53.2		1968	Lee Evans, USA	43.86	WR
1908	Wyndham Halswelle, GBR	50.0		1972	Vince Matthews, USA	44.66	
1912	Charlie Reidpath, USA	48.2	OR	1976	Alberto Juantorena, CUB	44.26	
1920	Bevil Rudd, S. Afr.	49.6		1980	Viktor Markin, USSR	44.60	
1924	Eric Liddell, GBR	47.6	OR	1984	Alonzo Babers, USA	44.27	
1928	Ray Barbuti, USA	47.8		1988	Steve Lewis, USA	43.87	
1932	Bill Carr, USA	46.2	WR	1992	Quincy Watts, USA	43.50	OR
1936	Archie Williams, USA	46.5		1996	Michael Johnson, USA	43.49	OR
1948	Arthur Wint, JAM	46.2		2000	Michael Johnson, USA	43.84	
1952	George Rhoden, JAM	45.9	OR	2004	Jeremy Wariner, USA	44.00	

800 meters

Year		Time		Year		Time	
1896	Teddy Flack, AUS	2:11.0		1956	Tom Courtney, USA	1:47.7	OR
1900	Alfred Tysoe, GBR	2:01.2		1960	Peter Snell, NZE	1:46.3	OR
1904	Jim Lightbody, USA	1:56.0	OR	1964	Peter Snell, NZE	1:45.1	OR
1906	Paul Pilgrim, USA	2:01.5		1968	Ralph Doubell, AUS	1:44.3	=WR
1908	Mel Sheppard, USA	1:52.8	WR	1972	Dave Wottle, USA	1:45.9	
1912	Ted Meredith, USA	1:51.9	WR	1976	Alberto Juantorena, CUB	1:43.50	WR
1920	Albert Hill, GBR	1:53.4		1980	Steve Ovett, GBR	1:45.4	
1924	Douglas Lowe, GBR	1:52.4		1984	Joaquim Cruz, BRA	1:43.00	OR
1928	Douglas Lowe, GBR	1:51.8	OR	1988	Paul Ereng, KEN	1:43.45	
1932	Tommy Hampson, GBR	1:49.7	WR	1992	William Tanui, KEN	1:43.66	
1936	John Woodruff, USA	1:52.9		1996	Vebjoern Rodal, NOR	1:42.58	OR
1948	Mal Whitfield, USA	1:49.2	OR	2000	Nils Schumann, GER	1:45.08	
1952	Mal Whitfield, USA	1:49.2	=OR	2004	Yuriy Borzakovskiy, RUS	1:44.45	

1500 meters

Year		Time		Year		Time	
1896	Teddy Flack, AUS	4:33.2		1956	Ron Delany, IRE	3:41.2	OR
1900	Charles Bennett, GBR	4:06.2	WR	1960	Herb Elliott, AUS	3:35.6	WR
1904	Jim Lightbody, USA	4:05.4	WR	1964	Peter Snell, NZE	3:38.1	
1906	Jim Lightbody, USA	4:12.0		1968	Kip Keino, KEN	3:34.9	OR
1908	Mel Sheppard, USA	4:03.4	OR	1972	Pekka Vasala, FIN	3:36.3	
1912	Arnold Jackson, GBR	3:56.8	OR	1976	John Walker, NZE	3:39.17	
1920	Albert Hill, GBR	4:01.8		1980	Sebastian Coe, GBR	3:38.4	
1924	Paavo Nurmi, FIN	3:53.6	OR	1984	Sebastian Coe, GBR	3:32.53	OR
1928	Harry Larva, FIN	3:53.2	OR	1988	Peter Rono, KEN	3:35.96	
1932	Luigi Beccali, ITA	3:51.2	OR	1992	Fermin Cacho, SPA	3:40.12	
1936	John Lovelock, NZE	3:47.8	WR	1996	Noureddine Morceli, ALG	3:35.78	
1948	Henry Eriksson, SWE	3:49.8		2000	Noah Ngeny, KEN	3:32.07	OR
1952	Josy Barthel, LUX	3:45.1	OR	2004	Hicham El Guerrouj, MOR	3:34.18	

5000 meters

Year		Time		Year		Time	
1912	Hannes Kolehmainen, FIN	14:36.6	WR	1968	Mohamed Gammoudi, TUN	14:05.0	
1920	Joseph Guillemot, FRA	14:55.6		1972	Lasse Viren, FIN	13:26.4	OR
1924	Paavo Nurmi, FIN	14:31.2	OR	1976	Lasse Viren, FIN	13:24.76	
1928	Ville Ritola, FIN	14:38.0		1980	Miruts Yifter, ETH	13:21.0	
1932	Lauri Lehtinen, FIN	14:30.0	OR	1984	Said Aouita, MOR	13:05.59	OR
1936	Gunnar Höckert, FIN	14:22.2	OR	1988	John Ngugi, KEN	13:11.70	
1948	Gaston Reiff, BEL	14:17.6	OR	1992	Dieter Baumann, GER	13:12.52	
1952	Emil Zátopek, CZE	14:06.6	OR	1996	Venuste Niyongabo, BUR	13:07.96	
1956	Vladimir Kuts, USSR	13:39.6	OR	2000	Millon Wolde, ETH	13:35.49	
1960	Murray Halberg, NZE	13:43.4		2004	Hicham El Guerrouj, MOR	13:14.39	
1964	Bob Schul, USA	13:48.8					

10,000 meters

Year		Time		Year		Time	
1912	Hannes Kolehmainen, FIN	31:20.8		1968	Naftali Temu, KEN	29:27.4	
1920	Paavo Nurmi, FIN	31:45.8		1972	Lasse Viren, FIN	27:38.4	WR
1924	Ville Ritola, FIN	30:23.2	WR	1976	Lasse Viren, FIN	27:40.38	
1928	Paavo Nurmi, FIN	30:18.8	OR	1980	Miruts Yifter, ETH	27:42.7	
1932	Janusz Kusocinski, POL	30:11.4	OR	1984	Alberto Cova, ITA	27:47.54	
1936	Ilmari Salminen, FIN	30:15.4		1988	Brahim Boutaib, MOR	27:21.46	OR
1948	Emil Zátopek, CZE	29:59.6	OR	1992	Khalid Skah, MOR	27:46.70	
1952	Emil Zátopek, CZE	29:17.0	OR	1996	Haile Gebrselassie, ETH	27:07.34	OR
1956	Vladimir Kuts, USSR	28:45.6	OR	2000	Haile Gebrselassie, ETH	27:18.20	
1960	Pyotr Bolotnikov, USSR	28:32.2	OR	2004	Kenenisa Bekele, ETH	27:05.10	OR
1964	Billy Mills, USA	28:24.4	OR				

Marathon

Year		Time		Year		Time	
1896	Spiridon Louis, GRE	2:58:50		1956	Alain Mimoun, FRA	2:25:00.0	
1900	Michel Théato, FRA	2:59:45		1960	Abebe Bikila, ETH	2:15:16.2	WB
1904	Thomas Hicks, USA	3:28:53		1964	Abebe Bikila, ETH	2:12:11.2	WB
1906	Billy Sherring, CAN	2:51:23.6		1968	Mamo Wolde, ETH	2:20:26.4	
1908	Johnny Hayes, USA*	2:55:18.4	OR	1972	Frank Shorter, USA	2:12:19.8	
1912	Kenneth McArthur, S. Afr.	2:36:54.8		1976	Waldemar Cierpinski, E. Ger	2:09:55.0	OR
1920	Hannes Kolehmainen, FIN	2:32:35.8	WB	1980	Waldemar Cierpinski, E. Ger	2:11:03.0	
1924	Albin Stenroos, FIN	2:41:22.6		1984	Carlos Lopes, POR	2:09:21.0	OR
1928	Boughéra El Ouafi, FRA	2:32:57.0		1988	Gelindo Bordin, ITA	2:10:32	
1932	Juan Carlos Zabala, ARG	2:31:36.0	OR	1992	Hwang Young-Cho, S. Kor	2:13:23	
1936	Sohn Kee-Chung, JPN†	2:29:19.2	OR	1996	Josia Thugwane, RSA	2:12:36	
1948	Delfo Cabrera, ARG	2:34:51.6		2000	Gezahenge Abera, ETH	2:10:11	
1952	Emil Zátopek, CZE	2:23:03.2	OR	2004	Stefano Baldini, ITA	2:10:55	

*Dorando Pietri of Italy placed first, but was disqualified for being helped across the finish line.
†Sohn was a Korean, but he was forced to compete under the name Kitei Son by Japan, which occupied Korea at the time.
Note: Marathon distances–40,000 meters (1896,1904); 40,260 meters (1900); 41,860 meters (1906); 42,195 meters (1908 and since 1924); 40,200 meters (1912); 42,750 meters (1920). Current distance of 42,195 meters measures 26 miles, 385 yards.

110-meter Hurdles

Year		Time		Year		Time	
1896	Tom Curtis, USA	17.6		1956	Lee Calhoun, USA	13.5	OR
1900	Alvin Kraenzlein, USA	15.4	OR	1960	Lee Calhoun, USA	13.8	
1904	Frederick Schule, USA	16.0		1964	Hayes Jones, USA	13.6	
1906	Robert Leavitt, USA	16.2		1968	Willie Davenport, USA	13.3	OR
1908	Forrest Smithson, USA	15.0	WR	1972	Rod Milburn, USA	13.24	=WR
1912	Frederick Kelly, USA	15.1		1976	Guy Drut, FRA	13.30	
1920	Earl Thomson, CAN	14.8	WR	1980	Thomas Munkelt, E. Ger	13.39	
1924	Daniel Kinsey, USA	15.0		1984	Roger Kingdom, USA	13.20	OR
1928	Syd Atkinson, S. Afr.	14.8		1988	Roger Kingdom, USA	12.98	OR
1932	George Saling, USA	14.6		1992	Mark McKoy, CAN	13.12	
1936	Forrest (Spec) Towns, USA	14.2		1996	Allen Johnson, USA	12.95	OR
1948	William Porter, USA	13.9	OR	2000	Anier Garcia, CUB	13.00	
1952	Harrison Dillard, USA	13.7	OR	2004	Liu Xiang, CHN	12.91	OR

400-meter Hurdles

Year		Time		Year		Time	
1900	Walter Tewksbury, USA	.57.6		1964	Rex Cawley, USA	.49.6	
1904	Harry Hillman, USA	.53.0		1968	David Hemery, GBR	.48.12	WR
1908	Charley Bacon, USA	.55.0	WR	1972	John Akii-Bua, UGA	.47.82	WR
1920	Frank Loomis, USA	.54.0	WR	1976	Edwin Moses, USA	.47.64	WR
1924	Morgan Taylor, USA	.52.6		1980	Volker Beck, E. Ger	.48.70	
1928	David Burghley, GBR	.53.4	OR	1984	Edwin Moses, USA	.47.75	
1932	Bob Tisdall, IRE	.51.7		1988	Andre Phillips, USA	.47.19	OR
1936	Glenn Hardin, USA	.52.4		1992	Kevin Young, USA	.46.78	WR
1948	Roy Cochran, USA	.51.1	OR	1996	Derrick Adkins, USA	.47.54	
1952	Charley Moore, USA	.50.8	OR	2000	Angelo Taylor, USA	.47.50	
1956	Glenn Davis, USA	.50.1	=OR	2004	Felix Sanchez, DOM	.47.63	
1960	Glenn Davis, USA	.49.3					

3000-meter Steeplechase

Year		Time		Year		Time	
1900	George Orton, CAN	.7:34.4		1964	Gaston Roelants, BEL	.8:30.8	OR
1904	Jim Lightbody, USA	.7:39.6		1968	Amos Biwott, KEN	.8:51.0	
1908	Arthur Russell, GBR	.10:47.8		1972	Kip Keino, KEN	.8:23.6	OR
1920	Percy Hodge, GBR	.10:00.4	OR	1976	Anders Gärderud, SWE	.8:08.2	WR
1924	Ville Ritola, FIN	.9:33.6	OR	1980	Bronislaw Malinowski, POL	.8:09.7	
1928	Toivo Loukola, FIN	.9:21.8	OR	1984	Julius Korir, KEN	.8:11.80	
1932	Volmari Iso-Hollo, FIN	.10:33.4*		1988	Julius Kariuki, KEN	.8:05.51	OR
1936	Volmari Iso-Hollo, FIN	.9:03.8	WR	1992	Matthew Birir, KEN	.8:08.84	
1948	Thore Sjöstrand, SWE	.9:04.6		1996	Joseph Keter, KEN	.8:07.12	
1952	Horace Ashenfelter, USA	.8:45.4	WR	2000	Reuben Kosgei, KEN	.8:21.43	
1956	Chris Brasher, GBR	.8:41.2	OR	2004	Ezekiel Kemboi, KEN	.8:05.81	
1960	Zdzislaw Krzyszkowiak, POL	.8:34.2	OR				

*Iso-Hollo ran one extra lap due to lap counter's mistake.

Note: Other steeplechase distances– 2500 meters (1900); 2590 meters (1904); 3200 meters (1908) and 3460 meters (1932).

4x100-meter Relay

Year		Time		Year		Time	
1912	Great Britain	.42.4		1968	United States	.38.23	WR
1920	United States	.42.2	WR	1972	United States	.38.19	WR
1924	United States	.41.0	=WR	1976	United States	.38.33	
1928	United States	.41.0	=WR	1980	Soviet Union	.38.26	
1932	United States	.40.0	WR	1984	United States	.37.83	WR
1936	United States	.39.8	WR	1988	Soviet Union	.38.19	
1948	United States	.40.6		1992	United States	.37.40	WR
1952	United States	.40.1		1996	Canada	.37.69	
1956	United States	.39.5	WR	2000	United States	.37.61	
1960	Germany	.39.5	=WR	2004	Great Britain	.38.07	
1964	United States	.39.0	WR				

4x400-meter Relay

Year		Time		Year		Time	
1908	United States	.3:29.4		1964	United States	.3:00.7	WR
1912	United States	.3:16.6	WR	1968	United States	.2:56.16	WR
1920	Great Britain	.3:22.2		1972	Kenya	.2:59.8	
1924	United States	.3:16.0	WR	1976	United States	.2:58.65	
1928	United States	.3:14.2	WR	1980	Soviet Union	.3:01.1	
1932	United States	.3:08.2	WR	1984	United States	.2:57.91	
1936	Great Britain	.3:09.0		1988	United States	.2:56.16	=WR
1948	United States	.3:10.4		1992	United States	.2:55.74	WR
1952	Jamaica	.3:03.9	WR	1996	United States	.2:55.99	
1956	United States	.3:04.8		2000	United States	.2:56.35	
1960	United States	.3:02.2	WR	2004	United States	.2:55.91	

20-kilometer Walk

Year		Time		Year		Time	
1956	Leonid Spirin, USSR	.1:31:27.4		1984	Ernesto Canto, MEX	.1:23:13	OR
1960	Vladimir Golubnichiy, USSR	.1:34:07.2		1988	Jozef Pribilinec, CZE	.1:19:57	OR
1964	Ken Matthews, GBR	.1:29:34.0	OR	1992	Daniel Plaza Montero, SPA	.1:21:45	
1968	Vladimir Golubnichiy, USSR	.1:33:58.4		1996	Jefferson Perez, ECU	.1:20:07	
1972	Peter Frenkel, E. Ger	.1:26:42.4	OR	2000	Robert Korzeniowski, POL	.1:18:59	OR
1976	Daniel Bautista, MEX	.1:24:40.6	OR	2004	Ivano Brugnetti, ITA	.1:19:40	
1980	Maurizio Damilano, ITA	.1:23:35.5	OR				

Track & Field (Cont.)

50-kilometer Walk

Year		Time		Year		Time	
1932	Thomas Green, GBR	4:50:10		1976	Not held		
1936	Harold Whitlock, GBR	4:30:41.4	OR	1980	Hartwig Gauder, E. Ger	3:49:24.0	OR
1948	John Ljunggren, SWE	4:41:52		1984	Raul Gonzalez, MEX	3:47:26	OR
1952	Giuseppe Dordoni, ITA	4:28:07.8	OR	1988	Vyacheslav Ivanenko, USSR	3:38:29	OR
1956	Norman Read, NZE	4:30:42.8		1992	Andrei Perlov, UT	3:50:13	
1960	Don Thompson, GBR	4:25:30.0	OR	1996	Robert Korzeniowski, POL	3:43:30	
1964	Abdon Pamich, ITA	4:11:12.4	OR	2000	Robert Korzeniowski, POL	3:42:22	
1968	Christoph Höhne, E. Ger	4:20:13.6		2004	Robert Korzeniowski, POL	3:38:46	
1972	Bernd Kannenberg, W. Ger	3:56:11.6	OR				

High Jump

Year		Height		Year		Height	
1896	Ellery Clark, USA	5-11¼		1956	Charley Dumas, USA	6-11½	OR
1900	Irving Baxter, USA	6- 2¾	OR	1960	Robert Shavlakadze, USSR	7- 1	OR
1904	Sam Jones, USA	5-11		1964	Valery Brumel, USSR	7- 1¾	OR
1906	Cornelius Leahy, GBR/IRE	5-10		1968	Dick Fosbury, USA	7- 4¼	OR
1908	Harry Porter, USA	6- 3	OR	1972	Yuri Tarmak, USSR	7- 3¾	
1912	Alma Richards, USA	6- 4	OR	1976	Jacek Wszola, POL	7- 4½	OR
1920	Richmond Landon, USA	6- 4	=OR	1980	Gerd Wessig, E. Ger	7- 8¾	WR
1924	Harold Osborn, USA	6- 6	OR	1984	Dietmar Mögenburg, W. Ger	7- 8½	
1928	Bob King, USA	6- 4½		1988	Gennady Avdeyenko, USSR	7- 9¾	OR
1932	Duncan McNaughton, CAN	6- 5½		1992	Javier Sotomayor, CUB	7- 8	
1936	Cornelius Johnson, USA	6- 8	OR	1996	Charles Austin, USA	7-10	OR
1948	John Winter, AUS	6- 6		2000	Sergey Klugin, RUS	7- 8½	
1952	Walt Davis, USA	6- 8½	OR	2004	Stefan Holm, SWE	7- 8¾	

Pole Vault

Year		Height		Year		Height	
1896	William Hoyt, USA	10-10		1956	Bob Richards, USA	14-11½	OR
1900	Irving Baxter, USA	10-10		1960	Don Bragg, USA	15- 5	OR
1904	Charles Dvorak, USA	11- 5¾		1964	Fred Hansen, USA	16- 8¾	OR
1906	Fernand Gonder, FRA	11- 5¾		1968	Bob Seagren, USA	17-8½	OR
1908	(TIE) Edward Cooke, USA	12- 2		1972	Wolfgang Nordwig, E. Ger	18- 0½	OR
	& Alfred Gilbert, USA	12- 2	OR	1976	Tadeusz Slusarski, POL	18- 0½	=OR
1912	Harry Babcock, USA	12-11½	OR	1980	Wladyslaw Kozakiewicz, POL	18-11½	WR
1920	Frank Foss, USA	13- 5	WR	1984	Pierre Quinon, FRA	18-10¼	
1924	Lee Barnes, USA	12-11½		1988	Sergey Bubka, USSR	19- 4¼	OR
1928	Sabin Carr, USA	13- 9¼		1992	Maksim Tarasov, UT	19-0¼	
1932	Bill Miller, USA	14-1¾	OR	1996	Jean Galfione, FRA	19- 5¼	OR
1936	Earle Meadows, USA	14- 3¼	OR	2000	Nick Hysong, USA	19-4¼	
1948	Guinn Smith, USA	14-1¼		2004	Timothy Mack, USA	19-6¼	OR
1952	Bob Richards, USA	14-11	OR				

Long Jump

Year		Distance		Year		Distance	
1896	Ellery Clark, USA	20-10		1956	Greg Bell, USA	25- 8¼	
1900	Alvin Kraenzlein, USA	23- 6¾	OR	1960	Ralph Boston, USA	26-7¾	OR
1904	Meyer Prinstein, USA	24- 1	OR	1964	Lynn Davies, GBR	26- 5¾	
1906	Meyer Prinstein, USA	23- 7½		1968	Bob Beamon, USA	29- 2½	WR
1908	Frank Irons, USA	24- 6½	OR	1972	Randy Williams, USA	27-0½	
1912	Albert Gutterson, USA	24-11¼	OR	1976	Arnie Robinson, USA	27- 4¾	
1920	William Petersson, SWE	23-5½		1980	Lutz Dombrowski, E. Ger	28- 0¼	
1924	De Hart Hubbard, USA	24- 5		1984	Carl Lewis, USA	28-0¼	
1928	Ed Hamm, USA	25- 4½	OR	1988	Carl Lewis, USA	28- 7¼	
1932	Ed Gordon, USA	25- 0¾		1992	Carl Lewis, USA	28- 5½	
1936	Jesse Owens, USA	26-5½	OR	1996	Carl Lewis, USA	27-10¾	
1948	Willie Steele, USA	25- 8		2000	Ivan Pedroso, CUB	28- 0¾	
1952	Jerome Biffle, USA	24-10		2004	Dwight Phillips, USA	28- 2¼	

Triple Jump

Year	Athlete	Distance	
1896	James Connolly, USA	44-11¾	
1900	Meyer Prinstein, USA	47-5¾	OR
1904	Meyer Prinstein, USA	47-1	
1906	Peter O'Connor, GBR/IRE	46-2¼	
1908	Timothy Ahearne, GBR/IRE	48-11¼	OR
1912	Gustaf Lindblom, SWE	48-5¼	
1920	Vilho Tuulos, FIN	47-7	
1924	Nick Winter, AUS	50-11¼	WR
1928	Mikio Oda, JPN	49-11	
1932	Chuhei Nambu, JPN	51-7	WR
1936	Naoto Tajima, JPN	52-6	WR
1948	Arne Ahman, SWE	50-6¼	
1952	Adhemar da Silva, BRA	53-2¾	WR
1956	Adhemar da Silva, BRA	53-7¾	OR
1960	Józef Schmidt, POL	55-2	
1964	Józef Schmidt, POL	55-3½	OR
1968	Viktor Saneyev, USSR	57-0¾	WR
1972	Viktor Saneyev, USSR	56-11¼	
1976	Viktor Saneyev, USSR	56-8¾	
1980	Jack Uudmäe, USSR	56-11¼	
1984	Al Joyner, USA	56-7½	
1988	Khristo Markov, BUL	57-9¼	OR
1992	Mike Conley, USA	59-7½ʷ	OR
1996	Kenny Harrison, USA	59-4¼	OR
2000	Jonathan Edwards, GBR	58-1¼	
2004	Christian Olsson, SWE	58-4½	

ʷindicates wind-aided.

Shot Put

Year	Athlete	Distance	
1896	Bob Garrett, USA	36-9¾	
1900	Richard Sheldon, USA	46-3¼	OR
1904	Ralph Rose, USA	48-7	WR
1906	Martin Sheridan, USA	40-5¼	
1908	Ralph Rose, USA	46-7½	
1912	Patrick McDonald, USA	50-4	OR
1920	Ville Pörhölä, FIN	48-7¼	
1924	Bud Houser, USA	49-2¼	
1928	John Kuck, USA	52-0¾	WR
1932	Leo Sexton, USA	52-6	OR
1936	Hans Woellke, GER	53-1¾	OR
1948	Wilbur Thompson, USA	56-2	OR
1952	Parry O'Brien, USA	57-1½	OR
1956	Parry O'Brien, USA	60-11¼	OR
1960	Bill Nieder, USA	64-6¾	OR
1964	Dallas Long, USA	66-8½	OR
1968	Randy Matson, USA	67-4¾	
1972	Wladyslaw Komar, POL	69-6	
1976	Udo Beyer, E. Ger	69-0¾	
1980	Vladimir Kiselyov, USSR	70-0½	OR
1984	Alessandro Andrei, ITA	69-9	
1988	Ulf Timmermann, E. Ger	73-8¾	OR
1992	Mike Stulce, USA	71-2½	
1996	Randy Barnes, USA	70-11¼	
2000	Arsi Harju, FIN	69-10¼	
2004	Yuriy Bilonog, UKR	69-5¼	

Discus Throw

Year	Athlete	Distance	
1896	Bob Garrett, USA	95-7½	
1900	Rudolf Bauer, HUN	118-3	OR
1904	Martin Sheridan, USA	128-10½	OR
1906	Martin Sheridan, USA	136-0	
1908	Martin Sheridan, USA	134-2	OR
1912	Armas Taipale, FIN	148-3	OR
1920	Elmer Niklander, FIN	146-7	
1924	Bud Houser, USA	151-4	OR
1928	Bud Houser, USA	155-3	OR
1932	John Anderson, USA	162-4	OR
1936	Ken Carpenter, USA	165-7	OR
1948	Adolfo Consolini, ITA	173-2	OR
1952	Sim Iness, USA	180-6	OR
1956	Al Oerter, USA	184-11	OR
1960	Al Oerter, USA	194-2	OR
1964	Al Oerter, USA	200-1	OR
1968	Al Oerter, USA	212-6	OR
1972	Ludvik Danek, CZE	211-3	
1976	Mac Wilkins, USA	221-5	
1980	Viktor Rashchupkin, USSR	218-8	
1984	Rolf Danneberg, W. Ger	218-6	
1988	Jürgen Schult, E. Ger	225-9	OR
1992	Romas Ubartas, LIT	213-8	
1996	Lars Riedel, GER	227-8	
2000	Virgilijus Alekna, LIT	227-4	
2004	Virgilijus Alekna, LIT*	229-3	OR

*Hungary's **Robert Fazekas** had a throw of 232 feet, 8 inches, and was initially declared the winner, but he was disqualified for failing to submit to a drug test following the competition.

Hammer Throw

Year	Athlete	Distance	
1900	John Flanagan, USA	163-1	
1904	John Flanagan, USA	168-1	OR
1908	John Flanagan, USA	170-4	OR
1912	Matt McGrath, USA	179-7	OR
1920	Pat Ryan, USA	173-5	
1924	Fred Tootell, USA	174-10	
1928	Pat O'Callaghan, IRE	168-7	
1932	Pat O'Callaghan, IRE	176-11	
1936	Karl Hein, GER	185-4	OR
1948	Imre Németh, HUN	183-11	
1952	József Csérmák, HUN	197-11	WR
1956	Harold Connolly, USA	207-3	OR
1960	Vasily Rudenkov, USSR	220-2	OR
1964	Romuald Klim, USSR	228-10	OR
1968	Gyula Zsivótzky, HUN	240-8	OR
1972	Anatoly Bondarchuk, USSR	247-8	OR
1976	Yuri Sedykh, USSR	254-4	OR
1980	Yuri Sedykh, USSR	268-4	WR
1984	Juha Tiainen, FIN	256-2	
1988	Sergey Litvinov, USSR	278-2	OR
1992	Andrei Abduvaliyev, UT	270-9	
1996	Balazs Kiss, HUN	266-6	
2000	Szymon Ziolkowski, POL	262-6	
2004	Koji Murofushi, JPN*	272-0	

Hungary's **Adrian Annus** was initially awarded the gold medal for his throw of 272-11, but after questions were raised about the legitimacy of his post-competition drug test, and he failed to submit to a follow-up test, he was disqualified and stripped of the gold.

Track & Field (Cont.)

Javelin Throw

Year		Distance		Year		Distance	
1908	Eric Lemming, SWE	179-10	WR	1964	Pauli Nevala, FIN	271- 2	
1912	Eric Lemming, SWE	198-11	WR	1968	Jänis Lüsis, USSR	295- 7	OR
1920	Jonni Myyrä, FIN	215-10		1972	Klaus Wolfermann, W. Ger	296-10	OR
1924	Jonni Myyrä, FIN	206- 7		1976	Miklos Németh, HUN	310- 4	WR
1928	Erik Lundkvist, SWE	218- 6	OR	1980	Dainis Kula, USSR	299- 2	
1932	Matti Järvinen, FIN	238- 6	OR	1984	Arto Härkönen, FIN	284- 8	
1936	Gerhard Stöck, GER	235- 8		1988	Tapio Korjus, FIN	276- 6	
1948	Kai Tapio Rautavaara, FIN	228-10		1992	Jan Zelezny, CZE	294- 2*	OR
1952	Cy Young, USA	242- 1	OR	1996	Jan Zelezny, CZR	289- 3	
1956	Egil Danielson, NOR	281- 2	WR	2000	Jan Zelezny, CZR	295- 10	OR
1960	Viktor Tsibulenko, USSR	277- 8		2004	Andreas Thorkildsen, NOR	283- 9	

*In 1986 the balance point of the javelin was modified and new records have been kept since.

Decathlon

Year		Points		Year		Points	
1904	Thomas Kiely, IRE	6036		1964	Willi Holdorf, GER	7887	
1906-08 Not held				1968	Bill Toomey, USA	8193	OR
1912	Jim Thorpe, USA	8412	WR	1972	Nikolai Avilov, USSR	8454	WR
1920	Helge Lövland, NOR	6803		1976	Bruce Jenner, USA	8617	WR
1924	Harold Osborn, USA	7711	WR	1980	Daley Thompson, GBR	8495	
1928	Paavo Yrjölä, FIN	8053	WR	1984	Daley Thompson, GBR	8798	=WR
1932	Jim Bausch, USA	8462	WR	1988	Christian Schenk, E. Ger	8488	
1936	Glenn Morris, USA	7900	WR	1992	Robert Zmelik, CZE	8611	
1948	Bob Mathias, USA	7139		1996	Dan O'Brien, USA	8824	
1952	Bob Mathias, USA	7887	WR	2000	Erki Nool, EST	8641	
1956	Milt Campbell, USA	7937	OR	2004	Roman Sebrle, CZE	8893	OR
1960	Rafer Johnson, USA	8392	OR				

WOMEN

At least 4 gold medals (including relays): Evelyn Ashford, Fanny Blankers-Koen, Betty Cuthbert and Bärbel Eckert Wöckel (4).

100 meters

Year		Time		Year		Time	
1928	Betty Robinson, USA	12.2	=WR	1972	Renate Stecher, E. Ger	11.07	
1932	Stella Walsh, POL*	11.9	=WR	1976	Annegret Richter, W. Ger	11.08	
1936	Helen Stephens, USA	11.5w		1980	Lyudmila Kondratyeva, USSR	11.06	
1948	Fanny Blankers-Koen, NED	11.9		1984	Evelyn Ashford, USA	10.97	OR
1952	Marjorie Jackson, AUS	11.5	=WR	1988	Florence Griffith Joyner, USA	10.54w	
1956	Betty Cuthbert, AUS	11.5		1992	Gail Devers, USA	10.82	OR
1960	Wilma Rudolph, USA	11.0w		1996	Gail Devers, USA	10.94	
1964	Wyomia Tyus, USA	11.4		2000	Ekaterina Thanou, GRE†	11.12	
1968	Wyomia Tyus, USA	11.08	WR	2004	Yuliya Nesterenko, BLR	10.93	

*An autopsy performed after Walsh's death in 1980 revealed that she was a man.
wIndicates wind-aided.
†Marion Jones won the gold (10.75) but later admitted to using performance-enhancing drugs and was stripped of the gold.

200 meters

Year		Time		Year		Time	
1948	Fanny Blankers-Koen, NED	24.4		1980	Bärbel Eckert Wockel, E. Ger	22.03	OR
1952	Marjorie Jackson, AUS	23.7	OR	1984	Valerie Brisco-Hooks, USA	21.81	OR
1956	Betty Cuthbert, AUS	23.4	=OR	1988	Florence Griffith Joyner, USA	21.34	WR
1960	Wilma Rudolph, USA	24.0		1992	Gwen Torrence, USA	21.81	
1964	Edith McGuire, USA	23.0	OR	1996	Marie-Jose Perec, FRA	22.12	
1968	Irena Szewinska, POL	22.5	WR	2000	Pauline Davis-Thompson, BAH†	22.27	
1972	Renate Stecher, E. Ger	22.40	=WR	2004	Veronica Campbell, JAM	22.05	
1976	Bärbel Eckert, E. Ger	22.37	OR				

†Marion Jones won the gold (21.84) but later admitted to using performance-enhancing drugs and was stripped of the gold.

400 meters

Year		Time		Year		Time	
1964	Betty Cuthbert, AUS	52.0		1988	Olga Bryzgina, USSR	48.65	OR
1968	Colette Besson, FRA	52.03	=OR	1992	Marie-Jose Perec, FRA	48.83	
1972	Monika Zehrt, E. Ger	51.08		1996	Marie-Jose Perec, FRA	48.25	OR
1976	Irena Szewinska, POL	49.29	WR	2000	Cathy Freeman, AUS	49.11	
1980	Marita Koch, E. Ger	48.88	OR	2004	Tonique Williams-Darling, BAH	49.41	
1984	Valerie Brisco-Hooks, USA	48.83	OR				

800 meters

Year		Time		Year		Time	
1928	Lina Radke, GER	2:16.8	WR	1980	Nadezhda Olizarenko, USSR	1:53.42	WR
1932-56 Not held				1984	Doina Melinte, ROM	1:57.60	
1960	Lyudmila Shevtsova, USSR	2:04.3	=WR	1988	Sigrun Wodars, E. Ger	1:56.10	
1964	Ann Packer, GBR	2:01.1	OR	1992	Ellen van Langen, NED	1:55.54	
1968	Madeline Manning, USA	2:00.9	OR	1996	Svetlana Masterkova, RUS	1:57.73	
1972	Hildegard Falck, W. Ger	1:58.55	OR	2000	Maria Mutola, MOZ	1:56.15	
1976	Tatyana Kazankina, USSR	1:54.94	WR	2004	Kelly Holmes, GBR	1:56.38	

1500 meters

Year		Time		Year		Time	
1972	Lyudmila Bragina, USSR	4:01.4	WR	1992	Hassiba Boulmerka, ALG	3:55.30	
1976	Tatyana Kazankina, USSR	4:05.48		1996	Svetlana Masterkova, RUS	4:00.83	
1980	Tatyana Kazankina, USSR	3:56.6	OR	2000	Nouria Merah-Benida, ALG	4:05.10	
1984	Gabriella Dorio, ITA	4:03.25		2004	Kelly Holmes, GBR	3:57.90	
1988	Paula Ivan, ROM	3:53.96	OR				

5000 meters

Year		Time		Year		Time	
1984	Maricica Puica, ROM	8:35.96		1996	Wang Junxia, CHN	14:59.88	
1988	Tatyana Samolenko, USSR	8:26.53	OR	2000	Gabriela Szabo, ROM	14:40.79	OR
1992	Elena Romanova, UT	8:46.04		2004	Meseret Defar, ETH	14:45.65	

Note: Event held over 3000 meters from 1984-92.

10,000 meters

Year		Time		Year		Time	
1988	Olga Bondarenko, USSR	31:05.21	OR	2000	Derartu Tulu, ETH	30:17.49	OR
1992	Derartu Tulu, ETH	31:06.02		2004	Xing Huina, CHN	30:24.36	
1996	Fernanda Ribeiro, POR	31:01.63	OR				

Marathon

Year		Time	Year		Time
1984	Joan Benoit, USA	2:24:52	1996	Fatuma Roba, ETH	2:26:05
1988	Rosa Mota, POR	2:25:40	2000	Naoko Takahashi, JPN	2:23:14
1992	Valentina Yegorova, UT	2:32:41	2004	Mizuki Noguchi, JPN	2:26:20

100-meter Hurdles

Year		Time		Year		Time	
1932	Babe Didrikson, USA	11.7	WR	1980	Vera Komisova, USSR	12.56	OR
1936	Trebisonda Valla, ITA	11.7		1984	Benita Fitzgerald-Brown, USA	12.84	
1948	Fanny Blankers-Koen, NED	11.2	OR	1988	Yordanka Donkova, BUL	12.38	OR
1952	Shirley Strickland, AUS	10.9	WR	1992	Paraskevi Patoulidou, GRE	12.64	
1956	Shirley Strickland, AUS	10.7	OR	1996	Ludmila Enquist, SWE	12.58	
1960	Irina Press, USSR	10.8		2000	Olga Shishigina, KAZ	12.65	
1964	Karin Balzer, GER	10.5w		2004	Joanna Hayes, USA	12.37	OR
1968	Maureen Caird, AUS	10.3	OR	w indicates wind-aided.			
1972	Annelie Ehrhardt, E. Ger	12.59	WR	**Note:** Event held over 80 meters from 1932-68.			
1976	Johanna Schaller, E. Ger	12.77					

400-meter Hurdles

Year		Time		Year		Time	
1984	Nawal El Moutawakel, MOR	54.61	OR	1996	Deon Hemmings, JAM	52.82	OR
1988	Debra Flintoff-King, AUS	53.17	OR	2000	Irina Privalova, RUS	53.02	
1992	Sally Gunnell, GBR	53.23		2004	Fani Halkia, GRE	52.82	

4x100-meter Relay

Year		Time		Year		Time	
1928	Canada	48.4	WR	1972	West Germany	42.81	WR
1932	United States	46.9	WR	1976	East Germany	42.55	OR
1936	United States	46.9		1980	East Germany	41.60	WR
1948	Holland	47.5		1984	United States	41.65	
1952	United States	45.9	WR	1988	United States	41.98	
1956	Australia	44.5	WR	1992	United States	42.11	
1960	United States	44.5		1996	United States	41.95	
1964	Poland	43.6		2000	Bahamas	42.20	
1968	United States	42.87	WR	2004	Jamaica	41.73	

Track & Field (Cont.)

4x400-meter Relay

Year		Time		Year		Time	
1972	East Germany	3:23.0	WR	1992	Unified Team	3:20.20	
1976	East Germany	3:19.23	WR	1996	United States	3:20.91	
1980	Soviet Union	3:20.2		2000	Jamaica†	3:23.25	
1984	United States	3:18.29	OR	2004	United States	3:19.01	
1988	Soviet Union	3:15.18	WR				

†The United States won the gold in Sydney but American Marion Jones would later admit to using performance-enhancing drugs and the United States relay squad (3:22.62) was stripped of the gold.

20-kilometer Walk

Year		Time	Year		Time
1992	Chen Yueling, CHN	44:32	2000	Wang Liping, CHN	1:29:05
1996	Yelena Ninikolayeva, RUS	41:49	2004	Athanasia Tsoumeleka, GRE	1:29:12

Note: Event was held over 10 kilometers from 1992-96.

Pole Vault

Year		Height		Year		Height	
2000	Stacy Dragila, USA	15- 1	OR	2004	Yelena Isinbayeva, RUS	16-1¼	WR

High Jump

Year		Height		Year		Height	
1928	Ethel Catherwood, CAN	5- 2½		1972	Ulrike Meyfarth, W. Ger	6- 3½	=WR
1932	Jean Shiley, USA	5- 5¼	WR	1976	Rosemarie Ackermann, E. Ger	6-4	OR
1936	Ibolya Csák, HUN	5- 3		1980	Sara Simeoni, ITA	6- 5½	OR
1948	Alice Coachman, USA	5- 6	OR	1984	Ulrike Meyfarth, W. Ger	6-7½	OR
1952	Esther Brand, RSA	5- 5¾		1988	Louise Ritter, USA	6- 8	OR
1956	Mildred McDaniel, USA	5- 9¼	WR	1992	Heike Henkel, GER	6-7½	
1960	Iolanda Balas, ROM	6-0¾		1996	Stefka Kostadinova, BUL	6- 8¾	
1964	Iolanda Balas, ROM	6- 2¾	OR	2000	Yelena Yelesina, RUS	6- 7	
1968	Miloslava Rezkova, CZE	5-11½		2004	Yelena Slesarenko, RUS	6- 9	OR

Long Jump

Year		Distance		Year		Distance	
1948	Olga Gyarmati, HUN	18- 8¼		1980	Tatyana Kolpakova, USSR	23-2	OR
1952	Yvette Williams, NZE	20- 5¾	OR	1984	Anisoara Cusmir-Stanciu, ROM	22-10	
1956	Elzbieta Krzesinska, POL	20-10	=WR	1988	Jackie Joyner-Kersee, USA	24-3¼	OR
1960	Vyera Krepkina, USSR	20-10¾		1992	Heike Drechsler, GER	23-5¼	
1964	Mary Rand, GBR	22- 2¼	WR	1996	Chioma Ajunwa, NGR	23-4½	
1968	Viorica Viscopoleanu, ROM	22- 4½	WR	2000	Heike Drechsler, GER	22-11¼	
1972	Heidemarie Rosendahl, W. Ger	22- 3		2004	Tatyana Lebedeva, RUS	23-2½	
1976	Angela Voigt, E. Ger	22-0¾					

Triple Jump

Year		Distance	Year		Distance
1996	Inessa Kravets, UKR	50-3½	2004	Francoise Mbango Etone, CMR	50-2½
2000	Tereza Marinova, BUL	49-10½			

Shot Put

Year		Distance		Year		Distance	
1948	Micheline Ostermeyer, FRA	45- 1½		1980	Ilona Slupianek, E. Ger	73- 6¼	OR
1952	Galina Zybina, USSR	50- 1¾	WR	1984	Claudia Losch, W. Ger	67-2¼	
1956	Tamara Tyshkevich, USSR	54-5	OR	1988	Natalia Lisovskaya, USSR	72- 11¾	
1960	Tamara Press, USSR	56- 10	OR	1992	Svetlana Krivaleva, UT	69- 1¼	
1964	Tamara Press, USSR	59- 6¼	OR	1996	Astrid Kumbernuss, GER	67-5½	
1968	Margitta Gummel, E. Ger	64- 4	WR	2000	Yanina Korolchik, BLR	67- 5½	
1972	Nadezhda Chizhova, USSR	69- 0	WR	2004	Yumileidi Cumba, CUB*	64-3¼	
1976	Ivanka Hristova, BUL	69-5¼	OR				

*Russia's Irina Korzhanenko (69- 1¼) was stripped of the gold for failing a post-competition drug test.

Discus Throw

Year		Distance		Year		Distance	
1928	Halina Konopacka, POL	129-11¾	WR	1972	Faina Melnik, USSR	218- 7	OR
1932	Lillian Copeland, USA	133- 2	OR	1976	Evelin Schlaak, E. Ger	226- 4	OR
1936	Gisela Mauermayer, GER	156- 3		1980	Evelin Schlaak Jahl, E. Ger	229- 6	OR
1948	Micheline Ostermeyer, FRA	137-6		1984	Ria Stalman, NED	214- 5	
1952	Nina Romaschkova, USSR	168- 8	OR	1988	Martina Hellmann, E. Ger	237- 2½	OR
1956	Olga Fikotová, CZE	176- 1	OR	1992	Maritza Marten, CUB	229-10	
1960	Nina Ponomaryeva, USSR	180- 9	OR	1996	Ilke Wyludda, GER	228-6	
1964	Tamara Press, USSR	187-10	OR	2000	Ellina Zvereva, BLR	224-5	
1968	Lia Manoliu, ROM	191- 2	OR	2004	Natalya Sadova, RUS	219-10	

Hammer Throw

Year		Distance	Year		Distance	
2000	Kamila Skolimowska, POL	233- 5¾	**OR**	2004	Olga Kuzenkova, RUS	246-1	**OR**

Javelin Throw

Year		Distance		Year		Distance	
1932	Babe Didrikson, USA	143- 4		1976	Ruth Fuchs, E. Ger	216- 4	**OR**
1936	Tilly Fleischer, GER	148- 3	**OR**	1980	Maria Colon Rueñes, CUB	224- 5	**OR**
1948	Herma Bauma, AUT	149- 6	**OR**	1984	Tessa Sanderson, GBR	228- 2	**OR**
1952	Dana Zátopková, CZE	165- 7	**OR**	1988	Petra Felke, E. Ger	245- 0	**OR**
1956	Ineze Jaunzeme, USSR	176- 8	**OR**	1992	Silke Renk, GER	224-2	
1960	Elvira Ozolina, USSR	183- 8	**OR**	1996	Heli Rantanen, FIN	222-11	
1964	Mihaela Penes, ROM	198- 7	**OR**	2000	Trine Hattestad, NOR	226-1	**OR**
1968	Angéla Németh, HUN	198- 0		2004	Osleidys Menendez, CUB	234-8	**OR**
1972	Ruth Fuchs, E. Ger	209- 7	**OR**				

Heptathlon

Year		Points		Year		Points	
1964	Irina Press, USSR	5246	**WR**	1988	Jackie Joyner-Kersee, USA	7291	**WR**
1968	Ingrid Becker, W. Ger	5098		1992	Jackie Joyner-Kersee, USA	7044	
1972	Mary Peters, GBR	4801	**WR**	1996	Ghada Shouaa, SYR	6780	
1976	Siegrun Siegl, E. Ger	4745		2000	Denise Lewis, GBR	6584	
1980	Nadezhda Tkachenko, USSR	5083	**WR**	2004	Carolina Kluft, SWE	6952	
1984	Glynis Nunn, AUS	6390	**OR**				

Note: Seven-event Heptathlon replaced five-event Pentathlon in 1984.

All-Time Leading Medal Winners – Single Games

Athletes who have won the most medals in a single Summer Olympics. Totals include individual, relay and team medals. U.S. athletes are in **bold** type.

MEN

No		Sport	G-S-B	No		Sport	G-S-B
8†	**Michael Phelps**, USA (2004)	Swim	6-0-2	6	Takashi Ono, JPN (1960)	Gym	3-1-2
8	Aleksandr Dityatin, USSR (1980)	Gym	3-4-1	6	Viktor Chukarin, USSR (1956)	Gym	4-2-0
7	**Mark Spitz**, USA (1972)	Swim	7-0-0	6	Konrad Frey, GER (1936)	Gym	3-1-2
7	**Willis Lee**, USA (1920)	Shoot	5-1-1	6	Ville Ritola, FIN (1924)	Track	4-2-0
7	**Matt Biondi**, USA (1988)	Swim	5-1-1	6	Hubert Van Innis, BEL (1920)	Arch	4-2-0
7	Boris Shakhlin, USSR (1960)	Gym	4-2-1	6	**Carl Osburn**, USA (1920)	Shoot	4-1-1
7	**Lloyd Spooner**, USA (1920)	Shoot	4-1-2	6	Louis Richardet, SWI (1906)	Shoot	3-3-0
7	Mikhail Voronin, USSR (1968)	Gym	2-4-1	6	**Anton Heida**, USA (1904)	Gym	5-1-0
7	Nikolai Andrianov, USSR (1976)	Gym	2-4-1	6	**George Eyser**, USA (1904)	Gym	3-2-1
6	Vitaly Scherbo, UT (1992)	Gym	6-0-0	6	**Burton Downing**, USA (1904)	Cycle	2-3-1
6	Li Ning, CHN (1984)	Gym	3-2-1	6	Alexei Nemov, RUS (1996)	Gym	2-1-3
6	Akinori Nakayama, JPN (1968)	Gym	4-1-1	6	Alexei Nemov, RUS (2000)	Gym	2-1-3

†Includes gold medal as preliminary member of 1st-place relay team.

WOMEN

No		Sport	G-S-B	No		Sport	G-S-B
7	Maria Gorokhovskaya, USSR (1952)	Gym	2-5-0	5	Nadia Comaneci, ROM (1976)	Gym	3-1-1
6	Kristin Otto, E. Ger (1988)	Swim	6-0-0	5	Karin Janz, E. Ger (1972)	Gym	2-2-1
6	Agnes Keleti, HUN (1956)	Gym	4-2-0	5	Ines Diers, E. Ger (1980)	Swim	2-2-1
6	Vera Cáslavská, CZE (1968)	Gym	4-2-0	5	**Shirley Babashoff**, USA (1976)	Swim	1-4-0
6	Larisa Latynina, USSR (1956)	Gym	4-1-1	5	**Mary Lou Retton**, USA (1984)	Gym	1-2-2
6	Larisa Latynina, USSR (1960)	Gym	3-2-1	5	**Shannon Miller**, USA (1992)	Gym	0-2-3
6	Daniela Silivas, ROM (1988)	Gym	3-2-1	5	**Marion Jones**†, USA (2000)	Track	3-0-2
6	Larisa Latynina, USSR (1964)	Gym	2-2-2	5	**Dara Torres**, USA (2000)	Swim	2-0-3
6	Margit Korondi, HUN (1956)	Gym	1-1-4	5	**Natalie Coughlin**, USA (2004)	Swim	2-2-1
5	Kornelia Ender, E. Ger (1976)	Swim	4-1-0				
5	Ecaterina Szabó, ROM (1984)	Gym	4-1-0				
5	Shane Gould, AUS (1972)	Swim	3-1-1				

†Jones admitted to using performance-enhancing drugs and has been stripped of her medals.

Most Individual Medals

Not including team competition.

MEN

No		Sport	G-S-B
12	Nikolai Andrianov, USSR	Gymnastics	6-3-3

WOMEN

No		Sport	G-S-B
15	Larissa Latynina, USSR	Gymnastics	7-5-3

All-Time Leading Medal Winners – Career

MEN

No		Sport	G-S-B	No		Sport	G-S-B
15	Nikolai Andrianov, USSR	Gymnastics	7-5-3	10	**Carl Lewis**, USA	Track/Field	9-1-0
13	Boris Shakhlin, USSR	Gymnastics	7-4-2	10	Aladár Gerevich, HUN	Fencing	7-1-2
13	Edoardo Mangiarotti, ITA	Fencing	6-5-2	10	Akinori Nakayama, JPN	Gymnastics	6-2-2
13	Takashi Ono, JPN	Gymnastics	5-4-4	10	Aleksandr Dityatin, USSR	Gymnastics	3-6-1
12	Paavo Nurmi, FIN	Track/Field	9-3-0	9	Vitaly Scherbo, BLR	Gymnastics	6-0-3
12	Sawao Kato, JPN	Gymnastics	8-3-1	9	**Gary Hall Jr.**, USA	Swimming	5-3-1
12	Alexei Nemov, RUS	Gymnastics	4-2-6	9*	**Martin Sheridan**, USA	Track/Field	5-3-1
11	**Mark Spitz**, USA	Swimming	9-1-1	9*	Zoltán Halmay, HUN	Swimming	3-5-1
11†	**Matt Biondi**, USA	Swimming	8-2-1	9	Giulio Gaudini, ITA	Fencing	3-4-2
11	Viktor Chukarin, USSR	Gymnastics	7-3-1	9	Mikhail Voronin, USSR	Gymnastics	2-6-1
11	**Carl Osburn**, USA	Shooting	5-4-2	9	Heikki Savolainen, FIN	Gymnastics	2-1-6
10*	**Ray Ewry**, USA	Track/Field	10-0-0	9	Yuri Titov, USSR	Gymnastics	1-5-3

†Includes gold medal as preliminary member of 1st-place relay team.

*Medals won by Ewry (2-0-0), Sheridan (2-3-0) and Halmay (1-1-0) at the 1906 Intercalated games are not officially recognized by the IOC.

Games Participated In

Andrianov (1972,76,80); **Biondi** (1984,88,92); **Chukarin** (1952,56); **Dityatin** (1976,80); **Ewry** (1900,04,06,08); **Gerevich** (1932,36,48,52,56,60); **Gaudini** (1928,32,36); **Hall Jr.** (1996,2000,04); **Halmay** (1900,04,06,08); **Kato** (1968,72,76); **Lewis** (1984,88,92,96); **Mangiarotti** (1936,48,52,56,60); **Nakayama** (1968,72); **Nemov** (1996,2000) **Nurmi** (1920,24,28); **Ono** (1952,56,60,64); **Osburn** (1912,20, 24); **Savolainen** (1928,32,36,48,52); **Scherbo** (1992,96): **Shakhlin** (1956,60,64); **Sheridan** (1904,06,08); **Spitz** (1968,72); **Titov** (1956,60,64); **Voronin** (1968,72).

WOMEN

No		Sport	G-S-B	No		Sport	G-S-B
18	Larissa Latynina, USSR	Gymnastics	9-5-4	8	**Shirley Babashoff**, USA	Swimming	2-6-0
12	**Jenny Thompson**, USA	Swimming	8-3-1	8	Sofia Muratova, USSR	Gymnastics	2-2-4
11	Vera Cáslavská, CZE	Gymnastics	7-4-0	8	Inge de Bruijn, NED	Swimming	4-2-2
10	Birgit Fischer, GER	Canoe/Kayak	7-3-0	7	Krisztina Egerszegi, HUN	Swimming	5-1-1
10	Agnes Keleti, HUN	Gymnastics	5-3-2	7	Irena Kirszenstein Szewinska, POL	Track/Field	3-2-2
10	Polina Astakhova, USSR	Gymnastics	5-2-3	7	Shirley Strickland, AUS	Track/Field	3-1-3
9	Nadia Comaneci, ROM	Gymnastics	5-3-1	7	Maria Gorokhovskaya, USSR	Gymnastics	2-5-0
9	Lyudmila Touricheva, USSR	Gymnastics	4-3-2	7	Ildiko Sagine-Ujlaki-Rejto, HUN	Fencing	2-3-2
9	**Dara Torres**, USA	Swimming	4-1-4	7	**Shannon Miller**, USA	Gymnastics	2-2-3
8	Kornelia Ender, E. Ger	Swimming	4-4-0	7	Susie O'Neill, AUS	Swimming	2-4-1
8	Dawn Fraser, AUS	Swimming	4-4-0	7	Merlene Ottey, JAM	Track/Field	0-2-5

Games Participated In

Astakhova (1956,60,64); **Babashoff** (1972,76); **Cáslavská** (1960,64,68); **Comaneci** (1976,80); **de Bruijn** (2000,04); **Egerszegi** (1988,92,96); **Ender** (1972,76); **Fischer** (1980,92,96,2000); **Fraser** (1956,60,64); **Gorokhovskaya** (1952); **Keleti** (1952,56); **Latynina** (1956,60,64); **Miller** (1992,96); **Muratova** (1956,60); **O'Neill** (1996,2000) **Ottey** (1980,84,88,92,96) **Sagine-Ujlaki-Rejto** (1960,64,68,72,76); **Strickland** (1948,52,56); **Szewinska** (1964,68,72,76,80); **Thompson** (1992,96,2000,04); **Torres** (1984,88,92,2000) **Touricheva** (1968, 72,76).

Most Gold Medals

MEN

No		Sport	G-S-B	No		Sport	G-S-B
10*	**Ray Ewry**, USA	Track/Field	10-0-0	7	Boris Shakhlin, USSR	Gymnastics	7-4-2
9	Paavo Nurmi, FIN	Track/Field	9-3-0	7	Viktor Chukarin, USSR	Gymnastics	7-3-1
9	**Mark Spitz**, USA	Swimming	9-1-1	7	Aladar Gerevich, HUN	Fencing	7-1-2
9	**Carl Lewis**, USA	Track/Field	9-1-0				
8	Sawao Kato, JPN	Gymnastics	8-3-1	*Medals won by Ewry (2-0-0) at the 1906 Intercalated games are not officially recognized by the IOC.
8†	**Matt Biondi**, USA	Swimming	8-2-1	
7	Nikolai Andrianov, USSR	Gymnastics	7-5-3	†Includes gold medal as preliminary member of 1st-place relay team.

WOMEN

No		Sport	G-S-B	No		Sport	G-S-B
9	Larissa Latynina, USSR	Gymnastics	9-5-4	4	Lyudmila Touricheva, USSR	Gymnastics	4-3-2
8	**Jenny Thompson**, USA	Swimming	8-3-1	4	**Dara Torres**, USA	Swimming	4-1-4
7	Vera Cáslavská, CZE	Gymnastics	7-4-0	4	**Evelyn Ashford**, USA	Track/Field	4-1-0
7	Birgit Fischer, GER	Canoe/Kayak	7-3-0	4	**Janet Evans**, USA	Swimming	4-1-0
6†	Kristin Otto, E. Ger	Swimming	6-0-0	4	Fu Mingxia, CHN	Diving	4-1-0
6†	**Amy Van Dyken**, USA	Swimming	6-0-0	4	Fanny Blankers-Koen, NED	Track/Field	4-0-0
5	Agnes Keleti, HUN	Gymnastics	5-3-2	4	Betty Cuthbert, AUS	Track/Field	4-0-0
5	Nadia Comaneci, ROM	Gymnastics	5-3-1	4	**Pat McCormick**, USA	Diving	4-0-0
5	Polina Astakhova, USSR	Gymnastics	5-2-3	4	Bärbel Eckert Wäckel, E. Ger.	Track/Field	4-0-0
5	Krisztina Egerszegi, HUN	Swimming	5-1-1	4	Inge de Bruijn, NED	Swimming	4-2-2
4	Kornelia Ender, E. Ger	Swimming	4-4-0				
4	Dawn Fraser, AUS	Swimming	4-4-0				

†Includes gold medal as preliminary member of 1st-place relay team.

Most Silver Medals

MEN				WOMEN			
No		Sport	G-S-B	No		Sport	G-S-B
6	Alexandr Dityatin, USSR	Gymnastics	3-6-1	6	**Shirley Babashoff**, USA	Swimming	2-6-0
6	Mikhail Voronin, USSR	Gymnastics	2-6-1	5	Larissa Latynina, USSR	Gymnastics	9-5-4
5	Nikolai Andrianov, USSR	Gymnastics	7-5-3	5	Maria Gorokhovskaya, USSR	Gymnastics	2-5-0
5	Edoardo Mangiarotti, ITA	Fencing	6-5-2	4	Vera Cáslavská, CZE	Gymnastics	7-4-0
5	Zoltán Halmay, HUN	Swimming	3-5-1	4	Kornelia Ender, E. Ger	Swimming	4-4-0
5	Gustavo Marzi, ITA	Fencing	2-5-0	4	Dawn Fraser, AUS	Swimming	4-4-0
5	Yuri Titov, USSR	Gymnastics	1-5-3	4	Erica Zuchold, E. Ger	Gymnastics	0-4-1
5	Viktor Lisitsky, USSR	Gymnastics	0-5-0				

Most Bronze Medals

MEN				WOMEN			
No		Sport	G-S-B	No		Sport	G-S-B
6	Alexei Nemov, RUS	Gymnastics	4-2-6	5	Merlene Ottey, JAM	Track/Field	0-2-5
6	Heikki Savolainen, FIN	Gymnastics	2-1-6	4	Larissa Latynina, USSR	Gymnastics	9-5-4
5	Daniel Revenu, FRA	Fencing	1-0-5	4	**Dara Torres**, USA	Swimming	4-1-4
5	Philip Edwards, CAN	Track/Field	0-0-5	4	Sofia Muratova, USSR	Gymnastics	2-2-4
5	Adrianus Jong, NED	Fencing	0-0-5				

All-Time Leading USA Medal Winners

Most Overall Medals

MEN

No		Sport	G-S-B	No		Sport	G-S-B
11	Mark Spitz	Swimming	9-1-1	6	Anton Heida	Gymnastics	5-1-0
11†	Matt Biondi	Swimming	8-2-1	6	Don Schollander	Swimming	5-1-0
11	Carl Osburn	Shooting	5-4-2	6	Johnny Weissmuller	Swim/Water Polo	5-0-1
10*	Ray Ewry	Track/Field	10-0-0	6	Alfred Lane	Shooting	5-0-1
10	Carl Lewis	Track/Field	9-1-0	6	Jim Lightbody	Track/Field	4-2-0
9	Gary Hall Jr.	Swimming	5-3-1	6	George Eyser	Gymnastics	3-2-1
9*	Martin Sheridan	Track/Field	5-3-1	6	Ralph Rose	Track/Field	3-2-1
8†	Michael Phelps	Swimming	6-0-2	6	Michael Plumb	Equestrian	2-4-0
8	Charles Daniels	Swimming	5-1-2	6	Burton Downing	Cycling	2-3-1
7‡	Tom Jager	Swimming	5-1-1	6	Bob Garrett	Track/Field	2-2-2
7	Willis Lee	Shooting	5-1-1				
7	Lloyd Spooner	Shooting	4-1-2				

†Includes gold medal as prelim. member of 1st-place relay team.
*Medals won by Ewry (2-0-0) and Sheridan (2-3-0) at the 1906 Intercalated games are not officially recognized by the IOC.
‡Includes 3 gold medals as prelim. member of 1st-place relay team.

Games Participated In

Biondi (1984,88,92); **Daniels** (1904,06,08); **Downing** (1904); **Ewry** (1900,04,06,08); **Eyser** (1904); **Garrett** (1896,1900); **Hall Jr.** (1996,2000,04) **Heida** (1904); **Jager** (1984,88,92); **Lane** (1912,20); **Lee** (1920); **Lewis** (1984,88,92,96); **Lightbody** (1904,06); **Osburn** (1912,20,24); **Phelps** (2004); **Plumb** (1960, 64,68,72,76,84); **Rose** (1904,08,12); **Schollander** (1964, 68); **Sheridan** (1904,06,08); **Spitz** (1968,72); **Spooner** (1920); **Weissmuller** (1924,28).

WOMEN

No		Sport	G-S-B	No		Sport	G-S-B
12	Jenny Thompson	Swimming	8-3-1	5	Evelyn Ashford	Track/Field	4-1-0
9	Dara Torres	Swimming	4-1-4	5	Janet Evans	Swimming	4-1-0
8	Shirley Babashoff	Swimming	2-6-0	5	Florence Griffith Joyner	Track/Field	3-2-0
7	Shannon Miller	Gymnastics	2-2-3	5†	Mary T. Meagher	Swimming	3-1-1
7	Amanda Beard	Swimming	2-4-1	5	Gwen Torrence	Track/Field	3-2-0
6†	Amy Van Dyken	Swimming	6-0-0	5	Marion Jones‡	Track/Field	3-0-2
6	Jackie Joyner-Kersee	Track/Field	3-1-2	5	Mary Lou Retton	Gymnastics	1-2-2
6	Angel Martino	Swimming	3-0-3	5	Natalie Coughlin	Swimming	2-2-1

†Includes gold medal as prelim. member of 1st-place relay team.
‡Jones admitted to using performance-enhancing drugs and has been stripped of her medals.

Games Participated In

Ashford (1976,84,88,92); **Babashoff** (1972,76); **Beard** (1996,2000,04); **Coughlin** (2004), **Evans** (1988,92,96); **Griffith Joyner** (1984,88); **Jones** (2000); **Joyner-Kersee** (1984,88,92,96); **Martino** (1992,96); **McCormick** (1952,56); **Meagher** (1984,88); **Miller** (1992, 96); **Retton** (1984); **Thompson** (1988,92,96,2000,04); **Torrence** (1988,92,96); **Torres** (1984,88,92,2000); **Van Dyken** (1996,2000).

Most Gold Medals

MEN

No		Sport	G-S-B
10*	Raymond Ewry	Track/Field	10-0-0
9	Mark Spitz	Swimming	9-1-1
9	Carl Lewis	Track/Field	9-1-0
8†	Matt Biondi	Swimming	8-2-1
6†	Michael Phelps	Swimming	6-0-2
5	Carl Osburn	Shooting	5-4-2
5*	Martin Sheridan	Track/Field	5-3-1
5	Charles Daniels	Swimming	5-1-2
5‡	Tom Jager	Swimming	5-1-1
5	Willis Lee	Shooting	5-1-1
5	Anton Heida	Gymnastics	5-1-0
5	Don Schollander	Swimming	5-1-0
5	Johnny Weissmuller	Swim/Water Polo	5-0-1
5	Alfred Lane	Shooting	5-0-1
5	Morris Fisher	Shooting	5-0-0
5	Gary Hall Jr.	Swimming	5-3-1
4	Jim Lightbody	Track/Field	4-2-0
4	Lloyd Spooner	Shooting	4-T-2
4	Greg Louganis	Diving	4-1-0
4	John Naber	Swimming	4-1-0
4	Meyer Prinstein	Track/Field	4-1-0
4	Mel Sheppard	Track/Field	4-1-0
4	Marcus Hurley	Cycling	4-0-1
4†	Jon Olsen	Swimming	4-0-1
4	Archie Hahn	Track/Field	4-0-0
4	Alvin Kraenzlein	Track/Field	4-0-0
4	Al Oerter	Track/Field	4-0-0
4	Jesse Owens	Track/Field	4-0-0

*Medals won by Ewry (2-0-0) and Sheridan (2-3-0) at the 1906 Intercalated games are not officially recognized by the IOC.
†Includes gold medal as preliminary member of 1st-place relay team.
‡Includes 3 gold medals as preliminary member of 1st-place relay teams.

WOMEN

No		Sport	G-S-B
8	Jenny Thompson	Swimming	8-3-1
6†	Amy Van Dyken	Swimming	6-0-0
4	Dara Torres	Swimming	4-1-4
4	Evelyn Ashford	Track/Field	4-1-0
4	Janet Evans	Swimming	4-1-0
4	Pat McCormick	Diving	4-0-0
3	Florence Griffith Joyner	Track/Field	3-2-0
3	Jackie Joyner-Kersee	Track/Field	3-1-2
3†	Mary T. Meagher	Swimming	3-1-1
3	Gwen Torrence	Track/Field	3-1-1
3	Marion Jones*	Track/Field	3-0-2
3	Valerie Brisco-Hooks	Track/Field	3-1-0
3	Nancy Hogshead	Swimming	3-1-0
3	Sharon Stouder	Swimming	3-1-0
3	Wyomia Tyus	Track/Field	3-1-0
3	Chris von Saltza	Swimming	3-1-0
3	Wilma Rudolph	Track/Field	3-0-1
3	Melissa Belote	Swimming	3-0-0
3	Ethelda Bleibtrey	Swimming	3-0-0
3	Tracy Caulkins	Swimming	3-0-0
3†	Nicole Haislett	Swimming	3-0-0
3	Helen Madison	Swimming	3-0-0
3	Debbie Meyer	Swimming	3-0-0
3	Sandra Neilson	Swimming	3-0-0
3	Martha Norelius	Swimming	3-0-0
3†	Carrie Steinseifer	Swimming	3-0-0
3‡	Ashley Tappin	Swimming	3-0-0

†Includes gold medal as preliminary member of 1st-place relay team.
‡Includes 3 gold medals as preliminary member of 1st-place relay teams.
*Jones was stripped of the five medals she won in 2000 after admitting to using performance-enhancing drugs.

Most Silver Medals

MEN

No		Sport	G-S-B
4	Carl Osburn	Shooting	5-4-2
4	Michael Plumb	Equestrian	2-4-0
3	Martin Sheridan	Track/Field	5-3-1
3	Burton Downing	Cycling	2-3-1
3	Irving Baxter	Track/Field	2-3-0

No		Sport	G-S-B
3	Earl Thomson	Equestrian	2-3-0
3	Alexander McKee	Swimming	0-3-0

WOMEN

No		Sport	G-S-B
6	Shirley Babashoff	Swimming	2-6-0

All-Time Medal Standings, 1896-2004

All-time Summer Games medal standings, based on *The Golden Book of the Olympic Games.* Medal counts include the 1906 Intercalated Games, which are not recognized by the IOC.

		G	S	B	Total
1	**United States**	907	697	615	2219
2	USSR (1952-88)	395	319	296	1010
3	Great Britain	189	242	237	668
4	France	199	202	230	631
5	Italy	189	154	168	511
6	Germany (1896-64,92–)	151	154	178	483
7	Sweden	140	157	179	476
8	Hungary	158	141	161	460
9	East Germany (1968-88)	159	150	136	445
10	Australia	119	126	154	399
11	Japan	113	106	114	333
12	West Germany (1968-88)	77	104	120	301
13	Finland	101	83	114	298
14	China	112	96	78	286
15	Romania	82	88	114	284
16	Poland	59	74	118	251
17	Russia (1896-1912, 96–)	85	79	84	248
18	Canada	54	87	101	242
19	Netherlands	65	76	94	234
20	Bulgaria	50	83	74	207
21	Switzerland	48	76	64	188
22	South Korea	55	64	65	184
23	Denmark	42	63	64	169
24	Cuba	64	51	49	164
25	Belgium	38	51	54	143
26	Czechoslovakia (1924-92)	49	49	44	142
	Greece	38	54	50	142
28	Norway	54	44	42	140
29	Unified Team (1992)	45	38	29	112
30	Spain	28	39	27	94
31	Yugoslavia (1924-88,96-2000)	28	32	33	93
	Austria	22	36	35	93
33	New Zealand	33	14	32	79
34	Brazil	16	22	38	76
35	Turkey	36	19	19	74
36	Rep. of S. Africa (1904-60, 92–)	20	23	26	69

#	Country	G	S	B	Total
37	Kenya	17	24	20	61
38	Argentina	15	23	22	60
39	Mexico	10	18	23	51
40	Iran	10	15	21	46
	Ukraine	12	15	19	46
42	Jamaica	7	21	14	42
43	North Korea	8	11	16	35
44	Belarus	5	9	18	32
45	Ethiopia	14	5	12	31
46	Estonia	8	7	14	29
47	Czech Republic	7	9	11	27
48	Ireland	9	6	6	21
	Egypt	7	6	8	21
50	Great Britain/Ireland	6	11	3	20
	Portugal	3	6	11	20
	Indonesia	5	8	7	20
53	Nigeria	2	8	9	19
	Morocco	6	4	9	19
55	India	8	4	5	17
	Thailand	5	2	10	17
57	Mongolia	0	5	10	15
	Chinese Taipei	2	6	7	15
	Kazakhstan	4	8	3	15
60	Latvia	1	10	3	14
	Slovakia	4	6	4	14
62	Algeria	4	1	7	12
	Trinidad & Tobago	1	3	8	12
	Lithuania	4	2	6	12
	Chile	2	6	4	12
	Georgia	2	2	8	12
	Croatia	3	4	5	12
68	Uzbekistan	3	3	5	11
69	Pakistan	3	3	4	10
	Uruguay	2	2	6	10
	Venezuela	1	2	7	10
	Slovenia	2	3	5	10
73	Azerbaijan	3	1	5	9
	Philippines	0	2	7	9
75	Bahamas	3	2	3	8
	Colombia	1	2	5	8
77	Uganda	1	3	2	6
	Tunisia	1	2	3	6
	Bohemia	0	1	5	6
	Puerto Rico	0	1	5	6
	Israel	1	1	4	6
82	Cameroon	2	1	1	4
	Zimbabwe	2	1	1	4
	Peru	1	3	0	4
	Costa Rica	1	1	2	4
	Namibia	0	4	0	4
	Lebanon	0	2	2	4
	Moldova	0	2	2	4
	Ghana	0	1	3	4
90	Luxembourg	2	1	0	3
	Armenia	1	1	1	3
	Iceland	0	1	2	3
	Malaysia	0	1	2	3
	Syria	1	1	1	3
95	Hong Kong	1	1	0	2
	Dominican Republic	1	0	1	2
	Japan/Korea	1	0	1	2
	Mozambique	1	0	1	2
	Surinam	1	0	1	2
	Serbia & Montenegro	0	2	0	2
	Tanzania	0	2	0	2
	Great Britain/USA	0	1	1	2
	Haiti	0	1	1	2
	Russia/Estonia	0	1	1	2
	Saudi Arabia	0	1	1	2
	United Arab Republic	0	1	1	2
	Zambia	0	1	1	2
	The Antilles	0	0	2	2
	Panama	0	0	2	2
	Qatar	0	0	2	2
111	Australia/New Zealand	1	0	0	1
	Burkina Faso	1	0	0	1
	Cuba/USA	1	0	0	1
	Denmark/Sweden	1	0	0	1
	Ecuador	1	0	0	1
	Gr. Britain/Ireland/Germany	1	0	0	1
	Gr. Britain/Ireland/USA	1	0	0	1
	Ireland/USA	1	0	0	1
	United Arab Emirates	1	0	0	1
	Belgium/Greece	0	1	0	1
	Ceylon	0	1	0	1
	France/USA	0	1	0	1
	France/Gr. Britain/Ireland	0	1	0	1
	Ivory Coast	0	1	0	1
	Netherlands Antilles	0	1	0	1
	Paraguay	0	1	0	1
	Senegal	0	1	0	1
	Singapore	0	1	0	1
	Smyrna	0	1	0	1
	Tonga	0	1	0	1
	Vietnam	0	1	0	1
	Virgin Islands	0	1	0	1
	Australia/Great Britain	0	0	1	1
	Barbados	0	0	1	1
	Bermuda	0	0	1	1
	Bohemia/Great Britain	0	0	1	1
	Djibouti	0	0	1	1
	Eritrea	0	0	1	1
	France/Great Britain	0	0	1	1
	Guyana	0	0	1	1
	Iraq	0	0	1	1
	Kuwait	0	0	1	1
	Kyrgyzstan	0	0	1	1
	Macedonia	0	0	1	1
	Mexico/Spain	0	0	1	1
	Niger	0	0	1	1
	Scotland	0	0	1	1
	Sri Lanka	0	0	1	1
	Thessalonika	0	0	1	1
	Wales	0	0	1	1

Combined totals:	G	S	B	Total
USSR/UT/Russia	525	436	409	1370
Germany/E. Ger/W. Ger	388	408	434	1230

Notes: Athletes from the USSR participated in the Summer Games from 1952-88, returned as the Unified Team in 1992 after the breakup of the Soviet Union (in 1991) and have competed as independent republics since the 1994 Winter Games. Germany was barred from the Olympics in 1924 and 1948 following World Wars I and II. Divided into East and West Germany after WWII, both countries competed together from 1952-64, then separately from 1968-88. Germany was reunified in 1990. Czechoslovakia split into Slovakia and the Czech Republic in 1993. Croatia and Bosnia-Herzegovina gained independence from Yugoslavia in 1991. Yugoslavia was not invited to the 1992 games (though Serbian and Montenegrin athletes were allowed to compete as independent athletes) but returned in 1996 and competed under the name Serbia & Montenegro starting in 2004. South Africa was banned from 1964-88 for using the apartheid policy in the selection of its teams. It returned in 1992 as the Republic of South Africa (RSA).

1924-2006
Through the Years

SPORTS ALMANAC

The Winter Olympics

The move toward a winter version of the Olympics began in 1908 when figure skating made an appearance at the Summer Games in London. Ten-time world champion Ulrich Salchow of Sweden, who originated the backwards, one revolution jump that bears his name, and Madge Syers of Britain were the first singles champions. Germans Anna Hubler and Heinrich Berger won the pairs competition.

Organizers of the 1916 Summer Games in Berlin planned to introduce a "Skiing Olympia," featuring nordic events in the Black Forest, but the Games were cancelled after the outbreak of World War I in 1914.

The Games resumed in 1920 at Antwerp, Belgium, where figure skating returned and ice hockey was added as a medal event. Sweden's Gillis Grafstrom and Magda Julin took individual honors, while Ludovika and Walter Jakobsson were the top pair. In hockey, Canada won the gold medal with the United States second and Czechoslovakia third.

Despite the objections of Modern Olympics' founder Baron Pierre de Coubertin and the resistance of the Scandinavian countries, which had staged their own Nordic championships every four or five years from 1901-26 in Sweden, the International Olympic Committee sanctioned an "International Winter Sports Week" at Chamonix, France, in 1924. The 11-day event, which included nordic skiing, speed skating, figure skating, ice hockey and bobsledding, was a huge success and was retroactively called the first Olympic Winter Games.

Seventy years after those first cold weather Games, the 17th edition of the Winter Olympics took place in Lillehammer, Norway, in 1994. The event ended the four-year Olympic cycle of staging both Winter and Summer Games in the same year and began a new schedule that calls for the two Games to alternate every two years.

Year	No	Location	Dates	Nations	Most medals	USA medals
1924	I	Chamonix, FRA	Jan. 25-Feb. 4	16	Norway (4-7-6–17)	1-2-1–4 (3rd)
1928	II	St. Moritz, SWI	Feb. 11-19	25	Norway (6-4-5–15)	2-2-2– 6 (2nd)
1932	III	Lake Placid, USA	Feb. 4-15	17	USA (6-4-2–12)	6-4-2–12 (1st)
1936	IV	Garmisch-Partenkirchen, GER	Feb. 6-16	28	Norway (7-5-3–15)	1-0-3– 4 (T-5th)
1940-**a**	–	Sapporo, JPN	Cancelled (WWII)			
1944	–	Cortina d'Ampezzo, ITA	Cancelled (WWII)			
1948	V	St. Moritz, SWI	Jan. 30-Feb. 8	28	Norway (4-3-3–10), Sweden (4-3-3–10) & Switzerland (3-4-3–10)	3-4-2– 9 (4th)
1952-**b**	VI	Oslo, NOR	Feb. 14-25	30	Norway (7-3-6–16)	4-6-1–11 (2nd)
1956-**c**	VII	Cortina d'Ampezzo, ITA	Jan. 26-Feb. 5	32	USSR (7-3-6–16)	2-3-2– 7 (T-4th)
1960	VIII	Squaw Valley, USA	Feb. 18-28	30	USSR (7-5-9–21)	3-4-3–10 (2nd)
1964	IX	Innsbruck, AUT	Jan. 29-Feb. 9	36	USSR (11-8-6–25)	1-2-3– 6 (7th)
1968-**d**	X	Grenoble, FRA	Feb. 6-18	37	Norway (6-6-2–14)	1-5-1– 7 (T-7th)
1972	XI	Sapporo, JPN	Feb. 3-13	35	USSR (8-5-3–16)	3-2-3– 8 (6th)
1976-**e**	XII	Innsbruck, AUT	Feb. 4-15	37	USSR (13-6-8–27)	3-3-4–10 (T-3rd)
1980	XIII	Lake Placid, USA	Feb. 14-23	37	E. Germany (9-7-7–23)	6-4-2–12 (3rd)
1984	XIV	Sarajevo, YUG	Feb. 7-19	49	USSR (6-10-9–25)	4-4-0– 8 (T-5th)
1988	XV	Calgary, CAN	Feb. 13-28	57	USSR (11-9-9–29)	2-1-3– 6 (T-8th)
1992-**f**	XVI	Albertville, FRA	Feb. 8-23	63	Germany (10-10-6–26)	5-4-2–11 (6th)
1994-**g**	XVII	Lillehammer, NOR	Feb. 12-27	67	Norway (10-11-5–26)	6-5-2–13 (T-5th)
1998	XVIII	Nagano, JPN	Feb. 7-22	72	Germany (12-9-8–29)	6-3-4–13 (5th)
2002	XIX	Salt Lake City, USA	Feb. 8-24	78	Germany (12-16-7–35)	10-13-11–34 (2nd)
2006	XX	Turin, ITA	Feb. 10-26	87	Germany (11-12-6–29)	9-9-7–25 (2nd)
2010	XXI	Vancouver, CAN	Feb. 12-28			
2014	XXII	Sochi, RUS	Feb. 7-23			

a–The 1940 Winter Games are originally scheduled for Sapporo, but Japan resigns as host in 1937 when the Sino-Japanese war breaks out. St. Moritz is the next choice, but the Swiss feel that ski instructors should not be considered professionals and the IOC withdraws its offer. Finally, Garmisch-Partenkirchen is asked to serve again as host, but the Germans invade Poland in 1939 and the Games are eventually cancelled.

b–Germany and Japan are allowed to rejoin the Olympic community for the first time since World War II. Though a divided country, the Germans send a joint East-West team through 1964.

c–The Soviet Union (USSR) participates in its first Winter Olympics and takes home the most medals, including the gold medal in ice hockey.

d–East Germany and West Germany officially send separate teams for the first time and will continue to do so through 1988.

e–The IOC grants the 1976 Winter Games to Denver in May 1970, but in 1972 Colorado voters reject a $5 million bond issue to finance the undertaking. Denver immediately withdraws as host and the IOC selects Innsbruck, the site of the 1964 Games, to take over.

f–Germany sends a single team after East and West German reunification in 1990 and the USSR competes as the Unified Team after the breakup of the Soviet Union in 1991.

g–The IOC moves the Winter Games' four-year cycle ahead two years in order to separate them from the Summer Games and alternate Olympics every two years.

Event-by-Event

Gold medal winners from 1924-2006 in the following events: Alpine Skiing, Biathlon, Bobsled, Cross Country Skiing, Curling, Figure Skating, Freestyle Skiing, Ice Hockey, Luge, Nordic Combined, Skeleton, Ski Jumping, Snowboarding and Speed Skating.

ALPINE SKIING

MEN

Multiple gold medals: Kjetil Andre Aamodt (4); Jean-Claude Killy, Toni Sailer and Alberto Tomba (3); Hermann Maier, Henri Oreiller, Benjamin Raich, Ingemar Stenmark and Markus Wasmeier (2).

Downhill

Year		Time	Year		Time
1948	Henri Oreiller, FRA	2:55.0	1980	Leonhard Stock, AUS	1:45.50
1952	Zeno Colò, ITA	2:30.8	1984	Bill Johnson, USA	1:45.59
1956	Toni Sailer, AUT	2:52.2	1988	Pirmin Zurbriggen, SWI	1:59.63
1960	Jean Vuarnet, FRA	2:06.0	1992	Patrick Ortlieb, AUT	1:50.37
1964	Egon Zimmermann, AUT	2:18.16	1994	Tommy Moe, USA	1:45.75
1968	Jean-Claude Killy, FRA	1:59.85	1998	Jean-Luc Cretier, FRA	1:50.11
1972	Bernhard Russi, SWI	1:51.43	2002	Fritz Strobl, AUT	1:39.13
1976	Franz Klammer AUT	1:45.73	2006	Antoine Deneriaz, FRA	1:48.80

Slalom

Year		Time	Year		Time
1948	Edi Reinalter, SWI	2:10.3	1980	Ingemar Stenmark, SWE	1:44.26
1952	Othmar Schneider, AUT	2:00.0	1984	Phil Mahre, USA	1:39.41
1956	Toni Sailer, AUT	3:14.7	1988	Alberto Tomba, ITA	1:39.47
1960	Ernst Hinterseer, AUT	2:08.9	1992	Finn Christian Jagge, NOR	1:44.39
1964	Pepi Stiegler, AUT	2:11.13	1994	Thomas Stangassinger, AUT	2:02.02
1968	Jean-Claude Killy, FRA	1:39.73	1998	Hans-Petter Buraas, NOR	1:49.31
1972	Francisco Ochoa, SPA	1:49.27	2002	Jean-Pierre Vidal, FRA	1:41.06
1976	Piero Gros, ITA	2:03.29	2006	Benjamin Raich, AUT	1:43.14

Giant Slalom

Year		Time	Year		Time
1952	Stein Eriksen, NOR	2:25.0	1984	Max Julen, SWI	2:41.18
1956	Toni Sailer, AUS	3:00.1	1988	Alberto Tomba, ITA	2:06.37
1960	Roger Staub, SWI	1:48.3	1992	Alberto Tomba, ITA	2:06.98
1964	Francois Bonlieu, FRA	1:46.71	1994	Markus Wasmeier, GER	2:52.46
1968	Jean-Claude Killy, FRA	3:29.28	1998	Hermann Maier, AUT	2:38.51
1972	Gustav Thöni, ITA	3:09.62	2002	Stephan Eberharter, AUT	2:23.28
1976	Heini Hemmi, SWI	3:26.97	2006	Benjamin Raich, AUT	2:35.00
1980	Ingemar Stenmark, SWE	2:40.74			

Super G

Year		Time	Year		Time
1988	Frank Piccard, FRA	1:39.66	1998	Hermann Maier, AUT	1:34.82
1992	Kjetil Andre Aamodt, NOR	1:13.04	2002	Kjetil Andre Aamodt, NOR	1:21.58
1994	Markus Wasmeier, GER	1:32.53	2006	Kjetil Andre Aamodt, NOR	1:30.65

Alpine Combined

Year		Points	Year		Time
1936	Franz Pfnür, GER	99.25	1994	Lasse Kjus, NOR	3:17.53
1948	Henri Oreiller, FRA	3.27	1998	Mario Reiter, AUT	3:08.06
1952-84	Not held		2002	Kjetil Andre Aamodt, NOR	3:17.56
1988	Hubert Strolz, AUT	36.55	2006	Ted Ligety, USA	3:09.35
1992	Josef Polig, ITA	14.58			

Athletes with Winter and Summer Medals

Only four athletes have won medals in **both** the Winter and Summer Olympics:

Eddie Eagan, USA—Light Heavyweight Boxing gold (1920) and Four-man Bobsled gold (1932).

Jacob Tullin Thams, Norway—Ski Jumping gold (1924) and 8-meter Yachting silver (1936).

Christa Luding-Rothenburger, East Germany—Speed Skating gold at 500 meters (1984) and 1,000m (1988), silver at 500m (1988) and bronze at 500m (1992) and Match Sprint Cycling silver (1988). Luding-Rothenburger is the only athlete to ever win medals in both Winter and Summer Games in the same year.

Clara Hughes, Canada—Cycling bronzes in Road Race and Time Trial (1996) and Speed Skating bronze at 5,000m (2002) and Speed Skating gold at 5,000m and silver in Team Pursuit (2006).

Gold Strike in the Mountains

With his age-defying gold medal performance at Sestriere, Italy in 2006, Norway's **Kjetil Andre Aamodt** became the first (and for 30 minutes only) skier in Olympic history to win four Alpine Skiing gold medals. The 34-year-old's gold at the 2006 Super G also made him the first Alpine skier to earn four medals in the same event (he won a bronze in 1994 to go with his three golds). Aamodt, is both the youngest *and* oldest alpine skier to win Olympic gold, first taking a gold medal in the Super G at 20 years old in 1992 at Albertville. Aamodt is also the only Alpine skier to win eight career Olympic medals.

Half an hour after Aamodt became the first Alpine skier to win four gold medals, **Janica Kostelic** of Croatia won the Alpine Combined to become the first woman to achieve the same feat. She also took the silver medal in the Super G and placed fourth in the slalom.

WOMEN

Multiple gold medals: Janica Kostelic (4), Deborah Compagnoni, Vreni Schneider and Katja Seizinger (3); Michaela Dorfmeister, Marielle Goitschel, Trude Jochum-Beiser, Petra Kronberger, Andrea Mead Lawrence, Rosi Mittermaier, Marie-Theres Nadig, Hanni Wenzel and Pernilla Wiberg (2).

Downhill

Year		Time	Year		Time
1948	Hedy Schlunegger, SWI	2:28.3	1980	Annemarie Moser-Pröll, AUT	1:37.52
1952	Trude Jochum-Beiser, AUT	1:47.1	1984	Michela Figini, SWI	1:13.36
1956	Madeleine Berthod, SWI	1:40.7	1988	Marina Kiehl, W. Ger	1:25.86
1960	Heidi Biebl, GER	1:37.6	1992	Kerrin Lee-Gartner, CAN	1:52.55
1964	Christl Haas, AUT	1:55.39	1994	Katja Seizinger, GER	1:35.93
1968	Olga Pall, AUT	1:40.87	1998	Katja Seizinger, GER	1:28.89
1972	Marie-Theres Nadig, SWI	1:36.68	2002	Carole Montillet, FRA	1:39.56
1976	Rosi Mittermaier, W. Ger	1:46.16	2006	Michaela Dorfmeister, AUT	1:56.49

Slalom

Year		Time	Year		Time
1948	Gretchen Fraser, USA	1:57.2	1980	Hanni Wenzel, LIE	1:25.09
1952	Andrea Mead Lawrence, USA	2:10.6	1984	Paoletta Magoni, ITA	1:36.47
1956	Renée Colliard, SWI	1:52.3	1988	Vreni Schneider, SWI	1:36.69
1960	Anne Heggtveit, CAN	1:49.6	1992	Petra Kronberger, AUT	1:32.68
1964	Christine Goitschel, FRA	1:29.86	1994	Vreni Schneider, SWI	1:56.01
1968	Marielle Goitschel, FRA	1:25.86	1998	Hilde Gerg, GER	1:32.40
1972	Barbara Cochran, USA	1:31.24	2002	Janica Kostelic, CRO	1:46.10
1976	Rosi Mittermaier, W. Ger	1:30.54	2006	Anja Paerson, SWE	1:29.04

Giant Slalom

Year		Time	Year		Time
1952	Andrea Mead Lawrence, USA	2:06.8	1984	Debbie Armstrong, USA	2:20.98
1956	Ossi Reichert, GER	1:56.5	1988	Vreni Schneider, SWI	2:06.49
1960	Yvonne Rügg, SWI	1:39.9	1992	Pernilla Wiberg, SWE	2:12.74
1964	Marielle Goitschel, FRA	1:52.24	1994	Deborah Compagnoni, ITA	2:30.97
1968	Nancy Greene, CAN	1:51.97	1998	Deborah Compagnoni, ITA	2:50.59
1972	Marie-Theres Nadig, SWI	1:29.90	2002	Janica Kostelic, CRO	2:30.01
1976	Kathy Kreiner, CAN	1:29.13	2006	Julia Mancuso, USA	2:09.19
1980	Hanni Wenzel, LIE	2:41.66			

Super G

Year		Time	Year		Time
1988	Sigrid Wolf, AUT	1:19.03	1998	Picabo Street, USA	1:18.02
1992	Deborah Compagnoni, ITA	1:21.22	2002	Daniela Ceccarelli, ITA	1:13.59
1994	Diann Roffe-Steinrotter, USA	1:22.15	2006	Michaela Dorfmeister, AUT	1:32.47

Alpine Combined

Year		Points	Year		Time
1936	Christl Cranz, GER	97.06	1994	Pernilla Wiberg, SWE	3:05.16
1948	Trude Beiser, AUT	6.58	1998	Katja Seizinger, GER	2:40.74
1952-84 Not held			2002	Janica Kostelic, CRO	2:43.28
1988	Anita Wachter, AUT	29.25	2006	Janica Kostelic, CRO	2:51.08
1992	Petra Kronberger, AUT	2.55			

BIATHLON

MEN

Multiple gold medals (including relays): Ole Einar Bjoerndalen (5); Aleksandr Tikhonov (4); Mark Kirchner, Michael Greis and Ricco Gross (3); Anatoly Alyabyev, Ivan Biakov, Sergei Chepikov, Sven Fischer, Halvard Hanevold, Frank Luck, Viktor Mamatov, Frank-Peter Roetsch, Magnar Solberg and Dmitri Vasilyev (2).

10 kilometers

Year		Time	Year		Time
1980	Frank Ulrich, E. Ger	32:10.69	1994	Sergei Chepikov, RUS	28:07.0
1984	Erik Kvalfoss, NOR	30:53.8	1998	Ole Einar Bjoerndalen, NOR	27:16.2
1988	Frank-Peter Roetsch, E. Ger	25:08.1	2002	Ole Einar Bjoerndalen, NOR	24:51.3
1992	Mark Kirchner, GER	26:02.3	2006	Sven Fischer, GER	26:11.6

12.5 kilometers

Year		Time	Year		Time
2002	Ole Einar Bjoerndalen, NOR	32:34.6	2006	Vincent Defrasne, FRA	35:20.2

15 kilometers

Year		Time
2006	Michael Greis, GER	47:20.0

20 kilometers

Year		Time	Year		Time
1960	Klas Lestander, SWE	1:33:21.6	1988	Frank-Peter Roetsch, E. Ger	56:33.3
1964	Vladimir Melanin, USSR	1:20:26.8	1992	Yevgeny Redkine, UT	57:34.4
1968	Magnar Solberg, NOR	1:13:45.9	1994	Sergei Tarasov, RUS	57:25.3
1972	Magnar Solberg, NOR	1:15:55.50	1998	Halvard Hanevold, NOR	56:16.4
1976	Nikolai Kruglov, USSR	1:14:12.26	2002	Ole Einar Bjoerndalen, NOR	51:03.3
1980	Anatoly Alyabyev, USSR	1:08:16.31	2006	Michael Greis, GER	54:23.0
1984	Peter Angerer, W. Ger	1:11:52.7			

4x7.5-kilometer Relay

Year		Time	Year		Time	Year		Time
1968	Soviet Union	2:13:02.4	1984	Soviet Union	1:38:51.7	1998	Germany	1:21:36.2
1972	Soviet Union	1:51:44.92	1988	Soviet Union	1:22:30.0	2002	Norway	1:23:42.3
1976	Soviet Union	1:57:55.64	1992	Germany	1:24:43.5	2006	Germany	1:21:51.5
1980	Soviet Union	1:34:03.27	1994	Germany	1:30:22.1			

WOMEN

Multiple gold medals (including relays): Myriam Bedard, Andrea Henkel, Svetlana Ishmouratova, Anfisa Reztsova and Kati Wilhelm (2). Note that Reztsova won a third gold medal in 1988 in the cross country 4x5-kilometer relay.

7.5 kilometers

Year		Time	Year		Time
1992	Anfisa Reztsova, UT	24:29.2	2002	Kati Wilhelm, GER	20:41.4
1994	Myriam Bedard, CAN	26:08.8	2006	Florence Baverel-Robert, FRA	22:31.4
1998	Galina Koukleva, RUS	23:08.0			

10 kilometers

Year		Time	Year		Time
2002	Olga Pyleva, RUS	31:07.7	2006	Kati Wilhelm, GER	36:43.6

12.5 kilometers

Year		Time
2006	Anna Carin Olofsson, SWE	40:36.5

15 kilometers

Year		Time	Year		Time
1992	Antje Misersky, GER	51:47.2	2002	Andrea Henkel, GER	47:29.1
1994	Myriam Bedard, CAN	52:06.6	2006	Svetlana Ishmouratova, RUS	49:24.1
1998	Ekaterina Dafovska, BUL	54:52.0			

4x7.5-kilometer Relay

Year		Time	Year		Time
1992	France	1:15:55.6	2002	Germany	1:27:55.0
1994	Russia	1:47:19.5	2006	Russia	1:16:12.5
1998	Germany	1:40:13.6	**Note:** Event featured three skiers per team in 1992.		

BOBSLED

A two-woman bobsled event was added in 2002. Only drivers are listed in parentheses.

Multiple gold medals: DRIVERS–Andre Lange and Meinhard Nehmer (3); Billy Fiske, Wolfgang Hoppe, Christoph Langen, Eugenio Monti, Andreas Ostler and Gustav Weder (2). CREW–Bernard Germeshausen (3); Donat Acklin, Luciano De Paolis, Cliff Gray, Lorenz Nieberl and Dietmar Schauerhammer (2).

Two-Man

Year		Time	Year		Time
1932	United States (Hubert Stevens)	8:14.74	1980	Switzerland (Erich Schärer)	4:09.36
1936	United States (Ivan Brown)	5:29.29	1984	East Germany (Wolfgang Hoppe)	3:25.56
1948	Switzerland (Felix Endrich)	5:29.2	1988	Soviet Union (Janis Kipurs)	3:54.19
1952	Germany (Andreas Ostler)	5:24.54	1992	Switzerland I (Gustav Weder)	4:03.26
1956	Italy (Lamberto Dalla Costa)	5:30.14	1994	Switzerland I (Gustav Weder)	3:30.81
1960	Not held		1998	(TIE) Italy I (Guenther Huber)	3:37.24
1964	Great Britain (Anthony Nash)	4:21.90		& Canada I (Pierre Lueders)	3:37.24
1968	Italy (Eugenio Monti)	4:41.54	2002	Germany I (Christoph Langen)	3:10.11
1972	West Germany (Wolfgang Zimmerer)	4:57.07	2006	Germany I (Andre Lange)	3:43.38
1976	East Germany (Meinhard Nehmer)	3:44.42			

Two-Woman

Year		Time	Year		Time
2002	United States II (Jill Bakken)	1:37.76	2006	Germany I (Sandra Kiriasis)	3:49.98

Four-Man

Year		Time	Year		Time
1924	Switzerland (Eduard Scherrer)	5:45.54	1972	Switzerland (Jean Wicki)	4:43.07
1928	United States (Billy Fiske)	3:20.5	1976	East Germany (Meinhard Nehmer)	3:40.43
1932	United States (Billy Fiske)	7:53.68	1980	East Germany (Meinhard Nehmer)	3:59.92
1936	Switzerland (Pierre Musy)	5:19.85	1984	East Germany (Wolfgang Hoppe)	3:20.22
1948	United States (Francis Tyler)	5:20.1	1988	Switzerland (Ekkehard Fasser)	3:47.51
1952	Germany (Andreas Ostler)	5:07.84	1992	Austria I (Ingo Appelt)	3:53.90
1956	Switzerland (Franz Kapus)	5:10.44	1994	Germany II (Harald Czudaj)	3:27.78
1960	Not held		1998	Germany II (Christoph Langen)	2:39.41
1964	Canada (Vic Emery)	4:14.46	2002	Germany II (Andre Lange)	3:07.51
1968	Italy (Eugenio Monti)	2:17.39	2006	Germany I (Andre Lange)	3:40.42

Note: Five-man sleds were used in 1928.

CROSS COUNTRY SKIING

Starting with the 1988 Winter Games in Calgary, the classical and freestyle (i.e., skating) techniques were designated for specific events. The Pursuit race was introduced in 1992 and revamped after the 1998 Nagano Games. The Sprint was added in 2002 and the distances have differed slightly (1.5k in 2002 and 1.4k in 2006). The Team Sprint was added in 2006

MEN

Multiple gold medals (including relays): Bjorn Dählie (8); Thomas Alsgaard, Sixten Jernberg, Gunde Svan, Thomas Wassberg and Nikolai Zimyatov (4); Veikko Hakulinen, Eero Mäntyranta and Vegard Ulvang (3); Hallgeir Brenden, Harald Grönningen, Thorleif Haug, Bjoern Lind, Johann Muehlegg, Jan Ottoson, Kristen Skjeldal, Pål Tyldum, Andrus Veerpalu and Vyacheslav Vedenine (2).

Multiple gold medals (including Nordic Combined): Johan Gröttumsbråten and Thorleif Haug (3).

Sprint
Held as a freestyle event.

Year		Time	Year		Time
2002	Tor Arne Hetland, NOR	2:56.9	2006	Bjoern Lind, SWE	2:26.5

Team Sprint (3x1.4 km)
Held as a classical event.

Year		Time
2006	Sweden	17:02.9

10 kilometers
Held as a classical event.

Year		Time	Year		Time
1992	Vegard Ulvang, NOR	27:36.0	1998	Bjorn Dählie, NOR	27:24.5
1994	Bjorn Dählie, NOR	24:20.1	2002	discontinued	

Combined Pursuit

From 1992-98 the pursuit included a 10-km classical race and a 15-km freestyle race contested on separate days. In 2002, the pursuit was shortened to two 10-km races held on the same day. In 2006, the Combined Pursuit was comprised of back-to-back 15-km classical and freestyle races.

Year		Time	Year		Time
1992	Bjorn Dählie, NOR	1:05:37.9	2002	Johann Muehlegg, SPA	49:20.4
1994	Bjorn Dählie, NOR	1:00:08.8	2006	Eugeni Dementiev, RUS	1:17:00.8
1998	Thomas Alsgaard, NOR	1:07:01.7			

15 kilometers

Held over 18 kilometers from 1924-52. Held as a classical event from 1956-88, and since 2002. Replaced by the 15-km combined pursuit (1992-98).

Year		Time	Year		Time
1924	Thorleif Haug, NOR	1:14:31.0	1968	Harald Grönningen, NOR	47:54.2
1928	Johan Gröttumsbräten, NOR	1:37:01.0	1972	Sven-Ake Lundback, SWE	45:28.24
1932	Sven Utterström, SWE	1:23:07.0	1976	Nikolai Bazhukov, USSR	43:58.47
1936	Erik-August Larsson, SWE	1:14:38.0	1980	Thomas Wassberg, SWE	41:57.63
1948	Martin Lundström, SWE	1:13:50.0	1984	Gunde Svan, SWE	41:25.6
1952	Hallgeir Brenden, NOR	1:01:34.0	1988	Mikhail Devyatyarov, USSR	41:18.9
1956	Hallgeir Brenden, NOR	49:39.0	1992-98 Not held		
1960	Hakon Brusveen, NOR	51:55.5	2002	Andrus Veerpalu, EST	37:07.4
1964	Eero Mäntyranta, FIN	50:54.1	2006	Andrus Veerpalu, EST	38:01.3

30 kilometers

Held as a freestyle event from 1956-94, and in 2002. Held as a classical event in 1998.

Year		Time	Year		Time
1956	Veikko Hakulinen, FIN	1:44:06.0	1984	Nikolai Zimyatov, USSR	1:28:56.3
1960	Sixten Jernberg, SWE	1:51:03.9	1988	Alexei Prokurorov, USSR	1:24:26.3
1964	Eero Mäntyranta, FIN	1:30:50.7	1992	Vegard Ulvang, NOR	1:22:27.8
1968	Franco Nones, ITA	1:35:39.2	1994	Thomas Alsgaard, NOR	1:12:26.4
1972	Vyacheslav Vedenine, USSR	1:36:31.15	1998	Mika Myllylae, FIN	1:33:55.8
1976	Sergei Saveliev, USSR	1:30:29.38	2002	Johann Muehlegg, SPA	1:09:28.9
1980	Nikolai Zimyatov, USSR	1:27:02.80	2006	discontinued	

50 kilometers

Held as a classical event from 1924-94, and since 2002. Held as a freestyle event in 1998.

Year		Time	Year		Time
1924	Thorleif Haug, NOR	3:44:32.0	1972	Päl Tyldum, NOR	2:43:14.75
1928	Per Erik Hedlund, SWE	4:52:03.0	1976	Ivar Formo, NOR	2:37:30.05
1932	Veli Saarinen, FIN	4:28:00.0	1980	Nikolai Zimyatov, USSR	2:27:24.60
1936	Elis Wiklund, SWE	3:30:11.0	1984	Thomas Wassberg, SWE	2:15:55.8
1948	Nils Karlsson, SWE	3:47:48.0	1988	Gunde Svan, SWE	2:04:30.9
1952	Veikko Hakulinen, FIN	3:33:33.0	1992	Bjorn Dählie, NOR	2:03:41.5
1956	Sixten Jernberg, SWE	2:50:27.0	1994	Vladimir Smirnov, KAZ	2:07:20.3
1960	Kalevi Hämäläinen, FIN	2:59:06.3	1998	Bjorn Dählie, NOR	2:05:08.2
1964	Sixten Jernberg, SWE	2:43:52.6	2002	Mikhail Ivanov, RUS*	2:06:20.8
1968	Ole Ellefsaeter, NOR	2:28:45.8	2006	Giorgio Di Centa, ITA	2:06:11.8

*Ivanov finished second to Johann Muehlegg of Spain, who was disqualified for failing a drug test.

4x10-kilometer Mixed Relay

Two classical and two freestyle legs.

Year		Time	Year		Time	Year		Time
1936	Finland	2:41:33.0	1968	Norway	2:08:33.5	1992	Norway	1:39:26.0
1948	Sweden	2:32:08.0	1972	Soviet Union	2:04:47.94	1994	Italy	1:41:15.0
1952	Finland	2:20:16.0	1976	Finland	2:07:59.72	1998	Norway	1:40:55.7
1956	Soviet Union	2:15:30.0	1980	Soviet Union	1:57:03.46	2002	Norway	1:32:45.5
1960	Finland	2:18:45,6	1984	Sweden	1:55:06.3	2006	Italy	1:43:45.7
1964	Sweden	2:18:34.6	1988	Sweden	1:43:58.6			

WOMEN

Multiple gold medals (including relays): Lyubov Egorova (6); Larissa Lazutina (5); Galina Kulakova and Raisa Smetanina (4); Claudia Boyarskikh, Olga Danilova and Marja-Liisa Hämäläinen and Elena Valbe (3); Stefania Belmondo, Manuela Di Centa, Nina Gavriluk, Toini Gustafsson, Barbara Petzold, Kristina Smigun and Julija Tchepalova (2).

Multiple gold medals (including relays and Biathlon): Anfisa Reztsova (2).

Cross Country (Cont.)

Sprint

The Sprint was added in 2002 and the distances have differed slightly (1.5km in 2002 and 1.2km in 2006). The Team Sprint was added in 2006

Year	Time	Year	Time
2002 Julija Tchepalova, RUS	3:10.6	2006 Chandra Crawford, CAN	2:12.3

Team Sprint (3x1.2km)

Year	Time
2006 Sweden	16:36.9

5 kilometers

Held as a classical event from 1964-98. From 1992-98 it was half of the combined pursuit event. Discontinued after 1998.

Year	Time	Year	Time
1964 Claudia Boyarskikh, USSR	17:50.5	1984 Marja-Liisa Hämäläinen, FIN	17:04.0
1968 Toini Gustafsson, SWE	16:45.2	1988 Marjo Matikainen, FIN	15:04.0
1972 Galina Kulakova, USSR	17:00.50	1992 Marjut Lukkarinen, FIN	14:13.8
1976 Helena Takalo, FIN	15:48.69	1994 Lyubov Egorova, RUS	14:08.8
1980 Raisa Smetanina, USSR	15:06.92	1998 Larissa Lazutina, RUS	17:37.9

Combined Pursuit

From 1992-98 the pursuit consisted of a 10-km freestyle race in which the starting order was determined by order of finish in the 5-km classical race contested on separate days. In 2002, the pursuit was shortened to a 5-km classical race followed by a 5-km freestyle race contested on the same day. The 5-km classical is no longer a separate medal event. In 2006, the Combined Pursuit was comprised of back-to-back 7½-km classical and freestyle races.

Year	Time	Year	Time
1992 Lyubov Egorova, UT	40:07.7	2002 Olga Danilova, RUS	24:52.1
1994 Lyubov Egorova, RUS	41:38.1	2006 Kristina Smigun, EST	42:48.7
1998 Larissa Lazutina, RUS	46:06.9		

10 kilometers

Held as a classical event from 1952-88, and since 2002. Replaced by 10-km combined pursuit from 1992-98.

Year	Time	Year	Time
1952 Lydia Wideman, FIN	41:40.0	1980 Barbara Petzold, E. Ger	30:31.54
1956 Lyubov Kosyreva, USSR	38:11.0	1984 Marja-Liisa Hämäläinen, FIN	31:44.2
1960 Maria Gusakova, USSR	39:46.6	1988 Vida Venciene, USSR	30:08.3
1964 Claudia Boyarskikh, USSR	40:24.3	1992-98 Not held	
1968 Toini Gustafsson, SWE	36:46.5	2002 Bente Skari, NOR	28:05.6
1972 Galina Kulakova, USSR	34:17.82	2006 Kristina Smigun, EST	27:51.4
1976 Raisa Smetanina, USSR	30:13.41		

15 kilometers

Held as a freestyle event from 1992-94, and 2002. Held as a classical event in 1998.

Year	Time	Year	Time
1992 Lyubov Egorova, UT	42:20.8	1998 Olga Danilova, RUS	46:55.4
1994 Manuela Di Centa, ITA	39:44.5	2002 Stefania Belmondo, ITA	39:54.4

20 kilometers

Held as a classical event from 1984-88. Discontinued in 1992 and replaced by the 30-kilometer freestyle.

Year	Time	Year	Time
1984 Marja-Liisa Hämäläinen, FIN	1:01:45.0	1988 Tamara Tikhonova, USSR	55:53.6

30 kilometers

Replaced 20-km classical event in 1992. Held as a freestyle event 1992-98 and 2006. Held as a classical event in 2002.

Year	Time	Year	Time
1992 Stefania Belmondo, ITA	1:22:30.1	2002 Gabriella Paruzzi, ITA*	1:30:57.1
1994 Manuela Di Centa, ITA	1:25:41.6	2006 Katerina Neumannova, CZE	1:22:25.4
1998 Julija Tchepalova, RUS	1:22:01.5		

*Paruzzi finished second to Larissa Lazutina of Russia, who was disqualified after failing a drug test.

4x5-kilometer Relay

Two classical and two freestyle legs since 1992. Event featured three skiers per team from 1956-72.

Year	Time	Year	Time	Year	Time
1956 Finland	1:09:01.0	1976 Soviet Union	1:07:49.75	1994 Russia	57:12.5
1960 Sweden	1:04:21.4	1980 East Germany	1:02:11.10	1998 Russia	55:13.5
1964 Soviet Union	59:20.2	1984 Norway	1:06:49.7	2002 Germany	49:30.6
1968 Norway	57:30.0	1988 Soviet Union	59:51.1	2006 Russia	54:47.7
1972 Soviet Union	48:46.15	1992 Unified Team	59:34.8		

CURLING

MEN		WOMEN	
Year		**Year**	
1998	**Switzerland**, Canada, Norway	1998	**Canada**, Denmark, Sweden
2002	**Norway**, Canada, Switzerland	2002	**Great Britain**, Switzerland, Canada
2006	**Canada**, Finland, United States	2006	**Sweden**, Switzerland, Canada

FIGURE SKATING

MEN

Multiple gold medals: Gillis Grafström (3); Dick Button and Karl Schäfer (2).

Year		Year		Year	
1908	Ulrich Salchow ....SWE	1952	Dick Button ....USA	1984	Scott Hamilton ....USA
1912	Not held	1956	Hayes Alan Jenkins ......USA	1988	Brian Boitano ....USA
1920	Gillis Grafström ......SWE	1960	David Jenkins ....USA	1992	Victor Petrenko ....UT
1924	Gillis Grafström ......SWE	1964	Manfred Schnelldorfer ....GER	1994	Alexei Urmanov ....RUS
1928	Gillis Grafström ......SWE	1968	Wolfgang Schwarz ......AUT	1998	Ilia Kulik ....RUS
1932	Karl Schäfer ....AUT	1972	Ondrej Nepela ....CZE	2002	Alexei Yagudin ....RUS
1936	Karl Schäfer ....AUT	1976	John Curry ....GBR	2006	Yevgeny Plushenko ....RUS
1948	Dick Button ....USA	1980	Robin Cousins ....GBR		

WOMEN

Multiple gold medals: Sonja Henie (3); Katarina Witt (2).

Year		Year		Year	
1908	Madge Syers ....GBR	1952	Jeanette Altwegg ....GBR	1984	Katarina Witt ....E. Ger
1912	Not held	1956	Tenley Albright ....USA	1988	Katarina Witt ....E. Ger
1920	Magda Julin-Mauroy ....SWE	1960	Carol Heiss ....USA	1992	Kristi Yamaguchi ....USA
1924	Herma Planck-Szabö .....AUT	1964	Sjoukje Dijkstra ....NED	1994	Oksana Baiul ....UKR
1928	Sonja Henie ....NOR	1968	Peggy Fleming ....USA	1998	Tara Lipinski ....USA
1932	Sonja Henie ....NOR	1972	Beatrix Schuba ....AUT	2002	Sarah Hughes ....USA
1936	Sonja Henie ....NOR	1976	Dorothy Hamill ....USA	2006	Shizuka Arakawa ....JPN
1948	Barbara Ann Scott ......CAN	1980	Anett Poetzsch ....E. Ger		

Pairs

Multiple gold medals: MEN–Pierre Brunet, Artur Dmitriev, Sergei Grinkov, Oleg Protopopov and Aleksandr Zaitsev (2). WOMEN–Irina Rodnina (3); Ludmila Belousova, Ekaterina Gordeeva and Andree Joly Brunet (2).

Year			Year		
1908	Anna Hübler & Heinrich Burger	Germany	1968	Ludmila Belousova & Oleg Protopopov ......USSR	
1912	Not held		1972	Irina Rodnina & Aleksei Ulanov ....USSR	
1920	Ludovika & Walter Jakobsson ....Finland		1976	Irina Rodnina & Aleksandr Zaitsev ....USSR	
1924	Helene Engelmann & Alfred Berger ....Austria		1980	Irina Rodnina & Aleksandr Zaitsev ....USSR	
1928	Andrée Joly & Pierre Brunet ....France		1984	Elena Valova & Oleg Vasiliev ....USSR	
1932	Andrée & Pierre Brunet ....France		1988	Ekaterina Gordeeva & Sergei Grinkov .....USSR	
1936	Maxi Herber & Ernst Baier ....Germany		1992	Natalia Mishkutienok & Arthur Dmitriev ......UT	
1948	Micheline Lannoy & Pierre Baugniet .....Belgium		1994	Ekaterina Gordeeva & Sergei Grinkov ......RUS	
1952	Ria & Paul Falk ....Germany		1998	Oksana Kazakova & Artur Dmitriev ....RUS	
1956	Elisabeth Schwartz & Kurt Oppelt ....Austria		2002	Elena Berezhnaya & Anton Sikharulidze ......RUS	
1960	Barbara Wagner & Robert Paul ....Canada			Jamie Sale & David Pelletier* ....CAN	
1964	Ludmila Belousova & Oleg Protopopov ....USSR		2006	Tatyana Totmiyanina & Maxim Marinin ......RUS	

*Originally awarded silver medals, Sale & Pelletier later had them upgraded to gold after an investigation by the International Olympic Committee and the International Skating Union concluded that a judge was guilty of misconduct.

Ice Dancing

Multiple gold medals: Oksana Grishuk & Yevgeny Platov (2).

Year		Year		
1976	Lyudmila Pakhomova & Aleksandr Gorshkov ..USSR	1994	Oksana Grishuk & Yevgeny Platov ....RUS	
1980	Natalia Linichuk & Gennady Karponosov ...USSR	1998	Oksana Grishuk & Yevgeny Platov ....RUS	
1984	Jayne Torvill & Christopher Dean .....Great Britain	2002	Marina Anissina & Gwendal Peizerat ....FRA	
1988	Natalia Bestemianova & Andrei Bukin ......USSR	2006	Tatyana Navka & Roman Kostomarov ....RUS	
1992	Marina Klimova & Sergei Ponomarenko ....UT			

FREESTYLE SKIING

MEN

Aerials

Year		Points
1994	Andreas Schoebaechler, SWI	234.67
1998	Eric Bergoust, USA	255.64
2002	Ales Valenta, CZR	257.02
2006	Xiaopeng Han, CHN	250.77

Moguls

Year		Points
1994	Jean-Luc Brassard, CAN	27.24
1998	Jonny Moseley, USA	26.93
2002	Janne Lahtela, FIN	27.97
2006	Dale Begg-Smith, AUS	26.77

WOMEN

Aerials

Year		Points
1994	Lina Cherjazova, UZB	166.84
1998	Nikki Stone, USA	193.00
2002	Alisa Camplin, AUS	193.47
2006	Evelyne Leu, SWI	202.55

Moguls

Year		Points
1994	Stine Lise Hattestad, NOR	25.97
1998	Tae Satoya, JPN	25.06
2002	Kari Traa, NOR	25.94
2006	Jennifer Heil, CAN	26.50

ICE HOCKEY

MEN

Multiple gold medals: Soviet Union/Unified Team (8); Canada (7); Sweden and United States (2).

Year	
1920	**Canada**, United States Czechoslovakia
1924	**Canada**, United States, Great Britain
1928	**Canada**, Sweden, Switzerland
1932	**Canada**, United States, Germany
1936	**Great Britain**, Canada, United States
1948	**Canada**, Czechoslovakia, Switzerland
1952	**Canada**, United States, Sweden
1956	**Soviet Union**, United States, Canada
1960	**United States**, Canada, Soviet Union
1964	**Soviet Union**, Sweden, Czechoslovakia
1968	**Soviet Union**, Czechoslovakia, Canada
1972	**Soviet Union**, United States, Czechoslovakia
1976	**Soviet Union**, Czechoslovakia, West Germany
1980	**United States**, Soviet Union, Sweden
1984	**Soviet Union**, Czechoslovakia, Sweden
1988	**Soviet Union**, Finland, Sweden
1992	**Unified Team**, Canada, Czechoslovakia
1994	**Sweden**, Canada, Finland
1998	**Czech Republic**, Russia, Finland
2002	**Canada**, United States, Russia
2006	**Sweden**, Finland, Czech Republic

WOMEN

Year	
1998	**United States**, Canada, Finland
2002	**Canada**, United States, Sweden
2006	**Canada**, Sweden, United States

U.S. Gold Medal Hockey Teams

MEN

1960

Forwards: Billy Christian, Roger Christian, Billy Cleary, Gene Grazia, Paul Johnson, Bob McVey, Dick Meredith, Weldy Olson, Dick Rodenheiser and Tom Williams. **Defensemen:** Bob Cleary, Jack Kirrane (captain), John Mayasich, Bob Owen and Rod Paavola. **Goaltenders:** Jack McCartan and Larry Palmer. **Coach:** Jack Riley.

1980

Forwards: Neal Broten, Steve Christoff, Mike Eruzione (captain), John Harrington, Mark Johnson, Rob McClanahan, Mark Pavelich, Buzz Schneider, Dave Silk, Eric Strobel, Phil Verchota and Mark Wells. **Defensemen:** Bill Baker, Dave Christian, Ken Morrow, Jack O'Callahan, Mike Ramsey and Bob Suter. **Goaltenders:** Jim Craig and Steve Janaszak. **Coach:** Herb Brooks.

WOMEN

1998

Forwards: Laurie Baker, Alana Blahoski, Lisa Brown-Miller, Karen Bye, Tricia Dunn, Cammi Granato, Katie King, Shelley Looney, A.J. Mleczko, Jenny Schmidgall, Gretchen Ulion, Sandra Whyte. **Defensemen:** Chris Bailey, Colleen Coyne, Sue Mertz, Tara Mounsey, Vicki Movessian, Angela Ruggiero. **Goaltenders:** Sarah DeCosta and Sarah Tueting. **Coach:** Ben Smith.

LUGE
MEN

Multiple gold medals: (including doubles): Georg Hackl (3); Jan Behrendt, Norbert Hahn, Paul Hildgartner, Thomas Köhler, Stefan Krausse, Hans Rinn and Armin Zoeggeler (2).

Singles

Year		Time	Year		Time
1964	Thomas Köhler, GER	3:26.77	1988	Jens Müller, E. Ger	3:05.548
1968	Manfred Schmid, AUT	2:52.48	1992	Georg Hackl, GER	3:02.363
1972	Wolfgang Scheidel, E. Ger	3:27.58	1994	Georg Hackl, GER	3:21.571
1976	Dettlef Günther, E. Ger	3:27.688	1998	Georg Hackl, GER	3:18.436
1980	Bernhard Glass, E. Ger	2:54.796	2002	Armin Zoeggeler, ITA	2:57.941
1984	Paul Hildgartner, ITA	3:04.258	2006	Armin Zoeggeler, ITA	3:26.088

Doubles

Year		Time	Year		Time
1964	Josef Feistmantl & Manfred Stengl, AUT	1:41.62	1988	Joerg Hoffmann & Jochen Pietzsch, E. Ger.	1:31.940
1968	Klaus Bonsack & Thomas Köhler, E. Ger.	1:35.85	1992	Jan Behrendt & Stefan Krausse, GER	1:32.053
1972	(TIE) Paul Hildgartner/Walter Plaikner, ITA	1:28.35	1994	Kurt Brugger & Wilfred Huber, ITA	1:36.720
	& Richard Bredow/Horst Hornlein, E. Ger.	1:28.35	1998	Jan Behrendt & Stefan Krausse, GER	1:41.105
1976	Norbert Hahn & Hans Rinn, E. Ger.	1:25.604	2002	Patric-Fritz Leitner & Alexander Resch, GER	1:26.082
1980	Norbert Hahn & Hans Rinn, E. Ger.	1:19.331	2006	Andreas Linger & Wolfgang Linger, AUT	1:34.497
1984	Hans Stangassinger & Franz Wembacher, W. Ger.	1:23.620			

WOMEN

Multiple gold medals: Sylke Otto and Steffi Martin Walter (2).

Singles

Year		Time	Year		Time
1964	Ortrun Enderlein, GER	3:24.67	1988	Steffi Martin Walter, E. Ger	3:03.973
1968	Erica Lechner, ITA	2:28.66	1992	Doris Neuner, AUT	3:06.696
1972	Anna-Maria Müller, E. Ger	2:59.18	1994	Gerda Weissensteiner, ITA	3:15.517
1976	Margit Schumann, E. Ger	2:50.621	1998	Silke Kraushaar, GER	3:23.779
1980	Vera Zozulya, USSR	2:36.537	2002	Sylke Otto, GER	2:52.464
1984	Steffi Martin, E. Ger	2:46.570	2006	Sylke Otto, GER	3:07.979

NORDIC COMBINED

Ski jumping followed by a cross country race. Judges stopped converting cross country times into points after the 1994 Games. The times listed are final cross country times adjusted to include the competitors' staggered start time. The staggered start is determined by the Gundersen Method, which is a table that converts final ski jumping point differentials into time intervals.

Multiple gold medals: Samppa Lajunen and Ulrich Wehling (3); Bjarte Engen Vik, Felix Gottwald, Johan Gröttumsbråten, Fred Boerre Lundberg, Takanori Kono and Kenji Ogiwara (2).

Individual

Year		Points	Year		Points
1924	Thorleif Haug, NOR	18.906	1976	Ulrich Wehling, E. Ger	423.39
1928	Johan Gröttumsbråten, NOR	17.833	1980	Ulrich Wehling, E. Ger	432.200
1932	Johan Gröttumsbråten, NOR	446.00	1984	Tom Sandberg, NOR	422.595
1936	Oddbjörn Hagen, NOR	430.3	1988	Hippolyt Kempf, SWI	432.230
1948	Heikki Hasu, FIN	448.80	1992	Fabrice Guy, FRA	426.470
1952	Simon Slattvik, NOR	451.621	1994	Fred Boerre Lundberg, NOR	457.970
1956	Sverre Stenersen, NOR	455.000			**Time**
1960	Georg Thoma, GER	457.952	1998	Bjarte Engen Vik, NOR	41:21.1
1964	Tormod Knutsen, NOR	469.28	2002	Samppa Lajunen, FIN	39:11.7
1968	Franz Keller, W. Ger	449.04	2006	Georg Hettich, GER	39:44.6
1972	Ulrich Wehling, E. Ger	413.340			

Sprint
New event in 2002.

Year		Time	Year		Time
2002	Samppa Lajunen, FIN	16:40.1	2006	Felix Gottwald, AUT	18:29.0

Team

Year		Points			Time
1988	West Germany	792.08	1998	Norway	54:11.5
1992	Japan	1247.180	2002	Finland	48:42.2
1994	Japan	1368.860	2006	Austria	49:52.6

SKELETON

MEN
Singles

Year		Time
1928	Jennison Heaton, USA	3:01.8
1932-36	Not held	
1948	Nino Bibbia, ITA	5:23.2
1952-98	Not held	
2002	Jim Shea, USA	1:41.96
2006	Duff Gibson, CAN	1:55.88

WOMEN
Singles

Year		Time
2002	Tristan Gale, USA	1:45.11
2006	Maya Pedersen, SWI	1:59.83

Note: This event was called Cresta when it was held in 1928 and 1948.

SKI JUMPING

Multiple gold medals (including team jumping): Matti Nykänen (4); Jens Weissflog (3); Simon Ammann, Birger Ruud, Thomas Morgenstern and Toni Nieminen (2).

Normal Hill (90 Meters)

Year		Points
1924-60	Not held	
1964	Veikko Kankkonen, FIN	229.9
1968	Jiri Raska, CZE	216.5
1972	Yukio Kasaya, JPN	244.2
1976	Hans-Georg Aschenbach, E. Ger	252.0
1980	Anton Innauer, AUT	266.3
1984	Jens Weissflog, E. Ger	215.2
1988	Matti Nykänen, FIN	229.1
1992	Ernst Vettori, AUT	222.8
1994	Espen Bredesen, NOR	282.0
1998	Jani Soininen, FIN	234.5
2002	Simon Ammann, SWI	269.0
2006	Lars Bystoel, NOR	266.5

Note: Jump held at 70 meters from 1964-92.

Large Hill (120 Meters)

Year		Points
1924	Jacob Tullin Thams, NOR	18.960
1928	Alf Andersen, NOR	19.208
1932	Birger Ruud, NOR	228.1
1936	Birger Ruud, NOR	232.0
1948	Petter Hugsted, NOR	228.1
1952	Arnfinn Bergmann, NOR	226.0
1956	Antti Hyvärinen, FIN	227.0
1960	Helmut Recknagel, GER	227.2
1964	Toralf Engan, NOR	230.7
1968	Vladimir Beloussov, USSR	231.3
1972	Wojciech Fortuna, POL	219.9
1976	Karl Schäabl, AUT	234.8
1980	Jouko Törmänen, FIN	271.0
1984	Matti Nykänen, FIN	231.2
1988	Matti Nykänen, FIN	224.0
1992	Toni Nieminen, FIN	239.5
1994	Jens Weissflog, GER	274.5
1998	Kazuyoshi Funaki, JPN	272.3
2002	Simon Ammann, SWI	281.4
2006	Thomas Morgenstern, AUT	276.9

Note: Jump held at various lengths from 1924-56; at 80 meters from 1960-64; and at 90 meters from 1968-88.

Team (Large Hill)

Year		Points
1988	Finland	634.4
1992	Finland	644.4
1994	Germany	970.1
1998	Japan	933.0
2002	Germany	974.1
2006	Austria	984.0

Skicross In for 2010 Games

Men's and Women's **Skicross** will be the only new event to make its debut at the 2010 Winter Games in Vancouver, Canada. Women's ski jumping, which was thought to have a decent chance at inclusion, was passed over.

The Vancouver skicross events will feature 32 men and 16 women competing in the same format as the snowboard version, where multiple skiers race down a winding, banked course side-by-side. The two gold medals will bring the total of medal events in Vancouver to 86.

Ski jumping, and by extension nordic combined, remain the only Winter Olympic sports that do not have events for women. The IOC also denied a proposed team event in Alpine skiing, mixed relay in biathlon, team competitions in bobsled and skeleton, a team luge competition and mixed doubles in curling. In other Winter Olympic news from 2007, **Sochi, Russia** was named the host city for the 2014 Games. Sochi beat out competing bids from Salzburg, Austria and PyeongChang, South Korea.

SNOWBOARDING

Multiple gold medals: Philipp Schoch (2).

MEN

Halfpipe

Year		Points
1998	Gian Simmen, SWI	.85.2
2002	Ross Powers, USA	.46.1
2006	Shaun White, USA	.46.8

Giant Slalom

Discontinued after 1998, replaced by Parallel Giant Slalom.

Year		Time
1998	Ross Rebagliati, CAN	.2:03.96

Parallel Giant Slalom

Year		
2002	Philipp Schoch	.SWI
2006	Philipp Schoch	.SWI

Snowboard Cross

Added in 2006.

Year		
2006	Seth Wescott	.USA

WOMEN

Halfpipe

Year		Points
1998	Nicola Thost, GER	.74.6
2002	Kelly Clark, USA	.47.9
2006	Hannah Teter, USA	.46.4

Giant Slalom

Discontinued after 1998, replaced by Parallel Giant Slalom.

Year		Time
1998	Karine Ruby, FRA	.2:17.34

Parallel Giant Slalom

Year		
2002	Isabelle Blanc	.FRA
2006	Daniela Meuli	.SWI

Snowboard Cross

Added in 2006.

Year		
2006	Tanja Frieden	.SWI

SPEED SKATING

MEN

Multiple gold medals: Eric Heiden and Clas Thunberg (5); Ivar Ballangrud, Yevgeny Grishin and Johann Olav Koss (4); Hjalmar Andersen, Tomas Gustafson, Irving Jaffee and Ard Schenk (3); Gaétan Boucher, Enrico Fabris, Knut Johannesen, Erhard Keller, Uwe-Jens Mey, Gianni Romme, Jack Shea and Jochem Uytdehaage (2). Note that Thunberg's total includes the All-Around, which was contested for the only time in 1924.

500 meters

Year		Time		Year		Time	
1924	Charles Jewtraw, USA	.44.0		1972	Erhard Keller, W. Ger	.39.44	OR
1928	(TIE) Bernt Evensen, NOR	.43.4	OR	1976	Yevgeny Kulikov, USSR	.39.17	OR
	& Clas Thunberg, FIN	.43.4	OR	1980	Eric Heiden, USA	.38.03	OR
1932	Jack Shea, USA	.43.4	=OR	1984	Sergei Fokichev, USSR	.38.19	
1936	Ivar Ballangrud, NOR	.43.4	OR	1988	Uwe-Jens Mey, E. Ger	.36.45	WR
1948	Finn Helgesen, NOR	.43.1	OR	1992	Uwe-Jens Mey, GER	.37.14	
1952	Ken Henry, USA	.43.2		1994	Aleksandr Golubev, RUS	.36.33	OR
1956	Yevgeny Grishin, USSR	.40.2	=WR	1998	Hiroyashu Shimizu, JPN	.71.35*	OR
1960	Yevgeny Grishin, USSR	.40.2	=WR	2002	Casey FitzRandolph, USA	.69.23	OR
1964	Terry McDermott, USA	.40.1	OR	2006	Joey Cheek, USA	.69.76	
1968	Erhard Keller, W. Ger	.40.3					

*The two-race final was introduced; skater with the lowest combined time wins gold.

1000 meters

Year		Time		Year		Time	
1924-72 Not held				1992	Olaf Zinke, GER	.1:14.85	
1976	Peter Mueller, USA	.1:19.32		1994	Dan Jansen, USA	.1:12.43	WR
1980	Eric Heiden, USA	.1:15.18	OR	1998	Ids Postma, NED	.1:10.64	OR
1984	Gaétan Boucher, CAN	.1:15.80		2002	Gerard van Velde, NED	.1:07.18	WR
1988	Nikolai Gulyaev, USSR	.1:13.03	OR	2006	Shani Davis, USA	.1:08.89	

1500 meters

Year		Time		Year		Time	
1924	Clas Thunberg, FIN	.2:20.8		1968	Kees Verkerk, NED	.2:03.4	OR
1928	Clas Thunberg, FIN	.2:21.1		1972	Ard Schenk, NED	.2:02.96	OR
1932	Jack Shea, USA	.2:57.5		1976	Jan Egil Storholt, NOR	.1:59.38	OR
1936	Charles Mathisen, NOR	.2:19.2	OR	1980	Eric Heiden, USA	.1:55.44	OR
1948	Sverre Farstad, NOR	.2:17.6	OR	1984	Gaétan Boucher, CAN	.1:58.36	
1952	Hjalmar Andersen, NOR	.2:20.4		1988	Andre Hoffman, E. Ger	.1:52.06	WR
1956	(TIE) Yevgeny Grishin, USSR	.2:08.6	WR	1992	Johann Olav Koss, NOR	.1:54.81	
	& Yuri Mikhailov, USSR	.2:08.6	WR	1994	Johann Olav Koss, NOR	.1:51.29	WR
1960	(TIE) Roald Aas, NOR	.2:10.4		1998	Aadne Sondral, NOR	.1:47.87	WR
	& Yevgeny Grishin, USSR	.2:10.4		2002	Derek Parra, USA	.1:43.95	WR
1964	Ants Antson, USSR	.2:10.3		2006	Enrico Fabris, ITA	.1:45.97	

5000 meters

Year		Time			Year		Time	
1924	Clas Thunberg, FIN	8:39.0			1972	Ard Schenk, NED	7:23.61	
1928	Ivar Ballangrud, NOR	8:50.5			1976	Sten Stensen, NOR	7:24.48	
1932	Irving Jaffee, USA	9:40.8			1980	Eric Heiden, USA	7:02.29	OR
1936	Ivar Ballangrud, NOR	8:19.6	OR		1984	Tomas Gustafson, SWE	7:12.28	
1948	Reidar Liaklev, NOR	8:29.4			1988	Tomas Gustafson, SWE	6:44.63	WR
1952	Hjalmar Andersen, NOR	8:10.6	OR		1992	Geir Karlstad, NOR	6:59.97	
1956	Boris Shilkov, USSR	7:48.7	OR		1994	Johann Olav Koss, NOR	6:34.96	WR
1960	Viktor Kosichkin, USSR	7:51.3			1998	Gianni Romme, NED	6:22.20	WR
1964	Knut Johannesen, NOR	7:38.4	OR		2002	Jochem Uytdehaage, NED	6:14.66	WR
1968	Fred Anton Maier, NOR	7:22.4	WR		2006	Chad Hedrick, USA	6:14.68	

10,000 meters

Year		Time			Year		Time	
1924	Julius Skutnabb, FIN	18:04.8			1972	Ard Schenk, NED	15:01.35	OR
1928	Irving Jaffee, USA*	18:36.5			1976	Piet Kleine, NED	14:50.59	OR
1932	Irving Jaffee, USA	19:13.6			1980	Eric Heiden, USA	14:28.13	WR
1936	Ivar Ballangrud, NOR	17:24.3	OR		1984	Igor Malkov, USSR	14:39.90	
1948	Ake Seyffarth, SWE	17:26.3			1988	Tomas Gustafson, SWE	13:48.20	WR
1952	Hjalmar Andersen, NOR	16:45.8	OR		1992	Bart Veldkamp, NED	14:12.12	
1956	Sigvard Ericsson, SWE	16:35.9	OR		1994	Johann Olav Koss, NOR	13:30.55	WR
1960	Knut Johannesen, NOR	15:46.6	WR		1998	Gianni Romme, NED	13:15.33	WR
1964	Jonny Nilsson, SWE	15:50.1			2002	Jochem Uytdehaage, NED	12:58.92	WR
1968	Johnny Höglin, SWE	15:23.6	OR		2006	Bob De Jong, NED	13:01.57	

*Unofficial, according to the IOC. Jaffee recorded the fastest time, but the event was called off in progress due to thawing ice.

Team Pursuit
Added in 2006.

Year	
2006	**Italy**, Canada, Netherlands

WOMEN

Multiple gold medals: Lydia Skoblikova (6); Bonnie Blair (5); Claudia Pechstein (4); Karin Enke, Gunda Niemann-Stirnemann and Yvonne van Gennip (3); Tatiana Averina, Catriona Lemay-Doan, Christa Rothenburger and Marianne Timmer (2).

500 meters

Year		Time			Year		Time	
1960	Helga Haase, GER	45.9			1988	Bonnie Blair, USA	39.10	WR
1964	Lydia Skoblikova, USSR	45.0	OR		1992	Bonnie Blair, USA	40.33	
1968	Lyudmila Titova, USSR	46.1			1994	Bonnie Blair, USA	39.25	
1972	Anne Henning, USA	43.33	OR		1998	Catriona Lemay-Doan, CAN	76.60*	OR
1976	Sheila Young, USA	42.76	OR		2002	Catriona Lemay-Doan, CAN	74.75	OR
1980	Karin Enke, E. Ger	41.78	OR		2006	Svetlana Zhurova, RUS	76.57	
1984	Christa Rothenburger, E. Ger	41.02	OR					

*The two-race final was introduced; skater with the lowest combined time wins gold.

1000 meters

Year		Time			Year		Time	
1960	Klara Guseva, USSR	1:34.1			1988	Christa Rothenburger, E. Ger	1:17.65	WR
1964	Lydia Skoblikova, USSR	1:33.2	OR		1992	Bonnie Blair, USA	1:21.90	
1968	Carolina Geijssen, NED	1:32.6	OR		1994	Bonnie Blair, USA	1:18.74	
1972	Monika Pflug, W. Ger	1:31.40	OR		1998	Marianne Timmer, NED	1:16.51	OR
1976	Tatiana Averina, USSR	1:28.43	OR		2002	Chris Witty, USA	1:13.83	WR
1980	Natalia Petruseva, USSR	1:24.10	OR		2006	Marianne Timmer, NED	1:16.05	
1984	Karin Enke, E. Ger	1:21.61	OR					

1500 meters

Year		Time			Year		Time	
1960	Lydia Skoblikova, USSR	2:25.2	WR		1988	Yvonne van Gennip, NED	2:00.68	OR
1964	Lydia Skoblikova, USSR	2:22.6	OR		1992	Jacqueline Börner, GER	2:05.87	
1968	Kaija Mustonen, FIN	2:22.4	OR		1994	Emese Hunyady, AUT	2:02.19	
1972	Dianne Holum, USA	2:20.85	OR		1998	Marianne Timmer, NED	1:57.58	WR
1976	Galina Stepanskaya, USSR	2:16.58	OR		2002	Anni Friesinger, GER	1:54.02	WR
1980	Annie Borckink, NED	2:10.95	OR		2006	Cindy Klassen, CAN	1:55.27	
1984	Karin Enke, E. Ger	2:03.42	WR					

Speed Skating (Cont.)

3000 meters

Year		Time		Year		Time	
1960	Lydia Skoblikova, USSR	5:14.3		1988	Yvonne van Gennip, NED	4:11.94	WR
1964	Lydia Skoblikova, USSR	5:14.9		1992	Gunda Niemann, GER	4:19.90	
1968	Johanna Schut, NED	4:56.2	OR	1994	Svetlana Bazhanova, RUS	4:17.43	
1972	Christina Baas-Kaiser, NED	4:52.14	OR	1998	Gunda Niemann-Stirnemann, GER	4:07.29	OR
1976	Tatiana Averina, USSR	4:45.19	OR	2002	Claudia Pechstein, GER	3:57.70	WR
1980	Bjorg Eva Jensen, NOR	4:32.13	OR	2006	Ireen Wust, NED	4:02.43	
1984	Andrea Schöne, E. Ger	4:24.79	OR				

5000 meters

Year		Time		Year		Time	
1960-84 Not held				1998	Claudia Pechstein, GER	6:59.61	WR
1988	Yvonne van Gennip, NED	7:14.13	WR	2002	Claudia Pechstein, GER	6:46.91	WR
1992	Gunda Niemann, GER	7:31.57		2006	Clara Hughes, CAN	6:59.07	
1994	Claudia Pechstein, GER	7:14.37					

Team Pursuit
Added in 2006.

Year	
2006	**Germany**, Canada, Russia

SHORT TRACK SPEED SKATING

MEN
Multiple gold medals (including relays): Hyun-Soo Ahn, Marc Gagnon and Kim Ki-Hoon (3); Apolo Anton Ohno (2).

WOMEN
Multiple gold medals (including relays): Chun Lee-Kyung (4); Sun-Yu Jin (3); Kim Yun-Mi, Annie Perrault, Cathy Turner, Won Hye-Kyung and Yang Yang (A) (2)

500 meters
added in 1994.

Year		Time	
1994	Chae Ji-Hoon, S. Kor.	43.45	
1998	Takafumi Nishitani, JPN	42.862	
2002	Marc Gagnon, CAN	41.802	OR
2006	Apolo Anton Ohno, USA	41.935	

500 meters

Year		Time	
1992	Cathy Turner, USA	47.04	
1994	Cathy Turner, USA	45.98	OR
1998	Annie Perrault, CAN	46.568	
2002	Yang Yang (A), CHN	44.187	
2006	Meng Wang, CHN	44.345	

1000 meters

Year		Time	
1992	Kim Ki-Hoon, S. Kor.	1:30.76	WR
1994	Kim Ki-Hoon, S. Kor.	1:34.57	
1998	Kim Dong-Sung, S. Kor.	1:32.375	
2002	Steven Bradbury, AUS	1:29.109	
2006	Hyun-Soo Ahn, S. Kor.	1:26.739	

1000 meters
added in 1994.

Year		Time
1994	Chun Lee-Kyung, S. Kor.	1:36.87
1998	Chun Lee-Kyung, S. Kor.	1:42.776
2002	Yang Yang (A), CHN	1:36.391
2006	Sun-Yu Jin, S. Kor.	1:32.859

1500 meters
added in 2002.

Year		Time
2002	Apolo Anton Ohno, USA*	2:18.541
2006	Hyun-Soo Ahn, S. Kor.	2:25.341

*Ohno finished second to South Korea's Kim Dong-Sung, who was disqualifed for cross-tracking.

1500 meters
added in 2002.

Year		Time
2002	Ko Gi-Hyun, S. Kor.	2:31.581
2006	Sun-Yu Jin, S. Kor.	2:23.494

5000-m Relay

Year		Time	
1992	South Korea	7:14.02	WR
1994	Italy	7:11.74	OR
1998	Canada	7:06.075	
2002	Canada	6:51.579	
2006	South Korea	6:43.376	

3000-m Relay

Year		Time	
1992	Canada	4:36.62	
1994	South Korea	4:26.64	WR
1998	South Korea	4:16.260	WR
2002	South Korea	4:12.793	WR
2006	South Korea	4:17.040	

All-Time Leading Medal Winners

MEN

No		Sport	G-S-B
12	Bjorn Dählie, NOR . . . . .Cross Country		8-4-0
9	Sixten Jernberg, SWE . . . . . .Cross Country		4-3-2
8	Kjetil Andre Aamodt, NOR . . . . .Alpine		4-2-2
7	Clas Thunberg, FIN . . . . .Speed Skating		5-1-1
7	Ivar Ballangrud, NOR . . . . . .Speed Skating		4-2-1
7	Ricco Gross, GER . . . . .Biathlon		3-3-1
7	Veikko Hakulinen, FIN . . . . . .Cross Country		3-3-1
7	Eero Mäntyranta, FIN . . . . . .Cross Country		3-2-2
7	Bogdan Musiol, E. Ger/GER . . . . . .Bobsled		1-5-1
6	Ole Einar Bjoerndalen, NOR . . . . . .Biathlon		5-1-0
6	Thomas Alsgaard, NOR . . . . . .Cross Country		4-2-0
6	Gunde Svan, SWE . . . . .Cross Country		4-1-1
6	Vegard Ulvang, NOR . . . . . . .Cross Country		3-2-1
6	Johan Gröttumsbräten, NOR . . . . . . .Nordic		3-1-2
6	Wolfgang Hoppe, E. Ger/GER . . . . .Bobsled		2-3-1
6	Eugenio Monti, ITA . . . . .Bobsled		2-2-2
6	Felix Gottwald, AUT . . . . .Nordic		2-1-3
6	Vladimir Smirnov, USSR/UT/KAZ . . .X-country		1-4-1
6	Mika Myllylae, FIN . . . . .Cross Country		1-1-4
6	Roald Larsen, NOR . . . . .Speed Skating		0-2-4
6	Harri Kirvesniemi, FIN . . . . . .Cross Country		0-0-6
5	**Eric Heiden, USA** . . . . .Speed Skating		5-0-0
5	Yevgeny Grishin, USSR . . . . .Speed Skating		4-1-0
5	Johann Olav Koss, NOR . . . . .Speed Skating		4-1-0
5	Matti Nykänen, FIN . . . . .Ski Jumping		4-1-0
5	Aleksandr Tikhonov, USSR . . . . .Biathlon		4-1-0
5	Nikolai Zimyatov, USSR . . . . . .Cross Country		4-1-0
5	Georg Hackl, GER . . . . .Luge		3-2-0
5	Samppa Lajunen, FIN . . . . . .Cross Country		3-2-0
5	Alberto Tomba, ITA . . . . .Alpine		3-2-0
5	Marc Gagnon, CAN . . . . .ST Sp. Skating		3-0-2
5	Harald Grönningen, NOR . . . .Cross Country		2-3-0
5	Frank Luck, GER . . . . .Biathlon		2-3-0
5	Päl Tyldum, NOR . . . . .Cross Country		2-3-0
5	Sven Fischer, GER . . . . .Biathlon		2-2-1
5	Knut Johannesen, NOR . . . . .Speed Skating		2-2-1
5	Lasse Kjus, NOR . . . . .Alpine		1-3-1
5	Peter Angerer, W. Ger/GER . . . . . . .Biathlon		1-2-2
5	Juha Mieto, FIN . . . . .Cross Country		1-2-2
5	Fritz Feierabend, SWI . . . . .Bobsled		0-3-2
5	Rintje Ritsma, NED . . . . .Speed Skating		0-2-3

WOMEN

No		Sport	G-S-B
10	Raisa Smetanina, USSR/UT . . . .Cross Country		4-5-1
9	Lyubov Egorova, UT/RUS . . . . .Cross Country		6-3-0
9	Larissa Lazutina, UT/RUS . . . . .Cross Country		5-3-1
9	Stefania Belmondo, ITA . . . . . .Cross Country		2-3-4
8	Galina Kulakova, USSR . . . . .Cross Country		4-2-2
8	Karin (Enke) Kania, E. Ger . . . .Speed Skating		3-4-1
8	Gunda Neimann- Stirnemann, GER . . . . .Speed Skating		3-4-1
8	Ursula Disl, GER . . . . .Biathlon		2-4-2
7	Claudia Pechstein, GER . . . . . .Speed Skating		4-1-2
7	Marja-Liisa (Hämäläinen) Kirvesniemi, FIN . . . . .Cross Country		3-0-4
7	Elena Valbe, UT/RUS . . . . . . .Cross Country		3-0-4
7	Andrea (Mitscherlich, Schöne) Ehrig, E. Ger . . . . .Speed Skating		1-5-1
6	Lydia Skoblikova, USSR . . . . . .Speed Skating		6-0-0
6	**Bonnie Blair, USA** . . . . .Speed Skating		5-0-1
6	Janica Kostelic, CRO . . . . .Alpine		4-2-0
6	Manuela Di Centa, ITA . . . . . .Cross Country		2-2-2
6	Cindy Klassen, CAN . . . . .Speed Skating		1-2-3
5	Lee-Kyung Chun, S. Kor . . . . . .ST Sp. Skating		4-0-1
5	Olga Danilova, RUS . . . . .Cross Country		3-2-0
5	Antisa Reztsova, USSR/UT . . . . .CC/Biathlon		3-1-1
5	Vreni Schneider, SWI . . . . .Alpine		3-1-1
5	Katja Seizinger, GER . . . . .Alpine		3-0-2
5	Kati Wilhelm, GER . . . . .Biathlon		2-3-0
5	Helena Takalo, FIN . . . . .Cross Country		1-3-1
5	Bente (Martinsen) Skari, NOR . .Cross Country		1-2-2
5	Alevtina Kolchina, USSR . . . . . .Cross Country		1-1-3
5	Anja Paerson, SWE . . . . .Alpine		1-1-3
5	Yang Yang (S), CHN . . . . .ST Sp. Skating		0-4-1
5	Anita Moen, NOR . . . . .Cross Country		0-3-2

Games Medaled In

MEN—Aamodt (1992,94,2002,2006); **Alsgaard** (1994,98,2002); **Angerer** (1980,84,88); **Ballangrud** (1928,32,36); **Bjoerndalen** (1998,2002); **Dählie** (1992,94,98); **Feierabend** (1936,48,52); **Fischer** (1994,98,2002); **Gagnon** (1994,98,2002); **Gottwald** (2002,06); **Grishin** (1956,60,64); **Gross** (1992,94,98,2002); **Gröttumsbräten** (1924,28,32); **Grönningen** (1960,64,68); **Hackl** (1988,92,94,98,2002) **Hakulinen** (1952,56,60); **Heiden** (1980); **Hoppe** (1984,88,92,94); **Jernberg** (1956,60,64); **Johannesen** (1956,60,64); **Kirvesniemi** (1980,84,92,94,98); **Kjus** (1994,98,2002); **Koss** (1992,94); **Lajunen** (1998,2002);**Larsen** (1924,28); **Luck** (1994,98,2002); **Mäntyranta** (1960,64,68); **Mieto** (1976,80,84); **Musiol** (1980,84,88,92); **Myllylae** (1994,98); **Nykänen** (1984,88); **Ritsma** (1994,98); **Smirnov** (1988,92,94,98); **Svan** (1984,88); **Thunberg** (1924,28); **Tikhonov** (1968,72,76,80); **Tomba** (1988,92,94); **Tyldum** (1968,72,76); **Ulvang** (1988,92,94); **Zimyatov** (1980,84).

WOMEN—Belmondo (1992,94,98,2002); **Blair** (1988,92,94); **Chun** (1994,98); **Danilova** (1998,2002); **Di Centa** (1992,94); **Disl** (1992,94,98,2002); **Egorova** (1992,94); **Ehrig** (1976,80,84,88); **Kania** (1980,84,88); **Kirvesniemi** (1984,88,94); **Klassen** (2002,06); **Kolchina** (1956,64,68); **Kulakova** (1968,72,76,80); **Lazutina** (1992,94,98,2002); **Moen** (1994,98,2002); **Niemann-Stirnemann** (1992,94,98); **Paerson** (2002,06); **Pechstein** (1992,94,98,2002); **Reztsova** (1988,92,94); **Schneider** (1988,92,94); **Seizinger** (1992,94,98); **Skari** (1998,2002); **Skoblikova** (1960,64); **Smetanina** (1976,80,84,88,92); **Takalo** (1972,76,80); **Valbe** (1992,94,98); **Wilhelm** (2002,06); **Yang** (1998,2002).

All-Time Leading USA Medalists
MEN

No		Sport	G-S-B	No		Sport	G-S-B
5	Eric Heiden	Speed Skating	5-0-0	2	Terry McDermott	Speed Skating	1-1-0
5	Apolo Anton Ohno	ST Sp. Skating	2-1-2	2	Dick Meredith	Ice Hockey	1-1-0
3*	Irving Jaffee	Speed Skating	3-0-0	2	Tommy Moe	Alpine	1-1-0
3	Pat Martin	Bobsled	1-2-0	2	Weldy Olson	Ice Hockey	1-1-0
3	Joey Cheek	Speed Skating	1-1-1	2	Derek Parra	Speed Skating	1-1-0
3	Chad Hendrick	Speed Skatng	1-1-1	2	Dick Rodenheiser	Ice Hockey	1-1-0
3	John Heaton	Bobsled/Skeleton	0-2-1	2	Shani Davis	Speed Skating	1-1-0
2	Dick Button	Figure Skating	2-0-0	2	Ross Powers	Snowboarding	1-0-1
2†	Eddie Eagan	Boxing/Bobsled	2-0-0	2	Stan Benham	Bobsled	0-2-0
2	Billy Fiske	Bobsled	2-0-0	2	Herb Drury	Ice Hockey	0-2-0
2	Cliff Gray	Bobsled	2-0-0	2	Eric Flaim	Sp. Skate/ST Sp. Skate	0-2-0
2	Jack Shea	Speed Skating	2-0-0	2	Bode Miller	Alpine	0-2-0
2	Billy Cleary	Ice Hockey	1-1-0	2	Frank Synott	Ice Hockey	0-2-0
2	Jennison Heaton	Bobsled/Skeleton	1-1-0	2	Danny Kass	Snowboarding	0-2-0
2	David Jenkins	Figure Skating	1-1-0	2	John Garrison	Ice Hockey	0-1-1
2	John Mayasich	Ice Hockey	1-1-0	2	Rusty Smith	ST Sp. Skating	0-0-2

*Jaffee is generally given credit for a third gold medal in the 10,000-meter Speed Skating race of 1928. He had the fastest time before the race was cancelled due to thawing ice. The IOC considers the race unofficial.

†Eagan won the light heavyweight boxing title at the 1920 Summer Games in Antwerp and the four-man Bobsled at the 1932 Winter Games in Lake Placid. He is the only athlete ever to win gold medals in both the Winter and Summer Olympics.

WOMEN

No		Sport	G-S-B	No		Sport	G-S-B
6	Bonnie Blair	Speed Skating	5-0-1	2	Cammi Granato	Ice Hockey	1-1-0
4	Cathy Turner	ST Sp. Skating	2-1-1	2	Carol Heiss	Figure Skating	1-1-0
4	Dianne Holum	Speed Skating	1-2-1	2	Shelley Looney	Ice Hockey	1-1-0
3	Chris Witty	Speed Skating	1-1-1	2	Sue Merz	Ice Hockey	1-1-0
3	Sheila Young	Speed Skating	1-1-1	2	A.J. Mleczko	Ice Hockey	1-1-0
3	Angela Ruggiero	Ice Hockey	1-1-1	2	Tara Mounsey	Ice Hockey	1-1-0
3	Katie King	Ice Hockey	1-1-1	2	Diann Roffe-Steinrotter	Alpine	1-1-0
3	Tricia Dunn	Ice Hockey	1-1-1	2	Picabo Street	Alpine	1-1-0
3	Jenny Potter	Ice Hockey	1-1-1	2	Sarah Teuting	Ice Hockey	1-1-0
3	Leah Poulos Mueller	Speed Skating	0-3-0	2	Anne Henning	Speed Skating	1-0-1
3	Beatrix Loughran	Figure Skating	0-2-1	2	Penny Pitou	Alpine	0-2-0
3	Amy Peterson	ST Sp. Skating	0-2-1	2	Nancy Kerrigan	Figure Skating	0-1-1
2	Andrea Mead Lawrence	Alpine	2-0-0	2	Michelle Kwan	Figure Skating	0-1-1
2	Tenley Albright	Figure Skating	1-1-0	2	Jean Saubert	Alpine	0-1-1
2	Chris Bailey	Ice Hockey	1-1-0	2	Nikki Ziegelmeyer	ST Sp. Skating	0-1-1
2	Laurie Baker	Ice Hockey	1-1-0	2	Jennifer Rodriguez	Speed Skating	0-0-2
2	Karyn Bye	Ice Hockey	1-1-0				
2	Sara DeCosta	Ice Hockey	1-1-0				
2	Gretchen Fraser	Alpine	1-1-0				

Note: The term ST Sp. Skating refers to Short Track (or pack) Speed Skating.

Most Gold Medals

MEN

No		Sport	G-S-B
8	Bjorn Dählie, NOR	Cross Country	8-4-0
5	Clas Thunberg, FIN	Speed Skating	5-1-1
5	Ole Einar Bjoerndalen, NOR	Biathlon	5-1-0
5	**Eric Heiden, USA**	Speed Skating	5-0-0
4	Sixten Jernberg, SWE	Cross Country	4-3-2
4	Kjetil Andre Aamodt, NOR	Alpine	4-2-2
4	Ivar Ballangrud, NOR	Speed Skating	4-2-1
4	Thomas Alsgaard, NOR	Cross Country	4-2-0
4	Gunde Svan, SWE	Cross Country	4-1-1
4	Yevgeny Grishin, USSR	Speed Skating	4-1-0
4	Johann Olav Koss, NOR	Speed Skating	4-1-0
4	Matti Nykänen, FIN	Ski Jumping	4-1-0
4	Aleksandr Tikhonov, USSR	Biathlon	4-1-0
4	Nikolai Zimyatov, USSR	Cross Country	4-1-0
4	Thomas Wassberg, SWE	Cross Country	4-0-0

WOMEN

No		Sport	G-S-B
6	Lyubov Egorova, UT/RUS	Cross Country	6-3-0
6	Lydia Skoblikova, USSR	Speed Skating	6-0-0
5	Larissa Lanina, USSR/UT	Cross Country	4-5-1
4	Galina Kulakova, USSR	Cross Country	4-2-2
4	Janica Kostelic, CRO	Alpine	4-2-0
4	Claudia Pechstein, GER	ST Sp. Skating	4-1-2
4	Lee-Kyung Chun, S. Kor.	ST Sp. Skating	4-0-1

All-Time Medal Standings, 1924-2006

All-time Winter Games medal standings, according to *The Golden Book of the Olympic Games*. Medal counts include figure skating medals (1908 and '20) and hockey medals (1920) awarded at the Summer Games. National medal standings for the Winter and Summer Games are not recognized by the IOC.

		G	S	B	Total
1	Norway	96	102	84	282
2	**United States**	78	81	59	218
3	Soviet Union (1956-88)	78	57	59	194
4	Austria	50	64	71	185
5	Germany (1928-36, 52-64, 1992–)	58	58	38	154
6	Finland	42	57	52	151
7	Sweden	46	32	44	122
8	Canada	38	38	44	120
9	East Germany (1968-88)	43	39	36	118
10	Switzerland	37	37	43	117
11	Italy	36	31	33	100
12	France	25	24	32	81
13	Russia (1994–)	33	26	19	80
14	Netherlands	25	30	23	78
15	West Germany (1968-88)	18	20	19	57
16	China	4	16	13	33
17	Japan	9	10	13	32
18	South Korea	17	8	6	31
19	Great Britain	8	5	14	27
20	Czechoslovakia (1924-92)	2	8	16	26
21	Unified Team (1992)	9	6	8	23
22	Czech Republic (1998–)	3	3	3	9
23	Liechtenstein	2	2	5	9
24	Poland	1	3	4	8
25	Estonia	4	1	1	6
	Hungary	0	2	4	6
	Bulgaria	1	2	3	6
	Belarus (1994–)	0	3	3	6
	Australia	3	0	3	6
30	Kazakhstan (1994–)	1	2	2	5
	Belgium	1	1	3	5
	Ukraine (1994–)	1	1	3	5
33	Croatia	3	1	0	4
	Spain	3	0	1	4
	Yugoslavia (1924-88)	0	3	1	4
	Slovenia	0	0	4	4
	Slovenia (1992–)	0	0	3	3
38	Luxembourg	0	2	0	2
	North Korea	0	1	1	2
40	Uzbekistan (1994–)	1	0	0	1
	Slovakia	0	1	0	1
	Denmark	0	1	0	1
	New Zealand	0	1	0	1
	Romania	0	0	1	1
	Latvia	0	0	1	1

Combined totals	G	S	B	Total
Germany/East Germany/West Germany	119	117	93	329
USSR/Unified Team/Russia	122	89	86	297

Notes: Athletes from the USSR participated in the Winter Games from 1956-88, returned as the Unified Team in 1992 after the breakup of the Soviet Union (in 1991) and then competed for the independent republics of Belarus, Kazakhstan, Russia, Ukraine, Uzbekistan and three others in 1994. Yugoslavia divided into Croatia and Bosnia-Herzegovina in 1992, while Czechoslovakia split into Slovakia and the Czech Republic in 1993.

Germany was barred from the Olympics in 1924 and 1948 as an aggressor nation in both World Wars I and II. Divided into East and West Germany after WWII, both countries competed under one flag from 1952-64, then as separate teams from 1968-88. Germany was reunified in 1990.

SOCCER

2006 / 2007 YEAR IN REVIEW

In a bit of a surprise, USA goalkeeper **Hope Solo** was benched before the team's semifinal loss to Brazil in the Women's World Cup.

NO HOPE FOR USA

A controversial lineup change for Team USA and the ensuing turmoil made headlines, but it was Germany and Brazil that made the biggest highlights at the 2007 Women's World Cup in China.

AS CURIOUS A DECISION AS IT WAS, THE GOALKEEPER WASN'T THE PROBLEM.

Hope Solo, unless she was going to start scoring goals instead of saving them, wouldn't have made much, if any, of a difference in Team USA's 4-0 loss to Brazil in the semifinals of the Women's World Cup in China.

Coach Greg Ryan made a stunning decision to bench his undefeated starting keeper, and her 300-minute scoreless streak, in favor of veteran backup Briana Scurry.

Suddenly, it was the news of the tournament.

Scurry has an impressive resume dating back to the glory days of American soccer in the 1990s but hasn't played as much in recent years and hadn't yet appeared in the tournament.

The Samba Queens of Brazil did a dance with which the Americans were obviously not familiar. And late in the second half, the footwork was taken to a beautiful new level by Marta, Brazil's brilliant striker, when she scored one of the most spectacular goals you'll ever see.

Getting the ball on the left side of the box, she flicked it around USA defender Tina Ellertson with her left heel, spun around to the ball and shook a second defender (Cat Whitehill) way off balance and blasted it low past Scurry.

It was a goal that would have got past a Jersey barrier, let alone Hope Solo.

As beautiful as it was, Marta's goal was just a capper.

The game went wrong early when Leslie Osbourne headed a corner kick into the net for an own goal. Bad got worse just before halftime when Shannon Boxx was sent off by the referee with her second yellow card in what could be one of the worst calls in women's soccer history, forcing the USA to play short-handed for the rest of the game. Boxx, running near the

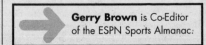

Gerry Brown is Co-Editor of the ESPN Sports Almanac.

AP/Wide World Photos

FIFA president **Sepp Blatter** presents German captain **Birgit Prinz** with the trophy at the Women's World Cup following Germany's 2-0 win over Brazil in the final.

sideline, had her heel clipped from behind by Brazil's Cristiane and they both went tumbling.

The talented Brazilians played their best game of the tournament and the Americans had no Hope.

Solo couldn't contain herself and her emotional outburst in a postgame interview made a lousy situation even worse. In the interview, she publicly criticized coach Ryan for the move (deserved), trashed a teammate (undeserved) and dismissed the team's past accomplishments (unwise).

She was shunned for the public display of rejection and was not welcomed back into the fold for the team's third-place game with Norway after Coach Ryan reportedly conferred with members of the team.

Next up for Brazil was the rock solid, unscored upon German squad in the tournament final in Shanghai. Still, as good as they looked against the U.S., many expected them to dance their way past the defending champions on their way to the trophy.

It was not to be.

Perhaps folks should have looked back a couple of weeks to the Cup opener for a clue on what was in store for Brazil.

Germany set the tone for their title defense right away with their star-

Marta's play was fierce at the 2007 Women's World Cup for the Brazilians, who beat Team USA in the semis before losing to Germany in the finals.

Birgit Prinz, whose mantle as the world's greatest female player had been taken by Marta in recent days, that scored the winning goal on a one-timer in the second half.

Late in the game Simone Laudehr scored the clincher with her head on a corner kick to make it 2-0. That score would stand.

And the Germans stand as the first Women's World Cup champs to successfully defend the title. Along the way they became the first team to go through a major competition without yielding a goal, outscoring the opposition 21-0.

The Berlin Wall still stands.

Women's soccer has come far since the first World Cup in 1991. The future looks positive for the women's game globally. Just ask FIFA president Sepp Blatter, the man who came under fire a few years ago for his sexist ideas for increasing the appeal of the women's game.

"Let the women play in more feminine clothes like they do in volleyball," said Blatter in 2004.

"They could, for example, have tighter shorts."

Blatter has moved on a bit from his fashion concerns and in 2007 he even expressed a desire to add teams to future Women's World Cups and actually expand the size of the tournament, if not the uniforms.

tling 11-0 win over Argentina.

While the final margin was dissimilar, Germany's defense was still too much for Brazil in the Cup finale.

Grand opening. Grand closing.

Marta, who defied physics against the U.S. in the semifinals, couldn't even convert a potential game-tying penalty kick when it was deflected by diving German keeper Nadine Angerer.

Furthermore it was the woman,

BECKHAM GOES TO HOLLYWOOD

This British invasion was very nearly repelled.

David Beckham's highly publicized grand tour of the United States was all but over before it began.

After joining Major League Soccer's Los Angeles Galaxy in mid-season, bringing with him from Britain a glam waif wife, a gimpy left ankle, and the dreams of an entire League, Becks limped out of the blocks.

After signing what was originally reported as a $250 million contract (in reality his salary is reportedly something just short of $10 million per season) the expectations were high.

But Beckham is now past his prime as a playmaking superstar at home among the world's top players. Still, his movie star good looks and his free kick made famous in the film "Bend it like Beckham" were what most casual fans were looking for.

Nevertheless "Mend it like Beckham" was the mantra for the American public after he played sparingly for most of the season.

"Becks" sustained an injury to his right knee on a game on Aug. 29 and only appeared in five MLS games all season for the L.A. Galaxy, failing to score a single goal in league play.

The Galaxy finished with a disappointing 9-14-7 record but stayed alive in the playoff hunt into the season's final weekend.

While his impact on the field may have been minimal during his "Coming To America" season, it was anything but at the box office where ticket sales jumped dramatically wherever the Galaxy appeared. Sellouts were the norm. Merchandise moved at an incredible rate. The Galaxy sold 250,000 Beckham jerseys, roughly $20 million worth, before they were even put on display.

The big splash that league officials hoped for rippled through the nation where, if only briefly, soccer displaced football and baseball on the front of the sports pages.

More than 30 years after Pele, another high-profile import arrived on American shores to sow the soccer seed in this country. Beckham made only a series of token appearances in his first season and has yet to really deliver on the bill of goods fans across the country were sold. He has four more years on his contract and big things are expected.

Still, the buzz was deafening.

–GB

THE BIGGEST

10 ⬇

Stories of the **Year in Soccer.**

10 UCSB takes title. Unseeded UC Santa Barbara wins the 2006 NCAA Men's College Cup with a 2-1 victory over UCLA. The Gauchos had only beaten the Bruins once in 32 previous meetings—25 years ago—but put the past behind them and erased the memory of their shootout loss to Indiana in the 2004 College Cup final.

09 Tar Heel Invitational. North Carolina and head coach Anson Dorrance take their umpteenth (actually 18th out of a possible 25) NCAA Women's College Cup title, beating Notre Dame and national player of the year Kerri Hanks, 2-1.

08 ¡Albicelestes! The White and Sky Blue of Argentina win their second straight (and sixth all-time) Under-20 World Cup, coming from behind to beat the Czech Republic in Canada.

07 Brazil! Brazil! Brazil! Sporting Club Internacional keeps Brazil three-for-three all-time at the FIFA Club World Championship with their 1-0 win over Barcelona in December 2006.

06 Chelsea has no Peer. The Blues of Chelsea beat Manchester United, 1-0, on a stoppage-time goal by Didier Drogba at the first FA Cup final at the brand new Wembley Stadium in London.

05 MLS Cup Shoot-out. The Houston Dynamo quell the New England Revolution, 4-3, on penalty kicks in the 2006 MLS Cup. After a scoreless end to regulation and the first OT, the Revs' Taylor Twellman scores in the game's 113th minute but Houston's Brian Ching matches him with a header less than a minute later sending the game to a shoot-out for the first time.

04 Solo all alone. After inexplicably getting benched at the World Cup in China, USA goalkeeper Hope Solo publicly criticizes her coach and teammate. She pays the price when her team sends her a message by dismissing her for their final match.

03 Brazil beats Team USA, 4-0, in the semifinals of the Women's World Cup. Marta puts the exclamation point on the win, scoring one of the greatest goals in World Cup history.

02 Cup Defended. Germany captures its second straight Women's World Cup, beating Brazil, 2-0. Team USA edges Norway in the third-place game.

01 Immigrant makes it big. David Beckham arrives in Los Angeles to play (a little anyway) for the MLS' L.A. Galaxy.

2006-2007
Season in Review

SPORTS ALMANAC

2007 FIFA Women's World Cup Tournament

The FIFA Women's World Cup is held every four years to determine the best women's national team in the world. In 2007 it was contested for the fifth time since its inception in 1991. Held Sept. 10-30, 2007 in China.

First Round

Round robin; each team played the other three teams in its group once. Note that three points were awarded for a win and one point for a tie. (*) indicates team advanced to second round.

Group A	W	L	T	Pts	GF	GA
*Germany	2	0	1	7	13	0
*England	1	0	2	5	8	3
Japan	1	1	1	4	3	4
Argentina	0	3	0	0	1	18

Results

Date	Site	Result
Sept. 10	Shanghai	Germany 11, Argentina 0
Sept. 11	Shanghai	Japan 2, England 2
Sept. 14	Shanghai	Japan 1, Argentina 0
Sept. 14	Shanghai	England 0, Germany 0
Sept. 17	Hangzhou	Germany 2, Japan 0
Sept. 17	Chengdu	England 6, Argentina 1

Group B	W	L	T	Pts	GF	GA
*USA	2	0	1	7	5	2
*North Korea	1	1	1	4	5	4
Sweden	1	1	1	4	3	4
Nigeria	0	2	1	1	1	4

Results

Date	Site	Result
Sept. 11	Chengdu	USA 2, North Korea 2
Sept. 11	Chengdu	Nigeria 1, Sweden 1
Sept. 14	Chengdu	USA 2, Sweden 0
Sept. 14	Chengdu	North Korea 2, Nigeria 0
Sept. 18	Shanghai	USA 1, Nigeria 0
Sept. 18	Tianjin	Sweden 2, North Korea 1

Group C	W	L	T	Pts	GF	GA
*Norway	2	0	1	7	10	4
*Australia	1	0	2	5	7	4
Canada	1	1	1	4	7	4
Ghana	0	3	0	0	3	15

Results

Date	Site	Result
Sept. 12	Hangzhou	Australia 4, Ghana 1
Sept. 12	Hangzhou	Noway 2, Canada 1
Sept. 15	Hangzhou	Canada 4, Ghana 0
Sept. 15	Hangzhou	Australia 1, Norway 1
Sept. 20	Hangzhou	Norway 7, Ghana 2
Sept. 20	Chengdu	Australia 2, Canada 2

Group D	W	L	T	Pts	GF	GA
*Brazil	3	0	0	9	10	0
*China	2	1	0	6	5	6
Denmark	1	2	0	3	4	4
New Zealand	0	3	0	0	0	9

Results

Date	Site	Result
Sept. 12	Wuhan	Brazil 5, New Zealand 0
Sept. 12	Wuhan	China 3, Denmark 2
Sept. 15	Wuhan	Denmark 2, New Zealand 0
Sept. 15	Wuhan	Brazil 4, China 0
Sept. 20	Wuhan	China 2, New Zealand 0
Sept. 20	Hangzhou	Brazil 1, Denmark 0

Quarterfinals

Date	Site	Result
Sept. 22	Wuhan	Germany 3, North Korea 0
Sept. 22	Tianjin	USA 3, England 0
Sept. 23	Wuhan	Norway 1, China 0
Sept. 23	Tianjin	Brazil 3, Australia 2

Semifinals

Date	Site	Result
Sept. 26	Tianjin	Germany 3, Norway 0
Sept. 27	Hangzhou	Brazil 4, USA 0

Third Place

Date	Site	Result
Sept. 30	Shanghai	USA 4, Norway 1

Final

Date	Site	Result
Sept. 30	Shanghai	Germany 2, Brazil 0

Goals: GER—Birgit Prinz (52'), Simone Laudehr (86').

Referee: Tammy Ogston, Australia;

Assistant Referees: Maria Isabel Tovar, Mexico; Rita Munoz, Mexico.

Attendance: 31,000

Tournament Leaders

Leading Goal Scorers	Gms	Goals
Marta, Brazil	6	7
Abby Wambach, USA	6	6
Ragnhild Gulbrandsen, Norway	6	6
Cristiane, Brazil	6	5
Birgit Prinz, Germany	6	5
Renate Lingor, Germany	6	4
Lisa De Vanna, Australia	4	4
Kelly Smith, England	4	4

Most Valuable Player Voting	Pct. of Vote
Marta, Brazil	51%
Birgit Prinz, Germany	17%
Cristiane, Brazil	10%

All-Tournament Team

GK: Nadine Angerer, Germany and Bente Nordby, Norway. **DEF:** Li Jie, China; Kerstin Stegemann, Germany; Ariane Hingst, Germany; Ane Stangeland Horpestad, Norway; **MF:** Daniela, Brazil; Formiga, Brazil; Kelly Smith, England; Renate Lingor, Germany; Ingvild Stensland, Norway; Kristine Lilly, USA; **FWD:** Lisa De Vanna, Australia; Marta, Brazil; Cristiane, Brazil; Birgit Prinz, Germany.

FIFA Top 50 World Rankings

FIFA announced a new monthly world ranking system on Aug. 13, 1993 designed to "provide a constant international comparison of national team performances." The rankings are based on a mathematical formula that weighs strength of schedule, importance of matches and goals scored for and against. Games considered include World Cup qualifying and final rounds, Continental championship qualifying and final rounds, and friendly matches.

The formula has been altered somewhat over the years. Following a change in July 2006, the rankings now take into account all International "A" matches from the last four years. At the end of the year, FIFA designates a Team of the Year. Teams of the Year so far have been Germany (1993), Brazil (1994-2000, 2002-06) and France (2001). The USA reached their highest-ever ranking (6th) in July 2005.

2006

#	Team	Points	2005 Rank	#	Team	Points	2005 Rank	#	Team	Points	2005 Rank
1	Brazil	1588	1	18	Ivory Coast	919	42	35	Paraguay	745	30
2	Italy	1560	12	19	Romania	912	27	36	Mali	732	63
3	Argentina	1551	4	20	Mexico	883	5	37	Slovakia	621	42
4	France	1523	5	21	Denmark	865	13	38	Iran	716	19
5	England	1359	9	22	Russia	858	34	39	Australia	703	48
6	Germany	1350	19	23	Guinea	856	79		Morocco	703	36
7	Netherlands	1305	3	24	Poland	854	22	41	Senegal	700	30
8	Portugal	1258	10	25	Scotland	847	60		Chile	700	64
9	Nigeria	1244	24	26	Turkey	845	11	43	Bulgaria	684	39
10	Czech Republic	1190	2	27	Egypt	835	32	44	Israel	667	36
11	Cameroon	1160	23	28	Ghana	816	50	45	Uzbekistan	645	59
12	Spain	1154	5	29	Uruguay	806	18	46	Cuba	641	75
13	Ukraine	1054	40	30	Ecuador	802	37	47	Japan	640	15
14	Sweden	958	14	31	USA	792	8	48	Northern Ireland	625	103
15	Croatia	948	20	32	Tunisia	790	28	49	Ireland	596	24
16	Greece	945	16	33	Serbia	765	47	50	Norway	587	38
17	Switzerland	937	35	34	Colombia	758	24				

2007 (as of Sept. 19)

#	Team	Points	2006 Rank	#	Team	Points	2006 Rank	#	Team	Points	2006 Rank
1	Italy	1488	2	18	USA	897	31	35	Bulgaria	727	43
2	Argentina	1451	3	19	Uruguay	889	29	36	Northern Ireland	707	48
3	Brazil	1444	1	20	Sweden	888	14	37	Tunisia	692	32
4	Germany	1330	6	21	Turkey	883	26	38	Morocco	688	39
5	Netherlands	1246	7	22	Serbia	877	33	39	Bosnia-Herzegovina	686	59
6	France	1220	4	23	Nigeria	867	9	40	Iran	685	38
7	Spain	1178	12	24	Colombia	862	34		Senegal	685	41
8	Portugal	1169	8	25	Cameroon	856	11	42	Switzerland	683	17
9	England	1165	5	26	Russia	851	22	43	Egypt	679	27
10	Croatia	1151	15	27	Ivory Coast	806	18	44	Finland	678	52
11	Czech Republic	1190	10	28	Denmark	794	21	45	Ghana	671	28
12	Romania	1037	19	29	Norway	763	50	46	Slovakia	663	37
13	Mexico	1026	13	30	Guinea	752	23	47	Chile	624	41
14	Scotland	1025	25	31	Paraguay	750	35	48	Australia	620	39
15	Greece	940	16	32	Ireland	733	49	49	Mali	613	36
16	Poland	926	24	33	Israel	732	44	50	South Korea	605	51
17	Ukraine	900	13	34	Japan	731	47				

FIFA Women's World Rankings

As part of its growing recognition of women's soccer FIFA began ranking the women's national teams in 2002 following the inaugural FIFA Women's U19 World Championship in Canada. The rankings are currently released four times a year and are calculated in a similar manner to the men's rankings. The first women's international was held on April 17, 1971 (France vs. the Netherlands). The Top 30 teams are listed below.

2007 (as of Oct. 5)

#	Team	Points	2006 Rank	#	Team	Points	2006 Rank	#	Team	Points	2006 Rank
1	Germany	2201	1	11	Japan	1943	10	21	Iceland	1793	21
2	USA	2192	2	12	Australia	1928	15	22	Mexico	1771	22
3	Brazil	2082	6	13	China	1918	9	23	New Zealand	1720	24
4	Sweden	2070	4	14	Italy	1910	13	24	Nigeria	1720	25
5	Norway	2035	3	15	Russia	1903	14	25	South Korea	1710	23
6	North Korea	2029	5	16	Finland	1877	16	26	Scotland	1687	26
7	France	1993	7	17	Ukraine	1846	17	27	Poland	1680	28
8	Denmark	1973	8	18	Netherlands	1833	18	28	Argentina	1658	31
9	Canada	1950	11	19	Czech Republic	1812	19		Chinese Taipei	1658	27
10	England	1944	12	20	Spain	1802	20	30	Switzerland	1650	29

2007 FIFA Under-20 Men's World Cup

Officially the FIFA World Youth Championship, contested for the 16th time since its inception in 1977. Held June 30-July 22, 2007 in Canada.

First Round

Round robin; each team played the other three teams in its group once. Note that three points were awarded for a win and one point for a tie. (*) indicates team advanced to second round.

Group A	W	L	T	Pts	GF	GA
*Chile	2	0	1	7	6	0
*Austria	1	0	2	5	2	1
Congo	1	1	1	4	3	4
Canada	0	3	0	0	0	6

Group B	W	L	T	Pts	GF	GA
*Spain	2	0	1	7	8	5
*Zambia	1	1	1	4	4	3
*Uruguay	1	1	1	4	3	4
Jordan	0	2	1	1	3	6

Group C	W	L	T	Pts	GF	GA
*Mexico	3	0	0	9	7	2
*Gambia	2	1	0	6	3	4
*Portugal	1	2	0	3	4	4
New Zealand	0	3	0	0	1	5

Group D	W	L	T	Pts	GF	GA
*USA	2	0	1	7	9	3
*Poland	1	1	1	4	3	7
Brazil	1	2	0	3	4	5
South Korea	0	1	2	2	4	5

Group E	W	L	T	Pts	GF	GA
*Argentina	2	0	1	7	7	0
*Czech Republic	1	0	2	5	4	3
North Korea	0	1	2	2	2	4
Panama	0	2	1	1	1	8

Group F	W	L	T	Pts	GF	GA
*Japan	2	0	1	7	4	1
*Nigeria	2	0	1	7	3	0
Costa Rica	1	2	0	3	2	3
Scotland	0	3	0	0	2	7

Round of 16

Date	Site	Result
July 11	Edmonton	Austria 2, Gambia 1
July 11	Toronto	USA 2, Uruguay 1 OT
July 11	Burnaby	Spain 4, Brazil 2 OT
July 11	Victoria	Czech Republic 2, Japan 2

Czech Republic advances on shoot-out, 4-3

Date	Site	Result
July 12	Edmonton	Chile 1, Portugal 0
July 12	Ottawa	Nigeria 2, Zambia 1
July 12	Toronto	Argentina 3, Poland 1
July 12	Montreal	Mexico 3, Congo 0

Quarterfinals

Date	Site	Result
July 14	Toronto	Austria 2, USA 1 OT
July 14	Edmonton	Czech Republic 1, Spain 1

Czech Republic advances on shoot-out, 4-3

Date	Site	Result
July 15	Montreal	Chile 4, Nigeria 0
July 15	Ottawa	Argentina 1, Mexico 0

Semifinals

Date	Site	Result
July 18	Edmonton	Czech Republic 2, Austria 0
July 19	Toronto	Argentina 3, Chile 0

Third Place

Date	Site	Result
July 22	Toronto	Chile 1, Austria 0

Final

Date	Site	Result
July 22	Toronto	Argentina 2, Czech Republic 1

Leading Goal Scorers

	Gms	Goals
Sergio Aguero, Argentina	7	6
Adrian Lopez, Spain	5	5
Maximiliano Moralez, Argentina	7	4
Josmer Altidore, USA	5	4
Nine tied at 3 each.		

2007 FIFA Under-17 Men's World Cup

Contested for the 12th time since its inception in 1985. Held Aug. 18-Sept. 9, 2007 in South Korea.

Round of 16

Date	Site	Result
Aug. 29	Ulsan	Spain 3, North Korea 0
Aug. 29	Changwon	France 3, Tunisia 1 OT
Aug. 29	Suwon	Peru 1, Tajikistan 1

Peru advances on shoot-out, 5-4

Date	Site	Result
Aug. 29	Gwangyang	Ghana 1, Brazil 0
Aug. 30	Goyan City	Argentina 2, Costa Rica 0
Aug. 30	Gwangyang	Nigeria 2, Colombia 1
Aug. 30	Jeju	England 3, Syria 1
Aug. 30	Cheonan	Germany 2, USA 1

Quarterfinals

Date	Site	Result
Sept. 1	Jeju	Spain 1, France 1

Czech Republic advances on shoot-out, 5-4

Date	Site	Result
Sept. 1	Changwon	Ghana 2, Peru 0
Sept. 2	Cheonan	Nigeria 2, Argentina 0
Sept. 2	Goyang City	Germany 4, England 1

Semifinals

Date	Site	Result
Sept. 5	Ulsan	Spain 2, Ghana 1 OT
Sept. 6	Suwon	Nigeria 3, Germany 1

Third Place

Date	Site	Result
Sept. 9	Seoul	Germany 2, Ghana 1

Final

Date	Site	Result
Sept. 9	Seoul	Nigeria 3, Spain 0

Leading Goal Scorers

	Gms	Goals
Macauley Chrisantus, Nigeria	7	7
Ransford Osei, Ghana	7	6
Toni Kroos, Germany	6	5
Bojan, Spain	5	5
Damien Le Tallec, France	5	4
Richard Sukuta-Pasu, Germany	7	4
Sadick Adams, Ghana	6	4

U.S. Men's National Team
2007 Schedule and Results

Through Oct. 17, 2007. Games in **bold** type are from the 2007 Copa America in Venezuela.

Date		Result	USA Goals	Site	Attendance
Jan. 20	Denmark	W, 3-1	Donovan, Bronsterin, Cooper	Carson, Calif.	10,048
Feb. 7	Mexico	W, 2-0	Conrad, Donovan	Glendale, Ariz.	62,426
Mar. 25	Ecuador	W, 3-1	Donovan (3)	Tampa, Fla.	31,547
Mar. 28	Guatemala	T, 0-0	—	Frisco, Tex.	10,932
June 2	China	W, 4-1	Beasley, Feilhaber, Dempsey Onyewu	San Jose, Calif.	20,821
June 7	Guatemala	W, 1-0	Dempsey	Carson, Calif.	20,821
June 9	Trinidad & Tobago	W, 2-0	Chang, Johnson	Carson, Calif.	27,000
June 12	El Salvador	W, 4-0	Beasley (2), Donovan, Twellman	Foxboro, Mass.	26,523
June 16	Panama	W, 2-1	Donovan, Bocanegra	Foxboro, Mass.	22,412
June 21	Canada	W, 2-1	Hejduk, Donovan	Chicago, Ill.	50,760
June 24	Mexico	W, 2-1	Donovan, Feilhaber	Chicago, Ill.	60,000
June 28	**Argentina**	L, 1-4	Johnson	Maracaibo, Venezuela	37,000
July 2	**Paraguay**	L, 1-3	Clark	Barinas, Venezuela	25,000
July 5	**Colombia**	L, 0-3	—	Barquisimeto, Venezuela	35,000
Oct. 17	Switzerland	W, 1-0	Bradley	Basel, Switzerland	16,500
Nov. 17	South Africa			Johannesburg, S. Africa	

Overall record: 11-3-1. **Team scoring:** Goals for–28; Goals against–16.

U.S. Women's National Team
2007 Schedule and Results

Games in **bold** type are from the 2007 Women's World Cup in China.

Date		Result	USA Goals	Site	Attendance
Jan. 26	Germany	T, 0-0	—	Guangzhou, China	1,500
Jan. 28	England	T, 1-1	Reilly	Guangzhou, China	3,000
Jan. 30	China	W, 2-0	Chalupny, Kai	Guangzhou, China	8,000
Mar. 7	China	W, 2-1	Lilly, Floyd	Silves, Portugal	500
Mar. 9	Finland @	W, 1-0	Lloyd	Ferreiras, Portugal	500
Mar. 12	Sweden @	W, 3-2	Wambach (2), Lloyd	VR de SA, Portugal	1,000
Mar. 14	Denmark @	W, 2-0	Lilly, Lloyd	VR de SA, Portugal	1,000
Apr. 14	Mexico	W, 5-0	Wambach, Tarpley, Lilly (2), Cheney	Foxboro, Mass.	18,184
May 12	Canada	W, 6-2	Wambach (2), Tarpley, Chalupny, Lilly, O'Reilly	Frisco, Texas	8,569
June 16	China	W, 2-0	Wambach (2)	Cleveland, Ohio	8,888
June 23	Brazil	W, 2-0	Lilly, Wambach	East Rutherford, N.J.	16,856
July 14	Norway	W, 1-0	Lloyd	Hartford, Conn.	9,957
July 28	Japan	W, 4-1	Boxx, Own Goal, Lilly, Wambach	San Jose, Calif.	11,290
Aug. 12	New Zealand	W, 6-1	Wambach (2), Lloyd (2), Lilly, Tarpley	Chicago, Ill.	7,015
Aug. 25	Finland	W, 4-0	Boxx, Lilly, Tarpley, O'Reilly	Carson, Calif.	7,118
Sept. 11	**North Korea**	T, 2-2	Wambach, O'Reilly	Chengdu, China	35,100
Sept. 14	**Sweden**	W, 2-0	Wambach (2)	Chengdu, China	35,500
Sept. 18	**Nigeria**	W, 1-0	Chalupny	Shanghai, China	6,500
Sept. 22	**England**	W, 3-0	Wambach, Boxx, Lilly	Tianjin, China	29,586
Sept. 27	**Brazil**	L, 0-4	—	Hangzhou, China	47,818
Sept. 30	**Finland**	W, 4-1	Wambach (2), Chalupny, O'Reilly	Shanghai, China	34,000
Oct. 13	Mexico	W, 5-1	O'Reilly, Wambach (2), Lilly, Lloyd	St. Louis, Mo.	10,861
Oct. 17	Mexico	W, 4-0	Lilly, Wambach, Kai, Lloyd	Portland, Ore.	10,006
Oct. 20	Mexico	T, 1-1	O'Reilly	Albuquerque, N.M.	8,972

Overall record: 19-1-4. **Team Scoring:** Goals for–63; Goals against–17.

Awards
2006 FIFA World Players of the Year

As determined by a global vote of national team coaches and captains from FIFA member associations. Top three vote-getters listed below. USA national team player in **bold** type.

MEN	Pts		WOMEN	Pts
1 Fabio Cannavaro, Italy	498	1	Marta, Brazil	475
2 Zinedine Zidane, France	494	2	**Kristine Lilly**, USA	388
3 Ronaldinho, Brazil	380	3	Renate Lingor, Germany	305

Club Team Competition
2006 FIFA Club World Championship

The FIFA Club World Championship (now officially the FIFA Club World Championship TOYOTA Cup Japan) merged with the Toyota Cup (a.k.a European/South American Cup) in 2005 and is now open to the champions from the African, Asian, Oceanic and North/Central American soccer federations as well as Europe and South America. The four newcomers will play-off for the right to face the seeded European and South American sides in the semi-finals. Like the Toyota Cup, the new six-team knockout tournament will still be held each December in Japan. The previous edition of the FIFA Club World Championship was played once (held in 2000 and won by Brazil's Corinthians) but it fell apart while the Toyota Cup continued uninterrupted.

The 2006 FIFA Club World Championship TOYOTA Cup took place December 10-17. The teams representing their continents were as follows: EUROPE—**FC Barcelona** (Spain), NORTH/CENTRAL AMERICA—**CF America** (Mexico), SOUTH AMERICA—**Sport Club Internacional de Porto Alegre** (Brazil), OCEANIA—**Auckland City FC** (New Zealand), ASIA—**Jeonbuk Hyundai** (South Korea), AFRICA—**Al Ahly** (Egypt). As the European and South American teams, respectively, Liverpool and Sao Paulo received byes into the semifinals.

Quarterfinals
Ahly Sporting Club 2 . . . . .Auckland City FC 0
CF America 1 . . . . Jeonbuk Hyundai 0

Semifinals
Sport Club Internacional 2 . . . . . . .Ahly Sporting Club 1
FC Barcelona 4 .CF America 0

5th Place Match
Jeonbuk Hyundai 3 . . . . .Auckland City FC 0

3rd Place Match
Ahly Sporting Club 2 . . . . .CF America 1

Final
Dec. 17 at Yokohoma, Japan.
Attendance: 67,128

Sport Cub Internacional 1 . . . . FC Barcelona 0

Scoring
SC Internacional—Vieira Adriano 82'

SOUTH AMERICA

2007 Libertadores Cup

Contested by the league champions of South America's football union. Two-leg Semifinals and two-leg Final; home teams listed first. Boca Juniors of Argentina qualified for the 2007 FIFA Club World Championship in Japan in December.

Final Four: Grêmio (Brazil), Santos (Brazil), Boca Juniors (Argentina) and Cúcuta Deportivo (Colombia).

Semifinals

Santos vs. Grêmio
Grêmio 2 . . . . .Santos FC 0
Santos FC 3 . . . . .Grêmio 1
Aggregate tied 3-3, Grêmio advanced on away goals

Boca Juniors vs. Cúcuta Deportivo
Cúcuta Deportivo 3 . . . . .Boca Juniors 1
Boca Juniors 3 . . . . .Cúcuta Deportivo 0
Boca Juniors won 4-3 on aggregate

Final

Matches played June 13 in Buenos Aires, Argentina and June 20 in Porto Alegre, Brazil.

Boca Juniors 3 . . . . .Gremio 0
Gremio 0 . . . . .Boca Juniors 2
Boca Juniors won 5-0 on aggregate

2007 Lamar Hunt U.S. Open Cup

Dating back to 1914, the U.S. Open Cup is the oldest soccer competition in the United States and is among the oldest in the world. The U.S. Open Cup is a single-elimination tournament open to all amateur and professional teams in the United States. Forty teams (24 professional and 16 amateur) competed in the 2007 Lamar Hunt U.S. Open Cup. The tournament was renamed for the U.S. Soccer pioneer and MLS Team owner in 1999. All teams listed below are from the MLS unless otherwise noted.

Third Round
Harrisburg City Islanders (USL-2) def. D.C. United, 1-0
N.E. Revolution def. Rochester Raging Rhinos (USL-1), 4-2
Richmond Kickers (USL-2) def. Los Angeles Galaxy, 1-0
Carolina RailHawks (USL-1) def. Chicago Fire, 1-0
FC Dallas def. Atlanta Silverbacks (USL-1) on PKs
Charleston Battery (USL-1) def. Houston Dynamo, 1-0

Quarterfinals
N.E. Revolution def. Harrisburg City Islanders, 2-1
Carolina RailHawks def. Richmond Kickers, 1-0
FC Dallas def. Charleston Battery, 2-1
Seattle Sounders def. Colorado Rapids, 5-0

Semifinals
New England Revolution def. Carolina RailHawks, 2-1
FC Dallas def. Seattle Sounders, 2-1

Final (Oct. 3, 2007)
New England Revolution def. FC Dallas, 3-2

There are two major European club competitions sanctioned by the Union of European Football Associations (UEFA). The constantly evolving **Champions League** is currently a 74-team tournament made up from UEFA member countries. The teams are ranked 1-74 depending on how they finish in their own domestic leagues. UEFA ranks the quality of the 52 European national football associations (from number one Spain to number 52 San Marino) and assigns each association a number weighted by their respective ranking (UEFA calls this number a coefficient). Each team's domestic league finish is then multiplied by the coefficient and the teams are finally ranked (countries can enter a maximum of four teams).

The defending champions and the other 15 highest-ranked teams form Group 1 and are given a direct entry into the League but the remaining 16 teams are determined by dividing teams 17-74 into three groups—Group 2 (teams 17-34), Group 3 (35-50) and Group 4 (51-74). The 24 teams in the lowest Group (Group 4) play two-leg, total goal elimination series. The 12 survivors advance to the Second Qualifying Phase and join the 16 teams from Group 3 to play 14 two-leg, total goal elimination series. The 14 clubs that survive this phase join the 18 teams from Group 2 to play in the Third Qualifying Phase. The winning clubs from the 16 two-leg, total goal elimination series advance to the Champions League for the right to play against the top-ranked 16 teams in Europe.

The 32 teams are separated into eight groups of four and play a round-robin series of home-and-home matches. Starting for the 2003-04 Champions League, the eight group winners and eight group runners-up advance to the next round where they are paired and play two home-and-home matches. The home-and-home series are played through the semifinals until ultimately ah single championship match for the European club championship is held.

The updated **UEFA Cup**, which is basically a combination of the what was known as the Cup Winners' Cup (played between national cup champions) and the old UEFA Cup (sort of a "best of the rest" tournament), is single-elimination throughout and features 121 additional teams plus teams that have been already eliminated from the Champions League.

2006-07 Champions League

Round of 16
Two legs, total goals; home team listed first.

Chelsea vs. Porto
Feb. 21 Porto 1 . . . . .Chelsea 1
Mar. 6 Chelsea 2 .Porto 1
Chelsea wins 3-2 on aggregate

Celtic vs. AC Milan
Feb. 20 Celtic 0 .AC Milan 0
Mar. 7 AC Milan 1 . . . . . . .OT . . . . .Celtic 0
AC Milan wins 1-0 on aggregate

Liverpool vs. Barcelona
Feb. 21 Barcelona 1 . . . . .Liverpool 2
Mar. 6 Liverpool 0 . . . . .Barcelona 1
Aggregate tied 2-2, Liverpool wins on away goals

PSV Eindhoven vs. Arsenal
Feb. 20 PSV Eindhoven 1 . . . . .Arsenal 0
Mar. 7 Arsenal 1 . . . . .PSV Eindhoven 1
PSV Eindhoven wins 2-1 on aggregate

Inter Milan vs. Valencia
Feb. 21 Inter Milan 2 . . . . .Valencia 2
Mar. 6 Valencia 0 . . . . .Inter Milan 0
Aggregate tied 2-2, Valencia wins on away goals

Manchester United vs. Lille
Feb. 22 Lille 0 . . . . .Manchester United 1
Mar. 7 Manchester United 1 . . . . .Lille 0
Manchester United wins 2-0 on aggregate

AS Roma vs. Olympique Lyon
Feb. 21 AS Roma 0 . . . . .Olympique Lyon 0
Mar. 6 Olympique Lyon 0 . . . . .AS Roma 2
AS Roma wins 2-0 on aggregate

Internazionale vs. Valencia
Feb. 22 Internazionale 2 . . . . .Valencia 2
Mar. 7 Valencia 0 . . . . .Internazionale 0
Aggregate tied 2-2, Valencia wins on away goals

Quarterfinals
Two legs, total goals; home team listed first.

AC Milan vs. FC Bayern
Apr. 3 AC Milan 2 . . . . .FC Bayern 2
Apr. 10 FC Bayern 0 . . . . .AC Milan 2
AC Milan wins 4-2 on aggregate

Chelsea vs. Valencia
Apr. 3 AC Milan 2 . . . . .FC Bayern 2
Apr. 10 FC Bayern 0 . . . . .AC Milan 2
AC Milan wins 4-2 on aggregate

PSV Eindhoven vs. Liverpool
Apr. 3 Liverpool 3 . . . . .PSV Eindhoven 0
Apr. 10 PSV Eindhoven 0 . . . . .Liverpool 1
Liverpool wins 4-0 on aggregate

Manchester United vs. Roma
Apr. 4 Roma 2 . . . . .Manchester United 1
Apr. 11 Manchester United 7 . . . . .Roma 1
Manchester United wins 8-3 on aggregate

Semifinals
Two legs, total goals; home team listed first.

Liverpool vs. Chelsea
Apr. 24 Chelsea 1 . . . . .Liverpool 0
May 1 Liverpool 1 . . . . .Chelsea 0
Aggregate tied 1-1, Liverpool wins 4-1 on PKs

AC Milan vs. Manchester United
Apr. 25 Manchester United 3 . . . . .AC Milan 2
May 2 AC Milan 3 . . . . .Manchestern United 1
AC Milan wins 5-3 on aggregate

2007 Champions League Final

AC Milan vs. Liverpool

May 23, 2007 at Olympic Stadium in Athens. **Attendance:** 74,000

AC Milan 2 . . . . .Liverpool 1

Scoring:

AC MILAN—Filippo Inzaghi (45', 82'); LIVERPOOL— Dirk Kuyt (89')

Referee: Herbet Fandel, Germany

2007 UEFA Cup

Two-leg Quarterfinals and Semifinals, one-game Final; home team listed first.

Final Eight: Alkmaar Zaanstreek (The Netherlands), Sevilla (Spain), Werder Bremen (Germany), Bayer Leverkusen (Germany), Osasuna (Spain), Tottenham Hotspur (England), Benfica (Portugal), Espanyol (Spain).

Quarterfinals

AZ vs. Werder Bremen

Apr. 5   AZ 0 . . . . .Werder Bremen 0
Apr. 12 Werder Bremen 4 . . . . .AZ 1
   Werded Bremen wins 4-1 on aggregate

Sevilla vs. Tottenham Hotspur

Apr. 5   Sevilla 2 . . . . .Tottenham Hotspur 1
Apr. 12 Tottenham Hotspur 2 . . . . .Sevilla 2
   Sevilla wins 4-3 on aggregate

Bayer Leverkusen vs. Osasuna

Apr. 5   Bayer Leverkusen 0 . . . . .Osasuna 3
Apr. 12 Osasuna 1 . . . . .Bayer Leverkusen 0
   Osasuna wins 4-0 on aggregate

Espanyol vs. Benfica

Apr. 5   Espanyol 3 .Benfica 2
Apr. 12 Benfica 0 .Espanyol 0
   Espanyol wins 3-2 on aggregate

Semifinals

Espanyol vs. Werder Bremen

Apr. 26 Espanyol 3 . . . . .Werder Bremen 0
May 3   Werder Bremen 1 . . . . .Espanyol 2
   Espanyol wins 5-1 on aggregate

Sevilla vs. Osasuna

Apr. 26 Osasuna 1 .Sevilla 0
May 3   Sevilla 2 .Osasuna 0
   Sevilla wins 2-1 on aggregate

Final

Sevilla vs. Espanyol

May 16, 2007 in Hampden Park, Glasgow. **Attendance:** 52,000

Espanyol 2 . . . . .Sevilla 2

Scoring:

ESPANYOL—Riera (28'), Jonatas (115'); SEVILLA—Adriano (18'), Kanoute (105')

Sevilla wins UEFA Cup, 3-1, on PKs

2007 FA Cup

May 19, 2007 at Wembley Stadium, London, England. **Attendance:** 89,826

Chelsea 1 .OT . . . . .Manchester United 0

Scoring:

CHELSEA—Didier Drogba (116')

International Soccer events scheduled for Late 2007 and 2008

Dates	Tournament
Nov. 1-11, 2007	FIFA Beach Soccer World Cup (Rio de Janeiro)
Nov. 25, 2007	Preliminary Draw for 2010 FIFA World Cup (Durban, South Africa)
June 7-29, 2008	European Soccer Championships (Swtizerland/Austria)AC
Aug. 6-23, 2008	Men's and Women's Olympic Soccer Tournament (Beijing, China)
Oct. 30-Nov. 16, 2008	FIFA U-17 Women's World Cup (New Zealand)
Nov. 16-20, 2008	FIFA Futsal (Indoor Soccer) World Cup (Brazil)

Major League Soccer

2007 Final Regular Season Standings

Conference champions (*) and playoff qualifiers (†) are noted. Teams receive three points for a win and one for a tie. The GF and GA columns refer to Goals For and Goals Against in regulation play. Number of seasons listed after each head coach refers to current tenure with club through the 2007 season.

Eastern Conference

Team	W	L	T	Pts	GF	GA
*D.C. United	16	7	7	55	56	34
†N.E. Revolution	14	8	8	50	51	43
†New York Red Bulls	12	11	7	43	47	45
†Chicago Fire	10	10	10	40	31	36
†Kansas City Wizards	11	12	7	40	45	45
Columbus Crew	9	11	10	37	39	44
Toronto FC	6	17	7	25	25	49

Head Coaches: DC—Tom Soehn (1st season); **NE**—Steve Nicol (7th); **NY**—Bruce Arena (2nd); **KC**—Curt Onalfo (1st); **Chi**—Dave Sarachan (5th, 4-6-2) was fired on June 20 and replaced by assistant Denis Hamlett (0-1-2) on an interim basis then Juan Carlos Osorio (6-3-6); **Clb**—Sigi Schmid (2nd); **Tor**—Mo Johnston (1st).

Western Conference

Team	W	L	T	Pts	GF	GA
*Chivas USA	15	7	8	53	46	28
†Houston Dynamo	15	8	7	52	43	23
†FC Dallas	13	12	5	44	37	44
Colorado Rapids	9	13	8	35	29	34
Los Angeles Galaxy	9	14	7	34	38	48
Real Salt Lake	6	15	9	27	31	45

Head Coaches: Chv—Preki (1st season); **Hou**—Dominic Kinnear (4th); **Dal**—Steve Morrow (2nd); **Colo**—Fernando Clavijo (3rd); **LA**—Frank Yallop (2nd); **RSL**—John Ellinger (3rd, 0-2-2) was fired on May 3 and replaced by player Jason Kreis (6-13-7).

Leading Scorers

Goals

	Gm	No
Luciano Emilio, DC	29	20
Juan Pablo Angel, NY	24	19
Taylor Twellman, NE	26	16
Eddie Johnson, KC	24	15
Maykel Galindo, Chv	28	12
Ante Razov, Chv	26	11
Christian Gomez, DC	27	10
Josy Altidore, NY	22	9
Landon Donovan, LA	25	8
Robbie Findley, RSL	25	8

Assists

	Gm	No
Steve Ralston, NE	26	14
Landon Donovan, LA	25	13
Sacha Kljestan, Chv	25	13
Guillermo Barros Schelotto, Clb	22	11
Davy Arnaud, KC	28	9
Christian Gomez, DC	27	9
Fred, DC	26	8
Ante Razov, Chv	26	8
Dave van den Bergh, NY	29	8

Seven players tied with 7 each.

Shots

	Gm	No
Juan Pablo Angel, NY	24	97
Taylor Twellman, NE	26	90
Ante Razov, Chv	26	85
Christian Gomez, DC	27	82
Luciano Emilio, DC	27	79
Eddie Johnson, KC	24	75
Davy Arnaud, KC	28	74
Dwayne De Rosario, Hou	24	62
Arturo Alvarez, Dal	27	61

Three players tied with 59 each.

Shots on Goal

	Gm	No
Taylor Twellman, NE	26	55
Juan Pablo Angel, NY	24	53
Luciano Emilio, DC	29	47
Christian Gomez, DC	27	44
Eddie Johnson, KC	24	43
Ante Razov, Chv	26	42
Chad Barrett, Chi	30	37
Eddie Gaven, Clb	27	33
Alejandro Moreno, Clb	29	32

Multi-Goal Games

	Gm	MGG
Juan Pablo Angel, NY	24	5
Luciano Emilio, DC	29	5
Maykel Galindo, Chv	28	3
Eddie Johnson, KC	24	3
Taylor Twellman, NE	26	3
Jozy Altidore, NY	22	2
Ben Olsen, DC	24	2
Scott Sealey, KC	18	2

Twenty-seven players tied with 1 each.

Hat Tricks

	Gm	Hats
Eddie Johnson, KC	24	2
Brad Davis, Hou	17	1
Nate Jaqua, Hou	25	1
Ben Olsen, DC	24	1

Consecutive Games with Goals

6	Juan Pablo Angel, NY	5/19 to 6/16
5	Luciano Emilio, DC	6/10 to 7/4
4	Chris Rolfe, Chi	4/21 to 5/12
4	Ante Razov, Chv	9/6 to 9/22
4	Eddie Johnson, KC	5/26 to 7/22

MLS All-Star Game

MLS 2, Celtic 0

Played Saturday, July 19, 2007 at Dick's Sporting Goods Park in Commerce City, Colo. between a team of MLS All-Stars and Scottish Premier League team Celtic FC.

Attendance: 18,661; **MVP:** Juan Pablo Angel, New York Red Bulls, F

	1	2	Final
Celtic	0	0	−0
MLS All-Stars	2	0	−2

Scoring

1st Half: MLS—Juan Pablo Angel (Dwayne De Rosario), 36'; Juan Toja (unassisted), 44'.

Discipline

CEL—Steven Pressley (yellow), 27'
CEL—Scott Brown (yellow), 49'

Fouls Committed

	Gm	No
Juan Toja, Dal	.27	83
Eddie Robinson, Hou	.25	70
Maurice Edu, Tor	.25	65
Jeff Larentowicz, NE	.28	61
Ryan Cochrane, Hou	.25	55
Shalrie Joseph, NE	.27	55
Alejandro Moreno, Clb	.29	54
Dane Richards, NY	.28	50
Carl Robinson, Tor	.26	50
Ben Olsen, DC	.24	49

Fouls Suffered

	Gm	No
Alejandro Moreno, Clb	.29	93
Guillermo Barros Schelotto, Clb	.22	65
Eddie Robinson, Hou	.25	64
Davy Arnaud, KC	.28	63
Cuauhtemoc Blanco, Chi	.14	61
Joseph Ngwenya, Hou	.30	60
Eddie Johnson, KC	.24	57
Brian Mullan, Hou	.28	55
Maykel Galindo, Chv	.28	53
Shalrie Joseph, NE	.27	52

Offsides

	Gm	Offs
Joseph Ngwenya, Hou	.30	55
Eddie Johnson, KC	.24	50
Juan Pablo Angel, NY	.24	42
Chad Barrett, Chi	.30	37
Jeff Cunningham, Tor	.23	33
Alejandro Moreno, Clb	.29	32
Pat Noonan, NE	.27	32
Maykel Galindo, Chv	.28	30
Ante Razov, Chv	.26	30
Carlos Pavan, LA	.18	24

Cautions (Yellow Cards)

	Gm	No
Eddie Robinson, Hou	.25	11
Kyle Beckerman, RSL	.28	9
Alecko Eskandarian, RSL	.23	9
Jesse Marsch, Chv	.28	9
Carlos Ruiz, Dal	.22	9
Three players tied with 8 each.		

Ejections (Red Cards)

	Gm	No
Andrew Boyens, Tor	.23	2
Ugo Ihemelu, Col	.25	2
Kyle Martino, LA	.26	2
Clint Mathis, NY	.26	2
Forty-six players tied with 1 each.		

Corner Kicks

	Gm	CKs
Steve Ralston, NE	.26	130
Terry Cooke, Col	.29	101
Landon Donovan, LA	.25	80
Guillermo Barros Schelotto, Clb	.22	73
Brad Davis, Hou	.17	62
Davy Arnaud, KC	.28	61
Carlos Marinelli, KC	.26	57
Richard Mulrooney, Hou	.30	55
Cuauhtemoc Blanco, Chi	.14	51
Eddie Gaven, Clb	.27	50

Game-Winning Goals

	Gm	GWG
Eddie Johnson, KC	.24	6
Juan Pablo Angel, NY	.24	5
Maykel Galindo, Chv	.28	5
Taylor Twellman, NE	.26	5
Luciano Emilio, DC	.29	4
Ante Razov, Chv	.26	4

Game-Winning Assists

	Gm	GWA
Christian Gomez, DC	.27	5
Shalrie Joseph, NE	.27	4
Ante Razov, Chv	.26	4
Eight players tied with 3 each.		

Minutes Played

	Mins
Chris Klein, LA	.2880
Kevin Hartman, KC	.2700
Matt Reis, NE	.2700
Bouna Coundoul, Col	.2668
Wade Barrett, Hou	.2649
Joe Cannon, LA	.2610
Troy Perkins, DC	.2610
C.J. Brown, Chi	.2565
Kerry Zavagnin, KC	.2564

Leading Goaltenders

Goals Against Average

	Gm	Min	Shts	Svs	GAA	W-L-T
Pat Onstad, Hou	.27	2418	107	85	**0.82**	13-8-6
Brad Guzan, Chv	.27	2430	112	87	**0.93**	14-6-7
Bouna Coundoul, Col	.30	2668	152	120	**1.08**	9-12-8
Jon Conway, NY	.14	1143	71	57	**1.10**	6-5-2
Troy Perkins, DC	.29	2610	149	117	**1.10**	16-6-7
Matt Pickens, Chi	.27	2430	133	102	**1.15**	9-8-10
Nick Rimando, RSL	.27	2430	183	146	**1.37**	6-13-8
Matt Reis, NE	.30	2700	163	120	**1.43**	14-8-8
Will Hesmer, Clb	.20	1800	100	71	**1.45**	8-7-5
Kevin Hartman, KC	.30	2700	155	110	**1.50**	11-12-7
Joe Cannon, LA	.29	2610	165	119	**1.59**	9-13-7
Dario Sala, Dal	.18	1620	93	64	**1.61**	8-7-3

Save Percentage

	Svs	SOG	SV Pct
Pat Onstad, Hou	.85	109	78.0
Nick Rimando, RSL	.146	191	76.4
Bouna Coundoul, Col	.120	158	75.9
Troy Perkins, DC	.117	155	75.5
Matt Pickens, Chi	.102	137	74.5
Brad Guzan, Chv	.87	119	73.1
Jon Conway, NY	.57	79	72.2

Saves

	Gm	No
Nick Rimando, RSL	.27	146
Bouna Coundoul, Col	.30	120
Matt Reis, NE	.30	120
Joe Cannon, LA	.29	119
Troy Perkins, DC	.29	117

Shutouts

	Gm	No
Brad Guzan, Chv	.27	13
Pat Onstad, Hou	.27	11
Matt Pickens, Chi	.27	10
Matt Reis, NE	.30	10
Bouna Coundoul, Col	.30	9

Wins

	Gm	No
Troy Perkins, DC	.29	16
Brad Guzan, Chv	.27	14
Matt Reis, NE	.30	14
Pat Onstad, Hou	.27	13
Kevin Hartman, KC	.30	11
Three tied with 9 each.		

Major League Soccer (Cont.)
Team-by-Team Statistics
Players who played with more than one club during the season are listed with final team.

Eastern Conference

Chicago Fire

(min. 10 Gms)	Pos	Gm	Min	G	A	Sht
Chad Barrett	F	30	1983	7	2	59
Chris Rolfe	F	19	1451	6	3	38
Cuauhtemoc Blanco	F	14	1233	4	7	26
Calen Carr	F	27	1136	3	2	33
Paulo Wanchope	F	12	932	2	0	26
Ivan Guerrero	M/D	19	1490	1	2	12
Logan Pause	M	23	1905	1	0	2
Dasan Robinson	D	23	1820	1	0	11
Gonzalo Segares	D	27	2406	1	1	15
Chris Armas	M	25	2194	0	2	7
C.J. Brown	D	29	2565	0	0	7
Jim Curtin	D	11	856	0	0	3
Thiago	M	13	569	0	1	10
Diego Gutierrez	M	23	1890	0	1	10
Justin Mapp	M	13	808	0	1	15
Bakary Soumare	M	19	1072	0	0	4

Top Goalkeepers	Gm	Min	W-L-T	Shts	Svs	GAA
Matt Pickens	27	2430	9-8-10	137	102	1.15
Jon Busch	3	270	1-2-0	15	15	1.67

Columbus Crew

(min. 10 Gms)	Pos	Gm	Min	G	A	Sht
Alejandro Moreno	F	25	2205	7	7	52
Guillermo Barros Schelotto	M/F	22	1605	5	11	39
Eddie Gaven	M/F	27	1923	5	7	59
Andy Herron	F	18	794	4	2	19
Ned Grabavoy	M	26	2093	3	3	37
Stefani Miglioranzi	D/M	23	1622	3	2	18
Robbie Rogers	F	10	598	3	1	15
Kei Kamara	F	17	475	2	0	16
Chad Marshall	D	12	1020	2	0	8
Jason Garey	F	11	447	1	0	13
Marcos Gonzalez	D	27	2356	1	1	21
Ezra Hendrickson	D	23	1851	1	0	11
Duncan Oughton	M	19	1231	1	4	9
Frankie Hejduk	D	24	2160	0	3	10
Danny O'Rourke	M	27	2426	0	1	11
Rusty Pierce	D	21	1580	0	1	1

Top Goalkeepers	Gm	Min	W-L-T	Shts	Svs	GAA
Will Hesmer	20	1800	8-7-5	99	71	1.45
Andy Gruenebaum	10	900	1-4-5	53	35	1.50

D.C. United

(min. 10 Gms)	Pos	Gm	Min	G	A	Sht
Luciano Emilio	F	29	2410	20	1	79
Christian Gomez	M	27	2272	10	9	82
Fred	M	26	2097	7	8	28
Jaime Moreno	F	21	1440	7	6	34
Ben Olsen	M	24	1881	7	7	29
Nicholas Addlery	F	11	456	1	2	9
Marc Burch	D	18	1362	1	3	9
Rod Dyachenko	F	14	378	1	0	5
Joshua Gros	M/D	22	1854	1	1	11
Bobby Boswell	D	23	1963	0	2	7
Brian Carroll	M	28	1801	0	4	7
Facundo Erpen	D	11	881	0	2	5
Guy-Roland Kpene	F	15	626	0	2	18
Devon McTavish	D	22	1825	0	0	7
Domenic Mediate	M	10	330	0	0	3
Bryan Namoff	D	24	2089	0	0	3
Clyde Simms	M/D	25	1505	0	3	15
Greg Vanney	D	15	1261	0	0	2

Top Goalkeepers	Gm	Min	W-L-T	Shts	Svs	GAA
Troy Perkins	29	2610	16-6-7	155	117	1.10
Jay Nolly	1	90	0-1-0	9	7	2.00

Kansas City Wizards

(min. 10 Gms)	Pos	Gm	Min	G	A	Sht
Eddie Johnson	F	24	2149	15	6	75
Scott Sealy	F	18	1194	7	2	33
Yura Movsisyan	F	18	666	5	0	32
Davy Arnaud	F/M	28	2489	4	9	74
Michael Harrington	M	29	2422	3	4	15
Kerry Zavagnin	M	29	2564	3	2	16
Jose Burciaga Jr.	D	23	1826	2	4	26
Jack Jewsbury	M	28	2316	2	3	25
Sasha Victorine	M	29	2135	2	7	37
Eloy Colombano	M/F	10	310	1	1	6
Carlos Marinelli	M	26	1674	1	5	42
Jimmy Conrad	D	25	2172	0	0	13
Nick Garcia	D	27	2420	0	1	2
Kurt Morsink	M	21	895	0	0	10
Ryan Pore	F	17	456	0	0	11
Ryan Raybould	D/M	10	424	0	2	1

Top Goalkeeper	Gm	Min	W-L-T	Shts	Svs	GAA
Kevin Hartman	30	2700	11-12-7	159	110	1.50

New England Revolution

(min. 10 Gms)	Pos	Gm	Min	G	A	Sht
Taylor Twellman	F	26	2283	16	3	90
Andy Dorman	M	30	2699	7	2	48
Pat Noonan	F	27	1738	7	4	48
Adam Cristman	F	28	1421	4	4	40
Shalrie Joseph	M	27	2366	4	5	42
Steve Ralston	M	26	2337	4	14	33
Jeff Larentowicz	M	28	2455	3	4	21
Khano Smith	M	29	2216	2	6	36
Jay Heaps	D	28	2475	1	0	16
Michael Parkhurst	D	25	2197	1	0	1
Wells Thompson	M	27	1217	1	0	16
Avery John	D	19	1559	0	1	2
James Riley	D/F	26	2131	0	0	4

Goalkeeper	Gm	Min	W-L-T	Shts	Svs	GAA
Matt Reis	30	2700	14-8-8	169	120	1.43

New York Red Bulls

(min. 8 Gms)	Pos	Gm	Min	G	A	Sht
Juan Pablo Angel	F	24	2125	19	5	97
Jozy Altidore	F	22	1399	9	4	43
Clint Mathis	M/F	26	1723	6	2	47
John Wolyniec	F	21	1032	3	2	24
Francis Doe	F	8	428	2	1	17
Dema Kovalenko	M	19	1378	2	1	21
Dane Richards	M	28	2335	2	6	24
Dave van den Bergh	M	29	2228	2	8	36
Hunter Freeman	D/M	16	1342	1	1	6
Kevin Goldthwaite	D	9	662	0	0	3
Chris Leitch	D	12	1018	0	0	2
Carlos Mendes	D	23	1709	0	0	0
Jeff Parke	D	28	2246	0	1	10
Claudio Reyna	M	21	1723	0	3	14
Seth Stammler	M/D	29	2547	0	2	26
Sinisa Ubiparipovic	F/M	12	233	0	1	4
Joe Vide	M	16	1107	0	0	10

Goalkeepers	Gm	Min	W-L-T	Shts	Svs	GAA
Ronald Waterreus	18	1557	6-6-5	89	59	1.79
Jon Conway	14	1143	6-5-2	79	57	1.10

Toronto FC

(min. 8 Gms)	Pos	Gm	Min	G	A	Sht
Danny Dichio	.F	17	1175	6	1	20
Maurice Edu	.M	25	2180	4	1	24
Jeff Cunningham	.F	16	1034	3	1	21
Collin Samuel	.F	18	1510	3	0	41
Carl Robinson	.M	26	2340	2	4	14
Andrew Boyens	.D	23	1825	1	1	4
Jim Brennan	.D	27	2430	1	0	13
Miguel Canizalez	.D	12	414	1	0	5
Kevin Goldthwaite	.D	9	801	1	1	8
Andy Welsh	.M	20	1335	1	3	14
Adam Braz	.D	13	773	0	0	1
Edson Buddle	.F	10	481	0	2	9
Todd Dunivant	.D	18	1600	0	0	13
Andrea Lombardo	.F	16	726	0	1	17
Tyrone Marshall	.D	16	1440	0	0	9
Ronnie O'Brien	.M	13	1139	0	4	22
Chris Pozniak	.M	22	1498	0	3	9
Marco Reda	.D	8	573	0	0	1
Marvell Wynne	.D	22	1873	0	3	9

Goalkeepers	Gm	Min	W-L-T	Shts	Svs	GAA
Kenny Stamatopoulos	.12	1080	1-8-3	61	41	1.67
Greg Sutton	.8	720	2-5-1	53	36	1.88
Srdjan Djekanovic	.8	635	2-3-2	34	22	1.28

Western Conference

Club Deportivo Chivas USA

(min. 9 Gms)	Pos	Gm	Min	G	A	Sht
Maykel Galindo	.F	28	2021	12	5	55
Ante Razov	.F	26	2041	11	8	85
Sacha Kljestan	.M	25	2186	4	13	40
John Cunliffe	.F	15	494	3	1	16
Claudio Suarez	.D	25	2153	3	1	14
Jesse Marsch	.M	28	2425	2	4	15
Francisco Mendoza	.M	28	2459	2	4	36
Paulo Nagamura	.M	22	1818	2	2	15
Jonathan Bornstein	.D	23	2070	1	1	14
Laurent Merlin	.F	22	806	1	2	15
Orlando Perez	.D	15	1033	1	1	3
Matt Taylor	.F	11	159	1	0	5
Lawson Vaughn	.D	24	1901	1	2	5
Jason Hernandez	.D	21	930	0	0	0
Shavar Thomas	.D	23	2037	0	0	1
Alex Zotinca	.D	22	1667	0	3	15

Goalkeepers	Gm	Min	W-L-T	Shts	Svs	GAA
Brad Guzan	.27	2430	14-6-7	119	87	0.93
Preston Burpo	.3	270	1-1-1	16	13	1.00

Colorado Rapids

(min. 10 Gms)	Pos	Gm	Min	G	A	Sht
Jovan Kirovski	.M	28	2161	6	1	36
Herculez Gomez	.M/F	20	1537	4	2	51
Roberto Brown	.F	13	696	3	0	14
Conor Casey	.F	15	977	2	3	12
Colin Clark	.M	16	1321	2	2	26
Omar Cummings	.F	11	182	2	0	10
Kyle Beckerman	.M	13	1125	1	2	19
Jose Cancela	.M	11	611	1	0	15
Facundo Erpen	.D	15	1175	1	0	6
Nicolas Hernandez	.F	21	1474	1	1	29
Ugo Ihemelu	.D	25	2018	1	0	7
Jacob Peterson	.M	24	1118	1	0	24
Mike Petke	.D	24	2018	1	0	4
Terry Cooke	.M	29	2288	0	7	21
Dan Gargan	.D	15	1029	0	0	4
Pablo Mastroeni	.M/D	23	1865	0	1	9
Brandon Prideaux	.D	21	1770	0	0	7

Goalkeepers	Gm	Min	W-L-T	Shts	Svs	GAA
Bouna Coundoul	.30	2668	9-12-8	158	120	1.08
Zach Thornton	.1	32	0-1-0	3	1	5.62

FC Dallas

(min. 10 Gms)	Pos	Gm	Min	G	A	Sht
Carlos Ruiz	.F	22	1722	7	2	59
Juan Toja	.M	27	2388	6	1	33
Abe Thompson	.F	24	1227	5	4	19
Kenny Cooper	.F	14	1068	4	2	33
Arturo Alvarez	.M	27	1898	3	3	61
Ramon Nunez	.M	13	1001	3	2	36
Dominic Oduro	.F	29	1163	3	2	24
Drew Moor	.D	28	2495	2	0	7
Chris Gbandi	.D	21	1701	1	2	5
Clarence Goodson	.D	27	2297	1	1	9
Dax McCarty	.M	25	1604	1	7	13
Aaron Pitchkolan	.M/D	16	1142	0	0	6
Bobby Rhine	.M	19	862	0	0	5
Pablo Ricchetti	.M	19	1600	0	3	6
Marcelo Saragosa	.M	13	800	0	2	3
Adrian Serioux	.D	10	806	0	0	6
David Wagenfuhr	.D	13	828	0	0	1
Alex Yi	.D	15	1178	0	0	0

Goalkeepers	Gm	Min	W-L-T	Shts	Svs	GAA
Dario Sala	.18	1620	8-7-3	97	64	1.61
Ray Burse	.6	540	3-2-1	29	23	1.00
Shaka Hislop	.6	540	2-3-1	32	23	1.50

Houston Dynamo

(min. 9 Gms)	Pos	Gm	Min	G	A	Sht
Corey Ashe	.M	22	811	0	4	10
Wade Barrett	.D	30	2649	0	2	3
Brian Ching	.F	20	1590	7	2	48
Ricardo Clark	.M	19	1635	3	3	28
Ryan Cochrane	.D	25	2059	1	0	6
Brad Davis	.M	17	1275	3	3	27
Dwayne De Rosario	.M	24	1973	6	4	62
Stuart Holden	.M	22	1030	5	5	24
Patrick Ianni	.D	16	961	1	0	1
Nate Jaqua	.F	15	1002	6	2	26
Brian Mullan	.M	28	2407	1	3	19
Richard Mulrooney	.M	28	2341	0	5	8
Joseph Ngwenya	.F	25	1944	7	3	35
Eddie Robinson	.D	25	2187	2	2	10
Craig Waibel	.D	21	1639	0	2	7
Chris Wondolowski	.F	16	307	1	1	6

Goalkeeper	Gm	Min	W-L-T	Shts	Svs	GAA
Pat Onstad	.27	2418	13-8-6	109	85	0.82
Zach Wells	.4	282	2-0-1	9	8	0.32

Major League Soccer (Cont.)

Los Angeles Galaxy

(min. 10 Gms and "Becks") Pos	Gm	Min	G	A	Sht
Landon Donovan ....F	25	2191	8	13	44
Edson Buddle ....F	16	770	5	0	38
Gavin Glinton ....F	19	711	4	0	19
Cobi Jones ....M	25	1679	4	5	19
Alan Gordon ....F	14	828	3	0	19
Kyle Martino ....M	26	1928	3	1	29
Carlos Pavon ....F	18	978	3	0	29
Troy Roberts ....D	16	1140	2	0	4
Kevin Harmse ....M	17	1171	1	0	6
Nat Jaqua ....F	10	770	1	0	23
Chris Klein ....M	21	1890	1	3	18
David Beckham ....M	5	252	0	2	8
Ty Harden ....D	24	2086	0	0	1
Ante Jazic ....D	18	1397	0	0	0
Quavas Kirk ....D	11	438	0	0	1
Mike Randolph ....D	19	1451	0	1	1
Peter Vagenas ....M	24	1786	0	5	13
Abel Xavier ....D	10	900	0	1	4

Top Goalkeeper	Gm	Min	W-L-T	Shts	Svs	GAA
Joe Cannon 29	2610	9-13-7	171	119	1.59	
Steve Cronin 1	90	0-1-0	8	6	2.00	

Real Salt Lake

(min. 9 Gms) Pos	Gm	Min	G	A	Sht
Robbie Findley ....F	16	974	6	0	20
Chris Brown ....M/F	22	1084	5	0	23
Carey Talley ....M	26	2195	3	1	28
Kyle Beckerman ....M	15	1305	2	1	33
Fabian Espindola ....F	12	602	2	2	13
Freddy Adu ....M	11	899	1	2	24
Alecko Eskandarian ....F	17	1428	1	3	47
Chris Klein ....M	11	990	1	1	22
Matias Mantilla ....D	10	828	1	0	2
Eddie Pope ....D	27	2248	1	0	5
Andy Williams ....M	24	1277	1	3	19
Mehdi Ballouchy ....M	14	1239	0	0	23
Willis Forko ....D	12	990	0	0	0
Atiba Harris ....M/F	21	1259	0	1	8
Jean-Martial Kipre ....D/M	18	1427	0	0	7
Ritchie Kotschau ....D	20	1664	0	0	3
Chris Lancos ....M/D	14	811	0	1	3
Jack Stewart ....D	13	1006	0	1	2
Daniel Torres ....D	10	825	0	0	4
Chris Wingert ....D	16	1144	0	2	3

Top Goalkeeper	Gm	Min	W-L-T	Shts	Svs	GAA
Nick Rimando 27	2430	6-13-8	191	146	1.37	
Chris Seitz 3	270	0-2-1	14	6	2.67	

SuperLiga

Created in 2007, the SuperLiga is a competition between teams from Major League Soccer and Mexico's Primera Division. Eight clubs—four each from MLS and the Primera Division—took part in the inaugural competition held July 24-Aug. 29. Though the first edition of SuperLiga was set up by invitation to specific teams, qualification will determine future SuperLiga berths. The games were played at American stadiums. The winning club, CF Pachuca of Mexico, received $1 million. (*) denotes that club advanced to the knockout stage.

Group Stage

Group A	W	L	T	Pts
*LA. Galaxy (MLS) 2	1	0	6	
*CF Pachuca (Primera) 1	1	1	4	
CD Guadalajara (Primera) 1	1	1	4	
FC Dallas (MLS) 0	1	2	2	

RESULTS: July 24–FC Dallas 1, CD Guadalajara 1; July 24–L.A. Galaxy 2, CF Pachuca 1; July 28–FC Dallas 1, CF Pachuca 1; July 28–CD Guadalajara 2, L.A. Galaxy 1; July 31–L.A. Galaxy 6, FC Dallas 5; July 31– CF Pachuca 1, CD Guadalajara 0.

Group B	W	L	T	Pts
*Houston Dynamo (MLS) 2	0	1	7	
*D.C. United (MLS) 1	1	1	4	
Club America (Primera) 1	2	0	3	
Monarcas Morelia (Primera) 0	1	2	2	

RESULTS: July 25–Monarcas Morelia 1, D.C. United 1; July 25–Houston Dynamo 1, Club America 0; July 29–D.C. United 1, Club America 0; July 29–Monarcas Morelia 1, Houston Dynamo 1; Aug. 1–Houston Dynamo 1, D.C. United 1; Aug. 1–Club America 3, Monarcas Morelia 2.

Semifinals

Aug. 14

CF Pachuca 4 ....at Houston Dynamo 3

Aug. 15

at L.A. Galaxy 2 .................D.C. United 0

Final

Aug. 29 at the Home Depot Center, Carson, Calif.

CF Pachuca 1 ....................L.A. Galaxy 1

Pachuca wins, 4-3, on penalty kicks

Scoring

1st Half: PAC–Own Goal (Peter Vagena) 28th;
2nd Half: LA–Chris Klein (Troy Roberts), 93rd.

SHOOTOUT

Pachuca	Los Angeles
Rafael Marquez Lugo (Goal),	Peter Vagenas (Saved)
Luis Gabriel Rey (Goal)	Cobi Jones (Goal)
Gabriel Caballero (Saved)	Chris Klein (Goal)
Julio Mansur (Goal)	Edson Buddle (Goal)
Marvin Cabrera (Crossbar)	Landon Donovan (Saved)
Carlos Rodriguez (Goal)	Abel Xavier (Wide right)

Colleges

MEN

2006 NCAA Division I Tournament

First Round (Nov. 11-12)

Rhode Island 1 . . . . .2 OT . . . . .Rutgers
Rhode Island advanced on PKs
Gardner-Webb 1 . . . . .2 OT . . . . .UAB 1
Gardner-Webb advanced on PKs
Harvard 2 . . . . .Binghamton 1
St. John's 1 . . . . .Monmouth 0
Ill-Chicago 3 . . . . .Western Illinois 0
New Mexico 1 . . . . .San Francisco 0
Bucknell 1 . . . . .OT . . . .George Mason 0
UC Santa Barbara 2 . . . . .San Diego St. 1
Old Dominion 0 . . . . .2 OT . . . . .Winthrop 0
Old Dominion advanced on PKs
Northwestern 3 . . . . .Cincinnati 0
NC-Greensboro 2 . . . . .Virginia Tech 1
Northern Ill. 1 . . . . .OT . . . . .Loyola-IL 0
Washington 3 .Creighton 0
Fairfield 2 . . . . .Connecticut 1
Hofstra 2 . . . . .Providence 0

Second Round (Nov. 15-16)

Duke 2 . . . . .Brown 0
Lehigh 1 . . . . .2OT . . . . . .Rhode Island 1
Lehigh advanced on PKs
Clemson 3 .Gardner-Webb 1
UCLA 3 . . . . .Harvard 0
Maryland 2 . . . . .St. John's 0
Notre Dame 1 . . . . .Ill-Chicago 0
California 3 . . . . .New Mexico 1
Virginia 4 . . . . .Bucknell 0
UC Santa Barbara 3 .SMU 1
Old Dominion 1 . . . . .North Carolina 0
Northwestern 1 .St. Louis 0
NC-Greensboro 2 . . . . .2 OT . . . . . .West Virginia 1
Indiana 2 . . . . .Northern Ill. 0
Santa Clara 3 . . . . .OT . . . . . . .Washington 2
Towson 2 . . . . .Fairfield 1
Wake Forest 5 . . . . .Hofstra 1

Third Round (Nov. 18-19)

Duke 3 . . . . .Lehigh 0
UCLA 3 . . . . .Clemson 0
Notre Dame 1 . . . . .2 OT . . . . . . .Maryland 0
Virginia 2 . . . . .California 1
UC Santa Barbara 2 . . . . .Old Dominion 1
Northwestern 2 . . . . .NC-Greensboro 1
Santa Clara 0 . . . . .2 OT . . . . .Indiana 0
Santa Clara advanced on PKs
Wake Forest 2 .Towson 1

Quarterfinals (Nov. 24-26)

UCLA 3 . . . . .OT . . . . .Duke 2
Virginia 3 .Notre Dame 2
UC Santa Barbara 3 . . . . .Northwestern 2
Wake Forest 3 . . . . .Santa Clara 1

2006 College Cup
at St. Louis, Mo (Dec. 2 & 3)

Semifinals

UCLA 4 . . . . .Virginia 0
UC Santa Barbara 0 . . .2OT . . . . . . .Wake Forest 0
UC Santa Barbara advanced on PKs

Championship

UC Santa Barbara 2 . . . . .UCLA 1

Scoring

1st Half: UCSB—Nick Perera (Tyler Rosenlund), 2:12;
2nd Half: UCSB—Eric Avila (Perera, Bryan Byrne),
60:01; UCLA—Jason Leopoldo (Tony Beltran), 78:56.

Attendance: 5,948
Final records: UCSB (17-7-1), UCLA (14-6-4).
Most Outstanding Off. Player: Nick Perera, UCSB
Most Outstanding Def. Player: Andy Iro, UCSB

2006 Annual Awards

Men's Players of the Year

M.A.C. Hermann Trophy . . Joseph Lapira, Notre Dame, F
Soccer America . . . . Joseph Lapira, Notre Dame, F

NSCAA Coach of the Year

Men's Div. I . . . . .Tim Vom Steeg, UC Santa Barbara

Division I All-America Teams
MEN

The 2006 first team All-America selections of the National
Soccer Coaches Association of America (NSCAA).

GOALKEEPER—Nick Noble, West Virginia.

DEFENDERS—Andrew Boyens, New Mexico; Julies James,
Connecticut; Jay Needham, SMU; John O'Reilly, Lehigh.

MIDFIELDERS—Greg Dalby, Notre Dame; Maurice Edu,
Maryland; Ryan Maduro, Providence.

FORWARDS—Omar Cummings, Cincinnati; Charlie Davies,
Boston College; Edson Elcock, Old Dominion; Joseph Lapira,
Notre Dame.

Individual Leaders

Points Per Game

	Gm	G	A	Pts	PPG
Charlie Davies, Boston Coll.	.16	15	6	36	2.25
Tommy Krizanovic, Jacksonville	15	14	5	33	2.20
Joseph Lapira, Notre Dame	.23	22	6	50	2.17
Steven Holloway, Monmouth	.20	18	4	40	2.00
Patrick Nyarko, Va. Tech	.20	16	8	40	2.00
Jarrod Smith, West Virginia	.16	14	4	32	2.00
Saidi Isaac, Winthrop	.21	17	6	40	1.90
Riley O'Neill, Kentucky	.20	17	4	38	1.90
Josh Trott, Holy Cross	.17	15	2	32	1.88

Goals Against Average

	Gm	Mins	GA	GAA
Joe Zimka, Northern Ill.	.15	1304	3	.207
Billy Chiles, Towson	.13	1081	4	.333
Elvir Prasovic, Fairleigh Dickinson	.11	974	4	.369
Jovan Bubonja, Ill-Chicago	.21	1930	8	.373
Daniel Schenkel, Monmouth	.21	1970	10	.457

WOMEN

2006 NCAA Division I Tournament

First Round (Nov. 10)

at North Carolina 7 . . . . .NC-Asheville 0
Navy 0 . . . . .William & Mary 0
Navy advanced on PKs
Duke 0 . . . . .Louisville 0
Duke advanced on PKs
at Tennessee 4 . . . . .UAB 0
at Wake Forest 4 . . . . .Old Dominion 0
Virginia 2 . . . . .at West Virginia 0
at SMU 2 . . . . .McNeese St. 0
at Texas A&M 5 . . . . .Grambling 0
at UCLA 6 . . . . .UNLV 1
CS Fullerton 3 . . . . .Loyola Marymount 0
at Marquette 1 . . . . .Purdue 0
Florida 2 . . . . .Loyola-IL 0
at Utah 3 . . . . .2 OT . . . . .Idaho St. 2
Portland 2 . . . . .BYU 1
at Connecticut 2 . . . . .Columbia-Barnard 1
at Texas 4 . . . . .Long Island 0
USC 1 . . . . .at Santa Clara 0
Stanford 2 . . . . .Nevada 1
at Clemson 1 . . . . .Vanderbilt 1
Clemson advanced on PKs
at Oklahoma St. 2 . . . . .NC-Greensboro 0
Illinois 2 . . . . .SE Missouri St. 0
at St. Louis 2 . . . . .Drake 0
California 3 . . . . .Auburn 0
at Florida St. 6 .Jacksonville 0
at Penn St. 3 . . . . .Niagara 1
Villanova 5 . . . . .Toledo 0
Boston College 3 . . . . .Boston University 0
at Rutgers 3 . . . . .Hartford 0
at Colorado 2 . . . . .Colorado College 1
Denver 2 . . . . .Kentucky 0
Wisconsin-Milwaukee 0 . . . . .Michigan 0
Wisconsin-Milwaukee advanced on PKs
at Notre Dame 7 . . . . .Oakland 1

Second Round (Nov. 12)

at North Carolina 4 . . . . .Navy 0
Tennessee 0 . . . . .Duke 0
Tennessee advanced on PKs
Virginia 2 . . . . .Wake Forest 0
at Texas A&M 4 . . . . .SMU 0
at UCLA 3 . . . . .CS Fullerton 1
Florida 0 . . . . .Marquette 0
Florida advanced on PKs

2006 Annual Awards

Women's Players of the Year

M.A.C. Hermann Trophy . . . . .Kerri Hanks, Notre Dame, F
Soccer America . . . . . .Heather O'Reilly, North Carolina, F

NSCAA Coach of the Year

Women's Div. I . . . . . . .Anson Dorrance, North Carolina

Division I All-America Teams

The 2006 first team All-America selections of the National Soccer Coaches Association of America (NSCAA).
GOALKEEPER—Jillian Loyden, Villanova.
DEFENDERS—Ali Krieger, Penn St.; Kasey Moore, Texas; Kelly Rowland, Florida St.
MIDFIELDERS—Yael Averbuch, North Carolina; Christina DiMartino, UCLA; Yolanda Odenyo, Oklahoma St.
FORWARDS—Lauren Cheney, UCLA; Kerri Hanks, Notre Dame; Heather O'Reilly, North Carolina; India Trotter, Florida St.

Portland 3 . . . . .Utah 0
at Texas 1 . . . . .Connecticut 1
Texas advanced on PKs
at Stanford 2 . . . . .USC 0
at Clemson 0 .Oklahoma St. 0
Illinois 4 . . . . .St. Louis 1
at Florida St. 3 . . . . .California 1
at Penn St. 2 . . . . .Villanova 0
Boston College 0 . . . . .Rutgers 0
Boston College advanced on PKs
Colorado 2 . . . . .Denver 1
at Notre Dame 1 . . . .*. . . . .Wisconsin-Milwaukee 0

Third Round (Nov. 18 or 20)

at North Carolina 6 . . . . .Tennessee 2
at Texas A&M 2 . . . . .Virginia 1
UCLA 3 . . . . .Florida 2
Portland 2 . . . . .Texas 0
Clemson 0 . . . . .Stanford 0
Clemson advanced on PKs
Florida St. 1 . . . . .Illinois 0
Penn St. 1 .Boston College 0
at Notre Dame 3 . . . . .Colorado 0

Quarterfinals (Nov. 24, 25 or 26)

North Carolina 3 . . . . .Texas A&M 2
UCLA 2 . . . . .Portland 1
Florida St. 2 . . . . .Clemson 1
Notre Dame 4 . . . . .Penn St. 0

2006 College Cup

at Cary, North Carolina (Dec. 1 & 3)

Semifinals

North Carolina 2 . . . . .UCLA 0
Notre Dame 2 .Florida St. 1

Championship

North Carolina 2 . . . . .Notre Dame 1

Scoring

1st Half: NC—Heather O'Reilly (Casey Nogueira), 17:57.

2nd Half: NC—Casey Nogueira (Whitney Engen), 46:28. ND—Brittany Bock (Kerri Hanks), 80:30.

Attendance: 8,349

Final records: Notre Dame (25-1-1), North Carolina (27-1-0).

Individual Leaders

Points Per Game

	Gm	G	A	Pts	PPG
Belinda Kanda, Ala. A&M	16	20	9	49	3.06
Kala Morgan, Mid. Tenn.	21	22	8	52	2.48
Kerri Hanks, Notre Dame	27	22	22	66	2.44
Brittany Bisnott, Niagara	20	21	3	45	2.25
Kathryn Moos, Brown	17	15	6	36	2.12
Dean Everrett, West Va.	21	18	7	43	2.05
Holly Grogan, Mid. Tenn.	21	15	12	42	2.00
Michele Weissenhofer, N.D.	27	18	17	53	1.96
Ali Wean, St. Joseph's	17	14	5	33	1.94

Goals Against Average

	Gm	Mins	GA	GAA
Lizzie Barnes, Navy	23	1852	6	.292
Jasmine Phillips, Maine	20	1882	8	.383
Anna Rodenbough, N. Carolina	28	2301	10	.391
Lauren Karas, Notre Dame	23	2214	10	.406
Staci Pugh, Kennesaw St.	17	1600	8	.450

1900-2007
Through the Years

SPORTS ALMANAC

The World Cup

The Federation Internationale de Football Association (FIFA) began the World Cup championship tournament in 1930 with a 13-team field in Uruguay. Sixty-four years later, 138 countries competed in qualifying rounds to fill 24 berths in the 1994 World Cup finals. FIFA increased the World Cup '98 tournament field from 24 to 32 teams, and it remained at 32 in 2006 including automatic berths for defending champion Brazil and host Germany. The other 30 slots were allotted by region: Europe (12), Africa (5), South America (4), CONCACAF (3), Asia (4), the two remaining positions were determined via two home-and-away playoff series. One was between the #4 CONCACAF team (Trinidad & Tobago) and the #5 Asian team (Bahrain) and the other was between the #5 South American team (Uruguay) and the champion of Oceania (Australia).

Tournaments have been played once in Asia (Japan/South Korea), three times in North America (Mexico 2 and U.S.), four times in South America (Argentina, Chile, Brazil and Uruguay) and nine times in Europe (France 2, Italy 2, England, Spain, Sweden, Switzerland and West Germany). Following an outcry when Germany was awarded the 2006 World Cup over South Africa, FIFA announced that, starting in 2010, the World Cup will be rotated among six continents.

Brazil retired the first World Cup (called the Jules Rimet Trophy after FIFA's first president) in 1970 after winning it for the third time. The new trophy, first presented in 1974, is known as simply the World Cup.

Multiple winners: Brazil (5); Italy (4); West Germany (3); Argentina and Uruguay (2).

Year	Champion	Manager	Score	Runner-up	Host Country	Third Place
1930	Uruguay	Alberto Suppici	4-2	Argentina	Uruguay	No game
1934	Italy	Vittório Pozzo	2-1*	Czechoslovakia	Italy	Germany 3, Austria 2
1938	Italy	Vittório Pozzo	4-2	Hungary	France	Brazil 4, Sweden 2
1942-46 Not held						
1950	Uruguay	Juan Lopez	2-1	Brazil	Brazil	No game
1954	West Germany	Sepp Herberger	3-2	Hungary	Switzerland	Austria 3, Uruguay 1
1958	Brazil	Vicente Feola	5-2	Sweden	Sweden	France 6, W. Ger. 3
1962	Brazil	Aimoré Moreirà	3-1	Czechoslovakia	Chile	Chile 1, Yugoslavia 0
1966	England	Alf Ramsey	4-2*	W. Germany	England	Portugal 2, USSR 1
1970	Brazil	Mario Zagalo	4-1	Italy	Mexico	W. Ger. 1, Uruguay 0
1974	West Germany	Helmut Schoen	2-1	Netherlands	W. Germany	Poland 1, Brazil 0
1978	Argentina	Cesar Menotti	3-1*	Netherlands	Argentina	Brazil 2, Italy 1
1982	Italy	Enzo Bearzot	3-1	W. Germany	Spain	Poland 3, France 2
1986	Argentina	Carlos Bilardo	3-2	W. Germany	Mexico	France 4, Belgium 2*
1990	West Germany	Franz Beckenbauer	1-0	Argentina	Italy	Italy 2, England 1
1994	Brazil	Carlos Parreira	0-0†	Italy	USA	Sweden 4, Bulgaria 0
1998	France	Aimé Jacquet	3-0	Brazil	France	Croatia 2, Netherlands 1
2002	Brazil	Luiz Felipe Scolari	2-0	Germany	Japan/S. Korea	Turkey 3, S. Korea 2
2006	Italy	Marcelo Lippi	1-1‡	France	Germany	Germany 3, Portugal 1
2010	at South Africa (June 11-July 11)					
2014	at Brazil (TBD)					

*Winning goals scored in overtime (no sudden death); †Brazil def. Italy in shootout (3-2); ‡Italy def. France in shootout (5-3).

All-Time World Cup Leaders

Career Goals

World Cup scoring leaders through 2006. Years listed are years played in World Cup.

	No
Ronaldo, Brazil (1994, 98, 2002, 06)	15
Gerd Müller, West Germany (1970, 74)	14
Just Fontaine, France (1958)	13
Pelé, Brazil (1958, 62, 66, 70)	12
Sandor Kocsis, Hungary (1954)	11
Juergen Klinsmann, Germany (1990, 94, 98)	11
Six Players tied with 10 each.	

Most Valuable Player

Officially, the Golden Ball Award, the Most Valuable Player of the World Cup tournament has been selected since 1982 by a panel of international soccer journalists.

Year		Year	
1982	Paolo Rossi, Italy	1998	Ronaldo, Brazil
1986	Diego Maradona, Arg.	2002	Oliver Kahn, Germany
1990	Toto Schillaci, Italy	2006	Zinedine Zidane, France
1994	Romario, Brazil		

Single Tournament Goals

Year		Gm	No
1930	Guillermo Stabile, Argentina	4	8
1934	Angelo Schiavio, Italy	3	4
	Oldrich Nejedly, Czechoslovakia	4	4
	Edmund Conen, Germany	4	4
1938	Leônidas, Brazil	3	8
1950	Ademir, Brazil	6	7
1954	Sandor Kocsis, Hungary	5	11
1958	Just Fontaine, France	6	13
1962	Drazen Jerkovic, Yugoslavia	6	5
1966	Eusébio, Portugal	6	9
1970	Gerd Müller, West Germany	6	10
1974	Grzegorz Lato, Poland	7	7
1978	Mario Kempes, Argentina	7	6
1982	Paolo Rossi, Italy	7	6
1986	Gary Lineker, England	5	6
1990	Toto Schillaci, Italy	7	6
1994	Oleg Salenko, Russia	3	6
	Hristo Stoitchkov, Bulgaria	7	6
1998	Davor Suker, Croatia	7	6
2002	Ronaldo, Brazil	7	8
2006	Miroslav Klose, Germany	7	5

All-Time World Cup Ranking Table

Since the first World Cup in 1930, Brazil is the only country to play in all 17 final tournaments. The FIFA all-time table below ranks all nations that have ever qualified for a World Cup final tournament by points earned through 2006. Victories, which earned two points from 1930-90, were awarded three points starting in 1994. Note that Germany's appearances include 10 made by West Germany from 1954-90. Participants in the 2006 World Cup final are in **bold** type.

		App	Gm	W	L	T	Pts	GF	GA			App	Gm	W	L	T	Pts	GF	GA
1	**Brazil**	18	92	64	14	14	**153**	201	84	43	Norway	2	8	2	3	3	**7**	7	8
2	**Germany**	16	92	56	18	19	**142**	190	110	44	East Germany	1	6	2	2	2	**6**	5	5
3	**Italy**	16	76	56	17	19	**115**	122	68		South Africa	2	6	1	2	3	**6**	8	11
4	**Argentina**	14	64	33	20	12	**83**	113	74		**Saudi Arabia**	4	13	2	9	2	**6**	9	32
5	**England**	12	55	27	14	16	**71**	74	47		**Tunisia**	4	12	1	7	4	**6**	8	17
6	**Spain**	12	49	23	16	10	**63**	80	57		**Ghana**	1	3	2	0	1	**6**	4	3
	France	12	51	25	17	9	**63**	95	64	49	Algeria	2	6	2	3	1	**5**	6	10
8	**Sweden**	11	46	16	17	12	**47**	74	69		Wales	1	5	1	1	3	**5**	4	4
9	**Netherlands**	8	34	16	10	10	**44**	59	38		**Australia**	2	6	1	4	2	**5**	5	11
10	Russia	9	37	17	14	6	**41**	64	44	52	**Iran**	3	9	1	6	2	**4**	6	18
11	Yugoslavia	9	37	16	13	8	**40**	60	46	53	North Korea	1	4	1	2	1	**3**	5	9
	Uruguay	10	40	15	15	10	**40**	65	57		Cuba	1	3	1	1	1	**3**	5	12
13	**Poland**	7	31	15	11	5	**37**	44	40		Jamaica	1	3	1	2	0	**3**	3	9
	Mexico	13	44	11	22	12	**37**	48	85		**Ivory Coast**	1	3	1	2	0	**3**	5	6
15	Hungary	9	32	15	14	3	**33**	87	57	57	Egypt	2	4	0	2	2	**2**	3	6
16	Belgium	11	36	10	17	9	**30**	46	63		Honduras	1	3	0	1	2	**2**	2	3
	Czech Republic	9	33	12	16	5	**30**	47	49		Israel	1	3	0	1	2	**2**	1	3
18	Austria	7	29	12	13	4	**28**	43	47		**Angola**	1	3	0	1	2	**2**	1	2
19	**Portugal**	4	19	12	7	0	**27**	31	19	61	Bolivia	3	6	0	5	1	**1**	1	20
20	**Switzerland**	8	26	8	14	4	**22**	37	51		Kuwait	1	3	0	2	1	**1**	2	6
21	Romania	7	21	8	8	5	**21**	30	32		**Trinidad & Tobago**	1	3	0	2	1	**1**	0	4
	Paraguay	7	22	6	10	6	**21**	27	36	64	El Salvador	2	6	0	6	0	**0**	1	22
	South Korea	7	24	5	13	6	**21**	22	53		Canada	1	3	0	3	0	**0**	0	5
24	Chile	7	25	7	12	6	**20**	31	40		East Indies	1	1	0	1	0	**0**	0	6
25	Denmark	3	13	7	4	2	**18**	24	18		Greece	1	3	0	3	0	**0**	0	10
26	**USA**	8	25	6	16	3	**17**	27	51		Haiti	1	3	0	3	0	**0**	2	14
27	Cameroon	5	17	4	6	7	**16**	15	29		Iraq	1	3	0	3	0	**0**	1	4
28	Scotland	8	23	4	12	7	**15**	25	41		Slovenia	1	3	0	2	1	**0**	2	7
	Turkey	2	10	4	4	1	**15**	20	17		New Zealand	1	3	0	2	1	**0**	2	12
	Croatia	3	13	6	5	2	**15**	15	11		UAE	1	3	0	3	0	**0**	2	11
31	Bulgaria	7	26	3	15	8	**14**	22	53		China	1	3	0	3	0	**0**	0	9
32	Ireland	3	13	2	4	7	**12**	10	10		Zaire	1	3	0	3	0	**0**	0	14
33	Peru	4	15	4	8	3	**11**	19	31		**Serbia & Montenegro**	1	3	0	3	0	**0**	2	10
	No. Ireland	3	13	3	5	5	**11**	13	23		**Togo**	1	3	0	3	0	**0**	1	6
35	Nigeria	3	11	4	6	1	**9**	14	16										
	Ukraine	1	5	3	2	0	**9**	5	7										
37	Morocco	4	13	2	7	4	**8**	12	18										
	Colombia	4	13	3	8	2	**8**	14	23										
	Costa Rica	3	10	3	6	1	**8**	12	21										
	Senegal	1	5	2	1	2	**8**	7	6										
	Japan	3	10	2	6	2	**8**	8	14										
	Ecuador	2	7	3	4	0	**8**	7	8										

The United States in the World Cup

While the United States has fielded a national team every year of the World Cup, only seven of those teams have been able to make it past the preliminary competition and qualify for the final World Cup tournament. The 1994 national team automatically qualified because the U.S. served as host of the event for the first time. The U.S. played in three of the first four World Cups (1930, '34 and '50) and each of the last five (1990, '94, '98, 2002 and 2006). The Americans have a record of 6-16-3 in 25 World Cup matches.

1930

1st Round Matches

United States 3 . . . . Belgium 0
United States 3 . . . . Paraguay 0

Semifinals

Argentina 6 . . . . United States 1

U.S. Scoring—Bert Patenaude (3), Bart McGhee (2), James Brown and Thomas Florie.

1934

1st Round Match

Italy 7 . . . . United States 1

U.S. Scoring—Buff Donelli (who later became a noted college and NFL football coach).

1950

1st Round Matches

Spain 3 . . . . United States 1
United States 1 . . . . England 0
Chile 5 . . . . United States 2

U.S. Scoring—Joe Gaetjens, Joe Maca, John Souza and Frank Wallace.

1990

1st Round Matches

Czechoslovakia 5 . . . . United States 1
Italy 1 . . . . United States 0
Austria 2 . . . . United States 1

U.S. Scoring—Paul Caligiuri and Bruce Murray.

1994
1st Round Matches
United States 1 . . . . .Switzerland 1
United States 2 . . . . .Colombia 1
Romania 1 . . . . .United States 0

Round of 16
Brazil 1 . . . . .United States 0
U.S. Scoring–Eric Wynalda, Earnie Stewart and own goal
(Colombia defender Andres Escobar).

1998
1st Round Matches
Germany 2 . . . . .United States 0
Iran 2 . . . . .United States 1
Yugoslavia 1 . . . . .United States 0
U.S. Scoring–Brian McBride.

2002
1st Round Matches
United States 3 . . . . .Portugal 2
United States 1 . . . . .So. Korea 1
Poland 3 . . . . .United States 1

Round of 16
United States 2 . . . . .Mexico 0

Round of 8
Germany 1 . . . . .United States 0
U.S. Scoring– Landon Donovan (2), Brian McBride (2),
John O'Brien, own goal (Portugal defender Jorge Costa) and
Clint Mathis.

2006
1st Round Matches
Czech Republic 3 . . . . .United States 0
Italy 1 . . . . .United States 1
Ghana 2 . . . . .United States 1
U.S. Scoring–own goal (Italian defender Christian Zaccardo), Clint Dempsey.

World Cup Finals

Brazil and Germany (formerly West Germany) have played in the most Cup finals with seven but faced each other for the first time in a final in 2002. Note that a four-team round robin determined the 1950 championship–the deciding game turned out to be the last one of the tournament between Uruguay and Brazil.

1930
Uruguay 4, Argentina 2
(at Montevideo, Uruguay)

	1	2–T
July 30 Uruguay (4-0) 1		3–4
Argentina (4-1) 2		0–2

Goals: Uruguay–Pablo Dorado (12th minute), Pedro Cea (54th), Santos Iriarte (68th), Castro (89th); Argentina–Carlos Peucelle (20th), Guillermo Stabile (37th).
Uruguay–Ballesteros, Nasazzi, Mascheroni, Andrade, Fernandez, Gestido, Dorado, Scarone, Castro, Cea, Iriarte.
Argentina–Botasso, Della Torre, Paternoster, J. Evaristo, Monti, Suarez, Peucelle, Varallo, Stabile, Ferreira, M. Evaristo.
Attendance: 90,000. **Referee:** Langenus (Belgium).

1934
Italy 2, Czechoslovakia 1 (OT)
(at Rome)

	1	2	OT–T
June 10 Italy (4-0-1) 0		1	1–2
Czechoslovakia (3-1) 0		1	0–1

Goals: Italy–Raimondo Orsi (80th minute), Angelo Schiavio (95th); Czechoslovakia–Puc (70th).
Italy–Combi, Monzeglio, Allemandi, Ferraris IV, Monti, Bertolini, Guaita, Meazza, Schiavio, Ferrari, Orsi.
Czechoslovakia–Planicka, Zenisek, Ctyroky, Kostalek, Cambal, Krcil, Junek, Svoboda, Sobotka, Nejedly, Puc.
Attendance: 55,000. **Referee:** Eklind (Sweden).

1938
Italy 4, Hungary 2
(at Paris)

	1	2–T
June 19 Italy (4-0) 3		1–4
Hungary (3-1) 1		1–2

Goals: Italy–Gino Colaussi (5th minute), Silvio Piola (16th), Colaussi (35th), Piola (82nd); Hungary–Titkos (7th), Georges Sarosi (70th).
Italy–Olivieri, Foni, Rava, Serantoni, Andreolo, Locatelli, Biavati, Meazza, Piola, Ferrari, Colaussi.
Hungary–Szabo, Polgar, Biro, Szalay, Szucs, Lazar, Sas, Vincze, G. Sarosi, Szengeller, Titkos.
Attendance: 65,000. **Referee:** Capdeville (France).

1950
Uruguay 2, Brazil 1
(at Rio de Janeiro)

	1	2–T
July 16 Uruguay (3-0-1) 0		2–2
Brazil (4-1-1) 0		1–1

Goals: Uruguay–Juan Schiaffino (66th minute), Chico Ghiggia (79th); Brazil–Friaca (47th).
Uruguay–Maspoli, M. Gonzales, Tejera, Gambetta, Varela, Andrade, Ghiggia, Perez, Miguez, Schiaffino, Moran.
Brazil–Barbosa, Augusto, Juvenal, Bauer, Danilo, Bigode, Friaca, Zizinho, Ademir, Jair, Chico.
Attendance: 199,854. **Referee:** Reader (England).

DID YOU KNOW?

*Italy won the last **World Cup** (in 1938) before World War II and held the trophy until the return of the tournament in 1950. **Did you know** that during the war Dr. Ottorino Barassi, the Italian Vice President of FIFA, actually hid the World Cup trophy in a shoe box under his bed to save it from falling into the hands of occupying troops?*

World Cup Finals (Cont.)

1954
West Germany 3, Hungary 2
(at Berne, Switzerland)

		1	2–T
July 4	West Germany (4-1) 2		1–3
	Hungary (4-1) 2		0–2

Goals: West Germany–Max Morlock (10th minute), Helmut Rahn (18th), Rahn (84th); Hungary–Ferenc Puskas (4th), Zoltan Czibor (9th).

West Germany–Turek, Posipal, Liebrich, Kohlmeyer, Eckel, Mai, Rahn, Morlock, O. Walter, F. Walter, Schaefer.

Hungary–Grosics, Buzansky, Lorant, Lantos, Bozsik, Zakarias, Czibor, Kocsis, Hidegkuti, Puskas, J. Toth.

Attendance: 60,000. **Referee:** Ling (England).

1958
Brazil 5, Sweden 2
(at Stockholm)

		1	2–T
June 29	Brazil (5-0-1) 2		3–5
	Sweden (4-1-1) 1		1–2

Goals: Brazil–Vava (9th minute), Vava (32nd), Pelé (55th), Mario Zagalo (68th), Pelé (90th); Sweden–Nils Liedholm (3rd), Agne Simonsson (80th).

Brazil–Gilmar, D. Santos, N. Santos, Zito, Bellini, Orlando, Garrincha, Didi, Vava, Pelé, Zagalo.

Sweden–Svensson, Bergmark, Axbom, Boerjesson, Gustavsson, Parling, Hamrin, Gren, Simonsson, Liedholm, Skoglund.

Attendance: 49,737. **Referee:** Guigue (France).

1962
Brazil 3, Czechoslovakia 1
(at Santiago, Chile)

		1	2–T
June 17	Brazil (5-0-1) 1		2–3
	Czechoslovakia (3-2-1) 1		0–1

Goals: Brazil–Amarildo (17th minute), Zito (68th), Vava (77th); Czechoslovakia–Josef Masopust (15th).

Brazil–Gilmar, D. Santos, N. Santos, Zito, Mauro, Zozimo, Garrincha, Didi, Vava, Amarildo, Zagalo.

Czechoslovakia–Schroiff, Tichy, Novak, Pluskal, Popluhar, Masopust, Pospichal, Scherer, Kvasniak, Kadraba, Jelinek.

Attendance: 68,679. **Referee:** Latishev (USSR).

1966
England 4, West Germany 2 (OT)
(at London)

		1	2	OT–T
July 30	England (5-0-1) 1		1	2–4
	West Germany (4-1-1) 1		1	0–2

Goals: England–Geoff Hurst (18th minute), Martin Peters (78th), Hurst (101st), Hurst (120th); West Germany–Helmut Haller (12th), Wolfgang Weber (90th).

England–Banks, Cohen, Wilson, Stiles, J. Charlton, Moore, Ball, Hurst, B. Charlton, Hunt, Peters.

West Germany–Tilkowski, Hottges, Schnellinger, Beckenbauer, Schulz, Weber, Haller, Seeler, Held, Overath, Emmerich.

Attendance: 93,802. **Referee:** Dienst (Switzerland).

1970
Brazil 4, Italy 1
(at Mexico City)

		1	2–T
June 21	Brazil (6-0) 1		3–4
	Italy (3-1-2) 1		0–1

Goals: Brazil–Pelé (18th minute), Gerson (65th), Jairzinho (70th), Carlos Alberto (86th); Italy–Roberto Boninsegna (37th).

Brazil–Felix, C. Alberto, Everaldo, Clodoaldo, Brito, Piazza, Jairzinho, Gerson, Tostão, Pelé, Rivelino.

Italy–Albertosi, Burgnich, Facchetti, Bertini (Juliano, 73rd), Rosato, Cera, Domenghini, Mazzola, Boninsegna (Rivera, 84th), De Sisti, Riva.

Attendance: 107,412. **Referee:** Glockner (E. Germany).

1974
West Germany 2, Netherlands 1
(at Munich)

		1	2–T
July 7	West Germany (6-1) 2		0–2
	Netherlands (5-1-1) 1		0–1

Goals: West Germany–Paul Breitner (25th minute, penalty kick), Gerd Müller (43rd); Netherlands–Johan Neeskens (1st, penalty kick).

West Germany–Maier, Beckenbauer, Vogts, Breitner, Schwarzenbeck, Overath, Bonhof, Hoeness, Grabowski, Muller, Holzenbein.

Netherlands–Jongbloed, Suurbier, Rijsbergen (De Jong, 58th), Krol, Haan, Jansen, Van Hanegem, Neeskens, Rep, Cruyff, Rensenbrink (R. Van de Kerkhof, 46th).

Attendance: 77,833. **Referee:** Taylor (England).

1978
Argentina 3, Netherlands 1 (OT)
(at Buenos Aires)

		1	2	OT–T
June 25	Argentina (5-1-1) 1		0	2–3
	Netherlands (3-2-2) 0		1	0–1

Goals: Argentina–Mario Kempes (37th minute), Kempes (104th), Daniel Bertoni (114th); Netherlands–Dirk Nanninga (81st).

Argentina–Fillol, Olguin, L. Galvan, Passarella, Tarantini, Ardiles (Larrosa, 65th), Gallego, Kempes, Luque, Bertoni, Ortiz (Houseman, 77th).

Netherlands–Jongbloed, Jansen (Suurbier, 72nd), Brandts, Krol, Poortvliet, Haan, Neeskens, W. Van de Kerkhof, R. Van de Kerkhof, Rep (Nanninga, 58th), Rensenbrink.

Attendance: 77,260. **Referee:** Gonella (Italy).

1982
Italy 3, West Germany 1
(at Madrid)

		1	2–T
July 11	Italy (4-0-3) 0		3–3
	West Germany (4-2-1) 0		1–1

Goals: Italy–Paolo Rossi (57th minute), Marco Tardelli (68th), Alessandro Altobelli (81st); West Germany–Paul Breitner (83rd).

Italy–Zoff, Scirea, Gentile, Cabrini, Collovati, Bergomi, Tardelli, Oriali, Conti, Rossi, Graziani (Altobelli, 8th, and Causio, 89th).

West Germany–Schumacher, Stielike, Kaltz, Briegel, K.H. Forster, B. Forster, Breitner, Dremmler (Hrubesch, 61st), Littbarski, Fischer, Rummenigge (Muller, 69th).

Attendance: 90,080. **Referee:** Coelho (Brazil).

1986
Argentina 3, West Germany 2
(at Mexico City)

		1	2-T
June 29	Argentina (6-0-1)	1	2–3
	West Germany (4-2-1)	0	2–2

Goals: Argentina–Jose Brown (22nd minute), Jorge Valdano (55th), Jorge Burruchaga (83rd); West Germany–Karl-Heinz Rummenigge (73rd), Rudi Voller (81st).

Argentina–Pumpido, Cuciuffo, Olarticoechea, Ruggeri, Brown, Batista, Burruchaga (Trobbiani, 89th), Giusti, Enrique, Maradona, Valdano.

West Germany–Schumacher, Jakobs, B. Forster, Berthold, Briegel, Eder, Brehme, Matthaus, Rummenigge, Magath (Hoeness, 61st), Allofs (Voller, 46th).

Attendance: 114,590. **Referee:** Filho (Brazil).

1990
West Germany 1, Argentina 0
(at Rome)

		1	2-T
July 8	West Germany (6-0-1)	0	1–1
	Argentina (4-2-1)	0	0–0

Goals: West Germany–Andreas Brehme (85th minute, penalty kick).

West Germany–Illgner, Berthold (Reuter, 73th), Kohler, Augenthaler, Buchwald, Brehme, Haessler, Matthaus, Littbarski, Klinsmann, Voller.

Argentina: Goycoechea, Ruggeri (Monzon, 46th), Simon, Serrizuela, Lorenzo, Basualdo, Troglio, Burruchaga (Calderon, 53rd), Sensini, Dezotti, Maradona.

Attendance: 73,603. **Referee:** Codesal (Mexico).

1994
Brazil 0, Italy 0 (Shoot-out)
(at Pasadena, Calif.)

		1	2	OT- T
July 17	Brazil (6-0-1)	0	0	0–0*
	Italy (4-2-1)	0	0	0–0

*Brazil wins shootout, 3-2.

Shootout (five shots each, alternating): ITA–Baresi (miss, 0-0); BRA–Santos (blocked, 0-0); ITA– Albertini (goal, 1-0); BRA–Romario (goal, 1-1); ITA–Evani (goal, 2-1); BRA–Branco (goal, 2-2); ITA–Massaro (blocked, 2-2); BRA–Dunga (goal, 2-3); ITA–R. Baggio (miss, 2-3).

Brazil–Taffarel, Jorginho (Cafu, 21st minute), Branco, Aldair, Santos, Mazinho, Silva, Dunga, Zinho (Viola, 106th), Bebeto, Romario.

Italy–Pagliuca, Mussi (Apolloni, 35th minute), Baresi, Benarrivo, Maldini, Albertini, D. Baggio (Evani, 95th), Berti, Donadoni, R. Baggio, Massaro.

Attendance: 94,194. **Referee:** Puhl (Hungary).

1998
France 3, Brazil 0
(at Paris)

		1	2- T
July 12	Brazil (6-1)	0	0– 0
	France (7-0)	2	1– 3

Goals: France–Zinedine Zidane (27th and 46th minutes), Petit (92).

Brazil–Taffarel, Cafu, Aldair, Baiano, Carlos, Sampaio (Edmundo, 74th minute), Dunga, Rivaldo, Leonardo (Denilson, 46th minute), Bebeto, Ronaldo.

France–Barthez, Lizarazu, Desailly, Thuram, Leboeuf, Djorkaeff (Viera, 75th minute), Deschamps, Zidane, Petit, Karembeu (Boghossian, 57th minute), Guivarc'h, Dugarry.

Attendance: 75,000. **Referee:** Belqola (Morocco).

2002
Brazil 2, Germany 0
(at Yokohama, Japan)

		1	2- T
June 30	Germany (5-2)	0	0– 0
	Brazil (7-0)	0	2– 2

Goals: Brazil–Ronaldo (67th and 79th minutes).

Germany–Kahn, Linke, Ramelow, Neuville, Hamann, Klose (Bierhoff, 74th minute), Jeremies (Asamoah, 77th minute), Bode (Ziege, 84th minute), Schneider, Metzelder, Frings.

Brazil–Marcos, Cafu, Lucio, Junior, Edmilson, Carlos, Silva, Ronaldo (Denilson, 90th minute), Rivaldo, Ronaldinho (Paulista, 85th minute), Kleberson.

Attendance: 69,029. **Referee:** Collina (Italy).

2006
Italy 1, France 1 (Shoot-out)
(at Berlin)

		1	2	OT- T
July 9	Italy (5-2)	1	0	0–1*
	France (7-0)	1	0	0–1

*Italy wins shootout, 5-4.

Goals: France–Zinedine Zidane (7th minute); Italy–Marco Materazzi (19th).

Shootout (five shots each, alternating): ITA–Pirlo (goal, 1-0); FRA–Wiltord (goal, 1-1); ITA– Materazzi (goal, 2-1); FRA–Trezeguet miss, 1-2); ITA– De Rossi (goal, 3-1); FRA–Abidal (goal, 2-3); ITA– Del Piero (goal, 4-2); FRA–Sagnol (goal, 3-4); ITA–Grosso (goal, 5-3).

Italy–Buffon, Gross, Cannavaro, Gattuso, Toni, Totti (De Rossi, 61st minute), Camoranesi (Del Piero, 86th), Zambrotta, Perrotta (Iaquinta), Pirlo, Materazzi.

France–Barthez, Abidal, Vieira (Diarra, 56th minute), Gallas, Makelele, Malouda, Zidane, Henry (Wiltord 107th), Thuram, Sagnol, Ribery (Trezeguet 100th).

Attendance: 69,000. **Referee:** Elizondo (Argentina).

World Cup Shoot-outs
Introduced in 1982; winning sides in **bold** type.

Year	Round		Final	SO	Year	Round		Final	SO
1982	Semi	**W. Germany** vs. France	3-3	(5-4)	1998	Second	**Argentina** vs. England	2-2	(4-3)
1986	Quarter	**Belgium** vs. Spain	1-1	(5-4)		Quarter	**France** vs. Italy	0-0	(4-3)
	Quarter	**France** vs. Brazil	1-1	(4-3)	2002	Second	**Spain** vs. Ireland	1-1	(3-2)
	Quarter	**W. Germany** vs. Mexico	0-0	(4-1)		Quarter	**So. Korea** vs. Spain	0-0	(5-3)
1990	Second	**Ireland** vs. Romania	0-0	(5-4)	2006	Second	**Ukraine** vs. Switzerland	0-0	(3-0)
	Quarter	**Argentina** vs.Yugoslavia	0-0	(3-2)		Quarter	**Germany** vs. Argentina	1-1	(4-2)
	Semi	**Argentina** vs. Italy	1-1	(4-3)		Quarter	**Portugal** vs. England	0-0	(3-1)
	Semi	**W. Germany** vs. England	1-1	(4-3)		Final	**Italy** vs. France	1-1	(5-3)
1994	Second	**Bulgaria** vs. Mexico	1-1	(3-1)					
	Quarter	**Sweden** vs. Romania	2-2	(5-4)					
	Final	**Brazil** vs. Italy	0-0	(3-2)					

World Cup (Cont.)
Year-by-Year Comparisons

How the 18 World Cup tournaments have compared in nations qualifying, matches played, players participating, goals scored, average goals per game, overall attendance and attendance per game.

Year	Host	Continent	Nations	Matches	Players	Scored	Goals Per Game	Attendance Overall	Per Game
1930	Uruguay	So. America	13	18	189	70	3.8	589,300	32,739
1934	Italy	Europe	16	17	208	70	4.1	361,000	21,235
1938	France	Europe	15	18	210	84	4.7	376,000	20,889
1942-46	Not held								
1950	Brazil	So. America	13	22	192	88	4.0	1,044,763	47,489
1954	Switzerland	Europe	16	26	233	140	5.3	872,000	33,538
1958	Sweden	Europe	16	35	241	126	3.6	819,402	23,411
1962	Chile	So. America	16	32	252	89	2.8	892,812	27,900
1966	England	Europe	16	32	254	89	2.8	1,464,944	45,780
1970	Mexico	No. America	16	32	270	95	3.0	1,690,890	52,840
1974	West Germany	Europe	16	38	264	97	2.6	1,809,953	47,630
1978	Argentina	So. America	16	38	277	102	2.7	1,685,602	44,358
1982	Spain	Europe	24	52	396	146	2.8	2,108,723	40,552
1986	Mexico	No. America	24	52	414	132	2.5	2,393,031	46,020
1990	Italy	Europe	24	52	413	115	2.2	2,516,354	48,391
1994	United States	No. America	24	52	437	140	2.7	3,587,088	68,982
1998	France	Europe	32	64	704	171	2.7	2,775,400	43,366
2002	Japan/So. Korea	Asia	32	64	736	161	2.5	2,705,197	42,269
2006	Germany	Europe	32	64	736	147	2.3	3,353,655	52,401

OTHER WORLDWIDE COMPETITION

The Olympic Games

Held every four years since 1896, except during World War I (1916) and World War II (1940-44). Soccer was not a medal sport in 1896 at Athens or in 1932 at Los Angeles. By agreement between FIFA and the IOC, Olympic soccer competition is currently limited to players 23 years old and under with a few exceptions.

Multiple winners: England and Hungary (3); Soviet Union and Uruguay (2).

MEN

Year		Year	
1900	**England**, France, Belgium	1964	**Hungary**, Czechoslovakia, Germany
1904	**Canada**, USA I, USA II	1968	**Hungary**, Bulgaria, Japan
1906	**Denmark**, Smyrna (Int'l entry), Greece	1972	**Poland**, Hungary, East Germany & Soviet Union
1908	**England**, Denmark, Netherlands	1976	**East Germany**, Poland, Soviet Union
1912	**England**, Denmark, Netherlands	1980	**Czechoslovakia**, East Germany, Soviet Union
1920	**Belgium**, Spain, Netherlands	1984	**France**, Brazil, Yugoslavia
1924	**Uruguay**, Switzerland, Sweden	1988	**Soviet Union**, Brazil, West Germany
1928	**Uruguay**, Argentina, Italy	1992	**Spain**, Poland, Ghana
1936	**Italy**, Austria, Norway	1996	**Nigeria**, Argentina, Brazil
1948	**Sweden**, Yugoslavia, Denmark	2000	**Cameroon**, Spain, Chile
1952	**Hungary**, Yugoslavia, Sweden	2004	**Argentina**, Paraguay, Italy
1956	**Soviet Union**, Yugoslavia, Bulgaria	2008	(at Beijing, China)
1960	**Yugoslavia**, Denmark, Hungary		

WOMEN

Multiple winners: United States (2).

Year		Year	
1996	**USA**, China, Norway	2004	**USA**, Brazil, Germany
2000	**Norway**, USA, Germany	2008	(at Beijing, China)

The Under-20 World Cup

Held every two years since 1977. Officially, the FIFA World Youth Championship.

Multiple winners: Argentina (6); Brazil (3); Portugal (2).

Year		Year		Year		Year	
1977	Soviet Union	1985	Brazil	1993	Brazil	2001	Argentina
1979	Argentina	1987	Yugoslavia	1995	Argentina	2003	Brazil
1981	West Germany	1989	Portugal	1997	Argentina	2005	Argentina
1983	Brazil	1991	Portugal	1999	Spain	2007	Argentina

The Under-17 World Cup

Held every two years since 1985. Officially, the FIFA U-17 World Championship.

Multiple winners: Brazil and Nigeria (3); Ghana (2).

Year		Year	
1985	Nigeria	1997	Brazil
1987	Soviet Union	1999	Brazil
1989	Saudi Arabia	2001	France
1991	Ghana	2003	Brazil
1993	Nigeria	2005	Mexico
1995	Ghana	2007	Nigeria

Indoor World Championship

First held in 1989. Officially, the FIFA Futsal World Championship.

Multiple winners: Brazil (3), Spain (2).

Year		Year	
1989	Brazil	2000	Spain
1992	Brazil	2004	Spain
1996	Brazil	2008	(at Brazil)

Women's World Cup

First held in 1991. Officially, the FIFA Women's World Championship.

Multiple winner: Germany and United States (2).

Year		Year	
1991	United States	2003	Germany
1995	Norway	2007	Germany
1999	United States		

Confederations Cup

First held in 1992. Contested by the Continental champions of Africa, Asia, Europe, North America and South America and originally called the Intercontinental Championship for the King Fahd Cup until it was redubbed the FIFA/Confederations Cup for the King Fahd Trophy in 1997.

Multiple winners: Brazil and France (2).

Year		Year	
1992	Argentina	2001	France
1995	Denmark	2003	France
1997	Brazil	2005	Brazil
1999	Mexico		

CONTINENTAL COMPETITION

European Championship

Held every four years since 1960. Officially, the European Football Championship. Winners receive the Henri Delaunay trophy, named for the Frenchman who first proposed the idea of a European Soccer Championship in 1927. The first one would not be played until five years after his death in 1955.

Multiple winners: Germany/West Germany (3); France (2).

Year		Year		Year		Year	
1960	Soviet Union	1976	Czechoslovakia	1988	Netherlands	2000	France
1964	Spain	1980	West Germany	1992	Denmark	2004	Greece
1968	Italy	1984	France	1996	Germany	2008	(at Switzerland/ Austria)
1972	West Germany						

Copa America

Held irregularly since 1916. Unofficially, the Championship of South America.

Multiple winners: Argentina and Uruguay (14); Brazil (8); Paraguay and Peru (2).

Year		Year		Year		Year		Year	
1916	Uruguay	1926	Uruguay	1946	Argentina	1963	Bolivia	1995	Uruguay
1917	Uruguay	1927	Argentina	1947	Argentina	1967	Uruguay	1997	Brazil
1919	Brazil	1929	Argentina	1949	Brazil	1975	Peru	1999	Brazil
1920	Uruguay	1935	Uruguay	1953	Paraguay	1979	Paraguay	2001	Colombia
1921	Argentina	1937	Argentina	1955	Argentina	1983	Uruguay	2004	Brazil
1922	Brazil	1939	Peru	1956	Uruguay	1987	Uruguay	2007	Brazil
1923	Uruguay	1941	Argentina	1957	Argentina	1989	Brazil		
1924	Uruguay	1942	Uruguay	1958	Argentina	1991	Argentina		
1925	Argentina	1945	Argentina	1959	Uruguay	1993	Argentina		

African Nations Cup

Contested since 1957 and held every two years since 1968.

Multiple winners: Egypt (5); Cameroon and Ghana (4); Congo/Zaire (3); Nigeria (2).

Year		Year		Year		Year		Year	
1957	Egypt	1970	Sudan	1982	Ghana	1994	Nigeria	2004	Tunisia
1959	Egypt	1972	Congo	1984	Cameroon	1996	South Africa	2006	Egypt
1962	Ethiopia	1974	Zaire	1986	Egypt	1998	Egypt	2008	(at Ghana)
1963	Ghana	1976	Morocco	1988	Cameroon	2000	Cameroon		
1965	Ghana	1978	Ghana	1990	Algeria	2002	Cameroon		
1968	Zaire	1980	Nigeria	1992	Ivory Coast				

CONCACAF Gold Cup

The Confederation of North, Central American and Caribbean Football Championship. Contested irregularly from 1963-81 and revived as CONCACAF Gold Cup in 1991.

Multiple winners: Mexico (7); Costa Rica and United States (2).

Year		Year		Year		Year		Year	
1963	Costa Rica	1969	Costa Rica	1977	Mexico	1993	Mexico	2000	Canada
1965	Mexico	1971	Mexico	1981	Honduras	1996	Mexico	2003	Mexico
1967	Guatemala	1973	Haiti	1991	United States	1998	Mexico	2005	United States

CLUB COMPETITION

FIFA Club World Championship

The FIFA Club World Championship merged with the Toyota Cup in 2005. The Toyota Cup held each December in Japan had previously served as the unofficial world club championship and was played between the champions of Europe and South America. But FIFA took over the tournament starting in 2005 and is now open to the champions from the African, Asian, Oceanic and North/Central American soccer federations as well as Europe and South America. From now on the new six-team tournament will be played each December in Japan. Note that FIFA held an eight-team world club championship tournament in 2000 but the tournament was not held again until late 2005 when it officially merged with the Toyota Cup.

Year	Year	Year
2000 Corinthians (Brazil)	2005 São Paulo (Brazil)	2006 SC Internacional (Brazil)

Toyota Cup

Also known as the **European/South American Cup** and Intercontinental Cup. Until 2005, it was contested annually in December between the winners of the European Champions League (formerly European Cup) and South America's Copa Libertadores for the unofficial World Club Championship. Four European Cup winners refused to participate in the championship match in the 1970s and were replaced each time by the European Cup runner-up: Panathinaikos (Greece) for Ajax Amsterdam (Netherlands) in 1971; Juventus (Italy) for Ajax in 1973; Atlético Madrid (Spain) for Bayern Munich (West Germany) in 1974; and Malmo (Sweden) for Nottingham Forest (England) in 1979. Another European Cup winner, Marseille of France, was prohibited by the Union of European Football Associations (UEFA) from playing for the 1993 Toyota Cup because of its involvement in a match-rigging scandal. Best-of-three game format from 1960-68, then a two-game/total goals format from 1969-79. Toyota became Cup sponsor in 1980, changed the format to a one-game championship and moved it to Toyko.

Multiple winners: AC Milan, Boca Juniors, Nacional, Penarol and Real Madrid (3); Ajax Amsterdam, Bayern Munich, FC Porto, Independiente, Inter Milan, Juventus, Santos and Sao Paulo (2).

Year	Year	Year
1960 Real Madrid (Spain)	1975 Not held	1990 AC Milan (Italy)
1961 Penarol (Uruguay)	1976 Bayern Munich (W. Germany)	1991 Red Star (Yugoslavia)
1962 Santos (Brazil)	1977 Boca Juniors (Argentina)	1992 Sao Paulo (Brazil)
1963 Santos (Brazil)	1978 Not held	1993 Sao Paulo (Brazil)
1964 Inter Milan (Italy)	1979 Olimpia (Paraguay)	1994 Velez Sarsfield (Argentina)
1965 Inter Milan (Italy)	1980 Nacional (Uruguay)	1995 Ajax Amsterdam (Netherlands)
1966 Penarol (Uruguay)	1981 Flamengo (Brazil)	1996 Juventus (Italy)
1967 Racing Club (Argentina)	1982 Penarol (Uruguay)	1997 Borussia Dortmund (Germany)
1968 Estudiantes (Argentina)	1983 Gremio (Brazil)	1998 Real Madrid (Spain)
1969 AC Milan (Italy)	1984 Independiente (Argentina)	1999 Manchester United (England)
1970 Feyenoord (Netherlands)	1985 Juventus (Italy)	2000 Boca Juniors (Argentina)
1971 Nacional (Uruguay)	1986 River Plate (Argentina)	2001 Bayern Munich (Germany)
1972 Ajax Amsterdam (Netherlands)	1987 FC Porto (Portugal)	2002 Real Madrid (Spain)
1973 Independiente (Argentina)	1988 Nacional (Uruguay)	2003 Boca Juniors (Argentina)
1974 Atlético Madrid (Spain)	1989 AC Milan (Italy)	2004 FC Porto (Portugal)

European Cup/UEFA Champions League

Contested annually since the 1955-56 season by the league champions of the member countries of the Union of European Football Associations (UEFA). In 1999, UEFA announced the formation of a new competition called the UEFA Champions League to take the place of the Cup competition.

Multiple winners: Real Madrid (9); AC Milan (7); Ajax Amsterdam, Bayern Munich and Liverpool (4); Barcelona, Benfica, FC Porto, Inter Milan, Juventus and Nottingham Forest (2).

Year	Year	Year
1956 Real Madrid (Spain)	1974 Bayern Munich (W. Germany)	1992 Barcelona (Spain)
1957 Real Madrid (Spain)	1975 Bayern Munich (W. Germany)	1993 Marseille (France)*
1958 Real Madrid (Spain)	1976 Bayern Munich (W. Germany)	1994 AC Milan (Italy)
1959 Real Madrid (Spain)	1977 Liverpool (England)	1995 Ajax Amsterdam (Netherlands)
1960 Real Madrid (Spain)	1978 Liverpool (England)	1996 Juventus (Italy)
1961 Benfica (Portugal)	1979 Nottingham Forest (England)	1997 Borussia Dortmund (Germany)
1962 Benfica (Portugal)	1980 Nottingham Forest (England)	1998 Real Madrid (Spain)
1963 AC Milan (Italy)	1981 Liverpool (England)	1999 Manchester United (England)
1964 Inter Milan (Italy)	1982 Aston Villa (England)	2000 Real Madrid (Spain)
1965 Inter Milan (Italy)	1983 SV Hamburg (W. Germany)	2001 Bayern Munich (Germany)
1966 Real Madrid (Spain)	1984 Liverpool (England)	2002 Real Madrid (Spain)
1967 Glasgow Celtic (Scotland)	1985 Juventus (Italy)	2003 AC Milan (Italy)
1968 Manchester United (England)	1986 Steaua Bucharest (Romania)	2004 FC Porto (Portugal)
1969 AC Milan (Italy)	1987 FC Porto (Portugal)	2005 Liverpool (England)
1970 Feyenoord (Netherlands)	1988 PSV Eindhoven (Netherlands)	2006 Barcelona (Spain)
1971 Ajax Amsterdam (Netherlands)	1989 AC Milan (Italy)	2007 AC Milan (Italy)
1972 Ajax Amsterdam (Netherlands)	1990 AC Milan (Italy)	*title vacated
1973 Ajax Amsterdam (Netherlands)	1991 Red Star Belgrade (Yugo.)	

European Cup Winner's Cup

Contested annually from the 1960-61 season through the 1999-2000 season by the cup winners of the member countries of the Union of European Football Associations (UEFA). The Cup Winner's Cup was absorbed by the UEFA Cup in 2000.

Multiple winners: Barcelona (4); AC Milan, RSC Anderlecht, Chelsea and Dinamo Kiev (2).

Year		Year		Year	
1961	Fiorentina (Italy)	1974	FC Magdeburg (E. Germany)	1987	Ajax Amsterdam (Netherlands)
1962	Atletico Madrid (Spain)	1975	Dinamo Kiev (USSR)	1988	Mechelen (Belgium)
1963	Tottenham Hotspur (England)	1976	RSC Anderlecht (Belgium)	1989	Barcelona (Spain)
1964	Sporting Lisbon (Portugal)	1977	SV Hamburg (W. Germany)	1990	Sampdoria (Italy)
1965	West Ham United (England)	1978	RSC Anderlecht (Belgium)	1991	Manchester United (England)
1966	Borussia Dortmund (W.Germany)	1979	Barcelona (Spain)	1992	Werder Bremen (Germany)
1967	Bayern Munich (W. Germany)	1980	Valencia (Spain)	1993	Parma (Italy)
1968	AC Milan (Italy)	1981	Dinamo Tbilisi (USSR)	1994	Arsenal (England)
1969	Slovan Bratislava (Czech.)	1982	Barcelona (Spain)	1995	Real Zaragoza (Spain)
1970	Manchester City (England)	1983	Aberdeen (Scotland)	1996	Paris St. Germain (France)
1971	Chelsea (England)	1984	Juventus (Italy)	1997	Barcelona (Spain)
1972	Glasgow Rangers (Scotland)	1985	Everton (England)	1998	Chelsea (England)
1973	AC Milan (Italy)	1986	Dinamo Kiev (USSR)	1999	Lazio (Italy)

UEFA Cup

Contested annually since the 1957-58 season by teams other than league champions and cup winners of the Union of European Football Associations (UEFA). Teams selected by UEFA based on each country's previous performance in the tournament. Teams from England were banned from UEFA Cup play from 1985-90 for the criminal behavior of their supporters. In 1999, with the formation of the new Champions League, UEFA announced that the UEFA Cup would be expanded and include any teams that would have normally played in the Cup Winner's Cup.

Multiple winners: Barcelona, Inter Milan, Juventus, Liverpool and Valencia (3); Borussia Mönchengladbach, Feyenoord, IFK Göteborg, Leeds United, Parma, Real Madrid and Tottenham Hotspur (2).

Year		Year		Year	
1958	Barcelona (Spain)	1976	Liverpool (England)	1994	Inter Milan (Italy)
1959	Not held	1977	Juventus (Italy)	1995	Parma (Italy)
1960	Barcelona (Spain)	1978	PSV Eindhoven (Netherlands)	1996	Bayern Munich (Germany)
1961	AS Roma (Italy)	1979	Borussia Mönchengladbach (W.	1997	Schalke 04 (Germany)
1962	Valencia (Spain)		Germany)	1998	Inter Milan (Italy)
1963	Valencia (Spain)	1980	Eintracht Frankfurt (W. Germany)	1999	Parma (Italy)
1964	Real Zaragoza (Spain)	1981	Ipswich Town (England)	2000	Galatasaray (Turkey)
1965	Ferencvaros (Hungary)	1982	IFK Göteborg (Sweden)	2001	Liverpool (England)
1966	Barcelona (Spain)	1983	RSC Anderlecht (Belgium)	2002	Feyenoord (Netherlands)
1967	Dinamo Zagreb (Yugoslavia)	1984	Tottenham Hotspur (England)	2003	FC Porto (Portugal)
1968	Leeds United (England)	1985	Real Madrid (Spain)	2004	Valencia (Spain)
1969	Newcastle United (England)	1986	Real Madrid (Spain)	2005	CSKA Moscow (Russia)
1970	Arsenal (England)	1987	IFK Göteborg (Sweden)	2006	Sevilla (Spain)
1971	Leeds United (England)	1988	Bayer Leverkusen (W. Germany)	2007	Espanyol (Spain)
1972	Tottenham Hotspur (England)	1989	Napoli (Italy)		
1973	Liverpool (England)	1990	Juventus (Italy)		
1974	Feyenoord (Netherlands)	1991	Inter Milan (Italy)		
1975	Borussia Mönchengladbach (W. Germany)	1992	Ajax Amsterdam (Netherlands)		
		1993	Juventus (Italy)		

Copa Libertadores

Contested annually since the 1955-56 season by the league champions of South America's football union.

Multiple winners: Independiente (7); Boca Juniors and Peñarol (5); Estudiantes, Nacional-Uruguay, Olimpia and São Paulo (3); Cruzeiro, Gremio, River Plate and Santos (2).

Year		Year		Year	
1960	Peñarol (Uruguay)	1976	Cruzeiro (Brazil)	1992	São Paulo (Brazil)
1961	Peñarol (Uruguay)	1977	Boca Juniors (Argentina)	1993	São Paulo (Brazil)
1962	Santos (Brazil)	1978	Boca Juniors (Argentina)	1994	Velez Sarsfield (Argentina)
1963	Santos (Brazil)	1979	Olimpia (Paraguay)	1995	Gremio (Brazil)
1964	Independiente (Argentina)	1980	Nacional (Uruguay)	1996	River Plate (Argentina)
1965	Independiente (Argentina)	1981	Flamengo (Brazil)	1997	Cruzeiro (Brazil)
1966	Peñarol (Uruguay)	1982	Peñarol (Uruguay)	1998	Vasco da Gama (Brazil)
1967	Racing Club (Argentina)	1983	Gremio (Brazil)	1999	Palmeiras (Brazil)
1968	Estudiantes de la Plata (Argentina)	1984	Independiente (Argentina)	2000	Boca Juniors (Argentina)
1969	Estudiantes de la Plata (Argentina)	1985	Argentinos Jrs. (Argentina)	2001	Boca Juniors (Argentina)
1970	Estudiantes de la Plata (Argentina)	1986	River Plate (Argentina)	2002	Olimpia (Paraguay)
1971	Nacional (Uruguay)	1987	Peñarol (Uruguay)	2003	Boca Juniors (Argentina)
1972	Independiente (Argentina)	1988	Nacional (Uruguay)	2004	Once Caldas (Colombia)
1973	Independiente (Argentina)	1989	Nacional Medellin (Colombia)	2005	São Paulo (Brazil)
1974	Independiente (Argentina)	1990	Olimpia (Paraguay)	2006	Internacional (Brazil)
1975	Independiente (Argentina)	1991	Colo Colo (Chile)	2007	Boca Juniors (Argentina)

Annual Awards
World Player of the Year

Presented by FIFA, the European Sports Magazine Association (ESM) and Adidas, the sports equipment manufacturer, since 1991. Winners are selected by national team coaches and captains from around the world.

Multiple winners: Ronaldo and Zinedine Zidane (3); Ronaldinho (2).

Year		Nat'l Team	Year		Nat'l Team
1991	Lothar Matthäus, Inter Milan	Germany	1999	Rivaldo, Barcelona	Brazil
1992	Marco Van Basten, AC Milan	Netherlands	2000	Zinedine Zidane, Juventus	France
1993	Roberto Baggio, Juventus	Italy	2001	Luis Figo, Real Madrid	Portugal
1994	Romario, Barcelona	Brazil	2002	Ronaldo, Real Madrid	Brazil
1995	George Weah, AC Milan	Liberia	2003	Zinedine Zidane, Real Madrid	France
1996	Ronaldo, Barcelona	Brazil	2004	Ronaldinho, Barcelona	Brazil
1997	Ronaldo, Inter Milan	Brazil	2005	Ronaldinho, Barcelona	Brazil
1998	Zinedine Zidane, Juventus	France	2006	Fabio Cannavaro, Juventus/Real Madrid	Italy

Women's World Player of the Year

Presented by FIFA since 2001. Winners are selected by national team coaches from around the world.

Multiple winners: Birgit Prinz (3), Mia Hamm (2).

Year		Nat'l Team	Year		Nat'l Team
2001	Mia Hamm, Washington Freedom	USA	2004	Birgit Prinz, FFC Frankfurt	Germany
2002	Mia Hamm, Washington Freedom	USA	2005	Birgit Prinz, FFC Frankfurt	Germany
2003	Birgit Prinz, FFC Frankfurt	Germany	2006	Marta, Umea IK	Brazil

European Player of the Year

Officially, the "Ballon d'Or," or "Golden Ball," and presented by *France Football* magazine since 1956. Candidates are limited to European players in European leagues and winners are selected by a poll of European soccer journalists.

Multiple winners: Johan Cruyff, Michel Platini and Marco Van Basten (3); Franz Beckenbauer, Alfredo di Stéfano, Kevin Keegan, Ronaldo and Karl-Heinz Rummenigge (2).

Year		Nat'l Team	Year		Nat'l Team
1956	Stanley Matthews, Blackpool	England	1982	Paolo Rossi, Juventus	Italy
1957	Alfredo di Stéfano, Real Madrid	Arg./Spain	1983	Michel Platini, Juventus	France
1958	Raymond Kopa, Real Madrid	France	1984	Michel Platini, Juventus	France
1959	Alfredo di Stéfano, Real Madrid	Arg./Spain	1985	Michel Platini, Juventus	France
1960	Luis Suarez, Barcelona	Spain	1986	Igor Belanov, Dinamo Kiev	Soviet Union
1961	Enrique Sivori, Juventus	Arg./Italy	1987	Ruud Gullit, AC Milan	Netherlands
1962	Josef Masopust, Dukla Prague	Czech.	1988	Marco Van Basten, AC Milan	Netherlands
1963	Lev Yashin, Dinamo Moscow	Soviet Union	1989	Marco Van Basten, AC Milan	Netherlands
1964	Denis Law, Manchester United	Scotland	1990	Lothar Matthäus, Inter Milan	W. Ger.
1965	Eusébio, Benfica	Portugal	1991	Jean-Pierre Papin, Marseille	France
1966	Bobby Charlton, Manchester United	England	1992	Marco Van Basten, AC Milan	Netherlands
1967	Florian Albert, Ferencvaros	Hungary	1993	Roberto Baggio, Juventus	Italy
1968	George Best, Manchester United	No. Ireland	1994	Hristo Stoitchkov, Barcelona	Bulgaria
1969	Gianni Rivera, AC Milan	Italy	1995	George Weah, AC Milan	Liberia
1970	Gerd Müller, Bayern Munich	W. Ger.	1996	Matthias Sammer, Bor. Dortmund	Germany
1971	Johan Cruyff, Ajax Amsterdam	Netherlands	1997	Ronaldo, Inter Milan	Brazil
1972	Franz Beckenbauer, Bayern Munich	W. Ger.	1998	Zinedine Zidane, Juventus	France
1973	Johan Cruyff, Barcelona	Netherlands	1999	Rivaldo, Barcelona	Brazil
1974	Johan Cruyff, Barcelona	Netherlands	2000	Luis Figo, Real Madrid	Portugal
1975	Oleg Blokhin, Dinamo Kiev	Soviet Union	2001	Michael Owen, Liverpool	England
1976	Franz Beckenbauer, Bayern Munich	W. Ger.	2002	Ronaldo, Real Madrid	Brazil
1977	Allan Simonsen, B. Mönchengladbach	Denmark	2003	Pavel Nedved, Juventus	Czech Republic
1978	Kevin Keegan, SV Hamburg	England	2004	Andriy Schevchenko, AC Milan	Ukraine
1979	Kevin Keegan, SV Hamburg	England	2005	Ronaldinho, Barcelona	Brazil
1980	K.H. Rummenigge, Bayern Munich	W. Ger.	2006	Fabio Cannavaro, Juventus/Real Madrid	Italy
1981	K.H. Rummenigge, Bayern Munich	W. Ger.			

U.S. Player of the Year

Presented by Honda and the Spanish-speaking radio show "Futbol de Primera" since 1991. Candidates are limited to American players who have played with the U.S. National Team and winners are selected by a panel of U.S. soccer journalists.

Multiple winners: Landon Donovan (4); Clint Dempsey and Eric Wynalda (2).

Year		Year		Year		Year	
1991	Hugo Perez	1996	Eric Wynalda	2001	Earnie Stewart	2006	Clint Dempsey
1992	Eric Wynalda	1997	Eddie Pope	2002	Landon Donovan	2007	Landon Donovan
1993	Thomas Dooley	1998	Cobi Jones	2003	Landon Donovan		
1994	Marcelo Balboa	1999	Kasey Keller	2004	Landon Donovan		
1995	Alexi Lalas	2000	Claudio Reyna	2005	Clint Dempsey		

South American Player of the Year

Presented by *El Mundo* of Venezuela from 1971-1985 and *El Pais* of Uruguay since 1986. Candidates are limited to South American players in South American leagues and winners are selected by a poll of South American sports editors.

Multiple winners: Elías Figueroa, Carlos Tevez and Zico (3); Enzo Francescoli, Diego Maradona and Carlos Valderrama (2).

Year		Nat'l Team	Year		Nat'l Team
1971	Tostao, Cruzeiro	Brazil	1989	Bebeto, Vasco da Gama	Brazil
1972	Teofilo Cubillas, Alianza Lima	Peru	1990	Raul Amarilla, Olimpia	Paraguay
1973	Pelé, Santos	Brazil	1991	Oscar Ruggeri, Velez Sarsfield	Argentina
1974	Elias Figueroa, Internacional	Chile	1992	Rai, Sao Paulo	Brazil
1975	Elias Figueroa, Internacional	Chile	1993	Carlos Valderrama, Atl. Junior	Colombia
1976	Elias Figueroa, Internacional	Chile	1994	Cafu, Sao Paulo	Brazil
1977	Zico, Flamengo	Brazil	1995	Enzo Francescoli, River Plate	Uruguay
1978	Mario Kempes, Valencia	Argentina	1996	Jose Luis Chilavert, Velez Sarsfield	Paraguay
1979	Diego Maradona, Argentinos Juniors	Argentina	1997	Marcelo Salas, River Plate	Chile
1980	Diego Maradona, Boca Juniors	Argentina	1998	Martin Palermo, Boca Juniors	Argentina
1981	Zico, Flamengo	Brazil	1999	Javier Saviola, River Plate	Argentina
1982	Zico, Flamengo	Brazil	2000	Romario, Vasco da Gama	Brazil
1983	Socrates, Corinthians	Brazil	2001	Juan Roman Riquelme, Boca Juniors	Argentina
1984	Enzo Francescoli, River Plate	Uruguay	2002	Jose Cardozo, Toluca	Paraguay
1985	Julio Cesar Romero, Fluminense	Paraguay	2003	Carlos Tevez, Boca Juniors	Argentina
1986	Antonio Alzamendi, River Plate	Uruguay	2004	Carlos Tevez, Boca Juniors	Argentina
1987	Carlos Valderrama, Deportivo Cali	Colombia	2005	Carlos Tevez, Corinthians	Argentina
1988	Ruben Paz, Racing Buenos Aires	Uruguay	2006	Matias Fernandez, Colo Coco	Chile

Asian Player of the Year

Presented by the Asian Football Confederation since 1994. Prior to 1994 it was awarded unoffically.

Multiple winners: Kim Joo-Sung (3); Hidetoshi Nakata (2).

Year		Year		Year	
1988	Ahmed Radhi, Iraq	1995	Masami Ihara, Japan	2002	Shinji Ono, Japan
1989	Kim Joo-Sung, South Korea	1996	Khodadad Azizi, Iran	2003	Mehdi Mahdavikia, Iran
1990	Kim Joo-Sung, South Korea	1997	Hidetoshi Nakata, Japan	2004	Ali Karimi, Iran
1991	Kim Joo-Sung, South Korea	1998	Hidetoshi Nakata, Japan	2005	Hamad Al-Montashari, S. Arabia
1992	no award	1999	Ali Daei, Iran		
1993	Kazuyoshi Miura, Japan	2000	Nawaf Al-Temyat, S. Arabia	2006	Khalfan Ibrahim, Qatar
1994	Saeed Al-Owairan, S. Arabia	2001	Fan Zhiyi, China		

African Player of the Year

Officially, the African "Ballon d'Or" and presented by *France Football* magazine from 1970-96. The Arican Player of the Year award has been presented by the CAF (African Football Confederation) since 1997. All African players are eligible for the award.

Multiple winners: George Weah and Abedi Pelé (3); El Hadji Diouf, Samuel Eto'o, Nwankwo Kanu, Roger Milla and Thomas N'Kono (2).

Year		Year		Year	
1970	Salif Keita, Mali	1983	Mahmoud Al-Khatib, Egypt	1996	Nwankwo Kanu, Nigeria
1971	Ibrahim Sunday, Ghana	1984	Theophile Abega, Cameroon	1997	Victor Ikpeba, Nigeria
1972	Cherif Souleymane, Guinea	1985	Mohamed Timoumi, Morocco	1998	Mustapha Hadji, Morocco
1973	Tshimimu Bwanga, Zaire	1986	Badou Zaki, Morocco	1999	Nwankwo Kanu, Nigeria
1974	Paul Moukila, Congo	1987	Rabah Madjer, Algeria	2000	Patrick Mboma, Cameroon
1975	Ahmed Faras, Morocco	1988	Kalusha Bwalya, Zambia	2001	El Hadji Diouf, Senegal
1976	Roger Milla, Cameroon	1989	George Weah, Liberia	2002	El Hadji Diouf, Senegal
1977	Dhiab Tarak, Tunisia	1990	Roger Milla, Cameroon	2003	Samuel Eto'o, Cameroon
1978	Abdul Razak, Ghana	1991	Abedi Pelé, Ghana	2004	Samuel Eto'o, Cameroon
1979	Thomas N'Kono, Cameroon	1992	Abedi Pelé, Ghana	2005	Samuel Eto'o, Cameroon
1980	Jean Manga Onguene, Cameroon	1993	Abedi Pelé, Ghana	2006	Didier Drogba, Ivory Coast
1981	Lakhdar Belloumi, Algeria	1994	George Weah, Liberia		
1982	Thomas N'Kono, Cameroon	1995	George Weah, Liberia		

U.S. PRO LEAGUES

OUTDOOR
Major League Soccer

Sanctioned by U.S. Soccer and FIFA, the international soccer federation. MLS was founded on the heels of the successful 1994 World Cup tournament hosted by the United States and it remains the only FIFA-sanctioned division I outdoor league in the United States. The annual MLS title game is known as the MLS Cup.

Multiple winners: D.C. United (4); Los Angeles and San Jose (2).

MLS Cup

Year	Winner	Head Coach	Score	Loser	Head Coach	Site
1996	D.C. United	Bruce Arena	3-2 OT	Los Angeles Galaxy	Lothar Osiander	Foxboro, Mass.
1997	D.C. United	Bruce Arena	2-1	Colorado Rapids	Glen Myernick	Washington, D.C.
1998	Chicago Fire	Bob Bradley	2-0	D.C. United	Bruce Arena	Pasadena, Calif.
1999	D.C. United	Thomas Rongen	2-0	Los Angeles Galaxy	Sigi Schmid	Foxboro, Mass.
2000	Kansas City Wizards	Bob Gansler	1-0	Chicago Fire	Bob Bradley	Washington, D.C.
2001	San Jose Earthquakes	Frank Yallop	2-1 OT	Los Angeles Galaxy	Sigi Schmid	Columbus, Ohio
2002	Los Angeles Galaxy	Sigi Schmid	1-0 2OT	N.E. Revolution	Steve Nicol	Foxboro, Mass.
2003	San Jose Earthquakes	Frank Yallop	4-2	Chicago Fire	Dave Sarachan	Carson, Calif.
2004	D.C. United	Peter Nowak	3-2	Kansas City Wizards	Bob Gansler	Carson, Calif.
2005	Los Angeles Galaxy	Steve Sampson	1-0 OT	N.E. Revolution	Steve Nicol	Frisco, Texas
2006	Houston Dynamo	Dominic Kinnear	1-1 2OT*	N.E. Revolution	Steve Nicol	Frisco, Texas

*Dynamo won on penalty kicks, 4-3.

MLS Cup '96
D.C. United, 3-2 (OT)
Oct. 20 at Foxboro Stadium, Foxboro, Mass.
Attendance: 34,643

	1	2	OT	
Los Angeles Galaxy	1	1	0	—2
D.C. United	0	2	1	—3

First Half: LA–Eduardo Hurtado (Mauricio Cienfuegos), 5th minute.
Second Half: LA–Chris Armas (unassisted), 56th; DC–Tony Sanneh (Marco Etcheverry), 73rd; DC–Shawn Medved (unassisted), 82nd.
Overtime: DC–Eddie Pope (Etcheverry), 94th.
MVP: Marco Etcheverry, D.C. United, Midfielder

MLS Cup '97
D.C. United, 2-1
Oct. 26 at RFK Stadium, Washington, D.C.
Attendance: 57,431

	1	2	
Colorado Rapids	0	1	—1
D.C. United	1	1	—2

First Half: DC–Jaime Moreno (Tony Sanneh, David Vaudreuil), 37th minute.
Second Half: DC–Sanneh (John Harkes, Richie Williams), 68th; COL–Adrian Paz (David Patino, Matt Kmosko), 75th.
MVP: Jaime Moreno, D.C. United, Forward

MLS Cup '98
Chicago Fire, 2-0
Oct. 25 at the Rose Bowl, Pasadena, Calif.
Attendance: 51,350

	1	2	
D.C. United	0	0	—0
Chicago	2	0	—2

First Half: CHI–Jerzy Podbrozny (Peter Nowak, Ante Razov), 29th minute; CHI–Diego Gutierrez (Nowak), 45th.
MVP: Nowak, Chicago, Midfielder

MLS Cup '99
D.C. United, 2-0
Nov. 21 at Foxboro Stadium, Foxboro, Mass.
Attendance: 44,910

	1	2	
D.C. United	2	0	—2
Los Angeles	0	0	—0

First Half: DC–Jaime Moreno (Roy Lassiter), 19th minute; DC–Ben Olsen (unassisted), 48th
MVP: Olsen, D.C. United, Midfielder

MLS Cup 2000
Kansas City Wizards, 1-0
Oct. 15 at RFK Stadium, Washington, D.C.
Attendance: 39,159

	1	2	
Chicago	0	0	—0
Kansas City	1	0	—1

First Half: DC– Miklos Molnar (Chris Klein), 11th minute.
MVP: Tony Meola, Kansas City, Goalkeeper

MLS Cup 2001
San Jose Earthquakes, 2-1 (OT)
Oct. 21 at Crew Stadium, Columbus, Ohio
Attendance: 21,626

	1	2	OT	
San Jose	1	0	1	—2
Los Angeles	1	0	0	—1

First Half: LA–Luis Hernandez (Greg Vanney, Kevin Hartman), 21st minute; SJ–Landon Donovan (Ian Russell, Richard Mulrooney), 43rd. **Overtime:** SJ–Dwayne DeRosario (Ronnie Ekelund, Zak Ibsen), 96th.
MVP: Dwayne DeRosario, San Jose, Forward

MLS Cup 2002
Los Angeles Galaxy, 1-0 (2 OT)
Oct. 20 at Gillette Stadium, Foxboro, Mass.
Attendance: 61,316

	1	2	1OT	2OT	
Los Angeles	0	0	0	1	—1
New England	0	0	0	0	—0

2nd OT: LA–Carlos Ruiz, (Tyrone Marshall, Chris Albright), 113th minute.
MVP: Carlos Ruiz, Los Angeles, F

MLS Cup 2003
San Jose Earthquakes, 4-2
Nov. 23 at Home Depot Center, Carson, Calif.
Attendance: 27,000

	1	2	
San Jose	2	2	—4
Chicago	0	2	—2

First Half: SJ— Ronnie Ekelund (unassisted), 5th minute; SJ–Landon Donovan (Jamil Walker), 38th.

Second Half: CHI–DaMarcus Beasley (Andy Williams), 49th; SJ–Richard Mulrooney (Craig Waibel), 50th; CHI–own goal (Chris Roner), 54th; SJ–Donovan (Dwayne De Rosario, Brian Mullan), 71st.

MVP: Landon Donovan, San Jose, F

MLS Cup 2004
D.C. United, 3-2
Nov. 14 at Home Depot Center, Carson, Calif.
Attendance: 25,797

	1	2	
D.C. United	3	0	—3
Kansas City	1	1	—2

First Half: KC— Jose Burciaga Jr. (unassisted), 6th minute; DC–Alecko Eskandarian (Brian Carroll), 19th. DC–Alecko Eskandarian (unassisted), 23rd. DC–own goal (Alex Zotinca), 26th.

Second Half: KC–Josh Wolff (penalty kick), 58th.

MVP: Alecko Eskandarian, D.C. United, F

MLS Cup 2005
Los Angeles Galaxy, 1-0 (OT)
Nov. 13 at Pizza Hut Park, Frisco, Texas
Attendance: 21,193

	1	2	OT	
Los Angeles	1	0	1	—1
New England	0	0	0	—0

Overtime: LA–Guillermo Ramirez (unassisted), 107th.

MVP: Guillermo "Pando" Ramirez, Los Angeles, F

MLS Cup 2006
Houston Dynamo, 1-1 (2OT)
won on penalty kicks, 4-3
Nov. 12 at Pizza Hut Park, Frisco, Texas
Attendance: 22,427

	1	2	OT	2OT	
New England	0	0	0	1	—1
Houston	0	0	0	1	—1

2nd Overtime: NE–Taylor Twellman, 113th. HOU–Brian Ching, 114th.

MVP: Brian Ching, Houston, F

MLS Cup 2007
The 2007 MLS Cup was scheduled for Nov. 18, 2007 at RFK Stadium, Washington, D.C.

Regular Season

Most Valuable Player
Multiple winner: Preki (2).
1996 Carlos Valderrama, Tampa Bay
1997 Preki, Kansas City
1998 Marco Etcheverry, D.C.
1999 Jason Kreis, Dallas
2000 Tony Meola, Kansas City
2001 Alex Pineda Chacón, Miami
2002 Carlos Ruiz, LA
2003 Preki, Kansas City
2004 Amado Guevara, MetroStars
2005 Taylor Twellman, New England
2006 Christian Gomez, D.C. United

Coach of the Year
Multiple winner: Bob Bradley (2).
1996 Thomas Rongen, Tampa Bay
1997 Bruce Arena, D.C.
1998 Bob Bradley, Chicago
1999 Sigi Schmid, Los Angeles
2000 Bob Gansler, Kansas City
2001 Frank Yallop, San Jose
2002 Steve Nicol, New England
2003 Dave Sarachan, Chicago
2004 Greg Andrulis, Columbus
2005 Dominic Kinnear, San Jose
2006 Bob Bradley, Chivas USA

Defender of the Year
Multiple winners: Carlos Bocanegra (2).
1996 John Doyle, San Jose
1997 Eddie Pope, D.C.
1998 Lubos Kubik, Chicago
1999 Robin Fraser, Los Angeles
2000 Peter Vermes, Kansas City
2001 Jeff Agoos, San Jose
2002 Carlos Bocanegra, Chicago
2003 Carlos Bocanegra, Chicago
2004 Robin Fraser, Columbus
2005 Jimmy Conrad, Kansas City
2006 Bobby Bosewell, D.C. United

Leading Scorer
Multiple winners: Preki and Taylor Twellman (2).

	G	A	Pts
1996 Roy Lassiter, Tampa Bay	27	4	58
1997 Preki, Kansas City	12	17	41
1998 Stern John, Columbus	26	5	57
1999 Jason Kreis, Dallas	18	15	51
2000 Mamadou Diallo, Tampa Bay	26	4	56
2001 Alex Pineda Chacón, Miami	19	9	47
2002 Taylor Twellman, New England	23	6	52
2003 Preki, Kansas City	12	17	41
2004 Pat Noonan, New England	11	8	30
& Amado Guevara, MetroStars	10	10	30
2005 Taylor Twellman, New England	17	7	41
2006 Jeff Cunningham, Real Salt Lake	16	11	43

Goalkeeper of the Year
Multiple winners: Joe Cannon and Pat Onstad (2).
1996 Mark Dodd, Dallas
1997 Brad Friedel, Columbus
1998 Zach Thornton, Chicago
1999 Kevin Hartman, Los Angeles
2000 Tony Meola, Kansas City
2001 Tim Howard, MetroStars
2002 Joe Cannon, San Jose
2003 Pat Onstad, San Jose
2004 Joe Cannon, Colorado
2005 Pat Onstad, San Jose
2006 Troy Perkins, D.C. United

Rookie of the Year
1996 Steve Ralston, Tampa Bay
1997 Mike Duhaney, Tampa Bay
1998 Ben Olsen, D.C.
1999 Jay Heaps, Miami
2000 Carlos Bocanegra, Chicago
2001 Rodrigo Faria, MetroStars
2002 Kyle Martino, Columbus
2003 Damani Ralph, Chicago
2004 Clint Dempsey, New England
2005 Michael Parkhurst, New England
2006 Jonathan Bornstein, Chivas USA

Other U.S. Pro Leagues (Cont.)
National Professional Soccer League (1967)

Not sanctioned by FIFA, the international soccer federation. The NPSL recruited individual players to fill the rosters of its 10 teams. The league lasted only one season.

	Playoff Final			Regular Season			
Year	Winner	Scores	Loser	Leading Scorer	G	A	Pts
1967	Oakland Clippers	0-1, 4-1	Baltimore Bays	Yanko Daucik, Toronto 20	8	48	

United Soccer Association (1967)

Sanctioned by FIFA. Originally called the North American Soccer League, it became the USA to avoid being confused with the National Professional Soccer League (see above). Instead of recruiting individual players, the USA imported 12 entire teams from Europe to represent its 12 franchises. It, too, only lasted a season. The league champion Los Angeles Wolves were actually Wolverhampton of England and the runner-up Washington Whips were Aberdeen of Scotland.

	Playoff Final			Regular Season			
Year	Winner	Score	Loser	Leading Scorer	G	A	Pts
1967	Los Angeles Wolves	6-5 (OT)	Washington Whips	Roberto Boninsegna, Chicago 10	1	21	

North American Soccer League (1968-84)

The NPSL and USA merged to form the NASL in 1968 and the new league lasted through 1984. The NASL championship was known as the Soccer Bowl from 1975-84. One game decided the NASL title every year but five. There were no playoffs in 1969; a two-game/aggregate goals format was used in 1968 and '70; and a best-of-three games format was used in 1971 and '84; (*) indicates overtime and (†) indicates game decided by shootout.

Multiple winners: NY Cosmos (5); Chicago (2).

	Playoff Final			Regular Season			
Year	Winner	Score(s)	Loser	Leading Scorer	G	A	Pts
1968	Atlanta Chiefs	0-0,3-0	San Diego Toros	John Kowalik, Chicago 30	9	69	
1969	Kansas City Spurs	No game	Atlanta Chiefs	Kaiser Motaung, Atlanta 16	4	36	
1970	Rochester Lancers	3-0,1-3	Washington Darts	Kirk Apostolidis, Dallas 16	3	35	
1971	Dallas Tornado	1-2*,4-1,2-0	Atlanta Chiefs	Carlos Metidieri, Rochester 19	8	46	
1972	New York Cosmos	2-1	St. Louis Stars	Randy Horton, New York 9	4	22	
1973	Philadelphia Atoms	2-0	Dallas Tornado	Kyle Rote Jr., Dallas 10	10	30	
1974	Los Angeles Aztecs	3-3†	Miami Toros	Paul Child, San Jose 15	6	36	
1975	Tampa Bay Rowdies	2-0	Portland Timbers	Steve David, Miami 23	6	52	
1976	Toronto Metros	3-0	Minnesota Kicks	Giorgio Chinaglia, New York 19	11	49	
1977	New York Cosmos	2-1	Seattle Sounders	Steve David, Los Angeles 26	6	58	
1978	New York Cosmos	3-1	Tampa Bay Rowdies	Giorgio Chinaglia, New York 34	11	79	
1979	Vancouver Whitecaps	2-1	Tampa Bay Rowdies	Oscar Fabbiani, Tampa Bay 25	8	58	
1980	New York Cosmos	3-0	Ft. Laud. Strikers	Giorgio Chinaglia, New York 32	13	77	
1981	Chicago Sting	0-0†	New York Cosmos	Giorgio Chinaglia, New York 29	16	74	
1982	New York Cosmos	1-0	Seattle Sounders	Giorgio Chinaglia, New York 20	15	55	
1983	Tulsa Roughnecks	2-0	Toronto Blizzard	Roberto Cabanas, New York 25	16	66	
1984	Chicago Sting	2-1,3-2	Toronto Blizzard	Steve Zungul, Golden Bay 20	10	50	

Note: In 1969, Kansas City won the NASL regular season championship with 110 points to 109 for Atlanta. There were no playoffs.

Regular Season MVP
Regular season Most Valuable Player as designated by the NASL.

Multiple winner: Carlos Metidieri (2).

Year		Year		Year	
1967	Rueben Navarro, Phila (NPSL)	1973	Warren Archibald, Miami	1979	Johan Cruyff, Los Angeles
1968	John Kowalik, Chicago	1974	Peter Silvester, Baltimore	1980	Roger Davies, Seattle
1969	Cirilio Fernandez, KC	1975	Steve David, Miami	1981	Giorgio Chinaglia, New York
1970	Carlos Metidieri, Rochester	1976	Pelé, New York	1982	Peter Ward, Seattle
1971	Carlos Metidieri, Rochester	1977	Franz Beckenbauer, New York	1983	Roberto Cabanas, New York
1972	Randy Horton, New York	1978	Mike Flanagan, New England	1984	Steve Zungul, Golden Bay

USL First Division/A-League

The American Professional Soccer League was formed in 1990 with the merger of the Western Soccer League and the New American Soccer League. The APSL was officially sanctioned as an outdoor pro league in 1992 and changed its name to the A-League in 1995. The league was reorganized under the umbrella of the United Soccer Leagues and renamed the USL First Division in 2005.

Multiple winners: Seattle (4); Rochester (3); Colorado, Milwaukee and Montreal (2).

Year		Year		Year	
1990	Maryland Bays	1996	Seattle Sounders	2002	Milwaukee Rampage
1991	SF Bay Blackhawks	1997	Milwaukee Rampage	2003	Charleston Battery
1992	Colorado Foxes	1998	Rochester Rhinos	2004	Montreal Impact
1993	Colorado Foxes	1999	Minnesota Thunder	2005	Seattle Sounders
1994	Montreal Impact	2000	Rochester Rhinos	2006	Vancouver Whitecaps
1995	Seattle Sounders	2001	Rochester Rhinos	2007	Seattle Sounders

Women's United Soccer Association (2001-03)

The eight-team WUSA was formed in 2000 as the top women's outdoor professional league and play began in 2001. The league championship game is known as the Founders Cup. The league folded following the 2003 season.

Founders Cup

Year	Winner	Score	Loser	Site
2001	Bay Area CyberRays	3-3*	Atlanta Beat	Foxboro, Mass.
2002	Carolina Courage	3-2	Washington Freedom	Atlanta, Ga.
2003	Washington Freedom	2-1 OT	Atlanta Beat	San Diego, Calif.

*Bay Area won shoot-out, 4-2.

Regular Season

WUSA Most Valuable Player

2001 Tiffeny Milbrett, New York
2002 Marinette Pichon, Philadelphia
2003 Maren Meinert, Boston

WUSA Leading Scorer

		G	A	Pts
2001	Tiffeny Milbrett, New York	16	3	35
2002	Katia, San Jose	15	5	35
2003	Mia Hamm, Washington	11	11	33
	& Abby Wambach, Washington	13	7	33

INDOOR

Major Soccer League (1978-92)

Originally the Major Indoor Soccer League from 1978-79 season through 1989-90. The MISL championship was decided by one game in 1980 and 1981; a best-of-three games series in 1979, best-of-five games in 1982 and 1983; and best-of-seven games since 1984. The MSL folded after the 1991-92 season.

Multiple winners: San Diego (8); New York (4).

Playoff Final / Regular Season

Year	Winner	Series	Loser	Leading Scorer	G	A	Pts
1979	New York Arrows	2-0	Philadelphia	Fred Grgurev, Philadelphia	46	28	74
1980	New York Arrows	7-4 (1 game)	Houston	Steve Zungul, New York	90	46	136
1981	New York Arrows	6-5 (1 game)	St. Louis	Steve Zungul, New York	108	44	152
1982	New York Arrows	3-2 (LWWLW)	St. Louis	Steve Zungul, New York	103	60	163
1983	San Diego Sockers	3-2 (WWLLW)	Baltimore	Steve Zungul, NY/Golden Bay	75	47	122
1984	Baltimore Blast	4-1 (LWWWW)	St. Louis	Stan Stamenkovic, Baltimore	34	63	97
1985	San Diego Sockers	4-1 (WWLWW)	Baltimore	Steve Zungul, San Diego	68	68	136
1986	San Diego Sockers	4-3 (WLLLWWW)	Minnesota	Steve Zungul, Tacoma	55	60	115
1987	Dallas Sidekicks	4-3 (LLWWLWW)	Tacoma	Tatu, Dallas	73	38	111
1988	San Diego Sockers	4-0	Cleveland	Eric Rasmussen, Wichita	55	57	112
1989	San Diego Sockers	4-3 (LWWWLLW)	Baltimore	Preki, Tacoma	51	53	104
1990	San Diego Sockers	4-2 (LWWWLW)	Baltimore	Tatu, Dallas	64	49	113
1991	San Diego Sockers	4-2 (WLWLWW)	Cleveland	Tatu, Dallas	78	66	144
1992	San Diego Sockers	4-2 (WWWLLW)	Dallas	Zoran Karic, Cleveland	39	63	102

Playoff MVPs

MSL playoff Most Valuable Players, selected by a panel of soccer media covering the playoffs.

Multiple winners: Steve Zungul (4); Brian Quinn (2).

Year		Year	
1979	Shep Messing, NY	1986	Brian Quinn, SD
1980	Steve Zungul, NY	1987	Tatu, Dallas
1981	Steve Zungul, NY	1988	Hugo Perez, SD
1982	Steve Zungul, NY	1989	Victor Nogueira, SD
1983	Juli Veee, SD	1990	Brian Quinn, SD
1984	Scott Manning, Bal.	1991	Ben Collins, SD
1985	Steve Zungul, SD	1992	Thompson Usiyan, SD

Regular Season MVPs

MSL regular season Most Valuable Players, selected by a panel of soccer media from every city in the league.

Multiple winners: Steve Zungul (6); Victor Nogueira and Tatu (2).

Year		Year	
1979	Steve Zungul, NY	1986	Steve Zungul, SD/Tac.
1980	Steve Zungul, NY	1987	Tatu, Dallas
1981	Steve Zungul, NY	1988	Erik Rasmussen, Wich.
1982	Steve Zungul, NY	1989	Preki, Tacoma
	& Stan Terlecki, Pit.	1990	Tatu, Dallas
1983	Alan Mayer, SD	1991	Victor Nogueira, SD
1984	Stan Stamenkovic, Bal.	1992	Victor Nogueira, SD
1985	Steve Zungul, SD		

NASL Indoor Champions (1980-84)

The North American Soccer League started an indoor league in the fall of 1979. The indoor NASL, which featured many of the same teams and players who played in the outdoor NASL, crowned champions from 1980-82 before suspending play. It was revived for the 1983-84 indoor season but folded for good in 1984. The NASL held indoor tournaments in 1975 (San Jose Earthquakes won) and 1976 (Tampa Bay Rowdies won) before the indoor league was started.

Multiple winner: San Diego (2).

Year		Year		Year		Year	
1980	Tampa Bay Rowdies	1982	San Diego Sockers	1983	Play suspended	1984	San Diego Sockers
1981	Edmonton Drillers						

Major Indoor Soccer League

The winter indoor MISL began as the American Indoor Soccer Association in 1984-85, then changed its name to the National Professional Soccer League in 1989-90 and was known as the NPSL until 2001 when the name was changed again and the league was relaunched as the MISL.

Multiple winners: Canton (5); Milwaukee (4); Baltimore and Cleveland (3); Kansas City and Philadelphia (2).

Year		Year		Year		Year	
1985	Canton (OH) Invaders	1991	Chicago Power	1997	Kansas City Attack	2003	Baltimore Blast
1986	Canton Invaders	1992	Detroit Rockers	1998	Milwaukee Wave	2004	Baltimore Blast
1987	Louisville Thunder	1993	Kansas City Attack	1999	Cleveland Crunch	2005	Milwaukee Wave
1988	Canton Invaders	1994	Cleveland Crunch	2000	Milwaukee Wave	2006	Baltimore Blast
1989	Canton Invaders	1995	St. Louis Ambush	2001	Milwaukee Wave	2007	Philadelphia Kixx
1990	Canton Invaders	1996	Cleveland Crunch	2002	Philadelphia Kixx		

Continental Indoor Soccer League (1993-97)

The summer indoor CISL played its first season in 1993 and folded following the 1997 season.

Multiple winner: Monterrey (2).

Year		Year		Year	
1993	Dallas Sidekicks	1995	Monterrey La Raza	1997	Seattle Seadogs
1994	Las Vegas Dustdevils	1996	Monterrey La Raza		

U.S. COLLEGES

NCAA Men's Division I Champions

NCAA Division I champions since the first title was contested in 1959. The championship has been shared three times—in 1967, 1968 and 1989. There was a playoff for third place from 1974-81.

Multiple winners: Saint Louis (10); Indiana (7); San Francisco and Virginia (5); UCLA (4); Clemson, Connecticut, Howard and Michigan St. (2).

Year	Winner	Head Coach	Score	Runner-up	Host/Site	Semifinalists
1959	Saint Louis	Bob Guelker	5-2	Bridgeport	Connecticut	West Chester, CCNY
1960	Saint Louis	Bob Guelker	3-2	Maryland	Brooklyn	West Chester, Connecticut
1961	West Chester	Mel Lorback	2-0	Saint Louis	Saint Louis	Bridgeport, Rutgers
1962	Saint Louis	Bob Guelker	4-3	Maryland	Saint Louis	Mich. St., Springfield
1963	Saint Louis	Bob Guelker	3-0	Navy	Rutgers	Army, Maryland
1964	Navy	F.H. Warner	1-0	Michigan St.	Brown	Army, Saint Louis
1965	Saint Louis	Bob Guelker	1-0	Michigan St.	Saint Louis	Army, Navy
1966	San Francisco	Steve Negoesco	5-2	LIU-Brooklyn	California	Army, Mich. St.
1967-a	Michigan St. & Saint Louis	Gene Kenney Harry Keough	0-0	—	Saint Louis	LIU-Bklyn, Navy
1968-b	Michigan St. & Maryland	Gene Kenney Doyle Royal	2-2 (2 OT)	—	Ga. Tech	Brown, San Jose St.
1969	Saint Louis	Harry Keough	4-0	San Francisco	San Jose St.	Harvard, Maryland
1970	Saint Louis	Harry Keough	1-0	UCLA	SIU-Ed'sville	Hartwick, Howard
1971-c	Howard	Lincoln Phillips	3-2	Saint Louis	Miami	Harvard, San Fran.
1972	Saint Louis	Harry Keough	4-2	UCLA	Miami	Cornell, Howard
1973	Saint Louis	Harry Keough	2-1 (OT)	UCLA	Miami	Brown, Clemson

Year	Winner	Head Coach	Score	Runner-up	Host/Site	Third Place
1974	Howard	Lincoln Phillips	2-1 (4OT)	Saint Louis	Saint Louis	Hartwick 3, UCLA 1
1975	San Francisco	Steve Negoesco	4-0	SIU-Ed'sville	SIU-Ed'sville	Brown 2, Howard 0
1976	San Francisco	Steve Negoesco	1-0	Indiana	Penn	Hartwick 4, Clemson 3
1977	Hartwick	Jim Lennox	2-1	San Francisco	California	SIU-Ed'sville 3, Brown 2
1978-d	San Francisco	Steve Negoesco	4-3 (OT)	Indiana	Tampa	Clemson 6, Phi. Textile 2
1979	SIU-Ed'sville	Bob Guelker	3-2	Clemson	Tampa	Penn St. 2, Columbia 1
1980	San Francisco	Steve Negoesco	4-3 (OT)	Indiana	Tampa	Ala. A&M 2, Hartwick 0
1981	Connecticut	Joe Morrone	2-1 (OT)	Alabama A&M	Stanford	East. Ill. 4, Phi. Textile 2

Year	Winner	Head Coach	Score	Runner-up	Host/Site	Semifinalists
1982	Indiana	Jerry Yeagley	2-1 (8 OT)	Duke	Ft. Lauderdale	Connecticut, SIU-Ed'sville
1983	Indiana	Jerry Yeagley	1-0 (2 OT)	Columbia	Ft. Lauderdale	Connecticut, Virginia
1984	Clemson	I.M. Ibrahim	2-1	Indiana	Seattle	Hartwick, UCLA
1985	UCLA	Sigi Schmid	1-0 (8 OT)	American	Seattle	Evansville, Hartwick
1986	Duke	John Rennie	1-0	Akron	Tacoma	Fresno St., Harvard
1987	Clemson	I.M. Ibrahim	2-0	San Diego St.	Clemson	Harvard, N. Carolina
1988	Indiana	Jerry Yeagley	1-0	Howard	Indiana	Portland, S. Carolina
1989-e	Santa Clara & Virginia	Steve Sampson Bruce Arena	1-1 (2 OT)	—	Rutgers	Indiana, Rutgers
1990-f	UCLA	Sigi Schmid	0-0 (PKs)	Rutgers	South Fla.	Evansville, N.C. State
1991-g	Virginia	Bruce Arena	0-0 (PKs)	Santa Clara	Tampa	Indiana, Saint Louis
1992	Virginia	Bruce Arena	2-0	San Diego	Davidson	Davidson, Duke
1993	Virginia	Bruce Arena	2-0	South Carolina	Davidson	CS-Fullerton, Princeton

Year	Winner	Head Coach	Score	Runner-up	Host/Site	Semifinalists
1994	Virginia	Bruce Arena	1-0	Indiana	Davidson	Rutgers, UCLA
1995	Wisconsin	Jim Launder	2-0	Duke	Richmond	Portland, Virginia
1996	St. John's	Dave Masur	4-1	Fla. International	Richmond	Creighton, NC-Charlotte
1997	UCLA	Sigi Schmid	2-0	Virginia	Richmond	Indiana, Saint Louis
1998	Indiana	Jerry Yeagley	3-1	Stanford	Richmond	Maryland, Santa Clara
1999	Indiana	Jerry Yeagley	1-0	Santa Clara	Charlotte	Connecticut, UCLA
2000	Connecticut	Ray Reid	2-0	Creighton	Charlotte	Indiana, Southern Methodist
2001	North Carolina	Elmar Bolowich	2-0	Indiana	Columbus	St. John's, Stanford
2002	UCLA	Tom Fitzgerald	1-0	Stanford	Dallas	Creighton, Maryland
2003	Indiana	Jerry Yeagley	2-1	St. John's	Columbus	Maryland, Santa Clara
2004-h	Indiana	Mike Freitag	1-1 (PKs)	UCSB	Carson, Calif.	Duke, Maryland
2005	Maryland	Sasho Cirovski	1-0	New Mexico	Cary, N.C.	Clemson, SMU
2006	UCSB	Tim Vom Steeg	2-1	UCLA	St. Louis, Mo.	Virginia, Wake Forest

a–game declared a draw due to inclement weather after regulation time; **b**–game declared a draw after two overtimes; **c**–Howard vacated title for using ineligible player; **d**–San Francisco vacated title for using ineligible player; **e**–game declared a draw due to inclement weather after two overtimes. **f**–UCLA wins on penalty kicks (4-3) after four overtimes; **g**–Virginia wins on penalty kicks (3-1) after four overtimes; **h**–Indiana wins on penalty kicks (3-2) after two overtimes.

Women's NCAA Division I Champions

NCAA Division I women's champions since the first tournament was contested in 1982.

Multiple winner: North Carolina (18).

Year	Winner	Coach	Score	Runner-up	Host/Site
1982	North Carolina	Anson Dorrance	2-0	Central Florida	Central Florida
1983	North Carolina	Anson Dorrance	4-0	George Mason	Central Florida
1984	North Carolina	Anson Dorrance	2-0	Connecticut	North Carolina
1985	George Mason	Hank Leung	2-0	North Carolina	George Mason
1986	North Carolina	Anson Dorrance	2-0	Colorado College	George Mason
1987	North Carolina	Anson Dorrance	1-0	Massachusetts	Massachusetts
1988	North Carolina	Anson Dorrance	4-1	N.C. State	North Carolina
1989	North Carolina	Anson Dorrance	2-0	Colorado College	N.C. State
1990	North Carolina	Anson Dorrance	6-0	Connecticut	North Carolina
1991	North Carolina	Anson Dorrance	3-1	Wisconsin	North Carolina
1992	North Carolina	Anson Dorrance	9-1	Duke	North Carolina
1993	North Carolina	Anson Dorrance	6-0	George Mason	North Carolina
1994	North Carolina	Anson Dorrance	5-0	Notre Dame	Portland
1995	Notre Dame	Chris Petrucelli	1-0 (3OT)	Portland	North Carolina
1996	North Carolina	Anson Dorrance	1-0 (2OT)	Notre Dame	Santa Clara
1997	North Carolina	Anson Dorrance	2-0	Connecticut	NC-Greensboro
1998	Florida	Becky Burleigh	1-0	North Carolina	NC-Greensboro
1999	North Carolina	Anson Dorrance	2-0	Notre Dame	San Jose, Calif.
2000	North Carolina	Anson Dorrance	2-1	UCLA	San Jose, Calif.
2001	Santa Clara	Jerry Smith	1-0	North Carolina	Dallas
2002	Portland	Clive Charles	2-1 (2OT)	Santa Clara	Austin
2003	North Carolina	Anson Dorrance	6-0	Connecticut	Cary, N.C.
2004-a	Notre Dame	Randy Waldrum	1-1 (PKs)	UCLA	Cary, N.C.
2005	Portland	Bill Irwin	4-0	UCLA	College Station, Tex.
2006	North Carolina	Anson Dorrance	2-1	Notre Dame	Cary, N.C.

a–Notre Dame wins on penalty kicks (4-3) after two overtimes.

Annual Awards
MEN
Hermann Trophy

College Player of the Year. Voted on by Division I college coaches and selected sportswriters and first presented in 1967 in the name of Robert Hermann, one of the founders of the North American Soccer League.

Multiple winners: Mike Fisher, Mike Seerey, Ken Snow and Al Trost (2).

Year		Year		Year	
1967	Dov Markus, LIU	1981	Armando Betancourt, Indiana	1995	Mike Fisher, Virginia
1968	Manuel Hernandez, San Jose St.	1982	Joe Ulrich, Duke	1996	Mike Fisher, Virginia
1969	Al Trost, Saint Louis	1983	Mike Jeffries, Duke	1997	Johnny Torres, Creighton
1970	Al Trost, Saint Louis	1984	Amr Aly, Columbia	1998	Wojtek Krakowiak, Clemson
1971	Mike Seerey, Saint Louis	1985	Tom Kain, Duke	1999	Ali Curtis, Duke
1972	Mike Seerey, Saint Louis	1986	John Kerr, Duke	2000	Chris Gbandi, Connecticut
1973	Dan Counce, Saint Louis	1987	Bruce Murray, Clemson	2001	Luchi Gonzalez, SMU
1974	Farrukh Quraishi, Oneonta St.	1988	Ken Snow, Indiana	2002	Alecko Eskandarian, Virginia
1975	Steve Ralbovsky, Brown	1989	Tony Meola, Virginia	2003	Chris Wingert, St. John's
1976	Glenn Myernick, Hartwick	1990	Ken Snow, Indiana	2004	Danny O'Rourke, Indiana
1977	Billy Gazonas, Hartwick	1991	Alexi Lalas, Rutgers	2005	Jason Garey, Maryland
1978	Angelo DiBernardo, Indiana	1992	Brad Friedel, UCLA	2006	Joseph Lapira, Notre Dame
1979	Jim Stamatis, Penn St.	1993	Claudio Reyna, Virginia		
1980	Joe Morrone, Jr. Connecticut	1994	Brian Maisonneuve, Indiana		

Missouri Athletic Club Award

College Player of the Year. Voted on by men's team coaches around the country from Division I to junior college level and first presented in 1986 by the Missouri Athletic Club of St. Louis.

Multiple winners: Claudio Reyna and Ken Snow (2).

Year		Year		Year	
1986	John Kerr, Duke	1992	Claudio Reyna, Virginia	1998	Jay Heaps, Duke
1987	John Harkes, Virginia	1993	Claudio Reyna, Virginia	1999	Sasha Victorine, UCLA
1988	Ken Snow, Indiana	1994	Todd Yeagley, Indiana	2000	Ali Curtis, Duke
1989	Tony Meola, Virginia	1995	Matt McKeon, St. Louis	2001	Luchi Gonzalez, SMU
1990	Ken Snow, Indiana	1996	Mike Fisher, Virginia	2002	merged with Hermann Trophy.
1991	Alexi Lalas, Rutgers	1997	Johnny Torres, Creighton		

Coach of the Year

Men's Coach of the Year. Voted on by the National Soccer Coaches Association of America. From 1973-81 all Senior College coaches were eligible. In 1982, the award was split into several divisions. The Division I Coach of the Year is listed since 1982.

Multiple winner: Jerry Yeagley (6), Tim Vom Steeg (2).

Year		Year		Year	
1973	Robert Guelker, SIU-Edwardsville	1985	Peter Mehlert, American	1997	Sigi Schmid, UCLA
1974	Jack MacKenzie, Quincy College	1986	Steve Parker, Akron	1998	Jerry Yeagley, Indiana
1975	Paul Reinhardt, Vermont	1987	Anson Dorrance, N. Carolina	1999	Jerry Yeagley, Indiana
1976	Jerry Yeagley, Indiana	1988	Keith Tucker, Howard	2000	Ray Reid, Connecticut
1977	Klass Deboer, Cleveland St.	1989	Steve Sampson, Santa Clara	2001	Elmar Bolowich, North Carolina
1978	Cliff McCrath, Seattle Pacific	1990	Bob Reasso, Rutgers	2002	Tom Fitzgerald, UCLA
1979	Walter Bahr, Penn St.	1991	Mitch Murray, Santa Clara	2003	Jerry Yeagley, Indiana
1980	Jerry Yeagley, Indiana	1992	Charles Slagle, Davidson	2004	Tim Vom Steeg, UCSB
1981	Schellas Hyndman, E. Illinois	1993	Bob Bradley, Princeton	2005	Sasho Cirovski, Maryland
1982	John Rennie, Duke	1994	Jerry Yeagley, Indiana	2006	Tim Vom Steeg, UCSB
1983	Dieter Ficken, Columbia	1995	Jim Launder, Wisconsin		
1984	James Lennox, Hartwick	1996	Dave Masur, St. John's		

WOMEN
Hermann Trophy

Women's College Player of the year. Voted on by Division I college coaches and selected sportswriters and first presented in 1988 in the name of Robert Hermann, one of the founders of the North American Soccer League.

Multiple winners: Mia Hamm, Cindy Parlow and Christine Sinclair (2).

Year		Year		Year	
1988	Michelle Akers, Central Fla.	1995	Shannon McMillan, Portland	2002	Aly Wagner, Santa Clara
1989	Shannon Higgins, N. Carolina	1996	Cindy Daws, Notre Dame	2003	Catherine Reddick, N. Carolina
1990	April Kater, Massachusetts	1997	Cindy Parlow, N. Carolina	2004	Christine Sinclair, Portland
1991	Kristine Lilly, N. Carolina	1998	Cindy Parlow, N. Carolina	2005	Christine Sinclair, Portland
1992	Mia Hamm, N. Carolina	1999	Mandy Clemens, Santa Clara	2006	Kerri Hanks, Notre Dame
1993	Mia Hamm, N. Carolina	2000	Anne Makinen, Notre Dame		
1994	Tisha Venturini, N. Carolina	2001	Christie Welsh, Penn St.		

Missouri Athletic Club Award

Women's College Player of the Year. Voted on by women's team coaches around the country from Division I to junior college level and first presented in 1991 by the Missouri Athletic Club of St. Louis.

Multiple winners: Mia Hamm and Cindy Parlow (2).

Year		Year		Year	
1991	Kristine Lilly, N. Carolina	1995	Shannon McMillan, Portland	1999	Mandy Clemens, Santa Clara
1992	Mia Hamm, N. Carolina	1996	Cindy Daws, Notre Dame	2000	Anne Makinen, Notre Dame
1993	Mia Hamm, N. Carolina	1997	Cindy Parlow, N. Carolina	2001	Christie Welsh, Penn St.
1994	Tisha Venturini, N. Carolina	1998	Cindy Parlow, N. Carolina	2002	merged with Hermann Trophy.

Coach of the Year

Women's Coach of the Year. Voted on by the National Soccer Coaches Association of America. From 1982-87 all Senior College coaches were eligible. In 1988, the award was split into several divisions. The Division I Coach of the Year is listed since 1988.

Multiple winners: Anson Dorrance (4); Kalenkeni M. Banda and Chris Petrucelli (2).

Year		Year		Year	
1982	Anson Dorrance, N. Carolina	1991	Greg Ryan, Wisc-Madison	2000	Jillian Ellis, UCLA
1983	David Lombardo, Keene St.	1992	Bell Hempen, Duke	2001	Jerry Smith, Santa Clara
1984	Phillip Picince, Brown	1993	Jac Cicala, George Mason	2002	Clive Charles, Portland
1985	Kalenkeni M. Banda, UMass	1994	Chris Petrucelli, Norte Dame	2003	Anson Dorrance, N. Carolina
1986	Anson Dorrance, N. Carolina	1995	Chris Petrucelli, Norte Dame	2004	Julie Shackford, Princeton
1987	Kalenkeni M. Banda, UMass	1996	John Walker, Nebraska	2005	Paula Wilkins, Penn St.
1988	Larry Gross, N.C. State	1997	Len Tsantiris, Connecticut	2006	Anson Dorrance, N. Carolina
1989	Austin Daniels, Hartford	1998	Becky Burleigh, Florida		
1990	Lauren Gregg, Virginia	1999	Patrick Farmer, Penn St.		

ACTION
SPORTS

2006 / 2007 YEAR IN REVIEW

Skateboarder **Jake Brown** had nowhere to go but down once he lost his board 45 feet up at X Games 13.

BIG AIR

Jake Brown's wild crash landing reminded us all just how much today's athletes push the envelope and risk it all every time out.

THIS YEAR, THANKS TO YOUTUBE, CNN AND JAKE BROWN, THE WHOLE WORLD SAW WHAT IT IS LIKE TO BE A SKATEBOARDER.

At Summer X Games 13, Brown, a 32-year-old Aussie, took the slam of his life on his fifth and final run in the Big Air event at the Staples Center in Los Angeles.

After landing his first ever 720 over a 70-foot gap on the mega ramp quarterpipe, Brown lost control of his board and fell 45 feet to flat, losing consciousness—and his shoes—upon impact. He was down for almost 10 minutes, but eventually managed to walk off (in his socks) with the help of medical staff, despite a broken wrist, fractured vertebrae and bruised liver and lung.

Having logged hours all summer on his own personal mega ramp, Bob Burnquist swept the Big Air with a switch backside 180 over the 70-foot gap to huge frontside rodeo 540, squeezing Brown out of the gold medal spot—but certainly not the spotlight—by three-tenths of a point.

In other, somewhat less life-threatening action, not-so-hush-hush whisper tricks were the buzz of the Moto X Best Trick contest. Two weeks before X Games 13, X-rookie and virtual unknown Scott Murray made the trek from Michigan in a retired ambulance after a video of him throwing a double backflip hit the Web. Murray was sent home early after he broke his bike by under-rotating the trick on his first run, but another X-rookie, Kyle Loza, came through with the volt, a new body varial, for the gold.

Another X-rookie, Ricky Carmichael came to L.A. with 15

Mary Fenton
is an Editor at EXPN.com

ESPN Media

→ **Steve Fisher** (center) took gold in the star-studded Superpipe at Winter X Games 11. Olympic champion **Shaun White** (left) settled for the silver.

AMA National Championships. For the X Games debut of Moto X Racing, it was only proper that Carmichael add a gold medal to his trophy house.

Somebody else added a first summer gold to their usually snow-filled repertoire. After three back-to-back skate vert wins and a commanding lead at the Dew Tour (a track record not dissimilar from Ryan Sheckler's), Shaun White finally sacked a Summer X gold.

Three points separated The Game between Team U.S.A. and Team World at the first ladies edition of X Games Surfing at Puerto Escondido, Mexico. The U.S. boys rounded out a red, white and blue Fourth of July when they came out less than one point ahead of the World.

On surfing's World Championship Tour, two Aussies headed the rankings going into the last events of the season. Mick Fanning, who, should he win in December will be the first Aussie to win a world title in eight years, has racked up seven podium finishes on the 10-stop tour and leads 8-time world champ Kelly Slater by 1000 points. Stephanie Gilmore has held down two

Action sports icon **Shaun White** finally nailed a Summer X Games gold medal in 2007, taking top prize in the men's skateboard vert.

victories so far and leads the women's rankings by more than 100 points.

The ladies from Down Under can hold their own up north, too. Aussie Torah Bright nailed a Snowboard SuperPipe win at Winter X 11 and went on to win the World Superpipe Championships, the Nippon Open and take third at the U.S. Open. She also came in second in Slopestyle behind Lake Tahoe's 16-year-old Jamie Anderson.

While Anderson was slaying every event she entered, older sister Joanie was on the boardercross course giving Lindsey Jacobellis Winter Olympic déjà vu and taking the win out from under her nose on a course that redefined the word carnage.

Despite throwing a record-breaking, 106-foot backflip at the first Winter X Freestyle Snowmobile contest, Aleksander Nordgaard went home with the silverware while Chris Burandt, having not made a Winter X appearance since his 16th-place finish in 2004's Hillcross, brought home the gold.

Shaun White saw his latest Winter X pipe dream vanish when Steve Fisher out-tricked him in Snowboard SuperPipe finals, forcing White to settle for silver, and then bronze in Slopestyle. Simon Dumont also got hit with the silver bullet when Tanner Hall took him out in the Ski SuperPipe finals in a hotly contested series of runs. The final score this time around was 95-94.

Biggest Stories of the Year in **Action Sports**

10 *Event X-Change.* 2007 saw the exodus and arrival of eight X Games disciplines. Starting at Winter X 11 in January, engines were swapped – Moto X was out and Freestyle Snowmobiling was in. Winter gained a Mono Skier X event and a Snowboard Best Trick contest, while summer lost both Skateboard Vert Best Trick and BMX Vert Best Trick. The two-wheeled groups also bid adieu to BMX Dirt, but welcomed in Moto X Racing and the first X appearance of Supercross star Ricky Carmichael. Women's Surfing was also added to X Games 12, as was Skateboard Street Best Trick.

09 **Jamie Anderson.** For the eight Anderson siblings, snowboarding runs deep. For 17-year-old South Lake Tahoe snowboard prodigy Jamie Anderson, it's only the beginning. As the only athlete to compete in all three snowboard disciplines at the 2006 Winter X Games, Anderson became the youngest medalist in Winter X history when she took the three-spot in Slopestyle. Anderson earned a Transworld Rookie of the Year nomination for '06 and took eight podiums in '07, including her first Winter X gold in Slopestyle.

08 **Andreas Wiig Double Gold.** Upon moving from Norway to California's Mammoth Mountain in 2001, Andreas Wiig took the snowboard video world by storm. He made his first Winter X appearance in 2004 and went home with a Slopestyle bronze, but it wasn't until 2007 that Wiig brought out his filming guns to take golds in both Slopestyle and Best Trick (a frontside 1080 to beat Travis Rice in the final showdown). Wiig won the 2007 Vans Cup and Honda Sessions, and he also earned nominations for a 2007 ESPY award for Best Male Action Sports Athlete, as well as for 2006's Transworld Rider of the Year.

07 **Surreality.** MTV made action sports waves with two highly successful series. Rob & Big, starring skateboarder Rob Dyrdek and his bodyguard/best friend Christopher Boykin, ranked number one in its time slot, reaching 70 million viewers and earning MTV2 their highest-rated day ever in January. Life of Ryan, a show about skateboarder Ryan Sheckler, is MTV's highest-rated new show of 2007, with 30 million viewers so far in its first season.

06 **Double Back, Part Two.** Two weeks before the 2007 X Games, a home video began circulating on the web. The clip was of Scott Murray, a 29-year-old Michigan native, doing a freestyle motocross double backflip. Previously a rider in monster truck demos, Murray, the only person to land the trick since Travis Pastrana, earned an immediate invite to the X Games Moto X Best Trick competition. The sponsor-less Murray under-rotated his trick on his first run, breaking his bike and sending him home empty-handed.

05 Shaun's Golden Summer. After five years skating at the X Games, Shaun White finally took his first summer gold in Skateboard Vert. With 10 medals already under his belt from Winter X's past, as well as a Skate Vert silver from 2005 summer X, White put down a flawless final run to finish with a commanding lead over silver medalist Pierre-Luc Gagnon. After having won three back-to-back '07 Dew Tour skate vert wins, White also had a 100-point overall lead going into the 5th and final stop of the Dew Tour in not-so-snowy Orlando.

04 Tragedies. The action sports community suffered a serious 1-2 blow with the deaths of 21-year-old Australian skateboarder Shane Cross and 39-year-old World Rally Champion Colin McRae. In March, Cross was killed in a motorcycle accident in Australia, and in September, McRae and his 5-year-old son were killed in a helicopter crash near his home in Scotland. Also in September, BMX rider-turned-mountain biker, Tara Lllanes crashed in the Jeep King of the Mountain finals, becoming paralyzed from the waist down. This came less than three months after BMX rider Stephan Murray became paralyzed from the chest down after crashing at Baltimore's Dew Tour opener.

03 Clean Slates. After securing an unprecedented eighth surfing world title in October 2006 in Spain, the only remaining elite surf-ing record for Kelly Slater to break was Tom Curren's 16-year-old mark of 33 WCT event victories. At this year's contest at Trestles, California, Slater didn't just break the record, he raked up enough Tour points to qualify him for a ninth world title. With two events to go, Slater sat 1,000 points below ratings-leader Mick Fanning.

02 Fisher King. After dipping under the radar for two seasons (and buying a new condo on a golf course), Breckenridge-local Steve Fisher came back to the ultra-competitive halfpipe circuit in '07 to nearly-shadow a particular red-head's '06 season. Fish became only the third person to win a second halfpipe event at Winter X, overshadowing Shaun White with one of the cleanest pipe runs ever seen. He also won one stop of the '07 Grand Prix and the Progression Session at another, taking third overall.

01 Shoes Off, Lights Out: The Crash Felt Around the World. With 3-time X Games Skateboard Big Air winner Danny Way out of contention at the 2007 X Games, the ramp was up for the taking. Standing in first place with one run to go, Aussie Jake Brown flew over the 70-foot gap, landing his first ever 720. Upon hitting the quarterpipe, Brown's skateboard came out from under his feet, and he fell 45 feet to flatbottom. Brown miraculously walked off the ramp with assistance and was later diagnosed with two fractured wrists and a lacerated liver. He went home with a silver medal.

2006-2007
Season in Review

SPORTS ALMANAC

Summer X Games 13

The annual action sports showcase originally founded by ESPN in 1995. The 13th edition of the Summer X Games was held Aug. 2-5, 2007 at the Staples Center and Home Depot Center in Los Angeles, Calif. Medal winners from each event listed below.

Multiple Medal Winners: TWO—Chris Cole (two golds), Kevin Robinson (one gold, one bronze).

Skateboarding

Men's Street
		Score
1	Chris Cole, USA	94.33
2	Greg Lutzka, USA	93.41
3	Jereme Rogers, USA	87.41

Women's Street
		Score
1	Marisa Dal Santo, USA	86.08
2	Elissa Streamer, USA	80.33
3	Amy Caron, USA	80.16

Men's Vert
		Best Run
1	Shaun White, USA	95.75
2	Pierre Luc Gagnon, CAN	91.25
3	Mathias Ringstrom, SWE	88.25

Women's Vert
1 Lyn-Z Adams Hawkins, USA
2 Mimi Knoop, USA
3 Cara-Beth Burnside, USA

Vert Best Trick
1 Chris Cole, USA
2 Andrew Reynolds, USA
3 Eric Koston, USA

Big Air
		Score
1	Bob Burnquist, USA	95.66
2	Jake Brown, AUS	95.33
3	Pierre Luc Gagnon, CAN	93.00

Amateur Vert
		Best Run
1	Ben Hatchell, USA	87.50
2	Josh Stafford, USA	86.50
3	Paul Luc Ronchetti, ENG	83.50

Rally Car Racing
1 Tanner Foust & Christine Beavis, USA
2 Ken Block & Alex Gelsomino, USA
3 Travis Pastrana & Christian Edstrom, USA

BMX

Vert
		Score
1	Jamie Bestwick, ENG	93.66
2	Simon Tabron, ENG	92.66
3	Kevin Robinson, USA	88.33

Park
		Score
1	Daniel Dhers, VEN	91.66
2	Scotty Cranmer, USA	90.33
3	Dave Mirra, USA	88.00

Big Air
		Score
1	Kevin Robinson, USA	95.33
2	Steve McCann, AUS	93.00
3	Anthony Napolitan, USA	92.66

Moto X

Freestyle
		Score
1	Adam Jones, USA	94.40
2	Nate Adams, USA	93.60
3	Jeremy Stenberg, USA	

Step Up
		Height
1	Ronnie Renner, USA	33-0
2	Brian Deegan, USA	32-0
	Tommy Clowers, USA	32-0
	Matt Buyten, USA	32-0

SuperMoto
1 Mark Burkhart, USA
2 Jeff Ward, USA
3 David Pingree, USA

Racing
1 Ricky Carmichael, USA
2 Grant Langston, USA
3 Kevin Windham, USA

Surfing

Held July 5, 2007 at Zicatela Beach
in Puerto Escondido, Mexico

Men
Team USA def. Team World, 81:75-81.00

Women
Team USA def. Team World, 55-52

Winter X Games 11

Held January 25-28, 2007 at Aspen, Colorado. Medal winners from each event listed below.
Multiple Medal Winners: TWO—Andreas Wiig (two golds), Shaun White (one silver, one bronze),

Snowboarding

Men's Snowboarder X

		Winning Time
1	Nate Holland, USA	.64.796
2	Xavier de le Rue, FRA	
3	Seth Wescott, USA	

Women's Snowboarder X

		Winning Time
1	Joanie Anderson, USA	.71.387
2	Lindsey Jacobellis, USA	
3	Maelle Ricker, CAN	

Men's Slopestyle

		Score
1	Andreas Wiig, NOR	.89.00
2	Jussi Oksanen, FIN	.84.66
3	Shaun White, USA	.83.33

Women's Slopestyle

		Score
1	Jamie Anderson, USA	85.33
2	Hana Beaman, USA	78.33
3	Chanelle Sladics, USA	76.33

Men's SuperPipe

		Score
1	Steve Fisher, USA	.92.00
2	Shaun White, USA	.91.00
3	Mason Aguirre, USA	.90.66

Women's SuperPipe

		Score
1	Torah Bright, AUS	.94.66
2	Gretchen Bleiler, USA	.91.00
3	Elena Hight, USA	.88.00

Best Trick

Gold Medal Match (loser wins Silver)—Andreas Wiig, NOR def. Travis Rice, USA 90.00-45.00; **Bronze Medal**—Antti Autti, FIN def. Danny Davis, USA 85.00-70.00.

Skiing

Men's Skier X

		Winning Time
1	Casey Puckett, USA	.57.958
2	Jack Fiala, USA	
3	Enak Gavaggio, FRA	

Women's Skier X

		Winning Time
1	Ophelie David, FRA	.65.367
2	Valentine Scuotto, FRA	
3	Meryll Boulandgeat, FRA	

Men's SuperPipe

		Score
1	Tanner Hall, USA	.95.00
2	Simon Dumont, USA	.94.00
3	Peter Olenick, USA	.90.00

Women's SuperPipe

		Score
1	Sarah Burke, CAN	.90.00
2	Grete Eliassen, USA	.86.33
3	Jen Hudak, USA	.66.33

Moto X Best Trick

		Score
1	Jeremy Stenberg, USA	.93.00
2	Mat Rebeaud, SUI	.92.40
3	Ronnie Faisst, USA	.90.60

Men's Slopestyle

		Score
1	Candide Thovex, FRA	.95.00
2	Sammy Carlson, USA	.92.33
3	Colby West, USA	.90.00

Mono Skier X

		Score
1	Tyler Walker, USA	.84.868
2	Kevin Connolly, USA	.84.930
3	Kees-Jan van der Klooster, NED	.93.480

Snowmobiling

SnoCross

		Time (seconds)
1	Tucker Hibbert, USA	.186.226
2	Ryan Simmons, CAN	.186.543
3	T.J. Gulla, USA	.192.684

Freestyle

Gold Medal Match (loser wins Silver)—Chris Burandt, USA def. Aleksander Nordgaard, NOR, 96.33-93.66; **Bronze Medal**—Heath Frisby, USA def. Daniel Bodin, SWE, 89.33-78.33.

2007 U.S. Open of Snowboarding

Held March 16-17 at Stratton Mountain, Vermont

Men's Halfpipe

1 Shaun White
2 Danny Davis
3 Markus Malin

Women's Halfpipe

1 Kelly Clark
2 Gretchen Bleiler
3 Tora Bright

Men's Slopestyle

1 Travis Rice
2 Janne Korpi
3 Shaun White

Women's Slopestyle

1 Jamie Anderson
2 Torah Bright
3 Jenny Jones

Mountain Dew Action Sports Tour

2007 Dew Tour Locations: Panasonic Open, Baltimore, Md. (June 21-24); Right Guard Open, Cleveland, Ohio (July 19-22); Vans Invitational, Portland, Ore. (Aug. 16-19); Toyota Challenge, Salt Lake City, Utah (Sept. 20-23); Playstation Pro, Orlando, Fla. (Oct. 18-21).

Panasonic Open
June 21-24 at Baltimore, Md.

Skate Vert
		Score
1	Shaun White	94.25
2	Bob Burnquist	91.00
3	Andy Macdonald	87.50

Skate Park
		Score
1	Ryan Sheckler	94.00
2	Greg Lutzka	85.53
3	Carlos De Andrade	81.17

BMX Vert
		Score
1	Jamie Bestwick	89.17
2	Chad Kagy	88.67
3	Jimmy Walker	87.67

BMX Park
		Score
1	Daniel Dhers	93.17
2	Mike Spinner	92.67
3	Dennis Enarson	90.67

BMX Dirt
		Score
1	Ryan Nyquist	89.42
2	Cameron White	88.42
3	Chris Doyle	88.25

FMX
		Score
1	Nate Adams	95.67
2	Blake Williams	93.83
3	Mike Mason	92.17

Right Guard Open
July 19-22 at Cleveland, Ohio

Skate Vert
		Score
1	Shaun White	90.25
2	Bucky Lasek	89.00
3	Bob Burnquist	87.00

Skate Park
		Score
1	Ryan Sheckler	94.00
2	Rodolfo Ramos	87.92
2	Carlos De Andrade	86.17

BMX Vert
		Score
1	Simon Tabron	91.67
2	Steven McCann	90.83
3	Chad Kagy	90.67

BMX Park
		Score
1	Daniel Dhers	93.62
2	Ryan Nyquist	93.25
3	Garrett Reynolds	90.75

BMX Dirt
		Score
1	Ryan Nyquist	91.08
2	Corey Bohan	90.42
2	Luke Parslow	89.67

FMX
		Score
1	Nate Adams	92.67
2	Takayuki Higashino	91.67
3	Jeremy Stenberg	90.50

Vans Invitational
Aug. 16-19 at Portland, Ore.

Skate Vert
		Score
1	Shaun White	91.25
2	Pierre-Luc Gagnon	89.00
3	Bob Burnquist	87.75

BMX Dirt
		Score
1	Dennis Enarson	93.17
2	Diogo Canina	92.92
2	Anthony Napolitan	92.00

Skate Park
		Score
1	Greg Lutzka	90.67
2	Ryan Sheckler	89.83
3	Fabricio Santos	86.17

BMX Park
		Score
1	Mike Spinner	94.00
2	Dave Mirra	93.50
3	Daniel Dhers	92.33

BMX Vert
		Score
1	Jamie Bestwick	94.67
2	Simon Tabron	92.67
3	Kevin Robinson	92.00

FMX
		Score
1	Adam Jones	91.17
2	Nate Adams	90.83
3	Mike Mason	89.57

Mountain Dew Action Sports Tour (Cont.)

Toyota Challenge
Sept. 20-23 at Salt Lake City, Utah

Skate Vert
	Score
1 Pierre-Luc Gagnon	93.00
2 Bucky Lasek	91.00
3 Shaun White	89.00

BMX Dirt
	Score
1 James Foster	93.25
2 Cameron White	92.92
3 Mike Aitken	90.50

Skate Park
	Score
1 Ryan Sheckler	87.58
2 Rodolfo Ramos	82.58
3 Rodil Araujo Jr.	82.08

BMX Park
	Score
1 Scotty Cranmer	93.17
2 Ryan Guettler	92.50
3 Ryan Nyquist	91.67

BMX Vert
	Score
1 Jamie Bestwick	94.00
2 Simon Tabron	92.50
3 Steve McCann	91.00

FMX
	Score
1 Nate Adams	93.33
2 Todd Potter	89.67
3 Jeremy Lusk	89.50

PlayStation Pro
Oct. 18-21 at Orlando, Fla.

Skate Vert
	Score
1 Bucky Lasek	95.50
2 Pierre-Luc Gagnon	94.00
3 Shaun White	91.00

Skate Park
	Score
1 Greg Lutzka	90.83
2 Ryan Sheckler	89.58
3 Rodil Araujo Jr.	85.08

BMX Vert
	Score
1 Chad Kagy	92.67
2 Jamie Bestwick	92.67
3 Steve McCann	92.33

BMX Park
	Score
1 Daniel Dhers	94.67
2 Mike Spinner	94.17
3 Ryan Nyquist	92.67

BMX Dirt
	Score
1 Luke Parslow	88.17
2 Dennis Enarson	88.09
3 Anthony Napolitan	87.83

FMX
	Score
1 Nate Adams	93.17
2 Jeremy Stenberg	92.33
3 Todd Potter	91.50

2007 Mountain Dew Tour Final Points Standings

In each discipline (SKATE, BMX and FMX), athletes who qualify into each event (Vert, Park, Dirt or FMX) receive points based on the Final results from that event. Riders are awarded points corresponding to their final placing.

Skate Vert
	Pts
1 Shaun White	426
2 Bucky Lasek	343
3 Pierre-Luc Gagnon	337
4 Bob Burnquist	288
5 Andy Macdonald	277

BMX Park
	Pts
1 Daniel Dhers	418
2 Mike Spinner	332
3 Ryan Nyquist	299
4 Scotty Cranmer	227
5 Dave Mirra	225

Skate Park
	Pts
1 Ryan Sheckler	450
2 Greg Lutzka	356
3 Rodolfo Ramos	277
4 Austen Seaholm	242
5 Carlos De Andrade	224

BMX Dirt
	Pts
1 Ryan Nyquist	331
2 Cameron White	278
3 Dennis Enarson	275
4 Luke Parslow	273
5 James Foster	237

BMX Vert
	Pts
1 Jamie Bestwick	418
2 Simon Tabron	343
3 Steve McCann	311
4 Chad Kagy	259
5 Jimmy Walker	240

FMX
	Pts
1 Nate Adams	475
2 Adam Jones	276
3 Mike Mason	257
4 Jeremy Lusk	256
5 Todd Potter	246

Surfing
2007 ASP World Championship Tour
MEN

Quiksilver Pro at Gold Coast

Finals		Pts
1	Mick Fanning	16.17
2	Bede Durbridge	12.00

Rip Curl Pro at Bells Beach

Finals		Pts
1	Taj Burrow	16.83
2	Andy Irons	14.73

Billabong Pro Teahupoo

Finals		Pts
1	Damien Hobgood	16.60
2	Mick Fanning	16.20

Rip Curl Pro at Arica, Chile

Finals		Pts
1	Andy Irons	16.84
2	Damien Hobgood	8.67

Billabong Pro at Jeffreys Bay

Finals		Pts
1	Taj Burrow	16.50
2	Kelly Slater	6.17

Boost Mobile Pro at Trestles

Finals		Pts
1	Kelly Slater	13.40
2	Pancho Sullivan	10.60

Quiksilver Pro France

Finals		Pts
1	Mick Fanning	18.43
2	Greg Emslie	11.63

Billabong Pro Spain

Finals		Pts
1	Bobby Martinez	16.44
2	Taj Burrow	16.16

Ratings
through Billabong Pro Spain (Oct. 14)

		Pts
1	Mick Fanning, AUS	7346
2	Kelly Slater, USA	6326
3	Taj Burrow, AUS	6275
4	Joel Parkinson, AUS	5505
5	Andy Irons, HAW	4966
6	Bobby Martinez, USA	4582
7	Jeremy Flores, FRA	4580
8	Bede Durbridge, AUS	4424
9	Pancho Sullivan, HAW	4287
10	Damien Hobgood, USA	4274

Remaining Men's Events: Hang Loose Santa Catarina Pro, Oct. 30-Nov. 7; Billabong Pipeline Masters at Oahu, Dec. 8-20.

WOMEN

Roxy Pro at Gold Coast

Finals		Pts
1	Chelsea Hedges	11.33
2	Carissa Moore	6.70

Rip Curl Pro at Bells Beach

Finals		Pts
1	Stephanie Gilmore	16.50
2	Sofia Mulanovich	11.93

Billabong Girls at Praia da Tiririca

Finals		Pts
1	Samantha Cornish	12.00
2	Silvana Lima	8.10

Rip Curl Girls Festival at Spain

Finals		Pts
1	Sofia Mulanovich	15.55
2	Silvana Lima	14.00

NAB Beachley Classic at Sydney

Finals		Pts
1	Stephanie Gilmore	16.43
2	Silvana Lima	15.33

Ratings
through NAB Beachley Classic (Oct. 14)

		Pts
1	Stephanie Gilmore, AUS	4308
2	Silvana Lima, BRA	4226
3	Sofia Mulanovich, PER	3811
4	Samantha Cornish, AUS	3504
5	Chelsea Hedges, AUS	3326
6	Layne Beachley, AUS	2882
	Amee Donohoe, AUS	2882
8	Rebecca Woods, AUS	2448
9	Jessi Miley-Dyer, AUS	2347
10	Melanie Redman-Carr, AUS	2232

Remaining Women's Events: Mancora Peru Classic, Oct. 30-Nov. 4; Roxy Pro at Sunset Beach, Nov. 23-Dec. 6; Billabong Pro at Honolua Bay, Dec. 8-20.

Snowboarding
Chevrolet Grand Prix Series

Breckenridge, Colo. (Dec. 16, 2006); Mt. Bachelor, Ore. (Feb. 3, 2007); Tamarack Resort, Idaho (Feb. 24-25, 2007)

Breckenridge

Men's Pipe Finals
1 Danny Davis
2 Mason Aguirre
3 Jarret Thomas

Women's Pipe Finals
1 Kelly Clark
2 Elena Hight
3 Lindsey Jacobellis

Mt. Bachelor

Men's Pipe Finals
1 Steve Fisher
2 Louie Vito
3 Tommy Czeschin

Women's Pipe Finals
1 Kelly Clark
2 Elena Hight
3 Gretchen Bleiler

Men's Slopestyle Finals
1 Ian Thorley
2 Tim Humphreys
3 Scott Lago

Women's Slopestyle Finals
1 Jenniver Jones
2 Jordan Karlinski
3 Ellery Hollingsworth

Tamarack

Men's Pipe Finals
1 Tommy Czeschin
2 Louie Vito
3 Matthew Ladley

Women's Pipe Finals
1 Gretchen Bleiler
2 Lindsey Jacobellis
3 Tricia Byrnes

Men's Boarder Cross Finals
1 Nick Baumgartner
2 Alex Deibold
3 Graham Watanabe

Women's Boarder Cross Finals
1 Callan Chythlook-Sifsof
2 Jordan Karlinski
3 Kim Krahulec

See the **International Sports** chapter for Results from the 2007 Snowboarding World Championships and World Cup.

1995-2007
Through the Years

SPORTS ALMANAC

X GAMES

The ESPN Extreme Games, originally envisioned as a biannual showcase for "alternative" sports, were first held June 24-July 1, 1995 in Newport and Providence, R.I. and Mt. Snow, Vt. The success of the inaugural event prompted organizers to make it an annual competition. Newport would again serve as host for the redubbed X Games in 1996. The X Games has evolved rapidly since its inception and have been held in several cities since. New sports and events have been added while others have been dropped.

SUMMER X GAMES

Summer X Games sites: 1995-Newport/Providence, R.I. (and Mt. Snow, Vt.); 1996-Newport/Providence, R.I.; 1997-San Diego; 1998-San Diego; 1999-San Francisco; 2000-San Francisco; 2001-Phiadelphia; 2002-Philadelphia; 2003-Los Angeles; 2004-Los Angeles; 2005-Los Angeles; 2006-Los Angeles; 2007-Los Angeles.

BMX

Multiple winners: Dave Mirra (13); Jamie Bestwick and Ryan Nyquist (4); Corey Bohan, Martti Kuoppa and Trevor Meyer (3); Matt Hoffman, T.J. Lavin, Brandon Meadows and Kevin Robinson (2)

Year	Vert
1995	Matt Hoffman
1996	Matt Hoffman
1997	Dave Mirra
1998	Dave Mirra
1999	Dave Mirra
2000	Jamie Bestwick
2001	Dave Mirra
2002	Dave Mirra
2003	Jamie Bestwick
2004	Dave Mirra
2005	Jamie Bestwick
2006	Chad Kagy
2007	Jamie Bestwick

Year	Vert Best Trick
2005	Jamie Bestwick
2006	Kevin Robinson
2007	not held

Year	Street/Stunt Park
1996	Dave Mirra
1997	Dave Mirra
1998	Dave Mirra
1999	Dave Mirra
2000	Dave Mirra
2001	Bruce Crisman
2002	Ryan Nyquist
2003	Ryan Nyquist
2004	Dave Mirra
2005	Dave Mirra
2006	Scotty Cranmer
2007	Daniel Dhers

Year	Big Air
2006	Kevin Robinson
2007	Kevin Robinson

Year	Downhill
2001	Brandon Meadows
2002	Robbie Miranda
2003	Brandon Meadows
2004	event discontinued

Year	Dirt
1995	Jay Miron
1996	Joey Garcia
1997	T.J. Lavin
1998	Brian Foster
1999	T.J. Lavin
2000	Ryan Nyquist
2001	Stephen Murray
2002	Allan Cooke
2003	Ryan Nyquist
2004	Corey Bohan
2005	Corey Bohan
2006	Corey Bohan
2007	not held

Year	Flatland
1997	Trevor Meyer
1998	Trevor Meyer
1999	Trevor Meyer
2000	Martti Kuoppa
2001	Martti Kuoppa
2002	Martti Kuoppa
2003	Simon O'Brien
2004	event discontinued

Moto X

Year	Freestyle
1999	Travis Pastrana
2000	Travis Pastrana
2001	Travis Pastrana
2002	Mike Metzger
2003	Travis Pastrana
2004	Nate Adams
2005	Travis Pastrana
2006	Jeremy Stenberg
2007	Adam Jones

Year	Step Up
2001	Tommy Clowers
2002	Tommy Clowers
2003	Matt Buyten
2004	Jeremy McGrath
2005	Tommy Clowers
2006	Matt Buyten
2007	Ronnie Renner

Year	Racing
2007	Ricky Carmichael

Year	Big Air
2001	Kenny Bartman
2002	Mike Metzger
2003	Brian Deegan

Year	Super Moto
2004	Ben Bostrom
2005	Doug Henry
2006	Jeff Ward
2007	Mark Burkhart

Year	Best Trick
2004	Chuck Carothers
2005	not held
2006	Travis Pastrana
2007	Adam Jones

Rally Car Racing

Year	
2006	Travis Pastrana/Christian Edstrom
2007	Tanner Foust/Christine Beavis

Skateboarding

Multiple winners: Tony Hawk (9); Andy Macdonald (8); Bucky Lasek (6); Bob Burnquist (4); Rodil de Araujo Jr., Pierre-Luc Gagnon and Danny Way (3); Cara-Beth Burnside, Sandro Dias, Paul Rodriguez and Chris Senn (2).

Year	Vert Singles	Year	Vert Doubles	Year	Women's Street
1995	Tony Hawk	1997	Hawk/Macdonald	2004	Elissa Steamer
1996	Andy Macdonald	1998	Hawk/Macdonald	2005	Elissa Steamer
1997	Tony Hawk	1999	Hawk/Macdonald	2006	Elissa Steamer
1998	Andy Macdonald	2000	Hawk/Macdonald	2007	Marisa Dal Santo
1999	Bucky Lasek	2001	Hawk/Macdonald	**Year**	**Big Air**
2000	Bucky Lasek	2002	Hawk/Macdonald	2004	Danny Way
2001	Bob Burnquist	2003	Lasek/Burnquist	2005	Danny Way
2002	Pierre-Luc Gagnon	2004	event discontinued	2006	Danny Way
2003	Bucky Lasek	**Year**	**Vert Best Trick**	2007	Bob Burnquist
2004	Bucky Lasek	2000	Bob Burnquist	**Year**	**Street/Park**
2005	Pierre-Luc Gagnon	2001	Matt Dove	1995	Chris Senn
2006	Sandro Dias	2002	Pierre-Luc Gagnon	1996	Rodil de Araujo Jr.
2007	Shaun White	2003	Tony Hawk	1997	Chris Senn
Year	**Women's Vert**	2004	Sandro Dias	1998	Rodil de Araujo Jr.
2004	L. Adams Hawkins	2005	Bob Burnquist	1999	Chris Senn
2005	Cara-Beth Burnside	2006	Bucky Lasek	2000	Eric Koston
2006	Cara-Beth Burnside	2007	not held	2001	Kerry Getz
2007	Lyn-Z Adams Hawkins	**Year**	**Park**	2002	Rodil de Araujo Jr.
Year	**Street Best Trick**	2003	Ryan Sheckler	2003	event discontinued
2001	Kerry Getz	2004	event discontinued	**Year**	**Street**
2002	Rodil de Araujo Jr.	**Year**	**Women's Park**	2003	Eric Koston
2003	Chad Muska	2003	Vanessa Torres	2004	Paul Rodriguez
2004	event discontinued	2004	event discontinued	2005	Paul Rodriguez
				2006	Chris Cole
				2007	Chris Cole

Street Luge

Multiple winners: Biker Sherlock (5); Dennis Derammelaere and Rat Sult (2).

Year	Dual	Year	Mass	Year	Super Mass
1995	Bob Pereyra	1995	Shawn Gilbert	1997	Biker Sherlock
1996	Shawn Goular	1996	Biker Sherlock	1998	Rat Sult
1997	Biker Sherlock	1997	Biker Sherlock	1999	David Rogers
1998	Biker Sherlock	1998	Rat Sult	2000	Bob Pereyra
1999	Dennis Derammelaere	1999	event discontinued	2001	Brent DeKeyser
2000	Bob Ozman	**Year**	**King of the Hill**	2002	event discontinued
2001	event discontinued	2001	Dennis Derammelaere		
		2002	event discontinued		

Sportclimbing

Multiple winners: Katie Brown, Hans Florine and Elena Ovtchinnikova (3); Maxim Stenkovoy (2).

Year	Men's Difficulty	Year	Men's Speed	Year	Women's Speed
1995	Ian Vickers	1995	Hans Florine	1995	Elena Ovtchinnikova
1996	Arnaud Petit	1996	Hans Florine	1996	Cecile Le Flem
1997	Francois Legrand	1997	Hans Florine	1997	Elena Ovtchinnikova
1998	Christian Core	1998	Vladimir Netsvetaev	1998	Elena Ovtchinnikova
1999	Chris Sharma	1999	Aaron Shamy	1999	Renata Piszczek
2000	event discontinued	2000	Vladimir Zakharov	2000	Etti Hendrawati
Year	**Women's Difficulty**	2001	Maxim Stenkovoy	2001	Elena Repko
1995	Robyn Erbersfield	2002	Maxim Stenkovoy	2002	Tori Allen
1996	Katie Brown	2003	event discontinued	2003	event discontinued
1997	Katie Brown				
1998	Katie Brown				
1999	Stephanie Bodet				
2000	event discontinued				

	X-Venture Race		Bungee Jumping		Big-Air Snowboarding
Year		**Year**		**Year**	**Men**
1995	Team Threadbo	1995	Doug Anderson	1997	Peter Line
1996	Team Kobeer	1996	Peter Bihun	1998	Kevin Jones
1997	Team Presidio	1997	event discontinued	1999	Peter Line
1998	event discontinued			**Year**	**Women**
				1997	Tina Dixon
				1998	Janet Matthews
				1999	Barrett Christy

Note: Snowboarding was held at the Summer X Games from 1997-99.

Summer X Games (Cont.)

In-Line Skating

Multiple winners: Fabiola da Silva (7); Eito Yasutoko (3), Derek Downing, Jaren Grob, Martina Svobodova, Gypsy Tidwell (2).

Year	Men's Vert
1995	Tom Fry
1996	Rene Hulgreen
1997	Tim Ward
1998	Cesar Mora
1999	Eito Yasutoko
2000	Eito Yasutoko
2001	Taig Khris

Year	Women's Vert
1995	Tash Hodgeson
1996	Fabiola da Silva
1997	Fabiola da Silva
1998	Fabiola da Silva
1999	Ayumi Kawasaki
2000	Fabiola da Silva
2001	Fabiola da Silva

Year	Combined Vert
2002	Takeshi Yasutoko
2003	Eito Yasutoko
2004	Takeshi Yasutoko
2005	event discontinued

Note: In 2002 the men's and women's vert events were combined.

Year	Men's Park
1995	Matt Salerno
1996	Arlo Eisenberg
1997	Arron Feinberg
1998	Jonathan Bergeron
1999	Nicky Adams
2000	Sven Boekhorst
2001	Jaren Grob
2002	Jaren Grob
2003	Bruno Lowe
2004	event discontinued

Year	Women's Park
1997	Sayaka Yabe
1998	Jenny Curry
1999	Sayaka Yabe
2000	Fabiola da Silva
2001	Martina Svobodova
2002	Martina Svobodova
2003	Fabiola da Silva
2004	event discontinued

Year	Vert Triples
1998	Malina/Fogarty/Popa
1999	Khris/Bujanda/Boekhorst
2000	event discontinued

Year	Men's Downhill
1995	Derek Downing
1996	Dante Muse
1997	Derek Downing
1998	Patrick Naylor
1999	event discontinued

Year	Women's Downhill
1995	Julie Brandt
1996	Gypsy Tidwell
1997	Gypsy Tidwell
1998	Julie Brandt
1999	event discontinued

Watersports

Multiple winners: Dallas Friday and Danny Harf (4); Parks Bonifay, Peter Fleck, Tara Hamilton and Darin Shapiro (2).

Year	Barefoot Waterski Jumping
1995	Justin Seers
1996	Ron Scarpa
1997	Peter Fleck
1998	Peter Fleck
1999	event discontinued

Year	Men's Wakeboarding
1996	Parks Bonifay
1997	Jeremy Kovak
1998	Darin Shapiro
1999	Parks Bonifay
2000	Darin Shapiro
2001	Danny Harf
2002	Danny Harf
2003	Danny Harf
2004	Phillip Soven
2005	Danny Harf
2006	event discontinued

Year	Women's Wakeboarding
1997	Tara Hamilton
1998	Andrea Gaytan
1999	Meaghan Major
2000	Tara Hamilton
2001	Dallas Friday
2002	Emily Copeland
2003	Dallas Friday
2004	Dallas Friday
2005	Dallas Friday
2006	event discontinued

Year	Skysurfing
1995	Fradet/Zipser
1996	Furrer/Scmid
1997	Hartman/Pappadato
1998	Rozov/Burch
1999	Fradet/Iodice
2000	Klaus/Rogers
2001	event discontinued

Surfing

Year	Men	Year	Women
2003	East Coast	2007	Team USA
2003	East Coast		
2004	East Coast		
2005	East Coast		
2006	West Coast		
2007	Team USA		

Note: The X Games surfing competition was held between teams from the East and West Coasts (2003-2006) and between Team USA and Team World (2007).

WINTER X GAMES

Winter X Games sites: 1997–Snow Summit Mountain Resort, Big Bear Lake, Calif.; 1998–Crested Butte, Colo.; 1999–Crested Butte, Colo.; 2000– Mt. Snow, Vt.; 2001–Mt. Snow, Vt.; 2002–Aspen, Colo.; 2003–Aspen, Colo.; 2004–Aspen, Colo.; 2005–Aspen, Colo; 2006–Aspen, Colo; 2007–Aspen, Colo.

Snowboarding

Multiple winners: Tara Dakides and Shaun White (5); Janna Meyen (4); Lindsey Jacobellis and Shaun Palmer (3); Gretchen Bleiler, Barrett Christy, Kelly Clark, Steve Fisher, Kevin Jones, Ueli Kestenholz, Todd Richards and Maelle Ricker (2).

Year	Men's Big Air
1997	Jimmy Halopoff
1998	Jason Borgstede
1999	Kevin Sansalone
2000	Peter Line
2001	Jussi Oksanen

Year	Women's Big Air
1997	Barrett Christy
1998	Tina Basich
1999	Barrett Christy
2000	Tara Dakides
2001	Tara Dakides

Year	Best Trick
2007	Andreas Wiig

Year	Men's Boarder X	Year	Women's Boarder X	Year	Men's Slopestyle	Year	Women's Slopestyle
1997	Shaun Palmer	1997	Jennie Waara	1997	Daniel Franck	1997	Barrett Christy
1998	Shaun Palmer	1998	Tina Dixon	1998	Ross Powers	1998	Jennie Waara
1999	Shaun Palmer	1999	Maelle Ricker	1999	Peter Line	1999	Tara Dakides
2000	Drew Neilson	2000	Leslee Olson	2000	Kevin Jones	2000	Tara Dakides
2001	Scott Gaffney	2001	Line Oestvold	2001	Kevin Jones	2001	Jaime MacLeod
2002	Philippe Conte	2002	Ine Poetzl	2002	Travis Rice	2002	Tara Dakides
2003	Ueli Kestenholz	2003	Lindsey Jacobellis	2003	Shaun White	2003	Janna Meyen
2004	Ueli Kestenholz	2004	Lindsey Jacobellis	2004	Shaun White	2004	Janna Meyen
2005	Xavier de le Rue	2005	Lindsey Jacobellis	2005	Shaun White	2005	Janna Meyen
2006	Nate Holland	2006	Maelle Ricker	2006	Shaun White	2006	Janna Meyen
2007	Nate Holland	2007	Joanie Anderson	2007	Andreas Wiig	2007	Jamie Anderson

Year	Men's Halfpipe	Year	Women's Halfpipe
1997	Todd Richards	1997	Shannon Dunn
1998	Ross Powers	1998	Cara-Beth Burnside
1999	Jimi Scott	1999	Michele Taggart
2000	Todd Richards	2000	S. Brun Kjeldaas

Year	Men's Superpipe	Year	Women's Superpipe
2001	Dan Kass	2001	Shannon Dunn
2002	J.J. Thomas	2002	Kelly Clark
2003	Shaun White	2003	Gretchen Bleiler
2004	Steve Fisher	2004	Hannah Teter
2005	Antti Autti	2005	Gretchen Bleiler
2006	Shaun White	2006	Kelly Clark
2007	Steve Fisher	2007	Torah Bright

X GAMES TO STAY IN COLORADO

The Winter X Games will be contested at Aspen/Snowmass through 2010. **Winter X Games 12** will be held at Aspen/Snowmass' Buttermilk Mountain on January 24-28, 2008. It will be the seventh straight year that Aspen/Snowmass has served as the event's host.

WINTER X GAMES

Skiing

Multiple winners: Aleisha Cline (4); Simon Dumont (3); Reggie Crist, Grete Eliassen, Tanner Hall, Lars Lewen (2).

Year	Men's Big Air	Year	Women's Skier X	Year	Women's SuperPipe
1999	J.F. Cusson	1999	Aleisha Cline	2005	Grete Eliassen
2000	Candide Thovex	2000	Anik Demers	2006	Grete Eliassen
2001	Tanner Hall	2001	Aleisha Cline	2007	Sarah Burke
2002	event discontinued	2002	Aleisha Cline	**Year**	**Men's Speed**
Year	**Men's Skier X**	2003	Aleisha Cline	1997	Phil Tintsman
1998	Dennis Rey	2004	Karin Huttary	1998	Jurgen Beneke
1999	Enak Gavaggio	2005	Sanna Tidstrand	1999	event discontinued
2000	Shaun Palmer	2006	Karin Huttary	**Year**	**Men's Slopestyle**
2001	Zach Crist	2007	Ophelie David	2002	Tanner Hall
2002	Reggie Crist	**Year**	**SuperPipe**	2003	Not held
2003	Lars Lewen	2002	Jon Olsson	2004	Simon Dumont
2004	Casey Puckett	2003	Candide Thovex	2005	Charles Gagnier
2005	Reggie Crist	2004	Simon Dumont	2006	not held
2006	Lars Lewen	**Year**	**Men's SuperPipe**	2007	Candide Thovex
2007	Casey Puckett	2005	Simon Dumont	**Year**	**Women's Speed**
Year	**Mono Skier X** (Coed)	2006	Tanner Hall	1997	Cheri Elliott
2007	Tyler Walker	2007	Tanner Hall	1998	Elke Brutsaert
				1999	event discontinued

Snomobiling

Year	Snocross	Year	Hillcross
1998	Toni Haikonen	2001	Carl Kuster
1999	Chris Vincent	2002	Carl Kuster
2000	Tucker Hibbert	2003	T.J. Kullas
2001	Blair Morgan	2003	Mike Metzger
2002	Blair Morgan	2004	Levi LaVallee
2003	Not held	2005	event discontinued
2004	Michael Island		
2005	Blair Morgan	**Year**	**Freestyle**
2006	Blair Morgan	2007	Chris Burandt
2007	Tucker Hibbert		

Ice Climbing

Year	Men's Difficulty
1997	Jaren Ogden
1998	Will Gadd
1999	Will Gadd
2000	event discontinued

Year	Women's Difficulty
1997	Bird Lew
1998	Kim Csizmazia
1999	Kim Csizmazia
2000	event discontinued

Year	Men's Speed
1997	Jared Ogden
1998	Will Gadd
1999	event discontinued

Year	Women's Speed
1997	Bird Lew
1998	Kim Csizmazia
1999	event discontinued

Snow Mountain Bike Racing

Year	Men's Downhill	Year	Men's Biker X
1997	Shaun Palmer	1999	Steve Peat
1998	Andrew Shandro	2000	Myles Rockwell
1999	event discontinued	2001	event discontinued

Year	Women's Downhill	Year	Women's Biker X
1997	Missy Giove	1999	Tara Llanes
1998	Marla Streb	2000	Katrina Miller
1999	event discontinued	2001	event discontinued

Winter X Games (Cont.)

Super-modified Shovel Racing

Year
1997 Don Adkins
1999 event discontinued

CrossOver

Year
1997 Brian Patch
1998 event discontinued

Skiboarding

Year
1998 Mike Nick
1999 Chris Hawks
2000 Neal Lyons
2001 event discontinued

Moto X

Year	Big Air
2001	Mike Jones
2002	Brian Deegan

Year	Best Trick
2004	Caleb Wyatt
2005	Jeremy Stenberg
2006	Jeremy Stenberg

UltraCross

Year
2000 McLain/Lind
2001 Palmer/Takizawa
2002 Wescott/Lind
2003 Delerue/Zackrisson
2004 Holland/Crist
2005 Huser/Andersson
2006 event discontinued

Mountain Dew Action Sports Tour
All-Time Winners

Panasonic Open

Skate Vert
2005 Bucky Lasek   2007 Shaun White
2006 Bob Burnquist

Skate Park
2005 Ryan Sheckler   2007 Ryan Sheckler
2006 Ryan Sheckler

BMX Vert
2005 Jamie Bestwick 2007 Jamie Bestwick
2006 Simon Tabron

BMX Park
2005 Ryan Guettler   2007 Daniel Dhers
2006 Scotty Cranmer

BMX Dirt
2005 Ryan Guettler   2007 Ryan Nyquist
2006 Anthony Napolitan

FMX
2005 Kenny Batram   2007 Nate Adams
2006 Nate Adams

Righ Guard Open

Skate Vert
2005 Bucky Lasek   2007 Shaun White
2006 Shaun White

Skate Park
2005 Ryan Sheckler   2007 Ryan Sheckler
2006 Jereme Rogers

BMX Vert
2005 Jamie Bestwick 2007 Simon Tabron
2006 Jamie Bestwick

BMX Park
2005 Ryan Guettler   2007 Daniel Dhers
2006 Daniel Dhers

BMX Dirt
2005 Ryan Guettler   2007 Ryan Nyquist
2006 Ryan Nyquist

FMX
2005 Kenny Batram   2007 Nate Adams
2006 Travis Pastrana

Vans Invitational

Skate Vert
2005 Bucky Lasek   2007 Shaun White
2006 Sandro Dias

Skate Park
2005 Greg Lutzka   2007 Greg Lutzka
2006 Ryan Sheckler

BMX Vert
2005 Jamie Bestwick 2007 Jamie Bestwick
2006 Jamie Bestwick

BMX Park
2005 Ryan Nyquist   2007 Mike Spinner
2006 Ryan Nyquist

BMX Dirt
2005 Ryan Guettler   2007 Dennis Earson
2006 Cameron White

FMX
2005 Kenny Batram   2007 Adam Jones
2006 Travis Pastrana

Toyota Challenge

Skate Vert
2005 Pierre-Luc Gagnon 2007 Pierre-Luc Gagnon
2006 Bucky Lasek

Skate Park
2005 Ryan Sheckler   2007 Ryan Sheckler
2006 Ryan Sheckler

BMX Vert
2005 Jamie Bestwick 2007 Jamie Bestwick
2006 Jamie Bestwick

BMX Park
2005 Dave Mirra   2007 Scotty Cranmer
2006 Scotty Cranmer

BMX Dirt
2005 Ryan Guettler   2007 James Foster
2006 Ryan Guettler

FMX
2005 Jeremy Stenberg 2007 Nate Adams
2006 Nate Adams

Playstation Pro

Skate Vert
2005 Pierre-Luc Gagnon 2007 Bucky Lasek
2006 Bucky Lasek

Skate Park
2005 Jereme Rogers   2007 Greg Lutzka
2006 Jereme Rogers

BMX Vert
2005 Jamie Bestwick 2007 Chad Kagy
2006 Jamie Bestwick

BMX Park
2005 Scotty Cranmer 2007 Daniel Dhers
2006 Daniel Dhers

BMX Dirt
2005 Ryan Nyquist   2007 Luke Parslow
2006 Anthony Napolitan

FMX
2005 Kenny Bartram   2007 Nate Adams
2006 Mike Mason

HORSE RACING

2006 / 2007 YEAR IN REVIEW

Trainer **Todd Pletcher** and jockey **John Velazquez** celebrate Rags to Riches' win in the Belmont Stakes.

TRIPLE CROWN DROUGHT

With three different winners in the Kentucky Derby, Preakness and Belmont, the wait continues for a Triple Crown winner.

AND SO THE DROUGHT CONTINUES – 29 YEARS AND COUNTING, SINCE AFFIRMED AND JOCKEY STEVE CAUTHEN swept the Kentucky Derby, Preakness and Belmont Stakes to win thoroughbred racing's Triple Crown in 1978.

To put that in perspective, in 1978 the average cost for a gallon of gas was about 65 cents, YMCA and Stayin' Alive were burning up the pop charts, Tiger Woods appeared on the Mike Douglas Show...as a two-year-old, and the Chicago Cubs were only 70 years into their current 99-year rebuilding period.

Sure, plenty of horses have come close. Ten times since 1978, a horse has won the first two legs, only to be thwarted at the 1½-mile Belmont (see list of near misses on page 788). Still, as the 133rd running of the Kentucky Derby approached in early May, race fans were hopeful.

The early Derby money was on Steve Asmussen-trained Curlin, who was attempting to become the first horse since Apollo in 1882 (yes...1882!) to win the Run For the Roses despite not having raced at all as a 2-year-old. After cruising to wins in the first three races of his career by a combined 28½ lengths, including a record-setting 10½-length whupping at the Arkansas Derby three weeks before the Derby, Curlin was firmly entrenched as the 7-2 pre-race favorite.

Just behind Curlin was Street Sense at 4-1. Trained by Carl Nafzger who saddled 1990 Derby winner Unbridled, Street Sense grabbed everyone's attention as a 2-year-old with his stunning 10-length romp at the Breeders' Cup Juvenile at Churchill Downs in November. He returned to Kentucky with high hopes but had history working against him, as no horse had ever won the Juvenile and then went on to win the Derby.

It was a clean start as Hard Spun and jockey Mario Pino shot to the lead right out of the gate and held firm through the half-mile mark. The

 Michael Morrison is Co-Editor of the ESPN Sports Almanac.

Curlin, left, ridden by Robby Albarado, passes **Street Sense**, right, ridden by Calvin Borel, to win the 132nd running of the Preakness Stakes in Baltimore, Saturday, May 19, 2007.

race favorites were nowhere to be found. "I backed him up a little bit," Street Sense jockey Calvin Borel would later say. A little bit? Street Sense was 19th, seemingly focused more on Curlin, who was caught in traffic and in 13th place, than he was on the leaders.

As the race neared the halfway point, Street Sense struck. Powering along the rail, he left the field in his dust, moving from 17th place to 3rd in only a quarter-mile. Hard Spun valiantly tried to hang on, but was no match as Borel guided Street Sense into the lead at the stretch, then drove to the victory by 2¼ lengths. Hard Spun placed second, while Curlin rallied to finish third.

Despite entering five horses in the 20-horse field, Todd Pletcher, the sport's best trainer over the past several years, and arguably one of the top trainers of all time, once again went home without a Triple Crown win. Pletcher, who earlier stood at the podium of a pre-race press conference and quipped, "My name is Todd Pletcher...and I've never won the Kentucky Derby," ran his personal Derby mark to 0-for-19 and his Triple Crown streak to 0-for-26.

Immediately, Street Sense was pegged as the 7-5 favorite for the Preakness, with Curlin not far behind at 7-2. Borel was confident in his horse, claiming, "I don't think he can get beat. Something very bad would

Jockey **Russell Baze**, left, celebrates with former jockey **Laffit Pincay Jr.**, after Baze won the fourth race at Bay Meadows in San Mateo, Calif., Dec. 1, 2006. It was Baze's 9,531st victory, eclipsing Pincay's career record as racing's winningest jockey.

have to happen, a fall or something. If he don't fall, no way he'll get beat."

A record crowd of 121,263 jammed into Pimlico to see the two favorites battle it out with just seven other horses. They didn't leave disappointed.

As he did at the Derby two weeks earlier, Street Sense held back and ran comfortably in the eighth spot for the first half-mile. Curlin, who had nearly fallen to his knees after stumbling out of the gate, quickly recovered and stalked the leaders from the 6-spot.

At the stretch, the duel was on, with Street Sense and Curlin running 1-2 and just 1½ lengths apart. Curlin, under jockey Robby Albarado, made a bold move, circling five-wide to pull even with his rival. At the finish line, Curlin made a last surge and a head bob, and it was enough to beat Street Sense by a head. Derby runner-up Hard Spun placed third.

"What I really wanted most of all was for everyone to know how good Curlin is," Asmussen said. "It was hard to be quiet after the Derby and let others question him. But now it won't happen again."

Continued on page 782

THE TOP

10

Stories of the Year in
Horse Racing

10 Hot To Trot

With wins in harness racing's Hambletonian, Kentucky Futurity and finally the Yonkers Trot in November 2006, Glidemaster becomes the eighth horse to win the Trotting Triple Crown.

09 That's Rich

Invasor, the 2006 Horse of the Year and Breeders' Cup Classic champ, continued where he left off in 2007, winning the Donn Handicap at Gulfstream and then the $6 million Dubai World Cup in March.

08 Maybe Next Year

The Kentucky Derby, Preakness and Belmont Stakes have three different winners, meaning thoroughbred racing's Triple Crown drought extends another year. It's been 29 years since Affirmed won in 1978.

07 Barbaro Loses Battle

After an eight-month struggle following his injury at the 2006 Preakness, Barbaro is euthanized in late January.

06 Where Is Everyone?

With a small 7-horse field and no chance of a Triple Crown winner, the Belmont Stakes sees its lowest attendance total in 11 years (46,870) and a 2.9 television rating, the lowest since 2000.

05 Baze Is Best

Russell Baze wins his 9,531st race on Dec. 1, 2006, eclipsing Laffit Pincay Jr.'s career record as racing's all-time winningest jockey.

04 Easy Street

Less than six months after his stunning 10-length victory at the Breeders' Cup Juvenile as a 2-year-old, Street Sense, under jockey Calvin Borel, bides his time then roars to a 2¼-length win at the Kentucky Derby.

03 Filly Fanatic

Rags to Riches makes her move at the mile mark, takes the lead and holds on to nip pre-race favorite Curlin at the wire to becomes the first filly in 102 years to win the Belmont Stakes.

02 Curlin is Sterling

After a second-place finish at the Kentucky Derby, Curlin, under jockey Robby Albarado, battles Street Sense down the stretch and wins the Preakness by a head.

01 Finally!

Rags to Riches' victory in the Belmont Stakes (see #3) removes the monkey from Todd Pletcher's back, giving the trainer extraordinaire his first Triple Crown victory in 29 tries.

With the possibility of a Triple Crown winner now wiped away, the Belmont Stakes struggled for national attention. A crowd of only 46,870 (the smallest in 11 years) watched just seven horses compete on the 1½-mile track. Street Sense skipped the race to prepare for the Travers Stakes and Breeders' Cup Classic, but Curlin and Hard Spun were in attendance.

Also in attendance was the impressive filly Rags to Riches, who was attempting to become the third filly (Ruthless in 1867 and Tanya in 1905) ever to win the Belmont Stakes, and the first in 102 years.

Like Curlin three weeks prior, Rags to Riches gave everyone a scare when she stumbled to her knees out of the gate. "My heart stopped," said jockey John Velazquez. She regained her composure and hung tight behind Curlin as the two made their move at the mile mark. With a blazing 48.51-second final half-mile, Rags to Riches showed the boys who was boss, edging Curlin by a head and entering the history books in the process. Tiago placed third, while Hard Spun came in fourth.

Trainer Pletcher had decided to run Rags to Riches just four days before the race and was rewarded with his first Triple Crown victory, snapping his 0-for-28 drought. The win was also the first for Velazquez, who ended his 0-for-20 drought.

"It's a special feeling no matter when you do it," Pletcher said after the race. "But when you do it with a filly for the first time in 102 years, it's really special."

Two droughts over. One major drought still going strong.

Stable Relationships

A selection of successful thoroughbreds with sports-inspired names

Horse	Years	Earnings	Horse	Years	Earnings
Grand Slam	1997-98	$971,292	Hook and Ladder	1999-03	$338,120
Bowl Game	1977-80	907,083	Splendid Splinter	1996-03	259,906
Power Play	1994-98	469,176	Home Run Hitter	2002-06	228,438
Fifty Six Ina Row	1983-86	355,650	K.O. Punch	1997	212,870
Rockchalk Jayhawk	2000-04	351,032	Tubby Cat	1999-05	173,476

...and some others that are just kind of cool:

Horse	Years	Earnings	Horse	Years	Earnings
Beatmichiganagain	1999-01	$144,452	Knuckleball	2001-06	$97,258
Brett's Favrette	2005-06	79,498	Lambeau Leap	1999-01	n/a
Clear the Bases	2003-06	115,060	Red Sox Parade	2005-06	67,110
Flushing Meadows	2003-06	113,431	Tiger on Tour	2004-05	n/a
It's Awesome Baby	2003-05	n/a	Touchdown USC	2004-06	96,525

Source: *23 Ways To Get To First Base: The ESPN Uncyclopedia*

2006-2007
Season in Review

Thoroughbred Racing
Major Stakes Races

Winners of major stakes races from Nov. 25, 2006 through Sept. 30, 2007; (T) indicates turf race course; F indicates furlongs.

Late 2006

Date	Race	Track	Miles	Winner	Jockey	Purse
Nov. 4	Breeders' Cup Classic	Churchill Downs	1¼	Invasor (ARG)	Fernando Jara	$5,000,000
Nov. 4	Breeders' Cup Turf	Churchill Downs	1½ (T)	Red Rocks (IRE)	Frankie Dettori	3,000,000
Nov. 4	Breeders' Cup Distaff	Churchill Downs	1⅛	Round Pond	Edgar Prado	2,000,000
Nov. 4	Breeders' Cup Mile	Churchill Downs	1 (T)	Miesque's Approval	Eddie Castro	2,000,000
Nov. 4	Breeders' Cup Sprint	Churchill Downs	6 F	Thor's Echo	Corey Nakatani	2,000,000
Nov. 4	Breeders' Cup Filly/Mare Turf	Churchill Downs	1⅜ (T)	Ouija Board (GB)	Frankie Dettori	2,000,000
Nov. 4	Breeders' Cup Juvenile	Churchill Downs	1¹⁄₁₆	Street Sense	Calvin Borel	2,000,000
Nov. 4	Breeders' Cup Juvenile Fillies	Churchill Downs	1¹⁄₁₆	Dreaming of Anna	Rene Douglas	2,000,000
Nov. 24	Clark Handicap	Churchill Downs	1⅛	Premium Tap	Kent Desormeaux	572,000

2007 (through Sept. 30)

Date	Race	Track	Miles	Winner	Jockey	Purse
Jan. 27	Sunshine Millions Classic	Gulfstream	1⅛	McCann's Mojave	Frank Alvarado	$1,000,000
Feb. 3	Charles H. Strub Stakes	Santa Anita	1⅛	Arson Squad	Garrett Gomez	300,000
Feb. 3	Donn Handicap	Gulfstream	1⅛	Invasor (ARG)	Fernando Jara	500,000
Feb. 10	Santa Maria Handicap	Santa Anita	1¹⁄₁₆	Sugar Shake	David Flores	250,000
Mar. 3	Fountain of Youth Stakes	Gulfstream	1⅛	Scat Daddy	John Velazquez	350,000
Mar. 3	Santa Anita Handicap	Santa Anita	1¼	Lava Man	Corey Nakatani	1,000,000
Mar. 10	Santa Margarita Handicap	Santa Anita	1⅛	Balance	Victor Espinoza	300,000
Mar. 11	Santa Anita Oaks	Santa Anita	1¹⁄₁₆	Rags to Riches	Garrett Gomez	300,000
Mar. 17	San Felipe Stakes	Santa Anita	1¹⁄₁₆	Cobalt Blue	Victor Espinoza	250,000
Mar. 17	Rebel Stakes	Oaklawn	1¹⁄₁₆	Curlin	Robby Albarado	300,000
Mar. 17	Tampa Bay Derby	Tampa Bay	1¹⁄₁₆	Street Sense	Calvin Borel	300,000
Mar. 18	WinStar Derby	Sunland	1⅛	Song of Navarone	Victor Espinoza	600,000
Mar. 24	Lane's End Stakes	Turfway	1⅛	Hard Spun	Mario Pino	500,000
Mar. 31	Dubai World Cup	Nad al-Sheba	1¼	Invasor (ARG)	Fernando Jara	6,000,000
Mar. 31	Dubai Golden Shaheen	Nad al-Sheba	¾	Kelly's Landing	Frankie Dettori	2,000,000
Mar. 31	Dubai Duty Free	Nad al-Sheba	1⅛	Admire Moon	Yutaka Take	5,000,000
Mar. 31	Dubai Sheema Classic	Nad al-Sheba	1½	Vengeance of Rain	Anthony Delpech	5,000,000
Mar. 31	UAE Derby	Nad al-Sheba	1⅛	Asiatic Boy	Weichong Marwing	2,000,000
Mar. 31	Florida Derby	Gulfstream	1⅛	Scat Daddy	Edgar Prado	1,000,000
Apr. 7	Santa Anita Derby	Santa Anita	1⅛	Tiago	Mike Smith	750,000
Apr. 7	Ashland Stakes	Keeneland	1¹⁄₁₆	Christmas Kid	Rene Douglas	500,000
Apr. 7	Oaklawn Handicap	Oaklawn	1⅛	Lawyer Ron	Edgar Prado	500,000
Apr. 7	Apple Blossom Handicap	Oaklawn	1¹⁄₁₆	Ermine	Eddie Castro	500,000
Apr. 7	Illinois Derby	Hawthorne	1⅛	Cowtown Cat	Fernando Jara	500,000
Apr. 7	Wood Memorial	Aqueduct	1⅛	Nobiz Like Shobiz	Cornelio Velazquez	750,000
Apr. 14	Blue Grass Stakes	Keeneland	1⅛	Dominican	Rafael Bejarano	750,000
Apr. 14	Arkansas Derby	Oaklawn	1⅛	Curlin	Robby Albarado	1,000,000
Apr. 21	Coolmore Lexington Stakes	Keeneland	1¹⁄₁₆	Slew's Tizzy	Robby Albarado	325,000
Apr. 29	Queen Elizabeth II Cup	Sha Tin	1¼ (T)	Viva Pataca (HK)	Michael Kinane	1,789,200
May 4	Kentucky Oaks	Churchill Downs	1⅛	Rags to Riches	Garrett Gomez	500,000
May 5	**Kentucky Derby**	Churchill Downs	1¼	Street Sense	Calvin Borel	2,000,000
May 5	Woodford Reserve Classic	Churchill Downs	1⅛ (T)	Sky Conqueror	Javier Castellano	500,000
May 18	Black-Eyed Susan Stakes	Pimlico	1⅛	Panty Raid	Edgar Prado	250,000
May 19	**Preakness Stakes**	Pimlico	1³⁄₁₆	Curlin	Robby Albarado	1,000,000
May 28	Gamely BC Handicap	Hollywood Park	1⅛ (T)	Citronnade	David Flores	300,000
May 28	Shoemaker BC Mile	Hollywood Park	1 (T)	The Tin Man	Victor Espinoza	300,000
May 28	Metropolitan Handicap	Belmont	1	Corinthian	Kent Desormeaux	600,000
June 2	Epsom Derby	Epsom Downs	1½ (T)	Authorized	Frankie Dettori	2,470,000
June 9	**Belmont Stakes**	Belmont	1½	Rags to Riches	John Velazquez	1,000,000
June 9	Manhattan Handicap	Belmont	1¼ (T)	Better Talk Now	Ramon Dominguez	400,000
June 9	Acorn Stakes	Belmont	1	Cotton Blossom	John Velazquez	250,000
June 9	Charles Whittingham H	Hollywood Park	1¼ (T)	After Market	Alex Solis	300,000

Major Stakes Races (Cont.)

Date	Race	Track	Miles	Winner	Jockey	Purse
June 16	Stephen Foster Handicap	Churchill Downs	1⅛	Flashy Bull	Robby Albarado	$750,000
June 16	Ogden Phipps Handicap	Belmont	1¹⁄₁₆	Take D'Tour	Eibar Coa	300,000
June 22	Colonial Turf Cup Stakes	Colonial Downs	1³⁄₁₆ (T)	Summer Doldrums	Jose Lezcano	750,000
June 24	Queen's Plate	Woodbine	1¼	Mike Fox	Emma-Jayne Wilson	1,000,000
June 30	Suburban Handicap	Belmont	1¼	Political Force	Cornelio Velasquez	400,000
June 30	Mother Goose Stakes	Belmont	1⅛	Octave	John Velazquez	250,000
June 30	Hollywood Gold Cup	Hollywood Park	1¼	Lava Man	Corey Nakatani	750,000
July 6	CashCall Mile	Hollywood Park	1 (T)	Lady of Venice	Julien Leparoux	1,000,000
July 7	American Oaks	Hollywood Park	1¼ (T)	Panty Raid	Edgar Prado	750,000
July 7	United Nations Stakes	Monmouth Park	1⅜ (T)	English Channel	John Velazquez	750,000
July 7	Princess Rooney Handicap	Calder	6 F	River's Prayer	Clinton Potts	500,000
July 7	Smile Sprint Handicap	Calder	6 F	Mach Ride	Elvis Trujillo	500,000
July 9	Irish Derby	Curragh	1½ (T)	Soldier Of Fortune	Seamus Heffernan	2,119,812
July 14	Swaps BC Stakes	Hollywood Park	1⅛	Tiago	Mike Smith	350,000
July 14	Delaware Oaks	Delaware	1¹⁄₁₆	Moon Catcher	Carlos Marquez Jr.	500,000
July 15	Delaware Handicap	Delaware	1¼	Unbridled Belle	Ramon Dominguez	1,000,000
July 21	Virginia Derby	Colonial Downs	1¼ (T)	Red Giant	Horacio Karamanos	1,000,000
July 21	Coaching Club Am. Oaks	Belmont	1¼	Octave	John Velazquez	300,000
July 22	Eddie Read Handicap	Del Mar	1⅛ (T)	After Market	Alex Solis	400,000
July 28	K. George VI and Q. Elizabeth Diamond Stakes	Ascot	1½ (T)	Dylan Thomas	Johnny Murtagh	1,500,000
July 28	Diana Stakes	Saratoga	1⅛ (T)	My Typhoon	Eddie Castro	500,000
July 28	Go for Wand Handicap	Saratoga	1⅛	Ginger Punch	Rafael Bejarano	250,000
July 28	Whitney Handicap	Saratoga	1⅛	Lawyer Ron	John Velazquez	750,000
July 29	Jim Dandy Stakes	Saratoga	1⅛	Street Sense	Calvin Borel	500,000
Aug. 4	John C. Mabee Handicap	Del Mar	1⅛ (T)	Precious Kitten	Rafael Bejarano	400,000
Aug. 4	Test Stakes	Saratoga	7 F	Dream Rush	Eibar Coa	250,000
Aug. 4	West Virginia Derby	Mountaineer Park	1⅛	Zanjero	Shaun Bridgmohan	750,000
Aug. 5	Haskell Invitational	Monmouth	1⅛	Any Given Sunday	Garrett Gomez	1,000,000
Aug. 11	Sword Dancer Invitational	Saratoga	1½ (T)	Grand Couturier	Calvin Borel	500,000
Aug. 11	Arlington Million	Arlington	1¼ (T)	Jambalaya	Robby Albarado	1,000,000
Aug. 11	Beverly D. Stakes	Arlington	1³⁄₁₆ (T)	Royal Highness	Rene Douglas	750,000
Aug. 11	Secretariat Stakes	Arlington	1¼ (T)	Shamdinan	Julien Leparoux	400,000
Aug. 18	Alabama Stakes	Saratoga	1¼	Lady Joanne	Calvin Borel	600,000
Aug. 19	Pacific Classic	Del Mar	1¼	Student Council	Richard Migliore	1,000,000
Aug. 24	Personal Ensign Handicap	Saratoga	1¼	Miss Shop	Javier Castellano	400,000
Aug. 25	Travers Stakes	Saratoga	1¼	Street Sense	Calvin Borel	1,000,000
Sept. 1	The Woodward Stakes	Saratoga	1⅛	Lawyer Ron	John Velazquez	500,000
Sept. 3	Pennsylvania Derby	Philadelphia	1⅛	Timber Reserve	Javier Castellano	1,000,000
Sept. 8	Man o' War Stakes	Belmont	1⅜ (T)	Doctor Dino	Olivier Peslier	500,000
Sept. 8	Irish Champion Stakes	Leopardstown	1¼ (T)	Dylan Thomas	Kieren Fallon	1,360,000
Sept. 8	Ruffian Handicap	Belmont	1¹⁄₁₆	Ginger Punch	Rafael Bejarano	300,000
Sept. 15	Futurity Stakes	Belmont	7 F	Tale of Ekati	Eibar Coa	250,000
Sept. 16	Woodbine Mile	Woodbine	1 (T)	Shakespeare	Garrett Gomez	1,000,000
Sept. 22	Super Derby	Louisiana Downs	1⅛	Going Ballistic	M. Clifton Berry	500,000
Sept. 29	Hawthorne Gold Cup	Hawthorne	1¼	Student Council	Richard Migliore	500,000
Sept. 29	Goodwood Handicap	Santa Anita	1⅛	Tiago	Mike Smith	500,000
Sept. 30	Jockey Club Gold Cup	Belmont	1¼	Curlin	Robby Albarado	750,000

NTRA National Thoroughbred Poll

The NTRA Thoroughbred Poll conducted by National Thoroughbred Racing Association, covering races through Sept. 30, 2007. Rankings are based on the votes of horse racing media representatives on a 10-9-8-7-6-5-4-3-2-1 basis. First place votes are in parentheses.

		Pts	Age	Sex	'07 Record Sts—1-2-3	Owner	Trainer
1	Curlin (7)	149	3	Colt	8—5-1-2	G. Bolton, Stonestreet & Padua	Steven Asmussen
2	Street Sense (5)	131	3	Colt	7—4-3-0	Jim Tafel LLC	Carl Nafzger
3	Lawyer Ron (1)	117	4	Colt	7—4-2-1	Hines Racing LLC	Todd Pletcher
4	Hard Spun	104	3	Colt	9—4-2-1	Fox Hill Farms, Inc.	J. Larry Jones
5	Any Given Sunday (2)	90	3	Colt	7—4-1-1	WinStar Farm & Padua Stables	Todd Pletcher
6	Rags to Riches (1)	60	3	Filly	6—5-1-0	Michael Tabor & Derrick Smith	Todd Pletcher
7	Nashoba's Key	42	4	Filly	7—7-0-0	Warren Williamson	Carla Gaines
8	English Channel	38	5	Horse	6—3-2-0	James Scatuorchio	Todd Pletcher
9	Tiago	22	3	Colt	7—4-0-1	Mr. & Mrs. Jerome S. Moss	John Shirreffs
10	Invasor	17	5	Horse	2—2-0-0	Shadwell Stable	Kiaran McLaughlin

Others receiving votes: Lava Man (15); Fabulous Strike and Lady Joanne (11); Shakespeare (10); Student Council (9); Awesome Gem (8); After Market (7); Political Force (6); Brass Hat and The Tin Man (5); Gottcha Gold and Midnight Lute (4); Majestic Warrior (3); Awfully Smart, Corinthian, Dream Rush and Lear's Princess (2); Danzon, Hystericalady, On The Acorn and Smokey Stover (1).

The 2007 Triple Crown

133RD KENTUCKY DERBY

Grade I for three-year-olds; 10th race at Churchill Downs in Louisville. **Date**—May 5, 2007; **Distance**—1¼ miles; **Stakes Purse**—$2,210,000 ($1,450,000 to winner; $400,000 for 2nd; $200,000 for 3rd; $100,000 for 4th; $60,000 for 5th); **Track**—Fast; **Off**—6:16 p.m. EDT; **Favorite**—Curlin (7-2 odds). **Winner**—Street Sense; **Field**—20 horses; **Time**—2:02.17; **Start**—Good; **Won**—Driving; **Sire**—Street Cry (Machiavellian); **Dam**—Bedazzle (Dixieland Band); **Record** (going into race)—7 starts, 3 wins, 2 seconds, 2 thirds; **Last start**—2nd in Blue Grass Stakes (Apr. 14); **Breeder**—Jim Tafel.

Order of Finish	Jockey	PP	1/4	1/2	3/4	Mile	Stretch	Finish	To $1
Street Sense	Calvin Borel	7	18-1½	19-5	17-hd	3-hd	1-1	1-2¼	4.90
Hard Spun	Mario Pino	8	1-hd	1-1	1-2	1-3	2-4	2-5¾	10.00
Curlin	Robby Albarado	2	13-1½	13-2½	14-11½	8-hd	6-1	3-½	5.00
Imawildandcrazyguy	Mark Guidry	5	20	20	20	16-½	11-1½	4-½	28.90
Sedgefield	Julien Leparoux	1	.5-½	5-1½	3-hd	2-½	3-hd	5-nk	58.60
Circular Quay	John Velazquez	16	19-3	18-1	16-hd	13-½	8-½	6-¾	11.40
Tiago	Mike Smith	15	17-hd	17-½	18-4	15-1	12-hd	7-½	14.80
Any Given Sunday	Garrett Gomez	18	8-1½	9-1½	9-1	4-hd	4-2½	8-2½	13.60
Sam P.	Ramon Dominguez	13	9-1½	12-1½	12-1½	7-hd	7-1½	9-1¾	43.70
Nobiz Like Shobiz	Cornelio Velasquez	12	6-1½	6-1½	6-1	5-hd	5-hd	10-3	10.40
Dominican	Rafael Bejarano	19	11-½	10-hd	10-hd	10-½	14-2½	11-nk	24.90
Zanjero	Shaun Bridgmohan	3	16-2	15-3	13-hd	11-½	10-½	12-2¾	36.00
Great Hunter	Corey Nakatani	20	12-2½	11-2½	11-1½	6-½	9-hd	13-1¾	25.30
Liquidity	David Flores	9	10-½	8-½	7-½	9-hd	13-1	14-¾	40.00
Bwana Bull	Javier Castellano	11	14-2	14-hd	15-1	19-½	16-2	15-1	50.30
Storm in May	Juan Leyva	4	15-1½	16-hd	19-2½	18-2	15-½	16-11½	27.20
Teuflesberg	Stewart Elliott	10	4-1½	3-½	2-½	12-hd	17-½	17-2¾	51.90
Scat Daddy	Edgar Prado	14	7-½	7-hd	8-hd	20	20	18-6¼	7.20
Stormello	Kent Desormeaux	17	2-hd	4-1	5-hd	14-1½	18-1½	19-7¼	44.80
Cowtown Cat	Fernando Jara	6	3-½	2-½	4-1	17-1½	19-½	20	19.80

Times—22.96; 46.26; 1:11.13; 1:37.04; 2:02.17.

$2 Mutuel Prices—#7 Street Sense ($11.80, $6.40, $4.60); #8 Hard Spun ($9.80, $7.00); #2 Curlin ($5.60). **Exacta**—(7-8) for $101.80; **Trifecta**—(7-8-2) for $440.00; **$2 Superfecta**—(7-8-2-5) for $29,046.40; **Scratched**—none; **Overweights**—none. **Attendance**—156,635; **TV Rating**—8.7 (NBC).

Trainers & Owners (by finish): **1**—Carl Nafzger & Jim Tafel LLC; **2**—J. Larry Jones & Fox Hill Farms Inc.; **3**—Steven Asmussen & Stonestreet, Padua, Midnight Cry Stables and George Bolton; **4**—William Kaplan & Lewis Pell and Michael Eigner; **5**—Darrin Miller & Silverton Hill LLC; **6**—Todd Pletcher & Michael and Doreen Tabor; **7**—John Shirreffs & Mr. and Mrs. Jerome S. Moss; **8**—Todd Pletcher & WinStar Farm and Padua Stables; **9**—Todd Pletcher & Starlight Stable and Donald Lucarelli; **10**—Barclay Tagg & Elizabeth Valando; **11**—Darrin Miller & Silverton Hill LLC; **12**—Steven Asmussen & Winchell Thoroughbreds LLC; **13**—Doug O'Neill & J. Paul Reddam; **14**—Doug O'Neill & J. Paul Reddam; **15**—Jerry Hollendorfer & Mark DeDomenico, Dan Jelladian and Dan and George Todaro; **16**—William Kaplan & William Kaplan, Teresa and David Palmer andFelicity Waugh; **17**—Jamie Sanders & Jeff Singer, Jamie Sanders, Donnie Kelly and Gary Logsdon; **18**—Todd Pletcher & James Scatuorchio, Michael Tabor and Derrick Smith; **19**—William Currin & William Currin and Al Eisman; **20**—Todd Pletcher & WinStar Farm and Gulf Coast Farms.

132ND PREAKNESS STAKES

Grade I for three-year-olds; 12th race at Pimlico in Baltimore. **Date**—May 19, 2007; **Distance**—1³⁄₁₆ miles; **Stakes Purse**—$1,000,000 ($600,000 to winner; $200,000 for 2nd; $110,000 for 3rd; $60,000 for 4th; $30,000 for 5th); **Track**—Fast; **Off**—6:18 p.m. EDT; **Favorite**—Street Sense (7-5 odds). **Winner**—Curlin; **Field**—9 horses; **Time**—1:53.46; **Start**—Good; **Won**—Driving; **Sire**—Smart Strike (Mr. Prospector); **Dam**—Sheriff's Deputy (Deputy Minister); **Record** (going into race)—4 starts, 3 wins, 0 seconds, 1 third; **Last start**—3rd in Kentucky Derby (May 5); **Breeder**—Fares Farms, Inc. (Ky.).

Order of Finish	Jockey	PP	1/4	1/2	3/4	Stretch	Finish	To $1
Curlin	Robby Albarado	4	6-hd	7-2	6-3	2-hd	1-hd	3.40
Street Sense	Calvin Borel	8	8-2½	8-3	7-hd	1-1½	2-4	1.30
Hard Spun	Mario Pino	7	3-1½	3-2½	1-2	3-1½	3-1½	4.10
C P West	Edgar Prado	9	5-3	4-1½	3-2½	4-5	4-1¼	24.90
Circular Quay	John Velazquez	3	9	9	9	5-hd	5-3¾	6.00
King of the Roxy	Garrett Gomez	5	4-½	5-4	5-1	6-6	6-6½	14.20
Mint Slewlep	Alan Garcia	1	7-1	6-½	8-2½	7-3	7-8½	40.10
Xchanger	Ramon Dominguez	2	1-½	1-1	2-hd	8-5	8-4½	23.00
Flying First Class	Mark Guidry	6	2-3	2-3½	4-1	9	9	16.60

Times—22.83; 45.75; 1:09.80; 1:34.68; 1:53.46.

$2 Mutuel Prices—#4 Curlin ($8.80, $3.80, $2.80); #8 Street Sense ($3.00, $2.40); #7 Hard Spun ($3.00). **Exacta**—(4-8) for $23.20; **Trifecta**—(4-8-7) for $50.00; **$1 Superfecta**—(4-8-7-9) for $340.30; **Scratched**—none; **Overweights**—none. **Attendance**—121,263; **TV Rating**—3.8 (NBC).

Trainers & Owners (by finish): **1**—Steven Asmussen & Stonestreet, Padua, Midnight Cry Stables and George Bolton; **2**—Carl Nafzger & Jim Tafel LLC; **3**—J. Larry Jones & Fox Hill Farms Inc.; **4**—Nick Zito & Robert LaPenta; **5**—Todd Pletcher & Michael and Doreen Tabor; **6**—Todd Pletcher & Team Valor Stables; **7**—W. Robert Bailes & Marshall Dowell; **8**—Mark Shuman & Circle Z Stables; **9**—D. Wayne Lukas & Ellwood W. Johnston.

The 2007 Triple Crown (Cont.)

139TH BELMONT STAKES

Grade I for three-year-olds; 11th race at Belmont Park in Elmont, N.Y. **Date**—June 9, 2007; **Distance**—1½ miles; **Stakes Purse**—$1,000,000 ($600,000 to winner; $200,000 for 2nd; $110,000 for 3rd; $60,000 for 4th; $30,000 for 5th); **Track**—Fast; **Off**—6:29 p.m. EDT; **Favorite**—Curlin (6-5 odds). **Winner**—Rags to Riches; **Field**—7 horses; **Time**—2:28.74; **Start**—Good for all but Rags to Riches (7); **Won**—Driving; **Sire**—A.P. Indy (Seattle Slew); **Dam**—Better Than Honour (Deputy Minister); **Record** (going into race)—5 starts, 4 wins, 0 seconds, 0 thirds; **Last Start**—1st in Kentucky Oaks (May 4); **Breeder**—Skara Glen Stables (Ky.).

Order of Finish	Jockey	PP	1/4	1/2	Mile	1-1/4	Stretch	Finish	To $1
Rags to Riches	John Velazquez	7	6-7	5-1	5-1½	1-hd	1-hd	1-hd	4.30
Curlin	Robby Albarado	3	3-hd	4-½	4-½	2-hd	2-5	2-5½	1.10
Tiago	Mike Smith	2	5-hd	6-6	6-7	5-8	3-2½	3-5½	6.80
Hard Spun	Garrett Gomez	6	4-1	3-½	3-½	3-1½	4-3½	4-4¼	4.90
C P West	Edgar Prado	4	1-hd	1-hd	1-hd	4-1	5-6	5-1¾	12.40
Imawildandcrazyguy	Mark Guidry	1	7	7	7	7	6-8	6-17	9.30
Slew's Tizzy	Rafael Bejarano	5	2-1½	2-1	2-½	6-1½	7	7	18.30

Times—24.74; 50.14; 1:15.32; 1:40.23; 2:04.91; 2:28.74.

$2 Mutuel Prices—#7 Rags to Riches ($10.60, $4.40, $3.20); #3 Curlin ($3.00, $2.30); #2 Tiago ($3.70).
Exacta—(7-3) for $25.20; **Trifecta**—(7-3-2) for $131.50; **Superfecta**—(7-3-2-6) for $242.50; **Scratched**—none; **Overweights**—none; **Attendance**—46,870; **TV Rating**—2.9 (ABC).

Trainers & Owners (by finish): **1**—Todd Pletcher & Michael Tabor and Derrick Smith; **2**—Steven Asmussen & Stonestreet, Padua, Midnight Cry Stables and George Bolton; **3**—John Shirreffs & Mr. and Mrs. Jerome S. Moss; **4**—J. Larry Jones & Fox Hill Farms Inc.; **5**—Nick Zito & Robert LaPenta; **6**—William Kaplan & Lewis Pell and Michael Eigner; **7**—Gregory Fox & Joseph Lacombe Stable Inc.

2006-07 Money Leaders

Official Top 10 standings for 2006 and unofficial Top 10 standings for 2007, through Sept. 30. Results are based on North American races plus select international races. Source: *Equibase Company.*

FINAL 2006				2007 (Through Sept. 30)			
HORSES Age	Sts	1-2-3	**Earnings**	**HORSES** Age	Sts	1-2-3	**Earnings**
Invasor (ARG) 4	4	4-0-0	$3,690,000	Invasor (ARG) 5	2	2-0-0	$3,900,000
Bernardini 3	8	6-1-0	3,060,480	Street Sense 3	4	4-3-0	2,950,000
Lava Man 5	8	7-0-0	2,770,000	Curlin 3	8	5-1-2	2,402,800
Barbaro 3	5	4-0-0	2,203,200	Hard Spun 3	9	4-2-1	1,572,500
Miesque's Approval 7	7	5-1-0	1,906,405	Lava Man 6	5	3-1-0	1,405,000
Red Rocks (IRE) 3	1	1-0-0	1,620,000	Rags to Riches 3	6	5-1-0	1,340,028
Showing Up 3	9	7-0-1	1,610,500	Lawyer Ron 4	7	4-2-1	1,320,000
Bluegrass Cat 3	7	2-4-0	1,547,500	Kelly's Landing 6	3	2-0-0	1,263,000
English Channel 4	7	4-0-1	1,507,937	Premium Tap 5	1	0-1-0	1,200,000
Fleet Indian 5	7	6-0-0	1,473,720	Nobiz Like Shobiz 3	8	5-1-1	1,184,200
JOCKEYS	Mts	1st	**Earnings**	**JOCKEYS**	Mts	1st	**Earnings**
Garrett Gomez 1270	261		$20,122,592	Garrett Gomez 985	199		$16,455,724
Edgar Prado 1303	248		19,762,813	John Velazquez 907	170		13,556,385
Victor Espinoza 1285	259		16,138,004	Robby Albarado 910	191		13,069,397
John Velazquez 944	218		15,562,828	Edgar Prado 979	181		12,314,024
Ramon Dominguez 1417	385		14,410,463	Ramon Dominguez 1051	266		11,895,339
Corey Nakatani 735	145		13,604,210	Rafael Bejarano 1186	186		10,751,878
Eibar Coa 1612	321		12,743,612	Cornelio Velasquez 1315	211		10,607,858
Julien Leparoux 1740	403		12,491,316	Eibar Coa 1254	217		10,377,441
Cornelio Velasquez 1519	237		12,393,715	Victor Espinoza 897	156		9,875,088
Rafael Bejarano 1481	275		12,369,078	Kent Desormeaux 869	159		9,859,023
TRAINERS	Sts	1st	**Earnings**	**TRAINERS**	Sts	1st	**Earnings**
Todd Pletcher 1168	294		$26,820,243	Todd Pletcher 983	233		$22,463,273
Doug O'Neill 968	163		11,247,756	Steven Asmussen 1689	356		15,687,138
Bobby Frankel 585	139		9,786,673	Kiaran McLaughlin 396	93		10,005,809
Scott Lake 2158	528		9,565,656	Doug O'Neill 810	128		9,082,894
Kiaran McLaughlin 406	80		8,499,166	Bobby Frankel 403	97		7,787,931
Bob Baffert 392	91		8,136,567	Scott Lake 1769	357		7,363,978
Richard Dutrow Jr. 686	156		7,842,357	Bill Mott 574	120		7,253,844
Bill Mott 640	120		7,831,106	Gary Contessa 970	141		6,105,235
Steven Asmussen 1141	241		7,715,373	Richard Dutrow Jr. 520	133		5,989,862
Scott Blasi 998	198		6,719,236	Jerry Hollendorfer 722	182		5,098,607

The $23 million Breeders' Cup World Championships were held October 26-27 at Monmouth Park in New Jersey. See Updates chapter (973-975) for results.

Breeders' Cup
WORLD
CHAMPIONSHIPS

Harness Racing

2006-07 Major Stakes Races

Winners of major stakes races from Oct. 14, 2006 through Sept. 30, 2007; all paces and trots cover one mile; (BC) indicates year-end Breeders' Crown series.

Late 2006

Date	Race	Raceway	Winner	Time	Driver	Purse
Oct. 28	BC 3-Yr-Old Colt Pace	Woodbine	Shark Gesture	1:49$\frac{4}{5}$	George Brennan	$694,485
Oct. 28	BC 3-Yr-Old Filly Pace	Woodbine	My Little Dragon	1:52$\frac{3}{5}$	Brian Sears	569,250
Oct. 28	BC 3-Yr-Old Colt Trot	Woodbine	Majestic Son	1:54$\frac{2}{5}$	Trevor Ritchie	569,250
Oct. 28	BC 3-Yr-Old Filly Trot	Woodbine	Susies Magic	1:55$\frac{4}{5}$	David Miller	569,250
Oct. 28	BC 2-Yr-Old Colt Pace	Woodbine	Charley Barley	1:53$\frac{3}{5}$	Mike Lachance	683,100
Oct. 28	BC 2-Yr-Old Filly Pace	Woodbine	Calgary Hanover	1:55$\frac{4}{5}$	Mike Lachance	683,100
Oct. 28	BC 2-Yr-Old Colt Trot	Woodbine	Donato Hanover	1:56	Ron Pierce	683,100
Oct. 28	BC 2-Yr-Old Filly Trot	Woodbine	Possess The Magic	1:57$\frac{2}{5}$	Mike Lachance	683,100
Nov. 25	**Yonkers Trot**	Yonkers	Glidemaster	1:55$\frac{4}{5}$	George Brennan	728,930
Nov. 25	**Messenger Stakes**	Yonkers	Palone Ranger	1:54$\frac{3}{5}$	Ron Pierce	546,830

2007 (through Sept. 30)

Date	Race	Raceway	Winner	Time	Driver	Purse
June 2	New Jersey Classic	Meadowlands	Fresh Deck	1:49$\frac{4}{5}$	John Campbell	$500,000
June 16	North America Cup	Mohawk	Tell All	1:50$\frac{3}{5}$	Jody Jamieson	1,410,000
June 2	Art Rooney Pace	Yonkers	Southwind Lynx	1:52$\frac{3}{5}$	Tim Tetrick	1,000,000
July 7	William Haughton Open Pace	Meadowlands	Mister Big	1:48$\frac{2}{5}$	David Miller	650,000
July 14	Meadowlands Pace	Meadowlands	Southwind Lynx	1:49$\frac{1}{5}$	Tim Tetrick	1,000,000
Aug. 2	Peter Haughton Memorial	Meadowlands	Blue York Yankee	1:57$\frac{2}{5}$	Brian Sears	467,000
Aug. 2	Merrie Annabelle Final	Meadowlands	Muscovite	1:57	Mike Lachance	458,550
Aug. 3	Sweetheart Pace	Meadowlands	McArts N Crafts	1:53$\frac{2}{5}$	Steve Smith	441,750
Aug. 3	Woodrow Wilson Pace	Meadowlands	Dali	1:50$\frac{2}{5}$	Luc Ouellette	415,000
Aug. 4	**Hambletonian**	Meadowlands	Donato Hanover	1:53$\frac{2}{5}$	Ron Pierce	1,500,000
Aug. 4	Hambletonian Oaks	Meadowlands	Danae	1:54$\frac{2}{5}$	Tim Tetrick	750,000
Aug. 4	Mistletoe Shalee	Meadowlands	Hana Hanover	1:49$\frac{3}{5}$	George Brennan	320,000
Aug. 4	Nat Ray	Meadowlands	Corleone Kosmos	1:51$\frac{2}{5}$	John Campbell	300,000
Aug. 4	U.S. Pacing Championship	Meadowlands	Mr. Big	1:47$\frac{4}{5}$	David Miller	342,000
Aug. 18	Canadian Pacing Derby	Mohawk	Lis Mara	1:49$\frac{4}{5}$	Brian Sears	739,000
Aug. 19	Confederation Cup	Flamboro	Laughing Art	1:53$\frac{3}{5}$	Jody Jamieson	600,000
Aug. 25	**Yonkers Trot**	Yonkers	Green Day	1:56	Cat Manzi	644,770
Sept. 1	BC Open Pace	Mohawk	Artistic Fella	1:49$\frac{2}{5}$	Tim Tetrick	500,000
Sept. 1	BC Mare Trot	Mohawk	Mystical Sunshine	1:54$\frac{2}{5}$	Daniel Dube	250,000
Sept. 1	BC Open Trot	Mohawk	Equinox Bi	1:52	Trevor Ritchie	726,000
Sept. 1	BC Mare Pace	Mohawk	Moving Pictures	1:51$\frac{2}{5}$	Mark MacDonald	363,000
Sept. 1	World Trotting Derby	DuQuoin	Donato Hanover	1:51$\frac{2}{5}$	Ron Pierce	600,000
Sept. 1	Metro Pace	Mohawk	Somebeachsomewhere	1:49$\frac{3}{5}$	Paul MacDonell	1,018,382
Sept. 3	**Cane Pace**	Freehold	Always A Virgin	1:51$\frac{1}{5}$	Brian Sears	297,500
Sept. 15	Maple Leaf Trot	Mohawk	Equinox Bi	1:53$\frac{4}{5}$	Trevor Ritchie	706,248
Sept. 15	Canadian Trotting Classic	Mohawk	Donato Hanover	1:54	Ron Pierce	1,018,382
Sept. 20	**Little Brown Jug**	Delaware	Tell All	1:52	Jody Jamieson	480,000

2006-07 Money Leaders

Official Top 10 standings for 2006 and unofficial Top 10 standings for 2007 through Sept. 30.

FINAL 2006

HORSES	Age	Sts	1-2-3	Earnings
Glidemaster	3th	15	8-7-0	$1,918,701
Total Truth	3ph	19	8-3-4	1,494,222
Majestic Son	3tr	19	14-0-2	1,208,236
Sand Vic	5th	18	10-3-1	1,130,380
Passionate Glide	3tm	15	13-1-1	1,087,900
Lis Mara	4ph	17	10-5-1	967,485
Artistic Fella	3ph	18	11-1-0	941,385
Darlin's Delight	3pm	15	10-3-1	940,352
My Little Dragon	3pm	13	6-7-0	898,627
Chocolatier	3th	13	6-3-0	816,550

DRIVERS	Mts	1st	Earnings
Ron Pierce	2667	456	$14,439,087
Brian Sears	2255	442	12,053,789
David Miller	2864	362	10,225,938
Mark MacDonald	3562	745	10,182,217
George Brennan	2047	346	9,094,354
Jody Jamieson	3035	587	9,005,804
John Campbell	1427	183	8,790,864
Anthony Morgan	4133	1004	8,478,313
Cat Manzi	3573	698	7,978,980
Yannick Gingras	2483	368	7,178,013

2007 (through Sept. 30)

HORSES	Age	Sts	1-2-3	Earnings
Donato Hanover	3th	9	9-0-0	$1,908,000
Tell All	3ph	18	10-2-3	1,386,747
Southwind Lynx	3ph	11	4-3-0	1,191,130
Mister Big	4ph	24	11-8-2	1,168,724
Lis Mara	5ph	15	8-2-1	922,855
Equinox Bi	6th	10	5-1-0	866,757
Moving Pictures	4pm	17	9-2-2	826,577
Southwind Tempo	3pm	19	15-2-2	826,104
Pampered Princess	3tm	10	6-3-0	804,021
Adrian Chip	3th	10	6-3-1	774,891

DRIVERS	Mts	1st	Earnings
Tim Tetrick	3422	890	$13,573,370
Ron Pierce	2042	331	10,468,288
Brian Sears	1684	315	9,678,323
David Miller	2070	298	8,262,995
Jody Jamieson	1875	324	7,612,277
Anthony Morgan	2955	654	7,550,936
Yannick Gingras	2159	388	7,332,021
John Campbell	904	142	6,963,047
Andy Miller	2647	390	6,767,845
George Brennan	1761	279	6,643,301

1867-2007
Through the Years

SPORTS ALMANAC

Thoroughbred Racing

The Triple Crown

The term "Triple Crown" was coined by sportswriter Charles Hatton while covering the 1930 victories of Gallant Fox in the Kentucky Derby, Preakness Stakes and Belmont Stakes. Before then, only Sir Barton (1919) had won all three races in the same year. Since then, nine horses have won the Triple Crown. Two trainers, James (Sunny Jim) Fitzsimmons and Ben A. Jones, have saddled two Triple Crown champions, while Eddie Arcaro is the only jockey to ride two champions.

Year		Jockey	Trainer	Owner	Sire/Dam
1919	**Sir Barton**	Johnny Loftus	H. Guy Bedwell	J.K.L. Ross	Star Shoot/Lady Sterling
1930	**Gallant Fox**	Earl Sande	J.E. Fitzsimmons	Belair Stud	Sir Gallahad III/Marguerite
1935	**Omaha**	Willie Saunders	J.E. Fitzsimmons	Belair Stud	Gallant Fox/Flambino
1937	**War Admiral**	Charley Kurtsinger	George Conway	Samuel Riddle	Man o' War/Brushup
1941	**Whirlaway**	Eddie Arcaro	Ben A. Jones	Calumet Farm	Blenheim II/Dustwhirl
1943	**Count Fleet**	Johnny Longden	Don Cameron	Mrs. J.D. Hertz	Reigh Count/Quickly
1946	**Assault**	Warren Mehrtens	Max Hirsch	King Ranch	Bold Venture/Igual
1948	**Citation**	Eddie Arcaro	Ben A. Jones	Calumet Farm	Bull Lea/Hydroplane II
1973	**Secretariat**	Ron Turcotte	Lucien Laurin	Meadow Stable	Bold Ruler/Somethingroyal
1977	**Seattle Slew**	Jean Cruguet	Billy Turner	Karen Taylor	Bold Reasoning/My Charmer
1978	**Affirmed**	Steve Cauthen	Laz Barrera	Harbor View Farm	Exclusive Native/Won't Tell You

Note: Gallant Fox (1930) is the only Triple Crown winner to sire another Triple Crown winner, Omaha (1935). Wm. Woodward Sr., owner of Belair Stud, was breeder-owner of both horses and both were trained by Sunny Jim Fitzsimmons.

Triple Crown Near Misses

Forty-nine horses have won two legs of the Triple Crown. Of those, eighteen won the Kentucky Derby (KD) and Preakness Stakes (PS) only to be beaten in the Belmont Stakes (BS). Two others, Burgoo King (1932) and Bold Venture (1936), won the Derby and Preakness, but were forced out of the Belmont with the same injury—a bowed tendon—that effectively ended their racing careers. In 1978, Alydar finished second to Affirmed in all three races, the only time that has happened. Note that the Preakness preceded the Kentucky Derby in 1922, '23 and '31; (*) indicates won on disqualification.

Year		KD	PS	BS	Year		KD	PS	BS
1877	**Cloverbrook**	DNS	won	won	1966	**Kauai King**	won	won	4th
1878	**Duke of Magenta**	DNS	won	won	1967	**Damascus**	3rd	won	won
1880	**Grenada**	DNS	won	won	1968	**Forward Pass**	won*	won	2nd
1881	**Saunterer**	DNS	won	won	1969	**Majestic Prince**	won	won	2nd
1895	**Belmar**	DNS	won	won	1971	**Canonero II**	won	won	4th
1920	**Man o' War**	DNS	won	won	1972	**Riva Ridge**	won	4th	won
1922	**Pillory**	DNS	won	won	1974	**Little Current**	5th	won	won
1923	**Zev**	won	12th	won	1976	**Bold Forbes**	won	3rd	won
1931	**Twenty Grand**	won	2nd	won	1979	**Spectacular Bid**	won	won	3rd
1932	**Burgoo King**	won	won	DNS	1981	**Pleasant Colony**	won	won	3rd
1936	**Bold Venture**	won	won	DNS	1984	**Swale**	won	7th	won
1939	**Johnstown**	won	5th	won	1987	**Alysheba**	won	won	4th
1940	**Bimelech**	2nd	won	won	1988	**Risen Star**	3rd	won	won
1942	**Shut Out**	won	5th	won	1989	**Sunday Silence**	won	won	2nd
1944	**Pensive**	won	won	2nd	1991	**Hansel**	10th	won	won
1949	**Capot**	2nd	won	won	1994	**Tabasco Cat**	6th	won	won
1950	**Middleground**	won	2nd	won	1995	**Thunder Gulch**	won	3rd	won
1953	**Native Dancer**	2nd	won	won	1997	**Silver Charm**	won	won	2nd
1955	**Nashua**	2nd	won	won	1998	**Real Quiet**	won	won	2nd
1956	**Needles**	won	2nd	won	1999	**Charismatic**	won	won	3rd
1958	**Tim Tam**	won	won	2nd	2001	**Point Given**	5th	won	won
1961	**Carry Back**	won	won	7th	2002	**War Emblem**	won	won	8th
1963	**Chateaugay**	won	2nd	won	2003	**Funny Cide**	won	won	3rd
1964	**Northern Dancer**	won	won	3rd	2004	**Smarty Jones**	won	won	2nd
					2005	**Afleet Alex**	3rd	won	won

The Triple Crown Challenge (1987-93)

Seeking to make the Triple Crown more than just a media event and to insure that owners would not be attracted to more lucrative races, officials at Churchill Downs, the Maryland Jockey Club and the New York Racing Association created Triple Crown Productions in 1985 and announced that a $1 million bonus would be given to the horse that performs best in the Kentucky Derby, Preakness Stakes and Belmont Stakes. Furthermore, a bonus of $5 million would be presented to any horse winning all three races.

Revised in 1991, the rules stated that the winning horse must: 1. finish all three races; 2. earn points by finishing first, second, third or fourth in at least one of the three races; and 3. earn the highest number of points based on the following system–10 points to win, five to place, three to show and one to finish fourth. In the event of a tie, the $1 million is distributed equally among the top point-getters. From 1987-90, the system was five points to win, three to place and one to show. The Triple Crown Challenge was discontinued in 1994.

Year		KD	PS	BS	Pts
1987	1 **Bet Twice**	2nd	2nd	1st–	11
	2 Alysheba	1st	1st	4th–	10
	3 Cryptoclearance	4th	3rd	2nd–	4
1988	1 **Risen Star**	3rd	1st	1st–	11
	2 Winning Colors	1st	3rd	6th–	6
	3 Brian's Time	6th	2nd	3rd–	4
1989	1 **Sunday Silence**	1st	1st	2nd–	13
	2 Easy Goer	2nd	2nd	1st–	11
	3 Hawkster	5th	5th	5th–	0
1990	1 **Unbridled**	1st	2nd	4th–	8
	2 Summer Squall	2nd	1st	DNR–	8
	3 Go and Go	DNR	DNR	1st–	5
	(Unbridled was only horse to run all three races.)				
1991	1 **Hansel**	10th	1st	1st–	20
	2 Strike the Gold	1st	6th	2nd–	15
	3 Mane Minister	3rd	3rd	3rd–	9
1992	1 **Pine Bluff**	5th	1st	3rd–	13
	2 Casual Lies	2nd	3rd	5th–	8
	(No other horses ran all three races.)				
1993	1 **Sea Hero**	1st	5th	7th–	10
	2 Wild Gale	3rd	8th	3rd–	6
	(No other horses ran all three races.)				

Kentucky Derby

For three-year-olds. Held the first Saturday in May at Churchill Downs in Louisville, Ky. Inaugurated in 1875. Originally run at 1½ miles (1875-95), shortened to present 1¼ miles in 1896.

Trainers with most wins: Ben Jones (6); D. Wayne Lukas and Dick Thompson (4); Bob Baffert, Sunny Jim Fitzsimmons and Max Hirsch (3).

Jockeys with most wins: Eddie Arcaro and Bill Hartack (5); Bill Shoemaker (4); Angel Cordero Jr., Issac Murphy, Earl Sande and Gary Stevens (3).

Winning fillies: Regret (1915), Genuine Risk (1980) and Winning Colors (1988).

Year	Winner (Margin)	Time	Jockey	Trainer	2nd place	3rd place
1875	**Aristides** (1)	2:37¾	Oliver Lewis	Ansel Anderson	Volcano	Verdigris
1876	**Vagrant** (2)	2:38¼	Bobby Swim	James Williams	Creedmore	Harry Hill
1877	**Baden-Baden** (2)	2:38	Billy Walker	Ed Brown	Leonard	King William
1878	**Day Star** (2)	2:37¼	Jimmy Carter	Lee Paul	Himyar	Leveler
1879	**Lord Murphy** (1)	2:37	Charlie Shauer	George Rice	Falsetto	Strathmore
1880	**Fonso** (1)	2:37½	George Lewis	Tice Hutsell	Kimball	Bancroft
1881	**Hindoo** (4)	2:40	Jim McLaughlin	James Rowe Sr.	Lelex	Alfambra
1882	**Apollo** (½)	2:40¼	Babe Hurd	Green Morris	Runnymede	Bengal
1883	**Leonatus** (3)	2:43	Billy Donohue	John McGinty	Drake Carter	Lord Raglan
1884	**Buchanan** (2)	2:40¼	Isaac Murphy	William Bird	Loftin	Audrain
1885	**Joe Cotton** (nk)	2:37¼	Babe Henderson	Alex Perry	Bersan	Ten Booker
1886	**Ben Ali** (½)	2:36½	Paul Duffy	Jim Murphy	Blue Wing	Free Knight
1887	**Montrose** (2)	2:39¼	Isaac Lewis	John McGinty	Jim Gore	Jacobin
1888	**MacBeth II** (1)	2:38¼	George Covington	John Campbell	Gallifet	White
1889	**Spokane** (ns)	2:34½	Thomas Kiley	John Rodegap	Proctor Knott	Once Again
1890	**Riley** (2)	2:45	Isaac Murphy	Edward Corrigan	Bill Letcher	Robespierre
1891	**Kingman** (1)	2:52¼	Isaac Murphy	Dud Allen	Balgowan	High Tariff
1892	**Azra** (ns)	2:41½	Lonnie Clayton	John Morris	Huron	Phil Dwyer
1893	**Lookout** (5)	2:39¼	Eddie Kunze	Wm. McDaniel	Plutus	Boundless
1894	**Chant** (2)	2:41	Frank Goodale	Eugene Leigh	Pearl Song	Sigurd
1895	**Halma** (3)	2:37½	Soup Perkins	Byron McClelland	Basso	Laureate
1896	**Ben Brush** (ns)	2:07¾	Willie Simms	Hardy Campbell	Ben Eder	Semper Ego
1897	**Typhoon II** (hd)	2:12½	Buttons Garner	J.C. Cahn	Ornament	Dr. Catlett
1898	**Plaudit** (nk)	2:09	Willie Simms	John E. Madden	Lieber Karl	Isabey
1899	**Manuel** (2)	2:12	Fred Taral	Robert Walden	Corsini	Mazo
1900	**Lieut. Gibson** (4)	2:06¼	Jimmy Boland	Charles Hughes	Florizar	Thrive
1901	**His Eminence** (2)	2:07¾	Jimmy Winkfield	F.B. Van Meter	Sannazarro	Driscoll
1902	**Alan-a-Dale** (ns)	2:08¾	Jimmy Winkfield	T.C. McDowell	Inventor	The Rival
1903	**Judge Himes** (¾)	2:09	Hal Booker	J.P. Mayberry	Early	Bourbon
1904	**Elwood** (½)	2:08½	Shorty Prior	C.E. Durnell	Ed Tierney	Brancas
1905	**Agile** (3)	2:10¾	Jack Martin	Robert Tucker	Ram's Horn	Layson
1906	**Sir Huon** (2)	2:08⅘	Roscoe Troxler	Pete Coyne	Lady Navarre	James Reddick
1907	**Pink Star** (2)	2:12⅗	Andy Minder	W.H. Fizer	Zal	Ovelando
1908	**Stone Street** (1)	2:15⅕	Arthur Pickens	J.W. Hall	Sir Cleges	Dunvegan
1909	**Wintergreen** (4)	2:08⅕	Vincent Powers	Charles Mack	Miami	Dr. Barkley

Kentucky Derby (Cont.)

Year	Winner (Margin)	Time	Jockey	Trainer	2nd place	3rd place
1910	**Donau** (½)	2:06⅖	Fred Herbert	George Ham	Joe Morris	Fighting Bob
1911	**Meridian** (¾)	2:05	George Archibald	Albert Ewing	Governor Gray	Colston
1912	**Worth** (nk)	2:09⅖	C.H. Shilling	Frank Taylor	Duval	Flamma
1913	**Donerail** (½)	2:04⅘	Roscoe Goose	Thomas Hayes	Ten Point	Gowell
1914	**Old Rosebud** (8)	2:03⅖	John McCabe	F.D. Weir	Hodge	Bronzewing
1915	**Regret** (2)	2:05⅖	Joe Notter	James Rowe Sr.	Pebbles	Sharpshooter
1916	**George Smith** (nk)	2:04	Johnny Loftus	Hollie Hughes	Star Hawk	Franklin
1917	**Omar Khayyam** (2)	2:04⅗	Charles Borel	C.T. Patterson	Ticket	Midway
1918	**Exterminator** (1)	2:10⅘	William Knapp	Henry McDaniel	Escoba	Viva America
1919	**SIR BARTON** (5)	2:09⅘	Johnny Loftus	H. Guy Bedwell	Billy Kelly	Under Fire
1920	**Paul Jones** (hd)	2:09	Ted Rice	Billy Garth	Upset	On Watch
1921	**Behave Yourself** (hd)	2:04⅕	Charles Thompson	Dick Thompson	Black Servant	Prudery
1922	**Morvich** (1½)	2:04⅗	Albert Johnson	Fred Burlew	Bet Mosie	John Finn
1923	**Zev** (1½)	2:05⅖	Earl Sande	David Leary	Martingale	Vigil
1924	**Black Gold** (½)	2:05⅕	John Mooney	Hanly Webb	Chilhowee	Beau Butler
1925	**Flying Ebony** (1½)	2:07⅗	Earl Sande	William Duke	Captain Hal	Son of John
1926	**Bubbling Over** (5)	2:03⅘	Albert Johnson	Dick Thompson	Bagenbaggage	Rock Man
1927	**Whiskery** (hd)	2:06	Linus McAtee	Fred Hopkins	Osmand	Jock
1928	**Reigh Count** (3)	2:10⅖	Chick Lang	Bert Michell	Misstep	Toro
1929	**Clyde Van Dusen** (2)	2:10⅘	Linus McAtee	Clyde Van Dusen	Naishapur	Panchio
1930	**GALLANT FOX** (2)	2:07⅗	Earl Sande	Jim Fitzsimmons	Gallant Knight	Ned O.
1931	**Twenty Grand** (4)	2:01⅘	Charley Kurtsinger	James Rowe Jr.	Sweep All	Mate
1932	**Burgoo King** (5)	2:05⅕	Eugene James	Dick Thompson	Economic	Stepenfetchit
1933	**Brokers Tip** (ns)	2:06⅘	Don Meade	Dick Thompson	Head Play	Charley O.
1934	**Cavalcade** (2½)	2:04	Mack Garner	Bob Smith	Discovery	Agrarian
1935	**OMAHA** (1½)	2:05	Willie Saunders	Jim Fitzsimmons	Roman Soldier	Whiskolo
1936	**Bold Venture** (hd)	2:03⅗	Ira Hanford	Max Hirsch	Brevity	Indian Broom
1937	**WAR ADMIRAL** (1¾)	2:03⅕	Charley Kurtsinger	George Conway	Pompoon	Reaping Reward
1938	**Lawrin** (1)	2:04⅘	Eddie Arcaro	Ben Jones	Dauber	Can't Wait
1939	**Johnstown** (8)	2:03⅖	James Stout	Jim Fitzsimmons	Challedon	Heather Broom
1940	**Gallahadion** (1½)	2:05	Carroll Bierman	Roy Waldron	Bimelech	Dit
1941	**WHIRLAWAY** (8)	2:01⅖	Eddie Arcaro	Ben Jones	Staretor	Market Wise
1942	**Shut Out** (2½)	2:04⅖	Wayne Wright	John Gaver	Alsab	Valdina Orphan
1943	**COUNT FLEET** (3)	2:04	Johnny Longden	Don Cameron	Blue Swords	Slide Rule
1944	**Pensive** (4½)	2:04⅕	Conn McCreary	Ben Jones	Broadcloth	Stir Up
1945	**Hoop Jr** (6)	2:07	Eddie Arcaro	Ivan Parke	Pot O'Luck	Darby Dieppe
1946	**ASSAULT** (8)	2:06⅗	Warren Mehrtens	Max Hirsch	Spy Song	Hampden
1947	**Jet Pilot** (hd)	2:06⅘	Eric Guerin	Tom Smith	Phalanx	Faultless
1948	**CITATION** (3½)	2:05⅖	Eddie Arcaro	Ben Jones	Coaltown	My Request
1949	**Ponder** (3)	2:04⅕	Steve Brooks	Ben Jones	Capot	Palestinian
1950	**Middleground** (1¼)	2:01⅗	William Boland	Max Hirsch	Hill Prince	Mr. Trouble
1951	**Count Turf** (4)	2:02⅗	Conn McCreary	Sol Rutchick	Royal Mustang	Ruhe
1952	**Hill Gail** (2)	2:01⅗	Eddie Arcaro	Ben Jones	Sub Fleet	Blue Man
1953	**Dark Star** (hd)	2:02	Hank Moreno	Eddie Hayward	Native Dancer	Invigorator
1954	**Determine** (1½)	2:03	Raymond York	Willie Molter	Hasty Road	Hasseyampa
1955	**Swaps** (1½)	2:01⅘	Bill Shoemaker	Mesh Tenney	Nashua	Summer Tan
1956	**Needles** (¾)	2:03⅖	David Erb	Hugh Fontaine	Fabius	Come On Red
1957	**Iron Liege** (ns)	2:02⅕	Bill Hartack	Jimmy Jones	Gallant Man	Round Table
1958	**Tim Tam** (½)	2:05	Ismael Valenzuela	Jimmy Jones	Lincoln Road	Noureddin
1959	**Tomy Lee** (ns)	2:02⅕	Bill Shoemaker	Frank Childs	Sword Dancer	First Landing
1960	**Venetian Way** (3½)	2:02⅖	Bill Hartack	Victor Sovinski	Bally Ache	Victoria Park
1961	**Carry Back** (¾)	2:04	John Sellers	Jack Price	Crozier	Bass Clef
1962	**Decidedly** (2¼)	2:00⅖	Bill Hartack	Horatio Luro	Roman Line	Ridan
1963	**Chateaugay** (1¼)	2:01⅘	Braulio Baeza	James Conway	Never Bend	Candy Spots
1964	**Northern Dancer** (nk)	2:00	Bill Hartack	Horatio Luro	Hill Rise	The Scoundrel
1965	**Lucky Debonair** (nk)	2:01⅕	Bill Shoemaker	Frank Catrone	Dapper Dan	Tom Rolfe
1966	**Kauai King** (½)	2:02	Don Brumfield	Henry Forrest	Advocator	Blue Skyer
1967	**Proud Clarion** (1)	2:00⅗	Bobby Ussery	Loyd Gentry	Barbs Delight	Damascus
1968	**Forward Pass*** (nk)	—	Ismael Valenzuela	Henry Forrest	Francie's Hat	T.V. Commercial
1969	**Majestic Prince** (nk)	2:01⅘	Bill Hartack	Johnny Longden	Arts and Letters	Dike
1970	**Dust Commander** (5)	2:03⅖	Mike Manganello	Don Combs	My Dad George	High Echelon
1971	**Canonero II** (3¼)	2:03⅕	Gustavo Avila	Juan Arias	Jim French	Bold Reason
1972	**Riva Ridge** (3¼)	2:01⅘	Ron Turcotte	Lucien Laurin	No Le Hace	Hold Your Peace
1973	**SECRETARIAT** (2½)	1:59⅖	Ron Turcotte	Lucien Laurin	Sham	Our Native
1974	**Cannonade** (2¼)	2:04	Angel Cordero Jr.	Woody Stephens	Hudson County	Agitate
1975	**Foolish Pleasure** (1¾)	2:02	Jacinto Vasquez	LeRoy Jolley	Avatar	Diabolo
1976	**Bold Forbes** (1)	2:01⅗	Angel Cordero Jr.	Laz Barrera	Honest Pleasure	Elocutionist
1977	**SEATTLE SLEW** (1¾)	2:02⅕	Jean Cruguet	Billy Turner	Run Dusty Run	Sanhedrin
1978	**AFFIRMED** (1½)	2:01⅕	Steve Cauthen	Laz Barrera	Alydar	Believe It

Year	Winner (Margin)	Time	Jockey	Trainer	2nd place	3rd place
1979	**Spectacular Bid** (2¾)	2:02⅖	Ron Franklin	Bud Delp	General Assembly	Golden Act
1980	**Genuine Risk** (1)	2:02	Jacinto Vasquez	LeRoy Jolley	Rumbo	Jaklin Klugman
1981	**Pleasant Colony** (¾)	2:02	Jorge Velasquez	John Campo	Woodchopper	Partez
1982	**Gato Del Sol** (2½)	2:02⅖	E. Delahoussaye	Eddie Gregson	Laser Light	Reinvested
1983	**Sunny's Halo** (2)	2:02⅕	E. Delahoussaye	David Cross Jr.	Desert Wine	Caveat
1984	**Swale** (3¼)	2:02⅖	Laffit Pincay Jr.	Woody Stephens	Coax Me Chad	At The Threshold
1985	**Spend A Buck** (5¼)	2:00⅕	Angel Cordero Jr.	Cam Gambolati	Stephan's Odyssey	Chief's Crown
1986	**Ferdinand** (2¼)	2:02⅘	Bill Shoemaker	Chas. Whittingham	Bold Arrangement	Broad Brush
1987	**Alysheba** (¾)	2:03⅖	Chris McCarron	Jack Van Berg	Bet Twice	Avies Copy
1988	**Winning Colors** (nk)	2:02⅕	Gary Stevens	D. Wayne Lukas	Forty Niner	Risen Star
1989	**Sunday Silence** (2½)	2:05	Pat Valenzuela	Chas. Whittingham	Easy Goer	Awe Inspiring
1990	**Unbridled** (3½)	2:02	Craig Perret	Carl Nafzger	Summer Squall	Pleasant Tap
1991	**Strike the Gold** (1¾)	2:03	Chris Antley	Nick Zito	Best Pal	Mane Minister
1992	**Lil E. Tee** (1)	2:03	Pat Day	Lynn Whiting	Casual Lies	Dance Floor
1993	**Sea Hero** (2½)	2:02⅖	Jerry Bailey	Mack Miller	Prairie Bayou	Wild Gale
1994	**Go For Gin** (2)	2:03⅗	Chris McCarron	Nick Zito	Strodes Creek	Blumin Affair
1995	**Thunder Gulch** (2¼)	2:01⅕	Gary Stevens	D. Wayne Lukas	Tejano Run	Timber Country
1996	**Grindstone** (ns)	2:01	Jerry Bailey	D. Wayne Lukas	Cavonnier	Prince of Thieves
1997	**Silver Charm** (hd)	2:02⅖	Gary Stevens	Bob Baffert	Captain Bodgit	Free House
1998	**Real Quiet** (½)	2:02⅕	Kent Desormeaux	Bob Baffert	Victory Gallop	Indian Charlie
1999	**Charismatic** (nk)	2:03⅕	Chris Antley	D. Wayne Lukas	Menifee	Cat Thief
2000	**Fusaichi Pegasus** (1½)	2:01⅕	Kent Desormeaux	Neil Drysdale	Aptitude	Impeachment
2001	**Monarchos** (4¾)	1:59⅘	Jorge Chavez	John Ward Jr.	Invisible Ink	Congaree
2002	**War Emblem** (4)	2:01	Victor Espinoza	Bob Baffert	Proud Citizen	Perfect Drift
2003	**Funny Cide** (1¾)	2:01	Jose Santos	Barclay Tagg	Empire Maker	Peace Rules
2004	**Smarty Jones** (2¾)	2:04	Stewart Elliott	John Servis	Lion Heart	Imperialism
2005	**Giacomo** (½)	2:02¾	Mike Smith	John Shirreffs	Closing Argument	Afleet Alex
2006	**Barbaro** (6½)	2:01⅖	Edgar Prado	Michael Matz	Blue Grass Cat	Steppenwolfer
2007	**Street Sense** (2¼)	2:02⅕	Calvin Borel	Carl Nafzger	Hard Spun	Curlin

*Dancer's Image finished first (in 2:02⅕), but was disqualified after traces of prohibited medication were found in his system.

Preakness Stakes

For three-year-olds. Held two weeks after the Kentucky Derby at Pimlico Race Course in Baltimore. Inaugurated 1873. Note that the 1918 race was held over two divisions. Originally run at 1½ miles (1873-88), then at 1¼ miles (1889), 1½ miles (1890), 1 1/16 miles (1894-1900), 1 mile & 70 yards (1901-07), 1 1/16 miles (1908), 1 mile (1909-1910), 1⅛ miles (1911-24), and the present 1 3/16 miles since 1925.

Trainers with most wins: Robert W. Walden (7); T.J. Healey and D. Wayne Lukas (5); Bob Baffert, Sunny Jim Fitzsimmons and Jimmy Jones (4); J. Whalen (3).

Jockeys with most wins: Eddie Arcaro (6); Pat Day (5); G. Barbee, Bill Hartack and Lloyd Hughes (3).

Winning fillies: Flocarline (1903), Whimsical (1906), Rhine Maiden (1915) and Nellie Morse (1924).

Year	Winner (Margin)	Time	Jockey	Trainer	2nd place	3rd place
1873	**Survivor** (10)	2:43	G. Barbee	A.D. Pryor	John Boulger	Artist
1874	**Culpepper** (¾)	2:56½	W. Donohue	H. Gaffney	King Amadeus	Scratch
1875	**Tom Ochiltree** (2)	2:43½	L. Hughes	R.W. Walden	Viator	Bay Final
1876	**Shirley** (4)	2:44¾	G. Barbee	W. Brown	Rappahannock	Compliment
1877	**Cloverbrook** (2)	2:45½	C. Holloway	J. Walden	Bombast	Lucifer
1878	**Duke of Magenta** (2)	2:41¾	C. Holloway	R.W. Walden	Bayard	Albert
1879	**Harold** (1)	2:40½	L. Hughes	R.W. Walden	Jericho	Rochester
1880	**Grenada** (¾)	2:40½	L. Hughes	R.W. Walden	Oden	Emily F.
1881	**Saunterer** (½)	2:40½	T. Costello	R.W. Walden	Compensation	Baltic
1882	**Vanguard** (nk)	2:44½	T. Costello	R.W. Walden	Heck	Col. Watson
1883	**Jacobus** (4)	2:42½	G. Barbee	R. Dwyer	Parnell	(2-horse race)
1884	**Knight of Ellerslie** (2)	2:39½	S. Fisher	T.B. Doswell	Welcher	(2-horse race)
1885	**Tecumseh** (2)	2:49	Jim McLaughlin	C. Littlefield	Wickham	John C.
1886	**The Bard** (3)	2:45	S. Fisher	J. Huggins	Eurus	Elkwood
1887	**Dunboyne** (1)	2:39½	W. Donohue	W. Jennings	Mahoney	Raymond
1888	**Refund** (3)	2:49	F. Littlefield	R.W. Walden	Bertha B.*	Glendale
1889	**Buddhist** (8)	2:17½	W. Anderson	J. Rogers	Japhet	(2-horse race)
1890	**Montague** (3)	2:36¾	W. Martin	E. Feakes	Philosophy	Barrister
1891-93	Not held					
1894	**Assignee** (3)	1:49¼	F. Taral	W. Lakeland	Potentate	Ed Kearney
1895	**Belmar** (1)	1:50½	F. Taral	E. Feakes	April Fool	Sue Kittie
1896	**Margrave** (1)	1:51	H. Griffin	Byron McClelland	Hamilton II	Intermission
1897	**Paul Kauvar** (1½)	1:51¼	T. Thorpe	T.P. Hayes	Elkins	On Deck
1898	**Sly Fox** (2)	1:49¾	W. Simms	H. Campbell	The Huguenot	Nuto
1899	**Half Time** (1)	1:47	R. Clawson	F. McCabe	Filigrane	Lackland
1900	**Hindus** (hd)	1:48⅖	H. Spencer	J.H. Morris	Sarmatian	Ten Candles
1901	**The Parader** (2)	1:47⅕	F. Landry	T.J. Healey	Sadie S.	Dr. Barlow
1902	**Old England** (ns)	1:45⅘	L. Jackson	G.B. Morris	Maj. Daingerfield	Namtor
1903	**Flocarline** (½)	1:44⅘	W. Gannon	H.C. Riddle	Mackey Dwyer	Rightful

Preakness Stakes (Cont.)

Year	Winner (Margin)	Time	Jockey	Trainer	2nd place	3rd place
1904	**Bryn Mawr** (1)	1:44⅕	E. Hildebrand	W.F. Presgrave	Wotan	Dolly Spanker
1905	**Cairngorm** (hd)	1:45⅘	W. Davis	A.J. Joyner	Kiamesha	Coy Maid
1906	**Whimsical** (4)	1:45	Walter Miller	T.J. Gaynor	Content	Larabie
1907	**Don Enrique** (1)	1:45⅖	G. Mountain	J. Whalen	Ethon	Zambesi
1908	**Royal Tourist** (4)	1:46⅖	Eddie Dugan	A.J. Joyner	Live Wire	Robert Cooper
1909	**Effendi** (1)	1:39⅘	Willie Doyle	F.C. Frisbie	Fashion Plate	Hill Top
1910	**Layminster** (½)	1:40⅗	R. Estep	J.S. Healy	Dalhousie	Sager
1911	**Watervale** (1)	1:51	Eddie Dugan	J. Whalen	Zeus	The Nigger
1912	**Colonel Holloway** (5)	1:56⅗	C. Turner	D. Woodford	Bwana Tumbo	Tipsand
1913	**Buskin** (nk)	1:53⅖	James Butwell	J. Whalen	Kleburne	Barnegat
1914	**Holiday** (¾)	1:53⅘	A. Schuttinger	J.S. Healy	Brave Cunarder	Defendum
1915	**Rhine Maiden** (1½)	1:58	Douglas Hoffman	F. Devers	Half Rock	Runes
1916	**Damrosch** (1½)	1:54⅘	Linus McAtee	A.G. Weston	Greenwood	Achievement
1917	**Kalitan** (2)	1:54⅖	E. Haynes	Bill Hurley	Al M. Dick	Kentucky Boy
1918	**War Cloud** (¾)	1:53⅗	Johnny Loftus	W.B. Jennings	Sunny Slope	Lanius
1918	**Jack Hare Jr** (2)	1:53⅖	Charles Peak	F.D. Weir	The Porter	Kate Bright
1919	**SIR BARTON** (4)	1:53	Johnny Loftus	H. Guy Bedwell	Eternal	Sweep On
1920	**Man o' War** (1½)	1:51⅗	Clarence Kummer	L. Feustel	Upset	Wildair
1921	**Broomspun** (¾)	1:54⅕	F. Coltiletti	James Rowe Sr.	Polly Ann	Jeg
1922	**Pillory** (hd)	1:51⅗	L. Morris	Thomas Healey	Hea	June Grass
1923	**Vigil** (1¼)	1:53⅗	B. Marinelli	Thomas Healey	General Thatcher	Rialto
1924	**Nellie Morse** (1½)	1:57⅕	John Merimee	A.B. Gordon	Transmute	Mad Play
1925	**Coventry** (4)	1:59	Clarence Kummer	William Duke	Backbone	Almadel
1926	**Display** (hd)	1:59⅘	John Maiben	Thomas Healey	Blondin	Mars
1927	**Bostonian** (½)	2:01⅗	Whitey Abel	Fred Hopkins	Sir Harry	Whiskery
1928	**Victorian** (ns)	2:00⅕	Sonny Workman	James Rowe Jr.	Toro	Solace
1929	**Dr. Freeland** (1)	2:01⅗	Louis Schaefer	Thomas Healey	Minotaur	African
1930	**GALLANT FOX** (¾)	2:00⅗	Earl Sande	Jim Fitzsimmons	Crack Brigade	Snowflake
1931	**Mate** (1½)	1:59	George Ellis	J.W. Healy	Twenty Grand	Ladder
1932	**Burgoo King** (hd)	1:59⅘	Eugene James	Dick Thompson	Tick On	Boatswain
1933	**Head Play** (4)	2:02	Charley Kurtsinger	Thomas Hayes	Ladysman	Utopian
1934	**High Quest** (ns)	1:58⅕	Robert Jones	Bob Smith	Cavalcade	Discovery
1935	**OMAHA** (6)	1:58⅖	Willie Saunders	Jim Fitzsimmons	Firethorn	Psychic Bid
1936	**Bold Venture** (ns)	1:59	George Woolf	Max Hirsch	Granville	Jean Bart
1937	**WAR ADMIRAL** (hd)	1:58⅖	Charley Kurtsinger	George Conway	Pompoon	Flying Scot
1938	**Dauber** (7)	1:59⅘	Maurice Peters	Dick Handlen	Cravat	Menow
1939	**Challedon** (1¼)	1:59⅘	George Seabo	Louis Schaefer	Gilded Knight	Volitant
1940	**Bimelech** (3)	1:58⅗	F.A. Smith	Bill Hurley	Mioland	Gallahadion
1941	**WHIRLAWAY** (5½)	1:58⅘	Eddie Arcaro	Ben Jones	King Cole	Our Boots
1942	**Alsab** (1)	1:57	Basil James	Sarge Swenke	Requested & Sun Again (dead heat)	
1943	**COUNT FLEET** (8)	1:57⅖	Johnny Longden	Don Cameron	Blue Swords	Vincentive
1944	**Pensive** (¾)	1:59⅕	Conn McCreary	Ben Jones	Platter	Stir Up
1945	**Polynesian** (2½)	1:58⅘	W.D. Wright	Morris Dixon	Hoop Jr.	Darby Dieppe
1946	**ASSAULT** (nk)	2:01⅖	Warren Mehrtens	Max Hirsch	Lord Boswell	Hampden
1947	**Faultless** (1¼)	1:59	Doug Dodson	Jimmy Jones	On Trust	Phalanx
1948	**CITATION** (5½)	2:02⅖	Eddie Arcaro	Jimmy Jones	Vulcan's Forge	Bovard
1949	**Capot** (hd)	1:56	Ted Atkinson	J.M. Gaver	Palestinian	Noble Impulse
1950	**Hill Prince** (5)	1:59⅕	Eddie Arcaro	Casey Hayes	Middleground	Dooly
1951	**Bold** (7)	1:56⅖	Eddie Arcaro	Preston Burch	Counterpoint	Alerted
1952	**Blue Man** (3½)	1:57⅖	Conn McCreary	Woody Stephens	Jampol	One Count
1953	**Native Dancer** (nk)	1:57⅘	Eric Guerin	Bill Winfrey	Jamie K.	Royal Bay Gem
1954	**Hasty Road** (nk)	1:57⅖	Johnny Adams	Harry Trotsek	Correlation	Hasseyampa
1955	**Nashua** (1)	1:54⅗	Eddie Arcaro	Jim Fitzsimmons	Saratoga	Traffic Judge
1956	**Fabius** (¾)	1:58⅖	Bill Hartack	Jimmy Jones	Needles	No Regrets
1957	**Bold Ruler** (2)	1:56⅕	Eddie Arcaro	Jim Fitzsimmons	Iron Liege	Inside Tract
1958	**Tim Tam** (1½)	1:57⅕	Ismael Valenzuela	Jimmy Jones	Lincoln Road	Gone Fishin'
1959	**Royal Orbit** (4)	1:57	William Harmatz	R. Cornell	Sword Dancer	Dunce
1960	**Bally Ache** (4)	1:57⅗	Bobby Ussery	Jimmy Pitt	Victoria Park	Celtic Ash
1961	**Carry Back** (¾)	1:57⅗	Johnny Sellers	Jack Price	Globemaster	Crozier
1962	**Greek Money** (ns)	1:56⅕	John Rotz	V.W. Raines	Ridan	Roman Line
1963	**Candy Spots** (3½)	1:56⅕	Bill Shoemaker	Mesh Tenney	Chateaugay	Never Bend
1964	**Northern Dancer** (2¼)	1:56⅘	Bill Hartack	Horatio Luro	The Scoundrel	Hill Rise
1965	**Tom Rolfe** (nk)	1:56⅕	Ron Turcotte	Frank Whiteley	Dapper Dan	Hail To All
1966	**Kauai King** (1¾)	1:55⅖	Don Brumfield	Henry Forrest	Stupendous	Amberoid
1967	**Damascus** (2¼)	1:55⅕	Bill Shoemaker	Frank Whiteley	In Reality	Proud Clarion
1968	**Forward Pass** (6)	1:56⅘	Ismael Valenzuela	Henry Forrest	Out Of the Way	Nodouble
1969	**Majestic Prince** (hd)	1:55⅗	Bill Hartack	Johnny Longden	Arts and Letters	Jay Ray
1970	**Personality** (nk)	1:56⅕	Eddie Belmonte	John Jacobs	My Dad George	Silent Screen
1971	**Canonero II** (1½)	1:54	Gustavo Avila	Juan Arias	Eastern Fleet	Jim French

AP/Wide World Photos

Affirmed *(with jockey Steve Cauthen) wins the 103rd running of the Preakness on May 20, 1978 by a neck over Alydar. Affirmed is the last horse to win the Triple Crown.*

Year	Winner (Margin)	Time	Jockey	Trainer	2nd place	3rd place
1972	**Bee Bee Bee** (1¼)	1:55⅗	Eldon Nelson	Red Carroll	No Le Hace	Key To The Mint
1973	**SECRETARIAT** (2½)	1:54⅖	Ron Turcotte	Lucien Laurin	Sham	Our Native
1974	**Little Current** (7)	1:54⅗	Miguel Rivera	Lou Rondinello	Neapolitan Way	Cannonade
1975	**Master Derby** (1)	1:56⅖	Darrel McHargue	Smiley Adams	Foolish Pleasure	Diabolo
1976	**Elocutionist** (3½)	1:55	John Lively	Paul Adwell	Play The Red	Bold Forbes
1977	**SEATTLE SLEW** (1½)	1:54⅖	Jean Cruguet	Billy Turner	Iron Constitution	Run Dusty Run
1978	**AFFIRMED** (nk)	1:54⅖	Steve Cauthen	Laz Barrera	Alydar	Believe It
1979	**Spectacular Bid** (3½)	1:54⅕	Ron Franklin	Bud Delp	Golden Act	Screen King
1980	**Codex** (4¾)	1:54⅕	Angel Cordero Jr.	D. Wayne Lukas	Genuine Risk	Colonel Moran
1981	**Pleasant Colony** (1)	1:54⅗	Jorge Velasquez	John Campo	Bold Ego	Paristo
1982	**Aloma's Ruler** (½)	1:55⅖	Jack Kaenel	John Lenzini Jr.	Linkage	Cut Away
1983	**Deputed Testamony** (2¾)	1:55⅖	Donald Miller Jr.	Bill Boniface	Desert Wine	High Honors
1984	**Gate Dancer** (1½)	1:53⅗	Angel Cordero Jr.	Jack Van Berg	Play On	Fight Over
1985	**Tank's Prospect** (hd)	1:53⅖	Pat Day	D. Wayne Lukas	Chief's Crown	Eternal Prince
1986	**Snow Chief** (4)	1:54⅘	Alex Solis	Melvin Stute	Ferdinand	Broad Brush
1987	**Alysheba** (½)	1:55⅘	Chris McCarron	Jack Van Berg	Bet Twice	Cryptoclearance
1988	**Risen Star** (1¼)	1:56⅕	E. Delahoussaye	Louie Roussel III	Brian's Time	Winning Colors
1989	**Sunday Silence** (ns)	1:53⅘	Pat Valenzuela	Chas. Whittingham	Easy Goer	Rock Point
1990	**Summer Squall** (2¼)	1:53⅗	Pat Day	Neil Howard	Unbridled	Mister Frisky
1991	**Hansel** (7)	1:54	Jerry Bailey	Frank Brothers	Corporate Report	Mane Minister
1992	**Pine Bluff** (¾)	1:55⅗	Chris McCarron	Tom Bohannan	Alydeed	Casual Lies
1993	**Prairie Bayou** (½)	1:56⅗	Mike Smith	Tom Bohannan	Cherokee Run	El Bakan
1994	**Tabasco Cat** (¾)	1:56⅖	Pat Day	D. Wayne Lukas	Go For Gin	Concern
1995	**Timber Country** (½)	1:54⅖	Pat Day	D. Wayne Lukas	Oliver's Twist	Thunder Gulch
1996	**Louis Quatorze** (3¼)	1:53⅖	Pat Day	Nick Zito	Skip Away	Editor's Note
1997	**Silver Charm** (hd)	1:54⅖	Gary Stevens	Bob Baffert	Free House	Captain Bodgit
1998	**Real Quiet** (2¼)	1:54⅘	Kent Desormeaux	Bob Baffert	Victory Gallop	Classic Cat
1999	**Charismatic** (1½)	1:55⅕	Chris Antley	D. Wayne Lukas	Menifee	Badge
2000	**Red Bullet** (3¾)	1:56	Jerry Bailey	Joe Orseno	Fusaichi Pegasus	Impeachment
2001	**Point Given** (2¼)	1:55⅖	Gary Stevens	Bob Baffert	A P Valentine	Congaree
2002	**War Emblem** (¾)	1:56⅕	Victor Espinoza	Bob Baffert	Magic Weisner	Proud Citizen
2003	**Funny Cide** (9¾)	1:55⅗	Jose Santos	Barclay Tagg	Midway Road	Scrimshaw
2004	**Smarty Jones** (11½)	1:55⅖	Stewart Elliott	John Servis	Rock Hard Ten	Eddington
2005	**Afleet Alex** (4¾)	1:55	Jeremy Rose	Tim Ritchey	Scrappy T	Giacomo
2006	**Bernardini** (5¼)	1:54⅗	Javier Castellano	Thomas Albertrani	Sweetnorthernsaint	Hemingway's Key
2007	**Curlin** (hd)	1:53⅖	Robby Albarado	Steven Asmussen	Street Sense	Hard Spun

* Later named Judge Murray.

Belmont Stakes

For three-year-olds. Held three weeks after Preakness Stakes at Belmont Park in Elmont, N.Y. Inaugurated in 1867 at Jerome Park, moved to Morris Park in 1890 and then to Belmont Park in 1905.

Originally run at 1 mile and 5 furlongs (1867-89), then 1¼ miles (1890-1905), 1⅜ miles (1906-25), and the present 1½ miles since 1926.

Trainers with most wins: James Rowe Sr. (8); Sam Hildreth (7); Sunny Jim Fitzsimmons (6); Woody Stephens (5); Max Hirsch, D. Wayne Lukas and Robert W. Walden (4); Elliott Burch, Lucien Laurin, F. McCabe and D. McDaniel (3).

Jockeys with most wins: Eddie Arcaro and Jim McLaughlin (6); Earl Sande and Bill Shoemaker (5); Braulio Baeza, Pat Day, Laffit Pincay Jr., Gary Stevens and James Stout (3).

Winning fillies: Ruthless (1867), Tanya (1905) and Rags to Riches (2007).

Year	Winner (Margin)	Time	Jockey	Trainer	2nd place	3rd place
1867	**Ruthless** (½)	3:05	J. Gilpatrick	A.J. Minor	DeCourcey	Rivoli
1868	**General Duke** (2)	3:02	Bobby Swim	A. Thompson	Northumberland	Fanny Ludlow
1869	**Fenian** (6)	3:04¼	C. Miller	J. Pincus	Glenelg	Invercauld
1870	**Kingfisher** (nk)	2:59½	W. Dick	R. Colston	Foster	Midday
1871	**Harry Bassett** (3)	2:56	W. Miller	D. McDaniel	Stockwood	By the Sea
1872	**Joe Daniels** (¾)	2:58¼	James Roe	D. McDaniel	Meteor	Shylock
1873	**Springbok** (¾)	3:01¾	James Roe	D. McDaniel	Count d'Orsay	Strachino
1874	**Saxon** (nk)	2:39½	G. Barbee	W. Prior	Grinstead	Aaron Pennington
1875	**Calvin** (2)	2:42¼	Bobby Swim	A. Williams	Aristides	Milner
1876	**Algerine** (½)	2:40½	Billy Donohue	Major Doswell	Fiddlesticks	Barricade
1877	**Cloverbrook** (1)	2:46	C. Holloway	J. Walden	Loiterer	Baden-Baden
1878	**Duke of Magenta** (2)	2:43½	L. Hughes	R.W. Walden	Bramble	Sparta
1879	**Spendthrift** (6)	2:42¾	George Evans	T. Puryear	Monitor	Jericho
1880	**Grenada** (nk)	2:47	L. Hughes	R.W. Walden	Ferncliffe	Turenne
1881	**Saunterer** (nk)	2:47	T. Costello	R.W. Walden	Eole	Baltic
1882	**Forester** (5)	2:43	Jim McLaughlin	L. Stuart	Babcock	Wyoming
1883	**George Kinney** (3)	2:42½	Jim McLaughlin	James Rowe Sr.	Trombone	Renegade
1884	**Panique** (nk)	2:42	Jim McLaughlin	James Rowe Sr.	Knight of Ellerslie	Himalaya
1885	**Tyrant** (3)	2:43	Paul Duffy	W. Claypool	St. Augustine	Tecumseh
1886	**Inspector B** (1)	2:41	Jim McLaughlin	F. McCabe	The Bard	Linden
1887	**Hanover** (15)	2:43½	Jim McLaughlin	F. McCabe	Oneko	(2-horse race)
1888	**Sir Dixon** (15)	2:40¼	Jim McLaughlin	F. McCabe	Prince Royal	(2-horse race)
1889	**Eric** (½)	2:47¼	W. Hayward	J. Huggins	Diablo	Zephyrus
1890	**Burlington** (2)	2:07¾	Pike Barnes	A. Cooper	Devotee	Padishah
1891	**Foxford** (nk)	2:08¾	Ed Garrison	M. Donavan	Montana	Laurestan
1892	**Patron** (6)	2:12	W. Hayward	L. Stuart	Shellbark	(2-horse race)
1893	**Commanche** (hd)	1:53¼	Willie Simms	G. Hannon	Dr. Rice	Rainbow
1894	**Henry of Navarre** (1½)	1:56½	Willie Simms	B. McClelland	Prig	Assignee
1895	**Belmar** (hd)	2:11½	Fred Taral	E. Feakes	Counter Tenor	Nanki Poo
1896	**Hastings** (hd)	2:24½	H. Griffin	J.J. Hyland	Handspring	Hamilton II
1897	**Scottish Chieftain** (1)	2:23¼	J. Scherrer	M. Byrnes	On Deck	Octagon
1898	**Bowling Brook** (6)	2:32	F. Littlefield	R.W. Walden	Previous	Hamburg
1899	**Jean Beraud** (hd)	2:23	R. Clawson	Sam Hildreth	Half Time	Glengar
1900	**Ildrim** (ns)	2:21¼	Nash Turner	H.E. Leigh	Petruchio	Missionary
1901	**Commando** (2)	2:21	H. Spencer	James Rowe Sr.	The Parader	All Green
1902	**Masterman** (2)	2:22⅗	John Bullman	J.J. Hyland	Renald	King Hanover
1903	**Africander** (2)	2:21¾	John Bullman	R. Miller	Whorler	Red Knight
1904	**Delhi** (4)	2:06⅗	George Odom	James Rowe Sr.	Graziallo	Rapid Water
1905	**Tanya** (½)	2:08	E. Hildebrand	J.W. Rogers	Blandy	Hot Shot
1906	**Burgomaster** (4)	2:20	Lucien Lyne	J.W. Rogers	The Quail	Accountant
1907	**Peter Pan** (1)	N/A	G. Mountain	James Rowe Sr.	Superman	Frank Gill
1908	**Colin** (hd)	N/A	Joe Notter	James Rowe Sr.	Fair Play	King James
1909	**Joe Madden** (8)	2:21⅗	E. Dugan	Sam Hildreth	Wise Mason	Donald MacDonald
1910	**Sweep** (6)	2:22	James Butwell	James Rowe Sr.	Duke of Ormonde	(2-horse race)
1911-12	Not held					
1913	**Prince Eugene** (½)	2:18	Roscoe Troxler	James Rowe Sr.	Rock View	Flying Fairy
1914	**Luke McLuke** (8)	2:20	Merritt Buxton	J.F. Schorr	Gainer	Charlestonian
1915	**The Finn** (4)	2:18⅖	George Byrne	E.W. Heffner	Half Rock	Pebbles
1916	**Friar Rock** (3)	2:22	E. Haynes	Sam Hildreth	Spur	Churchill
1917	**Hourless** (10)	2:17⅘	James Butwell	Sam Hildreth	Skeptic	Wonderful
1918	**Johren** (2)	2:20⅖	Frank Robinson	A. Simons	War Cloud	Cum Sah
1919	**SIR BARTON** (5)	2:17⅖	John Loftus	H. Guy Bedwell	Sweep On	Natural Bridge
1920	**Man o' War** (20)	2:14⅕	Clarence Kummer	L. Feustel	Donnacona	(2-horse race)
1921	**Grey Lag** (3)	2:16⅘	Earl Sande	Sam Hildreth	Sporting Blood	Leonardo II
1922	**Pillory** (2)	2:18⅘	C.H. Miller	T.J. Healey	Snob II	Hea
1923	**Zev** (1½)	2:19	Earl Sande	Sam Hildreth	Chickvale	Rialto
1924	**Mad Play** (2)	2:18⅘	Earl Sande	Sam Hildreth	Mr. Mutt	Modest
1925	**American Flag** (8)	2:16⅘	Albert Johnson	G.R. Tompkins	Dangerous	Swope
1926	**Crusader** (1)	2:32⅕	Albert Johnson	George Conway	Espino	Haste

Year	Winner (Margin)	Time	Jockey	Trainer	2nd place	3rd place
1927	**Chance Shot** (1$\frac{1}{2}$)	2:32$\frac{2}{5}$	Earl Sande	Pete Coyne	Bois de Rose	Flambino
1928	**Vito** (3)	2:33$\frac{1}{5}$	Clarence Kummer	Max Hirsch	Genie	Diavolo
1929	**Blue Larkspur** ($\frac{3}{4}$)	2:32$\frac{4}{5}$	Mack Garner	C. Hastings	African	Jack High
1930	**GALLANT FOX** (3)	2:31$\frac{3}{5}$	Earl Sande	Jim Fitzsimmons	Whichone	Questionnaire
1931	**Twenty Grand** (10)	2:29$\frac{3}{5}$	Charley Kurtsinger	James Rowe Jr.	Sun Meadow	Jamestown
1932	**Faireno** (1$\frac{1}{2}$)	2:32$\frac{4}{5}$	Tom Malley	Jim Fitzsimmons	Osculator	Flag Pole
1933	**Hurryoff** (1$\frac{1}{2}$)	2:32$\frac{3}{5}$	Mack Garner	H. McDaniel	Nimbus	Union
1934	**Peace Chance** (6)	2:29$\frac{1}{5}$	W.D. Wright	Pete Coyne	High Quest	Good Goods
1935	**OMAHA** (1$\frac{1}{2}$)	2:30$\frac{3}{5}$	Willie Saunders	Jim Fitzsimmons	Firethorn	Rosemont
1936	**Granville** (ns)	2:30	James Stout	Jim Fitzsimmons	Mr. Bones	Hollyrood
1937	**WAR ADMIRAL** (3)	2:28$\frac{3}{5}$	Charley Kurtsinger	George Conway	Sceneshifter	Vamoose
1938	**Pasteurized** (nk)	2:29$\frac{2}{5}$	James Stout	George Odom	Dauber	Cravat
1939	**Johnstown** (5)	2:29$\frac{3}{5}$	James Stout	Jim Fitzsimmons	Belay	Gilded Knight
1940	**Bimelech** ($\frac{3}{4}$)	2:29$\frac{3}{5}$	Fred Smith	Bill Hurley	Your Chance	Andy K.
1941	**WHIRLAWAY** (2$\frac{1}{2}$)	2:31	Eddie Arcaro	Ben Jones	Robert Morris	Yankee Chance
1942	**Shut Out** (2)	2:29$\frac{1}{5}$	Eddie Arcaro	John Gaver	Alsab	Lochinvar
1943	**COUNT FLEET** (25)	2:28$\frac{1}{5}$	Johnny Longden	Don Cameron	Fairy Manhurst	Deseronto
1944	**Bounding Home** ($\frac{1}{2}$)	2:32$\frac{1}{5}$	G.L. Smith	Matt Brady	Pensive	Bull Dandy
1945	**Pavot** (5)	2:30$\frac{1}{5}$	Eddie Arcaro	Oscar White	Wildlife	Jeep
1946	**ASSAULT** (3)	2:30$\frac{4}{5}$	Warren Mehrtens	Max Hirsch	Natchez	Cable
1947	**Phalanx** (5)	2:29$\frac{2}{5}$	R. Donoso	Syl Veitch	Tide Rips	Tailspin
1948	**CITATION** (8)	2:28$\frac{1}{5}$	Eddie Arcaro	Jimmy Jones	Better Self	Escadru
1949	**Capot** ($\frac{1}{2}$)	2:30$\frac{1}{5}$	Ted Atkinson	John Gaver	Ponder	Palestinian
1950	**Middleground** (1)	2:28$\frac{3}{5}$	William Boland	Max Hirsch	Lights Up	Mr. Trouble
1951	**Counterpoint** (4)	2:29	David Gorman	Syl Veitch	Battlefield	Battle Morn
1952	**One Count** (2$\frac{1}{2}$)	2:30$\frac{1}{5}$	Eddie Arcaro	Oscar White	Blue Man	Armageddon
1953	**Native Dancer** (nk)	2:28$\frac{3}{5}$	Eric Guerin	Bill Winfrey	Jamie K.	Royal Bay Gem
1954	**High Gun** (nk)	2:30$\frac{4}{5}$	Eric Guerin	Max Hirsch	Fisherman	Limelight
1955	**Nashua** (9)	2:29	Eddie Arcaro	Jim Fitzsimmons	Blazing Count	Portersville
1956	**Needles** (nk)	2:29$\frac{4}{5}$	David Erb	Hugh Fontaine	Career Boy	Fabius
1957	**Gallant Man** (8)	2:26$\frac{3}{5}$	Bill Shoemaker	John Nerud	Inside Tract	Bold Ruler
1958	**Cavan** (6)	2:30$\frac{1}{5}$	Pete Anderson	Tom Barry	Tim Tam	Flamingo
1959	**Sword Dancer** ($\frac{3}{4}$)	2:28$\frac{2}{5}$	Bill Shoemaker	Elliott Burch	Bagdad	Royal Orbit
1960	**Celtic Ash** (5$\frac{1}{2}$)	2:29$\frac{1}{5}$	Bill Hartack	Tom Barry	Venetian Way	Disperse
1961	**Sherluck** (2$\frac{1}{4}$)	2:29$\frac{1}{5}$	Braulio Baeza	Harold Young	Globemaster	Guadalcanal
1962	**Jaipur** (ns)	2:28$\frac{4}{5}$	Bill Shoemaker	B. Mulholland	Admiral's Voyage	Crimson Satan
1963	**Chateaugay** (2$\frac{1}{2}$)	2:30$\frac{1}{5}$	Braulio Baeza	James Conway	Candy Spots	Choker
1964	**Quadrangle** (2)	2:28$\frac{2}{5}$	Manuel Ycaza	Elliott Burch	Roman Brother	Northern Dancer
1965	**Hail to All** (nk)	2:28$\frac{2}{5}$	John Sellers	Eddie Yowell	Tom Rolfe	First Family
1966	**Amberoid** (2$\frac{1}{2}$)	2:29$\frac{3}{5}$	William Boland	Lucien Laurin	Buffle	Advocator
1967	**Damascus** (2$\frac{1}{2}$)	2:28$\frac{4}{5}$	Bill Shoemaker	F.Y. Whiteley Jr.	Cool Reception	Gentleman James
1968	**Stage Door Johnny** (1$\frac{1}{4}$)	2:27$\frac{1}{5}$	Gus Gustines	John Gaver	Forward Pass	Call Me Prince
1969	**Arts and Letters** (5$\frac{1}{2}$)	2:28$\frac{4}{5}$	Braulio Baeza	Elliott Burch	Majestic Prince	Dike
1970	**High Echelon** ($\frac{3}{4}$)	2:34	John Rotz	John Jacobs	Needles N Pens	Naskra
1971	**Pass Catcher** ($\frac{3}{4}$)	2:30$\frac{2}{5}$	Walter Blum	Eddie Yowell	Jim French	Bold Reason
1972	**Riva Ridge** (7)	2:28	Ron Turcotte	Lucien Laurin	Ruritania	Cloudy Dawn
1973	**SECRETARIAT** (31)	2:24	Ron Turcotte	Lucien Laurin	Twice A Prince	My Gallant
1974	**Little Current** (7)	2:29$\frac{1}{5}$	Miguel Rivera	Lou Rondinello	Jolly Johu	Cannonade
1975	**Avatar** (nk)	2:28$\frac{1}{5}$	Bill Shoemaker	Tommy Doyle	Foolish Pleasure	Master Derby
1976	**Bold Forbes** (nk)	2:29	Angel Cordero Jr.	Laz Barrera	McKenzie Bridge	Great Contractor
1977	**SEATTLE SLEW** (4)	2:29$\frac{3}{5}$	Jean Cruguet	Billy Turner	Run Dusty Run	Sanhedrin
1978	**AFFIRMED** (hd)	2:26$\frac{4}{5}$	Steve Cauthen	Laz Barrera	Alydar	Darby Creek Road
1979	**Coastal** (3$\frac{1}{4}$)	2:28$\frac{3}{5}$	Ruben Hernandez	David Whiteley	Golden Act	Spectacular Bid
1980	**Temperence Hill** (2)	2:29$\frac{4}{5}$	Eddie Maple	Joseph Cantey	Genuine Risk	Rockhill Native
1981	**Summing** (nk)	2:29	George Martens	Luis Barerra	Highland Blade	Pleasant Colony
1982	**Conquistador Cielo** (14)	2:28$\frac{1}{5}$	Laffit Pincay Jr.	Woody Stephens	Gato Del Sol	Illuminate
1983	**Caveat** (3$\frac{1}{2}$)	2:27$\frac{4}{5}$	Laffit Pincay Jr.	Woody Stephens	Slew o' Gold	Barberstown
1984	**Swale** (4)	2:27$\frac{1}{5}$	Laffit Pincay Jr.	Woody Stephens	Pine Circle	Morning Bob
1985	**Creme Fraiche** ($\frac{1}{2}$)	2:27	Eddie Maple	Woody Stephens	Stephan's Odyssey	Chief's Crown
1986	**Danzig Connection** (1$\frac{1}{4}$)	2:29$\frac{4}{5}$	Chris McCarron	Woody Stephens	Johns Treasure	Ferdinand
1987	**Bet Twice** (14)	2:28$\frac{1}{5}$	Craig Perret	Jimmy Croll	Cryptoclearance	Gulch
1988	**Risen Star** (14$\frac{3}{4}$)	2:26$\frac{2}{5}$	E. Delahoussaye	Louie Roussel III	Kingpost	Brian's Time
1989	**Easy Goer** (8)	2:26	Pat Day	Shug McGaughey	Sunday Silence	Le Voyageur
1990	**Go And Go** (8$\frac{1}{4}$)	2:27$\frac{1}{5}$	Michael Kinane	Dermot Weld	Thirty Six Red	Baron de Vaux
1991	**Hansel** (hd)	2:28	Jerry Bailey	Frank Brothers	Strike the Gold	Mane Minister
1992	**A.P. Indy** ($\frac{3}{4}$)	2:26	E. Delahoussaye	Neil Drysdale	My Memoirs	Pine Bluff
1993	**Colonial Affair** (2)	2:29$\frac{4}{5}$	Julie Krone	Scotty Schulhofer	Kissin Kris	Wild Gale
1994	**Tabasco Cat** (2)	2:26$\frac{4}{5}$	Pat Day	D. Wayne Lukas	Go For Gin	Strodes Creek
1995	**Thunder Gulch** (2)	2:32	Gary Stevens	D. Wayne Lukas	Star Standard	Citadeed
1996	**Editor's Note** (1)	2:28$\frac{4}{5}$	Rene Douglas	D. Wayne Lukas	Skip Away	My Flag
1997	**Touch Gold** ($\frac{3}{4}$)	2:28$\frac{4}{5}$	Chris McCarron	David Hofmans	Silver Charm	Free House

Belmont Stakes (Cont.)

Year	Winner (Margin)	Time	Jockey	Trainer	2nd place	3rd place
1998	**Victory Gallop** (ns)	2:29	Gary Stevens	Elliott Walden	Real Quiet	Thomas Jo
1999	**Lemon Drop Kid** (hd)	2:27⅘	Jose Santos	Scotty Schulhofer	Vision and Verse	Charismatic
2000	**Commendable** (1½)	2:31⅕	Pat Day	D. Wayne Lukas	Aptitude	Unshaded
2001	**Point Given** (12¼)	2:26⅖	Gary Stevens	Bob Baffert	A P Valentine	Monarchos
2002	**Sarava** (½)	2:29⅗	Edgar Prado	Ken McPeek	Medaglia d'Oro	Sunday Break
2003	**Empire Maker** (¾)	2:28⅕	Jerry Bailey	Bobby Frankel	Ten Most Wanted	Funny Cide
2004	**Birdstone** (1)	2:27⅖	Edgar Prado	Nick Zito	Smarty Jones	Royal Assault
2005	**Afleet Alex** (7)	2:28⅗	Jeremy Rose	Tim Ritchey	Andromeda's Hero	Nolan's Cat
2006	**Jazil** (1¼)	2:27⅘	Fernando Jara	Kiaran McLaughlin	Bluegrass Cat	Sunriver
2007	**Rags to Riches** (hd)	2:28⅘	John Velazquez	Todd Pletcher	Curlin	Tiago

Breeders' Cup World Championships

Inaugurated on Nov. 10, 1984, the Breeders' Cup World Championships consists of eight races on one track on one day late in the year to determine thoroughbred racing's principle champions.

The Breeders' Cup has been (will be) held at the following tracks: Aqueduct Racetrack (N.Y.) in 1985; Arlington Park (Ill.) in 2002; Belmont Park (N.Y.) in 1990, '95, 2001 and '05; Churchill Downs (Ky.) in 1988, '91, '94, '98, 2000 and '06; Gulfstream Park (Fla.) in 1989, '92 and '99; Hollywood Park (Calif.) in 1984, '87 and '97; Lone Star Park (Texas) in 2004; Monmouth Park (N.J.) in 2007; Santa Anita Park (Calif.) in 1986, '93, 2003 and '08; and Woodbine (Toronto) in 1996.

Horses with most wins: Bayakoa, Da Hoss, High Chaparral, Lure, Miesque and Tiznow (2).

Trainers with most wins: D. Wayne Lukas (18); Shug McGaughey (9); Neil Drysdale and Richard Mandella (6); Bill Mott (5); Andre Fabre, Bobby Frankel, Ron McAnally (4); Bob Baffert, Pascal Bary, Francois Boutin, Patrick Byrne, Julio Canani, Aidan O'Brien and Sir Michael Stoute (3).

Jockeys with most wins: Jerry Bailey (15); Pat Day (12); Mike Smith (10); Chris McCarron (9); Gary Stevens (8); Eddie Delahoussaye, Corey Nakatani, Laffit Pincay Jr., Jose Santos and Pat Valenzuela (7); Frankie Dettori and John Velazquez (6); Angel Cordero Jr. and Craig Perret (4); David Flores, Michael Kinane, Edgar Prado, Randy Romero and Alex Solis (3).

Juvenile

Distances: one mile (1984-85, 87); 1$\frac{1}{16}$ miles (1986, 1988-2001, 2003–), 1⅛ miles (2002).

Year	Winner (Margin)	Time	Jockey	Trainer	2nd place	3rd place
1984	**Chief's Crown** (¾)	1:36⅕	Don MacBeth	Roger Laurin	Tank's Prospect	Spend A Buck
1985	**Tasso** (ns)	1:36⅕	Laffit Pincay Jr.	Neil Drysdale	Storm Cat	Scat Dancer
1986	**Capote** (1¼)	1:43⅘	Laffit Pincay Jr.	D. Wayne Lukas	Qualify	Alysheba
1987	**Success Express** (1¾)	1:35⅕	Jose Santos	D. Wayne Lukas	Regal Classic	Tejano
1988	**Is It True** (1¼)	1:46⅗	Laffit Pincay Jr.	D. Wayne Lukas	Easy Goer	Tagel
1989	**Rhythm** (2)	1:43⅗	Craig Perret	Shug McGaughey	Grand Canyon	Slavic
1990	**Fly So Free** (3)	1:43⅖	Jose Santos	Scotty Schulhofer	Take Me Out	Lost Mountain
1991	**Arazi** (4¾)	1:44⅗	Pat Valenzuela	Francois Boutin	Bertrando	Snappy Landing
1992	**Gilded Time** (¾)	1:43⅖	Chris McCarron	Darrell Vienna	It'sali'lknownfact	River Special
1993	**Brocco** (5)	1:42⅘	Gary Stevens	Randy Winick	Blumin Affair	Tabasco Cat
1994	**Timber Country** (½)	1:44⅖	Pat Day	D. Wayne Lukas	Eltish	Tejano Run
1995	**Unbridled's Song** (nk)	1:41⅗	Mike Smith	James Ryerson	Hennessy	Editor's Note
1996	**Boston Harbor** (nk)	1:43⅖	Jerry Bailey	D. Wayne Lukas	Acceptable	Ordway
1997	**Favorite Trick** (5½)	1:41⅖	Pat Day	Patrick Byrne	Dawson's Legacy	Nationalore
1998	**Answer Lively** (hd)	1:44	Jerry Bailey	Bobby Barnett	Aly's Alley	Cat Thief
1999	**Anees** (2½)	1:42⅕	Gary Stevens	Alex Hassinger Jr.	Chief Seattle	High Yield
2000	**Macho Uno** (ns)	1:42	Jerry Bailey	Joe Orseno	Point Given	Street Cry
2001	**Johannesburg** (2¼)	1:42⅕	Michael Kinane	Aidan O'Brien	Repent	Siphonic
2002	**Vindication** (2¾)	1:49⅗	Mike Smith	Bob Baffert	Kafwain	Hold That Tiger
2003	**Action This Day** (2¼)	1:43⅗	David Flores	Richard Mandella	Minister Eric	Chapel Royal
2004	**Wilko** (¾)	1:42	Frankie Dettori	Jeremy Noseda	Afleet Alex	Sun King
2005	**Stevie Wonderboy** (1¼)	1:41⅗	Garrett Gomez	Doug O'Neill	Henny Hughes	First Samurai
2006	**Street Sense** (10)	1:43⅘	Calvin Borel	Carl Nafzger	Circular Quay	Great Hunter

Breeders' Cup Leaders

The all-time money-winning horses and jockeys in the history of the Breeders' Cup through 2006.

Top 10 Horses

		Sts	1-2-3	Earnings
1	Tiznow	2	2-0-0	$4,560,400
2	Ouija Board	3	2-1-0	2,833,200
3	Invasor	1	1-0-0	2,700,000
4	Awesome Again	1	1-0-0	2,662,400
5	Pleasantly Perfect	2	1-0-1	2,520,000
6	Saint Liam	1	1-0-0	2,433,600
7	Skip Away	2	1-0-0	2,288,000
8	Cat Thief	3	1-0-1	2,200,000
9	Alysheba	3	1-1-1	2,133,000
10	Three tied with $2,080,000.			

Top 10 Jockeys

		Sts	1-2-3	Earnings
1	Pat Day	117	12-17-11	$23,033,360
2	Jerry Bailey	102	15-12-14	22,006,440
3	Chris McCarron	101	9-12-7	17,669,600
4	Gary Stevens	99	8-15-11	13,723,910
5	Mike Smith	54	10-6-3	10,760,760
6	Corey Nakatani	65	7-8-9	9,965,480
7	Frankie Dettori	42	6-2-4	9,841,910
8	John Velazquez	63	6-6-9	8,929,800
9	Jose Santos	65	7-2-4	8,008,800
10	Eddie Delahoussaye	68	7-3-6	7,775,000

Juvenile Fillies

Distances: one mile (1984-85, 87); 1¹⁄₁₆ miles (1986, 1988-2001, 2003–); 1¹⁄₈ miles (2002).

Year	Winner (Margin)	Time	Jockey	Trainer	2nd place	3rd place
1984	Outstandingly*	1:37⁴⁄₅	Walter Guerra	Pancho Martin	Dusty Heart	Fine Spirit
1985	Twilight Ridge (1)	1:35¹⁄₅	Jorge Velasquez	D. Wayne Lukas	Family Style	Steal A Kiss
1986	Brave Raj (5¹⁄₂)	1:43¹⁄₅	Pat Valenzuela	Melvin Stute	Tappiano	Saros Brig
1987	Epitome (ns)	1:36²⁄₅	Pat Day	Phil Hauswald	Jeanne Jones	Dream Team
1988	Open Mind (1³⁄₄)	1:46³⁄₅	Angel Cordero Jr.	D. Wayne Lukas	Darby Shuffle	Lea Lucinda
1989	Go for Wand (2³⁄₄)	1:44¹⁄₅	Randy Romero	Wm. Badgett Jr.	Sweet Roberta	Stella Madrid
1990	Meadow Star (5)	1:44	Jose Santos	LeRoy Jolley	Private Treasure	Dance Smartly
1991	Pleasant Stage (nk)	1:46²⁄₅	E. Delahoussaye	Chris Speckert	La Spia	Cadillac Women
1992	Eliza (nk)	1:42⁴⁄₅	Pat Valenzuela	Alex Hassinger	Educated Risk	Boots 'n Jackie
1993	Phone Chatter (hd)	1:43	Laffit Pincay Jr.	Richard Mandella	Sardula	Heavenly Prize
1994	Flanders (hd)	1:45¹⁄₅	Pat Day	D. Wayne Lukas	Serena's Song	Stormy Blues
1995	My Flag (¹⁄₂)	1:42²⁄₅	Jerry Bailey	Shug McGaughey	Cara Rafaela	Golden Attraction
1996	Storm Song (4¹⁄₂)	1:43³⁄₅	Craig Perret	Nick Zito	Love That Jazz	Critical Factor
1997	Countess Diana (8¹⁄₂)	1:42¹⁄₅	Shane Sellers	Patrick Byrne	Career Collection	Primaly
1998	Silverbulletday (¹⁄₂)	1:43³⁄₅	Gary Stevens	Bob Baffert	Excellent Meeting	Three Ring
1999	Cash Run (1¹⁄₄)	1:43¹⁄₅	Jerry Bailey	D. Wayne Lukas	Chilukki	Surfside
2000	Caressing (¹⁄₂)	1:42³⁄₅	John Velazquez	David Vance	Platinum Tiara	She's a Devil Due
2001	Tempera (1¹⁄₂)	1:41²⁄₅	David Flores	Eoin Harty	Imperial Gesture	Bella Bellucci
2002	Storm Flag Flying (¹⁄₂)	1:49³⁄₅	John Velazquez	Shug McGaughey	Composure	Santa Catarina
2003	Halfbridled (2¹⁄₂)	1:42³⁄₅	Julie Krone	Richard Mandella	Ashado	Victory U.S.A.
2004	Sweet Catomine (3³⁄₄)	1:41³⁄₅	Corey Nakatani	Julio Canani	Balletto	Runway Model
2005	Folklore (1¹⁄₄)	1:43⁴⁄₅	Edgar Prado	D. Wayne Lukas	Wild Fit	Original Spin
2006	Dreaming of Anna (1¹⁄₂)	1:43⁴⁄₅	Rene Douglas	Wayne Catalano	Octave	Cotton Blossom

*In 1984, winner Fran's Valentine was disqualified for interference in the stretch and placed 10th.

Sprint

Distance: six furlongs (since 1984).

Year	Winner (Margin)	Time	Jockey	Trainer	2nd place	3rd place
1984	Eillo (ns)	1:10¹⁄₅	Craig Perret	Budd Lepman	Commemorate	Fighting Fit
1985	Precisionist (³⁄₄)	1:08²⁄₅	Chris McCarron	L.R. Fenstermaker	Smile	Mt. Livermore
1986	Smile (1¹⁄₄)	1:08²⁄₅	Jacinto Vasquez	Scotty Schulhofer	Pine Tree Lane	Bedside Promise
1987	Very Subtle (4)	1:08⁴⁄₅	Pat Valenzuela	Melvin Stute	Groovy	Exclusive Enough
1988	Gulch (³⁄₄)	1:10²⁄₅	Angel Cordero Jr.	D. Wayne Lukas	Play The King	Afleet
1989	Dancing Spree (nk)	1:09	Angel Cordero Jr.	Shug McGaughey	Safely Kept	Dispersal
1990	Safely Kept (nk)	1:09³⁄₅	Craig Perret	Alan Goldberg	Dayjur	Black Tie Affair
1991	Sheikh Albadou (nk)	1:09¹⁄₅	Pat Eddery	Alexander Scott	Pleasant Tap	Robyn Dancer
1992	Thirty Slews (nk)	1:08¹⁄₅	Eddie Delahoussaye	Bob Baffert	Meafara	Rubiano
1993	Cardmania (nk)	1:08³⁄₅	Eddie Delahoussaye	Derek Meredith	Meafara	Gilded Time
1994	Cherokee Run (nk)	1:09²⁄₅	Mike Smith	Frank Alexander	Soviet Problem	Cardmania
1995	Desert Stormer (nk)	1:09	Kent Desormeaux	Frank Lyons	Mr. Greeley	Lit de Justice
1996	Lit de Justice (1¹⁄₄)	1:08²⁄₅	Corey Nakatani	Jenine Sahadi	Paying Dues	Honour and Glory
1997	Elmhurst (¹⁄₂)	1:08¹⁄₅	Corey Nakatani	Jenine Sahadi	Hesabull	Bet On Sunshine
1998	Reraise (2)	1:09	Corey Nakatani	Craig Dollase	Grand Slam	Kona Gold
1999	Artax (¹⁄₂)	1:07⁴⁄₅	Jorge Chavez	Louis Albertrani	Kona Gold	Big Jag
2000	Kona Gold (¹⁄₂)	1:07³⁄₅	Alex Solis	Bruce Headley	Honest Lady	Bet On Sunshine
2001	Squirtle Squirt (¹⁄₂)	1:08²⁄₅	Jerry Bailey	Bobby Frankel	Xtra Heat	Caller One
2002	Orientate (¹⁄₂)	1:08⁴⁄₅	Jerry Bailey	D. Wayne Lukas	Thunderello	Crafty C.T.
2003	Cajun Beat (2¹⁄₄)	1:07³⁄₅	Cornelio Velasquez	Stephen Margolis	Bluesthestandard	Shake You Down
2004	Speightstown (1¹⁄₄)	1:08	John Velazquez	Todd Pletcher	Kela	My Cousin Matt
2005	Silver Train (hd)	1:08⁴⁄₅	Edgar Prado	Richard Dutrow Jr.	Taste of Paradise	Lion Tamer
2006	Thor's Echo (4)	1:08⁴⁄₅	Corey Nakatani	Doug O'Neill	Friendly Island	Nightmare Affair

Mile

Year	Winner (Margin)	Time	Jockey	Trainer	2nd place	3rd place
1984	Royal Heroine (1¹⁄₂)	1:32³⁄₅	Fernando Toro	John Gosden	Star Choice	Cozzene
1985	Cozzene (2¹⁄₄)	1:35	Walter Guerra	Jan Nerud	Al Mamoon*	Shadeed
1986	Last Tycoon (hd)	1:35¹⁄₅	Yves St.-Martin	Robert Collet	Palace Music	Fred Astaire
1987	Miesque (3¹⁄₂)	1:32⁴⁄₅	Freddie Head	Francois Boutin	Show Dancer	Sonic Lady
1988	Miesque (4)	1:38³⁄₅	Freddie Head	Francois Boutin	Steinlen	Simply Majestic
1989	Steinlen (³⁄₄)	1:37¹⁄₅	Jose Santos	D. Wayne Lukas	Sabona	Most Welcome
1990	Royal Academy (nk)	1:35¹⁄₅	Lester Piggott	M.V. O'Brien	Itsallgreektome	Priolo
1991	Opening Verse (2¹⁄₄)	1:37²⁄₅	Pat Valenzuela	Dick Lundy	Val des Bois	Star of Cozzene
1992	Lure (3)	1:32¹⁄₅	Mike Smith	Shug McGaughey	Paradise Creek	Brief Truce
1993	Lure (2¹⁄₄)	1:33²⁄₅	Mike Smith	Shug McGaughey	Ski Paradise	Fourstars Allstar
1994	Barathea (hd)	1:34²⁄₅	Frankie Dettori	Luca Cumani	Johann Quatz	Unfinished Symph.
1995	Ridgewood Pearl (2)	1:43³⁄₅	John Murtagh	John Oxx	Fastness	Sayyedati
1996	Da Hoss (1¹⁄₂)	1:35⁴⁄₅	Gary Stevens	Michael Dickinson	Spinning World	Same Old Wish
1997	Spinning World (2)	1:32³⁄₅	Cash Asmussen	Jonathan Pease	Geri	Decorated Hero
1998	Da Hoss (hd)	1:35¹⁄₅	John Velazquez	Michael Dickinson	Hawksley Hill	Labeeb

Breeders' Cup Championship (Cont.)

Mile (Cont.)

Year	Winner (Margin)	Time	Jockey	Trainer	2nd place	3rd place
1999	**Silic** (nk)	1:34 1/5	Corey Nakatani	Julio Canani	Tuzla	Docksider
2000	**War Chant** (nk)	1:34 3/5	Gary Stevens	Neil Drysdale	North East Bound	Dansili
2001	**Val Royal** (1 3/4)	1:32	Jose Valdivia	Julio Canani	Forbidden Apple	Bach
2002	**Domedriver** (3/4)	1:36 4/5	Thierry Thulliez	Pascal Bary	Rock of Gibraltar	Good Journey
2003	**Six Perfections** (3/4)	1:33 4/5	Jerry Bailey	Pascal Bary	Touch of the Blues	Century City
2004	**Singletary** (1/2)	1:36 4/5	David Flores	Donald Chatlos Jr.	Antonius Pius	Six Perfections
2005	**Artie Schiller** (3/4)	1:36 1/5	Garrett Gomez	James Jerkens	Leroidesanimaux	Gorella
2006	**Miesque's Approval** (4)	1:34 3/5	Eddie Castro	Martin Wolfson	Aragorn	Badge of Silver

*In 1985, 2nd place finisher Palace Music was disqualified for interference and placed 9th.

Distaff

Distances: 1 1/4 miles (1984-87); 1 1/8 miles (since 1988).

Year	Winner (Margin)	Time	Jockey	Trainer	2nd place	3rd place
1984	**Princess Rooney** (7)	2:02 2/5	Eddie Delahoussaye	Neil Drysdale	Life's Magic	Adored
1985	**Life's Magic** (6 1/4)	2:02	Angel Cordero Jr.	D. Wayne Lukas	Lady's Secret	DontstopThemusic
1986	**Lady's Secret** (2 1/2)	2:01 1/5	Pat Day	D. Wayne Lukas	Fran's Valentine	Outstandingly
1987	**Sacahuista** (2 1/4)	2:02 4/5	Randy Romero	D. Wayne Lukas	Clabber Girl	Oueee Bebe
1988	**Personal Ensign** (ns)	1:52	Randy Romero	Shug McGaughey	Winning Colors	Goodbye Halo
1989	**Bayakoa** (1 1/2)	1:47 2/5	Laffit Pincay Jr.	Ron McAnally	Gorgeous	Open Mind
1990	**Bayakoa** (6 3/4)	1:49 1/5	Laffit Pincay Jr.	Ron McAnally	Colonial Waters	Valay Maid
1991	**Dance Smartly** (1/2)	1:50 4/5	Pat Day	Jim Day	Versailles Treaty	Brought to Mind
1992	**Paseana** (4)	1:48	Chris McCarron	Ron McAnally	Versailles Treaty	Magical Maiden
1993	**Hollywood Wildcat** (ns)	1:48 1/5	Eddie Delahoussaye	Neil Drysdale	Paseana	Re Toss
1994	**One Dreamer** (nk)	1:50 3/5	Gary Stevens	Thomas Proctor	Heavenly Prize	Miss Dominique
1995	**Inside Information** (13 1/2)	1:46	Mike Smith	Shug McGaughey	Heavenly Prize	Lakeway
1996	**Jewel Princess** (1 1/2)	1:48 1/5	Corey Nakatani	Wallace Dollase	Serena's Song	Different
1997	**Ajina** (2)	1:47 1/5	Mike Smith	Bill Mott	Sharp Cat	Escena
1998	**Escena** (ns)	1:49 4/5	Gary Stevens	Bill Mott	Banshee Breeze	Keeper Hill
1999	**Beautiful Pleasure** (3/4)	1:47 2/5	Jorge Chavez	John Ward Jr.	Banshee Breeze	Heritage of Gold
2000	**Spain** (1 1/2)	1:47 3/5	Victor Espinoza	D. Wayne Lukas	Surfside	Heritage of Gold
2001	**Unbridled Elaine** (hd)	1:49 1/5	Pat Day	Dallas Stewart	Spain	Two Item Limit
2002	**Azeri** (5)	1:48 3/5	Mike Smith	Laura de Seroux	Farda Amiga	Imperial Gesture
2003	**Adoration** (4 1/2)	1:49 1/5	Pat Valenzuela	David Hofmans	Elloluv	Got Koko
2004	**Ashado** (1 1/4)	1:48 1/5	John Velazquez	Todd Pletcher	Storm Flag Flying	Stellar Jayne
2005	**Pleasant Home** (9 1/4)	1:48 2/5	Cornelio Velasquez	Shug McGaughey	Society Selection	Ashado
2006	**Round Pond** (5 1/2)	1:50 2/5	Edgar Prado	Michael Matz	Asi Siempre	Happy Ticket

Turf

Distance: 1 1/2 miles (since 1984).

Year	Winner (Margin)	Time	Jockey	Trainer	2nd place	3rd place
1984	**Lashkari** (nk)	2:25 1/5	Yves St.-Martin	de Royer-Dupre	All Along	Raami
1985	**Pebbles** (nk)	2:27	Pat Eddery	Clive Brittain	StrawberryRoad II	Mourjane
1986	**Manila** (nk)	2:25 2/5	Jose Santos	Leroy Jolley	Theatrical	Estrapade
1987	**Theatrical** (1/2)	2:24 2/5	Pat Day	Bill Mott	Trempolino	Village Star II
1988	**Gt. Communicator** (1/2)	2:35 1/5	Ray Sibille	Thad Ackel	Sunshine Forever	Indian Skimmer
1989	**Prized** (hd)	2:28	Eddie Delahoussaye	Neil Drysdale	Sierra Roberta	Star Lift
1990	**In The Wings** (1/2)	2:29 3/5	Gary Stevens	Andre Fabre	With Approval	El Senor
1991	**Miss Alleged** (2)	2:30 4/5	Eric Legrix	Pascal Bary	Itsallgreektome	Quest for Fame
1992	**Fraise** (ns)	2:24	Pat Valenzuela	Bill Mott	Sky Classic	Quest for Fame
1993	**Kotashaan** (1/2)	2:25	Kent Desormeaux	Richard Mandella	Bien Bien	Luazur
1994	**Tikkanen** (1 1/2)	2:26 2/5	Mike Smith	Jonathan Pease	Hatoof	Paradise Creek
1995	**Northern Spur** (nk)	2:42	Chris McCarron	Ron McAnally	Freedom Cry	Carnegie
1996	**Pilsudski** (1 1/4)	2:30 1/5	Walter Swinburn	Sir Michael Stoute	Singspiel	Swain
1997	**Chief Bearhart** (3/4)	2:24	Jose Santos	Mark Frostad	Borgia	Flag Down
1998	**Buck's Boy** (1 1/4)	2:28 3/5	Shane Sellers	Noel Hickey	Yagli	Dushyantor
1999	**Daylami** (2 1/2)	2:24 3/5	Frankie Dettori	Saeed bin Suroor	Royal Anthem	Buck's Boy
2000	**Kalanisi** (1/2)	2:26 4/5	John Murtagh	Sir Michael Stoute	Quiet Resolve	John's Call
2001	**Fantastic Light** (3/4)	2:24 1/5	Frankie Dettori	Saeed bin Suroor	Milan	Timboroa
2002	**High Chaparral** (1 1/4)	2:30 1/5	Michael Kinane	Aidan O'Brien	With Anticipation	Falcon Flight
2003	**High Chaparral***	2:24 1/5	Michael Kinane	Aidan O'Brien	—	Falbrav
	& **Johar***	2:24 1/5	Alex Solis	Richard Mandella		
2004	**Better Talk Now** (1 3/4)	2:29 3/5	Ramon Dominguez	H. Graham Motion	Kitten's Joy	Powerscourt
2005	**Shirocco** (1 3/4)	2:29 2/5	Christophe Soumillon	Andre Fabre	Ace	Azamour
2006	**Red Rocks** (1/2)	2:27 1/5	Frankie Dettori	Brian Meehan	Better Talk Now	English Channel

*in 2003, High Chaparral and Johar finished in a dead heat, the first in Breeders' Cup history.

Filly & Mare Turf

Distance: 1⅜ miles (1999-2000, 2004–); 1¼ miles (2001-03).

Year	Winner (Margin)	Time	Jockey	Trainer	2nd place	3rd place
1999	**Soaring Softly** (¾)	2:13⅘	Jerry Bailey	James J. Toner	Coretta	Zomarradah
2000	**Perfect Sting** (¾)	2:13	Jerry Bailey	Joe Orseno	Tout Charmant	Catella
2001	**Banks Hill** (5½)	2:00⅕	Olivier Peslier	Andre Fabre	Spook Express	Spring Oak
2002	**Starine** (1½)	2:03⅗	John Velazquez	Bobby Frankel	Banks Hill	Islington
2003	**Islington** (nk)	1:59	Kieren Fallon	Sir Michael Stoute	L'Ancresse	Yesterday
2004	**Ouija Board** (1½)	2:18⅕	Kieren Fallon	Edward Dunlop	Film Maker	Wonder Again
2005	**Intercontinental** (1¼)	2:02⅖	Rafael Bejarano	Bobby Frankel	Ouija Board	Film Maker
2006	**Ouija Board** (2¼)	2:14⅖	Frankie Dettori	Edward Dunlop	Film Maker	Honey Ryder

Classic

Distance: 1¼ miles (since 1984).

Year	Winner (Margin)	Time	Jockey	Trainer	2nd place	3rd place
1984	**Wild Again** (hd)	2:03⅖	Pat Day	Vincent Timphony	Slew o' Gold	Gate Dancer*
1985	**Proud Truth** (hd)	2:00⅘	Jorge Velasquez	John Veitch	Gate Dancer	Turkoman
1986	**Skywalker** (1¼)	2:00⅖	Laffit Pincay Jr.	M. Whittingham	Turkoman	Precisionist
1987	**Ferdinand** (ns)	2:01⅖	Bill Shoemaker	C. Whittingham	Alysheba	Judge Angelucci
1988	**Alysheba** (ns)	2:04⅘	Chris McCarron	Jack Van Berg	Seeking the Gold	Waquoit
1989	**Sunday Silence** (½)	2:00⅕	Chris McCarron	C. Whittingham	Easy Goer	Blushing John
1990	**Unbridled** (1)	2:02⅕	Pat Day	Carl Nafzger	Ibn Bey	Thirty Six Red
1991	**Black Tie Affair** (1¼)	2:02⅘	Jerry Bailey	Ernie Poulos	Twilight Agenda	Unbridled
1992	**A.P. Indy** (2)	2:00⅕	Eddie Delahoussaye	Neil Drysdale	Pleasant Tap	Jolypha
1993	**Arcangues** (2)	2:00⅘	Jerry Bailey	Andre Fabre	Bertrando	Kissin Kris
1994	**Concern** (nk)	2:02⅖	Jerry Bailey	Richard Small	Tabasco Cat	Dramatic Gold
1995	**Cigar** (2½)	1:59⅖	Jerry Bailey	Bill Mott	L'Carriere	Unaccounted For
1996	**Alphabet Soup** (ns)	2:01	Chris McCarron	David Hofmans	Louis Quatorze	Cigar
1997	**Skip Away** (6)	1:59⅕	Mike Smith	Hubert Hine	Deputy Commander	Dowty
1998	**Awesome Again** (¾)	2:02	Pat Day	Patrick Byrne	Silver Charm	Swain
1999	**Cat Thief** (1¼)	1:59⅖	Pat Day	D. Wayne Lukas	Budroyale	Golden Missile
2000	**Tiznow** (nk)	2:00⅗	Chris McCarron	Jay Robbins	Giant's Causeway	Captain Steve
2001	**Tiznow** (ns)	2:00⅗	Chris McCarron	Jay Robbins	Sakhee	Albert the Great
2002	**Volponi** (6½)	2:01⅖	Jose Santos	Philip Johnson	Medaglia d'Oro	Milwaukee Brew
2003	**Pleasantly Perfect** (1½)	1:59⅘	Alex Solis	Richard Mandella	Medaglia d'Oro	Dynever
2004	**Ghostzapper** (3)	1:59	Javier Castellano	Bobby Frankel	Roses in May	Pleasantly Perfect
2005	**Saint Liam** (1)	2:01⅖	Jerry Bailey	Richard Dutrow Jr.	Flower Alley	Perfect Drift
2006	**Invasor** (1)	2:02	Fernando Jara	Kiaran McLaughlin	Bernardini	Premium Tap

*In 1984, 2nd place finisher Gate Dancer was disqualified for interference and placed 3rd.

Annual Money Leaders

Horses

Annual money-leading horses since 1910, according to *The American Racing Manual*.

Multiple leaders: Round Table, Buckpasser, Alysheba and Cigar (2).

Year		Age	Sts	1-2-3	Earnings
1910	Novelty	2	16	11–	$72,630
1911	Worth	2	13	10–	16,645
1912	Star Charter	4	17	6–	14,655
1913	Old Rosebud	2	14	12–	19,057
1914	Roamer	3	16	12–	29,105
1915	Borrow	7	9	4–	20,195
1916	Campfire	2	9	6–	49,735
1917	Sun Briar	2	9	5–	59,505
1918	Eternal	2	8	6–	56,173
1919	Sir Barton	3	13	8-3-2	88,250
1920	Man o' War	3	11	11-0-0	166,140
1921	Morvich	2	11	11-0-0	115,234
1922	Pillory	3	7	4-1-1	95,654
1923	Zev	3	14	12-1-0	272,008
1924	Sarzen	3	12	8-1-1	95,640
1925	Pompey	2	10	7-2-0	121,630
1926	Crusader	3	15	9-4-0	166,033
1927	Anita Peabody	2	7	6-0-1	111,905
1928	High Strung	2	6	5-0-0	153,590
1929	Blue Larkspur	3	6	4-1-0	153,450
1930	Gallant Fox	3	10	9-1-0	308,275
1931	Gallant Flight	2	7	7-0-0	219,000
1932	Gusto	3	16	4-3-2	145,940
1933	Singing Wood	2	9	3-2-2	88,050
1934	Cavalcade	3	7	6-1-0	111,235
1935	Omaha	3	9	6-1-2	142,255
1936	Granville	3	11	7-3-0	$110,295
1937	Seabiscuit	4	15	11-2-2	168,580
1938	Stagehand	3	15	8-2-3	189,710
1939	Challedon	3	15	9-2-3	184,535
1940	Bimelech	3	7	4-2-1	110,005
1941	Whirlaway	3	20	13-5-2	272,386
1942	Shut Out	3	12	8-2-0	238,872
1943	Count Fleet	3	6	6-0-0	174,055
1944	Pavot	2	8	8-0-0	179,040
1945	Busher	3	13	10-2-1	273,735
1946	Assault	3	15	8-2-3	424,195
1947	Armed	6	17	11-4-1	376,325
1948	Citation	3	20	19-1-0	709,470
1949	Ponder	3	21	9-5-2	321,825
1950	Noor	5	12	7-4-1	346,940
1951	Counterpoint	3	15	7-2-1	250,525
1952	Crafty Admiral	4	16	9-4-1	277,225
1953	Native Dancer	3	10	9-1-0	513,425
1954	Determine	3	15	10-3-2	328,700
1955	Nashua	3	12	10-1-1	752,550
1956	Needles	3	8	4-2-0	440,850
1957	Round Table	3	22	15-1-3	600,383
1958	Round Table	4	20	14-4-0	662,780
1959	Sword Dancer	3	13	8-4-0	537,004
1960	Bally Ache	3	15	10-3-1	445,045
1961	Carry Back	3	16	9-1-3	565,349

Annual Money Leaders (Cont.)

Horses (Cont.)

Year		Age	Sts	1-2-3	Earnings	Year		Age	Sts	1-2-3	Earnings
1962	Never Bend	2	10	7-1-2	$402,969	1985	Spend A Buck	3	7	5-1-1	$3,552,704
1963	Candy Spots	3	12	7-2-1	604,481	1986	Snow Chief	3	9	6-1-1	1,875,200
1964	Gun Bow	4	16	8-4-2	580,100	1987	Alysheba	3	10	3-3-1	2,511,156
1965	Buckpasser	2	11	9-1-0	568,096	1988	Alysheba	4	9	7-1-0	3,808,600
1966	Buckpasser	3	14	13-1-0	669,078	1989	Sunday Silence	3	9	7-2-0	4,578,454
1967	Damascus	3	16	12-3-1	817,941	1990	Unbridled	3	11	4-3-2	3,718,149
1968	Forward Pass	3	13	7-2-0	546,674	1991	Dance Smartly	3	8	8-0-0	2,876,821
1969	Arts and Letters	3	14	8-5-1	555,604	1992	A.P. Indy	3	7	5-0-1	2,622,560
1970	Personality	3	18	8-2-1	444,049	1993	Kotashaan (FRA)	5	10	6-3-0	2,619,014
1971	Riva Ridge	2	9	7-0-0	503,263	1994	Paradise Creek	5	11	8-2-1	2,610,187
1972	Droll Role	4	19	7-3-4	471,633	1995	Cigar	5	10	10-0-0	4,819,800
1973	Secretariat	3	12	9-2-1	860,404	1996	Cigar	6	8	5-2-1	4,910,000
1974	Chris Evert	3	8	5-1-2	551,063	1997	Skip Away	4	11	4-5-2	4,089,000
1975	Foolish Pleasure	3	11	5-4-1	716,278	1998	Silver Charm	4	9	6-2-0	4,696,506
1976	Forego	6	8	6-1-1	401,701	1999	Almutawakel	4	4	1-1-1	3,290,000
1977	Seattle Slew	3	7	6-1-1	641,370	2000	Dubai Millennium (GBR)	4	1	1-0-0	3,600,000
1978	Affirmed	3	11	8-2-0	901,541	2001	Captain Steve	4	6	2-1-1	4,201,200
1979	Spectacular Bid	3	12	10-1-1	1,279,334	2002	Street Cry (IRE)	4	3	2-1-0	4,266,615
1980	Temperence Hill	3	17	8-3-1	1,130,452	2003	Moon Ballad (IRE)	4	3	1-0-0	3,651,101
1981	John Henry	6	10	8-0-0	1,798,030	2004	Smarty Jones	3	7	6-1-0	7,563,535
1982	Perrault (GBR)	5	8	4-1-2	1,197,400	2005	Saint Liam	5	6	4-1-0	3,696,960
1983	All Along (FRA)	4	7	4-1-1	2,138,963	2006	Invasor (ARG)	4	4	4-0-0	3,690,000
1984	Slew o' Gold	4	6	5-1-0	2,627,944						

Jockeys

Annual money-leading jockeys since 1910, according to *The American Racing Manual*.

Multiple leaders: Bill Shoemaker (10); Laffit Pincay Jr. (7); Eddie Arcaro and Jerry Bailey (6); Braulio Baeza (5); Chris McCarron and Jose Santos (4); Angel Cordero Jr. and Earl Sande (3); Ted Atkinson, Pat Day, Laverne Fator, Mack Garner, Bill Hartack, Charley Kurtsinger, Johnny Longden, Mike Smith, Gary Stevens, John Velazquez, Sonny Workman and Wayne Wright (2).

Year		Mts	Wins	Earnings	Year		Mts	Wins	Earnings
1910	Carroll Shilling	506	172	$176,030	1946	Ted Atkinson	1377	233	$1,036,825
1911	Ted Koerner	813	162	88,308	1947	Douglas Dodson	646	141	1,429,949
1912	Jimmy Butwell	684	144	79,843	1948	Eddie Arcaro	726	188	1,686,230
1913	Merritt Buxton	887	146	82,552	1949	Steve Brooks	906	209	1,316,817
1914	J. McCahey	824	155	121,845	1950	Eddie Arcaro	888	195	1,410,160
1915	Mack Garner	775	151	96,628	1951	Bill Shoemaker	1161	257	1,329,890
1916	John McTaggart	832	150	155,055	1952	Eddie Arcaro	807	188	1,859,591
1917	Frank Robinson	731	147	148,057	1953	Bill Shoemaker	1683	485	1,784,187
1918	Lucien Luke	756	178	201,864	1954	Bill Shoemaker	1251	380	1,876,760
1919	John Loftus	177	65	252,707	1955	Eddie Arcaro	820	158	1,864,796
1920	Clarence Kummer	353	87	292,376	1956	Bill Hartack	1387	347	2,343,955
1921	Earl Sande	340	112	263,043	1957	Bill Hartack	1238	341	3,060,501
1922	Albert Johnson	297	43	345,054	1958	Bill Shoemaker	1133	300	2,961,693
1923	Earl Sande	430	122	569,394	1959	Bill Shoemaker	1285	347	2,843,133
1924	Ivan Parke	844	205	290,395	1960	Bill Shoemaker	1227	274	2,123,961
1925	Laverne Fator	315	81	305,775	1961	Bill Shoemaker	1256	304	2,690,819
1926	Laverne Fator	511	143	361,435	1962	Bill Shoemaker	1126	311	2,916,844
1927	Earl Sande	179	49	277,877	1963	Bill Shoemaker	1203	271	2,526,925
1928	Linus McAtee	235	55	301,295	1964	Bill Shoemaker	1056	246	2,649,553
1929	Mack Garner	274	57	314,975	1965	Braulio Baeza	1245	270	2,582,702
1930	Sonny Workman	571	152	420,438	1966	Braulio Baeza	1341	298	2,951,022
1931	Charley Kurtsinger	519	93	392,095	1967	Braulio Baeza	1064	256	3,088,888
1932	Sonny Workman	378	87	385,070	1968	Braulio Baeza	1089	201	2,835,108
1933	Robert Jones	471	63	226,285	1969	Jorge Velasquez	1442	258	2,542,315
1934	Wayne Wright	919	174	287,185	1970	Laffit Pincay Jr.	1328	269	2,626,526
1935	Silvio Coucci	749	141	319,760	1971	Laffit Pincay Jr.	1627	380	3,784,377
1936	Wayne Wright	670	100	264,000	1972	Laffit Pincay Jr.	1388	289	3,225,827
1937	Charley Kurtsinger	765	120	384,202	1973	Laffit Pincay Jr.	1444	350	4,093,492
1938	Nick Wall	658	97	385,161	1974	Laffit Pincay Jr.	1278	341	4,251,060
1939	Basil James	904	191	353,333	1975	Braulio Baeza	1190	196	3,674,398
1940	Eddie Arcaro	783	132	343,661	1976	Angel Cordero Jr.	1534	274	4,709,500
1941	Don Meade	1164	210	398,627	1977	Steve Cauthen	2075	487	6,151,750
1942	Eddie Arcaro	687	123	481,949	1978	Darrel McHargue	1762	375	6,188,353
1943	Johnny Longden	871	173	573,276	1979	Laffit Pincay Jr.	1708	420	8,183,535
1944	Ted Atkinson	1539	287	899,101	1980	Chris McCarron	1964	405	7,666,100
1945	Johnny Longden	778	180	981,977	1981	Chris McCarron	1494	326	8,397,604

Year		Mts	Wins	Earnings
1982	Angel Cordero Jr.	1838	397	$9,702,520
1983	Angel Cordero Jr.	1792	362	10,116,807
1984	Chris McCarron	1565	356	12,038,213
1985	Laffit Pincay Jr.	1409	289	13,415,049
1986	Jose Santos	1636	329	11,329,297
1987	Jose Santos	1639	305	12,407,355
1988	Jose Santos	1867	370	14,877,298
1989	Jose Santos	1459	285	13,847,003
1990	Gary Stevens	1504	283	13,881,198
1991	Chris McCarron	1440	265	14,456,073
1992	Kent Desormeaux	1568	361	14,193,006
1993	Mike Smith	1510	343	14,024,815
1994	Mike Smith	1484	317	15,979,820
1995	Jerry Bailey	1367	287	$16,311,876
1996	Jerry Bailey	1187	298	19,465,376
1997	Jerry Bailey	1136	269	18,206,013
1998	Gary Stevens	869	178	19,358,840
1999	Pat Day	1265	254	18,092,845
2000	Pat Day	1219	267	17,479,838
2001	Jerry Bailey	912	227	22,597,720
2002	Jerry Bailey	833	214	22,871,814
2003	Jerry Bailey	776	206	23,354,960
2004	John Velazquez	1327	335	22,248,661
2005	John Velazquez	1148	251	24,459,923
2006	Garrett Gomez	1270	261	20,122,592

Trainers

Annual money-leading trainers since 1908, according to *The American Racing Manual.*

Multiple Leaders: D. Wayne Lukas (14); Sam Hildreth (9); Charlie Whittingham (7); Sunny Jim Fitzsimmons and Jimmy Jones (5); Bob Baffert, Laz Barrera, Ben Jones and Willie Molter (4); Hirsch Jacobs, Eddie Neloy, Todd Pletcher and James Rowe Sr. (3); H. Guy Bedwell, Bobby Frankel, Jack Gaver, John Schorr, Humming Bob Smith, Silent Tom Smith and Mesh Tenney (2).

Year		Wins	Earnings
1908	James Rowe Sr.	50	$284,335
1909	Sam Hildreth	73	123,942
1910	Sam Hildreth	84	148,010
1911	Sam Hildreth	67	49,418
1912	John Schorr	63	58,110
1913	James Rowe Sr.	18	45,936
1914	R.C. Benson	45	59,315
1915	James Rowe Sr.	19	75,596
1916	Sam Hildreth	39	70,950
1917	Sam Hildreth	23	61,698
1918	H. Guy Bedwell	53	80,296
1919	H. Guy Bedwell	63	208,728
1920	Louis Feustel	22	186,087
1921	Sam Hildreth	85	262,768
1922	Sam Hildreth	74	247,014
1923	Sam Hildreth	75	392,124
1924	Sam Hildreth	77	255,608
1925	G.R. Tompkins	30	199,245
1926	Scott Harlan	21	205,681
1927	W.H. Bringloe	63	216,563
1928	John Schorr	65	258,425
1929	James Rowe Jr.	25	314,881
1930	Sunny Jim Fitzsimmons	47	397,355
1931	Big Jim Healy	33	297,300
1932	Sunny Jim Fitzsimmons	68	266,650
1933	Humming Bob Smith	53	135,720
1934	Humming Bob Smith	43	249,938
1935	Bud Stotler	87	303,005
1936	Sunny Jim Fitzsimmons	42	193,415
1937	Robert McGarvey	46	209,925
1938	Earl Sande	15	226,495
1939	Sunny Jim Fitzsimmons	45	266,205
1940	Silent Tom Smith	14	269,200
1941	Ben Jones	70	475,318
1942	Jack Gaver	48	406,547
1943	Ben Jones	73	267,915
1944	Ben Jones	60	601,660
1945	Silent Tom Smith	52	510,655
1946	Hirsch Jacobs	99	560,077
1947	Jimmy Jones	85	1,334,805
1948	Jimmy Jones	81	1,118,670
1949	Jimmy Jones	76	978,587
1950	Preston Burch	96	637,754
1951	Jack Gaver	42	616,392
1952	Ben Jones	29	662,137
1953	Harry Trotsek	54	1,028,873
1954	Willie Molter	136	1,107,860
1955	Sunny Jim Fitzsimmons	66	1,270,055
1956	Willie Molter	142	1,227,402
1957	Jimmy Jones	70	1,150,910
1958	Willie Molter	69	$1,116,544
1959	Willie Molter	71	847,290
1960	Hirsch Jacobs	97	748,349
1961	Jimmy Jones	62	759,856
1962	Mesh Tenney	58	1,099,474

Year		Sts	Wins	Earnings
1963	Mesh Tenney	192	40	$860,703
1964	Bill Winfrey	287	61	1,350,534
1965	Hirsch Jacobs	610	91	1,331,628
1966	Eddie Neloy	282	93	2,456,250
1967	Eddie Neloy	262	72	1,776,089
1968	Eddie Neloy	212	52	1,233,101
1969	Elliott Burch	156	26	1,067,936
1970	Charlie Whittingham	551	82	1,302,354
1971	Charlie Whittingham	393	77	1,737,115
1972	Charlie Whittingham	429	79	1,734,020
1973	Charlie Whittingham	423	85	1,865,385
1974	Pancho Martin	846	166	2,408,419
1975	Charlie Whittingham	487	3	2,437,244
1976	Jack Van Berg	2362	496	2,976,196
1977	Laz Barrera	781	127	2,715,848
1978	Laz Barrera	592	100	3,307,164
1979	Laz Barrera	492	98	3,608,517
1980	Laz Barrera	559	99	2,969,151
1981	Charlie Whittingham	376	74	3,993,302
1982	Charlie Whittingham	410	63	4,587,457
1983	D. Wayne Lukas	595	78	4,267,261
1984	D. Wayne Lukas	805	131	5,835,921
1985	D. Wayne Lukas	1140	218	11,155,188
1986	D. Wayne Lukas	1510	259	12,345,180
1987	D. Wayne Lukas	1735	343	17,502,110
1988	D. Wayne Lukas	1500	318	17,842,358
1989	D. Wayne Lukas	1398	305	16,103,998
1990	D. Wayne Lukas	1396	267	14,508,871
1991	D. Wayne Lukas	1497	289	15,942,223
1992	D. Wayne Lukas	1349	230	9,806,436
1993	Bobby Frankel	345	79	8,933,252
1994	D. Wayne Lukas	693	147	9,247,457
1995	D. Wayne Lukas	837	194	12,834,483
1996	D. Wayne Lukas	1006	192	15,966,344
1997	D. Wayne Lukas	824	169	9,993,569
1998	Bob Baffert	538	139	15,000,870
1999	Bob Baffert	735	169	16,934,607
2000	Bob Baffert	678	146	11,831,605
2001	Bob Baffert	660	138	16,354,996
2002	Bobby Frankel	480	117	17,748,340
2003	Bobby Frankel	413	114	19,143,289
2004	Todd Pletcher	948	240	17,511,923
2005	Todd Pletcher	1039	257	20,867,842
2006	Todd Pletcher	1168	294	26,820,243

All-Time Leaders

The all-time leading horses, trainers and jockeys of North America. Records are courtesy of the *Equibase Company* and include all available earnings from races in foreign countries. Horses must have had at least one start in the United States or Canada. Note that horses, jockeys and trainers who were active in 2007 are in **bold** type.

Records are through Sept. 30, 2007.

Top 20 Horses—Earnings

		Sts	1st	2nd	3rd	Earnings
1	Cigar	33	19	4	5	$9,999,815
2	Skip Away	38	18	10	6	9,616,360
3	Fantastic Light	25	12	5	3	8,486,957
4	**Invasor** (ARG)	12	11	0	0	7,804,070
5	Pleasantly Perfect	18	9	3	2	7,789,880
6	Smarty Jones	9	8	1	0	7,613,155
7	Silver Charm	24	12	7	2	6,944,369
8	Captain Steve	25	9	3	7	6,828,356
9	Alysheba	26	11	8	2	6,679,242
10	John Henry	83	39	15	9	6,591,860

Top 10 Jockeys—Races Won

		Yrs	Wins	Earnings
1	**Russell Baze**	34	9855	$150,216,846
2	Laffit Pincay Jr.	37	9530	237,120,625
3	Bill Shoemaker	42	8833	123,375,524
4	Pat Day	33	8803	297,912,019
5	David Gall	43	7396	24,972,821
6	Chris McCarron	29	7141	263,985,505
7	Angel Cordero Jr.	35	7057	164,570,227
8	Jorge Velasquez	33	6795	125,544,379
9	Sandy Hawley	31	6449	88,681,292
10	**Earlie Fires**	33	6428	85,330,314

Top 10 Jockeys—Earnings

		Yrs	Wins	Earnings
1	Pat Day	33	8803	$297,912,019
2	Jerry Bailey	31	5893	296,104,129
3	Chris McCarron	29	7141	263,985,505
4	Laffit Pincay Jr.	37	9530	237,120,625
5	Gary Stevens	27	4888	221,207,064
6	Alex Solis	27	4518	204,598,947
7	**Edgar Prado**	21	5952	199,566,285
8	**Kent Desormeaux**	22	4848	196,687,143
7	Eddie Delahoussaye	36	6384	195,884,940
8	**John Velazquez**	18	3787	192,019,197

Top 10 Trainers—Races Won

		Wins	Earnings
1	**Dale Baird**	9416	$34,924,445
2	**Jack Van Berg**	6378	81,783,484
3	**King Leatherbury**	6218	56,055,229
4	**Jerry Hollendorfer**	4944	91,374,070
5	**Richard Hazelton**	4687	39,432,931
6	**D. Wayne Lukas**	4450	249,061,700
7	Frank Merrill Jr.	3974	16,980,632
8	**Scott Lake**	3966	70,176,033
9	**Steven Asmussen**	3793	100,411,723
10	**H. Allen Jerkens**	3716	96,641,078

Top 10 Trainers—Earnings

		Wins	Earnings
1	**D. Wayne Lukas**	4450	$249,061,700
2	**Bobby Frankel**	3495	205,862,118
3	**Bill Mott**	3665	159,521,690
4	**Todd Pletcher**	1934	136,892,905
5	**Bob Baffert**	1694	124,742,489
6	**Ron McAnally**	2514	119,279,841
7	Charles Whittingham	2534	109,215,527
8	**Richard Mandella**	1749	107,135,898
9	**Steven Asmussen**	3793	100,411,723
10	**H. Allen Jerkens**	3716	96,641,078

Horse of the Year (1936-70)

In 1971, the *Daily Racing Form*, the Thoroughbred Racing Associations, and the National Turf Writers Assn. joined forces to create the Eclipse Awards. Before then, however, the *Racing Form* (1936-70) and the TRA (1950-70) issued separate selections for Horse of the Year. Their picks differed only four times from 1950-70 and are so noted. Horses listed in CAPITAL letters are Triple Crown winners; (f) indicates female.

Multiple winners: Kelso (5); Challedon, Native Dancer and Whirlaway (2).

Year	Year	Year	Year
1936 Granville	1946 ASSAULT	1955 Nashua	1964 Kelso
1937 WAR ADMIRAL	1947 Armed	1956 Swaps	1965 Roman Brother (DRF)
1938 Seabiscuit	1948 CITATION	1957 Bold Ruler (DRF)	Moccasin (TRA)
1939 Challedon	1949 Capot	Dedicate (TRA)	1966 Buckpasser
1940 Challedon	1950 Hill Prince	1958 Round Table	1967 Damascus
1941 WHIRLAWAY	1951 Counterpoint	1959 Sword Dancer	1968 Dr. Fager
1942 Whirlaway	1952 One Count (DRF)	1960 Kelso	1969 Arts and Letters
1943 COUNT FLEET	Native Dancer (TRA)	1961 Kelso	1970 Fort Marcy (DRF)
1944 Twilight Tear (f)	1953 Tom Fool	1962 Kelso	Personality (TRA)
1945 Busher (f)	1954 Native Dancer	1963 Kelso	

Eclipse Awards

The Eclipse Awards, honoring the Horse of the Year and other champions of the sport, are sponsored by the National Thoroughbred Racing Association (NTRA), *Daily Racing Form* and the National Turf Writers Assn. In 1998, the NTRA replaced the Thoroughbred Racing Associations of North America as co-sponsor.

The awards are named after the 18th century racehorse and sire, Eclipse, who began racing at age five and was unbeaten in 18 starts (eight wins were walkovers). As a stallion, Eclipse sired winners of 344 races, including three Epsom Derby champions.

Horses listed in CAPITAL letters won the Triple Crown that year. Age of horse in parentheses where necessary.

Multiple winners: (horses): Forego (8); John Henry (7); Affirmed, Lonesome Glory and Secretariat (5); Azeri, Cigar, Flatterer, Seattle Slew, Skip Away and Spectacular Bid (4); Ack Ack, McDynamo, Susan's Girl, Tiznow and Zaccio (3); All Along, Alysheba, Ashado, Bayakoa, Black Tie Affair, Cafe Prince, Charismatic, Conquistador Cielo, Desert Vixen, Favorite Trick, Ferdinand, Flawlessly, Flat Top, Ghostzapper, Go for Wand, High Chaparral, Holy Bull, Housebuster, Invasor, Kotashaan, Lady's Secret, Life's Magic, Miesque, Mineshaft, Morley Street, Open Mind, Ouija Board, Paseana, Point Given, Riva Ridge, Saint Liam, Silverbulletday, Slew o' Gold and Spend A Buck (2).

Multiple winners: (people): Jerry Bailey (7); Juddmonte Farms and Laffit Pincay Jr. (6); Bobby Frankel (5); Laz Barrera, Pat Day, John Franks, D. Wayne Lukas, Allen Paulson, Ogden Phipps and Frank Stronach (4); Adena Springs, Bob Baffert, Steve Cauthen, Harbor View Farm, Fred W. Hooper, Nelson Bunker Hunt, Mr. & Mrs. Gene Klein, Dan Lasater, John & Betty Mabee, Paul Mellon, Todd Pletcher, Bill Shoemaker, Edward Taylor and Charlie Whittingham (3); Braulio Baeza, C.T. Chenery, Claiborne Farm, Angel Cordero Jr., Kent Desormeaux, Richard Englander, William S. Farish, John W. Galbreath, Chris McCarron, Bill Mott, Mike Smith and John Velazquez (2).

Horse of the Year

Year		Year		Year		Year	
1971	Ack Ack (5)	1980	Spectacular Bid (4)	1989	Sunday Silence (3)	1998	Skip Away (5)
1972	Secretariat (2)	1981	John Henry (6)	1990	Criminal Type (5)	1999	Charismatic (3)
1973	SECRETARIAT (3)	1982	Conquistador Cielo (3)	1991	Black Tie Affair (5)	2000	Tiznow (3)
1974	Forego (4)	1983	All Along (4)	1992	A.P. Indy (3)	2001	Point Given (3)
1975	Forego (5)	1984	John Henry (9)	1993	Kotashaan (5)	2002	Azeri (4)
1976	Forego (6)	1985	Spend A Buck (3)	1994	Holy Bull (3)	2003	Mineshaft (4)
1977	SEATTLE SLEW (3)	1986	Lady's Secret (4)	1995	Cigar (5)	2004	Ghostzapper (4)
1978	AFFIRMED (3)	1987	Ferdinand (4)	1996	Cigar (6)	2005	Saint Liam (5)
1979	Affirmed (4)	1988	Alysheba (4)	1997	Favorite Trick (2)	2006	Invasor (4)

Older Male

Year		Year		Year		Year	
1971	Ack Ack (5)	1980	Spectacular Bid (4)	1989	Blushing John (4)	1998	Skip Away (5)
1972	Autobiography (4)	1981	John Henry (6)	1990	Criminal Type (5)	1999	Victory Gallop (4)
1973	Riva Ridge (4)	1982	Lemhi Gold (4)	1991	Black Tie Affair (5)	2000	Lemon Drop Kid (4)
1974	Forego (4)	1983	Bates Motel (4)	1992	Pleasant Tap (5)	2001	Tiznow (4)
1975	Forego (5)	1984	Slew o' Gold (4)	1993	Bertrando (4)	2002	Left Bank (5)
1976	Forego (6)	1985	Vanlandingham (4)	1994	The Wicked North (4)	2003	Mineshaft (4)
1977	Forego (7)	1986	Turkoman (4)	1995	Cigar (5)	2004	Ghostzapper (4)
1978	Seattle Slew (4)	1987	Ferdinand (4)	1996	Cigar (6)	2005	Saint Liam (5)
1979	Affirmed (4)	1988	Alysheba (4)	1997	Skip Away (4)	2006	Invasor (4)

Older Female

Year		Year		Year		Year	
1971	Shuvee (5)	1980	Glorious Song (4)	1989	Bayakoa (5)	1998	Escena (5)
1972	Typecast (6)	1981	Relaxing (5)	1990	Bayakoa (6)	1999	Beautiful Pleasure (4)
1973	Susan's Girl (4)	1982	Track Robbery (6)	1991	Queena (5)	2000	Riboletta (5)
1974	Desert Vixen (4)	1983	Amb. of Luck (4)	1992	Paseana (5)	2001	Gourmet Girl (6)
1975	Susan's Girl (6)	1984	Princess Rooney (4)	1993	Paseana (6)	2002	Azeri (4)
1976	Proud Delta (4)	1985	Life's Magic (4)	1994	Sky Beauty (4)	2003	Azeri (5)
1977	Cascapedia (4)	1986	Lady's Secret (4)	1995	Inside Information (4)	2004	Azeri (6)
1978	Late Bloomer (4)	1987	North Sider (5)	1996	Jewel Princess (4)	2005	Ashado (4)
1979	Waya (5)	1988	Personal Ensign (4)	1997	Hidden Lake (4)	2006	Fleet Indian (5)

3-Year-Old Male

Year		Year		Year		Year	
1971	Canonero II	1980	Temperence Hill	1989	Sunday Silence	1998	Real Quiet
1972	Key to the Mint	1981	Pleasant Colony	1990	Unbridled	1999	Charismatic
1973	SECRETARIAT	1982	Conquistador Cielo	1991	Hansel	2000	Tiznow
1974	Little Current	1983	Slew o' Gold	1992	A.P. Indy	2001	Point Given
1975	Wajima	1984	Swale	1993	Prairie Bayou	2002	War Emblem
1976	Bold Forbes	1985	Spend A Buck	1994	Holy Bull	2003	Funny Cide
1977	SEATTLE SLEW	1986	Snow Chief	1995	Thunder Gulch	2004	Smarty Jones
1978	AFFIRMED	1987	Alysheba	1996	Skip Away	2005	Afleet Alex
1979	Spectacular Bid	1988	Risen Star	1997	Silver Charm	2006	Bernardini

Eclipse Awards (Cont.)

3-Year-Old Filly

Year		Year		Year		Year	
1971	Turkish Trousers	1980	Genuine Risk	1989	Open Mind	1998	Banshee Breeze
1972	Susan's Girl	1981	Wayward Lass	1990	Go for Wand	1999	Silverbulletday
1973	Desert Vixen	1982	Christmas Past	1991	Dance Smartly	2000	Surfside
1974	Chris Evert	1983	Heartlight No. One	1992	Saratoga Dew	2001	Xtra Heat
1975	Ruffian	1984	Life's Magic	1993	Hollywood Wildcat	2002	Farda Amiga
1976	Revidere	1985	Mom's Command	1994	Heavenly Prize	2003	Bird Town
1977	Our Mims	1986	Tiffany Lass	1995	Serena's Song	2004	Ashado
1978	Tempest Queen	1987	Sacahuista	1996	Yanks Music	2005	Smuggler
1979	Davona Dale	1988	Winning Colors	1997	Ajina	2006	Wait a While

2-Year-Old Male

Year		Year		Year		Year	
1971	Riva Ridge	1980	Lord Avie	1989	Rhythm	1998	Answer Lively
1972	Secretariat	1981	Deputy Minister	1990	Fly So Free	1999	Anees
1973	Protagonist	1982	Roving Boy	1991	Arazi	2000	Macho Uno
1974	Foolish Pleasure	1983	Devil's Bag	1992	Gilded Time	2001	Johannesburg
1975	Honest Pleasure	1984	Chief's Crown	1993	Dehere	2002	Vindication
1976	Seattle Slew	1985	Tasso	1994	Timber Country	2003	Action This Day
1977	Affirmed	1986	Capote	1995	Maria's Mon	2004	Declan's Moon
1978	Spectacular Bid	1987	Forty Niner	1996	Boston Harbor	2005	Stevie Wonderboy
1979	Rockhill Native	1988	Easy Goer	1997	Favorite Trick	2006	Street Sense

2-Year-Old Filly

Year		Year		Year		Year	
1971	Numbered Account	1980	Heavenly Cause	1990	Meadow Star	2000	Caressing
1972	La Prevoyante	1981	Before Dawn	1991	Pleasant Stage	2001	Tempera
1973	Talking Picture	1982	Landaluce	1992	Eliza	2002	Storm Flag Flying
1974	Ruffian	1983	Althea	1993	Phone Chatter	2003	Halfbridled
1975	Dearly Precious	1984	Outstandingly	1994	Flanders	2004	Sweet Catomine
1976	Sensational	1985	Family Style	1995	Golden Attraction	2005	Folklore
1977	Lakeville Miss	1986	Brave Raj	1996	Storm Song	2006	Dreaming of Anna
1978	(TIE) Candy Eclair & It's in the Air	1987	Epitome	1997	Countess Diana		
		1988	Open Mind	1998	Silverbulletday		
1979	Smart Angle	1989	Go for Wand	1999	Chilukki		

Champion Turf Horse

Year		Year		Year		Year	
1971	Run the Gantlet (3)	1973	SECRETARIAT (3)	1975	Snow Knight (4)	1977	Johnny D (3)
1972	Cougar II (6)	1974	Dahlia (4)	1976	Youth (3)	1978	Mac Diarmida (3)

Champion Male Turf Horse

Year		Year		Year		Year	
1979	Bowl Game (5)	1986	Manila (3)	1993	Kotashaan (5)	2000	Kalanisi (4)
1980	John Henry (5)	1987	Theatrical (5)	1994	Paradise Creek (5)	2001	Fantastic Light (5)
1981	John Henry (6)	1988	Sunshine Forever (3)	1995	Northern Spur (4)	2002	High Chaparral (3)
1982	Perrault (5)	1989	Steinlen (6)	1996	Singspiel (4)	2003	High Chaparral (4)
1983	John Henry (8)	1990	Itsallgreektome (3)	1997	Chief Bearhart (4)	2004	Kitten's Joy (3)
1984	John Henry (9)	1991	Tight Spot (4)	1998	Buck's Boy (5)	2005	Leroidesanimaux (5)
1985	Cozzene (4)	1992	Sky Classic (5)	1999	Daylami (5)	2006	Miesque's Approval (7)

Champion Female Turf Horse

Year		Year		Year		Year	
1979	Trillion (5)	1986	Estrapade (6)	1993	Flawlessly (5)	2000	Perfect Sting (4)
1980	Just A Game II (4)	1987	Miesque (3)	1994	Hatoof (5)	2001	Banks Hill (3)
1981	De La Rose (3)	1988	Miesque (4)	1995	Possibly Perfect (5)	2002	Golden Apples (4)
1982	April Run (4)	1989	Brown Bess (7)	1996	Wandesta (5)	2003	Islington (4)
1983	All Along (4)	1990	Laugh and Be Merry (5)	1997	Ryafan (3)	2004	Ouija Board (3)
1984	Royal Heroine (4)	1991	Miss Alleged (4)	1998	Fiji (4)	2005	Intercontinental (5)
1985	Pebbles (4)	1992	Flawlessly (4)	1999	Soaring Softly (4)	2006	Ouija Board (5)

Sprinter

Year		Year		Year		Year	
1971	Ack Ack (5)	1980	Plugged Nickle (3)	1990	Housebuster (3)	2000	Kona Gold (6)
1972	Chou Croute (4)	1981	Guilty Conscience (5)	1991	Housebuster (4)	2001	Squirtle Squirt (3)
1973	Shecky Greene (3)	1982	Gold Beauty (3)	1992	Rubiano (5)	2002	Orientate (4)
1974	Forego (4)	1983	Chinook Pass (4)	1993	Cardmania (7)	2003	Aldebaran (5)
1975	Gallant Bob (3)	1984	Eillo (4)	1994	Cherokee Run (4)	2004	Speightstown (6)
1976	My Juliet (4)	1985	Precisionist (4)	1995	Not Surprising (4)	2005	Lost in the Fog (3)
1977	What a Summer (4)	1986	Smile (4)	1996	Lit de Justice (6)	2006	Thor's Echo (4)
1978	(TIE) Dr. Patches (4)	1987	Groovy (4)	1997	Smoke Glacken (3)		
	& J.O. Tobin (4)	1988	Gulch (4)	1998	Reraise (3)		
1979	Star de Naskra (4)	1989	Safely Kept (3)	1999	Artax (4)		

Steeplechase or Hurdle Horse

Year		Year		Year		Year	
1971	Shadow Brook (7)	1980	Zaccio (4)	1989	Highland Bud (4)	1998	Flat Top (5)
1972	Soothsayer (5)	1981	Zaccio (5)	1990	Morley Street (6)	1999	Lonesome Glory (11)
1973	Athenian Idol (5)	1982	Zaccio (6)	1991	Morley Street (7)	2000	All Gong (6)
1974	Gran Kan (8)	1983	Flatterer (4)	1992	Lonesome Glory (4)	2001	Pompeyo (8)
1975	Life's Illusion (4)	1984	Flatterer (5)	1993	Lonesome Glory (5)	2002	Flat Top (9)
1976	Straight and True (6)	1985	Flatterer (6)	1994	Warm Spell (6)	2003	McDynamo (6)
1977	Cafe Prince (7)	1986	Flatterer (7)	1995	Lonesome Glory (7)	2004	Hirapour (8)
1978	Cafe Prince (8)	1987	Inlander (6)	1996	Correggio (5)	2005	McDynamo (8)
1979	Martie's Anger (4)	1988	Jimmy Lorenzo (6)	1997	Lonesome Glory (9)	2006	McDynamo (9)

Outstanding Jockey

Year		Year		Year		Year	
1971	Laffit Pincay Jr.	1980	Chris McCarron	1989	Kent Desormeaux	1998	Gary Stevens
1972	Braulio Baeza	1981	Bill Shoemaker	1990	Craig Perret	1999	Jorge Chavez
1973	Laffit Pincay Jr.	1982	Angel Cordero Jr.	1991	Pat Day	2000	Jerry Bailey
1974	Laffit Pincay Jr.	1983	Angel Cordero Jr.	1992	Kent Desormeaux	2001	Jerry Bailey
1975	Braulio Baeza	1984	Pat Day	1993	Mike Smith	2002	Jerry Bailey
1976	Sandy Hawley	1985	Laffit Pincay Jr.	1994	Mike Smith	2003	Jerry Bailey
1977	Steve Cauthen	1986	Pat Day	1995	Jerry Bailey	2004	John Velazquez
1978	Darrel McHargue	1987	Pat Day	1996	Jerry Bailey	2005	John Velazquez
1979	Laffit Pincay Jr.	1988	Jose Santos	1997	Jerry Bailey	2006	Edgar Prado

Outstanding Apprentice Jockey

Year		Year		Year		Year	
1971	Gene St. Leon	1981	Richard Migliore	1991	Mickey Walls	2000	Tyler Baze
1972	Thomas Wallis	1982	Alberto Delgado	1992	Rosemary Homeister	2001	Jeremy Rose
1973	Steve Valdez	1983	Declan Murphy	1993	Juan Umana	2002	Ryan Fogelsonger
1974	Chris McCarron	1984	Wesley Ward	1994	Dale Beckner	2003	Eddie Castro
1975	Jimmy Edwards	1985	Art Madrid Jr.	1995	Ramon B. Perez	2004	Brian Hernandez Jr.
1976	George Martens	1986	Allen Stacy	1996	Neil Poznansky	2005	Emma-Jayne Wilson
1977	Steve Cauthen	1987	Kent Desormeaux	1997	Roberto Rosado	2006	Julien Leparoux
1978	Ron Franklin	1988	Steve Capanas		& Philip Teator		
1979	Cash Asmussen	1989	Michael Luzzi	1998	Shaun Bridgmohan		
1980	Frank Lovato Jr.	1990	Mark Johnston	1999	Ariel Smith		

Outstanding Trainer

Year		Year		Year		Year	
1971	Charlie Whittingham	1980	Bud Delp	1989	Charlie Whittingham	1998	Bob Baffert
1972	Lucien Laurin	1981	Ron McAnally	1990	Carl Nafzger	1999	Bob Baffert
1973	H. Allen Jerkens	1982	Charlie Whittingham	1991	Ron McAnally	2000	Bobby Frankel
1974	Sherill Ward	1983	Woody Stephens	1992	Ron McAnally	2001	Bobby Frankel
1975	Steve DiMauro	1984	Jack Van Berg	1993	Bobby Frankel	2002	Bobby Frankel
1976	Laz Barrera	1985	D. Wayne Lukas	1994	D. Wayne Lukas	2003	Bobby Frankel
1977	Laz Barrera	1986	D. Wayne Lukas	1995	Bill Mott	2004	Todd Pletcher
1978	Laz Barrera	1987	D. Wayne Lukas	1996	Bill Mott	2005	Todd Pletcher
1979	Laz Barrera	1988	Shug McGaughey	1997	Bob Baffert	2006	Todd Pletcher

Outstanding Owner

Year		Year		Year		Year	
1971	Mr. & Mrs. E.E. Fogleson	1980	Mr. & Mrs. B. Firestone	1989	Ogden Phipps	1998	Frank Stronach
1972-73	No award	1981	Dotsam Stable	1990	Frances Genter	1999	Frank Stronach
1974	Dan Lasater	1982	Viola Sommer	1991	Sam-Son Farms	2000	Frank Stronach
1975	Dan Lasater	1983	John Franks	1992	Juddmonte Farms	2001	Richard Englander
1976	Dan Lasater	1984	John Franks	1993	John Franks	2002	Richard Englander
1977	Maxwell Gluck	1985	Mr. & Mrs. Gene Klein	1994	John Franks	2003	Juddmonte Farms
1978	Harbor View Farm	1986	Mr. & Mrs. Gene Klein	1995	Allen Paulson	2004	Ken & Sarah Ramsey
1979	Harbor View Farm	1987	Mr. & Mrs. Gene Klein	1996	Allen Paulson	2005	Michael Gill
		1988	Ogden Phipps	1997	Carolyn Hine	2006	Darley & Lael Stables

Eclipse Awards (Cont.)
Outstanding Breeder

Year		Year		Year		Year	
1971	Paul Mellon	1980	Mrs. Henry Paxson	1989	North Ridge Farm	1998	John & Betty Mabee
1972	C.T. Chenery	1981	Golden Chance Farm	1990	Calumet Farm	1999	William S. Farish
1973	C.T. Chenery	1982	Fred W. Hooper	1991	John & Betty Mabee	2000	Frank Stronach
1974	John W. Galbreath	1983	Edward P. Taylor	1992	William S. Farish	2001	Juddmonte Farms
1975	Fred W. Hooper	1984	Claiborne Farm	1993	Allan Paulson	2002	Juddmonte Farms
1976	Nelson Bunker Hunt	1985	Nelson Bunker Hunt	1994	William T. Young	2003	Juddmonte Farms
1977	Edward P. Taylor	1986	Paul Mellon	1995	Juddmonte Farms	2004	Adena Springs
1978	Harbor View Farm	1987	Nelson Bunker Hunt	1996	Farnsworth Farms	2005	Adena Springs
1979	Claiborne Farm	1988	Ogden Phipps	1997	John & Betty Mabee	2006	Adena Springs

Award of Merit

Year		Year		Year		Year	
1976	Jack J. Dreyfus	1987	J.B. Faulconer	1995	Ted Bassett III	2003	Richard Duchossois
1977	Steve Cauthen	1988	John Forsythe	1996	Allen Paulson	2004	Oaklawn Park &
1978	Dinny Phipps	1989	Michael Sandler	1997	Bob & Beverly Lewis		the Cella family
1979	Jimmy Kilroe	1990	Warner L. Jones	1998	D.G. Van Clief Jr.	2005	Penny Chenery
1980	John D. Shapiro	1991	Fred W. Hooper	2000	Jim McKay	2006	John Nerud
1981	Bill Shoemaker	1992	Joe Hirsch	2001	Pete Pederson		
1984	John Gaines		& Robert P. Strub		& Harry T. Mangurian		
1985	Keene Daingerfield	1993	Paul Mellon	2002	Ogden Phipps		
1986	Herman Cohen	1994	Alfred G. Vanderbilt		& Howard Battle		

Special Award

Year		Year		Year		Year	
1971	Robert J. Kleberg	1987	Anheuser-Busch	1998	Oak Tree Racing	2004	Dale Baird
1974	Charles Hatton	1988	Edward J. DeBartolo Sr.		Association	2005	Cash is King Stable
1976	Bill Shoemaker	1989	Richard Duchossois	1999	Laffit Pincay Jr.	2006	Roy & Gretchen
1980	John T. Landry	1994	Eddie Arcaro	2000	John Hettinger		Jackson
	& Pierre E. Bellocq		& John Longden	2001	Sheikh Mohammed		
1984	C.V. Whitney	1995	Russell Baze		al-Maktoum		
1985	Arlington Park			2002	Keeneland Library		

HARNESS RACING

Triple Crown Winners
PACERS

Ten three-year-olds have won the Cane Pace, Little Brown Jug and Messenger Stakes in the same year since the Pacing Triple Crown was established in 1956. No trainer or driver has won it more than once.

Year		Driver	Trainer	Owner
1959	**Adios Butler**	Clint Hodgins	Paige West	Paige West & Angelo Pellillo
1965	**Bret Hanover**	Frank Ervin	Frank Ervin	Richard Downing
1966	**Romeo Hanover**	Bill Myer & George Sholty*	Jerry Silverman	Lucky Star Stables & Morton Finder
1968	**Rum Customer**	Billy Haughton	Billy Haughton	Kennilworth Farms & L.C. Mancuso
1970	**Most Happy Fella**	Stanley Dancer	Stanley Dancer	Egyptian Acres Stable
1980	**Niatross**	Clint Galbraith	Clint Galbraith	Niagara Acres, Niatross Stables & Clint Galbraith
1983	**Ralph Hanover**	Ron Waples	Stew Firlotte	Waples Stable, Pointsetta Stable, Grant's Direct Stable & P.J. Baugh
1997	**Western Dreamer**	Mike Lachance	Bill Robinson Stable	Matthew, Daniel and Patrick Daly
1999	**Blissful Hall**	Ron Pierce	Benn Wallace	Daniel Plouffe
2003	**No Pan Intended**	David Miller	Ivan Sugg	Bob Glazer

*Myer drove Romeo Hanover in the Cane, Sholty in the other two races.

TROTTERS

Eight three-year-olds have won the Yonkers Trot, Hambletonian and Kentucky Futurity in the same year since the Trotting Triple Crown was established in 1955. Stanley Dancer is the only driver/trainer to win it twice.

Year		Driver/Trainer	Owner
1955	**Scott Frost**	Joe O'Brien	S.A. Camp Farms
1963	**Speedy Scot**	Ralph Baldwin	Castleton Farms
1964	**Ayres**	John Simpson Sr.	Charlotte Sheppard
1968	**Nevele Pride**	Stanley Dancer	Nevele Acres & Lou Resnick
1969	**Lindy's Pride**	Howard Beissinger	Lindy Farms
1972	**Super Bowl**	Stanley Dancer	Rachel Dancer & Rose Hild Breeding Farm
2004	**Windsong's Legacy**	Trond Smedshammer	Fredrick Lindegaard
2007	**Glidemaster**	John Campbell & George Brennan*	Bob Burgess, Karin Olsson-Burgess, Marsha Cohen & Brittany Farms

*Brennan drove Glidemaster in the Yonkers Trot, Campbell in the other two races.

Triple Crown Near Misses
PACERS

Nine horses have won the first two legs of the Triple Crown, but not the third. The Cane Pace (CP), Little Brown Jug (LBJ), and Messenger Stakes (MS) have not always been run in the same order so numbers after races won indicate sequence for that year.

Year		CP	LBJ	MS	Year		CP	LBJ	MS
1957	**Torpid**	won, 1	won, 2	DNF*	1990	**Jake and Elwood**	won, 1	NE	won, 2
1960	**Countess Adios**	won, 2	NE	won, 1	1992	**Western Hanover**	won, 1	2nd*	won, 2
1971	**Albatross**	won, 2	2nd*	won, 1	1993	**Rijadh**	won, 1	2nd*	won, 2
1976	**Keystone Ore**	won, 1	won, 2	2nd*	1998	**Shady Character**	won, 1	won, 2	6th*
1986	**Barberry Spur**	won, 1	won, 2	2nd*					

*Winning horses: Meadow Lands (1957), Nansemond (1971), Windshield Wiper (1976), Amity Chef (1986), Fake Left (1992), Life Sign (1993), Fit for Life (1998).

Note: Torpid (1957) scratched before the final heat; Countess Adios (1960) and Jake and Elwood (1990) not eligible for Little Brown Jug.

TROTTERS

Eight horses have won the first two legs of the Triple Crown— the Yonkers Trot (YT) and the Hambletonian (Ham)—but not the third. The winner of the Kentucky Futurity (KF) is listed.

Year		YT	Ham	KF	Year		YT	Ham	KF
1962	**A.C.'s Viking**	won	won	Safe Mission	1987	**Mack Lobell**	won	won	Napoletano
1976	**Steve Lobell**	won	won	Quick Pay	1993	**American Winner**	won	won	Pine Chip
1977	**Green Speed**	won	won	Texas	1996	**Continentalvictory**	won	won	Running Sea
1978	**Speedy Somolli**	won	won	Doublemint	1998	**Muscles Yankee**	won	won	Trade Balance

Note: Green Speed (1977) was not eligible for the Kentucky Futurity; Continentalvictory (1996) was withdrawn from the Kentucky Futurity due to a leg injury.

The Hambletonian

For three-year-old trotters. Inaugurated in 1926 and has been held in Syracuse, N.Y.; Lexington, Ky.; Goshen, N.Y.; Yonkers, N.Y.; Du Quoin, Ill.; and since 1981 at The Meadowlands in East Rutherford, N.J.

Run at one mile since 1947. Winning horse must win two heats.

Drivers with most wins: John Campbell (6); Stanley Dancer, Billy Haughton, Mike Lachance and Ben White (4); Howard Beissinger, Del Cameron and Henry Thomas (3).

Year	Horse	Driver	Fastest Heat	Year	Horse	Driver	Fastest Heat
1926	**Guy McKinney**	Nat Ray	2:04¾	1960	**Blaze Hanover**	Joe O'Brien	1:59⅗
1927	**Iosola's Worthy**	Marvin Childs	2:03¾	1961	**Harlan Dean**	James Arthur	1:58⅖
1928	**Spencer**	W.H. Lessee	2:02½	1962	**A.C.'s Viking**	Sanders Russell	1:59⅗
1929	**Walter Dear**	Walter Cox	2:02¾	1963	**Speedy Scot**	Ralph Baldwin	1:57⅗
1930	**Hanover's Bertha**	Tom Berry	2:03	1964	**Ayres**	John Simpson Sr.	1:56⅘
1931	**Calumet Butler**	R.D. McMahon	2:03¼	1965	**Egyptian Candor**	Del Cameron	2:03⅘
1932	**The Marchioness**	Will Caton	2:01¼	1966	**Kerry Way**	Frank Ervin	1:58⅘
1933	**Mary Reynolds**	Ben White	2:03¾	1967	**Speedy Streak**	Del Cameron	2:00
1934	**Lord Jim**	Doc Parshall	2:02¾	1968	**Nevele Pride**	Stanley Dancer	1:59⅖
1935	**Greyhound**	Sep Palin	2:02¼	1969	**Lindy's Pride**	Howard Beissinger	1:57⅗
1936	**Rosalind**	Ben White	2:01¾	1970	**Timothy T**	John Simpson Jr.	1:58⅖
1937	**Shirley Hanover**	Henry Thomas	2:01½	1971	**Speedy Crown**	Howard Beissinger	1:57⅖
1938	**McLin Hanover**	Henry Tomas	2:02¼	1972	**Super Bowl**	Stanley Dancer	1:56⅖
1939	**Peter Astra**	Doc Parshall	2:04¼	1973	**Flirth**	Ralph Baldwin	1:57⅕
1940	**Spencer Scott**	Fred Egan	2:02	1974	**Christopher T**	Billy Haughton	1:58⅗
1941	**Bill Gallon**	Lee Smith	2:05	1975	**Bonefish**	Stanley Dancer	1:59
1942	**The Ambassador**	Ben White	2:04	1976	**Steve Lobell**	Billy Haughton	1:56⅖
1943	**Volo Song**	Ben White	2:02½	1977	**Green Speed**	Billy Haughton	1:55⅗
1944	**Yankee Maid**	Henry Thomas	2:04	1978	**Speedy Somolli**	Howard Beissinger	1:55
1945	**Titan Hanover**	Harry Pownall Sr.	2:04	1979	**Legend Hanover**	George Sholty	1:56⅕
1946	**Chestertown**	Thomas Berry	2:02½	1980	**Burgomeister**	Billy Haughton	1:56⅗
1947	**Hoot Mon**	Sep Palin	2:00	1981	**Shiaway St. Pat**	Ray Remmen	2:01⅕
1948	**Demon Hanover**	Harrison Hoyt	2:02	1982	**Speed Bowl**	Tommy Haughton	1:56⅘
1949	**Miss Tilly**	Fred Egan	2:01⅖	1983	**Duenna**	Stanley Dancer	1:57⅖
1950	**Lusty Song**	Del Miller	2:02	1984	**Historic Freight**	Ben Webster	1:56⅖
1951	**Mainliner**	Guy Crippen	2:02⅗	1985	**Prakas**	Bill O'Donnell	1:54⅗
1952	**Sharp Note**	Bion Shively	2:02⅗	1986	**Nuclear Kosmos**	Ulf Thoresen	1:55⅖
1953	**Helicopter**	Harry Harvey	2:01⅗	1987	**Mack Lobell**	John Campbell	1:53⅗
1954	**Newport Dream**	Del Cameron	2:02⅖	1988	**Armbro Goal**	John Campbell	1:54⅗
1955	**Scott Frost**	Joe O'Brien	2:00⅗	1989	**Park Avenue Joe** & **Probe** *	Ron Waples / Bill Fahy	1:54⅗
1956	**The Intruder**	Ned Bower	2:01⅖				
1957	**Hickory Smoke**	John Simpson Sr.	2:00⅕	1990	**Harmonious**	John Campbell	1:54⅕
1958	**Emily's Pride**	Flave Nipe	1:59⅘	1991	**Giant Victory**	Jack Moiseyev	1:54⅘
1959	**Diller Hanover**	Frank Ervin	2:01⅕	1992	**Alf Palema**	Mickey McNichol	1:56⅖
				1993	**American Winner**	Ron Pierce	1:53⅕

*In 1989, Park Avenue Joe and Probe finished in a dead heat in the race-off. They were later declared co-winners, but Park Avenue Joe was awarded 1st place money because his three-race summary (2-1-1) was better than Probe's (1-9-1).

The Hambletonian (Cont.)

Year		Driver	Fastest Heat	Year		Driver	Fastest Heat
1994	**Victory Dream**	Mike Lachance	1:54⅕	2001	**Scarlet Knight**	Stefan Melander	1:53⅘
1995	**Tagliabue**	John Campbell	1:54⅘	2002	**Chip Chip Hooray**	Eric Ledford	1:53⅗
1996	**Continentalvictory**	Mike Lachance	1:52⅘	2003	**Amigo Hall**	Mike Lachance	1:54
1997	**Malabar Man**	Mal Burroughs	1:55	2004	**Windsong's Legacy**	T. Smedshammer	1:54⅕
1998	**Muscles Yankee**	John Campbell	1:52⅖	2005	**Vivid Photo**	Roger Hammer	1:52⅗
1999	**Self Possessed**	Mike Lachance	1:51⅗	2006	**Glidemaster**	John Campbell	1:51⅕
2000	**Yankee Paco**	Trevor Ritchie	1:53⅖	2007	**Donato Hanover**	Ron Pierce	1:53⅖

The Little Brown Jug

Harness racing's most prestigious race for three-year-old pacers. Inaugurated in 1946 and held annually at the Delaware, Ohio County Fairgrounds. Winning horse must win two heats.

Year		Year		Year		Year	
1946	Ensign Hanover	1962	Lehigh Hanover	1978	Happy Escort	1994	Magical Mike
1947	Forbes Chief	1963	Overtrick	1979	Hot Hitter	1995	Nick's Fantasy
1948	Knight Dream	1964	Vicar Hanover	1980	Niatross	1996	Armbro Operative
1949	Good Time	1965	Bret Hanover	1981	Fan Hanover	1997	Western Dreamer
1950	Dudley Hanover	1966	Romeo Hanover	1982	Merger	1998	Shady Character
1951	Tar Heel	1967	Best Of All	1983	Ralph Hanover	1999	Blissful Hall
1952	Meadow Rice	1968	Rum Customer	1984	Colt Fortysix	2000	Astreos
1953	Keystoner	1969	Laverne Hanover	1985	Nihilator	2001	Bettor's Delight
1954	Adios Harry	1970	Most Happy Fella	1986	Barberry Spur	2002	Million Dollar Cam
1955	Quick Chief	1971	Nansemond	1987	Jaguar Spur	2003	No Pan Intended
1956	Noble Adios	1972	Strike Out	1988	B.J. Scoot	2004	Timesarechanging
1957	Torpid	1973	Melvin's Woe	1989	Goalie Jeff	2005	P-Forty-Seven
1958	Shadow Wave	1974	Armbro Omaha	1990	Beach Towel	2006	Mr. Feelgood
1959	Adios Butler	1975	Seatrain	1991	Precious Bunny	2007	Tell All
1960	Bullet Hanover	1976	Keystone Ore	1992	Fake Left		
1961	Henry T. Adios	1977	Governor Skipper	1993	Life Sign		

Annual Awards

Harness Horse of the Year

Selected since 1947 by U.S. Trotting Association and the U.S. Harness Writers Association; age of winning horse is noted; (t) indicates trotter and (p) indicates pacer. **Multiple winners:** Bret Hanover and Nevele Pride (3); Adios Butler, Albatross, Cam Fella, Good Time, Mack Lobell, Moni Maker, Niatross and Scott Frost (2).

Year		Year		Year		Year	
1947	Victory Song (4t)	1962	Su Mac Lad (8t)	1977	Green Speed (3t)	1992	Artsplace (4p)
1948	Rodney (4t)	1963	Speedy Scot (3t)	1978	Abercrombie (3p)	1993	Staying Together (4p)
1949	Good Time (3p)	1964	Bret Hanover (2p)	1979	Niatross (2p)	1994	Cam's Card Shark (3p)
1950	Proximity (8t)	1965	Bret Hanover (3p)	1980	Niatross (3p)	1995	CR Kay Suzie (3t)
1951	Pronto Don (6t)	1966	Bret Hanover (4p)	1981	Fan Hanover (3p)	1996	Continentalvictory (3t)
1952	Good Time (6p)	1967	Nevele Pride (2t)	1982	Cam Fella (3p)	1997	Malabar Man (3t)
1953	Hi Lo's Forbes (5p)	1968	Nevele Pride (3t)	1983	Cam Fella (4p)	1998	Moni Maker (5t)
1954	Stenographer (3t)	1969	Nevele Pride (4t)	1984	Fancy Crown (3t)	1999	Moni Maker (6t)
1955	Scott Frost (3t)	1970	Fresh Yankee (7t)	1985	Nihilator (3p)	2000	Gallo Blue Chip (3p)
1956	Scott Frost (4t)	1971	Albatross (3p)	1986	Forrest Skipper (4p)	2001	Bunny Lake (3p)
1957	Torpid (3p)	1972	Albatross (4p)	1987	Mack Lobell (3t)	2002	Real Desire (4p)
1958	Emily's Pride (3t)	1973	Sir Dalrae (4p)	1988	Mack Lobell (4t)	2003	No Pan Intended (3p)
1959	Bye Bye Byrd (4p)	1974	Delmonica Hanover (5t)	1989	Matt's Scooter (4p)	2004	Rainbow Blue (3p)
1960	Adios Butler (4p)	1975	Savoir (7t)	1990	Beach Towel (3p)	2005	Rocknroll Hanover (3p)
1961	Adios Butler (5p)	1976	Keystone Ore (3p)	1991	Precious Bunny (3p)	2006	Glidemaster (3t)

Driver of the Year

Determined by Universal Driving Rating System (UDR) and presented by the Harness Tracks of America since 1968. Eligible drivers must have at least 1,000 starts for the season. **Multiple winners:** Herve Filion (10); Dave Palone (4); John Campbell, Walter Case Jr. and Mike Lachance (3); Tony Morgan, Bill O'Donnell, Luc Ouellette and Ron Waples (2).

Year		Year		Year		Year	
1968	Stanley Dancer	1979	Ron Waples	1991	Walter Case Jr.	2002	Tony Morgan
1969	Herve Filion	1980	Ron Waples	1992	Walter Case Jr.	2003	Dave Palone
1970	Herve Filion	1981	Herve Filion	1993	Jack Moiseyev	2004	Dave Palone
1971	Herve Filion	1982	Bill O'Donnell	1994	Dave Magee	2005	Cat Manzi
1972	Herve Filion	1983	John Campbell	1995	Luc Ouellette	2006	Jim Morrill Jr.
1973	Herve Filion	1984	Bill O'Donnell	1996	Tony Morgan & Luc Ouellette		
1974	Herve Filion	1985	Mike Lachance	1997	Tony Morgan		
1975	Joe O'Brien	1986	Mike Lachance	1998	Walter Case Jr.		
1976	Herve Filion	1987	Mike Lachance	1999	Dave Palone		
1977	Donald Dancer	1988	John Campbell	2000	Dave Palone		
1978	Carmine Abbatiello & Herve Filion	1989	Herve Filion	2001	Stephane Bouchard		
		1990	John Campbell				

TENNIS

2006 / 2007 YEAR IN REVIEW

Venus Williams can't hide her excitement after winning her fourth Wimbledon singles title.

HISTORY
IN THE MAKING

Federer grabs three more Grand Slam singles titles in 2007, but still can't solve rival Nadal at the French Open.

ROGER FEDERER IS GREAT. THIS MUCH WE KNOW.

But that just doesn't cut it, does it? As sports fans, we need more. We need comparisons. We need rankings. We need historical perspective. We need debates. And we can't help it.

With each passing year, the "Is Roger Federer the greatest tennis player of all time" debate is gaining more and more steam...and with each passing Grand Slam title, it's becoming more and more one-sided.

In 2007, Federer added to his growing legend, and continued to climb up the list of career men's Grand Slam singles titles with his tenth, 11th and 12th. In doing so, he tied Roy Emerson for second on the all-time list and now trails only Pete Sampras' 14 (see page 830 for more).

He carried a winning streak into 2007 that reached 41 matches, the fifth longest streak in history (Guillermo Vilas' streak of 46 is highest), before finally losing to Guillermo Canas at Indian Wells in March. He did his best to downplay the loss —

"It was just a normal loss, like I've had about 100 times on tour," Federer said.

But when Federer loses, it's never normal. Shocking is more like it.

Through October 7, Federer had lost just six matches out of 60 played in 2007 — and strangely enough, that could almost be considered a down year, given his 92-5 mark in 2006 and his astounding 81-4 record in 2005.

He kicked off his 2007 Grand Slam quest in dominant fashion, toying with the rest of the field at the Australian Open, and becoming the first man in 27 years (since Bjorn Borg at the 1980 French Open) to win a major tournament without losing a set — 21 straight victories. He rolled through Tommy Robredo in the quarters, then Andy Roddick in the semis, and then he dispatched the game but overmatched Fernando Gonzalez, 7-6, 6-4, 6-4, in the finals.

 Michael Morrison is Co-Editor of the ESPN Sports Almanac.

Switzerland's **Roger Federer**, left, holds the winning trophy and **Rafael Nadal** the runners-up plate, after Federer won his fifth straight Wimbledon singles title.

The French Open, however, was a different story...and it was the same story as the 2006 French Open as No. 2 ranked Rafael Nadal defeated Federer in four sets for the second straight year.

The only black mark on Federer's otherwise gleaming resume is his inability to take down Nadal on the clay courts of Roland Garros. His confidence was riding high after defeating Nadal in Hamburg two weeks earlier. It was Federer's first victory over Nadal on clay, and it ended the energetic Spaniard's all-time record of 81 straight wins on the surface.

But alas, it was Nadal who etched his name into the history books, becoming only the second man since 1914 to win three straight French Open titles (he also defeated Mariano Puerta in 2005).

The two men squared off again less than a month later in the Wimbledon final, a five-set, back-and-forth epic battle won by Federer, 7-6, 4-6, 7-6, 2-6, 6-2. The victory gave him five Wimbledon titles in a row, and it extended his grass-court win streak to 54 matches.

Two months later, he added his 12th Grand Slam title with a hard fought, albeit straight-set win over rising star Novak Djokovic at the U.S. Open. The win gave him four straight U.S. Open titles, and he became the

AP/Wide World Photos

 She may not recieve the attention of some of her peers, but **Justine Henin** has quietly become the most dominant player on the women's tour. She now has seven major titles.

first man since Bill Tilden in the 1920s to accomplish that feat.

So is he the best ever? As you might expect, opinions vary, but judging from the following quotes, many players, past and present, believe that's exactly where he's headed:

"He's the most physically gifted I've played against." — Andy Roddick.

"What we're seeing right now is unprecedented in men's tennis." — commentator and four-time Grand Slam winner Jim Courier.

"Federer is the best player in history, no other player has ever had such quality." — Rafael Nadal, after beating Federer at the 2006 French Open.

"He's fun to watch. Just his athletic ability, what he's able to do on the run. I think he can and will break every tennis record out there." — Pete Sampras.

"The best way to beat him would be to hit him over the head with a racket. Roger could win the Grand Slam if he keeps playing the way he

Continued on page 814

THE TOP

Stories of the Year in **Tennis**

10 Rising Star.
Up-and-coming 20-year-old Serbian Novak Djokovic stakes his claim as the third-ranked men's tennis player on the ATP Tour with four wins through early October. He advances to the finals of the U.S. Open where he, like many others, loses to Roger Federer.

09 Davis Cup Dreams.
Buoyed by star Andy Roddick and doubles gurus Bob and Mike Bryan, the U.S. Davis Cup squad powers to the finals against Russia in November.

08 Newport News.
All-time greats Pete Sampras and Arantxa Sanchez-Vicario are inducted into the International Tennis Hall of Fame.

07 She's Baaack.
Serena Williams, unseeded and ranked 81st in the world, crushes Maria Sharapova, 6-1, 6-2, in the finals of the Australian Open for her eighth Grand Slam singles title.

06 He's Human.
Roger Federer's streak of 41 consecutive matches won comes to a surprising end with a straight-set loss to Guillermo Canas at Indian Wells.

05 Model Clay Performer.
Rafael Nadal has his record clay court winning streak snapped at 81 matches, then defeats Roger Federer at Roland Garros to win his third straight French Open title.

04 Uh oh.
Match-fixing suspicions arise when irregular betting patterns cause an online gambling site to void bets on a match in August between Nikolay Davydenko and Martin Vassallo.

03 Venus Envy.
Venus Williams becomes the lowest-ranked woman ever to win Wimbledon (No. 31) with a 6-4, 6-1 win over Marion Bartoli. It is her fourth Wimbledon title.

02 Quietly Dominant.
Justine Henin captures two Grand Slam singles finals — the French and U.S. Opens — and is now moving very quietly up the all-time list with seven total.

01 Roger Rules.
Roger Federer adds three more Grand Slam championships to his resume — the Australian Open, Wimbledon and U.S. Open — and now has 12 total, behind only Pete Sampras' 14.

is and, if he does that, it will equate to the two Grand Slams that I won because standards are much higher these days." — Rod Laver

"I'd like to be in his shoes for one day to know what it feels like to play that way," — Mats Wilander, who by the way has seven Grand Slam titles on his resume.

"He's the most gifted player that I've ever seen in my life. I've seen a lot of people play. I've seen the [Rod] Lavers, I played against some of the great players — Sampras, Becker, Connors, Borg. You name it. This guy could be the greatest of all time." — John McEnroe

Federer has now won 12 of the last 18 Grand Slam titles. And the scary thing is...he may be getting better! It's a foregone conclusion that he'll break Sampras' all-time Grand Slam record, quite possibly in 2008. At just 26 years old, he has mentioned that his goal is to play for at least another nine or ten years.

Are 20 majors a possibility? 30? Suffice to say, if that were the case, there would no longer be any hint of a debate.

Clay Master

Roger Federer's 2-6, 6-2, 6-0, victory over Rafael Nadal at the Hamburg Masters in May snapped Nadal's record of 81 straight wins on clay. Listed are the top five clay-court streaks during the ATP's open era (since 1968).

	Dates	Wins
Rafael Nadal	Apr. 05—May 07	81
Guillermo Villas	May 77—Sept. 77	53
Bjorn Borg	Oct. 77—May 79	46
Thomas Muster	Feb. 95—June 95	40
Thomas Muster	Aug. 95—Apr. 96	38
Ilie Nastase	May 73—Oct. 73	38

Mano-y-Mano

While Roger Federer has the obvious edge in all-time Grand Slam titles, No. 2 Rafael Nadal still boasts the better head-to-head mark between the two, thanks mostly to his success vs. Federer on clay. Listed are the results of their head-to-head matchups by court surface (through October 7, 2007).

	Federer	Nadal
Clay wins	1	6
Hardcourt wins	2	2
Grass wins	2	0
Total	5	8

Source: *ATP Tennis Weekly*

2006-2007
Season in Review

ESPN
SPORTS ALMANAC

Tournament Results

Winners of men's and women's pro singles championships from Nov. 5, 2006 through Oct. 7, 2007.

Men's ATP Tour

Late 2006

Finals	Tournament	Winner	Earnings	Runner-Up	Score
Nov. 5	TMS—Paris	Nikolay Davydenko	$480,230	D. Hrbaty	61 62 62
Nov. 19	Tennis Masters Cup (Shanghai)	Roger Federer	700,000	J. Blake	60 63 64
Dec. 3	Davis Cup Final (Moscow)	Russia	—	Argentina	3-2

2007 (through Oct. 7)

Finals	Tournament	Winner	Earnings	Runner-Up	Score
Jan. 6	Qatar ExxonMobil Open (Doha)	Ivan Ljubicic	$142,000	A. Murray	64 64
Jan. 7	Next Generation Hardcourts (Adelaide)	Novak Djokovic	64,800	C. Guccione	63 67 64
Jan. 7	Chennai Open	Xavier Malisse	65,850	S. Koubek	61 63
Jan. 13	Medibank International (Sydney)	James Blake	68,800	C. Moya	63 57 61
Jan. 13	Heineken Open (Auckland)	David Ferrer	65,850	T. Robredo	64 62
Jan. 28	**Australian Open** (Melbourne)	Roger Federer	1,281,000	F. Gonzalez	76 64 64
Feb. 4	PBZ Zagreb Indoors	Marcos Baghdatis	76,250	I. Ljubicic	76 46 64
Feb. 4	Movistar Open (Vina Del Mar)	Luis Horna	67,110	N. Massu	75 63
Feb. 5	Delray Beach Int'l Champs	Xavier Malisse	64,800	J. Blake	57 64 64
Feb. 18	SAP Open (San Jose)	Andy Murray	68,850	I. Karlovic	67 64 76
Feb. 18	Brasil Open (Costa Do Sauipe)	Guillermo Canas	73,000	J. C. Ferrero	76 62
Feb. 18	Open 13 (Marseille)	Gilles Simon	93,800	M. Baghdatis	64 76
Feb. 25	Copa Telmex (Buenos Aires)	Juan Monaco	66,450	A. Di Mauro	61 62
Feb. 25	Regions Morgan Keegan Champs (Memphis)	Tommy Haas	156,550	A. Roddick	63 62
Feb. 25	ABN/AMRO World Tennis Tournament (Rotterdam)	Mikhail Youzhny	193,000	I. Ljubicic	62 64
Mar. 3	Mexican Open (Acapulco)	Juan Ignacio Chela	156,550	C. Moya	63 76
Mar. 3	Dubai Tennis Championships	Roger Federer	300,000	M. Youzhny	64 63
Mar. 4	Tennis Channel Open (Las Vegas)	Lleyton Hewitt	61,850	J. Melzer	64 76
Mar. 18	TMS—Pacific Life Open (Indian Wells)	Rafael Nadal	500,000	N. Djokovic	62 75
Apr. 1	TMS—Sony Ericsson Open (Miami)	Novak Djokovic	533,350	G. Canas	63 62 64
Apr. 15	Valencia Open	Nicolas Almagro	78,600	P. Starace	46 62 61
Apr. 15	U.S. Clay Court Championships (Houston)	Ivo Karlovic	68,850	M. Zabaleta	64 61
Apr. 22	TMS—Monte Carlo Open	Rafael Nadal	460,000	R. Federer	64 64
Apr. 29	Grand Prix Hassan II (Casablanca)	Paul-Henri Mathieu	75,000	A. Montanes	61 61
Apr. 29	Open Seat Godo (Barcelona)	Rafael Nadal	184,000	G. Canas	63 64
May 6	Estoril Open	Novak Djokovic	100,000	R. Gasquet	76 06 61
May 6	BMW Open (Munich)	Phillip Kohlschreiber	75,000	M. Youzhny	26 63 64
May 13	TMS—Internazionali BNL d'Italia (Rome)	Rafael Nadal	480,000	F. Gonzalez	62 62
May 20	TMS—Hamburg	Roger Federer	480,000	R. Nadal	26 62 60
May 26	Hypo Group Tennis Int'l (Portschach)	Juan Monaco	78,600	G. Monfils	76 60
May 26	World Team Championship (Dusseldorf)	Argentina	—	Czech Republic	2-1
June 10	**French Open** (Roland Garros)	Rafael Nadal	1,413,000	R. Federer	63 46 63 64
June 17	Gerry Weber Open (Halle)	Tomas Berdych	135,700	M. Baghdatis	75 64
June 17	Stella Artois Championships (London)	Andy Roddick	107,000	N. Mahut	46 76 76
June 23	Red Letter Days Open (Nottingham)	Ivo Karlovic	78,600	A. Clement	36 64 64
June 23	Ordina Open ('s-Hertogenbosch)	Ivan Ljubicic	78,600	P. Wessels	76 46 76
July 8	**Wimbledon** (London)	Roger Federer	1,429,645	R. Nadal	76 46 76 26 62
July 15	Allianz Swiss Open (Gstaad)	Paul-Henri Mathieu	83,000	A. Seppi	67 64 75
July 15	Hall of Fame Championships (Newport)	Fabrice Santoro	65,850	N. Mahut	64 64
July 15	Catella Swedish Open (Bastad)	David Ferrer	78,600	N. Almagro	61 62
July 22	Dutch Open (Amersfoort)	Steve Darcis	78,600	W. Eschauer	61 76
July 22	Mercedes Cup (Stuttgart)	Rafael Nadal	188,350	S. Wawrinka	64 75
July 22	Countrywide Classic (Los Angeles)	Radek Stepanek	73,000	J. Blake	76 57 62
July 29	Indianapolis Tennis Championships	Dmitry Tursunov	73,000	F. Dancevic	64 75
July 29	Croatia Open (Umag)	Carlos Moya	73,000	A. Pavel	64 62
July 29	Generali Open (Kitzbuhel)	Juan Monaco	156,200	P. Starace	57 63 64

Tournament Results (Cont.)

Finals	Tournament	Winner	Earnings	Runner-Up	Score
Aug. 5	Orange Prokom Open (Sopot)	Tommy Robredo	$83,700	J. Acasuso	75 60
Aug. 5	Legg Mason Classic (Washington D.C.)	Andy Roddick	74,250	J. Isner	64 76
Aug. 12	TMS—Rogers Masters (Toronto)	Novak Djokovic	400,000	R. Federer	76 26 76
Aug. 19	TMS—Western & Southern Financial Group Masters (Cincinnati)	Roger Federer	400,000	J. Blake	61 64
Aug. 25	Pilot Pen (New Haven)	James Blake	84,000	M. Fish	75 64
Sept. 9	**U.S. Open** (Flushing)	Roger Federer	1,400,000	N. Djokovic	76 76 64
Sept. 16	China Open (Beijing)	Fernando Gonzalez	69,200	T. Robredo	61 36 61
Sept. 16	BCR Romanian Open (Bucharest)	Gilles Simon	78,600	V. Hanescu	46 63 62
Sept. 30	Thailand Open (Bangkok)	Dmitry Tursunov	76,500	B. Becker	62 61
Sept. 30	Kingfisher Airlines Open (Mumbai)	Richard Gasquet	65,850	O. Rochus	63 64
Oct. 7	Open de Moselle (Metz)	Tommy Robredo	78,600	A. Murray	06 62 63
Oct. 7	AIG Japan Open (Tokyo)	David Ferrer	145,000	R. Gasquet	61 62

Note: TMS indicates tournament is part of the ATP Tennis Masters Series.

Women's WTA Tour

Late 2006

Finals	Tournament	Winner	Earnings	Runner-Up	Score
Nov. 5	Gaz de France Stars (Hasselt)	Kim Clijsters	$28,000	K. Kanepi	63 36 64
Nov. 5	Bell Challenge (Quebec)	Marion Bartoli	28,000	O. Poutchkova	60 60
Nov. 12	Sony Ericsson Championships (Madrid)	J. Henin-Hardenne	1,000,000	A. Mauresmo	64 63

2007 (through Oct. 7)

Finals	Tournament	Winner	Earnings	Runner-Up	Score
Jan. 6	Mondial Australian Hardcourts (Gold Coast)	Dinara Safina	$25,840	M. Hingis	63 36 75
Jan. 6	ASB Bank Classic (Auckland)	Jelena Jankovic	21,140	V. Zvonareva	76 57 63
Jan. 12	Moorilla International (Hobart)	Anna Chakvetadze	23,700	V. Bardina	63 76
Jan. 12	Medibank International (Sydney)	Kim Clijsters	88,265	J. Jankovic	46 76 64
Jan. 28	**Australian Open** (Melbourne)	Serena Williams	1,281,000	M. Sharapova	61 62
Feb. 4	Toray Pan Pacific Open (Tokyo)	Martina Hingis	182,000	A. Ivanovic	64 62
Feb. 11	Pattaya Open (Pattaya City)	Sybille Bammer	23,700	G. Dulko	75 36 75
Feb. 11	Open Gaz de France (Paris)	Nadia Petrova	88,265	L. Safarova	46 61 64
Feb. 18	Proximus Diamond Games (Antwerp)	Amelie Mauresmo	88,265	K. Clijsters	64 76
Feb. 18	Sony Ericsson International (Bangalore)	Yaroslava Shvedova	25,840	M. Santangelo	64 64
Feb. 24	Dubai Women's Duty Free Open	Justine Henin	231,080	A. Mauresmo	64 75
Feb. 24	Regions Morgan Keegan Championships and Cellular South Cup (Memphis)	Venus Williams	25,840	S. Peer	61 61
Feb. 25	Copa Colsanitas (Bogota)	Roberta Vinci	25,840	T. Garbin	67 64 03 (ret.)
Mar. 3	Qatar Total Open (Doha)	Justine Henin	222,000	S. Kuznetsova	64 62
Mar. 3	Abierto Mexicano de Tenis (Acapulco)	Emilie Loit	25,845	F. Pennetta	76 64
Mar. 18	Pacific Life Open (Indian Wells)	Daniela Hantuchova	306,890	S. Kuznetsova	63 64
Apr. 1	Sony Ericsson Open (Miami)	Serena Williams	492,950	J. Henin	06 75 63
Apr. 8	Bausch & Lomb Championships (Amelia Island)	Tatiana Golovin	88,265	N. Petrova	62 61
Apr. 15	Family Circle Cup (Charleston)	Jelena Jankovic	196,000	D. Safina	62 62
Apr. 29	Budapest Grand Prix	Gisela Dulko	25,840	S. Cirstea	67 62 62
May 6	J&S Cup (Warsaw)	Justine Henin	88,265	A. Bondarenko	61 63
May 6	Estoril Open	Greta Arn	21,140	V. Azarenka	26 61 76
May 13	Qatar Total German Open (Berlin)	Ana Ivanovic	181,980	S. Kuznetsova	36 64 76
May 13	ECM Prague Open	Akiko Morigami	21,140	M. Bartoli	61 63
May 20	Grand Prix De S.A.R. (Fes)	Milagros Sequera	21,140	A. Wozniak	61 63
May 20	Internazionali BNL d'Italia (Rome)	Jelena Jankovic	181,890	S. Kuznetsova	75 61
May 26	Strasbourg International	A. Medina Garrigues	25,865	A. Mauresmo	64 46 64
May 26	Istanbul Cup	Elena Dementieva	28,180	A. Rezai	76 30 (ret.)
June 10	**French Open** (Roland Garros)	Justine Henin	1,340,000	A. Ivanovic	61 62
June 16	Barcelona KIA	M. Shaughnessy	21,140	E. Gallovits	63 62
June 17	DFS Classic (Birmingham)	Jelena Jankovic	21,140	M. Sharapova	46 63 75
June 23	Ordina Open ('s-Hertogenbosch)	Anna Chakvetadze	25,865	J. Jankovic	76 36 63
June 23	International Women's Open (Eastbourne)	Justine Henin	88,265	A. Mauresmo	75 67 76
July 7	**Wimbledon** (London)	Venus Williams	1,429,645	M. Bartoli	64 61
July 22	Western & Southern Open (Cincinnati)	Anna Chakvetadze	25,840	A. Morigami	61 63
July 22	Palermo International	Agnes Szavay	21,140	M. Muller	60 61
July 29	Bank of the West Classic (Stanford)	Anna Chakvetadze	88,265	S. Mirza	63 62
July 29	Gastein Ladies (Bad Gastein)	Francesca Schiavone	25,840	Y. Meusburger	61 64
Aug. 5	Acura Classic (San Diego)	Maria Sharapova	181,980	P. Schnyder	62 36 60

Finals	Tournament	Winner	Earnings	Runner-Up	Score
Aug. 6	Nordea Nordic Light Open (Stockholm) . . .	Agnieska Radwanska	$21,140	V. Dushevina	61 61
Aug. 12	East West Bank Classic (Los Angeles)	Ana Ivanovic	88,265	N. Petrova	75 64
Aug. 19	Rogers Cup (Toronto)	Justine Henin	181,980	J. Jankovic	76 75
Aug. 25	Pilot Pen Tennis (New Haven)	Svetlana Kuznetsova	88,265	A. Szavay	46 60 (ret.)
Aug. 25	Forest Hills Women's Tennis Classic	Gisela Dulko	20,550	V. Razzano	62 62
Sept. 9	**U.S. Open** (Flushing)	Justine Henin	1,400,000	S. Kuznetsova	61 63
Sept. 16	2007 Fed Cup Final (Moscow)	Russia	—	Italy	4-0
Sept. 16	Commonwealth Bank Classic (Bali)	Lindsay Davenport	32,340	D. Hantuchova	64 36 62
Sept. 23	Banka Koper Slovenia Open (Portoroz)	Tatiana Golovin	21,140	K. Srebotnik	26 64 64
Sept. 23	Sunfeast Open (Kolkata)	Maria Kirilenko	25,855	M. Koryttseva	60 62
Sept. 23	China Open (Beijing)	Agnes Szavay	88,265	J. Jankovic	67 75 62
Sept. 30	Fortis Championships (Luxembourg)	Ana Ivanovic	88,265	D, Hantuchova	36 64 64
Sept. 30	Guangzhou International	Virginie Razzano	25,855	T. Obziler	60 63
Sept. 30	Hansol Korea Open (Seoul)	Venus Williams	21,140	M. Kirilenko	63 16 64
Oct. 6	AIG Japan Open (Tokyo)	Virginie Razzano	25,840	V. Williams	46 76 64
Oct. 7	Porsche Grand Prix (Stuttgart)	Justine Henin	92,410	T. Golovin	26 62 61
Oct. 7	Tashkent Open	Pauline Parmentier	21,165	V. Azarenka	75 62

2007 Grand Slam Tournaments
Australian Open

MEN'S SINGLES

FINAL EIGHT—# 1 Roger Federer; #2 Rafael Nadal; #3 Nikolay Davydenko; #6 Andy Roddick; #7 Tommy Robredo; #10 Fernando Gonzalez; #12 Tommy Haas; plus unseeded Mardy Fish.

Quarterfinals

Roddick def. Fish 62 62 62
Haas def. Davydenko 63 26 16 61 75
Federer def. Robredo . . . . .63 76(2) 75
Gonzalez def. Nadal 62 64 63

Semifinals

Federer def. Roddick 64 60 62
Gonzalez def. Haas 61 63 61

Final

Federer def. Gonzalez . . . . .76(2) 64 64

WOMEN'S SINGLES

FINAL EIGHT—#1 Maria Sharapova; #4 Kim Clijsters; #6 Martina Hingis; #10 Nicole Vaidisova; #12 Anna Chakvetadze; #16 Shahar Peer; plus unseeded Lucie Safarova and Serena Williams.

Quarterfinals

Vaidisova def. Safarova 61 64
Sharapova def. Chakvetadze . . . . .76(5) 75
Williams def. Peer 63 62 86
Clijsters def. Hingis 36 64 63

Semifinals

Williams def. Vaidisova . . . . .76(5) 64
Sharapova def. Clijsters 64 62

Final

Williams def. Sharapova 61 62

DOUBLES FINALS

Men—#1 Bob Bryan & Mike Bryan def. #2 Jonas Bjorkman & Max Mirnyi, 7-5, 7-5.

Women—#3 Cara Black & Liezel Huber def. #Chin-Wei Chan & Chia-Jung Chuang, 6-4, 6-7 (4-7), 6-1.

Mixed—Elena Likhovtseva & Daniel Nestor def. Victoria Azarenka & Max Mirnyi, 6-4, 6-4.

French Open

MEN'S SINGLES

FINAL EIGHT—#1 Roger Federer; #2 Rafael Nadal; #4 Nikolay Davydenko; #6 Novak Djokovic; #9 Tommy Robredo; #19 Guillermo Canas; #23 Carlos Moya; plus unseeded Igor Andreev.

Quarterfinals

Federer def. Robredo 75 16 61 62
Nadal def. Moya 64 63 60
Davydenko def. Canas 75 64 64
Djokovic def. Andreev 63 63 63

Semifinals

Federer def. Davydenko . . . . .75 76(5) 76(7)
Nadal def. Djokovic 75 64 62

Final

Nadal def. Federer 63 46 63 64

WOMEN'S SINGLES

FINAL EIGHT—#1 Justine Henin; #2 Maria Sharapova; #3 Svetlana Kuznetsova; #4 Jelena Jankovic; #6 Nicole Vaidisova; #7 Ana Ivanovic; #8 Serena Williams; #9 Anna Chakvetadze.

Quarterfinals

Henin def. Williams 64 63
Sharapova def. Chakvetadze 63 64
Ivanovic def. Kuznetsova 60 36 61
Jankovic def. Vaidisova 63 75

Semifinals

Henin def. Jankovic 62 62
Ivanovic def. Sharapova 62 61

Final

Henin def. Ivanovic 61 62

DOUBLES FINALS

Men—Mark Knowles & Daniel Nestor def. #9 Lukas Diouhy & Pavel Vizner, 2-6, 6-3, 6-4.

Women—Alicia Molik & Mara Santangelo def. #7 Katarina Srebotnik & Ai Sugiyama, 7-6 (7-5), 6-4.

Mixed—#8 Nathalie Dechy & Andy Ram def. #6 Katarina Srebotnik & Nenad Zimonjic, 7-5, 6-3.

2007 Grand Slam Tournaments (Cont.)
Wimbledon

MEN'S SINGLES

FINAL EIGHT—#1 Roger Federer; #2 Rafael Nadal; #3 Andy Roddick; #4 Novak Djokovic; #7 Tomas Berdych; #10 Marcos Baghdatis; #12 Richard Gasquet; #20 Juan Carlos Ferrero.

Quarterfinals

Federer def. Ferrero . . . . .76(2) 36 61 63
Nadal def. Berdych .76(1) 64 62
Gasquet def. Roddick . . . . .46 46 76(2) 76(3) 86
Djokovic def. Baghdatis . . . . . . .76(4) 76(9) 67(3) 46 75

Semifinals

Federer def. Gasquet 75 63 64
Nadal def. Djokovic . . . . .36 61 41 (ret.)

Final

Federer def. Nadal . . . . .76(7) 46 76(3) 26 62

WOMEN'S SINGLES

FINAL EIGHT—#1 Justine Henin; #5 Svetlana Kuznetsova; #6 Ana Ivanovic; #7 Serena Williams; #14 Nicole Vaidisova; #18 Marion Bartoli; #23 Venus Williams; #31 Michaella Krajicek.

Quarterfinals

Henin def. S. Williams 64 36 63
V. Williams def. Kuznetsova 63 64
Ivanovic def. Vaidisova 46 62 75
Bartoli def. Krajicek 36 63 62

Semifinals

V. Williams def. Ivanovic 62 64
Bartoli def. Henin .16 75 61

Final

V. Williams def. Bartoli 64 61

DOUBLES FINALS

Men—#10 Arnaud Clement & Michael Llodra def. #1 Bob Bryan & Mike Bryan, 6-7 (5-7), 6-3, 6-4, 6-4.

Women—#2 Cara Black & Liezel Huber def. Katarina Srebotnik & Ai Sugiyama, 3-6, 6-3, 6-2.

Mixed—Jelena Jankovic & Jamie Murray def. Alicia Molik & Jonas Bjorkman, 6-4, 3-6, 6-1.

U.S. Open

MEN'S SINGLES

FINAL EIGHT—#1 Roger Federer; #3 Novak Djokovic; #4 Nikolay Davydenko; #5 Andy Roddick; #10 Tommy Haas; #15 David Ferrer; #17 Carlos Moya; #20 Juan Ignacio Chela.

Quarterfinals

Federer def. Roddick . . . . .76(5) 76(4) 62
Djokovic def. Moya . . . . .64 76(7) 61
Davydenko def. Haas 63 63 64
Ferrer def. Chela 62 63 75

Semifinals

Federer def. Davydenko 75 61 75
Djokovic def. Ferrer 64 64 63

Final

Federer def. Djokovic . . . . .76(4) 76(2) 64

WOMEN'S SINGLES

FINAL EIGHT—#1 Justine Henin; #3 Jelena Jankovic; #4 Svetlana Kuznetsova; #6 Anna Chakvetadze; #8 Serena Williams; #12 Venus Williams; #18 Shahar Peer; unseeded Agnes Szavay.

Quarterfinals

Henin def. S. Williams . . . . .76(3) 61
V. Williams def. Jankovic . . . . .46 61 76(4)
Kuznetsova def. Szavay 61 64
Chakvetadze def. Peer 64 61

Semifinals

Henin def. V. Williams . . . . .76(2) 64
Kuznetsova def. Chakvetadze 36 61 61

Final

Henin def. Kuznetsova 61 63

DOUBLES FINALS

Men—#10 Simon Aspelin & Julian Knowle def. #9 Lukas Diouhy & Pavel Vizner, 7-5, 6-4.

Women—#7 Nathalie Dechy & Dinara Safina def. #5 Yung-Jan Chan & Chia-Jung Chuang, 6-4, 6-2.

Mixed—Victoria Azarenka & Max Mirnyi def. Meghann Shaughnessy & Leander Paes, 6-4, 7-6 (8-6).

2007 Fed Cup

Originally the Federation Cup and started in 1963 by the International Tennis Federation as the Davis Cup of women's tennis.

Quarterfinals (April 21-22)

Winner	Loser
at United States 5	Belgium 0
at Russia 5	Spain 0
at France 5	Japan 0
at Italy 5	China 0

Semifinals (July 14-15)

Winner	Loser
Russia 3	at United States 2
at Italy 3	France 2

Finals
(in Moscow, Russia, Sept. 15-16)

Russia 4, Italy 0

Singles—Anna Chakvetadze (RUS) def. Francesca Schiavone (ITA) 6-4, 4-6, 6-4; Svetlana Kuznetsova (RUS) def. Mara Santangelo (ITA) 6-1, 6-2; Kuznetsova (RUS) def. Schiavone (ITA) 4-6, 7-6 (7), 7-5; Elena Vesnina (RUS) def. Santangelo (ITA) 6-2, 6-4.

Doubles—Not played.

Singles Leaders

Official Top 20 rankings and money leaders of men's and women's tours for 2006 and unofficial rankings for 2007 (through Oct. 7), as compiled by the ATP Tour (Association of Tennis Professionals) and WTA (Women's Tennis Association). Note that money lists include doubles earnings.

Final 2006 Rankings and Money Won

Listed are events won and times a finalist and semifinalist (Finish, 1-2-SF), match record (W-L), and earnings for the year.

MEN

		Finish 1-2-SF	W-L	Earnings
1	Roger Federer	12-4-0	92-5	$8,343,885
2	Rafael Nadal	5-1-3	59-12	3,746,360
3	Nikolay Davydenko	5-2-3	68-28	2,026,845
4	James Blake	5-3-0	59-25	1,894,295
5	Ivan Ljubicic	3-2-1	61-20	1,713,167
6	Andy Roddick	1-2-3	49-20	2,214,890
7	Tommy Robredo	2-1-3	49-29	1,454,675
8	David Nalbandian	1-0-6	41-16	1,420,040
9	Mario Ancic	2-3-1	55-18	1,276,265
10	Fernando Gonzalez	0-3-5	49-22	1,124,630
11	Tommy Haas	3-0-4	49-21	947,035
12	Marcos Baghdatis	1-1-2	37-20	1,155,495
13	Tomas Berdych	0-2-3	48-24	1,023,135
14	David Ferrer	1-0-1	41-26	886,135
15	Jarkko Nieminen	1-1-3	55-27	894,565
16	Novak Djokovic	2-1-1	40-18	644,940
17	Andy Murray	1-1-2	40-25	677,802
18	Richard Gasquet	3-1-0	34-21	770,310
19	Radek Stepanek	1-1-1	30-15	820,460
20	Lleyton Hewitt	1-2-0	33-15	646,680

WOMEN

		Finish 1-2-SF	W-L	Earnings
1	Justine Henin-Hardenne	6-4-2	57-8	$4,204,810
2	Maria Sharapova	5-2-6	59-10	3,674,501
3	Amelie Mauresmo	4-3-3	50-14	3,281,737
4	Svetlana Kuznetsova	3-2-8	61-20	1,904,502
5	Kim Clijsters	3-2-5	41-12	1,395,542
6	Nadia Petrova	5-2-2	48-19	1,288,045
7	Martina Hingis	2-2-3	53-19	1,103,326
8	Elena Dementieva	2-1-4	45-21	1,158,169
9	Patty Schnyder	0-2-5	47-25	746,293
10	Nicole Vaidisova	1-0-6	35-17	699,458
11	Dinara Safina	0-2-2	44-21	672,467
12	Jelena Jankovic	0-1-4	45-28	640,576
13	Anna Chakvetadze	2-0-2	37-20	581,693
14	Ana Ivanovic	1-0-0	36-18	585,778
15	Francesca Schiavone	0-3-0	35-23	476,006
16	Anastasia Myskina	0-3-1	31-18	544,201
17	Marion Bartoli	3-1-1	45-28	365,785
18	Daniela Hantuchova	0-1-1	35-25	500,572
19	Anna-Lena Groenefeld	1-0-2	30-26	446,838
20	Shahar Peer	3-0-1	38-20	386,549

2007 Tour Rankings (through Oct. 7)

Listed are tournaments won and times a finalist and semifinalist (Finish, 1-2-SF), match record (W-L), and points earned (Pts). The **Indesit ATP Race** replaced the men's pro tennis tour's 27-year-old computer ranking system in 2000. Under the new system players start from zero on Jan. 1 and accumulate points during the calendar year with the player accumulating the most points becoming the World No. 1. Points are awarded in 18 tournaments: nine Tennis Masters Series events, four Grand Slams and five other International Series events. The Tennis Master Cup will count as a 19th tournament for those that qualify.

MEN

Final ATP Tour singles rankings will be based on points earned from 18 tournaments played in 2007. Tournaments, titles and match won-lost records are for 2007 only.

Rank 07	(06)		Finish 1-2-SF	W-L	Pts
1	1	Roger Federer	6-3-0	54-6	1171
2	2	Rafael Nadal	6-2-2	62-11	1012
3	16	Novak Djokovic	4-2-3	60-14	802
4	3	Nikolay Davydenko	0-0-6	45-27	485
5	6	Andy Roddick	2-1-4	51-13	466
6	14	David Ferrer	3-0-2	55-19	424
7	10	Fernando Gonzalez	1-2-0	30-18	331
8	7	Tommy Robredo	2-2-1	47-23	327
9	4	James Blake	2-3-1	47-20	321
10	18	Richard Gasquet	1-2-2	44-19	320
11	13	Tomas Berdych	1-0-4	43-21	317
12	11	Tommy Haas	1-0-2	35-14	316
13	43	Carlos Moya	1-2-3	42-20	315
14	5	Ivan Ljubicic	2-2-2	40-19	314
15	24	Mikhail Youzhny	1-2-2	43-19	281
16	—	Guillermo Canas	1-2-2	36-17	280
17	32	Juan Ignacio Chela	1-0-2	38-21	279
18	20	Lleyton Hewitt	1-0-3	35-16	273
19	17	Andy Murray	1-2-3	33-11	261
20	12	Marcos Baghdatis	1-2-1	40-18	258

WOMEN

WTA Tour singles ranking system based on total Round and Quality Points for each tournament played during the last 12 months (capped at 17 tournaments). Tournaments, titles and match won-lost records, however, are for 2007 only.

Rank 07	(06)		Finish 1-2-SF	W-L	Pts
1	1	Justine Henin	8-1-3	54-4	5500
2	4	Svetlana Kuznetsova	1-5-3	52-15	3650
3	12	Jelena Jankovic	4-4-7	72-20	3475
4	2	Maria Sharapova	1-2-4	36-9	3235
5	14	Ana Ivanovic	3-2-2	49-15	3175
6	13	Anna Chakvetadze	4-0-4	56-16	2890
7	95	Serena Williams	2-0-0	32-7	2466
8	48	Venus Williams	3-1-2	47-9	2405
9	18	Daniela Hantuchova	1-2-5	46-25	2177
10	6	Nadia Petrova	1-2-1	38-19	2121
11	3	Amelie Mauresmo	1-3-1	27-13	1995
12	17	Marion Bartoli	0-2-4	41-27	1991
13	10	Nicole Vaidisova	0-0-2	29-10	1735
14	8	Elena Dementieva	1-0-3	36-17	1727
15	9	Patty Schnyder	0-1-1	39-22	1694
16	20	Shahar Peer	0-1-2	44-20	1689
17	11	Dinara Safina	1-1-1	39-19	1665
18	22	Tatiana Golovin	2-1-2	42-16	1624
19	7	Martina Hingis	1-1-0	24-13	1577
20	—	Agnes Szavay	2-1-1	51-14	1363

2007 Money Winners

Amounts include singles and doubles earnings through Oct. 7, 2007.

MEN

	Earnings			Earnings			Earnings
1 Roger Federer	$7,063,620	11 Tommy Haas	$896,300	21 Lleyton Hewitt	$662,075
2 Rafael Nadal	4,344,435	12 Ivan Ljubicic	893,045	22 Andy Murray	646,155
3 Novak Djokovic	3,057,150	13 Mikhail Youzhny	889,625	23 Arnaud Clement	631,640
4 Nikolay Davydenko	1,417,775	14 Juan Ignacio Chela	871,515	24 Juan Monaco	623,695
5 Andy Roddick	1,224,120	15 James Blake	853,985	25 Fabrice Santoro	623,550
6 David Ferrer	1,178,452	16 Carlos Moya	832,265	26 Juan Carlos Ferrero	614,585
7 Fernando Gonzalez	1,106,430	17 Guillermo Canas	812,915	27 Jonas Bjorkman	584,690
8 Tomas Berdych	1,055,320	18 Mike Bryan	737,185	28 Radek Stepanek	579,815
9 Richard Gasquet	957,290	19 Bob Bryan	733,360	29 Nicolas Almagro	562,480
10 Tommy Robredo	906,197	20 Marcos Baghdatis	712,755	30 Michael Llodra	560,050

WOMEN

	Earnings			Earnings			Earnings
1 Justine Henin	$4,185,086	11 Dinara Safina	$793,372	21 Ai Sugiyama	$594,122
2 Serena Williams	1,960,721	12 Nicole Vaidisova	768,503	22 Samantha Stosur	563,712
3 Svetlana Kuznetsova	1,881,812	13 Shahar Peer	768,070	23 Amelie Mauresmo	556,854
4 Venus Williams	1,835,097	14 Mara Santangelo	669,662	24 Alicia Molik	537,547
5 Jelena Jankovic	1,669,032	15 Nadia Petrova	655,962	25 Agnes Szavay	527,866
6 Ana Ivanovic	1,645,224	16 Katarina Srebotnik	655,452	26 Elena Dementieva	504,371
7 Maria Sharapova	1,243,420	17 Liezel Huber	644,084	27 Nathalie Dechy	494,419
8 Anna Chakvetadze	1,116,371	18 Patty Schnyder	633,607	28 Sybille Bammer	477,490
9 Marion Bartoli	1,068,195	19 Martina Hingis	625,295	29 Tatiana Golovin	473,570
10 Daniela Hantuchova	930,452	20 Cara Black	621,892	30 Lucie Safarova	439,325

Davis Cup

2006 FINAL

Russia 3, Argentina 2

at Moscow, Russia (Dec. 1-3)

Day One—Nikolay Davydenko (RUS) def. Juan Ignacio Chela (ARG) 6-1, 6-2, 5-7, 6-4; David Nalbandian (ARG) def. Marat Safin (RUS) 6-4, 6-4, 6-4.

Day Two—Safin & Dmitry Tursunov (RUS) def. Agustin Calleri & Nalbandian (ARG) 6-2, 6-3, 6-4.

Day Three—Nalbandian (ARG) def. Davydenko (RUS) 6-2, 6-2, 4-6, 6-4; Safin (RUS) def. Jose Acasuso (ARG) 6-3, 3-6, 6-3, 7-6(5).

2007

FIRST ROUND
(February 9-11)

Winner	Loser
Russia 3	at Chile 2
at France 4	Romania 1
at Germany 3	Croatia 2
at Belgium 3	Australia 2
United States 4	at Czech Republic 1
Spain 3	at Switzerland 2
Sweden 3	at Belarus 2
Argentina 4	at Austria 1

QUARTERFINALS
(April 6-8)

Winner	Loser
at Russia 3	France 2
Germany 3	at Belgium 2
at United States 4	Spain 1
at Sweden 4	Argentina 1

SEMIFINALS

Russia 3, Germany 2

at Moscow, Russia (Sept. 21-23)

Day One—Igor Andreev (RUS) def. Tommy Haas (GER) 6-2, 6-2, 6-2; Philipp Kohlschreiber (GER) def. Nikolay Davydenko (RUS) 6-7(5), 6-2, 6-2, 4-6, 7-5.

Day Two—Philipp Petzschner & Alexander Waske (GER) def. Dmitry Tursunov & Mikhail Youzhny (RUS) 6-3, 3-6, 7-6(4), 7-6(5).

Day Three—Youzhny (RUS) def. Petzschner (GER) 6-4, 6-4, 3-6, 6-3; Andreev (RUS) def. Kohlschreiber (GER) 6-3, 3-6, 6-0, 6-3.

United States 4, Sweden 1

at Goteborg, Sweden (Sept. 21-23)

Day One—Andy Roddick (USA) def. Joachim Johansson (SWE) 7-6(4), 7-6(3), 6-3; Thomas Johansson (SWE) def. James Blake (USA) 6-4, 6-2, 3-6, 6-3.

Day Two—Bob Bryan & Mike Bryan (USA) def. Simon Aspelin & Jonas Bjorkman (SWE) 7-6(11), 6-2, 6-3.

Day Three—Roddick (USA) def. Bjorkman (SWE) 6-2, 7-6(3), 6-4; Blake (USA) def. Aspelin (SWE) 6-1, 6-3.

2007 FINAL

United States vs. Russia: scheduled for Nov. 30 - Dec. 2 at the Memorial Coliseum in Portland, Oregon.

1877-2007
Through the Years

SPORTS ALMANAC

Grand Slam Championships
Australian Open
MEN

Became an Open Championship in 1969. Two tournaments were held in 1977; the first in January, the second in December. Tournament moved back to January in 1987, so no championship was decided in 1986. **Surface:** Synpave Rebound Ace (hardcourt surface composed of polyurethane and synthetic rubber).

Multiple winners: Roy Emerson (6); Andre Agassi, Jack Crawford and Ken Rosewall (4); James Anderson, Roger Federer, Rod Laver, Adrian Quist, Mats Wilander and Pat Wood (3); Boris Becker, Jack Bromwich, Ashley Cooper, Jim Courier, Stefan Edberg, Rodney Heath, Johan Kriek, Ivan Lendl, John Newcombe, Pete Sampras, Frank Sedgman, Guillermo Vilas and Tony Wilding (2).

Year	Winner	Loser	Score	Year	Winner	Loser	Score
1905	Rodney Heath	A. Curtis	46 63 64 64	1960	Rod Laver	N. Fraser	57 36 63 86 86
1906	Tony Wilding	H. Parker	60 64 64	1961	Roy Emerson	R. Laver	16 63 75 64
1907	Horace Rice	H. Parker	63 64 64	1962	Rod Laver	R. Emerson	86 06 64 64
1908	Fred Alexander	A. Dunlop	36 36 60 62 63	1963	Roy Emerson	K. Fletcher	63 63 61
1909	Tony Wilding	E. Parker	61 75 62	1964	Roy Emerson	F. Stolle	63 64 62
1910	Rodney Heath	H. Rice	64 63 62	1965	Roy Emerson	F. Stolle	79 26 64 75 61
1911	Norman Brookes	H. Rice	61 62 63	1966	Roy Emerson	A. Ashe	64 68 62 63
1912	J. Cecil Parke	A. Beamish	36 63 16 61 75	1967	Roy Emerson	A. Ashe	64 61 61
1913	Ernie Parker	H. Parker	26 61 62 63	1968	Bill Bowrey	J. Gisbert	75 26 97 64
1914	Pat Wood	G. Patterson	64 63 57 61	1969	Rod Laver	A. Gimeno	63 64 75
1915	Gordon Lowe	H. Rice	46 61 61 64	1970	Arthur Ashe	D. Crealy	64 97 62
1916-18	Not held World War I			1971	Ken Rosewall	A. Ashe	61 75 63
1919	A.R.F. Kingscote	E. Pockley	64 60 63	1972	Ken Rosewall	M. Anderson	76 63 75
1920	Pat Wood	R. Thomas	63 46 68 61 63	1973	John Newcombe	O. Parun	63 67 75 61
1921	Rhys Gemmell	A. Hedeman	75 61 64	1974	Jimmy Connors	P. Dent	76 64 46 63
1922	James Anderson	G. Patterson	60 36 36 63 62	1975	John Newcombe	J. Connors	75 36 64 75
1923	Pat Wood	C.B. St. John	61 61 63	1976	Mark Edmondson	J. Newcombe	67 63 76 61
1924	James Anderson	R. Schlesinger	63 64 36 57 63	1977	Roscoe Tanner	G. Vilas	63 63 63
1925	James Anderson	G. Patterson	11-9 26 62 63		Vitas Gerulaitis	J. Lloyd	63 76 57 36 62
1926	John Hawkes	J. Willard	61 63 61	1978	Guillermo Vilas	J. Marks	64 64 36 63
1927	Gerald Patterson	J. Hawkes	36 64 36 18-16 63	1979	Guillermo Vilas	J. Sadri	76 63 62
1928	Jean Borotra	R.O. Cummings	64 61 46 57 63	1980	Brian Teacher	K. Warwick	75 76 63
1929	John Gregory	R. Schlesinger	62 62 57 75	1981	Johan Kriek	S. Denton	62 76 67 64
1930	Gar Moon	H. Hopman	63 61 63	1982	Johan Kriek	S. Denton	63 63 62
1931	Jack Crawford	H. Hopman	64 62 26 61	1983	Mats Wilander	I. Lendl	61 64 64
1932	Jack Crawford	H. Hopman	46 63 36 63 61	1984	Mats Wilander	K. Curren	67 64 76 62
1933	Jack Crawford	K. Gledhill	26 75 63 62	1985	Stefan Edberg	M. Wilander	64 63 63
1934	Fred Perry	J. Crawford	63 75 61	1986	Not held		
1935	Jack Crawford	F. Perry	26 64 64 64	1987	Stefan Edberg	P. Cash	63 64 36 57 63
1936	Adrian Quist	J. Crawford	62 63 46 36 97	1988	Mats Wilander	P. Cash	63 67 36 61 86
1937	Viv McGrath	J. Bromwich	63 16 60 26 61	1989	Ivan Lendl	M. Mecir	62 62 62
1938	Don Budge	J. Bromwich	64 62 61	1990	Ivan Lendl	S. Edberg	46 76 52 (ret.)
1939	Jack Bromwich	A. Quist	64 61 63	1991	Boris Becker	I. Lendl	16 64 64 64
1940	Adrian Quist	J. Crawford	63 61 62	1992	Jim Courier	S. Edberg	63 36 64 62
1941-45	Not held World War II			1993	Jim Courier	S. Edberg	62 61 26 75
1946	Jack Bromwich	D. Pails	57 63 75 36 62	1994	Pete Sampras	T. Martin	76 64 64
1947	Dinny Pails	J. Bromwich	46 64 36 75 86	1995	Andre Agassi	P. Sampras	46 61 76 64
1948	Adrian Quist	J. Bromwich	64 36 63 26 63	1996	Boris Becker	M. Chang	62 64 26 62
1949	Frank Sedgman	J. Bromwich	63 63 62	1997	Pete Sampras	C. Moya	62 63 63
1950	Frank Sedgman	K. McGregor	63 64 46 61	1998	Petr Korda	M. Rios	62 62 62
1951	Dick Savitt	K. McGregor	63 26 63 61	1999	Yevgeny Kafelnikov	T. Enqvist	46 60 63 76
1952	Ken McGregor	F. Sedgman	75 12-10 26 62	2000	Andre Agassi	Y. Kafelnikov	36 63 62 64
1953	Ken Rosewall	M. Rose	60 63 64	2001	Andre Agassi	A. Clement	64 62 62
1954	Mervyn Rose	R. Hartwig	62 06 64 62	2002	Thomas Johansson	M. Safin	36 64 64 76
1955	Ken Rosewall	L. Hoad	97 64 64	2003	Andre Agassi	R. Schuettler	62 62 61
1956	Lew Hoad	K. Rosewall	64 36 64 75	2004	Roger Federer	M. Safin	76 64 62
1957	Ashley Cooper	N. Fraser	63 9-11 64 62	2005	Marat Safin	L. Hewitt	16 63 64 64
1958	Ashley Cooper	M. Anderson	75 63 64	2006	Roger Federer	M. Baghdatis	57 75 60 62
1959	Alex Olmedo	N. Fraser	61 62 36 63	2007	Roger Federer	F. Gonzalez	76 64 64

WOMEN

Became an Open Championship in 1969. Two tournaments were held in 1977, the first in January, the second in December. Tournament moved back to January in 1987, so no championship was decided in 1986.

Multiple winners: Margaret Smith Court (11); Nancye Wynne Bolton (6); Daphne Akhurst (5); Evonne Goolagong Cawley, Steffi Graf and Monica Seles (4); Joan Hartigan, Martina Hingis, Martina Navratilova and Serena Williams (3); Coral Buttsworth, Jennifer Capriati, Chris Evert Lloyd, Thelma Long, Hana Mandlikova, Mall Molesworth and Mary Carter Reitano (2).

Year	Winner	Loser	Score	Year	Winner	Loser	Score
1922	Mall Molesworth	E. Boyd	63 10-8	1968	Billie Jean King	M. Smith	61 62
1923	Mall Molesworth	E. Boyd	61 75	1969	Margaret Court	B.J. King	64 61
1924	Sylvia Lance	E. Boyd	63 36 64	1970	Margaret Court	K. Melville	61 63
1925	Daphne Akhurst	E. Boyd	16 86 64	1971	Margaret Court	E. Goolagong	26 76 75
1926	Daphne Akhurst	E. Boyd	61 63	1972	Virginia Wade	E. Goolagong	64 64
1927	Esna Boyd	S. Harper	57 61 62	1973	Margaret Court	E. Goolagong	64 75
1928	Daphne Akhurst	E. Boyd	75 62	1974	Evonne Goolagong	C. Evert	76 46 60
1929	Daphne Akhurst	L. Bickerton	61 57 62	1975	Evonne Goolagong	M. Navratilova	63 62
1930	Daphne Akhurst	S. Harper	10-8 26 75	1976	Evonne Cawley	R. Tomanova	62 62
1931	Coral Buttsworth	M. Crawford	16 63 64	1977	Kerry Reid	D. Balestrat	75 62
1932	Coral Buttsworth	K. Le Messurier	97 64		Evonne Cawley	H. Gourlay	63 60
1933	Joan Hartigan	C. Buttsworth	64 63	1978	Chris O'Neil	B. Nagelsen	63 76
1934	Joan Hartigan	M. Molesworth	61 64	1979	Barbara Jordan	S. Walsh	63 63
1935	Dorothy Round	N. Lyle	16 61 64	1980	Hana Mandlikova	W. Turnbull	60 75
1936	Joan Hartigan	N. Wynne	64 64	1981	Martina Navratilova	C. Evert Lloyd	67 64 75
1937	Nancye Wynne	E. Westacott	63 57 64	1982	Chris Evert Lloyd	M. Navratilova	63 26 63
1938	Dorothy Bundy	D. Stevenson	63 62	1983	Martina Navratilova	K. Jordan	62 76
1939	Emily Westacott	N. Hopman	61 62	1984	Chris Evert Lloyd	H. Sukova	67 61 63
1940	Nancye Wynne	T. Coyne	57 64 60	1985	Martina Navratilova	C. Evert Lloyd	62 46 62
1941-45	Not held World War II			1986	Not held		
1946	Nancye Bolton	J. Fitch	64 64	1987	Hana Mandlikova	M. Navratilova	75 76
1947	Nancye Bolton	N. Hopman	63 62	1988	Steffi Graf	C. Evert	61 76
1948	Nancye Bolton	M. Toomey	63 61	1989	Steffi Graf	H. Sukova	64 64
1949	Doris Hart	N. Bolton	63 64	1990	Steffi Graf	M.J. Fernandez	64 64
1950	Louise Brough	D. Hart	64 36 64	1991	Monica Seles	J. Novotna	57 63 61
1951	Nancye Bolton	T. Long	61 75	1992	Monica Seles	M.J. Fernandez	62 63
1952	Thelma Long	H. Angwin	62 63	1993	Monica Seles	S. Graf	46 63 62
1953	Maureen Connolly	J. Sampson	63 62	1994	Steffi Graf	A.S. Vicario	60 62
1954	Thelma Long	J. Staley	63 64	1995	Mary Pierce	A.S. Vicario	63 62
1955	Beryl Penrose	T. Long	64 63	1996	Monica Seles	A. Huber	64 61
1956	Mary Carter	T. Long	36 62 97	1997	Martina Hingis	M. Pierce	62 62
1957	Shirley Fry	A. Gibson	63 64	1998	Martina Hingis	C. Martinez	63 63
1958	Angela Mortimer	L. Coghlan	63 64	1999	Martina Hingis	A. Mauresmo	62 63
1959	Mary Reitano	R. Schuurman	62 63	2000	Lindsay Davenport	M. Hingis	61 75
1960	Margaret Smith	J. Lehane	75 62	2001	Jennifer Capriati	M. Hingis	64 63
1961	Margaret Smith	J. Lehane	61 64	2002	Jennifer Capriati	M. Hingis	46 76 62
1962	Margaret Smith	J. Lehane	60 62	2003	Serena Williams	V. Williams	76 36 62
1963	Margaret Smith	J. Lehane	62 62	2004	J. Henin-Hardenne	K. Clijsters	63 46 63
1964	Margaret Smith	L. Turner	62 63	2005	Serena Williams	L. Davenport	26 63 60
1965	Margaret Smith	M. Bueno	57 64 52 (ret)	2006	Amelie Mauresmo	J. Henin-Hardenne	61 20 (ret)
1966	Margaret Smith	N. Richey	walkover	2007	Serena Williams	M. Sharapova	61 62
1967	Nancy Richey	L. Turner	61 64				

French Open
MEN

From 1891 to 1925, entry was restricted to members of French clubs. Became an Open Championship in 1968, but closed to contract pros in 1972. Note that Max Decugis won eight tournaments before 1925 (1903-04, 1907-09, 1912-14) to lead all men. **Surface:** Red clay.

Multiple winners (since 1925): Bjorn Borg (6); Henri Cochet (4); Gustavo Kuerten, Rene Lacoste, Ivan Lendl, Rafael Nadal and Mats Wilander (3); Sergi Bruguera, Jim Courier, Jaroslav Drobny, Roy Emerson, Jan Kodes, Rod Laver, Frank Parker, Nicola Pietrangeli, Ken Rosewall, Manuel Santana, Tony Trabert and Gottfried von Cramm (2).

Year	Winner	Loser	Score	Year	Winner	Loser	Score
1925	Rene Lacoste	J. Borotra	75 61 64	1939	Don McNeill	B. Riggs	75 60 63
1926	Henri Cochet	R. Lacoste	62 64 63	1940-45	Not held World War II		
1927	Rene Lacoste	B. Tilden	64 46 57 63 11-9	1946	Marcel Bernard	J. Drobny	36 26 61 64 63
1928	Henri Cochet	R. Lacoste	57 63 61 63	1947	Joseph Asboth	E. Sturgess	86 75 64
1929	Rene Lacoste	J. Borotra	63 26 60 26 86	1948	Frank Parker	J. Drobny	64 75 57 86
1930	Henri Cochet	B. Tilden	36 86 63 61	1949	Frank Parker	B. Patty	63 16 61 64
1931	Jean Borotra	C. Boussus	26 64 75 64	1950	Budge Patty	J. Drobny	61 62 36 57 75
1932	Henri Cochet	G. de Stefani	60 64 46 63	1951	Jaroslav Drobny	E. Sturgess	63 63 63
1933	Jack Crawford	H. Cochet	86 61 63	1952	Jaroslav Drobny	F. Sedgman	62 60 36 64
1934	Gottfried von Cramm	J. Crawford	64 79 36 75 63	1953	Ken Rosewall	V. Seixas	63 64 16 62
1935	Fred Perry	G. von Cramm	63 36 61 63	1954	Tony Trabert	A. Larsen	64 75 61
1936	Gottfried von Cramm	F. Perry	60 26 62 26 60	1955	Tony Trabert	S. Davidson	26 61 64 62
1937	Henner Henkel	H. Austin	61 64 63	1956	Lew Hoad	S. Davidson	64 86 63
1938	Don Budge	R. Menzel	63 62 64	1957	Sven Davidson	H. Flam	63 64 64

Year	Winner	Loser	Score	Year	Winner	Loser	Score
1958	Mervyn Rose	L. Ayala	63 64 64	1983	Yannick Noah	M. Wilander	62 75 76
1959	Nicola Pietrangeli	I. Vermaak	36 63 64 61	1984	Ivan Lendl	J. McEnroe	36 26 64 75 75
1960	Nicola Pietrangeli	L. Ayala	36 63 64 46 63	1985	Mats Wilander	I. Lendl	36 64 62 62
1961	Manuel Santana	N. Pietrangeli	46 61 36 60 62	1986	Ivan Lendl	M. Pernfors	63 62 64
1962	Rod Laver	R. Emerson	36 26 63 97 62	1987	Ivan Lendl	M. Wilander	75 62 36 76
1963	Roy Emerson	P. Darmon	36 61 64 64	1988	Mats Wilander	H. Leconte	75 62 61
1964	Manuel Santana	N. Pietrangeli	63 61 46 75	1989	Michael Chang	S. Edberg	61 36 46 64 62
1965	Fred Stolle	T. Roche	36 60 62 63	1990	Andres Gomez	A. Agassi	63 26 64 64
1966	Tony Roche	I. Gulyas	61 64 75	1991	Jim Courier	A. Agassi	36 64 26 61 64
1967	Roy Emerson	T. Roche	61 64 26 62	1992	Jim Courier	P. Korda	75 62 61
1968	Ken Rosewall	R. Laver	63 61 26 62	1993	Sergi Bruguera	J. Courier	64 26 62 36 63
1969	Rod Laver	K. Rosewall	64 63 64	1994	Sergi Bruguera	A. Berasategui	63 75 26 61
1970	Jan Kodes	Z. Franulovic	62 64 60	1995	Thomas Muster	M. Chang	75 62 64
1971	Jan Kodes	I. Nastase	86 62 26 75	1996	Yevgeny Kafelnikov	M. Stich	76 75 76
1972	Andres Gimeno	P. Proisy	46 63 61 61	1997	Gustavo Kuerten	S. Bruguera	63 64 62
1973	Ilie Nastase	N. Pilic	63 63 60	1998	Carlos Moya	A. Corretja	63 75 63
1974	Bjorn Borg	M. Orantes	26 67 60 61 61	1999	Andre Agassi	A. Medvedev	16 26 64 63 64
1975	Bjorn Borg	G. Vilas	62 63 64	2000	Gustavo Kuerten	M. Norman	62 63 26 76
1976	Adriano Panatta	H. Solomon	61 64 46 76	2001	Gustavo Kuerten	A. Corretja	67 75 62 60
1977	Guillermo Vilas	B. Gottfried	60 63 60	2002	Albert Costa	J. C. Ferrero	61 60 46 63
1978	Bjorn Borg	G. Vilas	61 61 63	2003	Juan Carlos Ferrero	M. Verkerk	61 63 62
1979	Bjorn Borg	V. Pecci	63 61 67 64	2004	Gaston Gaudio	G. Coria	06 36 64 61 86
1980	Bjorn Borg	V. Gerulaitis	64 61 62	2005	Rafael Nadal	M. Puerta	67 63 61 75
1981	Bjorn Borg	I. Lendl	61 46 62 36 61	2006	Rafael Nadal	R. Federer	16 61 64 76
1982	Mats Wilander	G. Vilas	16 76 60 64	2007	Rafael Nadal	R. Federer	63 46 63 64

WOMEN

From 1897 to 1925, entry was restricted to members of French clubs. Became an Open Championship in 1968, but closed to contract pros in 1972. Note that Suzanne Lenglen won two titles prior to 1925, giving her six total.

Multiple winners (since 1925): Chris Evert Lloyd (7); Steffi Graf (6); Margaret Smith Court (5); Justine Henin and Helen Wills Moody (4); Arantxa Sanchez Vicario, Monica Seles and Hilde Sperling (3); Maureen Connolly, Margaret Osborne du Pont, Doris Hart, Ann Haydon Jones, Suzanne Lenglen, Simone Mathieu, Margaret Scriven, Martina Navratilova and Lesley Turner (2).

Year	Winner	Loser	Score	Year	Winner	Loser	Score
1925	Suzanne Lenglen	K. McKane	61 62	1969	Margaret Court	A. Jones	61 46 63
1926	Suzanne Lenglen	M. Browne	61 60	1970	Margaret Court	H. Niessen	62 64
1927	Kea Bouman	I. Peacock	62 64	1971	Evonne Goolagong	H. Gourlay	63 75
1928	Helen Wills	E. Bennett	61 62	1972	Billie Jean King	E. Goolagong	63 63
1929	Helen Wills	S. Mathieu	63 64	1973	Margaret Court	C. Evert	67 76 64
1930	Helen Moody	H. Jacobs	62 61	1974	Chris Evert	O. Morozova	61 62
1931	Cilly Aussem	B. Nuthall	86 61	1975	Chris Evert	M. Navratilova	26 62 61
1932	Helen Moody	S. Mathieu	75 61	1976	Sue Barker	R. Tomanova	62 06 62
1933	Margaret Scriven	S. Mathieu	62 46 64	1977	Mima Jausovec	F. Mihai	62 67 61
1934	Margaret Scriven	H. Jacobs	75 46 61	1978	Virginia Ruzici	M. Jausovec	62 62
1935	Hilde Sperling	S. Mathieu	62 61	1979	Chris Evert Lloyd	W. Turnbull	62 60
1936	Hilde Sperling	S. Mathieu	63 64	1980	Chris Evert Lloyd	V. Ruzici	60 63
1937	Hilde Sperling	S. Mathieu	62 64	1981	Hana Mandlikova	S. Hanika	62 64
1938	Simone Mathieu	N. Landry	60 63	1982	Martina Navratilova	A. Jaeger	76 61
1939	Simone Mathieu	J. Jedrzejowska	63 86	1983	Chris Evert Lloyd	M. Jausovec	61 62
1940-45	Not held World War II			1984	Martina Navratilova	C. Evert Lloyd	63 61
1946	Margaret Osborne	P. Betz	16 86 75	1985	Chris Evert Lloyd	M. Navratilova	63 67 75
1947	Patricia Todd	D. Hart	63 36 64	1986	Chris Evert Lloyd	M. Navratilova	26 63 63
1948	Nelly Landry	S. Fry	62 06 60	1987	Steffi Graf	M. Navratilova	64 46 86
1949	Margaret du Pont	N. Adamson	75 62	1988	Steffi Graf	N. Zvereva	60 60
1950	Doris Hart	P. Todd	64 46 62	1989	A. Sanchez Vicario	S. Graf	76 36 75
1951	Shirley Fry	D. Hart	63 36 63	1990	Monica Seles	S. Graf	76 64
1952	Doris Hart	S. Fry	64 64	1991	Monica Seles	A.S. Vicario	63 64
1953	Maureen Connolly	D. Hart	62 64	1992	Monica Seles	S. Graf	62 36 10-8
1954	Maureen Connolly	G. Bucaille	64 61	1993	Steffi Graf	MJ. Fernandez	46 62 64
1955	Angela Mortimer	D. Knode	26 75 10-8	1994	A. Sanchez Vicario	M. Pierce	64 64
1956	Althea Gibson	A. Mortimer	60 12-10	1995	Steffi Graf	A.S. Vicario	76 46 60
1957	Shirley Bloomer	D. Knode	61,63	1996	Steffi Graf	A.S. Vicario	63 67 10-8
1958	Suzi Kormoczi	S. Bloomer	64 16 62	1997	Iva Majoli	M. Hingis	64 62
1959	Christine Truman	S. Kormoczi	64 75	1998	A. Sanchez Vicario	M. Seles	76 06 62
1960	Darlene Hard	Y. Ramirez	63 64	1999	Steffi Graf	M. Hingis	46 75 62
1961	Ann Haydon	Y. Ramirez	62 61	2000	Mary Pierce	C. Martinez	62 75
1962	Margaret Smith	L. Turner	63 36 75	2001	Jennifer Capriati	K. Clijsters	16 64 1210
1963	Lesley Turner	A. Jones	26 63 75	2002	Serena Williams	V. Williams	75 63
1964	Margaret Smith	M. Bueno	57 61 62	2003	J. Henin-Hardenne	K. Clijsters	60 64
1965	Lesley Turner	M. Smith	63 64	2004	Anastasia Myskina	E. Dementieva	61 62
1966	Ann Jones	N. Richey	63 61	2005	J. Henin-Hardenne	M. Pierce	61 61
1967	Francoise Durr	L. Turner	46 63 64	2006	J. Henin-Hardenne	S. Kuznetsova	64 64
1968	Nancy Richey	A. Jones	57 64 61	2007	Justine Henin	A. Ivanovic	61 62

Wimbledon
MEN

Officially called "The Lawn Tennis Championships" at the All England Club, Wimbledon. Challenge round system (defending champion qualified for following year's final) used from 1877-1921. Became an Open Championship in 1968, but closed to contract pros in 1972. **Surface:** Grass.

Multiple winners: Willie Renshaw and Pete Sampras (7); Bjorn Borg, Laurie Doherty and Roger Federer (5); Reggie Doherty, Rod Laver and Tony Wilding (4); Wilfred Baddeley, Boris Becker, Arthur Gore, John McEnroe, John Newcombe, Fred Perry and Bill Tilden (3); Jean Borotra, Norman Brookes, Don Budge, Henri Cochet, Jimmy Connors, Stefan Edberg, Roy Emerson, John Hartley, Lew Hoad, Rene Lacoste, Gerald Patterson and Joshua Pim (2).

Year	Winner	Loser	Score	Year	Winner	Loser	Score
1877	Spencer Gore	W. Marshall	61 62 64	1947	Jack Kramer	T. Brown	61 63 62
1878	Frank Hadow	S. Gore	75 61 97	1948	Bob Falkenburg	J. Bromwich	75 06 62 36 75
1879	John Hartley	V. St. L. Goold	62 64 62	1949	Ted Schroeder	J. Drobny	36 60 63 46 64
1880	John Hartley	H. Lawford	60 62 26 63	1950	Budge Patty	F. Sedgman	61 8-10 62 63
1881	Willie Renshaw	J. Hartley	60 61 61	1951	Dick Savitt	K. McGregor	64 64 64
1882	Willie Renshaw	E. Renshaw	61 26 46 62 62	1952	Frank Sedgman	J. Drobny	46 62 63 62
1883	Willie Renshaw	E. Renshaw	26 63 63 46 63	1953	Vic Seixas	K. Nielsen	97 63 64
1884	Willie Renshaw	H. Lawford	60 64 97	1954	Jaroslav Drobny	K. Rosewall	13-11 46 62 97
1885	Willie Renshaw	H. Lawford	75 62 46 75	1955	Tony Trabert	K. Nielsen	63 75 61
1886	Willie Renshaw	H. Lawford	60 57 63 64	1956	Lew Hoad	K. Rosewall	62 46 75 64
1887	Herbert Lawford	E. Renshaw	16 63 36 64 64	1957	Lew Hoad	A. Cooper	62 61 62
1888	Ernest Renshaw	H. Lawford	63 75 60	1958	Ashley Cooper	N. Fraser	36 63 64 13-11
1889	Willie Renshaw	E. Renshaw	64 61 36 60	1959	Alex Olmedo	R. Laver	64 63 64
1890	Willoughby Hamilton	W. Renshaw	68 62 36 61 61	1960	Neale Fraser	R. Laver	64 36 97 75
1891	Wilfred Baddeley	J. Pim	64 16 75 60	1961	Rod Laver	C. McKinley	63 61 64
1892	Wilfred Baddeley	J. Pim	46 63 63 62	1962	Rod Laver	M. Mulligan	62 62 61
1893	Joshua Pim	W. Baddeley	36 61 63 62	1963	Chuck McKinley	F. Stolle	97 61 64
1894	Joshua Pim	W. Baddeley	10-8 62 86	1964	Roy Emerson	F. Stolle	64 12-10 46 63
1895	Wilfred Baddeley	W. Eaves	46 26 86 62 63	1965	Roy Emerson	F. Stolle	64 64 64
1896	Harold Mahony	W. Baddeley	62 68 57 86 63	1966	Manuel Santana	D. Ralston	64 11-9 64
1897	Reggie Doherty	H. Mahony	64 64 63	1967	John Newcombe	W. Bungert	63 61 61
1898	Reggie Doherty	L. Doherty	63 63 26 57 61	1968	Rod Laver	T. Roche	63 64 62
1899	Reggie Doherty	A. Gore	16 46 62 63 63	1969	Rod Laver	J. Newcombe	64 57 64 64
1900	Reggie Doherty	S. Smith	68 63 61 62	1970	John Newcombe	K. Rosewall	57 63 62 36 61
1901	Arthur Gore	R. Doherty	46 75 64 64	1971	John Newcombe	S. Smith	63 57 26 64 64
1902	Laurie Doherty	A. Gore	64 63 36 60	1972	Stan Smith	I. Nastase	46 63 63 46 75
1903	Laurie Doherty	F. Riseley	75 63 60	1973	Jan Kodes	A. Metreveli	61 98 63
1904	Laurie Doherty	F. Riseley	61 75 86	1974	Jimmy Connors	K. Rosewall	61 61 64
1905	Laurie Doherty	N. Brookes	86 62 64	1975	Arthur Ashe	J. Connors	61 61 57 64
1906	Laurie Doherty	F. Riseley	64 46 62 63	1976	Bjorn Borg	I. Nastase	64 62 97
1907	Norman Brookes	A. Gore	64 62 62	1977	Bjorn Borg	J. Connors	36 62 61 57 64
1908	Arthur Gore	R. Barrett	63 62 46 36 64	1978	Bjorn Borg	J. Connors	62 62 63
1909	Arthur Gore	M. Ritchie	68 16 62 62 62	1979	Bjorn Borg	R. Tanner	67 61 36 63 64
1910	Tony Wilding	A. Gore	64 75 46 62	1980	Bjorn Borg	J. McEnroe	16 75 63 67 86
1911	Tony Wilding	R. Barrett	64 46 26 62 (ret)	1981	John McEnroe	B. Borg	46 76 76 64
1912	Tony Wilding	A. Gore	64 64 46 64	1982	Jimmy Connors	J. McEnroe	36 63 67 76 64
1913	Tony Wilding	M. McLoughlin	86 63 10-8	1983	John McEnroe	C. Lewis	62 62 62
1914	Norman Brookes	T. Wilding	64 64 75	1984	John McEnroe	J. Connors	61 61 62
1915-18 Not held World War I				1985	Boris Becker	K. Curren	63 67 76 64
1919	Gerald Patterson	N. Brookes	63 75 62	1986	Boris Becker	I. Lendl	64 63 75
1920	Bill Tilden	G. Patterson	26 63 62 64	1987	Pat Cash	I. Lendl	76 62 75
1921	Bill Tilden	B. Norton	46 26 61 60 75	1988	Stefan Edberg	B. Becker	46 76 64 62
1922	Gerald Patterson	R. Lycett	63 64 62	1989	Boris Becker	S. Edberg	60 76 64
1923	Bill Tilden	F. Hunter	60 63 61	1990	Stefan Edberg	B. Becker	62 62 36 36 64
1924	Jean Borotra	R. Lacoste	61 36 61 36 64	1991	Michael Stich	B. Becker	64 76 64
1925	Rene Lacoste	J. Borotra	63 63 46 86	1992	Andre Agassi	G. Ivanisevic	67 64 64 16 64
1926	Jean Borotra	H. Kinsey	86 61 63	1993	Pete Sampras	J. Courier	76 76 36 63
1927	Henri Cochet	J. Borotra	46 46 63 64 75	1994	Pete Sampras	G. Ivanisevic	76 76 60
1928	Rene Lacoste	H. Cochet	61 46 64 62	1995	Pete Sampras	B. Becker	67 62 64 62
1929	Henri Cochet	J. Borotra	64 63 64	1996	Richard Krajicek	M. Washington	63 64 63
1930	Bill Tilden	W. Allison	63 97 64	1997	Pete Sampras	C. Pioline	64 62 64
1931	Sidney Wood	F. Shields	walkover	1998	Pete Sampras	G. Ivanisevic	67 76 64 36 62
1932	Ellsworth Vines	H. Austin	64 63 60	1999	Pete Sampras	A. Agassi	63 64 75
1933	Jack Crawford	E. Vines	46 11-9 62 26 64	2000	Pete Sampras	P. Rafter	67 76 64 62
1934	Fred Perry	J. Crawford	63 60 75	2001	Goran Ivanisevic	P. Rafter	63 36 63 26 97
1935	Fred Perry	G. von Cramm	62 64 64	2002	Lleyton Hewitt	D. Nalbandian	61 63 62
1936	Fred Perry	G. von Cramm	61 61 60	2003	Roger Federer	M. Philippoussis	76 62 76
1937	Don Budge	G. von Cramm	63 64 62	2004	Roger Federer	A. Roddick	46 75 76 64
1938	Don Budge	H. Austin	61 60 63	2005	Roger Federer	A. Roddick	62 76 64
1939	Bobby Riggs	E. Cooke	26 86 36 63 62	2006	Roger Federer	R. Nadal	60 76 67 63
1940-45 Not held World War II				2007	Roger Federer	R. Nadal	76 46 76 26 62
1946	Yvon Petra	G. Brown	62 64 79 57 64				

WOMEN

Officially called "The Lawn Tennis Championships" at the All England Club, Wimbledon. Challenge round system (defending champion qualified for following year's final) used from 1877-1921. Became an Open Championship in 1968, but closed to contract pros in 1972.

Multiple winners: Martina Navratilova (9); Helen Wills Moody (8); Dorothea Douglass Chambers and Steffi Graf (7); Blanche Bingley Hillyard, Billie Jean King and Suzanne Lenglen (6); Lottie Dod and Charlotte Cooper Sterry (5); Louise Brough and Venus Williams (4); Maria Bueno, Maureen Connolly, Margaret Smith Court and Chris Evert Lloyd (3); Evonne Goolagong Cawley, Althea Gibson, Kitty McKane Godfree, Dorothy Round, May Sutton, Maud Watson and Serena Williams (2).

Year	Winner	Loser	Score
1884	Maud Watson	L. Watson	68 63 63
1885	Maud Watson	B. Bingley	61 75
1886	Blanche Bingley	M. Watson	63 63
1887	Lottie Dod	B. Bingley	62 60
1888	Lottie Dod	B. Hillyard	63 63
1889	Blanche Hillyard	L. Rice	46 86 64
1890	Lena Rice	M. Jacks	64 61
1891	Lottie Dod	B. Hillyard	62 61
1892	Lottie Dod	B. Hillyard	61 61
1893	Lottie Dod	B. Hillyard	68 61 64
1894	Blanche Hillyard	E. Austin	61 61
1895	Charlotte Cooper	H. Jackson	75 86
1896	Charlotte Cooper	A. Pickering	62 63
1897	Blanche Hillyard	C. Cooper	57 75 62
1898	Charlotte Cooper	L. Martin	64 64
1899	Blanche Hillyard	C. Cooper	62 63
1900	Blanche Hillyard	C. Cooper	46 64 64
1901	Charlotte Sterry	B. Hillyard	62 62
1902	Muriel Robb	C. Sterry	75 61
1903	Dorothea Douglass	E. Thomson	46 64 62
1904	Dorothea Douglass	C. Sterry	60 63
1905	May Sutton	D. Douglass	63 64
1906	Dorothea Douglass	M. Sutton	63 97
1907	May Sutton	D. Chambers	61 64
1908	Charlotte Sterry	A. Morton	64 64
1909	Dora Boothby	A. Morton	64 46 86
1910	Dorothea Chambers	D. Boothby	62 62
1911	Dorothea Chambers	D. Boothby	60 60
1912	Ethel Larcombe	C. Sterry	63 61
1913	Dorothea Chambers	R. McNair	60 64
1914	Dorothea Chambers	E. Larcombe	75 64
1915-18 Not held World War I			
1919	Suzanne Lenglen	D. Chambers	10-8 46 97
1920	Suzanne Lenglen	D. Chambers	63 60
1921	Suzanne Lenglen	E. Ryan	62 60
1922	Suzanne Lenglen	M. Mallory	62 60
1923	Suzanne Lenglen	K. McKane	62 62
1924	Kitty McKane	H. Wills	46 64 64
1925	Suzanne Lenglen	J. Fry	62 60
1926	Kitty Godfree	L. de Alvarez	62 46 63
1927	Helen Wills	L. de Alvarez	62 64
1928	Helen Wills	L. de Alvarez	62 63
1929	Helen Wills	H. Jacobs	61 62
1930	Helen Moody	E. Ryan	62 62
1931	Cilly Aussem	H. Krahwinkel	62 75
1932	Helen Moody	H. Jacobs	63 61
1933	Helen Moody	D. Round	64 68 63
1934	Dorothy Round	H. Jacobs	62 57 63
1935	Helen Moody	H. Jacobs	63 36 75
1936	Helen Jacobs	H.K. Sperling	62 46 75
1937	Dorothy Round	J. Jedrzejowska	62 26 75
1938	Helen Moody	H. Jacobs	64 60
1939	Alice Marble	K. Stammers	62 60
1940-45 Not held World War II			
1946	Pauline Betz	L. Brough	62 64
1947	Margaret Osborne	D. Hart	62 64
1948	Louise Brough	D. Hart	63 86
1949	Louise Brough	M. du Pont	10-8 16 10-8

Year	Winner	Loser	Score
1950	Louise Brough	M. du Pont	61 36 61
1951	Doris Hart	S. Fry	61 60
1952	Maureen Connolly	L. Brough	75 63
1953	Maureen Connolly	D. Hart	86 75
1954	Maureen Connolly	L. Brough	62 75
1955	Louise Brough	B. Fleitz	75 86
1956	Shirley Fry	A. Buxton	63 61
1957	Althea Gibson	D. Hard	63 62
1958	Althea Gibson	A. Mortimer	86 62
1959	Maria Bueno	D. Hard	64 63
1960	Maria Bueno	S. Reynolds	86 60
1961	Angela Mortimer	C. Truman	46 64 75
1962	Karen Susman	V. Sukova	64 64
1963	Margaret Smith	B.J. Moffitt	63 64
1964	Maria Bueno	M. Smith	64 79 63
1965	Margaret Smith	M. Bueno	64 75
1966	Billie Jean King	M. Bueno	63 36 61
1967	Billie Jean King	A. Jones	63 64
1968	Billie Jean King	J. Tegart	97 75
1969	Ann Jones	B.J. King	36 63 62
1970	Margaret Court	B.J. King	14-12 11-9
1971	Evonne Goolagong	M. Court	64 61
1972	Billie Jean King	E. Goolagong	63 63
1973	Billie Jean King	C. Evert	60 75
1974	Chris Evert	O. Morozova	60 64
1975	Billie Jean King	E. Cawley	60 61
1976	Chris Evert	E. Cawley	63 46 86
1977	Virginia Wade	B. Stove	46 63 61
1978	Martina Navratilova	C. Evert	26 64 75
1979	Martina Navratilova	C. Evert Lloyd	64 64
1980	Evonne Cawley	C. Evert Lloyd	61 76
1981	Chris Evert Lloyd	H. Mandlikova	62 62
1982	Martina Navratilova	C. Evert Lloyd	61 36 62
1983	Martina Navratilova	A. Jaeger	60 63
1984	Martina Navratilova	C. Evert Lloyd	76 62
1985	Martina Navratilova	C. Evert Lloyd	46 63 62
1986	Martina Navratilova	H. Mandlikova	76 63
1987	Martina Navratilova	S. Graf	75 63
1988	Steffi Graf	M. Navratilova	57 62 61
1989	Steffi Graf	M. Navratilova	62 67 61
1990	Martina Navratilova	Z. Garrison	64 61
1991	Steffi Graf	G. Sabatini	64 36 86
1992	Steffi Graf	M. Seles	62 61
1993	Steffi Graf	J. Novotna	76 16 64
1994	Conchita Martinez	M. Navratilova	64 36 63
1995	Steffi Graf	A.S. Vicario	46 61 75
1996	Steffi Graf	A.S. Vicario	63 75
1997	Martina Hingis	J. Novotna	26 63 63
1998	Jana Novotna	N. Tauziat	64 76
1999	Lindsay Davenport	S. Graf	64 75
2000	Venus Williams	L. Davenport	63 76
2001	Venus Williams	J. Henin	61 36 60
2002	Serena Williams	V. Williams	76 63
2003	Serena Williams	V. Williams	46 64 62
2004	Maria Sharapova	S. Williams	61 64
2005	Venus Williams	L. Davenport	46 76 97
2006	Amelie Mauresmo	J. Henin-Hardenne	26 63 64
2007	Venus Williams	M. Bartoli	64 61

U.S. Open
MEN

Challenge round system (defending champion qualified for following year's final) used from 1884 to 1911. Known as the Patriotic Tournament in 1917 during World War I. Amateur and Open Championships held in 1968 and '69. Became an exclusively Open Championship in 1970. **Surface:** Decoturf II (acrylic cement).

Multiple winners: Bill Larned, Richard Sears and Bill Tilden (7); Jimmy Connors and Pete Sampras (5); Roger Federer, John McEnroe and Robert Wrenn (4); Oliver Campbell, Ivan Lendl, Fred Perry and Malcolm Whitman (3); Andre Agassi, Don Budge, Stefan Edberg, Roy Emerson, Neale Fraser, Pancho Gonzales, Bill Johnston, Jack Kramer, Rene Lacoste, Rod Laver, Maurice McLoughlin, Lindley Murray, John Newcombe, Frank Parker, Patrick Rafter, Bobby Riggs, Ken Rosewall, Frank Sedgman, Henry Slocum Jr., Tony Trabert, Ellsworth Vines and Dick Williams (2).

Year	Winner	Loser	Score	Year	Winner	Loser	Score
1881	Richard Sears	W. Glyn	60 63 62	1946	Jack Kramer	T. Brown, Jr.	97 63 60
1882	Richard Sears	C. Clark	61 64 60	1947	Jack Kramer	F. Parker	46 26 61 60 63
1883	Richard Sears	J. Dwight	62 60 97	1948	Pancho Gonzales	E. Sturgess	62 63 14-12
1884	Richard Sears	H. Taylor	60 16 60 62	1949	Pancho Gonzales	F. Schroeder	16-18 26 61 62 64
1885	Richard Sears	G. Brinley	63 46 60 63	1950	Arthur Larsen	H. Flam	63 46 57 64 63
1886	Richard Sears	R. Beeckman	46 61 63 64	1951	Frank Sedgman	V. Seixas	64 61 61
1887	Richard Sears	H. Slocum Jr.	61 63 62	1952	Frank Sedgman	G. Mulloy	61 62 63
1888	Henry Slocum Jr.	H. Taylor	64 61 60	1953	Tony Trabert	V. Seixas	63 62 63
1889	Henry Slocum Jr.	Q. Shaw	63 61 46 62	1954	Vic Seixas	R. Hartwig	36 62 64 64
1890	Oliver Campbell	H. Slocum Jr.	62 46 63 61	1955	Tony Trabert	K. Rosewall	97 63 63
1891	Oliver Campbell	C. Hobart	26 75 79 61 62	1956	Ken Rosewall	L. Hoad	46 62 63 63
1892	Oliver Campbell	F. Hovey	75 36 63 75	1957	Mal Anderson	A. Cooper	10-8 75 64
1893	Robert Wrenn	F. Hovey	64 36 64 64	1958	Ashley Cooper	M. Anderson	62 36 46 10-8 86
1894	Robert Wrenn	M. Goodbody	68 61 64 64	1959	Neale Fraser	A. Olmedo	63 57 62 64
1895	Fred Hovey	R. Wrenn	63 62 64	1960	Neale Fraser	R. Laver	64 64 97
1896	Robert Wrenn	F. Hovey	75 36 60 16 61	1961	Roy Emerson	R. Laver	75 63 62
1897	Robert Wrenn	W. Eaves	46 86 63 26 62	1962	Rod Laver	R. Emerson	62 64 57 64
1898	Malcolm Whitman	D. Davis	36 62 62 61	1963	Rafael Osuna	F. Froehling	75 64 62
1899	Malcolm Whitman	P. Paret	61 62 36 75	1964	Roy Emerson	F. Stolle	64 62 64
1900	Malcolm Whitman	B. Larned	64 16 62 62	1965	Manuel Santana	C. Drysdale	62 79 75 61
1901	Bill Larned	B. Wright	62 68 64 64	1966	Fred Stolle	J. Newcombe	46 12-10 63 64
1902	Bill Larned	R. Doherty	46 62 64 86	1967	John Newcombe	C. Graebner	64 64 86
1903	Laurie Doherty	B. Larned	60 63 10-8	1968	Am-Arthur Ashe	B. Lutz	46 63 8-10 60 64
1904	Holcombe Ward	B. Clothier	10-8 64 97		Op-Arthur Ashe	T. Okker	14-12 57 63 36 63
1905	Beals Wright	H. Ward	62 61 11-9	1969	Am-Stan Smith	B. Lutz	97 63 61
1906	Bill Clothier	B. Wright	63 60 64		Op-Rod Laver	T. Roche	79 61 63 62
1907	Bill Larned	R. LeRoy	62 62 64	1970	Ken Rosewall	T. Roche	26 64 76 63
1908	Bill Larned	B. Wright	62 62 64	1971	Stan Smith	J. Kodes	36 63 62 76
1909	Bill Larned	B. Clothier	61 62 57 16 61	1972	Ilie Nastase	A. Ashe	36 63 67 64 63
1910	Bill Larned	T. Bundy	61 57 60 68 61	1973	John Newcombe	J. Kodes	64 16 46 62 63
1911	Bill Larned	M. McLoughlin	64 64 62	1974	Jimmy Connors	K. Rosewall	61 60 61
1912	Maurice McLoughlin	W.F. Johnson	36 26 62 64 62	1975	Manuel Orantes	J. Connors	64 63 63
1913	Maurice McLoughlin	R. Williams	64 57 63 61	1976	Jimmy Connors	B. Borg	64 36 76 64
1914	Dick Williams	M. McLoughlin	63 86 10-8	1977	Guillermo Vilas	J. Connors	26 63 76 60
1915	Bill Johnston	M. McLoughlin	16 60 75 10-8	1978	Jimmy Connors	B. Borg	64 62 62
1916	Dick Williams	B. Johnston	46 64 06 62 64	1979	John McEnroe	V. Gerulaitis	75 63 63
1917	Lindley Murray	N. Niles	57 86 63 63	1980	John McEnroe	B. Borg	76 61 67 57 64
1918	Lindley Murray	B. Tilden	63 61 75	1981	John McEnroe	B. Borg	46 62 64 63
1919	Bill Johnston	B. Tilden	63 61 64	1982	Jimmy Connors	I. Lendl	63 62 46 64
1920	Bill Tilden	B. Johnston	61 16 75 57 63	1983	Jimmy Connors	I. Lendl	63 67 75 60
1921	Bill Tilden	W. Johnson	61 63 61	1984	John McEnroe	I. Lendl	63 64 61
1922	Bill Tilden	B. Johnston	46 36 62 63 64	1985	Ivan Lendl	J. McEnroe	76 63 64
1923	Bill Tilden	B. Johnston	64 61 64	1986	Ivan Lendl	M. Mecir	64 62 60
1924	Bill Tilden	B. Johnston	61 97 62	1987	Ivan Lendl	M. Wilander	67 60 76 64
1925	Bill Tilden	B. Johnston	46 11-9 63 46 63	1988	Mats Wilander	I. Lendl	64 46 63 57 64
1926	Rene Lacoste	J. Borotra	64 60 64	1989	Boris Becker	I. Lendl	76 16 63 76
1927	Rene Lacoste	B. Tilden	11-9 63 11-9	1990	Pete Sampras	A. Agassi	64 63 62
1928	Henri Cochet	F. Hunter	46 64 36 75 63	1991	Stefan Edberg	J. Courier	62 64 60
1929	Bill Tilden	F. Hunter	36 63 46 62 64	1992	Stefan Edberg	P. Sampras	36 64 76 62
1930	John Doeg	F. Shields	10-8 16 64 16-14	1993	Pete Sampras	C. Pioline	64 64 63
1931	Ellsworth Vines	G. Lott Jr.	79 63 97 75	1994	Andre Agassi	M. Stich	61 76 75
1932	Ellsworth Vines	H. Cochet	64 64 64	1995	Pete Sampras	A. Agassi	64 63 46 75
1933	Fred Perry	J. Crawford	63 11-13 46 60 61	1996	Pete Sampras	M. Chang	61 64 76
1934	Fred Perry	W. Allison	64 63 16 86	1997	Patrick Rafter	G. Rusedski	63 62 46 75
1935	Wilmer Allison	S. Wood	62 62 63	1998	Patrick Rafter	M. Philippoussis	63 36 62 60
1936	Fred Perry	D. Budge	26 62 86 16 10-8	1999	Andre Agassi	T. Martin	64 67 63 63 62
1937	Don Budge	G. von Cramm	61 79 61 36 61	2000	Marat Safin	P. Sampras	64 63 63
1938	Don Budge	G. Mako	63 68 62 61	2001	Lleyton Hewitt	P. Sampras	76 61 61
1939	Bobby Riggs	S.W. van Horn	64 62 64	2002	Pete Sampras	A. Agassi	63 64 57 64
1940	Don McNeill	B. Riggs	46 68 63 63 75	2003	Andy Roddick	J.C. Ferrero	63 76 63
1941	Bobby Riggs	F. Kovacs	57 61 63 63	2004	Roger Federer	L. Hewitt	60 76 60
1942	Fred Schroeder	F. Parker	86 75 36 46 62	2005	Roger Federer	A. Agassi	63 26 76 61
1943	Joe Hunt	J. Kramer	63 68 10-8 60	2006	Roger Federer	A. Roddick	62 46 75 61
1944	Frank Parker	B. Talbert	64 36 63 63	2007	Roger Federer	N. Djokovic	76 76 64
1945	Frank Parker	B. Talbert	14-12 61 62				

WOMEN

Challenge round system used from 1887-1918. Five set final played from 1887 to 1901. Amateur and Open Championships held in 1968 and '69. Became an exclusively Open Championship in 1970.

Multiple winners: Molla Bjurstedt Mallory (8); Helen Wills Moody (7); Chris Evert Lloyd (6); Margaret Smith Court and Steffi Graf (5); Pauline Betz, Maria Bueno, Helen Jacobs, Billie Jean King, Alice Marble, Elisabeth Moore, Martina Navratilova and Hazel Hotchkiss Wightman (4); Juliette Atkinson, Mary Browne, Maureen Connolly and Margaret Osborne du Pont (3); Tracy Austin, Mabel Cahill, Sarah Palfrey Cooke, Althea Gibson, Darlene Hard, Doris Hart, Justine Henin, Marion Jones, Monica Seles, Bertha Townsend, Serena Williams and Venus Williams (2).

Year	Winner	Loser	Score
1887	Ellen Hansell	L. Knight	61 60
1888	Bertha Townsend	E. Hansell	63 65
1889	Bertha Townsend	L. Voorhes	75 62
1890	Ellen Roosevelt	B. Townsend	62 62
1891	Mabel Cahill	E. Roosevelt	64 61 46 63
1892	Mabel Cahill	E. Moore	57 63 64 46 62
1893	Aline Terry	A. Schultz	61 63
1894	Helen Hellwig	A. Terry	75 36 60 36 63
1895	Juliette Atkinson	H. Hellwig	64 62 61
1896	Elisabeth Moore	J. Atkinson	64 46 62 62
1897	Juliette Atkinson	E. Moore	63 63 46 36 63
1898	Juliette Atkinson	M. Jones	63 57 64 26 75
1899	Marion Jones	M. Banks	61 61 75
1900	Myrtle McAteer	E. Parker	62 62 60
1901	Elisabeth Moore	M. McAteer	64 36 75 26 62
1902	Marion Jones	E. Moore	61 10(ret)
1903	Elisabeth Moore	M. Jones	75 86
1904	May Sutton	E. Moore	64 62
1905	Elisabeth Moore	H. Homans	64 57 61
1906	Helen Homans	M. Barger-Wallach	64 63
1907	Evelyn Sears	C. Neely	63 62
1908	Maud B. Wallach	Ev. Sears	63 16 63
1909	Hazel Hotchkiss	M. Barger-Wallach	60 61
1910	Hazel Hotchkiss	L. Hammond	64 62
1911	Hazel Hotchkiss	F. Sutton	8-10 61 97
1912	Mary Browne	E. Sears	64 62
1913	Mary Browne	D. Green	62 75
1914	Mary Browne	M. Wagner	62 16 61
1915	Molla Bjurstedt	H. Wightman	46 62 60
1916	Molla Bjurstedt	L. Raymond	60 61
1917	Molla Bjurstedt	M. Vanderhoef	46 60 62
1918	Molla Bjurstedt	E. Goss	64 63
1919	Hazel Wightman	M. Zinderstein	61 62
1920	Molla Mallory	M. Zinderstein	63 61
1921	Molla Mallory	M. Browne	46 64 62
1922	Molla Mallory	H. Wills	63 61
1923	Helen Wills	M. Mallory	62 61
1924	Helen Wills	M. Mallory	61 63
1925	Helen Wills	K. McKane	36 60 62
1926	Molla Mallory	E. Ryan	46 64 97
1927	Helen Wills	B. Nuthall	61 64
1928	Helen Wills	H. Jacobs	62 61
1929	Helen Wills	P. Watson	64 62
1930	Betty Nuthall	A. Harper	61 64
1931	Helen Moody	E. Whittingstall	64 61
1932	Helen Jacobs	C. Babcock	62 62
1933	Helen Jacobs	H. Moody	86 36 30(ret)
1934	Helen Jacobs	S. Palfrey	62 64
1935	Helen Jacobs	S. Fabyan	62 64
1936	Alice Marble	H. Jacobs	46 63 62
1937	Anita Lizana	J. Jedrzejowska	64 62
1938	Alice Marble	N. Wynne	60 63
1939	Alice Marble	H. Jacobs	60 8-10 64
1940	Alice Marble	H. Jacobs	62 63
1941	Sarah Cooke	P. Betz	75 62
1942	Pauline Betz	L. Brough	46 61 64
1943	Pauline Betz	L. Brough	63 57 63
1944	Pauline Betz	M. Osborne	63 86
1945	Sarah Cooke	P. Betz	36 86 64
1946	Pauline Betz	P. Canning	11-9 63
1947	Louise Brough	M. Osborne	86 46 61
1948	Margaret du Pont	L. Brough	46 64 15-13
1949	Margaret du Pont	D. Hart	64 61
1950	Margaret du Pont	D. Hart	64 63
1951	Maureen Connolly	S. Fry	63 16 64
1952	Maureen Connolly	D. Hart	63 75
1953	Maureen Connolly	D. Hart	62 64
1954	Doris Hart	L. Brough	68 61 86
1955	Doris Hart	P. Ward	64 62
1956	Shirley Fry	A. Gibson	63 64
1957	Althea Gibson	L. Brough	63 62
1958	Althea Gibson	D. Hard	36 61 62
1959	Maria Bueno	C. Truman	61 64
1960	Darlene Hard	M. Bueno	64 10-12 64
1961	Darlene Hard	A. Haydon	63 64
1962	Margaret Smith	D. Hard	97 64
1963	Maria Bueno	M. Smith	75 64
1964	Maria Bueno	C. Graebner	61 60
1965	Margaret Smith	B.J. Moffitt	86 75
1966	Maria Bueno	N. Richey	63 61
1967	Billie Jean King	A. Jones	11-9 64
1968	Am-Margaret Court	M. Bueno	62 62
	Op-Virginia Wade	B.J. King	64 62
1969	Am-Margaret Court	V. Wade	46 63 60
	Op-Margaret Court	N. Richey	62 62
1970	Margaret Court	R. Casals	62 26 61
1971	Billie Jean King	R. Casals	64 76
1972	Billie Jean King	K. Melville	63 75
1973	Margaret Court	E. Goolagong	76 57 62
1974	Billie Jean King	E. Goolagong	36 63 75
1975	Chris Evert	E. Cawley	57 64 62
1976	Chris Evert	E. Cawley	63 60
1977	Chris Evert	W. Turnbull	76 62
1978	Chris Evert	P. Shriver	75 64
1979	Tracy Austin	C. Evert Lloyd	64 63
1980	Chris Evert Lloyd	H. Mandlikova	57 61 61
1981	Tracy Austin	M. Navratilova	16 76 76
1982	Chris Evert Lloyd	H. Mandlikova	63 61
1983	Martina Navratilova	C. Evert Lloyd	61 63
1984	Martina Navratilova	C. Evert Lloyd	46 64 64
1985	Hana Mandlikova	M. Navratilova	76 16 76
1986	Martina Navratilova	H. Sukova	63 62
1987	Martina Navratilova	S. Graf	76 61
1988	Steffi Graf	G. Sabatini	63 36 61
1989	Steffi Graf	M. Navratilova	36 75 61
1990	Gabriela Sabatini	S. Graf	62 76
1991	Monica Seles	M. Navratilova	76 61
1992	Monica Seles	A.S. Vicario	63 63
1993	Steffi Graf	H. Sukova	63 63
1994	A. Sanchez Vicario	S. Graf	16 76 64
1995	Steffi Graf	M. Seles	76 06 63
1996	Steffi Graf	M. Seles	75 64
1997	Martina Hingis	V. Williams	60 64
1998	Lindsay Davenport	M. Hingis	63 75
1999	Serena Williams	M. Hingis	63 75
2000	Venus Williams	L. Davenport	64 75
2001	Venus Williams	S. Williams	62 64
2002	Serena Williams	V. Williams	64 63
2003	J. Henin-Hardenne	K. Clijsters	75 61
2004	Svetlana Kuznetsova	E. Dementieva	63 75
2005	Kim Clijsters	M. Pierce	63 61
2006	Maria Sharapova	J. Henin-Hardenne	64 64
2007	Justine Henin	S. Kuznetsova	61 63

Grand Slam Summary

Singles winners of the four Grand Slam tournaments–Australian, French, Wimbledon and United States–since the French was opened to all comers in 1925. Note that there were two Australian Opens in 1977 and none in 1986.

MEN

Three wins in one year: Jack Crawford (1933); Fred Perry (1934); Tony Trabert (1955); Lew Hoad (1956); Ashley Cooper (1958); Roy Emerson (1964); Jimmy Connors (1974); Mats Wilander (1988); Roger Federer (2004, 2006-07).

Two wins in one year: Roy Emerson and Pete Sampras (4 times); Bjorn Borg (3 times); Rene Lacoste, Ivan Lendl, John Newcombe and Fred Perry (twice); Andre Agassi, Boris Becker, Don Budge, Henri Cochet, Jimmy Connors, Jim Courier, Roger Federer, Neale Fraser, Jack Kramer, John McEnroe, Alex Olmedo, Budge Patty, Bobby Riggs, Ken Rosewall, Dick Savitt, Frank Sedgman and Guillermo Vilas (once).

Year	Australian	French	Wimbledon	U.S.	Year	Australian	French	Wimbledon	U.S.
1925	Anderson	Lacoste	Lacoste	Tilden	1967	Emerson	Emerson	Newcombe	Newcombe
1926	Hawkes	Cochet	Borotra	Lacoste	1968	Bowrey	Rosewall	Laver	Ashe
1927	Patterson	Lacoste	Cochet	Lacoste	1969	**Laver**	**Laver**	**Laver**	**Laver**
1928	Borotra	Cochet	Lacoste	Cochet	1970	Ashe	Kodes	Newcombe	Rosewall
1929	Gregory	Lacoste	Cochet	Tilden	1971	Rosewall	Kodes	Newcombe	Smith
1930	Moon	Cochet	Tilden	Doeg	1972	Rosewall	Gimeno	Smith	Nastase
1931	Crawford	Borotra	Wood	Vines	1973	Newcombe	Nastase	Kodes	Newcombe
1932	Crawford	Cochet	Vines	Vines	1974	Connors	Borg	Connors	Connors
1933	Crawford	Crawford	Crawford	Perry	1975	Newcombe	Borg	Ashe	Orantes
1934	Perry	von Cramm	Perry	Perry	1976	Edmondson	Panatta	Borg	Connors
1935	Crawford	Perry	Perry	Allison	1977	Tanner	Vilas	Borg	Vilas
1936	Quist	von Cramm	Perry	Perry		& Gerulaitis			
1937	McGrath	Henkel	Budge	Budge	1978	Vilas	Borg	Borg	Connors
1938	**Budge**	**Budge**	**Budge**	**Budge**	1979	Vilas	Borg	Borg	McEnroe
1939	Bromwich	McNeill	Riggs	Riggs	1980	Teacher	Borg	Borg	McEnroe
1940	Quist	—	—	McNeill	1981	Kriek	Borg	McEnroe	McEnroe
1941	—	—	—	Riggs	1982	Kriek	Wilander	Connors	Connors
1942	—	—	—	Schroeder	1983	Wilander	Noah	McEnroe	Connors
1943	—	—	—	Hunt	1984	Wilander	Lendl	McEnroe	McEnroe
1944	—	—	—	Parker	1985	Edberg	Wilander	Becker	Lendl
1945	—	—	—	Parker	1986	—	Lendl	Becker	Lendl
1946	Bromwich	Bernard	Petra	Kramer	1987	Edberg	Lendl	Cash	Lendl
1947	Pails	Asboth	Kramer	Kramer	1988	Wilander	Wilander	Edberg	Wilander
1948	Quist	Parker	Falkenburg	Gonzales	1989	Lendl	Chang	Becker	Becker
1949	Sedgman	Parker	Schroeder	Gonzales	1990	Lendl	Gomez	Edberg	Sampras
1950	Sedgman	Patty	Patty	Larsen	1991	Becker	Courier	Stich	Edberg
1951	Savitt	Drobny	Savitt	Sedgman	1992	Courier	Courier	Agassi	Edberg
1952	McGregor	Drobny	Sedgman	Sedgman	1993	Courier	Bruguera	Sampras	Sampras
1953	Rosewall	Rosewall	Seixas	Trabert	1994	Sampras	Bruguera	Sampras	Agassi
1954	Rose	Trabert	Drobny	Seixas	1995	Agassi	Muster	Sampras	Sampras
1955	Rosewall	Trabert	Trabert	Trabert	1996	Becker	Kafelnikov	Krajicek	Sampras
1956	Hoad	Hoad	Hoad	Rosewall	1997	Sampras	Kuerten	Sampras	Rafter
1957	Cooper	Davidson	Hoad	Anderson	1998	Korda	Moya	Sampras	Rafter
1958	Cooper	Rose	Cooper	Cooper	1999	Kafelnikov	Agassi	Sampras	Agassi
1959	Olmedo	Pietrangeli	Olmedo	Fraser	2000	Agassi	Kuerten	Sampras	Safin
1960	Laver	Pietrangeli	Fraser	Fraser	2001	Agassi	Kuerten	Ivanisevic	Hewitt
1961	Emerson	Santana	Laver	Emerson	2002	Johansson	Costa	Hewitt	Sampras
1962	**Laver**	**Laver**	**Laver**	**Laver**	2003	Agassi	Ferrero	Federer	Roddick
1963	Emerson	Emerson	McKinley	Osuna	2004	Federer	Gaudio	Federer	Federer
1964	Emerson	Santana	Emerson	Emerson	2005	Safin	Nadal	Federer	Federer
1965	Emerson	Stolle	Emerson	Santana	2006	Federer	Nadal	Federer	Federer
1966	Emerson	Roche	Santana	Stolle	2007	Federer	Nadal	Federer	Federer

Men's, Women's & Mixed Doubles Grand Slam

The tennis Grand Slam has only been accomplished in doubles competition six times in the same calendar year. Here are the doubles teams to accomplish the feat. The two men and three women to win the singles Grand Slam are noted in the Grand Slam Summary tables.

Men's Doubles

1951 . . . . .Frank Sedgman, Australia
& Ken McGregor, Australia

Mixed Doubles

1963 .Ken Fletcher, Australia
& Margaret Smith, Australia
1967 . . . . .Owen Davidson and two partners*

*Davidson's partners: AUS–Lesley Turner; FR, WIM, U.S.–Billie Jean King.

Women's Doubles

1960 . . . . .Maria Bueno, Brazil & two partners†
1984 . . . : . . . . .Martina Navratilova, USA
& Pam Shriver, USA
1998 . . . .Martina Hingis, Switzerland & two partners#

†Bueno's partners: AUS–Christine Truman; FR, WIM, U.S.–Darlene Hard.

#Hingis' partners: AUS–Mirjana Lucic; FR, WIM, U.S.–Jana Novotna.

WOMEN

Three in one year: Helen Wills Moody (1928 and '29); Margaret Smith Court (1962, '65, '69 and '73); Billie Jean King (1972); Martina Navratilova (1983 and '84); Steffi Graf (1989, '93, '95 and '96); Monica Seles (1991 and '92); Martina Hingis (1997) and Serena Williams (2002).

Two in one year: Chris Evert Lloyd (5 times); Helen Wills Moody and Martina Navratilova (3 times); Maria Bueno, Maureen Connolly, Margaret Smith Court, Althea Gibson, Justine Henin, Billie Jean King and Venus Williams (twice); Cilly Aussem, Pauline Betz, Louise Brough, Jennifer Capriati, Evonne Goolagong Cawley, Margaret Osborne du Pont, Shirley Fry, Darlene Hard, Suzanne Lenglen, Alice Marble, Amelie Mauresmo, Arantxa Sanchez Vicario and Serena Williams (once).

Year	Australian	French	Wimbledon	U.S.
1925	Akhurst	Lenglen	Lenglen	Wills
1926	Akhurst	Lenglen	Godfree	Mallory
1927	Boyd	Bouman	Wills	Wills
1928	Akhurst	Wills	Wills	Wills
1929	Akhurst	Wills	Wills	Wills
1930	Akhurst	Moody	Moody	Nuthall
1931	Buttsworth	Aussem	Aussem	Moody
1932	Buttsworth	Moody	Moody	Jacobs
1933	Hartigan	Scriven	Moody	Jacobs
1934	Hartigan	Scriven	Round	Jacobs
1935	Round	Sperling	Moody	Jacobs
1936	Hartigan	Sperling	Jacobs	Marble
1937	Wynne	Sperling	Round	Lizana
1938	Bundy	Mathieu	Moody	Marble
1939	Westacott	Mathieu	Marble	Marble
1940	Wynne	—	—	Marble
1941	—	—	—	Cooke
1942	—	—	—	Betz
1943	—	—	—	Betz
1944	—	—	—	Betz
1945	—	—	—	Cooke
1946	Bolton	Osborne	Betz	Betz
1947	Bolton	Todd	Osborne	Brough
1948	Bolton	Landry	Brough	du Pont
1949	Hart	du Pont	Brough	du Pont
1950	Brough	Hart	Brough	du Pont
1951	Bolton	Fry	Hart	Connolly
1952	Long	Hart	Connolly	Connolly
1953	**Connolly**	**Connolly**	**Connolly**	**Connolly**
1954	Long	Connolly	Connolly	Hart
1955	Penrose	Mortimer	Brough	Hart
1956	Carter	Gibson	Fry	Fry
1957	Fry	Bloomer	Gibson	Gibson
1958	Mortimer	Kormoczi	Gibson	Gibson
1959	Reitano	Truman	Bueno	Bueno
1960	Smith	Hard	Bueno	Hard
1961	Smith	Haydon	Mortimer	Hard
1962	Smith	Smith	Susman	Smith
1963	Smith	Turner	Smith	Bueno
1964	Smith	Smith	Bueno	Bueno
1965	Smith	Turner	Smith	Smith
1966	Smith	Jones	King	Bueno
1967	Richey	Durr	King	King
1968	King	Richey	King	Wade
1969	Court	Court	Jones	Court
1970	**Court**	**Court**	**Court**	**Court**
1971	Court	Goolagong	Goolagong	King
1972	Wade	King	King	King
1973	Court	Court	King	Court
1974	Goolagong	Evert	Evert	King
1975	Goolagong	Evert	King	Evert
1976	Cawley	Barker	Evert	Evert
1977	Reid & Cawley	Jausovec	Wade	Evert
1978	O'Neil	Ruzici	Navratilova	Evert
1979	Jordan	Evert Lloyd	Navratilova	Austin
1980	Mandlikova	Evert Lloyd	Cawley	Evert Lloyd
1981	Navratilova	Mandlikova	Evert Lloyd	Austin
1982	Evert Lloyd	Navratilova	Navratilova	Evert Lloyd
1983	Navratilova	Evert Lloyd	Navratilova	Navratilova
1984	Evert Lloyd	Navratilova	Navratilova	Navratilova
1985	Navratilova	Evert Lloyd	Navratilova	Mandlikova
1986	–	Evert Lloyd	Navratilova	Navratilova
1987	Mandlikova	Graf	Navratilova	Navratilova
1988	**Graf**	**Graf**	**Graf**	**Graf**
1989	Graf	Vicario	Graf	Graf
1990	Graf	Seles	Navratilova	Sabatini
1991	Seles	Seles	Graf	Seles
1992	Seles	Seles	Graf	Seles
1993	Seles	Graf	Graf	Graf
1994	Graf	Vicario	Martinez	Vicario
1995	Pierce	Graf	Graf	Graf
1996	Seles	Graf	Graf	Graf
1997	Hingis	Majoli	Hingis	Hingis
1998	Hingis	Vicario	Novotna	Davenport
1999	Hingis	Graf	Davenport	S. Williams
2000	Davenport	Pierce	V. Williams	V. Williams
2001	Capriati	Capriati	V. Williams	V. Williams
2002	Capriati	S. Williams	S. Williams	S. Williams
2003	S. Williams	H-Hardenne	S. Williams	H-Hardenne
2004	H-Hardenne	Myskina	Sharapova	Kuznetsova
2005	S. Williams	H-Hardenne	V. Williams	Clijsters
2006	Mauresmo	H-Hardenne	Mauresmo	Sharapova
2007	S. Williams	Henin	V. Williams	Henin

Overall Leaders

All-Time Grand Slam titleists including all singles and doubles championships at the four major tournaments. Titles listed under each heading are singles, doubles and mixed doubles.

MEN

		Career	Australian	French	Wimbledon	U.S.	S-D-M	Total Titles
1	Roy Emerson	1959-71	6-3-0	2-6-0	2-3-0	2-4-0	12-16-0	28
2	John Newcombe	1965-76	2-5-0	0-3-0	3-6-0	2-3-1	7-17-1	25
3	Frank Sedgman	1949-52	2-2-2	0-2-2	1-3-2	2-2-2	5-9-8	22
	Todd Woodbridge	1988-2005	0-3-1	0-1-1	0-9-1	0-3-3	0-16-6	22
5	Bill Tilden	1913-30	*	0-0-1	3-1-0	7-5-4	10-6-5	21
6	Rod Laver	1959-71	3-4-0	2-1-1	4-1-2	2-0-0	11-6-3	20
7	Jack Bromwich	1938-50	2-8-1	0-0-0	0-2-2	0-3-1	2-13-4	19
	Neale Fraser	1957-62	0-3-1	0-3-0	1-2-1	2-3-3	3-11-5	19
9	Ken Rosewall	1953-72	4-3-0	2-2-0	0-2-0	2-2-1	8-9-1	18
	Jean Borotra	1925-36	1-1-1	1-5-2	2-3-1	0-0-1	4-9-5	18
	Fred Stolle	1962-69	0-3-1	1-2-0	0-2-3	1-3-2	2-10-6	18
12	Four tied with 17 total titles each.							

Grand Slam Overall Leaders (Cont.)
WOMEN

		Career	Australian	French	Wimbledon	U.S.	S-D-M	Total Titles
1	Margaret Smith Court	1960-75	11-8-2	5-4-4	3-2-5	5-5-8	24-19-19	62
2	Martina Navratilova	1974-95, 2000-06	3-8-1	2-7-2	9-7-4	4-9-3	18-31-10	59
3	Billie Jean King	1961-81	1-0-1	1-1-2	6-10-4	4-5-4	12-16-11	39
4	Margaret du Pont	1941-62	*	2-3-0	1-5-1	3-13-9	6-21-10	37
5	Louise Brough	1942-57	1-1-0	0-3-0	4-5-4	1-12-4	6-21-8	35
	Doris Hart	1948-55	1-1-2	2-5-3	1-4-5	2-4-5	6-14-15	35
7	Helen Wills Moody	1923-38	*	4-2-0	8-3-1	7-4-2	19-9-3	31
8	Elizabeth Ryan	1914-34	*	0-4-0	0-12-7	0-1-2	0-17-9	26
9	Suzanne Lenglen	1919-26	*	6-2-2	6-6-3	0-0-0	12-8-5	25
10	Steffi Graf	1982-99	4-0-0	6-0-0	7-1-0	5-0-0	22-1-0	23
11	Pam Shriver	1981-97	0-7-0	0-4-1	0-5-0	0-5-0	0-21-1	22
12	Chris Evert	1974-89	2-0-0	7-2-0	3-1-0	6-0-0	18-3-0	21
	Darlene Hard	1958-69	*	1-3-2	0-4-3	2-6-0	3-13-5	21
14	Natasha Zvereva	1989-2002	0-3-2	0-6-0	0-5-0	0-4-0	0-18-2	20
	Nancye Wynne Bolton	1935-52	6-10-4	0-0-0	0-0-0	0-0-0	6-10-4	20
	Maria Bueno	1958-68	0-1-0	0-1-1	3-5-0	4-5-0	7-12-1	20

All-Time Grand Slam Singles Titles

Men and women with the most singles championships in the Australian, French, Wimbledon and U.S. championships, through 2007. Note that (*) indicates player never played in that particular Grand Slam event; and players active in singles play in 2007 are in **bold** type.

Top 10 Men

		Aus	Fre	Wim	US	Total
1	Pete Sampras	2	0	7	5	14
2	Roy Emerson	6	2	2	2	12
	Roger Federer	3	0	5	4	12
4	Bjorn Borg	0	6	5	0	11
	Rod Laver	3	2	4	2	11
6	Bill Tilden	*	0	3	7	10
7	Andre Agassi	4	1	1	2	8
	Jimmy Connors	1	0	2	5	8
	Ivan Lendl	2	3	0	3	8
	Fred Perry	1	1	3	3	8
	Ken Rosewall	4	2	0	2	8

Top 10 Women

		Aus	Fre	Wim	US	Total
1	Margaret Smith Court	11	5	3	5	24
2	Steffi Graf	4	6	7	5	22
3	Helen Wills Moody	*	4	8	7	19
4	Chris Evert	2	7	3	6	18
	Martina Navratilova	3	2	9	4	18
6	Billie Jean King	1	1	6	4	12
	Suzanne Lenglen	*	6	6	0	12
8	Maureen Connolly	1	2	3	3	9
	Monica Seles	4	3	0	2	9
10	Molla Bjurstedt Mallory	*	*	0	8	8
	Serena Williams	3	1	2	2	8

Annual Number One Players

Unofficial world rankings for men and women determined by the London Daily Telegraph from 1914-72. Since then, official world rankings computed by men's and women's tours. Rankings included only amateur players from 1914 until the arrival of open (professional) tennis in 1968. No rankings were released during World Wars I and II.

MEN

Multiple winners: Pete Sampras and Bill Tilden (6); Jimmy Connors (5); Henri Cochet, Rod Laver, Ivan Lendl and John McEnroe (4); Roger Federer, John Newcombe and Fred Perry (3); Bjorn Borg, Don Budge, Ashley Cooper, Stefan Edberg, Roy Emerson, Neale Fraser, Lleyton Hewitt, Jack Kramer, Rene Lacoste, Ilie Nastase, Frank Sedgman and Tony Trabert (2).

Year		Year		Year		Year	
1914	Maurice McLoughlin	1939	Bobby Riggs	1966	Manuel Santana	1988	Mats Wilander
1915-18	No rankings	1940-45	No rankings	1967	John Newcombe	1989	Ivan Lendl
1919	Gerald Patterson	1946	Jack Kramer	1968	Rod Laver	1990	Stefan Edberg
1920	Bill Tilden	1947	Jack Kramer	1969	Rod Laver	1991	Stefan Edberg
1921	Bill Tilden	1948	Frank Parker	1970	John Newcombe	1992	Jim Courier
1922	Bill Tilden	1949	Pancho Gonzales	1971	John Newcombe	1993	Pete Sampras
1923	Bill Tilden	1950	Budge Patty	1972	Ilie Nastase	1994	Pete Sampras
1924	Bill Tilden	1951	Frank Sedgman	1973	Ilie Nastase	1995	Pete Sampras
1925	Bill Tilden	1952	Frank Sedgman	1974	Jimmy Connors	1996	Pete Sampras
1926	Rene Lacoste	1953	Tony Trabert	1975	Jimmy Connors	1997	Pete Sampras
1927	Rene Lacoste	1954	Jaroslav Drobny	1976	Jimmy Connors	1998	Pete Sampras
1928	Henri Cochet	1955	Tony Trabert	1977	Jimmy Connors	1999	Andre Agassi
1929	Henri Cochet	1956	Lew Hoad	1978	Jimmy Connors	2000	Gustavo Kuerten
1930	Henri Cochet	1957	Ashley Cooper	1979	Bjorn Borg	2001	Lleyton Hewitt
1931	Henri Cochet	1958	Ashley Cooper	1980	Bjorn Borg	2002	Lleyton Hewitt
1932	Ellsworth Vines	1959	Neale Fraser	1981	John McEnroe	2003	Andy Roddick
1933	Jack Crawford	1960	Neale Fraser	1982	John McEnroe	2004	Roger Federer
1934	Fred Perry	1961	Rod Laver	1983	John McEnroe	2005	Roger Federer
1935	Fred Perry	1962	Rod Laver	1984	John McEnroe	2006	Roger Federer
1936	Fred Perry	1963	Rafael Osuna	1985	Ivan Lendl		
1937	Don Budge	1964	Roy Emerson	1986	Ivan Lendl		
1938	Don Budge	1965	Roy Emerson	1987	Ivan Lendl		

WOMEN

Multiple winners: Helen Wills Moody (9); Steffi Graf (8); Margaret Smith Court and Martina Navratilova (7); Chris Evert Lloyd and Billie Jean King (5); Lindsay Davenport and Margaret Osborne du Pont (4); Maureen Connolly, Martina Hingis and Monica Seles (3); Maria Bueno, Althea Gibson, Justine Henin and Suzanne Lenglen (2).

Year	Year	Year	Year
1925 Suzanne Lenglen	1950 Margaret du Pont	1970 Margaret Court	1990 Steffi Graf
1926 Suzanne Lenglen	1951 Doris Hart	1971 Evonne Goolagong	1991 Monica Seles
1927 Helen Wills	1952 Maureen Connolly	1972 Billie Jean King	1992 Monica Seles
1928 Helen Wills	1953 Maureen Connolly	1973 Margaret Court	1993 Steffi Graf
1929 Helen Wills Moody	1954 Maureen Connolly	1974 Billie Jean King	1994 Steffi Graf
1930 Helen Wills Moody	1955 Louise Brough	1975 Chris Evert	1995 Steffi Graf
1931 Helen Wills Moody	1956 Shirley Fry	1976 Chris Evert	& Monica Seles*
1932 Helen Wills Moody	1957 Althea Gibson	1977 Chris Evert	1996 Steffi Graf
1933 Helen Wills Moody	1958 Althea Gibson	1978 Martina Navratilova	1997 Martina Hingis
1934 Dorothy Round	1959 Maria Bueno	1979 Martina Navratilova	1998 Lindsay Davenport
1935 Helen Wills Moody	1960 Maria Bueno	1980 Chris Evert Lloyd	1999 Martina Hingis
1936 Helen Jacobs	1961 Angela Mortimer	1981 Chris Evert Lloyd	2000 Martina Hingis
1937 Anita Lizana	1962 Margaret Smith	1982 Martina Navratilova	2001 Lindsay Davenport
1938 Helen Wills Moody	1963 Margaret Smith	1983 Martina Navratilova	2002 Serena Williams
1939 Alice Marble	1964 Margaret Smith	1984 Martina Navratilova	2003 Justine Henin-Hardenne
1940-45 No rankings	1965 Margaret Smith	1985 Martina Navratilova	2004 Lindsay Davenport
1946 Pauline Betz	1966 Billie Jean King	1986 Martina Navratilova	2005 Lindsay Davenport
1947 Margaret Osborne	1967 Billie Jean King	1987 Steffi Graf	2006 Justine Henin
1948 Margaret du Pont	1968 Billie Jean King	1988 Steffi Graf	
1949 Margaret du Pont	1969 Margaret Court	1989 Steffi Graf	

*Upon her return to the WTA Tour on Aug. 15, 1995, Seles retained her #1 ranking and was co-ranked at #1 through her first six tournaments (August '95–May '96). Seles was on leave since April 1993 when she was stabbed by a fan during a match.

Annual Top 10 World Rankings (since 1968)

Year by year Top 10 world computer rankings for men (ATP Tour) and women (WTA Tour) since the arrival of open tennis in 1968. Rankings from 1968-72 made by Lance Tingay of the *London Daily Telegraph*. Since 1973 the WTA Tour and ATP tour had compiled its own computer rankings. Since 2000, the men's rankings reflect the final standings of the ATP Champions Race.

MEN

1968
1 Rod Laver
2 Arthur Ashe
3 Ken Rosewall
4 Tom Okker
5 Tony Roche
6 John Newcombe
7 Clark Graebner
8 Dennis Ralston
9 Cliff Drysdale
10 Pancho Gonzales

1969
1 Rod Laver
2 Tony Roche
3 John Newcombe
4 Tom Okker
5 Ken Rosewall
6 Arthur Ashe
7 Cliff Drysdale
8 Pancho Gonzales
9 Andres Gimeno
10 Fred Stolle

1970
1 John Newcombe
2 Ken Rosewall
3 Tony Roche
4 Rod Laver
5 Arthur Ashe
6 Ilie Nastase
7 Tom Okker
8 Roger Taylor
9 Jan Kodes
10 Cliff Richey

1971
1 John Newcombe
2 Stan Smith
3 Rod Laver
4 Ken Rosewall
5 Jan Kodes
6 Arthur Ashe
7 Tom Okker
8 Marty Riessen
9 Cliff Drysdale
10 Ilie Nastase

1972
1 Stan Smith
2 Ken Rosewall
3 Ilie Nastase
4 Rod Laver
5 Arthur Ashe
6 John Newcombe
7 Bob Lutz
8 Tom Okker
9 Marty Riessen
10 Andres Gimeno

1973
1 Ilie Nastase
2 John Newcombe
3 Jimmy Connors
4 Tom Okker
5 Stan Smith
6 Ken Rosewall
7 Manuel Orantes
8 Rod Laver
9 Jan Kodes
10 Arthur Ashe

1974
1 Jimmy Connors
2 John Newcombe
3 Bjorn Borg
4 Rod Laver
5 Guillermo Vilas
6 Tom Okker
7 Arthur Ashe
8 Ken Rosewall
9 Stan Smith
10 Ilie Nastase

1975
1 Jimmy Connors
2 Guillermo Vilas
3 Bjorn Borg
4 Arthur Ashe
5 Manuel Orantes
6 Ken Rosewall
7 Ilie Nastase
8 John Alexander
9 Roscoe Tanner
10 Rod Laver

1976
1 Jimmy Connors
2 Bjorn Borg
3 Ilie Nastase
4 Manuel Orantes
5 Raul Ramirez
6 Guillermo Vilas
7 Adriano Panatta
8 Harold Solomon
9 Eddie Dibbs
10 Brian Gottfried

1977
1 Jimmy Connors
2 Guillermo Vilas
3 Bjorn Borg
4 Vitas Gerulaitis
5 Brian Gottfried
6 Eddie Dibbs
7 Manuel Orantes
8 Raul Ramirez
9 Ilie Nastase
10 Dick Stockton

1978
1 Jimmy Connors
2 Bjorn Borg
3 Guillermo Vilas
4 John McEnroe
5 Vitas Gerulaitis
6 Eddie Dibbs
7 Brian Gottfried
8 Raul Ramirez
9 Harold Solomon
10 Corrado Barazzutti

1979
1 Bjorn Borg
2 Jimmy Connors
3 John McEnroe
4 Vitas Gerulaitis
5 Roscoe Tanner
6 Guillermo Vilas
7 Arthur Ashe
8 Harold Solomon
9 Jose Higueras
10 Eddie Dibbs

1980
1 Bjorn Borg
2 John McEnroe
3 Jimmy Connors
4 Gene Mayer
5 Guillermo Vilas
6 Ivan Lendl
7 Harold Solomon
8 Jose-Luis Clerc
9 Vitas Gerulaitis
10 Eliot Teltscher

1981
1 John McEnroe
2 Ivan Lendl
3 Jimmy Connors
4 Bjorn Borg
5 Jose-Luis Clerc
6 Guillermo Vilas
7 Gene Mayer
8 Eliot Teltscher
9 Vitas Gerulaitis
10 Peter McNamara

1982
1 John McEnroe
2 Jimmy Connors
3 Ivan Lendl
4 Guillermo Vilas
5 Vitas Gerulaitis
6 Jose-Luis Clerc
7 Mats Wilander
8 Gene Mayer
9 Yannick Noah
10 Peter McNamara

Annual Top 10 World Rankings (since 1968) (Cont.)

MEN

	1983		1989		1995		2001
1	John McEnroe	1	Ivan Lendl	1	Pete Sampras	1	Lleyton Hewitt
2	Ivan Lendl	2	Boris Becker	2	Andre Agassi	2	Gustavo Kuerten
3	Jimmy Connors	3	Stefan Edberg	3	Thomas Muster	3	Andre Agassi
4	Mats Wilander	4	John McEnroe	4	Boris Becker	4	Yevgeny Kafelnikov
5	Yannick Noah	5	Michael Chang	5	Michael Chang	5	Juan Carlos Ferrero
6	Jimmy Arias	6	Brad Gilbert	6	Yevgeny Kafelnikov	6	Sebastien Grosjean
7	Jose Higueras	7	Andre Agassi	7	Thomas Enqvist	7	Patrick Rafter
8	Jose-Luis Clerc	8	Aaron Krickstein	8	Jim Courier	8	Tommy Haas
9	Kevin Curren	9	Alberto Mancini	9	Wayne Ferreira	9	Tim Henman
10	Gene Mayer	10	Jay Berger	10	Goran Ivanisevic	10	Pete Sampras

	1984		1990		1996		2002
1	John McEnroe	1	Stefan Edberg	1	Pete Sampras	1	Lleyton Hewitt
2	Jimmy Connors	2	Boris Becker	2	Michael Chang	2	Andre Agassi
3	Ivan Lendl	3	Ivan Lendl	3	Yevgeny Kafelnikov	3	Marat Safin
4	Mats Wilander	4	Andre Agassi	4	Goran Ivanisevic	4	Juan Carlos Ferrero
5	Andres Gomez	5	Pete Sampras	5	Thomas Muster	5	Carlos Moya
6	Anders Jarryd	6	Andres Gomez	6	Boris Becker	6	Roger Federer
7	Henrik Sundstrom	7	Thomas Muster	7	Richard Krajicek	7	Jiri Novak
8	Pat Cash	8	Emilio Sanchez	8	Andre Agassi	8	Tim Henman
9	Eliot Teltscher	9	Goran Ivanisevic	9	Thomas Enqvist	9	Albert Costa
10	Yannick Noah	10	Brad Gilbert	10	Wayne Ferreira	10	Andy Roddick

	1985		1991		1997		2003
1	Ivan Lendl	1	Stefan Edberg	1	Pete Sampras	1	Andy Roddick
2	John McEnroe	2	Jim Courier	2	Patrick Rafter	2	Roger Federer
3	Mats Wilander	3	Boris Becker	3	Michael Chang	3	Juan Carlos Ferrero
4	Jimmy Connors	4	Michael Stich	4	Jonas Bjorkman	4	Andre Agassi
5	Stefan Edberg	5	Ivan Lendl	5	Yevgeny Kafelnikov	5	Guillermo Coria
6	Boris Becker	6	Pete Sampras	6	Greg Rusedski	6	Rainer Schuettler
7	Yannick Noah	7	Guy Forget	7	Carlos Moya	7	Carlos Moya
8	Anders Jarryd	8	Karel Novacek	8	Sergi Bruguera	8	David Nalbandian
9	Miloslav Mecir	9	Petr Korda	9	Thomas Muster	9	Mark Philippoussis
10	Kevin Curren	10	Andre Agassi	10	Marcelo Rios	10	Sebastien Grosjean

	1986		1992		1998		2004
1	Ivan Lendl	1	Jim Courier	1	Pete Sampras	1	Roger Federer
2	Boris Becker	2	Stefan Edberg	2	Marcelo Rios	2	Andy Roddick
3	Mats Wilander	3	Pete Sampras	3	Alex Corretja	3	Lleyton Hewitt
4	Yannick Noah	4	Goran Ivanisevic	4	Patrick Rafter	4	Marat Safin
5	Stefan Edberg	5	Boris Becker	5	Carlos Moya	5	Carlos Moya
6	Henri Leconte	6	Michael Chang	6	Andre Agassi	6	Tim Henman
7	Joakim Nystrom	7	Petr Korda	7	Tim Henman	7	Guillermo Coria
8	Jimmy Connors	8	Ivan Lendl	8	Karol Kucera	8	Andre Agassi
9	Miloslav Mecir	9	Andre Agassi	9	Greg Rusedski	9	David Nalbandian
10	Andres Gomez	10	Richard Krajicek	10	Richard Krajicek	10	Gaston Gaudio

	1987		1993		1999		2005
1	Ivan Lendl	1	Pete Sampras	1	Andre Agassi	1	Roger Federer
2	Stefan Edberg	2	Michael Stich	2	Yevgeny Kafelnikov	2	Rafael Nadal
3	Mats Wilander	3	Jim Courier	3	Pete Sampras	3	Andy Roddick
4	Jimmy Connors	4	Sergi Bruguera	4	Thomas Enqvist	4	Lleyton Hewitt
5	Boris Becker	5	Stefan Edberg	5	Gustavo Kuerten	5	Nikolay Davydenko
6	Miloslav Mecir	6	Andrei Medvedev	6	Nicolas Kiefer	6	David Nalbandian
7	Pat Cash	7	Goran Ivanisevic	7	Todd Martin	7	Andre Agassi
8	Yannick Noah	8	Michael Chang	8	Nicolas Lapentti	8	Guillermo Coria
9	Tim Mayotte	9	Thomas Muster	9	Marcelo Rios	9	Ivan Ljubicic
10	John McEnroe	10	Cedric Pioline	10	Richard Krajicek	10	Gaston Gaudio

	1988		1994		2000		2006
1	Mats Wilander	1	Pete Sampras	1	Gustavo Kuerten	1	Roger Federer
2	Ivan Lendl	2	Andre Agassi	2	Marat Safin	2	Rafael Nadal
3	Andre Agassi	3	Boris Becker	3	Pete Sampras	3	Nikolay Davydenko
4	Boris Becker	4	Sergi Bruguera	4	Magnus Norman	4	James Blake
5	Stefan Edberg	5	Goran Ivanisevic	5	Yevgeny Kafelnikov	5	Ivan Ljubicic
6	Kent Carlsson	6	Michael Chang	6	Andre Agassi	6	Andy Roddick
7	Jimmy Connors	7	Stefan Edberg	7	Lleyton Hewitt	7	Tommy Robredo
8	Jakob Hlasek	8	Alberto Berasategui	8	Alex Corretja	8	David Nalbandian
9	Henri Leconte	9	Michael Stich	9	Thomas Enqvist	9	Mario Ancic
10	Tim Mayotte	10	Todd Martin	10	Tim Henman	10	Fernando Gonzalez

WOMEN

1968
1 Billie Jean King
2 Virginia Wade
3 Nancy Richey
4 Maria Bueno
5 Margaret Court
6 Ann Jones
7 Judy Tegart
8 Annette du Plooy
9 Leslie Bowrey
10 Rosie Casals

1969
1 Margaret Court
2 Ann Jones
3 Billie Jean King
4 Nancy Richey
5 Julie Heldman
6 Rosie Casals
7 Kerry Melville
8 Peaches Bartkowicz
9 Virginia Wade
10 Leslie Bowrey

1970
1 Margaret Court
2 Billie Jean King
3 Rosie Casals
4 Virginia Wade
5 Helga Niessen
6 Kerry Melville
7 Julie Heldman
8 Karen Krantczke
9 Francoise Durr
10 Nancy R. Gunter

1971
1 Evonne Goolagong
2 Billie Jean King
3 Margaret Court
4 Rosie Casals
5 Kerry Melville
6 Virginia Wade
7 Judy Tegart
8 Francoise Durr
9 Helga N. Masthoff
10 Chris Evert

1972
1 Billie Jean King
2 Evonne Goolagong
3 Chris Evert
4 Margaret Court
5 Kerry Melville
6 Virginia Wade
7 Rosie Casals
8 Nancy R. Gunter
9 Francoise Durr
10 Linda Tuero

1973
1 Margaret S. Court
2 Billie Jean King
3 Evonne G. Cawley
4 Chris Evert
5 Rosie Casals
6 Virginia Wade
7 Kerry Reid
8 Nancy Richey
9 Julie Heldman
10 Helga Masthoff

1974
1 Billie Jean King
2 Evonne G. Cawley
3 Chris Evert
4 Virginia Wade
5 Julie Heldman
6 Rosie Casals
7 Kerry Reid
8 Olga Morozova
9 Lesley Hunt
10 Francoise Durr

1975
1 Chris Evert
2 Billie Jean King
3 Evonne G. Cawley
4 Martina Navratilova
5 Virginia Wade
6 Margaret S. Court
7 Olga Morozova
8 Nancy Richey
9 Francoise Durr
10 Rosie Casals

1976
1 Chris Evert
2 Evonne G. Cawley
3 Virginia Wade
4 Martina Navratilova
5 Sue Barker
6 Betty Stove
7 Dianne Balestrat
8 Mima Jausovec
9 Rosie Casals
10 Francoise Durr

1977
1 Chris Evert
2 Billie Jean King
3 Martina Navratilova
4 Virginia Wade
5 Sue Barker
6 Rosie Casals
7 Betty Stove
8 Dianne Balestrat
9 Wendy Turnbull
10 Kerry Reid

1978
1 Martina Navratilova
2 Chris Evert Lloyd
3 Evonne G. Cawley
4 Virginia Wade
5 Billie Jean King
6 Tracy Austin
7 Wendy Turnbull
8 Kerry Reid
9 Betty Stove
10 Dianne Balestrat

1979
1 Martina Navratilova
2 Chris Evert Lloyd
3 Tracy Austin
4 Evonne G. Cawley
5 Billie Jean King
6 Dianne Balestrat
7 Wendy Turnbull
8 Virginia Wade
9 Kerry Reid
10 Sue Barker

1980
1 Chris Evert Lloyd
2 Tracy Austin
3 Martina Navratilova
4 Hana Mandlikova
5 Evonne G. Cawley
6 Billie Jean King
7 Andrea Jaeger
8 Wendy Turnbull
9 Pam Shriver
10 Greer Stevens

1981
1 Chris Evert Lloyd
2 Tracy Austin
3 Martina Navratilova
4 Andrea Jaeger
5 Hana Mandlikova
6 Sylvia Hanika
7 Pam Shriver
8 Wendy Turnbull
9 Bettina Bunge
10 Barbara Potter

1982
1 Martina Navratilova
2 Chris Evert Lloyd
3 Andrea Jaeger
4 Tracy Austin
5 Wendy Turnbull
6 Pam Shriver
7 Hana Mandlikova
8 Barbara Potter
9 Bettina Bunge
10 Sylvia Hanika

1983
1 Martina Navratilova
2 Chris Evert Lloyd
3 Andrea Jaeger
4 Pam Shriver
5 Sylvia Hanika
6 Jo Durie
7 Bettina Bunge
8 Wendy Turnbull
9 Tracy Austin
10 Zina Garrison

1984
1 Martina Navratilova
2 Chris Evert Lloyd
3 Hana Mandlikova
4 Pam Shriver
5 Wendy Turnbull
6 Manuela Maleeva
7 Helena Sukova
8 Claudia Kohde-Kilsch
9 Zina Garrison
10 Kathy Jordan

1985
1 Martina Navratilova
2 Chris Evert Lloyd
3 Hana Mandlikova
4 Pam Shriver
5 Claudia Kohde-Kilsch
6 Steffi Graf
7 Manuela Maleeva
8 Zina Garrison
9 Helena Sukova
10 Bonnie Gadusek

1986
1 Martina Navratilova
2 Chris Evert Lloyd
3 Steffi Graf
4 Hana Mandlikova
5 Helena Sukova
6 Pam Shriver
7 Claudia Kohde-Kilsch
8 M. Maleeva-Fragniere
9 Zina Garrison
10 Gabriela Sabatini

1987
1 Steffi Graf
2 Martina Navratilova
3 Chris Evert
4 Pam Shriver
5 Hana Mandlikova
6 Gabriela Sabatini
7 Helena Sukova
8 M. Maleeva-Fragniere
9 Zina Garrison
10 Claudia Kohde-Kilsch

1988
1 Steffi Graf
2 Martina Navratilova
3 Chris Evert
4 Gabriela Sabatini
5 Pam Shriver
6 M. Maleeva-Fragniere
7 Natalia Zvereva
8 Helena Sukova
9 Zina Garrison
10 Barbara Potter

1989
1 Steffi Graf
2 Martina Navratilova
3 Gabriela Sabatini
4 Z. Garrison-Jackson
5 A. Sanchez Vicario
6 Monica Seles
7 Conchita Martinez
8 Helena Sukova
9 M. Maleeva-Fragniere
10 Chris Evert

1990
1 Steffi Graf
2 Monica Seles
3 Martina Navratilova
4 Mary Joe Fernandez
5 Gabriela Sabatini
6 Katerina Maleeva
7 A. Sanchez Vicario
8 Jennifer Capriati
9 M. Maleeva-Fragniere
10 Z. Garrison-Jackson

1991
1 Monica Seles
2 Steffi Graf
3 Gabriela Sabatini
4 Martina Navratilova
5 A. Sanchez Vicario
6 Jennifer Capriati
7 Jana Novotna
8 Mary Joe Fernandez
9 Conchita Martinez
10 M. Maleeva-Fragniere

1992
1 Monica Seles
2 Steffi Graf
3 Gabriela Sabatini
4 A. Sanchez Vicario
5 Martina Navratilova
6 Mary Joe Fernandez
7 Jennifer Capriati
8 Conchita Martinez
9 M. Maleeva-Fragniere
10 Jana Novotna

1993
1 Steffi Graf
2 A. Sanchez Vicario
3 Martina Navratilova
4 Conchita Martinez
5 Gabriela Sabatini
6 Jana Novotna
7 Mary Joe Fernandez
8 Monica Seles
9 Jennifer Capriati
10 Anke Huber

1994
1 Steffi Graf
2 A. Sanchez Vicario
3 Conchita Martinez
4 Jana Novotna
5 Mary Pierce
6 Lindsay Davenport
7 Gabriela Sabatini
8 Martina Navratilova
9 Kimiko Date
10 Natasha Zvereva

1995
1 Steffi Graf
Monica Seles*
2 Conchita Martinez
3 A. Sanchez Vicario
4 Kimiko Date
5 Mary Pierce
6 Magdalena Maleeva
7 Gabriela Sabatini
8 Mary Joe Fernandez
9 Iva Majoli
10 Anke Huber

1996
1 Steffi Graf
2 Monica Seles†
A. Sanchez Vicario
3 Jana Novotna
4 Martina Hingis
5 Conchita Martinez
6 Anke Huber
7 Iva Majoli
8 Kimiko Date
9 Lindsay Davenport
10 Barbara Paulus

Annual Top 10 World Rankings (since 1968) (Cont.)

WOMEN

1997	1999	2001	2003	2005
1 Martina Hingis	1 Martina Hingis	1 Lindsay Davenport	1 J. Henin-Hardenne	1 Lindsay Davenport
2 Jana Novotna	2 Lindsay Davenport	2 Jennifer Capriati	2 Kim Clijsters	2 Kim Clijsters
3 Lindsay Davenport	3 Venus Williams	3 Venus Williams	3 Serena Williams	3 Amelie Mauresmo
4 Amanda Coetzer	4 Serena Williams	4 Martina Hingis	4 Amelie Mauresmo	4 Maria Sharapova
5 Monica Seles	5 Mary Pierce	5 Kim Clijsters	5 Lindsay Davenport	5 Mary Pierce
6 Iva Majoli	6 Monica Seles	6 Serena Williams	6 Jennifer Capriati	6 J. Henin-Hardenne
7 Mary Pierce	7 Nathalie Tauziat	7 Justine Henin	7 Anastasia Myskina	7 Patty Schnyder
8 Irina Spirlea	8 Barbara Schett	8 Jelena Dokic	8 Elena Dementieva	8 Elena Dementieva
9 A. Sanchez Vicario	9 Julie Halard-Decugis	9 Amelie Mauresmo	9 Chanda Rubin	9 Nadia Petrova
10 Mary Joe Fernandez	10 Amelie Mauresmo	10 Monica Seles	10 Ai Sugiyama	10 Venus Williams

1998	2000	2002	2004	2006
1 Lindsay Davenport	1 Martina Hingis	1 Serena Williams	1 Lindsay Davenport	1 J. Henin-Hardenne
2 Martina Hingis	2 Lindsay Davenport	2 Venus Williams	2 Amelie Mauresmo	2 Maria Sharapova
3 Jana Novotna	3 Venus Williams	3 Jennifer Capriati	3 Anastasia Myskina	3 Amelie Mauresmo
4 A. Sanchez Vicario	4 Monica Seles	4 Kim Clijsters	4 Maria Sharapova	4 Svetlana Kuznetsova
5 Venus Williams	5 Conchita Martinez	5 J. Henin-Hardenne	5 Svetlana Kuznetsova	5 Kim Clijsters
6 Monica Seles	6 Serena Williams	6 Amelie Mauresmo	6 Elena Dementieva	6 Nadia Petrova
7 Mary Pierce	7 Mary Pierce	7 Monica Seles	7 Serena Williams	7 Martina Hingis
8 Conchita Martinez	8 Anna Kournikova	8 Daniela Hantuchova	8 J. Henin-Hardenne	8 Elena Dementieva
9 Steffi Graf	9 A. Sanchez Vicario	9 Jelena Dokic	9 Venus Williams	9 Patty Schnyder
10 Nathalie Tauziat	10 Nathalie Tauziat	10 Martina Hingis	10 Jennifer Capriati	10 Nicole Vaidisova

*Returning to the WTA Tour on Aug. 15, 1995, Seles was co-ranked #1 for her first six tournaments. Seles had been absent from the Tour since April 1993 when she was stabbed by a fan during a match. She was ranked #1 at the time of the stabbing.
†Seles' ranking was revised in May 1996. The revision stipulated that her new modified ranking would be calculated using a divisor of the actual number of tournaments she had played (13), and she would be co-ranked with the player whose average is immediately below her average (Sanchez Vicario).

All-Time Leaders

Tournaments Won (singles)

All-time tournament wins from the arrival of open tennis in 1968 through 2007 (through Oct. 7). Men's totals include ATP Tour, Grand Prix and WCT tournaments. Players active in singles play in 2007 are in **bold** type.

MEN

	Total		Total		Total
1 Jimmy Connors	109	11 Rod Laver	47	21 Tom Okker	31
2 Ivan Lendl	94	12 Thomas Muster	44	22 Vitas Gerulaitis	27
3 John McEnroe	77	13 Stefan Edberg	41	23 Yevgeny Kafelnikov	26
4 Pete Sampras	64	14 Stan Smith	39	**Lleyton Hewitt**	26
5 Bjorn Borg	62	15 Michael Chang	34	25 Jose-Luis Clerc	25
Guillermo Vilas	62	16 Arthur Ashe	33	Brian Gottfried	25
7 Andre Agassi	60	Mats Wilander	33	27 Jim Courier	23
8 Ilie Nastase	57	18 John Newcombe	32	Yannick Noah	23
9 **Roger Federer**	51	Manuel Orantes	32	**Andy Roddick**	23
10 Boris Becker	49	Ken Rosewall	32	**Rafael Nadal**	23

WOMEN

	Total		Total		Total
1 Martina Navratilova	167	11 **Justine Henin**	37	21 Nancy Richey	25
2 Chris Evert	154	12 **Venus Williams**	36	22 Jana Novotna	24
3 Steffi Graf	107	13 **Kim Clijsters**	34	**Amelie Mauresmo**	24
4 Margaret Smith Court	92	14 Conchita Martinez	33	24 Kerry Melville Reid	22
5 E. Goolagong Cawley	68	15 Olga Morozova	31	25 Pam Shriver	21
6 Billie Jean King	67	16 Tracy Austin	30	26 Julie Heldman	20
7 Virginia Wade	55	17 Arantxa Sanchez-Vicario	29	27 M. Maleeva-Fragniere	19
8 Monica Seles	53	18 **Serena Williams**	28	Nancy Richey	19
9 **Lindsay Davenport**	52	19 Hana Mandlikova	27	29 Mary Pierce	18
10 **Martina Hingis**	43	Gabriela Sabatini	27	30 Virginia Ruzici	17
				Regina Marsikova	17

Money Won

All-time money winners from the arrival of open tennis in 1968 through 2007 (through Oct. 7). Totals include doubles earnings.

MEN

		Earnings				Earnings				Earnings
1	Pete Sampras	$43,280,489	8	Goran Ivanisevic	$19,876,579	15	Andy Roddick	$12,984,526
2	Roger Federer	35,640,078	9	Michael Chang	19,145,632	16	Carlos Moya	12,833,329
3	Andre Agassi	31,152,975	10	Lleyton Hewitt	17,271,212	17	Rafael Nadal	12,681,374
4	Boris Becker	25,080,956	11	Gustavo Kuerten	14,748,338	18	Michael Stich	12,592,483
5	Yevgeny Kafelnikov	23,883,797	12	Jim Courier	14,034,132	19	John McEnroe	12,552,132
6	Ivan Lendl	21,262,417	13	Jonas Bjorkman	13,917,509	20	Thomas Muster	12,225,910
7	Stefan Edberg	20,630,941	14	Marat Safin	13,092,130			

WOMEN

		Earnings				Earnings				Earnings
1	Steffi Graf	$21,895,277	8	A. Sanchez-Vicario	$16,942,640	15	Mary Pierce	$9,793,119
2	Lindsay Davenport	21,823,477	9	Monica Seles	14,891,762	16	Maria Sharapova	9,716,272
3	Mart. Navratilova	21,626,089	10	Kim Clijsters	14,764,296	17	Chris Evert	8,896,195
4	Martina Hingis	20,130,657	11	Amelie Mauresmo	13,559,336	18	Gabriela Sabatini	8,785,850
5	Venus Williams	18,130,691	12	Conchita Martinez	11,527,977	19	Elena Dementieva	8,317,092
6	Serena Williams	17,967,313	13	Jana Novotna	11,249,284	20	Svetlana Kuznetsova	7,962,024
7	Justine Henin	17,758,405	14	Jennifer Capriati	10,206,639			

Year-end Tournaments

MEN

Tennis Masters Cup

The year-end championship featuring the top eight players in the Tennis Masters Series rankings. Two groups of four players square off in a round-robin tournament followed by a single-elimination semifinals and finals. Originally called the Masters in 1970, the tournament followed a round-robin format, but was revised in 1972 to include a round-robin to decide the four semifinalists then a single elimination format after that. Replaced by ATP Tour World Championship from 1990 through 1999.

Multiple Winners: Ivan Lendl and Pete Sampras (5); Ilie Nastase (4); Boris Becker, Roger Federer and John McEnroe (3); Bjorn Borg and Lleyton Hewitt (2).

Year	Winner	Runner-Up		Year	Winner	Loser	Score
1970	Stan Smith (4-1) *	Rod Laver (4-1)		1988	Boris Becker	I. Lendl	57 76 36 62 76
1971	Ilie Nastase (6-0)	Stan Smith (4-2)		1989	Stefan Edberg	B. Becker	46 76 63 61

Year	Winner	Loser	Score	Year	Winner	Loser	Score
				1990	Andre Agassi	S. Edberg	57 76 75 62
1972	Ilie Nastase	S. Smith	63 62 36 26 63	1991	Pete Sampras	J. Courier	36 76 63 64
1973	Ilie Nastase	T. Okker	63 75 46 63	1992	Boris Becker	J. Courier	64 63 75
1974	Guillermo Vilas	I. Nastase	76 62 36 36 64	1993	Michael Stich	P. Sampras	76 26 76 62
1975	Ilie Nastase	B. Borg	62 62 61	1994	Pete Sampras	B. Becker	46 63 75 64
1976	Manuel Orantes	W. Fibak	57 62 06 76 61	1995	Boris Becker	M. Chang	76 60 76
1978	Jimmy Connors	B. Borg	64 16 64	1996	Pete Sampras	B. Becker	36 76 76 67 64
1979	John McEnroe	A. Ashe	67 63 75	1997	Pete Sampras	Y. Kafelnikov	63 62 62
1980	Bjorn Borg	V. Gerulaitis	62 62	1998	Alex Corretja	C. Moya	36 36 75 63 75
1981	Bjorn Borg	I. Lendl	64 62 62	1999	Pete Sampras	A. Agassi	61 75 64
1982	Ivan Lendl	V. Gerulaitis	67 26 76 62 64	2000	Gustavo Kuerten	A. Agassi	64 64 64
1983	Ivan Lendl	J. McEnroe	64 64 62	2001	Lleyton Hewitt	S. Grosjean	63 63 64
1984	John McEnroe	I. Lendl	63 64 64	2002	Lleyton Hewitt	J.C. Ferrero	75 75 26 26 64
1985	John McEnroe	I. Lendl	75 60 64	2003	Roger Federer	A. Agassi	63 60 64
1986	Ivan Lendl	B. Becker	62 76 63	2004	Roger Federer	L. Hewitt	63 62 (rain)
1986	Ivan Lendl	B. Becker	64 64 64	2005	David Nalbandian	R. Federer	67 67 62 61 76
1987	Ivan Lendl	M. Wilander	62 62 63	2006	Roger Federer	J. Blake	60 63 64

*Smith was declared the winner because he beat Laver in their round-robin match (4-6, 6-3, 6-4).

Note: The tournament switched from December to January in 1977-78, then back to December in 1986.

Playing Sites

1970—Tokyo; **1971**—Paris; **1972**—Barcelona; **1973**—Boston; **1974**—Melbourne; **1975**—Stockholm; **1976, 2003-04**—Houston; **1977-89**—New York City; **1990-95**—Frankfurt, GER; **1996-99**—Hannover, GER; **2000**—Lisbon, POR; **2001**—Sydney, AUS; **2002, 2005-08**—Shanghai, CHN.

WCT Championship (1971-89)

World Championship Tennis was established in 1967 to promote professional tennis and led the way into the open era. Its major singles and doubles championships were held every May among the top eight regular season finishers on the circuit from 1971 until the WCT folded in 1989.

Multiple winners: John McEnroe (5), Jimmy Connors, Ivan Lendl and Ken Rosewall (2).

Year	Winner	Loser	Score	Year	Winner	Loser	Score
1971	Ken Rosewall	R. Laver	64 16 76 76	1976	Bjorn Borg	G. Vilas	16 61 75 61
1972	Ken Rosewall	R. Laver	46 60 63 67 76	1977	Jimmy Connors	D. Stockton	67 61 64 63
1973	Stan Smith	A. Ashe	63 63 46 64	1978	Vitas Gerulaitis	E. Dibbs	63 62 61
1974	John Newcombe	B. Borg	46 63 63 62	1979	John McEnroe	B. Borg	75 46 62 76
1975	Arthur Ashe	B. Borg	36 64 64 60	1980	Jimmy Connors	J. McEnroe	26 76 61 62

Year-end Tournaments (Cont.)

Year	Winner	Loser	Score	Year	Winner	Loser	Score
1981	John McEnroe	J. Kriek	61 62 64	1986	Anders Jarryd	B. Becker	67 61 61 64
1982	Ivan Lendl	J. McEnroe	62 36 63 63	1987	Miloslav Mecir	J. McEnroe	60 36 62 62
1983	John McEnroe	I. Lendl	62 46 63 67 76	1988	Boris Becker	S. Edberg	64 16 75 62
1984	John McEnroe	J. Connors	61 62 63	1989	John McEnroe	B. Gilbert	63 63 76
1985	Ivan Lendl	T. Mayotte	76 64 61				

WOMEN
WTA Championships

The WTA Tour's year-end tournament took place in March from 1972 until 1986 when the WTA decided to adopt a January-to-November playing season. Given the changeover, two championships were held in 1986. Held in Boca Raton (1972-73), Los Angeles (1974-76, 2002-05), New York (1977, 1979-2000), Oakland (1978), Munich (2001), Madrid (2006-07).

Multiple winners: Martina Navratilova (8); Steffi Graf (5); Chris Evert (4); Monica Seles (3); Kim Clijsters, Evonne Goolagong, Martina Hingis and Gabriela Sabatini (2).

Year	Winner	Loser	Score	Year	Winner	Loser	Score
1972	Chris Evert	K. Reid	75 64	1989	Steffi Graf	M. Navratilova	64 75 26 62
1973	Chris Evert	N. Richey	63 63	1990	Monica Seles	G. Sabatini	64 57 36 64 62
1974	Evonne Goolagong	C. Evert	63 64	1991	Monica Seles	M. Navratilova	64 36 75 60
1975	Chris Evert	M. Navratilova	64 62	1992	Monica Seles	M. Navratilova	75 63 61
1976	Evonne Goolagong	C. Evert	63 57 63	1993	Steffi Graf	A. S. Vicario	61 64 36 61
1977	Chris Evert	S. Barker	26 61 61	1994	Gabriela Sabatini	L. Davenport	63 62 64
1978	M. Navratilova	E. Goolagong	76 64	1995	Steffi Graf	A. Huber	61 26 61 46 63
1979	M. Navratilova	T. Austin	63 36 62	1996	Steffi Graf	M. Hingis	63 46 60 46 60
1980	Tracy Austin	M. Navratilova	62 26 62	1997	Jana Novotna	M. Pierce	76 62 63
1981	M. Navratilova	A. Jaeger	63 76	1998	Martina Hingis	L. Davenport	75 64 46 62
1982	Sylvia Hanika	M. Navratilova	16 63 64	1999	Lindsay Davenport	M. Hingis	64 62
1983	M. Navratilova	C. Evert	62 60	2000	Martina Hingis	M. Seles	67 64 64
1984	M. Navratilova	C. Evert	63 75 61	2001	Serena Williams	L. Davenport	walkover
1985	M. Navratilova	H. Sukova	63 75 64	2002	Kim Clijsters	S. Williams	75 63
1986	M. Navratilova	H. Mandlikova	62 60 36 61	2003	Kim Clijsters	A. Mauresmo	62 60
1986	M. Navratilova	S. Graf	76 63 62	2004	Maria Sharapova	S. Williams	46 62 64
1987	Steffi Graf	G. Sabatini	46 64 60 64	2005	Amelie Mauresmo	M. Pierce	57 76 64
1988	Gabriela Sabatini	P. Shriver	75 62 62	2006	J. Henin-Hardenne	A. Mauresmo	64 63

Note: The final was best-of-five sets from 1984-98 and best-of-three sets from 1972-83 and since 1999.

National Team Tournaments
Davis Cup

Established in 1900 as an annual international tournament by American player Dwight Davis. Originally called the International Lawn Tennis Challenge Trophy. Challenge round system until 1972. Since 1981, the top 16 nations in the world have played a straight knockout tournament over the course of a year. The format is a best-of-five match of two singles, one doubles and two singles over three days. Note that from 1900-24 Australia and New Zealand competed together as Australasia.

Multiple winners: USA (31); Australia (22); France (9); Sweden (7); Australasia (6); British Isles (5); Britain (4); Germany (3); Russia and Spain (2).

Challenge Rounds

Year	Winner	Loser	Score	Site	Year	Winner	Loser	Score	Site
1900	USA	British Isles	3-0	Boston	1929	France	USA	3-2	Paris
1901	Not held				1930	France	USA	4-1	Paris
1902	USA	British Isles	3-2	New York	1931	France	Britain	3-2	Paris
1903	British Isles	USA	4-1	Boston	1932	France	USA	3-2	Paris
1904	British Isles	Belgium	5-0	Wimbledon	1933	Britain	France	3-2	Paris
1905	British Isles	USA	5-0	Wimbledon	1934	Britain	USA	4-1	Wimbledon
1906	British Isles	USA	5-0	Wimbledon	1935	Britain	USA	5-0	Wimbledon
1907	Australasia	British Isles	3-2	Wimbledon	1936	Britain	Australia	3-2	Wimbledon
1908	Australasia	USA	3-2	Melbourne	1937	USA	Britain	4-1	Wimbledon
1909	Australasia	USA	5-0	Sydney	1938	USA	Australia	3-2	Philadelphia
1910	Not held				1939	Australia	USA	3-2	Philadelphia
1911	Australasia	USA	5-0	Christchurch, NZ	1940-45	Not held World War II			
1912	British Isles	Australasia	3-2	Melbourne	1946	USA	Australia	5-0	Melbourne
1913	USA	British Isles	3-2	Wimbledon	1947	USA	Australia	4-1	New York
1914	Australasia	USA	3-2	New York	1948	USA	Australia	5-0	New York
1915-18	Not held World War I				1949	USA	Australia	4-1	New York
1919	Australasia	British Isles	4-1	Sydney	1950	Australia	USA	4-1	New York
1920	USA	Australasia	5-0	Auckland, NZ	1951	Australia	USA	3-2	Sydney
1921	USA	Japan	5-0	New York	1952	Australia	USA	4-1	Adelaide
1922	USA	Australasia	4-1	New York	1953	Australia	USA	3-2	Melbourne
1923	USA	Australasia	4-1	New York	1954	USA	Australia	3-2	Sydney
1924	USA	Australia	5-0	Philadelphia	1955	Australia	USA	5-0	New York
1925	USA	France	5-0	Philadelphia	1956	Australia	USA	5-0	Adelaide
1926	USA	France	4-1	Philadelphia	1957	Australia	USA	3-2	Melbourne
1927	France	USA	3-2	Philadelphia	1958	USA	Australia	3-2	Brisbane
1928	France	USA	4-1	Paris	1959	Australia	USA	3-2	New York

Year	Winner	Loser	Score	Site	Year	Winner	Loser	Score	Site
1960	Australia	Italy	4-1	Sydney	1964	Australia	USA	3-2	Cleveland
1961	Australia	Italy	5-0	Melbourne	1965	Australia	Spain	4-1	Sydney
1962	Australia	Mexico	5-0	Brisbane	1966	Australia	India	4-1	Melbourne
1963	USA	Australia	3-2	Adelaide	1967	Australia	Spain	4-1	Brisbane

Final Rounds

Year	Winner	Loser	Score	Site	Year	Winner	Loser	Score	Site
1968	USA	Australia	4-1	Adelaide	1988	W. Germany	Sweden	4-1	Göteborg
1969	USA	Romania	5-0	Cleveland	1989	W. Germany	Sweden	3-2	Stuttgart
1970	USA	W. Germany	5-0	Cleveland	1990	USA	Australia	3-2	St. Petersburg
1971	USA	Romania	3-2	Charlotte	1991	France	USA	3-1	Lyon
1972	USA	Romania	3-2	Bucharest	1992	USA	Switzerland	3-1	Ft. Worth
1973	Australia	USA	5-0	Cleveland	1993	Germany	Australia	4-1	Dusseldorf
1974	So. Africa	India	walkover	Not held	1994	Sweden	Russia	4-1	Moscow
1975	Sweden	Czech.	3-2	Stockholm	1995	USA	Russia	3-2	Moscow
1976	Italy	Chile	4-1	Santiago	1996	France	Sweden	3-2	Malmo
1977	Australia	Italy	3-1	Sydney	1997	Sweden	USA	5-0	Göteborg
1978	USA	Britain	4-1	Palm Springs	1998	Sweden	Italy	4-1	Milan
1979	USA	Italy	5-0	San Francisco	1999	Australia	France	3-2	Nice
1980	Czech.	Italy	4-1	Prague	2000	Spain	Australia	3-1	Barcelona
1981	USA	Argentina	3-1	Cincinnati	2001	France	Australia	3-2	Melbourne
1982	USA	France	4-1	Grenoble	2002	Russia	France	3-2	Paris
1983	Australia	Sweden	3-2	Melbourne	2003	Australia	Spain	3-1	Melbourne
1984	Sweden	USA	4-1	Göteborg	2004	Spain	USA	3-2	Seville
1985	Sweden	W. Germany	3-2	Munich	2005	Croatia	Slovakia	3-2	Bratislava
1986	Australia	Sweden	3-2	Melbourne	2006	Russia	Argentina	3-2	Moscow
1987	Sweden	India	5-0	Göteborg					

Note: In 1974, India refused to play the final as a protest against the South African government's policies of apartheid.

Fed Cup

Originally the Federation Cup started by the International Tennis Federation as the Davis Cup of women's tennis. Played by 32 teams over one week at one site from 1963-94. Tournament changed to Davis Cup-style format of four rounds and home site in 1995. Currently 16 teams compete in a knockout format, with winners advancing to the quarterfinals, semifinals and finals.

Multiple winners: USA (17); Australia (7); Czechoslovakia and Spain (5); Russia (3); France and Germany (2).

Year	Winner	Loser	Score	Site	Year	Winner	Loser	Score	Site
1963	USA	Australia	2-1	London	1986	USA	Czech.	3-0	Prague
1964	Australia	USA	2-1	Philadelphia	1987	W. Germany	USA	2-1	Vancouver
1965	Australia	USA	2-1	Melbourne	1988	Czech.	USSR	2-1	Melbourne
1966	USA	W. Germany	3-0	Italy	1989	USA	Spain	3-0	Tokyo
1967	USA	Britain	2-0	W. Germany	1990	USA	USSR	2-1	Atlanta
1968	Australia	Holland	3-0	Paris	1991	Spain	USA	2-1	Nottingham
1969	USA	Australia	2-1	Athens	1992	Germany	Spain	2-1	Frankfurt
1970	Australia	Britain	3-0	W. Germany	1993	Spain	Australia	3-0	Frankfurt
1971	Australia	Britain	3-0	Perth	1994	Spain	USA	3-0	Frankfurt
1972	So. Africa	Britain	2-1	So. Africa	1995	Spain	USA	3-2	Valencia
1973	Australia	So. Africa	3-0	W. Germany	1996	USA	Spain	5-0	Atlantic City
1974	Australia	USA	2-1	Italy	1997	France	Netherlands	4-1	Netherlands
1975	Czech.	Australia	3-0	France	1998	Spain	Switzerland	3-2	Geneva
1976	USA	Australia	2-1	Philadelphia	1999	USA	Russia	4-1	Palo Alto
1977	USA	Australia	2-1	Eastbourne	2000	USA	Spain	5-0	Las Vegas
1978	USA	Australia	2-1	Melbourne	2001	Belgium	Russia	2-1	Madrid
1979	USA	Australia	3-0	Spain	2002	Slovakia	Spain	3-1	Canary Islands
1980	USA	Australia	3-0	W. Germany	2003	France	USA	4-1	Moscow
1981	USA	Britain	3-0	Tokyo	2004	Russia	France	3-2	Moscow
1982	USA	W. Germany	3-0	Santa Clara	2005	Russia	France	3-2	Paris
1983	Czech.	W. Germany	2-1	Zurich	2006	Italy	Belgium	3-2	Charleroi
1984	Czech.	Australia	2-1	Brazil	2007	Russia	Italy	4-0	Moscow
1985	Czech.	USA	2-1	Japan					

COLLEGES

NCAA team titles were not sanctioned until 1946. NCAA women's individual and team championships started in 1982.

Men's NCAA Individual Champions (1883-1945)

Multiple winners: Malcolm Chace and Pancho Segura (3); Edward Chandler, George Church, E.B. Dewhurst, Fred Hovey, Frank Guernsey, W.P. Knapp, Robert LeRoy, P.S. Sears, Cliff Sutter, Ernest Sutter and Richard Williams (2).

Year	Year	Year
1883 J. Clark, Harvard (spring)	1888 P.S. Sears, Harvard	1894 Malcolm Chace, Yale
H. Taylor, Harvard (fall)	1889 R.P. Huntington Jr., Yale	1895 Malcolm Chace, Yale
1884 W.P. Knapp, Yale	1890 Fred Hovey, Harvard	1896 Malcolm Whitman, Harvard
1885 W.P. Knapp, Yale	1891 Fred Hovey, Harvard	1897 S.G. Thompson, Princeton
1886 G.M. Brinley, Trinity, CT	1892 William Larned, Cornell	1898 Leo Ware, Harvard
1887 P.S. Sears, Harvard	1893 Malcolm Chace, Brown	1899 Dwight Davis, Harvard

Colleges (Cont.)

Year		Year		Year	
1900	Ray Little, Princeton	1915	Richard Williams, Harv.	1931	Keith Gledhill, Stanford
1901	Fred Alexander, Princeton	1916	G.C. Caner, Harvard	1932	Cliff Sutter, Tulane
1902	William Clothier, Harvard	1917-1918	Not held	1933	Jack Tidball, UCLA
1903	E.B. Dewhurst, Penn	1919	Charles Garland, Yale	1934	Gene Mako, USC
1904	Robert LeRoy, Columbia	1920	Lascelles Banks, Yale	1935	Wilbur Hess, Rice
1905	E.B. Dewhurst, Penn	1921	Philip Neer, Stanford	1936	Ernest Sutter, Tulane
1906	Robert LeRoy, Columbia	1922	Lucien Williams, Yale	1937	Ernest Sutter, Tulane
1907	G.P. Gardner Jr., Harvard	1923	Carl Fischer, Phi. Osteo.	1938	Frank Guernsey, Rice
1908	Nat Niles, Harvard	1924	Wallace Scott, Wash.	1939	Frank Guernsey, Rice
1909	Wallace Johnson, Penn	1925	Edward Chandler, Calif.	1940	Don McNeill, Kenyon
1910	R.A. Holden Jr., Yale	1926	Edward Chandler, Calif.	1941	Joseph Hunt, Navy
1911	E.H. Whitney, Harvard	1927	Wilmer Allison, Texas	1942	Ted Schroeder, Stanford
1912	George Church, Princeton	1928	Julius Seligson, Lehigh	1943	Pancho Segura, Miami-FL
1913	Richard Williams, Harv.	1929	Berkeley Bell, Texas	1944	Pancho Segura, Miami-FL
1914	George Church, Princeton	1930	Cliff Sutter, Tulane	1945	Pancho Segura, Miami-FL

NCAA Men's Division I Champions

Multiple winners (Teams): Stanford (17); UCLA and USC (16); Georgia (5); William & Mary (2). (Players): Matias Boeker, Alex Olmedo, Mikael Pernfors, Dennis Ralston and Ham Richardson (2).

Year	Team winner	Individual Champion	Year	Team winner	Individual Champion
1946	USC	Bob Falkenburg, USC	1977	Stanford	Matt Mitchell, Stanford
1947	Wm. & Mary	Gardner Larned, Wm.& Mary	1978	Stanford	John McEnroe, Stanford
1948	Wm. & Mary	Harry Likas, San Francisco	1979	UCLA	Kevin Curren, Texas
1949	San Francisco	Jack Tuero, Tulane	1980	Stanford	Robert Van't Hof, USC
1950	UCLA	Herbert Flam, UCLA	1981	Stanford	Tim Mayotte, Stanford
1951	USC	Tony Trabert, Cincinnati	1982	UCLA	Mike Leach, Michigan
1952	UCLA	Hugh Stewart, USC	1983	Stanford	Greg Holmes, Utah
1953	UCLA	Ham Richardson, Tulane	1984	UCLA	Mikael Pernfors, Georgia
1954	UCLA	Ham Richardson, Tulane	1985	Georgia	Mikael Pernfors, Georgia
1955	USC	Jose Aguero, Tulane	1986	Stanford	Dan Goldie, Stanford
1956	UCLA	Alex Olmedo, USC	1987	Georgia	Andrew Burrow, Miami-FL
1957	Michigan	Barry MacKay, Michigan	1988	Stanford	Robby Weiss, Pepperdine
1958	USC	Alex Olmedo, USC	1989	Stanford	Donni Leaycraft, LSU
1959	Tulane & Notre Dame	Whitney Reed, San Jose St.	1990	Stanford	Steve Bryan, Texas
1960	UCLA	Larry Nagler, UCLA	1991	USC	Jared Palmer, Stanford
1961	UCLA	Allen Fox, UCLA	1992	Stanford	Alex O'Brien Stanford
1962	USC	Rafael Osuna, USC	1993	USC	Chris Woodruff, Tennessee
1963	USC	Dennis Ralston, USC	1994	USC	Mark Merklein, Florida
1964	USC	Dennis Ralston, USC	1995	Stanford	Sargis Sargsian, Ariz. St.
1965	UCLA	Arthur Ashe, UCLA	1996	Stanford	Cecil Mamiit, USC
1966	USC	Charlie Pasarell, UCLA	1997	Stanford	Luke Smith, UNLV
1967	USC	Bob Lutz, USC	1998	Stanford	Bob Bryan, Stanford
1968	USC	Stan Smith, USC	1999	Georgia	Jeff Morrison, Florida
1969	USC	Joaquin Loyo-Mayo, USC	2000	Stanford	Alex Kim, Stanford
1970	UCLA	Jeff Borowiak, UCLA	2001	Georgia	Matias Boeker, Georgia
1971	UCLA	Jimmy Connors, UCLA	2002	USC	Matias Boeker, Georgia
1972	Trinity-TX	Dick Stockton, Trinity-TX	2003	Illinois	Amer Delic, Illinois
1973	Stanford	Alex Mayer, Stanford	2004	Baylor	Benjamin Becker, Baylor
1974	Stanford	John Whitlinger, Stanford	2005	UCLA	Benedikt Dorsch, Baylor
1975	UCLA	Bill Martin, UCLA	2006	Pepperdine	Benjamin Kohlleoffel, UCLA
1976	USC & UCLA	Bill Scanlon, Trinity-TX	2007	Georgia	Somdev Devvarman, Virginia

NCAA Women's Division I Champions

Multiple winners (Teams): Stanford (15); Florida (4); Georgia, Texas and USC (2). (Players): Sandra Birch, Patty Fendick, Laura Granville, Amber Liu and Lisa Raymond (2).

Year	Team winner	Individual Champion	Year	Team winner	Individual Champion
1982	Stanford	Alycia Moulton, Stanford	1995	Texas	Keri Phoebus, UCLA
1983	USC	Beth Herr, USC	1996	Florida	Jill Craybas, Florida
1984	Stanford	Lisa Spain, Georgia	1997	Stanford	Lilia Osterloh, Stanford
1985	USC	Linda Gates, Stanford	1998	Florida	Vanessa Webb, Duke
1986	Stanford	Patty Fendick, Stanford	1999	Stanford	Zuzana Lesenarova, S. Diego
1987	Stanford	Patty Fendick, Stanford	2000	Georgia	Laura Granville, Stanford
1988	Stanford	Shaun Stafford, Florida	2001	Stanford	Laura Granville, Stanford
1989	Stanford	Sandra Birch, Stanford	2002	Stanford	Bea Bielik, Wake Forest
1990	Stanford	Debbie Graham, Stanford	2003	Florida	Amber Liu, Stanford
1991	Stanford	Sandra Birch, Stanford	2004	Stanford	Amber Liu, Stanford
1992	Florida	Lisa Raymond, Florida	2005	Stanford	Zuzana Zemenova, Baylor
1993	Texas	Lisa Raymond, Florida	2006	Stanford	Suzi Babos, California
1994	Georgia	Angela Lettiere, Georgia	2007	Georgia Tech	Audra Cohen, Miami-FL

GOLF

Zach Johnson tries on his new green jacket, with the help of Phil Mickelson, after his 2007 Masters win.

TIGER APPROACHING

Tiger Woods' win at the PGA Championship at Southern Hills inches him closer to Jack Nicklaus' record of 18 majors.

ZACH JOHNSON, THE SELF-DESCRIBED "NORMAL GUY" FROM CEDAR RAPIDS, IOWA, WON THE MASTERS AND A 40-REGULAR GREEN JACKET.

Angel Cabrera, the cigarette-puffing, coachless, self-made pro from Argentina, won the U.S. Open.

Padraig Harrington, the unassuming career grinder from Ireland, won the British Open.

And yet the 2007 golf season belonged once again to—pause for yawn—a slightly balding, cut-and-buff, Sunday red-wearing, 31-year-old gajillionaire who changes diapers and record books on a regular basis. Yes, only Tiger Woods can overpower a golf year where so much changed and, by the sheer power of his performances, so much stayed the same.

Woods won "only" one major, the PGA Championship at Southern Hills Sauna/Country Club in the sweltering August heat of Tulsa, Okla. It was his 13th major victory and fifth in his last 12 tries. If he continues at this rate, Tiger mathematicians calculate that

Woods will slip past Jack Nicklaus' 18 majors as early as 2010, perhaps at St. Andrews.

If it happens, it will be the record that matters most to Woods. After all, Woods used to keep a list of Nicklaus' majors on his bedroom wall. But major by major, Woods moves closer to performing a golf eclipse of the great Nicklaus. The win at Southern Hills gives him four PGA Championships to go along with his four Masters, three British Opens and two (slacker) U.S. Opens.

"Well, when you first start your career, it's—18 [majors] is just a long way away," said Woods after the PGA Championship. "And even though I'm at 13, it's still a long way away. You can't get it done in one year."

It took Nicklaus more than 20 years to reach 18 majors. If Woods keeps up this pace, it would take him a little more than 14 years. Even

 Gene Wojciechowski is a senior writer for ESPN.com.

Tiger Woods won lucky major No. 13 at the PGA Championship and now has just five to go to tie Jack Nicklaus' record.

Nicklaus himself seems ready to concede the record to Woods.

"Oh, I think he probably will," said Nicklaus. "He probably should. He's got that in his mind and as a goal. I think he's as talented a player as I've ever seen. I think he's absolutely fantastic. Will he? Who knows, but I would say he has a lot of years to win not many more tournaments."

Woods won the PGA and finished second behind Johnson at Augusta and Cabrera at Oakmont. He wasn't much of a factor at Carnoustie, but the 12th-place finish didn't exactly send him into a funk.

He won four of his next five tournaments, including the PGA Championship and The Tour Championship (and with it, the inaugural FedExCup).

No wonder he's built like a free safety. You'd have biceps too if you had to lift all that hardware.

"If you would ask me that 12 years into my career, would I have had this many wins and this many majors, there's no way," Woods said.

"I've exceeded my own expectations and I'm certainly not against that."

There are no signs of a slump or boredom. He won without the presence of his father Earl, who died of cancer in May 2006. He won with the presence of his new daughter Sam Alexis, who was born a couple of months before the PGA

Championship victory. He won as rumors surfaced that the instructor-pupil relationship with his coach Hank Haney may be coming to a respectful end.

Woods finished atop the money list. Again. Woods finished atop the Player of the Year voting. Again. Woods was part of the U.S. team that won The Presidents Cup. Again. The likeable trio of Johnson, Cabrera and Harrington had their major moments, but Woods had most everything else. Again.

The unnerving prospect for the rest of the PGA Tour is that Woods says he's a better player than he was in 2000.

Better? Wasn't 2000 the year he carpet bombed the golf world by winning 11 tournaments, including the U.S. Open (by a mind-boggling 15 strokes), the British Open and the PGA?

"Yeah, by far," said Woods.

"Just experience. Understanding how to handle it and how to manage my game around the golf course. I have more shots than I did then just because [of] that many more years to learn them."

And more years (and championships) to come.

GENE WOJCIECHOWSKI'S

Biggest Stories of the Year in **Golf**

10 Peppery Language.

Golf Channel analyst Dottie Pepper, unaware that she was still on live air, calls the United States Solheim Cup team, "Chokin' freakin' dogs." The comment comes after the Americans squandered multiple chances against the Europeans, but still retained a one-point lead after Day Two.

The U.S. women eventually win the Cup, but Pepper's on-air gaffe isn't soon forgotten. European captain Helen Alfredsson calls it, "totally inappropriate." And Tiger Woods, when asked about it at The Tour Championship, dryly observes, "I don't think she's going to get a lot of interviews from the players."

09 FedEx Delivers (sort of).

The first-ever FedExCup, a season-long points scoring system and four-event Championship Series contrived by PGA Tour Commissioner Tim Finchem, receives mixed reviews. It's better than Silly Season golf, but it suffers from several flaws. The most glaring: the two most

important players on the Tour— Woods and Phil Mickelson—skip FedExCup events. It also doesn't help that some players think Finchem forced the late-season format on them. Woods wins The Tour Championship, but his $10 million bonus is deferred. Tour orders.

08 Drug Testing.

Finchem reverses his stance on instituting a drug testing policy for the PGA Tour. Against it in 2006, he announces that a policy could be in place in time for the 2008 season. The LPGA Tour also begins testing in 2008. The issue gains instant momentum when Gary Player tells the media during a British Open news conference that, "I know for a fact that some golfers are doing it. . . We're dreaming if we think it's not going to come into golf."

07 Zach Attack.

Iowan Zach Johnson, 31, who had one Tour win prior to 2007 and whose playing profile didn't fit many of the supposed criteria needed to win at 7,445-yard Augusta National, surprises the experts with a two-stroke Masters victory over Woods, Rory Sabbatini and Retief Goosen. Johnson, who shoots a record-tying high score of 289, overcomes the elements, the hellaciously fast greens, and the often-asphyxiating pressure of winning his first major. His course management is near perfect and his strategy of laying up on the four par-5s helps win him the tournament (he was a combined 11-under on the par 5s).

06 Wobbly Wie.
Teenage phenom Michelle Wie ventures dangerously close to cautionary tale as she becomes embroiled in controversies galore. She deals with a wrist injury, is criticized by such LPGA legends as Annika Sorenstam, and plays lousy golf. Her first-round withdrawal from the Ginn Tribute (hosted by Sorenstam) after 16 holes raises questions about the severity of her injury and whether she quit because she was 14 over par at the time and in danger of being barred from playing in any more 2007 LPGA events.

05 Harrington survives.
Ireland's Padraig Harrington becomes the first European in eight years to win the British Open, but only after a four-hole playoff and a Jean Van de Velde moment on Carnoustie's gruesome 18th hole during regulation.

Harrington hits two balls into Barry Burn on No. 18, costing him the late lead. But the whiny Sergio Garcia, who began the day with a three-stroke advantage over the field, shoots a two-over-par 73, including a bogey on 18 that costs him the tournament in regulation. Harrington birdies the first playoff hole and the lead holds up.

04 Oakmont and an Angel.
Oakmont Country Club and Angel Cabrera earn rave reviews during the U.S. Open. Oakmont gets them because of its timeless layout and its fair play. Cabrera receives major kudos for staring down eventual second-place finishers Tiger Woods and Jim Furyk. Cabrera shot a 5-over-par 285 for the tournament, but his Sunday round of 69 is a masterpiece under difficult circumstances.

03 Phil's new teacher.
Phil Mickelson, trying to shake his post-2006 U.S. Open hangover, parts ways with longtime instructor Rick Smith. In his place: former Tiger Woods instructor, Butch Harmon. He doesn't win a major, but he does win The Players Championship. A wrist injury hampers his season, though. Mickelson ties for 24th at The Masters, misses the cut at the U.S. Open and British Open, and finishes 32nd at the PGA Championship.

02 Ochoa Rules.
Lorena Ochoa easily laps her closest competitor on the LPGA money list, earning well over $3 million. She wins seven tournaments through mid-October, including three in a row in August that began with her first-ever major title at the British Open at St. Andrews.

01 This is a recording
Tiger Woods keeps chasing history...and continues to gain ground each year. This time he inches closer to Jack Nicklaus' record 18 majors victories, thanks to a PGA Championship win. Anybody who thinks marriage and fatherhood is going to cause a Tiger slump simply hasn't been paying attention.

2006-2007
Season In Review

SPORTS ALMANAC

Tournament Results

Schedules and results of PGA, LPGA, Champions and European PGA tournaments from Nov. 5, 2006 through Oct. 14, 2007.

PGA Tour
Late 2006

Last Rd	Tournament	Winner	Earnings	Runner-Up
Nov. 5	The Tour Championship	Adam Scott (269)	$1,170,000	J. Furyk (272)
Nov. 12@	Merrill Lynch Shootout	Jerry Kelly/ Rod Pampling (185)*	337,500 (each)	J. Leonard/ S. Verplank (185)
Dec. 10@	WGC: World Cup	Germany—Marcel Siem/ Bernhard Langer (268)*	700,000 (each)	Scotland—C. Montgomerie/ M. Warren (268)
Nov. 26@	LG Skins Game	Stephen Ames (8 skins)	590,000	F. Couples (9 skins)
Dec. 17@	Target World Challenge	Tiger Woods (272)	1,350,000	G. Ogilvy (276)

@ Unofficial PGA Tour money event.

*Playoffs: Merrill Lynch—Kelly/Pampling won on 1st hole; **World Cup**—Siem/Langer won on 1st hole.

2007 (through Oct. 14)

Last Rd	Tournament	Winner	Earnings	Runner-Up
Jan. 7	Mercedes-Benz Championships	Vijay Singh (278)	$1,100,000	A. Scott (280)
Jan. 14	Sony Open in Hawaii	Paul Goydos (266)	936,000	L. Donald & C. Howell III (267)
Jan. 21	Bob Hope Chrysler Classic	Charley Hoffman (343)*	900,000	J. Rollins (343)
Jan. 28	Buick Invitational	Tiger Woods (273)	936,000	C. Howell III (275)
Feb. 4	FBR Open	Aaron Baddeley (263)	1,080,000	J. Rollins (264)
Feb. 11	AT&T Pebble Beach Pro-Am	Phil Mickelson (268)	990,000	K. Sutherland (273)
Feb. 18	Nissan Open	Charles Howell III (268)*	936,000	P. Mickelson (268)
Feb. 25	WGC: Accenture Match Play Championship	Henrik Stenson (2&1)	1,350,000	G. Ogilvy
Feb. 25	Mayakoba Classic	Fred Funk (266)*	630,000	J. Coceres (266)
Mar. 4	Honda Classic	Mark Wilson (275)*	990,000	3-way tie (275)#
Mar. 11	PODS Championship	Mark Calcavecchia (274)	954,000	J. Senden & H. Slocum (275)
Mar. 18	Arnold Palmer Invitational	Vijay Singh (272)	990,000	R. Mediate (274)
Mar. 25	WGC: CA Championship	Tiger Woods (278)	1,350,000	B. Wetterich (280)
Apr. 1	Shell Houston Open	Adam Scott (271)	990,000	S. Appleby & B. Watson (274)
Apr. 8	**The Masters** (Augusta, Ga.)	Zach Johnson (289)	1,305,000	3-way tie (291)#
Apr. 15	Verizon Heritage	Boo Weekley (270)	972,000	E. Els (271)
Apr. 22	Zurich Classic of New Orleans	Nick Watney (273)	1,098,000	K. Duke (276)
Apr. 29	EDS Byron Nelson Championship	Scott Verplank (267)	1,134,000	L. Donald (268)
May 6	Wachovia Championship	Tiger Woods (275)	1,134,000	S. Stricker (277)
May 13	The Players Championship	Phil Mickelson (277)	1,620,000	S. Garcia (279)
May 20	AT&T Classic	Zach Johnson (273)*	972,000	R. Imada (273)
May 27	Crowne Plaza Invitational	Rory Sabbatini (266)*	1,080,000	J. Furyk & B. Langer (266)
June 3	The Memorial Tournament	K.J. Choi (271)	1,080,000	R. Moore (272)
June 10	Stanford St. Jude Championship	Woody Austin (267)	1,080,000	B. Davis (272)
June 17	**U.S. Open** (Oakmont, Pa.)	Angel Cabrera (285)	1,260,000	J. Furyk & T. Woods (286)
June 24	Travelers Championship	Hunter Mahan (265)*	1,080,000	J. Williamson (265)
July 1	Buick Open	Brian Bateman (273)	882,000	3-way tie (274)#
July 8	AT&T National	K.J. Choi (271)	1,080,000	S. Stricker (274)
July 15	John Deere Classic	Jonathan Byrd (266)	738,000	T. Clark (267)
July 22	U.S. Bank Championship	Joe Ogilvie (266)	720,000	T. Herron (270)
July 22	**British Open** (Carnoustie)	Padraig Harrington (277)*	1,542,450	S. Garcia (277)
July 29	Canadian Open	Jim Furyk (268)	900,000	V. Singh (269)
Aug. 5	Reno-Tahoe Open	Steve Flesch (273)	540,000	K. Stadler & C. Warren (278)
Aug. 5	WGC: Bridgestone Invitational	Tiger Woods (272)	1,350,000	J. Rose & R. Sabbatini (280)
Aug. 12	**PGA Championship** (Tulsa, Okla.)	Tiger Woods (272)	1,260,000	W. Austin (274)
Aug. 19	Wyndham Championship	Brandt Snedeker (266)	900,000	3-way tie (268)#
Aug. 26	The Barclays†	Steve Stricker (268)	1,260,000	K.J. Choi (270)
Sept. 3	Deutsche Bank Championship†	Phil Mickelson (268)	1,260,000	3-way tie (270)#
Sept. 9	BMW Championship†	Tiger Woods (262)	1,260,000	A. Baddeley (264)

PGA Tour Results (Cont.)

Last Rd	Tournament	Winner	Earnings	Runner-Up
Sept. 16	The Tour Championship†	Tiger Woods (257)	$1,260,000	M. Calcavecchia & Z. Johnson (265)
Sept. 23	Turning Stone Resort Championship	Steve Flesch (270)	1,080,000	M. Allen (272)
Sept. 30	Viking Classic	Chad Campbell (275)	630,000	J. Wagner (276)
Sept. 30	The Presidents Cup (Montreal)	United States (19½)	—	International (14½)
Oct. 7	Valero Texas Open	Justin Leonard (261)*	810,000	J. Parnevik (261)
Oct. 14	Frys.com Open	George McNeill (264)	720,000	D.J. Trahan (268)

† FedExCup Playoff event.

*Playoffs: Bob Hope Chrysler—Hoffman won on 1st hole; **Nissan**—Howell III won on 3rd hole; **Mayakoba**—Funk won on 2nd hole; **Honda**—Wilson won on 3rd hole; **PODS**—Calcavecchia won on 3rd hole; **AT&T Classic**—Johnson won on 1st hole; **Crowne Plaza**—Sabbatini won on 1st hole; **Travelers**—Mahan won on 1st hole; **British**—Harrington won the 4-hole playoff; **Valero Texas**—Leonard won on 3rd hole.

#Second place ties (3 players or more): 3-WAY—**Honda** (J. Coceres, B. Weekley, C. Villegas); **Masters** (T. Woods, R. Goosen, R. Sabbatini); **Buick Open** (J. Gore, J. Leonard, W. Austin); **Wyndham** (T. Petrovic, B. Mayfair, J. Overton); **Deutsche Bank** (B. Wetterich, T. Woods, A. Oberholser).

FedExCup

The top 144 players in the FedExCup Point Standings as of the Wyndham Championship on Aug. 19, played a four-week "playoff" for a shot at the inaugural FedExCup trophy and its accompanying $10 million bonus. The field narrowed during the first three playoff weeks until 30 were remaining for The Tour Championship on Sept. 16.

2007 Top 3	Events	Points
1 Tiger Woods	3	123,033
2 Steve Stricker	4	110,455
3 Phil Mickelson	3	109,358

PGA Majors

The Masters

Edition: 71st **Dates:** April 5–8
Site: Augusta National GC, Augusta, Ga.
Par: 36-36—72 (7445 yards) **Purse:** $7,418,464

		1 2 3 4	Tot	Earnings
1	Zach Johnson	71-73-76-69	289	$1,305,000
2	Tiger Woods	73-74-72-72	291	541,333
	Retief Goosen	76-76-70-69	291	541,333
	Rory Sabbatini	73-76-73-69	291	541,333
5	Justin Rose	69-75-75-73	292	275,500
	Jerry Kelly	75-69-78-70	292	275,500
7	Stuart Appleby	75-70-73-75	293	233,812
	Padraig Harrington	77-68-75-73	293	233,812
9	David Toms	70-78-74-72	294	210,250
10	Vaughn Taylor	71-72-77-75	295	181,250
	Luke Donald	73-74-75-73	295	181,250
	Paul Casey	79-68-77-71	295	181,250

Early round leaders: 1st—Rose & Brett Wetterich (69); 2nd—Wetterich & Tim Clark (142); 3rd—Appleby (218).
Top amateur: none.

British Open

Edition: 136th **Dates:** July 19–22
Site: Carnoustie Golf Club, Carnoustie, Scotland
Par: 36-35—71 (7112 yards) **Purse:** $8,637,720

		1 2 3 4	Tot	Earnings
1	Padraig Harrington*	69-73-68-67	277	$1,542,450
2	Sergio Garcia*	65-71-68-73	277	925,470
3	Andres Romero	71-70-70-67	278	596,414
4	Ernie Els	72-73-68-69	279	411,320
	Richard Green	72-73-70-64	279	411,320
6	Stewart Cink	69-73-68-70	280	299,235
	Hunter Mahan	73-73-69-65	280	299,235
8	K.J. Choi	69-69-72-71	281	194,863
	Ben Curtis	72-74-70-65	281	194,863
	Steve Stricker	71-72-64-74	281	194,863
	Mike Weir	71-68-72-70	281	194,863

Early round leaders: 1st—Garcia (65); 2nd—Garcia (136); 3rd—Garcia (204).
Top amateur: Rory McIlroy (289, tied for 42nd).

*Harrington (3-3-4-5—15) defeated Garcia (5-3-4-4—16) in a four-hole playoff (played on holes 1, 16, 17, 18).

U.S. Open

Edition: 107th **Dates:** June 14–17
Site: Oakmont Country Club, Oakmont, Pa.
Par: 35-35—70 (7355 yards) **Purse:** $7,000,000

		1 2 3 4	Tot	Earnings
1	Angel Cabrera	69-71-76-69	285	$1,260,000
2	Jim Furyk	71-75-70-70	286	611,336
	Tiger Woods	71-74-69-72	286	611,336
4	Niclas Fasth	71-71-75-70	287	325,923
5	David Toms	72-72-73-72	289	248,948
	Bubba Watson	70-71-74-74	289	248,948
7	Nick Dougherty	68-77-74-71	290	194,245
	Jerry Kelly	74-71-73-72	290	194,245
	Scott Verplank	73-71-74-72	290	194,245
10	Stephen Ames	73-69-73-76	291	154,093
	Paul Casey	77-66-72-76	291	154,093
	Justin Rose	71-71-73-76	291	154,093

Early round leaders: 1st—Nick Dougherty (68); 2nd—Cabrera (140); 3rd—Aaron Baddeley (212).
Top amateur: none.

PGA Championship

Edition: 89th **Dates:** Aug. 9–12
Site: Southern Hills Country Club, Tulsa, Oklahoma
Par: 35-35—70 (7131 yards) **Purse:** $7,000,000

		1 2 3 4	Tot	Earnings
1	Tiger Woods	71-63-69-69	272	$1,260,000
2	Woody Austin	68-70-69-67	274	756,000
3	Ernie Els	72-68-69-66	275	476,000
4	Arron Oberholser	68-72-70-69	279	308,000
	John Senden	69-70-69-71	279	308,000
6	Simon Dyson	73-71-72-64	280	227,500
	Trevor Immelman	75-70-66-69	280	227,500
	Geoff Ogilvy	69-68-74-69	280	227,500
9	Scott Verplank	70-66-74-71	281	170,333
	Kevin Sutherland	73-69-68-71	281	170,333
	Boo Weekley	76-69-65-71	281	170,333

Early round leaders: 1st—Graeme Storm (65); 2nd—Woods (134); 3rd—Woods (203).
Top amateur: none.

LPGA Tour
Late 2006

Last Rd	Tournament	Winner	Earnings	Runner-Up
Nov. 5	Mizuno Classic	Jarrie Webb (202)	$180,000	K. Higo (206)
Nov. 12	The Mitchell Company TOC	Lorena Ochoa (267)	150,000	J. Inkster & P. Creamer (277)
Nov. 19	ADT Tour Championship	Julieta Granada (68)†	1,000,000	L. Ochoa (70)
Dec. 17	Lexus Cup	Team Asia (12½)	50,000/member	Team International (11½)

† At the ADT Tour Championship, the top 8 players after 54 holes participate in a final-day shootout.

2007 (through Oct. 14)

Last Rd	Tournament	Winner	Earnings	Runner-Up
Jan 21	Women's World Cup of Golf	Paraguay (279)	$120,000	United States (286)
Feb. 17	SBS Open at Turtle Bay	Paula Creamer (207)	165,000	J. Granada (208)
Feb. 24	Fields Open in Hawaii	Stacy Prammanasudh (202)	180,000	J.Y. Lee (203)
Mar. 11	MasterCard Classic	Meaghan Francella (205)*	180,000	A. Sorenstam (205)
Mar. 25	Safeway International	Lorena Ochoa (270)	225,000	S. Pettersen (272)
Apr. 1	**Kraft Nabisco Championship** (Rancho Mirage, Calif.)	Morgan Pressel (285)	300,000	3-way tie (286)#
Apr. 15	Ginn Open	Brittany Lincicome (278)	390,000	L. Ochoa (279)
Apr. 29	Corona Championship	Silvia Cavalleri (272)	195,000	L. Ochoa & J. Granada (274)
May 6	SemGroup Championship	Mi Hyun Kim (210)*	210,000	J. Inkster (210)
May 13	Michelob Ultra Open	Suzann Pettersen (274)*	330,000	J.Y. Lee (274)
May 20	Sybase Classic	Lorena Ochoa (270)	210,000	S. Lee (273)
May 27	Corning Classic	Young Kim (268)	195,000	M.H. Kim & P. Creamer (271)
June 3	Ginn Tribute	Nicole Castrale (279)*	390,000	L. Ochoa (279)
June 10	**McDonald's LPGA Championship** (Havre de Grace, Md.)	Suzann Pettersen (274)	300,000	K. Webb (275)
June 24	Wegmans Rochester	Lorena Ochoa (280)*	270,000	I-K Kim (280)
July 1	**U.S. Women's Open** (Southern Pines, N.C.)	Cristie Kerr (279)	560,000	L. Ochoa & A. Park (281)
July 15	Jamie Farr Owens Corning Classic	Se Ri Pak (267)	195,000	M. Pressel (270)
July 22	HSBC Women's World Match Play	Seon Hwa Lee (2&1)	500,000	A. Miyazato
July 29	Evian Masters	Natalie Gulbis (284)*	450,000	J. Jang (284)
Aug. 5	**Ricoh Women's British Open** (St. Andrews, Scotland)	Lorena Ochoa (287)	320,512	J.Y. Lee & M. Hjorth (291)
Aug. 19	CN Canadian Women's Open	Lorena Ochoa (268)	337,500	P. Creamer (271)
Aug. 26	Safeway Classic	Lorena Ochoa (204)	255,000	4-way tie (209)*
Sept. 2	State Farm Classic	Sherri Steinhauer (271)	195,000	C. Kim (272)
Sept. 9	NW Arkansas Classic	Stacy Lewis (65)%	amateur	3-way tie (66)#
Sept. 16	The Solheim Cup (Halmstad, Sweden)	United States (16)	—	Europe (12)
Sept. 30	Navistar LPGA Classic	Maria Hjorth (274)	195,000	S. Prammanasudh (275)
Oct. 7	Longs Drugs Challenge	Suzann Pettersen (277)*	165,000	L. Ochoa (277)
Oct. 14	Samsung World Championship	Lorena Ochoa (270)	250,000	M. H. Kim (274)

% Rain-shortened from 54 holes to 18 holes. Money totals and stats are therefore unofficial.

*Playoffs: **MasterCard**—Francella won on 4th hole; **SemGroup**—Kim won on 1st hole; **Michelob Ultra**—Pettersen won on 3rd hole; **Ginn Tribute**—Castrale won on 1st hole; **Wegmans**—Ochoa won on 2nd hole; **Evian**—Gulbis won on 1st hole; **Longs Drug**—Pettersen won on 2nd hole.

#Second place ties (3 players or more): 4-WAY—**Safeway** (I-B Park, C. Kim, S. Gustafson, M. McKay). 3-WAY—**Kraft Nabisco** (C. Matthew, B. Lincicome, S. Pettersen); **NW Arkansas** (T. Lu, K. McPherson, K. Hull).

LPGA Majors

Kraft Nabisco Championship

Edition: 36th   **Dates:** March 29-April 1
Site: Mission Hills CC, Rancho Mirage, Calif.
Par: 36-36—72 (6673 yards)   **Purse:** $2,000,000

		1 2 3 4	Tot	Earnings
1	Morgan Pressel	74-72-70-69	285	$300,000
2	Catriona Matthew	70-73-72-71	286	140,945
	Brittany Lincicome	72-71-71-72	286	140,945
	Suzann Pettersen	72-69-71-74	286	140,945
5	a-Stacy Lewis	71-73-73-70	287	amateur
	Shi Hyun Ahn	68-73-74-72	287	69,688
	Stacy Prammanasudh	76-70-70-71	287	69,688
	Meaghan Francella	72-72-69-74	287	69,688
9	Maria Hjorth	70-73-72-73	288	50,114
10	Three tied at 289.			

Early round leaders: 1st—Ahn (68); 2nd—Lorena Ochoa & Paula Creamer (140); 3rd—Pettersen & Se Ri Pak (212).

McDonald's LPGA Championship

Edition: 53rd   **Dates:** June 7-10
Site: Bulle Rock Golf Course, Havre de Grace, Md.
Par: 36-36—72 (6596 yards)   **Purse:** $2,000,000

		1 2 3 4	Tot	Earnings
1	Suzann Pettersen	69-67-71-67	274	$300,000
2	Karrie Webb	68-69-71-67	275	179,038
3	Na On Min	71-70-65-70	276	129,880
4	Lindsey Wright	71-70-71-66	278	100,473
5	Angela Park	67-73-68-71	279	80,869
6	Paula Creamer	71-68-73-68	280	53,422
	Sophie Gustafson	70-71-71-68	280	53,422
	Brittany Lincicome	69-69-73-69	280	53,422
	Lorena Ochoa	71-71-69-69	280	53,422
10	Four tied at 281.			

Early round leaders: 1st—Kim Saiki-Maloney, Birdie Kim & Park (67); 2nd—Pettersen (136); 3rd—Min (206).
Top amateur: none.

LPGA Majors (Cont.)

U.S. Women's Open

Edition: 62nd **Dates:** June 28-July 1
Site: Pine Needles Lodge & Golf Club, Southern Pines, N.C.
Par: 35-36–71 (6664 yds) **Purse:** $3,100,000

		1 2 3 4	Tot	Earnings
1	Cristie Kerr	71-72-66-70	279	$560,000
2	Angela Park	68-69-74-70	281	271,022
	Lorena Ochoa	71-71-68-71	281	271,022
4	Se Ri Pak	74-72-68-68	282	130,549
	In-Bee Park	69-73-71-69	282	130,549
6	Ji-Yai Shin	70-69-71-74	284	103,581
7	Jee Young Lee	72-71-71-71	285	93,031
8	Mi Hyun Kim	71-75-70-70	286	82,464
	Jeong Jang	72-71-70-73	286	82,464
10	Four tied at 287.			

Early round leaders: 1st—Angela Park (68); 2nd—In-Bee Park (142); 3rd—Kerr (209).

Top amateur: Jennie Lee and Jennifer Song (294, tied for 39th).

Ricoh Women's British Open

Edition: 14th **Dates:** Aug. 2-5
Site: Old Course at St. Andrews, St. Andrews, Scotland
Par: 36-37–73 (6638 yards) **Purse:** $2,000,000

		1 2 3 4	Tot	Earnings
1	Lorena Ochoa	67-73-73-74	287	$320,512
2	Jee Young Lee	72-73-75-71	291	170,272
	Maria Hjorth	75-73-72-71	291	170,272
4	Reilley Rankin	73-74-74-71	292	110,176
5	Eun-Hee Ji	73-71-77-72	293	84,135
	Se Ri Pak	73-73-75-72	293	84,135
7	Miki Saiki	76-70-81-67	294	61,098
	Paula Creamer	73-75-74-72	294	61,098
	Catriona Matthew	73-68-80-73	294	61,098
	Linda Wessberg	74-73-72-75	294	61,098

Early round leaders: 1st—Ochoa (67); 2nd—Ochoa (140); 3rd—Ochoa (213).

Top amateur: Melissa Reid (296, t-16th place)

Champions Tour
(formerly Senior PGA Tour)

Late 2006

Last Rd	Tournament	Winner	Earnings	Runner-Up
Dec. 3@	Del Webb Father/Son Challenge	Bernhard/Stefan Langer (120)	$100,000 (each)	Bob/Kevin Tway & Vijay/Qass Singh (121)

2007 (through Oct. 14)

Last Rd	Tournament	Winner	Earnings	Runner-Up
Jan. 14@	Wendy's Champions Skins Game	Jack Nicklaus & Tom Watson (9 skins)	$320,000	G. Player & J. Haas (6)
Jan. 21	MasterCard Championship	Hale Irwin (193)	290,000	T. Kite & J. Thorpe (198)
Jan. 28	Turtle Bay Championship	Fred Funk (193)	240,000	5-way tie (204)#
Feb. 11	Allianz Championship	Mark James (201)	240,000	J. Haas (203)
Feb. 18	Outback Steakhouse Pro-Am	Tom Watson (209)	240,000	A. Bean & J. Haas (210)
Feb. 25	ACE Group Classic	Bobby Wadkins (201)	240,000	A. Doyle (202)
Mar. 11	Toshiba Classic	Jay Haas (194)	247,500	R.W. Eaks (196)
Mar. 18	AT&T Champions Classic	Tom Purtzer (206)*	240,000	L. Roberts (206)
Apr. 1	Ginn Championship	Keith Fergus (204)	375,000	H. Irwin & M. O'Meara (205)
Apr. 22	Liberty Mutual Legends of Golf	Jay Haas (207)*	395,000	T. Kite (207)
May 6	FedEx Kinko's Classic	Scott Hoch (201)	240,000	D.A. Weibring (203)
May 20	Regions Charity Classic	Brad Bryant (204)*	240,000	R.W. Eaks (204)
May 27	**Senior PGA Championship** (Kiawah Island, S.C.)	Denis Watson (279)	360,000	E. Romero (281)
June 3	Boeing Championship	Loren Roberts (197)	247,500	E. Romero (200)
June 10	The Principal Charity Classic	Jay Haas (201)	240,000	B. Bryant & R.W. Eaks (204)
June 24	Bank of America Championship	Jay Haas (203)	247,500	B. Bryant & L. Thompson (206)
July 1	Commerce Bank Championship	Lonnie Nielsen (199)	225,000	L. Roberts (201)
July 8	**U.S. Senior Open** (Kohler, Wis.)	Brady Bryant (282)	470,000	B. Crenshaw (285)
July 15	Dick's Sporting Goods Open	R.W. Eaks (199)	240,000	B. Vaughan (202)
July 29	**Senior British Open** (Muirfield, Scotland)	Tom Watson (284)	320,176	S. Ginn & M. O'Meara (285)
Aug. 5	3M Championship	D.A. Weibring (198)	262,500	J. Haas (199)
Aug. 19	**JELD-WEN Tradition** (Sunriver, Ore.)	Mark McNulty (272)	390,000	D. Edwards (277)
Aug. 26	Boeing Classic	Denis Watson (207)*	240,000	6-way tie (207)#
Sept. 2	Wal-Mart First Tee Open	Gil Morgan (202)	300,000	H. Irwin (204)
Sept. 16	Greater Hickory Classic	R.W. Eaks (199)	240,000	J. Haas & R. Spittle (201)
Sept. 23	SAS Championship	Mark Wiebe (198)	300,000	D. Quigley (201)
Oct. 7	**Senior Players Championship** (Baltimore, Md.)	Loren Roberts (267)	390,000	T. Watson (273)
Oct. 14	Administaff Small Business Classic	Bernhard Langer (191)	255,000	M. O'Meara (199)

%Weather-shortened.
@Unofficial Champions Tour money event.

*Playoffs: AT&T Championship—Purtzer won on 4th hole; Liberty Mutual Legends—Haas won on 1st hole; Regions Charity—Bryant won on 3rd hole.

#Second place tie (3 players or more): 6-WAY—Boeing Classic (G. Morgan, D. Quigley, R.W. Eaks, D. Eger, J. Ozaki, C. Stadler). 5-WAY—Turtle Bay (T. Kite, K. Murota, T. Putzer, L. Roberts, D. Watson).

Champions Tour Majors

Senior PGA Championship

Edition: 68th   **Dates:** May 24-27
Site: Kiawah Island Resort, Kiawah Island, S.C.
Par: 36-36—72 (7188 yards)   **Purse:** $2,000,000

		1 2 3 4	Tot	Earnings
1	Denis Watson	71-71-69-68 —	279	$360,000
2	Eduardo Romero	68-70-71-72 —	281	216,000
3	Nick Price	71-70-70-71 —	282	136,000
4	Joe Ozaki	69-71-72-72 —	284	96,000
5	Tim Simpson	76-71-69-70 —	286	76,000
6	Brad Bryant	71-72-73-71 —	287	66,000
7	Tom Kite	75-76-67-70 —	288	60,000
	Craig Stadler	72-75-70-71 —	288	60,000
9	Jay Haas	72-71-75-71 —	289	52,000
	Kong Meshiai	76-70-72-71 —	289	52,000

Early round leaders: 1st—Romero (68); 2nd—Romero (138); 3rd—Romero (209).

Top amateur: none.

U.S. Senior Open

Edition: 28th   **Dates:** July 5-8
Site: Whistling Straits, Kohler, Wis.
Par: 36-36—72 (7068 yards)   **Purse:** $2,600,000

		1 2 3 4	Tot	Earnings
1	Brad Bryant	71-72-71-68 —	282	$470,000
2	Ben Crenshaw	72-67-76-70 —	285	280,000
3	Loren Roberts	70-69-73-74 —	286	176,756
4	Tom Watson	70-66-73-78 —	287	123,175
5	Jay Haas	73-71-73-72 —	289	78,415
	Joe Ozaki	72-69-73-75 —	289	78,415
	Tom Purtzer	73-67-74-75 —	289	78,415
	Sam Torrance	73-69-71-76 —	289	78,415
	Denis Watson	74-73-67-75 —	289	78,415
	D.A. Weibring	72-68-74-75 —	289	78,415

Early round leaders: 1st—Eduardo Romero (66); 2nd—Watson (136); 3rd—Watson (209).

Top amateur: Danny Green & George Zahringer (296, tied for 33rd).

Senior British Open

Edition: 21st (5th as major)   **Dates:** July 26-29
Site: Muirfield Golf Club, Gullane, East Lothian, Scotland
Par: 35-36—71 (6970 yards)   **Purse:** $2,000,000

		1 2 3 4	Tot	Earnings
1	Tom Watson	70-71-70-73 —	284	$320,176
2	Stewart Ginn	71-70-69-75 —	285	166,885
	Mark O'Meara	72-71-70-72 —	285	166,885
4	Jay Haas	70-75-73-70 —	288	75,585
	Lonnie Nielsen	69-74-74-71 —	288	75,585
	Loren Roberts	74-72-71-71 —	288	75,585
	Eduardo Romero	70-71-73-74 —	288	75,585
8	John Ross	71-72-74-72 —	289	47,986
9	Donnie Hammond	73-71-71-75 —	290	43,055
10	Gordon Brand	68-73-74-76 —	291	34,351
	Tom Kite	70-76-74-71 —	291	34,351
	Des Smyth	70-70-77-74 —	291	34,351
	Sam Torrance	69-75-71-76 —	291	34,351

Early round leaders: 1st—4-way tie (68); 2nd—Smyth (140); 3rd—Ginn (210).

Top amateur: none.

JELD-WEN Tradition

Edition: 19th   **Dates:** Aug. 16-19
Site: Crosswater Golf Club, Sunriver, Oregon
Par: 36-36—72 (7683 yards)   **Purse:** $2,600,000

		1 2 3 4	Tot	Earnings
1	Mark McNulty	66-68-70-68 —	272	$390,000
2	David Edwards	67-65-72-73 —	277	227,760
3	D.A. Weibring	72-66-68-72 —	278	187,200
4	Tom Kite	70-69-68-73 —	280	140,400
	Loren Roberts	72-69-69-70 —	280	140,400
6	Keith Fergus	70-66-72-73 —	281	93,600
	Bob Gilder	72-71-72-66 —	281	93,600
	Tom Watson	68-72-67-74 —	281	93,600
9	R.W. Eaks	70-71-67-74 —	282	70,200
	Denis Watson	72-70-72-68 —	282	70,200

Early round leaders: 1st—McNulty & Mike Reid (66); 2nd—Edwards (132); 3rd—McNulty & Edwards (204).

Top amateur: none.

Sr. Players Championship

Edition: 25th   **Dates:** Oct. 4-7
Site: Baltimore Country Club, Timonium, Md.
Par: 35-35—70 (7037 yards)   **Purse:** $2,600,000

		1 2 3 4	Tot	Earnings
1	Loren Roberts	67-66-67-67 —	267	$390,000
2	Tom Watson	69-68-68-68 —	273	228,800
3	Fred Funk	68-69-66-71 —	274	171,600
	Scott Simpson	70-69-70-65 —	274	171,600
5	Danny Edwards	68-69-71-68 —	276	114,400
	D.A. Weibring	70-70-68-68 —	276	114,400
7	Keith Fergus	70-71-70-66 —	277	$72,800
	Scott Hoch	67-68-74-68 —	277	72,800
	Hale Irwin	69-71-68-69 —	277	72,800
	Eduardo Romero	73-66-70-68 —	277	72,800
	Mark Wiebe	67-70-69-71 —	277	72,800
	Fuzzy Zoeller	73-66-70-68 —	277	72,800

Early round leaders: 1st—5-way tie (67); 2nd—Roberts (133); 3rd—Roberts (200).

Top amateur: none.

European PGA Tour

Official money won on the European Tour is presented in euros (E).

Late 2006

Last Rd	Tournament	Winner	Earnings	Runner-Up
Nov. 12	HSBC Champions Tournament	Yong-eun Yang (274)	E655,883	T. Woods (276)
Nov. 19	UBS Hong Kong Open	Jose Manuel Lara (265)	259,178	J. Pagunsan (266)
Nov. 26	MasterCard Masters	Justin Rose (276)	170,353	G. Chalmers & R. Green (278)
Dec. 3	Blue Chip New Zealand Open	Nathan Green (279)	145,831	6-way tie (281)#
Dec. 10	Alfred Dunhill Championship	Alvaro Quiros (275)	158,500	C. Schwartzel (276)
Dec. 17	South African Airways Open	Ernie Els (264)	158,500	T. Immelman (267)

#Second place ties (3 players or more): 6-WAY—**New Zealand** (M. Campbell, N. Dougherty, M. Fraser, J. Moseley, W. Ormsby, B. Rumford).

2007 (through Oct. 14)

Last Rd	Tournament	Winner	Earnings	Runner-Up
Jan. 14	Joburg Open	Ariel Canete (266)	E158,500	A. McLardy (268)
Jan. 21	Abu Dhabi Championship	Paul Casey (271)	257,876	P. Hanson & M.A. Jimenez (272)
Jan. 28	Commercialbank Qatar Masters	Retief Goosen (273)	282,743	N. O'Hern (274)
Feb. 4	Dubai Desert Classic	Henrik Stenson (269)	309,862	E. Els (270)
Feb. 11	Maybank Malaysian Open	Peter Hedblom (280)	165,895	J-F Lucquin (281)
Feb. 18	Enjoy Jakarta HSBC Indonesia Open	Mikko Ilonen (275)	134,564	3-way tie (276)
Feb. 25	WGC: Accenture Match Play Championship	Henrik Stenson (2&1)	1,027,631	G. Ogilvy
Mar. 4	Johnnie Walker Classic	Anton Haig (275)*	310,801	R. Sterne & O. Wilson (275)
Mar. 11	Clariden Leu Singapore Masters	Wen-chong Liang (277)*	139,075	I. Steel (277)
Mar. 18	TCL Classic	Chapchai Nirat (266)	127,046	R. Echenique (269)
Mar. 25	WGC: CA Championship	Tiger Woods (278)	1,014,505	B. Wetterich (280)
Mar. 25	Madeira Island Open	Daniel Vancsik (270)	116,660	D. Frost & S. Luna (277)
Apr. 1	Portugal Open	Pablo Martin-Benavides (277)	amateur	R. Jacquelin (278)
Apr. 8	The Masters Tournament	Zach Johnson (289)	975,770	3-way tie (291)#
Apr. 15	Volvo China Open	Markus Brier (274)	249,125	3-way tie (279)#
Apr. 22	BMW Asian Open	Raphael Jacquelin (278)	283,570	S. Kjeldsen (280)
Apr. 29	Spanish Open	Charl Schwartzel (272)	333,330	J. Randhawa (273)
May 6	Telecom Italia Open%	G. Fernandez-Castano (200)*	283,330	M. Brier (200)
May 13	Valle Romano Andalucia Open	Lee Westwood (268)	166,660	F. Andersson Hed & P. Archer (270)
May 20	Irish Open	Padraig Harrington (283)*	416,660	B. Dredge (283)
May 27	BMW PGA Championship	Anders Hansen (280)*	725,000	J. Rose (280)
June 3	Celtic Manor Wales Open	Richard Sterne (263)	368,812	4-way tie (264)#
June 10	BA-CA Golf Open	Richard Green (268)*	216,660	J-F Remesy (268)
June 17	U.S. Open	Angel Cabrera (285)	943,182	J. Furyk & T. Woods (286)
June 17	Saint-Omer Open	Carl Suneson (276)	83,330	3-way tie (279)
June 24	BMW International Championship	Niclas Fasth (275)	333,330	B. Langer & J-F Lima (277)
July 1	French Open	Graeme Storm (277)	666,660	S. Hansen (278)
July 8	Smurfit Kappa European Open	Colin Montgomerie (269)	593,580	N. Fasth (270)
July 15	The Barclays Scottish Open	Gregory Havret (270)*	738,255	P. Mickelson (270)
July 22	British Open (Carnoustie)	Padraig Harrington (277)*	1,106,617	S. Garcia (277)
July 29	Deutsche Bank TPC	Andres Romero (269)	600,000	S. Hansen & O. Wilson (272)
Aug. 5	WGC: Bridgestone Invitational	Tiger Woods (272)	989,226	J. Rose & R. Sabbatini (280)
Aug. 5	The Russian Open	Per-Ulrik Johansson (265)	244,250	R-J Derksen (271)
Aug. 12	PGA Championship	Tiger Woods (272)	914,040	W. Austin (274)
Aug. 19	Scandinavian Masters	Mikko Ilonen (274)	266,660	5-way tie (276)#
Aug. 26	The KLM Open	Ross Fisher (268)	266,660	J. Luiten (269)
Sept. 2	Johnnie Walker Championship	Marc Warren (280)*	343,693	S. Wakefield (280)
Sept. 9	Omega European Masters	Brett Rumford (268)*	333,330	P. Archer (268)
Sept. 16	Mercedes-Benz Championship	Soren Hansen (271)	320,000	P. Archer & A. Forsyth (275)
Sept. 23	The Quinn Direct British Masters	Lee Westwood (273)	434,727	I. Poulter (278)
Sept. 30	Seve Trophy	Great Britain/Ireland (16½)	—	Europe (11½)
Oct. 7	Alfred Dunhill Links Championship	Nick Dougherty (270)	562,625	J. Rose (272)
Oct. 14	HSBC World Match Play	Ernie Els (6&4)	587,148	A. Cabrera
Oct. 14	Madrid Valle Romano	Mads Vibe-Hastrup (272)	150,000	A. Canizares (275)

% Weather-shortened.

*Playoffs: Johnnie Walker Classic—Haig won on 1st hole; **Singapore**—Liang won on 1st hole; **Italia**—Fernandez-Castano won on 2nd hole; **Irish**—Harrington won on 1st hole; **BMW PGA**—Hansen won on 1st hole; **BA-CA**—Green won on 1st hole; **Scottish**—Havret won on 1st hole; **British**—Harrington won the four-hole playoff; **Johnnie Walker Championship**—Warren won on 1st hole; **European**—Rumford won on 1st hole.

#Second place ties (3 players or more): 5-WAY—**Scandinavian** (C. Cevaer, N. Dougherty, J-B Gonnet, P. Hedblom, M. Kaymer). 4-WAY—**Wales** (B. Dredge, S. Kjeldsen, M. Mamat, M, Vibe-Hastrup). 3-WAY—**Indonesia** (S. Kapur, F. Minoza, A. Tampion); **Masters** (R. Goosen, R. Sabbatini, T. Woods); **Volvo China** (S. Hend, G. McDowell, A. McLardy); **Saint-Omer** (F. Calmels, P. Fowler, M. Higley).

The Official World Golf Ranking

Begun in 1986, the Official World Golf Ranking (formerly the Sony World Ranking) combines the best golfers on the world's six leading professional tours (U.S. PGA Tour, European Tour, Japan Golf Tour, South African PGA Tour, Asian PGA Tour and the PGA Tour of Australasia) in conjunction with the Canadian, Nationwide and Challenge Tours. Rankings are based on a rolling two-year period and weighted in favor of more recent results. Points are awarded after each worldwide tournament according to finish. Final points-per-tournament averages are determined by dividing a player's total points by the number of tournaments played over that two-year period (through Oct. 14, 2007).

		Avg			Avg			Avg
1	Tiger Woods, USA	23.60	6	Adam Scott, AUS	6.31	11	Vijay Singh, FIJ	5.41
2	Phil Mickelson, USA	9.54	7	Padraig Harrington, IRE	5.96	12	Justin Rose, ENG	5.40
3	Jim Furyk, USA	7.79	8	K.J. Choi, KOR	5.64	13	Geoff Ogilvy, AUS	5.36
4	Ernie Els, RSA	7.51	9	Sergio Garcia, ESP	5.61	14	Zach Johnson, USA	4.80
5	Steve Stricker, USA	7.18	10	Rory Sabbatini, RSA	5.55	15	Henrik Stenson, SWE	4.76

2007 Tour Statistics (through Oct. 14)

Statistical leaders on the PGA, LPGA, Champions and European PGA tours.

PGA

	Scoring	Avg		Putting	Avg		Driving Distance	Avg
1	Tiger Woods	67.79	1	Jonathan Byrd	1.728	1	Bubba Watson	316.4
2	Ernie Els	69.29	2	Fredrik Jacobson	1.730	2	John Daly	314.3
3	Justin Rose	69.30	3	Tiger Woods	1.733	3	J.B. Holmes	313.1
4	Steve Stricker	69.39	4	Tim Clark	1.741	4	Robert Garrigus	312.0
5	Phil Mickelson	69.42	5	Brian Gay	1.742	5	Scott Gutschewski	306.4
6	Jim Furyk	69.47	6	Jesper Parnevik	1.742	6	Tag Ridings	305.9
7	Sergio Garcia	69.48	7	Ryuji Ramada	1.743	7	Harrison Frazar	304.3
8	Vijay Singh	69.49	8	Steve Stricker	1.743	8	Matt Hendrix	303.7
9	K.J. Choi	69.61	9	Nathan Green	1.745	9	Brett Wetterich	303.7
10	Scott Verplank	69.71	10	Justin Rose	1.745	10	Charles Warren	303.2

LPGA

	Scoring	Avg		Putting	Avg		Driving Distance	Avg
1	Lorena Ochoa	69.73	1	Catriona Matthew	1.768	1	Karin Sjodin	275.8
2	Paula Creamer	70.99	2	Lorena Ochoa	1.769	2	Jee Young Lee	273.6
3	Suzann Pettersen	71.27	3	Se Ri Pak	1.769	3	Suzann Pettersen	272.7
4	Morgan Pressel	71.33	4	Natalie Gulbis	1.777	4	Lorena Ochoa	271.6
5	Mi Hyun Kim	71.37	5	Shi Hyun Ahn	1.778	5	Brittany Lincicome	271.1
6	Stacy Prammanasudh	71.38	6	Mi Hyun Kim	1.782	6	Sophie Gustafson	270.0
7	Se Ri Pak	71.40	7	Laura Davies	1.788	7	Laura Davies	268.5
8	Angela Park	71.47	8	Beth Bader	1.789	8	Maria Hjorth	266.5
9	Shi Hyun Ahn	71.58	9	Young Kim	1.789	9	Christina Kim	266.0
10	Angela Stanford	71.59	10	Morgan Pressel	1.792	10	Alena Sharp	264.0

Champions

	Scoring	Avg		Putting	Avg		Driving Distance	Avg
1	Jay Haas	69.30	1	Loren Roberts	1.720	1	Tom Purtzer	295.5
2	Loren Roberts	69.41	2	Joe Ozaki	1.724	2	Eduardo Romero	292.4
3	Eduardo Romero	70.02	3	D.A. Weibring	1.728	3	R.W. Eaks	287.4
4	D.A. Weibring	70.05	4	R.W. Eaks	1.734	4	Craig Stadler	287.2
5	Brad Bryant	70.28	5	Ben Crenshaw	1.739	5	Dick Mast	286.7

European PGA

	Scoring	Avg		Putting	Avg		Driving Distance	Avg
1	Ernie Els	70.10	1	Nick O'Hern	1.732	1	Alvaro Quiros	310.1
2	Richard Sterne	70.33	2	Marcus Fraser	1.739	2	Emanuele Canonica	302.1
3	Justin Rose	70.47	3	Marc Warren	1.745	3	Daniel Vancsik	301.8
4	Richard Green	70.52	4	Richard Green	1.746	4	Henrik Stenson	300.4
5	Mikko Ilonen	70.57	5	Ernie Els	1.746	5	Ricardo Gonzalez	299.8

Key: Scoring—average strokes per round adjusted to the average score of the field each week. If the field is under par, each player's score is adjusted upward a corresponding amount and vice-versa if the field is over par. This keeps a player from receiving an advantage for playing easier-than-average courses. **Putting**—average number of putts taken on greens hit in regulation; **Driving Distance**—average computed by charting exact distances of two tee shots on the most open par-4 or par-5 holes on both front and back nine.

Money Leaders

Official money leaders of PGA, LPGA, Champions and European PGA tours for 2006 and unofficial money leaders for 2007, through Oct. 14, as compiled by the PGA, LPGA and European PGA. Listed are tournaments played (TP), cuts made (CM), 1st, 2nd and 3rd place finishes and earnings for the year.

PGA

Arnold Palmer Award standings

	FINAL 2006	TP	CM	Finish 1-2-3	Earnings		2007 (through Oct. 14)	TP	CM	Finish 1-2-3	Earnings
1	Tiger Woods	15	14	8-1-1	$9,941,563	1	Tiger Woods	16	16	7-3-0	$10,867,052
2	Jim Furyk	24	22	2-4-3	7,213,316	2	Phil Mickelson	21	16	3-1-2	5,819,988
3	Adam Scott	19	17	1-3-3	4,978,858	3	Vijay Singh	27	25	2-1-0	4,728,376
4	Vijay Singh	27	25	1-2-0	4,602,416	4	Steve Stricker	23	19	1-2-1	4,663,077
5	Geoff Ogilvy	20	17	2-1-0	4,354,969	5	K.J. Choi	25	21	2-1-0	4,587,859
6	Phil Mickelson	19	18	2-1-0	4,256,505	6	Rory Sabbatini	23	18	1-2-3	4,550,040
7	Trevor Immelman	24	19	1-2-0	3,844,189	7	Jim Furyk	23	20	1-2-2	4,154,046
8	Stuart Appleby	23	20	2-0-0	3,470,457	8	Zach Johnson	23	18	2-1-0	3,922,338
9	Luke Donald	18	16	1-0-1	3,177,408	9	Sergio Garcia	19	17	0-2-1	3,721,185
10	Brett Wetterich	25	16	1-2-0	3,023,185	10	Aaron Baddeley	22	19	1-1-0	3,441,119

LPGA

	FINAL 2006	TP	CM	Finish 1-2-3	Earnings		2007 (through Oct. 14)	TP	CM	Finish 1-2-3	Earnings
1	Lorena Ochoa	25	25	6-6-2	$2,592,872	1	Lorena Ochoa	21	21	7-5-2	$3,318,421
2	Karrie Webb	21	20	5-3-1	2,090,113	2	Suzann Pettersen	19	16	3-1-0	1,367,059
3	Annika Sorenstam	20	19	3-5-1	1,971,741	3	Mi Hyun Kim	22	20	1-2-2	1,187,034
4	Julieta Granada	30	26	1-2-0	1,633,586	4	Paula Creamer	20	18	1-2-0	1,123,246
5	Cristie Kerr	26	26	3-3-0	1,578,362	5	Cristie Kerr	19	16	1-0-1	1,051,772
6	Mi Hyun Kim	30	27	2-0-1	1,332,274	6	Seon Hwa Lee	23	21	1-0-0	965,152
7	Juli Inkster	21	21	1-2-0	1,326,442	7	Angela Park	23	22	0-1-3	932,309
8	Jeong Jang	27	26	1-3-0	1,151,070	8	Morgan Pressel	21	19	1-1-1	927,484
9	Hee-Won Han	27	26	2-2-0	1,147,651	9	Jeong Jang	22	19	0-1-2	922,293
10	Pat Hurst	24	19	1-2-1	1,128,662	10	Jee Young Lee	20	16	0-3-0	916,851

Champions Tour

	FINAL 2006	TP	CM	Finish 1-2-3	Earnings		2007 (through Oct. 14)	TP	CM	Finish 1-2-3	Earnings
1	Jay Haas	21	21	4-2-3	$2,420,227	1	Jay Haas	25	25	4-4-0	$2,523,121
2	Loren Roberts	21	21	4-2-2	2,365,395	2	Loren Roberts	21	21	2-3-2	2,020,002
3	Brad Bryant	20	20	2-4-1	1,692,417	3	Brad Bryant	22	22	2-2-2	1,716,219
4	Tom Kite	25	25	2-2-0	1,643,348	4	R.W. Eaks	24	21	2-4-1	1,505,098
5	Gil Morgan	27	27	1-1-4	1,525,050	5	D.A. Weibring	25	25	1-1-1	1,473,131
6	Scott Simpson	27	27	1-2-3	1,340,676	6	Denis Watson	23	23	2-1-1	1,396,183
7	Jim Thorpe	26	26	1-1-0	1,296,784	7	Tom Watson	11	11	2-1-1	1,329,365
8	Tom Jenkins	27	26	1-1-2	1,287,666	8	Tom Kite	26	26	0-3-2	1,261,607
9	Bobby Wadkins	25	24	2-1-1	1,193,173	9	Tom Putzer	25	25	1-1-1	1,223,070
10	David Edwards	20	20	1-2-2	1,191,086	10	Hale Irwin	20	19	1-2-0	1,175,180

European PGA

Order of Merit standings. All amounts are listed in Euros (E).

	FINAL 2006	TP	CM	Finish 1-2-3	Earnings		2007 (through Oct. 14)	TP	CM	Finish 1-2-3	Earnings
1	Padraig Harrington	20	17	1-3-0	E2,489,337	1	Ernie Els	18	17	2-1-3	E2,496,237
2	Paul Casey	25	22	3-1-0	2,454,084	2	Padraig Harrington	14	13	2-0-0	2,278,942
3	David Howell	21	17	2-0-0	2,321,166	3	Justin Rose	10	10	1-3-0	2,247,535
4	Robert Karlsson	30	26	2-1-1	2,044,936	4	Henrik Stenson	16	12	2-0-1	1,986,191
5	Ernie Els	15	15	1-2-1	1,716,208	5	Niclas Fasth	21	19	1-1-1	1,855,439
6	Henrik Stenson	23	20	2-2-0	1,709,359	6	Angel Cabrera	13	12	1-1-0	1,753,024
7	Luke Donald	13	13	0-2-1	1,658,060	7	Andres Romero	21	14	1-0-1	1,672,157
8	Ian Poulter	22	19	1-1-1	1,589,074	8	Søren Hansen	24	17	1-2-1	1,631,654
9	Colin Montgomerie	26	19	1-1-2	1,534,748	9	Retief Goosen	20	15	1-1-1	1,447,495
10	Johan Edfors	25	18	3-0-0	1,505,583	10	Paul Casey	21	19	1-0-0	1,351,087

National Team Competition
2007 Solheim Cup

The 10th Solheim Cup tournament, Sept. 14-16, at Halmstad Golf Club, Halmstad, Sweden.

Rosters

The 2007 U.S. Team was chosen on the basis of points awarded for wins and top 20 finishes at official LPGA events over a two-year qualifying period. The top 10 finishers on the points list automatically qualified for the 12-member team, and U.S. Captain Betsy King selected the final two players.

The 2007 European Team players were chosen on the basis of points awarded weekly to the top 10 finishers at official Ladies European Tour (LET) events. The top nine players in the LET points standings automatically qualify for the 12-member team. European Team captain Helen Alfredsson selected the final three players.

United States: Qualifiers—Paula Creamer, Cristie Kerr, Morgan Pressel, Juli Inkster, Stacy Prammanasudh, Pat Hurst, Natalie Gulbis, Brittany Lincicome, Angela Stanford and Sherri Steinhauer; Captain's selections—Nicole Castrale and Laura Diaz.

Europe: Qualifiers—Gwladys Nocera (France), Trish Johnson (England), Bettina Hauert (Germany), Laura Davies (England), Becky Brewerton (Wales), Annika Sorenstam (Sweden), Suzann Pettersen (Norway), Catriona Matthew (Scotland) and Sophie Gustafson (Sweden); Captain's selections—Maria Hjorth (Sweden), Iben Tinning (Denmark) and Linda Wessberg (Sweden).

First Day

Foursome Match Results

Winner	Score	Loser
Hurst/Kerr	halved	Petterson/Gustafson
Steinhauer/Diaz	4&2	Sorenstam/Matthew
Inkster/Creamer	2&1	Davies/Brewerton
Nocera/Hjorth	3&2	Gulbis/Pressel

USA wins morning, 2½-1½

Four-Ball Match Results

Winner	Score	Loser
Matthew/Tinning	4&2	Hurst/Lincicome
Stanford/Prammanasudh	halved	Sorenstam/Hjorth
Castrale/Kerr	3&2	Gustafson/Nocera
Creamer/Pressel	halved	Johnson/Davies

Afternoon tied, 2-2 (USA leads, 4½-3½)

Second Day

Foursome Match Results

Winner	Score	Loser
Steinhauer/Diaz	halved	Hjorth/Nocera
Creamer/Inkster	halved	Gustafson/Pettersen
Hurst/Stanford	4&2	Tinning/Hauert
Matthew/Sorenstam	1-up	Castrale/Kerr

Morning tied, 2-2 (USA leads, 6½-5½)

Four-Ball Match Results

Winner	Score	Loser
Creamer/Lincicome	halved	Wessberg/Hjorth
Prammanasudh/Inkster	halved	Johnson/Tinning
Brewerton/Davies	2-up	Gulbis/Castrale
Sorenstam/Pettersen	3&2	Kerr/Pressel

Europe wins afternoon, 3-1 (Europe leads, 8½-7½)

Third Day

Singles Match Results

Winner	Score	Loser
Matthew	3&2	Diaz
Hurst	2&1	Gustafson
Prammanasudh	2-up	Pettersen
Inkster	4&3	Tinning
Steinhauer	halved	Brewerton
Stanford	3&2	Johnson

Winner	Score	Loser
Pressel	2&1	Sorenstam
Davies	4&3	Lincicome
Castrale	3&2	Hauert
Creamer	2&1	Hjorth
Wessberg	1-up	Kerr
Gulbis	4&3	Nocera

USA wins day, 8½-3½

USA wins Solheim Cup, 16-12

Overall Records

One point is awarded for a win. One-half point is awarded for a half.

United States

	W	L	H	Pts
Paula Creamer	2	0	3	3½
Juli Inkster	2	0	2	3
Pat Hurst	2	1	1	2½
Angela Stanford	2	0	1	2½
Sherri Steinhauer	1	0	2	2
Stacy Prammanasudh	1	0	2	2
Nicole Castrale	2	2	0	2
Laura Diaz	1	1	1	1½
Cristie Kerr	1	3	1	1½
Morgan Pressel	1	2	1	1½
Natalie Gulbis	1	2	0	1
Brittany Lincicome	0	2	1	½

Europe

	W	L	H	Pts
Catriona Matthew	3	1	0	3
Maria Hjorth	1	1	3	2½
Annika Sorenstam	2	2	1	2½
Suzann Pettersen	1	1	2	2
Iben Tinning	1	2	1	1½
Linda Wessberg	1	0	1	1½
Becky Brewerton	1	1	1	1½
Laura Davies	1	1	1	1½
Gwladys Nocera	1	2	1	1½
Sophie Gustafson	0	2	2	1
Trish Johnson	0	1	2	1
Bettina Hauert	0	2	0	0

1860-2007
Through the Years

SPORTS ALMANAC

Major Golf Championships
MEN
The Masters

The Masters has been played every year (except during World War II) since 1934 at the Augusta National Golf Club in Augusta, Ga. Both the course and the tournament were created by Bobby Jones; (*) indicates playoff winner.

Multiple winners: Jack Nicklaus (6); Arnold Palmer and Tiger Woods (4); Jimmy Demaret, Nick Faldo, Gary Player and Sam Snead (3); Seve Ballesteros, Ben Crenshaw, Ben Hogan, Bernhard Langer, Phil Mickelson, Byron Nelson, Jose Maria Olazabal, Horton Smith and Tom Watson (2).

Year	Winner	Score	Runner-up
1934	Horton Smith	284	Craig Wood (285)
1935	Gene Sarazen*	282	Craig Wood (282)
1936	Horton Smith	285	Harry Cooper (286)
1937	Byron Nelson	283	Ralph Guldahl (285)
1938	Henry Picard	285	Ralph Guldahl & Harry Cooper (287)
1939	Ralph Guldahl	279	Sam Snead (280)
1940	Jimmy Demaret	280	Lloyd Mangrum (284)
1941	Craig Wood	280	Byron Nelson (283)
1942	Byron Nelson*	280	Ben Hogan (280)
1943-45	Not held		World War II
1946	Herman Keiser	282	Ben Hogan (283)
1947	Jimmy Demaret	281	Frank Stranahan & Byron Nelson (283)
1948	Claude Harmon	279	Cary Middlecoff (284)
1949	Sam Snead	282	Lloyd Mangrum & Johnny Bulla (285)
1950	Jimmy Demaret	283	Jim Ferrier (285)
1951	Ben Hogan	280	Skee Riegel (282)
1952	Sam Snead	286	Jack Burke Jr. (290)
1953	Ben Hogan	274	Porky Oliver (279)
1954	Sam Snead*	289	Ben Hogan (289)
1955	Cary Middlecoff	279	Ben Hogan (286)
1956	Jack Burke Jr.	289	Ken Venturi (290)
1957	Doug Ford	283	Sam Snead (286)
1958	Arnold Palmer	284	Doug Ford & Fred Hawkins (285)
1959	Art Wall Jr.	284	Cary Middlecoff (285)
1960	Arnold Palmer	282	Ken Venturi (283)
1961	Gary Player	280	Arnold Palmer & Charles R. Coe (281)
1962	Arnold Palmer*	280	Dow Finsterwald & Gary Player (280)
1963	Jack Nicklaus	286	Tony Lema (287)
1964	Arnold Palmer	276	Jack Nicklaus & Dave Marr (282)
1965	Jack Nicklaus	271	Arnold Palmer & Gary Player (280)
1966	Jack Nicklaus*	288	Gay Brewer Jr. & Tommy Jacobs (288)
1967	Gay Brewer Jr.	280	Bobby Nichols (281)
1968	Bob Goalby	277	Roberto DeVicenzo (278)
1969	George Archer	281	Billy Casper, George Knudson & Tom Weiskopf (282)
1970	Billy Casper*	279	Gene Littler (279)
1971	Charles Coody	279	Jack Nicklaus & Johnny Miller (281)
1972	Jack Nicklaus	286	Bruce Crampton, Bobby Mitchell & Tom Weiskopf (289)

Year	Winner	Score	Runner-up
1973	Tommy Aaron	283	J.C. Snead (284)
1974	Gary Player	278	Tom Weiskopf, & Dave Stockton (280)
1975	Jack Nicklaus	276	Johnny Miller & Tom Weiskopf (277)
1976	Ray Floyd	271	Ben Crenshaw (279)
1977	Tom Watson	276	Jack Nicklaus (278)
1978	Gary Player	277	Hubert Green, Rod Funseth & Tom Watson (278)
1979	Fuzzy Zoeller*	280	Ed Sneed & Tom Watson (280)
1980	Seve Ballesteros	275	Gibby Gilbert & Jack Newton (279)
1981	Tom Watson	280	Jack Nicklaus & Johnny Miller (282)
1982	Craig Stadler*	284	Dan Pohl (284)
1983	Seve Ballesteros	280	Ben Crenshaw & Tom Kite (284)
1984	Ben Crenshaw	277	Tom Watson (279)
1985	Bernhard Langer	282	Curtis Strange, Seve Ballesteros & Ray Floyd (284)
1986	Jack Nicklaus	279	Greg Norman & Tom Kite (280)
1987	Larry Mize*	285	Seve Ballesteros & Greg Norman (285)
1988	Sandy Lyle	281	Mark Calcavecchia (282)
1989	Nick Faldo*	283	Scott Hoch (283)
1990	Nick Faldo*	278	Ray Floyd (278)
1991	Ian Woosnam	277	J.M. Olazabal (278)
1992	Fred Couples	275	Ray Floyd (277)
1993	Bernhard Langer	277	Chip Beck (281)
1994	J.M. Olazabal	279	Tom Lehman (281)
1995	Ben Crenshaw	274	Davis Love III (275)
1996	Nick Faldo	276	Greg Norman (281)
1997	Tiger Woods	270	Tom Kite (282)
1998	Mark O'Meara	279	Fred Couples & David Duval (280)
1999	J.M. Olazabal	280	Davis Love III (282)
2000	Vijay Singh	278	Ernie Els (281)
2001	Tiger Woods	272	David Duval (274)
2002	Tiger Woods	276	Retief Goosen (279)
2003	Mike Weir*	281	Len Mattiace (281)
2004	Phil Mickelson	279	Ernie Els (280)
2005	Tiger Woods*	276	Chris DiMarco (276)
2006	Phil Mickelson	281	Tim Clark (283)
2007	Zach Johnson	289	Tiger Woods, Retief Goosen & Rory Sabbatini (291)

*PLAYOFFS:

1935: Gene Sarazen (144) def. Craig Wood (149) in 36 holes. **1942:** Byron Nelson (69) def. Ben Hogan (70) in 18 holes. **1954:** Sam Snead (70) def. Ben Hogan (71) in 18 holes. **1962:** Arnold Palmer (68) def. Gary Player (71) and Dow Finsterwald (77) in 18 holes. **1966:** Jack Nicklaus (70) def. Tommy Jacobs (72) and Gay Brewer Jr. (78) in 18 holes. **1970:** Billy Casper (69) def. Gene Littler (74) in 18 holes. **1979:** Fuzzy Zoeller (4-3) def. Ed Sneed (4-4) and Tom Watson (4-4) on 2nd hole of sudden death. **1982:** Craig Stadler (4) def. Dan Pohl (5) on 1st hole of sudden death. **1987:** Larry Mize (4-3) def. Greg Norman (4-4) and Seve Ballesteros (5) on 2nd hole of sudden death. **1989:** Nick Faldo (5-3) def. Scott Hoch (5-4) on 2nd hole of sudden death. **1990:** Nick Faldo (4-4) def. Raymond Floyd (4) on 2nd hole of sudden death. **2003:** Mike Weir (5) def. Len Mattiace (6) on 1st hole of sudden death. **2005:** Tiger Woods (3) def. Chris DiMarco (4) on 1st hole of sudden death.

U.S. Open

Played at a different course each year, the U.S. Open was launched by the new U.S. Golf Association in 1895. The Open was a 36-hole event from 1895-97 and has been 72 holes since then. It switched from a 3-day, 36-hole Saturday finish to 4 days of play in 1965. Note that (*) indicates playoff winner and (a) indicates amateur.

Multiple winners: Willie Anderson, Ben Hogan, Bobby Jones and Jack Nicklaus (4); Hale Irwin (3); Julius Boros, Billy Casper, Ernie Els, Retief Goosen, Ralph Guldahl, Walter Hagen, Lee Janzen, John McDermott, Cary Middlecoff, Andy North, Gene Sarazen, Alex Smith, Payne Stewart, Curtis Strange, Lee Trevino and Tiger Woods (2).

Year	Winner	Score	Runner-up	Course	Location
1895	Horace Rawlins	173	Willie Dunn (175)	Newport GC	Newport, R.I.
1896	James Foulis	152	Horace Rawlins (155)	Shinnecock Hills GC	Southampton, N.Y.
1897	Joe Lloyd	162	Willie Anderson (163)	Chicago GC	Wheaton, Ill.
1898	Fred Herd	328	Alex Smith (335)	Myopia Hunt Club	Hamilton, Mass.
1899	Willie Smith	315	George Low, W.H. Way & Val Fitzjohn (326)	Baltimore CC	Baltimore
1900	Harry Vardon	313	J.H. Taylor (315)	Chicago GC	Wheaton, Ill.
1901	Willie Anderson*	331	Alex Smith (331)	Myopia Hunt Club	Hamilton, Mass.
1902	Laurie Auchterlonie	307	Stewart Gardner (313)	Garden City GC	Garden City, N.Y.
1903	Willie Anderson*	307	David Brown (307)	Baltusrol GC	Springfield, N.J.
1904	Willie Anderson	303	Gil Nicholls (308)	Glen View Club	Golf, Ill.
1905	Willie Anderson	314	Alex Smith (316)	Myopia Hunt Club	Hamilton, Mass.
1906	Alex Smith	295	Willie Smith (302)	Onwentsia Club	Lake Forest, Ill.
1907	Alec Ross	302	Gil Nicholls (304)	Phila. Cricket Club	Chestnut Hill, Pa.
1908	Fred McLeod*	322	Willie Smith (322)	Myopia Hunt Club	Hamilton, Mass.
1909	George Sargent	290	Tom McNamara (294)	Englewood GC	Englewood, N.J.
1910	Alex Smith*	298	Macdonald Smith & John McDermott (298)	Phila. Cricket Club	Chestnut Hill, Pa.
1911	John McDermott*	307	George Simpson & Mike Brady (307)	Chicago GC	Wheaton, Ill.
1912	John McDermott	294	Tom McNamara (296)	CC of Buffalo	Buffalo
1913	a-Francis Ouimet*	304	Harry Vardon & Ted Ray (304)	The Country Club	Brookline, Mass.
1914	Walter Hagen	290	a-Chick Evans (291)	Midlothian CC	Blue Island, Ill.
1915	a-John Travers	297	Tom McNamara (298)	Baltusrol GC	Springfield, N.J.
1916	a-Chick Evans	286	Jock Hutchinson (288)	Minikahda Club	Minneapolis
1917-18	Not held		World War I		
1919	Walter Hagen*	301	Mike Brady (301)	Brae Burn CC	West Newton, Mass.
1920	Ted Ray	295	Jock Hutchison, Jack Burke, Leo Diegel & Harry Vardon (296)	Inverness Club	Toledo, Ohio
1921	Jim Barnes	289	Walter Hagen & Fred McLeod (298)	Columbia CC	Chevy Chase, Md.
1922	Gene Sarazen	288	a-Bobby Jones & John Black (289)	Skokie CC	Glencoe, Ill.
1923	a-Bobby Jones*	296	Bobby Cruickshank (296)	Inwood CC	Inwood, N.Y.
1924	Cyril Walker	297	a-Bobby Jones (300)	Oakland Hills CC	Birmingham, Mich.
1925	Willie Macfarlane*	291	a-Bobby Jones (291)	Worcester CC	Worcester, Mass.
1926	a-Bobby Jones	293	Joe Turnesa (294)	Scioto CC	Columbus, Ohio
1927	Tommy Armour*	301	Harry Cooper (301)	Oakmont CC	Oakmont, Pa.
1928	Johnny Farrell*	294	a-Bobby Jones (294)	Olympia Fields CC	Matteson, Ill.
1929	a-Bobby Jones*	294	Al Espinosa (294)	Winged Foot CC	Mamaroneck, N.Y.
1930	a-Bobby Jones	287	Macdonald Smith (289)	Interlachen CC	Hopkins, Minn.
1931	Billy Burke*	292	George Von Elm (292)	Inverness Club	Toledo, Ohio
1932	Gene Sarazen	286	Bobby Cruickshank & Phil Perkins (289)	Fresh Meadow CC	Flushing, N.Y.
1933	a-Johnny Goodman	287	Ralph Guldahl (288)	North Shore GC	Glenview, Ill.
1934	Olin Dutra	293	Gene Sarazen (294)	Merion Cricket Club	Ardmore, Pa.
1935	Sam Parks Jr.	299	Jimmy Thomson (301)	Oakmont CC	Oakmont, Pa.
1936	Tony Manero	282	Harry E. Cooper (284)	Baltusrol GC	Springfield, N.J.
1937	Ralph Guldahl	281	Sam Snead (283)	Oakland Hills CC	Birmingham, Mich.
1938	Ralph Guldahl	284	Dick Metz (290)	Cherry Hills CC	Denver
1939	Byron Nelson*	284	Craig Wood & Denny Shute (284)	Philadelphia CC	Philadelphia

U.S. Open (Cont.)

Year	Winner	Score	Runner-up	Course	Location
1940	Lawson Little*	287	Gene Sarazen (287)	Canterbury GC	Cleveland
1941	Craig Wood	284	Denny Shute (287)	Colonial Club	Ft. Worth
1942-45	Not held		World War II		
1946	Lloyd Mangrum*	284	Byron Nelson & Vic Ghezzi (284)	Canterbury GC	Cleveland
1947	Lew Worsham*	282	Sam Snead (282)	St. Louis CC	Clayton, Mo.
1948	Ben Hogan	276	Jimmy Demaret (278)	Riviera CC	Los Angeles
1949	Cary Middlecoff	286	Clayton Heafner & Sam Snead (287)	Medinah CC	Medinah, Ill.
1950	Ben Hogan*	287	Lloyd Mangrum & George Fazio (287)	Merion Golf Club	Ardmore, Pa.
1951	Ben Hogan	287	Clayton Heafner (289)	Oakland Hills CC	Birmingham, Mich.
1952	Julius Boros	281	Porky Oliver (285)	Northwood Club	Dallas
1953	Ben Hogan	283	Sam Snead (289)	Oakmont CC	Oakmont, Pa.
1954	Ed Furgol	284	Gene Littler (285)	Baltusrol CC	Springfield, N.J.
1955	Jack Fleck*	287	Ben Hogan (287)	Olympic CC	San Francisco
1956	Cary Middlecoff	281	Ben Hogan & Julius Boros (282)	Oak Hill CC	Rochester, N.Y.
1957	Dick Mayer*	282	Cary Middlecoff (282)	Inverness Club	Toledo, Ohio
1958	Tommy Bolt	283	Gary Player (287)	Southern Hills CC	Tulsa
1959	Billy Casper	282	Bob Rosburg (283)	Winged Foot GC	Mamaroneck, N.Y.
1960	Arnold Palmer	280	Jack Nicklaus (282)	Cherry Hills CC	Denver
1961	Gene Littler	281	Doug Sanders & Bob Goalby (282)	Oakland Hills CC	Birmingham, Mich.
1962	Jack Nicklaus*	283	Arnold Palmer (283)	Oakmont CC	Oakmont, Pa.
1963	Julius Boros*	293	Arnold Palmer & Jacky Cupit (293)	The Country Club	Brookline, Mass.
1964	Ken Venturi	278	Tommy Jacobs (282)	Congressional CC	Bethesda, Md.
1965	Gary Player*	282	Kel Nagle (282)	Bellerive CC	St. Louis
1966	Billy Casper*	278	Arnold Palmer (278)	Olympic CC	San Francisco
1967	Jack Nicklaus	275	Arnold Palmer (279)	Baltusrol GC	Springfield, N.J.
1968	Lee Trevino	275	Jack Nicklaus (279)	Oak Hill CC	Rochester, N.Y.
1969	Orville Moody	281	Al Geiberger, Deane Beman & Bob Rosburg (282)	Champions GC	Houston
1970	Tony Jacklin	281	Dave Hill (288)	Hazeltine National GC	Chaska, Minn.
1971	Lee Trevino*	280	Jack Nicklaus (280)	Merion GC	Ardmore, Pa.
1972	Jack Nicklaus	290	Bruce Crampton (293)	Pebble Beach GL	Pebble Beach, Calif.
1973	Johnny Miller	279	John Schlee (280)	Oakmont CC	Oakmont, Pa.
1974	Hale Irwin	287	Forest Fezler (289)	Winged Foot GC	Mamaroneck, N.Y.
1975	Lou Graham*	287	John Mahaffey (287)	Medinah CC	Medinah, Ill.
1976	Jerry Pate	277	Al Geiberger & Tom Weiskopf (279)	Atlanta AC	Duluth, Ga.
1977	Hubert Green	278	Lou Graham (279)	Southern Hills CC	Tulsa
1978	Andy North	285	Dave Stockton & J.C. Snead (286)	Cherry Hills CC	Denver
1979	Hale Irwin	284	Gary Player & Jerry Pate (286)	Inverness Club	Toledo, Ohio
1980	Jack Nicklaus	272	Isao Aoki (274)	Baltusrol GC	Springfield, N.J.
1981	David Graham	273	George Burns & Bill Rogers (276)	Merion GC	Ardmore, Pa.
1982	Tom Watson	282	Jack Nicklaus (284)	Pebble Beach GL	Pebble Beach, Calif.
1983	Larry Nelson	280	Tom Watson (281)	Oakmont CC	Oakmont, Pa.
1984	Fuzzy Zoeller*	276	Greg Norman (276)	Winged Foot GC	Mamaroneck, N.Y.
1985	Andy North	279	Dave Barr, T.C. Chen & Denis Watson (280)	Oakland Hills CC	Birmingham, Mich.
1986	Ray Floyd	279	Lanny Wadkins & Chip Beck (281)	Shinnecock Hills GC	Southampton, N.Y.
1987	Scott Simpson	277	Tom Watson (278)	Olympic Club	San Francisco
1988	Curtis Strange*	278	Nick Faldo (278)	The Country Club	Brookline, Mass.
1989	Curtis Strange	278	Chip Beck, Ian Woosnam & Mark McCumber (279)	Oak Hill CC	Rochester, N.Y.
1990	Hale Irwin*	280	Mike Donald (280)	Medinah CC	Medinah, Ill.
1991	Payne Stewart*	282	Scott Simpson (282)	Hazeltine National GC	Chaska, Minn.
1992	Tom Kite	285	Jeff Sluman (287)	Pebble Beach GL	Pebble Beach, Calif.
1993	Lee Janzen	272	Payne Stewart (274)	Baltusrol GC	Springfield, N.J.
1994	Ernie Els*	279	Colin Montgomerie (279) & Loren Roberts (279)	Oakmont CC	Oakmont, Pa.
1995	Corey Pavin	280	Greg Norman (282)	Shinnecock Hills GC	Southampton, N.Y.

Year	Winner	Score	Runner-up	Course	Location
1996	Steve Jones	278	Davis Love III & Tom Lehman (279)	Oakland Hills CC	Bloomfield Hills, Mich.
1997	Ernie Els	276	Colin Montgomerie (277)	Congressional CC	Bethesda, Md.
1998	Lee Janzen	280	Payne Stewart (281)	Olympic Club	San Francisco
1999	Payne Stewart	279	Phil Mickelson (280)	Pinehurst CC	Pinehurst, N.C.
2000	Tiger Woods	272	Miguel Angel Jimenez & Ernie Els (287)	Pebble Beach GL	Pebble Beach, Calif.
2001	Retief Goosen*	276	Mark Brooks (276)	Southern Hills CC	Tulsa
2002	Tiger Woods	277	Phil Mickelson (280)	Bethpage Black	Farmingdale, N.Y.
2003	Jim Furyk	272	Stephen Leaney (275)	Olympia Fields CC	Olympia Fields, Ill.
2004	Retief Goosen	276	Phil Mickelson (278)	Shinnecock Hills GC	Southampton, N.Y.
2005	Michael Campbell	280	Tiger Woods (282)	Pinehurst CC	Pinehurst, N.C.
2006	Geoff Ogilvy	285	Jim Furyk, Colin Montgomerie & Phil Mickelson (286)	Winged Foot GC	Mamaroneck, N.Y.
2007	Angel Cabrera	285	Jim Furyk & Tiger Woods (286)	Oakmont CC	Oakmont, Pa.

*PLAYOFFS:

1901: Willie Anderson (85) def. Alex Smith (86) in 18 holes. **1903:** Willie Anderson (82) def. David Brown (84) in 18 holes. **1908:** Fred McLeod (77) def. Willie Smith (83) in 18 holes. **1910:** Alex Smith (71) def. John McDermott (75) & Macdonald Smith (77) in 18 holes. **1911:** John McDermott (80) def. Mike Brady (82) & George Simpson (85) in 18 holes. **1913:** Francis Ouimet (72) def. Harry Vardon (77) & Edward Ray (78) in 18 holes. **1919:** Walter Hagen (77) def. Mike Brady (78) in 18 holes. **1923:** Bobby Jones (76) def. Bobby Cruickshank (78) in 18 holes. **1925:** Willie Macfarlane (75-72—147) def. Bobby Jones (75-73—148) in 36 holes. **1927:** Tommy Armour (76) def. Harry Cooper (79) in 18 holes. **1928:** Johnny Farrell (70-73—143) def. Bobby Jones (73-71—144) in 36 holes. **1929:** Bobby Jones (141) def. Al Espinosa (164) in 36 holes. **1931:** Billy Burke (149-148) def. George Von Elm (149-149) in 72 holes. **1939:** Byron Nelson (68-70) def. Craig Wood (68-73) and Denny Shute (76) in 36 holes. **1940:** Lawson Little (70) def. Gene Sarazen (73) in 18 holes. **1946:** Lloyd Mangrum (72-72—144) def. Byron Nelson (72-73—145) and Vic Ghezzi (72-73—145) in 36 holes. **1947:** Lew Worsham (69) def. Sam Snead (70) in 18 holes.

1950: Ben Hogan (69) def. Lloyd Mangrum (73) & George Fazio (75) in 18 holes. **1955:** Jack Fleck (69) def. Ben Hogan (72) in 18 holes. **1957:** Dick Mayer (72) def. Cary Middlecoff (79) in 18 holes. **1962:** Jack Nicklaus (71) def. Arnold Palmer (74) in 18 holes. **1963:** Julius Boros (70) def. Jacky Cupit (73) & Arnold Palmer (76) in 18 holes. **1965:** Gary Player (71) def. Kel Nagle (74) in 18 holes. **1966:** Billy Casper (69) def. Arnold Palmer (73) in 18 holes. **1971:** Lee Trevino (68) def. Jack Nicklaus (71) in 18 holes. **1975:** Lou Graham (71) def. John Mahaffey (73) in 18 holes. **1984:** Fuzzy Zoeller (67) def. Greg Norman (75) in 18 holes. **1988:** Curtis Strange (71) def. Nick Faldo (75) in 18 holes. **1990:** Hale Irwin (74-3) def. Mike Donald (74-4) on 1st hole of sudden death after 18 holes. **1991:** Payne Stewart (75) def. Scott Simpson (77) in 18 holes. **1994:** Ernie Els (74-4-4) def. Loren Roberts (74-4-5) and Colin Montgomerie (78) on 2nd hole of sudden death after 18 holes; **2001:** Goosen (70) def. Brooks (72) in 18 holes.

Vardon Trophy

Awarded since 1937 by the PGA of America to the PGA Tour regular with the lowest adjusted scoring average, based on a minimum of 60 rounds. The award is named after Harry Vardon, the six-time British Open champion who also won the U.S. Open in 1900. A point system was used from 1937-41.

Multiple winners: Tiger Woods (6); Billy Casper and Lee Trevino (5); Arnold Palmer and Sam Snead (4); Ben Hogan, Greg Norman and Tom Watson (3); Fred Couples, Bruce Crampton, Tom Kite, Lloyd Mangrum and Nick Price (2).

Year		Pts	Year		Avg	Year		Avg
1937	Harry Cooper	500	1963	Billy Casper	70.58	1986	Scott Hoch	70.08
1938	Sam Snead	520	1964	Arnold Palmer	70.01	1987	Dan Pohl	70.25
1939	Byron Nelson	473	1965	Billy Casper	70.85	1988	Chip Beck	69.46
1940	Ben Hogan	423	1966	Billy Casper	70.27	1989	Greg Norman	69.49
1941	Ben Hogan	494	1967	Arnold Palmer	70.18	1990	Greg Norman	69.10
1942-46	No award		1968	Billy Casper	69.82	1991	Fred Couples	69.59
Year		**Avg**	1969	Dave Hill	70.34	1992	Fred Couples	69.38
1947	Jimmy Demaret	69.90	1970	Lee Trevino	70.64	1993	Nick Price	69.11
1948	Ben Hogan	69.30	1971	Lee Trevino	70.27	1994	Greg Norman	68.81
1949	Sam Snead	69.37	1972	Lee Trevino	70.89	1995	Steve Elkington	69.62
1950	Sam Snead	69.23	1973	Bruce Crampton	70.57	1996	Tom Lehman	69.32
1951	Lloyd Mangrum	70.05	1974	Lee Trevino	70.53	1997	Nick Price	68.98
1952	Jack Burke	70.54	1975	Bruce Crampton	70.51	1998	David Duval	69.13
1953	Lloyd Mangrum	70.22	1976	Don January	70.56	1999	Tiger Woods	68.43
1954	E.J. Harrison	70.41	1977	Tom Watson	70.32	2000	Tiger Woods	67.79
1955	Sam Snead	69.86	1978	Tom Watson	70.16	2001	Tiger Woods	68.81
1956	Cary Middlecoff	70.35	1979	Tom Watson	70.27	2002	Tiger Woods	68.56
1957	Dow Finsterwald	70.30	1980	Lee Trevino	69.73	2003	Tiger Woods	68.41
1958	Bob Rosburg	70.11	1981	Tom Kite	69.80	2004	Vijay Singh	68.84
1959	Art Wall	70.35	1982	Tom Kite	70.21	2005	Tiger Woods	68.66
1960	Billy Casper	69.95	1983	Ray Floyd	70.61	2006	Jim Furyk	68.86
1961	Arnold Palmer	69.85	1984	Calvin Peete	70.56			
1962	Arnold Palmer	70.27	1985	Don Pooley	70.36			

British Open

The oldest of the Majors, the Open began in 1860 to determine "the champion golfer of the world." While only professional golfers participated in the first year of the tournament, amateurs have been invited ever since. Competition was extended from 36 to 72 holes in 1892. Conducted by the Royal and Ancient Golf Club of St. Andrews, the Open is rotated among select golf courses in England and Scotland. Note that (*) indicates playoff winner and (a) indicates amateur winner.

Multiple winners: Harry Vardon (6); James Braid, J.H. Taylor, Peter Thomson and Tom Watson (5); Walter Hagen, Bobby Locke, Tom Morris Sr., Tom Morris Jr. and Willie Park (4); Jamie Anderson, Seve Ballesteros, Henry Cotton, Nick Faldo, Bob Ferguson, Bobby Jones, Jack Nicklaus, Gary Player and Tiger Woods (3); Harold Hilton, Bob Martin, Greg Norman, Arnold Palmer, Willie Park Jr. and Lee Trevino (2).

Year	Winner	Score	Runner-up	Course	Location
1860	Willie Park	174	Tom Morris Sr. (176)	Prestwick Club	Ayrshire, Scotland
1861	Tom Morris Sr.	163	Willie Park (167)	Prestwick Club	Ayrshire, Scotland
1862	Tom Morris Sr.	163	Willie Park (176)	Prestwick Club	Ayrshire, Scotland
1863	Willie Park	168	Tom Morris Sr. (170)	Prestwick Club	Ayrshire, Scotland
1864	Tom Morris Sr.	167	Andrew Strath (169)	Prestwick Club	Ayrshire, Scotland
1865	Andrew Strath	162	Willie Park (164)	Prestwick Club	Ayrshire, Scotland
1866	Willie Park	169	David Park (171)	Prestwick Club	Ayrshire, Scotland
1867	Tom Morris Sr.	170	Willie Park (172)	Prestwick Club	Ayrshire, Scotland
1868	Tom Morris Jr.	157	Robert Andrew (159)	Prestwick Club	Ayrshire, Scotland
1869	Tom Morris Jr.	154	Tom Morris Sr. (157)	Prestwick Club	Ayrshire, Scotland
1870	Tom Morris Jr.	149	Bob Kirk (161)	Prestwick Club	Ayrshire, Scotland
1871	Not held				
1872	Tom Morris Jr.	166	David Strath (169)	Prestwick Club	Ayrshire, Scotland
1873	Tom Kidd	179	Jamie Anderson (180)	St. Andrews	St. Andrews, Scotland
1874	Mungo Park	159	Tom Morris Jr. (161)	Musselburgh	Musselburgh, Scotland
1875	Willie Park	166	Bob Martin (168)	Prestwick Club	Ayrshire, Scotland
1876	Bob Martin*	176	David Strath (176)	St. Andrews	St. Andrews, Scotland
1877	Jamie Anderson	160	Bob Pringle (162)	Musselburgh	Musselburgh, Scotland
1878	Jamie Anderson	157	Bob Kirk (159)	Prestwick Club	Ayrshire, Scotland
1879	Jamie Anderson	169	Andrew Kirkaldy & James Allan (172)	St. Andrews	St. Andrews, Scotland
1880	Bob Ferguson	162	Peter Paxton (167)	Musselburgh	Musselburgh, Scotland
1881	Bob Ferguson	170	Jamie Anderson (173)	Prestwick Club	Ayrshire, Scotland
1882	Bob Ferguson	171	Willie Fernie (174)	St. Andrews	St. Andrews, Scotland
1883	Willie Fernie*	159	Bob Ferguson (159)	Musselburgh	Musselburgh, Scotland
1884	Jack Simpson	160	Douglas Rolland & Willie Fernie (164)	Prestwick Club	Ayrshire, Scotland
1885	Bob Martin	171	Archie Simpson (172)	St. Andrews	St. Andrews, Scotland
1886	David Brown	157	Willie Campbell (159)	Musselburgh	Musselburgh, Scotland
1887	Willie Park Jr.	161	Bob Martin (162)	Prestwick Club	Ayrshire, Scotland
1888	Jack Burns	171	David Anderson & Ben Sayers (172)	St. Andrews	St. Andrews, Scotland
1889	Willie Park Jr.*	155	Andrew Kirkaldy (155)	Musselburgh	Musselburgh, Scotland
1890	a-John Ball	164	Willie Fernie (167) & A. Simpson (167)	Prestwick Club	Ayrshire, Scotland
1891	Hugh Kirkaldy	166	Andrew Kirkaldy & Willie Fernie (168)	St. Andrews	St. Andrews, Scotland
1892	a-Harold Hilton	305	John Ball, Sandy Herd & Hugh Kirkaldy (308)	Muirfield	Gullane, Scotland
1893	Willie Auchterlonie	322	Johnny Laidley (324)	Prestwick Club	Ayrshire, Scotland
1894	J.H. Taylor	326	Douglas Rolland (331)	Royal St. George's	Sandwich, England
1895	J.H. Taylor	322	Sandy Herd (326)	St. Andrews	St. Andrews, Scotland
1896	Harry Vardon*	316	J.H. Taylor (316)	Muirfield	Gullane, Scotland
1897	a-Harold Hilton	314	James Braid (315)	Hoylake	Hoylake, England
1898	Harry Vardon	307	Willie Park Jr. (308)	Prestwick Club	Ayrshire, Scotland
1899	Harry Vardon	310	Jack White (315)	Royal St. George's	Sandwich, England
1900	J.H. Taylor	309	Harry Vardon (317)	St. Andrews	St. Andrews, Scotland
1901	James Braid	309	Harry Vardon (312)	Muirfield	Gullane, Scotland
1902	Sandy Herd	307	Harry Vardon (308)	Hoylake	Hoylake, England
1903	Harry Vardon	300	Tom Vardon (306)	Prestwick Club	Ayrshire, Scotland
1904	Jack White	296	James Braid (297)	Royal St. George's	Sandwich, England
1905	James Braid	318	J.H. Taylor (323) & Rowland Jones (323)	St. Andrews	St. Andrews, Scotland
1906	James Braid	300	J.H. Taylor (304)	Muirfield	Gullane, Scotland
1907	Arnaud Massy	312	J.H. Taylor (314)	Hoylake	Hoylake, England
1908	James Braid	291	Tom Ball (299)	Prestwick Club	Ayrshire, Scotland
1909	J.H. Taylor	295	James Braid (299)	Deal	Deal, England
1910	James Braid	299	Sandy Herd (303)	St. Andrews	St. Andrews, Scotland
1911	Harry Vardon*	303	Arnaud Massy (303)	Royal St. George's	Sandwich, England
1912	Ted Ray	295	Harry Vardon (299)	Muirfield	Gullane, Scotland
1913	J.H. Taylor	304	Ted Ray (312)	Hoylake	Hoylake, England

Year	Winner	Score	Runner-up	Course	Location
1914	Harry Vardon	306	J.H. Taylor (309)	Prestwick Club	Ayrshire, Scotland
1915-19	Not held		World War I		
1920	George Duncan	303	Sandy Herd (305)	Deal	Deal, England
1921	Jock Hutchison*	296	Roger Wethered (296)	St. Andrews	St. Andrews, Scotland
1922	Walter Hagen	300	George Duncan & Jim Barnes (301)	Royal St. George's	Sandwich, England
1923	Arthur Havers	295	Walter Hagen (296)	Royal Troon	Troon, Scotland
1924	Walter Hagen	301	Ernest Whitcombe (302)	Hoylake	Hoylake, England
1925	Jim Barnes	300	Archie Compston & Ted Ray (301)	Prestwick Club	Ayrshire, Scotland
1926	a-Bobby Jones	291	Al Watrous (293)	Royal Lytham	Lytham, England
1927	a-Bobby Jones	285	Aubrey Boomer (291)	St. Andrews	St. Andrews, Scotland
1928	Walter Hagen	292	Gene Sarazen (294)	Royal St. George's	Sandwich, England
1929	Walter Hagen	292	Johnny Farrell (298)	Muirfield	Gullane, Scotland
1930	a-Bobby Jones	291	Macdonald Smith & Leo Diegel (293)	Hoylake	Hoylake, England
1931	Tommy Armour	296	Jose Jurado (297)	Carnoustie	Carnoustie, Scotland
1932	Gene Sarazen	283	Macdonald Smith (288)	Prince's	Prince's, England
1933	Denny Shute*	292	Craig Wood (292)	St. Andrews	St. Andrews, Scotland
1934	Henry Cotton	283	Sid Brews (288)	Royal St. George's	Sandwich, England
1935	Alf Perry	283	Alf Padgham (287)	Muirfield	Gullane, Scotland
1936	Alf Padgham	287	Jimmy Adams (288)	Hoylake	Hoylake, England
1937	Henry Cotton	290	Reg Whitcombe (292)	Carnoustie	Carnoustie, Scotland
1938	Reg Whitcombe	295	Jimmy Adams (297)	Royal St. George's	Sandwich, England
1939	Dick Burton	290	Johnny Bulla (292)	St. Andrews	St. Andrews, Scotland
1940-45	Not held		World War II		
1946	Sam Snead	290	Bobby Locke (294) & Johnny Bulla (294)	St. Andrews	St. Andrews, Scotland
1947	Fred Daly	293	Frank Stranahan & Reg Horne (294)	Hoylake	Hoylake, England
1948	Henry Cotton	284	Fred Daly (289)	Muirfield	Gullane, Scotland
1949	Bobby Locke*	283	Harry Bradshaw (283)	Royal St. George's	Sandwich, England
1950	Bobby Locke	279	Roberto de Vicenzo (281)	Royal Troon	Troon, Scotland
1951	Max Faulkner	285	Tony Cerda (287)	Royal Portrush	Portrush, Ireland
1952	Bobby Locke	287	Peter Thomson (288)	Royal Lytham	Lytham, England
1953	Ben Hogan	282	Frank Stranahan, Dai Rees, Tony Cerda & Peter Thomson (286)	Carnoustie	Carnoustie, Scotland
1954	Peter Thomson	283	Sid Scott, Dai Rees & Bobby Locke (284)	Royal Birkdale	Southport, England
1955	Peter Thomson	281	Johny Fallon (283)	St. Andrews	St. Andrews, Scotland
1956	Peter Thomson	286	Flory Van Donck (289)	Hoylake	Hoylake, England
1957	Bobby Locke	279	Peter Thomson (282)	St. Andrews	St. Andrews, Scotland
1958	Peter Thomson*	278	Dave Thomas (278)	Royal Lytham	Lytham, England
1959	Gary Player	284	Flory Van Donck & Fred Bullock (286)	Muirfield	Gullane, Scotland
1960	Kel Nagle	278	Arnold Palmer (279)	St. Andrews	St. Andrews, Scotland
1961	Arnold Palmer	284	Dai Rees (285)	Royal Birkdale	Southport, England
1962	Arnold Palmer	276	Kel Nagle (282)	Royal Troon	Troon, Scotland
1963	Bob Charles*	277	Phil Rodgers (277)	Royal Lytham	Lytham, England
1964	Tony Lema	279	Jack Nicklaus (284)	St. Andrews	St. Andrews, Scotland
1965	Peter Thomson	285	Christy O'Connor & Brian Huggett (287)	Royal Birkdale	Southport, England
1966	Jack Nicklaus	282	Doug Sanders & Dave Thomas (283)	Muirfield	Gullane, Scotland
1967	Roberto de Vicenzo	278	Jack Nicklaus (280)	Hoylake	Hoylake, England
1968	Gary Player	289	Jack Nicklaus & Bob Charles (291)	Carnoustie	Carnoustie, Scotland
1969	Tony Jacklin	280	Bob Charles (282)	Royal Lytham	Lytham, England
1970	Jack Nicklaus*	283	Doug Sanders (283)	St. Andrews	St. Andrews, Scotland
1971	Lee Trevino	278	Lu Liang Huan (279)	Royal Birkdale	Southport, England
1972	Lee Trevino	278	Jack Nicklaus (279)	Muirfield	Gullane, Scotland
1973	Tom Weiskopf	276	Johnny Miller & Neil Coles (279)	Royal Troon	Troon, Scotland
1974	Gary Player	282	Peter Oosterhuis (286)	Royal Lytham	Lytham, England
1975	Tom Watson*	279	Jack Newton (279)	Carnoustie	Carnoustie, Scotland
1976	Johnny Miller	279	Seve Ballesteros & Jack Nicklaus (285)	Royal Birkdale	Southport, England
1977	Tom Watson	268	Jack Nicklaus (269)	Turnberry	Turnberry, Scotland
1978	Jack Nicklaus	281	Tom Kite, Ray Floyd, Ben Crenshaw & Simon Owen (283)	St. Andrews	St. Andrews, Scotland

British Open (Cont.)

Year	Winner	Score	Runner-up	Course	Location
1979	Seve Ballesteros	283	Jack Nicklaus & Ben Crenshaw (286)	Royal Lytham	Lytham, England
1980	Tom Watson	271	Lee Trevino (275)	Muirfield	Gullane, Scotland
1981	Bill Rogers	276	Bernhard Langer (280)	Royal St. George's	Sandwich, England
1982	Tom Watson	284	Peter Oosterhuis & Nick Price (285)	Royal Troon	Troon, Scotland
1983	Tom Watson	275	Hale Irwin & Andy Bean (276)	Royal Birkdale	Southport, England
1984	Seve Ballesteros	276	Bernhard Langer & Tom Watson (278)	St. Andrews	St. Andrews, Scotland
1985	Sandy Lyle	282	Payne Stewart (283)	Royal St. George's	Sandwich, England
1986	Greg Norman	280	Gordon J. Brand (285)	Turnberry	Turnberry, Scotland
1987	Nick Faldo	279	Paul Azinger & Rodger Davis (280)	Muirfield	Gullane, Scotland
1988	Seve Ballesteros	273	Nick Price (275)	Royal Lytham	Lytham, England
1989	Mark Calcavecchia*	275	Greg Norman & Wayne Grady (275)	Royal Troon	Troon, Scotland
1990	Nick Faldo	270	Payne Stewart & Mark McNulty (275)	St. Andrews	St. Andrews, Scotland
1991	Ian Baker-Finch	272	Mike Harwood (274)	Royal Birkdale	Southport, England
1992	Nick Faldo	272	John Cook (273)	Muirfield	Gullane, Scotland
1993	Greg Norman	267	Nick Faldo (269)	Royal St. George's	Sandwich, England
1994	Nick Price	268	Jesper Parnevik (269)	Turnberry	Turnberry, Scotland
1995	John Daly*	282	Costantino Rocca (282)	St. Andrews	St. Andrews, Scotland
1996	Tom Lehman	271	Mark McCumber & Ernie Els (273)	Royal Lytham	Lytham, England
1997	Justin Leonard	272	Jesper Parnevik & Darren Clarke (275)	Royal Troon	Troon, Scotland
1998	Mark O'Meara*	280	Brian Watts (280)	Royal Birkdale	Southport, England
1999	Paul Lawrie*	290	Justin Leonard & Jean Van de Velde (290)	Carnoustie	Carnoustie, Scotland
2000	Tiger Woods	269	Thomas Bjorn & Ernie Els (277)	St. Andrews	St. Andrews, Scotland
2001	David Duval	274	Niclas Fasth (277)	Royal Lytham	Lytham, England
2002	Ernie Els*	278	Thomas Levet, Stuart Appleby & Steve Elkington (278)	Muirfield	Gullane, Scotland
2003	Ben Curtis	283	Vijay Singh & Thomas Bjorn (284)	Royal St. George's	Sandwich, England
2004	Todd Hamilton*	274	Ernie Els (274)	Royal Troon	Troon, Scotland
2005	Tiger Woods	274	Colin Montgomerie (279)	St. Andrews	St. Andrews, Scotland
2006	Tiger Woods	270	Chris DiMarco (272)	Royal Liverpool	Hoylake, England
2007	Padraig Harrington*	277	Sergio Garcia (277)	Carnoustie	Carnoustie, Scotland

*PLAYOFFS:

1876: Bob Martin awarded title when David Strath refused playoff. **1883:** Willie Fernie (158) def. Robert Ferguson (159) in 36 holes. **1889:** Willie Park Jr. (158) def. Andrew Kirkaldy (163) in 36 holes. **1896:** Harry Vardon (157) def. John H. Taylor (161) in 36 holes. **1911:** Harry Vardon won when Arnaud Massy conceded at 35th hole. **1921:** Jock Hutchison (150) def. Roger Wethered (159) in 36 holes. **1933:** Denny Shute (149) def. Craig Wood (154) in 36 holes. **1949:** Bobby Locke (135) def. Harry Bradshaw (147) in 36 holes. **1958:** Peter Thomson (139) def. Dave Thomas (143) in 36 holes. **1963:** Bob Charles (140) def. Phil Rodgers (148) in 36 holes. **1970:** Jack Nicklaus (72) def. Doug Sanders (73) in 18 holes. **1975:** Tom Watson (71) def. Jack Newton (72) in 18 holes. **1989:** Mark Calcavecchia (4-3-3-3—13) def. Wayne Grady (4-4-4-4—16) and Greg Norman (3-3-4) in 4 holes. **1995:** John Daly (3-4-4-4—15) def. Costantino Rocca (4-5-7-3—19) in 4 holes. **1998:** Mark O'Meara (4-4-5-4—17) def. Brian Watts (5-4-5-5—19) in 4 holes. **1999:** Paul Lawrie (5-4-3-3—15) def. Justin Leonard (5-4-4-5—18) and Jean Van de Velde (6-4-3-5—18) in 4 holes. **2002:** Els (4-3-5-4—16) and Levet (4-2-5-5—16) remained tied after a four-hole playoff that also included Appleby (4-4-4-5—17) and Elkington (5-3-4-5—17). The pair moved on to sudden death, where Els (4) def. Levet (5) on the 1st hole. **2004:** Todd Hamilton (4-4-3-4—15) def. Ernie Els (4-4-4-4—16) in 4 holes. **2007:** Padraig Harrington (3-3-4-5—15) def. Sergio Garcia (5-3-4-4—16) in 4 holes.

PGA Championship

The PGA Championship began in 1916 as a professional golfers match play tournament, but switched to stroke play in 1958. Conducted by the PGA of America, the tournament is played on a different course each year.

Multiple winners: Walter Hagen and Jack Nicklaus (5); Tiger Woods (4); Gene Sarazen and Sam Snead (3); Jim Barnes, Leo Diegel, Ray Floyd, Ben Hogan, Byron Nelson, Larry Nelson, Gary Player, Nick Price, Paul Runyan, Denny Shute, Vijay Singh, Dave Stockton and Lee Trevino (2).

Year	Winner	Score	Runner-up	Course	Location
1916	Jim Barnes	1-up	Jock Hutchison	Siwanoy CC	Bronxville, N.Y.
1917-18	Not held		World War I		
1919	Jim Barnes	6 & 5	Fred McLeod	Engineers CC	Roslyn, N.Y.
1920	Jock Hutchison	1-up	J. Douglas Edgar	Flossmoor CC	Flossmoor, Ill.
1921	Walter Hagen	3 & 2	Jim Barnes	Inwood CC	Inwood, N.Y.

Year	Winner	Score	Runner-up	Course	Location
1922	Gene Sarazen	4 & 3	Emmet French	Oakmont CC	Oakmont, Pa.
1923	Gene Sarazen*	1-up/38	Walter Hagen	Pelham CC	Pelham, N.Y.
1924	Walter Hagen	2-up	Jim Barnes	French Lick CC	French Lick, Ind.
1925	Walter Hagen	6 & 5	Bill Mehlhorn	Olympia Fields CC	Matteson, Ill.
1926	Walter Hagen	5 & 3	Leo Diegel	Salisbury GC	Westbury, N.Y.
1927	Walter Hagen	1-up	Joe Turnesa	Cedar Crest CC	Dallas
1928	Leo Diegel	6 & 5	Al Espinosa	Five Farms CC	Baltimore
1929	Leo Diegel	6 & 4	John Farrell	Hillcrest CC	Los Angeles
1930	Tommy Armour	1-up	Gene Sarazen	Fresh Meadow CC	Flushing, N.Y.
1931	Tom Creavy	2 & 1	Denny Shute	Wannamoisett CC	Rumford, R.I.
1932	Olin Dutra	4 & 3	Frank Walsh	Keller GC	St. Paul, Minn.
1933	Gene Sarazen	5 & 4	Willie Goggin	Blue Mound CC	Milwaukee
1934	Paul Runyan*	1-up/38	Craig Wood	Park CC	Williamsville, N.Y.
1935	Johnny Revolta	5 & 4	Tommy Armour	Twin Hills CC	Oklahoma City
1936	Denny Shute	3 & 2	Jimmy Thomson	Pinehurst CC	Pinehurst, N.C.
1937	Denny Shute*	1-up/37	Harold McSpaden	Pittsburgh FC	Aspinwall, Pa.
1938	Paul Runyan	8 & 7	Sam Snead	Shawnee CC	Shawnee-on-Del, Pa.
1939	Henry Picard*	1-up/37	Byron Nelson	Pomonok CC	Flushing, N.Y.
1940	Byron Nelson	1-up	Sam Snead	Hershey CC	Hershey, Pa.
1941	Vic Ghezzi*	1-up/38	Byron Nelson	Cherry Hills CC	Denver
1942	Sam Snead	2 & 1	Jim Turnesa	Seaview CC	Atlantic City, N.J.
1943	Not held		World War II		
1944	Bob Hamilton	1-up	Byron Nelson	Manito G & CC	Spokane, Wash.
1945	Byron Nelson	4 & 3	Sam Byrd	Morraine CC	Dayton, Ohio
1946	Ben Hogan	6 & 4	Porky Oliver	Portland GC	Portland, Ore.
1947	Jim Ferrier	2 & 1	Chick Harbert	Plum Hollow CC	Detroit
1948	Ben Hogan	7 & 6	Mike Turnesa	Norwood Hills CC	St. Louis
1949	Sam Snead	3 & 2	John Palmer	Hermitage CC	Richmond, Va.
1950	Chandler Harper	4 & 3	Henry Williams Jr.	Scioto CC	Columbus, Ohio
1951	Sam Snead	7 & 6	Walter Burkemo	Oakmont CC	Oakmont, Pa.
1952	Jim Turnesa	1-up	Chick Harbert	Big Spring CC	Louisville
1953	Walter Burkemo	2 & 1	Felice Torza	Birmingham CC	Birmingham, Mich.
1954	Chick Harbert	4 & 3	Walter Burkemo	Keller GC	St. Paul, Minn.
1955	Doug Ford	4 & 3	Cary Middlecoff	Meadowbrook CC	Detroit
1956	Jack Burke	3 & 2	Ted Kroll	Blue Hill CC	Boston
1957	Lionel Hebert	2 & 1	Dow Finsterwald	Miami Valley CC	Dayton, Ohio
1958	Dow Finsterwald	276	Billy Casper (278)	Llanerch CC	Havertown, Pa.
1959	Bob Rosburg	277	Jerry Barber & Doug Sanders (278)	Minneapolis GC	St. Louis Park, Minn.
1960	Jay Hebert	281	Jim Ferrier (282)	Firestone CC	Akron, Ohio
1961	Jerry Barber**	277	Don January (277)	Olympia Fields CC	Matteson, Ill.
1962	Gary Player	278	Bob Goalby (279)	Aronimink GC	Newtown Square, Pa.
1963	Jack Nicklaus	279	Dave Ragan (281)	Dallas AC	Dallas
1964	Bobby Nichols	271	Jack Nicklaus & Arnold Palmer (274)	Columbus CC	Columbus, Ohio
1965	Dave Marr	280	Jack Nicklaus & Billy Casper (282)	Laurel Valley GC	Ligonier, Pa.
1966	Al Geiberger	280	Dudley Wysong (284)	Firestone CC	Akron, Ohio
1967	Don January**	281	Don Massengale (281)	Columbine CC	Littleton, Colo.
1968	Julius Boros	281	Arnold Palmer & Bob Charles (282)	Pecan Valley CC	San Antonio
1969	Ray Floyd	276	Gary Player (277)	NCR GC	Dayton, Ohio
1970	Dave Stockton	279	Arnold Palmer & Bob Murphy (281)	Southern Hills CC	Tulsa
1971	Jack Nicklaus	281	Billy Casper (283)	PGA National GC	Palm Beach Gardens, Fla.
1972	Gary Player	281	Jim Jamieson & Tommy Aaron (283)	Oakland Hills GC	Birmingham, Mich.
1973	Jack Nicklaus	277	Bruce Crampton (281)	Canterbury GC	Cleveland
1974	Lee Trevino	276	Jack Nicklaus (277)	Tanglewood GC	Winston-Salem, N.C.
1975	Jack Nicklaus	276	Bruce Crampton (278)	Firestone CC	Akron, Ohio
1976	Dave Stockton	281	Don January & Ray Floyd (282)	Congressional CC	Bethesda, Md.
1977	Lanny Wadkins**	282	Gene Littler (282)	Pebble Beach GL	Pebble Beach, Calif.
1978	John Mahaffey**	276	Jerry Pate & Tom Watson (276)	Oakmont CC	Oakmont, Pa.
1979	David Graham**	272	Ben Crenshaw (272)	Oakland Hills CC	Birmingham, Mich.
1980	Jack Nicklaus	274	Andy Bean (281)	Oak Hill CC	Rochester, N.Y.
1981	Larry Nelson	273	Fuzzy Zoeller (277)	Atlanta AC	Duluth, Ga.
1982	Ray Floyd	272	Lanny Wadkins (275)	Southern Hills CC	Tulsa
1983	Hal Sutton	274	Jack Nicklaus (275)	Riviera CC	Los Angeles
1984	Lee Trevino	273	Lanny Wadkins & Gary Player (277)	Shoal Creek	Birmingham, Ala.

PGA Championship (Cont.)

Year	Winner	Score	Runner-up	Course	Location
1985	Hubert Green	278	Lee Trevino (280)	Cherry Hills CC	Denver
1986	Bob Tway	276	Greg Norman (278)	Inverness Club	Toledo, Ohio
1987	Larry Nelson**	287	Lanny Wadkins (287)	PGA National	Palm Beach Gardens, Fla.
1988	Jeff Sluman	272	Paul Azinger 275)	Oak Tree GC	Edmond, Okla.
1989	Payne Stewart	276	Andy Bean, Mike Reid & Curtis Strange (277)	Kemper Lakes GC	Hawthorn Woods, Ill.
1990	Wayne Grady	282	Fred Couples (285)	Shoal Creek	Birmingham, Ala.
1991	John Daly	276	Bruce Lietzke (279)	Crooked Stick GC	Carmel, Ind.
1992	Nick Price	278	Nick Faldo, John Cook, Jim Gallagher & Gene Sauers (281)	Bellerive CC	St. Louis
1993	Paul Azinger**	272	Greg Norman (272)	Inverness Club	Toledo, Ohio
1994	Nick Price	269	Corey Pavin (275)	Southern Hills CC	Tulsa
1995	Steve Elkington**	267	Colin Montgomerie (267)	Riviera CC	Pacific Palisades, Calif.
1996	Mark Brooks**	277	Kenny Perry (277)	Valhalla GC	Louisville, Ky.
1997	Davis Love III	269	Justin Leonard (274)	Winged Foot GC	Mamaroneck, N.Y.
1998	Vijay Singh	271	Steve Stricker (273)	Sahalee CC	Redmond, Wash.
1999	Tiger Woods	277	Sergio Garcia (278)	Medinah CC	Medinah, Ill.
2000	Tiger Woods**	270	Bob May (270)	Valhalla GC	Louisville, Ky.
2001	David Toms	265	Phil Mickelson (266)	Atlanta AC	Duluth, Ga.
2002	Rich Beem	278	Tiger Woods (279)	Hazeltine National GC	Chaska, Minn.
2003	Shaun Micheel	276	Chad Campbell (278)	Oak Hill CC	Rochester, N.Y.
2004	Vijay Singh***	280	Chris DiMarco & Justin Leonard (280)	Whistling Straits	Kohler, Wis.
2005	Phil Mickelson	276	Steve Elkington & Thomas Bjorn (277)	Baltusrol GC	Springfield, N.J.
2006	Tiger Woods	270	Shaun Micheel (275)	Medinah CC	Medinah, Ill.
2007	Tiger Woods	272	Woody Austin (274)	Southern Hills CC	Tulsa

*While the PGA Championship was a match play tournament from 1916-57, the two finalists played 36 holes for the title. In the five years that a playoff was necessary, the match was decided on the 37th or 38th hole.

**PLAYOFFS:

1961: Jerry Barber (67) def. Don January (68) in 18 holes. **1967:** Don January (69) def. Don Massengale (71) in 18 holes. **1977:** Lanny Wadkins (4-4-4) def. Gene Littler (4-4-5) on 3rd hole of sudden death. **1978:** John Mahaffey (4-3) def. Jerry Pate (4-4) and Tom Watson (4-5) on 2nd hole of sudden death. **1979:** David Graham (4-4-2) def. Ben Crenshaw (4-4-4) on 3rd hole of sudden death. **1987:** Larry Nelson (5) def. Lanny Wadkins (5) on 1st hole of sudden death. **1993:** Paul Azinger (4-4) def. Greg Norman (4-5) on 2nd hole of sudden death. **1995:** Steve Elkington (3) def. Colin Montgomerie (4) on 1st hole of sudden death. **1996:** Mark Brooks (4) def. Kenny Perry (5) on 1st hole of sudden death. **2000:** Tiger Woods (3-4-5—12) won a three-hole playoff over Bob May (4-4-5—13). **2004:** Vijay Singh (3-3-4—10) won a three-hole playoff over Chris DiMarco (4-3-DNF) and Justin Leonard (4-3-DNF).

Grand Slam Summary

The only golfer ever to win a recognized Grand Slam—four major championships in a single season—was Bobby Jones in 1930. That year, Jones won the U.S. and British Opens as well as the U.S. and British Amateurs.

The men's professional Grand Slam—the Masters, U.S. Open, British Open and PGA Championship—did not gain acceptance until 30 years later when Arnold Palmer won the 1960 Masters and U.S. Open. The media wrote that the popular Palmer was chasing the "new" Grand Slam and would have to win the British Open and the PGA to claim it. He did not, but then nobody has before or since.

Three wins in one year (2): Ben Hogan (1953) and Tiger Woods (2000). **Two wins in one year** (21): Jack Nicklaus (5 times); Tiger Woods (4 times); Ben Hogan, Arnold Palmer and Tom Watson (twice); Nick Faldo, Mark O'Meara, Gary Player, Nick Price, Sam Snead, Lee Trevino and Craig Wood (once).

Year	Masters	US Open	Brit. Open	PGA	Year	Masters	US Open	Brit. Open	PGA
1934	H. Smith	Dutra	Cotton	Runyan	1952	Snead	Boros	Locke	Turnesa
1935	Sarazen	Parks	Perry	Revolta	1953	Hogan	Hogan	Hogan	Burkemo
1936	H. Smith	Manero	Padgham	Shute	1954	Snead	Furgol	Thomson	Harbert
1937	B. Nelson	Guldahl	Cotton	Shute	1955	Middlecoff	Fleck	Thomson	Ford
1938	Picard	Guldahl	Whitcombe	Runyan	1956	Burke	Middlecoff	Thomson	Burke
1939	Guldahl	B. Nelson	Burton	Picard	1957	Ford	Mayer	Locke	L. Hebert
1940	Demaret	Little	—	Ghezzi	1958	Palmer	Bolt	Thomson	Finsterwald
1941	Wood	Wood	—	Snead	1959	Wall	Casper	Player	Rosburg
1942	B. Nelson	—	—	Snead	1960	Palmer	Palmer	Nagle	J. Hebert
1943	—	—	—	—	1961	Player	Littler	Palmer	J. Barber
1944	—	—	—	Hamilton	1962	Palmer	Nicklaus	Palmer	Player
1945	—	—	—	B. Nelson	1963	Nicklaus	Boros	Charles	Nicklaus
1946	Keiser	Mangrum	Snead	Hogan	1964	Palmer	Venturi	Lema	Nichols
1947	Demaret	Worsham	F. Daly	Ferrier	1965	Nicklaus	Player	Thomson	Marr
1948	Harmon	Hogan	Cotton	Hogan	1966	Nicklaus	Casper	Nicklaus	Geiberger
1949	Snead	Middlecoff	Locke	Snead	1967	Brewer Jr.	Nicklaus	De Vicenzo	January
1950	Demaret	Hogan	Locke	Harper	1968	Goalby	Trevino	Player	Boros
1951	Hogan	Hogan	Faulkner	Snead	1969	Archer	Moody	Jacklin	Floyd

Year	Masters	US Open	Brit. Open	PGA	Year	Masters	US Open	Brit. Open	PGA
1970	Casper	Jacklin	Nicklaus	Stockton	1989	Faldo	Strange	Calcavecchia	Stewart
1971	Coody	Trevino	Trevino	Nicklaus	1990	Faldo	Irwin	Faldo	Grady
1972	Nicklaus	Nicklaus	Trevino	Player	1991	Woosnam	Stewart	Baker-Finch	J. Daly
1973	Aaron	J. Miller	Weiskopf	Nicklaus	1992	Couples	Kite	Faldo	Price
1974	Player	Irwin	Player	Trevino	1993	Langer	Janzen	Norman	Azinger
1975	Nicklaus	L. Graham	T. Watson	Nicklaus	1994	Olazabal	Els	Price	Price
1976	Floyd	J. Pate	Miller	Stockton	1995	Crenshaw	Pavin	Daly	Elkington
1977	T. Watson	H. Green	T. Watson	L. Wadkins	1996	Faldo	S. Jones	Lehman	Brooks
1978	Player	North	Nicklaus	Mahaffey	1997	Woods	Els	Leonard	Love
1979	Zoeller	Irwin	Ballesteros	D. Graham	1998	O'Meara	Janzen	O'Meara	Singh
1980	Ballesteros	Nicklaus	T. Watson	Nicklaus	1999	Olazabal	Stewart	Lawrie	Woods
1981	T. Watson	D. Graham	Rogers	L. Nelson	2000	Singh	Woods	Woods	Woods
1982	Stadler	T. Watson	T. Watson	Floyd	2001	Woods	Goosen	Duval	Toms
1983	Ballesteros	L. Nelson	T. Watson	Sutton	2002	Woods	Woods	Els	Beem
1984	Crenshaw	Zoeller	Ballesteros	Trevino	2003	Weir	Furyk	Curtis	Micheel
1985	Langer	North	Lyle	H. Green	2004	Mickelson	Goosen	Hamilton	Singh
1986	Nicklaus	Floyd	Norman	Tway	2005	Woods	Campbell	Woods	Mickelson
1987	Mize	S. Simpson	Faldo	L. Nelson	2006	Mickelson	Ogilvy	Woods	Woods
1988	Lyle	Strange	Ballesteros	Sluman	2007	Johnson	Cabrerea	Harrington	Woods

U.S. Amateur

Match play from 1895-64, stroke play from 1965-72, match play 1973-79, 36-hole stroke-play qualifying before match play since 1979.

Multiple winners: Bobby Jones (5); Jerry Travers (4); Walter Travis and Tiger Woods (3); Deane Beman, Charles Coe, Gary Cowan, H. Chandler Egan, Chick Evans, Lawson Little, Jack Nicklaus, Francis Ouimet, Jay Sigel, William Turnesa, Bud Ward, Harvie Ward, and H.J. Whigham (2).

Year		Year		Year		Year	
1895	Charles Macdonald	1924	Bobby Jones	1955	Harvie Ward	1983	Jay Sigel
1896	H.J. Whigham	1925	Bobby Jones	1956	Harvie Ward	1984	Scott Verplank
1897	H.J. Whigham	1926	George Von Elm	1957	Hillman Robbins	1985	Sam Randolph
1898	Findlay Douglas	1927	Bobby Jones	1958	Charles Coe	1986	Buddy Alexander
1899	H.M. Harriman	1928	Bobby Jones	1959	Jack Nicklaus	1987	Billy Mayfair
1900	Walter Travis	1929	Harrison Johnston	1960	Deane Beman	1988	Eric Meeks
1901	Walter Travis	1930	Bobby Jones	1961	Jack Nicklaus	1989	Chris Patton
1902	Louis James	1931	Francis Ouimet	1962	Labron Harris	1990	Phil Mickelson
1903	Walter Travis	1932	Ross Somerville	1963	Deane Beman	1991	Mitch Voges
1904	H. Chandler Egan	1933	George Dunlap	1964	Bill Campbell	1992	Justin Leonard
1905	H. Chandler Egan	1934	Lawson Little	1965	Bob Murphy	1993	John Harris
1906	Eben Byers	1935	Lawson Little	1966	Gary Cowan	1994	Tiger Woods
1907	Jerry Travers	1936	John Fischer	1967	Bob Dickson	1995	Tiger Woods
1908	Jerry Travers	1937	John Goodman	1968	Bruce Fleisher	1996	Tiger Woods
1909	Robert Gardner	1938	William Turnesa	1969	Steve Melnyk	1997	Matt Kuchar
1910	W.C. Fownes Jr.	1939	Bud Ward	1970	Lanny Wadkins	1998	Hank Kuehne
1911	Harold Hilton	1940	Richard Chapman	1971	Gary Cowan	1999	David Gossett
1912	Jerry Travers	1941	Bud Ward	1972	Vinny Giles	2000	Jeff Quinney
1913	Jerry Travers	1942-45	Not held	1973	Craig Stadler	2001	Bubba Dickerson
1914	Francis Ouimet	1946	Ted Bishop	1974	Jerry Pate	2002	Ricky Barnes
1915	Robert Gardner	1947	Skee Riegel	1975	Fred Ridley	2003	Nick Flanagan
1916	Chick Evans	1948	William Turnesa	1976	Bill Sander	2004	Ryan Moore
1917-18	Not held	1949	Charles Coe	1977	John Fought	2005	Edoardo Molinari
1919	Davidson Herron	1950	Sam Urzetta	1978	John Cook	2006	Richie Ramsay
1920	Chick Evans	1951	Billy Maxwell	1979	Mark O'Meara	2007	Colt Knost
1921	Jesse Guilford	1952	Jack Westland	1980	Hal Sutton		
1922	Jess Sweetser	1953	Gene Littler	1981	Nathaniel Crosby		
1923	Max Marston	1954	Arnold Palmer	1982	Jay Sigel		

Major Championship Leaders

Through 2007; active PGA players in **bold** type.

	US Open	British Open	PGA	Masters	US Am	British Am	Total
Jack Nicklaus	4	3	5	6	2	0	20
Tiger Woods	2	3	4	4	3	0	16
Bobby Jones	4	3	0	0	5	1	13
Walter Hagen	2	4	5	0	0	0	11
Ben Hogan	4	1	2	2	0	0	9
Gary Player	1	3	2	3	0	0	9
John Ball	0	1	0	0	0	8	9
Arnold Palmer	1	2	0	4	1	0	8
Tom Watson	1	5	0	2	0	0	8
Four tied with 7 wins each.							

British Amateur

Match play since 1885. **Multiple winners:** John Ball (8); Michael Bonallack (5); Harold Hilton (4); Joe Carr (3); Horace Hutchinson, Ernest Holderness, Trevor Homer, Johnny Laidley, Lawson Little, Peter McEvoy, Dick Siderowf, Frank Stranahan, Freddie Tait, Cyril Tolley and Gary Wolstenholme (2).

Year		Year		Year		Year	
1885	Allen MacFie	1914	J.L.C. Jenkins	1952	Harvie Ward	1981	Phillipe Ploujoux
1886	Horace Hutchinson	1915-19	Not held	1953	Joe Carr	1982	Martin Thompson
1887	Horace Hutchinson	1920	Cyril Tolley	1954	Douglas Bachli	1983	Philip Parkin
1888	John Ball	1921	William Hunter	1955	Joe Conrad	1984	Jose-Maria Olazabal
1889	Johnny Laidley	1922	Ernest Holderness	1956	John Beharrell	1985	Garth McGimpsey
1890	John Ball	1923	Roger Wethered	1957	Reid Jack	1986	David Curry
1891	Johnny Laidley	1924	Ernest Holderness	1958	Joe Carr	1987	Paul Mayo
1892	John Ball	1925	Robert Harris	1959	Deane Beman	1988	Christian Hardin
1893	Peter Anderson	1926	Jess Sweetser	1960	Joe Carr	1989	Stephen Dodd
1894	John Ball	1927	William Tweddell	1961	Michael Bonallack	1990	Rolf Muntz
1895	Leslie Balfour-Melville	1928	Thomas Perkins	1962	Richard Davies	1991	Gary Wolstenholme
1896	Freddie Tait	1929	Cyril Tolley	1963	Michael Lunt	1992	Stephen Dundas
1897	Jack Allan	1930	Bobby Jones	1964	Gordon Clark	1993	Ian Pyman
1898	Freddie Tait	1931	Eric Smith	1965	Michael Bonallack	1994	Lee James
1899	John Ball	1932	John deForest	1966	Bobby Cole	1995	Gordon Sherry
1900	Harold Hilton	1933	Michael Scott	1967	Bob Dickson	1996	Warren Bledon
1901	Harold Hilton	1934	Lawson Little	1968	Michael Bonallack	1997	Craig Watson
1902	Charles Hutchings	1935	Lawson Little	1969	Michael Bonallack	1998	Sergio Garcia
1903	Robert Maxwell	1936	Hector Thomson	1970	Michael Bonallack	1999	Graeme Storm
1904	Walter Travis	1937	Robert Sweeny Jr.	1971	Steve Melnyk	2000	Mikko Ilonen
1905	Arthur Barry	1938	Charles Yates	1972	Trevor Homer	2001	Michael Hoey
1906	James Robb	1939	Alexander Kyle	1973	Dick Siderowf	2002	Alejandro Larrazabal
1907	John Ball	1940-45	Not held	1974	Trevor Homer	2003	Gary Wolstenholme
1908	E.A. Lassen	1946	James Bruen	1975	Vinny Giles	2004	Stuart Wilson
1909	Robert Maxwell	1947	William Turnesa	1976	Dick Siderowf	2005	Brian McElhinney
1910	John Ball	1948	Frank Stranahan	1977	Peter McEvoy	2006	Julien Guerrier
1911	Harold Hilton	1949	Samuel McCready	1978	Peter McEvoy	2007	Drew Weaver
1912	John Ball	1950	Frank Stranahan	1979	Jay Sigel		
1913	Harold Hilton	1951	Richard Chapman	1980	Duncan Evans		

WOMEN

Kraft Nabisco Championship

Formerly known as the Colgate Dinah Shore (1972-81) and the Nabisco Dinah Shore (1982-99), the tournament became the LPGA's fourth designated major championship in 1983. Shore's name, which was dropped from the tournament in 2000, is preserved with the Nabisco Dinah Shore Trophy, which is awarded to the winner. The tourney has been played at Mission Hills CC in Rancho Mirage, Calif., since it began; (*) indicates playoff winner.

Multiple winners: (as a major): Amy Alcott, Betsy King and Annika Sorenstam (3); Juli Inkster, Dottie Pepper and Karrie Webb (2).

Year	Winner	Score	Runner-up	Year	Winner	Score	Runner-up
1972	Jane Blalock	.213	Carol Mann & Judy Rankin (216)	1991	Amy Alcott	.273	Dottie Pepper (281)
				1992	Dottie Pepper*	.279	Juli Inkster (279)
1973	Mickey Wright	.284	Joyce Kazmierski (286)	1993	Helen Alfredsson	.284	Amy Benz & Tina Barrett (286)
1974	Jo Anne Prentice*	.289	Jane Blalock & Sandra Haynie (289)	1994	Donna Andrews	.276	Laura Davies (277)
1975	Sandra Palmer	.283	Kathy McMullen (284)	1995	Nanci Bowen	.285	Susie Redman (286)
1976	Judy Rankin	.285	Betty Burfeindt (288)	1996	Patty Sheehan	.281	Kelly Robbins, Meg Mallon & Annika Sorenstam (276)
1977	Kathy Whitworth	.289	JoAnne Carner & Sally Little (290)	1997	Betsy King	.276	Kris Tschetter (278)
1978	Sandra Post*	.283	Penny Pulz (283)	1998	Pat Hurst	.281	Helen Dobson (282)
1979	Sandra Post	.276	Nancy Lopez (277)	1999	Dottie Pepper	.269	Meg Mallon (275)
1980	Donna Caponi	.275	Amy Alcott (277)	2000	Karrie Webb	.274	Dottie Pepper (284)
1981	Nancy Lopez	.277	Carolyn Hill (279)	2001	Annika Sorenstam	.281	Akiko Fukushima, Janice Moodie, Dottie Pepper, Rachel Teske
1982	Sally Little	.278	Hollis Stacy & Sandra Haynie (281)				
1983	Amy Alcott	.282	Beth Daniel & Kathy Whitworth (284)	2002	Annika Sorenstam	.280	Liselotte Neumann (281)
				2003	P. Meunier-Lebouc	.281	Annika Sorenstam (282)
1984	Juli Inkster*	.280	Pat Bradley (280)	2004	Grace Park	.277	Aree Song (278)
1985	Alice Miller	.275	Jan Stephenson (278)	2005	Annika Sorenstam	.273	Rosie Jones (281)
1986	Pat Bradley	.280	Val Skinner (282)	2006	Karrie Webb*	.279	Lorena Ochoa (279)
1987	Betsy King*	.283	Patty Sheehan (283)	2007	Morgan Pressel	.285	Catriona Matthew, Brittany Lincicome & Suzann Pettersen (286)
1988	Amy Alcott	.274	Colleen Walker (276)				
1989	Juli Inkster	.279	Tammie Green & JoAnne Carner (284)				
1990	Betsy King	.283	Kathy Postlewait & Shirley Furlong (285)				

*PLAYOFFS: 1974: Jo Ann Prentice def. Jane Blalock in sudden death. **1978:** Sandra Post def. Penny Pulz in sudden death. **1984:** Juli Inkster def. Pat Bradley in sudden death. **1987:** Betsy King def. Patty Sheehan in sudden death. **1992:** Dottie Pepper def. Juli Inkster in sudden death. **2006:** Karrie Webb def. Lorena Ochoa in sudden death.

U.S. Women's Open

The U.S. Women's Open began under the direction of the defunct Women's Professional Golfers Assn. in 1946, passed to the LPGA in 1949 and to the USGA in 1953. The tournament used a match play format its first year then switched to stroke play; (*) indicates playoff winner and (a) indicates amateur.

Multiple winners: Betsy Rawls and Mickey Wright (4); Susie Maxwell Berning, Annika Sorenstam, Hollis Stacy and Babe Zaharias (3); JoAnne Carner, Donna Caponi, Juli Inkster, Betsy King, Meg Mallon, Patty Sheehan, Louise Suggs and Karrie Webb (2).

Year	Winner	Score	Runner-up	Course	Location
1946	Patty Berg	5&4	Betty Jameson	Spokane CC	Spokane, Wash.
1947	Betty Jameson	295	a-Sally Sessions & a-Polly Riley (301)	Starmount Forest CC	Greensboro, N.C.
1948	Babe Zaharias	300	Betty Hicks (308)	Atlantic City CC	Northfield, N.J.
1949	Louise Suggs	291	Babe Zaharias (305)	Prince Georges CC	Landover, Md.
1950	Babe Zaharias	291	a-Betsy Rawls (300)	Rolling Hills CC	Wichita, Kan.
1951	Betsy Rawls	293	Louise Suggs (298)	Druid Hills GC	Atlanta, Ga.
1952	Louise Suggs	284	Marlene Hagge (291)	Bala GC	Philadelphia, Penn.
1953	Betsy Rawls*	302	Jackie Pung (302)	CC of Rochester	Rochester, N.Y.
1954	Babe Zaharias	291	Betty Hicks (303)	Salem CC	Peabody, Mass.
1955	Fay Crocker	299	Mary Lena Faulk (303)	Wichita CC	Wichita, Kan.
1956	Kathy Cornelius*	302	Barbara McIntire (302)	Northland CC	Duluth, Minn.
1957	Betsy Rawls	299	Patty Berg (305)	Winged Foot GC	Mamaroneck, N.Y.
1958	Mickey Wright	290	Louise Suggs (295)	Forest Lake CC	Detroit, Mich.
1959	Mickey Wright	287	Louise Suggs (289)	Churchill Valley CC	Pittsburgh, Penn.
1960	Betsy Rawls	292	Joyce Ziske (293)	Worcester CC	Worcester, Mass.
1961	Mickey Wright	293	Betsy Rawls (299)	Baltusrol GC	Springfield, N.J.
1962	Murle Breer	301	Jo Anne Prentice & Ruth Jessen (303)	Dunes GC	Myrtle Beach, S.C.
1963	Mary Mills	289	Sandra Haynie & Louise Suggs (292)	Kenwood CC	Cincinnati, Ohio
1964	Mickey Wright*	290	Ruth Jessen (290)	San Diego CC	Chula Vista, Calif.
1965	Carol Mann	290	Kathy Cornelius (292)	Atlantic City CC	Northfield, N.J.
1966	Sandra Spuzich	297	Carol Mann (298)	Hazeltine National GC	Chaska, Minn.
1967	a-Catherine LaCoste	294	Susie Berning & Beth Stone (296)	Hot Springs GC	Hot Springs, Va.
1968	Susie Berning	289	Mickey Wright (292)	Moselem Springs GC	Fleetwood, Penn.
1969	Donna Caponi	294	Peggy Wilson (295)	Scenic Hills CC	Pensacola, Fla.
1970	Donna Caponi	287	Sandra Haynie (288)	Muskogee CC	Muskogee, Okla.
1971	JoAnne Carner	288	Kathy Whitworth (295)	Kahkwa CC	Erie, Penn.
1972	Susie Berning	299	Kathy Ahern, Pam Barnett & Judy Rankin (300)	Winged Foot GC	Mamaroneck, N.Y.
1973	Susie Berning	290	Gloria Ehret (295)	CC of Rochester	Rochester, N.Y.
1974	Sandra Haynie	295	Carol Mann & Beth Stone (296)	La Grange CC	La Grange, Ill.
1975	Sandra Palmer	295	JoAnne Carner, a-Nancy Lopez & Sandra Post (299)	Atlantic City CC	Northfield, N.J.
1976	JoAnne Carner*	292	Sandra Palmer (292)	Rolling Green CC	Springfield, Penn.
1977	Hollis Stacy	292	Nancy Lopez (294)	Hazeltine National GC	Chaska, Minn.
1978	Hollis Stacy	289	JoAnne Carner & Sally Little (290)	CC of Indianapolis	Indianapolis, Ind.
1979	Jerilyn Britz	284	Debbie Massey & Sandra Palmer (286)	Brooklawn CC	Fairfield, Conn.
1980	Amy Alcott	280	Hollis Stacy (289)	Richland CC	Nashville, Tenn.
1981	Pat Bradley	279	Beth Daniel (280)	La Grange CC	La Grange, Ill.
1982	Janet Anderson	283	Beth Daniel, Sandra Haynie & Donna White (289)	Del Paso CC	Sacramento, Calif.
1983	Jan Stephenson	290	JoAnne Carner (291)	Cedar Ridge CC	Tulsa, Okla.
1984	Hollis Stacy	290	Rosie Jones (291)	Salem CC	Peabody, Mass.
1985	Kathy Baker	280	Judy Dickenson (283)	Baltusrol GC	Springfield, N.J.
1986	Jane Geddes*	287	Sally Little (287)	NCR GC	Dayton, Ohio
1987	Laura Davies*	285	Ayako Okamoto & JoAnne Carner (285)	Plainfield CC	Plainfield, N.J.
1988	Liselotte Neumann	277	Patty Sheehan (280)	Baltimore CC	Baltimore, Md.
1989	Betsy King	278	Nancy Lopez (282)	Indianwood GC	Lake Orion, Mich.
1990	Betsy King	284	Patty Sheehan (285)	Atlanta Athletic Club	Duluth, Ga.
1991	Meg Mallon	283	Pat Bradley (285)	Colonial CC	Ft. Worth, Texas
1992	Patty Sheehan*	280	Juli Inkster (280)	Oakmont CC	Oakmont, Penn.
1993	Lauri Merten	280	Donna Andrews & Helen Alfredsson (281)	Crooked Stick GC	Carmel, Ind.
1994	Patty Sheehan	277	Tammie Green (278)	Indianwood CC	Lake Orion, Mich.
1995	Annika Sorenstam	278	Meg Mallon (279)	The Broadmoor	Colorado Springs, Colo.
1996	Annika Sorenstam	272	Kris Tschetter (278)	Pine Needles Lodge & GC	Southern Pines, N.C.
1997	Alison Nicholas	274	Nancy Lopez (275)	Pumpkin Ridge GC	Cornelius, Ore.

U.S. Women's Open (Cont.)

Year	Winner	Score	Runner-up	Course	Location
1998	Se Ri Pak*	290	a-Jenny Chuasiriporn (290)	Blackwolf Run GC	Kohler, Wis.
1999	Juli Inkster	272	Sherri Turner (277)	Old Waverly GC	West Point, Miss.
2000	Karrie Webb	282	Cristie Kerr & Meg Mallon (287)	Merit Club	Libertyville, Ill.
2001	Karrie Webb	273	Se Ri Pak (281)	Pine Needles Lodge & GC	Southern Pines, N.C.
2002	Juli Inkster	276	Annika Sorenstam (278)	Prairie Dunes CC	Hutchinson, Kan.
2003	Hilary Lunke*	283	Angela Stanford & Kelly Robbins (283)	Pumpkin Ridge GC	North Plains, Ore.
2004	Meg Mallon	274	Annika Sorenstam (276)	Orchards GC	South Hadley, Mass.
2005	Birdie Kim	287	a-Brittany Lang & a-Morgan Pressel (289)	Cherry Hills CC	Cherry Hills Vill., Colo.
2006	Annika Sorenstam*	284	Pat Hurst (284)	Newport CC	Newport, R.I.
2007	Cristie Kerr	279	Angela Park & Lorena Ochoa (281)	Pine Needles Lodge & GC	Southern Pines, N.C.

*PLAYOFFS

1953: Betsy Rawls (70) def. Jackie Pung (77) in 18 holes. **1956:** Kathy Cornelius (75) def. Barbara McIntire (82) in 18 holes. **1964:** Mickey Wright (70) def. Ruth Jessen (72) in 18 holes. **1976:** JoAnne Carner (76) def. Sandra Palmer (78) in 18 holes. **1986:** Jane Geddes (71) def. Sally Little (73) in 18 holes. **1987:** Laura Davies (71) def. Ayako Okamoto (73) and JoAnne Carner (74) in 18 holes. **1992:** Patty Sheehan (72) def. Juli Inkster (74) in 18 holes. **1998:** Se Ri Pak def. Jenny Chuasiriporn on the second sudden death hole after both players were tied after an 18-hole playoff. **2003:** Hilary Lunke (70) def. Angela Stanford (71) and Kelly Robbins (73) in 18 holes. **2006:** Annika Sorenstam (70) def. Pat Hurst (74) in 18 holes.

LPGA Championship

Officially the McDonald's LPGA Championship since 1994 (Mazda was the title sponsor from 1987-93), the tournament began in 1955 and has had extended stays at the Stardust CC in Las Vegas (1961-66), Pleasant Valley CC in Sutton, Mass. (1967-68, 70-74), the Jack Nicklaus Sports Center at Kings Island, Ohio (1978-89), Bethesda CC in Maryland (1990-93), DuPont CC in Wilmington, Del. (1994-2004) and Bulle Rock GC in Havre de Grace, Md. (2005–); (*) indicates playoff winner, (a) amateur and (#) weather-shortened.

Multiple winners: Mickey Wright (4); Nancy Lopez, Se Ri Pak, Patty Sheehan, Annika Sorenstam and Kathy Whitworth (3); Donna Caponi, Laura Davies, Sandra Haynie, Juli Inkster, Mary Mills and Betsy Rawls (2).

Year	Winner	Score	Runner-up	Year	Winner	Score	Runner-up
1955	Beverly Hanson	220	Louise Suggs (223)	1982	Jan Stephenson	279	JoAnne Carner (281)
1956	Marlene Hagge*	291	Patty Berg (291)	1983	Patty Sheehan	279	Sandra Haynie (281)
1957	Louise Suggs	285	Wiffi Smith (288)	1984	Patty Sheehan	272	Beth Daniel & Pat Bradley (282)
1958	Mickey Wright	288	Fay Crocker (294)				
1959	Betsy Rawls	288	Patty Berg (289)	1985	Nancy Lopez	273	Alice Miller (281)
1960	Mickey Wright	292	Louise Suggs (295)	1986	Pat Bradley	277	Patty Sheehan (278)
1961	Mickey Wright	287	Louise Suggs (296)	1987	Jane Geddes	275	Betsy King (275)
1962	Judy Kimball	282	Shirley Spork (286)	1988	Sherri Turner	281	Amy Alcott (282)
1963	Mickey Wright	294	Mary Lena Faulk & Mary Mills (296)	1989	Nancy Lopez	274	Ayako Okamoto (277)
1964	Mary Mills	278	Mickey Wright (280)	1990	Beth Daniel	280	Rosie Jones (281)
1965	Sandra Haynie	279	Clifford A. Creed (280)	1991	Meg Mallon	274	Pat Bradley & Ayako Okamoto (275)
1966	Gloria Ehret	282	Mickey Wright (285)				
1967	Kathy Whitworth	284	Shirley Englehorn (285)	1992	Betsy King	267	JoAnne Carner, Karen Noble & Liselotte Neumann (278)
1968	Sandra Post	294	Kathy Whitworth (294)				
1969	Betsy Rawls	293	Susie Berning & Carol Mann (297)	1993	Patty Sheehan	275	Lauri Merten (276)
				1994	Laura Davies	279	Alice Ritzman (280)
1970	Shirley Englehorn	285	Kathy Whitworth (285)	1995	Kelly Robbins	274	Laura Davies (275)
1971	Kathy Whitworth	288	Kathy Ahern (292)	1996	Laura Davies#	213	Julie Piers (214)
1972	Kathy Ahern	293	Jane Blalock (299)	1997	Chris Johnson*	281	Leta Lindley (281)
1973	Mary Mills	288	Betty Burfeindt (289)	1998	Se Ri Pak	273	Donna Andrews & Lisa Hackney (276)
1974	Sandra Haynie	288	JoAnne Carner (290)				
1975	Kathy Whitworth	288	Sandra Haynie (289)	1999	Juli Inkster*	268	Liselotte Neumann (272)
1976	Betty Burfeindt	287	Judy Rankin (288)	2000	Juli Inkster*	281	Stefania Croce (281)
1977	Chako Higuchi	279	Pat Bradley, Sandra Post & Judy Rankin (282)	2001	Karrie Webb	270	Laura Diaz (272)
				2002	Se Ri Pak	279	Beth Daniel (282)
1978	Nancy Lopez	275	Amy Alcott (281)	2003	Annika Sorenstam*	278	Grace Park (278)
1979	Donna Caponi	279	Jerilyn Britz (282)	2004	Annika Sorenstam	271	Shi Hyun Ahn (274)
1980	Sally Little	285	Jane Blalock (288)	2005	Annika Sorenstam	277	a-Michelle Wie (280)
1981	Donna Caponi	280	Jerilyn Britz & Pat Meyers (281)	2006	Se Ri Pak*	280	Karrie Webb (280)
				2007	Suzann Pettersen	274	Karrie Webb (275)

*PLAYOFFS

1956: Marlene Hagge def. Patti Berg in sudden death. **1968:** Sandra Post (68) def. Kathy Whitworth (75) in 18 holes. **1970:** Shirley Englehorn def. Kathy Whitworth in sudden death. **1997:** Chris Johnson def. Leta Lindley in sudden death. **2000:** Juli Inkster def. Stefania Croce in sudden death. **2003:** Annika Sorenstam def. Grace Park in sudden death. **2006:** Se Ri Pak def. Karrie Webb in sudden death.

Women's British Open

Sponsored by Ricoh (Weetabix was title sponsor until 2007), this has been an official stop on the LPGA Tour since 1994, and it became the fourth designated major championship in 2001 when it replaced the du Maurier Classic.

Multiple winners Karrie Webb and Sherri Steinhauer (3); (as a major): none.

Year	Winner	Score	Runner-up	Course	Location
1994	Liselotte Neumann	.280	Dottie Mochrie & Annika Sorenstam (283)	Woburn G&CC	Milton Keynes, England
1995	Karrie Webb	.278	Annika Sorenstam & Jill McGill (284)	Woburn G&CC	Milton Keynes, England
1996	Emilee Klein	.277	Penny Hammel & Amy Alcott (284)	Woburn G&CC	Milton Keynes, England
1997	Karrie Webb	.269	Rosie Jones (277)	Sunningdale GC	Berkshire, England
1998	Sherri Steinhauer	.292	Sophie Gustafson & Brandie Burton (293)	Royal Lytham	Lytham, England
1999	Sherri Steinhauer	.283	Annika Sorenstam (284)	Woburn G&CC	Milton Keynes, England
2000	Sophie Gustafson	.282	Kirsty Taylor, Liselotte Neumann, Becky Iverson & Meg Mallon (284)	Royal Birkdale	Southport, England
2001	Se Ri Pak	.277	Mi Hyun Kim (279)	Sunningdale GC	Berkshire, England
2002	Karrie Webb	.273	Michelle Ellis & Paula Marti (275)	Turnberry GC	Turnberry, Scotland
2003	Annika Sorenstam	.278	Se Ri Pak (279)	Royal Lytham	Lytham, England
2004	Karen Stupples	.269	Rachel Teske (274)	Sunningdale GC	Berkshire, England
2005	Jeong Jang	.272	Sophie Gustafson (276)	Royal Birkdale GC	Merseyside, England
2006	Sherri Steinhauer	.281	Cristie Kerr & Sophie Gustafson (284)	Royal Lytham	Lytham, England
2007	Lorena Ochoa	.287	Jee Young Lee & Maria Hjorth (291)	St. Andrews	St. Andrews, Scotland

du Maurier Classic (1979-2000)

The du Maurier Classic was considered a major title on the women's tour from 1979 until it was discontinued in 2000; (*) indicates playoff winner. **Multiple winners** (as a major): Pat Bradley (3); Brandie Burton (2).

Year		Year		Year		Year	
1973	Jocelyne Bourassa	1980	Pat Bradley	1987	Jody Rosenthal	1994	Martha Nause
1974	Carole Jo Skala	1981	Jan Stephenson	1988	Sally Little	1995	Jenny Lidback
1975	JoAnne Carner	1982	Sandra Haynie	1989	Tammie Green	1996	Laura Davies
1976	Donna Caponi	1983	Hollis Stacy	1990	Cathy Johnston	1997	Colleen Walker
1977	Judy Rankin	1984	Juli Inkster	1991	Nancy Scranton	1998	Brandie Burton
1978	JoAnne Carner	1985	Pat Bradley	1992	Sherri Steinhauer	1999	Karrie Webb
1979	Amy Alcott	1986	Pat Bradley*	1993	Brandie Burton*	2000	Meg Mallon

Titleholders Championship (1937-72)

The Titleholders was considered a major title on the women's tour until it was discontinued after the 1972 tournament.

Multiple winners: Patty Berg (7); Louise Suggs (4); Babe Zaharias (3); Dorothy Kirby, Marilynn Smith, Kathy Whitworth and Mickey Wright (2).

Year		Year		Year		Year	
1937	Patty Berg	1947	Babe Zaharias	1955	Patty Berg	1963	Marilynn Smith
1938	Patty Berg	1948	Patty Berg	1956	Louise Suggs	1964	Marilynn Smith
1939	Patty Berg	1949	Peggy Kirk	1957	Patty Berg	1965	Kathy Whitworth
1940	Betty Hicks	1950	Babe Zaharias	1958	Beverly Hanson	1966	Kathy Whitworth
1941	Dorothy Kirby	1951	Pat O'Sullivan	1959	Louise Suggs	1967-71	Not held
1942	Dorothy Kirby	1952	Babe Zaharias	1960	Fay Crocker	1972	Sandra Palmer
1943-45	Not held	1953	Patty Berg	1961	Mickey Wright		
1946	Louise Suggs	1954	Louise Suggs	1962	Mickey Wright		

Western Open (1930-67)

The Western Open was considered a major title on the women's tour until it was discontinued after the 1967 tournament.

Multiple winners: Patty Berg (7); Louise Suggs and Babe Zaharias (4); Mickey Wright (3); June Beebe, Opal Hill, Betty Jameson and Betsy Rawls (2).

Year		Year		Year		Year	
1930	Mrs. Lee Mida	1940	Babe Zaharias	1950	Babe Zaharias	1960	Joyce Ziske
1931	June Beebe	1941	Patty Berg	1951	Patty Berg	1961	Mary Lena Faulk
1932	Jane Weiller	1942	Betty Jameson	1952	Betsy Rawls	1962	Mickey Wright
1933	June Beebe	1943	Patty Berg	1953	Louise Suggs	1963	Mickey Wright
1934	Marian McDougall	1944	Babe Zaharias	1954	Betty Jameson	1964	Carol Mann
1935	Opal Hill	1945	Babe Zaharias	1955	Patty Berg	1965	Susie Maxwell
1936	Opal Hill	1946	Louise Suggs	1956	Beverly Hanson	1966	Mickey Wright
1937	Betty Hicks	1947	Louise Suggs	1957	Patty Berg	1967	Kathy Whitworth
1938	Bea Barrett	1948	Patty Berg	1958	Patty Berg		
1939	Helen Dettweiler	1949	Louise Suggs	1959	Betsy Rawls		

Grand Slam Summary

From 1955-66, the U.S. Open, LPGA Championship, Western Open and Titleholders tournaments served as the Women's Grand Slam. From 1983-2000 the U.S. Open, LPGA, du Maurier Classic and Nabisco Championship were the major events. In 2001, the Weetabix Women's British Open replaced the du Maurier Classic as the tour's fourth major. No one has won a four-event Grand Slam on the women's tour.

Three wins in one year (3): Babe Zaharias (1950), Mickey Wright (1961) and Pat Bradley (1986).

Two wins in one year (19): Patty Berg and Mickey Wright (3 times); Juli Inkster, Annika Sorenstam, Louise Suggs and Karrie Webb (twice); Laura Davies, Sandra Haynie, Betsy King, Meg Mallon, Se Ri Pak, Betsy Rawls and Kathy Whitworth (once).

Year	LPGA	US Open	T'holders	Western
1937	—	—	Berg	Hicks
1938	—	—	Berg	Barrett
1939	—	—	Berg	Dettweiler
1940	—	—	Hicks	Zaharias
1941	—	—	Kirby	Berg
1942	—	—	Kirby	Jameson
1943	—	—	—	Berg
1944	—	—	—	Zaharias
1945	—	—	—	Zaharias
1946	—	Berg	Suggs	Suggs
1947	—	Jameson	Zaharias	Suggs
1948	—	Zaharias	Berg	Berg
1949	—	Suggs	Kirk	Suggs
1950	—	Zaharias	Zaharias	Zaharias
1951	—	Rawls	O'Sullivan	Berg
1952	—	Suggs	Zaharias	Rawls
1953	—	Rawls	Berg	Suggs
1954	—	Zaharias	Suggs	Jameson
1955	Hanson	Crocker	Berg	Berg
1956	Hagge	Cornelius	Suggs	Hanson
1957	Suggs	Rawls	Berg	Berg
1958	Wright	Wright	Hanson	Berg
1959	Rawls	Wright	Suggs	Rawls
1960	Wright	Rawls	Crocker	Ziske
1961	Wright	Wright	Wright	Faulk
1962	Kimball	Lindstrom	Wright	Wright
1963	Wright	Mills	M. Smith	Wright
1964	Mills	Wright	M. Smith	Mann
1965	Haynie	Mann	Whitworth	Maxwell
1966	Ehret	Spuzich	Whitworth	Wright
1967	Whitworth	a-LaCoste	—	Whitworth
1968	Post	Berning	—	—
1969	Rawls	Caponi	—	—
1970	Englehorn	Caponi	—	—
1971	Whitworth	Carner	—	—
1972	Ahern	Berning	Palmer	—
1973	Mills	Berning	—	—

Year	LPGA	US Open	T'holders	Western
1974	Haynie	Haynie	—	—
1975	Whitworth	Palmer	—	—
1976	Burfeindt	Carner	—	—
1977	Higuchi	Stacy	—	—
1978	Lopez	Stacy	—	—

Year	LPGA	US Open	duMaurier	Nabisco
1979	Caponi	Britz	Alcott	—
1980	Little	Alcott	Bradley	—
1981	Caponi	Bradley	Stephenson	—
1982	Stephenson	Anderson	Haynie	—
1983	Sheehan	Stephenson	Stacy	Alcott
1984	Sheehan	Stacy	Inkster	Inkster
1985	Lopez	Baker	Bradley	Miller
1986	Bradley	Geddes	Bradley	Bradley
1987	Geddes	Davies	Rosenthal	King
1988	Turner	Neumann	Little	Alcott
1989	Lopez	King	Green	Inkster
1990	Daniel	King	Johnston	King
1991	Mallon	Mallon	Scranton	Alcott
1992	King	Sheehan	Steinhauer	Pepper
1993	Sheehan	Merten	Burton	Alfredsson
1994	Davies	Sheehan	Nause	Andrews
1995	Robbins	Sorenstam	Lidback	Bowen
1996	Davies	Sorenstam	Davies	Sheehan
1997	Johnson	Nicholas	Walker	King
1998	Pak	Pak	Burton	Hurst
1999	Inkster	Inkster	Webb	Pepper
2000	Inkster	Webb	Mallon	Webb

Year	LPGA	US Open	Brit. Open	Nabisco
2001	Webb	Webb	Pak	Sorenstam
2002	Pak	Inkster	Webb	Sorenstam
2003	Sorenstam	Lunke	Sorenstam	Meunier-Lebouc
2004	Sorenstam	Mallon	Stupples	Park
2005	Sorenstam	Kim	Jang	Sorenstam
2006	Pak	Sorenstam	Steinhauer	Webb
2007	Pettersen	Kerr	Ochoa	Pressel

Major Championship Leaders

Through 2007; active LPGA players in **bold** type.

	US Open	LPGA	Nabisco	British Open	duM	Title	Western	US Am	Brit Am	Total
Patty Berg	1	0	0	0	0	7	7	1	0	**16**
Mickey Wright	4	4	0	0	0	2	3	0	0	**13**
Louise Suggs	2	1	0	0	0	4	4	1	1	**13**
Babe Didrikson Zaharias	3	0	0	0	0	3	4	1	1	**12**
Juli Inkster	2	2	2	0	1	0	0	3	0	**10**
Annika Sorenstam	3	3	3	1	0	0	0	0	0	**10**
Betsy Rawls	4	2	0	0	0	0	2	0	0	**8**
JoAnne Carner	2	0	0	0	0	0	0	5	0	**7**
Karrie Webb	2	1	2	1	1	0	0	0	0	**7**
Kathy Whitworth	0	3	0	0	0	2	1	0	0	**6**
Pat Bradley	1	1	1	0	3	0	0	0	0	**6**
Betsy King	2	1	3	0	0	0	0	0	0	**6**
Patty Sheehan	2	3	1	0	0	0	0	0	0	**6**
Glenna C. Vare	0	0	0	0	0	0	0	6	0	**6**

Tournaments: U.S. Open, LPGA Championship, Nabisco Championship, British Open, du Maurier Classic (1979-2000), Titleholders (1930-72), Western Open (1937-67), U.S. Amateur and British Amateur.

U.S. Women's Amateur

Stroke play in 1895, match play since 1896.

Multiple winners: Glenna Collett Vare (6); JoAnne Gunderson Carner (5); Margaret Curtis, Beatrix Hoyt, Dorothy Campbell Hurd, Juli Inkster, Alexa Stirling, Virginia Van Wie, Anne Quast Decker Welts (3); Kay Cockerill, Beth Daniel, Vicki Goetze, Katherine Harley, Genevieve Hecker, Betty Jameson, Kelli Kuehne and Barbara McIntire (2).

Year		Year		Year		Year	
1895	Mrs. C.S. Brown	1924	Dorothy C. Hurd	1955	Patricia Lesser	1983	Joanne Pacillo
1896	Beatrix Hoyt	1925	Glenna Collett	1956	Marlene Stewart	1984	Deb Richard
1897	Beatrix Hoyt	1926	Helen Stetson	1957	JoAnne Gunderson	1985	Michiko Hattori
1898	Beatrix Hoyt	1927	Miriam Burns Horn	1958	Anne Quast	1986	Kay Cockerill
1899	Ruth Underhill	1928	Glenna Collett	1959	Barbara McIntire	1987	Kay Cockerill
		1929	Glenna Collett			1988	Pearl Sinn
1900	Frances Griscom			1960	JoAnne Gunderson	1989	Vicki Goetze
1901	Genevieve Hecker	1930	Glenna Collett	1961	Anne Quast Decker		
1902	Genevieve Hecker	1931	Helen Hicks	1962	JoAnne Gunderson	1990	Pat Hurst
1903	Bessie Anthony	1932	Virginia Van Wie	1963	Anne Quast Welts	1991	Amy Fruhwirth
1904	Georgianna Bishop	1933	Virginia Van Wie	1964	Barbara McIntire	1992	Vicki Goetze
1905	Pauline Mackay	1934	Virginia Van Wie	1965	Jean Ashley	1993	Jill McGill
1906	Harriot Curtis	1935	Glenna Collett Vare	1966	JoAnne G. Carner	1994	Wendy Ward
1907	Margaret Curtis	1936	Pamela Barton	1967	Mary Lou Dill	1995	Kelli Kuehne
1908	Katherine Harley	1937	Estelle Lawson	1968	JoAnne G. Carner	1996	Kelli Kuehne
1909	Dorothy Campbell	1938	Patty Berg	1969	Catherine Lacoste	1997	Silvia Cavalleri
		1939	Betty Jameson			1998	Grace Park
1910	Dorothy Campbell			1970	Martha Wilkinson	1999	Dorothy Delasin
1911	Margaret Curtis	1940	Betty Jameson	1971	Laura Baugh		
1912	Margaret Curtis	1941	Elizabeth Hicks	1972	Mary Budke	2000	Marcy Newton
1913	Gladys Ravenscroft	1942-45	Not held	1973	Carol Semple	2001	Meredith Duncan
1914	Katherine Harley	1946	Babe D. Zaharias	1974	Cynthia Hill	2002	Becky Lucidi
1915	Florence Vanderbeck	1947	Louise Suggs	1975	Beth Daniel	2003	V. Nirapathpongporn
1916	Alexa Stirling	1948	Grace Lenczyk	1976	Donna Horton	2004	Jane Park
1917-18	Not held	1949	Dorothy Porter	1977	Beth Daniel	2005	Morgan Pressel
1919	Alexa Stirling			1978	Cathy Sherk	2006	Kimberly Kim
		1950	Beverly Hanson	1979	Carolyn Hill	2007	Maria Jose Uribe
1920	Alexa Stirling	1951	Dorothy Kirby	1980	Juli Inkster		
1921	Marion Hollins	1952	Jacqueline Pung	1981	Juli Inkster		
1922	Glenna Collett	1953	Mary Lena Faulk	1982	Juli Inkster		
1923	Edith Cummings	1954	Barbara Romack				

British Women's Amateur

Match play since 1893.

Multiple winners: Cecil Leitch and Joyce Wethered (4); May Hezlet, Lady Margaret Scott, Jessie Anderson Valentine, Brigitte Varangot and Enid Wilson (3); Rhona Adair, Pam Barton, Dorothy Campbell, Elizabeth Chadwick, Helen Holm, Rebecca Hudson, Marley Spearman, Louise Stahle, Frances Stephens and Michelle Walker (2).

Year		Year		Year		Year	
1893	Lady Margaret Scott	1924	Joyce Wethered	1956	Wiffi Smith	1983	Jill Thornhill
1894	Lady Margaret Scott	1925	Joyce Wethered	1957	Philomena Garvey	1984	Jody Rosenthal
1895	Lady Margaret Scott	1926	Cecil Leitch	1958	Jessie Valentine	1985	Lillian Behan
1896	Amy Pascoe	1927	Simone de la Chaume	1959	Elizabeth Price	1986	Marnie McGuire
1897	Edith Orr	1928	Nanette le Blan			1987	Janet Collingham
1898	Lena Thomson	1929	Joyce Wethered	1960	Barbara McIntire	1988	Joanne Furby
1899	May Hezlet			1961	Marley Spearman	1989	Helen Dobson
		1930	Diana Fishwick	1962	Marley Spearman		
1900	Rhona Adair	1931	Enid Wilson	1963	Brigitte Varangot	1990	Julie Wade Hall
1901	Mary Graham	1932	Enid Wilson	1964	Carol Sorenson	1991	Valerie Michaud
1902	May Hezlet	1933	Enid Wilson	1965	Brigitte Varangot	1992	Bernille Pedersen
1903	Rhona Adair	1934	Helen Holm	1966	Elizabeth Chadwick	1993	Catriona Lambert
1904	Lottie Dod	1935	Wanda Morgan	1967	Elizabeth Chadwick	1994	Emma Duggleby
1905	Bertha Thompson	1936	Pam Barton	1968	Brigitte Varangot	1995	Julie Wade Hall
1906	Mrs. W. Kennion	1937	Jessie Anderson	1969	Catherine Lacoste	1996	Kelli Kuehne
1907	May Hezlet	1938	Helen Holm			1997	Alison Rose
1908	Maud Titterton	1939	Pam Barton	1970	Dinah Oxley	1998	Kim Rostron
1909	Dorothy Campbell			1971	Michelle Walker	1999	Marine Monnet
		1940-45	Not held	1972	Michelle Walker		
1910	Eisie Grant-Suttie	1946	Jean Hetherington	1973	Ann Irvin	2000	Rebecca Hudson
1911	Dorothy Campbell	1947	Babe Zaharias	1974	Carol Semple	2001	Marta Prieto
1912	Gladys Ravenscroft	1948	Louise Suggs	1975	Nancy Roth Syms	2002	Rebecca Hudson
1913	Muriel Dodd	1949	Frances Stephens	1976	Cathy Panton	2003	Elisa Serramia
1914	Cecil Leitch			1977	Angela Uzielli	2004	Louise Stahle
1915-19	Not held	1950	Lally de St. Sauveur	1978	Edwina Kennedy	2005	Louise Stahle
		1951	Catherine MacCann	1979	Maureen Madill	2006	Belen Mozo
1920	Cecil Leitch	1952	Moira Paterson	1980	Anne Quast Sander	2007	Carlota Ciganda
1921	Cecil Leitch	1953	Marlene Stewart	1981	Belle Robertson		
1922	Joyce Wethered	1954	Frances Stephens	1982	Kitrina Douglas		
1923	Doris Chambers	1955	Jessie Valentine				

Vare Trophy

The Vare Trophy for best scoring average by a player on the LPGA Tour has been awarded since 1953 by the LPGA. The award is named after Glenna Collett Vare, winner of six U.S. women's amateur titles from 1922-35.

Multiple winners: Kathy Whitworth (7); Annika Sorenstam (6); JoAnne Carner and Mickey Wright (5); Patty Berg, Beth Daniel, Nancy Lopez, Judy Rankin and Karrie Webb (3); Pat Bradley and Betsy King (2).

Year		Avg	Year		Avg	Year		Avg
1953	Patty Berg	75.00	1971	Kathy Whitworth	72.88	1989	Beth Daniel	70.38
1954	Babe Zaharias	75.48	1972	Kathy Whitworth	72.38	1990	Beth Daniel	70.54
1955	Patty Berg	74.47	1973	Judy Rankin	73.08	1991	Pat Bradley	70.66
1956	Patty Berg	74.57	1974	JoAnne Carner	72.87	1992	Dottie Pepper	70.80
1957	Louise Suggs	74.64	1975	JoAnne Carner	72.40	1993	Betsy King	70.85
1958	Beverly Hanson	74.92	1976	Judy Rankin	72.25	1994	Beth Daniel	70.90
1959	Betsy Rawls	74.03	1977	Judy Rankin	72.16	1995	Annika Sorenstam	71.00
1960	Mickey Wright	73.25	1978	Nancy Lopez	71.76	1996	Annika Sorenstam	70.47
1961	Mickey Wright	73.55	1979	Nancy Lopez	71.20	1997	Karrie Webb	70.00
1962	Mickey Wright	73.67	1980	Amy Alcott	71.51	1998	Annika Sorenstam	69.99
1963	Mickey Wright	72.81	1981	JoAnne Carner	71.75	1999	Karrie Webb	69.43
1964	Mickey Wright	72.46	1982	JoAnne Carner	71.49	2000	Karrie Webb	70.05
1965	Kathy Whitworth	72.61	1983	JoAnne Carner	71.41	2001	Annika Sorenstam	69.42
1966	Kathy Whitworth	72.60	1984	Patty Sheehan	71.40	2002	Annika Sorenstam	68.70
1967	Kathy Whitworth	72.74	1985	Nancy Lopez	70.73	2003	Se Ri Pak	70.03
1968	Carol Mann	72.04	1986	Pat Bradley	71.10	2004	Grace Park	69.99
1969	Kathy Whitworth	72.38	1987	Betsy King	71.14	2005	Annika Sorenstam	69.25
1970	Kathy Whitworth	72.26	1988	Colleen Walker	71.40	2006	Lorena Ochoa	69.24

Champions Tour
(formerly Senior PGA Tour)

Senior PGA Championship

First played in 1937. Two championships played in 1979 and 1984.

Multiple winners: Sam Snead (6); Hale Irwin (4); Gary Player, Al Watrous and Eddie Williams (3); Julius Boros, Jock Hutchison, Don January, Arnold Palmer, Paul Runyan, Gene Sarazen and Lee Trevino (2).

Year		Year		Year		Year	
1937	Jock Hutchison	1956	Pete Burke	1974	Roberto De Vicenzo	1990	Gary Player
1938	Fred McLeod*	1957	Al Watrous	1975	Charlie Sifford*	1991	Jack Nicklaus
1939	Not held	1958	Gene Sarazen	1976	Pete Cooper	1992	Lee Trevino
1940	Otto Hackbarth*	1959	Willie Goggin	1977	Julius Boros	1993	Tom Wargo*
1941	Jack Burke	1960	Dick Metz	1978	Joe Jiminez*	1994	Lee Trevino
1942	Eddie Williams	1961	Paul Runyan	1979	Jack Fleck*	1995	Ray Floyd
1943-44	Not held	1962	Paul Runyan	1979	Don January	1996	Hale Irwin
1945	Eddie Williams	1963	Herman Barron	1980	Arnold Palmer*	1997	Hale Irwin
1946	Eddie Williams*	1964	Sam Snead	1981	Miller Barber	1998	Hale Irwin
1947	Jock Hutchison	1965	Sam Snead	1982	Don January	1999	Allen Doyle
1948	Charles McKenna	1966	Fred Haas	1983	Not held	2000	Doug Tewell
1949	Marshall Crichton	1967	Sam Snead	1984	Arnold Palmer	2001	Tom Watson
1950	Al Watrous	1968	Chandler Harper	1984	Peter Thomson	2002	Fuzzy Zoeller
1951	Al Watrous*	1969	Tommy Bolt	1985	Not held	2003	John Jacobs
1952	Ernest Newnham	1970	Sam Snead	1986	Gary Player	2004	Hale Irwin
1953	Harry Schwab	1971	Julius Boros	1987	Chi Chi Rodriguez	2005	Mike Reid*
1954	Gene Sarazen	1972	Sam Snead	1988	Gary Player	2006	Jay Haas*
1955	Mortie Dutra	1973	Sam Snead	1989	Larry Mowry	2007	Denis Watson

*PLAYOFFS:

1938: Fred McLeod def. Otto Hackbarth in 18 holes. **1940:** Otto Hackbarth def. Jock Hutchison in 36 holes. **1946:** Eddie Williams def. Jock Hutchison in 18 holes. **1951:** Al Watrous def. Jock Hutchison in 18 holes. **1975:** Charlie Sifford def. Fred Wampler on 1st extra hole **1978:** Joe Jiminez def. Paul Harney on 1st extra hole. **1979:** Jack Fleck def. Bill Johnston on 1st extra hole. **1980:** Arnold Palmer def. Paul Harney on 1st extra hole. **1993:** Tom Wargo def. Bruce Crampton on 2nd extra hole. **2005:** Mike Reid def. Dana Quigley and Jerry Pate on 1st extra hole. **2006:** Jay Haas def. Brad Bryant on 3rd extra hole.

Major Senior Championship Leaders

Through 2007. All players are still active. **Note:** The Senior British Open became the Champions Tour's fifth major in 2003.

		Sr. PGA	US Open	Sr. Play	Trad	Br. Open	Tot			Sr. PGA	US Open	Sr. Play	Trad	Br. Open	Tot
1	Jack Nicklaus	1	2	1	4	0	8	5	Allen Doyle	1	2	1	0	0	4
2	Hale Irwin	4	2	1	0	0	7		Ray Floyd	1	0	2	1	0	4
3	Gary Player	3	2	1	0	0	6		Lee Trevino	2	1	0	1	0	4
4	Tom Watson	1	0	0	1	3	5								

U.S. Senior Open

Established in 1980 for senior players 55 years old and over, the minimum age was dropped to 50 (the Champions Tour entry age) in 1981. Arnold Palmer, Billy Casper, Hale Irwin, Orville Moody, Jack Nicklaus and Lee Trevino are the only golfers who have won both the U.S. Open and U.S. Senior Open.

Multiple winners: Miller Barber (3); Allen Doyle, Hale Irwin, Jack Nicklaus and Gary Player (2).

Year		Year		Year		Year	
1980	Roberto De Vicenzo	1987	Gary Player	1994	Simon Hobday	2001	Bruce Fleisher
1981	Arnold Palmer*	1988	Gary Player*	1995	Tom Weiskopf	2002	Don Pooley*
1982	Miller Barber	1989	Orville Moody	1996	Dave Stockton	2003	Bruce Lietzke
1983	Bill Casper*	1990	Lee Trevino	1997	Graham Marsh	2004	Peter Jacobsen
1984	Miller Barber	1991	Jack Nicklaus*	1998	Hale Irwin	2005	Allen Doyle
1985	Miller Barber	1992	Larry Laoretti	1999	Dave Eichelberger	2006	Allen Doyle
1986	Dale Douglass	1993	Jack Nicklaus	2000	Hale Irwin	2007	Brad Bryant

*PLAYOFFS:

1981: Arnold Palmer (70) def. Bob Stone (74) and Billy Casper (77) in 18 holes. **1983:** Tied at 75 after 18-hole playoff, Casper def. Rod Funseth with a birdie on the 1st extra hole. **1988:** Gary Player (68) def. Bob Charles (70) in 18 holes. **1991:** Jack Nicklaus (65) def. Chi Chi Rodriguez (69) in 18 holes. **2002:** Don Pooley and Tom Watson remained tied after a three hole playoff and Pooley won on the second hole of sudden death.

Senior Players Championship

Sponsored by Ford since 1993. First played in 1983 and contested in Cleveland (1983-86), Ponte Vedra, Fla. (1987-89), Dearborn, Mich. (1990-2006), Baltimore, Md. (2007).

Multiple winners: Ray Floyd, Arnold Palmer and Dave Stockton (2).

Year		Year		Year		Year	
1983	Miller Barber	1990	Jack Nicklaus	1997	Larry Gilbert	2004	Mark James
1984	Arnold Palmer	1991	Jim Albus	1998	Gil Morgan	2005	Peter Jacobsen
1985	Arnold Palmer	1992	Dave Stockton	1999	Hale Irwin	2006	Bobby Wadkins
1986	Chi Chi Rodriguez	1993	Jim Colbert	2000	Ray Floyd	2007	Loren Roberts
1987	Gary Player	1994	Dave Stockton	2001	Allen Doyle*		
1988	Billy Casper	1995	J.C. Snead*	2002	Stewart Ginn		
1989	Orville Moody	1996	Ray Floyd	2003	Craig Stadler		

*PLAYOFFS:

1995: J.C. Snead def. Jack Nicklaus on 1st extra hole. **2001:** Allen Doyle def. Doug Tewell on 1st extra hole.

The Tradition

Sponsored by window and door manufacturer JELD-WEN since 2003, it was formerly called The Tradition at Desert Mountain (1989-91), The Tradition (1992-99) and The Countrywide Tradition (2000-02). Held at GC at Desert Mountain in Scottsdale, Ariz. (1989-2001), Superstition Mountain (Ariz.) G & CC (2002), The Reserve Vineyards & GC in Aloha, Ore. (2003-06) and Crosswater GC in Sunriver, Ore. (2007).

Multiple winners: Jack Nicklaus (4); Gil Morgan (2).

Year		Year		Year		Year	
1989	Don Bies	1994	Ray Floyd*	1999	Graham Marsh	2004	Craig Stadler
1990	Jack Nicklaus	1995	Jack Nicklaus*	2000	Tom Kite	2005	Loren Roberts*
1991	Jack Nicklaus	1996	Jack Nicklaus	2001	Doug Tewell	2006	Eduardo Romero*
1992	Lee Trevino	1997	Gil Morgan	2002	Jim Thorpe*	2007	Mark McNulty
1993	Tom Shaw	1998	Gil Morgan	2003	Tom Watson		

*PLAYOFFS:

1994: Ray Floyd def. Dale Douglass on 1st extra hole. **1995:** Jack Nicklaus def. Isao Aoki on 3rd extra hole. **2002:** Jim Thorpe def. John Jacobs on 1st extra hole. **2005:** Loren Roberts def. Dana Quigley on 2nd extra hole. **2006:** Eduardo Romero def. Lonnie Nielsen on 1st extra hole.

Senior British Open

First played in 1987 and contested in Turnberry, Scotland (1987-90, 2003), Lytham, England (1991-94), Portrush, Ireland (1995-99, 2004), Newcastle, Ireland (2000-02). Royal Aberdeen, Scotland (2005) and Muirfield, Scotland (2007). In 2003 it became the fifth designated major championship on the Champions Tour.

Multiple winners: Gary Player and Tom Watson (3); Brian Barnes, Bob Charles and Christy O'Connor Jr. (2). (as a major): Watson (3).

Year		Year		Year		Year	
1987	Neil Coles	1993	Bob Charles	1999	Christy O'Connor Jr.	2005	Tom Watson*
1988	Gary Player	1994	Tom Wargo	2000	Christy O'Connor Jr.	2006	Loren Roberts
1989	Bob Charles	1995	Brian Barnes	2001	Ian Stanley	2007	Tom Watson
1990	Gary Player	1996	Brian Barnes	2002	Noboru Sugai		
1991	Bobby Verwey	1997	Gary Player	2003	Tom Watson*		
1992	John Fourie	1998	Brian Huggett	2004	Pete Oakley		

*PLAYOFFS (as a Major):

2003: Tom Watson def. Carl Mason on 2nd extra hole. **2005:** Tom Watson def. Des Smyth on 3rd extra hole.

Champions Tour (Cont.)
Grand Slam Summary

The Senior Grand Slam had officially consisted of The Tradition, the Senior PGA Championship, the Senior Players Championship and the U.S. Senior Open from 1990-2002. In 2003, the Senior British Open was added. Jack Nicklaus won three of the four events in 1991, but no one has won all four (or now five) in one season.

Three wins in one year: Jack Nicklaus (1991). **Two wins in one year** (8): Gary Player (twice); Hale Irwin, Gil Morgan, Orville Moody, Jack Nicklaus, Arnold Palmer, Lee Trevino and Tom Watson (once).

Year	Tradition	Sr. PGA	Players	US Open	Year	Tradition	Sr. PGA	Players	US Open
1983	—	—	M. Barber	Casper	1993	Shaw	Wargo	Colbert	Nicklaus
1984	—	Palmer	Palmer	M. Barber	1994	Floyd	Trevino	Stockton	Hobday
1985	—	Thomson	Palmer	M. Barber	1995	Nicklaus	Floyd	Snead	Weiskopf
1986	—	Player	Rodriguez	Douglass	1996	Nicklaus	Irwin	Floyd	Stockton
1987	—	Rodriguez	Player	Player	1997	Morgan	Irwin	Gilbert	Marsh
1988	—	Player	Casper	Player	1998	Morgan	Irwin	Morgan	Irwin
1989	Bies	Mowry	Moody	Moody	1999	Marsh	Doyle	Irwin	Eichelberger
1990	Nicklaus	Player	Nicklaus	Trevino	2000	Kite	Tewell	Floyd	Irwin
1991	Nicklaus	Nicklaus	Albus	Nicklaus	2001	Tewell	T. Watson	Doyle	Fleisher
1992	Trevino	Trevino	Stockton	Laoretti	2002	Thorpe	Zoeller	Ginn	Pooley

Year	Tradition	Sr. PGA	Players	US Open	Sr. Brit. Open
2003	T. Watson	Jacobs	Stadler	Lietzke	T. Watson
2004	Stadler	Irwin	James	Jacobsen	Oakley
2005	Roberts	Reid	Jacobsen	Doyle	T. Watson
2006	Romero	Haas	Wadkins	Doyle	Roberts
2007	McNulty	D. Watson	Roberts	Bryant	T. Watson

Annual Money Leaders

Official annual money leaders on the PGA, European PGA, Champions and LPGA tours.

PGA

Multiple leaders: Jack Nicklaus (8); Tiger Woods (7); Ben Hogan and Tom Watson (5); Arnold Palmer (4); Greg Norman, Sam Snead and Curtis Strange (3); Julius Boros, Billy Casper, Tom Kite, Byron Nelson, Nick Price and Vijay Singh (2).

Year		Earnings	Year		Earnings	Year		Earnings
1934	Paul Runyan	$6,767	1959	Art Wall	$53,168	1984	Tom Watson	$476,260
1935	Johnny Revolta	9,543	1960	Arnold Palmer	75,263	1985	Curtis Strange	542,321
1936	Horton Smith	7,682	1961	Gary Player	64,540	1986	Greg Norman	653,296
1937	Harry Cooper	14,139	1962	Arnold Palmer	81,448	1987	Curtis Strange	925,941
1938	Sam Snead	19,534	1963	Arnold Palmer	128,230	1988	Curtis Strange	1,147,644
1939	Henry Picard	10,303	1964	Jack Nicklaus	113,285	1989	Tom Kite	1,395,278
1940	Ben Hogan	10,655	1965	Jack Nicklaus	140,752	1990	Greg Norman	1,165,477
1941	Ben Hogan	18,358	1966	Billy Casper	121,945	1991	Corey Pavin	979,430
1942	Ben Hogan	13,143	1967	Jack Nicklaus	188,998	1992	Fred Couples	1,344,188
1943	No records kept		1968	Billy Casper	205,169	1993	Nick Price	1,478,557
1944	Byron Nelson	37,968	1969	Frank Beard	164,707	1994	Nick Price	1,499,927
1945	Byron Nelson	63,336	1970	Lee Trevino	157,037	1995	Greg Norman	1,654,959
1946	Ben Hogan	42,556	1971	Jack Nicklaus	244,491	1996	Tom Lehman	1,780,159
1947	Jimmy Demaret	27,937	1972	Jack Nicklaus	320,542	1997	Tiger Woods	2,066,833
1948	Ben Hogan	32,112	1973	Jack Nicklaus	308,362	1998	David Duval	2,591,031
1949	Sam Snead	31,594	1974	Johnny Miller	353,022	1999	Tiger Woods	6,616,585
1950	Sam Snead	35,759	1975	Jack Nicklaus	298,149	2000	Tiger Woods	9,188,321
1951	Lloyd Mangrum	26,089	1976	Jack Nicklaus	266,439	2001	Tiger Woods	5,687,777
1952	Julius Boros	37,033	1977	Tom Watson	310,653	2002	Tiger Woods	6,912,625
1953	Lew Worsham	34,002	1978	Tom Watson	362,429	2003	Vijay Singh	7,573,907
1954	Bob Toski	65,820	1979	Tom Watson	462,636	2004	Vijay Singh	10,905,166
1955	Julius Boros	63,122	1980	Tom Watson	530,808	2005	Tiger Woods	10,628,024
1956	Ted Kroll	72,836	1981	Tom Kite	375,699	2006	Tiger Woods	9,941,563
1957	Dick Mayer	65,835	1982	Craig Stadler	446,462			
1958	Arnold Palmer	42,608	1983	Hal Sutton	426,668			

Note: In 1944-45, Nelson's winnings were in War Bonds.

Champions Tour

Multiple leaders: Hale Irwin and Don January (3); Miller Barber, Bob Charles, Jim Colbert, Dave Stockton and Lee Trevino (2).

Year		Earnings	Year		Earnings	Year		Earnings
1980	Don January	$44,100	1989	Bob Charles	$725,887	1998	Hale Irwin	$2,861,945
1981	Miller Barber	83,136	1990	Lee Trevino	1,190,518	1999	Bruce Fleisher	2,515,705
1982	Miller Barber	106,890	1991	Mike Hill	1,065,657	2000	Larry Nelson	2,708,005
1983	Don January	237,571	1992	Lee Trevino	1,027,002	2001	Allen Doyle	2,553,582
1984	Don January	328,597	1993	Dave Stockton	1,175,944	2002	Hale Irwin	3,028,304
1985	Peter Thomson	386,724	1994	Dave Stockton	1,402,519	2003	Tom Watson	1,853,108
1986	Bruce Crampton	454,299	1995	Jim Colbert	1,444,386	2004	Craig Stadler	2,306,066
1987	Chi Chi Rodriguez	509,145	1996	Jim Colbert	1,627,890	2005	Dana Quigley	2,170,258
1988	Bob Charles	533,929	1997	Hale Irwin	2,343,364	2006	Jay Haas	2,420,227

European PGA

Official money in the Volvo Order of Merit was awarded in British pounds from 1961-98 and euros (E) since 1999.

Multiple leaders: Colin Montgomerie (8); Seve Ballesteros (6); Sandy Lyle (3); Gay Brewer Jr., Ernie Els, Nick Faldo, Retief Goosen, Bernard Hunt, Bernhard Langer, Peter Thomson and Ian Woosnam (2).

Year		Earnings	Year		Earnings	Year		Earnings
1961	Bernard Hunt	£4,492	1977	Seve Ballesteros	£46,436	1993	Colin Montgomerie	£798,145
1962	Peter Thomson	5,764	1978	Seve Ballesteros	54,348	1994	Colin Montgomerie	920,647
1963	Bernard Hunt	7,209	1979	Sandy Lyle	49,233	1995	Colin Montgomerie	1,038,718
1964	Neil Coles	7,890	1980	Greg Norman	74,829	1996	Colin Montgomerie	1,034,752
1965	Peter Thomson	7,011	1981	Bernhard Langer	95,991	1997	Colin Montgomerie	1,583,904
1966	Bruce Devlin	13,205	1982	Sandy Lyle	86,141	1998	Colin Montgomerie	1,082,833
1967	Gay Brewer Jr.	20,235	1983	Nick Faldo	140,761	1999	C. Montgomerie	E2,066,885
1968	Gay Brewer Jr.	23,107	1984	Bernhard Langer	160,883	2000	Lee Westwood	3,125,147
1969	Billy Casper	23,483	1985	Sandy Lyle	254,711	2001	Retief Goosen	2,862,806
1970	Christy O'Connor	31,532	1986	Seve Ballesteros	259,275	2002	Retief Goosen	2,360,128
1971	Gary Player	11,281	1987	Ian Woosnam	439,075	2003	Ernie Els	2,975,374
1972	Bob Charles	18,538	1988	Seve Ballesteros	502,000	2004	Ernie Els	4,061,905
1973	Tony Jacklin	24,839	1989	Ronan Rafferty	465,981	2005	Colin Montgomerie	2,794,223
1974	Peter Oosterhuis	32,127	1990	Ian Woosnam	737,977	2006	Padraig Harrington	2,489,337
1975	Dale Hayes	20,507	1991	Seve Ballesteros	790,811			
1976	Seve Ballesteros	39,504	1992	Nick Faldo	1,220,540			

LPGA

Multiple leaders: Annika Sorenstam and Kathy Whitworth (8); Mickey Wright (4); Patty Berg, JoAnne Carner, Beth Daniel, Betsy King, Nancy Lopez and Karrie Webb (3); Pat Bradley, Judy Rankin, Betsy Rawls, Louise Suggs and Babe Zaharias (2).

Year		Earnings	Year		Earnings	Year		Earnings
1950	Babe Zaharias	$14,800	1969	Carol Mann	$49,152	1988	Sherri Turner	$350,851
1951	Babe Zaharias	15,087	1970	Kathy Whitworth	30,235	1989	Betsy King	654,132
1952	Betsy Rawls	14,505	1971	Kathy Whitworth	41,181	1990	Beth Daniel	863,578
1953	Louise Suggs	19,816	1972	Kathy Whitworth	65,063	1991	Pat Bradley	763,118
1954	Patty Berg	16,011	1973	Kathy Whitworth	82,864	1992	Dottie Pepper	693,335
1955	Patty Berg	16,492	1974	JoAnne Carner	87,094	1993	Betsy King	595,992
1956	Marlene Hagge	20,235	1975	Sandra Palmer	76,374	1994	Laura Davies	687,201
1957	Patty Berg	16,272	1976	Judy Rankin	150,734	1995	Annika Sorenstam	666,533
1958	Beverly Hanson	12,639	1977	Judy Rankin	122,890	1996	Karrie Webb	1,002,000
1959	Betsy Rawls	26,774	1978	Nancy Lopez	189,814	1997	Annika Sorenstam	1,236,789
1960	Louise Suggs	16,892	1979	Nancy Lopez	197,489	1998	Annika Sorenstam	1,092,748
1961	Mickey Wright	22,236	1980	Beth Daniel	231,000	1999	Karrie Webb	1,591,959
1962	Mickey Wright	21,641	1981	Beth Daniel	206,998	2000	Karrie Webb	1,876,853
1963	Mickey Wright	31,269	1982	JoAnne Carner	310,400	2001	Annika Sorenstam	2,105,868
1964	Mickey Wright	29,800	1983	JoAnne Carner	291,404	2002	Annika Sorenstam	2,863,904
1965	Kathy Whitworth	28,658	1984	Betsy King	266,771	2003	Annika Sorenstam	2,029,506
1966	Kathy Whitworth	33,517	1985	Nancy Lopez	416,472	2004	Annika Sorenstam	2,544,707
1967	Kathy Whitworth	32,937	1986	Pat Bradley	492,021	2005	Annika Sorenstam	2,588,240
1968	Kathy Whitworth	48,379	1987	Ayako Okamoto	466,034	2006	Lorena Ochoa	2,592,872

All-Time Leaders

PGA, Champions Tour and LPGA leaders through Oct. 14, 2007.

Tournaments Won

	PGA	No		Champions	No		LPGA	No
1	Sam Snead	82	1	Hale Irwin	45	1	Kathy Whitworth	88
2	Jack Nicklaus	73	2	Lee Trevino	29	2	Mickey Wright	82
3	Ben Hogan	64	3	Gil Morgan	25	3	Annika Sorenstam	69
4	Arnold Palmer	62	4	Miller Barber	24	4	Patty Berg	60
5	Tiger Woods	61	5	Bob Charles	23	5	Louise Suggs	58
6	Byron Nelson	52	6	Don January	22	6	Betsy Rawls	55
7	Billy Casper	51		Chi Chi Rodriguez	22	7	Nancy Lopez	48
8	Walter Hagen	44	8	Bruce Crampton	20	8	JoAnne Carner	43
9	Cary Middlecoff	40		Jim Colbert	20	9	Sandra Haynie	42
10	Gene Sarazen	39	10	George Archer	19	10	Babe Zaharias	41
	Tom Watson	39		Larry Nelson	19	11	Carol Mann	38
12	Lloyd Mangrum	36		Gary Player	19	12	Patty Sheehan	35
13	Horton Smith	32	13	Mike Hill	18		Karrie Webb	35
	Phil Mickelson	32		Bruce Fleisher	18	14	Betsy King	34
15	Harry Cooper	31	15	Dave Stockton	14	15	Beth Daniel	33
	Jimmy Demaret	31		Raymond Floyd	14	16	Pat Bradley	31
	Vijay Singh	31	17	Jim Dent	12		Juli Inkster	31
18	Leo Diegel	30		Jim Thorpe	12	18	Amy Alcott	29
19	Gene Littler	29	19	Six tied with 11 wins.		19	Jane Blalock	27
	Paul Runyan	29				20	Judy Rankin	26
	Lee Trevino	29					Marlene Hagge	26

All-Time Leaders (Cont.)
Money Won
All-time earnings through Oct. 14, 2007.

PGA

		Earnings				Earnings				Earnings
1	Tiger Woods	$76,579,376	10	Kenny Perry	$21,532,649		19	Sergio Garcia	$19,540,777
2	Vijay Singh	54,108,218	11	Stewart Cink	20,984,693		20	Fred Couples	19,172,199
3	Phil Mickelson	45,334,026	12	Scott Verplank	20,831,472		21	Scott Hoch	18,487,114
4	Davis Love III	35,630,313	13	Stuart Appleby	20,709,855		22	Retief Goosen	18,275,403
5	Jim Furyk	35,354,112	14	Fred Funk	20,668,565		23	Jeff Sluman	18,114,866
6	Ernie Els	31,126,111	15	Nick Price	20,551,208		24	Brad Faxon	17,656,554
7	David Toms	27,911,952	16	Mike Weir	19,939,988		25	David Duval	16,754,201
8	Justin Leonard	22,829,292	17	Tom Lehman	19,701,862				
9	Mark Calcavecchia	22,296,419	18	Chris DiMarco	19,660,264				

European PGA
Official earnings in Euros (E).

		Earnings				Earnings				Earnings
1	C. Montgomerie	E22,689,776	10	Vijay Singh	E11,666,837		19	Niclas Fasth	E8,458,052
2	Ernie Els	21,124,122	11	J.M. Olazabal	11,468,594		20	Paul Casey	8,189,380
3	Retief Goosen	17,309,667	12	Angel Cabrera	11,131,806		21	Nick Faldo	7,992,188
4	Padraig Harrington	16,771,644	13	Michael Campbell	10,954,497		22	Robert Karlsson	7,778,277
5	Darren Clarke	15,544,444	14	Sergio Garcia	10,407,438		23	Eduardo Romero	7,512,685
6	Lee Westwood	13,879,751	15	Ian Woosnam	9,584,347		24	Paul Lawrie	6,854,496
7	Bernhard Langer	12,497,358	16	David Howell	9,284,456		25	Henrik Stenson	6,826,852
8	Thomas Bjorn	12,166,140	17	Paul McGinley	9,257,173				
9	M. Angel Jimenez	11,932,725	18	Ian Poulter	8,565,371				

Champions Tour

		Earnings				Earnings				Earnings
1	Hale Irwin	$24,559,885	10	Tom Jenkins	$11,218,646		19	Jim Dent	$8,967,724
2	Gil Morgan	18,338,181	11	Dave Stockton	10,938,263		20	Bruce Summerhays	8,865,725
3	Dana Quigley	13,924,634	12	Tom Watson	10,015,484		21	Bob Gilder	8,744,556
4	Bruce Fleisher	13,513,100	13	Lee Trevino	9,837,242		22	John Jacobs	8,416,373
5	Larry Nelson	13,047,507	14	Raymond Floyd	9,449,519		23	Mike Hill	8,383,104
6	Allen Doyle	12,588,972	15	Jay Sigel	9,340,917		24	Vicente Fernandez	8,266,018
7	Jim Thorpe	12,026,861	16	Isao Aoki	9,295,043		25	Tom Wargo	7,732,914
8	Jim Colbert	11,620,231	17	Graham Marsh	9,060,848				
9	Tom Kite	11,403,576	18	Bob Charles	9,032,001				

LPGA

		Earnings				Earnings				Earnings
1	Annika Sorenstam	$20,718,680	10	Cristie Kerr	$7,765,401		19	Sherrie Steinhauer	$5,599,964
2	Karrie Webb	13,436,187	11	Betsy King	7,637,621		20	Patty Sheehan	5,513,409
3	Juli Inkster	11,671,175	12	Mi Hyun Kim	7,612,628		21	Nancy Lopez	5,320,877
4	Se Ri Pak	9,736,140	13	Dottie Pepper	6,827,284		22	Rachel Hetherington	5,315,943
5	Lorena Ochoa	9,137,643	14	Lorie Kane	6,635,611		23	Grace Park	5,228,650
6	Meg Mallon	8,871,495	15	Pat Hurst	5,847,181		24	Catriona Matthew	4,976,116
7	Beth Daniel	8,755,733	16	Pat Bradley	5,755,951		25	Michele Redman	4,917,030
8	Rosie Jones	8,355,068	17	Liselotte Neumann	5,721,425				
9	Laura Davies	7,975,664	18	Kelly Robbins	5,621,742				

Official World Golf Ranking

Begun in 1986, the Official World Golf Ranking (formerly the Sony World Ranking) combines the best golfers on the six pro men's tours which make up the International Federation of PGA Tours. Rankings are based on a rolling two-year period and weighed in favor of more recent results. While annual winners are not announced, certain players reaching No. 1 have dominated each year.

Multiple winners (at year's end): Tiger Woods (9); Greg Norman (6); Nick Faldo (3); Seve Ballesteros (2).

Year		Year		Year		Year	
1986	Seve Ballesteros	1991	Ian Woosnam	1997	Tiger Woods	2004	Vijay Singh
1987	Greg Norman	1992	Fred Couples	1998	Tiger Woods	2005	Tiger Woods
1988	Greg Norman		& Nick Faldo	1999	Tiger Woods	2006	Tiger Woods
1989	Seve Ballesteros	1993	Nick Faldo	2000	Tiger Woods		
	& Greg Norman	1994	Nick Price	2001	Tiger Woods		
1990	Nick Faldo	1995	Greg Norman	2002	Tiger Woods		
	& Greg Norman	1996	Greg Norman	2003	Tiger Woods		

Annual Awards

PGA of America Player of the Year

Awarded by the PGA of America; based on points scale that weighs performance in major tournaments, regular events, money earned and scoring average. **Note:** As of Oct. 14, Tiger Woods had already clinched the award for 2007.

Multiple winners: Tiger Woods (9); Tom Watson (6); Jack Nicklaus (5); Ben Hogan (4); Julius Boros, Billy Casper, Arnold Palmer and Nick Price.

Year		Year		Year		Year	
1948	Ben Hogan	1963	Julius Boros	1978	Tom Watson	1993	Nick Price
1949	Sam Snead	1964	Ken Venturi	1979	Tom Watson	1994	Nick Price
1950	Ben Hogan	1965	Dave Marr	1980	Tom Watson	1995	Greg Norman
1951	Ben Hogan	1966	Billy Casper	1981	Bill Rogers	1996	Tom Lehman
1952	Julius Boros	1967	Jack Nicklaus	1982	Tom Watson	1997	Tiger Woods
1953	Ben Hogan	1968	No award	1983	Hal Sutton	1998	Mark O'Meara
1954	Ed Furgol	1969	Orville Moody	1984	Tom Watson	1999	Tiger Woods
1955	Doug Ford	1970	Billy Casper	1985	Lanny Wadkins	2000	Tiger Woods
1956	Jack Burke	1971	Lee Trevino	1986	Bob Tway	2001	Tiger Woods
1957	Dick Mayer	1972	Jack Nicklaus	1987	Paul Azinger	2002	Tiger Woods
1958	Dow Finsterwald	1973	Jack Nicklaus	1988	Curtis Strange	2003	Tiger Woods
1959	Art Wall Jr.	1974	Johnny Miller	1989	Tom Kite	2004	Vijay Singh
1960	Arnold Palmer	1975	Jack Nicklaus	1990	Nick Faldo	2005	Tiger Woods
1961	Jerry Barber	1976	Jack Nicklaus	1991	Corey Pavin	2006	Tiger Woods
1962	Arnold Palmer	1977	Tom Watson	1992	Fred Couples	2007	Tiger Woods

PGA Tour Player of the Year

Award by the PGA Tour starting in 1990. Winner voted on by tour members from list of nominees. Winner receives the Jack Nicklaus Trophy, which originated in 1997.

Multiple winners: Tiger Woods (8); Fred Couples and Nick Price (2).

Year		Year		Year		Year	
1990	Wayne Levi	1995	Greg Norman	2000	Tiger Woods	2005	Tiger Woods
1991	Fred Couples	1996	Tom Lehman	2001	Tiger Woods	2006	Tiger Woods
1992	Fred Couples	1997	Tiger Woods	2002	Tiger Woods		
1993	Nick Price	1998	Mark O'Meara	2003	Tiger Woods		
1994	Nick Price	1999	Tiger Woods	2004	Vijay Singh		

PGA Tour Rookie of the Year

Awarded by the PGA Tour in 1990. Winner voted on by tour members from list of first-year nominees.

Year		Year		Year		Year	
1990	Robert Gamez	1995	Woody Austin	2000	Michael Clark II	2005	Sean O'Hair
1991	John Daly	1996	Tiger Woods	2001	Charles Howell III	2006	Trevor Immelman
1992	Mark Carnevale	1997	Stewart Cink	2002	Jonathan Byrd		
1993	Vijay Singh	1998	Steve Flesch	2003	Ben Curtis		
1994	Ernie Els	1999	Carlos Franco	2004	Todd Hamilton		

Champions Tour Player of the Year

Awarded by the Champions Tour starting in 1990. Winner voted on by tour members from list of nominees.

Multiple winner: Hale Irwin and Lee Trevino (3); Jim Colbert (2).

Year		Year		Year		Year	
1990	Lee Trevino	1994	Lee Trevino	1999	Bruce Fleisher	2004	Craig Stadler
1991	George Archer	1995	Jim Colbert	2000	Larry Nelson	2005	Dana Quigley
	& Mike Hill	1996	Jim Colbert	2001	Allen Doyle	2006	Jay Haas
1992	Lee Trevino	1997	Hale Irwin	2002	Hale Irwin		
1993	Dave Stockton	1998	Hale Irwin	2003	Tom Watson		

European Tour Golfer of the Year

Formerly the Ritz Club Trophy (1985-92), Johnnie Walker Trophy (1993-97) and Asprey Golfer of the Year (1998-2004); voting done by panel of European golf writers and tour members.

Multiple winners: Colin Montgomerie (4); Seve Ballesteros, Ernie Els, and Nick Faldo (3); Bernhard Langer and Lee Westwood (2).

Year		Year		Year		Year	
1985	Bernhard Langer	1991	Seve Ballesteros	1997	Colin Montgomerie	2003	Ernie Els
1986	Seve Ballesteros	1992	Nick Faldo	1998	Lee Westwood	2004	Vijay Singh
1987	Ian Woosnam	1993	Bernhard Langer	1999	Colin Montgomerie	2005	Michael Campbell
1988	Seve Ballesteros	1994	Ernie Els	2000	Lee Westwood	2006	Paul Casey
1989	Nick Faldo	1995	Colin Montgomerie	2001	Retief Goosen		
1990	Nick Faldo	1996	Colin Montgomerie	2002	Ernie Els		

LPGA Player of the Year

Sponsored by Rolex and awarded by the LPGA; based on performance points accumulated during the year.
Multiple winners: Annika Sorenstam (8); Kathy Whitworth (7); Nancy Lopez (4); JoAnne Carner, Beth Daniel and Betsy King (3); Pat Bradley, Judy Rankin and Karrie Webb (2).

Year		Year		Year		Year	
1966	Kathy Whitworth	1977	Judy Rankin	1988	Nancy Lopez	1999	Karrie Webb
1967	Kathy Whitworth	1978	Nancy Lopez	1989	Betsy King	2000	Karrie Webb
1968	Kathy Whitworth	1979	Nancy Lopez	1990	Beth Daniel	2001	Annika Sorenstam
1969	Kathy Whitworth	1980	Beth Daniel	1991	Pat Bradley	2002	Annika Sorenstam
1970	Sandra Haynie	1981	JoAnne Carner	1992	Dottie Mochrie	2003	Annika Sorenstam
1971	Kathy Whitworth	1982	JoAnne Carner	1993	Betsy King	2004	Annika Sorenstam
1972	Kathy Whitworth	1983	Patty Sheehan	1994	Beth Daniel	2005	Annika Sorenstam
1973	Kathy Whitworth	1984	Betsy King	1995	Annika Sorenstam	2006	Lorena Ochoa
1974	JoAnne Carner	1985	Nancy Lopez	1996	Laura Davies		
1975	Sandra Palmer	1986	Pat Bradley	1997	Annika Sorenstam		
1976	Judy Rankin	1987	Ayako Okamoto	1998	Annika Sorenstam		

LPGA Rookie of the Year

Sponsored by Rolex and awarded by the LPGA; based on performance points accumulated during the year. Winner receives Louise Suggs Trophy, which originated in 2000. Officially the Louise Suggs Rolex Rookie of the Year.

Year		Year		Year		Year	
1962	Mary Mills	1974	Jan Stephenson	1986	Jody Rosenthal	1998	Se Ri Pak
1963	Clifford Ann Creed	1975	Amy Alcott	1987	Tammie Green	1999	Mi Hyun Kim
1964	Susie Berning	1976	Bonnie Lauer	1988	Liselotte Neumann	2000	Dorothy Delasin
1965	Margie Masters	1977	Debbie Massey	1989	Pamela Wright	2001	Hee-Won Han
1966	Jan Ferraris	1978	Nancy Lopez	1990	Hiromi Kobayashi	2002	Beth Bauer
1967	Sharron Moran	1979	Beth Daniel	1991	Brandie Burton	2003	Lorena Ochoa
1968	Sandra Post	1980	Myra Van Hoose	1992	Helen Alfredsson	2004	Shi Hyun Ahn
1969	Jane Blalock	1981	Patty Sheehan	1993	Suzanne Strudwick	2005	Paula Creamer
1970	JoAnne Carner	1982	Patti Rizzo	1994	Annika Sorenstam	2006	Seon-Hwa Lee
1971	Sally Little	1983	Stephanie Farwig	1995	Pat Hurst		
1972	Jocelyne Bourassa	1984	Juli Inkster	1996	Karrie Webb		
1973	Laura Baugh	1985	Penny Hammel	1997	Lisa Hackney		

National Team Competition
MEN
Ryder Cup

The Ryder Cup was presented by British seed merchant and businessman Samuel Ryder in 1927 for competition between professional golfers from Great Britain and the United States. The British team was expanded to include Irish players in 1973 and the rest of Europe in 1979. The 2001 event was postponed due to the attacks on America, causing the event to switch from an odd- to even-year schedule. The United States leads the series 24-10-2 after 36 matches.

Year		Year		Year		Year	
1927	USA, 9½-2½	1953	USA, 6½-5½	1973	USA, 19-13	1993	USA, 15-13
1929	Britain-Ireland, 7-5	1955	USA, 8-4	1975	USA, 21-11	1995	Europe, 14½-13½
1931	USA, 9-3	1957	Britain-Ireland, 7½-4½	1977	USA, 12½-13½	1997	Europe, 14½-13½
1933	Great Britain, 6½-5½	1959	USA, 8½-3½	1979	USA, 17-11	1999	USA, 14½-13½
1935	USA, 9-3	1961	USA, 14½-9½	1981	USA, 18½-9½	2002	Europe, 15½-12½
1937	USA, 8-4	1963	USA, 23-9	1983	USA, 14½-13½	2004	Europe, 18½-9½
1939-45	Not held	1965	USA, 19½-12½	1985	Europe, 16½-11½	2006	Europe, 18½-9½
1947	USA, 11-1	1967	USA, 23½-8½	1987	Europe, 15-13		
1949	USA, 7-5	1969	Draw, 16-16	1989	Draw, 14-14		
1951	USA, 9½-2½	1971	USA, 18½-13½	1991	USA, 14½-13½		

Playing Sites

1927—Worcester CC (Mass.); **1929**—Moortown, England; **1931**—Scioto CC (Ohio); **1933**—Southport & Ainsdale, England; **1935**—Ridgewood CC (N.J.); **1937**—Southport & Ainsdale, England; **1939-45**—Not held. **1947**—Portland CC (Ore.); **1949**—Ganton GC, England; **1951**—Pinehurst CC (N.C.); **1953**—Wentworth, England; **1955**—Thunderbird Ranch & CC (Calif.); **1957**—Lindrick GC, England; **1959**—Eldorado CC (Calif.); **1961**—Royal Lytham & St. Annes, England; **1963**—East Lake CC (Ga.); **1965**—Royal Birkdale, England; **1967**—Champions GC (Tex.); **1969**—Royal Birkdale, England; **1971**—Old Warson CC (Mo.); **1973**—Muirfield, Scotland; **1975**—Laurel Valley GC (Pa.); **1977**—Royal Lytham & St. Annes, England; **1979**—The Greenbrier (W.Va.); **1981**—Walton Heath GC, England; **1983**—PGA National GC (Fla.); **1985**—The Belfry, England; **1987**—Muirfield Village GC (Ohio); **1989**—The Belfry, England; **1991**—Ocean Course (S.C.); **1993**—The Belfry, England; **1995**—Oak Hill CC (N.Y.); **1997**—Valderrama, Costa del Sol, Spain; **1999**—The Country Club (Mass.); **2002**— The Belfry, England; **2004**— Oakland Hills CC (Mich.); **2006**— Kildare Hotel & CC, Ireland; **2008**— Valhalla GC (Ky.); **2010**— Celtic Manor, Wales; **2012**— Medinah CC (Ill.); **2014**— Gleneagles, Scotland; **2016**—Hazeltine National GC (Minn); **2018**—TBA (Europe); **2020**—Whistling Straits (Wisc.).

Presidents Cup

The Presidents Cup is a biennial event played in non-Ryder Cup years in which the world's best non-European players compete against players from the United States. The U.S. leads the series, 5-1-1. In 2003 the match was called off due to darkness after three sudden-death playoff holes. It was deemed a tie with both teams sharing the Cup until 2005.

Year		Year		Year		Year	
1994	USA, 20-12	1998	Internat'l, 20½-11½	2003	Tie, 17-17	2007	USA, 19½-14½
1996	USA, 16½-15½	2000	USA, 21½-10½	2005	USA, 18½-15½		

Walker Cup

The Walker Cup was presented by American businessman George Herbert Walker in 1922 for competition between amateur golfers from Great Britain, Ireland and the United States. The U.S. leads the series against the combined Great Britain-Ireland team, 33-7-1, after 41 matches.

Year	Year	Year	Year
1922 USA, 8-4	1949 USA, 10-2	1973 USA, 14-10	1995 Britain-Ireland, 14-10
1923 USA, 6½-5½	1951 USA, 7½-4½	1975 USA, 15½-8½	1997 USA, 18-6
1924 USA, 9-3	1953 USA, 9-3	1977 USA, 16-8	1999 Britain-Ireland, 15-9
1926 USA, 6½-5½	1955 USA, 10-2	1979 USA, 15½-8½	2001 Britain-Ireland, 15-9
1928 USA, 11-1	1957 USA, 8½-3½	1981 USA, 15-9	2003 Britain-Ireland,
1930 USA, 10-2	1959 USA, 9-3	1983 USA, 13½-10½	12½-11½
1932 USA, 9½-2½	1961 USA, 11-1	1985 USA, 13-11	2005 USA, 12½-11½
1934 USA, 9½-2½	1963 USA, 14-10	1987 USA, 16½-7½	2007 USA, 12½-11½
1936 USA, 10½-1½	1965 Draw, 12-12	1989 Britain-Ireland,	
1938 Britain-Ireland, 7½-4½	1967 USA, 15-9	12½-11½	
1940-46 Not held	1969 USA, 13-11	1991 USA, 14-10	
1947 USA, 8-4	1971 Britain-Ireland, 13-11	1993 USA, 19-5	

WOMEN

Solheim Cup

The Solheim Cup was presented by the Karsten Manufacturing Co. in 1990 for competition between women professional golfers from Europe and the United States. The event was switched from even- to odd-numbered years after 2002 so it would not conflict with the men's Ryder Cup event. The U.S. leads the series, 7-3.

Year	Year	Year	Year
1990 USA, 11½-4½	1996 USA, 17-11	2002 USA, 15½-12½	2007 USA, 16-12
1992 Europe, 11½-6½	1998 USA, 16-12	2003 Europe, 17½-10½	
1994 USA, 13-7	2000 Europe, 14½-11½	2005 USA, 15½-12½	

Playing Sites

1990—Lake Nona CC (Fla.); **1992**—Dalmahoy CC, Scotland; **1994**—The Greenbrier (W. Va.); **1996**—Marriott St. Pierre Hotel G&CC, Wales; **1998**—Muirfield Village GC (Ohio); **2000**—Loch Lomond GC, Scotland; **2002**—Interlachen CC (Minn.); **2003**—Barseback G&CC, Sweden; **2005**—Crooked Stick GC (Ind.); **2007**—Halmstad GC (Sweden); **2009**—Rich Harvest Farms (Ill.).

Curtis Cup

Named after British golfing sisters Harriot and Margaret Curtis, the Curtis Cup was first contested in 1932 between teams of women amateurs from the United States and the British Isles.

Competed for every other year since 1932 (except during WWII). The U.S. leads the series, 25-6-3, after 34 matches.

Year	Year	Year	Year
1932 USA, 5½-3½	1956 British Isles, 5-4	1974 USA, 13-5	1992 British Isles, 10-8
1934 USA, 6½-2½	1958 Draw, 4½-4½	1976 USA, 11½-6½	1994 Draw, 9-9
1936 Draw, 4½-4½	1960 USA, 6½-2½	1978 USA, 12-6	1996 British Isles, 11½-6½
1938 USA, 5½-3½	1962 USA, 8-1	1980 USA, 13-5	1998 USA, 10-8
1940-46 Not held	1964 USA, 10½-7½	1982 USA, 14½-3½	2000 USA, 10-8
1948 USA, 6½-2½	1966 USA, 13-5	1984 USA, 9½-8½	2002 USA, 11-7
1950 USA, 7½-1½	1968 USA, 10½-7½	1986 British Isles, 13-5	2004 USA, 10-8
1952 British Isles, 5-4	1970 USA, 11½-6½	1988 British Isles, 11-7	2006 USA, 11½-6½
1954 USA, 6-3	1972 USA, 10-8	1990 USA, 14-4	

COLLEGES

Men's NCAA Division I Champions

College championships decided by match play from 1897-1964 and stroke play since 1965.

Multiple winners (Teams): Yale (21); Houston (16); Oklahoma St. (10); Stanford (8); Harvard (6); Florida, LSU and North Texas (4); Wake Forest (3); Arizona St., Georgia, Michigan, Ohio St. and Texas (2).

Multiple winners (Individuals): Ben Crenshaw and Phil Mickelson (3); Dick Crawford, Dexter Cummings, G.T. Dunlop, Fred Lamprecht and Scott Simpson (2).

Year	Team winner	Individual champion	Year	Team winner	Individual champion
1897	Yale	Louis Bayard, Princeton	1905	Yale	Robert Abbott, Yale
1898	Harvard (spring)	John Reid, Yale	1906	Yale	W.E. Clow Jr., Yale
1898	Yale (fall)	James Curtis, Harvard	1907	Yale	Ellis Knowles, Yale
1899	Harvard	Percy Pyne, Princeton	1908	Yale	H.H. Wilder, Harvard
1900	Not held		1909	Yale	Albert Seckel, Princeton
1901	Harvard	H. Lindsley, Harvard	1910	Yale	Robert Hunter, Yale
1902	Yale (spring)	Chas. Hitchcock Jr., Yale	1911	Yale	George Stanley, Yale
1902	Harvard (fall)	Chandler Egan, Harvard	1912	Yale	F.C. Davison, Harvard
1903	Harvard	F.O. Reinhart, Princeton	1913	Yale	Nathaniel Wheeler, Yale
1904	Harvard	A.L. White, Harvard	1914	Princeton	Edward Allis, Harvard

Colleges (Cont.)

Year	Team winner	Individual champion	Year	Team winner	Individual champion
1915	Yale	Francis Blossom, Yale	1963	Oklahoma St.	R.H. Sikes, Arkansas
1916	Princeton	J.W. Hubbell, Harvard	1964	Houston	Terry Small, San Jose St.
1917-18	Not held		1965	Houston	Marty Fleckman, Houston
1919	Princeton	A.L. Walker Jr., Columbia	1966	Houston	Bob Murphy, Florida
			1967	Houston	Hale Irwin, Colorado
1920	Princeton	Jess Sweetser, Yale	1968	Florida	Grier Jones, Oklahoma St.
1921	Dartmouth	Simpson Dean, Princeton	1969	Houston	Bob Clark, Cal St.-LA
1922	Princeton	Pollack Boyd, Dartmouth			
1923	Princeton	Dexter Cummings, Yale	1970	Houston	John Mahaffey, Houston
1924	Yale	Dexter Cummings, Yale	1971	Texas	Ben Crenshaw, Texas
1925	Yale	Fred Lamprecht, Tulane	1972	Texas	Ben Crenshaw, Texas
1926	Yale	Fred Lamprecht, Tulane			& Tom Kite, Texas
1927	Princeton	Watts Gunn, Georgia Tech	1973	Florida	Ben Crenshaw, Texas
1928	Princeton	Maurice McCarthy, G'town	1974	Wake Forest	Curtis Strange, W.Forest
1929	Princeton	Tom Aycock, Yale	1975	Wake Forest	Jay Haas, Wake Forest
			1976	Oklahoma St.	Scott Simpson, USC
1930	Princeton	G.T. Dunlap Jr., Princeton	1977	Houston	Scott Simpson, USC
1931	Yale	G.T. Dunlap Jr., Princeton	1978	Oklahoma St.	David Edwards, Okla. St.
1932	Yale	J.W. Fischer, Michigan	1979	Ohio St.	Gary Hallberg, Wake Forest
1933	Yale	Walter Emery, Oklahoma			
1934	Michigan	Charles Yates, Ga.Tech	1980	Oklahoma St.	Jay Don Blake, Utah St.
1935	Michigan	Ed White, Texas	1981	Brigham Young	Ron Commans, USC
1936	Yale	Charles Kocsis, Michigan	1982	Houston	Billy Ray Brown, Houston
1937	Princeton	Fred Haas Jr., LSU	1983	Oklahoma St.	Jim Carter, Arizona St.
1938	Stanford	John Burke, Georgetown	1984	Houston	John Inman, N.Carolina
1939	Stanford	Vincent D'Antoni, Tulane	1985	Houston	Clark Burroughs, Ohio St.
			1986	Wake Forest	Scott Verplank, Okla. St.
1940	Princeton & LSU	Dixon Brooke, Virginia	1987	Oklahoma St.	Brian Watts, Oklahoma St.
1941	Stanford	Earl Stewart, LSU	1988	UCLA	E.J. Pfister, Oklahoma St.
1942	LSU & Stanford	Frank Tatum Jr., Stanford	1989	Oklahoma	Phil Mickelson, Ariz. St.
1943	Yale	Wallace Ulrich, Carleton			
1944	Notre Dame	Louis Lick, Minnesota	1990	Arizona St.	Phil Mickelson, Ariz. St.
1945	Ohio State	John Lorms, Ohio St.	1991	Oklahoma St.	Warren Schuette, UNLV
1946	Stanford	George Hamer, Georgia	1992	Arizona	Phil Mickelson, Ariz. St.
1947	LSU	Dave Barclay, Michigan	1993	Florida	Todd Demsey, Ariz. St.
1948	San Jose St.	Bob Harris, San Jose St.	1994	Stanford	Justin Leonard, Texas
1949	North Texas	Harvie Ward, N.Carolina	1995	Oklahoma St.	Chip Spratlin, Auburn
			1996	Arizona St.	Tiger Woods, Stanford
1950	North Texas	Fred Wampler, Purdue	1997	Pepperdine	Charles Warren, Clemson
1951	North Texas	Tom Nieporte, Ohio St.	1998	UNLV	James McLean, Minnesota
1952	North Texas	Jim Vickers, Oklahoma	1999	Georgia	Luke Donald, Northwestern
1953	Stanford	Earl Moeller, Oklahoma St.			
1954	SMU	Hillman Robbins, Memphis St.	2000	Oklahoma St.	Charles Howell, Oklahoma St.
1955	LSU	Joe Campbell, Purdue	2001	Florida	Nick Gilliam, Florida
1956	Houston	Rick Jones, Ohio St.	2002	Minnesota	Troy Matteson, Georgia Tech
1957	Houston	Rex Baxter Jr., Houston	2003	Clemson	Alejandro Canizares, Ariz. St.
1958	Houston	Phil Rodgers, Houston	2004	California	Ryan Moore, UNLV
1959	Houston	Dick Crawford, Houston	2005	Georgia	James Lepp, Washington
1960	Houston	Dick Crawford, Houston	2006	Oklahoma St.	Jonathan Moore, Oklahoma St.
1961	Purdue	Jack Nicklaus, Ohio St.	2007	Stanford	Jamie Lovemark, USC
1962	Houston	Kermit Zarley, Houston			

Women's NCAA Division I Champions

College championships decided by stroke play since 1982.

Multiple winners (teams): Arizona St. (6); Duke (5); Arizona, Florida, San Jose St., Tulsa and UCLA (2).

Year	Team winner	Individual champion	Year	Team winner	Individual champion
1982	Tulsa	Kathy Baker, Tulsa	1995	Arizona St.	K. Mourgue d'Algue, Ariz. St.
1983	TCU	Penny Hammel, Miami	1996	Arizona	Marisa Baena, Arizona
1984	Miami-FL	Cindy Schreyer, Georgia	1997	Arizona St.	Heather Bowie, Texas
1985	Florida	Danielle Ammaccapane, Ariz.St.	1998	Arizona St.	Jennifer Rosales, USC
1986	Florida	Page Dunlap, Florida	1999	Duke	Grace Park, Arizona St.
1987	San Jose St.	Caroline Keggi, New Mexico	2000	Arizona	Jenna Daniels, Arizona
1988	Tulsa	Melissa McNamara, Tulsa	2001	Georgia	Candy Hannemann, Duke
1989	San Jose St.	Pat Hurst, San Jose St.	2002	Duke	Virada Nirapathpongporn, Duke
1990	Arizona St.	Susan Slaughter, Arizona	2003	USC	Mikaela Parmlid, USC
1991	UCLA	Annika Sorenstam, Arizona	2004	UCLA	Sarah Huarte, California
1992	San Jose St.	Vicki Goetze, Georgia	2005	Duke	Anna Grzebien, Duke
1993	Arizona St.	Charlotta Sorenstam, Ariz. St.	2006	Duke	Dewi Schreefel, USC
1994	Arizona St.	Emilee Klein, Ariz. St.	2007	Duke	Stacy Lewis, Arkansas

MOTOR SPORTS

2006 / 2007 YEAR IN REVIEW

Dario Franchitti celebrates his big win at the 2007 Indianapolis 500 as his wife Ashley Judd looks on.

FAMILY TROUBLE

In a surprising move, Dale Earnhardt Jr. splits from Dale Earnhardt, Inc. and will join Hendrick Motorsports in 2008.

DRIVERS CHANGING TEAMS IS CERTAINLY NOTHING NEW, BUT WITH EVERYTHING THAT'S HAPPENED, YOU'VE GOT TO CONSIDER DALE EARNHARDT JR. LEAVING DEI THE BIGGEST AUTO RACING STORY OF THE YEAR.

Leaving the family business, venturing out with Hendrick Motorsports and becoming teammates with Jeff Gordon, Jimmie Johnson and Casey Mears is a major deal for Dale Jr.

His year on the track was an enormous disappointment. He ran in the top five seemingly every single race, only to be let down by engine failures on numerous occasions and miss the Chase for the Nextel Cup.

One of the biggest stories about someone that actually *made* the Chase was the rise to prominence of Clint Bowyer. He hung in there all season long and actually had a chance to win the Nextel Cup. Before the season, nobody would have predicted that. Nobody saw him coming. Not only is he not making many mistakes, but he's running in the top 10 all the time, regardless of what's going on around him!

Bowyer has a pretty good fan following too. He runs all the dirt tracks and short tracks in America, all through Iowa and Kansas City and the other bullrings. Through all that racing all around the country, he's become quite a fan favorite.

While so much was made of Toyota coming into the Nextel Cup Series, their year was a huge disappointment. I think they never expected to have the problems that they've had, but they've shown some good signs as well, and are starting to see the light at the end of the tunnel with Michael Waltrip's team making races. I don't know that you can hang your hat on making races instead of running in the top-five and having a

Rusty Wallace is the 1989 NASCAR Winston Cup Series champion and winner of 55 career races. He is the lead auto racing analyst for ABC and ESPN.

Dale Earnhardt Jr., right, shares a laugh with new team owner **Rick Hendrick** during their news conference on June 13, 2007.

shot to win, but it's a start. At least their Busch Series teams ran well.

Looking forward to 2008, I really expect Tony Stewart to go right to Daytona and have a shot to win the race (in Joe Gibbs Racing's Toyota). The Car of Tomorrow is the Car of Tomorrow, so the Chevrolets that are running at the end of 2007 are the same cars Toyota will be running in 2008. All they'll do is pop a Toyota engine under the hood. So they'll be competitive right out of the box.

The issues surrounding the transition to the Car of Tomorrow was to be expected, but I'm really surprised at some of the off-the-wall things teams had to do to make the car handle properly.

I was pleasantly surprised when the car first came out, because it was putting on a pretty good race. Then, all of a sudden, the close racing stopped. It's almost as if the tire compounds were too hard and the tracks they went to weren't really suited for them. The great finishes we saw at Bristol, Martinsville and Phoenix stopped, and it turned into follow-the-leader racing. Because the tires don't wear, all the cars are so equal that they're basically running at the same speed. Something's got to give in order for these guys to be able to pass, but that's when trouble can occur.

In other news, Juan Pablo Montoya really impressed me this year. He's an

Lewis Hamilton, left, made a splash on the F-1 circuit in 2007, while Ferrari driver **Kimi Raikkonen**, right, won the World Driving Championship.

AP/Wide World Photos

absolute driver and I'm pleasantly surprised at how consistent he's been and how fast he is every single week. He truly looks like a seasoned veteran on the track, not someone who's only in his first full year in NASCAR.

If you have a world-class driver and stick them in great cars, they should run pretty well. Montoya is proving that even if you didn't grow up in the Southeast, or if you haven't been a stock car guy your whole life, that doesn't mean you can't compete and do well in the sport.

It won't surprise me at all to see Montoya and Dario Franchitti (coming over from the Indy Racing League) get better and better. I think Jacques Villeneuve is going to have a harder time at it because he's been out of racing at the highest level for a while. Franchitti, on the other hand, is coming over to NASCAR fresh off winning the IndyCar championship, and the Indianapolis 500. He's got a much better rhythm going.

Another top story off the track is all these team owners taking on business partners. It's a necessity really. And it's a long time coming. It just takes so much money to be successful, and the sponsors are so important. If you can partner up with somebody to help financially and to bring some smarter business people in to help some of these teams, it can make a major difference. And we'll continue to see that in the future.

THE TOP

10 ↓

Stories of the Year in **Motor Sports**

10 Crackdown on cheating.
NASCAR makes it clear it is going to take a tougher stance against cheating, as fines and crew chief suspensions begin in earnest at Daytona. A foreign substance in Michael Waltrip's fuel cell draws the most attention. In Formula One, McLaren is excluded from the World Constructors' Championship due to allegations of spying.

09 NHRA's tough season.
Top Fuel Funny Car driver Eric Medlen dies in March following an accident in Gainesville, Fla. Medlen earned six career wins while driving for John Force Racing. In September, Force sees his own season come to a premature close due to injuries suffered in a crash in Texas.

08 Sebastien Bourdais yet again.
Bourdais wins the Champ Car title for the fourth consecutive year, but he won't make it five in a row in 2008. That's because Bourdais will be moving to Formula One next year, opening the door for a new Champ Car champion.

07 Toyota's NASCAR struggles.
Many feared Toyota would instantly dominate NASCAR's Nextel Cup Series, but that was hardly the case. In fact, Toyota drivers spend virtually the entire season outside the top 35 in owner's points, meaning simply making the races was an achievement. The addition of Joe Gibbs Racing for 2008 should improve the manufacturer's fortunes.

06 Car of Tomorrow debuts.
While no one has argued that NASCAR's "Car of Tomorrow" would be safer for the drivers, many debated whether it would make the racing more competitive. That debate will carry over into 2008, when the car will be utilized in every race, after running in 16 events in 2007. Many drivers feel changes are needed to make the car handle better.

05 Juan Pablo Montoya settles in.
Montoya's move to NASCAR was highly scrutinized but he quickly establishes himself by winning a Busch Series race in Mexico City. In June, he wins the Nextel Cup race at Infineon Raceway. His move sparks an influx of open-wheel drivers to NASCAR for 2008.

 Mark Ashenfelter is an Associate Editor at ESPN and a frequent NASCAR contributor.

04 Franchitti's amazing year.

Dario Franchitti wins a rain-shortened Indianapolis 500 and shrugs off several horrific crashes to win the IndyCar title after Scott Dixon runs out of fuel on the last lap of the final race. Franchitti later announces he'd be moving to NASCAR full time in 2008.

03 Hamilton emerges, Raikkonen is champ.

With two wins and a rookie record nine consecutive podium finishes to open his career, Lewis Hamilton takes Formula One by storm. In the end, though, Kimi Raikkonen rallies in the year's final event to take the championship in his Ferrari.

02 Hendrick Motorsports dominates.

With all four of its drivers – Jeff Gordon, Jimmie Johnson, Kyle Busch and Casey Mears – winning Nextel Cup races, there was no denying that Hendrick Motorsports was the team to beat. Gordon, Johnson and Busch all make the Chase for the Nextel Cup, and Gordon and Johnson are in the thick of the championship race all season.

01 Dale Earnhardt Jr. bolts Dale Earnhardt Inc.

Tensions were evident between Dale Earnhardt Jr. and step-mother Teresa Earnhardt even before the season began. Still, many are shocked when the driver announces in May that he won't return to the team founded by his late father in 2008. In June, Earnhardt Jr. announces he'd be joining Hendrick Motorsports, and this leads to Kyle Busch later announcing his move to Joe Gibbs Racing for 2008.

NASCAR Series Name Changes for 2008

Beginning with the 2008 season, Sprint will replace Nextel as title sponsor of NASCAR's premiere racing series (Sprint actually owns Nextel), while Nationwide Insurance will replace Anheuser-Busch as title sponsor of NASCAR's second-tier series.

Names will be changed from the Nextel Cup Series to the Sprint Cup Series, and from the Busch Series to the Nationwide Series.

2006-2007
Season in Review

SPORTS ALMANAC

NASCAR RESULTS

Nextel Cup Series

Results of NASCAR Nextel Cup races from Nov. 5, 2006 through Oct. 21, 2007. **Note**: Earnings include bonus money. See *Updates* chapter (pages 973-975) for later results.

Late 2006

Date	Event	Location	Winner (Pos.)	Avg.mph	Earnings	Pole	Qual.mph
Nov. 5	Dickies 500	Ft. Worth	Tony Stewart (8)	134.891	$521,361	B. Vickers	196.235
Nov. 12	Checker Auto Parts 500	. . . . Phoenix	Kevin Harvick (2)	96.131	245,761	J. Gordon	134.464
Nov. 19	Ford 400	Homestead	Greg Biffle (22)	125.375	323,800	K. Kahne	178.259

Winning cars (entire 2006 season): CHEVROLET (23)—Harvick, Johnson and Stewart 5, J. Gordon and Hamlin 2, Burton, Ky. Busch, Earnhardt Jr., Vickers; DODGE (7)—Kahne 6, Ku. Busch; FORD (6)—Kenseth 4, Biffle 2.

2007 Season (through Oct. 21)

Date	Event	Location	Winner (Pos.)	Avg.mph	Earnings	Pole	Qual.mph
Feb. 18	**Daytona 500**	Daytona	Kevin Harvick (34)	149.335	$1,510,470	D. Gilliland	186.320
Feb. 25	Auto Club 500	Los Angeles	Matt Kenseth (25)	138.451	342,316	J. Gordon	185.735
Mar. 11	UAW-DaimlerChrysler 400	. . Las Vegas	Jimmie Johnson (23)	128.183	415,386	K. Kahne	128.183
Mar. 18	Kobalt Tools 500	Atlanta	Jimmie Johnson (3)	152.915	233,261	R. Newman	193.124
Mar. 25	Food City 500	Bristol	Kyle Busch (20)	81.969	173,400	J. Gordon	125.453
Apr. 1	Goody's Cool Orange 500	Martinsville	Jimmie Johnson (20)	70.258	198,736	D. Hamlin	95.103
Apr. 15	Samsung 500	Ft. Worth	Jeff Burton (2)	143.359	526,766	J. Gordon	—**
Apr. 21	Subway Fresh 500	Phoenix	Jeff Gordon (1)	107.710	251,411	J. Gordon	133.136
Apr. 29	Aaron's 499	Talladega	Jeff Gordon (1)	154.167	349,711	J. Gordon	192.069
May 5	Crown Royal 400	Richmond	Jimmie Johnson (4)	91.270	244,286	J. Gordon	126.251
May 12	Dodge Charger 500	Darlington	Jeff Gordon (10)	124.383	317,486	C. Bowyer	164.897
May 19@	Nextel All-Star Challenge . . .	Charlotte	Kevin Harvick (4)	89.091	1,031,539	M. Kenseth	133.442
May 27	**Coca-Cola 600**	Charlotte	Casey Mears (16)	130.222	371,425	R. Newman	185.312
June 3	Autism Speaks 400	Dover	Martin Truex Jr. (26)	118.950	295,045	R. Newman	152.925
June 10	Pocono 500	Pocono	Jeff Gordon (18)	135.608	238,286	R. Newman	170.062
June 17	Citizens Bank 400	Michigan	Carl Edwards (12)	148.072	177,850	J.J. Yeley	187.505
June 24	Dodge/Save Mart 350	Sonoma	J P Montoya (32)	74.547	310,600	J. McMurray	92.414
July 1	Lenox Industrial Tools 300 .	Loudon	Denny Hamlin (11)	108.215	235,775	D. Blaney	129.437
July 7	Pepsi 400	Daytona	Jamie McMurray (15)	138.983	302,500	J. Gordon	—**
July 15	USG Sheetrock 400	Chicago	Tony Stewart (19)	134.258	342,161	C. Mears	182.556
July 29	**Allstate 400/Brickyard** .	Indianapolis	Tony Stewart (14)	117.379	488,111	R. Sorenson	184.207
Aug. 5	Pennsylvania 500	Pocono	Kurt Busch (2)	131.627	206,008	D. Earnhardt Jr.	169.975
Aug. 12	Centurion Boats at the Glen	Watkins Glen	Tony Stewart (5)	77.535	239,286	J. Gordon	—**
Aug. 19	3M Performance 400	Michigan	Kurt Busch (15)	138.475	190,108	J. Gordon	189.026
Aug. 25	Sharpie 500	Bristol	Carl Edwards (6)	89.006	297,050	K. Kahne	119.805
Sept. 2	Sharp Aquos 500	Los Angeles	Jimmie Johnson (2)	131.502	289,411	Ku. Busch	182.399
Sept. 8	Chevy Rock & Roll 400	Richmond	Jimmie Johnson (1)	91.813	249,836	J. Johnson	126.298

— Chase for the Nextel Cup —

Date	Event	Location	Winner (Pos.)	Avg.mph	Earnings	Pole	Qual.mph
Sept. 16	Sylvania 300	Loudon	Clint Bowyer (1)	110.475	259,175	C. Bowyer	130.412
Sept. 23	Dodge Dealers 400	Dover	Carl Edwards (15)	101.846	229,250	J. Johnson	154.765
Sept. 30	LifeLock 400	Kansas City	Greg Biffle (7)	104.981	316,225	J. Johnson	175.063
Oct. 7	**UAW-Ford 500**	Talladega	Jeff Gordon (34)	143.438	246,036	M. Waltrip	189.070
Oct. 13	Bank of America 500	Charlotte	Jeff Gordon (4)	125.868	268,236	R. Newman	189.394
Oct. 21	Subway 500	Martinsville	Jimmie Johnson (4)	66.608	244,486	J. Gordon	94.974

@ A non-points exhibition event, formerly known as The Winston.
**Qualifying was canceled due to weather and the pole was awarded based on Owner points.

Winning Cars: CHEVROLET (23)—Johnson 7, J. Gordon 6, Stewart 3, Bowyer, Ky. Busch, Burton, Hamlin, Harvick, Mears and Truex Jr.; FORD (6)—Edwards 3, Biffle, Kenseth and McMurray; DODGE (3)—Ku. Busch 2 and Montoya.
Remaining Races (4): Pep Boys Auto 500 in Atlanta (Oct. 28); Dickies 500 in Fort Worth (Nov. 4); Checker Auto Parts 500 in Phoenix (Nov. 11); Ford 400 in Homestead (Nov. 18).

2007 Daytona 500

Date—Sunday, Feb. 18, 2007, at Daytona International Speedway. **Distance**—500 miles; **Course**—2.5 miles; **Field**—43 cars; **Average speed**—142.667 mph; **Margin of victory**—0.020 seconds; **Time of race**—3 hours, 22 minutes, 54 seconds.

Caution flags—6 for 26 laps; **Lead changes**—13 among 9 drivers; **Lap leaders**—Ku. Busch (95); Stewart (35); Martin (26); Gilliland (18); Truex Jr. (13); Kenseth (6); Harvick and Ky. Busch (4); Newman (1). **Pole sitter**—David Gilliland at 186.320 mph.

Attendance—185,000 (estimated). **Rating**—10.0/20. share (NBC). (r) indicates rookie driver.

	Driver	Start	Sponsor	Car	Laps	Ended	Earnings
1	Kevin Harvick	34	Shell	Chevrolet	202	Running	$1,510,469
2	Mark Martin	26	U.S. Army	Chevrolet	202	Running	1,120,416
3	Jeff Burton	7	Cingular Wireless	Chevrolet	202	Running	819,216
4	Mike Wallace	22	Miccosukee Resort	Chevrolet	202	Running	615,658
5	r-David Ragan	35	AAA	Ford	202	Running	529,350
6	Elliott Sadler	30	Dodge Dealers/UAW	Dodge	202	Running	407,153
7	Kasey Kahne	28	Dodge Dealers/UAW	Dodge	202	Running	386,074
8	David Gilliland	1	M&M's	Ford	202	Running	374,764
9	Joe Nemechek	18	Ginn Clubs & Resorts	Chevrolet	202	Running	302,008
10	Jeff Gordon	42	DuPont	Chevrolet	202	Running	371,679
11	David Stremme	6	Lone Star Steakhouse	Dodge	202	Running	294,758
12	J.J. Yeley	12	Interstate Batteries	Chevrolet	202	Running	308,541
13	Reed Sorenson	33	Target	Dodge	202	Running	296,833
14	Boris Said	23	No Fear	Ford	202	Running	265,375
15	Robby Gordon	39	Jim Beam	Ford	202	Running	268,475
16	Johnny Sauter	41	Haas Automation	Chevrolet	202	Running	262,675
17	Sterling Marlin	38	Ginn Clubs & Resorts	Chevrolet	202	Running	280,641
18	Clint Bowyer	11	Jack Daniel's	Chevrolet	202	Running	275,500
19	r-Juan Pablo Montoya	36	Texaco/Havoline	Dodge	202	Running	299,483
20	Casey Mears	17	GMAC	Chevrolet	202	Running	275,225
21	Bobby Labonte	27	Cheerios/Betty Crocker	Dodge	202	Running	300,436
22	Dale Jarrett	43	UPS	Toyota	202	Running	259,575
23	Carl Edwards	14	Office Depot	Ford	202	Running	273,383
24	Kyle Busch	8	Kellogg's	Chevrolet	202	Running	276,858
25	Greg Biffle	25	Ameriquest Mortgage	Ford	202	Running	276,075
26	Ricky Rudd	2	Snickers	Ford	202	Running	293,091
27	Matt Kenseth	10	DeWalt	Ford	202	Running	309,099
28	Denny Hamlin	9	FedEx Express	Chevrolet	201	Running	279,175
29	Martin Truex Jr.	13	Bass Pro Shops/Tracker	Chevrolet	201	Running	290,820
30	Michael Waltrip	15	NAPA Auto Parts	Toyota	200	Running	269,708
31	Jamie McMurray	24	Crown Royal	Ford	195	Accident	265,058
32	Dale Earnhardt Jr.	5	Budweiser	Chevrolet	195	Accident	315,733
33	Tony Raines	20	DLP HDTV	Chevrolet	195	Running	262,583
34	Dave Blaney	37	Caterpillar	Toyota	186	Parked	269,447
35	Ken Schrader	19	Motorcraft Genuine Parts	Ford	185	Accident	271,189
36	Jeff Green	31	Haas Automation/Best Buy	Chevrolet	181	Running	259,025
37	Scott Riggs	32	Stanley Tools/Valvoline	Dodge	179	Running	259,158
38	Ryan Newman	16	Alltel	Dodge	175	Engine	283,233
39	Jimmie Johnson	21	Lowe's	Chevrolet	173	Accident	298,886
40	r-David Reutimann	40	Burger King	Toyota	173	Accident	249,583
41	Kurt Busch	4	Miller Lite	Dodge	166	Running	300,816
42	Kyle Petty	29	Petty Enterprises/Victory Junction	Dodge	160	Running	248,050
43	Tony Stewart	3	The Home Depot	Chevrolet	152	Accident	334,931

Top 5 Finishing Order + Pole

2007 NEXTEL CUP SEASON (through Oct. 21)

No. Event	Winner	2nd	3rd	4th	5th	Pole
1 Daytona 500	K. Harvick	M. Martin	J. Burton	M. Wallace	D. Ragan	D. Gilliland
2 Auto Club 500	M. Kenseth	J. Gordon	J. Johnson	J. Burton	M. Martin	J. Gordon
3 UAW-DaimerChrysler 400	J. Johnson	J. Gordon	D. Hamlin	M. Kenseth	M. Martin	K. Kahne
4 Kobalt Tools 500	J. Johnson	T. Stewart	M. Kenseth	J. Burton	JP Montoya	R. Newman
5 Food City 500	Ky. Busch	J. Burton	J. Gordon	K. Harvick	G. Biffle	J. Gordon
6 Goody's Cool Orange 500	J. Johnson	J. Gordon	D. Hamlin	Ky. Busch	D. Earnhardt Jr.	D. Hamlin
7 Samsung 500	J. Burton	M. Kenseth	M. Martin	J. Gordon	J. McMurray	J. Gordon
8 Subway Fresh 500	J. Gordon	T. Stewart	D. Hamlin	J. Johnson	M. Kenseth	J. Gordon

No.	Event	Winner	2nd	3rd	4th	5th	Pole
9	Aaron's 499	J. Gordon	J. Johnson	Ku. Busch	D. Gilliland	J. McMurray	J. Gordon
10	Crown Royal 400	J. Johnson	Ky. Busch	D. Hamlin	J. Gordon	Ku. Busch	J. Gordon
11	Dodge Charger 500	J. Gordon	D. Hamlin	J. Johnson	R. Newman	C. Edwards	C. Bowyer
12	Coca-Cola 600	C. Mears	J.J. Yeley	K. Petty	R. Sorenson	B. Vickers	R. Newman
13	Autism Speaks 400	M. Truex Jr.	R. Newman	C. Edwards	D. Hamlin	M. Kenseth	R. Newman
14	Pocono 500	J. Gordon	R. Newman	M. Truex Jr.	C. Mears	T. Stewart	R. Newman
15	Citizens Bank 400	C. Edwards	M. Truex Jr.	T. Stewart	C. Mears	D. Earnhardt Jr.	J. J. Yeley
16	Dodge/Save Mart 350	JP Montoya	K. Harvick	J. Burton	C. Bowyer	G. Biffle	J. McMurray
17	Lenox Industrial Tools 300	D. Hamlin	J. Gordon	M. Truex Jr.	D. Earnhardt Jr.	J. Johnson	D. Blaney
18	Pepsi 400	J. McMurray	Ky. Busch	Ku. Busch	C. Edwards	J. Gordon	J. Gordon
19	USG Sheetrock 400	T. Stewart	M. Kenseth	C. Edwards	K. Harvick	C. Mears	C. Mears
20	Allstate 400 @ Brickyard	T. Stewart	JP Montoya	J. Gordon	Ky. Busch	R. Sorenson	R. Sorenson
21	Pennsylvania 500	Ku. Busch	D. Earnhardt Jr.	D. Hamlin	J. Gordon.	J. Johnson	D. Earnhardt Jr.
22	Cent. Boats at The Glen	T. Stewart	D. Hamlin	J. Johnson	R. Fellows	R. Gordon	J. Gordon
23	3M Performance 400	Ku. Busch	M. Truex Jr.	J. Johnson	M. Kenseth	D. Hamlin	J. Gordon
24	Sharpie 500	C. Edwards	K. Kahne	C. Bowyer	T. Stewart	D. Earnhardt Jr.	K. Kahne
25	Sharp Aquos 500	J. Johnson	C. Edwards	Ky. Busch	J. Burton	D. Earnhardt Jr.	Ku. Busch
26	Chevy Rock & Roll 400	J. Johnson	T. Stewart	D. Ragan	J. Gordon	J. Sauter	J. Johnson

— Chase for the Nextel Cup —

No.	Event	Winner	2nd	3rd	4th	5th	Pole
27	Sylvania 300	C. Bowyer	J. Gordon	T. Stewart	Ky. Busch	M. Truex Jr.	C. Bowyer
28	Dodge Dealers 400	C. Edwards	G. Biffle	D. Earnhardt Jr.	M. Martin	Ky. Busch	J. Johnson
29	LifeLock 400	G. Biffle	C. Bowyer	J. Johnson	C. Mears	J. Gordon	J. Johnson
30	UAW-Ford 500	J. Gordon	J. Johnson	D. Blaney	D. Hamlin	R. Newman	M. Waltrip
31	Bank of America 500	J. Gordon	C. Bowyer	Ky. Busch	J. Burton	C. Edwards	R. Newman
32	Subway 500	J. Johnson	R. Newman	J. Gordon	Ky. Busch	M. Kenseth	J. Gordon

Chase for the Nextel Cup Standings

Official NASCAR Chase for the Nextel Cup standings for 2006 and unofficial standings for 2007 as of Oct. 21 (with four races remaining). Points are awarded for all qualifying drivers (winner received 185) and lap leaders. Earnings include in-season bonuses. Listed are starts (Sts), top-5 finishes (1-2-3-4-5), poles won (PW) and points (Pts).

NASCAR's "Chase for the Nextel Cup" was implemented in 2004 to involve more drivers in the championship hunt, and intensify fan interest and drama during the season's stretch run. After the first 26 official races, the top 12 drivers in the point standings (was top 10 from 2004-06) are eligible for the "chase" over the final ten races of the season. All drivers will begin with 5,000 points; each will then receive a 10-point bonus for each victory during the first 26 events. Drivers not in the top 12 still participate in the final ten races, but are not eligible for the championship.

FINAL 2006

		Finishes		
	Sts	1-2-3-4-5	PW	Pts
1 Jimmie Johnson	36	5-6-1-1-0	1	6475
2 Matt Kenseth	36	4-3-3-2-3	0	6419
3 Denny Hamlin	36	2-2-2-2-0	3	6407
4 Kevin Harvick	36	5-1-4-1-4	1	6397
5 Dale Earnhardt Jr.	36	1-1-4-2-2	0	6328
6 Jeff Gordon	36	2-3-3-2-4	2	6256
7 Jeff Burton	36	1-1-1-2-2	0	6228
8 Kasey Kahne	36	6-1-1-4-0	6	6183
9 Mark Martin	36	0-1-1-2-3	0	6168
10 Kyle Busch	36	1-3-2-1-3	1	6027

2007 (through Race 32, Oct. 21)

		Finishes		
	Sts	1-2-3-4-5	PW	Pts
1 Jeff Gordon	32	6-5-3-4-2	7	6055
2 Jimmie Johnson	32	7-2-5-1-2	3	6002
3 Clint Bowyer	32	1-2-1-1-0	2	5940
4 Tony Stewart	32	3-3-2-1-1	0	5806
5 Carl Edwards	32	3-1-2-1-2	0	5770
6 Kyle Busch	32	1-2-2-4-1	0	5765
7 Kevin Harvick	32	1-1-0-2-0	0	5686
8 Denny Hamlin	32	1-2-5-2-1	1	5681
9 Jeff Burton	32	1-1-2-4-0	0	5646
10 Kurt Busch	32	2-0-2-0-1	1	5635
11 Martin Truex Jr.	32	1-2-2-0-1	0	5608
12 Matt Kenseth	32	1-2-1-2-3	0	5593

Note: Poles listed do not include those awarded for being points leader when qualification was canceled.

Jeff Gordon

Jimmie Johnson

Clint Bowyer

Tony Stewart

Nextel Cup Series (Cont.)
Money Leaders

	FINAL 2006	Earnings		2007 (through Oct. 21)	Earnings
1	Jimmie Johnson	$15,952,125	1	Kevin Harvick	$6,934,220
2	Matt Kenseth	9,544,966	2	Jeff Gordon	6,531,280
3	Tony Stewart	8,749,169	3	Jimmie Johnson	6,455,630
4	Kevin Harvick	8,231,406	4	Tony Stewart	5,835,280
5	Kasey Kahne	7,766,378	5	Jeff Burton	5,429,230
6	Jeff Gordon	7,486,447	6	Matt Kenseth	5,409,410
7	Dale Earnhardt Jr.	7,131,739	7	Dale Earnhardt Jr	4,725,780
8	Denny Hamlin	6,725,332	8	Kasey Kahne	4,623,000
9	Jeff Burton	6,439,995	9	Kurt Busch	4,598,390
10	Casey Mears	6,128,449	10	Ryan Newman	4,475,630

Busch Series

Results of NASCAR Busch Series races from Nov. 4, 2006 through Oct. 12, 2007.
Note: Earnings include bonus money. See *Updates* chapter (pages 973-975) for later results.

Late 2006

Date	Event	Location	Winner (Pos.)	Avg.mph	Earnings	Pole	Qual.mph
Nov. 4	O'Reilly Challenge 300	Ft. Worth	Kevin Harvick (4)	145.710	$65,625	M. Martin	192.589
Nov. 11	Arizona.Travel 200	Phoenix	Matt Kenseth (1)	91.902	59,850	M. Kenseth	132.144
Nov. 18	Ford 300	Homestead	Matt Kenseth (5)	126.523	86,200	K. Harvick	174.272

Winning cars (entire 2006 season): CHEVROLET (22)—Harvick 9, Burton, Earnhardt Jr. and Hamlin 2, Blaney, Bowyer, Ky. Busch, Gilliland, Menard, Stewart and Truex Jr.; FORD (8)—Edwards 4, Kenseth 3, Biffle; DODGE (5)—Ku. Busch and Kahne 2, Mears.

2007 Season (through Oct. 12)

Date	Event	Location	Winner (Pos.)	Avg.mph	Earnings	Pole	Qual.mph
Feb. 17	Orbitz 300	Daytona	Kevin Harvick (31)	156.227	$116,200	Aric Almirola	183.741
Feb. 24	Stater Bros. 300	Los Angeles	Matt Kenseth (2)	127.871	82,500	D. Blaney	180.410
Mar. 4	Telcel-Motorola 200	Mexico	J P Montoya (3)	74.969	113,100	S. Pruett	103.648
Mar. 10	Sam's Town 300	Las Vegas	Jeff Burton (6)	104.530	98,250	K. Harvick	181.111
Mar. 17	Nicorette 300	Atlanta	Jeff Burton (8)	127.201	55,625	Ky. Busch	191.080
Mar. 24	Sharpie Mini 300	Bristol	Carl Edwards (3)	64.038	59,200	S. Wallace	125.387
Apr. 7	Pepsi 300	Nashville	Carl Edwards (8)	128.051	53,650	D. Stremme	166.561
Apr. 14	O'Reilly 300	Ft. Worth	Matt Kenseth (10)	126.671	73,425	D. Ragan	191.063
Apr. 23	Bashas' Supermarkets 200	Phoenix	Clint Bowyer (2)	87.581	75,400	Ky. Busch	132.504
Apr. 30	Aaron's 312	Talladega	Bobby Labonte (34)	133.216	52,725	B. Coleman	184.299
May 4	Circuit City 250	Richmond	Clint Bowyer (8)	91.899	46,600	D. Hamlin	126.683
May 11	Diamond Hill Plywood 200	Darlington	Denny Hamlin (3)	92.370	52,575	D. Hamlin	166.993
May 26	Carquest Auto Parts 300	Charlotte	Kasey Kahne (32)	132.240	66,050	M. Kenseth	179.462
June 2	Dover 200	Dover	Carl Edwards (8)	92.975	49,575	D. Hamlin	153.564
June 9	Federated Auto Parts 300	Nashville	Carl Edwards (7)	129.949	55,700	S. Wallace	161.288
June 16	Meijer 300	Kentucky	Stephen Leicht (5)	117.698	103,823	R. Smith	177.026
June 23	AT&T 250	Milwaukee	Aric Almirola (1)	85.203	69,123	A. Almirola	121.589
June 30	Camping World 200	Loudon	Kevin Harvick (1)	100.669	55,250	K. Harvick	129.335
July 7	Winn-Dixie 300	Daytona	Kyle Busch (14)	139.091	87,425	J. Leffler	184.559
July 14	USG Durock 300	Chicago	Kevin Harvick (8)	135.661	86,400	D. Hamlin	179.503
July 21	Busch Series 250	Gateway	Reed Sorenson (2)	94.977	59,850	S. Wimmer	135.355
July 28	Kroger 200	Indianapolis	Jason Leffler (5)	80.143	61,266	A. Almirola	109.853
Aug. 4	NAPA Auto Parts 200	Montreal	Kevin Harvick (30)	64.671	109,450	P. Carpentier	95.531
Aug. 11	Zippo 200	Watkins Glen	Kevin Harvick (11)	90.768	52,125	Ku. Busch	121.540
Aug. 18	Carfax 250	Michigan	Denny Hamlin (5)	156.467	52,750	G. Biffle	186.548
Aug. 24	Food City 250	Bristol	Kasey Kahne (23)	76.119	57,525	J. Leffler	120.324
Sept. 1	Camping World 300	Los Angeles	Jeff Burton (5)	127.629	96,400	D. Hamlin	180.316
Sept. 7	Emerson Radio 250	Richmond	Kyle Busch (1)	93.913	42,250	Ky. Busch	126.399
Sept. 22	Roadloans.com 200	Dover	Denny Hamlin (4)	85.197	49,875	G. Biffle	154.440
Sept. 29	Yellow Transportation 300	Kansas City	Kyle Busch (6)	107.838	78,450	M. Kenseth	172:007
Oct. 12	Dollar General 300	Charlotte	Jeff Burton (13)	120.267	74,350	G. Biffle	183.511

Winning Cars: CHEVROLET (19)—Harvick 5, Burton 4, Ky. Busch 3, Hamlin 3, Bowyer 2, Almirola, Labonte; FORD (7)—Edwards 4, Kenseth 2, Leicht; DODGE (4)—Kahne 2, Montoya, Sorenson; TOYOTA (1)—Leffler.

Remaining Races (4): Sam's Town 250 in Memphis (Oct. 27); O'Reilly Challenge in Fort Worth (Nov. 3); Arizona.Travel 200 in Phoenix (Nov. 10); Ford 300 in Homestead (Nov. 17).

Top 5 Finishing Order + Pole

2007 BUSCH SERIES SEASON (through Oct. 12)

No.	Event	Winner	2nd	3rd	4th	5th	Pole
1	Orbitz 300	K. Harvick	D. Blaney	C. Edwards	C. Bowyer	M. Martin	A. Almirola
2	Stater Bros. 300	M. Kenseth	C. Mears	Ky. Busch	C. Edwards	G. Biffle	D. Blaney
3	Telcel-Motorola 200	JP Montoya	D. Hamlin	B. Said	C. Edwards	S. Pruett	S. Pruett
4	Sam's Town 300	J. Burton	Ky. Busch	T. Stewart	Ku. Busch	D. Stremme	K. Harvick
5	Nicorette 300	J. Burton	K. Harvick	Ky. Busch	C. Edwards	C. Mears	Ky. Busch
6	Sharpie Mini 300	C. Edwards	M. Kenseth	Ky. Busch	R. Newman	C. Bowyer	S. Wallace
7	Pepsi 300	C. Edwards	D. Reutimann	D. Blaney	J. Leffler	R. Smith	D. Stremme
8	O'Reilly 300	M. Kenseth	D. Hamlin	C. Edwards	C. Mears	D. Ragan	D. Ragan
9	Bashas' Supermarkets 200	C. Bowyer	M. Kenseth	J. Burton	D. Hamlin	C. Edwards	Ky. Busch
10	Aaron's 312	B. Labonte	T. Stewart	C. Mears	D. Ragan	K. Krisiloff	B. Coleman
11	Circuit City 250	C. Bowyer	M. Kenseth	J. Burton	K. Harvick	Ky. Busch	D. Hamlin
12	Diamond Hill Plywood 200	D. Hamlin	M. Martin	C. Edwards	J. Burton	C. Bowyer	D. Hamlin
13	Carquest Auto Parts 300	K. Kahne	C. Mears	C. Bowyer	J. Burton	R. Smith	M. Kenseth
14	Dover 200	C. Edwards	D. Hamlin	S. Wimmer	C. Mears	M. Kenseth	D. Hamlin
15	Federated Auto Parts 300	C. Edwards	C. Bowyer	J. Leffler	S. Wimmer	R. Smith	S. Wallace
16	Meijer 300	S. Leicht	B. Coleman	S. Wimmer	D. Stremme	S. Huffman	R. Smith
17	AT&T 250	A. Almirola	S. Wimmer	J. Leffler	B. Coleman	J. Keller	A. Almirola
18	Camping World 200	K. Harvick	C. Edwards	M. Kenseth	T. Stewart	D. Hamlin	K. Harvick
19	Winn-Dixie 250	Ky. Busch	K. Harvick	D. Blaney	T. Stewart	C. Bowyer	J. Leffler
20	USG Durock 300	K. Harvick	M. Kenseth	J. Burton	C. Bowyer	Ky. Busch	D. Hamlin
21	Busch Series 250	R. Sorenson	S. Wimmer	D. Reutimann	J. Leffler	D. Ragan	S. Wimmer
22	Kroger 200	J. Leffler	G. Biffle	D. Reutimann	C. Edwards	R. Hornaday	A. Almirola
23	NAPA Auto Parts 200	K. Harvick	P. Carpentier	M. Papis	R. Fellows	S. Leicht	P. Carpentier
24	Zippo 200	K. Harvick	J. Burton	Ku. Busch	P. Menard	B. Coleman	Ku. Busch
25	Carfax 250	D. Hamlin	M. Kenseth	K. Harvick	J. Burton	G. Biffle	G. Biffle
26	Food City 250	K. Kahne	J. Leffler	D. Reutimann	Ky. Busch	S. Wimmer	J. Leffler
27	Camping World 300	J. Burton	Ky. Busch	D. Hamlin	J. Johnson	C. Bowyer	D. Hamlin
28	Emerson Radio 250	Ky. Busch	C. Edwards	R. Newman	M. Kenseth	M. Bliss	Ky. Busch
29	Roadloans.com 200	D. Hamlin	M. Truex Jr.	M. Kenseth	M. Bliss	R. Sorenson	G. Biffle
30	Yellow Transportation 300	Ky. Busch	M. Kenseth	C. Mears	C. Bowyer	J. McMurray	M. Kenseth
31	Dollar General 300	J. Burton	Ky. Busch	D. Earnhardt Jr.	A. Almirola	D. Hamlin	G. Biffle

Busch Series Standings

Official Top 10 NASCAR Busch Series point leaders for 2006 and unofficial leaders for 2007 as of Oct. 12 (with five races remaining). Points are awarded for all qualifying drivers (winner received 180) and lap leaders. Earnings include in-season bonuses. Listed are starts (Sts), top-5 finishes (1-2-3-4-5), poles won (PW) and points (Pts).

FINAL 2006

		Finishes		
	Sts	1-2-3-4-5	PW	Pts
1 Kevin Harvick	35	9-6-5-1-2	1	5648
2 Carl Edwards	35	5-3-2-0-5	3	4824
3 Clint Bowyer	35	1-5-1-2-3	2	4683
4 Denny Hamlin	35	2-1-6-3-0	6	4667
5 J.J. Yeley	35	0-1-3-3-2	3	4487
6 Paul Menard	35	1-0-13-2	0	4075
7 Kyle Busch	34	1-0-2-1-0	2	3921
8 Johnny Sauter	35	0-0-0-1-1	1	3794
9 Greg Biffle	30	1-2-1-4-1	0	3789
10 Reed Sorenson	34	0-2-0-2-1	0	3670

2007 (through Oct. 12)

		Finishes		
	Sts	1-2-3-4-5	PW	Pts
1 Carl Edwards	31	4-2-3-4-1	0	4276
2 David Reutimann	31	0-1-3-0-0	0	3638
3 Kevin Harvick	23	5-2-1-1-0	2	3523
4 Jason Leffler	31	1-1-2-2-0	2	3451
5 David Ragan	31	0-0-0-1-2	1	3299
6 Bobby Hamilton Jr.	31	0-0-0-0-0	0	3264
7 Greg Biffle	28	0-1-0-0-2	3	3136
8 Stephen Leicht	31	1-0-0-0-1	0	3046
9 Marcos Ambrose	31	0-0-0-0-0	0	2987
10 Matt Kenseth	21	2-6-2-1-1	2	2981

Money Leaders

FINAL 2006

	Earnings
1 Kevin Harvick	$1,345,380
2 Johnny Sauter	1,226,650
3 Paul Menard	1,196,990
4 Denny Hamlin	1,099,010
5 Carl Edwards	1,093,470
6 Clint Bowyer	1,008,810
7 Jason Leffler	990,162
8 J.J. Yeley	954,604
9 Burney Lamar	925,613
10 Jon Wood	922,941

2007 (through Oct. 12)

	Earnings
1 Carl Edwards	$1,113,110
2 Jason Leffler	1,023,260
3 Kevin Harvick	985,170
4 David Reutimann	973,183
5 Stephen Leicht	944,298
6 Mike Wallace	858,416
7 Marcos Ambrose	852,831
8 Scott Wimmer	843,982
9 Bobby Hamilton Jr.	815,071
10 Kyle Krisiloff	794,321

Craftsman Truck Series

Results of NASCAR Craftsman Truck Series races from Nov. 3, 2006 through Oct. 20, 2007.
Note: Earnings include bonus money. See *Updates* chapter (pages 973-975) for later results.

Late 2006

Date	Event	Location	Winner (Pos.)	Avg.mph	Earnings	Pole	Qual.mph
Nov. 3	Silverado 350	Ft. Worth	Clint Bowyer (1)	124.895	$67.550	C. Bowyer	184.464
Nov. 10	Casino Arizona 150	Phoenix	Johnny Benson (1)	86.221	54,025	J. Benson	132.660
Nov. 17	Ford 200	Homestead	Mark Martin (6)	126.019	55,550	M. Skinner	171.865

Winning Trucks (entire 2006 season): TOYOTA (12)—Benson 5, Bodine 3, Sprague 2, Skinner and Starr; FORD (8)—Martin 6, Cook and Crawford; CHEVROLET (4)—Hornaday 2, Bliss and Ky. Busch.

2007 Season (through Oct. 20)

Date	Event	Location	Winner (Pos.)	Avg.mph	Earnings	Pole	Qual.mph
Feb. 16	Chevy Silverado HD 250	Daytona	Jack Sprague (1)	117.739	$93,375	J. Sprague	179.508
Feb. 23	San Bernardino County 200	Los Angeles	Mike Skinner (2)	130.933	64,725	C. Edwards	176.354
Mar. 16	Amer. Commercial Lines 200	Atlanta	Mike Skinner (1)	105.739	60,750	M. Skinner	181.926
Mar. 31	Kroger 250	Martinsville	Mike Skinner (1)	61.753	54,200	M. Skinner	95.985
Apr. 28	O'Reilly Auto Parts 250	Kansas City	Erik Darnell (10)	124.403	55,700	M. Skinner	170.729
May 18	Quaker Steak & Lube 200	Charlotte	Ron Hornaday (7)	122.809	57,550	M. Skinner	180.469
May 26	Ohio 250	Mansfield	Dennis Setzer (18)	52.873	52,150	M. Skinner	109.877
June 1	AAA Insurance 200	Dover	Ron Hornaday (15)	107.463	59,800	M. Skinner	155.420
June 8	Sam's Town 400	Ft. Worth	Todd Bodine (1)	118.060	75,600	T. Bodine	181.763
June 16	Michigan 200	Michigan	Travis Kvapil (1)	135.364	56,950	T. Kvapil	179.596
June 22	Toyota Tundra Milw. 200	Milwaukee	Johnny Benson (4)	95.503	59,400	M. Skinner	122.187
June 30	O'Reilly 200	Memphis	Travis Kvapil (10)	91.806	54,025	B. Keselowski	119.771
July 14	Built Ford Tough 225	Kentucky	Mike Skinner (1)	127.179	86,425	R. Mathews	172.995
July 27	Power Stroke Diesel 200	Indianapolis	Ron Hornaday (2)	76.438	54,775	M. Skinner	—**
Aug. 11	Toyota Tundra 200	Nashville	Travis Kvapil (1)	124.107	53,825	M. Skinner	159.635
Aug. 22	O'Reilly 200	Bristol	Johnny Benson (8)	71.331	60,300	T. Kvapil	121.136
Sept. 1	Dodge Dealers Ram Tough 200	Gateway	Johnny Benson (4)	103.657	61,375	M. Skinner	132.708
Sept. 15	New Hampshire 200	Loudon	Ron Hornaday (1)	109.780	58,575	R. Hornaday	—**
Sept. 22	Smith's Las Vegas 350	Las Vegas	Travis Kvapil (1)	115.061	54,100	T. Kvapil	175.387
Oct. 6	Mountain Dew 250	Talladega	Todd Bodine (1)	129.985	83,525	T. Bodine	181.811
Oct. 20	Kroger 200	Martinsville	Mike Skinner (4)	59.566	49,275	J. Sprague	95.656

**Qualifying was canceled due to weather and the pole was awarded based on Owner points.

Winning Trucks: TOYOTA (11)—Skinner 5, Benson 3, Bodine 2, Sprague; FORD (5)—Kvapil 4, Darnell; CHEVROLET (5)—Hornaday 4, Setzer.
Remaining Races (4): EasyCare Vehicle Service Contracts 200 in Atlanta (Oct. 28); Silverado 350 in Ft. Worth (Nov. 3); Phoenix 150 in Phoenix (Nov. 10); Ford 200 in Homestead (Nov. 17).

Top 5 Finishing Order + Pole

2007 CRAFTSMAN TRUCK SERIES SEASON (through Oct. 20)

No. Event	Winner	2nd	3rd	4th	5th	Pole
1 Chevy Silverado HD 250	J. Sprague	J. Benson	T. Kvapil	M. Skinner	T. Bodine	J. Sprague
2 San Bernardino Cty 200	M. Skinner	R. Hornaday	J. Sprague	C. Edwards	T. Musgrave	C. Edwards
3 Amer. Commer. Lines 200	M. Skinner	T. Bodine	M. Crafton	R. Crawford	C. Bowyer	M. Skinner
4 Kroger 250	M. Skinner	T. Bodine	R. Crawford	K. Harvick	T. Musgrave	M. Skinner
5 O'Reilly Auto Parts 250	E. Darnell	R. Crawford	J. Sprague	J. Benson	M. Skinner	M. Skinner
6 Quaker Steak & Lube 200	R. Hornaday	A. Allmendinger	T. Bodine	M. Martin	T. Musgrave	M. Skinner
7 Ohio 250	D. Setzer	J. Sprague	K. Schrader	M. Skinner	J. Benson	M. Skinner
8 AAA Insurance 200	R. Hornaday	S. Compton	T. Kvapil	J. Benson	M. Bliss	T. Bodine
9 Sam's Town 400	T. Bodine	M. Skinner	R. Crawford	R. Hornaday	D. Starr	T. Bodine
10 Michigan 200	T. Kvapil	Ky. Busch	B. Gaughan	M. Skinner	T. Musgrave	T. Kvapil
11 Toyota Tundra Milw. 200	J. Benson	R. Hornaday	T. Bodine	M. Skinner	R. Crawford	M. Skinner
12 O'Reilly 200, Memphis	T. Kvapil	J. Sprague	R. Hornaday	M. Skinner	A. Fike	B. Keselowski
13 Built Ford Tough 225	M. Skinner	T. Kvapil	T. Musgrave	R. Mathews	D. Green	R. Mathews
14 Power Stroke Diesel 200	R. Hornaday	J. Benson	T. Kvapil	R. Crawford	K. Schrader	M. Skinner
15 Toyota Tundra 200	T. Kvapil	R. Hornaday	M. Skinner	D. Starr	T. Bodine	M. Skinner
16 O'Reilly 200, Bristol	J. Benson	B. Gaughan	M. Martin	M. Skinner	R. Crawford	T. Kvapil
17 Ram Tough 200	J. Benson	R. Hornaday	T. Musgrave	T. Bodine	R. Smith	M. Skinner
18 New Hampshire 200	R. Hornaday	E. Darnell	M. Skinner	T. Bodine	M. Bliss	R. Hornaday
19 Smith's Las Vegas 350	T. Kvapil	J. Benson	J. Wood	T. Cook	E. Darnell	T. Kvapil
20 Mountain Dew 250	T. Bodine	R. Crawford	J. Benson	J. Leffler	D. Setzer	T. Bodine
21 Kroger 200	M. Skinner	J. Sprague	R. Hornaday	D. Starr	R. Crawford	J. Sprague

Craftsman Truck Series Standings

Official Top 10 NASCAR Craftsman Truck Series point leaders for 2006 and unofficial leaders for 2007 as of Oct. 20 (with four races remaining). Points are awarded for all qualifying drivers (winner received 180) and lap leaders. Earnings include in-season bonuses. Listed are starts (Sts), top-5 finishes (1-2-3-4-5), poles won (PW) and points (Pts).

FINAL 2006

		Sts	Finishes 1-2-3-4-5	PW	Pts
1	Todd Bodine	25	3-3-2-4-0	1	3666
2	Johnny Benson	25	5-0-1-4-3	1	3539
3	David Reutimann	25	0-0-1-3-3	2	3530
4	David Starr	25	1-1-1-1-2	0	3355
5	Jack Sprague	25	2-2-0-3-3	2	3328
6	Ted Musgrave	25	0-3-4-3-0	0	3314
7	Ron Hornaday	25	2-0-2-1-3	1	3313
8	Terry Cook	25	1-2-0-0-0	0	3265
9	Rick Crawford	25	1-2-1-0-1	0	3252
10	Mike Skinner	25	1-3-2-1-1	7	3219

2007 (through Oct. 20)

		Sts	Finishes 1-2-3-4-5	PW	Pts
1	Mike Skinner	21	5-1-2-6-1	9	3383
2	Ron Hornaday	21	4-4-2-1-0	0	3372
3	Travis Kvapil	21	4-1-3-0-0	3	3097
4	Todd Bodine	21	2-2-2-2-2	2	3048
5	Johnny Benson	21	3-3-1-2-1	0	2969
6	Rick Crawford	21	0-2-2-2-3	0	2949
7	Ted Musgrave	20	0-0-2-0-4	0	2616
8	Matt Crafton	21	0-0-1-0-0	0	2520
9	Erik Darnell	21	1-1-0-0-1	0	2515
10	Jack Sprague	21	1-3-2-0-0	2	2514

Money Leaders

FINAL 2006

		Earnings
1	Todd Bodine	$604,310
2	Johnny Benson	574,975
3	Mark Martin	519,125
4	Mike Skinner	496,630
5	Ted Musgrave	463,175
6	Jack Sprague	461,965
7	Ron Hornaday	446,015
8	Rick Crawford	441,520
9	Terry Cook	398,920
10	David Starr	383,815

2007 (through Oct. 20)

		Earnings
1	Mike Skinner	$663,075
2	Ron Hornaday	578,325
3	Travis Kvapil	539,350
4	Johnny Benson	528,885
5	Todd Bodine	515,750
6	Jack Sprague	412,860
7	Rick Crawford	380,875
8	Erik Darnell	327,200
9	Ted Musgrave	309,550
10	Dennis Setzer	296,380

INDY RACING LEAGUE RESULTS

IndyCar Series

Schedule and results of IndyCar Series events during the 2007 season.

2007 Season

Date	Event	Location	Winner (Pos.)	Time	Avg.mph	Pole	Qual.mph
Mar. 24	XM Satellite Radio 300	Homestead	Dan Wheldon (1)	1:48:06.8893	164.825	D. Wheldon	214.322
Apr. 1	Honda GP	St. Petersburg	Helio Castroneves (1)	2:01:07.3512	89.166	H. Castroneves	105.052
Apr. 21	Japan 300	Motegi	Tony Kanaan (3)	1:52:23.2574	162.295	H. Castroneves	205.393
Apr. 29	Kansas Lottery 300	Kansas City	Dan Wheldon (4)	1:36:56.0586	188.169	T. Kanaan	214.188
May 27	**Indianapolis 500**	Indianapolis	Dario Franchitti (3)	2:44:03.5608	151.774	H. Castroneves	225.817
June 3	A.J. Foyt 225	Milwaukee	Tony Kanaan (3)	1:47:42.4393	127.220	H. Castroneves	171.071
June 9	Bombardier Learjet 550k	Ft. Worth	Sam Hornish Jr. (2)	1:52:15.2873	177.314	S. Sharp	215.260
June 24	Iowa Corn 250	Iowa	Dario Franchitti (3)	1:48:14.1344	123.896	S. Dixon	182.360
June 30	SunTrust Challenge	Richmond	Dario Franchitti (1)	1:24:19.6684	133.408	D. Franchitti	—**
July 8	Watkins Glen GP	Watkins Glen	Scott Dixon (2)	1:43:51.5094	116.813	H. Castroneves	136.021
July 15	Firestone 200	Nashville	Scott Dixon (1)	1:35:06.2615	164.030	S. Dixon	204.414
July 22	Honda 200	Ohio	Scott Dixon (6)	1:47:24.0663	107.222	H. Castroneves	121.620
Aug. 5	Firestone 400	Michigan	Tony Kanaan (8)	2:49:38.0509	141.481	D. Franchitti	218.308
Aug. 11	Meijer 300	Kentucky	Tony Kanaan (1)	1:38:21.7078	180.558	T. Kanaan	218.086
Aug. 26	Motorola 300	Infineon	Scott Dixon (5)	1:51:58.5533	98.593	D. Franchitti	107.951
Sept. 2	Detroit Grand Prix	Belle Isle	Tony Kanaan (4)	2:11:50.5097	83.841	H. Castroneves	103.401
Sept. 9	Peak Antifreeze 300	Chicago	Dario Franchitti (1)	1:44:53.7950	173.886	D. Franchitti	214.646

**Qualifying was canceled due to inclement weather and the pole was awarded based on championship points.

Winning cars (Chassis/Engine): DALLARA/HONDA (17)—all.

Indy Racing League Results (Cont.)

91st Indianapolis 500

Date—Sunday, May 27, 2007, at Indianapolis Motor Speedway. **Distance**—415 miles (shortened from 500 due to rain); **Course**—2.5 mile oval; **Field**—33 cars; **Winner's average speed**—151.774 mph; **Margin of victory**—under caution; **Time of race**—2 hours, 44 minutes, 3.5608 seconds; **Caution flags**—11 for 55 laps; **Lead changes**—23 by 9 drivers; **Lap leaders**—Kanaan (83), Franchitti (34), Castroneves (19), Ma. Andretti (13), Dixon (11), Hornish Jr. (2), Lazier (2), Mi. Andretti (1), Simmons (1); **Pole Sitter**—Helio Castroneves at 225.817 mph; **Attendance**—400,000 (est.); **TV Rating**—4.3 (ABC). Note that (r) indicates rookie driver.

	Driver	Start	Country	Car	Laps	Ended	Earnings
1	Dario Franchitti	3	Scotland	D/H/F	166	Running	$1,645,233
2	Scott Dixon	4	New Zealand	D/H/F	166	Running	719,067
3	Helio Castroneves	1	Brazil	D/H/F	166	Running	646,303
4	Sam Hornish Jr.	5	United States	D/H/F	166	Running	360,389
5	Ryan Briscoe	7	Australia	D/H/F	166	Running	302,305
6	Scott Sharp	12	United States	D/H/F	166	Running	368,305
7	Tomas Scheckter	10	South Africa	D/H/F	166	Running	304,105
8	Danica Patrick	8	United States	D/H/F	166	Running	298,005
9	Davey Hamilton	20	United States	D/H/F	166	Running	268,905
10	Vitor Meira	19	Brazil	D/H/F	166	Running	280,305
11	Jeff Simmons	13	United States	D/H/F	166	Running	278,347
12	Tony Kanaan	2	Brazil	D/H/F	166	Running	414,319
13	Michael Andretti	11	United States	D/H/F	166	Running	238,247
14	A.J. Foyt IV	18	United States	D/H/F	165	Running	252,305
15	Alex Barron	26	United States	D/H/F	165	Running	249,305
16	Kosuke Matsuura	17	Japan	D/H/F	165	Running	245,305
17	Ed Carpenter	14	United States	D/H/F	164	Accident	246,305
18	Sarah Fisher	21	United States	D/H/F	164	Running	238,305
19	Buddy Lazier	22	United States	D/H/F	164	Running	216,805
20	Darren Manning	15	England	D/H/F	164	Running	232,305
21	Roger Yasukawa	23	United States	D/H/F	164	Running	234,305
22	Dan Wheldon	6	England	D/H/F	163	Accident	231,805
23	Richie Hearn	32	United States	D/H/F	163	Running	224,305
24	Marco Andretti	9	United States	D/H/F	162	Accident	229,351
25	Buddy Rice	16	United States	D/H/F	162	Accident	222,805
26	Al Unser Jr.	25	United States	D/H/F	161	Running	205,805
27	Jaques Lazier	28	United States	P/H/F	155	Accident	207,389
28	Marty Roth	30	Canada	D/H/F	148	Accident	216,305
29	r-Phil Giebler	33	United States	P/H/F	106	Accident	230,305
30	John Andretti	24	United States	D/H/F	95	Accident	204,305
31	r-Milka Duno	29	Venezuela	D/H/F	65	Accident	213,555
32	Jon Herb	27	United States	D/H/F	51	Accident	193,305
33	Roberto Moreno	31	Brazil	P/H/F	36	Accident	224,805

Car Legend: Chassis/Engine/Tires. D—Dallara, P—Panoz (chassis); H—Honda (engine); F—Firestone (tires).

Top 5 Finishing Order + Pole

2007 Season

No. Event	Winner	2nd	3rd	4th	5th	Pole
1 XM Satellite Radio 300	D. Wheldon	S. Dixon	S. Hornish Jr.	V. Meira	T. Kanaan	D. Wheldon
2 Honda GP of St. Pete	H. Castroneves	S. Dixon	T. Kanaan	Ma. Andretti	D. Franchitti	H. Castroneves
3 Japan 300	T. Kanaan	D. Wheldon	D. Franchitti	S. Dixon	S. Hornish Jr.	H. Castroneves
4 Kansas Lottery 300	D. Wheldon	D. Franchitti	H. Castroneves	S. Dixon	T. Scheckter	T. Kanaan
5 Indianapolis 500	D. Franchitti	S. Dixon	H. Castroneves	S. Hornish Jr.	R. Briscoe	H. Castroneves
6 AJ Foyt 225	T. Kanaan	D. Franchitti	D. Wheldon	D. Franchitti	V. Meira	H. Castroneves
7 Bombardier Learjet 500	S. Hornish Jr.	T. Kanaan	D. Patrick	D. Franchitti	V. Meira	S. Sharp
8 Iowa Corn 250	D. Franchitti	Ma. Andretti	S. Sharp	B. Rice	D. Manning	S. Dixon
9 SunTrust Challenge	D. Franchitti	S. Dixon	D. Wheldon	T. Kanaan	B. Rice	D. Franchitti
10 Watkins Glen GP	S. Dixon	S. Hornish Jr.	D. Franchitti	T. Kanaan	Ma. Andretti	H. Castroneves
11 Firestone 200	S. Dixon	D. Franchitti	D. Patrick	S. Hornish Jr.	Ma. Andretti	S. Dixon
12 Honda 200	S. Dixon	D. Franchitti	H. Castroneves	T. Kanaan	D. Patrick	H. Castroneves
13 Firestone 400	T. Kanaan	Ma. Andretti	S. Sharp	K. Matsuura	B. Rice	D. Franchitti
14 Meijer 300	T. Kanaan	S. Dixon	A.J. Foyt IV	Ma. Andretti	T. Scheckter	T. Kanaan
15 Motorola 300	S. Dixon	H. Castroneves	D. Franchitti	T. Kanaan	S. Hornish Jr.	D. Franchitti
16 Detroit GP	T. Kanaan	D. Patrick	D. Wheldon	D. Manning	K. Matsuura	H. Castroneves
17 Peak Antifreeze 300	D. Franchitti	S. Dixon	S. Hornish Jr.	H. Castroneves	S. Sharp	D. Franchitti

Final 2007 Indy Racing League Point Standings & Money Leaders

Final top-10 Indy Racing League driver points leaders and money leaders for 2007. Points are awarded for places 1 to 33 (winner receives 50) and overall lap leader. Listed are starts (Sts), top-5 finishes, poles won (PW) and points (Pts).

Points

		Sts	Finishes 1-2-3-4-5	PW	Pts
1	Dario Franchitti	17	4-4-3-1-1	4	637
2	Scott Dixon	17	4-6-0-3-0	2	624
3	Tony Kanaan	17	5-1-1-4-1	2	576
4	Dan Wheldon	17	2-1-3-0-0	1	466
5	Sam Hornish Jr.	17	1-1-2-2-2	0	465
6	Helio Castroneves	17	1-1-3-1-0	7	446
7	Danica Patrick	17	0-1-2-0-1	0	424
8	Scott Sharp	17	0-0-2-0-1	1	412
9	Buddy Rice	17	0-0-0-1-2	0	360
10	Tomas Scheckter	17	0-0-0-0-2	0	357

Earnings

		Earnings
1	Dario Franchitti	$4,017,583
2	Scott Dixon	2,152,417
3	Tony Kanaan	1,754,269
4	Helio Castroneves	1,659,603
5	Dan Wheldon	1,336,855
6	Sam Hornish Jr.	1,323,789
7	Scott Sharp	1,212,505
8	Danica Patrick	1,182,055
9	Tomas Scheckter	1,064,905
10	Marco Andretti	1,063,051

CHAMP CAR RESULTS

Schedule and results of Champ Car World Series races from Nov. 12, 2006 through Oct. 21, 2007.

Champ Car World Series

Late 2006

Date	Event	Location	Winner (Pos.)	Time	Avg.mph	Pole	Qual.mph
Nov. 12	Gran Premio Telmex-Tecate	Mexico City	Sebastien Bourdais (2)	1:51:31.146	98.504	J. Wilson	117.763

Winning cars (entire 2006 season): FORD-COSWORTH XFE/LOLA (14)—all.

2007 Season (through Oct. 21)

Date	Event	Location	Winner (Pos.)	Time	Avg.mph	Pole	Qual.mph
Apr. 8	Vegas GP	Las Vegas	Will Power (1)	1:45:13.637	94.607	W. Power	113.154
Apr. 15	Toyota GP	Long Beach	Sebastien Bourdais (1)	1:40:43.975	91.432	S. Bourdais	104.889
Apr. 22	GP of Houston	Houston	Sebastien Bourdais (2)	1:45:32.136	88.986	W. Power	105.545
June 10	GP of Portland	Portland	Sebastien Bourdais (3)	1:45:42.774	114.816	J. Wilson	121.903
June 24	GP of Cleveland pres. by LaSalle Bank	Cleveland	Paul Tracy (7)	1:45:10.860	106.921	S. Bourdais	134.514
July 1	Mont-Tremblant	Quebec	Robert Doornbos (5)	1:45:41.899	92.245	T. Gommendy	122.898
July 8	Steelback GP of Toronto	Toronto	Will Power (7)	1:45:58.568	72.534	S. Bourdais	108.393
July 22	Rexall GP of Edmonton	Edmonton	Sebastien Bourdais	1:45:41.953	107.517	W. Power	121.617
July 29	San Jose GP	San Jose	Robert Doornbos (15)	1:45:07.617	88.123	J. Wilson	105.932
Aug. 12	GP of Road America	Elkhart Lake	Sebastien Bourdais (1)	1:40:58.596	127.481	S. Bourdais	143.525
Aug. 26	GP of Belgium	Zolder	Sebastien Bourdais (1)	1:45:21.997	100.752	S. Bourdais	123.195
Sept. 2	Bavaria GP	Netherlands	Justin Wilson (2)	1:46:02.236	110.491	S. Bourdais	127.813
Oct. 21	Lexmark Indy 300	Queensland	Sebastien Bourdais (4)	1:45:49.318	96.669	W. Power	111.733

Winning cars (Engine/Chassis): COSWORTH XFE/DP01 (13)—all.
Remaining Races (1): Grand Premio de Mexico in Mexico City (Nov. 11).

Top 5 Finishing Order + Pole

2007 SEASON (through Oct. 21)

No.	Event	Winner	2nd	3rd	4th	5th	Pole
1	Vegas GP	W. Power	R. Doornbos	P. Tracy	A. Tagliani	T. Gommendy	W. Power
2	GP of Long Beach	S. Bourdais	O. Servia	W. Power	J. Wilson	A. Tagliani	S. Bourdais
3	GP of Houston	S. Bourdais	G. Rahal	R. Doornbos	O. Servia	S. Pagenaud	W. Power
4	GP of Portland	S. Bourdais	J. Wilson	R. Doornbos	W. Power	A. Tagliani	J. Wilson
5	GP of Cleveland	P. Tracy	R. Doornbos	N. Jani	J. Wilson	S. Pagenaud	S. Bourdais
6	Mont-Tremblant	R. Doornbos	S. Bourdais	W. Power	S. Pagenaud	J. Wilson	T. Gommendy
7	Steelback GP of Toronto	W. Power	N. Jani	J. Wilson	S. Pagenaud	B. Junqueira	S. Bourdais
8	GP of Edmonton	S. Bourdais	J. Wilson	G. Rahal	S. Pagenaud	P. Tracy	W. Power
9	GP of San Jose	R. Doornbos	N. Jani	O. Servia	W. Power	S. Bourdais	J. Wilson
10	GP of Road America	S. Bourdais	D. Clarke	G. Rahal	O. Servia	A. Tagliani	S. Bourdais
11	GP of Belgium	S. Bourdais	B. Junqueira	G. Rahal	W. Power	J. Wilson	S. Bourdais
12	Bavaria GP	J. Wilson	J. Heylen	B. Junqueira	T. Gommendy	N. Jani	S. Bourdais
13	Indy 300	S. Bourdais	J. Wilson	B. Junqueira	R. Doornbos	S. Pagenaud	W. Power

Champ Car Results (Cont.)
Champ Car Point Standings

Official Top 10 Champ Car World Series point leaders for 2006 and unofficial leaders for 2007 (through Oct. 21). Points are awarded for places 1 to 20, for the pole winner at oval events, fastest driver on each day of qualifying at road/street events, lap leaders and most positions gained. Listed are starts (Sts), top-5 finishes, poles won (PW) and points (Pts). (r) indicates rookie driver. **Note:** With one race remaining in 2007, Sebastien Bourdais had already accumulated enough points to clinch his third straight Champ Car World Series title.

FINAL 2006

		Sts	Finishes 1-2-3-4-5	PW	Pts
1	Sebastien Bourdais	14	7-1-3-0-0	7	387
2	Justin Wilson	13	1-1-1-1-2	2	298
3	A.J. Allmendinger	13	5-4-2-1-0	1	285
4	Nelson Philippe	14	1-0-2-2-1	0	231
5	Bruno Junqueira	14	0-3-0-2-0	1	219
6	r-Will Power	14	0-0-1-1-1	1	213
7	Paul Tracy	13	0-2-0-2-1	0	209
8	Alex Tagliani	13	0-0-2-1-2	0	205
9	Mario Dominguez	14	0-1-1-1-1	1	202
10	Andrew Ranger	14	0-0-0-0-1	0	200

2007 (through Oct. 21)

		Sts	Finishes 1-2-3-4-5	PW	Pts
1	Sebastien Bourdais	13	7-1-0-0-1	6	332
2	Justin Wilson	13	1-3-1-2-2	2	270
3	r-Robert Doornbos	13	2-2-2-1-0	0	262
4	Will Power	13	2-0-2-3-0	4	234
5	r-Graham Rahal	13	0-1-3-0-0	0	220
6	r-Neel Jani	13	0-2-1-0-1	0	218
7	Bruno Junqueira	13	0-1-2-0-1	0	216
8	r-Simon Pagenaud	13	0-0-0-3-3	0	213
9	Oriol Servia	12	0-1-1-2-0	0	212
10	Alex Tagliani	13	0-0-0-1-3	0	197

Money Leaders

FINAL 2006

		Earnings
1	Sebastien Bourdais	$757,500
2	A.J. Allmendinger	585,500
3	Justin Wilson	517,500
4	Nelson Philippe	407,500
5	Bruno Junqueira	393,000
6	Paul Tracy	386,500
7	Mario Dominguez	356,500
8	r-Will Power	339,000
9	Alex Tagliani	335,500
10	Oriol Servia	333,500

2007 (through Oct. 21)

		Earnings
1	Sebastien Bourdais	$686,000
2	r-Robert Doornbos	489,500
3	Justin Wilson	471,500
4	Will Power	439,000
5	r-Graham Rahal	361,500
6	r-Neel Jani	350,500
7	Bruno Junqueira	357,500
8	Oriol Servia	337,500
9	r-Simon Pagenaud	336,000
10	Alex Tagliani	313,500

FORMULA ONE RESULTS

Results of Formula One Grand Prix races in 2007

2007 Season

Date	Grand Prix	Location	Winner (Pos.)	Time	Avg.mph	Pole
Mar. 18	Australian	Melbourne	Kimi Raikkonen (6)	1:25:28.770	134.151	K. Raikkonen
Apr. 8	Malaysian	Kuala Lumpur	Fernando Alonso (2)	1:32:14.930	125.450	F. Massa
Apr. 15	Bahrain	Bahrain	Felipe Massa (1)	1:33:27.515	122.961	F. Massa
May 13	Spanish	Barcelona	Felipe Massa (1)	1:31:36.230	123.095	F. Massa
May 27	Monaco	Monte Carlo	Fernando Alonso (1)	1:40:29.329	96.655	F. Alonso
June 10	Canadian	Montreal	Lewis Hamilton (1)	1:44:11.292	109.236	L. Hamilton
June 17	U.S.	Indianapolis	Lewis Hamilton (1)	1:31:09.965	125.145	L. Hamilton
July 1	French	Magny-Cours	Kimi Raikkonen (3)	1:30:54.200	126.560	F. Massa
July 8	British	Silverstone	Kimi Raikkonen (2)	1:21:43.074	138.335	L. Hamilton
July 22	European	Nurburgring	Fernando Alonso (2)	2:06:26.358	91.072	K. Raikkonen
Aug. 5	Hungarian	Budapest	Lewis Hamilton (1)	1:35:52.991	119.239	L. Hamilton
Aug. 26	Turkish	Istanbul	Felipe Massa (1)	1:26:42.161	133.041	F. Massa
Sept. 9	Italian	Monza	Fernando Alonso (1)	1:18:37.806	145.430	F. Alonso
Sept. 16	Belgian	Spa-Francorchamps	Kimi Raikkonen (1)	1:20:39.066	142.402	K. Raikkonen
Sept. 30	Japanese	Fuji	Lewis Hamilton (1)	2:00:34.579	94.435	L. Hamilton
Oct. 7	Chinese	Shanghai	Kimi Raikkonen (1)	1:37:58.395	116.088	L. Hamilton
Oct. 21	Brazil	Sao Paolo	Kimi Raikkonen (3)	1:28:15.270	129.228	F. Massa

Winning Constructors: FERRARI (9)—Raikkonen 6, Massa 3; McLAREN MERCEDES (8)—Alonso 4, Hamilton 4.

Top 5 Finishing Order + Pole
2007 Season

No.	Event	Winner	2nd	3rd	4th	5th	Pole
1	Australian	K. Raikkonen	F. Alonso	L. Hamilton	N. Heidfeld	G. Fisichella	K. Raikkonen
2	Malaysian	F. Alonso	L. Hamilton	K. Raikkonen	N. Heidfeld	F. Massa	F. Massa
3	Bahrain	F. Massa	L. Hamilton	K. Raikkonen	N. Heidfeld	F. Alonso	F. Massa
4	Spanish	F. Massa	L. Hamilton	F. Alonso	R. Kubica	D. Coulthard	F. Massa
5	Monaco	F. Alonso	L. Hamilton	F. Massa	G. Fisichella	R. Kubica	F. Alonso
6	Canadian	L. Hamilton	N. Heidfeld	A. Wurz	H. Kovalainen	K. Raikkonen	L. Hamilton
7	U.S.	L. Hamilton	F. Alonso	F. Massa	K. Raikkonen	H. Kovalainen	L. Hamilton
8	French	K. Raikkonen	F. Massa	L. Hamilton	R. Kubica	N. Heidfeld	F. Massa
9	British	K. Raikkonen	F. Alonso	L. Hamilton	R. Kubica	F. Massa	L. Hamilton
10	European	F. Alonso	F. Massa	M. Webber	A. Wurz	D. Coulthard	K. Raikkonen
11	Hungarian	L. Hamilton	K. Raikkonen	N. Heidfeld	F. Alonso	R. Kubica	L. Hamilton
12	Turkish	F. Massa	K. Raikkonen	F. Alonso	N. Heidfeld	L. Hamilton	F. Massa
13	Italian	F. Alonso	L. Hamilton	K. Raikkonen	N. Heidfeld	R. Kubica	F. Alonso
14	Belgian	K. Raikkonen	F. Massa	F. Alonso	L. Hamilton	N. Heidfeld	K. Raikkonen
15	Japanese	L. Hamilton	H. Kovalainen	K. Raikkonen	D. Coulthard	G. Fisichella	L. Hamilton
16	Chinese	K. Raikkonen	F. Alonso	F. Massa	S. Vettel	J. Button	L. Hamilton
17	Brazil	K. Raikkonen	F. Massa	F. Alonso	N. Rosberg	R. Kubica	F. Massa

2007 Formula One Point Standings

Final top-10 Formula One World Drivers and Constructors Championship point leaders for 2007. Points are awarded for places 1 through 8 only (i.e., 10-8-6-5-4-3-2-1). Listed are starts (Sts), top-8 finishes, poles won (PW) and points (Pts). **Note:** Formula One does not keep money leader standings.

Drivers

		Sts	Finishes 1-2-3-4-5-6-7-8	PW	Pts
1	Kimi Raikkonen	17	6-2-4-1-1-0-0-1	3	110
2	Fernando Alonso	17	4-4-4-1-1-0-2-0	2	109
	Lewis Hamilton	17	4-5-3-1-1-0-1-0	6	109
4	Felipe Massa	17	3-4-3-0-2-2-0-0	6	94
5	Nick Heidfeld	17	0-1-1-5-2-4-1-0	0	61
6	Robert Kubica	16	0-0-0-3-4-1-2-1	0	39
7	Heikki Kovalainen	17	0-1-0-1-1-1-3-4	0	30
8	Giancarlo Fisichella	17	0-0-0-1-2-2-0-2	0	21
9	Nico Rosberg	17	0-0-0-1-0-3-3-0	0	20
10	David Coulthard	17	0-0-0-1-2-0-0-1	0	14

Constructors

		Pts
1	Ferrari	204
2	BMW	101
3	Renault	51
4	Williams-Toyota	33
5	Red Bull-Renault	24
6	Toyota	13
7	STR-Ferrari	8
8	Honda	6
9	Super Aguri-Honda	4
10	Spyker-Ferrari	1
—	McLaren-Mercedes	0

Note: McLaren was stripped of all 2007 constructors' points after being found to have been in possession of confidential Ferrari data.

Major 2007 Endurance Races

24 Hours of Daytona
Jan. 27-28, at Daytona Beach, Fla.

Officially the Rolex 24 at Daytona and first held in 1962 (as a 3-hour race). An IMSA Camel GT race for exotic prototype sports cars and contested over a 3.56-mile road course at Daytona International Speedway. Listed are qualifying position, drivers, chassis and laps completed.

1 (1) Scott Pruett, Salvador Duran and Juan Pablo Montoya; LEXUS RILEY; 668 laps (2,378 miles) at 99.020 mph; margin of victory—1 minute, 15.842 seconds.
2 (11) Milka Duno, Patrick Carpentier, Darren Manning and Ryan Dalziel; PONTIAC RILEY, 668 laps.
3 (10) Wayne Taylor, Max Angelelli, Jeff Gordon and Jan Magnussen; PONTIAC RILEY, 666 laps.
4 (59) Hurley Haywood, JC France, Joao Barbosa, Roberto Moreno and David Donohue; PORSCHE RILEY, 662 laps.
5 (61) Brian Frisselle, Mark Wilkins, Burt Frisselle and David Empringham; LEXUS RILEY, 657 laps.

Top qualifier: Scott Pruett, LEXUS RILEY, 119.856 mph.

24 Hours of Le Mans
June 16-17, at Le Mans, France

Officially the Le Mans Grand Prix d'Endurance and first held in 1923. Contested over the 8.48-mile Circuit de la Sarthe in Le Mans, France. Listed are qualifying position, drivers, car, and laps completed.

1 (4) Marco Werner, Emanuele Pirro and Frank Biela; AUDI R10; 369 laps (3,124.9 miles) at 129.961 mph.
2 (1) Stephane Sarrazin, Pedro Lamy and Sebastien Bourdais; PEUGEOT 908; 359 laps.
3 (6) Emmanuel Collard, Jean-Christophe Bouillion and Romain Dumas; PESCAROLO 01; 358 laps.
4 (8) Stuart Hall, Joao Barbosa and Martin Short; PESCAROLO 01; 347 laps.
5 (27) David Brabham, Darren Turner and Rickard Rydell; ASTON MARTIN DBR9; 343 laps.

Top qualifier: Sebastien Bourdais, PEUGEOT 908, 3:26.344 (147.965 mph).

NHRA RESULTS

Winners of National Hot Rod Association's POWERade Drag Racing events in the Top Fuel, Funny Car, Pro Stock and Pro Stock Motorcycle divisions through Oct. 7, 2007. All times are based on two cars/motorcycles racing head-to-head from a standing start over a straight line, quarter-mile course. Differences in reaction time account for apparently faster losing times.

2007 Season (through Oct. 7)

Top Fuel

Date	Event	Winner	Time	MPH	2nd Place	Time	MPH
Feb. 11	Carquest Winternationals	J.R. Todd	4.482	324.98	B. Bernstein	11.397	71.36
Feb. 25	Kragen Nationals	Rod Fuller	4.490	327.19	M. Troxel	4.536	325.61
Mar. 18	ACDelco Gatornationals	Tony Schumacher	4.542	325.14	L. Dixon	4.589	321.65
Apr. 1	O'Reilly Spring Nationals	J.R. Todd	4.603	313.80	J. Hartley	4.645	307.79
Apr. 15	SummitRacing.com Nationals	Brandon Bernstein	4.521	330.07	B. Vandergriff	4.828	298.87
Apr. 29	Southern Nationals	Brandon Bernstein	4.662	305.01	D. Herbert	4.714	297.02
May 6	O'Reilly Midwest Nationals	Melanie Troxel	4.741	274.33	C. McClenathan	5.355	254.52
June 3	O'Reilly Summer Nationals	Brandon Bernstein	4.582	320.51	J.R. Todd	4.667	299.86
June 10	Torco Racing Fuels Rt. 66 Nationals	Larry Dixon	4.579	322.11	R. Fuller	9.155	80.76
June 24	ProCare Rx SuperNationals	Larry Dixon	4.625	321.73	D. Herbert	4.675	316.30
July 1	Summit Racing Equipment Nationals	Tony Schumacher	4.537	322.04	R. Fuller	7.087	114.49
July 8	O'Reilly Thunder Valley Nationals	Brandon Bernstein	4.648	317.57	B. Vandergriff	9.236	100.08
July 15	Mopar Mile-High Nationals	Rod Fuller	4.683	312.93	W. Bazemore	4.770	308.35
July 22	Schuck's Auto Supply Nationals	Tony Schumacher	4.607	307.79	B. Bernstein	4.558	328.86
July 29	Fram-Autolite Nationals	Tony Schumacher	4.534	329.42	B. Vandergriff	4.597	305.84
Aug. 12	Lucas Oil Nationals	Brandon Bernstein	4.525	329.91	L. Dixon	4.586	323.35
Aug. 19	Toyo Tires Nationals	Doug Herbert	4.526	323.43	R. Fuller	4.709	324.98
Sept. 3	Mac Tools U.S. Nationals	Tony Schumacher	4.575	331.94	L. Dixon	4.748	268.44
Sept. 16	O'Reilly Mid-South Nationals	Melanie Troxel	4.728	313.22	D. Herbert	4.901	290.57
Sept. 23	O'Reilly Fall Nationals	Larry Dixon	4.629	310.91	B. Vandergriff	5.426	307.72
Oct. 7	Torco Racing Fuels Nationals	Doug Kalitta	4.647	316.08	M. Troxel	4.649	316.45

Funny Car

Date	Event	Winner	Time	MPH	2nd Place	Time	MPH
Feb. 11	Carquest Winternationals	Gary Scelzi	4.716	332.26	R. Hight		Broke
Feb. 25	Kragen Nationals	Tony Pedregon	4.803	326.32	R. Hight	9.723	84.75
Mar. 18	ACDelco Gatornationals	Ron Capps	4.773	323.27	P. Burkart	4.876	316.75
Apr. 1	O'Reilly Spring Nationals	Ron Capps	4.868	307.93	C. Pedregon	5.025	270.97
Apr. 15	SummitRacing.com Nationals	Robert Hight	5.126	282.90	R. Capps	5.592	178.57
Apr. 29	Southern Nationals	Robert Hight	4.882	314.61	M. Ashley	5.167	229.66
May 6	O'Reilly Midwest Nationals	Ron Capps	4.882	305.98	D. Worsham	4.918	308.50
June 3	O'Reilly Summer Nationals	Mike Ashley	4.896	310.70	J. Head	4.928	303.09
June 10	Torco Racing Fuels Rt. 66 Nationals	Gary Scelzi	4.838	321.42	R. Capps	4.850	318.39
June 24	ProCare Rx SuperNationals	Tommy Johnson	4.994	305.84	T. Pedregon	5.022	306.33
July 1	Summit Racing Equipment Nationals	Mike Ashley	4.823	321.88	K. Bernstein	12.080	80.40
July 8	O'Reilly Thunder Valley Nationals	John Force	4.993	284.62	C. Pedregon	5.024	279.73
July 15	Mopar Mile-High Nationals	Jack Beckman	4.932	312.86	R. Capps	5.001	307.86
July 22	Schuck's Auto Supply Nationals	Jack Beckman	4.829	320.97	J. Force	5.235	203.03
July 29	Fram-Autolite Nationals	John Force	4.831	320.58	D. Worsham	4.851	314.68
Aug. 12	Lucas Oil Nationals	John Force	4.794	316.60	K. Bernstein	4.801	320.43
Aug. 19	Toyo Tires Nationals	Tony Pedregon	6.061	151.99	J. Force	4.792	320.13
Sept. 3	Mac Tools U.S. Nationals	Mike Ashley	4.894	323.74	R. Hight	8.072	104.08
Sept. 16	O'Reilly Mid-South Nationals	Gary Scelzi	4.886	314.61	J. Beckman	4.892	310.55
Sept. 23	O'Reilly Fall Nationals	Tony Pedregon	5.010	254.86	C. Pedregon	6.882	131.31
Oct. 7	Torco Racing Fuels Nationals	Gary Scelzi	4.956	306.60	R. Capps	5.935	207.11

Pro Stock Car

Date	Event	Winner	Time	MPH	2nd Place	Time	MPH
Feb. 11	Carquest Winternationals	Greg Anderson	6.651	207.05	G. Stanfield	7.001	163.65
Feb. 25	Kragen Nationals	Kurt Johnson	6.694	206.67	J. Line	6.676	207.85
Mar. 18	ACDelco Gatornationals	Greg Anderson	6.577	211.06	L. Morgan	8.076	118.24
Apr. 1	O'Reilly Spring Nationals	Jason Line	6.661	207.75	A. Johnson	6.712	206.26
Apr. 15	SummitRacing.com Nationals	Greg Anderson	6.724	205.29	J. Coughlin	6.758	204.45
Apr. 29	Southern Nationals	Greg Anderson	6.671	207.62	W. Johnson	6.719	205.79
May 6	O'Reilly Midwest Nationals	Dave Connolly	6.663	206.99	J. Coughlin	6.695	206.64
June 3	O'Reilly Summer Nationals	Greg Anderson	6.704	206.86	D. Connolly	6.747	204.66
June 10	Torco Racing Fuels Rt. 66 Nationals	Jeg Coughlin	6.658	207.37	J. Line	6.656	208.07
June 24	ProCare Rx SuperNationals	Greg Anderson	6.617	209.52	J. Coughlin	6.879	169.66
July 1	Summit Racing Equipment Nationals	Dave Connolly	6.660	207.11	L. Morgan	6.718	205.54
July 8	O'Reilly Thunder Valley Nationals	Jeg Coughlin	6.809	203.22	K. Koretsky	6.839	201.82
July 15	Mopar Mile-High Nationals	Allen Johnson	7.132	192.47	R. Krisher	16.720	48.95
July 22	Schuck's Auto Supply Nationals	Dave Connolly	6.649	206.20	A. Johnson	6.682	206.23

Date	Event	Winner	Time	MPH	2nd Place	Time	MPH
July 29	Fram-Autolite Nationals	Greg Anderson	6.657	207.72	J. Line	6.688	204.08
Aug. 12	Lucas Oil Nationals	Jeg Coughlin	6.667	205.94	G. Anderson	6.669	207.24
Aug. 19	Toyo Tires Nationals	Dave Connolly	6.643	207.43	K. Johnson	6.857	206.80
Sept. 3	Mac Tools U.S. Nationals	Dave Connolly	6.710	206.32	G. Anderson	6.729	205.79
Sept. 16	O'Reilly Mid-South Nationals	Dave Connolly	6.648	207.59	G. Anderson	6.658	208.65
Sept. 23	O'Reilly Fall Nationals	Dave Connolly	8.553	112.17	G. Anderson		Broke
Oct. 7	Torco Racing Fuels Nationals	Dave Connolly	6.671	206.95	V. Gaines	6.679	206.92

Pro Stock Motorcycles

Date	Event	Winner	Time	MPH	2nd Place	Time	MPH
Mar. 18	ACDelco Gatornationals	Karen Stoffer	7.075	186.79	M. Smith	7.069	187.31
Apr. 1	O'Reilly Spring Nationals	Angelle Sampey	7.046	188.91	C. Treble	7.516	145.59
Apr. 29	Southern Nationals	Karen Stoffer	7.063	188.65	M. Smith		Broke
May 6	O'Reilly Midwest Nationals	Matt Smith	6.901	191.78	A. Sampey	7.132	162.67
June 10	Torco Racing Fuels Rt. 66 Nationals	Andrew Hines	6.959	192.11	M. Smith	7.014	187.18
June 24	ProCare Rx SuperNationals	Craig Treble	6.990	191.70	A. Hines	7.003	190.48
July 1	Summit Racing Equipment Nationals	Andrew Hines	6.988	190.46	M. Smith	10.961	70.13
July 15	Mopar Mile-High Nationals	Matt Smith	7.400	177.81	A. Sampey	7.481	177.65
July 29	Fram-Autolite Nationals	Matt Smith	6.992	189.10	E. Krawiec	7.090	190.16
Aug. 12	Lucas Oil Nationals	Andrew Hines	7.009	188.20	E. Krawiec	7.077	183.94
Aug. 19	Toyo Tires Nationals	Matt Guidera	6.971	188.02	A. Sampey		Broke
Sept. 3	Mac Tools U.S. Nationals	Craig Treble	7.037	190.83	M. Smith	6.977	189.63
Sept. 16	O'Reilly Mid-South Nationals	Andrew Hines	6.917	192.91	S. Johnson		Broke
Sept. 23	O'Reilly Fall Nationals	Peggy Llewellyn	7.020	190.00	A. Hines	7.007	191.16

Remaining Races (2): ACDelco Las Vegas Nationals (Oct. 28); Automobile Club of Southern California Finals in Pomona (Nov. 4).

2007 NHRA POWERade Point Standings (through Oct. 7)

Top Fuel

		Points
1	Larry Dixon	3030
2	Rod Fuller	3020
3	Tony Schumacher	3010
4	Brandon Bernstein	3000
5	Bob Vandergriff	2231
6	Doug Herbert	2209
7	Whit Bazemore	2182
8	J.R. Todd	2164
9	Melanie Troxel	1093
10	David Grubnic	910

Funny Car

		Points
1	Tony Pedregon	3030
2	Gary Scelzi	3020
3	Robert Hight	3010
4	Ron Capps	3000
5	Jack Beckman	2267
6	Mike Ashley	2212
7	John Force	2191
8	Jim Head	2082
9	Del Worsham	966
10	Tommy Johnson	896

Pro Stock Car

		Points
1	Dave Connolly	3030
2	Greg Anderson	3020
3	Jeg Coughlin	3010
4	Allen Johnson	3000
5	Kurt Johnson	2211
6	Jason Line	2202
7	Larry Morgan	2171
8	Warren Johnson	2112
9	Richie Stevens	948
10	V. Gaines	922

Pro Stock Motorcycle

		Points				Points
1	Andrew Hines	3030	6	Angelle Sampey		2179
2	Matt Smith	3020	7	Karen Stoffer		2157
3	Chip Ellis	3010	8	Ed Krawiec		2156
4	Peggy Llewellyn	3000	9	Steve Johnson		683
5	Craig Treble	2219	10	Chris Rivas		636

2007 AMA Motocross/Supercross
Final Championship Point Standings

Motocross

		Points
1	Grant Langston	439
2	Mike Alessi	423
3	Andrew Short	421
4	Timmy Ferry	417
5	Kevin Windham	363
6	Ricky Carmichael	291
7	James Stewart	290
8	Michael Byrne	230
9	Gavin Gracyk	218
10	David Vuillemin	207

Motocross Lites

		Points
1	Ryan Villopoto	544
2	Ben Townley	525
3	Josh Grant	346
4	Jason Lawrence	277
5	Ryan Dungey	267
6	Jake Weimer	255
7	Brett Metcalfe	242
8	Tommy Hahn	220
9	Martin Davalos	203
10	Broc Tickle	201

Supercross

		Points
1	James Stewart	385
2	Chad Reed	334
3	Timmy Ferry	276
4	Kevin Windham	240
5	Ivan Tedesco	197
6	David Vuillemin	196
7	Michael Byrne	189
8	Ricky Carmichael	160
	Heath Voss	160
10	Paul Carpenter	143

1909-2007
Through the Years

SPORTS ALMANAC

NASCAR CIRCUIT
Daytona 500

Held over 200 laps on 2.5-mile oval at Daytona International Speedway in Daytona Beach, Fla. First race in 1959, although stock car racing at Daytona dates back to 1936. Winners who started from pole position are in **bold** type.

Multiple winners: Richard Petty (7); Cale Yarborough (4); Bobby Allison; Jeff Gordon and Dale Jarrett (3); Bill Elliott, Sterling Marlin and Michael Waltrip (2). **Multiple poles:** Buddy Baker and Cale Yarborough (4); Bill Elliott, Dale Jarrett, Fireball Roberts and Ken Schrader (3); Donnie Allison (2).

Year	Winner	Car	Owner	MPH	Pole Sitter	MPH
1959	Lee Petty	Oldsmobile	Petty Enterprises	135.521	Bob Welborn	140.121
1960	Junior Johnson	Chevrolet	Ray Fox	124.740	Cotton Owens	149.892
1961	Marvin Panch	Pontiac	Smokey Yunick	149.601	Fireball Roberts	155.709
1962	**Fireball Roberts**	Pontiac	Smokey Yunick	152.529	Fireball Roberts	156.999
1963	Tiny Lund	Ford	Wood Brothers	151.566	Fireball Roberts	160.943
1964	Richard Petty	Plymouth	Petty Enterprises	154.334	Paul Goldsmith	174.910
1965-a	Fred Lorenzen	Ford	Holman-Moody	141.539	Darel Dieringer	171.151
1966-b	**Richard Petty**	Plymouth	Petty Enterprises	160.627	Richard Petty	175.165
1967	Mario Andretti	Ford	Holman-Moody	149.926	Curtis Turner	180.831
1968	**Cale Yarborough**	Mercury	Wood Brothers	143.251	Cale Yarborough	189.222
1969	Lee Roy Yarbrough	Ford	Junior Johnson	157.950	Buddy Baker	188.901
1970	Pete Hamilton	Plymouth	Petty Enterprises	149.601	Cale Yarborough	194.015
1971	Richard Petty	Plymouth	Petty Enterprises	144.462	A.J. Foyt	182.744
1972	A.J. Foyt	Mercury	Wood Brothers	161.550	Bobby Isaac	186.632
1973	Richard Petty	Dodge	Petty Enterprises	157.205	Buddy Baker	185.662
1974-c	Richard Petty	Dodge	Petty Enterprises	140.894	David Pearson	185.017
1975	Benny Parsons	Chevrolet	L.G. DeWitt	153.649	Donnie Allison	185.827
1976	David Pearson	Mercury	Wood Brothers	152.181	Ramo Stott	183.456
1977	Cale Yarborough	Chevrolet	Junior Johnson	153.218	Donnie Allison	188.048
1978	Bobby Allison	Ford	Bud Moore	159.730	Cale Yarborough	187.536
1979	Richard Petty	Oldsmobile	Petty Enterprises	143.977	Buddy Baker	196.049
1980	**Buddy Baker**	Oldsmobile	Ranier Racing	177.602*	Buddy Baker	194.099
1981	Richard Petty	Buick	Petty Enterprises	169.651	Bobby Allison	194.624
1982	Bobby Allison	Buick	DiGard Racing	153.991	Benny Parsons	196.317
1983	Cale Yarborough	Pontiac	Ranier Racing	155.979	Ricky Rudd	198.864
1984	**Cale Yarborough**	Chevrolet	Ranier Racing	150.994	Cale Yarborough	201.848
1985	**Bill Elliott**	Ford	Melling Racing	172.265	Bill Elliott	205.114
1986	Geoff Bodine	Chevrolet	Hendrick Motorsports	148.124	Bill Elliott	205.039
1987	**Bill Elliott**	Ford	Melling Racing	176.263	Bill Elliott	210.364†
1988	Bobby Allison	Buick	Stavola Brothers	137.531	Ken Schrader	198.823
1989	Darrell Waltrip	Chevrolet	Hendrick Motorsports	148.466	Ken Schrader	196.996
1990	Derrike Cope	Chevrolet	Bob Whitcomb	165.761	Ken Schrader	196.515
1991	Ernie Irvan	Chevrolet	Morgan-McClure	148.148	Davey Allison	195.955
1992	Davey Allison	Ford	Robert Yates	160.256	Sterling Marlin	192.213
1993	Dale Jarrett	Chevrolet	Joe Gibbs Racing	154.972	Kyle Petty	189.426
1994	Sterling Marlin	Chevrolet	Morgan-McClure	156.931	Loy Allen	190.158
1995	Sterling Marlin	Chevrolet	Morgan-McClure	141.710	Dale Jarrett	193.498
1996	Dale Jarrett	Ford	Robert Yates	154.308	Dale Earnhardt	189.510
1997	Jeff Gordon	Chevrolet	Hendrick Motorsports	148.295	Mike Skinner	189.813
1998	Dale Earnhardt	Chevrolet	Richard Childress	172.712	Bobby Labonte	192.415
1999	**Jeff Gordon**	Chevrolet	Hendrick Motorsports	161.551	Jeff Gordon	195.067
2000	**Dale Jarrett**	Ford	Robert Yates	155.669	Dale Jarrett	191.091
2001	Michael Waltrip	Chevrolet	Dale Earnhardt, Inc.	161.783	Bill Elliott	183.565
2002	Ward Burton	Dodge	Bill Davis	142.971	Jimmie Johnson	185.831
2003-d	Michael Waltrip	Chevrolet	Dale Earnhardt, Inc.	133.870	Jeff Green	186.606
2004	Dale Earnhardt Jr.	Chevrolet	Dale Earnhardt, Inc.	156.345	Greg Biffle	188.387
2005	Jeff Gordon	Chevrolet	Hendrick Motorsports	135.173	Dale Jarrett	188.312
2006	Jimmie Johnson	Chevrolet	Hendrick Motorsports	142.667	Jeff Burton	189.151
2007	Kevin Harvick	Chevrolet	Richard Childress	142.667	David Gilliland	186.320

*Track and race record for winning speed. †Track and race record for qualifying speed.
Notes: a—rain shortened 1965 race to 332.5 miles; **b**—rain shortened 1966 race to 495 miles; **c**—in 1974, race shortened 50 miles due to energy crisis; **d**—rain shortened 2003 race to 272.5 miles. **Also:** Pole sitters determined by pole qualifying race (1959-65); by two-lap average (1966-68); by fastest single lap (since 1969).

UAW-Ford 500

Held over 188 laps on 2.66-mile tri-oval at Talladega Superspeedway in Talladega, Ala.

Previously known as Winston 500 (1970-93, 1997-2000), Winston Select 500 (1994-96) and EA Sports 500 (2001-04). It became the UAW-Ford 500 in 2005. Winners who started from pole position are in **bold** type.

Multiple winners: Dale Earnhardt (4); Bobby Allison, Davey Allison, Buddy Baker, Dale Earnhardt Jr. and David Pearson (3); Dale Jarrett, Mark Martin, Darrell Waltrip and Cale Yarborough (2).

Year		Year		Year		Year	
1970	Pete Hamilton	1980	Buddy Baker	1990	**Dale Earnhardt**	2000	Dale Earnhardt
1971	**Donnie Allison**	1981	**Bobby Allison**	1991	Harry Gant	2001	Dale Earnhardt Jr.
1972	David Pearson	1982	Darrell Waltrip	1992	Davey Allison	2002	Dale Earnhardt Jr.
1973	David Pearson	1983	Richard Petty	1993	Ernie Irvan	2003	Michael Waltrip
1974	**David Pearson**	1984	**Cale Yarborough**	1994	Dale Earnhardt	2004	Dale Earnhardt Jr.
1975	**Buddy Baker**	1985	**Bill Elliott**	1995	**Mark Martin**	2005	Dale Jarrett
1976	Buddy Baker	1986	Bobby Allison	1996	Sterling Marlin	2006	Brian Vickers
1977	Darrell Waltrip	1987	Davey Allison	1997	Mark Martin	2007	Jeff Gordon
1978	**Cale Yarborough**	1988	Phil Parsons	1998	Dale Jarrett		
1979	Bobby Allison	1989	Davey Allison	1999	Dale Earnhardt		

Coca-Cola 600

Held over 400 laps on 1.5-mile oval at Lowe's Motor Speedway in Concord, N.C.

Previously known as World 600 (1960-85). It has been Coca-Cola 600 since 1986 (in 2002, sponsors announced a one-time-only name change to The Coca-Cola Racing Family 600). Winners who started from pole position are in **bold** type.

Multiple winners: Darrell Waltrip (5); Bobby Allison, Buddy Baker, Dale Earnhardt, Jeff Gordon, Jimmie Johnson and David Pearson (3); Neil Bonnett, Jeff Burton, Fred Lorenzen, Jim Paschal and Richard Petty (2).

Year		Year		Year		Year	
1960	Joe Lee Johnson	1972	Buddy Baker	1984	Bobby Allison	1996	Dale Jarrett
1961	David Pearson	1973	**Buddy Baker**	1985	Darrell Waltrip	1997	**Jeff Gordon***
1962	Nelson Stacy	1974	**David Pearson**	1986	Dale Earnhardt	1998	**Jeff Gordon**
1963	Fred Lorenzen	1975	Richard Petty	1987	Kyle Petty	1999	Jeff Burton
1964	Jim Paschal	1976	**David Pearson**	1988	Darrell Waltrip	2000	Matt Kenseth
1965	**Fred Lorenzen**	1977	Richard Petty	1989	Darrell Waltrip	2001	Jeff Burton
1966	Marvin Panch	1978	Darrell Waltrip	1990	Rusty Wallace	2002	Mark Martin
1967	Jim Paschal	1979	Darrell Waltrip	1991	Davey Allison	2003	Jimmie Johnson*
1968	Buddy Baker*	1980	Benny Parsons	1992	Dale Earnhardt	2004	**Jimmie Johnson**
1969	Lee Roy Yarbrough	1981	Bobby Allison	1993	Dale Earnhardt	2005	Jimmie Johnson
1970	Donnie Allison	1982	Neil Bonnett	1994	**Jeff Gordon**	2006	Kasey Kahne
1971	Bobby Allison	1983	Neil Bonnett	1995	Bobby Labonte	2007	Casey Mears

* rain-shortened.

Allstate 400 at the Brickyard

Held over 160 laps at 2.5-mile Indianapolis Motor Speedway in Indianapolis, Ind.

Previously known as Brickyard 400 (1994-2004). Winners who started from pole position are in **bold** type.

Multiple winners: Jeff Gordon (4); Dale Jarrett and Tony Stewart (2).

Year		Year		Year		Year		Year	
1994	Jeff Gordon	1997	Ricky Rudd	2000	Bobby Labonte	2003	**Kevin Harvick**	2006	Jimmie Johnson
1995	Dale Earnhardt	1998	Jeff Gordon	2001	Jeff Gordon	2004	Jeff Gordon	2007	Tony Stewart
1996	Dale Jarrett	1999	Dale Jarrett	2002	Bill Elliott	2005	Tony Stewart		

Mountain Dew Southern 500

Final race held in 2004. Held over 367 laps on 1.366-mile oval at Darlington International Raceway in Darlington, S.C.

Previously known as Southern 500 (1950-88); Heinz 500 (1989-91); and Pepsi Southern 500 (1998-2000). It was the Mountain Dew Southern 500 from 1992-97, and 2001-04. Winners who started from pole position are in **bold** type.

Multiple winners: Jeff Gordon and Cale Yarborough (5); Bobby Allison (4); Buck Baker, Dale Earnhardt, Bill Elliott, David Pearson and Herb Thomas (3); Harry Gant and Fireball Roberts (2).

Year		Year		Year		Year	
1950	Johnny Mantz	1964	Buck Baker	1978	Cale Yarborough	1992	Darrell Waltrip*
1951	Herb Thomas	1965	Ned Jarrett	1979	David Pearson	1993	Mark Martin*
1952	**Fonty Flock**	1966	Darel Dieringer	1980	Terry Labonte	1994	Bill Elliott
1953	Buck Baker	1967	**Richard Petty**	1981	Neil Bonnett	1995	Jeff Gordon
1954	Herb Thomas	1968	Cale Yarborough	1982	Cale Yarborough	1996	Jeff Gordon
1955	Herb Thomas	1969	Lee Roy Yarbrough*	1983	Bobby Allison	1997	Jeff Gordon*
1956	Curtis Turner	1970	Buddy Baker	1984	**Harry Gant**	1998	Jeff Gordon*
1957	Speedy Thompson	1971	**Bobby Allison**	1985	**Bill Elliott**	1999	Jeff Burton*
1958	Fireball Roberts	1972	**Bobby Allison**	1986	**Tim Richmond**	2000	Bobby Labonte*
1959	Jim Reed	1973	Cale Yarborough	1987	Dale Earnhardt*	2001	Ward Burton
1960	Buck Baker	1974	Cale Yarborough	1988	**Bill Elliott**	2002	Jeff Gordon
1961	Nelson Stacy	1975	Bobby Allison	1989	Dale Earnhardt	2003	Terry Labonte
1962	Larry Frank	1976	**David Pearson**	1990	**Dale Earnhardt**	2004	Jimmie Johnson
1963	Fireball Roberts	1977	David Pearson	1991	Harry Gant		* rain-shortened.

NASCAR Circuit (Cont.)
Nextel Cup Series Champions

Originally the Grand National Championship, 1949-70, then the Winston Cup Series Championship, 1971-2003, and based on official NASCAR records. Drivers listed since 2004 are winners of the Chase for the Nextel Cup, NASCAR's first playoff series run over the final ten races of the season. Note that earnings totals include bonus awards.

Multiple winners: (drivers) Dale Earnhardt and Richard Petty (7); Jeff Gordon (4); David Pearson, Lee Petty, Darrell Waltrip and Cale Yarborough (3); Buck Baker, Tim Flock, Ned Jarrett, Terry Labonte, Tony Stewart, Herb Thomas and Joe Weatherly (2).

Multiple winners: (cars) Chevrolet (24); Ford (7); Plymouth (5); Dodge, Oldsmobile and Pontiac (4); Buick and Hudson (3); and Chrysler (2).

Year	Car #	Driver	Car	Owner	Sts	Wins	Poles	Earnings
1949	22	Red Byron	Oldsmobile	Raymond Parks	5	2	1	$5,800
1950	60	Bill Rexford	Oldsmobile	Julian Buesink	17	1	0	6,175
1951	92	Herb Thomas	Hudson	Herb Thomas	34	7	4	18,200
1952	91	Tim Flock	Hudson	Ted Chester	33	8	4	20,210
1953	92	Herb Thomas	Hudson	Herb Thomas	37	11	10	27,300
1954	42	Lee Petty	Chrysler	Herb Thomas	34	7	3	26,706
1955	300	Tim Flock	Chrysler	Carl Kiekhaefer	38	18	19	33,750
1956	300B	Buck Baker	Chevrolet	Carl Kiekhaefer	48	14	12	29,790
1957	87	Buck Baker	Chevrolet	Buck Baker	40	10	5	24,712
1958	42	Lee Petty	Oldsmobile	Petty Enterprises	49	7	4	20,600
1959	42	Lee Petty	Plymouth	Petty Enterprises	42	10	2	45,570
1960	4	Rex White	Chevrolet	White-Clements	40	6	3	45,260
1961	11	Ned Jarrett	Chevrolet	W.G. Holloway Jr.	46	1	4	27,285
1962	8	Joe Weatherly	Pontiac	Bud Moore	52	9	6	56,110
1963	8	Joe Weatherly	Mercury	Wood Brothers	53	3	6	58,110
1964	43	Richard Petty	Plymouth	Petty Enterprises	61	9	8	98,810
1965	11	Ned Jarrett	Ford	Bondy Long	54	13	9	77,960
1966	6	David Pearson	Dodge	Cotton Owens	42	14	7	59,205
1967	43	Richard Petty	Plymouth	Petty Enterprises	48	27	18	130,275
1968	17	David Pearson	Ford	Holman-Moody	48	16	12	118,842
1969	17	David Pearson	Ford	Holman-Moody	51	11	14	183,700
1970	71	Bobby Isaac	Dodge	Nord Krauskopf	47	11	13	121,470
1971	43	Richard Petty	Plymouth	Petty Enterprises	46	21	9	309,225
1972	43	Richard Petty	Plymouth	Petty Enterprises	31	8	3	227,015
1973	72	Benny Parsons	Chevrolet	L.G. DeWitt	28	1	0	114,345
1974	43	Richard Petty	Dodge	Petty Enterprises	30	10	7	299,175
1975	43	Richard Petty	Dodge	Petty Enterprises	30	13	3	378,865
1976	11	Cale Yarborough	Chevrolet	Junior Johnson	30	9	2	387,173
1977	11	Cale Yarborough	Chevrolet	Junior Johnson	30	9	3	477,499
1978	11	Cale Yarborough	Oldsmobile	Junior Johnson	30	10	8	530,751
1979	43	Richard Petty	Chevrolet	Petty Enterprises	31	5	1	531,292
1980	2	Dale Earnhardt	Chevrolet	Rod Osterlund	31	5	0	588,926
1981	11	Darrell Waltrip	Buick	Junior Johnson	31	12	11	693,342
1982	11	Darrell Waltrip	Buick	Junior Johnson	30	12	7	873,118
1983	22	Bobby Allison	Buick	Bill Gardner	30	6	0	828,355
1984	44	Terry Labonte	Chevrolet	Billy Hagan	30	2	2	713,010
1985	11	Darrell Waltrip	Chevrolet	Junior Johnson	28	3	4	1,318,735
1986	3	Dale Earnhardt	Chevrolet	Richard Childress	29	5	1	1,783,880
1987	3	Dale Earnhardt	Chevrolet	Richard Childress	29	11	1	2,099,243
1988	9	Bill Elliott	Ford	Harry Meling	29	6	6	1,574,639
1989	27	Rusty Wallace	Pontiac	Raymond Beadle	29	6	4	2,247,950
1990	3	Dale Earnhardt	Chevrolet	Richard Childress	29	9	4	3,083,056
1991	3	Dale Earnhardt	Chevrolet	Richard Childress	29	4	0	2,396,685
1992	7	Alan Kulwicki	Ford	Alan Kulwicki	29	2	6	2,322,561
1993	3	Dale Earnhardt	Chevrolet	Richard Childress	30	6	2	3,353,789
1994	3	Dale Earnhardt	Chevrolet	Richard Childress	31	4	2	3,400,733
1995	24	Jeff Gordon	Chevrolet	Rick Hendrick	31	7	8	4,347,343
1996	5	Terry Labonte	Chevrolet	Rick Hendrick	31	2	4	4,030,648
1997	24	Jeff Gordon	Chevrolet	Rick Hendrick	32	10	1	6,375,658
1998	24	Jeff Gordon	Chevrolet	Rick Hendrick	33	13	7	9,306,584
1999	88	Dale Jarrett	Ford	Robert Yates	34	4	0	6,649,596
2000	18	Bobby Labonte	Pontiac	Joe Gibbs	34	4	2	7,361,387
2001	24	Jeff Gordon	Chevrolet	Rick Hendrick	36	6	6	10,879,757
2002	20	Tony Stewart	Pontiac	Joe Gibbs	36	3	2	9,163,761
2003	17	Matt Kenseth	Ford	Mark Martin	36	1	0	9,422,764
2004	97	Kurt Busch	Ford	Roush Racing	36	3	1	9,661,513
2005	20	Tony Stewart	Chevrolet	Joe Gibbs	36	5	3	13,578,168
2006	48	Jimmie Johnson	Chevrolet	Rick Hendrick	36	5	1	15,952,125

Nextel Cup Rookie of the Year

Sponsored by Raybestos, the official brake of NASCAR, and presented to rookie driver who accumulates the most Nextel Cup Series Raybestos Rookie of the Year points based on their best 17 finishes.

Year		Year		Year		Year	
1957	Ken Rush	1970	Bill Dennis	1983	Sterling Marlin	1996	Johnny Benson
1958	Shorty Rollins	1971	Walter Ballard	1984	Rusty Wallace	1997	Mike Skinner
1959	Richard Petty	1972	Larry Smith	1985	Ken Schrader	1998	Kenny Irwin
1960	David Pearson	1973	Lennie Pond	1986	Alan Kulwicki	1999	Tony Stewart
1961	Woodie Wilson	1974	Earl Ross	1987	Davey Allison	2000	Matt Kenseth
1962	Tom Cox	1975	Bruce Hill	1988	Ken Bouchard	2001	Kevin Harvick
1963	Billy Wade	1976	Skip Manning	1989	Dick Trickle	2002	Ryan Newman
1964	Doug Cooper	1977	Ricky Rudd	1990	Rob Moroso	2003	Jamie McMurray
1965	Sam McQuagg	1978	Ronnie Thomas	1991	Bobby Hamilton	2004	Kasey Kahne
1966	James Hylton	1979	Dale Earnhardt	1992	Jimmy Hensley	2005	Kyle Busch
1967	Donnie Allison	1980	Jody Ridley	1993	Jeff Gordon	2006	Denny Hamlin
1968	Pete Hamilton	1981	Ron Bouchard	1994	Jeff Burton		
1969	Dick Brooks	1982	Geoff Bodine	1995	Ricky Craven		

Manufacturers' Championship

Awarded to the most successful car manufacturer in the Nextel Cup Series since 1949. Manufacturers whose cars finish in the top six in each race are awarded points based on the following format: 9-6-4-3-2-1. **Note:** By early October, Chevrolet had already clinched the 2007 Manufacturers' Championship.

Multiple winners: Chevrolet (30); Ford (16); Oldsmobile (4); Dodge and Hudson (3); Buick and Pontiac (2).

Year		Year		Year		Year		Year	
1949	Oldsmobile	1961	Chevrolet	1973	Chevrolet	1985	Chevrolet	1996	Chevrolet
1950	Oldsmobile	1962	Pontiac	1974	Chevrolet	1986	Chevrolet	1997	Ford
1951	Oldsmobile	1963	Ford	1975	Dodge	1987	Chevrolet	1998	Chevrolet
1952	Hudson	1964	Ford	1976	Chevrolet	1988	Pontiac	1999	Ford
1953	Hudson	1965	Ford	1977	Chevrolet	1989	Chevrolet	2000	Ford
1954	Hudson	1966	Ford	1978	Chevrolet	1990	Chevrolet	2001	Chevrolet
1955	Oldsmobile	1967	Ford	1979	Chevrolet		& Ford	2002	Ford
1956	Ford	1968	Ford	1980	Chevrolet	1991	Chevrolet	2003	Chevrolet
1957	Ford	1969	Ford	1981	Buick	1992	Ford	2004	Chevrolet
1958	Chevrolet	1970	Dodge	1982	Buick	1993	Chevrolet	2005	Chevrolet
1959	Chevrolet	1971	Dodge	1983	Chevrolet	1994	Ford	2006	Chevrolet
1960	Chevrolet	1972	Chevrolet	1984	Chevrolet	1995	Chevrolet	2007	Chevrolet

Champion Crew Chiefs

Crew chiefs of Nextel Cup Series champions since 1949.

Multiple winners: Dale Inman (8); Kirk Shelmerdine (4); Ray Evernham and Lee Petty (3); Tim Brewer, Travis Carter, Jake Elder, Jeff Hammond, Bud Moore, Herb Nab, Andy Petree, Smokey Yunick and Greg Zipadelli (2).

Year		Year		Year		Year	
1949	Red Vogt	1964	Dale Inman	1979	Dale Inman	1994	Andy Petree
1950	Julian Buesink	1965	John Ervin	1980	Doug Richert	1995	Ray Evernham
1951	Smokey Yunick	1966	Cotton Owens	1981	Tim Brewer	1996	Gary DeHart
1952	B.B. Blackburn	1967	Dale Inman	1982	Jeff Hammond	1997	Ray Evernham
1953	Smokey Yunick	1968	Jake Elder	1983	Gary Nelson	1998	Ray Evernham
1954	Lee Petty	1969	Jake Elder	1984	Dale Inman	1999	Todd Parrott
1955	Carl Kiekhafer	1970	Harry Hyde	1985	Jeff Hammond	2000	Jimmy Makar
1956	Carl Kiekhafer	1971	Dale Inman	1986	Kirk Shelmerdine	2001	Robbie Loomis
1957	Bud Moore	1972	Dale Inman	1987	Kirk Shelmerdine	2002	Greg Zipadelli
1958	Lee Petty	1973	Travis Carter	1988	Ernie Elliott	2003	Robbie Reiser
1959	Lee Petty	1974	Dale Inman	1989	Barry Dodson	2004	Jimmy Fennig
1960	Louis Clements	1975	Dale Inman	1990	Kirk Shelmerdine	2005	Greg Zipadelli
1961	Bud Allman	1976	Herb Nab	1991	Kirk Shelmerdine	2006	Chad Knaus
1962	Bud Moore	1977	Herb Nab	1992	Paul Andrews		
1963	Bud Moore	1978	T Brewer/T. Carter	1993	Andy Petree		

Nextel All-Star Challenge

The NASCAR Nextel All-Star Challenge is a non-points event held each May at Lowe's Motor Speedway in Concord, N.C. It is open to race winners from the previous and current season, the winner of the Nextel Open qualifying race, former All-Star winners, former Nextel Cup champions and one driver chosen by fan vote. The Challenge winner earns $1 million.

Multiple winners: Dale Earnhardt and Jeff Gordon (3); Davey Allison, Jimmie Johnson, Terry Labonte and Mark Martin (2).

Year		Year		Year		Year	
1985	Darrell Waltrip	1991	Davey Allison	1997	Jeff Gordon	2003	Jimmie Johnson
1986	Bill Elliott	1992	Davey Allison	1998	Mark Martin	2004	Matt Kenseth
1987	Dale Earnhardt	1993	Dale Earnhardt	1999	Terry Labonte	2005	Mark Martin
1988	Terry Labonte	1994	Geoff Bodine	2000	Dale Earnhardt Jr.	2006	Jimmie Johnson
1989	Rusty Wallace	1995	Jeff Gordon	2001	Jeff Gordon	2007	Kevin Harvick
1990	Dale Earnhardt	1996	Michael Waltrip	2002	Ryan Newman		

NASCAR Circuit (Cont.)

Nextel Cup All-Time Leaders

NASCAR Nextel Cup's all-time Top 20 drivers in victories, pole positions and earnings based on records through Oct. 21, 2007. Drivers active in 2007 are in **bold** type.

Career

Victories

1	Richard Petty	200
2	David Pearson	105
3	Bobby Allison	84
	Darrell Waltrip	84
5	Cale Yarborough	83
6	**Jeff Gordon**	81
7	Dale Earnhardt	76
8	Lee Petty	55
	Rusty Wallace	55
10	Ned Jarrett	50
	Junior Johnson	50
12	Herb Thomas	48
13	Buck Baker	46
14	**Bill Elliott**	44
15	Tim Flock	40
16	Bobby Isaac	37
17	**Mark Martin**	35
18	Fireball Roberts	32
	Dale Jarrett	32
	Tony Stewart	32

Pole Positions

1	Richard Petty	126
2	David Pearson	113
3	Cale Yarborough	70
4	**Jeff Gordon**	63
5	Darrell Waltrip	59
6	Bobby Allison	57
7	**Bill Elliott**	55
8	Bobby Isaac	51
9	Junior Johnson	47
10	Buck Baker	44
11	**Ryan Newman**	42
12	**Mark Martin**	41
13	Buddy Baker	40
14	Tim Flock	39
	Herb Thomas	39
16	Geoff Bodine	37
17	**Rusty Wallace**	36
18	Ned Jarrett	35
	Fireball Roberts	35
	Rex White	35

Earnings

1	**Jeff Gordon**	$88,904,806
2	**Mark Martin**	63,249,045
3	**Tony Stewart**	63,051,898
4	**Dale Jarrett**	58,973,253
5	**Bobby Labonte**	54,900,340
6	**Jeff Burton**	52,327,566
7	**Jimmie Johnson**	50,667,346
8	**Rusty Wallace**	49,741,326
9	**Matt Kenseth**	48,511,064
10	**Dale Earnhardt Jr.**	47,691,315
11	**Sterling Marlin**	42,227,254
12	Dale Earnhardt	41,742,384
13	**Kurt Busch**	41,120,429
14	**Terry Labonte**	40,867,147
15	Ricky Rudd	40,696,133
16	**Kevin Harvick**	40,505,858
17	**Bill Elliott**	40,453,527
18	**Michael Waltrip**	36,535,942
19	**Ryan Newman**	36,293,359
20	**Ken Schrader**	33,942,203

Single Season (through 2006)

Victories

1	Richard Petty, '67	27
2	Richard Petty, '71	21
3	Tim Flock, '55	18
	Richard Petty, '70	18
5	Bobby Isaac, '69	17
6	David Pearson, '68	16
	Richard Petty, '68	16
8	Ned Jarrett, '64	15
	David Pearson, '66	15
10	Buck Baker, '56	14
	Richard Petty, '63	14

Modern Era (since 1972)

1	Richard Petty, '75	13
	Jeff Gordon, '98	13
3	Darrell Waltrip, '81	12
	Darrell Waltrip, '82	12
5	David Pearson, '73	11
	Bill Elliott, '85	11
	Dale Earnhardt, '87	11
8	Eight tied with 10 wins each, including twice by Cale Yarborough and Jeff Gordon.	

Pole Positions

1	Bobby Isaac, '69	20
2	Richard Petty, '67	19
3	Tim Flock, '55	18
4	Richard Petty, '66	16
5	Cale Yarborough, '80	14
6	David Pearson, '69	13
	Bobby Isaac, '70	13
8	Fonty Flock, '51	12
	David Pearson, '64	12
	David Pearson, '68	12
	Richard Petty, '68	12

Modern Era (since 1972)

1	Cale Yarborough, '80	14
2	Bobby Allison, '72	11
	David Pearson, '74	11
	Darrell Waltrip, '81	11
	Bill Elliott, 85	11
	Ryan Newman, '03	11
7	Geoff Bodine, '86	9
	Rusty Wallace, '00	9
	Ryan Newman, '04	9
10	Eight tied with 8 poles each.	

Earnings

1	Jimmie Johnson, '06	$15,952,125
2	Tony Stewart, '05	13,578,168
3	Jeff Gordon, '01	10,879,757
4	Kurt Busch, '04	9,677,543
5	Matt Kenseth, '06	9,544,966
6	Matt Kenseth, '03	9,422,764
7	Jeff Gordon, '98	9,306,584
8	Tony Stewart, '02	9,163,761
9	D. Earnhardt Jr., '04	8,913,510
10	Tony Stewart '06	8,749,169
11	Jeff Gordon, '04	8,439,382
12	Greg Biffle, '05	8,354,052
13	Jimmie Johnson, '05	8,336,712
14	Jimmie Johnson, '04	8,275,721
15	Kevin Harvick, '06	8,231,406
16	Jeff Gordon, '05	7,930,830
17	Tony Stewart, '04	7,830,807
18	Kasey Kahne, '06	7,766,378
19	Jimmie Johnson, '03	7,745,530
20	Mark Martin, '05	7,731,468

Richard Petty speeds through qualifying at the 1968 Daytona 500. Petty won 16 races in 1968, tied for 6th on the all-time single-season list and 11 behind his record of 27 set in 1967.

AP/Wide World Photos

Busch Series Champions

The Busch Series was founded in 1982 as the Budweiser Late Model Sportsman Series, and has since grown into the No. 2 motorsports series in the United States. The series emerged from NASCAR's old Sportsman Division, which was formed in 1950 as NASCAR's short track race division. The series switched sponsorship to the Busch brand in 1984 and became the Busch Grand National Series. Grand National was dumped from the series' title in 2003. Nationwide Insurance will take over sponsorship in 2008, and the series will be known as the NASCAR Nationwide Series. Note that earnings totals include bonus awards.

Multiple winners: (drivers) Sam Ard, Dale Earnhardt Jr., Kevin Harvick, Jack Ingram, Randy LaJoie, Larry Pearson and Martin Truex Jr. (2). **Multiple winners:** (cars) Chevrolet (15); Oldsmobile (5); Pontiac (4).

Year	Car #	Driver	Car	Owner	Sts	Wins	Poles	Earnings
1982	11	Jack Ingram	Olds/Pontiac	Aline Ingram	29	7	1	$122,100
1983	00	Sam Ard	Oldsmobile	Howard Thomas	35	10	10	192,362
1984	00	Sam Ard	Oldsmobile	Howard Thomas	28	8	7	217,531
1985	11	Jack Ingram	Pontiac	Aline Ingram	27	5	2	164,710
1986	21	Larry Pearson	Pontiac	David Pearson	31	1	1	184,344
1987	21	Larry Pearson	Chevrolet	David Pearson	27	6	3	256,372
1988	99	Tommy Ellis	Buick	John Jackson	30	3	5	200,003
1989	25	Rob Moroso	Oldsmobile	Dick Moroso	29	4	6	346,739
1990	63	Chuck Brown	Pontiac	Hubert Hensley	31	6	4	323,399
1991	44	Bobby Labonte	Oldsmobile	Bobby Labonte	31	2	2	246,368
1992	87	Joe Nemechek	Chevrolet	Joe Nemechek	31	2	1	285,008
1993	31	Steve Grissom	Chevrolet	Wayne Grissom	28	2	0	336,432
1994	44	David Green	Chevrolet	Bobby Labonte	28	1	9	391,670
1995	74	Johnny Benson	Chevrolet	William Baumgardner	26	2	0	469,129
1996	74	Randy LaJoie	Chevrolet	William Baumgardner	26	5	2	532,823
1997	74	Randy LaJoie	Chevrolet	William Baumgardner	30	5	2	1,105,201
1998	3	Dale Earnhardt Jr.	Chevrolet	Dale Earnhardt	31	5	3	1,332,701
1999	3	Dale Earnhardt Jr.	Chevrolet	Dale Earnhardt	32	6	3	1,680,549
2000	10	Jeff Green	Chevrolet	Greg Pollex	32	6	7	1,929,937
2001	2	Kevin Harvick	Chevrolet	Richard Childress	33	5	5	1,833,570
2002	60	Greg Biffle	Ford	Jack Roush	34	4	5	2,337,255
2003	5	Brian Vickers	Chevrolet	Ricky Hendrick	34	3	1	1,987,255
2004	8	Martin Truex Jr.	Chevrolet	T. Earnhardt/D. Earnhardt Jr.	34	6	7	2,537,171
2005	8	Martin Truex Jr.	Chevrolet	T. Earnhardt/D. Earnhardt Jr.	35	6	3	3,143,692
2006	21	Kevin Harvick	Chevrolet	Richard Childress	35	9	1	1,345,380

Busch Series Rookie of the Year

Sponsored by Raybestos, the official brake of NASCAR, and presented to rookie driver who accumulates the most Busch Series Raybestos Rookie of the Year points based on their best 16 finishes.

Year		Year		Year		Year	
1989	Kenny Wallace	1994	Johnny Benson	1999	Tony Raines	2004	Kyle Busch
1990	Joe Nemechek	1995	Jeff Fuller	2000	Kevin Harvick	2005	Carl Edwards
1991	Jeff Gordon	1996	Glenn Allen	2001	Greg Biffle	2006	Danny O'Quinn Jr.
1992	Ricky Craven	1997	Steve Park	2002	Scott Riggs		
1993	Hermie Sadler	1998	Andy Santerre	2003	David Stremme		

Manufacturers' Championship

Officially the Bill France Performance Cup and awarded each year to the most successful car manufacturer in the Busch Series. Manufacturers whose cars finish in the top four in each race are awarded points based on the following format: 9-6-4-3.

Multiple winners: Chevrolet (13); Ford (2).

Year		Year		Year		Year		Year	
1991	Oldsmobile	1995	Ford	1999	Chevrolet	2002	Ford	2005	Chevrolet
1992	Chevrolet	1996	Chevrolet	2000	Chevrolet	2003	Chevrolet	2006	Chevrolet
1993	Chevrolet	1997	Chevrolet	2001	Chevrolet	2004	Chevrolet		
1994	Chevrolet	1998	Chevrolet						

Busch Series All-Time Leaders

NASCAR Busch Series all-time Top 10 drivers in victories, pole positions and earnings based on records through Oct. 12, 2007.

Victories

1	Mark Martin	47
2	Jack Ingram	31
	Kevin Harvick	31
4	Jeff Burton	26
5	Tommy Houston	24
6	Matt Kenseth	23
7	Sam Ard	22
	Dale Earnhardt Jr.	22
	Tommy Ellis	22
10	Dale Earnhardt	21
	Harry Gant	21

Pole Positions

1	Mark Martin	30
2	Tommy Ellis	28
3	Sam Ard	24
4	Jeff Green	23
5	David Green	22
6	Tommy Houston	18
	Joe Nemechek	18
8	Brett Bodine	16
	Kevin Harvick	16
10	Jimmy Hensley	15
	Michael Waltrip	15

Earnings

1	Jason Keller	$11,198,290
2	Kevin Harvick	9,596,593
3	David Green	8,954,715
4	Greg Biffle	8,773,972
5	Randy LaJoie	7,702,143
6	Jeff Green	6,915,833
7	Matt Kenseth	6,860,315
8	Kenny Wallace	6,758,071
9	Mike McLaughlin	6,257,873
10	Martin Truex Jr.	6,169,757

NASCAR Circuit (Cont.)
Craftsman Truck Series Champions

The NASCAR Craftsman Truck Series features modified pickup trucks. The idea for the Series originated in 1993, when a group of off-road racers created a prototype for a NASCAR-style pickup truck. The trucks proved extremely popular and were first displayed during the 1994 Daytona 500. NASCAR created the series, first called the "SuperTruck Series," in 1995. The series became known as the Craftsman Truck Series in 1996. Note that earnings totals include bonus awards.

Multiple winners: (drivers) Jack Sprague (3); Ron Hornaday Jr. (2).

Multiple winners: (cars) Chevrolet (8); Dodge (2).

Year	Truck #	Driver	Car	Owner	Sts	Wins	Poles	Earnings
1995	3	**Mike Skinner**	Chevrolet	Richard Childress	20	8	10	$428,096
1996	16	**Ron Hornaday Jr.**	Chevrolet	Teresa Earnhardt	24	4	2	625,634
1997	24	**Jack Sprague**	Chevrolet	Rick Hendrick	26	3	5	880,835
1998	16	**Ron Hornaday Jr.**	Chevrolet	Teresa Earnhardt	27	6	2	915,407
1999	24	**Jack Sprague**	Chevrolet	Rick Hendrick	25	3	1	834,016
2000	50	**Greg Biffle**	Ford	Jack Roush	24	5	4	1,002,510
2001	24	**Jack Sprague**	Chevrolet	Rick Hendrick	24	4	7	967,493
2002	16	**Mike Bliss**	Chevrolet	Steve Coulter	22	5	4	894,388
2003	16	**Travis Kvapil**	Chevrolet	Steve Coulter	25	1	0	872,395
2004	4	**Bobby Hamilton**	Dodge	Debbie Hamilton	25	4	0	973,428
2005	1	**Ted Musgrave**	Dodge	Jim Smith	25	1	1	880,553
2006	30	**Todd Bodine**	Toyota	Stephen Germain	25	3	1	1,046,680

Craftsman Truck Series Rookie of the Year

Sponsored by Raybestos, the official brake of NASCAR, and presented to rookie driver who accumulates the most Craftsman Truck Series Raybestos Rookie of the Year points based on their best 14 finishes.

Year		Year		Year		Year	
1996	Bryan Reffner	1999	Mike Stefanik	2002	Brendan Gaughan	2005	Todd Kluever
1997	Kenny Irwin	2000	Kurt Busch	2003	Carl Edwards	2006	Erik Darnell
1998	Greg Biffle	2001	Travis Kvapil	2004	David Reutimann		

Manufacturers' Championship

Awarded each year to the most successful car manufacturer in the Craftsman Truck Series. Manufacturers whose cars finish in the top four in each race are awarded points based on the following format: 9-6-4-3.

Multiple winners: Chevrolet (6); Dodge (3); Ford (2).

Year		Year		Year		Year	
1995	Chevrolet	1998	Chevrolet	2001	Dodge	2004	Dodge
1996	Chevrolet	1999	Ford	2002	Chevrolet	2005	Chevrolet
1997	Chevrolet	2000	Ford	2003	Dodge	2006	Toyota

Craftsman Truck Series All-Time Leaders

NASCAR Craftsman Truck Series all-time Top 10 drivers in victories, pole positions and earnings based on records through Oct. 20, 2007.

Victories

1	Ron Hornaday Jr.	33
2	Jack Sprague	28
3	Mike Skinner	24
4	Dennis Setzer	17
5	Greg Biffle	16
	Ted Musgrave	16
7	Joe Ruttman	13
	Mike Bliss	13
9	Todd Bodine	12
10	Bobby Hamilton	10

Pole Positions

1	Mike Skinner	42
2	Jack Sprague	31
3	Mike Bliss	18
4	Joe Ruttman	17
5	Ron Hornaday Jr.	14
6	Greg Biffle	12
	Ted Musgrave	12
8	Jason Leffler	10
9	Stacy Compton	9
10	Terry Cook	8

Earnings

1	Jack Sprague	$6,709,744
2	Dennis Setzer	4,954,894
3	Ted Musgrave	4,642,517
4	Ron Hornaday Jr.	4,738,547
5	Rick Crawford	4,287,782
6	Terry Cook	3,579,744
7	Mike Bliss	3,335,316
8	Mike Skinner	3,301,907
9	Joe Ruttman	3,172,902
10	David Starr	2,900,809

Auto Racing Royalty

There must be something about auto racing that gets into a family's bloodstream. Generations of racers follow in each other's footsteps, working their way up the rungs of the ladder, starting in go-karts and graduating to the big time circuits. Is the need for speed in the genes? It certainly looks like it when you check out these fast-driving families, considered auto racing royalty in NASCAR and open-wheel racing.

The Allisons

Bobby (b. 12/3/1937): Collected 84 wins in 718 starts; won only Winston Cup title in 1983 at age 45; inducted into IMHOF in 1993; raced 1961-1988.

Donnie, Bobby's brother (b. 9/7/1939): Won 10 Grand National/Winston Cup races in 239 starts; raced from 1966 to 1988 on part-time basis.

Davey, Bobby's son (b. 2/25/1961, d. 7/13/1993): Won 19 Winston Cup races; killed in a 1993 helicopter accident at Talladega Superspeedway at age 32; inducted into IMHOF in 1998; raced from 1985-93.

Clifford, Bobby's son (b. 10/20/1964, d. 8/13/1992): Ran Busch Series from 1990-1992; killed in practice for a Busch Series race at Michigan in 1992 at age 27.

The Andrettis

Mario (b. 2/28/1940): Accumulated 111 career wins racing from 1961-2000; won four Champ Car titles, the 1978 Formula 1 title and the 1979 IROC crown; A.P. named him "Driver of the Century" along with A.J. Foyt.

Aldo, Mario's twin brother (b. 2/28/1940): After his second severe car crash, he retired from racing in 1969.

Michael, Mario's son (b. 10/5/1962): Raced from 1980-2003, won first Champ Car race in 1986 and joined his father's team in 1989; won only Champ Car crown in 1991; totaled 42 Champ Car wins.

Jeff, Mario's son (b. 4/14/1964): Joined father and brother in Champ Car in 1990; was 1991 Indy 500 and CART Rookie of the Year; raced from 1990-2000.

John, Aldo's son (b. 3/12/1963): Started racing in Champ Car in 1987, transitioned into NASCAR in 90's; won two Winston Cup races; currently racing in Nextel Cup Series.

Marco, Michael's son (b. 3/13/1987) Third-generation racer debuted as rookie in Indy in 2006; surprised watchers with second place finish at Indy 500; raced Indy 500 with father, who came out of retirement to join son.

The Earnhardts

Ralph (b. 2/23/1928, d. 9/26/1973): "Mr. Consistency" in Grand National; was inducted into IMHOF in 1997; raced from 1956-1964.

Dale, Ralph's son (b. 4/29/1951, d. 2/18/2001): "The Intimidator" won ROY in 1979, seven Winston Cup titles and 76 races; more than $27 million; career was cut short by fatal crash at the 2001 Daytona 500; raced from 1975-2001.

Dale Jr., Dale's son (b. 10/10/1974): "Little E" had won 17 races and won more than $47 million midway through his seventh full season. First full season in Nextel Cup was 2000.

The Jarretts

Ned (b. 10/12/1932): won two Grand National titles; won 50 races in 352 starts; nicknamed "Gentleman Ned"; inducted into IMHOF in 1991; raced from 1953-1966.

Dale, Ned's son (b. 11/26/1956): Started full-time in Winston Cup in 1987; won title in 1999; has 32 wins; with his Cup title, the Jarretts became the second father/son duo after the Pettys to grab titles; began racing in 1984.

The Labontes

Terry (b. 11/16/1956): First NASCAR start came in 1978; won Winston Cup crowns in 1984, 1996; broke Richard Petty's streak of 513 straight starts in 1996 (his eventual record of 655 consecutive starts was broken by Ricky Rudd in 2002).

Bobby, Terry's brother (b. 5/8/1964): Won the 2000 Winston Cup title; win gave the brothers the honor of being the first sibling tandem to win the title. He is the only driver to win both a Busch Series and Cup Series championship; began racing in 1991.

The Pettys

Lee (b. 3/14/1914, d. 4/5/2000): Won 54 strictly Stock/Grand National races, three titles; photo-finish winner of the first Daytona 500 in 1959; inducted into IMHOF in 1990; raced from 1953-1966.

Richard, Lee's son (b. 7/2/1937): "The King" was a seven-time Grand National/Winston Cup champ; 200 wins; seven-time winner of the Daytona 500; won single-season record 27 races in 1967; inducted into IMHOF in 1997; raced from 1958-1992.

Kyle, Richard's son (b. 6/2/1960): More than $24M in career earnings; more than 170 top-10 finishes; began racing in 1979.

Adam, Kyle's son (b. 7/10/1980, d. 5/12/2000): Killed at New Hampshire International Speedway in preparation for only his second Winston Cup start.

The Unsers

The Unser family tree continues to sprout branches of racing addicts. Eight Unsers (Jerry Jr., Louie, Bobby Sr., Al Sr., Johnny, Bobby Jr., Robby and Al Jr.) have spent time in the pits, while third-generation motorsports converts Jason Tanner and Al Unser III are trying their hand at advancing the Unser legacy.

Bobby (b. 2/20/1934): Three-time winner of the Indy 500 (1968, 1975, 1981); 1981 win was controversial, as Mario Andretti was declared winner because Unser passed cars during yellow flag, but Unser appealed and victory was restored; 35 CART wins; raced from 1949-1982.

Al Sr., Bobby's brother (b. 5/29/1939) "Big Al" won Indy 500 four times (1970, 1971, 1978, 1987); won 1987 Indy 500 at 47 years old, the oldest winner in history; posted 39 Indy wins; raced from 1957-1994.

Al Jr., Al's son (b. 4/19/1962): "Little Al" won the Indy 500 in 1992 and 1994; lost CART points title to his father by a single point in 1985; raced from 1982 to 2004.

The Waltrips

Darrell (b. 2/5/1947): Three-time Winston Cup champ, won 1989 Daytona 500; accumulated 84 Cup victories and 59 poles; inducted into IMHOF in 2005; raced 1972-2000.

Michael, Darrell's brother (b. 4/30/1963): two-time Daytona 500 winner; has earned more than $36 million; began racing in 1985.

INDY RACING LEAGUE CIRCUIT

Indianapolis 500

Held every Memorial Day weekend; 200 laps around a 2.5-mile oval at Indianapolis Motor Speedway. First race was held in 1911. The Indy Racing League began in 1996 and made the Indianapolis 500 its cornerstone event. Winning drivers are listed with starting positions. Winners who started from pole position are in **bold** type.

Multiple wins: A.J. Foyt, Rick Mears and Al Unser (4); Louis Meyer, Mauri Rose, Johnny Rutherford, Wilbur Shaw and Bobby Unser (3); Helio Castroneves, Emerson Fittipaldi, Gordon Johncock, Arie Luyendyk, Tommy Milton, Al Unser Jr., Bill Vukovich and Rodger Ward (2).

Multiple poles: Rick Mears (6); A.J. Foyt and Rex Mays (4); Mario Andretti, Arie Luyendyk, Johnny Rutherford and Tom Sneva (3); Scott Brayton, Helio Castroneves, Bill Cummings, Ralph DePalma, Leon Duray, Parnelli Jones, Jimmy Murphy, Duke Nalon, Eddie Sachs and Bobby Unser (2).

Year	Winner (Pos.)	Car	MPH	Pole Sitter	MPH
1911	Ray Harroun (28)	Marmon Wasp	74.602	Lewis Strang	–
1912	Joe Dawson (7)	National	78.719	Gil Anderson	–
1913	Jules Goux (7)	Peugeot	75.933	Caleb Bragg	–
1914	Rene Thomas (15)	Delage	82.474	Jean Chassagne	–
1915	Ralph DePalma (2)	Mercedes	89.840	Howard Wilcox	98.90
1916-a	Dario Resta (4)	Peugeot	84.001	John Aitken	96.69
1917-18	Not held	World War I			
1919	Howdy Wilcox (2)	Peugeot	88.050	Rene Thomas	104.78
1920	Gaston Chevrolet (6)	Monroe	88.618	Ralph DePalma	99.15
1921	Tommy Milton (20)	Frontenac	89.621	Ralph DePalma	100.75
1922	**Jimmy Murphy** (1)	Murphy Special	94.484	Jimmy Murphy	100.50
1923	**Tommy Milton** (1)	H.C.S. Special	90.954	Tommy Milton	108.17
1924	L.L. Corum & Joe Boyer (21)	Duesenberg Special	98.234	Jimmy Murphy	108.037
1925	Peter DePaolo (2)	Duesenberg Special	101.127	Leon Duray	113.196
1926-b	Frank Lockhart (20)	Miller Special	95.904	Earl Cooper	111.735
1927	George Souders (22)	Duesenberg	97.545	Frank Lockhart	120.100
1928	Louie Meyer (13)	Miller Special	99.482	Leon Duray	122.391
1929	Ray Keech (6)	Simplex Piston Ring Special	97.585	Cliff Woodbury	120.599
1930	**Billy Arnold** (1)	Miller-Hartz Special	100.448	Billy Arnold	113.268
1931	Louis Schneider (13)	Bowes Seal Fast Special	96.629	Russ Snowberger	112.796
1932	Fred Frame (27)	Miller-Hartz Special	104.144	Lou Moore	117.363
1933	Louie Meyer (6)	Tydol Special	104.162	Bill Cummings	118.530
1934	Bill Cummings (10)	Boyle Products Special	104.863	Kelly Petillo	119.329
1935	Kelly Petillo (22)	Gilmore Speedway Special	106.240	Rex Mays	120.736
1936	Louie Meyer (28)	Ring Free Special	109.069	Rex Mays	119.644
1937	Wilbur Shaw (2)	Shaw-Gilmore Special	113.580	Bill Cummings	123.343
1938	**Floyd Roberts** (1)	Burd Piston Ring Special	117.200	Floyd Roberts	125.681
1939	Wilbur Shaw (3)	Boyle Special	115.035	Jimmy Snyder	130.138
1940	Wilbur Shaw (2)	Boyle Special	114.277	Rex Mays	127.850
1941	Floyd Davis & Mauri Rose (17)	Noc-Out Hose Clamp Special	115.117	Mauri Rose	128.691
1942-45	Not held	World War II			
1946	George Robson (15)	Thorne Engineering Special	114.820	Cliff Bergere	126.471
1947	Mauri Rose (3)	Blue Crown Spark Plug Special	116.338	Ted Horn	126.564
1948	Mauri Rose (3)	Blue Crown Spark Plug Special	119.814	Rex Mays	130.577
1949	Bill Holland (4)	Blue Crown Spark Plug Special	121.327	Duke Nalon	132.939
1950-c	Johnnie Parsons (5)	Wynn's Friction Proofing	124.002	Walt Faulkner	134.343
1951	Lee Wallard (2)	Belanger Special	126.244	Duke Nalon	136.498
1952	Troy Ruttman (7)	Agajanian Special	128.922	Fred Agabashian	138.010
1953	**Bill Vukovich** (1)	Fuel Injection Special	128.740	Bill Vukovich	138.392
1954	Bill Vukovich (19)	Fuel Injection Special	130.840	Jack McGrath	141.033
1955	Bob Sweikert (14)	John Zink Special	128.213	Jerry Hoyt	140.045
1956	**Pat Flaherty** (1)	John Zink Special	128.490	Pat Flaherty	145.596
1957	Sam Hanks (13)	Belond Exhaust Special	135.601	Pat O'Connor	143.948
1958	Jimmy Bryan (7)	Belond AP Parts Special	133.791	Dick Rathmann	145.974
1959	Rodger Ward (6)	Leader Card 500 Roadster	135.857	Johnny Thomson	145.908
1960	Jim Rathmann (2)	Ken-Paul Special	138.767	Eddie Sachs	146.592
1961	A.J. Foyt (7)	Bowes Seal Fast Special	139.130	Eddie Sachs	147.481
1962	Rodger Ward (2)	Leader Card 500 Roadster	140.293	Parnelli Jones	150.370
1963	**Parnelli Jones** (1)	Agajanian-Willard Special	143.137	Parnelli Jones	151.153
1964	A.J. Foyt (5)	Sheraton-Thompson Special	147.350	Jim Clark	158.828
1965	Jim Clark (2)	Lotus Ford	150.686	A.J. Foyt	161.233
1966	Graham Hill (15)	American Red Ball Special	144.317	Mario Andretti	165.899
1967-d	A.J. Foyt (4)	Sheraton-Thompson Special	151.207	Mario Andretti	168.982
1968	Bobby Unser (3)	Rislone Special	152.882	Joe Leonard	171.559
1969	Mario Andretti (2)	STP Oil Treatment Special	156.867	A.J. Foyt	170.568
1970	**Al Unser** (1)	Johnny Lightning Special	155.749	Al Unser	170.221
1971	Al Unser (5)	Johnny Lightning Special	157.735	Peter Revson	178.696
1972	Mark Donohue (3)	Sunoco McLaren	162.962	Bobby Unser	195.940

Year	Winner (Pos.)	Car	MPH	Pole Sitter	MPH
1973-e	Gordon Johncock (11)	STP Double Oil Filters	159.036	Johnny Rutherford	198.413
1974	Johnny Rutherford (25)	McLaren	158.589	A.J. Foyt	191.632
1975-f	Bobby Unser (3)	Jorgensen Eagle	149.213	A.J. Foyt	193.976
1976-g	**Johnny Rutherford** (1)	Hy-Gain McLaren/Goodyear	148.725	Johnny Rutherford	188.957
1977	A.J. Foyt (4)	Gilmore Racing Team	161.331	Tom Sneva	198.884
1978	Al Unser (5)	FNCTC Chaparral Lola	161.363	Tom Sneva	202.156
1979	**Rick Mears** (1)	The Gould Charge	158.899	Rick Mears	193.736
1980	**Johnny Rutherford** (1)	Pennzoil Chaparral	142.862	Johnny Rutherford	192.256
1981-h	**Bobby Unser** (1)	Norton Spirit Penske PC-9B	139.084	Bobby Unser	200.546
1982	Gordon Johncock (5)	STP Oil Treatment	162.029	Rick Mears	207.004
1983	Tom Sneva (4)	Texaco Star	162.117	Teo Fabi	207.395
1984	Rick Mears (3)	Pennzoil Z-7	163.612	Tom Sneva	210.029
1985	Danny Sullivan (8)	Miller American Special	152.982	Pancho Carter	212.583
1986	Bobby Rahal (4)	Budweiser/Truesports/March	170.722	Rick Mears	216.828
1987	Al Unser (20)	Cummins Holset Turbo	162.175	Mario Andretti	215.390
1988	**Rick Mears** (1)	Pennzoil Z-7/Penske Chevy V-8	144.809	Rick Mears	219.198
1989	Emerson Fittipaldi (3)	Marlboro/Penske Chevy V-8	167.581	Rick Mears	223.885
1990	Arie Luyendyk (3)	Domino's Pizza Chevrolet	185.981*	Emerson Fittipaldi	225.301
1991	**Rick Mears** (1)	Marlboro Penske Chevy	176.457	Rick Mears	224.113
1992	Al Unser Jr. (12)	Valvoline Galmer '92	134.477	Roberto Guerrero	232.482
1993	Emerson Fittipaldi (9)	Marlboro Penske Chevy	157.207	Arie Luyendyk	223.967
1994	**Al Unser Jr.** (1)	Marlboro Penske Mercedes	160.872	Al Unser Jr.	228.011
1995	Jacques Villeneuve (5)	Player's Ltd. Reynard Ford	153.616	Scott Brayton	231.604
1996	Buddy Lazier (5)	Reynard Ford	147.956	Tony Stewart	233.100&
1997	**Arie Luyendyk** (1)	G-Force Olds Aurora	145.827	Arie Luyendyk	218.263
1998	Eddie Cheever Jr. (17)	Dallara Olds Aurora	145.155	Billy Boat	223.503
1999	Kenny Brack (8)	Dallara Olds Aurora	153.176	Arie Luyendyk	225.179
2000	Juan Montoya (2)	G-Force Olds Aurora	167.607	Greg Ray	223.471
2001	Helio Castroneves (11)	Dallara Olds Aurora	153.601	Scott Sharp	226.037
2002-i	Helio Castroneves (13)	Dallara Chevrolet	166.499	Bruno Junqueira	231.342
2003	Gil de Ferran (10)	G-Force Toyota	156.291	Helio Castroneves	231.725
2004-j	**Buddy Rice** (1)	G-Force Honda	138.518	Buddy Rice	222.024
2005	Dan Wheldon (16)	Dallara Honda	157.603	Tony Kanaan	227.566
2006	**Sam Hornish Jr.** (1)	Dallara Honda	157.085	Sam Hornish Jr.	228.985
2007-k	Dario Franchitti (3)	Dallara Honda	151.774	Helio Castroneves	225.817

*Track record for winning time.

& Scott Brayton won the pole position with an avg. mph of 233.718 but was killed in a practice run. Stewart was awarded pole position with the next fastest speed.

Notes: a—1916 race scheduled for 300 miles; **b**—rain shortened 1926 race to 400 miles; **c**—rain shortened 1950 race to 345 miles; **d**—1967 race postponed due to rain after 18 laps (May 30), resumed next day (May 31); **e**—rain shortened 1973 race to 332.5 miles; **f**—rain shortened 1975 race to 435 miles; **g**—rain shortened 1976 race to 255 miles; **h**—in 1981, runner-up Mario Andretti was awarded 1st place when winner Bobby Unser was penalized a lap after the race was completed for passing cars illegally under the caution flag. Unser and car-owner Roger Penske appealed the race stewards' decision to the U.S. Auto Club. Four months later, USAC overturned the ruling, saying that the penalty was too harsh and Unser should be fined $40,000 rather than stripped of his championship; **i**—Team Green, runner-up Paul Tracy's team, appealed Castroneves' victory, citing video evidence and driver testimonials that proved Tracy passed Castroneves moments before the caution flag on lap 199. The IRL denied the appeal the following day; **j**—rain shortened 2004 race to 450 miles; **k**—rain shortened 2007 race to 415 miles.

Indy 500 Rookie of the Year

Officially the Chase Rookie of the Year Award and voted on by a panel of auto racing media. Award does not necessarily go to highest-finishing first-year driver. Graham Hill won the race on his first try in 1966, but the rookie award went to Jackie Stewart, who led with 10 laps to go only to lose oil pressure and finish 6th.

Father and son winners: Mario and Michael Andretti (1965 and 1984); Michael and Marco Andretti (1984 and 2006); Bill and Billy Vukovich III (1968 and 1988).

Year		Year		Year		Year	
1952	Art Cross	1967	Denis Hulme	1982	Jim Hickman	1996	Tony Stewart
1953	Jimmy Daywalt	1968	Bill Vukovich	1983	Teo Fabi	1997	Jeff Ward
1954	Larry Crockett	1969	Mark Donohue	1984	Michael Andretti	1998	Steve Knapp
1955	Al Herman	1970	Donnie Allison		& Roberto Guerrero	1999	Robby McGehee
1956	Bob Veith	1971	Denny Zimmerman	1985	Arie Luyendyk	2000	Juan Montoya
1957	Don Edmunds	1972	Mike Hiss	1986	Randy Lanier	2001	Helio Castroneves
1958	George Amick	1973	Graham McRae	1987	Fabrizio Barbazza	2002	Alex Barron
1959	Bobby Grim	1974	Pancho Carter	1988	Billy Vukovich III		& Tomas Scheckter
1960	Jim Hurtubise	1975	Bill Puterbaugh	1989	Bernard Jourdain	2003	Tora Takagi
1961	Parnelli Jones	1976	Vern Schuppan		& Scott Pruett	2004	Kosuke Matsuura
	& Bobby Marshman	1977	Jerry Sneva	1990	Eddie Cheever	2005	Danica Patrick
1962	Jimmy McElreath	1978	Rick Mears	1991	Jeff Andretti	2006	Marco Andretti
1963	Jim Clark		& Larry Rice	1992	Lyn St. James	2007	Phil Giebler
1964	Johnny White	1979	Howdy Holmes	1993	Nigel Mansell		
1965	Mario Andretti	1980	Tim Richmond	1994	Jacques Villeneuve		
1966	Jackie Stewart	1981	Josele Garza	1995	Christian Fittipaldi		

Indy Racing League Circuit (Cont.)

IRL IndyCar Series Champions

The Indy Racing Leauge (IRL) split from the open-wheel CART series in 1994. Led by Indianapolis Motor Speedway President Tony George, the league's inaugural three-race series began in January 1996 and ended with the league's keystone event—the Indianapolis 500. Past series' sponsors include Pep Boys (1998-99) and Northern Light Technology, Inc., an Internet search engine (2000-01). **Multiple winner:** Sam Hornish Jr. (3).

Year	Driver	Car	Team	Sts	Wins	Poles	Earnings
1996	**Buzz Calkins**	Reynard Ford	A.J. Foyt Enterprises	3	1	0	$345,553
	Scott Sharp	Lola Ford	A.J. Foyt Enterprises	3	0	0	330,303
1997	**Tony Stewart**	Dallara Oldsmobile	Team Menard	10	1	4	1,142,450
1998	**Kenny Brack**	Dallara Oldsmobile	A.J. Foyt Enterprises	11	3	0	2,106,700
1999	**Greg Ray**	Dallara Oldsmobile	Team Menard	10	3	4	2,061,800
2000	**Buddy Lazier**	Dallara Oldsmobile	Hemelgarn Racing	9	2	1	2,176,200
2001	**Sam Hornish Jr.**	Dallara Oldsmobile	Panther Racing	13	3	0	2,477,025
2002	**Sam Hornish Jr.**	Dallara Oldsmobile	Panther Racing	15	5	2	2,470,615
2003	**Scott Dixon**	G-Force Toyota	Target Chip Ganassi	16	3	5	1,481,265
2004	**Tony Kanaan**	Dallara Honda	Andretti Green Racing	16	3	2	1,912,990
2005	**Dan Wheldon**	Dallara Honda	Andretti Green Racing	17	6	0	2,711,005
2006	**Sam Hornish Jr.**	Dallara Honda	Marlboro Team Penske	14	4	4	2,775,205
2007	**Dario Franchitti**	Dallara Honda	Andretti Green Racing	17	4	4	4,017,583

Note: In 1996, Calkins and Sharp were named co-champions after finishing the series tied in drivers' points (246).

IRL Rookie of the Year

Officially the Bombardier Rookie of the Year Award, presented to rookie driver who accumulates the most points in the IRL standings.

Year		Year		Year		Year	
1996	None	1999	Scott Harrington	2002	Laurent Redon	2005	Danica Patrick
1997	Jim Guthrie	2000	Airton Dare	2003	Dan Wheldon	2006	Marco Andretti
1998	Robby Unser	2001	Felipe Giaffone	2004	Kosuke Matsuura	2007	Ryan Hunter-Reay

All-Time IRL Leaders

IRL IndyCar Series all-time Top 10 drivers in victories, pole positions and earnings, based on records through the 2007 season. Earnings totals include season-ending contingency awards. Drivers active in 2007 are in **bold** type. (*) Denotes driver was active, but in NASCAR Nextel Cup Series.

Victories

1 **Sam Hornish Jr.** 19
2 **Dan Wheldon** 13
3 **Tony Kanaan** 12
  Helio Castroneves 12
5 **Scott Dixon** 10
6 **Scott Sharp** 9
7 **Buddy Lazier** 8
  Dario Franchitti 8
9 Eddie Cheever Jr. 5
  Greg Ray 5
  Gil de Ferran 5

Pole Positions

1 **Helio Castroneves** 24
2 Greg Ray 13
3 **Sam Hornish Jr.** 12
4 Billy Boat 9
5 Tomas Scheckter 8
6 Tony Stewart* 7
  Dario Franchitti 7
8 **Tony Kanaan** 8
  Scott Dixon 8
10 **Scott Sharp** 6

Earnings

1 **Sam Hornish Jr.** $14,466,094
2 **Helio Castroneves** 11,109,108
3 **Buddy Lazier** 10,405,214
4 **Scott Sharp** 10,306,963
5 **Dan Wheldon** 9,233,420
6 **Tony Kanaan** 9,151,299
7 **Scott Dixon** 7,948,982
8 **Dario Franchitti** . .7,720,798
9 Eddie Cheever Jr. . . .6,792,298
10 Greg Ray 6,250,690

CHAMP CAR CIRCUIT

Champ Car Series Champions

Formerly, AAA (American Automobile Assn., 1909-55), USAC (U.S. Auto Club, 1956-78), CART (Championship Auto Racing Teams, 1979-91). CART was renamed IndyCar in 1992 and then lost use of the name in 1997. It was known as the FedEx Championship Series from 1998-2002 and the "Bridgestone Presents The Champ Car World Series Powered by Ford" from 2003-06.

  Multiple titles: A.J. Foyt (7); Mario Andretti (4); Sebastien Bourdais, Jimmy Bryan, Earl Cooper, Ted Horn, Rick Mears, Louie Meyer, Bobby Rahal, Al Unser (3); Tony Bettenhausen, Gil de Ferran, Ralph DePalma, Peter DePaolo, Joe Leonard, Rex Mays, Tommy Milton, Ralph Mulford, Jimmy Murphy, Wilbur Shaw, Al Unser Jr., Bobby Unser, Rodger Ward and Alex Zanardi (2).

AAA

Year		Year		Year		Year	
1909	George Robertson	1920	Tommy Milton	1931	Louis Schneider	1942-45	No racing
1910	Ray Harroun	1921	Tommy Milton	1932	Bob Carey	1946	Ted Horn
1911	Ralph Mulford	1922	Jimmy Murphy	1933	Louie Meyer	1947	Ted Horn
1912	Ralph DePalma	1923	Eddie Hearne	1934	Bill Cummings	1948	Ted Horn
1913	Earl Cooper	1924	Jimmy Murphy	1935	Kelly Petillo	1949	Johnnie Parsons
1914	Ralph DePalma	1925	Peter DePaolo	1936	Mauri Rose	1950	Henry Banks
1915	Earl Cooper	1926	Harry Hartz	1937	Wilbur Shaw	1951	Tony Bettenhausen
1916	Dario Resta	1927	Peter DePaolo	1938	Floyd Roberts	1952	Chuck Stevenson
1917	Earl Cooper	1928	Louie Meyer	1939	Wilbur Shaw	1953	Sam Hanks
1918	Ralph Mulford	1929	Louie Meyer	1940	Rex Mays	1954	Jimmy Bryan
1919	Howard Wilcox	1930	Billy Arnold	1941	Rex Mays	1955	Bob Sweikert

USAC

Year		Year		Year		Year	
1956	Jimmy Bryan	1962	Rodger Ward	1968	Bobby Unser	1974	Bobby Unser
1957	Jimmy Bryan	1963	A.J. Foyt	1969	Mario Andretti	1975	A.J. Foyt
1958	Tony Bettenhausen	1964	A.J. Foyt	1970	Al Unser	1976	Gordon Johncock
1959	Rodger Ward	1965	Mario Andretti	1971	Joe Leonard	1977	Tom Sneva
1960	A.J. Foyt	1966	Mario Andretti	1972	Joe Leonard	1978	A.J. Foyt
1961	A.J. Foyt	1967	A.J. Foyt	1973	Roger McCluskey		

Champ Car World Series (formerly CART)

Year	Driver	Car	Team	Sts	Wins	Poles	Earnings
1979	**Rick Mears**	Penske Ford	Penske	14	3	2	$408,078
1980	**Johnny Rutherford**	Chaparral Ford	Chaparral	12	5	3	503,595
1981	**Rick Mears**	Penske Ford	Penske	11	6	2	323,670
1982	**Rick Mears**	Penske Ford	Penske	11	4	8	306,454
1983	**Al Unser**	Penske Ford	Penske	13	1	0	500,109
1984	**Mario Andretti**	Lola Ford	Newman/Haas	16	6	8	931,929
1985	**Al Unser**	March Ford	Penske	14	1	1	843,885
1986	**Bobby Rahal**	March Ford	TrueSports	17	6	2	1,488,049
1987	**Bobby Rahal**	Lola Ford	TrueSports	15	3	1	1,261,098
1988	**Danny Sullivan**	Penske Chevrolet	Penske	15	4	9	1,222,791
1989	**Emerson Fittipaldi**	Penske Chevrolet	Patrick	15	5	4	2,166,078
1990	**Al Unser Jr.**	Lola Chevrolet	Galles-Kraco	16	6	1	1,946,833
1991	**Michael Andretti**	Lola Chevrolet	Newman/Haas	17	8	8	2,461,734
1992	**Bobby Rahal**	Lola Chevrolet	Rahal-Hogan	16	4	3	2,235,298
1993	**Nigel Mansell**	Lola Ford	Newman/Haas	15	5	7	2,526,953
1994	**Al Unser Jr.**	Penske Ilmor	Marlboro Team Penske	16	8	4	3,535,813
1995	**Jacques Villeneuve**	Reynard Ford	Team Green	17	4	6	2,996,269
1996	**Jimmy Vasser**	Reynard Honda	Target Chip Ganassi	16	4	4	3,071,500
1997	**Alex Zanardi**	Reynard Honda	Target Chip Ganassi	16	5	4	2,096,250
1998	**Alex Zanardi**	Reynard Honda	Target Chip Ganassi	19	7	0	2,229,250
1999	**Juan Montoya**	Reynard Honda	Target Chip Ganassi	20	7	7	1,973,000
2000	**Gil de Ferran**	Reynard Honda	Marlboro Team Penske	20	2	5	1,677,000
2001	**Gil de Ferran**	Reynard Honda	Marlboro Team Penske	20	2	5	1,761,500
2002	**Cristiano da Matta**	Lola Toyota	Newman/Haas	19	7	7	2,053,000
2003	**Paul Tracy**	Lola Ford-Cosworth	Player's/Forsythe	18	7	6	1,007,000
2004	**Sebastien Bourdais**	Lola Ford-Cosworth	Newman/Haas	14	7	8	843,500
2005	**Sebastien Bourdais**	Lola Ford-Cosworth	Newman/Haas	13	6	5	668,500
2006	**Sebastien Bourdais**	DP01-Cosworth	Newman/Haas/Lanigan	14	7	7	757,500

Champ Car Rookie of the Year

Officially the Roshfrans Rookie of the Year Award and presented to the rookie who accumulates the most Champ Car Series points among first year drivers. Roshfrans is the official lubricant of Champ Car.

Year		Year		Year		Year	
1979	Bill Alsup	1986	Dominic Dobson	1993	Nigel Mansell	2000	Kenny Brack
1980	Dennis Firestone	1987	Fabrizio Barbazza	1994	Jacques Villeneuve	2001	Scott Dixon
1981	Bob Lazier	1988	John Jones	1995	Gil de Ferran	2002	Mario Dominguez
1982	Bobby Rahal	1989	Bernard Jourdain	1996	Alex Zanardi	2003	Sebastien Bourdais
1983	Teo Fabi	1990	Eddie Cheever	1997	Patrick Carpentier	2004	A.J. Allmendinger
1984	Roberto Guerrero	1991	Jeff Andretti	1998	Tony Kanaan	2005	Timo Glock
1985	Arie Luyendyk	1992	Stefan Johansson	1999	Juan Montoya	2006	Will Power

All-Time Champ Car Leaders

Champ Car's all-time Top 10 drivers in victories, pole positions and earnings, based on records through Oct. 21, 2007. Drivers active in 2007 are in **bold** type. Totals include victories, poles and earnings before Champ Car (then CART) was established in 1979. Earnings totals include year-end performance awards.

Victories

1	A.J. Foyt	67
2	Mario Andretti	52
3	Michael Andretti	42
4	Al Unser	39
5	Bobby Unser	35
6	Al Unser Jr.	31
	Paul Tracy	31
8	Rick Mears	29
	Sebastien Bourdais	29
10	Johnny Rutherford	27

Pole Positions

1	Mario Andretti	67
2	A.J. Foyt	53
3	Bobby Unser	49
4	Rick Mears	40
5	Michael Andretti	32
6	**Sebastien Bourdais**	31
7	Al Unser	27
8	**Paul Tracy**	25
9	Johnny Rutherford	23
10	Gordon Johncock	20

Earnings (unofficial)

1	Al Unser Jr.	$18,828,406
2	Michael Andretti	18,228,119
3	Bobby Rahal	16,344,008
4	Emerson Fittipaldi	14,293,625
5	Jimmy Vasser	12,125,726
6	Mario Andretti	11,552,154
7	**Paul Tracy**	11,497,270
8	Rick Mears	11,050,807
9	Danny Sullivan	8,884,126
10	Arie Luyendyk	7,732,188

FORMULA ONE CIRCUIT

United States Grand Prix

Federation Internationale Sportive Automobile (FISA) sanctioned two annual U.S. Grand Prix–USA/East and USA/West–from 1976-80 and 1983-84. Phoenix was the site of the U.S. Grand Prix from 1989-91. Indianapolis Motor Speedway has hosted the U.S. Grand Prix since 2000.

Indianapolis 500

Officially sanctioned as Grand Prix race from 1950-60 only. See page 902 for details.

U.S. Grand Prix—East

Held from 1959-80 and 1981-88 at the following locations: Sebring, Fla. (1959); Riverside, Calif. (1960); Watkins Glen, N.Y. (1961-80); and Detroit (1982-88). There was no race in 1981. Race discontinued in 1989.

Multiple winners: Jim Clark, Graham Hill and Ayrton Senna (3); James Hunt, Carlos Reutemann and Jackie Stewart (2).

Year		Car	Year		Car
1959	Bruce McLaren, NZE	Cooper Climax	1974	Carlos Reutemann, ARG	Brabham Ford
1960	Stirling Moss, GBR	Lotus Climax	1975	Niki Lauda, AUT	Ferrari
1961	Innes Ireland, GBR	Lotus Climax	1976	James Hunt, GBR	McLaren Ford
1962	Jim Clark, GBR	Lotus Climax	1977	James Hunt, GBR	McLaren Ford
1963	Graham Hill, GBR	BRM	1978	Carlos Reutemann, ARG	Ferrari
1964	Graham Hill, GBR	BRM	1979	Gilles Villeneuve, CAN	Ferrari
1965	Graham Hill, GBR	BRM	1980	Alan Jones, AUS	Williams Ford
1966	Jim Clark, GBR	Lotus BRM	1981	Not held	
1967	Jim Clark, GBR	Lotus Ford	1982	John Watson, GBR	McLaren Ford
1968	Jackie Stewart, GBR	Matra Ford	1983	Michele Alboreto, ITA	Tyrrell Ford
1969	Jochen Rindt, AUT	Lotus Ford	1984	Nelson Piquet, BRA	Brabham BMW Turbo
1970	Emerson Fittipaldi, BRA	Lotus Ford	1985	Keke Rosberg, FIN	Williams Honda Turbo
1971	Francois Cevert, FRA	Tyrrell Ford	1986	Ayrton Senna, BRA	Lotus Renault Turbo
1972	Jackie Stewart, GBR	Tyrrell Ford	1987	Ayrton Senna, BRA	Lotus Honda Turbo
1973	Ronnie Peterson, SWE	Lotus Ford	1988	Ayrton Senna, BRA	McLaren Honda Turbo

U.S. Grand Prix—West

Held from 1976-83 at Long Beach, Calif. Races also held in Las Vegas (1981-82), Dallas (1984) and Phoenix (1989-91). Race discontinued in 1992.

Multiple winners: Alan Jones and Ayrton Senna (2).

Year		Car	Year		Car
1976	Clay Regazzoni, SWI	Ferrari	1983	John Watson, GBR	McLaren Ford
1977	Mario Andretti, USA	Lotus Ford	1984	Keke Rosberg, FIN	Williams Honda Turbo
1978	Carlos Reutemann, ARG	Ferrari	1985-88	Not held	
1979	Gilles Villeneuve, CAN	Ferrari	1989	Alain Prost, FRA	McLaren Honda
1980	Nelson Piquet, BRA	Brabham Ford	1990	Ayrton Senna, BRA	McLaren Honda
1981	Alan Jones, AUS	Williams Ford	1991	Ayrton Senna, BRA	McLaren Honda
1982	Niki Lauda, AUT	McLaren Ford			

U.S. Grand Prix

Held since 2000 at Indianapolis Motor Speedway.

Multiple winner: Michael Schumacher (4).

Year		Car	Year		Car
2000	Michael Schumacher, GER	Ferrari	2004	Michael Schumacher, GER	Ferrari
2001	Mika Hakkinen, FIN	McLaren Mercedes	2005	Michael Schumacher, GER	Ferrari
2002	Rubens Barrichello, BRA	Ferrari	2006	Michael Schumacher, GER	Ferrari
2003	Michael Schumacher, GER	Ferrari	2007	Lewis Hamilton, GBR	McLaren-Mercedes

World Champions

Officially called the World Championship of Drivers and based on Formula One (Grand Prix) records through the 2007 season.

Multiple winners: Michael Schumacher (7); Juan-Manuel Fangie (5); Alain Prost (4); Jack Brabham, Niki Lauda, Nelson Piquet, Ayrton Senna and Jackie Stewart (3); Fernando Alonso, Alberto Ascari, Jim Clark, Emerson Fittipaldi, Mika Hakkinen and Graham Hill (2).

Year	Driver	Country	Car	Sts	Wins	Poles	Runner(s)-up
1950	**Guiseppe Farina**	Italy	Alfa Romeo	7	3	2	J.M. Fangio, ARG
1951	**Juan-Manuel Fangio**	Argentina	Alfa Romeo	8	3	4	A. Ascari, ITA
1952	**Alberto Ascari**	Italy	Ferrari	8	6	5	G. Farina, ITA
1953	**Alberto Ascari**	Italy	Ferrari	9	5	6	J.M. Fangio, ARG
1954	**Juan-Manuel Fangio**	Argentina	Maserati/Mercedes	9	6	5	F. Gonzalez, ARG
1955	**Juan-Manuel Fangio**	Argentina	Mercedes	7	4	3	S. Moss, GBR
1956	**Juan-Manuel Fangio**	Argentina	Lancia/Ferrari	8	3	5	S. Moss, GBR
1957	**Juan-Manuel Fangio**	Argentina	Maserati	8	4	4	S. Moss, GBR
1958	**Mike Hawthorn**	Great Britain	Ferrari	11	1	4	S. Moss, GBR
1959	**Jack Brabham**	Australia	Cooper Climax	9	2	1	T. Brooks, GBR
1960	**Jack Brabham**	Australia	Cooper Climax	10	5	3	B. McLaren, NZE

Year	Driver	Country	Car	Sts	Wins	Poles	Runner(s)-up
1961	Phil Hill	United States	Ferrari	8	2	5	W. von Trips, GER
1962	Graham Hill	Great Britain	BRM	9	4	1	J. Clark, GBR
1963	Jim Clark	Great Britain	Lotus Climax	10	7	7	G. Hill, GBR
							& R. Ginther, USA
1964	John Surtees	Great Britain	Ferrari	10	2	2	G. Hill, GBR
1965	Jim Clark	Great Britain	Lotus Climax	10	6	6	G. Hill, GBR
1966	Jack Brabham	Australia	Brabham Repco	9	4	3	J. Surtees, GBR
1967	Denis Hulme	New Zealand	Brabham Repco	11	2	0	J. Brabham, AUS
1968	Graham Hill	Great Britain	Lotus Ford	12	3	2	J. Stewart, GBR
1969	Jackie Stewart	Great Britain	Matra Ford	11	6	2	J. Ickx, BEL
1970	Jochen Rindt	Austria	Lotus Ford	13	5	3	J. Ickx, BEL
1971	Jackie Stewart	Great Britain	Tyrrell Ford	11	6	6	R. Peterson, SWE
1972	Emerson Fittipaldi	Brazil	Lotus Ford	12	5	3	J. Stewart, GBR
1973	Jackie Stewart	Great Britain	Tyrrell Ford	15	5	3	E. Fittipaldi, BRA
1974	Emerson Fittipaldi	Brazil	McLaren Ford	15	3	2	C. Regazzoni, SWI
1975	Niki Lauda	Austria	Ferrari	14	5	9	E. Fittipaldi, BRA
1976	James Hunt	Great Britain	McLaren Ford	16	6	8	N. Lauda, AUT
1977	Niki Lauda	Austria	Ferrari	17	3	2	J. Scheckter, RSA
1978	Mario Andretti	United States	Lotus Ford	16	6	8	R. Peterson, SWE
1979	Jody Scheckter	South Africa	Ferrari	15	3	1	G. Villeneuve, CAN
1980	Alan Jones	Australia	Williams Ford	14	5	3	N. Piquet, BRA
1981	Nelson Piquet	Brazil	Brabham Ford	15	3	4	C. Reutemann, ARG
1982	Keke Rosberg	Finland	Williams Ford	16	1	1	D. Pironi, FRA
							& J. Watson, GBR
1983	Nelson Piquet	Brazil	Brabham BMW Turbo	15	3	1	A. Prost, FRA
1984	Niki Lauda	Austria	McL. TAG Turbo	16	5	0	A. Prost, FRA
1985	Alain Prost	France	McL. TAG Turbo	16	5	2	M. Alboreto, ITA
1986	Alain Prost	France	McL. TAG Turbo	16	4	1	N. Mansell, GBR
1987	Nelson Piquet	Brazil	Williams Honda Turbo	16	3	4	N. Mansell, GBR
1988	Ayrton Senna	Brazil	McLaren Honda Turbo	16	8	13	A. Prost, FRA
1989	Alain Prost	France	McLaren Honda	16	4	2	A. Senna, BRA
1990	Ayrton Senna	Brazil	McLaren Honda	16	6	10	A. Prost, FRA
1991	Ayrton Senna	Brazil	McLaren Honda	16	7	8	N. Mansell, GBR
1992	Nigel Mansell	Great Britain	Williams Renault	16	9	14	R. Patrese, ITA
1993	Alain Prost	France	Williams Renault	16	7	13	A. Senna, BRA
1994	Michael Schumacher	Germany	Benetton Ford	14	8	6	D. Hill, GBR
1995	Michael Schumacher	Germany	Benetton Renault	17	9	4	D. Hill, GBR
1996	Damon Hill	Great Britain	Williams Renault	16	8	9	J. Villeneuve, CAN
1997	Jacques Villeneuve	Canada	Williams Renault	17	7	10	H.H. Frentzen, GER
1998	Mika Hakkinen	Finland	McLaren Mercedes	16	8	9	M. Schumacher, GER
1999	Mika Hakkinen	Finland	McLaren Mercedes	16	5	11	E. Irvine, GBR
2000	Michael Schumacher	Germany	Ferrari	17	9	9	M. Hakkinen, FIN
2001	Michael Schumacher	Germany	Ferrari	17	9	11	D. Coulthard, GBR
2002	Michael Schumacher	Germany	Ferrari	17	11	7	R. Barrichello, BRA
2003	Michael Schumacher	Germany	Ferrari	16	6	5	K. Raikkonen, FIN
2004	Michael Schumacher	Germany	Ferrari	18	13	8	R. Barrichello, BRA
2005	Fernando Alonso	Spain	Renault	19	7	6	K. Raikkonen, FIN
2006	Fernando Alonso	Spain	Renault	18	7	6	M. Schumacher, GER
2007	Kimi Raikkonen	Finland	Ferrari	17	6	3	F. Alonso, SPA
							& L. Hamilton, GBR

All-Time Leaders

The all-time Top 15 Grand Prix winning drivers, based on records through 2007. Listed are starts (Sts), poles won (Pole), wins (1st), second place finishes (2nd), and third (3rd). Drivers active in 2007 and career victories in **bold** type.

		Sts	Pole	1st	2nd	3rd			Sts	Pole	1st	2nd	3rd
1	Michael Schumacher	249	68	**91**	43	20	10	Damon Hill	99	20	**22**	15	5
2	Alain Prost	199	33	**51**	35	20	11	Mika Hakkinen	163	27	**20**	14	17
3	Ayrton Senna	161	65	**41**	23	16	12	**Fernando Alonso**	105	17	**19**	18	12
4	Nigel Mansell	187	32	**31**	17	11	13	Stirling Moss	66	16	**16**	5	3
5	Jackie Stewart	99	17	**27**	11	5	14	**Kimi Raikkonen**	88	14	**15**	16	13
6	Jim Clark	72	33	**25**	1	6	15	Jack Brabham	126	13	**14**	10	7
	Niki Lauda	171	24	**25**	20	9		Emerson Fittipaldi	144	6	**14**	13	8
8	Juan-Manuel Fangio	51	28	**24**	10	1		Graham Hill	176	13	**14**	15	7
9	Nelson Piquet	207	24	**23**	20	17							

ENDURANCE RACES
The 24 Hours of Le Mans

Officially, the Le Mans Grand Prix. First run May 22-23, 1923. All subsequent races have been held in June, except in 1956 (July) and 1968 (September). Originally contested on a 10.73-mile track, the circuit was shortened to 8.383 miles in 1932 and has fluxuated around 8.5 miles ever since.

Multiple winners: Tom Kristensen (7); Jacky Ickx (6); Derek Bell, Frank Biela and Emanuele Pirro (5); Yannick Dalmas, Oliver Gendebien and Henri Pescarolo (4); Woolf Barnato, Luigi Chinetti, Hurley Haywood, Phil Hill, Al Holbert, Klaus Ludwig and Marco Werner (3); Sir Henry Birkin, Ivoe Bueb, Rinaldo Capello, Ron Flockhart, Jean-Pierre Jaussaud, Gerard Larrousse, JJ Lehto, Andre Rossignol, Raymond Sommer, Hans Stuck, Gijs van Lennep, and Jean-Pierre Wimille (2).

Year	Drivers	Car	MPH
1923	Andre Lagache & Rene Leonard	Chenard & Walcker	57.21
1924	John Duff & Francis Clement	Bentley	53.78
1925	Gerard de Courcelles & Andre Rossignol	La Lorraine	57.84
1926	Robert Bloch & Andre Rossignol	La Lorraine	66.08
1927	J.D. Benjafield & Sammy Davis	Bentley	61.35
1928	Woolf Barnato & Bernard Rubin	Bentley	69.11
1929	Woolf Barnato & Sir Henry Birkin	Bentley Speed 6	73.63
1930	Woolf Barnato & Glen Kidston	Bentley Speed 6	75.88
1931	Earl Howe & Sir Henry Birkin	Alfa Romeo	78.13
1932	Raymond Sommer & Luigi Chinetti	Alfa Romeo	76.48
1933	Raymond Sommer & Tazio Nuvolari	Alfa Romeo	81.40
1934	Luigi Chinetti & Philippe Etancelin	Alfa Romeo	74.74
1935	John Hindmarsh & Louis Fontes	Lagonda	77.85
1936	Not held		
1937	Jean-Pierre Wimille & Robert Benoist	Bugatti 57G	85.13
1938	Eugene Chaboud & Jean Tremoulet	Delahaye	82.36
1939	Jean-Pierre Wimille & Pierre Veyron	Bugatti 57G	86.86
1940-48	Not held		
1949	Luigi Chinetti & Lord Selsdon	Ferrari	82.28
1950	Louis Rosier & Jean-Louis Rosier	Talbot-Lago	89.71
1951	Peter Walker & Peter Whitehead	Jaguar C	93.50
1952	Hermann Lang & Fritz Reiss	Mercedes-Benz	96.67
1953	Tony Rolt & Duncan Hamilton	Jaguar C	98.65
1954	Froilan Gonzalez & Maurice Trintignant	Ferrari 375	105.13
1955	Mike Hawthorn & Ivor Bueb	Jaguar D	107.05
1956	Ron Flockhart & Ninian Sanderson	Jaguar D	104.47
1957	Ron Flockhart & Ivor Bueb	Jaguar D	113.83
1958	Oliver Gendebien & Phil Hill	Ferrari 250	106.18
1959	Roy Salvadori & Carroll Shelby	Aston Martin	112.55
1960	Oliver Gendebien & Paul Fräre	Ferrari 250	109.17
1961	Oliver Gendebien & Phil Hill	Ferrari 250	115.88
1962	Oliver Gendebien & Phil Hill	Ferrari 250	115.22
1963	Lodovico Scarfiotti & Lorenzo Bandini	Ferrari 250	118.08
1964	Jean Guichel & Nino Vaccarella	Ferrari 275	121.54
1965	Masten Gregory & Jochen Rindt	Ferrari 250	121.07
1966	Bruce McLaren & Chris Amon	Ford Mk. II	125.37
1967	A.J. Foyt & Dan Gurney	Ford Mk. IV	135.46
1968	Pedro Rodriguez & Lucien Bianchi	Ford GT40	115.27
1969	Jacky Ickx & Jackie Oliver	Ford GT40	129.38
1970	Hans Herrmann & Richard Attwood	Porsche 917	119.28
1971	Gijs van Lennep & Helmut Marko	Porsche 917	138.13
1972	Graham Hill & Henri Pescarolo	Matra-Simca	121.45
1973	Henri Pescarolo & Gerard Larrousse	Matra-Simca	125.67
1974	Henri Pescarolo & Gerard Larrousse	Matra-Simca	119.27
1975	Derek Bell & Jacky Ickx	Mirage-Ford	118.98
1976	Jacky Ickx & Gijs van Lennep	Porsche 936	123.49
1977	Jacky Ickx, Jurgen Barth & Hurley Haywood	Porsche 936	120.95
1978	Jean-Pierre Jaussaud & Didier Pironi	Renault-Alpine	130.60
1979	Klaus Ludwig, Bill Wittington & Don Whittington	Porsche 935	108.10
1980	Jean-Pierre Jaussaud & Jean Rondeau	Rondeau-Cosworth	119.23
1981	Jacky Ickx & Derek Bell	Porsche 936	124.94
1982	Jacky Ickx & Derek Bell	Porsche 956	126.85
1983	Vern Schuppan, Hurley Haywood & Al Holbert	Porsche 956	130.70
1984	Klaus Ludwig & Henri Pescarolo	Porsche 956	126.88
1985	Klaus Ludwig, Paolo Barilla & John Winter	Porsche 956	131.75
1986	Derek Bell, Hans Stuck & Al Holbert	Porsche 962	128.75
1987	Derek Bell, Hans Stuck & Al Holbert	Porsche 962	124.06
1988	Jan Lammers, Johnny Dumfries & Andy Wallace	Jaguar XJR	137.75
1989	Jochen Mass, Manuel Reuter & Stanley Dickens	Sauber-Mercedes	136.39
1990	John Nielsen, Price Cobb & Martin Brundle	Jaguar XJR-12	126.71
1991	Volker Weider, Johnny Herbert & Bertrand Gachof	Mazda 787B	127.31

Year	Drivers	Car	MPH	Year	Drivers	Car	MPH
1992	Derek Warwick, Yannick Dalmas & Mark Blundell	Peugeot 905B	123.89	2000	Frank Biela, Tom Kristensen & Emanuele Pirro	Audi R8	128.34
1993	Geoff Brabham, Christophe Bouchut & Eric Helary	Peugeot 905	132.58	2001	Frank Biela, Tom Kristensen & Emanuele Pirro	Audi R8	129.66
1994	Yannick Dalmas, Hurley Haywood & Mauro Baldi	Porsche 962LM	129.82	2002	Frank Biela, Tom Kristensen & Emanuele Pirro	Audi R8	131.89
1995	Yannick Dalmas, JJ Lehto & Masanori Sekiya	McLaren BMW	105.00	2003	Tom Kristensen, Rinaldo Capello & Guy Smith	Bentley Speed 8	143.43
1996	Davy Jones, Manuel Reuter & Alexander Wurz	TWR Porsche	124.65	2004	Tom Kristensen, Rinaldo Capello & Seiji Ara	Audi R8	133.86
1997	Michele Alberto, Stefan Johansson & Tom Kristensen	TWR Porsche	126.88	2005	Tom Kristensen, JJ Lehto & Marco Werner	Audi R8	130.73
1998	Laurent Aiello, Allan McNish & Stephane Ortelli	Porsche 911 GT1	123.86	2006	Frank Biela, Emanuele Pirro & Marco Werner	Audi R10	133.85
1999	Yannick Dalmas, Joachim Winkelhock & Pierluigi Martini	BMW V-12 LMR	129.38	2007	Frank Biela, Emanuele Pirro & Marco Werner	Audi R10	129.96

The 24 Hours of Daytona

Officially, the Rolex 24 at Daytona. First run in 1962 as a three-hour race and won by Dan Gurney in a Lotus 19 Ford. Contested over a 3.56-mile course at Daytona (Fla.) International Speedway. There have been several distance changes since 1962: the event was a three-hour race (1962-63); a 2,000-kilometer race (1964-65); a 24-hour race (1966-71); a six-hour race (1972) and a 24-hour race again since 1973. The race was canceled in 1974 due to a national energy crisis.

Multiple winners: Hurley Haywood (5); Peter Gregg, Pedro Rodriguez and Bob Wollek (4); Derek Bell, Butch Leitzinger, Rolf Stommelen and Andy Wallace (3); Mauro Baldi, A.J. Foyt, Al Holbert, Ken Miles, John Paul Jr., Brian Redman, Elliott Forbes-Robinson, Lloyd Ruby, Wayne Taylor, Didier Theys and Al Unser Jr. (2).

Year	Drivers	Car	MPH	Year	Drivers	Car	MPH
1962	Dan Gurney	Lotus 19 Ford	104.101	1985	A.J. Foyt, Bob Wollek, Al Unser Sr. & Thierry Boutsen	Porsche 962	104.162
1963	Pedro Rodriguez	Ferrari GTO	102.074	1986	Al Holbert, Derek Bell & Al Unser Jr	Porsche 962	105.484
1964	Pedro Rodriguez & Phil Hill	Ferrari GTO	98.230	1987	Al Holbert, Derek Bell, Chip Robinson & Al Unser Jr	Porsche 962	111.599
1965	Ken Miles & Lloyd Ruby	Ford GT	99.944	1988	Raul Boesel, Martin Brundle & John Nielsen	Jaguar XJR-9	107.943
1966	Ken Miles & Lloyd Ruby	Ford Mk. II	108.020	1989	John Andretti, Derek Bell & Bob Wollek	Porsche 962	92.009
1967	Lorenzo Bandini & Chris Amon	Ferrari 330	105.688	1990	Davy Jones, Jan Lammers & Andy Wallace	Jaguar XJR-12	112.857
1968	Vic Elford & Jochen Neerpasch	Porsche 907	106.697	1991	Hurley Haywood, John Winter, Frank Jelinski, Henri Pescarolo & Bob Wollek	Porsche 962-C	106.633
1969	Mark Donohue & Chuck Parsons	Lola Chevrolet	99.268	1992	Masahiro Hasemi, Kazuyoshi Hoshino & Toshio Suzuki	Nissan R-91	112.897
1970	Pedro Rodriguez & Leo Kinnunen	Porsche 917	114.866	1993	P.J. Jones, Mark Dismore & Rocky Moran	Toyota Eagle	103.537
1971	Pedro Rodriguez & Jackie Oliver	Porsche 917K	109.203	1994	Paul Gentilozzi, Scott Pruett, Butch Leitzinger & Steve Millen	Nissan 300 ZXT	104.80
1972	Mario Andretti & Jacky Ickx	Ferrari 312P	122.573	1995	Jurgen Lassig, Christophe Bouchut, Giovanni Lavaggi & Marco Werner	Porsche Spyder	102.280
1973	Peter Gregg & Hurley Haywood	Porsche Carrera	106.225	1996	Wayne Taylor, Scott Sharp & Jim Pace	Olds Arness MK-III	103.32
1974	Not held			1997	Rob Dyson, James Weaver, Butch Leitzinger, Andy Wallace, John Paul Jr., Eliot Forbes-Robinson & John Schneider	Ford R&S MK-III	102.29
1975	Peter Gregg & Hurley Haywood	Porsche Carrera	108.531	1998	Mauro Baldi, Arie Luyendyk, Gianpiero Moretti & Didier Theys	Ferrari 333	105.40
1976	Peter Gregg, Brian Redman & John Fitzpatrick	BMW CSL	104.040	1999	Elliot Forbes-Robinson, Butch Leitzinger & Andy Wallace	Riley & Scott Ford	104.957
1977	Hurley Haywood, John Graves & Dave Helmick	Porsche Carrera	108.801	2000	Olivier Beretta, Dominique Dupuy & Karl Wendlinger	Dodge Viper	107.207
1978	Peter Gregg, Rolf Stommelen & Antoine Hezemans	Porsche Turbo	108.743	2001	Ron Fellows, Franck Freon, Chris Kneifel & Johnny O'Connell	Chevy Corvette	97.293
1979	Hurley Haywood, Ted Field & Danny Ongais	Porsche Turbo	109.249				
1980	Rolf Stommelen, Volkert Merl & Reinhold Joest	Porsche Turbo	114.303				
1981	Bobby Rahal, Brian Redman & Bob Garretson	Porsche Turbo	113.153				
1982	John Paul Sr., John Paul Jr. & Rolf Stommelen	Porsche Turbo	114.794				
1983	A.J. Foyt, Preston Henn, Bob Wollek & Claude Ballot-Lena	Porsche Turbo	98.781				
1984	Sarel van der Merwe, Tony Martin & Graham Duxbury	March Porsche	103.119				

The 24 Hours of Daytona (Cont.)

Year	Drivers	Car	MPH	Year	Drivers	Car	MPH
2002	Mauro Baldi, Fredy Lienhard, Max Papis & Didier Theys	Dallara LMP900	106.143	2005	Wayne Taylor, Max Angelelli & Emmanuel Collard	Pontiac Riley	105.204
2003	Kevin Buckler, Michael Schrom, Timo Bernhard & Jorg Bergmeister	Porsche GT3 RS	115.969	2006	Scott Dixon, Dan Wheldon & Casey Mears	Lexus Riley	108.826
2004	Terry Borcheller, Forest Barber, Andy Pilgrim & Christian Fittipaldi	Pontiac Doran	77.927	2007	Scott Pruett, Juan Pablo Montoya & Salvador Duran	Lexus Riley	99.020

NHRA DRAG RACING

NHRA Champions

Based on points earned during the NHRA POWERade Drag Racing series. The series, originally sponsored by the R.J. Reynolds Tobacco Company's Winston brand, began for Top Fuel, Funny Car and Pro Stock in 1975. The Coca-Cola Company's POWERade brand soft drink began a sponsorship deal with the series in 2002.

Top Fuel

Multiple winners: Joe Amato (5); Tony Schumacher (4); Don Garlits, Shirley Muldowney and Gary Scelzi (3); Kenny Bernstein, Larry Dixon and Scott Kalitta (2).

Year		Year		Year		Year	
1975	Don Garlits	1983	Gary Beck	1991	Joe Amato	1999	Tony Schumacher
1976	Richard Tharp	1984	Joe Amato	1992	Joe Amato	2000	Gary Scelzi
1977	Shirley Muldowney	1985	Don Garlits	1993	Eddie Hill	2001	Kenny Bernstein
1978	Kelly Brown	1986	Don Garlits	1994	Scott Kalitta	2002	Larry Dixon
1979	Rob Bruins	1987	Dick LaHaie	1995	Scott Kalitta	2003	Larry Dixon
1980	Shirley Muldowney	1988	Joe Amato	1996	Kenny Bernstein	2004	Tony Schumacher
1981	Jeb Allen	1989	Gary Ormsby	1997	Gary Scelzi	2005	Tony Schumacher
1982	Shirley Muldowney	1990	Joe Amato	1998	Gary Scelzi	2006	Tony Schumacher

Funny Car

Multiple winners: John Force (14); Don Prudhomme, Kenny Bernstein (4); Raymond Beadle (3); Frank Hawley (2).

Year		Year		Year		Year	
1975	Don Prudhomme	1983	Frank Hawley	1991	John Force	1999	John Force
1976	Don Prudhomme	1984	Mark Oswald	1992	Cruz Pedregon	2000	John Force
1977	Don Prudhomme	1985	Kenny Bernstein	1993	John Force	2001	John Force
1978	Don Prudhomme	1986	Kenny Bernstein	1994	John Force	2002	John Force
1979	Raymond Beadle	1987	Kenny Bernstein	1995	John Force	2003	Tony Pedregon
1980	Raymond Beadle	1988	Kenny Bernstein	1996	John Force	2004	John Force
1981	Raymond Beadle	1989	Bruce Larson	1997	John Force	2005	Gary Scelzi
1982	Frank Hawley	1990	John Force	1998	John Force	2006	John Force

Pro Stock

Multiple winners: Bob Glidden (9); Warren Johnson (6); Lee Shepherd (4); Greg Anderson (3); Darrell Alderman, Jeg Coughlin Jr. and Jim Yates (2).

Year		Year		Year		Year	
1975	Bob Glidden	1983	Lee Shepherd	1991	Darrell Alderman	1999	Warren Johnson
1976	Larry Lombardo	1984	Lee Shepherd	1992	Warren Johnson	2000	Jeg Coughlin Jr.
1977	Don Nicholson	1985	Bob Glidden	1993	Warren Johnson	2001	Warren Johnson
1978	Bob Glidden	1986	Bob Glidden	1994	Darrell Alderman	2002	Jeg Coughlin Jr.
1979	Bob Glidden	1987	Bob Glidden	1995	Warren Johnson	2003	Greg Anderson
1980	Bob Glidden	1988	Bob Glidden	1996	Jim Yates	2004	Greg Anderson
1981	Lee Shepherd	1989	Bob Glidden	1997	Jim Yates	2005	Greg Anderson
1982	Lee Shepherd	1990	John Myers	1998	Warren Johnson	2006	Jason Line

All-Time Leaders
Career Victories

All-time leaders through Oct. 7, 2007. Drivers active in 2007 are in **bold**.

	Top Fuel			Funny Car			Pro Stock	
1	Joe Amato	52	1	**John Force**	125	1	**Warren Johnson**	96
2	**Larry Dixon**	41	2	Don Prudhomme	35	2	Bob Glidden	85
3	**Tony Schumacher**	40		**Tony Pedregon**	35	3	**Greg Anderson**	50
4	Kenny Bernstein	39	4	Kenny Bernstein	30	4	**Jeg Coughlin**	37
5	Don Garlits	35	5	**Ron Capps**	24	5	**Kurt Johnson**	36

BOXING

2006 / 2007 YEAR IN REVIEW

Russian giant **Nikolai Valuev** outsized but couldn't outpoint challenger Ruslan Chagaev and lost his WBA heavyweight title in 2007.

OFF THE DECK

Boxing, decried as a fading relic of days gone by, was revived this year by one of the biggest fights in years.

BOXING, THE PUNCHING BAG FOR CRITICS WHO HAVE DECLARED IT DEAD TOO MANY TIMES TO COUNT, had once again been listed in critical condition. Standing ready to kick dirt on the grave was new kid on the block mixed martial arts, notably the Ultimate Fighting Championship, the fast-paced, slickly packaged extreme fighting genre with wide appeal to a younger, hipper demographic than grandfatherly boxing.

It was all the rage while boxing was supposedly petering out, its power brokers unable or unwilling to put together the biggest and best fights and a heavyweight division so faceless and woefully uninteresting that few cared anymore.

But a funny thing happened on the way to boxing's funeral: It once again got off the deck at the count of nine.

Although the heavyweight division, dominated by fighters from the former Soviet Union, remained a laughingstock, there was reason for encouragement.

How many sports supposedly gasping for life could produce the most financially successful event in its history?

That's what happened when Oscar De La Hoya, the "Golden Boy," and Floyd Mayweather Jr., the "Pretty Boy," squared off in a highly anticipated fight for De La Hoya's junior middleweight title and Mayweather's mythical pound-for-pound crown May 5 at the MGM Grand in Las Vegas.

It injected a dose of excitement and interest into the sweet science that hadn't been seen since the 1980s non-heavyweight heyday of Sugar Ray Leonard, Thomas Hearns, Marvelous Marvin Hagler and Roberto Duran. Suddenly boxing was on the front page of the sports section again and people were talking about "the fight."

 Dan Rafael covers boxing for ESPN.com.

AP/Wide World Photos

The Pretty Boy got the best of the Golden Boy in 2007 when **Floyd Mayweather** edged **Oscar de la Hoya** in their highly anticipated meeting in Las Vegas.

De La Hoya for years has been the face of the sport and its most bankable star while Mayweather was the flashy, pound-for-pound king with a blinding smile. From the moment the fight was signed in late 2006 until they met at center ring, it was an unparalleled rocket ride of anticipation.

The massive five-month buildup included an 11-city cross-country press tour and HBO's four-week reality series "24/7," which drew an average of 4.7 million viewers per week.

Ultimately, it was Mayweather who squeaked past De La Hoya via split decision in a fight that lacked the action many were hoping for. But it proved that with the right matchup boxing was still capable of delivering a gargantuan audience of casual sports fans and hard-core fight freaks alike.

The numbers were staggering as the fight shattered all box office records, which had previously been held by heavyweight matches.

- Total gross: $165 million, more than many Hollywood blockbusters draw during their entire run.

- Pay-per-view subscriptions: HBO PPV reported 2.4 million, which crushed the previous record of 1.99 million generated by the 1997 Evander Holyfield-Mike Tyson ear-biting fiasco.

- Pay-per-view gross: $134.4 million.

- Live gate: $18,419,200.

Kelly "The Ghost" Pavlik will be haunting the dreams of former undisputed middleweight champ **Jermain Taylor**—at least until a rematch.

Boy Promotions, settled a long-running feud with his former promoter, Top Rank's Bob Arum.

The truce allowed the companies to match their fighters for the first time since 2004. The result was a slate of quality fights, including a much-anticipated Nov. 10 showdown between welterweight titlist Miguel Cotto and popular former champ Shane Mosley.

Boxing had other fan-friendly fights, too, including one that delivered all the action fans had hoped for but didn't get from De La Hoya–Mayweather when No. 1 contender Kelly Pavlik seized the middleweight championship from Jermain Taylor, surviving a second-round knockdown and rallying for a thunderous seventh-round knockout in September.

That fight wasn't on pay-per-view. It was live on HBO and drew a very healthy 2 million-plus viewers, serving as a reminder of the words from Golden Boy Promotions CEO Richard Schaefer upon learning about the mind-boggling pay-per-view results of De La Hoya–Mayweather.

"It shows you," Schaefer said, "if you do the right fights, boxing is still very much alive."

During the promotion critics viewed De La Hoya-Mayweather as boxing's last gasp and had derisively called it "the fight to save boxing." Perhaps it didn't save the sport—how ridiculous is the notion that one fight could possibly "save" a sport that has been around for more than 120 years—but maybe the good feelings that followed helped nudge it in the right direction.

In its wake, De La Hoya, who also operates powerful Golden

AP/Wide World Photos

DAN RAFAEL'S

Biggest Stories of the Year in **Boxing**

10 **Five weeks, five fights postponed or canceled.**
Anemia forces Fernando Vargas to postpone a Sept. 8 showdown with Ricardo Mayorga to Nov. 23. An infected knuckle cut forces junior lightweight champion Juan Manuel Marquez's Sept. 15 defense against Rocky Juarez to shift to Nov. 3. A back injury to unretiring ex-heavyweight titleholder Vitali Klitschko forces him to cancel his Sept. 22 comeback against Jameel McCline. Light heavyweight Adrian Diaconu's bad hand knocked him out of a Sept. 29 shot at Chad Dawson. Heavyweight belt-holder Oleg Maskaev suffers a back injury and postpones an Oct. 6 defense against Samuel Peter, who defeats a replacement opponent -- the suddenly available McCline.

09 **Fans brace for three massive fall fights.** On Nov. 3 in Cardiff, Wales, more than 60,000 are expected at Millennium Stadium to see Welsh hero Joe Calzaghe and Danish icon Mikkel Kessler, a combined 82-0 with 61 knockouts, battle for super middleweight supremacy. On Nov. 10 at New York's Madison Square Garden, emerging star Miguel Cotto defends his welterweight belt against popular ex-champion Shane Mosley. On Dec. 8,

Floyd Mayweather defends the recognized welterweight world title against junior welterweight champion Ricky Hatton of England at Las Vegas' MGM Grand in a fight so anticipated that all 16,000 seats sell out in 30 minutes.

08 **The best fights often come in small packages.** The two rock 'em, sock 'em junior featherweight title fights between Israel Vazquez and Rafael Marquez are no exception. In March, bantamweight champ Marquez moves up one division and stops Vazquez, who retires after the seventh round with a badly broken nose. In the August rematch, Vazquez gains revenge via sixth-round knockout in another blazing battle. The rubber match: March 1, 2008.

07 **On the eve of New York's annual Puerto Rican Day parade**, welterweight titleholder Miguel Cotto, Puerto Rico's No. 1 fighter, and Brooklyn's Zab Judah, the former undisputed champion, pack Madison Square Garden with a record crowd of 20,658, which watches them wage a tremendously exciting fight. Cotto stops a dazed and bleeding Judah in the 11th round as the Garden rocks on one of the most memorable nights in the fabled arena's history.

06 **Heavyweight legend Rocky Marciano can rest easy** after Nikolai Valuev's run at his hallowed 49-0 mark ends. Valuev, the 7-foot, 320-pound Russian giant, is 46-0 and his German promoters are already starting to hype his march toward Marciano's milestone when he defends his title against Uzbekistan's Ruslan Chagaev April

14. Chagaev edges Valuev via majority decision, claims the belt and ends his run toward history.

05 **Kelly Pavlik emerges as a star** with a stirring comeback against Jermain Taylor to win the middleweight championship Sept. 29 in Atlantic City, N.J. Taylor, who owns a win against Pavlik in the 2000 U.S. Olympic trials, looks on his way to a successful defense when he knocks Pavlik down in the second round and is on the verge of stopping him. Pavlik survives and rallies to score a seventh-round knockout to win the title in dramatic fashion.

04 **Diego "Chico" Corrales, the former lightweight and junior lightweight champion, dies at age 29** in a May 7 motorcycle crash in Las Vegas. Corrales, who lives as hard as he fights, dies two years to the day after his greatest victory, a miraculous come-from-behind 10th-round knockout of Jose Luis Castillo in a lightweight unification bout that is one of the greatest fights in history. An autopsy reveals that Corrales is drunk at the time of the accident.

03 **Boxing says farewell to three of the most popular action stars of this era:** Arturo Gatti and bitter rivals Erik Morales and Marco Antonio Barrera, whose careers will forever be tied by their epic trilogy. Between July and October, the former multi-division champions announce their retirement after losses. Gatti is brutally knocked out by welterweight Alfonso Gomez, a former star of "The Contender" reality series; Morales is edged by David Diaz in a ferocious lightweight title battle; and Barrera drops a lopsided decision to junior lightweight star Manny Pacquiao in a much-anticipated rematch.

02 **Bob Arum's Top Rank and Oscar De La Hoya's Golden Boy Promotions reach a truce** in a protracted legal battle. The long-festering feud explodes when the sport's most powerful promoters each claim rights to Filipino star Manny Pacquiao, who signs contracts with both companies. The bad blood holds fans hostage because they refuse to match their fighters until mediation leads to peace in June. The result is a fall filled with matches between fighters from each stable.

01 **Pound-for-pound king Floyd Mayweather's victory against Oscar De La Hoya**, dubbed by many as "the fight to save boxing," is the event of the year. With star fighters, a massive five-month promotion and HBO's hit reality series "24/7" following the buildup, the showdown is the greatest money maker in boxing history. The May 5 junior middleweight title bout at Las Vegas' MGM Grand, waged in the face of mixed martial arts' increasing profile, proves boxing ain't dead yet. The fight blows away numerous all-time records, including total revenue (approximately $165 million), pay-per-view buys (2.4 million on HBO PPV), pay-per-view revenue ($134.4 million) and live gate ($18,419,200).

2006-2007
Season in Review

SPORTS ALMANAC

Current Champions

WBA, WBC, IBF and WBO Titleholders (through Oct. 31, 2007)

The champions of professional boxing's 17 principal weight divisions, as recognized by the Word Boxing Association (WBA), World Boxing Council (WBC), International Boxing Federation (IBF) and World Boxing Organization (WBO). Where applicable, records listed below fighters' names indicate wins-losses-draws-no contest (knockouts).

Weight Class (limit)	WBA	WBC	IBF	WBO
Heavyweight	Ruslan Chagaev 23-0-1 (17)	Oleg Maskaev* 34-5 (26)	Wladimir Klitschko 49-3 (44)	Sultan Ibragimov 22-0-1 (17)
Cruiserweight (190 lbs)	Virgil Hill* 50-6 (23)	Jean-Marc Mormeck* 33-3 (22)	Steve Cunningham 20-1 (10)	Enzo Maccarinelli 27-1 (20)
Light Heavyweight (175)	Stipe Drews 32-1 (13)	Chad Dawson 25-0 (17)	Clinton Woods 41-3-1 (24)	Zsolt Erdei 27-0 (17)
Super Middleweight (168)	Anthony Mundine* 29-3 (22)	Mikkel Kessler 39-0 (29)	Lucian Bute 21-0 (16)	Joe Calzaghe 43-0 (32)
Middleweight (160)	Felix Sturm 28-2-1 (12)	Kelly Pavlik 32-0 (29)	Arthur Abraham 24-0 (19)	Kelly Pavlik 32-0 (29)
Jr. Middleweight (154)	Joachim Alcine 29-0 (19)	Vernon Forrest 39-2 (28)	Cory Spinks 36-4 (21)	Sergei Dzindziruk 34-0 (22)
Welterweight (147)	Miguel Cotto 30-0 (25)	Floyd Mayweather Jr. 38-0 (24)	Kermit Cintron 28-1 (26)	Paul Williams 33-0 (24)
Jr. Welterweight (140)	Gavin Rees 27-0 (13)	Junior Witter 36-1-2 (21)	Paul Malignaggi 23-1 (5)	Ricardo Torres 32-1 (28)
Lightweight (135)	Juan Diaz 33-0 (16)	David Diaz* 33-1-1 (17)	Juan Diaz 33-0 (16)	Juan Diaz* 33-0 (16)
Jr. Lightweight (130)	Edwin Valero 22-0 (22)	Juan M. Marquez 47-3-1 (35)	Mzonke Fana 27-3 (10)	Alex Arthur 25-1 (19)
Featherweight (126)	Chris John 40-0-1 (21)	Jorge Linares 24-0 (15)	Robert Guerrero 20-2-1 (13)	Steven Luevano 33-1 (15)
Jr. Featherweight (122)	Celestino Caballero 27-2 (19)	Israel Vazquez 41-4 (30)	Steve Molitor 25-0 (10)	Daniel Ponce De Leon 33-1 (30)
Bantamweight (118)	Wladimir Sidorenko 20-0-2 (7)	Hozumi Hasegawa 22-2 (7)	Joseph Agbeko 25-1 (22)	Gerry Penalosa 52-6-2 (35)
Jr. Bantamweight (115)	Alexander Munoz 31-2 (27)	Cristian Mijares 31-3-2 (12)	Dmitri Kirilov 29-3 (9)	Fernando Montiel 34-2-1 (25)
Flyweight (112)	Takefumi Sakata 31-4-1 (15)	Daisuke Naito 32-2-2 (20)	Nonito Donaire 18-1 (11)	Omar Narvaez 25-0-2 (16)
Jr. Flyweight (108)	Juan Carlos Reveco 17-0 (8)	Edgar Sosa 29-5 (15)	Ulises Solis 25-1-2 (19)	Ivan Calderon 29-0 (6)
Minimumweight (105)	Yutaka Niida 22-1-3 (8)	Eagle Kyowa 17-1 (6)	Florante Condes 22-3-1 (20)	Donnie Nietes 22-1-3 (13)

*Samuel Peter is the WBC interim heavyweight champion; Jean-Marc Mormeck is the WBA cruiserweight "super world champion;" Firat Arslan is the WBA cruiserweight interim champion; Mikkel Kessler is the WBA super middleweight "super world champion;" Joel Casamayor is the WBC interim lightweight champion; Michael Katsidis is the WBO interim lightweight champion.

Note: The following weight divisions are also known by these names—**Cruiserweight** as Jr. Heavyweight; **Jr. Middleweight** as Super Welterweight; **Jr. Welterweight** as Super Lightweight; **Jr. Lightweight** as Super Featherweight; **Jr. Featherweight** as Super Bantamweight; **Jr. Bantamweight** as Super Flyweight; **Jr. Flyweight** as Light Flyweight; and **Minimumweight** as Strawweight or Mini-Flyweights.

Major Bouts, 2006-07

Division by division, from Nov. 1, 2006 through Oct. 31, 2007.

WBA, WBC and IBF champions are listed in **bold** type. Note the following Result colunm abbreviations (in alphabetical order): **Disq.** (won by disqualification); **KO** (knockout); **MDraw** (majority draw); **NC** (no contest); **SDraw** (split draw); **TDraw** (technical draw); **TKO** (technical knockout); **TWm** (won by technical majority decision); **TWs** (won by technical split decision); **TWu** (won by technical unanimous decision); **Wm** (won by majority decision); **Ws** (won by split decision) and **Wu** (won by unanimous decision).

Heavyweights

Date	Winner	Loser	Result	Title	Site
Nov. 10	Evander Holyfield	Fres Oquendo	Wu 12	—	San Antonio, Tex.
Nov. 11	**Wladimir Klitschko**	Calvin Brock	TKO 7	**IBF**	New York City
Dec. 10	**Oleg Maskaev**	Peter Okhello	Wu 12	**WBC**	Moscow, Russia
Jan. 20	**Nikolai Valuev**	Jameel McCline	TKO 3	**WBA**	Basel, Switzerland
Mar. 10	**Wladimir Klitschko**	Ray Austin	TKO 2	**IBF**	Mannheim, Germany
Mar. 10	Sultan Ibragimov	Javier Mota	KO 1	—	New York City
Mar. 17	Evander Holyfield	Vincent Maddalone	TKO 3	—	Corpus Christi, Tex.
Apr. 14	Ruslan Chagaev	**Nikolai Valuev**	Wm 12	**WBA**	Stuttgart, Germany
June 2	Sultan Ibragimov	Shannon Briggs	Wu 12	**WBO**	Atlantic City
June 30	Evander Holyfield	Lou Savarese	Wu 10	—	El Paso, Tex.
July 7	**Wladimir Klitschko**	Lamon Brewster	TKO 6	**IBF**	Cologne, Germany
Sept. 29	Nikolai Valuev	J.F. Bergeron	Wm 12	—	Oldenburg, Germany
Oct. 6	**Samuel Peter**	Jameel McCline	Wu 12	**WBC***	New York City
Oct. 13	**Sultan Ibragimov**	Evander Holyfield	Wu 12	**WBO**	Moscow, Russia
Oct. 27	Alexander Povetkin	Chris Byrd	TKO 11	—	Erfut, Germany

*Peter, who was originally scheduled to fight champion Oleg Maskaev on Oct. 6, retained the interim belt that he was awarded when Maskaev dropped out of the fight due to injury.

Cruiserweights (190 lbs)
(Jr. Heavyweights)

Date	Winner	Loser	Result	Title	Site
Nov. 25	Krzysztof Wlodarczyk	Steve Cunningham	Ws 12	**IBF***	Warsaw, Poland
Dec. 2	Valery Brudov	Luis Andrew Pineda	TKO 11	**WBA**†	Paris
Mar. 17	Jean-Marc Mormeck	**O'Neil Bell**	Wu 12	**WBA/WBC**	Levallois Perret, France
Mar. 26	Steve Cunningham	**K. Wlodarczyk**	Wm 12	**IBF**	Katowice, Poland
June 16	Firat Arslan	**Valery Brudov**	Ws 12	**WBA**†	Budapest, Hungary

*Wlodarczyk won the vacant IBF belt that was stripped from O'Neill Bell for failing to fight top-ranked contender Steve Cunnigham.
†interim belt.

Light Heavyweights (175 lbs)

Date	Winner	Loser	Result	Title	Site
Feb. 3	Chad Dawson	**Tomasz Adamek**	Wu 12	**WBC**	Kissimmee, Fla.
Apr. 28	Stipe Drews	**Silvio Branco**	Wu 12	**WBA**	Stuttgart, Germany
June 9	**Chad Dawson**	Jesus Ruiz	TKO 7	**WBC**	Hartford, Conn.
June 9	Antonio Tarver	Elvir Muriqi	Wm 12	—	Hartford, Conn.
July 14	Roy Jones Jr.	Anthony Hanshaw	Wu 12	—	Biloxi, Mississippi
July 21	Bernard Hopkins	Winky Wright	Wu 12	—	Las Vegas
Sept. 29	**Clinton Woods**	Julio Cesar Gonzalez	Wu 12	**IBF**	Sheffield, England
Sept. 29	**Chad Dawson**	Epifano Mendoza	TKO 4	**WBC**	Sacramento, Calif.

Super Middleweights (168 lbs)

Date	Winner	Loser	Result	Title	Site
Dec. 2	Jeff Lacy	Vitaly Tsypko	Wm 10	—	Tampa, Fla.
Mar. 3	Alejandro Berrio	Robert Stieglitz	TKO 3	**IBF***	Rostock, Germany
Mar. 7	Anthony Mundine	Sam Soliman	TKO 9	**WBA**†	Sydney, Australia
Mar. 24	**Mikkel Kessler**	Librando Andrade	Wu 12	**WBA/WBC**	Copenhagen, Denmark
Apr. 7	**Joe Calzaghe**	Peter Manfredo	TKO 3	**WBO**	Cardiff, Wales
June 27	**Anthony Mundine**	Pablo Nievas	Wu 12	**WBA**	Gold Coast, Australia
Oct. 19	Lucian Bute	**Alejandro Berrio**	KO 11	**IBF**	Montreal, Quebec

*Berrio won the IBF belt that was left vacant by Joe Calzaghe, who rather than fight mandatory challenger Robert Stieglitz, opted to fight a higher-profile opponent in Peter Manfredo, from "The Contender."
†Mundine won the WBA belt that was vacated when Mikkel Kessler was named "Super World Champion".

Middleweights (160 lbs)

Date	Winner	Loser	Result	Title	Site
Dec. 2	Mariano Natalio Carrera	**Javier Castillejo**	TKO 11*	WBA	Berlin
Dec. 2	Winky Wright	Ike Quartey	Wu 12	—	Tampa, Fla.
Dec. 9	**Jermain Taylor**	Kassim Ouma	Wu 12	WBC	N. Little Rock, Ark.
Jan. 27	Kelly Pavlik	Jose Luis Zertuche	KO 8	—	Anaheim, Calif.
Apr. 28	Felix Sturm	**Javier Castillejo**	Wu 12	WBA	Stuttgart, Germany
May 19	Kelly Pavlik	Edison Miranda	TKO 7	—	Memphis, Tenn.
May 19	**Jermain Taylor**	Cory Spinks	Ws 12	WBC	Memphis, Tenn.
May 26	**Arthur Abraham**	Sebastien Demers	TKO 3	IBF	Bamberg, Germany
June 30	Felix Sturm	Noe Alcoba	Wu 12	WBA	Stuttgart, Germany
Aug. 18	**Arthur Abraham**	Khoren Gevor	KO 11	IBF	Berlin, Germany
Sept. 29	Kelly Pavlik	**Jermain Taylor**	TKO 7	WBC	Atlantic City
Oct. 20	**Felix Sturm**	Randy Griffin	Draw 12	WBA	Halle, Germany

*Castillejo retained the belt when Carrera failed a post-fight drug test.

Junior Middleweights (154 lbs)
(Super Welterweights)

Date	Winner	Loser	Result	Title	Site
Jan. 6	Travis Simms	**Jose Antonio Rivera**	TKO 9	WBA	Hollywood, Fla.
Feb. 3	**Cory Spinks**	Rodney Jones	Wu 12	IBF	Kissimmee, Fla.
May 5	Floyd Mayweather Jr.	**Oscar de la Hoya**	Ws 12	WBC	Las Vegas
July 28	Vernon Forrest	Carlos Baldomir	Wu 12	WBC*	Tacoma, Wash.

*Forrest beat Baldomir for the WBC belt that Floyd Mayweather Jr. vacated to move back down to welterweight for his scheduled (Dec. 8, 2007) bout with fellow unbeaten Ricky Hatton.

Welterweights (147 lbs)

Date	Winner	Loser	Result	Title	Site
Nov. 4	Floyd Mayweather Jr.	**Carlos Baldomir**	Wu 12	WBC	Las Vegas
Dec. 2	Miguel Cotto	Carlos Quintana	TKO 5	WBA*	Atlantic City
Feb. 10	Shane Mosley	**Luis Collazo**	Wu 12	WBC†	Las Vegas
Feb. 10	Vivian Harris	Juan Lazcano	Wu 12	—	Las Vegas
Mar. 3	**Miguel Cotto**	Oktay Urkal	TKO 11	WBA	San Juan, Puerto Rico
June 9	**Miguel Cotto**	Zab Judah	TKO 11	WBA	New York City
July 14	Alfonso Gomez	Arturo Gatti	KO 7	—	Atlantic City
July 14	**Kermit Cintron**	Walter Dario Matthysse	KO 2	IBF	Atlantic City
July 14	Paul Williams	Antonio Margarito	Wu 12	—	Carson, Calif.

*Cotto won the WBA belt that was vacated by Ricky Hatton when he moved back down to the junior welterweight division.
†interim title.

Junior Welterweights (140 lbs)
(Super Lightweights)

Date	Winner	Loser	Result	Title	Site
Jan. 20	**Junior Witter**	Arturo Morua	TKO 9	WBC	London
Jan. 20	Ricky Hatton	**Juan Urango**	Wu 12	IBF	Las Vegas
Mar. 10	**Souleymane M'baye**	Andreas Kotelnik	Draw 12	WBA	Liverpool, England
June 16	Paul Malignaggi	Lovemore N'dou	Wu 12	IBF*	Mendoza, Argentina
June 23	Ricky Hatton	Jose Luis Castillo	KO 4	—	Las Vegas
July 21	Gavin Rees	**Souleymane M'baye**	Wu 12	WBA	Cardiff, Wales
Sept. 7	**Junior Witter**	Vivian Harris	KO 7	WBC	Brandford, England

*Malignaggi won the IBF title that was vacated when Ricky Hatton signed to fight Jose Luis Castillo rather than mandatory chalenger Lovemore N'dou.

Major Bouts Scheduled for Late 2006/Early 2007

Date	Division	Match-up	Title	Location
Nov. 3	super middleweight	Joe Calzaghe–Mikkel Kessler	WBO/WBC/WBA	Cardiff, Wales
Nov. 3	junior lightweight	Juan Manuel Marquez–Rocky Juarez	WBC	Tucson, Ariz.
Nov. 10	welterweight	Miguel Cotto–Shane Mosley	WBA	New York City
Nov. 10	cruiserweight	Jean-Marc Mormeck–David Haye	WBC/WBA	Paris
Nov. 17	junior lightweight	Joan Guzman–Humberto Soto	WBO	Atlantic City
Nov. 23	super middleweight	Fernando Vargas–Ricardo Mayorga	—	Los Angeles
Dec. 8	welterweight	Floyd Mayweather Jr.–Ricky Hatton	WBC	Las Vegas
Jan. 19	light heavyweight	Roy Jones Jr.–Felix Trinidad	—	New York City

Major Bouts, 2006-07 (Cont.)

Lightweights (135 lbs)

Date	Winner	Loser	Result	Title	Site
Nov. 4	**Juan Diaz**	Fernando Angulo	Wu 12	**WBA**	Phoenix, Ariz.
Feb. 3	Julio Diaz	**Jesus Chavez**	KO 3	**IBF**	Kissimmee, Fla.
Apr. 28	**Juan Diaz**	Acelino Freitas	TKO 8	**WBA**	Mashantucket, Conn.
May 11	Prawet Singwangcha	Jose Miguel Cotto	Draw 12	**WBA†**	Salinas, Puerto Rico
Aug. 4	**David Diaz**	Erik Morales	Wu 12	**WBC**	Chicago, Ill.
Oct. 13	**Juan Diaz**	**Julio Diaz**	TKO 9	**WBA/IBF**	Chicago, Ill.

†Singwangcha and Cotto fought to a draw in their fight for the WBA belt that was vacated when the WBA designated champion Juan Diaz "Super World Champion".

Junior Lightweights (130 lbs)
(Super Featherweights)

Date	Winner	Loser	Result	Title	Site
Nov. 4	Malcolm Klassen	**Gairy St. Clair**	Ws 12	**IBF**	Kempton Park, S. Africa
Nov. 18	Manny Pacquiao	Erik Morales	KO 3	—	Las Vegas
Jan. 3	**Edwin Valero**	Michael Lozada	TKO 1	**WBA**	Tokyo, Japan
Jan. 27	Jorge Arce	Julio Ler	Wu 12	—	Anaheim, Calif.
Mar. 17	Juan Manuel Marquez	**M. Antonio Barrera**	Wu 12	**WBC**	Las Vegas
Apr. 20	Mzonke Fana	**Malcolm Klassen**	Ws 12	**IBF**	Khayelitsha, S. Africa
Aug. 31	**Mzonke Fana**	Javier Osvaldo Alvarez	KO 9	**IBF**	Klerksdorp, S. Africa
Oct. 6	Manny Pacquiao	Marco Antonio Barrera	Wu 12	—	Las Vegas

Featherweights (126 lbs)

Date	Winner	Loser	Result	Title	Site
Nov. 4	Orlando Salido	**Robert Guerrero**	Wu 12	**IBF***	Phoenix, Ariz.
Nov. 25	Juan Manuel Marquez	Jimrex Jaca	KO 9	—	Hidalgo, Tex.
Dec. 17	In Jin Chi	**Rudy Lopez**	Wu 12	**WBC**	Seoul, S. Korea
Feb. 23	Robert Guerrero	Spend Abazi	TKO 9	**IBF**	Copenhagen, Denmark
Mar 3	**Chris John**	Jose Rojas	Wu 12	**WBA**	Jakarta, Indonesia
July 21	Jorge Linares	Oscar Larios	TKO 10	**WBC†**	Las Vegas
Aug. 19	**Chris John**	Zaiki Takemoto	TKO 9	**IBF**	Kobe, Japan

*Salido was stripped of his title when he tested positive in a post-fight drug test. Robert Guerrero won back the vacant IBF belt on Feb. 23.

†Linares won the interim WBC belt that was created when champ In Jin Chi left boxing to try his hand at mixed martial arts.

Junior Featherweights (122 lbs)
(Super Bantamweights)

Date	Winner	Loser	Result	Title	Site
Nov. 10	Steve Molitor	Michael Hunter	KO 5	**IBF***	Hartlepool, England
Mar. 3	Rafael Marquez	**Israel Vazquez**	TKO 7†	**WBC**	Carson, Calif.
Mar. 16	**Celestino Caballero**	Ricardo Castillo	TKO 9	**WBA**	Hollywood, Fla.
July 14	**Steve Molitor**	Takalani Ndlovu	TKO 9	**IBF**	Orilla, Ontario
Aug. 4	**Celestino Caballero**	Jorge Lacierva	Wu 12	**WBA**	Hidalgo, Texas
Aug. 4	Israel Vazquez	**Rafael Marquez**	TKO 6	**WBC**	Hidalgo, Texas
Oct. 27	**Steve Molitor**	Fashung 3K Battery	Wu 12	**IBF**	Rama, Ontario

*Molitor won the vacant IBF title.

†Vazquez asked his trainer to stop the fight because he was having trouble breathing.

Bantamweights (118 lbs)

Date	Winner	Loser	Result	Title	Site
Nov. 13	**Hozumi Hasegawa**	Genaro Garcia	Wu 12	**WBC**	Tokyo, Japan
Mar. 17	**Wladimir Sidorenko**	Ricardo Cordoba	Draw 12	**WBA**	Stuttgart, Germany
June 29	**Wladimir Sidorenko**	Jerome Arnould	TKO 7	**WBA**	Marseille, France
July 7	Luis Alberto Perez	Genaro Garcia	KO 7	**IBF***	Bridgeport, Conn.
Sept. 29	Joseph Agbeko	**Luis Alberto Perez**	TKO 7	**IBF**	Sacramento, Calif.

*Perez won the IBF title that was vacated by Rafael Maquez when he moved up to junior featherweight.

Junior Bantamweights (115 lbs)
(Super Flyweights)

Date	Winner	Loser	Result	Title	Site
Nov. 17	Cristian Mijares	Reynaldo Lopez	Wu 12	**WBC***	Torreon, Mexico
Dec. 2	**Nobuo Nashiro**	Eduardo Garcia	Wu 12	**WBA**	Osaka, Japan
Jan. 3	**Cristian Mijares**	Katsushige Kawashima	TKO 10	**WBC**	Tokyo, Japan
Apr. 14	**Cristian Mijares**	Jorge Arce	Wu 12	**WBC**	San Antonio, Texas
May 3	Alexander Munoz	**Nobuo Nashiro**	Wu 12	**WBA**	Tokyo, Japan
July 13	**Cristian Mijares**	Teppei Kikui	TKO 10	**WBC**	Durango, Mexico
Sept. 24	**Alexander Munoz**	Kuniyuki Aizawa	Wu 12	**WBA**	Tokyo, Japan
Oct. 13	Dmitri Kirilov	Jose Navarro	Wu 12	**IBF†**	Moscow, Russia
Oct. 20	**Cristian Mijares**	Franck Gorjux	TKO 1	**WBC**	Cancun, Mexcio

*interim title.

†Dmitri Kirilov won the belt that was vacated by former champ Luis Perez when he failed to make weight for his Nov. 4, 2006 scheduled bout against Ricardo Vargas. The fight was called off.

Flyweights (112 lbs)

Date	Winner	Loser	Result	Title	Site
Nov. 17	**P. Wonjongkam**	**M. Mhikiza Myekeni**	Wu 12	**WBC**	Korat, Thailand
Dec. 2	Roberto Vasquez	**Takefumi Sakata**	Ws 12	**WBA***	Paris
Mar. 3	**Vic Darchinyan**	Victor Burgos	TKO 12	**IBF**	Carson, Calif.
Mar. 19	Takefumi Sakata	**Lorenzo Parra**	TKO 3	**WBA**	Tokyo, Japan
Apr. 6	**P. Wonjongkam**	Tomonobu Shimizu	TKO 8	**WBC**	Saraburi, Thailand
July 1	**Takefumi Sakata**	Roberto Vasquez	Wu 12	**WBA**	Tokyo, Japan
July 7	Nonito Donaire	**Vic Darchinyan**	TKO 5	**IBF**	Bridgeport, Conn.
July 18	Daisuke Naito	**P. Wonjongkam**	Wu 12	**WBC**	Tokyo, Japan
Oct. 11	**Daisuke Naito**	Daiki Kameda	Wu 12	**WBC**	Tokyo, Japan

*Vasquez won the interim WBA belt.

Junior Flyweights (108 lbs)
(Light Flyweights)

Date	Winner	Loser	Result	Title	Site
Nov. 18	**Omar Nino**	Brian Viloria	MDraw 12*	**WBC**	Las Vegas
Dec. 20	**Koki Kameda**	Juan Jose Landaeta	Wu 12	**WBA**	Tokyo, Japan
Jan. 25	**Ulises Solis**	Will Grigsby	TKO 8	**IBF**	Las Vegas
Apr. 14	Edgar Sosa	Brian Viloria	Wm 12	**WBC†**	San Antonio, Texas
Mar. 19	**Ulises Solis**	Jose Antonio Aguirre	TKO 9	**IBF**	Guadalajara, Mexico
June 22	Juan Carlos Reveco	Nethra Sasiprapa	KO 8	**WBA‡**	Mendoza, Argentina
July 28	**Edgar Sosa**	Luis Lazarte	Disq. 10^	**WBC**	Cancun, Mexico
Aug. 4	**Ulises Solis**	Rodel Mayol	TKO 8	**IBF**	Chicago, Ill.
Sept. 16	**Edgar Sosa**	Lorenzo Trejo	KO 9	**WBC**	Las Vegas
Oct. 13	**Juan Carlos Reveco**	Humberto Pool	TKO 5	**WBA**	Buenos Aires, Argentina

*The Nino-Viloria bout was later ruled a no-contest after Nino failed a post-fight drug test. As a result of the positive drug test, Nino was stripped of the WBC belt.

†Sosa beat Viloria for the vacant WBC belt (see note above).

‡Reveco won the WBA belt that was left vacant by Koki Kameda when he moved up to flyweight.

^Lazarte was disqualified in the 10th for repeated low blows.

Minimumweights (105 lbs)
(Strawweights or Mini-Flyweights)

Date	Winner	Loser	Result	Title	Site
Nov. 7	Katsunari Takayama	Carlos Melo	TWu 9	**WBA***	Osaka, Japan
Nov. 13	**Eagle Kyowa**	Lorenzo Trejo	Wu 12	**WBC**	Tokyo, Japan
Dec. 23	**Muhammad Rachman**	Benjie Sorolla	TKO 7	**IBF**	Jakarta, Indonesia
Apr. 7	**Yutaka Niida**	Katsunari Takayama	Ws 12	**WBA†**	Tokyo, Japan
June 4	**Eagle Kyowa**	Akira Yaegashi	Wu 12	**WBC**	Yokohama, Japan
July 7	Florante Condes	**M. Rachman**	Ws 12	**IBF**	Jakarta, Indonesia
Sept. 1	**Yutaka Niida**	Eriberto Gejon	Wu 12	**WBA**	Tokyo, Japan

*Takayama won the the WBA interim when the fight was stopped in round nine following an unintentional head butt.

†Niida was the WBA titleholder while Takayama was the interim belt holder

1892-2007
Through the Years

SPORTS ALMANAC

World Heavyweight Championship Fights

Widely accepted world champions in **bold** type. Note following result abbreviations: KO (knockout), TKO (technical knockout), Wu (unanimous decision), Wm (majority decision), Ws (split decision), Ref (referee's decision), ND (no decision), Disq. (won on disqualification).

Year	Date	Winner	Age	Wgt	Loser	Wgt	Result	Location
1892	Sept. 7	James J. Corbett	26	178	John L. Sullivan	212	KO 21	New Orleans
1894	Jan. 25	**James J. Corbett**	27	184	Charley Mitchell	158	KO 3	Jacksonville, Fla.
1897	Mar. 17	Bob Fitzsimmons	34	167	**James J. Corbett**	183	KO 14	Carson City, Nev.
1899	June 9	James J. Jeffries	24	206	**Bob Fitzsimmons**	167	KO 11	Coney Island, N.Y.
1899	Nov. 3	**James J. Jeffries**	24	215	Tom Sharkey	183	Ref 25	Coney Island, N.Y.
1900	Apr. 6	**James J. Jeffries**	24	NA	Jack Finnegan	NA	KO 1	Detroit
1900	May 11	**James J. Jeffries**	25	218	James J. Corbett	188	KO 23	Coney Island, N.Y.
1901	Nov. 15	**James J. Jeffries**	26	211	Gus Ruhlin	194	TKO 6	San Francisco
1902	July 25	**James J. Jeffries**	27	219	Bob Fitzsimmons	172	KO 8	San Francisco
1903	Aug. 14	**James J. Jeffries**	28	220	James J. Corbett	190	KO 10	San Francisco
1904	Aug. 25	**James J. Jeffries***	29	219	Jack Munroe	186	TKO 2	San Francisco
1905	July 3	Marvin Hart	28	190	Jack Root	171	KO 12	Reno, Nev.
1906	Feb. 23	Tommy Burns	24	180	**Marvin Hart**	188	Ref 20	Los Angeles
1906	Oct. 2	**Tommy Burns**	25	NA	Jim Flynn	NA	KO 15	Los Angeles
1906	Nov. 28	**Tommy Burns**	25	172	Phila. Jack O'Brien	163½	Draw 20	Los Angeles
1907	May 8	**Tommy Burns**	25	180	Phila. Jack O'Brien	167	Ref 20	Los Angeles
1907	July 4	**Tommy Burns**	26	181	Bill Squires	180	KO 1	Colma, Calif.
1907	Dec. 2	**Tommy Burns**	26	177	Gunner Moir	204	KO 10	London
1908	Feb. 10	**Tommy Burns**	26	NA	Jack Palmer	NA	KO 4	London
1908	Mar. 17	**Tommy Burns**	26	NA	Jem Roche	NA	KO 1	Dublin
1908	Apr. 18	**Tommy Burns**	26	NA	Jewey Smith	NA	KO 5	Paris
1908	June 13	**Tommy Burns**	26	184	Bill Squires	183	KO 8	Paris
1908	Aug. 24	**Tommy Burns**	27	181	Bill Squires	184	KO 13	Sydney
1908	Sept. 2	**Tommy Burns**	27	183	Bill Lang	187	KO 6	Melbourne
1908	Dec. 26	Jack Johnson	30	192	**Tommy Burns**	168	TKO 14	Sydney
1909	Mar. 10	**Jack Johnson**	30	NA	Victor McLaglen	NA	ND 6	Vancouver
1909	May 19	**Jack Johnson**	31	205	Phila. Jack O'Brien	161	ND 6	Philadelphia
1909	June 30	**Jack Johnson**	31	207	Tony Ross	214	ND 6	Pittsburgh
1909	Sept. 9	**Jack Johnson**	31	209	Al Kaufman	191	ND 10	San Francisco
1909	Oct. 16	**Jack Johnson**	31	205½	Stanley Ketchel	170¼	KO 12	Colma, Calif.
1910	July 4	**Jack Johnson**	32	208	James J. Jeffries	227	KO 15	Reno, Nev.
1912	July 4	**Jack Johnson**	34	195½	Jim Flynn	175	TKO 9	Las Vegas, Nev.
1913	Dec. 19	**Jack Johnson**	35	NA	Jim Johnson	NA	Draw 10	Paris
1914	June 27	**Jack Johnson**	36	221	Frank Moran	203	Ref 20	Paris
1915	Apr. 5	Jess Willard	33	230	**Jack Johnson**	205½	KO 26	Havana
1916	Mar. 25	**Jess Willard**	34	225	Frank Moran	203	ND 10	NYC (Mad.Sq. Garden)
1919	July 4	Jack Dempsey	24	187	**Jess Willard**	245	TKO 4	Toledo, Ohio
1920	Sept. 6	**Jack Dempsey**	25	185	Billy Miske	187	KO 3	Benton Harbor, Mich.
1920	Dec. 14	**Jack Dempsey**	25	188¼	Bill Brennan	197	KO 12	NYC (Mad. Sq. Garden)
1921	July 2	**Jack Dempsey**	26	188	Georges Carpentier	172	KO 4	Jersey City, N.J.
1923	July 4	**Jack Dempsey**	28	188	Tommy Gibbons	175½	Ref 15	Shelby, Mont.
1923	Sept. 14	**Jack Dempsey**	28	192½	Luis Firpo	216½	KO 2	NYC (Polo Grounds)
1926	Sept. 23	Gene Tunney	29	189½	**Jack Dempsey**	190	Wu 10	Philadelphia
1927	Sept. 22	**Gene Tunney**	30	189½	Jack Dempsey	192½	Wu 10	Chicago
1928	July 26	**Gene Tunney****	31	192	Tom Heeney	203	TKO 11	NYC (Yankee Stadium)
1930	June 12	Max Schmeling	24	188	Jack Sharkey	197	Disq. 4	NYC (Yankee Stadium)
1931	July 3	**Max Schmeling**	25	189	Young Stribling	186½	TKO 15	Cleveland

*James J. Jeffries retired as champion on May 13, 1905, then came out of retirement to fight Jack Johnson for the title in 1910.
**Gene Tunney retired as champion in 1928.

Year	Date	Winner	Age	Wgt	Loser	Wgt	Result	Location
1932	June 21	Jack Sharkey	29	205	**Max Schmeling**	188	Ws 15	Long Island City, N.Y.
1933	June 29	Primo Carnera	26	260½	**Jack Sharkey**	201	KO 6	Long Island City, N.Y.
1933	Oct. 22	**Primo Carnera**	26	259½	Paulino Uzcudun	229¼	Wu 15	Rome
1934	Mar. 1	**Primo Carnera**	27	270	Tommy Loughran	184	Wu 15	Miami
1934	June 14	Max Baer	25	209½	**Primo Carnera**	263¼	TKO 11	Long Island City, N.Y.
1935	June 13	James J. Braddock	29	193¾	**Max Baer**	209	Wu 15	Long Island City, N.Y.
1937	June 22	Joe Louis	23.	197¼	**James J. Braddock**	197	KO 8	Chicago
1937	Aug. 30	**Joe Louis**	23	197	Tommy Farr	204¼	Wu 15	NYC (Yankee Stadium)
1938	Feb. 23	**Joe Louis**	23	200	Nathan Mann	193½	KO 3	NYC (Mad. Sq. Garden)
1938	Apr. 1	**Joe Louis**	23	202½	Harry Thomas	196	KO 5	Chicago
1938	June 22	**Joe Louis**	24	198¾	Max Schmeling	193	KO 1	NYC (Yankee Stadium)
1939	Jan. 25	**Joe Louis**	24	200¼	John Henry Lewis	180¾	KO 1	NYC (Mad. Sq. Garden)
1939	Apr. 17	**Joe Louis**	24	201¼	Jack Roper	204¾	KO 1	Los Angeles
1939	June 28	**Joe Louis**	25	200¾	Tony Galento	233¾	TKO 4	NYC (Yankee Stadium)
1939	Sept. 20	**Joe Louis**	25	200	Bob Pastor	183	KO 11	Detroit
1940	Feb. 9	**Joe Louis**	25	203	Arturo Godoy	202	Ws 15	NYC (Mad. Sq. Garden)
1940	Mar. 29	**Joe Louis**	25	201½	Johnny Paychek	187½	KO 2	NYC (Mad. Sq. Garden)
1940	June 20	**Joe Louis**	26	199	Arturo Godoy	201¼	TKO 8	NYC (Yankee Stadium)
1940	Dec. 16	**Joe Louis**	26	202¼	Al McCoy	180¾	TKO 6	Boston
1941	Jan. 31	**Joe Louis**	26	202½	Red Burman	188	KO 5	NYC (Mad. Sq. Garden)
1941	Feb. 17	**Joe Louis**	26	203½	Gus Dorazio	193½	KO 2	Philadelphia
1941	Mar. 21	**Joe Louis**	26	202	Abe Simon	254½	TKO 13	Detroit
1941	Apr. 8	**Joe Louis**	26	203½	Tony Musto	199½	TKO 9	St. Louis
1941	May 23	**Joe Louis**	27	201½	Buddy Baer	237½	Disq. 7	Washington, D.C.
1941	June 18	**Joe Louis**	27	199½	Billy Conn	174	KO 13	NYC (Polo Grounds)
1941	Sept. 29	**Joe Louis**	27	202¼	Lou Nova	202½	TKO 6	NYC (Polo Grounds)
1942	Jan. 9	**Joe Louis**	27	206¾	Buddy Baer	250	KO 1	NYC (Mad. Sq. Garden)
1942	Mar. 27	**Joe Louis**	27	207½	Abe Simon	255½	KO 6	NYC (Mad. Sq. Garden)
1942-45 World War II								
1946	June 9	**Joe Louis**	32	207	Billy Conn	187	KO 8	NYC (Yankee Stadium)
1946	Sept. 18	**Joe Louis**	32	211	Tami Mauriello	198½	KO 1	NYC (Yankee Stadium)
1947	Dec. 5	**Joe Louis**	33	211½	Jersey Joe Walcott	194½	Ws 15	NYC (Yankee Stadium)
1948	June 25	**Joe Louis***	34	213½	Jersey Joe Walcott	194¾	KO 11	NYC (Yankee Stadium)
1949	June 22	**Ezzard Charles**	27	181¾	Jersey Joe Walcott	195½	Wu 15	Chicago
1949	Aug. 10	**Ezzard Charles**	28	180	Gus Lesnevich	182	TKO 8	NYC (Yankee Stadium)
1949	Oct. 14	**Ezzard Charles**	28	182	Pat Valentino	188½	KO 8	San Francisco
1950	Aug. 15	**Ezzard Charles**	29	183¼	Freddie Beshore	184½	TKO 14	Buffalo
1950	Sept. 27	**Ezzard Charles**	29	184½	Joe Louis	218	Wu 15	NYC (Yankee Stadium)
1950	Dec. 5	**Ezzard Charles**	29	185	Nick Barone	178½	KO 11	Cincinnati
1951	Jan. 12	**Ezzard Charles**	29	185	Lee Oma	193	TKO 10	NYC (Mad. Sq. Garden)
1951	Mar. 7	**Ezzard Charles**	29	186	Jersey Joe Walcott	193	Wu 15	Detroit
1951	May 30	**Ezzard Charles**	29	182	Joey Maxim	181½	Wu 15	Chicago
1951	July 18	Jersey Joe Walcott	37	194	**Ezzard Charles**	182	KO 7	Pittsburgh
1952	June 5	**Jersey Joe Walcott**	38	196	Ezzard Charles	191½	Wu 15	Philadelphia
1952	Sept. 23	Rocky Marciano	29	184	**Jersey Joe Walcott**	196	KO 13	Philadelphia
1953	May 15	**Rocky Marciano**	29	184½	Jersey Joe Walcott	197¾	KO 1	Chicago
1953	Sept. 24	**Rocky Marciano**	30	185	Roland LaStarza	184¾	TKO 11	NYC (Polo Grounds)
1954	June 17	**Rocky Marciano**	30	187½	Ezzard Charles	185½	Wu 15	NYC (Yankee Stadium)
1954	Sept. 17	**Rocky Marciano**	31	187	Ezzard Charles	192½	KO 8	NYC (Yankee Stadium)
1955	May 16	**Rocky Marciano**	31	189	Don Cockell	205	TKO 9	San Francisco
1955	Sept. 21	**Rocky Marciano****	32	188¼	Archie Moore	188	KO 9	NYC (Yankee Stadium)
1956	Nov. 30	Floyd Patterson	21	182¼	Archie Moore	187¾	KO 5	Chicago
1957	July 29	**Floyd Patterson**	22	184	Tommy Jackson	192½	TKO 10	NYC (Polo Grounds)
1957	Aug. 22	**Floyd Patterson**	22	187¼	Pete Rademacher	202	KO 6	Seattle
1958	Aug. 18	**Floyd Patterson**	23	184½	Roy Harris	194	TKO 13	Los Angeles
1959	May 1	**Floyd Patterson**	24	182½	Brian London	206	KO 11	Indianapolis
1959	June 26	Ingemar Johansson	26	196	**Floyd Patterson**	182	TKO 3	NYC (Yankee Stadium)
1960	June 20	Floyd Patterson	25	190	**Ingemar Johansson**	194¾	KO 5	NYC (Polo Grounds)
1961	Mar. 13	**Floyd Patterson**	26	194¾	Ingemar Johansson	206½	KO 6	Miami Beach
1961	Dec. 4	**Floyd Patterson**	26	188½	Tom McNeeley	197	KO 4	Toronto
1962	Sept. 25	Sonny Liston	30	214	**Floyd Patterson**	189	KO 1	Chicago
1963	July 22	**Sonny Liston**	31	215	Floyd Patterson	194½	KO 1	Las Vegas
1964	Feb. 25	Cassius Clay**	22	210½	**Sonny Liston**	218	TKO 7	Miami Beach

*Joe Louis retired as champion on Mar. 1, 1949, then came out of retirement to fight Ezzard Charles for the title in 1950.
**Rocky Marciano retired as undefeated champion on Apr. 27, 1956.

World Heavyweight Championship Fights (Cont.)

Year	Date	Winner	Age	Wgt	Loser	Wgt	Result	Location
1965	Mar. 5	Ernie Terrell WBA	25	199	Eddie Machen	192	Wu 15	Chicago
1965	May 25	**Muhammad Ali**	23	206	Sonny Liston	215¼	KO 1	Lewiston, Maine
1965	Nov. 1	Ernie Terrell WBA	26	206	George Chuvalo	209	Wu 15	Toronto
1965	Nov. 22	**Muhammad Ali**	23	210	Floyd Patterson	196¾	TKO 12	Las Vegas
1966	Mar. 29	**Muhammad Ali**	24	214½	George Chuvalo	216	Wu 15	Toronto
1966	May 21	**Muhammad Ali**	24	201½	Henry Cooper	188	TKO 6	London
1966	June 28	Ernie Terrell WBA	27	209½	Doug Jones	187½	Wu 15	Houston
1966	Aug. 6	**Muhammad Ali**	24	209½	Brian London	201½	KO 3	London
1966	Sept. 10	**Muhammad Ali**	24	203½	Karl Mildenberger	194¼	TKO 12	Frankfurt, W. Ger.
1966	Nov. 14	**Muhammad Ali**	24	212¾	Cleveland Williams	210½	TKO 3	Houston
1967	Feb. 6	**Muhammad Ali**	25	212¼	Ernie Terrell WBA	212¼	Wu 15	Houston
1967	Mar. 22	**Muhammad Ali**	25	211½	Zora Folley	202½	KO 7	NYC (Mad. Sq. Garden)
1968	Mar. 4	Joe Frazier	24	204½	Buster Mathis	243½	TKO 11	NYC (Mad. Sq. Garden)
1968	Apr. 27	Jimmy Ellis	28	197	Jerry Quarry	195	Wm 15	Oakland
1968	June 24	Joe Frazier NY	24	203½	Manuel Ramos	208	TKO 2	NYC (Mad. Sq. Garden)
1968	Aug. 14	Jimmy Ellis WBA	28	198	Floyd Patterson	188	Ref 15	Stockholm
1968	Dec. 10	Joe Frazier NY	24	203	Oscar Bonavena	207	Wu 15	Philadelphia
1969	Apr. 22	Joe Frazier NY	25	204½	Dave Zyglewicz	190½	KO 1	Houston
1969	June 23	Joe Frazier NY	25	203½	Jerry Quarry	198½	TKO 8	NYC (Mad. Sq. Garden)
1970	Feb. 16	Joe Frazier NY	26	205	Jimmy Ellis WBA	201	TKO 5	NYC (Mad. Sq. Garden)
1970	Nov. 18	**Joe Frazier**	26	209	Bob Foster	188	KO 2	Detroit
1971	Mar. 8	**Joe Frazier**	27	205½	Muhammad Ali	215	Wu 15	NYC (Mad. Sq. Garden)
1972	Jan. 15	**Joe Frazier**	28	215½	Terry Daniels	195	TKO 4	New Orleans
1972	May 26	**Joe Frazier**	28	217½	Ron Stander	218	TKO 5	Omaha, Neb.
1973	Jan. 22	George Foreman	24	217½	**Joe Frazier**	214	TKO 2	Kingston, Jamaica
1973	Sept. 1	**George Foreman**	24	219½	Jose (King) Roman	196½	KO 1	Tokyo
1974	Mar. 26	**George Foreman**	25	224¾	Ken Norton	212¾	TKO 2	Caracas, Venezuela
1974	Oct. 30	Muhammad Ali	32	216½	**George Foreman**	220	KO 8	Kinshasa, Zaire
1975	Mar. 24	**Muhammad Ali**	33	223½	Chuck Wepner	225	TKO 15	Cleveland
1975	May 16	**Muhammad Ali**	33	224½	Ron Lyle	219	TKO 11	Las Vegas
1975	June 30	**Muhammad Ali**	33	224½	Joe Bugner	230	Wu 15	Kuala Lumpur, Malaysia
1975	Oct. 1	**Muhammad Ali**	33	224½	Joe Frazier	215	TKO 14	Manila, Philippines
1976	Feb. 20	**Muhammad Ali**	34	226	Jean Pierre Coopman	206	KO 5	San Juan, P.R.
1976	Apr. 30	**Muhammad Ali**	34	230	Jimmy Young	209	Wu 15	Landover, Md.
1976	May 24	**Muhammad Ali**	34	220	Richard Dunn	206½	TKO 5	Munich, W. Ger.
1976	Sept. 28	**Muhammad Ali**	34	221	Ken Norton	217½	Wu 15	NYC (Yankee Stadium)
1977	May 16	**Muhammad Ali**	35	221¼	Alfredo Evangelista	209¼	Wu 15	Landover, Md.
1977	Sept. 29	**Muhammad Ali**	35	225	Earnie Shavers	211¼	Wu 15	NYC (Mad. Sq. Garden)
1978	Feb. 15	Leon Spinks	24	197¼	**Muhammad Ali**	224¼	Ws 15	Las Vegas
1978	June 9	Larry Holmes	28	209	Ken Norton WBC††	220	Ws 15	Las Vegas
1978	Sept. 15	Muhammad Ali†	36	221	**Leon Spinks**	201	Wu 15	New Orleans
1978	Nov. 10	Larry Holmes WBC	29	214	Alfredo Evangelista	208¼	KO 7	Las Vegas
1979	Mar. 23	Larry Holmes WBC	29	214	Osvaldo Ocasio	207	TKO 7	Las Vegas
1979	June 22	Larry Holmes WBC	29	215	Mike Weaver	202	TKO 12	NYC (Mad. Sq. Garden)
1979	Sept. 28	Larry Holmes WBC	29	210	Earnie Shavers	211	TKO 11	Las Vegas
1979	Oct. 20	John Tate	24	240	Gerrie Coetzee	222	Wu 15	Pretoria, S. Africa
1980	Feb. 3	Larry Holmes WBC	30	213½	Lorenzo Zanon	215	TKO 6	Las Vegas
1980	Mar. 31	Mike Weaver	27	232	John Tate WBA	232	KO 15	Knoxville, Tenn.
1980	Mar. 31	Larry Holmes WBC	30	211	Leroy Jones	254½	TKO 8	Las Vegas
1980	July 7	Larry Holmes WBC	30	214¼	Scott LeDoux	226	TKO 7	Minneapolis
1980	Oct. 2	Larry Holmes WBC	30	211½	Muhammad Ali	217½	TKO 11	Las Vegas
1980	Oct. 25	Mike Weaver WBA	28	210	Gerrie Coetzee	226½	KO 13	Sun City, S. Africa
1981	Apr. 11	**Larry Holmes**	31	215	Trevor Berbick	215½	Wu 15	Las Vegas
1981	June 12	**Larry Holmes**	31	212½	Leon Spinks	200¼	TKO 3	Detroit
1981	Oct. 3	Mike Weaver WBA	29	215	James (Quick) Tillis	209	Wu 15	Rosemont, Ill.
1981	Nov. 6	**Larry Holmes**	32	213¼	Renaldo Snipes	215¾	TKO 11	Pittsburgh
1982	June 11	**Larry Holmes**	32	212½	Gerry Cooney	225½	TKO 13	Las Vegas
1982	Nov. 26	**Larry Holmes**	33	217½	Randall (Tex) Cobb	234¼	Wu 15	Houston
1982	Dec. 10	Michael Dokes	24	216	Mike Weaver WBA	209¾	TKO 1	Las Vegas

**After defeating Liston, Cassius Clay announced that he had changed his name to Muhammad Ali. He was later stripped of his title by the WBA and most state boxing commissions after refusing induction into the U.S. Army on Apr. 28, 1967.

† Muhammad Ali retired as champion on June 27, 1979, then came out of retirement to fight Larry Holmes for the title in 1980.

†† WBC recognized Ken Norton as world champion when Leon Spinks refused to meet Norton before Spinks' rematch with Muhammad Ali. Norton had scored a 15-round split decision over Jimmy Young on Nov. 5, 1977 in Las Vegas.

Year	Date	Winner	Age	Wgt	Loser	Wgt	Result	Location
1983	Mar. 27	**Larry Holmes**	33	221	Lucien Rodriguez	209	Wu 12	Scranton, Pa.
1983	May 20	Michael Dokes WBA	24	223	Mike Weaver	218½	Draw 15	Las Vegas
1983	May 20	**Larry Holmes**	33	213	Tim Witherspoon	219½	Wu 12	Las Vegas
1983	Sept. 10	**Larry Holmes**	33	223	Scott Frank	211¼	TKO 5	Atlantic City
1983	Sept. 23	Gerrie Coetzee	28	215	Michael Dokes WBA	217	KO 10	Richfield, Ohio
1983	Nov. 25	**Larry Holmes**	34	219	Marvis Frazier	200	TKO 1	Las Vegas
1984	Mar. 9	Tim Witherspoon*	26	220¼	Greg Page	239½	Wm 12	Las Vegas
1984	Aug. 31	Pinklon Thomas	26	216	Tim Witherspoon	217	Wm 12	Las Vegas
1984	Nov. 9	**Larry Holmes** IBF	35	221½	Bonecrusher Smith	227	TKO 12	Las Vegas
1984	Dec. 1	Greg Page	26	236½	Gerrie Coetzee WBA	218	KO 8	Sun City, S. Africa
1985	Mar. 15	**Larry Holmes** IBF	35	223½	David Bey	233¼	TKO 10	Las Vegas
1985	Apr. 29	Tony Tubbs	26	229	Greg Page WBA	239½	Wu 15	Buffalo
1985	May 20	**Larry Holmes** IBF	35	224¼	Carl Williams	215	Wu 15	Las Vegas
1985	June 15	Pinklon Thomas WBC	27	220¼	Mike Weaver	221¼	KO 8	Las Vegas
1985	Sept. 21	Michael Spinks	29	200	**Larry Holmes** IBF	221½	Wu 15	Las Vegas
1986	Jan. 17	Tim Witherspoon	28	227	Tony Tubbs WBA	229	Wm 15	Atlanta
1986	Mar. 22	Trevor Berbick	33	218½	Pinklon Thomas WBC	222¾	Wu 15	Las Vegas
1986	Apr. 19	**Michael Spinks** IBF	29	205	Larry Holmes	223	Ws 15	Las Vegas
1986	July 19	Tim Witherspoon WBA	28	234¾	Frank Bruno	228	TKO 11	Wembley, England
1986	Sept. 6	**Michael Spinks** IBF	30	201	Steffen Tangstad	214¾	TKO 4	Las Vegas
1986	Nov. 22	Mike Tyson	20	221¼	Trevor Berbick WBC	218½	TKO 2	Las Vegas
1986	Dec. 12	Bonecrusher Smith	33	228½	Tim Witherspoon WBA	233½	TKO 1	NYC (Mad. Sq. Garden)
1987	Mar. 7	Mike Tyson WBC	20	219	Bonecrusher Smith WBA	233	Wu 12	Las Vegas
1987	May 30	Mike Tyson	20	218¾	Pinklon Thomas	217¾	TKO 6	Las Vegas
1987	May 30	Tony Tucker**	28	221¼	Buster Douglas	227¼	TKO 10	Las Vegas
1987	June 15	**Michael Spinks**†	30	208¾	Gerry Cooney	238	TKO 5	Atlantic City
1987	Aug. 1	Mike Tyson	21	221	Tony Tucker IBF	221	Wu 12	Las Vegas
1987	Oct. 16	Mike Tyson	21	216	Tyrell Biggs	228¾	TKO 7	Atlantic City
1988	Jan. 22	Mike Tyson	21	215¾	Larry Holmes	225¾	TKO 4	Atlantic City
1988	Mar. 20	Mike Tyson	21	216¼	Tony Tubbs	238¼	KO 2	Tokyo
1988	June 27	Mike Tyson	21	218¼	**Michael Spinks**	212¼	KO 1	Atlantic City
1989	Feb. 25	**Mike Tyson**	22	218	Frank Bruno	228	TKO 5	Las Vegas
1989	July 21	**Mike Tyson**	23	219¼	Carl Williams	218	TKO 1	Atlantic City
1990	Feb. 10	Buster Douglas	29	231½	**Mike Tyson**	220½	KO 10	Tokyo
1990	Oct. 25	Evander Holyfield	28	208	**Buster Douglas**	246	KO 3	Las Vegas
1991	Apr. 19	**Evander Holyfield**	28	208	George Foreman	257	Wu 12	Atlantic City
1991	Nov. 23	**Evander Holyfield**	29	210	Bert Cooper	215	TKO 7	Atlanta
1992	June 19	**Evander Holyfield**	29	210	Larry Holmes	233	Wu 12	Las Vegas
1992	Nov. 13	Riddick Bowe	25	235	**Evander Holyfield**	205	Wu 12	Las Vegas
1993	Feb. 6	**Riddick Bowe**	25	243	Michael Dokes	244	TKO 1	NYC (Mad. Sq. Garden)
1993	May 8	Lennox Lewis WBC‡	27	235	Tony Tucker	235	Wu 12	Las Vegas
1993	May 22	**Riddick Bowe**	25	244	Jesse Ferguson	224	TKO 2	Washington, D.C.
1993	Oct. 1	Lennox Lewis WBC	28	233	Frank Bruno	238	TKO 7	Cardiff, Wales
1993	Nov. 6	Evander Holyfield	31	217	**Riddick Bowe** WBA/IBF	246	Wm 12	Las Vegas
1994	Apr. 22	Michael Moorer	26	214	**Evander Holyfield**	214	Wm 12	Las Vegas
1994	May 6	Lennox Lewis WBC	28	235	Phil Jackson	218	TKO 8	Atlantic City
1994	Sept. 25	Oliver McCall	29	231¼	**Lennox Lewis** WBC	238	TKO 2	London
1994	Nov. 5	George Foreman!	45	250	**Michael Moorer**	222	KO 10	Las Vegas
1995	Apr. 8	Oliver McCall WBC	29	231	Larry Holmes	236	Wu 12	Las Vegas
1995	Apr. 8	Bruce Seldon!	28	236	Tony Tucker	240	TKO 7	Las Vegas
1995	Apr. 22	**George Foreman**!	46	256	Axel Schulz	221	Ws 12	Las Vegas
1995	Aug. 19	Bruce Seldon WBA	28	234	Joe Hipp	223	TKO 10	Las Vegas
1995	Sept. 2	Frank Bruno	33	248	Oliver McCall WBC	235	Wu 12	London
1995	Dec. 9	Frans Botha*	27	237	Axel Schulz	222	Wu 12	Stuttgart, GER
1996	Mar. 16	Mike Tyson	29	220	Frank Bruno WBC	247	TKO 3	Las Vegas

*WBC recognized winner of Mar. 9, 1984 fight between Tim Witherspoon and Greg Page as world champion after Larry Holmes relinquished title in dispute. IBF then recognized Holmes.

**IBF recognized winner of May 30, 1987 fight between Tony Tucker and James (Buster) Douglas as world champion after Michael Spinks relinquished title in dispute.

†The July 15, 1987 Spinks-Cooney fight was not an official championship bout because it was not sanctioned by any boxing associations, councils or federations.

‡WBC recognized Lennox Lewis as world champion when Riddick Bowe gave up that portion of his title on Dec. 14, 1992, rather than fight Lewis, the WBC's mandatory challenger.

!George Foreman won WBA and IBF championships when he beat Michael Moorer on Nov. 5, 1994. He was stripped of WBA title on Mar. 4, 1995, when he refused to fight No. 1 contender Tony Tucker, and he relinquished IBF title on June 29, 1995, rather than give Axel Schulz a rematch. Tucker lost to Bruce Seldon in their April 8, 2001 fight for vacant WBA title.

World Heavyweight Championship Fights (Cont.)

Year	Date	Winner	Age	Wgt	Loser	Wgt	Result	Location
1996	June 22	Michael Moorer*	28	222	Axel Schulz	223	Ws 12	Dortmund, GER
1996	Sept. 7	Mike Tyson WBC†	30	219	Bruce Seldon WBA	229	TKO 1	Las Vegas
1996	Nov. 9	Evander Holyfield	34	215	**Mike Tyson** WBA	222	TKO 11	Las Vegas
1997	Feb. 7	Lennox Lewis†	31	251	Oliver McCall	237	TKO 5	Las Vegas
1997	Mar. 29	Michael Moorer IBF	29	212	Vaughn Bean	212	Wm 12	Las Vegas
1997	June 28	**Evander Holyfield** WBA‡	34	218	Mike Tyson	218	Disq. 3	Las Vegas
1997	July 12	Lennox Lewis WBC	31	242	Henry Akinwande	237½	Disq. 5	Stateline, Nev.
1997	Oct. 4	Lennox Lewis WBC	32	244	Andrew Golota	244	TKO 1	Atlantic City
1997	Nov. 8	Evander Holyfield WBA	35	214	Michael Moorer IBF	223	TKO 8	Las Vegas
1998	Mar. 28	Lennox Lewis WBC	32	243	Shannon Briggs	228	TKO 5	Atlantic City
1998	Sept. 19	**Evander Holyfield** WBA/IBF	35	217	Vaughn Bean	231	Wu 12	Atlanta
1998	Sept. 26	Lennox Lewis WBC	33	250	Zeljko Mavrovic	220	Wu 12	Uncasville, Conn.
1999	Mar. 13	Lennox Lewis WBC	33	246	**Evander Holyfield** WBA/IBF	215	Draw 12	NYC (Mad. Sq. Garden)
1999	Nov. 13	Lennox Lewis WBC	34	240	**Evander Holyfield** WBA/IBF	218	Wu 12	Las Vegas
2000	Apr. 29	**Lennox Lewis** WBC/IBF!	34	247	Michael Grant	250	KO 2	NYC (Mad. Sq. Garden)
2000	July 15	**Lennox Lewis** WBC/IBF	34	250	Frans Botha	237	TKO 2	London
2000	Aug. 12	Evander Holyfield	37	221	John Ruiz	224	Wu 12	Las Vegas
2000	Nov. 11	**Lennox Lewis** WBC/IBF	35	249	David Tua	245	Wu 12	Las Vegas
2001	Mar. 3	John Ruiz	29	227	Evander Holyfield	217	Wu 12	Las Vegas
2001	Apr. 22	Hasim Rahman	28	237	**Lennox Lewis** WBC/IBF	253	KO 5	Johannesburg, S. Africa
2001	Nov. 17	Lennox Lewis	36	247	**Hasim Rahman** WBC/IBF	236	KO 4	Las Vegas
2001	Dec. 15	**John Ruiz** WBA	29	232	Evander Holyfield	219	Draw 12	Mashantucket, Conn.
2002	June 8	**Lennox Lewis** WBC/IBF@	36	249	Mike Tyson	235	KO 8	Memphis, Tenn.
2002	July 27	**John Ruiz** WBA	30	233	Kirk Johnson	238	Disq. 10	Las Vegas
2002	Dec. 14	Chris Byrd	32	214	Evander Holyfield	220	Wu 12	Atlantic City
2003	Mar. 1	Roy Jones Jr.	34	193	**John Ruiz** WBA	226	Wu 12	Las Vegas
2003	June 21	**Lennox Lewis** WBC	37	257	Vitali Klitschko	248	TKO 6	Los Angeles
2003	Sept. 20	**Chris Byrd** IBF	33	212	Fres Oquendo	224	Wu 12	Uncasville, Conn.
2003	Dec. 13	John Ruiz WBA%	31	241	Hasim Rahman	246	Wu 12	Atlantic City
2004	Apr. 17	**John Ruiz** WBA	32	240	Fres Oquendo	222	TKO 11	NYC (Mad. Sq. Garden)
2004	Apr. 17	**Chris Byrd** IBF	33	210	Andrew Golota	237	Draw 12	NYC (Mad. Sq. Garden)
2004	Apr. 24	Vitali Klitschko WBC^	32	245	Corrie Sanders	236	TKO 8	Los Angeles
2004	Nov. 13	**John Ruiz** WBA	32	226	Andrew Golota	240	Wu 12	NYC (Mad. Sq. Garden)
2004	Nov. 13	**Chris Byrd** IBF	34	214	Jameel McCline	270	Wu 12	NYC (Mad. Sq. Garden)
2004	Dec. 11	**Vitali Klitschko** WBC	33	250	Danny Williams	270	TKO 8	Las Vegas
2005	Apr. 30	James Toney$	36	233	**John Ruiz** WBA	241	NC	NYC (Mad. Sq. Garden)
2005	Oct. 1	**Chris Byrd** IBF	35	213	DaVarryl Williamson	225	Wu 12	Reno, Nev.

*Frans Botha won the vacant IBF title with a controversial 12-round decision over Axel Schulz on Dec. 9, 1995, but after legal sparring, was eventually stripped of the IBF belt for using anabolic steroids. Moorer then claimed the revacated title with his June 22, 1996 win over Schulz.

†Mike Tyson won the WBC belt from Frank Bruno on Mar. 16, 1996 and still held it at the time of his Sept. 7, 1996 win over Bruce Seldon (although it was not at risk for that fight) but was forced to relinquish the title after the bout for not fighting mandatory challenge Lennox Lewis. Tyson also paid Lewis $4 million to step aside and allow the Tyson-Seldon bout to take place. Lewis then fought Oliver McCall for the vacant WBC belt. The fight was stopped 55 seconds into round 5 because, inexplicably, McCall was visibly distraught and stopped throwing punches.

‡Holyfield won the bout by disqualification and retained the WBA belt after Tyson spit out his mouthpiece and bit off a piece of Holyfield's ear. Tyson had received a two-point deduction from referee Mills Lane and after a stern warning and a short delay the fight was allowed to continue. Later in round 3, he bit Holyfield's other ear and Tyson was disqualified.

!Lewis was stripped of the WBA title for choosing to fight Michael Grant instead of John Ruiz, the WBA's #1 challenger. The WBA sanctioned the Evander Holyfield-John Ruiz August 12 bout for its vacant heavyweight belt.

@Lewis effectively sold his IBF title to promoter Don King for $1 million and a Range Rover in September 2002. Lewis stepped aside (in exchange for the car and substantial fee), relinquishing his IBF belt by declining to fight Chris Byrd the mandatory challenger. The IBF sanctioned the Dec. 14, 2002 fight between Byrd and Holyfield for its vacant heavyweight belt.

%Ruiz won the interim WBA title after Roy Jones Jr. declined to defend the title he won from Ruiz on Mar. 1, 2003. The interim tag was later dropped when Jones returned to the light heavyweight division.

^Klitschko won the WBC title vacated by the retirement of Lennox Lewis.

$Toney won a uaninmous 12-round decision but tested positive for steroids in a post-fight drug test.

Year	Date	Winner		Age	Wgt	Loser		Wgt	Result	Location
2005	Dec. 17	Nikolai Valuev		32	324	**John Ruiz** WBA		238	Wm 12	Berlin
2006	Mar. 18	**Hasim Rahman** WBC*		33	238	James Toney		237	MDraw 12	Atlantic City
2006	Apr. 22	Wladimir Klitschko		30	241	**Chris Byrd** IBF		231	TKO 7	Mannheim, Germany
2006	June 3	**Nikolai Valuev** WBA		32	321	Owen Beck		243	TKO 3	Hannover, Germany
2006	Aug. 12	Oleg Maskaev		37	238	**Hasim Rahman** WBC		235	TKO 12	Las Vegas
2006	Oct. 7	**Nikolai Valuev** WBA		33	330	Monte Barrett		229	TKO 11	Rosemont, Ill.
2006	Nov. 11	**W. Klitschko** IBF		30	241	Calvin Brock		224½	TKO 7	New York City
2006	Dec. 10	Oleg Maskaev WBC		37	240	Peter Okhello		255½	Wu 12	Moscow
2007	Jan. 20	**Nikolai Valuev** WBA		33	322⅓	Jameel McCline		268⅓	TKO 3	Basel, Switzerland
2007	Mar. 10	**W. Klitschko** IBF		30	246½	Ray Austin		247	TKO 2	Mannheim, Germany
2007	Apr. 14	Ruslan Chagaev		28	228	**Nikolai Valuev**		319	Wm 12	Stuttgart, Germany
2007	July 7	**W. Klitschko** IBF		31	243	Lamon Brewster		227	TKO 6	Cologne, Germany

*The WBC voted to award interim champ Rahman its heavyweight belt on Nov. 10, 2005 in the wake of the retirement of titleholder Vitali Klitschko who had previously postponed his scheduled rematch with Rahman four times.

AP/Wide World Photos

All-Time Heavyweight Upsets

Buster Douglas was a 42-1 underdog when he defeated previously unbeaten heavyweight champion Mike Tyson on Feb. 10, 1990. That 10th-round knockout ranks as the biggest upset in boxing history. By comparison, 45-year-old George Foreman was only a 3-1 underdog before he unexpectedly won the title from Michael Moorer on Nov. 5, 1994.

Here are the best-known upsets in the annals of the heavyweight division. All fights were for the world championship except the Max Schmeling-Joe Louis bout.

Date	Winner	Loser	Result	KO Time	Location
9/7/1892	James J. Corbett	John L. Sullivan	KO 21	1:30	Olympic Club, New Orleans
4/5/1915	Jess Willard	Jack Johnson	KO 26	1:26	Mariano Race Track, Havana
9/23/26	Gene Tunney	Jack Dempsey	Wu 10	–	Sesquicentennial Stadium, Phila.
6/13/35	James J. Braddock	Max Baer	Wu 15	–	Mad. Sq.Garden Bowl, L.I. City
6/19/36	Max Schmeling	Joe Louis	KO 12	2:29	Yankee Stadium, New York
7/18/51	Jersey Joe Walcott	Ezzard Charles	KO 7	0:55	Forbes Field, Pittsburgh
6/26/59	Ingemar Johansson	Floyd Patterson	TKO 3	2:03	Yankee Stadium, New York
2/25/64	Cassius Clay	Sonny Liston	TKO 7	*	Convention Hall, Miami Beach
10/30/74	Muhammad Ali	George Foreman	KO 8	2:58	20th of May Stadium, Zaire
2/15/78	Leon Spinks	Muhammad Ali	Ws 15	–	Hilton Pavilion, Las Vegas
9/21/85	Michael Spinks	Larry Holmes	Wu 15	–	Riviera Hotel, Las Vegas
2/10/90	Buster Douglas	Mike Tyson	KO 10	1:23	Tokyo Dome, Tokyo
11/5/94	George Foreman	Michael Moorer	KO 10	2:03	MGM Grand, Las Vegas
11/9/96	Evander Holyfield	Mike Tyson	TKO 11	0:37	MGM Grand, Las Vegas
4/22/2001	Hasim Rahman	Lennox Lewis	KO 5	2:32	Johannesburg, South Africa

*Liston failed to answer bell for Round 7.

Major Titleholders

Note the following sanctioning body abbreviations: NBA (National Boxing Association), WBA (World Boxing Association), WBC (World Boxing Council), GBR (Great Britain), IBF (International Boxing Federation), plus other national and state commissions. Fighters who retired as champion are indicated by (*) and champions who abandoned or relinquished their titles are indicated by (†).

Heavyweights

Widely accepted champions in CAPITAL letters. Current champions in **bold** type (as of Oct. 31, 2007).

Note: Muhammad Ali was stripped of his world title in 1967 after refusing induction into the Army (see Muhammad Ali's Career Pro Record). George Foreman was stripped of his WBA and IBF titles in 1995, but remained active as linear champion.

Champion	Held Title
JOHN L. SULLIVAN	1885–92
JAMES J. CORBETT	1892–97
BOB FITZSIMMONS	1897–99
JAMES J. JEFFRIES	1899–1905*
MARVIN HART	1905–06
TOMMY BURNS	1906–08
JACK JOHNSON	1908–15
JESS WILLARD	1915–19
JACK DEMPSEY	1919–26
GENE TUNNEY	1926–28*
MAX SCHMELING	1930–32
JACK SHARKEY	1932–33
PRIMO CARNERA	1933–34
MAX BAER	1934–35
JAMES J. BRADDOCK	1935–37
JOE LOUIS	1937–49*
EZZARD CHARLES	1949–51
JERSEY JOE WALCOTT	1951–52
ROCKY MARCIANO	1952–56*
FLOYD PATTERSON	1956–59
INGEMAR JOHANSSON	1959–60
FLOYD PATTERSON	1960–62
SONNY LISTON	1962–64
CASSIUS CLAY (MUHAMMAD ALI)	1964–67
Ernie Terrell (WBA)	1965–67
Joe Frazier (NY)	1968–70
Jimmy Ellis (WBA)	1968–70
JOE FRAZIER	1970–73
GEORGE FOREMAN	1973–74
MUHAMMAD ALI	1974–78
LEON SPINKS	1978
Ken Norton (WBC)	1978
Larry Holmes (WBC)	1978–80
MUHAMMAD ALI	1978–79*
John Tate (WBA)	1979–80
Mike Weaver (WBA)	1980–82
LARRY HOLMES	1980–85
Michael Dokes (WBA)	1982–83
Gerrie Coetzee (WBA)	1983–84
Tim Witherspoon (WBC)	1984
Pinklon Thomas (WBC)	1984–86
Greg Page (WBA)	1984–85

Champion	Held Title
MICHAEL SPINKS	1985–87
Tim Witherspoon (WBA)	1986
Trevor Berbick (WBC)	1986
Mike Tyson (WBC)	1986–87
James (Bonecrusher) Smith (WBA)	1986–87
Tony Tucker (IBF)	1987
MIKE TYSON (WBC, WBA, IBF)	1987–90
BUSTER DOUGLAS (WBC, WBA, IBF)	1990
EVANDER HOLYFIELD (WBC, WBA, IBF)	1990–92
RIDDICK BOWE (WBA, IBF)	1992–93
Lennox Lewis (WBC)	1992–94
EVANDER HOLYFIELD (WBA, IBF)	1993–94
MICHAEL MOORER (WBA, IBF)	1994
Oliver McCall (WBC)	1994–95
GEORGE FOREMAN (WBA, IBF)	1994–95
Bruce Seldon (WBA)	1995–96
GEORGE FOREMAN	1995–96
Frank Bruno (WBC)	1995–96
Mike Tyson (WBC)	1996†
Mike Tyson (WBA)	1996
Michael Moorer (IBF)	1996–1997
Evander Holyfield (WBA, IBF)	1996–2000
Lennox Lewis (WBC)	1997–2000
LENNOX LEWIS (WBA, WBC, IBF)	2000
Evander Holyfield (WBA)	2000–01
LENNOX LEWIS (WBC, IBF)	2000–01
John Ruiz (WBA)	2001-03
Hasim Rahman (WBC, IBF)	2001
LENNOX LEWIS (WBC, IBF)	2001–02†
LENNOX LEWIS (WBC)	2001–04*
Roy Jones Jr. (WBA)	2003–04
Chris Byrd (IBF)	2003–06
John Ruiz (WBA)	2004–05
Vitali Klitschko (WBC)	2004–05*
Hasim Rahman (WBC)	2005–06
Nikolai Valuev (WBA)	2005–07
Wladimir Klitschko (IBF)	2006—
Oleg Maskaev (WBC)	2006—
Ruslan Chagaev (WBA)	2007—

Note: John L. Sullivan held the Bare Knuckle championship from 1882-85.

Cruiserweights

Current champions in **bold** type.

Champion	Held Title
Marvin Camel (WBC)	1980
Carlos De Leon (WBC)	1980–82
Ossie Ocasio (WBA)	1982–84
S.T. Gordon (WBC)	1982–83
Carlos De Leon (WBC)	1983–85
Marvin Camel (IBF)	1983–84
Lee Roy Murphy (IBF)	1984–86
Piet Crous (WBA)	1984–85
Alfonso Ratliff (WBC)	1985
Dwight Braxton (WBA)	1985–86
Bernard Benton (WBC)	1985–86
Carlos De Leon (WBC)	1986–88
Evander Holyfield (WBA)	1986–88
Ricky Parkey (IBF)	1986–87
Evander Holyfield (WBA/IBF)	1987–88
Evander Holyfield	1988†

Champion	Held Title
Toufik Belbouli (WBA)	1989
Robert Daniels (WBA)	1989–91
Carlos De Leon (WBC)	1989–90
Glenn McCrory (IBF)	1989–90
Jeff Lampkin (IBF)	1990
Massimiliano Duran (WBC)	1990–91
Bobby Czyz (WBA)	1991–92†
Anaclet Wamba (WBC)	1991–95
James Pritchard (IBF)	1991
James Warring (IBF)	1991–92
Alfred Cole (IBF)	1992–96
Orlin Norris (WBA)	1993–95
Nate Miller (WBA)	1995–97
Marcelo Dominguez (WBC)	1996–98
Adolpho Washington (IBF)	1996–97
Uriah Grant (IBF)	1997

Champion	Held Title
Imamu Mayfield (IBF)	1997–98
Arthur Williams (IBF)	1998–99
Fabrice Tiozzo (WBA)	1997–2000
Juan Carlos Gomez (WBC)	1998–2002†
Vassiliy Jirov (IBF)	1999–2003
Virgil Hill (WBA)	2000–02
Jean-Marc Mormeck (WBA)	2002–06
Wayne Braithwaite (WBC)	2002–05

Champion	Held Title
James Toney (IBF)	2003†
Kelvin Davis (IBF)	2004–05
Jean-Marc Mormeck (WBA/WBC)	2005–06
O'Neil Bell (IBF)	2005–07
O'NEIL BELL (IBF/WBA/WBC)	2006–07
JEAN-MARC MORMECK (WBA/WBC)	2007–
Steve Cunningham (IBF)	2007–

Light Heavyweights

Widely accepted champions in CAPITAL letters. Current champions in **bold** type.

Champion	Held Title
JACK ROOT	1903
GEORGE GARDNER	1903
BOB FITZSIMMONS	1903–05
PHILADELPHIA JACK O'BRIEN	1905–12*
JACK DILLON	1914–16
BATTLING LEVINSKY	1916–20
GEORGES CARPENTIER	1920–22
BATTLING SIKI	1922–23
MIKE McTIGUE	1923–25
PAUL BERLENBACH	1925–26
JACK DELANEY	1926–27†
Jimmy Slattery (NBA)	1927
TOMMY LOUGHRAN	1927-29
JIMMY SLATTERY	1930
MAXIE ROSENBLOOM	1930–34
George Nichols (NBA)	1932
Bob Godwin (NBA)	1933
BOB OLIN	1934–35
JOHN HENRY LEWIS	1935–38
MELIO BETTINA (NY)	1939
Len Harvey (GBR)	1939–42
BILLY CONN	1939–40†
ANTON CHRISTOFORIDIS (NBA)	1941
GUS LESNEVICH	1941–48
Freddie Mills (GBR)	1942–46
FREDDIE MILLS	1948–50
JOEY MAXIM	1950–52
ARCHIE MOORE	1952–62
Harold Johnson (NBA)	1961
HAROLD JOHNSON	1962–63
WILLIE PASTRANO	1963–65
Eddie Cotton (Mich.)	1963–64
JOSE TORRES	1965–66
DICK TIGER	1966–68
BOB FOSTER	1968–74*
Vicente Rondon (WBA)	1971–72
John Conteh (WBC)	1974–77
Victor Galindez (WBA)	1974–78
Miguel A. Cuello (WBC)	1977–78
Mate Parlov (WBC)	1978
Mike Rossman (WBA)	1978–79
Marvin Johnson (WBC)	1978–79
Matthew (Franklin) Saad Muhammad (WBC)	1979–81
Marvin Johnson (WBA)	1979–80
Eddie (Gregory) Mustapha Muhammad (WBA)	1980–81

Champion	Held Title
Michael Spinks (WBA)	1981–83
Dwight (Braxton) Muhammad Qawi (WBC)	1981–83
MICHAEL SPINKS	1983–85†
J.B. Williamson (WBC)	1985–86
Slobodan Kacar (IBF)	1985–86
Marvin Johnson (WBA)	1986–87
Dennis Andries (WBC)	1986–87
Bobby Czyz (IBF)	1986–87
Leslie Stewart (WBA)	1987
Virgil Hill (WBA)	1987–91
Prince Charles Williams (IBF)	1987–93
Thomas Hearns (WBC)	1987
Donny Lalonde (WBC)	1987–88
Sugar Ray Leonard (WBC)	1988
Dennis Andries (WBC)	1989
Jeff Harding (WBC)	1989–90
Dennis Andries (WBC)	1990–91
Jeff Harding (WBC)	1991–94
Thomas Hearns (WBA)	1991–92
Iran Barkley (WBA)	1992†
Virgil Hill (WBA)	1992–97
Henry Maske (IBF)	1993–96
Virgil Hill (WBA/IBF)	1996–97
Mike McCallum (WBC)	1994–95
Fabrice Tiozzo (WBC)	1995–96
Roy Jones Jr. (WBC)	1996
Montell Griffin (WBC)	1996
D. Michaelczewski (WBA/IBF)	1997†
William Guthrie (IBF)	1997–98
Lou Del Valle (WBA)	1997–98
ROY JONES JR. (WBA/WBC)	1997–2003†
Reggie Johnson (IBF)	1998–99
ROY JONES JR. (WBA/WBC/IBF)	1999–2003†
Antonio Tarver (WBC/IBF)	2003
Mehdi Sahnoune (WBA)	2003
ROY JONES JR. (WBC)	2003–04
Silvio Branco (WBA)	2003–04
Antonio Tarver (WBC)	2003–04†
Glen Johnson (IBF)	2004†
Fabrice Tiozzo (WBA)	2004–06*
ANTONIO TARVER	2005–06†
Clinton Woods (IBF)	2006–
Tomasz Adamek (WBC)	2006–07
Silvio Branco (WBA)	2007
Chad Dawson (WBC)	2007–
Stipe Drews (WBA)	2007–

Super Middleweights

Current champions in **bold** type.

Champion	Held Title
Murray Sutherland (IBF)	1984
Chong-Pal Park (IBF)	1984–87
Chong-Pal Park (WBA)	1987–88
Graziano Rocchigiani (IBF)	1988–89
Fugencio Obelmejias (WBA)	1988–89
Ray Leonard (WBC)	1988–90†
In-Chut Baek (WBA)	1989–90
Lindell Holmes (IBF)	1990–91
Christophe Tiozzo (WBA)	1990–91
Mauro Galvano (WBC)	1990–92
Victor Cordova (WBA)	1991

Champion	Held Title
Darrin Van Horn (IBF)	1991–92
Iran Barkley (WBA)	1992
Nigel Benn (WBC)	1992–96
James Toney (IBF)	1992–94
Michael Nunn (WBA)	1992–94
Steve Little (WBA)	1994
Frank Liles (WBA)	1994–99
Roy Jones (IBF)	1994–96
Thulane Malinga (WBC)	1996
Vincenzo Nardiello (WBC)	1996
Robin Reid (WBC)	1996–97

Major Titleholders (Cont.)
Super Middleweights (Cont.)

Champion	Held Title	Champion	Held Title
Charles Brewer (IBF)	1997–98	Eric Lucas (WBC)	2001–03
Sven Ottke (IBF)	1998–2004*	Sven Ottke (IBF/WBA)	2003–04*
Thulane Malinga (WBC)	1997–98	Markus Beyer (WBC)	2003–04
Richie Woodhall (WBC)	1998–99	Anthony Mundine (WBA)	2004
Byron Mitchell (WBA)	1999–2000	Manny Siaca (WBA)	2004
Markus Beyer (WBC)	1999–2000	Cristian Sanavia (WBC)	2004
Glenn Gatley (WBC)	2000	Jeff Lacy (IBF)	2004–06
Dingaan Thobela (WBC)	2000	Markus Beyer (WBC)	2004–06
Bruno Girard (WBA)	2000–01†	**Mikkel Kessler** (WBA)	2004–
Dave Hilton (WBC)	2000†	Joe Calzaghe (IBF)	2006–07†
Byron Mitchell (WBA)	2001–03	**Mikkel Kessler** (WBA/WBC)	2006–

Middleweights

Widely accepted champions in CAPITAL letters. Current champions in **bold** type.

Champion	Held Title	Champion	Held Title
JACK (NONPAREIL) DEMPSEY	1884–91	Gene Fullmer (NBA)	1959–62
BOB FITZSIMMONS	1891–97	PAUL PENDER	1960–61
CHARLES (KID) McCOY	1897–98	TERRY DOWNES	1961–62
TOMMY RYAN	1898–1907	PAUL PENDER	1962–63
STANLEY KETCHEL	1908	Dick Tiger (WBA)	1962–63
BILLY PAPKE	1908	DICK TIGER	1963
STANLEY KETCHEL	1908–10	JOEY GIARDELLO	1963–65
FRANK KLAUS	1913	DICK TIGER	1965–66
GEORGE CHIP	1913–14	EMILE GRIFFITH	1966–67
AL McCOY	1914–17	NINO BENVENUTI	1967
Jeff Smith (AUS)	1914	EMILE GRIFFITH	1967–68
Mick King (AUS)	1914	NINO BENVENUTI	1968–70
Jeff Smith (AUS)	1914–15	CARLOS MONZON	1970–77*
Lee Darcy (AUS)	1915–17	Rodrigo Valdez (WBC)	1974–76
MIKE O'DOWD	1917–20	RODRIGO VALDEZ	1977–78
JOHNNY WILSON	1920–23	HUGO CORRO	1978–79
Wm. Bryan Downey (Ohio)	1921–22	VITO ANTUOFERMO	1979–80
Dave Rosenberg (NY)	1922	ALAN MINTER	1980
Jock Malone (Ohio)	1922–23	MARVELOUS MARVIN HAGLER	1980–87
Mike O'Dowd (NY)	1922	SUGAR RAY LEONARD	1987
Lou Bogash (NY)	1923	Frank Tate (IBF)	1987–88
HARRY GREB	1923–26	Sumbu Kalambay (WBA)	1987–89
TIGER FLOWERS	1926	Thomas Hearns (WBC)	1987–88
MICKEY WALKER	1926–31†	Iran Barkley (WBC)	1988–89
GORILLA JONES	1931–32	Michael Nunn (IBF)	1988–91
MARCEL THIL	1932–37	Roberto Duran (WBC)	1989–90*
Ben Jeby (NY)	1932–33	Mike McCallum (WBA)	1989–91
Lou Brouillard (NBA, NY)	1933	Julian Jackson (WBC)	1990–93
Vince Dundee (NBA, NY)	1933–34	James Toney (IBF)	1991–93†
Teddy Yarosz (NBA, NY)	1934–35	Reggie Johnson (WBA)	1992–93
Babe Risko (NBA, NY)	1935–36	Roy Jones Jr. (IBF)	1993–94†
Freddie Steele (NBA, NY)	1936–38	Gerald McClellan (WBC)	1993–95†
FRED APOSTOLI	1937–39	John David Jackson (WBA)	1993–94
Al Hostak (NBA)	1938	Jorge Castro (WBA)	1994–95
Solly Krieger (NBA)	1938–39	Julian Jackson (WBC)	1995
Al Hostak (NBA)	1939–40	Bernard Hopkins (IBF)	1995–
CEFERINO GARCIA	1939–40	Quincy Taylor (WBC)	1995–96
KEN OVERLIN	1940–41	Shinji Takehara (WBA)	1995–96
Tony Zale (NBA)	1940–41	William Joppy (WBA)	1996–98
BILLY SOOSE	1941	Keith Holmes (WBC)	1996–98
TONY ZALE	1941–47	Julio Cesar Green (WBA)	1997–98
ROCKY GRAZIANO	1947–48	William Joppy (WBA)	1998–2001
TONY ZALE	1948	Hassine Cherifi (WBC)	1998–99
MARCEL CERDAN	1948–49	Keith Holmes (WBC)	1999–2001
JAKE La MOTTA	1949–51	Bernard Hopkins (IBF/WBC)	2001–05
SUGAR RAY ROBINSON	1951	Felix Trinidad (WBA)	2001
RANDY TURPIN	1951	BERNARD HOPKINS (IBF/WBA/WBC)	2001–05
SUGAR RAY ROBINSON	1951–52*	JERMAIN TAYLOR (IBF/WBA/WBC)	2005–06†
CARL (BOBO) OLSON	1953–55	JERMAIN TAYLOR (WBA/WBC)	2005–07†
SUGAR RAY ROBINSON	1955–57	JERMAIN TAYLOR (WBC)	2005–07
GENE FULLMER	1957	**Arthur Abraham** (IBF)	2006–
SUGAR RAY ROBINSON	1957	Javier Castillejo (WBA)	2006–07
CARMEN BASILIO	1957–58	**Felix Sturm** (WBA)	2007–
SUGAR RAY ROBINSON	1958–60	**Kelly Pavlik** (WBC)	2007–

Junior Middleweights

Widely accepted champions in CAPITAL letters. Current champions in **bold** type.

Champion	Held Title
ERNILE GRIFFITH (EBU)	1962–63
DENNIS MOYER	1962–63
RALPH DUPAS	1963
SANDRO MAZZINGHI	1963–65
NINO BENVENUTI	1965–66
KI-SOO KIM	1966–68
SANDRO MAZZINGHI	1968
FREDDLIE LITTLE	1969–70
CARMELO BOSSI	1970–71
KOICHI WAJIMA	1971–74
OSCAR ALBARADO	1974–75
KOICHI WAJIMA	1975
Miguel de Oliveira (WBC)	1975–76
JAE-DO YUH	1975–76
Elisha Obed (WBC)	1975–76
KOICHI WAJIMA	1976
JOSE DURAN	1976
Eckhard Dagge (WBC)	1976–77
MIGUEL ANGEL CASTELLINI	1976–77
EDDIE GAZO	1977–78
Rocky Mattioli (WBC)	1977–79
MASASHI KUDO	1978–79
Maurice Hope (WBC)	1979–81
AYUB KALULE	1979–81
Wilfred Benitez (WBC)	1981–82
SUGAR RAY LEONARD	1981–82
Tadashi Mihara (WBA)	1981–82
Davey Moore (WBA)	1982–83
Thomas Hearns (WBC)	1982–84
Roberto Duran (WBA)	1983–84
Mark Medal (IBF)	1984
THOMAS HEARNS	1984–86
Mike McCallum (WBA)	1984–87
Carlos Santos (IBF)	1984–86
Buster Drayton (IBF)	1986–87
Duane Thomas (WBC)	1986–87
Matthew Hilton (IBF)	1987–88
Lupe Aquino (WBC)	1987
Gianfranco Rosi (WBC)	1987–88
Julian Jackson (WBA)	1987–90
Donald Curry (WBC)	1988–89
Robert Hines (IBF)	1988–89
Darrin Van Horn (IBF)	1989
Rene Jacquote (WBC)	1989
John Mugabi (WBC)	1989–90
Gianfranco Rosi (IBF)	1989–94
Terry Norris (WBC)	1990–94
Gilbert Dele (WBA)	1991
Vinny Pazienza (WBA)	1991–92
Julio Cesar Vasquez (WBA)	1992–95
Simon Brown (WBC)	1994
Terry Norris (WBC)	1994–
Vincent Pettway (IBF)	1994–95
Paul Vaden (IBF)	1995
Carl Daniels (WBA)	1995
Terry Norris (WBC)	1995–97
Terry Norris (IBF)	1995–96
Laurent Boudouani (WBA)	1996–99
Raul Marquez (IBF)	1997
Keith Mullings (WBC)	1997–99
Yori Boy Campas (IBF)	1997–98
Fernando Vargas (IBF)	1998–2000
Javier Castillejo (WBC)	1999–2001
David Reid (WBA)	1999–00
Felix Trinidad (WBA/IBF)	2000–01†
Oscar De La Hoya (WBC)	2001–03
Fernando Vargas (WBA)	2001–02
Winky Wright (IBF)	2001–
Oscar De La Hoya (WBA/WBC)	2002-03
Shane Mosley (WBA/WBC)	2003–04
WINKY WRIGHT (IBF/WBA/WBC)	2004
WINKY WRIGHT (WBA/WBC)	2004–05†
Kassim Ouma (IBF)	2004–05
Javier Castillejo (WBC)	2005
Roman Karmazin (IBF)	2005–06
Alejandro Garcia (WBA)	2005–06
Ricardo Mayorga (WBC)	2005–06
Jose Antonio Rivera (WBA)	2006–07
Oscar De La Hoya (WBC)	2006–07
Cory Spinks (IBF)	2006–
Travis Simms (WBA)	2007–
Floyd Mayweather Jr. (WBC)	2007†
Vernon Forrest (WBC)	2007–

Welterweights

Widely accepted champions in CAPITAL letters. Current champions in **bold** type.

Champion	Held Title
PADDY DUFFY	1888–90
MYSTERIOUS BILLY SMITH	1892–94
TOMMY RYAN	1894–98
MYSTERIOUS BILLY SMITH	1898–1900
MATTY MATTHEWS	1900
EDDIE CONNOLLY	1900
JAMES (RUBE) FERNS	1900
MATTY MATHEWS	1900–01
JAMES (RUBE) FERNS	1901
JOE WALCOTT	1901–04
THE DIXIE KID	1904–05
HONEY MELLODY	1906–07
Mike (Twin) Sullivan	1907–08†
Harry Lewis	1908–11
Jimmy Gardner	1908
Jimmy Clabby	1910–11
WALDEMAR HOLBERG	1914
TOM McCORMICK	1914
MATT WELLS	1914–15
MIKE GLOVER	1915
JACK BRITTON	1915
TED (KID) LEWIS	1915–16
JACK BRITTON	1916–17
TED (KID) LEWIS	1917–19
JACK BRITTON	1919–22
MICKEY WALKER	1922–26
PETE LATZO	1926–27
JOE DUNDEE	1927–29
JACKIE FIELDS	1929–30
YOUNG JACK THOMPSON	1930
TOMMY FREEMAN	1930–31
YOUNG JACK THOMPSON	1931
LOU BROUILLARD	1931–32
JACKIE FIELDS	1932–33
YOUNG CORBETT III	1933
JIMMY McLARNIN	1933–34
BARNEY ROSS	1934
JIMMY McLARNIN	1934–35
BARNEY ROSS	1935–38
HENRY ARMSTRONG	1938–40
FRITZIE ZIVIC	1940–41
Izzy Jannazzo (Md.)	1940–41
Freddie (Red) Cochrane	1941–46
MARTY SERVO	1946*
SUGAR RAY ROBINSON	1946–51†
Johnny Bratton	1951
KID GAVILAN	1951–54
JOHNNY SAXTON	1954–55
TONY DeMARCO	1955
CARMEN BASILIO	1955–56
JOHNNY SAXTON	1956
CARMEN BASILIO	1956–57†

Major Titleholders (Cont.)
Welterweights (Cont.)

Champion	Held Title	Champion	Held Title
VIRGIL AKINS	.1958	Mark Breland (WBA)	.1989–90
DON JORDAN	.1958–60	MARLON STARLING (WBC)	.1989–90
BENNY (KID) PARET	.1960–61	Aaron Davis (WBA)	.1990–91
EMILE GRIFFITH	.1961	Maurice Blocker (WBC)	.1990–91
BENNY (KID) PARET	.1961–62	Meldrick Taylor (WBA)	.1991–92
EMILE GRIFFITH	.1962–63	Simon Brown (WBC)	.1991
LUIS RODRIGUEZ	.1963	Maurice Blocker (IBF)	.1991–93
EMILE GRIFFITH	.1963–66†	Buddy McGirt (WBC)	.1991–93
Charlie Shipes (Calif.)	.1966–67	Crisanto Espana (WBA)	.1992–94
CURTIS COKES	.1966–69	Pernell Whitaker (WBC)	.1993–97
JOSE NAPOLES	.1969–70	Felix Trinidad (IBF)	.1993–99
BILLY BACKUS	.1970–71	Ike Quartey (WBA)	.1994–98†
JOSE NAPOLES	.1971–75	James Page (WBA)	.1998–2000†
Hedgemon Lewis (NY)	.1972–73	Oscar De La Hoya (WBC)	.1997–99
Angel Espada (WBA)	.1975–76	Felix Trinidad (WBC/IBF)	.1999–2000†
JOHN H. STRACEY	.1975–76	Oscar De La Hoya (WBC)	.2000
CARLOS PALOMINO	.1976–79	Shane Mosley (WBC)	.2000–00
Pipino Cuevas (WBA)	.1976–80	Andrew Lewis (WBA)	.2001–02
WILFREDO BENITEZ	.1979	Vernon Forrest (IBF)	.2001–02†
SUGAR RAY LEONARD	.1979–80	Vernon Forrest (WBC)	.2002–03
ROBERTO DURAN	.1980	Richard Mayorga (WBA)	.2002–03
Thomas Hearns (WBA)	.1980–81	Michele Piccirillo (IBF)	.2002–03
SUGAR RAY LEONARD	.1980–82	Richard Mayorga (WBA/WBC)	.2003
Donald Curry (WBA)	.1983–85	Cory Spinks (IBF)	.2003–05
Milton McCrory (WBC)	.1983–85	CORY SPINKS (IBF/WBA/WBC)	.2003–05
DONALD CURRY	.1985–86	ZAB JUDAH (IBF/WBA/WBC)	.2005–06
LLOYD HONEYGHAN	.1986–87	Zab Judah (IBF)	.2006
JORGE VACA (WBC)	.1987–88	Carlos Baldomir (WBC)	.2006
LLOYD HONEYGHAN (WBC)	.1988–89	Floyd Mayweather (IBF)	.2006†
Mark Breland (WBA)	.1987	Ricky Hatton (WBA)	.2006†
Marlon Starling (WBA)	.1987–88	**Floyd Mayweather (WBC)**	.2006–
Tomas Molinares (WBA)	.1988–89	**Miguel Cotto (WBA)**	.2006–
Simon Brown (IBF)	.1988–91	**Kermit Cintron (IBF)**	.2006–

Junior Welterweights

Widely accepted champions in CAPITAL letters. Current champions in **bold** type.

Champion	Held Title	Champion	Held Title
PINKEY MITCHELL	.1922–25	Antonio Cervantes (WBA)	.1977–80
RED HERRING	.1925	Sang-Hyun Kim (WBC)	.1978–80
MUSHY CALLAHAN	.1926–30	Saoul Mamby (WBC)	.1980–82
JACK (KID) BERG	.1930–31	Aaron Pryor (WBA)	.1980–83
TONY CANZONERI	.1931–32	Leroy Haley (WBC)	.1982–83
JOHNNY JADICK	.1932–33	Aaron Pryor (IBF)	.1983–85
Sammy Fuller	.1932–33	Bruce Curry (WBC)	.1983–84
BATTLING SHAW	.1933	Johnny Bumphus (WBA)	.1984
TONY CANZONERI	.1933	Bill Costello (WBC)	.1984–85
BARNEY ROSS	.1933–35	Gene Hatcher (WBA)	.1984–85
TIPPY LARKIN	.1946	Ubaldo Sacco (WBA)	.1985–86
CARLOS ORTIZ	.1959–60	Lonnie Smith (WBC)	.1985–86
DUILIO LOI	.1960–62	Patrizio Oliva (WBA)	.1986–87
EDDIE PERKINS	.1962	Gary Hinton (IBF)	.1986
DUILIO LOI	.1962–63	Rene Arredondo (WBC)	.1986
Roberto Cruz	.1963	Tsuyoshi Hamada (WBC)	.1986–87
EDDIE PERKINS	.1963–65	Joe Louis Manley (IBF)	.1986–87
CARLOS HERNANDEZ	.1965–66	Terry Marsh (IBF)	.1987
SANDRO LOPOPOLO	.1966–67	Juan Coggi (WBA)	.1987–90
PAUL FUJII	.1967–68	Rene Arredondo (WBC)	.1987
NICOLINO LOCHE	.1968–72	Roger Mayweather (WBC)	.1987–89
Pedro Adigue (WBC)	.1968–70	James McGirt (IBF)	.1988
Bruno Arcari (WBC)	.1970–74	Meldrick Taylor (IBF)	.1988–90
ALFONSO FRAZER	.1972	Julio Cesar Chavez (WBC)	.1989–94
ANTONIO CERVANTES	.1972–76	Julio Cesar Chavez (IBF)	.1990–91
Perico Fernandez (WBC)	.1974–75	Loreto Garza (WBA)	.1990–91
Saensak Muangsurin (WBC)	.1975–76	Juan Coggi (WBA)	.1991
WILFRED BENITEZ	.1976–79	Edwin Rosario (WBA)	.1991–92
Miguel Velasquez (WBC)	.1976	Rafael Pineda (IBF)	.1991–92
Saensak Muangsurin (WBC)	.1976–78	Akinobu Hiranaka (WBA)	.1992

Champion	Held Title
Pernell Whitaker (IBF)	1992–93†
Charles Murray (IBF)	1993–94
Jake Rodriguez (IBF)	1994–95
Juan Coggi (WBA)	1993–94
Frankie Randall (WBC)	1994
Frankie Randall (WBA)	1994–96
Juan Coggi (WBA)	1996
Julio Cesar Chavez (WBC)	1994–96
Kostya Tszyu (IBF)	1995–97
Frankie Randall (WBA)	1996–97
Oscar De La Hoya (WBC)	1996–97†
Khalid Rahilou (WBA)	1997–98
Sharmba Mitchell (WBA)	1998–2001
Vincent Phillips (IBF)	1997–99
Terronn Millet (IBF)	1999–00†

Champion	Held Title
Kostya Tszyu (WBC)	1999–2005
Zab Judah (IBF)	2000–01
Kostya Tszyu (WBA/WBC)	2001–04†
KOSTYA TSZYU (IBF/WBA/WBC)	2001–04†
KOSTYA TSZYU (IBF/WBC)	2004–05
Vivian Harris (WBA)	2004–05
Arturo Gatti (WBC)	2005
Ricky Hatton (IBF)	2005–07†
Ricky Hatton (IBF/WBA)	2005–06†
Carlos Maussa (WBA)	2005–06
Floyd Mayweather Jr. (WBC)	2005–06†
Junior Witter (WBC)	2006–
Souleymane M'baye (WBA)	2007
Gavin Rees (WBA)	2007–
Paul Malignaggi (IBF)	2007–

Lightweights

Widely accepted champions in CAPITAL letters. Current champions in **bold** type.

Champion	Held Title
JACK McAULIFFE	1886–94
GEORGE (KID) LAVIGNE	1896–99
FRANK ERNE	1899–02
JOE GANS	1902–04
JIMMY BRITT	1904–05
BATTLING NELSON	1905–06
JOE GANS	1906–08
BATTLING NELSON	1908–10
AD WOLGAST	1910–12
WILLIE RITCHIE	1912–14
FREDDIE WELSH	1915–17
BENNY LEONARD	1917–25*
JIMMY GOODRICH	1925
ROCKY KANSAS	1925–26
SAMMY MANDELL	1926–30
AL SINGER	1930
TONY CANZONERI	1930–33
BARNEY ROSS	1933–35†
TONY CANZONERI	1935–36
LOU AMBERS	1936–38
HENRY ARMSTRONG	1938–39
LOU AMBERS	1939–40
Sammy Angott (NBA)	1940–41
LEW JENKINS	1940–41
SAMMY ANGOTT	1941–42
Beau Jack (NY)	1942–43
Slugger White (Md.)	1943
Bob Montgomery (NY)	1943
Sammy Angott (NBA)	1943–44
Beau Jack (NY)	1943–44
Bob Montgomery (NY)	1944–47
Juan Zurita (NBA)	1944–45
IKE WILLIAMS	1947–51
JAMES CARTER	1951–52
LAURO SALAS	1952
JAMES CARTER	1952–54
PADDY DeMARCO	1954
JAMES CARTER	1954–55
WALLACE (BUD) SMITH	1955–56
JOE BROWN	1956–62
CARLOS ORTIZ	1962–65
Kenny Lane (Mich.)	1963–64
ISMAEL LAGUNA	1965
CARLOS ORTIZ	1965–68
CARLOS TEO CRUZ	1968–69
MANDO RAMOS	1969–70
ISMAEL LAGUNA	1970
KEN BUCHANAN	1970–72
Pedro Carrasco (WBC)	1971–72
Mando Ramos (WBC)	1972
ROBERTO DURAN	1972–79†
Chango Carmona (WBC)	1972
Rodolfo Gonzalez (WBC)	1972–74
Ishimatsu Suzuki (WBC)	1974–76
Esteban De Jesus (WBC)	1976–78

Champion	Held Title
Jim Watt (WBC)	1979–81
Ernesto Espana (WBA)	1979–80
Hilmer Kenty (WBA)	1980–81
Sean O'Grady (WBA, WAA)	1981
Alexis Arguello (WBC)	1981–82
Claude Noel (WBA)	1981
Andrew Ganigan (WAA)	1981–82
Arturo Frias (WBA)	1981–82
Ray Mancini (WBA)	1982–84
ALEXIS ARGUELLO	1982–83
Edwin Rosario (WBC)	1983–84
Choo Choo Brown (IBF)	1984
Livingstone Bramble (WBA)	1984–86
Harry Arroyo (IBF)	1984–85
Jose Luis Ramirez (WBC)	1984–85
Jimmy Paul (IBF)	1985–86
Hector Camacho (WBC)	1985–86
Edwin Rosario (WBA)	1986–87
Greg Haugen (IBF)	1986–87
Julio Cesar Chavez (WBA)	1987–88
Jose Luis Ramirez (WBC)	1987–88
JULIO CESAR CHAVEZ (WBC,WBA)	1988–89
Vinny Pazienza (IBF)	1987–88
Greg Haugen (IBF)	1988–89
Pernell Whitaker (IBF,WBC)	1989–90
Edwin Rosario (WBA)	1989–90
Juan Nazario (WBA)	1990
PERNELL WHITAKER (IBF, WBC, WBA)	1990–92†
Joey Gamache (WBA)	1992
Miguel A. Gonzalez (WBC)	1992–96
Tony Lopez (WBA)	1992–93
Dingaan Thobela (WBA)	1993
Fred Pendleton (IBF)	1993–94
Orzubek Nazarov (WBA)	1993–98
Rafael Ruelas (IBF)	1994–95
Oscar De La Hoya (IBF)	1995†
Phillip Holiday (IBF)	1995–97
Jean-Baptiste Mendy (WBC)	1996–97
Stevie Johnston (WBC)	1997–98
Shane Mosley (IBF)	1997–99†
Cesar Bazan (WBC)	1998–99
Jean-Baptiste Mendy (WBA)	1998–99
Julien Lorcy (WBA)	1999
Stevie Johnston (WBC)	1999–00
Stefano Zoff (WBA)	1999
Israel Cardona (IBF)	1999
Paul Spadafora (IBF)	1999–2004†
Gilberto Serrano (WBA)	1999–00
Takanori Hatakeyama (WBA)	2000–01
Jose Luis Castillo (WBC)	2000–02
Julien Lorcy (WBA)	2001
Raul Balbi (WBA)	2001–02
Leonard Dorin (WBA)	2002–03
Floyd Mayweather Jr. (WBC)	2002–04†
Javier Jauregui (IBF)	2003–04

Major Titleholders (Cont.)
Lightweights (Cont.)

Champion	Held Title	Champion	Held Title
Lakva Sim (WBA)	.2004	Jesus Chavez (IBF)	.2005–07
Juan Diaz (WBA)	.2004–	Joel Casamayor (WBC)	.2006–07†
Jose Luis Castillo (WBC)	.2004–05	Julio Diaz (IBF)	.2007
Julio Diaz (IBF)	.2004–05	**Juan Diaz** (WBA/IBF)	.2007–
Diego Corrales (WBC)	.2005–	**David Diaz** (WBC)	.2007–
Leavander Johnson (IBF)	.2005		

Junior Lightweights

Widely accepted champions in CAPITAL letters. Current champions in **bold** type.

Champion	Held Title	Champion	Held Title
JOHNNY DUNDEE	.1921–23	BRIAN MITCHELL	.1986–91
JACK BERNSTEIN	.1923	Rocky Lockridge (IBF)	.1987–88
JOHNNY DUNDEE	.1923–24	Azumah Nelson (WBC)	.1988–94
STEVE (KID) SULLIVAN	.1924–25	Tony Lopez (IBF)	.1988–89
MIKE BALLERINO	.1925	Juan Molina (IBF)	.1989–90
TOD MORGAN	.1925–29	Tony Lopez (IBF)	.1990–91
BENNY BASS	.1929–31	Joey Gamache (WBA)	.1991
KID CHOCOLATE	.1931–33	Brian Mitchell (IBF)	.1991
FRANKIE KLICK	.1933–34	Genaro Hernandez (WBA)	.1991–95
SANDY SADDLER	.1949–50	James Leija (WBC)	.1994
HAROLD GOMES	.1959–60	Juan Molina (IBF)	.1991–95
GABRIEL (FLASH) ELORDE	.1960–67	Gabriel Ruelas (WBC)	.1994–95
YOSHIAKI NUMATA	.1967	Eddie Hopson (IBF)	.1995
HIROSHI KOBAYASHI	.1967–71	Tracy Patterson (IBF)	.1995
Rene Barrientos (WBC)	.1969–70	Azumah Nelson (WBC)	.1995–97
Yoshiaki Numata (WBC)	.1970–71	Choi Yong-Soo (WBA)	.1995–98
ALFREDO MARCANO	.1971–72	Arturo Gatti (IBF)	.1995–98†
Ricardo Arredondo (WBC)	.1971–74	Genaro Hernandez (WBC)	.1997–98
BEN VILLAFLOR	.1972–73	Floyd Mayweather Jr. (WBC)	.1998–2002†
KUNIAKI SHIBATA	.1973	Takanori Hatakeyama (WBA)	.1998–99
BEN VILLAFLOR	.1973–76	Roberto Garcia (IBF)	.1998–99
Kuniaki Shibata (WBC)	.1974–75	Lavka Sim (WBA)	.1999
Alfredo Escalera (WBC)	.1975–78	Diego Corrales (IBF)	.1999–2001
SAMUEL SERRANO	.1976–80	Baek Jong-Kwon (WBA)	.1999–2000
Alexis Arguello (WBC)	.1978–80	Joel Casamayor (WBA)	.2000–02
YASUTSUNE UEHARA	.1980–81	Steve Forbes (IBF)	.2001–02†
Rafael Limon (WBC)	.1980–81	Acelino Freitas (WBA)	.2002–04†
Cornelius Boza-Edwards (WBC)	.1981	Sirimongkol Singmanassak (WBC)	.2002–03
SAMUEL SERRANO	.1981–83	Jesus Chavez (WBC)	.2003–04
Rolando Navarrete (WBC)	.1981–82	Carlos Hernandez (IBF)	.2003–04
Rafael Limon (WBC)	.1982	Erik Morales (WBC)	.2004
Bobby Chacon (WBC)	.1982–83	Erik Morales (IBF/WBC)	.2004
ROGER MAYWEATHER	.1983–84	Marco Antonio Barrera (WBC)	.2004–07
Hector Camacho (WBC)	.1983–84	Marco Antonio Barrera (IBF/WBC)	.2005–06
ROCKY LOCKRIDGE	.1984–85	Vicente Mosquera (WBA)	.2005–06
Hwan-Kil Yuh (IBF)	.1984–85	Cassius Baloyi (IBF)	.2006
Julio Cesar Chavez (WBC)	.1984–87	Gairy St. Clair (IBF)	.2006
Lester Ellis (IBF)	.1985	**Edwin Valero** (WBA)	.2006–
WILFREDO GOMEZ	.1985–86	Malcolm Klassen (IBF)	.2006-07
Barry Michael (IBF)	.1985–87	**Juan Manuel Marquez** (WBC)	.2007–
ALFREDO LAYNE	.1986	**Mzonke Fana** (IBF)	.2007–

Featherweights

Widely accepted champions in CAPITAL letters. Current champions in **bold** type.

Champion	Held Title	Champion	Held Title
TORPEDO BILLY MURPHY	.1890	JOHNNY KILBANE	.1912–23
YOUNG GRIFFO	.1890–92	Jem Driscoll (GBR)	.1912–13
GEORGE DIXON	.1892–97	EUGENE CRIQUI	.1923
SOLLY SMITH	.1897–98	JOHNNY DUNDEE	.1923–24†
Ben Jordan (GBR)	.1898–99	LOUIS (KID) KAPLAN	.1925–26†
Eddie Santry (GBR)	.1899–1900	Dick Finnegan (Mass.)	.1926–27
DAVE SULLIVAN	.1898	BENNY BASS	.1927–28
GEORGE DIXON	.1898–1900	TONY CANZONERI	.1928
TERRY McGOVERN	.1900–01	ANDRE ROUTIS	.1928–29
YOUNG CORBETT II	.1901–04	BATTLING BATTALINO	.1929–32†
JIMMY BRITT	.1904	Tommy Paul (NBA)	.1932–33
ABE ATTELL	.1904	Kid Chocolate (NY)	.1932–33
BROOKLYN TOMMY SULLIVAN	.1904–05	Freddie Miller (NBA)	.1933–36
ABE ATTELL	.1906–12	Baby Arizmendi (MEX)	.1935–36

Champion	Held Title
Mike Belloise (NY)	1936–37
Petey Sarron (NBA)	1936–37
HENRY ARMSTRONG	1937–38†
Joey Archibald (NY)	1938–39
Leo Rodak (NBA)	1938–39
JOEY ARCHIBALD (NBA)	1939–40
Petey Scalzo (NBA)	1940–41
Jimmy Perrin (La.)	1940–41
HARRY JEFFRA	1940–41
JOEY ARCHIBALD	1941
Richie Lemos (NBA)	1941
CHALKY WRIGHT	1941–42
Jackie Wilson (NBA)	1941–43
WILLIE PEP	1942–48
Jackie Callura (NBA)	1943
Phil Terranova (NBA)	1943–44
Sal Bartolo (NBA)	1944–46
SANDY SADDLER	1948–49
WILLIE PEP	1949–50
SANDY SADDLER	1950–57*
HOGAN (KID) BASSEY	1957–59
DAVEY MOORE	1959–63
ULTIMINIO (SUGAR) RAMOS	1963–64
VICENTE SALDIVAR	1964–67*
Howard Winstone (GBR)	1968
Raul Rojas (WBA)	1968
Jose Legra (WBC)	1968–69
Shozo Saijyo (WBA)	1968–71
JOHNNY FAMECHON (WBC)	1969–70
VICENTE SALDIVAR (WBC)	1970
KUNIAKI SHIBATA (WBC)	1970–72
Antonio Gomez (WBA)	1971–72
CLEMENTE SANCHEZ (WBC)	1972
Ernesto Marcel (WBA)	1972–74
JOSE LEGRA (WBC)	1972–73
EDER JOFRE (WBC)	1973–74
Ruben Olivares (WBA)	1974
Bobby Chacon (WBC)	1974–75
ALEXIS ARGUELLO (WBA)	1974–76†
Ruben Olivares (WBC)	1975
David (Poison) Kotey (WBC)	1975–76
DANNY (LITTLE RED) LOPEZ (WBC)	1976–80
Rafael Ortega (WBA)	1977
Cecilio Lastra (WBA)	1977–78
Eusebio Pedroza (WBA)	1978–85
SALVADOR SANCHEZ (WBC)	1980–82
Juan LaPorte (WBC)	1982–84
Wilfredo Gomez (WBC)	1984

Champion	Held Title
Min-Keun Oh (IBF)	1984–85
Azumah Nelson (WBC)	1984–88
Barry McGuigan (WBA)	1985–86
Ki-Young Chung (IBF)	1985–86
Steve Cruz (WBA)	1986–87
Antonio Rivera (IBF)	1986–88
Antonio Esparragoza (WBA)	1987–91
Calvin Grove (IBF)	1988
Jorge Paez (IBF)	1988–91†
Jeff Fenech (WBC)	1988–90†
Marcos Villasana (WBC)	1990–91
Yung-Kyun Park (WBA)	1991–93
Troy Dorsey (IBF)	1991
Manuel Medina (IBF)	1991–93
Paul Hodkinson (WBC)	1991–93
Tom Johnson (IBF)	1993–97
Goyo Vargas (WBC)	1993
Kevin Kelley (WBC)	1993–95
Eloy Rojas (WBA)	1993–96
Alejandro Gonzalez (WBC)	1995
Manuel Medina (IBF)	1995–96
Wilfredo Vasquez (WBA)	1996–98†
Luisito Espinosa (WBC)	1995–99
Naseem Hamed (IBF)	1997†
Hector Lizarraga (IBF)	1997–98
Freddie Norwood (WBA)	1998
Manuel Medina (IBF)	1998–99
Antonio Cermeno (WBA)	1998–99
Cesar Soto (WBC)	1999–00
Paul Ingle (IBF)	1999–2000
Mbuelo Botile (IBF)	2000–01
Guty Espadas (WBC)	2000–01
Freddie Norwood (WBA)	1999–00
Derrick Gainer (WBA)	2000–03
Erik Morales (WBC)	2001–02
Frankie Toledo (IBF)	2001
Manuel Medina (IBF)	2001–02
Johnny Tapia (IBF)	2002†
Erik Morales (WBC)	2002–03†
Juan Manuel Marquez (IBF)	2003–05†
Juan Manuel Marquez (WBA)	2003–06†
Chi In-jin (WBC)	2004–06
Chris John (WBA)	2006–
Takashi Koshimoto (WBC)	2006
Rudy Lopez (WBC)	2006
Robert Guerrero (IBF)	2006–
In Jin Chi (WBC)	2006–07†
Jorge Linares (WBC)	2007–

Junior Featherweights

Current champions in **bold** type.

Champion	Held Title
Jack (Kid) Wolfe	1922–23
Carl Duane	1923–24
Rigoberto Riasco (WBC)	1976
Royal Kobayashi (WBC)	1976
Dong-Kyun Yum (WBC)	1976–77
Wilfredo Gomez (WBC)	1977–83
Soo-Hwan Hong (WBA)	1977–78
Ricardo Cardona (WBA)	1978–80
Leo Randolph (WBA)	1980
Sergio Palma (WBA)	1980–82
Leonardo Cruz (WBA)	1982–84
Jaime Garza (WBC)	1983
Bobby Berna (IBF)	1983–84
Loris Stecca (WBA)	1984
Seung-Il Suh (IBF)	1984–85
Victor Callejas (WBA)	1984–85
Juan (Kid) Meza (WBC)	1984–85
Ji-Woo Kim (IBF)	1985–86
Lupe Pintor (WBC)	1985–86
Samart Payakaroon (WBC)	1986–87

Champion	Held Title
Seung-Hoon Lee (IBF)	1987–88
Louie Espinoza (WBA)	1987
Jeff French (WBA)	1987
Julio Gervacio (WBA)	1987–88
Daniel Zaragoza (WBC)	1988–90
Jose Sanabria (IBF)	1988–90
Bernardo Pinango (WBA)	1988
Juan Jose Estrada (WBA)	1988–89
Fabrice Benichou (IBF)	1989–90
Jesus Salud (WBA)	1989–90
Welcome Ncita (IBF)	1990–92
Paul Banke (WBC)	1990
Luis Mendoza (WBA)	1990–91
Raul Perez (WBA)	1992
Pedro Decima (WBC)	1990–91
Kiyoshi Hatanaka (WBC)	1991
Daniel Zaragoza (WBC)	1991–92
Tracy Patterson (WBC)	1992–94
Kennedy McKinney (IBF)	1993–94
Wilfredo Vasquez (WBA)	1992–95

Major Titleholders (Cont.)
Junior Featherweights (Cont.)

Champion	Held Title
Vuyani Bungu (IBF)	1994–99†
Hector Acero Sanchez (WBC)	1994–95
Antonio Cermeno (WBA)	1995–98†
Daniel Zaragoza (WBC)	1995–97
Erik Morales (WBC)	1997–00†
Enrique Sanchez (WBA)	1998
Nestor Garza (WBA)	1998–00
Lehlohonolo Ledwaba (IBF)	1999–2001
Clarence Adams (WBA)	2000–01†
Willie Jorrin (WBC)	2000–02
Manny Pacquiao (IBF)	2001–04†
Yorber Ortega (WBA)	2001–02

Champion	Held Title
Yoddamrong Sithyodthong (WBA)	2002
Osamu Sato (WBA)	2002
Salim Medjkoune (WBA)	2002–03
Oscar Larios (WBC)	2002–05
Mahyar Monshipour (WBA)	2003–06
Israel Vazquez (IBF)	2004–06
Israel Vazquez (IBF/WBC)	2005†
Israel Vazquez (WBC)	2005–07
Somsak Sithchatchawal (WBA)	2006
Celestino Caballero (WBA)	2006–
Rafael Marquez (WBC)	2007
Steve Molitor (IBF)	2007–
Israel Vazquez (WBC)	2007–

Bantamweights
Widely accepted champions in CAPITAL letters. Current champions in **bold** type.

Champion	Held Title
TOMMY (SPIDER) KELLY	1887
HUGHEY BOYLE	1887–88
TOMMY (SPIDER) KELLY	1889
CHAPPIE MORAN	1889–90
Tommy (Spider) Kelly	1890–92
GEORGE DIXON	1890–91
Billy Plummer	1892–95
JIMMY BARRY	1894–99
Pedlar Palmer	1895–99
TERRY McGOVERN	1899–1900
HARRY HARRIS	1901–02
DANNY DOUGHERTY	1900–01
HARRY FORBES	1901–03
FRANKIE NEIL	1903–04
JOE BOWKER	1904–05
JIMMY WALSH	1905–06†
OWEN MORAN	1907–08
MONTE ATTELL	1909–10
FRANKIE CONLEY	1910–11
JOHNNY COULON	1911–14
Digger Stanley (GBR)	1910–12
Charles Ledoux (GBR)	1912–13
Eddie Campi (GBR)	1913–14
KID WILLIAMS	1914–17
Johnny Ertle	1915–18
PETE HERMAN	1917–20
Memphis Pal Moore	1918–19
JOE LYNCH	1920–21
PETE HERMAN	1921
JOHNNY BUFF	1921–22
JOE LYNCH	1922–24
ABE GOLDSTEIN	1924
CANNONBALL EDDIE MARTIN	1924–25
PHIL ROSENBERG	1925–27
Teddy Baldock (GBR)	1927
BUD TAYLOR (NBA)	1927–28†
Willie Smith (GBR)	1927–28
Bushy Graham (NY)	1928–29
PANAMA AL BROWN	1929–35
Sixto Escobar (NBA)	1934–35
BALTAZAR SANGCHILLI	1935–36
Lou Salica (NBA)	1935
Sixto Escobar (NBA)	1935–36
TONY MARINO	1936
SIXTO ESCOBAR	1936–37
HARRY JEFFRA	1937–38
SIXTO ESCOBAR	1938–39*
Georgie Pace (NBA)	1939–40
LOU SALICA	1940–42
MANUEL ORTIZ	1942–47
HAROLD DADE	1947
MANUEL ORTIZ	1947–50
VIC TOWEEL	1950–52

Champion	Held Title
JIMMY CARRUTHERS	1952–54*
ROBERT COHEN	1954–56
Raul Macias (NBA)	1955–57
MARIO D'AGATA	1956–57
ALPHONSE HALIMI	1957–59
JOE BECERRA	1959–60*
Johnny Caldwell (EBU)	1961–62
EDER JOFRE	1961–65
MASAHIKO FIGHTING HARADA	1965–68
LIONEL ROSE	1968–69
RUBEN OLIVARES	1969–70
CHUCHO CASTILLO	1970–71
RUBEN OLIVARES	1971–72
RAFAEL HERRERA	1972
ENRIQUE PINDER	1972–73
ROMEO ANAYA	1973
Rafael Herrera (WBC)	1973–74
ARNOLD TAYLOR	1973–74
SOO-HWAN HONG	1974–75.
Rodolfo Martinez (WBC)	1974–76
ALFONSO ZAMORA	1975–77
Carlos Zarate (WBC)	1976–79
JORGE LUJAN	1977–80
Lupe Pintor (WBC)	1979–83
JULIAN SOLIS	1980
JEFF CHANDLER	1980–84
Albert Davila (WBC)	1983–85
RICHARD SANDOVAL	1984–86
Satoshi Shingaki (IBF)	1984–85
Jeff Fenech (IBF)	1985
Daniel Zaragoza (WBC)	1985
Miguel (Happy) Lora (WBC)	1985–88
GABY CANIZALES	1986
BERNARDO PINANGO	1986–87
Wilfredo Vasquez (WBA)	1987–88
Kevin Seabrooks (IBF)	1987–88
Kaokor Galaxy (WBA)	1988
Moon Sung-Kil (WBA)	1988–89
Kaokor Galaxy (WBA)	1989
Raul Perez (WBC)	1988–91
Orlando Canizales (IBF)	1988–94†
Luisito Espinosa (WBA)	1989–91
Greg Richardson	1991
Joichiro Tatsuyoshi (WBC)	1991–92
Israel Contreras (WBA)	1991–92
Eddie Cook (WBA)	1992
Victor Rabanales (WBC)	1992–93
Jorge Julio (WBA)	1992–93
Jung-Il Byun (WBC)	1993
Junior Jones (WBA)	1993–94
Yasuei Yakushiji (WBC)	1993–95
John M. Johnson (WBA)	1994
Daorung Chuvatana (WBA)	1994–95

Champion	Held Title
Harold Mestre (IBF)	1995
Mbuelo Botile (IBF)	1995–97
Wayne McCullough (WBC)	1995–96
Veeraphol Sahaprom (WBA)	1995–96
Nana Yaw Konadu (WBA)	1996
Daorung Chuvatana (WBA)	1996–97
Nana Yaw Konadu (WBA)	1997–98
Sirimongkol Singmanassak (WBC)	1996–97
Tim Austin (IBF)	1997–2003
Joichiro Tatsuyoshi (WBC)	1997–98

Champion	Held Title
Johnny Tapia (WBA)	1998–99
Veerapol Sahaprom (WBC)	1998–2005
Paulie Ayala (WBA)	1999–2001
Eidy Moya (WBA)	2001–02
Johnny Bredahl (WBA)	2002–04†
Rafael Marquez (IBF)	2003–07†
Wladimir Sidorenko (WBA)	2005–
Hozumi Hasegawa (WBC)	2005–
Luis Alberto Perez (IBF)	2007
Joseph Agbeko (IBF)	2007–

Junior Bantamweights

Widely accepted champions in CAPITAL letters. Current champions in **bold** type.

Champion	Held Title
Rafael Orono (WBC)	1980–81
Chul-Ho Kim (WBC)	1981–82
Gustavo Ballas (WBA)	1981
Rafael Pedroza (WBA)	1981–82
Jiro Watanabe (WBA)	1982–84
Rafael Orono (WBC)	1982–83
Payao Poontarat (WBC)	1983–84
Joo-Do Chun (IBF)	1983–85
JIRO WATANABE	1984–86
Kaosai Galaxy (WBA)	1984
Ellyas Pical (IBF)	1985–86
Cesar Polanco (IBF)	1986
GILBERTO ROMAN	1986–87
Ellyas Pical (IBF)	1986
Santos Laciar (WBC)	1987
Tae-Il Chang (IBF)	1987
Sugar Rojas (WBC)	1987–88
Ellyas Pical (IBF)	1987–89
Gilberto Roman (WBC)	1988–89
Juan Polo Perez (IBF)	1989–90
Nana Konadu (WBC)	1989–90
Sung-Kil Moon (WBC)	1990–93
Robert Quiroga (IBF)	1990–93
Julio Borboa (IBF)	1993–94
Katsuya Onizuka (WBA)	1993–94
Lee Hyung-Chul (WBA)	1994–95
Jose Luis Bueno (WBC)	1993–94

Champion	Held Title
Hiroshi Kawashima (WBC)	1994–97
Harold Grey (IBF)	1994–95
Alimi Goitia (WBA)	1995–96
Yokthai Sith-Oar (WBA)	1996–97
Carlos Salazar (IBF)	1995–96
Harold Grey (IBF)	1996
Danny Romero (IBF)	1996–97
Gerry Penalosa (WBC)	1997–98
Johnny Tapia (IBF)	1997–98†
Satoshi Iida (WBA)	1997–98
Cho In-Joo (WBC)	1998–00
Jesus Rojas (WBA)	1998–99
Mark Johnson (IBF)	1999–00†
Hideki Todaka (WBA)	1999–2000
Masanori Tokuyama (WBC)	2000–04
Felix Machado (IBF)	2000–03
Leo Gamez (WBA)	2000–01
Celes Kobayashi (WBA)	2001–02
Alexander Munoz (WBA)	2002–04
Luis Perez (IBF)	2003–06†
Katsushige Kawashima (WBC)	2004–05
Martin Castillo (WBA)	2004–06
Masmori Tokuyama (WBC)	2005–06
Nobuo Nashiro (WBA)	2006–07
Alexander Munoz (WBA)	2007–
Cristian Mijares (WBC)	2006–
Dmitri Kirilov (IBF)	2007–

Flyweights

Widely accepted champions in CAPITAL letters. Current champions in **bold** type.

Champion	Held Title
Sid Smith (GBR)	1913
Bill Ladbury (GBR)	1913–14
Percy Jones (GBR)	1914
Joe Symonds (GBR)	1914–16
JIMMY WILDE	1916–23
PANCHO VILLA	1923–25
FIDEL LaBARBA	1925–27*
FRENCHY BELANGER (NBA,IBU)	1927–28
Izzy Schwartz (NY)	1927–29
Johnny McCoy (Calif.)	1927–28
Newsboy Brown (Calif.)	1928
FRANKIE GENARO (NBA,IBU)	1928–29
Johnny Hill (GBR)	1928–29
SPIDER PLADNER (NBA,IBU)	1929
FRANKIE GENARO (NBA,IBU)	1929–31
Willie LaMorte (NY)	1929–30
Midget Wolgast (NY)	1930–35
YOUNG PEREZ (NBA,IBU)	1931–32
JACKIE BROWN (NBA,IBU)	1932–35
BENNY LYNCH	1935–38†
Small Montana (NY,Calif.)	1935–37
PETER KANE	1938–43
Little Dado (NBA,Calif.)	1938–40
JACKIE PATERSON	1943–48
RINTY MONAGHAN	1948–50*
TERRY ALLEN	1950
SALVADOR (DADO) MARINO	1950–52

Champion	Held Title
YOSHIO SHIRAI	1953–54
PASCUAL PEREZ	1954–60
PONE KINGPETCH	1960–62
MASAHIKO (FIGHTING) HARADA	1962–63
PONE KINGPETCH	1963
HIROYUKI EBIHARA	1963–64
PONE KINGPETCH	1964–65
SALVATORE BURRINI	1965–66
Horacio Accavallo (WBA)	1966–68
WALTER McGOWAN	1966
CHARTCHAI CHIONOI	1966–69
EFREN TORRES	1969–70
Hiroyuki Ebihara (WBA)	1969
Bernabe Villacampo (WBA)	1969–70
CHARTCHAI CHIONOI	1970
Berkrerk Chartvanchai (WBA)	1970
Masao Ohba (WBA)	1970–73
ERBITO SALAVARRIA	1970–73
Betulio Gonzalez (WBC)	1972
Venice Borkorsor (WBC)	1972–73
VENICE BORKORSOR	1973
Chartchai Chionoi (WBA)	1973–74
Betulio Gonzalez (WBA)	1973–74
Shoji Oguma (WBC)	1974–75
Susumu Hanagata (WBA)	1974–75
Miguel Canto (WBC)	1975–79
Erbito Salavarria (WBA)	1975–76

Major Titleholders (Cont.)
Flyweights (Cont.)

Champion	Held Title
Alfonso Lopez (WBA)	1976
Guty Espadas (WBA)	1976–78
Betulio Gonzalez (WBA)	1978–79
Chan-Hee Park (WBC)	1979–80
Luis Ibarra (WBA)	1979–80
Tae-Shik Kim (WBA)	1980
Shoji Oguma (WBC)	1980–81
Peter Mathebula (WBA)	1980–81
Santos Laciar (WBA)	1981
Antonio Avelar (WBC)	1981–82
Luis Ibarra (WBA)	1981
Juan Herrera (WBA)	1981–82
Prudencio Cardona (WBC)	1982
Santos Laciar (WBA)	1982–85
Freddie Castillo (WBC)	1982
Eleoncio Mercedes (WBC)	1982–83
Charlie Magri (WBC)	1983
Frank Cedeno (WBC)	1983–84
Soon-Chun Kwon (IBF)	1983–85
Koji Kobayashi (WBC)	1984
Gabriel Bernal (WBC)	1984
Sot Chitalada (WBC)	1984–88
Hilario Zapate (WBA)	1985–87
Chong-Kwan Chung (IBF)	1985–86
Bi-Won Chung (IBF)	1986
Hi-Sup Shin (IBF)	1986–87
Dodie Penalosa (IBF)	1987
Fidel Bassa (WBA)	1987–89
Choi Chang-Ho (IBF)	1987–88
Rolando Bohol (IBF)	1988
Yong-Kang Kim (WBC)	1988–89
Duke McKenzie (IBF)	1988–89
Dave McAuley (IBF)	1989–92
Sot Chitalada (WBC)	1989–91
Jesus Rojas (WBA)	1989–90
Yul-Woo Lee (WBA)	1990
Leopard Tamakuma (WBA)	1990–91
Muangchai Kittikasem (WBC)	1991–92
Yong-Kang Kim (WBA)	1991–92
Rodolfo Blanco (IBF)	1992
Yuri Arbachakov (WBC)	1992–97
Aquiles Guzman (WBA)	1992
Phichit Sithbangprachan (IBF)	1992–94†
David Griman (WBA)	1992–94
Saen Sor Ploenchit (WBA)	1994–96
Francisco Tejedor (IBF)	1995
Danny Romero (IBF)	1995–96
Mark Johnson (IBF)	1996–99†
Jose Bonilla (WBA)	1996–97
Chatchai Sasakul (WBC)	1997–98
Hugo Soto (WBA)	1998–99
Manny Pacquiao (WBC)	1998–99
Irene Pacheco (IBF)	1999–2005
Leo Gamez (WBA)	1999
Medgoen Lukchaopormasak (WBC)	1999–00
Sornpichai Kratindaenggym (WBA)	1999–00
Eric Morel (WBA)	2000–03
Malcolm Tunacao (WBC)	2000–01
Pongsaklek Wonjongkam (WBC)	2001–07
Lorenzo Parra (WBA)	2003–07
Vic Darchinyan (IBF)	2004–07
Takefumi Sakata (WBA)	2007–
Nonito Donaire (IBF)	2007–
Daisuke Naito (WBC)	2007–

Junior Flyweights
Current champions in **bold** type.

Champion	Held Title
Franco Udella (WBC)	1975
Jaime Rios (WBA)	1975–76
Luis Estaba (WBC)	1975–78
Juan Guzman (WBA)	1976
Yoko Gushiken (WBA)	1976–81
Freddy Castillo (WBC)	1978
Netrnoi Vorasingh (WBC)	1978
Sung-Jun Kim (WBC)	1978–80
Shigeo Nakajima (WBC)	1980
Hilario Zapata (WBC)	1980–82
Pedro Flores (WBA)	1981
Hwan-Jin Kim (WBA)	1981
Katsuo Tokashiki (WBA)	1981–83
Amado Urzua (WBC)	1982
Tadashi Tomori (WBC)	1982
Hilario Zapata (WBC)	1982–83
Jung-Koo Chang (WBC)	1983–88
Lupe Madera (WBA)	1983–84
Dodie Penalosa (IBF)	1983–86
Francisco Quiroz (WBA)	1984–85
Joey Olivo (WBA)	1985
Myung-Woo Yuh (WBA)	1985–91
Jum-Hwan Choi (IBF)	1986–88
Tacy Macalos (IBF)	1988–89
German Torres (WBC)	1988–89
Yul-Woo Lee (WBC)	1989
Muangchai Kittikasem (IBF)	1989–90
Humberto Gonzalez (WBC)	1989–90
Michael Carbajal (IBF)	1990–94
Rolando Pascua (WBC)	1990
Melchor Cob Castro (WBC)	1991
Humberto Gonzalez (WBC)	1991–93
Hirokia Ioka (WBA)	1991–92
Michael Carbajal (WBC)	1993–94
Myung-Woo Yuh (WBA)	1993
Leo Gamez (WBA)	1993–95
Humberto Gonzalez (WBC/IBF)	1994–95
Choi Hi-Yong (WBA)	1995–96
Saman Sor Jaturong (WBC/IBF)	1995–96
Carlos Murillo (WBA)	1996
Keiji Yamaguchi (WBA)	1996
Michael Carbajal (IBF)	1996–97
Saman Sor Jaturong (WBC)	1995–99
Phichit Chor Siriwat (WBA)	1996–00†
Mauricio Pastrana (IBF)	1997–98†
Will Grigsby (IBF)	1999
Choi Yo-Sam (WBC)	1999–2002
Ricardo Lopez (IBF)	1999–2003*
Beibis Mendoza (WBA)	2000–01
Rosendo Alvarez (WBA)	2001–04†
Jorge Arce (WBC)	2002–05†
Jose Victor Burgos (IBF)	2003–05
Eric Ortiz (WBC)	2005
Roberto Vasquez (WBA)	2005–06
Brian Viloria (WBC)	2005–06
Will Grigsby (IBF)	2005–06
Ulises Solis (IBF)	2006–
Koki Kameda (WBA)	2006–07†
Edgar Sosa (WBC)	2007–
Juan Carlos Reveco (WBA)	2007–

Strawweights

Current champions in **bold** type.

Champion	Held Title	Champion	Held Title
Franco Udella (WBC)	1975	Rolando Pascua (WBC)	1990
Jaime Rios (WBA)	1975–76	Melchor Cob Castro (WBC)	1991
Luis Estraba (WBC)	1975–78	Ricardo Lopez (WBC)	1990–98
Juan Guzman (WBA)	1976	Ratanapol Voraphin (IBF)	1992–97
Yoko Gushiken (WBA)	1976–81	Chana Porpaoin (WBA)	1993–95
Freddy Castillo (WBC)	1978	Rosendo Alvarez (WBA)	1995–98
Netrnoi Vorasingh (WBC)	1978	Ricardo Lopez (WBA/WBC)	1998–99†
Sung-Jun Kim (WBC)	1978–80	Zolani Petelo (IBF)	1997–2001†
Shigeo Nakajima (WBC)	1980	Wandee Chor Chareon (WBC)	1999–00
Hilario Zapata (WBC)	1980–82	Noel Arambulet (WBA)	1999–00†
Pedro Flores (WBA)	1981	Joma Gamboa (WBA)	2000
Hwan-Jin Kim (WBA)	1981	Keitaro Hoshino (WBA)	2000–01
Katsuo Tokashiki (WBA)	1981–83	Jose Antonio Aguirre (WBC)	2000–04
Amado Urzua (WBC)	1982	Chana Porpaoin (WBA)	2001
Tadashi Tomori (WBC)	1982	Robert Leyva (IBF)	2001–02
Hilario Zapata (WBC)	1982–83	Yutaka Niida (WBA)	2001*
Jung-Koo Chang (WBC)	1983–88	Keitaro Hoshino (WBA)	2002
Lupe Madera (WBA)	1983–84	Noel Arambulent (WBA)	2002–04
Dodie Penalosa (IBF)	1983–86	Miguel Barrera (IBF)	2002–03
Francisco Quiroz (WBA)	1984–85	Edgar Cardenas (IBF)	2003
Joey Olivo (WBA)	1985	Daniel Reyes (IBF)	2003–04
Myung-Woo Yuh (WBA)	1985–93	Eagle Kyowa (WBC)	2004
Jum-Hwan Choi (IBF)	1986–88	**Yutaka Niida** (WBA)	2004–
Tacy Macalos (IBF)	1988–89	Muhammad Rachman (IBF)	2004–07
German Torres (WBC)	1988–89	Isaac Bustos (WBA)	2004–05
Yul-Woo Lee (WBC)	1989	Katsunari Takayama (WBC)	2005
Muangchai Kittikasem (IBF)	1989–90	**Eagle Kyowa** (WBC)	2005–
Humberto Gonzalez (WBC)	1989–90	**Florante Condes** (IBF)	2007–
Michael Carbajal (IBF)	1990		

Annual Awards

Ring Magazine Fight of the Year

First presented in 1945 by Nat Fleischer, who started *The Ring* magazine in 1922.

Multiple matchups: Muhammad Ali vs. Joe Frazier, Marco Antonio Barrera vs. Erik Morales; Carmen Basilio vs. Sugar Ray Robinson, Arturo Gatti vs. Micky Ward and Rocky Graziano vs. Tony Zale (2).

Multiple fights: Muhammad Ali (6); Carmen Basilio (5); George Foreman, Arturo Gatti and Joe Frazier (4); Rocky Graziano, Rocky Marciano, Micky Ward and Tony Zale (3); Marco Antonio Barrera, Nino Benvenuti, Bobby Chacon, Ezzard Charles, Marvin Hagler, Thomas Hearns, Evander Holyfield, Sugar Ray Leonard, Erik Morales, Floyd Patterson, Sugar Ray Robinson, Jersey Joe Walcott (2).

Year	Winner	Loser	Result	Year	Winner	Loser	Result
1945	Rocky Graziano	Red Cochrane	KO 10	1972	Bob Foster	Chris Finnegan	KO 14
1946	Tony Zale	Rocky Graziano	KO 6	1973	George Foreman	Joe Frazier	KO 2
1947	Rocky Graziano	Tony Zale	KO 6	1974	Muhammad Ali	George Foreman	KO 8
1948	Marcel Cerdan	Tony Zale	KO 12	1975	Muhammad Ali	Joe Frazier	KO 14
1949	Willie Pep	Sandy Saddler	W 15	1976	George Foreman	Ron Lyle	KO 4
1950	Jake LaMotta	Laurent Dauthuille	KO 15	1977	Jimmy Young	George Foreman	W 12
1951	Jersey Joe Walcott	Ezzard Charles	KO 7	1978	Leon Spinks	Muhammad Ali	W 15
1952	Rocky Marciano	Jersey Joe Walcott	KO 13	1979	Danny Lopez	Mike Ayala	KO 15
1953	Rocky Marciano	Roland LaStarza	KO 11	1980	Saad Muhammad	Yaqui Lopez	KO 14
1954	Rocky Marciano	Ezzard Charles	KO 8	1981	Sugar Ray Leonard	Thomas Hearns	KO 14
1955	Carmen Basilio	Tony DeMarco	KO 12	1982	Bobby Chacon	Rafael Limon	W 15
1956	Carmen Basilio	Johnny Saxton	KO 9	1983	Bobby Chacon	C. Boza-Edwards	W 12
1957	Carmen Basilio	Sugar Ray Robinson	W 15	1984	Jose Luis Ramirez	Edwin Rosario	KO 4
1958	Sugar Ray Robinson	Carmen Basilio	W 15	1985	Marvin Hagler	Thomas Hearns	KO 3
1959	Gene Fullmer	Carmen Basilio	KO 14	1986	Stevie Cruz	Barry McGuigan	W 15
1960	Floyd Patterson	Ingemar Johansson	KO 5	1987	Sugar Ray Leonard	Marvin Hagler	W 12
1961	Joe Brown	Dave Charnley	W 15	1988	Tony Lopez	Rocky Lockridge	W 12
1962	Joey Giardello	Henry Hank	W 10	1989	Roberto Duran	Iran Barkley	W 12
1963	Cassius Clay	Doug Jones	W 10	1990	Julio Cesar Chavez	Meldrick Taylor	KO 12
1964	Cassius Clay	Sonny Liston	KO 7	1991	Robert Quiroga	Akeem Anifowoshe	W 12
1965	Floyd Patterson	George Chuvalo	W 12	1992	Riddick Bowe	Evander Holyfield	W 12
1966	Jose Torres	Eddie Cotton	W 15	1993	Michael Carbajal	Humberto Gonzalez	KO 7
1967	Nino Benvenuti	Emile Griffith	W 15	1994	Jorge Castro	John David Jackson	TKO 9
1968	Dick Tiger	Frank DePaula	W 10	1995	Saman Sorjaturong	Chiquita Gonzalez	KO 7
1969	Joe Frazier	Jerry Quarry	KO 7	1996	Evander Holyfield	Mike Tyson	TKO 11
1970	Carlos Monzon	Nino Benvenuti	KO 12	1997	Arturo Gatti	Gabriel Ruelas	KO 5
1971	Joe Frazier	Muhammad Ali	W 15	1998	Ivan Robinson	Arturo Gatti	W 10

Annual Awards (Cont.)

Ring Magazine Fight of the Year (Cont.)

Year	Winner	Loser	Result	Year	Winner	Loser	Result
1999	Paulie Ayala	Johnny Tapia	W 12	2004	Marco Antonio Barrera	Erik Morales	W 12
2000	Erik Morales	Marco Antonio Barrera	W 12	2005	Diego Corrales	Jose Luis Castillo	KO 10
2001	Micky Ward	Emanuel Burton	W 10	2006	Somsak Sithchatchawai	Mahyar Monshipour	TKO 10
2002	Micky Ward	Arturo Gatti	W 10				
2003	Arturo Gatti	Micky Ward	W 10				

Ring Magazine Fighter of the Year

First presented in 1928 by Nat Fleischer, who started *The Ring* magazine in 1922.

Multiple winners: Muhammad Ali (5); Joe Louis (4); Joe Frazier, Evander Holyfield and Rocky Marciano (3); Ezzard Charles, George Foreman, Marvin Hagler, Thomas Hearns, Ingemar Johansson, Sugar Ray Leonard, Tommy Loughran, Floyd Patterson, Sugar Ray Robinson, Barney Ross, Dick Tiger, James Toney and Mike Tyson (2).

Year		Year		Year	
1928	Gene Tunney	1955	Rocky Marciano	1981	Sugar Ray Leonard & Salvador Sanchez
1929	Tommy Loughran	1956	Floyd Patterson	1982	Larry Holmes
1930	Max Schmeling	1957	Carmen Basilio	1983	Marvin Hagler
1931	Tommy Loughran	1958	Ingemar Johansson	1984	Thomas Hearns
1932	Jack Sharkey	1959	Ingemar Johansson	1985	Donald Curry & Marvin Hagler
1933	No award	1960	Floyd Patterson	1986	Mike Tyson
1934	Tony Canzoneri & Barney Ross	1961	Joe Brown	1987	Evander Holyfield
1935	Barney Ross	1962	Dick Tiger	1988	Mike Tyson
1936	Joe Louis	1963	Cassius Clay	1989	Pernell Whitaker
1937	Henry Armstrong	1964	Emile Griffith	1990	Julio Cesar Chavez
1938	Joe Louis	1965	Dick Tiger	1991	James Toney
1939	Joe Louis	1966	No award	1992	Riddick Bowe
1940	Billy Conn	1967	Joe Frazier	1993	Michael Carbajal
1941	Joe Louis	1968	Nino Benvenuti	1994	Roy Jones Jr.
1942	Sugar Ray Robinson	1969	Jose Napoles	1995	Oscar De La Hoya
1943	Fred Apostoli	1970	Joe Frazier	1996	Evander Holyfield
1944	Beau Jack	1971	Joe Frazier	1997	Evander Holyfield
1945	Willie Pep	1972	Muhammad Ali & Carlos Monzon	1998	Floyd Mayweather Jr.
1946	Tony Zale	1973	George Foreman	1999	Paulie Ayala
1947	Gus Lesnevich	1974	Muhammad Ali	2000	Felix Trinidad
1948	Ike Williams	1975	Muhammad Ali	2001	Bernard Hopkins
1949	Ezzard Charles	1976	George Foreman	2002	Vernon Forrest
1950	Ezzard Charles	1977	Carlos Zarate	2003	James Toney
1951	Sugar Ray Robinson	1978	Muhammad Ali	2004	Glen Johnson
1952	Rocky Marciano	1979	Sugar Ray Leonard	2005	Ricky Hatton
1953	Carl (Bobo) Olson	1980	Thomas Hearns	2006	Manny Pacquiao
1954	Rocky Marciano				

Note: Cassius Clay changed his name to Muhammad Ali after winning the heavyweight title in 1964.

Dan Rafael's Annual Awards

ESPN.com's resident boxing expert Dan Rafael has been his handing out his annual awards since 2000.

Fighter of the Year

Year		Year		Year	
2000	Felix Trinidad	2003	James Toney	2006	Manny Pacquiao
2001	Bernard Hopkins	2004	Glen Johnson		
2002	Vernon Forrest	2005	Ricky Hatton		

Fight of the Year

Year	Winner	Loser	Result	Year	Winner	Loser	Result
2000	Felix Trinidad	Fernando Vargas	TKO 12	2004	Marco Antonio Barrera	Erik Morales	W 12
2001	Micky Ward	Emanuel Burton	W 10	2005	Diego Corrales	Jose Luis Castillo	KO 10
2002	Micky Ward	Arturo Gatti	W 10	2006	Somsak Sithchatchawal	Mahyar Monshipour	TKO 10
2003	Arturo Gatti	Micky Ward	W 10				

Round of the Year

Year	Winner	Loser	Round	Year	Winner	Loser	Round
2000	Erik Morales	Marco Antonio Barrera	5th	2004	Marco Antonio Barrera	Erik Morales	11th
2001	Micky Ward	Emanuel Burton	9th	2005	Diego Corrales	Jose Luis Castillo	10th
2002	Micky Ward	Arturo Gatti	9th	2006	Somsak Sithchatchawal	Mahyar Monshipour	9th
2003	Acelino Freitas	Jorge Barrios	11th				

Knockout of the Year

Year	Winner	Loser	Result	Year	Winner	Loser	Result
2000	Lennox Lewis	Frans Botha	TKO 2	2004	Antonio Tarver	Roy Jones Jr.	KO 2
2001	Lennox Lewis	Hasim Rahman	KO 4	2005	Allan Green	Jaidon Codrington	KO 1
2002	Roy Jones	Glenn Kelly	KO 7	2006	Calvin Brock	Zuri Lawrence	KO 6
2003	Rocky Juarez	Antonio "Chelo" Diaz	KO 10				

Prospect of the Year

Year		Year		Year		Year	
2000	Julio Diaz	2002	Miguel Cotto	2004	Samuel Peter	2006	Andre Berto
2001	Francisco Bojado	2003	Jermain Taylor	2005	Joel Julio		

All-Time Leaders

Based on rankings compiled by *The Ring Record Book and Encyclopedia.*

Knockouts

		Division	Career	No
1	Archie Moore	Lt. Heavy	1936–63	130
2	Young Stribling	Heavy	1921–33	126
3	Billy Bird	Welter	1920–48	125
4	George Odwel	Welter	1930–45	114
5	Sugar Ray Robinson	Middle	1940–65	110

Total Bouts

		Division	Career	No
1	Len Wickwar	Lt. Heavy	1928–47	463
2	Reggie Strickland	Lt. Heavy	1987–05	363
3	Jack Britton	Welter	1905–30	350
4	Johnny Dundee	Feather	1910–32	333
5	Billy Bird	Welter	1920–48	318

Triple Champions

Fighters who have won widely-accepted world titles in more than two divisions. Henry Armstrong is the only fighter listed to hold three titles simultaneously. Note that (*) indicates title claimant.

Sugar Ray Leonard (5) WBC Welterweight (1979-80,80-82); WBA Jr. Middleweight (1981); WBC Middleweight (1987); WBC Super Middleweight (1988-90); WBC Light Heavyweight (1988).

Floyd Mayweather Jr. (5) WBC Jr. Lighweight (1998-2002); WBC Lightweight (2002-04); WBC Jr. Welterweight (2005-06); WBC Welterweight (2006–); WBC Jr. Middleweight (2007).

Roy Jones Jr. (4) IBF Middleweight (1993-94); IBF Super Middleweight (1994-96); WBC Light Heavyweight (1996, 1997-2003); WBA Light Heavyweight (1998–); IBF Light Heavyweight (1999-2003); WBA Heavyweight (2003-04).

Oscar De La Hoya (4) IBF Lightweight (1995-96); WBC Super Lightweight (1996-97); WBC Welterweight (1997-99); WBC Jr. Middleweight (2001-03); WBA Jr. Middleweight (2002-03); WBC Middleweight (2006).

Roberto Duran (4) Lightweight (1972-79); WBC Welterweight (1980); WBA Jr. Middleweight (1983-84); WBC Middleweight (1989-90).

Leo Gamez (4) WBA Strawweight (1988-90); WBA Jr. Flyweight (1993-95); WBA Flyweight (1999); WBA Junior Bantamweight (2000-01).

Thomas Hearns (4) WBA Welterweight (1980-81); WBC Jr. Middleweight (1982-84); WBC Light Heavyweight (1987); WBC Middleweight (1987-88); WBA Light Heavyweight (1991).

James Toney (4) IBF Middleweight (1991-93); IBF Super Middleweight (1992-94); IBF Cruiserweight (2003); WBA Heavyweight† (2005).

Pernell Whitaker (4) IBF/WBC/WBA Lightweight (1989-92); IBF Jr. Welterweight (1992-93); WBC Welterweight (1993-97); WBC Jr. Middleweight (1995).

Alexis Arguello (3) WBA Featherweight (1974-77); WBC Jr. Lightweight (1978-80); WBC Lightweight (1981-83).

Henry Armstrong (3) Featherweight (1937-38); Welterweight (1938-40); Lightweight (1938-39).

Iran Barkley (3) WBC Middleweight (1988-89); IBF Super Middleweight (1992-93); WBA Light Heavyweight (1992).

Wilfredo Benitez (3) Jr. Welterweight (1976-79); Welterweight (1979); WBC Jr. Middleweight (1981-82).

Tony Canzoneri (3) Featherweight (1928); Lightweight (1930-33); Jr. Welterweight (1931-32,33).

Julio Cesar Chavez (3) WBC Jr. Lightweight (1984-87); WBA/WBC Lightweight (1987-89); WBC/IBF Jr. Welterweight (1989-91); WBC Jr. Welterweight (1991-94, 1994).

Jeff Fenech (3) IBF Bantamweight (1985); WBC Jr. Featherweight (1986-88); WBC Featherweight (1988-90).

Bob Fitzsimmons (3) Middleweight (1891-97); Light Heavyweight (1903-05); Heavyweight (1897-99).

Wilfredo Gomez (3) WBC Super Bantamweight (1977-83); WBC Featherweight (1984); WBA Jr. Lightweight (1985-86).

Emile Griffith (3) Welterweight (1961,62-63,63-66); Jr. Middleweight (1962-63); Middleweight (1966-67,67-68).

Mike McCallum (3) WBA Jr. Middleweight (1984-88); WBA Middleweight (1989-91); WBC Light Heavyweight (1994-95).

Terry McGovern (3) Bantamweight (1889-1900); Featherweight (1900-01); Lightweight* (1900-01).

Erik Morales (3) WBC Jr. Featherweight (1997-2000); WBC Featherweight (2001-02); IBF/WBC Jr. Lightweight (2004)

Barney Ross (3) Lightweight (1933-35); Jr. Welterweight (1933-35); Welterweight (1934, 35-38).

Johnny Tapia (3) IBF Jr. Bantamweight (1997-98); WBA Bantamweight (1998-99); IBF Featherweight (2002).

Felix Trinidad (3) IBF/WBC Welterweight (1993-2000); WBA/IBF Jr. Middleweight (2000-01); WBA Middleweight (2001).

Wilfredo Vazquez (3) WBA Bantamweight (1987-88); WBA Jr. Featherweight (1992-95); WBA Featherweight (1996-98).

†Toney won a uanimous 12-round decision over WBA champion John Ruiz but tested positive for steroids in a post-fight drug test and the fight was ruled a no-contest.

Muhammad Ali's Career Pro Record

Born Cassius Marcellus Clay, Jr. on Jan. 17, 1942, in Louisville; Amateur record of 100-5; won light-heavyweight gold medal at 1960 Olympic Games; Pro record of 56-5 with 37 KOs in 61 fights.

1960

Date	Opponent (location)	Result
Oct. 29	Tunney Hunsaker, Louisville	Wu 6
Dec. 27	Herb Siler, Miami Beach	TKO 4

1961

Date	Opponent (location)	Result
Jan. 17	Tony Esperti, Miami Beach	TKO 3
Feb. 7	Jim Robinson, Miami Beach	TKO 1
Feb. 21	Donnie Fleeman, Miami Beach	TKO 7
Apr. 19	Lamar Clark, Louisville	KO 2
June 26	Duke Sabedong, Las Vegas	Wu 10
July 22	Alonzo Johnson, Louisville	Wu 10
Oct. 7	Alex Miteff, Louisville	TKO 6
Nov. 29	Willi Besmanoff, Louisville	TKO 7

1962

Date	Opponent (location)	Result
Feb. 10	Sonny Banks, New York	TKO 4
Feb. 28	Don Warner, Miami Beach	TKO 4
Apr. 23	George Logan, Los Angeles	TKO 4
May 19	Billy Daniels, Los Angeles	TKO 7
July 20	Alejandro Lavorante, Los Angeles	KO 5
Nov. 15	Archie Moore, Los Angeles	KO 4

1963

Date	Opponent (location)	Result
Jan. 24	Charlie Powell, Pittsburgh	KO 3
Mar. 13	Doug Jones, New York	Wu 10
June 18	Henry Cooper, London	TKO 5

1964

Date	Opponent (location)	Result
Feb. 25	Sonny Liston, Miami Beach	TKO 7

(won World Heavyweight title)

After the fight, Clay announces he is a member of the Black Muslim religious sect and has changed his name to Muhammad Ali.

1965

Date	Opponent (location)	Result
May 25	Sonny Liston, Lewiston, Me	KO 1
Nov. 22	Floyd Patterson, Las Vegas	TKO 12

1966

Date	Opponent (location)	Result
Mar. 29	George Chuvalo, Toronto	Wu 15
May 21	Henry Cooper, London	TKO 6
Aug. 6	Brian London, London	KO 3
Sept.10	Karl Mildenberger, Frankfurt	TKO 12
Nov. 14	Cleveland Williams, Houston	TKO 3

1967

Date	Opponent (location)	Result
Feb. 6	Ernie Terrell, Houston	Wu 15
Mar. 22	Zora Folley, New York	KO 7
Apr. 28	Refuses induction into U.S. Army and is stripped of world title by WBA and most state commissions the next day.	
June 20	Found guilty of draft evasion in Houston; fined $10,000 and sentenced to 5 years; remains free pending appeals, but is barred from the ring.	

1968-69 (Inactive)

1970

Date	Opponent (location)	Result
Feb. 3	Announces retirement.	
Oct. 26	Jerry Quarry, Atlanta	TKO 3
Dec. 7	Oscar Bonavena, New York	TKO 15

1971

Date	Opponent (location)	Result
Mar. 8	Joe Frazier, New York	Lu 15

(for World Heavyweight title)

Date	Opponent (location)	Result
June 28	U.S. Supreme Court reverses Ali's 1967 conviction saying he had been drafted improperly.	
July 26	Jimmy Ellis, Houston	TKO 12

(won vacant NABF Heavyweight title)

Date	Opponent (location)	Result
Nov. 17	Buster Mathis, Houston	Wu 12
Dec. 26	Jurgen Blin, Zurich	KO 7

1972

Date	Opponent (location)	Result
Apr. 1	Mac Foster, Tokyo	Wu 15
May 1	George Chuvalo, Vancouver	Wu 12
June 27	Jerry Quarry, Las Vegas	TKO 7
July 19	Al (Blue) Lewis, Dublin, Ire	TKO 11
Sept.20	Floyd Patterson, New York	TKO 7
Nov. 21	Bob Foster, Stateline, Nev	TKO 8

1973

Date	Opponent (location)	Result
Feb. 14	Joe Bugner, Las Vegas	Wu 12
Mar. 31	Ken Norton, San Diego	Ls 12

(lost NABF Heavyweight title)

Date	Opponent (location)	Result
Sept.10	Ken Norton, Inglewood, Calif	Ws 12

(regained NABF Heavyweight title)

Date	Opponent (location)	Result
Oct. 20	Rudi Lubbers, Jakarta, Indonesia	Wu 12

1974

Date	Opponent (location)	Result
Jan. 28	Joe Frazier, New York	Wu 12
Oct. 30	George Foreman, Kinshasa, Zaire	KO 8

(regained World Heavyweight title)

1975

Date	Opponent (location)	Result
Mar. 24	Chuck Wepner, Cleveland	TKO 15
May 16	Ron Lyle, Las Vegas	TKO 11
June 30	Joe Bugner, Kuala Lumpur, Malaysia	Wu 15
Oct. 1	Joe Frazier, Manila, Philippines	TKO 14

1976

Date	Opponent (location)	Result
Feb. 20	Jean Pierre Coopman, San Juan	KO 5
Apr. 30	Jimmy Young, Landover, Md	Wu 15
May 24	Richard Dunn, Munich	TKO 5
Sept.28	Ken Norton, New York	Wu 15

1977

Date	Opponent (location)	Result
May 16	Alfredo Evangelista, Landover	Wu 15
Sept.29	Earnie Shavers, New York	Wu 15

1978

Date	Opponent (location)	Result
Feb. 15	Leon Spinks, Las Vegas	Ls 15

(lost World Heavyweight title)

Date	Opponent (location)	Result
Sept.15	Leon Spinks, New Orleans	Wu 15

(regained World Heavyweight title)

1979

Date		
June 27	Announces retirement.	

1980

Date	Opponent (location)	Result
Oct. 2	Larry Holmes, Las Vegas	TKO by 11

1981

Date	Opponent (location)	Result
Dec. 11	Trevor Berbick, Nassau	Lu 10

(retires after fight)

MISCELLANEOUS SPORTS

2006 / 2007 YEAR IN REVIEW

Joey Chestnut set a world record at the Nathan's Famous Hot Dog Eating Contest on July 4, 2007.

BOWLING

Major Championships
MEN
U.S. Open

Started in 1941 by the Bowling Proprietors' Association of America, 18 years before the founding of the Professional Bowlers Association. Originally the BPAA All-Star Tournament, it became the U.S. Open in 1971.

Multiple winners: Don Carter, Dick Weber and Pete Weber (4); Dave Husted (3); Del Ballard Jr., Marshall Holman, Junie McMahon, Connie Schwoegler, Andy Varipapa and Walter Ray Williams Jr. (2).

Year		Year		Year		Year	
1942	John Crimmins	1959	Billy Welu	1976	Paul Moser	1993	Del Ballard Jr.
1943	Connie Schwoegler	1960	Harry Smith	1977	Johnny Petraglia	1994	Justin Hromek
1944	Ned Day	1961	Bill Tucker	1978	Nelson Burton Jr.	1995	Dave Husted
1945	Buddy Bomar	1962	Dick Weber	1979	Joe Berardi	1996	Dave Husted
1946	Joe Wilman	1963	Dick Weber	1980	Steve Martin	1997	Not held
1947	Andy Varipapa	1964	Bob Strampe	1981	Marshall Holman	1998	Walter Ray Williams Jr.
1948	Andy Varipapa	1965	Dick Weber	1982	Dave Husted	1999	Bob Learn Jr.
1949	Connie Schwoegler	1966	Dick Weber	1983	Gary Dickinson	2000	Robert Smith
1950	Junie McMahon	1967	Les Schissler	1984	Mark Roth	2001	Miko Koivuniemi
1951	Dick Hoover	1968	Jim Stefanich	1985	Marshall Holman	2003	Walter Ray Williams Jr.
1952	Junie McMahon	1969	Billy Hardwick	1986	Steve Cook	2004	Pete Weber
1953	Don Carter	1970	Bobby Cooper	1987	Del Ballard Jr.	2005	Chris Barnes
1954	Don Carter	1971	Mike Limongello	1988	Pete Weber	2006	Tommy Jones
1955	Steve Nagy	1972	Don Johnson	1989	Mike Aulby	2007	Pete Weber
1956	Bill Lillard	1973	Mike McGrath	1990	Ron Palombi Jr.		
1957	Don Carter	1974	Larry Laub	1991	Pete Weber		
1958	Don Carter	1975	Steve Neff	1992	Robert Lawrence		

PBA World Championship

The Professional Bowlers Association was formed in 1958 and its first national championship tournament was held in Memphis in 1960. Formerly known as the PBA National Championship, the name was changed in 2002. The tournament was held in various locations (1960-80), Toledo, Ohio (1981-2002), Taylor, Mich. (2003-06) and Wyoming, Mich. (2007).

Multiple winners: Earl Anthony (6); Walter Ray Williams Jr. (3); Mike Aulby, Dave Davis, Mike McGrath, Pete Weber and Wayne Zahn (2).

Year		Year		Year		Year	
1960	Don Carter	1972	Johnny Guenther	1984	Bob Chamberlain	1996	Butch Soper
1961	Dave Soutar	1973	Earl Anthony	1985	Mike Aulby	1997	Rick Steelsmith
1962	Carmen Salvino	1974	Earl Anthony	1986	Tom Crites	1998	Pete Weber
1963	Billy Hardwick	1975	Earl Anthony	1987	Randy Pedersen	1999	Tim Criss
1964	Bob Strampe	1976	Paul Colwell	1988	Brian Voss	2000	Norm Duke
1965	Dave Davis	1977	Tommy Hudson	1989	Pete Weber	2001	Walter Ray Williams Jr.
1966	Wayne Zahn	1978	Warren Nelson	1990	Jim Pencak	2002	Doug Kent
1967	Dave Davis	1979	Mike Aulby	1991	Mike Miller	2003	Walter Ray Williams Jr.
1968	Wayne Zahn	1980	Johnny Petraglia	1992	Eric Forkel	2004	Tom Baker
1969	Mike McGrath	1981	Earl Anthony	1993	Ron Palombi Jr.	2005	Patrick Allen
1970	Mike McGrath	1982	Earl Anthony	1994	David Traber	2006	Walter Ray Williams Jr.
1971	Mike Limongello	1983	Earl Anthony	1995	Scott Alexander	2007	Doug Kent

Tournament of Champions

Originally the Firestone Tournament of Champions (1965-93), the tournament has also been sponsored by General Tire (1994), Brunswick Corp. (1995-2000) and Dexter (2002-). Held in Akron, Ohio in 1965, then Fairlawn, Ohio (1966-94), Lake Zurich, Ill. (1995-96, 2000), Reno, N.V. (1997), Overland Park, Kan. (1998-99) and Uncasville, Conn. (2002-).

Multiple winners: Jason Couch and Mike Durbin (3); Earl Anthony, Dave Davis, Jim Godman, Marshall Holman and Mark Williams (2).

Year		Year		Year		Year	
1965	Billy Hardwick	1976	Marshall Holman	1987	Pete Weber	1998	Bryan Goebel
1966	Wayne Zahn	1977	Mike Berlin	1988	Mark Williams	1999	Jason Couch
1967	Jim Stefanich	1978	Earl Anthony	1989	Del Ballard Jr.	2000	Jason Couch
1968	Dave Davis	1979	George Pappas	1990	Dave Ferraro	2001	Not held
1969	Jim Godman	1980	Wayne Webb	1991	David Ozio	2002	Jason Couch
1970	Don Johnson	1981	Steve Cook	1992	Marc McDowell	2003	Patrick Healey Jr.
1971	Johnny Petraglia	1982	Mike Durbin	1993	George Branham III	2005	Steve Jaros
1972	Mike Durbin	1983	Joe Berardi	1994	Norm Duke	2006	Chris Barnes
1973	Jim Godman	1984	Mike Durbin	1995	Mike Aulby	2007	Tommy Jones
1974	Earl Anthony	1985	Mark Williams	1996	Dave D'Entremont		
1975	Dave Davis	1986	Marshall Holman	1997	John Gant		

USBC Masters Tournament

Sponsored by the United States Bowling Congress, the Masters became an official PBA Tour title event in 1998. It is open to qualified pros and amateurs. The tournament was formerly known as the American Bowling Congress Masters.

Multiple winners: Mike Aulby (3); Earl Anthony, Billy Golembiewski, Dick Hoover and Billy Welu (2).

Year		Year		Year		Year	
1951	Lee Jouglard	1966	Bob Strampe	1981	Randy Lightfoot	1996	Ernie Schlegel
1952	Willard Taylor	1967	Lou Scalia	1982	Joe Berardi	1997	Jason Queen
1953	Rudy Habetler	1968	Pete Tountas	1983	Mike Lastowski	1998	Mike Aulby
1954	Red Elkins	1969	Jim Chestney	1984	Earl Anthony	1999	Brian Boghosian
1955	Buzz Fazio	1970	Don Glover	1985	Steve Wunderlich	2000	Mika Koivuniemi
1956	Dick Hoover	1971	Jim Godman	1986	Mark Fahy	2001	Parker Bohn III
1957	Dick Hoover	1972	Bill Beach	1987	Rick Steelsmith	2002	Brett Wolfe
1958	Tom Hennessey	1973	Dave Soutar	1988	Del Ballard Jr.	2003	Bryon Smith
1959	Ray Bluth	1974	Paul Colwell	1989	Mike Aulby	2004*	Walter Ray Williams Jr.
1960	Billy Golembiewski	1975	Eddie Ressler Jr.	1990	Chris Warren	2004*	Danny Wiseman
1961	Don Carter	1976	Nelson Burton Jr.	1991	Doug Kent	2005	Mike Scroggins
1962	Billy Golembiewski	1977	Earl Anthony	1992	Ken Johnson	2006	Doug Kent
1963	Harry Smith	1978	Frank Ellenburg	1993	Norm Duke		
1964	Billy Welu	1979	Doug Myers	1994	Steve Fehr	*held Jan. and Oct., 2004	
1965	Billy Welu	1980	Neil Burton	1995	Mike Aulby		

WOMEN
U.S. Open

Started by the Bowling Proprietors' Association of America in 1949. Originally the BPAA Women's All-Star Tournament (1949-70); and U.S. Open from 1971-2003. There were two BPAA All-Star tournaments in 1955, in January and December.

Multiple winners: Marion Ladewig (8); Donna Adamek, Paula Sperber Carter, Pat Costello, Dotty Fothergill, Liz Johnson, Dana Miller-Mackie, Aleta Sill and Sylvia Wene (2).

Year		Year		Year		Year	
1949	Marion Ladewig	1963	Marion Ladewig	1977	Betty Morris	1991	Anne Marie Duggan
1950	Marion Ladewig	1964	LaVerne Carter	1978	Donna Adamek	1992	Tish Johnson
1951	Marion Ladewig	1965	Ann Slattery	1979	Diana Silva	1993	Dede Davidson
1952	Marion Ladewig	1966	Joy Abel	1980	Patty Costello	1994	Aleta Sill
1953	Not held	1967	Gloria Simon	1981	Donna Adamek	1995	Cheryl Daniels
1954	Marion Ladewig	1968	Dotty Fothergill	1982	Shinobu Saitoh	1996	Liz Johnson
1955	Sylvia Wene	1969	Dotty Fothergill	1983	Dana Miller	1997	Not held
1955	Anita Cantaline	1970	Mary Baker	1984	Karen Ellingsworth	1998	Aleta Sill
1956	Marion Ladewig	1971	Paula Sperber	1985	Pat Mercatanti	1999	Kim Adler
1957	Not held	1972	Lorrie Koch	1986	Wendy Macpherson	2000	Tennelle Grijalva
1958	Merle Matthews	1973	Millie Martorella	1987	Carol Norman	2001	Kim Terrell
1959	Marion Ladewig	1974	Patty Costello	1988	Lisa Wagner	2002	Not held
1960	Sylvia Wene	1975	Paula Sperber Carter	1989	Robin Romeo	2003	Kelly Kulick
1961	Phyllis Notaro	1976	Patty Costello	1990	Dana Miller-Mackie	2004-06	Not held
1962	Shirley Garms					2007	Liz Johnson

WIBC Queens

Sponsored by the Women's International Bowling Congress, the Queens is open to qualified pros and amateurs. **Note**: Beginning in 2006, the tournament will be known as the USBC Queens, sponsored by the United States Bowling Congress.

Multiple winners: Wendy Macpherson and Millie Martorella (3); Donna Adamek, Dotty Fothergill, Aleta Sill and Katsuko Sugimoto (2).

Year		Year		Year		Year	
1961	Janet Harman	1973	Dotty Fothergill	1985	Aleta Sill	1997	Sandra Jo Odom
1962	Dorothy Wilkinson	1974	Judy Soutar	1986	Cora Fiebig	1998	Lynda Norry
1963	Irene Monterosso	1975	Cindy Powell	1987	Cathy Almeida	1999	Leanne Barrette
1964	D.D. Jacobson	1976	Pam Rutherford	1988	Wendy Macpherson	2000	Wendy Macpherson
1965	Betty Kuczynski	1977	Dana Stewart	1989	Carol Gianotti	2001	Carolyn Dorin-Ballard
1966	Judy Lee	1978	Loa Boxberger	1990	Patty Ann	2002	Kim Terrell
1967	Millie Martorella	1979	Donna Adamek	1991	Dede Davidson	2003	Wendy Macpherson
1968	Phyllis Massey	1980	Donna Adamek	1992	Cindy Coburn-Carroll	2004	Marianne DiRupo
1969	Ann Feigel	1981	Katsuko Sugimoto	1993	Jan Schmidt	2005	Tennelle Milligan
1970	Millie Martorella	1982	Katsuko Sugimoto	1994	Anne Marie Duggan	2006	Shannon Pluhowsky
1971	Millie Martorella	1983	Aleta Sill	1995	Sandra Postma	2007	Kelly Kulick
1972	Dotty Fothergill	1984	Kazue Inahashi	1996	Lisa Wagner		

Annual Leaders
Average
PBA Tour

The George Young Memorial Award, named after the late ABC Hall of Fame bowler. Based on at least 16 national PBA tournaments from 1959-78, and at least 400 games of tour competition since 1979.

Multiple winners: Mark Roth and Walter Ray Williams Jr. (6); Earl Anthony (5); Norm Duke and Marshall Holman (3); Parker Bohn III, Billy Hardwick, Don Johnson and Wayne Zahn (2).

Year	Avg	Year	Avg	Year	Avg
1962 Don Carter	212.84	1977 Mark Roth	218.17	1992 Dave Ferraro	219.70
1963 Billy Hardwick	210.35	1978 Mark Roth	219.83	1993 Walter Ray Williams Jr.	222.98
1964 Ray Bluth	210.51	1979 Mark Roth	221.66	1994 Norm Duke	222.83
1965 Dick Weber	211.90	1980 Earl Anthony	218.54	1995 Mike Aulby	225.49
1966 Wayne Zahn	208.63	1981 Mark Roth	216.70	1996 Walter Ray Williams Jr.	225.37
1967 Wayne Zahn	212.14	1982 Marshall Holman	216.15	1997 Walter Ray Williams Jr.	222.00
1968 Jim Stefanich	211.90	1983 Earl Anthony	216.65	1998 Walter Ray Williams Jr.	226.13
1969 Billy Hardwick	212.96	1984 Marshall Holman	213.91	1999 Parker Bohn III	228.04
1970 Nelson Burton Jr.	214.91	1985 Mark Baker	213.72	2000 Chris Barnes	220.93
1971 Don Johnson	213.98	1986 John Gant	214.38	2002 Parker Bohn III	221.54
1972 Don Johnson	215.29	1987 Marshall Holman	216.80	2003 Walter Ray Williams Jr.	224.94
1973 Earl Anthony	215.80	1988 Mark Roth	218.04	2004 Mika Koivuniemi	222.73
1974 Earl Anthony	219.34	1989 Pete Weber	215.43	2005 Walter Ray Williams Jr.	227.07
1975 Earl Anthony	219.06	1990 Amleto Monacelli	218.16	2006 Norm Duke	228.47
1976 Mark Roth	215.97	1991 Norm Duke	218.21		

Note: After its first nine events of 2001, the PBA instituted a new September-to-March schedule with the statistics for those first nine tournaments rolled over into players' final 2001-02 statistics.

PWBA Tour

The Professional Women's Bowling Association (PWBA) went by the name Ladies Professional Bowling Tour (LPBT) from 1981-97 and the Women's Professional Bowling Association prior to that. This table is based on at least 282 games of tour competition, with the expection of 2003 when the minimum was 122 games. In 2003 the fall season was unexpectedly cancelled, shortening the year to eight tournaments. There was no PWBA Tour in 2004, 2005 or 2006.

Multiple winners: Leanne Barrette (4); Nikki Gianulias, Wendy Macpherson and Lisa Rathgeber Wagner (3); Carolyn Dorin-Ballard, Anne Marie Duggan and Aleta Sill (2).

Year	Avg	Year	Avg	Year	Avg
1981 Nikki Gianulias	213.71	1989 Lisa Wagner	211.87	1997 Wendy Macpherson	214.68
1982 Nikki Gianulias	210.63	1990 Leanne Barrette	211.53	1998 Dede Davidson	217.25
1983 Lisa Rathgeber	208.50	1991 Leanne Barrette	211.48	1999 Wendy Macpherson	218.85
1984 Aleta Sill	210.68	1992 Leanne Barrette	211.36	2000 Cara Honeychurch	215.18
1985 Aleta Sill	211.10	1993 Tish Johnson	215.39	2001 Carolyn Dorin-Ballard	214.73
1986 Nikki Gianulias	213.89	1994 Anne Marie Duggan	213.47	2002 Leanne Barrette	216.45
1987 Wendy Macpherson	211.11	1995 Anne Marie Duggan	215.79	2003 Carolyn Dorin-Ballard	215.22
1988 Lisa Wagner	213.02	1996 Tammy Turner	215.23		

Money Won
PBA Tour

Multiple winners: Earl Anthony and Walter Ray Williams Jr. (6); Mark Roth and Dick Weber (4); Mike Aulby (3); Parker Bohn III, Don Carter and Norm Duke (2).

Year	Earnings	Year	Earnings	Year	Earnings
1959 Dick Weber	$7,672	1975 Earl Anthony	$107,585	1991 David Ozio	$225,585
1960 Don Carter	22,525	1976 Earl Anthony	110,833	1992 Marc McDowell	176,215
1961 Dick Weber	26,280	1977 Mark Roth	105,583	1993 Walter Ray Williams Jr.	296,370
1962 Don Carter	49,972	1978 Mark Roth	134,500	1994 Norm Duke	273,752
1963 Dick Weber	46,333	1979 Mark Roth	124,517	1995 Mike Aulby	219,792
1964 Bob Strampe	33,592	1980 Wayne Webb	116,700	1996 Walter Ray Williams Jr.	244,630
1965 Dick Weber	47,675	1981 Earl Anthony	164,735	1997 Walter Ray Williams Jr.	240,544
1966 Wayne Zahn	54,720	1982 Earl Anthony	134,760	1998 Walter Ray Williams Jr.	238,225
1967 Dave Davis	54,165	1983 Earl Anthony	135,605	1999 Parker Bohn III	232,595
1968 Jim Stefanich	67,375	1984 Mark Roth	158,712	2000 Norm Duke	136,900
1969 Billy Hardwick	64,160	1985 Mike Aulby	201,200	2002 Parker Bohn III	245,200
1970 Mike McGrath	52,049	1986 Walter Ray Williams Jr.	145,550	2003 Walter Ray Williams Jr.	419,700
1971 Johnny Petraglia	85,065	1987 Pete Weber	179,516	2004 Mika Koivuniemi	238,590
1972 Don Johnson	56,648	1988 Brian Voss	225,485	2005 Patrick Allen	350,740
1973 Don McCune	69,000	1989 Mike Aulby	298,237	2006 Doug Kent	200,530
1974 Earl Anthony	99,585	1990 Amleto Monacelli	204,775		

Note: After its first nine events of 2001, the PBA instituted a new September-to-March schedule with the statistics for those first nine tournaments rolled over into players' final 2001-02 statistics.

All-Time Leaders

All-time leading tournament winners on the PBA Tour, through Sept. 24, 2007. PBA figures date back to 1959.

PBA Top 20 Tournaments Won

		Titles
1	Walter Ray Williams Jr.	42
2	Earl Anthony	41
3	Mark Roth	34
	Pete Weber	34
5	Parker Bohn III	30
6	Mike Aulby	27
7	Don Johnson	26
	Dick Weber	26
	Norm Duke	26
10	Brian Voss	24

		Titles
11	Marshall Holman	22
12	Dick Ritger	20
	Wayne Webb	20
14	Amleto Monacelli	19
15	Dave Davis	18
16	Nelson Burton Jr.	17
	Billy Hardwick	17
	Carmen Salvino	17
	Dave Soutar	17
20	Steve Cook	15
	Jason Couch	15

Annual Awards

MEN

BWAA Bowler of the Year

Winners selected by Bowling Writers Association of America.

Multiple winners: Walter Ray Williams Jr. (8); Earl Anthony and Don Carter (6); Mark Roth (4); Mike Aulby and Dick Weber (3); Parker Bohn III, Buddy Bomar, Ned Day, Norm Duke, Billy Hardwick, Don Johnson and Steve Nagy (2).

Year		Year		Year		Year	
1942	John Crimmins	1958	Don Carter	1974	Earl Anthony	1990	Amleto Monacelli
1943	Ned Day	1959	Ed Lubanski	1975	Earl Anthony	1991	David Ozio
1944	Ned Day	1960	Don Carter	1976	Earl Anthony	1992	Marc McDowell
1945	Buddy Bomar	1961	Dick Weber	1977	Mark Roth	1993	Walter Ray Williams Jr.
1946	Joe Wilman	1962	Don Carter	1978	Mark Roth	1994	Norm Duke
1947	Buddy Bomar	1963	Dick Weber	1979	Mark Roth	1995	Mike Aulby
1948	Andy Varipapa	1964	Billy Hardwick	1980	Wayne Webb	1996	Walter Ray Williams Jr.
1949	Connie Schwoegler	1965	Dick Weber	1981	Earl Anthony	1997	Walter Ray Williams Jr.
1950	Junie McMahon	1966	Wayne Zahn	1982	Earl Anthony	1998	Walter Ray Williams Jr.
1951	Lee Jouglard	1967	Dave Davis	1983	Earl Anthony	1999	Parker Bohn III
1952	Steve Nagy	1968	Jim Stefanich	1984	Mark Roth	2000	Norm Duke
1953	Don Carter	1969	Billy Hardwick	1985	Mike Aulby	2001	Parker Bohn III
1954	Don Carter	1970	Nelson Burton Jr.	1986	Walter Ray Williams Jr.	2002	Walter Ray Williams Jr.
1955	Steve Nagy	1971	Don Johnson	1987	Marshall Holman	2003	Walter Ray Williams Jr.
1956	Bill Lillard	1972	Don Johnson	1988	Brian Voss	2004	Walter Ray Williams Jr.
1957	Don Carter	1973	Don McCune	1989	Mike Aulby	2005	Patrick Allen
						2006	Tommy Jones

PBA Player of the Year

Named after longtime broadcaster Chris Schenkel, winners are selected by members of Professional Bowlers Association. The PBA Player of the Year has differed from the BWAA Bowler of the Year four times—in 1963, '64, '89 and '92.

Multiple winners: Earl Anthony and Walter Ray Williams Jr. (6); Mark Roth (4); Mike Aulby, Parker Bohn III, Norm Duke, Billy Hardwick, Don Johnson and Amleto Monacelli (2).

Year		Year		Year		Year	
1963	Billy Hardwick	1974	Earl Anthony	1985	Mike Aulby	1996	Walter Ray Williams Jr.
1964	Bob Strampe	1975	Earl Anthony	1986	Walter Ray Williams Jr.	1997	Walter Ray Williams Jr.
1965	Dick Weber	1976	Earl Anthony	1987	Marshall Holman	1998	Walter Ray Williams Jr.
1966	Wayne Zahn	1977	Mark Roth	1988	Brian Voss	1999	Parker Bohn III
1967	Dave Davis	1978	Mark Roth	1989	Amleto Monacelli	2000	Norm Duke
1968	Jim Stefanich	1979	Mark Roth	1990	Amleto Monacelli	2002	Parker Bohn III
1969	Billy Hardwick	1980	Wayne Webb	1991	David Ozio	2003	Walter Ray Williams Jr.
1970	Nelson Burton Jr.	1981	Earl Anthony	1992	Dave Ferraro	2004	Mika Koivuniemi
1971	Don Johnson	1982	Earl Anthony	1993	Walter Ray Williams Jr.	2005	Patrick Allen
1972	Don Johnson	1983	Earl Anthony	1994	Norm Duke	2006	Tommy Jones
1973	Don McCune	1984	Mark Roth	1995	Mike Aulby	2007	Doug Kent

Note: After its first nine events of 2001, the PBA instituted a new September-to-March schedule with the statistics for those first nine tournaments rolled over into players' final 2001-02 statistics. Individual awards were handed out in 2002.

CHESS

World Champions

Garry Kasparov became the youngest man to win the world chess championship when he beat fellow Russian Anatoly Karpov in 1985 at age 22. In 1993, Kasparov and then-#1 challenger Nigel Short of England broke away from the established International Chess Federation (FIDE) to form the Professional Chess Association (the PCA was disbanded in 1998). FIDE retaliated by stripping Kasparov of the world title and arranging a playoff that was won by Karpov, the former title-holder. Karpov successfully defended the FIDE title several times before failing to show up for the 1999 FIDE World Championship Tournament that was won by Alexander Khalifman. Indian Viswanathan Anand won the 2000 FIDE World Championship.

In his first title defense in five years, Kasparov faced world #2 Vladimir Kramnik for 16 matches in the unofficial (though more widely recognized) world championship from Oct. 8-Nov. 4, 2000 in London. The 25-year-old Kramnik defeated the longtime world champion 8½-6½ in a stunning result. Kasparov failed to win a single game, but despite the loss was still the top-ranked player in the world. Ruslan Ponomariov of Ukraine won the 2002 FIDE title and a plan, known as the Prague Agreement, to unify the world chess championship was hatched. FIDE hosted a knockout tournament in 2003 which was won by the 18-year-old Ponomariov. Ponomariov was supposed to then play world No. 1 Kasparov. But Ponomariov could not agree to the terms set for his match with Kasparov and was stripped of his title.

Uzbekistan's Rustam Kasimdzhanov won the FIDE title in 2004 (however many of the world's top players didn't compete) and was scheduled to play Kasparov in 2005. The winner of that match was supposed to play the winner of the Kramnik-Peter Leko match (Kramnik retained his title in a 7-7 draw) but Kasparov withdrew from the Kasimdzhanov match in a financial dispute, effectively ending the Prague Agreement. In 2005, the FIDE championship was won by 30-year-old Bulgarian Veselin Topalov. The tournament included eight of the world's top players; each played two games against the others in a round-robin format. However, Kramnik, the linear world champion, did not compete.

Meanwhile, Kasparov stunned many when he announced his retirement from professional chess in March 2005 after winning the prestigious Linares tournament in Spain, claiming there are no real challenges on the horizon.

The 2006 FIDE Championship, designed to crown a unified champion, took place in Russia from Sept. 23-Oct. 13. Linear champ Vladimir Kramnik defeated the world's top-rated player, Veselin Topalov, 2½-1½ in a series of rapid tie-break games following a disputed 6-6 tie in the 12 games series. In a strange twist, the bathroom arrangements had an impact on the match when Topalov complained about Kramnik's frequent in-match bathroom breaks, seeming to imply Kramnik may be getting help from outside sources. Outraged at the accusations, Kramnik balked at playing game 5 and FIDE ruled it a forfeit. Despite that Kramnik prevailed in the tie-break. **Viswanathan Anand** of India won the 2007 FIDE World Championships in Mexico City and is considered the reigning world champion. A 2008 rematch between Anand and former champ Kramnik is planned.

Years		Years		Years	
1866-94	Wilhelm Steinitz, Austria	1957-58	Vassily Smyslov, USSR	1975-85	Anatoly Karpov, USSR
1894-1921	Emanuel Lasker, Germany	1958-59	Mikhail Botvinnik, USSR	1985-2000	Garry Kasparov, RUS
1921-27	Jose Capablanca, Cuba	1960-61	Mikhail Tal, USSR	2000-07	Vladimir Kramnik, RUS
1927-35	Alexander Alekhine, France	1961-63	Mikhail Botvinnik, USSR	2002-03	Ruslan Ponomariov, UKR
1935-37	Max Euwe, Holland	1963-69	Tigran Petrosian, USSR	2004-05	Rustam Kasimdzhanov, UZB
1937-46	Alexander Alekhine, France	1969-72	Boris Spassky, USSR	2005-06	Veselin Topalov, BUL
1948-57	Mikhail Botvinnik, USSR	1972-75	Bobby Fischer, USA*	2007—	Viswanathan Anand, IND

*Fischer defaulted the championship in 1975.

DOGS

Iditarod Trail Sled Dog Race

Lance Mackey, the 36-year-old son of 1978 Iditarod champion Dick Mackey, won the 2007 Iditarod, beating Paul Gebhardt to the finish by 2 hours, 19 minutes. Mackey made history as the first musher to win both the 1,000-mile Yukon Quest International Sled Dog Race and the Iditarod back-to-back, doing so with many of the same dogs. The Fairbanks resident and cancer survivor won the $69,000 prize for first place and a 2007 Dodge Ram Laramie truck valued at $40,980.

In even-numbered years the trail follows the 1,151-mile Northern Route, while in odd-numbered years, it takes a slightly different 1,161-mile Southern Route. The Iditarod, the longest sled dog race in the world, commemorates a 674-mile relay race from Nenana to Nome in 1925 when mushers and dog teams successfully delivered serum to stave off an outbreak of diphtheria among children.

Multiple winners: Rick Swenson (5); Martin Buser, Susan Butcher, Jeff King and Doug Swingley (4); Robert Sorlie (2).

Year		Elapsed Time	Year		Elapsed Time
1973	Dick Wilmarth	20 days, 00:49:41	1991	Rick Swenson	12 days, 16:34:39
1974	Carl Huntington	20 days, 15:02:07	1992	Martin Buser	10 days, 19:17:00
1975	Emmitt Peters	14 days, 14:43:45	1993	Jeff King	10 days, 15:38:15
1976	Gerald Riley	18 days, 22:58:17	1994	Martin Buser	10 days, 13:02:39
1977	Rick Swenson	16 days, 16:27:13	1995	Doug Swingley	9 days, 02:42:19
1978	Dick Mackey	14 days, 18:52:24	1996	Jeff King	9 days, 05:43:13
1979	Rick Swenson	15 days, 10:37:47	1997	Martin Buser	9 days, 08:31:45
1980	Joe May	14 days, 07:11:51	1998	Jeff King	9 days, 05:52:26
1981	Rick Swenson	12 days, 08:45:02	1999	Doug Swingley	9 days, 14:31:07
1982	Rick Swenson	16 days, 04:40:10	2000	Doug Swingley	9 days, 00:58:06
1983	Rick Mackey	12 days, 14:10:44	2001	Doug Swingley	9 days, 19:55:50
1984	Dean Osmar	12 days, 15:07:33	2002	Martin Buser	8 days, 22:46:02*
1985	Libby Riddles	18 days, 00:20:17	2003	Robert Sorlie	9 days, 15:47:36
1986	Susan Butcher	11 days, 15:06:00	2004	Mitch Seavey	9 days, 12:20:22
1987	Susan Butcher	11 days, 02:05:13	2005	Robert Sorlie	9 days, 18:39:31
1988	Susan Butcher	11 days, 11:41:40	2006	Jeff King	9 days, 11:11:36
1989	Joe Runyan	11 days, 05:24:34	2007	Lance Mackey	9 days, 05:08:41
1990	Susan Butcher	11 days, 01:53:23	*Race record.		

Westminster Kennel Club

Best in Show

The Best in Show prize at the 131st annual All-Breed Dog Show of the Westminster Kennel Club, held Feb. 12-13, 2007 at Madison Square Garden, went to Ch. Felicity's Diamond Jim, an English Springer Spaniel. The 6-year-old certified therapy dog who answers to the name James, was selected from more than 2,628 dogs in 165 breeds and varieties. Diamond Jim beat out a Dandie Dinmont terrier co-owned by Bill Cosby, among others, to win the 100th Best in Show award. It was his 51st best in show victory and likely his last, his owners planned to retire him from the show world to work as a therapy dog. The Westminster show is the most prestigious dog show in the country, and one of America's oldest annual sporting events.

Multiple winners: Ch. Warren Remedy (3); Ch. Chinoe's Adamant James, Ch. Comejo Wycollar Boy, Ch. Flornell Spicy Piece of Halleston; Ch. Matford Vic, Ch. My Own Brucie, Ch. Pendley Calling of Blarney, Ch. Rancho Dobe's Storm (2).

Year		Breed	Year		Breed
1907	Warren Remedy	Fox Terrier	1960	Chick T'Sun of Caversham	Pekingese
1908	Warren Remedy	Fox Terrier	1961	Cappoquin Little Sister	Toy Poodle
1909	Warren Remedy	Fox Terrier	1962	Elfinbrook Simon	W. Highland Terrier
1910	Sabine Rarebit	Fox Terrier	1963	Wakefield's Black Knight	English Springer Spaniel
1911	Tickle Em Jock	Scottish Terrier	1964	Courtenay Fleetfoot of Pennyworth	Whippet
1912	Kenmore Sorceress	Airedale	1965	Carmichaels Fanfare	Scottish Terrier
1913	Strathway Prince Albert	Bulldog	1966	Zeloy Mooremaides Magic	Fox Terrier
1914	Brentwood Hero	Old English Sheepdog	1967	Bardene Bingo	Scottish Terrier
1915	Matford Vic	Old English Sheepdog	1968	Stingray of Derryabah	Lakeland Terrier
1916	Matford Vic	Old English Sheepdog	1969	Glamoor Good News	Skye Terrier
1917	Comejo Wycollar Boy	Fox Terrier	1970	Arriba's Prima Donna	Boxer
1918	Haymarket Faultless	Bull Terrier	1971	Chinoe's Adamant James	E.S. Spaniel
1919	Briergate Bright Beauty	Airedale	1972	Chinoe's Adamant James	E.S. Spaniel
1920	Comejo Wycollar Boy	Fox Terrier	1973	Acadia Command Performance	Standard Poodle
1921	Midkiff Seductive	Cocker Spaniel	1974	Gretchenhof Columbia River	German SH Pointer
1922	Boxwood Barkentine	Airedale	1975	Sir Lancelot of Barvan	Old Eng. Sheepdog
1923	No best-in-show award		1976	Jo Ni's Red Baron of Crofton	Lakeland Terrier
1924	Barberryhill Bootlegger	Sealyham	1977	Dersade Bobby's Girl	Sealyham
1925	Governor Moscow	Pointer	1978	Cede Higgens	Yorkshire Terrier
1926	Signal Circuit	Fox Terrier	1979	Oak Tree's Irishtocrat	Irish Water Spaniel
1927	Pinegrade Perfection	Sealyham	1980	Sierra Cinnar	Siberian Husky
1928	Talavera Margaret	Fox Terrier	1981	Dhandy Favorite Woodchuck	Pug
1929	Land Loyalty of Bellhaven	Collie	1982	St. Aubrey Dragonora of Elsdon	Pekingese
1930	Pendley Calling of Blarney	Fox Terrier	1983	Kabik's The Challenger	Afghan Hound
1931	Pendley Calling of Blarney	Fox Terrier	1984	Seaward's Blackbeard	Newfoundland
1932	Nancolleth Markable	Pointer	1985	Braeburn's Close Encounter	Scottish Terrier
1933	Warland Protector of Shelterock	Airedale	1986	Marjetta National Acclaim	Pointer
1934	Flornell Spicy Bit of Halleston	Fox Terrier	1987	Covy Tucker Hill's Manhattan	German Shepherd
1935	Nunsoe Duc de la Terrace of Blakeen	Stan. Poodle	1988	Great Elms Prince Charming II	Pomeranian
1936	St. Margaret Magnificent of Clairedale	Sealyham	1989	Royal Tudor's Wild As The Wind	Doberman
1937	Flornell Spicy Bit of Halleston	Fox Terrier	1990	Wendessa Crown Prince	Pekingese
1938	Daro of Maridor	English Setter	1991	Whisperwind on a Carousel	Stan. Poodle
1939	Ferry v.Rauhfelsen of Giralda	Doberman	1992	Lonesome Dove	Fox Terrier
1940	My Own Brucie	Cocker Spaniel	1993	Salilyn's Condor	E.S. Spaniel
1941	My Own Brucie	Cocker Spaniel	1994	Chidley Willum	Norwich Terrier
1942	Wolvey Pattern of Edgerstoune	W. Highland Terrier	1995	Gaelforce Post Script	Scottish Terrier
1943	Pitter Patter of Piperscroft	Miniature Poodle	1996	Clussex Country Sunrise	Clumber Spaniel
1944	Flornell Rarebit of Twin Ponds	Welsh Terrier	1997	Parsifal di Casa Netzer	Standard Schnauzer
1945	Shieling's Signature	Scottish Terrier	1998	Fairewood Frolic	Norwich Terrier
1946	Hetherington Model Rhythm	Fox Terrier	1999	Loteki's Supernatural Being	Papillon
1947	Warlord of Mazelaine	Boxer	2000	Salilyn 'N Erin's Shameless	E.S. Spaniel
1948	Rock Ridge Night Rocket	Bedling. Terrier	2001	Special Times Just Right	Bichon Frise
1949	Mazelaine's Zazarac Brandy	Boxer	2002	Surrey Spice Girl	Miniature Poodle
1950	Walsing Winning Trick of Edgerstoune	Scot. Terrier	2003	Torums Scarf Michael	Kerry Blue Terrier
1951	Bang Away of Sirrah Crest	Boxer	2004	Darbydale's All Rise Pouchcove	Newfoundland
1952	Rancho Dobe's Storm	Doberman	2005	Kan-Point's VJK Autumn Roses	German SH Pointer
1953	Rancho Dobe's Storm	Doberman	2006	Rocky Top's Sundance Kid ROM	Colored Bull Terrier
1954	Carmor's Rise and Shine	Cocker Spaniel	2007	Felicity's Diamond Jim	English Springer Spaniel
1955	Kippax Fearnought	Bulldog			
1956	Wilber White Swan	Toy Poodle			
1957	Shirkhan of Grandeur	Afghan Hound			
1958	Puttencove Promise	Standard Poodle			
1959	Fontclair Festoon	Miniature Poodle			

FISHING

IGFA All-Tackle World Records

All-tackle records are maintained for the heaviest fish of any species caught on any line up to 130-lb (60 kg) class and certi-fied by the International Game Fish Association. Records logged through Oct. 1, 2007. **Address:** 300 Gulf Stream Way, Dania Beach, Fla. 33004. **Telephone:** (954) 927-2628. **Web:** www.igfa.org

FRESHWATER FISH

Species	Lbs-Oz	Where Caught	Date	Angler
Barramundi	83-7	N. Queensland, Australia	Sept. 23, 1999	David Powell
Bass, Guadalupe	3-11	Lake Travis, TX	Sept. 25, 1983	Allen Christenson Jr.
Bass, largemouth	22-4	Montgomery Lake, GA	June 2, 1932	George W. Perry
Bass, Roanoke	1-5	Nottoway River, VA	Nov. 11, 1991	Tom Elkins
Bass, rock	3-0	York River, Ontario	Aug. 1, 1974	Peter Gulgin
	3-0	Lake Erie, PA	June 18, 1998	Herbert G. Ratner Jr.
Bass, shoal	8-12	Apalachicola River, FL	Jan. 28, 1995	Carl W. Davis
Bass, smallmouth	11-15	Dale Hollow, TN	July 9, 1955	David Hayes
Bass, spotted	10-4	Pine Flat Lake, CA	Apr. 21, 2001	Bryan Shishido
Bass, striped (landlocked)	67-8	O'Neill Forebay, San Luis, CA	May 7, 1992	Hank Ferguson
Bass, Suwannee	3-14	Suwannee River, FL	Mar. 2, 1985	Ronnie Everett
Bass, white	6-13	Lake Orange, VA	July 31, 1989	Ronald L. Sprouse
Bass, whiterock	27-5	Greers Ferry Lake, AR	Apr. 24, 1997	Jerald C. Shaum
Bass, yellow	2-9	Duck River, TN	Feb. 27, 1998	John T. Chappell
Bass, yellow (hybrid)	4-0	Lake Fork, TX	Mar. 26, 2003	C. Runyan
Bluegill	4-12	Ketona Lake, AL	Apr. 9, 1950	T.S. Hudson
Bowfin	21-8	Florence, SC	Jan. 29, 1980	Robert L. Harmon
Buffalo, bigmouth	70-5	Bussey Brake, Bastrop, LA	Apr. 21, 1980	Delbert Sisk
Buffalo, black	63-6	Mississippi River, IA	Aug. 14, 1999	Jim Winters
Buffalo, smallmouth	82-3	Athens Lake, AL	June 6, 1993	Randy Collins
Bullhead, black	7-7	Mill Pond, NY	Aug. 25, 1993	Kevin Kelly
Bullhead, brown	6-5	Lake Mahopac, NY	Sept. 8, 2002	Ray Lawrence
Bullhead, yellow	6-6	Drevel, MO	May 27, 2006	John R. Irvin
Burbot	18-11	Angenmanelren, Sweden	Oct. 22, 1996	Margit Agren
Carp, bighead	90-0	Guntersville Lake, TN	June 2, 2005	Jeffrey J. Rorex
Carp, black	40-12	Chiba, Japan	Apr. 1, 2000	Kenichi Hosoi
Carp, common	75-11	St. Cassien, France	May 21, 1987	Leo van der Gugten
Carp, crucian	8-2	Seeland, Denmark	Sept. 20, 2005	Brian Jensen
Catfish, blue	124-0	Mississippi River, IL	May 21, 2005	Tim Pruitt
Catfish, channel	58-0	Santee-Cooper Res., SC	July 7, 1964	W.B. Whaley
Catfish, flathead	123-0	Elk City Reservoir, KS	Mar. 14, 1998	Ken Paulie
Catfish, flatwhiskered	16-15	Xingu River, Brazil	Aug. 7, 2001	Ian-Arthur de Sulocki
Catfish, gilded	85-8	Amazon River, Brazil	Nov. 15, 1986	Gilberto Fernandes
Catfish, redtail	108-14	Amazon River, Brazil	Oct. 8, 2006	Rolens Sonoda
Catfish, sharptoothed	79-5	Orange River, South Africa	Dec. 5, 1992	Hennie Moller
Catfish, white	19-5	Oakdale, CA	May 7, 2005	Russell D. Price
Char, Arctic	32-9	Tree River, Canada	July 30, 1981	Jeffery Ward
Crappie, black	5-0	Private Lake, MO	Apr. 21, 2006	John R. Horstman
Crappie, white	5-3	Enid Dam, MS	July 31, 1957	Fred L. Bright
Dolly Varden	20-14	Wulik River, AK	July 7, 2001	Raz Reid
Dorado	55-11	Uruguay River, Argentina	Jan. 1, 2006	Andre L. S. de Botton
Drum, freshwater	54-8	Nickajack Lake, TN	Apr. 20, 1972	Benny E. Hull
Gar, alligator	279-0	Rio Grande, TX	Dec. 2, 1951	Bill Valverde
Gar, Florida	10-0	The Everglades, FL	Jan. 28, 2002	Herbert G. Ratner Jr.
Gar, longnose	50-5	Trinity River, TX	July 30, 1954	Townsend Miller
Gar, shortnose	5-12	Rend Lake, IL	July 16, 1995	Donna K. Willmart
Gar, spotted	9-12	Lake Mexia, TX	Apr. 7, 1994	Rick Rivard
Goldfish	9-6	Lindo Lakes, CA	Nov. 29, 2002	Matthew Servant
Grayling, Arctic	5-15	Katseyedie River, N.W.T.	Aug. 16, 1967	Jeanne P. Branson
Inconnu	53-0	Pah River, AK	Aug. 20, 1986	Lawrence E. Hudnall
Kokanee	9-6	Okanagan Lake, Brit. Columbia	June 18, 1988	Norm Kuhn
Muskellunge	67-8	Hayward, WI	July 24, 1949	Cal Johnson
Muskellunge, tiger	51-3	Lac Vieux-Desert, WI-MI	July 16, 1919	John A. Knobla
Peacock, butterfly	12-9	Chiguao River, Venezuela	Jan. 6, 2000	Antonio Campa G.
Peacock, speckled	27-0	Rio Negro, Brazil	Dec. 4, 1994	Gerald (Doc) Lawson
Perch, Nile	230-0	Lake Nasser, Egypt	Dec. 20, 2000	William Toth
Perch, white	3-1	Forest Hill Park, NJ	May 6, 1989	Edward Tango
Perch, yellow	4-3	Bordentown, NJ	May, 1865	Dr. C.C. Abbot
Pickerel, chain	9-6	Homerville, GA	Feb. 17, 1961	Baxley McQuaig Jr.
Pickerel, grass	1-0	Dewart Lake, IN	June 9, 1990	Mike Berg
Pickerel, redfin	2-4	Gall Berry Swamp, NC	June 27, 1997	Edward C. Davis
Pike, northern	55-1	Lake of Grefeern, Germany	Oct. 16, 1986	Lothar Louis
Redhorse, greater	9-3	Salmon River, Pulaski, NY	May 11, 1985	Jason Wilson

Species	Lbs-Oz	Where Caught	Date	Angler
Redhorse, silver	11-7	Plum Creek, WI	May 29, 1985	Neal D.G. Long
Salmon, Atlantic	79-2	Tana River, Norway	1928	Henrik Henriksen
Salmon, chinook	97-4	Kenai River, AK	May 17, 1985	Les Anderson
Salmon, chum	35-0	Edye Pass, Brit. Columbia	July 11, 1995	Todd Johansson
Salmon, coho	33-4	Salmon River, Pulaski, NY	Sept. 27, 1989	Jerry Lifton
Salmon, pink	14-13	Monroe, WA	Sept. 30, 2001	Alexander Minerich
Salmon, sockeye	15-3	Kenai River, AK	Aug. 9, 1987	Stan Roach
Sauger	8-12	Lake Sakakawea, ND	Oct. 6, 1971	Mike Fischer
Shad, American	11-4	Conn. River, S. Hadley, MA	May 19, 1986	Bob Thibodo
Shad, gizzard	4-6	Lake Michigan, IN	Mar. 2, 1996	Mike Berg
Sturgeon, lake	168-0	Georgian Bay, Canada	May 29, 1982	Edward Paszkowski
Sturgeon, white	468-0	Benicia, CA	July 9, 1983	Joey Pallotta III
Tigerfish, giant	97-0	Zaire River, Kinshasa, Zaire	July 9, 1988	Raymond Houtmans
Tilapia, spotted	4-0	Plantation, FL	June 6, 2005	Reed McLane
Trout, Apache	5-3	White Mountain, AZ	May 29, 1991	John Baldwin
Trout, brook	14-8	Nipigon River, Ontario	July, 1916	Dr. W.J. Cook
Trout, brown	40-4	Little Red River, AR	May 9, 1992	Rip Collins
Trout, bull	32-0	Lake Pend Orielle, ID	Oct. 27, 1949	N.L. Higgins
Trout, cutthroat	41-0	Pyramid Lake, NV	Dec., 1925	John Skimmerhorn
Trout, golden	11-0	Cooks Lake, WY	Aug. 5, 1948	Charles S. Reed
Trout, lake	72-0	Great Bear Lake, N.W.T.	Aug. 19, 1995	Lloyd E. Bull
Trout, rainbow	43-10	Lake Deinfenbaker, Canada	June 5, 2007	Adam Konrad
Trout, tiger	20-13	Lake Michigan, WI	Aug. 12, 1978	Peter M. Friedland
Walleye	25-0	Old Hickory Lake, TN	Aug. 2, 1960	Mabry Harper
Warmouth	2-7	Guess Lake, Holt, FL	Oct. 19, 1985	Tony D. Dempsey
Whitefish, lake	14-6	Meaford, Ontario	May 21, 1984	Dennis M. Laycock
Whitefish, round	6-0	Putahow River, Manitoba	June 14, 1984	Allan J. Ristori
Zander	25-2	Trosa, Sweden	June 12, 1986	Harry Lee Tennison

SALTWATER FISH

Species	Lbs-Oz	Where Caught	Date	Angler
Albacore	88-2	Gran Canaria, Canary Islands	Nov. 19, 1977	Siegfried Dickemann
Amberjack, greater	155-12	Challenger Bank, Bermuda	Aug. 16, 1992	Larry Trott
Angelfish, gray	4-0	S.Beach Jetty, Miami, FL	July 12, 1999	Rene G. de Dios
Barracuda, great	85-0	Christmas Is., Rep. of Kiribati	Apr. 11, 1992	John W. Helfrich
Barracuda, Mexican	22-8	Pinas Bay, Panama	Nov. 11, 2005	Frank Ibarra
Barracuda, pickhandle	29-12	Malindi, Kenya	Nov. 7, 2002	Paul Gerritsen
Bass, barred sand	13-3	Huntington Beach, CA	Aug. 29, 1988	Robert Halal
Bass, black sea	10-4	Virginia Beach, VA	Jan. 1, 2000	Allan P. Paschall
Bass, European	20-14	Cap d'Agde, France	Sept. 8, 1999	Robert Mari
Bass, giant sea	563-8	Anacapa Island, CA	Aug. 20, 1968	J.D. McAdam Jr.
Bass, striped	78-8	Atlantic City, NJ	Sept. 21, 1982	Albert R. McReynolds
Bluefish	31-12	Hatteras, NC	Jan. 30, 1972	James M. Hussey
Bonefish	19-0	Zululand, South Africa	May 26, 1962	Brian W. Batchelor
Bonito, Atlantic	18-4	Faial Island, Azores	July 8, 1953	D. Gama Higgs
Bonito, Pacific	21-5	181 Spot, CA	Oct. 19, 2003	Kim Larson
Cabezon	23-0	Juan de Fuca Strait, WA	Aug. 4, 1990	Wesley Hunter
Cobia	135-9	Shark Bay, W. Australia	July 9, 1985	Peter W. Goulding
Cod, Atlantic	98-12	Isle of Shoals, NH	June 8, 1969	Alphonse Bielevich
Cod, Pacific	38-9	Kamoenia, Japan	Jan. 16, 2005	Atsunori Takahira
Conger	133-4	South Devon, England	June 5, 1995	Vic Evans
Dolphinfish	88-0	Highbourne Cay, Bahamas	May 5, 1998	Richard D. Evans
Drum, black	113-1	Lewes, DE	Sept. 15, 1975	Gerald M. Townsend
Drum, red	94-2	Avon, NC	Nov. 7, 1984	David G. Deuel
Eel, American	9-4	Cape May, NJ	Nov. 9, 1995	Jeff Pennick
Eel, marbled	36-1	Durban, South Africa	June 10, 1984	Ferdie van Nooten
Flounder, southern	20-9	Nassau Sound, FL	Dec. 23, 1983	Larenza Mungin
Flounder, summer	22-7	Montauk, NY	Sept. 15, 1975	Charles Nappi
Grouper, goliath	680-0	Fernandina Beach, FL	May 20, 1961	Lynn Joyner
Grouper, Warsaw	436-12	Gulf of Mexico, Destin, FL	Dec. 22, 1985	Steve Haeusler
Haddock	14-15	Saltraumen, Germany	Aug. 15, 1997	Heike Neblinger
Halibut, Atlantic	418-13	Vannaya Troms, Norway	July 28, 2004	Thomas Nielsen
Halibut, California	58-9	Santa Rosa Island, CA	June 26, 1999	Roger W. Borrell
Halibut, Pacific	459-0	Dutch Harbor, AK	June 11, 1996	Jack Tragis
Jack, almaco (Pacific)	132-0	La Paz, Baja Calif., Mexico	July 21, 1964	Howard H. Hahn
Jack, crevalle	58-6	Barra do Kwanza, Angola	Dec. 10, 2000	Nuno A.P. da Silva
Jack, horse-eye	29-8	Ascencion Island, South Atlantic	May 28, 1993	Mike Hanson
Kawakawa	29-0	Clarion Island, Mexico	Dec. 17, 1986	Ronald Nakamura
Lingcod	77-3	Homer, Alaska	July 5, 2006	Kindal Murry
Mackerel, cero	17-2	Islamorada, FL	Apr. 5, 1986	G. Michael Mills

FISHING (Cont.)

Species	Lbs-Oz	Where Caught	Date	Angler
Mackerel, king	.93-0	San Juan, Puerto Rico	Apr. 18, 1999	Steve Perez Graulau
Mackerel, Spanish	.13-0	Ocracoke Inlet, NC	Nov. 4, 1987	Robert Cranton
Marlin, Atlantic blue	1402-2	Vitoria, Brazil	Feb. 29, 1992	Paulo R.A. Amorim
Marlin, black	1560-0	Cabo Blanco, Peru	Aug. 4, 1953	A.C. Glassell Jr.
Marlin, Pacific blue	1376-0	Kaaiwi Point, Kona, HI	May 31, 1982	Jay W. deBeaubien
Marlin, striped	.494-0	Tutakaka, New Zealand	Jan. 16, 1986	Bill Boniface
Marlin, white	.181-14	Vitoria, Brazil	Dec. 8, 1979	Evandro Luiz Coser
Permit	.60-0	Paranagua, Brazil	Dec. 14, 2002	Renato Fiedler
Pollack, European	.27-6	Salcombe, Devon, England	Jan. 16, 1986	Robert S. Milkins
Pollock	.50-0	Salstraumen, Norway	Nov. 30, 1996	Thor-Magnus Lekang
Pompano, African	.50-8	Daytona Beach, FL	Apr. 21, 1990	Tom Sargent
Roosterfish	.114-0	La Paz, Baja Calif., Mexico	June 1, 1960	Abe Sackheim
Runner, blue	.11-2	Dauphin Island, AL	June 28, 1997	Stacey M. Moiren
Runner, rainbow	.37-9	Clarion Island, Mexico	Nov. 21, 1991	Tom Pfleger
Sailfish, Atlantic	.141-1	Luanda, Angola	Feb. 19, 1994	Alfredo de Sousa Neves
Sailfish, Pacific	.221-0	Santa Cruz Is., Ecuador	Feb. 12, 1947	C.W. Stewart
Seabass, white	.83-12	San Felipe, Mexico	Mar. 31, 1953	L.C. Baumgardner
Seatrout, spotted	.17-7	Ft. Pierce, FL	May 11, 1995	Craig F. Carson
Shark, blue	.528-0	Montauk Point, NY	Aug. 9, 2001	Joe Seidel
Shark, great white	.2664-0	Ceduna, S. Australia	Apr. 21, 1959	Alfred Dean
Shark, Greenland	.1708-9	Trondheimsfjord, Norway	Oct. 18, 1987	Terje Nordtvedt
Shark, hammerhead	.1280-0	Boca Grande, FL	May 23, 2006	Bucky Grande
Shark, shortfin mako	.1221-0	Chatham, MA	July 21, 2001	Luke Sweeney
Shark, porbeagle	.507-0	Pentland Firth, Scotland	Mar. 9, 1993	Christopher Bennet
Shark, bigeye thresher	.802-0	Tutukaka, New Zealand	Feb. 8, 1981	Dianne North
Shark, tiger	.1785-11	Ulladulla, Australia	Mar. 28, 2004	Kevin James Clapson
Snapper, cubera	.124-12	Garden Bank, LA	June 23, 2007	Marion Rose
Snapper, red	.50-4	Gulf of Mexico, LA	June 23, 1996	Capt. Doc Kennedy
Snook, Pacific black	.57-12	Rio Naranjo, Quepos, Costa Rica	Aug. 23, 1991	George Beck
Spearfish, Mediterranean	.90-13	Madeira Island, Portugal	June 2, 1980	Joseph Larkin
Swordfish	.1182-0	Iquique, Chile	May 7, 1953	Louis Marron
Tarpon	.283-4	Sherbro Is., Sierra Leone	Apr. 16, 1991	Yvon Victor Sebag
Tautog	.25-0	Ocean City, NJ	Jan. 20, 1998	Anthony R. Monica
Tuna, Atlantic bigeye	.392-6	Gran Canaria, Puerto Rico	July 25, 1996	Dieter Vogel
Tuna, blackfin	.49-6	Marathon, FL	April 6, 2006	Matthew E. Pullen
Tuna, bluefin	.1496-0	Aulds Cove, Nova Scotia	Oct. 26, 1979	Ken Fraser
Tuna, longtail	.79-2	Montague Is., NSW, Australia	Apr. 12, 1982	Tim Simpson
Tuna, Pacific bigeye	.435-0	Cabo Blanco, Peru	Apr. 17, 1957	Dr. Russell Lee
Tuna, skipjack	.45-4	Flathead Bank, Mexico	Nov. 16, 1996	Brian Evans
Tuna, southern bluefin	.348-5	Whakatane, New Zealand	Jan. 16, 1981	Rex Wood
Tuna, yellowfin	.388-12	San Benedicto Island, Mexico	Apr. 1, 1977	Curt Wiesenhutter
Tunny, little	.36-0	Washington Canyon, NJ	Nov. 5, 2006	Jess Lubert
Wahoo	.184-0	Cab San Lucas, Mexico	July 29, 2005	Sara Hayward
Weakfish	.19-2	Jones Beach, Long Island, NY	Oct. 11, 1984	Dennis R. Rooney
	19-2	Delaware Bay, DE	May 20, 1989	William E. Thomas

Bassmasters Classic

Boyd Duckett was the surprise winner of the 37th Bassmaster Classic, held on Alabama's Lay Lake, beating the second-place angler Skeet Reese by just six ounces. Duckett, who became the first Alabama native to win the Classic in his home state, credited his success to the fact that he went against conventional wisdom and properly anticipated where the fish would be given the changing weather conditions. It was his first appearance at the Classic and Duckett came from behind on the final day of competition to take home the $500,000 check for first place.

The 2008 Bassmasters Classic will be held Feb. 22-24 on Hartwell Lake in South Carolina.

The Bassmasters Classic, hosted by B.A.S.S. (Bass Anglers Sportsman Society), is professional bass fishing's world championship. Qualifiers for the three-day event include the 40 top pros on the CITGO Bassmaster Tour and the five top-ranked anglers from each of three CITGO Bassmasters Open circuits. Anglers may weigh only five bass per day and each bass must be at least 12 inches long. Only artificial lures are permitted. The first Classic, held at Lake Mead, Nev. in 1971, was a $10,000 winner-take-all event.

Multiple winners: Rick Clunn (4); George Cochran, Bobby Murray, Hank Parker and Kevin VanDam (2).

Year		Weight	Year		Weight
1971	Bobby Murray, Hot Springs, Ark	.43-11	1979	Hank Parker, Clover, S.C	.31-0
1972	Don Butler, Tulsa, Okla	.38-11	1980	Bo Dowden, Natchitoches, La	.54-10
1973	Rayo Breckenridge, Paragould, Ark	.52-8	1981	Stanley Mitchell, Fitzgerald, Ga	.35-2
1974	Tommy Martin, Hemphill, Tex	.33-7	1982	Paul Elias, Laurel, Miss	.32-8
1975	Jack Hains, Rayne, La	.45-4	1983	Larry Nixon, Hemphill, Tex	.18-1
1976	Rick Clunn, Montgomery, Tex	.59-15	1984	Rick Clunn, Montgomery, Tex	.75-9
1977	Rick Clunn, Montgomery, Tex	.27-7	1985	Jack Chancellor, Phenix City, Ala	.45-0
1978	Bobby Murray, Nashville, Tenn	.37-9	1986	Charlie Reed, Broken Bow, Okla	.23-9

Year		Weight	Year		Weight
1987	George Cochran, N. Little Rock, Ark	15-5	1998	Denny Brauer, Camdenton, Mo.	46-3
1988	Guido Hibdon, Gravois Mills, Mo	28-8	1999	Davy Hite, Prosperity, S.C.	55-10
1989	Hank Parker, Denver, N.C.	31-6	2000	Woo Daves, Spring Grove, Va.	27-13
1990	Rick Clunn, Montgomery, Tex	34-5	2001	Kevin VanDam, Kalamazoo, Mich.	32-5
1991	Ken Cook, Meers, Okla	33-2	2002	Jay Yelas, Tyler, Texas	45-13
1992	Robert Hamilton Jr., Brandon, Miss	59-6	2003	Michael Iaconelli, Woodbury Heights, N.J.	37-14
1993	David Fritts, Lexington, N.C.	48-6	2004	Takahiro Omori, Emory, Texas	39-2
1994	Bryan Kerchal, Newtown, Conn	36-7	2005	Kevin VanDam, Kalamazoo, Mich.	12-15
1995	Mark Davis, Mount Ida, Ark.	47-14	2006	Luke Clausen, Spokane Valley, Wash.	56-2
1996	George Cochran, Hot Springs, Ark.	31-14	2007	Boyd Duckett, Demopolis, Ala.	48-10
1997	Dion Hibdon, Stover, Mo.	34-13			

LITTLE LEAGUE BASEBALL

World Series

Warner Robbins, Ga., beat the boys from Tokyo, Japan, 3-2, on an extra-innnings home run to give the United States its first three-peat since 1966. Twelve-year-old Georgia slugger Dalton Carriker hit an opposite-field bomb off Japanese reliever Jun-sho Kiuchi in the eighth inning for the thrilling win. It was the second-straight LLWS win for the Peach State.

Lubbock, Texas won the third-place game on a combined no-hitter to beat Willemstad, Curacao, 1-0.

Played annually in late August in Williamsport, Penn. at Original Field in Williamsport, Penn. from 1947-1958 and at Howard J. Lamade Stadium since 1959 and also at newly constructed Volunteer Stadium starting in 2001.

In order to be invited to the World Series, teams must first win their regional tournaments. There are eight regions from the U.S. (Great Lakes, Midwest, Mid-Atlantic, New England, Northwest, Southeast, Southwest and West) and eight outside of the U.S. (Asia, Canada, Caribbean, European, Latin America, Mexico, Pacific and Trans-Atlantic). The eight U.S. regions then play each other and the the eight international regions play each other and the two winners from each meet in the championship game. This ensures that a team from the U.S. will always participate in the final game.

Multiple winners: Taiwan (16); Japan (6); California (5); Connecticut, New Jersey and Pennsylvania (4); Georgia and Mexico (3); New York, South Korea, Texas and Venezuela (2).

Year	Winner	Score	Loser	Year	Winner	Score	Loser
1947	Williamsport, PA	16-7	Lock Haven, PA	1978	Pin-Tung, Taiwan	11-1	Danville, CA
1948	Lock Haven, PA	6-5	St. Petersburg, FL	1979	Hsien, Taiwan	2-1†	Campbell, CA
1949	Hammonton, NJ	5-0	Pensacola, FL	1980	Hua Lian, Taiwan	4-3	Tampa, FL
1950	Houston, TX	2-1	Bridgeport, CT	1981	Tai-Chung, Taiwan	4-2	Tampa, FL
1951	Stamford, CT	3-0	Austin, TX	1982	Kirkland, WA	6-0	Hsien, Taiwan
1952	Norwalk, CT	4-3	Monongahela, PA	1983	Marietta, GA	3-1	Barahona, D. Rep.
1953	Birmingham, AL	1-0	Schenectady, NY	1984	Seoul, S. Korea	6-2	Altamonte, FL
1954	Schenectady, NY	7-5	Colton, CA	1985	Seoul, S. Korea	7-1	Mexicali, Mex.
1955	Morrisville, PA	4-3†	Merchantville, NJ	1986	Tainan Park, Taiwan	12-0	Tucson, AZ
1956	Roswell, NM	3-1	Merchantville, NJ	1987	Hua Lian, Taiwan	21-1	Irvine, CA
1957	Monterrey, Mexico	4-0	La Mesa, CA	1988	Tai Ping, Taiwan	10-0	Pearl City, HI
1958	Monterrey, Mexico	10-1	Kankakee, IL	1989	Trumbull, CT	5-2	Kaohsiung, Taiwan
1959	Hamtramck, MI	12-0	Auburn, CA	1990	Taipei, Taiwan	9-0	Shippensburg, PA
1960	Levittown, PA	5-0	Ft. Worth, TX	1991	Taichung, Taiwan	11-0	Danville, CA
1961	El Cajon, CA	4-2	El Campo, TX	1992	Long Beach, CA	6-0	Zamboanga, Phil.
1962	San Jose, CA	3-0	Kankakee, IL	1993	Long Beach, CA	3-2	Panama
1963	Granada Hills, CA	2-1	Stratford, CT	1994	Maracaibo, Venezuela	4-3	Northridge, CA
1964	Staten Island, NY	4-0	Monterrey, Mex.	1995	Tainan, Taiwan	17-3	Spring, TX
1965	Windsor Locks, CT	3-1	Stoney Creek, Can.	1996	Taipei, Taiwan	13-3	Cranston, RI
1966	Houston, TX	8-2	W. New York, NJ				(called after 5th inn.)
1967	West Tokyo, Japan	4-1	Chicago, IL	1997	Guadalupe, Mexico	5-4	Mission Viejo, CA
1968	Osaka, Japan	1-0	Richmond, VA	1998	Toms River, NJ	12-9	Kashima, Japan
1969	Taipei, Taiwan	5-0	Santa Clara, CA	1999	Osaka, Japan	5-0	Phenix City, AL
1970	Wayne, NJ	2-0	Campbell, CA	2000	Maracaibo, Venezuela	3-2	Bellaire, TX
1971	Tainan, Taiwan	12-3†	Gary, IN	2001	Tokyo, Japan	2-1	Apopka, FL
1972	Taipei, Taiwan	6-0	Hammond, IN	2002	Louisville, KY	1-0	Sendai, Japan
1973	Tainan City, Taiwan	12-0	Tucson, AZ	2003	Tokyo, Japan	10-1	Boynton Beach, FL
1974	Kao Hsiung, Taiwan	12-1	Red Bluff, CA	2004	Willemstad, Curacao	5-2	Thousand Oaks, CA
1975	Lakewood, NJ	4-3*	Tampa, FL	2005	West Oahu, HI	7-6†	Willemstad, Curacao
1976	Tokyo, Japan	10-3	Campbell, CA	2006	Columbus, GA	2-1	Kawaguchi City, Jap.
1977	Li-Teh, Taiwan	7-2	El Cajon, CA	2007	Warner Robbins, GA	3-2†	Tokyo, Japan

† extra innings.
* Foreign teams were banned from the tournament in 1975, but allowed back in the following year.

Note: In 1992, Zamboanga City of the Philippines beat Long Beach, 15-4, but was stripped of the title a month later when it was discovered that the team had used several players from outside the city limits. Long Beach was then awarded the title by forfeit, 6-0 (one run for each inning of the game).

Jerry Yang won $8.25 million at the 2007 World Series of Poker and pledged to give 10 percent of his haul to charity.

ESPN Media

POKER

World Series of Poker

Created by Benny Binion in 1970, the World Series of Poker is held each year at Binion's Horseshoe Casino in Las Vegas, Nev. and brings together the world's greatest poker players. The marquee event is the no-limit Texas hold-'em tournament. The first World Series was a seven-player tournament in which the champion Johnny Moss was chosen by a vote of his peers.

The 2007 World Champion was California psychologist Jerry Yang, who beat out 6,358 entrants over 12 days and won a first prize of $8.25 million—a larger payday than the winner of the Kentucky Derby, Wimbledon, Indianapolis 500 and the Masters combined. The 39-year-old Laotian immigrant and father of six entered the final table eighth in chips but quickly leapfrogged to first and proceeded to personally knock out seven of the other eight players at the table. In the end only Yang and Tuan Lam, a fellow South Asian refugee, were left. Yang caught a straight on the river to beat the queens that Lam flopped.

Anyone that's over 21 years old and can pay the $10,000 entry fee can compete.

No-Limit Texas Hold-'em Champions

Multiple winners: Johnny Moss and Stu Ungar (3); Doyle Brunson and Johnny Chan (2).

Year	Champion	Prize Money	Year	Champion	Prize Money
1970	Johnny Moss	n/a	1989	Phil Hellmuth Jr.	$ 755,000
1971	Johnny Moss	$ 30,000	1990	Mansour Matloubi	895,000
1972	"Amarillo Slim" Preston	80,000	1991	Brad Daugherty	1,000,000
1973	Puggy Pearson	130,000	1992	Hamid Datsmalchi	1,000,000
1974	Johnny Moss	160,000	1993	Jim Bechtel	1,000,000
1975	Sailor Roberts	210,000	1994	Russ Hamilton	1,000,000
1976	Doyle Brunson	220,000	1995	Dan Harrington	1,000,000
1977	Doyle Brunson	340,000	1996	Huck Seed	1,000,000
1978	Bobby Baldwin	210,000	1997	Stu Ungar	1,000,000
1979	Hal Fowler	270,000	1998	Scotty Nguyen	1,000,000
1980	Stu Ungar	385,000	1999	Noel Furlong	1,000,000
1981	Stu Ungar	375,000	2000	Chris Ferguson	1,500,000
1982	Jack Strauss	520,000	2001	Carlos Mortensen	1,500,000
1983	Tom McEvoy	580,000	2002	Robert Varkyoni	2,000,000
1984	Jack Keller	660,000	2003	Chris Moneymaker	2,500,000
1985	Bill Smith	700,000	2004	Greg Raymer	5,000,000
1986	Berry Johnston	570,000	2005	Joseph Hachem	7,500,000
1987	Johnny Chan	625,000	2006	Jamie Gold	12,000,000
1988	Johnny Chan	700,000	2007	Jerry Yang	8,250,000

PRO RODEO

All-Around Champion Cowboy

Trevor Brazile of Decatur, Tex., won his fourth career all-around world title, earning $329,924 during the 2006 campaign. Bull rider B.J. Schumacher of Hillsboro, Wisc., had a monster NFR, riding eight of 10 bulls and set a new record for single-event earnings and won $142,644 to ride away with his first word title.

The Professional Rodeo Cowboys Association (PRCA) title of all-around world champion cowboy goes to the rodeo athlete who wins the most prize money in a single year in two or more events, earning a minimum of $3,000 in each event. Only prize money earned in sanctioned PRCA rodeos is counted. From 1929-44, all-around champions were named by the Rodeo Association of America (earnings for those years are not available).

Multiple winners: Ty Murray (7); Tom Ferguson and Larry Mahan (6); Jim Shoulders (5); Trevor Brazile (4), Joe Beaver, Lewis Feild and Dean Oliver (3); Everett Bowman, Louis Brooks, Clay Carr, Bill Linderman, Phil Lyne, Gerald Roberts, Casey Tibbs and Harry Tompkins (2).

Year		Year		Year		Year	
1929	Earl Thode	1934	Leonard Ward	1939	Paul Carney	1944	Louis Brooks
1930	Clay Carr	1935	Everett Bowman	1940	Fritz Truan	1945	No award
1931	John Schneider	1936	John Bowman	1941	Homer Pettigrew	1946	No award
1932	Donald Nesbit	1937	Everett Bowman	1942	Gerald Roberts		
1933	Clay Carr	1938	Burel Mulkey	1943	Louis Brooks		

Year		Earnings	Year		Earnings	Year		Earnings
1947	Todd Whatley	$18,642	1967	Larry Mahan	$51,996	1987	Lewis Feild	$144,335
1948	Gerald Roberts	21,766	1968	Larry Mahan	49,129	1988	Dave Appleton	121,546
1949	Jim Shoulders	21,495	1969	Larry Mahan	57,726	1989	Ty Murray	134,806
1950	Bill Linderman	30,715	1970	Larry Mahan	41,493	1990	Ty Murray	213,772
1951	Casey Tibbs	29,104	1971	Phil Lyne	49,245	1991	Ty Murray	244,231
1952	Harry Tompkins	30,934	1972	Phil Lyne	60,852	1992	Ty Murray	225,992
1953	Bill Linderman	33,674	1973	Larry Mahan	64,447	1993	Ty Murray	297,896
1954	Buck Rutherford	40,404	1974	Tom Ferguson	66,929	1994	Ty Murray	246,170
1955	Casey Tibbs	42,065	1975	Tom Ferguson	50,300	1995	Joe Beaver	141,753
1956	Jim Shoulders	43,381	1976	Tom Ferguson	87,908	1996	Joe Beaver	166,103
1957	Jim Shoulders	33,299	1977	Tom Ferguson	65,981	1997	Dan Mortensen	184,559
1958	Jim Shoulders	32,212	1978	Tom Ferguson	83,734	1998	Ty Murray	264,673
1959	Jim Shoulders	32,905	1979	Tom Ferguson	96,272	1999	Fred Whitfield	217,819
1960	Harry Tompkins	32,522	1980	Paul Tierney	105,568	2000	Joe Beaver	225,396
1961	Benny Reynolds	31,309	1981	Jimmie Cooper	105,861	2001	Cody Ohl	296,419
1962	Tom Nesmith	32,611	1982	Chris Lybbert	123,709	2002	Trevor Brazile	273,998
1963	Dean Oliver	31,329	1983	Roy Cooper	153,391	2003	Trevor Brazile	294,839
1964	Dean Oliver	31,150	1984	Dee Pickett	122,618	2004	Trevor Brazile	253,170
1965	Dean Oliver	33,163	1985	Lewis Feild	130,347	2005	Ryan Jarrett	263,665
1966	Larry Mahan	40,358	1986	Lewis Feild	166,042	2006	Trevor Brazile	329,924

SOAP BOX DERBY

All-American Soap Box Derby

The 70th annual All-American Soap Box Derby was held on July 21, 2007 in Akron, Ohio. Over 500 kids from 43 states and three foreign countries competed.

The AASBD is a coasting race for small gravity-powered cars built by their drivers and assembled within strict guidelines on size, weight and cost. The Derby was started by Dayton, Ohio newsman Myron Scott after he witnessed several boys racing handmade carts down a hill while on a photographic assignment in 1933. Scott decided to start an organized race for kids and the first All-American Soap Box Derby was held in Dayton in 1934. The race got its name because early on most cars were built from wooden soap boxes. The following year, the race was moved to Akron because of its central location and hilly terrain. In 1936, town leaders saw the need for a permanent site for the growing event and with the help of the Works Progress Administration, Derby Downs was constructed.

Held every summer at Derby Downs in Akron, Ohio, the Soap Box Derby is open to all boys and girls from 8 to 17 years old who qualify. There are three competitive divisions: 1. Stock (ages 8-17)— made up of generic, prefab racers that come from Derby-approved kits, can be assembled in four hours and don't exceed 200 pounds when driver, car and wheels are weighed together; 2. Super Stock (ages 10-17)— the same as Stock only with a weight limit of 220 pounds; 3. Masters (ages 11-17)— made up of racers designed by the drivers, but constructed with Derby-approved hardware. The racing ramp at Derby Downs is 989 feet, four inches with an 11 percent grade.

One champion reigned at the All-American Soap Box Derby each year from 1934-75; Junior and Senior division champions from 1976-87; Kit and Masters champions from 1988-91; Stock, Kit and Masters champions from 1992-94; Stock, Super Stock and Masters champions starting in 1995.

Year		Hometown	Age	Year		Hometown	Age
1934	Robert Turner	Muncie, IN	11	1941	Claude Smith	Akron, OH	14
1935	Maurice Bale Jr.	Anderson, IN	13	1942-45	Not held		
1936	Herbert Muench Jr.	St. Louis	14	1946	Gilbert Klecan	San Diego	14
1937	Robert Ballard	White Plains, NY	12	1947	Kenneth Holmboe	Charleston, WV	14
1938	Robert Berger	Omaha, NE	14	1948	Donald Strub	Akron, OH	13
1939	Clifton Hardesty	White Plains, NY	11	1949	Fred Derks	Akron, OH	15
1940	Thomas Fisher	Detroit	12				

All-American Soap Box Derby (Cont.)

Year		Hometown	Age
1950	Harold Williamson	Charleston, WV	15
1951	Darwin Cooper	Williamsport, PA	15
1952	Joe Lunn	Columbus, GA	11
1953	Fred Mohler	Muncie, IN	14
1954	Richard Kemp	Los Angeles	14
1955	Richard Rohrer	Rochester, NY	14
1956	Norman Westfall	Rochester, NY	14
1957	Terry Townsend	Anderson, IN	14
1958	James Miley	Muncie, IN	15
1959	Barney Townsend	Anderson, IN	13
1960	Fredric Lake	South Bend, IN	11
1961	Dick Dawson	Wichita, KS	13
1962	David Mann	Gary, IN	14
1963	Harold Conrad	Duluth, MN	12
1964	Gregory Schumacher	Tacoma, WA	14
1965	Robert Logan	Santa Ana, CA	12
1966	David Krussow	Tacoma, WA	12
1967	Kenneth Cline	Lincoln, NE	13
1968	Branch Lew	Muncie, IN	11
1969	Steve Souter	Midland, TX	12
1970	Samuel Gupton	Durham, NC	13
1971	Larry Blair	Oroville, CA	13
1972	Robert Lange Jr.	Boulder, CO	14
1973	Bret Yarborough	Elk Grove, CA	11
1974	Curt Yarborough	Elk Grove, CA	11
1975	Karren Stead	Lower Bucks, PA	11
1976	JR: Phil Raber	Sugarcreek, OH	11
	SR: Joan Ferdinand	Canton, OH	14
1977	JR: Mark Ferdinand	Canton, OH	10
	SR: Steve Washburn	Bristol, CT	15
1978	JR: Darren Hart	Salem, OR	11
	SR: Greg Cardinal	Flint, MI	13
1979	JR: Russell Yurk	Flint, MI	10
	SR: Craig Kitchen	Akron, OH	14
1980	JR: Chris Fulton	Indianapolis	11
	SR: Dan Porul	Sherman Oaks, CA	12
1981	JR: Howie Fraley	Portsmouth, OH	11
	SR: Tonia Schlegel	Hamilton, OH	13
1982	JR: Carol A. Sullivan	Rochester, NH	14
	SR: Matt Wolfgang	Lehigh Val., PA	12
1983	JR: Tony Carlini	Del Mar, CA	10
	SR: Mike Burdgick	Flint, MI	14
1984	JR: Chris Hess	Hamilton, OH	11
	SR: Anita Jackson	St. Louis	15
1985	JR: Michael Gallo	Danbury, CT	12
	SR: Matt Sheffer	York, PA	14
1986	JR: Marc Behan	Dover, NH	9
	SR: Tami Jo Sullivan	Lancaster, OH	13
1987	JR: Matt Margules	Danbury, CT	11
	SR: Brian Drinkwater	Bristol, CT	14
1988	KIT: Jason Lamb	Des Moines, IA	10
	MAS: David Duffield	Kansas City	14

Year		Hometown	Age
1989	KIT: David Schiller	Dayton, OH	12
	MAS: Faith Chavarria	Ventura, CA	12

Year		Hometown	Age
1990	MAS: Sami Jones	Salem, OR	13
	KIT: Mark Mihal	Valparaiso, IN	12
1991	MAS: Danny Garland	San Diego, CA	14
	KIT: Paul Greenwald	Saginaw, MI	13
1992	MAS: Bonnie Thornton	Redding, CA	12
	KIT: Carolyn Fox	Sublimity, OR	11
	STK: Loren Hurst	Hudson, OH	10
1993	MAS: Dean Lutton	Delta, OH	14
	KIT: D.M. Del Ferraro	Stow, OH	12
	STK: Owen Yuda	Boiling Springs, PA	10
1994	MAS: D.M. Del Ferraro	Akron, OH	13
	KIT: Joel Endres	Akron, OH	14
	STK: Kristina Damond	Jamestown, NY	13
1995	MAS: J. Fensterbush	Kingman, AZ	11
	SS: Darcie Davisson	Kingman, AZ	11
	STK: Karen Thomas	Jamestown, NY	11
1996	MAS: Tim Scrofano	Conneaut, OH	12
	SS: Jeremy Phillips	Charlestown, WV	14
	STK: Matt Perez	No. Canton, OH	12
1997	MAS: Wade Wallace	Elk Hart, IN	11
	SS: Dolline Vance	Salem, OR	13
	STK: Mark Stephens	Waynesboro, VA	13
1998	MAS: James Marsh	Cleveland, OH	12
	SS: Stacy Sharp	Kingman, AZ	14
	STK: Hailey Simpson	Salem, OR	10
1999	MAS: Allan Endres	Barberton, OH	14
	SS: Alisha Ebner	Salem, OR	15
	STK: Justin Pillow	Deland, FL	12
2000	MAS: Cody Butler	Anderson, IN	12
	SS: Derek Etherington	Anderson, IN	11
	STK: Rachel Curran	Medina, OH	13
2001	MAS: Michael Flynn	Harrison Township, MI	12
	SS: James Rogers	Hilton, NY	15
	STK: Chad Eyerly	Alta Loma, CA	11
2002	MAS: Evan Griffin	Winter Park, FL	15
	SS: Roger Youmans Jr.	Spencerport, NY	13
	STK: Cameron Vannatta	Anderson, IN	12
2003	MAS: Anthony Marulli	Rochester, NY	14
	SS: Corey Harkins	Chicago	14
	STK: Nicholas Sibeto	New Castle, PA	12
2004	MAS: Hilary Pearson	Kansas City, MO	14
	SS: RickiLea Murphy	Mantua, OH	12
	STK: Perrin Norris	Tullahoma, TN	10
2005	MAS: Stephanie Inglezakis	Stow, OH	16
	SS: Tyler Gallagher	Mantua, OH	14
	STK: Nick Hoffman	Lancaster, OH	9
2006	MAS: Garrett Kysar	Martinsburg, WV	14
	SS: Sally Sue Thornton	Vallejo, CA	14
	STK: Michael Neely	North Canton, OH	14
2007	MAS: Kacie Rader	Washington, DC	16
	SS: Andrew Feldpausch	Saginaw, MI	15
	STK: Tyler Shoff	Akron, OH	13

Famous Americans who competed at the All-American Soap Box Derby

Johnny Carson, former entertainer and *Tonight Show* host
Frankie Muniz, Malcolm on Fox's *Malcolm in the Middle*
Richard Childress, 6-time NASCAR-winning owner
Cale Yarborough, 3-time NASCAR Cup champion
Jim France, NASCAR Vice Chairman/Executive Vice President
Mike Helton, NASCAR President
Tom Sneva, 1983 Indy 500 champion
Denny Zimmerman, 1971 Indy 500 rookie of the year
Paul Hornung, 1956 Heisman Trophy winner (Notre Dame)
Pete Dawkins, 1958 Heisman Trophy winner (Army)

source: www.aasbd.com

SOFTBALL

Men's national champions since 1933 in Major Fast Pitch and Major Slow Pitch. Sanctioned by the Amateur Softball Association of America.

MEN
Major Fast Pitch

Multiple winners: Clearwater Bombers (10); Raybestos Cardinals (5); Sealmasters (4); Briggs Beautyware, Decatur Pride, Pay'n Pak and Zollner Pistons (3); Billard Barbell, Farm Tavern, Frontier Players Casino, Hammer Air Field, Kodak Park, Meierhoffer, National Health Care, Penn Corp, Peterbilt Western and Tampa Bay Smokers (2).

Year	Year	Year
1933 J.L. Gill Boosters, Chicago	1961 Sealmasters	1987 Pay'n Pak
1934 Ke-Nash-A, Kenosha, WI	1962 Clearwater Bombers	1988 TransAire, Elkhart, IN
1935 Crimson Coaches, Toledo, OH	1963 Clearwater Bombers	1989 Penn Corp, Sioux City, IA
1936 Kodak Park, Rochester, NY	1964 Burch Tool, Detroit	1990 Penn Corp
1937 Briggs Body Team, Detroit	1965 Sealmasters	1991 Gianella Bros., Rohnert Park, CA
1938 The Pohlers, Cincinnati	1966 Clearwater Bombers	1992 National Health Care,
1939 Carr's Boosters, Covington, KY	1967 Sealmasters	Sioux City, IA
1940 Kodak Park	1968 Clearwater Bombers	1993 National Health Care
1941 Bendix Brakes, South Bend, IN	1969 Raybestos Cardinals	1994 Decatur (IL) Pride
1942 Deep Rock Oilers, Tulsa, OK	1970 Raybestos Cardinals	1995 Decatur Pride
1943 Hammer Air Field, Fresno, CA	1971 Welty Way, Cedar Rapids, IA	1996 Green Bay All-Car,
1944 Hammer Air Field	1972 Raybestos Cardinals	Green Bay, WI
1945 Zollner Pistons, Ft. Wayne, IN	1973 Clearwater Bombers	1997 Tampa Bay Smokers,
1946 Zollner Pistons	1974 Gianella Bros., Santa Rosa, CA	Tampa Bay, FL
1947 Zollner Pistons	1975 Rising Sun Hotel, Reading, PA	1998 Meierhoffer-Fleeman,
1948 Briggs Beautyware, Detroit	1976 Raybestos Cardinals	St. Joseph, MO
1949 Tip Top Tailors, Toronto	1977 Billard Barbell, Reading, PA	1999 Decatur Pride
1950 Clearwater (FL) Bombers	1978 Billard Barbell	2000 Meierhoffer
1951 Dow Chemical, Midland, MI	1979 McArdle Pontiac/Cadillac,	2001 Frontier Players Casino,
1952 Briggs Beautyware	Midland, MI	St. Joseph, MO
1953 Briggs Beautyware	1980 Peterbilt Western, Seattle	2002 Frontier Players Casino
1954 Clearwater Bombers	1981 Archer Daniels Midland,	2003 Farm Tavern, Madison, WI
1955 Raybestos Cardinals,	Decatur, IL	2004 Farm Tavern
1956 Clearwater Bombers	1982 Peterbilt Western	2005 Tampa Bay Smokers,
1957 Clearwater Bombers	1983 Franklin Cardinals,	Tampa Bay, FL
1958 Raybestos Cardinals	Stratford, CA	2006 Circle Tap, Denmark, WI
1959 Sealmasters, Aurora, IL	1984 California Kings, Merced, CA	2007 Patsy's, New York, NY
1960 Clearwater Bombers	1985 Pay'n Pak, Seattle	
	1986 Pay'n Pak	

Major Slow Pitch

Multiple winners: Gatliff Auto Sales, Riverside Paving and Skip Hogan A.C. (3); Campbell Carpets, Hamilton Tailoring, Howard's Furniture, Long Haul TPS and New Construction (2).

Year	Year	Year
1953 Shields Construction,	1973 Howard's Furniture,	1992 Vernon's, Jacksonville, FL
Newport, KY	Denver, NC	1993 Back Porch/Destin (FL) Roofing
1954 Waldneck's Tavern, Cincinnati	1974 Howard's Furniture	1994 Riverside Paving, Louisville
1955 Lang Pet Shop, Covington, KY	1975 Pyramid Cafe, Lakewood, OH	1995 Riverside Paving
1956 Gatliff Auto Sales, Newport, KY	1976 Warren Motors, J'ville, FL	1996 Bell II, Orlando, FL
1957 Gatliff Auto Sales	1977 Nelson Painting, Okla. City	1997 Long Haul TPS, Albertville, MN
1958 East Side Sports, Detroit	1978 Campbell Carpets,	1998 Chase Mortgage/Easton,
1959 Yorkshire Restaurant,	Concord, CA	Wilmington, NC
Newport, KY	1979 Nelco Mfg. Co., Okla. City	1999 Gasoline Heaven/Worth,
1960 Hamilton Tailoring, Cincinnati	1980 Campbell Carpets	Commack, NY
1961 Hamilton Tailoring	1981 Elite Coating, Gordon, CA	2000 Long Haul TPS
1962 Skip Hogan A.C., Pittsburgh	1982 Triangle Sports, Minneapolis	2001 New Construction
1963 Gatliff Auto Sales	1983 No.1 Electric & Heating,	2002 Twin States/Worth,
1964 Skip Hogan A.C.	Gastonia, NC	Montgomery, AL
1965 Skip Hogan A.C.	1984 Lilly Air Systems, Chicago	2003 New Construction/B&J/
1966 Michael's Lounge, Detroit	1985 Blanton's Fayetteville, NC	Snap-On, Metamora, IL
1967 Jim's Sport Shop, Pittsburgh	1986 Non-Ferrous Metals, Cleveland	2004 U.S. Vinyl, Houston, TX
1968 County Sports, Levittown, NY	1987 Stapath, Monticello, KY	2005 AM/Las Vegas/Benfield,
1969 Copper Hearth, Milwaukee	1988 Bell Corp/FAF, Tampa, FL	Bowling Green, KY
1970 Little Caesar's, Southgate, MI	1989 Ritch's Salvage, Harrisburg, NC	2006 discontinued
1971 Pile Drivers, Va. Beach, VA	1990 New Construction,	
1972 Jiffy Club, Louisville, KY	Shelbyville, IN	
	1991 Riverside Paving, Louisville	

EATING

Nathan's Famous Hot Dog Eating Contest

Contested since 1916, The Nathan's International July 4th Hot Dog Eating Contest brings some of the world's top competitive eaters together each July fourth at the world famous hot dog restaurant at Coney Island in Brooklyn, New York. Winner receives the Mustard Yellow Belt.

In 2007 at the 92nd annual contest the belt and $10,000 check for first place went to American Joey Chestnut who knocked off six-time defending champion Takeru "The Tsunami" Kobayashi of Japan. Chestnut became top dog by eating a world-record 66 hot dogs and buns in the contest's 12-minute span.

Note that **HDBs** in the list below refers to hot dogs and buns.

Year		HDBs	Year		HDBs
1999	Steve Keinter	.20¼	2004	Takeru Kobayashi	.53½
2000	Kazutoyo Arai	.25⅛	2005	Takeru Kobayashi	.49
2001	Takeru Kobayashi	.50	2006	Takeru Kobayashi	.53¾
2002	Takeru Kobayashi	.50½	2007	Joey Chestnut	.66
2003	Takeru Kobayashi	.44½			

OTHER NOTABLE EATING RECORDS:

Baked Beans
Don Lerman, 6 pounds; 1:48

Birthday Cake
Richard LeFevre, 5 pounds; 11:26

Butter
Don Lerman, 7 quarter-pound sticks (salted); 5:00

Cow Brains
Takeru Kobayashi
17.7 pounds; 15:00

Doughnuts
Eric Booker, 49 (glazed); 8:00

Hard-boiled Eggs
Sonya Thomas, 65; 6:40.

Mayonnaise
Oleg Zhornitskiy, Four 32-ounce bowls; 8:00

Meat Pies
Boyd Bulot, 16 six-ounce pies; 10:00

Pasta
Cookie Jarvis
6⅔ pounds (linguine); 10:00

SPAM
Richard LeFevre, 6 pounds; 12:00

Sweet Corn
Joe LaRue, 34 ears; 12:00

Watermelon
Jim Reeves, 13.22 pounds; 15:00

Source: 23 Ways to Get to First Base, The ESPN Uncyclopedia

TRIATHLON

World Championship

Contested since 1989, the Triathlon World Championship consists of a 1.5-kilometer swim, a 40-kilometer bike ride and a 10-kilometer run. The 2007 championship was held Sept. 1-2 in Hamburg, Germany.

Multiple winners: MEN—Simon Lessing (4); Peter Robertson (3); Spencer Smith (2). WOMEN—Emma Snowsill (3); Emma Carney, Michellie Jones and Karen Smyers (2).

MEN

Year		Time	Year		Time
1989	Mark Allen, United States	1:58:46	1999	Dimitry Gaag, Kazahkstan	1:45:25
1990	Greg Welch, Australia	1:51:37	2000	Oliver Marceau, France	1:51:41
1991	Miles Stewart, Australia	1:48:20	2001	Peter Robertson, Australia	1:48:01
1992	Simon Lessing, Great Britain	1:49:04	2002	Iván Raña, Spain	1:50:41
1993	Spencer Smith, Great Britain	1:51:20	2003	Peter Robertson, Australia	1:54:13
1994	Spencer Smith, Great Britain	1:51:04	2004	Bevan Docherty, New Zealand	1:41:04
1995	Simon Lessing, Great Britain	1:48:29	2005	Peter Robertston, Austrlia	1:49:31
1996	Simon Lessing, Great Britain	1:39:50	2006	Tim Don, Great Britain	1:51:32
1997	Chris McCormack, Australia	1:48:29	2007	Daniel Unger, Germany	1:43:18
1998	Simon Lessing, Great Britain	1:55:31			

WOMEN

Year		Time	Year		Time
1989	Erin Baker, New Zealand	2:10:01	1999	Loretta Harrop, Australia	1:55:28
1990	Karen Smyers, United States	2:03:33	2000	Nicole Hackett, Australia	1:54:43
1991	Joanne Ritchie, Canada	2:02:04	2001	Siri Lindley, United States	1:58:51
1992	Michellie Jones, Australia	2:02:08	2002	Leanda Cave, Wales	2:01:31
1993	Michellie Jones, Australia	2:07:41	2003	Emma Snowsill, Australia	2:06:40
1994	Emma Carney, Australia	2:03:19	2004	Sheila Taormina, United States	1:52:17
1995	Karen Smyers, USA	2:04:58	2005	Emma Snowsill, Australia	1:58:03
1996	Jackie Gallagher, Australia	1:50:52	2006	Emma Snowsill, Australia	2:04:03
1997	Emma Carney, Australia	1:59:22	2007	Vanessa Fernandes, Portugal	1:53:27
1998	Joanne King, Australia	2:07:25			

Ironman Championship

Contested in Hawaii since 1978, the Ironman Triathlon Championship consists of a 2.4-mile swim, a 112-mile bike ride and 26.2-mile run. The race begins at 7 A.M. and continues all day until the course is closed at midnight.

MEN

Multiple winners: Mark Allen and Dave Scott (6); Peter Reid (3); Tim DeBoom, Luc Van Lierde, Normann Stadler and Scott Tinley (2).

Year	Date	Winner	Time	Runner-up	Margin	Start	Finish	Location
I	2/18/78	Gordon Haller	11:46	John Dunbar	34:00	15	12	Waikiki Beach
II	1/14/79	Tom Warren	11:15:56	John Dunbar	48:00	15	12	Waikiki Beach
III	1/10/80	Dave Scott	9:24:33	Chuck Neumann	1:08	108	95	Ala Moana Park
IV	2/14/81	John Howard	9:38:29	Tom Warren	26:00	326	299	Kailua-Kona
V	2/6/82	Scott Tinley	9:19:41	Dave Scott	17:16	580	541	Kailua-Kona
VI	10/9/82	Dave Scott	9:08:23	Scott Tinley	20:05	850	775	Kailua-Kona
VII	10/22/83	Dave Scott	9:05:57	Scott Tinley	0:33	964	835	Kailua-Kona
VIII	10/6/84	Dave Scott	8:54:20	Scott Tinley	24:25	1036	903	Kailua-Kona
IX	10/25/85	Scott Tinley	8:50:54	Chris Hinshaw	25:46	1018	965	Kailua-Kona
X	10/18/86	Dave Scott	8:28:37	Mark Allen	9:47	1039	951	Kailua-Kona
XI	10/10/87	Dave Scott	8:34:13	Mark Allen	11:06	1380	1284	Kailua-Kona
XII	10/22/88	Scott Molina	8:31:00	Mike Pigg	2:11	1277	1189	Kailua-Kona
XIII	10/15/89	Mark Allen	8:09:15	Dave Scott	0:58	1285	1231	Kailua-Kona
XIV	10/6/90	Mark Allen	8:28:17	Scott Tinley	9:23	1386	1255	Kailua-Kona
XV	10/19/91	Mark Allen	8:18:32	Greg Welch	6:01	1386	1235	Kailua-Kona
XVI	10/10/92	Mark Allen	8:09:08	Cristian Bustos	7:21	1364	1298	Kailua-Kona
XVII	10/30/93	Mark Allen	8:07:45	Paulli Kiuru	6:37	1438	1353	Kailua-Kona
XVIII	10/15/94	Greg Welch	8:20:27	Dave Scott	4:05	1405	1290	Kailua-Kona
XIX	10/7/95	Mark Allen	8:20:34	Thomas Hellriegel	2:25	1487	1323	Kailua-Kona
XX	10/26/96	Luc Van Lierde	8:04:08	Thomas Hellriegel	1:59	1420	1288	Kailua-Kona
XXI	10/18/97	Thomas Hellriegel	8:33:01	Jurgen Zack	6:17	1534	1365	Kailua-Kona
XXII	10/3/98	Peter Reid	8:24:20	Luc Van Lierde	7:37	1487	1379	Kailua-Kona
XXIII	10/23/99	Luc Van Lierde	8:17:17	Peter Reid	5:37	1471	1419	Kailua-Kona
XXIV	10/14/00	Peter Reid	8:21:01	Tim DeBoom	2:09	1525	1426	Kailua-Kona
XXV	10/6/01	Tim DeBoom	8:31:18	Cameron Brown	14:52	1558	1364	Kailua-Kona
XXVI	10/19/02	Tim DeBoom	8:29:56	Peter Reid	3:10	1540	1457	Kailua-Kona
XXVII	10/18/03	Peter Reid	8:22:35	Rutger Beke	5:51	1647	1569	Kailua-Kona
XXVIII	10/16/04	Normann Stadler	8:33:29	Peter Reid	10:11	1728	1579	Kailua-Kona
XXIX	10/15/05	Faris Al-Sultan	8:14:17	Cameron Brown	5:19	1743	1688	Kailua-Kona
XXX	10/21/06	Normann Stadler	8:11:56	Chris McCormack	1:11	1689	1627	Kailua-Kona
XXXI	10/13/07	Chris McCormack	8:15:34	Craig Alexander	3:30	1787	1685	Kailua-Kona

WOMEN

Multiple winners: Paula Newby-Fraser (8); Natascha Badmann (6); Erin Baker, Lori Bowden and Sylviane Puntous (2).

Year	Winner	Time	Runner-up	Year	Winner	Time	Runner-up
1978	No finishers			1993	Paula Newby-Fraser	8:58:23	Erin Baker
1979	Lyn Lemaire	12:55.00	None	1994	Paula Newby-Fraser	9:20:14	Karen Smyers
1980	Robin Beck	11:21:24	Eve Anderson	1995	Karen Smyers	9:16:46	Isabelle Mouthon
1981	Linda Sweeney	12:00:32	Sally Edwards	1996	Paula Newby-Fraser	9:06:49	Natascha Badmann
1982	Kathleen McCartney	11:09:40	Julie Moss	1997	Heather Fuhr	9:31:43	Lori Bowden
1982	Julie Leach	10:54:08	Joann Dahlkoetter	1998	Natascha Badmann	9:24:16	Lori Bowden
1983	Sylviane Puntous	10:43:36	Patricia Puntous	1999	Lori Bowden	9:13:02	Karen Smyers
1984	Sylviane Puntous	10:25:13	Patricia Puntous	2000	Natascha Badmann	9:26:17	Lori Bowden
1985	Joanne Ernst	10:25:22	Liz Bulman	2001	Natascha Badmann	9:28:37	Lori Bowden
1986	Paula Newby-Fraser	9:49:14	Sylviane Puntous	2002	Natascha Badmann	9:07:54	Nina Kraft
1987	Erin Baker	9:35:25	Sylviane Puntous	2003	Lori Bowden	9:11:55	Natascha Badmann
1988	Paula Newby-Fraser	9:01:01	Erin Baker	2004	Natascha Badmann*	9:50:04	Heather Fuhr
1989	Paula Newby-Fraser	9:00:56	Sylviane Puntous	2005	Natascha Badmann	9:09:30	Michellie Jones
1990	Erin Baker	9:13:42	P. Newby-Fraser	2006	Michellie Jones	9:18:31	Desiree Ficker
1991	Paula Newby-Fraser	9:07:52	Erin Baker	2007	Chrissie Wellington	9:08:45	Samantha McGlone
1992	Paula Newby-Fraser	8:55:28	Julie Anne White				

*Nina Kraft of Germany was the first woman to cross the finish line in 2004 with her time of 9:33:25 but she was disqualified after failing a post-race drug test by testing positive for EPO. Badmann finished second but was awarded the title (and Canada's Heather Fuhr became runner-up) following the test.

MIXED MARTIAL ARTS
Ultimate Fighting Championship
Major Fights of 2007

Results Key: KO (knockout), TKO (technical knockout), Wu (Win by unanimous decision), Ws (win by split decision), Sub (win by submission).

Date	Event	Weight	Winner	Loser	Result (Rd.)	Site
Jan. 25	UFC Fight Night	205	Rashad Evans	Sean Salmon	KO 2	Hollywood, Fla.
		Hvy	Jake O'Brien	Heath Herring	Wu 3	Hollywood, Fla.
		155	Nate Marquardt	Hermes Franca	Wu 3	Hollywood, Fla.
Feb. 3	**UFC 67**	185	Anderson Silva	Travis Lutter	Sub 2	Las Vegas
		155	Roger Huerta	John Halverson	TKO 1	Las Vegas
		Hvy	Mirko Cro Cop	Eddie Sanchez	TKO 1	Las Vegas
		205	Quinton Jackson	Marvin Eastman	TKO 2	Las Vegas
Mar. 3	**UFC 68**	Hvy	Randy Couture	Tim Sylvia	Wu 5	Columbus, Ohio
		170	Matt Hughes	Chris Lytle	Wu 3	Columbus, Ohio
		185	Martin Kampmann	Drew McFedries	Sub 1	Columbus, Ohio
		185	Rich Franklin	Jason MacDonald	TKO 2	Columbus, Ohio
		205	Jason Lambert	Renato Sobral	TKO 2	Columbus, Ohio
Apr. 5	UFC Fight Night	155	Joe Stevenson	Melvin Guillard	Sub 1	Las Vegas
		Hvy	Justin McCully	Antoni Hardonk	Wu 3	Las Vegas
		155	Kenny Florian	Dokon. Mishima	Sub 3	Las Vegas
Apr. 7	**UFC 69**	170	Matt Serra	Georges St-Pierre	TKO 1	Houston, Tex.
		155	Roger Huerta	Leonard Garcia	Wu 3	Houston, Tex.
		170	Josh Koscheck	Diego Sanchez	Wu 3	Houston, Tex.
		185	Yushin Okami	Mike Swick	Wu 3	Houston, Tex.
Apr. 21	**UFC 70**	Hvy	Gabriel Gonzaga	Mirko Cro Cop	KO 1	Manchester, ENG
		205	Lyoto Machida	David Heath	Wu 3	Manchester, ENG
		205	Michael Bisping	Elvis Sinosic	TKO 2	Manchester, ENG
		Hvy	Andrei Arlovski	Fabricio Werdum	Wu 3	Manchester, ENG
		Hvy	Cheick Kongo	Assuerio Silva	Wm 3	Manchester, ENG
May 26	**UFC 71**	205	Quinton Jackson	Chuck Liddell	TKO 1	Las Vegas
		185	Terry Martin	Ivan Salaverry	TKO 1	Las Vegas
		170	Karo Parisyan	Josh Burkman	Wu 3	Las Vegas
		205	Houston Alexander	Keith Jardine	TKO 1	Las Vegas
		185	Kalib Starnes	Chris Leben	Wu 3	Las Vegas
June 12	UFC Fight Night	155	Spencer Fisher	Sam Stout	Wu 3	Hollywood, Fla.
		170	Jon Fitch	Roan Carneiro	Sub 2	Hollywood, Fla.
		185	Drew McFedries	Jordan Radev	KO 1	Hollywood, Fla.
June 16	**UFC 72**	185	Rich Franklin	Yushin Okami	Wu 3	Belfast, N. IRE
		205	Forrest Griffin	Hector Ramirez	Wu 3	Belfast, N. IRE
		185	Jason McDonald	Rory Singer	TKO 2	Belfast, N. IRE
		155	Tyson Griffin	Clay Guida	Ws 3	Belfast, N. IRE
		185	Ed Herman	Scott Smith	Sub 2	Belfast, N. IRE
June 23	Ultimate Fighter	155	B.J. Penn	Jens Pulver	Sub 2	Las Vegas
July 7	**UFC 73**	185	Anderson Silva	Nate Marquardt	TKO 1	Sacramento, Calif.
		155	Kenny Florian	Alvin Robinson	TKO 1	Sacramento, Calif.
		205	Tito Ortiz	Rashad Evans	Draw 3	Sacramento, Calif.
		155	Sean Sherk	Hermes Franca	Wu 5	Sacramento, Calif.
Aug. 25	**UFC 74**	Hvy	Randy Couture	Gabriel Gonzaga	TKO 3	Las Vegas
		155	Roger Huerta	Alberto Crane	TKO 3	Las Vegas
		170	Georges St-Pierre	Josh Koscheck	Wu 3	Las Vegas
		155	Joe Stevenson	Kurt Pellegrino	Wu 3	Las Vegas
		185	Patrick Cote	Kendall Grove	TKO 1	Las Vegas
Sept. 8	**UFC 75**	205	Quinton Jackson	Dan Henderson	Wu 5	London, ENG
		205	Michael Bisping	Matt Hamill	Ws 3	London, ENG
		Hvy	Cheick Kongo	Mirko Cro Cop	Wu 3	London, ENG
		170	Marcus Davis	Paul Taylor	Sub 1	London, ENG
		205	Houston Alexander	Alessio Sakara	TKO 1	London, ENG
Sept. 19	UFC Fight Night	155	Kenny Florian	Din Thomas	Sub 1	Las Vegas
		185	Chris Leben	Terry Martin	KO 3	Las Vegas
		155	Nate Diaz	Junior Assuncao	Sub 1	Las Vegas
		185	Nate Quarry	Pete Sell	KO 3	Las Vegas
Sept. 22	**UFC 76**	205	Keith Jardine	Chuck Liddell	Ws 3	Anaheim, Calif.
		205	Forrest Griffin	Mauricio Rua	Sub 3	Anaheim, Calif.
		170	Jon Fitch	Diego Sanchez	Ws 3	Anaheim, Calif.
Oct. 20	**UFC 77**	185	Anderson Silva	Rich Franklin	TKO 2	Cincinnati, Ohio
		Hvy	Tim Sylvia	Brandon Vera	Wu 3	Cincinnati, Ohio
		155	Alvin Robinson	Jorge Gurgel	Wu 3	Cincinnati, Ohio

YACHTING

The America's Cup

International yacht racing was launched in 1851 when England's Royal Yacht Squadron staged a 60-mile regatta around the Isle of Wight and offered a silver trophy to the winner. The 101-foot schooner *America*, sent over by the New York Yacht Club, won the race and the prize. Originally called the Hundred-Guinea Cup, the trophy was renamed The America's Cup after the winning boat's owners deeded it to the NYYC with instructions to defend it whenever challenged.

From 1870-1980, the NYYC successfully defended the Cup 25 straight times; first in large schooners and J-class boats that measured up to 140 feet in overall length, then in 12-meter boats. A foreign yacht finally won the Cup in 1983 when *Australia II* beat defender *Liberty* in the seventh and deciding race off Newport, R.I. Four years later, the San Diego Yacht Club's *Stars & Stripes* won the Cup back, sweeping the four races of the final series off Fremantle, Australia.

Then in 1988, New Zealand's Mercury Bay Boating Club, unwilling to wait the usual three- to four-year period between Cup defenses, challenged the SDYC to a match race, citing the Cup's 102-year-old Deed of Gift, which clearly stated that every challenge had to be honored. Mercury Bay announced it would race a 133-foot monohull. San Diego countered with a 60-foot catamaran. The resulting best-of-three series (Sept. 7-8) was a mismatch as the SDYC's catamaran *Stars & Stripes* won two straight by margins of better than 18 and 21 minutes. Mercury Bay syndicate leader Michael Fay protested the outcome and took the SDYC to court in New York State (where the Deed of Gift was first filed) claiming San Diego had violated the spirit of the deed by racing a catamaran instead of a monohull. N.Y. State Supreme Court judge Carmen Ciparick agreed and on March 28, 1989, ordered the SDYC to hand the Cup over to Mercury Bay. The SDYC refused, but did consent to the court's appointment of the New York Yacht Club as custodian of the Cup until an appeal was ruled on.

On Sept. 19, 1989, the Appellate Division of the N.Y. Supreme Court overturned Ciparick's decision and awarded the Cup back to the SDYC. An appeal by Mercury Bay was denied by the N.Y. Court of Appeals on April 26, 1990, ending three years of legal wrangling. To avoid the chaos of 1988-90, a new class of boat—75-foot monohulls with 110-foot masts—has been used by all competing countries since 1992. Note that (*) indicates skipper was also owner of the boat.

The America's Cup moved to Europe for the first time when the Swiss Alinghi Team beat Team New Zealand, 5-0, in the best-of-nine series in February and March 2003. Alinghi, under new skipper Brad Butterworth, successfully defended the title on Mediterranean waters off the Spanish city of Valencia in 2007. The next defense is currently scheduled for May 2009.

Schooners And J-Class Boats

Year	Winner	Skipper	Series	Loser	Skipper
1851	America	Richard Brown	—	—	—
1870	Magic	Andrew Comstock	1-0	Cambria, GBR	J. Tannock
1871	Columbia (2-1)	Nelson Comstock	4-0	Livonia, GBR	J.R. Woods
	& Sappho (2-0)	Sam Greenwood			
1876	Madeleine	Josephus Williams	2-0	Countess of Dufferin, CAN	J.E. Ellsworth
1881	Mischief	Nathanael Clock	2-0	Atalanta, CAN	Alexander Cuthbert*
1885	Puritan	Aubrey Crocker	2-0	Genesta, GBR	John Carter
1886	Mayflower	Martin Stone	2-0	Galatea, GBR	Dan Bradford
1887	Volunteer	Henry Haff	2-0	Thistle, GBR	John Barr
1893	Vigilant	William Hansen	3-0	Valkyrie II, GBR	Wm. Granfield
1895	Defender	Henry Haff	3-0	Valkyrie III, GBR	Wm. Granfield
1899	Columbia	Charles Barr	3-0	Shamrock I, GBR	Archie Hogarth
1901	Columbia	Charles Barr	3-0	Shamrock II, GBR	E.A. Sycamore
1903	Reliance	Charles Barr	3-0	Shamrock III, GBR	Bob Wringe
1920	Resolute	Charles F. Adams	3-2	Shamrock IV, GBR	William Burton
1930	Enterprise	Harold Vanderbilt*	4-0	Shamrock V, GBR	Ned Heard
1934	Rainbow	Harold Vanderbilt*	4-2	Endeavour, GBR	T.O.M. Sopwith
1937	Ranger	Harold Vanderbilt*	4-0	Endeavour II, GBR	T.O.M. Sopwith

12-Meter Boats

Year	Winner	Skipper	Series	Loser	Skipper
1958	Columbia	Briggs Cunningham	4-0	Sceptre, GBR	Graham Mann
1962	Weatherly	Bus Mosbacher	4-1	Gretel, AUS	Jock Sturrock
1964	Constellation	Bob Bavier & Eric Ridder	4-0	Sovereign, GBR	Peter Scott
1967	Intrepid	Bus Mosbacher	4-0	Dame Pattie, AUS	Jock Sturrock
1970	Intrepid	Bill Ficker	4-1	Gretel II, AUS	Jim Hardy
1974	Courageous	Ted Hood	4-0	Southern Cross, AUS	John Cuneo
1977	Courageous	Ted Turner	4-0	Australia	Noel Robins
1980	Freedom	Dennis Conner	4-1	Australia	Jim Hardy
1983	Australia II	John Bertrand	4-3	Liberty, USA	Dennis Conner
1987	Stars & Stripes	Dennis Conner	4-0	Kookaburra III, AUS	Iain Murray

60-ft Catamaran vs 133-ft Monohull

Year	Winner	Skipper	Series	Loser	Skipper
1988	Stars & Stripes	Dennis Conner	2-0	New Zealand, NZE	David Barnes

75-ft International America's Cup Class

Year	Winner	Skipper	Series	Loser	Skipper
1992	America [3]	Bill Koch* & Buddy Melges	4-1	Il Moro di Venezia, ITA	Paul Cayard
1995	Black Magic, NZE	Russell Coutts	5-0	Young America, USA	Dennis Conner & Paul Cayard
2000	Black Magic, NZE	Russell Coutts & Dean Barker	5-0	Luna Rossa, ITA	Francesco de Angelis
2003	Alinghi, SUI	Russell Coutts	5-0	New Zealand, NZE	Dean Barker
2007	Alinghi, SUI	Brad Butterworth	5-2	Emirates New Zealand, NZE	Dean Barker

Great Outdoor Games

Sites: Lake Placid, N.Y. (2000-02); Reno-Tahoe, Nev. (2003); Madison, Wis. (2004); Orlando, Fla. (2005).

Sporting Dogs

Year	Retriever Trials
2000	Barry Lyons & Skeet
2001	Jerry Day & Super Sue
2002	A. Washburn & Ticket
2003	Chris Akin & Boomer
2004	J.P. Jackson & Achilles

Year	Big Air
2000	Beth Gutteridge & Heidi
2001	Mike Wallace & Jerry
2002	Mike Jackson & Little Morgan
2003	Terry Casey & Skeeter
2004	Mike Jackson & Little Morgan
2005	Chris Piacun & Beau

Year	Agility (large dogs)
2000	D. Bommarito & Lacey
2001	Julie Daniels & Spring
2002	Olga Chaiko & Luz
2003	S. Kluever & Ransom
2004	Marcus Topps & Juice
2005	Marcus Topps & Juice

Year	Superweave (large)
2003	Ken Fairchild & Echo
2004	S. Kluever & Ransom
2005	Marcus Topps & Juice

Year	Agility (small dogs)
2001	Jean LaValley & Taz
2002	Erin Schaefer & Jag
2003	C. Frank & Kimie
2004	Renee King & Hamlet
2005	Susan Garrett & DeCaff

Year	Superweave (small)
2003	Jean LaValley & Taz
2004	Not held

Year	Disc Drive
2004	Tim Gelb & Lock-Eye Razzle

Year	Launch
2005	Angela Jones & Nestle

Year	Hot Zone
2005	Ron Watson & Split

ATV

Year	Terracross
2005	Marty Hart

Year	Four Wheel Frenzy
2005	John Natalie

Fishing

Year	Flyfishing
2000	Tom Rowland
2001	Chuck Farneth
2002	Peter Erickson
2003	Lance Egan
2004	Lance Egan

Year	Flycasting
2002	Carter Andrews
2003	Mike McFarland
2004	John Wilson

Year	Bass Fishing
2000	Peter Thliveros
2001	Peter Thliveros
2002	Shaw Grigsby
2003	S. Grigsby & G. Klein
2004	M. Gofron & D. Brauer

Target Sports

Year	Rifle
2000	Bob Mastroianni
2001	Jerry Miculek
2002	Jerry Miculek
2003	Doug Koenig
2004	Mike Cumming

Year	Shotgun
2000	Doug Fuller
2001	Dustin Long
2002	Robbie Purser
2003	Scott Robertson
2004	Travis Mears

Year	Archery
2000	Jackie Caudle
2001	Randy Hendrix
2002	Randy Hendrix
2003	Darren Collins
2004	Randy Hendrix
2005	Keith Brown

Timber Events

Year	Endurance (women)
2000	Sheree Taylor
2001	Penny Halvorson
2002	Sheree Taylor
2003	Peg Engasser
2004	Sheree Taylor
2005	Sheree Taylor

Year	Endurance (men)
2000	Jason Wynyard
2001	Jason Wynyard
2002	Matt Bush
2003	Jason Wynyard
2004	Jason Wynyard
2005	Dion Lane

Year	Hot Saw
2000	Harry Burnsworth
2001	Mel Lentz
2002	Mike Sullivan
2003	Mike Sullivan
2004	Matt Bush
2005	Harry Burnsworth

Year	Springboard
2000	Mitch Hewitt
2001	Mitch Hewitt
2002	Mitch Hewitt
2003	Dave Bolstad
2004	Dale Ryan

Year	Boom Run (men)
2000	J.R. Salzman
2001	J.R. Salzman
2002	Jamie Fischer
2003	Jamie Fischer
2004	J.R. Salzman
2005	Jamie Fischer

Year	Boom Run (women)
2000	Tina Salzman
2001	Mandy Erdmann
2002	Mandy Erdmann
2003	Abby Hosechler
2004	Mandy Erdmann
2005	Mandy Erdmann

Year	Boom Run (mixed)
2003	Jamie Fischer & Tanya Fischer
2004	J.R. Salzman & Shana Martin

Year	Log Rolling (men)
2000	J.R. Salzman
2001	J.R. Salzman
2002	Darren Hudson
2003	Jamie Fischer
2004	J.R. Salzman
2005	J.R. Salzman

Year	Log Rolling (women)
2000	Tina Salzman
2001	Tina Salzman
2002	Tina Bosworth
2003	Tina Bosworth
2004	Tina Bosworth
2005	Lizzie Hoeschler

Year	Speed Climbing
2000	Wade Stewart
2001	Brian Bartow
2002	Brian Bartow
2003	Brian Bartow
2004	Wade Stewart
2005	Brian Bartow

Year	Tree Topping
2000	Mick Lee
2001	Gregg Hart
2002	Wade Stewart
2003	Greg Hart
2004	Brian Bartow

Year	Team Relay
2001	Team Halvorson
2002	Team Clarke
2003	Team Wynard
2004	Team Zalewski
2005	Team USA East

Year	SuperJack
2005	Cassidy Scheer

Hall of Fame goalie **Gump Worsley**, who didn't wear a mask during most of his career, died in 2007.

Notable deaths in the world of sports from Nov. 1, 2006-Oct. 28, 2007.

Alex Agase, 85; three-time All-American guard and linebacker for Illinois (1942, 1946) and Purdue (1943). He transferred from Illinois to Purdue so that he could train for the Marine Corps. Returned to Illinois after fighting in World War II. Played six years for the Cleveland Browns and won three league championships before returning to the college ranks as a coach. He worked as an assistant to Ara Parseghian at Northwestern from 1956-63 before becoming head coach when Parseghian left for Notre Dame. Also was head coach at Purdue from 1973-76 and was later athletic director at Eastern Michigan for five years; named to the College Football Hall of Fame and was selected to the Walter Camp Foundation's All-Century Team in 1989; at a hospital near his home in Tarpon Springs, Fla.; May 3.

Paul Arizin, 78; Hall of Fame scorer with the NBA's Philadelphia Warriors; a 10-time All-Star and league MVP in 1952; named one of the NBA's 50 Greatest Players in 1996; credited with pioneering the jump shot explaining later that he couldn't plant his feet on the slippery courts; led the NBA in scoring twice (1952 and 1957); scored 16,266 points in 713 career games; played college ball at Villanova and was named The Sporting News player of the year as a senior; in his sleep; near Philadelphia, Penn.; Dec. 12, 2006.

Ed Bailey, 75; five-time All-Star catcher with the Cincinnati Reds (1956, 1957, 1960) and San Francisco Giants (1961 and 1963); also played for the Milwaukee Braves, the Chicago Cubs, and California Angels; of throat cancer; in Knoxville, Tenn.; Mar. 2.

Barbaro, 3; undefeated thoroughbred who won the 2006 Kentucky Derby but weeks later broke down early in the Preakness; his struggle in the nine months following his catastrophic injury garnered significant media attention and public sympathy; the bay colt broke his right hind leg in three spots but was spared (for a time) with a five-hour operation to fuse together two joints; was euthanized due to lingering complications from his injury; in Kennett Square, Pa.; Jan. 29.

Steve Barber, 67; former big-league pitcher for seven teams going 121-106 with a 3.36 ERA over 15 years; became the Baltimore Orioles' first 20-game winner, going 20-13 with a 2.75 ERA in 1963; from complications of pneumonia in Henderson, Nev.; Feb. 4.

Hank Bauer, 84; strong-armed three-time All-Star outfielder (1952-54) with the powerhouse New York Yankees who won seven World Series titles (and nine American League pennants) in 12 seasons, spanning the DiMaggio and Mantle eras; he set a World Series record hitting safely in 17 straight games (1956-58); hit four homers in the 1958 Series tied for most ever at that time; later managed the Baltimore Orioles to the 1966 World Series victory over the Koufax/Drysdale Los Angeles Dodgers; before joining the Major Leagues Bauer saw action with the Marines in the South Pacific dur-

ing World War II, winning two Bronze stars and two Purple Hearts; of cancer; in Shawnee Mission, Kan.; Feb. 9.

Rod Beck, 38; mustachioed hard-throwing relief pitcher who earned 286 career saves in 13 major league seasons; played for four teams and had a career record of 38-45 in 705 games from 1991-2004, with a 3.30 ERA; made the All-Star team three times; saved 51 games with the Chicago Cubs in 1998; battled drug addiction in recent years; of a heart attack; in Phoenix, Ariz.; June 23.

Willie Booker, 65; former Florida A&M basketball coach from 1984-93 who led the Rattlers to the Mid-Eastern Athletic Conference title in 1991; compiled a career record of 137-125; found dead in his home; in Orlando, Fla.; Aug. 7.

Gay Brewer, 75; PGA Tour golfer who shot a final round 67 to win the 1967 Masters by one stroke; a year before he failed to win the green jacket when he missed a six-foot par putt on the 18th green at Augusta and dropped into a three-way 18-hole playoff won by Jack Nicklaus; won 11 tournaments on the PGA Tour; of lung cancer; in Lexington, Ky.; Aug. 31.

Ed Brown, 78; former Pro Bowl quarterback who led the NFL in passing with the Chicago Bears in 1956; passed for 15,600 yards and 102 TDs in his pro career, including a career-best 2,982 yards and 21 TDs for the Pittsburgh Steelers in 1963; also led the University of San Francisco Dons to an undefeated season in 1951; in Kennewick, Wash.; of prostate cancer; Aug. 2.

Herb Carneal, 83; Hall of Fame broadcaster with the Minnesota Twins for 45 years; his mellow tone was familiar to baseball fans throughout the Upper Midwest; made the winning call for the 1987 World Series; was awarded the Ford Frick Award from the Baseball Hall of Fame in Cooperstown, N.Y., in 1996; of congestive heart failure; in Minneapolis, Minn.; Apr. 1.

Mike Coolbaugh, 35; first-base coach for the Texas League's Tulsa Drillers who was killed after being hit in the head with a line drive while standing in the coach's box; played 44 games in the big leagues for St. Louis and Milwaukee in parts of two seasons; in North Little Rock, Ark.; July 23.

Diego "Chico" Corrales, 29; former two-division world champion boxer; his legendary 2005 lightweight unification battle with Jose Luis Castillo will go down as one of the most exciting fights in boxing history; in an 11-year professional career Corrales compiled a 40-5 record with 33 knockouts, including the unforgettable one he scored after getting off the mat twice in the 10th round to KO Castillo two years to the day before dying in a motorcycle accident; beat Roberto Garcia for the IBF junior lightweight title in 1999 before moving up to lightweight; in Las Vegas; May 7.

Bing Devine, 90; St. Louis Cardinals general manager who helped put together two World Series

AP/Wide World Photos

Barbaro

NASCAR Media

Bill France Jr.

AP/Wide World Photos

Bowie Kuhn

champions; served as Cardinal GM from 1958-64 and 1968-78; acquired Hall of Fame pitcher Bob Gibson and outfielder Lou Brock among others; his shrewd acquisition of Brock from the Chicago Cubs for pitcher Ernie Broglio is widely recognized as one of the most lopsided trades in baseball history; also served as a scout and executive with several other Major League teams including a term as president of the New York Mets (1965-67) where he assembled many of the players–including most notably Tom Seaver–that would win the 1969 Series; at Barnes-Jewish Hospital in St. Louis; following an illness; Jan. 27.

Gaetan Duchesne, 44; former NHL veteran forward who played 14 seasons with five different teams, scoring 179 goals and 254 assists in 1,028 games; after collapsing while exercising; in Quebec; Apr. 16.

Eddie Feigner, 81; barnstorming softball pitching legend who toured the country for 50 years with his four-man team known as "The King and His Court"; reportedly threw 930 no-hitters and 238 perfect games and struck out 141,517 batters in more than 10,000 games; his fastball was once clocked at 104 mph; in 1964 he struck out major-leaguers Willie Mays, Willie McCovey, Maury Wills, Harmon Killebrew, Roberto Clemente and Brooks Robinson in order during a televised exhibition game; also had an arsenal of trick pitches, often throwing blindfolded, from his knees, between his legs, behind his back, from second base; from a respiratory ailment; in Huntsville, Ala.; Feb. 9.

Bill France Jr., 74; longtime NASCAR chairman (1972-2003) who oversaw and helped to engineer the massive growth of stock car racing over the last two decades including development of the Winston Cup season championship and big money network television deals; became NASCAR boss in 1972 when he replaced his father NASCAR founder Bill France Sr.; of cancer; in Daytona Beach, Fla.; June 4.

Eddie Griffin, 25; five-year NBA veteran forward who played most recently with the Minnesota Timberwolves; seventh overall pick by Houston in the 2001 NBA Draft out of Seton Hall; died in a fiery wreck when the SUV he was driving was hit by a freight train; tests later revealed his blood-alcohol level was more than three times the legal limit; in Houston, Texas; Aug. 18.

Elmer Gross, 90; took Penn State to the NCAA tournament as a player (1942) and later a coach when he led the Nittany Lions to the NCAAs in 1952 and all the way to the Final Four in 1954; finished with an 80-40 record in his five-year coaching career; won a Bronze Star and Purple Heart and took part in the Normandy invasion during World War II; in Chandler, Ariz.; June 29.

Bobby Hamilton, 49; veteran NASCAR driver who won the Nextel Cup's 2001 Talladega 500 and the 2004 Craftsman Truck Series championship; made 559 starts in NASCAR's top three series and won 15 times (four in Nextel Cup, one in the Busch Series and ten in Craftsman Truck); of cancer, in Nashville, Tenn.; Jan. 7.

Josh Hancock, 29; St. Louis relief pitcher who won a World Series with the Cardinals in 2006; a career record of 9-7 with a 4.20 ERA in 177.2 career innings over four Major League teams; in a car accident; Apr. 29.

Terry Hoeppner, 59; football coach at Indiana University since 2004; had a 57-39 record in eight seasons as a college coach at Indiana and Miami of Ohio; of complications from a brain tumor; in Bloomington, Ind.; June 19.

Lamar Hunt, 74; Hall of Fame Kansas City Chiefs owner who founded the American Football League and co-founded the North American Soccer League (1967-84) and Major League Soccer; when he founded the AFL after being rebuffed in his attempts to buy an NFL franchise, his franchise was named the Dallas Texans but would move the team to Kansas City for business reasons and rename them the Chiefs; coined the name "Super Bowl" for the AFL-NFL championship game while watching his children play with a Superball; also owned several MLS teams including the Columbus Crew and FC Dallas; of complications from prostate cancer; in Dallas, Texas; Dec. 13.

Stu Inman, 80; former vice president of player

personnel and the architect of the 1977 Portland Trail Blazers NBA championship team; also was GM of the Blazers when they drafted Sam Bowie ahead of Michael Jordan; of a heart attack; in Lake Oswego, Ore.; Jan. 30.

Dennis Johnson, 52; five-time NBA All-Star point guard with the Boston Celtics and Seattle SuperSonics; won three NBA championships with Seattle (1979) and Boston (1984 and 1986); "DJ" was named to the NBA All-Defensive First Team six times in 14 seasons; MVP of the 1979 Finals with Seattle; none other than fellow Celtic great Larry Bird once called him the best teammate he ever had; of a heart attack; in Austin, Texas; Feb. 22.

Ken Kavanaugh, 90; longtime coach and scout with the NFL's New York Giants; was a star receiver with the Chicago Bears in the 1940s but his playing career was interrupted during World War II where he served as a pilot and flew 30 missions over Germany, winning the Distinguished Flying Cross and Air Medal with four oak leaf clusters; played at LSU where he was the Southeastern Conference player of the year in 1939 and was elected to the College Football Hall of Fame in 1963; of complications from pneumonia; in Sarasota, Fla.; Jan. 26.

Buddy Kerr, 84; shortstop with the New York Giants and Boston Braves (1943-51); represented the Giants on the All-Star team in 1948; once played 68 straight games at shortstop without committing an error; worked as a scout for the New York Mets for 21 years (1975-96); after a short illness; at Memorial Sloan-Kettering Hospital in New York; Nov. 7, 2006.

Bowie Kuhn, 80; former MLB commissioner (1969-1984) whose turbulent 15-year tenure (second longest ever) spanned the birth of free agency in 1975, five work stoppages, and the dramatic rise in player salaries; was notably absent from the stands on the night Hank Aaron broke Babe Ruth's career home run record in 1974; regularly butted heads with owners and once suspended New York Yankees boss George Steinbrenner for 15 months for illegal campaign contributions he made to President Nixon's re-election campaign; following a short bout with pneumonia; at St. Luke's Hospital in Jacksonville, Fla.; Mar. 15.

Clem Labine, 80; former Major League pitcher who played most notably for the Brooklyn/Los Angeles Dodgers in the 1950's as a clutch part-time starter and effective reliever; threw a seven-hit shutout in Game 6 of the 1956 World Series against the New York Yankees; also pitched a six-hit shutout for the Dodgers to keep them alive in Game 2 of their three-game playoff with the New York Giants in 1951; led the league in saves in two All-Star seasons (1956 and '57); known for his nasty curve ball; also played for Detroit, Pittsburgh and the New York Mets in his 13-year career; while in a coma following brain surgery; in Vero Beach, Fla.; Mar 2.

Lamar Lundy, 71; standout defensive lineman for 13 seasons with the Los Angeles Rams (1957-69)

and part of the notorious "Fearsome Foursome" defensive line (along with Merlin Olsen, Deacon Jones and Roosevelt Grier); the Rams defensive set an NFL record for the fewest yards allowed in a season in 1968; after a long illness; in Richmond, Ind.; Feb. 24.

Max McGee; 75; former Green Bay Packers receiver who scored the first Super Bowl touchdown on a pass from Bart Starr in the Packers' 35-10 win over the Kansas City Chiefs in 1967; as a backup he wasn't expecting to play so snuck out for a night on the town on the eve of the big game but was inserted into the game when starter Boyd Dowler went down early with an injury; despite the hangover he would go on to make seven catches for 138 yards and two touchdowns; played 12 seasons in the NFL, finishing his career with 345 catches for 6,346 yards and 51 touchdowns; after falling from the roof of his home; in Deephaven, Minn.; Oct. 21.

Ray Mears, 80; former men's basketball coach at University of Tennessee who stalked the sidelines, often wearing a bright orange blazer, for 15 seasons (1962-78) compiling a 278-112 record; mentored future NBA players Bernard King and Ernie Grunfeld; won three SEC titles with the Vols; following a long illness; in Knoxville, Tenn.; June 11.

Eric Medlen, 33; up-and-coming NHRA Funny Car driver; won six times on the drag circuit and was named the top rookie of 2004; from a head injury sustained from a crash during testing; Gainesville, Fla.; Mar. 23.

Harry "Moose" Miller, 83; forward/center for the now defunct Toronto Huskies who played in the NBA first-ever game on Nov. 1, 1946 at Maple Leaf Gardens against the New York Knicks; from kidney failure, in Latrobe, Pa.; Apr. 18.

Damien Nash, 24; Denver Broncos running back who was a fifth-round draft pick by the Tennessee Titans in 2005; played college football at the University of Missouri; when he collapsed after playing in a charity basketball game; in St. Louis; Feb. 24.

Parry O'Brien, 75; two-time Olympic gold medal-winning shot-putter (1952 and 1956) who broke the world record 17 times; while a student at USC in 1951 he revolutionized the event with his new technique of starting with his back to the field and turning 180 degrees before releasing the shot; also won an Olympic silver medal in 1960; of a heart attack during a swimming race; in Santa Clarita, Calif.; Apr. 21.

Al Oerter, 71; four-time discus gold medalist (1956, 1960, 1964, 1968) for the USA; one of only two track and field athletes (Carl Lewis-long jump) in history to win gold in the same event in four straight Olympics; he broke the Olympic record and beat the current world record holder in each instance; of heart problems, at a hospital near his home in Fort Myers, Fla.; Sept. 25.

Benny Parsons, 65; the 1973 NASCAR Winston Cup champion who won 21 races, including the 1975 Daytona 500, and 20 poles in his 24-year Hall of Fame driving career; "BP" was well known

Eric Medlen
NHRA

Grambling State
Eddie Robinson

University of Michigan
Bo Schembechler

as the antithesis of the image of the surly, ill-tempered stock car driver, he notched 283 top-10 finishes in 526 starts from 1964-1988; of complications from lung cancer; in Charlotte, N.C.; Jan. 16.

Bryan Pata, 22; University of Miami senior defensive tackle who was shot and killed outside his apartment complex; a rare mix of size and speed, he was expected to be drafted in the first or second round of the 2007 NFL Draft; in Miami, Fla., Nov. 7, 2006.

Howard Porter, 58; three-time All-American basketball player at Villanova averaging 22.8 points and 14.8 rebounds in his career from 1968-71; led the Wildcats to the 1971 NCAA championship game, a 68-62 loss to UCLA; he was named the tourney's Most Outstanding Player despite the loss; drafted by Chicago in the 1971 NBA Draft and played with the Bulls, as well as the New York Knicks, Detroit Pistons and Nets; was found unconscious in an alley following an apparent beating; in Minneapolis, Minn.; May 26.

Skip Prosser, 56; men's basketball coach at Wake Forest since 2001; career coaching record of 291-146; was the 2003 ACC coach of the year with the Demon Deacons; before taking the job at Wake Forest he coached at Xavier for seven seasons; the only coach in history to lead three different schools (Loyola, Xavier, Wake Forest) to the NCAA Tournament in his first season at the school; of a heart attack while jogging; in Winston-Salem, N.C.; July 26.

Phil Rizzuto, 89; Hall of Fame shortstop and long-time TV and radio broadcaster for the New York Yankees; nicknamed "The Scooter," the 5-foot-6 infielder was known for his quick feet and quicker glove; 1952 American League MVP, hitting .328 that year; won seven World Series titles and was a five-time All-Star with New York; had his No. 10 retired by the Yankees; was elected to the Baseball Hall of Fame in 1994; his signature on-air catchphrase of "Holy Cow!" was familiar to generations of Yankee fans; in his sleep; West Orange, N.J.; Aug. 14.

Eddie Robinson, 88; legendary Hall of Fame football coach at Grambling State for 56 seasons; retired in 1997 as the winningest coach in college football history (since passed by John Gagliardi) with a record of 408-165-15, a .707 win percentage and 17 SWAC championships; had only eight losing seasons; of Alzheimer's disease; in Ruston, La.; Apr. 3.

Bo Schembechler, 77; longtime head football coach at Michigan (1969-89) who won 13 Big Ten titles and took the Wolverines to 10 Rose Bowls but never won a national championship; remains the winningest coach in program history, including a 11-9-1 record against arch-rival Ohio State (he went 5-4-1 against his former coach and mentor Woody Hayes); named the 1969 national coach of the year in his first year at Michigan and would never have a losing season, finishing #2 (to Oklahoma) in the final AP poll of 1985; also served as Michigan AD for almost two years (1988-90); following his coaching days he was named president of MLB's Detroit Tigers, serving two years before being fired in 1992; was an assistant coach in the 1950s to Ara Parseghian at Northwestern and Hayes at Ohio State before taking the head coaching job at Miami of Ohio (1963-68); after collapsing at a TV station where he filmed a segment on the eve of the annual Michigan-Ohio State game; Nov. 17, 2006.

Rollie Stiles, 100; former St. Louis Browns pitcher who, at the time of his death, was believed to be the oldest former big leaguer; played for the Browns in the 1930, 1931 and 1933 seasons compiling a 9-14 record and a 5.92 ERA; faced Babe Ruth among others; in his sleep; in St. Louis County; July 22.

Larry Staverman, 70; the first coach in Indiana Pacers history; lasted just over a season on the job after finishing 38-40 in the team's first season in the newly founded American Basketball Association; was fired after a 2-7 start in the following season; played in the NBA for several teams over five seasons; a long illness; July 11.

Daryl Stingley, 55; former New England Patriots wide receiver whose career ended tragically when he was paralyzed by a hit by Oakland

Raiders safety Jack Tatum after making a catch in a preseason game in 1978; first-round pick by the Pats in 1973; of bronchial pneumonia and heart disease complicated by quadriplegia; in Chicago; Apr. 5.

Cecil Travis, 93; shortstop/third baseman for the Washington Senator who piled up an American League-leading 218 hits in 1941—more than Ted Williams and Joe DiMaggio had that year. The same year Williams hit .406 and DiMaggio notched his recording setting 56-game hit streak; had a career batting average of .314–a record for AL shortstops—and was named an All-star three times (1938, 1940, 1941); in Riverdale, Ga.; Dec. 16, 2006.

Jose Uribe, 47; former San Francisco Giants shortstop and father of current Chicago White Sox shortstop Juan Uribe; career batting average of .241 in 10 seasons (1984-93) with the Giants, Cardinals and Astros; in a car crash in the Dominican Republic; Dec. 8.

Butch van Breda Kolff, 84; former Los Angeles Lakers coach (1967-69) who took the team (with a little help from Wilt Chamberlain, Jerry West and Elgin Baylor) to the NBA Finals twice (lost to the Boston Celtics in 1968 and 1969); also coached the NBA's Detroit Pistons and Phoenix Suns; coached 28 college seasons (compiled win-loss record of 482-272), mentoring Bill Bradley at Princeton and players at three other colleges; after a long illness; in Spokane, Wash.; Aug. 23.

Jimmy Walker, 63; former Providence College star guard who was the first pick in the 1967 NBA Draft by the Detroit Pistons; three-time AP All-American (1965-67) averaged 25.2 points per game in his college career; father of former NBA player Jalen Rose; of lung cancer; in Kansas City, Mo.; July 2.

Bill Walsh, 75; legendary head coach, general manager and president of the San Francisco 49ers who rose to the top of the league under his stewardship; coached the Niners to three Super Bowl championships (1982, 1985 and 1989), compiling a 10-year record of 102-63-1; two-time NFL coach of the year (1981 and 1984); father of the West Coast offense which–against conventional wisdom–successfully demonstrated the value of a passing game in setting up the run; served two stints as team GM (1982-1989 and 1999-2001); elected to the Pro Football Hall of Fame in 1993; also coached at Stanford twice (1977-78, 1992-94); following a long battle with leukemia; at his Bay Area home; July 30.

Andre Waters, 44; longtime defensive back with the Philadelphia Eagles (1984-93) known for his bone-jarring and often fine-inducing hits; was working as an assistant coach at Fort Valley State in Georgia at the time of his death; of a self-inflicted gunshot wound that has since been linked by some to the depression he dealt with as a result of brain damage he suffered during his playing days; in Tampa, Fla.; Nov. 20, 2006.

Darrent Williams, 24; Denver Broncos cornerback and punt returner; was a second-round draft pick out of Oklahoma State in 2005; killed in a drive-by shooting while sitting in a limousine on New Year's Eve; in Denver, Colo.; Jan. 1.

William Wirtz, 77; longtime owner/president of the NHL's Chicago Blackhawks who was often criticized for his spendthrift ways with the team's payroll in recent years; served as chairman of the NHL's Board of Governors for 18 years; the Wirtz family bought the team in 1954 and the Blackhawks, one of the league's "Original Six" franchises, won the Stanley Cup in 1961 but haven't in the 46 seasons since; in Chicago; of cancer; Sept. 26.

Bob Woolmer, 58; Pakistan's British-born cricket coach who was found dead in his hotel room following his team's stunning loss to upstart Ireland at the Cricket World Cup; initially ruled a murder by strangulation, the cause of Woolmer's death has been debated by authorities, many of whom believe he simply died of natural causes; in Kingston, Jamaica, Mar. 18.

Lorne "Gump" Worsley, 77; Hall of Fame goaltender who won the Stanley Cup four times (1965, 1966, 1968 and 1969) with the Montreal Canadiens; played 21 years and didn't wear a goalie mask until the final six games of his career; in 861 regular season games he finished with a 335-352-150 record and a 2.88 goal-against average in net; won the Calder Trophy as the NHL Rookie of the Year with the New York Rangers in 1953; of a heart attack; in Beloeil, Canada; Jan. 27.

Other notable sports deaths
Nov. 1, 2006-Oct. 29, 2007

Ralph Heywood, 85	Gene Oliver, 71
Max Lanier, 91	Mike Mooney, 37
Yelena Romanova, 43	George Webster, 61
Vern Ruhle, 55	Eddie Mayo, 96
Ray Beck, 75	Pat Dobson, 64
Mario Danelo, 21	Pete Suder, 90
"Dutch" Reibel, 76	Johnny Sain, 89
Don Massengale, 69	Chuck DeShane, 87
George Preas, 73	Ham Richardson, 73
Shelby Metcalf, 76	Michel Plasse, 58
Lew Burdette, 80	Chris Brown, 45
"Bucko" Kilroy, 86	Larry Sherry, 71
Dave Balon, 68	Bill Fisk, 90
Marquise Hill, 24	Bud Allin, 62
Ron Hall, 43	Don Dennis, 65
Charley Ane, 76	Ernie Wright, 67
Hugo Corro, 53	Bill Forester, 74
Jim Norton, 68	Ken MacAfee, 77
Sam Baker, 76	Joe Jimenez, 89
Clete Boyer, 70	Gato Del Sol, 28
Charles Johnson, 58	Max McNab, 83
Bill Robinson, 64	Russell Ellington, 96
Shag Crawford, 90	George Washington, 4
Johnny Perkins, 54	Jim Mitchell, 60
John Vukovich, 59	Edwyn Owen, 71

UPDATES

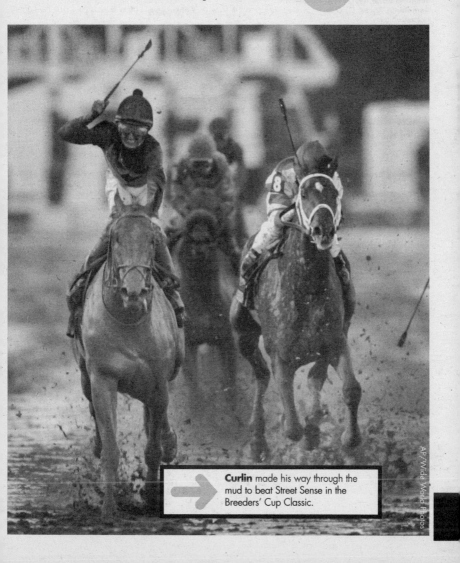

Curlin made his way through the mud to beat Street Sense in the Breeders' Cup Classic.

AP/Wide World Photos

AUTO RACING

Late 2007 Results
NASCAR
Chase for the Nextel Cup

Date	Event	Location	Winner (Pos)	Avg.mph	Earnings	Pole	Qual.mph
Oct. 29	Pep Boys Auto 500	Atlanta	Jimmie Johnson (6)	135.260	$349,561	G. Biffle	192.453

Winning Cars: CHEVROLET (1)—Johnson.
Remaining Races: (3): Dickies 500 in Texas (Nov. 4); Checker Auto Parts 500 in Phoenix (Nov. 11); Ford 400 in Homestead-Miami (Nov. 18).

Busch Series

Date	Event	Location	Winner (Pos)	Avg.mph	Earnings	Pole	Qual.mph
Oct. 27	Sam's Town 250	Memphis	David Reutimann (2)	62.487	$74,145	M. Ambrose	117.899

Winning Cars: TOYOTA (1)—Reutimann.
Remaining Races: (3) O'Reilly Challenge in Fort Worth (Nov. 3); Arizona.Travel 200 in Phoenix (Nov. 10); Ford 300 in Homestead (Nov. 17).

Craftsman Truck Series

Date	Event	Location	Winner (Pos)	Avg.mph	Earnings	Pole	Qual.mph
Oct. 28	EasyCare 200	Memphis	Kyle Busch (3)	127.381	$54,525	R. Hornaday Jr.	181.669

Winning Cars: CHEVROLET (1)—Busch.
Remaining Races: (3) Silverado 350 in Fort Worth (Nov. 2); Casino Arizona in Phoenix (Nov. 9); Ford 200 in Homestead (Nov. 16).

GOLF

Late 2007 Tournament Results
PGA Tour

Last Rd	Tournament	Winner	Earnings	Runner-Up
Oct. 21	Frys Electronics Open	Mike Weir (266)	$900,000	M. Hensby (267)
Oct. 28	Ginn sur Mer Classic at Tesoro	Daniel Chopra (273)	810,000	S. Maruyama & F. Jacobson (274)

Remaining Events (8): Children's Miracle Network Classic (Nov. 1-4); ADT Skills Challenge (Nov. 4-6); Wendy's 3 Tour Challenge (Nov. 12-13); OMEGA Mission Hills World Cup (Nov. 22-25); LG Skins Game (Nov. 24-25); PGA Tour Qualifying Tournament (Nov. 28-Dec. 3); Merrill Lynch Shootout (Dec. 7-9); Target World Challenge (Dec. 13-16).

European PGA Tour

Last Rd	Tournament	Winner	Earnings	Runner-Up
Oct. 21	Portugal Masters	Steve Webster (263)	E 500,000	R. Karlsson (265)
Oct. 28	Mallorca Classic	Gregory Bourdy (268)	333,330	S. Little (270)

Remaining Events (2): Volvo Masters (Nov. 1-4); OMEGA Mission Hills World Cup (Nov. 22-25).

Champions Tour

Last Rd	Tournament	Winner	Earnings	Runner-Up
Oct. 21	AT&T Championship	John Cook (198)	$240,000	M. O'Meara (200)
Oct. 28	Charles Schwab Cup Championship	Jim Thorpe (268)	442,000	F. Funk & D. Watson (271)

Remaining Events (3): Wendy's 3 Tour Challenge (Nov. 12-13); Champions Tour Q-School (Nov. 14-17); Del Webb Father-Son Challenge (Dec. 1-2).

LPGA Tour

Last Rd	Tournament	Winner	Earnings	Runner-Up
Oct. 21	Hana Bank-KOLON Championship	Suzanne Pettersen (141)*	$191,250	E-H Ji (142)
Oct. 28	Honda LPGA Thailand	Suzanne Pettersen (267)	195,000	L. Davies (268)

*The Hana Bank-KOLON Championship was cancelled after 36 holes due to unplayable course conditions caused by heavy rains.
Remaining Events (5): Mizuno Classic (Nov. 2-4); Mitchell Company Tournament of Champions (Nov. 8-11); ADT Championship (Nov. 15-18); Lexus Cup 2007 (Dec. 7-9); Wendy's 3 Tour Challenge (Dec. 21-23).

TENNIS

Late 2007 Tournament Results

Men's Tour

Finals	Tournament	Winner	Earnings	Loser	Score
Oct. 14	Kremlin Cup (Moscow)	Nikolay Davydenko	$142,000	P-H Mathieu	75 76 (2)
Oct. 14	BA-CA Tennis Trophy (Vienna)	Novak Djokovic	E 133,250	S. Wawarinka	64 60
Oct. 14	Stockholm Open	Ivo Karlovic	E 96,000	T. Johansson	63 36 61
Oct. 21	TMS—Madrid	David Nalbandian	E 340,000	R. Federer	16 63 63
Oct. 28	St. Petersburg Open	Mario Ancic	$142,000	T. Johansson	75 76(2)
Oct. 28	Swiss Indoors (Basel)	Roger Federer	E 120,750	F. Gonzalez	63 62 76 (3)
Oct. 28	Grand Prix of Tennis (Lyon)	Richard Gasquet	E 96,000	M. Gicquel	63 61

Remaining Events (3): BNP Paribas Paris Masters (Nov. 5); Tennis Masters Cup Shanghai (Nov. 26); Davis Cup Final **USA vs. Russia** (Dec. 2).

Women's Tour

Finals	Tournament	Winner	Earnings	Loser	Score
Oct. 14	Kremlin Cup (Moscow)	Elena Dementieva	$182,000	S. Williams	61 61
Oct. 14	PTT Bangkok Open	Flavia Pennetta	28,161	C. Yung-Jan	61 63
Oct. 22	Zurich Open	Justine Henin	182,000	T. Golovin	64 64
Oct. 29	Generali Open (Linz)	Daniela Hantuchova	88,265	P. Schnyder	64 62

Remaining Events (2): Bell Challenge (Nov. 5); WTA Tour Championships (Nov. 11).

THOROUGHBRED RACING

Late 2007 Major Stakes Races

Date	Race	Location	Miles	Winner	Jockey	Purse
Oct. 5	Darley Alcibiades Stakes	Keeneland	1 1/16	Country Star	Rafael Bejarano	$ 500,000
Oct. 6	Shadwell Turf Mile	Keeneland	1 (T)	Purim	Jamie Theriot	600,000
Oct. 6	Lane's End Breeders' Futurity	Keeneland	1 1/16	Wicked Style	Robby Albarado	500,000
Oct. 6	Champagne Stakes	Belmont	1	War Pass	Cornelio Velasquez	400,000
Oct. 6	Clement L. Hirsch Turf Championship Stakes	Santa Anita	1 1/4 (T)	Artiste Royal	Joseph Talamo	250,000
Oct. 6	Frizette Stakes	Belmont	1 1/16			
Oct. 7	Ancient Title	Oak Tree	6 F	Idiot Proof	David Flores	300,000
Oct. 7	Lady's Secret Handicap	Oak Tree	1 1/16	Tough Tiz's Sis	Victor Espinoza	250,000
Oct. 7	Juddmonte Spinster	Keeneland	1 1/8	Panty Raid	Garrett Gomez	500,000
Oct. 13	QE II Challenge Cup	Keeneland	1 1/8 (T)	Bill of Whimsy	Javier Castellano	500,000
Oct. 21	E.P. Taylor Stakes	Woodbine	1 1/4	Mrs. Lindsay	John Murtagh	1,000,000
Oct. 21	Canadian International*	Woodbine	1 1/2 (T)	Cloudy's Knight	Ramsey Zimmerman	2,000,000
Oct. 26	Breeders' Cup F & M Sprint	Monmouth	6 F	Maryfield	Elvis Trujillo	1,000,000
Oct. 26	Breeders' Cup Juvenile Turf	Monmouth	1	Nownownow	Julien Leparoux	1,000,000
Oct. 26	Breeders' Cup Dirt Mile	Monmouth	1	Corinthian	Kent Desormeaux	1,000,000
Oct. 27	Breeders' Cup Juvenile F.	Monmouth	1 1/16	Indian Blessing	Garrett Gomez	2,000,000
Oct. 27	Breeders' Cup Juvenile	Monmouth	1 1/16	War Pass	Cornelio Velasquez	2,000,000
Oct. 27	Breeders' Cup F & M Turf	Monmouth	1 3/8	Lahudood	Alan Garcia	2,000,000
Oct. 27	Breeders' Cup Sprint	Monmouth	6 F	Midnight Lute	Garrett Gomez	2,000,000
Oct. 27	Breeders' Cup Mile	Monmouth	1	Kip Deville	Cornelio Velasquez	2,000,000
Oct. 27	Breeders' Cup Distaff	Monmouth	1 1/8	Ginger Punch	Rafael Bejarano	2,000,000
Oct. 27	Breeders' Cup Turf	Monmouth	1 1/2	English Channel	John Velazquez	3,000,000
Oct. 27	Breeders' Cup Classic	Monmouth	1 1/4	Curlin	Robby Albarado	5,000,000

HARNESS RACING

Date	Race	Raceway	Winner	Driver	Purse
Oct. 6	**Kentucky Futurity**	Lexington	Donato Hanover	Ron Pierce	$742,000

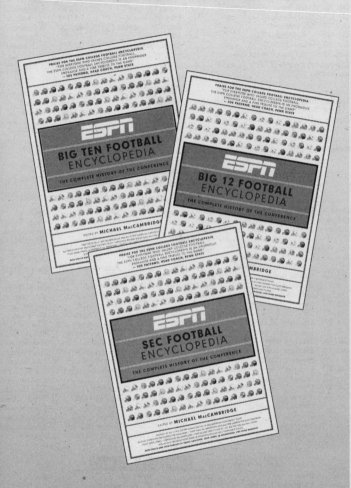